Concise HUTC[...]
GALLUP

INFO 94

Concise HUTCHINSON GALLUP INFO 94

Helicon

Helicon Publishing Ltd
42 Hythe Bridge Street Oxford OX1 2EP

Set in Helvetica and Times

Printed and bound in Great Britain by
The Bath Press Ltd, Bath, Avon

ISBN 0 09 178110 8

British Library Cataloguing in Publication Data
A catalogue record for this book is available from the British Library

Project Editor
Denise Dresner

Assistant Editor
Helen Maxey

Text Editors
Jane Anson, Lionel and Janet Browne,
Ingrid von Essen, Edith Harkness

Proofreaders
Frances Lass, Hazel Clark, Catherine Thompson

Researcher
Anna Farkas

Index
Clive and Ruth Barratt, Ann Barrett

Graphics
Ken Brooks

Gallup Liaison
Bob Wybrow

Page Make-up
Roger Walker, Graham Harmer

Production
Tony Ballsdon

Contributors
Owen Adikibi, Paul Bahn, David Bradley,
John Broad, Thomas Day, Celia Deane-Drummond,
Ian Derbyshire, J D Derbyshire, Michael Dewar,
Dougal Dixon, Nigel Dudley, Robert Dyer,
Ingrid von Essen, Eric Farge, Anna Farkas,
Barry Fox, Wendy Grossman, Charlotte Hardman,
Sian Jay, Peter Lafferty, James Le Fanu,
Robin Maconie, Tom McArthur, David Munro,
Joanna O'Brien, Maureen O'Connor, Robert Paisley,
Martin Palmer, Chris Pellant, Paulette Pratt,
Tim Pulleine, John Pym, Chris Rhys, Ian Ridpath,
Peter Rodgers, Julian Rowe, Emma Shackleton,
Adam Samuel, Jack Schofield, Steve Smyth,
Joe Staines, Calum Storrie, Chris Stringer,
Colin Tudge, Michael Walsh

CONTENTS

The Year

Quotes of the Year 3
Chronology of the Year 13
On This Day 30
Obituaries 38

Society

Clothes and Fashion 69
Education 74
Health and Medicine 82
International Organizations 108
Law 123
Media 138
Peoples and Languages 143
Politics 158
Religion 171
Sport 188
Transport 226
Warfare 235

Economics and Business

Business 255
International Economics 274

The Arts

Architecture and Building 289
Art 301
Books 317
Cinema 327
Dance 337
Music 341
Photography 358
Theatre 365

Science and Technology

Archaeology 379
Astronomy 390
Chemistry 414
Computing and Electronics 439

Earth Science 454
Energy 467
Environment and Conservation 474
Food and Agriculture 494
Life Sciences 511
Mathematics 530
Physics 543
Telecommunications and Video Technology 559

The World

History 571
Continents 596
Countries 602

Appendices

Conversion tables 719
Temperature scales 720
Currency exchange rates 721
Time zones and relative times 723
Islamic calendar 724
Jewish calendar 725
Christian festivals and holy days 726
Movable Christian feasts 726
Hindu festivals 727
Buddhist festivals 727
National holidays 728
Wedding anniversaries 734
Birthstones 734
Signs of the zodiac 734

Index 735

PREFACE

The ***Concise Hutchinson Gallup INFO 94*** is the first paperback edition of the successful INFO yearbook. It includes over 85% of the material in the unabridged INFO 94, the third and biggest-ever edition. Both almanac and encyclopedia in one, its aim is to provide the reader with concise and informed coverage of the issues of today as they affect us, including: current affairs and economics (the Bosnian crisis, the effect of the European recession on the UK recovery); health and medicine (the TB epidemic, the latest advances in gene therapy); environment and conservation (saving species from extinction, nuclear waste); business and finance (the biggest losses, new mergers); the sciences (aerogels, fossil DNA, patenting new forms of life); telecommunications (videophones, digital television); sport, media, and the arts.

Concise INFO 94 is designed for use by everyone who wants to keep in touch with today's world: its place is equally in the home, office, school, college, and library. We have made every effort to include the most up-to-date and informed expert opinion, together with the salient fact. Compiled with the help of more than fifty subject specialists, its aim is to inform the general reader in language free of pedantry or obscure technical jargon.

How it is different

Of course, ***Concise INFO 94*** includes the major events of the year – a chronology of events worldwide, notable deaths of the year, and memorable quotations – but it is more than just a yearbook. It is also an encyclopedia, an authoritative reference source that provides a glossary of terms for each subject, as well as full-page articles and shorter topic boxes on the most recent developments and trends in each area.

We have tried in every section to include not merely an undigested mass of statistics, lists, and figures, but to present information in a clear and easily understandable way. Graphics compiled expressly for the unabridged 1994 edition complement the text and display timely statistical data in a clear visual format.

With the aid of the extensive resources of Gallup Opinion Polls, ***Concise INFO 94*** also provides surveys of people's views on such issues as health, politics, the educational system, and the environment.

Extra appendices include conversion tables, temperature scales, currency exchange rates, national holidays worldwide, global time zones, and religious calendars and feast days.

How to use *Concise INFO 94*

Concise INFO 94 can be used in two ways. Look in the contents for the five major categories – Society, Economics and Business, The Arts, Science and Technology, and The World – which are in turn divided into forty subjects, each one forming a compact, alphabetically arranged section that includes key terms, dates, chronologies, and biographies.

Or use the index to help you find a specific entry or piece of information. The index has been expanded this year, and, besides listing the individual entries, contains additional references to topics elsewhere in the book, enabling you to find, for instance, information on 'extinction' in both the Environment and Life Sciences sections, as well as in articles that discuss the subject.

How you can help

Writing and compiling INFO 94 showed us that an encyclopedic yearbook can be fun; it can inform while being entertaining, and need not be a dull compilation of official titles and statistics. It can be packed with facts and figures but also be enlivened by topical opinion, illustrations, and a 'reader- friendly' format.

We are grateful to the readers who wrote in with suggestions to previous editions of INFO, all of which have helped make this year's edition the best yet. Please write to us with your comments on the new paperback format and let us know what you liked, what you didn't use, and what you think should be included in ***Concise INFO*** next time. Your letters will enable us to produce an improved second edition that corresponds more closely with what you, the reader, want to know.

ACKNOWLEDGEMENTS

We would like to thank the following for photographs supplied: Allsport; Greenpeace; Popperfoto; QA Photos Ltd; Rex Photos; Virgin Atlantic Airways.

We would also like to thank Lionel Browne for his help with the appendices; Ingrid von Essen for compiling the quotations; and Ruth Barratt for all her help with the tables.

Gallup

Gallup Social Surveys (Gallup Polls) Ltd have provided all the polls and surveys which appear in the book. The sample is representative of the adult population of the UK, aged 16 and over; all figures are percentages of people sampled unless stated otherwise. At the tabulating stage the sample has been weighted where necessary to give the correct proportion by sex by class within region. Any figures below 0.5% have been rounded down to zero. Percentages are rounded to the nearest whole number and consequently do not always add up to 100% exactly. To some questions contacts gave more than one reply; in such cases, therefore, the total of the replies exceeds 100%.

Statistics

It should be borne in mind that official statistics take a full year at the minimum to compile. We have provided the latest figures available at the time of going to press.

The Year

Quotes of the Year 3

Chronology of the Year 13

On This Day 30

Obituaries 38

QUOTES OF THE YEAR

We were promised a New Statesman, and what have we got instead? The Spectator.

JOHN SMITH *Labour Party leader, on John Major.*

Nobody is noticing how we are dismantling the old welfare state of Clement Attlee and completely rebuilding!

KENNETH CLARKE *as UK home secretary.*

To abandon Maastricht would be the most short-sighted act of foreign policy since Russia sold Alaska to the USA.

NORMAN FOWLER *Conservative Party chair, warning rebels in the House of Commons.*

We should stop trying to explain the Maastricht treaty, because it is unexplainable.

WILLY DE CLERCQ *former EC commissioner.*

I increasingly wonder whether paying unemployment benefit, without offering or requiring any activity in return, serves unemployed people or society well.

JOHN MAJOR *speech at Carlton Club.*

I regret that there are no vacancies here at present, but would suggest that you try finding work in France.

JOHN MAJOR *reply to unemployed man.*

To many it looks as if the NHS is falling away piece by piece like some cliff on the east coast.

JEREMY LEE-POTTER *chair of the council of the British Medical Association.*

We are not bouncing into dramatic speedy growth. And I do not want to because it will fall off the other end of the cliff again.

JOHN MAJOR *on his management of the economy.*

My wife said she had never heard me singing in the bath until last week.

NORMAN LAMONT *chancellor of the Exchequer, the week after the pound's Black Wednesday.*

Politics is about putting yourself in a state of grace.

PADDY ASHDOWN *leader of the Social and Liberal Democrats.*

Since I have become secretary of state, teaching has become an extremely appealing profession and people are entering it in record numbers.

JOHN PATTEN *education secretary, in the House of Commons.*

I always get my threes and fives muddled up.

NORMAN LAMONT *as chancellor of the Exchequer.*

I am the secretary for Trade and Industry.

PETER LILLEY *social-security secretary, introducing himself to a committee.*

I'm not an expert on the economy.

NORMAN LAMONT *as chancellor of the Exchequer.*

I hardly know the City.

KENNETH CLARKE *on being appointed chancellor of the Exchequer.*

Being a trade minister is rather like being a door-to-door salesman. You find yourself saying things like 'How are you off for aircraft?' and that sort of thing. I was always selling Hawk trainer jets to anybody I bumped into.

JOHN BIFFEN *remembering his official visits to Iraq in the 1980s.*

The point of selling Hawk aircraft to Indonesia is to give jobs to people in this country.

ARCHIE HAMILTON *armed-forces minister, addressing Parliament after the 1992 Indonesian massacre in East Timor.*

Economical with the actualité.

ALAN CLARK *former Conservative minister, on the government's attitude to exports of military equipment to Iraq.*

Anyone who thinks this country is turning the corner is going round the bend.

Norman Willis *secretary of the Trades Union Congress.*

I hold the establishment in the postwar British public services in very low regard.

Kenneth Clarke *home secretary.*

I am sure that I seem responsible for the sinking of the *Titanic*.

Norman Lamont *his last day as chancellor of the Exchequer.*

Chairman of the Coal Board — that was a job I could have had. I was offered it.

Arthur Scargill *miners' trade-union leader.*

Aren't their accents wonderful?

Kensington resident *watching miners' protest march.*

To write people off for short-term considerations about a market which you have rigged yourself means you must surely be immoral.

David Jenkins *bishop of Durham, on the government's coal policy.*

Desire and hope form no part of the statutory definition of remunerative work.

Social-security commissioner *ruling that unpaid writing did not disqualify a claimant from income support.*

First of all, it was ego. And secondly, I wanted to screw up the social-security system.

Lawrence Eagleburger *US Republican politician, on why he named each of his three sons Lawrence.*

The defence budget is more than a piggy bank for people who want to get busy beating swords into pork barrels.

George Bush *campaigning for re-election as US president.*

Don't mess with me, I got tanks.

Kim Campbell *as Canadian defence minister.*

I think there's a Trojan horse lurking in the weeds, ready to pull a fast one on the American people.

George Bush *campaigning for re-election as US president.*

We are America. Those other people are not.

Rich Bond *US Republican national chair, at his party's convention.*

However you define family, that's what we mean by family values.

Barbara Bush *as US First Lady.*

I think it is time we voted for senators with breasts. After all, we've been voting for boobs long enough.

Claire Sargent *US Democrat politician.*

I'm all ears.

Ross Perot *US presidential candidate.*

Hillary's husband elected.

Die Tageszeitung *headline in German newspaper on the US presidential election.*

This is the first coherent blueprint for the future of liberal politics, and it should not be allowed to fail.

Mario Soares *president of Portugal, on the election of Bill Clinton.*

There is nothing wrong with America that cannot be cured by what is right with America.

Bill Clinton *inaugural speech as US president.*

He is finished altogether as a person, as a criminal, thrown in humiliation behind the memory of the world.

Al-Jumhouriyah *Iraqi government newspaper, on the electoral defeat of George Bush.*

I'd like to be a positive influence on the president — a close and humanizing friend. I see myself as a kind of Sir Jack Falstaff to Clinton.

Jack Nicholson *US actor, asked if he has political ambitions.*

We have a very small stick and no carrots.

Boris Fyodorov *as Russian finance minister.*

In a way that's good, in a way that's not so good. Jobs way, it's tough. World peace, it's good.

GEORGE BUSH *as US president, on the collapse of the Soviet Union.*

I would bomb them. I would sail our large navy around their small island and if they so much as cheeped, I would nuke them.

VLADIMIR ZHIRINOVSKY *leader of Russian Liberal Democratic Party, on Japan.*

We Russians haven't forgotten English treachery during the war. You are a small island, so just you watch out, too.

VLADIMIR ZHIRINOVSKY *leader of Russian Liberal Democratic Party, on his foreign policy.*

I cannot bear responsibility for developments I can no longer influence. Nor do I want to be a barrier to historical developments, nor a mere time-serving bureaucrat.

VACLAV HAVEL *on his decision to resign as president of Czechoslovakia.*

The Czechs voted for the jungle, while the Slovaks voted for the zoo. It is clear that a compromise is impossible.

MILOS FORMAN *Czech-born film director, on the division of Czechoslovakia.*

Either you help us, or we will be on your doorstep. And I don't just mean the Poles and the Russians. Wait till the Chinese start their march. They'll be barefooted, so you won't even hear them until there are a thousand in your garden, all very hungry, eating the leaves from your trees. This is the danger that lies ahead.

LECH WALESA *president of Poland.*

Tito threw us together. We were like oil and water. While he shook us we stayed together. Once we were left alone, we separated.

RADOVAN KARADZIC *Bosnian Serb leader, on the coexistence of Serbs, Croats, and Muslims in Yugoslavia.*

Jesus said to love your neighbours. Well, I do love them. I love to kill them.

CROATIAN POLICE OFFICER.

Only criminals can live on what they earn now. The rest of us are living on the foreign money we have kept in our mattresses.

MILOS VLASIC *journalist, on life in Serbia.*

In his own way, he is interested in peace.

LORD OWEN *European Community negotiator, on Serb leader Slobodan Milosevic.*

I want to bring Californian lifestyle to Yugoslavia. Look at California, think of any race under the sun and you will find it living here, but nobody is killing anyone on ethnic grounds.

MILAN PANIC *formerYugoslavian prime minister.*

The faster you drive, the longer you live.

SARAJEVO RESIDENT *on avoiding snipers in traffic.*

The intent was to cripple, to break his bones so he would not be able to get up off the ground.

STACEY KOON *Los Angeles police sergeant, on beating Rodney King.*

Their actions may even have saved Mr King from being killed.

SERGEANT CHARLES L DUKE *of the Los Angeles police, speaking of his colleagues who beat up Rodney King, in testimony at the trial.*

People have to realize that what happened to Rodney King happens every day in the States.

SPIKE LEE *US film director.*

What are we supposed to do — beat a friendliness towards foreigners into people's heads?

HERMANN LUTZ *president of Germany's police union.*

I don't think black people and white people will ever really get on. The English will never like the French. That tunnel will collapse.

MORRISSEY *English pop singer.*

Some of these white kids are putting in a lot of work on their own people, and that's where revolution starts in. I think it's moving from a black/white thing to a rich/poor thing.

ICE CUBE *US rap musician.*

The poor are not just living off the crumbs from the rich man's table, they are being asked to put the crumbs back.

DAVID BRYER *Oxfam director.*

We may pretend that we're basically moral people who make mistakes, but the whole of history proves otherwise.

TERRY HANDS *English theatre director.*

Je ne regrette rien.

NORMAN LAMONT *chancellor of the Exchequer, on the Conservative defeat in the Newbury by-election.*

Given the choice, I would rather not have been born wealthy, but I never think of giving it up.

THE DUKE OF WESTMINSTER *on being the richest man in the UK.*

It would have been more sensible to make me a Commander of Milton Keynes — at least that exists.

SPIKE MILLIGAN *English comedian, on being made a Commander of the British Empire.*

No, I won't lend them my money. They wouldn't be able to pay it back.

PRESIDENT MOBUTU *of Zaire, who has become a billionaire in office, asked whether he would make some of his personal fortune available to his impoverished people.*

We should in our actions seek to make governments not just accountable to the international community, but to their people, so that change can come about from within.

PIERRE SANÉ *new secretary-general of Amnesty International.*

We want to dissociate ourselves from politics, but if after the election a new government is formed by lousy parties then the military has to intervene.

SUPREME COMMANDER *of the Thai armed forces.*

If you phoned hotel reception in India and asked them to send up the Treorchy Male Voice Choir someone would assure you that they would be sent up in five minutes. Assurances? They are shooting people on sight in Bombay.

GRAHAM GOOCH *English cricketer, on why he did not think it safe to play in India.*

The trouble with words is that you never know whose mouths they have been in.

DENNIS POTTER *English television playwright.*

I sometimes feel that I have nothing to say and I want to communicate this.

DAMIEN HIRST *English sculptor.*

Art is certain proof that there can be no God.

EDWARD BOND *English playwright.*

We went to the Moon and somehow forgot to keep going.

EUGENE CERNAN *US astronaut, on the decline of the space programme.*

We're working on that. It's three to five years away. After that, it's on to Mars.

SPACE MARKETING PRESIDENT *on putting hoardings on the Moon.*

In all musicians and artists there is always the fear that the game is going to be up for you sooner or later and somebody is going to say, 'What you do is now invalid and the conventional wisdom is that you shouldn't exist any more.' I had the distinct feeling that that day was imminent for quite some time, but I think that day has come and gone.

ELVIS COSTELLO *English rock musician.*

The thing I wanted to be was strong, independent, and jolly.

EMMA THOMPSON *English actress.*

The church has failed, education has gone to pot, and the family doctor has disappeared, so people turn to myself and Princess Diana.

BARBARA CARTLAND *English romantic novelist.*

The fact that she has to live in the public eye, I mean I would slit my wrists already. I can't understand how this poor girl can take it.

MADONNA *US singer, on Princess Diana.*

The Queen is all right and Princess Diana is a goddess, but the rest of them are so awful that it is quite a work to dredge out pejoratives strong enough to describe their vulgarity, brutishness, and maladroitness.

Alan Clark *former Conservative minister, on the royal family.*

It was time the Prince of Wales was cut down to size.

The Prince of Wales *on being 'shrunk' by camera for television.*

Only domestic servants apologize for what they've said.

Alan Clark *former Conservative minister, on publishing his outspoken diaries.*

There's more bad music in jazz than any other form. Maybe that's because the audience doesn't really know what's happening.

Pat Metheny *US jazz guitarist.*

A cat like Jimi Hendrix is a much more influential composer than Vivaldi in terms of the effect he has had on his contemporaries.

Nigel Kennedy *English violinist.*

I'd like to go into space with a band, have speakers on the outside of our spacecraft, see if we can communicate. Choose a really strange band.

Tom Waits *US musician.*

Sometimes it's good to combine high music with low music, orchestral guys with guys that play in the train station. Then, through the conflict of background you go to a new place.

Tom Waits *US musician and songwriter.*

We're certainly still very much opposed to any form of sponsorship. I'm not gonna make a moral point about it, but personally I think it makes you look like an utter schmuck.

Peter Buck *of US rock group REM.*

On my new album I was working with the general metaphor of a gorilla watching television.

Roger Waters *English rock musician, formerly of Pink Floyd.*

It's taken over 40 years to build up the language of film, and it's taken us four minutes to destroy it.

Keith McMillan *former director of pop videos.*

The imagination of television is dominated by male fantasies.

Lord Rees-Mogg *of the Broadcasting Standards Council.*

I suppose it's for political reasons. With a better image, the long shot becomes possible. Then we might see more than they want us to.

David Hockney *painter, on why Britain does not yet have high-definition television.*

I get my pleasure out of humiliating my opponent. I like to hurt him, to torture him slowly.

Nigel Short *English chess master.*

I accept it's unfortunate having to carry 420 lb over ice mountains to make a living.

Sir Ranulph Twistleton-Wykeham-Fiennes *English polar explorer.*

At some point I'll have to think about whether it's my responsibility as a musician to get into heavier drugs simply to find out more about music.

Nigel Kennedy *English violinist.*

I feel strongly that society needs to condemn a little more and understand a little less.

John Major *announcing a crackdown on crime.*

We cannot respond with demagogic promises to build more jails and put all the criminals away.

Janet Reno *US attorney general, on dealing with violent crime.*

The rehabilitative effect of punishment under our existing criminal justice system is now accepted as laughingly negligible, and has, in practice, been abandoned by our prison system as an objective.

Scotland Yard *discussion paper.*

Many prisoners like sharing cells, or they feel lonely.

Home Office *spokesperson on overcrowding at Strangeways prison.*

To have a good prison system, you have to put your political leaders in jail at some stage.

Stephen Tumim *British judge.*

His love of publicity and his lack of sophistication about what was being worked on him by the Americans were the cause of all his difficulties.

Lord Runcie *former archbishop of Canterbury, on his one-time envoy Terry Waite.*

It is nothing to do with celebrating the crime, it is celebrating the sensation of the robbery.

Ronnie Biggs *planning a Great Train Robbery 30th-anniversary bash.*

I don't believe in accidents. There are only encounters in history. There are no accidents.

ELIE WIESEL *US academic and human-rights campaigner.*

It was like looking for a needle in the haystack and finding the farmer's daughter.

GARETH ROBERTS *leader of the British team that uncovered the causes of Alzheimer's disease.*

You can't write songs about sex if you don't have it in the music. That's what was missing in the puzzle for U2.

BONO *of Irish rock group U2.*

I honestly think a lack of sex is vital to my writing process. I don't know if the same goes for Aerosmith.

BRETT ANDERSON *of English pop group Suede.*

In a way, I have fewer problems than Madonna.

SALMAN RUSHDIE *British writer, on no longer being recognized in public.*

My daily experience is optimistic, but I do observe that my species does many stupid things, and has an undeniable track record in that regard.

MICHAEL CRICHTON *author of* Jurassic Park.

They did not give me a lobotomy. They operated on the other end.

FRANÇOIS MITTERRAND *explaining that having prostate surgery would not cause him to resign.*

The quickest way to become a left-winger in the Labour Party today is to stand still for six months.

DAVE NELLIST *former Labour MP.*

The arguments for socialism are powerful. The social argument for socialism — the concept of the common good against individual greed — is not easy to refute.

ALAN CLARK *former Conservative minister.*

Socialism has nothing to offer the world and it is preposterous that this overblown bureaucratic flunkey should seek to ram socialism and workers' control down our throats.

WINSTON CHURCHILL *Conservative MP, on Jacques Delors, president of the European Commission.*

It will be in the history books: it may be a footnote.

SIR EDWARD HEATH *former Conservative prime minister, on Thatcherism.*

I am looking for some sort of lifeboat so I am not left on the beach while the cruise liner goes off with the corporate capital.

TIM POWELL *Lloyd's Name, on his liability for insurance losses.*

We will be going to a remote part of the airfield and absorbing the delay there.

PILOT *on flight from Heathrow.*

If Richard Branson had worn a pair of steel-rimmed glasses, a double-breasted suit and shaved off his beard, I would have taken him seriously. As it was, I underestimated him.

LORD KING *head of British Airways.*

So what if a few computer people hacked into somebody else's system? If it helped BA's profits none of the shareholders would complain. It's as simple as that. The Americans do it all the time. I really cannot understand what all the fuss is about.

SENIOR FINANCIER *on the City's view of the illegal activities of British Airways against Virgin Atlantic Airways.*

The quickest way to become a millionaire? Borrow fivers off everyone you meet.

RICHARD BRANSON *chair and founder of the Virgin group.*

It is much better to be a successful speculator and then apply your moral priorities elsewhere.

GEORGE SOROS *international financier.*

Christian teaching requires any worldly measure of success to be placed firmly in the perspective of the eternal values taught by Jesus Christ, who was himself a flop by worldly standards.

GEORGE CAREY *archbishop of Canterbury, attacking materialistic values.*

The simple issue is, do we want to live in a five-star world or not?

LORD FORTE *addressing a hoteliers' environmental conference.*

You will not be able to maintain a single market unless you have a single currency, because people will cheat. And by refusing to accept the social chapter, and therefore going for sweated labour, we're cheating.

SIR EDWARD HEATH *former Conservative prime minister.*

We cannot aspire to a classless society, whatever that means, if some children are disadvantaged the moment they open their mouths.

BARONESS JAMES *on English teaching.*

The quality of education will determine the quality of our country in the years ahead.

WALTER ANNENBERG *publishing billionaire, donating $365 million to US educational establishments.*

That's fine phonetically, but you're missing just a little bit.

DAN QUAYLE *as US vice president, instructing a schoolboy to spell 'potato' with an 'e' at the end.*

One in four pupils leaving secondary school can't read or write properly, and are not competent in arithmetic. What are they all to do? They can't all be prime minister.

JOHN MAJOR *addressing the Welsh Conservative Party conference.*

I don't think I know anything more than when I was 15, except on an experimental level. I only know things that I wish I didn't know.

ROBERT SMITH *of the Cure rock group.*

If a candidate for a library assistant post lists reading as a hobby this is counted against them. It is assumed that someone who likes reading will be introverted and unable to get on with the public.

PAT COLEMAN *director of library services in Birmingham.*

I have the British dry-cleaning industry close to my heart.

JOHN SELWYN GUMMER *secretary of state for the environment.*

We give the impression of being in office but not in power.

NORMAN LAMONT *in his resignation statement to the House of Commons.*

Far better that the Conservative Party should go through a purgation in decent relative obscurity rather than it should continue to make an embarrassing exhibition of its deep inner unhappiness at the expense of the effective government of the country.

LORD JENKINS OF HILLHEAD *former chancellor of the Exchequer.*

The Tory party is losing its marbles. It is perfectly clear they are acting like headless chickens under John Major.

SIR BERNARD INGHAM *Lady Thatcher's former press officer.*

There is an uncomfortable likelihood that many of us will live the rest of our lives under Conservative governments, which while discrediting not merely themselves but the whole political system, just manage to survive by default and in ignominy.

LORD JENKINS OF HILLHEAD *former chancellor of the Exchequer.*

I am no more a fascist than Mrs Thatcher ... And Hitler was a socialist.

JEAN-MARIE LE PEN *French right-wing politician, on being compared to Hitler.*

I'm not a believer in a totally free market. I think speculation does have harmful consequences and should be regulated.

GEORGE SOROS *successful speculator.*

Which country exactly am I supposed to have betrayed?

MARKUS WOLF *former East German spymaster.*

We must not get mixed up in civil wars.

SIR EDWARD HEATH *former Conservative prime minister, on Bosnia.*

There is a civil war. The patients have guns.

OFFICIAL *at Digfer Hospital, Mogadishu, Somalia.*

God protect us from cease-fires. It seems that whenever we have a cease-fire, the level of fighting goes up.

LEWIS MACKENZIE *Canadian major general, as United Nations commander in Bosnia.*

UNTAC now looks more and more like a pathetic monster caught in a tropical swamp. It's not the Father Christmas we had been led to believe.

CAMBODIAN *on the perceived failure of the United Nations Transitional Authority in Cambodia.*

I have spoken to God many times. But I have ceased to believe in the pope, priests, and the church.

DIEGO MARADONA *Argentine football player.*

I'm very much against terrorism. But our refugees are being spread all round the world. I'm worried that in Libya and Pakistan they won't be taking courses in classical music.

EJUP GANIC *Muslim vice president of Bosnia.*

There's nothing we can do with her. She thinks she can walk on water.

ALBERT REYNOLDS *Ireland's prime minister, on President Mary Robinson.*

The Vatican is an oppressive regime which, like a bat, fears the light.

FATHER LEONARDO BOFF *liberation theologian, leaving the Roman Catholic Church.*

As the low-fat diet unfolded, I really felt that God was showing me the way.

ROSEMARY CONLEY *British author of a series of diet books.*

If I give $500 to some guy who's running against someone who's funded by the Baptist church, I kinda see that as a civic duty. I think religion by and large is obscene, it's a joke.

PETER BUCK *of US rock group REM.*

Jesus' mother, Mary, was an unwed 16-year-old who, if she had been reading the Dublin newspapers when she was pregnant, would have had an abortion.

REVEREND DENIS FAUL *in an address at Knock, Ireland.*

I feel like meals on heels.

KATHY LETTE *writer, on breastfeeding.*

Being a rock 'n' roll star is like having a sex change. People treat you like a girl — they stare at you and follow you down the street. I now know what it's like to be a babe.

BONO *of Irish rock group U2.*

I do believe in reincarnation, but I wouldn't want to come back as a woman. Too complicated and I would have to deal with men like myself. No, I'd like to come back as a crow.

SYLVESTER STALLONE *US film actor.*

I've never understood why 90,000 people would want to come and see us. I could cynically say that they're waiting to see one of us keel over.

CHARLIE WATTS *of the Rolling Stones.*

If the listener believes that the singer has dipped his pen in the blood of his heart or whatever, then he has succeeded.

MICK JAGGER *of the Rolling Stones.*

I would rather have seen his pickled head in a jar. Then I would have felt like I got what I paid for.

TOM WAITS *US musician, on visiting Elvis Presley's home, Graceland.*

The music itself should be some kind of political statement. Lyrics are secondary to that.

KIM GORDON *of US art-rock group Sonic Youth.*

If you're getting booed for doing something that you want to do, you should remember that you want to do it. If you're an artist preoccupied with what people think, you may as well give up.

NEIL YOUNG *Canadian rock star.*

You make a record, you want people to buy your record. Period. Anybody who tells you 'I'm making a record because I want to be creative' is a liar.

WHITNEY HOUSTON *US pop singer.*

Men are absolutely hysterical about this because they know how they talk about women, they know what they do to women, and now they're thinking, Oh God, it can happen to me!

TANYA DOMI *US lesbian leader, on the controversy over gays in the military.*

He's a pot-smoking, draft-dodging, gay-loving womanizer ... and a wimp.

MAJOR GENERAL HAROLD CAMPBELL *on US president Bill Clinton.*

The military culture does not appear to be conducive to happy family life.

DES STOCKLEY *researcher finding that 37% of London's homeless young people came from service families.*

I think I was lucky — I was loved but not brought up.

BJÖRK GUDMUNDSDOTTIR *Icelandic pop singer, on her unconventional childhood.*

In institutions — including religious institutions — when people talk about unity, they're talking about keeping quiet.

DAVID JENKINS *bishop of Durham.*

We can't simply balance the budget on the backs of the old, the sick, and those who work hard but just barely make ends meet.

BILL CLINTON *US president.*

The concept of the undeserving poor — a peculiarly English heresy — is one of the most repulsive notions known to man.

ROY HATTERSLEY *Labour MP.*

The fact of the matter is that a contribution to the Conservative Party does not buy influence.

NORMAN FOWLER *chair of the party, on the more than £400,000 donated by Cypriot entrepreneur Asil Nadir.*

Most Tory money is raised by the selling of jam.

LORD MCALPINE *former Conservative Party treasurer.*

What I did was right and if I had done anything less it would have been wrong.

MICHAEL HESELTINE *secretary for trade and industry, on intervening on Asil Nadir's behalf with the attorney-general when the former was arrested for fraud.*

I thank God that there are people in Britain who are prepared to see justice prevail.

ASIL NADIR *bail-jumping Cypriot entrepreneur, on his supporters in the Conservative Party.*

If one cannot speak in this place about what is wrong with the system, then what is the point of being here?

MICHAEL MATES *Conservative minister, resigning over his role in the Asil Nadir affair.*

I would still defend to the death the right of Mr Latsis or anybody else who cares to take an interest in our country and support our political parties.

LORD MCALPINE *former Conservative Party treasurer.*

She was not entirely an angel herself.

JUDGE IAN STARFORTH HILL *on an eight-year-old sex-abuse victim, as he sentenced the attacker to two years' probation.*

It's a wonderful solution for the problems posed by surrogacy and a magnificent use of a corpse.

DR PAUL GERBER *ethicist, on using brain-dead women for surrogate pregnancies.*

If I hear the word Frankenstein again I shall throw up.

STEVE JONES *Welsh geneticist.*

The problem with technology is that it will not only save our lives, it will also eat our lunch, if we don't use it properly.

WHITE HOUSE OFFICIAL *in the Clinton administration.*

Smoking is a dying habit.

VIRGINIA BOTTOMLEY *health secretary.*

If they are buying my disc rather than cigarettes then I am saving lives all the time.

HENRYK GORECKI *Polish composer.*

If I'd been a European artist, the audience wouldn't have liked me.

FRANK ZAPPA *US musician.*

I have a brain like a sieve and enormous memory lapses. I have even thought about having my brain examined to see if there are any holes.

DAVID BOWIE *English rock star.*

Balance is the enemy of art.

RICHARD EYRE *English film and theatre director.*

It's been possible for giant squid to elude even highly motivated scientists.

SYLVIA EARLE *marine biologist.*

Western people see insects as almost universally repugnant, particularly as food items.

DICK VANE-WRIGHT *British entomologist.*

The basic rule of human nature is that powerful people speak slowly and subservient people quickly — because if they don't speak fast nobody will listen to them.

MICHAEL CAINE *English actor.*

There's a great deal to be said for Barbara Castle, and Barbara usually says it.

MICHAEL FOOT *on his former colleague in the Labour government.*

This administration will have cost as much as a major war, in terms of public finance.

LORD REES-MOGG *writing in the* Times.

I've never had a humble opinion. If you've got an opinion, why be humble about it?

JOAN BAEZ *singer and political activist.*

It doesn't matter what you become radicalized about. Once you are radicalized about something, you begin to see the connections between evils.

BENJAMIN SPOCK *US child-care expert and political activist.*

They can kill me, but they can't kill an energy. You can turn off the lights, but the electricity's still there.

ICE CUBE *US rap musician.*

I have sat in the cabinet for six years now. It just seems like sixty.

JOHN MAJOR.

Sixty years of progress, without change.

SAUDI ARABIA *slogan to promote the kingdom's 60th anniversary.*

The life of human beings is very short. We are all going to die. Why should we cling so much to power?

MOHAMMED BOUDIAF *Algerian president, seconds before he was assassinated.*

If we are lucky, mankind has about 50 years left.

LORD REES-MOGG *journalist.*

A good society relishes its problems.

EDWARD BOND *English playwright.*

CHRONOLOGY OF THE YEAR

June 1992

INTERNATIONAL

2 Voters in Denmark narrowly rejected the EC's Treaty on European Unity agreed at the 1991 EC summit in Maastricht, the Netherlands.

2 The military-backed government of Haiti nominated conservative politician Marc Bazin to become the country's new premier.

5 A revised version of the 1990 Conventional Forces in Europe treaty was signed by 29 nations in Oslo at a meeting of the North Atlantic Cooperation Council.

5 Poland's Sejm, or lower house of parliament, voted to confirm Waldemar Pawlak as premier. Pawlak was the first of Poland's post-Communist premiers with no previous ties to the Solidarity labour movement.

16–17 US President Bush and Russian President Yeltsin held the first official Russian-American Summit in Washington DC and reached a surprise agreement that went significantly beyond the 1991 Strategic Arms Reduction Treaty.

17 German relief workers Heinrich Struebig and Thomas Kemptner were freed by Lebanese Shiite guerrillas after more than three years in captivity. Struebig and Kemptner were the last Westerners known to be held hostage in Lebanon.

17 A band of armed marauders swept through the South African township of Boipatong, killing more than 40 blacks. According to survivors, the raid was carried out by about 200 Zulu men.

18 Irish voters approved the EC's Treaty on European Unity by a margin of more than two-to-one.

20 Czechoslovak federal Premier-designate Vaclav Klaus and Slovak Nationalist leader Vladimir Meciar agreed to the formation of a national caretaker government and on preparations for the transformation of the Czech lands and Slovakia into two separate countries.

26–27 Leaders of the 12 EC nations met in Lisbon, Portugal for their regular semiannual summit. The leaders agreed to push ahead toward implementation of the Maastricht Treaty.

23 The ANC's National Executive Committee met and decided to withdraw from constitutional negotiations at the 19-party Convention for a Democratic South Africa (Codesa) until the government took 'practical steps' to end the township violence.

23 Yitzhak Rabin's opposition Labour Party won a clear victory in Israeli national parliamentary elections, soundly defeating the Likud bloc led by Prime Minister Yitzak Shamir.

28 Socialist Giuliano Amato was sworn in as Italy's new premier.

29 Thirty-four lightly armed UN peacekeepers took charge of the airport of Sarajevo, the beseiged capital of Bosnia-Herzegovina. The airport had been held by Bosnian Serb Forces for nearly three months, preventing badly needed food and medicine from reaching the city.

29 Mohammed Boudiaf, the president of Algeria's ruling military council, was killed in a hail of machine-gun fire while giving a speech in the eastern coastal city of Annaba.

30 Fidel V Ramos was inaugurated as president of the Philippines.

NATIONAL

4 The Court of Appeal formally overturned the 1974 convictions of alleged IRA bomber Judith Ward, who had served more than 18 years in prison for crimes to which she had confessed out of apparent fantasies.

8 Social Security Secretary Peter Lilley announced a plan to provide £2.5 million in temporary aid to pensioners hurt by the collapse of companies controlled by the late publishing magnate Robert Maxwell.

15 Secretary of Defense Malcolm Rifkind announced that tactical nuclear weapons were to be removed from British navy ships and aircraft. The unilateral action would reduce Britain's nuclear stockpile by about 70 weapons.

18 Kevin and Ian Maxwell, sons of the late publisher Robert Maxwell, were arrested and charged with theft and fraud amounting to some £135 million.

GENERAL

1–9 John Demjanjuk, a Ukrainian-born US citizen who had been sentenced to death in 1988 for committing war crimes as a guard at a Nazi concentration camp during World War II, made a final appeal of his conviction before Israel's Supreme Court. Evidence produced at the hearing cast significant doubt on whether Demjanjuk was 'Ivan the Terrible', a notoriously cruel guard at the Treblinka death camp in Poland.

3 Australia's High Court in Sidney upheld land claims by Aborigines on the Murray Islands that predated European settlement in 1788.

3–14 The UN Conference on Environment and Development, more widely known as the Earth Summit, was held in Rio de Janeiro, Brazil.

Delegates from 178 countries reached accords at the talks on several landmark pacts intended to reconcile global economic development with environmental protection.

15 In a controversial decision, the US Supreme Court ruled that the US was entitled to kidnap criminal suspects from foreign countries for prosecution in the US, regardless of protests from the foreign countries or the terms of existing extradition treaties.

July 1992

INTERNATIONAL

2 After intense deliberation, Algeria's military-backed High State Council named Ali Kafi as its new president. Kafi replaced the nation's slain head of state, Mohammed Boudiaf.

3 Czechoslovak President Vaclav Hável failed to win reelection in the country's Federal Assembly (parliament).

4 The left-of-centre Social Democratic Party won a majority of seats in both houses of Nigeria's new National Assembly in general elections.

5–22 Tensions between Iraq and the UN over the UN's efforts to dismantle Iraq's arms-production programme were heightened, as Iraq refused to allow a UN inspection team to enter a ministry building in Baghdad where the team believed important records were stored.

7 The government of Macedonia resigned over its failure to convince other countries to unconditionally recognize Macedonian independence.

8 A meeting of the leaders of the G7 countries in Munich, Germany ended without a formal agreement on stalled international trade talks.

8 Thomas Klestil was sworn in as president of Austria. Klestil succeeded Kurt Waldheim, whose six-year tenure had been marked by a degree of isolation because of questions over his World War II service in the German army.

10 The Sejm, the lower house of Poland's parliament, confirmed Hanna Suchocka as premier and her 23-member parliament 11 July. Suchocka was Poland's first woman premier.

10 NATO and the Western European Union separately agreed to send warships to the Adriatic Sea to tighten the trade embargo imposed on Yugoslavia by the UN Security Council in May.

13 Serb forces in Bosnia-Herzegovina launched fresh military offensives. The date marked the 100th day of the Serb siege of Sarajevo, Bosnia-Herzegovina's capital.

13 The Israeli Knesset (parliament) voted 67-53, to confirm Yitzhak Rabin as Israel's prime minister and approve his coalition government.

14 The Yugoslav parliament confirmed Milan Panic, a Serbian-born US citizen, as Yugoslavia's premier.

16 Gov. Bill Clinton of Arkansas accepted the Democratic nomination for president at the close of the party's convention in New York City. Texas billionaire Ross Perot announced that he was dropping his US presidential bid.

16 The UN Security Council voted unanimously to send an emissary to South Africa to investigate violence in black townships.

19 Paolo Borsellino, the chief prosecutor in the Sicilian capital, Palermo, was killed there by a car bomb. The massive remote-controlled bomb also killed five of the magistrate's body guards; eighteen other people were injured.

19–23 US Secretary of State James Baker met with national leaders in the Middle East in an effort to restart the stalled Arab-Israeli peace talks.

21 Israeli Prime Minister Yitzhak Rabin travelled to Cairo for a meeting with Egyptian President Hosni Mubarak. Mubarak said he had accepted an invitation from Rabin to visit Israel.

23 Czech Premier Vaclav Klaus and Slovak Premier Vladimir Meciar agreed on a basic plan for a peaceful division of Czechoslovakia into two independent states by the end of Sept 1992.

24 Tensions between Georgia and Russia eased when Georgian State Council Chairman Shevardnadze, Russian President Yeltsin and leaders of the two Ossetian regions met at a resort in southern Russia and agreed to a cease-fire. Georgian and Russian peace-keeping troops had been deployed along Georgia's border with Ossetia, region of Georgia, 14 July in an attempt to halt fighting between Georgian guerrillas and Ossetian national guardsmen.

26 Iraq agreed to allow a team of UN arms experts to inspect an official building in Baghdad where the team believed information related to Iraq's nuclear-arms programme was stored. However, a search of the building revealed no arms-related evidence.

27 Estonian troops exchanged shots with Russian soldiers in the Estonian capital, Tallinn. The incident marked the latest serious episode in growing tensions over the issues of the continued presence in the Baltics of former Soviet troops and the rights of ethnic Russians in the region.

29 Eric Honecker, the leader of communist East Germany 1971–89, was flown to Berlin to stand trial on charges of manslaughter and misappropriating state funds.

NATIONAL

1 British Rail Corp. reported a loss of £44.7 million for its fiscal year through March.

7 Defense Secretary Malcolm Rifkind announced that the government would go ahead with its order for the fourth Trident nuclear-equipped submarine. Rifkind also presented an annual defense white paper outlining plans to keep annual defense spending in the £24 billion to £25 billion range through 1995.

10 Chancellor of the Exchequer Norman Lamont ruled out any devaluation of the pound, and expressed strong support for the exchange rate mechanism (ERM) of the European Monetary System.

14 The government issued a white paper outlining its plan to reduce government involvement in state-owned British Rail Corp.

18 John Smith was elected leader of the Labour Party. Smith, Labour's shadow chancellor of the Exchequer, had been the front-runner in the race since its start in mid-April after Neil Kinnock had announced his resignation.

24 The Labour Party unveiled its new shadow cabinet under John Smith. The new cabinet included five women.

GENERAL

5 Andre Agassi won his first Grand Slam tennis title when he triumphed in the men's final at Wimbledon. Steffi Graf defended her title by defeating Monica Seles of Yugoslavia 4 July.

9 The US space shuttle *Columbia* touched down at Cape Canaveral, Fla. The shuttle carried out a scientific mission devoted to testing the properties of various materials in the absence of gravity. The 14-day journey set a new endurance record for the shuttle program.

10 A judge in Miami sentenced former Panamanian leader Gen. Manuel Noriega to 40 years in prison on drug and racketeering charges.

19–24 The Eighth International Conference on AIDS was held in Amsterdam. The gathering, at which over 4,875 reports were heard, was dominated by reports of a mysterious illness whose victims had the symptoms of AIDS but did not test positive for the HIV virus that caused the disease.

22 Colombian drug baron Pablo Escobar broke out of prison in a battle with army soldiers that left six people dead. Escobar, a billionaire and the reputed head of the Medellin cartel, had surrendered to Colombian authorities in 1991 in exchange for a constitutional amendment prohibiting extradition and for permission to serve his sentence in a custom-built luxury prison.

31 All of the 113 passengers and crew aboard a Thai Airways jetliner were killed when the plane crashed in the Himalayan mountains northwest of Katmandu, Nepal, during a heavy rainstorm.

August 1992

INTERNATIONAL

2 Croatian President Franjo Tudjman was reelected in Croatia's first direct presidential election.

3 The US Senate voted in favour of legislation to impose an immediate moratorium and eventual ban on US nuclear testing.

3–4 Millions of blacks stayed home from work to pressure the South African government into accepting black majority rule. The strike brought industries to a standstill and emptied streets in the country's major cities. Township violence claimed the lives of at least 40 blacks 2-5 Aug.

4 The UN Security Council demanded that the International Red Cross and other relief agencies be allowed to inspect all detention centres in the former Yugoslavia. The demand followed an allegation of atrocities against Slavic Moslem and Croat civilians held in camps run by ethnic Serbs.

7 Yugoslav Premier Milan Panic vowed to close all Serb-run detention camps in Bosnia-Herzegovina. A British news team had filmed hundreds of detainees, mainly Moslems, at a Serb camp who appeared to be severely malnourished.

7 The warring factions in Mozambique's civil war agreed to a truce. The nation had been devastated by the 16-year-old conflict between the leftist government and the rightist Mozambique National Resistance.

11 Israeli Prime Minister Yitzhak Rabin and US President Bush announced that they had reached an agreement under which the US would grant $10 billion in loan guarantees to Israel. The loan guarantees had been a source of friction in US–Israeli relations since mid-1991.

13 The UN Security Council voted to authorize the use of military force to insure the delivery of humanitarian aid to Bosnia-Herzegovina. A second Security Council resolution, passed unanimously, condemned the Serbian policy of 'ethnic cleansing' through forced evacuations as a violation of international law.

18 Britain and France agreed to back a US plan to protect Shiite Moslems in Iraq from attacks by the Iraqi government. The 'no- fly zone' plan called for allied military aircraft to shoot down Iraqi fighter planes and helicopters that attempted to fly missions in predominantly Shiite southern Iraq.

20 President Bush accepted the Republican presidential nomination on the final night of the Republican National Convention in Houston.

22–26 Gangs of right-wing youths urging the expulsion of foreigners from Germany rioted on successive nights in the northeastern port city of

Rostock. About 150 people, half of them police officers, were injured and more than 200 arrests were made.

24 South Korea and China established diplomatic relations in a formal ceremony in Beijing. Taiwan broke diplomatic relations with South Korea following the formal announcement of the China-South Korea agreement.

25–26 About 1,500 ethnic Abkhaz militiamen and their allies from the ex-Soviet Caucasus area fought a fierce battle with Georgian troops near the town of Gagry in Western Georgia. The attack came eight days after Georgian troops had seized Sukhumi, the capital of Abkhazia, and set up an interim military government there.

26 The US, Britain and France ordered the Iraqi government to halt all aircraft flights over southern Iraq, as the 'no-fly zone' order went into effect.

27 The adversaries in the Yugoslav civil war agreed to comply with a framework accord aimed at bringing about peace. The accord was negotiated in London at a multilateral conference jointly sponsored by the EC and the UN. The agreements reached were, however, promptly undermined when it was revealed that there was no starting time in sight for the 96-hour deadline by which Bosnian Serbs agreed to place their heavy weapons under UN control.

28 Two unarmed UN military observers were shot and injured in Mogadishu, Somalia, during looting at the airport. The looters stole the UN's entire fuel stock, needed to deliver food to 4.5 million people facing starvation.

30 An artillery shell on an open marketplace killed at least 16 people in Sarajevo, capital of Bosnia-Herzegovina. The Serb attack was on a group of weekend shoppers, mainly women and children.

30 The ruling Liberal party of Quebec province gave its blessing to Canada's proposed constitution after a divisive debate at a two-day party convention in Quebec City.

NATIONAL

7 More than 2,500 passengers and crew abroad the Queen Elizabeth 2, the nation's best known cruise ship, were evacuated after the liner ran aground off the southern coast of Massachusetts, USA.

10 The government designated Northern Ireland's largest Protestant paramilitary group, the Ulster Defense Association, as an illegal organization.

11 A jury in London's Central Criminal Court convicted Simon Berkowitz of handling stolen property in connection with a document relating to an extramarital affair of Liberal Democratic leader Paddy Ashdown. The document's theft had prompted the politician to disclose the affair in February.

13 The Department of Employment released data showing that Britain's unemployment rate had risen to 9.7% of the work force in July. The rate marked a five-year high and was an indicator of Britain's persistent recession.

28 More than 2,000 job losses were announced by Swan Hunter, the shipbuilder, and Jaguar, the car maker, as the CBI said that economic pessimism among manufacturers had reached its worst level for 15 months.

GENERAL

5 The US Attorney in Los Angeles announced that a federal grand jury had indicted four white police officers on charges of violating the civil rights of Rodney King, a black motorist they had beaten in March 1991. The acquittal of three of the officers by a California jury in April had sparked riots in Los Angeles and other cities.

8 The US space shuttle *Atlantis* landed at Cape Canaveral, Florida. It had taken off 31 July on a troubled mission in which a European scientific probe initially missed its proper orbit and a tethered satellite failed to unreel to its full length.

16 The XXV Summer Olympic Games in Barcelona, Spain, concluded after two weeks of competition. Athletes from 12 former Soviet republics, competing as the 'Unified Team', won the most medals of any nation – 112.

24–26 Hurricane Andrew ravaged the US mainland, after striking the Bahamas 23 Aug. Damage estimates varied widely, but the storm was considered the costliest in US history.

September 1992

INTERNATIONAL

27 Aug–3 US and British warplanes began patrolling the skies above southern Iraq to enforce an allied ban on Iraqi military and civilian flights over the region.

3 An Italian military transport plane flying UN relief supplies to Sarajevo crashed on its approach to Sarajevo airport, killing all four crew members on board. Witnesses claimed that the plane had been brought down by at least one surface-to-air missile. The UN suspended all aid flights to Sarajevo (relief flights were resumed 13 Sept).

7 Soldiers in the nominally independent bantustan ('homeland') of Ciskei, South Africa, fired on ANC marchers who were demanding the ouster of the territory's military ruler – up to 28 people were killed and about 200 injured.

8 Two French UN peace-keeping soldiers were shot dead outside Sarajevo, the capital of Bosnia-Herzegovina.

12 Peruvian police captured Abimael Guzman Reynoso, the elusive leader of Sendero Luminoso (Shining Path), a Maoist guerrilla group that had waged a violent, 12-year insurrection against the government.

14 The first armed UN peace-keeping troops arrived in Somalia to insure that relief agencies were able to distribute food to the starving populace.

17 The Bank of Italy decided to withdraw the lira from the European Monetary System (EMS) after devaluation had failed to stabilize the currency, and Britain had decided 16 Sept to remove the pound from the EMS.

17 Ecuador officially withdrew from OPEC. OPEC's annual $2 million membership fee and strict production limits were cited as reasons for withdrawal.

22 The UN General Assembly expelled Yugoslavia from the UN for its alleged role in the war in Bosnia-Herzegovina. The resolution, pushed by EC states, marked the first time in the history of the UN that a sitting member had been ejected from the world body.

23 Chuan Leekpai, a pro-democracy activist, was named premier of Thailand. Chuan headed a fragile five-party coalition that emerged following 13 Sept parliamentary elections.

24 The sixth round of peace talks between Arab and Israeli negotiators concluded in Washington DC. Although amicable, the talks failed to result in a hoped-for agreement between Israel and Syria over control of the disputed Golan Heights region.

27 In protest against what he called the 'illegitimite' deals struck between South African President de Klerk and ANC President Mandela 26 Sept, Inkatha President Mangosuthu Buthelezi broke off relations with the government, withdrew from Codesa, and threatened to oppose the creation of an interim government.

29 A court in Tokyo fined Shin Kanemaru, one of Japan's leading political power brokers, 200,000 yen ($1,700) for improperly accepting a 500 million yen ($4 million) contribution from a former official of Tokyo Sagawa Kyubin Co, a Japanese transport company.

NATIONAL

3 Kevin Maxwell, the youngest son of the late media magnate Robert Maxwell, was declared bankrupt by the High Court. The sum Maxwell owed to his creditors, £406.5 million, made his case the biggest-ever personal bankruptcy in Britain.

7–10 The 124th annual Trades Union Congress was held in Blackpool. The meeting was marked by numerous delegates' acknowledgement of the declining influence of unions, and many union leaders signalled a shift away from left-wing economic policies towards the free-market principles of the Conservatives.

16 The British government suspended the pound from its participation in the European Monetary System (EMS).The decision was announced after the Bank of England had failed to stem the currency's fall below its floor in the EMS exchange rate mechanism (ERM) against the German mark, despite two sharp interest-rate increases during the day. The move had significant political importance because Prime Minister Major had staked his economic programme on defending the pound and preventing its devaluation.

22 The Bank of England engineered a one-percentage-point cut in Britain's base interest rate.

24 Prime Minister John Major defended his government's economic policies during an emergency debate in the House of Commons. Major had recalled Parliament from its recess in the wake of Britain's 16 Sept withdrawal from the ERM. Following the economic debate, Major won a vote of confidence by a narrow, but expected, margin of 330 to 288.

24 Dogged by reports of an extramarital affair and personal gifts from a member of a prominent Palestinian family, National Heritage Secretary David Mellor announced his resignation.

GENERAL

1 An earthquake under the Pacific Ocean floor hit Nicaragua, causing tidal waves along the breadth of the Pacific coast that reached a height of 50ft/15m; 116 people were killed, and over 16,000 made homeless.

1 Bobby Fischer emerged from self-imposed seclusion to attend a press conference in Sveti Stevan, Yugoslavia, the day before he was to begin playing his old rival, Boris Spassky, in an exhibition tournament with prize money totalling $5 million. Warned by the US Treasury Department that the match would be considered a breach of UN sanctions against Yugoslavia and that he could face up to 10 years in prison, Fischer spat on the warning letter during the conference.

8–18 Floods killed more than 2,000 people, damaged some two million acres of crops, and devastated villages throughout Pakistan. An additional 500 people were killed in northern sections of India.

13 Stefan Edberg of Sweden defeated Pete Sampras to win his second straight US Open tennis title; Monica Seles had defended her tournament title 12 Sept with a victory over Arantxa Sanchez Vicario of Spain.

25 The USA launched the *Mars Observer*, an unmanned spacecraft designed to orbit Mars and collect information about it.

28 Law-enforcement officials from the USA, Colombia, and Italy announced that they had arrested more than 165 people in six nations on charges related to a money-laundering scheme involving the Italian Mafia and the leading Colombian cocaine cartel. About $42 million, identified as illegal drug profits, had been seized in what the US Drug Enforcement Administartion described as the first instance of international cooperation on a case of this nature.

October 1992

INTERNATIONAL

1 Texas billionaire Ross Perot announced that he was reversing his 16 July decision not to run for president, and was re-entering the race as an independent.

1 The Bosnian government said that 14,364 people – including 1,447 children – had died in fighting in Bosnia since April 1992. The government claimed that 57,000 people, including 8,500 children, were missing.

2 Vice President Itamar Franco became acting president of Brazil following President Fernando Collor de Mello's 29 Sept impeachment on corruption charges.

4 The opposing factions in Mozambique's 16-year-old civil war formerly signed a peace accord in Rome. The two sides had agreed to the deal in principle in Aug.

5 Political opponents of Kuwait's ruling Sabah family won a majority of seats in the emirate's National Assembly, as Kuwait held its first parliamentary elections since 1985. The franchise was restricted to about 14% of all Kuwaiti citizens since the right to vote in Kuwait was reserved solely for men over 21 whose families had lived in Kuwait before 1921.

7 Hong Kong Governor Chris Patten unveiled his government's plans for the next five years in the run-up to China's scheduled takeover of the colony in 1997. Patten's speech included calls for increased democracy despite China's opposition. A statement issued by China's official press agency denounced the political implications of Patten's plan as 'irresponsible and imprudent'.

3–11 Tensions between Georgia and Russia rose amid allegations that the Russian military was arming, aiding, and encouraging secessionist Abkhaz guerrillas and their allies who, 2-6 Oct, reclaimed about one-half of Abkhazia in a surprise offensive against Georgian forces.

7–18 A hunger-strike by Palestinian prisoners provoked a wave of unrest and violence in Israel and Israeli-occupied territories.

16 The leaders of the 12 EC nations held a 'mini-summit' in Birmingham, England. The meeting, called in the wake of Sept's European monetary crisis, sought to rejuvenate the community's moves towards closer unity.

21 The Russian Supreme Soviet voted, 114-59, to reject a proposal by President Yeltsin to postpone the scheduled winter session of the Congress of People's Deputies. The rejection cleared the way for an anticipated showdown between law makers and the Yeltsin regime over economic reform.

21–28 Arab and Israeli negotiators gathered in Washington DC to begin their seventh round of bilateral peace talks; the discussions were hampered by uncertainty over the outcome of the US presidential elections.

22 Lebanese President Elias Hrawi named Sunni Moslem businessman Rafik Hariri to serve as Lebanon's premier.

25 The Democratic Labour Party, made up of reformed ex-Communists, won Lithuania's first post-Soviet parliamentary elections.

27 Special mediators Cyrus Vance of the UN and Lord Owen of the EC offered a power-sharing plan they hoped would bring peace to Bosnia-Herzegovina and preserve the country's territorial integrity. Under the plan, Bosnia would be divided into up to 10 ethnically mixed cantons, with built-in guarantees of power-sharing and human rights.

NATIONAL

28 Sept–2 The Labour Party held its annual conference in Blackpool. The conference, under the direction of new party leader John Smith, was generally characterized as a relatively calm one.

6–9 The Conservative Party held its annual conference in Brighton. The gathering was dominated by splits among the Tories on further European integration.

13 Secretary of Trade and Industry Michael Heseltine announced that the British Coal Co. would close 31 coal mines for economic reasons, putting 30,000 miners out of work. The plan was met with widespread public and ministerial criticism.

16 The Bank of England engineered a one-percentage-point cut in banks' base interest rates, to 8% from 9%. The decrease was widely seen as an attempt to deflect criticism from the government's coal plan.

21 Even after the government amended its proposal, announcing plans to shut only 10 mines, the plan was approved by the House of Commons by a slender margin of 320-307.

23 British Airways agreed to take over troubled Dan-Air Services Ltd carrier, Britain's oldest independent airline.

26 An elaborate pageant for Queen Elizabeth II, in celebration of the 40th anniversary of her accession to the throne, was held in the Earls Court Arena in London.

GENERAL

1–2 Scientists released the first two maps of human chromosomes, which were the carriers of genetic information. The achievement was part of the Human Genome Project, an international effort to determine the sequence of all human genes.

2 The Japanese government said it would allow a restaurant chain to import frozen sushi from the USA.

4 An Israeli El Al cargo plane crashed into an apartment complex in a suburb of Amsterdam, setting off a fire that ravaged the crowded complex. All four people aboard the plane died instantly, and scores were killed on the ground.

12 NASA began a systematic search of the universe for signs of intelligent extraterrestrial life. The project's commencement coincided with commemorations of the 500th anniversary of Christopher Columbus' arrival in the New World.

12 A strong earthquake wreaked havoc in and around the Egyptian capital, Cairo; 450 persons were killed and 4,000 injured. Most of the more than 160 buildings reported destroyed or badly damaged were located in low-income neighbourhoods, where much of the housing was poorly constructed.

23 A court in Paris convicted three French health officials on charges that they had knowingly allowed blood products tainted with the AIDS virus to be used for transfusions. An estimated 1,200 haemophiliacs had been infected with the HIV virus since the early 1980s, and more than 250 had died from the disease.

November 1992

INTERNATIONAL

1 A truce was established between the Angolan government and the Union of Total Independence of Angola (UNITA) following three days of heavy fighting in Luanda, the capital, in which at least 1,000 lives were claimed.

3 Arkansas Governor Bill Clinton (Democrat) was elected the 42nd president of the USA, ending 12 consecutive years of Republican control of the White House. Clinton, born in 1946, would be the first member of the post-war generation to lead the nation.

4 Voters chose military leader Jerry Rawlings to head a new civilian government in Ghana's first presidential elections since 1979.

5 Ireland's coalition government collapsed when Prime Minister Albert Reynolds lost a vote of confidence in the Dail (parliament).

5 The USA said it planned to add a 200% tariff on $300 million worth of export goods from the EC in retaliation for the EC's refusal to agree to US demands that it further reduce agricultural subsidies. The targeted items included white wine, wheat gluten, and rapeseed oil.

8 An estimated 350,000 people joined a demonstration in Berlin to protest a recent increase in right-wing violence against foreigners in Germany.

8 President Gaviria Trujillo declared a state of emergency to combat an avalanche of insurgent and drug-related terror that had shaken Colombia.

16 The UN Security Council authorized a naval blockade against Yugoslavia as a means of tightening sanctions imposed on the country by the council in May.

16–19 The South African government was rocked by revelations that the Defence Force had plotted a 'dirty tricks' campaign against the ANC May-Dec 1991. President de Klerk shuffled the top ranks of the military intelligence services and promised an internal investigation.

19 The UN Security Council approved an arms embargo against Liberia, and instructed the secretary general to send a special envoy their to report on its ongoing civil war.

19 Sweden's central bank, the Riksbank, announced it was ending the link between its currency, the krona, and the European curency unit (ECU). Sweden was not a member of the EC but was applying to join.

20 Trade officials from the USA and the EC reached agreement on a plan to reduce EC agricultural subsidies to oilseed producers. The accord eliminated a major obstacle hindering global trade talks.

22 The EC's finance committee agreed to devalue the currencies of Spain and Portugal within the exchange rate mechanism (ERM) of the European Monetary System. The ERM alignment was the third in 10 weeks.

23–30 The German government announced a series of measures designed to crack down on right-wing extremist violence against foreigners in Germany. The actions followed the deaths of two Turkish girls and a Turkish woman in a fire bombing 23 Nov.

30 China further escalated the conflict with Hong Kong's government over Governor Chris Patten's plan for democratic reform by warning that it would consider voiding all commercial agreements made by the Hong Kong government when the colony's sovereignty reverted to China in 1997.

30 The UN Security Council imposed a trade embargo on the areas of Cambodia controlled by the Khmer Rouge. The move was a response to the guerrilla group's refusal to cooperate with the terms of a peace accord signed in Paris in 1991.

NATIONAL

4 Prime Minister John Major narrowly won a key vote in the House of Commons concerning Britain's role in the EC. Major had forced a vote on a motion calling for Britain to 'play a leading role in the development of the European Community' in preparation for British ratification of the Maastricht Treaty.

10 The prime minister ordered an independent inquiry into allegations that the British government had permitted the sale of sophisticated manufacturing equipment to Iraq by British firms 1987–90, despite evidence that Iraq was using the equipment to make high-technology conventional weapons.

10 Talks aimed at forming a new system of government for Northern Ireland broke down. The talks, held on and off for 18 months amongst the British and Irish governments and Northern Ireland's leading political parties, produced no formal agreements.

11 The governing body of the Church of England narrowly voted to allow women to become priests.

12 The government outlined its spending plans for the 1993-94 fiscal year in the annual Autumn Economic Statement by the chancellor of the Exchequer. Lamont's plan included some immediate actions designed to stimulate the economy out of its recession – the longest since the 1930s – and announced that the base interest rate was being cut by one percentage point, to 7%.

26 Prime Minister Major announced that Queen Elizabeth II had decided to begin paying taxes on her personal income.

27 National Heritage Secretary Peter Brook announced that the government would provide funds to repair Windsor Castle, which belonged to the state rather than to the queen herself. The castle, 30m/50km west of London, had been heavily damaged 20 Nov by a fire in its 14th-century St George's Hall.

GENERAL

1 The US space shuttle *Columbia* touched down after carrying out a scientific mission in which an Italian probe to monitor the Earth's crust was deployed and a Canadian sensor for the winged craft's robot arm was tested.

5 Bobby Fischer, the former US world chess champion, completed his victory over Boris Spassky with a 10th win in the 30th game of their nine-week contest.

16 The Roman Catholic Church issued a new universal cathechism for the first time in more than four centuries. The new compendium of teachings reiterated traditional churh views, but was updated to address modern-day issues.

24 A Chinese airliner crashed into a mountain 15m/25km from its destination in the southern city of Guilin. All 141 passengers and crew aboard the Boeing 737 were killed in the crash.

25 Representatives of 93 nations agreed to speed up their efforts to phase out the production and use of chemicals that damaged the Earth's protective ozone layer. Under the agreement, reached by the 1987 Montreal Protocol, signatory nations would bring forward their deadlines for the elimination of some hazardous chemicals, and place regulations on others for the first time.

December 1992

INTERNATIONAL

6 Thousands of militant Hindus destroyed a 16th-century mosque in the north Indian city of Ayodhya, igniting a nationwide firestorm of sectarian conflict. By 9 Dec, the death toll in India exceeded 700 after three days of rioting between Moslems and Hindus.

9 About 1,800 US Marines arrived in the Somali capital of Mogadishu as the vanguard of 'Operation Restore Hope'. The UN Security Council had unanimously voted 3 Dec to send a large US-led military force to famine-stricken and war-torn Somalia to safeguard the delivery of food.

9 Russian President Boris Yeltsin suffered his most humiliating political setback when the Congress of People's Deputies voted against confirming Acting Premier Yegor Gaidar as premier. Gaidar was the chief architect of Russia's unpopular radical economic reforms.

11 The two main warlords in Mogadishu, the Somali capital, signed a US-brokered peace accord that took effect immediately. US marines began escorting food convoys into the city of Baidoa 16 Dec.

8–13 Police and armed forces in Egypt launched a crackdown on Islamic militants suspected of involvement in a wave of attacks on tourists.

11–13 The leaders of the 12 EC nations reached a series of compromise agreements at a semimannual summit in Edinburgh, Scotland, which included approval of limited participation of Denmark in closer union, and a budget accord aimed at helping poorer EC nations.

15 Bettino Craxi, the leader of Italy's Socialist Party, was informed that he was under investigation in a burgeoning corruption scandal that had racked the northern city of Milan.

16 US Secretary of State Lawrence Eagleberger made public a list of Serbs and Croats who he suggested should be brought before an international war-crimes tribunal for their alleged roles in atrocities in Bosnia-Herzegovina.

16 Japanese Premier Kiichi Miyazawa restructured his cabinet, in an attempt to boost public confidence in the ruling Liberal Democratic Party, which had been shaken by several severe political scandals.

16 The UN Security Council voted to send about 7,500 peace-keeping forces to Mozambique to monitor an Oct cease-fire and organize elections.

17 Israel deported 415 Palestinians to Lebanese territory in an unprecedented mass expulsion of suspected militants. The action came after a series of attacks by Arabs on Israeli security forces that culminated with the kidnapping and murder of a border guard. The expulsions were condemned by the US government and by the UN secretary general, and led to a Palestinian boycott of ongoing Arab–Israeli peace talks in Washington DC.

17 Leaders of the USA, Canada, and Mexico signed the North American Free Trade Agreement (NAFTA), to be ratified by their respective governments.

18 Former dissident Kim Young Sam, the candidate of the ruling Democratic Liberal Party, was elected president in the first all-civilian South Korean presidential elections in more than 30 years.

18 The UN Security Council voted unanimously to condemn Israel's expulsion of 415 Palestinians. The UN action came as Lebanon refused to allow the deportees to enter its territory, leaving them trapped in a no-man's land between Lebanese and Israeli army positions.

19 President de Klerk conceded for the first time that top members of the South African Defense Force had run a renegade 'third force' to foment violence in black townships and derail the transition to black majority rule.

20–28 US and European troops secured several key Somali towns as part of the ongoing, multinational 'Operation Restore Hope'.

21–29 The plight of the Palestinian deportees worsened when Israel and Lebanon refused to allow Red Cross and other relief groups to take food and medical supplies to their camps. On 28 Dec the Israeli army had announced that 10 of the Palestinians had been wrongly deported and would be allowed to return to Israel.

23 Russian President Yeltsin approved a new cabinet that included most members of the liberal economic-reform team of former Acting Premier Gaidar.

27 A US fighter plane shot down an Iraqi military aircraft that entered the 'no-fly zone' patrolled by the USA and its allies over southern Iraq.

28 Brazil, Argentina, Paraguay, and Uruguay agreed to form a common economic market effective 1 Jan 1995.

28 Khien Samphan, the nominal leader of the Khmer Rouge guerrilla faction, warned that UN personnel would be taken captive if they attempted to monitor UN sanctions in the Khmer Rouge-controlled area of Cambodia.

29 Yugoslav Premier Milan Panic was ousted from office by the country's nationalist-dominated parliament.

NATIONAL

5 Police in London disclosed that they had begun setting up roadblocks and conducting random searches of vehicles in an attempt to thwart a continuing bombing campaign by the IRA. In the largest recent bombing, more than 60 people were injured 3 Dec by two explosions about 90 minutes apart during the morning rush hour in Manchester; a bombing in a shopping district of Belfast, Northern Ireland, 1 Dec injured 27 people.

9 Prime Minister John Major announced that Charles and Diana, the prince and princess of Wales, had 'decided to separate'. The Church of England issued a statement saying that the separation would not prevent Charles from leading the Church.

17 The government reported that Britain's unemployment rate rose to 10.3% in November, reaching the highest level since May 1987.

21 The High Court ruled that the government's plan to close coal mines had not been reached in a legal manner. Nonetheless, the government and the British Coal Co. 22 Dec said it would not immediately reopen 10 mines closed or set for closure.

GENERAL

3 The Greek oil tanker *Aegean Sea* ran aground in bad weather near La Coruña, Spain. The ship split in two, caught fire and sank, creating an oil slick that within two days had spread along 60mi/100km of Spain's Atlantic coastline.

4 Representatives of 41 countries concluded a meeting in Montevideo, Uruguay, during which implementation of the 1989 Basel Convention restricting trade in toxic wastes was discussed. The pact, designed to prevent industrialized nations from dumping hazardous wastes in developing nations, had gone into effect in May, but among the USA, Japan, and the EC-12, only France had ratified the treaty.

6 The USA recaptured the Davis Cup by defeating Switzerland in the finals in Fort Worth, Texas.

12 A strong earthquake devastated the island of Flores, Indonesia. The death toll was placed at nearly 2,500.

15 The environment ministers of the EC agreed to end the production and use of the ozone-harming chemicals known as chlorofluorcarbons (CFCs) by Jan 1995 – one year earlier than the phase-out date set at an international conference in Nov.

21 A Dutch DC-10 jet crashed while landing at an airport in Faro, southern Portugal, killing 54 people aboard.

22 A Libyan Arab Airlines jetliner crashed on a domestic flight from Benghazi to Tripoli, Libya's capital, killing all 157 passengers and crew aboard the plane.

January 1993

INTERNATIONAL

1 Czechoslovakia split into two separate states, the Czech Republic and Slovakia. The peaceful division, engineered in 1992, was completed despite opinion polls indicating profoundly mixed feelings among Czechoslovaks.

2 A new round of peace talks aimed at ending the civil war in Bosnia-Herzegovina opened in Geneva. The leaders of the rival ethnic groups involved in the conflict failed to accept the Vance-Owen peace plan, which proposed to split Bosnia-Herzegovina into 10 semi-autonomous provinces.

3 US President George Bush and Russian President Boris Yeltsin signed the second Strategic Arms Reduction Treaty (START) in Moscow. The treaty called for both sides to slash their long-range nuclear arsenals to about one-third of their current levels, and would entirely eliminate land-based, multiple-warhead missiles.

3–21 Fighting between the Angolan government and the rebel UNITA took place in at least 12 towns, as the country appeared to be sliding back into full-scale civil war.

7 Four hundred US marines raided a camp belonging to one of Somalia's most powerful warlords, General Aidid, in the biggest clash to date in 'Operation Restore Hope'.

7–8 Bosnian President Izetbegovic visited the USA to plead his government's case for Western military aid and intervention to halt Serbian aggression.

12 Sectarian violence continued for the eighth consecutive day in Bombay, India, the newest focal point in nationwide clashes that had claimed 200 lives.

12 The Irish parliament approved the new coalition government of Prime Minister Albert Reynolds.

13 More than 100 US, British, and French warplanes attacked Iraqi batteries and radar stations, in response to stepped-up defiance of UN and allied peace-keeping measures by Iraqi President Hussein's regime.

13 Former East German leader Erich Honecker was freed from a Berlin prison after courts ruled that he was too ill to continue standing trial on charges of manslaughter. He flew to Chile where he was reunited with his wife.

19 The Iraqi government declared a cease-fire following a series of punitive attacks by the allies on Iraqi targets, and announced that it would no longer attack or harrass US and allied planes patrolling Kurdish and Shiite Moslem enclaves in Iraq.

20 William Jefferson Clinton took the oath of office to become the 42nd president of the USA.

20 The self-styled Serbian parliament of Bosnia-Herzegovina voted to approve the Vance-Owen peace plan proposed in Geneva. The vote came a week after the Bosnian Serb leader, Radovan Karadzic, heavily pressured by Serbian President Milosevic, had reversed himself and backed the peace plan.

22 The Croatian army launched a ground offensive against a Serbian-held enclave near the Adriatic Sea, and by 27 Jan the Serbs had begun a counter attack against the Croatian army. The fighting shattered a year-old UN-supervised truce, and threatened to derail ongoing peace talks in Geneva.

25 US and Belgian forces routed a column of Somali guerrillas who were apparently advancing on the city of Kismayu. It was the first time that foreign troops had used force to impose the cease-fire in Somalia.

27 The US Commerce Department imposed tariffs on steel imports from 19 countries. The move brought sharp criticism from the affected nations (which included some EC members) and further threatened the progress of ongoing world trade talks.

28 The Angolan government and UNITA met in Addis Ababa, the Ethiopian capital, for talks aimed at halting the fighting in Angola.

28–29 Fighting broke out in Kinshasa, the Zairean capital, when mutinous army soldiers went on a looting spree and battled troops loyal to President Mobutu Sese Seko.

30 Ireland devalued its currency, the punt, within the EC's exchange rate mechanism.

NATIONAL

3 Prime Minister John Major said that Britain would not rejoin the EC's exchange rate mechanism (ERM) in 1993.

11 British Airways agreed to pay libel damages to Richard Branson, head of Virgin Atlantic Airways, in connection with an alleged 'dirty tricks' scheme by BA against Virgin.

14 The government pledged to introduce legislation to criminalize invasions of privacy by the press, but was reluctant to pursue aspects of the contoversial Calcutt report, including the creation of a statutory tribunal. Much of the press coverage previously criticized as intrusive had been about the private lives of the British royal family.

21 The government reported that the number of unemployed workers in the country rose to a seasonally adjusted total of 2.97 million in Dec 1992, marking the 32nd consecutive monthly rise in the jobless total.

26 The Bank of England announced a one percentage point reduction in base lending rates. The new rate, of 6%, was the lowest since the fall of 1977.

28 Solicitors for Prime Minister John Major issued writs for libel against two magazines – the *New Statesman & Soc* and *Scallywag* – after they published stories detailing rumours of an alleged romantic affair between Major and Clare Latimer, a caterer. Both parties denied having a relationship.

GENERAL

5 A Japanese ship carrying more than a ton of plutonium arrived in Tokai, Japan following a two-month journey from France that had provoked criticism from several nations and environmental organizations.

5 The US-owned oil tanker *Braer* was driven aground by a heavy storm at the southern tip of the Shetland Islands, 100mi/160km north-northeast of Scotland in the North Sea. By 12 Jan, huge waves had shattered the ship's hull, spilling its cargo of 26 million gallons (100 million litres) of crude oil.

13 More than 120 nations, including the USA and Russia, in Paris began signing a landmark treaty that would outlaw the manufacture, stockpiling, and use of chemical weapons. The treaty, which represented the first verifiable disarmament treaty to eliminate an entire category of weapons of mass destruction, would take effect no earlier than 15 Jan 1995.

13–19 The US space shuttle *Endeavour* carried out a mission in which an information satellite was placed in orbit, and X-ray monitors studied the Milky Way galaxy.

14 A Polish ferry capsized in the Baltic Sea, killing dozens of passengers and crew.

15 Italian police announced that they had arrested Salvatore (Toto) Riina, said to be the 'boss of bosses' of Italian organized crime, and Italy's most wanted man.

19 International Business Machines Corp (IBM) announced a loss of US$4.97 billion for 1992, the largest single-year loss in US corporate history.

February 1993

INTERNATIONAL

29 Jan–2 The Cambodian government carried out a large-scale military offensive against Khmer Rouge guerrillas in north-central and western Cambodia. A UN spokesman declared that the government forces had 'exceeded their right of self-defense.'

1 The Israeli government announced that it would accept the return of about 100 of the more than 400 Palestinians it had deported to Lebanon, and would allow the remainder to return home within a year. Welcomed by the US government, the compromise was however criticized by Israeli right-wing leaders and by Arabs at the UN.

1 US Secretary of State Warren Christopher announced that he and UN Secretary General Boutros Boutros-Ghali had agreed that a UN peace-keeping force should replace US soldiers in Somalia 'in the relatively near future'.

4 Germany's central bank, the Bundesbank, cut two of its key interest rates. The action, which coincided with a lowering of interest rates in Japan, helped ease pressure on the EC's exchange rate mechanism.

7 Australian Prime Minister Paul Keating called a general election for 13 March. The government's most pressing problem was the nation's unemployment rate, which was at its highest level since the depression of the 1930s.

10 The USA announced that it would put 'full weight' behind the ongoing Bosnia peace process mediated by the UN and EC, ending weeks of speculation about what President Clinton's policy would be, and of hints that the USA would use military force against Serb belligerents.

12 After three days of talks, the South African government and the ANC reached an agreement on a transitional 'government of national unity' in which both parties would be partners for five years.

12 The Moslem-led Bosnian government announced that it would not accept further UN food and medical aid shipments to beseiged Sarajevo until the UN succeeded in getting relief convoys past Serbian blockades to Moslems trapped in eastern Bosnia-Herzegovina. The UN responded 13 Feb by suspending all relief flights to Sarajevo and, on 17 Feb, suspended most of its relief operations throughout Bosnia-Herzegovina.

14 Haiti's military junta allowed 40 human rights observers to enter Haiti under the first stage of a UN-brokered plan that sought to restore democracy to the country.

15 Algirdas Brazauskas, leader of the Democratic Labour Party (formerly the Communist Party), was declared the winner in Lithuania's presidential elections.

17 President Clinton presented his economic programme; his proposals included tax increases and spending reductions that would total US$ 493 billion over four years.

19–26 UN Secretary General Boutros Boutros-Ghali ordered the aid efforts in Bosnia-Herzegovina to resume. Serb forces finally permitted the UN convoy to reach the town of Zepa, and the Bosnian government then allowed relief flights to Sarajevo to resume. A second convoy was blocked by the Serbs for three days before it was allowed to continue to the town of Gorazde.

22 The UN Security Council unanimously approved the creation of an international cour to try war crimes committed in the former Yugoslavia.

24 Canadian Prime Minister Brian Mulroney resigned his leadership of the Progressive Conservative Party and, with it, the office of prime minister. Mulroney, who had been in office eight years, was chiefly motivated by a desire to give his party better prospects in a general election which would have to be held by November.

24–25 Mogadishu, the Somali capital, was hit by rioting and antiforeigner demonstrations led by supporters of General Mohammed Aidid, the country's most powerful warlord.

25 Some 80,000 police and paramilitary troops prevented Hindu nationalists from holding a mass rally in New Delhi, to demand the resignation of Prime Minister Rao and his government.

NATIONAL

8 Labour Party leader John Smith said that his party would force a vote on an amendment concerning the Treaty on European Union's 'Social Chapter' on labour restrictions, from which Britain was exempted. Labour's position threatened to derail Britain's ratification of treaty.

22 Two 10-year-old boys were arraigned in the Liverpool area and charged with the 12 Feb abduction and murder of a two-year-old boy, James Bulger. The murder attracted international attention and fanned widespread fears for the safety of children nationally as the public perceptions of a sharp increase of youth crime were heightened.

24–25 Prime Minister Major visited Washington DC and held talks with President Clinton. Major, who was the first European leader invited to the Clinton White House, was seeking to maintain the so-called special relationship between Britain and the USA.

25 A parliamentary subcommittee sharply criticized the Bank of England for its poor supervision of the coruption-ridden Bank of Commerce and Credit International.

GENERAL

4 Russian scientists unfurled a giant mirror in orbit and flashed a beam of sunlight across Europe during the night. The reflected ray, which had the intensity of several full moons, sped across the surface of the Atlantic Ocean, Europe, and Russia for eight minutes. Observers saw it only as an instantaneous flash.

8 All 132 passengers and crew aboard an Iran Air passenger jet were killed minutes after take-off when the plane collided with a military aircraft.

11 A gun-wielding Ethiopian student hijacked a Lufthansa Airbus 310 and forced it from Austria to New York City. The 20-year-old student surrendered without a struggle after landing in New York; none of the passengers and crew aboard the plane was injured.

26 A massive bomb exploded in a garage below the World Trade Center in New York City, killing five people. Mohammed Salameh, described as a Moslem fundamentalist, was arrested in connection with the bombing.

28 Four US federal agents were killed and more than a dozen wounded when law-enforcement officials launched an abortive raid on the compound of a cult, the Branch Davidians, near Waco, Texas. A stand-off between the authorities and heavily armed members of the religious cult, led by David Koresh, began.

March 1993

INTERNATIONAL

4–11 Despite continued promises by Serb leaders to allow relief convoys through, UN efforts to evacuate wounded Moslem civilians from eastern Bosnia-Herzegovina were frustrated as Serb militiamen pressed their attacks and blocked UN aid convoys.

7 Huambo, Angola's second-most-populous town, fell to rebel UNITA forces after a fierce 56–day battle. UNITA was now reported to control more than half of Angola's territory.

7 The leaders of eight rival Afghan military factions announced a peace agreement in Islamabad, Pakistan. The treaty was intended to end months of fighting to control Kabul, the capital, and other regions in Afghanistan.

9–10 At least 19 people died when Egyptian security forces conducted raids against alleged Islamic militants. The raids followed 6 March extremist attack on a Coptic Christian church in Aswan in which a soldier was killed.

10 Palestinian leaders rejected a US-Russian invitation to resume Arab-Israeli peace talks on 20 April, insisting that they would not return to peace negotiations until Israel ended its policy of deportations.

10–13 Russia's Congress of People's Deputies met in a special session and acted to limit powers that had been granted to President Yeltsin in a Dec 1992 compromise. The results of the meeting, which included a resolution canceling a referendum scheduled for 11 April, were widely viewed as having weakened Yeltsin in his power struggle with the congress. The president indicated that he would nonetheless proceed with the referendum on the division of powers, giving 25 April as the new date.

11 Indonesian President Suharto was sworn in for an uncontested sixth consecutive five-year term; Suharto had pursued autocratic rule since he came to power in 1966.

12 North Korea announced that it would withdraw from the Nuclear Non-proliferation Treaty, the international pact designed to limit the spread of nuclear arms sales.

12–30 As peace talks to end the civil war in Bosnia-Herzegovina faltered, UN relief and evacuation efforts in eastern Bosnia-Herzegovina had some small successes. On 28 March 20 UN trucks carrying food and medicine reached the beseiged town of Srebrenica, which had commanded international attention as the headquarters of General Morillon, commander of UN forces in Bosnia-Herzegovina.

13 The Australian Labour Party, led by Prime Minister Paul Keating, won an unprecedented fifth consecutive three-year term in national elections, defeating the Liberal Party–National Party opposition coalition, headed by John Hewson.

20 As the power struggle between Russian President Yeltsin and his parliament continued, Yeltsin claimed special emergency powers and confirmed 25 April as the date for a popular vote of confidence in him and his vice president, General Rutskoi.

24 President de Klerk revealed that South Africa had built six primitive atomic bombs during a secret 15-year programme, and that the weapons had been destroyed in 1990.

26 The UN Security Council unanimously approved a resolution to send the biggest peacekeeping force in UN history to Somalia. The contingent, which would take over from a US-led coalition that had been stationed in Somalia since Dec 1992, would include at least 28,000 peacekeeping soldiers, and 2,800 civilians who would take over the administration of the country.

27 Giulio Andreotti, seven-time premier of Italy, disclosed that he was under investigation in Sicily for possible associations with organized crime. The following day, five leading politicians in Naples were informed that they were under investigation for ties to the Camorra, the leading organized crime gang in that city.

28 Russian President Yeltsin narrowly survived an impeachment vote by the Congress of People's Deputies.

29 President François Mitterand named Edouard Balladur, a member of the neo-Gaullist Rally for the Republic party, premier of France following a general election landslide victory for the nation's conservative parties.

30 Israeli Prime Minister Yitzhak Rabin announced that Israel would indefinitely seal the West Bank and Gaza Strip following a month of heightened violence between Israelis and Palestinians.

NATIONAL

4 Authorities claimed that they had made significant gains against the IRA with a number of arrests of suspected IRA operatives in England.

8 Prime Minister Major suffered a setback when the House of Commons voted to amend legislation to ratify the EC's Treaty on European Union (or Maastricht Treaty). The minor amendment, proposed by the Labour Party, would require British representatives to a new EC European Committee of the Regions to be chosen from elected local officials. The passage of the amendment would delay the final passage of ratification legislation.

16 Chancellor of the Exchequer Norman Lamont delivered the government's 1993-94 budget, claiming that it would bring 'sustained recovery'. The budget planned steep tax increases, but deferred them until 1994-95 and beyond in order to nurture economic recovery. The most controversial aspect of Lamont's plan was an extension of VAT to domestic fuel and electricity.

18 The Department of Employment announced that the unemployment rate had declined in Feb for the first time since March 1990. Employment Secretary Gillian Shephard warned that the unemployment figures could be 'volatile' in coming months.

20 Two IRA bomb explosions at a shopping centre in Warrington killed two boys and wounded more than 50 other people. The attack prompted widespread outrage, including protests against the IRA in Dublin.

25 The government announced its revised plan on closing coal mines and moving toward the privatization of the industry. The plan would keep open, at least temporarily, 12 of the mines that had been previously scheduled for closure.

GENERAL

5 The World Meteorological Organization, a branch of the UN, reported that levels of ozone had fallen 20% below normal over Canada and Northern Europe.

5 Canadian sprinter Ben Johnson was banned for life from track and field after testing positive for drug use. Johnson had lost his world records and 1988 Olympic gold medal in the 100 metres after testing positive for anabolic steroids at the 1988 Olympics in Seoul.

10 A US doctor, David Gunn, was fatally shot during a demonstration outside an abortion clinic where he worked in Pensacola, Florida. The director of Rescue America, the anti-abortion group which had targeted the clinic, said 'While Gunn's death is unfortunate, it's also true that quite a number of babies' lives will be saved.'

12–19 A barrage of bombs jolted Bombay and Calcutta, India, leaving more than 300 people dead and 1,100 injured in the biggest wave of criminal violence in Indian history.

April 1993

INTERNATIONAL

3 Bosnian Serbs, meeting in Bileca, Bosnia-Herzegovina, rejected a UN-sponsored peace plan that would have left the Serbs in control of 43% of Bosnia-Herzegovina, compared with the 70% they then held.

3–11 Armenian forces consolidated their control of parts of Azerbaijan by occupying one western province and capturing a score of positions around a strategically important southern town.

4 On the last day of a two-day summit meeting with Russian President Yeltsin in Vancouver, Canada, US President Clinton pledged US$1.6 billion in immediate US aid to Russia.

8 Macedonia became the 181st member of the UN. Due to a continuing dispute with Greece over the name 'Macedonia', the nation entered the UN under the provisional name of The Former Yugoslav Republic of Macedonia.

8 Germany's highest court gave clearance for German personnel to participate in the enforcement of a 'no-fly zone' over Bosnia-Herzegovina, despite constitutional limits placed on the deployment of German forces outside their defensive obligations under NATO.

9 US planes and Iraqi anti-aircraft batteries exchanged fire over northern Iraq, the first such exchange in two months. None of the US planes were damaged.

10 Chris Hani, the secretary general of the South African Communist Party and a prominent ANC leader, was assassinated. His death provoked a surge of violence among his followers in the black townships, resulting in at least a dozen deaths. A white right-wing extremist was arrested in the killing.

12 After numerous violations, a two-week old cease-fire collapsed in Bosnia-Herzegovina as the Serbs renewed attacks on Sarajevo and Srebrenica.

15 The G-7 nations unveiled a $28.4 billion aid package for Russia at the conclusion of a two-day meeting in Tokyo.

16 Japanese Premier Miyazawa met with US President Clinton for the first time in Washington DC; the meeting was dominated by the contentious issue of the widening US–Japan trade imbalance.

18 President Khan of Pakistan ousted Prime Minister Nawaz Sharif and dissolved the National Assembly, capping a months-long power struggle between the two men. The president promised that new elections would be held within 90 days.

18-19 Amid an ever-growing political corruption scandal, Italians voted in a referendum to support a series of measures calling for government reform, including an end to Italy's strict system of proportional representation for elections to the Senate.

21 Negotiators representing Syria, Lebanon, Jordan, and the Palestinians announced that they had agreed to resume the Arab–Israeli peace talks, after the Palestinians dropped their insistence on the return of over 400 Palestinians deported to Lebanon by Israel in Dec 1992 as a precondition to resuming negotiations.

23–25 Voters in Eritrea, a province on the Red Sea coast of Ethiopia, overwhelmingly approved a referendum on declaring independence from Ethiopia, legitimizing a de facto sovereignty that had been in effect since 1991.

25 Popular support for Russian President Yeltsin was shown when 58% of voters participating in a country-wide referendum said they had confidence in him.

26 Italian President Scalfaro selected a political independent, central bank governor Carlo Azeglio

Ciampi, as the nation's new premier. He succeeded Giuliano Amato, who had resigned 22 April.

27 Tougher UN sanctions went into effect against Serbia and its ally Montenegro, after Serbs in Bosnia-Herzegovina, ignoring a UN deadline, refused a second time to endorse a peace plan based on the earlier proposed Vance–Owen one.

29 The heads of organizations representing the Chinese and Taiwanese governments signed four agreements specifying areas of cooperation between the rival nations, and calling for the assumption of regular dialogue between government officials.

30 US trade representatives threatened to impose unspecified sanctions on Japan unless it opened up its markets to US construction companies and superconductor manufacturers.

NATIONAL

2 Employees of British Rail and British Coal Corp. undertook separate one-day strikes. The rail action was taken in protest against government privatization plans; the coal strike was held by members of the National Union of Mineworkers, who were protesting government plans to shut down 19 state-owned coal mines.

16 Members of the National Union of Rail, Maritime and Transport Workers (RMT) held their second one-day strike in two weeks. The workers were seeking job guarantees in the face of a planned privatization scheme.

24 The IRA detonated a massive truck bomb in Bishopgate, in the City of London financial district. One man was killed, 40 people were injured, and dozens of buildings were damaged.

26 The government reported that the economy showed significant growth in the first quarter for the first time in two and a half years, data which seemed to confirm that the economy was heading out of its longest recession since the 1930s.

30 The Association of Teachers and Lecturers (ATL) announced that its members had voted to boycott a controversial government plan for national testing of primary and secondary students in England and Wales.

GENERAL

3 Results of the Grand National steeplechase were voided because of starting problems. The fiasco was described as one of the most embarassing incidents in British sporting history.

7 Swiss voters approved a referendum to allow gambling in their country. Money from casinos would be used to fund social security, with the government claiming 0.80% of their gross profits.

19 The compound of the Branch Davidians, a religious cult, near Waco, Texas, burned to the ground in what the FBI described as a mass suicide. The fire occured hours after federal agents in armoured vehicles had begun battering the compound's walls and pumping tear gas into the structure. The heavily armed cult had been in a stand-off with law-enforcement agents for 51 days. At least 72 people, including cult leader David Koresh, died in the fire.

30 Monica Seles, the world's top-ranked female tennis player, was stabbed in the back while resting at courtside between games of a match in Hamburg, Germany. The 19-year-old Yugoslav star was hospitalized with a half-inch puncture wound between her shoulder blades and was expected to be sidelined for at least a month.

May 1993

INTERNATIONAL

30 April–6 The Israeli government allowed 30 Palestinians deported between 1967 and 1987 to return to the Israeli-occupied territories from Jordan. The concession aimed to revive the Middle East peace talks.

1 President Ranasinghe Premadasa of Sri Lanka was assassinated by a suicide bomber in Colombo, the capital, during a state-sponsored May Day parade. Prime Minister Wijetunge took the oath of office as interim president.

1 Rioters fought running skirmishes with police in Moscow; about 570 people, including 355 policemen, were injured in the fracas which erupted after demonstrators began a march to mark May Day.

6 The self-proclaimed Bosnian Serb parliament rejected for a third time the UN-backed peace plan for Bosnia-Herzegovina, in spite of a US threat to use force in the region. Following the rejection Serbian President Milosevic ordered a halt to the movement of all supplies except food and medicine from Serbia to the defiant Bosnian Serbs in Bosnia-Herzegovina. The UN Security Council declared the Bosnian capital, Sarajevo, and the five remaining Moslem strongholds in the country – Bihac, Gorazde, Tuzla, Srebrenica and Zepa – to be 'safe areas'.

9 Juan Carlos Wasosy of the ruling Colorado Party won a close three-way race for the presidency in Paraguay's first multi-party, direct elections for a civilian head of state.

11 Russian President Yeltsin dismissed two top government officers who had opposed his program of political and economic reforms.

12 Rival Afghan factions renewed fighting for control of Kabul, the capital. The Red Cross reported 17 May that at least 700 people had been killed through the first six days of the ongoing battle.

13 The Arab and Israeli delegations to the Middle East peace talks completed a ninth round of negotiations in Washington DC. The talks produced few tangible results.

14 Nine of the 10 members of the Commonwealth of Independent States agreed to establish an economic union between them. Turkmenistan did not sign the accord.

14 Trade ministers from the USA, Japan, Canada, and the EC met in Toronto to discuss tariffs and other trade barriers they hoped to remove in other countries and at their own borders.

18 Danish citizens voted in a referendum to ratify the EC's Treaty on European Union, reversing a narrow defeat for the pact in May 1992 that had thrown the EC into turmoil.

18 The Moslems and Croats of Bosnia-Herzegovina agreed to begin observing parts of the UN-backed peace plan for the republic. Fighting between Croat and Moslem forces continued in the city of Mostar even as the agreement was being reached. Although Mostar was mostly calm 19 May, gun battles between the two sides resumed that day around Vitez in central Bosnia-Herzegovina.

19 The self-proclaimed Bosnian Serb parliament met to ratify the resounding 'no' turned in by voters in the 15-16 May referendum on the Vance-Owen plan.

21 Seven people were killed when a car bomb exploded in a crowded square in Cairo, Egypt. Although no group claimed responsibilty for the attack, observers blamed Islamic militants, who had blown up a Cairo cafe in Feb.

21 President Carlos Andres Perez was suspended from office, when Venezuela's Supreme Court was authorized to try him on charges of misappropriating government funds.

21 The rump Yugoslav Federation, consisting of Serbia and Montenegro, refused to accept an international presence to monitor compliance with the blockade against Bosnia.

22 The USA, Russia, the UK, France and Spain agreed on a joint policy on Bosnia-Herzegovina. The agreement represented the acquiescence of the USA in limited objectives and encouragement of a negotiated settlement favoured by Europe.

24 Thousands of Tibetans demonstrated in Lhasa, the capital, the first and most violent of five days of demonstrations against the Chinese government.

25 Iranian military planes attacked two opposition guerrilla bases deep inside Iraq.

27–30 Fighting intensified in Bosnia-Herzegovina in several areas identified by the UN as safe areas for Moslems fleeing Serb attacks.

28 The UN General Assembly admitted the African state of Eritrea and the European principality of Monaco, boosting its membership to 183.

29 Five members of a Turkish family died in the western German city of Solingen after their home was firebombed. A suspect, described as a right-wing extremist, was arrested. Germany's parliament had 26 and 28 May approved constitutional changes that would dilute the nation's guarantee of foreigners' rights to seek asylum in Germany.

NATIONAL

4 Asil Nadir, the former chairman of Polly Peck International PLC, jumped bail and flew to northern Cyprus. Nadir had been set to face trial in Sept on theft and false accounting charges stemming from the collapse of Polly-Peck in 1990.

5 The government agreed to accept an opposition amendment to legislation on ratifying the EC's Maastricht Treaty. The amendment would remove any reference to the Social Chapter from the ratification legislation being considered by the Parliament.

6 The Conservative Party lost a net total of 473 county council seats in local elections in England and Wales. The Conservatives also lost the Newbury by-election in west Berkshire, a seat that the party had held since 1924.

19 Three former police detectives involved in the investigation of a deadly 1974 pub bombing in Guildford, Surrey, were acquitted of fabricating evidence in the case.

20 The IRA launched a bombing campaign in Ulster with a truck bomb in central Belfast which injured 20 people and badly damaged the headquarters of the UUP. The damage caused by the Belfast bomb and three subsequent explosions 22–23 May would cost the government £22 million ($ 35 million). The bombings came in the wake of 19 May elections for local councils in Northern Ireland, which produced gains for both the Roman Catholic and Protestant extremist parties.

27 Prime Minister Major shuffled his cabinet and removed chancellor of the Exchequer Norman Lamont, who had borne the brunt of criticism for the nation's sputtering economy. The changes came amid widespread discontent with Major's government. Kenneth Clarke, formerly the home secretary, was named as Lamont's successor.

28 Beverly Allitt, a nurse, was sentenced to 13 life terms for the murders of four children in her care and attacks on nine others. The attacks were carried out over a two-month period in 1991 when Allitt worked at Granthamand Kesteven General Hospital.

GENERAL

13 The International Whaling Commission in Kyoto, Japan, rejected a motion to lift a moratorium on commercial whaling. The Japanese delegations to the IWC had proposed a partial lifting of the moratorium to permit the hunting of 50 minke whales per year.

15 A 46-hour hostage drama at a French nursery school ended when police commandos shot and killed the hostage-taker. Eric Schmitt had entered the school, in a Paris suburb, on the morning of 13 May and taken 21 children hostage, demanding 100 million francs ($18.5 million) in ransom.

22 Heavyweight boxing champion Riddick Bowe knocked out challenger Jess Ferguson 17 seconds into the second round of their title bout in Washington DC.

27 Five people were killed and at least two dozen people injured when a car bomb exploded near the Uffizi Gallery in Florence, Italy. The explosion, believed to be connected to the Mafia, also destroyed three paintings and damaged 30 others, including works by the Flemish painter Peter Paul Rubens.

30 Emerson Fittipaldi of Brazil won the 77th running of the Indianapolis 500 automobile race.

ON THIS DAY

January

1 The European Economic Community came into existence. *1958*
2 Frenchman Louis Daguerre took the first photograph of the Moon. *1839*
3 The Battle of Princeton took place in the War of Independence, in which George Washington defeated the British forces, led by Cornwallis. *1777*
4 The first pop-music chart was compiled, based on record sales published in New York in *The Billboard. 1936*
5 French premier Giscard d'Estaing promulgated a law making French the only language permitted in advertising. *1976*
6 English King Alfred defeated the Danes at the Battle of Ashdown. *871*
7 OPEC agreed to raise crude oil prices by 10%, which began a tidal wave of world economic inflation. *1975*
8 French General Charles de Gaulle became the first president of the Fifth Republic. *1959*
9 British prime minister William Pitt the Younger introduced income tax, at two shillings in the pound, to raise funds for the Napoleonic Wars. *1799*
10 The Treaty of Versailles was ratified, officially ending World War I with Germany. *1920*
11 The first disco, called the 'Whisky-go-go', opened in Los Angeles, USA. *1963*
12 The Boeing 747 aircraft touched down at London's Heathrow Airport at the end of its first transatlantic flight. *1970*
13 NASA selected its first women astronauts, 15 years after the USSR had a female astronaut orbit the Earth. *1978*
14 An earthquake killed over 1,000 people in Kingston, Jamaica, virtually destroying the capital. *1907*
15 The coronation of Queen Elizabeth I took place. *1559*
16 Leon Trotsky was dismissed as Chairman of the Revolutionary Council of the USSR. *1925*
17 The Papal See was transferred from Avignon back to Rome. *1377*
18 Captain Cook discovered the Sandwich Islands, now known as Hawaii. *1778*
19 The Japanese invaded Burma. *1942*
20 Terry Waite, the Archbishop of Canterbury's special envoy in the Middle East, disappeared on a peace mission in Beirut, Lebanon. *1987*
21 Louis XVI, King of France, was found guilty of treason and guillotined. *1793*
22 The Falkland Islands were ceded to Britain by Spain. *1771*
23 An earthquake in Shanxi Province, China, is thought to have killed some 830,000 people. *1556*
24 The US Supreme Court ruled that income tax is unconstitutional. *1916*
25 The first Winter Olympic Games were inaugurated in Chamonix in the French Alps. *1924*
26 Hong Kong was proclaimed a British sovereign territory. *1841*
27 The Vietnam cease-fire agreement was signed by North Vietnam and the USA. *1973*
28 Iceland became the first country to introduce legalized abortion. *1935*
29 Greenwich Mean Time was adopted by Scotland. *1848*
30 Adolf Hitler was appointed chancellor of Germany. *1933*
31 The executions of Winter, Rookwood, Keys, and Guy Fawkes, the Gunpowder Conspirators, took place in London. *1606*

February

1 The first edition of the Oxford English Dictionary was published. *1884*
2 The German army surrendered to the Soviet army at Stalingrad. *1943*
3 The Portuguese navigator Bartholomew Diaz landed at Mossal Bay in the Cape - the first European known to have landed on the southern extremity of Africa. *1488*
4 The Russo-Japanese War began after Japan laid seige to Port Arthur. *1904*
5 Laker Airways collapsed with debts of $270 million. *1982*
6 Maximilian I assumed the title of Holy Roman Emperor. *1508*
7 Austria and Prussia formed an alliance against France. *1792*
8 The 'Great Frost' of London ended (began 25 Dec 1739). *1740*
9 Explorer Charles Sturt discovered the termination of the Murray River in Australia. *1830*
10 Andrew Becker demonstrated his practical diving suit in the river Thames. *1774*
11 After more than 27 years in prison, ANC president Nelson Mandela walked to freedom from a prison near Cape Town, South Africa. *1990*
12 Lady Jane Grey, Queen of England for nine days, was executed on Tower Green for high treason. *1554*
13 The massacre of the Macdonalds at Glencoe in Scotland was carried out by their traditional enemies, the Campbells. *1692*
14 The naval Battle of St Vincent took place off SW Portugal, in which Captain Nelson and Admiral Jervis defeated the Spanish fleet. *1797*
15 The first session of the Permanent Court of International Justice in The Hague was held. *1922*
16 Leon Spinks beat Muhammad Ali to win the heavyweight boxing championship in Las Vegas, USA. *1978*
17 The inner chamber of the tomb of Tutankhamun was opened in the presence of

Egyptian government officials and leading archaeologists. *1923*
18 A direct telegraph line was established between Britain and New Zealand. *1876*
19 William K Kellogg formed the Battle Creek Toasted Cornflake Company to make a nourishing breakfast cereal he had invented for patients suffering from mental disorders. *1906*
20 John Glenn became the first American in orbit when he circled the Earth three times in the Mercury capsule *Friendship*. *1962*
21 American militant black Muslim leader Malcolm X was murdered in Manhattan. *1965*
22 The French landed in Britain at Fishguard, but were soon captured – it was the last foreign invasion of Britain. *1797*
23 The February Revolution began in Russia. *1917*
24 Galerius Valerius Maximianus issued the first edict of persecution against the Christians in Rome. *303*
25 Queen Elizabeth was excommunicated by Pope Pius V, who declared her a usurper. *1570*
26 Napoleon Bonaparte escaped from the island of Elba. *1815*
27 General Franco's rebel government in Spain was recognized by France and Britain. *1939*
28 Spain withdrew from Spanish Sahara. *1976*
29 Dr Jocelyn Burnell announced the discovery of the first 'pulsar' (pulsating radio source) in Cambridge, England. *1968*

March

1 The Soviet *Venus 3* spacecraft touched down on Venus – the first spacecraft to land on another planet. *1966*
2 Captain James Gallagher and his 13-man US Air Force crew completed the first round-the-world non-stop flight, in a little over 94 hours. *1949*
3 The first performance of Bizet's opera *Carmen* was staged at the Opéra Comique, Paris. *1875*
4 Lenin formed the Communist International, better known as Comintern. *1919*
5 The Boston Massacre took place, in which British troops opened fire on a crowd in Boston, Massachussets, killing five. *1770*
6 Ghana, formerly the Gold Coast, became the first British colony in Africa to achieve independence. *1957*
7 Germany occupied demilitarized zones in the Rhineland, violating the Treaty of Versailles. *1936*
8 Nearly 4,000 US Marines landed in South Vietnam. *1965*
9 Kissing in public was banned in Naples, contravention being punishable by death. *1562*
10 The *Rokeby Venus*, by Velazquez was damaged at the National Gallery by suffragettes. *1914*
11 *The Daily Courant*, the first successful English newspaper, was published. *1702*
12 Britain annexed Basutoland. *1868*
13 Tsar Alexander II of Russia was assassinated by anti-monarchists who threw a bomb at him near his palace. *1881*
14 Lake Albert (Nyanza) in Africa was discovered and named by Samuel Becker. *1864*
15 Hitler proclaimed the Third Reich in Germany; he said it would last a thousand years. *1933*
16 Arthur Evans revealed the ancient city of Knossos, Crete, which he began excavating in 1899. *1900*
17 Caesar defeated Pompey's supporters at the Battle of Munda. *45 BC*
18 Mahatma Gandhi was sentenced to six years' imprisonment for sedition. *1922*
19 The first eclipse ever recorded was observed by the Babylonians, according to Ptolemy. *721 BC*
20 Radar, developed by Dr Rudolf Kuhnold, was first demonstrated at Kiel Harbour. *1934*
21 A massive poll tax demonstration in Trafalgar Square, London, turned into a riot; 417 people were injured, 341 arrested. *1990*
22 The Pope abolished the Order of the Knights Templar. *1312*
23 The world's first nuclear-powered merchant vessel, the *Savannah*, was launched at Camden, New Jersey, USA. *1962*
24 The Oxford and Cambridge Boat Race ended in a dead heat for the first and only time. *1877*
25 Titan, a satellite of Saturn, was discovered by Christian Huyghens. *1655*
26 The British Road Traffic Act introduced the driving test for motor owners. *1934*
27 The Peace of Amiens was signed between France and Britain. *1802*
28 A radiation leak occurred at Three Mile Island nuclear station in Pennsylvania, USA. *1979*
29 The last US troops left South Vietnam. *1973*
30 *Sunflowers*, by Vincent Van Gogh, was sold at auction by Christie's in London for $24,750,000. *1987*
31 Japan opened its ports to US traders after the first US–Japan treaty was signed. *1854*

April

1 Ayatollah Khomeini declared Iran an Islamic republic. *1979*
2 Argentina invaded and occupied the Falkland Islands. *1982*
3 The Pony Express was first run – 3,218 km/2,000 mi from St Joseph, Missouri, to San Francisco. *1860*
4 Francis Drake, having returned from his circumnavigation of the world, was knighted by Queen Elizabeth I on board his ship, the *Golden Hind*. *1581*
5 *Ben Hur* won a record ten Oscars. *1960*
6 An earthquake badly damaged many of London's churches, including St Paul's Cathedral. *1580*

7 LSD (lysergic acid diethylamide) was first synthesized by Albert Hoffman in his Swiss Laboratory. *1943*
8 The League of Nations held its final meeting. *1946*
9 At Appotomax, General Robert E Lee surrendered to General Ulysses S Grant in the US Civil War. *1865*
10 Severe earthquakes in Iran killed over 3,000 people. *1972*
11 William III and Mary II were crowned joint monarchs of Great Britain by the Bishop of London. *1689*
12 Bill Haley and the Comets recorded *Rock Around the Clock. 1954*
13 John Dryden was appointed the first English Poet Laureate. *1668*
14 In New York Dr Henry Plotz discovered the typhus vaccine. *1903*
15 The first hand-held electronic pocket calculator was announced by Canon Business Machines of Japan. *1970*
16 Cambodia fell to the communist Khmer Rouge when the capital, Phnom Penh, surrendered. *1975*
17 Martin Luther was excommunicated by the Diet of Worms. *1521*
18 The Republic of Ireland was proclaimed, severing ties with Britain by leaving the Commonwealth. *1949*
19 The USSR launched the first space station, *Salyut. 1971*
20 At an exhibition in Paris 'Art Nouveau' was introduced. *1902*
21 Rome was founded by Romulus, according to the historian Varro. *735 BC*
22 Poison gas was used on the Western Front for the first time by German forces in World War I. *1915*
23 The Shakespeare Memorial Theatre, in Stratford-on-Avon, England, was opened. *1879*
24 The US Library of Congress, the largest in the world, was founded on Capitol Hill in Washington DC. *1800*
25 The Hubble Space Telescope was launched from the space shuttle *Discovery* and began sending back pictures on 20 May. *1990*
26 The world's worst nuclear accident occurred at Chernobyl nuclear power station near Kiev, USSR. *1986*
27 Ferdinand Magellan, Portuguese navigator, was killed by natives on the island of Mactan in the Philippines while on his voyage around the world. *1521*
28 The crew of the *Bounty*, led by Fletcher Christian, mutinied against Captain Bligh. *1789*
29 The Nazi concentration camp of Dachau, on the outskirts of Munich, Germany, was liberated by US troops. *1945*
30 General George Washington was inaugurated as the first president of the USA. *1789*

May

1 The Union of Scotland and England was proclaimed. *1707*
2 The Lebanese Civil War began when 29 people died as the army clashed with Palestinian refugees. *1973*
3 Columbus, on his second expedition, discovered Jamaica. *1494*
4 The Maori uprising against the British began in New Zealand. *1863*
5 SAS commandos stormed the beseiged Iranian embassy in London and released the hostages – all but one of the gunmen were killed. *1980*
6 Roger Bannister ran the first sub four-minute mile, on Iffley Road track in Oxford, England, in 3 min 59.4 sec. *1954*
7 The deaf Beethoven conducted the first performance of his *Ninth Symphony* in Vienna. *1823*
8 The volcano of Mount Pelée on the French Caribbean island of Martinique erupted – within three minutes the town of St Pierre was totally destroyed and about 30,000 people killed. *1902*
9 Joseph Bramah patented the beer pump handle. *1785*
10 The German and Italian warplanes stopped their blanket bombing of Malta after 11,000 missions. *1942*
11 Thailand was adopted as the new name for Siam. *1949*
12 The first H-bomb test on Eniwetok Atoll in the Pacific proved it was possible to destroy a city over 100 times the size of Hiroshima and Nagasaki. *1951*
13 Captain John Smith and 105 Cavaliers in three ships landed on the Virginia coast and started the first permanent English settlement in the New World, in Jamestown. *1607*
14 Edward Jenner made his first vaccination against smallpox, and laid the foundation for modern immunology. *1796*
15 The world's first machine gun was patented by its designer, James Puckle. *1718*
16 The Soviet spacecraft *Venus 5* touched down on Venus. *1969*
17 The first weekly comic paper, *Comic Cuts*, was published in London. *1890*
18 Karen Silkwood, a worker in a US nuclear plant, won $10.5 million for suffering nuclear contamination. *1979*
19 The Simplon rail tunnel between Switzerland and Italy was officially opened. *1909*
20 Vasco da Gama arrived at Calicut, S India, after discovering a route via the Cape of Good Hope, S Africa. *1498*
21 New Zealand was proclaimed a British colony. *1840*
22 The Lancastrians defeated the Yorkists at St Albans in the first battle of the English Wars of the Roses. *1455*

23 Bonnie (Parker) and Clyde (Barrow), notorious murderers and outlaws, were killed in an ambush near Gibland, Louisiana, USA. *1934*
24 The German battleship *Bismarck* sank HMS *Hood* off the Greenland coast – almost all of its 1,421 crew perished. *1941*
25 Philips, the electronics firm, introduced Laservision – laser discs and player unit. *1982*
26 Napoleon was crowned King of Italy, in Milan Cathedral. *1805*
27 The Habeas Corpus Act was passed in Britain. *1679*
28 Diego Maradona of Argentina was bought by Barcelona football club for £5 million. *1982*
29 *The Rites of Spring*, danced by Nijinsky, opened in Paris. *1913*
30 Jane Seymour became Henry VIII's third wife, 11 days after he had had Anne Boleyn beheaded. *1536*
31 Construction of the Trans-Siberian railway began. *1891*

June

1 Bob Dylan had purist fans booing at the Royal Albert Hall when he used an electric guitar for the first time on his British tour. *1966*
2 Lord George Gordon led the 'Gordon Riots' in protest against the ending of penalties against Roman Catholics. *1780*
3 The Duke of York defeated the Dutch fleet off the coast of Lowestoft. *1665*
4 Allied forces entered and liberated the city of Rome. *1944*
5 In Poland, Solidarity defeated the Communists in the first free elections since the end of World War II. *1989*
6 The three-mile coastal limit for territorial waters was established by the Hague Convention. *1882*
7 Norway gained independence from Sweden. *1905*
8 Kurt Waldheim was elected president of Austria amid widespread international criticism. *1986*
9 Donald Duck was 'born', in Walt Disney's *The Wise Little Hen. 1934*
10 The Six Day War ended when Israel agreed to observe the UN cease-fire. *1967*
11 The first oil was pumped ashore from Britain's North Sea oilfields. *1975*
12 Jean-Baptiste Denys of Montpellier University and personal physician to Louis XIV of France carried out a successful blood transfusion using sheep's blood. *1667*
13 Wat Tyler led the first popular rebellion in English history, called the Peasant's Revolt. *1381*
14 German troops entered and occupied Paris. *1940*
15 The first democratic elections for over 40 years were held in Spain. *1977*
16 The Battle of Dettingen took place in Bavaria, with King George II's forces defeating the French in the war of the Austrian Succession. *1743*
17 Joseph Lister performed the first operation under antiseptic conditions – on his sister Isabella, at the Glasgow Infirmary. *1867*
18 Prince Museid was publicly beheaded in Riyadh for the assassination of King Faisal of Saudi Arabia. *1975*
19 The General Council of Nicaea, which would settle rules for the computation of Easter, began. *325*
20 The White House and the Kremlin agreed to set up the 'hotline'. *1963*
21 The US Constitution came into force. *1788*
22 Charles the Bold was defeated by the Swiss at Morat. *1476*
23 The Battle of Plassey took place in Bengal, with victory for the British, under Robert Clive, over the Indian forces – so laying the foundations of the British Empire in India. *1757*
24 Picasso's first Paris exhibition had critics predicting a bright future for the young artist. *1901*
25 The Korean War began, when the Communist forces of North Korea crossed the 38th parallel and and invaded the South. *1050*
26 The Anglo-Chinese War ended with the Treaty of Tientsin. *1858*
27 A mutiny erupted aboard the Russian battleship Potemkin in the Black Sea when sailors were shot for complaining about bad food. *1905*
28 *Deutschland*, the first zeppelin airliner, crashed. *1910*
29 Julius Caesar defeated Pompey at Pharsalus to become the absolute ruler of Rome. *48 BC*
30 Charles Blondin made the earliest crossing of the Niagara Falls on a tightrope – 335 m/1,100 ft long and 50 m/160 ft above the Falls. *1859*

July

1 The first volume of Diderot's Encyclopédie was published in Paris. *1751*
2 At a revivalist meeting at Whitechapel, London, William Booth formed the Salvation Army. *1865*
3 The US *Vincennes*, patrolling in the Gulf during the Iraq-Iran conflict, mistook an Iranian civil airliner for a bomber and shot it down, killing all 290 people on board. *1988*
4 The first employment agency opened in Paris, charging a registration fee of three sous to both employer and employee. *1631*
5 Maria Callas, at the age of 41, gave her last stage performance singing *Tosca* at Covent Garden, London. *1965*
6 The first all-talking feature film, *Lights of New York*, was presented at thr Strand Theatre in New York City. *1928*
7 Christopher Stone became the first 'disc jockey' on British radio when he presented his 'Record Round-up' from Savoy Hill. *1927*

8 Jean Moulin, the French Resistance leader known as 'Max', was executed by the Gestapo. *1943*
9 The first Wimbledon Lawn Tennis championship was held at its original site at Worple Road. *1877*
10 Telstar, the world's first television telecommunications satellite, was launched in the USA. *1962*
11 Captain Cook sailed from Plymouth in the *Resolution*, accompanied by the *Discovery* on his third and last expedition. *1776*
12 Cyprus was ceded to British administration by Turkey. *1878*
13 Jean Paul Marat, French revolutionary leader, was stabbed to death in his bath by Charlotte Corday. *1793*
14 Alfred Nobel demonstrated dynamite for the first time at a quarry in Redhill, Surrey. *1867*
15 US *Mariner 4* transmitted the first close-up pictures of Mars. *1965*
16 The last Tsar of Russia, Nicholas II, along with his entire family, family doctor, servants, and even the pet dog, was murdered by Bolsheviks at Ekaterinburg. *1918*
17 The Potsdam Conference of Allied leaders Truman, Stalin, and Churchill (later replaced by Attlee) began. *1945*
18 Nero's great fire began in Rome and lasted for nine days. *64*
19 *Mary Rose*, the pride of Henry VIII's battle fleet, keeled over and sank in the Solent with the loss of 700 lives. (The ship was raised 11 Oct 1982 to be taken to Portsmouth Dockyard.) *1545*
20 Professional football was legalized in Britain. *1885*
21 The Battle of the Pyramids took place, in which Napoleon, soon after his invasion of Egypt, defeated an army of some 60,000 Mamelukes. *1798*
22 Wiley Post completed the first around the world solo aeroplane flight – the journey took 7 days, 18 hrs and 49.5 min. *1933*
23 In the heat of the mountain stage of the Tour de France, British cyclist Tony Simpson, 29, collapsed and died. *1967*
24 Jacques Cartier landed at Gaspé in Canada and claimed the territory for France. *1534*
25 The first test-tube baby in Britain was born – Louise Joy Brown, at Oldham General Hospital, Lancashire. *1978*
26 President Nasser of Egypt nationalized the Suez Canal which led to confrontation with Britain, France, and Israel. *1956*
27 The *Great Eastern* arrived at Heart's Content in Newfoundland, having successfully laid the transatlantic telegraph cable. *1866*
28 San Martin and his forces liberated Peru and proclaimed its independence from Spain. *1821*
29 Fingerprints were used for the first time as a means of identification by William Herschel. *1858*
30 'Penguin' paperback books, founded by Allen Lane, went on sale in Britain. *1935*
31 Columbus discovered Trinidad on his third voyage. *1498*

August

1 The kilogram was introduced in France as the first metric weight. *1793*
2 Right-wing terrorists exploded a bomb in the crowded Bologna Railway Station, northern Italy, killing 84 people. *1980*
3 Lake Victoria, the source of the Nile, was discovered by the English explorer John Speke. *1858*
4 The Battle of Evesham took place, in which Simon de Montfort was defeated by Royalist forces led by the future King Edward I, during the Barons' War. *1265*
5 The first American Express traveller's cheque was cashed. *1891*
6 Jamaica became independent after being a British colony for over 300 years. *1962*
7 Guadalcanal, in the southern Solomon Islands, was assaulted by US Marines in one of the most costly Pacific campaigns of World War II. *1942*
8 Hadrian became emperor of Rome following the death of his father Trajan. *117*
9 The second atom bomb of World War II was dropped on the Japanese city of Nagasaki. *1945*
10 The screw bottle top was patented by Dan Rylands of Hope Glass Works, Barnsley, Yorkshire. *1889*
11 The first Royal Ascot horserace meeting took place – attended by Queen Anne. *1711*
12 The quagga in Amsterdam Zoo died, the last of this zebra-like species in the world. *1883*
13 The border between East and West Berlin was sealed off by East Germany with the closure of the Brandenburg Gate to stop the exodus to the West. *1961*
14 France became the first country to introduce motor vehicle registration plates. *1893*
15 The Woodstock Music and Arts Fair began on a dairy farm in upstate New York. In the three days it lasted, 400,000 attended, two children were born, and three people died. *1969*
16 The earliest prize-ring code of boxing rules was formulated in England by the champion pugilist Jack Broughton. *1743*
17 Earthquakes and tidal waves in the Philippines resulted in the deaths of over 6,000 people. *1976*
18 South Africa was banned from participating in the Olympics because of its racial policies. *1964*
19 The coronation of Edward I took place. *1274*
20 The *Voyager I* spacecraft was launched on its journey via Jupiter and Saturn to become the first man-made object to leave the solar system. *1977*
21 The Cadillac Motor Company was formed in Detroit, Michigan, USA, named after the French explorer, Antoine Cadillac. *1901*

22 The British settlement in Sierra Leone was founded, the purpose of which was to secure a home in Africa for freed slaves and homeless Africans from England. *1788*
23 The Visigoths sacked Rome. *410*
24 Mount Vesuvius erupted and buried the cities of Pompeii and Herculaneum in hot volcanic ash. *79*
25 The space probe *Voyager 2*, launched 20 Aug 1977, reached Neptune and sent back pictures of Triton, its moon, which revealed two additional moons previously unknown to astronomers. *1989*
26 The French Assembly adopted the Declaration of the Rights of Man. *1789*
27 The Kellogg-Briand Peace Pact, renouncing war, was signed in Paris. *1928*
28 Liverpool was created a borough by King John I. *1207*
29 The Treaty of Nanking was signed, ending the Opium Wars between China and Britain, ceding Hong Kong to Britain. *1842*
30 The first tramway in Britain opened, at Birkenhead on Merseyside. *1860*
31 US swimmer Mark Spitz won five of the seven gold medals that he achieved at the Munich Olympics. *1972*

September

1 An earthquake took place in Japan, leaving the cities of Tokyo and Yokohama in ruins and nearly 100,000 people dead. *1923*
2 Roald Amundsen completed his sailing round Canada's Northwest Passage. *1906*
3 Great Britain and France declared war on Germany. *1939*
4 The wreck of the *Titanic* on the Atlantic seaboard was photographed by remote control. *1985*
5 Canterbury Cathedral was destroyed by fire. *1174*
6 Due to a computer error, 41,000 Parisians received letters charging them with murder, extortion, and organized prostitution instead of traffic violations. *1989*
7 Brazil proclaimed its independence from Portugal. *1822*
8 The first German V2 flying bombs fell in Britain. *1944*
9 Massive earthquakes in Mexico left more than 4,700 people dead and 30,000 injured. *1985*
10 The referendum held in Gibraltar resulted in an overwhelming vote to stay with Britain. *1967*
11 In the Crimean War, Sebastopol was taken by the Allies after capitulation by the Russians. *1855*
12 Henry Hudson sailed the sloop *Half Moon* into New York Harbour and up to Albany to discover the river named after him. *1609*
13 Little Richard recorded 'Tutti Frutti' in Los Angeles with cleaned-up lyrics. *1956*
14 Napoleon entered Moscow in his disastrous invasion of Russia. *1812*
15 Military tanks, designed by Ernest Swinton, were first used by the British Army, at Flers in the Somme offensive. *1916*
16 Malaysia became independent and a mob of over 100,000 burned down the British Embassy. *1963*
17 The Constitution of the United States of America was signed. *1787*
18 Japan seized Manchuria and set up a puppet state called Manchukuo - it was returned to China in 1945 after World War II. *1931*
19 New Zealand became the first nation to grant its female citizens the right to vote. *1893*
20 Ferdinand Magellan, with a fleet of five small ships, sailed from Seville on his expedition around the world. Only one ship returned, the *Vittoria*, on 6 Sept 1522. *1519*
21 Stonehenge and the surrounding 30 acres of land was sold at auction to Mr C H Chubb for £6,600. Mr Chubb presented it to the nation three years later. *1915*
22 Sir Robert Walpole became the first prime minister to occupy 10 Downing Street. *1735*
23 Chewing gum was first commercially produced by John Curtis on a stove in his home in Bangor, Maine, and sold under the name of 'State of Maine Pure Spruce Gum'. *1848*
24 The first nuclear-powered aircraft carrier, the *USS Enterprise*, was launched at Newport, Virginia. *1960*
25 Vasco Balboa, Spanish explorer, became the first European to sight the Pacific Ocean after crossing the Darien isthmus. *1513*
26 Alan Bond's *Australia II* won the America's Cup, the first non-US winner for 132 years. *1983*
27 Mexico achieved independence through the efforts of General Hubride, who declared himself Emperor Augustin I. *1821*
28 Britain, Russia, and Austria formed the Alliance of St Petersburg against France. *1794*
29 John D Rockefeller became the world's first billionaire during the share boom in the USA. *1916*
30 Jack the Ripper murdered two more women – Liz Stride, found behind 40 Berner Street and Kate Eddowes in Mitre Square, both in London's East End. *1888*

October

1 Alexander the Great defeated Darius III at Arbela. *331 BC*
2 The first telescope was demonstrated by the Dutch lens maker, Hans Lippershey. *1608*
3 SOS was established as an international distress signal, replacing the call sign CQD. *1906*
4 The USSR's *Sputnik 1*, the first space satellite, was launched. *1957*
5 Bulgaria declared its independence from Turkey. *1908*
6 The *Orient Express* completed its maiden run from Paris to Constantinople (now Istanbul) in nearly 78 hours. *1883*

7 The first photograph of the far side of the moon was transmitted from the USSR's *Lunik 2*. *1959*
8 The Great Fire of Chicago started. It burned until the 11th, killing over 250 people and making 95,000 homeless. *1871*
9 Ernesto 'Che' Guevara, Argentinian-born guerrilla leader and revolutionary, was murdered in Bolivia. *1967*
10 Mrs Emmeline Pankhurst formed the Women's Social & Political Union to fight for women's emancipation in Britain. *1903*
11 Pope Leo X conferred the title of 'Defender of the Faith' (Fidei Difensor) on Henry VIII for his book supporting Catholic principles. *1521*
12 Columbus sighted his first land in discovering the New World, calling it San Salvador. *1492*
13 Greenwich was adapted as the universal time meridian of longitude from which standard times throughout the world are calculated. *1884*
14 The largest mass wedding ceremony took place in Seoul, South Korea, when 5,837 couples were married simultaneously. *1982*
15 Mata Hari, Dutch spy, was shot in Paris, having been found guilty of espionage for the Germans. *1917*
16 Napoleon was exiled to the Atlantic island of St Helena. *1815*
17 Charles II, defeated by Cromwell at Worcester, fled to France, destitute and friendless. *1651*
18 Russia transferred Alaska to the USA for $7.2 million. *1887*
19 Lord Corwallis surrendered to General Washington at Yorktown, in Virginia, and marked the end of fighting in the American War of Independence. *1781*
20 The Battle of Navarino, off the coast of Greece, ended with the combined British, French, and Russian fleets completely destroying the Egyptian and Turkish fleets. *1827*
21 Niki Lauda became world motor racing champion for the third time. *1984*
22 US President Kennedy announced a naval blockade against Cuba in protest over the installation of Soviet missile bases on the island, beginning the Cuban Missile Crisis. *1962*
23 The Battle of Edgehill, in the Cotswolds, took place - the first major conflict of the English Civil War, between Charles I's Cavaliers and the Parliamentary Roundheads. *1642*
24 The Treaty of Westphalia was signed, ending the Thirty Years' War. *1648*
25 The Transvaal, a region in South Africa which is rich in minerals, especially gold, was annexed by the British. *1900*
26 The Erie Canal, linking the Niagara River with the Hudson River, was opened to traffic. *1825*
27 In Paris, a 'getaway car' was used for the first time, when thieves robbed a shop and sped away. *1901*
28 An earthquake demolished Lima and Callao in Peru. *1746*
29 Sir Walter Raleigh, English navigator, courtier, and once favourite of Elizabeth I, was beheaded at Whitehall for treason. *1618*
30 'Quakers', the more common name for the religious Society of Friends, came into being during a court case, at which George Fox, the founder, told the magistrate to 'quake and tremble at the word of God'. *1650*
31 Martin Luther nailed his theses on indulgences to the church door at Wittenberg, Germany. *1517*

November

1 A prehistoric painting was discovered in a cave in Lascaux in the Dordogne, France. *1940*
2 The first insubmersible lifeboat was patented by Lionel Lakin, a London coach builder. *1785*
3 A violent earthquake occurred in the Abruzzi, Italy, killing some 15,000 inhabitants. *1706*
4 The first fashion show was organized by Edna Woodman Chase of *Vogue* magazine and held at the Ritz-Carlton Hotel, New York. *1914*
5 The Gunpowder Plot of Guy Fawkes to blow up King James I and Parliament was foiled when 36 barrels of gunpowder were found in Parliament's cellar. *1605*
6 Construction of the Kariba High Dam, on the Zambezi River between Zambia and Zimbabwe, began. *1956*
7 The Bolshevik Revolution, led by Lenin, overthrew Prime Minister Alexander Kerensky's government. *1917*
8 William Rontgen discovered X-rays during an experiment at the University of Wurzburg. *1895*
9 Flogging in the British Army was abolished. *1859*
10 In the early hours, Nazis burned 267 synagogues and destroyed thousands of Jewish homes and businesses in Germany. The night is called 'Kristallnacht' because of the many shop windows that were smashed. *1938*
11 Angola gained independence from Portugal. *1975*
12 The Republic of Austria was declared, thus ending the Habsburg dynasty. *1918*
13 The Massacre of the Danes in the southern counties of England took place by order of Ethelred II. *1002*
14 The island of Surtsey off Iceland was 'born' by the eruption of an underwater volcano. *1963*
15 Pitman's system of shorthand was published, under the title *Stereographic Sound-Hand*. *1837*
16 Australian explorer Hamilton Hume discovered the Murray River, the longest river in Australia (2,589 km/1,609 mi). *1824*
17 The USSR's *Luna 17* landed on the Sea of Rains on the moon and released the first moonwalker vehicle. *1970*
18 William Caxton's *The Dictes or Sayinges of the Philosophres* was published – the first printed book in England bearing a date. *1477*

19 Alfred Tennyson became Poet Laureate. *1850*
20 The solar-powered *Solar Challenger* was flown for the first time, entirely under solar power. *1980*
21 Jean F Pilâtre de Rozier and the Marquis d'Arlandes made the first human flight when they lifted off from the Bois de Boulogne, Paris, in their hot-air balloon and flew for 25 min, covering just over 3 km/2 mi. *1783*
22 John F Kennedy, 35th US president, was assassinated in Dallas, Texas, allegedly by Lee Harvey Oswald. *1963*
23 Molière's *Le Bourgeois Gentilhomme* was performed for the first time in Paris. *1670*
24 The transit of Venus was first observed by Jeremiah Horrocks, in England. *1639*
25 The longest-running play, *The Mousetrap* by Agatha Christie, opened in London, at the Ambassador's Theatre. *1952*
26 French President de Gaulle opened the world's first tidal power station in Brittany. *1966*
27 Pope Urban began to preach the First Crusade at Clermont, France. *1095*
28 Edwin Land's first polaroid cameras went on sale in Boston. *1948*
29 US admiral Richard Byrd and his pilot, Bernt Balchen, became the first men to fly over the South Pole. *1929*
30 Charlie Chaplin made his film debut in *Making a Living*, a Mack Sennett one-reeler, without his trademark moustache and cane.*1914*

December

1 The Locarno Pact was signed in London, guaranteeing peace and frontiers in Europe. *1925*
2 The rebuilt St Paul's Cathedral in London was opened. *1697*
3 The Quebec Bridge, the world's longest cantilever, over the St Lawrence River, was opened – 87 lives were lost during its construction. *1917*
4 The first performance on Broadway of Tennessee Williams' *A Streetcar Named Desire* was staged, starring Marlon Brando and Jessica Tandy. *1947*
5 James Christie, founder of the famous auctioneers, held his first sale in London. *1766*
7 An earthquake hit Armenia, killing thousands and causing widespread destruction. *1988*
8 The USA, Britain, and Australia declared war on Japan, one day after the attack on Pearl Harbor. *1941*
9 The first episode of *Coronation Street* was screened on ITV. *1960*
10 Nobel prizes were first awarded. *1901*
11 The first motor show opened in Paris, with nine exhibitors. *1894*
12 Guglielmo Marconi gave the first public demonstration of radio at Toynbee Hall, London. *1896*
13 Francis Drake began his journey from Plymouth in the *Golden Hind* that was to take him around the world. *1577*
14 Professor Max Planck of Berlin University revealed his revolutionary Quantum Theory. *1900*
15 Gibraltar's frontier with Spain was opened to pedestrians after 13 years. *1982*
16 The Zulu chief Dingaan was defeated by a small force of Boers at Blood River – celebrated in South Africa as 'Dingaan's Day'. *1838*
17 Orville Wright made the first successful controlled flight in a powered aircraft, at Kill Devil Hill, near Kitty Hawk, North Carolina, USA. *1903*
18 Divorce became legal in Italy. *1970*
19 Air service between London and Moscow was inaugurated. *1957*
20 The ANZACS, Australian and New Zealand forces with British troops, were evacuated from Gallipoli after their expedition against the Turks went seriously wrong. *1915*
21 Walt Disney's *Snow White and the Seven Dwarfs* was shown in Los Angeles, to become the first full-length animated talking picture. *1937*
22 James Stuart, the 'Old Pretender', landed at Petershead after his exile in France. *1715*
23 The BBC began daily news broadcasts. *1922*
24 Afghanistan was invaded by Soviet troops as the Kabul government fell. *1979*
25 Charlemagne was crowned first Holy Roman Emperor in Rome by Pope Leo III. *800*
26 The first charity walk took place, along Icknield Way, in aid of the World Refugee Fund. *1959*
27 The Methuen Treaty was signed between Portugal and England, giving preference to the import of Portuguese wines into England. *1703*
28 Mexico's independence was recognized by Spain. *1836*
29 St Thomas à Becket, the 40th Archbishop of Canterbury, was murdered in his own cathedral by four knights acting on Henry II's orders. *1170*
30 King Michael of Romania abdicated in favour of a Communist Republic. *1947*
31 The window tax was imposed in Britain which resulted in many being bricked up. *1695*

Obituaries

Abe Kobo 1924–1993. Japanese writer. One of the most important post-war Japanese writers, known outside Japan particularly for his novel *The Woman of the Dunes* 1962 which was translated into 20 languages. The film version by avant-garde director Teshigahara Hiroshi became a classic of the Japanese cinema. Abe's treatment of 20th-century psychological themes – loneliness, alienation, nightmare fantasy, loss of identity and disintegration of personality – places him in the front rank of serious writers today.

Although born in Tokyo, Abe spent his childhood and adolescence in Japanese-occupied Manchuria where his father was a professor of medicine. His studies at Tokyo University Medical School were cut short by nervous exhaustion and a short period in a mental hospital. At the end of the war he was supporting himself as a street vendor while writing poems and short stories. He published his first book of poems, *Poems by an Unknown*, privately in 1947. Further poems, under the title *Road Sign at the End of a Road*, appeared in a magazine the following year. His first collection of short stories, published in 1951, won him the Akutagawa Prize, Japan's highest literary prize.

He achieved international recognition with his novel *Woman of the Dunes* 1962, about an entomologist tricked into entering a sand pit and, like a trapped insect, forced to shovel sand for the rest of his life. The hero of his equally disturbing second novel *The Face of Another* 1962 is a man whose face has been severely burnt. After learning the techniques of plastic surgery, he models himself a new, more handsome, face. Seducing his wife, he is not sure if he is lover or husband; she is not deceived but does not know if she loves him for his former self or as his new self. In *The Ruined Map* 1969 a detective searching for a missing man gets lost himself and loses his self-identity in a soulless, labyrinthine megalopolis: Abe's depiction of present-day Tokyo. Abe wrote many other novels and works on psychological themes for the stage, such as *Uniform* 1955 and *The Ghosts Are Here* 1958. He formed his own theatre group in 1967, and took a production of his play *You Too Are Guilty* on tour to the USA in 1979.

Alter Simha 1897–1992. Polish-born Israeli Hasidic rabbi. As head from 1977 of the Ger Hasidim, the largest Hasidic community in the world, he was also the most powerful man in Agudah, the Orthodox Religious Party of Israel, for whom all Ger Hasidim vote.

Alter was born in Gora (in Hebrew Ger, in Yiddish Gur) Kalwaria, a small town in Poland where in 1859 Rabbi Isaac Meir Alter, Simha Alter's great-great-grandfather, founded the family dynasty, and from which the Hasidic community takes its name. Hasidic Judaism arose from the revival of Judaism in Poland in the early 18th century under Rabbi Israel Bal Shemtov. Mystical, musical, and celebratory, Hasidic Judaism brought new energy and life to E European Judaism. Of the communities that emerged over the next 200 years, the Ger Hasidim are now the most numerous.

Rabbi Simha Alter was a quiet man, with a deep knowledge of Jewish mysticism, who had escaped the Holocaust in Poland and in 1940 moved to Israel, where he went into business. In 1977 he succeeded his brother as head of the Ger Hasidim. Through the Agudah, he tried on behalf of the Hasidim to make Israel a more overtly religious society.

Marian Anderson

Anderson Marian 1902–1993. US contralto; the first black singer to appear at the Metropolitan Opera House, New York. Mainly a solo singer and recitalist rather than an opera singer, she won people's hearts worldwide with her beautiful, vibrant voice and her warm personality. She was one of the most important non-political figures in the civil rights movement and fight against racism in the USA.

Anderson was born and grew up in Pennsylvania. She joined her local Baptist church choir when she was six. By the time she was a teenager she was singing in oratorio, specializing in Bach. Because of her colour she was not permitted to enter a Philadelphia music school. However, friends and sympathizers raised enough money to send her to New York to study. She gave recitals in and around New York and won a competition to sing with the New York Philharmonic Orchestra. This should have launched her on a successful career, but racial prejudice proved a serious obstacle. At the age of 30 she went to Europe, meeting an enthusiastic reception in every country including the USSR.

Back in New York by the mid-1930s her reputation was assured. Early in 1939 she was to appear at Constitution Hall in Washington but the Daughters of the American Revolution, who owned the building, refused to allow her to sing. Eleanor Roosevelt, the President's wife, arranged for her to sing at the Lincoln Memorial, which she did on Easter Day before an audience of 75,000: an historic occasion in the struggle for equal rights in the USA. She continued her career after World War II and made several tours in the 1950s including a tour of Asia. She made history again in 1955 when she sang Ulrica, the fortune teller, in Verdi's *A Masked Ball* at Metropolitan Opera. Her farewell concert was held at Carnegie Hall in 1965: appropriately enough, on Easter Day. She received the US Presidential Medal of Freedom in 1963 and on her 75th birthday was presented with a gold medal by the US Congress.

Andrews Dana 1909–1991. US actor. A performer who could convey both doggedness and sincerity beneath a deceptively impassive exterior, Andrews played in several major American films of the 1940s. He first attracted attention as one of the victims of a lynch mob in *The Oxbow Incident* 1943, then played a laconic detective in the mystery thriller *Laura* 1944, and the quietly determined sergeant in *A Walk in the Sun* 1946, widely regarded as one of the finest films to be made about World War II. His performance the same year as the disillusioned returning flyer in *The Best Years of Our Lives* demonstrated the versatility beneath his seemingly restricted acting range. He continued to play leading roles during the 1950s, but mainly in lesser films and to lesser effect, and a drinking problem further hindered his career.

Born in Mississippi, the son of a Baptist minister, he was initially destined for a career in accountancy, but opted instead for acting. He made his stage debut in 1935 and his first film in 1940. *Madison Avenue* 1961 was the last Hollywood film in which he had a starring role, but he subsequently made secondary appearances in a variety of productions, ranging from exploitation movies to expensive international undertakings like *Battle of the Bulge* 1965. One of his last screen appearances was as the film director 'Red Riding Hood' in the screen version of Scott Fitzgerald's *The Last Tycoon* 1976. Sadly, Andrews became a victim of Alzheimer's disease, and his final years were spent in obscurity.

Ascher, Zika (Zigmund) George 1910–1992. Czech fabric designer well known for producing scarves from designs by modern artists, and for designing cheesecloth, shaggy mohair, and lacy fabrics which became popular in the late 1950s to the early 1970s.

Born in Prague, Ascher moved to London in 1939 with his wife Lida, following the annexation of Czechoslovakia by Germany. During World War II he served in the British army while Lida began to design fabrics. In Paris in 1945 Ascher commissioned contemporary artists, including Braque, Picasso, and Matisse, to make designs for scarves. These three-foot silk squares were hand printed and became popular as glamorous scarves, skirts, and wraps. Designs were also made by other artists, including Henri Derain, Henry Moore, David Piper, and Jean Cocteau.

The Aschers' own fabric designs were popular with leading couturiers of the 1940s–60s such as Dior, Schiaparelli, Lanvin, Givenchy, and Saint-Laurent, and with the 1960s fashion designer Mary Quant. Continually experimenting, the Aschers produced neon-coloured shaggy-haired mohairs in 1957, followed by dress- and coat-weighted chenilles (fabric with a fine fur-like texture), and cheesecloth. Ascher continued working until his death, producing silk squares and fabric designs to order. He was always active, discussing new ideas with fashion designers, journalists, and friends. A retrospective exhibition of Zika and Lida Ascher's designs was held at the V&A Museum, London, in 1987.

Ashe Arthur Robert 1943–1993. US lawn tennis player who became the first black to win the Wimbledon men's singles title when he beat Jimmy Connors in the 1975 final.

Born in Richmond, Virginia, Ashe began playing tennis in an environment that was hostile to black participation in a traditionally white sport. He was at first refused entry to Richmond's junior tournaments because of his race; even at university (the University of California at Los Angeles) his tennis team excluded him when they played at fashionable country clubs. A conviction that sport could help overcome injustice grew within Ashe; as an established champion he made a point of visiting South Africa despite the opposition of many black South Africans. His involvement in anti-apartheid protests lead to his being arrested on two occasions. He also co-founded the Black Tennis Association. Ashe gained attention in 1968 when he won the US Open singles title. In 1970 he won the Australian Open singles as well as two grand-slam doubles titles. After his Wimbledon victory in 1975 Ashe played for a further four years, winning 33 singles and 18 doubles titles. His tennis career ended when he suffered his first heart attack, the result of a congenital heart defect. After a multiple bypass operation he contracted the HIV virus from a blood transfusion; the infection was diagnosed in 1988. From 1979 Ashe devoted himself to various tennis-related activities, to broadcasting, writing, and charity work. The Arthur

Arthur Ashe

Ashe Foundation for the Defeat of AIDS was launched on the eve of the 1992 US Open.

Auger Arleen 1939–1993. US soprano who sang at the wedding of Prince Andrew and Sarah Ferguson in Westminster Abbey in 1986 and was heard by a worldwide television audience of 500 million. Millions heard her again in December 1991 in the television broadcast of Mozart's *Requiem* live from Vienna in commemoration of the bicentenary of the composer's death. Yet she was really more a singer for the lover of 17th- and 18th-century opera and connoisseurs of *lieder*. She will be remembered especially as a superb recording artist, having made over 170 recordings and winning many awards in the process.

Auger was born and grew up in Long Beach, California. She studied singing and violin at California State University. In her mid-20s she won a competition to study in Vienna, where she was noticed by the influential conductor, Karl Böhm. She made her Vienna State Opera debut in 1967 as the Queen of the Night in Mozart's *The Magic Flute* and was chosen by Böhm to sing Constanze in his fine recording of the same composer's *Die Entführung aus dem Serail (Abduction from the Seraglio)*. She remained with the Vienna State Opera for seven years, singing many leading soprano roles, including the Countess in Mozart's *The Marriage of Figaro* and the Marschallin, or Field-Marshal's wife, in Richard Strauss's *Der Rosenkavalier (The Knight of the Rose)*. She also sang at most of the other major opera houses and festivals and regularly appeared at the Salzburg Festival. Her first London appearance was in 1985 at the Spitalfields Festival, where she sang the title role in Handel's *Alcina*, which she also sang in Paris, Geneva, and Los Angeles. She will be sorely missed by connoisseurs of *lieder*, who flocked to her recitals of songs by Schubert and other Viennese composers, like Alban Berg and Hugo Wolf.

Aurenche Jean 1904–1992. French screenwriter. He was a prolific writer, who over more than 40 years contributed to some 50 films, among them some of the finest the French cinema has produced. He worked, often in collaboration, on movies of almost every sort, but was especially noted for adaptations of major literary works. These included Stendhal's *Le Rouge et le Noir* 1954, Zola's *L'Assommoir* as *Gervaise* 1956, and Dostoievsky's *The Gambler* (*Le Joueur* 1958).

Born in Provence, Aurenche was a director of advertising films and documentaries before embarking on a screenwriting career in 1937. His first major success was *Hôtel du Nord* 1938, and from 1943 onwards much of his best writing was in collaborati on with Pierre Bost. In addition to the titles mentioned above, their joint credits notably included *Le Diable au Corps* 1947, with its romantic account of a love affair between a teenage boy and an older woman, and the anticlerical black comedy *L'Auberge Rouge* 1951 (which for six years was banned by the British censor). While the advent of the New Wave in the 1960s briefly caused the form of classical screen writing practised by Aurenche and Bost to become unfashionable, they returned to strength during the 1970s, in particular with *L'Horloger de St Paul* 1974, adapted from a Georges Simenon novel.

Bérégovoy Pierre 1925–1993. French Socialist politician, mayor of Nevers 1983–93, prime minister 1992–93. He committed suicide a month after his party lost the National Assembly elections.

Born in Deville-les-Rouen, son of a Ukrainian immigrant, Bérégovoy had a limited formal education and was largely self-taught. Like his friend and mentor, François Mitterrand, he served in the Resistance during World War II. Leaving school at 15 he worked in a textile factory and then on the railways. Here he supplemented his education by attending a school organized by the Communist Party. His tutor in Marxism and politics was Roland Leroy, later editor of *L'Humanité*. Moving to Gaz de France, Bérégovoy climbed swiftly up the managerial ladder. In 1981 François Mitterrand, now president, recognized his talents and made him secretary-general of his personal office. Various ministerial appointments followed, including social affairs 1982–84 and finance and economic affairs 1984–86 and 1988–92.

Bérégovoy masterminded Mitterrand's successful 1988 election campaign and expected to be made prime minister but did not attain this office until 1992. President Mitterrand, concerned about the Socialist Party's poor performance in the March 1992 elections, replaced Edith Cresson with Bérégovoy, hoping he would revive the party's fortunes. To do this within a year was an impossible task; in March 1993, when he realized the extent of the Socialist Party's defeat in the national assembly elections, he became deeply depressed. He blamed himself for the defeat; the now distant attitude of his mentor, Mitterrand, increased his depression and on 1 May 1993 he took his own life. *Le Monde* described him as the 'quintessence of political professionalism', and the *Financial Times* as 'a paragon of gravity, moderation and great experience'.

Bernstein Sidney Lewis, Lord 1899–1993. UK entrepreneur, film producer, and founder of Granada Television. As chair of the Granada group 1934–79 and president of the group until his death, he was a dominant influence on commercial television in the UK.

Bernstein was born in Ilford, Essex. He left school at 15 and quickly became responsible for the entertainment side of his father's property business, managing the picture palaces and music halls the company acquired near the housing estates it built. In 1922 Bernstein founded a chain of Granada cinemas, first acquiring derelict theatres and converting them. His first purpose-built cinema opened in Dover, Kent, 1927.

Bernstein was also active in the theatre, and built the Phoenix in Charing Cross Road, London, which opened in Sept 1930 with the premiere of Noël Coward's *Private Lives*. Although this production was successful, others were not, and Bernstein sold the theatre two years later.

During World War II, Bernstein was films adviser to the Ministry of Information, while his chain of 30 cinemas flourished. After the war, he spent five years in Hollywood, where he produced three films directed by Alfred Hitchcock: *Rope* 1948, *Under Capricorn* 1949, and *I Confess* 1953. In 1954, when the passage of the Television Act opened the way for commercial broadcasting, Bernstein applied for a licence, even though he was a long-time believer in public-service broadcasting. After struggles in the early years, the television company became hugely successful, and Granada diversified into TV-set rentals, motorway service centres, and publishing. Bernstein remained on the active board of the company until he was 80.

Bohm David 1917–1992. US-born physicist, professor of theoretical physics at Birkbeck College, London 1961–83. During the McCarthy era his radical political views led him to refuse to testify against colleagues when pressed to do so by the Un-American Activities Committee. He left the USA in 1951. Jobs in Brazil and Israel followed. He came to Birkbeck College in 1961.

His early work concerned the magnetic behaviour of plasma (hot ionized gas). With student Yakir Aharanov, Bohm predicted in 1958 that magnetic fields can affect plasma even when completely shielded from it. The Aharanov–Bohm effect has now been confirmed by experiment. In 1952 he produced a radical alternative version of quantum theory. In classical theory, an unobserved electron is seen as a jumble of wave states. When observed, it may behave as a particle or as a wave. This wave–particle duality is seen as an unavoidable feature of the microscopic world. Bohm proposed an alternative theory: particles are particles at all times, even when not observed. Their behaviour is determined by a hidden field or 'pilot wave' that produces the particles' wave-like behaviour.

When Bohm published his ideas, they were immediately rejected. French theoretician Louis de Broglie had proposed a similar theory 25 years earlier, but his work ran into difficulties because it implied that widely separated particles could instantaneously influence each other. Einstein ridiculed this 'spooky action at a distance'. Bohm, however, was unrepentant. He proposed an experiment that could demonstrate such action. In 1982, French physicists carried out Bohm's experiment, and demonstrated that quantum mechanics does indeed involve such spooky action. Throughout the 1980s Bohm continued to develop and advocate his ideas, but failed to persuade most physicists of his case. Recently, his ideas have enjoyed a revival, especially amongst quantum cosmologists, who attempt to describe the whole universe in quantum terms.

Brandt Willy. Adopted name of Karl Herbert Frahm 1913–1992. German socialist politician, federal chancellor of West Germany 1969–74. He played a key role in remoulding the Social Democratic Party (SPD) as a moderate socialist force and was leader 1964–87. As mayor of West Berlin 1957–66, Brandt became internationally famous during the Berlin Wall crisis 1961. He was awarded the Nobel Peace Prize 1971.

Born in Lubeck, he joined the SPD at 17. A fervent anti-Nazi, he fled to Norway 1933 where he changed his name, took Norwegian citizenship, attended Oslo University, and worked as a journalist. On the German occupation of Norway 1940 he went to Sweden where he continued as a journalist, supporting the anti-Nazi resistance movement.. He returned to West Germany 1945 and entered the Bundestag (federal parliament) 1949. In 1966 he took the SPD into the 'grand coalition' with the Christian Democrats under Kurt Kiesinger and, as foreign minister, introduced *ostpolitik*, a policy of reconciliation between west and east Europe. He continued the policy when he became federal chancellor 1969. It culminated in the 1972 signing of the basic treaty with what was then East Germany.

Willy Brandt

Brandt resigned the chancellorship 1974, when a close aide, Gunther Guillaume, was found to have been an East German spy. He continued to wield considerable influence in the SPD, particularly over the party's radical left wing. He chaired the Brandt Commission on Third World problems 1977–83, producing the notable report *North–South: A Programme for Survival* 1980, which advocated urgent action by the rich North to improve conditions in the poorer southern hemisphere. He was a member of the European Parliament 1979–83. He had not expected his *ostpolitik* to bring about the reunion of Germany so speedily but fortunately lived to see it happen. From 1976 he was president of the Socialist International (SI) but was too ill to attend its 1992 meeting in Berlin. He was buried in that city, where a memorial service was held, attended by leading politicians from throughout the world. His successor as chancellor, Helmut Schmidt, said of him: 'Willy Brandt made amends for a great deal of the blame that Germans had heaped on themselves through war, devastation, and genocide.'

Burkitt Denis Parsons 1911–1993. Irish surgeon and research scientist who discovered a form of cancer, Burkitt's lymphoma, and how to cure it. He also revolutionized nutrition, gastroenterology, and epidemiology when he established the importance of dietary fibre. Burkitt, untrained in scientific research, was elected a fellow of the Royal Society in 1972.

He received his medical training at Trinity College, Dublin. While a government surgeon in Uganda, he realized that all the young children brought to him with facial tumours came from the same part of the country. Burkitt, his intellectual curiosity aroused, devoted himself to finding out where such cases occurred. The evidence pointed to a 'lymphoma belt' across Africa. Using material provided by Burkitt, virologist Tony Epstein identified the virus that caused Burkitt's lymphoma. Burkitt continued to refine his knowledge of the disease's geography. It existed only in the hot, wet parts of Africa where malaria was endemic. Infected children therefore already had weakened immune systems. The virus, which ordinarily led to glandular fever, made lymphoid cells malignant in young malaria patients. Surgery was little use, so Burkitt experimented with chemotherapy. Remarkably, a single course of treatment caused the lymphoma to 'melt away'. Geography also played a role in Burkitt's second major discovery. Now working in London, he knew that few African patients s uffered from appendicitis, haemorrhoids, gallstones or other diseases prevalent in the West. He also knew that the food in rural Afr ica was high in fibre. He conducted a wide-ranging survey in rural areas of the Third World, and found that where sugar and white flour were eaten, so were the diseases of the West found rampant. This compelled scientists and the public to think about nutrition afresh.

Burkitt was a man of deep Christian faith to which his work bore witness. He held firmly that: 'Attitudes are more important than abilities, motives than methods and character than cleverness; and the heart takes precedence over the head.'

Cahn Sammy Adopted name of Samuel Cohen 1913–1993. US song lyricist whose career took him from Tin Pan Alley to Hollywood and Broadway. For over 20 years he provided Frank Sinatra with material, including 'Come Fly With Me' 1958 and 'My Kind of Town' 1964. His chief collaborators were composers Jule Styne (1905–) and Jimmy van Heusen (1913–1990).

Cahn, born in New York, began as a fiddle player in a dance band, where he met his first songwriting partner, Saul Chaplin (1912–). Their biggest success was the Andrews Sisters' 1937 hit 'Bei Mir Bist Du Schön' (based on a Yiddish folk song). The same year Cahn moved to Hollywood, writing songs for films, among them 'Three Coins in the Fountain' 1954 with Styne and 'The Tender Trap' 1955 with van Heusen, both for Sinatra. On Broadway Cahn fared less well: many of the shows for which he wrote lyrics were failures (for example, *Skyscraper* 1966 with van Heusen and *Look to the Lilies* 1970 with Styne). Cahn's favourite among his own songs was 'Call Me Irresponsible' 1963, which he described, with characteristic immodesty, as 'the epitome of matching words to music'.

Cahn prided himself on writing only for money and putting a lyric together in a few minutes. When his style went out of fashion, he began making appearances as a raconteur, performing his own songs. His autobiography is named after one of them: *I Should Care* 1974.

Cantinflas 1911–1993. Mexican comedian. Enormously popular in Latin America, he briefly achieved international fame when he was selected by the producer Mike Todd to play Passepartout, quizzical valet to the globetrotting Phineas Fogg, in the lavish screen version of Jules Verne's *Around the World in 80 Days* 1956. The film was an enormous popular success and led to Cantinflas being given the starring role in a subsequent American production, *Pepe* 1960, a comedy about a Mexican ranch-hand who lands up in Hollywood and has sundry adventures there. Unfortunately, this undertaking proved, partly because of the leading actor's inadequate command of English idiom, to be a complete failure, and Cantinflas never made another English-language picture.

Born in Mexico City, he was a tent-show entertainer and circus clown before making his Mexican film debut in 1936. He subsequently averaged at least one film a year, creating characterizations based on the notion of the resourceful 'little man'. His following was such that at one stage the Mexican government ordered as a precautionary measure that pawnshops should close on the day his films opened. After the debacle of *Pepe*, he returned to Mexico and continued his starring career in local films for many years, gaining immense wealth in the process.

Charteris Leslie 1907–1993. English–Chinese (naturalized American) author of crime and adventure stories and creator of 'The Saint', one of the most famous fictional adventurers, whose visiting card showing a little stick man with a halo above his head became his unmistakeable trademark. 'The Saint' also appeared in films, on radio and television, and in comic strips; the books themselves were translated into more than 15 different languages.

Charteris was born Leslie Charles Bowyer Yin in Singapore; his father was a Chinese surgeon and his mother an Englishwoman. He claimed direct descent from the Shang Dynasty (*c.* 1700 to *c.* 1100 BC) emperors of China. He could speak Chinese and Malay before he learnt English. He changed his name to Leslie Charteris when he decided to settle in Britain in 1928. For much of his early childhood he travelled around the world with his parents until, at the age of 12, he was sent to Rossall School in England. From there he went to King's College, Cambridge, where his interest in crime rapidly developed. He read everything he could find on criminology and every crime novel he could lay his hands on. Encouraged by the early publication of a story and a first novel, *Meet the Tiger* 1928, he made up his mind to be a professional writer. His father disapproved, however, and refused to support him. He pursued an exciting life for the next few years, working on a rubber plantation in Malaya (now Malaysia), prospecting for gold, pearl fishing, working as a seaman on a freighter, playing bridge professionally, until he wrote his first Saint novel, *Enter the Saint* 1930.

Thus began an industry in popular fiction and entertainment centring around the adventures of the principal character, Simon Templar, 'The Saint', a kind of latter-day Robin Hood. Charteris went to the USA in 1932, first to New York and then on to Hollywood where numerous Saint films were made with several different actors playing the role. The Saint made Charteris rich but stuck with him for the rest of his life as the ever-growing numbers of Saint enthusiasts demanded more and more. The last novel to appear was *Salvage for the Saint* 1983.

Les Dawson

Dawson Les 1934–1993. British comedian, who after a long apprenticeship in working men's clubs and similar venues, gained popularity on television, especially as host of the quiz show *Blankety Blank*, in which capacity he was apt to make mock of the celebrity guests. In mining a vein of determinedly glum humour, full of derogatory references to wives and mothers-in-law, Dawson was the natural successor to bygone exponents of northern working-class comedy like Norman Evans and Rob Wilton. However, his best routines possessed qualities of verbal elaboration and near-surreal fantasy such as to invoke in some admirers comparisons with such American humorists as Woody Allen.

Born in Manchester to an impoverished family, Dawson had early literary ambitions but left school at 14 to work at various jobs, including selling vacuum cleaners, washing dishes, and playing the piano in the bar of a Parisian bordello. Later, back in England, he would throw in an occasional joke during his appearances as a pianist and singer in Northern pubs and clubs. This met with little success until one evening in Hull, when he got drunk, forgot his scripted material, and improvised a stream of repartee at the expense of himself, his audience and life in general; this proved so popular that it set him on a new tack.

He gradually gained stardom on the variety theatre circuit and progressed to television, after winning *Opportunity Knocks* in 1967 and landing his own long-running series *Sez Les*. Although regarded by some as being a purveyor of cheap mother-in-law jokes, carrying misogynistic appeal, Dawson was most at home with his mock-Victorian word-spinning. For his best monologues he invested much thought, preparation, and scholarship. Besides his series, he appeared in TV plays and was also the author of 12 books. These included an autobiography, *One Clown Too Many* 1986, as well as several novels.

Dickens Monica Enid 1915–1992. Popular and prolific English writer and great-granddaughter of Charles Dickens. A close friend of the Samaritans' founder, Chad Varah, she was the founder of the Samaritans in the USA.

Dickens was born in London and went to St Paul's School for Girls, from which she was actually expelled for dropping her school uniform into the Thames from Hammersmith Bridge. She spent some time at a drama school but otherwise had no formal qualifications. She worked first as a cook in wealthy households, and the book she wrote about her experiences, *One Pair of Hands* 1939, which took her a mere six weeks to write, is still in print today. Her first novel, *Mariana*, was published the following year. In the early years of World War II she worked as a hospital nurse and then later as a fitter in a factory producing aircraft spare parts. Her experiences again provided material for her next books, *One Pair of Feet* 1942, *The Fancy* 1943, and *Thursday Afternoons* 1945, the last two being works of fiction that attracted much praise.

A whole stream of novels seemed to flow from her pen and she never stopped writing until the very end of her life. As a journalist she wrote for the magazine *Woman's Own* every week for 20 years and for a while was a reviewer for the *Sunday Chronicle*. In 1951 she married an American naval officer, Commander Roy Stratton, and settled in the USA until his death in 1985 when she returned to England. She tried her hand at writing for children and produced *The House at World's End* 1970, *Summer at World's End* 1971, *Follyfoot* 1971, *Spring Comes to World's End* 1972 and several other children's books. Novels continued to appear, and include *The Listeners* 1970, based on what she knew about the Samaritans, *Enchantment* 1989, *Closed at Dusk* 1990 and *Scarred* 1991. Her last novel *One of the Family* was published posthumously in 1993. Her work reflects the full life she led.

Diebenkorn Richard 1922–1993. US painter, a leading member of the second generation of Abstract Expressionists and also of the movement back to figurative art beginning in the mid-1950s. He achieved worldwide renown for his *Ocean Park* series, named after a district of Santa Monica, a sequence of mainly abstract canvases executed between 1966 and 1988.

Diebenkorn was born in Portland, Oregon but grew up from the age of two in San Francisco. He went to Stanford University and the University of California at Berkeley from 1940 to 1943 before joining the US Marines. After the war he studied for a time at the California School of Fine Arts and then spent a year in New York. His earliest work was representational and full of light, showing the influence of the older American artist, Edward Hopper. He had become an Abstract Expressionist by the time of his first one-man show in San Francisco 1948, and was regarded as one of the New York School artists, although he actually rejected their influences. He worked and taught in Albuquerque, New Mexico and Urbana, Illinois before returning in 1953 to San Francisco where he found the sun and the art gallery's colourful Matisses invigorating.

In 1955 he suddenly turned to painting still-lifes and landscapes and was thus occupied for the next ten years or so. His move to Santa Monica, Los Angeles, in 1967 marked his return to abstraction and the beginning of the *Ocean Park* paintings, quasi-abstracts of the Californian coast, that he worked on for much of the rest of his life. He represented the USA at the 1978 Venice Biennale but his work was otherwise not seen much in Europe until a retrospective exhibition held first at the Whitechapel Gallery in London 1991 and then in galleries in Germany and Spain.

Douglas Home Hon. William 1912–1992. Scottish playwright who entertained London's West End audiences and many others with over 40 plays. They were mostly in the long tradition of comedies set in the drawing rooms of country houses but often dealt with topical matters of more than passing interest.

Douglas Home was born in Edinburgh, son of the 13th Earl of Home and younger brother of Lord Home of the Hirsel, Sir Alec Douglas Home, the prime minister. He was educated at Eton and New College, Oxford. After Oxford, he was at the Royal Academy of Dramatic Art in London and acted for a while on the West End stage. During World War II he was a captain in the Royal Armoured Corps. A man of great principle, he disobeyed orders in 1944 by refusing to take part in the bombardment of Le Havre because the French civilian population had not been evacuated. More than 2,000 civilian lives were lost. Publicizing this fact and his action led to a court martial and a year in prison. He stood for Parliament a number of times under various banners but was never elected.

He had written two plays – *Great Possession* 1937 and *Passing By* 1940 – before his first real success with a play based on his prison experiences, *Now Barabbas*, written in a fortnight shortly after his release and produced two years later in London at the Boltons Theatre. Other plays include *The Chiltern Hundreds* 1949, *The Bad Samaritan* 1953, *Lloyd George Knew My Father* 1972, and *The Kingfisher* 1977. His last important work was *Portraits* 1987, about the relationship between a famous portrait painter, Augustus John, and three of his equally famous sitters; but it was also about the futility of war and the horror of nuclear weapons. He published a volume of autobiography *Half Term Report* in 1954 and another *Mr Home Pronounced Hume* in 1979. Two other works followed: *Sins of Commission* and *Old Men Remember* 1991.

Dubček Alexander 1922–1992. Slovak-born reform communist politician; leader of Czechoslovakia during the 1968 Prague Spring liberalization movement, of which he was the chief architect. After two decades in the political wilderness he returned to political office in 1989 following the downfall of the communist regime.

The son of Slovak communists who had earlier emigrated briefly to the USA, he grew up and was educated in the USSR. A committed socialist, he returned to Czechoslovakia 1938 and fought as a Slovak patriot against the Nazis 1944–45. In 1939 he joined the Communist Party and gradually rose through its hierarchy, becoming chief secretary of the regional committee 1953 and first secretary of the Slovak Commuist Party's Central Committee 1963. As Czechoslovakia's Communist Party leader from January 1968, he sought to popularize the system by introducing liberalizing economic, political, and cultural reforms, dubbed 'socialism with a human face'. This reform movement was crushed in August 1968 when Warsaw Pact forces invaded Czechoslovakia.

Initially, Dubček cooperated with the post-invasion, Soviet-directed 'normalization' process, but in 1969 was replaced as party leader by the more conservative Gustav Hasak. He served briefly as Czechoslovakia's ambassador to Turkey, but in 1970 was expelled from the Communist Party. Political banishment for two decades followed, with Dubček working as a clerk for the Slovakian forestry ministry. Though disenchanted with the cautious, stifling Husak regime, he retained his faith in the socialist dream and did not join the Charter 77 dissident movement formed by playwright Václav Havel. He returned to prominence November 1989, appearing with Havel on the balcony overlooking Prague's Wenceslas Square to acclaim the downfall of the communist regime. Dubček was subsequently elected as chairman (speaker) of the federal parliament. His popularity derived from his decency, dignity, good humour, and quiet courage, which he retained up to his death.

Eckstine Billy (William Clarence) 1913–1993. US jazz singer, bandleader, and trumpeter, whose mid-1940s orchestra included bebop greats Dizzy Gillespie and Charlie Parker, and singer Sarah Vaughan. He had several top-ten hits, including 'I Apologize' 1950 and 'Passing Strangers' 1957 (a duet with Vaughan).

Eckstine was born in Pittsburgh, Pennsylvania. With his deep baritone vibrato and liking for ballads, he began as a night-club singer and was always equally at home with pop and jazz. As the vocalist 1939–43 in the orchestra led by pianist Earl Hines, Eckstine learned to play trumpet and trombone, and had his first hit 1940 with 'Jelly, Jelly'. The big band he led 1944–47 became legendary for the number of outstanding jazz musicians it employed (the teenage Miles Davis and the drummer Art Blakey among them) and for its bebop innovation, but was not a commercial success. 'Anything the black man originates that cannot be copied right away by his white contemporaries is stepped on,' Eckstine explained. Returning to a solo career, he became the most popular vocalist in the USA, with hits like 'Blue Moon' 1948 and 'Caravan' 1949. In the late 1950s he disappeared from the charts and returned to night clubs.

In his heyday the handsome Mr B, as he was known, was noted for his sartorial style. Working with Duke Ellington's orchestra in 1966, Eckstine managed for four weeks to wear a different suit each evening.

Denholm Elliott

Elliott Denholm Mitchell 1922–1992. English actor of stage, film, and television. In his early career he was known especially for playing youthful parts and stiff-upper-lip Englishmen and then, as his good looks matured, for his portrayal of somewhat degenerate upper-class characters.

Elliott started acting at his Surrey preparatory school. He went on to Malvern College, Worcestershire. He studied for a year at the Royal Academy of Dramatic Art in London before joining RAF Bomber Command at the beginning of World War II. He spent the last three years of the war in a prisoner-of-war camp in Germany and acted in a number of camp productions. His professional career began in 1945 with a part in Victorian melodrama, *The Drunkard*, at the Amersham Playhouse. His first appearance in London's West End was a public schoolboy in *The Guinea Pig* by W Cheetham Strode, at the Criterion Theatre. In 1949 and 1950 he was Edgar, the son of the Duke of Altair, played by Lawrence Olivier, in Christopher Fry's *Venus Observed* at the St James's theatre. This won him the Clarence Derwent prize for best supporting performance. He went to New York later in 1950 to appear in *Ring Round the Moon* by the French playwright, Jean Anouilh. In 1953 he was in T S Eliot's *The Confidential Clerk* at the Edinburgh Festival and in London. He joined the Shakespeare Memorial Theatre, Stratford upon Avon, in 1960 and played Bassanio in *The Merchant of Venice*, Troilus in *Troilus and Cressida* and Valentine in *Two Gentlemen of Verona*.

His stage appearances became less frequent as his film career became more demanding. His first film part was that of the minor civil servant in *Dear Mr Prohack* 1949; then followed leading roles in *The Cruel Sea* 1953 and *The Heart of the Matter* 1953, and several minor roles until 1964 when his con man aristocrat in *Nothing but the Best*, instructing Alan Bates on how to get into high society, marked a turning point for him. In his first film for Hollywood he was a cynical prisoner in *King Rat* 1965. He followed this a year later with the part of the villainous back-street abortionist in *Alfie*. He played many villains in films after this. He will also be remembered as the conceited butler in *Trading Places* 1983, the Fleet Street hack in *Defence of the Realm* 1985, and as Mr Emerson in *A Room with a View* 1986. He appeared in many TV plays and series, including *Bleak House* 1987. He received the BAFTA award for best TV actor in 1981 and for best supporting film actor in 1984, 1985, and 1986.

Evans Geraint Llewellyn, Sir 1922–1992. Welsh operatic baritone who, in a career of 36 years, sang more than 70 roles. His successes abroad opened up a new era for post-war British singers. The warmth of his voice, the clarity of his diction, and his engaging stage presence endeared him to opera house audiences, television viewers, and recorded-music enthusiasts all over the world.

Evans was born and grew up in Cilfynydd, a Welsh mining village. His father was a miner and local choir leader. He left school at 14 and worked as a window-dresser in a ladies' fashion shop in Pontypridd. He studied at the Guildhall School of Music in London, but World War II had started and he became a radar operator in the RAF. By the end of the war he had joined the BBC British Forces network in Hamburg as a singer and producer. He studied singing in Hamburg with Theo Hermann and later in Geneva with Fernando Carpi. In 1948 he joined the struggling Covent Garden company and made his debut with them as the Nightwatchman in Wagner's *Die Meistersinger*. He made such an impression that he was given the title role in a new production of Mozart's *The Marriage of Figaro*, a role he sang throughout his career at Covent Garden, at the Salzburg Festival, and in many opera houses abroad. He was associated with several productions at Covent Garden of works by Benjamin Britten, the English composer. He created the role of Mr Flint, the sailing master, in Britten's *Billy Budd* 1951, sang Captain Balstrode in *Peter Grimes*, and Bottom in the first production of *A Midsummer Night's Dream* 1961.

He made his Glyndebourne debut in 1950 as Gulielmo, one of the lovers in Mozart's *Così Fan Tutte*. Other Mozart roles followed, including Papageno in *The Magic Flute* and Leporello in *Don Giovanni*. He will be always be remembered at Glyndebourne for his singing of the title role in Verdi's *Falstaff*, which he also sang and acted unforgettably at Covent Garden and elsewhere. Other roles he famously interpreted include Schaunard, the Bohemian musician in Puccini's *La Bohème*, with which he made his Vienna State Opera debut; Beckmesser in Wagner's *Die Meistersinger*, the first of many roles he sang for San Francisco; and Dulcamara, the quack seller of love potions in Donizetti's *L'Elisir d'Amore*, the role in which he made his farewell appearance at Covent Garden 1984. To coincide with this occasion he published his memoirs, *A Knight at the Opera*; he had been knighted in 1969.

Fowler Gerald (Gerry) 1935–1993. British politician and academic, influential in the educational and political camps of British policy-making during a period of intense change in higher education. In a career which took him from Parliament to academe and back several times, he was a doughty and at times unpredictable champion of equal access for all to higher education.

As a Labour MP, he had three periods as a junior minister at technology and education during an interrupted parliamentary career which extended from 1966 to 1979. The loss of his parliamentary seat in 1970 allowed him to experience life as an academic at the Open University and in the new polytechnics, two of the innovations in which he had been involved politically. Later, as rector of the Polytechnic of North London from 1982 until his early retirement in 1992, and as a combative chairman of the Committee of Directors of Polytechnics, he was involved in the transfer of the polytechnics from local government control and their elevation to university status in 1992. At NELP he was a staunch champion of education for disadvantaged groups in higher education.

Frink Elizabeth, Dame 1930–1993. English sculptor who, though uncompromising and unconcerned about fashion in the art world, achieved widespread popularity with her sculptures of dogs and horses and her striking images of the single naked male figure.

Frink was born in Thurlow, Suffolk. Her father was a brigadier in the Army, polo player and riding instructor, and she began riding at the age of four. World War II was another childhood influence on her work, particularly the sight of burning planes returning to the airfield close to the family home, and newsreels of Nazi concentration camps shown at the local cinema. After school at the Convent of The Holy Family, Exmouth, she studied at Guildford School of Art 1947–49 and Chelsea School of Art 1949–53, where she afterwards taught for several years. At Chelsea she explored two main themes in her sculpture: naked men on horses and predatory birds. She won a prize in the *Unknown Political Prisoner* international competition 1952. Amnesty International's work for prisoners of conscience was a strong concern of hers. She produced a series of busts of victims and martyrs of political injustice and this led on to her gaunt, somewhat larger than life-sized, male figures.

From 1967 to 1973 she lived in France and expressed her horror of the Algerian War and other troubles in North Africa in a series of 'goggle heads', resembling torturers in sunglasses, or the messengers of death in motor-cycle goggles in Jean Cocteau's film *Orphée*. In her later years, influenced by the *Riace* bronzes, Classical Greek figures found in the sea off the coast of southern Italy, her male figures became more aggressive, and the Aboriginal art she had seen on a visit to Australia induced her to produce startling colour effects. Frink will also be remembered for her public commissions, such as the *Dorset Martyrs* in Dorchester and the *Shepherd with Three Lambs* in Paternoster Square, London. She also undertook a few commissions for churches, the last being a bronze *Christ* for Liverpool Cathedral, unveiled only weeks before her death. She was created DBE 1982 and made a Companion of Honour 1992.

Frost Major General John Dutton, CB, DSO and Bar, MC, the commander of the 2nd Parachute Battalion, who held the bridge at Arnhem.

Frost was the son of Brigadier F D Frost. He was born in Poona on New Year's Eve 1912. He was educated at Wellington College, Monkton Combe School, and Sandhurst before being commissioned into the Cameronians (The Scottish Rifles) in 1932. His early service was in Palestine, and in 1938 he was seconded to the Iraq Levies with whom he served until 1941. Feeling that the war was passing him by, he engineered his return to England where he was posted to the newly formed 2nd Parachute Battalion. His distinguished wartime career included leading the Bruneval raid in February 1942 and service in North Africa and Sicily.

'Johnnie' Frost carved his name in the annals of Anglo-American military history by reaching and holding the bridge at Arnhem until his ammunition ran out in September 1944, although surrounded by SS Panzers. His name was later illuminated by Cornelius Ryan's book and Richard Attenborough's film *A Bridge Too Far*, in which he was portrayed by Anthony Hopkins. Frost's epic fight at Arnhem was but the climax of his wartime service with the 2nd Parachute Battalion. He was a founder member of '2 Para' and his indomitable leadership as adjutant, company commander and then commanding officer, established its fighting traditions.

Galinski Heinz 1912–1992. German Jewish community leader; survivor of the Auschwitz and Buchenwald death camps. He helped to re-establish a strong Jewish community in post-war Germany, becoming chairman of the Central Council of German Jews 1988–92.

Born in Marienburg, in what is now Poland, son of a German–Jewish businessman, as a young man in Berlin he witnessed Nazism's rise at first hand. When the regime took control, he was sent first to Auschwitz and then to Buchenwald. His first wife and parents were killed in the Holocaust, but Galinski survived, being moved eventually to Bergen-Belsen. In 1945 he was freed by the British army. Many fellow survivors left Germany for a new life in other western European countries or Israel, but he stayed in Germany to held rebuild the Jewish community, almost annihilated by the Nazis. Although slight of stature and physically unimpressive, his exceptional energy and fierce dedication made him unchallenged leader of German Jewry.

His methods were simple and direct. In West Berlin in 1949 he headed a tiny Jewish community, its morale severely dented by the experience of Nazism. By organizing old people's homes, and training rabbis and cantors to provide spiritual leadership, he revived spirits and restored self-esteem. His success led to a wider following and, eventually, a worldwide reputation. A fearless opponent of any revival of neo-Nazism and fascism, in 1975 he narrowly escaped a bomb attack by the far-left Red Army Faction, which objected to criticisms of extremism of all kinds. His relations with Israel were not always good, some Zionists arguing there was no place for Jews in Germany, yet on his death Israeli leaders applauded his devotion to the Jewish cause. In January 1992 he saw the establishment of a national memorial at the Wannsee Villa, Berlin, where Nazi leaders planned the Jews' extermination 50 years before. He hoped this would ensure that young Germans would always be made aware of the horrors perpetrated by the German nation.

Dizzy Gillespie

Gillespie Dizzy 1917–1993. US jazz trumpeter who, with saxophonist Charlie Parker, was the chief creator and exponent of the bebop style as well as a creator of Cu-bop, an Afro-Cuban fusion, both in the 1940s. He also campaigned for civil rights and multiculturalism. Gillespie influenced many modern jazz trumpeters, including Miles Davis.

Gillespie, born in South Carolina, moved first to Philadelphia and then, in 1937, to New York, where he made his first recordings as a soloist. He was a member of popular bandleader Cab Calloway's orchestra 1939–41, with shorter spells in other bands, and formed his own quartet 1942. The following year he first recorded with Parker (whom he described as 'the other side of my heartbeat') and jazz history was made.

The hipster image that Gillespie invented, with goatee, black beret, and sunglasses, was adopted by beboppers everywhere. He added an upturned trumpet (bent in an accident) and an amiable, clowning persona. Though his candidacy for US president 1964 was tongue in cheek (he promised to rename the White House the Blues House), Gillespie was a serious musician and internationalist. He toured widely on a cultural mission for the State Department in 1956, the first jazz musician to be so honoured. In 1968 he joined the Baha'i faith, which expects members to work for world peace. His formation of the United Nations Orchestra in the late 1980s, incorporating a strong Latin element, amounted almost to a summary of his life and work.

Gish Lillian 1893–1993. US actress. The preeminent actress of the American silent screen, Lillian Gish appeared in over 100 films. She is most readily associated with the masterpieces of D.W. Griffith, whose films gave the American cinema its early identity. Her pure style was far removed from the gesticulation often thought of as silent film acting. She was renowned for the lengths to which she was prepared to go in pursuit of physical conviction: for example, depriving herself of food and water for several days to make her death scene in *La Boheme* 1924 look authentic.

Born in Springfield, Ohio, she made her first stage appearance at the age of five. She and her sister Dorothy followed their mother into show business as a double act. In 1912 they were introduced to D.W. Griffith at Biograph's New York studio, and they (and their mother) made their first film appearances the same day. Over the next ten years Lillian acted for Griffith in numerous films, including the most celebrated and innovatory of their time: *Birth of a Nation* 1915, *Intolerance* 1916, *Broken Blossoms* 1919, *Way Down East* 1920, and *Orphans of the Storm* 1921.

After an amicable parting with Griffith, she appeared in such classics of the late-silent era as *The Scarlet Letter* 1926 and *The Wind* 1928. With the coming of sound her film career declined, but during the 1930s she played several classical roles on the Broadway stage. Later she occasionally returned to the cinema in subsidiary roles, notably in *Duel in the Sun* 1947 and *Night of the Hunter* 1955. She continued to work until almost the end of her life: her final film was *The Whales of August* 1987. In 1970 she received a special Academy Award for her contribution to films, and in 1984 the American Film Institute bestowed its life achievement award upon her.

Golding William Gerald, Sir 1911–1993. English novelist, essayist, and travel writer, winner of the 1983 Nobel Prize for Literature. His first and most well-known novel, *Lord of the Flies* 1954, although initially turned down by no less than 15 publishers, sold over 2,000,000 copies in ten years and has been translated into several languages. It became a cult book, especially in the USA, and is still today a prescribed text for almost every English literature course for young people. The film version, made by Peter Brook in 1962, was also highly successful.

Golding was born in St Columb Minor, Cornwall. He grew up in Marlborough, Wiltshire, and was educated at the grammar school there, where his father was a master. He was at Brasenose College, Oxford from 1932 to 1935. While still an undergraduate he published *Poems* 1934, a slim volume that he later did his best to disown. After Oxford he worked for a few years as an actor, writer and director for a number of small theatre companies and in 1939 joined the teaching staff at Bishop Wordsworth's School, Salisbury. He spend the war years between 1940 and 1945 in the

Royal Navy, as an officer in charge of a rocket ship and an instructor of naval cadets. He returned to his teaching post after the war, resigning in 1961 when the success of *Lord of the Flies* made it possible for him to write full-time.

Golding's novels were never about trivial or ephemeral matters. They dealt with universal themes and anxieties: evil, greed, guilt, primal instincts, unknown forces. His first childhood memory was of the terror and darkness he felt in the flint-walled cellar of the family's medieval house in Marlborough. Significant also was the proximity of numerous prehistoric sites, like Silbury Hill and Stonehenge. He thought of archaeologists as explorers of the darkness under the earth. He learnt ancient Greek during World War II and his study of the Greek myths, Homer and the tragedians was an important influence. In *Lord of the Flies*, a parody of R M Ballantyne's idealistic classic, *Coral Island* 1858, evil issues forth and the stranded schoolboys become savages. In *The Inheritors* 1955 savage *Homo sapiens* brutally defeat the inarticulate but feeling Neanderthals. *Pincher Martin* 1956 is about the desperate struggle of a man lost at sea and stranded on a rock. Among the other novels are *Freefall* 1959, *The Spire* 1964, *The Scorpion God* 1971, and *Darkness Visible* 1978, a disturbing book, full of symbolism, which won the James Tait Black Memorial Prize. Two important essay collections were published, *The Hot Gates and Other Occasional Pieces* 1966 and *A Moving Target* 1982, and a travel book *An Egyptian Journey* appeared in 1985.

William Golding

In his final period he wrote four more novels, *The Paper Men* 1984 about the trials of a writer's life, in particular his persecution by the biographer-critic, and a trilogy about a voyage to Australia in the early years of the 19th century, presenting a microcosm of English society at that time. The first novel of the trilogy, *Rites of Passage* 1980, won the Booker Prize. The other two, *Close Quarters* 1987 and *Fire Down Below* 1989, complete a masterpiece that leaves us in no doubt about Golding's greatness as a writer. He was knighted in 1988.

Hani Chris 1943–1993. South African black politician and guerrilla leader. An heroic and charismatic figure, he had the unique quality in the cauldron of South African politics of enjoying the support and trust of both militants and moderates, and especially the youth of his country. Next to Nelson Mandela he was the most popular and respected black politician and his assassination in April 1993 by white right-wing extremists left a void that will be difficult to fill.

Born in the Transkei, he joined the South African Communist Party (SACP) and ANC's guerrilla movement, Umkhonto we Sizwe (MK – Spear of the Nation) in 1962, after graduating as a classical scholar in Latin and English. He then left South Africa to be trained in Zimbabwe, with the guerrilla fighters of the African People's Union (ZAPU). After service in freedom movements in Botswana, Zambia, and Lesotho, Hani returned to South Africa in 1990 where, despite his military experience, he threw himself wholeheartedly into seeking a peaceful solution to his country's problems. Enormously popular among the mass of black South Africans, his breadth of culture also made him an attractive figure for moderate whites. He was seen by many as the natural successor to Nelson Mandela but his acceptance of the SACP leadership, in December 1991, seemed to reduce his chances of assuming Mandela's mantle. Hani was, however, following a longer-term strategy, with the aim of mobilizing working-class blacks, and perhaps even showing that a practical form of communism could succeed in a single country where it had failed internationally. He was seen as a key figure in the negotiations for constitutional change with the de Klerk government, a fact that provides an obvious reason for his untimely death by assassination.

Hawkes Christoher 1905–1992. Leading British archaeologist, professor of European archaeology at the University of Oxford. A pioneer in the study of the prehistoric periods of Britain and Europe, Hawkes helped to found international prehistory as a discipline in Britain in the late 1920s and early 1930s. Later, his interest in the application of scientific techniques to archaeological material led in 1955 to the creation of the Research Laboratory for Archaeology and the History of Art at Oxford.

Hawkes was a skilled excavator, whose work on Iron Age sites such as the hillfort of St Catherine's Hill and at Colchester often surpassed the standards of his contemporaries; but he will be remembered primarily for his writings, which have been extremely influential. He particularly specialized in the European late Bronze Age and early Iron Age, complex and formative periods that witnessed the interaction of barbarian communities with classical civilization. He focused on the problems of cultural change, and on the continuity between late prehistory and early civilization in Europe: for example, in the Celtic tradition of Europe and Britain.

Hawkes also made an important contribution to archaeological theory and the debate about the nature of archaeological evidence, insisting that there existed a 'ladder of inference': that is, one could safely use archaeological evidence to reconstruct the simpler and more material aspects of past societies, but that there were clear limitations on the amount of information about beliefs or social structure that could be inferred from these mute remains. This view has been intensively criticized by the more optimistic and idealistic (but perhaps less realistic) archaeologists of the past 30 years.

Hayes Helen 1900–1993. US actress. Although she gained wider fame in her latter years for her appearance as the stowaway passenger in the film *Airport* 1970, for which she won an Academy Award as best supporting actress, and for several subsequent Walt Disney productions, Helen Hayes was first and foremost a stage performer. She played her first role in the theatre at the age of six, and became a Broadway star in *Dear Brutus* in 1918. Over the next five decades, she consolidated a reputation as the 'first lady' of the American theatre, a regal association aptly underlined by her particular successes in the title roles of *Mary of Scotland* 1936 and *Victoria Regina* 1938–1939.

Born in Washington DC, the daughter of an actress, Helen Hayes appeared in several silent films and won an Academy Award for her first performance in a talkie, *The Sin of Madelon Claudet* 1931. However, she did not care for the atmosphere of Hollywood, and during the years of her Broadway eminence made only a few sorties into the cinema, of which the best remembered is probably the role of the dowager Empress in *Anastasia* 1956. In 1959 a Broadway theatre was named after her. She was married to the playwright Charles MacArthur (co-author of *The Front Page*) from 1928 until his death in 1956. Their son is the actor James MacArthur.

Hepburn Audrey 1929–1993. Professional name of Edda van Heemstra Hepburn-Ruston. US film actress. She won an Academy Award for her first starring role in the cinema, as the runaway princess in *Roman Holiday* 1953. Her innovative image, at once elfin and wistful, was highly influential in the spheres of modelling and fashion. She later ventured beyond this gamine appeal for more demanding roles, but turned down the title role in *The Diary of Anne Frank* 1959, saying that her memories of the Dutch Occupation would have made it too painful.

Born in Brussels to an English banker and a Dutch baroness, she was trapped in Arnhem with her mother when World War II began, and spent the war years there in hardship, though managing to train as a dancer. She subsequently appeared in revues in London's West End, plus small roles in several British films. Her break came when the novelist Colette insisted she play in the Broadway version of her novel *Gigi*. This led to her casting in *Roman Holiday* and to a succession of films during the 1950s and 1960s: mainly comedies, such as *Sabrina* 1954 and *Charade* 1963, but she also played Natasha in *War and Peace* 1956 and the doubting novice in *The Nun's Story* 1959. One of her most celebrated roles was the anarchic Holly Golightly in the bittersweet *Breakfast at Tiffany's* 1961.

In 1964 she played Eliza Doolittle in the film version of *My Fair Lady*: a controversial casting, as many had expected the part to be played by Julie Andrews, who created it on the stage. In the 1970s and 1980s Hepburn made occasional films, most significantly *Robin and Marian* 1976. Latterly she was active in a new career as special ambassador for the United Nations, and visited Somalia in the autumn of 1992. She was married twice: to the actor-director Mel Ferrer and to Italian psychiatrist Andrea Dotti.

Audrey Hepburn

Holley Robert William 1922–1993. Internationally-reputed American biochemist who, in addition to being a member of the team that first synthesized penicillin in the 1940s, shared the 1968 Nobel Prize for Physiology or Medicine for his pioneering work on the chemistry of the genetic code.

Working mainly at Cornell University, New York (where he gained his doctorate), and at the Salk Institute, California, Holley received over a dozen distinguished honours and awards. He was appointed to the National Academy of Sciences and to an American Cancer Society Research Professorship; he also received the Lasker Award for Basic Medical Research. At Cornell he became professor of biochemistry 1964 and was chairman of the department 1965–66. When he received the Nobel Prize, shared with Har Gobrind Khorana and Marshall Nirnberg, Holley was a visiting fellow at the Salk Institute.

The work of the three men, achieved independently, explained how the genes' 'language' – the information stored in a cell's DNA – ensures that amino acids are inserted into protein molecules in the correct order. This immensely complex project began in 1956 and took nine years to accomplish. Starting from 90 kg of baker's yeast, Holley painstakingly extracted 1 gram of pure RNA. For the first time, the sequence of a nucleic acid could be determined and the structure of a gene worked out. Holley then turned his attention to the way abnormalities in the growth of cells cause cancer. To this, as to all his scientific work, he brought a creative flair that showed itself in another of his talents: sculpture. A man of intellectual integrity and innate modesty, he said in his Nobel address: 'Without minimizing the pleasure of receiving awards and prizes, I think it is true that the greatest satisfaction for a scientist comes from carrying a major piece of research to a successful conclusion.'

Horszowski Mieczyslaw 1892–1993. Polish-born US pianist whose concert career of over 90 years is by far the longest ever. His technique and dexterity seemed to have diminished little, if at all, during his last years and his beautiful, expressive tone seemed, if anything, to have become even more remarkable. He remained a very fine interpreter of Bach, Beethoven, Schubert, and, of course, Chopin, and a champion of new music, particularly that of his compatriot, Karol Szymanowski.

Horszowski was a child progidy. At a very early age he studied with Hendryk Melcer at the Lwów Conservatory and when he was seven performed in public for the first time, playing by heart all of Bach's *Two-Part Inventions*. At this age also he went to Vienna to become a pupil of Theodor Leschetizky, the great Polish teacher who taught so many legendary pianists. He later went to Paris and studied with the composer Maurice Ravel, and the leading French pianist of the day, Alfred Cortot. In 1906 he toured the USA for the first time. Then followed a further period of study until 1913 when, now a mature artist, he launched himself on his extraordinary career. He was a noted chamber music player and formed duos and trios with the Catalan cellist, conductor and composer Pablo Casals, the Russian-born violinist Alexander Schneider and the Hungarian-born violinist Joseph Szigeti. He frequently took part in festivals, including the Prades Festival in southwest France, organized by Casals, the Marlboro Festival in Vermont, USA, and, in later years, the Aldeburgh Festival in the UK. In 1940 he emigrated to the USA where he taught at the Curtis Institute in Philadelphia. Among his most famous students are Eugene Istomin, Peter Serkin, Murray Perahia, and Andras Schiff.

Hunt James 1947–1993. English motor racing driver who won the World Formula One Drivers' Championship in 1976. He competed in 92 Grand Prix, winning ten.

A stockbroker's son, James Hunt was educated at Wellington College. His success as a driver began with the founding of the Hesketh Grand Prix team by Lord Hesketh in 1974. Previously, Hunt had struggled as a Formula Three driver; he had been involved in crashes so often that he was known as 'Hunt the Shunt'. Others claim the epithet derived from a punch that he threw at fellow competitor David Morgan after a collision at Crystal Palace in 1970. In 1975 Hunt won the Dutch Grand Prix for the Hesketh Team, beating the previously unstoppable Niki Lauda. In 1976 he moved to McLaren and won the world title by one point from Lauda, confirming his front-runner status. He scored a further three wins in 1977. The following year, Hunt was deeply affected by the death of his friend and fellow racing driver Ronnie Peterson, whom he had pulled from the blazing wreckage of his car at Monza. In 1979 he moved again, this time to the Wolf team, but he had clearly lost his enthusiasm for driving. Following the Monaco Grand Prix he announced his retirement. He became a successful motor-racing commentator when he joined Murray Walker on the BBC2 *Grand Prix* programme, affording him the opportunity to air his outspoken views.

Joseph Helen 1905–1992. Teacher and anti-racist campaigner in South Africa. A fearless fighter for racial tolerance and equality, she became a close friend of the leading figures in the African National Congress (ANC), including Nelson Mandela and Walter Sisulu, and, for her work with the ANC was awarded its highest honour.

Born Helen Fennell in Sussex, she left Britain in the 1920s to teach in India. She settled in South Africa in the early 1930s and then returned to her home country during World War II, serving in the Women's Auxiliary Air Force (WAAF). At the end of hostilities she returned to South Africa, mixing with the affluent white and Indian communities but quietly retaining her belief in the equality of man, irrespective of race or colour. Living in

Durban, she met and married a dentist, Billy Joseph, but the marriage was short-lived. She then moved to Johannesburg and became progressively active in trade union affairs and politics. Her abhorrence of apartheid and her campaigning for its removal earned her the respect of black African leaders and the contumely of the white minority government as she threw herself into the movement against apartheid and, especially, the promotion of the rights of black women. From the ANC she received its highest honour, Isithwalandwe-Seaparankoe, and from the government the fame of being the first South African woman to be placed under house arrest . Despite being diagnosed as having cancer in 1971, and eventually confined to a wheelchair, she continued her fight against oppression and became even closer to her friends whose cause she shared, referring to Winnie Mandela as 'the daughter I always wished I'd had'.

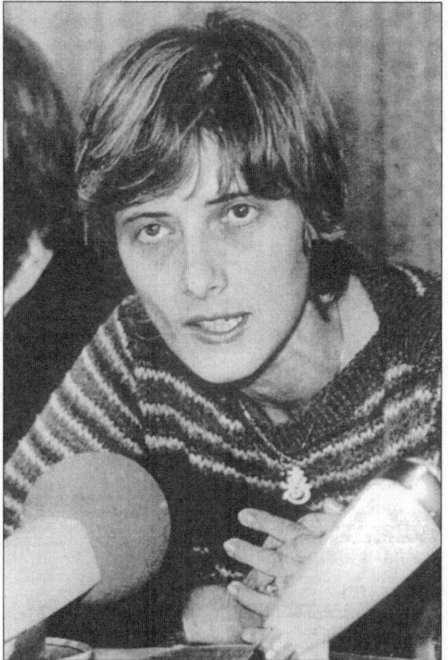

Petra Kelly

Kelly Petra Karin 1947–1992. German environmental activist, writer, and politician. She was a high-profile and effective campaigner against nuclear power and on other environmental issues, and helped found the German Green Party 1980. She died at the hands of her lover, the former general turned peace campaigner, Gert Bastian (1923–1992), who then killed himself with the same pistol he had used on her.

Born in Germany, Kelly, who took the name of her American stepfather (an army lieutenant-colonel), was brought up mainly in the United States, attending the American University in Washington, DC. She worked briefly in the office of Robert Kennedy, and in the presidential campaign of Hubert Humphrey, before returning to Germany and a job with the European Commission 1972. Deeply concerned with radioactivity in the environment, having seen the early death of her half-sister from leukemia, she carried out pioneering ecological work in this position. She co-founded the German Green Party (Die Grünen) 1980 and, with her fluency in English, emerged as its most prominent early spokesperson, and the leader of its pragmatic wing as the party split into its increasingly bitter divisions between 'realists' and 'fundamentalists'. She was elected a Green member of the German parliament 1983–1990, and she was one of the first – and certainly the best-known – Green MPs in the world. However, during her tenure she saw the fragmentation of the once powerful German Green Party and the rise of the far right. She was also severely criticized within the Greens for assuming too assertive and public a role. She met Gert Bastian in 1989, after he had been dismissed from the German army for opposing the stationing of American cruise missiles in the Federal Republic. He, too, subsequently became a Green Party Bundestag deputy. With the demise of unity within the Greens and experiencing poor health due to a kidney condition, Kelly grew increasingly introspective and paranoid. Her tragic death was not discovered until three weeks after the shootings and questions regarding the exact circumstances of the killings – whether there had been a suicide pact or whether Gert took the decision himself – remained unanswered.

King Albert. Adopted name of Albert Nelson 1923–1992. US blues guitarist and singer whose ringing tone influenced numerous rock guitarists. His recordings for the Stax label, such as 'Born Under a Bad Sign' and 'Crosscut Saw' (both 1967), became classics and made him popular beyond the blues circuit. His playing also shows psychedelic and funk influences.

King was born in Indianola, Mississippi. Left-handed, he learned to play on a standard guitar without restringing it, which contributed to his characteristic sound. His first recordings were made in Indiana, Chicago, and St Louis. In 1966 he signed with Stax Records in Memphis, then a leading blues and soul label, which provided him with first-rate backing musicians in Booker T and the MGs for the album *Born Under a Bad Sign* 1967. At that time many rock guitarists were discovering the blues, and King's strong electric guitar solos were much borrowed and imitated; King in turn gained a new audience in the rock clubs, and his next Stax album, *Live Wire/Blues Power* 1968, was recorded live at the fashionable Fillmore in San Francisco. 'My days of paying dues are over,' he concluded. 'Now it's my turn to do the collecting.'

Horn sections added a funk element to King's music in the 1970s, both before and after the demise of Stax; later he returned to a purer blues sound, as on *I'm in a Phone Booth, Baby* 1986, with its title track written by the younger blues musician Robert Cray.

Koresh David. Adopted name of Vernon Wayne Howell 1959–1993. US Christian religious leader of the Branch Davidians, an offshoot of the Seventh-Day Adventist Church that believes in the literal apocalyptic end of history, as described in the biblical Book of Revelation, prior to the second coming of Christ. With a number of coreligionists, he died in a fire at the cult's headquarters in Waco, Texas, as a result of military intervention.

Koresh, born in Houston, Texas, began as a Seventh-Day Adventist. He is said to have memorized the New Testament by the time he was 12, and as a teenager he would pray for hours; his mother thought he was a 'good boy'. But he was expelled from the Adventists as a 'bad influence on the young', and joined the Branch Davidians in 1981, rising to become leader. Identifying with his own understanding of Christ as a vengeful messiah, he stressed sacrifice and martyrdom and meted out corporal punishment to children who disobeyed. He married a 14-year-old girl, Rachel Jones, in 1983 and considered it his right to have sexual relations with any woman in the group or their children. The practices of the sect became increasingly repressive under Koresh's leadership, which led eventually to the siege of the Branch Davidians' camp in Waco by the Federal Bureau of Investigation in 1993. Their strong-arm military tactics fuelled the paranoia of the cult members, many of whom died when a fire broke out at the culmination of the siege.

Kroger Helen. Adopted name of Leoninta Cohen 1913–1992. Communist sympathizer and Soviet spy. Convicted in the UK of espionage in 1961, with her husband Morris Cohen, she was imprisoned and then released eight years later in a spy-swap deal, allowing her and her husband to settle in Moscow as guests of the Soviet government.

Born in Brooklyn, New York City, she married Morris Cohen, and instilled in him her deeply felt belief in the rightness of communism. Together they became active in the Soviet spy network in the USA and were suspected of involvement in the Rosenberg atomic espionage ring. When Julius Rosenberg was arrested in 1950 the Cohens disappeared. They moved to England, via Vienna, having acquired New Zealand passports and the names Peter and Helen Kroger. From a modest bungalow in Ruislip, Middlesex, where Peter supposedly had a small antiquarian book business, they operated a sophisticated radio station, passing vital defence information to Moscow. They were arrested, charged with espionage, and sentenced to 20 years' imprisonment at the Old Bailey in March 1961. Eight years later, however, they were released in exchange for the British university lecturer, Gerald Brooke, who had been imprisoned for spying in Moscow. At the time it was a major *cause célèbre* and provoked Hugh Whitemore to write the play *A Pack of Lies* 1983, which enjoyed success in Britain and the USA. After their release, Helen and her husband became the honoured guests of the Soviet government, living in some comfort in a dacha on the outskirts of Moscow. Although Morris later expressed some reservations about the totalitarian Soviet regime under Brezhnev, Helen retained her total commitment to communism to the end of her life.

MacMillan Kenneth 1929–1992. Leading British choreographer, dancer, and director, one of the most distinguished of the Royal Ballet's choreographers and probably its most prolific.

MacMillan was born in Dunfermline, Scotland, and suffered considerable hardship during his childhood. The family moved to Great Yarmouth, and MacMillan went to the grammar school there. He became interested in ballet on reading a dance magazine in the local public library and had the good fortune to find a teacher, Phyllis Adams, who took him on free of charge. At 16 he successfully auditioned for the Sadler's Wells Ballet School (now the Royal Ballet School) and about a year later, in 1946, joined the Sadler's Wells Theatre Ballet, which was just forming. The Sadler's Wells Ballet, the main company, had moved to Covent Garden and was to become the Royal Ballet. He danced for both companies from 1948. He began choreography in 1952 under Frederick Ashton. When Ashton became director of the Royal Ballet in 1963, MacMillan became resident choreographer. Between 1966 and 1969 he was director of ballet at the Deutsche Oper (German Opera House) in West Berlin. He returned to London in 1970 first as codirector, then director of the Royal Ballet, resigning in 1977 to become principal choreographer. Since 1984 he had been artistic associate of the American Ballet.

Among his most memorable ballets are: *Danses Concertantes* 1955, *Agon* 1958, *The Firebird* 1960, *The Rite of Spring* 1962, all to music by Igor Stravinsky; *Laiderette* 1954, to music by Frank Martin; Prokofiev's *Romeo and Juliet* 1965; a ballet to Mahler's *Song of the Earth* 1965, which he did for the Stuttgart company; *Anastasia* 1971, to music by Tchaikovsky and Martinu; *Elite Syncopations* 1974, to rags by Scott Joplin arranged by Richard Rodney Bennett; a new version of Benjamin Britten's *The Prince of the Pagodas* 1989; and *Winter Dreams* 1991, to music by Tchaikovsky. At the time of his death he was working on a revival of his extraordinarily rich, full-length ballet, *Mayerling*, and choreography for the dances in a revival of *Carousel*, the musical by Rodgers and Hammerstein, at the National Theatre in London. He received a knighthood in 1983.

Mankiewicz Joseph L(eo) 1909–1993. US film writer and director. He is celebrated as the writer-director of *All About Eve* 1950, a satirical melodrama about theatre people, that starred Bette Davis as a fading actress, and is generally considered one of the wittiest films ever to come out of Hollywood. Mankiewicz was noted for the quality of dialogue that graced his scripts.

He made his name with the social comedy *A Letter to Three Wives* 1949, and won writing and directing Academy Awards for this film and for *All about Eve*. His subsequent films were varied and often distinguished, but did not altogether sustain his early reputation.

Born in Wilkes Barr, Pennsylvania, son of an academic, he was the younger brother of Herman Mankiewicz (co-author of *Citizen Kane*), and through his brother's good offices entered films in 1929 as a staff writer at Paramount. He moved to MGM where he subsequently turned producer and was responsible for Fritz Lang's first American film *Fury* 1936 and for *Three Comrades* 1938, partly scripted by Scott Fitzgerald. After moving to Fox he began directing with *Dragonwyck* 1946, and directed films in several genres before making his name with *A Letter to Three Wives* and *All About Eve*. Back at MGM, he directed an acclaimed film of *Julius Caesar* 1953, and in Europe as an independent producer made *The Barefoot Contessa* 1954, which offered an acerbic view of the film industry, but was somewhat compromised by the requirements of censorship. His involvement with the epic *Cleopatra* 1963 was unhappy but made him rich, and he made only three subsequent films. His last was *Sleuth* 1972, an ingeniously theatrical thriller with only two performers, Laurence Olivier and Michael Caine. In his latter years he contemplated an autobiography, but sadly did not get round to writing it.

Mansoor Mallikarjun 1910–1992. Famous Indian classical singer who dominated Indian vocal music for almost 50 years, singing a combination of Hindustani (north Indian) and Carnatic (south Indian) music.

Mansoor was born in the village of Mansur, near Dharwed in the southern Indian state of Karnataka. He often played truant from school to watch the local drama troupe practising and eventually ran away from home to join them. He was a natural actor and often played leading roles. His artistic talent was spotted by Appayya Swami, a noted Carnatic singer, who gave him lessons in Carnatic music. He was also noticed by the Hindustani musician Neelakanthabua, who took him to his *gharana*, or music school, in the central Indian state of Gwalior. Somewhat later he became a disciple of Allaidya Khan, the pioneering musician and teacher of the Jaipir Atrauli *gharana* in Bombay. Allaidya Khan's sons, Manji and Brij Khan, were mainly responsible for instructing Mansoor, however. He made his first recording in 1933, for HMV, and by the 1940s his fame had spread across the whole of India. He became a music advisor to All India Radio in 1960. In 1962 he won the Karnataka Sangeet Natak Academy Award, which he was to win on three further occasions. A few months before he died he received the Padma Vibhushana, one of India's highest decorations.

Thurgood Marshall

Marshall Thurgood 1908–1993. US lawyer, campaigner for black civil rights, Solicitor General 1965–67, and first black Supreme Court justice 1967–91.

After exclusion from Maryland Law School for his colour, Marshall studied at Howard Law School, Washington DC, under Charles Houston, chief counsel of the National Association for the Advancement of Colored People. In 1936, he worked for the NAACP to remove the barriers set up for black people by the 1896 ruling that states could provide 'separate but equal' facilities for racial minorities. He also persuaded the Supreme Court to force the Maryland Law School to admit non-whites. Other universities were forced to admit and desegregate coloured students. Finally, in 1954, he led the Supreme Court to abandon the 'separate but equal' doctrine and forbid states from establishing separate schooling for black and white pupils.

Between 1944 and 1960, Marshall won 28 of his 32 Supreme Court cases, convincing the Court to ban 'whites only' democratic primaries, train waiting rooms, restaurants, rules restricting black bus passengers, and covenants preventing the sale of properties to minorities. From 1961 to 1965, as a Court of Appeals judge, none of his 112 opinions was reversed by the Supreme Court. He supported freedom of speech, passionately opposed the death penalty, and advocated affirmative action to cancel out the effects of racial prejudice. He also ended the use of 'whites-only' juries. As the court's liberal majority declined, Marshall found himself increasingly in the minority in over a fifth of cases during his last court term.

At the 1987 US Constitution bicentennial Marshall said that the original drafters 'could not have imagined, nor would then have accepted, that the document they were drafting would one day be construed by a Supreme Court to which had been appointed a woman and the descendant of an African slave.'

Maskell Dan 1908–1992. Tennis broadcaster, player, and coach. Dan Maskell was BBC Television's chief tennis commentator for 43 years and will always be remembered as the 'Voice of Wimbledon'. In 1982 he was appointed CBE for his services to tennis.

Born in Fulham, London, Maskell developed a love of tennis as a ball-boy at the nearby Queen's Club during his school holidays. He quickly progressed through the club's ranks, moving from professional ball-boy to teaching professional. By 1926 he had a five-year teaching contract at Queen's. Maskell became world professional champion in 1927, and in 1929 he moved to the All England Lawn Tennis and Croquet Club at Wimbledon as their first professional coach. During that time he coached the Davis Cup team to victory, in the great years of the tennis champion Fred Perry. By 1951 Maskell had won the British Professional Championships 16 times. Between 1947 and 1973 he was also the Lawn Tennis Association training manager, devoting himself to the transformation of its coaching and development work.

Maskell's broadcasting career began in 1949 when he became a radio commentator at Wimbledon. Two years later he moved into television coverage of the tournament. It was not long before his distinguished style of commentary became as much a part of Wimbledon as its strawberries and cream. Phrases such as 'Oh I say!' and 'That's a dream of a shot!', combined with his golden rule that 'A second's silence is worth a minute's talk' (a maxim he credited to golfing legend Henry Longhurst), helped make Dan Maskell a household name. He retired from commentating after the 1991 Wimbledon Championships.

McClintock Barbara 1902–1993. American geneticist who discovered mobile genetic elements or 'jumping genes'. Her demonstration that genes are not stable overturned one of the main tenets of heredity laid down by Gregor Mendel, the 19th century Moravian monk who founded genetics. It had enormous implications and explained, for example, how resistance to antibiotic drugs can be transmitted between entirely different bacterial types. Her Nobel Prize for Physiology or Medicine was awarded in 1983.

McClintock, the youngest of three sisters, enrolled in Cornell's College of Agriculture, New York. There she began, as an un dergraduate, to study the genetics of maize. Because the kernels are brightly coloured and variegated, maize is an ideal organism for genetic research. Subsequently her research was carried out at the Carnegie Institute of Washington, in Cold Spring Harbor, New York.

While working with maize seedlings, McClintock observed that the patterns on twin sectors were the inverse of one another. Further, the pigmentation of certain kernels did not correspond to their genetic makeup. She realized that as a single cell divided into sister cells, one gained what the other had lost. This meant that not all genes behave in the same way: some genes can switch others on and off. These genetic switches can move from one place to another on one chromosome, or even 'jump' from one chromosome to another. She explained her insight: 'When you suddenly see a problem, something happens. You have the answer – before you are able to put it into words... I know when to take it seriously. I'm absolutely sure... I'm just sure this is it.'

Moore Bobby 1941–1993. Footballer who captained England to victory in the 1966 World Cup Final. Moore became a British national hero, admired as much for his individualism and integrity as he was for his prowess on the football field. He was awarded an OBE in 1967.

Moore was born in Barking, East London. His footballing potential was first noticed by Malcolm Allison, then a player at West Ham United who was to become an outstanding coach. Moore went on to enjoy a 20-year league career for West Ham and Fulham, playing in 668 league games and representing his country in 108 internationals, 90 as captain. At club level he won the FA Cup with West Ham 1964 and the European Cup Winners' Cup a year later. He was named Footballer of the Year 1963–64. His behaviour on the pitch was low-key; he was not inclined towards the wild celebrations of goals. His nerves appeared steady even as he called the team out to the World Cup Final. It was his confidence and certainty of purpose, beyond his skill as a player, for which he gained such respect.

Moore retired from playing in 1977 and, after brief stints managing Oxford City and Southend United, where he was also a director, he concentrated on developing his sports marketing company and doing media work. He was disappointed in a number of business ventures. From 1986 to 1990 he was Sports Editor of the *Sunday Sport* and from 1990 to 1993 he was a regular commentator for London's Capital Radio station. Moore went public with his battle against cancer, which began in 1991, and continued to work until his death.

Nolan Sidney Robert, Sir 1917–1992. Australian painter, the first to deal with the essence and uniqueness of the continent's landscape and history. He became known internationally for his two series of paintings of the legendary outlaw and folk-hero, Ned Kelly.

Nolan was born in Carlton, a suburb of Melbourne. His family was poor, and he had to leave school at 14. He worked in the art studio of a hat firm, where he acquired useful skills in mixed media and paint spraying, and attended art classes in the evening at the Melbourne Gallery's school. His interest in European art developed in his early twenties and in 1938 he came to the notice of art patrons John and Sunday Reed, who supported him for several years. He did illustrations for the avant-garde magazine *Angry Penguins*. From 1942 he was in the army, stationed in a region of seemingly endless wheat fields. He took up landscape painting to relieve boredom, and observed how strong light isolates objects and events and imbues them with a timelessness. At the end of the war he began the first series of paintings on the life and exploits of Ned Kelly, depicting him in scrap-metal armour and a grotesque square helmet, almost comic yet vigorously masculine. Nolan worked on a second series in 1954–55 by which time he had already moved to Europe, eventually making the UK his base.

A visit to the Dardanelles resulted in over 100 paintings on the Gallipoli campaign of World War II, in which so many Australian soldiers lost their lives. Nolan's other works include the *Leda and the Swan* series 1960, and many paintings from his travels in Africa, America, Antartica, and China. His non-Australian paintings failed to excite the critics, and he suffered some neglect for 20 years or more until the showing of his famous earlier paintings at the *Angry Penguins* exhibition at the Hayward Gallery, London, in 1988 revived interest in his work. Nolan also produced designs and sets for opera and ballet, most notably for the 1981 production by fellow Australian, Elijah Moshinsky, of *Samson et Dalila* at the Royal Opera House, Covent Garden. He was knighted 1981 and appointed member of the Order of Merit 1983. In 1988 he was made Companion of the Order of Australia.

Nureyev Rudolf 1938–1993. Russian-born naturalized Austrian ballet dancer, choreographer, director, and producer. His athletic prowess, strikingly attractive appearance, and charismatic presence captivated audiences worldwide and made him one of the most remarkable figures in the history of dance. He danced all the important male roles in the ballet repertoire, and many others besides, and partnered most of the leading prima ballerinas of the past three or four decades. His partnership with Margot Fonteyn will remain unforgettable.

Nureyev was a Tatar. He was born near Lake Baikal, on a train journey, and grew up in Ufa in extreme poverty. A love of folk dancing and a sight of professional dancers at the town's small opera house led to lessons with Anna Udeltsova, who had been a member of the Diaghilev Ballet. At the age of 17 he entered the famous Vaganova Institute (also known as the Kirov Ballet School) in St Petersburg in the class of Aleksandr Pushkin, a brilliant teacher. Just three years later he joined the Kirov Ballet as a soloist, dancing with Natalya Dudinskaya (its top prima ballerina) for his first engagement. In 1961 the Kirov Ballet was in Paris on its first important tour of the West. Nureyev was highly praised but his socializing with French friends incurred the displeasure of the Soviet officials, who told him he had to return. Sensing that he would never again be allowed to leave the Soviet Union, he slipped his escort at Le Bourget Airport and sought political asylum – and a new career. In November 1961 he made his London debut at a gala in aid of the Royal Academy of Dancing with *Poème Tragique*, a short solo composed for him by Frederick Ashton, the English dancer, choreographer, and director of the Royal Ballet, and this led to an invitation to partner Margot Fonteyn, the academy's president, in *Giselle* at Covent Garden. Thus began the legendary partnership and a new lease of artistic life for Fonteyn, who was 19 years his senior.

Rudolf Nureyev

As well as dancing in the classics of the 19th century, he created many roles in modern works, most notably with Fonteyn in Ashton's *Marguerite and Armand*, first performed at Covent Garden 1963. He choreographed and staged ballets for nearly all the major companies, reviving works from the Russian repertoire like *Swan Lake*, *The Sleeping Beauty*, *The Nutcracker*, and *Raymonda*. In 1983 he was appointed director of the

Ballet at the Opéra in Paris, revitalized it, and gave much encouragement to young dancers. He appeared many times on TV and in films, including the feature *I Am a Dancer*, shown first in 1972. As a result of his tragically becoming a victim of AIDS, his physical powers inevitably declined but he was determined to continue working. He took up the new challenge of conducting in his last years and conducted (with considerable success) orchestras in Europe and the USA. His last appearance was a very emotional one at the Paris Opéra where he had been staging *La Bayadère*.

Nutter, Tommy 1943–1992. English trend-setting tailor whose suitings became famous in the 1960s–70s. Though employing conventional techniques he made a distinct break with traditional tailoring when he produced suits with wide lapels and flared trousers and experimented with fabrics by cutting pinstripes on the horizontal and mixing gamekeeper tweeds in three-piece suits.

Nutter initially went into the building trade aged 15 but changed career to join a traditional London tailoring company, and studied at the Tailor and Cutter Academy. However, he drew inspiration from the popular culture and night clubs of the 1960s. In 1969 he opened his own tailoring shop in Saville Row, London, where his clients included the Beatles, Mick and Bianca Jagger, Elton John, and the fashion designer Hardy Amies. Among his designs are the suits worn by John Lennon, Paul McCartney, and Ringo Starr on the cover of the Beatles' *Abbey Road* album.

Despite financial difficulties in the early 1970s he launched his first ready-to-wear line for Austin Reed in 1978, and in 1980 signed a five-year contract to design fabrics for a cloth manufacturer in Japan. He also produced two menswear collections for the Japanese department store Hankyu, and in 1989 created the outfits worn by the actor Jack Nicholson when he played the Joker in the film *Batman*. Although his designs questioned traditional conventions of tailoring Nutter was enthusiastic about the craftsmanship of tailoring and correct style; he would often write to journalists and clients with proposals for designs or comments on style.

Following his diagnosis as HIV-positive he campaigned actively in AIDS-related charity work.

Oort, Jan Hendrik 1900–1992. Dutch astronomer. He is recognized as one of the most influential astronomers of the 20th century for his work on the structure of our home galaxy and his deduction of the existence of a cloud of comets around our solar system, now known as the Oort Cloud.

Oort was born in Franeker, Friesland, and spent most of his working life at Leiden Observatory. In 1927 he used observations of the movement of stars in the Sun's neighbourhood to prove that the Galaxy rotates about a centre in the direction of the constellation Sagittarius, and he calculated that the Sun lies 30,000 light years from this centre. During World War II he turned his attention to the emerging science of radio astronomy, realizing that radio waves would make a powerful tool for mapping the Galaxy, since they were not blocked by intervening dust, unlike light waves. One of Oort's team, Hendrik van de Hulst, calculated that hydrogen gas (the most abundant substance in space) would emit radio waves of 21 cm wavelength and in 1951 Oort and his colleagues at Leiden succeeded in detecting these emissions. Subsequently Oort established radio observatories at Dwingeloo and Westerbork, which put the Netherlands in the forefront of radio astronomy. In 1950 came perhaps his most famous proposition, that billions of comets exist unseen in a vast swarm beyond the outermost planets of the Solar System, occasionally being disturbed onto new orbits so that they plunge towards the Sun where we can see them. The existence of the Oort Cloud, as it is known, is now generally accepted.

Ozal Turgut 1927–1993. Turkish politician, prime minister 1983–89, and president 1989–93, who died unexpectedly in office. His declared hope was to make Turkey the 'Japan of the Middle East'. He was often referred to as the Margaret Thatcher of Turkey for his commitment to free-market economic policies. Western leaders saw him as a dependable ally in one of the most volatile regions of the world, and his death has had repercussions far beyond his own country.

Born in Malaya and educated at Istanbul Technical University, he entered government service and became under-secretary for state planning 1967. From 1971 he worked for the World Bank and in 1979 joined the office of prime minister Bulent Ecevit. In 1980 he was deputy to prime minister Bulent Ulusu, within Kenan Evren's military regime. When multiparty politics returned in 1983, Ozal founded the Islamic, right-of-centre, Motherland Party (ANAP) and led it to a narrow election victory. He retained his parliamentary majority in the 1987 general election and in 1989 became Turkey's first civilian president for 30 years.

His working relationship with prime minister Suleyman Demirel owed more to French experience than normal parliamentary government, and observers often wondered who was really in control. This sometimes uneasy partnership made Ozal's reputation greater abroad than at home. For example, he was largely responsible for Turkey's involvement in the 1991 Desert Storm campaign against Saddam Hussein. He campaigned vigorously for the rights of Bosnian Muslims and the Azerbaijanis and, less overtly, for the Kurds on his country's remote southeast borders. Greece will also have cause to lament his loss because of his forward-looking and courageous *rapprochement* in 1988 with the then Greek prime minister, Andreas Papandreou. On many bases of evaluation Ozal was a significant figure whose loss will become more apparent as years go by.

Anthony Perkins

Perkins Anthony 1932–1992. US actor. Perkins will be associated more than anything with the role of Norman Bates, the homicidal motel keeper of Hitchcock's *Psycho* 1960, who butchers his female patrons while disguised as the mother he murdered years before. The edge of neurosis and half-sympathetic ambiguity that Perkins lent to the role contributed considerably to the film's achievement. At the same time, the characterization of Bates overshadowed its creator's acting career, even though he did not return to it for over 20 years, in two sequels made in 1983 and 1986, the latter directed by Perkins himself.

Born in New York City, son of the character actor Osgood Perkins, who died when Anthony was only five, he began acting at 15 and made his first film, *The Actress* 1953, a few years later. He appeared on Broadway and was nominated for an Academy Award for his second film, *Friendly Persuasion* 1956. After *Psycho* he gravitated to Europe, and during the 1960s appeared in a disparate selection of films, few of which won critical or commercial favour. Back in the USA, however, he turned successfully to character roles. Strangely, several of these had ecclesiastical overtones: he was the chaplain in *Catch-22* 1970, a bogus preacher in *The Life and Times of Judge Roy Bean* 1973, and a demented fundamentalist minister in *Crimes of Passion* 1984. Ken Russell, director of the last-named, described Perkins as the most dedicated actor he had ever worked with.

Pike Magnus Alfred 1908–1992. Food scientist and broadcaster who enjoyed an extraordinary period of celebrity following his retirement in 1973. Author of the standard work *The Manual of Nutrition* 1945, Pike ran Genochil Research Station in Scotland 1955–73. On his retirement, he became Secretary of the British Association for the Advancement of Science. Then, with Miriam Stoppard and David Bellamy, he made *Don't Ask Me* the most popular science series in British television. He said: 'I'm just a mediocre scientist,' but he had a genius for communication.

Pike referred to his period of fame as a television scientist as his Sixth Life. His Fifth Life was spent working for Distillers Co in Scotland and in bringing up his family; the Fourth was marked by the publication of his manual of nutrition. His Third Life was passed in Canada, working as a farm labourer in the summer, and studying at McGill University in the winter. Education at St Paul's School, London, marked his Second Life, while the First Life encompassed his early childhood in west London. Pike had a mission to explain, which he achieved brilliantly. At the time that chlorophyll was being (mistakenly) promoted for its properties as a deodorant, he responded with the memorable couplet:

The goat that reeks on yonder hill
Has browsed all day on chlorophyll.

Much in demand as a lecturer, Pike was tall, stooping and white-haired. His arms flailed as he sought the clearest answers to the questions his audience asked. Television viewers loved him for, clearly, here was the perfect television scientist. Recipient of honorary degrees from McGill and the universities of Lancaster and Stirling, his Seventh Life began when *Don't Just Sit There* – a further highly successful television programme – ended, and he did really retire, in 1980.

Plaidy Jean. Pen name of Eleanor Hibbert *c.* 1910–1993. Prolific English historical novelist who believed history should be told as a human story and not as a list of dry facts, and thus gave immense pleasure to thousands, perhaps millions, of readers all over the world.

Hibbert was born in London in about 1910 – she never revealed her date of birth nor her maiden name – and London remained her home for most of her life. In her determination to be a writer she sent short stories under various pseudonyms to the London *Evening Standard*. Her first novel, *Beyond the Blue Mountains*, was not published until 1947. It had been rejected by several publishers on grounds of excessive length before eventually being accepted by Robert Hale, whose early encouragement she gratefully acknowledged by having his firm publish all 90 of her Jean Plaidy novels. The name 'Plaidy' was taken from Plaidy Beach in Cornwall. She and her husband, George Hibbert, lived near Looe in Cornwall during World War II and she subsequently made frequent use of Cornish place-names in her fiction. The novels under this name were fictionalized English history and were often particularly concerned with episodes involving queens and princesses.

Jean Plaidy was by no means the only *nom de plume* employed by Hibbert. Under the name 'Victoria Holt' she published *Mistress of Mellyn* 1961, a Victorian gothic-style romance set in Cornwall. The author's identity was kept a closely guarded secret. Thirty more Victoria Holt novels were published, all of them set in the second half of the last century. A final novel, *The Black Opal*, her last book, will be published posthumously. She also wrote, under the name 'Philippa Car', a series of novels set in various historical periods from Tudor times to World War II, aiming to show how historical events affected the lives of individuals. The central character in each is an English gentlewoman, and the series became known as the 'Daughters of England'. An immensely popular writer, Hibbert received quantities of fan mail and apparently answered each letter personally.

Premadasa Ranasinghe 1924–1993. Sri Lankan prime minister 1978–88, president 1989–93. Sri Lanka's first political leader from outside the *goyigama* (high caste) elite, he was assassinated May 1993 by a Tamil separatist suicide-bomber.

A member of the lowly *hinaya* caste, he was born in a poor area of Colombo, but was educated at the prestigious Roman Catholic St Joseph's College. Originally a Labour Party member, after independence (1948) Premadasa became a municipal councillor and deputy mayor. In 1960 he was elected to parliament as a representative of the conservative United National Party (UNP) and became a protégé of J R Jayawardene, prime minister 1977–78 and president 1978–88. After serving as UNP chief whip 1965–68 and 1970–77, and minister of local government, housing, and construction 1968–70, Premadasa became prime minister 1978 under Jayawardene. He launched an initiative to provide universal housing and alleviate poverty. He also adopted a Sinhala nationalist stance in 1987 and refused to support the Indo–Sri Lankan Accord signed by Jayawardene and Indian prime minister Rajiv Gandhi.

An astute but ruthless politician, in December 1988 Premadasa was elected executive president to succeed Jayawardene. He negotiated the Indian peacekeeping force's withdrawal from the northern Jaffna peninsula and secured a 15-month ceasefire with the Tamil Tiger separatist forces. He sanctioned harsh action against the southern-based Marxist JVP movement, which cost at least 5,000 lives during August–September 1989. These forthright actions brought back political stability and revived Sri Lanka's economy. However, the price was high. Alienated by Premadasa's autocratic style, UNP rivals including former national security minister Lalith Athulathmudali (also assassinated 1993) and Gamani Dissanayake left to form the new Democratic United National Front. A leader with many enemies, Premadasa, like Rajiv Gandhi, was killed by a Tamil assassin in May 1993 in an explosion claiming 23 other lives.

Pucci, Emilio (Marchese di Barsento) 1914–1992. Italian couturier, champion skier, and politician. His designs were popular from the mid 1950s to the mid 1960s. Produced in bright colours, his designs became the symbol of new casual chic, and contributed to the growth of the Italian fashion industry in the post-war years.

Born of a noble Florentine family, he was a descendant of the Pucci family who were established as silk weavers in Florence in the 14th century. In 1934 he was a member of the Italian Olympic ski team, and shortly afterwards went to the USA to read social science at university. After returning to Florence and completing his studies in 1941 he enrolled in the Italian Air Force during World War II, where he rose to the rank of lieutenant colonel.

Pucci became known after photographs of him, wearing his own ski designs on the Italian ski slopes, appeared in *Harpers Bazaar* in 1948. In 1950 he established his own couture house at the family home, Palazzo Pucci. He became well known as a colourist and as an inventive user of fabrics, preferring soft silks and satins in bright acid colours and abstract patterns. His 'New Age' designs became synonymous with style and his trademarks – narrow-legged slacks and comfortable loose blouses – became the standard for the next decade. Among his customers were the actresses Marilyn Monroe and Elizabeth Taylor. Though the popularity of his designs declined after the mid 1960s, Pucci's influence was seen in Gianni Versace's 1991 collections.

In 1964 he stood for parliament and served as a deputy in Rome for nine years. He was also active in Florentine city politics.

Rice Peter 1935–1992. Structural engineer. One of the most imaginative engineers of his generation, he was responsible for some of the most exciting buildings of the last 25 years: the Sydney Opera House, the Pompidou Centre in Paris, and the Lloyd's building in London.

Born in Ulster, he studied engineering at Queen's University, Belfast and Imperial College, London. His first employment was with Ove Arup: at the age of 23 he was assigned to raise the sail-like roofs of the Sydney Opera House, designed by Finnish architect Jorn Utzon. There followed the Centre Pompidou, the Menil Art Collection Museum in Houston, the San Nicola World Cup Stadium in Bari, the Kansai International Airport in Osaka, and the Pavilion of the Future at the Seville Expo. In Britain he is known for the terminal at Stansted Airport as well as the Lloyd's building. The architects with whom he collaborated – notably Richard Rogers, Renzo Piano and Norman Foster – held him in high regard. Piano, the Italian architect with whom he built the Centre Pompidou and the Menil museum, said he designed structures 'like a pianist who can play with his eyes shut; he understands the basic nature of structures so well that he can afford to think in the darkness about what might be possible beyond the obvious'.

In July 1992 Rice received the UK's Royal Gold Medal for Architecture, an honour rarely awarded to engineers. In his acceptance speech, he remarked that structural engineers were often seen as reducing every soaring idea an architect might have by insisting on rationality in design. The structural engineer's true role, Rice said, was not to reduce and restrict, but to explore materials and structures as had the great Victorian engineers and medieval cathedral builders. Rigour and imagination could go hand in hand.

Ridley Nicholas. Lord Ridley of Liddlesdale 1929–1993. British Conservative politician. Personifying the patrician English gentleman, Nicholas Ridley held uncompromising views about Britain's place in the world and the need to get government off the backs of long-suffering taxpayers, that earned him the respect of like-minded Conservatives and the criticism of his opponents. He served under Edward Heath and Margaret Thatcher but always seemed very much his own man, who might not always follow the conventional party or government line.

He was born in Newcastle upon Tyne. After a privileged education at Eton and Balliol College, Oxford, he spent his early manhood in industry around Tyneside before entering politics. He entered Parliament as member for Tewkesbury 1959 and represented it until 1992. He held junior government posts before being made minister of state in the Department of Trade and Industry 1970–72 under Edward Heath. In his mistrust of Brussels bureaucracy, he was ideologically in tune with Margaret Thatcher, who gave him progressively senior portfolios, including transport 1983–86, environment 1986–89, and trade and industry 1989–90. Often apparently aloof and arrogant, he was frequently misunderstood, but well liked and respected by his close friends. He also earned the loyalty of the junior ministers and civil servants who worked under him. He seemed almost to want to avoid really high office, giving the impression that politics, and the compromises that its pursuit inevitably entails, were really beneath him He preferred brutal frankness to what he saw as 'fudge'. An article denigrating Germany in *The Spectator* in 1990 eventually cost him his ministerial post and his political career. Ridley was a gifted artist with a penchant for water colours, and his interests were wider than those of many of his political associates. A heavy smoker, he died from cancer at a relatively early age.

Nicholas Ridley

Roach Hal. Professional name of Harold Eugene Roach 1892–1992. US film producer. One of the great veterans of the American film industry, whose career stretches back virtually to that industry's inception, Roach was chiefly responsible not only for laun ching Harold Lloyd as a comedian but also for promoting the team of Laurel and Hardy. In later years, moving on from the sphere of two-reel comedies, he produced a wide variety of features, including the series inaugurated by *Topper* 1937 and the John Steinbeck adaptation *Of Mice and Men* 1939.

Born in Elmira, New York, he had an adventurous youth, including a spell as a gold prospector in Alaska, before entering films as a stunt man and bit player in 1912. He turned producer on the strength of a modest legacy in 1915. Directing many of his earlier efforts himself, he concentrated on two-reel shorts; these included vehicles for Charlie Chase and Zasu Pitts as well as the classic shorts of Laurel and Hardy, with whom he retained links after switching to feature-length production during the 1930s. After World War II, during which he produced training and propaganda films, he turned to television, with mixed fortunes. His production company folded up in the late 1950s, but he remained in good health, and sporadically active on the fringes of the film industry, until the end of his life.

Sabin Albert Bruce 1906–1993. Polish-American microbiologist who single-handedly developed the live-virus vaccine that effectively abolished poliomyelitis.

Emigrating with his parents to America in 1921, Sabin was educated at New York University. After a period at the Rockefeller Institute of Medical Research, he was appointed professor of paediatric medicine at the University of Cincinnati 1939. From 1970 to 1972 he worked at the Weizmann Institute, Israel, before moving to the Medical University of Southern Carolina as professor of biomedicine. Sabin was not first with a live vaccine. He knew from others' success in growing the polio virus in tissue culture that a 'live' polio vaccine was feasible. He had already helped develop vaccines against dengue fever and Japanese B encephalitis. Jonas Salk had developed a killed polio vaccine and tested it before Sabin's live vaccine became available. The Salk vaccine was administered by injection. Between 1956 and 1958, 200 million injections were performed without a single case of vaccine-induced paralysis. However, Sabin was unable to test his new vaccine in America because, at an earlier stage of the Salk vaccine's development in 1954, a faulty batch caused paralytic polio in some children. Sabin managed the extraordinary feat of interesting the Russians in his vaccine, and hence was able to report in 1959 that 4.5 million vaccinations had been successfully carried out. The way was now clear for the Sabin vaccine. It could be orally administered and, because it afforded a long-lasting immunity, required only a single dose. It rapidly replaced the Salk vaccine.

Sabin was completely goal-oriented and brilliant. These qualities enabled him, working in a small laboratory, without backing from established interests, to vanquish one of the world's most dreaded and infectious diseases. He was a renowned lecturer, and demanded much from his assistants, many of whom became prominent virologists.

Shuster Joseph (Joe) 1914–1992. Canadian-born US cartoonist who, with writer Jerry Siegel (1914–), created the world's first comic-strip superhero, Superman, 1938. It spawned 44 different comic-book series, radio shows, film serials, animated cartoons, television shows, and four of the highest-grossing films in cinema history.

Born in Toronto, Shuster grew up in Cleveland, Ohio, where as a boy he discovered strip cartoons, especially the Little Nemo fantasy series. Equally influenced by early science-fiction magazines, Shuster drew rocket ships and interplanetary cityscapes. When he was 15 his first strip was published in his school magazine. At 17 Shuster met Siegel, who was to become his lifelong partner. Together they designed strips of all kinds, most of which were rejected. Their first successes came in 1936, when Major Malcolm Wheeler Nicholson began publishing the first modern US comic books. Their dream, however, was to create a newspaper comic strip.

Superman was rejected by every syndicate in the business before it was finally recast and issued as *Action Comics* number 1. The book was an instant sell-out. In Jan 1939 Superman became a daily newspaper strip. Since then Superman has become one of the most widely known characters on Earth. Shuster and Siegel, however, reaped none of the benefits: they had signed away the rights to Superman to the publisher for the $130 they were paid for that first comic book.

Shuster and Siegel sued the publisher, now known as Superman DC, for a share of the profits as early as 1947. Eventually, younger artists took up the cause and when Warner Brothers, which had taken over Superman DC, launched the first Superman movie 1977, it settled with Shuster and Siegel, paying them an annual income of $20,000. With his wife, said to be the model for Superman's girlfriend, Lois Lane, Shuster moved from New York to Los Angeles, where he spent the rest of his life.

Shawn William (adopted name of William Chon) 1907–1992. US journalist, editor 1952–87 of the *New Yorker* cultural magazine, where he nurtured many outstanding writers. As managing editor 1939–52, responsible for the factual output, he helped establish the magazine's famous commitment to absolute accuracy. He was dismissed two years after the magazine was sold.

Shawn grew up in Chicago, where he was briefly the Midwest editor of the *International Illustrated News*. In 1933 he arrived at the *New Yorker*, starting as a reporter; he went on to become associate editor and (in 1939) managing editor, before succeeding the magazine's founding editor, Harold Ross, who died in 1951.

Shawn is generally credited with having transformed the *New Yorker* from being an entertaining magazine to being one of the USA's most influential cultural institutions. During his tenure as editor, some of the country's finest writers were contributors, including film critic Pauline Kael, fiction writers J D Salinger, John Cheever, and John Updike, and poets W H Auden and James Merrill. The magazine was also known for its cartoons, contributed by artists such as George Booth, Edward Koren, Saul Steinberg, and Charles Addams. 'Mr Shawn's ability to see to the core of each artist's creative self was the heart of his editorial gift,' one of the cartoonists observed, and the philosopher Hannah Arendt described him as having 'moral perfect pitch'. He also became legendary for his shyness and courtesy. To relax, he played jazz piano.

Shawn was held in great affection and respect by those who worked for him. When, in 1987, the Newhouse family of media magnates removed Shawn and appointed a new editor, Robert Gottlieb, 154 writers and contributors signed a letter asking Gottlieb to withdraw.

After he left the *New Yorker*, Shawn worked as a special editor for the publisher Farrar, Straus and Giroux.

Stark Freya, Dame 1893–1993. English traveller and writer in the great tradition of exploration and travel literature.

She was born in Paris to artist parents. Her early childhood was spent mostly in Dartmoor, in the West of England, and then the family moved to Asolo in Italy, near Venice, which later became her 'permanent' home. She entered Bedford College, London University at the age of 19, where she came under the wing of her godfather, the well-known English scholar and mountaineer, W.P. Ker. Her studies were cut short when World

War I broke out, and she served as a nurse on the Italian front. Her health suffered and for three years after the war she was bedridden. But she started to learn Arabic, eventually pursuing a course at the London School of Oriental Studies. Towards the end of 1927 she went out to the Near East for the first time. She stayed in Lebanon and journeyed through the Hebel Druze country before visiting Damascus, Jerusalem, and Cairo. and, two years later, based in Baghdad, she undertook difficult solo expeditions to Luristan in Iran and the Mazanderan mountains beyond the Caspian Sea, where she nearly died of malaria and dysentery. Her experiences are described in her most successful book, *The Valley of the Assassins* 1934. In 1935 and 1936 she ventured into Arabia, became almost fatally ill again and was rescued by the RAF. A second Arabian expedition followed soon after her recovery, however.

During World War II she was engaged in propaganda and publicity work in the Middle East and then in 1943 she returned to Italy where she worked for the British Embassy. After the war she began her autobiography. The first volume, *The Traveller's Prelude*, was published in 1950, followed by *Beyond Euphrates* 1951, *The Coast of Incense* 1953, and *Dust in the Lion's Paw* 1961. She also became interested in the history and archaeology of Asia Minor and, after learning the language, explored distant regions of Turkey. All this she wrote about in *Ionia: a Quest* 1954, *The Lycian Shore* 1956, and other books. In her 70s and 80s she travelled to Afghanistan and Nepal and again to Iraq, for a journey on a raft down the Euphrates. She continued writing; her last book, *Rivers in Time*, appeared in 1982. She was also an accomplished photographer, particularly of the people she knew and loved so well. She received many honours, including the Founder's Medal of the Royal Geographical Society, and was created DBE in 1972.

Sun Ra adopted name of Herman P Blount 1914–1993. US jazz keyboard player, bandleader, and composer, whose eccentricity matched his avant-garde experimental music. His big band, the Arkestra, formed in the 1950s, combined free-form and traditional jazz, African percussion, and synthesizer effects.

Blount was born in Birmingham, Alabama, studied piano at Alabama A&M University, and then moved to Chicago, where he worked 1946–47 as arranger and pianist for bandleader Fletcher Henderson. Initially known as Sonny, he eventually settled on calling himself Sun Ra, a tribute to the Egyptian god, and started claiming that he came from the planet Saturn, where aliens had taken him in his youth. ('Spaceship, yes! Censorship, no!' was one of his slogans.) The Arkestra, or Solar Arkestra, lived as a commune and dressed up in theatrical outer-space costumes to perform. In 1960 they relocated to New York.

Sun Ra's broad outlook and pioneering explorations of the Moog synthesizer led to a collaboration with US rock group the MC5 on their 1969 debut; other musicians who cite him as an influence range from funk master George Clinton to art rockers Sonic Youth, and British techno producers. Sun Ra's more than 300 compositions were often released on his own Saturn label. They include 'Brainville' 1956, 'Cosmic Explorer' 1970, and the albums *Sound of Joy* 1957 and *Heliocentric Worlds of Sun Ra* 1965. He never retired and the Arkestra is expected to continue.

Tambo Oliver 1917–1993. Black South African politician; close friend and colleague of Nelson Mandela. Tambo sustained the ANC and enhanced its reputation during Mandela's long imprisonment, despite himself spending 30 years in exile. He was a devout Christian, whose influence on the black cause in South Africa was undemonstrative but profound. He did not live to see the culmination of his struggle for a racially integrated country, but history will view his contribution as invaluable

Born in Bizana, Transkei, son of a peasant farmer, at 16 he travelled to Johannesburg to a school run by the Community for the Resurrection, where he came under Father Trevor Huddleston's influence. He first met Mandela at Fort Hare University. Although they came from the same region, their backgrounds were very different. They soon developed an understanding and friendship that strengthened and grew. Expelled from university for organizing a student protest, in 1944 Tambo joined the African National Congress

Oliver Tambo

(ANC). With Mandela he helped found the ANC Youth League, becoming its vice-president. He asked Father Huddleston to help him join the priesthood, but before being accepted as a candidate received a year's imprisonment for subversive activities in 1956. Meanwhile, he and Mandela had established South Africa's first black law practice. In 1960 Tambo, as ANC deputy president, was advised to go into exile. Before long the organization's main leaders had been imprisoned or killed. From his London base, Tambo worked tirelessly, acquiring, as ANC president, virtual head of state status in many world capitals. His return to South Africa in December 1990 was rapturously received, but a stroke suffered the previous year restricted his activities. Immediately after Tambo's death Nelson Mandela said, 'I will feel his loss in a unique manner. We are bleeding from the invisible wounds that are so difficult to heal.'

Todd Ann 1909–1993. British actress. She achieved lasting fame for her playing of the put-upon concert pianist heroine of the romantic melodrama *The Seventh Veil* 1945. The film was critically derided on its original release but proved a great popular success and has in subsequent years come to be regarded as a monument of kitsch. She subsequently went to Hollywood for one film, Hitchcock's *The Paradine Case* 1948, then played in three major British films directed by David Lean (her third husband, to whom she was married from 1947 to 1957). These were *The Passionate Friends* 1949, *Madeleine* 1950, and *The Sound Barrier* 1959, but they failed to establish her fully as a box-office name.

Ann Todd

Born in Hartford, Cheshire, she trained for the stage and rapidly achieved a West End reputation in a string of light comedies. Her film debut came in 1931, and of her pre-war films, the best remembered is probably *Things To Come* 1936. During the 1950s her screen appearances became sporadic, though she was active on the stage, including playing Lady Macbeth during the Old Vic season of 1954–55, and in television drama. A robbery during which she sustained injury dealt something of a blow to her career, but she went on to direct several travel films, and much later made a comeback to screen acting in *The Human Factor* 1979, based on the Graham Greene novel.

Treurnicht Andries 1921–1993. South African white, right-wing politician, former editor of the journal of the Dutch Reformed Church. He was leader of the National Party in the Transvaal 1978–82, founder of the Conservative Party, and its leader from 1982.

Born at Piketberg, he was a student at Stellenbosch and Cape Town universities, acquiring a doctorate in political philosophy. He was then ordained as a minister of the Dutch Reformed Church 1946–60, later becoming the editor of its influential journal *Die Kerkbode*. In this capacity he came to the attention of prime minister Hendrik Verwoerd, who was seeking some philosophical justification for the policy of apartheid. Treurnicht provided this and, having sampled the fringe of politics, decided to commit himself wholeheartedly, being elected MP for Waterbury 1971. He became leader of the National Party in the Transvaal, and there was speculation that he might eventually become the national leader. Entering government, he occupied a number of posts, including education and training 1976–78, plural relations and development 1978–79, public works, statistics and tourism 1979–80, and state administration and statistics 1980–82. He broke away from the National Party when it accepted a proposal to create a tricameral parliament in which whites, coloureds, and Indians would be represented in separate chambers. He then cofounded the right-wing Conservative Party, becoming its leader 1982. His courtesy and moderation in private affairs contrasted sharply with his public espousal of racist politics.

Wells Mary (Esther) 1943–1992. US pop and rhythm-and-blues singer, one of Motown Records' first stars. She had a number-one hit with 'My Guy' 1964, written and produced, like most of her material, by Smokey Robinson.

Wells began singing in school and in church in her native Detroit, Michigan, and auditioned for Berry Gordy, Motown's founder, in 1961 with her own song 'Bye Bye Baby', which became an R & B hit. Before Motown, she once said, young black women in Detroit had to choose between 'babies, the factories, or day [domestic] work'. She made a significant contribution to the early success of the company, backed by the production and songwriting skills of Robinson on clever midtempo numbers, like 'The One Who Really Loves You', 'You Beat Me to the Punch', 'Two Lovers' (all hits 1962), and 'Laughing Boy' 1963. But after 'My Guy', as she turned 21, she left Motown, and a legal battle ensued over her contract. Her unrealistic hopes of becoming a film star were crushed, she never again found the same chart success or even a label where she could settle, and she died in poverty.

Wells was also the first Motown artist to tour the UK, on a bill with the Beatles in 1964; later she was to record an album called *Love Songs to the Beatles*.

Weston Brett 1911–1993. US photographer of the American landscape and epic natural phenomena. He believed that Nature was the greatest artist.

Weston was the son of the more famous Edward and spent his teenage years serving an apprenticeship in his father's studio in Glendale (then Tropico), California, and travelling with him to Mexico in search of a photographer's paradise. He shared a studio with his father in San Francisco in 1928, Carmel in 1929, and Santa Monica in 1935. During the Depression of the 1930s he eked out a living as a portrait photographer and then worked as a government photographer, a movie cameraman, and a truck driver before joining the US Signal Corps in World War II. He returned to photography after the war, firstly in New York and then touring the USA, which the award of a Guggenheim fellowship enabled him to do. Unlike many post-war photographers, he had no interest in politics or social ills, his images being mostly of landscapes and abstracts of nature. His work is to be found in many US museums and other collections. His published portfolios include *San Francisco* 1938, *Japan* 1970, *Europe* 1973, and *Portraits of My Father* 1976.

Willis Ted, Lord Willis, 1914–1992. English writer and politician. The author of numerous entertaining novels, plays, and scripts for films, radio, and television, and the creator of one of British television's most popular characters, Constable Dixon (later Sergeant), the main character of a television series that ran for an amazing 22 years.

Willis was born in Tottenham, North London, and grew up there a working-class boy in a poor family. He was educated at Tottenham Central School. Early in the morning he delivered newspapers and, in the evening, bread, sneaking off to the local cinema whenever he could. He left school at 14 and worked as an office boy and a bookie's runner. His political life began with a resolve to oppose fascism. He became national leader of the Labour Party's League of Youth but in the later 1930s joined the Communist Party. He spend his war years with the Army Kinematographic Service, producing scripts for documentary films. His background and left-wing views led him to write about ordinary people. His first play, *Buster*, staged at the Arts Theatre in London in 1944, was a comedy about life in London's East End. He became theatre critic for the communist newspaper *The Daily Worker*, and producer and writer for the left-wing Unity Theatre. *No Trees in the Street*, a serious play about the London slums, was produced at the St James's Theatre in 1948.

A year later Willis and the Australian writer Jan Read submitted a play about the London police to Ealing Studios. The resulting film, *The Blue Lamp*, was Dixon's first appearance. Transferred to television in 1953, Dixon, as played by British actor Jack Warner, became everybody's friendly policeman and genial father-figure. Willis was also a scriptwriter for the long-running radio series *Mrs Dale's Diary*, and wrote several other scripts and plays for television, though none achieved the outstanding success of Dixon. His first book was his autobiography, *Whatever Happened to Tom Mix* 1970. After this he began a new career as a writer of thrillers, the first of which was *Death May Surprise Us* 1974, about the kidnapping of a prime minister. This was followed by *The Left-Handed Sleeper* 1975, *Man-Eater* 1976, *The Churchill Commando* 1977, *The Buckingham Palace Connexion* 1978 and many others, his last being *Bells of Autumn* 1990. His last book was another volume of autobiography, *Evening All*, published in 1991. He was made a Labour life peer in 1970, one of the first life peers. He was President of the Writers' Guild, which he had helped to found, from 1958 to 1968 and again from 1976 to 1979, being made Life President in 1988.

Wilson John Tuzo 1908–1993. Canadian geologist and geophysicist who, more than any other worker in the field, established and brought about a general understanding of the concept of plate tectonics.

Wilson was born in Ottawa, studied geology and physics – an original combination that led directly to the development of the science of geophysics – at the University of Toronto, and obtained his doctor's degree at Princeton University, New Jersey, USA. His particular interest was the movement of the continents across the Earth's surface – then a poorly understood and not widely accepted concept known as 'continental drift'. He spent 28 years as professor of geophysics at the University of Toronto, retiring 1974 just as interest in plate tectonics was catching on worldwide. From then on he was the director-general of the Ontario Science Centre and later the chancellor of York University, Toronto, finally retiring 1987. In 1957 he was the president of the International Union of Geodesy and Geophysics – the most senior administrative post in the field.

Wilson's great strength was in education. He pioneered hands-on interactive museum exhibits, and he could explain complex subjects like the movement of continents, the spreading of ocean floors, and the creation of island chains by using astonishingly simple models. He was a very active outdoor man, leading expeditions into the remote north of Canada, and he made the first ascent of Mount Hague in Montana, USA, 1935. The Wilson Range in Antarctica is named after him.

Zhen Wang 1908–1993. Chinese communist political leader. A veteran of the 'Long March' 1934–35 and vice-president from 1988. A hard-line Marxist, he strongly supported the June 1989 Tiananmen Square crackdown against the student-led pro-democracy movement and for four decades had been a scourge of liberal writers and intellectuals.

Born, like Mao Zedong, in the south-central province of Hunan, Wang began his career in the labour movement, working initially on the railways. He joined the Chinese Communist Party (CCP) in 1927 and until the 1950s was an important army commander and political officer. He took part in the 'Long March' of 1934–35 when the communists retreated northwards under the attack of the Nationalist forces. Following the communist victory in 1949 Wang directed the forced 'liberation' and Han Chinese colonization of the largely Muslim far-western province of Xinjiang. He became a full member of the CCP's influential central committee in 1956 and also agriculture minister. An unswerving Marxist, Wang escaped the purge during the ultra-leftist Cultural Revolution 1966–69. He was the only member of the subsequent reformist administration of Deng Xiaoping to do so. He became a vice-premier in 1975 and joined the CCP's Politburo in December 1978. Advancing age forced Wang to retire as vice-premier in 1980, but between 1985 and 1987 he served as vice-chairman of the Central Advisory Committee, a body set up by Deng to accommodate senior party figures, and in 1988 became vice-president. In his position as a party elder, he worked, via his protégés, to defend 'Mao's revolution'. In 1986 he was influential in securing the ousting of the liberal-minded CCP leader Hu Yaobang and in 1989 backed the harsh Tiananmen crackdown.

Zuckerman Solly. Baron Zuckerman of Burnham Thorpe 1904–1993. South African-born British zoologist, educationist, and establishment figure. He was chief scientific adviser to the British government 1964–71 and, as a member or chairman of numerous influential committees, had access to the very heart of government.

Born in Cape Town, where he was demonstrator in anatomy at the university, he came to London in the 1920s and soon established himself as a leading anatomist with the Zoological Society. He joined the faculty of Oxford University in 1934 and during World War II, as a government scientific adviser, investigated the biological effects of bomb blasts. He was made professor of anatomy at Birmingham University 1946–68 and chief scientific adviser to the government. In Harold Wilson's premiership he had his own office within the Cabinet Office, with direct access to the prime minister himself. He did extensive research on primates, publishing a number of books that became classics in their field, including *The Social Life of Monkeys and Apes* 1932 and *Functional Affinities of Man, Monkeys and Apes* 1933. He also published his autobiography *From Apes to Warlords* 1978. On a par with his influence in government, his life style was similarly spectacular. His wife was the daughter of a marquess, he lived well and his acquisition of honours and committee chairmanships was virtually unprecedented. He was created a peer in 1971.

Society

Clothes and Fashion 69

Education 74

Health and Medicine 82

International Organizations 108

Law 123

Media 138

Peoples and Languages 143

Politics 158

Religion 171

Sport 188

Transport 226

Warfare 235

CLOTHES AND FASHION

Designers of Today

Armani Giorgio 1935– . Italian fashion designer. He launched his first menswear collection 1974 and the following year started designing women's clothing. His work is known for understated styles, precise tailoring, and fine fabrics. He designs for young men and women under the Emporio label.

Cardin Pierre 1922– . French pioneering fashion designer whose clothes are bold and fantastic. He was the first to launch menswear (1960) and designer ready-to-wear collections (1963). His name has become well known as a label since he gave it to a perfume and luxury goods such as scarves and luggage.

Comme des Garçons trade name of Rei Kawakubo 1942– . Japanese fashion designer whose asymmetrical, seemingly shapeless designs, which are often sombre in colour and sometimes torn and crumpled, combine Eastern and Western ideas of clothing. She became a freelance designer 1966, after working in a Japanese textile company, and formed Comme des Garçons in 1969. In the early 1980s her avant-garde designs received acclaim in Paris and were widely influential. She continued to question conventions in 1993 when she produced outfits turned inside out, with unpicked seams and slashed hems, as well as jackets and coats with three sleeves.

Conran Jasper 1959– . English fashion designer known for using quality fabrics to create comfortable garments. He launched his first collection 1978 and has rarely altered the simple, successful style he then adopted. He has also designed costumes for the stage.

Courrèges André 1923– . French fashion designer who is credited with inventing the miniskirt 1964. His 'space-age' designs – square-shaped short skirts and trousers – were copied worldwide in the 1960s. He has become familiar since the 1960s for tailored designs often in pastel shades.

Dolce e Gabbana Domenico Dolce 1958– and Stefano Gabbana 1963– . Italian fashion designers, established 1982, who showed their first women's collection in 1985 and became well known for designs centring around bra-tops, corset-style dresses, and stretch leggings, inspired by Sicilian culture. They launched a menswear collection 1990 and in 1991 began designing the mainstream label Complice for the Milanese manufacturing company Girombelli.

The race is on

Advertising expenditure on footwear (UK, 1987–1991, £'000)*

	1987	*1988*	*1989*	*1990*	*1991*
Shoes	6,139	7,362	6,468	5,204	3,683
% change	–	+19.9	–12.1	–19.5	–29.2
Sports shoes	2,034	2,253	2,828	1,797	7,424
% change	–	+10.8	+25.5	–36.5	+313.1

In 1991 the balance of advertising expenditure shifted from general shoes to sports shoes. Since 1988 expenditure on shoe advertising has halved, while spending on sports shoe advertising has more than tripled. This trend culminated in 1991 when both Nike and Reebok dramatically increased their adspends, to establish brand leadership.

Leading advertisers (1990–1991, in £'000)*

Sports shoes	*1990*	*1991*
Nike	818	3,277
Reebok	385	2,854
Hi-Tec	594	864
Adidas	–	429

** year to Sept 1992*

Source: MEAL/Euromonitor

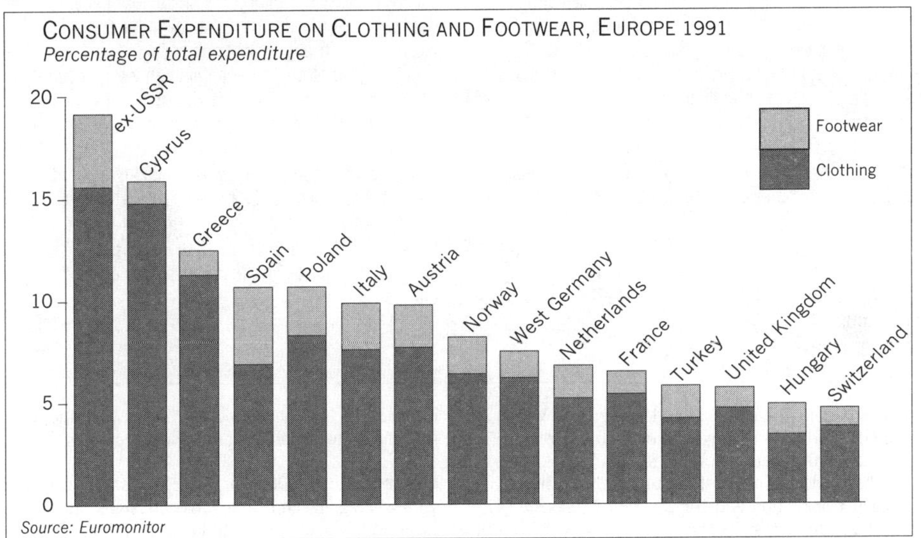

Dressing down

During a period in which it seemed that skirt lengths were the most important issue to fashion image makers, new influences and voices appeared on the catwalk to enliven and diversify the fashion debate.

The change of mood has come from both within and outside the fashion world. At the spring 1992 fashion show in Paris, Rei Kawakubo of Comme des Garçons, who was well known for questioning conventions of dress in the early 1980s, showed loose, shapeless designs, with raw seams and unpicked hems. Some of the outfits were turned inside out, while her jackets and coats contained extra sleeves.

Garments from Comme des Garçons collections and those of other designers, such as Helmut Lang and Martin Margiela, who were also producing collections that were not conventionally finished, have been labelled 'deconstructivist'. This term indicates the designers' practice of literally unpicking the seams, turning clothes inside out, slashing and recycling used fabrics, and destroying garments in order to make new ones.

Martin Margiela, who has attracted attention for his off-beat designs and unusual catwalks since he launched his first collection in 1988, continued to question the conventions of showing new designs when he showed his collection of outfits made from recycled fabrics and second-hand clothes in a Salvation Army used-furniture showroom.

Recycling used fabrics and garments has become a popular method of producing new clothing. In the UK Helen Storey launched a recycled collection, 'Second Life', alongside her main collection in July 1992. Taking second-hand clothes she added sequins and beads, or cut the garments and changed their shapes. Other designers recycle materials such as bedspreads and blankets to create an inexpensive range of clothing for the younger market.

Deconstruction designs and recycled collections indicate a move away from a preoccupation with status dressing and designer labels. In a sense the reaction has grown out of the recession; with less disposable income available, interest has moved away from the catwalks to street fashion, most notably in the form of the 1970s revival and 'grunge'.

Grunge originated in the late 1980s in Seattle, Washington, on the NW coast of the USA. Like punk, it initially focused on music – post-punk bands such as Sonic Youth, Butthole Surfers, and Nirvana. The impetus behind the movement was a rejection of 1980s values of attainment, a mood which in dress manifested itself as anti-fashion. Its hallmark is the layering of fabrics and misfitting clothes, such as loose T-shirts, flannel shirts, and big trousers worn on the hips. Stripes, checks, and floral patterns are combined and often worn with long, loose, lank hair, to create an unstructured appearance.

The clothes, many of which come from second-hand clothes shops, represent an alternative identity and attitude to clothing than that found in the mainstream fashion shops. As in the 1970s, people returned to second-hand clothes shops to seek distinctive, but inexpensive designs and accessories to create not only grunge, but also glamorous appearances.

However, in the same way that punk finally appeared on the catwalk, grunge has entered mainstream fashion. In the autumn 1992 designer-fashion shows in New York, Marc Jacobs, who designs for the fashion house Perry Ellis, and Christian Francis Roth showed 'grunge' collections – a plethora of patterns and layers of garments that were characteristically too large, or too small. Roth topped his outfits with a hat made from old socks.

Clearly grunge in its most obvious form will not be taken up by all designers, or worn by many of their customers, but grunge designs have appeared in *Vogue*, and its influence has permeated the fashion industry, even to Milan, where Gianni Versace translated the image into his elegant style, with a lacy décolleté evening dress, worn over a stripey T-shirt body.

Underground movements inevitably move overground as their popularity grows, but there is an irony in the contradiction between grunge-inspired outfits on the catwalk and those found on the street. Though grunge was originally created out of thrift shops, it has become part of a multimillion dollar industry. In effect therefore the fashion industry has defined an image out of an anti-fashion stance and in doing so has created another uniform.

ES

Farhi Nicole. French fashion designer who works in the UK producing understated easy-to-wear styles in natural earth-toned coloured fabrics and knitwear. She began designing for the mainstream fashion label French Connection and for Stephen Marks in 1973 (the Stephen Marks label was changed to Nicole Farhi in 1983). In 1989 she launched a menswear line, with soft unstructured jackets and casual separates.

Galliano John 1960– . British fashion designer whose elegant and innovative designs are often inspired by historical motifs (for example, 'Dickensian-style' clothing), the elements of which he redesigns to create progressive collections. He became known before graduating from St Martin's School of Art in 1984 for his technical expertise and imaginative flair. In 1990 he designed the costumes for a production of Ashley Page's ballet *Corrulao*, performed by the Ballet Rambert. In the same year he began showing his collections in Paris.

Gaultier Jean-Paul 1952– . French fashion designer who, after working for Pierre Cardin, launched his first collection in 1978, designing clothes that went against fashion trends, inspired by London's street style. He designed the costumes for Peter Greenaway's film *The Cook, the Thief, His Wife and Her Lover* 1989 and the singer Madonna's outfits for her world tour 1990, and launched a new denim line in 1993.

Hamnett Katharine 1948– . British fashion designer with her own business from 1979. Her oversized T-shirts promoting peace and environmental campaigns attracted attention 1984. She produces well-cut, inexpensive designs for men and women, predominantly in natural fabrics.

Jackson Betty 1940– . British fashion designer who produced her first collection 1981 and achieved an international reputation as a designer of young, up-to-the-minute clothes. She rescales separates into larger proportions and makes them in boldly coloured fabrics. In 1991 she launched her own accessory range.

Karan Donna 1948– . US fashion designer. For many years she worked for the Anne Klein company, producing Anne Klein sportswear until 1984 when she founded her own label. As well as trendy, wearable sportswear in bright colours, and tight, clingy clothes such as the bodysuit, she produced executive workwear. In 1989 she launched a second, less expensive, ready-to-wear line, DKNY. In 1992–93 she moved away from the structured look of the 1980s to produce lighter, casual, and more fluid outfits.

Kenzo trade name of Kenzo Takada 1940– . Japanese fashion designer, active in France from 1964. He opened his shop Jungle JAP 1970, and by 1972 was well established. He is known for unconventional designs based on traditional Japanese clothing. He also produces innovative designs in knitted fabrics.

Klein Calvin (Richard) 1942– . US fashion designer whose collections are characterized by the smooth and understated, often in natural fabrics – mohair, cashmere, wool, and suede in subtle colours. He set up his own business 1968 specializing in designing coats and suits, and expanded into sportswear in the mid-1970s. His designer jeans became a status symbol during the same period.

Klein Roland 1938– . French fashion designer, active in the UK from 1965. He opened his own-label shop 1979 and from 1991 designed menswear for the Japanese market.

Lacroix Christian 1951– . French fashion designer who opened his couture and ready-to-wear business in 1987, after working with Jean Patou 1981–87. He made headlines with his fantasy creations, including the short puffball skirt, rose prints, and low décolleté necklines.

Lagerfeld Karl (Otto) 1939– . German fashion designer, and a leading figure on the fashion scene from the early 1970s. As design director at Chanel for both the couture and ready-to-wear collections from 1983, he updated the Chanel look. He showed his first collection under his own label 1984.

Lauren Ralph 1939– . US fashion designer, producing menswear under the Polo label from 1968, womenswear from 1971, childrenswear, and home furnishings from 1983. He also designed costumes for the films *The Great Gatsby* 1973 and *Annie Hall* 1977.

Margiela Martin. Belgian fashion designer whose innovative 'deconstruction' designs have questioned conventions of dress since he launched his first collection in 1988. Taking used fabrics and second-hand clothes, he reworks the pieces, often making familiar garments into new outfits.

Missoni knitwear fashion label established in the UK 1953 by Italian designers Rosita and Ottavio Missoni. Producing individual pieces of knitwear, characterized by bold colours and geometric patterns, Missoni has become an international business and has raised the profile of knitwear on the fashion scene.

Miyake Issey 1938– . Japanese fashion designer, active in Paris from 1965. He showed his first collection in New York and Tokyo 1971, and has been showing in Paris since 1973. His 'anti-fashion' looks combined Eastern and Western influences: a variety of textured and patterned fabrics were layered and wrapped round the body to create linear and geometric shapes. His inspired designs have had a considerable influence on the fashion scene.

Montana Claude 1949– . French fashion designer who promoted the broad-shouldered look. He established his own business and launched his first collection 1977, becoming well known for black leather oufits with wide-shouldered jackets narrowed sharply at the waist, slim-fitting skirts, and trousers worn with chains. His designs were the antithesis of contemporary fashion and were widely influential. After 1984 he moved away from the structured look to softer, rounded shapes.

Mugler Thierry 1946– . French fashion designer who launched his first collection 1971 under the label Café de Paris. By 1973 he was designing under his own label. Strongly influenced by 1940s and 1950s fashion, his designs had broad shoulders and well-defined waists. His catwalk shows are often spectacular.

Muir Jean 1933– . British fashion designer who worked for Jaeger 1956–61 and set up her own fashion house 1961. In 1991 she launched a knitwear collection. Her clothes are characterized by soft, classic, tailored shapes in leather and soft fabrics.

Oldfield Bruce 1950– . English fashion designer who set up his own business 1975. His evening wear is worn by the British royal family, film stars, and socialites.

Ozbek Rifat 1953– . Turkish fashion designer whose opulent and influential clothing is often inspired by diverse cultures. He showed his first collection in London 1984, changed direction in 1990

The '70s revival

Alongside grunge the 1970s revival has been sweeping the fashion industry. Platform shoes, flared trousers, hot pants, tailored trouser suits, often in bold patterns, accompanied by crocheted berets, chokers, and wide-brimmed hats are some of the reworked outfits that became a familiar sight in 1992–93.

Like grunge the current revival originated on the street, as increasing numbers of people bought clothes from second-hand shops, made by well known 1960s and '70s designers such as Ossie Clark, Lee Bender, and Biba (the interest in second-hand clothing reflects the same tendency as the 1960s–70s when customers sought inspiration by searching through flea markets for 1930s designs).

Though considered a 1970s revival the movement has drawn inspiration from approximately 1964–74. The name that characterizes this period most strongly is Biba, a clothes shop and label which opened in 1963, prior to the craze for designer labels. The clothes were inexpensive and sold in a relaxed environment; outfits were often stored in piles on the floor. The fabrics tended to be heavily patterned, in rich colours or pastel shades, and the overall look was pale, languid, and skinny.

In 1992–93 the essence of the revival as seen on the catwalk comprised soft, draping, comfortable clothes in bold and contrasting patterns. Technological advances since the 1970s in fabric creation enable the materials used to be more refined and fluid, reducing the risk of being tripped up by your flares.

In the Milan autumn 1992 fashion shows Dolce e Gabbana incorporated the period by including in their collection narrow-tailed tailored suits, close-fitting jackets combined with fluid, loose trousers, open-necked, wide-lapelled shirts, and smocks. In New York Donna Karan, well known in the past for her executive workwear, showed looser, lighter, elegant designs, such as crepe or viscose cardigan tunics, long blouses with wide lapels, and slip dresses.

Although the 1970s revival offers a bolder and more colourful identity than grunge, it too highlights the general reaction away from the structured look of the 1980s. However, by its very boldness, it also offers an alternative appearance to the washed jeans and T-shirt 'dressing down' look that became popular at the end of the decade, with an identity that is imaginative, colourful, lively, and fun.

when he produced a collection that was entirely white, and began showing designs in Milan in 1991, with a collection inspired by native American dress.

Quant Mary 1934– . British fashion designer who popularized the miniskirt in the UK, and is well known for being one of the first designers to make clothes specifically for the teenage and early twenties market, producing bold, simple outfits that were in tune with the 1960s. In the 1970s she extended into cosmetics and textile design.

Red or Dead UK fashion design label established 1982 by Wayne Hemingway. Initially he sold clothing designed by his wife Geraldine, and customized heavy industrial footwear to make an anti-fashion statement, which was partly responsible for the trend for Doc Martens workwear boots. In 1987 he designed his own-label footwear range, and in 1988 launched clothing collections for men and women, which became popular in London's clubland.

Richmond John 1960– . British fashion designer who produces unconventional street and clubland designs. He worked in the partnership Richmond/Cornejo 1984–87, creating upmarket leather jackets and separates, before setting up his own fashion label 1987. He continued to experiment with leather, producing jackets with tattoo-printed sleeves in 1989 and jackets covered with graffiti in 1990. In 1989 he expanded his range with the 'Destroy' line which combines the basic elements of his signature with lower prices. He staged his first solo show in 1991.

Saint-Laurent Yves (Henri Donat Mathieu) 1936– . French fashion designer who has had an exceptional influence on fashion in the second half of the 20th century. He began working for Christian Dior 1955 and succeeded him as designer on Dior's death 1957. He established his own label 1962 and went on to create the first 'power-dressing' looks for men and women: classical, stylish city clothes.

Smith Paul 1946– . British menswear designer whose clothes are stylistically simple and practical. He opened his first shop 1970 and showed his first collection in Paris 1976. He launched a toiletry range in 1986 and a childrenswear collection 1991.

Storey Helen 1959– . British fashion designer who launched her own label 1984. She opened Boyd and Storey with fellow fashion designer Karen Boyd 1987, and in 1989 designed a range of shoes for Dr Martens UK. She staged her first solo catwalk show 1990 and launched a menswear collection 1991, followed by a '2nd Life' collection in 1992, made of second-hand clothes recycled to make new outfits.

Valentino Mario 1927–1991. Italian shoe designer. Born in Naples, he began his career designing specialist shoes, which brought him fame in the 1950s. His commercial flair steered him towards many different areas. By 1956 he had a shoe-manufacturing company in Naples and a number of shops around the world.

Versace Gianni 1946– . Fashion designer who opened his own business and presented a menswear collection 1978. He has diversified into womenswear, accessories, perfumes, furs, and costumes for opera, theatre, and ballet. He uses simple shapes and has a strong sense of colour.

Westwood Vivienne 1941– . British fashion designer who first attracted attention in the mid-1970s as co-owner of a shop with the rock-music entrepreneur Malcolm McLaren (1946–), which became a focus for the punk movement in London. Early in the 1980s her Pirate and New Romantics looks gained her international recognition. Westwood's dramatic clothes continue to have a wide influence on the public and other designers.

Yamamoto Yohji 1943– . Japanese fashion designer who formed his own company 1972 and showed his first collection 1976. He is an uncompromising, nontraditionalist designer who swathes and wraps the body in unstructured, loose, voluminous garments.

EDUCATION

Terms

adult education in the UK, voluntary classes and courses for adults provided mainly in further-education colleges, adult-education institutes, and school premises. Adult education covers a range of subjects from flower arranging to electronics and can lead to examinations and qualifications. The Open College, Open University, and Workers' Educational Association are adult-education bodies.

Most adult education is provided by Local Education Authorities (LEAs) and fees for classes are subsidized. In 1992 the government restricted subsidy to work-related courses, a proposal which met with strong opposition from bodies as diverse as the LEAs and the Women's Institute.

Assisted Places Scheme in UK education, a scheme established 1980 by which the government assists parents with the cost of fees at independent schools on a means-tested basis.

Baccalauréat French examination (or 'Bac') providing the school-leaving certificate and qualification, including vocational options, for university entrance.

The examination is also available on an international basis as an alternative to English A levels. The curriculum for the International Baccalauriat (IB) is much broader than the UK system, with a minimum of six compulsory subjects including a foreign language. The IB is offered in 52 countries. In the UK the IB can be taken in a growing number of colleges and sixth forms.

boarding school school offering board and lodging as well as tuition to its students. In the UK, most boarding education in the UK is provided in the private, fee-paying sector, but there are a number of state schools with boarding facilities. The number of boarding pupils in the UK is now in decline.

city technology college in the UK, one of a proposed network of some 20 schools, financed jointly by government and industry, designed to teach technological subjects in inner-city areas to students aged 11 to 18. By 1993 only 15 of the schools had opened, industry having proved reluctant to fund the scheme, which was abandoned in its original form.

CTCs have caused controversy (a) because of government plans to operate the schools independently of local education authorities; (b) because of selection procedures; and (c) because of the generous funds they receive in comparison with other schools. The government has been encouraging local authority and grant-maintained schools to opt for CTC status at reduced expense.

coeducation education of both boys and girls in one institution. In most countries coeducation has become favoured over single-sex education, although there is some evidence to suggest that girls perform better in a single-sex institution, particularly in maths and science. However, the new national curriculum in the UK will make it impossible for girls to drop science and technology at an early stage.

Education costs

UK government expenditure on education (1991/92 prices)

Financial year	*Net expenditure*	
	£ bn	*As a % of GDP*
1982–83	24.9	5.4
1983–84	25.1	5.2
1984–85	24.8	5.0
1985–86	24.4	4.7
1986–87	26.0	4.8
1987–88	26.9	4.8
1988–89	27.0	4.6
1989–90	28.3	4.8
1990–91	28.3	4.8
1991–92	29.6	5.1
1992–93*	31.2	5.4

** estimated*

Source: Department for Education

There has been a marked switch away from single-sex education in favour of coeducation over the last 20 years in the UK. In the USA, 90% of schools and colleges are coeducational. In 1954, the former USSR returned to its earlier coeducational system, which was partly abolished in 1944. In Islamic countries, coeducation is discouraged beyond the infant stage on religious principles.

college of higher education in the UK, a college in which a large proportion of the work undertaken is at degree level or above. Colleges of higher education are centrally funded by the Universities and Colleges Funding Council.

comprehensive school in the UK, a secondary school which admits pupils of all abilities, and therefore without any academic selection procedure. Most secondary education in the USA and the former USSR has always been comprehensive, but in W Europe most countries (including France and the UK) have switched from a selective to a comprehensive system within the last 20 years.

In England, the 1960s and 1970s saw slow but major reform of secondary education, in which most state-funded local authorities replaced selective grammar schools (those taking only the most academic 20% of children) and secondary modern schools (for the remainder), with comprehensive schools capable of providing suitable courses for children of all abilities. By 1987, only 3% of secondary pupils were still in grammar schools. Scotland and Wales have switched completely to comprehensive education, while Northern Ireland retains a largely selective system.

conductive education specialized method of training physically disabled children suffering from conditions such as cerebral palsy. The method was pioneered at the Peto Institute in Budapest, Hungary, and has been taken up elsewhere.

curriculum the range of subjects offered within an institution or course. Until 1988, the only part of the

Testing times for schools

The implementation of the National Curriculum and its associated assessment system ran into serious difficulties in the summer of 1993 when all three main teachers' unions voted by substantial majorities to boycott the tests scheduled for the summer term.

The seeds of the dispute were sown in 1988 when the Education Reform Act laid down a seven-year timetable for the implementation of the full programme of the curriculum change. This included the gradual introduction of external tests for children aged 7, 11, and 14. It soon became apparent that full implementation implied a greatly increased workload, especially for primary school teachers. The proposed assessments, which included teacher assessment and the external tests, also to be marked by teachers, also proved a significant burden. At the same time, teachers and parents became aware of the possibly damaging effects of school-against-school comparisons of test results in 'league tables'. Many teachers argued that such tables were inherently unfair.

The catalyst in 1993 proved to be the late, incompetent, and secretive introduction of English tests for 14-year-olds which, as the school year progressed, infuriated many previously moderate teachers. They discovered that although all children were expected to study a Shakespeare play, not all would be tested on it. They also objected to what they saw as an old-fashioned approach to language assessment and the imposition of a narrow reading anthology. As the spring term began and details of the content of the tests emerged, English staff opposing them won the backing of some head teachers and parents' groups, and the sympathy of many school governors.

Two other factors increased discontent within the profession and amongst parents' groups. The first was the refusal of the secretary of state, John Patten, to consult either with the teachers' unions or with parents' representatives. Well into the dispute he was still dismissing teachers as militants and parents as Luddites and 'Neanderthals', and refusing to attend meetings.

In several local authority areas opposition was also building up against the use of test results to compile league tables, something which the government regarded as an essential adjunct to their market approach to schools. Opponents argued that a great deal of the disparity between schools and local education authorities was the result of factors beyond anyone's control: social disadvantage, language difficulties, and the high levels of family mobility in some city areas. Parents in Bradford, West Yorkshire, dubbed by some newspapers 'the dunce of Britain' following publication of the first results, voted heavily against the use of their children's results to compile league tables.

School governors and head teachers' organizations also began to offer support to the dissaffected teachers in many parts of the country, in spite of pressure from the government to persuade them that their statutory duty was to implement the tests at all costs.

By March 1993, a ballot of members of the second largest teachers' union, the NAS/UWT, had come out in favour of a boycott of the tests on the grounds that they were causing staff excessive work. Legal attempts by the London Borough of Wandsworth, a high-profile Conservative-controlled council, to have the boycott declared illegal in the High Court and the Court of Appeal failed. The courts ruled that a boycott on the issue of workload was legal and that classroom teachers had no statutory duty to impose the tests. By May, a boycott of all tests had been approved by the National Union of Teachers and the normally moderate Association of Teachers and Lecturers, whose membership pressed initially reluctant officials into action.

In Parliament, John Patten, who had asked Sir Ron Dearing, already nominated head of the new curriculum and examinations body, to review the National Curriculum structure, announced significant reductions in the testing regime for 1994. He still insisted that the 1993 tests should go ahead. But neither local authorities, head teachers, nor boards of governors showed any inclination to impose sanctions on teachers taking part in the boycott. The momentum of the protest had become unstoppable.

Opinion polls showed that the teachers had support from parents. Parents were not opposed to assessment in principle but preferred it to be carried out by teachers and objected to league tables of schools. Many parents also felt that seven-year-olds were too young for external assessment. Outmanoeuvred ministers left Sir Ron Dearing's review to produce a more manageable National Curriculum and an assessment system more acceptable to teachers and parents for 1994.

MO

school curriculum prescribed by law in the UK was religious education. Growing concern about the low proportion of 14- and 16-year-olds opting to study maths, science, and technology, with a markedly low take-up rate among girls, led to the central government in the Education Reform Act 1988 introducing a compulsory national curriculum, which applies to all children of school age (5–16) in state schools. There are three core subjects in the curriculum – English, maths, and science – and seven foundation subjects: technology, history, geography, music, art, physical education, and a foreign language. A review of the national curriculum was made in 1993 after complaints that it was seriously loaded.

daycare all-day care for babies and young children, usually of working mothers. Daycare in the UK is not regarded as part of the education system but some daycare centres are now working in cooperation with schools to ensure that four- and five-year-olds are not excluded from nursery education. There is controversy among psychologists about the effects on children of spending so much time with their peers when very young. Some early research indicated that daycare for very young children could make them insecure and aggressive, but research in the USA in 1990 indicated beneficial effects.

distance learning home-based study by correspondence course or by radio, television, or audio or video tape. The establishment of the Open University 1969 put the UK in the forefront of distance learning. The Open College and individual institutions in the UK also offer distance-learning packages.

Eleven Plus examination test designed to select children for grammar school education in the UK, at the time when local authorities provided separate grammar, secondary modern, and occasionally technical schools for children over the age of 11. The examination became defunct on the introduction of comprehensive schools in Scotland, Wales, and most of England during the 1960s and 1970s, although certain education authorities retain the selective system and the Eleven Plus.

further education college college in the UK for students over school-leaving age that provides courses for skills towards an occupation or trade, and general education at a level below that of a degree course. FE colleges were removed from local authority control in 1993.

GCSE (***General Certificate of Secondary Education***) in the UK, from 1988, examination for 16-year-old pupils, superseding both GCE O level and CSE, and offering qualifications for up to 60% of school leavers in any particular subject. The GCSE includes more practical and course work than O level, although course work was reduced in syllabuses from 1993. GCSE subjects are organized as part of the national curriculum.

grammar school in the UK, a secondary school catering for children of high academic ability, about 20% of the total, usually measured by the Eleven Plus examination. Most grammar schools have now been replaced by comprehensive schools. By 1991 the proportion of English children in grammar schools was less than 3%.

Women staff and students

UK universities, 1991/2

	Old universities	*New universities**
Professors/senior posts		
Total	5,164	765
Men	4,916	673
Women	248 (4.8%)	92 (12%)
Academic staff		
Total	51,121	16,400
Men	39,964	12,429
Women	11,157 (21.8%)	3,971 (24%)
Students		
Men	51.4%	51.1%
Women	48.6%	48.9%

** Polytechnics renamed universities 1992*

Source: 1991–92 University Statistical Record

In the USA, the term is sometimes used for a primary school (also called elementary school).

grant-maintained school in the UK, a state school that has voluntarily withdrawn itself from local authority support (an action called ***opting out***), and instead is maintained directly by central government. The first was Skegness Grammar School in 1989. The schools are managed by their own boards of governors.

health education teaching and counselling on healthy living, including hygiene, nutrition, and sex education, and advice on alcohol and drug abuse, smoking, and other threats to health. Health education in most secondary schools is also included within a course of personal and social education, or integrated into subjects such as biology, home economics, or physical education.

higher education in most countries, education beyond the age of 18 leading to a university or college degree or similar qualification.

independent school school run privately without direct assistance from the state. In the UK, just over 7% of children attended private fee-paying schools in 1991. The proportion rose during the 1980s and fell back for the first time in a decade in 1993. The sector includes most boarding education in the UK. Although most independent secondary schools operate a highly selective admissions policy for entrants at the age of 11 or 13, some specialize in the teaching of slow learners or difficult children and a few follow particular philosophies of progressive education. A group of old-established and prestigious independent schools are known as public schools.

Ivy League eight long-established colleges and universities in the US with prestigious academic and social reputations: Brown, Columbia, Cornell, Dartmouth, Harvard, Pennsylvania, Princeton, and Yale. The members of the Ivy League compete in intercollegiate athletics.

literacy ability to read and write. The level at which functional literacy is set rises as society becomes more complex, and it becomes increasingly difficult for an illiterate person to find work and cope with the other demands of everyday life.

Nearly 1 billion adults in the world, most of them women, are unable to read or write. Africa has the world's highest illiteracy rate: 54% of the adult population. Asia has 666 million illiterates, 75% of the world total. Surveys in the USA, the UK, and France in the 1980s found far greater levels of functional illiteracy than official figures suggest, and revealed a lack of basic general knowledge, but no standard of measurement has been agreed.

magnet school school that specializes in a particular area of the curriculum; for example, science, sport, or the arts. Magnet schools were established in the USA from 1954 in some inner cities, with the aim of becoming centres of excellence in their particular field.

Critics maintain that magnet schools attract talented pupils and staff away from equally deserving schools in the surrounding neighbourhood. In the UK, the idea of introducing magnet schools has been discussed since 1987 but no action has been taken.

mixed-ability teaching practice of teaching children of all abilities in a single class. Although this is normal practice in British primary schools, most secondary schools begin to divide children according to ability, either in sets or, more rarely, streams, as they approach public examinations at age 16.

modular course a course, usually leading to a recognized qualification, that is divided into short and often optional units, which are assessed as they are completed. In the UK system, an accumulation of modular credits may lead to the award of a GCSE pass, a BTEC diploma, or a degree. Modular schemes are becoming increasingly popular as a means of allowing students to take a wider range of subjects.

multicultural education education aimed at preparing children to live in a multiracial society by giving them an understanding of the culture and history of different ethnic groups.

national curriculum in the UK from 1988, a course of study in ten subjects common to all primary and secondary state schools. The national curriculum is divided into three core subjects – English, maths, and science – and seven foundation subjects: geography, history, technology, a foreign language (for secondary school pupils), art, music, and physical education. There are four stages, on completion of which the pupil's work is assessed. The stages are for ages 5–7, 7–11, 11–14, and 14–16. The scheme were set up through the Education Reform Act 1988. The National Curriculum and testing system were reviewed in 1993 following teachers' compaints of over-load and a boycott of tests scheduled for June 1993.

national vocational qualification (NVQ) in the UK, a certificate of attainment of a standardized level of skill and competence. A national council for NVQs was set up 1986 in an effort by the government in cooperation with employers to rationalize the many unrelated vocational qualifications then on offer. The objective is to fit all qualifications to four levels of attainment, roughly equivalent to the GCSE, A level, and degree system of academic qualifications.

nursery school or ***kindergarten*** educational establishment for children aged three to five, initiated in the mid-19th century. In the UK, the Education Act 1944 did not make nursery school compulsory but increasing parental pressure from the 1960s led to a slow expansion. At the end of the 1980s the UK lagged behind most European countries in the provision of nursery-school places. Although 45% of three- and four-year-olds were in education in 1992, only half of these were in genuine nursery classes or schools; the rest were in primary classes.

Open College in the UK, a network launched by the former Manpower Services Commission 1987 to enable people to gain and update technical and vocational skills by means of distance teaching, such as correspondence courses, radio, and television.

Open University institution established in the UK 1969 to enable mature students without qualifications to study to degree level without regular attendance. Open University teaching is based on a mixture of correspondence courses, TV and radio lectures and demonstrations, personal tuition organized on a regional basis, and summer schools. It has been widely copied; by the National University Consortium in the USA, for example, set up in 1980.

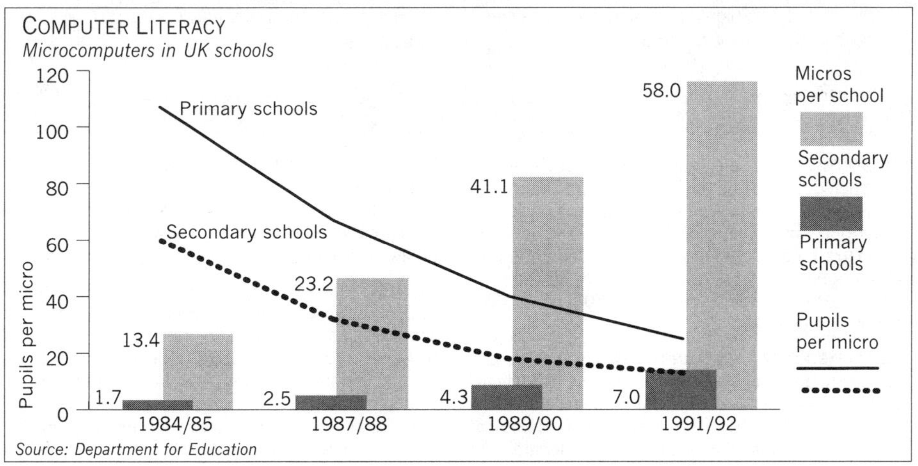

Source: Department for Education

Neglecting nurseries

In spite of a slow growth in the number of children in nursery education in the UK, Britain still lags well behind most other European countries in the proportion of children it educates before the start of compulsory schooling. Latest figures from the Department for Education show that numbers in nursery schools and classes – mostly on a part-time basis – increased from 250,000 (1983) to 330,000 (1992), a rise of one third. The rise between 1991 and 1992 was 12,000, or 4%.

Nursery educators welcomed this increase but pointed out that the proportion of three- and four-year-olds in publicly-funded education remained very low by European standards, at 26%. If four-year-olds admitted to primary school early are included, the UK proportion still only reaches 45%, lower than every other EC country except Portugal, which is building its nursery provision from a very low base.

The UK government prefers a much more generous interpretation of its statistics and likes to include another 40% of three- and four-year-olds who are catered for by voluntary nurseries and playgroups. But nursery experts counter that this comparison is unrealistic as there is no check on quality of care or qualification of personnel in playgroups, and many children attend for only a few hours per week.

In the rest of the EC, Belgium and France have the best record on nursery provision, with more than 95% of the over-threes catered for. Denmark and Luxembourg have places for more than 85% of their children, and the rest over 55%. Outside the EC, Norway and Sweden also have a very high proportion of children in nursery schools from three to school age. Much of the provision in Europe is on a full-time basis.

The UK also comes bottom of the league for the provision of publicly-funded daycare for the under-threes, but is not so isolated in this field. The majority of EC countries make little provision for this age group, with only Greece (14%), France and Belgium (20%), and Denmark (48%) reaching double figures.

Within the UK, nursery provision varies dramatically from one local education authority to another. In city areas, largely controlled by Labour councils, provision can be generous. The London borough of Merton has places for 57% of its three- and four-year-olds, Newham 58%, Cleveland 57%, Sandwell 56%, and Manchester 55%. At the other extreme, Gloucestershire has no publicly-funded places at all, while Bromley caters for 2%, Havering 4%, and Dorset, Hampshire, and Kent all counties where the Conservative Party has recently lost control of the education authority for 5%. There is speculation that some of the rural counties which have recently changed political control may now try to expand nursery provision for the first time.

Other pressure, however, seems more likely to reduce provision or worsen its quality. While there is increasing research evidence from the USA, from projects such as High Scope, and from within the UK that high-quality pre-school education is an excellent long-term investment because it reduces children's problems later, both in and out of school, in the UK the adult–teacher ratio in nursery education has been worsening steadily for a decade. In 1983 the ratio stood at 23:1; it deteriorated to 24:1 in 1991 and 25:1 in 1992. According to the National Children's Bureau these figures probably concealed the fact that, under financial pressure, nursery schools were reducing the numbers of trained teachers and increasing the numbers of less well-trained assistants.

In spite of recent slow growth in provision, nursery campaigners in the UK are gloomy about future prospects. There is no longer any government commitment to invest in nursery education and local authorities are complaining that legislation is making it increasingly difficult to sustain. Many experts predict that there are likely to be real cuts in provision over the next few years in some areas.

MO

opting out in UK education, schools that choose to be funded directly from the Department of Education and Science are said to be 'opting out' of local-authority control. The Education Act 1988 gave this option to all secondary schools and the larger primary schools, and in 1990 it was extended to all primary schools. However, by 1993 only 500 of 27,000 schools had opted out.

parent–teacher association (PTA) group attached to a school consisting of parents and teachers who support the school by fund-raising and other activities. In the UK, PTAs are organized into a national federation, the National Confederation of PTAs, which increasingly acts a pressure group for state schools.

Throughout the USA, PTAs are active as political pressure groups and as a way to involve parents in the public education process.

polytechnic formerly part of the UK educational system, an institution for higher education offering courses mainly at degree level and concentrating on full-time vocational courses, although many polytechnics provided a wide range of part-time courses at advanced levels.

In April 1989 the polytechnics in England and Wales became independent corporations. In 1992 all polytechnics and some colleges of higher education became universities. The new UK university sector consisted of 104 institutions.

preparatory school fee-paying independent school. In the UK, it is a junior school that prepares children for entry to a senior school at about age 13. In the USA, it is a school that prepares students for university entrance at about age 18.

primary education the education of children between the ages of 5 and 11 in the state school system in England and Wales, and up to 12 in Scotland.

private school alternative name in the UK for a fee-paying independent school.

progressive education teaching methods that take as their starting point children's own aptitudes and interests, encouraging children to follow their own investigations and lines of inquiry.

public school in England and Wales, a prestigious fee-paying independent school. In Scotland, the USA, and many other English-speaking countries, a 'public' school is a state-maintained school, and independent schools are generally known as 'private' schools.

remedial education special classes or teaching strategies that aim to help children with learning difficulties catch up with children within the normal range of achievement.

secondary education in the UK, education from the age of 11 (12 in Scotland) until school-leaving at 16 or later.

special education often in separate 'special schools', for children with specific physical or mental problems or disabilities.

statement in UK education, the results of an assessment of the special educational needs of a child with physical or mental disabilities. Under the Education Act 1981, less able children are entitled to such an assessment by various professionals to establish what their needs are and how they might be met. Approximately 2.5% children were in receipt of statements in 1992.

streaming the practice of dividing pupils for all classes according to an estimate of their overall ability, with arrangements for 'promotion' and 'demotion' at the end of each academic year.

student finance payment for higher education, whether by grants, loans, parents, or the student working part time. In the UK, students in higher education have their fees paid by their local education authority and are eligible for a maintenance grant, means-tested on their parents' income. In 1990 the government introduced a system of top-up loans intended gradually to replace 50% of the grant entitlement. At the same time students were debarred from previously available welfare benefits, and the National Union of Students argued that this left many worse off. In 1991–92 37% of higher education students applied for loans.

teacher training in the UK, teachers are trained by means of either a four-year Bachelor of Education (BEd) degree, which integrates professional training and the study of academic subjects, or a postgraduate Certificate of Education (PGCE), which provides one year of professional training to graduate students. The majority of BEd students train to teach in primary schools and two-thirds of PGCE students to teach specialist subjects in secondary schools.

In the 1970s the numbers of teacher training places fell sharply in line with school pupil numbers. By the late 1980s there were considerable difficulties in filling all training places, especially in such subjects as science, maths, and technology. By 1993, however, demand for training places had increased and the teacher shortage had largely disappeared as result of rising graduate unemployment.

tertiary college in the UK, a college for students over 16 that combines the work of a sixth form and a further education college.

Third Age late middle age and over. A Université du Troisième Age was established in France 1972 to

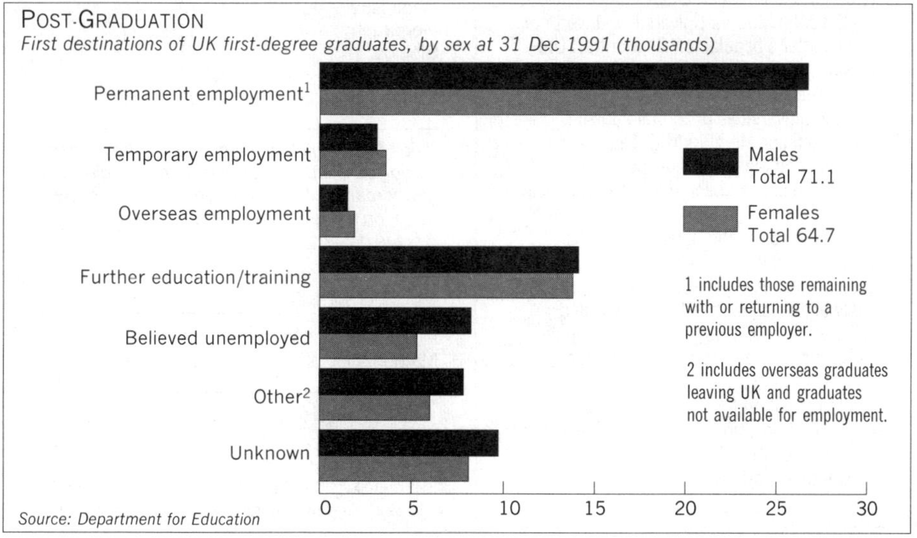

offer people over 50 the opportunity to continue their education. In the UK, the University of the Third Age established 1982 has no teachers and no qualifications for entry, but aims to help its 120 local groups to pursue any topics that interest them.

university institution of higher learning for those who have completed primary and secondary education.

The number of university students in the UK almost doubled after the major expansion of the 1960s to stand at 303,000 in 1991. There was an even greater increase in degree-level students in the public-sector colleges, which educated more graduates than the universities. In 1992, polytechnics and some colleges of higher education already awarding degrees became universities. The more generous funding of traditional universities was phased out and a joint funding council established. Research is funded separately from teaching, and the new universities have gained access to research funds for the first time.

The USA has both state universities (funded by the individual states) and private universities. The oldest and many of the most prestigious universities are private.

Recent innovations in secondary education include universities serving international areas – for example, the Middle East Technical University 1961 in Ankara, Turkey, supported by the United Nations; the United Nations University 1974 in Tokyo; and the British Open University 1969.

From poly to uni

In the academic year 1992–93 the number of universities in the UK more than doubled to over 100. This was achieved by granting university status to the former polytechnics and a handful of the largest colleges of education. With new charters came new names, including the John Moores University in Liverpool, named after a benefactor, De Montfort University in Leicester, named after a famous son of the city, and the more geographically inclined universities of central England, Greenwich and Huddersfield. The change consolidated the independence of these institutions, which had been removed from local authority control in 1991. The immediate benefits were psychological and financial. University status was felt to confirm an equality between institutions which had previously been real, in that they all awarded degrees, but not always apparent to applicants and the general public. In addition, equality of funding allowed the new universities to benefit on merit from research funding for the first time, in some cases to the extent of more than £1 million to support areas of outstanding work.

vocational education education relevant to a specific job or career. The term refers to medical and legal education in the universities as well as higher and further education courses in professional and craft skills. In the UK, the TVEI (Technical and Vocational Education Initiative) was intended to expand pre-vocational education in schools but was being run down in the early 1990s.

work experience the opportunity for pupils or students to gain practical experience of working within industry for a short period of time. Typically, 15–16 year olds spend 1–2 weeks in a work experience placement. It helps them gain some understanding of the world of work and of the opportunities that might be available to them when they leave full-time education.

Youth Training Scheme (YTS) in the UK, a one- or two-year course of job-training and work experience for unemployed school leavers aged 16 and 17, from 1989 provided by employer-led Training and Enterprise Councils at local levels and renamed Youth Training. On the basis of a government promise of training places for all school leavers without jobs, social security cover was withdrawn. However, places have not always matched demand, leaving some school leavers in financial difficulties.

Opponents of youth training argue that it is a form of cheap forced labour, that it does not provide young people with the high-technology skills that will be needed in the future, and that it is underpaid.

GALLUP POLL: Personal experience

For various reasons, the way we are taught at school can kill our interest in certain subjects. In which of these subjects did this happen to you, if at all?

Maths	20
French	15
History	15
Physics	13
Chemistry	12
Geography	11
Biology	7
English	7
None of these	39

It has been said that to understand the modern world you need a grounding both in English and Mathematics. How would you rate your grasp of each, on a 0 to 5 scale where zero is the worst and 5 is the best?

	Worst 0	1	2	3	4	Best 5
English	1	1	9	31	33	24
Mathematics	2	8	18	29	26	16

Can you spell the following six everyday words?

Necessary		*Business*	
Correct	58	Correct	65
Incorrect	30	Incorrect	26
Didn't attempt	12	Didn't attempt	9
Accommodation		*Separate*	
Correct	27	Correct	51
Incorrect	62	Incorrect	40
Didn't attempt	11	Didn't attempt	10
Sincerely		*Height*	
Correct	61	Correct	84
Incorrect	26	Incorrect	10
Didn't attempt	13	Didn't attempt	6

Standards

Is the quality of Britain's education system something that concerns you a great deal, a fair amount, or only a little?

A great deal	46
A fair amount	32
Only a little	22

Do you think that we in Britain are or are not giving enough attention to education?

	May 1993	Nov 1985	Jun 1984	Apr 1959
Yes, are	21	19	26	59
No, are not	73	75	69	34
Don't know	6	6	5	7

Thinking back over the last few years, in your opinion, have standards of achievement at schools gone up, gone down, or remained about the same?

	May 1993	Jan 1985
Gone up	16	16
Gone down	53	46
Same	22	21
Don't know	9	17

Over the last few years, in your opinion, have standards of discipline *at schools gone up, gone down or remained about the same?*

	May 1993	Jan 1985
Gone up	2	3
Gone down	82	69
Same	10	19
Don't know	5	9

From what you know, do you think that on the whole they have better systems of education in continental countries like France and Germany, or do we have a better system of education in this country?

Better in France/Germany	53
Better here	10
Both equal	6
Don't know	32

How confident are you that our educational system produces people sufficiently well trained to enable Britain to compete successfully with other countries: very confident, fairly confident, not very confident, or not at all confident?

Very confident	7
Fairly confident	36
Not very confident	38
Not at all confident	18

Priorities

Primary education is designed to give children a variety of skills. Thinking about the balance between different sorts of skills, which statement do you agree with most?

The main emphasis should be placed on the basics of reading, writing, and arithmetic	62
The main emphasis should be placed on developing childrens' broader potential such as their communication and creative skills	18
The balance is about right	18
Don't know	3

In general, do you think the education given in Britain is or is not satisfactory in respect of:

	May 1993	June 1988	Sept 1968
General culture?			
Is	30	34	61
Is not	57	55	23
Don't know	13	11	16
Formation of character?			
Is	24	26	53
Is not	65	50	32
Don't know	12	14	15
The preparation for a career/profession?			
Is	26	32	68
Is not	63	58	23
Don't know	11	10	9

HEALTH AND MEDICINE

Medical Terms

abortion ending of a pregnancy before the fetus is developed sufficiently to survive outside the uterus. Loss of a fetus at a later gestational age is termed premature stillbirth. Abortion may be accidental (miscarriage) or deliberate (termination of pregnancy).

Methods of deliberate abortion vary according to the gestational age of the fetus. Up to 12 weeks, the cervix is dilated and a suction curette passed into the uterus to remove its contents, a procedure called dilation and curretage (D and C). An alternative is the abortion pill mifepristone, licensed in the UK from 1991. Within 24 hours of ingestion, it leads to the expulsion of the foetus from the uterus, and can be used at an earlier stage in pregnancy than other methods. Over 12 weeks, a prostaglandin pessary is introduced into the vagina, which induces labour, producing a miscarriage.

Worldwide, an estimated 150,000 unwanted pregnancies are terminated each day by induced abortion. One-third of these abortions are performed outside the law in unsafe conditions, resulting in about 500 deaths a day.

allergy special sensitivity of the body that makes it react, with an exaggerated response of the natural immune defence mechanism, especially with histamines, to the introduction of an otherwise harmless foreign substance (allergen).

amniocentesis sampling the amniotic fluid surrounding a fetus in the womb for diagnostic purposes. It is used to detect Down's syndrome and other genetic abnormalities.

blood pressure pressure, or tension, of the blood against the inner walls of blood vessels, especially the arteries, due to the muscular pumping activity of the heart. Abnormally high blood pressure (see hypertension) may be associated with various conditions or arise with no obvious cause; abnormally low blood pressure (hypotension) occurs in shock and after excessive fluid or blood loss from any cause.

Caesarean section surgical operation to deliver a baby by cutting through the mother's abdominal and uterine walls. It may be recommended for almost any obstetric complication implying a threat to mother or baby. Britain's Caesarean rate of around 14% of births is one of the highest in Europe.

cervical smear removal of a small sample of tissue from the cervix (neck of the womb) to screen for changes implying a likelihood of cancer. The procedure is also known as the ***Pap test*** after its originator, George Papanicolau.

chemotherapy any medical treatment with chemicals. It usually refers to treatment of cancer with cytotoxic and other drugs. The term was coined by German bacteriologist Paul Ehrlich (1854–1915) for the use of synthetic chemicals against infectious diseases.

contraceptive any drug, device, or technique that prevents pregnancy. The contraceptive pill contains female hormones that interfere with egg production or the first stage of pregnancy. The 'morning-after' pill can be taken up to 72 hours after unprotected intercourse. Barrier contraceptives include condoms (sheaths) and diaphragms, also called caps or Dutch caps; they prevent the sperm entering the cervix (neck of the womb). Intrauterine devices, also known as IUDs or coils, cause a slight inflammation of the lining of the womb; this prevents the fertilized egg from becoming implanted. A sponge impregnated with spermicide inserted into the vagina kills the sperm.

Other contraceptive methods include sterilization (women) and vasectomy (men); these are usually nonreversible. 'Natural' methods include withdrawal of the penis before ejaculation (coitus interruptus), and avoidance of intercourse at the time of ovulation (rhythm method). These methods are unreliable and normally only used on religious grounds.

The effectiveness of a contraceptive method is often given as a percentage. To say that a method has 95% effectiveness means that, on average, out of 100 healthy couples using that method for a year, 95 will not conceive.

convulsion series of violent contractions of the muscles over which the patient has no control. It may be associated with loss of consciousness. Convulsions may arise from any one of a number of causes, including brain disease (such as epilepsy), injury, high fever, poisoning, and electrocution.

dermatology medical specialty concerned with the diagnosis and treatment of skin disorders. It is a rapidly expanding field owing to the proliferation of industrial chemicals affecting workers, and the universal use of household cleaners, cosmetics, and sun screens.

dialysis tecnhique for removing waste products from the blood in chronic or acute kidney failure. There are two main methods: haemodialysis and peritoneal dialysis.

endoscopy examination of internal organs or tissues by an instrument allowing direct vision. An endoscope is equipped with an eyepiece, lenses, and its own light source to illuminate the field of vision. The endoscope used to examine the digestive tract is a flexible fibreoptic instrument swallowed by the patient.

gallstone pebblelike, insoluble accretion formed in the human gall bladder or bile ducts from cholesterol or calcium salts present in bile. Gallstones may be symptomless or they may cause pain, indigestion, or jaundice. They can be dissolved with medication or removed, either by means of an endoscope or, along with the gall bladder, in an operation known as cholecystectomy.

geriatrics branch of medicine concerned with diseases and problems of the elderly.

gynaecology branch of medicine concerned with disorders of the female reproductive system.

haematology branch of medicine concerned with disorders of the blood.

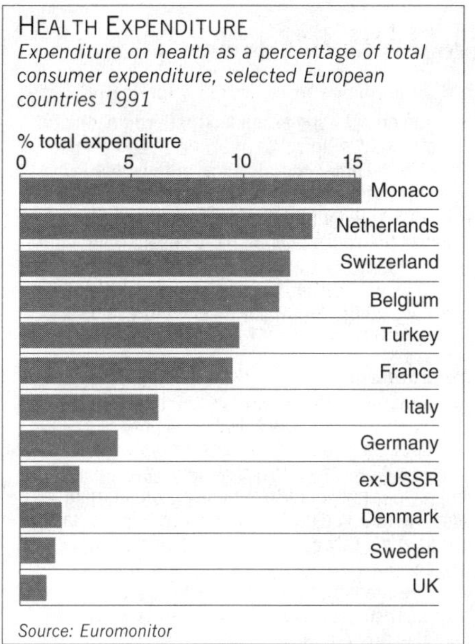

hormone-replacement therapy (HRT) use of oral oestrogen and progestogen to help limit the effects of the menopause in women. The treatment was first used in the 1970s.

hospice residential facility specializing in palliative care for terminally ill patients and their relatives.

hysterectomy surgical removal of all or part of the uterus (womb). The operation is performed to treat fibroids (benign tumours growing in the uterus) or cancer; also to relieve heavy menstrual bleeding. A woman who has had a hysterectomy will no longer menstruate and cannot bear children.

Instead of a full hysterectomy it is sometimes possible to remove the lining of the womb, the endometrium, using either diathermy or a laser.

immunization conferring immunity to infectious disease by artificial methods. The most widely used technique is vaccination. Four out of five children around the world were by 1991 immunized against six diseases: measles, tetanus, polio, diphtheria, whooping cough, and tuberculosis.

inflammation defensive reaction of the body tissues to disease or damage, including redness, swelling, and heat. Denoted by the suffix *-itis* (as in appendicitis), it may be acute or chronic, and may be accompanied by the formation of pus. It is an essential part of the healing process.

intrauterine device IUD or coil, a contraceptive device that is inserted into the womb (uterus). It is a tiny plastic object, sometimes containing copper. By causing a mild inflammation of the lining of the uterus it prevents fertilized eggs from becoming implanted. The success rate is about 98%, but there is a very small risk of a pelvic infection leading to infertility.

in vitro fertilization (IVF) ('fertilization in glass') allowing eggs and sperm to unite in a laboratory to form embryos. The embryos produced may then either be implanted into the womb of the otherwise infertile mother (an extension of artificial insemination), or used for research. The first baby to be produced by this method was born 1978 in the UK. In cases where the fallopian tubes are blocked, fertilization may be carried out by intra-vaginal culture, in which egg and sperm are incubated (in a plastic tube) in the mother's vagina, then transferred surgically into the uterus.

mammography X-ray procedure used to detect breast cancer at an early stage, before the tumours can be seen or felt.

nursing care of the sick, the very young, the very old, and the disabled. Organized training originated 1836 in Germany, and was developed in Britain by the work of Florence Nightingale (1820–1920), who, during the Crimean War, established standards of scientific, humanitarian care in military hospitals. Nurses give day-to-day care and carry out routine medical and surgical procedures under the supervision of a physician.

In the UK there are four National Boards (England, Scotland, Wales, and Northern Ireland) for Nursing, Midwifery and Health Visiting, and the Royal College of Nursing (1916) is the professional body.

nutrition the science of food, and its effect on health and disease. Nutrition is the study of the basic nutrients required to sustain life, their bioavailability in foods and overall diet, and the effects upon them of cooking and storage. ***Malnutrition*** can be caused by underfeeding, an imbalanced diet, and overfeeding.

obstetrics medical speciality concerned with the management of pregnancy, childbirth, and the immediate postnatal period.

oncology branch of medicine concerned with the diagnosis and treatment of neoplasms, especially cancer.

ophthalmology medical speciality concerned with diseases of the eye and its surrounding tissues.

orthopaedics branch of medicine concerned with the surgery of bones and joints.

pacemaker medical device implanted under the skin of a patient whose heart beats irregularly. It delivers minute electric shocks to stimulate the heart muscles at regular intervals and restores normal heartbeat. The latest pacemakers are powered by radioactive isotopes for long life and weigh no more than 15 g/0.5 oz.

paediatrics or ***pediatrics*** medical speciality concerned with the care of children.

pain sense that gives an awareness of harmful effects on or in the body. It may be triggered by stimuli such as trauma, inflammation, and heat. Pain is transmitted by specialized nerves and also has psychological components controlled by higher centres in the brain. Drugs that control pain are also known as analgesics.

paraplegia paralysis of the lower limbs, involving loss of both movement and sensation; it is usually due to spinal injury.

physiotherapy treatment of injury and disease by physical means such as exercise, heat, manipulation, massage, and electrical stimulation.

Medicine: the pace of progress slows down

Medical innovation has slowed down in recent years for two main reasons. Firstly, there is a limit to technological development. Once the ultimate operation of replacing a diseased heart with a healthy one has been achieved, as happened when the first transplant was performed in 1967, cardiac surgery cannot progress much further.

Secondly, medicine still remains remarkably ignorant about the causes and pathogenesis of most diseases, and this places an intellectual block on further development. Thus, although doctors can treat diabetes with insulin without understanding why diabetes occurs in the first place, it is difficult to know how to prevent it or cure it completely. The same is true for the common diseases of middle life – rheumatoid arthritis, multiple sclerosis, hypertension – and for the chronic degenerative diseases associated with ageing.

Surgery

Surgical techniques have been transformed in the last three years with the introduction of 'minimally invasive surgery'. This is best illustrated by the procedure for removal of the gall bladder – cholecystectomy – which is the commonest abdominal operation performed in the National Health Service. It is usually necessitated by the accumulation of gallstones, causing pain and recurrent infection. For decades the standard cholecystectomy entailed making a large incision in the abdominal wall, identifying the gall bladder nestling under the liver, tying off the bile duct and arteries, and removing it. Now the same operation can be performed by making four minute holes in the abdomen, one for the laparoscope through which the gall bladder is visualized, two through which the surgeon manipulates his delicate instruments, and one to remove any fluid and debris. Or, more simply, the gallstones can be removed through one tiny incision, leaving the gall bladder intact. The advantages to the patient are immeasurable – they are out of hospital in a couple of days and back to work within a fortnight.

Obstetrics

The most significant progress in obstetrics has paradoxically been a retreat from the high-tech management of labour, with its emphasis on induction and constant fetal monitoring, to a more 'natural' approach. The rate of Caesarean section remains high, though, as this is the best way of managing high-risk pregnancies where there is a threat to mother or baby.

The other main developments have been the improvements in ultrasound and amniocentesis to detect many more congenital abnormalities of the fetus early in pregnancy. With ultrasound it is now possible to diagnose not just spina bifida and hydrocephalus, but subtler abnormalities of the heart and kidneys. Doppler ultrasound is used to assess the blood flow through the placenta.

Amniocentesis – where cells are removed from the amniotic sac and examined for chromosomal defects such as Down's syndrome – can now be done much earlier in pregnancy, or the same information can be obtained by removing a few cells from the placenta (chorionic villus sampling). Early diagnosis obviates the trauma of late abortion if the fetus is found to be abnormal. The same procedure can be used to diagnose genetic disease when the specific genetic abnormality is known, as in sickle-cell disease and cystic fibrosis.

Infectious disease

Peptic ulcers of the stomach or duodenum used to be thought to arise from excess acid production. It now appears that in many cases the underlying causes are bacteria – *Helicobacter pylori* – which inhabit the lining of the gut while making it more sensitive to acid damage. Patients with *Helicobacter* can be effectively cured of their recurring ulcers if treated with a course of antibiotics and the anti-infective agent bismuth. Other chronic diseases, such as rheumatoid arthritis and multiple sclerosis, may also turn out to be caused by infectious agents.

Treatment of viral infections has been the other main development in this field, though antiviral drugs remain much less effective than antibiotics. The drug acyclovir, originally introduced for the treatment of genital herpes, has now been shown to modify the course of chickenpox and the related condition shingles, by reducing the duration of the illness. There is still no sign of a definitive cure for AIDS, thought the antiviral drug zidovudine may prolong life.

Heart disease

Heart disease is still the commonest cause of death in middle-aged males in the West, though its incidence has fallen for unknown reasons; changes in diet are not sufficient to account for it. Major progress has been made in the treatment of acute heart attack with the use of clot-busting drugs, such as streptokinase, which dissolve the thrombus that forms in the coronary arteries. Given early enough, it reduces the mortality rate by 50%, which works out as three lives saved for every 100 patients treated.

The other main form of heart disease, angina pectoris – caused by narrowing of the coronary arteries – is now increasingly treated by passing a wire with a balloon on the tip directly into the coronary arteries, dilating them. This is of course much less traumatic than open-heart bypass surgery.

Genetics

By far the greatest progress in medicine has been in the field of genetics. This has been made possible by the ability to identify specific genes, find out exactly what they do, discover the abnormalities in gene sequences that cause disease, and use genes to make hormones and – more speculatively – cure diseases. (See box on gene therapy in this section.)

JLF

poison or ***toxin*** any chemical substance that, when introduced into or applied to the body, is capable of injuring health or destroying life. The liver removes some poisons from the blood.

In the UK, the National Poisons Information Service, founded 1963, provides eight regional centres in the major city hospitals, where data on cases of poisoning is collected.

prematurity the condition of an infant born before the full term. In obstetrics, an infant born after less than 37 weeks' gestation is described as premature. In hospitals with advanced technology, specialized neonatal units can save babies born as early as 24 weeks.

prophylaxis any measure taken to prevent disease, including exercise and vaccination. Prophylactic (preventive) medicine is an aspect of public-health provision that is receiving increasing attention.

psychosomatic physical symptom or disease, thought to arise from emotional or mental factors. The term 'psychosomatic' has been applied to many conditions, including asthma, migraine, hypertension, and peptic ulcers. Whereas it is unlikely that these and other conditions are wholly due to psychological factors, emotional states such as anxiety or depression do have a distinct influence on the frequency and severity of illness.

radiotherapy treatment of disease by radiation from X-ray machines or radioactive sources. Radiation, which reduces the activity of dividing cells, is of special value for its effect on malignant tissues, certain nonmalignant tumours, and some diseases of the skin.

remission temporary disappearance of symptoms during the course of a disease.

resuscitation steps taken to revive anyone on the brink of death. The most successful technique for life-threatening emergencies, such as electrocution, near-drowning, or heart attack, is mouth-to-mouth resuscitation. Medical and paramedical staff are trained in cardiopulmonary resuscitation: the use of specialized equipment and techniques to attempt to restart the breathing and/or heartbeat and stabilize the patient long enough for more definitive treatment.

retrovirus any of a family (*Retroviridae*) of viruses containing the genetic material RNA rather than the more usual DNA. Retroviruses include those causing AIDS and some forms of leukaemia.

screening or ***health screening*** the systematic search for evidence of a disease, or of conditions that may precede it, in people who are not suffering from any symptoms. The aim of screening is to try to limit ill health from diseases that are difficult to prevent and might otherwise go undetected. Examples are hypothyroidism and phenylketonuria, for which all newborn babies in Western countries are screened; breast cancer and cervical cancer; and stroke, for which high blood pressure is a known risk factor.

spastic person with cerebral palsy. The term is also applied generally to limbs with impaired movement, stiffness, and resistance to passive movement, and to any body part (such as the colon) affected with spasm.

spermicide any cream, jelly, pessary, or other preparation that kills the sperm cells in semen. Spermicides are used for contraceptive purposes, usually in combination with a condom or diaphragm. Sponges impregnated with spermicide have been developed but are not yet in widespread use. Spermicide used alone is only 75% effective in preventing pregnancy.

sterilization any surgical operation to terminate the possibility of reproduction. In women, this is normally achieved by sealing or tying the Fallopian tubes (tubal ligation) so that fertilization can no longer take place. In men, the transmission of sperm is blocked by vasectomy.

tomography the obtaining of plane-section X-ray photographs, which show a 'slice' through any object. Crystal detectors and amplifiers can be used that have a sensitivity 100 times greater than X-ray film, and, in conjunction with a computer system, can detect, for example, the difference between a brain tumour and healthy brain tissue. In modern medical imaging there are several types, such as the CAT scan (computerized axial tomography).

transfusion intravenous delivery of blood or blood products (plasma, red cells) into a patient's circulation to make up for deficiencies due to disease, injury, or surgical intervention. Cross-matching is carried out to ensure the patient receives the right type of blood, unless a store of the patient's own blood is used.

transplant transfer of a tissue or organ from one human being to another or from one part of the body to another (skin grafting). In most organ transplants, the operation is for life-saving purposes, though the immune system tends to reject foreign tissue. Careful matching and immunosuppressive drugs must be used, but these are not always successful.

trauma painful emotional experience or shock with lasting psychic consequences; any physical damage or injury.

tumour overproduction of cells in a specific area of the body, often leading to a swelling or lump. Tumours are classified as ***benign*** or ***malignant*** (cancerous). Benign tumours grow more slowly, do not invade surrounding tissues, do not spread to other parts of the body, and do not usually recur after removal.

ultrasound scanning or ***ultrasonography*** the use of ultrasonic pressure waves to create a diagnostic image. It is a safe, noninvasive technique that often eliminates the need for exploratory surgery. An ultrasound beam can also be used to alleviate pain in joints and muscles.

vaccine any preparation of modified viruses or bacteria that is introduced into the body, usually either orally or by a hypodermic syringe, to induce the specific antibody reaction that produces immunity against a particular disease.

In the UK, children are routinely vaccinated against diphtheria, tetanus, whooping cough, polio, measles, mumps, German measles, and tuberculosis.

X-ray electromagnetic radiation with a short wavelength. X-rays pass through most body tissues, although dense areas such as bone prevent their passage, showing up as white areas on X-ray photographs. The X-rays used in radiotherapy have very short wavelengths that penetrate tissues deeply and destroy them. X-rays are dangerous and can cause cancer.

The Human Body

Achilles tendon tendon pinning the calf muscle to the heel bone. It is one of the largest in the human body.

adenoids masses of lymphoid tissue, similar to tonsils, located in the upper part of the throat, behind the nose. They are part of a child's natural defences against the entry of germs but usually shrink and disappear by the age of ten.

adrenal gland or ***suprarenal gland*** gland situated on top of the kidney. The adrenals are soft and yellow, and consist of two parts: the cortex and medulla. The ***cortex*** (outer part) secretes various steroid hormones, controls salt and water metabolism, and regulates the use of carbohydrates, proteins, and fats. The ***medulla*** (inner part) secretes the hormones adrenaline and noradrenaline which, during times of stress, cause the heart to beat faster and harder, increase blood flow to the heart and muscle cells, and dilate airways in the lungs, thereby delivering more oxygen to cells throughout the body and in general preparing the body for 'fight or flight'.

alimentary canal the tube through which food passes; it extends from the mouth to the anus. It is a complex organ, adapted for digestion. In adults, it is about 9 m/30 ft long, consisting of the mouth cavity, pharynx, oesophagus, stomach, and the small and large intestines.

antibody protein molecule produced in the blood by lymphocytes in response to the presence of foreign or invading substances (antigens); such substances include the proteins carried on the surface of infecting microorganisms. Antibody production is one aspect of immunity.

aorta the chief artery, the dorsal blood vessel carrying oxygenated blood from the left ventricle of the heart. It branches to form smaller arteries, which in turn supply all body organs except the lungs. Loss of elasticity in the aorta provides evidence of atherosclerosis, which may lead to heart disease.

artery vessel that carries blood from the heart to the rest of the body. It is built to withstand considerable pressure, having thick walls that are impregnated with muscle and elastic fibres. During contraction of the heart muscles, arteries expand in diameter to allow for the sudden increase in pressure that occurs; the resulting pulse or pressure wave can be felt at the wrist. Not all arteries carry oxygenated (oxygen-rich) blood; the pulmonary arteries convey deoxygenated (oxygen-poor) blood from the heart to the lungs.

blood liquid circulating in the arteries, veins, and capillaries. Blood carries nutrients and oxygen to individual cells and removes waste products, such as carbon dioxide. It is also important in the immune response and in the distribution of heat throughout the body.

Spending on health

Government expenditure on health

	Total health expenditure as % of GDP			*Percentage change in health expenditure*	
	1970	*1980*	*1990*	*1970–80*	*1980–90*
Belgium	4.1*	6.7	7.5	63*	12
France	5.8	7.6	8.8	31	16
Germany	5.9	8.4	8.1	42	-4
Ireland	5.6*	9.6	7.5	71*	-22
Netherlands	6.0	8.0	8.0	33	0
Spain	3.7	5.6	6.6	51	18
UK	4.5	5.8	6.2	29	7

** may be overestimated*

Source: OECD

bone marrow substance found inside the cavity of bones. In early life it produces red blood cells but later on lipids (fat) accumulate and its colour changes from red to yellow.

brain mass of interconnected nerve cells, forming the anterior part of the central nervous system, whose activities it coordinates and controls. In 1990 scientists at Johns Hopkins University, Baltimore, USA, succeeded in culturing human brain cells. (See ***Life Sciences*** for more.)

bronchus one of a pair of large tubes (bronchii) branching off from the windpipe and passing into the vertebrate lung. Cartilaginous rings give rigidity and prevent collapse during breathing movements. Numerous glands secrete a slimy mucus, which traps dust and other particles; the mucus is constantly being propelled upwards to the mouth by thousands of tiny hairs or cilia. The bronchus is adversely effected by several respiratory diseases and by smoking, which damages the cilia.

cranium the dome-shaped area of the skull, consisting of several fused plates, that protects the brain.

ear organ of hearing. It responds to the vibrations that constitute sound, and these are translated into nerve signals and passed to the brain. The ear consists of three parts: outer ear, middle ear, and inner ear. Three fluid-filled canals of the inner ear detect changes of position; this mechanism, with other sensory inputs, is responsible for the sense of balance.

eye organ of vision, a roughly spherical structure contained in a bony socket. Light enters it through the cornea, and passes through the circular opening (pupil) in the iris (the coloured part of the eye). The ciliary muscles act on the lens (the rounded transparent structure behind the iris) to change its shape, so that images of objects at different distances can be focused on the retina. This is at the back of the eye, and is packed with light-sensitive cells (rods and cones), connected to the brain by the optic nerve.

Fallopian tube or ***oviduct*** one of two tubes that carry eggs from the ovary to the uterus. An egg is fertilized by sperm in the Fallopian tubes, which are lined with cells whose cilia move the egg towards the uterus.

gall bladder small muscular sac, situated on the underside of the liver and connected to the small intestine by the bile duct. It stores bile from the liver.

the human body

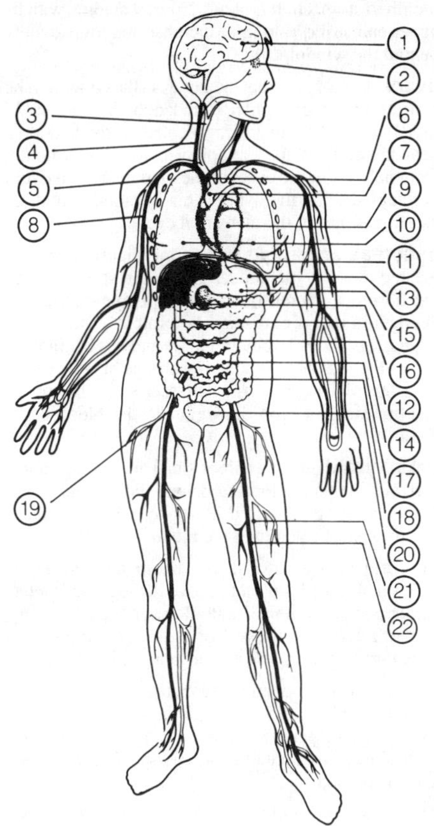

Key

1. brain
2. eye
3. carotid artery
4. jugular vein
5. subclavian artery
6. superior vena cava
7. aorta
8. subclavian vein
9. heart
10. lungs
11. diaphragm
12. liver
13. stomach
14. gall bladder
15. kidney
16. pancreas
17. small intestine
18. large intestine
19. appendix
20. bladder
21. femoral artery
22. femoral vein

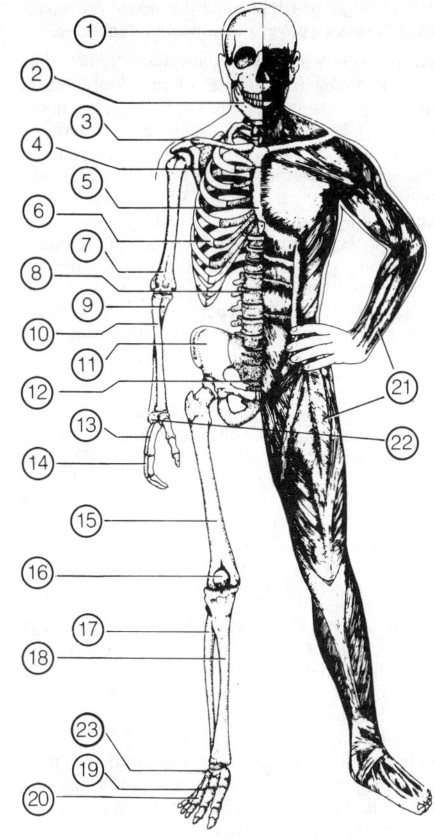

Key

1. cranium (skull)
2. mandible
3. clavicle
4. scapula
5. sternum
6. rib cage
7. humerus
8. vertebra
9. ulna
10. radius
11. pelvis
12. coccyx
13. metacarpals
14. phalanges
15. femur
16. patella
17. fibula
18. tibia
19. metatarsals
20. phalanges
21. superficial (upper) layer of muscles
22. carpals
23. tarsals

hair threadlike structure growing from the skin. Each hair grows from a pit-shaped follicle embedded in the second layer of the skin, the dermis. It consists of dead cells impregnated with the protein keratin. There are about a million hairs on the average person's head. Each grows at the rate of 5–10 mm/ 0.2–0.4 in per month, lengthening for about three years before being replaced by a new one. In 1990 scientists succeeded for the first time in growing human hair in vitro.

heart muscular organ that rhythmically contracts to force blood around the body. The beating of the heart is controlled by the autonomic nervous system and an internal control centre or pacemaker, the sinoatrial node.

hormone product of the endocrine glands, concerned with control of body functions. The main glands are the thyroid, parathyroid, pituitary, adrenal, pancreas, uterus, ovary, and testis. Hormones bring about changes in the functions of various organs according to the body's requirements. The pituitary gland, at the base of the brain, is a centre for overall coordination of hormone secretion; the thyroid hormones determine the rate of general body chemistry;

the adrenal hormones prepare the organism during stress for 'fight or flight'; and the sexual hormones such as oestrogen govern reproductive functions.

joint the point where two bones meet. Some joints allow no motion (the sutures of the skull), others allow a very small motion (the sacroiliac joints in the lower back), but most allow a relatively free motion. Of these, some allow a gliding motion (one vertebra of the spine on another), some have a hinge action (elbow and knee), and others allow motion in all directions (hip and shoulder joints) by means of a ball-and-socket arrangement. The ends of the bones at a moving joint are covered with cartilage for greater elasticity and smoothness, and enclosed in an envelope (capsule) of tough white fibrous tissue lined with a membrane which secretes a lubricating and cushioning synovial fluid. The joint is further strengthened by ligaments.

kidney one of a pair of organs responsible for water regulation, excretion of waste products, and maintaining the ionic composition of the blood. The kidneys are situated on the rear wall of the abdomen. Each one consists of a number of long tubules; the outer parts filter the aqueous components of blood, and the inner parts selectively reabsorb vital salts, leaving waste products in the remaining fluid (urine), which is passed through the ureter to the bladder.

liver large organ with many regulatory and storage functions. It is situated in the upper abdomen, and weighs about 2 kg/4.5 lb. It receives the products of digestion, converts glucose to glycogen (a long- chain carbohydrate used for storage), and breaks down fats. It removes excess amino acids from the blood, converting them to urea, which is excreted by the kidneys. The liver also synthesizes vitamins, produces bile and blood-clotting factors, and removes damaged red cells and toxins such as alcohol from the blood.

lung large cavity of the body, used for gas exchange. It is essentially a sheet of thin, moist membrane that is folded so as to occupy less space. The lung tissue, consisting of multitudes of air sacs and blood vessels, is very light and spongy, and functions by bringing inhaled air into close contact with the blood so that oxygen can pass into the organism and waste carbon dioxide can be passed out. The efficiency of lungs is enhanced by breathing movements, by the thinness and moistness of their surfaces, and by a constant supply of circulating blood.

lymph nodes small masses of lymphatic tissue in the body that occur at various points along the major lymphatic vessels. Tonsils and adenoids are large lymph nodes. As the lymph passes through them it is filtered, and bacteria and other microorganisms are engulfed by cells known as macrophages.

muscle contractile tissue that produces locomotion and maintains the movement of body substances. Muscle is made of long cells that can contract to between one-half and one-third of their relaxed length. (See ***Life Sciences*** for more.)

nerve strand of nerve cells enclosed in a sheath of connective tissue joining the central and the autonomic nervous systems with receptor and effector organs. A single nerve may contain both motor and sensory nerve cells, but they act independently.

oesophagus passage by which food travels from mouth to stomach. It is about 23 cm/9 in long, with its upper end at the bottom of the pharynx, immediately behind the windpipe.

ovary the organ that generates the ovum. The ovaries are two whitish rounded bodies about 25 mm/1 in by 35 mm/1.5 in, located in the abdomen near the ends of the Fallopian tubes. Every month, from puberty to the onset of the menopause, an ovum is released from the ovary. This is called ovulation, and forms part of the menstrual cycle.

pancreas accessory gland of the digestive system located close to the duodenum. When stimulated by the hormone secretin, it secretes enzymes into the duodenum that digest starches, proteins, and fats. In adults, it is about 18 cm/7 in long, and lies behind and below the stomach. It contains groups of cells called the islets of Langerhans, which secrete the hormones insulin and glucagon that regulate the blood sugar level.

parathyroid one of a pair of small endocrine glands. Two such pairs are located behind the thyroid gland. They secrete parathyroid hormone, which regulates the amount of calcium in the blood.

pelvis the lower area of the abdomen featuring the bones and muscles used to move the legs. The ***pelvic girdle*** is a set of bones that allows movement of the legs in relation to the rest of the body and provides sites for the attachment of relevant muscles.

penis male reproductive organ, used for internal fertilization; it transfers sperm to the female reproductive tract. The penis is made erect by vessels that fill with blood, and contains the urethra, through which urine is passed.

pharynx interior of the throat, the cavity at the back of the mouth. Its walls are made of muscle strengthened with a fibrous layer and lined with mucous membrane. The internal nostrils lead backwards into the pharynx, which continues downwards into the oesophagus and (through the epiglottis) into the windpipe. On each side, a Eustachian tube enters the pharynx from the middle ear cavity. The upper part (nasopharynx) is an airway, but the remainder is a passage for food.

prostate gland gland surrounding and opening into the urethra at the base of the bladder in males. The prostate gland produces an alkaline fluid that is released during ejaculation; this fluid activates sperm, and prevents their clumping together.

red blood cell or ***erythrocyte*** the most common type of blood cell, responsible for transporting oxygen around the body. It contains haemoglobin, which combines with oxygen from the lungs to form oxyhaemoglobin. When transported to the tissues these cells are able to release the oxygen because the oxyhaemoglobin splits into its original constituents.

rib long, usually curved bone that extends laterally from the spine in 12 pairs in the chest area. The ribs protect the lungs and heart, and allow the chest to expand and contract easily.

skull collection of flat and irregularly shaped bones (or cartilage) that enclose the brain and the organs of sight, hearing, and smell, and provide support for the

Gene therapy holds out promise

Excitement is growing over the potential of gene therapy as a weapon against inherited disease. Genes – basic units of hereditary material – code for proteins and it is the absence of particular proteins that is the problem in diseases such as cystic fibrosis, muscular dystrophy, and haemophilia. Scientists hope to cure these and many other distressing conditions by using healthy genes to alter or replace defective ones.

The first human being to undergo gene therapy, in Sept 1990, was one of the so-called 'bubble babies' – a four- year-old American girl suffering from a rare enzyme (ADA) deficiency that cripples the immune system. Unable to fight off infection, such children are nursed in a germ-free bubble; they usually die in early childhood. In the UK an eight-month-old baby with ADA deficiency began gene therapy in March 1993.

In this case, scientists isolate a healthy ADA gene and insert it into a virus that has been rendered harmless by removing its genetic code. The virus is then inserted into a blood-forming cell taken from the sick child's bone marrow. This cell is left to reproduce, creating millions of cells containing the missing gene. Finally, these cells are infused into the child's bloodstream, to be carried to the bone marrow, where they will produce healthy blood cells complete with the ADA gene.

Rival strategies are being developed to supply the gene missing in cystic fibrosis, the commonest inherited disorder and the one most keenly targeted by genetic engineers. Some researchers favour introducing the gene into the patient's lungs by way of a modified virus; others plan to package the normal gene in fat droplets, called liposomes, contained in an aerosol spray.

Gene therapy holds out the promise of a cure for various other conditions, including heart disease and some cancers. But it is not the final answer to inherited disease: it may cure the patient but it cannot prevent him or her from passing on the genetic defect to any children.

jaws. The skull consists of 22 bones joined by sutures. The floor of the skull is pierced by a large hole for the spinal cord and a number of smaller apertures through which other nerves and blood vessels pass.

spinal cord major component of the central nervous system. It is enclosed by the bones of the spine, and links the peripheral nervous system to the brain.

stomach the first cavity in the digestive system, a bag of muscle situated just below the diaphragm. Food enters it from the oesophagus, is digested by the acid and enzymes secreted by the stomach lining, and then passes into the duodenum.

testis (plural ***testes***) the organ that produces sperm in males. It is one of a pair of oval structures (testicles) that descend from the body cavity during development, to hang outside the abdomen in a scrotal sac.

throat passage that leads from the back of the nose and mouth to the trachea and oesophagus. It includes the pharynx and the larynx, the latter being at the top of the trachea.

thyroid endocrine gland situated in the neck in front of the trachea. It secretes several hormones, principally thyroxine, an iodine-containing hormone that stimulates growth, metabolism, and other functions of the body. The thyroid gland may be thought of as the regulator gland of the body's metabolic rate.

tongue muscular organ usually attached to the floor of the mouth. It has a thick root attached to a U-shaped bone (hyoid), and is covered with a mucous membrane containing nerves and taste buds. It directs food to the teeth and into the throat for chewing and swallowing. It is crucial for speech.

trachea or ***windpipe*** tube that forms an airway from the larynx to the upper part of the chest. Its diameter is about 1.5 cm/0.6 in and its length 10 cm/4 in. It is strong and flexible, and reinforced by rings of cartilage. In the upper chest, the trachea branches into two tubes: the left and right bronchi, which enter the lungs.

uterus hollow muscular organ of females, located between the bladder and rectum, and connected to the Fallopian tubes above and the vagina below. The embryo develops within the uterus, and is attached to it after implantation via the placenta and umbilical cord. The lining of the uterus changes during the menstrual cycle. The outer wall of the uterus is composed of smooth muscle, capable of powerful contractions (induced by hormones) during childbirth.

vagina the front passage in females, linking the uterus to the exterior. It admits the penis during sexual intercourse, and is the birth canal down which the fetus passes during delivery.

Psychological Disorders

agoraphobia phobia involving fear of open spaces and crowded places. The anxiety produced can be so severe that some sufferers are confined to their homes for many years.

anorexia lack of desire to eat, especially the pathological condition of ***anorexia nervosa***, usually found in adolescent girls and young women, who may be obsessed with the desire to lose weight. Compulsive eating, or bulimia, often accompanies anorexia. In anorexia nervosa, the patient refuses to eat and finally becomes unable to do so. The result is severe emaciation and, in rare cases, death.

anxiety emotional state of fear or apprehension. Anxiety is a normal response to potentially dangerous situations. Abnormal anxiety can either be free-floating, experienced in a wide range of situations, or it may be phobic, when the sufferer is excessively afraid of an object or situation.

behaviour therapy application of behavioural principles, derived from learning theories, to the treatment of clinical conditions such as phobias, obsessions, sexual and interpersonal problems. For example, in treating a phobia the person is taken into the feared situation in gradual steps. Over time, the fear typically reduces, and the problem becomes less acute.

claustrophobia phobia involving fear of enclosed spaces.

clinical psychology discipline dealing with the understanding and treatment of health problems, particularly mental disorders. The main problems dealt with include anxiety, phobias, depression, obsessions, sexual and marital problems, drug and alcohol dependence, childhood behavioural problems, psychoses (such as schizophrenia), mental handicap, and brain damage (such as dementia).

cognitive therapy treatment for emotional disorders, such as depression and anxiety, that encourages the patient to challenge the distorted and unhelpful thinking that is characteristic of these problems. The treatment includes behaviour therapy and has been most helpful for people suffering from depression.

delusion false belief that is unshakeably held. Delusions are a prominent feature of schizophrenia and paranoia, but may also occur in severe depression and manic depression.

depression emotional state characterized by sadness, unhappy thoughts, apathy, and dejection. Sadness is a normal response to major losses such as bereavement or unemployment. After childbirth, postnatal depression is common. However, clinical depression, which is prolonged or unduly severe, often requires treatment, such as antidepressant medication, cognitive therapy, or, in very rare cases, electroconvulsive therapy (ECT), in which an electrical current is passed through the brain.

drug and alcohol dependence physical or psychological craving for addictive drugs such as alcohol, nicotine (in cigarettes), tranquillizers, heroin, or stimulants (for example, amphetamines). Such substances can alter mood or behaviour. When dependence is established, sudden withdrawal from the drug can cause unpleasant physical and/or psychological reactions, which may be dangerous.

dyslexia malfunction in the brain's synthesis and interpretation of sensory information, popularly known as 'word blindness'. It results in difficulty with reading and writing. A similar disability with figures is called dyscalculia.

electroconvulsive therapy (ECT) or ***electroshock therapy*** treatment for schizophrenia and depression, given under anaesthesia and with a muscle relaxant. An electric current is passed through the brain to induce alterations in the brain's electrical activity. The treatment can cause distress and loss of concentration and memory, and so there is much controversy about its use and effectiveness.

hyperactivity condition of excessive activity in young children, combined with inability to concentrate and difficulty in learning. The cause is not known, although some food additives have come under suspicion. Modification of the diet may help, and in the majority of cases there is improvement at puberty.

hypnosis artificially induced state of relaxation in which suggestibility is heightened. Hypnosis is sometimes used to treat addictions to tobacco or overeating, or to assist amnesia victims.

hysteria according to the work of Austrian psychoanalyst Sigmund Freud (1856–1939), the conversion of a psychological conflict or anxiety feeling into a physical symptom, such as paralysis, blindness, recurrent cough, vomiting, and general malaise. The term is little used today in diagnosis.

manic depression mental disorder characterized by recurring periods of depression which may or may not alternate with periods of inappropriate elation (mania) or overactivity. Sufferers may be genetically predisposed to the condition. Some cases have been improved by taking prescribed doses of lithium.

mental handicap impairment of intelligence. It can be very mild, but in more severe cases, it is associated with social problems and difficulties in living independently. A person may be born with a mental handicap (for example, Down's syndrome) or may acquire it through brain damage. There are between 90 and 130 million people in the world suffering such disabilities.

nervous breakdown popular term for a reaction to overwhelming psychological stress. It has no equivalent in medicine: a patient said to be suffering from a nervous breakdown may in fact be going through an episode of depression, manic depression, anxiety, or even schizophrenia.

neurosis general term referring to emotional disorders, such as anxiety, depression, and obsessions. The main disturbance tends to be one of mood; contact with reality is relatively unaffected, in contrast to the effects of psychosis.

obsession repetitive unwanted thought or compulsive action that is often recognized by the sufferer as being irrational, but which nevertheless causes distress. It can be associated with the irresistible urge of an individual to carry out a repetitive series of actions.

paranoia mental disorder marked by delusions of grandeur or persecution. In popular usage, paranoia means baseless or exaggerated fear and suspicion.

phobia excessive irrational fear of an object or situation – for example, agoraphobia (fear of open spaces and crowded places), acrophobia (fear of heights), and claustrophobia (fear of enclosed places). Behaviour therapy is one form of treatment.

postnatal depression mood change occurring in many mothers a few days after the birth of a baby. It is usually a short-lived condition but can sometimes persist; the most severe form of postnatal depressive illness, ***puerperal psychosis***, requires hospital treatment. In mild cases, antidepressant drugs and hormone treatment may help.

psychiatry branch of medicine dealing with the diagnosis and treatment of mental disorder, normally divided into the areas of ***neurotic conditions***, including anxiety, depression, and hysteria, and ***psychotic disorders***, such as schizophrenia. Psychiatric treatment consists of analysis, drugs, or electroconvulsive therapy.

In practice there is considerable overlap between psychiatry and clinical psychology, the fundamental difference being that psychiatrists are trained medical doctors (holding an MD degree) and may therefore prescribe drugs, whereas psychologists may hold a PhD but do not need a medical qualification to practise.

psychoanalysis theory and treatment method for neuroses, developed by Austrian physician Sigmund Freud (1856–1939). The main treatment method involves the free association of ideas, and their interpretation by patient and analyst. It is typically prolonged and expensive and its effectiveness has been disputed.

psychology systematic study of human and animal behaviour. The first psychology laboratory was founded 1879 by Wilhelm Wundt (1832–1920) in Leipzig, Germany. The subject includes diverse areas of study and application, among them the roles of instinct, heredity, environment, and culture; the processes of sensation, perception, learning, and memory; the bases of motivation and emotion; and the functioning of thought, intelligence, and language.

psychosis or ***psychotic disorder*** general term for a serious mental disorder where the individual commonly loses contact with reality and may experience hallucinations (seeing or hearing things that do not exist) or delusions (fixed false beliefs). For example, in a paranoid psychosis an individual may believe that others are plotting against him or her. A major type of psychosis is schizophrenia (which may be biochemically induced).

psychotherapy treatment approaches for psychological problems involving talking rather than surgery or drugs. Examples include cognitive therapy and psychoanalysis.

schizophrenia psychosis of unknown origin that can lead to profound changes in personality and behaviour, including paranoia and hallucinations. Contrary to popular belief, it does not involve a split personality. Modern treatment approaches include drugs, family therapy, stress reduction, and rehabilitation.

senile dementia dementia associated with old age, often caused by Alzheimer's disease.

stress any event or situation that makes demands on a person's mental or emotional resources. Stress can be caused by overwork, anxiety about exams, money, or job security, unemployment, bereavement, poor relationships, marriage breakdown, sexual difficulties, poor living or working conditions, and constant exposure to loud noise.

Many changes that are apparently for the better, such as being promoted at work, going to a new school, moving house, and getting married, are also sources of stress. Stress can cause, or aggravate, physical illnesses, among them psoriasis, eczema, asthma, and stomach and mouth ulcers. Apart from removing the source of stress, acquiring some control over it and learning to relax when possible are the best treatments.

Diseases and Disorders

acne skin eruption, mainly occurring among adolescents and young adults, caused by inflammation of the sebaceous glands which secrete an oily substance (sebum), the natural lubricant of the skin. Sometimes the openings of the glands become blocked and they swell; the contents decompose and pimples form on the face, back, and chest.

AIDS (acronym for ***acquired immune deficiency syndrome***) the gravest of the sexually transmitted diseases, or STDs. It is caused by the human immunodeficiency virus (HIV), now known to be a retrovirus, an organism first identified 1983. HIV is transmitted in body fluids, mainly blood and sexual secretions.

The estimated incubation period between infection with HIV and outbreak of AIDS is 9.8 years. The effect of the virus in those who become ill is the devastation of the immune system, leaving the victim susceptible to (opportunistic) diseases that would not otherwise develop. Some AIDS victims die within a few months of the outbreak of symptoms, some survive for several years; roughly 50% are dead within three years. There is no cure for the disease.

By Feb 1991, 323,378 AIDS cases in 159 countries had been reported to the World Health Organization (WHO), which estimated that over 1.3 million cases might have occurred worldwide, of which about 400,000 were a result of transmission before, during, or shortly after birth. In the UK, 7,341 cases had been reported by April 1993, with 4,572 deaths. (See box on HIV in this section.)

alcoholism dependence on alcoholic liquor. It is characterized as an illness when consumption of alcohol interferes with normal physical or emotional health. Excessive alcohol consumption may produce physical and psychological addiction and lead to nutritional and emotional disorders. The direct effect is cirrhosis of the liver, nerve damage, and heart disease, and the condition is now showing genetic predisposition.

Alzheimer's disease common manifestation of dementia, thought to afflict one in 20 people over 65. Attacking the brain's 'grey matter', it is a disease of mental processes rather than physical function, characterized by memory loss and progressive intellectual impairment. The disease may result from a defective protein circulating in the blood; some forms of early-onset Alzheimer's disease, it was discovered 1991, are caused by a gene defect on chromosome 21.

anaemia condition caused by a shortage of haemoglobin, the oxygen-carrying component of red blood cells. The main symptoms are fatigue, pallor, breathlessness, palpitations, and poor resistance to infection. Treatment depends on the cause; untreated anaemia taxes the heart and may prove fatal.

AIDS and HIV figures

Cases and related deaths and HIV-positive reports in the UK to end June 1992

	AIDS						
	Cases		Related deaths		HIV – positive reports		
	Males	Females	Males	Females	Males	Females	Not known
Exposure category							
Sexual intercourse							
Between men	4,681		2,981		10,761		
Between men and women	340	219	172	96	1,011	1,117	12
Injecting drug user (IDU)	291	80	174	51	1,746	694	9
Blood							
Blood factor (eg haemophilia)	307	4	232	3	1,236	10	
Blood transfusion/tissue transfer	31	47	23	30	99	88	1
Mother to child	25	35	10	17	60	61	1
Other/undetermined	67	13	45	5	762	158	42
Total	***5,742***	***398***	***3,637***	***202***	***15,675***	***2,128***	***65***

Source: Social Trends 1993

angina or ***angina pectoris*** severe pain in the chest due to impaired blood supply to the heart muscle because a coronary artery is narrowed. Faintness and difficulty in breathing accompany the pain. Treatment is by drugs, such as nitroglycerin and amyl nitrite; rest is important.

appendicitis inflammation of the appendix, a small, blind extension of the bowel in the lower right abdomen. In an acute attack, the pus-filled appendix may burst, causing a potentially lethal spread of infection. Treatment is by removal (appendicectomy).

arthritis inflammation of the joints, with pain, swelling, and restricted motion. Many conditions may cause arthritis, including gout and trauma to the joint.

More common in women, ***rheumatoid arthritis*** usually begins in middle age in the small joints of the hands and feet, causing a greater or lesser degree of deformity and painfully restricted movement. It is alleviated by drugs, and surgery may be performed to correct deformity.

Osteoarthritis, a degenerative condition, tends to affect larger, load-bearing joints, such as the knee and hip. It appears in later life, especially in those whose joints may have been subject to earlier stress or damage; one or more joints stiffen and may give considerable pain. Joint replacement surgery is nearly always successful.

asthma difficulty in breathing due to spasm of the bronchi (air passages) in the lungs. Attacks may be provoked by allergy, infection, stress, or emotional upset. It may also be increasing as a result of air pollution and occupational hazards. Treatment is with bronchodilators to relax the bronchial muscles and thereby ease the breathing, and in severe cases by inhaled steroids that reduce inflammation of the bronchi.

Although the symptoms are similar to those of bronchial asthma, ***cardiac asthma*** is an unrelated condition and is a symptom of heart deterioration.

atherosclerosis thickening and hardening of the walls of the arteries, associated with atheroma.

autoimmunity condition where the body's immune responses are mobilized not against 'foreign' matter, such as invading germs, but against the body itself. Diseases considered to be of autoimmune origin include myasthenia gravis, rheumatoid arthritis, and lupus erythematosus. In 1990 in Israel a T-cell vaccine was produced that arrests the excessive reproduction of T-lymphocytes attacking healthy target tissues.

back pain aches in the region of the spine. Low back pain can be caused by a very wide range of medical conditions. About half of all episodes of back pain will resolve within a week, but severe back pain can be chronic and disabling. The causes include muscle sprain, a prolapsed intervertebral disc, and vertebral collapse due to osteoporosis or cancer. Treatment methods include rest, analgesics, physiotherapy, and exercises.

blindness complete absence or impairment of sight. It may be caused by heredity, accident, disease, or deterioration with age. Aids to the blind include the use of the Braille and Moon alphabets in reading and writing; electronic devices that convert print to recognizable mechanical speech; guide dogs; and sonic torches.

blood poisoning condition in which poisons are spread throughout the body by pathogens in the bloodstream.

bronchitis inflammation of the bronchi (air passages) of the lungs, usually caused initially by a viral infection, such as a cold or flu. It is aggravated by environmental pollutants, especially smoking, and results in a persistent cough, irritated mucus-secreting glands, and large amounts of sputum.

cancer group of diseases characterized by abnormal proliferation of cells. Cancer (malignant) cells are usually degenerate, capable only of reproducing themselves (tumour formation). Malignant cells tend to spread from their site of origin by travelling through the bloodstream or lymphatic system.

There are more than 100 types of cancer. Some, like lung or bowel cancer, are common; others are rare. The likely cause remains unexplained. Triggering agents (carcinogens) include chemicals such as those found in cigarette smoke, other forms of

HIV – worldwide statistics

Estimates released by the World Health Organization (WHO) in mid-1993 revealed that an estimated 14 million people had been infected by HIV, the human immuno-deficiency virus which causes AIDS. WHO estimated that, by the year 2000, between 30 and 40 million people will have been infected by the virus.

The worst affected area is sub-Saharan Africa, where WHO estimated that over eight million people had been infected. About half to two thirds of this total were in east and central Africa, an area that accounts for only about one sixth of the total population of the sub-Saharan region. The number of AIDS cases in Africa has also continued to increase. An estimated one and three quarter million people in sub-Saharan Africa have developed AIDS, two-thirds of the global figure. By the end of the century the cumulative total of AIDS cases in the region is expected to exceed five million.

The most alarming trends of HIV infection are in S and SE Asia, where the epidemic is spreading as fast as it was a decade ago in sub-Saharan Africa. The majority of the over one and a half million HIV infections estimated to have occurred in adults in these regions appeared in India and Thailand, but high rates of HIV spread have been seen elsewhere in S and SE Asia.

WHO estimates show that over one and a half million adult HIV infections have occurred in Latin America and the Caribbean since the epidemic began. The future course of the epidemic in the region depends greatly on the rate at which the virus spreads in Brazil, which has more AIDS cases than any other country outside Africa apart from the USA. More than 75,000 HIV infections are estimated to have occurred so far in the Middle East and North Africa. These figures are of particular concern because other factors, such as the presence of other sexually transmitted diseases and intravenous drug use, suggest that there is an increased exposure to the risk of HIV infection.

An estimated 50,000 adults in Eastern Europe and Central Asia have been infected with HIV. Current economic and social developments in these regions, together with rising drug use and prostitution, may spur the rate of transmission in the region.

WHO estimates that by the end of 1992 over 25,000 HIV infections had occurred in E Asia and the Pacific. By Jan 1993, 663 cumulative AIDS cases had been reported in these regions.

smoke, asbestos dust, exhaust fumes, and many industrial chemicals. Some viruses can also trigger the cancerous growth of cells, as can X-rays and radioactivity. Dietary factors are important in some cancers; for example, lack of fibre in the diet may predispose people to bowel cancer and a diet high in animal fats and low in fresh vegetables and fruit increases the risk of breast cancer. Psychological stress may increase the risk of cancer, more so if the person concerned is not able to control the source of the stress. In some families there is a genetic tendency towards a particular type of cancer.

Cancer is one of the leading causes of death in the industrialized world, yet it is by no means incurable, particularly in the case of certain tumours, including Hodgkin's disease, acute leukaemia, and testicular cancer. Cures are sometimes achieved with specialized treatments, such as surgery, chemotherapy with cytotoxic drugs, and irradiation, or a combination of all three. Monoclonal antibodies have been used therapeutically against some cancers, with limited success. There is also hope of combining a monoclonal antibody with a drug that will kill the cancer cell to produce a highly specific magic bullet drug. In 1990 it was discovered that the presence in some patients of a particular protein, p-glycoprotein, actively protects the cancer cells from drugs intended to destroy them. If this action can be blocked, the cancer should become far easier to treat. However, at present public health programmes are more concerned with prevention and early detection.

cataract eye disease in which the crystalline lens or its capsule becomes opaque, causing blindness. Fluid accumulates between the fibres of the lens and gives place to deposits of albumin. These coalesce into rounded bodies, the lens fibres break down, and areas of the lens or the lens capsule become filled with opaque products of degeneration. It is estimated (1991) that more than 25 million people around the world are blind because of cataracts. The treatment is surgical replacement of the opaque lens with an artificial implant.

chickenpox or ***varicella*** common acute disease, caused by a virus of the herpes group and transmitted by airborne droplets. Chickenpox chiefly attacks children under the age of ten. The incubation period is two to three weeks. One attack normally gives immunity for life.

cirrhosis any degenerative disease in an organ of the body, especially the liver, characterized by excessive development of connective tissue, causing scarring and painful swelling. Cirrhosis of the liver may be caused by an infection such as viral hepatitis, by chronic alcoholism or drug use, blood disorder, or malnutrition. If cirrhosis is diagnosed early, it can be arrested by treating the cause; otherwise it will progress to jaundice, oedema, vomiting of blood, coma, and death.

cot death or ***sudden infant death syndrome*** (SIDS) death of an apparently healthy baby during sleep. It is most common in the winter months, and strikes more boys than girls. The cause is not known.

cystic fibrosis hereditary disease characterized by the production of abnormally thick mucus and excessively salty sweat. In cystic fibrosis sufferers the airways become clogged, resulting in frequent, often severe infections; nutrition is impaired because mucus blockage of the pancreatic ducts inhibits the passage of digestive enzymes.

Unknown in Africans, cystic fibrosis is the commonest inherited disease among Caucasians. In the UK one person in 20 carries the defective gene. If both parents are carriers, there is a one-in-four chance of cystic fibrosis occurring in their child. Since the discovery of the cystic fibrosis gene in 1989, screening tests have been developed for carriers; the disease can be detected in the unborn child.

In the past, most cystic fibrosis sufferers died in infancy; today most survive into adulthood. Modern management is by diet and drugs, daily physiotherapy to keep the airways clear, and the use of antibiotics to combat infection; enzyme preparations are given to aid digestion. Some patients benefit from heart-lung transplants. Cystic fibrosis is seen as a promising test case for gene-replacement therapy. In 1992 the prospect of a cure improved greatly when a healthy version of the cystic-fibrosis gene was successfully introduced into the lung tissue of rats.

cystitis inflammation of the bladder, usually caused by bacterial infection, and resulting in frequent and painful urination. Treatment is by antibiotics and copious fluids with vitamin C.

deafness lack or deficiency in the sense of hearing, either inborn or caused by injury or disease of the middle or inner ear. Of assistance are hearing aids, lip-reading, a cochlear implant in the ear in combination with a special electronic processor, sign language (signs for concepts), and 'cued speech' (manual clarification of ambiguous lip movement during speech).

dementia mental deterioration as a result of physical changes in the brain. It may be due to degenerative change, circulatory disease, infection, injury, or chronic poisoning. ***Senile dementia***, a progressive loss of mental abilities such as memory and orientation, is typically a problem of old age, and can be accompanied by depression.

dermatitis inflammation of the skin, usually related to allergy. ***Dermatosis*** refers to any skin disorder and may be caused by contact or systemic problems.

diabetes disease *diabetes mellitus* in which a disorder of the islets of Langerhans in the pancreas prevents the body producing the hormone insulin, so that sugars cannot be used properly. Treatment is by strict dietary control and oral or injected insulin, depending on the type of diabetes. Experimental work is under way to transplant islets of Langerhans cells into diabetics. Without treatment the patient may go blind, ulcerate, lapse into diabetic coma, and die. Early-onset diabetes tends to be more severe than that developing in later years. In 1989 it was estimated that 4% of the world's population had diabetes.

diarrhoea excessive action of the bowels so that the faeces are fluid or semifluid. It is caused by intestinal irritants (including some drugs and poisons), infection with harmful organisms (as in dysentery, salmonella, or cholera), or allergies; most diarrhoea is viral in origin.

Diarrhoea is the biggest killer of children in the world. The World Health Organization estimates that 4.5 million children die each year from dehydration as a result of diarrhoeal disease in Third World countries. It can be treated by giving an accurately measured aqueous solution of salt and glucose by mouth in large quantities (to restore the electrolyte balance in the blood).

Down's syndrome condition caused by a chromosomal abnormality (the presence of an extra copy of chromosome 21) which in humans produces mental retardation, a flattened face, coarse and straight hair, and a fold of skin at the inner edge of the eye (hence the former name 'mongolism').

All people with Down's syndrome who live long enough eventually develop early-onset Alzheimer's disease, which led to the discovery in 1991 that some forms of early-onset Alzheimer's disease are caused by a gene defect on chromosome 21.

drug misuse illegal use of drugs for nonmedicinal purposes. Under the UK Misuse of Drugs Acts drugs used illegally comprise: (1) ***most harmful*** heroin, morphine, opium, and other narcotics; hallucinogens, such as mescalin and LSD, and injectable amphetamines, such as methedrine; (2) ***less harmful*** narcotics such as codeine and cannabis; stimulants of the amphetamine type, such as Benzedrine and barbiturates; (3) ***least harmful*** milder drugs of the amphetamine type. ***Designer drugs***, for example ecstasy, are usually modifications of the amphetamine molecule, altered in order to evade the law as well as for different effects. Crack, a smokable form of cocaine, became available to drug users in the 1980s.

eczema inflammatory skin condition, a form of dermatitis, marked by dryness, rashes, itching, the formation of blisters, and the exudation of fluid. It may be allergic in origin and is sometimes complicated by infection.

endometriosis common gynaecological complaint in which patches of endometrium (the lining of the womb) are found outside the uterus. Endometriosis may be treated with analgesics, hormone preparations, or surgery.

epilepsy disorder characterized by a tendency to develop fits, which are convulsions or abnormal feelings caused by abnormal electrical discharges in the cerebral hemispheres of the brain. Epilepsy can be controlled with a number of anticonvulsant drugs. Most epileptics have infrequent fits that have little impact on their daily lives. Epilepsy is common in the Third World, with up to 30 sufferers per 1,000 people in some areas; in industrialized countries the figure is 3–5 per 1,000.

food poisoning any acute illness characterized by vomiting and diarrhoea and caused by eating food contaminated with harmful bacteria (for example, listeriosis), poisonous food (for example, certain mushrooms, puffer fish), or poisoned food (such as lead or arsenic introduced accidentally during processing). A frequent cause of food poisoning is salmonella bacteria. These come in many forms, and strains are found in cattle, pigs, poultry, and eggs. The most dangerous food poison is the bacillus that causes botulism. This is rare but leads to muscle paralysis and, often, death. In 1992 in the UK, 64,882 cases of food poisoning were reported, compared with 52,543 in 1991.

gastroenteritis inflammation of the stomach and intestines, giving rise to abdominal pain, vomiting, and diarrhoea. It may be caused by food or other poisoning, allergy, or infection, and is dangerous in babies.

German measles or ***rubella*** mild, communicable virus disease, usually caught by children. It is marked by a sore throat, pinkish rash, and slight fever, and has an incubation period of two to three weeks. If a woman contracts it in the first three months of pregnancy, it may cause serious damage to the unborn child.

glandular fever or ***infectious mononucleosis*** viral disease characterized at onset by fever and painfully swollen lymph nodes (in the neck); there may also be digestive upset, sore throat, and skin rashes. Lassitude persists for months and even years, and recovery can be slow.

glaucoma condition in which pressure inside the eye (intraocular pressure) is raised abnormally as excess fluid accumulates. It occurs when the normal flow of intraocular fluid out of the eye is interrupted. As pressure rises, the optic nerve suffers irreversible damage, leading to a reduction in the field of vision and, ultimately, loss of eyesight.

gout hereditary form of arthritis, marked by an excess of uric acid crystals in the tissues, causing pain and inflammation in one or more joints (usually of the feet or hands), and posing a long-term threat to the blood vessels and kidneys. It is worsened by drinking alcohol. Acute attacks are treated with anti-inflammatories. The disease is ten times more common in men than women.

haemophilia any of several inherited diseases in which normal blood clotting is impaired. The sufferer experiences prolonged bleeding from the slightest wound, as well as painful internal bleeding without apparent cause. Haemophilias are nearly always sex-linked, transmitted through the female line only to male infants. Treatment is with a protein involved in the clotting of blood.

haemorrhoids or ***piles*** distended blood vessels (varicose veins) in the area of the anus.

hay fever allergic reaction to pollen, causing sneezing, inflammation of the eyes, and asthmatic symptoms. Sufferers experience irritation caused by powerful body chemicals related to histamine produced at the site of entry. Treatment is by antihistamine drugs.

heart attack sudden onset of gripping central chest pain, often accompanied by sweating and vomiting, caused by death of a portion of the heart muscle following obstruction of a coronary artery by thrombosis (formation of a blood clot). Half of all heart attacks result in death within the first two hours, but in the remainder survival has improved following the widespread use of streptokinase and aspirin to treat heart-attack victims.

heartburn burning sensation below the breastbone (sternum). It results from irritation of the lower oesophagus (gullet) by excessively acid stomach contents, as sometimes happens during pregnancy and in cases of duodenal ulcer or obesity. It is often due to a weak valve at the entrance to the stomach that allows its contents to well up into the oesophagus.

hepatitis any inflammatory disease of the liver, usually caused by a virus. Other causes include alcohol, drugs, gallstones, lupus erythematosus, and amoebic dysentery. Symptoms include weakness, nausea, and jaundice.

The viral disease ***hepatitis A*** (infectious or viral hepatitis) is spread by contaminated food, often seafood, and via the oro-faecal route. Incubation is about four weeks. The virus causing ***hepatitis B*** (serum hepatitis) is contained in all body fluids, and very easily transmitted. Some people become carriers. Those with the disease may be sick for weeks or months. The illness may be mild, or it may result in death from liver failure. A successful vaccine was developed in the late 1970s.

hernia or ***rupture*** protrusion of part of an internal organ through a weakness in the surrounding muscular wall, usually in the groin or navel. The appearance is that of a rounded soft lump or swelling.

herpes any of several infectious diseases caused by viruses of the herpes group. ***Herpes simplex I*** is the

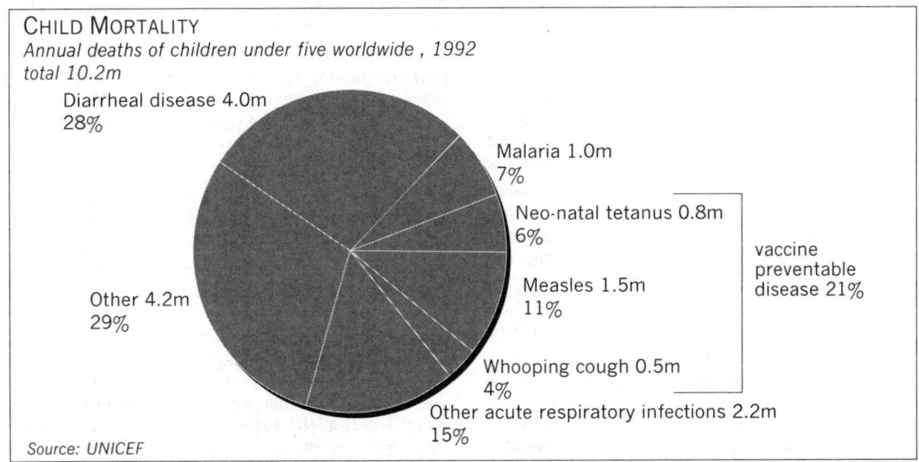

causative agent of a common inflammation, the cold sore. ***Herpes simplex II*** is responsible for genital herpes, a highly contagious, sexually transmitted disease characterized by painful blisters in the genital area. It can be transmitted in the birth canal from mother to newborn. ***Herpes zoster*** causes shingles; another herpes virus causes chickenpox. A number of antivirals treat these infections.

hypertension abnormally high blood pressure due to a variety of causes, leading to excessive contraction of the smooth muscle cells of the walls of the arteries. It increases the risk of kidney disease, stroke, and heart attack.

hypothermia condition in which the deep (core) temperature of the body spontaneously drops. If it is not discovered, coma and death ensue. Most at risk are the aged and babies (particularly if premature).

impotence physical inability to perform sexual intercourse (the term is not usually applied to women). Impotent men fail to achieve an erection, and this may be due to illness, the effects of certain drugs, or psychological factors.

incontinence failure or inability to control evacuation of the bladder or bowel (or both in the case of double incontinence). It may arise as a result of injury, childbirth, disease, or senility.

infection invasion of the body by disease-causing organisms (pathogens, or germs) that become established, multiply, and produce symptoms. Bacteria and viruses cause most diseases, but there are other microorganisms, protozoans, and other parasites.

Most pathogens enter and leave the body through the digestive or respiratory tracts. Polio, dysentery, and typhoid are examples of diseases contracted by ingestion of contaminated foods or fluids. Organisms present in the saliva or nasal mucus are spread by airborne or droplet infection; fine droplets or dried particles are inhaled by others when the affected individual talks, coughs, or sneezes. Diseases such as measles, mumps, and tuberculosis are passed on in this way. The common cold is passed from hand to hand, which then touches the eye or nose. A less common route of entry is through the skin, either by contamination of an open wound (as in tetanus) or by penetration of the intact skin surface, as in a bite from a malaria-carrying mosquito. Relatively few diseases are transmissible by skin-to-skin contact. Glandular fever and herpes simplex (cold sore) may be passed on by kissing, and the group now officially bracketed as sexually transmitted diseases (STDs) are mostly spread by intimate contact.

influenza any of various virus infections primarily affecting the air passages, accompanied by systemic effects such as fever, chills, headache, joint and muscle pains, and lassitude. Treatment is with bed rest and analgesic drugs such as aspirin and paracetamol. Vaccines are effective against known strains but will not give protection against newly evolving viruses.

jaundice yellow discolouration of the skin and whites of the eyes caused by an excess of bile pigment in the bloodstream. Mild jaundice is common in newborns, but a serious form occurs in rhesus disease. Bile pigment is normally produced by the liver from the breakdown of red blood cells, then excreted into the intestines. A build-up in the blood is due to abnormal destruction of red cells (as in some cases of anaemia), impaired liver function (as in hepatitis), or blockage in the excretory channels (as in gallstones or cirrhosis). The jaundice gradually recedes following treatment of the underlying cause.

laryngitis inflammation of the larynx, causing soreness of the throat, a dry cough, and hoarseness. The acute form is due to a virus or other infection, excessive use of the voice, or inhalation of irritating smoke, and may cause the voice to be completely lost. With rest, the inflammation usually subsides in a few days.

leukaemia any one of a group of cancers of the blood cells, with widespread involvement of the bone marrow and other blood-forming tissue. The central feature of leukaemia is runaway production of white blood cells that are immature or in some way abnormal. These rogue cells, which lack the defensive capacity of healthy white cells, overwhelm the normal ones, leaving the victim vulnerable to infection. Treatment is with radiotherapy and cytotoxic drugs to suppress replication of abnormal cells, or by bone-marrow transplantation.

malaria infectious parasitic disease of the tropics transmitted by mosquitoes, marked by periodic fever and an enlarged spleen. When a female mosquito of the *Anopheles* genus bites a human who has malaria, it takes in with the human blood one of four malaria protozoa of the genus *Plasmodium*. This matures within the insect and is then transferred when the mosquito bites a new victim. Malaria affects an estimated 267 million people (1993) in 103 countries, claiming up to 2 million lives a year. Quinine, the first drug used against malaria, has now been replaced by synthetics, such as chloroquine, used to prevent or treat the disease. However, chloroquine-resistant strains of the main malaria parasite, *Plasmodium fulciparum*, are spreading rapidly in many parts of the world.

Tests on a vaccine were begun 1986 in the USA. One experimental vaccine, devised in Colombia in the mid-1980s and widely tested in Latin America, is undergoing trials in Thailand, Tanzania, and the USA. (See box in this section.)

ME (abbreviation for ***myalgic encephalitis***) or ***postviral fatigue syndrome*** or ***chronic fatigue syndrome*** a debilitating condition still not universally accepted as a genuine disease. The condition occurs after a flulike attack and has a diffuse range of symptoms. These strike and recur for years and include extreme fatigue, muscular pain, weakness, and depression.

measles or ***rubeola*** acute virus disease spread by airborne infection. Symptoms are fever, severe catarrh, small spots inside the mouth, and a raised, blotchy red rash appearing for about a week after two weeks' incubation. Prevention is by vaccination.

In the UK a vaccination programme is under way, combining measles, mumps, and rubella (German measles) vaccine; this is given to children at age 15 months. A total of 10,264 cases of measles were notified 1992.

Malaria on the rise worldwide

The last few years have brought a dramatic increase in malaria, numerically the biggest of the tropical diseases and now claiming 2 million lives a year. Already some 280 million people are infected with the parasite and at least 110 million develop active disease each year. A further 2,100 million – almost half the world's population – are believed to be at risk, and the increase looks set to continue at the rate of at least 5% a year.

Africa, witnessing up to 1 million malaria deaths a year, is hardest hit, although in many parts of the continent local populations have developed some immunity. It is only when newcomers move into a region that epidemics occur. This has been vividly demonstrated in territories where there has been runaway exploitation of the tropical forest. In the Amazon basin and parts of SE Asia, for instance, malaria is now frankly out of control. Along Brazil's Trans-Amazonian Highway, up to a quarter of the population suffers an attack each year.

The emergency is compounded by the inexorable spread of drug-resistant parasites. First seen 30 years ago in Latin America and SE Asia, these are now found in almost every country where malaria flourishes. Chloroquine, the principal anti-malarial drug, has been rendered virtually useless in many countries. In parts of Thailand, one of the places where the disease is now rampant, half of all malaria cases are resistant to mefloquine, a drug licensed for use as recently as the mid-1980s.

The impact of malaria on a region with no natural immunity can be profound. This was borne out in the late 1980s by an outbreak in the interior of Madagascar, where the disease had not been seen for many years. Some 100,000 cases were reported and more than 20,000 people died; in some areas half of all those infected died.

Now, while several experimental vaccines are under development, there have been warnings that global warming could lead to a resurgence of malaria in temperate zones – including the British Isles – where it had previously been eradicated.

melanoma mole or growth containing the dark pigment melanin. Malignant melanoma is a type of skin cancer developing in association with a pre-existing mole. Unlike other skin cancers, it is associated with brief but excessive exposure to sunlight. Once rare, this disease is now frequent, owing to the increasing popularity of holidays in the sun. Most at risk are those with fair hair and light skin, and those who have had a severe sunburn in childhood.

meningitis inflammation of the meninges (membranes) surrounding the brain, caused by bacterial or viral infection. The severity of the disease varies from mild to rapidly lethal, and symptoms include fever, headache, nausea, neck stiffness, delirium, and (rarely) convulsions. Bacterial meningitis, though treatable by antibiotics, is the more serious threat. Diagnosis is by lumbar puncture. The treatment for viral meningitis is rest.

migraine acute, sometimes incapacitating headache (generally only on one side), accompanied by nausea, that recurs, often with advance symptoms such as flashing lights. No cure has been discovered, but ergotamine normally relieves the symptoms. Some sufferers learn to avoid certain foods, such as chocolate, which suggests an allergic factor.

In 1990 Hammersmith Hospital, London, reported successful treatment with goggles that turn down beta waves in the brain (associated with stress) and stimulate alpha waves (calming).

motor neuron disease or ***amyotrophic lateral sclerosis*** chronic disease in which there is progressive degeneration of the nerve cells (neurons) that instigate movement. It leads to weakness, wasting, and loss of muscle function, and usually proves fatal within two or three years of onset. Motor neuron disease occurs in both hereditary and sporadic forms, but its causes remain unclear. In the UK some 1,200 new cases are diagnosed each year.

multiple sclerosis (MS) incurable chronic disease of the central nervous system, occurring in young or middle adulthood. It is characterized by degeneration of the myelin sheath that surrounds nerves in the brain and spinal cord. It is also known as disseminated sclerosis. Its cause is unknown.

Depending on where the demyelination occurs – which nerves are affected – the symptoms of MS can mimic almost any neurological disorder. Typically seen are unsteadiness, ataxia (loss of muscular coordination), weakness, speech difficulties, and rapid involuntary movements of the eyes. The course of the disease is episodic, with frequent intervals of remission.

mumps virus infection marked by fever and swelling of the parotid salivary glands (such as those under the ears). It is usually minor in children, although meningitis is a possible complication. In adults the symptoms are severe and it may cause sterility in adult men. An effective vaccine against mumps, measles, and rubella (MMR vaccine) is now offered to children aged 18 months.

muscular dystrophy any of a group of inherited chronic muscle disorders marked by weakening and wasting of muscle. Muscle fibres degenerate, to be replaced by fatty tissue, although the nerve supply remains unimpaired. Death occurs in early adult life.

The commonest form, Duchenne muscular dystrophy, strikes boys, usually before the age of four. The child develops a waddling gait and an inward curvature (lordosis) of the lumbar spine. The muscles affected by dystrophy and the rate of progress vary. There is no cure, but physical treatments can minimize disability.

myalgic encephalomyelitis the full name of ME, or chronic fatigue syndrome.

osteoarthritis degenerative disease of the joints in later life, sometimes resulting in disabling stiffness and wasting of muscles. Formerly thought to be due to wear and tear, it has been shown to be less common in the physically active. It appears to be linked with crystal deposits (in the form of calcium phosphate) in cartilage.

osteoporosis disease in which the bone substance becomes porous and brittle. It is common in older people, affecting more women than men. It may be treated with calcium supplements and etidronate.

Osteoporosis may occur in women whose ovaries have been removed, unless hormone-replacement therapy (HRT) is instituted; it may also occur as a side effect of long-term treatment with corticosteroids. Early menopause in women, childlessness, small body build, lack of exercise, heavy drinking, smoking, and hereditary factors may be contributory factors.

otitis inflammation of the ear. *Otitis externa*, occurring in the outer ear canal, is easily treated with antibiotics. Inflamed conditions of the middle ear (*otitis media*) or inner ear (*otitis interna*) are more serious, carrying the risk of deafness and infection of the brain.

Parkinson's disease or ***parkinsonism*** or ***paralysis agitans*** degenerative disease of the brain characterized by a progressive loss of mobility, muscular rigidity, tremor, and speech difficulties. The condition is mainly seen in people over the age of 50.

Parkinson's disease destroys a group of cells called the *substantia nigra* ('black substance') in the upper part of the brainstem. These cells are concerned with the production of a neurotransmitter known as dopamine, which is essential to the control of voluntary movement. The almost total loss of these cells, and of their chemical product, produces the disabling effects.

The drug L-dopa, introduced in the 1960s, postpones the terminal phase of the disease. Brain grafts with dopamine-producing cells were pioneered in the early 1980s, and attempts to graft Parkinson's patients with fetal brain tissue have been made. In 1989 a large US study showed that the drug deprenyl may slow the rate at which disability progresses in patients with early Parkinson's disease.

pneumonia inflammation of the lungs, generally due to bacterial or viral infection but also to particulate matter or gases. It is characterized by a build-up of fluid in the alveoli, the clustered air sacs (at the end of the air passages) where oxygen exchange takes place.

Symptoms include fever and pain in the chest. With widespread availability of antibiotics, infectious pneumonia is much less common than it was. However, it remains a dire threat to patients whose immune systems are suppressed (including transplant recipients and AIDS and cancer victims) and to those who are critically ill or injured.

polio (***poliomyelitis***) viral infection of the central nervous system affecting nerves that activate muscles. The disease used to be known as infantile paralysis. Two kinds of vaccine are available, one injected and one given by mouth. The World Health Organization expects that polio will be eradicated by 2000.

premenstrual tension (PMT) or ***premenstrual syndrome*** medical condition caused by hormone changes and comprising a number of physical and emotional features that occur cyclically before menstruation and disappear with its onset. Symptoms include mood changes, breast tenderness, a feeling of bloatedness, and headache.

psoriasis chronic, recurring skin disease characterized by raised, red, scaly patches, usually on the scalp, back, arms, and/or legs. Tar preparations, steroid creams, and ultraviolet light are used to treat it, and sometimes it disappears spontaneously. Psoriasis may be accompanied by a form of arthritis (inflammation of the joints). It is a common disease, affecting 2% of the UK population.

puerperal fever infection of the genital tract of the mother after childbirth, due to lack of aseptic conditions. Formerly often fatal, it is now rare and treated with antibiotics.

rabies or ***hydrophobia*** disease of the central nervous system that can afflict all warm-blooded creatures. It is almost invariably fatal once symptoms have developed. Its transmission to humans is generally by a bite from an infected dog. Injections of rabies vaccine and antiserum may save those bitten by a rabid animal from developing the disease.

rheumatic fever or ***acute rheumatism*** acute or chronic illness characterized by fever and painful swelling of joints. Some victims also experience involuntary movements of the limbs and head, a form of chorea.

Rheumatic fever, which strikes mainly children and young adults, is always preceded by a streptococcal infection such as scarlet fever or a severe sore throat, usually occurring a couple of weeks beforehand. It is treated with bed rest, antibiotics, and painkillers. The most important complication of rheumatic fever is damage to the heart valve, producing rheumatic heart disease, which may lead to disability and death.

rubella technical term for German measles.

scabies contagious infection of the skin caused by the parasitic itch mite *Sarcoptes scaboi*, which burrows under the skin to deposit eggs. Treatment is by antiparasitic creams and lotions.

sciatica persistent pain in the leg, along the sciatic nerve and its branches. Causes of sciatica include inflammation of the nerve or pressure on, or inflammation of, a nerve root leading out of the lower spine.

septicaemia technical term for blood poisoning.

shingles common name for herpes zoster, a disease characterized by infection of sensory nerves, with pain and eruption of blisters along the course of the affected nerves.

shock circulatory failure marked by a sudden fall of blood pressure and resulting in pallor, sweating, fast (but weak) pulse, and sometimes complete collapse. Causes include disease, injury, and psychological trauma. Treatment depends on the cause. Rest is needed, and, in the case of severe blood loss, restoration of the normal circulating volume.

sickle-cell disease hereditary chronic blood disorder common among people of black African descent; also found in the E Mediterranean, parts of the Persian Gulf, and in NE India. It is characterized by distortion and fragility of the red blood cells, which are lost too rapidly from the circulation. This often results in anaemia.

sinusitis painful inflammation of one of the sinuses, or air spaces, that surround the nasal passages. Most cases clear with antibiotics and nasal decongestants, but some require surgical drainage.

spina bifida congenital defect in which part of the spinal cord and its membranes are exposed, due to incomplete development of the spine.

Spina bifida, usually present in the lower back, varies in severity. The most seriously affected babies may be paralysed below the waist. There is also a risk of mental retardation and death from hydrocephalus, which is often associated. Surgery is performed to close the spinal lesion shortly after birth, but this does not usually cure the disabilities caused by the condition.

stroke or ***cerebrovascular accident*** or ***apoplexy*** interruption of the blood supply to part of the brain due to a sudden bleed in the brain (cerebral haemhorrhage) or embolism or thrombosis. Strokes vary in severity from producing almost no symptoms to proving rapidly fatal. In between are those (often recurring) that leave a wide range of impaired function, depending on the size and location of the event. The disease of the arteries that predisposes to stroke is atherosclerosis. High blood pressure (hypertension) is also a precipitating factor. Strokes can sometimes be prevented by surgery (as in the case of some aneurysms), or by use of anticoagulant drugs or vitamin E or daily aspirin to minimize the risk of stroke due to blood clots.

syphilis venereal disease caused by the spiral-shaped bacterium (spirochete) *Treponema pallidum*. Untreated, it runs its course in three stages over many years, often starting with a painless hard sore, or chancre, developing within a month on the area of infection (usually the genitals). The second stage, months later, is a rash with arthritis, hepatitis, and/or meningitis. The third stage, years later, leads eventually to paralysis, blindness, insanity, and death. The Wassermann test is a diagnostic blood test for syphilis.

With widespread availability of antibiotics, syphilis is now increasingly cured in the industrialized world, at least to the extent that the final stage of the disease is rare. The risk remains that the disease may go undiagnosed or that it may be transmitted by a pregnant woman to her fetus.

tetanus or ***lockjaw*** acute disease caused by the toxin of the bacillus *Clostridium tetani*, which usually enters the body through a wound. The bacterium is chiefly found in richly manured soil. Untreated, in seven to ten days tetanus produces muscular spasm and rigidity of the jaw spreading to the other muscles, convulsions, and death. There is a vaccine, and the disease may be treatable with tetanus antitoxin and antibiotics.

thrombosis condition in which a blood clot forms in a vein or artery, causing loss of circulation to the area served by the vessel. If it breaks away, it often travels to the lungs, causing pulmonary embolism. Thrombosis in veins of the legs is often seen in association with phlebitis, and in arteries with atheroma. Thrombosis increases the risk of heart attack (myocardial infarct) and stroke. It is treated by surgery and/or anticoagulant drugs.

thrush or ***candidiasis*** infection usually of the mouth (particularly in infants), but also sometimes of the vagina, caused by a yeastlike fungus (genus *Candida*). It is seen as white patches on the mucous membranes. Thrush may be caused by antibiotics removing natural antifungal agents from the body. It is treated with a further antibiotic.

toxic shock syndrome rare condition marked by rapid onset of fever, vomiting, and low blood pressure, sometimes leading to death. It is caused by a toxin of the bacterium *Staphylococcus aureus*, normally harmlessly present in the body, which may accumulate, for example, if a tampon used during a period remains unchanged beyond four to six hours.

travel sickness nausea and vomiting caused by the motion of cars, boats, or other forms of transport. Constant vibration and movement may stimulate

FEWER BEDS

Availability of NHS hospital beds, England and Regional Health Authority areas (rates per '000 population)

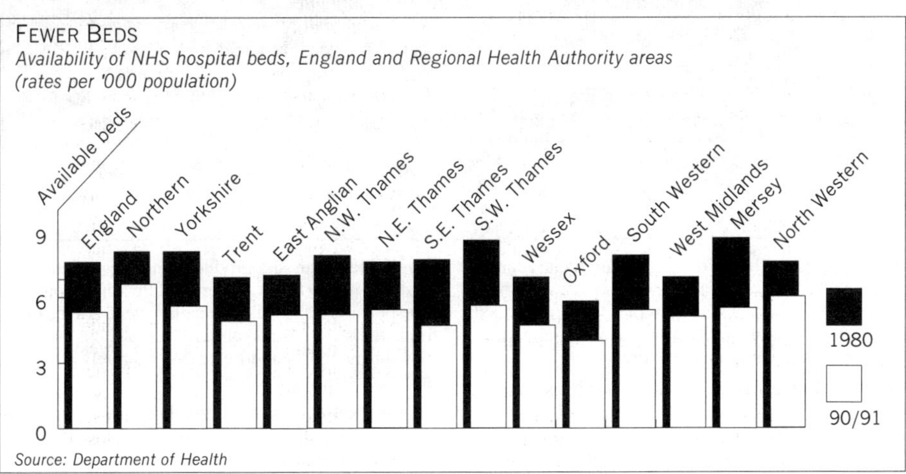

Source: Department of Health

Tuberculosis: a global emergency

The World Health Authority (WHO) has declared the growing threat of tuberculosis – already the world's foremost killer infection – a 'global emergency'. Currently TB strikes at the rate of 8 million new cases and 3 million deaths a year. Unless immediate action is taken, the WHO warned in April 1993, the disease will claim more than 30 million lives in the next decade.

The success of preventive programmes in the industrialized world has tended to obscure the fact that one-third of the global population is infected with TB. Mostly the bacterium (*Mycobacterium tuberculosis*) is kept in check by the body's immune system, but about 5% of those who are infected go on to develop active disease.

Traditionally the problem has always been most acute in the Third World, where 95% of all new cases and 98% of deaths occur. But the last decade or so has brought a resurgence in countries where previously the disease had been in decline for more than 30 years. In the UK the number of notified cases reached an all-time low in 1987, only to show a clear rise each year since then. In 1992, 5,861 new cases were reported, almost one-third of these in London.

TB has always been associated with poverty, overcrowding, and homelessness, and certainly in Britain, where there has been a rise in diseases of deprivation generally, many health professionals believe these factors are strongly implicated. Camberwell is a case in point. A depressed area in S London, it has a TB rate some five times the UK national average.

In the USA, too, where the incidence of TB has risen by 18% since 1985, it is in the deprived inner-city areas – the Bronx, Brooklyn, and Harlem in New York, and parts of Newark, New Jersey – that the increase is most marked. New York City has seen the steepest rise: almost 150% since 1980.

HIV: a trigger for TB

Besides adverse social conditions and lapsed public-health programmes, what has emerged, too, is a clear link between tuberculosis and HIV, the virus that causes AIDS. On the one hand dormant TB is activated by infection with HIV because the AIDS virus undermines the immune system; it also makes people who are free of the bacterium more susceptible to infection. Consequently, the spread of AIDS is expected to generate a continuing spiral in the number of cases of active TB.

A further sinister development throughout the last decade or so has been the spread of drug-resistant strains of the bacterium. Before 1980 resistance was relatively rare, and in the UK this is still the case, with only about 2% of cases showing resistance to one or more drugs. In New York, however, more than one-third of *M. tuberculosis* strains are resistant to one drug; almost one-fifth fail to respond to the two front-line drugs, isoniazid (or INH) and rifampicin; and some strains are resistant to every drug in the (admittedly small) anti-TB armamentarium. Multi-drug-resistant TB is, of course, virtually untreatable and many of its victims have died.

A big factor in the spread of multi-drug-resistant strains has been the failure of control programmes in the industrialized countries. This has meant that many patients embarking on treatment – a minimum of six months on a combination of drugs – lapse before the course is completed. If a patient carrying a resistant strain takes only one drug instead of the prescribed combination, or fails to complete the prescribed course, the effect is to promote resistant strains.

Urgent steps to combat resistance

Rare until its recent appearance in the USA, multi-drug-resistant TB is now spreading through a number of poorer countries, such as Tanzania and Thailand, bringing a worrying new element to the global situation. It is for this reason that the WHO is recommending urgent steps to detect and monitor drug resistance and to reinforce control programmes.

In the laboratory, meanwhile, scientists have been able to identify a gene that renders *M. tuberculosis* impervious to its foremost foe, the drug isoniazid. Besides enabling hospitals to diagnose drug-resistant strains without delay, this breakthrough should help in the development of a new generation of anti-TB drugs.

PP

changes in the fluids of the semicircular canals (responsible for balance) of the inner ear, to which the individual fails to adapt, and to which are added visual and psychological factors. Some proprietary remedies contain antihistamine drugs.

tropical disease any illness found mainly in hot climates. The most important tropical diseases worldwide are malaria, schistosomiasis, leprosy, and river blindness. Malaria kills about 1.5 million people each year, and produces chronic anaemia and tiredness in 100 times as many, while schistosomiasis is responsible for 1 million deaths a year. All the main tropical diseases are potentially curable, but the facilities for diagnosis and treatment are rarely adequate in the countries where they occur.

tuberculosis (TB) formerly known as ***consumption*** or ***phthisis*** infectious disease caused by the bacillus *Mycobacterium tuberculosis*. It takes several forms, of which pulmonary tuberculosis is by far the most common. A vaccine, BCG, was developed around 1920 and the first antituberculosis drug, streptomycin, in 1944.

In pulmonary TB, a patch of inflammation develops in the lung, with formation of an abscess. Often, this heals spontaneously, leaving only scar tissue. The dangers are of rapid spread through both lungs (what used to be called 'galloping consumption') or the development of miliary tuberculosis (spreading in the bloodstream to other sites) or tuberculous meningitis. In addition to streptomycin there are two other drugs used to treat TB: rifampicin and isoniazid.

Active tuberculosis is rare in the affluent parts of the world, although in the USA from 1985 there was a 16% rise each year (to 1992) in the number of TB cases, with a high proportion of drug-resistant strains of the disease. In the UK in 1991 there were 5,437 cases of TB notified, with 422 deaths. (See feature in this section.)

varicose veins or ***varicosis*** condition where the veins become swollen and twisted. The veins of the legs are most often affected; other vulnerable sites include the rectum (haemorrhoids) and testes. The affected veins can be injected with a substance that makes them shrink, or surgery may be needed.

vomiting expulsion of the contents of the stomach through the mouth. It may have numerous causes, including direct irritation of the stomach, severe pain, dizziness, and emotion. Sustained or repeated vomiting may indicate serious disease, and dangerous loss of water, salt, and acid may result (as in bulimia).

whooping cough or ***pertussis*** acute infectious disease, seen mainly in children, caused by colonization of the air passages by the bacterium *Bordetella pertussis*. There may be catarrh, mild fever, and loss of appetite, but the main symptom is violent coughing, associated with the sharp intake of breath that is the characteristic 'whoop', and often followed by vomiting and severe nose bleeds. The cough may persist for weeks.

Zidovudine

Up to 14 million people worldwide infected with HIV (human immunodeficiency virus) will have been devastated to learn that zidovudine does nothing to delay the onset of AIDS. The shock news about the hoped-for wonder drug emerged from a three-year Anglo-French trial known as Concorde. Publication of preliminary data, in March 1993, caused consternation in AIDS circles and an immediate slump in the shares of Wellcome, who manufacture the drug.

Zidovudine (formerly known as AZT) is one of a group of drugs known as nucleoside analogues. It is similar in structure to thymidine, one of the four chemical bases (nucleosides) that are the building blocks of DNA, the genetic code. The drug works by taking over the thymidine slot in the nucleoside chain, so blocking the replication of viral DNA.

Originally licensed in the UK for the treatment of full-blown AIDS, zidovudine clearly does prolong life in this patient group. However, in 1990 its licence was extended to cover people who had become infected with HIV but who remained symptom-free. Since the drug itself is quite toxic, this was undertaken in the belief that it could in fact delay the onset of what is after all a fatal disease.

Concorde, tracking 1,750 patients in the UK, Ireland, and France, set out to compare the fate of those who started taking zidovudine as soon as they were diagnosed HIV-positive with that of patients who only began treatment once the disease became apparent. The main finding was that there was no difference between the two patient groups in the rate of progression to AIDS.

Wellcome is contesting Concorde's findings and a larger- scale trial – featuring at least 10,000 subjects – is planned. Meanwhile, researchers are experimenting with combinations of zidovudine and related compounds to check the virus.

Types of Drugs

anabolic steroid any hormone of the steroid group that stimulates tissue growth. It is used to treat some anaemias and breast cancers, and may help to break up blood clots. Its use in sports to increase muscle bulk is widely condemned. Side effects include aggressive behaviour, masculinization in women, and, in children, reduced height.

anaesthetic drug that produces loss of sensation or consciousness; the resulting state is ***anaesthesia***, in which the patient is insensitive to stimuli. Anaesthesia may also happen as a result of nerve disorder.

Pain is felt when electrical stimuli travel along a nerve pathway, from peripheral nerve fibres to the brain via the spinal cord. An anaesthetic agent acts either by preventing stimuli from being sent (local), or by removing awareness of them (general). In cases where general anaesthesia is not called for, a substance may be applied to the skin or tissue surface; a local agent may be injected into the tissues under the skin in the area to be treated; or a regional block of sensation may be achieved by injection into a nerve. Spinal anaesthetic, such as epidural, is injected into the tissues surrounding the spinal cord, producing loss of feeling in the lower part of the body.

analgesic agent for relieving pain. Opiates alter the perception or appreciation of pain and are effective in controlling 'deep' visceral (internal) pain. Non-opiates, such as aspirin, paracetamol, and NSAIDs (nonsteroidal anti-inflammatory drugs), relieve musculoskeletal pain and reduce inflammation in soft tissues.

antibiotic drug that kills or inhibits the growth of bacteria and fungi. It is derived from living organisms such as fungi or bacteria, which distinguishes it from synthetic antimicrobials.

The earliest antibiotics, the penicillins, came into use from 1941. Each class and individual antibiotic acts in a different way and may be effective against either a broad spectrum or a specific type of disease-causing agent. Use of antibiotics has become more selective as side effects, such as toxicity, allergy, and resistance, have become better understood. Bacteria have the ability to develop immunity following repeated or subclinical (insufficient) doses, so more advanced and synthetic antimicrobials are continually required to overcome them.

antidepressant any drug used to relieve symptoms in depressive illness. The two main groups are the tricyclic antidepressants (TCADs) and the monoamine oxidase inhibitors (MAOIs), which act by altering chemicals available to the central nervous system. Both may produce serious side effects and are restricted.

anti-inflammatory any substance that reduces swelling in soft tissues. Antihistamines relieve allergic reactions; aspirin and NSAIDs are effective in joint and musculoskeletal conditions; rubefacients (counterirritant liniments) ease painful joints, tendons, and muscles. Steroids, because of their severe side effects, are only prescribed if other therapy is ineffective, or if a condition is life-threatening. A corticosteroid injection into the affected joint usually gives long-term relief from inflammation.

antiseptic any substance that kills or inhibits the growth of microorganisms. The use of antiseptics was pioneered by English surgeon Joseph Lister (1827–1912). He used carbolic acid (phenol), which is a weak antiseptic; substances such as TCP are derived from this.

antiviral any drug that acts against viruses, usually preventing them from multiplying. Most viral infections are not susceptible to antibiotics. Antivirals have been difficult drugs to develop, and do not necessarily cure viral diseases.

aspirin acetylsalicylic acid, a popular pain-relieving drug (analgesic) developed in the early 20th century for headaches and arthritis. It inhibits prostaglandins, and is derived from the white willow tree *Salix alba*. (See box in this section.)

beta-blocker any of a class of drugs that block impulses that stimulate certain nerve endings (beta receptors) serving the heart muscles. This reduces the heart rate and the force of contraction, which in turn reduces the amount of oxygen (and therefore the blood supply) required by the heart. Beta-blockers are banned from use in competitive sports. They may be useful in the treatment of angina, arrhythmia, and raised blood pressure, and following myocardial infarctions. They must be withdrawn from use gradually.

codeine opium derivative that provides analgesia in mild to moderate pain. It also suppresses the cough centre of the brain. It is an alkaloid, derived from morphine but less toxic and addictive.

corticosteroid any of several steroid hormones secreted by the cortex of the adrenal glands; also synthetic forms with similar properties. Corticosteroids have anti-inflammatory and immunosuppressive effects and may be used to treat a number of conditions including rheumatoid arthritis, severe allergies, asthma, some skin diseases, and some cancers. Side effects can be serious, and therapy must be withdrawn very gradually.

insulin protein hormone, produced by specialized cells in the islets of Langerhans in the pancreas, that regulates the metabolism (rate of activity) of glucose, fats, and proteins. Insulin was discovered by Cana-

A hundred years of headaches

What common drug was known to the Greeks and is currently being investigated for the treatment of cataracts, cancer of the colon, and senile dementia? It is a drug of proven efficacy in the treatment of heart disease, and 38 million tonnes of it are sold worldwide every year. The drug is aspirin. It has a simple chemical formula, and aspirin-like substances are found quite naturally in plants.

A hundred years ago, German chemist Felix Hoffmann was working for the Bayer company and wanted to help his father, who was painfully afflicted with arthritis. He already knew about salicylic acid and its ability to relieve pain. With his colleague Heinrich Dresser he developed aspirin, which Bayer patented in 1899. Aspirin is the acetylated form of salicylic acid. It is stable, and does not have the unpleasant taste, or cause the irritation of the mouth, of the parent compound. Successfully marketed, aspirin soon replaced cannabis, the pain reliever then widely used.

The wild flower meadowsweet contains salicin, a substance from which aspirin can be made. Aspirin got its name from meadowsweet, or *Spiraea ulmaria*: the German chemists simply added an 'a' (for acetyl) at the beginning.

To ease the pain of childbirth, Hippocrates recommended tea made from willow bark. Willow bark also contains salicin. The ability of a white willow brew to reduce fever was proved by a Cotswold parson, the Reverend Edmund Stone. Quite by accident, he noticed that the bark of the willow tree tasted bitter and wondered if it had the same properties as the bark of the cinchona, or fever tree, which also tasted bitter. It did; he tested his concoction on 50 people with considerable success and reported his results to the Royal Society in 1763.

Aspirin the painkiller now has many competitors, all more expensive. But aspirin retains a quarter of the market and, as new uses are found for it, will surely continue to be sold well into the next century.

dian physician Frederick Banting (1891–1941), who pioneered its use in treating diabetes.

Human insulin has now been produced from bacteria by genetic engineering techniques, but may increase the chance of sudden, unpredictable hypoglycaemia, or low blood sugar. In 1990 the Medical College of Ohio developed gelatine capsules and an aspirinlike drug which helps the insulin pass into the bloodstream.

L-dopa chemical, normally produced by the body, which is converted by an enzyme to dopamine in the brain. It is essential for integrated movement of individual muscle groups. As a treatment, it relieves the rigidity of Parkinson's disease but may have significant side effects, such as extreme mood changes, hallucinations, and uncontrolled writhing movements. It is often given in combination with other drugs to improve its effectiveness at lower doses.

mifepristone (formerly ***RU-486***) abortion pill first introduced in France 1989, and effective in 94% of patients up to 10 weeks pregnant when administered in conjunction with a prostaglandin. It was licensed in the UK in 1991.

oxytocin hormone that stimulates the uterus in late pregnancy to initiate and sustain labour. After birth, it stimulates the uterine muscles to contract, reducing bleeding at the site where the placenta was attached.

paracetamol analgesic, particularly effective for musculoskeletal pain. It is as effective as aspirin in reducing fever, and less irritating to the stomach, but has little anti-inflammatory action (as for joint pain). An overdose can cause severe, often irreversible or even fatal, liver and kidney damage.

penicillin any of a group of antibiotic (bacteria-killing) compounds obtained from filtrates of moulds of the genus *Penicillium* (especially *P. notatum*) or produced synthetically. Penicillin was the first antibiotic to be discovered (by Scottish bacteriologist Alexander Fleming, 1881–1955); it kills a broad spectrum of bacteria, many of which cause disease in humans.

pill, the commonly used term for any oral contraceptive pill, based on female hormones. The ***combined pill***, which contains synthetic hormones similar to oestrogen and progesterone, stops the production of eggs and makes the mucus produced by the cervix hostile to sperm. It is the most effective form of contraception apart from sterilization, being more than 99% effective. The ***minipill***, or progesterone-only pill, prevents implantation of a fertilized egg into the wall of the uterus. The minipill has a slightly higher failure rate, especially if not taken at the same time each day, but has fewer side effects and is considered safer for long-term use.

placebo any harmless substance, often called a 'sugar pill', that has no chemotherapeutic value. The use of placebos in medicine is limited to drug trials, where a placebo is given alongside the substance being tested, to compare effects. Placebos have been known to cause changes in blood pressure, perceived pain, and rates of healing.

premedication combination of drugs given before surgery to prepare a patient for general anaesthesia.

Root cures

Major drugs derived from plants

Plant	*Drug*	*Use*
Amazonian liana	Curare	Muscle relaxant
Annual mugwort	Artemisinin	Antimalarial
Autumn crocus	Colchicine	Antitumor agent
Belladonna	Atropine	Anticholinergic
Coca	Cocaine	Local anesthetic
Common thyme	Thymol	Antifungal
Ergot fungus	Ergotamine	Analgesic
Foxglove	Digitoxin, digitalis	Cardiotonic
Indian snakeroot	Reserpine	Antihypertensive
Meadowsweet	Salicylic acid*	Analgesic
Mexican yam	Diosgenin	Birth-control pill
Nux vomica	Strychnine	CNS stimulant
Opium poppy	Codeine, morphine	Analgesic (& antitussive)
Pacific yew	Taxol	Antitumor agent
Recured thornapple	Scopolamine	Sedative
Rosy periwinkle	Vincristine, vinblastine	Antileukemia
Velvet bean	L-Dopa	Antiparkinsonian
White willow	Salicin*	Analgesic
Yellow cinchona	Quinine	Antimalarial, Antipyretic

** Compound formed from salicylic acid and acetic acid is called acetylsalicylic acid: better known as aspirin.*

Source: Atlas of the Environment/WWF

steroid short for anabolic steroid.

warfarin poison that induces fatal internal bleeding in rats; neutralized with sodium hydroxide, it is used in medicine as an anticoagulant: it prevents blood clotting by inhibiting the action of vitamin K. It is often given as a preventive measure, to reduce the risk of thrombosis or embolism after major surgery. It can be taken orally and begins to act several days after the initial dose.

zidovudine (formerly ***AZT***) antiviral drug used in the treatment of AIDS. It is not a cure for AIDS but is effective in prolonging life; it does not, however, delay the onset of AIDS in people carrying the virus. Zidovudine was developed in the mid-1980s and approved for use by 1987. Taken every four hours, it reduces the risk of opportunistic infection and relieves many neurological complications. However, frequent blood monitoring is required to control anaemia, a potentially life-threatening side effect of zidovudine. Blood transfusions are often necessary, and the drug must be withdrawn if bone-marrow function is severely affected. (See box in this section.)

Alternative Medicine

acupuncture ancient Chinese medical art based on a theory of physiology that posits a network of life-energy pathways or 'meridians' in the human body and some 800 'acupuncture points' where metal needles may be inserted to affect the energy flow for purposes of preventive or remedial therapy or to produce a local anaesthetic effect. Numerous studies and surveys have attested the efficacy of the method, which is widely conceded by orthodox practitioners despite the lack of an acceptable scientific explanation.

Alexander technique method of correcting established bad habits of posture, breathing, and muscular tension which Australian therapist F M Alexander maintained cause many ailments. Back troubles, migraine, asthma, hypertension, and some gastric and gynaecological disorders are among the conditions said to be alleviated by the technique, which is also effective in the prevention of disorders, particularly those of later life. The technique also acts as a general health promoter, promoting relaxation and enhancing vitality.

applied kinesiology extension of chiropractic developed in the USA in the 1960s and 1970s, principally by US practitioner Dr George Goodheart. Relating to the science of kinesiology, or muscle testing, the Chinese principle that there exist energy pathways in the body and that disease results from local energy blockages or imbalances, Goodheart developed both diagnostic and therapeutic techniques, working on the body's musculature, which have proved particularly effective with stress-related ailments.

aromatherapy medicinal use of oils and essences derived from plants, flowers, and wood resins. Bactericidal properties and beneficial effects upon physiological functions are attributed to the oils, which are sometimes ingested but generally massaged into the skin. Aromatherapy was practised in the ancient world and revived in the 1960s in France, where today it is an optional component of some courses available to postgraduate medical students.

astrological diagnosis casting of a horoscope to ascertain a person's susceptibility to specific kinds of disease. From statistical evidence that offspring tend to have the same planetary positions in their charts as a parent, astrologers infer that there is a significant correlation between genetic and planetary influences, and that medical horoscopes, by pinpointing pathological tendencies, can be a useful tool of preventive medicine.

aura diagnosis ascertaining a person's state of health from the colour and luminosity of the aura, the 'energy envelope' of the physical body commonly claimed to be seen by psychics. A study carried out by the Charing Cross Hospital Medical School (London) confirmed that the aura can be viewed by high-frequency electrophotography techniques and is broadly indicative of states of health, but concluded that aura diagnosis cannot identify specific abnormalities.

autogenics system designed to facilitate mental control of biological and physiological functions generally considered to be involuntary. Effective in inducing relaxation, assisting healing processes, and relieving psychosomatic disorders, autogenics is regarded as a precursor of biofeedback. It was developed in the 1900s by German physician Johannes Schultz.

Bach flower healing homoeopathic system of therapy using extracts of wild flowers. It seeks to alleviate mental and emotional causes of disease rather than their physical symptoms. The system was developed in the 1920s by English physician Edward Bach.

A healthy business

Over-the-counter pharmacy sales of health supplements, UK 1991–92 (£m)

Product sectors	*1991*	*1992*
Cod liver & fish oils	56	59
Multivitamins	53	53
Evening primrose oil	17	32
Garlic	17	19
Homeopathic	10	12
Others, including single vitamins & royal jelly	48	52
Total	***201***	***227***

Source: Mintel

Bates eyesight training method developed by US opthalmologist William Bates (1860–1931) to enable people to correct problems of vision without wearing glasses. The method is of proven effectiveness in relieving all refractive conditions, correcting squints, lazy eyes, and similar problems, but does not claim to treat eye disease.

biochemic tissue salts therapy the correction of imbalances or deficiencies in the body's resources of essential mineral salts. There are 12 tissue salts in the body and the healthy functioning of cells depends on their correct balance, but there is scant evidence that disease is due to their imbalance and can be cured by supplements, as claimed by German physician W H Schuessler in the 1870s, though many people profess to benefit from the 'Schuessler remedies'.

bioenergetics extension of Reichian therapy principles designed to promote, by breathing, physical exercise, and the elimination of muscular blockages, the free flow of energy in the body and thus restore optimum health and vitality. Bioenergetics was developed in the 1960s by US physician Alexander Lowen.

biofeedback the use of electrophysiological monitoring devices to 'feed back' information about internal processes and thus facilitate conscious control. Developed in the USA in the 1960s, independently by neurophysiologist Barbara Brown and neuropsychiatrist Joseph Kamiya, the technique is effective in alleviating hypertension and preventing associated organic and physiological dysfunctions.

chiropractic technique of manipulation of the spine and other parts of the body, based on the principle that disorders are attributable to aberrations in the functioning of the nervous system, which manipulation can correct.

clinical ecology ascertaining environmental factors involved in illnesses, particularly those manifesting nonspecific symptoms such as fatigue, depression, allergic reactions, and immune system malfunctions, and prescribing means of avoiding or minimizing these effects.

colour therapy application of light of appropriate wavelength to alleviate ailments or facilitate healing. Coloured light affects not only psychological but also physiological states — for instance, long exposure to red light raises blood pressure and speeds up heartbeat and respiration rates, whereas exposure to blue has the reverse effect.

crystal therapy the application of crystals to diseased or disordered physical structures or processes to effect healing or stabilizing.

cupping ancient folk-medicine method of drawing blood to the surface of the body by applying cups or glasses in which a vacuum has been created, found to be effective in alleviating (though not curing) rheumatism, lumbago, arthritis, asthma, and bronchitis.

diatetics the prescription of dietary regimens to promote health or healing. Although no one quarrels with the general principle that diet affects health, the preventative or curative effects of specific diets, such as the raw vegetable diets sometimes prescribed for cancer patients, are disputed by orthodox medicine.

electrocrystal diagnosis technique recently developed by British biologist Harry Oldfield, based on the finding that stimulated electromagnetic fields of the human body resonate at a particular frequency which varies with individuals, and that actual or incipient disease can be pinpointed by a scanning device responsive to local deviations from the person's norm.

endogenous endocrinotherapy the fostering of hormonal balance in the body by regulating the activities of the endocrine glands by external manipulation, without recourse to introduced stimulants, suppressants, or supplements.

fasting total abstinence from food for a limited period. This is prescribed by some naturopaths to eliminate body toxins or make available for recuperative purposes the energy normally used by the digestive system. Prolonged fasting can be dangerous.

Gerson therapy radical nutritional therapy for degenerative diseases, particularly cancer, developed by German-born US physician Max Gerson (1881–1959).

hair analysis diagnostic technique for ascertaining deficiencies or excesses of mineral resources in the body, using a sophisticated analytic procedure called atomic-emission spectroscopy.

herbalism prescription and use of plants and their derivatives for medication. Herbal products are favoured by alternative practitioners as 'natural medicine', as opposed to modern synthesized medicines and drugs, which are regarded with suspicion because of the dangers of side- effects and dependence.

holistic medicine umbrella term for an approach that virtually all alternative therapies profess, which considers the overall health and lifestyle profile of a patient, and treats specific ailments not primarily as conditions to be alleviated but rather as symptoms of more fundamental disease.

homoeopathy or ***homeopathy*** system of medicine based on the principle that symptoms of disease are part of the body's self-healing processes, and on the practice of administering extremely diluted doses of natural substances found to produce in a healthy person the symptoms manifest in the illness being treated. Developed by German physician Samuel Hahnemann (1755-1843), the system is widely practised today as an alternative to allopathic medicine, and many controlled tests and achieved cures testify its efficacy.

hydrotherapy use of water, externally or internally, for health or healing. Programmed hot and/or cold applications or immersions, sometimes accompanied by local low-voltage stimulation, are used to alleviate tension and stress. Some hydrotherapists specialize in colonic or high colonic irrigation, the thorough washing-out and detoxification of the digestive system.

hypnotherapy use of hypnotic trance and post-hypnotic suggestions to relieve stress-related conditions such as insomnia and hypertension, or to break health-inimical habits or addictions.

ionization therapy enhancement of the atmosphere of an environment by instrumentally boosting the negative ion content of the air.

iridology diagnostic technique based on correspondences between specific areas of the iris and bodily functions and organs.

magnet therapy use of applied magnetic fields to regulate potentially pathogenic disorders in the electrical charges of body cells and structures.

megavitamin therapy administration of large doses of vitamins to combat conditions considered wholly or in part due to their deficiency.

music therapy use of music as an adjunct to relaxation therapy, or in psychotherapy to elicit expressions of suppressed emotions by prompting patients to dance, shout, laugh, cry, or whatever, in response.

naturopathy the facilitating of the natural self-healing processes of the body. Naturopaths are the GPs of alternative medicine and often refer clients to other specialists, particularly in manipulative therapies, to complement their own work of seeking — through diet, the prescription of natural medicines and supplements, and lifestyle counselling — to restore or augment the vitality of the body and thereby its optimum health.

osteopathy system of physical manipulation to treat mechanical stress. Osteopaths are generally consulted to treat problems of the musculo-skeletal structure such as back pain.

psionic medicine system of medical diagnosis and therapy developed by British physician George Lawrence in the 1930s and subsequently. Diagnosis is effected by dowsing a small blood sample with the aid of a pendulum to ascertain deficiencies or imbalances affecting the body's vitality, and treatment is by the administration of homoeopathic remedies.

pulsed high frequency (PHF) instrumental application of high-frequency radio waves in short bursts to damaged tissue to relieve pain, reduce bruising and swelling, and speed healing.

radionics healing method said to work on the 'subtle energy' level of the organism. Critics regard the radionic 'black box' — invented early in the century by US physician Albert Adams and later modified by his follower Ruth Drown — as a fraudulent quasi-scientific instrument, though practitioners maintain that it is an enabling device to effect psychic healing at a distance, and claim numerous successes, both diagnostic and curative

reflexology manipulation and massage of the feet to ascertain and treat disease or dysfunction elsewhere in the body.

Reichian therapy general term for a group of body-therapies based on the theory propounded in the 1930s by Wilhelm Reich, that many functional and organic illnesses are attributable to constriction of the flow of vital energies in the body by tensions that become locked into the musculature. Bioenergetics and Rolfing are related approaches.

relaxation therapy development of regular and conscious control of physiological processes and their related emotional and mental states, and of muscular tensions in the body, as a way of relieving stress and its results. Meditation, hypnotherapy, autogenics, and biofeedback are techniques commonly employed.

Rolfing technique of deep muscular manipulation developed in the 1960s and 1970s by US physiologist Ira Rolf. Also known as 'structural integration', the treatment is designed to correct gravitational imbalance in body postures and movements, and to relieve muscular rigidities and inflexibilities, thus enhancing general health and vitality.

shiatsu or *acupressure* Japanese method of massage derived from acupuncture which treats organic or physiological dysfunctions by applying finger or palm-of-the-hand pressure to parts of the body remote from the affected part.

sound therapy treatment based on the finding that human blood cells respond to sound frequencies by changing colour and shape, and the hypothesis that therefore sick or rogue cells can be healed or harmonized by sound. The therapy was in 1991 being developed and researched by French musician and acupuncturist Fabien Maman and US physicist Joel Sternheimer. It is claimed that sound frequencies applied to acupuncture points are as effective as needles.

spiritual healing or *psychic healing* the alleged transmission of energy from or through a healer, who may practise hand healing or absent healing through prayer or meditation.

thanatology study of the psychological aspects of the experiences of death and dying and its application in counselling and assisting the terminally ill. It was pioneered by US psychiatrist Elizabeth Kübler-Ross in the 1970s.

visualization use of guided mental imagery to activate and focus the body's natural self-healing processes. When used in the treatment of cancer patients, together with complementary techniques, some remarkable remissions have been attributed to visualization.

vitalistic medicine generic term for a range of therapies that base their practice on the theory that disease is engendered by energy deficiency in the organism as a whole or a dynamic dysfunction in the affected part. Such deficiencies or dysfunctions are regarded as antecedent to the biochemical effects in which disease becomes manifest and upon which orthodox medicine focuses. Acupuncture, crystal therapy, homoeopathy, magnet therapy, naturopathy, radionics, and Reichian therapy are all basically vitalistic.

zone therapy alternative name for reflexology.

GALLUP POLL: Physical health

What would you say was the state of your health in general?

Good	65
Fair	28
Rather poor	5
Very bad	1

Which one of these ailments do you personally fear most?

Cancer	39
Stroke	5
Heart disease	8
Alzheimer's/Senile dementia	15
Arthritis/Rheumatism	4
HIV/AIDS	15
Going deaf/blind	7
Any others	1
None of these	7

When you're climbing stairs or going up hills, how often would you say you get out of breath?

Always	8
Most of the time	7
Quite often	17
Rarely	42
Never	27

Are you currently trying to slim or have you ever tried to slim?

Currently trying	20
Not now but in the past	26
Never	54

Have you ever tried 'old wives' remedy for an illness?
If Yes: Did it work?

Yes – worked	24
Yes – did not work	7
No, never	70

How often, if at all, do you ask your chemist for advice about minor ailments?

Always	1
Most of the time	3
Quite often	12
Rarely	34
Never	51

Have you ever consulted any of these types of alternative practitioner?

Naturopath	0
Homeopath	6
Herbalist	3
Chiropractor	3
Osteopath	11
Acupuncturist	4
Reflexologist	1
Hypnotherapist	2
Aromatherapist	2
Other	1
No, never	76

Which, if any, of these would you say you are doing at present?

	March 1993	Jul 1992	Jul 1991	Sep 1988
Eating more fruit	52	40	48	42
Eating less or no fried foods	51	45	45	46
Eating less or no fatty foods	50	49	46	44
Taking less sugar with my meals	49	43	40	40
Eating more 'fibre' foods	42	34	34	39
Eating less or no butter	42	35	36	34
Taking less or no salt with my meals	39	32	37	33
Eating less or no red meat	39	32	35	31
Cutting down on the amount of alcohol I drink	24	19	17	17
Cutting down on all foods	23	17	20	18
Taking vitamin pills regularly	21	15	13	13
Cutting down on the amount I smoke	16	13	14	12
Eating no meat at all	7	7	6	5
None of these	12	15	15	17

In which country do you think people live longest?

Britain	12
USA	5
France	2
Japan	10
India	1
China	12
Russian Federation	3
Scandinavia	6
Other Western Europe	4
Other Far East	2
Other	10
Don't know	33

Mental health

Do you have the impression that most people in Britain suffer from stress or not? Would you say that you currently suffer from stress or not?

	Most people	Self
Suffer from stress	79	45
Do not	15	54
Don't know	6	2

Would you say you tend to be generally relaxed or anxious? Very or somewhat?

Relaxed – very	21
Relaxed – somewhat	45
Anxious – very	6
Anxious – somewhat	26
Don't know	3

In general, how happy would you say you are?

Very happy	37
Fairly happy	53
Not very happy	7
Very unhappy	2
Don't know	1

How often, if at all, do you feel tired, ill, or depressed when you wake up in the morning?

Always	6
Most of the time	8
Quite often	18
Rarely	48
Never	20

Would you say you are in love at the moment? If yes: very much or just somewhat?

Yes – very much	40
Yes – somewhat	24
No	36

INTERNATIONAL ORGANIZATIONS

International Organizations

Amazon Pact treaty signed 1978 by Bolivia, Brazil, Colombia, Ecuador, Guyana, Peru, Surinam, and Venezuela to protect and control the industrial or commercial development of the Amazon River.

Andean Group (Spanish ***Grupo Andino***) South American organization aimed at economic and social cooperation between member states. It was established under the Treaty of Cartagena 1969, by Bolivia, Chile, Colombia, Ecuador, and Peru; Venezuela joined 1973, but Chile withdrew 1976. The organization is based in Lima, Peru.

Antarctic Treaty international agreement aiming to promote scientific research and keep Antarctica free from conflict. It dates from 1961, and in 1991 a 50-year ban on mining activity was secured.

The treaty was signed 1959 between 12 nations with an interest in Antarctica, and came into force 1961, initially for a 30-year period. By 1993 a total of 38 countries were party to it. Its provisions (covering the area south of latitude 60°S) neither accepted nor rejected any nation's territorial claims, but barred any new ones; imposed a ban on military operations and large-scale mineral extraction; and allowed for free exchange of scientific data from bases. In 1980 the treaty was extended to conserve marine resources within the larger area bordered by the Antarctic Convergence.

Arab League organization of Arab states established in Cairo 1945 to promote Arab unity, primarily in opposition to Israel. The original members were Egypt, Syria, Iraq, Lebanon, Transjordan (Jordan 1949), Saudi Arabia, and Yemen. They were later joined by Algeria, Bahrain, Djibouti, Kuwait, Libya, Mauritania, Morocco, Oman, Palestine, Qatar, Somalia, Sudan, Tunisia, and the United Arab Emirates. In 1979 Egypt's membership was suspended and the league's headquarters transferred to Tunis in protest against the Egypt-Israeli peace, but Egypt was readmitted as a full member May 1989, and in March 1990 its headquarters returned to Cairo.

Arab Maghreb Union (AMU) association formed 1989 by Algeria, Libya, Mauritania, Morocco, and Tunisia to formulate common policies on military, economic, international, and cultural issues.

Asian and Pacific Council (ASPAC) organization established 1966 to encourage cultural and economic cooperation in Oceania and Asia. Its members include Australia, Japan, South Korea, Malaysia, New Zealand, the Philippines, Taiwan, and Thailand.

Asia-Pacific Economic Cooperation Conference (APEC) trade group comprising Pacific Asian countries, formed 1989 to promote multilateral trade and economic cooperation between member states. Its members are Australia, Brunei, Canada, China, Hong Kong, Indonesia, Japan, Malaysia, New Zealand, the Philippines, Singapore, South Korea, Thailand, and the USA.

Association of South East Asian Nations (ASEAN) regional alliance formed 1967; it took over the nonmilitary role of the Southeast Asia Treaty Organization 1975. Its members are Indonesia, Malaysia, the Philippines, Singapore, Thailand, and (from 1984) Brunei; its headquarters are in Jakarta, Indonesia. The six member states signed an agreement 1992 to establish an ASEAN free trade area (AFTA) by the beginning of 2008.

Benelux (acronym from ***Belgium, the Netherlands, and Luxembourg***) customs union agreed by Belgium, the Netherlands, and Luxembourg 1948, fully effective 1960. It was the precursor of the European Community.

Caribbean Community and Common Market (CARICOM) organization for economic and foreign policy coordination in the Caribbean region, established by the Treaty of Chaguaramas 1973 to replace the former Caribbean Free Trade Association. Its members are Antigua and Barbuda, Bahamas, Barbados, Belize, Dominica, Grenada, Guyana, Jamaica, Montserrat, St Christopher–Nevis, St Lucia, St Vincent and the Grenadines, and Trinidad and Tobago. The British Virgin Islands and the Turks and Caicos Islands are associate members, and the Dominican Republic, Haiti, Mexico, Puerto Rico, Surinam, and Venezuela are observers. CARICOM headquarters are in Kingston, Jamaica.

CERN nuclear research organization founded 1954 as a cooperative enterprise among European governments. It has laboratories at Meyrin, near Geneva, Switzerland. It was originally known as the ***Conseil Européen pour la Recherche Nucléaire*** but subsequently renamed ***Organisation Européenne pour la Recherche Nucléaire***, although still familiarly known as CERN. It houses the world's largest particle accelerator, the Large Electron–Positron Collider (LEP), with which notable advances have been made in particle physics.

Commonwealth of Independent States (CIS) successor body to the Union of Soviet Socialist Republics, established Jan 1992 by Armenia, Azerbaijan, Belarus, Kazakhstan, Kyrgyzstan, Moldova, the Russian Federation, Tajikistan, Turkmenistan, Ukraine, and Uzbekistan. It has no real, formal political institutions and its role is uncertain. Its headquarters are in Minsk (Mensk), Belarus.

Conference on Security and Cooperation in Europe (CSCE) international forum attempting to reach agreement in security, economics, science, technology, and human rights. The CSCE first met at the Helsinki Conference in Finland 1975. By the end of 1992, having admitted the former republics of the USSR, as well as Croatia, Slovenia, the Czech Republic, and Slovakia, its membership had risen to 52 states; Yugoslavia's membership was suspended 1992.

The second conference, in Paris Nov 1990, was hailed as marking the formal end of the Cold War. Reversing a long-standing policy of noninterference in members' internal affairs, the CSCE agreed in 1991 that fact-finding teams could be sent to investigate alleged human-rights abuses in any member country. A ministerial bureaucracy, an Office for Democratic Institutions, and a Conflict Prevention Centre were established 1992. A third conference, in Helsinki July 1992, debated the Yugoslav problem and gave the CSCE the power to authorize military responses of the North Atlantic Treaty Organization (NATO), the Western European Union (WEU), and the European Community (EC) within Europe.

Council of Europe body constituted 1949 in Strasbourg, France (still its headquarters), to secure 'a greater measure of unity between the European countries'. The widest association of European states, it has a ***Committee*** of foreign ministers, a ***Parliamentary Assembly*** (with members from national parliaments), and a ***European Commission*** investigating violations of human rights.

The first session of the ***Consultative Assembly*** opened Aug 1949, the members then being the UK, France, Italy, Belgium, the Netherlands, Sweden, Denmark, Norway, the Republic of Ireland, Luxembourg, Greece, and Turkey; Iceland, Germany, Austria, Cyprus, Switzerland, Malta, Portugal, Spain, Liechtenstein, Finland, and San Marino joined subsequently. With the collapse of communism in E Europe, the Council acquired a new role in assisting the establishment of Western- style democratic and accountable political systems in the region, and several countries applied for membership. Hungary joined 1990, Czechoslovakia and Poland 1991; Romania and Yugoslavia applied for membership 1991 and Albania for observer status.

Council of the Entente (CE, ***Conseil de l'Entente***) organization of W African states for strengthening economic links and promoting industrial development. It was set up 1959 by Benin, Burkina Faso, Ivory Coast, and Niger; Togo joined 1966 when a Mutual Aid and Loan Guarantee Fund was established. The headquarters of the CE are in Abidja'n, Ivory Coast.

Danube Commission organization that ensures the freedom of navigation on the river Danube, from Ulm in Germany to the Black Sea, to people, shipping, and merchandise of all states, in conformity with the Danube Convention 1948. The commission comprises representatives of all the states through which the Danube flows: Germany, Austria, Slovakia, Hungary, Bulgaria, and Romania. Its headquarters are in Budapest, Hungary.

Economic Community of Central African States (***Communauté Économique des États de l'Afrique Centrale*** CEEAC) organization formed 1983 to foster economic cooperation between member states, which include Burundi, Cameroon, Central African Republic, Chad, Congo, Equatorial Guinea, Gabon, Rwanda, São Tomé and Principe, and Zaire. Angola has observer status.

Economic Community of West African States (ECOWAS, ***Communauté Economique des Etats de l'Afrique de l'Ouest***) organization for the promotion of economic cooperation and development, established 1975 by the Treaty of Lagos. Its members include Benin, Burkina Faso, Cape Verde, Gambia, Ghana, Guinea, Guinea-Bissau, Ivory Coast, Liberia, Mali, Mauritania, Niger, Nigeria, Senegal, Sierra Leone, and Togo. Its headquarters are in Lagos, Nigeria.

Economic Cooperation Organization (ECO) Islamic regional grouping formed 1985 by Iran, Pakistan, and Turkey to reduce customs tariffs and promote commerce, with the aim of eventual customs union. In 1992 the newly independent republics of Azerbaijan, Kyrgyzstan, Tajikistan, Turkmenistan, and Uzbekistan were admitted into ECO.

European Free Trade Association (EFTA) organization established 1960 consisting of Austria, Finland, Iceland, Norway, Sweden, Switzerland, and (from 1991) Liechtenstein, previously a nonvoting associate member. There are no import duties between members.

Of the original members, Britain and Denmark left 1972 to join the European Community, as did Portugal 1985. In 1973 the EC signed agreements with EFTA members, setting up a free-trade area of over 300 million consumers. Trade between the two groups amounted to over half of total EFTA trade. A further pact signed 1991 between the EC and EFTA provided for a European Economic Area (EEA) to be set up, allowing EFTA greater access to the EC market by ending many of the restrictions. The area would span 19 nations and 380 million people. A Swiss referendum decision not to ratify postponed the implementation until mid-1993 at the earliest.

European Space Agency (ESA) organization of European countries (Austria, Belgium, Denmark, France, Germany, Ireland, Italy, the Netherlands, Norway, Spain, Sweden, Switzerland, and the UK) that engages in space research and technology. It was founded 1975, with headquarters in Paris.

G7 or ***Group of Seven*** the seven wealthiest nations in the world: the USA, Japan, Germany, France, the UK, Italy, and Canada. Since 1975 their heads of government have met once a year to discuss economic and, increasingly, political matters.

Group of Eight organization founded 1987 to develop a unified policy by Latin American debtor nations towards international creditors. Its members include Argentina, Brazil, Colombia, Mexico, Peru, and Uruguay. Panama was suspended from membership 1990.

Group of Rio international alliance formed 1987 from the Contadora Group to establish a general peace treaty for South America as 'a permanent mechanism for joint political action'. The original Contadora members – Colombia, Mexico, Panama, and Venezuela – were joined by Argentina, Bolivia, Brazil, Chile, Ecuador, Paraguay, Peru, and Uruguay.

Gulf Cooperation Council (GCC) Arab organization for promoting peace in the Persian Gulf area, established 1981. Its declared purpose is 'to bring about integration, coordination, and cooperation in economic, social, defence, and political affairs among Arab Gulf states'. Its members include Bahrain, Kuwait, Oman, Qatar, Saudi Arabia, and the United Arab Emirates; its headquarters are in Riyadh, Saudi Arabia.

Islamic Conference Organization (ICO) association of 44 states in the Middle East, Africa, and Asia, established 1971 to promote Islamic solidarity between member countries, and to consolidate economic, social, cultural, and scientific cooperation. Headquarters in Niger.

Latin American Economic System (LAES/SELA *Sistema Económico Latino-Americana*) international organization for economic, technological, and scientific cooperation in Latin America, aiming to create and promote multinational enterprises in the region and provide markets. It was founded 1975 as the successor to the Latin American Economic Coordination Commission; its members are Argentina, Barbados, Bahamas, Bolivia, Brazil, Chile, Colombia, Costa Rica, Cuba, Dominican Republic, Ecuador, El Salvador, Grenada, Guatemala, Guyana, Haiti, Honduras, Jamaica, Mexico, Nicaragua, Panama, Paraguay, Peru, Spain, Surinam, Trinidad and Togabo, Uruguay, and Venezuela. Its headquarters are in Caracas, Venezuela.

Latin American Integration Association (*Asociación Latino-Americana de Integración* ALADI) organization aiming to create a common market in Latin America; to promote trade it applies tariff reductions preferentially on the basis of the different stages of economic development that individual member countries have reached. It was formed in 1990 to replace the Latin American Free Trade Association, and its members are Argentina, Bolivia, Brazil, Chile, Colombia, Ecuador, Mexico, Paraguay, Peru, Uruguay, and Venezuela. Its headquarters are in Montevideo, Uruguay.

Lomé Convention convention in 1975 that established economic cooperation between the European Community and African, Caribbean, and Pacific countries. It was renewed 1979 and 1985.

Mercosur international organization formed 1991 to establish a South American common market by the end of 1994. Its members include Argentina, Brazil, Paraguay, and Uruguay.

North Atlantic Treaty Organization (NATO) association set up 1949 to provide for the collective defence of the major W European and North American states against the perceived threat from the USSR. Its chief body is the Council of Foreign Ministers (who have representatives in permanent session), and there is an international secretariat in Brussels, Belgium, and also Military Committee consisting of the Chiefs of Staff. The military headquarters SHAPE (Supreme Headquarters Allied Powers, Europe) is in Chièvres, near Mons, Belgium. After the E European Warsaw Pact was disbanded 1991, an adjunct to NATO, the ***North Atlantic Cooperation Council***, was established, including all the former Soviet republics, with the aim of building greater security in Europe. It was agreed July 1992 that the Conference on Security and Cooperation in Europe (CSCE) would in future authorize all NATO's military responses within Europe.

Organisation Commune Africaine et Mauricienne (OCAM; English 'Joint African and Mauritian Organization') organization founded 1965 to strengthen the solidarity and close ties between member states, raise living standards, and coordinate economic policies. The membership includes Benin, Burkina Faso, Central African Republic, Ivory Coast, Niger, Rwanda, Senegal, and Togo. Through the organization, members share an airline, a merchant fleet, and a common postal and communications system. The headquarters of OCAM are in Bangui in the Central African Republic.

Organization for Economic Cooperation and Development (OECD) international organization of 24 industrialized countries that provides a forum for discussion and coordination of member states' economic and social policies. Founded 1961, with its headquarters in Paris, the OECD superseded the Organization for European Economic Cooperation, which had been established 1948 to implement the Marshall Plan.

Organization of African Unity (OAU) association established 1963 to eradicate colonialism and improve economic, cultural, and political cooperation in Africa. Its membership expanded to 51 countries when Namibia joined after independence 1990. The secretary general is Salim Ahmed Salim of Tanzania. Its headquarters are in Addis Ababa, Ethiopia.

Organization of American States (OAS) association founded 1948 by a charter signed by representatives of 30 North, Central, and South American states. It aims to maintain peace and solidarity within the hemisphere, and is also concerned with the social and economic development of Latin America. By 1991, membership had expanded to 35. OAS headquarters are in Washington DC.

Organization of Arab Petroleum Exporting Countries (OAPEC) body established 1968 to safeguard the interests of its members and encourage cooperation in economic activity within the petroleum industry. Its members are Algeria, Bahrain, Egypt, Iraq, Kuwait, Libya, Qatar, Saudi Arabia, Syria, and the United Arab Emirates; headquarters in Kuwait.

Organization of Central American States (*Organización de Estados Centroamericanos* ODECA) international association, first established 1951 and superseded 1962, promoting common economic, political, educational, and military aims in Central America. The association was responsible for establishing the Central American Common Market 1960. Its members are Costa Rica, El Salvador, Guatemala, Honduras, and Nicaragua, provision being made for Panama to join at a later date. The permanent headquarters are in Guatemala City.

Organization of Petroleum-Exporting Countries (OPEC) body established 1960 to coordinate price and supply policies of oil-producing states. Its concerted action in raising prices in the 1970s triggered worldwide recession but also lessened demand so that its influence was reduced by the mid-1980s. OPEC members in 1991 were: Algeria, Ecuador, Gabon, Indonesia, Iran, Iraq, Kuwait, Libya, Nigeria, Qatar, Saudi Arabia, the United Arab Emirates, and Venezuela.

Preferential Trade Area for Eastern and Southern African States (PTA) organization established 1981 with the object of increasing economic and commercial cooperation between member states, harmonizing tariffs, and reducing trade barriers, with the eventual aim of creating a common market. Members include (1992) Angola, Burundi, Comoros, Djibouti, Ethiopia, Kenya, Lesotho, Malawi, Mauritius, Mozambique, Rwanda, Somalia, Sudan, Swaziland, Tanzania, Uganda, Zaire, Zambia, and Zimbabwe. The headquarters of the PTA are in Lusaka, Zambia.

Rarotonga Treaty agreement that formally declares the South Pacific a nuclear-free zone. The treaty was signed 1987 by Australia, Fiji, Indonesia, New Zealand, and the USSR.

South Asian Association for Regional Cooperation (SAARC) international organization formed 1985 to foster economic cooperation between its member states, which include Bangladesh, Bhutan, India, the Maldives, Nepal, Pakistan, and Sri Lanka. Its headquarters are in Delhi, India.

Southeast Asia Treaty Organization (SEATO) collective military system 1954–77 established by Australia, France, New Zealand, Pakistan, the Philippines, Thailand, the UK, and the USA, with Vietnam, Cambodia, and Laos as protocol states. After the Vietnam War SEATO was phased out.

Southern African Development Coordination Conference (SADCC) organization of countries in the region working together to reduce their economic dependence on South Africa. It was established 1980 and focuses on transport and communications, energy, mining, and industrial production. The member states are Angola, Botswana, Lesotho, Malawi, Mozambique, Namibia, Swaziland, Tanzania, Zambia, and Zimbabwe; headquarters in Gaborone, Botswana.

South Pacific Bureau for Economic Cooperation (SPEC) organization founded 1973 for the purpose of stimulating economic cooperation and the development of trade in the region. The headquarters of SPEC are in Suva, Fiji.

South Pacific Commission (SPC) organization to promote economic and social cooperation in the region, established 1948. Its members include (1993) American Samoa, Australia, Belau, Cook Islands, the Federated States of Micronesia, Fiji, France, French Polynesia, Guam, Kiribati, the Marshall Islands, Nauru, New Caledonia, New Zealand, Niue, Northern Marinas, Papua New Guinea, Pitcairn Islands, Solomon Islands, Tokelau, Tonga, Tuvalu, the UK, the USA, Vanuatu, Wallis and Fortuna, and Western Samoa. Its headquarters are in Nouméa, New Caledonia.

South Pacific Forum (SPF) association of states in the region to discuss common interests and develop common policies, created 1971 as an offshoot of the South Pacific Commission. Member countries include (1992) Australia, Cook Islands, Fiji, Kiribati, Marshall Islands, the Federated States of Micronesia, Nauru, New Zealand, Niue, Papua New Guinea, Solomon Islands, Tonga, Tuvalu, Vanuatu, and Western Samoa. In 1985 the forum adopted a treaty for creating a nuclear-free zone in the Pacific.

Unrepresented Nations' and Peoples' Organization (UNPO) international association founded 1991 to represent ethnic and minority groups unrecognized by the United Nations and to defend the right to self-determination of oppressed peoples around the world. The founding charter was signed by representatives of Tibet, the Kurds, Turkestan, Armenia, Estonia, Georgia, the Volga region, the Crimea, the Greek minority in Albania, North American Indians, Australian Aborigines, West Irians, West Papuans, the minorities of the Cordillera in the Philippines, and the non-Chinese in Taiwan.

Warsaw Pact or ***Eastern European Mutual Assistance Pact*** military alliance 1955–91 between the USSR and East European communist states, originally established as a response to the admission of West Germany into NATO. Its military structures and agreements were dismantled early in 1991; a political organization remained until the alliance was officially dissolved July 1991.

Western European Union (WEU) organization established 1955 as a consultative forum for military issues among the W European governments: Belgium, France, the Netherlands, Italy, Luxembourg, the UK, Germany, and (from 1988) Spain and Portugal.

World Council of Churches (WCC) international organization aiming to bring together diverse movements within the Christian church. Established 1945, it has a membership of more than 100 countries and more than 300 churches; headquarters in Geneva, Switzerland.

The European Community (EC)

The EC is a political and economic alliance consisting of the European Coal and Steel Community (1952), European Economic Community (EEC, popularly called the Common Market, 1957), and the European Atomic Energy Commission (Euratom,

Waiting to join

European countries applying for EC membership

Country	*Population 1990 (m)*	*Possible entry date*
EFTA		
Austria	7.7	1996
Switzerland	6.8	1996?
Norway	4.2	1996?
Sweden	8.6	1996
Iceland	0.3	?
Finland	5.0	1996
Central Europe		
Poland	38.2	c2000
Hungary	10.6	c2000
Czechoslovakia	15.7	c2000
Slovenia	2.0	c2000
Romania	23.2	?
Bulgaria	8.8	?
Albania	3.3	?
Baltic states	8.0	c2000
Mediterranean		
Cyprus	0.7	?
Malta	0.4	c2000
Turkey	56.1	?

Source: The Economist

1957). In 1992 there were more than 340 million people in the EC countries. A single market with free movement of goods and capital was established Jan 1993. A European Charter of Social Rights was approved at the Maastricht summit Dec 1991 by all members except the UK.

Member countries

The original six members – Belgium, France, West Germany, Italy, Luxembourg, and the Netherlands – were joined by the UK, Denmark, and the Republic of Ireland 1973, Greece 1981, and Spain and Portugal 1986. Association agreements – providing for free trade within ten years and the possibility of full EC membership – were signed with Czechoslovakia, Hungary, and Poland 1991, subject to ratification, and with Romania 1992.

Aims

The aims of the EC include the expansion of trade, reduction of competition, the abolition of restrictive trading practices, the encouragement of free movement of capital and labour within the community, and the establishment of a closer union among European people. The Maastricht Treaty 1991 provides the framework for closer economic and political union but there have been delays over its ratification.

Maastricht Treaty

The meeting in Maastricht Dec 1991 secured agreement on a treaty framework for European union, including political and monetary union, with a timetable for implementation, and for a new system of police and military EC cooperation. Compromises were agreed between all 12 nations at an Edinburgh summit Dec 1992, and the treaty was ratified by all member states 1993.

Budget

Almost 60% of the EC's budget in 1990 was spent on supporting farmers (about 4 million people); of this, £4 billion a year went to dairy farmers, because the dairy quotas, which were introduced 1984, were 14% greater than EC consumption. The EC sheep policy cost over £1.7 billion in 1990, and 30 million tonnes of excess grain were exported annually at a subsidized price. Altogether it cost member countries' taxpayers almost £9 billion in 1989–90 to maintain the international competitiveness of the EC's overpriced produce under the Common Agricultural Policy.

Constituent institutions

Common Agricultural Policy (CAP)
established 1962
purpose to ensure reasonable standards of living for farmers in member states by controlling outputs, giving financial grants, and supporting prices to even-out fluctuations

European Atomic Energy Commission (EURATOM)
established 1957
purpose the cooperation of member states in nuclear research and the development of large-scale nonmilitary nuclear energy

European Coal and Steel Community (ECSC)
established 1952
purpose the creation of a single European market for coal, iron ore, and steel by the abolition of customs duties and quantitative restrictions

European Court of Justice
established 1957
purpose to ensure the treaties that established the Community are observed and to adjudicate on disputes between members on the interpretation and application of the laws of the Community
base Luxembourg

European Economic Community (EEC) (popularly called the Common Market)
established 1957
purpose the creation of a single European market for the products of member states by the abolition of tariffs and other restrictions on trade

European Investment Bank (EIB)
established 1958
purpose to finance capital investment that will assist the steady development of the Community

European Monetary System (EMS)
established 1979
purpose to bring financial cooperation and monetary stability to the Community. Central to the EMS is the Exchange Rate Mechanism (ERM), which is a voluntary arrangement whereby members agreed to their currencies being fixed within certain limits. The value of each currency is related to the European Currency Unit (ECU), which, it is anticipated, will eventually become the single currency for all member states. If the currency of any one member state moves outside the agreed limits, its government must buy or sell to avert the trend

Central organs and methods of working of the Community

European Commission
membership 16: two each from France, Germany, Italy and the UK, and one each from Belgium, Denmark, Greece, Ireland, Luxembourg, the Netherlands, Portugal, and Spain. The members are nominated by each state for a four-year, renewable term of office. One member is chosen as president for a two-year, renewable term. The post of president is a mixture of head of government and head of the European civil service
operational methods the commissioners are drawn proportionately from member states, and each takes an oath on appointment not to promote national interests. They head a comparatively large bureaucracy, with 20 directorates-general, each responsible for a particular department
base Brussels

European commission presidents from 1958

term	*name*	*nationality*
1958–66	Walter Hallsein	German
1966–70	Jean Rey	Belgian
1970–72	Franco Malfatti	Italian
1972–73	Sicco Mansholt	Dutch
1973–77	François-Xavier Ortoll	French
1977–81	Roy Jenkins	British
1981–85	Gaston Thom	Luxembourgian
1985–	Jaques Delors	French

Council of Ministers
membership one minister from each of the 12 member countries

Europe: a catalogue of failures?

At the end of 1991, the twelve European Community leaders agreed, at Maastricht, a timetable towards political, economic, and monetary union. In June 1992 the Danes rejected the Maastricht Treaty; in September the UK and Italy withdrew from the exchange rate mechanism of the European Monetary System; and throughout the year Bosnia–Herzegovina tore itself apart while Western Europe looked on in helpless despair. Where were the high hopes of a year ago? Where were the common policies? Where was the leadership Europe desperately needed?

The European Community had a bad year, but so did most of its individual members. The German economy struggled to cope with the problems of unification and for once in the post-war period began to look frail. Following these problems came a wave of racial violence, more reminiscent of Nazism than of newly restored democratic liberalism. The UK government stumbled from crisis to crisis, the prime minister achieving the lowest poll ratings of any post-war leader. France, despite maintaining a strong economy, began to look leaderless, the Socialist Party showing clear signs of having lost its way. Italy, rocked by corruption scandals, revealed a government more in the pockets of the Mafia than esteem by the electorate. Spain's governing party also seemed doomed to defeat, as unemployment rose and economic growth fell. Only the smaller members showed signs of reasonable stability.

In 1992 the Community seemed obsessed with Maastricht and its aftermath, but the opportunity for a decisive contribution to Europe's wider problems was tragically missed. Politicians spoke optimistically of a new European order, with the Community gradually expanding to encompass a strong, stable continent that, with resources far greater than the world's present superpowers, would provide desperately needed leadership. But where was the strategy? Where were the leaders? Decisions were piecemeal and short-term. The vision was absent.

In January, Germany insisted that the Community formally recognize Croatia and Slovenia, but neglected the fate of the remnants of former Yugoslavia. In February, Commission President Jacques Delors announced spending proposals for 1993–98, which he argued were vital to maintain the momentum for greater integration and wider membership. The package's major contributors, Germany and the UK, were unenthusiastic.

In April, EC foreign ministers decided to recognize Bosnia–Herzegovina as an independent state, but this did not stop the spreading ethnic violence or the ambitions of ruthless politicians to create a Greater Serbia. In May, President Mitterrand and Chancellor Kohl announced the creation of a Franco–German defence force, as the embryo of a European force that would eventually replace NATO. The Americans and the British looked on with concern.

In June, Francois Mitterrand left the Community's Lisbon summit and flew to the Bosnian capital Sarajevo, now under violent siege by Serbian forces: a typically dramatic gesture that was not followed up by Community colleagues. In July, a new peace plan for Bosnia–Herzegovina by EC mediator Lord Carrington collapsed; in August he stepped down, to be replaced by former UK Labour foreign secretary, Lord Owen. Meanwhile, the current UK foreign secretary, Douglas Hurd, told the UN Security Council that his country and Germany were reluctant to commit ground troops to a peace-keeping role in Bosnia. The USA was similarly reluctant. Reports of atrocities in pursuance of a policy of 'ethnic cleansing' continued to come from the war-torn region. In August, prime minister John Major announced that 1,800 British troops would be sent to Bosnia under the UN flag to escort humanitarian aid convoys. Later that month, in London, he opened an international conference on the Yugoslav crisis. Still the fighting and 'cleansing' continued.

September saw the dramatic departure of Britain and Italy from the ERM, its effects rippling around the economies of the other ten members. The year ended with Switzerland's referendum rejection of closer links with the Community and Germany's decision to tighten the rules on admission of foreigners as alleged refugees.

1993 has shown few signs of improvement in the prestige and influence of the Community, but applications for membership continue. By 1995 Austria, Finland, Norway, and Sweden will probably have joined, and possibly some states of the former Soviet bloc. But will this make much difference? Will Europe realize the destiny that its founding fathers perceived? The omens are not propitious.

The Community lacks leadership: a commodity that is suddenly in short supply among European states. That much-needed leadership needs to be allied to vision and a long-term strategy to make Europe not only an economic superpower but an international force strong enough to make an indelible imprint on the continent's history. That leadership may well come not from the major members, each with its national axe to grind, but from the smaller states who have more to gain than lose from greater European cohesion.

JDD

Who's who at the EC Commission, 1993–94

President:	Jacques Delors (France)
Economic and financial affairs:	Henning Christophersen (Denmark)
Development:	Manuel Marin (Spain)
Industry:	Martin Bangemann (Germany)
External economic affairs:	Sir Leon Brittan (UK)
Energy, transport:	Abel Matutes (Spain)
Budget:	Peter Schmidhuber (German)
Customs, taxation:	Christiane Scrivener (France)
Regional policy:	Bruce Millan (UK)
Competition:	Karel Van Miert (Belgium)
External political relations:	Hans van den Broek (Netherlands)
Internal political relations:	Joao de Deus Pinheiro (Portugal)
Social affairs and employment:	Padraig Flynn (Ireland)
Science, research, & development:	Antonio Ruberti (Italy)
Agriculture:	René Steichen (Luxembourg)
Environment:	Ionnis Paleokrassas (Greece)
Single market:	Raniero Vanni d'Archirafi (Italy)

Source: Financial Times

operational methods it is the supreme decision-taking body of the Community. The representatives vary according to the subject matter under discussion. If it is economic policy it will be the finance ministers, if it is agricultural policy, the agriculture ministers. It is the foreign ministers, however, who tend to be the most active. The presidency of the Council changes hands at six-monthly intervals, each member state taking its turn
base Brussels

Committee of Permanent Representatives (COREPER)
membership a subsidiary body of officials, often called 'ambassadors', who act on behalf of the Council. The members of COREPER are senior civil servants who have been temporarily released by member states to work for the Community
operational methods COREPER receives proposals from the Council of Ministers for consideration in detail before the Council decides on action
base Brussels.

Economic and Social Committee
membership representatives from member countries covering a wide range of interests, including employers, trade unionists, professional people, and farmers
operational methods a consultative body advising the Council of Ministers and the Commission
base Brussels

European Parliament
membership determined by the populations of member states. The total number of seats is 518, of which France, Germany, Italy, and the UK have 81 each, Spain has 60, the Netherlands 25, Belgium, Greece, and Portugal 24 each, Denmark 16, Ireland 15, and Luxembourg 6. Members are elected for five-year terms in large Euro-constituencies. Voting is by a system of proportional representation in all countries except the UK

Presidency of the EC's Council of Ministers

The order until the end of 1998 is:

Denmark	1 January 1993–30 June 1993
Belgium	1 July 1993–31 December 1993
Greece	1 January 1994–30 June 1994
Germany	1 July 1994–31 December 1994
France	1 January 1995–30 June 1995
Spain	1 July 1995–31 December 1995
Italy	1 January 1996–30 June 1996
Ireland	1 July 1996–31 December 1996
Netherlands	1 January 1997–30 June 1997
Luxembourg	1 July 1997–31 December 1997
United Kingdom	1 January 1998–30 June 1998
Portugal	1 July 1998–31 December 199

Source: The European Companion 1993

role and powers mainly consultative, but it does have power to reject the Community budget and to dismiss the Commission if it has good grounds for doing so. It debates Community present and future policies and its powers will undoubtedly grow as the political nature of the Community becomes clearer
base Luxembourg and Strasbourg

United Nations

The UN is an association of states for international peace, security, and cooperation, with its headquarters in New York. The UN was established 1945 as a successor to the League of Nations, and has played a role in many areas, such as refugees, development assistance, disaster relief, and cultural cooperation. Its membership stands at 183 states (1993), and the total proposed budget for 1992/93 was $2,006 million. Boutros Boutros-Ghali became secretary general 1992.

Members contribute financially according to their resources, an apportionment being made by the General Assembly, with the addition of voluntary contributions from some governments to the funds of the UN. These finance the programme of assistance carried out by the UN intergovernmental agencies, the ***United Nations Children's Fund*** (UNICEF), the UN refugee organizations, and the ***United Nations Special Fund*** for developing countries. Total unpaid contributions of about $988 million had by the end of 1991 brought the UN to the brink of insolvency; fewer than half the members had paid their full contributions. By the deadline of 31 Jan 1993, only 18 member states had paid their annual dues in full; the UN was owed $500 million in arrears, approximately half of it from the USA.

The six official working languages are English, French, Russian, Spanish, Chinese, and Arabic.

Background
The UN charter was drawn up at the San Francisco Conference 1945, based on proposals drafted at the Dumbarton Oaks conference. The original intention was that the UN's Security Council would preserve the wartime alliance of the USA, USSR, and Britain (with France and China also permanent members) in order to maintain the peace. This never happened because of the outbreak of the Cold War.

The influence in the UN, originally with the Allied states of World War II, is now more widely spread. Although part of the value of the UN lies in recognition of member states as sovereign and equal, the rapid increase in membership of minor (in some cases minute) states was causing concern by 1980 (154 members) as lessening the weight of voting decisions. Taiwan, formerly a permanent member of the Security Council, was expelled 1971 on the admission of China. The breakup of the USSR and the increasing recongition of independent states throughout the world resulted in a further increase in UN membership between 1990 and 1992. The Russian Federation took over the Soviet permanent seat on the Security Council.

The USA regularly (often alone or nearly so) votes against General Assembly resolutions on aggression, international law, human-rights abuses, and disarmament, and has exercised its veto on the Security Council more times than any other member (the UK is second, France a distant third).

The UN suffers from a lack of adequate and independent funds and forces, the latter having been employed with varying success, for example, in Korea, Cyprus, and Sinai, and the intrusion of the Cold War which divided members into adherents of the East or West and the uncommitted. However, as secretary general 1982–91, Javier Pérez de Cuéllar was responsible for several successful peace initiatives, including the ending of the Iran-Iraq War and the withdrawal of South African and Cuban troops from Angola. The UN also responded promptly to the Iraqi invasion of Kuwait 1990 but has been less successful in its efforts to establish a permanent peace in the former republics of Yugoslavia. Its attempts at peacemaking in Somalia have also encountered problems and local criticism. In 1993, some 88,000 UN peacekeepers were deployed.

The principal UN institutions

All are based in New York except the International Court of Justice in The Hague.

General Assembly one member from each of 178 member states who meet annually for a session generally lasting from late Sept to the end of the year; it can be summoned at any time for an emergency session. Decisions are made by simple majority voting, but on certain important issues, such as the condemnation of an act by one of its members, a two-thirds majority is needed.

Security Council five permanent members (China, France, the UK, the USA, Russia) with the power of veto, so their support is requisite for all decisions, plus ten other members, elected for two-year terms by a two-thirds vote of the General Assembly; retiring members are not eligible for re-election. Any UN member may be invited to participate in the Security Council's discussions (though not to vote) if they bear on its interests. The council may undertake investigations into disputes and make recommendations to the parties concerned, and may call on all members to take economic or military measures to enforce its decisions; it has at its disposal a Military Staff Committee, composed of the chiefs of staff of the permanent member countries. The presidency of the Security Council is held for a month at a time by a representative of a member state, in English-language alphabetical order.

Economic and Social Council 54 members elected for three years, one-third retiring in rotation; presidency rotating on same system as Security Council. It initiates studies of international economic, social, cultural, educational, health, and related matters, and may make recommendations to the General Assembly. It operates largely through specialized commissions of international experts on economics, transport and communications, human rights, status of women, and so on, as well as regional commissions and hundreds of nongovernmental agencies that have been granted consultative status. It coordinates the activities of the ***Food and Agriculture Organization*** (FAO).

Trusteeship Council responsible for overseeing the administration of the UN trust territories. Its members are China, France, the Russian Federation, the UK, and the USA. It holds one regular session a year and can meet in special sessions if required.

International Court of Justice 15 independent judges, elected by the Security Council and the General Assembly on the basis of their competence in international law and irrespective of their nationalities, except that no two judges can be nationals of the same state. They serve for nine years and may be immediately re-elected. The president and vice president are elected by the court for three-year terms. Decisions are by majority vote of the judges present, and the president has a casting vote. Only states, not individuals, can be parties to cases before the court. There is no appeal.

United Nations Secretary Generals

term	*name*	*nationality*
1946–53	Trygve Lie	Norwegian
1953–61	Dag Hammarskjöld	Swedish
1961–71	U Thant	Burmese
1972–81	Kurt Waldheim	Austrian
1982–92	Javier Pérez de Cuéllar	Peruvian
1992–	Boutros Boutros Ghali	Egyptian

Secretariat the chief administrator of the UN is the secretary general, who has under- and assistant secretaries general and a large international staff. The secretary general is appointed by the General Assembly for a renewable five-year term.

UN specialized agencies

Food and Agriculture Organization (FAO)
established 1945
responsibilities to raise levels of nutrition and standards of living, to improve the production and distribution of food and agricultural products particularly for the less developed parts of the world, and to sponsor relief in emergency situations
headquarters Rome

General Agreement on Tariffs and Trade (GATT)
established 1948
responsibilities a multilateral treaty which lays down a common code of conduct in international trade, providing a forum for discussion of trade problems, with the object of reducing trade barriers.
headquarters Geneva

UN membership

Country	Year of admission	Contribution to UN budget (%)	Country	Year of admission	Contribution to UN budget (%)
Afghanistan	1946	0.01	Ghana	1957	0.01
Albania	1955	0.01	Greece†	1945	0.35
Algeria	1962	0.16	Grenada	1974	0.01
Angola	1976	0.01	Guatemala†	1945	0.02
Antigua & Barbuda	1981	0.01	Guinea	1958	0.01
Argentina†	1945	0.57	Guinea-Bissau	1974	0.01
Armenia	1992	0.13	Guyana	1966	0.01
Australia†	1945	1.51	Haiti†	1945	0.01
Austria	1955	0.75	Honduras†	1945	0.01
Azerbaijan	1992	0.22	Hungary	1955	0.18
Bahamas	1973	0.02	Iceland	1946	0.03
Bahrain	1971	0.03	India†	1945	0.36
Bangladesh	1974	0.01	Indonesia	1950	0.16
Barbados	1966	0.01	Iran†	1945	0.77
Belarus†	1945	0.48	Iraq†	1945	0.13
Belgium†	1945	1.06	Ireland	1955	0.18
Belize	1981	0.01	Israel	1949	0.23
Benin	1960	0.01	Italy	1955	4.29
Bhutan	1971	0.01	Jamaica	1962	0.01
Bolivia†	1945	0.01	Japan	1956	12.45
Bosnia-Herzegovina	1992	0.04	Jordan	1955	0.01
Botswana	1966	0.01	Kazakhstan	1992	0.35
Brazil†	1945	1.59	Kenya	1963	0.01
Brunei	1984	0.03	Kuwait	1963	0.25
Bulgaria	1955	0.13	Kyrgyzstan	1992	0.06
Burkina Faso	1960	0.01	Laos	1955	0.01
Burundi	1962	0.01	Latvia	1991	0.13
Cambodia	1955	0.01	Lebanon†	1945	0.01
Cameroon	1960	0.01	Lesotho	1966	0.01
Canada†	1945	3.11	Liberia†	1945	0.01
Cape Verde	1975	0.01	Libya	1955	0.24
Central African Republic	1960	0.01	Liechtenstein	1990	0.01
Chad	1960	0.01	Lithuania	1991	0.15
Chile†	1945	0.08	Luxembourg†	1945	0.06
China†	1945	0.77	Macedonia	1993	***
Colombia†	1945	0.13	Madagascar	1960	0.01
Comoros	1975	0.01	Malawi	1964	0.01
Congo	1960	0.01	Malaysia	1957	0.12
Costa Rica†	1945	0.01	Maldives	1965	0.01
Côte d'Ivoire	1960	0.02	Mali	1960	0.01
Croatia	1992	0.13	Malta	1964	0.01
Cuba†	1945	0.09	Marshall Islands	1991	0.01
Cyprus	1960	0.02	Mauritania	1961	0.01
Czech Republic	1993	***	Mauritius	1968	0.01
Denmark†	1945	0.65	Mexico†	1945	0.88
Djibouti	1977	0.01	Micronesia	1991	0.01
Dominica	1978	0.01	Moldova	1992	0.15
Dominican Republic†	1945	0.02	Monaco	1993	***
Ecuador†	1945	0.03	Mongolia	1961	0.01
Egypt†	1945	0.07	Morocco	1956	0.03
El Salvador†	1945	0.01	Mozambique	1975	0.01
Equatorial Guinea	1968	0.01	Myanmar (Burma)	1948	0.01
Eritrea	1993	***	Namibia	1990	0.01
Estonia	1991	0.07	Nepal	1955	0.01
Ethiopia†	1945	0.01	Netherlands†	1945	1.50
Fiji	1970	0.01	New Zealand†	1945	0.24
Finland	1955	0.57	Nicaragua†	1945	0.01
France†	1945	6.00	Niger	1960	0.01
Gabon	1960	0.02	Nigeria	1960	0.20
Gambia	1965	0.01	North Korea	1991	0.05
Georgia	1992	0.21	Norway†	1945	0.55
Germany **	1973/1990	8.93	Oman	1971	0.03

***UN membership** (cont.)*

Country	*Year of admission*	*Contribution to UN budget (%)*
Pakistan	1947	0.06
Panama†	1945	0.02
Papua New Guinea	1975	0.01
Paraguay†	1945	0.02
Peru†	1945	0.06
Philippines†	1945	0.07
Poland†	1945	0.47
Portugal	1955	0.20
Qatar	1971	0.05
Romania	1955	0.17
Russian Federation *	1945	6.71
Rwanda	1962	0.01
St Christopher–Nevis	1983	0.1
St Lucia	1979	0.01
St Vincent & Grenadines	1980	0.01
San Marino	1992	0.01
São Tomé e Principe	1975	0.01
Saudi Arabia†	1945	0.96
Senegal	1960	0.01
Seychelles	1976	0.01
Sierra Leone	1961	0.01
Singapore	1965	0.12
Slovak Republic	1993	***
Slovenia	1992	0.09
Solomon Isles	1978	0.01
Somalia	1960	0.01
South Africa†	1945	0.41
South Korea	1991	0.69
Spain	1955	1.98
Sri Lanka	1955	0.01
Sudan	1956	0.01
Surinam	1975	0.01
Swaziland	1968	0.01
Sweden	1946	1.11
Syria†	1945	0.04
Tajikistan	1992	0.05
Tanzania	1961	0.01
Thailand	1946	0.11
Togo	1960	0.01
Trinidad & Tobago	1962	0.05
Tunisia	1956	0.03
Turkey†	1945	0.27
Turkmenistan	1992	0.06
Uganda	1962	0.01
Ukraine†	1945	1.87
United Arab Emirates	1971	0.21
United Kingdom†	1945	5.02
United States of America†	1945	25.00
Uruguay†	1945	0.04
Uzbekistan	1992	0.26
Vanuatu	1981	0.01
Venezuela†	1945	0.49
Vietnam	1977	0.01
Western Samoa	1976	0.01
Yemen **	1947	0.01
Yugoslavia†	1945	0.16
Zaire	1960	0.01
Zambia	1964	0.01
Zimbabwe	1980	0.01

† *founder members*

* *Became a separate member upon the demise of the USSR which was a founder member 1945*

** *represented by two countries until unification 1990*

*** *contributions to be determined*

The sovereign countries that are not UN members are Andorra, Kiribati, Nauru, Switzerland, Taiwan, Tonga, Tuvalu, and Vatican City.

International Atomic Energy Agency (IAEA)
established 1957
responsibilities to accelerate and enlarge the contribution of atomic energy to peace, health and prosperity throughout the world and to prevent its diversion from peaceful purposes to military ends
headquarters Vienna

International Bank for Reconstruction and Development (IBRD) — (***World Bank***)
established 1945
responsibilities to provide funds and technical assistance to help the economies of the poorer nations of the world
headquarters Washington DC

International Civil Aviation Organization (ICAO)
established 1947
responsibilities to establish technical standards for safety and efficiency in air navigation, to develop regional plans for ground facilities and services for civil aviation, and generally provide advice to airline operators
headquarters Montréal

International Development Association (IDA)
established 1960
responsibilities as an agency of the World Bank, to provide financial and technical help to the poorest nations
headquarters Washington DC

International Finance Corporation (IFC)
established 1956
responsibilities as an affiliate of the World Bank, to make investments in companies, to assist their development, or provides loans
headquarters Washington DC

International Fund for Agricultural Development (IFAD)
established 1977
responsibilities to mobilize funds for agricultural and rural development
headquarters Rome

International Labour Organization (ILO)
established 1919, becoming part of the UN in 1946
responsibilities to improve labour conditions, raise living standards and promote productive employment through international cooperation

headquarters International Labour Conference, its supreme deliberative body, meets annually in Geneva; International Labour Office and International Institute for Labour Studies, both based permanently in Geneva; a training institution, particularly concerned with the needs of developing countries, based in Turin

International Maritime Organization (IMO)
established 1948
responsibilities to promote cooperation between governments on technical matters affecting merchant shipping, with the object of improving safety at sea
headquarters London

International Monetary Fund (IMF)
established 1945
responsibilities to promote international monetary cooperation and to help remedy any serious disequilibrium in a country's balance of payments by allowing it to draw on the resources of the Fund while it takes measures to correct the imbalance.
headquarters Washington DC

International Telecommunication Union (ITU)
established 1932
responsibilities to maintain and extend international cooperation in improving telecommunications of all kinds by promoting the development of technical skills and services and harmonizing national activities
headquarters Geneva

United Nations Centre for Human Settlements (UNCHS; Habitat)
established 1978
responsibilities to service the intergovernmental Commission on Human Settlements by providing planning, construction, land development, and finance
headquarters Nairobi

United Nations Children's Emergency Fund (UNICEF)
established 1953
responsibilities to meet the emergency needs of children in developing countries
headquarters New York

United Nations Conference on Trade and Development (UNCTAD)
established 1964
responsibilities to promote international trade, particularly in developing countries
headquarters Geneva

United Nations Development Programme (UNDP)
established 1961
responsibilities to promote higher standards of living in the poorer nations and to try to remedy the economic imbalance between industrialized and developing countries, to be achieved mainly by the economically advanced countries providing financial and technical help, and by adopting economic and commercial policies favouring the less advanced nations
headquarters New York.

United Nations Disaster Relief Coordinator (UNDRO)
established 1972.
responsibilities to provide a 24-hour service for monitoring natural disasters and emergencies; to promote disaster prevention; and to coordinate preparedness and relief
headquarters Geneva

United Nations Educational, Scientific and Cultural Organization (UNESCO)
established 1946
responsibilities to promote peace by encouraging international collaboration in education, science, and culture
headquarters Paris

United Nations Environment Programme (UNEP)
established 1972
responsibilities to monitor the state of the environment and to promote environmentally sound developments throughout the world
headquarters Nairobi

United Nations Fund for Population Activities (UNFPA)
established 1972
responsibilities to provide finance for projects in the areas of family planning, education, and research into population trends and the needs of particular age groups
headquarters New York

United Nations High Commissioner for Refugees (UNHCR)
established 1951
responsibilities to provide international protection for refugees and to find solutions to their problems
headquarters Geneva

United Nations Institute for Training and Research (UNITAR)
established 1965
responsibilities to improve the effectiveness of the UN through training and research
headquarters New York

United Nations Research Institute for Social Development (UNRISD)
established 1964
responsibilities to conduct research into problems and policies of social and economic development
headquarters Geneva

Universal Postal Union (UPU)
established 1875
responsibilities to improve the standards of postal services and promote international cooperation
headquarters Berne

World Food Council (WFC)
established 1974
responsibilities to stimulate national and international policies and programmes for alleviating world hunger, and to improve the global food system
headquarters Rome

World Food Programme (WFP)
established 1963
responsibilities to improve social and economic development through food aid, and to provide emergency relief
headquarters Rome

World Health Organization (WHO)
established 1948
responsibilities to assist all peoples in attaining the highest possible levels of health
headquarters Geneva

World Intellectual Property Organization (WIPO)
established 1974
responsibilities to protect intellectual property, which, in general, means patents and trademarks, throughout the world
headquarters Geneva

World Meteorological Organization (WMO)
established 1947
responsibilities to facilitate worldwide cooperation in the creation and maintenance of a network of stations for making meteorological observations and to ensure the rapid exchange of information
headquarters Geneva

United Nations Development Programme (UNDP)
Regional Commissions Established to promote cooperation between under- or less-developed countries, and to assist their economic and social development, through research and the coordination of national policies:

Economic Commission for Africa (ECA)
established 1958
membership 50 states, representing virtually the whole of north, central, and southern Africa.
headquarters Addis Ababa

Economic and Social Commission for Asia and the Pacific (ESCAP)
established 1947
membership 35 full and 10 associate members. Most of the full members are states in Asia or Oceania but other countries with interests in the regions, such as the USA, the UK, France, and the Netherlands also enjoy full membership. The associate members are the smaller countries of the region
headquarters Bangkok

Economic Commission for Europe (ECE).
established 1947
membership all European countries except Switzerland, which participates in a consultative capacity. The USA is also a consultant
headquarters Geneva

Economic Commission for Latin America (ECLA)
established 1948
membership 33 members, including, in addition to the countries of the region, Canada, France, the Netherlands, the UK, and the USA
headquarters Santiago

Economic Commission for Western Asia (ECWA)
established 1973
membership 14 members, which comprise 13 countries plus the Palestine Liberation Organization (PLO), all situated in the Middle East or north or central Africa
headquarters Amman

UN peacekeeping operations 1993

Location	*Year of establishment*	*Number of personnel*	*Annual cost $m*
Angola	1991	298	67
Bosnia	1991	23,000	222
Cambodia	1992	19,000	637
Cyprus	1964	1,500	31
El Salvador	1991	530	35
Iraq-Kuwait	1991	353	67
Lebanon	1978	5,643	144
Mozambique	1992	7,500	200
Palestine/Israel/ Golan Heights	1948/1974	74	64
Somalia	1992	30,800	1,500
Totals		***88,698***	***2,967***

The British Commonwealth

The British Commonwealth is a voluntary association of 50 countries and their dependencies that once formed part of the British Empire and are now independent sovereign states. They are all regarded as 'full members of the Commonwealth'. Additionally, there are some 20 territories that are not completely sovereign and remain dependencies of the UK or another of the fully sovereign members, and are regarded as 'Commonwealth countries'. Heads of government meet every two years, apart from those of Nauru and Tuvalu; however, Nauru and Tuvalu have the right to participate in all functional activities. The Commonwealth has no charter or constitution, and is founded more on tradition and sentiment than on political or economic factors.

Queen Elizabeth II was the formal head but not the ruler of 16 member states in 1992; 5 member states had their own monarchs; and 29 were republics. The Commonwealth secretariat, headed from Oct 1989 by Nigerian Emeka Anyaoko (1933–) as secretary general, is based in London. The secretariat's staff come from a number of member countries, which also pay its operating costs.

On 15 May 1917 Jan Smuts, representing South Africa in the imperial war cabinet of World War I, suggested that 'British Commonwealth of Nations' was the right title for the British Empire. The name was recognized in the Statute of Westminster 1931, but after World War II a growing sense of independent nationhood led to the simplification of the title to the Commonwealth.

Human-Rights and Relief Organizations

Action Aid
established 1972
objectives to help children, families, and communities in the world's poorest countries to overcome poverty, and to secure lasting improvements in the quality of their lives
areas of operation 18 countries in Africa, Asia, and Latin America
membership over 110,000 sponsors and supporters
annual budget (1990) £20,216,000
headquarters London

The British Commonwealth

Country	Capital	Date joined	Area in sq km	Constitutional status
in Africa				
Botswana	Gaborone	1966	582,000	sovereign republic
British Indian Ocean Territory	Victoria	1965	60	British dependent territory
Gambia	Banjul	1965	10,700	sovereign republic
Ghana	Accra	1957	238,300	sovereign republic
Kenya	Nairobi	1963	582,600	sovereign republic
Lesotho	Maseru	1966	30,400	sovereign constitutional monarchy
Malawi	Zomba	1964	118,000	sovereign republic
Mauritius	Port Louis	1968	2,000	sovereign republic
Namibia	Windhoek	1990	824,000	sovereign republic
Nigeria	Lagos	1960	924,000	sovereign republic
St Helena	Jamestown	1931	100	British dependent territory
Seychelles	Victoria	1976	450	sovereign republic
Sierra Leone	Freetown	1961	73,000	sovereign republic
Swaziland	Mbabane	1968	17,400	sovereign republic
Tanzania	Dodoma	1961	945,000	sovereign republic
Uganda	Kampala	1962	236,900	sovereign republic
Zambia	Lusaka	1964	752,600	sovereign republic
Zimbabwe	Harare	1980	390,300	sovereign republic
in the Americas				
Anguilla	The Valley	1931	155	British dependent territory
Antigua and Barbuda	St John's	1981	400	sovereign constitutional monarchy*
Bahamas	Nassau	1973	13,900	sovereign constitutional monarchy*
Barbados	Bridgetown	1966	400	sovereign constitutional monarchy*
Belize	Belmopan	1982	23,000	sovereign constitutional monarchy*
Bermuda	Hamilton	1931	54	British dependent territory
British Virgin Islands	Road Town	1931	153	British dependent territory
Canada	Ottawa	1931	9,958,400	sovereign constitutional monarchy*
Cayman Islands	Georgetown	1931	300	British dependent territory
Dominica	Roseau	1978	700	sovereign republic
Falkland Islands	Port Stanley	1931	12,100	British dependent territory
Grenada	St George's	1974	300	sovereign constitutional monarchy*
Guyana	Georgetown	1966	215,000	sovereign republic
Jamaica	Kingston	1962	11,400	sovereign constitutional monarchy*
Montserrat	Plymouth	1931	100	British dependent territory
St Christopher–Nevis	Basseterre	1983	300	sovereign constitutional monarchy*
St Lucia	Castries	1979	600	sovereign constitutional monarchy*
St Vincent and the Grenadines	Kingstown	1979	400	sovereign constitutional monarchy*
Trinidad and Tobago	Port of Spain	1962	5,100	sovereign republic
Turks and Caicos Islands	Grand Turk	1931	400	British dependent territory
in the Antarctic				
Australian Antarctic Territory	uninhabited	1936	5,403,000	Australian external territory
British Antarctic Territory	uninhabited	1931	390,000	British dependent territory
Falkland Islands Dependencies	uninhabited	1931	1,600	British dependent territories
Ross Dependency	uninhabited	1931	453,000	New Zealand associated territory
in Asia				
Bangladesh	Dhaka	1972	144,000	sovereign republic
Brunei	Bandar Seri Begawan	1984	5,800	sovereign monarchy
Hong Kong	Victoria	1931	1,100	British crown colony
India	Delhi	1947	3,166,800	sovereign republic
Malaysia	Kuala Lumpur	1957	329,800	sovereign constitutional monarchy
Maldives	Malé	1982	300	sovereign republic
Pakistan	Islamabad	1947†	803,900	sovereign republic
Singapore	Singapore	1965	600	sovereign republic
Sri Lanka	Colombo	1948	66,000	sovereign republic

***The British Commonwealth** (cont.)*

Country	*Capital*	*Date joined*	*Aea in sq km*	*Constitutional status*
in Australasia and the Pacific				
Australia	Canberra	1931	7,682,300	sovereign constitutional monarchy*
Cook Islands	Avarua	1931	300	New Zealand associated territory
Norfolk Island	Kingston	1931	34	Australian external territory
Kiribati	Tawawa	1979	700	sovereign republic
Nauru	Yaren	1968	21	sovereign republic
New Zealand	Wellington	1931	268,000	sovereign constitutional monarchy*
Niue	Alofi	1931	300	New Zealand associated territory
Papua New Guinea	Port Moresby	1975	462,800	sovereign constitutional monarchy*
Pitcairn Islands	Adamstown	1931	5	British dependent territory
Solomon Islands	Honiara	1978	27,600	sovereign constitutional monarchy*
Tokelau	Nukunonu	1931	10	New Zealand associated territory
Tonga	Nuku'alofa	1970	700	sovereign monarchy
Tuvalu	Funafuti	1978	24	sovereign constitutional monarchy*
Vanuatu	Villa	1980	15,000	sovereign republic
Western Samoa	Apia	1970	2,800	sovereign republic
in Europe				
Channel Islands		1931	200	UK crown dependencies
Cyprus	Nicosia	1961	9,000	sovereign republic
Gibraltar	Gibraltar	1931	6	British dependent territory
Malta	Valletta	1964	300	sovereign republic
Isle of Man	Douglas	1931	600	UK crown dependency
United Kingdom	London	1931	244,100	sovereign constitutional monarchy*
England	London			
Northern Ireland	Belfast			
Scotland	Edinburgh			
Wales	Cardiff			
Total			***33,089,900***	

** Queen Elizabeth II constitutional monarch and head of state*
† left 1972 and rejoined 1989

Amnesty International
established 1961
objectives to free all prisoners of conscience; to ensure fair and prompt trials for political prisoners; to abolish the death penalty, torture, and other cruel treatment of prisoners; to end extrajudicial executions and 'disappearances'. Amnesty International also opposes similar abuses by opposition groups. Politically unaligned
areas of operation organized sections in 47 countries (24 in Latin America, Asia, Africa, Middle East)
membership more than 6,000 volunteer groups active in more than 70 countries and 1,100,000 individual members, subscribers, and regular donors in more than 150 countries and territories
annual budget (1991) £12.9 million
headquarters international secretariat, London

Campaign for Nuclear Disarmament (CND)
established 1958
objectives to campaign for the dismantling of nuclear weapons, bases, and alliances; also campaigns against nuclear power. Politically unaligned
areas of operation mainly the UK
membership 60,000 plus affiliated organizations
annual budget (1990) £842,000 and £477,000 (publications wing)
headquarters London

Human Rights Watch *established* 1978
objectives to monitor and publicize human-rights abuses by governments, especially attacks on those who defend human rights in their own countries
areas of operation separate committees focus on one area each:
Africa Watch*, *Americas Watch*, *Asia Watch*, *Middle East Watch*; *Helsinki Watch monitors compliance with the 1975 Helsinki accords by the 35 signatory countries
annual budget does not accept financial support from governments or government-funded agencies
headquarters New York

Minority Rights Group
established 1965
objectives to promote human rights and increase awareness of minority issues
areas of operation Europe, Australia, North America, India
membership non-membership organization
headquarters London

Oxfam (Oxford Committee for Famine Relief)
established 1942
objectives to relieve poverty, distress, and suffering in any part of the world
areas of operation worldwide, particularly in developing countries
membership not a membership organization
annual budget (1990) £62m
headquarters Oxford

The Red Cross
established 1864 by the Geneva Convention; the

Muslim equivalent is the Red Crescent
objectives to assist the wounded and prisoners in war, and war-related victims such as refugees and the disabled; to aid victims of natural disasters — floods, earthquakes, epidemics, famine, and accidents — and to organize emergency relief operations worldwide
membership non-membership organization
annual budget (1991) £64 million
areas of operation worldwide
headquarters Geneva, Switzerland

Save the Children Fund
established 1919
objectives to promote the rights of children to care, good health, material welfare, and moral, spiritual, and educational development, throughout the world
areas of operation more than 50 Third World countries and the UK
membership over 850 branches in the UK
annual budget (1990) £52m
headquarters London

Survival International
established 1969
objectives to support tribal peoples and their right to decide their own future, and to help them protect their lands, environment, and way of life
areas of operation more than 60 countries worldwide
membership 12,000
annual budget (1990) £530,000
headquarters London

Voluntary Service Overseas (VSO)
established 1958
objectives to help Third World development by providing opportunities for people with skills to make a practical contribution as volunteers
areas of operation 40 developing countries worldwide
membership 45 local groups
annual budget (1990) £15.7m
headquarters London

War on Want
established 1952
objectives to support development work in developing countries and to campaign in Europe on world poverty
areas of operation Bangladesh, Cambodia, Vietnam, Sri Lanka, India, Philippines, South Africa, Namibia, Ethiopia, Eritrea, West Bank and Gaza Strip, Brazil, Chile, Nicaragua, El Salvador, Guatemala, Jamaica
membership (1992) 1,400 individual members and trade-union affiliations
annual budget (1992) £990,000
headquarters London

GALLUP POLL: United Nations

In general, do you feel the United Nations is doing a good job or a poor job in trying to solve the problems it has had to face?

	Feb 1993	Jun 1985	May 1985
Good	51	33	26
Poor	33	42	47
Do now	16	25	27

Do you think the United Nations does a better job at keeping peace or does it do a better job at helping poor countries to develop their economies?

	Feb 1993	Jun 1985	May 1985
Keeping peace	26	19	30
Helping poor countries	36	36	30
Does both well	10	8	7
Does neither well	11	17	16
Don't know	17	20	18

All things considered, do you think the world would be better off without the United Nations, or is better off with it?

	Feb 1993	Jun 1985	May 1985
Better without UN	7	12	11
Better with UN	78	71	69
Makes no difference	4	6	7
Don't know	11	12	13

European Community

Generally speaking, do you think that British membership of the European Community is a good thing, a bad thing, or neither good nor bad?

	Jan 1993	Sep 1992	Nov 1991
Good	41	42	49
Bad	29	27	22
Neither	19	22	20
Don't know	10	9	9

People hold different views about how they would like to see the European Community develop. Which of these statements comes closest to your own view?

	Jan 1993	Nov 1991	Nov 1990	Jun 1989
A fully integrated Europe with most major decision taken by a European government	9	11	13	13
A Europe more integrated than now, but with decisions that mainly affect Britain staying in British hands	44	48	56	48
The situation much as it is now with Britain retaining a veto over major policy changes it does not like	23	23	19	21
Complete British withdrawal from the European Community	17	12	8	12
Don't know	7	6	4	7

Source: Gallup

LAW

Terms

accessory a criminal accomplice who aids in commission of a crime that is actually committed by someone else. An accomplice may be either 'before the fact' (assisting, ordering, or procuring another to commit a crime) or 'after the fact' (giving assistance after the crime). An accomplice present when the crime is committed is an 'abettor'.

accomplice person who acts with another in the commission or attempted commission of a crime, either as a principal or as an accessory.

acquittal the setting free of someone charged with a crime after a trial. In English courts it follows a verdict of 'not guilty', but in Scotland the verdict may be either 'not guilty' or 'not proven'. Acquittal by the jury must be confirmed by the judge.

action any proceeding in a civil court of law, including an ecclesiastical court. Actions in the High Court are commenced by the plaintiff issuing a writ, which will usually include a concise statement about the nature of the claim and the damages being sought from the defendant.

act of God some sudden and irresistible act of nature that could not reasonably have been foreseen or prevented, such as floods, storms, earthquakes, or sudden death.

act of Parliament in Britain, a change in the law originating in Parliament and called a statute. Before an act receives the royal assent and becomes law it is a ***bill***. The US equivalent is an act of Congress.

An act of Parliament may be either public (of general effect), local, or private. The body of English statute law comprises all the acts passed by Parliament: the existing list opens with the Statute of Merton, passed in 1235. An act (unless it is stated to be for a definite period and then to come to an end) remains on the statute book until it is repealed.

How an act of Parliament becomes law: ***1 first reading of the bill*** The title is read out in the House of Commons (H of C) and a minister names a day for the second reading. ***2*** The bill is officially printed. ***3 second reading*** A debate on the whole bill in the H of C followed by a vote on whether or not the bill should go on to the next stage. ***4 committee stage*** A committee of MPs considers the bill in detail and makes amendments. ***5 report stage*** The bill is referred back to the H of C which may make further amendments. ***6 third reading*** The H of C votes whether the bill should be sent on to the House of Lords. ***7 House of Lords*** The bill passes through much the same stages in the Lords as in the H of C. (Bills may be introduced in the Lords, in which case the H of C considers them at this stage.) ***8 last amendments*** The H of C considers any Lords' amendments, and may make further amendments which must usually be agreed by the Lords. ***9 royal assent*** The Queen gives her formal assent. ***10*** The bill becomes an act of Parliament at royal assent, although it may not come into force until a day appointed in the act.

adjournment the postponement of the hearing of a case for later consideration. If a hearing is adjourned *sine die* ('without day') it is postponed for an indefinite period. If a party requests an adjournment, the court may find the costs of the adjournment have been unnecessarily incurred and make an order for costs against that party.

adoption permanent legal transfer of parental rights and duties in respect of a child from one person to another.

adultery voluntary sexual intercourse between a married person and someone other than his or her legal partner. It is one factor that may prove 'irretrievable breakdown' of marriage in actions for judicial separation or divorce in Britain.

advocate (Latin *advocatus*, one summoned to one's aid, especially in a lawcourt) professional pleader in a court of justice. A more common term for a professional advocate is barrister or counsel. In many tribunals lay persons may appear as advocates.

affidavit legal document, used in court applications and proceedings, in which a person swears that certain facts are true.

alibi a provable assertion that the accused was at some other place when a crime was committed.

alien a person who is not a citizen of a particular nation. In the UK, under the British Nationality Act 1981, an alien is anyone who is neither a British Overseas citizen (for example Commonwealth) nor a member of certain other categories; citizens of the Republic of Ireland are not regarded as aliens. Aliens may not vote or hold public office in the UK.

alimony in the USA, money allowance given by court order to a former spouse after separation or divorce. The right has been extended to relationships outside marriage and is colloquially termed palimony. Alimony is separate and distinct from court orders for child support.

PCs for PCs

The top five and bottom five police forces ranked by spending on computers as a percentage of overall budget, England and Wales

The top five forces	*IT budget 1992/93*	*% total force budget*
West Yorkshire	£5.7 million	5.1%
Kent	£6.4 million	4.7%
Surrey	£1.8 million	2.7%
Cleveland	£1.4 million	2.6%
Essex	£3.4 million	2.5%
The bottom five forces		
Northants	£0.4 million	0.73%
Lancashire	£0.9 million	0.67%
Durham	£0.3 million	0.64%
West Mercia	£0.5 million	0.62%
Suffolk	£0.3 million	0.56%

Source: Computing

amnesty release of political prisoners under a general pardon, or a person or group of people from criminal liability for a particular action; for example, the occasional amnesties in the UK for those who surrender firearms that they hold illegally.

appeal application for a re-hearing of all or part of an issue that has already been dealt with by a lower court or tribunal. The outcome can be a new decision on all or part of the points raised, or the previous decision may be upheld. In criminal cases, an appeal may be against conviction and either the prosecution or the defence may appeal against sentence. In the UK, summary trials (involving minor offences) are heard in the magistrates' court and appeals against conviction or sentence are heard in the crown court. The appeal in the crown court takes the form of a full retrial but no jury is present. Appeal against conviction or sentence in the crown court is heard by the criminal division of the Court of Appeal. The House of Lords is the highest appellate court within the UK. Further appeal may lie to either the European Court of Justice or the European Court of Human Rights. In 1991, 662 defendants were granted leave to appeal against conviction, and 878 were refused. Of those who appealed, 269 had their conviction quashed.

arbitration submission of a dispute to a third, unbiased party for settlement. It may be personal litigation, a trade-union issue, or an international dispute.

arrest apprehension and detention of a person suspected of a crime classified as sufficiently serious (an 'arrestable' offence). In Britain, an arrest may be made on a magistrate's warrant, but a police constable is empowered to arrest without warrant in all cases where he or she has reasonable ground for thinking a serious offence has been committed.

arson malicious and wilful setting fire to property. A capital offence until 1921, it still carries a maximum sentence of life imprisonment.

assault intentional act or threat of physical violence against a person. In English law it is both a crime and a tort (a civil wrong). The kinds of criminal assault are common (ordinary); aggravated (more serious, such as causing actual bodily harm); or indecent (of a sexual nature).

Attorney General in England, principal law officer of the crown and head of the English Bar; the post is one of great political importance. In England, Wales, and Northern Ireland, the consent of the Attorney General is required for bringing certain criminal proceedings where offences against the state or public order are at issue (for example incitement to racial hatred). Under the Criminal Justice Act 1988, cases can be referred to the Court of Appeal by the Attorney General if it appears to him or her that the sentencing of a person convicted of a serious offence has been unduly lenient.

bail the setting at liberty of a person in legal custody on an undertaking (usually backed by some security, given either by that person or by someone else) to attend at a court at a stated time and place. If the person does not attend, the bail may be forfeited.

barrister in the UK, a lawyer qualified by study at the Inns of Court to plead for a client in court. In Scotland such lawyers are called advocates. Barristers also undertake the writing of opinions on the prospects of a case before trial. They act for clients through the intermediary of solicitors. In the highest courts, only barristers can represent litigants but this distinction between barristers and solicitors seems likely to change in the 1990s. When pupil barristers complete their training they are 'called to the Bar': this being the name of the ceremony in which they are admitted as members of the profession. A Queen's Counsel (silk) is a senior barrister appointed on the recommendation of the Lord Chancellor.

bigamy the offence of marrying a person while already lawfully married to another. In some countries marriage to more than one wife or husband is lawful; see also polygamy.

blackmail criminal offence of extorting money with menaces or threats of detrimental action, such as exposure of some misconduct on the part of the victim.

blasphemy written or spoken insult directed against religious belief or sacred things with deliberate intent to outrage believers.

Breathalyzer trademark for an instrument for on-the-spot checking by police of the amount of alcohol consumed by a suspect driver. The driver breathes into a plastic bag connected to a tube containing a chemical that changes colour in the presence of alcohol. Another method is to use a gas chromatograph, again from a breath sample. Approximately 500,000 breath tests are carried out each year. Alcohol-related road-traffic accidents result in 22,000 casualties each year; 50% of those injured are victims of drunk drivers.

brief the written instructions sent by a solicitor to a barrister before a court hearing.

burden of proof in court proceedings, the duty of a party to produce sufficient evidence to prove that his or her case is true. In English and US law a higher standard of proof is required in criminal cases (beyond all reasonable doubt), than in civil cases (on the balance of probabilities).

burglary offence committed when a trespasser enters a building intending to steal, do damage to property, grievously harm any person, or rape a woman. Entry need only be effective so, for example, a person who puts their hand through a broken shop window to steal something may be guilty of burglary. In English and Welsh courts, burglary is considered a serious offence especially if committed during the hours of darkness. Where the burglary is aggravated by the use of weapons or explosives, the offender may be imprisoned for life. UK research 1991 suggested that the average age of burglars was 15 years. In England and Wales 1990, burglary formed 22% of all recorded crime, with 1,006,500 offences, an 11% increase from 1987 (these figures do not include theft from or of vehicles).

capital punishment punishment by death. Methods of execution include electrocution, lethal gas, hanging, shooting, lethal injection, garrotting, and decapitation. 44 countries have abolished the death penalty for all offences, and 17 (including the UK) have done so for all but exceptional crimes such as wartime crimes. 25 countries can be considered abolitionist *de facto*, that is they retain the death penalty in law but have not carried out any executions for the past ten years or more. Capital punishment is retained and used in 92 countries, including the USA (37 states), China, Islamic countries, and the ex-Soviet republics.

The International Covenant on Civil and Political Rights 1977 ruled out imposition of the death penalty on those under the age of 18. The covenant was signed by President Carter on behalf of the USA, but in 1989 the US Supreme Court decided that it could be imposed from the age of 16 for murder, and that the mentally retarded could also face the death penalty. In 1990, in the USA there were over 2,000 prisoners on death row (awaiting execution).

No to capital punishment

Countries that have abolished the death penalty since 1976

1976	Portugal*; Canada **
1978	Denmark*; Spain **
1979	Luxembourg, Nicaragua, Norway*; Brazil (1), Fiji, Peru**
1981	France*
1982	The Netherlands*
1983	Cyprus, El Salvador**
1984	Argentina (2), Australia**
1985	Australia*
1987	The Philippines, Haiti, Liechtenstein, German Democratic Republic*
1989	Cambodia, New Zealand, Romania*
1990	Andorra, Czech and Slovak Federative Republic, Hungary, Ireland, Mozambique, Namibia, São Tomé and Príncipe*; Nepal** (3)
1992	Switzerland
1993	Guinea-Bissau*

** for all offences ** for ordinary offences*

1. Brazil had abolished the death penalty in 1882 but reintroduced it in 1969 while under military rule.
2. Argentina had abolished the death penalty for all offences in 1921 and again in 1972 but reintroduced it 1976 following a military coup.
3. Nepal had abolished the death penalty for murder in 1946 but reintroduced it in 1985 after bomb explosions killed several people.

care order in Britain, a court order that places a child in the care of a local authority; this may be with foster parents or in a community home.

child abuse the molesting of children by parents and other adults. It can give rise to various criminal charges and has become a growing concern since the early 1980s. In the UK, a local authority can take abused children away from their parents by obtaining a care order from a juvenile court under the Children's and Young Persons Act 1969 (replaced by the Children's Act 1989). Controversial methods of diagnosing sexual abuse led to a public inquiry in Cleveland, England 1988, which severely criticized the handling of such cases. The standard of proof required for criminal proceedings is greater than that required for a local authority to take children into care. This has led to highly publicized cases where children have been taken into care but prosecutions have eventually not been brought, as in Rochdale, Lancashire, and the Orkneys, Scotland in 1990.

civil disobedience deliberate breaking of laws considered unjust, a form of nonviolent direct action; the term was coined by the US writer Henry Thoreau in an essay of that name 1849. It was advocated by Mahatma Gandhi to prompt peaceful withdrawal of British power from India. Civil disobedience has since been employed by, for instance, the US civil-rights movement in the 1960s and the peace movement in the 1980s.

civil law legal system based on Roman law. It is one of the two main European legal systems, English (common) law being the other. Civil law may also mean the law relating to matters other than criminal law, such as contract and tort. Inside the Commonwealth, Roman law forms the basis of the legal systems of Scotland and Québec and is also the basis of that of South Africa.

commissioner for oaths in English law, a person appointed by the Lord Chancellor with power to administer oaths or take affidavits. All practising solicitors have these powers but must not use them in proceedings in which they are acting for any of the parties or in which they have an interest.

committal proceedings in the UK, a preliminary hearing in a magistrate's court to decide whether there is a case to answer before a higher court. The media may only report limited facts about committal proceedings, such as the name of the accused and the charges, unless the defendant asks for reporting restrictions to be lifted.

common law that part of the English law not embodied in legislation. It consists of rules of law based on common custom and usage and on judicial decisions. English common law became the basis of law in the USA and many other English-speaking countries.

compulsory purchase in the UK, the right of the state and authorized bodies to buy land required for public purposes even against the wishes of the owner. Under the Land Compensation Act 1973, fair recompense is payable.

consent, age of age at which consent may legally be given to sexual intercourse by a girl or boy. In the UK it is 16 (21 for male homosexual intercourse).

consumer protection laws and measures designed to ensure fair trading for buyers. Responsibility for checking goods and services for quality, safety, and suitability has in the past few years moved increasingly away from the consumer to the producer.

contempt of court behaviour that shows lack of respect for the authority of a court of law, such as disobeying a court order, breach of an injunction, or improper use of legal documents. Behaviour that disrupts, prejudices, or interferes with court proceedings either inside or outside the courtroom may also be contempt. The court may punish contempt with a fine or imprisonment.

contract of employment the legal basis of an agreement between an employer and an employee.

How science is helping Poirot with his enquiries

The forensic scientist has to provide evidence that will stand scrutiny in a court of law. This is why crime laboratories need to keep up with the latest research and maintain the highest standards.

Every contact leaves a trace. The ordinary microscope is still a vital instrument for examining trace evidence – hairs, fibres, fragments of glass or paint – but the scanning electron microscope is also used. It provides high magnification with good resolution, and can also incorporate a microprobe that identifies the actual elements, particularly metallic ones, in the surface being examined. Surface elements absorb electrons and emit X-rays, which the microprobe converts into an X-ray emission spectrum whose characteristic pattern reveals the elements present. In this way, it is possible to detect and identify particles invisible to the optical microscope, such as those scattered from a firearm when discharged. These particles can indicate the type and make of ammunition used.

Anti-crime antibodies

Advances have also been made in analytical techniques called immunoassays, which use antibodies to detect and measure drugs, poisons, proteins, and even explosives such as TNT and Semtex. When a foreign chemical, such as a disease organism, enters the human body, antibodies are produced which recognize and react with the foreign substance. The same process occurs in animals, which can be used to produce antibodies against a wide variety of chemicals. An animal is injected with a target substance – cocaine, for example – and the resulting antibodies can be separated and used to recognize the substance against a background of body fluids, or in a body swab.

When trying to detect a target compound, such as the presence of explosive residue on a person's hands, it is vital to take account of possible contamination, since the substance might have been picked up casually. Also, it is important that the method used detects the target compound and no other. The value of antibodies is that they are specific to the compound which triggered their production. With other analytical methods, such as thin-layer chromatography, care has to be taken to eliminate other compounds that could show the same experimental result.

DNA fingerprinting

One impressive recent scientific advance is DNA profiling, or DNA fingerprinting. This has been used effectively in assault, rape, and murder cases, and paternity disputes. It involves using enzymes to cut up a sample of DNA extracted from body cells. The resulting bits are separated by gel electrophoresis, blotted onto a special membrane, marked radioactively and then visualized as a sequence of bars on an autoradiograph. Only a very small amount of DNA – from just a few cells – is needed; the polymerase chain reaction (PCR) can amplify it into sufficient material for a profile. A DNA profile on its own is not much good; there has to be another profile for comparison.

DNA profiling must be treated with caution. If two profiles match, they may not necessarily come from the same person. If two bands on adjacent profiles correspond, but not exactly, statistical analysis may be needed to decide if there is a match. However, there can still be doubts. For example, the DNA profiles of people from small communities with significant inbreeding can be similar, so it is possible to obtain deceptively similar bands on profiles from two different people.

ESDA (electrostatic document analysis) is a recent technique used for revealing indentations on paper. Left on an underlying sheet, these indicate what has been written on the paper above. The method uses a high electrostatic voltage to transfer the indentations onto imaging film where they are visualized by photographic toner. If the resulting impressions are markedly uneven – perhaps one half is more heavily indented than the other – then the writing under examination (on the top sheet) may have been written at two different times, showing that the document has been tampered with.

Computers on the beat

The increasing power of computers has been responsible for great advances in forensic science, as in other sciences. Computers have revolutionized the storage and retrieval of information. For example, all car registration numbers and owners' names are stored on computer for almost instant access. Information can be rapidly communicated to police officers in the field. This has increased the power of those who hold the information and, in addition to speeding the response to crime, has helped in the monitoring of 'undesirables' and in maintaining order on the streets.

Identification of a suspect fingerprint by comparison with thousands stored on file was once a time-consuming process. Nowadays, with a computer, the process takes minutes, even seconds. Even so, the final decision on fingerprint identification is still made visually by a trained expert. No matter how sophisticated the hardware, the human senses are still vital in forensic work.

JB

Crime and punishment

Criminal law: highest sentences 1990

judicial area	*murder*	*rape*	*tax fraud*	*armed robbery*	*soft drugs*
Canada	life	life	18 months	5 years	n/a
Denmark	life	3 years	10 months	6 years	fine
England and Wales	life	15 years	3 years	14 years	1 year
Greece	life	20 years	5 years	20 years	1 year
Hong Kong	death	life	3 years	life	life
India	death	10 years	n/a	7 years	n/a
Republic of Ireland	life	18 months	5 years	n/a	n/a
Kenya	death	life	life	3 years	death
Netherlands	life	5 years	1 year	6 years	n/a
New Zealand	life	6 years	large fine	9 years	n/a
Nigeria	death	life	7 years	death	21 years
Norway	21 years	5 years	6 months	2 years	n/a
Scotland	life	10 years	3 years	10 years	18 months
Spain	30 years	20 years	6 years	6 years	4 years
United Arab Emirates	death	life	n/a	life	10 years
Texas	death	50 years	99 years	99 years	1 year

copyright law applying to literary, musical, and artistic works (including plays, recordings, films, photographs, radio and television broadcasts, and, in the USA and the UK, computer programs), which prevents the reproduction of the work, in whole or in part, without the author's consent.

coroner official who investigates the deaths of persons who have died suddenly by acts of violence or under suspicious circumstances, by holding an inquest or ordering a postmortem examination (autopsy). The coroner's court aims not to establish liability but to find out how, where, and why the death occurred. A coroner must be a barrister, solicitor, or medical practitioner with at least five years' professional service. In Scotland similar duties are performed by the procurator-fiscal. The coroner alone decides which witnesses should be called, and legal aid is not available for representation in a coroner's court. Nor may any of the parties make a closing speech to the jury.

corporal punishment physical punishment of wrongdoers – for example, by whipping. It is still used as a punishment for criminals in many countries, especially under Islamic law. It was abolished as a punishment for criminals in Britain 1967 but only became illegal for punishing schoolchildren in state schools 1986. Corporal punishment of children by parents is illegal in some countries, including Sweden, Finland, Denmark, and Norway.

court martial court convened for the trial of persons subject to military discipline who are accused of violations of military laws.

criminal law body of law that defines the public wrongs (crimes) that are punishable by the state and establishes methods of prosecution and punishment. It is distinct from civil law, which deals with legal relationships between individuals (including organizations), for example contract law.

In England and Wales crimes are either: ***indictable offences*** (serious offences triable by judge and jury in a crown court); ***summary offences*** dealt with in magistrates' courts; or ***hybrid offences*** tried in either kind of court according to the seriousness of the case and the wishes of the defendant. Crown courts have power to punish more severely those found guilty than a magistrates' court. Punishments include imprisonment, fines, suspended terms of imprisonment (which only come into operation if the offender is guilty of further offences during a specified period), probation, and community service. Overcrowding in prisons and the cost of imprisonment have led to recent experiments with noncustodial sentences such as electronic tags fixed to the body to reinforce curfew orders on convicted criminals in the community. The total cost of criminal justice services for England and Wales was £7 billion in 1990, an increase of 77% in real terms from 1980.

custody the state of being held in confinement by the police or prison authorities. Following an arrest, a person may either be kept in custody or released on bail. Custody is also the legal guardianship of a child; a parent, guardian, or authority who has custody of a child usually exercises all parental rights.

In custody

Offenders imprisoned in the UK in 1990 (excluding fine defaulters)

	Males	*Females*	*Total*
Violent offences	6,699	217	6,916
Sexual offences	2,057	12	2,069
Burglary	8,991	99	9,090
Robbery	2,623	68	2,691
Theft, handling, fraud and forgery	10,167	822	10,989
Drugs offences	2,275	266	2,541
Other offences	9,811	381	10,192
Offences not recorded	6,113	250	6,363
Total	***48,736***	***2,115***	***50,851***

Source: NACRO

damages compensation for a tort (such as personal injuries caused by negligence) or breach of contract. In the case of breach of contract the complainant can claim all the financial loss he or she has suffered.

Damages for personal injuries include compensation for loss of earnings, as well as for the injury itself. The court might reduce the damages if the claimant was partly to blame. In the majority of cases, the parties involved reach an out-of-court settlement (a compromise without going to court).

decree nisi conditional order of divorce. A ***decree absolute*** is normally granted six weeks after the decree nisi, and from the date of the decree absolute the parties cease to be husband and wife.

deed legal document that passes an interest in property or binds a person to perform or abstain from some action. Deeds are of two kinds: indenture and deed poll. ***Indentures*** bind two or more parties in mutual obligations. A ***deed poll*** is made by one party only, such as when a person changes his or her name.

defamation an attack on a person's reputation by libel or slander.

defence collective term for the defendant and his or her legal advisors and representatives. It is also the case made in answer to the action or claim being made against the defendant.

defendant a person against whom court proceedings are brought.

Director of Public Prosecutions (DPP) in the UK, the head of the Crown Prosecution Service (established 1985), responsible for the conduct of all criminal prosecutions in England and Wales. The DPP was formerly responsible only for the prosecution of certain serious crimes, such as murder.

divorce legal dissolution of a lawful marriage. It is distinct from an annulment, which is a legal declaration that the marriage was invalid. The ease with which a divorce can be obtained in different countries varies considerably and is also affected by different religious practices.

easement rights that a person may have over the land of another. A common example is a right of way; others are the right to bring water over another's land and the right to a sufficient quantity of light.

ecclesiastical law church law. In England, the Church of England has special ecclesiastical courts to administer church law. Each diocese has a consistory court with a right of appeal to the Court of Arches (in the archbishop of Canterbury's jurisdiction) or the Chancery Court of York (in the archbishop of York's jurisdiction). They deal with the constitution of the Church of England, church property, the clergy, services, doctrine, and practice. These courts have no influence on churches of other denominations, which are governed by the usual laws of contract and trust.

employment law law covering the rights and duties of employers and employees. During the 20th century, statute law rather than common law has increasingly been used to give new rights to employees. Industrial tribunals are statutory bodies that adjudicate in disputes between employers and employees or trade unions and deal with complaints concerning unfair dismissal, sex or race discrimination, and equal pay. Discrimination against employees on the ground of their sex or race is illegal under the Sex Discrimination Act 1975 and the Race Relations Act 1976.

English law one of the major European legal systems, Roman law being the other. English law has spread to many other countries, including former English colonies such as the USA, Canada, Australia, and New Zealand.

equal opportunities the right to be employed or considered for employment without discrimination on the grounds of race, gender, physical or mental handicap.

equity system of law supplementing the ordinary rules of law where the application of these would operate harshly in a particular case; sometimes it is regarded as an attempt to achieve 'natural justice'. So understood, equity appears as an element in most legal systems, and in a number of legal codes judges are instructed to apply both the rules of strict law and the principles of equity in reaching their decisions.

escrow document sealed and delivered to a third party and not released or coming into effect until some condition has been fulfilled or performed, whereupon the document takes full effect.

executor a person appointed in a will to carry out the instructions of the deceased. A person so named has the right to refuse to act. The executor also has a duty to bury the deceased, prove the will, and obtain a grant of probate (that is, establish that the will is genuine and obtain official approval of his or her actions).

extradition surrender, by one state or country to another, of a person accused of a criminal offence in the state or country to which that person is extradited. When two nations are involved, extradition is usually governed by a treaty between the two countries concerned. A country usually will not allow extradition for political offences or an offence that it does not treat as a crime, even though it is a crime in the requesting country.

foreclosure the transfer of title of a mortgaged property from the mortgagor (borrower, usually a home owner) to the mortgagee (loaner, for example a bank) if the mortgagor is in breach of the mortgage agreement, usually by failing to make a number of payments on the mortgage (loan).

forgery the making of a false document, painting, or object with deliberate intention to deceive or defraud. The most common forgeries involve financial instruments such as cheques or credit-card transactions or money (counterfeiting). There are also literary forgeries, forged coins, and forged antiques.

fraud an act of deception resulting in injury to another. To establish fraud it has to be demonstrated that (1) a false representation (for example, a factually untrue statement) has been made, with the intention that it should be acted upon; (2) the person making the representation knows it is false or does not attempt to find out whether it is true or not; and (3) the person to whom the representation is made acts upon it to his or her detriment. A contract based on fraud can be declared void, and the injured party can sue for damages.

freehold in England and Wales, ownership of land for an indefinite period. It is contrasted with a leasehold, which is always for a fixed period. In practical effect, a freehold is absolute ownership.

grievous bodily harm (GBH) in English law, very serious physical damage suffered by the victim of a crime. The courts have said that judges should not try to define grievous bodily harm but leave it to the jury to decide.

hearsay evidence evidence given by a witness based on information passed to that person by others rather than evidence experienced at first hand by the witness. It is usually not admissible as evidence in criminal proceedings.

homicide the killing of a human being. This may be unlawful, lawful, or excusable, depending on the circumstances. Unlawful homicides include murder, manslaughter, infanticide, and causing death by dangerous driving. Lawful homicide occurs where, for example, a police officer is justified in killing a criminal in the course of apprehension or when a person is killed in self-defence or defence of others.

illegitimacy the status of a child born to a mother who is not legally married; a child may be legitimized by subsequent marriage of the parents. The nationality of the child is usually that of the mother.

indemnity an undertaking to compensate another for damage, loss, trouble, or expenses, or the money paid by way of such compensation – for example, under insurance agreements.

injunction court order that forbids a person to do something, or orders him or her to take certain action. Breach of an injunction is contempt of court.

inquest inquiry held by a coroner into an unexplained death. At an inquest, a coroner is assisted by a jury of between 7 and 11 people. Evidence is on oath, and medical and other witnesses may be summoned.

international law body of rules generally accepted as governing the relations between countries, pioneered by Hugo Grotius, especially in matters of human rights, territory, and war. The scope of the law is now extended to space – for example, the 1967 treaty that (among other things) banned nuclear weapons from space. ***The Genocide Convention*** 1948 declares that acts of killing, causing serious bodily harm, prevention of births, forcible transfer of children, the deliberate infliction of conditions of life calculated to bring about the physical destruction of a group, if those acts are 'committed with intent to destroy, in whole or in part, a national, ethnical, racial or religious group', are international crimes. ***The Geneva Convention*** is a series of international conventions on the laws of war. The Geneva Protocol of 1925 prohibits the use of gas and bacteriological warfare. The 1949 conventions include provision for the protection of sick and wounded soldiers, prisoners of war and certain groups of civilians; a Protocol of 1977 extends such protection and further regulates the law of bombing. Some of the Geneva conventions have been extended to cover civil wars and wars of national liberation.

intestacy absence of a will at a person's death. In law, special legal rules apply on intestacy for appointing administrators to deal with the deceased person's affairs, and for disposing of the deceased person's property in accordance with statutory provisions.

judge person invested with power to hear and determine legal disputes.

judicial review in English law, action in the High Court to review the decisions of lower courts, tribunals, and administrative bodies. Various court orders can be made: ***certiorari*** (which quashes the decision); ***mandamus*** (which commands a duty to be performed); ***prohibition*** (which commands that an action should not be performed because it is unauthorized); a ***declaration*** (which sets out the legal rights or obligations); or an ***injunction***.

jurisprudence the science of law in the abstract – that is, not the study of any particular laws or legal system, but of the principles upon which legal systems are founded.

jury body of lay people (usually 12) sworn to decide the facts of a case and reach a verdict in a court of law. Juries, used mainly in English-speaking countries, are implemented primarily in criminal cases, but also sometimes in civil cases; for example, inquests and libel trials.

In July 1991 a jury at the Old Bailey acquitted Michael Randle and Pat Pottle of helping the Soviet agent George Blake escape from prison in 1966. The two defendants were prosecuted 25 years after the escape following the publication of a book in which they admitted to their part in the escape. The judge told the jury that the two men had no defence in law. However, in an instance of reaching a 'perverse judgment', the jury adopted a common-sense rather than a strict letter-of-the-law approach and disobeyed the judge, acquitting both defendants. The case strengthened support for maintaining the jury system, in the face of abolitionist arguments.

juvenile offender young person who commits a criminal offence. In UK law, young people under the age of 17 are commonly referred to as juveniles,

Young offenders

Percentage of prison population under 21, Council of Europe countries on 1 Feb 1990

Country	*Total prison population*	*Percentage under 21*
Ireland	2,104	27.0
UK	53,182	20.7
Cyprus	225	16.0
Netherlands	6,405	14.5 (under 23)
France	46,798	11.1
Portugal	8,730	8.7
Spain	31,711	8.5
Finland	3,537	6.7
Norway	2,260	6.0 (on 1.9.90)
Iceland	101	5.9
Sweden	5,046	4.2
Turkey	46,357	2.8 (under 18; on 1.9.90)
Austria	6,294	2.3 (under 19)
Luxembourg	347	0.6
Belgium	7,001	0.3 (under 18)
Switzerland	5,074	0.1 (under 18; on 1.9.90)

Source: Council of Europe/NACRO

although for some purposes a distinction is made between 'children' (under the age of 14) and 'young persons' (14–16). A juvenile under the age of ten may not be found guilty of an offence. Most legal proceedings in respect of juveniles are brought in specially constituted magistrates' courts known as juvenile courts, where the procedure is simpler and less formal than in an adult magistrates' court. Members of the public are not admitted and the name of the juvenile may not be disclosed in any report of the proceedings.

King's Counsel in England, a barrister of senior rank; the term is used when a king is on the throne and ***Queen's Counsel*** when the monarch is a queen.

larceny in the USA, and formerly in the UK, theft, the taking of personal property without consent and with the intention of permanently depriving the owner of it. In the UK until 1827 larceny was divided into 'grand larceny', punishable by death or transportation for life, and 'petty larceny', when the stolen articles were valued at less than a shilling (one-twentieth of a pound; approximately two weeks' wages for a labourer at the time).

law lords in England, the ten Lords of Appeal in Ordinary who, together with the Lord Chancellor and other peers, make up the House of Lords in its judicial capacity. The House of Lords is the final court of appeal in both criminal and civil cases. Law lords rank as life peers.

leasehold land or property held by a tenant (lessee) for a specified period, (unlike freehold, outright ownership) usually at a rent from the landlord (lessor).

legacy gift of personal property made by a testator in a will and transferred on the testator's death to the legatee. ***Specific legacies*** are definite named objects; a ***general legacy*** is a sum of money or item not specially identified; a ***residuary legacy*** is all the remainder of the deceased's personal estate after debts have been paid and the other legacies have been distributed.

legal aid public assistance with legal costs. In Britain it is given only to those below certain thresholds of income and unable to meet the costs. There are separate provisions for civil and criminal cases. Since 1989 legal aid is administered by the Legal Aid Board.

libel defamation published in a permanent form, such as in a newspaper, book, or broadcast.

licensing laws laws governing the sale of alcoholic drinks. Most countries have some restrictions on the sale of alcoholic drinks, if not an outright ban, as in the case of Islamic countries.

lien the right to retain goods owned by another until the owner has satisfied a claim against him by the person in possession of the goods. For example, the goods may have been provided as security for a debt.

Lord Advocate chief law officer of the crown in Scotland who has ultimate responsibility for criminal prosecutions in Scotland. The Lord Advocate does not usually act in inferior courts, where prosecution is carried out by procurators-fiscal acting under the Lord Advocate's instructions.

Lord Chancellor UK state official, originally the royal secretary, today a member of the cabinet, whose office ends with a change of government. The Lord Chancellor acts as speaker of the House of Lords, may preside over the Court of Appeal, and is head of the judiciary.

magistrate in English law, a person who presides in a magistrates' court: either a justice of the peace (with no legal qualifications, and unpaid) or a stipendiary magistrate. Stipendiary magistrates are paid, qualified lawyers working mainly in London and major cities.

maintenance payments to support children or a spouse, under the terms of an agreement, or by a court order. In Britain, financial provision orders are made on divorce, but a court action can also be brought for maintenance without divorce proceedings. Applications for maintenance of illegitimate children are now treated in the same way as for legitimate children.

malpractice in US law, negligence by a professional person, usually a doctor, that may lead to an action for damages by the client. Such legal actions result in doctors having high insurance costs that are reflected in higher fees charged to their patients.

manslaughter in English law, the unlawful killing of a human being in circumstances less culpable than murder – for example, when the killer suffers extreme provocation, is in some way mentally ill (diminished responsibility), did not intend to kill but did so accidentally in the course of another crime or by behaving with criminal recklessness, or is the survivor of a genuine suicide pact that involved killing the other person.

maritime law that part of the law dealing with the sea: in particular, fishing areas, ships, and navigation. Seas are divided into ***internal waters*** governed by a state's internal laws (such as harbours, inlets); ***territorial waters*** (the area of sea adjoining the coast over which a state claims rights); the ***continental shelf*** (the seabed and subsoil that the coastal state is entitled to exploit beyond the territorial waters); and the ***high seas***, where international law applies.

martial law replacement of civilian by military authorities in the maintenance of order.

minor legal term for those under the age of majority, which varies from country to country but is usually between 18 and 21. In the USA (from 1971 for voting, and in some states for nearly all other purposes) and certain European countries (in Britain since 1970) the age of majority is 18. Most civic and legal rights and duties only accrue at the age of majority: for example, the rights to vote, to make a will, and (usually) to make a fully binding contract, and the duty to act as a juror.

motoring law law affecting the use of vehicles on public roads. It covers the licensing of vehicles and drivers, and the criminal offences that can be committed by the owners and drivers of vehicles.

murder unlawful killing of one person by another. In the USA, first-degree murder requires proof of premeditation; second-degree murder falls between first-degree murder and manslaughter.

negligence negligence consists in doing some act that a 'prudent and reasonable' person would not do, or omitting to do some act that such a person would do. Negligence may arise in respect of a person's duty towards an individual or towards other people in general. Breach of the duty of care that results in reasonably foreseeable damage is a tort. ***Contributory negligence*** is a defence sometimes raised where the defendant to an action for negligence claims that the plaintiff by his or her own action contributed to the cause of the action.

neighbourhood watch local crime-prevention scheme. Under the supervision of police, groups of residents agree to increase watchfulness in order to prevent crimes such as burglary and vandalism in their area.

oath solemn promise to tell the truth or perform some duty, combined with a declaration naming a deity or something held sacred.

obscenity law law established by the Obscene Publications Act 1959 prohibiting the publishing of any material that tends to deprave or corrupt.

parole conditional release of a prisoner from jail. The prisoner remains on licence until the date release would have been granted, and may be recalled if the authorities deem it necessary. Under the Criminal Justice Act 1991 parole is automatic for sentences under four years.

party a person who takes part in legal proceedings. Parties to a civil action may include one or more plaintiffs or defendants. In the UK, the parties in a criminal trial include the Crown (as prosecutor) and one or more defendants.

patent or ***letters patent*** documents conferring the exclusive right to make, use, and sell an invention for a limited period. Ideas are not eligible; neither is anything not new. In 1987 the USA began issuing patents for new animal forms (new types of livestock and assorted organisms) being created by gene splitting. The payment of $909.5 million by Eastman Kodak to Polaroid 1990 was a record sum for infringement of patent.

perjury the offence of deliberately making a false statement on oath (or affirmation) when appearing as a witness in legal proceedings, on a point material to the question at issue. In Britain and the USA it is punishable by a fine, imprisonment, or both.

perverting the course of justice the criminal offence of acting in such a way as to prevent justice being done. Examples are tampering with evidence, misleading the police or a court, and threatening witnesses or jurors.

picketing gathering of workers and their trade-union representatives to try to persuade others to support them in an industrial dispute. In the UK, the Employment Act 1980 restricted the right to picket to a striker's own place of work and outlawed secondary picketing (that is, at other workplaces). This allows employers or other persons picketed to sue pickets who are not at their own workplace and who are attempting to persuade other workers to break their contracts.

plaintiff person who brings a civil action in a court of law seeking relief (for example, damages).

poaching illegal hunting of game and fish on someone else's property.

police civil law-and-order force. In the UK it is responsible to the Home Office, with 56 autonomous police forces, generally organized on a county basis; mutual aid is given in circumstances such as mass picketing in the 1984–85 miners' strike, but there is no national police force or police riot unit (such as the French CRS riot squad). Unlike most other police forces, the British are armed only on special occasions, but arms issues grow more frequent.

Fewer crimes solved?

Number of crimes solved as a percentage of total recorded offences (by region, UK)

	1990	*1991*	*1992*
Avon	29	24	17
Bedfordshire	19	19	20
Cambridgeshire	38	36	27*
Cheshire	50	41	29
Cleveland	25	33	32
Cumbria	43	40	37
Devon & Cornwall	32	29	18*
Dorset	35	41	32
Durham	34	30	30
Gloucestershire	33	35	24
Hertfordshire	30	33	25
Leicestershire	36	29	29
Lincolnshire	43	46	38*
Northamptonshire	35	31	30
Northumbria	40	35	17
Thames Valley	26	22	20
Warwickshire	29	24	23*
West Mercia	46	35	34*
West Midlands	36	31	26
West Yorkshire	34	28	25
Wiltshire	44	40	37
Gwent	51	47	44*

** unpublished*

Source: Home Office

power of attorney legal authority to act on behalf of another, for a specific transaction, or for a particular period.

precedent common law principle that, in deciding a particular case, judges are bound to follow any applicable principles of law laid down by superior courts in earlier reported cases.

probate formal proof of a will. In the UK, if a will's validity is unquestioned, it is proven in 'common form'; the executor, in the absence of other interested parties, obtains at a probate registry a grant upon his or her own oath. Otherwise, it must be proved in 'solemn form': its validity established at a probate court (in the Chancery Division of the High Court), those concerned being made parties to the action.

probation the placing of offenders under supervision of probation officers in the community, as an alternative to prison.

procurator fiscal officer of a Scottish sheriff's court who (combining the role of public prosecutor and coroner) inquires into suspicious deaths and carries out the preliminary questioning of witnesses to crime.

prosecution the party instituting legal proceedings. In the UK, the prosecution of a criminal case is begun by bringing the accused (defendant) before a magistrate, either by warrant or summons, or by arrest without warrant. Most criminal prosecutions are conducted by the Crown Prosecution Service, although other government departments may also prosecute some cases; for example, the Department of Inland Revenue. An individual may bring a private prosecution, usually for assault.

provost chief magistrate of a Scottish burgh, approximate equivalent of an English mayor.

proxy person authorized to stand in another's place; also the document conferring this right. The term usually refers to voting at meetings, but marriages by proxy are possible.

public inquiry in English law, a legal investigation where witnesses are called and evidence is produced in a similar fashion to a court of law. Inquiries may be held as part of legal procedure, or into a matter of public concern.

quarter session former local criminal court in England, replaced 1972 by crown courts.

Queen's Counsel (QC) in England, a barrister appointed to senior rank by the Lord Chancellor. When the monarch is a king the term is ***King's Counsel (KC)***.

rape sexual intercourse without the consent of the subject. Most cases of rape are of women by men. A new ruling in 1991 made rape within marriage an offence; in the first prosecution of such a case a London man was found guilty of raping his wife and jailed for five years.

receiver person appointed by a court to collect and manage the assets of an individual, company, or partnership in serious financial difficulties. In the case of bankruptcy, the assets may be sold and distributed by a receiver to creditors.

redundancy rights in British law, the rights of employees to a payment (linked to the length of their employment) if they lose their jobs because they are no longer needed. The statutory right was introduced 1965, but payments are often made in excess of the statutory scheme.

remand the committing of an accused but not convicted person into custody or to release on bail pending a court hearing.

reply, right of right of a member of the public to respond to a media statement. A statutory right of reply, enforceable by a Press Commission, as exists in many Western European countries, failed to reach the statute book in the UK in 1989. There is no legal provision in the UK that any correction should receive the same prominence as the original statement and legal aid is not available in defamation cases, so that only the wealthy are able to sue. However, the major newspapers signed a Code of Practice in 1989 that promised some public protection.

reprieve legal temporary suspension of the execution of a sentence of a criminal court. It is usually associated with the death penalty. It is distinct from a pardon (extinguishing the sentence) and commutation (alteration) of a sentence (for example, from death to life imprisonment).

rule of law doctrine that no individual, however powerful, is above the law. The principle had a significant influence on attempts to restrain the arbitrary use of power by rulers and on the growth of legally enforceable human rights in many Western countries. It is often used as a justification for separating legislative from judicial power.

Scots law the legal system of Scotland. Owing to its separate development, Scotland has a system differing from the rest of the UK, being based on civil law. Its continued separate existence was guaranteed by the Act of Union with England in 1707.

settlement out of court a compromise reached between the parties to a legal dispute. Most civil legal actions are settled out of court, reducing legal costs and avoiding the uncertainty of the outcome of a trial.

sheriff in England and Wales, the crown's chief executive officer in a county for ceremonial purposes; in Scotland, the equivalent of the English county-court judge, but also dealing with criminal cases; and in the USA the popularly elected head law-enforcement officer of a county, combining judicial authority with administrative duties.

show trial public and well-reported trial of people accused of crimes against the state. In the USSR in the 1930s and 1940s, Stalin carried out show trials against economic saboteurs, Communist Party members, army officers, and even members of the Bolshevik leadership.

slander spoken defamatory statement; if written, or broadcast on radio or television, it constitutes libel.

solicitor in the UK, a member of one of the two branches of the English legal profession, the other being a barrister. A solicitor is a lawyer who provides all-round legal services (making wills, winding up estates, conveyancing, divorce, and litigation). A solicitor cannot appear at High Court level, but must brief a barrister on behalf of his or her client. Solicitors may become circuit judges and recorders. In the USA the general term is lawyer or attorney.

subpoena order requiring someone who might not otherwise come forward of his or her own volition to give evidence before a court or judicial official at a specific time and place. A witness who fails to comply with a subpoena is in contempt of court.

summons court order officially delivered, requiring someone to appear in court on a certain date.

tagging, electronic long-distance monitoring of the movements of people charged with or convicted of a crime, thus enabling them to be detained in their homes rather than in prison. In the UK, legislation passed 1991 allowed for its use as an aid to bail and as a means of enforcing punishment, for example a curfew. The system is in use in the USA.

telephone tapping listening in on a telephone conversation, without the knowledge of the participants; in the UK and the USA a criminal offence if done

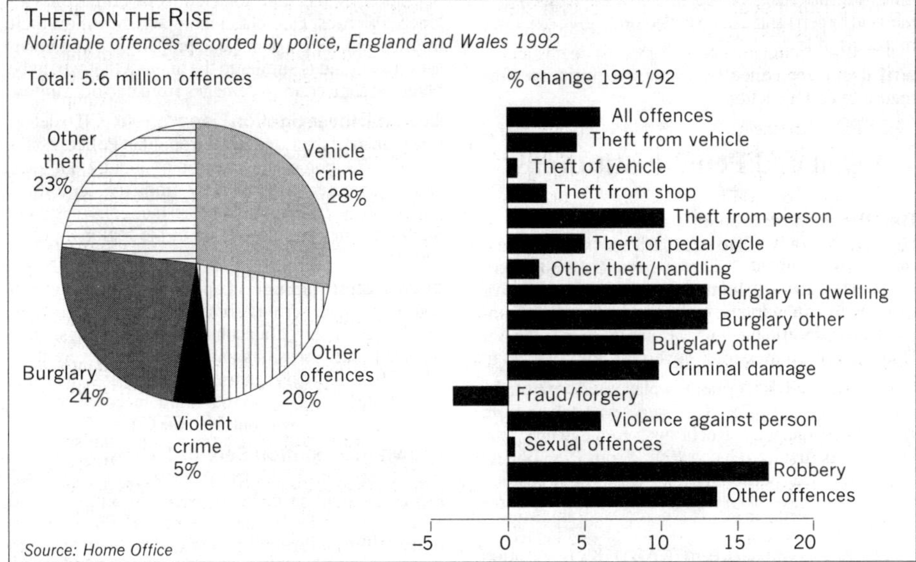

without a warrant or the consent of the person concerned. In the UK, the Interception of Communications Act 1985 allows a tribunal to investigate a complaint from any person believing they have been subject to an interception. Court of Human Rights for widespread telephone tapping by police.

theft dishonest appropriation of another's property with the intention of depriving him or her of it permanently. In Britain, under the Theft Act 1968, the maximum penalty is ten years' imprisonment. The act placed under a single heading forms of theft that had formerly been dealt with individually; for example, burglary and larceny.

tort wrongful act for which someone can be sued for damages in a civil court. It includes such acts as libel, trespass, injury done to someone (whether intentionally or by negligence), and inducement to break a contract (although breach of contract itself is not a tort). In general a tort is distinguished from a crime in that it affects the interests of an individual rather than of society at large, but some crimes can also be torts (for example, assault).

treason act of betrayal, in particular against the sovereign or the state to which the offender owes allegiance. Treason is punishable in Britain by death.

treasure trove in England, any gold or silver, plate or bullion, found concealed in a house or the ground, the owner being unknown. Normally, treasure originally hidden, and not abandoned, belongs to the crown, but if the treasure was casually lost or intentionally abandoned, the first finder is entitled to it against all but the true owner. Objects buried with no intention of recovering them, for example in a burial mound, do not rank as treasure trove, and belong to the owner of the ground.

trespass going on to the land of another without authority. In law, a landowner has the right to eject a trespasser by the use of reasonable force and can sue for any damage caused. A trespasser who refuses to leave when requested may, in certain circumstances, be committing a criminal offence under the Public Order Act 1986 (designed to combat convoys of caravans trespassing on farm land).

trial the determination of an accused person's innocence or guilt by means of the judicial examination of the issues of the case in accordance with the law of the land. The two parties in a trial, the defendant and plaintiff, or their counsels, put forward their cases and question the witnesses; on the basis of this evidence the jury or other tribunal body will decide on the innocence or guilt of the defendant.

tribunal strictly, a court of justice, but used in English law for a body appointed by the government to arbitrate in disputes, or investigate certain matters. Tribunals usually consist of a lawyer as chair, sitting with two lay assessors.

trust arrangement whereby a person or group of people (the trustee or trustees) hold property for others (the beneficiaries) entitled to the beneficial interest.

verdict a jury's decision, usually a finding of 'guilty' or 'not guilty'. In Scotland a third option is 'not proven' where the jury is not convinced either way. In Britain majority verdicts are acceptable if a unanimous verdict cannot be reached.

ward of court in the UK, a child whose guardian is the High Court. Any person may, by issuing proceedings, make the High Court guardian of any child within its jurisdiction. No important step in the child's life can then be taken without the court's leave.

will declaration of how a person wishes his or her property to be disposed of after death. It also appoints administrators of the estate (executors) and may contain wishes on other matters, such as place of burial or use of organs for transplant. Wills must comply with formal legal requirements of the local jurisdiction.

witness person who was present at some event (such as an accident, a crime, or the signing of a document) or has relevant special knowledge (such as a medical expert) and can be called on to give evidence in a court of law.

writ document issued by a court requiring performance of certain actions.

Legal and Penal Institutions

Bar, the the profession of barristers collectively. To be ***called to the Bar*** is to become a barrister. Prospective barristers in the UK must complete a course of study in law and be admitted to one of the four Inns of Court before they can be 'called'. The General Council of the Bar and of the Inns of Court (known as the Bar Council) is the professional governing body of the Bar.

borstal in the UK, formerly a place of detention for offenders aged 15–21. The name was taken from Borstal prison near Rochester, Kent, where the system was first introduced 1908. From 1983 borstal institutions were officially known as youth custody centres, and have been replaced by ***young offender institutions***.

Citizens' Advice Bureau (CAB) UK organization established 1939 to provide information and advice to the public on any subject, such as personal or financial problems, house purchase, or consumer rights. If required, the bureau will act on behalf of citizens, drawing on its own sources of legal and other experts. There are more than 900 bureaux located all over the UK.

county court English court of law created by the County Courts Act 1846 and now governed by the Act of 1984. It exists to try civil cases, such as actions on contract and tort where the claim does not exceed £5,000, and disputes about land, such as between landlord and tenant. County courts are presided over by one or more circuit judges. An appeal on a point of law lies to the Court of Appeal.

Court of Appeal UK court comprising two divisions: a Civil Division and a Criminal Division set up under the Criminal Appeals Act 1968. The Court of Appeal consists of 16 Lord Justices of Appeal and a number of ex-officio judges, for example, the Lord Chancellor, the Master of the Rolls, and the President of the Family Division. Usually, three judges sit, but where a case raises new or important issues, up to seven judges may form the court. The Criminal Division of the Court of Appeal has the power to revise sentences or quash a conviction on the grounds that in all the circumstances of the case the verdict is unsafe or unsatisfactory, or that the judgement of the original trial judge was wrong in law, or that there was a material irregularity during the course of the trial. The Court of Appeal in 1991 had a backlog of appeals by people charged and prosecuted by the West Midlands Serious Crime Squad, which was disbanded due to corruption.

Court of Protection in English law, a department of the High Court that deals with the estates of people who are incapable, by reason of mental disorder, of managing their own property and affairs.

Criminal Injuries Compensation Board UK board established 1964 to administer financial compensation by the state for victims of crimes of violence. Victims can claim compensation for their injuries, but not for damage to property. The compensation awarded is similar to the amount that would be obtained for a court in damages from personal injury.

Criminal Investigation Department (CID) detective branch of the London Metropolitan Police, established 1878, comprising a force of about 4,000 men and women recruited entirely from the uniformed police and controlled by an assistant commissioner. Such branches are also found in the regional police forces.

crown court in England and Wales, any of several courts that hear serious criminal cases referred from magistrates' courts after committal proceedings. They replaced quarter sessions and assizes, which were abolished 1971. Appeals against conviction or sentence at magistrates' courts may be heard in crown courts. Appeal from a crown court is to the Court of Appeal.

Crown Prosecution Service body established by the Prosecution of Offences Act 1985, responsible for prosecuting all criminal offences in England and Wales. It is headed by the Director of Public Prosecutions (DPP), and brings England and Wales in line with Scotland (which has a procurator fiscal) in having a prosecution service independent of the police.

European Court of Human Rights court that hears cases referred from the European Commission of Human Rights, if the commission has failed to negotiate a friendly settlement in a case where individuals' rights have been violated by a member state. The court sits in Strasbourg and comprises one judge for every state that is a party to the 1950 convention. Court rulings have forced the Republic of Ireland to drop its constitutional ban on homosexuality, and Germany to cease to exclude political left- and right-wingers from the civil service.

European Court of Justice the court of the European Community (EC), which is responsible for interpreting Community law and ruling on breaches by member states and others of such law. It sits in Luxembourg with judges from the member states.

Inns of Court four private legal societies in London, England: Lincoln's Inn, Gray's Inn, Inner Temple, and Middle Temple. All barristers (advocates in the English legal system) must belong to one of the Inns of Court. The main function of each Inn is the education, government, and protection of its members. Each is under the administration of a body of Benchers (judges and senior barristers).

International Court of Justice main judicial organ of the United Nations, in The Hague, the Netherlands. It hears international law disputes as well as playing an advisory role to UN organs. It was set up by the UN charter 1945 and superseded the World Court. There are 15 judges, each from a different member state.

Interpol (acronym for ***Inter***national Criminal ***Pol***ice Organization) agency founded following the Second International Judicial Police Conference 1923 with its headquarters in Vienna, and reconstituted after World War II with its headquarters in Paris. It has an international criminal register, fingerprint file, and methods index.

Land Registry, HM official body set up in 1925 to register legal rights to land in England and Wales. There has been a gradual introduction, since 1925, of compulsory registration of land in different areas of the country. This requires the purchaser of land to register details of his or her title and all other rights (such as mortgages and easements) relating to the land. Once registered, the title to the land is guaranteed by the Land Registry, subject to those interests that cannot be registered; this makes the buying and selling of land easier and cheaper. The records are open to public inspection (since Dec 1990).

Law Commission in the UK, either of two statutory bodies established in 1965 (one for England and Wales and one for Scotland) which consider proposals for law reform and publish their findings. They also keep British law under constant review, systematically developing and reforming it by, for example, the repeal of obsolete and unnecessary enactments.

law courts bodies that adjudicate in legal disputes. Civil and criminal cases are usually dealt with by separate courts. In many countries there is a hierarchy of courts that provide an appeal system.

In England and Wales the court system was reorganized under the Courts Act 1971. The higher courts are: the ***House of Lords*** (the highest court for the whole of Britain), which deals with both civil and criminal appeals; the ***Court of Appeal***, which is divided between criminal and civil appeal courts; the ***High Court of Justice*** dealing with important civil cases; ***crown courts***, which handle criminal cases; and ***county courts***, which deal with civil matters. ***Magistrates' courts*** deal with minor criminal cases and are served by justices of the peace or stipendiary (paid) magistrates; and ***juvenile courts*** are presided over by specially qualified justices. There are also special courts, such as the Restrictive Practices Court and the Employment Appeal Tribunal. The courts are organized in six circuits. The towns of each circuit are first-tier (High Court and circuit judges dealing with both criminal and civil cases), second-tier (High Court and circuit judges dealing with criminal cases only), or third-tier (circuit judges dealing with criminal cases only). Cases are allotted according to gravity among High Court and circuit judges and recorders (part-time judges with the same jurisdiction as circuit judges). In 1971 solicitors were allowed for the first time to appear in and conduct cases at the level of the crown courts, and solicitors as well as barristers of ten years' standing became eligible for appointment as recorders, who after five years become eligible as circuit judges. In 1989 a Green Paper proposed (1) omitting the Bar's monopoly of higher courts, removing demarcation between barristers and solicitors; (2) cases to be taken on a 'no win, no fee' basis (as already happens in Scotland). In the UK in 1989 there were 5,500 barristers and 47,000 solicitors. In Scotland, the supreme civil court is the Court of Session, with appeal to the House of Lords; the highest criminal court is the ***High Court of Justiciary***, with no appeal to the House of Lords.

magistrates' court in England and Wales, a local law court that mainly deals with minor criminal cases, but also decides, in committal proceedings, whether more serious criminal cases should be referred to the crown court. It deals with some civil matters, too, such as licensing certain domestic and matrimonial proceedings, and may include a juvenile court. A magistrates' court consists of between two and seven lay justices of the peace (who are advised on the law by a clerk to the justices), or a single paid lawyer called a stipendiary magistrate.

Old Bailey popular name for the Central Criminal Court in London, situated in a street of that name in the City of London, off Ludgate Hill.

Police Complaints Authority in the UK, an independent group of a dozen people set up under the Police and Criminal Evidence Act 1984 to supervise the investigation of complaints against the police by members of the public. When the investigation of a complaint is completed the authority must make a public declaration of its decision. It can order disci-

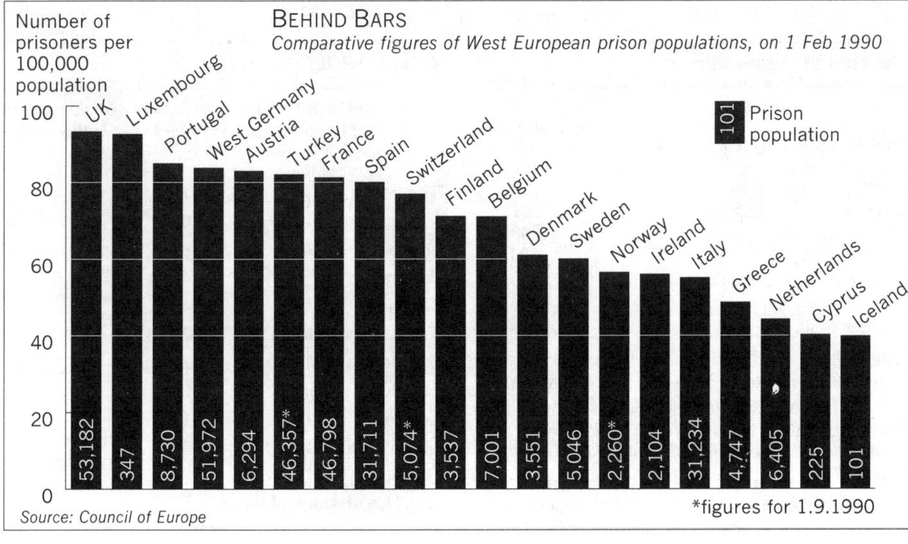

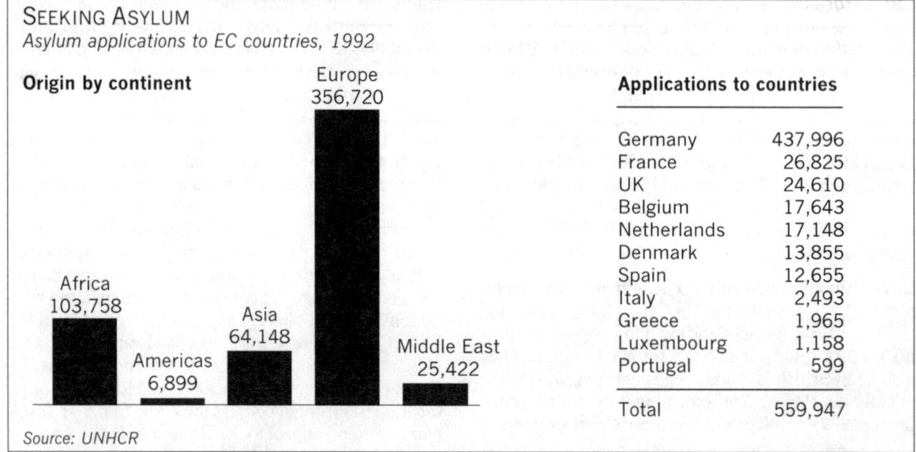

plinary action to be taken against police officers. Alternatively, a complainant may take a case to court. The number of successful civil actions against the police rises every year.

prison place of confinement for those convicted of contravening the laws of the state; most countries claim to aim also at rehabilitation. The approximate number of people in prison in the UK (1993) was 53,000. It costs 30 times more per year to keep a prisoner in custody than it would for 100 hours' community service.

Experiments have been made in Britain and elsewhere in 'open prisons' without bars, which included releasing prisoners in the final stages of their sentence to work in ordinary jobs outside the prison, and the provision of aftercare on release. Attempts to deal with the increasing number of young offenders include, from 1982, accommodation in community homes in the case of minor offences, with (in more serious cases) 'short, sharp shock' treatment in detention centres (although the latter was subsequently found to have little effect on reconviction rates).

In April 1992, The Wolds, Britain's first privatized prison, opened. Situated near Hull, it accommodates 320 remand prisoners.

Writers to the Signet society of Scottish solicitors. Their predecessors were originally clerks in the secretary of state's office entrusted with the preparation of documents requiring the signet, or seal. Scottish solicitors may be members of other societies, such as the Royal Faculty of Procurators in Glasgow.

young offender institution in the UK, establishment of detention for lawbreakers under 17 (juveniles) and 17–21 (young adults). The period of detention depends on the seriousness of the offence and on the age and sex of the offender. A number of statutory requirements support the principle that a custodial sentence in a young offender institution should be used only as a last resort. The institution was introduced by the Criminal Justice Act 1988.

The cost of imprisonment

	£
Local prisons and adult remand centres	388
Dispersal prisons	616
Category B training prisons	368
Category C training prisons	297
Open adult prisons	293
Closed youth establishments	390
Open youth establishments	550
Female establishments	563
Overall average	386

In the financial year 1990/91, the average cost of keeping a person in prison was £386 a week. The costs ranged from £293 a week for open prisons to £616 a week for maximum security dispersal prisons. Staff costs accounted for 83% of the net operating costs in penal establishments.

Source: NACRO

GALLUP POLL: Police

Which one of the following groups of people do you think most urgently needs to build trust in the eyes of the public?

The police	41
Politicians	28
Doctors	8
Journalists	4
Teachers	4
Trade union leaders	3
People in the City	2
Religious leaders	2
Lawyers	1
Military top brass	0
Scientists	0
Don't know/None of these	5

Fears for personal safety

On a different topic, how safe do you feel when you are alone during the day on your neighbourhood streets – very safe, somewhat safe, somewhat unsafe, or very unsafe?

	Very safe	Somewhat safe	Somewhat unsafe	Very unsafe	Don't know
July 1992	50	33	12	5	1
June 1986	63	28	6	2	2
And what about being out alone at night in your neighbourhood streets?					
July 1992	28	28	24	18	2
June 1986	33	28	21	14	3
And being out alone during the day in the local shopping area?					
July 1992	59	32	5	2	1
June 1986	72	22	3	1	1
And being alone at home during the day?					
July 1992	71	22	4	2	1
June 1986	81	15	2	1	2
And being alone at home at night?					
July 1992	56	26	12	5	1
June 1986	61	25	8	4	2

Rape

Would you classify each of the following statements as rape or not…

	Yes	No	Don't know
A married man has sex with his wife even though she does not want to	61	26	13
A man uses emotional pressure, but not physical force, to get a woman to have sex	35	50	15
A man has sex with a woman who has passed out after drinking too much	81	11	9
A man argues with a woman who does not want to have sex until she agrees to have sex	40	46	14
A man and a woman get drunk and have sex	7	84	9

Justice

Do you think our system of law and justice is or is not:

	Jun 1992	Feb 1985
Efficient?		
Is	27	51
Is not	66	45
Don't know	8	4
Fair to everybody?		
Is	15	34
Is not	78	62
Don't know	7	4

In your opinion, do the courts in this country dispense justice impartially or do they favour the rich and influential?

	Jun 1992	Feb 1985
Impartial	24	42
Favour the rich	64	50
Don't know	12	9

Capital punishment

Do you think that capital punishment (or the death penalty) should or should not be brought back for all persons convicted of murder? And for terrorists and bombers convicted of murder?

	All persons convicted of murder	Terrorists/bombers convicted of murder
Should	42	66
Should not	44	26
Don't know	14	8

If it were proved that an innocent man or woman had been wrongly convicted of a murder and hanged, would this alter your views about the death penalty? (All saying 'supported capital punishment for all persons and/or terrorists/bombers convicted of murder' = 100%)

No, would still support the death penalty	62
Yes, I would not want the death penalty brought back	23
Don't know	15

MEDIA

Press and TV Media

ABC American Broadcasting Company, absorbed 1986 into Capital Cities/ABC (see below).

Agence France-Presse the world's oldest and third largest news agency, founded in 1835. It is based in Paris and by 1992 had six 24-hour news wires in six languages, 200 bureaux, and 2,000 correspondents worldwide.

Associated Press (AP) the world's largest news service. It is a nonprofit cooperative wire news service, founded in 1848. AP has (1992) 16,200 print and broadcast subscribers in 110 countries; it is also available to individuals through on-line information services. It has 229 bureaux and more than 3,000 correspondents worldwide; headquarters in New York City.

British Broadcasting Corporation (BBC) UK state-owned broadcasting network, established as a private company 1922 and converted to a public body 1927. It operates television and national and local radio stations, and is financed solely by the sale of television viewing licences; it is not allowed to carry advertisements. Overseas radio broadcasts (World Service) have a government subsidy.

BSkyB (British Sky Broadcasting) British group of satellite TV channels, formed 1990 by a merger between Sky Television and British Satellite Broadcasting. In 1992 BSkyB operated six channels from the Astra satellite: Sky News, Sky One, Sky Movies Plus, the Movie Channel, the Comedy Channel, and Sky Sports. Rupert Murdoch's News Corporation holds a 50% interest.

Cable News Network (CNN) international television news channel; the 24-hour service was founded 1980 by US entrepreneur Ted Turner and has its headquarters in Atlanta, Georgia. CNN is owned by Turner Broadcasting – which also owns the satellite channels TBS, TNT, and Headline News (as well as the Atlanta Braves baseball team) – and had a 1992 turnover of $1,769.8 million. It established its global reputation in 1991 with eyewitness accounts from Baghdad of the beginning of the Gulf War.

Capital Cities/ABC US television and radio network, one of the three biggest in the country. The company owns eight TV and 21 radio stations, three cable TV channels, nine daily newspapers, as well as weekly papers, shopping guides, and magazines; its 1992 turnover was $5,344.1 million. ABC was founded 1943 when NBC was forced to sell off one of its two networks. It was taken over by Capital Cities in 1986.

CBC (Canadian Broadcasting Corporation or Société Radio-Canada) the national radio and television service of Canada. CBC was set up in 1936. It is primarily government-funded; the rest (about 30%) comes from advertising. It was the first system to use a geostationary satellite.

CBS (Columbia Broadcasting System) US television and radio network. Founded in 1927 as a rival radio network to NBC, CBS set up its first TV station in New York in 1931. It owns seven TV stations, 21 radio stations and, in 1991, acquired Midwest Communications, which included TV, radio stations, and a sports cable channel. The company's 1992 turnover was $3,503 million, with a profit of $81 million, after its 1991 $85.8 million loss.

Reaching consumers

UK advertising expenditure by media (at constant 1985 prices)

	1981 £m	*1981* %	*1991* £m	*1991* %
National newspapers	590	14.7	794	13.2
Regional newspapers	864	21.5	1,153	19.2
Consumer magazines	291	7.2	310	5.2
Business and professional	326	8.1	501	8.3
Directories	123	3.1	357	5.9
Press production costs*	185	4.6	295	4.9
Total press	***2,379***	***59.2***	***3,410***	***56.7***
Television	1,023	25.4	1,632	27.2
Direct mail	378	9.4	634	10.6
Poster and transport	145	3.6	189	3.1
Radio	76	1.9	106	1.8
Cinema	23	0.6	30	0.5
Total all advertising	***4,024***	***100.0+***	***6.001***	***100.0+***

** The production costs of advertisements are shown separately for the press but are included in the figures for the other media.*
+ Figures do not sum to 100 due to rounding.

Source: Advertising Association's Statistics Yearbook 1992

European Broadcasting Union (EBU) organization of W European public and national broadcasters, set up in 1950. The EBU manages Eurovision, founded 1954, a network for the exchange of programmes and news, and Euroradio, founded 1989.

Independent Television Commission (ITC) (formerly the Independent Broadcasting Authority) UK corporate body established by legislation to provide commercially funded television (ITV from 1955) and local radio (ILR from 1973) services. In the 1980s, services expanded to include the launching of Channel 4 (1982) and the provision of satellite television: services broadcast directly by satellite into homes (DBS).

ITAR-TASS (Information Telegraph Agency of Russia) Russian news service. Formerly TASS (the official Soviet news agency, founded in St Petersburg in 1925), ITAR-TASS supplies information in seven languages, and has bureaux in approximately 100 countries.

Maxwell Communications UK media group, broken up in 1991 after Robert Maxwell's death. Heavily debt-ridden, Maxwell Communications was the fifth largest European media group in 1991; by 1992 it was gone. Of its subsidiaries, Pergamon Press

56 channels and nothing on?

The changes to British broadcasting brought by the 1991 TV franchise auction were followed up in 1992 with a similar auction of two national commercial radio franchises. Of the unexpectedly few bidders who applied, Virgin and Classic FM were the two who won franchises. Classic had been outbid for the franchise by Showtime Radio, but won the franchise when Showtime failed to come up with the money in time.

Classic FM was the first to be launched, on 7 Sept 1992. Major shareholders are Time Warner (35%), Cray Electronics chair Sir Peter Michael (35%), and radio group GWR (17.5%), with small stakes held by Brian Brolly, a former managing director of Andrew Lloyd Webber's Really Useful Group (5%), and Associated Newspapers' Harmsworth Media (4.5%). Virgin Radio, launched on 30 April 1993, is jointly owned by Virgin and TV-am.

Both stations are part of a new era of competition for the BBC. Virgin, with its emphasis on classic rock, targets Radio One's audience, while Classic FM's popular-classics approach is intended to appeal to Radio Three listeners, said to be tired of the station's esoteric choice of programming. The two new national stations join more than 100 independent local radio stations, up from only 33 in 1980.

The growth in radio is paralleled by the proliferation of television channels. While Britain still has only four terrestrial TV channels, satellite TV burgeoned in 1991 and 1992. The biggest-selling satellite system, a fixed dish set up to receive signals from the Astra satellite, got a boost in 1992 when a second Astra satellite went up, raising the potential number of Astra channels to 32. A third Astra satellite, scheduled for the end of 1993, was to add another 16.

Not all the transponders are in use; nonetheless in 1992 British Astra viewers received a minimum of 19 German, Dutch, Scandinavian, and British channels, or 23 if they paid for BSkyB's premium channels: Sky Movies Plus, the Movie Channel, Sky Sports, and Sky Movies Gold. The BSkyB stations, plus CNN and the other English-language satellite channels, also got a boost from the increased availability of cable. What is often forgotten is that satellite also carries radio – the Astra satellites alone carry some 30 radio stations, including satellite feeds of BBC Radio One and Four, and CNN Radio. However, Britain still lagged far behind the USA, where by 1992 many areas were already receiving 60 to 100 TV channels.

1992 was not all growth. Eurosport, one of two free sports channels, first went off the air briefly, then was purchased by a European consortium, and finally merged with the other free sports channel, Screensport. Screensport's place on the satellite was taken by a new German channel, RTL-2, 17.5% of which is owned by Bertelsmann, which also owns a 38.9% stake in the established station RTL-Plus. Also new in 1992 was DSF, a German sports channel, in which majority shareholders are Fininvest (41%) and Axel Springer (25%). Axel Springer also owns 20% of the German station Sat 1.

Such cross-media ownership has generally characterized satellite television, but not British terrestrial television. At the beginning of 1993, however, that began to change: Pearson, owner of Penguin Books and the *Financial Times*, bid successfully to buy Thorn EMI's 59% stake in Thames TV. Thames, the shock loser in the 1991 TV franchise auction, is the producer of some of Britain's most popular and longest-running shows. Meanwhile Pearson, which also owns a 14% stake in Yorkshire/Tyne Tees, is a partner in BSkyB. Further changes to the shape of the industry are expected in the run-up to 1996, when the BBC's charter is up for renewal.

Arguments about the number and type of channels tend to revolve around the question of viewer choice: depending on what you believe, either more channels mean more choices, or more channels mean lower-quality programming. The truth is a combination of the two. A number of the satellite channels do offer material that is unavailable on existing channels – 24-hour news, minority-interest sporting events, uncut films, reruns of classic British shows. On the other hand, the mass of terrestrial viewers lose out when satellite channels outbid terrestrial channels for the popular programmes they have traditionally shown, such as football and boxing. It therefore worries terrestrial broadcasters that Britain's largest programme producer might fall into the hands of a company with a large stake in a satellite channel.

The proliferation of channels also has an unexpected social impact, as has already been seen in the USA: audiences are fragmented. It becomes harder for any single programme to have the widespread impact of old TV and radio soaps like *Coronation Street* and *The Archers*. The same does not apply to advertisements, which typically appear on more than one channel and even in more than one country. The hugely successful Gold Blend ads, which feature a couple seemingly always on the point of romance, appeared all over both British and US dials. The Gold Blend series made history in 1992 for another reason: it was the first series of ads to be made into a book.

WG

Global dailies

Number and circulation of daily newspapers worldwide

Continents, major areas	Number of dailies		Estimated circulation: Total m		Estimated circulation: per '000 inhabitants	
	1975	1990	1975	1990	1975	1990
Africa	170	200	5	11	12	17
Asia	2,190	3,580	128	198	55	64
Europe (including former USSR)	2,350	2,430	221	261	304	332
Oceania	120	110	6	5	299	206
Northern America	1,900	1,720	66	68	275	248
Latin America and the Caribbean	1,050	1,180	23	42	73	94
World total	***7,780***	***9,220***	***450***	***586***	***110***	***111***

Source: UNESCO

was sold to Elsevier, Maxwell Business Publishing was sold to EMAP, and the Mirror Group was floated on the London Stock Exchange as an independent company.

NBC (National Broadcasting Company) US television and radio network. NBC, founded 1926, is a wholly owned subsidiary of RCA (Radio Corporation of America), which was bought in 1985 by General Electric, which also owns the Financial News Network. Besides its broadcast network, NBC also has a 24-hour news channel, CNBC.

PBS (Public Broadcasting System) US public TV network of more than 300 stations. PBS and NPR (National Public Radio) were created by the Corporation for Public Broadcasting, which was set up by President Lyndon Johnson in 1967, to distribute programmes to educational TV and radio. Both are financed by a mix of government funding and public donations.

Reuters news and financial information service with (1992) 177 bureaux in 79 countries. It was founded 1851 by Baron Paul Julius von Reuter (1816–1899), and is based in London. Reuters is the largest shareholder in the television news service Visnews. Its 1991 turnover was £1,466.6 million.

RTE (Radio Telefis Eireann) the national radio and television service of the Republic of Ireland. Radio broadcasting began in Dublin 1926 and in Cork 1927. Television broadcasting started 1961. Both are financed by a mix of licence fees and advertising revenues.

United Press International (UPI) wire news service based in Washington DC. Originally founded in 1907 by publisher E W Scripps as United Press, it became UPI in 1958 after a merger with William Randolph Hearst's International News Service. In August 1991 it filed for bankruptcy; in 1992 the service was auctioned and sold to Saudi-owned Middle-East Broadcasting for $3.75 million.

Visnews TV news agency. Visnews, founded 1957 and based in London, has 35 bureaus worldwide, and provides international news to CBS, Fox, and NBC, which has a 37.5% stake in the company. Its other shareholders are Reuters, which is the majority shareholder, and the BBC. In late 1991, Visnews became the first international news agency from a noncommunist country to be approved to set up a bureau in Havana, Cuba.

Worldwide Television News TV news agency that supplies international news to CNN, PBS, ABC, and CBS, among others. It was founded in 1956, and is jointly owned by Capital Cities/ABC (80%), Nine Network Australia (10%), and Britain's Independent Television News (10%).

Europe's Top Ten Media Conglomerates

Reed/Elsevier UK-Dutch media conglomerate, created 1992 by a merger of Reed International and Elsevier. The group's turnover for 1992 was $4,003.5 million, $3,242.8 million of it from publishing and information services. Subsidiaries include IPC, Britain's largest magazine publisher, whose titles include *New Scientist* and *TV Times*.

Fininvest Italian media conglomerate. Owned by Sivio Berlusconi, Fininvest owns Italy's three largest commercial television channels, a group of Italian magazines, and has interests in television in Germany, France, and Spain; it also owns a substantial chunk of the Mondadori publishing company. Its

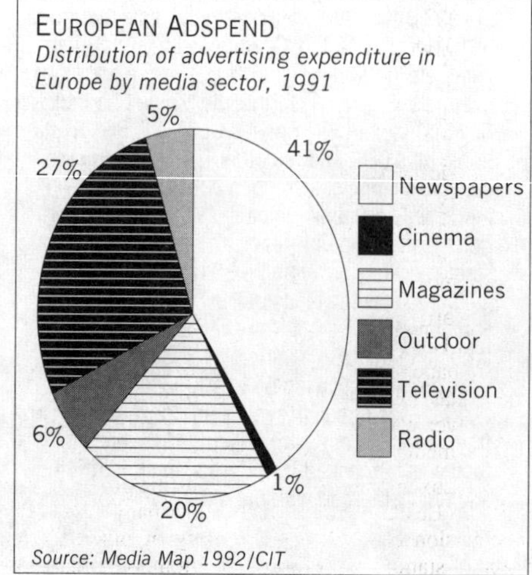

Viewer protection?

Advertising restrictions on European television

Products	*Benelux*	*Denmark*	*France*	*Germany*	*Greece*	*Ireland*	*Italy*	*Netherlands*	*Portugal*	*Spain*	*UK*
Cigarettes	×	×	×	×	×	×	×	×	×	×	×
Cigars	×	×	×	×	×	×	×	×	×	×	×
Beer/wine	√	×	×			√	√	√	√	√	
Spirits	√	×	×	√		×	√	√	√	√	×
Medical services		×		√		√	√	√	√		√
Pharmaceuticals	×	√	√	√	×	√	√	√	√	√	√
Family planning				×		×			√		√
Personal hygiene	√		√	√		√	√				√
Gambling			√	×		×			×		×
Loans			√			×					
Political parties	√	×		×	√	×		×		×	√
Religion	×	×		×	×	×		×		×	√
Travel agents			×				√				
Dieting			×	√				√			
Aimed at children	√	√	√	√	√		√	√		√	

× *TV advertising prohibited by law*

√ *TV advertising subject to restriction of copy/time of transmission*

Source: Media Map 1992/CIT

overall revenue for 1992 was $8,138.6 million, $2,929.6 million of it from its media interests.

Bertelsmann German-based international media conglomerate. With a 1992 turnover of $9,611.5 million (media: $2,171.7 million), Bertelsmann has a 38.9% stake in the German satellite TV station RTL-Plus and 24.9% of the channel Vox, new in 1993; it also owns German magazine publisher Grüner & Jahr and, in the USA, Doubleday, Bantam, Dell, and RCA Records. In the UK it owns Transworld Publishing.

Axel Springer German media conglomerate. It is Germany's largest newspaper publisher – it owns *Die Welt* and *Bild Zeitung* – and has stakes in the TV channels Sat 1, RTL-Plus, and Tele 5. It is also a major book publisher, and owns a variety of magazines and newspapers in E Europe. Its 1992 turnover was $2,217.6 million (media: $1,878.6 million).

Hachette French media conglomerate. With a 1992 turnover of $5,390.2 million (media: $1,699.3 million), Hachette is a major French book publisher, and owns *Elle* and French TV magazines, and the US publishers Grolier and Diamandis (*Women's Day*). Hachette merged at the beginning of 1993 with the missile, transport, and electronics company Matra.

Heinrich Bauer German media conglomerate, the country's largest publisher of consumer magazines. Bauer also publishes newspapers and the UK's *Take a Break* and *Bella*. Its 1992 turnover was $1,710.6 million (media: $1,602.7 million).

Hersant French media conglomerate, privately held. The Hersant family owns a number of French newspapers, including *Le Figaro* and *France Soir*, and has interests in TV and local radio. Its 1992 turnover was estimated at $1,431.2 million, all of it from media.

CLT Luxembourg-based broadcasting group. It owns Radio Luxembourg, 48.1% of Germany's RTL-Plus television channel, and a variety of other TV and radio stations in France, Belgium, Germany, the Netherlands, the Czech Republic, and Ireland, as well as several magazines. Its 1992 turnover was $1,438.3 million, $1,398.2 million of it from media.

United Newspapers British newspaper group. It owns the *Daily Express* and the *Daily Star* in Britain, and a variety of other newspapers in the USA and the UK, plus Yorkshire Post Newspapers, Link House (*Exchange & Mart*), Morgan Grampian, and Extel Financial. Its 1992 turnover was $1,438.3 million, $1,336.9 million of it from media.

RCS Editori Italian media group. RCS Editori controls about 30% of the Italian press; it also has interests in book publishing and women's magazines, and a 5% stake in the UK's Carlton Television. Its US arm is RCS Rizzoli, which owns the Rizzoli bookstores and is expanding into magazines. The 1992 turnover of RCS Editori was $2,062.7 million, $1,324.3 million of it from media.

Other Groups

News International/News Corporation one of the largest international media conglomerates, owned by Rupert Murdoch. Based in Australia, News Corporation owns 67% of the Australian press; *The Times* and the *Sun* in the UK; and *TV Guide* in the USA. It also owns the US Fox network and 50% of Britain's BSkyB satellite-channel group, plus the publisher Harper Collins. Rupert Murdoch controls 35%. Turnover for the year ending June 1992 was $7,612.2 million.

Pearson UK-based media group. Pearson owns publishers Pearson Longman, Pitman, Penguin, and Addison Wesley; it also owns the UK's *Financial Times*, 50% of *The Economist*, the Profile electronic newspaper database service, 20% of Yorkshire Television, and has a stake in BSkyB.

Time-Warner the world's biggest media conglomerate, formed by the 1989 merger between Time-Life and Warner Brothers. With a 1992 turnover of

$13,070 million, Time-Warner owns the US magazines *Time*, *People*, *Sports Illustrated*, and *Fortune*, and the USA's second biggest cable-TV operator and the satellite subscription service and film studio Home Box Office. It also has a 10% stake in Turner Broadcasting System, owner of CNN.

Chair and joint Chief Executive Officer Steven J Ross, who shaped the company, died in Dec 1992.

Dow Jones US media and financial services group. Based in New York, Dow Jones owns the *Wall Street Journal* and *Barron's* (weekly financial newspaper), and supplies financial news around the world in affiliation with Associated Press. Its 1992 turnover was $1,812.8 million.

Gannett US media group. Gannett owns the USA's largest newspaper chain plus *USA Today*, Harris polls, and a host of local TV and radio stations. Its 1992 turnover was $3,468.9 million.

UK Media Watchdogs

Advertising Standards Authority (ASA) organization founded by the UK advertising industry 1962 to promote higher standards of advertising in the media (excluding television and radio, which have their own authority). It is financed by the advertisers, who pay 0.1% supplement on the cost of advertisements. It advises the media not to publish advertisements that might breach the British Code of Advertising Practice, but has no statutory power.

Broadcasting Complaints Commission UK body responsible for dealing with complaints of invasion of privacy or unjust treatment on television or radio. It is a statutory body, formed 1981.

Broadcasting Standards Council UK body concerned with handling complaints on treatment of sex and violence. It was established 1988 and is responsible for drawing up a code on standards of taste and decency in TV and radio.

Press Complaints Commission (PCC) UK organization that replaced the Press Council (founded 1953) in 1991. It serves to preserve the freedom of the press, maintain standards, consider complaints, and report on monopoly developments.

In July 1992 it made a landmark ruling in favour of the right of the press to disclose information on public figures' personal lives, deeming such information to be in the public interest. The issue of whether or not to introduce privacy legislation was brought to the fore by press allegations of an affair between David Mellor, then secretary of state for national heritage, and actress Antonia de Sancha.

GALLUP POLL

How would you rate the overall quality of British TV programmes generally?

Excellent	5
Good	37
Middling	36
Poor	14
Very poor	7

How much confidence do you have in the BBC?

A great deal	13
Quite a lot	47
Not very much	31
None at all	10

Excluding hired videotapes, which kinds of TV broadcasts do you personally enjoy watching most? Choose two:

Comedy	32
Films	29
Soap operas	22
Drama (including series & serials)	20
Factual, documentaries	20
Wildlife, animals	20
News, current affairs	18
Sport	17
Game shows, quizzes	11
Arts magazines, concerts	3

Thinking of the kind of programme you enjoy most, which channel puts out the best programmes of that kind?

BBC1	37
BBC2	11
ITV	28
C4	10
Satellite, cable	4
Don't know	10

Source: Gallup

PEOPLES AND LANGUAGES

Ethnic Groups and Languages

Abkhazi member of a Muslim minority in Georgia. Abkhazia was a Georgian kingdom from the 4th century, and converted from Christianity to Islam in the 17th century. By the 1980s some 17% of the population were Muslims and two-thirds were of Georgian origin.

Afrikaans language an official language (with English) of the Republic of South Africa and Namibia. Spoken mainly by the Afrikaners – descendants of Dutch and other 17th-century colonists – it is a variety of the Dutch language, modified by circumstance and the influence of German, French, and other immigrant as well as local languages. It became a standardized written language about 1875.

Afro-Asiatic languages or ***Hamito-Semitic languages*** family of languages spoken throughout the world. There are two main branches, the ***Hamitic*** languages of N Africa and the ***Semitic*** languages originating in Syria, Mesopotamia, Palestine, and Arabia, but now found from Morocco in the west to the Persian Gulf in the east.

Ainu member of the aboriginal people of Japan, who were driven north in the 4th century AD by ancestors of the Japanese. The Ainu number about 25,000 (1986), inhabiting Japanese and Russian territory on Sakhalin, Hokkaido, and the Kuril Islands. Their language has no written form, and is unrelated to any other.

Algonquin member of the Algonquian-speaking hunting and fishing people formerly living around the Ottawa River in E Canada. Many now live on reservations in NE USA, E Ontario, and W Québec; others have chosen to live among the general populations of Canada and the USA.

Amhara member of an ethnic group comprising approximately 25% of the population of Ethiopia; 13 million (1987). The Amhara are traditionally farmers. They speak Amharic, a language of the Semitic branch of the Afro-Asiatic family. Most are members of the Ethiopian Christian Church.

Annamese member of the majority ethnic group in Vietnam, comprising 90% of the population. The Annamese language is distinct from Vietnamese, though it has been influenced by Chinese and has loan words from Khmer. Their religion combines elements of Buddhism, Confucianism, and Taoism, as well as ancestor worship.

Arab any of a Semitic people native to the Arabian peninsula, but now settled throughout North Africa and the nations of the Middle East. Arabic is the main Semitic language of the Afro-Asiatic family of W Asia and N Africa, originating among the Arabs of the Arabian peninsula. It is spoken by about 120 million people (1991). Arabic script is written from right to left.

Armenian member of the largest ethnic group inhabiting Armenia. There are Armenian minorities in Azerbaijan, as well as in Turkey and Iran. Christianity was introduced to the ancient Armenian kingdom in the 3rd century. There are 4–5 million speakers of Armenian, which belongs to the Indo-European family of languages.

Ashanti or ***Asante*** member of a people of central Ghana, west of Lake Volta. The Ashanti speak Akan (or Twi), which belongs to the Kwa branch of the Niger-Congo family of languages.

Australian Aborigine any of the 500 groups of indigenous inhabitants of the continent of Australia, who migrated to this region from S Asia about 40,000 years ago. They were hunters and gatherers, living throughout the continent in small kin-based groups before European settlement. Several hundred different languages developed, the most important being Aranda (Arunta), spoken in central Australia, and Murngin, spoken in Arnhem Land. There are about 227,645 Aborigines in Australia, making up about 1.5% of the country's population of 16 million.

Aymara member of an American Indian people of Bolivia and Peru, builders of a great culture, who were conquered first by the Incas and then by the Spaniards. Today 1.4 million Aymara farm and herd llamas and alpacas in the highlands; their language, belonging to the Andean-Equatorial language family, survives and their Roman Catholicism incorporates elements of their old beliefs.

Azerbaijani or ***Azeri*** native of the Azerbaijan region of Iran (population 5,500,000) or of the

Native peoples

Estimated populations of indigenous peoples, selected countries, 1992

Country	*Share of population[1] (million)*	*National population (percent)*
Papua New Guinea	3.0	77
Bolivia	5.6	70
Guatemala	4.6	47
Peru	9.0	40
Ecuador	3.8	38
Myanmar	14.0	33
Laos	1.3	30
Mexico	10.9	12
New Zealand	0.4	12
Chile	1.2	9
Philippines	6.0	9
India	63.0	7
Malaysia	0.8	4
Canada	0.9	4
Australia	0.4	2
Brazil	1.5	1
Bangladesh	1.2	1
Thailand	0.5	1
USA	2.0	1
ex-USSR	1.4	1

[1] *Generally excludes those of mixed ancestry*

Source: Worldwatch Institute

Republic of Azerbaijan (formerly a Soviet republic) (population 7,145,600). Azerbaijani is a Turkic language belonging to the Altaic family. Of the total population of Azerbaijanis, 70% are Shi'ite Muslims and 30% Sunni Muslims.

Bashkir member of the majority ethnic group of the autonomous republic of Bashkir in Russia. The Bashkirs have been Muslims since the 13th century. The Bashkir language belongs to the Turkic branch of the Altaic family, and has about 1 million speakers.

Basque member of a people inhabiting the Basque Country of central N Spain and the extreme SW of France. The Basques are a pre-Indo-European people who largely maintained their independence until the 19th century. Their language (***Euskara***), spoken by some half a million people, is unrelated to any other language. The Basque separatist movement ETA (*Euskadi ta Askatasuna*, 'Basque Nation and Liberty') and the French organization Iparretarrak ('ETA fighters from the North Side') have engaged in guerrilla activity from 1968 in an attempt to secure a united Basque state.

Bengali person of Bengali culture from Bangladesh or India (W Bengal, Tripura). There are 80–150 million speakers of Bengali, an Indo-Iranian language belonging to the Indo-European family. It is the official language of Bangladesh and of the state of Bengal, and is also used by emigrant Bangladeshi and Bengali communities in such countries as the UK and the USA. Bengalis in Bangladesh are predominantly Muslim, whereas those in India are mainly Hindu.

Bhil member of a semi-nomadic people of Dravidian origin, living in NW India and numbering about 4 million. They are hunter-gatherers and also practise shifting cultivation. The Bhili language belongs to the Indo-European family, as does Gujarati, which is also spoken by the Bhil. Their religion is Hinduism.

Bihari member of a N Indian people, also living in Bangladesh, Nepal, and Pakistan, and numbering over 40 million. The Bihari are mainly Muslim. The Bihari language is related to Hindi and has several widely varying dialects. It belongs to the Indic branch of the Indo-European family. Many Bihari were massacred during the formation of Bangladesh, which they opposed.

Burmen member of the largest ethnic group in Myanmar (formerly Burma). The Burmans, speakers of a Sino-Tibetan language, migrated from the hills of Tibet, settling in the areas around Mandalay by the 11th century AD.

Bushman former name for the Kung, San, and other hunter-gatherer groups (for example, the Gikwe, Heikom, and Sekhoin) living in and around the Kalahari Desert in southern Africa. They number approximately 50,000 and speak San and other languages of the Khoisan family. They are characteristically small-statured and brown-skinned.

Belarusian or ***Byelorussian*** or ***Belorussian*** 'White Russian' native of Belarus. Belarusian, a Balto-Slavonic language belonging to the Indo-European family, is spoken by about 10 million people, including some in Poland. It is written in the Cyrillic script. Belarusian literature dates from the 11th century AD.

Land rights

Areas legally controlled by indigenous peoples, selected countries 1992

Region	*Area legally controlled*[1] *('000 sq km)*	*Share of national territory (percent)*
Papua New Guinea	449	97
Fiji	15	83
Ecuador	190	41
Nicaragua	59	40
Sweden	137	31
Venezuela	234	26
Colombia	260	23
Canada	2,222	22
Australia	895	12
Panama	15	20
Mexico	160	8
Brazil	573	7
New Zealand	16	6
United States	365	4
Costa Rica	2	4

[1] *Figures are in most cases liberal. They include area over which, in principle, indigenous peoples have exclusive rights to use land and water bodies. Does not imply recognized indigenous ownership (many states retain ownership of indigenous reserves), or rights to minerals of petroleum (which states often retain). Does not necessarily imply effective state backing and full enforcement of rights. Some indigenous rights to use resources are limited (for example, Sweden recognizes indigenous peoples' rights only to graze reindeer). figures generally exclude private, individually owned farms of indigenous peoples, as in Andean countries and Mexico.*

Source: Worldwatch Institute

Celtic languages branch of the Indo-European family, divided into two groups: the ***Brythonic*** or ***P-Celtic*** (Welsh, Cornish, Breton, and Gaulish) and the ***Goidelic*** or ***Q-Celtic*** (Irish, Scottish, and Manx Gaelic). Celtic languages once stretched from the Black Sea to Britain, but have been in decline for centuries, limited to the so-called 'Celtic fringe' of western Europe.

Chinese native to or an inhabitant of China or Taiwan, or a person of Chinese descent. The Chinese comprise more than 25% of the world's population, and the Chinese language (Mandarin) is the largest member of the Sino-Tibetan family. Chinese traditions are ancient, many going back to at least 3000 BC. They include a range of philosophies and religions, including Confucianism, Taoism, and Buddhism. Descendants of Chinese migrants are found throughout SE Asia, the Pacific, Australia, North and South America, and Europe.

Chuang member of the largest minority group in China, numbering about 15 million. They live in S China, where they cultivate rice fields. Their religion includes elements of ancestor worship. The Chuang language belongs to the Tai family.

Chuvash member of the majority ethnic group inhabiting the autonomous republic of Chuvash, Russia. The Chuvash have lived in the middle Volga region since the 8th century. Their language belongs to the Altaic family, although whether it is a member of the Turkic branch or constitutes a branch on its own is not certain.

Copt descendant of those ancient Egyptians who adopted Christianity in the 1st century and refused to convert to Islam after the Arab conquest. They now form a small minority (about 5%) of Egypt's population. ***Coptic*** is a member of the Hamito-Semitic language family. It is descended from the language of the ancient Egyptians and is the ritual language of the Coptic Christian church. It is written in the Greek alphabet with some additional characters derived from demotic script.

creole language any pidgin language that has ceased to be simply a trade jargon in ports and markets and has become the mother tongue of a particular community. Many creoles have developed into distinct languages with literatures of their own; for example, Jamaican Creole, Haitian Creole, Krio in Sierra Leone, and Tok Pisin, now the official language of Papua New Guinea.

Croat member of the majority ethnic group in Croatia. Their language is generally considered to be identical to that of the Serbs, hence Serbo-Croatian. The Croats are mainly Roman Catholics.

Dariganga member of a Mongolian people numbering only 30,000. Their language is a dialect of Khalka, the official language of Mongolia. In the past, the Dariganga were nomads, and lived by breeding camels for use in the Chinese imperial army. With the rise of the communist regime in China they supported the new Mongolian state, and have become sedentary livestock farmers.

Dinka Nilotic minority group in S Sudan. Primarily cattle herders, the Dinka inhabit the lands around the river system that flows into the White Nile. Their language belongs to the Nilo-Saharan family. The Dinka's animist beliefs conflict with those of Islam, the official state religion; this has caused clashes between the Dinka and the Sudanese army. The Dinka number around 1-2 million.

Dogon member of the W African Dogon culture from E Mali and NW Burkina Faso. The Dogon number approximately 250,000 and their language belongs to the Voltaic (Gur) branch of the Niger-Congo family.

Dongxiang ethnic group living in NW China, numbering around 279,000 (1992). The Dongxiang farm in oases in the desert region of Gansu. They are Muslims, in spite of pressure from the state. Their language belongs to the Altaic family.

Estonian member of the largest ethnic group in Estonia. There are 1 million speakers of the Estonian language, a member of the Finno-Ugric branch of the Uralic family. Most live in Estonia.

Ewe member of a group of people inhabiting Ghana and Togo, and numbering about 2.5 million (1991). The Ewe live by fishing and farming, and practise an animist religion. Their language belongs to the Kwa branch of the Niger-Congo family.

Fang member of a W African people living in the rainforests of Cameroon, Equatorial Guinea, and NW Gabon, numbering about 2.5 million. The Fang language belongs to the Bantu branch of the Niger-Congo family.

Farsi or ***Persian*** language belonging to the Indo-Iranian branch of the Indo-European family, and the official language of Iran (formerly Persia). It is also spoken in Afghanistan, Iraq, and Tajikistan. It is written in Arabic script, from right to left.

Finno-Ugric group or family of more than 20 languages spoken by some 22 million people in scattered communities from Norway in the west to Siberia in the east and to the Carpathian mountains in the south. Members of the family include Finnish, Saami, and Hungarian.

Fon member of a people living mainly in Benin, and also in Nigeria, numbering about 2.5 million. The Fon language belongs to the Kwa branch of the Niger-Congo family. The Fon founded a kingdom which became powerful in the 18th and 19th centuries through the slave trade, and the region became known as the Slave Coast.

Fulani member of a W African culture from the southern Sahara and Sahel. Traditionally nomadic pastoralists and traders, Fulani groups are found in Senegal, Guinea, Mali, Burkina Faso, Niger, Nigeria, Chad, and Cameroon. The Fulani language is divided into four dialects and belongs to the W Atlantic branch of the Niger-Congo family; it has more than 10 million speakers.

Galla or ***Oromo*** nomadic pastoralists inhabiting S Ethiopia and NW Kenya. Galla is an Afro-Asiatic language, and is spoken by about 12 million people.

Ganda member of the Baganda people, the majority ethnic group in Uganda; the Baganda also live in Kenya. Until the 19th century they formed an independent kingdom, the largest in E Africa. Their language, Luganda, belongs to the Niger-Congo language family and has about 3 million speakers.

Georgian or ***Grazinian*** member of any of a number of related groups which make up the largest ethnic group in Georgia and the surrounding area. There are 3–4 million speakers of Georgian, a member of the Caucasian language family.

Germanic languages branch of the Indo-European language family, divided into ***East Germanic*** (Gothic, now extinct), ***North Germanic*** (Danish, Faroese, Icelandic, Norwegian, Swedish), and ***West Germanic*** (Afrikaans, Dutch, English, Flemish, Frisian, German, Yiddish).

Gond member of a heterogenous people of central India, about half of whom speak unwritten languages belonging to the Dravidian family. The rest speak Indo-European languages. There are over 4 million Gonds, most of whom live in Madhya Pradesh, E Maharashtra, and N Andra Pradesh, although some live in Orissa. Gond beliefs embrace Hinduism as well as a range of more ancient gods and spirits, and the society has a clan structure. Agriculture and livestock are the basis of their economy.

Guaraní member of a South American Indian people who formerly inhabited the area that is now Paraguay, S Brazil, and Bolivia. The Guaraní live mainly in reserves; few retain the traditional ways of hunting in the tropical forest, cultivation, and ritual warfare. About 1 million speak Guaraní, a member of the Tupian language group.

Gujarati inhabitant of Gujarat on the NW coast of India. The Gujaratis number approximately 30 million and speak their own Indo-European language, Gujarati, which has a long literary tradition. They are predominantly Hindu (90%), with Muslim (8%) and Jain (2%) minorities.

Hamito-Semitic languages former name for the Afro-Asiatic languages.

Han member of the majority ethnic group in China, numbering about 990 million. The Hans speak a wide variety of dialects of the same monosyllabic language, a member of the Sino-Tibetan family. Their religion combines Buddhism, Taoism, Confucianism, and ancestor worship.

Hausa member of an agricultural Muslim people of NW Nigeria, numbering 9 million. The Hausa language belongs to the Chadic subfamily of the Afro-Asiatic language group. It is used as a trade language throughout W Africa.

Hindi language member of the Indo-Iranian branch of the Indo-European language family, the official language of the Republic of India, although resisted as such by the Dravidian-speaking states of the south. Hindi proper is used by some 30% of Indians, in such northern states as Uttar Pradesh and Madhya Pradesh. Hindi has close historical and cultural links with Sanskrit, the classical language of Hinduism, and is written (from left to right) in Devanagari script.

Hmong member of a SE Asian highland people. They are predominantly hill farmers, rearing pigs and cultivating rice and grain, and many are involved in growing the opium poppy. Estimates of the size of the Hmong population vary between 1.5 million and 5 million, the greatest number being in China. Although traditional beliefs remain important, many have adopted Christianity. Their language belongs to the Sino-Tibetan family. The names ***Meo*** or ***Miao***, sometimes used to refer to the Hmong, are considered derogatory.

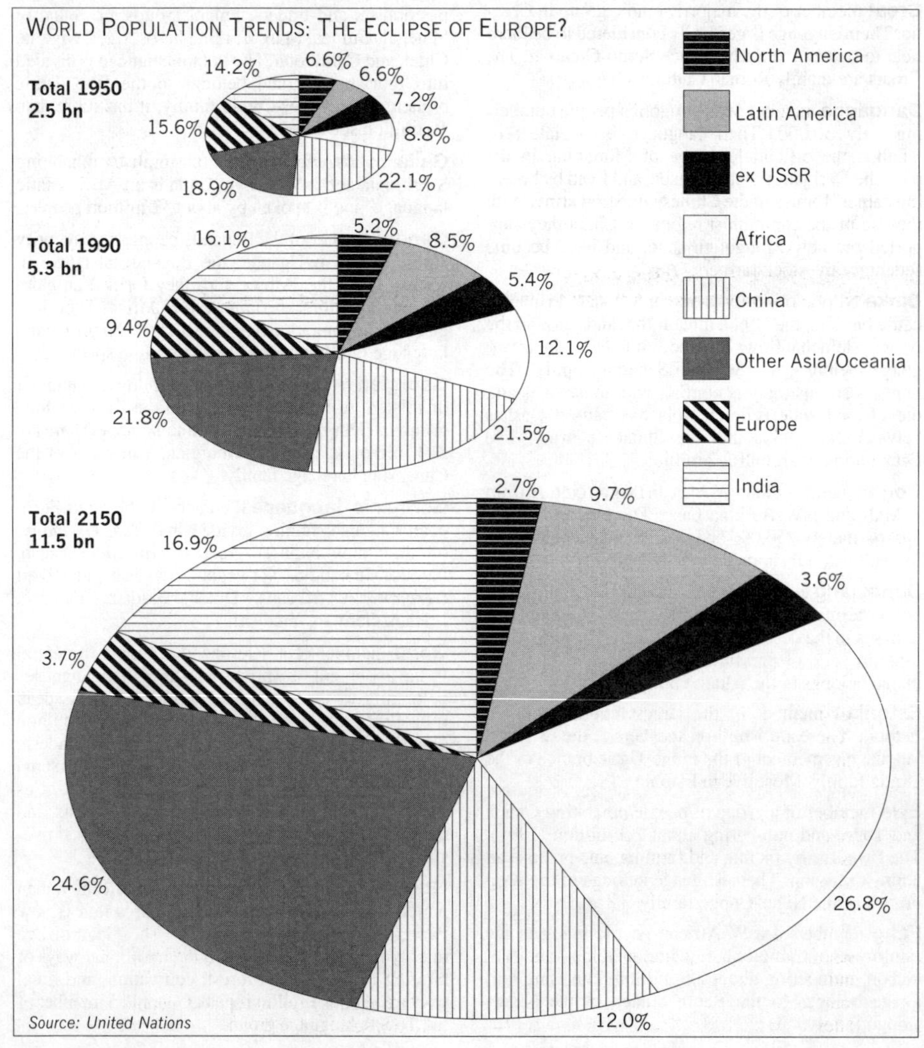

Hui member of one of the largest minority ethnic groups in China, numbering about 25 million. Members of the Hui live all over China, but are concentrated in the northern central region. They have been Muslims since the 10th century, for which they have suffered persecution both before and since the communist revolution.

Hutu member of the majority ethnic group of both Burundi and Rwanda, numbering around 9.5 million. The Hutu tend to live as peasant farmers, while the ruling minority, the Tutsi, are town dwellers. There is a long history of violent conflict between the two groups. The Hutu language belongs to the Bantu branch of the Niger-Congo family.

Iban or ***Sea Dyak*** member of a Dyak people of central Borneo. Approximately 250,000 Iban live in the interior uplands of Sarawak, while another 10,000 live in the border area of W Kalimantan. Traditionally the Iban live in long houses divided into separate family units, and practise shifting cultivation. Their languages belong to the Austronesian family.

Ibo or ***Igbo*** member of the W African Ibo culture group occupying SE Nigeria and numbering about 18 million. Primarily cultivators, they inhabit the richly forested tableland, bounded by the river Niger to the west and the river Cross to the east. They are divided into five main groups, and their languages belong to the Kwa branch of the Niger-Congo family.

Ifugao member of an indigenous people of N Luzon in the Philippines, numbering approximately 70,000. In addition to practising shifting cultivation on highland slopes, they build elaborate terraced rice fields. Their language belongs to the Austronesian family.

Indian languages traditionally, the languages of the subcontinent of India; since 1947, the languages of the Republic of India. These number some 200, depending on whether a variety is classified as a language or a dialect. They fall into five main groups, the two most widespread of which are the Indo-European languages (mainly in the north) and the Dravidian languages (mainly in the south).

Indo-European languages family of languages that includes some of the world's major classical languages (Sanskrit and Pali in India, Zend Avestan in Iran, Greek and Latin in Europe), as well as several of the most widely spoken languages (English worldwide; Spanish in Iberia, Latin America, and elsewhere; and the Hindi group of languages in N India). Indo-European languages were once located only along a geographical band from India through Iran into NW Asia, E Europe, the northern Mediterranean lands, N and W Europe and the British Isles.

Inuit people inhabiting the Arctic coasts of North America, the E islands of the Canadian Arctic, and the ice-free coasts of Greenland. ***Inuktitut***, their language, has about 60,000 speakers; it belongs to the Eskimo-Aleut group. The Inuit object to the name Eskimos ('eaters of raw meat') given them by the Algonquin Indians.

Jat member of an ethnic group living in Pakistan and N India, and numbering about 11 million; they are the largest group in N India. The Jat are predominantly farmers. They speak Punjabi, a language belonging to the Iranian branch of the Indo-European family. They are thought to be related to the Romany people.

Javanese member of the largest ethnic group in the Republic of Indonesia. There are more than 50 million speakers of Javanese, which belongs to the western branch of the Austronesian family. Although the Javanese have a Hindu-Buddhist heritage, they are today predominantly Muslim, practising a branch of Islam known as *Islam Jawa*, which contains many Sufi features.

Kannada or ***Kanarese*** language spoken in S India, the official state language of Karnataka; also spoken in Tamil Nadu and Maharashtra. There are over 20 million speakers of Kannada, which belongs to the Dravidian family. Written records in Kannada date from the 5th century AD.

Karen member of a group of SE Asian peoples, numbering 1.9 million. They live in E Myanmar (formerly Burma), Thailand, and the Irrawaddy delta. Their language belongs to the Thai division of the Sino-Tibetan family. In 1984 the Burmese government began a large-scale military campaign against the Karen National Liberation Army (KNLA), the armed wing of the Karen National Union (KNU).

Kazakh or ***Kazak*** member of a pastoral Kyrgyz people of Kazakhstan. Kazakhs also live in China (Xinjiang, Gansu, and Qinghai), Mongolia, and Afghanistan. There are 5–7 million speakers of Kazakh, a Turkic language belonging to the Altaic family. They are predominantly Sunni Muslim, although pre-Islamic customs have survived.

Khmer or ***Kmer*** member of the largest ethnic group in Cambodia, numbering about 7 million. Khmer minorities also live in E Thailand and S Vietnam. They practise Theravāda Buddhism and trace descent through both male and female lines. The Khmer language belongs to the Mon-Khmer family of Austro-Asiatic languages.

Khoikhoi (formerly ***Hottentot***) member of a people living in Namibia and the Cape Province of South Africa, and numbering about 30,000. Their language is related to San (spoken by the Kung) and belongs to the Khoisan family. Like the Kung, the Khoikhoi once inhabited a wider area, but were driven into the Kalahari Desert by invading Bantu peoples and Dutch colonists in the 18th century. They live as nomadic hunter-gatherers, in family groups, and have animist beliefs.

Khoisan the smallest group of languages in Africa. It includes fewer than 50 languages, spoken mainly by the people of the Kalahari Desert (including the Khoikhoi and Kung). Two languages from this group are spoken in Tanzania. The Khoisan languages are known for their click consonants (clicking sounds made with the tongue, which function as consonants).

Kikuyu member of Kenya's dominant ethnic group, numbering about 3 million. The Kikuyu are primarily cultivators, although many are highly educated and have entered the professions. Their language belongs to the Bantu branch of the Niger-Congo family.

Kirghiz member of a pastoral people numbering approximately 1.5 million. They inhabit the central

Out of Africa and the Eve hypothesis

Most palaeoanthropologists recognize the existence of two human species during the last million years – *Homo erectus*, now extinct, and *Homo sapiens* (including recent or 'modern' humans). In general, they believe that *H. erectus* was the ancestor of *H. sapiens*. How did the transition occur?

The multiregional model

There are two opposing views. The multiregional model says that *H. erectus* gave rise to *H. sapiens* across its whole range, which, about 700,000 years ago, included Africa, China, Java (Indonesia), and, probably, Europe. *H. erectus*, following an African origin about 1.7 million years ago, dispersed around the Old World, developing the regional variation that lies at the roots of modern 'racial' variation. Particular features in a given region persisted in the local descendant populations of today.

For example, Chinese *H. erectus* specimens had the same flat faces, with prominent cheekbones, as modern Oriental populations. Javanese *H. erectus* had robustly built cheekbones and faces that jutted out from the braincase, characteristics found in modern Australian Aborigines. No definite representatives of *H. erectus* have yet been discovered in Europe. Here, the fossil record does not extend back as far as those of Africa and eastern Asia, although a possible *H. erectus* jawbone more than 1 million years old was recently excavated in Georgia. Nevertheless, the multiregional model claims that European *H. erectus* did exist, and evolved into a primitive form of *H. sapiens*. Evolution in turn produced the Neanderthals: the ancestors of modern Europeans. Features of continuity in this European lineage include prominent noses and midfaces.

The multiregional model was first described in detail by Franz Weidenreich, a German palaeoanthropologist. It was developed further by the American Carleton Coon, who tended to regard the regional lineages as genetically separate. Most recently the model has become associated with such researchers as Milford Wolpoff (USA) and Alan Thorne (Australia), who have re-emphasized the importance of gene flow between the regional lines. In fact they regard the continuity in time and space between the various forms of *H. erectus* and their regional descendants to be so complete that they should be regarded as representing only one species – *H. sapiens*.

The Garden of Eden ...

The opposing view is that *H. sapiens* had a restricted origin in time and space. This is an old idea. Early in this century workers such as Marcellin Boule (France) and Arthur Keith (UK) believed that the lineage of *H. sapiens* was very ancient, having developed in parallel with that of *H. erectus* and the Neanderthals. However, much of the fossil evidence used to support their ideas has been re-evaluated and few workers now accept the idea of a very ancient and separate origin for modern *H. sapiens*.

Modern proponents of this approach focus on a recent and restricted origin for modern *H. sapiens*. This was dubbed the 'Garden of Eden' or 'Noah's Ark' model by the US anthropologist William Howells in 1976 because of the idea that all modern human variation had a localized origin from one centre. Howells did not specify the centre of origin, but research since 1976 points to Africa as especially important in modern human origins.

The consequent 'Out of Africa' model claims that *H. erectus* evolved into modern *H. sapiens* in Africa about 100,000–150,000 years ago. Part of the African stock of early modern humans spread from the continent into adjoining regions and eventually reached Australia, Europe, and the Americas (probably by 45,000, 40,000 and 15,000 years ago respectively). Regional ('racial') variation only developed during and after the dispersal so that there is no continuity of regional features between *H. erectus* and present counterparts in the same regions.

Like the multiregional model this view accepts that *H. erectus* evolved into new forms of human in inhabited regions outside Africa but argues that these non-African lineages became extinct without evolving into modern humans. Some, such as the Neanderthals, were displaced and then replaced by the spread of modern humans into their regions.

... and an African Eve?

In 1987, research on the genetic material called mitochondrial DNA (mtDNA) in living humans led to the reconstruction of a hypothetical female ancestor for all present-day humanity. This 'Eve' was believed to have lived in Africa about 200,000 years ago. Recent re-examination of the 'Eve' research has cast doubt on this hypothesis but further support for an 'Out of Africa' model has come from genetic studies of nuclear DNA, which also point to a recent African origin for present-day *H. sapiens*.

Studies of fossil material of the last 50,000 years also seem to indicate that many 'racial' features in the human skeleton have developed only over the last 30,000 years, in line with the 'Out of Africa' model, and at odds with the million-year timespan expected from the multiregional model.

CS

Asian region bounded by the Hindu Kush, the Himalayas, and the Tian Shan mountains. The Kirghiz are Sunni Muslims, and their Turkic language belongs to the Altaic family.

Kung (formerly ***Bushman***) member of a small group of hunter-gatherer peoples of the NE Kalahari, southern Africa, still living to some extent nomadically. Their language belongs to the Khoisan family.

Kurd member of the Kurdish culture, living mostly in the Taurus and Sagros mountains of W Iran and N Iraq in the region called Kurdistan. Although divided among more powerful states, the Kurds have nationalist aspirations; there are some 8 million in Turkey (where they suffer from discriminatory legislation), 5 million in Iran, 4 million in Iraq, 500,000 in Syria, and 500,000 in Azerbaijan, Armenia, and Georgia. Several million live elsewhere in Europe. Some 2 million Kurds became refugees from Iraq between 1984 and 1991. The Kurdish languages (Kurmanji, Sorani Kurdish, Guraní, and Zaza) are members of the Indo-Iranian branch of the Indo-European family, and the Kurds are a non-Arab, non-Turkic ethnic group. The Kurds are predominantly Sunni Muslims, although there are some Shi'ites in Iran.

Lahnda language spoken by 15–20 million people in Pakistan and N India. It is closely related to Punjabi and Romany, and belongs to the Indo-Iranian branch of the Indo-European language family.

Latvian (or ***Lett***) member of the majority ethnic group living in Latvia. The region has been Christian since the 13th century. The Latvian language is also known as ***Lettish***; with Lithuanian, it is one of the two surviving members of the Baltic branch of the Indo-European family.

Lithuanian member of the majority ethnic group living in Lithuania, comprising 80% of the population. The Lithuanian language belongs to the Baltic branch of the Indo-European family and is closely related to Latvian. It acquired a written form in the 16th century, using the Latin alphabet, and is currently spoken by about 3–4 million people.

Makua member of a people living to the north of the Zambezi River in Mozambique. With the Lomwe people they make up the country's largest ethnic group. The Makua are mainly farmers, living in villages ruled by chiefs. The Makua language belongs to the Niger-Congo family, and has about 5 million speakers.

Malagasy inhabitant of or native to Madagascar. The Malagasy language has about 9 million speakers; it belongs to the Austronesian family.

Malayalam southern Indian language, the official language of the state of Kerala. Malayalam is closely related to Tamil, also a member of the Dravidian language family; it is spoken by about 20 million people. Written records in Malayalam date from the 9th century AD.

Maori member of the indigenous Polynesian people of New Zealand, numbering 294,200 (1986), about 10% of the total population. Their language, Maori, belongs to the eastern branch of the Austronesian family. Only one-third use the Maori language today, but in recent years there has been increased Maori consciousness.

Maratha or ***Mahratta*** member of a people living mainly in Maharashtra, W India. There are about 40 million speakers of Marathi, a language belonging to the Indo-European family. The Maratha are mostly farmers, and practise Hinduism. In the 17th and 18th centuries the Maratha formed a powerful military confederacy in rivalry with the Mogul emperors.

Masai member of an E African people whose territory is divided between Tanzania and Kenya, and who number about 250,000. They were originally warriors and nomads, breeding humped zebu cattle, but some have adopted a more settled life. Their cooperation is being sought by the Kenyan authorities to help in wildlife conservation. They speak a Nilotic language belonging to the Nilo-Saharan family.

Mende member of a W African people living in the rainforests of central east Sierra Leone and W Liberia. They number approximately 1 million. The Mende are farmers as well as hunter-gatherers, and each of their villages is led by a chief and a group of elders. The Mende language belongs to the Niger-Congo family.

Moldavian member of the majority ethnic group living in Moldova, comprising almost two-thirds of the population; also, an inhabitant of the Romanian province of Moldavia. The Moldavian language is a dialect of Romanian, and belongs to the Romance group of the Indo-European family.

Mon (or ***Talaing***) member of a minority ethnic group living in Myanmar (Burma) and Thailand. The Mon established kingdoms in the area as early as the 7th century. Much of their culture was absorbed by the Khmer and Thai invaders who conquered them. The Mon language belongs to the Mon-Khmer branch of the Austro-Asiatic family. They are Buddhists, but also retain older animist beliefs.

Mordvin Finnish people inhabiting the middle Volga Valley in W Asia. They are known to have lived in the region since the 1st century AD. There are 1 million speakers of Mordvin scattered throughout W Russia, about one-third of whom live in the Mordvinian republic. Mordvin is a Finno-Ugric language belonging to the Uralic family.

Mossi member of the majority ethnic group living in Burkina Faso. Their social structure, based on a monarchy and aristocracy, was established in the 11th century. The Mossi have been prominent traders, using cowrie shells as currency. There are about 4 million speakers of Mossi, a language belonging to the Gur branch of the Niger-Congo family.

Munda member of any one of several groups living in NE and central India, numbering about 5 million (1983). Their most widely spoken languages are Santali and Mundari, languages of the Munda group, an isolated branch of the Austro-Asiatic family. The Mundas were formerly nomadic hunter-gatherers, but now practise shifting cultivation. They are Hindus, but retain animist beliefs.

Naga member of any of the various peoples who inhabit the highland region near the India–Myanmar (Burma) border; they number approximately 800,000. These peoples do not possess a common name; some of the main groups are Ao, Konyak,

Sangtam, Lhota, Sema, Rengma, Chang, and Angami. They live by farming, hunting, and fishing. Their languages belong to the Sino-Tibetan family.

Nahuatl member of any of a group of Mesoamerican Indian peoples (Mexico and Central America), of which the best-known group were the Aztecs. The Nahuatl are the largest ethnic group in Mexico, and their languages, which belong to the Uto-Aztecan (Aztec-Tanoan) family, are spoken by over 1 million people today.

Natchez member of a North American Indian people of the Mississippi area, one of the Moundbuilder group of peoples. They had a highly developed caste system unusual in North America, headed by a ruler priest (the 'Great Sun'). Members of the highest caste always married members of the lowest caste. The system lasted until French settlers colonized the area 1731. Only a few Natchez now survive in Oklahoma. Their Muskogean language is extinct.

Navajo or ***Navaho*** (Tena *Navahu* 'large planted field') member of a North American Indian people related to the Apache, and numbering about 200,000, mostly in Arizona. They speak an Athabaskan language, belonging to the Na-Dené family. The Navajo were traditionally cultivators; many now herd sheep and earn an income from tourism, making and selling rugs, blankets, and silver and turquoise jewellery. The Navajo refer to themselves as ***Dineh***, 'people'.

Niger-Congo languages the largest group of languages in Africa. It includes about 1,000 languages and covers a vast area south of the Sahara desert, from the west coast to the east, and down the east coast as far as South Africa. It is divided into groups and subgroups; the most widely spoken Niger-Congo languages are Swahili (spoken on the east coast), the members of the Bantu group (southern Africa), and Yoruba (Nigeria).

Nuba member of a minority ethnic group living in S Sudan, numbering about 1 million (1991). They speak related dialects of Nubian, which belongs to the Chari-Nile family. Forced Islamization threatens their cultural identity, and thousands were killed in the Sudan civil war.

Nyanja member of a central African people living mainly in Malawi, and numbering about 400,000 (1984). The Nyanja are predominantly farmers, living in villages under a hereditary monarchy. They speak a Bantu language belonging to the Niger-Congo family.

Oriya member of the majority ethnic group living in the Indian state of Orissa. Oriya is Orissa's official language; it belongs to the Eastern group of the Indo-Iranian branch of the Indo-European family.

Oromo member of any of a group of E African peoples, especially of S Ethiopia, who speak an Afro-Asiatic language.

Palikur member of a South American Indian people living in N Brazil and numbering about 1 million (1980). Formerly a warlike people, they occupied a vast area between the Amazon and Orinoco rivers.

Pathan member of a people of NW Pakistan and Afghanistan, numbering about 14 million (1984). The majority are Sunni Muslims. The Pathans comprise distinct groups, some living as nomads with herds of goats and camels, while others are farmers. The Pakistani Pathans are now claiming independence, with the Afghani Pathans, in their own state of Pakhtoonistan, although this has not yet been recognized. The Pathans speak Pashto, a member of the Indo-Iranian branch of the Indo-European family.

pidgin language any of various trade jargons, contact languages, or lingua francas arising in ports and markets where people of different linguistic backgrounds meet for commercial and other purposes. Usually a pidgin language is a rough blend of the vocabulary of one (often dominant) language with the syntax or grammar of one or more other (often dependent) groups. Pidgin English in various parts of the world, *français petit negre*, and Bazaar Hindi or Hindustani are examples of pidgins that have served long-term purposes to the extent of being acquired by children as one of their everyday languages. At this point they become creole languages.

Potiguara member of a group of South American Indians living in NW Brazil, and numbering about 1 million (1983). Their language belongs to the Tupi-Guaraní family. Their religion is centred around a shaman, who mediates between the people and the spirit world.

Punjabi member of the majority ethnic group living in the Punjab. Approximately 37 million live in the Pakistan half of Punjab while another 14 million live on the Indian side of the border. In addition to Sikhs there are Rajputs in Punjab, some of whom have adopted Islam. The Punjabi language belongs to the Indo-Iranian branch of the Indo-European family. It is considered by some to be a variety of Hindi, by others to be a distinct language.

Pygmy (sometimes ***Negrillo***) member of any of several groups of small-statured, dark-skinned peoples of the rainforests of equatorial Africa. They were probably the aboriginal inhabitants of the region, before the arrival of farming peoples from elsewhere. They live nomadically in small groups, as hunter-gatherers; they also trade with other, settled people in the area.

Quechua or ***Quichua*** or ***Kechua*** member of the largest group of South American Indians. The Quechua live in the Andean region. Their ancestors included the Inca, who established the Quechua language in the region. Quechua is the second official language of Peru and is widely spoken as a lingua franca in Ecuador, Bolivia, Columbia, Argentina, and Chile; it belongs to the Andean-Equatorial family.

Romance languages branch of Indo-European languages descended from the Latin of the Roman Empire ('popular' or 'vulgar' as opposed to 'classical' Latin). The present-day Romance languages with national status are French, Italian, Portuguese, Romanian, and Spanish.

Romany member of a nomadic people, also called ***Gypsy*** (a corruption of 'Egyptian', since they were erroneously thought to come from Egypt). They are now believed to have originated in NW India, and live throughout the world. The Romany language, spoken in several different dialects, belongs to the Indic branch of the Indo-European family.

Russian member of the majority ethnic group living in Russia. Russians are also often the largest minority in neighbouring republics. The Russian language is a member of the East Slavonic branch of the Indo-European language family and was the official language of the USSR, with 130–150 million speakers. It is written in the Cyrillic alphabet. The ancestors of the Russians migrated from central Europe between the 6th and 8th centuries AD.

Saami (or ***Lapp***) member of a group of herding people living in N Scandinavia and the Kola Peninsula, and numbering about 46,000 (1983). Some are nomadic, others lead a more settled way of life. They live by herding reindeer, hunting, fishing, and producing handicrafts. Their language belongs to the Finno-Ugric family. Their religion is basically animist, but incorporates elements of Christianity.

Serb member of Yugoslavia's largest ethnic group, found mainly in Serbia, but also in the neighbouring independent republics of Bosnia-Herzegovina and Croatia. Their language is generally recognized to be the same as Croat and hence known as Serbo-Croatian. The Serbs are predominantly Greek Orthodox Christians.

Serbo-Croatian (or ***Serbo-Croat***) the most widely spoken language in Yugoslavia, with more than 17 million speakers. It is a member of the South Slavonic branch of the Indo-European family. The different dialects of Serbo-Croatian tend to be written by the Serbs in the Cyrillic script, and by the Croats in the Latin script.

Shona member of a Bantu-speaking people of southern Africa, comprising approximately 80% of the population of Zimbabwe. They also occupy the land between the Save and Pungure rivers in Mozambique, and smaller groups are found in South Africa, Botswana, and Zambia. The Shona are mainly farmers, living in scattered villages. The Shona language belongs to the Niger-Congo family.

Sindhi member of the majority ethnic group living in the Pakistani province of Sind. The Sindhi language is spoken by about 15 million people.

Sinhalese member of the majority ethnic group of Sri Lanka (70% of the population). Sinhalese is the official language of Sri Lanka; it belongs to the Indo-Iranian branch of the Indo-European family, and is written in a script derived from the Indian Pali form. The Sinhalese are Buddhists.

Sino-Tibetan languages group of languages spoken in SE Asia. This group covers a large area, and includes Chinese and Burmese, both of which have numerous dialects. Some classifications include the Tai group of languages (including Thai and Lao) in the Sino-Tibetan family.

Slav member of an Indo-European people in central and E Europe, the Balkans, and parts of N Asia, speaking closely related Slavonic languages. The ancestors of the Slavs are believed to have included the Sarmatians and Scythians. Moving west from Central Asia, they settled in E and SE Europe during the 2nd and 3rd millennia BC.

Slavonic languages or ***Slavic languages*** branch of the Indo-European language family spoken in central and E Europe, the Balkans, and parts of N Asia. The family comprises the ***southern group*** (Slovene, Serbo-Croatian, Macedonian, and Bulgarian); the ***western group*** (Czech and Slovak, Sorbian in Germany, and Polish and its related dialects); and the ***eastern group*** (Russian, Ukrainian, and Belarusian).

Slovene member of the Slavonic people of Slovenia and parts of the Austrian Alpine provinces of Styria and Carinthia. There are 1.5–2 million speakers of Slovene, a language belonging to the South Slavonic branch of the Indo-European family. The Slovenes use the Roman alphabet and the majority belong to the Roman Catholic Church.

Sotho member of a large ethnic group in southern Africa, numbering about 7 million (1987) and living mainly in Botswana, Lesotho, and South Africa. The Sotho are predominantly farmers, living in small village groups. They speak a variety of closely related languages belonging to the Bantu branch of the Niger-Congo family. With English, Sotho is the official language of Lesotho.

Sundanese member of the second largest ethnic group in the Republic of Indonesia. There are more than 20 million speakers of Sundanese, a member of the western branch of the Austronesian family. Like their neighbours, the Javanese, the Sundanese are predominantly Muslim.

Swahili language belonging to the Bantu branch of the Niger-Congo family, widely used in east and central Africa. Swahili originated on the E African coast as a *lingua franca* used among traders, and contains many Arabic loan words. It is an official language in Kenya and Tanzania. The name Swahili is also used for a member of an African people using the language, especially someone living in Zanzibar and adjoining coastal areas of Kenya and Tanzania. The Swahili are not an isolated group, but are part of a mixed coastal society engaged in fishing and trading.

Tagalog member of the majority ethnic group living around Manila on the island of Luzon, in the Philippines, and numbering about 10 million (1988). The Tagalog live by fishing and trading. In its standardized form, known as Pilipino, Tagalog is the official language of the Philippines, and belongs to the Western branch of the Austronesian family. The Tagalogs' religion is a mixture of animism, Christianity, and Islam.

Tajik or ***Tadzhik*** member of the majority ethnic group living in Tajikistan. Tajiks also live in Afghanistan and parts of Pakistan and W China. The Tajiki language belongs to the West Iranian subbranch of the Indo-European family, and is similar to Farsi; it is written in the Cyrillic script, however. The majority of the Tajik people are Sunni Muslims; there is a Shi'ite minority in Afghanistan.

Tamil member of the majority ethnic group living in the Indian state of Tamil Nadu (formerly Madras). Tamils also live in S India, N Sri Lanka, Malaysia, Singapore, and South Africa, totalling 35–55 million worldwide. Tamil belongs to the Dravidian family of languages; written records in Tamil date from the 3rd century BC. The 3 million Tamils in Sri Lanka are predominantly Hindu, although some are Muslims, unlike the Sinhalese majority, who are mainly Buddhist. The ***Tamil Tigers***, most prominent of the various Tamil groupings, are attempting to create a separate homeland in N Sri Lanka through both political and military means.

Tatar or ***Tartar*** member of a Turkic people, the descendants of the mixed Mongol and Turkic followers of Genghis Khan, called the Golden Horde because of the wealth they gained by plunder. The vast Tatar state was conquered by Russia 1552. The Tatars now live mainly in the Russian autonomous republic of Tatarstan, W Siberia, Turkmenistan, and Uzbekistan (where they were deported from the Crimea 1944). There are over 5 million speakers of the Tatar language, which belongs to the Turkic branch of the Altaic family. The Tatar people are mainly Muslim, although some have converted to the Orthodox Church.

Telugu language spoken in SE India. It is the official language of Andhra Pradesh, and is also spoken in Malaysia, giving a total number of speakers of around 50 million. Written records in Telugu date from the 7th century AD. Telugu belongs to the Dravidian family.

Thai member of the majority ethnic group living in Thailand and N Myanmar (Burma). Thai peoples also live in SW China, Laos, and N Vietnam. They speak Thai languages, all of which belong to the Sino-Tibetan language family. There are over 60 million speakers (1991), the majority of whom live in Thailand. Most Thais are Buddhists, but the traditional belief in spirits, *phi*, remains.

Tibetan member of a Mongolian people inhabiting Tibet, who practise Lamaism, a form of Mahāyāna Buddhism, introduced in the 7th century. Until Tibet's annexation by China 1959, it was a theocratic state. The Tibetans claim to be victims of 'cultural genocide' as result of Chinese immigration and economic colonization, and refugee communities have formed in India and Nepal. The Tibetan language belongs to the Sino-Tibetan language family.

Tigré people of N Ethiopia. The Tigré language is spoken by about 2.5 million people; it belongs to the SE Semitic branch of the Afro-Asiatic family. ***Tigrinya*** is a closely related language spoken slightly to the south.

Consumer culture invades Tibet

Annexed by Chinain 1950 and renamed the Xizang Autonomous Region, Tibet was soon overrun by Han Chinese administrators, Communist Party officials, and military personnel. The Sin-cization of the Tibetans followed, with Chinese communist ideals being imposed. Buddhism, controlled by the lamas (priests) and supported by an aristocratic social order, had been the traditional corner stone of Tibetan culture since the 13th century. The Chinese began systematically dismantling both systems, resulting in an uprising in 1959 that attempted to reassert traditional values. This was brutally suppressed and the Dalai Lama – the spiritual and political leader of Tibet, chosen within the Buddhist community – led thousands of his followers into exile.

Chinese-run schools were opened, where the children were taught in Chinese and encouraged to despise traditional social and ideological values. Collectivization of agriculture was introduced, undermining village life. During the Cultural Revolution 1966–69 more than 3,500 monasteries and temples were destroyed and practising Buddhists cruelly persecuted. An influx of zealous young Chinese in Tibetan villages forced people to attend political lectures and encouraged them to denounce politically 'suspect' Tibetans. Village shrines were torn down and people discouraged from wearing their traditional costumes.

In spite of Chinese domination many Tibetans clung to their traditional ways. When Chinese policy towards Tibet softened in the late 1970s there was a general return to Buddhist practice. The Chinese government has continued to modernize Tibetan towns and develop large-scale infrastructure projects that inevitably alter the Tibetan way of life. Chinese immigration has increased, with consequent tensions. In 1987 a major uprising occurred in Lhasa; the demonstrators, who included large numbers of clergy, protested against Chinese influence and the erosion of traditional values. Martial law was imposed and many Tibetans imprisoned. Since then the Chinese authorities have attempted to engineer economic growth, which they hope will dilute political tensions.

The policy appears to have been successful, with a consumer culture emerging. A generation of young Tibetans who have not known the Dalai Lama have come to value sports shoes, jeans, and video recorders rather than prayer wheels and homespun coats. Chinese factories and compounds surround the old city of Lhasa, which has doubled in size in the last six years. Poor Chinese from over-populated regions have flocked to Tibet to benefit from commercial opportunities and they now outnumber the Tibetans in many towns. The Buddhist clergy remain in opposition, believing that the Dalai Lama will soon return to lead an independent Tibet. Young Tibetans who choose to remain true to their culture continue to enter the monasteries, but more have adopted Western dress and behaviour. Lhasa became in 1992 a special economic zone, attracting thousands more Han Chinese and continuing the move towards a consumer-led culture.

Tswana member of the majority ethnic group living in Botswana. The Tswana are divided into four subgroups: the Bakwena, the Bamangwato, the Bangwaketse, and the Batawana. Traditionally they are rural-dwelling farmers, though many now leave their homes to work as migrant labourers in South African industries. The Tswana language belongs to the Bantu branch of the Niger-Congo family.

Tuareg Arabic name given to nomadic stockbreeders from west and central Sahara and Sahel (Algeria, Libya, Mali, Niger, and Burkina Faso). The eight Tuareg groups refer to themselves by their own names. Their language, ***Tamashek***, belongs to the Berber branch of the Afro-Asiatic family and is spoken by 500,000–850,000 people. It is written in a noncursive script known as *tifinagh*, derived from ancient Numidian.

Turkoman or ***Turkman*** member of the majority ethnic group in Turkmenistan. They live to the E of the Caspian Sea, around the Kara Kum desert, and along the borders of Afghanistan and Iran. Traditionally the Turkomen were tent-dwelling pastoral nomads, though the majority are now sedentary farmers. Their language belongs to the Turkic branch of the Altaic family. They are predominantly Sunni Muslims.

Tutsi member of a minority ethnic group living in Rwanda and Burundi. Although fewer in number, they have traditionally been politically dominant over the Hutu majority and the Twa (or Pygmies). The Tutsi are traditionally farmers; they also hold virtually all positions of importance in Burundi's government and army. They have carried out massacres in response to Hutu rebellions, notably in 1972 and 1988. In Rwanda the balance of power is more even.

Twa member of an ethnic group comprising 1% of the populations of Burundi and Rwanda. The Twa are the aboriginal inhabitants of the region. They are a pygmoid people, and live as nomadic hunter-gatherers in the forests.

Uigur member of a Turkic people living in NW China and Kazakhstan; they form about 80% of the population of the Chinese province of Xinjiang Uigur. There are about 5 million speakers of Uigur, a language belonging to the Turkic branch of the Altaic family; it is the official language of the province. The Uigur are known to have lived in the region since the 3rd century AD, and converted to Islam in the 14th century.

Ukrainian member of the majority ethnic group living in Ukraine; there are minorities in Siberian Russia, Kazakhstan, Poland, the Slovak Republic, and Romania. There are 40–45 million speakers of Ukrainian, a member of the East Slavonic branch of the Indo-European family, closely related to Russian. Ukrainian-speaking communities are also found in Canada and the USA.

Urdu language member of the Indo-Iranian branch of the Indo-European language family, related to Hindi and written not in Devanagari but in Arabic script. Urdu is strongly influenced by Farsi (Persian) and Arabic. It is the official language of Pakistan and is used by Muslims in India.

Uzbek member of the majority ethnic group (almost 70%) living in Uzbekistan; minorities live in Turkmenistan, Tajikistan, Kazakhstan, and Afghanistan. There are 10–14 million speakers of the Uzbek language, which belongs to the Turkic branch of the Altaic family. Uzbeks are predominantly Sunni Muslims.

Vedda member of the aboriginal peoples of Sri Lanka, who occupied the island before the arrival of the Aryans c. 550 BC. Formerly cave-dwelling hunter-gatherers, they have now almost died out or merged with the rest of the population. They speak a Sinhalese language, belonging to the Indo-European family.

Wolof member of the majority ethnic group living in Senegal. There is also a Wolof minority in Gambia. There are about 2 million speakers of Wolof, a language belonging to the Niger-Congo family. The Wolof are Muslims. The remnants of a three-tiered social structure comprising aristocracy, artisans, and slaves can still be seen.

Xhosa member of a Bantu people of southern Africa, living mainly in the Black National State of Transkei. Traditionally, the Xhosa were farmers and pastoralists, with a social structure based on a monarchy. Many are now town-dwellers, and provide much of the labour in South African mines and factories. Their Bantu language belongs to the Niger-Congo family.

Yanamamo or ***Yanomamo*** (plural ***Yanamami***) member of a semi-nomadic South American Indian people, numbering approximately 15,000, who live in S Venezuela and N Brazil. The Yanamamo language belongs to the Macro-Chibcha family. In Nov 1991 Brazil granted the Yanamami possession of their original land, 58,395 km/36,293 sq mi on its northern border.

Yao member of a people living in S China, N Vietnam, N Laos, Thailand, and Myanmar (Burma), and numbering about 4 million (1984). The Yao language may belong to either the Sino-Tibetan or the Thai language family. The Yao incorporate elements of ancestor worship in their animist religion. Most are hill-dwelling farmers.

Yi member of a people living in S China; there are also Yi populations in Laos, Thailand, and Vietnam, totalling about 5.5 million (1987). The Yi are farmers, producing both crops and livestock. Their language belongs to the Sino-Tibetan family; their religion is animist.

Yoruba member of the majority ethnic group living in SW Nigeria; there is a Yoruba minority in E Benin. They number approximately 20 million in all, and their language belongs to the Kwa branch of the Niger-Congo family. The Yoruba established powerful city states in the 15th century.

Zulu member of a group of southern African peoples mainly from Natal, South Africa. Their present homeland, KwaZulu, represents the nucleus of the once extensive and militaristic Zulu kingdom. Today many Zulus work in the industrial centres around Johannesburg and Durban. The Zulu language, closely related to Xhosa, belongs to the Bantu branch of the Niger-Congo family.

Grammar and Usage

adjective grammatical part of speech for words that describe nouns (for example, *new* and *beautiful*, as in 'a new hat' and 'a beautiful day'). Adjectives generally have three degrees (grades or levels for the description of relationships): the positive degree (*new, beautiful*) the comparative degree (*newer, more beautiful*), and the superlative degree (*newest, most beautiful*).

Some adjectives do not normally need comparative and superlative forms; one person cannot be 'more asleep' than someone else, a lone action is unlikely to be 'the most single-handed action ever seen', and many people dislike the expression 'most unique' or 'almost unique', because something unique is supposed to be the only one that exists. For purposes of emphasis or style these conventions may be set aside ('I don't know who is more unique; they are both remarkable people'). Double comparatives such as 'more bigger' are not grammatical in Standard English, but Shakespeare used a double superlative ('the most unkindest cut of all'). Some adjectives may have both the comparative and superlative forms (*commoner* and *more common*; *commonest* and *most common*), usually shorter words take on the suffixes *-er/-est* but occasionally they may be given the *more/most* forms for emphasis or other reasons ('Which of them is the *most clear*?').

When an adjective comes before a noun it is attributive; when it comes after noun and verb (for example, 'It looks *good*') it is predicative. Some adjectives can only be used predicatively ('The child was asleep', but not 'the asleep child'). The participles of verbs are regularly used adjectivally ('a *sleeping* child', '*boiled* milk'), often in compound forms ('a *quick-acting* medicine', 'a *glass-making* factory'; 'a *hard-boiled* egg', '*well-trained* teachers'). Adjectives are often formed by adding suffixes to nouns (sand: sand*y*; nation: nation*al*).

adverb grammatical part of speech for words that modify or describe verbs ('She ran *quickly*'), adjectives ('a *beautifully* clear day'), and adverbs ('They did it *really* well'). Most adverbs are formed from adjectives or past participles by adding *-ly* (*quick: quickly*) or *-ally* (*automatic: automatically*).

Sometimes adverbs are formed by adding *-wise* (*likewise* and *clockwise*, as in 'moving *clockwise*'; in 'a *clockwise* direction', *clockwise* is an adjective). Some adverbs have a distinct form from their partnering adjective; for example, *good/well* ('It was *good* work; they did it *well*'). Others do not derive from adjectives (*very*, in '*very* nice'; *tomorrow*, in 'I'll do it *tomorrow*'); and some are unadapted adjectives (*pretty*, as in 'It's *pretty* good'). Sentence adverbs modify whole sentences or phrases: '*Generally*, it rains a lot here'; '*Usually*, the town is busy at this time of year.' Sometimes there is controversy in such matters. *Hopefully* is universally accepted in sentences like 'He looked at them *hopefully*' (= in a hopeful way), but some people dislike it in '*Hopefully*, we'll see you again next year' (= We hope that we'll see you again next year).

apostrophe mark (') used in written English and some other languages. In English it serves primarily to indicate either a missing letter (*mustn't* for *must not*) or number (*'47* for *1947*), or grammatical possession ('*John's* camera', '*women's* dresses'). It is often omitted in proper names (Publishers Association, Actors Studio, *Collins Dictionary*). Many people otherwise competent in writing have great difficulty with the apostrophe, which has never been stable at any point in its history.

An apostrophe may precede the plural *s* used with numbers and abbreviations (*the 1970's, a group of P.O.W.'s*) but is equally often omitted (*the 1970s, a group of POWs*). For possessives of certain words ending with *s*, usage is split, as between *James's book* and *James' book*. Names and dates used adjectivally are not usually followed by an apostrophe ('a *1950s* car', 'a *Beatles* record'). The use of an apostrophe to help indicate a plural (as in a shopkeeper's *Apple's* and *Tomato's*, followed by their prices) is regarded by many as semiliterate.

article grammatical part of speech. There are two articles in English: the ***definite article*** *the*, which serves to specify or identify a noun (as in 'This is *the* book I need'), and the ***indefinite article*** *a* or (before vowels) *an*, which indicates a single unidentified noun ('They gave me *a* piece of paper and *an* envelope').

Some people use the form 'an' before *h* ('an historic building'); this practice dates from the 17th century, when an initial *h* was often not pronounced (as in '*h*onour'), and is nowadays widely considered rather grandiose.

asterisk starlike punctuation mark (*) used to link the asterisked word with a note at the bottom of a page, and to indicate that certain letters are missing from a word (especially a taboo word such as 'f**k').

An asterisk is also used to indicate that a word or usage is nonexistent; for example, 'In English we say three boys and not three *boy'.

colon punctuation mark (:) intended to direct the reader's attention forward, usually because what follows explains or develops what has just been written (for example, *The farmer owned the following varieties of dogs: a spaniel, a pointer, a terrier, a border collie, and three mongrels*).

comma punctuation mark (,) intended to provide breaks or pauses within a sentence; commas may come at the end of a clause, to set off a phrase, or in lists (for example, *apples, pears, plums, and pineapples*).

Some writers, uncertain where sentences properly end, use a comma instead of a period (or full stop), writing *We saw John last night, it was good to see him again*, rather than *We saw John last night. It was good to see him again.* The meaning is entirely clear in both cases. One solution in such situations is to use a ***semicolon*** (;), which bridges the gap between the close association of the comma and the sharp separation of the period. For parenthetical commas, see parenthesis.

conjunction grammatical part of speech that serves to connect words, phrases, and clauses; for example *and* in 'apples and pears' and *but* in 'we're going but they aren't'.

exclamation mark or *exclamation point* punctuation mark (!) used to indicate emphasis or strong emotion ('That's terrible!'). It is appropriate after

Common roots

The similarities of six words in Indo-European languages contrast with their differences in other language groups

English	*month*	*mother*	*new*	*night*	*nose*	*three*
Welsh	mis	mam	newydd	nos	trwyn	tri
Gaelic	mí	máthair	nua	oíche	srón	trí
French	mois	mère	nouveau	nuit	nez	trois
Spanish	mes	madre	nuevo	noche	nariz	tres
Portuguese	mês	mãe	novo	noite	nariz	três
Italian	mese	madre	nuovo	notte	naso	tre
Latin	mensis	mater	novus	nox	nasus	tres
German	Monat	Mutter	neu	Nacht	Nase	drei
Dutch	maand	moeder	nieuw	nacht	neus	drie
Icelandic	mánudur	módir	nýr	nótt	nef	brír
Swedish	månad	moder	ny	natt	näsa	tre
Polish	miesiąc	matka	nowy	noc	nos	trzy
Czech	měsć	matka	nový	noc	nos	tři
Rumanian	lună	mamă	nou	noapte	nas	trei
Albanian	muaj	nënë	iri	natë	hundë	tre,tri
Greek	men	meter	neos	nux	rhïs	treis
Russian	mesyats	mat'	novy	noch'	nos	tri
Lithuanian	menuo	motina	naujas	naktis	nosis	trys
Armenian	amis	mayr	nor	kisher	kit	yerek
Persian	mãh	mãdar	nau	shab	bini	se
Sanskrit	mãs	matar	nava	nakt	nãs	trayas
NON-INDO-EUROPEAN LANGUAGES						
	(month)	*(mother)*	*(new)*	*(night)*	*(nose)*	*(three)*
Basque	hilabethe	ama	berri	gai	sãdãr	hirur
Finnish	kuukausi	äiti	uusi	yö	nenä	kolme
Hungarian	hónap	anya	új	éjszaka	orr	három
Turkish	ay	anne	yeni	gece	burun	úç

Source: Katzner, Kenneth/The Languages of the World/Routledge & Kegan Paul, London 1986

interjections ('Rats!'), emphatic greetings ('Yo!'), and orders ('Shut up!'), as well as those sentences beginning *How* or *What* that are not questions ('How embarrassing!', 'What a surprise!').

The exclamation mark is most often seen in dialogue. Its use is kept to a minimum in narrative prose and technical writing.

Within a quotation an exclamation mark may be placed in square brackets to indicate that the writer or editor is surprised by something. The convention that all sentences in comic books end with an exclamation mark is on the wane.

grammar the rules of combining words into phrases, clauses, sentences, and paragraphs. Emphasis on the standardizing impact of print has meant that spoken or colloquial language is often perceived as less grammatical than written language, but all forms of a language, standard or otherwise, have their own grammatical systems of differing complexity. People often acquire several overlapping grammatical systems within one language; for example, one formal system for writing and standard communication and one less formal system for everyday and peer-group communication.

Originally 'grammar' was an analytical approach to writing, intended to improve the understanding and the skills of scribes, philosophers, and writers. When compared with Latin, English has been widely regarded as having less grammar or at least a simpler grammar; it would be truer, however, to say that English and Latin have different grammars, each complex in its own way. In linguistics (the contemporary study of language) grammar, or syntax, refers to the arrangement of the elements in a language for the purposes of acceptable communication in speech, writing, and print.

All forms of a language, standard or otherwise, have their grammars or grammatical systems, which children acquire through use; a child may acquire several overlapping systems within one language (especially a nonstandard form for everyday life and a standard form linked with writing, school, and national life). Not even the most comprehensive grammar book (or grammar) of a language like English, French, Arabic, or Japanese completely covers or fixes the implicit grammatical system that people use in their daily lives. The rules and tendencies of natural grammar operate largely in nonconscious ways but can, for many social and professional purposes, be studied and developed for conscious as well as inherent skills. See also parts of speech.

Recent theories of the way language functions include ***phrase structure grammar***, ***transformational grammar***, and ***case grammar***.

hyphen punctuation mark (-) with two functions: to join words, parts of words, syllables, and so on, for particular purposes; and to mark a word break at the end of a line. Adjectival compounds (see adjective) are hyphenated because they modify the noun jointly rather than separately ('a small-town boy' is a boy from a small town; 'a small town boy' is a small boy from a town). The use of hyphens with adverbs is redundant unless an identical adjective exists (*well, late, long*): 'late-blooming plant' but 'brightly blooming plant'.

Phrasal verbs are not hyphenated ('things *turned out* well', 'it *washed up* on the beach') unless used adjectivally ('a well-*turned-out* crowd', 'a *washed-up* athlete'). Nouns formed from phrasal verbs are hyphenated or joined together ('a good *turnout* tonight', 'please do the *washing-up*'). In the use of certain prefixes, modern style is moving towards omitting the hyphen (*noncooperation*).

The hyphenation of compound nouns in English is by no means clear cut; the same person may inadvertently in one article write, for example *world view, worldview* and *world-view*.

Here, conventional hyphenation is a first stage in bringing two words together; if their close association is then generally agreed, the two words are written or printed as one (*teapot*, as opposed to *tea-pot* or *tea pot*), or are kept apart for visual and aesthetic reasons (*coffee pot* rather than *coffee-pot* or *coffeepot*). Practice does, however, vary greatly.

inflection or ***inflexion*** in grammatical analysis, an ending or other element in a word that indicates its grammatical function (whether plural or singular, masculine or feminine, subject or object, and so on).

In a highly inflected language like Latin, nouns, verbs, and adjectives have many inflectional endings (for example, in the word *amabunt* the base *am* means 'love' and the complex *abunt* indicates the kind of verb, the future tense, indicative mood, active voice, third person, and plurality). English has few inflections: for example, the *s* for plural forms (as in *the books*) and for the third person singular of verbs (as in *He runs*).

noun grammatical part of speech that names a person, animal, object, quality, idea, or time. Nouns can refer to objects such as *house, tree* (***concrete nouns***); specific persons and places such as *John Alden*, the *White House* (**proper nouns**); ideas such as *love, anger* (**abstract nouns**). In English many simple words are both noun and verb (*jump, reign, rain*). Adjectives are sometimes used as nouns ('a *local* man', 'one of the *locals*').

A common noun does not begin with a capital letter (*child, cat*), whereas a proper noun does, because it is the name of a particular person, animal, or place (*Jane, Rover, Norfolk*). A concrete noun refers to things that can be sensed (*dog, box*), whereas an abstract noun relates to generalizations abstracted from life as we observe it (*fear, condition, truth*). A ***countable noun*** can have a plural form (*book: books*), while an ***uncountable noun*** or mass noun cannot (*dough*). Many English nouns can be used both countably and uncountably (*wine*: 'Have some *wine*; it's one of our best *wines*'). A ***collective noun*** is singular in form but refers to a group (*flock, group, committee*), and a ***compound noun*** is made up of two or more nouns (*teapot, baseball team, car-factory strike committee*). A ***verbal noun*** is formed from a verb as a gerund or otherwise (*build: building; regulate: regulation*).

participle in grammar, a form of the verb; in English either a ***present participle*** ending in *-ing* (for example, 'work*ing*' in 'They were *working*', '*working* men', and 'a hard-*working* team') or a ***past participle*** ending in *-ed* in regular verbs (for example, 'train*ed*' in 'They have been *trained* well', '*trained* soldiers', and 'a well- *trained* team').

In irregular verbs the past participle has a special form (for example, drive/*driven*; light/*lit*, burn/*burned, burnt*). The participle is used to open such constructions as '*Coming* down the stairs, she paused and ...' and '*Angered* by the news, he ...'. Such constructions, when not logically formed, may have irritating or ambiguous results. '*Driving* along a country road, a stone broke my windscreen' suggests that the stone was driving along the road. This illogical usage is a ***misplaced participle***. A ***dangling*** or ***hanging participle*** has nothing at all to relate to: 'While *driving* along a country road there was a loud noise under the car.' Such sentences need to be completely re-expressed, except in some well-established usages where the participle can stand alone (for example, '*Taking* all things into consideration, your actions were justified').

part of speech the grammatical function of a word, described in the grammatical tradition of the Western world, based on Greek and Latin. The four major parts of speech are the noun, verb, adjective, and adverb; the minor parts of speech vary according to schools of grammatical theory, but include the article, conjunction, preposition, and pronoun.

In languages like Greek and Latin, the part of speech of a word tends to be invariable (usually marked by an ending, or inflection); in English, it is much harder to recognize the function of a word simply by its form. Some English words may have only one function (for example, *and* as a conjunction). Others may have several functions (for example, *fancy*, which is a noun in the phrase 'flights of *fancy*', a verb in '*Fancy* that!', and an adjective in 'a *fancy* hat').

period punctuation mark (.). The term 'period' is universally understood in English and is the preferred usage in North America; ***full stop*** is the preferred term in the UK. The period has two functions: to mark the end of a sentence and to indicate that a word has been abbreviated. It is also used in mathematics to indicate decimals and is then called a ***point***.

Such abbreviations as acronyms are unlikely to have periods (NATO rather than N.A.T.O.), and contractions (incorporating the last letter of the word, for example Dr for 'doctor') may or may not have periods. In such contexts as fictional dialogue and advertising, periods sometimes follow incomplete sentences in an effort to represent speech more faithfully or for purposes of emphasis.

preposition in grammar, a part of speech coming before a noun or a pronoun to show a location (*in, on*), time (*during*), or some other relationship (for example, figurative relationships in phrases like '*by* heart' or '*on* time').

In the sentence 'Put the book *on* the table', *on* is a preposition governing the noun 'table' and relates the verb 'put' to the phrase 'the table', indicating where the book should go. Some words of English that are

Common spelling errors

These are the 50 most commonly misspelled words in English:

accommodation
appearance
address
amount
achieve

beautiful
bicycle
biscuit
business
beginning

committee
competition

definitely
disappoint
disappear
describe

embarrass
exaggerate
excellent
excitement

finally
foreign
fulfil
friend

grammar
government

handkerchief
humorous
height

immediately

library
literature
league

minute

necessary
neither

occasion

parallel
prejudice
possess
profession
parliament

receive

sincerely
solemn
sergeant
soldier

unusual
until

vicious

often prepositional in function may, however, be used adverbially, as in the sentences, 'He picked the book *up*' and 'He picked *up* the book', in which the ordering is different but the meaning the same. In such cases *up* is called an ***adverbial particle*** and the form *pick up* is a ***phrasal verb***.

pronoun in grammar, a part of speech that is used in place of a noun, usually to save repetition of the noun (for example 'The people arrived around nine o'clock. *They* behaved as though we were expecting *them*').

They, them, he, and *she* are ***personal pronouns*** (representing people); *this/these*, and *that/those* are ***demonstrative pronouns*** (demonstrating or pointing to something: '*this* book and not *that* book'. Words like *that* and *who* can be ***relative pronouns*** in sentences like 'She said *that* she was coming' and 'Tell me *who* did it' relating one clause to another), and *myself* and *himself* are ***reflexive pronouns*** (reflecting back to a person, as in 'He did it *himself*').

punctuation the system of conventional signs (punctuation marks) and spaces by means of which written and printed language is organized in order to be as readable, clear, and logical as possible.

It contributes to the effective layout of visual language; if a work is not adequately punctuated, there may be problems of ambiguity and unclear association among words. Conventions of punctuation differ from language to language, and there are preferred styles in the punctuation of a language like English. Some people prefer a fuller use of punctuation, while others punctuate lightly; comparably, the use of punctuation will vary according to the kind of passage being produced: a personal letter, a newspaper article, and a technical report are all laid out and punctuated in distinctive ways.

Standard punctuation marks and conventions include the period (full stop or point), comma, colon, semicolon, exclamation mark (or point), question mark, apostrophe, asterisk, hyphen, and parenthesis (including dashes, brackets, and the use of parenthetical commas).

question mark punctuation mark (?) used to indicate enquiry or doubt. When indicating enquiry, it is placed at the end of a *direct question* ('Who is coming?') but never at the end of an *indirect question* ('He asked us who was coming'). When indicating doubt, it usually appears between brackets, to show that a writer or editor is puzzled or uncertain about quoted text.

semicolon punctuation mark (;) with a function halfway between the separation of sentence from sentence by means of a period, or full stop, and the gentler separation provided by a comma. It also helps separate items in a complex list: 'pens, pencils, and paper; staples, such as rice and beans; tools, various; and rope'.

Rather than the abrupt 'We saw Mark last night. It was good to see him again', and the casual (and often condemned) 'We saw Mark last night, it was good to see him again', the semicolon reflects a link in a two-part statement and is considered good style: *We saw Mark last night; it was good to see him again.* In such cases an alternative is to use a comma followed by *and* or *but*.

verb the grammatical part of speech for what someone or something does (*to go*), experiences (*to live*), or is (*to be*). Verbs involve the grammatical categories known as number (singular or plural: 'He *runs*; they *run*'), voice (active or passive: 'She *writes* books; it *is written*'), mood (statements, questions, orders, emphasis, necessity, condition), aspect (completed or continuing action: 'She *danced*; she *was dancing*'), and tense (variation according to time: simple present tense, present progressive tense, simple past tense, and so on).

Many verbs are formed from nouns and adjectives by adding affixes (prison: *imprison*; light: *enlighten*; fresh: *freshen up*; pure: *purify*). Some words function as both nouns and verbs (*crack, run*), both adjectives and verbs (*clean*; *ready*), and as nouns, adjectives, and verbs (*fancy*). In the sentences 'They *saw* the accident', 'She *is working* today', and 'He *should have been trying to meet* them', the words in italics are verbs (and, in the last case) two verb groups together; these sentences show just how complex the verbs of English can be.

POLITICS

Political Ideologies

absolutism or ***absolute monarchy*** system of government in which the ruler or rulers have unlimited power. The principle of an absolute monarch, given a right to rule by God (the divine right of kings), was extensively used in Europe during the 17th and 18th centuries. Absolute monarchy is contrasted with limited or constitutional monarchy, in which the sovereign's powers are defined or limited.

anarchism political belief that society should have no government, laws, police, or other authority, but should be a free association of all its members. It does not mean 'without order'; most theories of anarchism imply an order of a very strict and symmetrical kind, but they maintain that such order can be achieved by cooperation. Anarchism must not be confused with nihilism (a purely negative and destructive activity directed against society); anarchism is essentially a pacifist movement.

authoritarianism rule of a country by a dominant elite who repress opponents and the press to maintain their own wealth and power. They are frequently indifferent to activities not affecting their security, and rival power centres, such as trade unions and political parties, are often allowed to exist, although under tight control. An extreme form is totalitarianism.

collectivism position in which the collective (such as the state) has priority over its individual members. It is the opposite of individualism, which is itself a variant of anarchy.

communism revolutionary socialism based on the theories of the political philosophers Karl Marx (1818–1883) and Friedrich Engels (1820–1895), emphasizing common ownership of the means of production and a planned economy. The principle held is that each should work according to their capacity and receive according to their needs. Politically, it seeks the overthrow of capitalism through a proletarian revolution.

The first communist state was the USSR after the revolution of 1917. Revolutionary socialist parties and groups united to form communist parties in other countries (in the UK 1920). After World War II, communism was enforced in those countries that came under Soviet occupation. China emerged after 1961 as a rival to the USSR in world communist leadership, and other countries attempted to adapt communism to their own needs. The late 1980s saw a movement for more individual freedoms in many communist countries, culminating in the abolition or overthrow of communist rule in Eastern European countries and Mongolia, and further state repression in China. The failed hard-line coup in the USSR against President Gorbachev 1991 resulted in the effective abandonment of communism there.

conservatism approach to government favouring the maintenance of existing institutions and identified with a number of Western political parties, such as the British Conservative, US Republican, German Christian Democratic, and Australian Liberal parties. It tends to be explicitly nondoctrinaire and pragmatic but generally emphasizes free-enterprise capitalism, minimal government intervention in the economy, rigid law and order, and the importance of national traditions.

democracy government by the people, usually through elected representatives. In the modern world democracy has developed from the American and French revolutions.

In ***direct democracy*** the whole people meets for the making of laws or the direction of executive officers, for example in Athens in the 5th century BC (and allegedly in modern Libya). Direct democracy today is represented mainly by the use of the referendum, as in the UK, France, Switzerland, and certain states of the USA.

The two concepts underlying ***liberal democracy*** are the right to representative government and the right to enjoy individual freedom. In practice the principal features of a liberal democratic system include representative institutions based on majority rule, through free elections and a choice of political parties; accountability of the government to the electorate; freedom of expression, assembly, and the individual, guaranteed by an independent judiciary; and limitations on the power of government.

It is estimated that almost one-third (1.6 billion) of the world's population live within political systems founded on liberal democracy. While it is an ideology that has been successfully implemented in all parts of the world, this type of political system tends to flourish best in high-income, First World states.

Social democracy is founded on the belief in the gradual evolution of a democratic socialism within existing political structures. The earliest was the German *Sozialdemokratische Partei* (SPD), today one of the two main German parties, created in 1875 from August Bebel's earlier German Social Democratic Workers' Party, founded 1869. Parties along the lines of the German model were founded in the last two decades of the 19th century in a number of countries, including Austria, Belgium, the Netherlands, Hungary, Poland, and Russia. The British Labour Party is in the social democratic tradition.

egalitarianism belief that all citizens in a state should have equal rights and privileges. Interpretations of this can vary, from the notion of equality of opportunity to equality in material welfare and political decision-making. Some states clearly reject any thought of egalitarianism; most accept the concept of equal opportunities but recognize that people's abilities vary widely. Even those states that claim to be socialist find it necessary to have hierarchical structures in the political, social, and economic spheres. Egalitarianism was one of the principles of the French Revolution.

fascism political ideology that denies all rights to individuals in their relations with the state; specifically, the totalitarian nationalist movement founded in Italy 1919 by Benito Mussolini and followed by Adolf Hitler's Germany 1933. The fascist party, the ***Partitio Nazionale Fascista***, controlled Italy 1922–43.

Fascism was essentially a product of the economic and political crisis of the years after World War I. Fascism protected the existing social order by forcible suppression of the working-class movement and by providing scapegoats for popular anger such as outsiders who lived within the state: Jews, foreigners, or blacks; it also prepared the citizenry for the economic and psychological mobilization of war.

imperialism policy of extending the power and rule of a government beyond its own boundaries. A country may attempt to dominate others by direct rule or by less obvious means such as control of markets for goods or raw materials. The latter is often called neo-colonialism.

individualism view in which the individual takes precedence over the collective: the opposite of collectivism. The term ***possessive individualism*** has been applied to the writings of John Locke (1632–1704) and Jeremy Bentham (1748–1832), describing society as comprising individuals interacting through market relations.

liberalism political and social theory that favours representative government, freedom of the press, speech, and worship, the abolition of class privileges, the use of state resources to protect the welfare of the individual, and international free trade. It is historically associated with the Liberal Party in the UK and the Democratic Party in the USA.

Liberalism developed during the 17th–19th centuries as the distinctive theory of the industrial and commercial classes in their struggle against the power of the monarchy, the church, and the feudal landowners. The classical statement of liberal principles is found in *On Liberty* 1859 and other works of the British philosopher J S Mill (1806–1873).

Maoism form of communism based on the ideas and teachings of Chinese communist leader Mao Zedong (1893–1976). It involves an adaptation of Marxism to suit conditions in China and apportions a much greater role to agriculture and the peasantry in the building of socialism, thus effectively bypassing the capitalist (industrial) stage envisaged by Marx.

Marxism or ***dialectical materialism*** philosophical system, developed by the 19th-century German social theorists Karl Marx (1818–1883) and Friedrich Engels (1820–1895). As applied to history it supposes that human society, having passed through successive stages of slavery, feudalism, and capitalism, must advance to communism. The stubborn resistance of any existing system to change necessitates its complete overthrow in the ***class struggle*** – in the case of capitalism, by the proletariat (working class) – rather than gradual modification. Marxism is the basis of communism.

nationalism movement that consciously aims to unify a nation, create a state, or liberate it from foreign or imperialistic rule. Nationalist movements became a potent factor in European politics during the 19th century; since 1900 nationalism has become a strong force in Asia and Africa and in the late 1980s revived strongly in E Europe.

neo-nazism or ***neo-fascism*** term applied to the upsurge in radical and political intolerance occuring in Western Europe from the 1980s. In Austria, Belgium, France, Germany, and Italy the growth of extreme right-wing political groupings, coupled with racial violence – particularly in Germany – has revived memories of the Nazi period, which post-war politicians have vowed must never be allowed to happen again. Sparked in part by a rapid influx of immigrants at a time of world recession, xenophobia took on new and violent extremes, particularly in the hands of previously marginalized political parties. Another factor that influenced the recent rise in neo-nazism has been the liberalization of politics in the post-cold war world, unleashing anti-liberal forces that were previously kept in check by authoritarian regimes.

The German neo-Nazi movement, consisting of dozens of competing groups, claimed approximately 80,000 members in 1993.

pluralism the view that decision-making in contemporary liberal democracies is the outcome of competition among several interest groups in a political system characterized by free elections, representative institutions, and open access to the organs of power. This concept is opposed by corporatism and other approaches that perceive power to be centralized in the state and its principal elites (the Establishment).

socialism movement aiming to establish a classless society by substituting public for private ownership of the means of production, distribution, and exchange. The term has been used to describe positions as widely apart as anarchism and social democracy. Socialist ideas appeared in classical times; in early Christianity; among later Christian sects such as the Anabaptists and Diggers; and, in the 18th and early 19th centuries, were put forward as systematic political aims by Jean-Jacques Rousseau (1712–1778), Claude Saint-Simon (1760–1825), François Fourier (1772-1837), and Robert Owen (1771–1858), among others. Most countries in W Europe have a strong socialist party; for example, in Germany the Social Democratic Party and in Britain the Labour Party.

Thatcherism political outlook comprising a belief in the efficacy of market forces, the need for strong central government, and a conviction that self-help is preferable to reliance on the state, combined with a strong element of nationalism. The ideology is associated with Margaret Thatcher but stems from an individualist view found in Britain's 19th-century Liberal and 20th-century Conservative parties, and is no longer confined to Britain.

theocracy political system run by priests, as was once found in Tibet. In practical terms it means a system where religious values determine political decisions. The closest modern example was Iran during the period when Ayatollah Khomeini was its religious leader, 1979–89.

totalitarianism government control of all activities within a country, overtly political or otherwise, as in fascist or communist dictatorships. Examples of totalitarian regimes are Italy under Benito Mussolini 1922–45; Germany under Adolph Hitler 1933–45; the USSR under Joseph Stalin from the 1930s until his death in 1953; more recently Romania under Nicolae Ceauşescu 1974–89.

Trotskyism form of Marxism advocated by the Russian Leon Trotsky (1879–1940). Its central concept is that of ***permanent revolution***. In his view a proletarian revolution, leading to a socialist society, could not be achieved in isolation, so it would be necessary to spark off further revolutions throughout Europe and ultimately worldwide. This was in direct opposition to the Stalinist view that socialism should be built and consolidated within individual countries.

Political Terms

affirmative action government policy of positive discrimination that favours members of minority ethnic groups and women in such areas as employment and education, designed to counter the effects of long-term discrimination against them. In Europe, Sweden, Belgium, the Netherlands, and Italy actively promote affirmative action through legal and financial incentives.

alliance agreement between two or more states to come to each other's assistance in the event of war. Alliances were criticized after World War I as having contributed to the outbreak of war, but NATO has been a major part of the post-1945 structure of international relations (as was the Warsaw Pact until its dissolution 1991).

ambassador officer of the highest rank in the diplomatic service, who represents the head of one sovereign state at the court or capital of another.

apartheid racial-segregation policy of the government of South Africa, which was legislated 1948, when the Afrikaner National Party gained power, and partly repealed 1991. Nonwhites (classified as Bantu, coloured or mixed, or Indian) do not share full rights of citizenship with the 4.5 million whites (for example, the 23 million black people cannot vote in parliamentary elections), and many public facilities and institutions were until 1990 (and in some cases remain) restricted to the use of one race only; the establishment of Black National States ('homelands') was another manifestation of apartheid. In 1991 President de Klerk repealed the key elements of apartheid, and democratic elections were set for 1994.

The term has also been applied to similar movements and other forms of racial separation, for example social or educational, in other parts of the world.

arms control attempts to limit the arms race between the superpowers by reaching agreements to restrict the production of certain weapons. (See *disarmament* in ***Warfare*** for more.)

autonomy political self-government of a state or, more commonly, a subdivision of a state. Autonomy may be based upon cultural or ethnic differences and often leads eventually to independence.

ballot the process of voting in an election. In political elections in democracies ballots are usually secret: voters indicate their choice of candidate on a voting slip that is placed in a sealed ballot box. ***Ballot rigging*** is a term used to describe elections that are fraudulent because of interference with the voting process or the counting of votes.

blockade cutting-off of a place by hostile forces by land, sea, or air so as to prevent any movement to or fro, in order to compel a surrender without attack or to achieve some other political aim (for example, the Berlin blockade 1948 by the USSR).

cabinet the group of ministers holding a country's highest executive offices who decide government policy. In Britain the cabinet system originated under the Stuarts. Under William III it became customary for the king to select his ministers from the party with a parliamentary majority. The US cabinet, unlike the British, does not initiate legislation, and its members, appointed by the president, must not be members of Congress.

citizenship status as a member of a state. In most countries citizenship may be acquired either by birth or by naturalization. The status confers rights, such as voting and the protection of the law, and also imposes responsibilities, such as military service, in some countries.

coalition association of political groups, usually for some limited or short-term purpose, such as fighting an election or forming a government when one party has failed to secure a majority in a legislature.

Khmer Rouge: a historic defeat?

Feared and loathed for its role in the genocidal 'killing-fields' purges of the Pol Pot era 1976–79, which claimed the lives of up to a quarter of Cambodia's population, the Khmer Rouge was challenged successfully in May 1993 by the silent force of the ballot box. The Maoist guerrillas, fearing humiliation, were determined to boycott and disrupt the National Assembly election, which, held under UN auspices, was the first truly democratic contest in the nation's history. Attacks were launched on civilians and UN personnel, claiming more than a hundred lives between March and May 1993. Yet, despite this intimidation, an astonishing 90% of the country's 4.7 million registered voters cast their ballots, some walking for up to 30 km/20 mi to reach the polling booths. The clear victor of the election was Prince Norodom Sihanouk (70), whose son's royalist party, Funcinpec (the United Front for an Independent, Neutral, Peaceful and Cooperative Cambodia), secured victory over the ruling, former communist Cambodian People's Party (CPP). After the election a Funcinpec–CPP coalition government was proposed. The Khmer Rouge was threatened with political isolation but remained a dangerous guerrilla force. Well-entrenched in the north and west of the country and refusing to disarm, it continued to wage a brutal struggle within the rural hinterlands and launched 'ethnic cleansing' campaigns against ethnic Vietnamese immigrants.

constitution body of fundamental laws of a state, laying down the system of government and defining the relations of the legislature, executive, and judiciary to each other and to the citizens. Since the French Revolution almost all countries (the UK is an exception) have adopted written constitutions; that of the USA (1787) is the oldest.

council in local government in England and Wales, a popularly elected local assembly charged with the government of the area within its boundaries. Under the Local Government Act 1972, they comprise three types: county councils, district councils, and parish councils.

coup d'état or ***coup*** forcible takeover of the government of a country by elements from within that country, generally carried out by violent or illegal means. It differs from a revolution in typically being carried out by a small group (for example, of army officers or opposition politicians) to install its leader as head of government, rather than being a mass uprising by the people.

détente (French) reduction of political tension and the easing of strained relations between nations – for example, the ending of the Cold War 1989–90, although it was first used in the 1970s to describe the easing East–West relations, trade agreements, and cultural exchanges.

dictatorship term or office of an absolute ruler, overriding the constitution. Although dictatorships were common in Latin America during the 19th century, the only European example during this period was the rule of Napoleon III. The crises following World War I produced many dictatorships, including the regimes of Kemal Atatürk in Turkey and Józef Piłsudski in Poland (nationalist); Benito Mussolini in Italy, Adolf Hitler in Germany, Miguel Primo de Rivera and Francisco Franco in Spain, and Antonio Salazar in Portugal (all right-wing); and Joseph Stalin in the USSR (communist).

diplomacy process by which states attempt to settle their differences through peaceful means such as negotiation or arbitration.

dissident in one-party states, a person intellectually dissenting from the official line. Dissidents have been sent into exile, prison, labour camps, and mental institutions, or deprived of their jobs. In China the number of prisoners of conscience increased after the 1989 Tiananmen Square massacre, and in South Africa, despite the release of Nelson Mandela in 1990, numerous political dissidents have remained in jail.

ethnic cleansing the forced expulsion of one ethnic group by another. The term has been frequently used in relation to the Serbian policy toward Moslems in Bosnia-Herzegovina during 1992 and thereafter. The practice of ethnic cleansing has been formally condemned by the United Nations.

federalism system of government in which two or more separate states unite under a common central government while retaining a considerable degree of local autonomy. A federation should be distinguished from a ***confederation***, a looser union of states for mutual assistance. Switzerland, the USA, Canada, Australia, and Malaysia are all examples of federal government, and many supporters of the European Community see it as the forerunner of a federal Europe.

glasnost former Soviet leader Mikhail Gorbachev's policy of liberalizing various aspects of Soviet life, such as introducing greater freedom of expression and information and opening up relations with Western countries. Glasnost was introduced and adopted by the Soviet government 1986.

high commissioner representative of one independent Commonwealth country in the capital of another, ranking with ambassador.

judiciary in constitutional terms, the system of courts and body of judges in a country. The independence of the judiciary from other branches of the central authority is generally considered to be an essential feature of a democratic political system. This independence is often written into a nation's constitution and protected from abuse by politicians.

left wing the socialist parties of the political spectrum. The term originated in the French National Assembly of 1789, where the nobles sat in the place of honour to the right of the president, and the commons sat to the left. This arrangement has become customary in European parliaments, where the progressives sit on the left and the conservatives on the right. It is also usual to speak of the right, left, and centre, when referring to the different elements composing a single party.

lobby individual or pressure group that sets out to influence government action. The lobby is prevalent in the USA, where the term originated in the 1830s from the practice of those wishing to influence state policy waiting for elected representatives in the lobby of the Capitol.

local government that part of government dealing mainly with matters concerning the inhabitants of a particular area or town, usually financed at least in part by local taxes. In the USA and UK, local government has comparatively large powers and responsibilities.

mandate in politics, the right (given by the electors) of an elected government to carry out its programme of policies.

In history, mandate referred to a territory whose administration was entrusted to Allied states by the League of Nations under the Treaty of Versailles after World War I. Mandated territories were former German and Turkish possessions (including Iraq, Syria, Lebanon, and Palestine). When the United Nations replaced the League of Nations 1945, mandates that had not achieved independence became known as trust territories.

manifesto published prospectus of a political party, setting out the policies that the party will pursue if elected to govern. When elected to power a party will often claim that the contents of its manifesto constitute a mandate to introduce legislation to bring these policies into effect.

militia body of civilian soldiers, usually with some military training, who are on call in emergencies, distinct from professional soldiers. In Switzerland, the militia is the national defence force, and every able-

Bosnia: an unending crisis?

The bitter civil war in Bosnia–Herzegovina erupted in April 1992 when Bosnian Serb militia units, reacting to the recognition by the European Community and the USA of the new state's declaration of independence, seized control of a chain of small towns in eastern Bosnia and launched mortar attacks on the capital, Sarajevo. By summer 1992 the outside world was outraged by harrowing television images of emaciated prisoners held in detention camps, notoriously Trnopolje and Omarska, in northern Bosnia; by relevations of gang rapings of thousands of Bosnian Muslim women; and by the sight and consequences of the forced evacuation of numerous villages. Seeking 'purification' of their core regions, the chilling phrase 'ethnic cleansing' entered the modern lexicon. Memories of Nazi genocide and of brutal medieval European religious pogroms were reawakened. To outside west European observers the conflict appeared to be both unbelievable and senseless. Yet, as the spiral of revenge killings escalated, hopes of its speedy resolution became increasingly remote.

As early as the spring of 1992, EC-sponsored talks were convened between the three principal ethnic communities who lived, often intermingled, in the patchwork, quilt former Yugoslavian province: the Bosnian Muslims, forming 44% of the population; the Bosnian Serbs (32%); and the Bosnian Catholic Croats (18%). A Swiss-style confederation was proposed and a UN protection force sent into beleaguered Sarajevo. However, the proposed settlement was summarily rejected by the Bosnian Serbs. Led by the unpredictable poet–psychiatrist Radovan Karadzic (47), and encouraged initially by the nationalist-minded leadership of neighbouring Serbia, they sought to carve out their own sovereign, Serb-controlled regions in preparation for a future Anschluss into a 'Greater Serbia' proper. By the close of 1992, the Serb 'Chetnik' militias, aided by regular troops, had succeeded in their prime goal. They had occupied seven-tenths of Bosnian territory. A further 20% had been annexed by equally nationalist Croat forces. This left the ill-armed, mostly secular, hapless Bosnian Muslims in control of just a tenth of the land area. The bitter fighting, with civilians as specific targets, had claimed at least 150,000 lives, including an estimated 20,000 in the notorious detention camps. More than 1.7 million – 40% of the population – had been made refugees. This constituted the largest forced movement of Europeans since World War II.

The UN special envoy, Cyrus Vance, and EC representative Lord Owen worked tirelessly for a solution, proposing in January 1993 a far-from-perfect but, in the circumstances, realistic peace plan, based around agreement to a ceasefire and the creation of a new state embracing ten ethnically determined, semi-autonomous provinces. To back this plan Western economic sanctions imposed against Serbia since May 1992 were tightened, US relief food and medical aid was air-dropped into starving, isolated eastern Bosnia from March 1993 and, a month later, a no-fly zone, which had been declared by the UN Security Council in October 1992, began to be enforced by American, French, and Dutch warplanes. Accepted by Bosnia's Muslim and Croat leaders, its implementation was thwarted, however, by the stubborn defiance of Bosnia's Serbian minority, unwilling to cut back their territorial holdings from 70% to the Vance–Owen plan's 43%.

Conditioned by the experience of the centuries of tutelage by Muslims, which followed Old Serbia's defeat at Ottoman Turk hands at the Battle of Kosovo (1389), and traumatized more recently by the slaughter of around 500,000 of their kinfolk by Croatia's fascist Ustasha regime during World War II, the Orthodox Christian Serbs retained a powerful sense of national identity. Essentially a defensive and inward-looking sense of nationhood, characterized by deep mistrust of the outside world, it had survived half a century of communist anti-nationalist propaganda. In recent years, it had been skilfully exploited by Serbia's socialist–nationalist strongman president, Slobodan Milosevic, who, like Saddam Hussein during the Gulf War crisis, used the party-controlled media to foment a siege mentality amongst the Serbian people during a period of severe, sanctions-induced, economic austerity.

The Bosnian crisis, like the Balkan Wars of the early 20th century, threatened to have seriously destabilizing consequences for Western Europe as the brutal, revenge-driven conflict showed no signs of abating. The outflow of refugees had heightened already strained racial tensions in states such as Germany. In addition, a real threat existed that, if their displacement became permanent, Bosnia's Muslim community might become the Palestinians of the 1990s: an embittered, stateless focus for a new wave of international terrorism. However, apart from providing humanitarian relief, establishing protected 'safe areas' for the Muslims, exerting economic pressure on Serbia and encouraging political dialogue between the three warring communities, it was difficult to see what else the West could do to bring the conflict to a speedy and successful end. Direct military intervention, involving the clear taking of sides, threatened only to fan its flames.

JJD

bodied man is liable for service in it. In the UK the ***Territorial Army*** and in the USA the ***National Guard*** have supplanted earlier voluntary militias.

nationalization policy of bringing a country's essential services and industries under public ownership. It was pursued, for example, by the UK Labour government 1945–51. In recent years the trend has in many countries (the UK, France, and Japan, for example) reversed (privatization). Assets in the hands of foreign governments or companies may also be nationalized; for example, Iran's oil industry, the Suez Canal, and US- owned fruit plantations in Guatemala, all in the 1950s.

parliament legislative body of a country. The world's oldest parliament is the Icelandic Althing, which dates from about 930. The UK Parliament is usually dated from 1265.

In the UK, Parliament is the supreme legislature, comprising the ***House of Commons*** and the ***House of Lords***. The origins of Parliament are in the 13th century, but its powers were not established until the late 17th century. The powers of the Lords were curtailed 1911, and the duration of parliaments was fixed at five years, but any parliament may extend its own life, as happened during both world wars. The UK Parliament meets in the Palace of Westminster, London.

perestroika in Soviet politics, the wide-ranging economic and political reforms initiated from 1985 by Mikhail Gorbachev, finally leading to the demise of the USSR. Originally, in the economic sphere, *perestroika* was conceived as involving 'intensive development' concentrating on automation and improved labour efficiency. It evolved to attend increasingly to market indicators and incentives ('market socialism') and the gradual dismantling of the Stalinist central-planning system, with decision-taking being devolved to self-financing enterprises.

president the usual title of the head of state in a republic; the power of the office may range from the equivalent of a constitutional monarch to the actual head of the government.

prime minister or ***premier*** head of a parliamentary government, usually the leader of the largest party. In countries with an executive president, the prime minister is of lesser standing, whereas in those with dual executives, such as France, power is shared with the president.

privatization policy or process of selling or transferring state-owned or public assets and services (notably nationalized industries) to private investors. Privatization of services involves the government contracting private firms to supply services previously supplied by public authorities. The term 'privatization' is used even when the state retains a majority share of an enterprise.

The policy has been pursued by the post-1979 Conservative administration in the UK, and by recent governments in France, Japan, Italy, New Zealand, and elsewhere. By 1988 the practice had spread worldwide with communist countries such as China and Cuba selling off housing to private tenants.

propaganda systematic spreading (propagation) of information or disinformation, usually to promote a religious or political doctrine with the intention of instilling particular attitudes or responses. Examples of the use of propaganda are the racial doctrines put forth by Nazism in World War II, and some of the ideas and strategies propagated by the USA and the USSR during the Cold War (1945–90).

Hong Kong

Hong Kong is at present a UK dependency, administered by Crown-appointed governor Chris Patten, former Conservative Party chairman. It is the richest country in the Asia–Pacific area, with a per capita GNP of $18,800, compared with Australia's $17,320 and China's $399. It is destined to be handed over to China 1 July 1997.

The transfer, agreed in 1984, guarantees the continuation of a capitalist way of life, under the concept of 'one nation, two systems', but the inhabitants of Hong Kong have their doubts. The colony has historically enjoyed very little democracy. The new governor wants to increase Hong Kong's democracy, but China's communist leaders are suspicious of such political freedoms spilling over on to the mainland.

Will Chris Patten succeed in his plans for greater democracy? Can Hong Kong's capitalist strength survive after 1997? A game of political poker is being played. China needs a stable and prosperous Hong Kong, but a politically servile one as well. The UK wants to protect the interests of its colonial subjects but also wants good relations with China. Patten's gamble is that by 1997 the experience of eastern Europe will be repeated in Asia but, even if this were to happen, could it be accomplished without bloodshed? The rewards are great but the stakes are high.

purge removal (for example, from a political party) of suspected opponents or persons regarded as undesirable (often by violent means). During the 1930s purges were conducted in the USSR under Joseph Stalin, carried out by the secret police against political opponents, Communist Party members, minorities, civil servants, and large sections of the armed forces' officer corps. Some 10 million people were executed or deported to labour camps from 1934 to 1938.

rainbow coalition or ***rainbow alliance*** loose, left-of-centre alliance of people from several different sections of society that are traditionally politically underrepresented, such as nonwhite ethnic groups. Its aims include promoting minority rights and equal opportunities.

referendum procedure whereby a decision on proposed legislation is referred to the electorate for settlement by direct vote of all the people. A referendum was held in the UK for the first time 1975 on the issue of membership of the European Community. In 1992 several European countries (Ireland, Denmark, France) held referenda on whether or not to ratify the Maastricht Treaty on closer European economic and political union.

A similar device is the ***recall***, whereby voters are given the opportunity of demanding the dismissal from office of officials.

refugee person fleeing from oppressive or dangerous conditions (such as political, religious, or military persecution) and seeking refuge in a foreign country. Their numbers grow every year: in 1970 they numbered 2.5 million; in 1985, 10 million; in 1987, 12 million; in 1990, 15 million; in 1991, 17 million. In 1993 there were an estimated 19 million refugees worldwide, whose resettlement and welfare were the responsibility of the United Nations High Commission for Refugees (UNHCR). An estimated average of 3,000 people a day become refugees.

Major refugee movements in 20th-century Europe include: Jews from the pogroms of Russia 1881–1914 and again after the Revolution; White Russians from the USSR after 1917; Jews from Germany and other Nazi-dominated countries 1933–45; the displaced people of World War II; and from 1991 victims of the the civil wars in Croatia and Bosnia-Herzegovina.

World refugee population, 1991/92

	31.12.91	*31.12.92*
Africa	5,067,932	5,030,467
Asia and Oceania	835,093	1,092,931
Europe	1,202,568	4,407,461
North America	1,020,055	1,041,238
Latin American and the Caribbean	883,319	885,525
South West Asia, North Africa and the Middle East	7,998,516	6,441,107
Total	***17,007,483***	***18,898,729***

Source: UNHCR

right wing the more conservative or reactionary section of a political party or spectrum. It originated in the French national assembly 1789, where the nobles sat in the place of honour on the president's right, whereas the commons were on his left (hence left wing).

sanction economic or military measure taken by a state or number of states to enforce international law. The first use of sanctions was the attempted economic boycott of Italy (1935–36) during the Abyssinian War by the League of Nations; a current example is the sanctions against South Africa on human-rights grounds by the UN and other organizations from 1985.

shuttle diplomacy in international relations, the efforts of an independent mediator to achieve a compromise solution between belligerent parties, travelling back and forth from one to the other.

sovereignty absolute authority within a given territory. The possession of sovereignty is taken to be the distinguishing feature of the state, as against other forms of community. The term has an internal aspect, in that it refers to the ultimate source of authority within a state, such as a parliament or monarch, and an external aspect, where it denotes the independence of the state from any outside authority.

state territory that forms its own domestic and foreign policy, acting through laws that are typically decided by a government and carried out, by force if necessary, by agents of that government. It can be argued that growth of regional international bodies such as the European Community means that states no longer enjoy absolute sovereignty.

summit or ***summit conference*** meeting of heads of government to discuss common interests, especially the US–Soviet summits 1959–90, of which there were 15. The term was first used during World War II; and the Yalta Conference and Potsdam Conference 1945 were summits that did much to determine the political structure of the postwar world. Later summits have been of varying importance, being partly used as public-relations exercises.

terrorism systematic violence in the furtherance of political aims, often perpetrated by small guerrilla groups.

trade union organization of employed workers formed to undertake collective bargaining with employers and to try to achieve improved working conditions for its members. Attitudes of government to unions and of unions to management vary greatly from country to country. Probably the most effective trade-union system is that of Sweden, and the internationally best known is Poland's Solidarity.

unilateralism support for ***unilateral nuclear disarmament***: scrapping a country's nuclear weapons without waiting for other countries to agree to do so at the same time.

veto (Latin 'I forbid') exercise by a sovereign, branch of legislature, or other political power, of the right to prevent the enactment or operation of a law, or the taking of some course of action. At the United Nations, members of the Security Council can exercise a veto on resolutions.

vote expression of opinion by ballot, show of hands, or other means. In systems that employ direct vote, the plebiscite and referendum are fundamental mechanisms. In parliamentary elections the results can be calculated in a number of ways. The main electoral systems are: ***simple plurality*** or ***first past the post***, with single-member constituencies (USA, UK, India, Canada); ***absolute majority***, achieved for example by the ***alternative vote***, where the voter, in single-member constituencies, chooses a candidate by marking preferences (Australia), or by the ***second ballot***, where, if a clear decision is not reached immediately, a second ballot is held (France, Egypt); ***proportional representation***, achieved for example by the ***party list*** system (Israel, most countries of Western Europe, and several in South America), the ***additional member*** system (Germany), the ***single transferable vote*** (Ireland and Malta), and the ***limited vote*** (Japan).

All British subjects over 18, except peers, the insane, and felons, are entitled to vote in UK local government and parliamentary elections. A register

The Clinton presidency: is it living up to its promise?

Hailed *Time* magazine's 'Man of the Year' in December 1992, six months later Bill Clinton's public approval rating stood at just 36%. This was the lowest-ever figure for a new president just four months into office. Already political commentators were beginning to dub Clinton a 'second Carter': a skilled campaigner but not an administrator, destined to be a one-term failure. So disappointing was his early performance that Republican opponents had begun to prepare their challenges for 1996. What had gone wrong for this new Lochinvar who had promised a new era of progressive social change and economic renewal? Was the Clinton presidency already doomed, or could this slump in public support be made temporary and overcome with policy, personnel, and presentational changes?

An equivocal mandate – a chameleon personality

The roots of these problems could be traced to the gruelling year-long election campaign from which, through sheer single-minded determination and the greater weaknesses of his own Democratic Party and Republican rivals, he had emerged victorious on 3 November 1992. During the campaign he withstood charges of womanizing, and 'draft dodging' during the Vietnam War. He was repeatedly branded by Republican opponents as a traditional big-spending liberal. Unlike his 1988 Democrat predecessor Michael Dukakis, Clinton refused to buckle. This is why he secured *Time*'s accolade. However, although he became the first Democrat to secure the presidency in 12 years, Clinton's share of the national vote was just 43%: the lowest for a successful presidential candidate since Woodrow Wilson. The election witnessed a decisive rejection of the unpopular incumbent, George Bush, with 38% of the national vote compared with 53% in 1988. But the electorate clearly had reservations, splitting support between Clinton and maverick independent Ross Perot, who captured 19% of the vote, the strongest showing of any third-party candidate since 1912.

Despite projecting himself as the Kennedy-esque representative of a young, new political generation and a moderate 'New Democratic Party', 46-year-old Clinton failed to convince. A former Rhodes Scholar at Oxford University and a successful, long-serving governor of the southern state of Arkansas, Clinton had the political intellect and experience for the Oval Office. But did he have a clear vision: a core of firmly held principles and beliefs to give purpose to his presidency?

Early mistakes

During the pre-inauguration period of November 1992–January 1993, president-elect Clinton assembled the core of an impressively experienced cabinet team. Lloyd Bentsen (71), Democratic vice-presidential candidate in 1988, was appointed treasury secretary, while Warren Christopher (67), deputy secretary of state under President Carter, was placed in charge of foreign policy. But the new president's concern for a true gender and ethnic balance caused inordinate delays in filling many portfolios, as well as the humiliating withdrawals of his first two female designates as attorney-general.

In his first address to a joint session of Congress, in February 1993, Clinton impressed, unveiling an ambitious five-year federal deficit reduction and economic stimulation package. The plan combined tax increases for the wealthy with public spending cuts, and was swiftly set upon by interest-group representatives within Congress.

Determined to avoid the mistakes of the 'foreign policy president' George Bush during his first months, Clinton deliberately put diplomatic activities on the back burner. This led to taunts of 'indecisiveness' as Serb atrocities mounted in Bosnia-Herzegovina. And in implementing a campaign pledge to end the ban on the employment of gays in the armed forces, the president alienated the military's high command.

By the late spring of 1993 Clinton had the image of another Jimmy Carter: a leader so engrossed with policy details and so ready to see all sides of an issue that he could not take clear decisions and chart a strategic course. To compound matters, his public standing was lowered by a number of miscalculations and gaffes, perhaps the most notorious being the enforced closure, in May 1993, of two runways at Los Angeles International Airport for an hour while the presidential locks were trimmed by Cristophe, a Beverly Hills hair stylist.

The way back

Alert to the mounting unease with his presidency, Clinton responded in June 1993 by appointing as his chief spokesman David Gergen, an astute Republican veteran of the Nixon and Reagan White Houses. The aim was for a clearer, more coherent public image to be projected for the president and his sponsored programmes. One of the key initiatives, a radical overhaul of the health care system, was being superintended by the president's formidable wife, Hillary Rodham Clinton. On the success of this programme, and on the performance of the slowly reviving US economy, much of the future of the Clinton presidency rested.

JDD

is prepared annually, and since 1872 voting has been by secret ballot. Under the Corrupt and Illegal Practices Act 1883, any candidate attempting to influence voters by gifts, loans or promises, or by intimidation, is liable to a fine or imprisonment. The voting system is by a simple majority in single-member constituencies.

welfare state political system under which the state (rather than the individual or the private sector) has responsibility for the welfare of its citizens. Services such as unemployment and sickness benefits, family allowances and income supplements, pensions, medical care, and education may be provided and financed through state insurance schemes and taxation.

Internationally, the aim of creating a welfare state has been adopted in several countries, particularly in Scandinavia. The welfare-state concept was built into the political structures of communist states, led by the USSR, but even here economic realities tempered its practical implementation.

UK Central Government

Central government in the UK is currently based on 16 major departments of state, each headed by a minister who is a member of the cabinet, and 16 minor departments or subdepartments.

MAJOR DEPARTMENTS

Ministry of Agriculture, Fisheries and Food
Ministry of Defence
Department for Education
Department of Employment
Department of the Environment Foreign and Commonwealth Office
Department of Health Department for National Heritage
Home Office
Northern Ireland Office
Scottish Office
Department of Social Security
Department of Trade and Industry
Department of Transport
Treasury *
Welsh Office

* The Treasury is the one department with two cabinet representatives, the chancellor of the Exchequer and the chief secretary to the Treasury, and, since the prime minister is formally also First Lord of the Treasury, it can be argued that the cabinet representation is threefold.

MINOR DEPARTMENTS

Board of Inland Revenue
Central Office of Information
Department of National Savings
Export Credits Guarantee Department
H M Customs and Excise Department
Her Majesty's Household
Her Majesty's Stationery Office
Law Officers' Department
Lord Advocate's Department
Lord Chancellor's Department
Office of Arts and Libraries
Office of the Minister for the Civil Service
Overseas Development Administration
Parliamentary Counsel's Office
Paymaster General's Office
Privy Council Office*

* Direct representation in the cabinet.

NONDEPARTMENTAL CABINET MEMBERS

Apart from the prime minister, there are three members of the cabinet without specific departmental responsibilities : Lord President of the Council, who is Leader of the House of Commons; Lord Privy Seal, who is Leader of the House of Lords; and Chancellor of the Duchy of Lancaster, who is responsible for the implementation of the Citizens' Charter, for science, and for civil-service reform.

MINISTERIAL GRADINGS

The top-ranking ministers are members of the cabinet. Most cabinet ministers heading departments are now styled secretary of state. The exceptions are: the minister of Agriculture, Fisheries, and Food; the Lord Chancellor; the chancellor of the Exchequer; and the President of the Board of Trade.

The other ministers, in descending order of rank, are:

minister of state who may be of cabinet rank (may sometimes be styled minister of state and sometimes minister)

undersecretary of state (may sometimes be styled minister)

parliamentary undersecretary (in the cases of Agriculture, Fisheries, and Food; and the Treasury; styled parliamentary secretary)

When the minister heading a major department is styled secretary of state, junior ministers in that department are styled parliamentary undersecretaries. In other cases they are styled parliamentary secretaries.

CIVIL-SERVICE GRADINGS

The three most senior grades in the home civil service, found in all major departments, are: permanent secretary, deputy secretary, undersecretary.

TYPICAL STRUCTURE OF A DEPARTMENT

All departments have specific, distinctive features but most conform to the following pattern:

political head: secretary of state, supported by one or more ministers of state and junior ministers

nonpolitical head: permanent secretary, supported by administrative, executive, and clerical staff.

MAJOR DEPARTMENTS

Ministry of Agriculture, Fisheries, and Food
established 1955, through combination of existing agriculture, fisheries, and food ministries
responsibilities agriculture, horticulture, fisheries, and food policies

ministerial team minister, one minister of state, two parliamentary secretaries
head Gillian Shephard
permanent staff 10,400
administrative headquarters Whitehall Place, London SW1

Ministry of Defence

established 1964, when Admiralty, War Office, and Air Defence were brought together in one ministry
responsibilities national defence, including overall control of the Royal Navy, Army, and Royal Air Force, and arms procurement
ministerial team secretary of state, two ministers of state, one parliamentary undersecretary
head Malcolm Rifkind
permanent staff 98,000, including Royal Ordnance factories
administrative headquarters Whitehall, London SW1

Department for Education

established 1944, as the Ministry of Education
responsibilities education and scientific research policies
ministerial team secretary of state, one minister of state, one parliamentary undersecretary
head John Patten
permanent staff 2,600
administrative headquarters York Road, London SE1

Department of Employment

established 1970 in its present form. The original Ministry of Labour was formed in 1917
responsibilities employment and training policies
ministerial team secretary of state, one minister of state, two parliamentary undersecretaries
head David Hunt
permanent staff 53,700
administrative headquarters Tothill Street, London SW1

Department of the Environment

established 1970, bringing together ministries of Housing and Local Government, Transport, and Building and Works. Transport returned to an independent status in 1975
responsibilities housing, construction, local government, sport and recreation policies, and preservation of the environment
ministerial team secretary of state, three ministers of state, one parliamentary undersecretary
head John Selwyn Gummer
permanent staff 19,400
administrative headquarters Marsham Street, London SW1

Foreign and Commonwealth Office

established 1782, as the Foreign Office
responsibilities conduct of foreign policy, representation of British interests abroad, relations with other members of the Commonwealth, overseas aid policy and administration
ministerial team secretary of state, four ministers of state, one parliamentary undersecretary
head Douglas Hurd
permanent staff 8,300
administrative headquarters Downing Street, London SW1

Department of Health

established 1988, following the division of the Department of Health and Social Security into two separate departments. Ministry of Health formed in 1919
responsibilities operation of the national health service and overall policies on health
ministerial team secretary of state, one minister of state, three parliamentary undersecretaries
head Virginia Bottomley
permanent staff 11,400, excluding NHS staff
administrative headquarters Whitehall, London SW1

Department for National Heritage

established 1992
responsibilities broadcasting and the media, the arts, sport and recreation, the national lottery
ministerial team secretary of state, one minister of state
head Peter Brooke
permanent staff not yet known
administrative headquarters Whitehall, London SW1

Home Office

established 1782
responsibilities administration of justice, penal system (including the prison and probation services), police, fire, civil defence, licensing (including marriage, liquor, theatres, and cinemas), radio and television broadcasting, immigration and nationality policies
ministerial team secretary of state, two ministers of state, two parliamentary undersecretaries
head Michael Howard
permanent staff 45,000
administrative headquarters Queen Anne's Gate, London SW1

Northern Ireland Office

established 1972
responsibilities direct government of Northern Ireland, including administration of security, law and order, and economic, industrial, and social policies
ministerial team secretary of state, one minister of state, one parliamentary undersecretary
head Patrick Mayhew
permanent staff 29,500
administrative headquarters Whitehall, London SW1, and Belfast

Scottish Office

established 1707 in England, 1938 in Scotland
responsibilities administration for Scotland of policies on agriculture and fisheries, education, industrial development, law and order, and health
ministerial team secretary of state, two ministers of state, two parliamentary undersecretaries
head Ian Lang
permanent staff 13,000
administrative headquarters Whitehall, London SW1, and Edinburgh

Department of Social Security

established 1988, after being part of the Department of Health and Social Security
responsibilities administration of social-service policies, including pensions, unemployment, income support, and disability benefits

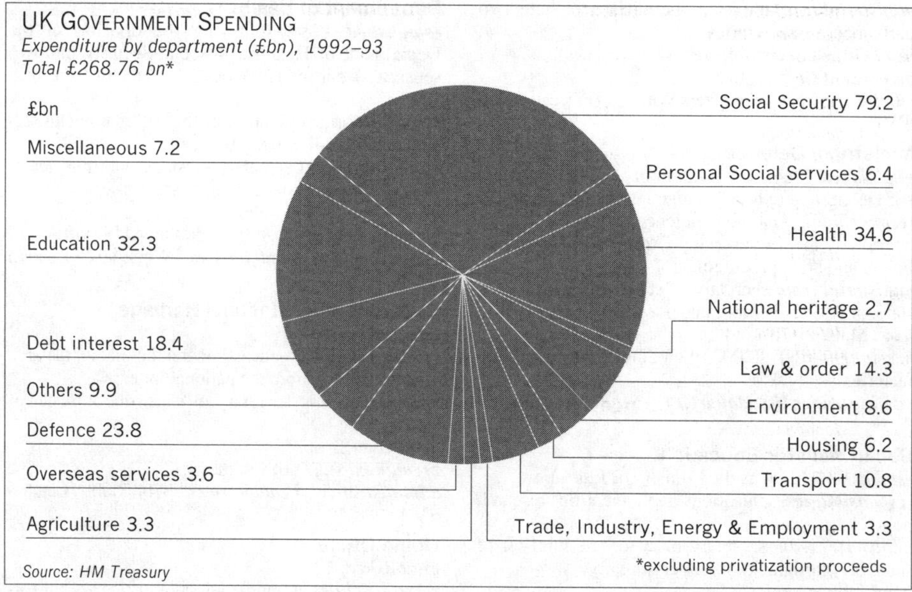

ministerial team secretary of state, one minister of state, three parliamentary undersecretaries
head Peter Lilley
permanent staff 78,000
administrative headquarters Whitehall, London SW1

Department of Trade and Industry
established 1970, bringing together the Board of Trade, founded in 1786, and the Ministry of Technology, formed in 1964; took over the responsibilities of the Department of Energy in 1992
responsibilities administration of policies on international trade, industry, competition, industrial research and assistance to exporters
ministerial team President of the Board of Trade (secretary of state), three ministers of state, three parliamentary undersecretaries
head Michael Heseltine
permanent staff 12,500
administrative headquarters Marsham Street, London SW1

Department of Transport
established 1975, in its present form
responsibilities land, sea, and air transport policies, including sponsorship of British Rail, and construction and maintenance of motorways and trunk roads
ministerial team secretary of state, two ministers of state, two parliamentary undersecretaries
head John MacGregor
permanent staff 16,000
administrative headquarters Victoria Street, London SW1

Treasury
established 1612
responsibilities control of public expenditure, national economic policy, including monetary and fiscal measures, efficiency in the public sector, international finance, and oversight of the financial system
ministerial team chancellor of the Exchequer, chief secretary (of cabinet rank), three ministers of state rank (paymaster general, financial secretary, and economic secretary), one parliamentary secretary
chancellor Kenneth Clarke
chief secretary Michael Portillo
permanent staff 3,200
administrative headquarters Parliament Street, London SW1

Welsh Office
established 1951
responsibilities administration for Wales of policies on agriculture, education, health and social services, local government, planning, sport, and tourism. It is also responsible for promoting the Welsh language and culture
ministerial team secretary of state, one minister of state, one parliamentary undersecretary
head John Redwood
permanent staff 2,300
administrative headquarters Whitehall, London SW1, and Cardiff

MINOR DEPARTMENTS

Board of Inland Revenue
parent department Treasury
responsibilities collection of central government taxes, other than VAT and customs and excise duties, throughout the UK

Cabinet Office
parent department Cabinet
responsibilities services the cabinet and all its committees and subcommittees; it organizes meetings; prepares and distributes agendas and cabinet papers, including minutes; and decides, with the prime minister, which issues should go to the full cabinet and which to one of its committees or subcommttees

Central Office of Information (COI)
parent department Treasury
resposibilities operation of government information services

Customs and Excise Department
parent department Treasury
responsibilities collection of customs and excise duties, including VAT

Department of National Savings
parent department Treasury
responsibilities management of government savings schemes

Exports Credits Guarantee Department
parent department Department of Trade and Industry
responsibilities management of government scheme to underwrite finance for exporters

Her Majesty's Household
parent department Lord Chamberlain
responsibilities management of the affairs of the royal household

Her Majesty's Stationery Office (HMSO)
parent department Treasury
responsibilities production and sale of government publications

Law Officers' Department
parent department freestanding, under Attorney General
responsibilities legal advice to the government and representation of the Crown in court

Lord Advocate's Department
parent department freestanding
responsibilities administration of law in Scotland

Lord Chancellor's Department
parent department freestanding, under Lord Chancellor
responsibilities administration of civil law in England and Wales, including the appointment of the judiciary in lower courts and advice on appointments in the higher courts

The Lord Chancellor also presides over sittings in the House of Lords

Office of Arts and Libraries
parent department Privy Council Office, under Lord President of the Council
responsibilities promotion of the arts

Office of the Minister for the Civil Service
parent department prime minister
responsibilities management of the home civil service

Overseas Development Administration (ODA)
parent department Foreign and Commonwealth Office
responsibilities administration of development assistance to overseas countries

Parliamentary Counsel's Office
parent department freestanding
responsibilities drafting of parliamentary legislation

Paymaster General's Office
parent department Treasury
responsibilities administration of payment of government financial liabilities

Privy Council Office
parent department freestanding, under Lord President of the Council
responsibilities a miscellany of duties, including management of the civil service and promotion of the arts

GALLUP POLL: Political Parties

How much confidence do you have in the following institutions?

	Feb 1993	Dec 1992	Mar 1992	Dec 1989	Nov 1987
Parliament					
A great deal	5	3	6	7	8
Quite a lot	25	22	41	31	36
Not very much	47	45	43	43	40
None at all	22	30	10	19	16
The Civil Service					
A great deal	4	4	5	6	6
Quite a lot	32	30	36	37	39
Not very much	48	45	48	42	43
None at all	16	22	10	15	12

On the whole, how much confidence do you have in Conservative politicians to deal wisely with Britain's problems – very great, considerable, little, or very little?

	Mar 1993	Jul 1992	Oct 1990	Nov 1989	Aug 1987
Very great	3	4	3	8	7
Considerable	18	28	30	33	36
Little	20	27	20	22	20
Very little	26	18	25	20	20
None at all	32	19	19	15	15
Don't know	2	3	2	2	3

On the whole, how much confidence do you have in Labour politicians to deal wisely with Britain's problems – very great, considerable, little, or very little?

	Mar 1993	Jul 1992	Oct 1990	Nov 1989	Aug 1987
Very great	4	3	5	8	6
Considerable	29	25	26	31	21
Little	28	25	25	23	26
Very little	19	22	22	18	23
None at all	17	21	17	17	20
Don't know	4	4	5	3	4

On the whole, how much confidence do you have in Liberal Democrat politicians to deal wisely with Britain's problems – very great, considerable, little, or very little?

	Mar 1993	Jul 1992	Oct 1990
Very great	1	1	2
Considerable	17	19	16
Little	31	31	26
Very little	19	18	19
None at all	24	22	22
Don't know	8	9	15

Taking everything into account, which party has the best policies?

	Mar 1993	Apr 1992	June 1987	June 1983	May 1979
Conservative	28	35	38	42	37
Labour	38	30	29	21	32
Liberal Democrat	12	13	17	20	14
Scottish Nationalist/ Plaid Cymru (Welsh Nationalist)	1	2	1	1	2
Other	2	1	1	1	1
None of them/don't know	19	19	15	16	14

Here is a list of politicians' names. Could you tell me whether you trust each of them or not? Or, to put it another way, would you buy a used car from this person or not?

	Trust, Yes, buy	Do not trust, not buy	Don't know
John Major	40	56	4
Michael Heseltine	18	75	7
Robin Cook	28	49	23
Norman Lamont	14	79	7
John Smith	57	34	9
Virginia Bottomley	34	56	10
Tony Blair	26	34	40
Kenneth Clarke	22	62	16
Margaret Beckett	27	34	39
Douglas Hurd	42	46	12
Gordon Brown	30	35	36
Paddy Ashdown	54	38	9

In political matters people talk of 'the left' and 'the right'. How would you place your views on this scale?

	Feb 1993	Mar 1992	Jan 1991
Far left	2	2	2
Substantially left	2	4	4
Moderately left	14	12	12
Slightly left	13	14	15
All left	31	32	33
Slightly right	18	17	15
Moderately right	20	21	17
Substantially right	4	4	4
Far right	2	2	2
All right	44	44	38
Middle of the road*	9	11	12
Don't know	15	14	17

* Volunteered

Britain and Europe

Irrespective of your own views, how do you see Britain's future over the next decade or two? Will Britain be a great world power, a major power within Europe, a relatively minor power within Europe, or will Britain have very little influence anywhere in the world?

World power	3
Major power in Europe	33
Minor power in Europe	37
Very little influence	20
Don't know	7

Do you want Parliament to ratify – that is, formally approve – the Maastricht Treaty or not?

Yes	30
No	27
Don't know	43

Do you think we should or should not have a referendum, as in Denmark and France, on whether we should ratify, formally approve, the Maastricht Treaty?

Should	71
Should not	14
Don't know	14

As a result of the coming of the single European Market, which of these do you think will happen?

People will buy more wines and spirits on the Continent to bring home	71
More people from Britain will look for jobs on the Continent	53
People travelling to the Continent from Britain will no longer have to carry passports	44
More goods that do not meet British standards will be imported into Britain	41
More people from the Continent, apart from refugees, will come to work in Britain	39
VAT will soon be extended to things like food, books, travel, and children's clothing	39
More refugees from eastern Europe will come into this country	35
The pound will become part of a single currency	32
Cars will become cheaper to buy in Britain	27
British exporters will be more successful in competing in Continental markets	26
Air fares in Europe will be reduced	23
Don't know	7

RELIGION

Religious Traditions

BCE/CE before the common era (BCE) and common era (CE) are abbreviations used in this section to replace, respectively, before Christ (BC) and anno Domini (AD).

African religions there is a wide variety of belief and practice in African religion. Most indigenous African religions are basically polytheistic (believing in a number of gods), but there is often a concept of one High God, generally a creator who has withdrawn from interaction with the world. There are also many spirits, which are present in all natural objects: water is seen as a particularly powerful force. Dead ancestors are very important in African religions, and are consulted before major undertakings. If offended, they can cause natural disasters and sterility, so they must be placated with offerings. In society, healers are highly regarded, as they deal with supernatural powers, as do diviners, but the most powerful human figure is the chief-king, who is surrounded by prohibitions because he is so dangerous: he is the life of the tribe incarnate, though because of this he may be required to sacrifice himself to preserve the health of his people.

Australian Aboriginal religion the creation story of the Australian Aborigines is recorded in the ***Dreamtime*** stories. These reveal how giant human and other animals sprang from the earth, sea, and sky and criss-crossed the empty continent of Australia on a journey known as Dreamtime. At the end of their journey they returned into the earth where it is believed their spirits still exist. The places where they travelled or sank back into the land became mountain ranges, rocks, and sites full of sacred meaning.

Every sacred site has its own Dreamtime story that is part of the sacred law and must be re-enacted at certain times of the year in order to maintain the life of the land and the Dreamtime. Each Australian Aborigine has their own particular Dreamtime Ancestor although they are related to many other ancestors through kinship. When hunting, Aborigines are careful never to trap, maim, or kill the animals who are associated with their kinship ancestors.

Buddhism one of the great world religions, which originated in India about 500 BCE. It derives from the teaching of Buddha, who is regarded as one of a series of such enlightened beings; there are no gods. The chief doctrine is that of ***karma***, good or evil deeds meeting an appropriate reward or punishment either in this life or (through reincarnation) a long succession of lives. The main divisions in Buddhism are ***Theravāda*** (or ***Hīnayāna***) in SE Asia and ***Mahāyāna*** in N Asia; ***Lamaism*** in Tibet and ***Zen*** in Japan are among the many Mahāyāna sects. Its symbol is the lotus. There are approximately 315 million (1992) Buddhists worldwide.

scriptures The only complete canon of the Buddhist scriptures is that of the Sinhalese (Sri Lanka) Buddhists, in Pāli, but other schools have essentially the same canon in Sanskrit. The scriptures, known as *pitakas* (baskets), date from the 2nd to 6th centuries CE. There are three divisions: ***vinaya*** (discipline), listing offences and rules of life; the sūtras (discourse), or ***dharma*** (doctrine), the exposition of Buddhism by Buddha and his disciples; and ***abhidharma*** (further doctrine), later discussions on doctrine.

beliefs The self is not regarded as permanent, as it is subject to change and decay. It is attachment to the things that are essentially impermanent that cause delusion, suffering, greed, and aversion, the origin of karma, and they in turn create further karma and the sense of self is reinforced. Actions which incline towards selflessness are called 'skilful karma' and they are on the path leading to enlightenment. In the ***Four Noble Truths*** the Buddha acknowledged the existence and source of suffering, and showed the way of deliverance from it through the ***Eightfold Path***. The aim of following the Eightfold Path is to break the chain of karma and achieve dissociation from the body by attaining ***nirvana*** ('blowing out') – the eradication of all desires, either in annihilation or by absorption of the self in the infinite. Supreme reverence is accorded to the historical Buddha (Śākyamuni, or, when referred to by his clan name, Gautama), who is seen as one in a long and ongoing line of Buddhas, the next one (Maitreya) being due *c.* CE 3000.

divisions: Theravāda Buddhism, the School of the Elders, also known as ***Hīnayāna*** or Lesser Vehicle, prevails in SE Asia (Sri Lanka, Thailand, and Burma), and emphasizes the mendicant, meditative life as the way to break the cycle of ***samsāra***, or death and rebirth. Its three alternative goals are *arahat*: one who has gained insight into the true nature of things; *Paccekabuddha*, an enlightened one who lives alone and does not teach; and fully awakened *Buddha*. Its scriptures are written in ***Pāli***, an Indo-Aryan language with its roots in N India. In India itself Buddhism had virtually died out by the 13th century, and was replaced by Hinduism. However, it has 5 million devotees in the 20th century and is still growing.

Mahāyāna, or Greater Vehicle arose at the beginning of the Christian era. This tradition emphasised the eternal, formless principle of the Buddha as the essence of all things. It exhorts the individual not merely to attain personal nirvana, but to become a trainee Buddha, or ***bodhisattva***, and so save others; this meant the faithful could be brought to enlightenment by a bodhisattva without following the austeri-

Followers of major faiths (1992)

Christianity	1,833,022,000
Islam	1,025,585,000
Hinduism	732,812,000
Buddhism	314,939,000
Sikhism	18,000,000
Judaism	17,822,000
Confucianism	8,028,000
Jainism	3,794,000
Baha'ism	3,517,000
Shintoism	3,222,800

Source: David B. Barrett

The ordination of women

The recent crisis in the Church of England over the ordination of women has threatened to break up the church, with fears that a large number of those opposed to the General Synod's decision to ordain women would leave. Without doubt the vote on 11 Nov 1992 was a victory for those who had campaigned for many years to allow women to become priests in the Church of England, a vote that had already been passed in other parts of the Anglican Communion such as the USA, Canada, and New Zealand. The Church of England remains a stronghold of those Anglicans opposed to the ordination of women. The threat of the retired bishop of London, Graham Leonard, was that those Anglicans leaving over the issue would seek to form a separate Uniate church. This church would retain the characteristics of Anglican liturgy, but would be received into the Roman Catholic communion.

The crisis claimed by those who were against ordination was that the real issue was one of authority: what right had the Church of England to go back on hundreds of years of history and tradition of the wider church; that is, the Catholic church? The allegiance of the anti-ordination lobby is predominantly Anglo-Catholic; that is, those who are aware of the historical rootedness of the Anglican church in the Catholic faith. These Anglicans are not prepared to accept the authority of either their own archbishop or the General Synod.

The irony is that the church to which the rebels are seeking union is still open as far as the ordination of women is concerned. Pope Paul VI ensured that both the role of women and the possibility of women's ordination remain questions to be explored for the future. In 1975, US feminist Betty Friedan told the pope that 'during his papacy he had done more to give women a voice than in the 1,900 previous years'. The Catholic Commission on Women set up by the pope as far back as 1976 concluded that the New Testament was ambiguous over the possible accession of women to the priesthood. Even though the pope was personally opposed to the ordination of women, he had a reluctance to commit the Catholic church to irrevocable courses of action.

Other arguments against the ordination of women have been used, such as: How can a female represent Christ at the altar? George Carey, while bishop of Bath and Wells, stirred up a public commotion when he roundly dismissed this argument with 'the idea that only a male can represent Christ at the altar is a serious heresy'. He did not claim that those opposed to ordination were heretics, but his statements generated hostility against him by those who opposed ordination. Cries of 'Get rid of George Carey' were heard at a rally of the anti-ordination lobby, Forward in Faith, in May 1993. Those who are in favour of women's ordination stress that if Christ cannot be represented by women at the altar, how can he represent women at the cross? In other words, arguments such as these imply Christ came to save one half of humanity.

How have those who were bitterly disappointed by the vote on women's ordination been received in their overtures to Rome? As might be expected, the Roman church was cautious in allowing Anglicans entry into the Catholic church simply because they rejected women's ordination. The Conference of Roman Catholic Bishops which met at the end of April 1993 decided that each and every person and priest who sought to become Roman Catholic should go through the usual period of testing and instruction. The number of those originally cited by Forward in Faith as likely to leave the Church of England for Rome has dropped from 3,000 to a few hundred. Cardinal Hulme, head of the Catholic church in England, was sympathetic to the problems over authority felt by the dissident members of the Church of England. However, he insisted that the goal of their reception would be 'their eventual total integration into the full life of the Catholic church'. The authority of the Catholic church also could not recognize the official validity of Anglican ministerial orders, which rules out an automatic transfer from Anglican to Catholic priesthood. This lack of official recognition of any priesthood other than that of the Roman Catholic Church is particularly painful for those Anglicans who reject the priestly ministry of women because it is out of line with the accepted practice of the Roman church. For them, staying and leaving both seem equally painful and equally impossible.

The strong Anglican ability for compromise was once again apparent in the decision in May 1993 of Bishop Hope of London to allow women to serve as priests in the London diocese. The plans that were drawn up by the Anglican Bishops' Conference in Manchester early in the year allowed certain areas to be havens of male priesthood. There were fears that some dioceses would be no-go areas for women. His proposal would allow women to be ordained by those bishops who agreed with women's ordination and would be given special licence to function in a diocese where the acting bishop was opposed. His statements came in the same week that John Austin Baker, the bishop of Salisbury, suggested that no one should be ordained who did not accept women's ordination. His statements are likely to continue to fuel the debate. However, the perceived split in the Anglican church forecast earlier in the year has not materialized.

The issue has helped to create the atmosphere of debate on the role of women and the whole question of women's ministry.

At its best, this could be an opportunity to discuss the model of priesthood accepted by the Anglican church as well as the role of women generally. The feminist theologian Sara Maitland, who chose in 1993 to be received into the Roman Catholic Church, remarked that the vote to ordain women was 'a moment of liberation', believing that 'much of the best feminist theology in Britain is coming from Roman Catholicism'. The small number of those deciding to become Roman Catholic over the issue is perhaps a victory for common sense. Like all churches, the Roman church is seeking to expand and develop its ministerial tasks for women. To do otherwise would amount to a failure to keep in touch with contemporary society.

CDD

ties of Theravāda, and the cults of various Buddhas and bodhisattvas arose. Mahāyāna Buddhism also emphasises ***shunyata***, or the experiential understanding of the emptiness of all things, even Buddhist doctrine.

Mahāyāna Buddhism prevails in N Asia (China, Korea, Japan, and Tibet). In the 6th century CE Mahāyāna spread to China with the teachings of Bodhidharma and formed Ch'an, which became established in Japan from the 12th century as ***Zen Buddhism***. Zen emphasises silent meditation with sudden interruptions from a master to encourage awakening of the mind. Japan also has the lay organization ***Sōka Gakkai*** (Value Creation Society), founded 1930, which equates absolute faith with immediate material benefit; by the 1980s it was followed by more than 7 million households.

Esoteric, Tantric, or Diamond Buddhism became popular in Tibet and Japan, and holds that enlightenment is already within the disciple and with the proper guidance, (that is privately passed on by a master) can be realised.

Christianity world religion derived from the teaching of Jesus in the first third of the 1st century, with a present-day membership of about 1 billion. It is divided into different groups or denominations which differ in some areas of belief and practice. Its main divisions are the Roman Catholic, Eastern Orthodox, and Protestant churches. There are approximately 1,833 million (1992) Christian believers worldwide.

beliefs Christianity is based on the belief that the man Jesus, born about 2000 years ago, is 'the Christ', the Son of God, and that his death and resurrection broke down the barrier that human sinfulness put between humanity and God. Christians believe in one God with three aspects or persons: God the Father, God the Son (Jesus), and God the Holy Spirit, who is the power of God working in the world. Christians believe in God the Creator, who came to Earth as Jesus, was crucified, resurrected three days after his death, appeared to his disciples, and then ascended into heaven.

Christians believe that Jesus is alive and present in the world as the Holy Spirit. The main commandments are to love God and to love one's neighbour as oneself, which, if followed successfully, lead to an afterlife in heaven.

divisions: Orthodox Church or ***Eastern Orthodox Church*** or ***Greek Orthodox Church*** a federation of self-governing Christian churches mainly found in E and SE Europe, Russia, and parts of Asia. The centre of worship is the Eucharist. There is a married clergy, except for bishops; the Immaculate Conception is not accepted. The highest rank in the church is that of Ecumenical Patriarch, or Bishop of Istanbul. There are approximately 135 million (1990) adherents.

The church's teaching is based on the Bible, and the Nicene Creed (as modified by the Council of Constantinople 381) is the only confession of faith used. The celebration of the Eucharist has changed little since the 6th century. The ritual is elaborate, and accompanied by singing in which both men and women take part, but no instrumental music is used. Besides the seven sacraments, the prayer book contains many other services for daily life. During the marriage service, the bride and groom are crowned.

Its adherents include Greeks, Russians, Romanians, Serbians, Bulgarians, Georgians, and Albanians. In the last 200 years the Orthodox Church has spread into China, Korea, Japan, and the USA, as well as among the people of Siberia and central Asia. Some of the churches were founded by the apostles and their disciples; all conduct services in their own languages and follow their own customs and traditions, but are in full communion with one another. There are many monasteries, for example Mount Athos in Greece, which has flourished since the 10th century. The senior church of Eastern Christendom is that of Constantinople (Istanbul).

Protestantism one of the main divisions of Christianity, which emerged from Roman Catholicism at the Reformation. The chief denominations are the Anglican Communion (Episcopalian in the USA), Baptists, Lutherans, Methodists, Pentecostals, and Presbyterians, with a total membership of about 327 million (1990).

Protestantism takes its name from the protest of Luther and his supporters at the Diet of Spires 1529 against the decision to reaffirm the edict of the Diet of Worms against the Reformation. The first conscious statement of Protestantism as a distinct movement was the Confession of Augsburg 1530. The chief characteristics of original Protestantism are the acceptance of the Bible as the only source of truth, the universal priesthood of all believers, and forgiveness of sins solely through faith in Jesus Christ. The Protestant church minimalises the liturgical aspects of Christianity and emphasizes the preaching and hearing of the word of God before sacramental faith and practice. The many interpretations of doctrine and practice are reflected in the various denominations. The ecumenical movement of the 20th century has unsuccessfully attempted to reunite various Protestant denominations and, to some extent, the Protestant churches and the Catholic church. During the last 20 years there has been a worldwide upsurge in Christianity taking place largely outside the established church.

Roman Catholicism one of the main divisions of the Christian religion, separate from the Eastern Orthodox Church from 1054, and headed by the pope. For history and beliefs, see Christianity. Membership is about 920 million worldwide (1990), concentrated in S Europe, Latin America, and the Philippines.

The Protestant churches separated from the Catholic with the Reformation in the 16th century, to which the Counter-Reformation was a response. An attempt to update Catholic doctrines in the late 19th century was condemned by Pope Pius X in 1907, and more recent moves have been rejected by John Paul II.

doctrine The focus of liturgical life is the Mass or Eucharist, and attendance is obligatory on Sundays and Feasts of Obligation such as Christmas or Easter. The Roman Catholic differs from the other Christian churches in that it acknowledges the supreme jurisdiction of the pope, infallible when he speaks *ex cathedra* ('from the throne'); in the doctrine of the Immaculate Conception (which states that the Virgin Mary, the mother of Jesus, was conceived without the original sin with which all other human beings are born); and in according a special place to the Virgin Mary.

Evangelists invade the CIS

The collapse of communism opened the former USSR to a wave of religious missionaries. The main church of Russia, the Eastern Orthodox Church, has expressed concern about the number of new religious movements, such as the Hare Krishnas, and the many evangelical and fundamentalist Christian groups entering the country. This concern is shared by all the established mainstream churches, such as the Roman Catholics and the Baptists.

More than 300 US missionary groups are now active in Russia alone, and one of them is sending more than 2,000 missionaries a year into the Commonwealth of Independent States (CIS) and E Europe. These groups bring with them a very different creed from that taught and practised by the older churches of the country. For many such missionary groups, the older churches are not valid Christian churches anyway and part of the missionary zeal comes from a conviction that these older churches are either apostate or even the work of the Devil.

Many of the groups bring the assumption that the American way of life is the fullest expression of true Christian living. This is proving very tempting to people who long to have the consumer lifestyle of the West. However, leaders of the mainstream churches fear that these values will not only force increased division in the expression of Christianity in the CIS, but also undermine core traditional religious values of community and solidarity that have survived the communist persecution only to run the risk now of falling to US evangelical consumerism.

organization Since the Second Vatican Council 1962–66, major changes have taken place. They include the use of vernacular or everyday language instead of Latin in the liturgy, and increased freedom amongst the religious and lay orders. The pope has an episcopal synod of 200 bishops elected by local hierarchies to collaborate in the government of the church. The priesthood is celibate and there is a strong emphasis on the monastic orders.

Confucianism the body of beliefs and practices that are based on the Chinese classics and supported by the authority of the philosopher Confucius (Kong Zi). The origin of things is seen in the union of ***yin*** and ***yang***, the passive and active principles. Human relationships follow the patriarchal pattern. For more than 2,000 years Chinese political government, social organization, and individual conduct was shaped by Confucian principles. In 1912, Confucian philosophy, as a basis for government, was dropped by the state. There are approximately 8 million Confucian believers (1992) worldwide.

The writings on which Confucianism is based include the ideas of a group of traditional books edited by Confucius, as well as his own works, such as the *Analects*, and those of some of his pupils. The *I Ching* is included among the Confucianist texts.

doctrine Until 1912 the emperor of China was regarded as the father of his people, appointed by heaven to rule. The Superior Man was the ideal human and filial piety was the chief virtue. Accompanying a high morality was a kind of ancestor worship.

practices Under the emperor, sacrifices were offered to heaven and earth, the heavenly bodies, the imperial ancestors, various nature gods, and Confucius himself. These were abolished at the Revolution in 1912, but ancestor worship (better expressed as reverence and remembrance) remained a regular practice in the home.

Under communism Confucianism continued. The defence minister Lin Biao was associated with the religion, and although the communist leader Mao Zedong undertook an anti-Confucius campaign 1974–76, this was not pursued by the succeeding regime.

Hinduism religion originating in N India about 4,000 years ago, which is superficially and in some of its forms polytheistic, but has a concept of the supreme spirit, Brahman, above the many divine manifestations. These include the triad of chief gods (the Trimurti): Brahma, Vishnu, and Siva (creator, preserver, and destroyer). Central to Hinduism are the beliefs in reincarnation and karma; the oldest scriptures are the *Vedas*. Temple worship is almost universally observed and there are many festivals. There are approximately 732 million (1992) Hindus worldwide. Women are not regarded as the equals of men but should be treated with kindness and respect. Muslim influence in N India led to the veiling of women and the restriction of their movements from about the end of the 12th century.

roots Hindu beliefs originated in the Indus Valley civilization dating from about 4500 years ago. Much of the tradition that is now associated with Hinduism stems from the ritual and religion of the Aryans who invaded N India about 3000 years ago.

scriptures The *Veda* collection of hymns, compiled by the Aryans, was followed by the philosophical *Upanishads*, centring on the doctrine of Brahman, and the epics *Rāmāyana* and *Mahābhārata* (which includes the *Bhagavad-Gītā*), all from before the Christian era.

beliefs Hindu belief and ritual can vary greatly even between villages. Some deities achieve widespread popularity such as Krishna, Hanuman, Lakshmi, and Durga; others, more localised and specialised, are referred to particularly in times of sickness or need. Some deities manifest themselves in different incarnations or avatars such as Rama or Krishna: both avatars of the god Vishnu. Underlying this multifaceted worship is the creative strength of Brahman, the Supreme Being. Hindus believe that all living things are part of Brahman: they are sparks of atman or divine life that transmute from one body to another, sometimes descending into the form of a plant or an insect, sometimes the body of a human. This is all according to its karma or past actions which are the cause of its sufferings or joy as it rises and falls in *samsara* (the endless cycle of birth and death). Humans have the opportunity, through knowledge and devotion, to break the karmic chain and achieve final liberation or moksha. The atman is then free to return to Brahman.

The creative force of the universe is recognised in the god Brahma, once he has brought the cosmos into being it is sustained by Vishnu and then annihilated by the god Shiva, only to be created once more by Brahma. Vishnu and Shiva are, respectively, the forces of light and darkness, preservation and destruction, with Brahma as the balancing force that enables the existence and interaction of life. The cosmos is seen as both real and an illusion (*maya*), since its reality is not lasting; the cosmos is itself personified as the goddess Maya.

practice Hinduism has a complex of rites and ceremonies performed within the framework of the *jati* or caste system under the supervision of the Brahman priests and teachers. In India, caste is traditionally derived from the four classes of early Hindu society: brahmans (priests), kshatriyas (nobles and warriors), vaisyas (traders and cultivators), and sudras (servants). A fifth class, the untouchables, regarded as polluting in its origins, remained (and still largely remains) on the edge of Hindu society. The Indian Constituent Assembly 1947 made discrimination against the Schedules Castes or Depressed Classes illegal, but strong prejudice continues.

Western influence The International Society for Krishna Consciousness (ISKON), the western organization of the Hare Krishna movement, was introduced to the west by Swami Prabhupada (1896–1977). Members are expected to lead ascetic lives. It is based on devotion to Krishna which includes study of the *Bhagavad-Gītā*, temple and home ritual, and the chanting of the name Hare (saviour) Krishna. Members are expected to avoid meat, eggs, alcohol, tea, coffee, drugs, and gambling. Sexual relationships should be for procreation within the bonds of marriage.

Islam religion founded in the Arabian peninsula in the early 7th century CE. It emphasizes the oneness of God, his omnipotence, benificence, and inscrutability. The sacred book is the ***Koran*** of the prophet Muhammad, the Prophet or Messenger of Allah. There are two main Muslim sects: ***Sunni*** and ***Shi'ite***. Other schools include ***Sufism***, a mystical movement originating in the 8th century. There are over 1,025 million Muslims (1992) worldwide.

beliefs The fundamental beliefs of Islam are contained in the Adhan: 'I bear witness that there is no God but Allah and Muhammad is the Prophet of Allah.' Creation, Fall of Adam, angels and jinns, heaven and hell, Day of Judgment, God's predestination of good and evil, and the succession of scriptures revealed to the prophets, including Moses and Jesus, but of which the perfect, final form is the ***Koran*** or ***Quran***, divided into 114 ***suras*** or chapters, said to have been divinely revealed to Muhammad; the original is said to be preserved beside the throne of Allah in heaven.

Islamic law Islam embodies a secular law (the ***Shari'a*** or 'Highway'), which is clarified for Shi'ites by reference to their own version of the ***sunna***, 'practice' of the Prophet as transmitted by his companions and embodied in the Hadith; the Sunni sect also take into account ***ijma'***, the endorsement by universal consent of practices and beliefs among the faithful. For the Sufi, the ***Shari'a***, is the starting point on the 'Sufi Path' to self-enlightenment. A ***mufti*** is a legal expert who guides the courts in their interpretation. (In Turkey until the establishment of the republic 1924 the mufti had supreme spiritual authority.)

organization There is no organized church or priesthood, although Muhammad's descendants (the Hashim family) and popularly recognized holy men, mullahs, and ayatollahs are accorded respect.

observances The Shari'a includes the observances known as 'The Five Pillars of the Faith', which are binding on all adult believers. The observances include: *shahada* or profession of the faith; *salat* or worship five times a day facing the holy city of Mecca (the call to prayer is given by a muezzin, usually from the minaret or tower of a mosque); *zakat* or obligatory almsgiving; *saum* or fasting dawn to sunset through Ramadan (ninth month of the year, which varies with the calendar); and the *hajj* or pilgrimage to Mecca at least once in a lifetime.

history Islam began as a militant and missionary religion, and between 711 and 1492 spread east into India, west over N Africa, then north across Gibraltar into the Iberian peninsula. During the Middle Ages, Islamic scholars preserved ancient Greco-Roman learning, while the Dark Ages prevailed in Christian Europe. Islam was seen as an enemy of Christianity by European countries during the Crusades, and Christian states united against a Muslim nation as late as the Battle of Lepanto 1571. Driven from Europe, Islam remained established in N Africa and the Middle East.

Islam is a major force in the Arab world and is a focus for nationalism among the peoples of Soviet Central Asia. It is also a significant factor in Pakistan, Indonesia, Malaysia, and parts of Africa. It is the second largest religion in the UK. Since World War II there has been a resurgence of fundamentalist Islam Iran, Libya, Afghanistan, and elsewhere. In the UK 1987 the manifesto *The Muslim Voice* demanded rights for Muslim views on education (such as single-sex teaching) and on the avoidance of dancing, mixed bathing, and sex education.

divisions: Shi'ite or ***Shiah*** member of a sect of Islam who believe that Ali was Muhammad's first true successor. The term Shi'ite originally referred to shi'a ('the partisans') of Ali. They are doctrinally opposed to the Sunni Muslims. They developed their own law differing only in minor directions, such as inheritance and the status of women. Holy men have greater authority in the Shi'ite sect than in the Sunni sect. They are prominent in Iran, the Lebanon, and Indo-Pakistan, and are also found in Iraq, Bahrain, and the eastern province of Saudi Arabia. In the aftermath of the Gulf War 1991, many thousands of Shi'ites in Iraq were forced to take refuge in the marshes of S Iraq, after unsuccessfully rebelling against Saddam Hussein. Shi'ite sacred shrines were desecrated and atrocities committed by the armed forces on civilians.

There are approximately 129 million Shi'ites (1990) worldwide.

Breakaway sub-sects include the ***Alawite*** sect, to which the ruling party in Syria belongs; the ***Ismaili*** sect, with the Aga Khan IV (1936–) as its spiritual head; and the Baha'i religion founded from a Muslim splinter group.

Sufism a mystical movement of Islam which originated in the 8th century. Sufis believe that deep intuition is the only real guide to knowledge. The movement has a strong strain of asceticism. The name derives from the *suf*, a rough woollen robe worn as an indication of disregard for material things. There are a number of groups or brotherhoods within Sufism, each with its own method of meditative practice, one of which is the whirling dance of the dervishes.

Sunni a member of the larger of the two main sects of Islam. Sunni Muslims believe that the first three caliphs were all legitimate successors of the prophet Muhammad, and that guidance on belief and life should come from the Koran and the Hadith, and from the Shari'a, not from a human authority or spiritual leader. Imams in Sunni Islam are educated lay teachers of the faith and prayer leaders. The name derives from the *Sunna*, Arabic 'code of behaviour', the body of traditional law evolved from the teaching and acts of Muhammad. There are approximately 690 million (1990) Sunni Muslims worldwide.

Jainism ancient Indian religion, sometimes regarded as an offshoot of Hinduism. Jains believe that non-injury to living beings is the highest religion, and their code of ethics is based on sympathy and compassion for all forms of life. They also believe in karma. In Jainism there is no deity and, like Buddhism, it is a monastic, ascetic religion. There are two main sects: the Digambaras and the Swetambaras. Jainism practises the most extreme form of non-violence (*ahimsā*) of all Indian sects, and influenced the philosophy of Mahātmā Gāndhī. Jains number approximately 4 million (1992); there are Jain communities throughout the world but the majority live in India.

Jainism's sacred books record the teachings of Mahavira (*c.* 540–468 BCE), the last in a line of 24 great masters called Tirthankaras (or *jinas*, 'those who overcome'). Mahavira was born in Vessali (now Bihar), E India. He became an ascetic at the age of 30, achieved enlightenment at 42, and preached for 30 years.

During the 3rd century BCE two divisions arose regarding the extent of austerities. The Digambaras ('sky-clad') believe that enlightenment can only occur when all possessions have been given up, including clothes, and that it can only be achieved when a soul is born into a human male body. Monks of this sect go naked on the final stages of their spiritual path. The Swetambaras ('white-clad') believe that both human sexes can achieve enlightenment and that nakedness is not a prerequisite. Jain derives its name from ancient prophets known as jinas ('those who overcome').

Judaism the religion of the ancient Hebrews and their descendents the Jews, based, according to the Old Testament, on a covenant between God and Abraham about 2000 BCE, and the renewal of the covenant with Moses about 1200 BCE. It rests on the concept of one eternal, invisible God, whose will is revealed in the *Torah* and who has a special relationship with the Jewish people. The Torah comprises the first five books of the Bible (the Pentateuch), which contains the history, laws, and guide to life for correct behaviour. Besides those living in Israel, there are large Jewish populations today in the USA, the ex-USSR, the UK and Commonwealth nations, and in Jewish communities throughout the world. There are approximately 18 million Jews (1992), with about 9 million in the Americas, 5 million in Europe, and 4 million in Asia, Africa, and the Pacific.

scriptures The *Talmud* combines the *Mishna*, rabbinical commentary on the law handed down orally from CE 70 and put in writing about 200, and the *Gemara*, legal discussions in the schools of Palestine and Babylon from the 3rd and 4th centuries. The *Haggadah* is a part of the Talmud dealing with stories of heroes. The *Midrash* is a collection of commentaries on the scriptures written 400–1200, mainly in Palestine. Along with the *Torah* they are regarded as authoritative sources of Jewish ritual, worship, and practice.

observances The *synagogue* (in US non-Orthodox usage ***temple***) is the local building for congregational worship (originally simply the place where the Torah was read and expounded); its characteristic feature is the Ark, the enclosure where the Torah scrolls are kept. *Rabbis* are ordained teachers schooled in the Jewish law and ritual who act as spiritual leaders and pastors of their communities; some devote themselves to study. Religious practices include: circumcision, daily services in Hebrew, observance of the *Sabbath* (sunset on Friday to sunset Saturday) as a day of rest, and, among Orthodox Jews, strict dietary laws. High Holy days include *Rosh Hashanah* marking the Jewish New Year (first new moon after the autumn equinox) and, a week later, the religious fast *Yom Kippur* (Day of Atonement). Other holidays are celebrated throughout the year to commemorate various events of Biblical history.

history In the late Middle Ages when Europe and Western Asia were divided into Christian and Islamic countries, the Jewish people also found itself divided into two main groups. Jews in central and eastern Europe, namely in Germany and Poland, were called *Ashkenazi*. *Sefardic* Jews can trace their tradition back to the Mediterranean countries, particularly Spain and Portugal under Muslim rule. When they were expelled in 1492 they settled in north Africa, the Levant, the Far East, and northern Europe. The two traditions differ in a number of ritual and cultural ways but their theology and basic Jewish practice is the same. The Hassidic sects of eastern Europe and some north African and Oriental countries also differ from other groups in their rites but they, too, maintain the concept of divine authority.

divisions In the 19th and early 20th centuries there was a move by some Jewish groups away from traditional or orthodox observances. This trend gave rise to a number of groups within Judaism. ***Orthodox Jews***, who form the majority, assert the supreme authority of the Torah, adhere to all the traditions of Judaism, including the strict dietary laws and the segregation of women in the synagogue. ***Reform***

Judaism rejects the idea that Jews are the chosen people, has a liberal interpretation of the dietary laws, and takes a critical attitude toward the Torah. ***Conservative Judaism*** is a compromise between Orthodox and Reform in its acceptance of the traditional law, making some allowances for modern conditions, although its services and ceremonies are closer to Orthodox than to Reform. ***Liberal Judaism***, or ***Recontructionism***, goes further than Reform in attempting to adapt Judaism to the needs of the modern world and to interpret the Torah in the light of current scholarship. In all the groups except Orthodox, women are not segregated in the synagogue, and there are female rabbis in both Reform and Liberal Judaism. In the 20th century many people who call themselves Jews prefer to identify Judaism with a historical and cultural tradition rather than with strict religious observance, and a contemporary debate (complicated by the history of non-Jewish attitudes towards Jews) centres on the question of how to define a Jew. As in other religions, fundamentalist movements have emerged, for example, Gush Emunim.

North American indigenous religions these form a wide variety, but have some features in common, especially a belief that everything in nature is alive and contains powerful forces which can be helpful or harmful to humans. If the forces are to be helpful, they must be treated with respect, and so hunting and other activities require ritual and preparation. Certain people are believed to be in contact with or possessed by the spirit world and so to have special powers; but each individual can also seek power and vision through ordeals and fasting.

Shinto the indigenous religion of Japan. It combines an empathetic oneness with natural forces and loyalty to the reigning dynasty as descendants of the Sun goddess, Amaterasu-Omikami. Traditional Shinto followers stressed obedience and devotion to the emperor, and an aggressive nationalistic aspect was developed by the Meiji rulers. Today Shinto has discarded these aspects. There are about 3.2 million (1992) adherents worldwide.

Shinto is the Chinese transliteration of the Japanese ***Kami-no-Michi***. Shinto ceremonies appeal to the Kami, the mysterious forces of nature manifest in topographical features such as mountains, trees, stones, springs, and caves. Shinto focuses on purity, devotion, and sincerity; aberrations can be cleansed through purification rituals. In addition, purification procedures make the worshipper presentable and acceptable when making requests before the Kami.

Shinto's holiest shrine is at Ise, near Kyoto, where in the temple of the Sun Goddess is preserved the mirror that she is supposed to have given to Jimmu, the first emperor, in the 7th century BCE. Sectarian Shinto consists of 130 sects; the sects are officially recognized but not state-supported (as was state Shinto until its disestablishment after World War II and Emperor Hirohito's disavowal of his divinity 1946).

There is no Shinto philosophical literature although there are texts on mythologies, ceremonial and administrative procedures, religious laws, and chronicles or ruling families and temple construction.

Sikhism religion professed by 14 million Indians, living mainly in the Punjab. Sikhism was founded by Nanak (1469–*c.* 1539). Sikhs believe in a single God who is the immortal creator of the universe and who has never been incarnate in any form, and in the equality of all human beings; Sikhism is strongly opposed to caste divisions. There are approximately 18 million (1992) adherents worldwide.

Their holy book is the *Guru Granth Sahib*. Guru Gobind Singh (1666–1708) instituted the *Khanda-di-Pahul*, (the Baptism of the Sword), and established the *Khalsa* ('pure'), the company of the faithful. The Khalsa wear the five Ks: *kes*, long hair; *kangha*, a comb; *kirpan*, a sword; *kachh*, short trousers; and *kara*, a steel bracelet. Sikh men take the last name 'Singh' ('lion') and women 'Kaur' ('princess').

beliefs Human beings can make themselves ready to find God by prayer and meditation but can achieve closeness to God only as a result of God's *nadar* (grace). Sikhs believe in reincarnation and that the ten human gurus were teachers through whom the spirit of Guru Nanak was passed on to live today in the *Guru Granth Sahib* and the Khalsa.

practice Sikhs do not have a specific holy day, but hold their main services on the day of rest of the country in which they are living. Daily prayer is important in Sikhism, and the gurdwara functions as a social as well as religious centre; it contains a kitchen, the *langar*, where all, male and female, Sikh and non-Sikh, may eat together as equals. Sikh women take the same role as men in religious observances, for example, in reading from the *Guru Granth Sahib* at the gurdwara. Festivals in honour of the ten human gurus include a complete reading of the *Guru Granth Sahib*; Sikhs also celebrate at the time of some of the major Hindu festivals, but their emphasis is on aspects of Sikh belief and the example of the gurus. Sikhs avoid the use of all nonmedicinal drugs and, in particular, tobacco.

history On Nanak's death he was followed as guru by a succession of leaders who converted the Sikhs (the word means 'disciple') into a military confraternity which established itself as a political power. The last of the gurus, Guru Gobind Singh, instituted the *Khanda-di-Pahul* ('baptism of the sword') and established the Khalsa. Gobind Singh was assassinated by a Muslim 1708, and since then the *Guru Granth Sahib* has taken the place of a leader.

Upon the partition of India many Sikhs migrated from W to E Punjab, and in 1966 the efforts of Sant Fateh Singh (*c.* 1911–1972) led to the creation of a Sikh state within India by partition of the Punjab. However, the Akali separatist movement agitates for a completely independent Sikh state, Khalistan, and a revival of fundamentalist belief and was headed from 1978 by Sant Jarnail Singh Bhindranwale (1947–1984), killed in the siege of the Golden Temple, Amritsar. In retaliation for this, the Indian prime minister Indira Gandhi was assassinated in Oct of the same year by her Sikh bodyguards. Heavy rioting followed, in which 1,000 Sikhs were killed. Mrs Gandhi's successor, Rajiv Gandhi, reached an agreement for the election of a popular government in the Punjab and for state representatives to the Indian parliament with the moderate Sikh leader Sant Harchand Singh Longowal, who was himself killed 1985 by Sikh extremists.

South American indigenous religions religious beliefs and practice are diverse and since early Indian contact with whites there has been some reconciliation between Christian and local belief, and also the emergence of new religious movements. Many of the local religions have the concept of a supreme religious force or god, but this force is often so remote or great that it is not worshipped directly. There are many powerful spirits, including souls of the ancestors, that inhabit and influence the natural environment and the lives of humans. To maintain harmony with the forest, rivers, or animals, these spirits are respected and frequently associated with creation myths or as the harbingers of fortune or suffering, and as such are not hunted – for example, the anaconda snake amongst the Sarema people of the Amazonian rainforest.

Taoism Chinese philosophical system, traditionally founded by the Chinese philosopher Lao Zi 6th century BCE. He is also attributed authorship of the scriptures, *Tao Te Ching*, which were apparently compiled 3rd century BCE. The 'tao' or 'way' denotes the hidden principle of the universe, and less stress is laid on good deeds than on harmonious interaction with the environment, which automatically ensures right behaviour. The second major work is that of Zhuangzi (*c.* 389–286 BCE), *The Way of Zhuangzi*. The magical side of Taoism is illustrated by the *I Ching* or *Book of Changes*, a book of divination. There are approximately 190 million (1990) Taoists worldwide.

beliefs The universe is believed to be kept in balance by the opposing forces of yin and yang that operate in dynamic tension between themselves. Yin is female and watery: the force in the moon and rain which reached its peak in the winter; yang is masculine and solid: the force in the sun and earth which reaches its peak in the summer. The interaction of yin and yang is believed to shape all life.

This magical, ritualistic aspect of Taoism developed from the 2nd century CE and was largely responsible for its popular growth; it stresses physical immortality, which was attempted by means ranging from dietary regulation and fasting to alchemy. By the 3rd century, worship of gods had begun to appear, including that of the stove god Tsao Chun. From the 4th century, rivalry between Taoists and Mahāyāna Buddhists was strong in China, leading to persecution of one religion by the other; this was resolved by mutual assimilation, and Taoism developed monastic communities similar to those of the Buddhists.

Taoist texts record the tradition of mental and physical discipline, and methods to use in healing, exorcism, and the quest for immortality.

Zoroastrianism pre-Islamic Persian religion founded by the Persian prophet Zarathustra or Zoroaster (Greek), and still practised by the Parsees in India. The *Zendavesta* are the sacred scriptures of the faith. The theology is dualistic, ***Ahura Mazda*** or ***Ormuzd*** (the good God) being perpetually in conflict with ***Ahriman*** (the evil God), but the former is assured of eventual victory. There are approximately 150,000 (1990) adherents worldwide.

beliefs Humanity has been given free will to choose between the two powers, thus rendering believers responsible for their fate after death in heaven or hell. Moral and physical purity is central to all aspects of Zoroastrianism *yasna* or worship: since life and work are part of worship, there should be purity of action. Fire is considered sacred, and Ahura Mazda believed to be present when the ritual flame is worshipped at home or in the temple. It is believed that there will be a second universal judgement at *Frashokereti*, a time when the dead will be raised and the world cleansed of unnatural impurity.

The Parsee community in Bombay is now the main centre of Zoroastrianism, but since conversion is generally considered impossible, the numbers in India have been steadily decreasing at the rate of 10% per decade since 1947. Parsee groups, mainly in Delhi and outside India have been pushing for the acceptance of converts, but the concern of the majority in Bombay is that their religious and cultural heritage will be lost.

Religious Movements

Baha'i movement founded in 19th century Persia by a Muslim splinter group, Babis. It evolved into the Baha'i religion under the leadership of Baha'ullah. His message in essence was that all great religious leaders are manifestations of the unknowable God and all scriptures are sacred. There is no priesthood: all Baha'is are expected to teach, and to work towards world unification. There are about 4.5 million (1990) Baha'is worldwide.

Jehovah's Witness member of a religious organization originating in the USA 1872 under Charles Taze Russell (1852–1916). Jehovah's Witnesses attach great importance to Christ's second coming, which Russell predicted would occur 1914, and which Witnesses still believe is imminent. All Witnesses are expected to take part in house-to-house preaching; there are no clergy. There are approximately 6.75 million (1990) adherents worldwide.

Mormon or ***Latter-day Saint*** member of a Christian sect, the ***Church of Jesus Christ of Latter-day Saints***, founded at Fayette, New York, in 1830 by Joseph Smith. According to Smith, Mormon was an ancient prophet in North America whose *Book of Mormon*, of which Smith claimed divine revelation, is accepted by Mormons as part of the Christian scriptures. In the 19th century the faction led by Brigham Young was polygamous. It is a missionary church with headquarters in Utah and a worldwide membership of about 5 million.

Rajneesh meditation meditation based on the teachings of the Indian Shree Rajneesh (born Chaadra Mohan Jain), established in the early 1970s. Until 1989 he called himself ***Bhagwan*** (Hindi 'God'). His followers, who number about half a million worldwide, regard themselves as Sannyas, or Hindu ascetics; they wear orange robes and carry a string of prayer beads. They are not expected to observe any specific prohibitions but to be guided by their instincts.

Rastafarianism religion originating in the West Indies, based on the ideas of Marcus Garvey, who called on black people to return to Africa and set up a

Cults – or new religious movements

Hardly any religious group would describe itself as a cult. The word 'cult' is used mainly by those who wish to identify particular groups as dangerous. This definition of the term has been mainly promoted by the Christian counter-cult movement (whose members see 'cults' as everything that departs from their version of Christianity) and by secular anti-cultists (whose definition of 'cult' emerged from the active campaigns of parents worried by how their children changed when they joined particular religious groups). To avoid the negative connotations implicit in the word 'cult', sociologists of religion prefer the term 'new religious movement' (NRM) for any of those broadly religious groups that have come into being in the second half of the 20th century. However, the more widespread use of the term 'NRM' is beginning to carry with it some of the negativity and sinister overtones that 'cult' conveys. Members of NRMs often deny they are new or religious or a movement. They emphasize instead that their beliefs are based on old traditions, and that they offer a philosophy, an education, a healing process, or a particular 'way of life'.

The wish to disclaim the terms 'cult' and 'new religious movement' has become particularly strong since the Branch Davidian tragedy in Texas, which reaffirmed the Jonestown message of 15 years ago that 'cults' and 'cult leaders' are dangerous. (Strikingly, however, the People's Temple was not labelled a cult until after the mass suicide of the members in Guyana, and the Branch Davidians could be said to have been closer to a fundamentalist sect – one of several splinter groups whose extremist leader broke with the main Davidic Seventh-Day Adventists.)

'New religious movements' or 'cults' are not a new phenomenon. Throughout history small, unconventional religious groups have emerged, as Christianity and other now accepted mainstream religions once did. What is new is the rapid growth in the number of these groups in the 1960s and 1970s, with some 1,000 now in existence in the UK (though inevitably there are problems of definition). To put the groups in perspective, the number of committed members of all NRMs in the UK – those who have dedicated their whole lives to a movement – is unlikely to exceed 15,000.

It is impossible to generalize about the beliefs and practices of the NRMs. They have adopted ideas from a wide range of traditions, many of which were, until recently, strange to the West. Of all the new religious groups, a few may be said to be benevolent and a few malevolent but the majority have both positive and negative attributes. Moreover, the individual members may be said to share characteristics with the rest of the population; if anything, they have a larger proportion of young people with high ideals who want to bring about improvements to themselves and the world.

The popular image of a 'cult', and one that has been adopted by the tabloid press in particular, is of a group of brainwashed followers of a corrupt leader who encourages them to use deceptive practices to secure more members to satisfy his or her greed for money, power, or sexual gratification, and who allows or even encourages the abuse of children, political conspiracy, drug-trafficking, and even murder. Although a few of these activities may be practised by some of the new groups or may have been practised in the past, the implication that this is standard practice of all NRMs is inaccurate and highly misleading. Many of the groups have changed, and continue to develop in response to internal and external influences. The disaster at Waco, Texas, with its armed fortress and zealot leader, David Koresh, was much publicized hence poplarly perceived as typical of a 'cult', whereas the morally acceptable activities of members of many of the new religious movements remain unseen.

Another widely accepted notion about 'cults' is that their members are all innocent victims who are members because they were rendered incapable of making a decision about joining. Much has been written by sociologists of religion on this topic. They point out, for example, the high turnover rate, which is incompatible with the notion of brainwashing. Although recruitment practices may sometimes be deceptive or highly persuasive (such as 'love-bombing', by which prospective members are showered with affection, attention, and instant friendship), research shows that most people are capable of resisting the encouragements to join if they do not wish to do so. Once they have joined, some members are subjected to techniques that may affect their powers of reasoning, yet even in these situations people do leave the group. The attachment of a particular member to a particular group is a process far more complex than the brainwashing thesis suggests, and to understand why any individual has joined a new religious movement it is crucial to look closely at both the individual and the group he or she has joined.

CH

black-governed country there. When Haile Selassie (***Ras Tafari***, 'Lion of Judah') was crowned emperor of Ethiopia 1930, this was seen as a fulfilment of prophecy and Rastafarians acknowledged him as the Messiah, the incarnation of God (***Jah***). The use of ganja (marijuana) is a sacrament. There are no churches. There were about one million Rastafarians by 1990.

Scientology (Latin *scire* 'to know' and Greek *logos* 'branch of learning') an 'applied religious philosophy' based on dianetics, founded in California in 1954 by L Ron Hubbard as the ***Church of Scientology***. Through a form of psychotherapy it claims to 'increase man's spiritual awareness', but its methods of recruiting and retaining converts have met criticism. Its headquarters from 1959 have been in Sussex, England.

Seventh Day Adventist, often called an ***Adventist***. A member of the Protestant religious sect of the same name. It originated in the US in the fervent expectation of Christ's Second Coming, or advent, that swept across New York State following William Miller's prophecy that Christ would return on Oct 22, 1844. When this failed to come to pass, a number of Millerites, as his followers were called, reinterpreted his prophetic speculations and continued to maintain that the millennium was imminent. Adventists observe Saturday as the Sabbath and emphasize healing, temperance, and diet; many are vegetarians. The sect has about 500,000 members in the US.

transcendental meditation (TM) technique of focusing the mind, based in part on Hindu meditation. Meditators are given a *mantra* (a special word or phrase) to repeat over and over to themselves; such meditation is believed to benefit the practitioner by relieving stress and inducing a feeling of well-being and relaxation. It was introduced to the West by Maharishi Mahesh Yogi and popularized by the Beatles in the late 1960s.

Unification Church or ***Moonies*** church founded in Korea 1954 by the Reverend Sun Myung Moon. The theology unites Christian and Taoist ideas and is based on Moon's book *Divine Principle*, which teaches that the original purpose of creation was to set up a perfect family, in a perfect relationship with God. The church has met with criticism over its recruiting methods and use of finances. The number of members (often called 'moonies') is about 200,000 worldwide.

Unitarianism a Christian denomination that rejects the orthodox doctrine of the Trinity and gives a preeminent position to Jesus as a religious teacher, while denying his deity. Unitarians believe in individual conscience and reason as a guide to right action, rejecting the doctrines of original sin, the atonement, and eternal punishment. There are approximately 750,000 adherents (1990) worldwide.

Rites of Passage

Most religions mark certain important stages in a person's life, such as birth, initiation, marriage, and death, by special ceremonies or rites of passage. These rituals provide a way of publicly recognizing a change of status; they are also a time for the whole community to reaffirm its faith.

Birth rites Birth is often a time of rejoicing, but it is also a time of new responsibility. The rituals associated with birth mark the child's entrance into a new community and the adult's commitment to that child.

Hindu birth rites begin with the choice of a suitable day for conception, and continue through pregnancy; the mother-to-be must avoid certain foods and recite verses from the Hindu holy books. When the baby is born, there are a number of further ceremonies including naming the child, the calculation of a horoscope, and the inscription of the word 'aum' (the elemental sound of the universe) in honey on the child's tongue. The last of these ceremonies, the shaving of the child's hair, may take place up to two years after the birth. Hindus believe that these ceremonies will help the child towards a better rebirth.

Sikh birth rites Sikhs believe that the first words a child should hear are those of the Mool Mantra, the beginning of the Sikh holy book, and so, as soon as the baby is born, it is washed and the words of the Mool Mantra whispered into its ear. A few weeks later the child is taken to the gurdwara, the Sikh place of worship, to be named. The initial of the name is chosen by opening the *Guru Granth Sahib* at random and choosing the first letter of the hymn on the left hand page.

Muslim birth rites the first words which a Muslim baby will hear are those of the call to prayer, which is used to call Muslims to the mosque or place of worship each day; these words, which contain the basic beliefs of Islam, are whispered into its ears. Seven days later, the child is named. This ceremony involves the shaving of the baby's head. If the child is a boy, he will also be circumcised at this time, to recall Abraham and his son Ismail.

Jewish birth rites the surgical operation of ***circumcision*** consists of the removal of a small part of the foreskin. All Jewish boys must be circumcised on the eighth day after birth, as long as health permits. During circumcision a prayer is said which recalls the covenant or agreement God made with Abraham and the ceremony marks the boy's entry into this covenant. If the child is a girl, her name is announced in the synagogue (the Jewish place of worship) by the father on the first Sabbath after her birth.

Christian birth rites universal in the Christian church from its beginning has been the religious initiation rite of ***baptism*** (Greek 'to dip'), involving immersion in or sprinkling with water. In the baptismal ceremony, sponsors or godparents make vows on behalf of the child which are renewed by the child at confirmation. Baptism was originally administered to adults by immersion, and infant baptism has been common only since the 6th century. In some of the Protestant churches, adults are still baptized by immersion in a pool of water. The immersion symbolizes death and new life.

Chinese birth rites Chinese babies are not named for the first month after birth; then the Full Month ceremony is held, with special foods, including red eggs which are symbols of luck and new life. The name given to the baby is a nickname designed to convince any malevolent spirits that the child is not worth stealing.

Initiation rites Initiation is a passage into full membership of a group, whether religious or social. It gives the individual both rights and responsibilities.

Sikh initiation rites the tenth guru of Sikhism, Guru Gobind Singh, set up a brotherhood of dedicated Sikhs, the Khalsa; any sufficiently mature and dedicated Sikh may apply to join the Khalsa. The ceremony is conducted by five members of the Khalsa in the presence of the *Guru Granth Sahib*, the Sikh holy book; it involves special prayers, the sharing of karah parshad (a sweet mixture) to symbolize the equality of Sikhs, and the drinking and sprinkling of amrit (sugar and water). Those initiated in the Khalsa should always wear five things known as the Five K's: uncut hair; a steel bracelet; a short sword; a comb; and kaccha, a type of shorts.

Jewish initiation is marked by the ***bar mitzvah*** (Hebrew 'son of the commandment'), initiation of a boy at the age of 13 into the adult Jewish community; less common is the bat mitzvah for girls. In the synagogue, the boy says a special bar mitzvah prayer promising to keep God's commandments, and accept responsibility for his actions before God, he then reads a passage from the Torah in the synagogue on the Sabbath. After this, he is regarded as a full member of the congregation.

Christian initiation is marked by ***confirmation***, a rite by which a previously baptized person is admitted to full membership of the Christian church.

It consists of the laying on of hands by a bishop in order that the confirmed person may receive the gift of the Holy Spirit, the third aspect of the Trinity. Among Anglicans, the rite is deferred until the child is able to comprehend the fundamental beliefs of Christian doctrine.

Marriage rites Marriage involves not only a change in status for the two people concerned, but also a new set of relationships for their families and the probability of children. In many cultures the choice of marriage partner is made by the parents, though the participants usually have some say in the matter.

Hindu marriage rites Hindu weddings may take place at the bride's home or in a temple. The bride usually wears a red sari and her hands and feet are painted with patterns in henna, an orange dye. Offerings are made before a sacred fire and prayers said; the bride and groom take seven steps around the fire, which symbolize food, strength, wealth, good fortune, children, the seasons, and everlasting friendship.

Sikh wedding rites a Sikh wedding may be held anywhere, as long as the *Guru Granth Sahib* is present. During the ceremony, the couple show their assent to the marriage by bowing to the holy book. The couple walk together round the *Guru Granth Sahib* four times as a hymn written by the fourth Guru is sung: this hymn contains all the basic teachings of Sikhism.

Jewish wedding rites the ceremony usually takes place in the synagogue, the place of worship. The bride and groom, with their parents, stand under a canopy or chupah. Blessings are recited by the rabbi, the religious leader, and the groom gives the bride a ring. The couple are now legally married and the *ketubah* or marriage contract, is read out. At the end of the ceremony the groom steps on and shatters a glass as a reminder, amidst the happiness, of the destruction of the Temple at Jerusalem.

Christian marriage rites Christian marriages are usually celebrated at the place of worship (church or chapel). The groom is accompanied by a helper, or best man, while the bride is escorted by her father, who officially 'gives' her to her new husband, and by attendants (bridesmaids). The couple make promises to love, honour and care for each other, and exchange rings.

Muslim marriage rites Muslim weddings may take place in the bride's home or in the place of worship, the mosque. The bride and groom are normally in separate rooms throughout the short ceremony. There is often a reading from the Koran, and a talk on the duties of marriage. The couple must both consent to the marriage, and rings are exchanged.

Chinese wedding rites in Chinese weddings, the concept of yin and yang, the two complementary forces which make up the universe, plays a prominent part; among their other attributes yin is seen as female and yang as male. There is a series of rituals leading up to the wedding, including the giving of gifts, an exchange of horoscopes (a prediction of a person's fortune), and a payment to the bride's family. The ceremony itself involves offerings and prayers to the bridegroom's ancestors and the household gods.

Death rites Death rites fulfil three main purposes: to comfort and strengthen the dying person, to comfort those left behind, and to ensure the best possible outcome for the deceased person in the next world or next birth. In several religions, such as Sikhism, Judaism, and Islam, people are encouraged to speak a declaration of faith before death, and Sikhs and Muslims read from their holy books to the dying person. Some religions discourage mourning, because they feel that death should not be regarded as a tragedy for the individual, especially after a long life, while others, such as Judaism, set time aside for the family to grieve. There are many ways in which religions try to help the deceased in the afterlife. The Chinese offer practical help: since the afterlife may have resemblances to this life, replicas of useful goods, cars, washing machines, and money, are burnt at the funeral for the use of the deceased who will, with the other ancestors, now watch over the family.

Holy Books

Many religions have a book or books which are regarded as holy or as providing special wisdom. These books are treated with great reverence and copies may be kept in a place particularly set aside or have specific ceremonies associated with them. Such books are sometimes referred to as scriptures.

Buddhist Buddhist literature is divided into two groups, the teachings and discourses of the Buddha himself, and the teachings of saints, sages, and scholars. Since Buddhism was transmitted by word of mouth for about five hundred years after the death of the Buddha, it is difficult to say which of these writings contain the original word of the Buddha and which are later additions. One of the fundamental differences between the Hīnayāna and Mahāyāna schools is the attribution of the Buddha's word to the various texts. The Buddha's words are assembled in the ***Tipitaka*** or ***Tripitaka*** (three baskets) containing sutra (discourses), vinaya (rules of discipline), abhidharma (further knowledge). Important texts in this group include the commentaries on the Buddha's word by Buddhagosa in the Theravāda tradition and Nagarjuna and Asanga in the early Indian Mahāyāna tradition.

Chinese Since Chinese religion is a mixture of Buddhism, Confucianism and Taoism, the Chinese generally respect the writings of all three. The main text of Taoism is the *Tao Te Ching*, attributed to the traditional founder of Taoism, Lao Tzu, although its date and authorship are obscure. Confucianism's main writings are those of Confucius himself, especially the *Analects* or 'selected sayings'. Confucius is traditionally the author of the Five Classics: ***Su Ching***, ***Shi Ching***, ***Li Chi***, ***I Ching***, and the annals of ***Lu***.

Christian The Christian ***Bible*** (Greek *ta biblia* 'the books') consists of the ***Old Testament***, the first five books of the Hebrew Bible, and the ***New Testament***, originally written in Greek, containing the Gospels, Acts of the Apostles, Letters, and Revelation. It is believed that the books of the New Testament were written within a hundred years of the death of Christ, and from the 4th century were recognized by the Christian church as canonical. Early church history is recorded in the ***Acts of the Apostles***, the life of Jesus Christ in the four ***Gospels***, the epistles are the letters of St Paul and other Christian leaders to fellow Christians, and the New Testament closes with the ***Book of Revelation*** which records St John's vision of the end of time and Christ's second coming.

Hindu ***Veda*** (Sanskrit, divine knowledge). The most sacred of the Hindu scriptures, hymns written in an old form of Sanskrit; the oldest may date from 1500 or 2000 BCE. The four main collections are: the Rigveda (hymns and praises); Yajurveda (prayers and sacrificial formulae); Sāmaveda (hymns); and Atharvaveda, (spells, charms, and chants).

Rāmāyana Hindu epic of 24,000 stanzas written in Sanskrit. It was assembled in its received form between the 1st century BCE and 1st century CE. The story reveals how Rama, an incarnation of the god Vishnu, and his friend Hanuman (the monkey chieftain) strive to recover Rama's wife, Sita, abducted by the demon king Ravana. It upholds the Hindu ideal of a relationship between a man and woman.

Mahābhārata Sanskrit ('great poem of the Bharatas') Hindu epic of 90,000 stanzas probably written between the 2nd century BCE and the end of the 1st century CE. With the Rāmāyana, it forms the two great epics of Hindu literature. The story is set on the Upper Ganges plain and deals with the fortunes of two rival families, the Kauravas and the Pandavas. It reveals the ethical values of ancient Hindu society and individual responsibility in particular. The central and most popular part is the *Bhagavad-Gītā* or *Song of the Blessed One*, a religious and philosophical poem delivered by Krishna to the hero Arjuna. The *Bhagavad-Gītā* is regarded as one of the essential Hindu religious texts.

Jain The Swetabaras' canon is the ***Siddhanta*** assembled in the 5th century CE which includes accounts of the monastic discipline and teachings of Mahavira. The Digambaras' canon is made of two early Pakrit texts (Indian vernacular language) supplemented by commentaries from later scholars. There is also a large body of literature, dating from the 8th century CE, including narratives, commentaries, and cosmologies on existing texts. This later material is generally accepted by both Jain groups.

Jewish The ***Torah*** contains the first five books of the Hebrew Bible and it is given absolute religious authority by orthodox Jews. As well as referring to the first five books of Moses, the ***Torah*** is sometimes used as a term for the whole Hebrew Bible. The First Five Books of Moses contain 613 laws covering social and religious customs and histories of the early patriarchs of the Jewish nation. The Hebrew Bible contains two further sections, the Prophets and the Writings.

The Oral Law, traditionally revealed to Moses on Mount Sinai alongside the Written Law, is codified in the Mishna which was compiled after the destruction of the Temple CE 70. Further debates and interpretations by rabbis on the Torah's law and guidance are recorded in the Gemara and Midrash. The combined texts of the Mishna, Gemara, and Midrash, together with later rabbinical commentaries, are recorded in the ***Talmud***, the main compilation of traditional Jewish thought.

Muslim ***Koran*** more properly, Quran, though both are transliterations; the sacred book of Islam. Written in the purest Arabic, it contains 114 suras or chapters, and is stated to have been divinely revealed to the prophet Muhammad from Allah through the angel Jibra'el; the original is supposed to be preserved beside the throne of Allah in heaven.

Sikh The Sikh holy book is the ***Guru Granth Sahib***, also known as the ***Adi Granth*** ('first book'). It is a collection of hymns by the Sikh gurus or teachers, as well as by Muslim and Hindu writers, which was compiled largely by the fifth guru, Guru Arjan, and completed by the tenth guru, Guru Gobind Singh. On

The new catechism

Published on 8 December 1992, the *Catechism of the Catholic Church* is a book of some 700 pages containing the essential teaching of the Roman Catholic Church. It is the first 'universal' catechism since that produced in 1566 in the aftermath of the Protestant reformation. This new catechism follows the Second Vatican Council 1961–64, but the initiative to produce it was only taken in 1985. The book is not in the traditional question and answer form, but contains commentaries on the Creed, the Ten Commandments, the Lord's Prayer, and other topics, the target readership being bishops and teachers of religion rather than the laity in general.

the death of the tenth guru, the *Guru Granth Sahib* took over the role of teacher and leader of the Sikhs. Guidance is sought by opening the holy book at random and reading verses. Any copy of the *Guru Granth Sahib* must have a special room to itself; people entering the room must cover their heads and remove their shoes. All copies of the holy book are identical, having 1,430 pages, and written in Gurmukhi, the written form of Punjabi.

Religious Figures

Abraham *c.* 2300 BCE. in the Old Testament, founder of the Jewish nation. Jehovah promised him heirs and land for his people in Canaan (Israel), renamed him Abraham ('father of many nations'), and tested his faith by a command (later retracted) to sacrifice his son Isaac. Jehovah's promise to Abraham was fulfilled when the descendants of Abraham's grandson, Jacob, were led out of Egypt by Moses.

Abu Bakr or ***Abu-Bekr*** 573–634. 'Father of the virgin', name used by Abd-el-Ka'aba from about 618 when the prophet Muhammad married his daughter Ayesha. He was a close adviser to Muhammad in the period 622–32. On the prophet's death, he became the first caliph, adding Mesopotamia to the Muslim world and instigating expansion into Iraq and Syria.

Ali *c.* 598–660. 4th caliph of Islam. He was born in Mecca, the son of Abu Talib, uncle to the prophet Muhammad, who gave him his daughter Fatima in marriage. On Muhammad's death 632, Ali had a claim to succeed him, but this was not conceded until 656. After a stormy reign, he was assassinated. Around Ali's name the controversy has raged between the Sunni and the Shi'ites, the former denying his right to the caliphate and the latter supporting it.

Asoka lived *c.* 273–238 BCE. Indian emperor, and Buddhist convert from Hinduism. He issued edicts, carved on pillars and rock faces throughout his dominions, promoting wise government and the cultivation of moral virtues according to Buddhist teachings. Many still survive,and are amongst the oldest deciphered texts in India. In Patna there are the remains of a hall built by him.

Augustine, St ?–605. First archbishop of Canterbury, England. He was sent from Rome to convert England to Christianity by Pope Gregory I. He landed at Ebbsfleet in Kent 597, and soon after baptized Ethelbert, king of Kent, along with many of his subjects. He was consecrated bishop of the English at Arles in the same year, and appointed archbishop 601, establishing his see at Canterbury. Feast day 26 May.

Bodhidharma 6th century CE. Indian Buddhist and teacher. He entered China from S India about 520, and was the founder of the Ch'an school (Zen is the Japanese derivation). Ch'an focuses on contemplation leading to intuitive meditation, a direct pointing to and stilling of the human mind. In the 20th century, Zen has attracted many followers in the west.

Buddha 'enlightened one', title of Prince ***Gautama***

Popes of the last 500 years

1492–1503	Alexander VI	1676–89	Innocent XI
1503	Pius III	1689–91	Alexander VIII
1503–13	Julius II	1691–1700	Innocent XII
1513–21	Leo X	1700–21	Clement XI
1522–3	Hadrian VI	1721–4	Innocent XIII
1523–34	Clement VII	1724–30	Benedict XIII
1534–49	Paul III	1730–40	Clement XII
1550–5	Julius III	1740–58	Benedict XIV
1555	Marcellus II	1758–69	Clement XIII
1555–9	Paul IV	1769–74	Clement XIV
1559–65	Pius IV	1775–99	Pius VI
1566-72	Pius V	1800–23	Pius VII
1572–85	Gregory XIII	1823–9	Leo XII
1585–90	Sixtus V	1829–30	Pius VIII
1590	Urban VII	1831–46	Gregory XVI
1590–1	Gregory XIV	1846–78	Pius IX
1591	Innocent IX	1878–1903	Leo XIII
1592–1605	Clement VIII	1903–14	Pius X
1605	Leo XI	1914–22	Benedict XV
1605–21	Paul V	1922–39	Pius XI
1621–3	Gregory XV	1939–58	Pius XII
1623–44	Urban VIII	1958–63	John XXIII
1644-55	Innocent X	1963–78	Paul VI
1655–67	Alexander VII	1978	John Paul I
1667–9	Clement IX	1978–	John Paul II
1670–6	Clement X		

Siddhārtha *c.*563–483 BCE. Religious leader, founder of Buddhism, born at Lumbini in Nepal. At the age of 29, he left his wife and son and a life of luxury, to escape from the material burdens of existence. After six years of austerity he realized that asceticism, like overindulgence, was futile, and chose the middle way of meditation. He became enlightened under a bo or bodhi tree in Bihar, India. He began teaching at Varanasi, and founded the Sangha, or order of monks. He spent the rest of his life travelling around N India, and died at Kusinagara in Uttar Pradesh.

Confucius Latinized form of ***K'ung Tzu***, 'Kong the master' 551–479 BCE. Chinese sage whose name is given to Confucianism. He devoted his life to relieving suffering among the poor through governmental and administrative reform. His emphasis on tradition and ethics attracted a growing number of pupils during his lifetime. *The Analects of Confucius*, a compilation of his teachings, was published after his death. Within three hundred years of the death of Confucius his teaching was adopted by the Chinese state, and remained so until 1912.

Ghazzali, al- 1058–1111. Muslim philosopher and one of the most celebrated Sufis (Muslim mystics). He was responsible for easing the conflict between the Sufi and the Ulama, a body of Muslim religious and legal scholars.

Gobind Singh 1666–1708. Indian religious leader, the tenth and last guru (teacher) of Sikhism, 1675–1708, and founder of the Sikh brotherhood known as the Khalsa. On his death, the Sikh holy book, the *Guru Granth Sahib*, replaced the line of human gurus as the teacher and guide of the Sikh community.

Jesus *c.* 4 BCE–CE 29 or 30. Hebrew preacher on

whose teachings Christianity was founded. According to the accounts of his life in the four Gospels, he was born in Bethlehem, Palestine, son of God and the Virgin Mary, and brought up by Mary and her husband Joseph as a carpenter in Nazareth. After adult baptism, he gathered 12 disciples, but his preaching antagonized the Roman authorities and he was executed by crucifixion. Three days later there came reports of his resurrection and, later, his ascension to heaven.

Lao Zi or ***Lao Tzu*** *c.* 604–531 BCE. Chinese philosopher, commonly regarded as the founder of Taoism, with its emphasis on the Tao, the inevitable and harmonious way of the universe. Nothing certain is known of his life, and he is variously said to have lived in the 6th or the 4th century BCE. The *Tao Tê Ching*, the Taoist scripture, is attributed to him but apparently dates from the 3rd century BCE.

Luther Martin 1483–1546. German Christian church reformer, a founder of Protestantism. While he was a priest at the University of Wittenberg, he wrote an attack on the sale of indulgences (remissions of punishment for sin) in 95 theses which he nailed to a church door 1517, in defiance of papal condemnation. The Holy Roman Emperor Charles V summoned him to the Diet of Worms 1521, where he refused to retract his objections. Originally intending reform, his protest led to schism, with the emergence, following the Augsburg Confession 1530, of a new Protestant church. Luther is regarded as the instigator of the Protestant revolution, and Lutherism is now the major religion of many north European countries including Germany, Sweden, and Denmark.

Mahavira *c.* 540–468 BCE. Indian teacher and scholar. He was born into the warrior-king caste in Vessili (now Bihar). He became an ascetic at 30, achieved enlightenment at 42, and preached for 30 years. He was last in a line of 24 Jain masters called *Tirthankaras* or jinas ('those who overcome').

Maimonides Moses (Moses Ben Maimon) 1135–1204. Jewish rabbi and philosopher, born in Córdoba, Spain. Known as one of the greatest Hebrew scholars, he attempted to reconcile faith and reason. He was author of the *Thirteen Principles of Faith*.

Moses *c.* 13th century BCE. Hebrew lawgiver and judge who led the Israelites out of Egypt to the promised land of Canaan. On Mount Sinai he claimed to have received from Jehovah the oral and written Law, including the ***Ten Commandments*** engraved on tablets of stone. The first five books of the Old Testament – in Judaism, the *Torah* – are ascribed to him.

Muhammad or ***Mohammed, Mahomet*** *c.* 570–632. Prophet of Islam, born in Mecca on the Arabian peninsula. He began his prophetic mission *c.* 610 CE when it is believed he began to receive the revelations of the *Koran*, revealed to him by God (it was later written down by his followers) through the angel Jibra'el (Gabriel). He fled from persecution to the town now known as Medina in 622: the flight, ***Hegira***, marks the beginning of the Islamic era.

Nanak 1469–*c.* 1539. Indian guru and founder of Sikhism, a religion based on the unity of God and the equality of all human beings. He was strongly opposed to caste divisions. He was the first of ten human gurus in the Sikh faith.

Paul, St *c.* 3–*c.* CE 68. Christian missionary and martyr; in the New Testament, one of the apostles and author of 13 epistles. He is said to have been converted by a vision on the road to Damascus. His emblems are a sword and a book; feast day 29 June.

Shankara 799–833. Hindu philosopher who wrote commentaries on some of the major Hindu scriptures, as well as hymns and essays on religious ideas. Shankara was responsible for the final form of the Advaita Vedanta school of Hindu philosophy, which teaches that Brahman, the supreme being, is all that exists in the universe, everything else is illusion. Shankara was fiercely opposed to Buddhism and may have influenced its decline in India.

Zoroaster or ***Zarathustra*** 6th century BCE. Persian prophet and religious teacher, founder of Zoroastrianism. Zoroaster believed that he had seen God, Ahura Mazda, in a vision. His first vision came at the age of 30 and, after initial rejection and violent attack, he converted King Vishtaspa. Subsequently, his teachings spread rapidly, becoming the official religion of the kingdom. Zoroastrianism was a dualistic theology: the god of absolute purity and goodness, Ahura Mazda, being opposed by the twin spirit of violence and death: Angra Mainyu. According to tradition, Zoroaster was murdered at the age of 70 while praying at the altar.

Holy Places

The concept of ***pilgrimage***, a journey to sacred places inspired by religious devotion, is common to many religions. For Hindus the holy places include Benares and the purifying Ganges; for Buddhists, Bodhgaya, the site of the Buddha's enlightenment; the Tooth of the Buddha in Sri Lanka; and numerous temples and sacred mountains throughout China and south-east Asia; for the ancient Greeks, the shrines at Delphi, Ephesus, among others; for the Jews, the Western Wall at Jerusalem; and for Muslims, Mecca. Among Christians, pilgrimages were common by the second century, and as a direct result of the established necessity of making pilgrimages there arose the numerous hospices catering for pilgrims, the religious orders of knighthood, and the Crusades. The great centres of Christian pilgrimages have been, or are, Jerusalem, Rome, the tomb of St James of Compostella in Spain, the shrine of Becket at Canterbury, and the holy places at La Salette and Lourdes in France.

Amritsar city in the Punjab, India, founded 1577. It is the religious centre of the Sikhs and contains the Golden Temple and Guru Nanak University 1969, named after the first Sikh Guru.

Jerusalem ancient city of Palestine, which is a holy place for Jews, Christians, and Muslims. It was divided in 1948 between the new republic of Israel and Jordan. In 1950, the western New City was proclaimed as the Israeli capital, and following the Israeli capture of the eastern Old City in 1967 from the Jordanians, it was affirmed in 1980 that the united city was the country's capital, but the United Nations does not recognize the claim.

history by 1400 BCE Jerusalem was ruled by a king

subject to Egypt, but *c.* 1000 BCE David, the second king of Israel, made it the capital of a united Jewish kingdom. It was captured by Nebuchadnezzar 586 BCE, who deported its population. Later conquerors include Alexander the Great and Pompey (63 BCE), and it was under Roman rule that Jesus Christ was executed. In 70 CE a Jewish revolt led to its complete destruction by Titus. It was first conquered by Islam in 637; was captured by Crusaders, Christians who were fighting the Muslims in Israel, 1099, and recaptured by Saladin 1187, to remain under almost unbroken Islamic rule until the British occupation of Palestine in 1917.

Notable buildings include the Church of the Holy Sepulchre (built 335), and the mosque of the Dome of the Rock. The latter was built on the site of Solomon's Temple, and the Western ('wailing') Wall, held sacred by Jews, is part of the walled platform on which the Temple once stood.

Temple the centre of Jewish national worship at Jerusalem. Three temples occupied the site: Solomon's Temple, which was destroyed by Nebuchadnezzar; Zerubbabel's Temple, built after the return from Babylon; and Herod's Temple, which was destroyed by the Romans in 70 CE. The Mosque of Omar occupies the site. The Wailing Wall is the surviving part of the western wall of the platform of the enclosure of the Temple of Herod, so-called by tourists because of the chanting style of the Jews in their prayers there. Under Jordanian rule Jews had no access to the place, but took this part of the city in the 1967 campaign.

Mecca city of Saudi Arabia, the holiest city of the Muslim world, where the Prophet was born. It stands in the desert, in a valley about 72 km/45 mi east of Jidda, its port on the Red Sea, with which it is linked by a motorway, and long before the time of Muhammad was a commercial centre, caravan junction, and place of pilgrimage. In the centre of Mecca is the Great Mosque, in whose courtyard is the Kaaba; it also contains the well Zam-Zam, associated by tradition with Ishmael, the son of Abraham, and his mother Hagar, and the Maqām Ibrāhīm, a holy stone believed to bear the imprint of Abraham's foot.

kaaba the oblong building in the quadrangle of the Great Mosque at Mecca into the south-east corner of which is built the black stone declared by Muhammad to have been given to Abraham by Gabriel, and devoutly revered by Muslim pilgrims. The name means chamber.

Medina city in Saudi Arabia, about 355 km/220 mi north of Mecca. To Muslims it is a holy city second only to Mecca, since Muhammad lived here for many years after he fled from Mecca, and died here. The Mosque of the Prophet is believed to contain Muhammad's tomb, and those of the caliphs or Muslim leaders Abu Bakr, Omar, and Fatima, Muhammad's daughter.

Varanasi or Benares Indian city on the sacred Ganges river in Uttar Pradesh. It is holy to Hindus with a 5 km/3 mi frontage of stairways (ghats), leading up from the river to innumerable streets, temples, and the 1,500 golden shrines. The ritual of purification is practised daily by thousands of devout Hindus, who bathe from the ghats in the sacred river. At the burning ghats, the ashes, following cremation, are scattered on the river, a ritual followed to ensure a favourable reincarnation.

Festivals

Buddhist festivals

Wesak the day of the Buddha's birth, enlightenment, and death. A large act of worship is held and gifts given to monks; captive animals may be freed.

Dhammacakka celebrates the preaching of the Buddha's first sermon. Visits are made to monasteries and gifts are given to the monks.

Bodhi Day Mahāyāna Buddhist celebration of the Buddha's enlightenment.

Chinese festivals

New Year time when the Kitchen God, whose picture is in every home, returns to heaven to report on the family's behaviour during the year. There are elaborate lion dances and fireworks, and vegetarian feasts are eaten.

Ching Ming a time for visiting ancestral tombs, making offerings and remembering the dead.

Dragon Boat Festival celebrates the story of a brave official who persuaded a harsh emperor to relent over his crippling taxation of the people by drowning himself. Races are held between boats carved to resemble dragons, in memory of the boat chase to save the official's body from being eaten by dragons and demons.

Moon Festival commemorates the story of a brave woman who defied her husband, a wicked king, to stop him obtaining immortality, and was carried off by the gods to live on the moon. The festival is held at the harvest full moon and the moon is greeted with incense, lanterns and feasting.

Winter Festival time of feasting to build up strength for the winter ahead.

Christian festivals

Epiphany annual festival (6 Jan) of the Christian church, celebrating the coming of the Magi or wise men to Bethlehem with gifts for the infant Christ, and symbolizing the manifestation of Christ to the world. It is the twelfth day after Christmas, and marks the end of the Christmas festivities. In many countries the night before, called ***Twelfth Night***, is marked by the giving of gifts.

Shrove Tuesday the day before Ash Wednesday. The name comes from the Anglo-Saxon *scrifan*, to shrive, and in former times it was the time for confession before Lent. Another name for it is Pancake Tuesday; the pancakes are a survival of merry-making in anticipation of Lenten abstinence.

Ash Wednesday first day of Lent, the period in the Christian calendar leading up to Easter; in the Catholic church the foreheads of the congregation are marked with a cross in ash, as a sign of penitence.

Lent in the Christian church, the forty days' period of fasting which precedes Easter, beginning on Ash Wednesday, but omitting Sundays.

Palm Sunday the Sunday before Easter, and first day of Holy Week; so-called to commemorate Christ's entry into Jerusalem, when the crowd strewed palm

Religious festivals

Date	Festival	Religion	Event commemorated
6 Jan	Epiphany	Western Christian	coming of the Magi
6–7 Jan	Christmas	Orthodox Christian	birth of Jesus
18–19 Jan	Epiphany	Orthodox Christian	coming of the Magi
Jan–Feb	New Year	Chinese	Return of Kitchen god to heaven
Feb–Mar	Shrove Tuesday	Christian	day before Lent
	Ash Wednesday	Christian	first day of Lent
	Purim	Jewish	story of Esther
	Mahashivaratri	Hindu	Siva
Mar–Apr	Palm Sunday	Western Christian	Jesus's entry into Jerusalem
	Good Friday	Western Christian	crucifixion of Jesus
	Easter Sunday	Western Christian	resurrection of Jesus
	Passover	Jewish	escape from slavery in Egypt
	Holi	Hindu	Krishna
	Holi Mohalla	Sikh	(coincides with Holi)
	Rama Naumi	Hindu	birth of Rama
	Ching Ming	Chinese	remembrance of the dead
13 Apr	Baisakhi	Sikh	founding of the Kalsa
Apr–May	Easter	Orthodox Christian	death and resurrection of Jesus
	Lailut ul-Isra wal Mi'raj	Muslim	Prophet Muhammad's journey to Jerusalem and then up to Heaven
	Lailat ul-Bara'h	Muslim	forgiveness before Ramadan
May–Jun	Shavuot	Jewish	giving of Ten Commandments to Moses
	Lailat ul-Qadr	Muslim	revelation of the Qur'an to Muhammad
	Eid ul-Fitr	Muslim	end of Ramadan
	Pentecost (Whitsun)	Christian	Jesus's followers receiving the Holy Spirit
	Wesak	Buddhist	day of Buddha's birth, enlightenment, and death
	Martyrdom of Guru Arjan	Sikh	death of fifth guru of Sikhism
June	Dragon Boat Festival	Chinese	Chinese martyr
Jul	Dhammacakka	Buddhist	preaching of Buddha's first sermon
	Eid ul-Adha	Muslim	Abraham's willingness to sacrifice his son
Aug	Raksha Bandhan	Hindu	family
Aug–Sept	Janmashtami	Hindu	birthday of Khrishna
Sept	Moon Festival	Chinese	Chinese hero
Sept–Oct	Rosh Hashanah	Jewish	start of Jewish New Year
	Yom Kippur	Jewish	Day of Atonement
	Succot	Jewish	Israelites' time in the wilderness
Oct	Dusshera	Hindu	goddess Devi
Oct–Nov	Divali	Hindu	goddess Lakshmi
	Divali	Sikh	release of Guru Hargobind from prison
Nov	Guru Nanak's Birthday	Sikh	founder of Sikhism
1 Nov	All Saint's Day	Christian	deceased Christian saints and holy people
2 Nov	All Soul's Day	Christian	Christian deceased
	Bodhi Day	Buddhist (Mahāyāna)	Buddha's enlightenment
Dec	Hanukkah	Jewish	recapture of Temple of Jerusalem
	Winter Festival	Chinese	time of feasting
25 Dec	Christmas	Western Christian	birth of Christ
Dec–Jan	Birthday of Guru Gobind Sind	Sikh	last (tenth) human guru of Sikhism
	Martyrdom of Guru Tegh Bahadur	Sikh	ninth guru of Sikhism

leaves in his path.

Good Friday (probably a corruption of God's Friday). In the Christian church, the Friday before Easter, which is kept in memory of the Crucifixion (the death of Jesus).

Easter feast of the Christian church, commemorating the Resurrection of Christ. It usually falls around the time of the Jewish Passover since Christ's crucifixion coincided with the time of this festival. The English name derives from Eostre, Anglo-Saxon goddess of spring, who was honoured in April. Eggs are given at this time as a symbol of new life.

Whitsun celebrates the filling of the followers of Jesus with the Holy Spirit, which Christians believe to be the third aspect of God, after Jesus had returned to heaven. As the disciples went out and told everyone about Jesus, so at Whitsun many Christians go on processions around the parish boundaries.

Advent the time leading up to Christmas; a time of preparation for Christians.

Christmas day on which the birth of Christ is celebrated by Christians. Although the actual birth date is unknown, the choice of a date near the winter solstice owned much to missionary desire to facilitate conversion of pagans, for example in Britain 25 Dec had been kept as a festival long before the introduction of Christianity. Many of its customs also have a non-Christian origin.

Hindu festivals

Mahashivaratri Festival of Siva, who is celebrated as lord of the dance, dancing on the demon of ignorance.

Holi a harvest time festival in honour of Krishna, when bonfires are lit; people throw coloured water at each other and play games and tricks as a reminder of Krishna's mischievous behaviour.

Rama Naumi celebration of the Birth of Rama. An eight-day fast during which the Rāmāyana is recited; the fast is broken on the ninth day with fruit and nuts, and offerings are made to Rama.

Raksha Bandhan a family festival in which sisters present their brothers with a bracelet of thread to protect them from harm, in return for which the brothers promise to look after their sisters.

Janmashtami celebration of the birthday of Krishna. Children act out stories of Krishna, and a statue of the young Krishna is used in the celebrations.

Dusshera a festival (also known as Durga Puja) which lasts ten days; the great goddess Devi is worshipped in her many forms.

Divali a new year festival which honours Lakshmi, goddess of fortune. Lights are lit in every window.

Jewish festivals

Purim celebrates the story of Esther, a Jewish woman who risked her life to save her people from treacherous slaughter. The story is read from a scroll in the synagogue, and the congregation boo and hiss when the villain's name is read out. It is a time for noisy parties and merriment.

Passover (Pesach) festival which commemorates the escape from slavery in Egypt. A special meal, the seder meal, is eaten and the story of how the Jews were saved by God from this bondage is told.

Shavuot or Pentecost commemorates the giving of the ten commandments to Moses.

Rosh Hashanah the two-day festival at the start of the Jewish New Year (first new moon after the autumn equinox), a time for repentence and forgiveness. This reflective period is brought to a close nine days later at Yom Kippur. Rosh Hashanah begins on the first day of the month of Tishri (Sept–Oct), the seventh month of the Jewish year.

Yom Kippur (Day of Atonement) day of Jewish religious fast held on the tenth day of Tishri. Final forgiveness is sought for past deeds and the Kol Nidrei is sung in the synagogue to end the old vows of the past year and to prepare for the demands of the coming year. The festival ends with the blowing of the shofar, the ram's horn.

Succot the feast of Tabernacles (tents), a reminder of the time the Israelites spent wandering in the wilderness. Temporary homes of branches are built at the synagogue and sometimes at home.

Hanukkah celebrates the recapture and rededication of the Temple of Jerusalem by Judah Maccabee in 165 BCE. The festival lasts eight days; each day, a new candle is lit on a special candlestick or menorah.

Muslim festivals

The Muslim calendar is lunar, and correspondences with the Western calendar cannot be given; festivals fall 11–12 days earlier each year.

Lailat ul-Isra Wal Mi'raj celebrates Muhammad's night journey by horse to Jerusalem and up to heaven.

Lailat ul-Barah the night of forgiveness; a time to prepare for Ramadan.

Ramadan the ninth month of the Muslim year, throughout which a strict fast is observed during the hours of daylight.

Lailat ul-Qadr commemorates the night the Koran was first revealed to Muhammad.

Eid ul-Fitr the end of the fast of Ramadan. Gifts are given to charity, new clothes are worn and sweets are given.

Eid ul-Adha celebrates the faith of the prophet Abraham, who was prepared to sacrifice his son Ismail when Allah asked him to. Lamb is eaten and shared with the poor, as a reminder of the sheep which Allah provided as a sacrifice instead of Ismail.

Day of Hijra commemorates the journey of Muhammad from Mecca to Medina.

Sikh festivals

Hola Mohalla a three-day festival held at the time of the Hindu festival Holi. Sporting competitions and other tests of skill take place.

Baisakhi originally a harvest festival, it now celebrates the founding of the Khalsa, the Sikh brotherhood, and commemorates those Sikhs killed by British troops in Amritsar on Baisakhi, 1919.

Martyrdom of Guru Arjan commemorates the death of the fifth guru, Guru Arjan, who built the Golden Temple at Amritsar and compiled the main part of the Sikh holy book.

Divali celebrates the release from prison of the sixth guru, Guru Hargobind, who also managed to secure the release of 51 Hindu princes who were imprisoned with him.

Guru Nanak's birthday celebrates the birth of the founder of the first guru of Sikhism.

Martyrdom of Guru Tegh Bahadur the ninth guru, martyred for the faith.

Birthday of Guru Gobind Singh The tenth and last human guru of Sikhism, and the founder of the Khalsa.

GALLUP POLL

How much confidence you have in the Church (as an institution)?

	Feb 1993	Dec 1992	Mar 1991	Dec 1989	Nov 1987
A great deal	12	11	11	15	17
Quite a lot	25	27	25	28	28
Not very much	40	36	42	41	36
None at all	23	26	19	16	19

SPORT

Events and Records

angling fishing with rod and line. ***Freshwater fishing*** embraces game fishing, in which members of the salmon family, such as salmon and trout, are taken by spinners (revolving lures) and flies (imitations of adult or larval insects); and coarse fishing, in which members of the carp family, pike, perch, and eels are taken by baits or lures, and (in the UK) are returned to the water virtually unharmed. In ***sea fishing*** the catch includes flatfish, bass, and mackerel; big-game fishes include shark, tuna or tunny, marlin, and swordfish. World championships take place for most branches of the sport.

WORLD FRESHWATER CHAMPIONSHIPS

first held 1957

individual
1982 Kevin Ashurst *(England)*
1983 Wolf-Rüdiger Kremkus *(West Germany)*
1984 Bobby Smithers *(England)*
1985 Dave Roper *(England)*
1986 Lud Wever *(Holland)*
1987 Clive Branson *(Wales)*
1988 Jean-Pierre Fouquet *(France)*
1989 Tom Pickering *(England)*
1990 Bob Nudd *(England)*
1991 Bob Nudd *(England)*
1992 David Wesson *(Australia)*

team
1982 Holland
1983 Belgium
1984 Luxembourg
1985 England
1986 Italy
1987 England
1988 England
1989 Wales
1990 France
1991 England
1992 Italy

---

archery shooting with a bow and arrow at a circular target made up of ten concentric scoring zones. The highest score (10 points) is obtained by hitting the central, gold-coloured zone. Competitions usually take the form of Double FITA (Fédération Internationale de Tir à l'Arc) rounds – that is, 72 arrows are fired at each of four targets from distances of 90, 70, 50, and 30 m (70, 60, 50, and 30 m for women). The highest possible score is 2,880.

WORLD CHAMPIONSHIP

first held 1931; now contested every two years

men: individual
1983 Richard McKinney *(USA)*
1985 Richard McKinney *(USA)*
1987 Vladimir Asheyer *(USSR)*
1989 Stanislav Zabrodsky *(USSR)*
1991 Simon Fairweather *(Australia)*

men: team
1983 USA
1985 South Korea
1987 South Korea
1989 USSR
1991 South Korea

women: individual
1983 Jin-Ho Kim *(South Korea)*
1985 Irina Soldatova *(USSR)*
1987 Ma Xiagjuan *(China)*
1989 Soo Nyung-Kim *(South Korea)*
1991 Soo Nyung-Kim *(South Korea)*

women: team
1983 South Korea
1985 USSR
1987 China
1989 South Korea
1991 South Korea

---

athletics competitive track and field events consisting of running, throwing, and jumping disciplines. ***Running events*** range from sprint races (100 metres) and hurdles to the marathon (26 miles 385 yards). ***Jumping events*** are the high jump and long jump, and, for men only, the triple jump and pole vault. ***Throwing events*** are javelin, discus, shot put, and hammer throw (men only).

OLYMPIC GAMES

events staged since 1896

Barcelona Olympics 1992 (25th Olympic Games)

track and field
men/women
100 metres: Linford Christie *(UK)*/Gail Devers *(USA)*
200 metres: Michael Marsh *(USA)*/Gwen Torrence *(USA)*
400 metres: Quincy Watts *(USA)*/Marie-Jose Perec *(France)*
800 metres: William Tanui *(Kenya)*/Ellen van Langen *(Netherlands)*
1,500 metres: Fermin Cacho *(Spain)*/Hassiba Boulmerka *(Algeria)*
3,000 metres: — /Yelina Romanova *(Unified Team*)*
5,000 metres: Dieter Baumann *(Germany)*/ —
10,000 metres: Khalid Skah *(Morocco)*/Derartu Tulu *(Ethiopia)*
marathon: Hwang Young Cho *(South Korea)*/Valentina Yegorova *(Unified Team)*
110-metre hurdles: Mark McCoy *(Canada)*/Paraskevi Patoulidou *(Greece)*
400-metre hurdles: Kevin Young *(USA)*/Sally Gunnell *(UK)*
3,000-metre steeplechase: Matthew Birir *(Kenya)*/ —
10,000-metre walk: — /Chen Yueling *(China)*
20,000-metre walk: Daniel Plaza Montero *(Spain)*/ —
50,000-metre walk: Andrei Perlov *(Unified Team)*/ —
400-metre relay: USA/USA
1,600-metre relay: USA/Unified Team
high jump: Javier Sotomayor *(Cuba)*/ Heike Henkel *(Germany)*
long jump: Carl Lewis *(USA)*/Heike Drechsler *(Germany)*
triple jump: Mike Conley *(USA)*/ —
pole vault: Maksim Tarassov *(Unified Team)*/ —
javelin: Jan Zelezny *(Czechoslovakia)*/Silke Renke *(Germany)*

hammer: Andrei Abduvaliyev *(Unified Team)*/ —
discus: Romas Ubartas *(Lithuania)*/Maritza Marten Garcia *(Cuba)*
shot put: Mike Stulce *(USA)*/Svetlana Kriveleva *(Unified Team)*
decathlon: Robert Zmelik *(Czechoslovakia)*/ —
heptathlon: — /Jackie Joyner-Kersee *(USA)*
* *Commonwealth of Independent States plus Georgia*

WORLD RECORDS
at 16 August 1992

men
100 metres: 9.86 sec Carl Lewis *(USA)*
200 metres: 19.72 sec Pietro Mennea *(Italy)*
400 metres: 43.29 sec Butch Reynolds *(USA)*
800 metres: 1 min 41.73 sec Sebastian Coe *(UK)*
1,000 metres: 2 min 12.18 sec Sebastian Coe *(UK)*
1,500 metres: 2 min 28.82 sec Noureddine Morceli *(Morocco)*
mile: 3 min 46.32 sec Steve Cram *(UK)*
2,000 metres: 4 min 50.81 sec Said Aouita *(Morocco)*
3,000 metres: 7 min 28.96 sec Moses Kiptanui *(Kenya)*
5,000 metres: 12 min 58.39 sec Said Aouita *(Morocco)*
10,000 metres: 27 min 08.23 sec Arturo Barrios *(Mexico)*
20,000 metres: 56 min 55.6 sec Arturo Barrios *(Mexico)*
20,994 metres: 1 hr Jos Hermans *(Holland)*
25,000 metres: 1 hr 13 min 55.8 sec Toshihiko Seko *(Japan)*
30,000 metres: 1 hr 29 min 18.8 sec Toshihiko Seko *(Japan)*
110-metre hurdles: 12.92 sec Roger Kingdom *(USA)*
400-metre hurdles: 46.78 sec Kevin Young *(USA)*
3,000-metre steeplechase: 8 min 2.08 sec Moses Kiptanui *(Kenya)*
400-metre relay: 37.40 sec USA
1,600-metre relay: 2 min 55.74 sec USA
3,200-metre relay: 7 min 03.89 sec UK
6,000-metre relay: 14 min 38.8 sec West Germany
high jump: 2.44 metres Javier Sotomayor *(Cuba)*
pole vault: 6.13 metres Sergey Bubka *(USSR)*
long jump: 8.95 metres Mike Powell *(USA)*
triple jump: 17.97 metres Willie Banks *(USA)*
shot: 23.12 metres Randy Barnes *(USA)*
discus: 74.08 metres Jurgen Schult *(East Germany)*
hammer: 86.74 metres Yuriy Sedykh *(USSR)*
javelin: 95.54 metres Jan Zelezny *(RCS)*
decathlon: 8,891 points Dan O'Brien *(USA)*
marathon: 2 hr 6 min 50 sec Belayneh Dinsamo *(Ethiopia)*

women
100 metres: 10.49 sec Florence Griffith-Joyner *(USA)*
200 metres: 21.34 sec Florence Griffith-Joyner *(USA)*
400 metres: 47.60 sec Marita Koch *(East Germany)*
800 metres: 1 min 53.28 sec Jarmila Kratochvilova *(Czechoslovakia)*
1,500 metres: 3 min 52.47 sec Tatyana Kazankina *(USSR)*
mile: 4 min 15.61 sec Paula Ivan *(Romania)*
2,000 metres: 5 min 28.69 sec Maricica Puica *(Romania)*
3,000 metres: 8 min 22.62 sec Tatyana Kazankini *(USSR)*
5,000 metres: 14 min 37.33 sec Ingrid Kristiansen *(Norway)*
10,000 metres: 30 min 13.74 sec Ingrid Kristiansen *(Norway)*
20,000 metres: 1 hr 29 min 29.2 sec Karolina Szabo *(Hungary)*
30,000 metres: 1 hr 49 min 5.6 sec Karolina Szabo *(Hungary)*
100-metre hurdles: 12.21 sec Yordanka Donkova *(Bulgaria)*
400-metre hurdles: 52.94 sec Marina Stepanova *(USSR)*
400-metre relay: 41.37 sec *(East Germany)*
800-metre relay: 1 min 28.15 sec *(East Germany)*
1,600-metre relay: 3 min 15.17 sec *(USSR)*

WORLD CROSS-COUNTRY CHAMPIONSHIP

men: individual
1988 John Ngugi *(Kenya)*
1989 John Ngugi *(Kenya)*
1990 Khaled Skah *(Morocco)*
1991 Khaled Skah *(Morocco)*
1992 John Ngugi *(Kenya)*
1993 William Sigei *(Kenya)*

women: individual
1988 Ingrid Kristiansen *(Norway)*
1989 Annette Sergant *(France)*
1990 Lynn Jennings *(USA)*
1991 Lynn Jennings *(USA)*
1992 Lynn Jennings *(USA)*
1993 Albertina Dias *(Portugal)*

men: team
1988 Kenya
1989 Kenya
1990 Kenya
1991 Kenya
1992 Kenya
1993 Kenya

women: team
1988 USSR
1989 USSR
1990 USSR
1991 Kenya/Ethiopia
1992 Kenya
1993 Kenya

badminton indoor racket game, similar to lawn tennis but played with a shuttlecock (a half sphere of cork or plastic with a feather or nylon skirt) instead of a ball. It may be played by two or four players. The game takes place on a court 13.4 m/44 ft long and 5.2 m/17 ft wide (6.1 m/20 ft wide for doubles), with a raised net across the middle. The object of the game is to prevent the opponent from being able to return the shuttlecock.

WORLD CHAMPIONSHIP
first held 1977; now contested every two years

men
1983 Icuk Sugiarto *(Indonesia)*
1985 Han Jian *(China)*
1987 Yang Yang *(China)*
1989 Yang Yang *(China)*
1991 Zao Zinhua *(China)*
1993 Joko Suprianto *(Indonesia)*

women
1983 Li Lingwei *(China)*
1985 Han Aiping *(China)*
1987 Han Aiping *(China)*
1989 Li Lingwei *(China)*
1991 Tang Jiu Hong *(China)*
1993 Susi Susanti *(Indonesia)*

THOMAS CUP

men's team championship, first held 1949
1970 Indonesia
1973 Indonesia
1976 Indonesia
1979 Indonesia
1982 China
1984 Indonesia
1986 China
1988 China
1990 China
1992 Malaysia

UBER CUP

women's team championship, first held 1957
1969 Japan
1972 Japan
1975 Indonesia
1978 Japan
1981 Japan
1984 China
1986 China
1988 China
1990 China
1992 China

baseball national summer game of the USA, derived in the 19th century from the English game of rounders. Baseball is a bat-and-ball game played between two teams, each of nine players. The field is marked out in the form of a diamond, with a base at each corner. The ball is struck with a cylindrical bat, and the players try to score ('make a run') by circuiting the bases. A 'home run' is a circuit on one hit.

WORLD SERIES

first held 1903 as an end-of-season game between the winners of the two professional leagues, the National League and the American League, and established as a series of seven games 1905
1982 St Louis Cardinals
1983 Baltimore Orioles
1984 Detroit Tigers
1985 Kansas City Royals
1986 New York Mets
1987 Minnesota Twins
1988 Los Angeles Dodgers
1989 Oakland Athletics
1990 Cincinatti Reds
1991 Minnesota Twins
1992 Toronto Blue Jays

basketball ball game between two teams of five players on a rectangular enclosed court. The object is to throw the large inflated ball through a circular hoop and net positioned at the end of each courts, 3.05 m/10 ft above the ground. Players move the ball by passing it or by dribbling it (bouncing it on the floor) while running.

WORLD CHAMPIONSHIPS

first held 1950 for men, 1953 for women; contested every four years

men
1954 USA
1959 Brazil
1963 Brazil
1967 USSR
1970 Yugoslavia
1974 USSR
1978 Yugoslavia
1982 USSR
1986 USA
1990 Yugoslavia

women
1957 USA
1959 USSR
1964 USSR
1967 USSR
1971 USSR
1975 USSR
1979 USA
1983 USSR
1986 USA
1990 USA

NBA (NATIONAL BASKETBALL ASSOCIATION) CHAMPIONSHIP

US end-of-season contest, first held 1947, between the top teams of the two professional leagues, the Western Conference and the Eastern Conference
1982 Los Angeles Lakers
1983 Philadelphia 76ers
1984 Boston Celtics
1985 Los Angeles Lakers
1986 Boston Celtics
1987 Los Angeles Lakers
1988 Los Angeles Lakers
1989 Detroit Pistons
1990 Detroit Pistons
1991 Chicago Bulls
1992 Chicago Bulls
1993 Chicago Bulls

billiards indoor game played, normally by two players, with tapered poles (cues) and composition balls (one red, two white) on a rectangular table covered with a green feltlike cloth (baize). The table has six pockets, one at each corner and in each of the long sides at the middle. Scoring strokes are made by potting the red ball, potting the opponent's ball, or potting another ball off one of these two. The cannon (when the cue ball hits the two other balls on the table) is another scoring stroke.

WORLD PROFESSIONAL CHAMPIONSHIP

instituted 1870, on a challenge basis, and restored as an annual tournament 1980
1982 Rex Williams *(England)*
1983 Rex Williams *(England)*
1984 Mark Wildman *(England)*
1985 Ray Edmonds *(England)*
1986 Robert Foldvari *(Australia)*
1987 Norman Dagley *(England)*
1988 Norman Dagley *(England)*
1989 Mike Russell *(England)*
1990 Mike Russell *(England)*
1991 Mike Russell *(England)*
1992 Geet Sethi *(India)*

bobsleighing or ***bobsledding*** racing steel-bodied, steerable toboggans, crewed by two or four people, down mountain ice-chutes at speeds of up to 130 kph/80 mph.

WORLD CHAMPIONSHIP

four-crew championship introduced 1924, two-crew 1931; Olympic winners automatically become world champions

two-person/four-person
1983 Switzerland/Switzerland
1984 East Germany/East Germany
1985 East Germany/East Germany
1986 East Germany/Switzerland
1987 Switzerland/Switzerland
1988 USSR/Switzerland
1989 East Germany/Switzerland
1990 Switzerland/Switzerland
1991 Germany/Germany
1992 Switzerland/Switzerland
1993 Germany/Switzerland

---

bowls outdoor and indoor game popular in Commonwealth countries. The outdoor game is played on a finely cut grassed area called a rink, with biased bowls 13 cm/5 in in diameter. It is played as either singles, pairs, triples, or fours. The object is to position one's bowl (or bowls) as near as possible to the jack (target). ***Lawn bowls*** is played on a flat surface; ***crown green bowls*** is played on a rink with undulations and a crown at the centre of the green.

WORLD OUTDOOR CHAMPIONSHIP

first held 1966 for men, and 1969 for women

men: singles
1972 Maldwyn Evans *(Wales)*
1976 Doug Watson *(South Africa)*
1980 David Bryant *(England)*
1984 Peter Bellis *(New Zealand)*
1988 David Bryant *(England)*
1992 Tony Allcock *(England)*

women: singles
1973 Elsie Wilke *(New Zealand)*
1977 Elsie Wilke *(New Zealand)*
1981 Norma Shaw *(England)*
1985 Merle Richardson *(Australia)*
1988 Janet Ackland *(Wales)*
1992 Margaret Johnston *(Ireland)*

WORLD INDOOR CHAMPIONSHIP

first held 1979 for men, 1988 for women

men: singles
1988 Hugh Duff *(Scotland)*
1989 Richard Corsie *(Scotland)*
1990 John Price *(Wales)*
1991 Richard Corsie *(Scotland)*
1992 Ian Schuback *(Australia)*
1993 Richard Corsie *(Scotland)*

women: singles
1988 Margaret Johnston *(Ireland)*
1989 Margaret Johnston *(Ireland)*
1990 Fleur Bougourd *(England)*
1991 Mary Price *(England)*
1992 Sarah Gourlay *(Scotland)*

WATERLOO HANDICAP

crown green tournament first held 1907
1982 Dennis Mercer
1983 Stan Frith
1984 Steve Ellis
1985 Tommy Johnstone
1986 Brian Duncan
1987 Brian Duncan
1988 Ingham Gregory
1989 Brian Duncan
1990 John Bancroft
1991 John Eccles
1992 Brian Duncan

---

boxing fighting with gloved fists, almost entirely a male sport. Contests take place in a square, roped ring 4.3—6.1 m/14—20 ft square. All rounds last 3 minutes. Amateur bouts last three rounds and professional championship bouts for as many as 12 or 15 rounds. Boxers are classified according to weight and may not fight in a division lighter than their own. The weight divisions in professional boxing range from straw-weight (also known as paperweight and mini-flyweight), under 49 kg/108 lb, to heavyweight, over 88 kg/195 lb.

WORLD CHAMPIONSHIP

(WBC = World Boxing Council; WBA = World Boxing Association; IBF = International Boxing Federation; WBO = World Boxing Organization)

heavyweight
1986 Tim Witherspoon (*USA*, WBA)
1986 Trevor Berbick (*Canada*, WBC)
1986 Mike Tyson (*USA*, WBC)
1986 James Smith (*USA*, WBA)
1987 Mike Tyson (*USA*, WBA)
1987 Tony Tucker (*USA*, IBF)
1987 Mike Tyson (*USA*, undisputed)
1989 Francesco Damiani (*Italy*, WBO)
1990 James Douglas (*USA*, undisputed)
1990 Evander Holyfield (*USA*, undisputed)
1992 Riddick Bowe (*(USA)*, WBA, IBF)
1992 Lennox Lewis (*(UK)*, WBC)
1992 Michael Moorer (*(USA)*, WBO)
1993 Tommy Morrison (*(USA)*, WBO)

great heavyweight champions include:
John L Sullivan (bare-knuckle champion) 1882–92
Jim Corbett (first Marquess of Queensberry champion) 1892–97
Jack Dempsey 1919–26
Joe Louis 1937–49
Rocky Marciano 1952–56
Muhammad Ali 1964–67, 1974–78, 1978–79
Larry Holmes 1978–85
Mike Tyson 1986–1990

---

canoeing propelling a lightweight, shallow boat, pointed at both ends, by paddles or sails. Currently, canoes are made from fibreglass, but original boats were of wooden construction covered in bark or skin. Two types of canoe are used: the *kayak*, and the *Canadian-style* canoe. The kayak, derived from the Eskimo model, has a keel and the canoeist sits. The Canadian style canoe has no keel and the canoeist kneels.

OLYMPIC GAMES

event introduced 1936
men: kayak singles
500 metres
1980 Vladimir Parfenovich *(USSR)*

1984 Ian Ferguson *(New Zealand)*
1988 Zsolt Gyulay *(Hungary)*
1992 Mikko Kolehmainen *(Finland)*

1,000 metres
1980 Rudiger Helm *(East Germany)*
1984 Alan Thompson *(New Zealand)*
1988 Greg Barton *(USA)*
1992 Clint Robinson *(Australia)*

kayak pairs
500 metres
1980 USSR
1984 New Zealand
1988 New Zealand
1992 Germany

1,000 metres
1980 USSR
1984 Canada
1988 USA
1992 Germany

kayak fours
1,000 metres
1980 East Germany
1984 New Zealand
1988 Hungary
1992 Germany

Canadian singles
500 metres
1980 Sergey Postrekhin *(USSR)*
1984 Larry Cain *(Canada)*
1988 Olaf Heukrodt *(East Germany)*
1992 Nikolai Bukhalov *(Germany)*

1,000 metres
1980 Lubomir Lubenov *(Bulgaria)*
1984 Ulrich Eicke *(West Germany)*
1988 Ivan Klementiev *(USSR)*
1992 Nikolai Bukhalov *(Germany)*

Canadian pairs
500 metres
1980 Hungary
1984 Yugoslavia
1988 USSR
1992 Unified Team*

1,000 metres
1980 Romania
1984 Romania
1988 USSR
1992 Germany

women: kayak singles
500 metres
1980 Birgit Fischer *(East Germany)*
1984 Agneta Anderson *(Sweden)*
1988 Vania Guecheva *(Bulgaria)*
1992 Birgit Schmidt *(Germany)*

kayak pairs
500 metres
1980 East Germany
1984 Sweden
1988 East Germany
1992 Germany

* *Commonwealth of Independent States plus Georgia*

cricket bat-and-ball game between two teams of 11 players each. It is played with a small solid ball and long flat-sided wooden bats, on a round or oval field, at the centre of which is a finely mown pitch, 20 m/22 yd long. At each end of the pitch is a wicket made up of three upright wooden sticks (stumps), surmounted by two smaller sticks (bails). The object of the game is to score more runs than the opposing team. A run is normally scored by the batsman striking the ball and exchanging ends with his or her partner until the ball is returned by a fielder, or by hitting the ball to the boundary line for an automatic four or six runs.

COUNTY CHAMPIONSHIP

first held officially 1890
1983 Essex
1984 Essex
1985 Middlesex
1986 Essex
1987 Nottinghamshire
1988 Worcestershire
1989 Worcestershire
1990 Middlesex
1991 Essex
1992 Essex

AXA EQUITY AND LAW LEAGUE

(formerly Refuge Assurance League), first held 1969
1982 Sussex
1983 Yorkshire
1984 Essex
1985 Essex
1986 Hampshire
1987 Worcestershire

Sites of summer Olympic Games*

1896	Athens, Greece
1900	Paris, France
1904	St Louis, USA
1908	London, England
1912	Stockholm, Sweden
1920	Antwerp, Belgium
1924	Paris, France
1928	Amsterdam, Netherlands
1932	Los Angeles, USA
1936	Berlin, Germany
1948	London, England
1952	Helsinki, Finland
1956	Melbourne, Australia
1960	Rome, Italy
1964	Tokyo, Japan
1968	Mexico City, Mexico
1972	Munich, W Germany
1976	Montreal, Canada
1980	Moscow, USSR
1984	Los Angeles, USA
1988	Seoul, S Korea
1992	Barcelona, Spain
1996	Atlanta, USA

* *Winter Olympic Games were started in 1924.*

The 1906 Games were not recognized by the International Olympic Committee. In 1916, 1940, and 1944 the Games were not held because of the two World Wars. Sixty-two nations, including the USA, boycotted the 1980 Games; the 1984 Games were boycotted by the USSR and most of Eastern Europe. In 1992, athletes from the 12 former Soviet republics formed the Unified Team, while the Independent Olympic Participants (I.O.P.) consisted of athletes from Serbia, Montenegro, and Macedonia.

Cricket heights

Leading scorers in tests	*Dates*	*Tests*	*Runs*	*Average*
A R Border (Aus)	1978–	139	10,161	51.31
S M Gavaskar (Ind)	1970–1987	125	10,122	51.51
Javed Miandad (Pak)	1976–	118	8,569	54.23
I V A Richards (WI)	1974–1991	121	8,540	50.23
D I Gower (Eng)	1978–	117	8,231	44.25
G Boycott (Eng)	1964–1982	108	8,114	47.72
G Sobers (WI)	1953–1974	93	8,032	57.78
M C Cowdrey (Eng)	1954–1975	114	7,624	44.06
G A Gooch (Eng)	1975–	101	7,620	43.05
C G Greenidge (WI)	1974–1991	108	7,558	44.72
C H Lloyd (WI)	1966–1985	110	7,515	46.67
W R Hammond (Eng)	1928–1947	85	7,249	58.46
G S Chappell (Aus)	1970–1983	87	7,110	53.86
D G Bradman (Aus)	1928–1948	52	6,996	99.94

Source: The Independent, May 1993

1988 Worcestershire
1989 Lancashire
1990 Derbyshire
1991 Nottinghamshire
1992 Middlesex

NATWEST TROPHY

(formerly the Gillette Cup), first held 1963
1983 Somerset
1984 Middlesex
1985 Essex
1986 Sussex
1987 Nottinghamshire
1988 Middlesex
1989 Warwickshire
1990 Lancashire
1991 Hampshire
1992 Northamptonshire

BENSON AND HEDGES CUP

first held 1972
1983 Middlesex
1984 Lancashire
1985 Leicestershire
1986 Middlesex
1987 Yorkshire
1988 Hampshire
1989 Nottinghamshire
1990 Lancashire
1991 Worcestershire
1992 Hampshire

WORLD CUP

first held 1975, contested every four years
1975 West Indies
1979 West Indies
1983 India
1987 Australia
1992 Pakistan

curling game resembling bowls that is played on ice, between two teams of four players each. Each player has two disclike stones, of equal size, fitted with a handle. The object of the game is to slide the stones across the ice so that they are positioned as near as possible to a target object (the tee), those nearest scoring. The stone may be curled in one direction or another according to the twist given as it leaves the hand. The match is played for an agreed number of heads or shots, or by time.

WORLD CHAMPIONSHIP

first held 1959 for men, 1979 for women

men
1988 Norway
1989 Canada
1990 Canada
1991 Scotland
1992 Switzerland
1993 Canada

women
1988 West Germany
1989 Canada
1990 Norway
1991 Norway
1992 Sweden
1993 Canada

cycling cycle racing can take place on oval artificial tracks, on the road,or across country (cyclo-cross). ***Stage races*** are run over gruelling terrain and can last anything from three to five days up to three and a half weeks, as in the Tour de France, Tour of Italy, and Tour of Spain. ***Criteriums*** are fast, action-packed races around the closed streets of town or city centres. ***Road races*** are run over a prescribed circuit, which the riders will lap several times. Such a race will normally cover a distance of approximately 100 mi/160 km. ***Track racing*** takes place on a concrete or wooden banked circuit, either indoors or outdoors. In ***time trialing*** each rider races against the clock, with all the competitors starting at different intervals.

TOUR DE FRANCE

first held 1903
1983 Laurent Fignon *(France)*
1984 Laurent Fignon *(France)*
1985 Bernard Hinault *(France)*
1986 Greg LeMond *(USA)*
1987 Stephen Roche *(Ireland)*
1988 Pedro Delgado *(Spain)*
1989 Greg LeMond *(USA)*
1990 Greg LeMond *(USA)*

1991 Miguel Indurain *(Spain)*
1992 Miguel Indurain *(Spain)*
1993 Miguel Indurain *(Spain)*

TOUR OF BRITAIN

(formerly the Milk Race), first held 1951
1982 Yuri Kashirin *(USSR)*
1983 Matt Eaton *(USA)*
1984 Oleg Czougeda *(USSR)*
1985 Erik van Lancker *(Belgium)*
1986 Joey McLoughlin *(UK)*
1987 Malcolm Elliott *(UK)*
1988 Vasily Zhdanov *(USSR)*
1989 Brian Walton *(Canada)*
1990 Shane Sutton *(Australia)*
1991 Chris Walker *(UK)*
1992 Conor Henry *(Ireland)*
1993 Chris Lillywhite *(UK)*

WORLD PROFESSIONAL ROAD RACE CHAMPIONS

first held 1927
1982 Giuseppe Saroni *(Italy)*
1983 Greg LeMond *(USA)*
1984 Claude Criquielon *(Belgium)*
1985 Joop Zoetemelk *(Holland)*
1986 Moreno Argentin *(Italy)*
1987 Stephen Roche *(Ireland)*
1988 Maurizio Fondriest *(Italy)*
1989 Greg LeMond *(USA)*
1990 Rudy Dhaenens *(Belgium)*
1991 Gianni Bugno *(Italy)*
1992 Gianni Bugno *(Italy)*

---

darts indoor game played on a circular board. Darts about 13 cm/5 in long are thrown at segmented targets, and score points according to their landing place.

WORLD CHAMPIONSHIP

first held 1978
1983 Keith Deller *(England)*
1984 Eric Bristow *(England)*
1985 Eric Bristow *(England)*
1986 Eric Bristow *(England)*
1987 John Lowe *(England)*
1988 Bob Anderson *(England)*
1989 Jocky Wilson *(Scotland)*
1990 Phil Taylor *(England)*
1991 Dennis Priestley *(England)*
1992 Phil Taylor *(England)*
1993 John Lowe *(England)*

---

diving sport of entering water either from a springboard (3 m/10 ft) above the water, or from a platform, or highboard, (10 m/33 ft) above the water. Various starts are adopted, and twists and somersaults may be performed in midair. Points are awarded and the level of difficulty of each dive is used as a multiplying factor.

OLYMPIC GAMES

springboard diving
men
1980 Aleksandr Portnov *(USSR)*
1984 Greg Louganis *(USA)*
1988 Greg Louganis *(USA)*
1992 Mark Lenzi *(USA)*
women
1980 Irina Kalinina *(USSR)*
1984 Sylvie Bernier *(Canada)*
1988 Gao Min *(China)*
1992 Gao Min *(China)*
platform diving
men
1980 Falk Hoffmann *(East Germany)*
1984 Greg Louganis *(USA)*
1988 Greg Louganis *(USA)*
1992 Sun Shuwei *(China)*
women
1980 Martina Jäschke *(East Germany)*
1984 Zhou Jihong *(China)*
1988 Xu Yanmei *(China)*
1992 Fu Mingxia *(China)*

---

equestrianism skill in horse riding, as practised under International Equestrian Federation rules. ***Showjumping*** is horse-jumping over a course of fences. The winner is usually the competitor with fewest 'faults' (penalty marks given for knocking down or refusing fences), but in timed competitions it is the competitor completing the course most quickly, additional seconds being added for mistakes. ***Dressage*** tests the horse's obedience skills, and the rider's control. Tests consist of a series of movements at walk, trot, canter, with each movement marked by judges who look for suppleness, balance, and the special harmony between rider and horse. ***Three-Day Eventing*** tests the all-round abilities of a horse and rider in dressage, cross-country, and showjumping.

WORLD CHAMPIONSHIP

show jumping; first held 1953 for men, 1965 for women; since 1978 men and women have competed together
men
1953 Francisco Goyoago *(Spain)*
1954 Hans-Günter Winkler *(West Germany)*
1955 Hans-Günter Winkler *(West Germany)*
1956 Raimondo D'Inzeo *(Italy)*
1960 Raimondo D'Inzeo *(Italy)*
1966 Pierre d'Oriola *(France)*
1970 David Broome *(UK)*
1974 Hartwig Steenken *(West Germany)*
women
1965 Marion Coakes *(UK)*
1970 Janou Lefebvre *(France)*
1974 Janou Tissot (born Lefebvre) *(France)*
mixed
1978 Gerd Wiltfang *(West Germany)*
1982 Norbert Koof *(West Germany)*
1986 Gail Greenough *(Canada)*
1990 Eric Navet *(France)*

EUPOPEAN CHAMPIONSHIP

show jumping; first held 1957 with men and women competing separately; since 1975 they have competed together
1977 Johan Heins *(Holland)*
1979 Gerd Wiltfang *(West Germany)*
1981 Paul Schockemohle *(West Germany)*
1983 Paul Schockemohle *(West Germany)*
1985 Paul Schockemohle *(West Germany)*
1987 Pierre Durand *(France)*

1989 John Whitaker *(UK)*
1991 Eric Navet *(France)*

BRITISH SHOWJUMPING CHAMPIONSHIP

first held 1961
1982 Paul Schockemohle *(West Germany)*
1983 John Whitaker *(UK)*
1984 John Ledingham *(Ireland)*
1985 Paul Schockemohle *(West Germany)*
1986 Paul Schockemohle *(West Germany)*
1987 Nick Skelton *(UK)*
1988 Nick Skelton *(UK)*
1989 Nick Skelton *(UK)*
1990 Joe Turi *(UK)*
1991 Michael Whitaker *(UK)*
1992 Michael Whitaker *(UK)*

THREE-DAY EVENTING WORLD CHAMPIONSHIP

1974 Bruce Davidson *(USA)*
1978 Bruce Davidson *(USA)*
1982 Lucinda Green (born Prior-Palmer) *(UK)*
1986 Virginia Leng (born Holgate) *(UK)*
1990 Blyth Tait *(New Zealand)*

BADMINTON HORSE TRIALS

three-day eventing; first held 1949
1983 Lucinda Green *(UK)*
1984 Lucinda Green *(UK)*
1985 Virginia Holgate *(UK)*
1986 Ian Stark *(UK)*
1987 cancelled
1988 Ian Stark *(UK)*
1989 Virginia Leng *(UK)*
1990 Nicola McIrvine *(UK)*
1991 Rodney Powell *(UK)*
1992 Mary Thompson *(UK)*
1993 Virginia Leng *(UK)*

---

fencing sport of fighting with swords including the ***foil***, derived from the light weapon used in practice duels; the ***épée***, a heavier weapon derived from the duelling sword proper; and the ***sabre***, with a curved handle and narrow V-shaped blade. In sabre fighting, cuts count as well as thrusts. Masks and protective jackets are worn, and hits are registered electronically in competitions.

WORLD CHAMPIONSHIP

first held 1921; Olympic winners automatically become world champions

foil: men
1988 Stefano Cerioni *(Italy)*
1989 Alexandr Koch *(West Germany)*
1990 Philippe Omnes *(France)*
1991 Ingo Weissenborn *(Germany)*
1992 Philippe Omnes *(France)*

foil: women
1988 Anja Fichtel *(West Germany)*
1989 Olga Velichko *(USSR)*
1990 Anja Fichtel *(Germany)*
1991 Giovanna Trillini *(Italy)*
1992 Giovanna Trillini *(Italy)*

épée: men
1988 Arnd Schmitt *(West Germany)*
1989 Manuel Pereira *(Spain)*
1990 Thomas Gerull *(Germany)*
1991 Andrei Chouvalov *(USSR)*
1992 Eric Srecki *(France)*

épée: women
1989 Anja Straub *(Switzerland)*
1990 Taimi Chappe *(Cuba)*
1991 Mariann Horvath *(Hungary)*
1992 not an Olympic event

sabre: men
1988 Jean-François Lamour *(France)*
1989 Grigoriy Kirienko *(USSR)*
1990 Gyorgy Nebald *(Hungary)*
1991 Grigoriy Kirienko *(USSR)*
1992 Bence Szabo *(Hungary)*

---

football, American contact sport played between two teams of 11 players, with an inflated oval ball. Players are well padded for protection and wear protective helmets. The game is played on a field 91.4 m/100 yd long and 48.8 m/53.3 yd wide, marked out with a series of parallel lines giving a gridiron effect. There is a goalpost at each end of the field, and beyond this an endzone 9 m/10 yd long. Points are scored by running or passing the ball across the goal line (touchdown); by kicking it over the goal's crossbar after a touchdown (conversion or point after touchdown), or from the field during regular play (field goal); or by tackling an offensive player who has the ball in the end zone, or blocking an offensive team's kick so it goes out of bounds from the end zone (safety). A touchdown counts 6 points, a field goal 3, a safety 2, and a conversion 1. Games are divided into four quarters of 15 minutes each.

SUPER BOWL

first held 1967
1983 Washington Redskins
1984 Los Angeles Raiders
1985 San Francisco 49ers
1986 Chicago Bears
1987 New York Giants
1988 Washington Redskins
1989 San Francisco 49ers
1990 San Francisco 49ers
1991 New York Giants
1992 Washington Redskins
1993 Dallas Cowboys

---

football, association or ***soccer*** form of football originating in the UK, popular in Europe and Latin America. It is played between two teams each of 11 players, on a field 90–120 m/100–130 yd long and 45–90 m/ 50–100 yd wide, with an inflated spherical ball. The object of the game is to kick or head the ball into the opponents' goal, an area 7.31 m/8 yd wide and 2.44 m/8 ft high. Games are divided into two halves of 45 minutes each, the teams changing ends at half-time.

In the UK the game is played according to the rules laid down by the Football Association, founded 1863. Slight amendments to the rules take effect in certain competitions and overseas matches as laid down by the sport's world governing body, Fédération Internationale de Football Association (FIFA, 1904).

WORLD CUP

first held 1930; contested every four years
1954 West Germany

1958 Brazil
1962 Brazil
1966 England
1970 Brazil
1974 West Germany
1978 Argentina
1982 Italy
1986 Argentina
1990 West Germany

EUROPEAN CHAMPIONSHIP

instituted 1958, first final 1960; contested every four years
1960 USSR
1964 Spain
1968 Italy
1972 West Germany
1976 Czechoslovakia
1980 West Germany
1984 France
1988 Holland
1992 Denmark

EUROPEAN CHAMPIONS CUP

first held 1955
1983 SV Hamburg *(West Germany)*
1984 Liverpool *(England)*
1985 Juventus *(Italy)*
1986 Steaua Bucharest *(Romania)*
1987 FC Porto *(Portugal)*
1988 PSV Eindhoven *(Holland)*
1989 AC Milan *(Italy)*
1990 AC Milan *(Italy)*
1991 Red Star Belgrade *(Yugoslavia)*
1992 Barcelona *(Spain)*
1993 Marseille *(France)*

EUROPEAN CUP WINNERS' CUP

first held 1960
1983 Aberdeen *(Scotland)*
1984 Juventus *(Italy)*
1985 Everton *(England)*
1986 Dinamo Kiev *(USSR)*
1987 Ajax *(Holland)*
1988 Mechelen *(Belgium)*
1989 Barcelona *(Spain)*
1990 Sampdoria *(Italy)*
1991 Manchester United *(England)*
1992 Werder Bremen *(Germany)*
1993 Parma *(Italy)*

UEFA CUP

(formerly Inter Cities Fairs Cup) first held 1955
1983 Anderlecht *(Belgium)*
1984 Tottenham Hotspur *(England)*
1985 Real Madrid *(Spain)*
1986 Real Madrid *(Spain)*
1987 IFK Gothenburg *(Sweden)*
1988 Bayer Leverkusen *(West Germany)*
1989 Napoli *(Italy)*
1990 Juventus *(Italy)*
1991 Internazionale Milan *(Italy)*
1992 Ajax *(Holland)*
1993 Juventus *(Italy)*

UK CHAMPIONSHIPS

FA CUP

a knockout club competition, first held 1872
1983 Manchester United
1984 Everton
1985 Manchester United
1986 Liverpool
1987 Coventry City
1988 Wimbledon
1989 Liverpool
1990 Manchester United
1991 Tottenham Hotspur
1992 Liverpool
1993 Arsenal

FOOTBALL LEAGUE CUP

(currently known as the Coca-Cola Cup, formerly the Rumbelows Cup, the Milk Cup and the Littlewoods Cup) first final 1961 in two stages, now a single game
1983 Liverpool
1984 Liverpool
1985 Norwich City
1986 Oxford United
1987 Arsenal
1988 Luton Town
1989 Nottingham Forest
1990 Nottingham Forest
1991 Sheffield Wednesday
1992 Manchester United
1993 Arsenal

PREMIER LEAGUE CHAMPIONS

(Formerly Division One Champions), Football League founded 1888—89
1982—83 Liverpool
1983—84 Liverpool
1984—85 Everton
1985—86 Liverpool
1986—87 Everton
1987—88 Liverpool
1988—89 Arsenal
1989—90 Liverpool
1990—91 Arsenal
1991—92 Leeds United
1992—93 Manchester United

SCOTTISH PREMIER DIVISION

Scottish League formed 1899—91, reformed into three divisions 1975—76
1982—83 Dundee United
1983—84 Aberdeen
1984—85 Aberdeen
1985—86 Celtic
1986—87 Rangers
1987—88 Celtic
1988—89 Rangers
1989—90 Rangers
1990—91 Rangers
1991—92 Rangers
1992—93 Rangers

SCOTTISH FA CUP

first final held 1874
1983 Aberdeen
1984 Aberdeen
1985 Celtic
1986 Aberdeen
1987 St Mirren
1988 Celtic
1989 Celtic
1990 Aberdeen
1991 Motherwell

1992 Rangers
1993 Rangers

football, Australian Rules game that combines aspects of Gaelic football, rugby, and association football; it is played between two teams of 18 players, with an inflated oval ball. It is unique to Australia. The game is played on an oval pitch, 164.4 m/180 yd long and 137 m/150 yd wide, with a pair of goalposts, 6 m/19 ft high, at each end. On either side of each pair of goalposts is a smaller post. Each team is placed in five lines of three persons each, and three players follow the ball all the time. Points are scored by kicking the ball between the goalposts, without its being touched on the way (goal, 6 points), or by passing the ball between a goalpost and one of the smaller posts, or causing it to hit a post (behind, 1 point).

VICTORIA FOOTBALL LEAGUE PREMIERSHIP TROPHY

first contested 1897
1982 Carlton
1983 Hawthorn
1984 Essendon
1985 Essendon
1986 Hawthorn
1987 Carlton
1988 Hawthorn
1989 Hawthorn
1990 Collingwood
1991 Hawthorn
1992 West Coast

football, Gaelic kicking and catching game played mainly in Ireland, between two teams of 15 players each. It is played with an inflated spherical ball, on a field 76–91 m/ 84–100 yd long and 128–146 m/ 140–160 yd wide. At each end is a set of goalposts 4.88 m/16 ft high, with a crossbar 2.44 m/8 ft above the ground, and a net across its lower half. Goals are scored by kicking the ball into the net (3 points) or over the crossbar (1 point).

ALL-IRELAND CHAMPIONSHIP

first played 1887
1982 Offaly
1983 Dublin
1984 Kerry
1985 Kerry
1986 Kerry
1987 Meath
1988 Meath
1989 Cork
1990 Cork
1991 Down
1992 Donegal

golf outdoor game in which a small rubber-cored ball is hit with a wooden- or iron-faced club. Its object is to sink the ball in a hole that can be anywhere between 90 m/100 yd and 457 m/500 yd away, using the least number of strokes. The faces of the clubs have varying angles and are styled for different types of shot.

Most golf courses consist of 18 holes and are approximately 5,500 m/6,000 yd in length. Each hole is made up of distinct areas: the ***tee***, from where plays start at each hole; the ***green***, a finely manicured area where the hole is located; the ***fairway***, the grassed area between the tee and the green, not cut as finely as the green; and the ***rough***, the perimeter of the fairway, which is left to grow naturally. Natural hazards such as trees, bushes, and streams make play more difficult, and there are additional artificial hazards in the form of sand-filled bunkers.

BRITISH OPEN

first held 1860
1983 Tom Watson *(USA)*
1984 Severiano Ballesteros *(Spain)*
1985 Sandy Lyle *(UK)*
1986 Greg Norman *(Australia)*
1987 Nick Faldo *(UK)*
1988 Severiano Ballesteros *(Spain)*
1989 Mark Calcavecchia *(USA)*
1990 Nick Faldo *(UK)*
1991 Ian Baker-Finch *(Australia)*
1992 Nick Faldo *(UK)*
1993 Greg Norman *(Australia)*

UNITED STATES OPEN

first held 1895
1983 Larry Nelson *(USA)*
1984 Fuzzy Zoeller *(USA)*
1985 Andy North *(USA)*
1986 Ray Floyd *USA)*
1987 Scott Simpson *(USA)*
1988 Curtis Strange *(USA)*
1989 Curtis Strange *(USA)*
1990 Hale Irwin *(USA)*
1991 Payne Stewart *(USA)*
1992 Tom Kite *(USA)*
1993 Lee Janzen *(USA)*

MASTERS

first held 1934
1983 Severiano Ballesteros *(Spain)*
1984 Ben Crenshaw *(USA)*
1985 Bernhard Langer *(West Germany)*
1986 Jack Nicklaus *(USA)*
1987 Larry Mize *(USA)*
1988 Sandy Lyle *(UK)*
1989 Nick Faldo *(UK)*
1990 Nick Faldo *(UK)*
1991 Ian Woosnam *(UK)*
1992 Fred Couples *(USA)*
1993 Bernard Langer *(Germany)*

UNITED STATES PGA

first held 1916
1982 Ray Floyd *(USA)*
1983 Hal Sutton *(USA)*
1984 Lee Trevino *(USA)*
1985 Hubert Green *(USA)*
1986 Bob Tway *(USA)*
1987 Larry Nelson *(USA)*
1988 Jeff Sluman *(USA)*
1989 Payne Stewart *(USA)*
1990 Wayne Grady *(Australia)*
1991 John Daly *(USA)*
1992 Nick Price *(Zimbabwe)*
1993 Paul Azinger *(USA)*

greyhound racing spectator sport, invented in 1919 in the USA, that has a number of greyhounds pursuing a mechanical hare around a circular or oval track. It is popular in the UK and Australia, attracting much on- and offcourse betting.

GREYHOUND DERBY

UK, first held 1927
1983 I'm Slippy
1984 Whisper Wishes
1985 Pagan Swallow
1986 Tico
1987 Signal Park
1988 Hit the Lid
1989 Lartigue Note
1990 Slippy Blue
1991 Ballinderry Ash
1992 Farloe Melody

---

gymnastics competitive physical exercises. ***Men's gymnastics*** includes exercises on apparatus such as the horizontal bar, parallel bars, horse vault, pommel horse, and rings, and on an area of floor 12 m/13 yd square. ***Women's gymnastics*** includes work on the asymmetric bars, side horse vault, and beam, and floor exercises. Each exercise is marked out of ten by a set of judges, who look for suppleness, balance, control, and innovation. ***Rhythmic gymnastics***, is choreographed to music and performed by individuals or six-woman teams, with small hand apparatus such as a ribbon, ball, or hoop.

WORLD CHAMPIONSHIP

first held 1903 for men, 1934 for women; contested every two years; Olympic champions automatically become world champions

men: individual/team
1974 Shigeru Kasamatsu *(Japan)*/Japan
1978 Nikolai Adrianov *(USSR)*/Japan
1979 Aleksandr Ditiatin *(USSR)*/USSR
1981 Yuri Korolev *(USSR)*/USSR
1983 Dimitri Belozertchev *(USSR)*/China
1985 Yuri Korolev *(USSR)*/USSR
1987 Dimitri Belozertchev *(USSR)*/USSR
1989 Igor Korobichensky *(USSR)*/USSR
1991 Gregori Misutin (*USSR*)/USSR
1992 Vitaly Scherbo (*Unified Team* *)/Unified Team
1993 Vitaly Scherbo (*Belarus*)/Belarus

women: individual/team
1974 Ludmila Tourischeva *(USSR)*/USSR
1978 Elena Mukhina *(USSR)*/USSR
1979 Nelli Kim *(USSR)*/Romania
1981 Olga Bitcherova *(USSR)*/USSR
1983 Natalia Yurchenko *(USSR)*/USSR
1985 Elena Shoushounova *(USSR)* and Oksana Omeliantchik *(USSR)*/USSR
1987 Aurelia Dobre *(Romania)*/Romania
1989 Svetlana Boginskaya *(USSR)*/USSR
1991 Kim Zmeskal (*USA*)/USSR
1992 Tatyana Gutsu (*Unified Team*)/Unified Team
1993 Shannon Miller *(USA)*/USA

**Commonwealth of Independent States plus Georgia*

---

handball game resembling football, but played with the hands instead of the feet. The indoor game has seven players in a team; the outdoor version (field handball) has 11. The indoor court is 40 m/43.8 yd long and 20 m/21.9 yd wide, with goals 2 m/6.6 ft high and 3 m/9.8 ft wide.

OLYMPIC GAMES

indoor event introduced 1972 for men, 1976 for women

men
1972 Yugoslavia
1976 USSR
1980 East Germany
1984 Yugoslavia
1988 USSR
1992 Unified Team*

women
1976 USSR
1980 USSR
1984 Yugoslavia
1988 South Korea
1992 South Korea

** Commonwealth of Independent States plus Georgia*

---

hockey or ***field hockey*** stick-and-ball game played by two teams of 11 players each. Its object is to strike the solid white ball, by means of a hooked stick, into the opposing team's goal. The game is played on a pitch 91.5 m/100 yd long and 54.9 m/60 yd wide, with a goal, 2.13 m/7 ft high and 3.65 m/4 yd wide, at each end. All shots at goal must be made from within a striking 'circle', a semicircle of 14.64 m/16 yd radius in front of each goal. The game is divided into two 35-minute periods.

OLYMPIC GAMES

event introduced 1908 for men, 1980 for women

men
1980 India
1984 Pakistan
1988 Great Britain
1992 Germany

women
1980 Zimbabwe
1984 Netherlands
1988 Australia
1992 Spain

WORLD CUP

men's tournament first held 1971 and contested every four years; women's tournament first held 1974 and contested every four years

men
1971 Pakistan
1973 Holland
1975 India
1978 Pakistan
1982 Pakistan
1986 Australia
1990 Holland

women
1974 Holland
1976 West Germany
1978 Holland
1981 West Germany
1983 Holland
1986 Holland
1990 Holland

horse racing the sport of racing mounted or driven horses. Two popular forms in Britain are ***flat racing***, for thoroughbred horses over a flat course, and ***National Hunt racing***, in which the horses have to clear obstacles. Forms of National Hunt racing include ***steeplechasing***, a development of foxhunting, in which horses jump over fixed fences 0.9—1.2 m/3—4 ft high (the amateur version is point-to-point), and ***hurdling***, in which the horses negotiate less taxing, and movable, fences. ***Harness racing*** is popular in North America. It is for standard-bred horses pulling a two- wheeled 'sulky' on which the driver sits. Leading races include The Hambletonian and Little Brown Jug.

DERBY

first held 1780; 1 mi 4 furlongs long

horse/jockey

1983 Teenoso/Lester Piggott
1984 Secreto/Christy Roche
1985 Slip Anchor/Steve Cauthen
1986 Shahrastani/Walter Swinburn
1987 Reference Point/Steve Cauthen
1988 Kahyasi/Ray Cochrane
1989 Nashwan/Willie Carson
1990 Quest for Fame/Pat Eddery
1991 Generous/Alan Munro
1992 Dr Devious/John Reid
1993 Commander In Chief/Michael Kinane

OAKS

first held 1779; 1 mi 4 furlongs long

horse/jockey

1982 Time Charter/Billy Newnes
1983 Sun Princess/Willie Carson
1984 Circus Plume/Lester Piggott
1985 Oh So Sharp/Steve Cauthen
1986 Midway Lady/Ray Cochrane
1987 Unite/Walter Swinburn
1988 Diminuendo/Steve Cauthen
1989 Snow Bride/Steve Cauthen
1990 Salsabil/Willie Carson
1991 Jet Ski Lady/Christy Roche
1992 User Friendly/George Duffield
1993 Intrepidity/Michael Roberts

1,000 GUINEAS

first held 1814; 1 mi long

horse/jockey

1983 Ma Biche/Freddy Head
1984 Pebbles/Philip Robinson
1985 Oh So Sharp/Steve Cauthen
1986 Midway Lady/Ray Cochrane
1987 Miesque/Freddy Head
1988 Ravinella/Gary Moore
1989 Musical Bliss/Walter Swinburn
1990 Salsabil/Willie Carson
1991 Shadayid/Willie Carson
1992 Hatoof/Walter Swinburn
1993 Sayyedati/Walter Swinburn

2,000 GUINEAS

first held 1809; 1 mi long

horse/jockey

1983 Lomond/Pat Eddery
1984 El Gran Senor/Pat Eddery
1985 Shadeed/Lester Piggott
1986 Dancing Brave/Greville Starkey
1987 Don't Forget Me/Willie Carson
1988 Doyoun/Walter Swinburn
1989 Nashwan/Walter Swinburn
1990 Tirol/Michael Kinane
1991 Mystiko/Michael Roberts
1992 Rodrigo de Triano/Lester Piggott
1993 Zafonic/Pat Eddery

Twenty years of Derby winners and favourites

Year	*Winner*	*Time*	*Favourite*	*Favourite finished*
1993	Commander In Chief (15-2)	2m 34.51s	Tenby (4-5)	Tenth
1992	Dr Devious (8-1)	2m 36.19s	Rodrigo De Triano (13-2)	Ninth
1991	Generous (9-1)	2m 34.00s	Corrupt (4-1)	Sixth
			Toulon (4-1)	Ninth
1990	Quest For Fame (7-1)	2m 37.26s	Razeen (9-2)	Fourteenth
1989	Nashwan (5-4)	2m 34.90s	Nashwan	First
1988	Kahyasi (11-1)	2m 33.84s	Red Glow (5-2)	Fourth
1987	Reference Point (6-4)	2m 33.90s	Reference Point	First
1986	Shahrastani (11-2)	2m 37.13s	Dancing Brave (2-1)	Second
1985	Slip Anchor (9-4)	2m 36.23s	Slip Anchor	First
1984	Secreto (14-1)	2m 39.12s	El Gran Senor (8-11)	Second
1983	Teenoso (9-2)	2m 49.07s	Teenoso	First
1982	Golden Fleece (3-1)	2m 34.27s	Golden Fleece	First
1981	Shergar (10-11)	2m 44.21s	Shergar	First
1980	Henbit (7-1)	2m 34.77s	Nikolai (4-1)	Eighth
1979	Troy (6-1)	2m 36.59s	Ela-Mana-Mou (9-2)	Fourth
1978	Shirley Heights (8-1)	2m 35.30s	Inkerman (4-1)	Twenty-First
1977	The Minstrel (5-1)	2m 36.44s	Blushing Groom (9-4)	Third
1976	Empery (10-1)	2m 35.69s	Wollow (11-10)	Fifth
1975	Grundy (5-1)	2m 35.35s	Green Dancer (6-4)	Sixth
1974	Snow Knight (50-1)	2m 35.04s	Nonoalco (9-4)	Seventh
1973	Morston (25-1)	2m 35.92s	Ksar (5-1)	Fourth

Source: The Independent

ST LEGER

the oldest English classic, first held 1776; 1 mi 6 furlongs 127 yd long

horse/jockey
1982 Touching Wood/Paul Cook
1983 Sun Princess/Willie Carson
1984 Commanche Run/Lester Piggott
1985 Oh So Sharp/Steve Cauthen
1986 Moon Madness/Pat Eddery
1987 Reference Point/Steve Cauthen
1988 Minster Son/Willie Carson
1989 Michelozza/Steve Cauthen
1990 Snurge/Richard Quinn
1991 Toulon/Pat Eddery
1992 User Friendly/George Duffield

GRAND NATIONAL

steeplechase; first held 1847; 4 mi 4 furlongs long

horse/jockey (amateurs are shown as Mr)
1983 Corbiere/Ben De Haan
1984 Hallo Dandy/Neale Doughty
1985 Last Suspect/Hywel Davies
1986 West Tip/Richard Dunwoody
1987 Maori Venture/Steve Knight
1988 Rhyme N'Reason/Brendan Powell
1989 Little Polveir/Jimmy Frost
1990 Mr Frisk/Marcus Armytage
1991 Seagram/Nigel Hawke
1992 Party Politics/Carl Llewellyn
1993 void

PRIX DE L'ARC DE TRIOMPHE

first held 1920; 2,400 m long

horse/jockey
1983 All Along/Walter Swinburn
1984 Sagace/Yves Saint-Martin
1985 Rainbow Quest/Pat Eddery
1986 Dancing Brave/Pat Eddery
1986 Lieutenant's Lark/Robbie Davis
1987 Trempolino/Pat Eddery
1988 Tony Bin/John Reid
1989 Caroll House/Michael Kinane
1990 Saumarez/Gerald Mosse
1991 Suave Dancer/Cash Asmussen
1992 Subotica/Thierry Jarnet

---

hurling or ***hurley*** stick-and-ball game played between two teams of 15 players each, popular in Ireland. Its object is to hit the ball, by means of a curved stick, into the opposing team's goal. If the ball passes under the goal's crossbar 3 points are scored; if it passes above the crossbar 1 point is scored.

ALL-IRELAND CHAMPIONSHIP

first held 1887
1982 Kilkenny
1983 Kilkenny
1984 Cork
1985 Offaly
1986 Cork
1987 Galway
1988 Galway
1989 Tipperary
1990 Cork
1991 Tipperary
1992 Limerick

---

ice hockey game played on ice between two teams of six, developed in Canada from hockey. A rubber disc (puck) is used in place of a ball. Players wear skates and protective clothing.

OLYMPIC GAMES

event introduced 1920
1976 USSR
1980 United States
1984 USSR
1988 USSR
1992 Unified Team*

** Commonwealth of Independent States plus Georgia*

STANLEY CUP

end-of-season playoff tournament conducted between the top teams of the Canadian and US National Hockey League conferences
1988 Edmonton Oilers
1989 Calgary Flames
1990 Edmonton Oilers
1991 Pittsburgh Penguins
1992 Pittsburgh Penguins
1993 Montreal Canadiens

---

judo form of wrestling of Japanese origin. The two combatants wear loose-fitting, belted jackets and trousers to facilitate holds, and falls are broken by a square mat; when one has established a painful hold that the other cannot break, the latter signifies surrender by slapping the ground with a free hand. Degrees of proficiency are indicated by the colour of the belt: for novices, white; after examination, brown (three degrees); and finally, black (nine degrees).

WORLD CHAMPIONSHIP

first held 1956 for men, 1980 for women; contested every two years

men: open class
1983 Angelo Parisi *(France)*
1985 Yoshimi Masaki *(Japan)*
1987 Noayo Ogawa *(Japan)*
1989 Noayo Ogawa *(Japan)*
1991 Noayo Ogawa *(Japan)*

women: open class
1984 Ingrid Berghmans *(Belgium)*
1986 Ingrid Berghmans *(Belgium)*
1987 Fengliang Gao *(China)*
1989 Estela Rodriguez *(Cuba)*
1991 Zhuang Xiaoyan *(China)*

---

lacrosse Canadian ball game, adopted from the North American Indians, and named from a fancied resemblance of the lacrosse stick (crosse) to a bishop's crosier. Thongs across the curved end of the crosse form a pocket to carry the small rubber ball. The field is approximately 100 m/110 yd long and a minimum 55 m/60 yd wide in the men's game, which is played with ten players per side; the women's field is larger, and there are twelve players per side. The goals are just under 2 m/6 ft square, with loose nets.

WORLD CHAMPIONSHIP

first held 1967 for men, 1969 for women

men
1967 USA

1974 USA
1978 Canada
1982 USA
1986 USA
1990 USA
women
1969 UK
1974 USA
1978 Canada
1982 USA
1986 Australia
1989 USA

motorcycle racing speed contests on motorcycles. It has many different forms: ***road racing*** over open roads; ***circuit racing*** over purpose-built tracks; ***speedway*** over oval-shaped dirt tracks; ***motocross*** (or ***scrambling***) over natural terrain, incorporating hill climbs; and ***trials***, also over natural terrain, but with the addition of artificial hazards. For finely tuned production machines, there exists a season-long world championship Grand Prix series with various categories for machines with engine sizes 125–500 cc.

WORLD CHAMPIONSHIP

Grand Prix racing; first held 1949
500cc class
rider/manufacturer
1982 Franco Uncini/Suzuki *(Italy)*
1983 Freddie Spencer/Honda *(USA)*
1984 Eddie Lawson/Yamaha *(USA)*
1985 Freddie Spencer/Honda *(USA)*
1986 Eddie Lawson/Yamaha *(USA)*
1987 Wayne Gardner/Honda *(Australia)*
1988 Eddie Lawson/Yamaha *(USA)*
1989 Eddie Lawson/Honda *(USA)*
1990 Wayne Rainey/Yamaha *(USA)*
1991 Wayne Rainey/Yamaha *(USA)*
1992 Wayne Rainey/Yamaha *(USA)*

ISLE OF MAN TOURIST TROPHY

road race; first held 1907
Senior TT
rider/manufacturer
1983 Rob McElnea/Suzuki *(UK)*
1984 Rob McElnea/Suzuki *(UK)*
1985 Joey Dunlop/Honda *(Ireland)*
1986 Roger Burnett/Honda *(UK)*
1987 Joey Dunlop/Honda *(Ireland)*
1988 Joey Dunlop/Honda *(Ireland)*
1989 Steve Hislop/Honda *(UK)*
1990 Carl Fogarty/Honda *(UK)*
1991 Steve Hislop/Honda *(UK)*
1992 Steve Hislop/Norton *(UK)*
1993 Joey Dunlop/Honda *(Ireland)*

WORLD CHAMPIONSHIP

speedway; first held 1936
individual
1982 Bruce Penhall *(USA)*
1983 Egon Müller *(West Germany)*
1984 Erik Gundersen *(Denmark)*
1985 Erik Gundersen *(Denmark)*
1986 Hans Nielsen *(Denmark)*
1987 Hans Nielsen *(Denmark)*
1988 Erik Gundersen *(Denmark)*
1989 Hans Nielsen *(Denmark)*
1990 Per Jonsson *(Sweden)*
1991 Jan Pedersen *(Denmark)*
1992 Gary Havelock *(England)*
pairs
event introduced 1970
1982 Dennis Sigalos and Bobby Schwartz *USA)*
1983 Kenny Carter and Peter Collins *(England)*
1984 Peter Collins and Chris Morton *(England)*
1985 Erik Gundersen and Tommy Knudsen *Denmark)*
1986 Erik Gundersen and Hans Nielsen *(Denmark)*
1987 Erik Gundersen and Hans Nielsen *(Denmark)*
1988 Erik Gundersen and Hans Nielsen *(Denmark)*
1989 Erik Gundersen and Hans Nielsen *(Denmark)*
1990 Hans Nielsen and Jan Pedersen *(Denmark)*
1991 Hans Nielsen, Jan Pedersen, and Tommy Knudsen *(Denmark)*
1992 Grey Hancock, Sam Ermolenko, and Ronnie Correy *(USA)*
team
event introduced 1960
1982 USA
1983 Denmark
1984 Denmark
1985 Denmark
1986 Denmark
1987 Denmark
1988 Denmark
1989 England
1990 USA
1991 Denmark
1992 USA

WORLD CHAMPIONSHIP

motocross; first held 1957
500cc class
rider/manufacturer
1982 Brad Lackey/Suzuki *(USA)*
1983 Håkan Carlqvist/Yamaha *(Sweden)*
1984 André Malherbe/Honda *(Belgium)*
1985 Dave Thorpe/Honda *(UK)*
1986 Dave Thorpe/Honda *(UK)*
1987 Georges Jobé/Honda *(Belgium)*
1988 Eric Geboers/Honda *(Belgium)*
1989 Dave Thorpe/Honda *(UK)*
1990 Eric Geboers *(Belgium)*
1991 Georges Jobé *(Belgium)*
1992 Georges Jobé *(Belgium)*

motor racing competitive racing of motor vehicles. It has forms as diverse as hill-climbing, stock-car racing, rallying, sports-car racing, and Formula One Grand Prix racing. The first organized race was from Paris to Rouen 1894.

WORLD DRIVERS' CHAMPIONSHIP

Formula One Grand Prix racing; instituted 1950
driver/manufacturer
1983 Nelson Piquet/Ferrari *(Brazil)*
1984 Niki Lauda/McLaren *(Austria)*
1985 Alain Prost/McLaren *(France)*
1986 Alain Prost/Williams *(France)*
1987 Nelson Piquet/Williams *(Brazil)*
1988 Ayrton Senna/McLaren *(Brazil)*
1989 Alain Prost/McLaren *(France)*
1990 Ayrton Senna/McLaren *(Brazil)*

1991 Ayrton Senna/McLaren *(Brazil)*
1992 Nigel Mansell/Williams *(UK)*

LE MANS GRAND PRIX D'ENDURANCE

(Le Mans 24-Hour Race) first held 1923
1983 Vern Schuppan *(Austria)*, Al Holbert *(USA)*, and Hurley Haywood *(USA)*
1984 Klaus Ludwig *(West Germany)* and Henri Pescarolo *(France)*
1985 Klaus Ludwig *(West Germany)*, 'John Winter' *(West Germany)*, and Paolo Barilla *(Italy)*
1986 Hans Stuck *(West Germany)*, Derek Bell *(UK)*, and Al Holbert *(USA)*
1987 Hans Stuck *(West Germany)*, Derek Bell *(UK)*, and Al Holbert *(USA)*
1988 Jan Lammers *(Holland)*, Johnny Dumfries *(UK)*, and Andy Wallace *(UK)*
1989 Jochen Mass *(West Germany)*, Manuel Reuter *(West Germany)*, and Stanley Dickens *(Sweden)*
1990 John Nielsen *(Denmark)*, Price Cobb *(USA)*, and Martin Brundle *(UK)*
1991 Volker Weidler *(Germany)*, John Herbert *(UK)*, and Bertrand Gachot *(Belgium)*
1992 Derek Warwick *(UK)*, Yannick Dalmas *(France)*, and Mark Blundell *(UK)*
1993 Geoff Brabham *(Australia)*, Christophe Bouchut *(France)*, Eric Helary *(France)*

INDIANAPOLIS 500

first held 1911

driver/manufacturer
1983 Tom Sneva/March—Cosworth *(USA)*
1984 Rick Mears/March—Cosworth *(USA)*
1985 Danny Sullivan/March—Cosworth *(USA)*
1986 Bobby Rahal/March—Cosworth *(USA)*
1987 Al Unser, Jr/March—Cosworth *(USA)*
1988 Rick Mears/Penske—Chevrolet *(USA)*
1989 Emerson Fittipaldi/Penske—Chevrolet *(Brazil)*.
1990 Arie Luyendyk/Lola—Chevrolet *(Holland)*
1991 Rick Mears/Penske—Chevrolet *(USA)*
1992 Al Unser, Jr/Galmer—Chevy A *(USA)*
1993 Emerson Fittipaldi/Penske—Chevrolet *(Brazil)*

MONTE CARLO RALLY

1983 Walter Röhrl *(West Germany)*
1984 Walter Röhrl *(West Germany)*
1985 Ari Vatanen *(Finland)*
1986 Henri Toivonen *(Finland)*
1987 Mikki Biasion *(Italy)*
1988 Bruno Saby *(France)*
1989 Mikki Biasion *(Italy)*
1990 Didier Auriol *(France)*
1991 Carlos Sainz *(Spain)*
1992 Didier Auriol *(France)*
1993 Didier Auriol *(France)*

LOMBARD– RAC RALLY

(formerly RAC International Rally of Great Britain) first held 1927
1982 Hannu Mikkola *(Finland)*
1983 Stig Blomqvist *(Sweden)*
1984 Ari Vatanen *(Finland)*
1985 Henri Toivonen *(Finland)*
1986 Timo Salonen *(Finland)*
1987 Juha Kankkunen *(Finland)*
1988 Markku Alén *(Finland)*
1989 Pentti Arikkala *(Finland)*
1990 Carlos Sainz *(Spain)*
1991 Juha Kankkunen *(Finland)*
1992 Carlos Sainz *(Spain)*

netball a women's game, developed from basketball, played by two teams of seven players each. It is played on a hard court 30.5 m/100 ft long and 15.25 m/50 ft wide. At each end is a goal, consisting of a post 3.05 m/10 ft high, at the top of which is attached a circular hoop and net. The object of the game is to pass an inflated spherical ball through the opposing team's net. The ball is thrown from player to player; no contact is allowed between players, and none may run with the ball.

WORLD CHAMPIONSHIP

first held 1963; contested every four years
1963 Australia
1967 New Zealand
1971 Australia
1975 Australia
1979 Australia, New Zealand, and Trinidad and Tobago
1983 Australia
1987 New Zealand
1991 Australia

orienteering sport of cross-country running and route-finding. Competitors set off at one-minute intervals and have to find their way, using map and compass, to various checkpoints (approximately 0.8 km/0.5 mi apart), where their control cards are marked.

WORLD CHAMPIONSHIP

first held 1966

individual (men/women)
1983 Morten Berglia *(Norway)*/Annichen Kringstad *(Norway)*
1985 Kari Sallinen *(Finland)*/Annichen Kringstad *(Norway)*
1987 Kent Olsson *(Sweden)*/Arja Hannus *(Sweden)*
1989 Peter Thoresen *(Norway)*/Marita Skogum *(Sweden)*
1991 Jorgen Martensson *(Sweden)*/Katarina Olch *(Hungary)*

relay (men/women)
1983 Norway/Sweden
1985 Norway/Sweden
1987 Norway/Norway
1989 Norway/Sweden
1991 Switzerland/Sweden

polo stick-and-ball game played between two teams of four on horseback. It is played on the largest pitch of any game, measuring up to 274 m/300 yd by 182 m/200 yd. A small solid ball is struck with the side of a long-handled mallet through goals at each end of the pitch. A typical match lasts about an hour, and is divided into 'chukkas' of $7^1/_2$ minutes each. No pony is expected to play more than two chukkas in the course of a day.

COWDRAY PARK GOLD CUP

British Open Championship; first held 1956
1982 Southfield
1983 Falcons
1984 Southfield
1985 Maple Leafs

1986 Tramontana
1987 Tramontana
1988 Tramontana
1989 Tramontana
1990 Hildon
1991 Tramontana
1992 Black Bears

rowing propulsion of a boat by oars, either by one rower with two oars (sculling) or by crews (two, four, or eight persons) with one oar each, often with a coxswain.

WORLD CHAMPIONSHIP

first held 1962 for men, 1974 for women; Olympic winners automatically become world champions

men—-single sculls
1983 Peter-Michael Kolbe *(West Germany)*
1984 Pertti Karppinen *(Finland)*
1985 Pertti Karppinen *(Finland)*
1986 Peter-Michael Kolbe *(West Germany)*
1987 Thomas Lange *(East Germany)*
1988 Thomas Lange *(East Germany)*
1989 Thomas Lange *(East Germany)*
1990 Uri Janson *(USSR)*
1991 Thomas Lange *(Germany)*
1992 Thomas Lange *(Germany)*

women—-single sculls
1983 Jutta Hampe *(East Germany)*
1984 Valeria Racila *(Romania)*
1985 Cornelia Linse *(East Germany)*
1986 Jutta Hampe *(East Germany)*
1987 Magdalena Georgeyeva *(Bulgaria)*
1988 Jutta Hampe *(East Germany)*
1989 Elisabeta Lipa *(Romania)*
1990 Birgit Peter *(Germany)*
1991 Silke Laumann *(Canada)*
1992 Elisabeta Lipa *(Romania)*

THE BOAT RACE

first held 1829; rowed annually by crews from Oxford and Cambridge Universities, between Putney and Mortlake on the river Thames
1986 Cambridge
1987 Oxford
1988 Oxford
1989 Oxford
1990 Oxford
1991 Oxford
1992 Oxford
1993 Cambridge

wins
Cambridge 70
Oxford 68

rugby league the professional form of rugby football founded in England 1895 as the Northern Union when a dispute about pay caused northern clubs to break away from the Rugby Football Union. The game is similar to rugby union, but the number of players is reduced from 15 to 13, and other rule changes have made the game more open and fast-moving.

CHALLENGE CUP

first held 1897
1983 Featherstone Rovers
1984 Widnes
1985 Wigan
1986 Castleford
1987 Halifax
1988 Wigan
1989 Wigan
1990 Wigan
1991 Wigan
1992 Wigan
1993 Wigan

PREMIERSHIP TROPHY

introduced at the end of the 1974—75 season; a knockout competition involving the top eight clubs in the first division
1983 Widnes
1984 Hull Kingston Rovers
1985 St Helens
1986 Warrington
1987 Wigan
1988 Widnes
1989 Widnes
1990 Widnes
1991 Hull
1992 Wigan
1993 St Helens

rugby union the amateur form of rugby football in which there are 15 players on each side. It is played with an inflated oval ball, on a field 69 m/75 yd long and 100 m/110 yd wide. At each end of the field is an H-shaped set of goalposts 5.6 m/18.5 ft wide, with a crossbar 3 m/10 ft above the ground. Points are scored by 'touching down', or grounding, the ball beyond the goal line (try, 4 points), or by kicking it over the goal's crossbar after a touchdown (conversion, 2 points), from the field during regular play (dropped goal, 3 points), or in response to a penalty against the opposing team (3 points).

WORLD CUP

William Webb Ellis Trophy; first held 1987
1987 New Zealand
1991 Australia

INTERNATIONAL CHAMPIONSHIP

instituted 1884, now a tournament between England, France, Ireland, Scotland, and Wales
1983 France and Ireland
1984 Scotland
1985 Ireland
1986 France
1987 France
1988 France and Wales
1989 France
1990 Scotland
1991 England
1992 England
1993 France

COUNTY CHAMPIONSHIP

first held 1889
1983 Gloucestershire
1984 Gloucestershire
1985 Middlesex
1986 Warwickshire
1987 Yorkshire
1988 Lancashire

1989 Durham
1990 Lancashire
1991 Cornwall
1992 Lancashire
1993 Lancashire

PILKINGTON CUP

formerly the John Player Special Cup, the English club knockout tournament, first held 1971—72
1983 Bristol
1984 Bath
1985 Bath
1986 Bath
1987 Bath
1988 Harlequins
1989 Bath
1990 Bath
1991 Harlequins
1992 Bath
1993 Leicester

SCOTTISH CLUB CHAMPIONSHIP

first held 1974

Division One
1983 Gala
1984 Hawick
1985 Hawick
1986 Hawick
1987 Hawick
1988 Kelso
1989 Kelso
1990 Melrose
1991 Boroughmuir
1992 Melrose
1993 Melrose

SWALEC WELSH CUP

(formerly the Schweppes Welsh Cup), the Welsh club knockout tournament, first held 1971—72
1983 Pontypool
1984 Cardiff
1985 Llanelli
1986 Cardiff
1987 Cardiff
1988 Llanelli
1989 Neath
1990 Neath
1991 Llanelli
1992 Llanelli
1993 Llanelli

---

shinty (Gaelic *camanachd*) stick-and-ball game, resembling hurling, popular in the Scottish Highlands. It is played between two teams of 12 players each, on a field 132–183 m/144–200 yd long and 64–91 m/70–99 yd wide. A curved stick (caman) is used to propel a leather-covered cork-and-worsted ball into the opposing team's goal (hail).

CAMANACHD CUP

instituted 1896
1983 Kyles Athletic
1984 Kingussie
1985 Newtonmore
1986 Newtonmore
1987 Kingussie
1988 Kingussie
1989 Kingussie
1990 Skye
1991 Kingussie
1992 Fort William
1993 Kingussie

---

skating self-propulsion on ice by means of bladed skates, or on other surfaces by skates with small rollers. The chief competitive ice-skating events are figure skating, for singles or pairs, ice-dancing, and simple speed skating.

WORLD CHAMPIONSHIP

ice-skating; first held 1896

men
1988 Brian Boitano *(USA)*
1989 Kurt Browning *(Canada)*
1990 Kurt Browning *(Canada)*
1991 Kurt Browning *(Canada)*
1992 Viktor Petrenko *(USSR)*
1993 Kurt Browning *(Canada)*

women
1988 Katarina Witt *(East Germany)*
1989 Midoria Ito *(Japan)*
1990 Jill Trenary *(USA)*
1991 Kristi Yamaguchi *(USA)*
1992 Kristi Yamaguchi *(USA)*
1993 Oksana Baiul *(Ukraine)*

pairs
1988 Oleg Vasilyev and Yelena Valova *(USSR)*
1989 Sergey Grinkov and Ekaterina Gordeeva *(USSR)*
1990 Sergey Grinkov and Ekaterina Gordeeva *(USSR)*
1991 Artur Dmitriev and Natalya Mishkuteniok *(USSR)*
1992 Artur Dmitriev and Natalya Mishkuteniok *(USSR)*
1993 Lloyd Eisler and Isabelle Brasseur *(Canada)*

ice dance
1988 Andrei Bukin and Natalia Bestemianova *(USSR)*
1989 Sergey Ponomarenko and Marina Klimova *(USSR)*
1990 Sergey Ponomarenko and Marina Klimova *(USSR)*
1991 Paul Duchesnay and Isabelle Duchesnay *(France)*
1992 Sergey Ponomarenko and Marina Klimova *(USSR)*
1993 Alexandr Zhulin and Maia Usova *(Russia)*

---

skiing self-propulsion on snow by means of elongated runners (skis) for the feet, slightly bent upward at the tip. Events include downhill; slalom, in which a series of turns between flags have to be negotiated; cross-country racing; and ski jumping, when jumps of over 150 m/490 ft are achieved from ramps up to 90 m/295 ft high. Speed-skiing uses skis approximately $^1/_3$ longer and wider than normal, with which speeds of up to 200 kmph have been recorded.

OLYMPIC GAMES

events introduced 1936

men : downhill
1976 Franz Klammer *(Austria)*
1980 Leonhard Stock *(Austria)*
1984 William Johnson *(USA)*
1988 Pirmin Zurbriggen *(Switzerland)*
1992 Patrick Ortlieb *(Austria)*

men : slalom
1976 Piero Gros *(Italy)*
1980 Ingemar Stenmark *(Sweden)*
1984 Phil Mahre *(USA)*

1988 Alberto Tomba *(Italy)*
1992 Christian Jagge *(Norway)*

women : downhill
1976 Rosi Mittermaier *(West Germany)*
1980 Annemarie Moser-Proll *(Austria)*
1984 Michela Figini *(Switzerland)*
1988 Marina Kiehl *(Germany)*
1992 Kerrin Lee-Gartner *(Canada)*

women : slalom
1976 Rosi Mittermaier *(West Germany)*
1980 Hanni Wenzel *(Liechtenstein)*
1984 Paoletta Magoni *(Italy)*
1988 Vreni Schneider *(Switzerland)*
1992 Petra Krönberger *(Austria)*

ALPINE WORLD CUP

first held 1967

men - overall
1983 Phil Mahre *(USA)*
1984 Pirmin Zurbriggen *(Switzerland)*
1985 Marc Girardelli *(Luxembourg)*
1986 Marc Girardelli *(Luxembourg)*
1987 Pirmin Zurbriggen *(Switzerland)*
1988 Pirmin Zurbriggen *(Switzerland)*
1989 Marc Girardelli *(Luxembourg)*
1990 Pirmin Zurbriggen *(Switzerland)*
1991 Marc Girardelli *(Luxembourg)*
1992 Paul Accola *(Switzerland)*
1993 Marc Girardelli *(Luxembourg)*

women - overall
1983 Tamara McKinney *(USA)*
1984 Erika Hess *(Switzerland)*
1985 Michela Figini *(Switzerland)*
1986 Maria Walliser *(Switzerland)*
1987 Maria Walliser *(Switzerland)*
1988 Michela Figini *(Switzerland)*
1989 Vreni Schneider *(Switzerland)*
1990 Petra Krönberger *(Austria)*
1991 Petra Krönberger *(Austria)*
1992 Petra Krönberger *(Austria)*
1993 Anita Wachter *(Austria)*

snooker indoor game derived from billiards. It is played with 22 balls: 15 red, one each of yellow, green, brown, blue, pink, and black, and one white cueball. Red balls are worth one point when sunk, while the coloured balls have ascending values from two points for the yellow to seven points for the black.

WORLD PROFESSIONAL CHAMPIONSHIP

first held 1927
1983 Steve Davis *(England)*
1984 Steve Davis *(England)*
1985 Dennis Taylor *(Northern Ireland)*
1986 Joe Johnson *(England)*
1987 Steve Davis *(England)*
1988 Steve Davis *(England)*
1989 Steve Davis *(England)*
1990 Stephen Hendry *(Scotland)*
1991 John Parrott *(England)*
1992 Stephen Hendry *(Scotland)*
1993 Stephen Hendry *(Scotland)*

WORLD AMATEUR CHAMPIONSHIP

first held 1963
1980 Jimmy White *(England)*
1982 Terry Parsons *(Wales)*
1984 O B Agrawal *(India)*
1985 Paul Mifsud *(Malta)*
1986 Paul Mifsud *(Malta)*
1987 Darren Morgan *(Wales)*
1988 James Wattana *(Thailand)*
1989 Ken Doherty *(Ireland)*
1990 Stephen O'Connor *(Ireland)*
1991 Noppadon Noppachom *(Thailand)*
1992 Neil Mosley *(England)*
1993 Neil Mosley *(England)*

softball a form of baseball played with similar equipment. The two main differences are the distances between the bases (18.29 m/60 ft) and that the ball is pitched underhand in softball. There are two forms of the game, ***fast pitch*** and ***slow pitch***; in the latter the ball must be delivered to home plate in an arc that must not be less than 2.4 m/8 ft at its height.

WORLD CHAMPIONSHIP

fast pitch; introduced 1965 for women, 1966 for men; now contested every four years

men
1966 USA
1968 USA
1972 Canada
1976 Canada, New Zealand, and USA
1980 USA
1984 New Zealand
1988 USA
1992 Canada

women
1965 Australia
1970 Japan
1974 USA
1978 USA
1982 New Zealand
1986 USA
1990 USA

squash or ***squash rackets*** racket-and-ball game usually played by two people on an enclosed court. Each player hits the small rubber ball against the front wall of the court alternately. The object is to win points by playing shots the opponent cannot return to the wall. There are two forms of the game: the American form, which is played in North and some South American countries and the English, which is played mainly in Europe, Pakistan, and Commonwealth countries such as Australia and New Zealand. In English singles, the court is 6.4 m/21 ft wide and 10 m/32 ft long. Doubles squash is played on a larger court.

WORLD OPEN CHAMPIONSHIP

first held 1975

men
1982 Jahangir Khan *(Pakistan)*
1983 Jahangir Khan *(Pakistan)*
1984 Jahangir Khan *(Pakistan)*
1985 Jahangir Khan *(Pakistan*
1986 Ross Norman *(New Zealand)*
1987 Jansher Khan *(Pakistan)*
1988 Jahangir Khan *(Pakistan)*

1989 Jansher Khan *(Pakistan)*
1990 Jansher Khan *(Pakistan)*
1991 Rodney Martin *(Australia)*
1992 Jansher Khan *(Pakistan)*

women
1981 Rhonda Thorne *(Australia)*
1983 Vicky Cardwell *(Australia)*
1985 Sue Devoy *(New Zealand)*
1987 Sue Devoy *(New Zealand)*
1989 Martine Le Moignan *(UK)*
1990 Sue Devoy *(New Zealand)*
1991 Sue Devoy *(New Zealand)*
1992 Sue Devoy *(New Zealand)*

---

surfing riding on the crest of large waves while standing on a narrow, keeled surfboard, usually of a light synthetic material such as fibreglass, about 1.8 m/6 ft long (or 2.4–7 m/8–9 ft known as the Malibu), as first developed in Hawaii and Australia.

OWRLD PROFESSIONAL CHAMPIONSHIP
first held 1970

men
1987 Damien Hardman *(Australia)*
1988 Barton Lynch *(Australia)*
1989 Martin Potter *(UK)*
1990 Tommy Curren *(USA)*
1991 Damien Hardman *(Australia)*
1992 Kelly Slater *(USA)*

women
1987 Wendy Botha *(South Africa)*
1988 Frieda Zamba *(USA)*
1989 Wendy Botha *(South Africa)*
1990 Pam Burridge *(Australia)*
1991 Wendy Botha *(South Africa)*
1992 Wendy Botha *(Australia ex-South Africa)*

WORLD AMATEUR CHAMPIONSHIP
first held 1964

men
1982 Tommy Curren *(USA)*
1984 Scott Farnsworth *(USA)*
1986 Mark Sainsbury *(Australia)*
1988 Fabio Gouveia *(Brazil)*
1990 Heifara Tahutini *(Tahiti)*

women
1982 Jenny Gill *(Australia)*
1984 Janice Aragon *(USA)*
1986 Connie Nixon *(Australia)*
1988 Pauline Menczer *(Australia)*
1990 Kathy Newman *(Australia)*

---

swimming self-propulsion of the body through water. There are four strokes in competitive swimming: ***freestyle*** (or ***front crawl***), the fastest stroke; ***breaststroke***, the slowest stroke; ***backstroke***; and ***butterfly***, the newest stroke, developed in the USA from breaststroke. Swimmers enter the water with a 'racing plunge' (a form of dive) with the exception of the backstroke, when competitors start in the water. Distances of races vary between 50 m/54.7 yd and 1,500 m/1,641 yd. Olympic-size pools are 50 m/55 yd long and have eight lanes. ***Synchronized swimming*** is a form of 'ballet' performed in and under water.

OLYMPIC GAMES
event introduced 1896 for men, 1912 for women
Barcelona Olympics 1992 (25th Olympic Games)

men/women
100 metres backstroke: Mark Tewkesbury *(Canada)*/Kristina Egerszegi *(Hungary)*
200 metres backstroke: Martin Lopez-Zubero *(Spain)*/Kristina Egerszegi *(Hungary)*
100 metres breaststroke: Nelson Diebel *(USA)*/Yelena Roudkovskaya *(Unified Team*)*
200 metres breaststroke: Mike Barrowman *(USA)*/Kyoko Iwasaki *(Japan)*
100 metres butterfly: Pablo Morales *(USA)*/Qian Hong *(China)*
200 metres butterfly: Melvin Stewart *(USA)*/Summer Sanders *(USA)*
50 metres freestyle: Aleksandr Popov *(Unified Team)*/Yang Wenyi *(China)*
100 metres freestyle: Aleksandr Popov *(Unified Team)*/Zhuang Yong *(China)*
200 metres freestyle: Yevgeny Sadovyi *(Unified Team)*/Nicole Haislett *(USA)*
400 metres freestyle: Yevgeny Sadovyi *(Unified Team)*/Dagmar Hase *(Germany)*
800 metres freestyle: — /Janet Evans *(USA)*
1,500 metres freestyle: Kieren Perkins *(Australia)*/ —
200 metres individual medley: Tamás Darnyi *(Hungary)*/Lin Li *(China)*
400 metres individual medley: Tamás Darnyi *(USA)*/Kristina Egerszegi *(Hungary)*
400 metres freestyle relay: USA/USA
800 metres freestyle relay: Unified Team/ —
400 metres medley relay: USA/USA
synchronized swimming (individual): — /Kristen Babb-Sprague *(USA)*
synchronized swimming (duet): — /Karen Josephson and Sarah Josephson *(USA)*

** Commonwealth of Independent States plus Georgia*

most gold medals:
9 Mark Spitz *(USA)* 1968, 1972
8 Matt Biondi *(USA)* 1984, 1988, 1992
6 Kristin Otto *(East Germany)* 1988
5 Charles Daniels *(USA)* 1904, 1908
5 Johnny Weissmuller *(USA)* 1924, 1928
5 Don Schollander *(USA)* 1964, 1968
4 Henry Taylor *(UK)* 1906, 1908
4 Murray Rose *(Australia)* 1956, 1960
4 Dawn Fraser *(Australia)* 1956, 1960, 1964
4 Roland Matthes *(East Germany)* 1968, 1972
4 John Naber *(USA)* 1976
4 Kornelia Ender *(East Germany)* 1976
4 Vladimir Salnikov *(USSR)* 1980, 1988
4 Tamás Darnyi *(Hungary)* 1988, 1992
4 Janet Evans *(USA)* 1988, 1992

most medals:
11 Mark Spitz *(USA)* 1968, 1972
11 Matt Biondi *(USA)* 1984, 1988, 1992
8 Charles Daniels *(USA)* 1904, 1908
8 Roland Matthes *(East Germany)* 1968, 1972
8 Henry Taylor *(UK)* 1906, 1908, 1912, 1920
8 Dawn Fraser *(Australia)* 1956, 1960, 1964
8 Kornelia Ender *(East Germany)* 1972, 1976
8 Shirley Babashoff *(USA)* 1972, 1976

table tennis or ***ping pong*** indoor game played on a rectangular table by two or four players. Play takes place on a table measuring 2.74 m/9 ft long by 1.52 m/5 ft wide. Across the middle is a 15.25 cm/6 in high net over which the ball must be hit. The players use small, wooden paddles covered in sponge or rubber. Points are scored by forcing the opponent(s) into an error. The first to score 21 wins the game. A match may consist of three or five games. Volleying is not allowed. In doubles play, the players must hit the ball in strict rotation.

WORLD CHAMPIONSHIP

first held 1926, now contested every two years

men's team
1983 China
1985 China
1987 China
1989 Sweden
1991 Sweden
1993 Sweden

women's team
1983 China
1985 China
1987 China
1989 China
1991 Korea
1993 China

men's singles
1983 Guo Yue-Hua *(China)*
1985 Jiang Jialiang *(China)*
1987 Jiang Jialiang *(China)*
1989 Jan-Ove Waldner *(Sweden)*
1991 Jorgen Persson *(Sweden)*
1993 Jean-Philippe Gatien *(France)*

women's singles
1983 Cao Yan-Hua *(China)*
1985 Cao Yan-Hua *(China)*
1987 He Zhili *(China)*
1989 Qiuo Hong *(China)*
1991 Deng Yalping *(China)*
1993 Hyun Jung-hwa *(South Korea)*

---

tennis, lawn racket-and-ball game for two or four players, invented towards the end of the 19th century. It may be played on a grass, wood, shale, clay, or concrete surface. The object of the game is to strike the ball into the prescribed area of the court, with oval-headed rackets (strung with gut or nylon), in such a way that it cannot be returned. The game is won by those first winning four points (called 15, 30, 40, game), unless both sides reach 40 (deuce), when two consecutive points are needed to win. A set is won by winning six games with a margin of two over opponents, though a tie-break system operates, that is at six games to each side (or in some cases eight) except in the final set.

The Grand Slam events are the Wimbledon Championship, the United States Open, French Open, and Australian Open.

WIMBLEDOM CHAMPIONSHIPS

All-England Lawn Tennis Club championships; first held 1877; grass surface

men's singles
1983 John McEnroe *(USA)*
1984 John McEnroe *(USA)*
1985 Boris Becker *(West Germany)*
1986 Boris Becker *(West Germany)*
1987 Pat Cash *(Australia)*
1988 Stefan Edberg *(Sweden)*
1989 Boris Becker *(West Germany)*
1990 Stefan Edberg *(Sweden)*
1991 Michael Stich *(Germany)*
1992 Andre Agassi *(USA)*
1993 Pete Sampras *(USA)*

women's singles
1983 Martina Navratilova *(USA)*
1984 Martina Navratilova *(USA)*
1985 Martina Navratilova *(USA)*
1986 Martina Navratilova *(USA)*
1987 Martina Navratilova *(USA)*
1988 Steffi Graf *(West Germany)*
1989 Steffi Graf *(West Germany)*
1990 Martina Navratilova *(USA)*
1991 Steffi Graf *(Germany)*
1992 Steffi Graf *(Germany)*
1993 Steffi Graf *(Germany)*

UNITED STATES OPEN

first held 1881 as the United States Championship; became the United States Open 1968; concrete surface

men's singles
1983 Jimmy Connors *(USA)*
1984 John McEnroe *(USA)*
1985 Ivan Lendl *(Czechoslovakia)*
1986 Ivan Lendl *(Czechoslovakia)*
1987 Ivan Lendl *(Czechoslovakia)*
1988 Mats Wilander *(Sweden)*
1989 Boris Becker *(West Germany)*
1990 Pete Sampras *(USA)*
1991 Stefan Edberg *(Sweden)*
1992 Stefan Edberg *(Sweden)*

women's singles
1983 Martina Navratilova *(USA)*
1984 Martina Navratilova *(USA)*
1985 Hana Mandlikova *(Czechoslovakia)*
1986 Martina Navratilova *(USA)*
1987 Martina Navratilova *(USA)*
1988 Steffi Graf *(West Germany)*
1989 Steffi Graf *(West Germany)*
1990 Gabriela Sabatini *(Argentina)*
1991 Monica Seles *(Yugoslavia)*
1992 Monica Seles *(Yugoslavia)*

FRENCH OPEN

first held 1891 (a national championship until 1924); clay surface

men's singles
1983 Yannick Noah *(France)*
1984 Ivan Lendl *(Czechoslovakia)*
1985 Mats Wilander *(Sweden)*
1986 Ivan Lendl *(Czechoslovakia)*
1987 Ivan Lendl *(Czechoslovakia)*
1988 Mats Wilander *(Sweden)*
1989 Michael Craig *(USA)*
1990 Andres Gomez *(Ecuador)*
1991 Jim Courier *(USA)*
1992 Jim Courier *(USA)*
1993 Sergi Bruguera *(Spain)*

women's singles
1983 Chris Evert-Lloyd *(USA)*
1984 Martina Navratilova *(USA)*

1985 Chris Evert-Lloyd *(USA)*
1986 Chris Evert-Lloyd *(USA)*
1987 Steffi Graf *(West Germany)*
1988 Steffi Graf *(West Germany)*
1989 Arantxa Sanchez Vicario *(Spain)*
1990 Monica Seles *(Yugoslavia)*
1991 Monica Seles *(Yugoslavia)*
1992 Monica Seles *(Yugoslavia)*
1993 Steffi Graf *(West Germany)*

AUSTRALIAN OPEN

first held 1905 (a national championship until 1925); clay surface

men's singles
1983 Mats Wilander *(Sweden)*
1984 Mats Wilander *(Sweden)*
1985 Stefan Edberg *(Sweden)*
1987 Stefan Edberg *(Sweden)*
1988 Mats Wilander *(Sweden)*
1989 Ivan Lendl *(Czechoslovakia)*
1990 Ivan Lendl *(Czechoslovakia)*
1991 Boris Becker *(Germany)*
1992 Jim Courier *(USA)*
1993 Jim Courier *(USA)*
women's singles
1983 Martina Navratilova *(USA)*
1984 Chris Evert-Lloyd *(USA)*
1985 Martina Navratilova *(USA)*
1987 Hana Mandlikova *(Czechoslovakia)*
1988 Steffi Graf *(West Germany)*
1989 Steffi Graf *(West Germany)*
1990 Steffi Graf *(West Germany)*
1991 Monica Seles *(Yugoslavia)*
1992 Monica Seles *(Yugoslavia)*
1993 Monica Seles *(Yugoslavia)*

DAVIS CUP

first contested 1900
1982 USA
1983 Australia
1984 Sweden
1985 Sweden
1986 Australia
1987 Sweden
1988 West Germany
1989 West Germany
1990 USA
1991 France
1992 USA

---

trampolining gymnastics performed on a sprung canvas sheet that allows the performer to reach great heights before landing again. Marks are gained for carrying out difficult manoeuvres. Synchronized trampolining and tumbling are also popular forms of the sport.

WORLD CHAMPIONSHIP

first held 1964

men
1974 Richard Tisson *(France)*
1976 Richard Tisson *(France)* and Evgeni Janes *(USSR)*
1978 Evgeni Janes *(USSR)*
1980 Stewart Matthews *(UK)*
1982 Carl Furrer *(UK)*
1984 Lionel Pioline *(France)*
1986 Lionel Pioline *(France)*
1988 Vadim Krasonchapka *(USSR)*
1990 Alexandr Moskalenko *(USSR)*
1992 Alexandr Moskalenko *(USSR)*
women
1974 Alexandra Nicholson *(USA)*
1976 Svetlana Levina *(USSR)*
1978 Tatyana Anisimova *(USSR)*
1980 Ruth Keller *(Switzerland)*
1982 Ruth Keller *(Switzerland)*
1984 Sue Shotton *(UK)*
1986 Tatyana Lushina *(USSR)*
1988 Khoperla Rusudum *(USSR)*
1990 Elena Merkulova *(USSR)*
1992 Elena Merkulova *(USSR)*

---

volleyball an indoor and outdoor game played between two teams of six players each. The court measures 18 m/59 ft by 9 m/29 ft 6 in, and has a raised net drawn across its centre. Players hit an inflated spherical ball over the net with their hands or arms, the aim being to ground the ball in the opponents' court. The ball may not be hit more than three times on one team's side of the net.

WORLD CHAMPIONSHIP

first held 1949 for men, 1952 for women; Olympic winners automatically become world champions

men
1974 Poland
1976 Poland
1978 USSR
1980 USSR
1982 USSR
1984 USA
1986 USA
1988 USA
1990 Italy
1992 Brazil
women
1974 Japan
1976 Japan
1978 Cuba
1980 USSR
1982 China
1984 China
1986 USA
1988 USSR
1990 USSR
1992 Cuba

---

water polo (formerly ***soccer-in-water***) sport played in a swimming pool, between two teams of seven players each. An inflated ball is passed among the players, who must swim around the pool without touching the bottom. Goals are scored when the ball is thrown past the opposing team's goalkeeper and into a net.

WORLD CHAMPIONSHIP

first held 1973; contested every four years since 1978
1973 Hungary
1975 USSR
1978 Italy
1982 USSR
1986 Yugoslavia
1990/91 Yugoslavia

water skiing sport in which a person is towed across water on a ski or skis, by means of a rope (23 m/75 ft long) attached to a speedboat. Competitions are held for overall performances, slalom, tricks, and jumping.

WORLD CHAMPIONSHIP

first held 1949; contested every two years

men—-overall
1973 George Athans *(Canada)*
1975 Carlos Suarez *(Venezuela)*
1977 Mike Hazelwood *(UK)*
1979 Joel McClintock *(Canada)*
1981 Sammy Duvall *(USA)*
1983 Sammy Duvall *(USA)*
1985 Sammy Duvall *(USA)*
1987 Sammy Duvall *(USA)*
1989 Patrice Martin *(France)*
1991 Patrice Martin *(France)*

women—-overall
1973 Lisa St John *(USA)*
1975 Liz Allan-Shetter *(USA)*
1977 Cindy Todd *(USA)*
1979 Cindy Todd *(USA)*
1981 Karin Roberge *(USA)*
1983 Ana-Maria Carrasco *(Venezuela)*
1985 Karen Neville *(Australia)*
1987 Deena Brush *(USA)*
1989 Deena Mapple (née Brush) *(USA)*
1991 Karen Neville *(Australia)*

---

weightlifting the sport of lifting the heaviest possible weight above one's head to the satisfaction of judges. In international competitions there are two standard lifts: snatch and jerk. In the ***snatch***, the bar and weights are lifted from the floor to a position with the arms outstretched and above the head in one continuous movement. The arms must be locked for two seconds for the lift to be good. The ***jerk*** is a two-movement lift: from the floor to the chest, and from the chest to the outstretched position. The aggregate weight of the two lifts counts.

OLYMPIC GAMES

Barcelona Olympics (25th Olympics) 1992
52 kg: Ivan Ivanov *(Bulgaria)*
56 kg: Chun Byung-Kwan *(South Korea)*
60 kg: Naim Suleymanoglu *(Turkey)*
67.5 kg: Israel Militossyan *(Unified Team*)*
75 kg: Fyodor Kassapu *(Unified Team)*
82.5 kg: Pyrros Dimas *(Greece)*
90 kg: Kakhi Kakhiashvili *(Unified Team)*
100 kg: Viktor Tregubov *(Unified Team)*
110 kg: Ronny Weller *(Germany)*
110+ kg: Aleksandr Kurlovich *(Unified Team)*

** Commonwealth of Independent States plus Georgia*

---

wrestling fighting without the use of fists. The two main modern international styles are ***Greco-Roman***, concentrating on above-waist holds, and ***freestyle***, which allows the legs to be used to hold or trip; in both, the aim is to throw the opponent to the ground. Competitors are categorized according to weight: there are ten weight divisions in each style of wrestling, ranging from light-flyweight (under 48 kg) to super-heavyweight (over 100 kg). The professional form of the sport has become popular, partly due to television coverage, but is regarded by purists as an extension of show-business. Many countries have their own forms of wrestling. ***Glima*** is unique to Iceland; ***kushti*** is the national style practised in Iran; ***schwingen*** has been practised in Switzerland for hundreds of years; and ***sumo*** is the national sport of Japan.

OLYMPIC GAMES

Barcelona Olympics (25th Olympics) 1992
Greco-Roman
light-flyweight (48 kg): Oleg Koutherenko *(Unified Team*)*
flyweight (52 kg): Jon Ronningen *(Norway)*
bantamweight (57 kg): An Han Bong *(South Korea)*
featherweight (62 kg): M Akif Pirim *(Turkey)*
lightweight (68 kg): Attila Repka *(Hungary)*
welterweight (74 kg): Mnatsakan Iskandaryan *(Unified Team)*
middleweight (82 kg): Peter Farkas *(Hungary)*
light-heavyweight (90 kg): Maik Bullmann *(Germany)*
heavyweight (100 kg): Hector Milian Perez *(Cuba)*
super-heavyweight (over 100 kg): Aleksandr Karelin *(Unified Team)*

freestyle
light-flyweight: Kim Il *(North Korea)*
flyweight: Li Hak Son *(North Korea)*
bantamweight: Alejandro Puerto Diaz *(Cuba)*
featherweight: John Smith *(USA)*
lightweight: Arsen Fadzyev *(Unified Team)*
welterweight: Park Jang Sun *(South Korea)*
middleweight: Kevin Jackson *(USA)*
light-heavyweight: Makharbek Khadartsev *(Unified Team)*
heavyweight: Lery Khabelov *(Unified Team)*
super-heavyweight: Bruce Baumgartner *(USA)*

** Commonwealth of Independent States plus Georgia*

---

yachting racing a small, light sailing vessel. At the Olympic Games, seven categories exist: Soling, Flying Dutchman, Star, Finn, Tornado, 470, and Windglider (or windsurfing/boardsailing), which was introduced at the 1984 Los Angeles games. The Finn and Windglider are solo events; the Soling class is for three-person crews; all other classes are for crews of two.

AMERICA'S CUP

first held 1870; now contested approximately every four years; all winners have been US boats, except for *Australia II* 1983
1962 *Weatherly*
1964 *Constellation*
1967 *Intrepid*
1970 *Intrepid*
1974 *Courageous*
1977 *Courageous*
1980 *Freedom*
1983 *Australia II*
1987 *Stars and Stripes*
1988 *Stars and Stripes*
1992 *America 3*

ADMIRAL'S CUP

first held 1957; national teams consisting of three boats compete over three inshore courses and two offshore courses; contested every two years

1973 West Germany
1975 UK
1977 UK
1979 Australia
1981 UK
1983 West Germany
1985 West Germany
1987 New Zealand
1989 UK
1991 France

Biographies

Agostini Giacomo 1943– . Italian motorcyclist who won a record 122 grand prix and 15 world titles. His world titles were at 350cc and 500cc and he was five times a dual champion. In addition he was ten times winner of the Isle of Man Tourist Trophy (TT) races; a figure only bettered by Mike Hailwood and Joey Dunlop.

CAREER HIGHLIGHTS

world titles
350cc: 1968–73 (MV Agusta), 1974 (Yamaha)
500cc: 1966–72 (MV Agusta), 1975 (Yamaha)
Isle of Man TT wins
Junior TT: 1966, 1968–70, 1972 (all MV Agusta)
Senior TT: 1968–72 (all MV Agusta)

Alexeev Vasiliy 1942– . Soviet weightlifter who broke 80 world records 1970–77, a record for any sport. He was Olympic super-heavyweight champion twice, world champion seven times, and European champion on eight occasions. At one time the most decorated man in the USSR, he was regarded as the strongest man in the world. He carried the Soviet flag at the 1980 Moscow Olympics opening ceremony, but retired shortly afterwards.

CAREER HIGHLIGHTS

Olympic champion: 1972, 1976
world champion: 1970–71, 1973–75, 1977
European champion: 1970–78

Ali Muhammad. Adopted name of Cassius Marcellus Clay, Jr 1942– . US boxer. Olympic light-heavyweight champion 1960, he went on to become world professional heavyweight champion 1964, and was the only man to regain the title twice. Ali had his title stripped from him 1967 for refusing to be drafted into the US Army. He was known for his fast footwork and extrovert nature.

CAREER HIGHLIGHTS

fights: 61
wins: 56 (37 knockouts)
draws: 0
defeats: 5
first professional fight: 29 Oct 1960 v. Tunny Hunsaker *(USA)*
last professional fight: 11 Dec 1981 v. Trevor Berbick *(Canada)*

Aouita Said 1960– . Moroccan runner. Outstanding at middle and long distances, he won the 1984 Olympic and 1987 World Championship 5,000-metres title. In 1985 he held world records at both 1,500 and 5,000 metres, the first person for 30 years to hold both. He has since broken the 2 miles, 3,000 metres, and 2,000 metres world records.

CAREER HIGHLIGHTS

Olympic Games
1984: gold 5,000 metres
world records
1985: 1,500 metres, 5,000 metres
1987: 2,000 metres, 3,000 metres, 5,000 metres
1989: 3,000 metres
world championships
1987: gold 5,000 metres
world best
2 miles: 1987

Ashe Arthur Robert, Jr 1943–1993. US tennis player and coach, renowned for his exceptionally strong serve. He won the US national men's singles title at Forest Hills and the first US Open 1968. He won the Australian men's title 1970 and Wimbledon 1975. Cardiac problems ended his playing career 1979, but he continued his involvement with the sport as captain of the US Davis Cup team.

Ballesteros Seve(riano) 1957– . Spanish golfer who came to prominence 1976 and has won several leading tournaments in the USA, including the Masters Tournament 1980 and 1983. He has also won the British Open three times: in 1979, 1984, and 1988.

CAREER HIGHLIGHTS

British Open: 1979, 1984, 1988
Ryder Cup (individual): 1979, 1983, 1985, 1987, 1989, 1991
Ryder Cup (team): 1985,1987, tie 1989
PGA Championship: 1983, 1991
US Masters: 1980, 1983
World Match-Play Championship: 1981–82, 1984–85, 1991

Bannister Roger Gilbert 1929– . English track and field athlete, the first person to run a mile in under four minutes. He achieved this feat at Oxford, England, on 6 May 1954 in a time of 3 min 59.4 sec. Bannister also broke the four-minute barrier at the 1954 Commonwealth Games in Vancouver, Canada.

Beckenbauer Franz 1945– . German football player who made a record 103 appearances for his country. He captained West Germany to the 1972 European Championship and the 1974 World Cup, and was twice European Footballer of the Year. After retiring as a player, he became West Germany's team manager, taking them to the runners-up spot in the 1986 World Cup and victory in the 1990 World Cup. He is the only person both to captain and manage a winning World Cup team.

CAREER HIGHLIGHTS

as player
World Cup: 1974

European Championship: 1972
European Cup: 1974–76
European Footballer of the Year: 1972, 1976
as manager
World Cup: 1990

Becker Boris 1967– . German tennis player. In 1985 he became the youngest winner of a singles title at Wimbledon at the age of 17. He has won the title three times and helped West Germany to win the Davis Cup 1988 and 1989. He also won the US Open 1989 and the Grand Prix Masters/ATP Tour World Championship 1992.

CAREER HIGHLIGHTS

Wimbledon
singles: 1985, 1986, 1989
US Open
singles: 1989
Australian Open
singles: 1991
Grand Prix Masters
1988

Best George 1946– . Irish footballer. He won two League championship medals and was a member of the Manchester United side that won the European Cup in 1968. Best joined Manchester United as a youth and made his debut at 17; seven months later he made his international debut for Northern Ireland. Trouble with managers, fellow players, and the media led to his early retirement.

CAREER HIGHLIGHTS

Football League
appearances: 411
goals: 147
League championship: 1965, 1967
Footballer of the Year: 1968
internationals
appearances: 37
goals: 9
European Cup: 1968
European Footballer of the Year: 1968

Blanco Serge 1958– . French rugby union player, renowned for his pace, skill, and ingenuity on the field. Blanco played a world-record 93 internationals before his retirement in 1991, scoring 38 tries of which 34 were from full back – another world record. He was instrumental in France's Grand Slam wins of 1981 and 1987.

Border Allan 1955– . Left-handed batsman and captain of the Australian cricket team since 1985. At the start of the 1993 Ashes series, he held world records for most runs in test cricket (10,262), most appearances in test matches (141) and most appearances in one day internationals (256). Plays in Australia for Queensland after starting career with NSW, and has also played for Gloucestershire and Essex in England.

CAREER HIGHLIGHTS

Test cricket runs: 10,262 average: 51.05 best: 205 not out v. New Zealand 1987–88 wickets: 38 average: 38.53 best: 7 for 4 v. West Indies 1988–89

Borg Bjorn 1956– . Swedish tennis player who won the men's singles title at Wimbledon five times 1976–80, a record since the abolition of the challenge system 1922. He also won six French Open singles titles. In 1990 Borg announced plans to return to professional tennis, but he enjoyed little competitive success.

CAREER HIGHLIGHTS

Wimbledon
singles: 1976–80
French Open
singles: 1974–75, 1978–81
Davis Cup
1975 (member of winning Sweden team)
Grand Prix Masters
1980–81
WCT Champion
1976
ITF World Champion
1978–80

Botham Ian (Terrence) 1955– . English cricketer whose test record places him among the world's greatest all-rounders. He has played county cricket for Somerset, Worcestershire, and Durham as well as playing in Australia. He played for England 1977-89 and returned to the England side 1991. He retired from cricket in 1993. Botham has raised money for leukaemia research with walks from John o'Groats to Land's End in the UK, and across the Alps.

CAREER HIGHLIGHTS

all first-class matches (to start of 1992 season)
runs: 18,983
average: 34.20
best: 228 (Somerset v. Gloucestershire 1980)
wickets: 1,159
average: 27.08
best: 8 for 34 (England v. Pakistan 1978)
test cricket
appearances: 102
runs: 5,200
average: 33.54
best: 208 (England v. India 1982)
wickets: 383
average: 28.40
best: 8 for 34 (England v. Pakistan 1978)
catches: 120

Boycott Geoffrey 1940– . English cricketer born in Yorkshire, England's most prolific run-maker with 8,114 runs in test cricket until overtaken by David Gower in 1992. He played in 108 test matches and in 1981 overtook Gary Sobers' world record total of test runs. Twice, in 1971 and 1979, his average was over 100 runs in an English season. Boycott was banned as a test player in 1982 for taking part in matches against South Africa. He was released by Yorkshire after a dispute in 1986 and has not played first-class cricket since.

CAREER HIGHLIGHTS

all first-class matches
runs: 48,426
average: 56.83
best: 261 not out (MCC v. WIBC President's X I 1973–74)
test cricket
runs: 8,114
average: 47.72
best: 246 not out (England v. India 1967)

Bradman Don (Donald George) 1908– . Australian test cricketer with the highest average in test history. From 52 test matches he averaged 99.94 runs per innings. He only needed four runs from his final test innings to average 100 but was dismissed at second ball. Bradman played for Australia for 20 years and was captain 1936–48. He twice scored triple centuries against England and in 1930 scored 452 not out for New South Wales against Queensland, the highest first-class innings until 1959.

CAREER HIGHLIGHTS

all first-class matches
runs: 28,067
average: 95.14
best: 452 not out (New South Wales v. Queensland 1930)
test cricket
runs: 6,996
average: 99.94
best: 334 (Australia v. England 1930)

Bristow Eric 1957– . English darts player nicknamed 'the Crafty Cockney'. He has won all the game's major titles, including the world professional title a record five times between 1980 and 1986.

CAREER HIGHLIGHTS

world professional champion: 1980–81, 1984–86
World Masters: 1977, 1979, 1981, 1983–84
World Cup (individual): 1983, 1985, 1987, 1989
World Cup (team): 1979, 1981, 1983, 1985, 1987, 1989
British Open: 1978, 1981, 1983, 1985–86
News of the World: 1983–84
World Pairs: 1987 (with Peter Locke)

Bryant David 1931– . English flat-green (lawn) bowls player. He has won every honour the game has offered, including four outdoor world titles (three singles and one triples) 1966–88 and three indoor titles 1979–81.

CAREER HIGHLIGHTS

world outdoor champion: 1966, 1980, 1988
world indoor champion: 1979–81
Commonwealth Games
singles: 1962, 1970, 1974, 1978
fours: 1962
English Bowling Association titles
singles: 1960, 1966, 1971–73, 1975
pairs: 1965, 1969, 1974
triples: 1966, 1977
fours: 1957, 1968–69, 1971

Budge Donald 1915– . US tennis player. He was the first to perform the Grand Slam when he won the Wimbledon, French, US, and Australian championships all in 1938. He won 14 Grand Slam events in all, including Wimbledon singles twice.

CAREER HIGHLIGHTS

Wimbledon
singles: 1937–38
doubles: 1937–38
mixed: 1937–38
US Open
singles: 1937–38
doubles: 1936, 1938
mixed: 1937–38
French Open
singles: 1938
Australian Open
singles: 1938

Campese David– . 1962 Australian rugby union player, one of the outstanding entertainers of the game. He holds the world record for the most tries scored in international rugby (52 international tries by 1 June 1993). Australia's most capped player, he was a key element in their 1991 World Cup victory.

Carson Willie (William Hunter) 1942– . Scottish jockey who has ridden three Epsom Derby winners as well as the winners of most major races worldwide. The top flat-race jockey on five occasions, Carson has had over 3,000 wins in Britain. For many years he rode for the royal trainer, Major Dick Hern. To the start of the 1993 season, he has ridden 16 Classic winners and ridden 3,434 winners since 1962.

CAREER HIGHLIGHTS

Champion Jockey
1972–73, 1978, 1980, 1983
Derby
1979 (Troy)
1980 (Henbit)
1989 (Nashwan)

Caslavska Vera 1943– . Czechoslovak gymnast, the first of the great present-day stylists. She won a record 21 world, Olympic, and European gold medals 1959-68; she also won eight silver and three bronze medals.

CAREER HIGHLIGHTS

Olympic champion
overall individual: 1964, 1968
beam: 1964, 1968
vault: 1964, 1968
floor exercise: 1968
world champion
overall individual: 1966
vault: 1962, 1966

Charlton Bobby (Robert) 1937– . English footballer, younger brother of Jack Charlton, who scored a record 49 goals in 106 appearances. An elegant midfield player who specialized in fierce long-range shots, Charlton spent most of his playing career with Manchester United. On retiring he had an unsuccessful spell as manager of Preston North End. He later became a director of Manchester United.

CAREER HIGHLIGHTS

Football League appearances: 644; goals: 206
international appearances: 106; goals: 49
World Cup: 1966
Football League championship: 1965, 1967
FA Cup: 1963
European Cup: 1968
Footballer of the Year: 1966
European Footballer of the Year: 1966

Christie Linford 1960– . Jamaican-born English sprinter who won a gold medal in the 100-metres event in the 1992 Barcelona Olympics. In 1986, Christie won the European 100-metres championship and finished second to Ben Johnson in the Commonwealth Games. At the 1988 Seoul Olympics, he won two silver medals in the 100 metres and 400-metre relay. In 1990 he won gold medals in the Commonwealth Games for the 100 metres and 400-metre relay.

CAREER HIGHLIGHTS

Olympic games
1988: silver 100 metres; silver 400-metre relay
1992: gold 100 metres
Commonwealth games
1990: gold 100 metres; gold 400-metre relay
European championships
1986: gold 100 metres
1990: gold 100 metres
World Cup
1989: gold 100 metres
1992: gold 100 metres
World Athletic Championships
1993: gold 100 metres

Clark Jim (James) 1936–1968. Scottish-born motor-racing driver who was twice world champion 1963 and 1965. He spent all his Formula One career with Lotus. Clark won 25 Formula One Grand Prix races, a record at the time, before losing his life at Hockenheim, West Germany, in April 1968 during a Formula Two race.

CAREER HIGHLIGHTS

world champion
1963 (Lotus)
1965 (Lotus)
Formula One Grand Prix
races: 72
wins: 25

Cobb Ty(rus Raymond), nicknamed 'the Georgia Peach' 1886–1961. US baseball player, one of the greatest batters and base runners of all time. He played for Detroit and Philadelphia 1905–28, and won the American League batting average championship 12 times. He holds the record for runs scored (2,254) and batting average (0.367). He had 4,191 hits in his career – a record that stood for almost 60 years.

Coe Sebastian 1956– . English middle-distance runner, Olympic 1,500-metre champion 1980 and 1984. Coe became Britain's most prolific world-record breaker with eight outdoor world records and three indoor world records 1979–81. After his retirement in 1990 he pursued a political career with the Conservative party, and in 1992 was elected member of Parliament for Falmouth and Camborne in Cornwall.

CAREER HIGHLIGHTS

Olympic Games
1980: gold 1,500 metres, silver 800 metres
1984: gold 1,500 metres, silver 800 metres
world records
1979: 800 metres, one mile, 1,500 metres
1980: 1,000 metres
1981: 800 metres, 1,000 metres, one mile (twice)
1982: 3,200-metre relay

Comaneci Nadia 1961– . Romanian gymnast. She won three gold medals at the 1976 Olympics at the age of 14, and was the first gymnast to record a perfect score of 10 in international competition. Upon retirement she became a coach of the Romanian team, but defected to Canada 1989.

CAREER HIGHLIGHTS

Olympic Games
1976: gold beam, vault, floor exercise
1980: gold beam, parallel bars

Connolly Maureen 1934–1969. US tennis player, nicknamed 'Little Mo' because she was just 157 cm/5 ft 2 in tall. In 1953 she became the first woman to complete the Grand Slam by winning all four major tournaments. All her singles titles (at nine major championships) and her Grand Slam titles were won between 1951 and 1954. Her career ended 1954 after a riding accident.

CAREER HIGHLIGHTS

Wimbledon
singles: 1952–54
US Open
singles: 1951–53
French Open
singles: 1953–54
doubles: 1954
mixed: 1954
Australian Open
singles: 1953
doubles: 1953

Connors Jimmy 1952– . US tennis player who won the Wimbledon title 1974, and subsequently won ten Grand Slam events. He was one of the first players to popularize the two-handed backhand.

CAREER HIGHLIGHTS

Wimbledon
singles: 1974, 1982
doubles: 1973
US Open
singles: 1974, 1976, 1978, 1982–83
doubles: 1975

Australian Open
singles: 1974
Grand Prix Masters
1978

Court Margaret (born Smith) 1942– . Australian tennis player. The most prolific winner in the women's game, she won a record 64 Grand Slam titles, including 25 at singles. Court was the first from her country to win the ladies title at Wimbledon 1963, and the second woman after Maureen Connolly to complete the Grand Slam 1970.

CAREER HIGHLIGHTS
Wimbledon
singles: 1963, 1965, 1970
doubles: 1964, 1969
mixed: 1963, 1965–66, 1968, 1975
US Open
singles: 1962, 1965, 1968–70, 1973
doubles: 1963, 1968–70, 1973, 1975
mixed: 1961–65, 1969–70, 1972
French Open
singles: 1962, 1964, 1969–70, 1973
doubles: 1964–66, 1973
mixed: 1963–65, 1969
Australian Open
singles: 1960–66, 1969–71, 1973
doubles: 1961–63, 1965, 1969–71, 1973
mixed: 1963–64

Cruyff Johan 1947– . Dutch football player, an outstanding European player in the 1970s. He was capped 48 times by his country, scoring 33 goals. He spent most of his career playing with Ajax and Barcelona and was named European Footballer of the Year on three occasions. As a coach he took both clubs to domestic and European honours.

CAREER HIGHLIGHTS
as player:
European Cup
1971–73 (with Ajax)
as coach:
European Cup Winners Cup
1987 (with Ajax)
1989 (with Barcelona)
European Cup
1992 (with Barcelona)
European Footballer of the Year
1971, 1973, 1974
World Club Champions
1972 (with Ajax)

Davis Steve 1957– . English snooker player, who has won every major honour in the game since turning professional 1978. Davis won his first major title 1980 when he won the Coral UK Championship. He has been world champion six times, and has also won world titles at pairs and with the England team.

CAREER HIGHLIGHTS
UK Open
1980–81, 1984–87, 1993
World Professional Champion
1981, 1983–84, 1987–89
World Pairs Championship (with Tony Meo)
1982–83, 1985–86
Benson & Hedges Masters
1982, 1988
World Team Championship
1981, 1983, 1988–89
Rothmans Grand Prix
1985, 1988–89

Dempsey Jack 1895–1983. US heavyweight boxing champion, nicknamed 'the Manassa Mauler'. He beat Jess Willard 1919 to win the title and held it until 1926, when he lost it to Gene Tunney. In a re-match the following year (the 'Battle of the Long Count') Dempsey narrowly lost his chance to regain the title, when after knocking out Tunney in the seventh round he failed to return to a neutral corner, and thereby obliged the referee to delay the start of the count.

CAREER HIGHLIGHTS
fights: 79
wins: 64
draws: 9
defeats: 6

DiMaggio Joe 1914– . US baseball player with the New York Yankees 1936–51. In 1941 he set a record by getting hits in 56 consecutive games. He was an outstanding fielder, played centre field, hit 361 home runs, and had a career average of 0.325. He was once married to the actress Marilyn Monroe.

Edberg Stefan 1966– . Swedish lawn-tennis player, twice winner of Wimbledon 1988 and 1990. He won the junior Grand Slam 1983 and his first Grand Slam title – the Australian Open – 1985, repeated 1987. Other Grand Slam singles titles include the US Open 1991 and 1992. At Wimbledon in 1987 he became the first male player in 40 years to win a match without conceding a game.

CAREER HIGHLIGHTS
Wimbledon
singles: 1988, 1990
Australian Open
singles: 1985, 1987
doubles: 1987
US Open
singles: 1991, 1992
doubles: 1987
Grand Prix Masters
1989

Edwards Gareth 1947– . Welsh rugby union player. He was appointed captain of his country when only 20 years old. Edwards appeared in seven championship winning teams, five Triple Crown winning teams, and two Grand Slam winning teams. In 53 international matches he scored a record 20 tries.

CAREER HIGHLIGHTS
international championship: 1969, 1970*, 1971,

1975–76, 1978
Triple Crown: 1969, 1971, 1976–78
Grand Slam: 1971, 1976, 1978
British Lions tours: 1968 to South Africa, 1971 to New Zealand, 1974 to South Africa

** denotes title shared*

Evert Chris(tine) 1954– . US tennis player renowned for her outstanding two-handed backhand and baseline technique. She won her first Wimbledon title 1974, and has since won 21 Grand Slam titles. From 1974–89 she never failed to reach the quarter-finals at Wimbledon. She became the first woman tennis player to win $1 million in prize money.

CAREER HIGHLIGHTS

Wimbledon
singles: 1974, 1976, 1981
doubles: 1976

US Open
singles: 1975–78, 1980, 1982

French Open
singles: 1974–75, 1979–80, 1983, 1985–86
doubles: 1974–75

Australian Open
singles: 1982, 1984

Faldo Nick 1957– . English golfer who was the first Briton in 54 years to win three British Open titles, and the only person after Jack Nicklaus to win two successive US Masters titles (1989 and 1990). He is one of only six golfers to win the Masters and British Open in the same year.

CAREER HIGHLIGHTS

British Open: 1987, 1989, 1992
US Masters: 1989, 1990
PGA Championship: 1978, 1980-81, 1989
Ryder Cup winning team: 1985, 1987, tie 1989
World Match-Play Championship: 1989, 1992
European Open: 1992

Ferrari Enzo 1898–1988. Italian founder of the Ferrari car manufacturing company, which specializes in Grand Prix racing cars and high-quality sports cars. He was a racing driver for Alfa Romeo in the 1920s, went on to become one of their designers and in 1929 took over their racing division. In 1947 the first 'true' Ferrari was seen. The Ferrari car has won more world championship Grands Prix than any other car.

Finney Tom (Thomas) 1922– . English footballer, known as the 'Preston Plumber'. His only Football League club was his home-town team, Preston North End. He played for England 76 times, in every forward position. He was celebrated for his ball control and goal-scoring skills, and was the first person to win the Footballer of the Year award twice.

CAREER HIGHLIGHTS

Football League appearances: 433; goals: 187
international appearances: 76; goals: 30
FA Cup (runners-up medal): 1954
Footballer of the Year: 1954, 1957

Francome John 1952– . English jockey who holds the record for the most National Hunt winners (over hurdles or fences). Between 1970 and 1985 he rode 1,138 winners from 5,061 mounts – the second person (after Stan Mellor) to ride 1,000 winners. He took up training after retiring from riding.

CAREER HIGHLIGHTS

Champion Jockey: 1979, 1981–85 (shared title 1982)
Cheltenham Gold Cup: 1978
Champion Hurdle: 1981
Hennessy Cognac Gold Cup: 1983–84
King George VI Chase: 1982

Gascoigne Paul ('Gazza') 1967– . English footballer who has played for Tottenham Hotspur 1988–91 and for Lazio, Italy, from 1992. At the 1990 World Cup semifinal against West Germany, he committed a foul for which he was booked (cautioned by the referee), meaning that he would be unable to play in the final, should England win. His tearful response drew public sympathy, and he was subsequently lionized by the British press.

Gavaskar Sunil Manohar 1949– . Indian cricketer. Between 1971 and 1987 he scored a record 10,122 test runs in a record 125 matches (including 106 consecutive tests) until overtaken by Allan Border in 1993.

CAREER HIGHLIGHTS

all first-class matches
runs: 25,834
average: 51.46
best: 340 (Bombay v. Bengal, 1981–82)

test cricket
runs: 10,122
average: 51.12
best: 236 not out (India v. West Indies, 1983–84)

Gooch Graham Alan 1953– . English cricketer who plays for Essex county and England. He made his first-class cricket debut in 1973, and was first capped for England two years later. Banned for three years for captaining a team for a tour of South Africa in 1982, he was later re-instated as England captain in 1989. He scored a world record 456 runs in a test match against India in 1990. In 1993 he joined the select band of cricketers to reach the milestone of 100 centuries.

CAREER HIGHLIGHTS

all first-class matches (to end of 1992 season)
runs: 36,126
average: 48.16
best: 333 (England v. India 1990)
wickets: 231
average: 34.77
best: 7-14 (Essex v. Worcestershire 1982)

test cricket (to start of 1993 season)
appearances: 101
runs: 7,620
average: 43.05
best: 333 (England v. India 1990)
wickets: 22
average: 40.63
best: 3-39 (England v. Pakistan 1992)

Gower David 1957– . English left-handed cricketer who played for Leicestershire 1975–89 and for Hampshire from 1990. In 1992, during the third test against Pakistan, he became England's highest-scoring batsman in test cricket, surpassing Geoffrey Boycott's record of 8,114 runs.

CAREER HIGHLIGHTS

all first-class matches (to start of 1993 season)
runs: 25,203
average: 40.00
best: 228 (Leicestershire v. Glamorgan 1989)
test cricket (to start of 1993 season)
appearances (to April 1991): 117
runs: 8,231
average: 44.25
best: 215 (England v. Australia 1985)

Grace W(illiam) G(ilbert) 1848–1915. English cricketer. By profession a doctor, he became the best batsman in England. He began playing first-class cricket at the age of 16, scored 152 runs in his first test match, and scored the first triple century 1876. Throughout his career, which lasted nearly 45 years, he scored more than 54,000 runs.

CAREER HIGHLIGHTS

all first-class matches
runs: 54,896
average: 39.55
best: 344 MCC v. Kent, 1876
wickets: 2,876
average: 17.92
best: 10-49 MCC v. Oxford University, 1886
test cricket
runs: 1,098
average: 32.29
best: 170 v. Australia, 1886
wickets: 9
average: 26.22
best: 2-12 v Australia, 1890

Graf Steffi 1969– . German tennis player who brought Martina Navratilova's long reign as the world's number-one female player to an end. Graf reached the semifinal of the US Open 1985 at the age of 16, and won five consecutive Grand Slam singles titles 1988–89.

CAREER HIGHLIGHTS

Wimbledon
singles: 1988–89, 1991, 1992, 1993
doubles: 1988
US Open
singles: 1988–89
French Open
singles: 1987–88, 1993
Australian Open
singles: 1988–90
Olympics
gold: 1988

Green Lucinda (born Prior-Palmer) 1953– . English three-day eventer. She has won the Badminton Horse Trials a record six times 1973–84 and was world individual champion 1982.

Gretzky Wayne 1961– . Canadian ice-hockey player, probably the best in the history of the National Hockey League (NHL). Gretsky played with the Edmonton Oilers 1979–88 and with the Los Angeles Kings from 1988. He took just 11 years to break the NHL scoring record of 1,850 goals (accumulated by Gordie Howe over 26 years) and won the Hart Memorial Trophy as the NHL's most valuable player of the season a record nine times (1980–87, 1990–91).

CAREER HIGHLIGHTS

Stanley Cup: 1984, 1985, 1987, 1988
Hart Memorial Trophy (NHL's most valuable player): 1980–87, 1989
Ross Trophy (most points in regular season): 1981–87

Griffith-Joyner (born Griffith) Delorez Florence 1959– . US track athlete, nicknamed 'Flo-Jo', who won three gold medals at the 1988 Seoul Olympics, the 100 and 200 metres and the sprint relay. Her time in the 200 metres was a world record 21.34 seconds.

Hadlee Richard John 1951– . New Zealand cricketer. In 1987 he surpassed Ian Botham's world record of 373 wickets in test cricket and went on to set the record at 431 wickets. He played for Canterbury and Nottinghamshire in England, and retired from international cricket 1990.

CAREER HIGHLIGHTS

all first-class matches
runs: 12,052
average: 31.78
best: 210 not out (Nottinghamshire v. Middlesex 1984)
wickets: 1,490
average: 18.11
best: 9 for 52 (New Zealand v. Australia 1985–86)
test cricket
appearances: 86
runs: 3,124
average: 27.16
best: 151 not out (New Zealand v. Sri Lanka 1986–87)
wickets: 431
average: 22.29
best: 9 for 52 (New Zealand v. Australia 1985–86)

Hanley Ellery 1965– . English rugby league player, a regular member of the Great Britain team since 1984 and the inspiration behind Wigan's domination of the sport in the 1980s. Hanley started his career in 1981 with Bradford Northern before his transfer to Wigan 1985 for a then world record £85,000. He has since won all the top honours of the game in Britain as well as earning a reputation in Australia, the world's top rugby league nation. He joined Leeds in 1991.

CAREER HIGHLIGHTS

Challenge Cup: 1985, 1988–91
Division One Championship: 1987, 1990–91
Regal Trophy: 1986–87, 1989–90
Lancashire County Cup: 1986–89
Premiership Trophy: 1987

Hendry Stephen 1970– . Scottish snooker player. Hendry was the youngest winner ever of a professional tournament when he claimed the 1986 Scottish professional title, and won his first ranking event in the 1987 Rothmans Grand Prix. During the 1989–90 season he replaced Steve Davis as the top-ranking player, and became the youngest world champion ever.

CAREER HIGHLIGHTS

Embassy World Professional Championship: 1990, 1992, 1993
Rothmans Grand Prix: 1987, 1990, 1991
MIM/Pearl Assurance British Open: 1988, 1991
Benson and Hedges Masters: 1989–91, 1992, 1993
UK Open: 1989–90

Hick Graeme 1966– . Rhodesian-born cricketer who became Zimbabwe's youngest professional cricketer at the age of 17. A prolific batsman, he joined Worcestershire, England, in 1984. He achieved the highest score in England in the 20th century in 1988 against Somerset with 405 not out. He made his test debut for England in 1991 after a seven-year qualification period.

CAREER HIGHLIGHTS

all first-class cricket (to end of 1992 season)
runs: 19,083
average: 59.08
best: 405 (Worcestershire v. Somerset 1988)
test cricket (to start of 1993 season)
appearances: 15
runs: 716
average: 28.64
best: 178 (England v. India 1993)

Hill Graham 1929–1975. English motor-racing driver. He won the Dutch Grand Prix in 1962, progressing to the world driver's title in 1962 and 1968. In 1972 he became the first world driver's champion to win the Le Mans Grand Prix d' Endurance (Le Mans 24-Hour Race). Hill started his Formula One career with Lotus 1958, went to BRM 1960–66, returned to Lotus 1967–69, moved to Brabham 1970–72, and formed his own team, Embassy Shadow, 1973–75. He was killed in an air crash.

CAREER HIGHLIGHTS

world champion
1962 BRM
1968 Lotus
Formula One Grand Prix
races: 176
wins: 14
Le Mans Grand Prix d'Endurance
1972 Matra-Simca
Indianapolis 500
1966 Lola Ford

Hobbs Jack (John Berry) 1882–1963. English cricketer who represented his country 61 times. In first-class cricket he scored a world record 61,237 runs, including a record 197 centuries, in a career that lasted nearly 30 years.

CAREER HIGHLIGHTS

all first-class matches
runs: 61,237
average: 50.65
test cricket
runs: 5,410
average: 56.94
best: 211 v. South Africa, 1924

Howe Gordie 1926– . Canadian ice- hockey player who played for the Detroit Red Wings (National Hockey League) 1946–71 and then the New England Whalers (World Hockey Association). In the NHL, he scored more goals (801), assists (1,049), and points (1,850) than any other player in ice- hockey history until beaten by Wayne Gretsky. Howe played professional hockey until he was over 50.

Hutton Len (Leonard) 1916–1990. English cricketer. He captained England in 23 test matches 1952–56 and was England's first professional captain. In 1938 at the Oval he scored 364 against Australia, a world record test score until beaten by Gary Sobers 1958.

CAREER HIGHLIGHTS

all first-class matches
runs: 40,140
average: 55.51
best: 364 England v. Australia, 1938
test cricket
runs: 6,971
average: 55.51
best: 364 (England v. Australia, 1938)

Johnson Jack 1878–1968. US heavyweight boxer. He overcame severe racial prejudice to become the first black heavyweight champion of the world 1908 when he travelled to Australia to challenge Tommy Burns. The US authorities wanted Johnson 'dethroned' because of his colour but could not find suitable challengers until 1915, when he lost the title in a dubious fight decision to the giant Jess Willard.

CAREER HIGHLIGHTS

fights: 107
wins: 86
draws: 11
defeats: 10

Jones Bobby (Robert Tyre) 1902–1971. US golfer who was the game's greatest amateur player. He never turned professional but won 13 major amateur and professional tournaments, including the Grand Slam of the amateur and professional opens of both the USA and Britain 1930. Jones finished playing competitive golf 1930, but maintained his contacts with the sport and was largely responsible for inaugurating the US Masters.

CAREER HIGHLIGHTS

British Open: 1926–27, 1930
US Open: 1923, 1926, 1929–30
British Amateur: 1930
US Amateur: 1924–25, 1927–28, 1930

US Walker Cup (team): 1922, 1924, 1926, 1928*, 1930*
** indicates playing captain*

Khan Imran 1952– . Pakistani cricketer. He played county cricket for Worcestershire and Sussex in the UK, and made his test debut for Pakistan 1971, subsequently playing for his country 85 times. In first-class cricket he has scored over 16,000 runs and taken over 1,200 wickets. He captained Pakistan to victory in the 1992 World Cup.

CAREER HIGHLIGHTS

test cricket
appearances: 88
runs: 3,807
average: 37.69
best: 136 (Pakistan v. Australia 1989–90)
wickets: 362
average: 22.81
best: 8–58 (Pakistan v. Sri Lanka 1981–82)

Khan Jahangir 1963– . Pakistani squash player who won the world open championship a record six times 1981–85 and 1988. He was ten times British Open champion 1982–91, and World Amateur champion 1979, 1983, and 1985. After losing to Geoff Hunt of Australia in the final of the 1981 British Open he did not lose again until Nov 1986 when he lost to Ross Norman of New Zealand in the World Open final. He announced his retirement 1993.

King Billie Jean (born Moffitt) 1943– . US tennis player. She won a record 20 Wimbledon titles between 1961 and 1979 (including six singles titles), and her 39 Grand Slam events at singles and doubles are third only to Navratilova and Margaret Court.

CAREER HIGHLIGHTS

Wimbledon
singles: 1966–68, 1972–73, 1975
doubles: 1961–62, 1965, 1967–68, 1970–73, 1979
mixed: 1967, 1971, 1973–74

US Open
singles: 1967, 1971–72, 1974
doubles: 1964, 1967, 1974, 1978, 1980
mixed: 1967, 1971, 1973, 1976

French Open
singles: 1972
doubles: 1972
mixed: 1967, 1970

Australian Open
singles: 1968
mixed: 1968

Klammer Franz 1953– . Austrian skier who won a record 35 World Cup downhill races between 1974 and 1985. He was the combined world champion 1974, Olympic gold medallist 1976, and the World Cup downhill champion 1975–78 and 1983.

Korbut Olga 1955– . Soviet gymnast who attracted world attention at the 1972 Olympic Games with her lively floor routine. She won gold medals for the beam and floor exercises, a silver for the parallel bars, and another gold as member of the winning Soviet team.

CAREER HIGHLIGHTS

Olympic Games
1972: gold beam, floor exercise, team
1976: team

Kristiansen Ingrid 1956– . Norwegian athlete, an outstanding long-distance runner of 5,000 metres, 10,000 metres, marathon, and cross-country races. She has won all the world's leading marathons. In 1986 she knocked 45.68 seconds off the world 10,000 metres record. She was the world cross-country champion 1988 and won the London marathon 1984–85 and 1987–88.

Latynina Larissa Semyonovna 1935– . Soviet gymnast, winner of more Olympic medals than any person in any sport. She won 18 between 1956 and 1964, including nine gold medals. During her career she won a total of 12 individual Olympic and world championship gold medals.

CAREER HIGHLIGHTS

Olympic champion
team: 1956, 1960, 1964
overall individual: 1956, 1960
floor exercise: 1956*, 1960, 1964
vault: 1956

world championship
team: 1958, 1962
overall individual: 1958, 1962
vault: 1958
beam: 1958
floor exercise: 1962
asymmetric bars: 1958
** denotes shared title*

Lauda Niki 1949– . Austrian motor racing driver who won the world championship in 1975, 1977 and 1984. He was also runner-up in 1976 just six weeks after a serious accident at Nurburgring, Germany, which left him badly burned. Lauda was Formula Two champion in 1972, and drove for March, BRM, Ferrari, and Brabham before his retirement in 1978. He returned to the sport in 1984 and won his third world title in a McLaren before eventually retiring in 1985 to concentrate on his airline business, Lauda-Air.

CAREER HIGHLIGHTS

world champion
1975 Ferrari
1977 Ferrari
1984 McLaren

Formula One Grand Prix
races: 171
wins: 25

Laver Rod(ney George) 1938– . Australian tennis player. He was one of the greatest left-handed players, and the only player to perform the Grand Slam twice (1962 and 1969). He won four Wimbledon singles titles, the Australian title three times, the US Open twice, and the French Open twice. He turned professional after winning Wimbledon in 1962 but returned when the championships were opened to professionals in 1968.

CAREER HIGHLIGHTS

Wimbledon
singles: 1961–62, 1968–69
doubles: 1971
mixed: 1959–60

US Open
singles: 1962, 1969

French Open
singles: 1962, 1969
doubles: 1961
mixed: 1961

Australian Open
singles: 1960, 1962, 1969
doubles: 1959–61, 1969

Leonard Sugar Ray 1956– . US boxer. In 1988 he became the first man to have won world titles at five officially recognized weights. He was Olympic light-welterweight champion 1976, and won his first professional title in 1979 when he beat Wilfred Benitez for the WBC welterweight title. He later won titles at junior middleweight (WBA version) 1981, middleweight (WBC) 1987, light-heavyweight (WBC) 1988, and super-middleweight (WBC) 1988. He retired 1992.

Lewis Carl (Frederick Carlton) 1961– . US track and field athlete who won eight gold medals and one silver in three successive Olympic Games 1984, 1988, and 1992. At the 1984 Olympic Games he equalled the performance of Jesse Owens, winning gold medals in the 100 and 200 metres, 400-metre relay, and long jump.

CAREER HIGHLIGHTS

Olympic Games
1984: gold 100 metres, 200 metres, 400-metre relay, long jump
1988: gold 100 metres, long jump; silver 200 metres
1992: gold long jump, 400-metre relay

Lewis Lennox 1966– . British-born heavyweight boxer who represented Canada in the super-heavyweight division. Turning professional in 1989, he won the European heavyweight title in 1990 and British title in 1991. In 1992 he became the first British-born boxer this century to win the world heavyweight title, when reigning champion Riddick Bowe refused to fight him. He then successfully defended his WBC crown against Tony Tucker in 1993.

Lillee Dennis 1949– . Australian cricketer regarded as the best fast bowler of his generation. He made his test debut in the 1970–71 season and subsequently played for his country 70 times. Lillee was the first to take 300 wickets in test cricket. He played Sheffield Shield cricket for Western Australia and at the end of his career made a comeback with Tasmania.

CAREER HIGHLIGHTS

test cricket (to the beginning of the 1992 season)
appearances: 70
wickets: 355
average: 23.92

Lineker Gary 1960– . English footballer who scored over 250 goals in 550 games for Leicester, Everton, Barcelona, and Tottenham. With 48 goals in 80 internationals he failed by one goal to equal Bobby Charlton's record of 49 goals for England. Lineker was elected Footballer of the Year in 1986 and 1992 and was leading scorer at the 1986 World Cup finals. In 1993 he moved to Japan to play for Nagoya Grampus Eight.

CAREER HIGHLIGHTS

FA Cup: 1991 (with Tottenham)
European Cup Winners Cup: 1989 (with Barcelona)
Footballer of the Year: 1986, 1992

Lopez Nancy 1957– . US golfer who turned professional in 1977 and in 1979 became the first woman to win $200,000 in a season. She has won the US LPGA title three times 1978, 1985, and 1989, and has won over 35 tour events, and $3 million in prize money.

Louis Joe. Assumed name of Joseph Louis Barrow 1914–1981. US boxer, nicknamed 'the Brown Bomber'. He was world heavyweight champion between 1937 and 1949 and made a record 25 successful defences (a record for any weight). Louis was the longest-reigning world heavyweight champion at 11 years and 252 days before announcing his retirement in 1949. He made a comeback and lost to Ezzard Charles in a world title fight in 1950.

CAREER HIGHLIGHTS

professional fights: 66
wins: 63
knockouts: 49
defeats: 3
1st professional fight: 4 July 1934 v. Jack Kracken
last professional fight: 26 Oct 1951 v. Rocky Marciano

McBride Willie John 1940– . Irish rugby union player. He was capped 63 times by Ireland, and won a record 17 British Lions caps. He played on five Lions tours 1962, 1966, 1968, 1971, and in 1974 as captain when they returned from South Africa undefeated.

CAREER HIGHLIGHTS

British Lions tours
1962 South Africa
1966 Australia and New Zealand
1968 South Africa
1971 Australia and New Zealand
1974 South Africa (captain)
1983 New Zealand (manager)

McEnroe John Patrick 1959– . US tennis player whose brash behaviour and fiery temper on court dominated the men's game in the early 1980s. He was three times winner of the Wimbledon men's title 1981, 1983, and 1984. He also won three successive US Open titles 1979–81 and again in 1984. A fine doubles player, McEnroe also won ten Grand Slam doubles titles, seven in partnership with Peter Fleming.

CAREER HIGHLIGHTS

Wimbledon
singles: 1981, 1983, 1984
doubles: 1979, 1981, 1983, 1984, 1992
US Open
singles: 1979–81, 1984
doubles: 1979, 1981, 1983, 1989
French Open
mixed doubles: 1977
Grand Prix Masters
singles: 1979, 1984, 1985
doubles: 1979–85

Mansell Nigel 1954– . English motor-racing driver. Runner-up in the world championship on two occasions, he became world champion in 1992 and in the same year announced his retirement from Formula One racing. He won 30 Grand Prix races – more than any other British driver. Mansell started his Formula One career with Lotus 1980 and won the European Grand Prix 1985. He drove for the Williams team 1985–88, then for Ferrari 1989–90, before returning to Williams 1991–92. He joined the Newman-Haas team in 1993 to compete in the Indycar Championships.

Mantle Mickey (Charles) 1931– . US baseball player. Signed by the New York Yankees, he broke into the major leagues 1951. A powerful switch-hitter (able to bat with either hand), he also excelled as a centre-fielder. In 1956 he won baseball's Triple Crown, leading the American League in batting average, home runs, and runs batted in. He retired 1969 after 18 years with the Yankees and seven World Series championships.

Maradona Diego 1960– . Argentine footballer who was voted the best player of the 1980s by the world's press. He has won over 80 international caps, and helped his country to two successive World Cup finals. Maradona played for Argentinos Juniors and Boca Juniors before leaving South America for Barcelona, Spain, 1982, for a transfer fee of approximately £5 million. He moved to Napoli, Italy, for £6.9 million 1984, and contributed to their first Italian League title. In 1992 he moved to Spanish club Seville.

CAREER HIGHLIGHTS

World Cup: 1986
UEFA Cup: 1989
Italian League: 1987, 1990
Italian Cup: 1987
Spanish Cup: 1983
South American footballer of the year: 1979, 1980

Marciano Rocky (Rocco Francis Marchegiano) 1923–1969. US boxer, world heavyweight champion 1952–56. He retired after 49 professional fights, the only heavyweight champion to retire undefeated. He was killed in a plane crash.

CAREER HIGHLIGHTS

professional fights: 49
wins: 49
knockouts: 43
defeats: 0
1st professional fight: 17 March 1947 v. Lee Epperson *(USA)*
last professional fight: 21 Sept 1955 v. Archie Moore (USA)

Matthews Stanley 1915– . English footballer who played for Stoke City, Blackpool, and England. An outstanding right-winger, he won the nickname 'the Wizard of the Dribble' because of his ball control. Matthews played nearly 700 Football League games, and won 54 international caps. He continued to play first-division football after the age of 50. He was the first European Footballer of the Year 1956.

CAREER HIGHLIGHTS

Football League appearances: 698, goals: 71
international appearances: 54, goals: 11
FA Cup: 1953
Footballer of the Year: 1948, 1963
European Footballer of the Year: 1956

Merckx Eddie 1945– . Belgian cyclist, known as 'the Cannibal', who won the Tour de France a joint record five times 1969–74. Merckx turned professional 1966 and won his first classic race, the Milan–San Remo, the same year. He went on to win 24 classics as well as the three major tours (of Italy, Spain, and France) a total of 11 times.

He was world professional road-race champion three times and in 1971 won a record 54 races in the season. He rode 50 winners in a season four times. He retired in 1977.

CAREER HIGHLIGHTS

Tour de France: 1969–72, 1974
Tour of Italy: 1968, 1970, 1972–74
Tour of Spain: 1973
world professional champion: 1967, 1971, 1974
world amateur champion: 1964

Miandad Javed 1957– . Pakistani test cricketer, his country's leading run-maker. He scored a century on his test debut in 1976 and has since become one of a handful of players to make 100 test appearances. He has captained his country and helped Pakistan to win the 1992 World Cup. His highest score of 311 was made when he was aged 17.

CAREER HIGHLIGHTS

test cricket (to end of 1992 season)
appearances: 117
runs: 8,465
average: 54.26
best: 280 not out v. India 1982–83

Montana Joe 1956– . US football player who has appeared in four winning Super Bowls as quarterback for the San Francisco 49ers 1982, 1985, 1989, and 1990, winning the Most Valuable Player award in 1982, 1985, and 1990. He had a record five touchdown passes in the 1990 Super Bowl.

Moore Bobby (Robert Frederick) 1941–1993. English footballer who led the England team to victory against West Germany in the 1966 World Cup final at Wembley Stadium. A superb defender, he played 108 games for England 1962–70 (until 1978, a world-record number of international appearances) and was captain 90 times. His Football League career, spent at West Ham 1968–74 and Fulham 1974–77, spanned 19 years and 668 matches.

CAREER HIGHLIGHTS

Football League appearances: 668; goals: 25
international appearances: 108; goals: 2
World Cup: 1966
European Cup Winners Cup: 1965
FA Cup: 1964
Footballer of the Year: 1964
World Cup Player of Players: 1966

Namath Joe (Joseph William) 1943– . US football player. In 1965 Namath signed with the New York Jets of the newly established American Football League. In 1969 Namath led the Jets to a historic upset victory over the Baltimore Colts in the Super Bowl. After leaving the Jets 1977, Namath joined the Los Angeles Rams; however, knee injuries forced his retirement as a player the following year. He later became a sports broadcaster and actor.

Navratilova Martina 1956– . Czech tennis player who became a naturalized US citizen 1981. The most outstanding woman player of the 1980s, she had 55 Grand Slam victories by 1991, including 18 singles titles. She has won the Wimbledon singles title a record nine times, including six in succession 1982–87.

CAREER HIGHLIGHTS

Wimbledon
singles: 1978–79, 1982–87, 1990
doubles: 1976, 1979, 1981–84, 1986
mixed: 1985
US Open
singles: 1983–84, 1986–87
doubles: 1977–78, 1980, 1983–84, 1986–90
mixed: 1985, 1987
French Open
singles: 1982, 1984
doubles: 1975, 1982, 1984–88
mixed: 1974, 1985
Australian Open
singles: 1981, 1983, 1985
doubles: 1980, 1982–85, 1987–89

Nicklaus Jack (William) 1940– . US golfer, nicknamed 'the Golden Bear'. He won a record 20 major titles, including 18 professional majors between 1962 and 1986. He played for the US Ryder Cup team six times 1969–81 and was nonplaying captain 1983 and 1987 when the event was played over the course he designed at Muirfield Village, Ohio. In 1988 he was voted Golfer of the Century.

CAREER HIGHLIGHTS

US Amateur: 1959, 1961
US Open: 1962, 1967, 1972, 1980
British Open: 1966, 1970, 1978
US Masters: 1963, 1965–66, 1972, 1975, 1986
US PGA Championship: 1963, 1971, 1973, 1975, 1980
US Ryder Cup (team): 1969, 1971, 1973, 1975, 1977

Owens Jesse (James Cleveland) 1913–1980. US track and field athlete who excelled in the sprints, hurdles, and the long jump. At the 1936 Berlin Olympics he won four gold medals, and the Nazi leader Hitler is said to have stormed out of the stadium in disgust at the black man's triumph. Owens held the world long-jump record for 25 years 1935–60. At Ann Arbor, Michigan, on 25 May 1935, he broke six world records in less than an hour.

CAREER HIGHLIGHTS

Olympic Games
1936: gold 100 metres, 200 metres, 400-metre relay, long jump
world records:
1935: 100 yards, 200 metres, 220 yards, 200-metre hurdles, 220-yd hurdles, long jump
1936: 100 metres, 100 yards, 400-metre relay (US National team)

Palmer Arnold (Daniel) 1929– . US golfer who helped to popularize the professional sport in the USA in the 1950s and 1960s. He won the US amateur title 1954, and went on to win all the world major professional trophies except the US PGA Championship. In the 1980s he enjoyed a successful career on the US Seniors Tour.

CAREER HIGHLIGHTS

US Open: 1960
British Open: 1961–62
Masters: 1958, 1960, 1962, 1964
World Match-Play: 1964, 1967
US Ryder Cup: 1961, 1963*, 1965, 1967, 1971, 1973, 1975**

** playing captain; ** nonplaying captain*

Pelé Adopted name of Edson Arantes do Nascimento 1940– . Brazilian soccer player who was celebrated as one of the finest inside-forwards in the history of the game. A prolific goal scorer, he appeared in four World Cup competitions 1958–70 and led Brazil to three championships 1958, 1962, and 1970. He spent most of his playing career with the Brazilian team Santos, before ending it with the New York Cosmos in the USA.

Piggott Lester 1935– . English jockey. He has adopted a unique high riding style and is renowned as a brilliant tactician. A champion jockey 11 times between 1960 and 1982, he has ridden a record nine Derby winners. He retired from riding 1985 and took up training. In 1987 he was imprisoned for tax evasion. He returned to racing in 1990 and has ridden

4,435 winners, including a record 30 Classics, in Britain to the start of the 1993 season.

CAREER HIGHLIGHTS

Champion Jockey: 1960, 1964–71, 1981–82
Derby: 1954, 1957, 1960, 1968, 1970, 1972, 1976–77, 1983
Oaks: 1957, 1959, 1966, 1975, 1981, 1984
St Leger: 1960–61, 1967–68, 1970–72, 1984
1,000 Guineas: 1970, 1981
2,000 Guineas: 1957, 1968, 1970, 1985, 1992
Irish 2,000 Guineas: 1992

Platini Michel 1955– . French football player who was the inspiration of the French team that won the 1984 European Championship. He represented his country on 72 occasions, scoring a record 41 goals and playing in three World Cups, and was the first to be elected European Footballer of the Year on three successive years 1983–85. He became manager of the French national team in 1988.

CAREER HIGHLIGHTS

European Championship: 1984
French Cup: 1978 (with Nancy)
French Championship: 1981 (with St Etienne)
Italian Championship: 1984, 1986 (with Juventus)
European Cup: 1985 (with Juventus)
European Cup Winners Cup: 1984 (with Juventus)
European Footballer of the Year: 1983–85

Prost Alain 1955– . French motor-racing driver who was world champion 1985, 1986, and 1989, the first French world drivers' champion. He raced in Formula One events from 1980 and had his first Grand Prix win 1981, driving a Renault. In 1984 he began driving for the McLaren team. To the start of the 1993 season he had won 44 Grands Prix from 184 starts.

CAREER HIGHLIGHTS

world champion
1985 Marlboro McLaren–TAG
1986 Marlboro McLaren–TAG
1989 Marlboro McLaren–Honda
Formula One Grand Prix (to start of 1993 season)
races: 184
wins: 44 (record)

Rhodes Wilfred 1877–1973. English cricketer who took more wickets than anyone else in the game – 4,187 wickets from 1898 to 1930 – and also scored 39,802 first-class runs. Playing for Yorkshire, Rhodes made a record 763 appearances in the county championship. He took 100 wickets in a season 23 times and completed the 'double' of 1,000 runs and 100 wickets in a season 16 times (both records). He played his 58th and final game for England, against the West Indies 1930, when he was 52 years old, the oldest ever test cricketer.

CAREER HIGHLIGHTS

all first-class matches
runs: 39,802
average: 30.83
best: 267 not out Yorkshire v. Leicestershire, 1921
wickets: 4,187
average: 16.71
best: 9-24 C I Thornton's XI v. Australians, 1899
test cricket
runs: 2,325
average: 30.19
best: 179 v. Australia, 1911-12
wickets: 127
average: 26.96
best: 8-68 v. Australia, 1903-04

Richards Gordon 1905–1986. English jockey and trainer who was champion on the flat a record 26 times between 1925 and 1953. He started riding 1920 and rode 4,870 winners from 21,834 mounts before retiring 1954 and taking up training. He rode the winners of all the classic races but only once won the Derby (on Pinza 1953). In 1947 he rode a record 269 winners in a season.

CAREER HIGHLIGHTS

Champion Jockey: 1925, 1927-29, 1931-40, 1942-53
Derby: 1953
Oaks: 1930, 1942
St Leger: 1930, 1937, 1940, 1942, 1944
1,000 Guineas: 1942, 1948, 1951
2,000 Guineas: 1938, 1942, 1947

Richards Viv (Isaac Vivian Alexander) 1952– . West Indian cricketer, captain of the West Indies team 1986–91. He has played for the Leeward Islands and, in the UK, for Somerset and Glamorgan. A prolific run-scorer, he holds the record for the greatest number of runs made in test cricket in one calendar year (1,710 runs in 1976). He retired from international cricket after the West Indies tour of England in 1991.

CAREER HIGHLIGHTS

all first-class cricket (to start of 1993 season)
runs: 34,977
average: 49.40
best: 322 (Somerset v. Warwickshire 1985)
wickets: 219
average: 44.90
best: 5 for 88 (West Indies v. Queensland 1981-82)
test cricket
appearances: 121
runs: 8,540
average: 50.23
best: 291 (v. England 1976)
wickets: 32
average: 61.37
best: 2 for 17 (v. Pakistan 1988)

Rodnina Irina 1949– . Soviet ice skater. Between 1969 and 1980 she won 23 world, Olympic, and European gold medals in pairs competitions. Her partners were Alexei Ulanov and then Alexsandr Zaitsev.

CAREER HIGHLIGHTS

Olympic champion: 1972, 1976, 1980
world champion: 1969-78
European champion: 1969-78

Ruth Babe (George Herman) 1895–1948. US baseball player, regarded by many as the greatest of all time. He played in ten World Series and hit 714 home runs, a record that stood from 1935 to 1974 and led to the nickname 'Sultan of Swat'. He is still the holder of the record for most bases in a season: 457 in 1921. Yankee Stadium is known as 'the house that Ruth built' because of the money he brought into the club.

CAREER HIGHLIGHTS

games: 2,503
runs: 2,174
home runs: 714
average: .342
World Series wins: 1915–16, 1918, 1923, 1927–28, 1932

Sawchuk Terry (Terrance Gordon) 1929–1970. Canadian ice-hockey player, often considered the greatest goaltender of all time. He played for Detroit, Boston, Toronto, Los Angeles, and New York Rangers 1950–67, and holds the National Hockey League record of 103 shut-outs (games in which he did not concede a goal).

Scudamore Peter 1958– . English National Hunt jockey who was champion jockey 1982 (shared with John Francome) and from 1986 to 1992. In 1988–89 he rode a record 221 winners. In April 1993 he announced his retirement from the sport with a world record of 1,677 winners.

Seles Monica 1973– . Yugoslavian tennis player who won her first Grand Slam title, the French Open, at the age of 16. She dominated the major events in 1991 but withdrew from Wimbledon and consequently missed the chance to achieve the Grand Slam. In the same year she became the youngest woman player ever to achieve number-one ranking. In 1993 she was stabbed by a spectator during the Hamburg Open. The enforced break from the game meant her missing most major tournaments.

CAREER HIGHLIGHTS

US Open
singles: 1991, 1992
French Open
singles: 1990–92
Australian Open
singles: 1991, 1992, 1993

Senna Ayrton 1960– . Brazilian motor-racing driver. He had his first Grand Prix win in the 1985 Portuguese Grand Prix, and progressed to the world driver's title in 1988, 1990, and 1991. By the beginning of the 1993 season he had 36 wins in 142 starts.

Shilton Peter 1949– . English international footballer, an outstanding goalkeeper, who has set records for the highest number of Football League appearances (991 to start of 1993–94 season) and England caps (125). First capped by England 1970 he announced his retirement from international football in 1990, after the England–West Germany World Cup semifinal. In 1992 he became manager of Plymouth Argyle.

Shoemaker Willie (William Lee) 1931– . US jockey whose career, from 1949 to 1990, was outstandingly successful. He rode 8,833 winners from 40,351 mounts and his earnings exceeded $123 million. He retired Feb 1990 after finishing fourth on Patchy Groundfog at Santa Anita, California.

CAREER HIGHLIGHTS

Kentucky Derby: 1955, 1959, 1965, 1986
Preakness Stakes: 1963, 1967
Belmont Stakes: 1957, 1959, 1962, 1967, 1975
leading US money winner: 1951, 1953–54, 1958–64

Sobers Gary (Garfield St Aubrun) 1936– . West Indian test cricketer. One of the game's great all-rounders, he holds the record for the highest test innings (365 not out). Sobers played English county cricket with Nottinghamshire and while playing for them against Glamorgan at Swansea in 1968, he established a world record by scoring six 6s in one over. He played for the West Indies 93 times.

CAREER HIGHLIGHTS

all first-class cricket
runs: 28,315
average: 54.87
best: 365 not out West Indies v. Pakistan 1957–58
wickets: 1,043
average: 27.74
best: 9-49 West Indies v. Kent 1966
test cricket
runs: 8,032
average: 57.78
best: 365 not out v. Pakistan 1957–58
wickets: 235
average: 34.03
best: 6-73 v. Australia 1968–69

Spitz Mark Andrew 1950– . US swimmer. He won a record seven gold medals at the 1972 Olympic Games, all in world record times. He won 11 Olympic medals in total (four in 1968) and set 26 world records between 1967 and 1972. After retiring in 1972 he became a movie actor, two of his films being elected candidates for 'The Worst of Hollywood'.

CAREER HIGHLIGHTS

Olympic medals
1968: gold – 400 metres freestyle relay, 800 metres freestyle relay; silver – 100 metres butterfly; bronze – 100 metres freestyle
1972: gold – 100 metres freestyle, 200 metres freestyle, 100 metres butterfly, 200 metres butterfly, 400 metres freestyle relay, 800 metres freestyle relay, 400 metres medley relay

---

Stewart Jackie (John Young) 1939– . Scottish motor-racing driver. Until surpassed by Alain Prost in 1987, Stewart held the record for the most Formula One Grand Prix wins (27). With manufacturer Ken Tyrrell, Stewart built up one of the sport's great partnerships. His last race was the 1973 Canadian Grand Prix. He pulled out of the next race (which would have been his 100th) because of the death of his team-mate François Cevert. He is now a motor-racing commentator.

CAREER HIGHLIGHTS

world champion
1969 Matra
1971 Tyrrell
1973 Tyrrell
Formula One Grand Prix
races: 99
wins: 27
first: 1965 (South African Grand Prix; BRM)
last: 1973 (Canadian Grand Prix; Tyrrell)

Thompson Daley (Francis Morgan) 1958– . English decathlete who has broken the world record four times since winning the Commonwealth Games decathlon title 1978. He has won two more Commonwealth titles (1982, 1986), two Olympic gold medals (1980, 1984), three European medals (silver 1978; gold 1982, 1986), and a world title (1983).

Torvill and Dean English ice-dance champions Jayne Torvill (1957–) and Christopher Dean (1959–). They won the world title four times 1981–84 and were the 1984 Olympic champions. They turned professional upon ending their competitive careers.

Tyson Mike (Michael Gerald) 1966– . US heavyweight boxer, undisputed world champion from Aug 1987 to Feb 1990 (when he was defeated by James 'Buster' Douglas). He won the World Boxing Council heavyweight title 1986 when he beat Trevor Berbick to become the youngest world heavyweight champion ever. He beat James 'Bonecrusher' Smith for the World Boxing Association title 1987 and later that year became the first undisputed champion since 1978 when he beat Tony Tucker for the International Boxing Federation title. Of Tyson's first 25 opponents, 15 were knocked out in the first round. In 1992 he was imprisoned for rape.

Witt Katarina 1965– . German ice-skater. She was 1984 Olympic champion (representing East Germany) and by 1990 had won four world titles (1984–85, 1987–88) and six consecutive European titles (1983–88). After four years as a professional she returned to competitive skating in 1993.

Woosnam Ian 1958– . Welsh golfer who, in 1987, became the first UK player to win the World Match-Play Championship. He has since won many tournaments, including the World Cup 1987, World Match-Play 1990, and US Masters 1991. Woosnam was Europe's leading money-winner in 1987 (as a result of winning the $1 million Sun City Open in South Africa) and again in 1990. He was ranked Number One in the world for 50 weeks in 1991–92.

CAREER HIGHLIGHTS

Ryder Cup (individual): 1983, 1985, 1987, 1989, 1991
Ryder Cup (team): 1985,1987, tie 1989
US Masters: 1991
World Match-Play Championship: 1987, 1990
World Cup (individual): 1987, 1991
World Cup (team): 1987 (Wales)

Governing bodies of Olympic sports affiliated to the British Olympic Association

archery: Grand National Archery Society, Seventh Street, National Agricultural Centre, Stoneleigh, Kenilworth, Warwickshire CV8 2LG Tel: (0203) 696631

athletics: British Athletic Federation, Edgbaston House, 3 Duchess Place, Hagley Road, Edgbaston, Birmingham B16 8NM Tel: 021-456 4050

badminton: British Badminton Olympic Committee, 2 Broadstrood, Loughton, Essex IG10 2SE Tel: 081-508 7218

baseball: British Baseball Federation, 19 Troutsdale Grove, Southcoates Lane, Hull HU9 3SD Tel: (0482) 792337

basketball: British and Irish Basketball Federation, The Carnegie National Sports Development Centre, Beckett Park, Leeds LS6 3QS Tel: (0532) 832600 x 3574

bobsleigh: British Bobsleigh Association, Springfield House, Woodstock Road, Couldsdon, Surrey CR5 3HS Tel: (0737) 555152

boxing: British Amateur Boxing Association, Francis House, Francis Street, London SW1P 1DE Tel: 071-828 8568

canoeing: British Canoe Union, John Dudderidge House, Adbolton Lane, West Bridgford, Nottingham NG2 5AS Tel: (0602) 821100

cycling: British Cycling Federation, 36 Rockingham Road, Kettering, Northamptonshire NN16 8HG Tel: (0536) 412211

equestrianism: British Equestrian Federation, British Equestrian Centre, Stoneleigh, Kenilworth, Warwickshire CV8 2LR Tel: (0203) 696697

fencing: Amateur Fencing Association, 1 Barons Gate, 33–35 Rothschild Road, London W4 5HT Tel: 081-742 3032

football, association: Football Association, 16 Lancaster Gate, London W2 3LW Tel: 071-262 4542

gymnastics: British Amateur Gymnastics Association, Ford Hall, Lilleshall National Sports Centre, Newport, Shropshire TF10 9ND Tel: (0952) 820330

handball: British Handball Association, 60 Church Street, Radcliffe, Manchester M26 8SQ Tel: 061-724 9656

hockey: Great Britain Olympic Hockey Board, Coventry Farmhouse, Hankins Lane, London NW7 3AJ Tel: 081-959 2339

ice hockey: British Ice Hockey Association, 517 Christchurch Road, Boscombe, Bournemouth, Dorset Tel: (0202) 303946

judo: British Judo Association, 7A Rutland Street, Leicester LE1 1RB Tel: (0533) 559669

luge: Great Britain Luge Association, 1 Highfield House, Hampton Bishop, Hereford HR1 4JN Tel: (0432) 353920

pentathlon, modern: Modern Pentathlon Association of Great Britain, Wessex House, Silchester Road, Tadley, Basingstoke, Hampshire Tel: (0734) 810111

rowing: Amateur Rowing Association, The Priory, 6 Lower Mall, London W6 9DJ Tel: 081-748 3632

shooting: Great Britain Target Shooting Federation, Lord Roberts House, Bisley Camp, Brookwood, Woking, Surrey GU24 0NP Tel: (0483) 476969

skating: National Skating Association of Great Britain, 15–27 Gee Street, London EC1V 3RE Tel: 071-253 3824

skiing: British Ski Federation, 258 Main Street, East Calder, Livingston, West Lothian EH53 0EE Tel: (0506) 884343

swimming: Amateur Swimming Federation of Great Britain, Harold Fern House, Derby Square, Loughborough, Leicestershire LE11 0AL Tel: (0509) 230431

table tennis: British Olympic Table Tennis Committee, Third Floor, Queensbury House, Havelock Road, Hastings, East Sussex TN34 1HF Tel: (0424) 722525

tennis, lawn: Lawn Tennis Association, Queens Club, Barons Court, West Kensington, London W14 9EG Tel: 071-385 2366

volleyball: British Volleyball Association, 27 South Road, West Bridgford, Nottingham Tel: (0602) 816324

weightlifting: British Amateur Weightlifters' Association, 3 Iffley Turn, Oxford OX4 4DU Tel: (0865) 778319

wrestling: British Amateur Wrestling Association, 41 Great Clowes Street, Salford, Lancashire M7 9RQ Tel: 061- 832 9209

yachting: Royal Yachting Association, RYA House, Romsey Road, Eastleigh, Hampshire SO5 4YA Tel: (0703) 629962

Other sporting bodies affiliated to the British Olympic Association

athletics: Scottish Amateur Athletic Association, Caledonia House, South Gyle, Edinburgh EH12 9DQ Tel: 031-317 7320

Universities Athletic Union, Suite 36, London Fruit Exchange, Brushfield Street, London E1 6EU Tel: 071-247 3066

Welsh Amateur Athletic Association, Morfa Stadium, Landore, Swansea, West Glamorgan SA1 7DF Tel: (0792) 456237

Women's Amateur Athletic Association, Francis House, Francis Street, London SW1P 1DE Tel: 071-828 4731

boxing: Scottish Amateur Boxing Association, 96 High Street, Lochee, Dundee, Tayside Tel: (0382) 611412

Welsh Amateur Boxing Association, 8 Erw Wen, Rhiwbina, Cardiff, South Glamorgan Tel: (0222) 623506

clay pigeon shooting: Clay Pigeon Shooting Association, 107 Epping New Road, Buckhurst Hill, Essex IG9 5TQ Tel: 081-505 6221

cross-country running: Welsh Cross Country Association, Harries Haunt, 40 Twyni-Teg, Killay, Swansea SA2 7NS

karate: British Karate Federation, Smalldrink, Parsonage Lane, Begelly, Kilgetty, Dyfed SA68 0YL Tel: (0834) 813776

lacrosse: English Lacrosse Union, Winton House, Winton Road, Bowdon, Altrincham, Cheshire WA14 Tel: 061-928 9600

netball: All England Netball Association, Netball House, 9 Paynes Park, Hitchin, Hertfordshire SG5 1EH Tel: (0462) 442344

orienteering: British Orienteering Federation, Riversdale, Dale Road North, Darley Dale, Matlock, Derbyshire DE4 2HX Tel: (0629) 734042

race walking: Race Walking Association, Hustlers, Herds Lane, Shenfield, Brentwood, Essex CM15 0SH

swimming: Scottish Amateur Swimming Association, Holmhills Farm, Greenlees Road, Cambusleng, Glasgow G72 8DT Tel: 041-641 8818

Welsh Amateur Swimming Association, Wales Empire Pool, Wood Street, Cardiff, South Glamorgan Tel: (0222) 342201

taekwondo: British Taekwondo Control Board (WTF), 53 Geary Road, London NW10 1HJ Tel: 081-450 3818

tenpin bowling: British Tenpin Bowling Association, 114 Balfour Road, Ilford, Essex IG1 4JD Tel: 081-478 1745

water skiing: British Water Ski Federation, 390 City Road, London EC1V 2QA Tel: 071-833 2855

Army Sport Control Board Ministry of Defence, Clayton Barracks, Thornhill Road, Aldershot, Hampshire GU11 2BG Tel: (0252) 348569

British Association of Sport and Medicine c/o The National Sports Medicine Institute, Medical College of St Bartholomew's Hospital, Charterhouse Square, London EC1M 6BQ Tel: 071-253 3244

Central Council of Physical Recreation Francis House, Francis Street, London SW1P 1DE Tel: 071-828 3163

Civil Service Sports Council 7–8 Buckingham Place, Bellfield House, High Wycombe, Buckinghamshire Tel: (0494) 461800

TRANSPORT

Air Transport

People first took to the air in balloons and began powered flight in airships, but the history of flying is dominated by the aeroplane. The aeroplane is a development of the model glider, first flown by Sir George Cayley (1773–1857) in 1804. It was not until the invention of the petrol engine that powered flight become feasible. The Wright brothers in the USA first achieved success, when they flew their biplane *Flyer* on 17 Dec 1903. In Europe, France led the way in aviation – the Voisin brothers pioneered aeroplane design and much publicity was attracted by Louis Blériot who crossed the Channel in 1909 and by the Reims air races of that year. The first powered flight in the UK was made by S F Cody in 1908. In 1912 Sopwith and Bristol both built small biplanes.

The stimulus of World War I (1914–18) and the rapid development of the petrol engine led to increased power, and speeds rose to 320 kph/200 mph. Streamlining the body of planes became imperative: the body, wings, and exposed parts were reshaped to reduce drag. Eventually the biplane was superseded by the internally braced monoplane structure – for example, the Hawker Hurricane and Supermarine Spitfire fighters and the Avro Lancaster and Boeing Flying Fortress bombers of World War II (1939–45).

The German Heinkel 178, built 1939, ushered in a new era in aviation. It was the first jet plane, driven, not as all planes before it, with a propeller, but by a jet of hot gases. The first British jet aircraft, the Gloster E.28/39 flew from Cranwell, Lincolnshire, on 15 May 1941, powered by a jet engine invented by Frank Whittle. Twin-jet Meteor fighters were in use by the end of the war. The rapid development of the jet plane led to enormous increases in power and speed until air-compressibility effects were felt near the speed of sound, which at first seemed to be the limit for flight speed (the sound barrier). To exceed supersonic speed, streamlining only the aircraft body became insufficient: wings were swept back, engines buried in wings and tail units, and bodies were even eliminated in all-wing delta designs.

In the 1950s the first jet airliners, such as the Comet, were introduced into service. Today jet planes dominate both military and civilian aviation, although many light planes still use piston engines and propellers. The late 1960s saw the introduction of the jumbo jet, and in 1976 the Anglo-French Concorde, which makes a transatlantic crossing in under three hours, came into commercial service.

During the 1950s and 1960s research was done on V/STOL (vertical and/or short take-off and landing) aircraft. The British Harrier jet fighter has been the only VTOL aircraft to achieve commercial success, but STOL technology has fed into subsequent generations of aircraft. The 1960s and 1970s also saw the development of variable geometry ('swing-wing') aircraft, whose wings can be swept back in flight to achieve higher speeds. In the 1980s much progress has been made in 'fly-by-wire' aircraft with computer-aided controls.

International partnerships have developed both civilian and military aircraft. The Panavia Tornado is a joint project of British, German, and Italian aircraft companies. It is an advanced swing-wing craft with multiple military functions – interception, strike, ground support, and reconnaissance. The Airbus is a wide-bodied airliner built jointly by companies from France, Germany, the UK, the Netherlands, and Spain.

aeroplane heavier-than-air craft supported in flight by fixed wings: it may be unpowered (a glider) or powered, when it is propelled by the thrust of a jet engine or propeller. It must be designed aerodynamically, since streamlining ensures maximum flight efficiency. The shape of a plane depends on its use and operating speed – aircraft operating at well below the speed of sound need not be as streamlined as supersonic aircraft.

Efficient streamlining prevents the formation of shock waves over the body surface and wings, which would cause instability and power loss. The wing of an aeroplane has the cross-sectional shape of an aerofoil, being broad and curved at the front, flat underneath, curved on top, and tapered to a sharp point at the rear. The wings' shape is such that air passing above them is speeded up, reducing pressure below atmospheric pressure, while that above is slowed. This results in a force acting vertically upwards, called lift, which counters the aircraft's weight. In level flight, lift equals weight. The wings develop sufficient lift to support the plane when they move quickly through the air. The thrust that causes propulsion comes from the reaction to the air stream accel-

Virgin strikes back

UK entrepreneur Richard Branson's airline Virgin launched its latest attack on British Airways in May 1993 by suing BA over the misuse of computer information. The writ was the first move in an elaborate strategy by Virgin that could see the two airlines confront each other in British, European, and US courts.

The allegations suggest that it is easier to gain access to supposedly restricted computer information than the computer industry would have us believe. Virgin's writ claims BA gained access to details of Virgin's passengers and other confidential information from the computers of Virgin's handling agent at Gatwick Airport, England. It is also alleged that BA employees impersonated Virgin employees to persuade the handling agents into releasing sensitive information. It seems that, when faced with a winning smile or a persuasive chat-up, computer security may easily fall apart.

flight: chronology

1783	First human flight, by Jean F Pilâtre de Rozier and the Marquis d'Arlandes, in Paris, using a hot-air balloon made by Joseph and Etienne Montgolfier; first ascent in a hydrogen-filled balloon by Jacques Charles and M N Robert in Paris.
1785	Jean-Pierre Blanchard and John J Jeffries made the first balloon crossing of the English Channel.
1852	Henri Giffard flew the first steam-powered airship over Paris.
1853	George Cayley flew the first true aeroplane, a model glider 1.5 m/5 ft long.
1891-96	Otto Lilienthal piloted a glider in flight.
1903	First powered and controlled flight of a heavier-than-air craft (aeroplane) by Orville Wright, at Kitty Hawk, North Carolina, USA.
1908	First powered flight in the UK by Samuel Cody.
1909	Louis Blériot flew across the English Channel in 36 minutes.
1914-18	World War I stimulated improvements in speed and power.
1919	First E–W flight across the Atlantic by Albert C Read, using a flying boat; first nonstop flight across the Atlantic E–W by John William Alcock and Arthur Whitten Brown in 16 hours, 27 minutes; first complete flight from Britain to Australia by Ross Smith and Keith Smith.
1923	Juan de la Cieva flew the first autogiro with a rotating wing.
1927	Charles Lindbergh made the first W–E solo nonstop flight across the Atlantic.
1928	First transpacific flight, from San Francisco to Brisbane, by Charles Kinsford Smith and C T P Ulm.
1930	Frank Whittle patented the jet engine; Amy Johnson became the first woman to fly solo from England to Australia.
1937	The first fully pressurized aircraft, the Lockheed XC-35, came into service.
1939	Erich Warsitz flew the first Heinkel jet plane, in Germany; Igor Sikorsky designed the first helicopter, with a large main rotor and a smaller tail rotor.
1939-45	World War II – developments included the Hawker Hurricane and Supermarine Spitfire Fighters, and Avro Lancaster and Boeing Flying Fortress bombers.
1947	A rocket-powered plane, the Bell X-1, was the first aircraft to fly faster than the speed of sound.
1949	The de Havilland Comet, the first jet airliner, entered service; James Gallagher made the first nonstop round-the-world flight, in a Boeing Superfortress.
1953	The first vertical takeoff aircraft, the Rolls-Royce 'Flying Bedstead', was tested.
1968	The world's first supersonic airliner, the Russian TU-144, flew for the first time.
1970	The Boeing 747 jumbo jet entered service, carrying 500 passengers.
1976	Anglo-French Concorde, making a transatlantic crossing in under three hours, came into commercial service. A Lockheed SR-17A, piloted by Eldon W Joersz and George T Morgan, set the world air-speed record of 3,529.56 kmh/2,193.167 mph over Beale Air Force Base, California, USA.
1978	A US team made the first transatlantic crossing by balloon, in the helium-filled *Double Eagle II*.
1979	First crossing of the English Channel by a human-powered aircraft, *Gossamer Albatross*, piloted by Bryan Allen.
1981	The solar-powered *Solar Challenger* flew across the English Channel, from Paris to Kent, taking 5 hours for the 262 km/162.8 mi journey.
1986	Dick Rutan and Jeana Yeager made the first nonstop flight around the world without refuelling, piloting *Voyager*, which completed the flight in 9 days, 3 minutes, 44 seconds.
1987	Richard Branson and Per Lindstrand made the first transatlantic crossing by hot-air balloon, in *Virgin Atlantic Challenger*.
1988	*Daedelus*, a human-powered craft piloted by Kanellos Kanellopoulos, flew 118 km/74 mi across the Aegean Sea.
1991	Richard Branson and Per Lindstrand crossed the Pacific Ocean in the hot-air balloon *Virgin Otsouka Pacific Flyer* from the southern tip of Japan to NW Canada in 46 hours, 15 minutes.
1992	US engineers demonstrated a model radio-controlled ornithopter, the first aircraft to be successfully propelled and manoeuvred by flapping wings.

erated backwards by the propeller or the gases shooting backwards from the jet exhaust. In flight the engine thrust must overcome the air resistance, or ◊drag. Drag depends on frontal area (large in the case of an airliner; small in the case of a fighter plane) and shape (drag coefficient); in level flight, drag equals thrust. The drag is reduced by streamlining the plane, resulting in higher speed and reduced fuel consumption for a given power. Carrying less fuel for a given distance means a larger payload (cargo or passengers) can be carried.

Planes are constructed using light but strong aluminium alloys such as duralumin (with copper, magnesium, and so on). For supersonic planes special stainless steel and titanium may be used in areas subjected to high heat loads. The structure of the plane, or the airframe (wings, fuselage, and so on) consists of a surface skin of alloy sheets supported at intervals by struts known as ribs and stringers. The structure is bonded together by riveting or by powerful adhesives such as ◊epoxy resins. In certain critical areas, which have to withstand very high stresses (such as the wing roots), body panels are machined from solid metal for extra strength.

Fastest aeroplane – the Lockheed SR-71, holder of the world air-speed record of 3,529 kph/2,193 mph (over Mach 3.3).

Missile technology to aid airliners

Technology from cruise missiles could stop airliners from flying into mountains. In 1992 there were 26 accidents of this type, known in the trade as 'controlled flight into terrain'. Over 80% of all civil aviation deaths are caused by aircraft flying into mountains or cliffs even though there is nothing wrong with their navigation or control systems.

A new initiative aims at improving the current generation of ground proximity warning systems (GPWS) using cruise missile and satellite technology. Current GPWS use radio altimeters and other aircraft instruments to calculate whether the aircraft is dropping too rapidly during a landing, or when the ground is rising too rapidly during level flight. However, these devices only monitor the ground directly beneath the aircraft and cannot detect a cliff or mountain straight ahead. Also, they may be triggered by electricity pylons or buildings on the flight path, and give false alarms.

A British company is preparing a database containing digital maps of the terrain around all airports. The new GPWS would compare the information from altimeters with the information in the database and establish the aircraft's position. On feeding the aircraft's course into the system, it would calculate if there was danger ahead. The technology is similar to that used by cruise missiles to find their way. The new GPWS will be supplemented by a satellite system that locates the aircraft and switches on the digital system when the aircraft approaches the airport.

Fastest airliner – Concorde, which can cruise at up to 2,333 kph/1,450 mph (Mach 2.2).

Largest airliner – Boeing 747, with a wingspan of 59.6 m/195.7 ft and a length of 70.7 m/231.8 ft.

Largest volume aeroplane – the Guppy-201, with a usable volume of 1,104 cu m/39,000 cu ft.

airship a power-driven balloon. All airships have streamlined envelopes or hulls, which contain the inflation gas, and are either non-rigid, semi-rigid, or rigid. In 1900, Count Ferdinand von Zeppelin pioneered the rigid type, named after him, which were later used for bombing raids on the UK in World War I. The destruction by fire of the British R101 in 1930 halted airship building in Britain, but the Germans continued and built the 248-m/812-ft-long *Hindenburg*. However, this airship exploded at Lakehurst, New Jersey 1937, marking the effective end of airship travel. The early airships were vulnerable because they used hydrogen for inflation. It is the lightest gas, but highly flammable. After World War II, interest grew in airships using the nonflammable gas helium. They cause minimum noise, can lift enormous loads, and are economical on fuel. In 1987, the US Navy commissioned the British airship industry to build large numbers of airships for use in coastguard patrol. In recent years, airships have also been used commercially for the promotion of products and services.

balloon bag or envelope of impermeable fabric that rises from the ground when filled with a gas that is lighter than the surrounding air. In 1783, the first successful human ascent was piloted by Pilâtre de Rozier in Paris, in a hot-air balloon designed by the Montgolfier brothers. During the French Revolution balloons were used for observation; in World War II they were used to defend London against low-flying aircraft. Balloons continue in use for sport, and as an economical means of meteorological, infrared, gamma-ray, and ultraviolet observation. The first transatlantic crossing by gas balloon (from Presque Isle, Maine to Miserey, France) was made 11–17 Aug 1978 by a US team.

helicopter an aircraft that achieves both lift and propulsion by means of a rotary wing, or rotor, on top of the fuselage. It can take off and land vertically, move in any direction, or remain stationary in the air. Igor Sikorsky built the first practical single rotor craft, in the USA 1939. The rotor of a helicopter has two or more blades, which are of aerofoil cross-section, like an aeroplane's wings. Lift and propulsion are achieved by angling the blades as they rotate. A single-rotor helicopter must also have a small tail rotor to counter the tendency of the body to spin in the opposite direction to the main rotor. Twin-rotor helicopters, like the Boeing Chinook, have their rotors turning in opposite directions, and this prevents the body from spinning.

Helicopters are now widely used in passenger service, rescue missions on land and sea, police pursuits and traffic control, firefighting, and agriculture. In war they carry troops and equipment into difficult terrain, make aerial reconnaissance and attacks, and carry wounded to aid stations. Helicopters are increasingly being associated with naval aircraft carriers, as many as 30 helicopters being used on larger carriers, in combination with V/STOL aircraft, such as Harriers. The helicopter may possess depth charges and homing torpedoes guided to submarine or surface targets beyond the carrier's attack range. It may also use dunking sonar to find targets beyond the carrier's own radar horizon.

jet propulsion a method of propulsion in which an object is propelled in one direction by a jet, or stream of gases, moving in the other. This follows from Newton's celebrated third law of motion 'to every action, there is an equal and opposite reaction'. The most widespread application of the jet principle is in the jet engine, the commonest kind of aero-engine.

The jet engine is a type of gas turbine. Air, after passing through a forward-facing intake, is compressed by a compressor, or fan, and fed into a combustion chamber. Fuel (usually kerosene) is sprayed in and ignited. The hot gas produced expands rapidly rearwards, spinning a turbine that drives the compressor before being finally ejected from a rearward-facing tail pipe, or nozzle, at very high speed. Reaction to the jet of gases streaming backwards produces a propulsive thrust forwards, which acts on the aircraft through its engine-mountings, not from any pushing of the hot gas stream against the static air.

rocket a projectile driven by the reaction of gases produced by a fast-burning fuel. Unlike the jet engine, which is also a reaction engine, the rocket engine carries its own oxygen supply to burn its fuel and is totally independent of any surrounding atmosphere. As rockets are the only form of propulsion available that can function in a vacuum, they are essential to the exploration of outer space. Multistage rockets have to be used for this, consisting of a number of rockets joined together. In the 1990s, the most powerful rocket system is the Russian Energiya, capable of placing 100 tonnes/110 tons into low Earth orbit.

Rail Transport

Tracks to carry goods waggons were in use at collieries in the 18th century, but the first practical public passenger service was that between Stockton and Darlington in 1825, under the power of Stephenson's engine 'Locomotion'. A railway boom ensued, and railways were the major form of land transport for passengers and goods until after World War II when the private car, coach services, internal air services, and road haulage door-to-door destroyed their monopoly. In the UK the railways (known as British Rail from 1965) were nationalized in 1948, and the network shrank steadily. In the USA and Canada railways made the 19th-century exploitation of the central and western territories possible, and in the USA underpinned the victory of the north in the Civil War, the 'Railway War'.

In countries with less developed road systems and large areas of difficult terrain, the railway is still important, as in India, China, South America, and Russia. Electrification, or the use of diesel electric engines, has superseded the steam engine in most countries, and there has been some revival in the popularity of the train for longer distance 'inter-city' services.

rail transport: chronology

1500s Tramways – wooden tracks along which trolleys ran – were in use in mines.

1804 Richard Trevithick built the first steam locomotive and ran it on a track at the Pen-y-darren ironworks in South Wales.

1825 British engineer George Stephenson built the first public railway to carry steam trains – the Stockton and Darlington line.

1829 Stephenson designed his locomotive *Rocket*, which trounced its rivals at the Rainhill trials.

1830 Stephenson completed the Liverpool and Manchester Railway, the first steam passenger line; the first US-built locomotive, *Best Friend of Charleston*, went into service on the South Carolina Railroad.

1835 Germany pioneered steam railways in Europe, using *Der Adler*, a locomotive built by Stephenson.

1863 Robert Fairlie, a Scot, patented a locomotive with pivoting driving bogies, allowing tight curves in the track (this was later applied in the Garratt locomotives); London opened the world's first underground railway, powered by steam.

1869 The first US transcontinental railway was completed at Promontory, Utah, when the Union Pacific and the Central Pacific railroads met; George Westinghouse of the USA invented the compressed-air brake.

1879 Werner von Siemens demonstrated an electric train in Germany; Volk's Electric Railway along the Brighton seafront was the world's first public electric railway.

1883 Charles Lartique built the first monorail, in Ireland.

1885 The trans-Canada continental railway was completed, from Montreal in the east to Port Moody, British Columbia, in the west.

1890 The first electric underground railway opened in London.

1901 The world's most successful monorail, the Wuppertal Schwebebahn, went into service.

1912 The first diesel locomotive took to the rails in Germany.

1938 The British steam locomotive *Mallard* set a steam-rail speed record of 201 kph/125 mph.

1941 Swiss Federal Railways introduced a gas-turbine locomotive.

1964 Japan National Railways inaugurated the 512- km/320-mi New Tokaido line between Osaka and Tokyo, on which run the 210-kph/130-mph 'bullet' trains.

1973 British Rail's High Speed Train (HST) set a diesel rail speed record of 229 kph/143 mph.

1979 Japan National Railways' maglev test vehicle ML-500 attained a speed of 517 kph/321 mph.

1981 France's TGV superfast trains began operation between Paris and Lyons, regularly attaining a peak speed of 270 kph/168 mph.

1987 British Rail set a new diesel-traction speed record of 238.9 kph/148.5 mph, on a test run between Darlington and York; France and the UK began work on the Channel Tunnel, a railway link connecting the two countries, running beneath the English Channel. Japanese maglev MUV- 001 test train reaches speed with passengers of 400 kph/249 mph.

1988 The West German Intercity Experimental train reached 405 kph/252 mph on test run between Würzburg amd Fulda.

1990 A new rail-speed record of 515 kph/320 mph was established by a French TGV train, on a stretch of line between Tours and Paris.

1991 British and French twin tunnels met 23 km/14 mi out to sea to form the Channel tunnel.

1992 Trams returned to the streets of Manchester, England, after an absence of 40 years; towns in France and the US followed suit.

Fuel economy on the road

A small French car, called the Micro-Joule, recently travelled 2,630 km/1,634 mi on a single litre of petrol (equivalent to over 8,000 miles per gallon) at Silverstone race track, near Towcester, Northamptonshire, England. The distance breaks the world record distance for a litre of fuel held since 1988 by a Honda. The record-breaking Micro-Joule only weighs 36 kg/80 lb and has two tiny 32cc engines. The driver lies flat on the floor in the low, streamlined cab. An important feature of the design was special tubeless tyres made for extra speed by Michelin. The car was the result of eight years' work by pupils and teachers at Saint Joseph school in Nantes, in west France, helped by Michelin and the French aerospace firm Aérospatiale.

No one expects this sort of fuel economy to be matched, or even approached, in the family car, but production cars are becoming more efficient: between 1978 and 1987 the average fuel consumption of a new car improved by nearly 25%. Currently the average fuel consumption of a new car is 29 miles per gallon. Cars under development by Ford, Volkswagen, Peugeot, Toyota, and General Motors will be capable of between 80 and 120 miles per gallon.

Research into fuel economy is concentrating on three areas: aerodynamics and weight, engines, and electronics. The aerodynamics of a car is the most obvious focus for reducing fuel consumption. Cars are becoming sleeker and more streamlined each year. The average drag coefficient of cars has fallen from 0.45 in 1973 to around 0.35, and could be halved again by the end of the decade. A 10% reduction in drag results in a 3% saving in fuel. The Fiat CNR Energetica 2 with 30% less drag than the Fiat Tempra produces a 17% fuel saving overall (with the same engine and gearbox in each car). At 120 kph/75 mph, there is a 35% fuel saving.

Weight savings call for lighter, stronger materials. The Honda NSX sports car produces excellent performance on a relatively modest engine thanks to the use of aluminium rather than steel. Weight savings achieved by using aluminium can reduce a vehicle's weight by about a quarter and a similar reduction in fuel consumption. Toyota have shown a small two-seater city car, making extensive use of aluminium and magnesium, which weighed 450 kg/1,000 lb – less than half the weight of a family hatchback. Racing cars use exotic carbon fibre and other composite material panels to form very light and strong body sections. The drawback is that these materials are very expensive.

Better engines offer potential for fuel savings of between 5% and 15%. The diesel engine has built-in fuel economy over the petrol engine, because fuel combustion using compression is more efficient. Fuel injection also improves economy over the petrol engine. The most economical cars today are generally small diesels such as the Daihatsu Charade, the Citroen AX140, and Rover's Montego Diesel, all of which can do over 60 miles per gallon. The lean-burn engine uses higher air-to-fuel ratios – 20: 1 compared with 15:1 in a standard engine – and so offers better fuel economy. However, at these ratios catalytic converters are ineffective and EC pollution standards cannot be met. Toyota, Honda, and Mitsubishi have developed electronic engine control systems, which switch the engine to lean-burn at low power outputs. These systems give fuel economies which approach those of the diesel engine while meeting emission regulations.

Electronic control can improve the fuel economy of any engine. In a diesel, accurate control of the fuel injection timing and rate can reduce exhaust pollution and noise. In lean-burn and two-stroke engines, precise control of ignition timing and the air–fuel mixture is necessary for optimum economy. Electronic engine-management systems for petrol engines have been developed by Ford and Saab. The Ford system, installed in the Zeta engine in the new Escort and Mondeo, has a microprocessor or computer chip that can perform 1.25 million computations each second. The engine has 10 sensors that monitor engine performance, and the temperature and oxygen content of the exhaust. The system controls the fuel injection, spark timing, idle speed, and compensates for wear and ageing. It even allows for changes in atmospheric pressure. The Saab system is the most powerful engine control system ever developed for a mass-produced car. Its microprocessor is more powerful than the computers used during the Apollo mission to send men to the Moon. It can perform two million calculations each second. In the Saab, the driver may press down on the accelerator, but the control system decides the most efficient way of speeding up, even choosing the gear to be in.

PL

The 1970s saw diesel high-speed trains (HSTs) introduced in the UK, followed by super-fast networks in Japan and France.

monorail a railway that runs on a single (mono) rail. It was invented in 1882 to carry light loads, and when run by electricity was called a ***telpher***. The most successful monorail, the Wuppertal Schwebebahn, has been running in Germany since 1901. It is a suspension monorail, where the passenger cars hang from an arm fixed to a trolley that runs along the rail. Today most monorails are of the straddle type, where the passenger cars run on top of the rail. They are used to transport passengers between terminals at some airports – as at Birmingham, where the monorail works on the maglev (magnetic levitation) principle.

tramway a transport system for use in cities, by which wheeled vehicles run along parallel rails. It originated in collieries in the 18th century. The earliest passenger system was established in 1832, in New York, and by the 1860s horse-drawn trams plied in London and Liverpool. Trams are now powered either by electric conductor rails below ground, or conductor arms connected to overhead wires, but their use on public roads is very limited because of their lack of manoeuvrability. Greater flexibility is achieved with the ***trolleybus***, similarly powered by conductor arms overhead but without tracks. In the 1990s both trams and trolley buses were being revived in some areas. Both vehicles have the advantage of being nonpolluting to the local environment.

Road Transport

Specially constructed, reinforced tracks became necessary with the invention of wheeled vehicles in about 3000 BC and most ancient civilizations had some form of road network. The Romans developed engineering techniques that were not equalled for another 1,400 years. Until the late 18th century most European roads were haphazardly maintained, making winter travel difficult. In the UK the turnpike system of collecting tolls created some improvement. The Scottish engineers Thomas Telford and John McAdam introduced sophisticated construction methods in the early 19th century. Recent developments have included durable surface compounds and machinery for rapid ground preparation.

The world's top car producers (1992)

Company	*Country*	*Worldwide production (m vehicles)*
General Motors	USA	7.0
Ford	USA	5.4
Toyota	Japan	4.7
Volkswagen	Germany	3.1
Nissan	Japan	3.1
Fiat	Italy	2.5
Peugeot-Citroën	France	2.1
Honda	Japan	2.0
Mitsubishi Motors	Japan	1.9
Renault	France	1.8
Mazda	Japan	1.6
Chrysler	USA	1.5

Source: Automotive News

bicycle a pedal-driven two-wheeled vehicle. It consists of a metal frame mounted on two large wire-spoked wheels, with handlebars in front and a seat between the front and back wheels. The first pedal-bicycle was invented by Kirkpatrick Macmillan, a Scot, in about 1840, pneumatic tyres being added from 1846, and by 1888 these had been improved by J B Dunlop to boost the cycling craze of the turn of the century. Design changes were then minor until the small-wheeled Moulton bicycle appeared after World War II. The bicycle is an energy-efficient, nonpolluting form of transport and it is estimated that 800 million bicycles are in use throughout the world – outnumbering cars three to one. China, India, Denmark, and the Netherlands are countries with a high use of bicycles.

car a small self-propelled vehicle able to be run and be steered on normal roads. Most are four-wheeled and have water-cooled, piston-type internal-combustion engines fuelled by petrol or diesel.

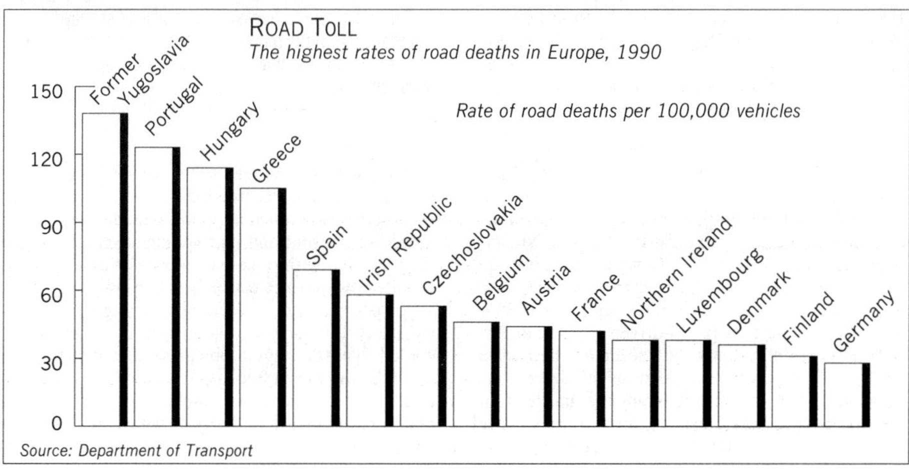

car: chronology

1769 Nicholas-Joseph Cugnot in France built a steam tractor.
1860 Jean Etienne Lenoir built a gas-fuelled internal-combustion engine.
1831 The British government passed the 'Red Flag' Act, requiring a man to precede a 'horseless carriage' with a red flag.
1876 Nikolaus August Otto improved the gas engine, making it a practical power source.
1885 Gottlieb Daimler developed a successful lightweight petrol engine and fitted it to a bicycle to create the prototype of the modern motorbike; Karl Benz fitted his lightweight petrol engine to a three-wheeled carriage to pioneer the motor car.
1886 Gottlieb Daimler fitted his engine to a four-wheeled carriage to produce a four-wheeled motor car.
1891 René Panhard and Emile Levassor established the modern design of cars by putting the engine in front.
1896 Frederick Lanchester introduced epicyclic gearing, which foreshadowed automatic transmission.
1901 The first Mercedes took to the roads. It was the direct ancestor of the modern car; Ransome Olds in the USA introduced mass production on an assembly line.
1906 Rolls-Royce introduced the legendary Silver Ghost, which established their reputation for superlatively engineered cars.
1908 Henry Ford used assembly-line production to manufacture his famous Model T, nicknamed the Tin Lizzie because lightweight steel sheets were used for the body, which looked 'tinny'.
1911 Cadillac introduced the electric starter and dynamo lighting.
1913 Ford introduced the moving conveyor belt to the assembly line, further accelerating production of the Model T.
1920 Duesenberg began fitting four-wheel hydraulic brakes.
1922 The Lancia Lambda featured unitary (all-in-one) construction and independent front suspension.
1928 Cadillac introduced the synchromesh gearbox, greatly facilitating gear changing.
1934 Citroën pioneered front-wheel drive in their 2CV model.
1936 Fiat introduced their baby car, the Topolino, 500 cc.
1938 Germany produced their 'people's car', the Volkswagen 'beetle'.
1948 Jaguar launched the XK120 sports car; Michelin introduced the radial-ply tyre; Goodrich produced the tubeless tyre.
1950 Dunlop announced the disc brake.
1951 Buick and Chrysler in the USA introduced power steering.
1952 Rover's gas-turbine car set a speed record of 243 kph/152 mph.
1954 Bosch introduced fuel-injection for cars.
1955 Citroën produced the advanced DS-19 'shark-front' car with hydropneumatic suspension.
1957 Felix Wankel built his first rotary petrol engine.
1959 BMC (now Rover) introduced the Issigonis-designed Mini, with front-wheel drive, transverse engine, and independent rubber suspension.
1966 California introduced legislation regarding air pollution by cars.
1972 Dunlop introduced safety tyres, which sealed themselves after a burst.
1979 American Sam Barrett exceeded the speed of sound in the rocket-engined *Budweiser Rocket*, reaching 1,190.377 kph/739.666 mph, a speed not officially recognized as a record because of timing difficulties.
1980 The first mass-produced car with four-wheel drive, the Audi Quattro, was introduced; Japanese car production overtook that of the USA.
1981 BMW introduced the on-board computer, which monitored engine performance and indicated to the driver when a service was required.
1983 British driver Richard Noble set an official speed record in the jet-engined *Thrust 2* of 1,019.4 kph/ 633.468 mph; Austin Rover introduced the Maestro, the first car with a 'talking dashboard' that alerted the driver to problems.
1987 The solar-powered *SunRaycer* travelled 3,000 km/1,864 mi from Darwin to Adelaide, Australia, in six days.
1990 Fiat of Italy, and Peugeot of France launched electric passenger cars on the market; the solar-powered *Spirit of Biel-Bienne* won a 3,000-km/1,864-mi race, travelling from Darwin to Adelaide, Australia, in six days.
1991 European Parliament voted to adopt stringent controls of car emissions.

Although it is recorded that in 1479 one Gilles de Dom was paid 25 livres by the treasurer of Antwerp for supplying a self-propelled vehicle, the forerunner of the automobile is generally agreed to be Nicolas-Joseph Cugnot's cumbrous steam carriage 1769, still preserved in Paris. Another Parisian,Étienne Lenoir, made the first gas engine in 1860, and in 1885 Benz built and ran the first petrol-driven motor car. Panhard 1890 (front radiator, engine under the bonnet, sliding-pinion gearbox, wooden ladder-chassis) and Mercedes 1901 (honeycomb radiator, in-line four-cylinder engine, gate-change gearbox, pressed-steel chassis) set the pattern for the modern car.

A typical modern medium-sized saloon car has a semi-monocoque construction in which the body panels, suitably reinforced, support the road loads through independent front and rear sprung suspension, with seats located within the wheelbase for comfort. It is usually powered by a petrol engine using a carburettor to mix petrol and air for feeding to the engine cylinders (typically four or six). The engine is usually water cooled. From the engine, power is transmitted through a clutch to a four- or five-speed gearbox and thence, in a front-engine rear-drive car, through a drive (propeller) shaft to a differential gear, which drives the rear wheels. In a front-engine front-wheel drive car, clutch,

World production of cars in selected countries

	1991	*1988*	*1985*
France	3,187,634	3,223,987	2,632,366
Germany, West	4,659,480	4,346,283	4,166,686
Italy	1,632,904	1,884,313	1,389,156
United Kingdom	1,236,900	1,226,835	1,047,973
Sweden	269,431	407,117	400,748
Canada	890,847	1,024,807	1,077,935
Czechoslovakia	172,726	163,834	177,068
India	209,082	195,079	129,332
Japan*	9,753,069	8,198,400	7,646,816
Korea (South)	1,158,245	872,074	264,458
USA	5,438,579	7,110,728	8,184,821
USSR	1,029,000 e	1,318,866	1,305,000 e

** Excludes 3 wheelers*
e Estimated

Source: Society of Motor Manufacturers & Traders Ltd

gearbox, and final drive are incorporated with the engine unit. An increasing number of high-performance cars are being offered with four-wheel drive. This gives vastly superior roadholding in wet and icy conditions.

internal-combustion engine a heat engine in which fuel is burned inside the engine, contrasting with an external-combustion engine (such as the steam engine) in which fuel is burned in a separate unit. The petrol and diesel engine are both internal-combustion engines. They are reciprocating piston engines in which pistons move up and down in cylinders to effect the engine operating cycle. This may be a four-stroke cycle or a two-stroke cycle. Gas turbines and jet and rocket engines are sometimes also considered to be internal-combustion engines because they burn their fuel inside their combustion chambers.

motorcycle or ***motorbike*** a two-wheeled vehicle propelled by a petrol engine. Gottlieb Daimler, who went on to produce the motorcar, created the first motorcycle when he installed his lightweight petrol engine in a bicycle frame in 1885. The first really successful two-wheel design was devised by Michael and Eugene Werner in France 1901. They adopted the classic motorcycle layout with the engine low down between the wheels. Harley Davidson in the USA and Triumph in the UK began manufacture 1903. Road races like the Isle of Man TT (Tourist Trophy), established in 1907, helped improve motorcycle design and it soon evolved into more or less its present form. Today Japanese motorcycles, such as Honda, Suzuki, Yamaha, and Kawasaki, dominate the world market. The Japanese make a wide variety of machines, from mopeds (lightweights with pedal assistance) to streamlined superbikes capable of speeds up to 250 kph/160 mph.

Sea Transport

People have travelled on and across the seas, for various purposes, throughout history. The Greeks and Phoenicians built wooden ships, propelled by oar or sail, to transport themselves and their goods across the sea. The Romans and Carthaginians built war galleys equipped with rams and several tiers of oars. The oak ships of the Vikings were designed for rough seas, and propelled by oar and sail. The Crusader fleet of Richard the Lionheart was largely of sail. By 1840 iron had largely replaced wood, although fast-sailing clippers, introduced in the mid-1800s, made effective use of wooden planks on iron frames. The USA and the UK experimented with steam propulsion as the 19th century opened. The paddle-wheel-propelled *Comet* appeared 1812, the Canadian *Royal William* crossed the Atlantic 1833, and the English *Great Western* steamed from Bristol to New York 1838. Pettit Smith first used the screw propeller in the *Archimedes* 1839, and after 1850 the paddle-wheel became largely obsolete, its use being confined to the inland waterways, particularly the great American rivers. The introduction of the internal-combustion engine and turbine completed the revolution in propulsion until the advent after World War II of nuclear-powered vessels, chiefly submarines.

More recently hovercraft and wave-piercing catamarans (vessels with a long pointed main hull and two outriggers) have been developed for specialized purposes, particularly as short-distance ferries – for example, the catamarans introduced 1991 by Hoverspeed cross the English Channel from Dover to Calais in 35 min, cruising at a speed of 35 knots (84.5 kph/52.5 mph). Sailing ships in automated form for cargo purposes, and maglev (magnetic-levitation) ships, are in development.

Largest ship – the oil tanker *Happy Giant*, which is 458 m/1,505 ft long, with a beam of 69 m/226 ft. Of 564,739 tonnes deadweight, she was launched 1979.

Longest and largest passenger liner – the *Norway*, launched 1961 as the *France*. Of 70,202 gross tonnage, she measures 316 m/1,035 ft long.

hovercraft a vehicle that rides on a cushion of high-pressure air, free from all contact with the surface beneath, invented by British engineer Christopher Cockerell 1959. Hovercraft need a smooth terrain when operating overland, and are best adapted to use on lakes, sheltered coastal waters, river estuaries and swamps. They are useful in places where harbours have not been established. Large hovercraft (SR-N4) operate a swift car-ferry service across the English Channel, taking only about 35 minutes between Dover and Calais.

hydrofoil boat a boat whose hull rises out of the water when it travels at speed. The boat gets its lift from a set of hydrofoils, wings which are partially submerged underwater. The hydrofoils develop lift in the water in much the same way that aeroplane wings develop lift in the air, enabling the boat to skim the water's surface.

jetfoil an advanced type of hydrofoil boat built by Boeing, propelled by water jets. It features horizontal, fully submerged hydrofoils fore and aft, and has a sophisticated computerized control system to maintain its stability in all waters. Jetfoils have been in service worldwide since 1975. A jetfoil service currently operates between Dover and Ostend, with a passage time of 1 hr 40 min.

sea transport: chronology

8000–7000 BC	Reed boats developed in Mesopotamia and Egypt; dug-out canoes used in NW Europe.
4000–3000 BC	Egyptians used single-masted square-rigged ships on Nile.
1200 BC	Phoenicians built keeled boats with hulls of wooden planks.
1st century BC	Chinese invented the rudder.
AD 200	Chinese built ships with several masts.
200–300	Arabs and Romans developed fore-and-aft rigging that allowed boats to sail across the direction of wind.
800–900	Square-rigged Viking longboats crossed the North Sea to Britain, the Faroe Islands, and Iceland.
1090	Chinese invented the magnetic compass.
1400–1500	Three-masted ships devleoped in western Europe, stimulating voyages of exploration.
1620	Dutch engineer Cornelius Drebbel invented the submarine.
1776	US engineer David Bushnell built a handpowered submarine, *Turtle*, with buoyancy tanks.
1777	The first boat with an iron hull built in Yorkshire, England.
1783	French engineer Jouffroy d'Abbans built the first paddle-driven steam boat.
1802	Scottish engineer William Symington launched the first stern paddle-wheel steamer *Charlotte Dundas*.
1836	The screw propeller was patented, by Francis Pettit Smith in the UK.
1838	British engineer Isambard Kingdom Brunel's *Great Western*, the first steamship built for crossing the Atlantic, sailed from Bristol to New York in 15 days.
1845	*Great Britain*, also built by Isambard Kingdom Brunel, became the first propeller-driven iron ship to cross the Atlantic.
1845	The first clipper ship, *Rainbow*, was launched in the USA.
1863	*Plongeur*, the first submarine powered by an air-driven engine was launched in France.
1866	The British clippers *Taeping* and *Ariel* sailed, laden with tea, from China to London in 99 days.
1886	German engineer Gottlieb Daimler built the first boat powered by an internal-combustion engine.
1897	English engineer Charles Parson fitted a steam turbine to *Turbinia*, making it the fastest boat of the time.
1900	Irish-American John Philip Holland designed the first modern submarine *Holland VI*, fitted with an electric motor for underwater sailing and an internal-combustion engine for surface travel; E Forlanini of Italy built the first hydrofoil.
1902	The French ship *Petit-Pierre* became the first boat to be powered by a diesel engine.
1955	The first nuclear-powered submarine, *Nautilus*, was built; the hovercraft was patented by British inventor Christopher Cockerell.
1959	The first nuclear-powered ship, the Soviet ice-breaker *Lenin*, was commissioned; the US *Savannah* became the first nuclear-powered merchant (passenger and cargo) ship.
1980	Launch of the first wind-assisted commercial ship for half a century, the Japanese tanker *Shin-Aitoku-Maru*.
1983	German engineer Ortwin Fries invented a hinged ship designed to bend into a V-shape in order to scoop up oil spillages in its jaws.
1989	*Gentry Eagle* set a record for the fastest crossing of the Atlantic by a power vessel, taking 2 days, 14 hours, 7 minutes.
1990	*Hoverspeed Great Britain*, a wave-piercing catamaran, crossed the Atlantic in 3 days, 7 hours, 52 minutes, setting a record for the fastest crossing by a passenger vessel. The world's largest car and passenger ferry the *Silja Serenade* entered service between Stockholm and Helsinki, carrying 2500 passengers and 450 cars.

submarine an underwater ship, especially a warship. The first underwater boat was constructed for King James I of England by the Dutch scientist Cornelius van Drebbel 1620. A century and a half later, David Bushnell in the USA designed a submarine called *Turtle* for attacking British ships. In both world wars submarines, from the oceangoing to the midget type, played a vital role. The conventional submarine of this period was driven by diesel engine on the surface and by battery-powered electric motors underwater. The diesel engine also drove a generator that produced electricity to charge the batteries.

In 1955 the USA launched the first nuclear-powered submarine, *Nautilus*. The US nuclear submarine *Ohio*, USA, in service from 1981, is 170 m/560 ft long and carries 24 Trident missiles, each with 12 independently targetable nuclear warheads. The nuclear warheads on US submarines have a range that is being extended to 11,000 km/6.750 mi. Operating depth is usually up to 300 m/1,000 ft, and nuclear power speeds of 30 knots (i.e. 55 kph/34 mph) are reached. As in all nuclear submarines, propulsion is by steam turbine driving a propellor. The steam is raised using the heat given off by the nuclear reactor.

WARFARE

Military Terms

admiral highest-ranking naval officer. In the UK Royal Navy and the US Navy, in descending order, the ranks of admiral are: admiral of the fleet (fleet admiral in the USA), admiral, vice admiral, and rear admiral.

air force a nation's fighting aircraft and the organization that maintains them.

history The emergence of the aeroplane at first brought only limited recognition of its potential value as a means of waging war. Like the balloon, used since the American Civil War, it was considered a way of extending the vision of ground forces. A unified air force was established in the UK 1918, Italy 1923, France 1928, Germany 1935 (after repudiating the arms limitations of the Versailles treaty), and the USA 1947 (it began as the Aeronautical Division of the Army Signal Corps in 1907, and evolved into the Army's Air Service Division by 1918; by 1926 it was the Air Corps and in World War II the Army Air Force). The main specialized groupings formed during World War I – such as ***combat***, ***bombing***, ***reconnaissance***, and ***transport*** – were adapted and modified in World War II; activity was extended, with self-contained tactical air forces to meet the needs of ground commanders in the main theatres of land operations and for the attack on and defence of shipping over narrow seas.

During the period 1945–60 piston-engine aircraft were superseded by jet aircraft. Computerized guidance systems lessened the difference between missile and aircraft, and flights of unlimited duration became possible with air-to-air refuelling. For example, the US Strategic Air Command's bombers were capable of patrolling 24 hours a day armed with thermonuclear weapons. It was briefly anticipated that the pilot might become obsolete, but the continuation of conventional warfare and the evolution of tactical nuclear weapons led in the 1970s and 1980s to the development of advanced combat aircraft able to fly supersonically beneath an enemy's radar on strike and reconnaissance missions, as well as so-called stealth aircraft that cannot be detected by radar.

Allied Mobile Force (AMF) permanent multinational military force established 1960 to move immediately to any NATO country under threat of attack. Its headquarters are in Heidelberg, Germany.

Allies, the in World War I, the 23 countries allied against the Central Powers (Germany, Austria-Hungary, Turkey, and Bulgaria), including France, Italy, Russia, the UK, Australia and other Commonwealth nations, and, in the latter part of the war, the USA; and in World War II, the 49 countries allied against the Axis powers (Germany, Italy, and Japan), including France, the UK, Australia and other Commonwealth nations, the USA, and the USSR. In the 1991 Gulf War, there were 28 countries in the Allied coalition.

Armistice Day anniversary of the armistice signed 11 Nov 1918, ending World War I.

armour body protection worn in battle. Chain mail was developed in the Middle Ages but the craft of the armourer in Europe reached its height in design in the 15th century, when knights were completely encased in plate armour that still allowed freedom of movement. Medieval Japanese armour was articulated, made of iron, gilded metal, leather, and silk. Contemporary bulletproof vests and riot gear are forms of armour. The term is used in a modern context to refer to a mechanized armoured vehicle, such as a tank. Since World War II armour for tanks and ships has been developed beyond an increasing thickness of steel plate, becoming an increasingly light, layered composite, including materials such as ceramics.

arms trade sale of arms from a manufacturing country to another nation. It is estimated that 56% of the world's arms exports end up in Third World countries. The proportion of global military expenditure accounted for by Third World countries was about 18% in 1993 (up from 6% in 1965, but down from 24% in 1989). Arms exports are known in the trade as 'arms transfers'. In the UK, the Defence Export Services, a department of the Ministry of Defence, is responsible for British arms exports. Its annual budget is about £10 million.

army organized military force for fighting on the ground. A national army is used to further a political policy by force either within the state or on the territory of another state. Most countries have a national army, maintained at the expense of the state, and raised either by conscription (compulsory military service) or voluntarily (paid professionals). Private armies may be employed by individuals and groups. Following the ending of the Cold War, the US, and the former Soviet and European armies are to be substantially cut by the mid-1990s. The UK army will be cut from 155,000 to 119,000.

artillery collective term for military firearms too heavy to be carried. Artillery can be mounted on tracks, wheels, ships, or aeroplanes and includes cannons and rocket launchers.

AWACS (acronym for ***Airborne Warning And Control System***) surveillance system that incorporates a long-range surveillance and detection radar mounted on a Boeing E-3 sentry aircraft. It was used with great success in the 1991 Gulf War.

battalion or ***unit*** basic personnel unit in the military system, usually consisting of four or five companies and about 600–700 soldiers. A battalion is commanded by a lieutenant colonel. Several battalions form a brigade.

battleship class of large warships with the biggest guns and heaviest armour. In 1991, four US battleships were in active service. They are now all decommissioned.

biological warfare the use of living organisms, or of infectious material derived from them, to bring about death or disease in humans, animals, or plants. It was condemned by the Geneva Convention 1925, to which the United Nations has urged all states to adhere. Nevertheless research in this area continues; the Biological

The arms trade

The leading exporters and importers of major conventional weapons, 1987-91

Exporters	*1987*	*1988*	*1989*	*1990*	*1991*	*1987-91*
USSR	17,745	15,115	14,887	9,663	3,930	61,339
USA	13,691	11,867	11,969	11,234	11,195	59,957
France	3,232	2,374	2,861	1,950	804	11,220
UK	2,171	1,690	2,661	1,575	999	9,097
China	2,917	1,930	929	954	1,127	7,857
Germany, FR	784	1,309	780	1,226	2,015	6,115
Czechoslovakia	954	927	715	669	0	3,264
Italy	599	732	225	149	172	1,878
Netherlands	317	631	459	142	208	1,758
Brazil	666	507	288	165	2	1,629
Sweden	474	585	302	103	59	1,524
Israel	408	155	382	108	119	1,172
Spain	169	231	602	80	47	1,128
Yugoslavia	3	4	0	60	661	728
Egypt	234	277	78	42	5	636
Others	1,506	983	1,089	883	771	5,233
Total	***45,870***	***39,317***	***38,228***	***29,004***	***22,114***	***174,532***
To the developing world						
Total	***32,162***	***24,054***	***21,735***	***16,720***	***12,336***	***107,007***
To the industralized world						
Total	***13,708***	***15,263***	***16,492***	***12,284***	***9,778***	***67,525***
Importers						
India	5,475	4,009	4,461	1,607	2,009	17,561
Saudi Arabia	2,617	2,441	1,914	2,487	1,138	10,597
Iraq	5,438	2,759	1,526	596	0	10,319
Japan	1,644	2,177	2,795	2,094	1,040	9,750
Afghanistan	901	1,275	2,615	2,419	1,220	8,430
Turkey	1,203	1,419	1,138	1,067	1,559	6,384
Egypt	2,850	493	248	1,203	667	5,461
Spain	1,457	1,681	912	674	231	4,955
Czechoslovakia	1,167	1,197	1,557	716	47	4,684
Korea, North	751	1,734	1,518	612	15	4,631
Israel	1,940	604	120	228	1,676	4,567
Greece	92	819	1,471	929	1,081	4,393
Poland	1,012	1,247	1,225	334	137	3,954
Angola	1,599	1,171	88	748	0	3,606
Korea, South	720	1,184	1,101	370	177	3,551
Others	17,005	15,106	15,539	12,919	11,119	71,687
Total	***45,870***	***39,317***	***38,228***	***29,004***	***22,114***	***174,532***

Source: SIPRI Yearbook

Weapons Convention 1972 permits research for defence purposes but does not define how this differs from offensive-weapons development. In 1990 the US Department of Defense allocated $60 million to research, develop, and test defence systems. Advances in genetic engineering make the development of new varieties of potentially offensive biological weapons more likely. At least ten countries have this capability.

Russian president Boris Yeltsin signed a decree to comply with the treaty in 1992. Although the treaty was originally ratified by the Kremlin three months after its original signing, national laws ensuring compliance were never passed.

bomb container filled with explosive or chemical material and generally used in warfare. There are also incendiary bombs and nuclear bombs and missiles. Any object designed to cause damage by explosion can be called a bomb (car bombs, letter bombs). Initially dropped from aeroplanes (from World War I), bombs were in World War II also launched by rocket (V1, V2). The 1960s saw the development of missiles that could be launched from aircraft, land sites, or submarines. Although high explosive is increasingly delivered by means of missiles, free fall and so- called 'smart' or laser-guided munitions are still widely used.

The rapid development of ***laser guidance systems*** in the 1970s meant that precise destruction of small but vital targets could be more effectively achieved with standard 450 kg/1,000 lb high-explosive bombs. The laser beam may be directed at the target by the army from the ground, or alternatively from high-performance aircraft accompanying the bombers, for example, the Laser Ranging Marker Target System (LRMTS). The effectiveness of these systems was demonstrated during the Gulf War of 1991.

brigade military formation consisting of a minimum of two battalions, but more usually three or more, as well as supporting arms. There are typically about 5,000 soldiers in a brigade, which is commanded by a brigadier. Two or more brigades form a division.

carrier warfare naval warfare involving aircraft carriers. Carrier warfare was conducted during World War II in the battle of the Coral Sea May 1942, which stopped the Japanese advance in the South Pacific, and in the battle of Midway Islands June 1942, which weakened the Japanese navy through the loss of four aircraft carriers. The US Navy deployed six aircraft carriers during the Gulf War 1991.

Central Command military strike force consisting of units from the US army, navy, and air force, which operates in the Middle East and North Africa. Its headquarters are in Fort McDill, Florida. It was established 1979, following the Iranian hostage crisis and the Soviet invasion of Afghanistan, and was known as the Rapid Deployment Force until 1983. It commanded coalition forces in the Gulf War 1991.

chemical warfare use in war of gaseous, liquid, or solid substances intended to have a toxic effect on humans, animals, or plants. Together with biological warfare, it was banned by the Geneva Convention 1925, although this has not always been observed. In 1989, when the 149-nation Conference on Chemical Weapons unanimously voted to outlaw chemical weapons, the total US stockpile was estimated at 30,000 tonnes and the Soviet stockpile variously at 30,000 and 300,000 tonnes.

In a deal with the USA, the USSR offered to eliminate its stocks; the USA began replacing its stocks with new binary nerve-gas weapons. In 1990 President Bush offered to destroy all US chemical weapons if the convention to outlaw them, signed in Paris on 13 Jan 1993, were ratified. The Conventional Weapons Convention (CWC) will enter into force 180 days after the 65th signatory has ratified the convention, but in no case earlier than 13 Jan 1995. By mid-Feb 1993, 136 countries had signed the convention. Some 20 nations currently hold chemical weapons, including Iraq, Iran, Israel, Syria, Libya, South Africa, China, Ethiopia, North Korea, Myanmar, Taiwan, and Vietnam.

civil defence or ***civil protection*** organized activities by the civilian population of a state to mitigate the effects of enemy attack on them. The threat of nuclear weapons in the post-World War II period led to the building of fallout shelters in the USA, the USSR, and elsewhere. China has networks of tunnels in cities that are meant to enable the population to escape nuclear fallout and reach the countryside, but which do not protect against the actual blast. Sweden and Switzerland have highly developed civil-defence systems.

A new structure of 'Home Defence' is now being created in Britain, in which the voluntary services, local authorities, the Home Service Force, and the Territorial Army would cooperate. Regulations came into force 1983 compelling local authorities to take part in civil-defence exercises. Councils have to provide blast-proof bunkers and communication links, train staff, and take part in the exercises. In July 1991 it was announced that much of the Home Defence infrastructure would be severely cut back since the Cold War had ended.

COIN acronym for ***co**unter **in**surgency*, the suppression by a state's armed forces of uprisings against the state. Also called internal security (IS) operations of counter-revolutionary warfare (CRW). The British army has been engaged in COIN operations in Northern Ireland since 1969.

commando member of a specially trained, highly mobile military unit. The term originated in South Africa in the 19th century, where it referred to Boer military reprisal raids against Africans and, in the South African Wars, against the British. Commando units have often carried out operations behind enemy lines.

company a subunit of a battalion. It consists of about 120 soldiers, and is commanded by a major in the British army, a captain or major in the US army. Four or five companies make a battalion.

conscription legislation for all able-bodied male citizens (and female in some countries, such as Israel) to serve with the armed forces. It originated in France 1792, and in the 19th and 20th centuries became the established practice in almost all European states. Modern conscription systems often permit alternative national service for conscientious objectors.

In Britain conscription was introduced in March 1916 but was abolished after World War I. It was introduced for the first time in peace April 1939, when all men aged 20 became liable to six months' military training. The National Service Act, passed Sept 1939, made all men between 18 and 41 liable to military service, and in 1941 women also became liable to be called up for the women's services as an alternative to industrial service. Men reaching the age of 18 continued to be called up until 1960. Conscription remains the norm for most NATO and Warsaw Pact countries as well as neutral states. In the USSR 21% of those called up in 1990 failed to respond. It is also practised by governments in the Third World. In South Africa, the penalty for evading conscription is up to six years' imprisonment.

corps a military formation consisting of 2-5 divisions. Its strength is between 50,000 and 120,000 men. All branches of the army are represented. A corps is commanded by a lieutenant general or, in the USA, a three-star general. Two or more corps form an army group.

deception the use of dummies, decoys, and electronics to trick the enemy into believing in and preparing to defend against armies that do not exist. The Allied ground offensive in the 1991 Gulf War was launched 160 km/100 mi W of where the Iraqi army was led to believe it would take place. The deception techniques used completely wrong-footed the Iraqi forces.

Delta Force US antiguerrilla force, based at Fort Bragg, North Carolina, and modelled on the British Special Air Service.

destroyer small, fast warship designed for antisubmarine work. Destroyers played a critical role in the convoy system in World War II. Modern destroyers often carry guided missiles and displace 3,700–5,650 tonnes.

Disarmament: a timetable for peace?

1930s	League of Nations attempt to achieve disarmament failed.
1968	US president Johnson's proposals for Strategic Arms Limitation Talks (SALT) were delayed by the Soviet invasion of Czechoslovakia.
1972-77	SALT I was in effect.
1979-85	SALT II, signed by the Soviet and US leaders Brezhnev and Carter, was never ratified by the US Senate, but both countries abided by it.
1986	US president Reagan revoked this pledge, against the advice of his European NATO partners.
1987	Reagan and the Soviet leader Gorbachev agreed to reduce their nuclear arsenals by 4% by scrapping intermediate-range nuclear weapons.
1990	Treaty signed between the USA and the USSR limiting both NATO and the Warsaw Pact to much reduced conventional weapons systems in Europe.
Jan 1991	President Bush announced decision to halve US military presence in Europe.
July 1991	Bush and Soviet president Gorbachev signed Strategic Arms Reduction Treaty (START) which limited both sides to no more than 6,000 nuclear warheads.
Sept-Oct 1991	Bush announced the unilateral reduction of about 2,400 US nuclear weapons, asking the USSR to respond in kind. Gorbachev offered a package of unilateral cuts and proposals that surpassed the broad arms-control initiative presented by Bush.
Jan 1992	Bush and Russia's president, Boris Yeltsin, promised additional (60-80%) cuts in land- and sea-based long-range nuclear missiles. In addition, Bush promised an accelerated withdrawal of US troops from Europe and the halting of future production of the advanced B-2 bomber. Yeltsin announced that Russian long-range missiles would no longer be targetted on US cities.
June 1992	Yeltsin consented to the abandonment of strategic parity (equal balance of arms) and announced, with Bush, bilateral cuts in long-term nuclear weapons that far surpassed the terms of the 1991 START treaty. By 2003, it was promised, US warheads would be cut from 9,986 to 3,500, and Russian warheads from 10,237 to 3,000.
Jan 1993	START II treaty signed by Bush and Yeltsin in Moscow, committing both countries to reduce long-range nuclear weapons by two-thirds by the year 2003 and to do away with land-based, multiple warheads.

disarmament reduction of a country's weapons of war. Most disarmament talks since World War II have been concerned with nuclear-arms verification and reduction, but biological, chemical, and conventional weapons have also come under discussion at the United Nations and in other forums.

division military formation consisting of two or more brigades. A major general at divisional headquarters commands the brigades and also additional artillery, engineers, attack helicopters, and other logistic support. There are 10,000 or more soldiers in a division. Two or more divisions form a corps.

early warning advance notice of incoming attack, often associated with nuclear attack. There are early-warning radar systems in the UK (Fylingdales), Alaska, and Greenland. ***Airborne early warning*** (AEW) is provided by sentry planes; NATO has such a system.

explosive any material capable of a sudden release of energy and the rapid formation of a large volume of gas, leading when compressed to the development of a high-pressure wave (blast). Examples include gelignite, dynamite, nitroglycerin, nitrobenzine, TNT (trinitoluene), and RDX (Research Department Explosive).

fallout harmful radioactive material released into the atmosphere in the debris of a nuclear explosion and descending to the surface of the Earth. Such material can enter the food chain, cause radiation sickness, and last for hundreds of thousands of years.

field marshal the highest rank in many European armies. A British field marshal is equivalent to a 5-star US general (of the army).

firearm weapon from which projectiles are discharged by the combustion of an explosive. Firearms are generally divided into two main sections: ***artillery*** (ordnance or cannon), with a bore greater than 2.54 cm/1 in, and ***small arms***, with a bore of less than 2.54 cm/1 in. Although gunpowder was known in Europe 60 years previously, the invention of guns dates from 1300–25, and is attributed to Berthold Schwartz, a German monk.

frigate escort warship smaller than a destroyer. Before 1975 the term referred to a warship larger than a destroyer but smaller than a light cruiser. In the 18th and 19th centuries a frigate was a small, fast sailing warship.

general senior military rank, the ascending grades being major general, lieutenant general, and general. The US rank of general of the army, or 5-star general, is equivalent to the British field marshal.

guerrilla irregular soldier fighting in a small unofficial unit, typically against an established or occupying power, and engaging in sabotage, ambush, and the like, rather than pitched battles against an opposing army. Guerrilla tactics have been used both by resistance armies in wartime (for example, the Vietnam War) and in peacetime by national liberation groups and militant political extremists (for example the PLO; Tamil Tigers).

Political activists who resort to violence, particularly ***urban guerrillas***, tend to be called 'freedom fighters' by those who support their cause, 'terrorists' by those who oppose it. Efforts by governments to put a stop to their activities have had only sporadic success. The Council of Europe has set up the European Convention on the Suppression of Terrorism, to

Bosnia–Herzegovina: no arms from the West

By mid-1993 the conflict in Bosnia seemed to have reached a watershed. After 18 months of agonizing, prevarication, indecision, and hesitation the international community decided in May not to intervene in any meaningful way. If ever full-scale military intervention was a practicable option, that time is now past. To occupy and pacify every town and village within Bosnia-Herzegovina would involve many hundreds of thousands of troops for many years. Even supposing the political will to undertake such an operation existed – which it clearly does not – the military victory that would undoubtedly be achieved would be unlikely, given the history of the region, to lead to a political solution. It would be impossible to eradicate the inevitable Serbian-backed guerrilla action, and any imposed political solution would depend upon continuing occupation.

President Clinton's plan for lifting the arms embargo on the Bosnian Muslims whilst at the same time initiating air strikes against the Bosnian Serbs, was rejected outright by his European allies. Although significant damage could have been inflicted on Serbian militias, air strikes, as the Gulf War clearly showed, are only effective with subsequent action by ground troops. The terrain in Bosnia is unsuited to ground attack missions and civilian casualties would be high. Moreover, the British and French were aware that air attacks would endanger UN forces, causing their withdrawal and an end to humanitarian aid. More importantly, air strikes would be unlikely to halt Serb aggression altogether, seriously deplete their weapon or ammunition stocks, or encourage them to negotiate.

As for arming the Muslims, it can be argued that the Bosnian Muslims have a right to defend themselves. They are at a serious disadvantage, having virtually no heavy weapons. However, Russia was never likely to agree to reverse the UN arms embargo; and even if it did, it would take time to supply enough arms and more to train the recipients to use them. Arguably, it would encourage the Serbs and the Croats to seek more arms, although the Serbs already have a surplus. Such a course of action would not only complicate things for President Yeltsin – something the West wishes to avoid – but would also lead to the withdrawal of UN forces and possibly to a widening of the conflict. Calibrating air strikes and arms supplies to create a precise balance rather than fuelling the conflict would be impossible.

However, both the USA and its European allies endorsed a plan to maintain designated UN 'safe areas', though not calling them 'safe havens' leaves in some doubt the degree of protection that would be afforded them. 'Safe havens' worked well in Kurdistan in 1991, where clear ethnic boundaries existed on the ground and exclusion zones could be created in the air. Moreover a neighbouring NATO country provided convenient military bases and temporary refuge for the displaced. The relatively open terrain allowed the allies to keep a defeated Saddam Hussein at bay.

None of these conditions apply in Bosnia. Moreover, the UN's commitment to the 'safe areas' seems half-hearted. The USA is not prepared to contribute ground troops and the Europeans are nervous that meaningful security guarantees to the Muslim enclaves could lead to inextricable involvement. Thus it seems that pragmatism has prevailed: the 'safe areas' will be given humanitarian aid and a degree of protection and monitors may be deployed on the Serbian border to enforce the arms embargo on the Serb militias in Bosnia. UN troops will remain in Macedonia, and the Vance-Owen plan will be kept in reserve should a political settlement ever be brokered. What looks likely, however, is that a Greater Croatia and a Greater Serbia will emerge from this war. Whether it will be possible for a rump Bosnian Muslim state to survive as well remains to be seen. The international community may be willing to accept a solution which incorporates sufficient guarantees for a Muslim minority in enlarged Croatian and Serbian states. In fact the de facto partition of Bosnia may in many ways be preferable to a rump Muslim state which would almost certainly not be viable and would be dependent on outside aid. It would in effect mean the creation of a Balkan 'Gaza Strip', something which the international community could well do without. What is now certain is that the last chance for intervention passed in early spring 1993. When faced with the possibility of being involved in a civil war indefinitely, both Europe and the USA stepped back from the brink. They accepted the unpalatable truth that when people are determined to fight each other, there is precious little that the outside world can do to stop them.

MD

which many governments are signatories. In the UK the Prevention of Terrorism Act 1984 is aimed particularly at the Irish Republican Army (IRA). The Institute for the Study of Terrorism was founded in London 1986.

Gurkha member of a people living in the mountains of Nepal, whose young men have been recruited since 1815 for the British and Indian armies. There are currently five battalions of Gurkhas in the British Army (though the cuts of July 1991 will reduce these to two by 1996). There are many more Gurkhas in the Indian Army.

Home Service Force (HSF) military unit established in the UK 1982, linked to the Territorial Army (TA) and recruited from volunteers aged 18-60 with previous army (TA or regular) experience. It was introduced to guard key points and installations likely to be the target of enemy 'special forces' and saboteurs, so releasing other units for mobile defence roles. It was stood down in 1992.

ICBM abbreviation for ***intercontinental ballistic missile***.

Luftwaffe German air force. In World War I and, as reorganized by the Nazi leader Hermann Goering in 1933, in World War II. The Luftwaffe also covered anti-aircraft defence and the launching of the flying bombs V1 and V2.

manoeuvre to move around the battlefield so as to gain an advantage over the enemy. It implies rapid movement, shock action, and surprise. Bold manoeuvre warfare can be synonymous with Blitzkrieg or a swift military campaign. An example of manoeuvre warfare was the wide-ranging encirclement of the Iraqi army by coalition forces in the 1991 Gulf War.

marines fighting force that operates both on land and at sea. The ***US Marine Corps*** (1775) is constituted as an arm of the US Navy. It is made up of infantry and air support units trained and equipped for amphibious landings under fire. The ***Corps of Royal Marines*** founded by Charles I in 1664 is the British equivalent, numbering approximately 7,000 (1993). It is part of the Royal Navy.

mercenary soldier hired by the army of another country or by a private army. Mercenary military service originated in the 14th century, when cash payment on a regular basis was the only means of guaranteeing soldiers' loyalty. In the 20th century mercenaries have been common in wars and guerrilla activity in Asia, Africa, and Latin America.

Article 47 of the 1977 Additional Protocols to the Geneva Convention stipulates that 'a mercenary shall not have the right to be a combatant or a prisoner of war' but leaves a party to the Protocols the freedom to grant such status if so wished.

minesweeper small naval vessel for locating and destroying mines at sea. A typical minesweeper weighs about 725 tonnes, and is built of reinforced plastic (immune to magnetic and acoustic mines). Remote-controlled miniature submarines may be used to lay charges next to the mines and destroy them.

mobilization preparation of armed forces (land, sea, air) for active service.

MRBM abbreviation for ***medium-range ballistic missile***, such as the French M-5 ballistic missile.

navy fleet of ships, usually a nation's warships and the organization to maintain them. In the early 1990s, the UK had a force of small carriers, destroyers, frigates, and submarines. In the light of 1991 Armed Forces reductions, the Royal Navy is to be reduced from around 50 to 40 destroyers and frigates, and the submarine fleet to be cut by 50%.

NBC abbreviation for ***nuclear, biological, and chemical warfare*** term used to describe the form of warfare fought with weapons of mass destruction. The only case of nuclear warfare to date was the dropping of two nuclear weapons on Hiroshima and Nagasaki by the US Air Force in 1945, with the purpose of forcing Japan to surrender in World War II. Biological warfare is a weapon that is difficult to use in the field of battle but which could be used as a strategic weapon to poison water supplies or cause epidemics. Chemical weapons were first used during World War I in the form of mustard gas, and they have been used since in Vietnam, Afghanistan, and during the Iran–Iraq war by the Iraqis.

North Atlantic Treaty Organization (NATO) association set up 1949 to provide for the collective defence of the major W European and North American states against the perceived threat from the USSR. Its chief body is the Council of Foreign Ministers (who have representatives in permanent session), and there is an international secretariat in Brussels, Belgium, and also the Military Committee consisting of the Chiefs of Staff. The military headquarters SHAPE (Supreme Headquarters Allied Powers, Europe) is in Chièvres, near Mons, Belgium. In Oct 1991, it was agreed that NATO's nuclear arsenal in Europe would be reduced by 80%. There were also plans for NATO forces to be reduced by up to 30% by the mid-1990s. It was agreed July 1992 that the Conference on Security and Cooperation in Europe (CSCE) would in future authorize all NATO's military responses within Europe. After the E European Warsaw Pact was disbanded 1991, the ***North Atlantic Cooperation Council***, was established, including all the former Soviet republics, with the aim of building greater security in Europe. In May 1991 a meeting of NATO defence ministers endorsed the creation of a UK-commanded, 100,000-strong 'rapid-reaction corps' (RRC) adaptable to post-Cold War contingencies. The new force is to be operational from late 1994 and to be used solely inside NATO territory, unless otherwise agreed by all members of the alliance.

nuclear warfare war involving the use of nuclear weapons. Nuclear-weapons research began in Britain 1940, but was transferred to the USA after it entered World War II. The research programme, known as the Manhattan Project, was directed by J Robert Oppenheimer. The first test explosion was at Alamogordo, New Mexico, 16 July 1945; the first use in war was by the USA against Japan 6 Aug 1945 over Hiroshima and three days later at Nagasaki. ***atom bomb*** The original weapon relied on use of a chemical explosion to trigger a chain reaction. ***hydrogen bomb*** A much more powerful weapon than the atom bomb, it relies on the release of thermonuclear energy by the condensation of hydrogen nuclei to helium nuclei (as happens in the Sun). The first detonation was at Eniwetok Atoll, Pacific Ocean, 1952 by the USA. ***neutron bomb*** or ***e***nhanced ***r***adiation ***w***eapon (ERW) a very small hydrogen bomb that has relatively high radiation but relatively low blast, designed to kill (in up to six days) by a brief neutron radiation that leaves buildings and weaponry intact. ***nuclear methods of attack*** now include aircraft bombs, missiles (long- or short-range, surface to surface, air to surface, and surface to air), depth charges, and high-powered landmines ('atomic demolition munitions') to destroy bridges and roads.

The major subjects of disarmament negotiations are ***intercontinental ballistic missiles*** (ICBMs), which have from 1968 been equipped with clusters of warheads (which can be directed to individual targets) and are known as multiple independently targetable re-entry vehicles (MIRVs). The 1980s US-designed MX (Peacekeeper) carries up to ten warheads in each missile. In 1989, the UK agreed to purchase submarine-launched Trident missiles from the USA. Each warhead has eight independently targetable re-entry vehicles (each nuclear-armed) with a range of about 6,400 km/4,000 mi to eight separate targets within about 240 km/150 mi of the central aiming point. The Trident system was scheduled to enter service within the Royal Navy in the mid-1990s.

nuclear methods of defence include: ***antiballistic missile*** (ABM) Earth-based systems with two types of missile, one short-range with high acceleration, and one comparatively long-range for interception above the atmosphere; ***Strategic Defense Initiative*** (announced by the USA 1983 to be operative from 2000; popularly known as the 'Star Wars' programme) 'directed energy weapons' firing laser beams would be mounted on space stations, and by burning holes in incoming missiles would either collapse them or detonate their fuel tanks.

The worldwide total of nuclear weapons in 1990 was about 50,000, and the number of countries possessing nuclear weapons stood officially at five – USA, USSR, UK, France, and China – although some other nations were thought either to have a usable stockpile of these weapons (Israel) or the a bility to produce them quickly (Brazil, India, Pakistan, South Africa). Successive arms-reduction treaties between 1990 and 1993 have, however, resulted in agreements to reduce the worldwide figure to approximately 10,000 by 2003. In the 1991 Minsk Agreement – 'The Creation of the Commonwealth of Independent States' – Belarus, Ukraine, and Kazakhstan declared they would become non-nuclear.

The UK nuclear warhead programme costs £607 million a year.

platoon in the army, the smallest infantry subunit. It contains 30–40 soldiers and is commanded by a lieutenant or second lieutenant. There are three or four platoons in a company.

prisoner of war (POW) person captured in war, who has fallen into the hands of, or surrendered to, an opponent. Such captives may be held in prisoner-of-war camps. The treatment of POWs is governed by the Geneva Convention.

Rapid Reaction Force (or ***RRF***) any military unit that is maintained at a high state of readiness to react to an emergency. Specifically, it refers to the corps-sized unit, the formation of which was announced by NATO in May 1991 to meet threats anywhere in its area of responsibility.

reconnaissance the gathering of information about a military objective. This can be carried out by a reconnaissance ('recce') patrol or from a small, fast-moving vehicle or an aircraft configured for reconnaissance, or a remotely piloted vehicle (RPV). The SAS (Special Air Service) carried out invaluable reconnaissance work in the 1991 Gulf War. Less precise information was provided by satellites.

Red Army name of the army of the USSR until 1946; later known as the ***Soviet Army***. It developed from the Red Guards, volunteers who carried out the Bolshevik revolution, and took its name from the red flag under which it fought. The Chinese revolutionary army was also called the Red Army.

regiment military formation equivalent to a battalion in parts of the British army, and to a brigade in the armies of many other countries. In the British infantry, a regiment may include more than one battalion, and soldiers belong to the same regiment throughout their career.

Royal Air Force (RAF) the air force of Britain. The RAF was formed 1918 by the merger of the Royal Naval Air Service and the Royal Flying Corps. It numbers approximately 85,000 (1991), with some 48 front-line squadrons of aircraft out of approximately 600 aircraft. The 1991 defence cuts will reduce this by 15 squadrons and by 75,000 personnel.

Royal British Legion full name of the British Legion, a nonpolitical body promoting the welfare of war veterans and their dependants.

Royal Marines British military force trained for amphibious warfare.

services, armed the air, sea, and land forces of a country; also called the armed forces.

SHAPE acronym for ***Supreme Headquarters Allied Powers Europe***, situated near Mons, Belgium, and the headquarters of NATO's Supreme Allied Command Europe (SACEUR).

SLBM abbreviation for ***submarine-launched ballistic missile***.

Special Air Service (SAS) specialist British regiment recruited from regiments throughout the army. It has served in Malaysia, Oman, Yemen, the Falklands, Northern Ireland, and during the 1991 Gulf War, as well as against international urban guerrillas, as in the siege of the Iranian embassy in London 1980.

Strategic Defense Initiative (SDI) also called ***Star Wars*** attempt by the USA to develop a defence system against incoming nuclear missiles, based in part outside the Earth's atmosphere. The essence of the SDI is to attack enemy missiles at several different stages of their trajectory, using advanced laser and particle-beam technology, thus increasing the chances of disabling them. It was announced by President Reagan in March 1983, and the research had by 1990 cost over $16.5 billion. In 1988, the joint Chiefs of Staff announced that they expected to be able to intercept no more than 30% of incoming missiles. Israel, Japan, and the UK are among the nations assisting in SDI research and development. In 1987 President Gorbachev acknowledged that the USSR was developing a similar defence system.

The SDI programme was subsequently scaled down dramatically, and it is now certain that the original concept will not be deployed. The scaled-down version is known as Global Protection Against Limited Strikes (GPALS). The overall programme was renamed the Ballistic Missile Defence Organization (BMDO) in May 1993.

tank armoured fighting vehicle that runs on tracks and is fitted with weapons systems capable of defeating other tanks and destroying life and property. The term was originally a code name for the first effective tracked and armoured fighting vehicle, invented by the British soldier and scholar Ernest Swinton, and used in the battle of the Somme 1916. A tank consists of a body or hull of thick steel, on which are mounted machine guns and a larger gun. The hull contains the crew (usually consisting of a commander, driver, and one or two soldiers), engine, radio, fuel tanks, and ammunition. The tank travels on caterpillar tracks that enable it to cross rough ground and debris. It is known today as an MBT (main battle tank).

Territorial Army British force of volunteer soldiers, created from volunteer regiments (incorporated 1872) as the ***Territorial Force*** 1908. It was raised and administered by county associations, and intended primarily for home defence. It was renamed Territorial Army 1922. Merged with the Regular Army in World War II, it was revived 1947, and replaced by a smaller, more highly trained Territorial and Army Volunteer Reserve, again renamed Territorial Army 1979.

war act of force, usually on behalf of the state, intended to compel a declared enemy to obey the will of the other. The aim is to render the opponent incapable of further resistance by destroying its capability and will to bear arms in pursuit of its own aims. War is therefore a continuation of politics carried on with violent and destructive means, as an instrument of policy. The estimated figure for loss of life in Third World wars since 1945 is 17 million.

War is generally divided into ***strategy***, the planning and conduct of a war, and ***tactics***, the deployment of forces in battle. Types of war include: ***guerrilla war*** the waging of low-level conflict by irregular forces against an occupying army or against the rear of an enemy force. Examples include Mao Zedong's campaign against the Nationalist Chinese and T E Lawrence's Arab revolt against the Turks. ***low-intensity conflict*** US term for its interventions in the Third World, ranging from drug-running to funding and training guerrillas, and fought with political, economic, and cultural weapons as well as by military means. ***civil war*** the waging of war by opposing parties, or members of different regions, within a state. The American Civil War 1861–65, the English Civil War of the 17th century, and the Spanish Civil War 1936–39 are notable examples. ***limited war*** the concept that a war may be limited in both geographical extent and levels of force exerted and have aims that stop short of achieving the destruction of the enemy. The Korean War 1950–53 falls within this category. ***total war*** the waging of war against both combatants and noncombatants, taking the view that no distinction should be made between them. The Spanish Civil War marked the beginning of this type of warfare, in which bombing from the air included both civilian and military targets. ***absolute war*** the view that there should be no limitations, such as law, compassion, or prudence, in the application of force, the sole aim being to achieve the complete annihilation of one's opponent. Such a concept contradicts the notion, formulated by Clausewitz, of war as an instrument of political dialogue since it implies that no dialogue is actually intended. It has been claimed that nuclear warfare would assume such proportions and would be in accordance with the doctrine of mutually assured destruction (MAD).

warship fighting ship armed and crewed for war. The supremacy of the battleship at the beginning of the 20th century was rivalled during World War I by the development of submarine attack, and was rendered obsolescent in World War II with the advent of long-range air attack. Today the largest and most important surface warships are the aircraft carriers.

aircraft carriers The large-scale aircraft carrier was temporarily out of favour, as too vulnerable, until the resumption of building, especially by the USSR, in the late 1970s and 1980s. The USS *Carl Vinson* (1982) weighs 81,600 tonnes. Some countries, such as the UK, have opted for ***mini-carriers*** with vertical takeoff aircraft and long-range helicopters. Minicarriers evolved in the early 1970s and have been advocated by US military reformers. ***submarines*** The first nuclear-powered submarine was the US *Nautilus* 1955; the first Polaris was the *George Washington* 1960. Submarines fall into two classes: the specially designed, almost silent ***attack submarine***, intended to release its fast torpedoes and missiles at comparatively close range, and the ***ballistic- missile submarine*** with guided missiles of such long range that the submarine itself is virtually undetectable to the enemy. For the USA these submarines form one leg of the strategic 'triad' of land-based missiles, crewed bombers, and submarine-launched missiles. ***battleships*** The US Navy has recommissioned and modernized several World War II battleships for shore bombardment and force projection purposes. These were used with great effect during the 1991 Gulf War. They have since been decommissioned.

withdrawal an orderly movement of forces in a rearward direction in order to occupy more favourable ground. It is voluntary and controlled, unlike a retreat.

women's services the organized military use of women on a large scale, a 20th-century development. First, women replaced men in factories, on farms, and in noncombat tasks during wartime; they are now found in combat units in many countries, including the USA, Cuba, the UK, Russia, and Israel.

Treaties and Conferences

Georgetown, Declaration of call, at a conference in Guyana of nonaligned countries 1972, for a multipolar system to replace the two world power blocs, and for the Mediterranean Sea and Indian Ocean to be neutral.

Helsinki Conference international meeting 1975 at which 35 countries, including the USSR and the USA, attempted to reach agreement on cooperation in security, economics, science, technology, and human rights.

INF abbreviation for ***intermediate nuclear forces***, as in the Intermediate Nuclear Forces Treaty.

Intermediate Nuclear Forces Treaty agreement signed 8 Dec 1987 between the USA and the USSR to eliminate all ground-based nuclear missiles in Europe that were capable of hitting only European targets (including European Russia). It reduced the countries' nuclear arsenals by some 2,000 (4% of the total). The treaty included provisions for each country to inspect the other's bases.

Paris, Treaty of any of various peace treaties signed in Paris. In the 20th century these have included: ***1919–20*** the conference preparing the Treaty of Versailles at the end of World War I was held in Paris; ***1946*** after World War II, the peace treaties between the Allies and Italy, Romania, Hungary, Bulgaria, and Finland; ***1951*** treaty signed by France, West Germany, Italy, Belgium, Netherlands, and Luxembourg, embodying the Schuman Plan to set up a single coal and steel authority; ***1973*** ending US participation in the Vietnam War.

SALT abbreviation for ***Strategic Arms Limitation Talks***, a series of US–Soviet negotiations 1969–79.

START acronym for ***Strategic Arms Reduction Talks***.

Strategic Arms Limitation Talks (SALT) series of US–Soviet discussions 1969–79 aimed at reducing the rate of nuclear-arms build-up. The talks, delayed by the Soviet invasion of Czechoslovakia 1968, began in 1969 between the US president Lyndon Johnson and the Soviet leader Leonid Brezhnev. Neither the SALT I accord (effective 1972–77) nor SALT II called for reductions in nuclear weaponry, merely a limit on the expansion of these forces. SALT II was mainly negotiated by US president Ford before 1976 and signed by Brezhnev and US president Carter in Vienna in 1979. It was never fully ratified because of the Soviet occupation of Afghanistan, although the terms of the accord were respected by both sides until US president Reagan exceeded its limitations during his second term 1985–89. SALT talks were superseded by START negotiations under Reagan, and the first significant reductions began under Soviet president Gorbachev.

Strategic Arms Reduction Talks (START) phase in peace discussions dealing with disarmament, initially involving the USA and the Soviet Union and from 1992 the USA and Russia. It began with talks in Geneva 1983, leading to the signing of the Intermediate Nuclear Forces (INF) Treaty 1987. Reductions of about 30% in strategic nuclear weapons systems were agreed 1991 (START I). More significant cuts were agreed 3 Jan 1993 (START II), when Presidents Bush and Yeltsin brought the START process to a dramatic conclusion by signing the START II Treaty, agreeing to reduce their strategic nuclear warheads to 3,000–3,500 weapons each by 2003. The treaty will be put into effect in two stages, with interim ceilings to be reached in the first seven years after the treaty enters into force. The treaty has yet to be ratified.

Versailles, Treaty of peace treaty after World War I between the Allies and Germany, signed 28 June 1919. It established the League of Nations. Germany surrendered Alsace-Lorraine to France, and large areas in the east to Poland, and made smaller cessions to Czechoslovakia, Lithuania, Belgium, and Denmark. The Rhineland was demilitarized, German rearmament was restricted, and Germany agreed to pay reparations for war damage. The treaty was never ratified by the USA, which made a separate peace with Germany and Austria 1921.

Yalta Conference in 1945, a meeting at which the Allied leaders Churchill (UK), Roosevelt (USA), and Stalin (USSR) completed plans for the defeat of Germany in World War II and the foundation of the United Nations. It took place in Yalta, a Soviet holiday resort in the Crimea.

Wars and Leaders

Alamein, El, Battles of in World War II, two decisive battles in the western desert, N Egypt. In the ***First Battle of El Alamein*** 1–27 July 1942 the British 8th Army under Auchinleck held the German and Italian forces under Rommel. In the ***Second Battle of El Alamein*** 23 Oct–4 Nov 1942 Montgomery defeated Rommel.

Arab-Israeli Wars series of wars between Israel and various Arab states in the Middle East since the founding of the state of Israel 1948. ***First Arab-Israeli War*** 15 May 1948–13 Jan/24 March 1949. As soon as the independent state of Israel had been proclaimed by the Jews, it was invaded by combined Arab forces. The Israelis defeated them and went on to annex territory until they controlled 75% of what had been Palestine under British mandate. ***Second Arab-Israeli War*** 29 Oct–4 Nov 1956. After Egypt had taken control of the Suez Canal and blockaded the Straits of Tiran, Israel, with British and French support, invaded and captured Sinai and the Gaza Strip, from which it withdrew under heavy US pressure after the entry of a United Nations force. ***Third Arab-Israeli War*** 5–10 June 1967, the ***Six Day War***. It resulted in the Israeli capture of the Golan Heights from Syria; the eastern half of Jerusalem and the West Bank from Jordan; and, in the south, the Gaza Strip and Sinai peninsula as far as the Suez Canal. ***Fourth Arab-Israeli War*** 6-24 Oct 1973, the 'October War' or ***Yom Kippur War***, so called because the Israeli forces were attacked by Egypt and Syria on the Day of Atonement, the holiest day of the Jewish year. After nearly three weeks of heavy fighting, with heavy losses, a cease-fire was agreed. ***Fifth Arab-Israeli War*** From 1978 the presence of Palestinian guerrillas in Lebanon led to Arab raids on Israel and Israeli retaliatory incursions, but on 6 June 1982 Israel launched a full-scale invasion. By 14 June Beirut was encircled, and Palestine Liberation Organization (PLO) and Syrian forces were evacuated (mainly to Syria) 21–31 Aug, but in Feb 1985 there was a unilateral Israeli withdrawal from the country without any gain or losses incurred. Israel maintains

Defence spending: the cost of restructuring

When the Berlin Wall came down in 1989, when communism failed and the Cold War ended, it seemed that peace had broken out in Europe and beyond. There was much discussion of a 'peace dividend' – a transfer of resources from defence spending to areas such as education, health, and social security. Now there is a degree of disillusion as we look back on the Gulf War, intervention in Kurdistan, strife in South Africa, famine and war in Somalia, Sudan, and Ethiopia, conflict in Moldova, Georgia, Tajikistan, and Azerbaijan, and civil war in Angola, Cambodia, and Bosnia – to mention only a few of the 73 'hot spots' extant in 1993. This figure includes 26 conflicts raging where two or more countries are at war, 23 areas where ethnic tensions and rivalries between nations or within a nation could give way to fighting, and 24 other areas where tension exists. What went wrong?

Arguably nothing 'went wrong'. The world had simply returned to normal. For 40 years it was as if Europe had been in a deep freeze. When communism failed the power source that had kept Europe frozen ceased to flow. Ethnic, religious, and nationalist tensions that had been suppressed for a generation and more re-emerged. Conflict was suppressed outside Europe too. Client states tended to pay homage to one or other superpower, and change occurred slowly in a bipolar world. Now that these artificial constraints have been removed the world is a much more untidy and unstable place.

But despite this return to 'normality', the collapse of the Soviet Union is an historic political and military watershed. The world has witnessed the disintegration of a nuclear superpower; the monolithic threat presented to Western Europe by the Warsaw Pact, which necessitated a high level of defence spending by NATO countries for 40 years, has evaporated. Conventional and nuclear arms control agreements have transformed the security environment. The Conventional Forces in Europe (CFE) Treaty, the Strategic Arms Reduction Treaty (START I and II), and other unilateral proposals made by both Russia and the USA, have resulted in agreements to slash weapon holdings by over 50%. Similarly armed forces personnel in Europe and in USA are being cut by about 25%, though some smaller nations such as Belgium, Denmark, and Holland are undertaking cuts of up to 50%.

So, despite widespread instability, moves have been made to cut defence spending. But reorganizations are expensive, and savings are unlikely to show before 1995. Reducing force levels means reorganizing force structures. It is not until the new structure is functioning smoothly that savings are made. In the UK, for instance, defence spending has increased in the financial year 1992–93 to £24 billion, from £22.85 billion in the previous year. A planned reduction from around 5% of GDP allocated to defence to about 3.5% is unlikely to be achieved in the UK until the late 1990s. Similarly, in the USA cuts of around 25% to the armed forces are taking place. But closing bases and relocating troops from Europe to the USA will be costly in the short term. Russia is finding the decommissioning of its nuclear arsenal a prohibitively expensive business, which is why the US Congress allocated $400 million in 1992 to help Russia undertake its disarmament programme.

Although some savings will be possible in the longer term, they may not be as great as was hoped in 1989. The international community is likely to feel obliged to attempt to minimize conflict where it can. Thus much effort is likely to be put into peacekeeping and peacemaking efforts through the auspices of the UN and other suitable ad hoc coalitions. Although it would be impossible to address every problem, there are situations where military intervention is practicable (such as Kurdistan and Somalia); equally there are some where it is not (such as Bosnia). Even Germany is overcoming its history: it deployed non-combat troops to Somalia in May 1993 and Japan did likewise to Cambodia in early 1993. Both these nations seem set on a path, albeit a cautious one, to becoming great powers in the full sense of the word. As such they realize they have to do more than just contribute economically to the international peacekeeping effort. In any event it is likely to be some years before either nation can bring itself to deploy combat troops, even for peacekeeping duties.

Defence spending will decrease in time, but not until the massive post-Cold War reorganization of defence structure is complete. Even then the new demands of peacekeeping will ensure that defence budgets will remain sizeable. The 'new world order' of peace and stability that we imagined might emerge in the wake of the Cold War has not materialized. While the threat of nuclear Armageddon has receded, nuclear proliferation remains a threat, and the world's energies must be turned towards defusing this new threat to peace.

MD

a 'security zone' in S Lebanon and supports the South Lebanese Army militia as a buffer against Palestinian guerrilla incursions.

Arnhem, Battle of in World War II, airborne operation by the Allies, 17–26 Sept 1944, to secure a bridgehead over the Rhine, thereby opening the way for a thrust towards the Ruhr and a possible early end to the war. It was only partially successful, with 7,600 casualties. Arnhem is a city in the Netherlands, on the Rhine SE of Utrecht.

Arras, Battle of battle of World War I, April–May 1917. It was an effective but costly British attack on German forces in support of a French offensive, which was only partially successful, on the Siegfried Line. British casualties totalled 84,000 as compared to 75,000 German casualties.

Atlantic, Battle of the continuous battle fought in the Atlantic Ocean during World War II by the sea and air forces of the Allies and Germany, to control the supply routes to the UK. The number of U-boats destroyed by the Allies during the war was nearly 800. At least 2,200 convoys of 75,000 merchant ships crossed the Atlantic, protected by US naval forces. Before the US entry into the war 1941, destroyers were supplied to the British under the Lend-Lease Act 1941. Fiftieth anniversary celebrations took place in Liverpool, England, in late May 1993.

Bataan peninsula in Luzon, the Philippines, which was defended against the Japanese in World War II by US and Filipino troops under General MacArthur 1 Jan–9 April 1942. MacArthur was evacuated, but some 67,000 Allied prisoners died on the ***Bataan Death March*** to camps in the interior.

Bradley Omar Nelson 1893–1981. US general in World War II. In 1943 he commanded the 2nd US Corps in their victories in Tunisia and Sicily, leading to the surrender of 250,000 Axis troops, and in 1944 led the US troops in the invasion of France. His command, as the 12th Army Group, grew to 1.3 million troops, the largest US force ever assembled.

Britain, Battle of World War II air battle between German and British air forces over Britain lasting 10 July–31 Oct 1940. At the outset the Germans had the advantage because they had seized airfields in the Netherlands, Belgium, and France, which were basically safe from attack and from which SE England was within easy range. On 1 Aug 1940 the Luftwaffe had about 4,500 aircraft of all kinds, compared to about 3,000 for the RAF. The Battle of Britain had been intended as a preliminary to the German invasion plan *Seelöwe* (Sea Lion), which Hitler indefinitely postponed 17 Sept and abandoned 10 Oct, choosing instead to invade the USSR.

Bulge, Battle of the or ***Ardennes offensive*** in World War II, Hitler's plan, code-named 'Watch on the Rhine', for a breakthrough by his field marshal Rundstedt aimed at the US line in the Ardennes 16 Dec 1944–28 Jan 1945. There were 77,000 Allied casualties and 130,000 German, including Hitler's last powerful reserve, his Panzer elite. Although US troops were encircled for some weeks at Bastogne, the German counteroffensive failed.

Caporetto former name of Kobarid (see entry), a village in Slovenia.

Cassino town in S Italy, 80 km/50 mi NW of Naples, at the foot of Monte Cassino; population (1981) 31,139. It was the scene of heavy fighting during World War II 1944, when most of the town was destroyed. It was rebuilt 1.5 km/1 mi to the N. The abbey on the summit of Monte Cassino, founded by St Benedict 529, was rebuilt 1956.

Clausewitz Karl von 1780–1831. Prussian officer and writer on war, born near Magdeburg. His book *Vom Kriege/On War* 1833, translated into English 1873, gave a new philosophical foundation to the art of war and put forward a concept of strategy that was influential until World War I.

D-day 6 June 1944, the day of the Allied invasion of Normandy under the command of General Eisenhower, with the aim of liberating Western Europe from German occupation. The Anglo-American invasion fleet landed on the Normandy beaches on the stretch of coast between the Orne River and St Marcouf. Artificial harbours known as 'Mulberries' were constructed and towed across the Channel so that equipment and armaments could be unloaded onto the beaches. After overcoming fierce resistance the allies broke through the German defences; Paris was liberated on 25 Aug, and Brussels on 2 Sept.

de Gaulle Charles André Joseph Marie 1890–1970. French general and first president of the Fifth Republic 1958-69. He organized the Free French troops fighting the Nazis 1940-44, was head of the provisional French government 1944-46, and leader of his own Gaullist party. In 1958 the national assembly asked him to form a government during France's economic recovery and to solve the crisis in Algeria. He became president at the end of 1958, having changed the constitution to provide for a presidential system, and served until 1969.

Desert Storm, Operation codename of the military action to eject the Iraqi army from Kuwait 1991. The build-up phase was codenamed ***Operation Desert Shield*** and lasted from Aug 1990, when Kuwait was first invaded by Iraq, to Jan 1991 when Operation Desert Storm was unleashed, starting the Gulf War. Desert Storm ended with the defeat of the Iraqi army in the Kuwaiti theatre of operations late Feb 1991. The cost of the operation was $53 billion.

Dönitz Karl 1891–1980. German admiral, originator of the wolf-pack submarine technique, which sank 15 million tonnes of Allied shipping in World War II. He succeeded Hitler in 1945, capitulated, and was imprisoned 1946–56.

Dunkirk (French ***Dunkerque***) seaport on the north coast of France, in Nord *département*, on the Strait of Dover. Dunkirk was close to the front line during much of World War I, and in World War II, 337,131 Allied troops (including about 110,000 French) were evacuated from the beaches as German forces approached.

Falklands War war between Argentina and Britain over disputed sovereignty of the Falkland Islands. It was initiated when Argentina invaded and occupied the islands 2 April 1982, declaring the Falkland Islands and other British-held South Atlantic islands part of the new Argentine province of Tierra del Fuego. On the following day, the United Nations

Security Council passed a resolution calling for Argentina to withdraw. A British task force was immediately dispatched and, after a fierce conflict in which over 1,000 Argentine and British lives were lost, 12,000 Argentine troops surrendered and the islands were returned to British rule 14-15 June 1982. The cost of the Falklands War was £1.6 billion.

Fuchs Klaus (Emil Julius) 1911–1988. German spy who worked on atom-bomb research in the USA in World War II, and subsequently in the UK. He was imprisoned 1950–59 for passing information to the USSR, and resettled in eastern Germany.

Fuller John Frederick Charles 1878–1966. British major general and military theorist who propounded the concept of armoured warfare which, when interpreted by the Germans, became ***blitzkrieg*** in 1940.

Gallipoli port in European Turkey. In World War I, at the instigation of Winston Churchill, an unsuccessful attempt was made Feb 1915–Jan 1916 by Allied troops to force their way through the Dardanelles and link up with Russia. The campaign was fought mainly by Australian and New Zealand (ANZAC) forces, who suffered heavy losses. An estimated 36,000 Commonwealth troops died during the nine-month campaign.

Galtieri Leopoldo 1926– . Argentine general, president 1981–82. A leading member from 1979 of the ruling right-wing military junta and commander of the army, Galtieri became president in 1981. Under his leadership the junta ordered the seizure 1982 of the Falkland Islands (Malvinas), a British colony in the SW Atlantic claimed by Argentina. After the surrender of his forces he resigned as army commander and was replaced as president. He and his fellow junta members were tried for abuse of human rights and court-martialled for their conduct of the war; he was sentenced to 12 years in prison in 1986.

Gulf War war 16 Jan–28 Feb 1991 between Iraq and a coalition of 28 nations led by the USA. The invasion and annexation of Kuwait by Iraq on 2 Aug 1990 provoked a build-up of US troops in Saudi Arabia, eventually totalling over 500,000. The UK subsequently deployed 42,000 troops, Egypt 20,000, France 15,000, and other nations smaller contingents. An air offensive lasting six weeks, in which 'smart' weapons came of age, destroyed about one-third of Iraqi equipment and inflicted massive casualties. A 100-hour ground war followed, which effectively destroyed the remnants of the 500,000-strong Iraqi army in or near Kuwait. The cost of the war is estimated to be $60–70 billion. A sum approximating $54.5 billion was donated by the Japanese, Germans, and Saudi Arabians towards the cost of conducting the war.

Hiroshima industrial city and port on the south coast of Honshu Island, Japan, destroyed by the first wartime use of an atomic bomb 6 Aug 1945. The city has largely been rebuilt since the war. Towards the end of World War II the city was utterly devastated by the US atomic bomb. More than 10 sq km/4 sq mi were obliterated, with very heavy damage outside that area. Casualties totalled at least 137,000 out of a population of 343,000: 78,150 were found dead, others died later.

Iwo Jima largest of the Japanese Volcano Islands in the W Pacific Ocean, 1,222 km/760 mi S of Tokyo; area 21 sq km/8 sq mi. Annexed by Japan 1891, it was captured by the USA 1945 after fierce fighting. It was returned to Japan 1968.

Jutland, Battle of naval battle of World War I, fought between England and Germany on 31 May 1916, off the W coast of Jutland. Its outcome was indecisive, but the German fleet remained in port for the rest of the war.

Khe Sanh in the Vietnam War, US Marine outpost near the Laotian border and just south of the demilitarized zone between North and South Vietnam. Garrisoned by 4,000 Marines, it was attacked unsuccessfully by 20,000 North Vietnamese troops 21 Jan–7 April 1968.

Kobarid formerly ***Caporetto*** village on the river Isonzo in NW Slovenia. Originally in Hungary, it was in Italy from 1918, and in 1947 became Kobarid. During World War I, German-Austrian troops defeated Italian forces there 1917.

Liddell Hart Basil 1895–1970. British military strategist. He was an exponent of mechanized warfare, and his ideas were adopted in Germany in 1935 in creating the 1st Panzer Division, combining motorized infantry and tanks. From 1937 he advised the UK War Office on army reorganization.

Marne, Battles of the in World War I, two unsuccessful German offensives. In the ***First Battle*** 6–9 Sept 1914, von Moltke's advance was halted by the British Expeditionary Force and the French under Foch; in the ***Second Battle*** 15 July–4 Aug 1918, Ludendorff's advance was defeated by British, French, and US troops under the French general Pétain, and German morale crumbled.

Montgomery Bernard Law, 1st Viscount Montgomery of Alamein 1887–1976. British field marshal. In World War II he commanded the 8th Army in N Africa in the Second Battle of El Alamein 1942. As commander of British troops in N Europe from 1944, he received the German surrender 1945.

Okinawa largest of the Japanese Ryuku Islands in the W Pacific; area 2,250 sq km/869 sq mi. It was captured by the USA in the ***Battle of Okinawa*** 1 Apr–21 June 1945, with 47,000 US casualties (12,000 dead) and 60,000 Japanese (only a few hundred survived as prisoners); the island was returned to Japan 1972.

Passchendaele village in W Flanders, Belgium, near Ypres. The Passchendaele ridge before Ypres was the object of a costly and unsuccessful British offensive in World War I, between July and Nov 1917; British casualties numbered nearly 400,000.

Patton George (Smith) 1885–1945. US general in World War II, known as 'Blood and Guts'. He was appointed to command the 2nd Armored Division 1940 and became commanding general of the First Armored Corps 1941. In 1942 he led the Western Task Force that landed at Casablanca, Morocco. After commanding the 7th Army, he led the 3rd Army across France and into Germany, and in 1945 took over the 15th Army.

Current regional conflicts

Europe	Northern Ireland (vs IRA); Spain (vs Basque separatist organization, ETA); Croatia (vs Serbian irregulars); Bosnia-Herzegovina (vs Serbian irregulars)
Middle East	Iran (vs Kurdish irregulars); Iraq (vs Kurdish irregulars and Shi'ite Muslim irregulars); Lebanon (Southern Lebanon, a battleground for Israeli–Palestinian conflict); Turkey (vs Kurdish irregulars)
Former USSR	Georgia (civil war); Armenia (vs Azerbaijan); Azerbaijan (vs Armenians in Nogorno-Karabakh); Tajikistan (civil war); Moldova (civil war)
South Asia	Afghanistan (civil war); Bangladesh (antigovernment insurgency); India (Hindu–Muslim clashes); India–Pakistan (over Kashmir); Myanmar (the Sha, Kachin, Karen secessionists, and prodemocracy rebellions); Sri Lanka (antigovernment insurgency by Tamil Tigers)
Pacific Asia	Cambodia (fragile ceasefire between four Cambodian factions maintained by UN peacekeeping force); Indonesia (continuing resistance to government in East Timor and Aceh independence movement in northern Sumatra); Philippines (armed communist and Muslim insurgency); Spratley Islands (contested by China, Vietnam, Brunei, Malaysia, Taiwan, and the Philippines; some islands occupied by Chinese and Vietnamese troops; clashes have occurred); Korea (spasmodic incidents on N Korea/S Korea border; 1.4 million troops facing each other across demilitarized zone)
Africa	Algeria (suppression of fundamentalist rebellion); Chad (intermittent antigovernment insurgency); Zaire (antigovernment insurgency); Morocco/Western Sahara (to establish independence for Western Sahara); Liberia (civil war); Somalia (civil war); South Africa (Inkatha–ANC violence and antigovernment insurgency); Sudan (civil war); Sierra Leone (antigovernment rebellion); Uganda (sporadic violence)
Central and South America	Columbia (narco-terrorism); El Salvador (UN peacekeeping force maintaining fragile peace between FMLN and government forces); Guatemala (antigovernment insurgency); Nicaragua (former Contra soldiers staging occasional violence); Peru (antigovernment insurgency by Shining Path terrorists)

Pearl Harbor US Pacific naval base in Oahu, Hawaii, USA, the scene of a Japanese aerial attack 7 Dec 1941, which brought the USA into World War II. The attack took place while Japanese envoys were holding so-called peace talks in Washington. More than 2,000 members of US armed forces were killed, and a large part of the US Pacific fleet was destroyed or damaged. The local commanders Admiral Kummel and Lt-Gen Short were relieved of their posts and held responsible for the fact that the base was totally unprepared at the time of the attack, but recent information indicates that warnings of the attack given to the USA (by British intelligence and others) were withheld from Kummel and Short by President Roosevelt. US public opinion was very much against entering the war, and Roosevelt wanted an excuse to change popular sentiments and take the USA into the war.

Rommel Erwin 1891–1944. German field marshal. He served in World War I, and in World War II he played an important part in the invasions of central Europe and France. He was commander of the N African offensive from 1941 (when he was nicknamed 'Desert Fox') until defeated in the Battles of El Alamein. Rommel was commander in chief for a short time against the Allies in Europe 1944 but (as a sympathizer with the Stauffenberg plot against Hitler) was forced to commit suicide.

Russo-Japanese War war between Russia and Japan 1904–05, which arose from conflicting ambitions in Korea and Manchuria, specifically, the Russian occupation of Port Arthur (modern Lüda) 1896 and of the Amur province 1900. Japan successfully besieged Port Arthur May 1904–Jan 1905, took Mukden (modern Shenyang) on 29 Feb–10 March, and on 27 May defeated the Russian Baltic fleet, which had sailed halfway around the world to Tsushima Strait. A peace was signed 23 Aug 1905. Russia surrendered its lease on Port Arthur, ceded S Sakhalin to Japan, evacuated Manchuria, and recognized Japan's interests in Korea.

Schwarzkopf (H) Norman (nicknamed 'Stormin' Norman') 1934– . US general who was supreme commander of the Allied forces in the Gulf War 1991. He planned and executed a blitzkrieg campaign, 'Desert Storm', sustaining remarkably few casualties in the liberation of Kuwait. He was a battalion commander in the Vietnam War and deputy commander of the 1983 US invasion of Grenada. A graduate of the military academy at West Point, Schwarzkopf obtained a master's degree in guided-missile engineering. He became an infantryman and later a paratrooper, and did two tours of service in Vietnam. Maintaining the 28-member Arab–Western military coalition against Iraq 1991 extended his diplomatic skills, and his success in the Gulf War made him a popular hero in the USA. He retired from the army Aug 1991.

Sevastopol or ***Sevastopol***, a port, resort, and fortress in the Crimea, Ukraine. It is the base of the (former) Black Sea fleet. It was besieged by the English and French during the Crimean War (Oct 1854–Sept 1855) and in World War II by the Germans (Nov 1941–July 1942, but was retaken by the USSR in 1944.

Sinai Egyptian peninsula, at the head of the Red Sea; area 65,000 sq km/25,000 sq mi. Resources include oil, natural gas, manganese, and coal; irrigation water from the river Nile is carried under the Suez Canal. Sinai was occupied by Israel 1967–82. After the Battle of Sinai 1973, Israel began a gradual withdrawal from the area, under the disengagement agreement 1975 and the Camp David peace treaty 1979, and restored the whole of Sinai to Egyptian control by April 1982.

Sino-Japanese Wars two wars waged by Japan against China 1894–95 and 1931–45 to expand to the mainland. Territory gained in the First Sino-Japanese War (Korea) and in the 1930s (Manchuria, Shanghai) was returned at the end of World War II. ***First Sino-***

Japanese War 1894–95. Under the treaty of Shimonoseki, Japan secured the 'independence' of Korea, cession of Taiwan and the nearby Pescadores Islands, and the Liaodong peninsula (for a naval base). France, Germany, and Russia pressured Japan into returning the last-named, which Russia occupied 1896 to establish Port Arthur (now Lüda); this led to the Russo-Japanese War 1904–05. ***Second Sino-Japanese War*** 1931–45. 1931– 37 The Japanese occupied Manchuria, which they formed into the puppet state of Manchukuo. They also attacked Shanghai, and moved into NE China. 1937 Chinese leaders Chiang Kai-shek and Mao Zedong allied to fight the Japanese; war was renewed as the Japanese overran NE China and seized Shanghai and Nanjing. 1938 Japanese capture of Wuhan and Guangzhou was followed by the transfer of the Chinese capital to Chongqing; a period of stalemate followed. 1941 Japanese attack on the USA (see Pearl Harbor) led to the extension of lend-lease aid to China and US entry into war against Japan and its allies. 1944 A Japanese offensive threatened Chongqing. 1945 The Chinese received the Japanese surrender at Nanjing in Sept, after the Allies had concluded World War II.

Stalingrad former name (1925–61) of the Russian city of Volgograd (see entry).

Tirpitz Alfred von 1849–1930. German admiral. As secretary for the navy 1897–1916, he created the German navy and planned the World War I U-boat campaign.

Tonkin Gulf Incident clash that triggered US entry into the Vietnam War in Aug 1964. Two US destroyers (USS *C Turner Joy* and USS *Maddox*) reported that they were fired on by North Vietnamese torpedo boats. It is unclear whether hostile shots were actually fired, but the reported attack was taken as a pretext for making air raids against North Vietnam. On 7 Aug the US Congress passed the ***Tonkin Gulf Resolution***, which allowed President Johnson to 'take all necessary steps, including the use of armed forces' to help SEATO (South-East Asia Treaty Organization) members 'defend their freedom'. This resolution formed the basis for the considerable increase in US military involvement in the Vietnam War; it was repealed 1970 in the light of evidence that the Johnson administration contrived to deceive Congress about the incident.

Verdun fortress town in NE France on the Meuse. During World War I it became the symbol of French resistance, withstanding a German onslaught 1916.

Vietnam War 1954–75. War between communist North Vietnam and US-backed South Vietnam. 200,000 South Vietnamese soldiers, 1 million North Vietnamese soldiers, and 500,000 civilians were killed. 56,555 US soldiers were killed 1961–75, a fifth of them by their own troops. The war destroyed 50% of the country's forest cover and 20% of agricultural land. Cambodia, a neutral neighbour, was bombed by the US 1969–75, with 1 million killed or wounded.

Volgograd formerly (until 1925) ***Tsaritsyn*** and (1925–61) ***Stalingrad***, an industrial city (metal goods, machinery, sawmills, oil refining) in SW Russia, on the river Volga; population (1987) 988,000. Its successful defence 1942–43 against Germany was a turning point in World War II. The German 6th army under field marshal Friedrich Paulus captured Stalingrad 1943, but was forced to surrender to the USSR under marshal Georgi Zhukov. After intense fighting, the Germans lost 70,000 men.

World War I 1914–1918. War between the Central European Powers (Germany, Austria-Hungary, and allies) on one side and the Triple Entente (Britain and the British Empire, France, and Russia) and their allies, including the USA (which entered 1917), on the other side. An estimated 10 million lives were lost and twice that number were wounded.

World War II 1939–1945. War between Germany, Italy, and Japan (the Axis powers) on one side, and Britain, the Commonwealth, France, the USA, the USSR, and China (the Allied powers) on the other. An estimated 55 million lives were lost, 20 million of them citizens of the USSR. The war was fought in the Atlantic and Pacific theatres. In May 1945 Germany surrendered, but Japan fought on until the USA dropped atomic bombs on Hiroshima and Nagasaki in August.

Ypres (Flemish ***Ieper***) Belgian town in W Flanders, 40 km/25 mi S of Ostend, a site of three major battles 1914–17 fought in World War I. The Menin Gate 1927 is a memorial to British soldiers lost in these battles.

Zhukov Georgi Konstantinovich 1896–1974. Marshal of the USSR in World War II and minister of defence 1955–57. As chief of staff from 1941, he defended Moscow 1941, counterattacked at Stalingrad (now Volgograd) 1942, organized the relief of Leningrad (now St Petersburg) 1943, and led the offensive from the Ukraine March 1944 which ended in the fall of Berlin. He subsequently commanded the Soviet occupation forces in Germany.

Weapons and Equipment

aircraft carrier sea-going base for military aircraft. After World War II the cost and vulnerability of such large vessels were thought to have outweighed their advantages. However, by 1980 the desire to have a means of destroying enemy aircraft beyond the range of a ship's own weapons, especially on convoy duty, led to a widespread revival of aircraft carriers of 20,000–30,000 tonnes. Aircraft carriers are equipped with combinations of fixed-wing aircraft, helicopters, missile launchers, and anti-aircraft guns.

armoured personnel carrier (APC) wheeled or tracked military vehicle designed to transport up to ten people. Armoured to withstand small-arms fire and shell splinters, it is used on battlefields.

assault ship naval vessel designed to land and support troops and vehicles under hostile conditions.

bayonet short sword attached to the muzzle of a firearm. The new British Army rifle, the SA-80, is fitted with a bayonet; its predecessor, the SLR, was similarly equipped and used, with its bayonet, during the 1982 Falklands conflict.

binary weapon weapon consisting of two substances that in isolation are harmless but when mixed together form a poisonous nerve gas. They are loaded into the delivery system separately and combine after launch.

enhanced radiation weapon another name for the neutron bomb.

fuel-air explosive warhead containing a highly flammable petroleum and oxygen mixture; when released over a target, this mixes with the oxygen in the atmosphere and produces a vapour which, when ignited, causes a blast approximately five times more powerful than conventional high explosives. Fuel-air explosives were used by the US Air Force in the 1991 Gulf War to flatten Iraqi defensive positions.

Harrier the only truly successful vertical takeoff and landing fixed-wing aircraft, often called the ***jump jet***. Built in Britain, it made its first flight 1966. It has a single jet engine and a set of swivelling nozzles. These deflect the jet exhaust vertically downwards for takeoff and landing, and to the rear for normal flight. Designed to fly from confined spaces with minimal ground support, it can refuel in midair.

incendiary bomb a bomb containing inflammable matter. Usually dropped by aircraft, incendiary bombs were used in World War I, and were a major weapon in attacks on cities in World War II. To hinder firefighters, delayed-action high-explosive bombs were usually dropped with them. In the Vietnam War, US forces used napalm in incendiary bombs.

machine gun rapid-firing automatic gun. The forerunner of the modern machine gun was the Gatling (named after its US inventor R J Gatling 1818–1903), perfected in the USA in 1860 and used in the American Civil War. The Maxim of 1884 was recoil-operated, but some later types have been gas-operated (Bren) or recoil assisted by gas (some versions of the Browning). The ***sub-machine gun***, exploited by Chicago gangsters in the 1920s, was widely used in World War II; for instance the Thompson, often called the Tommy gun.

mechanized infantry combat vehicle (MICV) tracked military vehicle designed to fight as part of an armoured battle group; that is, with tanks. It is armed with a quick-firing cannon and one or more machine guns. MICVs have replaced armoured personnel carriers.

mine explosive charge on land or sea, or in the atmosphere, designed to be detonated by contact, vibration (for example, from an enemy engine), magnetic influence, or a timing device. Countermeasures include metal detectors (useless for plastic types), specially equipped helicopters, and (at sea) minesweepers.

missile rocket-propelled weapon, which may be nuclear-armed. Modern missiles are often classified according to range into ***intercontinental ballistic missiles*** (ICBMs, capable of reaching targets over 5,500 km/3,400 mi), ***intermediate-range missiles*** (1,100 km/680 mi–2,750 km/1,700 mi), and ***short-range missiles*** (under 1,100 km/680 mi). They are also categorized as ***surface-to-surface missiles*** (SSM), ***air-to-air missiles*** (AAM), ***surface-to-air missiles*** (SAM), or ***air-to-surface missiles*** (ASM).

A ***ballistic missile*** is one whose trajectory is governed by gravity once the power is shut off. The first long-range ballistic missile used was the V2 launched by Germany against Britain in World War II. Outside the industrialized countries, 22 states had active ballistic-missile programmes by 1989, and 17 had deployed these weapons: Afghanistan, Argentina, Brazil, Cuba, Egypt, India, Iran, Iraq, Israel, North Korea, South Korea, Libya, Pakistan, Saudi Arabia, South Africa, Syria, and Taiwan.

A ***cruise missile*** is in effect a pilotless, computer-guided aircraft; it can be sea-launched from submarines or surface ships, or launched from the air or the ground. Tomahawk cruise missiles launched from both US submarines and battleships lying offshore were devastatingly effective and accurate against targets deep within Iraq during the 1991 Gulf War.

Battlefield missiles used in the 1991 Gulf War include anti-tank missiles and short-range attack missiles. NATO announced in 1990 that it was phasing out ground-launched nuclear battlefield missiles, and these are being replaced by types of tactical air-to-surface missile (TASM), also with nuclear warheads.

European defence

Expenditure and personnel, selected countries, 1991 ($m/persons)

Forces	*Defence spending*	*% of GDP*	*Regular forces*	*Reserve forces*
Austria	1,680	1.0	44,000	242,000
Belgium	3,250	1.6	85,450	234,000
Denmark	2,850	2.2	29,400	72,300
Finland	2,420	1.9	31,800	700,000
France	37,340	3.1	453,100	419,000
Germany	34,360	2.4	476,300	1,009,400
Greece	4,520	6.8	158,500	406,000
Ireland	553	1.3	12,900	16,100
Italy	21,310	1.9	361,400	584,000
Luxembourg	100	1.1	800	0
Netherlands	8,290	2.9	101,400	152,400
Norway	3,760	3.5	32,700	285,000
Portugal	1,540	2.6	61,800	190,000
Spain	8,970	1.8	257,400	2,400,000
Sweden	6,240	2.7	63,000	709,000
Switzerland	4,100	1.8	3,500	625,000
UK	43,559	4.3	300,100	347,200

Source: Eurostat

mortar method of projecting a bomb via a high trajectory at a target up to 6–7 km/3–4 mi away. A mortar bomb is stabilized in flight by means of tail fins. The high trajectory results in a high angle of attack and makes mortars more suitable than artillery for use in built-up areas or mountains; mortars are less accurate, however. Artillery also differs in firing a projectile through a rifled barrel, thus creating greater muzzle velocity.

napalm fuel used in flamethrowers and incendiary bombs. Produced from jellied petrol, it is a mixture of ***na***phthenic and ***palm***itic acids. Napalm causes extensive burns because it sticks to the skin even when aflame. It was widely used by the US Army during the Vietnam War.

Patriot missile ground-to-air medium-range missile system used in air defence. It has high-altitude coverage, electronic jamming capability, and excellent mobility. US Patriot missiles were tested in battle against Scud missiles fired by the Iraqis in the 1991 Gulf War, successfully intercepting 24 missiles out of about 85 attempts.

periscope optical instrument designed for observation from a concealed position such as a submerged submarine. In its basic form it consists of a tube with parallel mirrors at each end, inclined at 45° to its axis. The periscope attained prominence in naval and military operations of World War I.

remotely piloted vehicle (RPV) crewless mini-aircraft used for military surveillance and to select targets in battle. RPVs barely show up on radar, so they can fly over a battlefield without being shot down, and they are equipped to transmit TV images to an operator on the ground. RPVs were used by Israeli forces in 1982 in Lebanon and by the Allies in the 1991 Gulf War. The US system is called Aquila and the British system Phoenix.

rifle firearm that has spiral grooves (rifling) in its barrel. When a bullet is fired, the rifling makes it spin, thereby improving accuracy. Rifles were first introduced in the late 18th century.

Scud surface-to-surface missile designed and produced in the USSR, that can be armed with a nuclear, chemical, or conventional warhead. The ***Scud-B***, deployed on a mobile launcher, was the version most commonly used by the Iraqi army in the Gulf War 1991. It is a relatively inaccurate weapon. The Scud-B has a range of 300 km/180 mi; modified by the Iraqi army into the ***al-Hussayn***, it was capable of projecting a smaller payload (about 500 kg/1,100 lb) for a distance of up to 650 km/400 mi, and was used during the Gulf War to hit Israel and Saudi Arabia.

Semtex plastic explosive, manufactured in the Czech Republic. It is safe to handle (it can only be ignited by a detonator) and difficult to trace, since it has no smell. It has been used by extremist groups in the Middle East and by the IRA in Northern Ireland. 0.5kg of Semtex is thought to have been the cause of an explosion that destroyed a Pan-American Boeing 747 in flight over Lockerbie, Scotland, in Dec 1988, killing 270 people.

small arms one of the two main divisions of firearms: guns that can be carried by hand. The first small arms were portable handguns in use in the late 14th century, supported on the ground and ignited by hand. Today's small arms range from breech-loading single-shot rifles and shotguns to sophisticated automatic and semiautomatic weapons. In 1980, there were 11,522 deaths in the USA caused by hand-held guns; in the UK, there were 8. From 1988 guns accounted for more deaths among teenage US males than all other causes put together.

smart weapon programmable bomb or missile that can be guided to its target by laser technology, TV homing technology, or terrain-contour matching (TERCOM). A smart weapon relies on its pinpoint accuracy to destroy a target rather than on the size of its warhead. Examples are the cruise missile (Tomahawk), laser-guided artillery shells (Copperhead), laser-guided bombs, and short-range TV-guided missiles (SLAM). Smart weapons were first used on the battlefield in the Gulf War 1991, but only 3% of all the bombs dropped or missiles fired were smart. Of that 3%, it was estimated that 50–70% hit their targets, which is a high accuracy rate.

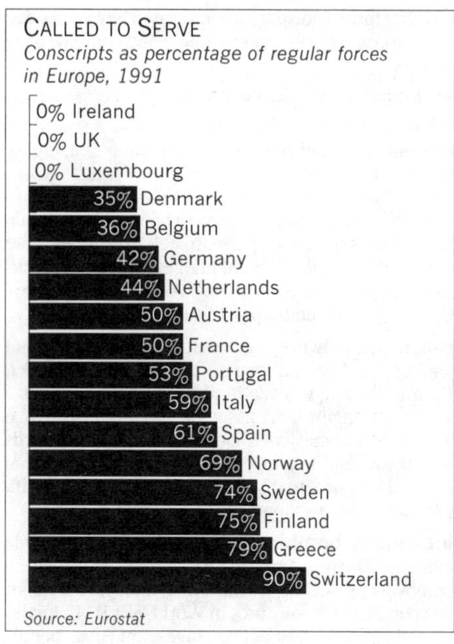

stealth technology methods used to make an aircraft as invisible as possible, primarily to radar detection but also to detection by visual means and heat sensors. This is achieved by a combination of aircraft-design elements: smoothing off all radar-reflecting sharp edges; covering the aircraft with radar-absorbent materials; fitting engine coverings that hide the exhaust and heat signatures of the aircraft; and other, secret technologies.

The US F-117A stealth fighter-bomber was used during the 1991 Gulf War to attack targets in Baghdad completely undetected. The B-2 bomber, a larger stealth aircraft, is being put into limited production.

TASM (abbreviation for ***tactical air-to-surface missile***) missile with a range of under 500 km/300 mi and a nuclear warhead. TASMs are being developed independently by the USA and France to replace the surface-to-surface missiles being phased out by NATO from 1990.

torpedo self-propelled underwater missile, invented 1866 by British engineer Robert Whitehead. Modern torpedoes are homing missiles; some resemble mines in that they lie on the seabed until activated by the acoustic signal of a passing ship. A television camera enables them to be remotely controlled, and in the final stage of attack they lock on to the radar or sonar signals of the target ship.

U-2 US military reconnaissance aeroplane, used in secret flights over the USSR from 1956 to photograph military installations. In 1960 a U-2 was shot down over the USSR and the pilot, Gary Powers, was captured and imprisoned. He was exchanged for a US-held Soviet agent two years later.

U-boat German submarine. The title was used in both world wars.

vertical takeoff and landing craft (VTOL) aircraft that can take off and land vertically. Helicopters, airships, and balloons can do this, as can a few fixed-wing aeroplanes, like the convertiplane.

GALLUP POLL

How much confidence do you have in the armed forces?

A great deal	33	27	52	31	35
Quite a lot	51	52	39	46	48
Not very much	12	14	7	14	12
None at all	4	7	2	9	4

Would you say that you worry a lot or very little about the possibility of another war?

	Dec 1992	Mar 1986	Apr 1983
Lot	11	20	20
Little	29	26	32
Not at all	60	53	48

Which of the following would you prefer to see happen to Northern Ireland? Would you prefer Northern Ireland to...?

	Mar 1993	Jul 1992	Jan 1988	May 1986
Remain part of the UK	27	28	26	26
Become part of the Republic of Ireland	15	20	21	24
Become independent from both the UK and the Republic of Ireland	41	36	36	35
Don't know/don't care	17	16	16	15

Which of these statements comes closest to the way you, yourself, feel about the presence of British troops in Northern Ireland?

	Mar 1993	Jul 1992	Jan 1988	Aug 1981	Mid Sep 1979
We should withdraw our troops immediately	27	29	24	34	44
We should withdraw our troops within 5 years	18	22	20	17	15
British troops should remain in Northern Ireland till a settlement is reached	44	37	42	33	27
We should not withdraw our troops	6	6	7	7	7
Don't know	5	6	7	6	7

Source: Gallup

ECONOMICS & BUSINESS

Business 255

International Economics 274

BUSINESS

Business Terms

added value or ***value added*** the sales revenue from selling a firm's products less the cost of the materials or purchases used in those products. An increasingly used indicator of relative efficiency within and between firms, although in the latter case open to distortion where mark-up varies between standard and premium-priced segments of a market.

adverse variance a difference between actual and budgeted spending or income that results in the organization having less money than planned.

alpha share on the stock market, a share in any of the companies most commonly traded – that is, the larger companies.

amortization the ending of a debt by paying it off gradually, over a period of time. The term is used to describe either the paying-off of a cash debt or the accounting procedure by which the value of an asset is progressively reduced ('depreciated') over a number of years.

annual accounts summary of the records of a company's financial activities, prepared by an accountant and in most countries made available for public inspection. Annual accounts include a balance sheet and a profit/loss or income/expenditure account.

annual general meeting (AGM) yearly meeting of the shareholders of a company or the members of an organization, at which business including consideration of the annual report and accounts, the election of officers, and the appointment of auditors is normally carried out.

annual percentage rate (APR) charge (including interest) for granting consumer credit, expressed as an equivalent once-a-year percentage figure of the amount of the credit granted. It is usually approximately double the flat rate of interest, or simple interest. In the UK, lenders are legally required to state the APR when advertising loans.

arbitrageur person who buys securities (such as currency or commodities) in one country or market for immediate resale in another market, to take advantage of different prices. Arbitrage became widespread during the 1970s and 1980s with the increasing deregulation of financial markets. The effect of arbitrage is to lessen or eliminate the price differentials among the markets. The term took on additional meaning with the increase in corporate buy-outs in the deregulated atmosphere of the late 1980s. Arbitrageurs speculated on target companies, buying stock and reselling it at the higher buy-out price.

articles of association in the UK, the rules governing the relationship between a registered company, its members (the shareholders), and its directors. The articles of association are deposited with the Registrar of Companies along with the memorandum of association.

asset in business accounting, a term that covers the land or property of a company or individual, payments due from bills, investments, and anything else owned that can be turned into cash. On a company's balance sheet, total assets must be equal to liabilities (money and services owed). An ***intangible asset*** is one that is not physical, for example a brand name or a list of business contacts. A ***fixed asset*** is a possession or valuable that is used over a long period of time. Examples of physical fixed assets include factories, offices, machinery, lorries, company cars, and office equipment.

asset stripping sale or exploitation by other means of the assets of a business, often one that has been taken over for that very purpose. The parts of the business may be potentially more valuable separately than together. Asset stripping is a major force for the more efficient use of assets.

audit official inspection of a company's accounts by a qualified accountant as required by law each year to ensure that the company balance sheet reflects the true state of its affairs.

bad debt bill or debt that has not been paid and is most unlikely to be paid. Bad debts eventually have to be 'written off' on the profit and loss account. They are counted as a provision and are deducted from the account.

balance sheet statement of the financial position of a company or individual on a specific date, showing both assets and liabilities.

bankruptcy process by which the property of a person (in legal terms, an individual or corporation) unable to pay debts is taken away under a court order and divided fairly among the person's creditors, after preferential payments such as taxes and wages. Proceedings may be instituted either by the debtor (voluntary bankruptcy) or by any creditor for a substantial sum (involuntary bankruptcy). Until 'discharged', a bankrupt is severely restricted in financial activities.

base rate the rate of interest to which most bank lending is linked, the actual rate depending on the status of the borrower. A prestigious company might command a rate only 1% above base rate, while an individual would be charged several points above.

bear speculator who sells stocks or shares on the stock exchange expecting a fall in the price in order to buy them back at a profit; the opposite of a bull. In a bear market, prices fall and bears prosper.

beta share on the stock exchange, a share traded less actively than an alpha share.

bill of exchange form of commercial credit instrument, or IOU, used in international trade. In Britain, a bill of exchange is defined by the Bills of Exchange Act 1882 as an unconditional order in writing addressed by one person to another, signed by the person giving it, requiring the person to whom it is addressed to pay on demand or at a fixed or determinable future time a certain sum in money to or to the order of a specified person, or to the bearer.

bill of lading document giving proof of particular goods having been loaded on a ship. The person to whom the goods are being sent normally needs to show the bill of lading in order to obtain the release of the goods. For air freight, there is an ***airway bill***.

blue chip stock that is considered strong and reliable in terms of the dividend yield and capital value. Blue-chip companies are favoured by stock-market investors more interested in security than risk taking.

bond security issued by a government, local authority, company, bank, or other institution on fixed interest. Usually a long-term security, a bond may be irredeemable (with no date of redemption), secured (giving the investor a claim on the company's property or on a part of its assets), or unsecured (not protected by a lien). Property bonds are non-fixed securities with the yield fixed to property investment.

brand named good that in the perception of the buyer is different from other similar goods in the market; its name and logo, or ***trademark***. A ***brand leader*** is a branded product that has the largest share of the market for all products of that type.

breakeven the level of output where costs equal revenue and no profit or loss is made.

broker intermediary who arranges the sale of financial products (shares, insurance, mortgages, and so on) to the public for a commission or brokerage fee.

budget estimate of income and expenditure for some future period, used in financial planning.

bull speculator who buys stocks or shares on the stock exchange expecting a rise in the price in order to sell them later at a profit; the opposite of a bear. In a bull market, prices rise and bulls profit.

business plan key management tool that focuses on business objectives, the products or services involved, estimated market potential, expertise in the firm, projected financial results, the money required from investors, and the likely investment return.

call demand for money, especially instalments of part-paid securities.

capacity the maximum amount that can be produced when all the resources in an economy, industry, or firm are employed as fully as possible. Capacity constraints can be caused by lack of investment and skills shortages, and spare capacity can be caused by lack of demand.

capital employed the total assets of a company (excluding intangibles, such as good will) less its current liabilities (including overdrafts, short-term loans, trade and other creditors).

capital expenditure spending on fixed assets such as plant and equipment, trade investments, or the purchase of other businesses.

capital flight transfer of funds from a particular national economy or out of a particular currency in anticipation of less attractive investment conditions.

cartel agreement among national or international firms to fix prices for their products. A cartel may restrict supply (output) to raise prices in order to increase member profits. It therefore represents a form of oligopoly.

cash flow input of cash required to cover all expenses of a business, whether revenue or capital. Alternatively, the actual or prospective balance between the various outgoing and incoming movements which are designated in total, positive or negative according to which is greater.

commodity something produced for sale. Commodities may be consumer goods, such as radios, or producer goods, such as copper bars. ***Commodity markets*** deal in raw or semi-raw materials that are amenable to grading and that can be stored for considerable periods without deterioration.

company a number of people grouped together as a business enterprise. Types of company include public limited companies, partnerships, joint ventures, sole proprietorships, and branches of foreign companies. Most companies are private and, unlike public companies, cannot offer their shares to the general public.

consumer person who purchases goods and services. Consumers demand goods which businesses provide, and they need to be protected by law from unfair traders; hence the need for consumer protection acts and the work of consumer bodies such as the Consumers' Association.

consumer durable any commodity for personal use that has a long life, such as furniture and electrical goods, as opposed to food and drink, which are ***perishables*** and have to be replaced frequently.

consumer sovereignty a situation where consumers decide what is to be produced by producers. In a market economy, this is achieved through companies being forced to compete to attract the spending of consumers. The opposite of consumer sovereignty is producer sovereignty, the situation where producers decide what consumers can buy. In a market economy, this could be the result of monopoly power, or the use of advertising which manipulates the desires of consumers for products.

convertible loan stock stock or bond (paying a fixed interest) that may be converted into a stated number of shares at a specific date.

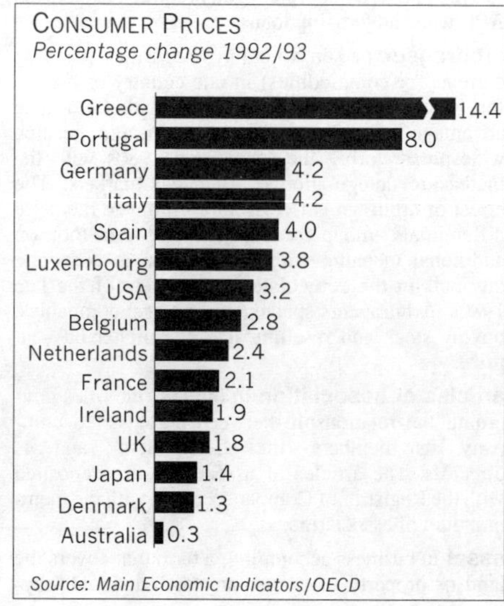

The top 25 European companies

Ranking 1992	1991	Company	Country	Market capital ($m)
1	1	Royal Dutch/Shell	Netherlands/UK	76,049.7
2	3	Glaxo Holdings	UK	38,315.5
3	2	BT	UK	35,909.7
4	5	Unilever plc/NV	Netherlands/UK	31,589.6
5	8	Nestlé	Switzerland	27,918.6
6	18	Roche Holding	Switzerland	25,018.2
7	6	Allianz Holding	Germany	22,570.7
8	9	Siemens	Germany	21,269.0
9	15	BAT Industries	UK	20,520.9
10	12	Deutsche Bank	Germany	20,329.3
11	17	Smithkline Beecham	UK	20,238.9
12	4	British Petroleum	UK	19,229.5
13	10	Daimler-Benz	Germany	17,789.0
14	7	British Gas	UK	17,516.9
15	14	Guinness	UK	17,502.2
16	11	Hanson	UK	17,122.5
17	23	Alcatel Alsthom	France	16,702.1
18	13	Elf Aquitaine	France	16,413.4
19	0	HSBC Holdings	UK	16,293.8
20	29	Sandoz	Switzerland	15,612.7
21	22	BTR	UK	15,510.2
22	20	Marks and Spencer	UK	14,810.3
23	24	Generali (Assicurazioni)	Italy	13,805.2
24	26	Ciba-Geigy	Switzerland	13,794.6
25	30	Union Bank of Switzerland	Switzerland	13,786.6

Source: Financial Times

corporate strategy the way an organization intends to meet its objectives. This may be set out in a document of its principles, its situation, and the environment in which it expects to operate.

cost for a business, the amount of money it has to spend in order to produce goods and services for sale. ***Direct costs*** are costs that vary directly with output, such as raw material inputs. ***Indirect costs*** are costs that change as output changes but not in direct proportion. ***Overhead costs*** are the costs of running the business, which do not change as output changes. In economics, these three cost concepts are called variable, semi-variable, and fixed costs. ***Total cost*** is the sum of all costs incurred in producing a given level of output.

cost–benefit analysis process whereby a project is assessed for its social and welfare benefits in addition to considering the financial return on investment. For example, this might take into account the environmental impact of an industrial plant or convenience for users of a new railway. A major difficulty is finding a way to quantify net social costs and benefits.

cost of sales the cost incurred directly by a business in making sales. This may include the cost of raw materials or goods bought for resale and labour costs incurred in producing goods. It does not include overhead costs.

creditor individual or business organization that is owed money by another individual or business. Money owed to creditors by a company is a current liability on the company's balance sheet.

critical-path analysis procedure used in the management of complex projects to minimize the amount of time taken. The analysis shows which subprojects can run in parallel with each other, and which have to be completed, in which order, before other subprojects can follow on. Complex projects may involve hundreds of subprojects, and computer applications packages for critical-path analysis are widely used to help reduce the time and effort involved in their analysis.

cumulative preference share preference share whose entitlement to dividend is carried forward to a subsequent year whenever a dividend is not paid.

current asset or ***circulating*** or ***floating asset*** any asset of a business that could be turned into cash in a limited period of time, generally less than a year. Current assets include stocks, accounts receivable or billings, short-term investments, and cash.

current liability any debt of a business that falls due within one year. Current liabilities include creditors (including employees), bank overdrafts, and interest.

current ratio or ***working capital ratio*** in a company, the ratio of current assets to current liabilities. It is a general indication of the solvency of a company, the adequacy of its working capital and its ability to meet day-to-day calls upon it.

dawn raid sudden and unexpected buying of a significant proportion of a company's shares, usually as a prelude to a takeover bid. The aim is to prevent the target company from having time to organize opposition to the takeover.

debenture or ***company stock*** long-term loan raised by a company through the issue of debenture certificates, using its assets as security for repayment.

debt something that is owed by a person, organization, or country, usually money, goods, or services. Debt usually occurs as a result of borrowing credit. ***Debt servicing*** is the payment of interest on a debt. A ***debtor*** is an individual, business organization, or government that owes money to another. (For *international debt*, see ***International Economics***.)

deferred share on the stock market, a share that typically warrants a dividend only after a specified dividend has been paid on the ordinary shares; it may, however, be entitled to a dividend on all the profits after that point.

depreciation the decline of a currency's value in relation to other currencies. Depreciation also describes the fall in value of an asset (such as factory machinery) resulting from age, wear and tear, or other circumstances. It is an important factor in assessing company profits and tax liabilities.

director person who is elected to the board of directors of a company by shareholders at the annual general meeting of the company. Directors are by law responsible for protecting the interests of shareholders in a company. They appoint managers to run the company on a day-to-day basis.

diseconomies of scale increase in the average cost of production as output increases in the long run. Diseconomies of scale are said to arise because larger businesses find it more difficult to manage their resources, particularly their workers, than small firms. For example, a large firm may employ too many managers, which pushes up their average costs.

diversification corporate strategy of entering distinctly new products or markets, as opposed to simply adding to an existing product range. A company may diversify in order to spread its risks or because its original area of operation is becoming less profitable.

dividend the amount of money that company directors decide should be taken out of net profits for distribution to shareholders. It is usually declared as a percentage or fixed amount per share.

earnings pay including basic pay plus any additional payments such as overtime pay or bonus payments. ***Gross earnings*** are earnings before deductions such as income tax and national insurance contributions have been taken away. ***Net earnings*** are earnings after deductions.

economies of scale increase in production capacity at a financial cost that is more than compensated for by the greater volume of output. For example, there would be economies of scale present if a car manufacturer could manufacture cars at £5,000 per car if it produced 100,000 cars per year, but at £4,000 per car if it produced 200,000 cars per year.

EFTPOS (acronym for ***electronic funds transfer at point of sale***) transfer of funds from one bank account to another by electronic means. For example, a customer inserts a plastic card into a point-of-sale computer terminal in a supermarket, and telephone lines are used to make an automatic debit from the customer's bank account to settle the bill.

end-use certificate in shipping, a document intended to assure authorities of the eventual application (generally also the final customer and destination) of a particular actual or intended shipment. End-use certificates are needed in cases where there are political controls on exports, such as advanced military weapons.

equal-opportunity policy plan of action that spells out what constitutes unfair discrimination in order to guide employment practices and to ensure that the organization is working within the legislation on equal pay, sex and race discrimination.

equity a company's assets, less its liabilities, which are the property of the owner or shareholders. Popularly, equities are stocks and shares which do not pay interest at fixed rates but pay dividends based on the company's performance. The value of equities tends to rise over the long term, but in the short term they are a risk investment because prices can fall as well as rise. Equity is also used to refer to the paid value of mortgaged real property, most commonly a house.

Eurobond bond underwritten by an international syndicate and sold in countries other than the country of the currency in which the issue is denominated. It provides longer-term financing than is possible with loans in Eurodollars.

executive director company director who is also an employee of the company.

experience curve observed effect of improved performance of individuals and organizations as experience of a repeated task increases.

external economies of scale fall in the average cost of production for a firm arising from the growth of the industry in which the firm operates. For example, growth in an industry might lead to an increase in the number of component supply firms for that industry, which might lead to a fall in the price of components.

factoring lending money to a company on the security of money owed to that company; this is often done on the basis of collecting those debts. The lender is known as the factor. Factoring may also describe acting as a commission agent for the sale of goods.

favourable variance difference between actual and budgeted spending or income that results in an organization having more money than planned.

Financial Times indices scales for measuring aspects of the stock market, published by the *Financial Times* of London. They are: FT ordinary, FT- SE 100, FT-Actuaries All Share, FT Government Securities, FT Fixed Interest, FT-SE Eurotrack 200, FT-Actuaries World Index and Indices of National and Regional Markets.

financial year in the UK, from 6 April one year to 5 April the following year. The financial year of a company (its accounting year) may differ from this. A company can choose any 12-month period for its accounting year.

fixed cost or ***overhead cost*** cost that does not vary directly with output, but remains constant as output increases. For example, a company may increase its output by one third; variable costs will increase in

The cost of clean water

Europe's water industry is in crisis as it counts the costs of new EC directives at a time when its neglected systems are struggling to cope with recurring drought and rising demand. Under pressure from Brussels and badgered by environmentalists and consumer groups, Europe's water suppliers need lots of money to protect, provide, and deliver clean and high-quality water.

Already, most European consumers are worse off than their US counterparts. In the USA, water charges average under $0.50 per cu m. Equivalent charges in Europe range from $0.75 in Ireland to $1.25 in Germany; only Norway and Italy's water is cheaper. Yet demands on water supplies in Europe are becoming ever more stringent, which is bound to send costs even higher.

The EC standards demand better water quality, which means that more water will have to be treated. The directives require that major water purification treatment plants should be installed in towns of more than 15,000 inhabitants by the end of the century. The scale of the task is daunting, but even stricter laws are expected to come into force by the year 2005, when similar purification plants will be required for towns of more than 2,000 inhabitants. Even with the help of EC structural funding, the cost of implementing these directives and achieving the targets will be phenomenal. The question that arises is: who picks up the extra bill?

Perhaps a lesson can be learned from the experience in France, where privatization provided French companies with the flexibility to adapt to stricter EC standards without undue pain. The water industry in France allows the private sector to operate effectively under only limited control. Water companies tender for water provision and treatment contracts from local, regional, and departmental authorities. Winning bidders are then licensed to charge a set rate on all the water supply or treatment in the area. A French water authority monitors pricing and water-quality levels and can rescind licences if it finds that a firm is breaking its contractual obligations. Price regulation is flexible enough for companies to make good returns. Current prices of about $1 per cu m compare well with the rest of Europe.

Two large companies, Générale des Eaux and Lyonnaise des Eaux Dumez, dominate the French water market. In recent years, both have diversified into different sectors, such as construction and cable television, and have taken interests in foreign private water firms, mainly in Britain. Latin America, Eastern Europe, and Asia are other regions where both firms have expanded and bought large water interests. Profits in the core water interests of both companies at home and abroad have been healthy, although the larger of the two companies, Générale des Eaux, has fared much better over the past few years. Profits there hovered around $560 million in 1992, up about 11% on the previous year. In France, water treatment and purification offer the best prospects for expansion and higher margins. Returns from the new treatment services, for example, are expected to be higher than the margins that can be achieved in water supply.

The overall verdict on the French water business suggests that utility companies will enjoy increased profits and general growth in the years ahead. It is not surprising that despite the seemingly persistent drought in the South, acid rain in the North, appalling pollution in the East, and increasing demand everywhere, Europe's water companies are poised to jump in to ensure that there is enough to wash the baby and the family car, the household laundry and the dishes, and also to satisfy the insatiable thirst of farmers and industry.

But the cost of keeping water or making waste water clean and safe to drink can be measured only in billions of dollars. Many companies believe that the EC quality standards and the cost of complying are too high. What is the alternative: to be penny wise and pound foolish?

OA

proportion with this but fixed costs will stay the same.

Fordism mass production characterized by a high degree of job specialization, as typified by Ford motor company's early use of assembly lines. ***Post-Fordism*** management theory and practice emphasizes flexibility and autonomy of decision-making for nonmanagerial staff. It is concerned more with facilitating and coordinating tasks than with control.

franchise the right given by one company to another to manufacture, distribute, or provide its products. Examples of franchise operations in the UK include Benetton and the Body Shop. Many US companies use franchises to distribute their products.

future contract to buy or sell a specific quantity of a particular commodity or currency (or even a purely notional sum, such as the value of a particular stock index) at a particular date in the future. There is usually no physical exchange between buyer and seller. It is only the difference between the ground value and the market value that changes. Such transactions are a function of the ***futures market***.

gearing ratio ratio of a company's permanent loan capital (preference shares and long-term loans) to its equity (ordinary shares plus reserves). If the gearing ratio is above 100%, then the company is considered to be highly geared. It has more long-term debt than equity, so if the company goes through bad trading conditions, it will face more difficulties than a company with a lower gearing ratio; this is because the company with the higher gearing ratio will have to carry on paying interest on its loans, whereas a company with a lower gearing but the same amount of loans plus equity can cut the dividends paid to shareholders. The burden of the higher interest payments could push the company into bankruptcy.

GmbH abbreviation for *Gesellshaft mit beschrankter Haftung* (German 'limited liability company').

golden share share, often with overriding voting powers, issued by governments to control privatized companies.

greenmail payment made by a target company to avoid a takeover; for example, buying back a portion of its own shares from a potential predator (either a person or a company) at an inflated price.

grey market dealing in shares using methods that are legal but perhaps officially frowned upon – for example, before issue and flotation.

gross a particular figure or price, calculated before the deduction of specific items such as commission, discounts, interest, and taxes. The opposite is net.

gross profit the difference between sales revenue and the direct cost of production for a business. It does not take account of the overheads of the business. The gross profit is usually shown in the profit and loss account of the company.

human-resource management or ***personnel management*** recruitment, selection, and training of staff, and efforts to involve them in the company. Japanese firms, in particular, invest heavily in human-resource management.

indirect cost or ***semi-variable cost*** cost that changes as output changes, but not in direct proportion. For example, the costs of running an office are indirect costs for a manufacturing company. Day-to-day changes in output in the factory will not affect office costs. However, a permanent 20% increase in output may lead to a need for more office staff and hence higher indirect costs.

indirect tax tax on products or services. VAT (value-added tax) and excise duties are examples of indirect taxes. The opposite of an indirect tax is a direct tax, a tax on income.

industrial tribunal independent panel which decides on legal cases brought before it including employment issues such as unfair dismissal, redundancy, equal opportunities, and discrimination at work.

inflation accounting method of accounting that allows for the changing purchasing power of money due to inflation.

insider trading or ***insider dealing*** illegal use of privileged information in dealing on a stock exchange; for example, when a company takeover bid is imminent. Insider trading is in theory detected by the Securities and Investment Board (SIB) in the UK, and the Securities and Exchange Commission (SEC) in the USA. Neither agency, however, has any legal powers other than public disclosure and they do not bring prosecutions themselves.

insolvency inability to pay debts, which may lead to bankruptcy.

internal economies of scale fall in the average cost of production for a firm arising from a change in the scale of production by that firm.

inventory list of goods owned. The owner of a furnished house that is rented out is likely to have an inventory of all the furniture, fixtures, and fittings in the house. In business studies, an inventory usually refers to the stocks of goods held by a company.

investment the purchase of any asset with the potential to yield future financial benefit to the purchaser (such as a house, a work of art, stocks and shares, or even a private education).

Target cities

The leading equity cities and their environs ranked by institutional equity holdings, end 1991 (US $bn)

City	US $bn
Tokyo	1,691.6
New York	506.9
London	476.8
Geneva	253.4
Zurich	246.2
Boston	229.9
Paris	159.7
Frankfurt	143.9
San Francisco	141.2
Los Angeles	101.1
Philadelphia	98.8
Chicago	91.6
Toronto	89.9
Edinburgh	78.3
Hartford/Greater Connecticut*	65.2
Hong Kong	53.7
Minneapolis/St Paul	48.0
Basle	47.1
Montreal	45.9
Houston	45.2
Atlanta	44.1
Milan	42.0
Amsterdam	41.9
Stockholm	38.2
Brussels	35.2

** Bridgeport/Greenwich/Stamford*

Source: The Banker

investment trust public company that makes investments in other companies on behalf of its shareholders. It may issue shares to raise capital and issue fixed interest securities.

issued capital the nominal value of those shares in a company that have been allotted. The issued capital is equivalent to the amount invested, provided the issue has not been at a premium price.

job enrichment initiative or incentive that makes a job more satisfying to perform. For example, giving workers more control over how a task is to be completed often leads to job enrichment because workers can think out their own way of tackling the task, change their pattern of working when they want, and feel more responsible for achieving the end product.

joint venture undertaking in which an individual or legal entity of one country forms a company with those of another country, with risks being shared.

junk bond derogatory term for a security officially rated as 'below investment grade'. It is issued in order to raise capital quickly, typically to finance a takeover to be paid for by the sale of assets once the company is acquired. Junk bonds have a high yield, but are a high-risk investment.

just-in-time (JIT) production management practice requiring that incoming supplies arrive at the time when they are needed by the customer, most typically in a manufacturer's assembly operations. JIT requires considerable cooperation between supplier and customer, but can reduce expenses and improve efficiency, for example by reducing stock levels and by increasing the quality of goods supplied.

key-results analysis management procedure involving the identification of performance components critical to a particular process or event, the necessary level of performance required from them, and the methods of monitoring to be used.

learning curve graphical representation of the improvement in performance of a person executing a new task.

leveraged buyout purchase of a controlling proportion of the shares of a company by its own management, financed almost exclusively by borrowing. It is so called because the ratio of a company's long-term debt to its equity (capital assets) is known as its 'leverage'.

limited company company for whose debts the members are liable only to a limited extent. The capital of a limited company is divided into small units, and profits are distributed according to shareholding. It is the usual type of company formation in the UK.

limited liability legal safeguard that allows shareholders to be liable for their company's debts only up to and including the value of their shareholding. For example, if a limited liability company goes bankrupt with debts of 1 million, the shareholders are not liable for any of that debt, although the value of their shares in the company would be worthless.

liquidation the winding-up of a company by converting all its assets into money to pay off its liabilities.

loan form of borrowing by individuals, businesses, and governments. Individuals and companies usually obtain loans from banks. The loan with interest is typically paid back in fixed monthly instalments over a period of between one and five years in the UK, although longer-term loans and different repayment conditions may be negotiated. Debentures and mortgages are specific forms of loan. In business, loans are the second most important way (after retained profit) in which firms finance their expansion.

loss the opposite of profit, when revenues are less than costs.

management accounting the use of financial accounts in the process of decision-making within a business organization. Examples would include finding out which business activities were least profitable and then making a decision about whether to continue with these activities.

management buyout purchase of control of a company by its management, generally with debt funding, making it a leveraged buyout.

management information system computer system used for converting company data from internal and external sources into appropriate information, and then communicating it to managers at all levels, enabling them to carry out their work.

managing director the director of a company who is also its most senior manager. The managing director is therefore responsible for the day-to-day running of the company and has a seat on the board. The managing director may also be the chair of the company, but in large companies the role of chair is likely to be separate from that of managing director.

market capitalization market value of a company, based on the market price of all its issued securities – a price that would be unlikely to apply, however, if a bid were actually made for control of them.

marketing mix the factors that help a firm to sell its products. Four elements – the ***four Ps*** – are normally distinguished: getting the right ***product*** to the market, at the right ***price***; ensuring that the ***promotion*** in terms of advertising and marketing for the product is right; and ensuring that the product is distributed to the most convenient ***place*** for customers to buy it.

market maker in the UK, a stockbroker entitled to deal directly on the stock exchange. The role was created in Oct 1986, when the jobber (intermediary) disappeared from the stock exchange. Market makers trade in the dual capacity of broker and jobber.

market segment portion of a market characterized by such similarity of customers, their requirements and/or buying behaviour, that those who sell the products or services bought by these customers can aim their marketing effort specifically at this segment.

market share the proportion of a market taken by one producer. Market share can be measured in terms of volume of sales; for example, company X sold 40% of all the cars sold last month in the UK market. Or it can be measured as the value of sales; for example, company X sold 30% of the total value of all cars sold in the UK market last month. Or it could be measured in terms of output by volume or value; for example, company X could have produced 50% of all the cars made in the UK even though its UK market share was 30% because it exported cars to other markets while some cars sold in the UK were produced in other countries.

memorandum of association document that defines the purpose of a company and the amount and different classes of share capital. In the UK, the memorandum is drawn up on formation of the company, together with the articles of association.

merger linking of two or more companies, either by creating a new organization by consolidating the original companies or by absorption by one company of the others. Unlike a takeover, which is not always a voluntary fusion of the parties, a merger is the result of an agreement.

minority interest item in the consolidated accounts of a holding company that represents the value of any shares in its subsidiaries that it does not itself own.

multinational corporation company or enterprise operating in several countries, usually defined as one that has 25% or more of its output capacity located outside its country of origin.

In 1992, the world's 500 largest companies, generally multinationals, controlled at least 70% of world trade, 80% of foreign investment, and 30% of global GDP.

national insurance in the UK, state social-security scheme that provides child allowances, maternity benefits, and payments to the unemployed, sick, and retired, and also covers medical treatment. It is paid for by weekly or monthly contributions from employees and employers.

net of a particular figure or price, calculated after the deduction of specific items such as commission, discounts, interest, and taxes. The opposite is gross.

net assets either the total assets of a company less its current liabilities (that is, the capital employed) or the total assets less current liabilities, debt capital, long-term loans and provisions, which would form the amount available to ordinary shareholders if the company were to be wound up.

net current assets current assets minus current liabilities. A company is only solvent if its net current assets are positive.

net worth the total assets of a company less its total liabilities, equivalent to the interest of the ordinary shareholders in the company.

nonexecutive director member of the board of a company who is not an employee of the company. A nonexecutive director can provide a wider perspective to the outlook of the board, but may be limited by not having access to informal sources of information.

nonvoting share ordinary share in a company that is without entitlement to vote at shareholders' meetings. Shares are often distinguished as A-shares (voting) and B-shares (nonvoting).

option contract giving the owner the right (as opposed to the obligation, as with futures contracts) to buy or sell a specific quantity of a particular commodity or currency at a future date and at an agreed price, in return for a premium. The buyer or seller can decide not to exercise the option if it would prove disadvantageous.

ordinary share type of share in a company. Ordinary shareholders receive a variable rate of dividend. When company profits are high, the dividends will be high also. If the company is doing badly, it may well reduce or even stop paying any dividend to ordinary shareholders. Ordinary shareholders have only second claim on dividends after preference shareholders.

overhead any of the fixed costs in a business that do not vary in the short term. These might include property rental, heating and lighting, insurance, and administration costs.

patent certificate issued by the government through the Patent Office giving a person or business organization the exclusive right to make, use, or sell a newly invented product. The patent normally lasts 25 years from the day it is granted. Patents are important because they enable a business organization to generate profits from its research and development by preventing other companies from copying the process or product.

PAYE abbreviation for ***Pay-As-You- Earn*** in the UK, a system of tax collection in which income tax is deducted on a regular basis by the employer before wages are paid. PAYE tax deductions are calculated so that when added up they will approximately equal the total amount of tax likely to be due in that year. In the USA it is called ***withholding tax***.

performance-related pay the element of a wage or salary that is linked to the working performance of an individual or working group, according to a prior arrangement.

piggyback export scheme firm already established in the export field making its services available without charge to a small firm just entering the market. The small firm thus obtains the assistance of the large firm's good will, experience, and know-how, and is saved the trouble and expense of setting up its own export department.

poison pill tactic to avoid hostile business takeover by making the target unattractive. For example, a company may give a certain class of shareholders the right to have their shares redeemed at a very good price in the event of the company being taken over, thus involving the potential predator in considerable extra cost.

preference share share in a company with rights in various ways superior to those of ordinary shares; for example, priority to a fixed dividend and priority over ordinary shares in the event of the company being wound up.

premium price difference between the current market price of a security and its issue price (where the current price is the greater).

price/earnings ratio or ***p/e ratio*** a company's share price divided by its earnings per share after tax.

price elasticity of demand responsiveness of changes in quantity demanded to a change in the price of a product. It is measured by the formula: percentage change in quantity demanded/percentage change in price. For example, if the price of butter is reduced by 10% and the demand increases by 20%, the price elasticity of demand is 2.

pricing strategy the decision a business organization has to make about the price at which it will sell its products. Pricing strategies include creaming, penetration pricing, profit maximization, price capturing, price discrimination, range pricing, and loss leading.

prime rate the interest rate charged by commercial banks to their best customers. It is the lowest interest or base rate on which other rates are calculated according to the risk involved. Only borrowers who have the highest credit rating qualify for the prime rate.

profit amount by which total revenue exceeds total cost. It is the reward for risk-taking for shareholders in a business organization. ***Gross profit*** is the difference between sales revenue and the direct cost of production. ***Net profit*** is total revenue minus total direct and indirect cost (for example, overheads, the cost of running the business).

profit and loss account in a set of accounts, the account that compares all revenues and all costs of a business organization in order to arrive at a figure for net profit (or loss). The credit side of the account starts with a figure for gross profit – the difference between turnover and cost of products sold. Other revenues added to gross profit might include interest on investments and rent from let properties. All costs other than the cost of new stock purchased (already taken into account when calculating gross profit) are placed on the debit side of the account. The costs include overhead costs.

profit-sharing scheme in a company, arrangements for some or all the employees to receive cash or shares related to the profits of the company.

public relations (PR) promotion of a positive image about itself to the general public by a business or other organization. Public relations departments deal with critical letters from the public about the business. They also attempt to get free media publicity; for example, by providing stories or photographs to the press.

put option on the stock market, the right to sell a specific number of shares at a specific price on or before a specific date.

quality circle small group of production workers concerned with problems relating to the quality, safety, and efficiency of their product. Key characteristics of quality circles are size (8–12 members); voluntary membership; natural work groups, rather than artificially created ones; autonomy in setting their own agenda; access to senior managers; and a relatively permanent existence. Quality circles were popularized in Japan.

quality control steps taken to ensure that products are of a minimum acceptable standard for buyers of the product. In manufacturing, quality control should be achieved through inspection of products at each stage of the manufacturing process. In services, quality control is just as important but quality of service is often more difficult to define and measure. Quality control can cost money if products are poorly made and end up being rejected. Poor quality also leads to a poor image for a business organization and lower sales.

rate of return the income from an investment expressed as a percentage of the cost of that investment.

receiver in law, a person appointed by a court to collect and manage the assets of an individual, company, or partnership in serious financial difficulties. In the case of bankruptcy, the assets may be sold and distributed by a receiver to creditors.

redeemable preference share share in a company that the company has a right to buy back at a specific price.

research and development (R&D) process undertaken by a business organization before the launch of a product. Research is usually scientific research into materials and production processes. Product development is application of that research to the development of existing or new products.

Large companies may have a research and development department with its own budget and staff. Smaller companies are less likely to be able to afford R&D. The relatively low expenditure on R&D by UK civilian manufacturing companies compared to their competitors abroad is one possible reason for the low rate of economic growth of the UK economy and for deindustrialization in the UK.

Investing in the future

International ranking of the top 20 companies by research and development expenditure, 1992

	Current spending (£'000)	*% change 1991/92*
1 General Motors, USA	3,908,120	1
2 Daimler-Benz, Germany	3,796,941	11
3 Siemens, Germany	3,418,960	6
4 IBM, USA	3,357,331	2
5 Ford, USA	2,861,294	16
6 Hitachi, Japan	2,748,809	6
7 Toyota Motor, Japan	2,365,079	4
8 Matsushita Electric, Japan	2,212,015	9
9 Fujitsu, Japan	2,073,465	19
10 AT&T, USA	1,922,721	–7
11 Toshiba, Japan	1,682,703	6
12 NEC, Japan	1,600,000	8
13 Asea Brown Boveri, Switzerland/Sweden	1,575,957	2
14 Nippon Telegraph, Japan	1,517,920	5
15 Philips, Netherlands	1,328,493	–5
16 Sony, Japan	1,272,968	17
17 Nissan Motor, Japan	1,269,841	2
18 Bayer, Germany	1,262,385	3
19 VW, Germany	1,223,241	11
20 Boeing, USA	1,219,286	30

Source: Standard & Poor's Compustat Global Vantage

revenue money received from the sale of a product. ***Total revenue*** can be calculated by multiplying the average price received by the total quantity sold. ***Average revenue*** is the average price received and is calculated by dividing total revenue by total quantity sold. ***Marginal revenue*** is the revenue gained from the sale of an additional unit of output.

reverse takeover a company selling itself to another (a white knight) to avoid being the target of a purchase by an unwelcome predator.

rights issue new shares offered to existing shareholders to raise new capital. Shareholders receive a discount on the market price while the company benefits from not having the costs of a relaunch of the new issue.

risk capital or ***venture capital*** finance provided by venture capital companies, individuals, and merchant banks for medium- or long-term business ventures that are not their own and in which there is a strong element of risk.

sales promotion selling technique used by a business organization to persuade customers to buy its products in the short term. ***Below-the-line promotion***, or merchandising, includes special offers such as gifts, discounts, competitions, better-value offers (for example, 500 grams for the price of 400 grams), and trade-ins. ***Above-the-line promotion*** is advertising.

scrip issue or ***subscription certificate*** UK term for bonus issue.

sequestrator person or organization appointed by a court of law to control the assets of another person or organization within the jurisdiction of that court.

shareholder owner of part of the share capital of a company. Shareholders own shares in order to make a return on them. They do this partly by receiving dividends, a share of any profit made by the company, and partly by seeing the price of their shares rise over time if the value of the company increases.

solvency state of a business when its current assets exceed its current liabilities, in other words, when it has positive net current assets or positive working capital. This means that it has enough liquid assets to pay off its debts in the short term.

spreadsheet software package that enables the user to analyse data because it will perform calculations and routine mathematical operations. A cash-flow forecast could be prepared on a spreadsheet.

stag subscriber for new share issues who expects to profit from a rise in price on early trading in the shares.

stakeholder any person or group that has a stake in an organization: primarily, shareholders, employees, management, customers, and suppliers.

Standard and Poor's Stock Price Index or ***S & P 500*** index of the US stock market covering 500 stocks broken down into sectors.

stocks and shares investment holdings (securities) in private or public undertakings. Although distinctions have become blurred, in the UK stock usually means fixed-interest securities – for example, those issued by central and local government – while shares represent a stake in the ownership of a trading company which, if they are ordinary shares, yield to the owner dividends reflecting the success of the company. In the USA the term 'stock' generally signifies what in the UK is an ordinary share.

supply curve diagrammatic illustration of the relationship between the price of a good and the quantity that producers will supply at that price. It is said to be upward-sloping because the higher the price, the more profitable existing production becomes, attracting new companies into the industry and thus increasing the quantity supplied.

SWOT analysis breakdown of an organization into its *s*trengths and *w*eaknesses (the internal analysis), with an assessment of the *o*pportunities open to it and the *t*hreats confronting it. SWOT analysis is commonly used in marketing and strategic studies.

takeover acquisition by one company of a sufficient number of shares in another company to have effective control of that company – usually 51%, although a controlling stake may be as little as 30%.

Takeovers may be agreed or contested; methods employed include the ***dawn raid***, and methods of avoiding an unwelcome takeover include ***reverse takeover***, ***poison pills***, or inviting a ***white knight*** to make a takeover bid.

TESSA (acronym for ***tax-exempt special savings account***) UK scheme, introduced 1991, to encourage longer-term savings by making interest tax-free on deposits of up to £9,000 over five years.

trading account in a set of accounts, the account that deals with turnover (the value of sales) and the cost of new stock purchased. The trading account enables a business organization to calculate gross profit, the difference between the value of sales and the cost of new stock.

turnover the value of sales of a business organization over a period of time. For example, if a shop sells 10,000 items in a week at an average price of 2 each, then its weekly turnover is 20,000. Profit of a company is not only affected by the total turnover but also by the rate of turnover.

unit trust company that invests its clients' funds in other companies. The units it issues represent holdings of shares, which means unit shareholders have a wider spread of capital than if they bought shares on the stock market.

venture capital or ***risk capital*** money put up by investors such as merchant banks to fund a new company or expansion of an established company. The organization providing the money receives a share of the company's equity and seeks to make a profit by rapid growth in the value of its stake, as a result of expansion by the start-up company or 'venture'.

white knight company invited by the target of a takeover bid to make a rival bid. The company invited to bid is usually one that is already on good terms with the target company.

working capital current assets minus current liabilities of a business organization. It is the assets that are left free, after liabilities have been covered, for the business to use or put to work if it feels that it should take that risk.

yield the annual percentage return from an investment; on ordinary shares it is the dividend expressed as a percentage.

zero-based budgeting management technique requiring that no resources for a new period of a programme are approved and/or released unless their justification can be demonstrated against alternative options.

Business News

(The exchange rates may vary according to the date of the transaction.)

MTV Europe declines offer

The burgeoning pop music satellite channel MTV Europe, has declined the offer of being included in the new Sky pay package. MTV Europe would have been forced to encrypt the output from its satellite transponder beamed at the UK, but that would have meant losing audiences in Scandinavia.

MuZ motorcycles survive disaster

A two-year battle for survival came to an unexpected and happy ending for Motorrad und Zwelwerk GmbH (MuZ), one of the world's oldest and best-loved motorcycle manufacturers. MuZ, which was founded in 1907 and was the largest and most progressive motorcycle company in the world at that time, was declared officially closed by the prime minister of the state of Saxony in December 1991. But the federal government and the state of Saxony agreed to guarantee most of a DM32.6 million ($20 million) loan to save the company. This is the first such action taken by both the federal and Saxony state governments to save an East German company. MuZ has made an excellent inroad into China, a market that is hungry to purchase transport vehicles, and its current workforce of about 240 workers (compared with 3,000 under communist rule) has a production goal of 6,000 motorcycles and revenue of DM40 million for 1993. Under communist rule, 200,000 units were produced annually.

BCH takes full control of Banco de Fomento

Banco Central Hispano (BCH), the Spanish bank, is to acquire full ownership of Banco de Fomento, in which it has a 66% shareholding, with a view to disposing of the subsidiary bank's 165-branch network. BCH, which will be employing equity from its own treasury stock for the takeover, will be offering one of its shares for every two of Fomento's in an acquisition representing Pta10.3 billion ($82 million). Brokers recommended the bid, noting that BCH paid a dividend of Pta210 per share in 1992, against Fomento's Pta90 share payout. BCH said that following the takeover it would put aside Fomento's cash flow, which stood at Pta5.9 billion in 1982, for 1992 pension funds and reserves. In 1992, Fomento's coverage of non-performing loans stood at 70.5%, down from 84.4% the year before. Analysts saw BCH's decision to strengthen Fomento's balance sheet as heralding a disposal of the bank network.

Tetra Laval sells B&L

Tetra Laval, the Swedish food packaging and equipment group, has made its first big disposal since the takeover of Alfa-Laval in 1991. It has sold German-based Bran & Luebbe in a DM210 million ($130 million) leveraged buyout. CWB Capital Partners, a London-based acquisition fund, is buying B&L, one of the world's leading suppliers of dosing pumps, industrial analysers, and electronics for industrial weighing and process automation. The deal is believed to be the largest leveraged buyout in Germany in three years. Bank financing is being provided by Dresdner Bank, Deutsche Bank and Citibank. Rhein Donau Capital Partners, a fund managed by Goldman Sachs, has taken a substantial minority stake in the transaction, and Hancock International Private Equity Partners has also made a minority investment.

Carlton moves into Asian television market

Carlton Communications, the broadcasting and television services group, plans expansion into the Asian television market. Nigel Walmsley, managing director of Carlton Television, the weekend ITV company for the London region, has had talks with leading broadcasters in the Asian region. Carlton, already well known to Asian broadcasters through Quantel, its broadcasting equipment division, is now keen to explore everything from equity stakes in Asian broadcasters to joint ventures on new channels. Carlton had talks in Hong Kong with Star TV, the Asian Satellite venture that claims more than 45 million viewers in 38 countries, and with the Hong Kong domestic broadcasters Television Broadcasts (TVB) and Asia TV. Carlton is also looking at the potential of television investments in Singapore and mainland China.

Supreme Court upholds cigarette decision

The Supreme Court, the highest judicial authority in the USA, has affirmed a lower court decision that threw out a $148.8-million jury award against Brown & Williamson, the US-based cigarette manufacturer and a subsidiary of the UK's BAT Industries. The decision came after almost a decade of legal wrangling. The case against B&W was brought by Liggett Group, a rival US tobacco company now called Brooke Group, and centred on anti-trust issues. The suit was first filed by Liggett/Brooke in 1984. Brooke claimed that B&W had used 'predatory' pricing to limit Brooke's ability to compete in the burgeoning market for low-priced 'generic' cigarettes. Brooke had introduced some ultra-cheap cigarettes, sold in plain black-and-white packaging, and was successfully wooing smokers from other brands. B&W retaliated with its own generic brand, and offered wholesalers bigger volume-based rebates than its smaller competitor. Brooke sued, and in 1990 a jury in North Carolina awarded Brooke just under $50 million. Damages, in US anti-trust cases, are automatically tripled. However, a federal appeal court in Richmond, Virginia, sided with B&W, and the Supreme Court, by a six-to-three vote, has affirmed that ruling.

Banks to save Canary Wharf

Banks financing London's troubled Canary Wharf office complex have agreed in principle to put up an extra £500 million ($793 million) in credit to get the project back into operation under their ownership. All but one of the 11 banks involved in existing loans to the Docklands real-estate venture, now totalling around £600 million, have agreed to participate. Only National Bank of Canada has decided against providing further loans, because of its already extensive exposure to Olympia & York Developments Ltd. O&Y, the Canadian developer of Canary Wharf, collapsed last year in one of the biggest corporate failures ever. Banks that have agreed to press ahead with the rescue operation hope that by getting the project out of administration, they will be able to operate it as a viable commercial entity. In addition to National Bank of Canada and Credit Suisse, the other lenders to Canary Wharf are Canadian Imperial Bank of Commerce, Barclays plc, Commerzbank AG, Credit Lyonnais, Lloyds Bank plc, Chemical Bank, Royal Bank of Canada, Citibank and Kansallis Osake Pankki.

Enso-Gutzeit expands to Germany

Enso-Gutzeit, one of Finland's largest papermakers, plan to build a DM800 million ($493 million) recycling plant in the eastern German state of Saxony, the biggest single foreign investment so far in the region. This move is aimed at expanding into the German market and, later, into eastern Europe. Germany

Lloyd's of London losses

Lloyd's of London, the world's largest insurance syndicate, became the biggest loser in terms of net earnings in 1992. Lloyd's had reported losses of £510 million for 1988, £2.06 billion for 1989 and £2.9 billion in 1990. In 1992 this loss had increased still further, by far the biggest single loss by a corporate organization in 1992/93. The losses stem from a succession of huge insurance claims, following the *Piper Alpha* disaster, Hurricane Hugo, the *Exxon Valdez* oil spill, and many other mishaps. The indicators, such as the gross capacity, number of Names, and net claims, suggest that Lloyd's will take some time to recover and get their balance sheet back into the black.

Loss of capital

Almost universally at Lloyd's, an influx of incorporated capital – which would have limited liability – is seen as essential for halting the decline in the market's capacity to compete in international commercial insurance and reinsurance markets. The market's traditional capital supply – individual Names trading on the basis of unlimited liability – is drying up in the wake of losses of some £6 billion in the past five years. Capital supplied by Names is expected to fall to less than £8 billion in 1994, compared with £11.1 billion in 1991.

New sources needed

Corporate capital could come from several sources. Existing wealthy Names can now form companies with limited liability. To do this, though, an individual Name would need assets of at least £1.5 million, compared with the £250,000 required by existing Names. Members' agencies are also working on schemes that would allow existing less wealthy Names to form groups trading on a limited liability basis. Two Lloyd's agencies have set up 'consortium' arrangements, in which an insurance company underwrites business alongside the Lloyd's syndicate. Japanese insurance companies are understood to be expressing tentative interest. A number of investment banks, mainly from the USA, are looking to venture capitalists to back new funds, through private placements. They would trade at the Lloyd's of London market as corporate Names. They will be encouraged by the backing offered by private US investors such as Texas-based financier Richard Rainwater and Vermont-based Jack Byrne to new Bermudan reinsurance companies over the past year.

A number of agents hope to establish funds backed by institutional investors or directly by individuals, who would buy shares in investment trusts sold on the retail market. There are hopes that some of these new funds and new companies could be listed on the New York or London stock exchanges, making the investments more liquid and providing capital with an exit route.

US investment banks like JP Morgan and Salomon Brothers, and international insurance brokers like Marsh McLennan and Johnson & Higgins, are most active in exploring these new ventures. The banks believe that sharply increased insurance rates create attractive opportunities for profit, while the brokers are keen to find new sources of capacity to allow them to place clients' business more easily. Morgan and Marsh have already teamed up a number of new Bermuda-based ventures, including one that will supply reinsurance exclusively to Lloyd's syndicates.

Plans for stricter control

Matters should become clearer when Lloyd's publishes a rule book in the summer, providing more details on legal and accounting arrangements, as well as on the regulatory and tax implications for incorporated Names. Lloyd's plans to control the amount of capital that comes into the market, to avoid the growth of capacity, which led to disastrous rate competition in the 1980s. This will possibly be achieved through a bidding system, although the rules as to how this will work have still to be spelled out. Some agents fear that the new rules will be too late to allow any corporate Name to participate in 1994.

Lloyd's must surmount a number of obstacles if its plans are to be successful. It still has to convince the markets that billions of dollars of old liabilities from US asbestosis and pollution claims can be isolated in a new reinsurance company, whose formation is a centrepiece of the new business plan. Many investors will also want to see evidence that a settlement of the litigation dogging the market is on the horizon before they commit themselves. Moreover, many agents and syndicates may still have ground to make up before they can meet the much tougher standards of professionalism and disclosure that corporate investors will demand.

OA

already accounts for 15% of the net sales of the Enso-Gutzeit Group, which in 1992 totalled DM10.2 billion ($16.8 billion). The plant, situated east of Leipzig, will start operating in September 1994 with an initial workforce of 300 people.

Royal Dutch/Shell Group in China
The Royal Dutch/Shell Group has signed a contract with a Chinese company to prospect for oil in East China's Jiangsu province. Under the terms of the agreement with China National Oil & Gas Exploration & Development Corporation, the Anglo/Dutch oil company will assume the risk in prospecting and sinking wells. The licence allows Shell to prospect for seven years and sink wells for 15 years over an area in Jiangsu. Seismic prospecting will begin in September 1993. The contract gives the Chinese side 51% of the shares and the British side 49%.

Apple Computer's $5.5 billion copyright claim dismissed
Apple Computer's $5.5 billion copyright infringement suit against Microsoft and Hewlett-Packard was dismissed by a federal judge in San Francisco. The case was the biggest copyright infringement claim in the history of the computer industry. Apple agreed not to contest a motion for dismissal of the case, filed by Microsoft and HP. However, Apple said that it now intends to take the case to the appeals court. In its suit, filed five years ago, Apple charged that Microsoft's Windows program, which has since become a top seller used on millions of personal computers, infringes copyrights on Apple's Macintosh programs. Apple also charged that an HP program, New Wave, infringes Macintosh copyrights. The case has been closely watched because the outcome could have a broad impact on the computer industry, limiting the publication of 'look-alike' programs and programs that incorporate features of existing products. The case was also seen as a threat to the development of easy-to-use graphical interface programs for IBM-compatible PCs. Microsoft said, however, that having won the case in the trial court, it would 'vigorously defend this result through any appeal'.

ICI–Zeneca demerger
Imperial Chemical Industries (ICI) plc, the UK's largest manufacturer, has split into two units: a chemicals unit to be known as ICI and a drugs and bioscience business to be known as Zeneca Group plc. The demerger comes with a £1.3 billion-rights issue by Zeneca, which is quoted at 705p ($11.18) per share, and the new ICI shares at 525p a share. Although ICI and Zeneca stress that the priority in the rights issue is that it should be a normal domestic issue – preserving pre-emption rights and raising capital for Zeneca on suitable terms – they are also believed to be keen to take the opportunity to put Zeneca into the international arena. Only about 5% of ICI's shares are held in the USA. Zeneca will go for a New York Stock Exchange listing and will register the rights in the USA so that investors there can take them in.

Eastman Kodak accuses Sony of patent infringement
Eastman Kodak has filed a suit against Sony, one of Japan's leading electronics manufacturers, in a patent infringement dispute that could have broad implications throughout the consumer electronics industry. Kodak alleges that Sony's video cassette recorders, camcorders (video cameras), and other audio and video recording products infringe upon a patent that the US company obtained in 1981 covering a new type of recording head for magnetic recording devices. The same technology is widely used throughout the consumer electronics industry. According to the complaint, which was filed in Texas, Kodak has been attempting to reach a licensing agreement with Sony since the late 1980s. Kodak is asking the court to issue an injunction to prevent Sony from selling products in the USA that allegedly infringe its patent. The US company is also seeking treble damages, although it does not specify the amount, and has asked for a jury trial. Sony's sales in the USA last year were over $6 billion, of which VCRs and video cameras represented a significant portion.

Nestlé sells US hotel business
Nestlé, the world's largest food group, is to sell Stouffer Hotel Holdings, its US hotel business, to a private company owned by the family of Cheng Yu-Tung of Hong Kong. The sale, to be finalized before 1 June, will complete Nestlé's withdrawal from the hotel and catering business in different parts of the world. Last year, it sold the Stouffer restaurants, and three years ago withdrew from a hotel joint venture with Swissair. Stouffer owns or manages 24 upmarket hotels in the USA, Mexico, and the Caribbean.

Pilkington expands insulation side
Pilkington Insulation, a subsidiary of the glass group, has acquired Ecomax (UK). The purchase price was not disclosed, but Pilkington said that the acquisition represented less than 1% of group assets. Ecomax is a sales and marketing organization previously owned by Rockwool of Sweden, a division of Partek of Finland.

Sainsbury sales top £10 billion
J Sainsbury, Britain's biggest retailer, reported in July 1993 a 16.7% increase in full-year pretax profits. The results of the group, whose sales exceeded £10 billion for the first time, compare with the 6.5% profit gain posted by its rival, Tesco. Sainsbury's pretax profits in the year to 13 March, increased to £732.8 million from £628 million the previous year on sales that grew by 11.6% to £10.27 billion (from £9.2 billion), including £584.2 million of VAT and US sales taxes. The profit improvement, which was nevertheless at the low end of market expectations, was underpinned by a small increase in like-for-like sales volumes in the group's UK supermarkets and Savacentre hypermarkets, and by higher operating margins and a 0.7 percentage point gain in UK market share to 11.3%. In the UK, supermarket and Savacentre sales increased by 12.6% to £8.9 billion, with 23 new stores contributing 8.8 percentage points of the gain – the largest contribution from new space for 10 years. Eight stores were closed and like-for-like sales rose 3.8% which, with price inflation of 2.5%, resulted in a real volume gain. Another 23 new stores are due to open this year at an average cost of £17 million each and 14 stores will close. The foodstores' operating profits were 19.1% higher at £752.2 million. Sunday trading at 160 supermarkets was only marginally profitable.

Tory MPs are Lloyd's losers

At least 46 Conservative members of parliament are reported to have lost substantial amounts of money on the insurance market as a result of being Lloyd's 'Names'. Among prominent Tories listed by *The Times* of 1 June 1993 as having lost heavily are Mr Hunt, Employment Secretary; Mr Brooke, Heritage Secretary; Mr Lang, Scottish Secretary; Sir Nicholas Lyell QC, Attorney General; and Sir Norman Fowler, party chairman. Sir Nicholas said: 'I have suffered some losses and I shall pay them. I am certainly not facing bankruptcy.' He added that the implications for the Government had been overstated but declined to comment further or disclose the extent of his personal losses. Sir Richard Body, MP for Holland with Boston, who is understood to have lost a significant sum, agreed that some MPs faced bills likely to exceed £500,000 and would find the consequences 'extremely difficult'. He did not believe they would be driven to bankruptcy.

Most of the MPs are likely to have taken out stop-loss insurance to avoid catastrophic financial loss. In addition, payments will be eased for some by the right to set losses against tax and by arrangements allowing Names to put some 1993 profits towards their bill. It was suggested at Westminster that some members will have sought to limit financial damage by other means, including transferring shares, antiques, works of art, and holiday homes into their wives' names. A Lloyd's spokesman said that some investors chose bankruptcy as a neater way of divesting themselves of financial responsibility. However, the view at Westminster was that MPs 'would need their heads examining' if they opted for a solution that would destroy their political careers.

Unilever expansion in China
Unilever, the Anglo-Dutch consumer company, plans to expand its presence in China by building a fabric detergents plant and an ice cream factory with local partners. The total initial cost is $60 million (£40 million), which is likely to double in the near future. The detergents plant is being built by Unilever Shanghai, in which Unilever has 70% and Shanghai Daily Chemical and Shanghai Detergents each hold 15%. Unilever began selling imported Omo concentrated detergent in Shanghai in February and said the potential market for washing powder was huge. The ice cream factory will be built in Beijing by Wall's Beijing, 85% owned by Unilever with the state-owned Sumstar holding the balance. The factory will make products under the Wall's name. Unilever already has three joint ventures in the Shanghai region making soap and shampoos, bakery fats, and skin care products.

Apple ranks third in Japan PC market
Apple Computer, the US company, has overtaken Toshiba as the third-largest supplier in the Japanese personal computer market, according to Dataquest, the market research group. Apple has concluded sales agreements with distributors, including Minolta Camera and Mitsubishi Corporation, the trading house. It has worked closely with third-party software developers to localize software applications. In 1992, it increased its share of the Japanese market by 2.9 percentage points to 8.3%, against a share of 7.6% for Toshiba. This puts it in third place after NEC, which took a 53.4% share of the market, and Fujitsu with 9.8%. Apple was significantly ahead of IBM Japan.

Dresdner Bank opens in China
Dresdner Bank will be the first German bank to establish a branch in China when it opens for business in Shanghai in late 1993. Approval for a Shanghai branch was given at the end of April after the bank had made an application late last year. Dresdner has also applied to open branches in Guangzhou and in Shenzen, the booming development zone next to Hong Kong, as part of its strategy to capture a share of growing business opportunities in Asia. Approval is expected.

Ferranti pulls out of USA
Ferranti, the British defence electronics company whose former US deputy chairman is now in prison for fraud and illegal arms sales, is winding up one of its US companies and seeking buyers for its remaining US assets. Ferranti's US assets, which still employ nearly 1,000 people and have an annual turnover of close to $100 million (£65 million), represent about one quarter of the group's worldwide turnover. In the year ended 31 March 1992, the US businesses contributed £113.9 million of total group turnover of £409 million. The US company being wound up is Ferranti International Simulation and Training, a small part of the group's Pennsylvania-based operations that featured in criminal proceedings last year against James Guerin, the former group deputy chairman.

Rothschild group opens in Mexico
The Rothschild group of the UK has been given permission to open a financial advisory company in Mexico, making it the first foreign investment bank to win such authority. The holding company of NM Rothschild, with the Chilean bank BICE and Mexican partners, have been granted authorization to open Rothschild Mexico, a financial boutique that will advise Mexican companies on corporate finance issues, such as mergers and acquisitions, privatizations, project finance, and international equity offerings. Under Mexican law, foreigners cannot own a bank or brokerage, although this will be changed when and if the North American Free Trade Agreement is implemented. Until now, foreign investment banks like Rothschild have had to make do with representative offices, from which they can offer offshore the full range of corporate finance advice, but cannot be incorporated under Mexican law.

Russian Ilyushin wins big order in West

The first airliner jointly built by Russian and US companies has won its first Western order, at the Paris Air Show. Partnairs, an Amsterdam-based company, has placed an order for up to ten Ilyushin IL-96M, worth about $700 million (£454.5 million). The aircraft is Russia's challenge to the new generation of long-haul airliners from the European Airbus consortium and Boeing and McDonnell Douglas of the USA. Deliveries of the 318-seat Russian aircraft, powered by four US Pratt & Whitney engines and fitted with advanced US fly-by-wire technology and digital flight navigation equipment produced by Rockwell Collins, are due to begin in 1996. United Technologies (UTC), Pratt & Whitney's parent company, said Partnairs had placed five firm orders for the new aircraft and taken options on an additional five. The deal was worth about $280 million for Pratt & Whitney. Ilyushin, together with the rest of the Russian aerospace industry, has been seeking to introduce Western engines and avionics on Russian airliners to gain access to Western markets and badly needed hard currency. Tupolev has equipped its TU-204 midrange 200-seater twin jet airliner with Rolls-Royce engines. Russian airframe manufacturers could eventually pose a longer-term challenge to Western manufacturers because their products are priced about 25-30% lower than equivalent Western jets.

EC widens ERM band

European Community (EC) finance ministers agreed on 2 August 1993 to allow ERM currencies, except the Deutschmark and the guilder, to fluctuate by 15% on either side of their central rates. Until the change, the fluctuation band was only 2.25% on either side of the central rate and that was considered very tight for some weak currencies. The recent agreement was necessitated by the weakening of many European currencies, including the French franc, in the Exchange Rate Mechanism (ERM) against the Deutschmark and the reluctance of the German government to reduce key interest rates to bail out the sinking currencies. In late 1992, UK sterling was forced out of the ERM for similar reasons even after devaluation. The new wider fluctuation band, however, may lead to interest rate cuts in Europe, which would stimulate business and economic recovery. Despite the currency turmoil and the crisis in the ERM, all EC states reaffirmed their determination to put the Maastricht treaty on European economic and monetary union into operation as soon as its ratification was completed.

Mergers, Acquisitions, and Takeovers

BAe sale of jet business

British Aerospace has sold its corporate jet business for £250 million to Raytheon, the US company that makes Beechcraft aircraft. This was against a proposed management buyout led by Richard Hooke, a former BAe executive, which BAe described as 'unworkable and unfocused'. Part of the deal includes Raytheon supplying airframe assemblies from BAe's division for a minimum of three years from completion. The transaction was structured on the basis that net assets are worth £194 million. BAe's shares rose by 16p to 355p after the confirmation of the deal in June 1993 and the announcement that in 1992, the corporate jet business made an operating profit before interest and launch costs of £6 million on sales of £308 million.

Microsoft and Xerox in PC partnership

Microsoft, the leading personal computer software company, has formed a partnership with Xerox, the office products and imaging company, to develop technology aimed at integrating copying machines and other office document products into PC networks. PCs and document products are most often unconnected or incompatible, hindering workflow and productivity. Microsoft and Xerox have agreed to deliver a new generation of document products and PC software. The two companies hope to define and develop software products that streamline processes for the creation, production, and distribution of documents. As well as jointly developing technology, the companies will cooperate in marketing, sales, and promotional activities. Specific terms are subject to negotiation of a final agreement between the companies. The agreement between Microsoft and Xerox came on the eve of a Microsoft announcement that included partnership agreements with several other office products companies, including Hewlett-Packard, Compaq Computer, Minolta, Ricoh and Ericsson.

Brewery merger in Europe

The UK cidermaker HP Bulmer has purchased the Belgian Cidrerie Stassen in a Bfr 414-million merger that is bound to bubble up the European cider market in a couple of years. The merger opens the UK market to an upmarket range of fruit-flavoured ciders, while beefy British brands like Strongbow and Scrumpty Jack will invade Belgium, the Netherlands, and France. Stassen has seen tremendous growth since launching its fruit-flavoured ciders in 1987. Sales have risen from two million bottles a year to 12 million. The first Stassen ciders in Britain will be Les Brut de Péche; Les Brut de Parfait d'Oranges; and the low alcohol Degré Zero.5 brands.

Danka first step into Europe

Danka Business Systems, the acquisitive US-based office equipment supplier quoted in London, made its first move into Europe with the £9 million purchase of the Saint Group, a private UK copier company. Danka states that the purchase of the Saint Group marks the beginning of an acquisition campaign in the UK. The Saint Group, which distributes Canon, NEC, Konica, and Risograph equipment, reported pretax profits of £752,000 on sales of £13 million in 1992. The Saint Group will now be called Danka (UK).

Hoechst and Schering of Germany

Hoechst and Schering, two of Germany's leading chemicals groups, are to merge their plant protection divisions in a joint venture with annual sales of about DM3.4 billion ($2.1 billion). The Berlin-based merger starts operation at the beginning of 1994. The move, an important further step in the consolidation of the international chemicals industry, has been forced by the combined effects of recession and reforms of the common agricultural policy (CAP). The Hoechst division, employing 5,350 people, had sales of DM2.1 billion last year (1992), about 5% of the group's total. At Schering, 3,900 are employed in plant protection, which had sales of DM1.3 billion, accounting for 20% of group turnover.

Applied Materials and Komatsu in joint venture
Applied Materials of the USA, the world's largest maker of semiconductor manufacturing equipment, and Komatsu, the Japanese construction machinery maker, are setting up a joint venture to develop, manufacture, and market equipment to make liquid crystal displays. Applied Materials and Komatsu will each take a 50% stake in the joint venture, which will be established in Japan. The new company will take over the business of Applied Displays Technology, a subsidiary of Applied Materials established in Japan in 1991 to develop equipment to manufacture LCD panels. The market for LCD panels, which are used in laptop computers and compact televisions, is expected to show strong growth.

Siemens Nixdorf and Fujitsu extend alliance
Siemens Nixdorf, the German information technology group, and Fujitsu, Japan's largest computer maker, are extending their cooperation in mainframe computers to include the next generation of machines. Fujitsu will supply Siemens with high-performance semiconductor manufacturing technology to be used in Siemens' entry-level and mid-range machines, while Siemens will provide Fujitsu with the central processing unit technology for Fujitsu's entry-level range. Siemens and Fujitsu will work together on operating systems software and on components. The tie-up extends the relationship that the two companies have had in mainframes, for which Fujitsu has supplied Siemens with high-end mainframe computers. The extended relationship underlines both companies' belief that high costs need to be reduced in view of the length of time it takes to develop mainframe computers. Fujitsu is one of the largest makers of mainframes in Japan, but this is a shrinking business, with users increasingly switching to equally powerful but much cheaper networked workstations and PCs.

Renault and Volvo to merge
Intensive talks are under way between Renault, the state-owned French car and truck maker, and Volvo of Sweden, on turning their three-year old alliance into a merger. The negotiations have been accelerated by the new French government's privatization policy and the resolution of an 18-month dispute between Volvo and the Swedish government over the future of Procordia, a drugs and food group jointly controlled by Volvo and the state. The companies and the French finance ministry refused to comment publicly on a report in *Libèration*, the French newspaper, that the French finance and industry ministries had given their agreement in principle to the structure of a merger. Renault and Volvo would form a joint holding company, which in turn would take 55% of a publicly quoted Renault–Volvo manufacturing company. The rest of the latter joint company's equity would be held directly by AB Volvo and a new company, Renault Investissement. At present, Renault holds 8% of Volvo and Volvo has 20% of Renault, and both companies have cross-holdings in their respective car and truck divisions.

Saudi Arabian oil companies merge
Saudi Arabia is to merge its two main oil companies, creating the largest integrated oil concern in the world. Samerec, the kingdom's refining and marketing arm, will be merged into the oil production company, Saudi Aramco. 'It will give the company more energy to look at expanding outside Saudi Arabia and compete head-on with the oil majors. Its potential power as a joint company is profound,' said Robin West, who runs Petroleum Finance Company, an energy consulting group in Washington. Saudi Arabia is looking to expand its downstream outlets for oil through deals in Europe and Asia as well as continuing to expand its production capacity beyond 10 million barrels a day. The company's drive to become involved in the industry worldwide will put it into direct competition with multinational oil companies such as Royal Dutch/Shell and Exxon. Aramco is already the world's largest exporter with current output of 8 million barrels/day and current production capacity of 9 millions barrels/day. The company is also custodian of the kingdom's 295 billion barrels of proven oil reserves. Samarec will bring to the merger 1.23 million barrels/day refining capacity from three wholly owned and three joint-venture refineries in Saudi Arabia. This will take the joint company into all stages of the oil industry: production, refining, transport, and marketing.

Gillette acquires Parker Pen for £285 million
The £285-million bid for Parker Pen by Gillette, the US shaving and toiletries manufacturer, was cleared by Michael Heseltine, UK trade and industry secretary, after a Monopolies and Mergers Commission inquiry found that the deal would not operate against the public interest. According to the MMC, Parker supplies about half the value of UK sales of refillable pens, while the Waterman and PaperMate brands, which Gillette already owns, account for a further 7%. The MMC found that any attempt by the enlarged company to exploit its position in the retail market would be constrained by numerous competitors and the bargaining power of larger retailers. The proposed Parker acquisition, agreed in September 1992, is still being studied in the USA.

Fyffes in Spanish joint venture
Fyffes Group, the Dublin-based fruit wholesaler, has entered into a joint venture with Coplaca (Group Regional de Cooperatives del Archipielago Canario), the largest banana-producing cooperative in the Canary Islands. The two companies are establishing a Spanish company on a 50:50 basis to market, distribute, and ripen bananas from the Canaries in continental Europe. The new company is expected to have annual sales of $100m (£65m).

Problems and Troubles

New car sales down in western Europe
New car sales in western Europe plunged by 16.7% in February, continuing January's steep downturn and steering 1993 towards what some in the industry say could be its sharpest sales decline since 1974. Car registrations in February totalled 921,257, down from 1,105,595 the year earlier. Volkswagen AG forecasts a 15% market retraction for all of 1993. If

this occurs, the plunge could be worse than the 13.9% slump recorded in 1974 under the weight of an oil crisis.

John Labatt losses deepen
John Labatt, the Canadian brewing and consumer product group, posted a loss of C$240 million (US$159.3 million) on revenues of C$446 million in the fourth quarter ended April. A year earlier, Labatt posted a loss of C$23 million on revenues of C$379 million. The latest loss stems mainly from continuing problems with Labatt's US diary business. The loss included a C$173 million write-down in the value of this operation. For the whole of 1992–93, the loss was C$70 million against a profit of C$101 million a year earlier. Revenues were C$2.1 billion against C$1.7 billion. Brewing had an operating profit of C$218 million for the year, up from C$178 million. Labatt recently spun off its Canadian diary products operations and classified its US diary business as a discontinued operation while attempts are made to sell it.

UK's 'Big 6' accounting firms in trouble
Five of the UK's 'Big 6' accounting firms – Coopers & Lybrand, KPMG Peat Marwick, Ernst & Young, Andersen, Price Waterhouse, and Touche Ross – suffered a fall in fee income in 1992. Only Andersen – comprising Arthur Andersen and Andersen Consulting – managed to increase its income, which jumped by 17.5% to £388.6 million in the year to 31 March 1993. That caused the firm to rise from sixth to fourth in terms of fee income, just £2 million behind Ernst & Young. Price Waterhouse fell from third to fifth and Touche Ross became the smallest of the Big 6. Coopers & Lybrand remained the largest, but also reported the biggest decline, down 4.2% to £553 million in the year to 1 May 1993. In 1991–92, it was the only one of the Big 6 to report a decline. Total fee income generated by the firms rose by just £2.5 million to nearly £2.6 billion. The number of partners across the firms fell by 1.4% to 2,797 and the number of other professional staff by 6.4% to 29,601. Audit, tax, and consulting services performed least well across most of the firms, generally offset by rises from insolvency and corporate reconstruction work.

Alpine (Double Glazing) ceases trading
Alpine (Double Glazing), one of the oldest names in the UK window industry, has ceased trading. Once owned by ADT, Alpine went into administration in August 1991. The administrators sold the business for £900,000 in February 1992 to a group backed by the Midlands entrepreneur, Clive Smith. Alpine sent a letter to staff stating that it had suffered 'substantial bad debts'. Alpine's directors included James Berry, associated with Mr Smith through his role at Corporate Broking Services, which collapsed in 1991. Mr Smith held a substantial stake in CBS.

Moulinex (SA) swings to losses
Moulinex SA, the French home appliance company, swung to a loss for 1992, blaming a 'recession' in its industry sector and financial charges from its purchase of Germany's Robert Krups GmbH. The net loss swelled to FFr115 million ($21.5 million) last year, against a net profit in 1991 of FFr171 million. The acquisition of Krups in early 1991 is the main reason for Moulinex's serious debt problems. The

IBM shake-up after record loss

One of the great shocks of 1992 was IBM's annual results: the technology giant announced the first corporate loss in its 80-year history, a whopping $4.97 billion, the highest corporate loss ever recorded at the time. A week later General Motors topped this record with an even bigger loss. IBM stock plunged to a ten-year low, below $50. Chair John Akers slashed the dividend by 55% and announced job losses for 1993 of 25,000, on top of the 40,000 shed from the workforce in 1992, leaving the company with 300,000 worldwide.

All this bad news came only a year after Akers's dramatic restructuring plan, which split the company into 13 semi-autonomous businesses. It was not a surprise, therefore, when, on 26 Jan 1993, Akers stepped down as chair. A two-month worldwide search resulted in the appointment of a former chair of RJR Nabisco, Louis V Gerstner, Jr, the first outsider to run IBM in the company's history.

Most industry observers attribute IBM's losses to its failure to adapt to the changing marketplace created by the runaway success of the personal-computer standard it created in 1983. The company was heavily dependent on declining mainframe sales and management-heavy, and its continuing development of excellent technology was offset by its being too slow at turning its inventions into products.

Even with its deficits, IBM dominates the computer industry from sheer size: it is a $65-billion-a-year company which invests $5 billion a year in research and development. Besides its best-known products – personal, mini, and mainframe computers – it makes UNIX workstations and has a traditional strength in low-cost manufacturing. Recent new products include RISC-based massively parallel supercomputers, visualization systems, workstation-based speech recognition, and Thinkpad notebook computers.

One big change in IBM's approach in the early 1990s was its formation of partnerships with other technology companies: Apple, Motorola, Toshiba, and many more. Most of these projects were expected to bear fruit in the mid-1990s.

group's non-operational loss from financial transactions was FFr345 million in 1992, widening from FFr270 million in the prior year. On an operating level, the group remained profitable, although profit declined to FFr235 million from FFr499 million. Revenue, at FFr8.22 billion, fell well short of the company's target of FFr9 billion. Moulinex also noted that, with 80% revenue posted outside France, it was hit hard by the currency devaluations in the UK, Italy, and Spain.

NedCar's losses deepen

Netherlands Car (NedCar), the Dutch carmaker owned jointly by Mitsubishi Motors of Japan, Volvo of Sweden, and the Dutch government, suffered a net loss of Fl 243.6 million ($133.9 million) in 1992, its third year of rising losses. The 1992 financial performance, burdened by restricting cost of Fl 117 million, was a further sharp deterioration from a net loss of Fl 74.1 million in 1991 and Fl 76.1 million in 1990. NedCar was formed in 1991 when Mitsubishi Motors acquired a one-third equity stake in Volvo Cat BV, which had been controlled 70/30 by Dutch state interests and Volvo respectively. The company, which makes the Volvo 400 series, was hit last year by the continuing weakness of demand in its main markets and by significant currency losses after the European exchange rate fluctuations in the autumn of 1992. Car production rose last year to 94,019 from 84,507 in 1991, but output remained well below the breakeven level of more than 100,000 cars a year. Turnover rose to Fl 1.98 billion from Fl 1.74 billion in 1991. The NedCar workforce fell to 6,109 people at the end of 1992 from 6,521 a year earlier and is expected to fall sharply to around 4,500 by the end of 1993. Mitsubishi and Volvo are investing around Fl 3 billion in NedCar for the development of a new range of cars to be launched in 1995–96 and the doubling of capacity to 200,000 cards.

Fiat cuts dividend as profits fall

Fiat, Italy's biggest private company, bowed to the pressures of a depressed car market and heavy investment spending by slashing its dividend by more than half to L100 ($4^1/_2$ pence)for ordinary shares and L130 for non-voting savings stock. The heavy cut, for the second year in succession, was accompanied by news that net profits at Fiat Auto, the group's mainstream car subsidiary, fell to just L161 billion (£7.02 million) last year from L415 billion in 1991. Group net profits in 1992, buoyed by Fiat's profitable non-industrial activities and extraordinary earnings from asset sales, dropped by more than half to L551 billion after minority interests from L1,114 billion in 1991. Turnover rose by about 4.6% to L59,106 billion. In spite of the pressure on earnings, Fiat appears intent on pursuing its ambitious investment plans, which pushed net group indebtedness to L3,849 billion (£1.75 billion) in 1992. The company confirmed its L40,000 billion investment programme for 1992–95 and revealed that investment and R&D spending in 1992, mostly on developing new models and plant, rose to L8,526 billion, representing 14.4% of sales.

Taylor Woodrow goes deeper into the red

Losses on several problem contracts and further write-downs in property and land values sent Taylor Woodrow, the UK construction group, much deeper into the red last year. The final dividend was slashed to 0.5p to leave a 1p total down from 9.5p. Pretax losses of £66.1 million, against £2.7 million, followed £66.4 million of exceptional charges as housing land and property values were cut further. Before exceptionals, profits fell from £43.8 million to £300,000. Contracting, which accounted for 71% of the group's £1.23 billion sales, increased its losses from £19.6 million to £32.5 million. Problem contracts include: the Channel tunnel, for which £8.5 million was provided; the Storebaelt project in Denmark; EuroDisney in Paris; John Wayne airport in the USA; and a newly disclosed £4.2 million shortfall in Saudi Arabia. Action taken to cut £20 million from annual overhead costs included shedding 1,400 jobs – among them 30 subsidiary directors as 30 companies were eliminated. Sixteen buildings had been vacated, releasing 150,000 sq ft/14,000 sq m for sale, rent or surrender.

EuroDisney plans to ease burden

EuroDisney, the leisure group that has incurred heavy losses since opening the EuroDisneyland theme park outside Paris in April 1993, plans to try to alleviate its difficulties by restructuring its finances. The group was doing a lot of thinking and considering a number of different options to reduce the cost of servicing its net debt of FFr18 billion ($3.2 billion). EuroDisney, which announced that it had attracted 10 million visitors to EuroDisneyland since it opened, pays fixed interest rates on FFr8.5 billion of its debt and floating rates in the remaining FFr9.5 billion. EuroDisney made a pre-tax loss of FFr339 million in its last full financial year to 30 September 1992, lost FFr492 million in the first quarter of 1993, and has confirmed that it will stay in the red for the full financial year. Rebecca Winnington-Ingram, European leisure analyst at Morgan Stanley in London, expects EuroDisney to produce a loss of FFr650 million in the second quarter of 1993 and a profit of FFr375 million in the second half, reducing its projected loss for the full financial year to FFr769 million.

Ford (Europe) posts record loss

Ford's European automotive operations made a record loss last year of $1.3 billion, compared with a loss of $1.079 billion in 1991. The loss was largely incurred by Ford's operations in the UK, including Jaguar. The loss in Europe included a $419 million one-off charge for restructuring, while adverse currency fluctuations added exchange rate losses of more than $200 million. Ford of Europe announced late in 1992 that it was planning to cut more than 10,000 jobs by the end of 1993. The workforce of its European automotive operations, excluding Jaguar, had already been cut by 19% from 115,000 in 1990 to 93,000 in late 1992 and is set to fall to 83,000 by the end of 1993. Jaguar, which was taken over by Ford at the end of 1989, said that its loss in 1992 was little changed under US accounting rules, at $394.9 million, compared with a loss of $402.2 million in 1991. Under UK accounting rules, the loss was cut to £189.5 million ($286 million) from £226.2 million a year earlier. The Jaguar UK workforce has also been sharply reduced, to only 6,481 at the end of 1992 from 7,520 a year earlier and 11,661 at the end of 1990. Jaguar's retail sales worldwide fell last year by 12.4% to 22,478. This was the lowest level since 1982. Production dropped last year by 10.5% to 20,593 – the lowest since 1981.

Sears, Roebuck sinks to $3.9 billion loss

Sears, Roebuck, the troubled US retail group, reported a plunge into net losses of $3.93 billion for 1992 from profits of $1.3 billion the year before. This is one of the biggest reversals in US corporate history, and rivals IBM recently reported record loss of $4.96 billion for the year. However, the result had been expected by Wall Street, as Sears had previously disclosed that it would take a $1.72 billion charge for restructuring its merchandising operations and a $206.7-million write-down on its Homart Development property business. Sears also took a $1.65-billion after-tax charge for losses incurred by its Allstrate Insurance subsidiary from catastrophe claims relating to hurricanes Andrew and Iniki. Analysts had expected a $1.25-billion charge. The group recorded a $1.87-billion charge for required accounting changes, and a gain of $86.6 million on the sale of minority interests in two companies. For the fourth quarter, Sears' net losses came to $1.80 billion, compared with profits of $5,133.1 million.

Ferruzzi-Montedison of Italy in trouble

Ferruzzi-Montedison, the Italian chemicals, energy, and agroindustrial group, which recently reported record losses, is facing the most testing period in its history. It is negotiating the restructuring of its L15,123 billion ($10 billion) borrowings, a deal that could involve Italy's first debt-for-equity swap. Under new rules proposed by the Bank of Italy, the creditor committee of five banks, headed by Mediobanca, may seek to convert some of the loans into shares. Action is urgently needed to stop Ferruzzi-Montedison buckling under the weight of debt and losses. Ferruzzi Finanziaria (Ferfin), the holding company, lost L1,519 billion (£675 million) in 1992, compared with net profits of L115 billion in 1991. Montedison, its main operating subsidiary, lost L1,244 billion against net profits of L168 billion. The group is Italy's second biggest private-sector company, with revenues of L19,900 billion in 1992. It has mushroomed from its origins in farming and commodities trading. When the founder, Serafino Ferruzzi, died in 1979, leadership passed to the charismatic and domineering Raul Gardini. He led the group into chemicals (Montedison), cement (Calcestruzzi), insurance (Fondiaria), and a string of other operations, including a barely profitable national newspaper (*Il Messagero*) and a heavily loss-making TV station (Telemontecarlo). The takeovers created an increasingly indebted conglomerate, with few synergies and too little management talent. The strains were masked by the booming 1980s, but became impossible to hide in a recession.

INTERNATIONAL ECONOMICS

Terms

aid, development money given or lent on concessional terms to developing countries or spent on maintaining agencies for this purpose. In the late 1980s official aid from governments of richer nations amounted to $45–60 billion annually, whereas voluntary organizations in the West received about $2.4 billion a year for the Third World. The World Bank is the largest dispenser of aid. In 1992 it transferred $49.7 million to developing countries. All industrialized United Nations (UN) member countries devote a proportion of their gross national product to aid, ranging from 0.20% of GNP (Ireland) to 1.10% (Norway) (1988 figures). Each country spends more than half this contribution on direct bilateral assistance to countries with which they have historical or military links or hope to encourage trade. The rest goes to international organizations such as UN and World Bank agencies, which distribute aid multilaterally.

The UK development-aid budget in 1990 was 0.31% of GNP, with India and Kenya among the principal beneficiaries. The European Development Fund (an arm of the European Community) and the International Development Association (an arm of the World Bank) receive approximately 5% and 8% respectively of the UK development-aid budget. The Overseas Development Administration is the department of the Foreign Office that handles bilateral aid.

In 1990, the US development-aid budget was 0.15% of GNP, with Israel and Egypt among the principal beneficiaries; Turkey, Pakistan, and the Philippines are also major beneficiaries. The United States Agency for International Development (USAID) is the State Department body responsible for bilateral aid. The USA is the largest contributor to, and thus the most powerful member of, the International Development Association.

The combined overseas development aid of all EC member countries is less than the sum ($20 billion) the EC spends every year on storing surplus food produced by European farmers.

balance of payments account of a country's debit and credit transactions with other countries. Items are divided into the ***current account***, which includes both visible trade (imports and exports of goods) and invisible trade (services such as transport, tourism, interest, and dividends), and the ***capital account***, which includes investment in and out of the country, international grants, and loans. Deficits or surpluses on these accounts are brought into balance by buying and selling reserves of foreign currencies.

A ***balance of payments crisis*** arises when a country's current account deteriorates because the cost of imports exceeds income from exports. Persistent trade deficits often result in heavy government borrowing overseas, which in turn leads to a debt crisis.

bank financial institution that uses funds deposited with it to lend money to companies or individuals, and also provides financial services to its customers. A ***central bank*** (in the UK, the Bank of England) issues currency for the government, in order to provide cash for circulation and exchange.

Big Bang popular term for the changes instituted in late 1986 to the organization and practices of the City of London as Britain's financial centre, including the liberalization of the London Stock Exchange. This involved merging the functions of jobber (dealer in stocks and shares) and broker (who mediates between the jobber and the public), introducing negotiated commission rates, and allowing foreign banks and financial companies to own British brokers/jobbers, or themselves to join the London Stock Exchange.

capital accumulated or inherited wealth held in the form of assets (such as stocks and shares, property, and bank deposits). In stricter terms, capital is defined as the stock of goods used in the production of other goods, and may be ***fixed capital*** (such as buildings, plant, and machinery) that is durable, or ***circulating capital*** (raw materials and components) that is used up quickly.

collective bargaining process whereby management, representing an employer, and a trade union, representing employees, agree to negotiate jointly terms and conditions of employment. Agreements can be company-based or industry-wide.

comparative advantage law of international trade first elaborated by English economist David Ricardo (1772–1823) showing that trade becomes worthwhile if the cost of production of particular items differs between one country and another.

consumption the purchase of goods and services for final use, as opposed to spending by firms on capital goods, known as capital formation.

cost of living cost of goods and services needed for an average standard of living. In Britain the cost-of-living index was introduced 1914 and based on the expenditure of a working-class family of a man, woman, and three children; the standard is 100. Known from 1947 as the Retail Price Index (RPI), it is revised to allow for inflation.

cost-push inflation theory stating that inflation is caused by increases in the costs of production. A rise in wages, profit levels, or product inputs to the firm will push up its costs. It responds by increasing its prices. This then contributes to inflation in the economy.

credit means by which goods or services are obtained without immediate payment, usually by agreeing to pay interest. The three main forms are ***consumer credit*** (usually extended to individuals by retailers), ***bank credit*** (such as overdrafts or personal loans), and ***trade credit*** (common in the commercial world both within countries and internationally). Consumer credit is increasingly used to pay for goods. In the USA in 1991 it amounted to $756 billion, with about 18% of disposable income expended on hire-purchase and credit card payments.

In the UK in 1992, net lending to consumers amounted to approximately £35 billion.

crowding out situation in which an increase in government expenditure results in a fall in private-sector investment, either because it causes inflation or a rise in interest rates (as a result of increased government borrowing) or because it reduces the efficiency of production as a result of government intervention. Crowding out has been used in recent years as a justification of supply-side economics such as the privatization of state-owned industries and services.

currency the type of money in use in a country; for example, the US dollar, the Australian dollar, the UK pound sterling, the German Deutschmark, and the Japanese yen.

debt, international money owed by one country to another. It began on a large scale with the investment in foreign countries by newly industrialized countries in the late 19th to early 20th centuries. International debt became a global problem as a result of the oil crisis of the 1970s.

The World Bank was established 1945 as an agency of the United Nations to finance international development, by providing loans where private capital was not forthcoming. Loans were made largely at prevailing market rates ('hard loans') and therefore generally to the developed countries, who could afford them. In 1960 the International Development Association (IDA) was set up as an offshoot of the World Bank to provide interest-free ('soft') loans over a long period to finance the economies of developing countries and assist their long-term development. The cash surpluses of Middle Eastern oil-producing countries were channelled by Western banks to Third World countries. However, a slump in the world economy, and increases in interest rates, resulted in the debtor countries paying an ever-increasing share of their national output in debt servicing (paying off the interest on a debt, rather than paying off the debt itself). As a result, many loans had to be ***rescheduled*** (renegotiated so that repayments were made over a longer term).

The debtor countries paid more than $1,300 billion 1982–90, yet their debt increased by 61%. Africa transferred $10 billion a year (1993) to the rich countries in debt repayments. Banks in the creditor countries had received $44–$50 billion in tax relief on bad debts by 1993.

In 1980–81 Poland ceased making repayments on international debts. Today, the countries most at risk include Mexico and Brazil, both of which have a ***debt-servicing ratio*** (proportion of export earnings which is required to pay off the debt) of more than 50%. In May 1987 the world's largest bank, Citibank of New York, announced that it was writing off $3 billion of international loans, mainly due to Brazil's repeated rescheduling of debt repayments. The dangers of the current scale of international debt (the so-called ***debt crisis***) is that the debtor country can only continue to repay its existing debts by means of further loans; for the Western countries, there is the possibility of a confidence crisis causing panic withdrawals of deposits and consequent collapse of the banking system.

deficit financing planned excess of expenditure over income, dictated by government policy, creating a shortfall of public revenue which is met by borrowing. The decision to create a deficit is made to stimulate an economy by increasing consumer purchasing and at the same time to create more jobs.

demand-pull inflation rise in prices (inflation) caused by excess aggregate demand (total demand for goods and services) in the economy. For example, when the economy is in boom, aggregate demand tends to be rising quickly, but inflation also rises quickly.

deregulation US term for freeing markets from protection, with the aim of improving competitiveness. It often results in greater monopoly control. An example is the deregulation of the US airline industry 1978, after which 14 new companies began flying. By 1991 only one was left. In Britain, the major changes in the City of London 1986 (the Big Bang) were in part deregulation.

devaluation lowering of the official value of a currency against other currencies, so that exports become cheaper and imports more expensive. Used when a country is badly in deficit in its balance of trade, it results in the goods the country produces being cheaper abroad, so that the economy is stimulated by increased foreign demand. ***Revaluation*** is the opposite process.

Devaluation of important currencies upsets the balance of the world's money markets and encourages speculation. The increased cost of imported food, raw materials, and manufactured goods as a consequence of devaluation may stimulate an acceleration in inflation, especially when commodities are rising in price because of increased world demand.

disinvestment withdrawal of investments in a country for political reasons. The term is also used to describe non-replacement of stock as it wears out.

It is generally applied to the removal of funds from South Africa in recent years by some multinational companies, and to the withdrawal of private investment funds (by universities, pension funds, and other organizations) from portfolios doing business in South Africa. Disinvestment may be motivated by fear of loss of business in the home market caused by adverse publicity or by fear of loss of foreign resources if the local government changes.

Dow Jones Index (***Dow Jones Industrial 30 Share Index***) scale for measuring the average share price and percentage change of 30 major US industrial companies. It has been calculated and published since 1897 by the financial news publisher Dow Jones and Co.

economic growth rate of growth of output of all goods and services in an economy, usually measured as the percentage increase in gross domestic product or gross national product from one year to the next. It

Growth of real GNP/GDP in the G7 countries

Seasonally adjusted at annual rates (%)

	Percentage change from previous year		
	1991	*1992*	*1993*
USA	−1.2	1.8	2.4
Japan	4.4	1.8	2.3
Germany	3.7	1.4	1.2
France	1.2	1.9	1.6
Italy	1.4	1.2	0.8
UK	−2.2	−1.0	1.3
Canada	−1.7	1.3	3.2

Source: OECD Economic Outlook

is regarded as an indicator of the rate of increase or decrease in the standard of living; it is negative in a recession, as it was in the UK in 1991 and 1992, when economic growth was –2.5% and –0.4% respectively.

exchange rate the price at which one currency is bought or sold in terms of other currencies, gold, or accounting units such as the special drawing right of the International Monetary Fund. Exchange rates may be fixed by international agreement or by government policy; or they may be wholly or partly allowed to 'float' (that is, find their own level) in world currency markets.

Central banks, as large holders of foreign currency, often intervene to buy or sell particular currencies in an effort to maintain some stability in exchange rates.

exchange-rate policy policy of government towards the level of the exchange rate of its currency. It may want to influence the exchange rate by using its gold and foreign currency reserves held by its central bank to buy and sell its currency. It can also use interest rates (monetary policy) to alter the value of the currency.

excise duty indirect tax levied on certain goods produced within a country, such as petrol, alcohol, and tobacco. It is collected by the government's Customs and Excise department.

export goods or service produced in one country and sold to another. Exports may be visible (goods physically exported) or invisible (services provided in the exporting country but paid for by residents of another country).

Export markets

Countries' international exports by region, 1991 (percentage of total)

	EC	*Western hemisphere*	*Asia/ Pacific*	*Others*
Benelux	74.9	5.6	5.6	13.9
Denmark	54.3	7.4	7.4	30.1
France	62.0	10.6	7.3	20.1
Germany	54.2	9.0	8.1	28.7
Greece	63.8	10.7	2.8	26.5
Ireland	73.6	10.7	4.8	10.9
Italy	59.2	10.0	7.5	23.3
Portugal	75.2	5.1	2.3	17.4
Spain	71.6	8.9	4.1	15.4
UK	56.6	14.1	10.6	18.7
USA	24.4	35.2	29.7	10.7
Japan	18.9	35.5	36.1	9.5

Source: IMF

Financial Times Index (FT Index) indicator measuring the daily movement of 30 major industrial share prices on the London Stock Exchange (1935 = 100), issued by the UK *Financial Times* newspaper. Other FT indices cover government securities, fixed-interest securities, gold mine shares, and Stock Exchange activity.

fiscal policy that part of government policy devoted to raising revenue, notably through taxation, and deciding on government borrowing (the public sector borrowing requirement), and the priorities and purposes governing its expenditure.

Fiscal policy can also be used to direct the economy. For example, value-added tax (VAT) and excise duty on tobacco discourages cigarette smoking; mortgage tax relief encourages people to buy their own home. At a macroeconomic level, more public spending and less taxation will stimulate total spending in the economy, leading probably to a fall in unemployment but a rise in inflation.

free-enterprise economy another term for free-market economy.

free-market economy or ***free-enterprise economy*** economic system where the factors of production are mainly owned by private individuals or organizations, and where resource allocation takes place through the market mechanism. Government plays a relatively small role in providing goods and services, but it is responsible for upholding laws which protect rights to own property, and for maintaining a stable currency.

gilt-edged securities stocks and shares issued and guaranteed by the British government to raise funds and traded on the Stock Exchange. A relatively risk-free investment, gilts bear fixed interest and are usually redeemable on a specified date. The term is now used generally to describe securities of the highest value.

gross domestic product (GDP) value of the output of all goods and services produced within a nation's borders, normally given as a total for the year. It thus includes the production of foreign-owned firms within the country, but excludes the income from domestically owned firms located abroad.

Since output is derived from expenditure on goods and services by firms, consumers, and government net of imports; and income (in the form of wages, salaries, interest, rent, and profits) is derived from the production of goods and services, GDP can be measured either by the sum of total output or expenditure or incomes. However, in practice there is usually a slight discrepancy between the three because of the highly complex calculations involved. GDP fluctuates in relation to the trade cycle and standard of living.

In the UK, the percentage increase in GDP from one year to the next is the standard measure of economic growth.

gross national product (GNP) the most commonly used measurement of the wealth of a country. GNP is defined as the total value of all goods and services produced by firms owned by the country concerned. It is measured as the gross domestic product plus income from abroad, minus income earned during the same period by foreign investors within the country.

hyperinflation rapid and uncontrolled inflation, or increases in prices, usually associated with political and/or social instability (as in Germany in the 1920s).

import product or service that one country purchases from another for domestic consumption, or for processing and re-exporting (Hong Kong, for example, is heavily dependent on imports for its export busi-

Recovery in the UK and recession in Europe?

As the UK recovers from recession in 1993, attention has turned to the rate and sustainability of the recovery.

Forecasts for economic growth, inflation, and the balance of payments

	Real GDP % change		*Consumer prices % increase*		*Current account as % of GDP*	
	1993	*1994*	*1993*	*1994*	*1993*	*1994*
Belgium	−0.2	+1.2	2.5	2.4	+2.1	+2.1
France	−0.2	+1.6	2.3	2.1	−0.1	−0.3
Germany*	−1.5	+1.1	3.8	2.8	−1.2	−1.0
Netherlands	−0.1	+1.5	2.4	2.3	+3.0	+2.9
Italy	−0.5	+1.0	4.7	4.5	−1.6	−1.2
Spain	−0.5	+1.2	4.7	4.3	−3.9	−4.0
UK	+1.4	+2.5	2.1	4.1	−2.8	−3.1

**Current account figures are on all-German basis; others western Germany only.*

Source: *The Economist*

The table shows that the European economy is relatively stagnant. The percentage change in real GDP (gross domestic product) is the change in the value of the output of all goods and services after allowing for increases in the average level of prices (inflation). For example, if the value of all goods and services rises by 3.5% in 1993, and the rate of inflation is 2.1%, real GDP increases by 1.4%. The UK is likely to be the only country of those shown that will have positive growth in 1993. Its real GDP will still be below the 1990 level by the end of 1993. This is in contrast to the experience of the rest of Europe, which had positive growth in1992, is in recession in 1993, and is likely to return to positive growth in 1994.

The recession in the rest of Europe partly explains the fragility of the UK recovery in 1993. About 55% of the UK's exports of goods are sold in the European Community, and the European recession has significantly weakened the demand for UK products. However, this has to some extent been offset by the significant fall in the value of the pound since it left the exchange rate mechanism in September 1992. This has made UK exports cheaper and foreign imports into the UK more expensive. The immediate effect of more expensive imports and cheaper exports is to increase the balance of payments current account deficit (the amount by which imports of goods and services exceeds exports), but then, as the demand for exports and imports adjusts to the price changes, exports rise and imports fall, the balance of payments improves and the demand for UK goods and services rises.

A recurring problem of the UK economy is that recovery tends not to be sustainable at rates of over 2.5%, in contrast to many other developed economies. The general recovery of the European economy is shown in 1994, when all the economies are expected to return to positive growth, and with them Britain's export markets. However, the balance of payments deficit is forecast to increase, as a large proportion of the increased income generated from the rising UK economic growth shown from1993 to 1994 is spent on imports.

Another indicator of the inability of producers to keep up with accelerating demand in the UK is the expected rise in inflation. The fall in the value of the pound since September 1992 has brought a significant increase in UK import prices. In fact, in the last three months of 1992, import prices rose by 8%. These increases were not passed on in the first half of 1993 as a result of the low levels of demand faced by producers and retailers. However, as the economy picks up, these cost increases will be passed on, and inflation is expected to rise back to 4.1% in 1994. Beyond 1994, inflationary pressure is likely to increase further, as history suggests that whenever the UK rate of growth exceeds 2.5% for any length of time, inflation rises significantly. In 1988, real GDP grew by 4.5%, but this was not sustainable as inflation rose, and the economy subsequently slowed down and went into deep recession. This'boom and bust' or 'stop–go' cycle has been a feature of the UK economy for the last 30 years. Other countries have fluctuations in output, as the table shows, but they seem to be less violent. France and Germany have been able to sustain rates of growth above 3%, while Japan has been able to sustain even higher rates. It has been argued that the UK economy has been less susceptible to high rates of inflation since the mid 1980s as the boom resulted in a peak of inflation of 10% compared with the 25% experienced in the mid 1970s. However, there has not been the same dramatic increase in oil prices seen in that period.

The table shows the very significant problems being experienced by Germany, with relatively high rates of inflation (compared with previous German rates) and a relatively stagnant economy. It remains to be seen whether the strains of adjusting to unification have dealt a long-term blow to German economic success, or whether the productive potential of an enlarged area and skilled workforce can be harnessed by the efficient productive techniques that have been developed in the post-war period.

RP

ness). Imports may be visible (goods) or invisible (services). If an importing country does not have a counterbalancing value of exports, it may experience balance-of-payments difficulties and accordingly consider restricting imports by some form of protectionism (such as an import tariff or import quotas).

import control control that limits the number of imports entering the country. One type of import control is an import quota.

incomes policy government-initiated exercise to curb inflation by restraining rises in incomes, on either a voluntary or a compulsory basis; often linked with action to control prices, in which case it becomes a prices and incomes policy.

income tax direct tax levied on personal income, mainly wages and salaries, but which may include the value of receipts other than in cash. It is one of the main instruments for achieving a government's income redistribution objectives. In contrast, ***indirect taxes*** are duties payable whenever a specific product is purchased; examples include VAT and customs duties.

Most countries impose income taxes on company (corporation) profits and on individuals (personal), although the rates and systems differ widely from country to country. In the case of companies in particular, income tax returns are prepared by an accountant, who will take advantage of the various exemptions, deductions, and allowances available. Personal income taxes are usually progressive so that the poorest members of society pay little or no tax, while the rich make much larger contributions.

inflation rise in the general level of prices. The many causes include increased production costs (***cost-push inflation***); ***demand-pull inflation*** results when overall demand exceeds supply. Suppressed inflation occurs in controlled economies and is reflected in rationing, shortages, and black-market prices. Deflation, a fall in the general level of prices, is the reverse of inflation.

interest sum of money paid by a borrower to a lender in return for the loan, usually expressed as a percentage per annum. ***Simple interest*** is interest calculated as a straight percentage of the amount loaned or invested. In ***compound interest***, the interest earned over a period of time (for example, per annum) is added to the investment, so that at the end of the next period interest is paid on that total.

invisible trade international trade in services. In a balance of payments account, invisible exports are exports of services and invisible imports are imports of services.

laissez faire theory that the state should not intervene in economic affairs, except to break up a monopoly. The degree to which intervention should take place is one of the chief problems of economics. Scottish economist Adam Smith (1723–1790) justified the theory in *The Wealth of Nations* 1776.

The 20th century has seen an increasing degree of state intervention to promote social benefits, which after World War II in Europe was extended into the field of nationalization of leading industries and services. However, from the 1970s, laissez-faire policies were again pursued in the UK and the USA.

market any situation where buyers and sellers are in contact with each other. This could be a street market or a world market where buyers and sellers communicate via letters, faxes, telephones, and representatives. In a perfect or ***free market***, there are many buyers and sellers, so that no single buyer or seller is able to influence the price of the product; there is therefore perfect competition in the market. In an ***imperfect market*** either a few buyers or sellers (or even just one) dominates the market.

market economy free-market economy where most resources are allocated through markets rather than through state planning.

market forces the forces of demand (a want backed by the ability to pay) and supply (the willingness and ability to supply).

Some economists argue that resources are allocated most efficiently when producers are able to respond to consumer demand without intervention from 'distortions' such as governments and trade unions, and that profits and competition between firms and individuals provide sufficient incentives to produce efficiently (monetarism). Critics of this view suggest that market forces alone may not be efficient because they fail to consider social costs and benefits, and may also fail to provide for the needs of the less well off, since private firms aiming to make a profit respond to the ability to pay.

monetarism economic policy, advocated by the economist Milton Friedman (1912–) and the Chicago school of economists, that proposes control of a country's money supply to keep it in step with the country's ability to produce goods, with the aim of curbing inflation. Cutting government spending is advocated, and the long-term aim is to return as much of the economy as possible to the private sector, allegedly in the interests of efficiency.

LONG-TERM INTEREST RATES*
(percent per annum, 1992)

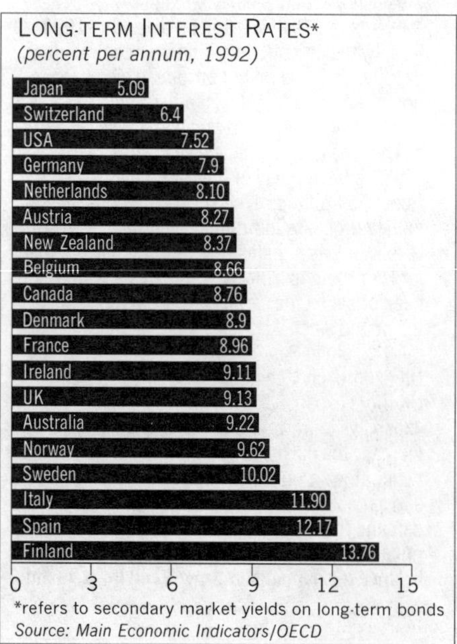

*refers to secondary market yields on long-term bonds
Source: Main Economic Indicators/OECD

Central banks use the discount rate and other tools to restrict or expand the supply of money to the economy. Additionally, credit is restricted by high interest rates, and industry is not cushioned against internal market forces or overseas competition (with the aim of preventing 'overstaffing', 'restrictive' union practices, and 'excessive' wage demands). Unemployment may result from some efforts to withdraw government safety nets, but monetarists claim it is less than eventually occurs if the methods of Keynesian economics are adopted. Monetarist policies were widely adopted in the 1980s in response to the inflation problems caused by spiralling oil prices in 1979.

monetary policy economic policy aimed at controlling the amount of money in circulation, usually through controlling the level of lending or credit. Increasing interest rates is an example of a contractionary monetary policy, which aims to reduce inflation by reducing the rate of growth of spending in the economy.

money any common medium of exchange acceptable in payment for goods or services or for the settlement of debts; legal tender. Money is usually coinage (invented by the Chinese in the second millennium BC) and paper notes (used by the Chinese from about AD 800). Developments such as the cheque and credit card fulfil many of the traditional functions of money.

money supply quantity of money in circulation in an economy at any given time. It can include notes, coins, and clearing-bank and other deposits used for everyday payments. Changes in the quantity of lending are a major determinant of changes in the money supply. One of the main principles of monetarism is that increases in the money supply in excess of the rate of economic growth are the chief cause of inflation.

In Britain there are several definitions of money supply. M0 was defined as notes and coins in circulation, together with the operational balance of clearing banks with the Bank of England. M1 encompasses M0 plus current-account deposits; M2, now rarely used, covers the M1 items plus deposit accounts; M3 covers M2 items plus all other deposits held by UK citizens and companies in the UK banking sector. In May 1987 the Bank of England introduced M4 (M3 plus building-society deposits) and M5 (M4 plus Treasury bills and local-authority deposits).

monopoly the domination of a market for a particular product or service by a single company, which can therefore restrict competition and keep prices high. In practice, a company can be said to have a monopoly when it controls a significant proportion of the market (technically an oligopoly).

In the UK, monopoly was originally a royal grant of the sole right to manufacture or sell a certain article. The Fair Trading Act 1973 defines a monopoly supplier as one having 'a quarter of the market', and the Monopolies and Mergers Commission controls any attempt to reach this position (in the USA 'antitrust laws' are similarly used). The Competition Act of 1980 covers both private monopolies and possible abuses in the public sector. A ***monopsony*** is a situation in which there is only one buyer; for example, most governments are the only legal purchasers of military equipment inside their countries.

multiplier theoretical concept, formulated by John Maynard Keynes (1883–1946), of the effect on national income or employment by an adjustment in overall demand. For example, investment by a company in a new plant will stimulate new income and expenditure, which will in turn generate new investment, and so on, so that the actual increase in national income may be several times greater than the original investment.

national debt debt incurred by the central government of a country to its own people and institutions and also to overseas creditors. A government can borrow from the public by means of selling interest-bearing bonds, for example, or from abroad. Traditionally, a major cause of national debt was the cost of war but in recent decades governments have borrowed heavily in order to finance development or nationalization, to support an ailing currency, or to avoid raising taxes.

At the end of the financial year 1992–93, the UK national debt was approximately £127 billion. This represented a rise in the national debt since 1991–92, caused by a budget deficit, or public sector borrowing requirement (PSBR) of £35 billion in the year 1992–93.

newly industrialized country (NIC) country that has in recent decades experienced a breakthrough into manufacturing and rapid export-led economic growth. The prime examples are Taiwan, Hong Kong, Singapore, and South Korea. Their economic development during the 1970s and 1980s was partly due to a rapid increase of manufactured goods in their exports.

oligopoly situation in which a few companies control the major part of a particular market and concert their actions to perpetuate such control. This may include an agreement to fix prices (a cartel).

poll tax tax levied on every individual, without reference to income or property. Being simple to administer, it was among the earliest sorts of tax (introduced in England 1377), but because it is a regressive tax, in that it falls proportionately more on poorer people, it has often proved unpopular. The ***community charge***, a type of poll tax, was introduced in the UK 1989–90 but replaced by a 'council tax' 1993–94. The combined cost of its collection and abolition was estimated at £4 billion.

privatization policy or process of selling or transferring state-owned or public assets and services (notably nationalized industries) to private investors. Privatization of services involves the government contracting private firms to supply services previously supplied by public authorities.

Supporters of privatization argue that the public benefits from theoretically greater efficiency from firms already in the competitive market, and the release of resources for more appropriate use by government. Those against privatization believe that it transfers a country's assets from all the people to a controlling minority, that public utilities such as gas and water become private monopolies, and that a profit-making state-owned company raises revenue for the government.

In many cases the trend towards privatization has been prompted by dissatisfaction with the high level

Measuring the quality of life

*Human development index, 1993**

Overall top-ranked countries	*Top developing nations (overall ranking)*
1. Japan	1. Barbados (20)
2. Canada	2. Hong Kong (24)
3. Norway	3. Cyprus (27)
4. Switzerland	4. Uruguay (30)
5. Sweden	5. Trinidad and Tobago (31)
6. United States	6. Bahamas (32)
7. Australia	7. S Korea (33)
8. France	8. Chile (36)
9. Netherlands	9. Costa Rica (42)
10. Britain	10. Singapore (43)
11. Iceland	11. Brunei (44)
12. Germany	12. Argentina (46)
13. Denmark	13. Venezuela (50)
14. Finland	14. Dominica (51)
15. Austria	15. Kuwait (52)
16. Belgium	16. Mexico (53)
17. New Zealand	17. Qatar (55)
18. Luxembourg	18. Mauritius (56)
19. Israel	19. Malaysia (57)
	20. Bahrain (58)
	21. Grenada (59)
	22. Antigua and Barbuda (60)

* *The index is based on income and quality of life, a factor that measures life expectancy, literacy, ability to take part in society's institutions, and real purchasing power. The above rankings are included in the UN Development Programme's fourth annual report on human development. According to the report, 90 % of the world's population have no control over institutions affecting their lives, and the gap between rich and poor is continuing to widen across the globe.*

Source: UNDP

of subsidies being given to often inefficient state enterprise. The term 'privatization' is used even when the state retains a majority share of an enterprise.

The policy has been pursued by the post-1979 Conservative administration in the UK, and by recent governments in France, Japan, Italy, New Zealand and elsewhere. By 1988 the practice had spread worldwide, with communist countries such as China and Cuba selling off housing to private tenants.

productivity the output produced by a given quantity of labour, usually measured as output per person employed in the firm, industry, sector, or economy concerned. Productivity is determined by the quality and quantity of the fixed capital used by labour, and the effort of the workers concerned.

The level of productivity is a major determinant of cost-efficiency: higher productivity tends to reduce average costs of production. Increases in productivity in a whole economy are a major determinant of economic growth. It is important to distinguish between the rate of growth of productivity and the level of productivity, since at lower levels of productivity, higher rates of productivity growth may be achieved.

profit-sharing system whereby an employer pays the workers a fixed share of the company's profits. It originated in France in the early 19th century and was widely practised for a time within the cooperative movement.

public-sector borrowing requirement (PSBR) the amount of money needed by a government to cover any deficit in financing its own activities.

The PSBR includes loans to local authorities and public corporations, and also the funds raised by local authorities and public corporations from other sources. It is financed chiefly by sales of debt to the public outside the banking system (gilt-edged stocks, national savings, and local-authority stocks and bonds), by external transactions with other countries, and by borrowing from the banking system. In the UK, after the 1986 budget, this measure was changed to the ***public-sector financial deficit (PSFD)***, which is net of the asset sales due to privatization, which are thought to distort the PSBR.

public-sector debt repayment (PSDR) the amount of money left over when government expenditure (public spending) is subtracted from government receipts. This occurs only when government spending is less than government receipts. A PSDR enables a government to repay some of the national debt.

quantity theory of money economic theory claiming that an increase in the amount of money in circulation causes a proportionate increase in prices. The theory dates from the 17th century and was elaborated by US economist Irving Fisher (1867–1947). Supported and developed by US economist Milton Friedman (1912–), it forms the theoretical basis of monetarism.

recession fall in business activity lasting more than a few months, causing stagnation in a country's output. A serious recession is called a ***slump***.

reserve currency a country's holding of internationally acceptable means of payment (major foreign currencies or gold); central banks also hold the ultimate reserve of money for their domestic banking sector. On the asset side of company balance sheets, undistributed profits are listed as reserves.

retail price index (RPI) indicator of variations in the cost of living.

savings unspent income, after deduction of tax. In economics a distinction is made between investment, involving the purchase of capital goods, such as buying a house, and saving (where capital goods are not directly purchased; for example, buying shares).

Say's law the 'law of markets' formulated by Jean-Baptiste Say (1767–1832) to the effect that supply creates its own demand and that resources can never be underused.

self-sufficiency situation where no trade takes place between an individual or a group and others. If an economy were self-sufficient, it would not export or import. In a modern economy, there is very little self-sufficiency because specialization enables individuals to enjoy a much higher standard of living then if they were self-sufficient.

slump in the business or trade cycle, the period of time when the economy is in depression, unemployment is very high, and national income is well below its full employment level. In the UK, the economy

Job crisis in western Europe

Western Europe's recession might begin easing in 1994, but a deepening jobs crisis could continue to frustrate policymakers as Europe falls behind the global competition curve. Some 22 million western Europeans, nearly one in nine workers, are out of work. A million more are expected to join them next year as industry sheds thousands of jobs. Increasingly, it appears that without structural reform Europe cannot generate enough growth to create jobs.

Most governments are locked into policies that rule out massive fiscal stimulus packages and deep cuts in interest rates – the classic remedies for faltering economies. Industry is calling for deregulated labour markets but, so far, unpopular arguments for lower wages, longer working weeks and fewer unemployment and social benefits are gaining only grudging political support.

Unless competitiveness improves, economists expect that Europe's recession will be replaced by anaemic growth and even longer jobless rolls in the mid-1990s. The seeming powerlessness of governments erodes trust in Europe's political leadership and feeds the confidence crisis of consumers and industry, threatening to shelve more investment plans and kill off even more jobs.

The painful 1990s: samples of job cuts in western Europe

Company	*Country*	*Sector*	*Period*	*Job cuts*
Phillips	Netherlands	electronics	1990–93	75,000
Bundesbahn	Germany	railway	1993–93	50,700
Ferrovie D. Stato	Italy	railway	1993–95	43,100
BT	UK	telecommunications	1992–93	39,800
ICI	UK	energy	1992	31,000
Daimler-Benz	Germany	chemicals	1991–93	21,000
Volkswagen	Germany	automobiles	1992–93	33,000
Volkswagen	Germany	automobiles	1993–94	30,000
Telekom	Germany	telecommunications	1993–96	20,000
Fiat	Italy	automobiles	1993	20,000
Michelin	France	tyres, rubber	1991–94	20,000
Electrolux	Sweden	appliances	1990–91	15,000
SKF	Sweden	ball bearings	1990–93	14,000
Siemens	Germany	electrical Engineering	1993	13,000
ABB	Sweden	energy	1993	12,000
Volvo	Sweden	automobiles	1990–93	11,000
Renault	France	automobiles	1991–93	10,600
CSI	Spain	steel	1993–94	9,700
Mannesmann	Germany	steel, machinery	1992–93	9,600
Ford	Europe	automobiles	1993	9,500
Bayer	Germany	chemicals	1992–93	9,200
Thyssen	Germany	steel, machinery	1993–94	9,000
Stora	Sweden	paper, pulp	1991–93	9,000
Usinor-Sacilor	France	steel	1991–93	7,300
Hoechst	Germany	chemicals	1992–93	7,100
British Rail	UK	railways	1991–93	7,000
Fag Kugel	Germany	ball bearings	1993	6,500
Daf	UK	trucks	1993	6,000
Oerlikon	Switzerland	conglomerate	1990–92	6,000
British Gas	UK	energy	1993	5,200
Hoogovens	Netherlands	steel	1993	5,000
Ciba-Geigy	Switzerland	chemicals	1991–93	5,000
Veba	Germany	energy, chemicals	1991–94	5,000
Iberia	Spain	airline	1992–93	4,700
BASF	Germany	chemicals	1993–94	4,400
Sabena	Belgium	airline	1991–94	3,200

Source: The Wall Street Journal (Europe)

OA

experienced a slump in the 1930s (the Great Depression), in 1980–81, and 1990–92.

social costs and benefits the costs and benefits to society as a whole that result from economic decisions. These include private costs (the financial cost of production incurred by firms) and benefits (the profits made by firms and the value to people of consuming goods and services) and external costs and benefits (affecting those not directly involved in production or consumption); pollution is one of the external costs.

Transport policy provides a clear example of the need to take external costs and benefits into account, where increases in the demand for private road transport generate considerable external costs in the form of pollution, road repairs, and extra costs to firms using transport networks and to medical services as a result of traffic congestion.

stagflation economic condition (experienced in Europe in the 1970s) in which rapid inflation is accompanied by stagnating, even declining, output and by increasing unemployment. Its cause is often sharp increases in costs of raw materials and/or labour.

stock exchange institution for the buying and selling of stocks and shares (securities). The world's largest stock exchanges are London, New York (Wall Street), and Tokyo. The oldest stock exchanges are Antwerp 1460, Hamburg 1558, Amsterdam 1602, New York 1790, and London 1801.

trade cycle or ***business cycle*** period of time that includes a peak and trough of economic activity, as measured by a country's national income. In Keynesian economics, one of the main roles of the government is to smooth out the peaks and troughs of the trade cycle by intervening in the economy, thus minimizing 'overheating' and 'stagnation'. This is accomplished by regulating interest rates and government spending.

Treasury bill in Britain, borrowing by the government in the form of a promissory note to repay the bearer 91 days from the date of issue; such bills represent a flexible and relatively cheap way for the government to borrow money for immediate needs.

unemployment lack of paid employment. The unemployed are usually defined as those out of work who are available for and actively seeking work. Unemployment is measured either as a total or as a percentage of those who are available for work, known as the working population or labour force. Periods of widespread unemployment in Europe and the USA in the 20th century include 1929–1930s and the years since the mid-1970s.

Unemployment is, generally, subdivided into ***frictional unemployment***, the inevitable temporary unemployment of those moving from one job to another; ***cyclical unemployment***, caused by a downswing in the business cycle; ***seasonal unemployment***, in an area where there is high demand only during holiday periods, for example; and ***structural unemployment***, where changing technology or other long-term change in the economy results in large numbers without work.

Many Third World countries suffer from severe unemployment and underemployment; the problem is exacerbated by rapid growth of population and lack of skills. In industrialized countries, unemployment has been a phenomenon since the mid-1970s, when the rise in world oil prices caused a downturn in economic activity, and greater use of high technology has improved output without the need for more jobs. The average unemployment rate in industrialized countries (the members of the OECD) was 8% in 1993 compared with only 3% in 1970, with some countries, such as Spain and Ireland, suffering over 15%. In the USA, the unemployment rate was 7% in 1993. In China, nearly a quarter of the urban labour force is unemployed.

In Britain, deflationary economic measures have tended to exacerbate the trend, and in the mid-1980s the unemployment rate had risen to 14% (although the basis on which it is calculated has in recent years been changed several times and many commentators argue that the real rate is higher). Since Sept 1988 it has been measured as the total or percentage of the working population unemployed and claiming benefit, but this only includes people aged 18 or over, since the under-18s are assumed to be in full-time education or training. As the British economy experienced significant economic growth between 1986 and 1989, the rate of unemployment fell to a low of 5.6% in April 1990 (using the post-1988 definition) but rose again during the subsequent recession, standing at 10.4% in May 1993.

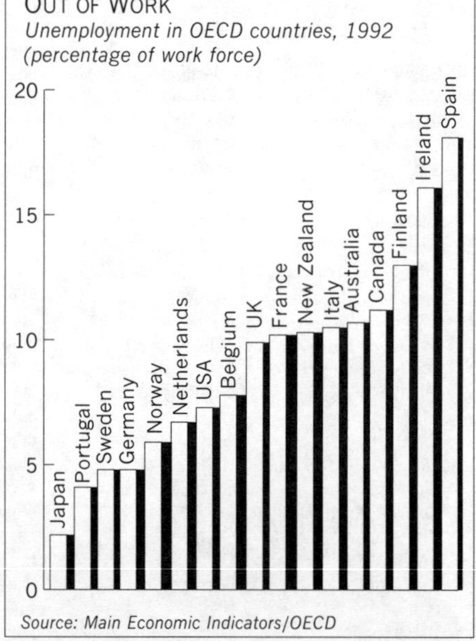

unlisted securities market market for the shares of companies that are not included in the official list of the main market of the stock exchange. These lower-tier markets are less stringently regulated than the main markets and provide an intermediate step for new or small companies trying to reach the main markets.

visible trade international trade in goods. Trade in visibles is put on the current account of the balance of payments. Visible exports minus visible imports gives the balance of trade.

Institutions and Organizations

African Development Bank (ADB) international organization founded 1963 to promote and finance economic development across the continent. Members include 51 African and 25 non-African countries. Its headquarters are in Abidja'n, Cote d'Ivoire.

Arab Common Market organization providing for the abolition of customs duties on agricultural products, and reductions on other items, between the member states: Egypt, Iraq, Jordan, and Syria. It was founded 1965.

Arab Monetary Fund (AMF) money reserve established 1976 by 20 Arab states plus the Palestine Liberation Organization to provide a mechanism for promoting greater stability in exchange rates and to coordinate Arab economic and monetary policies. It operates mainly by regulating petrodollars within the Arab community to make member countries less dependent on the West for the handling of their surplus money. The fund's headquarters are in Abu Dhabi in the United Arab Emirates.

Asian Development Bank (ADB) bank founded 1966 to stimulate growth in Asia and the Far East by administering direct loans and technical assistance. Members include 30 countries within the region and 14 countries of W Europe and North America. The headquarters are in Manila, Philippines.

Bank for International Settlements (BIS) bank established 1930 to handle German reparations settlements from World War I. The BIS (based in Basel, Switzerland) is today a centre for economic and monetary research and assists cooperation of central banks. It also has important trustee duties. Its place in the international financial world was superseded from 1944 by the International Monetary Fund.

Bank of England UK central bank founded by act of Parliament 1694. It was entrusted with issuing bank notes 1844 and nationalized 1946. It is banker to the clearing banks and the UK government.

As the government's bank, it manages and arranges the financing of the public sector borrowing requirement and the national debt, implements monetary policy and exchange-rate policy by intervening in foreign-exchange markets, and supervises the UK banking system.

Central American Common Market CACM (***Mercado Común Centroamericana*** MCCA) economic alliance established 1960 by El Salvador, Guatemala, Honduras (seceded 1970), and Nicaragua; Costa Rica joined 1962. Formed to encourage economic development and cooperation between the smaller Central American nations and to attract industrial capital, CACM failed to live up to early expectations: nationalist interests remained strong and by the mid-1980s political instability in the region and border conflicts between members were hindering its activities.

Colombo Plan plan for cooperative economic and social development in Asia and the Pacific, established 1950. The 26 member countries are Afghanistan, Australia, Bangladesh, Bhutan, Cambodia, Canada, Fiji, India, Indonesia, Iran, Japan, South Korea, Laos, Malaysia, Maldives, Myanmar (Burma), Nepal, New Zealand, Pakistan, Papua New Guinea, Philippines, Singapore, Sri Lanka, Thailand, UK, and USA. They meet annually to discuss economic and development plans such as irrigation, hydroelectric schemes, and technical training.

Comecon (acronym for ***Council for Mutual Economic Assistance***, or ***CMEA***) economic organization 1949–91, linking the USSR with Bulgaria, Czechoslovakia, Hungary, Poland, Romania, East Germany (1950–90), Mongolia (from 1962), Cuba (from 1972), and Vietnam (from 1978), with Yugoslavia as an associated member. Albania also belonged 1949–61. Its establishment was prompted by the Marshall Plan.

In Jan 1991 it was agreed that Comecon should be effectively disbanded and replaced by a new body, the Organization for International Economic Cooperation (OIEC), to be based probably in Budapest. The OIEC would act as a 'clearing house' for mutual E European trade, and would coordinate E European policy towards the European Community.

European Bank for Reconstruction and Development (EBRD) international organization founded 1990 to assist the economic reconstruction of E Europe by financing industrial and economic expansion, using loan guarantees, equity investment, and underwriting, to promote the transition to free-market capitalist systems. The bank was originally proposed by French president François Mitterand, and his former adviser Jacques Attali became its first president in 1990; he resigned in 1993. Its headquarters are in London.

Members include Albania, Armenia, Australia, Austria, Azerbaijan, Belarus, Belgium, Bulgaria, Canada, Cyprus, the Czech Republic, Denmark, Egypt, Estonia, Finland, France, Georgia, Germany, Greece, Hungary, Iceland, Ireland, Israel, Italy, Japan, Kazakhstan, South Korea, Kyrgyzstan, Latvia, Liechtenstein, Lithuania, Luxembourg, Malta, Mexico, Moldova, Morocco, the Netherlands, New Zealand, Norway, Poland, Portugal, Romania, Russia,

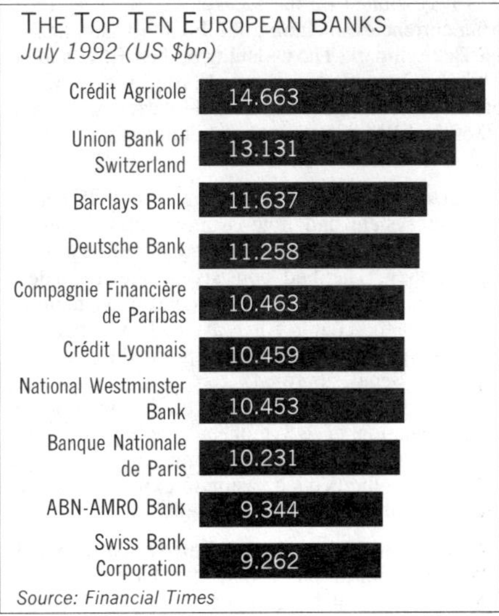

Slovakia, Spain, Sweden, Switzerland, Tajikistan, Turkey, Turkmenistan, Ukraine, the UK, the USA, Uzbekistan, Yugoslavia, the Commission of the European Community, and the European Investment Bank.

European Free Trade Association (EFTA) organization established 1960 consisting of Austria, Finland, Iceland, Norway, Sweden, Switzerland, and (from 1991) Liechtenstein, previously a nonvoting associate member. There are no import duties between members.

In 1973 the EC signed agreements with EFTA members, setting up a free-trade area of over 300 million consumers. Trade between the two groups amounted to over half of total EFTA trade. A further pact signed 1991 between the EC and EFTA provided for a European Economic Area to be set up, allowing EFTA greater access to the EC market by ending many of the restrictions. The area would span 19 nations and 380 million people.

European Monetary System (EMS) attempt by the European Community to bring financial cooperation and monetary stability to Europe. It was established 1979 in the wake of the 1974 oil crisis, which brought growing economic disruption to European economies because of floating exchange rates. Central to the EMS is the ***Exchange Rate Mechanism*** (ERM), a voluntary system of semi-fixed exchange rates based on the European Currency Unit (ECU).

Each currency has a central rate with every other currency and with the ECU which is maintained within a band of fluctuation. The UK entered the ERM in Oct 1990, and left in Sept 1992, when doubts about the prospects for movement towards a single European currency caused speculators to sell the weaker ERM currencies, particularly sterling. This forced sterling out of its ERM band. Between Oct 1990 and Sept 1992, sterling's central rate with the Deutschmark was £1 = DM2.95 and the central rate with the ECU was £1 = 1.43 ECU.

In August 1993, the ERM band was allowed to fluctuate by 15% on either side for all ERM currencies except the Deutschmark and guilder; this move was necessitated by the weakening of many European currencies, including the French franc, against the Deutschmark. The widening of the ERM band put back the timetable for a single European currency, as one of the conditions for a single currency was that all of the ERM currencies had to fall within the original narrow band of 2.5%.

Federal Reserve System (the 'Fed') US central banking system and note-issuing authority, established 1913 to regulate the country's credit and monetary policy. The Fed consists of the 12 federal reserve banks, their 25 branches and other facilities throughout the country; it is headed by a board of governors in Washington DC, appointed by the president with Senate approval.

The Fed plays a major role in the formulation and implementation of US monetary policy. Inflation, interest rates, and overall economic activity can be governed by the Fed's decision to expand or restrict the supply of money to the economy.

General Agreement on Tariffs and Trade (GATT) organization within the United Nations founded 1948 with the aim of encouraging free trade between nations through low tariffs, abolitions of quotas, and curbs on subsidies.

The latest rounds of talks, begun in Uruguay in 1986, intended to cut restrictions on trade of manufactured goods, agriculture, textiles, and services. The Uruguay round was scheduled to end in 1990, but reached a deadlock in Dec 1990 after negotiators failed to agree on a plan to reduce farm subsidies. However, in Nov 1992, the EC negotiator agreed to a scaled-down reduction in agricultural subsidies, but without the support of the French government. Farmers in France and other EC countries demonstrated against these cuts.

Inter-American Development Bank (IADB) bank founded 1959, at the instigation of the Organization of American States, to finance economic and social development, particularly in the less wealthy regions of the Americas. Its membership includes the states of Central and Southern America, the Caribbean, and the USA, as well as Austria, Belgium, Canada, Denmark, Finland, France, Germany, Israel, Italy, Japan, the Netherlands, Spain, Sweden, Switzerland, and the UK. Its headquarters are in Washington DC.

International Monetary Fund (IMF) specialized agency of the United Nations, headquarters Washington DC, established under the 1944 Bretton Woods agreement and operational since 1947. It seeks to promote international monetary cooperation and the growth of world trade, and to smooth multilateral payment arrangements among member states. IMF standby loans are available to members in balance-of-payments difficulties (the amount being governed by the member's quota), usually on the basis that the country must agree to take certain corrective measures.

The Fund also operates other drawing facilities, including several designed to provide preferential credit to developing countries with liquidity problems. Having previously operated in US dollars linked to gold, since 1972 the IMF has used the special drawing right (SDR) as its standard unit of account, valued in terms of a weighted 'basket' of major currencies. Since the 1971 Smithsonian agreement permitting wider fluctuations from specified currency parities, IMF rules have been progressively adapted to the increasing prevalence of fully floating exchange rates.

LIFFE (acronym for ***London International Financial Futures Exchange***) one of the exchanges in London where futures contracts are traded. It opened 1982 and began options trading in 1985.

Monopolies and Mergers Commission (MMC) UK government body re-established 1973 under the Fair Trading Act and, since 1980, embracing the Competition Act. Its role is to investigate and report when there is a risk of creating a monopoly by a company merger or takeover, or when a newspaper or newspaper assets are transferred. It also investigates companies, nationalized industries, or local authorities that are suspected of operating in a noncompetitive way. The US equivalent is the ***Federal Trade Commission*** (FTC).

Organization for Economic Cooperation and Development (OECD) international organization of 24 industrialized countries that provides a forum for discussion and coordination of member states' economic and social policies. Founded 1961, with its headquarters in Paris, the OECD superseded the Organization for European Economic Cooperation (established 1948 to implement the Marshall Plan) when the USA and Canada became members and its scope was extended to include development aid.

The OECD members are: Australia, Austria, Belgium, Canada, Denmark, Finland, France, Germany, Greece, Iceland, Ireland, Italy, Japan, Luxembourg, Netherlands, New Zealand, Norway, Portugal, Spain, Sweden, Switzerland, Turkey, UK, and USA.

Organization of Petroleum-Exporting Countries (OPEC) body established 1960 to coordinate price and supply policies of oil-producing states. Its concerted action in raising prices in the 1970s triggered worldwide recession but also lessened demand so that its influence was reduced by the mid-1980s. OPEC members in 1991 were: Algeria, Ecuador, Gabon, Indonesia, Iran, Iraq, Kuwait, Libya, Nigeria, Qatar, Saudi Arabia, the United Arab Emirates, and Venezuela.

OPEC's importance in the world market was reflected in its ability to implement oil price increases from $3 a barrel 1973 to $30 a barrel 1980. In the 1980s, OPEC's dominant position was undermined by reduced demand for oil in industrialized countries, increased non-OPEC oil supplies, and production of alternative energy. These factors contributed to the dramatic fall in world oil prices to $10 a barrel in July 1986 from $28 at the beginning of the year. OPEC's efforts to stabilize oil prices through mandatory reduced production have been resisted by various members.

Securities and Exchange Commission (*SEC*) official US agency created 1934 to ensure full disclosure to the investing public and protection against malpractice in the securities (stocks and bonds) and financial markets (such as insider trading). The SEC is also an impartial adviser to federal courts in bankruptcy cases involving publicly held corporations. Since 1988, the SEC has been authorized to pay bounties for information leading to conviction of inside traders.

Securities and Investment Board UK body with the overall responsibility for policing financial dealings in the City of London. Introduced in 1987 following the deregulation process of the so-called Big Bang, it acts as an umbrella organization to such self-regulating bodies as the Stock Exchange.

World Bank popular name for the ***International Bank for Reconstruction and Development*** specialized agency of the United Nations that borrows in the commercial market and lends on commercial terms. It was established 1945 under the 1944 Bretton Woods agreement, which also created the International Monetary Fund. The ***International Development Association*** is an arm of the World Bank.

The World Bank now earns almost as much money from interest and loan repayments as it hands out in new loans every year. Over 60% of the bank's loans go to suppliers outside the borrower countries for such things as consultancy services, oil, and machinery. Control of the bank is vested in a board of executives representing national governments, whose votes are apportioned according to the amount they have funded the bank. Thus the USA has nearly 20% of the vote and always appoints the board's president.

In 1992 the World Bank made a net transfer of $49.7 million to developing countries.

GALLUP POLL: The rich

Describe briefly, in your own words, what sorts of things do you think of when you think of rich people?

Property (houses, cars etc)	52
Lifestyle (travel, luxury living etc)	37
Wealth in total cash value	23
State of well being (freedom from worry, happiness)	12
Annual income	5
Occupation (businessman, banker etc)	5
Snobbery	5
Not having to work	3
Envy	4
Power over others	3
How they became rich	3
Private education	2
Other unfavourable	5
Other favourable	1
Other	14
Don't know	6

How much money would someone have to have coming in each year before you thought of him or her as being really rich?

Less than £15,000	1
£15,000-£19,000	1
£20,000-£29,999	6
£30,000-£49,999	15
£50,000-£99,000	24
£100,000-£249,000	23
£250,000-£499,000	6
£500,000-£999,999	5
£1 million and over	7
Don't know	12

Do you personally know anybody you consider to be rich?

Yes - I am	3
Yes - others	40
No, nobody	57

Financial worries

Would you say that you worry a lot or a little about...:

	Dec 1992	Mar 1986	Apr 1983
Making both ends meet?			
Lot	33	32	21
Little	35	37	33
Not at all	32	31	46
Keeping your (your husband's) job?			
Lot	28	26	24
Little	20	18	16
Not at all	52	57	60
Having enough money in your old age ?			
Lot	26	28	14
Little	32	28	26
Not at all	42	43	60

Wage/price expectations

Over the next 12 months what, if any, percentage increase do you expect to get in your wages or salary?

	May 1993
Nil	28
1 or 2%	26
3 or 4	18
5 or 6	8
7 or 8	2
9 or 10	3
11 or 12	0
13 or 14	0
15–20	0
Over 20	0
Don't know	15
Average 2.3	

Bearing in mind the present economic situation, inflation and unemployment, what level of wage or salary increase do you think workers should aim for?

	May 1993
Nil	2
1 or 2%	5
3 or 4	23
5 or 6	26
7 or 8	9
9 or 10	11
11 or 12	1
13 or 14	0
15-20	2
Over 20	1
Don't know	21
Average 6.0	

Over the next twelve months, what percentage increase in prices do you expect?

	May 1993
Nil	5
1 or 2%	12
3 or 4	26
5 or 6	20
7 or 8	5
9 or 10	7
11 or 12	1
13 or 14	0
15–20	2
Over 20	1
Don't know	21
Average 5.1	

Government policies

Now, thinking about the general economic situation in this country over the past twelve months, do you think the Government's policies have had a good effect, a bad effect, or that they really haven't made much of a difference?

	Mar 1993
Good effect	5
Bad effect	53
No difference	33
Mixed	6
Don't know	3

What about the financial situation of your household over the past twelve months? Do you think the Government's policies have had a good effect, a bad effect, or that they really haven't made much of a difference?

	Mar 1993
Good effect	4
Bad effect	45
No difference	42
Mixed	5
Don't know	3

The Arts

Architecture and Building 289

Art 301

Books 317

Cinema 327

Dance 337

Music 341

Photography 358

Theatre 365

ARCHITECTURE AND BUILDING

History

Architecture is the art of designing structures. The term covers the design of the visual appearance of structures; their internal arrangements of space; selection of external and internal building materials; design or selection of natural and artificial lighting systems, as well as mechanical, electrical, and plumbing systems; and design or selection of decorations and furnishings. Architectural style may emerge from evolution of techniques and styles particular to a culture in a given time period with or without identifiable individuals as architects, or may be attributed to specific individuals or groups of architects working together on a project.

early architecture little remains of the earliest forms of architecture, but archaeologists have examined remains of prehistoric sites and documented Stone Age villages of wooden post buildings with aboveground construction of organic materials such as mud or wattle and daub from the Upper Paleolithic, Mesolithic, and Neolithic periods in Asia, the Middle East, Europe, and the Americas. More extensive remains of stone-built structures have given clues to later Neolithic farming communities as well as habitations, storehouses, and religious and civic structures of early civilizations. The best documented are those of ancient Egypt, where exhaustive work in the 19th and 20th centuries revealed much about ordinary buildings, the monumental structures such as the pyramid tombs near modern Cairo, and the temple and tomb complexes concentrated at Luxor and Thebes.

Classical this architecture evolved its basic forms in Greece between the 16th and 2nd centuries BC. Its hallmark characteristic is its post-and-lintel construction of temples and public structures, classified into the Doric, Ionic, and Corinthian orders, defined by simple, scrolled, and acanthus-leaf capitals for support columns, respectively. The Romans copied and expanded on Greek Classical forms, notably introducing bricks and concrete and inventing the vault, arch, and dome for public buildings and aqueducts.

Byzantine this architecture developed primarily in the E Roman Empire from the 4th century, with its centre at Byzantium (later named Constantinople, now Istanbul). Its most notable feature was construction of churches, some very large, based on the Greek cross plan (Hagia Sophia, Istanbul; St Mark's, Venice), with formalized painted and mosaic decoration.

Islamic this architecture developed from the 8th century, when the Islamic religion spread from its centre in the Middle East west to Spain and E to China and parts of the Philippine Islands. Notable features are the development of the tower with dome and the pointed arch. Islamic architecture, chiefly through Spanish examples such as the Great Mosque at Córdoba and the Alhambra in Granada, profoundly influenced Christian church architecture – for example, by adoption of the pointed arch into the Gothic arch.

Romanesque this architecture is associated with Western European Christianity from the 8th to the 12th centuries. It is marked by churches with massive walls for structural integrity, rounded arches, small windows, and resulting dark volumes of interior space. In England this style is generally referred to as Norman architecture (Durham Cathedral). The style enjoyed a renewal of interest in Europe and the USA in the late 19th and early 20th centuries.

Gothic this architecture emerged out of Romanesque, since the pointed arch and flying buttress made it possible to change from thick supporting walls to lighter curtain walls with extensive expansion of window areas (and stained-glass artwork) and resulting increases in interior light. Gothic architecture was developed particularly in France from the 12th to 16th centuries. The style is divided into Early Gothic (Sens Cathedral), High Gothic (Chartres Cathedral), and Late or Flamboyant Gothic. In England the corresponding divisions are Early English (Salisbury Cathedral), Decorated (Wells Cathedral), and Perpendicular (Kings College Chapel, Cambridge). Gothic was also developed extensively in Germany and neighbouring countries and in Italy.

Renaissance this architecture of 15th- and 16th-century Europe saw the rebirth of Classical form and motifs in the Italian Neo-Classical movement. A major source of inspiration was the work of the 1st-century BC Roman engineer Vitruvius for Palladio, Alberti, Brunelleschi, Bramante, and Michelangelo – the major Renaissance architects. The Palladian style was extensively used later in England by Inigo Jones and the Classical idiom by Christopher Wren. Classical or Neo-Classical style and its elements have been popular in the USA from the 18th century, as evidenced in much of the civic and commercial architecture since the time of the early republic (the US Capitol and Supreme Court buildings in Washington; many state capitols).

Baroque European architecture of the 17th and 18th centuries elaborated on Classical models with exuberant and extravagant decoration. In large-scale public buildings, the style is best seen in the innovative work of Giovanni Bernini and Francesco Borromini in Italy and later by John Vanbrugh, Nicholas Hawksmoor, and Christopher Wren in England. There were numerous practitioners in France and the German-speaking countries; Vienna is rich in Baroque work.

Rococo this architecture extends the Baroque style with an even greater extravagance of design motifs, using a new lightness of detail and naturalistic elements, such as shells, flowers, and trees.

Neo-Classical European architecture of the 18th and 19th centuries again focused on the more severe Classical idiom (inspired by archaeological finds), producing, for example, the large-scale rebuilding of London by Robert Adam and John Nash and later of Paris by Georges Haussman.

Neo-Gothic the later part of the 19th century saw a Gothic revival in Europe and the USA, most evident in churches and public buildings (such as the Houses of Parliament in London, designed by Charles Barry).

Art Nouveau was a new movement arising at the end of the 19th century, characterized by sinuous, flowing shapes, informal room plans, and particular attention to interior as well as architectural design. The style is best seen in England in the work of Charles Rennie Mackintosh (Glasgow Art School), in Paris at the entrances to the Metro and in Spain by the work of Antonio Gaudí.

Modernism an increasing emphasis on rationalism and reduction of ornament led to Modernism (also known as Functionalism or the International Style) in the 1930s. Seeking to exclude everything that did not have a purpose, the latest technological advances in glass, steel, and concrete were used to full advantage. Major architects included Frank Lloyd Wright, Mies van der Rohe, Le Corbusier, and Alvar Aalto.

Brutalism architectural style of the 1950s and 1960s that evolved from the work of Le Corbusier and Mies van der Rohe. It stressed functionalism and honesty to materials; steel and concrete were favoured. In the UK the style was developed by Alison and Peter Smithson.

Post-Modernism in the 1980s a Post-Modernist movement emerged, which split into two camps:

High Tech, represented in Britain by architects such as Norman Foster, Richard Rogers, and James Stirling (Hong Kong and Shanghai Bank, Hong Kong, Lloyd's, London, *Staatsgalerie Stuttgart* respectively); and architects using elements from the architecture of previous times, either following certain tenets of the Classical orders – Neo-Classicism yet again – such as Quinlan Terry, or using such elements at whim, such as Michael Graves.

Deconstruction a style that fragments forms and space by taking the usual building elements of floors, walls, and ceilings and sliding them apart to create a sense of disorientation and movement. Its proponents include Zaha Hadid (1950–) in the UK, Frank Gehry (1929–) and Peter Eisenman (1932–) in the USA, and Co-op Himmelbau in Austria.

Terms

arch curved structure of masonry that supports the weight of material over an open space, as in a bridge or doorway. It originally consisted of several wedge-shaped stones supported by their mutual pressure. The term is also applied to any curved structure that is an arch in form only.

atrium an inner, open courtyard. Originally the central court or main room of an ancient Roman house, open to the sky, often with a shallow pool to catch water.

bailey open space or court of a stone-built castle.

basilica type of Roman public building; a large roofed hall flanked by columns, generally with an aisle on each side, used for judicial or other public business. The earliest known basilica, at Pompeii, dates from the 2nd century BC. This architectural form was adopted by the early Christians for their churches.

buttress reinforcement in brick or masonry, built against a wall to give it strength. A ***flying buttress*** is an arc transmitting the force of the wall to be supported to an outer buttress, common in Gothic architecture.

cantilever beam or structure that is fixed at one end only, though it may be supported at some point along its length; for example, a diving board. The cantilever principle, widely used in construction engineering, eliminates the need for a second main support at the free end of the beam, allowing for more elegant structures and reducing the amount of materials required. Many large-span bridges have been built on the cantilever principle.

caryatid building support or pillar in the shape of a woman, the name deriving from the Karyatides, who were priestesses at the temple of Artemis at Karyai; the male equivalent is a ***telamon*** or ***atlas***.

castle private fortress of a king or noble during the Middle Ages. At first a building on a mound surrounded by a wooden fence, this was later copied in stone. The earliest castles in Britain were built following the Norman Conquest, and the art of castle building reached a peak in the 13th century. By the 15th century, the need for castles for domestic defence had largely disappeared, and the advent of gunpowder made them largely useless against attack.

cathedral Christian church containing the throne of a bishop or archbishop, which is usually situated on the south side of the choir. There are cathedrals in most of the chief cities of Europe; UK cathedrals include Canterbury Cathedral (spanning the Norman to Perpendicular periods), Exeter Cathedral (13th-century Gothic), and Coventry Cathedral (rebuilt after World War II, consecrated 1962).

château term originally applied to a French medieval castle, but now used to describe a country house or important residence in France. The château was first used as a domestic building in the late 15th century; by the reign of Louis XIII (1610–43) fortifications such as moats and keeps were no longer used for defensive purposes, but merely as decorative features. The Loire valley contains some fine examples of châteaux.

church building designed as a Christian place of worship. Churches were first built in the 3rd century, when persecution ceased under the Holy Roman emperor Constantine. The original church design was based on the Roman basilica, with a central nave, aisles either side, and an apse at one end.

cloister a covered walk within a convent or monastery, often opening onto a courtyard.

colonnade row of columns supporting arches or an entablature.

column a structure, round or polygonal in plan, erected vertically as a support for some part of a building. Cretan paintings reveal the existence of wooden columns in Aegean architecture, about 1500 BC. The Hittites, Assyrians, and Egyptians also used wooden columns, and they are a feature of the monumental architecture of China and Japan. In Classical architecture there are five principal types (or orders) of column: Doric, Ionic, Corinthian, Tuscan, and Composite.

community architecture movement enabling people to work directly with architects in the design and building of their own homes and neighbourhoods. It is an approach strongly encouraged by the Prince of Wales.

conservation, architectural attempts to maintain the character of buildings and historical areas. In England this is subject to a growing body of legislation that has designated more listed buildings. There are now over 6,000 conservation areas throughout England alone.

curtain wall in buildings, a light-weight wall of glass or aluminium that is not load-bearing and is hung from a metal frame rather than built up from the ground like a brick wall. Curtain walls are typically used in high-rise blocks.

garden city in the UK, a town built in a rural area and designed to combine town and country advantages, with its own industries, controlled developments, private and public gardens, and cultural centre. The idea was proposed by Sir Ebenezer Howard (1850–1928), who in 1899 founded the Garden City Association, which established the first garden city, Letchworth (in Hertfordshire).

gargoyle spout projecting from the roof gutter of a building with the purpose of directing water away from the wall. The term is usually applied to the ornamental forms found in Gothic architecture; these were carved in stone in the form of fantastic animals, angels, or human heads.

geodesic dome spherical dome whose surface is formed by an arrangement of short rods arranged in triangles. The rods lie on geodesics (the shortest lines joining two points on a curved surface). This dome allows large spaces to be enclosed using the minimum of materials, and was patented by US engineer Buckminster Fuller 1954.

green belt area surrounding a large city, officially designated not to be built on but preserved where possible as open space (for agricultural and recreational use). In the UK the first green belts were established from 1938 around conurbations such as London in order to prevent urban sprawl. New towns were set up to take the overspill population.

ha-ha in landscape gardening, a sunken boundary wall permitting an unobstructed view beyond a garden; a device much used by Capability Brown in the 18th century.

listed building in Britain, a building officially recognized as having historical or architectural interest and therefore legally protected from alteration or demolition. In England the listing is drawn up by the Secretary of State for the Environment under the advice of the English Heritage organization, which provides various resources for architectural conservation.

mezzanine architectural term for a storey with a lower ceiling placed between two main storeys, usually between the ground and first floors of a building.

minaret slender turret or tower attached to a Muslim mosque or to buildings designed in that style. It has one or more balconies, from which the *muezzin* calls the people to prayer five times a day.

Virtual views

Virtual reality computer technology will soon allow prospective tenants to check the view from their bedroom window before they buy a property. Developers of the East Quayside complex, in Newcastle upon Tyne, England, have commissioned a virtual reality system, called Superscape, which displays a computer model of the complex and its surroundings. As the complex is built over the next five years, new buildings and roads will be added to the model to keep up with 'real' reality. Prospective tenants will be able to move about the model, checking the views, using a computer mouse.

misericord or ***miserere*** in church architecture, a projection on the underside of a hinged seat of the choir stalls, used as a rest for a priest when standing during long services. Misericords are often decorated with carvings.

obelisk tall, tapering column of stone, much used in ancient Egyptian and Roman architecture. Examples are Cleopatra's Needles 1475 BC, one of which is in London, the other in New York.

order in classical architecture, the column (including capital, shaft, and base) and the entablature, considered as an architectural whole. The five orders are Doric, Ionic, Corinthian, Tuscan, and Composite.

pantheon originally a temple for worshipping all the gods, such as that in ancient Rome, rebuilt by the emperor Hadrian and still used as a church. In more recent times, the name has been used for a building where famous people are buried (Panthéon, Paris).

pediment the triangular part crowning the fronts of buildings in Classical styles. The pediment was a distinctive feature of Greek temples.

peristyle range of columns surrounding a building or open courtyard.

piano nobile the main floor of a house, containing the main reception room.

portico porch with a pediment and columns.

pyramid four-sided building with triangular sides used in ancient Egypt to enclose a royal tomb; for example, the Great Pyramid of Khufu/Cheops at Gîza, near Cairo, 230 m/755 ft square and 147 m/481 ft high. In Babylon and Assyria broadly stepped pyramids (ziggurats) were used as the base for a shrine to a god: the Tower of Babel was probably one of these.

satellite town new town planned and built to serve a particular local industry, or as a dormitory or overspill town for people who work in a nearby metropolis. New towns in Britain include Port Sunlight near Birkenhead (Cheshire), built to house workers at Lever Brothers soap factories. More recent examples include Welwyn Garden City (1948), Cumbernauld (1955), and Milton Keynes (1967).

sick building syndrome malaise diagnosed in the early 1980s among office workers and thought to be caused by such pollutants as formaldehyde (from furniture and insulating materials), benzene (from paint), and the solvent trichloroethene, concentrated in air-conditioned buildings. Symptoms include headache, sore throat, tiredness, colds, and flu. Studies have found that it can cause a 40% drop in productivity and a 30% rise in absenteeism.

skyscraper building so tall that it appears to 'scrape the sky', developed 1868 in New York, USA, where land prices were high and the geology allowed such methods of construction. Skyscrapers are now found in cities throughout the world. The world's tallest free-standing structure is the CN (Canadian National) Tower, Toronto, 555 m/1,821 ft.

town planning the design of buildings or groups of buildings in a physical and social context, concentrating on the relationship between various buildings and their environment, as well as on their uses.

urban renewal the adaptation of existing buildings and neighbourhoods in towns and cities to meet changes in economic, social, and environmental requirements, rather than demolishing them. Since the early 1970s, when it became less expensive to renew than to build, urban renewal has increased.

vault arched ceiling or roof built mainly of stone or bricks.

Building and Construction

adobe Spanish name for sun-baked earth bricks, or buildings made with them. The material commonly consists of sandy clay or loam mixed with straw or grass. Another less common form of adobe is made from dampened earth which is pressed within moulds (*pisé de terre*). The techniques are commonly found in Spain, Latin America, and the southwestern USA – areas where the climate is warm and dry. Modern adobe houses are covered with stucco, a type of plaster.

brick common building material, rectangular in shape, made of clay that has been fired in a kiln. Bricks are made by kneading a mixture of crushed clay and other materials into a stiff mud and extruding it into a ribbon. The ribbon is cut into individual bricks, which are fired at a temperature of up to about 1,000°C/1,800°F. In wall building, bricks are either laid out as stretchers (long side facing out) or as headers (short side facing out). The two principle patterns of brickwork are ***English bond***, in which alternate courses, or layers, are made up of stretchers or headers only; and ***Flemish bond***, in which stretchers and headers alternate within courses.

bridge structure that provides a continuous path or road over water, valleys, ravines, or above other roads. The basic designs and composites of these are based on the way they bear the weight of the structure and its load. Bridges may be classified into the following main groups: ***arch*** bridges, thrusting outwards but downwards at their ends, in compression (Sydney Harbour bridge, Australia, for example); ***beam***, or ***girder*** bridges, supported at each end by the ground with the weight thrusting downwards (Rio Niterói bridge, Guanabara Bay, Brazil); ***cable-stayed*** bridges, relying on diagonal cables connected directly between the bridge deck and supporting towers at each end (Alex Fraser

The world's most remarkable bridges

Name	*Location*	*Type and length*
Angostura	Cuidad Bolivar, Venezuela	suspension-type bridge; span 712 m/2,336 ft; total length 1,678 m/5,507 ft
Bendorf Bridge	Coblenz, Germany	three-span cement girder bridge; main span 208 m/682 ft; total length 1,030 m/3,378 ft
Bosphorous Bridge	Istanbul, Turkey (linking Europe to Asia)	suspension bridge; total length 1,074 m/ 3,524 ft
Gladsville Bridge	Sydney Australia	concrete arch bridge; 305 m/1,000 ft – world's longest concrete arch
Humber Bridge	Kingston upon Hull, England	suspension bridge; total span 1,410 m/4,628 ft – world's longest suspension bridge
Ikuchi Bridge	Honshu/Shikoku, Japan	cable-stayed bridge; 490 m/1,608 ft span
Lake Pontchartrain Bridge	New Orleans, USA	multiple-span; 38,421 m/126,055 ft – world's longest multiple span
Oosterscelderbrug	Flushing/Rotterdam, The Netherlands	traffic causeway over Zeeland sea arm total length 19 km/31.25 mi
Rio-Niteroi	Guanabara Bay, Brazil	continuous box and plate girder bridge; 14 km/8.7 mi – world's longest box girder bridge
Tagus River Bridge	Lisbon, Portugal	main span 1,013 m/3,323 ft
Zoo Bridge	Cologne, Germany	steel box girder bridge; main span 259 m/850 ft

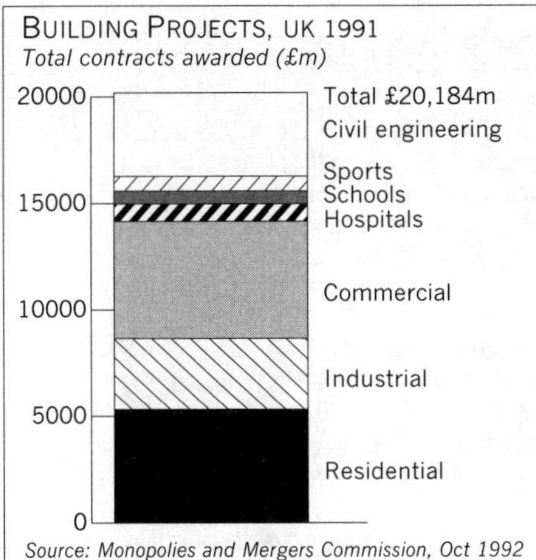

Source: Monopolies and Mergers Commission, Oct 1992

bridge, Fraser River, British Columbia) – sometimes having movable parts, like swing and draw bridges, to allow traffic to pass beneath; ***cantilever*** bridges, a complex form of girder bridge (Quebec bridge, St Lawrence River, Canada); ***suspension*** bridges, using cables under tension to pull inwards against anchorages on either side of the span, so that the roadway hangs from the main cables by a network of vertical cables (Golden Gate Bridge, San Francisco, USA).

cement any bonding agent used to unite particles in a single mass or to cause one surface to adhere to another. ***Portland cement*** is a powder obtained from burning together a mixture of lime (or chalk) and clay, and when mixed with water and sand or gravel, turns into mortar or concrete. In geology, a chemically precipitated material such as carbonate that occupies the interstices of clastic rocks is called cement.

cladding thin layer of external covering on a building; for example, tiles, wood, stone, concrete.

concrete building material composed of cement, stone, sand, and water. It has been used since Egyptian and Roman times. During the 20th century, it has been increasingly employed as an economical alternative to materials such as brick and wood. From the 1980s, however, there has been a move away from concrete in house-building due to its comparatively short life span.

dam a structure built to hold back water in order to prevent flooding, provide water for irrigation and storage, and to provide hydroelectric power. The biggest dams are of the earth- and rock-fill type, also called ***embankment dams***. Such dams are generally built on broad valley sites. Deep, narrow gorges dictate a ***concrete dam***, where the strength of reinforced concrete can withstand the water pressures involved. Many concrete dams are triangular in cross-section, with their vertical face pointing upstream. Their sheer weight holds them in position, and they are called ***gravity dams***. Other concrete dams, however, are more slight and are built in the shape of an arch, with the curve facing upstream: the ***arch dam*** derives its strength from the arch shape, just as an arch bridge does. A valuable development in arid regions, as in parts of Brazil, is the ***underground dam***, where water is stored on a solid rock base, with a wall to ground level, so avoiding rapid evaporation.

masonry the craft of constructing stonework walls. The various styles of masonry include ***random rubblework***, irregular stones arranged according to fit; ***coursed rubblework***, irregular stones arranged in broad horizontal bands, or courses; ***ashlar masonry***, smooth square-cut stones arranged in courses; ***Cyclopean masonry***, large polygonal stones cut to fit eachother; ***rustification***, large stones separated by deep joints and chiselled or hammered into a variety of styles. Rustification is usually employed at the base of buildings, on top of an ashlar base, to give an appearance of added strength.

module a standard or unit that governs the form of the rest: for example, Japanese room sizes are traditionally governed by multiples of standard tatami floor mats; today prefabricated buildings are mass-produced in a similar way. The components of a spacecraft are designed in coordination; for example, for the Apollo Moon landings the craft comprised a command module (for working, eating, sleeping), service module (electricity generators, oxygen supplies, manoeuvring rocket), and lunar module (to land and return the astronauts).

prefabricated building the use of large elements, such as walls, floors, and roofs, that are factory produced and subsequently assembled on site.

The world's highest dams

Name	*Country*	*Height above lowest formation*
Rogun*	Tajikistan	335 m/1,099 ft
Nurek	Tajikistan	300 m/984 ft
Grand Dixence	Switzerland	285 m/935 ft
Inguri	Georgia	272 m/892 ft
Boruca*	Costa Rica	267 m/875 ft
Chicoasen	Mexico	261 m/856 ft
Tehri*	India	261 m/856 ft
Kambaratinsk*	Kyrgyzstan	255 m/836 ft
Kishau*	India	253 m/830 ft
Sayano-Shushensk*	Russia	245 m/804 ft
Guavio	Colombia	243 m/797 ft
Mica	Canada	242 m/794 ft
Ertan*	China	240 m/787 ft
Mauvoisin	Switzerland	237 m/778 ft
Chivor	Colombia	237 m/778 ft
Kishau*	India	236 m/774 ft
El Cajon	Honduras	234 m/768 ft
Chirkey	Russian Federation	233 m/765 ft
Oroville	USA	230 m/754 ft
Bekhme*	Iraq	230 m/754 ft
Bhakra	India	226 m/741 ft
Hoover	USA	221 m/738 ft
Contra	Switzerland	220 m/772 ft
Mratinje	Yugoslavia	220 m/772 ft

** under construction*

Rebuilding after the terrorists

On 24 April 1993, an IRA bomb exploded in the Bishopsgate area of central London, killing one person and injuring 46. The explosion was a repeat of another blast almost exactly a year earlier. At 9.20 pm on 10 April 1992, a bomb exploded near the Baltic Exchange building, only streets away from the latest blast. The 1,000 lb/450 kg bomb was the largest on the UK mainland since World War II. Three people died, 91 were injured, and £800 million damage caused. A year after the blast, rebuilding and repair of the damaged buildings is under way. Some of the problems of repairing damage from a major explosion are only now coming to light; the lessons learned will help heal the damage caused by the latest blast.

A large explosion causes three 'layers' of damage around the centre of the blast. In the centre, within a short distance of where the bomb explodes, the damage is total. Beyond the inner area, buildings suffer damage from the pressure wave travelling out from the blast. A third outer ring of damage, spread over a wide area around the blast, is caused by flying fragments spreading out from the explosion.

Demolition job

The 1992 bomb was placed outside the Exchequer Court building in St Mary Axe. This building, the Chamber of Shipping building opposite, and the nearby Baltic Exchange, all suffered the full close-range effects of the blast. The damage inflicted on the Exchequer Court was devastating. The precast concrete cladding, composite steel and concrete floors, and steel frame were so badly damaged that the building is being demolished and rebuilt. The Chamber of Shipping was so badly damaged that its front section had to be demolished immediately after the blast.

The Baltic Exchange was severely damaged but was repairable. Only the front section is being demolished and rebuilt. Repair work is concentrating on preparing temporary trading facilities for the Exchange in the basement, built as a bomb shelter during the Cold War era, of a next-door building. Another priority task is to dismantle the severely damaged front entrance. The dismantling work has revealed greater damage to the building than was immediately apparent. Demolition revealed steel joists bowed upwards by 200 mm/8 in when the blast tore through the building. Roof joists that looked undamaged proved to be split along their length. Hairline cracks in masonry blocks were found to extend right through the blocks. The façade columns were pockmarked by lumps of molten metal from the van that held the bomb. Tests have shown that this damage could not be repaired by polishing as was hoped early on.

No stone unturned

As the façade stonework is removed, it is labelled and logged onto a computer-aided design system to show the original position. The stone goes to a mason for redressing. Every piece possible is being re-used, since the quarry which originally supplied it has closed long ago. Even if replacement stone can be found it will be a different colour from the original, which has discoloured over the 90 years since the building was erected. Inside the vast trading hall, large portions of marble cladding were blasted from the walls. Much of the remaining cladding is cracked and damaged. The interior repair work is so far limited to rescuing and recording any marble fragments that can be re-used.

Vacuum follows blast

Beyond the inner area of severe damage, the effects of the pressure blast were felt. A high-explosive blast causes a sudden increase in air pressure over a wide area. The rise in pressure is very sudden and envelopes whole buildings. Consequently, the windows of buildings in the high-pressure area are all blown inwards. The increased pressure is dissipated just as quickly and, in some cases, the effect of the vacuum created is just as damaging as the initial pressure blast; some buildings are built to withstand positive pressures but not the suction forces created by the subsequent vacuum. Because the pressure wave effects are so transient, the damage caused depends upon the inertia or lightness of the material involved. Lightweight cladding and glass fail more easily than heavier concrete or stone blocks.

Two churches were damaged by pressure wave effects from the Baltic Exchange blast. However, because the churches had heavy masonry walls, they withstood the blast well. The windows and stone tracework were most severely damaged, damaging the interior as they fell. The roof of one church was lifted from its seating by the blast and dropped down. In places it did not settle into its original position.

PL

World's tallest buildings

Tallest inhabited buildings and tallest structures

Building and location	*Year completed*	*Height m/ft*	*Storeys*
Sears Tower, Chicago	1974	443/1,454*	110
World Trade Centre (twin towers), New York	1972	417/1,368*	110
Empire State Building, New York	1931	381/1,250*	102
Bank of China, Hong Kong	1989	368/1,209	72
Amoco Building, Chicago	1971	346/1,136	80
John Hancock Centre, Chicago	1967	344/1,127	100
Chrysler Building, New York	1930	319/1,046	77
First Interstate World Center, Los Angeles	1989	310/1,017	73
Texas Commerce Tower, Houston	1981	305/1,002	75
Allied Bank Plaza, Houston	1983	302/992	71
Messe Turin Building, Frankfurt	1991	256/841	70
Canary Wharf Tower, London	1990	244/800	56

** excluding TV antennae*

Tallest structures

Structure and location	*Height m/ft*
Warszawa Radio Mast,** Konstantynow, Poland	646/2,120
KTHI-TV Mast, Fargo, North Dakota	629/2,063
CN Tower, Metro Center, Toronto	555/1,822

*** collapsed during renovation, Aug 1991*

prestressed concrete reinforced concrete in which ducts enclose mechanically tensioned steel cables. This allows the most efficient use of the tensile strength of steel with the compressive strength of concrete.

pylon steel lattice tower that supports high-tension electrical cables. In ancient Egyptian architecture, a pylon is one of a pair of inward-sloping towers that flank an entrance.

space-frame lightweight, triangulated, structural framework, designed to be of uniform load resistance and used principally in large-span constructions, such as exhibition halls, stadia, and aircraft hangars. The Eiffel Tower, Paris 1899, is of space-frame constructoin. A contemporary development is Buckminster Fuller's ***geodesic dome***, a shell-like space-frame covered in plastic, plywood, or metal sheeting.

tunnel passageway through a mountain, under a body of water, or under ground. Tunnelling is an increasingly important branch of civil engineering in mining, transport and other areas. In the 19th century there were two major advances: the use of compressed air within underwater tunnels to balance the external pressure of water, and, on land, the development of the tunnel shield to support the rockface and assist excavation. In recent years there have been notable developments in linings, such as concrete segments and steel liner plates, and in the use of rotary diggers and cutters, and explosives.

Major tunnels include: ***Orange–Fish River*** (South Africa) 1975, longest irrigation tunnel, 82 km/51 mi; ***Chesapeake Bay Bridge–Tunnel*** (USA) 1963, combined bridge, causeway, and tunnel structure, 28 km/17.5 mi; ***St Gotthard*** (Switzerland–Italy) 1980, longest road tunnel, 16.3 km/10.1 mi; ***Seikan*** (Japan) 1964–85, longest rail tunnel, Honshu–Hokkaido, under Tsugaru Strait, 53.9 km/33.5 mi, 23.3 km/14.5

World's longest railway tunnels

Tunnel	*Location*	*Date*	*Km/mi*
Seikan*	Japan	1985	54/33.5
Dai-shimizu	Japan	1979	23/14
Simplon No. 1 and 2	Switzerland – Italy	1906, 1922	19/12
Kanmon	Japan	1975	19/12
Apennine	Italy	1934	18/11
Rokko	Japan	1972	16/10
Mt MacDonald	Canada	1989	15/9.1
Gotthard	Switzerland	1882	14/9
Lotschberg	Switzerland	1913	14/9
Hokuriku	Japan	1962	14/9
Mont Canis (Frejus)	France – Italy	1871	13/8
Shin-Shimizu	Japan	1961	13/8
Aki	Japan	1975	13/8
Cascade	USA	1929	13/8
Flathead	USA	1970	13/8
Keijo	Japan	1970	11/7
Lierasen	Norway	1973	11/7
Santa Lucia	Italy	1977	10/6
Arlberg	Austria	1884	10/6
Moffat	USA	1928	10/6
Shimizu	Japan	1931	10/6

** Longest sub-aqueous rail*

mi undersea (however, a bullet-train service is no longer economical); ***Simplon*** (Switzerland–Italy) 1906, longest rail tunnel on land, 19.8 km/12.3 mi; ***Rogers Pass*** (Canada) 1989, longest tunnel in the western hemisphere, 35 km/22 mi long, through the Selkirk Mountains, British Columbia. Plans for the ***Channel tunnel*** linking England and France were approved by the French and British governments in 1986, and work is under way with a schedule for completion in early 1994.

Biographies

Aalto Alvar 1898–1976. Finnish architect and designer. One of Finland's first Modernists, he had a unique architectural style, characterized by asymmetry, curved walls, and contrast of natural materials. His buildings include the Hall of Residence at the Massachusetts Institute of Technology, Cambridge, Massachusetts, 1947–49; Technical High School, Otaniemi, 1962–65; and Finlandia Hall, Helsinki, 1972. He invented a new form of laminated bent-plywood furniture 1932 and won many design awards for household and industrial items.

Adam family of Scottish architects and designers. ***William Adam*** (1689–1748) was the leading Scottish architect of his day, and his son ***Robert Adam*** (1728–1792) is considered one of the greatest British architects of the late 18th century, who transformed the prevailing Palladian fashion in architecture to a Neo-Classical style. He designed interiors for many great country houses and earned a considerable reputation as a furniture designer.

Alberti Leon Battista 1404–1472. Italian Renaissance architect and theorist who recognized the principles of Classical architecture and their modification for Renaissance practice in *On Architecture* 1452.

Archigram London-based group of English architects in the 1960s whose work was experimental and polemical; architecture was to be technological and flexible. The group included Peter Cook (1936–), Dennis Crompton (1935–), David Greene (1937–), Ron Herron (1930–), and Mike Webb (1937–).

Barry Charles 1795–1860. English architect of the Neo-Gothic Houses of Parliament at Westminster, London, 1840–60, in collaboration with Augustus Pugin.

Berlage Hendrikus 1856–1934. Dutch architect of the Amsterdam Stock Exchange 1897–1903. His individualist style marked a move away from 19th-century historicism and towards Dutch Expressionism.

Bernini Giovanni Lorenzo 1598–1680. Italian sculptor, architect, and painter, a leading figure in the development of the Baroque style. His work in Rome includes the colonnaded piazza in front of St Peter's Basilica (1656), fountains (as in the Piazza Navona), and papal monuments. His sculpture includes *The Ecstasy of St Theresa* 1645–52 (Sta Maria della Vittoria, Rome) and numerous portrait busts.

Borromini Francesco 1599–1667. Italian Baroque architect, one of the two most important (with Bernini, his main rival) in 17th-century Rome. Whereas Bernini designed in a florid, expansive style, his pupil Borromini developed a highly idiosyncratic and austere use of the Classical language of architecture. His genius may be seen in the cathedrals of San Carlo 1641 and San Ivo 1660, and the oratorio of St Filippo Neri 1650.

Bramante Donato c. 1444–1514. Italian Renaissance architect and artist. Inspired by Classical designs, he was employed by Pope Julius II in rebuilding part of the Vatican and St Peter's in Rome.

Breuer Marcel 1902–1981. Hungarian-born architect and designer who studied and taught at the Bauhaus school in Germany. His tubular steel chair 1925 was the first of its kind. He moved to England, then to the USA, where he was in partnership with Walter Gropius 1937–40. His buildings show an affinity with natural materials; the best known is the Bijenkorf, Rotterdam, the Netherlands 1953.

Brunelleschi Filippo 1377–1446. Italian Renaissance architect. One of the earliest and greatest Renaissance architects, he pioneered the scientific use of perspective. He was responsible for the construction of the dome of Florence Cathedral (completed 1438), a feat deemed impossible by many of his contemporaries.

Burlington Richard Boyle, 3rd Earl of Burlington 1694–1753. British architectural patron and architect; one of the premier exponents of the Palladian style in Britain. His buildings, such as Chiswick House, London, 1725–29, are characterized by absolute adherence to the Classical rules. His major protégé was William Kent.

Butterfield William 1814–1900. English Gothic Revival architect. His work is characterized by vigorous, aggressive forms and multicoloured striped and patterned brickwork, as in the church of All Saints, Margaret Street, London 1850–59, and Keble College, Oxford 1867–83.

Casson Hugh 1910– . British architect, professor at the Royal College of Art 1953–75, and president of the Royal Academy 1976–84. His books include *Victorian Architecture* 1948. He was director of architecture for the Festival of Britain 1948–51.

Chambers William 1726–1796. British architect and popularizer of Chinese influence (for example, the pagoda in Kew Gardens, London) and designer of Somerset House, London.

Coates Nigel 1949– . British architect. While teaching at the Architectural Association in London in the early 1980s, Coates and a group of students founded NATO (***N****arrative* ***A****rchitecture* ***To****day*) and produced an influential series of manifestos and drawings on the theme of the imaginative regeneration of derelict areas of London.

Eyck Aldo van 1918– . Dutch architect with a strong commitment to social architecture. His works include an Orphans' Home 1957–60, and a refuge for single mothers, Mothers' House 1978; both are in Amsterdam.

Farrell Terry 1938– . British architect working in a Post-Modern idiom, largely for corporate clients seeking an alternative to the rigours of High Tech or

Modernist office blocks. His Embankment Place scheme 1991 sits theatrically on top of Charing Cross station in Westminster, London, and has been likened to a giant jukebox.

Foster Norman 1935– . English architect of the high-tech school. His buildings include the Willis Faber office, Ipswich, 1978, the Sainsbury Centre for Visual Arts at the University of East Anglia 1974 (opened 1978), the headquarters of the Hong Kong and Shanghai Bank, Hong Kong, 1986, and Stansted Airport, Essex, 1991.

Fuller (Richard) Buckminster 1895–1983. US architect, engineer, and futurist social philosopher who embarked on an unorthodox career in an attempt to maximize energy resources through improved technology. In 1947 he invented the lightweight geodesic dome, a half-sphere of triangular components independent of buttress or vault.

Gaudí Antonio 1852–1926. Spanish architect distinguished for his flamboyant Art Nouveau style. Gaudí worked almost exclusively in Barcelona, designing both domestic and industrial buildings. He introduced colour, unusual materials, and audacious technical innovations. His spectacular Church of the Holy Family, Barcelona, begun 1883, is still under construction.

Gehry Frank 1929– . US architect, based in Los Angeles. His architecture approaches abstract art in its use of collage and montage techniques.

Gibbs James 1682–1754. Scottish Neo-Classical architect whose works include St Martin-in-the-Fields, London, 1722–26, Radcliffe Camera, Oxford, 1737–49, and Bank Hall, Warrington, Cheshire, 1750.

Gilbert Cass 1859–1934. US architect, major developer of the skyscraper. His designed the Woolworth Building, New York, 1913, the highest building in America (868 ft/265 m) when built and famous for its use of Gothic decorative detail.

Grimshaw Nicholas 1939– . English architect whose work has developed along distinctly High Tech lines, diverging sharply from that of his former partner, Terry Farrell. His Financial Times printing works, London 1988, is an uncompromising industrial building, exposing machinery to view through a glass outer wall. He created the British Pavilion for Expo'92 in Seville in similar vein, but also addressed problems of climatic control, incorporating a huge wall of water in its façade and sail-like mechanisms on the roof.

Gropius Walter Adolf 1883–1969. German architect who lived in the USA from 1937. He was an early exponent of the international modern style defined by glass curtain walls, cubic blocks, and unsupported corners – for example, the model factory and office building at the 1914 Cologne Werkbund exhibition. A founder-director of the Bauhaus school in Weimar 1919–28, he advocated teamwork in design and artistic standards in industrial production.

Haussmann Georges Eugène, Baron Haussmann 1809–1891. French administrator who replanned medieval Paris 1853–70 to achieve the current city plan, with wide boulevards and parks. The cost of his scheme and his authoritarianism caused opposition, and he was made to resign.

Hawksmoor Nicholas 1661–1736. English architect, assistant to Christopher Wren in designing London churches and St Paul's Cathedral; joint architect with John Vanbrugh of Castle Howard and Blenheim Palace. His genius is displayed in a quirky and uncompromising style incorporating elements from both Gothic and Classical sources. The original west towers of Westminster Abbey, long attributed to Wren, were designed by Hawksmoor.

Howard Ebenezer 1850–1928. English town planner and founder of the ideal of the garden city, through his book *Tomorrow* 1898 (republished as *Garden Cities of Tomorrow* 1902).

Isozaki Arata 1931– . Japanese architect. One of Kenzo Tange's team 1954–63, his Post-Modernist works include Ochanomizu Square, Tokyo (retaining the existing facades), and buildings for the 1992 Barcelona Olympics.

Jellicoe Geoffrey 1900– . English architect, landscape architect, and historian. His contribution to 20th-century thinking on landscapes and gardens has been mainly through his writings, notably *Landscape of Man* 1975. However, he has also made an impact as a designer, working in a comtemplative and poetic vein and frequently incorporating water and sculptures. Representative of his work are the Kennedy Memorial at Runnymede, Berkshire 1965, and the gardens at Sutton Place, Sussex, 1980–84.

Jencks Charles 1939– . US architectural theorist and furniture designer. He coined the term 'Post-Modern architecture' and wrote *The Language of Post-Modern Architecture* 1984.

Johnson Philip (Cortelyou) 1906– . US architect who coined the term 'international style'. Originally designing in the style of Mies van der Rohe, he later became an exponent of Post-Modernism. He designed the giant AT&T building in New York 1978, a pink skyscraper with a Chippendale-style cabinet top. He was director of architecture and design at the Museum of Modern Art, New York 1932–54, where he built the annexe and sculpture court.

Jones Inigo 1573–*c*. 1652. English classical architect. Born in London, he studied in Italy and was influenced by the works of Palladio. He was employed by James I to design scenery for Ben Jonson's masques. He designed the Queen's House, Greenwich, 1616–35 and his English Renaissance masterpiece, the Banquet House in Whitehall, London, 1619–22.

Kahn Louis 1901–1974. US architect, born in Estonia. A follower of Mies van de Rohe, he developed a classically romantic style, in which functional 'servant' areas, such as stairwells and air ducts, featured prominently, often as towerlike structures surrounding the main living and working, or 'served', areas. His projects are characterized by an imaginative use of concrete and brick and include the Salk Institute for Biological Studies, La Jolla, California, and the British Art Center at Yale University.

Lasdun Denys 1914– . British architect. He designed the Royal College of Surgeons in Regent's Park, London 1960–64, some of the buildings at the University of East Anglia, Norwich, and the National

Theatre 1976–77 on London's South Bank. He was knighted 1976.

Le Corbusier assumed name of Charles-Édouard Jeanneret 1887–1965. Swiss architect. His functionalist approach to town planning in industrial society was based on the interrelationship between machine forms and the techniques of modern architecture. His concept, *La Ville radieuse*, developed in Marseille, France (1945–50) and Chandigarh, India, placed buildings and open spaces with related functions in a circular formation, with buildings based on standard-sized units mathematically calculated according to the proportions of the human figure.

Ledoux Claude-Nicolas 1736–1806. French Neo-Classical architect, stylistically comparable to E L Boullée in his use of austere, geometric forms, exemplified in his toll houses for Paris; for instance, the Barrière de la Villette in the Place de Stalingrad.

Lethaby William Richard 1857–1931. English architect. An assistant to Norman Shaw, he embraced the principles of William Morris and Philip Webb in the Arts and Crafts movement, and was cofounder and first director of the Central School of Arts and Crafts from 1894. He wrote a collection of essays entitled *Form in Civilization* 1922.

Lutyens Edwin Landseer 1869–1944. English architect. His designs ranged from picturesque to Renaissance-style country houses and ultimately evolved into a Classical style as in the Cenotaph, London, and the Viceroy's House, New Delhi.

Mackintosh Charles Rennie 1868–1928. Scottish architect, designer, and painter, whose chief work includes the Glasgow School of Art 1896, various Glasgow tea rooms 1897 to about 1911, and Hill House, Helensburg, 1902–03. His early work is Art Nouveau; he subsequently developed a unique style, both rational and expressive. Influenced by the Arts and Crafts Movement, he designed furniture and fittings, cutlery, and lighting to go with his interiors. Although initially influential, Mackintosh was not successful in his lifetime and has only recently come to be regarded as a pioneeer of modern design.

Meier Richard 1934– . US architect whose white designs spring from the poetic modernism of the Le Corbusier villas of the 1920s. His abstract style is at its most mature in the Museum für Kunsthandwerk (Museum of Arts and Crafts), Frankfurt, Germany, which was completed 1984. He is the architect for the Getty Museum, Los Angeles.

Mendelsohn Erich 1887–1953. German Expressionist architect who designed the Einstein Tower, Potsdam, 1919–20. His later work fused Modernist and Expressionist styles; in Britain he built the de la Warr Pavilion 1935–36 in Bexhill-on-Sea, East Sussex. In 1941 he settled in the USA, where he built the Maimonides Hospital, San Francisco, 1946–50.

Mies van der Rohe Ludwig 1886–1969. German architect who practised in the USA from 1937. He succeeded Walter Gropius as director of the Bauhaus 1929–33. He designed the bronze-and-glass Seagram building in New York City 1956–59 and numerous apartment buildings.

Moore Charles 1925– . US architect with an eclectic approach to design. He was an early exponent of Post-Modernism in, for example, his students' housing for Kresge College, University of California at Santa Cruz, 1973–74, and the Piazza d'Italia in New Orleans, 1975–78, which is one of the key monuments of Post-Modernism.

Nash John 1752–1835. English architect. He laid out Regent's Park, London, and its approaches. Between 1813 and 1820 he planned Regent Street (later rebuilt), repaired and enlarged Buckingham Palace (for which he designed Marble Arch), and rebuilt Brighton Pavilion in flamboyant oriental style.

Nervi Pier Luigi 1891–1979. Italian architect who used soft steel mesh within concrete to give it flowing form. For example, the Turin exhibition hall 1949, the UNESCO building in Paris 1952, and the cathedral at New Norcia, near Perth, Australia, 1960.

Neutra Richard Joseph 1892–1970. Austrian-born architect who became a US citizen 1929. His works, often in impressive landscape settings, include Lovell Health House, Los Angeles (1929), and Mathematics Park, Princeton, New Jersey.

Niemeyer Oscar 1907– . Brazilian architect, joint designer of the United Nations headquarters in New York and of many buildings in Brasília, capital of Brazil.

Olbrich Joseph Maria 1867–1908. Viennese architect who worked under Otto Wagner and was opposed to the overornamentation of Art Nouveau. His major buildings, however, remain Art Nouveau in spirit: the Vienna Sezession 1897–98, the Hochzeitsturm 1907, and the Tietz department store in Düsseldorf, Germany.

Palladio Andrea 1518–1580. Italian Renaissance architect noted for his harmonious and balanced classical structures. He designed numerous country houses in and around Vicenza, Italy, making use of Roman classical forms, symmetry, and proportion. The Villa Malcontenta and the Villa Rotonda are examples of houses designed from 1540 for patrician families of the Venetian Republic; he also designed churches in Venice. His ideas were revived in England in the early 17th century by Inigo Jones and in the 18th century by Lord Burlington and later by architects in Italy, Holland, Germany, Russia, and the USA. Examples of Neo-Classical architecture influenced by 'Palladian' buildings include Washington's home at Mount Vernon, USA, the palace of Tsarskoe Selo in Russia, and Prior Park, England.

Paxton Joseph 1801–1865. English architect, garden superintendent to the Duke of Devonshire from 1826 and designer of the Great Exhibition building 1851 (the Crystal Palace), which was revolutionary in its structural use of glass and iron.

Pei Ieoh Ming 1917– . Chinese-born US Modernist/High Tech architect, noted for the use of glass walls. His buildings include the Bank of China Tower, Hong Kong, 1987; the glass pyramid in front of the Louvre, Paris, 1989; East Building, National Gallery of Art, Washington DC, 1978; and the John Hancock Tower, Boston 1979.

Piranesi Giambattista 1720–1778. Italian architect, most significant for his powerful etchings of Roman antiquities and as a theorist of architecture, advocating imaginative use of Roman models. Only one of his designs was built, Sta Maria del Priorato, Rome.

Pugin Augustus Welby Northmore 1812–1852. English architect, collaborator with Charles Barry in the detailed design of the Houses of Parliament. He did much to revive Gothic architecture in England.

Rogers Richard 1933– . British architect. His works include the Centre Pompidou in Paris 1977 (jointly with Renzo Piano) and the Lloyd's building in London 1986.

Saarinen Eero 1910–1961. Finnish-born US architect distinguished for a wide range of innovative modern designs using a variety of creative shapes for buildings. His works include the US embassy, London, the TWA terminal, New York, and Dulles Airport, Washington DC. He collaborated on a number of projects with his father, Eliel Saarinen.

Saarinen Eliel 1873–1950. Finnish architect and town planner, founder of the Finnish Romantic school. In 1923 he emigrated to the USA, where he contributed to US skyscraper design by his work in Chicago, and later turned to functionalism.

Sant'Elia Antonio 1888–1916. Italian architect. His drawings convey a Futurist vision of a metropolis with skyscrapers, traffic lanes, and streamlined factories.

Schinkel Karl Friedrich 1781–1841. Prussian Neo-Classical architect. Major works include the Old Museum, Berlin, 1823–30, the Nikolaikirche in Potsdam 1830–37, and the Roman Bath 1833 in the park of Potsdam.

Scott (George) Gilbert 1811–1878. English architect. As the leading practical architect in the mid-19th-century Gothic revival in England, Scott was responsible for the building or restoration of many public buildings, including the Albert Memorial, the Foreign Office, and St Pancras Station, all in London.

Serlio Sebastiano 1475–1554. Italian architect and painter, author of *L'Architettura* 1537–51, which set down practical rules for the use of the Classical orders, and was used by architects of the Neo-Classical style throughout Europe.

Shaw (Richard) Norman 1831–1912. British architect. He was the leader of the trend away from Gothic and Tudor styles back to Georgian lines. His buildings include Swan House, Chelsea, 1876.

Sinan 1489–1588. Ottoman architect, chief architect from 1538 to Suleiman the Magnificent. Among the hundreds of buildings he designed are the Suleimaniye in Istanbul, a mosque complex, and the Topkapi Saray, palace of the sultan (now a museum).

Smirke Robert 1780–1867. English Classical architect, designer of the British Museum, London (1823–47).

Smithson Alison 1928– . and Peter 1923– . British architects, teachers, and theorists, best known for their development in the 1950s and 1960s of the style known as Brutalism, for example in Hunstanton School, Norfolk, 1954; the Economist Building, London, 1964; and Robin Hood Gardens, London, 1968–72.

Soane John 1753–1837. English architect whose individual Neo-Classical designs anticipated contemporary taste. He designed his own house in Lincoln's Inn Fields, London, now the ***Soane Museum***. Little remains of his extensive work at the Bank of England, London.

Speer Albert 1905–1981. German architect and minister in the Nazi government during World War II. Commissioned by Hitler, Speer, like his counterparts in Fascist Italy, chose an overblown Classicism to glorify the state, as, for example, in his plan for the Berlin and Nuremberg Party Congress Grounds 1934.

Stirling James 1926–1992. British architect, associated with collegiate and museum architecture. His works include the engineering building at Leicester University, and the Clore Gallery (the extension to house the Turner collection) at the Tate Gallery, London, opened in 1987.

Sullivan Louis Henry 1856–1924. US architect, a leader of the Chicago school of architects and an early developer of the skyscraper. His skyscrapers include the Wainwright Building, St Louis, 1890 and the Guaranty Building, Buffalo, 1894. He was the teacher of Frank Lloyd Wright.

Tange Kenzo 1913– . Japanese architect. His works include the National Gymnasium, Tokyo, for the 1964 Olympics, and the city of Abuja, planned to replace Lagos as the capital of Nigeria.

Terry (John) Quinlan 1937– . British Neo-Classical architect. His work includes country houses, for example Merks Hall, Great Dunmow, Essex, 1982, and the larger-scale Richmond, London, riverside project, commissioned 1984.

Vanbrugh John 1664–1726. English Baroque architect and dramatist. He designed Blenheim Palace, Oxfordshire, and Castle Howard, Yorkshire, and wrote the comic dramas *The Relapse* 1696 and *The Provok'd Wife* 1697.

Venturi Robert 1925– . US architect. He pioneered Post-Modernism through his books *Complexity and Contradiction in Architecture* 1967 (Pulitzer Prize 1991) and *Learning from Las Vegas* 1972. In 1986 he was commissioned to design the extension to the National Gallery, London, opened 1991.

Vitruvius (Marcus Vitruvius Pollio) 1st century BC. Roman architect whose ten-volume interpretation of Roman architecture *De architectura* influenced Leon Battista Alberti and Andrea Palladio.

Voysey Charles Francis Annesley 1857–1941. English architect and designer. He designed country houses which were characteristically asymmetrical with massive buttresses, long sloping roofs, and rough-cast walls. He also designed textiles and wallpaper.

Wagner Otto 1841–1918. Viennese architect. Initially designing in the Art Nouveau style, for example Vienna Stadtbahn 1894–97, he later rejected ornament for rationalism, as in the Post Office Savings Bank, Vienna, 1904–06. He influenced such Viennese architects as Josef Hoffmann, Adolf Loos, and Joseph Olbrich.

Waterhouse Alfred 1830–1905. English architect. He was a leading exponent of Victorian Neo-Gothic using, typically, multicoloured tiles and bricks. His works include the Natural History Museum in London 1868.

Webb Philip (Speakman) 1831–1915. English architect. He mostly designed private houses, including the Red House, Bexley Heath, Sussex, for William Morris, and was one of the leading figures, with Richard Norman Shaw and C F A Voysey, in the revival of domestic English architecture in the late 19th century.

Wren Christopher 1632–1723. English architect, designer of St Paul's Cathedral, London, built 1675–1710; many London churches including St Bride's, Fleet Street, and St Mary-le-Bow, Cheapside; the Royal Exchange; Marlborough House; and the Sheldonian Theatre, Oxford. After the Great Fire of London 1666, he prepared a plan for rebuilding the city, but it was not adopted. Instead, Wren was commissioned to rebuild 51 City churches and St Paul's Cathedral. The west towers of Westminster Abbey, often attributed to him, were the design of his pupil Hawksmoor.

Wright Frank Lloyd 1869–1959. US architect who rejected Neo-Classicist styles for 'organic architecture', in which buildings reflected their natural surroundings. Among his buildings are his Wisconsin home Taliesin East 1925; Falling Water, near Pittsburgh, Pennsylvania, 1936, a house built straddling a waterfall; and the Guggenheim Museum, New York, 1959. Wright also designed buildings in Japan from 1915 to 1922, most notably the Imperial Hotel in Tokyo 1922.

ART

History of Western Art

In the visual arts of Western civilization, painting and sculpture have been the dominant forms for many centuries. This has not always been the case in other cultures. Islamic art, for example, is one of ornament, as artists were forbidden to portray living creatures. In some cultures masks, tattoos, pottery, and metalwork have been the main forms of visual art. In the recent past technology has made new art forms possible, such as photography and cinema, and today electronic media – computer graphics, computer-aided animation and 'painting', and other imaging techniques – have led to entirely new ways of creating and presenting visual images.

ANCIENT ART

prehistoric art 25,000–1000 BC. The history of the fine arts, painting and sculpture, begins about 21,000 BC in the Paleolithic, or Old Stone Age. Vivid, lifelike images of animals and humans have been found incised, painted or sculpted on the walls deep inside the caves where our ancestors sheltered, mostly in Spain and in southwestern France, but also in Portugal, Sicily, and Russia. The images of reindeer, mammoth, horses and bison are most common, varying from very small to almost lifesize. It is thought that they served as part of a 'magic' ritual to ensure a successful hunt. Paintings such as those at the caves of *Lascaux* in France show great skill in drawing, with vigorous and sweepingly graceful outlines. Stone Age people also used flint tools to carve small figurines in bone, horn, or stone. The most famous of these is the so-called *Venus of Willendorf*, a limestone statuette 4.5 in high, found in lower Austria and dating from about 21,000 BC. Her exaggeratedly bulbous form makes clear her magic significance as a fertility figure.

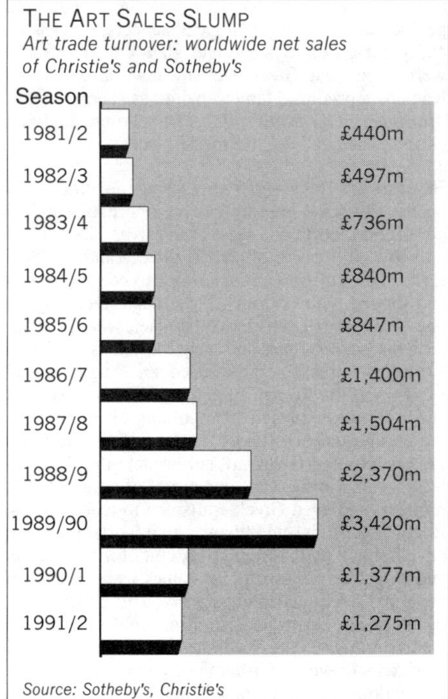

art of early civilizations 14,000–300 BC. Architecture became the new art form when people began to settle in communities as farmers rather than as hunters. They decorated their buildings with sculpture, imposing a sense of pattern and order on them, although Stonehenge in Britain (1800–1400 BC) had not achieved this sophistication. In Europe, ***Celtic art*** ornamented tombs, crosses, metalwork and pottery with stylized animal and plant forms in swirling curvilinear patterns. Pottery had reached Europe from the Near East where it began as early as 5500 BC in Mesopotamia, where sign pictures also grew into cuneiform (wedge-shaped) writing. The Near and Middle East produced many highly developed urban civilizations, including the ***Sumerian*** (4000 BC), and the ***Persian*** (550 BC). In these cultures, sculptures and reliefs of people, gods, and animals decorated palaces, temples, and tombs telling stories or praising their gods and rulers. A fine example is the grand stairway of the *Persian royal palace*, Persepolis, from 518–6 BC. Outstanding examples of precious metalwork, glassware, and pottery also survive, of which there are splendid collections in the British Museum and the Louvre.

Egyptian art 3000–200 BC. *The Great Sphinx at Giza* (2680–2565 BC), a gigantic human-headed lion carved from an outcropping of natural rock, is the supreme example of Egyptian sculpture. 185 ft long and 63 ft high, it was meant to guard for eternity the god-king's pyramid tomb nearby. Most Egyptian art is funerary, largely consisting of sculptured relief panels painted in bright, lifelike colours covering the walls of tombs and temples. They depend on strong, simple outlines, the main aim being clarity: to portray the dead in their idealized prime, their servants and families, and the objects, animals, foods and activities they enjoyed in life, so that these could be magically transported into the afterworld to be enjoyed forever.

Human forms are recomposed almost diagrammatically to show the whole of a person, face and legs in profile, upper torso in front view, hips three-quarters and with the eye magnified. If anything needed further description a hieroglyphic label would be added. Statues, whether of wood or stone, were also generally painted. They retain a strong cubic sense of the block from which they were hewn, with the figures facing straight ahead, the arms in a single unit with the body. The serene vision of eternity found in all Egyptian art is epitomized in the beautiful portrait head of *Queen Nefertiti* in the Staatlich Museum, Berlin, dating from about 1360 BC.

art of Aegean civilizations 2800–100 BC. The ***Minoan*** and ***Mycenean*** civilizations flourished in the area of the Aegean Sea from about 2800 BC. Based on the island of Crete, Minoan society was pleasure-loving and open, and its major monument, the new *palace at Knossos* (1700 BC), was decorated with cheerful frescoes of scenes from daily life, plants, birds, and leaping fish and dolphins. Their pottery was painted in the same fresh, spontaneous style with plant and animal motifs curving to suit the form of the vases. In 1400 they were conquered by the Mycenaeans from the Peloponnese, whose art reflected its more warlike society. Instead of airy palaces, they constructed fortified citadels such as Mycenae itself, which was entered through the *Lion Gate* (1330), named for the remarkable monumental sculpture that adorns it. In the nearby Cyclades Islands a unique art form emerged about 2800: the small marble *Cycladic figures* much admired today, which represent the Great Mother Goddess in such streamlined simplicity that her face is simply an elongated oval with a triangular nose.

Many of the ideas and art forms of these early seafaring civilizations were to be adapted by the Greeks who came from Central Asia between 2000–1000 BC to establish their own splendid culture that was to dominate Western taste and thought for many centuries.

CLASSICAL ART

Greek art 1000–400 BC. Greek temples are almost sculptures in themselves, designed not to be entered but to be looked at. The sculptured reliefs which decorated them, such as the *Elgin Marbles* (now in the British Museum) which came from the Parthenon in Athens, show perfectly the Greek artistic ideal: the human form at its most beautiful.

The major periods of Greek art can be divided into the Archaic (late 8th century–480 BC), Classical (480–323 BC), and Hellenistic (323–27 BC). No large-scale painting survives, although colour was very important, and even the white marble sculptures we admire today were originally brightly painted.

In the ***Archaic*** period the statues of naked standing men *kouroi* and draped females *korai* show an Egyptian influence in their rigid frontality. By about 500 BC the figure was allowed to relax its weight onto one leg and immediately seemed to come alive. The archaic smile which gave these early figures a certain cheerful sameness vanished in the ***Classical*** period when expressions assumed a dignified serenity. Further movement was introduced in new poses such as in Myron's bronze *Diskobolus/The Discus Thrower* (460–50 BC), and in the rhythmic Parthenon reliefs of men and horses supervised by Phidias. Artists were no longer anonymous and among sculptors whose work is known are **Praxiteles**, **Scopas**, **Lysippus**, and **Polykleitos**, whose *Doryphoros/The Spear Carrier* (450–440) was of such harmony and poise that it set a standard for beautiful proportions which is still in use today. Praxiteles introduced the female nude into the sculptural repertory with the graceful *Aphrodite of Knidos*, (*c.* 350 BC). It was easier to express movement in bronze, hollow-cast by the lost wax method, but few bronze sculptures survive and many are known only through Roman copies in marble.

The ***Hellenistic*** period, when the Greek Empire under Alexander the Great spread to Egypt and beyond Iraq, produced such sculptures as the *Winged Victory of Samothrace* with its dramatic drapery, the expressive *Dying Gaul* and the tortured *Laocoon*, which explored the effects of movement and of deeply-felt emotion.

Vase painting is the one form of Greek painting which has survived the centuries. Good, even great, artists worked as both potters and painters until the 5th century BC and the works they signed were exported throughout the Empire. Made in several standard shapes and sizes, the pottery served as functional containers for wine, water, and oil. The first decoration took the form of simple lines and circles, from which the ***'Geometric style'*** emerged near Athens in the 10th century BC. It consisted of precisely drawn patterns, the most characteristic being the key meander. Gradually the bands of decoration multiplied and the human figure, geometrically stylized, was added.

About 700 BC the potters of Corinth invented the ***black figure*** technique in which the unglazed red clay was painted in black with mythological scenes, gods and battles in a narrative frieze. About 530 BC Athenian potters reversed the process and developed the more sophisticated ***red figure*** pottery, which allowed for more detailed and elaborate painting of the figures in red against a black background. This grew increasingly naturalistic, with lively scenes of daily life. The finest examples date from the mid-6th century–mid-5th century BC at Athens. Later painters tried to follow major art trends and represent spatial depth, dissipating the unique quality of their fine linear technique.

The ancient Greeks excelled in carving gems and cameos, and in jewellery and metalwork. They also invented the pictorial mosaic and from the 5th century BC onwards floors were paved with coloured pebbles depicting mythological subjects. Later, specially cut cubes of stone and glass called *tesserae* were used, and Greek craftsmen working for the Romans reproduced famous paintings such as that of *Alexander at the Battle of Issus* from Pompeii, giving us some idea of these lost masterpieces.

Roman art 753 BC–410 AD. During the 8th century BC the Etruscans appeared as the first native Italian civilization, north and west of the river Tiber. Their art shows influences of archaic Greece and the Near East. Their coffins (*sarcophagi*), carved with reliefs and topped with portraits of the dead, reclining on one elbow as if at an eternal banquet, were to influence the later Romans and early Christians.

Under Julius Caesar's successor Augustus (27 BC–14 AD) the Roman Empire was established. Art and architecture played an important role in unifying the European nations under Roman rule. The Romans greatly admired Greek art and became the first collectors, importing vast quantities of marbles and bronzes, and even Greek craftsmen to make copies. Realistic portrait sculpture was an important original development by the Romans. A cult of heroes began and in public places official statues were erected of generals, rulers and philosophers. The portrait bust developed as a new art form from about 75 BC; these were serious, factual portraits of a rugged race of patriarchs to whose wisdom and authority their subject nations should reasonably submit.

The interactive museum becomes a virtual reality

First, imagine the museum: a dusty receptacle for scholars and ancient artefacts. Then think of the technology of the present and the near future: for instance, the laser disc and computer graphics. These two stereotypes may be far apart in the popular imagination, but in the 1990s they are coming together rapidly to create a new interactive environment.

One meaning of 'interactive', in the museum context, connotes the movement towards increased public access to collections; visitors can handle actual objects under the benevolent supervision of knowledgeable museum staff. The other meaning, which concerns us here, derives from the world of high technology. It involves responsive computers with stores of information accessible to visitors. In both senses, interactivity challenges the traditional museum approach.

There are examples of the interactive approach in museums worldwide, from the USA, through much of continental Europe, to Australia. The Powerhouse Museum in Sydney has pioneered the use of interactive technology in its exhibitions. For example, visitors are given the opportunity to design their own room using the furniture exhibits. In France, the concept of the 'exploded museum' has grown out of the experience of the Pompidou Centre, where a library, exhibition spaces, a museum, and sound laboratories were put together in a single complex in an attempt to break down the divisions between disciplines. The 'exploded museum' forms a resource centre for a town and uses technology to ease access to information. The Carré d'Art, Nimes, designed by Norman Foster, is an excellent example.

In the USA, most large museums are involved in development work on programmes at different levels. The Chicago Institute of Arts has produced a videodisk aimed at five year olds. It looks at four particular Impressionist paintings without written instruction and is, in effect, a game about pictures. In striking contrast is the work being done at the new Warhol Museum project in Pittsburgh. This combines everyday information retrieval with education, in an attempt to develop programmes that will assist both administrators and museum visitors. Eventually, this system will encompass the whole of Warhol's output, from paintings and prints to film and video.

Similar trends are apparent in the UK. For example, the Micro Gallery in the National Gallery, London, is intended as a resource for casual visitors and students alike. It allows users to plan a route through the gallery taking in paintings of particular subjects, and gives information more detailed than that found on the paintings' labels. The interactive video is linked to printers, so the system can generate hard copy. The Micro Gallery is tucked away on a mezzanine floor, and is more like an office than an art gallery.

Other institutions have been bolder about integrating equipment into their displays. The Imperial War Museum has used interactive systems, projected video, sound installations and 'experiences' alongside static objects in showcases. The Victoria and Albert Museum, in its new Chinese and Korean galleries, uses small interactive monitors integrated into the displays, as does the Natural History Museum.

Another side of this work is the design and production of interactive material for use in the classroom and eventually in the home. The Tate Gallery in Liverpool and the British Museum are both involved in the development of such material.

Meanwhile, virtual reality is waiting in the wings. It is rumoured that at least one UK museum will have a virtual reality installation by the end of 1993. The user, in effect, enters a computer-generated environment in which there are degrees of control of movement. At the moment this involves wearing awkward gloves and a headset; but development in this field are often rapid and it is impossible to anticipate technological developments.

Probably, in the long run, interactive media don't belong in the gallery, at least not in their current forms. The touchscreen monitor may end up as archaic as the chained library. Once books were precious objects, the product of what seemed like infinite labour; now they sit on the shelves of museum bookshops waiting to be bought by whoever has the money to pay. No doubt a similar fate awaits interactive software. The museum of the future will still contain real things, but perhaps the labels will discretely interact, and the gift-shop shelves will be full of laser discs alongside the books and souvenir pencils.

In the meantime, every museum needs to take account of that flickering screen and discover what it can do for them. The children of the late 20th century are probably more computer-literate than book-literate; they understand and feel comfortable with the touchscreens and keyboards. Ultimately the museums are theirs. It's not that museums are in competition with the games arcade and Super Mario, but the curators are having to learn to use that language to constructive ends.

CS

Narrative relief sculpture also flourished in Rome, again linked to the need to commemorate publicly the glorious victories of their heroes. These appeared on monumental altars, triumphal arches and giant columns such as *Trajan's Column* 106–113 AD which records his historic battles like a strip cartoon, winding its way around the column for 656 ft. Strict realism in portraiture gave way to a certain amount of Greek-style idealization in the propaganda statues of the emperors, befitting their semi-divine status. Gods and allegorical figures feature with Rome's heroes on such narrative relief sculptures as those on Augustus's giant altar to peace, the *Ara Pacis* 13–9 BC.

Very little ***Roman painting*** has survived, and much of what has is due to the volcanic eruption of Mount Vesuvius in AD 79 which buried the southern Italian seaside towns of Pompeii and Herculaneum under ash, thus preserving the lively and impressionistic wall paintings (frescoes) which decorated the holiday villas of an art-loving elite. Favourite motifs were illusionistic and still-life. A type of interior decoration known as ***Grotesque***, rediscovered in Rome during the Renaissance, combined swirling plant motifs, strange animals and tiny fanciful scenes. Grotesque was much used in later decorative schemes whenever it was fashionable to quote the Classical period.

The art of ***mosaic*** was universally popular throughout the Roman Empire. It was introduced from Greece and used for floors as well as walls and vaults, in *trompe l'oeil* effects, geometric patterns and scenes from daily life and mythology.

MEDIEVAL ART

early Christian and Byzantine art 330–1453 AD. In 312 the Emperor Constantine was converted to Christianity and made it one of the official religions of the Roman State. Churches were built, and artistic traditions adapted to the portrayal of the new Christian saints and symbols. Roman burial chests *(sarcophagi)* were adopted by the Christians and their imagery of pagan myths gradually changed into biblical themes.

Byzantine style developed in the East in Constantinople which in 330 became the headquarters of the Roman Empire, and an Eastern Christian tradition was maintained there until 1453 when Constantinople was conquered by the Turks. The use of mosaic came to be associated with both Byzantine art and early Christian church decoration in the West. Ravenna became the Western imperial capital in the 5th century, and the ecclesiastical buildings there, built in the 5th and 6th centuries, are a glorious tribute to the art of mosaic, presenting powerful religious images on walls and vaults in brilliant, glittering colour. Byzantine art moved away from the natural portrayal of people and became highly stylized, symbolizing the divine. Ornament became flattened into intricate lacework patterns. Oriental, highly decorative, and unchanging, the Byzantine style can be seen in the icons – often thought to be capable of working miracles – which have remained for centuries the main religious art of Greece and Russia.

art of the Dark Ages 400–800 AD. The 400 years between the fall of the Roman Empire and the establishment of Charlemagne's new Holy Roman Empire in 800 are traditionally known as the Dark Ages, and the art of that period as belonging to the Migration Period. Through a time of turmoil and invasion, with the northern 'barbarians' overrunning the old Mediterranean civilizations, the Christian church maintained its stability and the interchange of artistic traditions fostered creativity.

The art of the migrant peoples consisted mainly of portable objects, articles of personal use or adornment. They excelled in metalwork and jewellery, often in gold with garnet or enamel inlays and ornamented with highly stylized, animal-based interlace patterns. This type of ornament was translated into manuscript illumination such as the decorated pages of the *Lindisfarne Gospel* (British Museum, London) which dates from the 7th century, or the 8th century *Book of Kells* (Trinity College, Dublin). With Charlemagne's Christian Empire modelled on that of ancient Rome, a cultural renaissance ensued, drawing its inspiration from the late Classical artistic traditions of the early Christians. At Charlemagne's capital, Aachen, the human figure was re-introduced into art and continuous narrative was rediscovered in the *Tours Bibles* produced there. They in turn influenced the sculptured reliefs on the bronze doors at St Michael's Church, Hildesheim, Germany, dating from 1015, the first doors cast in one piece in the West since Roman times.

art of the Middle Ages 800–1300 AD. Under the unifying force of the Latin Church, a new civilization spread across Europe which during the 10th century produced a style in art called ***Romanesque***, and, in England, ***Norman***. Chiefly evident in relief sculpture surrounding church portals, on capitals and corbels, it translated manuscript illuminations into stone, combining naturalistic elements from the antique Roman style with the fantastic, poetical, and pattern-loving Celtic and Germanic tradition. Imaginary beasts, monsters, saints, and sinners mingle with humour and innocence in an enchanted world of biblical themes. Fine examples remain in Burgundy and southwest France, extending down into Spain on the pilgrimage route to Santiago de Compostela.

Gothic during the late 12th and 13th centuries European cities began to raise great cathedrals, and sculptural decoration became more monumental. The cathedrals of Chartres and Reims in France had such extensive sculptural programmes that many artists came from far afield to work and learn there. A new interest in the natural world is shown in such examples as the strikingly life-like founder figures of Naumberg Cathedral, East Germany, (*c.* 1245) or in the naturalistic foliage on the capitals at Southwell in England.

With the increased height of the cathedrals, stained glass windows became their new glory. Chartres, where an entire set of stained glass is preserved, awesomely illustrates the magical effect of coloured light seemingly suspended within its dark interior. Both windows and sculpture, by depicting the lives of the saints and texts from the bible, gave the faithful an encyclopedic view of the Christian history of the world.

Art patronage, although still mainly concerned with religious imagery, now burgeoned in the many small courts of Europe and under this influence art became more stylized, delicate and refined. Even the Virgin Mary was portrayed as an elegant young queen. In her most characteristic pose, holding the Christ child in her arms, her weight shifts gracefully onto one hip causing her body to form an S-curve and her drapery to fall into elegant folds. This figure stance, the 'Gothic sway', became a hallmark of the period. Court patronage produced exquisite small ivories, precious goldsmith's work, devotional books illustrated with miniatures, and tapestries which warmed cold castle walls, depicting romantic tales or the joys of springtime.

In Italy, the monumentality of the antique Roman past subdued the spread of northern Gothic ideas. A type of ***Gothic Classicism*** was developed by the sculptors Nicola and Giovanni **Pisano** (working 1258–1314) whose four great pulpits carved in relief (Siena, Pisa, Pistoia) show the influence of antique sarcophagi but also that of French Gothic in the dramatic expressiveness of their figures.

An innovative group of painters brought the art of ***fresco painting***, always important in Italy, to a new height. **Giotto**'s (1267–1337) cycle of the lives of Mary and Christ in the Arena Chapel, Padua (*c.* 1300) set a new standard for figural naturalism, seen as proto-Renaissance, and in the Town Hall of Siena Ambrogio **Lorenzetti** (*c.* 1306–1345) illustrated the effects of *Good and Bad Government* (1337) in panoramic townscapes and landscapes.

Panel painting, in jewel-like colours on a gold background, developed from Byzantine models, and the Sienese painter **Duccio**'s (*c.* 1255/60–*c.* 1318) *Maestá* for the High Altar of Siena Cathedral (1308–11) achieved a peak of expressive power of line and colour. Simone **Martini** (*c.* 1284–1344) developed this into courtly refinement in both frescoes (for example Assisi, Siena) and panel paintings, and became a major influence on the ***International Gothic*** style which in the years around 1400 achieved the perfect mix of French courtliness and the Italian command of form, together with a delight in the observed details of nature. A magnificent example of this moment in art can be seen in the miniatures painted for the devotional book, the *Très Riches Heures du Duc de Berry*, by the Flemish **Limbourg** brothers in about 1415.

THE ITALIAN RENAISSANCE

Florence the rebirth or 'Renaissance' of Classical art and learning began in Florence in the early 15th century. The self-made men of Florence, merchants and bankers, saw themselves as direct descendants of the great men of ancient Rome and, led by the Medici family, vied with each other in patronage of all the arts, building palaces and churches filled with sculptured and painted monuments to themselves. In this new age of humanism, people – and the aesthetic delights of the world they lived in – were suddenly important.

The most far-reaching artistic innovation of the period, which was one of continual discovery and rediscovery, was that of scientific ***perspective*** by Filippo **Brunelleschi** (1377–1446), the architect who later built the dome of Florence Cathedral. Perspective allowed artists to create an authentic three-dimensional space, correctly sized to the figures within their paintings. **Masaccio** (1401–28) used this new style to superb effect in his frescoes in the Brancacci Chapel, Santa Maria del Carmine, in which the apostles look like Roman gods. The sculptor **Donatello** (*c.* 1386–1466) used perspective in his relief sculptures. His bronze statues, like the youthful *David* (1430–2), the first free-standing nude since antiquity, or his equestrian statue of the mercenary General Gattamelata (1443, Padua) look back to Classical prototypes but have the alert liveliness of all early Renaissance art. In his later work, such as his wood-carving of the aged Mary Magdalene (1445), he sought dramatic expression through distortion, even ugliness. His only real rival was the goldsmith and bronze sculptor Lorenzo **Ghiberti** (1378–1455), who only gradually adapted his graceful **International Gothic** style to Renaissance ideals in such works as the gilt-bronze Baptistery doors which Michelangelo called 'The Gates of Paradise'.

Paolo **Uccello**'s (1397–1475) decorative paintings reflect an obsessive interest in mathematical perspective. **Fra Angelico** (*c.* 1400–55) used delicate colours and a simple style to express his religious feeling. Andrea del **Castagno**'s (c. 1421–1457) style was fiercely linear. The antithesis of his violent suffering figures are Piero **della Francesca**'s (*c.* 1420–1492) strangely silent ones. Solidly rounded in pale light, immobile within perfect perspective spaces, they express an enigmatic timelessness. His mastery of geometry, proportion, form, and colour is breathtakingly evident in his frescoes of *The Legend of the True Cross* in San Francesco in Arezzo (1452–66).

Many sculptors produced public statues, grandiose tombs, Roman-style portrait busts and innumerable versions of the Madonna and Child. The Florentines enjoyed seeing themselves in religious paintings and they appear in crowd scenes in many magnificent frescoes in the churches of their city, such as those by Domenico del **Ghirlandaio** (c. 1449–1494). He was the most popular painter in Florence in the latter part of the 15th century, respected for his honesty, which is epitomized in his portrait of *An Old Man with a Child* (*c.* 1480) in the Louvre. His contemporaries included Antonio **Pollaiuolo** (c. 1432–1498), whose interest centres on the nude in action; Andrea del **Verrocchio** (1435–1488), famous for the equestrian statue of Bartolomeo Colleoni in Venice (1481–96); and **Botticelli** (1445–1510), whose poetic, gracefully linear paintings of Madonnas and mythological subjects such as *The Birth of Venus* (1482) show the Florentine ideal of female beauty. Almost every art work produced included some reference to antiquity, either in form or content.

Leonardo da Vinci 1452–1519. Through his genius, the art of the early 16th century became the ***High Renaissance***, attaining a grandeur that appealed particularly to the popes, who now became the leading art patrons in their attempt to build the 'New Rome'. Leonardo's enquiring scientific mind led him to investigate every aspect of the natural world from anatomy to aerodynamics. His notebooks and drawings remain his finest legacy, but his experiments also revolutionized painting style. Instead of a white background, he used a dark one to allow the overlying colour a more three-dimensional existence. He invented 'aerial perspective' whereby the misty atmosphere (*sfumato*) blurs and changes the colours of the landscape as it dissolves into the distance. His principle of grouping figures within an imaginary pyramid, linked by their gestures and emotions, became a High Renaissance compositional rule. His *Madonna of the Rocks* (Louvre) exemplifies all these ideas.

Michelangelo Buonarroti 1475–1564. His giant talent dominated the High Renaissance and led his contemporaries to label him 'Divine'. No other artist could escape his influence. He said of his stone carvings, such as the monumental *David* in Florence (1501–4), that he was simply revealing the figure hidden within the block. His massive figure style was translated into paint in the *Sistine Chapel frescoes* (Vatican, Rome) covering the ceiling with human figures, mostly nude, all grandly Classical, telling the Old Testament story from Genesis to the Deluge (1508–11) and finishing on the altar wall with a titanic *Last Judgement* (1541).

Raphael (Raffaello Sanzio) 1483–1520. He quickly mastered the innovations of Leonardo and Michelangelo and in 1509 was commissioned to fresco the *Stanza della Segnature* in the Vatican, where his classicist *School of Athens* is his masterpiece. Immensely prolific and popular, he combined both delicacy and grandeur in his work.

Mannerism Giulio **Romano** (c. 1499–1546), Raphael's principal follower, exaggerated his style into an individual one of his own, heralding the next major art movement, Mannerism. This flouted the 'rules' of Renaissance order and harmony by striving for idiosyncratic, sometimes alarming, effects. The Florentine Andrea **del Sarto** (1486–1531) and his assistants **Pontormo** (1494–1556) and **Rosso** Fiorentino (1494–1540) each pursued self-consciously mannered styles, as did Giorgio **Vasari** (1511–1574), who is chiefly remembered for his book *The Lives of the Most Excellent Architects, Painters and Sculptors* (1550), in which he coined the term 'Mannerist' and laid down the chronology of the history of art which is still in use today. Mannerism appealed particularly to courtly patrons and it became increasingly effete. The Medici, now grand dukes, employed such artists as the sculptor Benvenuto **Cellini** (1500–71), as famous for his racy autobiography as for the gilt salt cellar he made for the King of France; Agnolo **Bronzino** (1503–1572), whose patrician portraits display a stony hauteur; and Giovanni da **Bologna** (Giambologna) (1529–1608), whose elegant small bronze statuettes were widely reproduced.

Venice the Venetian Renaissance was slow in coming because of the city's traditional links with the East. Two non-Venetians were influential: Antonello **da Messina** (*c.* 1430–79), who in 1475 brought to Venice the new Flemish technique of oil painting, and Andrea **Mantegna** (*c.* 1431–1506), an archaeologically-minded painter whose figures looked like antique sculptures. Giovanni **Bellini** (*c.* 1430–1516) specialized in devotional pictures of the Madonna, but his sensitive appreciation of light and colour introduced that element of sensuality to Venetian talent which later made **Titian** (Tiziano Vecellio) (1487–1576) the preferred painter of Emperor Charles V and his son Philip II of Spain. His fellow-painter **Giorgione** (*c.* 1478–1510) died young, leaving only a few securely attributed works, but who nevertheless made an innovative mark with his small, intimate, easel paintings and a new treatment of figures in a landscape. **Veronese** (*c.* 1528–88) and Jacopo **Tintoretto** (1518–94) worked on a much larger scale, Veronese excelling in sumptuous *trompe l'oeil* interior decorations and Tintoretto in dramatic religious paintings, spectacularly lit and composed with daring foreshortening. His paintings for the Venetian Scuola di San Rocco (1566–88) foreshadow, in their exciting exuberance, the next major movement, the **Baroque**.

THE 15TH AND 16TH CENTURIES

Northern European artists took their inspiration from Gothic sources, but shared with the Italians an insatiable interest in realistic portrayals of themselves and their world.

Netherlands one of the first examples of the new ***humanism*** was the work of Claus **Sluter** (*c.* 1380–1406). His mourning figures on the tomb of Philip the Bold, Duke of Burgundy, their faces hidden by the hoods of their robes, are poignantly mute but solidly real people.

In Flanders where the patrons were wealthy merchants, Robert **Campin** (1378–1444) put his *Madonna and Child before a Firescreen* (1420–30, National Gallery, London) into an ordinary living room and through its open window showed a Flemish town. Mary's halo is replaced by the circular firescreen behind her, an example of disguised symbolism, making the supernatural seem real.

Among Campin's followers, all marvellous draughtsmen, was Jan **van Eyck** (d.1441) whose strength lay in his detailed analysis of the beauty of the world around him. His innovative recipe for oil painting makes his colours glow like precious jewels. In his *Arnolfini Wedding* (1434, National Gallery, London) the bride and groom appear in a domestic interior crammed with disguised symbols, in a kind of pictorial marriage certificate. Flemish realism reached Italy with the Portinari Altarpiece, an *Adoration of the Shepherds* by Hugo **van der Goes** (d. 1481). Commissioned by the Medici agent in Bruges, it was sent to Florence where it had a considerable effect on Italian artists. The quietly contemplative portraits of Hans **Memlinc** (d. 1481) sum up the achievement of 15th- century Netherlands painters.

Individual styles proliferated in the 16th century. Hieronymous **Bosch** (*c.* 1450–1516) painted nightmarish scenes filled with diminutive human figures caught in a surrealist demonic world. Pieter **Brueghel** the Elder (1525/30–69) treated biblical subjects as contemporary events, viewing with compassion a miserable humanity. In his paintings of the seasons (1565) he brilliantly evokes both winter's icy silence and the golden warmth of summer.

Germany the giant among German artists was Albrecht **Dürer** (1471–1528). His intellectual powers put him in line with the great Italian masters and their influence introduced a new solidity of form into his basically Gothic style. Particularly important as a graphic artist, he was widely influential through woodcuts and engravings. Mathias **Grünewald** (*c.* 1460–1528), a tragic visionary, used colour symbolically in the *Isenheim Altar* (1512–15, Colmar), painted for hospital patients to see the crucified Christ, covered with festering wounds, sharing their suffering. Lucas **Cranach** the Elder (1473–1538) painted self-conscious courtly nudes, and Albrecht **Altdorfer** (*c.*1489–1538) painted landscapes in which tiny human figures are dwarfed by nature's immensity.

Spain Philip II did not care for the work of **El Greco** (1541–1614), the painter who really established Spain as an artistic centre. Trained in Venice, and particularly influenced by Tintoretto, he developed his hallucinatory style in Toledo, where his patrons were ecclesiastics and the intelligentsia. In his *Burial of Count Orgaz* (1586) the flame-like figures and unearthly colours blend mystic vision and reality.

England Renaissance ideas arrived with the German Hans Holbein the Younger (1497–1543), who was by 1536 court painter to Henry VIII. His piercing portraits of the king and his wives, and his delicate portrait drawings, give a superb pictorial record of the Tudor court. The court of Elizabeth I comes to life for us through the art of the miniature. Nicholas **Hilliard** (*c.* 1547–1619) developed an unparalleled technique, delicate, refined and often lyrically poetic as in his *Young Man amid Roses* (*c.* 1590, Victoria and Albert Museum, London).

France Jean **Fouquet** (*c.* 1420–81) painted miniatures as well as altarpieces in which Italian influences take tangible shape. Jean **Clouet** (d. 1541) and his son François (d. 1572) were court painters to King Francis I. Jean's portrait of the king splendidly expresses the king's concern with elegance and decoration, and François' half-nude portrait of Diane de Poitiers, *The Lady in Her Bath*, is a piece of refined eroticism. His style reflects Italian Mannerist ideas as developed by the so-called ***School of Fontainebleau*** founded by Rosso and **Primaticcio** (1504/5–1570) who came to decorate the royal hunting lodge in the 1530s. They devised a unique type of stucco decoration combining figures in high relief with decorative swags, cartouches and strapwork. These Mannerist motifs were copied all over northern Europe, where they were called 'Renaissance'.

THE 17TH CENTURY

Italy in Rome, the Counter-Reformation of the Catholic church against Protestantism launched an exciting, emotionally appealing new style, the ***Baroque***. The sculptor and architect Gianlorenzo **Bernini** (1598–1680) was its principal exponent, revitalizing Rome with his exuberantly dramatic masterpieces. His *Ecstasy of St Teresa* at Santa Maria della Vittoria is a theatrical set-piece in which supernatural light pours from a hidden window to illuminate the rapturous saint, whose body seems to shudder as an angel prepares to pierce her heart with the arrow of divine love.

Large-scale illusionistic fresco painting transformed ceilings into heavens, thronged with flying saints and angels. A spectacular example is Pietro **da Cortona**'s colossal *Allegory of Divine Providence* (1629–37) in the Barberini Palace, glorifying the pope and his family. Hundreds of figures are drawn upwards toward God's golden light, aswarm with bees, the Barberini family emblem.

Balancing this flamboyant artistic stream were the ***Classicists***, who even in religious commissions looked back to the concepts of harmony and order of antiquity. Annibale **Carracci** (1560–1609) in the years around 1600 decorated Cardinal Farnese's gallery of antique sculpture in the Farnese Palace, turning the walls and ceiling into a *trompe l'oeil* classical picture gallery. He also introduced the landscape as a new category of art with his *Flight into Egypt* (1603), which has as its real subject an idealized vision of the classical Roman countryside, harmonious and calm.

Among Carracci's assistants who became famous in their own right were the consistently classicizing **Domenichino** (1581–1641) and Guido **Reni** (1575–1642) who often succumbed to popular taste with emotive paintings of repentant sinners rolling tearful eyes toward heaven. The work of Michelangelo Merisi da **Caravaggio** (1573–1619) introduced something totally different and unique, a harsh realism in which ordinary folk with dirty feet appear as saints and apostles, lit by a raking spotlight as if God's piercing eye had picked them out from the surrounding blackness of sin. One of his most striking followers was Georges **de la Tour** (1593–1652), a French artist whose simplified figures assume a spiritual purity, modelled by God's light in the form of a single candle shining in the darkness.

France art was used to establish the splendour of Louis XIV's centralized authority and divine kingship. Although grandiose in the extreme, the decorative schemes, portraits, and history paintings produced by the members of the new artists' Academy (formed 1648) were based on Classical rules, rigidly controlled by Charles **Lebrun** (1619–90), who was appointed First Painter to the King in 1662. He was the first Director of the Academy and of the Gobelins Manufactory, which employed its members to produce the art, tapestries, and furnishings for Louis's new Palace of Versailles.

The two major French artists of the century lived in Rome, escaping the constricting grip of the Academy. Claude **Lorrain** (1600–82) was the first painter to specialize entirely in landscapes, reducing the storytelling elements to small foreground figures. The romantic suggestiveness of the Classical past appealed to him, and he created an enchanting idyllic world, luminous and poetic. The intellectual Nicolas **Poussin** (1594–1665) composed his classical landscapes with mathematical precision but his people remained important, noble and heroic. Not even his religious works escape the pervasive influence of antiquity. In his *Last Supper* (1647, Edinburgh), Christ and the disciples lounge on couches as if at a Roman banquet.

Spain as in Rome, art in Spain aimed to excite Counter-Reformation zeal. José **Ribera** (1591–1652) carried a Caravaggesque style to brutal extremes to shock people into identifying with the sufferings inherent in Christian history. Francisco **Zurbarán** (1598–1664) expressed religious feeling in the opposite way, with solemn, silent monks and saints lost in a private world of meditation. Bartolomé Estebán **Murillo** (1617–82) painted sentimental *Holy Families* and sugar-sweet *Madonnas* fluently, cheerfully, and with a feather-light touch and lovely colours.

Diego Rodriguez de Silva **Velázquez** (1599–1660) was the giant of Spanish painting, reflecting many aspects of the 17th-century Spanish world. By 1623 he was court painter to Philip IV in Madrid, where he was influenced by Philip's collection of 16th century Venetian paintings. The most fascinating of his life-like portraits of the Spanish court is *Las Meninas/The Ladies-in-Waiting* (1655, Prado, Madrid), a complex group portrait which includes Velázquez himself at his easel, and the king and queen as pale reflections in a mirror.

Netherlands Peter Paul **Rubens** (1577–1640) brought the sensual exuberance of the Italian Baroque to the Netherlands. A many-sided genius, artist, scholar and diplomat, he used his powerful pictorial imagination to create, with an army of assistants, innumerable religious and allegorical paintings for the churches and palaces of Catholic Europe. His largest commission was the cycle of 21 enormous canvases allegorizing the life of Marie de Medici, Queen of France (Louvre, Paris). His sheer delight in life can be seen in his magnificent colours, opulent nudes, and expansive landscapes.

Rubens's Grand Baroque style did not suit the Protestant merchants of the new Dutch Republic, who wanted small paintings reflecting their own lives and interests. Among the artists who responded to this demand, the towering genius was **Rembrandt** van Rijn (1606–69), all of whose paintings hint at some inner drama. In his portraits and biblical scenes he saw light as a spiritual mystery which momentarily allows his characters to loom out of the surrounding shadows. His self-portraits (nearly 100 in number) touchingly trace the drama of his own passage through life and even the large group portrait, *The Night Watch* (1642) becomes a suspense story. A master draughtsman and printmaker, over 1,000 drawings survive.

The greatest of the straightforward portraitists was Frans **Hals** (*c.* 1581–1666), whose free brushstrokes caught fleeting moments brilliantly in such paintings as the so-called *Laughing Cavalier* (1624, Wallace Collection, London).

Genre pictures, scenes of daily life, merrymakers and peasants – often uncouth, comic, or satirical – were the speciality of such painters as Jan **Steen** (1626–79), in whose anecdotal scenes of traditional festivals or slovenly households the pleasures of drink, gluttony, and wantonness hold sway.

During the 1650s genre painters took a different view of their society. Instead of depicting boisterous low-life, painters like Pieter de **Hooch** (1629–84) chose scenes of domestic virtue, well-ordered households where families live in harmony in quiet sunlit rooms. Jan **Vermeer** (1632–75) was the greatest master of these scenes of peaceful prosperity, arranging domestic interiors as if they were abstract forms and enclosing his characters within an enamelled world of pearly light. *A Young Woman Standing at a Virginal* (*c.* 1670, National Gallery, London) is a superb example of the small group of paintings he produced, each one a masterpiece.

The Dutch specialities of seascape and landscape made giant strides during the century, based on low horizons with emphasis on a great expanse of sky. Experts in this were Aelbert **Cuyp** (1620–91) who bathed his views in a golden light, and Jacob van **Ruisdael** (1638/9–1709), who painted in many moods, responding to the shifting patterns of light and shade in nature.

Still-life painting also burgeoned: fruit, flowers, fish, banquets, breakfasts, groaning boards of every kind, in which the artist displayed skill in painting inanimate objects, often with a hidden religious significance.

England Charles I had employed Rubens to paint the ceiling of the Banqueting House at Whitehall 1629–30. Rubens's assistant Anthony **van Dyck** (1599–1641) became Court Painter in 1632 and created magnificent portraits of the aristocracy, cool and elegant in shimmering silks. The German Peter **Lely** (1618–80) succeeded him under the Restoration to depict a society that exudes an air of well-fed decadence. By contrast, the English-born Samuel **Cooper** (1609–72), painter to the Parliamentarians and most famous for his portraits of Oliver Cromwell ('warts and all'), was a miniaturist whose serious, objective portraits raised the status of his art to that of oil painting.

THE 18TH CENTURY

France the beginning of the 18th century saw the start of a frivolous new style in art, the ***Rococo***. Jean-Antoine **Watteau** (1684–1721) devised for his aristocratic patrons the *Fête Gallante*, a type of painting in which amorous couples in poetic landscapes contemplate the transience of life and love.

The more overtly sensual work of François **Boucher** (1703–70), First Painter to Louis XV, included voluptuous scenes of naked gods and goddesses. Painting at the same time, but completely against the mainstream, was Jean-Baptiste-Siméon **Chardin** (1699–1779), whose still-lifes and genre scenes have a masterful dignity. Jean-Honoré **Fragonard** (1732–1806) continued with the Rococo theme under Louis XVI, light-heartedly reflecting the licentiousness of courtly life. But all this changed with the Revolution and in 1789 Neo-Classicism became the dominant style under the Republic. Its artistic dictator, Jacques-Louis **David** (1748–1825) in his *Death of Marat* (1793) turned a political murder into a classical tragedy. Later, under Napoleon's Empire, David painted heroic portraits and scenes celebrating its glory.

Italy Antonio **Canova** (1757–1822), the sculptor, also exalted Napoleon and his family in classicizing portraits, and the vogue for this style dominated most English and European sculpture right through the Victorian era. Rococo illusionistic fresco-painting in Italy was the special province of Giovanni-Battista **Tiepolo** (1696–1770), a Venetian who decorated palaces and churches there and elsewhere in Europe. His painted ceilings became vast, airy regions whose delicate colour shadings made the sky seem endless.

The *vedutisti* (view-painters) produced souvenir views for young English gentlemen making the Grand Tour to complete their education with first-hand viewing of Renaissance and Classical art. In Venice, Francesco **Guardi** (1712–93) painted atmospheric visions of the floating city, pulsating with life. The views of (Giovanni) Antonio **Canaletto** (1697–1768), though faithfully observed, are static in comparison.

In Rome, Giovanni Battista **Piranesi** (1720–78) produced etchings inspired by his feelings for the evocative quality of ruins. His most original work, however, was a series which turned the ruins into images of terrifying imaginary prisons, fantasies of architectural madness.

Spain produced one artist of enormous talent and versatility, Francisco de **Goya** y Lucientes (1746–1828), whose work expresses a wide range of feeling and emotion and explores a variety of themes. Court Painter to Charles IV and later to Joseph Bonaparte under the French occupation of Spain, his portraits were acutely perceptive, his war scenes savagely dramatic, his religious paintings believable and his strange late fantasies powerfully imaginative. He is often seen as the source of 20th century art.

England produced a memorable group of fine artists, each expressing the varied interests of the age. Joseph **Wright** of Derby (1734–97), scientifically-minded, painted such scenes as *Experiment with an Air Pump* (1768). George **Stubbs** (1724–1806) specialized in horse paintings, based on painstaking scientific investigation. Sir Joshua **Reynolds** (1723–92), first President of the Royal Academy (founded 1768), wanted to introduce the European Grand Manner into English painting with history paintings on exalted themes of heroism, but the demand was for portraits; his were confident but lacking in spontaneity, based more on theory than on inspiration.

Thomas **Gainsborough** (1727–88) was also a popular portraitist, although he would have preferred to paint landscapes and made much of them in the backgrounds of his pictures. William **Hogarth** (1697–1764) is best known through engravings of his satirical series of paintings, such as *The Rake's Progress* (1735).

Reacting against the academic theorizing of Reynolds, the poet William **Blake** (1757–1827) illustrated his writings with mystical visions, and the imaginative Henry **Fuseli** (1741–1825) plumbed the depths of his subconscious for grotesque and fantastic dream images in such paintings as *The Nightmare* (1782).

THE 19TH CENTURY

France vast historical, religious, and mythological pictures were no longer greatly in demand, and after the fall of Napoleon in 1814 French artists trained in the Academic Grand Manner had to seek new dramatic themes. They looked to the world around them; Theodore **Géricault** (1791–1824) found his subject in the gruesome sufferings of the survivors of a recent shipwreck, which he portrayed in his huge *Raft of the Medusa* (1816, Louvre, Paris). His desire to express and evoke emotion put Géricault among the ***Romantics***, whose art sought to speak passionately to the heart in contrast to the ***Classicists*** who appealed to the intellect. These two opposing approaches dominated much of the art of the century.

Eugène **Delacroix** (1798–1863) became the best-known Romantic painter. His *Massacre of Chios* (1824, Louvre) shows Greeks enslaved by wild Turkish horsemen, a contemporary atrocity. Admired as a colourist, he used a technique of divided brushwork – adjacent brush marks of contrasting colour which the eye mixes as it scans – that anticipates the Impressionists. He learned this from seeing Constable's *Hay Wain*, when it was exhibited in Paris in 1824.

By contrast, the brushwork is invisible in the enamelled paintings of Jean-Auguste-Dominique **Ingres** (1780–1867), the leading exponent of French Neo-Classicism. Drawing was the foundation of his style, emphasizing line and control at the expense of colour and expression.

Gustave **Courbet** (1819–77), reacting against both Classicists and Romantics, set out to establish a new ***Realism***, based solely on direct observation of the things around him. His *Burial at Ornans* (1850) showed ordinary working people gathered round a village grave, and shocked the Establishment art world with its 'vulgarity' and 'coarseness'. Another Realist was Honoré **Daumier** (1808–79) whose lithographs of the 1830s dissected Parisian society with a surgeon's scalpel.

Throughout Europe, 19th-century artists found their ideal subject matter in the landscape. In France, Jean-Baptiste-Camille **Corot** (1796–1875) made it acceptable by recomposing his open-air studies into a harmonious, classical whole, although a romantic mood pervades his later misty confections. Theodore **Rousseau** (1812–67) led a group of artists who in 1844 sought refuge from the Industrial Revolution in the woods of Barbizon, near Paris. Their close observation of nature produced a new awareness of its changing moods. Jean-François **Millet** (1814–75) also settled at Barbizon but his romantic landscapes, such as *The Angelus* (1857–9, Louvre), introduce idealized peasants who manage to commune with nature while toiling to wrest from it their daily bread.

Germany a different, more melancholy Romantic sensibility invaded the landscapes of a small group of painters working in Germany. Seeking to express the mystery of God in nature and people's oneness with it, the evocative paintings of Caspar David **Friedrich** (1774–1840) usually include a small poetic figure contemplating distant mountain peaks or moonlit seashores.

England the two greatest artists of the century were landscapists – Joseph Mallord William **Turner** (1775–1851) and John **Constable** (1776–1837), both finding inspiration in the thriving English watercolour school. Turner was the master painter of English Romanticism.

Not concerned with the human figure, it was always through nature itself that he could express human feeling, as in the poignant last voyage of the ship *The Fighting Temeraire* (1839, Tate Gallery, London). His increasing obsession with light and its deep emotional significance turned his late pictures into misty abstract visions. Reputedly his dying words were 'The sun is God'.

Constable too was fascinated with the effects of light. He made innumerable painted sketches of the changing windy sky and in his *Hay Wain* used white marks like snowflakes to express the way light gave the landscape its freshness and sparkle.

Although primarily interested in romantic literary or biblical themes, the ***Pre-Raphaelites*** led by Dante Gabriel **Rossetti** (1828–82) in the 1840s and 50s took a detailed look at nature, in their claim to a realistic vision; from this influence the medievalist designer-artist William **Morris** (1834–96) developed his stylized patterns of leaves and flowers for fabrics and wallpapers.

The opposition to the Pre-Raphaelites was led by two Establishment artists, Frederic, Lord **Leighton** (1830–96) and Sir Lawrence **Alma-Tadema** (1836–1912), whose equally romantic view pretended to Classicism by centring on pseudo-genre scenes of daily life in ancient Greece and Rome. This pleased their educated patrons enough to earn knighthoods for them both.

Impressionism in the second half of the century France took an innovative look at nature. A direct precursor was Edouard **Manet** (1832–83), who carried on Courbet's scientific spirit of realism, making the eye the sole judge of reality. Stylistically, he gave up modelling forms in volume in favour of *suggesting* them by juxtaposed colours and gradations of tones, and, like Courbet, the subject matter of his pictures was always modern life. His *Déjeuner sur l'herbe/Luncheon on the Grass* (Louvre) updated a Renaissance prototype to 1862.

The Impressionists delighted in painting real life but the scenes and objects they painted became increasingly less important than the way they were affected by the ever-changing play of light. Evolving in the 1860s, the Impressionist group painted out of doors, capturing the immediacy and freshness of light on rippling water or on moving leaves. To catch these fleeting moments they broke up the forms they painted into fragments of pure colour laid side by side directly on the canvas, rather than mixing them on a palette. The members of the group were Alfred **Sisley** (1839–99), Camille **Pissarro** (1831–1903), Claude **Monet** (1840–1926) whose *Impression, Sunrise* of 1872 (Musée Marmottan, Paris) gave the movement its name, Pierre-Auguste **Renoir** (1841–1919), and Edgar **Degas** (1834–1917).

By the late 1870s they had each gone on to pursue individual interests, and the acceptance of a common purpose had had its day. Sisley and Pissarro continued painting landscapes, but Renoir became more interested in the female nude and Degas in 'snapshot' studies of dancers and jockeys. Degas hardly ever painted landscapes but instead concentrated on the spectacle of the racetrack and the ballet in oddly angled compositions influenced by snapshot photography. Monet remained obsessed with the optical effects of light on colour and carried his original fragmented technique to the final extreme in series of paintings such as those of the façade of Rouen Cathedral (1894) or his famous water lilies, showing the changing colour effects at different times of day. With these variations on a theme the actual subject did not matter at all, and in this he anticipated the abstract art of the 20th century.

Post-Impressionism other artists of the same generation who used the innovations of the Impressionists as a basis for developing their own styles are

A controversial sale

In Feb 1993 the University of London's Royal Holloway College sold a painting by Turner to a foreign buyer, raising ethical concerns as well as badly needed funds. The painting, *Van Tromp, going about to please his masters, ships at sea, a good meeting,* 1844, was sold to the John Paul Getty Museum in California for £11 million, the highest amount ever paid for a work by an English artist. The sale of the work will be used to establish an endowment fund for the maintenence and refurbishment of the college, and for the security of its collection.

Controversy had surrounded the sale since the college first announced its intentions, which were in contravention of the wishes of the donor, philanthropist Thomas Holloway (1800–83), who founded the college and gave it an art collection. However, outrage over the breaking of the trust of a donor, and the anger expressed by the art world over the move, did not prevent the Charity Commissioners from allowing the sale to go ahead. Nor did appeals to the attorney general and the parliamentary ombudsman succeed in halting it.

A senior academic resigned from the college's governing body in protest at the sale. Geoffrey Alderman, professor of politics and contemporary history, said the loss of the painting would do untold damage to the institution and he was particularly irritated with the Charity Commission for allowing the college to sell part of a collection whose 'inalienability had been confirmed in several Acts of Parliament,' one as recently as 1985.

The outcome of the controversial sale provoked fears in the art world that it had paved the way for other cash-starved universities to raise funds by selling art. There are an estimated 400 university collections throughout Britain, including multi-million pound collections as fine as the Ashmolean in Oxford, Fitzwilliam in Cambridge, and Hunterian in Glasgow. The Royal Holloway is not the first to sell works – precedents include the highly protested 1985 sale by Newcastle of the George Brown collection of 3,000 items to the National Museum of Ethnology in Osaka, Japan.

The Royal Holloway College has claimed that financial concerns left it with no other choice, and that it will continue to sell; it is now inviting offers for its Gainsborough.

Ten highest prices ever paid for works of art at auction

Artist	*Title of work*	*Auction house/date of sale*	*Auction price ($m)*
Van Gogh	*Portrait of Dr Gachet*	Christie's, May 1990	82.5
Renoir	*Au Moulin de la Galette*	Sotheby's, May 1990	78.1
Van Gogh	*Irises*	Sotheby's, Nov 1987	53.9
Picasso	*Les Noces de Pierette*	Binoche et Godeau, Nov 1989	51.9
Picasso	*Self portrait – Yo Picasso*	Sotheby's, May 1989	47.8
Picasso	*Au Lapine Agile*	Sotheby's, Nov 1989	40.7
Van Gogh	*Sunflowers*	Christie's, Mar 1987	40.3
Picasso	*Acrobate et Jeune Arlequin*	Christie's, May 1989	38.9
Pontormo	*Portrait of Duke Cosimo I de Medici*	Christie's, Nov 1988	35.2
Cézanne	*Nature Morte – Les Grosses Pommes*	Sotheby's May 1993	28.6

Source: Christie's/Sotheby's

called the Post-Impressionists. They include Paul **Cézanne** (1839–1906), who infused something more permanent into their spontaneous vision by using geometrical shapes to form a solid scaffolding for his pictorial compositions; and Georges **Seurat** (1859–91), who achieved greater structure in his landscapes through the technique of ***pointillism*** (also known as Neo-Impressionism) which turns the Impressionist's separate brush-strokes into minute points of pure colour. The eye then mixes these for itself. Green grass, for instance, is made up of closely packed points of blue and yellow. In this painstaking method any idea of spontaneity vanishes, and the effect is stable and serene.

Henri de **Toulouse-Lautrec** (1864–1901) portrayed the low-life of Parisian bars and music halls without sentiment or judgement. Like Degas, he recorded contemporary life in informal poses from odd angles and his bold, colourful posters show the influence of Japanese colour prints.

The great Dutch individualist Vincent **van Gogh** (1853–90) longed to give visible form to every emotion and used violent rhythmic brushwork and brilliant unnatural colours to express his inner passions, even in something as simple as a pot of sunflowers. Paul **Gauguin** (1848–1903) also went beyond the Impressionists' notion of reality, seeking a more direct experience of life in the magical rites of so-called primitive peoples in his colourful works from the South Seas.

Symbolism was a movement initiated by poets as a reaction to materialist values, and their 1886 Manifesto sought to re-establish the imagination in art. Their most admired painter was Gustave **Moreau** (1826–98) whose paintings of biblical and mythological subjects contain psychological overtones expressed through exotic settings, strange colours and eerie light. Odilon **Redon** (1840–1916) translated dreams into bizarre and striking visual images. In the paintings of the Norwegian Edvard **Munch** (1863–1944), a particularly northern sense of fear and alienation is given extreme expression in such painings as *The Scream* (1893).

The Nabis (from Hebrew 'prophet') were followers of Gauguin who used simple forms and flat colours as he did for emotional effect, in a new style called *synthetisme*. Among the Nabis, Pierre **Bonnard** (1867–1947) and Edouard **Vuillard** (1868–1940) were less concerned with mystical ideas and found that with contemporary domestic interiors they could develop their interest in sumptuously coloured and patterned surfaces. Their work was dubbed *intimisme*.

sculpture the work of the Parisian Auguste **Rodin** (1840–1917) shows an extraordinary technical facility and a deep understanding of the human form. A romantic realist who infused his forms with passion, such famous sculptures as *The Thinker* and *The Kiss* were originally designed for a never-completed giant set of bronze doors, *The Gates of Hell*, with themes taken from Dante's *Divine Comedy*. The Musée Rodin in Paris houses many examples of his work and their preparatory drawings.

THE 20TH CENTURY

The 20th century has been an age of experimentation, with the boundaries of art being continually stretched by a succession of avant-garde movements. The anti-naturalism of the Symbolists and the Post-Impressionists, which attempted to reveal the essential reality behind the mere appearance of things, was continued in the first decade by Picasso, Matisse, and other artists before finally developing into complete abstraction.

Fauvism, a short-lived movement, began in France around 1905 and ended just three years later. The painters were nicknamed *Les Fauves* ('wild beasts') because of the extreme brilliance of the colours, which were often applied in jarring combinations to heighten the emotional impact. Henri **Matisse**

Impressive prices

Overall performance at auction of the five major impressionists (Oct 1970–July 1992)

Artist	*Number of works recorded*	*Total turnover (£ m)*	*Highest price (£ m)*	*Overall average price (£)*
Cezanne	324	92.9	10.0	286,700
Degas	988	147.5	6.8	145,300
Manet	120	63.9	15.5	532,400
Monet	546	344.2	13.0	612,100
Renoir	1,833	392.8	42.0	208,600

Source: Art Sales Index

(1869–1954), the major figure of the movement, spent his life refining this expressive use of pure colour partially influenced by the pattern-making of North African decorative art. André **Derain** (1880–1954) at this time enlarged the brushstrokes of Neo-Impressionism to produce a vibrant mosaic of colour, whereas Maurice **de Vlaminck** (1876–1958) was more influenced by the violent intensity of van Gogh. Georges **Rouault** (1871–1958), though associated with the group, employed more sombre colours enclosed by thick dark outlines reminiscent of stained glass.

Cubism was invented by Pablo **Picasso** (1881–1973) and the former Fauvist Georges **Braque** (1882–1963). By fragmenting the objects they depicted, then reconstructing them as a series of almost geometric facets that overlap and interlock with each other, they attempted to explode the harmonious and unified perspective of the Renaissance. In its place is an image of multiple viewpoints seen simultaneously. Initially the work grew out of Picasso's fascination with African sculpture as in his *Les Demoiselles d'Avignon* (1907, MOMA, New York). The influence of Cézanne can also be found in the simplification of forms and the ambiguity of the picture space. Emotion and narrative were avoided, colours were muted, and anti-illusionistic devices such as stencilled writing and collage were introduced. The two artists worked closely together from 1907 to 1914 but neither believed in theorizing about their work. This was done by later followers Juan Gris, Albert Gleizes, Jean Metzinger, Fernand Léger, and Robert **Delaunay** (1885–1941), the last named forming his own, more sensual and poetic variant of Cubism known as ***Orphism***.

Futurism The Italian poet Filippo **Marinetti** (1876–1944) published the *Futurist Manifesto* in 1909, which demanded a new art to celebrate the age of the machine. He called for the destruction of the museums and eulogized the modern world and the 'beauty of speed and energy'. The most talented of the artists inspired by his ideas was the painter and sculptor Umberto **Boccioni** (1882–1916), who wrote his own *Technical Manifesto of Painting* the following year. But it was not until a trip to Paris and contact with Cubism that the Futurist artists managed to create a sufficiently dynamic style to match their rhetoric. Giacomo **Balla** (1871–1958) produced the painting *Dog on a Leash* which attempted to convey sequential movement in the manner of the photographers Muybridge and Marey. Gino **Severini** (1883–1966) painted a topsy-turvy landscape as if seen from the moving window of a *Suburban Train Arriving at Paris* (1915, Tate Gallery, London). Boccioni's sculpture *Unique Forms of Continuity in Space* (1913, Tate Gallery) shows the dynamic interaction between a striding figure and its surrounding space.

Expressionism Germany was the scene of two successive Expressionist groups. In 1905 a group of artists in Dresden, with obvious parallels to the Fauves, founded *Die Brücke* ('the bridge'). Led by Ernst Ludwig **Kirchner** (1880–1938), they sought to express their 'inner convictions ... with spontaneity and sincerity'. This raw subjectivity is best seen in Kirchner's vivid scenes of the Berlin streets and in the prints of Karl **Schmidt-Rotluff** (1884–1976). The woodcut was a favourite medium of the group because of its primitive simplicity. In Munich *Der Blaue Reiter* ('the blue rider') group was set up in 1911 by Wassily **Kandinsky** (1866–1944). Influenced by the spiritual ideas of the Theosophists, Kandinsky believed that precise emotional and spiritual ideas could be conveyed by form and colour. He evolved a highly subjective style which finally became purely abstract. His colleague Franc **Marc** (1880–1916), partially inspired by Orphism, produced pantheistic celebrations of nature in which animals, particularly horses, dominate.

Suprematism After working in a manner that fused Cubism and Futurism with Russian folk styles, Kasimir **Malevich** (1878–1935) developed an abstract language of simple geometrical forms which he called Suprematism. In 1913, he painted a black square on a white ground as a rejection of 'ordinary objective life'. A white square on a white ground represented the ultimate in spiritual enlightenment, uniting the viewer with the infinite.

Constructivism was another Russian movement that also employed a nonobjective visual language, but in the service of the Revolution rather than the spiritual. *Beat the Whites with the Red Wedge* (1919) by **El Lissitsky** (1890–1941) (a student of Malevich) has an easily understandable and overtly political message. Vladimir **Tatlin** (1885–1953) designed a *Monument to the Third International* as a vast, skeletal, rotating tower, symbolic of technical endeavour and aspiration – it was never built. Naum **Gabo** (1890–1977) was less political than Tatlin but as important in pioneering the new 'constructed' architectural sculpture that employed materials like plastic to reveal the structural logic of the form. Stalin denounced these artists as bourgeois formalists and instead favoured a highly academic, official style known as Socialist Realism.

Neo-Plasticism Dutch painter Piet **Mondrian** (1872–1944), like Malevich, tried to express the 'truths of the universe' through pure aesthetics. Using primary colours, black, white, and grey, he painted parallel horizontal lines that intersected vertical ones. The perfection described by the parallel lines, the right-angle intersections, and the rectangles of pure colour were meant to mirror the ultimate perfection of the universe. In 1917 he headed a group called *De Stijl* ('the style') which included Theo **van Doesburg** (1883–1931) and the furniture designer Gerrit **Rietveld** (1888–1964). Like the Constructivists, with whom they had links, they believed in the artist as 'designer' with responsibilities to enhance every aspect of modern life by their work.

Many of the ideas of these seemingly disparate Modern groups were propagated at the ***Bauhaus***, an influential German school of art and design, where several major artists, including Kandinsky, taught.

Dada, so called for its infantile associations, was considerably less positive and utopian in its aims. Born at the Cabaret Voltaire, Zürich, Switzerland, in 1916, it was an anarchic series of gestures that aimed to shock by undermining the sanctity of art with all its rules and values. Tristan **Tzara** 'created' poems by tearing out words from newspapers, then drawing

High prices for the choosy, low prices for the lucky?

A calculated bid

An early 19th-century German mechanical calculator, estimated at £15,000–£20,000, was sold at Christie's in May 1993 for £7.7 million. The gilt and lacquered brass piece, made by J C Schuster (b. 1789) in the 1820s, was bought by a Swiss clock dealer, Edgar Mannheimer, over the telephone. He engaged in unprecedented competitive bidding, battling against an unidentified German bidder representing a German museum. Christie's described the final figure as the highest ever paid for any 'non fine or applied work of art'.

A work of art as well as a working scientific instrument, the calculator's mechanism is so complex that it took Schuster two years to construct it. A predecessor of the modern calculator, it has a series of 20 enamelled dials that can be set by the operator using a winding handle to multiply, subtract, add, calculate square roots, and carry out many more operations. Few believed that Mannheimer, the bidder, had bought it for himself. One source suggested that the actual purchaser was US businessman Bill Gates, founder of Microsoft, the computer software company, and the world's richest businessman.

Man Ray's *Glass Tears* became the world's most expensive photograph when it fetched £122,500 at Sotheby's in May 1993. It multiplied the £20,000–£30,000 estimate roughly five times.

Car-boots and bin-liners

In an extreme case of getting a good return on one's investment, a painting purchased by an American tourist for £2 at a car-boot sale in Bristol sold at auction in New York in May 1993 for £67,226. The tourist, niggled by the thought that it might be valuable, took it into Christie's in London to discover his suspicions were well founded. The London expert who identified the painting – *Ruby Throats with Apple Blossoms*, by US painter Martin Johnson Heade (1819–1904) – said the tourist was pleasantly surprised.

In March 1993 Gainsborough's portrait of Judge Sir John Skynner, rolled up and wrapped in a bin-liner, was bought at a London market for a very reasonable £85. The amateur art expert who made the purchase also picked up a portrait of Francis Hargrave, by Joshua Reynolds, for £60. The two paintings – along with Gainsborough's *William Pitt the Younger* – were stolen from Lincoln's Inn Fields three years ago, and were valued by the police at £6 million.

At Sotheby's, where the new 'owner' turned up, the paintings were immediately recognized and detectives called in. The police were unable to trace the third stolen painting, which might well have been bought on the same day. The street-market shopper let Sotheby's keep the paintings, though on paper they belong to the insurers who paid out £100,000 to Lincoln's Inn Fields.

them out of a hat. Similarly, Hans **Arp** (1887–1966) made collages by randomly dropping pieces of paper, then fixing them where they landed. Chance was more valid than choice. At the same time in New York, Marcel **Duchamp** (1887–1968) exhibited 'ready-made' art works: a snow shovel bought in a hardware store, a bicycle wheel mounted on a stool, a urinal.

Surrealism succeeded Dada. In 1922 the French writer André **Breton** (1896–1966) made it a coherent and organized group, precisely what Dada rejected. Freud's investigations into the unconscious were an inspiration, as were the strange empty townscapes of the Italian painter Giorgio **de Chirico** (1888–1978). Some Surrealist artists, like André **Masson** (1896–) and Joan **Miro** (1893–1983), attempted to connect with the unconscious through automatic drawing. Others, like Salvador **Dali** (1904–1989) and René **Magritte** (1898–1967), used a more realistic style to create an imagery of dreams. In both cases, thought and creativity were liberated by the absence of reason. Even Picasso was regarded as a Surrealist by Breton and certainly his work of the late 1920s and the 1930s explored the destructive human impulses. This is most dramatically seen in **Guernica** (1936, Prado, Madrid), in which his horrified reaction to the German Luftwaffe's bombing of a Basque town during the Spanish Civil War has the quality of an epic nightmare.

The impact of Surrealism was widespread. In Britain the landscapes of Paul **Nash** (1889–1946) became even more haunted and mysterious. The Swiss painter Paul **Klee** (1879–1940) painted quirky semiabstract pictures and Marc **Chagall** (1881–1955) evoked the memories of his Jewish-Russian childhood. Both artist delved into the imagination for their visions in a way that paralleled Surrealism.

Abstract Expressionism Many European artists moved to the USA in the years around World War II. New York became the centre of world art and Abstract Expressionism its first major movement. Influenced by Mondrian as well as by Surrealism, US avant-garde painting divided into two groups: the Gesture painters (or Action painters) and the Colour Field painters. Jackson **Pollock** (1912–1956) led the Gesture painters. By putting his canvas on the floor and swirling paint on it, he created a complex web of multicoloured trails which spectators could retrace with their eyes, thereby reliving the artist's dynamic act of creation. The Colour Field painter Mark **Rothko** (1903–1970) filled large canvases with shimmering blocks of solid colour, the contemplation of which offered the spectator a transcendent experience.

Highest prices paid for works by living artists at auction (1988–90)

	Artist	Title of work	Auction house/year of sale	Auction price ($m)
1	de Kooning	*Interchange**	Sotheby's, 1989	20.68
2	Johns	*False Start*	Sotheby's, 1988	17.05
3	de Kooning	*July*	Christie's, 1990	8.8
4	Lichtenstein	*Torpedo Los!*	Christie's, 1990	6.8
5	Lichtenstein	*Kiss II*	Christie's, 1990	6.05

** holds record price for a work by a living artist.*

Pop art was to some extent a reaction against the anguished soul-searching of Abstract Expressionism as well as being a celebration of consumerism and popular culture. Pop artists plundered the mass media, employing the imagery of advertising, comic strips, and the movies. Jasper **Johns** (1930–) gave us paintings of targets and the American flag in endless permutations. Andy **Warhol** (1928–1987), through the medium of the screen print, transformed celebrities and events, from Marilyn Monroe to the electric chair, into contemporary icons. Roy **Lichtenstein** (1923–), in paintings like *Whaam!* (1963, Tate Gallery, London) presents a comic-strip moment in a wittily depersonalized parody of its original style. In the UK, artists like Richard **Hamilton** (1922–) and Eduoardo **Paolozzi** (1924–)had a similar disregard for the division between high and low culture. In Paolozzi's case this meant using almost any material that came to hand, making his collages and sculptures almost archaeological concentrates of the late 20th century.

Op art The paintings of Victor **Vasarely** (1908–) and Bridget **Riley** (1931–) use abstraction to create optical illusions, confusing the spectator's eye with coloured lines and dots that appear to jump, blend, and waver.

In sculpture the influence of Rodin dominated the early years of the century. Matisse, Émile-Antoine **Bourdelle** (1861–1929), and the Cubist sculptors extended Rodin's liberated attitude to the human form as a complex and dynamic surface. The raw directness of African sculpture affected the work of Jacob **Epstein** (1880–1959), Henri **Gaudier-Brzeska** (1891–1915), and Amedeo **Modigliani** (1884–1920), while in Germany Ernst **Barlach** (1870–1938) derived similar inspiration from late Gothic sculpture. Constantin **Brancusi** (1876–1957) in his carvings gradually refined and simplified his work into pure, almost abstract forms, like the ovoid *Prometheus* (1911). Henry **Moore** (1898–1957) created a more rugged reduction of the human form which reflects the full and flowing contours of nature. At the other extreme, the elongated and emaciated figures of Alberto **Giacometti** (1901–1966) emit a sense of spiritual and existential isolation. Both Dada and Cubist collage encouraged a more varied and untraditional choice and use of materials, evident in the work of the Russian Constructivists. In the 1930s Picasso and Julio **Gonzalez** (1876–1972) made highly linear 'drawings in space' by welding sheets and strips of metal together. This direction was pursued in a more dramatic and monumental way by David **Smith** (1906–1965) and his fellow American Alexander **Calder** (1989–1976), who invented mobiles, flat shapes attached in patterns to rods that hang from the ceiling and move gently in the air. More recently Jean **Tinguely** (1925–) has employed electricity to create movement in his elaborate, whimsical machine constructions.

contemporary trends Since the freethinking 1960s, a bewildering number of new trends and movements have appeared, many of which stress the intellectual and material processes behind an art work's creation.

Minimalism reacted to the promiscuity of Pop art by reducing the art object to a bare and essential purity, devoid of any exterior reference or meaning. *Equivalent VIII* (1966) by Carl **Andre** (1935–), two layers of bricks laid on the floor, caused great controversy when purchased by the Tate Gallery, London.

Super Realism or *Photo Realism* imitates reality through exact, illusionistic copies of colour photographs in the work of Richard **Estes** (1932–)and waxworklike sculptures in the work of Duane **Hanson** (1925–). Meaning and intention are obscured by the clinical detachment of the execution and the banality of the subject matter.

Conceptualism Here the actual art object is challenged and sometimes replaced by the ideas behind it. Documentation in the form of statements and photographs may be presented on gallery walls.

Performance art is the staging of events by artists. It may be theatrical but it differs from theatre in its emphasis on visual complexity rather than on a text. In ***Body art*** the artist uses his or her own body as a vehicle for often confrontational ideas. ***Land art*** or ***Earth art*** involves the direct interaction of the artist with the environment. It is usually ephemeral and so preserved only in documentation. **Christo** Javacheff (1935–) has wrapped up part of the Australian coastline (1979), erected a curtain in a Colorado valley (1981), and a long running fence across California (1986). Richard **Long** (1945–) maps and photographs his landscape journeys, displaying them in galleries with works made from natural materials collected en route.

Although these developments undermined the conventional notion of the art work as permanent and unique, traditional forms like figurative oil painting have, even so, continued to thrive since World War II, albeit in increasingly extreme manifestations. In the work of the painter Francis **Bacon** (1909-1992), scenes of horror and brutality are presented as the typical condition of modern humans. Since the 1970s, other painters, the so-called ***Neo-Expressionists*** or ***Bad painters***, like Julian **Schnabel** (1951–), Anselm **Kiefer** (1945–), Georg **Baselitz**

(1938–), and Francesco **Clemente** (1952–), have created an equally direct and lurid visual language in order to explore issues of personal and national history and mythology.

Eastern Art

Chinese art From the Bronze Age to the Cultural Revolution, Chinese art shows a stylistic unity unparalleled in any other culture. From about the 1st century AD Buddhism inspired much sculpture and painting. The ***Han dynasty*** (206 BC–AD 220) produced outstanding metalwork, ceramics, and sculpture. The ***Song dynasty*** (960–1278) established standards of idyllic landscape and nature painting in a delicate calligraphic style.

Neolithic Period Accomplished pottery dates back to about 2500 BC, already showing a distinctive Chinese approach to form.

Bronze Age Rich burial goods, with bronzes and jade carvings, survive from the second millennium BC, decorated with hieroglyphs and simple stylized animal forms. Astonishing life-size terracotta figures from the Qin period (about 221–206 BC) guard the tomb of Emperor Shi Huangdi in the old capital of Xian. Bronze horses, naturalistic but displaying the soft curving lines of the Chinese style, are a feature of the Han dynasty.

Early Buddhism Once Buddhism was established in China it inspired a monumental art, with huge rock-cut Buddhas and graceful linear relief sculptures at the monasteries of Yungang, about 460–535, and Longmen. Bronze images show the same curving lines and rounded forms.

Tang dynasty (618–907) Art during the Tang dynasty shows increasing sophistication in idealized images and naturalistic portraits, such as the carved figures of Buddhist monks (Luohan). This period also produced brilliant metalwork and delicate ceramics. It is known that the aims and, broadly speaking, the style of Chinese painting were already well established, but few paintings survive, with the exception of some Tang scrolls and silk paintings.

Song dynasty The golden age of painting was during the Song dynasty (960–1278). The imperial court created its own workshop, fostering a fine calligraphic art, mainly devoted to natural subjects – landscape, mountains, trees, flowers, birds, and horses – though genre scenes of court beauties were also popular. Scrolls, albums, and fans of silk or paper were painted with watercolours and ink, using soft brushes that produced many different textures. Painting was associated with literature, and painters added poems or quotations to their work to intensify the effect. Ma Yuan (*c.* 1190–1224) and Xia Gui (active *c.* 1180–1230) are among the painters; Muqi (1180–*c.* 1270) was a monk known for exquisite brushwork. The Song dynasty also produced the first true porcelain, achieving a classic simplicity and delicacy in colouring and form.

Ming dynasty (1368–1644) Painters of this period continued the landscape tradition, setting new standards in idealized visions. The painter Dong Qichang wrote a history and theory of Chinese painting. The Song style of porcelain gradually gave way to increasingly elaborate decorative work, and pale shades were superseded by rich colours, as in Ming blue-and- white patterned ware.

Qing dynasty (1644–1911) During the Qing dynasty the so-called Individualist Spirits emerged, painters who developed bolder, personal styles of brushwork.

20th century The strong spirit that supported traditional art began to fade in the 19th and 20th centuries, but attempts to incorporate modernist ideas have been frowned on by the authorities. Not directly concerned with the representation of political events, Chinese art took some years before responding to the political upheavals of this century. Subsequently, response to offical directives produced a period of Soviet-style realism followed by a reversion to a peasant school of painting, which was the officially favoured direction for art during the Cultural Revolution. Mao Zedong was a calligrapher and calligraphy remains, perhaps, the most flourishing art form in China.

Influence Chinese art had a great impact on surrounding countries. The art of Korea was almost wholly inspired by Chinese example for many centuries. Along with Buddhism, Chinese styles of art were established in Japan in the 6th–7th centuries BC and continued to exert a profound influence, though Japanese culture soon developed an independent style.

Indian art Indian art dates back to the ancient Indus Valley civilization of about 3000 BC. Sophisticated artistic styles emerged from the 1st century AD. Buddhist art includes sculptures and murals. Hindu artists created sculptural schemes in caves and huge temple complexes; the Hindu style is lively, with voluptuous nude figures. The Islamic Mogul Empire of the 16th-17th centuries created an exquisite style of miniature painting, inspired by Persian examples.

Buddhist art In NW India the Gandhara kingdom produced the first known images of the Buddha in a monumental soft and rounded style that was exported, with the Buddhist religion, to China, Korea, and Japan. The Kusana and Andhra periods (1st-4th centuries AD) led to the mature and voluptuous art of the Gupta period, which spread widely over SE Asia. The Gupta kingdom emerged around the 4th century AD in the Ganges plain; Mathura, Sarnath, Ajanta, and Aurangabad were centres of Buddhist sculpture. The caves of Ajanta have extensive remains of murals of the 5th and 6th centuries as well as sculpture. The same tradition led in the 6th and 7th centuries to the painting of frescoes, usually depicting incidents in the legends of the Buddhist, Hindu, and Jain religions.

Hindu art Hinduism advanced further in central and S India. Influenced by Buddhist art, Hindu artists created brilliant sculptural schemes in rock-cut caves at Mamallapuram, and huge temple complexes: for example, in Orissa, Konarak, and Khajuraho. The caves at Ellora are known for their ensemble of religious art (Buddhist, Hindu, and Jain) dating from the 6th and 7th centuries. By the 13th century Hinduism became the major religion. The figures of its many exotic deities are rounded and sensuous, their poses based on religious dance movements. Eroticism enters with exuberantly amorous couples symbolizing the unity of the divine. Sculpture was generally of a religious character, but the Gujarat school also excelled in decorating dwelling houses.

Mogul art dates from the Muslim invasion of NW India in the Middle Ages. The invaders destroyed Buddhist and Hindu temple art and introduced their own styles. An early example of their work is the Q'utb mosque of about 1200 in Delhi. They introduced a school of painting based on Persian forms; Indian artists absorbed and expanded this art with great technical virtuosity. Court artists excelled in miniature painting, particularly in the reigns of Jehangir and Shah Jahan (*c.* 1566-1658). Their subjects ranged from portraiture and histories to birds, animals, and flowers. After a period of decline, Indian art has enjoyed a renaissance in modern times, for example the work of Abanindranath Tagore, Amrita Sher-Gil, Jamini Roy, and Sailoz Mookherjee.

Japanese art Early Japanese art was influenced by China. Painting later developed a distinct Japanese character, bolder and more angular, with the spread of Zen Buddhism in the 12th century. Ink painting and calligraphy flourished, followed by book illustration and decorative screens. Japanese prints developed in the 17th century, with multicolour prints invented around 1765. Buddhist sculpture proliferated from 580, and Japanese sculptors excelled at portraits. Japanese pottery stresses simplicity.

The ***Jōmon*** period (10,000–300 BC) was characterized by cord-marked pottery. In the ***Yayoi*** period (300 BC–AD 300) elegant pottery with geometric designs and *dōtaku*, bronze bells decorated with engravings, were the dominant *objets d'art*. During the ***Kofun*** period (300–552) burial mounds held *haniwa*, clay figures, some of which show Chinese influence. The ***Asuka*** period (552–646) is characterized by Buddhist art, introduced from Korea 552, which flourished in sculpture, metalwork, and embroidered silk banners. Painters' guilds were formed. During the ***Nara*** period (646–794) religious and portrait sculptures were made of bronze, clay, or dry lacquer. A few painted scrolls, screens, and murals survive. Textiles were decorated with batik, tie-dye, stencils, embroidery, and brocade. In the ***Heian*** period (794–1185) Buddhist statues became formalized and were usually made of wood. Shinto images emerged. A native style of secular painting (*Yamato-e*) developed, especially in scroll painting, with a strong emphasis on surface design. Lacquerware was also decoratively stylized. In the ***Kamakura*** period (1185–1392) sculpture and painting became vigorously realistic. Portraits were important, as were landscapes and religious, narrative, and humorous picture scrolls. During the ***Ashikaga*** or ***Muromachi*** period (1392–1568) the rapid ink sketch in line and wash introduced by Zen priests from China became popular. Pottery gained in importance from the spread of the tea ceremony. Masks and costumes were made for Nō theatre. Artists of the ***Momoyama*** period (1568–1615) produced beautiful screens to decorate palaces and castles. The arrival of Korean potters also inspired new styles. The ***Tokugawa*** or ***Edo*** period (1615–1867) is characterized by the print (*ukiyo-e*) which originated in genre paintings of 16th- and 17th-century kabuki actors and teahouse women. It developed into the woodcut and after 1740 the true colour print, while its range of subject matter expanded. *Ukiyo-e* artists include Utamaro and Hokusai. Lacquer and textiles became more sumptuous. Tiny *netsuke* figures were mostly carved from ivory or wood. In the ***Meiji*** period (1868–1912) painting was influenced by styles of Western art, for example Impressionism. Most recently, in the ***Shōwa*** period (1926–89), attempts were made to revive the traditional Japanese painting style and to combine traditional and foreign styles.

Books

Great Writers

Abú Nuwás Hasan ibn Háni 762–*c.* 815. Arab poet celebrated for the freedom, eroticism, and ironic lightness of touch he brought to traditional forms.

Andersen Hans Christian 1805–1875. Danish writer. His fairy tales such as 'The Ugly Duckling', 'The Emperor's New Clothes', and 'The Snow Queen', gained him international fame and have been translated into many languages.

Ariosto Ludovico 1474–1533. Italian poet, born in Reggio. He wrote Latin poems and comedies along Classical lines, including the poem *Orlando Furioso* 1516, 1532, an epic treatment of the *Roland* story, and considered to be the perfect poetic expression of the Italian Renaissance.

Machado de Assis Joaquim Maria 1839–1908. Brazilian writer and poet. He is regarded as the greatest Brazilian novelist. His sceptical, ironic wit is well displayed in his 30 volumes of novels and short stories, including *Epitaph for a Small Winner* 1880 and *Dom Casmurro* 1900.

Asturias Miguel Ángel 1899–1974. Guatemalan author and diplomat. He published poetry, Guatemalan legends, and novels, such as *El Señor Presidente/The President* 1946, *Men of Corn* 1949, and *Strong Wind* 1950, attacking Latin-American dictatorships and 'Yankee imperialism'. Nobel prize 1967.

Atwood Margaret (Eleanor) 1939– . Canadian novelist, short-story writer, and poet. Her novels, which often treat feminist themes with wit and irony, include *The Edible Woman* 1969, *Life Before Man* 1979, *Bodily Harm* 1981, *The Handmaid's Tale* 1986, and *Cat's Eye* 1989.

Austen Jane 1775–1817. English novelist whose books are set within the confines of middle-class provincial society, and show her skill at drawing characters and situations with delicate irony. Her principal works are *Sense and Sensibility* 1811 (like its successors, published anonymously), *Pride and Prejudice* 1813, *Mansfield Park* 1814, *Emma* 1816, *Persuasion* 1818, and *Northanger Abbey* 1818. She died at Winchester and is buried in the cathedral.

Baldwin James 1924–1987. US writer, born in New York City, who portrayed the condition of black Americans in contemporary society. His works include the novels *Go Tell It on the Mountain* 1953, *Another Country* 1962, and *Just Above My Head* 1979; the play *The Amen Corner* 1955; and the autobiographical essays *Notes of a Native Son* 1955 and *The Fire Next Time* 1963. He was active in the civil rights movement.

Balzac Honoré de 1799–1850. French novelist. His first success was *Les Chouans/The Chouans* and *La Physiologie du mariage/The Physiology of Marriage* 1829, inspired by Scott. This was the beginning of the long series of novels *La Comédie humaine/The Human Comedy* (planned as 143 volumes, of which 80 were completed), depicting vice and folly in contemporary French society. He also wrote the Rabelaisian *Contes drolatiques/Ribald Tales* 1833.

Bashō Pen name of Matsuo Munefusa 1644–1694. Japanese poet who was a master of the ***haiku***, a 17-syllable poetic form with lines of 5, 7, and 5 syllables, which he infused with subtle allusiveness and made the accepted form of poetic expression in Japan. His most famous work is *Oku-no-hosomichi/The Narrow Road to the Deep North* 1694, an account of a visit to northern Japan, which consists of haikus interspersed with prose passages.

Baudelaire Charles Pierre 1821–1867. French poet, whose work combined rhythmical and musical perfection with a morbid romanticism and eroticism, finding beauty in decadence and evil. His first book of verse, *Les Fleurs du mal/Flowers of Evil* 1857, was condemned by the censor as endangering public morals, but was enormously influential, paving the way for Arthur Rimbaud, Paul Verlaine, and the symbolist school.

Bellow Saul 1915– . Canadian-born US novelist of Russian descent, whose finely styled works and skilled characterizations of life, especially contemporary Jewish-American life, won him the Nobel Prize for Literature 1976. His works usually portray an individual's frustrating relationship with the ongoing events of an indifferent society, and include the picaresque *The Adventures of Augie March* 1953, the philosophically speculative *Herzog* 1964, *Humboldt's Gift* 1975, *The Dean's December* 1982, and *The Bellarosa Connection* 1989.

Blake William 1757–1827. English poet, painter, and mystic, a leading figure in the Romantic period. His visionary, symbolic poems include *Songs of Innocence* 1789 and *Songs of Experience* 1794. He engraved the text and illustrations for his works and hand-coloured them, mostly in watercolour. He also illustrated works by John Milton and William Shakespeare.

Boccaccio Giovanni 1313–1375. Italian poet, chiefly known for the collection of tales called the *Decameron* 1348–53. The bawdiness and exuberance of this work, as well as its narrative skill and characterization, made the work enormously popular and influential, inspiring Chaucer, Shakespeare, Dryden, and Keats, among many others.

Böll Heinrich 1917–1985. West German novelist. A radical Catholic and anti-Nazi, he attacked Germany's political past and the materialism of its contemporary society. His many publications include poems, short stories, and novels which satirize German society, for example *Billard um Halbzehn/Billiards at Half-Past Nine* 1959 and *Gruppenbild mit Dame/Group Portrait with Lady* 1971. Nobel Prize for Literature 1972.

Borges Jorge Luis 1899–1986. Argentinian poet and short-story writer. In 1961 he became director of the National Library, Buenos Aires, and was professor of English literature at the university there. He is known for his fantastic and paradoxical work *Ficciones/Fictions* 1944.

Brontë family of English writers, including the three sisters ***Charlotte*** (1816–55), ***Emily Jane*** (1818–48) and ***Anne*** (1820–49), and their brother ***Patrick Branwell*** (1817–48). Their most enduring works are Charlotte Brontë's *Jane Eyre* 1847 and Emily Brontë's *Wuthering Heights* 1847. Later works include Anne's *The Tenant of Wildfell Hall* 1848 and Charlotte's *Shirley* 1849 and *Villette* 1853.

Burns Robert 1759–1796. Scottish poet who used the Scots dialect at a time when it was not considered suitably 'elevated' for literature. Burns's first volume, *Poems, Chiefly in the Scottish Dialect*, appeared in 1786. In addition to his poetry Burns wrote or adapted many songs, including 'Auld Lang Syne'.

Byron George Gordon, 6th Baron Byron 1788–1824. English poet who became the symbol of Romanticism and political liberalism throughout Europe in the 19th century. His reputation was established with the first two cantos of *Childe Harold* 1812. Later works include *The Prisoner of Chillon* 1816, *Beppo* 1818, *Mazeppa* 1819, and, most notably, *Don Juan* 1819–24. He left England in 1816, spending most of his later life in Italy. In 1823 he sailed for Greece to further the Greek struggle for independence, but died of fever at Missolonghi.

Camoëns or ***Camões***, Luís Vaz de 1524–1580. Portuguese poet and soldier. He went on various military expeditions, and was shipwrecked in 1558. His poem, *Os Lusiades/The Lusiads*, published 1572, tells the story of the explorer Vasco da Gama and incorporates much Portuguese history; it has become the country's national epic. His posthumously published lyric poetry is also now valued.

Camus Albert 1913–1960. Algerian-born French writer. A journalist in France, he was active in the Resistance during World War II. His novels, which owe much to existentialism, include *L'Etranger/The Outsider* 1942, *La Peste/The Plague* 1948, and *L'Homme Révolté/The Rebel* 1952. He was awarded the Nobel Prize for Literature 1957.

Cao Chan or ***Ts'ao Chan*** 1719–1763. Chinese novelist. His tragic love story *Hung Lou Meng/The Dream of the Red Chamber* published 1792, involves the downfall of a Manchu family and is semi-autobiographical.

Carroll Lewis. Pen name of Charles Lutwidge Dodgson 1832–1898. English mathematician and writer of children's books, including the classics *Alice's Adventures in Wonderland* 1865 and its sequel *Through the Looking Glass* 1872. He also published mathematics books under his own name.

Cervantes Saavedra, Miguel de 1547–1616. Spanish novelist, playwright, and poet, whose masterpiece, *Don Quixote* (in full *El ingenioso hidalgo Don Quixote de la Mancha*) was published 1605. In 1613, his *Novelas Ejemplares/Exemplary Novels* appeared, followed by *Viaje del Parnaso/The Voyage to Parnassus* 1614. A spurious second part of *Don Quixote* prompted Cervantes to bring out his own second part in 1615, often considered superior to the first in construction and characterization.

Chaucer Geoffrey *c.* 1340–1400. English poet, the greatest and most influential English poet of the Middle Ages. In his masterpiece, *The Canterbury Tales* (*c.* 1387), a collection of tales told by pilgrims on their way to the shrine of Thomas à Becket, he showed his genius for metre and characterization. His other work includes the French-influenced *Romance of the Rose* and an adaptation of Boccaccio's *Troilus and Criseyde*. The great popularity of his work assured the dominance of the southern English dialect in literature.

Conrad Joseph 1857–1924. English novelist of Polish parentage, born Teodor Jozef Konrad Korzeniowski in the Ukraine. His novels include *Almayer's Folly* 1895, *Lord Jim* 1900, *Heart of Darkness* 1902, *Nostromo* 1904, *The Secret Agent* 1907, and *Under Western Eyes* 1911. His works vividly evoke the mysteries of sea life and exotic foreign settings and explore the psychological isolation of the 'outsider'.

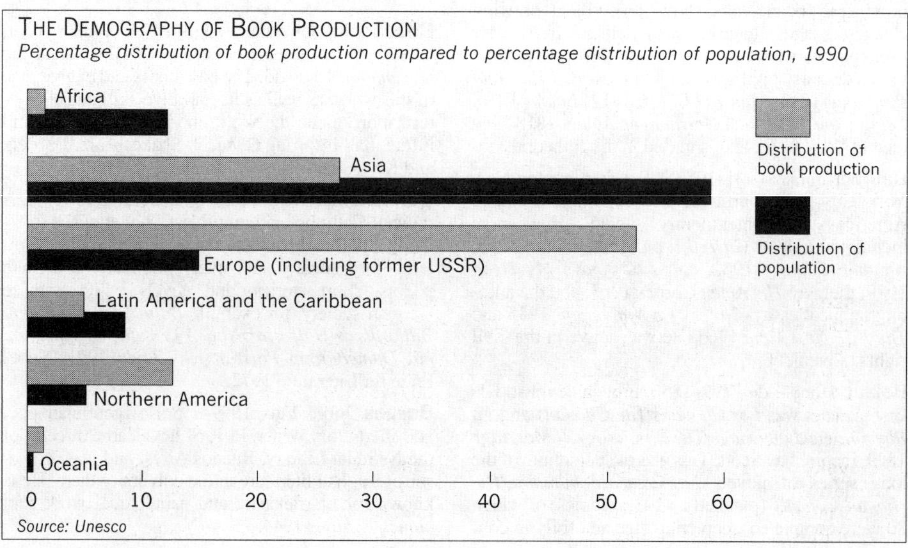

Dante Alighieri 1265–1321. Italian poet. His masterpiece *La Divina Commedia/The Divine Comedy* 1307–21, the greatest poem of the Middle Ages, is an epic account in three parts of his journey through Hell, Purgatory, and Paradise, during which he is guided part of the way by the poet Virgil; on a metaphorical level the journey is also one of Dante's own spiritual development. Other works include the philosophical prose treatise *Convivio/The Banquet* 1306–08, the first major work of its kind to be written in Italian rather than Latin; *Monarchia/On World Government* 1310–13, expounding his political theories; *De vulgari eloquentia/Concerning the Vulgar Tongue* 1304–06, an original Latin work on Italian, its dialects, and kindred languages; and *Canzoniere/Lyrics*, containing his scattered lyrics.

Darío Rubén. Pen name of Félix Rubén García Sarmiento 1867–1916. Nicaraguan poet. His first major work *Azul/Azure* 1888, a collection of prose and verse influenced by French Symbolism, created a sensation. He went on to establish *modernismo*, the Spanish-American modernist literary movement, distinguished by an idiosyncratic and deliberately frivolous style that broke away from the prevailing Spanish provincialism and adapted French poetic models. His vitality and eclecticism influenced every poet writing in Spanish after him, both in the New World and in Spain.

Defoe Daniel 1660–1731. English novelist and journalist. His best-known work, *Robinson Crusoe* 1719, was greatly influential in the development of the novel. An active pamphleteer and political critic, he was imprisoned 1702–04 following publication of the ironic *The Shortest Way With Dissenters*. Fictional works include *Moll Flanders* 1722 and *A Journal of the Plague Year* 1724. Altogether he produced over 500 books, pamphlets, and journals.

Dickens Charles 1812–1870. English novelist, popular for his memorable characters and his portrayal of the social evils of Victorian England. In 1836 he published the first number of the *Pickwick Papers*, followed by *Oliver Twist* 1838, the first of his 'reforming' novels; *Nicholas Nickleby* 1839; *Barnaby Rudge* 1840; *The Old Curiosity Shop* 1841; and *David Copperfield* 1849. Among his later books are *Hard Times* 1854; *Little Dorritt* 1857; *A Tale of Two Cities* 1859; and *Great Expectations* 1861.

Donne John 1571–1631. English metaphysical poet whose work is characterized by subtle imagery and figurative language. In 1615 Donne took orders in the Church of England and as dean of St Paul's Cathedral, London, was noted for his sermons. His poetry includes the sonnets 'Batter my heart, three person'd God' and 'Death be not proud', elegies, and satires.

Dos Passos John 1896–1970. US author. He made his reputation with the war novels *One Man's Initiation* 1919 and *Three Soldiers* 1921. His major work is the trilogy *U.S.A.* 1930–36, which gives a panoramic view of US life through the device of placing fictitious characters against the setting of real newspaper headlines and contemporary events.

Dostoievsky Fyodor Mihailovich 1821–1881. Russian novelist. Remarkable for their profound psychological insight, Dostoievsky's novels have greatly influenced Russian writers, and since the beginning of the 20th century have been increasingly influential abroad. In 1849 he was sentenced to four years' hard labour in Siberia, followed by army service, for printing socialist propaganda. *The House of the Dead* 1861 recalls his prison experiences, followed by his major works *Crime and Punishment* 1866, *The Idiot* 1868–69, and *The Brothers Karamazov* 1880.

Duras Marguerite 1914– . French writer. Her works include short stories (*Des Journèes entières dans les arbres*), plays (*La Musica*), film scripts (*Hiroshima mon amour* 1960), and novels such as *Le Vice-Consul* 1966, evoking an existentialist world from the setting of Calcutta, and *Emily L.* 1989. *La vie materielle* (published in France 1987) appeared in England as *Practicalities* 1990. Her autobiographical novel, *La Douleur*, is set in Paris in 1945.

Eliot George. Pen name of Mary Ann Evans 1819–1880. English novelist who portrayed Victorian society, including its intellectual hypocrisy, with realism and irony. In 1857 she published the story 'Amos Barton', the first of the *Scenes of Clerical Life*. This was followed by the novels *Adam Bede* 1859, *The Mill on the Floss* 1860, and *Silas Marner* 1861. *Middlemarch* 1872 is now considered one of the greatest novels of the 19th century. Her final book *Daniel Deronda* 1876 was concerned with anti-Semitism. She also wrote poetry.

Eliot T(homas) S(tearns) 1888–1965. US poet, playwright, and critic who lived in London from 1915. His first volume of poetry, *Prufrock and Other Observations* 1917, introduced new verse forms and rhythms, and expressed the disillusionment of the generation affected by World War I; further collections include *The Waste Land* 1922, which established his central position in modern poetry; *The Hollow Men* 1925, and *Old Possum's Book of Practical Cats* 1939. *Four Quartets* 1943 revealed his religious vision. His plays include *Murder in the Cathedral* 1935 and *The Cocktail Party* 1949. He was also an influential literary critic, and helped to reassess the importance of Donne. He was awarded the Nobel Prize for Literature in 1948.

Faulkner William 1897–1962. US novelist who wrote in an experimental stream-of-consciousness style. His works include *The Sound and the Fury* 1929, dealing with a Southern US family in decline; *As I Lay Dying* 1930; *Light in August* 1932, a study of segregation; *The Unvanquished* 1938, stories of the Civil War; and *The Hamlet* 1940, *The Town* 1957, and *The Mansion* 1959, a trilogy covering the rise of the materialist Snopes family. He was awarded the Nobel Prize for Literature in 1949.

Fielding Henry 1707–1754. English novelist whose narrative power influenced the form and technique of the novel and helped to make it the most popular form of literature in England. In 1742 he parodied Richardson's novel *Pamela* in his *Joseph Andrews*, which was followed by *Jonathan Wild the Great* 1743; his masterpiece *Tom Jones* 1749, which he described as a 'comic epic in prose'; and *Amelia* 1751.

Firdawsi Mansûr Abu'l-Qâsim *c.* 935–*c.* 1020. Persian poet, the greatest epic poet of Persia. His *Shahnama/The Book of Kings* relates the history of Persia in 60,000 verses, and includes the legend of Sohrab and Rustum, in which the father unknowingly kills the son in battle.

Fitzgerald F(rancis) Scott (Key) 1896–1940. US novelist and short-story writer. His early autobiographical novel *This Side of Paradise* 1920 made him known in the postwar society of the East Coast, and *The Great Gatsby* 1925 epitomizes the Jazz Age.

Flaubert Gustave 1821–1880. French novelist, one of the greatest of the 19th century. His masterpiece, noted for its psychological realism, is *Madame Bovary* 1857. He entered Paris literary circles 1840, but in 1846 moved to Rouen, where he remained for the rest of his life. *Salammbô* 1862 earned him the Legion of Honour 1866, and was followed by *L'Education sentimentale/Sentimental Education* 1869, and *La Tentation de Saint Antoine/The Temptation of St Anthony* 1874. Flaubert also wrote the short stories *Trois contes/Three Tales* 1877.

García Márquez Gabriel 1928– . Colombian novelist. His sweeping novel *Cien años de soledad/One Hundred Years of Solitude* 1967 (which tells the story of a family over a period of six generations) is an example of magic realism, a technique used to heighten the intensity of realistic portrayal of social and political issues by introducing grotesque or fanciful material. His other books include *El amor en los tiempos del célera/Love in the Time of Cholera* 1985. Nobel Prize for Literature 1982.

Gide André 1869–1951. French novelist, born in Paris. His work is largely autobiographical and concerned with the dual themes of self-fulfilment and renunciation. It includes *L'Immoraliste/The Immoralist* 1902, *La Porte étroite/Strait Is the Gate 1909, Les Caves du Vatican/The Vatican Cellars* 1914, and *Les Faux-monnayeurs/The Counterfeiters* 1926; and an almost lifelong *Journal*. Nobel Prize for Literature 1947.

Goethe Johann Wolfgang von 1749–1832. German poet, novelist, and dramatist, generally considered the founder of modern German literature, and leader of the Romantic *Sturm und Drang* movement. His works include the autobiographical *Die Leiden des Jungen Werthers/The Sorrows of the Young Werther* 1774 and *Faust* 1808, his masterpiece. A visit to Italy 1786–88 inspired the classical dramas *Iphigenie auf Tauris/Iphigenia in Tauris* 1787 and *Tasso* 1790.

Gogol Nicolai Vasilyevich 1809–1852. Russian writer. His first success was a collection of stories, *Evenings on a Farm near Dikanka* 1831–32, followed by *Mirgorod* 1835. Later works include *Arabesques* 1835, the comedy play *The Inspector General* 1836, and the picaresque novel *Dead Souls* 1842, which satirizes Russian provincial society.

Grass Günter 1927– . German writer. Born in Danzig, he studied at the art academies of Düsseldorf and Berlin, worked as a writer and sculptor (first in Paris and later in Berlin), and in 1958 won the coveted 'Group 47' prize. The grotesque humour and socialist feeling of his novels *Die Blechtrommel/The Tin Drum* 1959 and *Der Butt/The Flounder* 1977 are also characteristic of many of his poems.

Greene (Henry) Graham 1904–1991. English writer, whose novels of guilt, despair, and penitence, include *The Man Within* 1929, *Brighton Rock* 1938,

Booker Prize for Fiction *(British)*

1980 William Golding *Rites of Passage*
1981 Salman Rushdie *Midnight's Children*
1982 Thomas Keneally *Schindler's Ark*
1983 J M Coetzee *Life and Times of Michael K*
1984 Anita Brookner *Hotel du Lac*
1985 Keri Hulme *The Bone People*
1986 Kingsley Amis *The Old Devils*
1987 Penelope Lively *Moon Tiger*
1988 Peter Carey *Oscar and Lucinda*
1989 Kazuo Ishiguro *Remains of the Day*
1990 A S Byatt *Possession*
1991 Ben Okri *The Famished Road*
1992 Bary Unsworth *Sacred Hunger*; Michael Ondaatje *The English Patient (joint winners)*

Nobel Prize for Literature *(International)*

1980 Czeslaw Milosz (Polish-American)
1981 Elias Canetti (Bulgarian-British)
1982 Gabriel García Márquez (Columbian-Mexican)
1983 William Golding (British)
1984 Jaroslav Seifert (Czechoslovakian)
1985 Claude Simon (French)
1986 Wole Soyinka (Nigerian)
1987 Joseph Brodsky (Soviet)
1988 Naguib Mahfouz (Egyptian)
1989 Camilo Jose Cela (Spanish)
1990 Octavio Paz (Mexican)
1991 Nadine Gordimer (South African)
1992 Derek Walcott (St Lucia)

Prix Goncourt *for fiction (French)*

1980 Yves Navarre *Le Jardin d'acclimation*
1981 Lucien Bodard *Anne Marie*
1982 Dominique Fernandez *Dans la Main de l'ange*
1983 Frederick Tristan *Les Égares*
1984 Marguerite Duras *L'Amant*
1985 Yann Queffelec *Les Noces barbares*
1986 Michel Host *Valet de Nuit*
1987 Tahir Ben Jelloun *LA Nuit Sacrée*
1988 Erik Orsenna *L'Exposition Coloniale*
1989 Jean Vautrin *Un Grand Pas Vers le Bon Dieu*
1990 Jean Rouault *Les Champs d'Honneur*
1991 Pierre Combescot *Les Filles du Calvaire*
1992 Patrick Chamoisean *Texaco*

Pulitzer Prize for Fiction *(American)*

1980 Norman Mailer *The Executioner's Song*
1981 John Kennedy Toole *A Confederacy of Dunces*
1982 John Updike *Rabbit is Rich*
1983 Alice Walker *The Color Purple*
1984 William Kennedy *Ironweed*
1985 Alison Lurie *Foreign Affairs*
1986 Larry McMurtry *Lonesome Dove*
1987 Peter Taylor *A Summer to Memphis*
1988 Toni Morrison *Beloved*
1989 Anne Tyler *Breathing Lessons*
1990 Oscar Hijelos *The Mambo Kings Play Songs of Love*
1991 John Updike *Rabbit at Rest*
1992 Jane Smiley *A Thousand Acres*
1993 Robert Olen Butler *A Good Scent from a Strange Mountain*

The Power and the Glory 1940, *The Heart of the Matter* 1948, *The Third Man* 1950, *The Honorary Consul* 1973, *Monsignor Quixote* 1982, and *The Captain and the Enemy* 1988.

Hâfiz Shams al-Din Muhammad *c.* 1326–1390. Persian lyric poet, who was born in Shiraz and taught in a Dervish college there. His *Diwan*, a collection of short odes, extols the pleasures of life and satirizes his fellow Dervishes.

Hardy Thomas 1840–1928. English novelist and poet. His novels, set in rural 'Wessex' (his native West Country), portray intense human relationships played out in a harshly indifferent natural world. They include *Far From the Madding Crowd* 1874, *The Return of the Native* 1878, *The Mayor of Casterbridge* 1886, *The Woodlanders* 1887, *Tess of the D'Urbervilles* 1891, and *Jude the Obscure* 1895. The latter, portraying social attitudes towards education, marriage, divorce, and suicide, aroused great antagonism, which reinforced his decision to confine himself to verse. His poetry includes the *Wessex Poems* 1898, and several volumes of lyrics.

Heine Heinrich 1797–1856. German romantic poet and journalist, who wrote *Reisebilder* 1826 and *Buch der Lieder/Book of Songs* 1827. From 1831 he lived mainly in Paris, working as a correspondent for German newspapers. Schubert and Schumann set many of his lyrics to music.

Hemingway Ernest 1898–1961. US writer. War, bullfighting, and fishing were used symbolically in his writings to represent honour, dignity, and primitivism – prominent themes in his short stories and novels, which included *A Farewell to Arms* 1929, *For Whom the Bell Tolls* 1940, and *The Old Man and the Sea* 1952. His deceptively simple writing styles attracted many imitators. He received the Nobel Prize for Literature in 1954.

Homer lived *c.* 8th century BC. Legendary Greek epic poet. According to tradition he was a blind minstrel and the author of the *Iliad* and the *Odyssey*, which are probably based on much older stories, passed on orally, concerning war with Troy in the 12th century BC.

Horace 65–8 BC. Roman lyric poet and satirist. He became a leading poet under the patronage of Emperor Augustus. His works include *Satires* 35–30 BC; the four books of *Odes* about 25–24 BC; *Epistles*, a series of verse letters; and a critical work, *Ars poetica*.

Hugo Victor (Marie) 1802–1885. French poet, novelist, and dramatist. The *Odes et poésies diverses* appeared 1822, and his verse play *Hernani* 1830 established him as the leader of French Romanticism. More volumes of verse followed between his series of dramatic novels, which included *The Hunchback of Notre Dame* 1831 and *Les Misérables* 1862.

Huxley Aldous (Leonard) 1894–1963. English writer. The satirical disillusionment of his first novel, *Crome Yellow* 1921, continued throughout *Antic Hay* 1923, *Those Barren Leaves* 1925, *Point Counter Point* 1928, and *Brave New World* 1932, in which human beings are mass-produced in laboratories and rendered incapable of freedom by indoctrination and drugs.

Iqbāl Muhammad 1875–1938. Islamic poet and thinker. His literary works, in Urdu and Persian, were mostly verse in the classical style, suitable for public recitation. He sought through his writings to arouse Muslims to take their place in the modern world.

Ishiguro Kazuo 1954– . Japanese-born British novelist. His novel *An Artist of the Floating World* won the 1986 Whitbread Prize, and *The Remains of the Day* won the 1989 Booker Prize.

James Henry 1843–1916. US novelist, who lived in Europe from 1875 and became a naturalized British subject 1915. His novels deal with the impact of sophisticated European culture on the innocent American. They include *The Portrait of a Lady* 1881, *Washington Square* 1881, *The Bostonians* 1886, *The Ambassadors* 1903, and *The Golden Bowl* 1904. He also wrote more than a hundred shorter works of fiction, notably the supernatural tale *The Turn of the Screw* 1898.

Johnson Samuel, known as 'Dr Johnson', 1709–1784. English lexicographer, author, and critic, also a brilliant conversationalist and the dominant figure in 18th-century London literary society. His *Dictionary*, published 1755, remained authoritative for over a century, and is still remarkable for the vigour of its definitions. In 1764 he founded the 'Literary Club', whose members included Reynolds, Burke, Goldsmith, Garrick, and Boswell, Johnson's biographer.

Joyce James (Augustine Aloysius) 1882–1941. Irish writer, born in Dublin, who revolutionized the form of the English novel with his 'stream of consciousness' technique. His works include *Dubliners* 1914 (short stories), *Portrait of the Artist as a Young Man* 1916, *Ulysses* 1922, and *Finnegans Wake* 1939.

Kafka Franz 1883–1924. Czech novelist, born in Prague, who wrote in German. His three unfinished allegorical novels *Der Prozess/The Trial* 1925, *Der Schloss/The Castle* 1926, and *Amerika/America* 1927 were posthumously published despite his instructions that they should be destroyed. His short stories include 'Die Verwandlung/The Metamorphosis' 1915, in which a man turns into a huge insect.

Kālidāsa lived 5th century AD. Indian epic poet and dramatist. His works, in Sanskrit, include the classic drama *Sakuntala*, the love story of King Dushyanta and the nymph Sakuntala.

Keats John 1795–1821. English poet, a leading figure of the Romantic movement. He published his first volume of poetry 1817; this was followed by *Endymion*, *Isabella*, and *Hyperion* 1818, 'The Eve of St Agnes', his odes 'To Autumn', 'On a Grecian Urn', and 'To a Nightingale', and 'Lamia' 1819. His final volume of poems appeared in 1820.

Kerouac Jack 1923–1969. US novelist who named and epitomized the Beat Generation of the 1950s. His books, all autobiographical, include *On the Road* 1957, *Big Sur* 1963, and *Desolation Angel* 1965.

Kipling (Joseph) Rudyard 1865–1936. English writer, born in India. His stories for children include the *Jungle Books* 1894–1895, *Stalky and Co* 1899, and the *Just So Stories* 1902. Other works include the novel *Kim* 1901, the short story 'His Gift', poetry, and the unfinished autobiography *Something of Myself* 1937. In his heyday he enjoyed enormous popularity, and although subsequently denigrated for alleged 'jingoist imperialism', his work is increasingly valued for its complex characterization and subtle moral viewpoints. Nobel prize 1907.

La Fontaine Jean de 1621–1695. French poet. He was born at Château-Thierry, and from 1656 lived largely in Paris, the friend of Molière, Racine, and Boileau. His works include *Fables* 1668–94 and *Contes* 1665–74, a series of witty and bawdy tales in verse.

Lafontaine Oskar 1943– . German socialist politician, federal deputy chair of the Social Democrat Party (SPD) from 1987. Leader of the Saar regional branch of the SPD from 1977 and former mayor of Saarbrucken, West Germany, he was dubbed 'Red Oskar' because of his radical views on military and environmental issues. His attitude became more conservative once he had become minister-president of Saarland in 1985.

Lawrence D(avid) H(erbert) 1885–1930. English writer whose work expresses his belief in emotion and the sexual impulse as creative and true to human nature. His novels include *Sons and Lovers* 1913, *The Rainbow* 1915, *Women in Love* 1921, and *Lady Chatterley's Lover* 1928 (the latter was banned as obscene in the UK until 1960). Lawrence also wrote short stories (for example 'The Woman Who Rode Away') and poetry.

Leopardi Giacomo, Count Leopardi 1798–1837. Italian romantic poet. The first collection of his uniquely pessimistic poems, *I Versi/Verses*, appeared in 1824, and was followed by his philosophical *Operette morali/Minor Moral Works* 1827, in prose, and *I Canti/Lyrics* 1831.

Levi Primo 1919–1987. Italian novelist. He joined the anti-Fascist resistance during World War II, was captured, and sent to the concentration camp at Auschwitz. He wrote of these experiences in *Se questo è un uomo/If This Is a Man* 1947.

Lewis (Harry) Sinclair 1885–1951. US novelist. He made a reputation with satirical novels: *Main Street* 1920, depicting American small-town life; *Babbitt* 1922, the story of a real-estate dealer of the Midwest caught in the conventions of his milieu; *Arrowsmith* 1925, a study of the pettiness in medical science; and *Elmer Gantry* 1927, a satiric portrayal of evangelical religion. *Dodsworth*, a gentler novel of a US industrialist, was published 1929. He was the first American to be awarded the Nobel Prize for Literature 1930.

Li Po 705–762. Chinese poet. He used traditional literary forms, but his exuberance, the boldness of his imagination, and the intensity of his feeling have won him recognition as perhaps the greatest of all Chinese poets. Although he was mostly concerned with higher themes, he is also remembered for his celebratory verses on drinking.

London Jack (John Griffith) 1876–1916. US novelist, author of the adventure stories *The Call of the Wild* 1903, *The Sea Wolf* 1904, and *White Fang* 1906.

Lorca Federico García 1898–1936. Spanish poet and playwright, born in Granada. *Romancero gitano/Gipsy Ballad-book* 1928 shows the influence of the Andalusian songs of the area. In 1929–30 Lorca visited New York, and his experiences are reflected in *Poeta en Nuevo York* 1940. His poems include *Lament*, written for the bullfighter Mejías. He was shot by the Falangists during the Spanish Civil War.

Machado de Assis Joaquim Maria 1839–1908. Brazilian writer and poet. He is regarded as the greatest Brazilian novelist. His sceptical, ironic wit is well displayed in his 30 volumes of novels and short stories, including *Epitaph for a Small Winner* 1880 and *Dom Casmurro* 1900.

Mann Thomas 1875–1955. German novelist and critic, concerned with the theme of the artist's relation to society. His first novel was *Buddenbrooks* 1901, which, followed by *Der Zauberberg/The Magic Mountain* 1924, led to a Nobel prize 1929. Later works include *Dr Faustus* 1947 and *Die Bekenntnisse des Hochstaplers Felix Krull/Confessions of Felix Krull* 1954. Notable among his works of short fiction is *Der Tod in Venedig/Death in Venice* 1913.

Manzoni Alessandro, Count Manzoni 1785–1873. Italian poet and novelist, author of the historical romance, *I promessi sposi/The Betrothed* 1825–27, set in Spanish-occupied Milan during the 17th century. Verdi's *Requiem* commemorates him.

Maupassant Guy de 1850–1893. French author who established a reputation with the short story 'Boule de Suif/Ball of Fat' 1880 and wrote some 300 short stories in all. His novels include *Une Vie/A Woman's Life* 1883 and *Bel-Ami* 1885. He was encouraged as a writer by Flaubert.

Melville Herman 1819–1891. US writer, whose *Moby-Dick* 1851 was inspired by his whaling experiences in the South Seas. These experiences were also the basis for earlier fiction, such as *Typee* 1846 and *Omoo* 1847. He published several volumes of verse, as well as short stories (*The Piazza Tales* 1856). *Billy Budd* was completed just before his death and published 1924. Although most of his works were unappreciated during his lifetime, today he is one of the most highly regarded of US authors.

Milton John 1608–1674. English poet. His early poems include the pastoral *L'allegro* and *Il penseroso* 1632, the masque *Comus* 1633, and the elegy *Lycidas* 1637. His middle years were devoted to the Puritan

Volume trade

Largest exporters of books to the USA, 1991–92 (in US $m)

Country	*1991*	*1992*	*% change*
UK	187.0	205.9	10.1
Hong Kong	156.3	187.3	19.8
Japan	88.6	91.5	3.3
Singapore	76.4	88.7	16.0
Canada	57.7	86.3	49.8
Italy	82.2	63.5	–23.1
Germany	47.8	49.6	3.7
Spain	29.7	30.8	3.8

Source: US Department of Commerce

cause and pamphleteering, including one advocating divorce, and another (*Areopagitica*) freedom of the press. From 1649 he was (Latin) secretary to the Council of State, his assistants (as his sight failed) including Marvell. The masterpieces of his old age are his epic poems on biblical themes, *Paradise Lost* 1667, *Paradise Regained* 1677, and the classic drama *Samson Agonistes* 1677.

Mishima Yukio 1925–1970. Japanese novelist whose work often deals with sexual desire and perversion, as in *Confessions of a Mask* 1949 and *The Temple of the Golden Pavilion* 1956. He committed hara-kiri (ritual suicide) as a protest against what he saw as the corruption of the nation and the loss of the samurai warrior tradition.

Montaigne Michel Eyquem de 1533–1592. French writer, regarded as the creator of the essay form. In 1580 he published the first two volumes of his *Essais*, the third volume appeared in 1588. Montaigne deals with all aspects of life from an urbanely sceptical viewpoint. Through the translation by John Florio in 1603 he influenced Shakespeare and other English writers.

Musil Robert 1880–1942. Austrian novelist, author of the unfinished *Der Mann ohne Eigenschaften/The Man without Qualities* (three volumes, 1930–43). Its hero shares the author's background of philosophical study and scientific and military training, and is preoccupied with the problems of the self viewed from a mystic but agnostic viewpoint.

Nabokov Vladimir 1899–1977. US writer who left his native Russia 1917 and began writing in English in the 1940s. His most widely known book is *Lolita* 1955, the story of the middle-aged Humbert Humbert's infatuation with a precocious child of 12. His other books include *Laughter in the Dark* 1938, *The Real Life of Sebastian Knight* 1945, *Pnin* 1957, and his memoirs *Speak, Memory* 1947.

Naipaul V(idiadhar) S(urajprasad) 1932– . British writer, born in Trinidad of Hindu parents. His novels include *A House for Mr Biswas* 1961, *The Mimic Men* 1967, *A Bend in the River* 1979, and *Finding the Centre* 1984. His brother ***Shiva(dhar) Naipaul*** (1940–85) was also a novelist (*Fireflies* 1970) and journalist.

Neruda Pablo. Pen name of Neftalí Ricardo Reyes y Basualto 1904–1973. Chilean poet and diplomat. His work includes lyrics and the epic poem of the American continent *Canto General* 1950. Nobel Prize for Literature 1971. He served as consul and ambassador to many countries.

Orwell George. Pen name of Eric Arthur Blair 1903–1950. English author. His books include the satire *Animal Farm* 1945, which included such sayings as 'All animals are equal, but some are more equal than others', and the prophetic *Nineteen Eighty-Four* 1949, portraying the dangers of excessive state control over the individual. Other works include *Down and Out in Paris and London* 1933 and *Homage to Catalonia* 1938.

Ovid (Publius Ovidius Naso) 43 BC–AD 17. Roman poet. His poetry deals mainly with the themes of love (*Amores* 20 BC), (*Ars amatoria* 1 BC), mythology (*Metamorphoses* AD 2), and exile (*Tristia* AD 9–12).

Pasternak Boris Leonidovich 1890–1960. Russian poet and novelist. His novel *Dr Zhivago* 1957 was banned in the USSR as a 'hostile act', and followed by a Nobel prize (which he declined). *Dr Zhivago* has since been unbanned and Pasternak posthumously rehabilitated.

Paz Octavio 1914– . Mexican poet and essayist. His works reflect many influences, including Marxism, surrealism, and Aztec mythology. His celebrated poem *Piedra del sol/Sun Stone* 1957 uses contrasting images, centring upon the Aztec Calendar Stone (representing the Aztec universe), to symbolize the loneliness of individuals and their search for union with others. Nobel Prize for Literature 1990.

Perrault Charles 1628–1703. French author of the fairy tales *Contes de ma mère l'oye/Mother Goose's Fairy Tales* 1697, which include 'Sleeping Beauty', 'Little Red Riding Hood', 'Blue Beard', 'Puss in Boots', and 'Cinderella'.

Pessoa Fernando 1888–1935. Portuguese poet. Born in Lisbon, he was brought up in South Africa and was bilingual in English and Portuguese. His verse is considered to be the finest written in Portuguese this century. He wrote under three assumed names, which he called 'heteronyms' – Alvaro de Campos, Ricardo Reis, and Alberto Caeiro – for each of which he invented a biography.

Petrarch (Italian ***Petrarca***) Francesco 1304–1374. Italian poet, born in Arezzo, a devotee of the Classical tradition. His *Il Canzoniere* is composed of sonnets in praise of his idealized love 'Laura', whom he first saw 1327 (she was a married woman and refused to become his mistress). His 14-line sonnets, in a form which was given the name Petrarchan, were influential for centuries.

Poe Edgar Allan 1809–1849. US writer and poet. His short stories are renowned for their horrific atmosphere (as in *The Fall of the House of Usher* 1839) and acute reasoning (for example, *The Gold Bug* 1843 and *The Murders in the Rue Morgue* 1841, in which the investigators Legrand and Dupin anticipate Conan Doyle's Sherlock Holmes). His most famous poem is 'The Raven' 1844.

Pope Alexander 1688–1744. English poet and satirist. He established his reputation with the precocious *Pastorals* 1709 and *Essay on Criticism* 1711, which were followed by a parody of the heroic epic *The Rape of the Lock* 1712–14 and 'Eloisa to Abelard' 1717. Other works include a highly Neo-Classical translation of Homer's *Iliad* and *Odyssey* 1715–26.

Pound Ezra 1885–1972. US poet who lived in London from 1908. His *Personae* and *Exultations* 1909 established the principles of the Imagist movement. His largest work was the series of *Cantos* 1925–1969 (intended to number 100), which attempted a massive reappraisal of history.

Proust Marcel 1871–1922. French novelist and critic. His immense autobiographical work *À la recherche du temps perdu/Remembrance of Things Past* 1913–27, consisting of a series of novels, is the expression of his childhood memories coaxed from his subconscious; it is also a precise reflection of life in provincial France at the end of the 19th century.

Pushkin Aleksandr 1799–1837. Russian poet and writer. He was exiled 1820 for his political verse and in 1824 was in trouble for his atheistic opinions. He wrote ballads such as *The Gypsies* 1827, and the novel in verse *Eugene Onegin* 1823–31. Other works include the tragic drama *Boris Godunov* 1825, and the prose pieces *The Captain's Daughter* 1836 and *The Queen of Spades* 1834. Pushkin's range was wide, and his willingness to experiment freed later Russian writers from many of the archaic conventions of the literature of his time.

Pynchon Thomas 1937– . US novelist who created a bizarre, labyrinthine world in his books, the first of which was *V* 1963. *Gravity's Rainbow* 1973 represents a major achievement in 20th-century literature, with its fantastic imagery and esoteric language, drawn from mathematics and science.

Rabelais François 1495–1553. French satirist, monk, and physician, whose name has become synonymous with bawdy humour. He was educated in the Renaissance humanist tradition and was the author of satirical allegories, including *La Vie inestimable de Gargantua/The Inestimable Life of Gargantua* 1535 and *Faits et dits héroïques du grand Pantagruel/Deeds and Sayings of the Great Pantagruel* 1533, about two giants (father and son), Gargantua and Pantagruel.

Richardson Samuel 1689–1761. English novelist, one of the founders of the modern novel. *Pamela* 1740–41, written in the form of a series of letters and containing much dramatic conversation, was sensationally popular all across Europe, and was followed by *Clarissa* 1747–48 and *Sir Charles Grandison* 1753–54.

Rilke Rainer Maria 1875–1926. Austrian writer, born in Prague. His prose works include the semi-autobiographical *Die Aufzeichnungen des Malte Laurids Brigge/Notebook of Malte Laurids Brigge* 1910, and his poetical works include *Die Sonnette an Orpheus/Sonnets to Orpheus* 1923 and *Duisener Elegien/Duino Elegies* 1923. His verse is characterized by a form of mystic pantheism that seeks to achieve a state of ecstasy in which existence can be apprehended as a whole.

Rimbaud (Jean Nicolas) Arthur 1854–1891. French Symbolist poet. His verse was chiefly written before the age of 20, notably *Les Illuminations* published 1886. From 1871 he lived with Verlaine.

Rousseau Jean-Jacques 1712–1778. French social philosopher and writer, born in Geneva, Switzerland. *Discourses on the Origins of Inequality* 1754 made his name: he denounced civilized society and postulated the paradox of the superiority of the 'noble savage'. *Social Contract* 1762 emphasized the rights of the people over those of the government, and stated that a government could be legitimately overthrown if it failed to express the general will of the people. It was a significant influence on the French Revolution. In the novel *Emile* 1762 he outlined a new theory of education, based on natural development and the power of example, to elicit the unspoiled nature and abilities of children. *Confessions*, published posthumously 1782, was a frank account of his occasionally immoral life and was a founding work of autobiography.

Salinger J(erome) D(avid) 1919– . US writer, author of the classic novel of mid-20th-century adolescence *The Catcher in the Rye* 1951. He also wrote short stories about a Jewish family named Glass, including *Franny and Zooey* 1961.

Sartre Jean-Paul 1905–1980. French author and philosopher, a leading proponent of existentialism in postwar philosophy. He published his first novel, *La Nausée/Nausea*, 1937, followed by the trilogy *Les Chemins de la Liberté/Roads to Freedom* 1944–45 and many plays, including *Huis Clos/In Camera* 1944.

Scott Walter 1771–1832. Scottish novelist and poet. His first works were translations of German ballads, followed by poems such as 'The Lady of the Lake' 1810 and 'Lord of the Isles' 1815. He gained a European reputation for his historical novels such as *Heart of Midlothian* 1818, *Ivanhoe* 1819, and *The Fair Maid of Perth* 1828. His last years were marked by frantic writing to pay off his debts, after the bankruptcy of his publishing company in 1826.

Shakespeare William 1564–1616. English dramatist and poet, the greatest English playwright; he also wrote numerous sonnets. (See entry in *Theatre* section for more.)

Shelley Percy Bysshe 1792–1822. English lyric poet, a leading figure in the Romantic movement. Expelled from Oxford university for atheism, he fought all his life against religion and for political freedom. This is reflected in his early poems such as *Queen Mab* 1813. He later wrote tragedies including *The Cenci* 1818, lyric dramas such as *Prometheus Unbound* 1820, and lyrical poems such as 'Ode to the West Wind'. He drowned while sailing in Italy.

Singer Isaac Bashevis 1904– . Polish-born US novelist and short-story writer. His works, written in Yiddish, then translated into English, often portray traditional Jewish life in Poland and the USA, and the loneliness of old age. They include *Gimpel the Fool* 1957, *The Slave* 1960, *Shosha* 1978, *Old Love* 1979, *Lost in America* 1981, *The Image and Other Stories* 1985, and *The Death of Methuselah* 1988. He has also written plays and books for children. In 1978 he was awarded the Nobel Prize for Literature.

Solzhenitsyn Alexander (Isayevich) 1918– . Soviet novelist, a US citizen from 1974. After military service, he was in prison and exile 1945–57 for anti-Stalinist comments. Much of his writing is semi-autobiographical and highly critical of the system, including *One Day in the Life of Ivan Denisovich* 1962 which deals with the labour camps under Stalin, and *The Gulag Archipelago* 1973, an exposé of the whole Soviet labour camp network. This led to his expulsion from the USSR 1974.

Soyinka Wole 1934– . Nigerian author who was a political prisoner in Nigeria 1967–69. His works include the play *The Lion and the Jewel* 1963; his prison memoirs *The Man Died* 1972; *Aké, The Years of Childhood* 1982, an autobiography, and *Isara*, a fictionalized memoir 1989. He was the first African to receive the Nobel Prize for Literature, in 1986.

Spenser Edmund *c.* 1552–1599. English poet, who has been called the 'poet's poet' because of his rich imagery and command of versification. He is known for his moral allegory *The Faerie Queene*, of which six books survive (three published 1590 and three 1596). Other books include *The Shepheard's Calendar* 1579, *Astrophel* 1586, the love sonnets *Amoretti* and the *Epithalamion* 1595.

Steinbeck John (Ernst) 1902–1968. US novelist. His realist novels, such as *In Dubious Battle* 1936, *Of Mice and Men* 1937, and *The Grapes of Wrath* 1939 (Pulitzer prize 1940), portray agricultural life in his native California, where migrant farm laborers from the Oklahoma dust bowl struggled to survive. He received the Nobel Prize for Literature in 1962.

Stendhal pen name of Marie Henri Beyle 1783–1842. French novelist. His novels *Le Rouge et le noir/The Red and the Black* 1830 and *La Chartreuse de Parme/The Charterhouse of Parme* 1839 were pioneering works in their treatment of disguise and hypocrisy; a review of the latter by Balzac in 1840 furthered Stendhal's reputation.

Sterne Laurence 1713–1768. Irish writer, creator of the comic anti-hero Tristram Shandy. *The Life and Opinions of Tristram Shandy, Gent* 1760–67, an eccentrically whimsical and bawdy novel, foreshadowed many of the techniques and devices of 20th-century novelists, including James Joyce. His other works include *A Sentimental Journey through France and Italy* 1768.

Stevenson Robert Louis 1850–1894. Scottish novelist and poet, author of the adventure novel *Treasure Island* 1883. Later works included the novels *Kidnapped* 1886, *The Master of Ballantrae* 1889, *Dr Jekyll and Mr Hyde* 1886, and the anthology *A Child's Garden of Verses* 1885.

Swift Jonathan 1667–1745. Irish satirist and Anglican cleric, author of *Gulliver's Travels* 1726, an allegory describing travel to lands inhabited by giants, miniature people, and intelligent horses. Other works include *The Tale of a Tub* 1704, attacking corruption in religion and learning; contributions to the Tory paper *The Examiner*, of which he was editor 1710–11; the satirical *A Modest Proposal* 1729, which suggested that children of the poor should be eaten; and many essays and pamphlets.

Tagore Rabindranath 1861–1941. Bengali Indian writer, born in Calcutta, who translated into English his own verse *Gitanjali* ('song offerings') 1912 and his verse play *Chitra* 1896. Nobel prize 1913.

Tennyson Alfred, 1st Baron Tennyson 1809–1892. English poet, poet laureate 1850–96, whose verse has a majestic, musical quality. His works include 'The Lady of Shalott', 'The Lotus Eaters', 'Ulysses', 'Break, Break, Break', 'The Charge of the Light Brigade'; the longer narratives *Locksley Hall* 1832 and *Maud* 1855; the elegy *In Memoriam* 1850; and a long series of poems on the Arthurian legends *The Idylls of the King* 1857–85.

Thackeray William Makepeace 1811–1863. English novelist and essayist, born in Calcutta, India. He was a regular contributor to *Fraser's Magazine* and *Punch*. *Vanity Fair* 1847–48 was his first novel, followed by *Pendennis* 1848, *Henry Esmond* 1852 (and its sequel *The Virginians* 1857–59), and *The Newcomes* 1853–55, in which Thackeray's tendency to sentimentality is most marked.

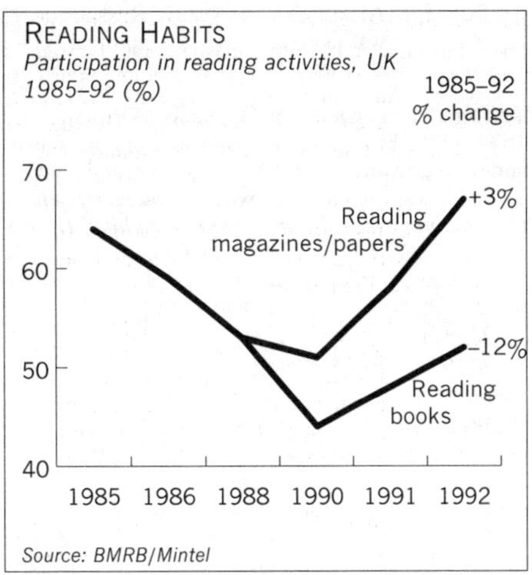

Tolstoy Leo Nikolaievich 1828–1910. Russian novelist who wrote *Tales from Sebastopol* 1856, *War and Peace* 1863–69, and *Anna Karenina* 1873–77. From 1880 Tolstoy underwent a profound spiritual crisis and took up various moral positions, including passive resistance to evil, rejection of authority (religious or civil) and private ownership, and a return to basic mystical Christianity. He was excommunicated by the Orthodox Church, and his later works were banned.

Turgenev Ivan Sergeievich 1818–1883. Russian writer, notable for poetic realism, pessimism, and skill in characterization. His works include the play *A Month in the Country* 1849, and the novels *A Nest of Gentlefolk* 1858, *Fathers and Sons* 1862, and *Virgin Soil* 1877. His series *A Sportsman's Sketches* 1852 criticized serfdom.

Twain Mark. Pen name of Samuel Langhorne Clemens 1835–1910. US writer. He established his reputation with the comic masterpiece *The Innocents Abroad* 1869 and two classic American novels, in dialect, *The Adventures of Tom Sawyer* 1876 and *The Adventures of Huckleberry Finn* 1885. He also wrote satire, as in *A Connecticut Yankee at King Arthur's Court* 1889.

Verlaine Paul 1844–1896. French lyric poet who was influenced by the poets Baudelaire and Rimbaud. His volumes of verse include *Poèmes saturniens/Saturnine Poems* 1866, *Fêtes galantes/Amorous Entertainments* 1869 and *Romances sans paroles/Songs without Words* 1874. In 1873 he was imprisoned for attempting to shoot Rimbaud. His later works reflect his attempts to lead a reformed life. He was acknowledged as leader of the Symbolist poets.

Villon François 1431– *c.* 1465. French poet who used satiric humour, pathos, and lyric power in works written in *argot* (slang) of the time. Very little of his work survives, but it includes the *Ballade des dames du temps jadis/Ballad of the Ladies of Former Times*, *Petit Testament* 1456, and *Grand Testament* 1461.

Virgil (Publius Vergilius Maro) 70–19 BC. Roman poet who wrote the *Eclogues* 37 BC, a series of pastoral poems; the *Georgics* 30 BC, four books on the art of farming; and his epic masterpiece, the *Aeneid* 29–19 BC.

Voltaire Pen name of François-Marie Arouet 1694–1778. French writer who believed in deism, and devoted himself to tolerance, justice, and humanity. He was threatened with arrest for *Lettres philosophiques sur les anglais/Philosophical Letters on the English* 1733 (essays in favour of English ways, thought, and political practice) and had to take refuge. Other writings include *Le Siècle de Louis XIV/The Age of Louis XIV* 1751; *Candide* 1759, a parody on Leibniz's 'best of all possible worlds'; and *Dictionnaire philosophique* 1764.

Walker Alice 1944– . US poet, novelist, critic, and essay writer. She was active in the US civil-rights movement in the 1960s and, as a black woman, wrote about the double burden of racist and sexist oppression that such women bear. Her novel *The Color Purple* 1983 (film, 1985) won the Pulitzer Prize.

Wharton Edith (born Jones) 1862–1937. US novelist. Her work, known for its subtlety and form and influenced by her friend Henry James, was mostly set in New York society. It includes *The House of Mirth* 1905, which made her reputation; the grim, uncharacteristic novel of New England *Ethan Frome* 1911; *The Custom of the Country* 1913, and *The Age of Innocence* 1920.

Whitman Walt(er) 1819–1892. US poet who published *Leaves of Grass* 1855, which contains the symbolic 'Song of Myself'. It used unconventional free verse (with no rhyme or regular rhythm) and scandalized the public by its frank celebration of sexuality.

Woolf Virginia (née Virginia Stephen) 1882–1941. English novelist and critic. Her first novel, *The Voyage Out* 1915, explored the tensions experienced by women who want marriage and a career. In *Mrs Dalloway* 1925 she perfected her 'stream of consciousness' technique. Among her later books are *To the Lighthouse* 1927, *Orlando* 1928, and *The Years* 1937, which considers the importance of economic independence for women.

Wordsworth William 1770–1850. English Romantic poet. In 1797 he moved with his sister Dorothy to Somerset to be near Coleridge, collaborating with him on *Lyrical Ballads* 1798 (which included 'Tintern Abbey'). From 1799 he lived in the Lake District, and later works include *Poems* 1807 (including 'Intimations of Immortality') and *The Prelude* (written by 1805, published 1850). He was appointed poet laureate in 1843.

Yeats W(illiam) (B)utler 1865–1939. Irish poet. He was a leader of the Celtic revival and a founder of the Abbey Theatre in Dublin. His early work was romantic and lyrical, as in the poem 'The Lake Isle of Innisfree' and plays *The Countess Cathleen* 1892 and *The Land of Heart's Desire* 1894. His later books of poetry include *The Wild Swans at Coole* 1917 and *The Winding Stair* 1929. He was a senator of the Irish Free State 1922–28. Nobel prize 1923.

Zola Émile Edouard Charles Antoine 1840–1902. French novelist and social reformer. With *La Fortune des Rougon/The Fortune of the Rougons* 1867 he began a series of some 20 naturalistic novels, portraying the fortunes of a French family under the Second Empire. They include *Le Ventre de Paris/The Underbelly of Paris* 1873, *Nana* 1880, and *La Débâcle/The Debacle* 1892. In 1898 he published *J'accuse/I Accuse*, a pamphlet indicting the persecutors of Dreyfus, for which he was prosecuted for libel but later pardoned.

CINEMA

Great Directors

Allen Woody. Adopted name of Allen Stewart Konigsberg 1935– . US film writer, director, and actor, known for his cynical, witty, often self-deprecating parody and offbeat humor.

His films include *Sleeper* 1973, *Annie Hall* 1977 (for which he won three Academy Awards), *Manhattan* 1979, and *Hannah and Her Sisters* 1986, all of which he directed, wrote, and appeared in. From the late 1970s, Allen has mixed his output of comedies with straight dramas, such as *Interiors* 1978 and *Another Woman* 1988, but *Crimes and Misdemeanors* 1990 broke with tradition by combining humour and straight drama.

Other films include *Take the Money and Run* 1969, *Sleeper* 1973, *Love and Death* 1975, *Stardust Memories* 1982, *Zelig* 1983, *Purple Rose of Cairo* 1985, and *Night and Fog* 1991.

Altman Robert 1925– . US maverick film director. His antiwar comedy *M.A.S.H.* 1970 was a critical and commercial success; subsequent films include *McCabe and Mrs Miller* 1971, *The Long Goodbye* 1973, *Nashville* 1975, and *Popeye* 1980.

Antonioni Michelangelo 1912– . Italian film director, whose work evinces both formal innovation and an acute power to analyse the effects of affluence and technology on contemporary sensibility. He began as a maker of documentaries and directed his first feature film, *Cronaca di un Amore* in 1950, gradually developing the elliptical approach to narrative seen in *L'Avventura* 1960 and its successors. His other films include *Blow Up* 1966, filmed in England, the US-made *Zabriskie Point* 1970, *The Passenger* 1974, and *Identification of a Woman* 1982.

Bergman Ingmar 1918– . Swedish stage producer (from the 1930s) and film director (from the 1950s). His work deals with complex moral, psychological, and metaphysical problems and is tinged with pessimism. His films include *Wild Strawberries* 1957, *The Seventh Seal* 1957, *Persona* 1966, *Cries and Whispers* 1972, *The Serpent's Egg* and *Autumn Sonata* both 1978, and *Fanny and Alexander* 1982. He is one of the greatest directors of acting performances.

Buñuel Luis 1900–1983. Spanish Surrealist film director. He collaborated with Salvador Dali on *Un Chien andalou* 1928 and *L'Age d'or/The Golden Age* 1930, and established his solo career in Mexico with *Los olvidados/The Young and the Damned* 1950. His works are often anticlerical, with black humour and erotic imagery.

Later, he worked in France with higher budgets on such films as *Le Charme discret de la bourgeoisie/The Discreet Charm of the Bourgeoisie* 1972 (Academy Award winner) and *Cet Obscur Objet du désir/That Obscure Object of Desire* 1977.

Capra Frank 1897–1991. Italian-born US film director. His satirical, populist comedies, which often have idealistic heroes, were hugely successful in the 1930s, and he won Academy Awards for *It Happened One Night* 1934, *Mr Deeds Goes to Town* 1936, and *Mr Smith Goes to Washington* 1939.

Capra began as a gagman for silent comedies, then directed several films with Harry Langdon (1884–1944). An instinctive craftsman, his popular success continued after World War II with the sentimental and imaginative *It's a Wonderful Life* 1946, but subsequently waned. His later work included *A Hole in the Head* 1959 and *A Pocketful of Miracles* 1961.

Carné Marcel 1909– . French director known for the romantic fatalism of such films as *Drôle de Drame* 1936, *Hôtel du Nord* 1938, *Le Quai des brumes/Port of Shadows* 1938, and *Le Jour se lève/Daybreak* 1939. His masterpiece, *Les Enfants du paradis/The Children of Paradise* 1943–45, was made with his longtime collaborator, the poet and screenwriter Jacques Prévert (1900-1977).

Chaplin Charlie (Charles Spencer) 1889–1977. English film actor and director. He made his reputation as a tramp with a smudge moustache, bowler hat, and twirling cane in silent comedies from the mid-1910s, including *The Rink* 1916, *The Kid* 1920, and *The Gold Rush* 1925. His work often contrasts buffoonery with pathos, and his later films combine dialogue with mime and music, as in *The Great Dictator*

The rise of an English rose

When Emma Thompson won the best actress Academy Award for *Howards End,* and marked the occasion by declaring herself 'very, very gobsmacked', the seal was set on her position as first lady of British show business. She was born into a theatrical family – her mother is the actress Phylida Law and her father was Eric Thompson, creator of the cult children's TV series *Magic Roundabout* – and versatility has been her hallmark. She made a name in the Footlights theatre group at Cambridge, and later appeared in the West End musical *Me and My Girl,* despite having no training in either song or dance. But it was playing the independent-minded heroine of the TV miniseries *Fortunes of War* that properly made her reputation. In private – and not so private – life, she is Mrs Kenneth Branagh, and has acted in all the films made by her husband, including the double role of blonde amnesiac and voluptuous murder victim in *Dead Again.* Her 'solo' outing in *Howards End* decisively established her as an independent force, and renders into definitive understatement her comment on the discovery attendant upon appearing in a student revue: 'Gosh, I thought, this is wonderful – I can do something.'

Academy Awards: recent winners

1971 Best Picture: *The French Connection*; Best Director: William Friedkin *The French Connection*; Best Actor: Gene Hackman *The French Connection*; Best Actress: Jane Fonda *Klute*
1972 Best Picture: *The Godfather*; Best Director: Bob Fosse *Cabaret*; Best Actor: Marlon Brando *The Godfather*; Best Actress: Liza Minnelli *Cabaret*
1973 Best Picture: *The Sting*; Best Director: George Roy Hill *The Sting*; Best Actor: Jack Lemmon *Save the Tiger*; Best Actress: Glenda Jackson *A Touch of Class*
1974 Best Picture: *The Godfather II*; Best Director: Francis Ford Coppola *The Godfather II*; Best Actor: Art Carney *Harry and Tonto*; Best Actress: Ellen Burstyn *Alice Doesn't Live Here Anymore*
1975 Best Picture: *One Flew Over the Cuckoo's Nest*; Best Director: Milos Forman *One Flew Over the Cuckoo's Nest*; Best Actor: Jack Nicholson *One Flew Over the Cuckoo's Nest*; Best Actress: Louise Fletcher *One Flew Over the Cuckoo's Nest*
1976 Best Picture: *Rocky*; Best Director: John G Avildsen *Rocky*; Best Actor: Peter Finch *Network*; Best Actress: Faye Dunaway *Network*
1977 Best Picture: *Annie Hall*; Best Director: Woody Allen *Annie Hall*; Best Actor: Richard Dreyfuss *The Goodbye Girl*; Best Actress: Diane Keaton *Annie Hall*
1978 Best Picture: *The Deer Hunter*; Best Director: Michael Cimino *The Deer Hunter*; Best Actor: Jon Voight *Coming Home*; Best Actress: Jane Fonda *Coming Home*
1979 Best Picture: *Kramer vs Kramer*; Best Director: Robert Benton *Kramer vs Kramer*; Best Actor: Dustin Hoffman *Kramer vs Kramer*; Best Actress: Sally Field *Norma Rae*
1980 Best Picture: *Ordinary People*; Best Director: Robert Redford *Ordinary People*; Best Actor: Robert De Niro *Raging Bull*; Best Actress: Sissy Spacek *Coal Miner's Daughter*
1981 Best Picture: *Chariots of Fire*; Best Director: Warren Beatty *Reds*; Best Actor: Henry Fonda *On Golden Pond*; Best Actress: Katharine Hepburn *On Golden Pond*
1982 Best Picture: *Gandhi*; Best Director: Richard Attenborough *Gandhi*; Best Actor: Ben Kingsley *Gandhi*; Best Actress: Meryl Streep *Sophie's Choice*
1983 Best Picture: *Terms of Endearment*; Best Director: James L Brooks *Terms of Endearment*; Best Actor: Robert Duvall *Tender Mercies*; Best Actress: Shirley MacLaine *Terms of Endearment*
1984 Best Picture: *Amadeus*; Best Director: Milos Forman *Amadeus*; Best Actor: F Murray Abraham *Amadeus*; Best Actress: Sally Field *Places in the Heart*
1985 Best Picture: *Out of Africa*; Best Director: Sidney Pollack *Out of Africa*; Best Actor: William Hurt *Kiss of the Spiderwoman*; Best Actress: Geraldine Page *The Trip to Bountiful*
1986 Best Picture: *Platoon*; Best Director: Oliver Stone *Platoon*; Best Actor: Paul Newman *The Color of Money*; Best Actress: Marlee Matlin *Children of a Lesser God*
1987 Best Picture: *The Last Emperor*; Best Director: Bernardo Bertolucci *The Last Emperor*; Best Actor: Michael Douglas *Wall Street*; Best Actress: Cher *Moonstruck*
1988 Best Picture: *Rain Man*; Best Director: Barry Levinson *Rain Man*; Best Actor: Dustin Hoffman *Rain Man*; Best Actress: Jodie Foster *The Accused*
1989 Best Picture: *Driving Miss Daisy*; Best Director: Oliver Stone *Born on the 4th of July*; Best Actor: Daniel Day-Lewis *My Left Foot*; Best Actress: Jessica Tandy *Driving Miss Daisy*
1990 Best Picture: *Dances with Wolves*; Best Director: Kevin Costner *Dances with Wolves*; Best Actor: Jeremy Irons *Reversal of Fortune*; Best Actress: Kathy Bates *Misery*
1991 Best Picture: *The Silence of the Lambs*; Best Director: Jonathan Demme *The Silence of the Lambs*; Best Actor: Anthony Hopkins *The Silence of the Lambs*; Best Actress: Jodie Foster *The Silence of the Lambs*
1992 Best Picture: *Unforgiven*; Best Director: Clint Eastwood *Unforgiven*; Best Actor: Al Pacino *Scent of a Woman*; Best Actress: Emma Thompson *Howards End*

1940 and *Limelight* 1952 (the latter won an Oscar for Chaplin's musical theme). His other films include *City Lights* 1931, *Modern Times* 1936, and *Monsieur Verdoux* 1947. He was one of cinema's most popular and greatest stars, and his "Little Tramp' character became recognized and loved the world over.

Chaplin was born in south London and first appeared on the stage at the age of five. In 1913 he joined Mack Sennett's Keystone Company in Los Angeles, and from 1915 he took artistic control of all his films. When accused of communist sympathies during the McCarthy witchhunt, he left the USA 1952 and moved to Switzerland. He received special Oscars 1928 and 1972.

Coppola Francis Ford 1939– . US film director and screenwriter. He directed *The Godfather* 1972, which became one of the biggest money-making films of all time, and its sequels *The Godfather Part II* 1974, which garnered seven Academy Awards, and *The Godfather Part III* 1990. His other films include *Apocalypse Now* 1979, *One From the Heart* 1982, *Rumblefish* 1983, *The Outsiders* 1983, and *Tucker: The Man and His Dream* 1988.

After working on horror B-films, his first successes were *Finian's Rainbow* 1968 and *Patton* 1969, for which his screenplay won an Academy Award. Among his other films are *The Conversation* 1972, *The Cotton Club* 1984, and *Gardens of Stone* 1987.

De Mille Cecil B(lount) 1881–1959. US film director and producer. He entered films 1913 with Jesse L Lasky (with whom he later established Paramount Pictures), and was one of the founders of Hollywood. He specialized in biblical epics, such as *The Sign of* *the Cross* 1932 and *The Ten Commandments* 1923; remade 1956. He also made the 1952 Academy Award-winning circus movie *The Greatest Show on Earth*.

De Sica Vittorio 1902–1974. Italian director and actor. He won his first Oscar with *Bicycle Thieves* 1948, a film of subtle realism. Later films included *Umberto D* 1952, *Two Women* 1960, and *The Garden of the Finzi-Continis* 1971. His considerable acting credits include *Madame de ...* 1953 and *The Millionaires* 1960.

Disney Walt(er Elias) 1901–1966. US filmmaker and animator, a pioneer of family entertainment. He established his own studio in Hollywood 1923, and his first Mickey Mouse cartoons (*Plane Crazy*, which was silent, and *Steamboat Willie*, which had sound) appeared 1928. In addition to short cartoons, the studio made feature-length animated films, including *Snow White and the Seven Dwarfs* 1938, *Pinocchio* 1940, *Fantasia* 1940, *Dumbo* 1941, *Bambi* 1942, *Cinderella* 1950, *Alice in Wonderland* 1952, and *Peter Pan* 1953. Disney's cartoon figures also appeared in comic books, magazines, books, and records, which helped make his animated characters loved throughout the world.

The Disney studio also made nature-study films such as *The Living Desert* 1953, which have been criticized for their fictionalization of nature: wild animals were placed in unnatural situations to create "drama'. Feature films with human casts were made from 1946, such as *Davy Crockett* 1955, *The Swiss Family Robinson* 1960, and *Mary Poppins* 1964.

Disney produced the first television series in colour in 1961. He also conceived the idea of theme parks, of which Disneyland, California was the first (1955). Walt Disney World, near Orlando, Florida, 1971, included the Epcot (Experimental Prototype Community of Tomorrow) Center 1982, a cross between a science museum and a theme park. There is also a park in Tokyo, Japan, and – opened in 1992 – the EuroDisney park in Paris, France.

Dreyer Carl Theodor 1889–1968. Danish film director. His wide range of films include the austere silent classic *La Passion de Jeanne d'Arc/The Passion of Joan of Arc* 1928 and the Expressionist horror film *Vampyr* 1932, after the failure of which Dreyer made no full-length films until *Vredens Dag/Day of Wrath* 1943. His two late masterpieces are *Ordet/The Word* 1955 and *Gertrud* 1964.

Eisenstein Sergei Mikhailovich 1898–1948. Latvian film director who pioneered film theory and introduced the use of montage (the juxtaposition of shots to create a particular effect) as a means of propaganda, as in *The Battleship Potemkin* 1925.

The Soviet dictator Stalin banned the second part of Eisenstein's projected trilogy *Ivan the Terrible* 1944–46. The last part was never made. His other films include *Strike* 1925, *October* 1928, *Que Viva Mexico!* 1931–32, and *Alexander Nevsky* 1938.

Fellini Federico 1920– . Italian film director whose films combine dream and fantasy sequences with satire and autobiographical details. His films include *I vitelloni/The Young and the Passionate* 1953, *La Strada* 1954 (Academy Award 1956), *Le notti di Cabiria/The Nights of Cabiria* 1956, *La dolce vita* 1960, *Otto e mezzo/8 ½* 1963, *Giulietta degli spiriti/Juliet of the Spirits* 1965, *Satyricon* 1969, *Roma/Fellini's Roma* 1972, *Amarcord* 1974, *Casanova* 1976, and *La città delle donne/City of Women* 1980.

Ford John. Adopted name of Sean O'Feeney 1895–1973. US film director. Active from the silent film era, he was one of the early creators of the 'Western', directing *The Iron Horse* 1924; *Stagecoach* 1939 became his masterpiece. But he also worked in many other genres, and won Academy Awards for

Awards for Best Film from four top festivals

Cannes Film Festival

Palme d'Or for Best Film

1985	*When Father Was Away on Business* (Yug)
1986	*The Mission* (UK)
1987	*Under the Sun of Satan* (Fr)
1988	*Pelle the Conqueror* (Den)
1989	*sex, lies and videotape* (US)
1990	*Wild at Heart* (US)
1991	*Barton Fink* (US)
1992	*The Best Intentions* (Swe)
1993	*The Piano* (NZ/Australia); *Farewell to My Concubine* (Hong Kong/China)

Venice Film Festival

Golden Lion for Best Film

1985	*Sans toit ni loi* (aka *Vagabonde*) (Fr)
1986	*Le Rayon Vert* (Fr)
1987	*Au Revoir les Enfants* (Fr)
1988	*La Leggenda del Santo Bevitore (The Legend of the Holy Drinker)* (It)
1989	*Beiqing Chengshi (City of Sadness)* (Taiwan)
1990	*Rosencrantz and Guildenstern are Dead* (UK)
1991	*Urga* (Russia)
1992	*Story of Qiu Ju* (China)

Berlin Film Festival

Golden Bear for Best Film

1985	*Wetherby* (UK); *Die Frau und der Fremde* (FRG)
1986	*Stammheim* (FRG)
1987	*The Theme* (USSR)
1988	*Red Sorghum* (China)
1989	*Rain Man* (US)
1990	*Skylarks on a String* (Czech); *Music Box* (US)
1991	*La Casa del Sorriso (House of Smiles)* (It)
1992	*Grand Canyon* (USA)
1993	*Woman from the Lake of Centred Souls* (China); *Wedding Banquet* (Taiwan)

British Academy of Film and Television Arts (BAFTA)

Best Film Awards

1985	*The Killing Fields* (UK)
1986	*The Purple Rose of Cairo* (US)
1987	*A Room with a View* (UK)
1988	*Jean de Florette* (Fr)
1989	*The Last Emperor* (US)
1990	*Dead Poets Society* (US)
1991	*GoodFellas* (US)
1992	*The Commitments* (UK)
1993	*Howards End* (UK)

cinema: chronology

1826–34	Various machines invented to show moving images: the stroboscope, zoetrope, and thaumatrope.
1872	Eadweard Muybridge demonstrated movement of horses' legs by using 24 cameras.
1877	Invention of Praxinoscope; developed as a projector of successive images on screen 1879 in France.
1878–95	Marey, a French physiologist, developed various types of camera for recording human and animal movements.
1887	Augustin le Prince produced the first series of images on a perforated film; Thomas A Edison, having developed the phonograph, took the first steps in developing a motion-picture recording and reproducing device to accompany recorded sound.
1888	William Friese-Greene (1855-1921) showed the first celluloid film and patented a movie camera.
1889	Edison invented 35-mm film.
1890–94	Edison, using perforated film, developed his Kinetograph camera and Kinetoscope individual viewer; developed commercially in New York, London, and Paris.
1895	The Lumière brothers projected, to a paying audience, a film of an oncoming train arriving at a station. Some of the audience fled in terror.
1896	Charles Pathé introduced the Berliner gramophone, using discs in synchronization with film. Lack of amplification, however, made the performances ineffective.
1900	Attempts to synchronize film and disc were made by Leon Gaumont (1863–1946) in France and Goldschmidt in Germany, leading later to the Vitaphone system of the USA.
1902	Georges Méliès made *Le Voyage dans la Lune/A Trip to the Moon.*
1903	The first Western was made in the USA: *The Great Train Robbery* by Edwin Porter.
1906	The earliest colour film (Kinemacolor) was patented in Britain by George Albert Smith (1864–1959).
1907–11	The first films shot in the Los Angeles area called Hollywood. In France, Emile Cohl (1857–1938) experimented with film animation.
1911	The first Hollywood studio, Horsley's Centaur Film Company, was established, followed in 1915 by Carl Laemmle's Universal City and Thomas Ince's studio.
1912	In Britain, Eugene Lauste designed experimental 'sound on film' systems.
1914–18	Full newsreel coverage of World War I.
1915	*The Birth of a Nation*, D W Griffith's epic on the American Civil War, was released in the USA.
1917	35 mm was officially adopted as the standard format for motion picture film by the Society of Motion Picture Engineers of America.
1918–19	A sound system called Tri-Ergon was developed in Germany, which led to sound being recorded on film photographically. Photography with sound was also developed in the USA by Lee De Forest in his Phonofilm system.
1923	First sound film (as Phonofilm) demonstrated.
1926	*Don Juan*, a silent film with a synchronized music score, was released.
1927	Release of the first major sound film, *The Jazz Singer*, consisting of some songs and a few moments of dialogue, by Warner Brothers, New York City. The first Academy Awards (Oscars) were presented.
1928	Walt Disney released his first Mickey Mouse cartoon, *Steamboat Willie*. The first all-talking film, *Lights of New York*, was released.
1930	*The Big Trail*, a Western filmed and shown in 70-mm rather than the standard 35-mm format, was released. 70 mm is still used, mainly for big-budget epics such as *Lawrence of Arabia.*
1932	Technicolor (three-colour) process introduced and used for a Walt Disney cartoon film.
1935	*Becky Sharp*, the first film in three-colour Technicolor was released.
1937	Walt Disney released the first feature-length (82 minutes) cartoon, *Snow White and the Seven Dwarfs.*
1939	*Gone With the Wind*, regarded as one of Hollywood's greatest achievements, was released.
1952	Cinerama, a wide-screen presentation using three cameras and three projectors, was introduced in New York.
1953	Commercial 3-D (three-dimensional) cinema and wide-screen CinemaScope were launched in the USA. CinemaScope used a single camera and projector to produce a wide-screen effect with an anamorphic lens. The 3-D cameras were clumsy and the audiences disliked wearing the obligatory glasses. The new wide-screen cinema was accompanied by the introduction of Stereographic sound, which eventually became standard.
1959	The first film in Smell-O-Vision, *The Scent of Mystery*, was released. The process did not catch on.
1980	Most major films were released in Dolby stereo.
1981	Designated 'the Year of Color Film' by director Martin Scorsese in a campaign to draw attention to, and arrest, the deterioration of colour film shot since 1950.
1982	One of the first and most effective attempts at feature-length, computer-generated animation was *Tron*, Walt Disney's $20-million bid to break into the booming fantasy market. 3-D made a short-lived comeback.
1987	US House Judiciary Committee petitioned by leading Hollywood filmmakers to protect their work from electronic 'colorization', the new process by which black-and-white films were tinted for television transmission.
1988	Robert Zemeckis's (1952–) *Who Framed Roger Rabbit* set new technical standards in combining live action with cartoon animation.

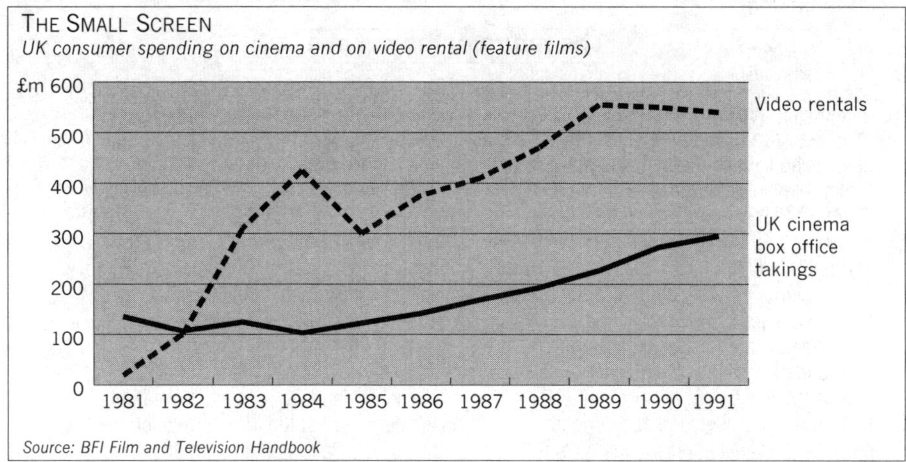

The Informer 1935, *The Grapes of Wrath* 1940, *How Green Was My Valley* 1941, and *The Quiet Man* 1952.

Other films include *They Were Expendable* 1945, *She Wore a Yellow Ribbon* 1949, *Rio Grande* 1950, *The Last Hurrah* 1958, and *The Man Who Shot Liberty Valance* 1962.

Gance Abel 1889–1981. French film director who was one of the great innovators of the French silent cinema. His romantic epic *Napoléon* 1927 (restored in 1980 and subsequently widely shown) was the high point of his career. One of the most ambitious silent epic films, it features colour and triple-screen sequences, as well as multiple-exposure shots.

An actor in films from 1909 and a director from 1912, Gance showed his inclination for experiment in films such as *J'Accuse* 1919 and *La Roue* 1922. The process culminated in *Napoléon*, with its extravagant use of hand-held cameras, rapid cutting, and superimpositions. The arrival of sound seemed to stifle his creative output, though he continued to work, mainly on historical films, until the 1960s. Later films included *Lucreze Borgia* 1935 and *Austerlitz* 1960.

Godard Jean-Luc 1930– . French film director, one of the leaders of New Wave cinema. His works are often characterized by experimental techniques and an unconventional dramatic form, as well as by political allusions. His films include *A bout de souffle* 1959, *Vivre sa Vie* 1962, *Pierrot le fou* 1965, *Weekend* 1968, and *Je vous salue, Marie* 1985.

Griffith D(avid) W(ark) 1875–1948. US film director, one of the most influential figures in the development of cinema as an art. He made hundreds of "one-reelers' 1908–13, in which he pioneered the techniques of masking, fade-out, flashback, crosscut, close-up, and long shot. After much experimentation, his masterpiece as a director emerged, *The Birth of a Nation* 1915, about the aftermath of the Civil War, later criticized as degrading to blacks.

Other films include the epic *Intolerance* 1916, *Broken Blossoms* 1919, *Way Down East* 1920, *Orphans of the Storm* 1921, and *The Struggle* 1931. He was a cofounder of United Artists 1919. With the advent of sound, his reputation was eclipsed, and he lived forgotten in Hollywood until his death.

Hawks Howard 1896–1977. US director and producer. In a career spanning over four decades, Hawks worked in virtually all the popular American genres – westerns, thrillers, screwball comedies, among others – and brought to them a skill and professionalism that made him the arch-exponent of Hollywood filmmaking.

Hawks had been an aviator and racing driver before entering the cinema, and films as varied as *Scarface* 1932, *The Big Sleep* 1946, and *Rio Bravo* 1959 are concerned with both danger and the need for functional expertise. At the same time, uniquely fast-talking comedies like *His Girl Friday* 1940 turned the preoccupations of his action movies on their head by dramatising the lure of irresponsibility. His other films include *Bringing Up Baby* 1938 and *Gentlemen Prefer Blondes* 1953. His final film was *Rio Lobo* 1970.

Hitchcock Alfred 1899–1980. British film director who became a US citizen in 1955. A master of the suspense thriller, he was noted for his meticulously drawn storyboards that determined his camera angles and for his cameo 'walk-ons' in his own films. His *Blackmail* 1929 was the first successful British talking film; *The Thirty-Nine Steps* 1935 and *The Lady Vanishes* 1939 are British suspense classics.

He went to Hollywood 1940, where his films included *Rebecca* 1940, *Notorious* 1946, *Strangers on a Train* 1951, *Rear Window* 1954, *Vertigo* 1958, *Psycho* 1960, and *The Birds* 1963. His last film was *Family Plot* 1976. He also hosted two US television mystery series, *Alfred Hitchcock Presents* 1955-62 and *The Alfred Hitchcock Hour* 1963-65.

Huston John 1906–1987. US film director, screenwriter, and actor. An impulsive and individualistic film maker, he often dealt with the themes of greed, treachery in human relationships, and the loner. His works as a director include *The Maltese Falcon* 1941 (his debut), *The Treasure of the Sierra Madre* 1948 (in which his father Walter Huston starred and for which both won Academy Awards), *Key Largo* 1948, *The African Queen* 1951, *Moby Dick* 1956, *The Misfits* 1961, *Fat City* 1972, *Prizzi's Honor* 1984, and his last, *The Dead* 1987. His daughter is the actress Anjelica Huston.

The return of the remake

A characteristic of recent US cinema, evident to anyone scrutinizing the small print in credit titles, is how many films are adaptations of foreign-language originals. For example, *Sommersby* derives from *Le Retour de Martin Guerre* 1982, *Scent of a Woman* from *Profumo di donna* 1975, *The Assassin* from *Nikita* 1990, *The Vanishing* from the Dutch film *Spoorloos* 1988.

This phenomenon needs, however, to be placed in perspective. Remakes have always been a staple element in commercial filmmaking in Hollywood and, indeed, elsewhere, even if in recent years semi-remakes of successful movies have been passed off as sequels. A well-known title possesses built-in appeal and in the days of the studio system it was cheaper to revisit a property to which the studio already held the rights. (As a random example, Warners remade *The Mouthpiece* 1932 under different titles in 1940 and 1955.) Established directors did not scorn the process: John Ford and Alfred Hitchcock each undertook a remake of one of his own earlier films.

Nor was it unusual for Hollywood to purchase the rights to European successes. By an odd coincidence, two of the films Fritz Lang made in the USA were derived from French films by Jean Renoir (*Scarlet Street* 1945 from *La Chienne* 1932; *Human Desire* 1954 from *La Bëte humaine* 1938), while Lang's German classic *M* 1931 underwent a US remake in 1951. The American *M*, in fact, succeeded strikingly because its style was wholly different from that of its source. But to remake an acknowledged classic is rendered riskier than ever by a shift in underlying cultural assumptions: *Sorcerer* 1977 was a lamentable US version of Henri-Georges Clouzot's *La Salaire de la peur/The Wages of Fear* 1953.

Even when, as in the recent instances, the original is not a particularly celebrated one, pitfalls still exist, as became evident in the Robert De Niro vehicle *Night and the City*, derived from a 1950 film *noir* of the same name. The problem is not one of direct comparison, which by now only a handful of movie buffs would be qualified to make, but more basically that when the storyline has been wrenched out of its original context – in this instance that of the postwar London underworld – and relocated in contemporary North America, it does not retain much in the way of individuality or conviction.

Something of the same problem may attach to *Sommersby*, which adapts to the post-Civil War American South a story (with a basis in historical records) of 16th-century France. The appeal of the original substantially lay in evoking the texture of a remote time, and while *Sommersby* attempts its own show of heightened atmosphere, the era being depicted is much more familiar, to the detriment of the film. Moreover, the new film's elaboration of the dramatic intrigue changes the emphasis of the courtroom scenes and in doing so renders them somewhat unsatisfactory. The spectator may be left wondering whether the story might have worked better had it been made up from scratch.

With contemporary thrillers like *The Assassin* and *The Vanishing*, where narrative is much more central, difficulties of cultural translation are abated, though it may be questioned whether the former's storyline is of any special interest once bereft of the stylistic attributes of the original director, Luc Besson.

The Dutch original of *The Vanishing* possessed both an ingenious plot and an adaptable veneer of social observation, though in respect of the former, the horrific final twist was evidently deemed too strong for US audiences, who have been regaled with a more upbeat conclusion.

What further distinguishes *The Vanishing* is that the remake has been directed by George Sluizer, who made the original. This represents a logical variation on the traditional Hollywood practice of absorbing international talent. What might rather be considered cause for concern is that if such remakes become instant – and reportedly some US producers have purchased rights to foreign properties while the native versions are still in production – films made outside North America will find it even more difficult than at present to get on to US screens. Thus, one more disincentive is created for filmmaking in the countries of Europe and elsewhere, and a further impetus provided for US domination of the worldwide box office.

TP

Transatlantic exchange

Original European films and their US remakes (in $US)

Original (year of release in USA)	*US gross*	*Remake (year)*	*US gross*
3 Men and A Cradle ('86)	2,150,000	3 Men and A Baby ('87)	168,000,000
Profumo di Donna ('76)	200,000	Scent of a Woman ('92)	57,000,000*
The Toy ('79)	700,000	The Toy ('82)	50,000,000
Le Retour de Martin Guerre ('83)	4,000,000	Sommersby ('93)	44,500,000*
Les Fugitifs (unreleased in US)	-	Three Fugitives ('89)	40,000,000
La Femme Nikita ('91)	5,000,000	The Assassin ('93)	25,000,000*
Pardon Mon Affaire ('77)	1,700,000	Woman in Red ('84)	24,000,000
La Chevre ('75)	2,100,000	Pure Luck ('91)	22,000,000
One Wild Moment ('81)	150,000	Blame It on Rio ('83)	21,000,000
Cousin, Cousine ('76)	8,500,000	Cousins ('88)	20,000,000
Le Grand Chemin ('88)	750,000	Paradise ('91)	19,000,000
The Vanishing ('90)	800,000	The Vanishing ('93)	14,000,000
The Man Who Loved Women ('77)	2,000,000	The Man Who Loved Women ('83)	10,000,000
Tall Blond Man With 1 Black Shoe ('73)	1,400,000	The Man With 1 Red Shoe ('85)	9,000,000
A Pain in the A.. ('75)	1,200,000	Buddy, Buddy ('81)	7,000,000
La Vie continue ('82)	800,000	Men Don't Leave ('90)	6,100,000
Happy New Year ('73)	600,000	Happy New Year ('87)	100,000

** still in release April 1993.*

Source: Variety

Jennings Humphrey 1907–1950. British documentary filmmaker who introduced a poetic tone and subjectivity to factually based material. He was active in the General Post Office Film Unit from 1934 and his wartime films vividly portrayed London in the Blitz: *London Can Take It* 1940, *This Is England* 1941, and *Fires Were Started* 1943.

Kubrick Stanley 1928– . US director and producer. His films include *Paths of Glory* 1957, *Dr Strangelove* 1964, *2001: A Space Odyssey* 1968, *A Clockwork Orange* 1971, and *The Shining* 1979.

A former photographer for *Life* magazine, he forged an early reputation with several low-budget features, notably *The Killing* 1956, and subsequently relocated to England. More than any of his American contemporaries, he achieved complete artistic control over his projects, which have been eclectic in subject matter and ambitious in scale and technique. His other films include *Lolita* 1962, and *Full Metal Jacket* 1987.

Kurosawa Akira 1929– . Japanese director whose film *Rashomon* 1950 introduced Western audiences to Japanese cinema. Epics such as *Shichinin no samurai/Seven Samurai* 1954 combine spectacle with intimate human drama. His other films include *Drunken Angel* 1948, *Yojimbo* 1961, *Kagemusha* 1981, and *Ran* 1985.

Lang Fritz 1890–1976. Austrian film director whose films are characterized by a strong sense of fatalism and moral inquiry. His German films include *Metropolis* 1927, *M* 1931, in which Peter Lorre starred as a child-killer, and the series of Dr Mabuse films, after which he fled from the Nazis to Hollywood in 1936. His US films include *Fury* 1936, *You Only Live Once* 1937, *Scarlet Street* 1945, *Rancho Notorious* 1952, and *The Big Heat* 1953. He returned to Germany and directed a third picture in the Dr Mabuse series in 1960.

Lean David 1908–1991. British film director. His films, noted for their storytelling flair and atmospheric quality, include early work codirected with playwright Noël Coward. *Brief Encounter* 1946 established Lean as a leading talent. Among his later films are such accomplished epics as *The Bridge on the River Kwai* 1957 (Academy Award), *Lawrence of Arabia* 1962 (Academy Award), and *Dr Zhivago* 1965. The critics' antipathy to *Ryan's Daughter* 1970 caused him to withdraw from filmmaking for over a decade, but *A Passage to India* 1984 represented a return to form.

Méliès Georges 1861–1938. French film pioneer. From 1896 to 1912 he made over 1,000 films, many of them imaginative fantasies (*Le Voyage dans la Lune/A Trip to the Moon* 1902). He developed trick effects, slow motion, double exposure, and dissolves, and in 1897 built Europe's first film studio at Montreuil.

Born in Paris, Méliès started out as a stage magician. His interest in cinema was sparked by the Lumière brothers' *cinématographe*, premiered 1895. He constructed a camera and founded a production company, Star Film. Méliès failed to develop as a filmmaker and he went bankrupt 1913.

Ophuls Max. Adopted name of Max Oppenheimer 1902–1957. German film director, initially in the theatre, whose style is characterized by a bitter-sweet tone and intricate camera movement. He worked in Europe and the USA, attracting much critical praise for such films as *Letter from an Unknown Woman* 1948, *La Ronde* 1950, and *Lola Montes* 1955. His son is the documentary filmmaker Marcel Ophuls (1927–).

Ozu Yasujiro 1903–1963. One of Japan's leading film director who became known in the West only in his last years. *Tokyo Monogatari/Tokyo Story* 1953 illustrates his typical low camera angles and his predominant theme of middle-class family life. Other major films include *Late Spring* 1949 and *Autumn Afternoon* 1962.

Returns from abroad

US films at home and abroad: foreign gross versus domestic gross, 1992 (in US $m)

Title	*Foreign/US distrib*	*Foreign gross*	*US gross*
Basic Instinct	Indies/TriStar	235	117
Hook	Columbia TriStar/TriStar	180	120
Alien 3	20th Century Fox	125	55
JFK	Warner Brothers	120	70
Patriot Games	UIP/Paramount	85	83
Beethoven	UIP/Universal	85	57
Far and Away	UIP/Universal	66	59
My Girl	Columbia TriStar/Columbia	65	58
Universal Soldier	Indies/TriStar	59	36
Final Analysis	Warner	46	29
1492	Indies/Paramount	40	7

Source: Variety

Pasolini Pier Paolo 1922–1975. Italian director, poet, and novelist. His early work is coloured by his experience of life in the poor districts of Rome, where he lived from 1950, and illustrates the decadence and inequality of society from a Marxist viewpoint. Among his films are *Accattone!* 1961, *Mamma Roma* 1962, *Il vangelo secondo Mateo/The Gospel According to St Matthew* 1964, *Decameron* 1970, *I racconti de Canterbury/The Canterbury Tales* 1972, and *Salò/The 120 Days of Sodom* 1975.

Porter Edwin Stanton 1869–1941. US director, a pioneer of film narrative. His 1903 film *The Great Train Robbery* lasted 12 minutes – then an unusually long time for a film – and contained an early use of the close-up. More concerned with the technical than the artistic side of his films, which include *The Teddy Bears* 1907 and *The Final Pardon* 1912, Porter abandoned filmmaking 1916.

Powell Michael 1905–1990. English film director and producer. Some of his most memorable films were made in collaboration with Hungarian screenwriter Emeric Pressburger (1902–1988), with whom he formed a company, the Archers, in 1942. They produced a succession of ambitious and richly imaginative films, including *The Life and Death of Colonel Blimp* 1943, *A Matter of Life and Death* 1946, *Black Narcissus* 1947, *The Red Shoes* 1948, and the opera movie *The Tales of Hoffman* 1951. On his own, Powell later made *Peeping Tom* 1960, a voyeuristic horror film which attracted widespread criticism.

Ray Satyajit 1921–1992. Indian film director, internationally known for his trilogy of life in his native Bengal: *Pather Panchali*, *Unvanquished*, and *The World of Apu* 1955–59. Later films include *The Music Room* 1958, *Charulata* 1964, *The Chess Players* 1977, and *The Home and the World* 1984.

Reed Carol 1906–1976. British film producer and director, an influential figure in the British film industry of the 1940s. His films include *Odd Man Out* 1947, *The Fallen Idol* and *The Third Man* both 1950 (both written by Graham Greene), and *Our Man in Havana* 1959. His later films included the Academy Award-winning *Oliver!* 1968.

Renoir Jean 1894–1979. French director whose films, characterized by their humanism and naturalistic technique, include *Boudu sauvé des eaux/Boudu Saved from Drowning* 1932, *La Grande Illusion* 1937, and *La Règle du Jeu/The Rules of the Game* 1939. In 1975 he received an honorary Academy Award for his life's work. He was the son of the painter Pierre-Auguste Renoir.

Rossellini Roberto 1906–1977. Italian film director. His World War II trilogy, *Roma città aperta/Rome, Open City* 1945, *Paisà/Paisan* 1946, and *Germania anno zero/Germany Year Zero* 1947, had a quality of direct realism which made it a landmark of European cinema.

In 1949 he made *Stromboli*, followed by other films in which his wife Ingrid Bergman appeared. After their divorce he made *General della Rovere* 1959 and embarked on television work including a feature-length film for French TV *La Prise de Pouvoir par Louis XIV/The Rise of Louis XIV* 1966. He and Ingrid Bergman were the parents of actress Isabella Rossellini (1952–).

Scorsese Martin 1942– . US director whose films concentrate on complex characterization and the themes of alienation and guilt. His influential and forceful work includes *Mean Streets* 1973, *Taxi Driver* 1976, *Raging Bull* 1980, *The Color of Money* 1986, *After Hours* 1987, *The Last Temptation of Christ* 1988, and *Cape Fear* 1991.

Spielberg Steven 1947– . US director, writer, and producer of such films as *Jaws* 1975, *Close Encounters of the Third Kind* 1977, *Raiders of the Lost Ark* 1981, and *ET* 1982. Immensely successful, his films usually combine cliff-hanging suspense with heartfelt sentimentality. He also directed *Indiana Jones and the Temple of Doom* 1984, *The Color Purple* 1985, *Empire of the Sun* 1987, *Indiana Jones and the Last Crusade* 1989, *Hook* 1992, and Jurassic Park 1993.

Sternberg Josef von 1894–1969. Austrian film director, in the USA from childhood. He is best remembered for his seven films with Marlene Dietrich, including *The Blue Angel/Der blaue Engel* 1930, *Blonde Venus* 1932, and *The Devil Is a Woman* 1935, all of which are marked by his expressive use of light and shadow. His subsequent career was sporadic, culminating in the Japanese-made *Saga of Anatahan* 1953.

Downed by law

In March 1993, a California court ruling bankrupted actress Kim Basinger by requiring her to pay $6 million damages (reduced on appeal to $5 million) to the producers of *Boxing Helena* for abruptly withdrawing from the picture, putting paid to Samuel Goldwyn's maxim that a verbal contract is not worth the paper it is printed on. The Basinger case threatens the culture of Hollywood deal-making in the US state where verbal agreements are legally binding. Carl Mazzocone, president of Main Line, producers of *Boxing Helena*, said after the jury ruled that Basinger had acted with fraud and malice: 'I think it will alert actors and actresses that when they commit, they commit.' Basinger, star of *Batman* and the explicit *9½ Weeks*, said she decided not to play in the film because she only considered roles involving 'artistic' rather than 'graphic' nudity. Not the least unexpected aspect of the affair is that the writer-director of *Boxing Helena*, whose heroine is kept in a box after her arms and legs are amputated, is a woman: Jennifer Lynch.

Stroheim Erich von. Assumed name of Erich Oswald Stroheim 1885–1957. Austrian actor and director, in Hollywood from 1914. He was successful as an actor in villainous roles, then embarked on a career as a director. Such films as *Foolish Wives* 1922 won widespread praise, but his progress foundered on his extravagance (*Greed* 1923), and he returned to acting in such international films as *La Grande Illusion* 1937 and *Sunset Boulevard* 1950.

Sturges Preston. Adopted name of Edmond Biden 1898–1959. US film director and writer who enjoyed great success with a series of satirical comedies in the early 1940s, including *Sullivan's Travels* 1941, *The Palm Beach Story* 1942, and *The Miracle of Morgan's Creek* 1943. His last film *Diary of Major Thompson* 1955 was made in France.

Tarkovsky Andrei 1932–1986. Soviet film director whose work is characterized by an epic style combined with intense personal spirituality. His films include *Solaris* 1972, *Mirror* 1975, *Stalker* 1979, and *The Sacrifice* 1986. The last was made in Sweden, following his exile from the USSR in 1984.

Tati Jacques. Stage name of Jacques Tatischeff 1908–1982. French comic actor, director, and writer. He portrayed Monsieur Hulot, the embodiment of polite opposition to modern mechanization, in a series of films starting with *Les Vacances de M Hulot/Monsieur Hulot's Holiday* 1953, and including *Mon Oncle/My Uncle* 1959 and *Playtime* 1968.

Truffaut François 1932–1984. French New Wave film director and actor, formerly a critic. A popular, romantic, and intensely humane filmmaker, he wrote and directed a series of semi-autobiographical films starring Jean-Pierre Léaud, beginning with *Les Quatre Cent Coups/The 400 Blows* 1959. His other films include *Jules et Jim* 1961, *Fahrenheit 451* 1966, *L'Enfant sauvage/The Wild Child* 1970, and *La Nuit américaine/Day for Night* 1973 (Academy Award).

His love of cinema led to a job as film critic for *Cahiers du Cinema* during the 1950s before embarking on his career as director. His later work includes *The Story of Adèle H* 1975 and *The Last Metro* 1980. He was influenced by Alfred Hitchcock, and also by French comic traditions.

Vigo Jean. Adopted name of Jean Almereida 1905–1934. French director of intensely lyrical and semi-surrealist films. He made only two shorts, *A Propos de Nice* 1930 and *Taris Champion de Natation* 1934; and two feature films, *Zéro de conduite/Nothing for Conduct* 1933 and *L'Atalante* 1934. His promising career was tragically cut short by leukemia.

Visconti Luchino 1906–1976. Italian film, opera, and theatre director. The film *Ossessione* 1942 pioneered neorealist cinema despite being subject to censorship problems from the fascist government; later works include *Rocco and His Brothers* 1960,

Made in the UK?

UK feature films produced in 1991 (by type of production)

	Number of films	*Total production cost (£m)*	*UK share of total production cost (£m)*
Films shot wholly or partly in the UK by British production companies	23	48.80	46.74
Films shot wholly or partly in the UK by foreign production companies	7	81.00	43.80
British films and co-productions shot wholly or partly outside the UK	18	79.98	27.85
Sub total	48	209.78	118.39
Co-productions shot outside the UK with no British cast or crew	11	33.46	–
Total – all UK films	***59***	***243.24***	***118.39***

Source: Cultural Trends/PSI

The Leopard 1963, *The Damned* 1969, and *Death in Venice* 1971. His powerful social commentary led to clashes with the Italian government and Roman Catholic Church.

Wajda Andrzej 1926– . Polish film and theatre director, one of the major figures in postwar European cinema. His films are often concerned with the predicament and disillusionment of individuals caught up in political events. His works include *Ashes and Diamonds* 1958, *Man of Marble* 1977, *Man of Iron* 1981, *Danton* 1982, and *Korczak* 1990. He has also worked in television and theatre. He made a television film version of Joseph Conrad's *The Shadow Line* 1976.

Welles (George) Orson 1915–1985. US actor and film and theatre director, whose first film was *Citizen Kane* 1941, which he produced, directed, and starred in. Using innovative lighting, camera angles and movements, he made it a landmark in the history of cinema, yet he directed very few films subsequently in Hollywood, and later worked mostly in Europe. His performances as an actor include the character of Harry Lime in *The Third Man* 1949.

In 1937 he founded the Mercury Theater, New York, with John Houseman, where their repertory productions included a modern-dress version of *Julius Caesar*. Welles's realistic radio broadcast of H G Wells's *The War of the Worlds* 1938 caused panic and fear of Martian invasion in the USA. He directed the films *The Magnificent Ambersons* 1942, *The Lady from Shanghai* 1948 with his wife Rita Hayworth, *Touch of Evil* 1958, and *Chimes at Midnight* 1967, a Shakespeare adaptation. As his career declined he became a familiar voice and face in US television commercials, and made guest appearances on TV shows.

Dance

African traditional dance tribal and regional African dances with a primarily ritualistic function. These rhythmically complex dances are performed to celebrate the important events in people's lives and are part of their everyday experience. In most cases the dance focuses on the circle, with soloists splitting off and then returning to the main group. Movement is generally directed towards the ground rather than upwards.

avant-garde dance experimental dance form that rejects the conventions of modern dance. It is often performed in informal spaces – museums, rooftops, even scaling walls.

In the USA, avant-garde dance stemmed mainly from the collaboration between Merce Cunningham in New York and musician Robert Dunn, which resulted in the Judson Dance Theater. While retaining technique and rhythm, Cunningham deleted the role of choreographer, thus giving dancers a new freedom. The Judson collective went further, denying even the necessity for technique and concentrating on the use of everyday movements – walking, spinning, jumping. In the UK, leading exponents of avant- garde dance techniques include Michael Clark from the mid-1980s and Rosemary Butcher. In Germany, Pina Bausch with her Wuppertal Tanztheater (dance theatre), established 1974, has been considered the most compelling influence in European dance since Diaghilev. Her works, often several hours long, blend dance, music, dialogue, gesture, psychology, comedy, and stark fear, and may be performed on floors covered with churned earth, rose petals, or water..

Avant-garde dance repertory

Date	*Title*	*Choreographer*	*Place*
1969	*Moving Earth*	Kei Takei	New York
1970	*Walking on the Wall*	Trisha Brown	New York
1971	*Education of the Girlchild*	Meredith Monk	New York
1978	*Café Müller*	Pina Bausch	Essen
1986	*The Watteau Duet*	Karole Armitage	New York
1988	*I Am Curious Orange*	Michael Clark	Amsterdam

ballet theatrical representation in stylized dance form in which music also plays a major part in telling a story or conveying a mood. Some such form of entertainment existed in ancient Greece, but Western ballet as we know it today first appeared in Italy. From there it was brought by Catherine de' Medici to France in the form of a spectacle combining singing, dancing, and declamation. In the 20th century Russian ballet has had a vital influence on the Classical tradition in the West, and ballet developed further in the USA through the work of George Balanchine and American Ballet Theater, and in the UK through the influence of Marie Rambert. Modern dance is a separate development.

history The first important dramatic ballet, the *Ballet comique de la reine*, was produced 1581 by the Italian Balthasar de Beaujoyeux at the French court and was performed by male courtiers, with ladies of the court forming the *corps de ballet*. In 1661 Louis XIV founded *L'Académie royale de danse*, to which all subsequent ballet activities throughout the world can be traced. Long, flowing court dress was worn by the dancers until the 1720s when Marie-Anne Camargo, the first great ballerina, shortened her skirt to reveal her ankles, thus allowing greater movement *à terre* and the development of dancing *en l'air*. It was not until the early 19th century that a Paris costumier, Maillot, invented tights, thus allowing complete muscular freedom. The first of the great ballet masters was Jean-Georges Noverre, and great contemporary dancers were Teresa Vestris, Anna Friedrike Heinel, Jean Dauberval, and Maximilien Gardel. Carlo Blasis is regarded as the founder of Classical ballet since he defined the standard conventional steps and accompanying gestures.

Romantic ballet The great Romantic era of Taglioni, Elssler, Grisi, Grahn, and Cerrito began about 1830 but survives today only in the ballets *Giselle* 1841 and *La Sylphide* 1832. Characteristics of this era were the new calf-length Romantic white dress and the introduction of dancing on the toes, *sur les pointes*. The technique of the female dancer was developed, but the role of the male dancer was reduced to that of her partner.

Russian ballet was introduced to the West by Sergei Diaghilev, who set out for Paris 1909, at about the same time that Isadora Duncan, a fervent opponent of classical ballet, was touring Europe. Associated with Diaghilev were Mikhail Fokine, Vaslav Nijinsky, Anna Pavlova, Léonide Massine, George Balanchine, and Serge Lifar. Ballets presented by his company, before its break-up after his death 1929, included *Les Sylphides*, *Schéhérazade*, *Petrouchka*, and *Blue Train*. Diaghilev and Fokine pioneered a new and exciting combination of the perfect technique of imperial Russian dancers and the appealing naturalism favoured by Isadora Duncan. In Russia ballet continues to flourish, the two chief companies being the Kirov and the Bolshoi. Best-known ballerinas are Galina Ulanova and Maya Plisetskaya, and male dancers include the late Rudolf Nureyev, Mikhail Baryshnikov, and Alexander Godunov, now dancing in the West, as are the husband-and-wife team Vyacheslav Gordeyev and Nadezhda Pavlova.

American ballet was firmly established by the founding of Balanchine's School of American Ballet 1934, and by de Basil's Ballets Russes de Monte Carlo and Massine's Ballet Russe de Monte Carlo, which also carried on the Diaghilev tradition. In 1939 Lucia Chase and Richard Pleasant founded American Ballet Theater. From 1948 the New York City Ballet, under the guiding influence of Balanchine, developed a genuine American Neo-Classic style.

British ballet Marie Rambert initiated 1926 the company that developed into the Ballet Rambert, and launched the careers of choreographers such as Frederick Ashton and Anthony Tudor. The national company, the Royal Ballet (so named 1956), grew from

dance: chronology

1000 BC	King David danced 'with all his might' before the ark of the Covenant in Jerusalem – one of the earliest known instances of ritual dance.
405	*Bacchants* by Euripides was staged in Athens. The play demanded a considerable amount of dancing.
142	Consul Scipio Aemilianus Africanus closed the burgeoning dance schools of Rome in a drive against hedonism.
774 AD	Pope Zacharias forbade dancing.
1050	The *Ruodlieb*, a poem written by a monk at Tegernsee, Bavaria, contained the first European reference to dancing in couples.
1313	Rabbi Hacén ben Salomo of Zaragoza, in Aragon, like many other Jews in medieval times, was the local dancing master.
1489	A rudimentary allegorical ballet was performed in honour of the marriage of the Duke of Milan, at Tortona, Italy.
1581	In Paris, the first modern-style unified ballet, the *Ballet Comique de la Reine*, was staged at the court of Catherine de' Medici.
1588	Dance and ballet's first basic text, *L'Orchésographie*, by the priest Jehan Tabouret, was printed in Langres, near Dijon.
1651	In London, John Playford published *The English Dancing Master*. The 18th edition (1728) described 900 country dances.
1661	Louis XIV founded L'Académie Royale de Danse in Paris.
1670	The first classic ballet, *Le Bourgeois Gentilhomme*, was produced in Chambord, France.
1681	La Fontaine, the first professional female ballet dancer, made her debut in *Le Triomphe de L'amour* at the Paris Opéra.
1734	The dancer Marie Sallé adopted the gauze tunic, precursor to the Romantic tutu, and Marie Camargo shortened her skirts.
1738	The Kirov Ballet was established in St Petersburg, Russia.
1760	The great dancer and choreographer Jean-Georges Noverre published in Lyons *Lettres sur la Danse et sur les Ballets*, one of the most influential of all ballet books.
1776	The Bolshoi Ballet was established in Moscow.
1778	Noverre and Mozart collaborated on *Les Petits Riens* in Paris. The cast included the celebrated Auguste Vestris.
late 1700s	The waltz originated in Austria and Germany from a popular folk dance, the *Ländler*.
1820	Carlo Blasis, teacher and choreographer, published his *Traité élémentaire théoretique et pratique de l'arte de la danse* in Milan which, together with his later works of dance theory, codified techniques for future generations of dancers.
1821	The first known picture of a ballerina *sur les pointes*, the French Fanny Bias by F Waldeck, dates from this year.
1832	The first performance of *La Sylphide* at the Paris Opéra opened the Romantic era of ballet and established the central significance of the ballerina. Marie Taglioni, the producer's daughter, who created the title role, wore the new-style Romantic tutu.
1841	Ballet's Romantic masterpiece *Giselle*, with Carlotta Grisi in the leading role, was produced in Paris.
1845	Four great rival ballerinas of the Romantic era – Taglioni, Grisi, Fanny Cerrito, and Lucille Grahn – appeared together in Perrot's *Pas de Quatre* in London.
1866	*The Black Crook*, the ballet extravaganza from which US vaudeville and musical comedy developed, began its run of 474 performances in New York.
1870	*Coppélia*, 19th-century ballet's comic masterpiece, was presented in Paris.
1877	*La Bayadère* and *Swan Lake* were premiered in Moscow, but the latter failed through poor production and choreography. The Petipa-Ivanov version, in which Pierina Legnani performed 32 *fouettés*, established the work 1895.
1897	Anna Pavlova made her debut in St Petersburg with the Imperial Russian Ballet.
1905	Isadora Duncan appeared in Russia, making an immense impression with her 'antiballet' innovations derived from Greek dance.
1906	Vaslav Nijinsky made his debut in St Petersburg.
1909	The first Paris season given by Diaghilev's troupe of Russian dancers, later to become known as the Ballets Russes, marked the beginning of one of the most exciting periods in Western ballet.
1913	The premiere of Stravinsky's *The Rite of Spring* provoked a scandal in Paris.
1914	The foxtrot developed from the two-step in the USA.
1915	The Denishawn School of Modern Dance was founded in Los Angeles.
1926	Martha Graham, one of the most innovative figures in Modern dance, gave her first recital in New York. In England, students from the Rambert School of Ballet, opened by Marie Rambert in 1920, gave their first public performance in *A Tragedy of Fashion*, the first ballet to be choreographed by Frederick Ashton.
1928	The first performance of George Balanchine's *Apollon Musagète* in Paris, by the Ballets Russes, marked the birth of Neo-Classicism in ballet.

dance: chronology *(cont.)*

1931	Ninette de Valois's Vic-Wells Ballet gave its first performance in London. In 1956 the company became the Royal Ballet.
1933	The Hollywood musical achieved artistic independence through Busby Berkeley's kaleidoscopic choreography in *Forty-Second Street* and Dave Gould's airborne finale in *Flying Down to Rio*, in which Fred Astaire and Ginger Rogers appeared together for the first time.
1939	The American Ballet Theater was founded in New York.
1940	The Dance Notation Bureau was established in New York for recording ballets and dances.
1948	The New York City Ballet was founded with George Balanchine as artistic director and principal choreographer. The film *The Red Shoes* appeared, choreographed by Massine and Robert Helpmann, starring Moira Shearer.
1950	The Festival Ballet, later to become the London Festival Ballet, was created by Alicia Markova and Anton Dolin, who had first danced together with the Ballets Russes de Monte Carlo 1929.
1952	Gene Kelly starred and danced in the film *Singin' in the Rain*.
1953	The US experimental choreographer Merce Cunningham, who often worked with the composer John Cage, formed his own troupe.
1956	The Bolshoi Ballet opened its first season in the West at Covent Garden in London, with Galina Ulanova dancing in *Romeo and Juliet*.
1957	Jerome Robbins conceived and choreographed the musical *West Side Story*, demonstrating his outstanding ability to work in both popular and Classical forms.
1960	The progressive French choreographer Maurice Béjart became director of the Brussels-based *Ballet du XXième Siècle* company.
1961	Rudolf Nureyev defected from the USSR while dancing with the Kirov Ballet in Paris. He was to have a profound influence on male dancing in the West. The South African choreographer John Cranko became director and chief choreographer of the Stuttgart Ballet, transforming it into a major company.
1962	Glen Tetley's ballet *Pierrot Lunaire*, in which he was one of the three dancers, was premiered in New York. In the same year he joined the Nederlands Dans Theater.
1965	US choreographer Twyla Tharp produced her first works.
1966	The School of Contemporary Dance was founded in London, from which Robin Howard and the choreographer Robert Cohan created the London Contemporary Dance Theatre, later to become an internationally renowned company. The choreographer Norman Morrice rejoined the Ballet Rambert as director and the company began to concentrate on contemporary works.
1968	Arthur Mitchell, the first black principal dancer to join the New York City Ballet, founded the Dance Theatre of Harlem.
1974	Mikhail Baryshnikov defected from the USSR while dancing with the Kirov Ballet in Toronto, and made his US debut with the American Ballet Theater.
1977	The release of Robert Stigwood's film *Saturday Night Fever* popularized disco dancing worldwide.
1980	Natalia Makarova, who had defected from the USSR 1979, staged the first full-length revival of Petipa's *La Bayadère* in the West with the American Ballet Theater in New York.
1981	Wayne Sleep, previously principal dancer with the Royal Ballet, starred as lead dancer in Andrew Lloyd-Webber's musical *Cats*, choreographed by Gillian Lynne.
1983	Peter Martins, principal dancer with the New York City Ballet, became choreographer and codirector with Jerome Robbins on the death of Balanchine. Break dancing became widely popular in Western inner cities.
1984	The avant-garde group Michael Clark and Company made its debut in London.
1990	*Maple Leaf Rag*, Martha Graham's final work, was premiered in New York City.

foundations laid by Ninette de Valois and Frederick Ashton 1928. British dancers include the late Margot Fonteyn, Alicia Markova, Anton Dolin, Antoinette Sibley, Anthony Dowell, David Wall, Merle Park, and Lesley Collier; Britain's leading choreographer was the late Kenneth MacMillan.

belly dancing Westernized form of ***rakshaki***, a traditional Egyptian dance form that has spread through the Middle East. It is characterized by the primary use of the hips, spine, shoulders, and stomach muscles rather than the legs, although jumps, turning, and precise footwork are features of the original form. The dance is now usually performed by women and is accompanied by traditional instruments. Traditionally, *rakshaki* was performed by both women and men; different forms exist for the two sexes.

butoh dance Japanese *ankoku butō* 'dance of darkness'. Japanese avant-garde dance. Developed by Tatsumi Hijikata in the 1960s, the form draws on both Japanese traditions and the European avant-garde. It is characterized by stillness, which is contrasted with frantic movements and an emotional intensity represented in a highly stylized manner. The dancers' faces and bodies are often painted white.

contact improvisation improvised movement sequences often in avant-garde dance. The sequences are the result of intuitive communication leading to contact between two or more dancers, which is used to explore the changes in the flow of movement between them. Contact improvisation is used both as a choreographic tool and as a form of therapy through movement.

dervish dance religious dance of Islam. Part of the mystical Sufi tradition, its aim is to reach spiritual awareness with a trance-like state created by continual whirling. This spinning symbolizes the Earth's orbit of the Sun.

flamenco music and dance of the Andalusian gypsies of S Spain, evolved from Andalusian and Arabic folk music. The *cante* (song) is sometimes performed as a solo but more often accompanied by guitar music and passionate improvised dance. Hand clapping, finger clicking (castanets are a more recent addition), and enthusiastic shouts are all features. Male flamenco dancers excel in powerful, rhythmic footwork while the female dancers place emphasis on the graceful and erotic movements of their hands and bodies.

folk dance dance characteristic of a particular people, nation, or region. Many European folk dances are derived from the dances accompanying the customs and ceremonies of pre-Christian times. Some later became ballroom dances (for example, the minuet and waltz). Once an important part of many rituals, folk dance has tended to die out in industrialized countries. Examples of folk dance are Morris dance, farandole, and jota.

jazz dance dance based on African techniques and rhythms, developed by black Americans around 1917. It entered mainstream dance in the 1920s, mainly in show business, and from the 1960s the teachers and choreographers Matt Mattox and Luigi expanded its vocabulary. Contemporary choreographers as diverse as Jerome Robbins and the late Alvin Ailey have used it in their work.

modern dance 20th-century dance idiom developed in reaction against the rigidity of traditional ballet by those seeking a freer and more immediate means of dance expression. Leading exponents include Martha Graham and Merce Cunningham in the USA, Isadora Duncan, and Loie Fuller in Europe. The first generation of modern dance – Martha Graham, Doris Humphrey, and Charles Weidman – emerged from Ruth St Denis and Ted Shawn's Denishawn School in Los Angeles 1915. Doris Humphrey opened a school and performing group in New York 1928. The Humphrey-Weidman technique was based on the kinetic theory of ***fall and recovery***. Humphrey's most famous protégé was José Limón. In the UK, the London Contemporary Dance Theatre and school was set up 1967 by Graham's pupil, Robert Cohan. It is the only European institute authorized to teach Graham Technique. In Germany, the originators of a modernist movement known as Central European dance were Jacques Dalcroze and Rudolph Laban. The leading exponents, Mary Wigman, Harald Kreutzberg, and Kurt Jooss, had some influence on modern dance.

Martha Graham's distinctive technique is based on ***contraction and release***, using the stomach and pelvic area as a dynamic centre of movement. From her company and School of Contemporary Dance, opened 1927 in New York, a long line of dancers and choreographers continues to emerge. Among them, Erick Hawkins, Merce Cunningham, Glenn Tetley, Paul Taylor, and Dan Waggoner have each evolved his own style.

tap dancing rapid step dance, derived from clog dancing. Its main characteristic is the tapping of toes and heels accentuated by steel 'taps' affixed to the shoes. It was popularized in vaudeville and in 1930s films by such dancers as Fred Astaire and Bill 'Bojangles' Robinson.

MUSIC

Musical Terms

a cappella choral music sung without instrumental accompaniment. It is characteristic of gospel music, doo-wop, and the evangelical Christian church movement.

acoustics in general, the experimental and theoretical science of sound and its transmission; in particular, that branch of the science that has to do with the phenomena of sound in a particular space such as a room or theatre.

alto voice or instrument between tenor and soprano. The sound of the traditional high male alto voice (also known as ***countertenor***) is trumpetlike and penetrating; the low-register female ***contralto*** is rich and mellow in tone. The alto range is centred on the octave above middle C on the piano. Alto is also another name for the French viola.

anthem short, usually elaborate, religious choral composition, sometimes accompanied by the organ; also a song of loyalty and devotion.

aria solo vocal piece in an opera or oratorio, often in three sections, the third repeating the first after a contrasting central section.

atonality music in which there is an apparent absence of key; often associated with an expressionist style.

bagatelle short character piece, often for piano.

bar or ***measure*** modular unit of rhythm, shown in notation by vertical 'barring' of the musical continuum into sections of usually constant duration and rhythmic content.

barbershop a style of unaccompanied close-harmony singing of sentimental ballads, revived in the USA during the 19th century. Traditionally sung by four male voices, since the 1970s it has developed as a style of a cappella choral singing for both male and female voices.

baritone male voice pitched between bass and tenor, centred in the octave below middle C and rising to the F or G above. The range is well suited to lieder.

bass (1) lowest range of male voice; (2) lower regions of musical pitch; (3) in the violin family, a double bass.

bel canto Italian style of singing with emphasis on perfect technique and beautiful tone. The style began in the 18th century and reached its peak in the operas of Gioacchino Rossini, Gaetano Donizetti (1797–1848), and Vincenzo Bellini (1801–1835).

cadence termination of a musical line or phrase, expressed rhythmically and harmonically.

cadenza unaccompanied bravura passage (requiring elaborate, virtuoso execution) in the style of an improvisation for the soloist during a concerto.

canon echo form for two or more parts repeating and following a leading melody at regular time intervals to achieve a harmonious effect. It is often found in classical music; for example, Vivaldi and J S Bach employed it.

cantata extended work for voices, from the Italian, meaning 'sung', as opposed to sonata ('sounded') for instruments. A cantata can be sacred or secular, sometimes uses solo voices, and usually has orchestral accompaniment. The first printed collection of sacred cantata texts dates from 1670.

capriccio short instrumental piece, often humorous or whimsical in character.

chamber music music suitable for performance in a small room or chamber, rather than in the concert hall, and usually written for instrumental combinations, played with one instrument to a part, as in the string quartet.

clef symbol used to indicate the pitch of the lines of the staff in musical notation.

coda concluding section of a movement, added to indicate finality.

coloratura rapid ornamental vocal passage with runs and trills. A ***coloratura soprano*** is a light, high voice suited to such music.

concerto composition, usually in three movements, for solo instrument (or instruments) and orchestra. It developed during the 18th century from the ***concerto grosso*** form for string orchestra, in which a group of solo instruments is contrasted with a full orchestra.

contralto low-registered female voice; also called an ***alto***.

counterpoint the art of combining different forms of an original melody with apparent freedom and yet to harmonious effect. Giovanni Palestrina and J S Bach were masters of counterpoint.

diatonic scale consisting of the seven notes of any major or minor key.

encore (French 'again') unprogrammed extra item, usually short and well known, played at the end of a concert to please an enthusiastic audience.

étude musical exercise designed to develop technique.

finale the last movement or section of a composition, by implication resolute in character.

fret inlaid ridge of ivory or metal, or of circlets of nylon, marking positions in the fingerboard of a plucked or bowed string instrument indicating changes of pitch.

fugue contrapuntal form (with two or more melodies) for a number of parts or 'voices', which enter successively in imitation of each other. It was raised to a high art by J S Bach.

gamelan Indonesian orchestra employing tuned gongs, xylophones, metallophones (with bars of metal), cymbals, drums, flutes, and fiddles, the music of which has inspired such Western composers as Debussy, Benjamin Britten, and Philip Glass (1937–).

Gregorian chant any of a body of plainsong choral chants associated with Pope Gregory the Great (540–604), which became standard in the Roman Catholic Church.

Classical music using unusual instruments

Instrument	*Composer and work*
accordion	Gerhard Nonet, *Metamorphoses*
antique cymbals	Debussy, *L'Après-midi d'un faune*
anvils	Wagner, *Das Rheingold*; Verdi, *Il Trovatore*; Varèse, *Ionisation*
basset horn (tenor clarinet)	Mozart, *Masonic Funeral Music*; Stockhausen, *Donnerstag aus LICHT*
bass tuba	Vaughan Williams, *Concerto in F minor*
bell plates	Boulez, *Rituel in Memoriam Maderna*
brake drums	John Cage, *First Construction in Metal*
castanets	Manuel de Falla, *The Three-Cornered Hat*, Ravel, *Alborada del Gracioso*
celesta	Tchaikovsky, *Nutcracker Suite*; Bartók, *Music for Strings, Percussion and Celesta*
cimbalom	Kodály, *Háry János*; Stravinsky, *Renard*
concertina	Regondi, *Concerto in D*
cowbell	Richard Strauss, *Alpen Symphony*; Mahler, Symphonies No 6 and 7
electric guitar	Martin, *Trois Poèmes de Villon*
flexatone	Schoenberg, *Variations Opus 31 for Orchestra*
glass armonica	Mozart, Beethoven (attributed)
guero	Stravinsky, *Rite of Spring*
harmonium	Schoenberg, *Herzgewächse*; Saint-Saëns, *L'Assassination du Duc de Guise*
heckelphone (baritone oboe)	Richard Strauss, *Salome*
Japanese tuned bowls (*rin*)	Stockhausen, *Inori*
Jew's harp	Albrechtsberger, *Concerto*
lion roar (cord or friction drum)	Varèse, *Ionisation*
marimbula	H W Henze, *El Cimarrón*
mouth organ	Vaughan Williams, *Romanza in D flat*; concertos by George Benjamin, Darius Milhaud
musical saw	George Crumb, *Ancient Voices of Children*
musical top	Stockhausen, *Zodiac*
musical toys (trumpet, drum, rattle, cuckoo, bird warbler, and so on)	Leopold Mozart, *'Toy' Symphony*
ondes Martenot	Messiaen, *Turangalîla Symphony*
panpipes	Mozart, *The Magic Flute*
prepared piano	John Cage, *Sonatas and Interludes*; Ravel, *L'Enfant et les Sortilèges*
piano roll	Stravinsky, *Les Noces*; Conlon Nancarrow (various compositions)
ratchet	Beethoven, *Wellington's Victory*; Schoenberg, *Gurrelieder*
sarrusaphone (contrabass oboe)	Stravinsky, *Threni*
saxophone	Richard Strauss, *'Domestic' Symphony*; Webern, *Quartet Opus 22*
slapstick (whip)	Britten, *The Burning Fiery Furnace*
Swanee whistle	Ravel, *L'Enfant et les sortilèges*
typewriter (manual, acoustic)	Satie, *Parade*
vibraphone	Alban Berg, *Lulu*; Pierre Boulez, *Le Marteau sans maître*
wind machine	Richard Strauss, *Don Quixote*; Messiaen, *Des Canyons aux étoiles*
xylophone	Saint-Saëns, *Danse macabre*

harmonics series of partial vibrations that combine to form a musical tone. The number and relative prominence of harmonics produced determines an instrument's tone colour (timbre). An oboe is rich in harmonics; a flute has few. Harmonics conform to successive divisions of the sounding air column or string: their pitches are harmonious.

impromptu short instrumental piece that suggests spontaneity. Composers of piano impromptus include Schubert and Chopin.

intermezzo short orchestral interlude often used between the acts of an opera to denote the passage of time; by extension, a short piece for an instrument to be played between other more substantial works.

key the diatonic scale around which a piece of music is written; for example, a passage in the key of C major will mainly use the notes of the C major scale. The term is also used for the lever activated by a keyboard player, such as a piano key.

libretto the text of an opera or other dramatic vocal work, or the scenario of a ballet.

lied musical setting of a poem, usually for solo voice and piano; referring to Romantic songs of Schubert, Schumann, Brahms, and Hugo Wolf.

madrigal form of secular song in four or five parts, usually sung without instrumental accompaniment. It originated in 14th-century Italy. Madrigal composers include Monteverdi and Thomas Morley (1557–1602).

melody distinctive sequence of notes. A melody may be a tune in its own right, or it may form a theme running through a longer piece of music.

metre accentuation pattern characteristic of a musical line; the regularity underlying musical rhythm.

mezzo-soprano female singing voice halfway between soprano and contralto.

middle C white note at the centre of the piano keyboard, indicating the division between left- and right-hand regions and between the treble and bass staves of printed music.

minuet European courtly dance of the 17th century, later used with the trio as the third movement in a classical symphony.

modulation movement from one key to another.

movement section of a large work, such as a symphony, which is often complete in itself.

nocturne lyrical, dreamy piece, often for piano, introduced by John Field (1782–1837) and adopted by Chopin.

opera dramatic musical work in which singing takes the place of speech. In opera, the music accompanying the action has paramount importance, although dancing and spectacular staging may also play their parts. Opera originated in late 16th-century Florence when the musical declamation, lyrical monologues, and choruses of Classical Greek drama were reproduced in current forms.

operetta light form of opera, with music, dance, and spoken dialogue. The story line is romantic and sentimental, often employing farce and parody. Its origins lie in the 19th-century *opéra comique* and is intended to amuse. Examples of operetta are Offenbach's (1819–1880) *Orphée aux enfers/Orpheus in the Underworld* 1858, Johann Strauss's *Die Fledermaus/The Bat* 1874, and *Pirates of Penzance* 1879 and *The Mikado* 1885 by W S Gilbert (1836–1911) and Arthur Sullivan (1842–1900).

opus term, used with a figure, to indicate the numbering of a composer's works, usually in chronological order.

oratorio dramatic, non-scenic musical setting of religious texts, scored for orchestra, chorus, and solo voices. Its origins lie in the *Laudi spirituali* performed by St Philip Neri's Oratory in Rome in the 16th century. The form reached perfection in such works as J S Bach's *Christmas Oratorio* and Handel's *Messiah*.

orchestration scoring of a composition for orchestra; the choice of instruments of a score expanded for orchestra (often by another hand). A work may be written for piano, and then transferred to an orchestral score.

overture piece of instrumental music, usually preceding an opera. There are also overtures to suites and plays, ballets, and 'concert' overtures, such as Elgar's *Cockaigne*.

prelude composition intended as the preface to further music, to set a mood for a stage work, as in Wagner's *Lohengrin*; as used by Chopin, a short piano work.

requiem in the Roman Catholic church, a mass for the dead. Musical settings include those by Palestrina, Mozart, Berlioz, and Verdi.

rhapsody instrumental fantasia, often based on folk melodies, such as Franz Lizst's *Hungarian Rhapsodies* 1853–54.

rhythm the patterning of music in movement; a recurring unit of long and short time values.

rondo form of instrumental music in which the principal section returns like a refrain. Rondo form is often used for the last movement of a sonata or concerto.

Top 10 classical albums (1992)

1	*The Essential Kiri*	Kiri Te Kanawa
2	*Essential Opera*	Various
3	*In Concert*	Carreras/Domingo/ Pavarotti
4	*Pavarotti In Hyde Park*	Luciano Pavarotti
5	*The Classic Romance*	Various
6	*The Essential Pavarotti*	Luciano Pavarotti
7	*The Classic Experience*	Various
8	*Take 2*	Various
9	*Essential Pavarotti II*	Luciano Pavarotti
10	*Beethoven Violin Concerto*	Nigel Kennedy/Klaus Tennstedt

scale sequence of pitches that establishes a key, and in some respects the character of a composition. A scale is defined by its starting note and may be ***major*** or ***minor*** depending on the order of intervals. A ***chromatic*** scale is the full range of 12 notes: it has no key because there is no fixed starting point.

scherzo lively piece, usually in rapid triple (3/4) time; often used for the third movement of a symphony, sonata, or quartet.

serenade musical piece for chamber orchestra or wind instruments in several movements, originally intended for evening entertainment, such as Mozart's *Eine kleine Nachtmusik/A Little Night Music*.

sonata piece of instrumental music written for a soloist or a small ensemble and consisting of a series of related movements.

soprano the highest range of the female voice, about an octave higher than a contralto. Its range stretches from F above middle C to the C an octave and half above; however, some operatic roles require the extended upper range of a coloratura soprano.

suite set of instrumental pieces, sometimes assembled from a stage work, such as Tchaikovsky's *Nutcracker Suite* 1891–92. Formerly, the term meant a grouping of old dance forms.

symphonic poem term originated by Liszt for his 13 one-movement orchestral works that interpret a story from literature or history, also used by many other composers. Richard Strauss preferred the term 'tone poem'.

symphony musical composition for orchestra, traditionally in four separate but closely related movements. It developed from the smaller sonata form, the Italian overture, and the dance suite of the 18th century.

syncopation the deliberate upsetting of rhythm by shifting the accent to a beat that is normally unaccented.

tempo the speed at which a piece is played.

tenor the highest range of adult male voice when not using falsetto. It covers a two-octave range centred on middle C and is the preferred voice for operatic heroic roles.

timbre the tone colour of an instrument.

tonality the observance of a key structure; that is, the recognition of the importance of a tonic or key note and of the diatonic scale built upon it.

vibrato slight but rapid fluctuation of intensity or pitch in voice or instrument.

Great Composers

Bach Johann Sebastian 1685–1750. German composer. He was a master of counterpoint, and his music epitomizes the Baroque polyphonic style. His orchestral music includes the six *Brandenburg Concertos*, other concertos for keyboard instrument and violin, and four orchestral suites. Bach's keyboard music, for clavier and organ, his fugues, and his choral music are of equal importance. He also wrote chamber music and songs.

Bartók Béla 1881–1945. Hungarian composer who developed a personal musical language, combining folk elements with mathematical concepts of tone and rhythmic proportion. His large output includes six string quartets, concertos, an opera, and graded teaching pieces for piano.

Beethoven Ludwig van 1770–1827. German composer and pianist whose mastery of musical expression in every genre made him the dominant influence on 19th-century music. Beethoven's repertoire includes concert overtures; the opera *Fidelio*; five piano concertos and two for violin (one unfinished); 32 piano sonatas, including the *Moonlight* and *Appassionata*; 17 string quartets; the *Mass in D* (*Missa solemnis*); and nine symphonies, as well as many youthful works. He usually played his own piano pieces and conducted his orchestral works until he was hampered by deafness 1801; nevertheless he continued to compose.

Berg Alban 1885–1935. Austrian composer. He studied under Arnold Schoenberg and was associated with him as one of the leaders of the serial, or 12-tone, school of composition. His output includes orchestral, chamber, and vocal music as well as two operas, *Wozzeck* 1925, a grim story of working-class life, and the unfinished *Lulu* 1929–35.

Berlioz (Louis) Hector 1803–1869. French Romantic composer, the founder of modern orchestration. Much of his music was inspired by drama and literature and has a theatrical quality. He wrote symphonic works, such as *Symphonie fantastique* 1830-31 and *Roméo et Juliette* 1839; dramatic cantatas, including *La Damnation de Faust* 1846 and *L'Enfance du Christ* 1854; sacred music; and three operas.

Brahms Johannes 1833–1897. German composer, pianist, and conductor who is considered one of the greatest composers of symphonic music and songs. His works include four symphonies; lieder (songs); concertos for piano and for violin; chamber music; sonatas; and the choral *A German Requiem* 1868.

Britten (Edward) Benjamin 1913–1976. English composer. He often wrote for the individual voice; for example, the role in the opera *Peter Grimes* 1945, based on verses by George Crabbe, was created for English tenor Peter Pears (1910–1986). Among his many works are the *Young Person's Guide to the Orchestra* 1946; the chamber opera *The Rape of Lucretia* 1946; *Billy Budd* 1951; *A Midsummer Night's Dream* 1960; and *Death in Venice* 1973.

Bruckner (Joseph) Anton 1824–1896. Austrian Romantic composer. He was cathedral organist at Linz 1856–68, and from 1868 he was professor at the Vienna Conservatoire. His works include many choral pieces and 11 symphonies, the last unfinished. His compositions were influenced by Richard Wagner and Beethoven.

Chopin Frédéric (François) 1810–1849. Polish composer and pianist. He made his debut as a pianist at the age of eight. As a performer, Chopin revolutionized the technique of pianoforte-playing, turning the hands outwards and favouring a light, responsive touch. His compositions for piano, which include two concertos and other works with orchestra, are characterized by great volatility of mood, and rhythmic fluidity.

Debussy (Achille-) Claude 1862–1918. French composer. He broke with the dominant tradition of German Romanticism and introduced new qualities of melody and harmony based on the whole-tone scale, evoking oriental music. His work includes *Prélude à l'après-midi d'un faune* 1894 and the opera *Pelléas et Mélisande* 1902.

Dvořák Antonin (Leopold) 1841–1904. Czech composer. International recognition came with his series of *Slavonic Dances* 1877–86, and he was director of the National Conservatory, New York, 1892–95. Works such as his *New World Symphony* 1893 reflect his interest in American folk themes, including black and native American. He wrote nine symphonies; tone poems; operas, including *Rusalka* 1900; large-scale choral works; the *Carnival* 1891–92 and other overtures; violin and cello concertos; chamber music; piano pieces; and songs. His Romantic music extends the Classical tradition of Beethoven and Brahms and displays the influence of Czech folk music.

Elgar Edward (William) 1857–1934. English composer. His *Enigma Variations* appeared 1899, and although his choral work, the oratorio setting of John Henry Newman's *The Dream of Gerontius*, was initially a failure, it was well received in Düsseldorf, Germany, in 1902. Many of his earlier works were then performed, including the *Pomp and Circumstance* marches.

Franck César Auguste 1822–1890. Belgian composer. His music, mainly religious and Romantic in style, includes the Symphony in D minor 1866–68, *Symphonic Variations* 1885 for piano and orchestra, the *Violin Sonata* 1886, the oratorio *Les Béatitudes/The Beatitudes* 1879, and many organ pieces.

Grieg Edvard Hagerup 1843–1907. Norwegian composer. Much of his music is small-scale, particularly his songs, dances, sonatas, and piano works. Among his orchestral works are the *Piano Concerto* 1869 and the incidental music for Henrik Ibsen's drama *Peer Gynt* 1876.

Handel Georg Friedrich 1685–1759. German composer who became a British subject 1726. His first opera, *Almira*, was performed in Hamburg 1705. In 1710 he was appointed Kapellmeister to the elector of Hanover (the future George I of England). In 1712 he settled in England, where he established his popularity with such works as the *Water Music* 1717 (written for George I). His great choral works include the *Messiah* 1742 and the later oratorios *Samson* 1743, *Belshazzar* 1745, *Judas Maccabaeus* 1747, and *Jephtha* 1752.

Haydn Franz Joseph 1732–1809. Austrian composer. A teacher of Mozart and Beethoven, he was a major exponent of the classical sonata form in his numerous chamber and orchestral works (he wrote more than 100 symphonies). He also composed choral music, including the oratorios *The Creation* 1798 and *The Seasons* 1801. He was the first great master of the string quartet.

Janáček Leoš 1854–1928. Czech composer. He became director of the Conservatoire at Brno in 1919 and professor at the Prague Conservatoire in 1920. His music, highly original and influenced by Moravian folk music, includes arrangements of folk songs, operas (*Jenůfa* 1904, *The Cunning Little Vixen* 1924), and the choral *Glagolitic Mass* 1926.

Liszt Franz 1811–1886. Hungarian pianist and composer. An outstanding virtuoso of the piano, he was an established concert artist by the age of 12. His expressive, romantic, and frequently chromatic works include piano music (*Transcendental Studies* 1851), symphonies, piano concertos, and organ music. Much of his music is programmatic; he also originated the symphonic poem.

Mahler Gustav 1860–1911. Austrian composer and conductor whose work displays a synthesis of Romanticism and new uses of chromatic harmonies and musical forms. He composed 14 symphonies, including three unnumbered (as a student), nine massive repertoire symphonies, the titled *Das Lied von der Erde/Song of the Earth* 1909, and the incomplete *Symphony No. 10*. He also wrote song cycles.

Mendelssohn (-Bartholdy) (Jakob Ludwig) Felix 1809–1847. German composer, also a pianist and conductor. As a child he composed and performed with his own orchestra and as an adult was helpful to Schumann's career. Among his best-known works are *A Midsummer Night's Dream* 1827; the *Fingal's Cave* overture 1832; and five symphonies, which include the Reformation 1830, the Italian 1833, and the Scottish 1842. He was instrumental in promoting the revival of interest in J S Bach's music.

Messiaen Olivier 1908–1992. French composer and organist. His music is mystical in character, vividly coloured, and incorporates transcriptions of birdsong. Among his works are the *Quartet for the End of Time* 1941, the large-scale *Turangalîla Symphony* 1949, and solo organ and piano pieces.

Monteverdi Claudio (Giovanni Antonio) 1567–1643. Italian composer. He contributed to the development of the opera with *Orfeo* 1607 and *The Coronation of Poppea* 1642. He also wrote madrigals, motets, and sacred music, notably the *Vespers* 1610.

Mozart Wolfgang Amadeus 1756–1791. Austrian composer and performer who showed astonishing precocity as a child and was an adult virtuoso. He was trained by his father, ***Leopold Mozart*** (1719–1787). From an early age he composed prolifically, his works including 27 piano concertos, 23 string quartets, 35 violin sonatas, and more than 50 symphonies including the E flat K543, G minor K550, and C major K551 ('Jupiter') symphonies, all composed 1788. His operas include *Idomeneo* 1781, *Le Nozze di Figaro/The Marriage of Figaro* 1786, *Don Giovanni* 1787, *Così fan tutte/Thus Do All Women* 1790, and *Die Zauberflöte/The Magic Flute* 1791. Strongly influenced by Haydn, Mozart's music marks the height of the Classical age in its purity of melody and form.

Mussorgsky Modest Petrovich 1839–1881. Russian composer who was largely self-taught. His opera *Boris Godunov* was completed in 1869, although not produced in St Petersburg until 1874. Some of his works were 'revised' by Rimsky-Korsakov, and only recently has their harsh original beauty been recognized.

Nielsen Carl (August) 1865–1931. Danish composer. His works show a progressive tonality, as in his opera *Saul and David* 1902 and six symphonies.

Palestrina Giovanni Pierluigi da 1525–1594. Italian composer of secular and sacred choral music. Apart from motets and madrigals, he also wrote 105 masses, including *Missa Papae Marcelli*.

Prokofiev Sergey (Sergeyevich) 1891–1953. Russian composer. His music includes operas such as *The Love for Three Oranges* 1921; ballets, including *Romeo and Juliet* 1935; seven symphonies, including the *Classical Symphony* 1916–17; music for films; piano and violin concertos; songs and cantatas (for example, that composed for the 30th anniversary of the October Revolution); and *Peter and the Wolf* 1936.

Puccini Giacomo (Antonio Domenico Michele Secondo Maria) 1858–1924. Italian opera composer whose music shows a strong gift for melody and dramatic effect and whose operas combine exotic plots with elements of *verismo* (realism). They include *Manon Lescaut* 1893, *La Bohème* 1896, *Tosca* 1900, *Madame Butterfly* 1904, and the unfinished *Turandot* 1926.

Purcell Henry 1659–1695. English Baroque composer. His work can be highly expressive; for example, the opera *Dido and Aeneas* 1689 and music for Dryden's *King Arthur* 1691 and for *The Fairy Queen* 1692. He wrote more than 500 works, ranging from secular operas and incidental music for plays to cantatas and church music.

Rachmaninov Sergei (Vasilevich) 1873–1943. Russian composer, conductor, and pianist. After the 1917 Revolution he went to the USA. His dramatically emotional Romantic music has a strong melodic basis and includes operas, such as *Francesca da Rimini* 1906, three symphonies, four piano concertos, piano pieces, and songs. Among his other works are the *Prelude in C-Sharp Minor* 1882 and *Rhapsody on a Theme of Paganini* 1934 for piano and orchestra.

Ravel (Joseph) Maurice 1875–1937. French composer. His work is characterized by its sensuousness, unresolved dissonances, and tone colour. Examples are the piano pieces *Pavane pour une infante défunte* 1899 and *Jeux d'eau* 1901, and the ballets *Daphnis et Chloë* 1912 and *Boléro* 1928.

Some musical expressions

Expression	*Meaning*
accelerando	gradually faster
adagio, adagietto	easy-going
agitato	agitated
alla breve	four beat as two to the bar
allargando	spreading out in tempo
allegro, allegretto	with lightness of action
andante, andantino	with movement
brio, con	with spirit
calando	winding down, slower and softer
cantabile	singing
capo (da)	from the top (beginning)
concerto	the solo (group)
crescendo	gradually louder
deciso	firmly
diminuendo	gradually softer
divisi a 2, 3, etc.	divided in 2, 3, etc. parts
dolce, dolcissimo	soft and sweetly
doloroso	mournfully
espressivo	with expression
flatterzunge	(German) fluttertongue
fuoco, con	with fire
giocoso	with fun
grave	with gravity
largo, larghetto	expansively
legato	smoothly
lento	slowly
l'istesso (tempo)	the same (tempo)
loco	in (its usual) place
lungo, lunga	long
misterioso	mysteriously
molto	much, very
pesante	weightily
poco, pochissimo	a little, very little
portamento	lifting (note to note)
presto, prestissimo	at speed, at high speed

Expression	*Meaning*
quasi	sort of, rather
ripieno	the accompanying ensemble
ritardando	gradually coming to a stop
ritenuto	pulling back
ritornello	refrain
rubato	borrowed (time)
secco	with a dry tone
segno	cue sign
segue	follow on
sempre	always
sforzato, sforzando	with a forced tone
smorzando	smothering, stifling the tone
sotto voce	in an undertone
spiccato	bounced (of the bow off the string)
staccato, -issimo	short, very short
subito	sudden, suddenly
Takt	(German) beat, metre, bar (measure)
tema	theme
tenuto	holding back
tessitura	range of instrument or voice
tranquillo	calmly
tanto	so much
troppo	too much
via	remove (eg mute)
veloce	at speed
vivo, vivace	with life
voce, voci	voice, voices
volante	as though flying
wieder	(German) again
Zeitmass	(German) tempo
zingaresca	gipsy
zu 2	(German) 1. for 2 players; 2. in 2 parts

Rimsky-Korsakov Nikolay Andreyevich 1844–1908. Russian composer. He used Russian folk idiom and rhythms in his Romantic compositions and published a text on orchestration. His operas include *The Maid of Pskov* 1873, *The Snow Maiden* 1882, *Mozart and Salieri* 1898, and *The Golden Cockerel* 1907, a satirical attack on despotism that was banned until 1909.

Rossini Gioacchino (Antonio) 1792–1868. Italian composer. His first success was the opera *Tancredi* 1813. In 1816 his 'opera buffa' *Il barbiere di Siviglia/The Barber of Seville* was produced in Rome. During 1815–23 he produced 20 operas, and took a leading part in creating the 19th-century Italian operatic style.

Saint-Saëns (Charles) Camille 1835–1921. French composer, pianist and organist. Among his many lyrical Romantic pieces are concertos, the symphonic poem *Danse macabre* 1875, the opera *Samson et Dalila* 1877, and the orchestral *Carnaval des animaux/Carnival of the Animals* 1886.

Schoenberg Arnold (Franz Walter) 1874–1951. Austro-Hungarian composer, a US citizen from 1941. After Romantic early works such as *Verklärte Nacht/Transfigured Night* 1899 and the *Gurrelieder/Songs of Gurra* 1900–11, he experimented with atonality (absence of key), producing works such as *Pierrot Lunaire* 1912 for chamber ensemble and voice, before developing the 12-tone system of musical composition. This was further developed by his pupils Alban Berg and Anton Webern (1883–1945).

Schubert Franz (Peter) 1797–1828. Austrian composer. His ten symphonies include the incomplete eighth in B minor (the 'Unfinished') and the 'Great' in C major. He wrote chamber and piano music, including the 'Trout Quintet', and over 600 lieder (songs) combining the Romantic expression of emotion with pure melody. They include the cycles *Die schöne Müllerin/The Beautiful Maid of the Mill* 1823 and *Die Winterreise/The Winter Journey* 1827.

Schumann Robert Alexander 1810–1856. German Romantic composer. His songs and short piano pieces show simplicity combined with an ability to portray mood and emotion. Among his compositions are four symphonies, a violin concerto, a piano con-

orchestra setting

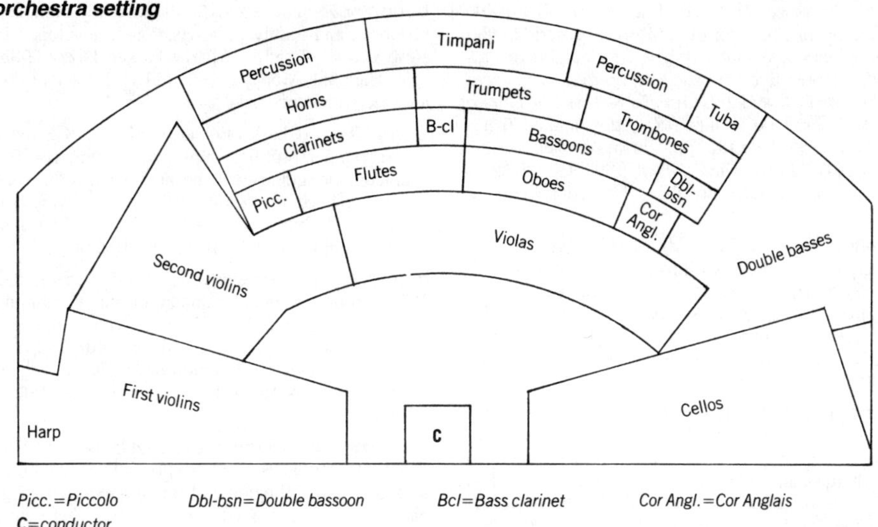

Picc.=Piccolo *Dbl-bsn=Double bassoon* *Bcl=Bass clarinet* *Cor Angl.=Cor Anglais*
***C**=conductor*

Orchestra: Setting most usual today. It is unbalanced – the bass instruments tend to the right, treble instruments to the left.

certo, sonatas, and song cycles, such as *Dichterliebe/Poet's Love* 1840. Felix Mendelssohn championed many of his works.

Shostakovich Dmitry (Dmitriyevich) 1906–1975. Soviet composer. His music is tonal, expressive, and sometimes highly dramatic; it was not always to official Soviet taste. He wrote 15 symphonies, chamber music, ballets, and operas, the latter including *Lady Macbeth of Mtsensk* 1934, which was suppressed as 'too divorced from the proletariat', but revived as *Katerina Izmaylova* 1963.

Sibelius Jean (Christian) 1865–1957. Finnish composer. His works include nationalistic symphonic poems such as *En saga* 1893 and *Finlandia* 1900, a violin concerto 1904, and seven symphonies.

Smetana Bedřich 1824–1884. Czech composer whose music has a distinct national character, as in, for example, the operas *The Bartered Bride* 1866 and *Dalibor* 1868, and the symphonic suite *My Country* 1875–80.

Stockhausen Karlheinz 1928– . German composer of avant-garde music who has continued to explore new musical sounds and compositional techniques since the 1950s. His major works include *Gesang der Jünglinge* 1956, *Kontakte* 1960 (electronic music), and *Sirius* 1977. Since 1977 all his works have been part of *LICHT*, a cycle of seven musical ceremonies intended for performance on the evenings of a week. He completed the fourth, *Dienstag*, 1992.

Strauss Johann (Baptist) 1825–1899. Austrian conductor and composer, the son of composer ***Johann Strauss*** (1804–1849). In 1872 he gave up conducting and wrote operettas, such as *Die Fledermaus* 1874, and numerous waltzes, such as *The Blue Danube* and *Tales from the Vienna Woods*, which gained him the title 'the Waltz King'.

Strauss Richard (Georg) 1864–1949. German composer and conductor. He followed the German Romantic tradition but had a strongly personal style, characterized by his bold, colourful orchestration. He first wrote tone poems such as *Don Juan* 1889, *Till Eulenspiegel's Merry Pranks* 1895, and *Also sprach Zarathustra* 1896. He then moved on to opera with *Salome* 1905 and *Elektra* 1909, both of which have elements of polytonality. He reverted to a more traditional style with *Der Rosenkavalier* 1911.

Stravinsky Igor 1882–1971. Russian composer, later of French (1934) and US (1945) nationality. He studied under Rimsky-Korsakov and wrote the music for the ballets *The Firebird* 1910, *Petrushka* 1911, and *The Rite of Spring* 1913 (controversial at the time for their unorthodox rhythms and harmonies). His versatile work ranges from his Neo-Classical ballet *Pulcinella* 1920 to the choral- orchestral *Symphony of Psalms* 1930. He later made use of serial techniques in such works as the *Canticum Sacrum* 1955 and the ballet *Agon* 1953–57.

Tchaikovsky Pyotr Il'yich 1840–1893. Russian composer. His strong sense of melody, personal expression, and brilliant orchestration are clear throughout his many Romantic works, which include six symphonies, three piano concertos, a violin concerto, operas (for example, *Eugene Onegin* 1879), ballets (for example, *The Nutcracker* 1892), orchestral fantasies (for example, *Romeo and Juliet* 1870), and chamber and vocal music.

Varèse Edgard 1885–1965. French composer who settled in New York 1916 where he founded the New Symphony Orchestra 1919 to advance the cause of modern music. His work is experimental and often dissonant, combining electronic sounds with orchestral instruments, and includes *Hyperprism* 1923, *Intégrales* 1931, and *Poème Electronique* 1958.

Verdi Giuseppe (Fortunino Francesco) 1813–1901. Italian opera composer of the Romantic period, who took his native operatic style to new heights of dramatic expression. In 1842 he wrote the opera *Nabucco*, followed by *Ernani* 1844 and *Rigoletto* 1851. Other works include *Il Trovatore* and *La Traviata* both 1853, *Aida* 1871, and the masterpieces of his old age, *Otello* 1887 and *Falstaff* 1893. His *Requiem* 1874 commemorates novelist Alessandro Manzoni (1785–1873).

Vivaldi Antonio (Lucio) 1678–1741. Italian Baroque composer, violinist, and conductor. He wrote 23 symphonies, 75 sonatas, over 400 concertos, including the *Four Seasons* (*c.* 1725) for violin and orchestra, over 40 operas, and much sacred music. His work was largely neglected until the 1930s.

Wagner Richard 1813–1883. German opera composer. He revolutionized the 19th-century conception of opera, envisaging it as a wholly new art form in which musical, poetic, and scenic elements should be unified through such devices as the leitmotiv (recurring theme). His operas include *Tannhäuser* 1845, *Lohengrin* 1850, and *Tristan und Isolde* 1865. In 1872 he founded the Festival Theatre in Bayreuth; his masterpiece *Der Ring des Nibelungen/The Ring of the Nibelung*, a sequence of four operas, was first performed there in 1876. His last work, *Parsifal*, was produced in 1882.

Popular Music and Jazz

Armstrong Louis ('Satchmo') 1901–1971. US jazz cornet and trumpet player and singer. His Chicago recordings in the 1920s with the Hot Five and Hot Seven brought him recognition for his warm and pure trumpet tone, his skill at improvisation, and his quirky, gravelly voice. From the 1930s he also appeared in films.

Beach Boys, the US pop group formed 1961. They began as exponents of vocal-harmony surf music with Chuck Berry guitar riffs (their hits include 'Surfin' USA' 1963 and 'Help Me, Rhonda' 1965) but the compositions, arrangements, and production by Brian Wilson (1942–) became highly complex under the influence of psychedelic rock, peaking with 'Good Vibrations' 1966. Wilson spent most of the next 20 years in retirement but returned with a solo album 1988.

Beatles, the English pop group 1960–70. The members, all born in Liverpool, were John Lennon (1940–80, rhythm guitar, vocals), Paul McCartney (1942– , bass, vocals), George Harrison (1943– , lead guitar, vocals), and Ringo Starr (Richard Starkey, 1940– , drums). Using songs written largely by Lennon and McCartney, the Beatles dominated rock music and pop culture in the 1960s.

beat music pop music that evolved in the UK in the early 1960s, known in its purest form as Mersey beat, and as British Invasion in the USA. The beat groups characteristically had a simple, guitar-dominated line-up, vocal harmonies, and catchy tunes. They included the Beatles (1960–70), the Hollies (1962–), and the Zombies (1962–67).

bebop or ***bop*** hot jazz style, rhythmically complex, virtuosic, and highly improvisational, developed in New York 1940–55 by Charlie Parker, Dizzy Gillespie, Thelonius Monk, and other black musicians disaffected with dance bands.

Berry Chuck (Charles Edward) 1926– . US rock-and-roll singer, prolific songwriter, and guitarist. His characteristic guitar riffs became staples of rock music, and his humorous storytelling lyrics were also emulated. He had a string of hits in the 1950s and 1960s beginning with 'Maybellene' 1955.

bhangra pop music evolved in the UK in the late 1970s from traditional Punjabi music, combining electronic instruments and ethnic drums. Bhangra bands include Holle Holle, Alaap, and Heera. A 1990s development is ***bhangramuffin***, a ragga-bhangra fusion popularized by Apache Indian (Steve Kapur, 1967–).

big-band jazz swing music created in the late 1930s and 1940s by bands of 13 or more players, such as those of Duke Ellington and Benny Goodman. Big-band jazz relied on fixed arrangements, where there is more than one instrument to some of the parts, rather than improvisation. Big bands were mainly dance bands, and they ceased to be economically viable in the 1950s.

blues African-American music that originated in the rural American South in the late 19th century, characterized by a 12-bar construction and frequently melancholy lyrics. The guitar has been the dominant instrument; harmonica and piano are also common. Blues guitar and vocal styles have played a vital part in the development of jazz, rock, and pop music in general.

1920s–30s The ***rural*** or ***delta blues*** was usually performed solo with guitar or harmonica, by such artists as Robert Johnson (*c.* 1912–1938) and Bukka White (1906–1977), but the earliest recorded style, ***classic blues***, by such musicians as W C Handy (1873–1958) and Bessie Smith (1894–1937), was sung with a small band.

1940s–50s The urban blues, using electric amplification, emerged in the northern cities, chiefly Chicago. As exemplified by Howlin' Wolf (1910–1976), Muddy Waters (1915–1983), and John Lee Hooker (1917–), urban blues became ***rhythm and blues***.

1960s The jazz-influenced smooth guitar style of B B King (1925–) inspired many musicians of the ***British blues boom***, including Eric Clapton.

1980s The 'blues *noir*' of Robert Cray (1953–) contrasted with the rock-driven blues playing of Stevie Ray Vaughan (1955–1990).

boogie-woogie jazz played on the piano, using a repeated motif for the left hand. It was common in the USA from around 1900 to the 1950s. Boogie-woogie players included Pinetop Smith (1904–1929), Meade 'Lux' Lewis (1905–1964), and Jimmy Yancey (1898–1951). Rock-and-roll pianist Jerry Lee Lewis adapted the style.

Bowie David. Stage name of David Jones 1947– . English pop singer, songwriter, and actor whose career has been a series of image changes. His hits

What price CD now?

The price of compact discs was the subject of an inquiry by the House of Commons Select Committee for National Heritage in the spring of 1993. The record industry was told that CDs are unjustifiably expensive compared with other formats and with the price of CDs elsewhere, especially in the USA.

The committee heard evidence from retailers and from the record companies' representative body, the British Phonographic Institute (BPI). The main points of their argument were that CDs are significantly more expensive to manufacture than other formats, and that profits are invested in the high-risk activity of fostering new talent.

There was a great deal of public scepticism over the latter claim, since new acts generally appear on small independent labels while the industry majors have focused on established million-selling acts and on reissuing material from the vaults. The amount of royalties received by artists was also a contested issue.

A study in April 1993 showed that the average price of a new CD was £13.12 in London and the equivalent of £8.74 in New York. This may explain why over 50% of all CDs sold in the UK are in the cut-price bracket. At £525 million in 1992, CD sales in the UK had overtaken sales for all other formats. Record retailers paid £7.18 for a CD that would sell at full price, compared with £5.17 for a cassette. The most recent breakdown of costs supplied by the BPI dated from 1989 gave the cost of manufacture and packaging as £1.28 per CD.

A 1992 inquiry by the Office of Fair Trading had cleared the industry and retailers of price collusion, but the select committee concluded otherwise and the question was referred to the Monopolies and Mergers Commission.

Compact discs: facts and figures

CD retail prices, 1993 (£)

Tower Records store	*New York**	*London*
Diva, Annie Lennox	7.78	10.99
Lady in Satin, Billie Holiday	9.07	11.99
Dark Side of the Moon, Pink Floyd	9.72	13.99
The Bodyguard, The Original Soundtrack, Whitney Houston	7.78	10.99
Don Carlos, Verdi (3 CDs)	30.38	40.99
Symphonie fantastique, Berlioz	10.12	13.99
Contes d'Hoffmann, Offenbach, with Placido Domingo (2 CDs)	20.25	27.99

** excluding sales tax of 8.25%*

Source: Consumers' Association

Costs breakdown of full-price CDs

	%
Advertising & promotion	3.7
Overhead contribution	9.8
Artist royalty	11.5
Mechanical royalty	5.1
Design & packaging	2.0
Dealer margin	23.5
Distribution/dealer discount	9.7
Manufacturing costs	9.1
Profit per unit	8.3
Other A & R costs	4.2
VAT @ 15%	13.1
Total	***100.0***

Source: BPI Yearbook 1989/90

include 'Jean Genie' 1973, 'Rebel, Rebel' 1974, 'Golden Years' 1975, and 'Underground' 1986. He has acted in plays and films, including Nicolas Roeg's *The Man Who Fell to Earth* 1976. His 1993 album was *Black Tie White Noise*.

Brown James 1928– . US rhythm-and-blues and soul singer, a pioneer of funk. Staccato horn arrangements and shouted vocals characterize his hits, which include 'Please, Please, Please' 1956, 'Papa's Got a Brand New Bag' 1965, and 'Say It Loud, I'm Black and I'm Proud' 1968. In that year his TV appearance appealing for calm succeeded in restraining race riots in US cities. In the 1980s and 1990s his records were subject to much electronic sampling by rap musicians.

Byrds, the US pioneering folk-rock group 1964–73. Emulated for their 12-string guitar sound, as on the hits 'Mr Tambourine Man' (a 1965 version of Bob Dylan's song) and 'Eight Miles High' 1966, they moved towards country rock in the late 1960s, setting another trend.

Cajun music originating in the French-speaking community of Louisiana, USA. It has a lively rhythm and features steel guitar, fiddle, and accordion. Since the 1930s Cajun has fed into and drawn from country-and-western music. Cajun musicians include accordionist Nathan Abshire (1913–1981) and the Balfa Brothers Band (1946–1978).

calypso West Indian satirical ballad with a syncopated beat. Calypso is a traditional song form of Trinidad, a feature of its annual carnival, with roots in W African praise singing. It was first popularized in the USA by Harry Belafonte (1927–) in 1956. Mighty Sparrow (1935–) is Trinidad's best-known calypso singer.

Charles Ray 1930– . US singer, songwriter, and pianist whose first hits were 'I've Got A Woman'

1955, 'What'd I Say' 1959, and 'Georgia On My Mind' 1960. He has recorded gospel, blues, rock, soul, country, and rhythm and blues.

Clapton Eric 1945– . English blues and rock guitarist, singer, and songwriter. Originally a blues purist, then one of the pioneers of heavy rock with Cream 1966-68, he returned to the blues after making the landmark album *Layla and Other Assorted Love Songs* 1970 by Derek and the Dominos. Solo albums include *Journeyman* 1989 and the acoustic *Unplugged* 1992.

Coleman Ornette 1930– . US alto saxophonist and jazz composer. In the late 1950s he rejected the established structural principles of jazz for free avant-garde improvisation. He has worked with small and large groups, ethnic musicians of different traditions, and symphony orchestras. His albums include *The Shape of Jazz to Come* 1959, *Chappaqua Suite* 1965, and *Skies of America* 1972.

Coltrane John (William) 1926–1967. US jazz saxophonist who first came to prominence 1955 with the Miles Davis quintet, later playing with Thelonious Monk 1957. He was a powerful and individual artist, whose performances featured much experimentation. His 1960s quartet was highly regarded for its innovations in melody and harmony.

Costello Elvis. Stage name of Declan McManus 1954– . English rock singer, songwriter, and guitarist whose intricate yet impassioned lyrics have made him one of Britain's foremost songwriters. The great stylistic range of his work was evident from his 1977 debut *My Aim Is True* and was further extended 1993 when he collaborated with the classical Brodsky Quartet on the song cycle *The Juliet Letters*.

country and western or ***country music*** the popular music of the white US South and West; it evolved from the folk music of the English, Irish, and Scottish settlers and has a strong blues influence. Characteristic instruments are slide guitar, mandolin, and fiddle. Lyrics typically extol family values and traditional sex roles, and often have a strong narrative element. Country music encompasses a variety of regional styles, and ranges from mournful ballads to fast and intricate dance music.

history

1920s Jimmie Rodgers (1897–1933) wrote a series of 'Blue Yodel' songs that made him the first country-music recording star.

1930s Nashville, Tennessee, became a centre for the country-music industry, with the Grand Ole Opry a showcase for performers. The Carter Family arranged and recorded hundreds of traditional songs. Hollywood invented the singing cowboy.

1940s Hank Williams (1923–1953) emerged as the most significant singer and songwriter; ***western swing*** spread from Texas.

1950s The ***honky-tonk*** sound; Kentucky ***bluegrass***; ballad singers included Jim Reeves (1923–1964) and Patsy Cline (1932–1963).

1960s Songs of the Bakersfield, California, school, dominated by Buck Owens (1929–) and Merle Haggard (1937–), contrasted with lush Nashville productions of singers such as George Jones (1931–) and Tammy Wynette (1942–).

Top 10 CDs (1992)

1	*Stars*	Simply Red
2	*Back To Front*	Lionel Richie
3	*Glittering Prize 81/92*	Simple Minds
4	*Cher's Greatest Hits: 1965–1992*	Cher
5	*Diva*	Annie Lennox
6	*We Can't Dance*	Genesis
7	*Pop! – The First 20 Hits*	Erasure
8	*Divine Madness*	Madness
9	*Timeless (The Classics)*	Michael Bolton
10	*Gold – Greatest Hits*	Abba

1970s Dolly Parton (1946–) and Emmylou Harris (1947–); the Austin, Texas, ***outlaws*** Willie Nelson (1933–) and Waylon Jennings (1937–); ***country rock*** pioneered by Gram Parsons (1946–1973).

1980s Neotraditionalist ***new country*** represented by Randy Travis (1963–), Dwight Yoakam (1957–), and k d lang (1961–).

1990s US pop charts invaded by cowboy-hat-wearing singers like Garth Brooks (1961–).

Crosby Bing (Harry Lillis) 1904–1977. US film actor and singer who achieved world success with his distinctive style of crooning in such songs as 'Pennies from Heaven' 1936 (featured in a film of the same name) and 'White Christmas' 1942. He won an acting Oscar for *Going My Way* 1944, and made a series of 'road' film comedies with Dorothy Lamour and Bob Hope, the last being *Road to Hong Kong* 1962.

Davis Miles (Dewey, Jr) 1926–1991. US jazz trumpeter, composer, and bandleader, one of the most influential and innovative figures in jazz. He pioneered bebop with Charlie Parker 1945, cool jazz in the 1950s, and jazz-rock fusion from the late 1960s. His albums include *Birth of the Cool* 1957 (recorded 1949 and 1950), *Sketches of Spain* 1959, *Bitches Brew* 1970, and *Tutu* 1985.

Dire Straits UK rock group formed 1977 by guitarist, singer, and songwriter Mark Knopfler (1949–). Their tasteful musicianship was tailor-made for the new compact-disc audience, and their 1985 LP *Brothers in Arms* went on to sell 20 million copies. Other albums include *On Every Street* 1991. Knopfler is also much in demand as a producer.

disco music international style of dance music of the 1970s with a heavily emphasized beat, derived from ***funk***. It was designed to be played in discotheques rather than performed live; hence the production was often more important than the performer, and drum machines came to dominate. Disco music was celebrated in the 1977 film *Saturday Night Fever*.

Dixieland jazz jazz style that originated in New Orleans, USA, in the early 20th century, dominated by cornet, trombone, and clarinet. The trumpeter Louis Armstrong emerged from this style. The ***trad jazz*** movement in the UK in the 1940s–50s was a Dixieland revival. The Rebirth Brass Band of New Orleans plays a funky 1990s version.

Doors, the US psychedelic rock group formed 1965 in Los Angeles with Jim Morrison (1943–1971) on vocals. Their first hit was 'Light My Fire' from their debut album *The Doors* 1967. They were noted for Morrison's poetic lyrics and flamboyant performance.

Dylan Bob. Adopted name of Robert Allen Zimmerman 1941– . US singer and songwriter whose lyrics provided catchphrases for a generation and influenced innumerable songwriters. He began in the folk-music tradition. His early songs, as on his albums *Freewheelin'* 1963 and *The Times They Are A-Changin'* 1964, were associated with the US civil-rights movement and antiwar protest. From 1965 he worked in an individualistic rock style, as on the albums *Highway 61 Revisited* 1965 and *Blonde on Blonde* 1966. Later work includes *Blood on the Tracks* 1975 and *Good As I Been to You* 1992.

Ellington Duke (Edward Kennedy) 1899–1974. US pianist who had an outstanding career as a composer and arranger of jazz. He wrote numerous pieces for his own jazz orchestra, accentuating the strengths of individual virtuoso instrumentalists, and became one of the leading figures in jazz over a 55-year period. Some of his most popular compositions include 'Mood Indigo', 'Sophisticated Lady', 'Solitude', and 'Black and Tan Fantasy'. He was one of the founders of big-band jazz.

Fitzgerald Ella 1918– . US jazz singer, recognized as one of the finest, most lyrical voices in jazz, both in solo work and with big bands. She is celebrated for her smooth interpretations of George and Ira Gershwin and Cole Porter songs.

funk dance music of black US origin, relying on heavy percussion in polyrhythmic patterns. Leading exponents include James Brown and George Clinton (1940–).

Gershwin George 1898–1937. US composer who wrote both 'serious' music, such as the tone poem *Rhapsody in Blue* 1924 and *An American in Paris* 1928, and popular musicals and songs, many with lyrics by his brother ***Ira Gershwin*** (1896–1983), including 'I Got Rhythm', ''S Wonderful', and 'Embraceable You'. His opera *Porgy and Bess* 1935 incorporated jazz rhythms and popular song styles in an operatic format.

Gillespie Dizzy (John Birks) 1917–1993. US jazz trumpeter who, with Charlie Parker, was the chief creator and exponent of the bebop style (*Groovin' High* is a CD reissue of their seminal 78-rpm recordings).

Goodman Benny (Benjamin David) 1909–1986. US clarinetist, nicknamed the 'King of Swing' for the new jazz idiom he introduced with arranger Fletcher Henderson (1897–1952). In 1934 he founded his own 12-piece band, which combined the expressive improvisatory style of black jazz with disciplined precision ensemble playing. He is associated with such numbers as 'Blue Skies' and 'Let's Dance'.

gospel music vocal music developed in the 1920s in the black Baptist churches of the US South from spirituals. Outstanding among the early gospel singers was Mahalia Jackson, but from the 1930s to the mid-1950s male harmony groups predominated, among them the Dixie Hummingbirds, the Swan Silvertones, and the Five Blind Boys of Mississippi. The style they developed was continued into the 1990s.

grunge rock-music style of the early 1990s, characterized by a thick, abrasive, distorted sound. Grunge evolved from punk in the Seattle, Washington, USA, area and came to prominence with the chart success of the band Nirvana 1991. The Melvins (formed in Seattle early 1980s) pioneered grunge with their turbid, slow-moving sound. Pearl Jam (formed in Seattle 1990), with their powerful singer, have been the most commercially successful grunge-inspired group in the wake of Nirvana.

Guthrie Woody (Woodrow Wilson) 1912–1967. US folk singer and songwriter whose left-wing protest songs, 'dustbowl ballads', and 'talking blues' influenced, among others, Bob Dylan; they include 'Deportees', 'Hard Travelin'', and 'This Land Is Your Land'.

hardcore of any music style, the more extreme and generally less commercial end of the spectrum: hardcore techno is a minimalist electronic dance music; hardcore rap is aggressive or offensive; hardcore punk jettisons form and melody for speed and noise.

Hawkins Coleman (Randolph) 1904–1969. US virtuoso tenor saxophonist. He was, until 1934, a soloist in the swing band led by Fletcher Henderson (1898–1952), and was an influential figure in bringing the jazz saxophone to prominence as a solo instrument.

heavy metal rock style characterized by histrionic guitar solos and a macho swagger. Heavy metal developed out of the hard rock of the late 1960s and early 1970s, was performed by such groups as Led Zeppelin and Deep Purple, and enjoyed a resurgence in the late 1980s. Bands include Van Halen (formed 1974), Def Leppard (formed 1977), and Guns n' Roses (formed 1987).

Hendrix Jimi (James Marshall) 1942–1970. US rock guitarist, songwriter, and singer, legendary for his virtuoso experimental technique. *Are You Experienced?* 1967 was his first album. He greatly expanded the vocabulary of the electric guitar and influenced both rock and jazz musicians.

hip-hop popular music originating in New York in the early 1980s, created with scratching (a percussive effect obtained by manually rotating a vinyl record) and heavily accented electronic drums behind a rap vocal. Within a decade, digital sampling had largely superseded scratching. The term 'hip-hop' also comprises break dancing and graffiti.

Holiday Billie ('Lady Day'). Stage name of Eleanora Gough McKay 1915–1959. US jazz singer, known for her emotionally charged delivery and idiosyncratic phrasing; she brought a blues feel to performances with swing bands. Songs she made her own include 'Stormy Weather', 'Strange Fruit' and 'I Cover the Waterfront'.

Holly Buddy. Stage name of Charles Hardin Holley 1936–1959. US rock-and-roll singer, guitarist, and songwriter, born in Lubbock, Texas. Holly had a distinctive, hiccuping vocal style and was an early experimenter with recording techniques. Many of his hits with his band, the Crickets, such as 'That'll Be the Day' 1957, 'Peggy Sue' 1957, and 'Maybe Baby' 1958, have become classics.

The king, the president, and the VP's wife

Secret Service crew protecting Bill Clinton during his presidential campaign are said to have worn T-shirts with the slogan 'Elvis Tour 1992'. And it is no secret that Clinton's appearance on the Arsenio Hall TV talk show to play 'Heartbreak Hotel' on the saxophone was a factor in endearing the candidate to some voters. Clinton also took time out to vote for Elvis: in the choice between two images of the singer proposed for a postage stamp, he told *Rolling Stone* magazine that he voted and even campaigned for the younger Elvis – who duly appeared on the nation's letters from 8 January 1993. In acknowledgement of the power of a dead king of rock and roll to influence the election of a live president of the USA, there was an Elvis Presley float in the inaugural parade, complete with an impersonator.

But what does he sing in the bath?

The campaign theme was a Fleetwood Mac song, 'Don't Stop Thinking About Tomorrow' (for which Clinton aides initially forgot to get permission). In California, his rallies finished with a burst of the Beach Boys' 'Good Vibrations'; in Illinois, they opened with the gospel number 'Oh Happy Day'; in Georgia, the crowds obligingly sang along to Mary Wells's 'My Guy'. Younger audiences were wooed with records by Hammer (in fact a Republican) and the English techno-rock band Jesus Jones. For each rally, campaign staff would compile a play list. It was appropriate, therefore, that Clinton should become the beneficiary of Music Television's Rock the Vote campaign for voter registration: the majority of first-time voters came out for the Democrat.

They too

Although not his constituents, the Irish rock band U2 played a part in Clinton's election. While on stage during the Zoo TV tour, the singer, Bono, used to phone the White House as a stunt and ask for George Bush. Bush did not reply, but Clinton took the initiative to phone U2 and their conversation was syndicated on US radio. Later, when his campaign trail crossed the route of the U2 tour and they were staying in the same hotel, he accepted the band's invitation to a meeting – but they are not believed to have jammed together.

Having provided the theme tune, Fleetwood Mac (who started life as an English band) re-formed specially for the Clinton inauguration bash. 'If John Lennon were alive, we'd have tried for a Beatles reunion,' said one of the planners in a fit of hubris.

Even without the Beatles, the occasion was celebrated with a four-day all-star rock-and-roll party in Washington DC and Little Rock, Arkansas, as well as other places. Steel Pulse, a reggae band from Birmingham, had the distinction of being the first British band to play at a US presidential inauguration, being favourites of Vice President Al Gore; the English singer Robyn Hitchcock appeared at one of the unofficial events. Ireland was again represented by members of U2, who played with members of REM at MTV's ball.

Taking the rap

Clinton's relationship with popular music had had its rocky moment during the campaign when he commented disapprovingly on a controversial remark made by the militant black rapper Sister Souljah: 'If black people kill black people every day, why not have a week and kill white people?' Clinton was later criticized for not making clear that Sister Souljah had been speaking from the hypothetical point of view of a Los Angeles rioter, and not actually advocating homicide herself.

And in Clinton's own camp, Tipper Gore, the wife of his vice-presidential nominee, was the target of ridicule for the campaign she started in 1985 to put 'parental-advisory' stickers on albums with lyrics that she and her associates considered unsuitable. The punk band the Ramones addressed her on their 1992 album in a song: 'Ah, Tipper, come on, it's just a smoke-screen for the real problems / S & L deficit, the homeless, the environment.' She took the hint, dissociated herself from the campaign, and let it be known that she was not so square: she had once played drums in a band called the Wildcats.

Keep on pushing

In the spring of 1993, musicians continued to keep an eye on the new president. Neil Young played a concert in Portland, Oregon, to draw attention to a meeting Clinton was having there with representatives of the clashing environmentalists and loggers. And at the White House the party was not over. Clinton decided to host the graduation dance of Georgetown University's class of 1968, which had originally been cancelled owing to the assassination of Robert Kennedy. Chuck Berry, the Temptations, and the Four Tops were now booked to perform.

IVE

house music dance music of the 1980s originating in the inner-city clubs of Chicago, USA, combining funk with European high-tech pop (techno), and using dub, digital sampling, and cross-fading. ***Acid house*** has minimal vocals and melody, instead surrounding the mechanically emphasized 4/4 beat with stripped-down synthesizer riffs and a wandering bass line. Other variants include ***hip house***, with rap elements, and ***acid jazz***.

indie (short for ***independent***) any record label that is neither owned nor distributed by one of the large conglomerates ('majors') that dominate the industry. Without a corporate bureaucratic structure, the independent labels are often quicker to respond to new trends and more idealistic in their aims. What has become loosely known as ***indie music*** therefore tends to be experimental, amateurish, or at the cutting edge of street fashion.

Jackson Michael 1958– . US rock singer and songwriter whose videos and live performances are meticulously choreographed. His first solo hit was 'Got to Be There' 1971; his worldwide popularity peaked with the albums *Thriller* 1982 and *Bad* 1987. The follow-up was *Dangerous* 1991.

jazz polyphonic, syncopated music characterized by solo virtuosic improvisation, which developed in the USA at the turn of the 20th century. Initially music for dancing, often with a vocalist, it had its roots in black American and other popular music. As jazz grew increasingly complex and experimental, various distinct forms evolved. Seminal musicians include Louis Armstrong, Charlie Parker, and John Coltrane.

jazz chronology

1880–1900 Originated chiefly in New Orleans from ragtime.

1920s During Prohibition, the centre of jazz moved to Chicago (Louis Armstrong, Bix Beiderbecke) and St Louis. By the end of the decade the focus had shifted to New York City (Art Tatum, Fletcher Henderson), to radio and recordings.

1930s The ***swing*** bands used call-and-response arrangements with improvised solos of voice and instruments (Paul Whiteman, Benny Goodman).

1940s Swing grew into the ***big-band*** era with jazz composed as well as arranged (Glenn Miller, Duke Ellington); rise of ***West Coast*** jazz (Stan Kenton) and rhythmically complex, highly improvised ***bebop*** (Charlie Parker, Dizzy Gillespie, Thelonius Monk).

1950s Jazz had ceased to be dance music; ***cool jazz*** (Stan Getz, Miles Davis, Lionel Hampton, Modern Jazz Quartet) developed in reaction to the insistent, 'hot' bebop and ***hard bop***.

1960s Free-form or ***free jazz*** (Ornette Coleman, John Coltrane).

1970s Jazz rock (US group Weather Report, formed 1970; British guitarist John McLaughlin, 1942–); jazz funk (US saxophonist Grover Washington Jr, 1943–); more eclectic free jazz (US pianist Keith Jarrett, 1945–).

1980s Resurgence of tradition (US trumpeter Wynton Marsalis, 1962– ; British saxophonist Courtney Pine, 1965–) and avant-garde (US chamber-music Kronos Quartet, formed 1978; anarchic British group Loose Tubes, 1983–89).

karaoke amateur singing in public to prerecorded backing tapes. Karaoke originated in Japan and spread to other parts of the world in the 1980s. Karaoke machines are jukeboxes of backing tracks to well-known popular songs, usually with a microphone attached and lyrics displayed on a video screen.

Lennon John (Ono) 1940–1980. UK rock singer, songwriter, and guitarist, in the USA from 1971; a founder member of the Beatles. Both before the band's break-up 1969 and in his solo career, he collaborated intermittently with his wife ***Yoko Ono*** (1933–). 'Give Peace a Chance', a hit 1969, became an anthem of the peace movement. His solo work alternated between the confessional and the political, as on the album *Imagine* 1971. He was shot dead by a fan.

Madonna Stage name of Madonna Louise Veronica Ciccone 1958– . US pop singer and actress who presents herself on stage and in videos with an exaggerated sexuality. Her first hit was 'Like a Virgin' 1984; others include 'Material Girl' 1985 and 'Like a Prayer' 1989. Her films include *Desperately Seeking Susan* 1985, *Dick Tracy* 1990, and the documentary *In Bed with Madonna* 1991. Her dance album *Erotica* 1992 coincided with the publication of her book *Sex*.

Marley Bob (Robert Nesta) 1945–1981. Jamaican reggae singer and songwriter, a Rastafarian whose songs, many of which were topical and political, popularized reggae worldwide in the 1970s. They include 'Get Up, Stand Up' 1973 and 'No Woman No Cry' 1974; his albums include *Natty Dread* 1975 and *Exodus* 1977.

Factory closure

One of the most influential independent British record companies, the Manchester-based Factory Records, was forced into receivership in November 1992. Factory was founded in 1978 by a local television reporter, Anthony Wilson. One of his first and crucial signings was the gloomy post-punk band Joy Division, later, as New Order, a mainstay of the label.

Much of the blame for the crash is pinned on the 1990 chart success Happy Mondays, whose second album was delayed as they ran up a recording bill of £300,000. Album sales declined by 50% as Factory struggled through its last year without the hoped-for new releases from Happy Mondays and New Order. An attempt to strike a bail-out deal with London Records, a division of Polygram, failed when London discovered the chaotic state of Factory's accounts.

Manchester's most successful club, the Hacienda, co-owned by Factory, remains open.

Miller Glenn 1904–1944. US trombonist and, as bandleader, exponent of the big-band swing sound from 1938. He composed his signature tune 'Moonlight Serenade' (a hit 1939). Miller became leader of the US Army Air Force Band in Europe 1942, made broadcasts to troops throughout the world during World War II, and disappeared without a trace on a flight between England and France.

Mingus Charles 1922–1979. US jazz bassist and composer. He played with Louis Armstrong, Duke Ellington, and Charlie Parker. Based on the West Coast until 1951, he took part in the development of cool jazz, and his experimentation with atonality and dissonant effects opened the way for the new style of free collective jazz improvisation of the 1960s.

Monk Thelonious (Sphere) 1917–1982. US jazz pianist and composer who took part in the development of bebop. He had a highly idiosyncratic style, but numbers such as 'Round Midnight' and 'Blue Monk' have become standards. Monk worked in New York during the Depression, and became popular in the 1950s.

Morrison Van (George Ivan) 1945– . Northern Irish singer and songwriter whose jazz-inflected Celtic soul style was already in evidence on *Astral Weeks* 1968 and has been highly influential. Among other albums are *Tupelo Honey* 1971, *Veedon Fleece* 1974, and *Hymns to the Silence* 1991.

New Age instrumental or ambient music of the 1980s, often semi-acoustic or electronic; less insistent than rock.

New Wave style that evolved parallel to punk in the second half of the 1970s. It shared the urban aggressive spirit of punk but was musically and lyrically more sophisticated; examples are the early work of Elvis Costello and Talking Heads.

Parker Charlie (Charles Christopher 'Bird', 'Yardbird') 1920–1955. US alto saxophonist and jazz composer, associated with the trumpeter Dizzy Gillespie in developing the bebop style. His skilful improvisations inspired performers on all jazz instruments.

pop music or ***popular music*** any contemporary music not categorizable as jazz or classical. Pop became distinct from folk music with the advent of sound-recording techniques, and has incorporated blues, country and western, and music-hall elements; electronic amplification and other technological innovations have played a large part in the creation of new styles. The traditional format is a song of roughly three minutes with verse, chorus, and middle eight bars.

1910s The singer Al Jolson was one of the first recording stars. Ragtime was still popular.

1920s In the USA Paul Whiteman and his orchestra played jazz that could be danced to, country singer Jimmie Rodgers reached a new record-buying public, the blues was burgeoning; in the UK popular singers included Al Bowlly (1899–1941, born in Mozambique).

1930s Crooner Bing Crosby and vocal groups such as the Andrews Sisters were the alternatives to swing bands.

1940s ***Rhythm and blues*** evolved in the USA while Frank Sinatra was a teen idol and Glenn Miller played dance music; the UK preferred such singers as Vera Lynn.

1950s In the USA ***doo-wop*** group vocalizing preceded ***rockabilly*** and the rise of ***rock and roll*** (Elvis Presley, Chuck Berry). British pop records were often cover versions of US originals.

1960s The Beatles and the ***Mersey beat*** transcended UK borders, followed by the Rolling Stones, ***hard rock*** (the Who, Led Zeppelin), and ***art rock*** (Genesis, Yes). In the USA ***surf music*** (group harmony vocals or guitar-based instrumentals) preceded ***Motown***, ***folk rock*** (the Byrds, Bob Dylan), and ***blues rock*** (Jimi Hendrix, Janis Joplin). ***Psychedelic rock*** evolved from 1966 on both sides of the Atlantic (the Doors, Pink Floyd, Jefferson Airplane).

1970s The first half of the decade produced ***glitter rock*** (David Bowie), ***heavy metal***, and ***disco***; in the UK also ***pub rock*** (a return to basics, focusing on live performance); ***reggae*** spread from Jamaica. From 1976 ***punk*** was ascendant; the US term ***New Wave*** encompassed bands not entirely within the punk idiom (Talking Heads, Elvis Costello).

1980s Punk continued as ***hardcore*** or mutated into ***gothic***; dance music developed regional US variants: ***hip-hop*** (New York), ***go-go*** (Washington DC), and ***house*** (Chicago). Live audiences grew, leading to anthemic ***stadium rock*** (U2, Bruce Springsteen) and increasingly elaborate stage performances (Michael Jackson, Prince, Madonna). An interest in ***world music*** sparked new fusions.

1990s ***Rap***, hard rock, and heavy metal predominated in the USA at the start of the decade; on the UK ***indie*** scene, dance music (Happy Mondays, Primal Scream) and a new wave of guitar groups (Ride, Lush) drew on the psychedelic era. Germany in particular produced minimalist ***techno*** dance music. Reggae gave way to ***ragga***. ***Grunge*** emerged from Seattle, Washington, USA.

Porter Cole (Albert) 1892–1964. US composer and lyricist, mainly of musical comedies. His witty, sophisticated songs like 'Let's Do It' 1928, 'I Get a Kick Out of You' 1934, and 'Don't Fence Me In' 1944 have been widely recorded and admired. His shows, many of which were made into films, include *The Gay Divorcee* 1932 and *Kiss Me Kate* 1948.

Presley Elvis (Aron) 1935–1977. US singer and acoustic guitarist, the most influential performer of the rock-and-roll era. With his recordings for Sun Records in Memphis, Tennessee, 1954–55 and early hits such as 'Heartbreak Hotel', 'Hound Dog', and 'Love Me Tender', all 1956, he created an individual vocal style, influenced by Southern blues, gospel music, country music, and rhythm and blues. His records continued to sell in their millions into the 1990s.

Prince Stage name of Prince Rogers Nelson 1960– . US pop musician who composes, arranges, and produces his own records and often plays all the instruments. His albums, including *1999* 1982, *Purple Rain* 1984, and the 1992 release with a symbol instead of a name, contain elements of rock, funk, and jazz. His stage shows are energetic and extravagant. He has also starred in several films, including *Graffiti Bridge* 1990. In 1993, Prince announced that he had changed his name to that of the symbol used on his 1992 album.

Top 10 singles (1992)

1	*I Will Always Love You*	Whitney Houston
2	*Rhythm Is A Dancer*	Snap
3	*Would I Lie To You?*	Charles & Eddie
4	*Stay*	Shakespears Sister
5	*Please Don't Go*	KWS
6	*End Of The Road*	Boyz II Men
7	*Abba-esque* (EP)	Erasure
8	*Ain't No Doubt*	Jimmy Nail
9	*Heal The World*	Michael Jackson
10	*Goodnight Girl*	Wet Wet Wet

psychedelic rock or ***acid rock*** pop music that usually involves advanced electronic equipment for both light and sound. The free-form improvisations and light shows that appeared about 1966, attempting to suggest or improve on mind-altering drug experiences, had by the 1980s evolved into stadium performances with lasers and other special effects.

punk rock style of the late 1970s that stressed aggressive, amateurish performance within a three-chord, three-minute format, as exemplified by the Sex Pistols. The lyrics and associated fashions were designed to shock or intimidate. Punk rock began in the UK but drew heavily on earlier US garage bands. Hardcore punk and grunge are derivations.

ragga type of reggae music with a rhythmic, rapid-fire, semi-spoken vocal line. A macho swagger is a common element in the lyrics. Influenced by rap, ragga developed around 1990 from toasting, the earliest talkover style. Performers and fans of ragga call themselves ***ragamuffins***. Ragga performers include the Jamaicans Shabba Ranks, Anthony Red Rose, and Ninja Man; the ragga-rapper Daddy Freddy entered the *Guinness Book of Records* for cramming 528 syllables into 60 seconds (May 1991).

ragtime syncopated music ('ragged time') in 2/4 rhythm, usually played on piano. It developed in the USA among black musicians in the late 19th century; it was influenced by folk tradition, minstrel shows, and marching bands, and was later incorporated into jazz. Scott Joplin was a leading writer of ragtime pieces, called 'rags'.

raï Algerian pop music developed in the 1970s from the Bedouin song form *melhoun*, using synthesizers and electronic drums. Singers often take the name Cheb or Cheba ('young'); for example, Cheb Khaled, Cheb Mami.

rap music rapid, rhythmic chant over a prerecorded repetitive backing track. Rap emerged in New York 1979 as part of the hip-hop culture, although the macho, swaggering lyrics that initially predominated have ancient roots in ritual boasts and insults. By the 1990s, the main schools were gangsta rap (violent) and conscious rap (extolling peaceful coexistence), divided more by content than style, and the more relaxed jazz rap.

Reed Lou 1942– . US rock singer, songwriter, and guitarist; member (1965–70 and 1993–) of the New York avant-garde group ***the Velvet Underground***, one of the most influential bands of the 1960s. His solo work deals largely with urban alienation and angst, and includes the albums *Berlin* 1973, *Street Hassle* 1978, and *New York* 1989.

reggae predominant West Indian popular music of the 1970s and 1980s, characterized by a heavily accented offbeat and a thick bass line. The lyrics often refer to Rastafarianism. Musicians include Bob Marley, Lee 'Scratch' Perry (1940– , performer and producer), and the group Black Uhuru (1974–). Reggae is also played in the UK, South Africa, and elsewhere.

remix the studio practice of reassembling a recording from all or some of its individual components, often with the addition of new elements. As a commercial concept, remixes accompanied the rise of the 12-inch single in the 1980s.

rhythm and blues (R & B) US popular music of the 1940s–60s, which drew on swing and jump-jazz rhythms and blues vocals, and was a progenitor of rock and roll. It diversified into soul, funk, and other styles. R & B artists include Bo Diddley (1928–), Jackie Wilson (1934–84), and Etta James (*c.* 1938–).

Robinson Smokey (William) 1940– . US singer, songwriter, and record producer, associated with Motown records from its conception. He was lead singer of the Miracles 1957–72 (hits include 'Shop Around' 1961, 'The Tears of a Clown' 1970) and his solo hits include 'Cruisin'' 1979 and 'Being With You' 1981. His light tenor voice and wordplay characterize his work.

rock and roll pop music born of a fusion of rhythm and blues and country and western and based on electric guitar and drums. In the mid-1950s, with the advent of Elvis Presley, it became the heartbeat of teenage rebellion in the West and also had considerable impact on other parts of the world. It found perhaps its purest form in late-1950s rockabilly, the style of white Southerners in the USA; the blanket term 'rock' later came to comprise a multitude of styles.

Rolling Stones, the British band formed 1962, once notorious as the 'bad boys' of rock. Original members included Mick Jagger (1943–), Keith Richards (1943–), and Brian Jones (1942–1969). Classic early hits like 'Satisfaction' 1965 and the albums from *Beggars Banquet* 1968 to *Exile on Main Street* 1972 have been rated among their best work; other albums include *Some Girls* 1978 and *Steel Wheels* 1989. A rock-and-roll institution, the Rolling Stones were still performing and recording in the 1990s.

salsa Latin big-band dance music popularized by Puerto Ricans in New York City in the 1970s–80s and by, among others, the Panamanian singer Rubén Blades (1948–).

Simon Paul 1942– . US pop singer and songwriter. In a folk-rock duo with Art Garfunkel (1942–), he had such hits as 'Mrs Robinson' 1968 and 'Bridge Over Troubled Water' 1970. Simon's solo work includes the critically acclaimed album *Graceland* 1986, for which he drew on Cajun and African music, and *The Rhythm of the Saints* 1990.

Sinatra Frank (Francis Albert) 1915– . US singer and film actor, celebrated for his phrasing and emotion, especially on love ballads. He is particularly

Remember when...?

UK best-selling singles, 1956-1992

1956	*I'll Be Home*	Pat Boone
1957	*Love Letters in the Sand*	Pat Boone
1958	*All I Have To Do Is Dream*	The Everly Brothers
1959	*Livin' Doll*	Cliff Richard
1960	*Cathy's Clown*	The Everly Brothers
1961	*Runaway*	Del Shannon
1962	*Stranger On The Shore*	Acker Bilk
1963	*From Me To You*	The Beatles
1964	*I Love You Because*	Jim Reeves
1965	*I'll Never Find Another You*	The Seekers
1966	*Distant Drum*	Jim Reeves
1967	*Release Me*	Engelbert Humperdinck
1968	*What A Wonder World*	Louis Armstrong
1969	*My Way*	Frank Sinatra
1970	*The Wonder Of You*	Elvis Presley
1971	*My Sweet Lord*	George Harrison
1972	*Amazing Grace*	Royal Scots Dragoon Guards
1973	*Tie A Yellow Ribbon*	Dawn
1974	*Tiger Feet*	Mud
1975	*Bye Bye Baby*	Bay City Rollers
1976	*Save Your Kisses For Me*	Brotherhood of Man
1977	*Don't Give Up On Us*	David Soul
1978	*Rivers Of Babylon/Brown Girl In The Ring*	Boney M
1979	*Bright Eyes*	Art Garfunkel
1980	*Don't Stand So Close To Me*	The Police
1981	*Tainted Love*	Soft Cell
1982	*Come On Eileen*	Dexys Midnight Runners
1983	*Karma Chameleon*	Culture Club
1984	*Do They Know It's Christmas*	Band Aid
1985	*The Power Of Love*	Jennifer Rush
1986	*Don't Leave Me This Way*	The Communards
1987	*Never Gonna Give You Up*	Rick Astley
1988	*Mistletoe And Wine*	Cliff Richard
1989	*Ride On Time*	Black Box
1990	*Unchained Melody*	The Righteous Brothers
1991	*Everything I Do (I Do It For You)*	Bryan Adams
1992	*I Will Always Love You*	Whitney Houston

Source: The Independent

associated with the song 'My Way'. His films from 1941 include *From Here to Eternity* 1953 (Academy Award) and *Guys and Dolls* 1955. He was still performing in the 1980s.

Smiths, the English four-piece rock group (1982–87) from Manchester. Their songs, with lyrics by singer Morrissey (1959–) and tunes by guitarist Johnny Marr (1964–), drew on diverse sources such as rockabilly and Mersey beat, with confessional humour and images of urban desolation. They had an intensely dedicated following in Britain and were one of the most popular indie bands. Morrissey went on to a solo career and Marr became a part-time member of The The and Electronic.

soca Latin Caribbean dance music, a mixture of ***so****ul* and ***ca****lypso* but closer to the latter. A soca band is likely to include conga drums, synthesizer, and a small horn section, as well as electric guitar, bass, and drums. Soca originated on Trinidad in the 1970s.

Sondheim Stephen (Joshua) 1930– . US composer and lyricist. He wrote the lyrics of Leonard Bernstein's *West Side Story* 1957 and composed witty and sophisticated musicals, including *A Little Night Music* 1973, *Pacific Overtures* 1976, *Sweeney Todd* 1979, *Into the Woods* 1987, and *Sunday in the Park with George* 1989.

soul music emotionally intense style of rhythm and blues sung by, among others, Sam Cooke (1935–1964), Aretha Franklin (1942–), and Al Green (1946–). With elements of blues, gospel music, and jazz, it emerged in the 1950s. Sometimes all popular music made by African-Americans is labelled soul music.

Spector Phil 1940– . US record producer, known for the 'wall of sound', created using a large orchestra, distinguishing his work in the early 1960s with vocal groups such as the Crystals and the Ronettes. He withdrew into semi-retirement in 1966 but his influence can still be heard.

Springsteen Bruce 1949– . US rock singer, songwriter, and guitarist, born in New Jersey. His work combines music in traditional rock idiom and reflective lyrics about working-class life and the pursuit of the American dream on such albums as *Born to Run* 1975, *Born in the USA* 1984, and *Human Touch* 1992.

stadium rock epic style of rock music developed in the 1980s. As live audiences grew, performers had to adapt their delivery and material to the size of the auditorium. Stadium rock is a music of broad gesture, windswept and brooding. The Irish U2 and Scottish Simple Minds (formed 1977) are formative stadium-rock bands.

steel band musical ensemble common in the West Indies, consisting mostly of percussion instruments made from oil drums that give a sweet, metallic ringing tone.

Supremes, the US vocal group, pioneers of the Motown sound, formed 1959 in Detroit. Beginning in 1962, the group was a trio comprising, initially, Diana Ross (1944–), Mary Wilson (1944–), and Florence Ballard (1943–1976). The most successful female group of the 1960s, they had a string of pop hits beginning with 'Where Did Our Love Go?' 1964 and 'Baby Love' 1964. Diana Ross left to pursue a solo career 1969.

swing music jazz style popular in the 1930s–40s, a big-band dance music with a simple harmonic base of varying tempo from the rhythm section (percussion, guitar, piano), harmonic brass and woodwind sections (sometimes strings), and superimposed solo melodic line from, for example, trumpet, clarinet, or saxophone. Exponents included Benny Goodman, Duke Ellington, and Glenn Miller, who introduced jazz to a mass white audience.

syncopation the deliberate upsetting of rhythm by shifting the accent to a beat that is normally unaccented.

Velvet Underground, the US avant-garde rock group formed 1965, dissolved 1969–72; reformed 1993. Their experiments with dissonance and abrasive noise proved highly influential in subsequent decades, as did the street-smart lyrics of guitarist and vocalist Lou Reed. Their albums include *The Velvet Underground and Nico* 1967, *White Light/White Heat* 1968, and *Loaded* 1970. Songs like 'Waiting for the Man' and 'Sweet Jane' have become classics, and the Velvet Underground's sound, image, and attitude have been endlessly imitated and invoked. A Velvet Underground reunion took place with the original line-up in Paris 1991 and led to a European tour 1993.

world music or ***roots music*** any music whose regional character has not been lost in the melting pot of the pop industry. Examples are W African *mbalax*, E African soukous, S African mbaqanga, French Antillean zouk, Javanese gamelan, Latin American salsa and lambada, Cajun music, European folk music, and rural blues, as well as combinations of these (flamenco guitar and kora; dub polka).

1920s Afro-Cuban dance music popularized in the USA by bandleader Xavier Cugat (1900–1990). Highlife music developed in W Africa.

1930s Latin American dances like samba and rumba became Western ballroom dances.

1940s Afro-Cuban rhythms fused with American jazz to become Cubop.

1950s The cool-jazz school imported bossa nova from Brazil. US bandleader Tito Puente (1923–) popularized Latin dances mambo and cha-cha-cha. Calypso appeared in the pop charts.

1960s Miriam Makeba took South African folk and pop to the West. The Beatles introduced Indian sitar music. Folk-rock recycled traditional songs.

1970s Jamaican reggae became international and was an influence on punk. Cuban singer Celia Cruz established herself in the USA as the 'queen of salsa'. Malian guitarist Ali Farka Touré (1939–) brought a blues feel to traditional African melodies.

1980s World music was embraced by several established pop stars and various African, Latin American, Bulgarian, Yemenite, and other styles became familiar in the West. Zairean Papa Wemba was one of many Third World singers recording in France.

1990s New fusions, such as Afro-Gaelic, punk Ukrainian, and bhangramuffin, appeared.

Young Neil 1945– . Canadian rock guitarist, singer, and songwriter, in the USA from 1966. His high, plaintive voice and loud, abrasive guitar make his work instantly recognizable, despite abrupt changes of style throughout his career. His albums include *Rust Never Sleeps* 1979 (with the group Crazy Horse), *Harvest Moon* 1992 (a nod to his best-selling *Harvest* 1972), and *Unplugged* 1993.

zydeco dance music originating in Louisiana, USA, similar to Cajun but more heavily influenced by blues and West Indian music. Zydeco is fast and bouncy, using instruments like accordion, saxophone, and washboard. It was widely popularized by singer and accordion player Clifton Chenier (1925–1987).

PHOTOGRAPHY

Terms

aperture in a camera, an opening that allows light to pass through the lens to strike the film. Controlled by shutter speed and the iris diaphragm, it can be set mechanically or electronically at various diameters.

ASA numbering system for rating the speed of films, devised by the American Standards Association. It has now been superseded by ***ISO***, the International Standards Organization.

autochrome single-plate additive colour process devised by the Lumière brothers 1903. It was the first commercially available process, in use 1907–35.

calotype paper-based photograph using a wax paper negative, the first example of the negative/positive process invented by the English photographer Fox Talbot around 1834.

camera apparatus used in photography, consisting of a lens system set in a light-proof box inside of which a sensitized film or plate can be placed. The lens collects rays of light reflected from the subject and brings them together as a sharp image on the film; it has apertures marked with f-numbers, or f-stops, that reduce or increase the amount of light. Apertures also control depth of field. A shutter controls the amount of time light has to affect the film. There are small-, medium-, and large-format cameras; the format refers to the size of recorded image and the dimensions of the print obtained.

A simple camera has a fixed shutter speed and aperture, chosen so that on a sunny day the correct amount of light is admitted. More complex cameras allow the shutter speed and aperture to be adjusted; most have a built-in exposure meter to help choose the correct combination of shutter speed and aperture for the ambient conditions and subject matter. The most versatile camera is the single-lens reflex (SLR) which allows the lens to be removed and special lenses attached. A pin-hole camera has a small (pin-sized) hole instead of a lens. It must be left on a firm support during exposures, which are up to ten seconds with slow film, two seconds with fast film, and five minutes for paper negatives in daylight. The pin-hole camera gives sharp images from close-up to infinity.

camera obscura darkened box with a tiny hole for projecting the inverted image of the scene outside on to a screen inside.

Cibachrome process of printing photographs directly from transparencies. It can be home-processed and the rich, saturated colours are highly resistant to fading. It was introduced 1963.

cine camera camera that takes a rapid sequence of still photographs – 24 frames (pictures) each second. When the pictures are projected one after the other at the same speed on to a screen, they appear to show movement, because our eyes hold on to the image of one picture before the next one appears.

The cine camera differs from an ordinary still camera in having a motor that winds the film on. The film is held still by a claw mechanism while each frame is exposed. When the film is moved between frames, a semicircular disc slides between the lens and the film and prevents exposure.

daguerreotype single-image process using mercury vapour and an iodine-sensitized silvered plate; it was invented by Louis Daguerre 1838.

developing process that produces a visible image on exposed photographic film, involving the treatment of the exposed film with a chemical developer.

The developing liquid consists of a reducing agent that changes the light-altered silver salts in the film into darker metallic silver. The developed image is made permanent with a fixer, which dissolves away any silver salts which were not affected by light. The developed image is a negative, or reverse image: darkest where the strongest light hit the film, lightest where the least light fell. To produce a positive image the negative is itself photographed, and the development process reverses the shading, producing the final print. Colour and black-and-white film can be obtained as direct reversal, slide, or transparency material. Slides and transparencies are used for projection or printing with a positive-to-positive process such as Cibachrome.

dye-transfer print print made by a relatively permanent colour process that uses red, yellow, and blue separation negatives printed together.

exposure meter instrument used in photography for indicating the correct exposure – the length of time the camera shutter should be open under given light conditions. Meters use substances such as cadmium sulphide and selenium as light sensors. These materials change electrically when light strikes them, the change being proportional to the intensity of the incident light. Many cameras have a built-in exposure meter that sets the camera controls automatically as the light conditions change.

film, photographic strip of transparent material (usually cellulose acetate) coated with a light-sensitive emulsion, used in cameras to take pictures. The emulsion contains a mixture of light-sensitive silver halide salts (for example, bromide or iodide) in gelatin. When the emulsion is exposed to light, the silver salts are invisibly altered, giving a latent image, which is then made visible by the process of developing. Films differ in their sensitivities to light, this being indicated by their speeds. Colour film consists of several layers of emulsion, each of which records a different colour in the light falling on it.

In ***colour film*** the front emulsion records blue light, then comes a yellow filter, followed by layers that record green and red light respectively. In the developing process the various images in the layers are dyed yellow, magenta (red), and cyan (blue), respectively. When they are viewed, either as a transparency or as a colour print, the colours merge to produce the true colour of the original scene photographed.

f-number or ***f-stop*** measure of the relative aperture of a telescope or camera lens; it indicates the light-gathering power of the lens. In photography, each successive f-number represents a halving of exposure speed.

photography: chronology

1515 Leonardo da Vinci described the camera obscura.
1750 The painter Canaletto used a camera obscura as an aid to his painting in Venice.
1790 Thomas Wedgwood in England made photograms – placing objects on leather, sensitized using silver nitrate.
1826 Nicephore Niépce (1765–1833), a French doctor, produced the world's first photograph from nature on pewter plates with a camera obscura and an eight-hour exposure.
1835 Niépce and L J M Daguerre produced the first Daguerreotype camera photograph.
1839 Daguerre was awarded an annuity by the French government and his process given to the world.
1840 Invention of the Petzval lens, which reduced exposure time by 90%. Herschel discovered sodium thiosulphate as a fixer for silver halides.
1841 Fox Talbot's calotype process was patented – the first multicopy method of photography using a negative/positive process, sensitized with silver iodide.
1844 Fox Talbot published the first photographic book, *The Pencil of Nature*.
1845 Hill and Adamson began to use calotypes for portraits in Edinburgh.
1851 Fox Talbot used a one-thousandth of a second exposure to demonstrate high-speed photography. Invention of the wet-collodion-on-glass process and the waxed-paper negative. Photographs were displayed at the Great Exhibition in London.
1852 The London Society of Arts exhibited 779 photographs.
1855 Roger Fenton made documentary photographs of the Crimean War from a specially constructed caravan with portable darkroom.
1859 Nadar in Paris made photographs underground using battery-powered arc lights.
1860 Queen Victoria was photographed by Mayall. Abraham Lincoln was photographed by Matthew Brady for political campaigning.
1861 The single-lens reflex plate camera was patented by Thomas Sutton. The principles of three-colour photography were demonstrated by Scottish physicist James Clerk Maxwell.
1862 Nadar took aerial photographs over Paris.
1870 Julia Margaret Cameron used long lenses for her distinctive portraits.
1871 Gelatin-silver bromide was developed.
1878 In the USA Eadweard Muybridge analysed the movements of animals through sequential photographs, using a series of cameras.
1879 The photogravure process was invented.
1880 A silver bromide emulsion was fixed with hypo. Photographs were first reproduced in newspapers in New York using the half-tone engraving process. The first twin-lens reflex camera was produced in London. Gelatin-silver chloride paper was introduced.
1884 George Eastman produced flexible negative film.
1889 The Eastman Company in the USA produced the Kodak No 1 camera and roll film, facilitating universal, hand-held snapshots.
1891 The first telephoto lens. The interference process of colour photography was developed by the French doctor Gabriel Lippmann.
1897 The first issue of Alfred Stieglitz's *Camera Notes* in the USA.
1902 In Germany, Deckel invented a prototype leaf shutter and Zeiss introduced the Tessar lens.
1904 The autochrome colour process was patented by the Lumière brothers.
1905 Alfred Stieglitz opened the gallery '291' in New York promoting photography. Lewis Hine used photography to expose the exploitation of children in US factories, causing protective laws to be passed.
1907 The autochrome process began to be factory-produced.
1914 Oskar Barnack designed a prototype Leica camera for Leitz in Germany.
1924 Leitz launched the first 35mm camera, the Leica, delayed because of World War I. It became very popular with photojournalists because it was quiet, small, dependable, and had a range of lenses and accessories.
1929 Rolleiflex produced a twin-lens reflex camera in Germany.
1935 In the USA, Mannes and Godowsky invented Kodachrome transparency film, which produced sharp images and rich colour quality. Electronic flash was invented in the USA.
1936 *Life* magazine, significant for its photojournalism, was first published in the USA.
1938 *Picture Post* magazine was introduced in the UK.
1940 Multigrade enlarging paper by Ilford was made available in the UK.
1942 Kodacolour negative film was introduced.
1945 The zone system of exposure estimation was published in the book *Exposure Record* by Ansel Adams.
1947 Polaroid black and white instant process film was invented by Dr Edwin Land, who set up the Polaroid corporation in Boston, Massachusetts. The principles of holography were demonstrated in England by Dennis Gabor.
1955 Kodak introduced Tri-X, a black and white 200 ASA film.
1959 The zoom lens was invented by the Austrian firm of Voigtlander.
1960 The laser was invented in the USA, making holography possible. Polacolor, a self-processing colour film, was introduced by Polaroid, using a 60-second colour film and dye diffusion technique.
1963 Cibachrome, paper and chemicals for printing directly from transparencies, was made available by Ciba-Geigy of Switzerland. One of the most permanent processes, it is marketed by Ilford in the UK.

***photography: chronology** (cont.)*

1966	The International Center of Photography was established in New York.
1969	Photographs were taken on the Moon by US astronauts.
1970	A charge-coupled device was invented at Bell Laboratories in New Jersey, USA, to record very faint images (for example in astronomy). *Rencontres Internationales de la Photographie*, the annual summer festival of photography with workshops, was founded in Arles, France.
1971	Opening of the Photographers' Gallery, London, and the Photo Archive of the Bibliothéque Nationale, Paris.
1972	The SX70 system, a single-lens reflex camera with instant prints, was produced by Polaroid.
1975	The Center for Creative Photography was established at the University of Arizona.
1980	Ansel Adams sold an original print, *Moonrise: Hernandez*, for $45,000, a record price, in the USA. *Voyager 1* sent photographs of Saturn back to Earth across space.
1983	The National Museum of Photography, Film and Television opened in Bradford, England.
1985	The Minolta Corporation in Japan introduced the Minolta 7000 – the world's first body-integral autofocus single-lens reflex camera.
1988	The electronic camera, which stores pictures on magnetic disc instead of on film, was introduced in Japan.
1990	Kodak introduced PhotoCD which converts 35mm camera pictures (on film) into digital form and stores them on compact disc (CD) for viewing on TV.
1992	Japanese company Canon introduced a camera with autofocus controlled by the user's eye. The camera focuses on whatever the user is looking at.
1993	Man Ray's *Glass Tears* became world's most expensive photograph when it fetched £122,500 at Sotheby's

focus the distance that a lens must be moved in order to focus a sharp image on the light-sensitive film at the back of the camera. The lens is moved away from the film to focus the image of closer objects. The focusing distance is often marked on a scale around the lens; however, some cameras now have an automatic focusing (autofocus) mechanism that uses an electric motor to move the lens.

f-stop another name for f-number.

hypo sodium thiosulphate, discovered 1819 by John Herschel, and used as a fixative for photographic images since 1837.

ISO numbering system for rating the speed of films, devised by the International Standards Organization.

negative/positive reverse image, which when printed is again reversed, restoring the original scene. It was invented by Fox Talbot about 1834.

orthochromatic photographic film or paper of decreased sensitivity, which can be processed with a red safelight. Using it, blue objects appear lighter and red ones darker because of increased blue sensitivity.

panchromatic film highly sensitive black-and-white film made to render all visible spectral colours in correct grey tones. Panchromatic film is always developed in total darkness.

photogram picture produced on photographic material by exposing it to light, but without using a camera.

photography process for reproducing images on sensitized materials by various forms of radiant energy, including visible light, ultraviolet, infrared, X-rays, atomic radiations, and electron beams. Photography was developed in the 19th century; among the pioneers were L J M Daguerre in France and Fox Talbot in the UK. Colour photography dates from the early 20th century.

The most familiar photographic process depends upon the fact that certain silver compounds (called halides) are sensitive to light. A photographic film is coated with these compounds and, in a camera, is exposed to light. An image, or picture, of the scene before the camera is formed on the film because the silver halides become activated (light-altered) where light falls but not where light does not fall. The image is made visible by the process of developing, made permanent by fixing, and, finally, is usually printed on paper. Motion-picture photography uses a camera that exposes a roll of film to a rapid succession of views that, when developed, are projected in equally rapid succession to provide a moving image.

Polaroid camera instant-picture camera, invented by Edwin Land in the USA 1947; colour Polaroid cameras were introduced 1963. A modern camera produces black-and-white prints in a few seconds, and colour prints in less than a minute. It ejects a piece of film on paper immediately after the picture has been taken. The film consists of layers of emulsion and colour dyes together with a pod of chemical developer. When the film is ejected the pod bursts and processing occurs in the light.

rangefinder instrument for determining the range or distance of an object from the observer; used to focus a camera or to sight a gun accurately. A ***rangefinder camera*** has a rotating mirror or prism that alters the image seen through the viewfinder, and a secondary window. When the two images are brought together into one, the lens is sharply focused.

reflex camera camera that uses a mirror and prisms to reflect light passing through the lens into the viewfinder, showing the photographer the exact scene that is being shot. When the shutter button is released the mirror springs out of the way, allowing light to reach the film. The most common type is the single-lens reflex (SLR) camera. The twin-lens reflex (TLR) camera has two lenses: one has a mirror for viewing, the other is used for exposing the film.

SLR abbreviation for ***single-lens reflex***, a type of camera in which the image can be seen through the lens before a picture is taken. A small mirror directs light entering the lens to the viewfinder. When a picture is taken the mirror moves rapidly aside to allow the light to reach the film. The SLR allows different lenses, such as close-up or zoom lenses, to be used because the photographer can see exactly what is being focused on.

telephoto lens photographic lens of longer focal length than normal that takes a very narrow view and gives a large image through a combination of telescopic and ordinary photographic lenses.

thaumatrope disc with two different pictures at opposite ends of its surface. The images combine into one when rapidly rotated because of the persistence of visual impressions.

35 mm width of photographic film, the most popular format for the camera today. The 35-mm camera falls into two categories, the single-lens reflex (SLR) and the rangefinder.

TLR camera twin-lens reflex camera that has a viewing lens of the same angle of view and focal length mounted above and parallel to the taking lens.

transparency picture on slide film. This captures the original in a positive image (direct reversal) and can be used for projection or printing on positive-to-positive print material; for example, by the Cibachrome or Kodak R-type process. Slide film is usually colour but can be obtained in black and white.

wide-angle lens photographic lens of shorter focal length than normal, taking in a wider angle of view.

zoetrope optical toy with a series of pictures on the inner surface of a cylinder. When the pictures are rotated and viewed through a slit, it gives the impression of continuous motion.

zone system system of exposure estimation invented by Ansel Adams that groups infinite tonal gradations into ten zones, zone 0 being black and zone 10 white. An f-stop change in exposure is required from zone to zone.

zoom lens photographic lens that, by variation of focal length, allows speedy transition from long shots to close-ups.

Famous Photographers

Abbott Berenice 1898–1991. US photographer best known for her portrait studies of artists in the 1920s and for her comprehensive documentation of New York City in the 1930s, culminating in the publication of *Changing New York* 1939. Her straightforward style was partially influenced by French photograher Eugène Atget, whose work she rescued from obscurity.

Adams Ansel 1902–1984. US photographer known for his printed images of dramatic landscapes and organic forms of the American West. Light and texture were important elements in his photographs. He was associated with the zone system of exposure estimation and was a founder member (with Imogen Cunningham and Edward Weston) of the 'f/64' group, which advocated precise definition. The Yosemite National Park and the High Sierras in California featured prominently in his work throughout his life.

Adamson Robert. Scottish photographer who collaborated with David Octavius Hill.

Arbus Diane 1923–1971. US photographer. Although she practised as a fashion photographer for 20 years, Arbus is best known for her later work, which examined the fringes of American society, the misfits, the eccentrics, and the bizarre. Her work has been attacked as cruel and voyeuristic, but it is essentially sympathetic in its unflinching curiosity. *A Box of Ten Photographs*, a limited edition of her work, was published 1970.

Atget Eugène 1857–1927. French photographer. He took up photography at the age of 40, and for 30 years documented urban Paris, leaving some 10,000 images. His photographs were sometimes used by painters and he was admired by the Surrealists. After his death his work was rescued and promoted by the photographer Berenice Abbott.

Avedon Richard 1923– . US photographer. A fashion photographer with *Harper's Bazaar* magazine in New York from the mid-1940s, he moved to *Vogue* 1965. He later became the highest-paid fashion and advertising photographer in the world. His work consists of intensely realistic images, chiefly portraits, made with large-format cameras.

Bailey David 1938– . British fashion photographer. His work for *Vogue* magazine in the 1960s and his black-and-white portraits of celebrities did much to define the image of 'swinging London'. He has published several books, including *Box of Pin-Ups* 1965 and *Goodbye Baby and Amen* 1969.

Beaton Cecil 1904–1980. English photographer whose elegant and sophisticated fashion pictures and society portraits often employed exotic props and settings. He adopted a simpler style for his wartime photographs of bomb-damaged London. He also worked as a stage and film designer.

Bourke-White Margaret 1906–1971. US photographer. As an editor of *Fortune* magazine 1929–33, she travelled extensively in the USSR, publishing several collections of photographs. Later, with husband Erskine Caldwell, she also published photo collections of American and European subjects. She began working for *Life* magazine 1936, and covered combat in World War II and documented India's struggle for independence.

Brady Mathew B *c.* 1823–1896. US photographer. Famed for his skill in photographic portraiture, he published *The Gallery of Illustrious Americans* 1850. With the outbreak of the US Civil War 1861 Brady and his staff became the foremost photographers of battle scenes and military life. Although his war photos were widely reproduced Brady later suffered a series of financial reverses and died in poverty.

Brandt Bill 1905–1983. British photographer, born in Germany. During the 1930s he made a series of social records contrasting the lives of the rich and the poor, some of which were presented in his book *The English at Home* 1936. During World War II he documented conditions in London in the Blitz. The strong contrasts in his black-and-white prints often produced a gloomy and threatening atmosphere. His outstanding creative work was his treatment of the nude, published in *Perspective of Nudes* and *Shadows of Light*, both 1966.

Brassäi adopted name of Gyula Halesz 1899–1986. French photographer of Hungarian origin who chronicled, mainly by flash, the nightlife of Paris: prostitutes, street cleaners, and criminals. These pictures were published as *Paris by Night* 1933. Later he turned to more abstract work.

Cameron Julia Margaret 1815–1879. British photographer who made lively and dramatic portraits of the Victorian intelligentsia, often posed as historical or literary figures. Her sitters included her friends Sir John Herschel and the poet Alfred Lord Tennyson, whose *Idylls of the King* she illustrated 1872, and Charles Darwin. She used a large camera, five-minute exposures, and wet plates.

Capa Robert. Adopted name of André Friedmann 1913–1954. US photographer, born in Hungary, who specialized in war photography. He covered the Spanish Civil War as a freelance and World War II for *Life* and *Collier's* magazines. His pictures emphasize the human tragedy of war. He was a founder member of the Magnum photographic agency, a cooperative. He died while on an assignment in Vietnam.

Cartier-Bresson Henri 1908– . French photographer, considered one of the greatest photographic artists. His documentary work was shot in black and white, using a small-format Leica camera. His work is remarkable for its tightly structured composition and his ability to capture the decisive moment. He was a cofounder (with Robert Capa and others) of the cooperative photo agency Magnum.

Cunningham Imogen 1883–1976. US photographer. Her early photographs were romantic but she gradually rejected pictorialism, producing clear and detailed plant studies 1922–29. With Ansel Adams and Edward Weston, she was a founder member of the 'f/64' group which advocated precise definition. From the mid-1930s she concentrated on portraiture.

Daguerre Louis Jacques Mande 1789–1851. French pioneer of photography. Together with Joseph Niépce, he is credited with the invention of photography (though others were reaching the same point simultaneously). In 1838 he invented the daguerreotype, a single image process superseded ten years later by Fox Talbot's negative/positive process.

Doisneau Robert 1912– . French photographer known for his sensitive and often witty depictions of ordinary people and everyday situations within the environs of Paris. His most famous image, *Baiser de l'Hôtel de Ville/The Kiss at the Hôtel de Ville*, was produced for *Life* magazine 1950.

Eggleston William 1937– . US photographer whose banal scenes of life in the deep South are transformed by his use of the dye-transfer technique into intense, superreal images of richly saturated colour. In 1984 he documented Elvis Presley's home, Graceland.

Evans Walker 1903–1975. US photographer best known for his documentary photographs of people in the rural American South during the Great Depression. Many of his photographs appeared in James Agee's book *Let Us Now Praise Famous Men* 1941.

Fenton Roger 1819–1869. English photographer, best known for his comprehensive documentation of the Crimean War 1855. He was a founder member of the Photographic Society (later the Royal Photographic Society) in London 1853 but completely gave up photography 1860.

Hill David Octavius 1802–1870 and Robert R Adamson 1821–1848. Scottish photographers who worked together 1843–48, making extensive use of the calotype process in their portraits of leading members of the Free Church of Scotland and their views of Edinburgh and the Scottish fishing village of Newhaven. They produced around 2,500 calotypes. Their work was rediscovered around 1900.

Hine Lewis 1874–1940. US sociologist and photographer. His dramatic photographs of child-labour conditions in US factories at the beginning of the 20th century led to changes in state and local labour laws. His photographs of immigrants arriving at New York's Ellis Island, their tenement homes and the sweatshops in which they worked, published 1908, are considered the first photo story.

Hosking Eric (John) 1909–1990. English wildlife photographer known for his documentation of British birds, especially owls. Beginning at the age of eight and still photographing in Africa at 80, he covered all aspects of birdlife and illustrated a large number of books, published between 1940 and 1990.

Karsh Yousuf 1908– . Canadian portrait photographer, born in Armenia. He is known for his formal and dramatically lit studies of the famous, in which he attempts to capture their 'inward power'. His most notable picture is the defiant portrait of Winston Churchill which appeared on the cover of *Life* magazine 1941.

Kertész André 1894–1986. Hungarian-born US photographer whose spontaneity had a great impact on photojournalism. A master of the 35-mm-format camera, he recorded his immediate environment (Paris, New York) with wit and style.

Koudelka Josef 1939– . Czech photographer best known for his photographs of East European Romanies, whose vanishing way of life he has recorded. He also photographed the Soviet invasion of Czechoslovakia 1968 and the inauguration of Václav Havel as president of Czechoslovakia 1989.

Land Edwin Herbert 1909–1991. US inventor of the Polaroid Land camera 1947, which developed the film in one minute inside the camera and produced an 'instant' photograph.

Lange Dorothea 1895–1965. US photographer who was hired in 1935 by the federal Farm Security Administration to document the westward migration of farm families from the Dust Bowl of the S central USA. Her photographs, characterized by a gritty realism, were widely exhibited and subsequently published as *An American Exodus: A Record of Human Erosion* 1939.

Le Gray Gustave 1820–1882. French photographer who in 1850 invented the waxed-paper negative, a more efficient version of the calotype, where the paper is waxed before being coated with silver iodide. He also experimented with printing images using more than one negative, notably in his detailed seascapes which use a separate negative for sea and sky.

Leibovitz Annie 1950– . US photographer whose elaborately staged portraits of American celebrities appeared first in *Rolling Stone* magazine and later in *Vanity Fair*. The odd poses in which her sitters allow themselves to be placed suggest an element of self-mockery.

McCullin Don(ald) 1935– . British war photographer who started out as a freelance photojournalist for Sunday newspapers. His coverage of hostilities in the Congo 1967, Vietnam 1968, Biafra 1968 and 1970, and Cambodia 1970 is notable for his pessimistic vision. He has published several books of his work, among them *Destruction Business*.

Man Ray adopted name of Emmanuel Rudnitsky 1890–1977. US photographer, painter, and sculptor, active mainly in France; associated with the Dada movement. His pictures often showed Surrealist images, like the photograph *Le Violon d'Ingres* 1924.

In 1922 he invented the ***rayograph***, a black-and-white image obtained without a camera by placing objects on sensitized photographic paper and exposing them to light; he also used the technique of solarization (partly reversing the tones on a photograph). His photographs include portraits of many artists and writers.

Mapplethorpe Robert 1946–1989. US art photographer known for his use of racial and homoerotic imagery in chiefly fine platinum prints. He developed a style of polished elegance in his gallery art works, whose often culturally forbidden subject matter caused controversy.

Meiselas Susan 1948– . US freelance war photographer who has covered conflicts in Nicaragua and El Salvador. Her brilliant cibachrome prints seem anti-heroic in their intention.

Modotti Tina 1896–1942 Italian photographer who studied with Edward Weston and went to Mexico with him 1923. As well as her sensitive studies of Mexican women, she recorded the work of the Mexican muralists and made near-abstract prints of stairs and flowers.

Moholy-Nagy Laszlo 1895–1946. US photographer, born in Hungary. He lived in Germany 1923–29, where he was a member of the Bauhaus school, and fled from the Nazis 1935. Through the publication of his illuminating theories and practical experiments, he had great influence on 20th-century photography and design.

Munkácsi Martin 1896–1963. US photographer born in Hungary. After a successful career in Budapest and then Berlin, where he was influenced by the New Photography movement, he moved to the USA 1934. There he worked as a fashion photographer pioneering a more lively and natural style of photograph for such magazines as *Harper's Bazaar* and *Ladies' Home Journal*.

Muybridge Eadweard. Adopted name of Edward James Muggeridge 1830–1904. British photographer. He made a series of animal locomotion photographs in the USA in the 1870s and proved that, when a horse trots, there are times when all its feet are off the ground. He also explored motion in birds and humans.

Nadar adopted name of Gaspard-Félix Tournachon 1820–1910. French portrait photographer and caricaturist. He took the first aerial photographs (from a balloon 1858) and was the first to take flash photographs (using magnesium bulbs).

Namuth Hans 1915–1990. German-born US photographer who specialized in portraits and documentary work. He began as a photojournalist in Europe in the 1930s and opened a portrait studio in New York in 1950. His work includes documentation of the Guatemalan Mam Indians (published as *Los Todos Santeros* 1989) and of US artists from the 1950s (published as *Artists 1950–1981*). He also carried out assignments for magazines.

Parkinson Norman. Adopted name of Ronald William Parkinson Smith 1913–1990. English fashion and portrait photographer who caught the essential glamour of each decade from the 1930s to the 1980s. Long associated with the magazines *Vogue* and *Queen*, he was best known for his colour work, and from the late 1960s took many official portraits of the royal family.

Penn Irving 1917– . US fashion, advertising, portrait, editorial, and fine art photographer. In 1948 he took the first of many journeys to Africa and the Far East, resulting in a series of portrait photographs of local people, avoiding sophisticated technique. He was associated for many years with *Vogue* magazine in the USA.

Renger-Patzsch Albert 1897–1966. German photographer. He was a leading figure of the New Photography movement which emphasized objectivity of vision. His influential book *Die Welt ist schön/The World is Beautiful* 1928 was a disparate collection of objects, from plants to industrial machinery, all photographed in the same way.

Rodchenko Alexander 1891–1956. Russian avant-garde painter and designer who took up photography 1924. The aim of his work, in all media, was to create a visual language that would reflect the new revolutionary times. In his photographs everyday objects were presented in close-up, from strange angles, or from high viewpoints, an approach similar to that of the Hungarian Laszlo Moholy-Nagy.

Sander August 1876–1964. German portrait photographer whose long-term project was to create a vast composite portrait, *Man of the Twentieth Century*. Concentrating on German society, he turned his dispassionate gaze on every walk of life – from butchers to bankers – in a way that combined the individual with the archetypal. Much of his work was destroyed when his Cologne studio was bombed 1944.

Siskind Aaron 1903–1991. US art photographer who began as a documentary photographer and in 1940 made a radical change towards a poetic exploration of forms and planes, inspired by the Abstract Expressionist painters.

Steichen Edward 1897–1973. Luxembourg-born US photographer, who with Alfred Stieglitz helped to establish photography as an art form. His style evolved during his career from painterly impressionism to realism.

During World War I he helped to develop aerial photography, and in World War II he directed US naval-combat photography. He turned to fashion and advertising 1923–38, working mainly for *Vogue* and *Vanity Fair* magazines. He was in charge of the Museum of Modern Art's photography collection 1947–62, where in 1955 he organized the renowned 'Family of Man' exhibition.

Stieglitz Alfred 1864–1946. US photographer who was mainly responsible for the recognition of photography as an art form. After forming the multimedia Photo-Secession Group at 291 Fifth Avenue, New York, with Edward Steichen, he began the magazine *Camera Work* 1902–17. His cloud series, the portraits of the painter Georgia O'Keeffe (whom he married 1924), and his studies of New York City, are his most famous works. Through exhibitions, competitions, and publication at his galleries, he helped establish a photographic esthetic.

Strand Paul 1890–1976. US photographer and film maker who studied with Lewis Hine and was encouraged by Alfred Stieglitz. After his early, near-abstract studies of New York, he turned to predominantly rural subjects which celebrate human dignity in a clear and straightforward manner. His portfolios, which include *Photographs of Mexico* 1940 and *Time in New England*, were always meticulously printed.

Talbot William Henry Fox 1800–1877. English pioneer of photography. He invented the paper-based calotype process, the first negative/positive method. Talbot made photograms several years before Louis Daguerre's invention was announced. In 1851 he made instantaneous photographs and in 1852 photo engravings. *The Pencil of Nature* 1844–46 was the first book of photographs published.

Weston Edward 1886–1958. US photographer. A founding member of the 'f/64' group (after the smallest lens opening), a school of photography advocating sharp definition. He is noted for the technical mastery, composition, and clarity in his California landscapes, clouds, gourds, cactuses, and nude studies.

In his photography, Weston aimed for realism. He never used artificial light and seldom enlarged, cropped, or retouched his negatives. His aesthetic principle dominated American photography for many years.

Woolcott Marion Post 1910–1990. US documentary photographer best known for her work for the Farm Security Administration (with Walker Evans and Dorothea Lange), showing the conditions of poor farmers in the late 1930s in Kentucky and the deep South.

THEATRE

Genres

Absurd, Theatre of the avant-garde drama originating with a group of playwrights in the 1950s, including Beckett, Ionesco, Genet, and Pinter. Their work expressed the belief that in a godless universe human existence has no meaning or purpose and therefore all communication breaks down. Logical construction and argument gives way to irrational and illogical speech and to its ultimate conclusion, silence, as in Beckett's play *Breath* 1970.

autos sacramentales Spanish 'religious plays'. Spanish drama form, related to the mystery plays in England, and well established by the 13th century. These traditional performances were redeveloped in the 17th century by dramatists Lope de Vega and Calderón, whose masterpiece in this form is *El gran teatro del mundo/The Great Theatre of the World* 1641.

burlesque in the 17th and 18th centuries, a form of satirical comedy parodying a particular play or dramatic genre. For example, John Gay's *The Beggar's Opera* 1728 is a burlesque of 18th-century opera, and Richard Brinsley Sheridan's *The Critic* 1777 satirizes the sentimentality in contemporary drama. In the USA from the mid-19th century, burlesque referred to a sex and comedy show invented by Michael Bennett Leavitt 1866 with acts including acrobats, singers, and comedians. During the 1920s striptease was introduced in order to counteract the growing popularity of the movies; Gypsy Rose Lee was the most famous stripper. Burlesque was frequently banned in the USA.

cabaret theatrical revue traditionally combining satire and song in cafés or bars. Originating in Paris in the late 19th century in venues such as the Moulin Rouge, cabaret was embraced by avant-garde writers and artists. In Germany in the 1920s, Berlin became a centre for an increasingly political cabaret, later suppressed by the Nazis. In Britain, satirical revue was revived by the Cambridge Footlights theatre group in *Beyond the Fringe* 1961, before cabaret and alternative comedy combined to provide a new generation of stand-up entertainers during the 1980s, notably from the Comedy Store group in London.

circus entertainment, often held in a large tent ('big top'), involving performing animals, acrobats, and clowns. In 1871 Phineas T Barnum created the 'Greatest Show on Earth' in the USA. The popularity of animal acts decreased in the 1980s. Originally, in Roman times, a circus was an arena for chariot races and gladiatorial combats.

comedy drama that aims to make its audience laugh, usually with a happy or amusing ending, as opposed to tragedy. The comic tradition was established by the Greek dramatists Aristophanes and Menander, and the Roman writers Terence and Plautus. In medieval times, the Vices and Devil of the Morality plays developed into the stock comic characters of the Renaissance ***comedy of humours*** with such notable villains as Ben Jonson's Mosca, in *Volpone*. The timeless comedies of Shakespeare and Molière were followed in England during the 17th century by the witty ***comedy of manners*** of Restoration writers such as George Etherege, William Wycherley, and William Congreve. Their often coarse but always vital comedies were toned down in the later Restoration dramas of Richard Sheridan and Oliver Goldsmith. Sentimental comedy dominated most of the 19th century, though little is remembered in the late 20th century, which prefers the realistic tradition of Shaw and the elegant social comedies of Wilde. The polished comedies of Nöel Coward and Terence Rattigan from the 1920s to 1940s were eclipsed during the late 1950s and the 1960s by a trend towards satire and cynicism as seen in the works of Joe Orton and Peter Nichols, alongside absurdist comedies by Samuel Beckett and Jean Genet. From the 1970s the 'black comedies' of Alan Ayckbourn have dominated the English stage. Genres of comedy include pantomime, satire, farce, black comedy, and commedia dell'arte.

commedia dell'arte popular form of Italian improvised comic drama in the 16th and 17th centuries, performed by trained troupes of actors and involving stock characters and situations. It exerted considerable influence on writers such as Molière and Carlo Goldoni, and on the genres of pantomime, harlequinade, and the Punch and Judy show. It laid the foundation for a tradition of mime, strong in France, that has continued with the contemporary mime of Jean-Louis Barrault and Marcel Marceau.

Cruelty, Theatre of theory advanced by Antonin Artaud in his book *Le Theâtre et son double* 1938 and adopted by a number of writers and directors. It aims to shock the audience into an awareness of basic, primitive human nature through the release of feelings usually repressed by conventional behaviour. In the UK Artaud's ideas particularly influenced the producer and director Peter Brook.

farce a broad form of comedy involving stereotyped characters in complex, often improbable situations frequently revolving around extramarital relationships (hence the term 'bedroom farce'). Originating in the physical knockabout comedy of Greek satyr plays and the broad humour of medieval religious drama, the farce was developed and perfected during the 19th century by Eugène Labiche (1815–1888) and Georges Feydeau (1862–1921) in France and Arthur Pinero in England.

fringe theatre plays that are anti-establishment or experimental, and performed in informal venues, in contrast to mainstream commercial theatre. In the UK, the term originated in the 1960s from the activities held on the 'fringe' of the Edinburgh Festival. Notable 'fringe' writers include Howard Brenton and David Hare. Fringe groups that tour the country include Belt and Braces, Hull Truck, and Joint Stock. The US equivalent is off-off-Broadway (off-Broadway is mainstream theatre that is not on Broadway).

kabuki drama originating in late 16th-century Japan, drawing on Nō, puppet plays, and folk dance. Kabuki was first popularized 1603; its colourful, lively spectacle became popular through the 17th and 18th centuries, although from 1629 only men were allowed to act, in the interests of propriety. The art was modernized and its following revived in the 1980s by Ennosuke III (1940–). Unlike Nō actors, kabuki actors do not wear masks; and many specialize in particular types of character, female impersonators (*onnagata*) being the biggest stars.

masque spectacular and essentially aristocratic entertainment with a fantastic or mythological theme in which music, dance, and extravagant costumes and scenic design figured larger than plot. Originating in Italy, it reached its height of popularity at the English court between 1600 and 1640, with the collaboration of Ben Jonson as writer and Inigo Jones as stage designer. The masque powerfully influenced the development of ballet and opera, and the elaborate frame in which it was performed developed into the proscenium arch.

melodrama play or film with romantic and sensational plot elements, often unsubtly acted. Originally it meant a play accompanied by music. The early melodramas used extravagant theatrical effects to heighten violent emotions and actions artificially. By the end of the 19th century, melodrama had become a popular genre of stage play.

mime type of acting in which gestures, movements, and facial expressions replace speech. It has developed as a form of theatre, particularly in France, where Marcel Marceau and Jean Louis Barrault have continued the traditions established in the 19th century by Deburau and the practices of the commedia dell'arte in Italy. In ancient Greece, mime was a crude, realistic comedy with dialogue and exaggerated gesture.

morality play didactic medieval European verse drama, in part a development of the mystery play (or miracle play), in which human characters are replaced by personified virtues and vices, the limited humorous elements being provided by the Devil. Morality plays, such as *Everyman*, flourished in the 15th century. They exerted an influence on the development of Elizabethan drama.

musical 20th-century form of dramatic musical performance, combining elements of song, dance, and the spoken word, often characterized by lavish staging and large casts. It developed from the operettas and musical comedies of the 19th century.

The ***operetta*** is a light-hearted entertainment with extensive musical content: Jacques Offenbach, Johann Strauss, Franz Lehár, and Gilbert and Sullivan all composed operettas. The ***musical comedy*** is an anglicization of the French *opéra bouffe*, of which the first was *A Gaiety Girl* 1893, mounted by George Edwardes (1852–1915) at the Gaiety Theatre, London. Typical musical comedies of the 1920s were *The Student Prince* 1924 and *The Desert Song* 1926, by Sigmund Romberg. The 1930s and 1940s were an era of sophisticated musical comedies with many filmed examples and a strong US presence (Irving Berlin, Jerome Kern, Cole Porter, and George Gershwin). In 1943 the word 'comedy' was dropped and the era of the 'musical' arrived with Rodgers and Hammerstein's *Oklahoma!*; this show introduced an integration of plot and music, which was developed in Lerner and Loewe's *My Fair Lady* 1956 and Leonard Bernstein's *West Side Story* 1957. In England in the 1930s and 1940s Noël Coward and Ivor Novello also wrote stylish musicals. Sandy Wilson's *The Boy Friend* 1953 revived the British musical and was followed by hits such as Lionel Bart's *Oliver!* 1960. Musicals began to branch into religious and political themes with *Oh What a Lovely War!* 1963, produced by Joan Littlewood and Charles Chiltern, and the Andrew Lloyd Webber musicals *Jesus Christ Superstar* 1970 and *Evita* 1978. Another category of musical, substituting a theme for conventional plotting, includes Stephen Sondheim's *Company* 1970, Hamlisch and Kleban's *A Chorus Line* 1975, and Lloyd Webber's *Cats* 1981, using verses by T S Eliot. In the 1980s 19th-century melodrama was popular, for example *Phantom of the Opera* 1986 and *Les Misérables* 1987 (both Lloyd Webber.)

music hall British light theatrical entertainment, in which singers, dancers, comedians, and acrobats perform in 'turns'. Music hall originated in the 17th century, when tavern-keepers acquired the organs that the Puritans had banished from churches. On certain nights organ music was played, and this resulted in a weekly entertainment known as the 'free and easy'. The music hall's heyday was at the beginning of the 20th century, with such artistes as Marie Lloyd, Harry Lauder, and George Formby. The US equivalent is vaudeville.

mystery play or ***miracle play*** medieval religious drama based on stories from the Bible. Mystery plays were performed around the time of church festivals, reaching their height in Europe during the 15th and 16th centuries. A whole cycle running from the Creation to the Last Judgement was performed in separate scenes on mobile wagons by various town guilds. Four English cycles survive: Coventry, Wakefield (or Townley), Chester, and York. Versions are still performed, such as the York cycle in York.

Nō or ***Noh*** the classical, aristocratic Japanese drama, which developed from the 14th to the 16th centuries and is still performed. There is a repertory of some 250 pieces, of which five, one from each of the several classes devoted to different subjects, may be put on in a performance lasting a whole day. Dance, mime, music, and chanting develop the mythical or historical themes. All the actors are men, some of whom wear masks and elaborate costumes; scenery is limited. Nō developed from popular rural entertainments and religious performances staged at shrines and temples by travelling companies. The leader of one of these troupes, Kan'ami (1333–1384), and his son and successor Zeami (1363–1443/4) wrote a number of Nō plays and are regarded as the founders of the form. Symbolism and suggestion dominate action, and the slow, stylized dance is the strongest element. Flute, drums, and chorus supply the music. Nō influenced kabuki drama.

pageant originally the wagon on which medieval mystery plays were performed. The term was later applied to the street procession of songs, dances, and historical tableaux that became fashionable during the 1920s and exist today in forms such as the Lord Mayor's Show in London, England. The open-air entertainment *Son et Lumière* is related to the pageant.

Recent award winners

American Theater Wing Antoinette Perry (Tony) Awards, 1986–1993 (Best Play, Best Musical, and Best Revival production)

1986	*I'm Not Rappaport, The Mystery of Edwin Drood, Sweet Charity*
1987	*Fences, Les Miserables, All My Sons*
1988	*M. Butterfly, The Phantom of the Opera, Anything Goes*
1989	*The Heidi Chronicles, Jerome Robbins' Broadway, Our Town*
1990	*The Grapes of Wrath, City of Angels, Gypsy*
1991	*Lost in Yonkers, The Will Rogers Follies, Fiddler on the Roof*
1992	*Dancing at Lughnasa, Crazy for You, Guys and Dolls*
1993	*Angels in America: Kiss of the Spider Women, Anna Christie*

The Laurence Olivier Awards, presented by The Society of West End Theatre (Best Play, Best Musical, and Best Comedy)

1986	*Les Liaisons Dangereuses, The Phantom of the Opera, When We Are Married*
1987	*Serious Money, Follies, Three Men on a Horse*
1988	*Our Country's Good, Candide, Shirley Valentine*
1989/90	*Racing Demon, Return to the Forbidden Planet, Single Spies*
1991	*Dancing at Lughnasa, Sunday in the Park with George, Out of Order*
1992	*Death and the Maiden, Carmen Jones, La Bête*
1993	*Six Degrees of Separation, Crazy for You, The Rise and Fall of Little Voice*

Evening Standard Drama Awards (Best Play, Best Musical, and Best Comedy)

1986	*Les Liaisons Dangereuses, The Phantom of the Opera, A Month of Sundays*
1987	*A Small Family Business, Follies, Serious Money*
1988	*Aristocrats*, (award for Best Musical was not presented), *Lettice and Lovage*
1989	*Ghetto, Miss Saigon, Henceforward*
1990	*Shadowlands, Into the Woods, Man of the Moment* and *Jeffrey Bernard is Unwell* (joint award)
1991	*Dancing at Lughnasa, Carmen Jones, Kvetch*
1992	*Angels in America, Kiss of the Spider Woman, The Rise and Fall of Little Voice*

pantomime in the British theatre, a traditional Christmas entertainment with its origins in the harlequin spectacle of the 18th century and burlesque of the 19th century, which gave rise to the tradition of the principal boy being played by an actress and the dame by an actor. The harlequin's role diminished altogether as themes developed on folktales such as *The Sleeping Beauty* and *Cinderella*, and with the introduction of additional material such as popular songs, topical comedy, and audience participation. The term 'pantomime' was also applied to Roman dumbshows performed by a masked actor, to 18th-century ballets with mythical themes, and, in 19th-century France, to the wordless Pierrot plays from which modern mime developed.

puppet theatre drama performed with puppets manipulated by usually unseen operators. By the 16th and 17th centuries refined versions of the travelling puppet shows became popular with the aristocracy, and puppets were extensively used in caricature and satire until the 19th century. There has been a revival of interest in the 20th century, partly stimulated by the influence of the *joruri* tradition in Japan, and by leading exponents of rod puppets such as Obraztsov and his Moscow Puppet Theatre, and by Fluck and Law, whose satirical *Spitting Image* puppets, caricaturing public figures, have appeared on British television.

Wayang Kulit is Indonesian shadow puppet theatre, with characters drawn from the Sanskrit epic tradition contrasted with grotesque demons and clowns. Performances, with jointed puppets cut from leather, are accompanied by the brass gong orchestra known as the gamelan, and may last all through the night, on private or public celebrations. Similar forms of shadow puppet theatre are found in India and Malaya.

revue stage presentation involving short satirical and topical items in the form of songs, sketches, and monologues; it originated in the late 19th century. In Britain the first revue seems to have been *Under the Clock* 1893 by Seymour Hicks (1871–1949) and Charles Brookfield. The 1920s revues were spectacular entertainments, but the 'intimate revue' became increasingly popular, employing writers such as Noël Coward. During the 1960s the satirical revue took off with the Cambridge Footlights' production *Beyond the Fringe*, establishing the revue tradition among the young and at fringe theatrical events.

theatre-in-the-round theatrical performance that has the audience watching from all sides. In a reaction against the picture-frame stage of the 19th century, a movement began in the mid-20th century to design theatres with the performing area placed centrally in the auditorium. Notable examples are The Arena Stage in Washington DC, USA 1961 and the Royal Exchange in Manchester, England 1976. The concept was promoted in productions by Margo Jones (1913–1955) in Dallas, USA, who wrote a book on her work, *Theater-in-the-Round* 1951.

tragedy a play dealing with a serious theme, traditionally one in which a character meets disaster as a result either of personal failings or circumstances beyond his or her control. Historically the Greek view of tragedy, as defined by Aristotle and expressed by the great tragedians Aeschylus, Euripides, and Sophocles, has been predominant in the western tradition. In the 20th century, tragedies in the narrow Greek sense – that is, concerned with exalted personages and written in an elevated manner – have virtually died out. Tragedy has been replaced by dramas with 'tragic' implications or overtones, as in the work of Ibsen, O'Neill, Tennessee Williams, Pinter, and Osborne, for example, or by the hybrid tragicomedy. ***Revenge tragedy*** was a form of Elizabeth and Jacobean drama in which revenge formed the mainspring of the action. Characterized by bloody deeds, intrigue, and high melodrama, it was pioneered by Thomas Kyd with *The Spanish Tragedy c.* 1589, Shakespeare's *Titus Andronicus c.* 1592, and Cyril Tourneur's *The Revenger's Tragedy c.* 1606. Its influence is apparent in tragedies such as Shakespeare's *Hamlet* and *Macbeth*.

Biographies

Aeschylus *c.* 525–*c.* 456 BC. Athenian dramatist, who developed Greek tragedy by introducing the second actor, thus enabling true dialogue and dramatic action to occur independently of the chorus. Ranked with Euripides and Sophocles as one of the three great tragedians, Aeschylus composed some 90 plays between 500–456 BC, of which seven survive in his name: *Persians* 472 BC, *Seven Against Thebes* 467, *Suppliants* 463, the *Oresteia* trilogy, and *Prometheus Bound* (the last, although attributed to him, is of uncertain authorship).

Albee Edward 1928– . US playwright. His internationally performed plays are associated with the Theatre of the Absurd and include *The Zoo Story* 1960, *The American Dream* 1961, *Who's Afraid of Virginia Woolf?* 1962 (his most successful play; also filmed with Elizabeth Taylor and Richard Burton as the quarrelling, alcoholic, academic couple 1966), and *Tiny Alice* 1965. *A Delicate Balance* 1966 and *Seascape* 1975 both won Pulitzer prizes.

Anouilh Jean 1910–1987. French dramatist. His plays, influenced by the Neo-Classical tradition, include *Antigone* 1942, *L'Invitation au château/Ring Round the Moon* 1947, *Colombe* 1950, and *Becket* 1959, about St Thomas à Becket and Henry II.

Aristophanes *c.* 448–380 BC. Greek comedic dramatist. Of his 11 extant plays (of a total of over 40), the early comedies are remarkable for the violent satire with which he ridiculed the democratic war leaders. He also satirized contemporary issues such as the new learning of Socrates in *The Clouds* 423 BC and the power of women in *Lysistrata* 411 BC. The chorus plays a prominent role, frequently giving the play its title, as in *The Wasps* 422 BC, *The Birds* 414 BC, and *The Frogs* 405 BC.

Artaud Antonin 1896–1948. French theatre director. Although his play, *Les Cenci/The Cenci* 1935, was a failure, his concept of the ***Theatre of Cruelty***, intended to release feelings usually repressed in the unconscious, has been an important influence on modern dramatists such as Albert Camus and Jean Genet and on directors and producers. Declared insane 1936, Artaud was confined in an asylum.

Ayckbourn Alan 1939– . English playwright. His prolific output, characterized by comic dialogue and experiments in dramatic structure, includes the trilogy *The Norman Conquests* 1974, *A Woman in Mind* 1986, *Henceforward* 1987, and *Man of the Moment* 1988.

Barker Howard 1946– . English playwright whose plays, renowned for their uncompromising and poetically dense language, confront the issues of private ambition and the exploitation of power. Among his works are *Victory* 1982; *The Castle* 1985; *The Last Supper*, *The Possibilities*, and *The Bite of the Night*, all 1988; and *Seven Lears* 1989. Essentially, his plays examine the human spirit when it is subjected to dictatorship, whether mental or physical.

Baylis Lilian 1874–1937. English theatre manager, who was responsible for re-opening Sadler's Wells Theatre, London 1931. From 1934 Sadler's Wells specialized in productions of opera and ballet: the resultant companies eventually became the Royal Ballet and the English National Opera.

Beckett Samuel 1906–1989. Irish novelist and dramatist who wrote in French and English. His *En attendant Godot/Waiting for Godot* 1952 is possibly the most universally known example of Theatre of the Absurd, in which life is taken to be meaningless. This genre is taken to further extremes in *Fin de Partie/Endgame* 1957 and *Happy Days* 1961. Nobel Prize for Literature 1969.

Berkoff Steven 1937– . English dramatist and actor whose abrasive and satirical plays, often informed by classical literature, include *East* 1975, *Greek* 1979, and *West* 1983. Berkoff's production of Oscar Wilde's *Salome* was staged 1991. In 1968 he set up the London Theatre Group, whose highly physical productions have included Berkoff's adaptations of Kafka's *Metamorphosis* 1969 and *The Trial* 1970, and Poe's *The Fall of the House of Usher* 1974.

Bond Edward 1935– . English dramatist. His early work aroused controversy because of the savagery of some of his imagery, for example, the brutal stoning of a baby by bored youths in *Saved* 1965. Other works include *Early Morning* 1968, the last play to be banned in the UK by the Lord Chamberlain; *Lear* 1972, a reworking of Shakespeare's play; *Bingo* 1973, an account of Shakespeare's last days; and *The War Plays* 1985.

Boucicault Dion(ysus) Larner 1822–1890. Irish dramatist and actor. His first success was with the social comedy *London Assurance* 1841, and during his long career he wrote or adapted about 200 plays, many of them melodramas, including *The Corsican Brothers* 1852 and *Louis XI* 1855. He moved to the USA 1872 where *The Poor of New York* 1857, *The Octoroon* 1859, and *The Colleen Bawn* 1860 had been produced.

Branagh Kenneth 1960– . British actor and director. He cofounded, with David Parfitt, the Renaissance Theatre Company 1987, was a notable Hamlet and Touchstone in 1988, and in 1989 directed and starred in a film of Shakespeare's *Henry V*.

Brecht Bertolt 1898–1956. German dramatist and poet who aimed to destroy the 'suspension of disbelief' usual in the theatre – to this end he developed a number of 'alienation techniques' – and to express Marxist ideas. He adapted John Gay's *Beggar's Opera* as *Die Dreigroschenoper/The Threepenny Opera* 1928, set to music by Kurt Weill. Later plays include *Galileo* 1938, *Mutter Courage/Mother Courage* 1941, set during the Thirty Years' War, and *Der kaukasische Kreidekreis/The Caucasian Chalk Circle* 1949. In 1949 he established the Berliner Ensemble theatre group in East Germany.

Brook Peter 1925– . English director renowned for his experimental productions. His work with the Royal Shakespeare Company included a production of Shakespeare's *A Midsummer Night's Dream* 1970, set in a white gymnasium and combining elements of circus and commedia dell'arte. In the same year he established Le Centre International de Créations Théâtrales/The International Centre for Theatre Research in Paris. Brook's later productions transcend Western theatre conventions and include *The Conference of the Birds* 1973, based on a Persian story, and *The Mahabharata* 1985–88, a cycle of three plays based on the Hindu epic. His films include *Lord of the Flies* 1962 and *Meetings with Remarkable Men* 1979.

Büchner Georg 1813–1837. German dramatist. His characters were often individuals pitted against the forces of society. Büchner's plays include *Danton's Death* 1835, which chronicles the power struggle between Danton and Robespierre during the French Revolution; and *Woyzeck* 1836, unfinished at his death, which depicts the despair of a common soldier, crushed by his social superiors. Büchner's third play is the comedy *Leonce and Lena* 1836. Unperformed until well after his death, his plays have been repeatedly produced in the 20th century.

Chekhov Anton (Pavlovich) 1860–1904. Russian dramatist and writer of short stories. His plays concentrate on the creation of atmosphere and delineation of internal development, rather than external action. His first play, *Ivanov* 1887, was a failure, as was *The Seagull* 1896 until revived by Stanislavsky 1898 at the Moscow Art Theatre, for which Chekhov went on to write his finest plays: *Uncle Vanya* 1899, *The Three Sisters* 1901, and *The Cherry Orchard* 1904.

Churchill Caryl 1938– . English playwright. Her predominantly radical and feminist works include *Top Girls* 1982, a study of the hazards encountered by 'career' women throughout history; *Serious Money* 1987, which satirized the world of London's brash young financial brokers; and *Mad Forest* 1990, set in Romania during the overthrow of the Ceauşescu regime.

Congreve William 1670–1729. English dramatist and poet. His first success was the comedy *The Old Bachelor* 1693, followed by *The Double Dealer* 1694, *Love for Love* 1695, the tragedy *The Mourning Bride* 1697, and *The Way of the World* 1700. His plays, which satirize the social affectations of the time, are characterized by elegant wit and wordplay.

Corneille Pierre 1606–1684. French dramatist. His many tragedies, such as *Oedipe* 1659, glorify the strength of will governed by reason, and established the French classical dramatic tradition for the next two centuries. His first play, *Mélite*, was performed 1629, followed by others that gained him a brief period of favour with Cardinal Richelieu. *Le Cid* 1636 was attacked by the Academicians, although it received public acclaim. Later plays were based on Aristotle's unities; Louis XIV approved, and he was elected to the Académie 1647 .

Coward Noël 1899–1973. English playwright, actor, producer, director, and composer, who epitomized the witty and sophisticated man of the theatre. From his first success with *The Young Idea* 1923, he wrote and appeared in plays and comedies on both sides of the Atlantic such as *Hay Fever* 1925, *Private Lives* 1930 with Gertrude Lawrence, *Design for Living* 1933, and *Blithe Spirit* 1941. Coward also wrote for and acted in films, including the patriotic *In Which We Serve* 1942 and the sentimental *Brief Encounter* 1945.

de Filippo Eduardo 1900–1984. Italian actor and dramatist. He founded his own company in Naples 1932, which was strongly influenced by the commedia dell'arte, and for which he wrote many plays. These include his finest comedies, *Filumena Marturano* 1946, *Napoli milionaria!* 1945, *Questi fantasmi!/These Ghosts!* 1946, *Grande magia/Grand Magic* 1951, and *Saturday, Sunday, Monday* 1959.

Donellan Declan 1953– . British theatre director, cofounder of the ***Cheek by Jowl*** theatre company 1981, and associate director of the National Theatre from 1989. His irreverent and audacious productions include many classics, such as Racine's *Andromaque* 1985, Corneille's *Le Cid* 1987, and Ibsen's *Peer Gynt* 1990; and Stephen Sondheim's musical *Sweeney Todd* 1993.

Euripides *c.* 485–*c.* 406 BC. Athenian tragic dramatist, ranked with Aeschylus and Sophocles as one of the three great tragedians, though he had more influence on the development of later drama than either Aeschylus or Sophocles. Drawing on the sophists, he transformed tragedy with unheroic themes. He wrote about 90 plays, of which 18 and some long fragments survive. These include *Alcestis* 438 BC, *Medea* 431, *Hippolytus* 428, the satyr-drama *Cyclops* about 424-423, *Electra, Trojan Women* 415, *Iphigenia in Tauris* 413, *Iphigenia in Aulis* about 414-412, and *The Bacchae* about 405 (the last two were produced shortly after his death).

Eyre Richard (Charles Hastings) 1943– . English stage and film director who succeeded Peter Hall as artistic director of the National Theatre, London, 1988. His stage productions include *Guys and Dolls* 1982, *Bartholomew Fair* 1988, and *Richard III* 1990, which he set in 1930s Britain. His films include *The Ploughman's Lunch* 1983 and *Laughterhouse* (US *Singleton's Pluck*) 1984.

Feydeau Georges 1862–1921. French comic dramatist. He is the author of over 60 farces and light comedies, which have been repeatedly revived in France at the Comédie Française and abroad. These include *La dame de chez Maxim/The Girl from Maxim's* 1899, *Une puceà l'oreille/A Flea in her Ear* 1907, *Feu la mère de Madame/My Late Mother-in-Law*, and *Occupe-toi d'Amélie/Look after Lulu*, both 1908.

Fo Dario 1926– . Italian playwright and actor. His plays are predominantly political satires, combining

theatre: chronology

c. 3200 BC	Beginnings of Egyptian religious drama, essentially ritualistic.
c. 600 BC	Choral performances (dithyrambs) in honour of Dionysus formed the beginnings of Greek tragedy, according to Aristotle.
500–300 BC	Great age of Greek drama which included tragedy, comedy, and satyr plays (grotesque farce).
468 BC	Sophocles' first victory at the Athens festival. His use of a third actor altered the course of the tragic form.
458 BC	Aeschylus' *Oresteia* were first performed.
c. 425–388 BC	Comedies of Aristophanes including *The Birds* 414, *Lysistrata* 411, and *The Frogs* 405. In tragedy the importance of the chorus diminished under Euripides, author of *The Bacchae* 405.
c. 350 BC	Menander's 'New Comedy' of social manners developed.
c. 240 BC–AD 500	Emergence of Roman drama, adapted from Greek originals. Plautus, Terence, and Seneca were the main playwrights.
c. AD 375	Kālidāsa's *Sakuntalā* marked the height of Sanskrit drama in India.
c. 1250–1500	European mystery (or miracle) plays flourished, first in the churches, later in marketplaces, and were performed in England by town guilds.
c. 1375	Nō (or Noh) drama developed in Japan.
c. 1495	*Everyman*, the best known of all the morality plays, was first performed.
1500–1600	Italian commedia dell'arte troupes performed popular, improvised comedies; they were to have a large influence on Molière and on English harlequinade and pantomime.
c. 1551	Nicholas Udall wrote *Ralph Roister Doister*, the first English comedy.
c. 1576	The first English playhouse, The Theatre, was built by James Burbage in London.
1587	Christopher Marlowe's play *Tamburlaine the Great* marked the beginning of the great age of Elizabethan and Jacobean drama in England.
c. 1589	Thomas Kyd's play *Spanish Tragedy* was the first of the 'revenge' tragedies.
c. 1590–1612	Shakespeare's greatest plays, including *Hamlet* and *King Lear*, were written.
1604	Inigo Jones designed *The Masque of Blackness* for James I, written by Ben Jonson.
1614	Lope de Vega's *Fuenteovejuna* marked the Spanish renaissance in drama. Other writers include Calderón de la Barca.
1637	Pierre Corneille's *Le Cid* established classical tragedy in France.
1642	An act of Parliament closed all English theatres.
1660	With the restoration of Charles II to the English throne, dramatic performances recommenced. The first professional actress appeared as Desdemona in Shakespeare's *Othello*.
1664	Molière's *Tartuffe* was banned for three years by religious factions.
1667	Jean Racine's first success, *Andromaque*, was staged.
1680	The Comédie Française was formed by Louis XIV.
1700	William Congreve, the greatest exponent of Restoration comedy, wrote *The Way of the World*.
1716	The first known American theatre was built in Williamsburg, Virginia.
1728	John Gay's *The Beggar's Opera* was first performed.
1737	The Stage Licensing Act in England required all plays to be approved by the Lord Chamberlain before performance.
1747	The actor David Garrick became manager of the Drury Lane Theatre, London.
1773	In England, Oliver Goldsmith's *She Stoops to Conquer* and Richard Sheridan's *The Rivals* 1775 established the 'comedy of manners'. Goethe's *Götz von Berlichingen* was the first *Sturm und Drang* (literally, storm and stress) play.
1781	Friedrich Schiller's *Die Räuber/The Robbers*.
1784	Beaumarchais's *Le Mariage de Figaro/The Marriage of Figaro* (written 1778) was first performed.
1830	Victor Hugo's *Hernani* caused riots in Paris. His work marked the beginning of a new Romantic drama, changing the course of French theatre.
1878	Henry Irving became actor-manager of the Lyceum with Ellen Terry as leading lady.
1879	Henrik Ibsen's *A Doll's House*, an early example of realism in European theatre.
1888	August Strindberg wrote *Miss Julie*.
1893	George Bernard Shaw wrote *Mrs Warren's Profession* (banned until 1902 because it deals with prostitution). Shaw's works brought the new realistic drama to Britain and introduced social and political issues as subjects for the theatre.
1895	Oscar Wilde's comedy *The Importance of Being Earnest*. Alfred Jarry's *Ubu Roi*, a forerunner of Surrealism.
1896	The first performance of Anton Chekhov's *The Seagull* failed.
1899	The Abbey Theatre, Dublin, founded by W B Yeats and Lady Gregory, marked the beginning of an Irish dramatic revival.
1904	Chekhov's *The Cherry Orchard*. The Academy of Dramatic Art (Royal Academy of Dramatic Art 1920) was founded in London to train young actors.
1919	The Theater Guild was founded in the USA to perform less commercial new plays.
1920	*Beyond the Horizon*, Eugene O'Neill's first play, marked the beginning of serious theatre in the USA.

theatre: chronology *(cont.)*

1921	Luigi Pirandello's *Six Characters in Search of an Author* introduced themes of the individual and exploration of reality and appearance.
1928	Bertolt Brecht's *Die Dreigroschenoper/The Threepenny Opera* with score by Kurt Weill; other political satires by Karel Čapek and Elmer Rice. In the USA Jerome Kern's *Show Boat* with Paul Robeson, and other musical comedies by Cole Porter, Irving Berlin, and George Gershwin, became popular.
1930s	US social-protest plays of Clifford Odets, Lillian Hellman, Thornton Wilder, and William Saroyan.
1935	T S Eliot's *Murder in the Cathedral.*
1935–39	WPA Federal Theater Project in the USA.
1938	Publication of Antonin Artaud's *Theatre and Its Double.*
1943	The first of the musicals, *Oklahoma!*, opened.
1944–45	Jean-Paul Sartre's *Huis Clos/In Camera*; Jean Anouilh's *Antigone*; Arthur Miller's *Death of a Salesman.*
post-1945	Resurgence of German-language theatre, including Wolfgang Borchert, Max Frisch, Friedrich Dürrenmatt, and Peter Weiss.
1947	Tennessee Williams's *A Streetcar Named Desire.* First Edinburgh Festival, Scotland, with fringe theatre events.
1953	Arthur Miller's *The Crucible* opened in the USA; *En attendant Godot/Waiting for Godot* by Samuel Beckett exemplified the Theatre of the Absurd.
1956	The English Stage Company was formed at the Royal Court Theatre to provide a platform for new dramatists. John Osborne's *Look Back in Anger* was included in its first season.
1957	Leonard Bernstein's *West Side Story* opened in New York.
1960	Harold Pinter's *The Caretaker* was produced in London.
1960s	Off-off-Broadway theatre, a more daring and experimental type of drama, began to develop in New York.
1961	The Royal Shakespeare Company was formed in the UK under the directorship of Peter Hall.
1963–64	The UK National Theatre Company was formed at the Old Vic under the directorship of Laurence Olivier.
1967	Success in the USA of *Hair*, the first of the 'rock' musicals; Tom Stoppard's *Rosencrantz and Guildenstern are Dead* was produced at the Old Vic, London.
1968	Abolition of theatre censorship in the UK.
1975	*A Chorus Line*, to become the longest-running musical, opened in New York.
1980	Howard Brenton's *The Romans in Britain* led in the UK to a private prosecution of the director for obscenity.
1987	The Japanese Ninagawa Company performed Shakespeare's *Macbeth* in London.
1989	Discovery of the remains of the 16th-century Rose and Globe theatres, London.
1990	The Royal Shakespeare Company suspended its work at the Barbican Centre, London, for six months, pleading lack of funds.
1993	Agatha Christie's *The Mousetrap* entered its 41st year in the West End, London, the longest-running play in the world.

black humour with slapstick. They include *Morte accidentale di un anarchico/Accidental Death of an Anarchist* 1970, and *Non si paga non si paga/Can't Pay? Won't Pay!* 1975/1981.

Ford John 1586–*c.* 1640. English poet and dramatist. His play *'Tis Pity She's a Whore* (performed about 1626, printed 1633) is a study of incest between brother and sister.

Friel Brian 1929– . Northern Irish dramatist whose work often deals with the social and historical pressures that contribute to the Irish political situation. His first success was with *Philadelphia, Here I Come!* 1964, which dealt with the theme of exile. In 1980 he founded the Field Day Theatre Company, which produced *Translations* 1981, a study of British cultural colonialism in 19th-century Ireland. Other plays include *The Freedom of the City* 1973, about victims of the Ulster conflict, *Faith Healer* 1980, and the critically acclaimed *Dancing at Lughnasa* 1990.

Genet Jean 1910–1986. French dramatist, novelist, and poet, an exponent of the Theatre of Cruelty. His turbulent life and early years spent in prison are reflected in his drama, characterized by ritual, role-play, and illusion, in which his characters come to act out their bizarre and violent fantasies. His plays include *Les Bonnes/The Maids* 1947, *Le Balcon/The Balcony* 1957, and two plays dealing with the Algerian situation: *Les Nègres/The Blacks* 1959 and *Les Paravents/The Screens* 1961.

Goethe Johann Wolfgang von 1749–1832. German poet, novelist, and dramatist, generally considered the founder of modern German literature, and leader of the Romantic *Sturm und Drang* ('storm and stress') movement. His works include the autobiographical *Die Leiden des Jungen Werthers/The Sorrows of Young Werther* 1774 and *Faust* 1808, his masterpiece. A visit to Italy 1786–88 inspired the classical dramas *Iphigenie auf Tauris/Iphigenia in Tauris* 1787 and *Torquato Tasso* 1790.

Goldoni Carlo 1707–1793. Italian dramatist, born in Venice. He wrote popular comedies for the Sant'Angelo theatre, including *La putta onorata/The Respectable Girl* 1749, *I pettegolezzi delle donne/Women's Gossip* 1750, and *La locandiera/Mine*

Hostess 1753. In 1761 he moved to Paris, where he directed the Italian theatre and wrote more plays, including *L'Eventail/The Fan* 1763.

Grotowski Jerzy 1933– . Polish theatre director. His ascetic theory of performance in *Towards a Poor Theatre* 1968 has had a great influence on experimental theatre in the USA and Europe. His most famous productions were *Akropolis* 1962, *The Constant Prince* 1965, and *Apocalypsis cum Figuris* 1969, which he toured widely.

Guthrie Tyrone 1900–1971. British theatre director, notable for his experimental approach. Administrator of the Old Vic and Sadler's Wells theatres 1939–45, he helped found the Ontario (Stratford) Shakespeare Festival 1953 and the Minneapolis theatre now named after him.

Hall Peter (Reginald Frederick) 1930– . English theatre, opera, and film director. He was director of the Royal Shakespeare Theatre in Stratford-on-Avon 1960–68 and developed the Royal Shakespeare Company 1968–73 until appointed director of the National Theatre 1973–88, succeeding Laurence Olivier. He was appointed artistic director of opera at Glyndebourne 1984. He founded the Peter Hall Company 1988.

Hare David 1947– . British dramatist and director, whose plays include *Slag* 1970, *Teeth 'n' Smiles* 1975, *Pravda* 1985 (with Howard Brenton), and *Wrecked Eggs* 1986.

Ibsen Henrik (Johan) 1828–1906. Norwegian playwright and poet, whose realistic and often controversial plays revolutionized European theatre. Driven into exile 1864–91 by opposition to the satirical *Love's Comedy* 1862, he wrote the verse dramas *Brand* 1866 and *Peer Gynt* 1867, followed by realistic plays dealing with social issues, including *Pillars of Society* 1877, *A Doll's House* 1879, *Ghosts* 1881, *An Enemy of the People* 1882, and *Hedda Gabler* 1891. By the time he returned to Norway, he was recognized as the country's greatest living writer. His later plays, which are more symbolic, include *The Master Builder* 1892, *Little Eyolf* 1894, *John Gabriel Borkman* 1896, and *When We Dead Awaken* 1899.

Ionesco Eugène 1912– . Romanian-born French dramatist, a leading exponent of the Theatre of the Absurd. Most of his plays are in one act and concern the futility of language as a means of communication. These include *La Cantatrice chauve/The Bald Prima Donna* 1950 and *La Leçon/The Lesson* 1951. Later full-length plays include *Rhinocéros* 1958 and *Le Roi se meurt/Exit the King* 1961.

Jonson Ben(jamin) 1572–1637. English dramatist, poet, and critic. *Every Man in his Humour* 1598 established the English 'comedy of humours', in which each character embodies a 'humour', or vice, such as greed, lust, or avarice. This was followed by *Every Man out of his Humour* 1599, *Cynthia's Revels* 1600 and *Poetaster* 1601. His first extant tragedy is *Sejanus* 1603, with Burbage and Shakespeare as members of the original cast. The plays of his middle years include *Volpone, or The Fox* 1606, *The Alchemist* 1610, and *Bartholomew Fair* 1614.

Kantor Tadeusz 1915–1990. Polish theatre director and scene designer. He founded his experimental theatre Cricot 2 in 1955, and produced such plays as the *Dead Class* 1975, with which he became internationally known. Later productions include *Wielopole, Wielopole* 1980, *Let the Artists Die* 1985, and *I Shall Never Return* 1988.

Kazan Elia 1909– . US stage and film director, a founder of the Actors Studio 1947. Plays he directed include *The Skin of Our Teeth* 1942, *A Streetcar Named Desire* 1947, and *Cat on a Hot Tin Roof* 1955; films include *Gentlemen's Agreement* 1948, *East of Eden* 1954, and *The Visitors* 1972.

Littlewood Joan 1914– . English theatre director. She was responsible for many vigorous productions at the Theatre Royal, Stratford (London) 1953–75, such as *A Taste of Honey* 1959, *The Hostage* 1959–60, and *Oh, What a Lovely War* 1963. She established the Theatre Workshop 1945.

Lorca Federico García 1898–1936. Spanish poet and playwright, born in Granada. His plays include *Bodas de sangre/Blood Wedding* 1933 and *La casa de Bernarda Alba/The House of Bernarda Alba* 1936. His poems include *Lament*, written for the bullfighter Mejías. Lorca was shot by the Falangists during the Spanish Civil War.

Mamet David 1947– . US playwright. His plays, with their vivid, freewheeling language and sense of ordinary US life, include *American Buffalo* 1977, *Sexual Perversity in Chicago* 1978, *Glengarry Glen Ross* 1984 (filmed 1992), *Speed-the-Plow* 1988, and *Oleanna* 1992, about a sexual harrassment case.

Marlowe Christopher 1564–1593. English poet and dramatist. His work includes the blank-verse plays *Tamburlaine the Great c.* 1587, *The Jew of Malta c.* 1589, *Edward II* and *Dr Faustus*, both *c.* 1592, the poem *Hero and Leander* 1598, and a translation of Ovid's *Amores*.

McGrath John 1935– . Scottish dramatist and director. He founded the socialist 7:84 Theatre Companies in England 1971 and Scotland 1973, and is the author of such plays as *Events Guarding the Bofors Gun* 1966; *The Cheviot, the Stag, and the Black, Black Oil* 1973, a musical account of the economic exploitation of the Scottish highlands; and *The Garden of England* 1985.

Matura Mustapha 1939– . Trinidad-born British dramatist. Cofounder of the Black Theatre Cooperative 1978, his plays deal with problems of ethnic diversity and integration. These include *As Time Goes By* 1971, *Play Mas* 1974, and *Meetings* 1981. Other works include *Playboy of the West Indies* 1984 and *Trinidad Sisters* 1988, his adaptations of plays by Synge and Chekhov, and *The Coup* 1991.

Meyerhold Vsevolod 1874–1940. Russian actor and director. Before the revolution of 1917 he developed a strong interest in commedia dell'arte and stylized acting. He developed a system of actor-training known as bio-mechanics, which combined insights drawn from sport, the circus, and modern studies of time and motion. A member of the Moscow Art Theatre, he was briefly director of its Studio theatre under Stanislavsky 1905. He produced the Russian poet Mayakovsky's futurist *Mystery-Bouffe* 1918 and 1921, and later his *The Bed Bug* 1929.

Miller Arthur 1915– . US playwright. His plays deal with family relationships and contemporary American values, and include *Death of a Salesman* 1949 and *The Crucible* 1953, based on the Salem witch trials and reflecting the communist witch-hunts of Senator Joe McCarthy. He was married 1956–61 to the film star Marilyn Monroe, for whom he wrote the film *The Misfits* 1960. Among other plays are *All My Sons* 1947, *A View from the Bridge* 1955, and *After the Fall* 1964, based on his relationship with Monroe.

Mnouchkine Ariane 1939– . French theatre director. She founded the Theatre du Soleil 1964, which established a reputation with a vigorous production of Arnold Wesker's *The Kitchen* 1967. After 1968, the company began to devise its own material, firstly with *The Clowns* 1969, which was followed by *1789* 1970, an exploration of the French Revolution, and *L'Age d'Or* 1975, concerning the exploitation of immigrant workers. She has also collaborated with the writer Helene Cixous on *Sihanouk* 1985, a production about Cambodia, and directed *Les Atrides* 1992, a version of Aeschylus' *Oresteia*.

Molière Pen name of Jean Baptiste Poquelin 1622–1673. French satirical playwright from whose work modern French comedy developed. One of the founders of the Illustre Théâtre 1643, he was later its leading actor. In 1655 he wrote his first play, *L'Etourdi*, followed by *Les Précieuses Ridicules* 1659. His satires include *L'Ecole des femmes* 1662, *Le Misanthrope* 1666, *Le Bourgeois Gentilhomme* 1670, and *Le Malade imaginaire* 1673. Other satiric plays include *Tartuffe* 1664 (banned until 1697 for attacking the hypocrisy of the clergy), *Le Médecin malgré lui* 1666, and *Les Femmes savantes* 1672.

Müller Heiner 1929– . German dramatist whose scripts have played a leading role in contemporary avant-garde theatre in Germany and abroad. Early political works, showing the influence of Brecht, (*The Scab* 1950, and *The Correction* 1958) were followed by *Mauser* 1970, *Cement* 1972 (on the Russian revolution), *Hamletmachine* 1977, and *Medea-material* 1982.

O'Casey Sean. Adopted name of John Casey 1884–1964. Irish dramatist. His early plays are tragicomedies, blending realism with symbolism and poetic with vernacular speech: *The Shadow of a Gunman* 1922, *Juno and the Paycock* 1925, *The Plough and the Stars* 1926, and *The Silver Tassie* 1929. Later plays include *Red Roses for Me* 1946 and *The Drums of Father Ned* 1960.

Odets Clifford 1906–1963. US playwright, associated with the Group Theater and the most renowned of the social-protest playwrights of the Depression era. His plays include *Waiting for Lefty* 1935, about a taxi drivers' strike, *Awake and Sing* 1935, *Golden Boy* 1937, and *The Country Girl* 1950. In the late 1930s he became a successful Hollywood film writer and director, but he continued to write plays.

Olivier Laurence (Kerr), Baron Olivier 1907–1989. English actor and director. For many years associated with the Old Vic theatre, he was director of the National Theatre company 1962–73. His stage roles include Henry V, Hamlet, Richard III, and Archie Rice in John Osborne's *The Entertainer*. His acting and direction of filmed versions of Shakespeare's plays received critical acclaim – for example, *Henry V* 1944 and *Hamlet* 1948.Olivier, appeared on screen in many films, including *Wuthering Heights* 1939, *Sleuth* 1972, and *The Boys from Brazil* 1978.

O'Neill Eugene (Gladstone) 1888–1953. US playwright, the leading dramatist between World Wars I and II. His plays include *Anna Christie* 1922, *Desire under the Elms* 1924, *The Iceman Cometh* 1946, and the posthumously produced autobiographical drama *Long Day's Journey into Night* 1956 (written 1940). Other plays include *Strange Interlude* 1928 (which lasts five hours) and *Mourning Becomes Electra* 1931 (a trilogy on the theme of Orestes from Greek mythology). He was awarded the Nobel prize for Literature 1936.

Orton Joe 1933–1967. English dramatist in whose black comedies surreal and violent action takes place in genteel and unlikely settings. Plays include *Entertaining Mr Sloane* 1964, *Loot* 1966, and *What the Butler Saw* 1968. His diaries deal frankly with his personal life. He was murdered by his lover Kenneth Halliwell.

Osborne John (James) 1929– . English dramatist. He became one of the first Angry Young Men (anti-establishment writers of the 1950s) of British theatre with his debut play, *Look Back in Anger* 1956. Other plays include *The Entertainer* 1957, *Luther* 1960, and *Watch It Come Down* 1976.

Ostrovsky Alexander Nikolaevich 1823–1886. Russian playwright, founder of the modern Russian theatre. He dealt satirically with the manners of the middle class in numerous plays – for example, *A Family Affair* 1850. His fairy-tale play *The Snow Maiden* 1873 inspired the composers Tchaikovsky and Rimsky-Korsakov.

Pinter Harold 1930– . English dramatist, originally an actor. He specializes in the tragicomedy of the breakdown of communication, broadly in the tradition of the Theatre of the Absurd – for example, *The Birthday Party* 1958 and *The Caretaker* 1960. Later plays include *The Homecoming* 1965, *Old Times* 1971, *Betrayal* 1978, and *Mountain Language* 1988. Pinter's work is known for its pauses, allowing the audience to read between the lines. He writes for radio and television, and his screenplays include *The Go-Between* 1969 and *The French Lieutenant's Woman* 1982.

Pirandello Luigi 1867–1936. Italian writer. His plays include *La morsa/The Vice* 1912, *Sei personaggi in cerca d'autore/Six Characters in Search of an Author* 1921, and *Enrico IV/Henry IV* 1922. The themes and treatment of his plays anticipated the work of Brecht, O'Neill, Anouilh, and Genet. Nobel Prize 1934.

Piscator Erwin 1893–1966. German theatre director. He introduced the idea of epic theatre, using slide-projection, music, dance, and film to create a revolutionary social drama in the *Red Revue* 1921 and in *Hoppla, That's Life!* 1927. While in the USA 1939–51 he produced an adaptation of Tolstoy's *War and Peace* 1942, but returned to directing in Germany 1951, and produced plays by Ralf Hochhuth.

Planchon Roger 1931– . French theatre director, actor, and dramatist. After early productions of the plays of Adamov and Brecht he established a theatre company in Villeurbanne, outside Lyon, France 1957; it inherited the name Théâtre National Populaire in 1973. Major productions of Shakespeare (*Henry V* 1957) and Molière (*Tartuffe* 1962 and 1973) were followed by Pinter's *No Man's Land* 1979 and Racine's *Athalie* 1980.

Racine Jean 1639–1699. French dramatist and exponent of the classical tragedy in French drama. His subjects came from Greek mythology and he observed the rules of classical Greek drama. Most of his tragedies have women in the title role, for example *Andromaque* 1667, *Iphigénie* 1674, and *Phèdre* 1677. After the failure of *Phèdre* in the theatre he no longer wrote for the secular stage, but wrote two religious dramas, *Esther* 1689 and *Athalie* 1691, which achieved posthumous success.

Reinhardt Max 1873–1943. Austrian producer and director, whose Expressionist style was predominant in German theatre and film during the 1920s and 1930s. Directors such as Murnau and Lubitsch, and actors such as Dietrich worked with him. He co-directed the US film *A Midsummer Night's Dream* 1935.

Saint-Denis Michel 1897–1971. French director and actor. He founded both the Compagnie des Quinze 1930, and the London Theatre Studio 1936-39. From 1946–52 he was director of the Old Vic Theatre school, and became an artistic adviser for the Lincoln Centre in New York 1957, and later for the Royal Shakespeare Company in Britain 1962.

Schiller Johann Christoph Friedrich von 1759–1805. German dramatist, poet, and historian. He wrote *Sturm und Drang* verse and became the foremost German dramatist with his classic dramas *Wallenstein*, *Maria Stuart* 1800, *Die Jungfrau von Orleans/The Maid of Orleans* 1801, and *Wilhelm Tell/William Tell* 1804. He also wrote essays on aesthetics. Much of his work concerns the aspirations for political freedom and the avoidance of mediocrity.

Shakespeare William 1564–1616. English dramatist and poet. Established in London by 1589 as an actor and a playwright, he was England's unrivalled dramatist until his death, and is considered the greatest English playwright. His plays, written in blank verse, can be broadly divided into lyric plays, including *Romeo and Juliet* and *A Midsummer Night's Dream*; comedies, including *The Comedy of Errors*, *As You Like It*, *Much Ado About Nothing*, and *Measure For Measure*; historical plays, such as *Henry VI* (in three parts), *Richard III*, and *Henry IV* (in two parts), which often showed cynical political wisdom; and tragedies, such as *Hamlet*, *Macbeth*, and *King Lear*. He also wrote numerous sonnets.

Shaw George Bernard 1856–1950. Irish dramatist. He was also a critic and novelist, and an early member of the socialist Fabian Society. His plays combine comedy with political, philosophical, and polemic aspects, aiming to make an impact on his audience's social conscience as well as their emotions. They include *Arms and the Man* 1894, *Devil's Disciple* 1897, *Man and Superman* 1905, *Pygmalion* 1913, and *St Joan* 1924. Nobel prize 1925. Altogether Shaw wrote more than 50 plays and became a byword for wit. His theories were further explained in the voluminous prefaces to the plays, and in books.

Shepard Sam 1943– . US dramatist and actor. His work combines colloquial American dialogue with striking visual imagery, and includes *The Tooth of Crime* 1972 and *Buried Child* 1978, for which he won a Pulitzer Prize. *Seduced* 1979 is based on the life of the recluse Howard Hughes. He has acted in a number of films, including *The Right Stuff* 1983, *Fool for Love* 1986, based on his play of the same name, and *Steel Magnolias* 1989.

Shakespeare: the plays

Title	*Performed*
Early plays	
Henry VI Part I	1589–92
Henry VI Part II	1589–92
Henry VI Part III	1589–92
The Comedy of Errors	1592–93
The Taming of the Shrew	1593–94
Titus Andronicus	1593–94
The Two Gentlemen of Verona	1594–95
Love's Labours Lost	1594–95
Romeo and Juliet	1594–95
Histories	
Richard III	1592–93
Richard II	1593–96
King John	1596–97
Henry IV Part I	1597–98
Henry IV Part II	1597–98
Henry V	1599
Roman plays	
Julius Caesar	1599–1600
Antony and Cleopatra	1607–08
Coriolanus	1607–08
The 'great' or 'middle' comedies	
A Midsummer Night's Dream	1595–96
The Merchant of Venice	1596–97
Much Ado About Nothing	1598–99
As You Like It	1599–1600
The Merry Wives of Windsor	1600–01
Twelfth Night	1601–02
The great tragedies	
Hamlet	1600–01
Othello	1604–05
King Lear	1605–06
Macbeth	1605–06
Timon of Athens	1607–08
The 'dark' comedies	
Troilus and Cressida	1601–02
All's Well That Ends Well	1602–03
Measure for Measure	1604–05
Late plays	
Pericles	1608–09
Cymbeline	1609–10
The Winter's Tale	1610–11
The Tempest	1611–12
Henry VIII	1612–13

Sheridan Richard Brinsley 1751–1816. Irish dramatist and politician, born in Dublin. His social comedies include *The Rivals* 1775, celebrated for the character of Mrs Malaprop, *The School for Scandal* 1777, and *The Critic* 1779. In 1776 he became lessee of the Drury Lane Theatre. He became a member of Parliament in 1780.

Simon (Marvin) Neil 1927– . US playwright. His stage plays (which were made into films) include the wryly comic *Barefoot in the Park* 1963, *The Odd Couple* 1965, and *The Sunshine Boys* 1972, and the more serious, autobiographical trilogy *Brighton Beach Memoirs* 1983, *Biloxi Blues* 1985, and *Broadway Bound* 1986. He has also written screenplays and co-written musicals, including *Sweet Charity* 1966, *Promises, Promises* 1968, and *They're Playing Our Song* 1978.

Sophocles *c.* 496–406 BC. Athenian dramatist, attributed with having developed tragedy by introducing a third actor and scene-painting, and ranked with Aeschylus and Euripides as one of the three great tragedians. He wrote some 120 plays, of which seven tragedies survive. These are *Antigone* 441 BC, *Oedipus the King*, *Electra*, *Ajax*, *Trachiniae*, *Philoctetes* 409 BC, and *Oedipus at Colonus* 401 (produced after his death). In his tragedies heroic determination leads directly to violence unless, as in *Philoctetes* and *Oedipus at Colonus*, it contains an element of resignation.

Stanislavsky Konstantin Sergeivich 1863–1938. Russian actor, director, and teacher of acting. He rejected the declamatory style of acting in favour of a more realistic approach, concentrating on the psychological basis for the development of character. His ideas, which he described in *My Life in Art* 1924 and other works, had considerable influence on acting techniques in Europe and the USA. The Actors Studio is based on this approach.

Stein Peter 1937– . German theatre director. Artistic director of the politically radical Berlin Schaubühne 1970–85, Stein's early productions included Edward Bond's *Saved* 1967 and Goethe's *Torquato Tasso* 1969. These foreshadowed the spectacular staging of Ibsen's *Peer Gynt* 1971, and his exploratory show *Shakespeare's Memory* 1976. His final productions for the Schaubühne included Genet's *The Blacks* 1983 and Chekhov's *Three Sisters* 1984.

Stoppard Tom 1937– . Czechoslovak-born British playwright whose works use wit and wordplay to explore logical and philosophical ideas. His play *Rosencrantz and Guildenstern are Dead* 1966 was followed by comedies including *The Real Inspector Hound* 1968, *Jumpers* 1972, *Travesties* 1974, *Dirty Linen* 1976, *The Real Thing* 1982, *Hapgood* 1988, and *Arcadia* 1993. He has also written for radio, television, and the cinema.

Strasberg Lee 1902–1982. US actor and artistic director of the Actors Studio from 1948, who developed Method acting from Stanislavsky's system; pupils have included Marlon Brando, Paul Newman, Julie Harris, Kim Hunter, Geraldine Page, Al Pacino, and Robert de Niro.

Strindberg August 1849–1912. Swedish playwright and novelist. His plays, influential in the development of dramatic technique, are in a variety of styles including historical plays, symbolic dramas (the two-part *Dödsdansen/The Dance of Death* 1901), and 'chamber plays', such as *Spöksonaten/The Ghost [Spook] Sonata* 1907. *Fadren/The Father* 1887 and *Fröken Julie/Miss Julie* 1888 are among his works.

Synge J(ohn) M(illington) 1871–1909. Irish playwright, a leading figure in the Irish dramatic revival of the early 20th century. His six plays reflect the speech patterns of the Aran Islands and W Ireland. They include *In the Shadow of the Glen* 1903, *Riders to the Sea* 1904, and *The Playboy of the Western World* 1907, which caused riots at the Abbey Theatre, Dublin, when first performed.

Vega Lope Felix de (Carpio) 1562–1635. Spanish poet and dramatist, one of the founders of modern Spanish drama. He wrote epics, pastorals, odes, sonnets, novels, and, reputedly, over 1,500 plays (of which 426 are still in existence), mostly tragicomedies. He set out his views on drama in *Arte nuevo de hacer comedias/The New Art of Writing Plays* 1609, while reaffirming the classical form. *Fuenteovejuna* 1614 has been acclaimed as the first proletarian drama.

Webster John *c.* 1580–1634. English dramatist who ranks after Shakespeare as the greatest tragedian of his time and is the Jacobean whose plays are most frequently performed today. His two great plays *The White Devil* 1608 and *The Duchess of Malfi* 1614 are dark, violent tragedies obsessed with death and decay and infused with poetic brilliance.

Wedekind Frank 1864–1918. German dramatist. He was a forerunner of Expressionism with *Frühlings Erwachen/The Awakening of Spring* 1891, and *Der Erdgeist/The Earth Spirit* 1895 and its sequel *Der Marquis von Keith. Die Büchse der Pandora/Pandora's Box* 1904 was the source for Berg's opera *Lulu.*

Wilde Oscar (Fingal O'Flahertie Wills) 1854–1900. Irish writer. With his flamboyant style and quotable conversation, he dazzled London society and, on his lecture tour 1882, the USA. He published his only novel, *The Picture of Dorian Gray*, 1891, followed by the elegant, witty social comedies including *Lady Windermere's Fan* 1892, *A Woman of No Importance* 1893, *The Importance of Being Earnest* and *An Ideal Husband*, both 1895. The drama *Salome* 1893, based on the biblical character, was written in French; considered scandalous by the British censor, it was first performed in Paris 1896 with the actress Sarah Bernhardt in the title role. In 1895 he was imprisoned for two years for homosexual offences; he died in exile.

Wilder Thornton (Niven) 1897–1975. US playwright and novelist. He won Pulitzer prizes for the novel *The Bridge of San Luis Rey* 1927, and for the plays *Our Town* 1938 and *The Skin of Our Teeth* 1942. His farce *The Matchmaker* 1954 was filmed 1958. In 1964 it was adapted into the hit stage musical *Hello, Dolly!*, also made into a film.

Williams Tennessee (Thomas Lanier) 1911–1983. US playwright, born in Mississippi. His work is characterized by fluent dialogue and searching analysis of the psychological deficiencies of his characters. His plays, usually set in the Deep South against a background of decadence and degradation, include *The Glass Menagerie* 1945, *A Streetcar Named Desire* 1947, and *Cat on a Hot Tin Roof* 1955, the last two of which earned Pulitzer Prizes.

Wilson Robert 1944– . US avant-garde theatre director who specializes in non-narrative, elaborately visual theatre productions such as *Deafman Glance* 1971, *Ka Mountain* at the Shiraz Festival, Iran 1972, and *The Life and Times of Joseph Stalin* 1973. Later productions include *Einstein on the Beach* 1976 and 1992, operatic productions of Euripides' tragedies *Medea* 1984 and *Alcestis* 1986, *The Black Rider* 1990, and *Alice* 1992.

SCIENCE AND TECHNOLOGY

Archaeology 379

Astronomy 390

Chemistry 414

Computing and Electronics 439

Earth Science 454

Energy 467

Environment and Conservation 474

Food and Agriculture 494

Life Sciences 511

Mathematics 530

Physics 543

Telecommunications and Video Technology 559

ARCHAEOLOGY

Terms and Techniques

absolute dating the determination of age in calendar years by reference to a fixed time scale. Also called chronometric dating, it usually incorporates a measure of uncertainty, expressed as a standard deviation.

accelerator mass spectrometry (AMS) a new radiocarbon dating method that determines the actual number of carbon-14 atoms in a sample rather than the small numbers of carbon-14 atoms that decay radioactively during the measurement time of the conventional method. This method requires only a tiny sample, and its measurement time is only about one hour (as opposed to days for radiocarbon dating), but it is expensive.

aerial photography or ***aerial archaeology*** taking photographs from a high level, a technique used in archaeology to detect surface features (such as crop marks, soil marks, shadow marks) that are not clearly visible from ground level and which indicate the presence of ancient features; for example, crops will show differences in growth and colour if they are growing over a buried wall foundation or other stone feature.

aerial reconnaissance technique used primarily for the recording and interpretation of archaeological sites from the air, though at times it can also be useful in discovering new sites. ***Thermal prospection*** (also called thermography) is an expensive remote-sensing method that uses heat sensors in aircraft which scan the varying temperatures of remains below ground. Images produced from LANDSAT satellites have been used to discover ancient sites and landscapes (in particular Mayan sites in Mesoamerica); SLAR (sideways looking aerial radar) from NASA aircraft has also been used to reveal ancient sites and field systems.

anthropology the study of humanity's physical characteristics and culture, generally divided into the three subdisciplines of physical (biological) anthropology, social (cultural) anthropology, and archaeology.

archaeology the study of the human past through the systematic recovery and analysis of material remains. Its aims are to recover, describe, and classify this material, to describe the form and behaviour of past societies, and to understand the reasons for this behaviour. A truly inter-disciplinary subject, it has borrowed many of its major theoretical and methodological concepts and approaches from history and anthropology.

methods Principal activities include preliminary field (or site) surveys, excavation (where necessary), and the classification, dating, and interpretation of finds. Related disciplines that have been useful in archaeological reconstruction include stratigraphy (the study of geological strata), dendrochronology (the establishment of chronological sequences through the study of tree rings), palaeobotany (the study of ancient pollens, seeds, and grains), epigraphy (the study of inscriptions), and numismatics (the study of coins). Since 1958 radiocarbon dating has been used and refined to establish the age of archaeological strata and associated materials.

archaeomagnetic dating dating technique based on the palaeomagnetism of archaeological materials such as baked clay structures (hearths, kilns, ovens). When originally heated, their magnetic particles realigned with the Earth's magnetic field at the time, and since that field changes over time, local and regional chronologies of field-direction can be built up and independently dated. In England for example such curves have been established for the last 2000 years, allowing for any sample to be dated within that span to within approximately 50 years.

archaeozoology or ***zooarchaeology*** branch of archaeology involving the analysis of animal remains for information on physiology and ecology; for the interpretation of these remains in association with artefacts and people; and for data on subsistence, dietary and butchering patterns, animal domestication, and palaeoenvironment.

artefact any movable object that has been used, modified, or manufactured by humans, such as a tool, weapon, or vessel.

assemblage a collection of artefacts that can be considered a single analytic unit, occurring together at a particular time and place. Frequently repeated assemblages that represent a broad range of human activity are termed an archaeological culture.

atomic absorption spectrometry technique used to determine quantitatively the chemical composition of artefactual metals, minerals, and rocks, in order to identify raw material sources, to relate artefacts of the same material, or to trace trade routes. A sample of the material is atomized in a flame, and its light intensity measured. The method is slow and destructive.

attribute characteristic element of a particular archaeological culture or group; or a specific element of an individual artefact, such as the rim of a pot or the base of a projectile point, or a type of decoration, raw material, or colour.

auger tool used to collect sediment and soil samples below ground without hand excavation, or to determine the depth and type of archaeological deposits. The auger may be hand- or machine-powered.

bosing locating buried pits or ditches by striking the surface of the ground with a heavy wooden mallet; a duller sound is produced over any disturbance.

Bronze Age stage of prehistory and early history when copper and bronze became the first metals worked extensively and used for tools and weapons. It developed out of the Stone Age, preceded the Iron Age, and may be dated 5000–1200 BC in the Middle East and about 2000–500 BC in Europe. Mining and metalworking were the first specialized industries, and the invention of the wheel during this time revolutionized transport. Agricultural productivity (which began during the Neolithic period, about 10,000 BC), and hence the size of the population that could be supported, was transformed by the ox-drawn plough.

Spanish cave art proved a fake

The Ice Age art in the cave of Zubialde, in northern Spain, whose discovery was announced in March 1991, has been pronounced a fake.

When colour photographs of the cave art were first published in newspapers, the great majority of Paleolithic art specialists outside Spain expressed profound scepticism: even allowing for distortion of these photographs caused by the narrowness of the cave and the shape of the walls, the 102 figures painted in black manganese or red iron oxide simply did not look or 'feel' right. Unlike authentic Ice Age images, the 22 animal figures seemed clumsy, even ugly; and the range of motifs was positively bizarre. Apart from horses and bison, there were two woolly rhinos and a mammoth, species which were extremely rare in northern Spain; and whereas abstract 'signs' have specific chronological and regional distributions in Ice Age art, this cave appeared to possess an anthology of every type plus a few never seen before.

However, subjective assessments from press photographs are no basis for a solid diagnosis, and the cave – located near Vitoria in the Basque region – therefore underwent an intensive programme of analyses. Meanwhile, the local Basque authorities had awarded the discoverer – a history student and caver named Serafin Ruiz – with 10 million pesetas (approximately £47,000), and planned to make a replica of the cave which tourists might visit.

Almost all the figures on the cave's walls proved to contain mistakes in their proportions or anatomical details. Analysis of the pigments revealed the presence not only of insect legs, which could not have survived in the paint since the Ice Age, but also of synthetic fibres from a known type of abrasive kitchen sponge which had clearly been used to apply the paint to the walls. None of the figures were covered even partially by calcite: all seemed fresh. The clinching evidence, however, was the fact that new figures had appeared on the walls after Serafin Ruiz's first photographs had been taken in 1990, and their pigments were identical to those of the rest.

Recent discoveries in Thailand suggest that the Far East, rather than the Middle East, was the cradle of the Bronze Age.

cognitive archaeology the study of past ways of thought from material remains, and of the meanings evoked by the symbolic nature of material culture.

computerized axial tomography (CAT) a technique for looking inside bodies or mummies without disturbing them. X-ray scans made at intervals produce a series of cross-sectional 'slices' that the computer can reformat to create images from any angle.

context an artefact's matrix (the sediment or material surrounding it), its provenance (its three- dimensional position within that matrix), and its association with other artefacts in the matrix.

contract archaeology archaeological survey and/or excavation undertaken under the aegis of state legislation, most often in advance of highway construction or urban development.

core solid cylinder of sediment or soil collected with a coring device and used to evaluate the geological context and stratigraphy of archaeological material or to obtain palaeobotanical samples. Core can also mean the tool used to extract a core sample from the ground, or a stone blank from which flakes or blades are removed.

cross-dating demonstrating the degree to which cultural groups were contemporary by establishing links between them. For example, objects produced by one group might be found in the remains of another.

cultural anthropology or ***social anthropology*** subdiscipline of anthropology that analyses human culture and society, the nonbiological and behavioural aspects of humanity. Two principal branches are ethnography (the study at first hand of living cultures) and ethnology (the comparison of cultures using ethnographic evidence).

cultural resource management the legally mandated protection of archaeological sites located on public lands that are threatened by destruction, usually through development. The term is mainly used in the USA.

dating means employed to establish a chronological ordering of past cultures and events, and a timescale against which to set that sequence. Dating is an integral part of the discipline, and the success of much archaeological analysis depends on the precision of dating that can be achieved.

Relative dating methods – such as stratigraphy and seriation – are used to order archaeological material into sequences, placing earlier before later, but without linking these sequences to dates in calendar years. ***Absolute dating*** methods – such as radiocarbon dating, thermoluminescence, potassium-argon dating, electron spin resonance, fission track dating, archaeomagnetism, dendrochronology – are those that determine age in calendar years by reference to a fixed time scale, but often incorporate a degree of uncertainty, expressed as a standard deviation.

Archaeological dating is at its most reliable when relative and absolute methods are used together, for example when the relative sequence assigned to layers in an excavation can be confirmed by absolute dates for each layer. Where circumstances permit, results from one absolute method should be cross-checked by those from another, for example radiocarbon by dendrochronology or by thermoluminescence.

dendrochronology dating technique that uses tree-ring sequences to date timbers and other logs from archaeological structures and sites. This technique is based on the principle that every year trees add a ring of growth, and by counting these rings their age can be determined. An unbroken series of rings can be built up and extended back for centuries by 'overlapping' identical sequences preserved on modern and ancient timbers; subsequently, any piece of wood found in the area can have its rings checked against the master sequence and its precise age established. 'Floating' chronologies, which do not extend to the present day, have been built up in many regions worldwide and allow for relative dating between structures and sites.

In North America, sequences of tree rings extending back over 8,000 years have been obtained by using cores from the bristle-cone pine (*Pinus aristata*), which can live for over 4,000 years. Such sequences have proved very useful for calibrating, or correcting, radiocarbon dates, which were found to have serious discrepancies due to a differences in the atmosphere's carbon-14 content over time.

diffusion the spread of ideas, objects or cultural traits from one culture or society to another, rather than their independent invention; for example a diffusionist school of thought held that Egypt was the source of metallurgy and megalithic building, whereas it is now accepted that these traits arose independently in different areas.

dowsing unconventional and controversial method for locating subsurface features by holding out a twig, rod, or pendulum and waiting for it to move. Although used at times in archaeology, it is not taken seriously by most archaeologists.

electrolysis a cleaning process in archaeological conservation, especially of material from underwater archaeology, involving immersing the object in a chemical solution, and passing a weak current between it and a surrounding metal grill. Corrosive salts move slowly from the object (cathode) to the grill (anode), leaving the artifact clean.

electron spin resonance (ESR) is a non-destructive dating method applicable to teeth, bone, heat-treated flint, ceramics, sediments and stalagmitic concretions. It enables electrons, displaced by natural radiation and then trapped in the structure, to be measured; their number indicate the age of the specimen.

environmental archaeology a subfield of archaeology aimed at identifying processes, factors and conditions of past biological and physical environmental systems and how they relate to cultural systems. It is an eminently inter-disciplinary field, where archaeologists and natural scientists combine to reconstruct the human uses of plants and animals and how societies adapted to changing environmental conditions.

eolith naturally shaped or fractured stone found in Lower Pleistocene deposits and once believed by some scholars to be the oldest known artefact type, dating to the pre-Palaeolithic era. They are now recognized as not having been made by humans.

ethnoarchaeology the study of human behaviour and the material culture of living societies, in order to see how materials enter the archaeological record, and that way to provide hypotheses explaining the production, use, and disposal patterns of ancient material culture.

ethnography study of living cultures, using anthropological techniques, like participant observation (where the anthropologist lives in the society being studied) and a reliance on informants. Ethnography has provided many data of use to archaeologists as analogies.

ethnology study of contemporary peoples, concentrating on their geography and culture, as distinct from their social systems. Ethnologists make a comparative analysis of data from different cultures to understand how cultures work and why they change, with a view to deriving general principles about human society.

excavation or ***dig*** the systematic recovery of data through the exposure of buried sites and artefacts. Excavation is destructive, and is therefore accompanied by a comprehensive recording of all material found and its three-dimensional locations (its context). As much material and information as possible must be recovered from any dig. A full record of all the techniques employed in the excavation itself must also be made, so that future archaeologists will be able to evaluate the results of the work accurately.

Besides being destructive, excavation is also costly. For both these reasons, it should be used only as a last resort. It can be partial, with only a sample of the site investigated, or total. Samples are chosen either intuitively, in which case excavators investigate those areas they feel will be most productive, or statistically, in which case the sample is drawn using various statistical techniques, so as to ensure that it is representative. An important goal of excavation is a full understanding of a site's stratigraphy; that is, the vertical layering of a site. These layers or levels can be defined naturally (for example, soil changes), culturally (for example, different occupation levels), or arbitrarily (for example, 10 cm levels). Excavation can also be done horizontally, to uncover larger areas of a particular layer and reveal the spatial relationships between artefacts and features in that layer. This is known as open-area excavation and is used especially where single-period deposits lie close to the surface, and the time dimension is represented by lateral movement rather than by the placing of one building on top of the preceding one.

Most excavators employ a flexible combination of vertical and horizontal digging, adapting to the nature of their site and the questions they are seeking to answer.

experimental archaeology the controlled replication of ancient technologies and behaviour in order to provide hypotheses that can be tested by actual archaeological data. Experiments can range in size from the reproduction of ancient tools in order to learn about their processes of manufacture and use, and their effectiveness, to the construction of whole villages and ancient subsistence practices in long-term experiments.

faunal dating imprecise method of relative dating based on evolutionary changes in particular species of animals so as to form a chronological sequence.

CHRONOLOGICAL CHART SHOWING MAJOR CULTURAL DEVELOPMENTS WORLDWIDE

Years AD/BC	*North Europe*	*Mediterranean*	*Near East*	*Egypt and Africa*
1,500				Great Zimbabwe
1,000	Medieval states	BYZANTINE EMPIRE		
500			ISLAM	
AD	ROMAN EMPIRE	ROMAN EMPIRE		Towns (*Africa*) AXUM
BC				
500	IRON AGE	CLASSICAL GREECE	PERSIA BABYLON	LATE PERIOD
1,000			ASSYRIA	
1,500		Iron	HITITES	NEW KINGDOM
2,000	BRONZE AGE (*Stonehenge*)	MYCENAE	Iron	MIDDLE KINGDOM
2,500		MINOAN		OLD KINGDOM (*Pyramids*)
3,000			SUMER	EARLY DYNASTIC
3,500			Writing Cities Wheeled vehicles	Towns (*Egypt*)
4,000				
4,500	Megaliths	Copper (*Balkans*)		
5,000	Farming, pottery			
5,500			Irrigation	
6,000				
6,500		Farming, pottery	Copper	Cattle (*North Africa*)
7,000			Pottery	
7,500			Wheat, rye etc	Pottery (*Sudan*)
8,000				
8,500				
9,000			Sheep	
9,500				
10,000				

Information supplied by Paul Bahn

feature nonportable element of a site, such as a hearth, wall, post-hole, or activity area. Some are constructed (e.g. houses, storerooms, burial features), while others simply form over time, such as heaps of shells, or quarry areas.

field survey the examination of the surface of the earth for evidence of archaeological remains, without recourse to excavation. Surveys can be carried out unsystematically, where ***field walking*** takes place over areas suspected of having archaeological material, and the location of any finds or surface features encountered is plotted; or systematically, where the area is divided into a grid and a sample of its sectors is walked, making the survey more representative of the whole and hence more accurate.

fission-track dating dating method based on the natural and spontaneous nuclear fission of uranium-238 and its physical product, linear atomic displacements (tracks) created along the trajectory of released energized fission fragments. Knowing the rate of fission (a constant), the uranium content of the material, and by counting the number of fission tracks, the age of the material can be determined. The method is most widely used to date volcanic deposits adjacent to archaeological material.

India	*East Asia and Pacific*	*North America*	*Meso-America*	*South America*	*Years AD/BC*
				INCA	1,500
			AZTEC		
		Cahokia			1,000
	New Zealand	Chaco	"TOLTEC"	CHIMU	
	settled	HOPEWELL			500
	States (*Japan*)		MAYA		
		PUEBLOS			AD
	Great Wall		TEOTIHUACAN	MOCHE	
MAURYAN	(*China*)				BC
	Cast iron				
Iron	(*China*)				500
	Lapita	Maize		CHAVIN	1,000
	(*Polynesia*)	(*Southwest*)	OLMEC		
	SHANG (*China*)				1,500
					2,000
INDUS					
	Walled villages				2,500
	(*China*)			Temple-mounds	
					3,000
				Maize, llama	
				cotton	3,500
					4,000
					4,500
					5,000
	Rice-millet		Maize		
	(*China*)			Manioc	5,500
				Pottery	
				(*Amazonia*)	6,000
			Beans, squash,	Beans, squash	
			peppers	peppers	6,500
Farming	Gardens				
	(*New Guinea*)				7,000
					7,500
					8,000
					8,500
					9,000
					9,500
	Pottery (*Japan*)				
					10,000

grid system excavation technique that aims to include both the vertical and horizontal dimensions by retaining intact baulks (standing sections) of earth between the excavated squares of the grid so that different layers can be traced and correlated across the site of the vertical profiles.

historical archaeology the archaeological study of historically documented cultures, especially in America and Australia, where it is directed at colonial and post-colonial settlements. The European equivalent is medieval and post-medieval archaeology.

hoard valuables or prized possessions that have been deliberately buried, often in times of conflict or war, and never reclaimed. Coins, objects in precious metals, and scrap metal are the most common objects found in hoards. In July 1991 the largest hoard found in Britain was discovered, consisting of 7,000 15th-century coins; it was declared a treasure trove.

Iron Age developmental stage of human technology when weapons and tools were made from iron. Iron was produced in Thailand by about 1600 BC but was considered inferior in strength to bronze until about 1000 BC when metallurgical techniques improved and the alloy steel was produced by adding carbon during the smelting process. In Europe, it begins around 1100 BC, and early Iron Age cultures are represented by the

Roman treasure

One of the most spectacular Roman treasure hoards ever uncovered has been found near Hoxne, in Suffolk, England. It was discovered by Eric Lawes, a 69-year-old retired gardener, who was using his metal detector in a ploughed field in November 1992 to find a hammer lost there by the tenant farmer. He first discovered a silver coin, which led to the unearthing of more silver and gold items beneath. The authorities were contacted and a subsequent excavation by archaeologists uncovered the rest.

The treasure seems to have been buried in a (now rotted) chest, perhaps by a wealthy Christian family during civil unrest at the end of Roman rule in Britain, in the early 5th century AD. It comprised about 1,000 gold and 5,000 silver coins; around 100 silver spoons and small strainers, some bearing Latin words and the Christian Chi-Rho symbol; gold jewellery, including three neck chains, fifteen bracelets, two rings, and a three-foot body chain; a silver bowl, and silver figurines including a tigress and a small female bust. One gold chain has an emperor's head on it and is encrusted with jewels. The earliest coins date back to the Emperor Julian (AD 360–408) and the latest to Honorius (393–423). The treasure came to the surface because the farmer ploughed a little deeper than normal that year. It is now being cleaned, conserved, and catalogued at the British Museum. Estimates of its value range from £1 million–£6 million.

Mr Lawes also recovered the hammer.

Villanovans in Italy and Hallstatt in La Téne in central and western Europe; it is also the time when Celtic art flourished. The end of the period overlaps with the expansion of imperial Rome around the 1st century BC, but beyond the borders of the Empire it is generally taken to end much later, around the 4th-6th centuries AD.

isotopic analysis the analysis of ratios of the principal isotopes preserved in human bone in order to reconstruct ancient diet, based on the principle that different food categories (for example, marine resources) leave specific chemical signatures in the body.

landscape archaeology the study of human occupation and activities on landscapes, in particular the patterning of settlements and sites within that broad perspective through time.

magnetometer device for measuring the intensity of the Earth's magnetic field; distortions in this field occur when archaeological structures such as kilns and hearths are present, or pits and ditches. The technique allows for such features to be located without disturbing the ground, and for excavation to be focused on the most likely area.

material culture the physical, human-made remains of past societies (tools, buildings, and so on) which constitute the major source of evidence for archaeology.

matrix the physical material within which cultural debris or fossils are contained or embedded.

Mesolithic the Middle Stone Age developmental stage of human technology and of prehistory, following the Paleolithic and preceding the Neolithic. While the environment changed with the withdrawal of the Pleistocene ice sheets around 10,000 years ago, the old Palaeolithic hunting and gathering way of life continued during the Mesolithic; changes in the tool assemblages however reflect adaptations to environmental changes, with the flint industries of this period characterized by microliths (very small flint tools) in great number. With the introduction of farming and stock-rearing the Mesolithic gave way to the Neolithic (occurring in Britain around 4000 BC).

metal detector electronic device for detecting metal on or beneath the surface of the ground. It is used to survey areas for buried metallic objects, occasionally by archaeologists. However, their indiscriminate use by treasure hunters has led to their being banned on recognized archaeological sites in some countries; in Britain the law forbids the use of metal detectors on 'scheduled' (that is, nationally important) sites.

metallographic examination method of analysing the manufacturing techniques of metal artefacts. A cross-sectional slice of an artefact is polished, etched to highlight internal structures, and examined under a metallurgical microscope. The reflected light of the microscope enhances uneven surfaces, revealing grain size, shape, and boundaries, inclusions, fabric, defects, and other detail.

microwear analysis or ***usewear analysis*** the examination of the surface and working edge of an artefact for signs of use (such as damage or residue), often by means of a high-powered microscope. The technique is principally used in the study of stone tools, which suffer diagnostic damage or polishing when used to cut, saw, or pierce other materials.

Neolithic last period of the Stone Age, characterized by settled communities based on agriculture and domesticated animals, and identified by sophisticated, finely honed stone tools, and ceramic wares. The earliest Neolithic communities appeared about 9000 BC in the Middle East, followed by Egypt, India, and China. In Europe farming began in about 6500 BC in the Balkans and Aegean, spreading north and east by 1000 BC. Sometimes called the Neolithic Revolution, the period marks the most important single development of humanity as it brought with it sedentarism, which in turn encouraged growth and greater specialization.

New Archaeology development in the 1960s aimed at making archaeology more scientific, now more often referred to as Processual Archaeology. It proposed that archaeology should openly state its assumptions and use specific scientific procedures

New dates for cave paintings

The study of cave art and rock art has entered an exciting phase, as new techniques for analysis of pigments have revealed a greater use of organic materials (notably charcoal) than was hitherto realised. Since radiocarbon dating by accelerator mass spectrometry requires only minute quantities of material for analysis, it has proved possible to remove samples of paint from drawings and to obtain a direct date from them for the first time.

In the past, drawings on rocks or cave walls could be dated only by comparison with figures in portable works of art which were securely dated through their stratigraphic position or, if they were on materials such as bone or antler, through radiocarbon analysis. The new results have surprised archaeologists and shown that a style-based chronology is unreliable: several styles may coexist in any period, a style may last longer than expected, or styles which appear similar may in fact have been widely separated in space and time.

The first direct dating of Ice Age cave art in Europe has been carried out in three French and two Spanish caves. Pigment analysis in the caves of the Quercy region of France revealed that charcoal – rather than manganese dioxide, as had been assumed – had been used to produce a number of black figures in the cave of Cougnac. A 100-mg sample of black pigment produced a radiocarbon date of 14,300 years ago.

Pigment samples from red figures on Cougnac's walls were compared with a deposit of red ochre on the cave floor, and with ochre sources outside the cave and 15 km away. Analysis showed that the floor deposit was probably related to production of the red figures, and the ochre used probably came from local clays. Large red animal figures in the cave were drawn with the same pigment, and were therefore probably produced around the same time. But whereas stylistic studies had assigned Cougnac to the early Magdalenian period (about 18,000–16,000 years ago), the charcoal points to a later period, while new dates for the cave's giant deer figures are several millennia earlier than expected.

Similar results have emerged from the cave of Niaux in the Pyrenees. A number of different mixtures of pigments and minerals have been detected. In Niaux's famous 'Salon Noir' sanctuary, most of the animal figures were first sketched in charcoal, with manganese paint added on top. This was clearly a special place where the figures were carefully planned whereas the other figures in the cave were done without preliminary sketches.

In the past the whole of Niaux's decoration was assigned, on stylistic grounds, to about 14,000 years ago; however, charcoal from two bison figures in the Salon Noir has now been radiocarbon dated, and produced strikingly different results: one bison was dated to 13,850 years ago, as expected, but the other produced a date of 12,890 years ago: in other words, Niaux's decoration was built up in at least two separate phases.

In Spain, charcoal was discovered in some of the bison paintings from the cave of Altamira; three of them have been dated, and produced results that average out at about 14,000 years ago. However, similar paintings from the nearby cave of El Castillo were dated to about 12,990 years ago, a millennium later than expected.

Doubts about the authenticity of the Cosquer Cave near Marseille, S France, discovered in 1991, led to the taking of pigment and charcoal samples, making it the best-dated cave of all, with charcoal from a black hand stencil giving a date of 27,110 years ago – the oldest dated cave art in the world – and some animal figures dating from around 19,000 years ago.

These breakthroughs are already being overshadowed by results from some Australian rock-shelter paintings that have been found to contain human blood in their pigments, and radiocarbon dates from this material at two sites have produced results of 10,730 and 20,320 years. Red paint in the rock shelter of Sandy Creek 2, in Queensland, dates from 24,600 years ago.

The most startling evidence, however, is coming from petroglyphs – motifs pecked into rocks in the open air. Once thought to be undatable except by style, they are now proving to be suitable for a new technique of dating which involves the rock varnish which has formed over them. This varnish sometimes has microscopic organic inclusions trapped beneath it, and when these are dated by accelerator mass spectrometry they provide a minimum age for the motif under them. A petroglyph from Wharton Hill, South Australia, produced a minimum age of more than 42,700 years; while one at Panaramitee North has yielded a result of 43,140 years. These two dates constitute the greatest minimum radiocarbon ages for rock art anywhere in the world.

PB

archaeology: chronology

14th–16th centuries	The Renaissance revived interest in Classical Greek and Roman art and architecture, including ruins and buried art and artefacts.
1748	The buried Roman city of Pompeii was discovered under lava from Vesuvius.
1784	Thomas Jefferson excavated an Indian burial mound on the Rivanna River in Virginia and wrote a report on his finds.
1790	John Frere identified Old Stone Age (Palaeolithic) tools together with large extinct animals.
1822	Jean François Champollion deciphered Egyptian hieroglyphics.
1836	Christian Thomsen devised the Stone, Bronze, and Iron Age classification.
1840s	Austen Layard excavated the Assyrian capital of Nineveh.
1868	The Great Zimbabwe ruins in E Africa were first seen by Europeans.
1871	Heinrich Schliemann began excavations at Troy.
1879	Stone Age paintings were first discovered at Altamira, Spain.
1880s	Augustus Pitt-Rivers developed the concept of stratigraphy (identification of successive layers of soil within a site with successive archaeological stages; the most recent at the top).
1891	Flinders Petrie began excavating Akhetaton in Egypt.
1899–1935	Arthur Evans excavated Minoan Knossos in Crete.
1900–44	Max Uhle began the systematic study of the civilizations of Peru.
1911	The Inca city of Machu Picchu was discovered by Hiram Bingham in the Andes.
1911–12	The Piltdown skull was 'discovered'; it was proved to be a fake 1949.
1914–18	Osbert Crawford developed the technique of aerial survey of sites.
1917–27	John Eric Thompson (1898-1975) discovered the great Mayan sites in Yucatán, Mexico.
1922	Tutankhamen's tomb in Egypt was opened by Howard Carter.
1926	A kill site in Folsom, New Mexico, was found with human-made spearpoints in association with ancient bison.
1935	Dendrochronology (dating events in the distant past by counting tree rings) was developed by A E Douglas.
1939	An Anglo-Saxon ship-burial treasure was found at Sutton Hoo, England.
1947	The first of the Dead Sea Scrolls was discovered.
1948	The *Proconsul* prehistoric ape was discovered by Mary Leakey in Kenya.
1950s–1970s	Several early hominid fossils were found by Louis Leakey in Olduvai Gorge.
1953	Michael Ventris deciphered Minoan Linear B.
1960s	Radiocarbon and thermoluminescence measurement techniques were developed as aids for dating remains.
1961	The Swedish warship *Wasa* was raised at Stockholm.
1963	Walter Emery pioneered rescue archaeology at Abu Simbel before the site was flooded by the Aswan Dam.
1969	Human remains found at Lake Mungo, Australia, were dated at 26,000 years; earliest evidence of ritual cremation.
1974	The Tomb of Shi Huangdi was discovered in China. The footprints of a hominid called 'Lucy', 3 to 3.7 million years old, were found at Laetoli in Ethiopia.
1978	The tomb of Philip II of Macedon (Alexander the Great's father) was discovered in Greece.
1979	The Aztec capital Tenochtitlán was excavated beneath a zone of Mexico City.
1982	The English king Henry VIII's warship *Mary Rose* of 1545 was raised and studied with new techniques in underwater archaeology.
1985	The tomb of Maya, Tutankhamen's treasurer, was discovered at Saqqara, Egypt.
1988	The Turin Shroud was established as being of medieval origin by radiocarbon dating.
1989	The remains of the Globe and Rose Theatres, where many of Shakespeare's plays were originally performed, were discovered in London.
1991	Body of man from 5,300 years ago, with clothing, bow, arrows, a copper axe, and other implements, found preserved in Italian Alps.
1992	The world's oldest surviving wooden structure, a well 15 m/49 ft deep made of huge oak timbers at Kückhoven, Germany, was dated by tree-rings to 5,300 BC.
1993	Drawings done in charcoal on the walls of the Cosquer Cave (whose underwater entrance near Marseilles, France, was discovered in 1991), were dated by radiocarbon to 27,110 and *c.* 19,000 years ago, making this the oldest directly dated cave art in the world.

derived from Positivism. Some adherents of New Archaeology believed that laws of human behaviour were obtainable by using the correct methodologies.

palaeobotany or ***palaeoethnobotany*** or ***archaeobotany*** the recovery and identification of plant remains from archaeological contexts, and their use in the reconstruction of past environments and economies.

Palaeolithic earliest stage of human technology and development of the Stone Age, beginning with the emergence of hominids and the production of the earliest stone tools (approximately three million years ago), and lasting till the retreat of the ice sheets about 10,000 years ago. Its subdivisions are the Lower Palaeolithic, in which the earliest hominids appear (*Australopithecus* and *Homo erectus*; the Middle

Palaeolithic, the age of Neanderthals; and the Upper Paleolithic, marked by the appearance of *Homo sapiens* and the remarkable cave art of western Europe (for example the caves at Lascaux). The final stage also saw the colonization of the New World and Australia.

palaeontology the study of ancient life that encompasses the structure of ancient organisms and their environment, evolution, and ecology, as revealed by their fossils.

phosphate analysis the regular sampling and chemical analysis of phosphorus levels in the soil around archaeological sites in order to locate concentrations of human bone and excrement, and hence areas of human activity, settlements, and burial grounds.

physical anthropology or ***biological anthropology*** subdiscipline of anthropology that studies human biological or physical characteristics and how they evolved.

pollen analysis or ***palynology*** the study of fossil and living pollen and spores, utilized in palaeoenvironmental and palaeoclimatic reconstruction, identifying natural and humanly induced vegetation changes, and developing relative chronologies.

potassium-argon dating an isotopic dating method based on the radioactive decay of potassium-40 to the stable isotope argon-40. The method is used primarily to date volcanic layers in stratigraphic sequences with archaeological deposits, and the palaeomagnetic reversal timescale. Ages are based on the known half-life of 40K, and the ratio of 40K/40Ar. The method is routinely applied from about 100,000 to 30 million years ago.

prehistory human cultures before the use of writing. It constitutes the longest segment of the human past, and is the major object of study of archaeology. A classification system was devised 1816 by Danish archaeologist Christian Thomsen, based on the predominant materials used by early humans for tools and weapons: Stone Age, Bronze Age, Iron Age. Prehistory and history can overlap in time – for example, prehistoric Iron Age cultures existed at the same time as the historic Roman culture; and in our own age, 'prehistoric' societies have existed contemporaneously with modern ones, for example the Kung Bushmen or the Australian aborigines.

protohistory period following prehistory but prior to the appearance of history as documented in written records.

radiocarbon dating or ***carbon dating*** a radiometric dating technique used for determining the age of carbon-bearing materials including wood and plant remains, bone, peat, and shell. It is based on the radioactive decay of the carbon-14 isotope in the sample to nitrogen, with the release of (beta) particles that is initiated when an organism dies and ceases to exchange carbon-14 with the atmosphere. After death the carbon-14 content is a function of time and is determined by counting (beta) particles with either a proportional gas or a liquid scintillation counter for a period of time.

The method yields reliable ages back to *c.* 30,000 years, but its results require correction since the atmospheric production rate of carbon-14 has not been constant through time. Radiocarbon dates from tree rings showed that material before 1000 BC had been exposed to greater concentrations of carbon-14. Now radiocarbon dates are calibrated against calendar dates obtained from tree rings, or, for earlier periods, against uranium/thorium dates obtained from coral. A new advance, AMS (accelerator mass spectrometry) requires only tiny samples of the material being dated, and counts the atoms of carbon-14 directly, disregarding their decay.

relative dating dating methods that measure differences in age utilizing an ordinal scale. For example, they include sequencing of events or objects relative to one another but without linkage to ages in calendar years.

remote sensing gathering and recording information from a distance. Space probes have sent back photographs and data about planets as distant as Neptune. In archaeology, surface survey techniques provide information without disturbing subsurface deposits.

rescue archaeology or ***salvage archaeology*** the location and recording (usually by rapid excavation) of archaeological sites before they are destroyed by contemporary construction or other developments. Salvage archaeology is also concerned with the various laws enacted to mitigate the threat.

resistivity survey geophysical survey method used to locate buried features and structures with a resistivity meter. An electrical current is passed through the soil between electrodes and the resistance (normally a consequence of moisture content) is recorded. In this way buried features can be detected through their differential retention of groundwater – so, for example, a stone feature will show greater resistance than the soil around it, and a damp pit will show less.

seriation relative dating technique in which artefacts are temporally organized, according to their relative popularity. Evolutionary seriation is based on changes that represent essentially technological improvements, while stylistic seriation is based on gradual changes in the frequencies of stylistic attributes, so that the greater the similarity in style, the closer in age artefacts are to each other.

site any location where there is evidence for past human behaviour. A site can be as small as an isolated find, which is either a single artefact or a small number of artefacts, or as large as an ancient city. Sites are classified according to function: major types include domestic/habitation sites, kill sites, and processing/butchering sites.

site catchment analysis (SCA) the definition of the site catchment, the total area from which the site's contents have been derived (i.e. the full inventory of its artefactual and non-artefactual remains, and their sources), and an assessment of the catchment's economic potential.

site exploitation territory the territory surrounding a site that was habitually exploited by the site's inhabitants. Territories are normally seen as having a radius of one hour's walking distance for farmers, and a two-hour distance for hunter-gatherers.

Celtic burials

By a remarkable coincidence the spectacular graves of what seem to be members of the Celtic nobility were found in 1992 in two SE England locations, at St Albans (Roman Verulamium) and Colchester (Roman Camolodunum). The St Albans burial was particularly sumptuous: in an underground timber mortuary chamber the body was apparently laid on a couch, and rich belongings and a funeral feast were set out around it. The corpse was then taken out and, together with many of the grave goods, cremated on a huge pyre 10 m/30 ft to the north. After this the funerary chamber and its contents were smashed to bits. The ashes and fragments from the pyre were placed in a cremation pit alongside the chamber. This burial lay within a huge, 2-ha/5-acre rectangular enclosure, 115 m/375 ft by 170 m/560 ft in size. Within the chamber archaeologists found the remains of 30 or 40 broken pots, mainly of southern Gaulish Samian, Gallo-Belgic ware, or local imitations, and dating to about AD 45–50; as well as three or four Italian wine amphorae. Within the cremation pit a layer of molten metal and numerous fragments reveal that the grave goods included a large amount of bronze sheet and over a pound of silver, as well as iron bars and nails, and parts of a horse harness. There was also a large folded bundle of iron chain mail, which constitutes a whole knee-length tunic.

The site of this burial continued to be venerated for 200 years, and 50 years after the event a Romano-Celtic temple was built on the site of the pyre. The scale of the enclosure is far greater than that of all other burials of the period and suggests that the deceased may have been a member of the ruling Catuvellaunian family, perhaps a tribal leader or client king who ruled immediately after the invasion of AD 43 and died early in the Roman period.

The graves found at Colchester are similar and appear to represent the same kind of rite, probably for members of the royal family of the Trinovantes. Five large, ditched enclosures occur in two groups; two of them held sunken mortuary chambers in the form of large timber boxes. The first contained fragments of dozens of smashed imported pots and some fragments of human bone from a cremation that took place nearby. Drips of molten metal again point to the burning of grave goods. The second was similar, though the presence of beads from a broken necklace suggests a female occupant. Two secondary graves were also found nearby, one of them containing rich grave goods including a set of gaming pieces and fine glassware. The male burial has been provisionally dated to about AD 35; the secondary burials are later, about AD 43–60, while the female is post-conquest, possibly AD 60–75.

sondage deep test-pit used to investigate a site's stratigraphy (layered arrangement of deposits) before carrying out larger-scale excavation.

spectrographic analysis technique used to analyse the component elements of a chemical compound; it is based on the principle that the light given off when the compound is vaporized will break up into a distinctive pattern when split into a spectrum by a prism. By analyzing the pattern of lines in the spectrum the elements present in the compound can be determined. The technique has been especially useful in metal analysis, but is also applied to pottery, obsidian, and glass.

step-trenching excavation technique used on very deep sites such as Middle Eastern 'tells' (mounds) where a large area opened at the top gradually narrows as the dig descends in a series of large steps.

Stone Age the developmental stage of humans in prehistory before the use of metals, when tools and weapons were made chiefly of stone, especially flint. The Stone Age is subdivided into the Old or Palaeolithic, the Middle or Mesolithic, and the New or Neolithic. The people of the Old Stone Age were hunters and gatherers, whereas the Neolithic people took the first steps in agriculture, the domestication of animals, weaving, and pottery.

stratigraphy the study of the formation, composition, sequence, and correlation of stratified sediment, soils, and rocks. Stratigraphy is the principal means by which the context of archaeological deposits is evaluated, chronologies are constructed, and events are sequenced. It is invaluable for interpreting the sequence of deposition of the site and thereby the relative age of artefacts, features, and other phenomena in the site.

thermoluminescence (TL) is used to date fired archaeological material such as pottery and burned flint tools. When the material was originally fired, any electrons trapped in it by radiation escaped, emitting light known as thermoluminescence, and thereby setting the TL clock to zero. By measuring the amount of TL emitted when the material is reheated, and knowing its radioactive content, one can calculate the lapse of time since the original firing.

thin-section analysis technique using a sample chip – ground down to a paper-thin sheet and mounted on a glass slide – that is utilized in petrological analysis of the mineralogical composition of ceramics, stone artefacts, and soils.

Three Age System scheme first formulated by Christian Thomsen (1788–1865) in 1816–19 to divide prehistory into a Stone Age, Bronze Age, and Iron

Age. Further subdivisions followed, with the Stone Age being divided into the Old and the New (the Palaeolithic and Neolithic), a Middle (Mesolithic) Stone Age added later, and the Copper Age added between the New Stone Age and Bronze Age. While providing a valuable and valid classification system for prehistoric material, it did not provide dates but only a sequence of developmental stages, which, furthermore, were not necessarily followed in that order by different societies.

trace element analysis the study (e.g. by neutron activation analysis or X-ray fluorescence) of elements that occur naturally in minor amounts in minerals in soil and sediment. Trace elements can be identified by various analyses and may serve as 'fingerprints' for some artifact raw material sources.

typology the systematic organization of artifacts into types on the basis of their shared attributes. The two objectives are classification, i.e. grouping objects according to their shape, leading to a type series; and, through the comparison of different types, to discover how these types relate to each other. The latter process can lead to seriation, which demonstrates the development of a type of artifact (the development may be related to function, technological advance, fashion, etc.). Such information requires an independent dating source for at least several examples in the series in order to establish the rate of change.

underwater reconnaissance geophysical methods of underwater survey including the proton magnetometer, towed behind a survey vessel to detect iron and steel objects that distort the earth's magnetic field; side-scan sonar, that transmits sound waves in a fan-shaped beam to produce a graphic image of subsurface features on the sea-bed; and a sub-bottom profiler that emits sound pulses that bounce back from features and objects buried under the sea-floor.

X-ray diffraction analysis a physical technique used to identify the mineralogy of material such as ceramics, stone, sediments and weathering products on metals. The sample is ground to powder, and exposed to X-rays at various angles; the diffraction patterns produced are compared with reference standards for identification.

X-ray fluorescence spectrometry (XRF) a physical technique used to determine the major and trace elements in the chemical composition of materials such as ceramics, obsidian and glass that may help in identifying the material source. The sample is bombarded with X-rays, and the wavelengths of the released energy, or fluorescent X-rays, are detected and measured. Different elements have unique wavelengths, while their concentrations can be estimated from the intensity of the released X-rays.

ASTRONOMY

Space Exploration

Ames Research Center US space-research (NASA) installation at Mountain View, California, USA, for the study of aeronautics and life sciences. It has managed the Pioneer series of planetary probes and is involved in the search for extraterrestrial life.

Apollo project US space project to land a person on the Moon, achieved 20 July 1969, when Neil Armstrong was the first to set foot there. He was accompanied on the Moon's surface by Col Edwin E Aldrin Jr; Michael Collins remained in the orbiting command module.

Apollo–Soyuz test project joint US-Soviet space mission in which an Apollo and a Soyuz craft docked while in orbit around the Earth on 17 July 1975. The craft remained attached for two days and crew members were able to move from one craft to the other through an airlock attached to the nose of the Apollo. The mission was designed to test rescue procedures as well as having political significance.

Ariane launch vehicle built in a series by the European Space Agency (first flight 1979). The launch site is at Kourou in French Guiana. Ariane is a three-stage rocket using liquid fuels. Since 1984 it has been operated commercially by Arianespace, a private company financed by European banks and aerospace industries.

Ariel series of six UK satellites launched by the USA 1962–79, the most significant of which was *Ariel 5*, 1974, which made a pioneering survey of the sky at X-ray wavelengths.

astronaut person making flights into space; the term ***cosmonaut*** is used in the West for any astronaut from the former Soviet Union.

astronautics the science of space travel.

astronomy the science of the celestial bodies: the Sun, the Moon, and the planets; the stars and galaxies; and all other objects in the universe. It is concerned with their positions, motions, distances, and physical conditions; and with their origins and evolution. Astronomy thus divides into fields such as astrophysics, celestial mechanics, and cosmology.

Cape Canaveral promontory on the Atlantic coast of Florida, USA, 367 km/228 mi N of Miami, used as a rocket launch site by NASA. It was known as Cape Kennedy 1963–73. The Kennedy Space Center is nearby.

Cassini joint space probe of NASA and the European Space Agency to the planet Saturn. *Cassini* is scheduled to be launched in Oct 1997 and will go into orbit around Saturn in June 2004, dropping off a sub-probe, *Huygens*, to land on Saturn's largest moon, Titan.

communications satellite relay station in space for sending telephone, television, telex, and other messages around the world. Messages are sent to and from the satellites via ground stations. Most communications satellites are in geostationary orbit, appearing to hang fixed over one point on the Earth's surface. The first satellite to carry TV signals across the Atlantic Ocean was *Telstar* 1962.

Cosmos name used from the early 1960s for nearly all Soviet artificial satellites. Over 2,200 Cosmos satellites had been launched by the end of 1992.

Delta rocket US rocket used to launch many scientific and communications satellites since 1960, based on the Thor ballistic missile. Several increasingly powerful versions, produced as satellites, became larger and heavier. Solid-fuel boosters were attached to the first stage to increase lifting power.

Edwards Air Force Base military USAF centre in California, situated on a dry lake bed, often used as a landing site by the space shuttle.

Energiya the most powerful Soviet space rocket, capable, with the use of strap-on boosters, of launching payloads of up to 190 tonnes into Earth orbit. It was first launched 15 May 1987.

European Space Agency (ESA) organization of European countries (Austria, Belgium, Denmark, France, Germany, Ireland, Italy, the Netherlands, Norway, Spain, Sweden, Switzerland, and the UK) that engages in space research and technology. It was founded 1975, with headquarters in Paris. ESA is working on its own space-shuttle project, Hermes.

Explorer series of US scientific satellites. *Explorer 1*, launched Jan 1958, was the first US satellite in orbit and discovered the Van Allen radiation belts around the Earth.

Galileo spacecraft launched from the space shuttle *Atlantis* Oct 1989, on a six-year journey to Jupiter. It flew past Venus in Feb 1990 and passed within 970 km/600 mi of Earth in Dec 1990, using the gravitational fields of these two planets to increase its velocity. The craft flew past Earth again 1992 to receive its final boost towards Jupiter. It flew past the asteroid Gaspra in Oct 1991, taking close-up photographs.

Spending on space

Comparison of world space budgets (in US $m)

Year	*Europe*	*USA*	*Japan*	*Canada*	*USSR*
1981	1,404.2	9,165.5	539.8	89.8	15,000.0
1982	1,266.2	10,466.2	578.7	114.7	16,000.0
1983	1,301.9	12,590.4	527.3	108.5	17,000.0
1984	1,495.0	14,726.1	555.6	126.5	18,000.0
1985	1,397.1	19,583.5	565.6	121.6	20,000.0
1986	1,413.4	23,322.6	524.7	108.4	25,000.0
1987	2,161.9	26,612.6	833.1	128.2	30,000.0
1988	2,993.1	24,381.0	975.7	128.2	33,000.0
1989	3,265.3	26,868.0	1,066.8	144.6	33,000.0
1990	3,794.9	30,710.0	1,499.4	206.4	33,000.0
1991	4,948.3	34,450.0	1,430.0	245.2	–

The USA and USSR figures include military space expenditures, but the European figures do not.

USSR figures are highly hypothetical.

Source: European Space Directory 1992

Gemini project US space programme (1965–66) in which astronauts practised rendezvous and docking of spacecraft, and working outside their spacecraft, in preparation for the Apollo Moon landings.

Giotto space probe built by the European Space Agency to study Halley's comet. Launched by an Ariane rocket in July 1985, *Giotto* passed within 600 km/375 mi of the comet's nucleus on 13 March 1986. On 2 July 1990 it flew 23,000 km/14,300 mi from Earth, which – by means of the phenomenon known as gravity assist – diverted its path to encounter another comet, Grigg-Skjellerup, on 10 July 1992.

Goddard Space Flight Center NASA installation at Greenbelt, Maryland, USA, responsible for the operation of NASA's crewless scientific satellites, including the Hubble Space Telescope. It is also home of the National Space Science Data Center, a repository of data collected by satellites.

Hipparcos (acronym for ***high-precision parallax collecting satellite***) satellite launched by the European Space Agency Aug 1989. It is the world's first astrometry satellite and is providing precise positions, distances, colours, brightnesses, and apparent motions for over 100,000 stars. It is named after the Greek astronomer Hipparchus.

Hubble Space Telescope (HST) telescope placed into orbit around the Earth, at an altitude of 610 km/380 mi, by a US space shuttle in April 1990. It has a main mirror 2.4 m/94 in wide, which suffers from spherical aberration and so cannot be focused properly. Yet, because it is above the atmosphere, the HST outperforms ground-based telescopes. Computer techniques are being used to improve the images from the telescope until the arrival of a maintenance mission to install corrective optics. The HST carries four scientific instruments.

Intelsat International Telecommunications Satellite Organization, established 1964 to operate a worldwide system of communications satellites. More than 100 countries are members of Intelsat. Intelsat satellites are stationed in geostationary orbit (maintaining their positions relative to the Earth) over the Atlantic, Pacific, and Indian Oceans. The first Intelsat satellite was *Early Bird*, launched 1965.

IRAS Infrared Astronomy Satellite, a joint US-UK-Dutch satellite launched 1983 to survey the sky at infrared wavelengths, studying areas of star formation, distant galaxies, possible embryo planetary systems around other stars; it discovered five new comets in our own Solar System.

Jet Propulsion Laboratory NASA installation in Pasadena, California, operated by the California Institute of Technology. It is the command centre for NASA's deep-space probes such as the Voyager, Magellan, and Galileo missions, with which it communicates via the Deep Space Network of radio telescopes in Goldstone, California; Madrid, Spain; and Canberra, Australia.

Johnson Space Center NASA installation in Houston, Texas, home of mission control for crewed space missions. It is the main centre for the selection and training of astronauts.

Kennedy Space Center NASA launch site on Merritt Island, near Cape Canaveral, Florida, used for Apollo and space-shuttle launches. The first flight to land on the Moon (1969) and *Skylab*, the first orbiting laboratory (1973), were launched here.

Steadily ascending

Civilian UK space expenditure (in £m)

	1987–88	*1988–89*	*1989–90*	*1990–91*
Non ESA programmes:*				
Earth observation	23	25	30	31
Science	9	11	12	12
Communications	2	2	2	2
Technology support	7	9	11	9
Total	41	47	55	54
ESA:				
Earth observation	22	25	18	23
Science	20	23	24	24
Communications	22	21	22	28
Technology support	–	–	–	–
ESA general budget	12	16	19	17
Launchers	5	5	5	2
Total	81	90	88	94
Grand Total	***122***	***137***	***143***	***148***

** European Space Agency*

Source: European Space Directory 1992

Kourou town in French Guiana, NW of Cayenne, site of the ***Guiana Space Centre*** of the European Space Agency. Situated near the equator, it is an ideal site for launching satellites into geostationary orbit.

Landsat series of satellites used for monitoring Earth resources. The first was launched in 1972.

Magellan NASA space probe to Venus, launched May 1989. It went into orbit around Venus in Aug 1990 to make a detailed map of the planet by radar. It revealed volcanoes, meteorite craters, and fold mountains on the planet's surface.

Mariner spacecraft series of US space probes that explored the planets Mercury, Venus, and Mars 1962–75. *Mariner 9* 1971 mapped the entire Martian surface, and photographed Mars' moons. *Mariner 10* 1974–75 took close-up photographs of Mercury and Venus, and measured temperature, radiation, and magnetic fields.

Marshall Space Flight Center NASA installation at Huntsville, Alabama, where the series of Saturn rockets and the space-shuttle engines were developed. It also manages various payloads for the space shuttle, including the *Spacelab* space station.

Mars Observer NASA space probe launched 1992 to orbit Mars and survey the planet, its atmosphere, and the polar caps. It was also scheduled to communicate information from the robot vehicles delivered by Russia's Mars 94 mission. The $1 billion project miscarried, however, when the probe unaccountably stopped transmitting Aug 1993, three days before it was due to drop into orbit

Mir Soviet space station, the core of which was launched 20 Feb 1986. It has been enlarged by adding extra sections to it. Cosmonauts have spent up to a year at a time aboard *Mir*, with visits from other crews.

Space diary – main launches June 1992 – May 1993

Launch date	*Flight*	*Remarks*
1992		
7 June	*EUVE*	*Extreme Ultraviolet Explorer* scientific satellite launched from Cape Canaveral to study the sky at ultraviolet wavelengths
25 June	*STS 50*	Space Shuttle *Columbia* carried US Microgravity Laboratory on the longest shuttle flight to date, 13 days. Crew: Richard Richards, Kenneth Bowersox, Carl Meade, Ellen Baker, Bonnie Dunbar, Lawrence Delucas, Eugene Trinh. Landed at Kennedy Space Center on 9 July
27 July	*Soyuz TM-15*	Michel Tognini of France launched with Anatoli Solovyov and Sergey Avdeyev to *Mir* space station. Tognini returned on 10 Aug in *Soyuz TM-14* with Aleksandr Viktorenko and Aleksandr Kalery. Solovyov and Avdeyev remained aboard *Mir* until 1 Feb 1993
31 July	*STS 46*	Space Shuttle *Atlantis* launched Eureca (European recoverable carrier) and Tethered Satellite. Crew: Loren Shriver, Andrew Allen, Franklin Chang-Diaz, Jeffrey Hoffman, Claude Nicollier (ESA), Marsha Ivins, Franco Malerba (Italy). Landed at Kennedy Space Center 8 Aug
12 Sept	*STS 47*	Space Shuttle *Endeavor* launched Japanese *Spacelab* mission. Crew: Robert Gibson, Curtis Brown, Jan Davis Jerome Apt, Mae Jemison, Mark Lee, Mamoru Mohri (Japan). Landed Kennedy Space Center 20 Sept
25 Sept	*Mars Observer*	Mars probe launched by Titan rocket from Cape Canaveral. Due to go into orbit around Mars in Aug 1993
22 Oct	*STS 52*	Space Shuttle *Columbia* launched Lageos 2 geology satellite and carried US materials processing experiments and Canadian experiments. Crew: James Wetherbee, Michael Baker, William Shepherd, Tamara Jernigan, Charles Veach, Steven MacLean (Canada). Landed at Kennedy Space Center 1 Nov
2 Dec	*STS 53*	Space Shuttle *Discovery* launched Department of Defense satellite. Crew: David Walker, Robert Cabana, Guion Bluford, James Voss, Michael Clifford. Landed at Edwards Air Force Base 9 Dec
1993		
13 Jan	*STS 54*	Space Shuttle *Endeavor* launched TDRS-F communications satellite. Crew: John Casper, Donald McMonagle, Gregory Harbaugh, Mario Runco, Susan Helms. Landed at Kennedy Space Center 19 Jan
24 Jan	*Soyuz TM-16*	Gennady Manakov and Aleksandr Poleshchuk launched to *Mir* space station
8 April	*STS 56*	Space Shuttle *Discovery* carried ATLAS 2 atmospheric science laboratory. Crew: Kenneth Cameron, Stephen Oswald, Michael Foale, Kenneth Cockrell, Ellen Ochoa. Landed at Kennedy Space Center 17 April
26 April	*STS 55*	Space Shuttle *Columbia* carried second German *Spacelab* mission. Crew: Steven Nagel, Tom Henricks, Jerry Ross, Charles Precourt, Bernard Harris, Ulrich Walter (Germany), Hans Schlegel (Germany). Landed at Edwards Air Force Base 6 May

Moon probe crewless spacecraft used to investigate the Moon. Early probes flew past the Moon or crash-landed on it, but later ones achieved soft landings or went into orbit. Soviet probes included the Luna/Lunik series. US probes (Ranger, Surveyor, Lunar Orbiter) prepared the way for the Apollo crewed flights. The first space probe to hit the Moon was the Soviet *Luna 2*, on 13 Sept 1959.

NASA ***National Aeronautics and Space Administration*** US government agency, founded 1958, for space-flight and aeronautical research. Its main installation is at the Kennedy Space Center in Florida. NASA's Apollo project took the first people to the Moon 1969.

Pioneer probe any of a series of US Solar-System space probes 1958–78. *Pioneer 5*, launched 1960, was the first of a series to study the solar wind between the planets. *Pioneer 10*, launched 1972, was the first probe to reach Jupiter 1973 and to leave the Solar System 1983. *Pioneer 11*, launched 1973, passed Jupiter 1974, and was the first probe to reach Saturn 1979, before also leaving the Solar System.

Plesetsk rocket-launching site 170 km/105 mi S of Archangel, Russia. From 1966 the USSR launched artificial satellites from here, mostly military.

Proton rocket Soviet space rocket introduced 1965, used to launch heavy satellites, space probes, and the Salyut and *Mir* space stations.

Redstone rocket short-range US military missile, modified for use as a space launcher. Redstone rockets launched the first two flights of the Mercury project. A modified Redstone, *Juno 1*, launched the first US satellite, *Explorer 1*, in 1958.

rocket projectile driven by the reaction of gases produced by a fast-burning fuel. Unlike jet engines, which are also reaction engines, modern rockets carry their own oxygen supply to burn their fuel and do not require any surrounding atmosphere. Being the only form of propulsion available that can function in a vacuum, rockets are essential to exploration in outer space. Multistage rockets have to be used, consisting of a number of rockets joined together.

ROSAT joint US-German-UK satellite launched

astronomy: chronology

2300 BC	Chinese astronomers made their earliest observations.
2000	Babylonian priests made their first observational records.
1900	Stonehenge was constructed: first phase.
365	The Chinese observed the satellites of Jupiter with the naked eye.
3rd century	Aristarchus argued that the Sun is the centre of the Solar System.
2nd century AD	Ptolemy's complicated Earth-centred system was promulgated, which dominated the astronomy of the Middle Ages.
1543	Copernicus revived the ideas of Aristarchus in *De Revolutionibus*.
1608	Hans Lippershey invented the telescope, which was first used by Galileo 1609.
1609	Johannes Kepler's first two laws of planetary motion were published (the third appeared 1619).
1632	The world's first official observatory was established in Leiden in the Netherlands.
1633	Galileo's theories were condemned by the Inquisition.
1675	The Royal Greenwich Observatory was founded in England.
1687	Isaac Newton's *Principia* was published, including his 'law of universal gravitation'.
1705	Edmond Halley correctly predicted that the comet that had passed the Earth in 1682 would return in 1758; the comet was later to be known by his name.
1781	William Herschel discovered Uranus and recognized stellar systems beyond our Galaxy.
1796	Pierre Laplace elaborated his theory of the origin of the Solar System.
1801	Giuseppe Piazzi discovered the first asteroid, Ceres.
1814	Joseph von Fraunhofer first studied absorption lines in the solar spectrum.
1846	Neptune was identified by Johann Galle, following predictions by John Adams and Urbain Leverrier.
1859	Gustav Kirchhoff explained dark lines in the Sun's spectrum.
1887	The earliest photographic star charts were produced.
1889	Edward Barnard took the first photographs of the Milky Way.
1908	Fragment of comet fell at Tunguska, Siberia.
1920	Arthur Eddington began the study of interstellar matter.
1923	Edwin Hubble proved that the galaxies are systems independent of the Milky Way, and by 1930 had confirmed the concept of an expanding universe.
1930	The planet Pluto was discovered by Clyde Tombaugh at the Lowell Observatory, Arizona, USA.
1931	Karl Jansky founded radio astronomy.
1945	Radar contact with the Moon was established by Z Bay of Hungary and the US Army Signal Corps Laboratory.
1948	The 5-m/200-in Hale reflector telescope was installed at Mount Palomar, California, USA.
1957	The Jodrell Bank telescope dish in England was completed.
1957	The first Sputnik satellite (USSR) opened the age of space observation.
1962	The first X-ray source was discovered in Scorpius.
1963	The first quasar was discovered.
1967	The first pulsar was discovered by Jocelyn Bell and Antony Hewish.
1969	The first crewed Moon landing was made by US astronauts.
1976	A 6-m/240-in reflector telescope was installed at Mount Semirodniki, USSR.
1977	Uranus was discovered to have rings.
1977	The spacecrafts *Voyager 1* and *2* were launched, passing Jupiter and Saturn 1979–81.
1978	The spacecrafts *Pioneer Venus 1* and *2* reached Venus.
1978	A satellite of Pluto, Charon, was discovered by James Christy of the US Naval Observatory.
1986	Halley's comet returned. *Voyager 2* flew past Uranus and discovered six new moons.
1987	Supernova SN1987A flared up, becoming the first supernova to be visible to the naked eye since 1604. The 4.2-m/165-in William Herschel Telescope on La Palma, Canary Islands, and the James Clerk Maxwell Telescope on Mauna Kea, Hawaii, began operation.
1988	The most distant individual star was recorded – a supernova, 5 billion light years away, in the AC118 cluster of galaxies.
1989	*Voyager 2* flew by Neptune and discovered eight moons and three rings.
1990	Hubble Space Telescope was launched into orbit by the US space shuttle.
1991	The space probe *Galileo* flew past the asteroid Gaspra, approaching it to within 26,000 km/16,200 mi.
1992	COBE satellite detected ripples from the Big Bang that mark the first stage in the formation of galaxies. NASA began 10-year search for radio signals from extraterrestial beings.

1990 to study cosmic sources of X-rays and extremely short ultraviolet wavelengths.

Salyut series of seven space stations launched by the USSR 1971–82. Salyut was cylindrical in shape, 15 m/50 ft long, and weighed 19 tonnes/21 tons. It housed two or three cosmonauts at a time, for missions lasting up to eight months.

satellite any small body that orbits a larger one, either natural or artificial. Natural satellites that orbit planets are called moons. The first ***artificial satellite***, *Sputnik 1*, was launched into orbit around the Earth by the USSR 1957. Artificial satellites are used for scientific purposes, communications, weather forecasting, and military applications. The largest artificial satellites can be seen by the naked eye.

At any time, there are several thousand artificial satellites orbiting the Earth, including active satellites, satellites that have ended their working lives, and discarded sections of rockets.

Saturn rocket family of large US rockets, developed by Wernher von Braun (1912–1977) for the Apollo project. The two-stage *Saturn IB* was used for launching Apollo spacecraft into orbit around the Earth. The three-stage *Saturn V* sent Apollo spacecraft to the Moon and launched the *Skylab* space station. The liftoff thrust of a *Saturn V* was 3,500 tonnes. After Apollo and *Skylab*, the Saturn rockets were retired in favour of the space shuttle.

Skylab US space station, in orbit 1973–79, made from the adapted upper stage of a *Saturn V* rocket. At 75 tonnes/82.5 tons, it was the heaviest object ever put into space, and was 25.6 m/84 ft long. *Skylab* contained a workshop for carrying out experiments in weightlessness, an observatory for monitoring the Sun, and cameras for photographing the Earth's surface.

Soyuz Soviet series of spacecraft, capable of carrying up to three cosmonauts. Soyuz spacecraft consist of three parts: a rear section containing engines; the central crew compartment; and a forward compartment that gives additional room for working and living space. They are now used for ferrying crews up to space stations, though they were originally used for independent space flight.

Spacelab small space station built by the European Space Agency, carried in the cargo bay of the US space shuttle, in which it remains throughout each flight, returning to Earth with the shuttle. The first *Spacelab* mission lasted ten days Nov–Dec 1983. *Spacelab* consists of a pressurized module in which astronauts can work, and a series of pallets, open to the vacuum of space, on which equipment is mounted.

space probe any instrumented object sent beyond Earth to collect data from other parts of the solar system and from deep space. The first probe was the Soviet *Lunik 1*, which flew past the Moon 1959. The first successful planetary probe was the US *Mariner 2*, which flew past Venus 1962, using transfer orbit. The first space probe to leave the Solar System was *Pioneer 10* 1983. Space probes include *Galileo*, *Giotto*, *Magellan*, *Mars Observer*, *Ulysses*, the Moon probes, and the Mariner, Pioneer, Viking, and Voyager series. Japan launched its first space probe 1990.

space shuttle reusable crewed spacecraft. The first was launched 12 April 1981 by the USA. It was developed by NASA to reduce the cost of using space for commercial, scientific, and military purposes. After leaving its payload in space, the space-shuttle orbiter can be flown back to Earth to land on a runway, and is then available for reuse.

The first Soviet shuttle, *Buran*, was launched without a crew by the *Energiya* rocket 15 Nov 1988. In Japan, development of a crewless shuttle began 1986.

space sickness or ***space adaptation syndrome*** feeling of nausea, sometimes accompanied by vomiting, experienced by about 40% of all astronauts during their first few days in space. It is akin to travel sickness, and is thought to be caused by confusion of the body's balancing mechanism, located in the inner ear, by weightlessness. The sensation passes after a few days as the body adapts.

space station any large structure designed for human occupation in space for extended periods of time. Space stations are used for carrying out astronomical observations and surveys of Earth, as well as for biological studies and the processing of materials in weightlessness. The first space stations were the Soviet *Salyut 1* 1971 and the US *Skylab* 1973–79.

NASA plans to build a larger space station, to be called *Freedom*, and place it in orbit during the 1990s, in cooperation with other countries, including the European Space Agency, which is building a module called *Columbus*, and Japan, also building a module.

space suit protective suit worn by astronauts and cosmonauts in space. It provides an insulated, air-conditioned cocoon in which people can live and work for hours at a time outside the spacecraft. Inside the suit is a cooling garment that keeps the body at a comfortable temperature even during vigorous work. The suit provides air to breathe, and removes exhaled carbon dioxide and moisture. The suit's outer layers insulate the occupant from the extremes of hot and cold in space (–150°C/–240°F in the shade to +180°C/+350°F in sunlight) and from the impact of small meteorites. Some space suits have a jet-propelled backpack, which the wearer can use to move about.

Sputnik series of ten Soviet Earth-orbiting satellites. *Sputnik 1* was the first artificial satellite, launched 4 Oct 1957. It weighed 84 kg/185 lb, with a 58 cm/23 in diameter, and carried only a simple radio transmitter which allowed scientists to track it as it orbited Earth. It burned up in the atmosphere 92 days later. Sputniks were superseded in the early 1960s by the Cosmos series.

Telstar US communications satellite, launched 10 July 1962, which relayed the first live television transmissions between the USA and Europe. *Telstar* orbited the Earth in 158 minutes, and so had to be tracked by ground stations, unlike the geostationary satellites of today.

Titan rocket family of US space rockets, developed from the Titan intercontinental missile. Two-stage Titan rockets launched the Gemini crewed missions. More powerful Titans, with additional stages and strap-on boosters, were used to launch spy satellites and space probes, including the *Viking* and *Voyager* probes and *Mars Observer*.

Ulysses space probe to study the Sun's poles, launched 1990 by a US space shuttle. It is a joint project by NASA and the European Space Agency. In Feb 1992, the gravity of Jupiter swung *Ulysses* on to a path that loops it first under the Sun's south pole in 1994 and then over the north pole in 1995 to study the Sun and solar wind at latitudes not observable from the Earth.

Vanguard early series of US Earth-orbiting satellites and their associated rocket launcher. *Vanguard 1* was the second US satellite, launched 17 March 1958 by the three-stage Vanguard rocket. Tracking of its orbit revealed that Earth is slightly pear-shaped. The series ended Sept 1959 with *Vanguard 3*.

The space probe that lived again

In March 1968, the European space probe *Giotto* plunged into the head of Halley's comet, passing 500 km/310 mi from the 'dirty snowball' nucleus, and confounded predictions by emerging in working order. Almost immediately, plans were laid to send it towards another comet, plans which reached fruition in the summer of 1992.

After the Halley encounter, mission controllers at the European Space Operations Centre in Darmstadt, Germany, had commanded *Giotto* into a state of hibernation. It was following a course that would bring it back to the vicinity of the Earth four years later. In July 1990, *Giotto* sped 23,000 km/14,300 mi above the Earth, and the Earth's gravity swung the probe onto a new path towards the comet Grigg-Skjellerup, named after the two astronomers who discovered it earlier this century.

Unlike the big and bright Halley, Grigg-Skjellerup is a small and relatively inactive comet with a nucleus estimated to be no more than about 1 km across, against the 8 × 16 km/5 × 10 mi of Halley. The contrast between the two types of comet would, it was hoped, be instructive.

In May 1992, ground controllers re-established radio contact with the distant probe and began to switch on its various systems. Of the original ten experiments, three were undamaged and another four were partly usable. The biggest loss was the camera, which had been put out of action by the hail of dust particles near Halley's nucleus. Fortunately, the Grigg-Skjellerup encounter would be less dangerous, for the closing speed between the comet and the spacecraft was only 14 km/8.7 mi per second, one-fifth that at Halley.

On 10 July, eight years after launch, *Giotto* duly met its second comet. About 20,000 km/12,500 mi from the nucleus it entered the dusty coma, ten minutes before its closest approach. Shortly after the closest approach, three dust particles hit the spacecraft, the largest estimated to be a few millimetres across. This was in contrast to the heavy battering experienced from Halley.

From their instrument readings, scientists concluded that *Giotto* had passed through the tail of comet Grigg-Skjellerup, passing within 200 km/125 mi of its nucleus, even closer than to the nucleus of Halley. *Giotto* emerged unscathed from its second cometary encounter, but it is unlikely that it will be sent to visit a third comet. It has told scientists much about these frozen vagabonds of the Solar System, and they are now planning new probes that will bring back samples from a comet's nucleus to Earth.

Viking probes two US space probes to Mars, each one consisting of an orbiter and a lander. They were launched 20 Aug and 9 Sept 1975 and touched down about a year later. They transmitted colour pictures and analysed the soil. No definite signs of life were found.

Voskhod Soviet spacecraft used in the mid-1960s; it was modified from the single-seat *Vostok*, and was the first spacecraft capable of carrying two or three cosmonauts. During *Voskhod 2*'s flight 1965, Aleksi Leonov made the first space walk.

Vostok first Soviet spacecraft, used 1961–63. Vostok was a metal sphere 2.3 m/7.5 ft in diameter, capable of carrying one cosmonaut. It made flights lasting up to five days. *Vostok 1* carried the first person into space, Yuri Gagarin (1934–1968).

Voyager probes two US space probes, originally Mariners. *Voyager 1*, launched 5 Sept 1977, passed Jupiter March 1979, and reached Saturn Nov 1980. *Voyager 2* was launched earlier, 20 Aug 1977, on a slower trajectory that took it past Jupiter July 1979, Saturn Aug 1981, Uranus Jan 1986, and Neptune Aug 1989. Like the Pioneer probes, the Voyagers are on their way out of the Solar System. As of mid-1993 *Voyager 1* was 8 billion km/5 billion mi from the Sun, and *Voyager 2* over 6 billion km/3.8 billion mi from the Sun. Their tasks now include helping scientists to locate the position of the heliopause, the boundary at which the influence of the Sun gives way to the forces exerted by other stars.

weightlessness condition in which there is no gravitational force acting on a body, either because gravitational force is cancelled out by equal and opposite acceleration, or because the body is so far outside a planet's gravitational field that it no force is exerted upon it. Astronauts in space, though seemingly 'weightless', do not experience zero gravity because of the motion of their spacecraft.

The Solar System

Apollo asteroid member of a group of asteroids whose orbits cross that of the Earth. They are named after the first of their kind, Apollo, discovered 1932 and then lost until 1973. Apollo asteroids are so small and faint that they are difficult to see except when close to Earth (Apollo is about 2 km/1.2 mi across).

asteroid or ***minor planet*** any of many thousands of small bodies, composed of rock and iron, that orbit the Sun. Most lie in a belt between the orbits of Mars and Jupiter, and are thought to be fragments left over from the formation of the Solar System. About 100,000 may exist, but their total mass is only a few hundredths the mass of the Moon.

aurora coloured light in the night sky near the Earth's magnetic poles, called ***aurora borealis***, 'northern lights', in the northern hemisphere and ***aurora australis*** in the southern hemisphere. An aurora is usually in the form of a luminous arch with its apex towards the magnetic pole followed by arcs, bands, rays, curtains, and coronas, usually green but often showing shades of blue and red, and sometimes yellow or white. Auroras are caused at heights of over 100 km/60 mi by a fast stream of charged particles from solar flares and low-density 'holes' in the Sun's corona. These are guided by the Earth's magnetic field towards the north and south magnetic poles, where they enter the upper atmosphere and bombard the gases in the atmosphere, causing them to emit visible light.

Baily's beads bright spots of sunlight seen around the edge of the Moon for a few seconds immediately before and after a total eclipse of the Sun, caused by sunlight shining between mountains at the Moon's edge. Sometimes one bead is much brighter than the others, producing the so-called ***diamond ring*** effect. The effect was described 1836 by English astronomer Francis Baily (1774–1844).

Callisto the second largest moon of Jupiter, 4,800 km/3,000 mi in diameter, orbiting every 16.7 days at a distance of 1.9 million km/1.2 million mi from the planet. Its surface is covered with large craters.

Ceres the largest asteroid, 940 km/584 mi in diameter, and the first to be discovered (by Italian astronomer Giuseppe Piazzi 1801). Ceres orbits the Sun every 4.6 years at an average distance of 414 million km/257 million mi. Its mass is about one-seventieth of that of the Moon.

Chiron unusual Solar-System object orbiting between Saturn and Uranus, discovered 1977 by US astronomer Charles T Kowal (1940–). Initially classified as an asteroid, it is now believed to be a giant cometary nucleus about 200 km/120 mi across, composed of ice with a dark crust of carbon dust.

chromosphere layer of mostly hydrogen gas about 10,000 km/6,000 mi deep above the visible surface of the Sun (the photosphere). It appears pinkish red during eclipses of the Sun.

comet small, icy body orbiting the Sun, usually on a highly elliptical path. A comet consists of a central nucleus a few kilometres across, and has been likened to a dirty snowball because it consists mostly of ice mixed with dust. As the comet approaches the Sun the nucleus heats up, releasing gas and dust which form a tenuous coma, up to 100,000 km/60,000 mi wide, around the nucleus. Gas and dust stream away from the coma to form one or more tails, which may extend for millions of kilometres. A dozen or more comets are discovered every year.

corona faint halo of hot (about 2,000,000°C/3,600,000°F) and tenuous gas around the Sun, which boils from the surface. It is visible at solar eclipses or through a ***coronagraph***, an instrument that blocks light from the Sun's brilliant disc. Gas flows away from the corona to form the solar wind.

crater bowl-shaped depression, usually round and with steep sides. Craters are formed by explosive events such as the eruption of a volcano or by the impact of a meteorite. The Moon has more than 300,000 craters over 1 km/6 mi in diameter, formed by meteorite bombardment.

crescent curved shape of the Moon when it appears less than half-illuminated.

Deimos one of the two moons of Mars. It is irregularly shaped, 15 × 12 × 11 km/9 × 7.5 × 7 mi, orbits at a height of 24,000 km/15,000 mi every 1.26 days, and is not as heavily cratered as the other moon, Phobos. Deimos was discovered 1877 by US astronomer Asaph Hall (1829–1907), and is thought to be an asteroid captured by Mars's gravity.

Earth the third planet from the Sun. It is almost spherical, flattened slightly at the poles, and is composed of three concentric layers: the core, the mantle, and the crust. 70% of the surface (including the north

Major comets

Name	*First recorded sighting*	*Orbital period (years)*	*Interesting facts*
Halley's comet	240 BC	76	Parent of Eta Aquarid and Orionid meteor showers
Comet Tempel-Tuttle	AD 1366	33	Parent of Leonid meteors
Biela's comet	1772	6.6	Broke in half 1846; not seen since 1852
Encke's comet	1786	3.3	Parent of Taurid meteors
Comet Swift-Tuttle	1862	130	Parent of Perseid meteors; reappeared 1992
Comet Ikeya-Seki	1965	880	So-called 'Sun-grazing' comet, passed 500, 000 km/300,000 mi above surface of Sun on 21 Oct 1965
Comet Kohoutek	1973		Observed from space by *Skylab* astronauts; period too long to calculate accurately
Comet West	1975	500,000	Nucleus broke into four parts
Comet Bowell	1980		Ejected from Solar System after close encounter with Jupiter
Comet IRAS-Araki-Alcock	1983		Passed only 4.5 million km/2.8 million mi from Earth on 11 May 1983; period too long to calculate accurately
Comet Austin	1989		Passed 32 million km/20 million mi from Earth 1990

Smiley and Karla are out in the cold

Where do comets come from? In 1992 and 1993, astronomers caught their first glimpses of a previously unseen ring of comets beyond the outermost planets. The discovery of this comet belt finally lays to rest all hopes of finding a tenth planet beyond Pluto.

Since 1950 it has been accepted that there is a vast store of billions upon billions of comets at the edge of the Solar System, extending partway to the nearest star. This cometary store is called the Oort cloud, after the Dutch astronomer Jan Oort who proposed its existence, and it accounts very well for comets that approach the Sun on highly elongated orbits that take millions of years to complete.

But there is also a group of comets on much shorter orbits, reappearing every couple of centuries or less, and these comets are thought to come from a closer source, just beyond the outermost planet, Pluto. This inner band of comets is termed the Kuiper belt after Gerard Kuiper, a Dutch-US astronomer who proposed its existence in 1951.

For the past four decades the reality of this belt has been a debating point for theorists – that is, until 30 August 1992, when David Jewitt and Jane Luu spotted a faint, slow-moving object using a 2.2-m/7-ft telescope on Mauna Kea in Hawaii. Calculations showed that the new object lay about a billion kilometres beyond Pluto – exactly where the Kuiper belt was expected to be. Officially, it was labelled 1992 QB1, but Jewitt and Luu nicknamed it Smiley, after the spymaster in the novels of John le Carré. Its estimated diameter is about 200 km/125 mi.

Seven months later, in March 1993, they found another such object at a similar distance, officially, catalogued as 1993 FW but nicknamed Karla after John le Carré's fictional East German spymaster. Probably there are countless millions of these cometlike objects orbiting unseen in the icy darkness, consisting of material left over from the formation of the planets.

The outer planets of the Solar System are thought to have been built up from objects like those in the Kuiper belt. The existence of the Kuiper belt of comets shows that planetary formation stopped at Pluto.

and south polar icecaps) is covered with water. The Earth is surrounded by a life-supporting atmosphere and is the only planet on which life is known to exist.

mean distance from the Sun 149,500,000 km/ 92,860,000 mi.

equatorial diameter 12,756 km/7,923 mi.

circumference 40,070 km/24,900 mi.

rotation period 23 hr 56 min 4.1 sec.

year (complete orbit, or sidereal period) 365 days 5 hr 48 min 46 sec. Earth's average speed around the Sun is 30 kps/18.5 mps; the plane of its orbit is inclined to its equatorial plane at an angle of 23.5°, the reason for the changing seasons.

atmosphere nitrogen 78.09%; oxygen 20.95%; argon 0.93%; carbon dioxide 0.03%; and less than 0.0001% neon, helium, krypton, hydrogen, xenon, ozone, radon.

surface land surface 150,000,000 sq km/57,500,000 sq mi (greatest height above sea level 8,872 m/ 29,118 ft Mount Everest); water surface 361,000,000 sq km/139,400,000 sq mi (greatest depth 11,034 m/ 36,201 ft Mariana Trench in the Pacific). The interior is thought to be an inner core about 2,600 km/1,600 mi in diameter, of solid iron and nickel; an outer core about 2,250 km/1,400 mi thick, of molten iron and nickel; and a mantle of mostly solid rock about 2,900 km/1,800 mi thick, separated by the Mohorovičić discontinuity from the Earth's crust. The crust and the topmost layer of the mantle form about 12 major moving plates, some of which carry the continents. The plates are in constant, slow motion, called tectonic drift.

satellite the Moon.

age 4.6 billion years. The Earth was formed with the rest of the Solar System by consolidation of interstellar dust. Life began about 3.5 billion years ago.

eclipse passage of an astronomical body through the shadow of another. The term is usually employed for solar and lunar eclipses, which may be either partial or total, but also, for example, for eclipses by Jupiter of its satellites. An eclipse of a star by a body in the Solar System is called an occultation. A ***solar eclipse*** occurs when the Moon passes in front of the Sun as seen from Earth, and can happen only at new Moon. A total solar eclipse can last up to 7.5 minutes. Between two and five solar eclipses occur each year. A ***lunar eclipse*** occurs when the Moon passes into the shadow of the Earth, becoming dim until emerging from the shadow. Lunar eclipses may be partial or total, and they can happen only at full Moon. Total lunar eclipses last for up to 100 minutes; the maximum number each year is three.

Encke's comet comet with the shortest known orbital period, 3.3 years. It is named after German mathematician and astronomer Johann Franz Encke (1791–1865), who calculated its orbit in 1819 from earlier sightings.

Eros the first asteroid to be discovered (1898) that has an orbit coming within that of Mars. It can pass 22 million km/14 million mi from the Earth, as

Solar and lunar eclipses until 2000*

Date	Type of eclipse	Time of maximum eclipse (UT)	Main area of visibility
1994			
10 May	Sun annular	17h 12m	North and Central America
3 November	Sun total	13h 40m	South America, southern Africa
1995			
29 April	Sun annular	17h 33m	South and Central America
24 October	Sun total	04h 33m	India, SE Asia, Oceania, northern Australia
1996			
3/4 April	Moon total	00h 10m	Eastern North America, Central and South America, Europe, Africa, western Asia
17 April	Sun partial	22h 38m	New Zealand, southern Pacific Ocean
27 September	Moon total	02h 54m	The Americas, Europe, Africa, western Asia
12 October	Sun partial	14h 03m	NE Canada, Greenland, western Europe, North Africa
1997			
9 March	Sun total	01h 25m	E Asia, Japan
1/2 September	Sun partial	00h 05m	Australia, New Zealand
16 September	Moon total	18h 47m	Europe, Africa, Asia, Australasia
1998			
26 February	Sun total	17h 29m	S and E USA, Central America, northern South America
22 August	Sun annular	02h 07m	SE Asia, Oceania, Australasia
1999			
16 February	Sun annular	06h 35m	Southern Indian Ocean, Antarctica, Australia
11 August	Sun total	11h 04m	Europe, North Africa, Arabia, western Asia
2000			
21 January	Moon total	04h 44m	The Americas, Europe, Africa, western Asia
5 February	Sun partial	12h 50m	Antarctica
1 July	Sun partial	19h 34m	SE Pacific Ocean
16 July	Moon total	13h 56m	SE Asia, Australasia
31 July	Sun partial	02h 14m	Arctic regions
25 December	Sun partial	17h 36m	USA, eastern Canada, Central America, Caribbean

* Except partial eclipses of the Moon

observed in 1975. It measures about 36 × 12 km/22 × 7 mi and orbits the Sun every 1.8 years.

Europa the fourth largest moon of the planet Jupiter, diameter 3,140 km/1,950 mi, orbiting 671,000 km/417,000 mi from the planet every 3.55 days. It is covered by ice and criss-crossed by thousands of thin cracks, each some 50,000 km/30,000 mi long.

Ganymede the largest moon of the planet Jupiter, and the largest moon in the Solar System, 5,260 km/3,270 mi in diameter (larger than the planet Mercury). It orbits Jupiter every 7.2 days at a distance of 1.1 million km/700,000 mi. Its surface is a mixture of cratered and grooved terrain.

Halley's comet comet that orbits the Sun about every 76 years, named after English scientist Edmund Halley (1656–1742), who calculated its orbit. It is the brightest and most conspicuous of the periodic comets. Recorded sightings go back over 2,000 years. It travels around the Sun in the opposite direction to the planets. Its orbit is inclined at almost 20° to the main plane of the Solar System and ranges between the orbits of Venus and Neptune. It will next reappear 2061.

heliosphere region of space through which the solar wind flows outwards from the Sun. The ***heliopause*** is the boundary of this region, believed to lie about 100 astronomical units from the Sun, where the flow of the solar wind merges with the interstellar gas.

Icarus Apollo asteroid 1.5 km/1 mi in diameter, discovered 1949. It orbits the Sun every 409 days at a distance of 28–300 million km/18–186 million mi (0.19–2.0 astronomical units). It was the first asteroid known to approach the Sun closer than does the planet Mercury. In 1968 it passed 6 million km/4 million mi from the Earth.

inferior planet planet (Mercury or Venus) whose orbit lies within that of the Earth, best observed when at its greatest elongation from the Sun, either at eastern elongation in the evening (setting after the Sun) or at western elongation in the morning (rising before the Sun).

interplanetary matter gas and dust thinly spread through the Solar System. The gas flows outwards from the Sun as the solar wind. Fine dust lies in the plane of the Solar System, scattering sunlight to cause the zodiacal light. Swarms of dust shed by comets enter the Earth's atmosphere to cause meteor showers.

Io the third largest moon of the planet Jupiter, 3,630 km/2,260 mi in diameter, orbiting in 1.77 days at a distance of 422,000 km/262,000 mi. It is the most volcanically active body in the Solar System, covered by hundreds of vents that erupt not lava but sulphur, giving Io an orange-coloured surface.

Jupiter the fifth planet from the Sun, and the largest in the Solar System (equatorial diameter 142,800 km/88,700 mi), with a mass more than twice that of all the other planets combined, 318 times that of the Earth's. It takes 11.86 years to orbit the Sun, at an average distance of 778 million km/484 million mi, and has at least 16 moons. It is largely composed of hydrogen and helium, liquefied by pressure in its interior, and probably with a rocky core larger than the Earth. Its main feature is the Great Red Spot, a cloud of rising gases, revolving anticlockwise, 14,000 km/8,500 mi wide and some 30,000 km/ 20,000 mi long.

Kuiper belt a ring of small, icy bodies orbiting the Sun beyond the outermost planet. The Kuiper belt, named after the American astronomer Gerard Kuiper who proposed its existence in 1951, is thought to be the source of comets that orbit the Sun with periods of less than 200 years.

The first member of the Kuiper belt was seen in 1992.

Lagrangian points five locations in space where the centrifugal and gravitational forces of two bodies neutralize each other; a third, less massive body located at any one of these points will be held in equilibrium with respect to the other two. Three of the points, L1–L3, lie on a line joining the two large bodies. The other two points, L4 and L5, which are the most stable, lie on either side of this line. Their existence was predicted in 1772 by French mathematician Joseph Louis Lagrange (1736–1813).

magnetosphere volume of space surrounding a planet, controlled by the planet's magnetic field and acting as a magnetic 'shell'. The Earth's magnetosphere extends 64,000 km/40,000 mi towards the Sun, but many times this distance on the side away from the Sun.

mare (plural ***maria***) dark lowland plain on the Moon. The name comes from Latin 'sea', because these areas were once wrongly thought to be water.

Mars the fourth planet from the Sun, average distance 227.9 million km/141.6 million mi. It revolves around the Sun in 687 Earth days, and has a rotation period of 24 hr 37 min. It is much smaller than Venus or Earth, with a diameter 6,780 km/4,210 mi, and mass 0.11 that of Earth. Mars is slightly pearshaped, with a low, level northern hemisphere, which is comparatively uncratered and geologically 'young', and a heavily cratered 'ancient' southern hemisphere.

Mercury the closest planet to the Sun, at an average distance of 58 million km/36 million mi. Its diameter is 4,880 km/3,030 mi, its mass 0.056 that of Earth. Mercury orbits the Sun every 88 days, and spins on its axis every 59 days. On its sunward side the surface temperature reaches over 400°C/752°F, but on the 'night' side it falls to –170°C/–274°F. Mercury has an atmosphere with minute traces of argon and helium; it has no moons.

meteor flash of light in the sky, popularly known as a ***shooting*** or ***falling star***, caused by a particle of dust, a ***meteoroid***, entering the atmosphere at speeds up to 70 kps/45 mps and burning up by friction at a height of around 100 km/60 mi. On any clear night, several ***sporadic meteors*** can be seen each hour; more than 500,000 meteors visible to the naked eye burn up in Earth's atmosphere every day.

meteorite piece of rock or metal from space that reaches the surface of the Earth, Moon, or other body. Most meteorites are thought to be fragments from asteroids, although some may be pieces from the heads of comets. Most are stony, although some are made of iron and a few have a mixed rock-iron composition. Meteorites provide evidence for the nature of the Solar System and may be similar to the Earth's core and mantle, neither of which can be observed directly. The Earth sweeps up an estimated 16,000 tonnes of meteoric material every year.

moon any natural satellite that orbits a planet. Mercury and Venus are the only planets in the Solar System that do not have moons.

Moon the natural satellite of Earth, 3,476 km/2,160 mi in diameter, with a mass 0.012 (approximately one-eightieth) that of Earth. Its surface gravity is only 0.16 (one-sixth) that of Earth. Its average distance from Earth is 384,400 km/238,855 mi, and it orbits in a west-to-east direction every 27.32 days (the ***sidereal month***). It spins on its axis with one side permanently turned towards Earth. The Moon has no atmosphere or water.

Neptune the eighth planet in average distance from the Sun. Neptune orbits the Sun every 164.8 years at an average distance of 4.497 billion km/2.794 billion mi. It is a giant gas (hydrogen, helium, methane) planet, with a diameter of 48,600 km/30,200 mi and a mass 17.2 times that of Earth. Its rotation period is 16 hours 7 minutes. The methane in its atmosphere absorbs red light and gives the planet a blue colouring. It is believed to have a central rocky core covered by a layer of ice. Neptune has eight known moons.

occultation temporary obscuring of a star by a body in the Solar System. Occultations are used to provide information about changes in an orbit, and the structure of objects in space, such as radio sources.

Oort cloud spherical cloud of comets beyond Pluto, extending out to about 100,000 astronomical units (1.5 light years) from the Sun. The gravitational effect of passing stars and the rest of our Galaxy disturbs comets from the cloud so that they fall in towards the Sun on highly elongated orbits, becoming visible from Earth. As many as 10 trillion comets may reside in the Oort cloud, named after Dutch astronomer Jan Oort (1900–1992) who postulated it 1950.

Phobos one of the two moons of Mars, discovered 1877 by US astronomer Asaph Hall (1829–1907). It is an irregularly shaped lump of rock, cratered by meteorite impacts. Phobos is 27 × 22 × 19 km/17 × 13 × 12 mi across, and orbits Mars every 0.32 days at a distance of 9,400 km/5,840 mi from the planet's centre. It is thought to be an asteroid captured by Mars's gravity.

photosphere visible surface of the Sun, which emits light and heat. About 300 km/200 mi deep, it consists of incandescent gas at a temperature of 5,800K (5,530°C/9,980°F).

planet large celestial body in orbit around a star, composed of rock, metal, or gas. There are nine plan-

Planets

Planet	*Main constituents*	*Atmosphere*	*Average distance from Sun in millions of km*	*Time for one orbit in Earth-years*	*Diameter in thousands of km*	*Average density if density of water is 1 unit*
Mercury	rocky, ferrous	–	58	0.241	4.88	5.4
Venus	rocky, ferrous	carbon dioxide	108	0.615	12.10	5.2
Earth	rocky, ferrous	nitrogen, oxygen	150	1.00	12.76	5.5
Mars	rocky	carbon dioxide	228	1.88	6.78	3.9
Jupiter	liquid hydrogen, helium	–	778	11.86	142.80	1.3
Saturn	hydrogen, helium	–	1,427	29.46	120.00	0.7
Uranus	icy, hydrogen, helium	hydrogen, helium	2,870	84.00	50.80	1.3
Neptune	icy, hydrogen, helium	hydrogen, helium	4,497	164.80	48.60	1.8
Pluto	icy, rocky	methane	5,900	248.50	2.25	about 2

ets in the solar system: Mercury, Venus, Earth, Mars, Jupiter, Saturn, Neptune, Uranus, and Pluto. The inner four, called the ***terrestrial planets***, are small and rocky, and include the planet Earth. The outer planets, with the exception of Pluto, are called the giant planets, large balls of rock, liquid, and gas; the largest is Jupiter, which contains more than twice as much mass as all the other planets combined. Planets do not produce light, but reflect the light of their parent star.

Pluto the smallest and, usually, outermost planet of the Solar System. The existence of Pluto was predicted by calculation by Percival Lowell and the planet was located by Clyde Tombaugh in 1930. It orbits the Sun every 248.5 years at an average distance of 5.8 billion km/3.6 billion mi. Its highly elliptical orbit occasionally takes it within the orbit of Neptune, as in 1979–99. Pluto has a diameter of about 2,300 km/1,400 mi, and a mass about 0.002 of that of Earth. It is of low density, composed of rock and ice, with frozen methane on its surface and a thin atmosphere. It has one moon, Charon, half its own diameter.

prominence bright cloud of gas projecting from the Sun into space 100,000 km/60,000 mi or more. ***Quiescent prominences*** last for months, and are held in place by magnetic fields in the Sun's corona. ***Surge prominences*** shoot gas into space at speeds of 1,000 kps/600 mps. ***Loop prominences*** are gases falling back to the Sun's surface after a solar flare.

satellite any small body that orbits a larger one, either natural or artificial. Natural satellites that orbit planets are called moons. The first ***artificial satellite***, *Sputnik 1*, was launched into orbit around the Earth by the USSR 1957. Artificial satellites are used for scientific purposes, communications, weather forecasting, and military applications. The largest artificial satellites can be seen by the naked eye.

Saturn the second-largest planet in the Solar System, sixth from the Sun, and encircled by bright and easily visible equatorial rings. Viewed through a telescope it is ochre. Saturn orbits the Sun every 29.46 years at an average distance of 1,427,000,000 km/886,700,000 mi. Its equatorial diameter is 120,000 km/ 75,000 mi, but its polar diameter is 12,000 km/7,450 mi smaller, a result of its fast rotation and low density, the lowest of any planet. Saturn spins on its axis every 10 hours 14 minutes at its equator, slowing to 10 hours 40 minutes at high latitudes. Its mass is 95 times that of Earth, and its magnetic field 1,000 times stronger. Saturn is believed to have a small core of rock and iron, encased in ice and topped by a deep layer of liquid hydrogen. There are 18 known moons, its largest being Titan. The rings visible from Earth begin about 14,000 km/ 9,000 mi from the planet's cloudtops and extend out to about 76,000 km/47,000 mi. Made of small chunks of ice and rock (averaging 1 m/3 ft across), they are 275,000 km/170,000 mi rim to rim, but only 100 m/ 300 ft thick. The Voyager probes showed that the rings actually consist of thousands of closely spaced ringlets, looking like the grooves in a gramophone record.

solar flare brilliant eruption on the Sun above a sunspot, thought to be caused by release of magnetic energy. Flares reach maximum brightness within a few minutes, then fade away over about an hour. They eject a burst of atomic particles into space at up to 1,000 kps/600 mps. When these particles reach Earth they can cause radio blackouts, disruptions of the Earth's magnetic field, and auroras.

solar spicules short-lived jets of hot gas in the upper chromosphere of the Sun. Spiky in appearance, they move at high velocities along lines of magnetic force to which they owe their shape, and last for a few minutes each. Spicules appear to disperse material into the corona.

Solar System the Sun (a star) and all the bodies orbiting it: the nine planets (Mercury, Venus, Earth, Mars, Jupiter, Saturn, Uranus, Neptune, and Pluto), their moons, the asteroids, and the comets. It is thought to have formed from a cloud of gas and dust in space about 4.6 billion years ago. The Sun contains 99% of the mass of the Solar System.

solar wind stream of atomic particles, mostly protons and electrons, from the Sun's corona, flowing outwards at speeds of between 300 kps/200 mps and 1,000 kps/600 mps.

Sun the star at the centre of the Solar System. Its diameter is 1,392,000 km/865,000 mi; its temperature at the surface is about 5,800K (5,530°C/9,980°F), and at the centre 15,000,000K (15,000,000°C/27,000,000°F). It is composed of about 70% hydrogen and 30% helium,

Largest natural planetary satellites

Planet	*Satellite*	*Diameter in km*	*Mean distance from centre of primary in km*	*Orbital period in days*	*Reciprocal mass (planet = 1)*
Jupiter	Ganymede	5,262	1,070,000	7.16	12,800
Saturn	Titan	5,150	1,221,800	15.95	4,200
Jupiter	Callisto	4,800	1,883,000	16.69	17,700
Jupiter	Io	3,630	421,600	1.77	21,400
Earth	Moon	3,476	384,400	27.32	81.3
Jupiter	Europa	3,138	670,900	3.55	39,700
Neptune	Triton	2,700	354,300	5.88	770

with other elements making up less than 1%. The Sun's energy is generated by nuclear fusion reactions that turn hydrogen into helium at its centre. The gas core is far denser than mercury or lead on Earth. The Sun is about 4.7 billion years old, with a predicted lifetime of 10 billion years.

sunspot dark patch on the surface of the Sun, actually an area of cooler gas, thought to be caused by strong magnetic fields that block the outward flow of heat to the Sun's surface. Sunspots consist of a dark central ***umbra***, about 4,000K (3,700°C/6,700°F), and a lighter surrounding ***penumbra***, about 5,500K (5,200°C/9,400°F). They last from several days to over a month, ranging in size from 2,000 km/1,250 mi to groups stretching for over 100,000 km/62,000 mi. The number of sunspots visible at a given time varies from none to over 100 in a cycle averaging 11 years.

superior planet planet that is farther away from the Sun than the Earth is; that is, Mars, Jupiter, Saturn, Uranus, Neptune, and Pluto.

tektite small, rounded, glassy stone, found in certain regions of the Earth, such as Australasia. Tektites are probably the scattered drops of molten rock thrown out by the impact of a large meteorite.

Titan the largest moon of the planet Saturn, with a diameter of 5,150 km/3,200 mi and a mean distance from Saturn of 1,222,000 km/759,000 mi. It is the second largest moon in the Solar System (Ganymede, of Jupiter, is larger), and the only moon in the Solar System with a substantial atmosphere (mostly nitrogen).

Uranus the seventh planet from the Sun, discovered by William Herschel 1781. It is twice as far out as the sixth planet, Saturn. Uranus has a diameter of 50,800 km/31,600 mi and a mass 14.5 times that of Earth. It orbits the Sun in 84 years at an average distance of 2.9 billion km/1.8 billion mi. The spin axis of Uranus is tilted at 98°, so that one pole points towards the Sun, giving extreme seasons. It has 15 moons, and thin rings around its equator.

Venus the second planet from the Sun. It orbits the Sun every 225 days at an average distance of 108.2 million km/67.2 million mi and can approach the Earth to within 38 million km/24 million mi, closer than any other planet. Its diameter is 12,100 km/7,500 mi and its mass is 0.82 that of Earth. Venus rotates on its axis more slowly than any other planet, once every 243 days and from east to west, the opposite direction to the other planets (except Uranus and possibly Pluto). Venus is shrouded by clouds of sulphuric acid droplets that sweep across the planet from east to west every four days. The atmosphere is almost entirely carbon dioxide, which traps the Sun's heat by the greenhouse effect and raises the planet's surface temperature to 480°C/900°F, with an atmospheric pressure of 90 times that at the surface of the Earth.

zodiacal light cone-shaped light sometimes seen extending from the Sun along the ecliptic, visible after sunset or before sunrise. It is due to thinly spread dust particles in the central plane of the Solar System. It is very faint, and requires a dark, clear sky to be seen.

Stars, Galaxies, and the Universe

Algol or ***Beta Persei*** eclipsing binary, a pair of rotating stars in the constellation Perseus, one of which eclipses the other every 69 hours, causing its brightness to drop by two-thirds.

Alpha Centauri or ***Rigil Kent*** brightest star in the constellation Centaurus and the third brightest star in the sky. It is actually a triple star: three stars orbiting round their common centre of mass. The two brighter stars orbit each other every 80 years, and the third, Proxima Centauri, is the closest star to the Sun, 4.2 light years away, 0.1 light years closer than the other two.

Andromeda galaxy galaxy 2.2 million light years away from Earth in the constellation Andromeda, and the most distant object visible to the naked eye. It is the largest member of the Local Group of galaxies. Like the Milky Way, it is a spiral orbited by several companion galaxies but contains about twice as many stars. It is about 200,000 light years across.

Barnard's star second closest star to the Sun, six light years away in the constellation Ophiuchus. It is a faint red dwarf of 10th magnitude, visible only through a telescope. It is named after US astronomer Edward E Barnard (1857–1923), who discovered 1916 that it has the fastest proper motion of any star, crossing 1 degree of sky every 350 years.

Big Bang the hypothetical 'explosive' event that marked the origin of the universe as we know it. At the time of the Big Bang, the entire universe was squeezed into a hot, superdense state. The Big Bang explosion threw this compacted material outwards, producing the expanding universe. The cause of the Big Bang is unknown; observations of the current

The Comet of Doom and the search for ET

Comet sightings do not usually make headlines. At least two dozen are seen every year, about half of them reappearances of known objects. However, Comet Swift-Tuttle created a stir in 1992 when astronomers calculated that it might hit the Earth in August 2126. Newspapers christened it the Comet of Doom and announced the end of the world. Fortunately, the truth is not so alarming.

The comet was discovered in 1862 by US astronomers Lewis Swift and Horace Tuttle. Like all comets, it goes round the Sun in an elliptical orbit that regularly brings it back into view. It was expected to reappear around 1982 but, despite careful searches, nothing was seen. Was it lost or simply late?

Careful work by Dr Brian Marsden of the Harvard-Smithsonian Center for Astrophysics, Cambridge, Massachusetts, showed that the comet was probably the same as one seen in 1737. If so, its orbital period was nearer 130 years than the 120 previously calculated, so it would not return until late 1992.

The wanderer returns

Evidence of Swift-Tuttle's return came from observations of a shower of meteors (shooting stars) caused by dust in the comet's orbit. Visible in August every year, they are known as the Perseids, because they seem to radiate from the constellation Perseus. Amateur astronomers have recorded increasing numbers of Perseids over recent years, fuelling speculation that their parent comet was near.

In September 1992, Japanese comet hunter Tsuruhiko Kiuchi spotted a faint comet near the Big Dipper. Its direction of motion gave it away as Comet Swift-Tuttle, returning as predicted by Marsden. The ten-year hunt was over.

Swift-Tuttle's orbit was difficult to calculate because jets of gas and dust, escaping from its central nucleus, push the comet off course like little rockets. New calculations by Marsden showed that if the comet were only two weeks later than expected next time round – not much, given the ten-year error this time – then the comet would strike in August 2126, during the Perseid meteor shower.

The consequences would be disastrous. The Earth would be shrouded in dust and water vapour, changing the climate and bringing famine to those parts that had escaped the earthquakes, tidal waves, and fires from the initial cometary strike. The death of the dinosaurs is believed to have resulted from a similar impact 65 million years ago; next time, it would be us that faced extinction.

So astronomers watched Comet Swift-Tuttle's passage round the Sun in 1992 with close interest. Analysis of these observations will help astronomers decide whether the comet could hit us on its next orbit or whether, as seems likely, the Comet of Doom is just another scare story.

NASA listens for extraterrestrials

In Steven Spielberg's film *ET*, the extraterrestrial landed on Earth and then tried to phone home. Perhaps he should have phoned Earth before setting out; radio communication is easier than interstellar travel. That is the thinking behind NASA's search for extraterrestrial intelligence, which started on 12 October 1992, the 500th anniversary of Columbus' arrival in America.

NASA's survey uses two approaches. In an all-sky survey, radio telescopes will listen in all directions for signals at frequencies with least background noise, between 1,000 and 10,000 megahertz. The survey began with the 34-m/111-ft radio dish of NASA's Goldstone tracking station in California; the southern sky will be covered later by a similar dish at Canberra, Australia.

A targeted search will listen to a thousand stars like the Sun within 100 light-years' distance, using large radio telescopes worldwide. First observations were made with the world's largest radio dish, the 305-m/1,000-ft radio telescope at Arecibo, Puerto Rico.

The targeted search can pick up fainter signals, but might miss a transmission from some unexpected source, which the all-sky survey would pick up. The all-sky survey is less sensitive and might miss faint signals from a nearby star, which the targeted search would hear. Sophisticated electronics have been developed to recognize a genuine alien message while filtering out terrestrial interference.

Is there anybody there?

No previous attempt to pick up alien radio messages has been as comprehensive. 'In the first few minutes, more searching will be accomplished than in all previous searches combined,' said John Billingham at NASA's Ames Research Center in California.

If a seemingly artificial signal is detected, the searchers will notify other radio observatories worldwide to check the discovery. If it is genuine rather than a false alarm, the world will be told. No attempt will be made to answer except by international agreement.

If the search succeeds, says Carl Sagan, 'we will have transformed our civilization and our concept of ourselves forever'; if nothing is heard, that will reveal 'something about the rarity and preciousness of life on our planet.' The survey will probably continue for ten years at a total cost of around $100 million. By early next century, we may know whether or not we are alone.

IR

rate of expansion of the universe suggest that it took place about 10 to 20 billion years ago. The Big Bang theory began modern cosmology.

binary star pair of stars moving in orbit around their common centre of mass. Observations show that most stars are binary, or even multiple; for example, the nearest star system to the Sun, Alpha Centauri.

black hole object in space whose gravity is so great that nothing can escape from it, not even light. Thought to form when massive stars shrink at the ends of their lives, a black hole sucks in more matter, including other stars, from the space around it. Matter that falls into a black hole is squeezed to infinite density at the centre of the hole. Black holes can be detected because gas falling towards them becomes so hot that it emits X-rays. Four have been identified in our Galaxy.

brown dwarf hypothetical object less massive than a star, but heavier than a planet. Brown dwarfs would not have enough mass to ignite nuclear reactions at their centres, but would shine by heat released during their contraction from a gas cloud. Because of the difficulty of detection, no brown dwarfs have been spotted with certainty, but some astronomers believe that vast numbers of them may exist throughout the Galaxy.

Cepheid variable yellow supergiant star that varies regularly in brightness every few days or weeks as a result of pulsations. The time that a Cepheid variable takes to pulsate is directly related to its average brightness; the longer the pulsation period, the brighter the star.

constellation one of the 88 areas into which the sky is divided for the purposes of identifying and naming celestial objects. The first constellations were simple, arbitrary patterns of stars in which early civilizations visualized gods, sacred beasts, and mythical heroes.

cosmic background radiation or *3° radiation* electromagnetic radiation left over from the original formation of the universe in the Big Bang around 15 billion years ago. It corresponds to an overall background temperature of 3K (–270°C/–454°F), or 3°C above absolute zero. In 1992 the Cosmic Background Explorer satellite, COBE, detected slight ripples in the strength of the background radiation that are believed to mark the first stage in the formation of galaxies.

dark matter hypothetical matter that, according to current theories of cosmology, makes up 90–99% of the mass of the universe but so far remains undetected.

double star two stars that appear close together. Most double stars attract each other through gravity, and orbit each other, forming a genuine binary star, but other double stars are at different distances from Earth, and lie in the same line of sight only by chance. Through a telescope both types of double star look the same.

eclipsing binary binary (double) star in which the two stars periodically pass in front of each other as seen from Earth.

galaxy congregation of millions or billions of stars, held together by gravity. ***Spiral galaxies***, such as the Milky Way, are flattened in shape, with a central bulge of old stars surrounded by a disc of younger stars, arranged in spiral arms like a Catherine wheel. ***Barred spirals*** are spiral galaxies that have a straight bar of stars across their centre, from the ends of which the spiral arms emerge. The arms of spiral galaxies contain gas and dust from which new stars are still forming. ***Elliptical galaxies*** contain old stars and very little gas. They include the most massive galaxies known, containing a trillion stars. At least some elliptical galaxies are thought to be formed by mergers between spiral galaxies. There are also irregular galaxies. Most galaxies occur in clusters, containing anything from a few to thousands of members.

globular cluster spherical or near–spherical star cluster containing from approximately 10,000 to millions of stars. More than a hundred globular clusters are distributed in a spherical halo around our Galaxy. They consist of old stars, formed early in the Galaxy's history. Globular clusters are also found around other galaxies.

interstellar molecules over 50 different types of molecule existing in gas clouds in our Galaxy. Most have been detected by their radio emissions, but some have been found by the absorption lines they produce in the spectra of starlight. The most complex molecules, many of them based on carbon, are found in the dense clouds where stars are forming. They may be significant for the origin of life elsewhere in space.

Local Group cluster of about 30 galaxies that includes our own, the Milky Way. Like other groups of galaxies, the Local Group is held together by the gravitational attraction among its members, and does not expand with the expanding universe. Its two largest galaxies are the Milky Way and the Andromeda galaxy; most of the others are small and faint.

Magellanic Clouds the two galaxies nearest to our own Galaxy. They are irregularly shaped, and appear as detached parts of the Milky Way, in the southern constellations Dorado and Tucana.

Milky Way faint band of light crossing the night sky, consisting of stars in the plane of our Galaxy. The name Milky Way is often used for the Galaxy itself. It is a spiral galaxy, about 100,000 light years in diameter, containing at least 100 billion stars. The Sun is in one of its spiral arms, about 25,000 light years from the centre.

Mira or ***Omicron Ceti*** the brightest long-period pulsating variable star, located in the constellation Cetus. Mira was the first star discovered to vary periodically in brightness.

nebula (plural ***nebulae***) cloud of gas and dust in space. Nebulae are the birthplaces of stars, but some (planetary) nebulae are produced by gas thrown off from dying stars. Nebulae are classified depending on whether they emit, reflect, or absorb light.

An ***emission nebula***, such as the Orion nebula, glows brightly because its gas is energized by stars that have formed within it. In a ***reflection nebula***, starlight reflects off grains of dust in the nebula, such as surround the stars of the Pleiades cluster. A ***dark nebula*** is a dense cloud, composed of molecular hydrogen, which partially or completely absorbs light behind it. Examples include the Coalsack nebula in Crux and the Horsehead nebula in Orion.

Going out with a bang

Astronomers excitedly turned their telescopes towards an exploding star, a supernova, that erupted in a nearby galaxy in March 1993, marking the dramatic death of a formerly massive star. Supernovae are important because, in their thermonuclear eruptions, they produce the chemical elements from which planets and life can form. In fact, the atoms of our bodies were produced by supernovae that erupted before our Sun was born.

This new supernova was spotted on 28 March by a Spanish amateur astronomer, Francisco García, who immediately alerted professionals. The supernova, labelled 1993J, occurred in the spiral galaxy M81, about 10 million light years away in the constellation Ursa Major.

Because of the early warning and the relative closeness of the galaxy, astronomers regarded it as the second most important supernova of the century, beaten only by supernova 1987A, which was too far south to be seen from most observatories in the northern hemisphere.

M81 is so close that astronomers were able to identify the star that exploded from photographs of M81 taken before the outburst. As predicted by theories of stellar evolution, it turned out to have been a large and brilliant star that had swollen up into a red supergiant, bigger even than the size of the Earth's orbit.

'It's a very exciting result and a tremendous advance for stellar astronomy,' said Dr George Sonneborn, of NASA's Goddard Space Flight Center, Greenbelt, Maryland. 'It has long been suspected that red supergiants explode to become supernovae. Now we have first-hand evidence of that.' Photographs in archives will help astronomers study the behaviour of this star before it exploded.

Over the next few nights after its discovery the supernova brightened rapidly before beginning its slow and irregular fade back to obscurity. As it fades, there is one other prediction that supernova 1993J can help verify. According to the theory, a supernova explosion should leave behind a pulsar or a black hole. Astronomers will be watching with interest to see what appears as the debris clears.

neutron star very small, superdense star composed mostly of neutrons. They are thought to form when massive stars explode as supernovae, during which the protons and electrons of the star's atoms merge, owing to intense gravitational collapse, to make neutrons. A neutron star may have the mass of up to three Suns, compressed into a globe only 20 km/12 mi in diameter. If its mass is any greater, its gravity will be so strong that it will shrink even further to become a black hole. Being so small, neutron stars can spin very quickly. The rapidly flashing radio stars called pulsars are believed to be neutron stars. The flashing is caused by a rotating beam of radio energy similar in behaviour to a lighthouse beam of light.

nova (plural ***novae***) faint star that suddenly erupts in brightness by 10,000 times or more. Novae are believed to occur in close binary star systems, where gas from one star flows to a companion white dwarf. The gas ignites and is thrown off in an explosion at speeds of 1,500 kps/930 mps or more. Unlike a supernova, the star is not completely disrupted by the outburst. After a few weeks or months it subsides to its previous state; it may erupt many more times.

Olbers' paradox question put forward 1826 by German astronomer Heinrich Olbers (1758–1840), who asked: If the universe is infinite in extent and filled with stars, why is the sky dark at night? The answer is that the stars do not live infinitely long, so there is not enough starlight to fill the universe. A wrong answer, frequently given, is that the expansion of the universe weakens the starlight.

oscillating universe theory that states that the gravitational attraction of the mass within the universe will eventually slow down and stop the expansion of the universe. The outward motions of the galaxies will then be reversed, eventually resulting in a 'Big Crunch' where all the matter in the universe would be contracted into a small volume of high density. This could undergo a further Big Bang, thereby creating another expansion phase. The theory suggests that the universe would alternately expand and collapse through alternate Big Bangs and Big Crunches.

planetary nebula shell of gas thrown off by a star at the end of its life. Planetary nebulae have nothing to do with planets. They were named by William Herschel, who thought their rounded shape resembled the disc of a planet. After a star such as the Sun has expanded to become a red giant, its outer layers are ejected into space to form a planetary nebula, leaving the core as a white dwarf at the centre.

Plaskett's Star the most massive binary star known, consisting of two supergiants of about 40 and 50 solar masses, orbiting each other every 14.4 days. Plaskett's star lies in the constellation Monoceros and is named after Canadian astronomer John S Plaskett (1865–1941), who identified it as a binary star and discovered its massive nature in 1922.

Polaris or ***Pole Star*** or ***North Star*** the bright star closest to the north celestial pole, and the brightest star in the constellation Ursa Minor. Its position is indicated by the 'pointers' in Ursa Major. Polaris is a yellow supergiant about 500 light years away.

Proxima Centauri the closest star to the Sun, 4.2 light years away. It is a faint red dwarf, visible only with a telescope, and is a member of the Alpha Centauri triple-star system.

pulsar celestial source that emits pulses of energy at regular intervals, ranging from a few seconds to a few thousandths of a second. Pulsars are thought to be rapidly rotating neutron stars, which flash at radio and other wavelengths as they spin. They were discovered in 1967. Over 500 radio pulsars are now known in our Galaxy, although a million or so may exist.

quasar (from ***quas****i-stell****ar*** object or QSO) starlike object emitting more energy than 100 giant galaxies. Quasars are the most distant extragalactic objects known (up to 10 billion light years away), and were discovered 1964–65. They are thought to be at the centre of galaxies, their brilliance emanating from the stars and gas falling towards an immense black hole at their nucleus. Quasar light shows a large red shift, indicating that they are very distant. Some quasars emit radio waves but most are radio-quiet.

radio galaxy galaxy that is a strong source of electromagnetic waves of radio wavelengths. All galaxies, including our own, emit some radio waves, but radio galaxies are up to a million times more powerful.

red dwarf any star that is cool, faint, and small (about one-tenth the mass and diameter of the Sun). Red dwarfs burn slowly, and have estimated lifetimes of 100 billion years. They may be the most abundant type of star, but are difficult to see because they are so faint. Two of the closest stars to the Sun, Proxima Centauri and Barnard's Star, are red dwarfs.

red giant any large bright star with a cool surface. It is thought to represent a late stage in the evolution of a star like the Sun, as it runs out of hydrogen fuel at its centre. Red giants have diameters between 10 and 100 million times that of the Sun. They are very bright because they are so large, although their surface temperature is lower than that of the Sun, about 2,000–3,000K (1,700–2,700°C/3,000°–5,000°F).

Seyfert galaxy galaxy whose small, bright centre is caused by hot gas moving at high speed around a massive central object, possibly a black hole. Almost all Seyferts are spiral galaxies. They seem to be closely related to quasars, but are about 100 times fainter. They are named after their discoverer Carl Seyfert (1911–1960).

star luminous globe of gas, mainly hydrogen and helium, which produces its own heat and light by nuclear reactions. The surface temperatures of stars range from 2,000°C/3,600°F to 200,000°C/360,000°F and the corresponding colours range from red to blue-white. When, after billions of years, all the hydrogen at the core has been converted into helium, the star swells to become a ***red giant***, its core collapses in on itself to form a small and very dense body called a ***white dwarf***, which eventually fades away.

Some very large stars do not end their lives as white dwarfs. They pass through their cycle quickly, becoming red supergiants that eventually explode into brilliant supernovae. Part of the core remaining after such an explosion may collapse to form a small superdense neutron star.

star cluster group of related stars, usually held together by gravity. Members of a star cluster are thought to form together from one large cloud of gas in space. ***Open clusters*** such as the Pleiades contain from a dozen to many hundreds of young stars, loosely scattered over several light years. Globular clusters are larger and much more densely packed, containing perhaps 100,000 old stars.

steady-state theory theory that claims that the universe has no origin but is expanding because new matter is being created continuously throughout the universe. The theory was proposed 1948 by Hermann Bondi (1919–), Thomas Gold (1920–), and Fred Hoyle (1915–), but was dealt a severe blow in 1965 by the discovery of cosmic background radiation (radiation left over from the formation of the universe) and is now largely rejected in favour of the Big Bang theory.

supernova the explosive death of a star, which temporarily attains a brightness of 100 million Suns or more, so that it can shine as brilliantly as a small galaxy for a few days or weeks. Astronomers have catalogued about 150 supernovae in our galaxy.

universe all of space and its contents, the study of which is called cosmology. The universe is thought to be between 10 billion and 20 billion years old, and is mostly empty space, dotted with galaxies for as far as telescopes can see. The most distant detected galaxies and quasars lie 10 billion light years or more from Earth, and are moving farther apart as the universe expands. The most widely accepted explanation of how the universe came into being and evolved is the Big Bang theory of an expanding universe.

variable star star whose brightness changes, either regularly or irregularly, over a period ranging from a few hours to months or even years. The Cepheid variables regularly expand and contract in size every few days or weeks.

white dwarf small, hot star, the last stage in the life of a star such as the Sun. White dwarfs have a mass similar to that of the Sun, but only 1% of the Sun's diameter, similar in size to the Earth. Most have surface temperatures of 8,000°C/14,400°F or more, hotter than the Sun. Yet, being so small, their overall luminosities may be less than 1% of that of the Sun. The Milky Way contains an estimated 50 billion white dwarfs.

Technical Terms

aberration of starlight apparent displacement of a star from its true position, due to the combined effects of the speed of light and the speed of the Earth in orbit around the Sun (about 30 km per second/18.5 mi per second).

albedo the fraction of the incoming light reflected by a body such as a planet. A body with a high albedo, near 1, is very bright, while a body with a low albedo, near 0, is dark. The Moon has an average albedo of 0.12, Venus 0.65, Earth 0.37.

aphelion the point at which an object, travelling in an elliptical orbit around the Sun, is at its farthest from the Sun.

apogee the point at which an object, travelling in an elliptical orbit around the Earth, is at its farthest from the Earth.

arc minute, arc second units for measuring small angles, used in geometry, surveying, map-making, and astronomy. An arc minute (symbol ') is one-sixtieth of a degree, and an arc second (symbol ") is one-sixtieth of an arc minute. Small distances in the sky, as between two close stars or the apparent width of a planet's disc, are expressed in minutes and seconds of arc.

astrometry measurement of the precise positions of stars, planets, and other bodies in space. Such information is needed for practical purposes including accurate timekeeping, surveying and navigation, and calculating orbits and measuring distances in space.

astronomical unit unit (symbol AU) equal to the mean distance of the Earth from the Sun: 149,597,870 km/92,955,800 mi. It is used to describe planetary distances. Light travels this distance in approximately 8.3 minutes.

astrophotography use of photography in astronomical research. The first successful photograph of a celestial object was the daguerreotype plate of the Moon taken by John W Draper (1811–1882) of the USA in March 1840. The first photograph of a star, Vega, was taken by US astronomer William C Bond (1789–1859) in 1850.

celestial mechanics the branch of astronomy that deals with the calculation of the orbits of celestial bodies, their gravitational attractions (such as those that produce the Earth's tides), and also the orbits of artificial satellites and space probes. It is based on the laws of motion and gravity laid down by Isaac Newton (1642–1727).

celestial sphere imaginary sphere surrounding the Earth, on which the celestial bodies seem to lie. The positions of bodies such as stars, planets, and galaxies are specified by their coordinates on the celestial sphere. The equivalents of latitude and longitude on the celestial sphere are called declination and right ascension (which is measured in hours from 0 to 24). The ***celestial poles*** lie directly above the Earth's poles, and the ***celestial equator*** lies over the Earth's equator. The celestial sphere appears to rotate once around the Earth each day, actually a result of the rotation of the Earth on its axis.

charge-coupled device (CCD) device for forming images electronically, using a layer of silicon that releases electrons when struck by incoming light. The electrons are stored in pixels and read off into a computer at the end of the exposure. CCDs have now almost entirely replaced photographic film in astrophotography because they are 30 times more sensitive to light than a photographic plate and can reveal objects millions of times fainter than can be seen with the naked eye.

conjunction the alignment of two celestial bodies as seen from Earth. A superior planet (or other object) is in conjunction when it lies behind the Sun. An inferior planet (or other object) comes to ***inferior conjunction*** when it passes between the Earth and the Sun; it is at ***superior conjunction*** when it passes behind the Sun. ***Planetary conjunction*** takes place when a planet is closely aligned with another celestial object, such as the Moon, a star, or another planet.

cosmology study of the structure of the universe. Modern cosmology began in the 1920s with the discovery that the universe is expanding, which suggested that it began in an explosion, the Big Bang. An alternative view, now discarded, the steady-state theory, claimed that the universe has no origin, but is expanding because new matter is being continually created.

declination the coordinate on the celestial sphere (imaginary sphere surrounding the Earth) that corresponds to latitude on the Earth's surface. Declination runs from 0° at the celestial equator to 90° at the north and south celestial poles.

ecliptic the path, against the background of stars, that the Sun appears to follow each year as the Earth orbits the Sun. It can be thought of as the plane of the Earth's orbit projected on to the celestial sphere (imaginary sphere around the Earth).

elongation the angular distance between the Sun and a planet or other Solar-System object. This angle is 0° at conjunction, 90° at quadrature, and 180° at opposition.

equinox the points in spring and autumn at which the Sun's path, the ecliptic, crosses the celestial equator, so that the day and night are of approximately equal length. The ***vernal equinox*** occurs about 21 March and the ***autumnal equinox***, 23 Sept.

escape velocity minimum velocity with which an object must be projected for it to escape from the gravitational pull of a planetary body. In the case of the Earth, the escape velocity is 11.2 kps/6.9 mps; the Moon 2.4 kps/1.5 mps; Mars 5 kps/3.1 mps; and Jupiter 59.6 kps/37 mps.

exobiology study of life forms that may possibly exist elsewhere in the universe, and of the effects of extraterrestrial environments on Earth organisms.

geostationary orbit circular path 35,900 km/22,300 mi above the Earth's equator on which a satellite takes 24 hours, moving from west to east, to complete an orbit, thus appearing to hang stationary over one place on the Earth's surface. Geostationary orbits are particularly used for communications satellites and weather satellites. They were first thought of by the author Arthur C Clarke. A ***geosynchronous orbit*** lies at the same distance from Earth but is inclined to the equator.

gravitational lensing bending of light by a gravitational field, predicted by Albert Einstein's general theory of relativity. The effect was first detected 1917 when the light from stars was found to be bent as it passed the totally eclipsed Sun. More remarkable is the splitting of light from distant quasars into two or more images by intervening galaxies. In 1979 the first double image of a quasar produced by gravitational lensing was discovered and a quadruple image of another quasar was later found.

gravity force of attraction that arises between objects by virtue of their masses. On Earth, gravity is the force of attraction between any object in the Earth's gravitational field and the Earth itself. It is regarded as one of the four fundamental forces of nature, the other three being the electromagnetic force, the strong nuclear force, and the weak nuclear force. The gravitational force is the weakest of the four forces, but it acts over great distances. The particle that is postulated as the carrier of the gravitational force is the graviton.

Greenwich Mean Time (GMT) local time on the zero line of longitude (the ***Greenwich meridian***), which passes through the Old Royal Observatory in Greenwich, London. It was replaced 1986 by coordinated universal time (UTC), but continued to be used to measure longitudes and the world's standard time zones.

Hertzsprung–Russell diagram graph on which the surface temperatures of stars are plotted against their luminosities. Most stars, including the Sun, fall into a narrow band called the ***main sequence***. When a star grows old it moves from the main sequence to the upper right part of the graph, into the area of the giants and supergiants. At the end of its life, as the star shrinks to become a white dwarf, it moves again, to the bottom left area. It is named after the Dane Ejnar Hertzsprung (1873–1967) and the American Henry Norris Russell (1877–1957), who independently devised it in the years 1911–13.

Hubble's constant measure of the rate at which the universe is expanding, named after US astronomer Edwin Hubble (1889–1953). Observations suggest that galaxies are moving apart at a rate of 50–100 kps/30–60 mps for every million parsecs of distance. This means that the universe, which began at one point according to the Big Bang theory, is between 10 billion and 20 billion years old (probably closer to 20).

Hubble's law law that relates a galaxy's distance from us to its speed of recession as the universe expands, announced in 1929 by Edwin Hubble. He found that galaxies are moving apart at speeds that increase in direct proportion to their distance apart. The rate of expansion is known as Hubble's constant.

inclination the angle between the ecliptic and the plane of the orbit of a planet, asteroid, or comet. In the case of satellites orbiting a planet, it is the angle between the plane of orbit of the satellite and the equator of the planet.

light year the distance travelled by a beam of light in a vacuum in one year, approximately 9.46 trillion (million million) km/5.88 trillion mi.

luminosity or ***brightness*** the amount of light emitted by a star, measured in magnitudes. The apparent brightness of an object decreases in proportion to the square of its distance from the observer. The luminosity of a star or other body can be expressed in relation to that of the Sun.

magnitude measure of the brightness of a star or other celestial object. The larger the number denoting the magnitude, the fainter the object. Zero or first magnitude indicates some of the brightest stars. Still brighter are those of negative magnitude, such as Sirius, whose magnitude is –1.46. ***Apparent magnitude*** is the brightness of an object as seen from Earth; ***absolute magnitude*** is the brightness at a standard distance of 10 parsecs (32.6 light years).

nadir the point on the celestial sphere vertically below the observer and hence diametrically opposite the ***zenith***.

nutation slight 'nodding' of the Earth in space, caused by the varying gravitational pulls of the Sun and Moon. Nutation changes the angle of the Earth's axial tilt (average 23.5°) by about 9 seconds of arc to either side of its mean position, a complete cycle taking just over 18.5 years.

opposition the moment at which a body in the Solar System lies opposite the Sun in the sky as seen from the Earth and crosses the meridian at about midnight.

orbit path of one body in space around another, such as the orbit of Earth around the Sun, or the Moon around Earth. When the two bodies are similar in mass, as in a binary star, both bodies move around their common centre of mass. The movement of objects in orbit follows the laws of German astronomer Johann Kepler (1571–1630), which apply to artificial satellites as well as to natural bodies.

parallax the change in the apparent position of an object against its background when viewed from two different positions. In astronomy, nearby stars show a shift owing to parallax when viewed from different positions on the Earth's orbit around the Sun. A star's parallax is used to deduce its distance.

parsec unit (symbol pc) used for distances to stars and galaxies. One parsec is equal to 3.2616 light years, 2.063×10^5 astronomical units, and 3.086×10^{13} km.

perigee the point at which an object, travelling in an elliptical orbit around the Earth, is at its closest to the Earth. The point at which it is farthest from the Earth is the apogee.

perihelion the point at which an object, travelling in an elliptical orbit around the Sun, is at its closest to the Sun. The point at which it is farthest from the Sun is the aphelion.

phase the apparent shape of the Moon or a planet when all or part of its illuminated hemisphere is facing Earth. The Moon undergoes a full cycle of phases from new (when between Earth and the Sun) through first quarter (when at 90° eastern elongation from the Sun), full (when opposite the Sun), and last quarter (when at 90° western elongation from the Sun).

precession slow wobble of the Earth on its axis, like that of a spinning top. The gravitational pulls of the Sun and Moon on the Earth's equatorial bulge cause the Earth's axis to trace out a circle on the sky every 25,800 years. The position of the celestial poles (see celestial sphere) is constantly changing owing to precession, as are the positions of the equinoxes (the points at which the celestial equator intersects the Sun's path around the sky). The ***precession of the equinoxes*** means that there is a gradual westward drift in the ecliptic – the path that the Sun appears to follow – and in the coordinates of objects on the celestial sphere.

proper motion gradual change in the position of a star that results from its motion in orbit around our Galaxy, the Milky Way. Proper motions are slight and undetectable to the naked eye, but can be accurately measured on telescopic photographs taken many years apart.

red shift the lengthening of the wavelengths of light from an object as a result of the object's motion away from us. It is an example of the Doppler effect. The red shift in light from galaxies is evidence that the universe is expanding. A strong gravitational field can also produce a red shift in light; this is termed ***gravitational red shift***.

right ascension the coordinate on the celestial sphere that corresponds to longitude on the surface of the Earth. It is measured in hours, minutes, and seconds eastwards from the point where the Sun's path, the ecliptic, once a year intersects the celestial equator; this point is called the ***vernal equinox***.

sidereal period the orbital period of a planet around the Sun, or a moon around a planet, with reference to a background star. The sidereal period of a planet is in effect a 'year'. A synodic period is a full circle as seen from Earth.

singularity the point at the centre of a black hole at which it is predicted that the infinite gravitational forces will compress the infalling mass of the collapsing star to infinite density. It is a point in space-time at which the known laws of physics break down. In the Big Bang theory, it is the point from which the expansion of the universe began.

solstice either of the points at which the Sun is farthest north or south of the celestial equator each year. The ***summer solstice***, when the Sun is farthest north, occurs around June 21; the ***winter solstice*** around Dec 22.

speckle interferometry technique whereby large telescopes can achieve high resolution of astronomical objects despite the adverse effects of the atmosphere through which light from the object under study must pass. It involves the taking of large numbers of images, each under high magnification and with short exposure times. The pictures are then combined to form the final picture.

synodic period the time taken for a planet or moon to return to the same position in its orbit as seen from the Earth; that is, from one opposition to the next. It differs from the sidereal period because the Earth is moving in orbit around the Sun.

transfer orbit elliptical path followed by a spacecraft moving from one orbit to another, designed to save fuel although making the journey time longer.

transit the passage of a smaller object across the visible disc of a larger one. Transits of the inferior planets occur when they pass directly between the Earth and the Sun, and are seen as tiny dark spots against the Sun's disc.

universal time (UT) another name for Greenwich Mean Time. It is based on the rotation of the Earth, which is not quite constant. Since 1972, UT has been replaced by ***coordinated universal time*** (UTC), which is based on uniform atomic time.

zenith uppermost point of the celestial horizon, immediately above the observer; the nadir is below, diametrically opposite.

zodiac zone of the heavens containing the paths of the Sun, Moon, and planets. When this was devised by the ancient Greeks, only five planets were known, making the zodiac about 16° wide. In astrology, the zodiac is divided into 12 signs, each 30° in extent: Aries, Taurus, Gemini, Cancer, Leo, Virgo, Libra, Scorpio, Sagittarius, Capricorn, Aquarius, and Pisces. These do not cover the same areas of sky as the astronomical constellations.

Telescopes and Observatories

Algonquin Radio Observatory site in Ontario, Canada, of the radio telescope, 46 m/150 ft in diameter, of the National Research Council of Canada, opened 1966.

Arecibo site in Puerto Rico of the world's largest single-dish radio telescope, 305 m/1,000 ft in diameter. It is built in a natural hollow and uses the rotation of the Earth to scan the sky. It has been used both for radar work on the planets and for conventional radio astronomy, and is operated by Cornell University, USA.

Australia Telescope giant radio telescope in New South Wales, Australia, operated by the Commonwealth Scientific and Industrial Research Organization (CSIRO). It consists of six 22-m/72-ft antennae at Culgoora, a similar antenna at Siding Spring Mountain, and the 64-m/210-ft Parkes radio telescope – the whole simulating a dish 300 m/186 mi across.

David Dunlap Observatory Canadian observatory at Richmond Hill, Ontario, operated by the University of Toronto, with a 1.88-m/74-in reflector, the largest optical telescope in Canada, opened 1935.

Dominion Astrophysical Observatory Canadian observatory near Victoria, British Columbia, the site of a 1.85-m/73-in reflector opened 1918, operated by the National Research Council of Canada. The associated Dominion Radio Astrophysical Observatory at Penticton, British Columbia, operates a 26-m/84-ft radio dish and an aperture synthesis radio telescope.

Effelsberg site near Bonn, Germany, of the world's largest fully steerable radio telescope, the 100-m/328-ft radio dish of the Max Planck Institute for Radio Astronomy, opened 1971.

European Southern Observatory observatory operated jointly by Belgium, Denmark, France, Germany, Italy, the Netherlands, Sweden, and Switzerland. Its telescopes, located at La Silla, Chile, include a 3.6-m/142-in reflector opened 1976 and the 3.58-m/141-in New Technology Telescope opened 1990. By 1988 work began on the Very Large Telescope, consisting of four 8-m/315-in reflectors mounted independently but capable of working in combination.

Jodrell Bank site in Cheshire, England, of the Nuffield Radio Astronomy Laboratories of the University of Manchester. Its largest instrument is the 76-m/250-ft radio dish (the Lovell Telescope), completed 1957 and modified 1970. A 38 × 25 m/125 × 82 ft elliptical radio dish was introduced 1964, capable of working at shorter wavelengths. These radio telescopes are used in conjunction with six smaller dishes up to 230 km/143 mi apart in an array called MERLIN (***m***ulti-***e***lement ***r***adio-***l***inked ***i***nterferometer ***n***etwork) to produce detailed maps of radio sources.

Keck Telescope world's largest optical telescope, situated on Mauna Kea, Hawaii, USA. It has a primary mirror 10 m/33 ft in diameter, unique in that it consists of 36 hexagonal sections, each controlled and adjusted by a computer to generate single images

Space mirror lights up the night

From the ground, it looked like a dazzling star brighter than the Moon, speeding behind the clouds above Europe towards Asia. To the cosmonauts Gennady Manakov and Aleksandr Poleshchuk aboard the *Mir* space station, it looked like a shiny daisy, reflecting the Sun's rays to Earth 400 km/250 mi below.

It was no UFO, but a Russian space experiment to test the idea of using giant mirrors in orbit to brighten the long Arctic nights and spotlight disaster areas or industrial sites, thereby saving electricity. The experiment, called Znamya ('Banner'), was mounted aboard *Progress M-15*, a cargo craft that had been docked to *Mir*. On 4 Feb 1993 the *Progress* craft separated from *Mir* and a drum on one end of *Progress* began to spin rapidly, unfolding the sections of the mirror by centrifugal force. The metal-coated plastic sheets were supposed to open into a disc 20 m/65.5 ft wide but instead took on the form of a daisy, which Russian space scientists said was more effective than the planned shape.

From *Mir*, the cosmonauts Manakov and Poleshchuk saw a pool of light 4 km/2.5 mi wide scudding across the night side of Earth from France towards Russia at a speed of nearly 30,000 km/18,600 mi per hour. The mirror was later detached from *Progress* and burned up in the atmosphere.

Full-scale mirrors planned for the future will be hundreds of metres wide and will focus as much light as dozens of full Moons onto selected areas of Earth for up to 40 minutes at a time. A series of such reflectors could give continuous illumination at night if needed – assuming there are no clouds in the way, as there were during this experiment.

However, Western scientists have been horrified at the scheme, as they are already fighting against light pollution from artificial sources on the ground. 'If this is true, it is terrible,' said the British astronomer Sir Bernard Lovell of Jodrell Bank. 'It will be just one more step towards ruining the night skies for astronomy.' There is also concern over the effects of permanent daylight on nocturnal animals and plant growth.

of the objects observed. It received its first images Nov 1990. An identical telescope, to be named Keck II, is under construction next to it and is due for completion 1996. Both telescopes are jointly owned by the California Institute of Technology and the University of California.

Kitt Peak National Observatory US observatory in the Quinlan Mountains near Tucson, Arizona, operated by AURA (Association of Universities for Research into Astronomy). Its main telescopes are the 4-m/158-in Mayall reflector, opened 1973, and the McMath Solar Telescope, opened 1962, the world's largest of its type. Among numerous other telescopes on the site is a 2.3-m/90-in reflector owned by the Steward Observatory of the University of Arizona.

Las Campanas Observatory site in Chile of the 2.5-m/100-in Du Pont telescope of the Carnegie Institution of Washington, opened 1977.

Lick Observatory observatory of the University of California on Mount Hamilton, California, USA. Its main instruments are the 3.04-m/120-in Shane reflector, opened 1959, and a 91-cm/36-in refractor, opened 1888, the second-largest refractor in the world.

Lowell Observatory US observatory in Flagstaff, Arizona, with a 61-cm/24-in refractor opened in 1896. The observatory now operates other telescopes at a nearby site on Anderson Mesa, including the 1.83-m/72-in Perkins reflector of Ohio State and Ohio Wesleyan universities.

McDonald Observatory observatory of the University of Texas on Mount Locke, Texas, USA. It is the site of a 2.72-m/107-in reflector opened 1969 and a 2.08-m/82-in reflector opened 1939.

Mauna Kea observatory in Hawaii, USA, built on a dormant volcano at 4,200 m/13,784 ft above sea level. Because of its elevation high above clouds, atmospheric moisture, and artificial lighting, Mauna Kea is ideal for infrared astronomy. The first telescope on the site was installed 1970. Several countries now operate telescopes there, and the world's largest optical telescope, the Keck Telescope, is also situated on Mauna Kea.

Mills Cross type of radio telescope consisting of two rows of aerials at right angles to each other, invented 1953 by the Australian radio astronomer Bernard Mills (1920–). The cross-shape produces a narrow beam useful for pinpointing the positions of radio sources.

Mount Palomar US observatory 80 km/50 mi NE of San Diego, California. It has a 5-m/200-in diameter reflector called the Hale. Completed 1948, it was the world's premier observatory during the 1950s.

Mount Wilson site near Los Angeles, California, of the 2.5-m/100-in Hooker telescope, opened 1917, with which Edwin Hubble discovered the expansion of the universe. It was closed in 1985 when the Carnegie Institution withdrew its support. Two solar telescopes in towers 18.3 m/60 ft and 45.7 m/150 ft tall, and a 1.5-m/60-in reflector opened 1908, still operate there.

Mullard Radio Astronomy Observatory radio observatory of the University of Cambridge, England. Its main instrument is the Ryle Telescope, eight dishes 12.8 m/42 ft wide in a line 5 km/3 mi long, opened 1972.

Multiple Mirror Telescope telescope on Mount Hopkins, Arizona, USA, opened 1979, consisting of six 1.83-m/72-in mirrors mounted in a hexagon, the light-collecting area of which equals that of a single mirror of 4.5 m/176 in diameter. It is planned to replace the six mirrors with a single mirror 6.5 m/256 in wide.

New Technology Telescope optical telescope that forms part of the European Southern Observatory, La Silla, Chile; it came into operation 1991. It has a thin, lightweight mirror, 3.38 m/141 in across, which is kept in shape by computer-adjustable supports to produce a sharper image than is possible with conventional mirrors. Such a system is termed ***active optics***.

observatory site or facility for observing astronomical or meteorological phenomena. The earliest recorded observatory was in Alexandria, N Africa, built by Ptolemy Soter in about 300 BC. The modern observatory dates from the invention of the telescope. Observatories may be ground-based, carried on aircraft, or sent into orbit as satellites, in space stations, and on the space shuttle.

The most powerful optical telescopes covering the sky are at Mauna Kea, Hawaii; Mount Palomar, California; Kitt Peak National Observatory, Arizona; La Palma, Canary Islands; Cerro Tololo Inter-American Observatory, and the European Southern Observatory, Chile; Siding Spring Mountain, Australia; and Zelenchukskaya in the Caucasus. Radio astronomy observatories include Jodrell Bank, Cheshire, England; the Mullard Radio Astronomy Observatory, Cambridge, England; Arecibo, Puerto Rico; Effelsberg, Germany; and Parkes, Australia. The Hubble Space Telescope was launched into orbit April 1990. The Very Large Telescope is under construction by the European Southern Observatory in the mountains of N Chile, for completion by 1999.

Parkes site in New South Wales of the Australian National Radio Astronomy Observatory, featuring a radio telescope of 64-m/210-ft aperture, run by the Commonwealth Scientific and Industrial Research Organization.

planetarium optical projection device by means of which the motions of stars and planets are reproduced on a domed ceiling representing the sky.

radio telescope instrument for detecting radio waves from the universe in radio astronomy. Radio telescopes usually consist of a metal bowl that collects and focuses radio waves the way a concave mirror collects and focuses light waves. Radio telescopes are much larger than optical telescopes, because the wavelengths they are detecting are much longer than the wavelength of light. The largest single dish is 305 m/1,000 ft across, at Arecibo, Puerto Rico

Royal Greenwich Observatory the national astronomical observatory of the UK, founded 1675 at Greenwich, E London, England, to provide navigational information for sailors. After World War II it was moved to Herstmonceux Castle, Sussex; in 1990 it was transferred to Cambridge. It also operates telescopes on La Palma in the Canary Islands, including the 4.2-m/165-in William Herschel Telescope, commissioned 1987.

Schmidt Telescope reflecting telescope used for taking wide-angle photographs of the sky. It was invented 1930 by Estonian astronomer Bernhard Schmidt (1879–1935), and has an added corrector lens to help focus the incoming light. Examples are the 1.2-m/48-in Schmidt telescope on Mount Palomar and the UK Schmidt telescope, of the same size, at Siding Spring.

Siding Spring Mountain peak 400 km/250 mi NW of Sydney, site of the UK Schmidt Telescope, opened 1973, and the 3.9-m/154-in Anglo-Australian Telescope, opened 1975, which was the first big telescope to be fully computer-controlled. It is one of the most powerful telescopes in the southern hemisphere.

South African Astronomical Observatory national observatory of South Africa at Sutherland, founded 1973 after the merger of the Royal Observatory, Cape Town, and the Republic Observatory, Johannesburg, and operated by the Council for Scientific and Industrial Research of South Africa. Its main telescope is a 1.88-m/74-in reflector formerly at the Radcliffe Observatory, Pretoria.

telescope optical instrument that magnifies images of faint and distant objects; any device for collecting and focusing light and other forms of electromagnetic radiation. It is a major research tool in astronomy and is used to sight over land and sea; small telescopes can be attached to cameras and rifles. A telescope with a large aperture, or opening, can distinguish finer detail and fainter objects than one with a small aperture. The ***refracting telescope*** uses lenses, and the ***reflecting telescope*** uses mirrors. A third type, the ***catadioptric telescope***, with a combination of lenses and mirrors, is used increasingly.

United Kingdom Infrared Telescope (UKIRT) 3.8-m/150-in reflecting telescope for observing at infrared wavelengths, opened in 1978 on Mauna Kea, Hawaii, USA, and operated by the Royal Observatory, Edinburgh, Scotland.

US Naval Observatory US government observatory in Washington DC, which provides the nation's time service and publishes almanacs for navigators, surveyors, and astronomers. It contains a 66-cm/26-in refracting telescope opened 1873. A 1.55-m/61-in reflector for measuring positions of celestial objects was opened 1964 at Flagstaff, Arizona.

Very Large Array (VLA) largest and most complex single-site radio telescope in the world. It is located on the Plains of San Augustine, 80 km/50 mi W of Socorro, New Mexico, USA. It consists of 27 dish antennae, each 25 m/82 ft in diameter, arranged along three equally spaced arms forming a Y-shaped array. Two of the arms are 21 km/13 mi long, and the third, to the north, is 19 km/11.8 mi long. The dishes are mounted on railway tracks, enabling the configuration and size of the array to be altered as required.

Yerkes Observatory astronomical centre in Wisconsin, USA, founded 1897. It houses the world's largest refracting optical telescope, with a lens of 102 cm/40 in diameter.

Zelenchukskaya site of the world's largest single-mirror optical telescope, with a mirror of 6 m/236 in diameter, in the Caucasus Mountains of Russia. At the same site is the RATAN 600 radio telescope, consisting of radio reflectors in a circle of 600 m/2,000 ft diameter. Both instruments are operated by the Academy of Sciences in St Petersburg.

Astronomers and Astronauts

Adams John Couch 1819–1892. English astronomer who mathematically deduced the existence of the planet Neptune 1845 from the effects of its gravitational pull on the motion of Uranus, although it was not found until 1846 by J G Galle. Adams also studied the Moon's motion, the Leonid meteors, and terrestrial magnetism.

Airy George Biddell 1801–1892. English astronomer who installed a transit telescope at the Royal Observatory at Greenwich, England, and accurately measured Greenwich Mean Time by the stars as they crossed the meridian.

Aldrin Edwin (Eugene 'Buzz') 1930– . US astronaut who landed on the Moon with Neil Armstrong during the *Apollo 11* mission in July 1969, becoming the second person to set foot on the Moon.

Anaximander *c.* 610–*c.* 546 BC. Greek astronomer and philosopher. He claimed that the Earth was a cylinder three times wider than it is deep, motionless at the centre of the universe, and the celestial bodies were fire seen through holes in the hollow rims of wheels encircling the Earth. He is thought to have been the first to determine solstices and equinoxes.

Aristarchus of Samos *c.* 320–*c.* 250 BC. Greek astronomer. The first to argue that the Earth moves around the Sun, he was ridiculed for his beliefs. He was also the first astronomer to estimate the sizes of the Sun and Moon and their distances from the Earth.

Armstrong Neil Alden 1930– . US astronaut. In 1969, he became the first person to set foot on the Moon, and said, 'That's one small step for a man, one giant leap for mankind.' The Moon landing was part of the Apollo project.

Baade Walter 1893–1960. German-born US astronomer who made observations that doubled the scale and age of the universe. Baade worked at Mount Wilson Observatory, USA, and discovered that stars are in two distinct populations according to their age, known as Population I (the younger) and Population II (the older). Later, he found that Cepheid variable stars of Population I are brighter than had been supposed, and hence farther away.

Bessel Friedrich Wilhelm 1784–1846. German astronomer and mathematician, the first person to find the approximate distance to a star by direct methods when he measured the parallax (annual displacement) of the star 61 Cygni in 1838.

Bode Johann Elert 1747–1826. German astronomer who published the first atlas of all stars visible to the naked eye, *Uranographia* 1801. He devised Bode's law, a numerical sequence that gives the approximate distance of the planets from the Sun.

Bradley James 1693–1762. English astronomer who in 1728 discovered the aberration of starlight. From the amount of aberration in star positions, he was able to calculate the speed of light. In 1748, he announced the discovery of nutation (variation in the Earth's axial tilt).

Brahe Tycho 1546–1601. Danish astronomer who made accurate observations of the planets from which German astronomer and mathematician Johannes Kepler proved that planets orbit the Sun in ellipses. His discovery and report of the 1572 supernova brought him recognition, and his observations of the comet of 1577 proved that it moved on an orbit among the planets, thus disproving the Greek view that comets were in the Earth's atmosphere.

Cannon Annie Jump 1863–1941. US astronomer who, from 1896, worked at Harvard College Observatory and carried out revolutionary work on the classification of stars by examining their spectra. Her system, still used today, has spectra arranged according to temperature and runs from O through B, A, F, G, K, and M. O-type stars are the hottest, with surface temperatures of over 25,000 K.

Cassini Giovanni Domenico 1625–1712. Italian-French astronomer who discovered four moons of Saturn and the gap in the rings of Saturn now called the ***Cassini division***.

Chandrasekhar Subrahmanyan 1910– . Indian-born US astrophysicist who made pioneering studies of the structure and evolution of stars. The ***Chandrasekhar limit*** of 1.4 Suns is the maximum mass of a white dwarf before it turns into a neutron star. Nobel Prize for Physics 1983.

Copernicus Nicolaus 1473–1543. Polish astronomer who believed that the Sun, not the Earth, is at the centre of the Solar System, thus defying the Christian church doctrine of the time. For 30 years he worked on the hypothesis that the rotation and the orbital motion of the Earth were responsible for the apparent movement of the heavenly bodies. His great work *De Revolutionibus Orbium Coelestium/About the Revolutions of the Heavenly Spheres* was not published until the year of his death.

Eddington Arthur Stanley 1882–1944. British astrophysicist who studied the motions, equilibrium, luminosity, and atomic structure of the stars. In 1919 his observation of stars during an eclipse confirmed Einstein's prediction that light is bent when passing near the Sun. In *The Expanding Universe* 1933 he

Astronomers royal

John Flamsteed	1675–1719
Edmond Halley	1720–1742
James Bradley	1742–1762
Nathaniel Bliss	1762–1764
Nevil Maskelyne	1765–1811
John Pond	1811–1835
George Airy	1835–1881
William Christie	1881–1910
Frank Dyson	1910–1933
Harold Spencer Jones	1933–1955
Richard Woolley	1956–1971
Martin Ryle	1972–1982
F Graham Smith	1982–1990
Arnold Wolfendale	1991–

expressed the theory that in the spherical universe the outer galaxies or spiral nebulae are receding from one another.

Flamsteed John 1646–1719. English astronomer who began systematic observations of the positions of the stars, Moon, and planets at the Royal Observatory he founded at Greenwich, London, 1676. His observations were published 1725.

Gagarin Yuri (Alexeyevich) 1934–1968. Soviet cosmonaut who in 1961 became the first human in space, aboard the spacecraft *Vostok 1*, completing one orbit of the Earth.

Galle Johann Gottfried 1812–1910. German astronomer who located the planet Neptune 1846, close to the position predicted by French astronomer Urbain Leverrier.

Glenn John (Herschel), Jr 1921– . US astronaut and politician. On 20 Feb 1962, he became the first American to orbit the Earth, doing so three times in the Mercury spacecraft *Friendship 7*, in a flight lasting 4 hr 55 min. After retiring from NASA, he was elected to the US Senate as a Democrat from Ohio 1974.

Hale George Ellery 1868–1938. US astronomer who made pioneer studies of the Sun and founded three major observatories. In 1889 he invented the spectroheliograph, a device for photographing the Sun at particular wavelengths. In 1897 he founded the Yerkes Observatory in Wisconsin, and in 1917 he established on Mount Wilson, California, a 2.5-m/100-in reflector, the world's largest telescope until superseded 1948 by the 5-m/200-in reflector on Mount Palomar, which Hale had planned just before he died.

Halley Edmond 1656–1742. English atronomer who not only identified 1705 the comet that was later to be known by his name, but also compiled a star catalogue, detected the proper motion of stars using historical records, and began a line of research that – after his death – resulted in a reasonably accurate calculation of the astronomical unit.

Herschel John Frederick William 1792–1871. English scientist and astronomer, son of William Herschel. He discovered thousands of close double stars, clusters, and nebulae, reported 1847. His inventions include astronomical instruments.

Herschel William 1738–1822. German-born English astronomer. He was a skilled telescope maker, and pioneered the study of binary stars and nebulae. He discovered the planet Uranus 1781 and infrared solar rays 1801. He catalogued over 800 double stars, and found over 2,500 nebulae, catalogued by his sister ***Caroline Herschel*** (1750–1848); this work was continued by his son John Herschel. By studying the distribution of stars, William established the basic form of our Galaxy, the Milky Way.

Hewish Antony 1924– . British radio astronomer who was awarded, with Martin Ryle, the Nobel Prize for Physics 1974 for his work on pulsars, rapidly rotating neutron stars that emit pulses of energy.

Hipparchus *c.* 190–*c.* 120 BC. Greek astronomer who invented trigonometry, calculated the lengths of the solar year and the lunar month, discovered the precession of the equinoxes, made a catalogue of 800 fixed stars, and advanced Eratosthenes' method of determining the situation of places on the Earth's surface by lines of latitude and longitude.

Hoyle Fred(erick) 1915– . English astronomer and writer. In 1948 he joined with Hermann Bondi (1919–) and Thomas Gold (1920–) in developing the steady-state theory. In 1957, with Geoffrey and Margaret Burbidge (1925– and 1919–) and William Fowler (1911–), he showed that chemical elements heavier than hydrogen and helium are built up by nuclear reactions inside stars. He has suggested that life originates in the gas clouds of space and is delivered to the Earth by passing comets.

Hubble Edwin Powell 1889–1953. US astronomer who discovered the existence of other galaxies outside our own, and classified them according to their shape. In 1929 he announced ***Hubble's law***, which states that the galaxies are moving apart at a rate that increases with their distance.

Jansky Karl Guthe 1905–1950. US radio engineer who discovered that the Milky Way Galaxy emanates radio waves; he did not follow up his discovery, but it marked the birth of radioastronomy.

Kepler Johannes 1571–1630. German mathematician and astronomer. He formulated what are now called ***Kepler's laws*** of planetary motion: (1) the orbit of each planet is an ellipse with the Sun at one of the foci; (2) the radius vector of each planet sweeps out equal areas in equal times; (3) the squares of the periods of the planets are proportional to the cubes of their mean distances from the Sun.

Laplace Pierre Simon, Marquis de Laplace 1749–1827. French astronomer and mathematician. In 1796, he theorized that the Solar System originated from a cloud of gas (the nebular hypothesis). He studied the motion of the Moon and planets, and published a five-volume survey of celestial mechanics, *Traité de méchanique céleste* 1799–1825. Among his mathematical achievements was the development of probability theory.

Leavitt Henrietta Swan 1868–1921. US astronomer who in 1912 discovered the ***period–luminosity law*** that links the brightness of a Cepheid variable star to its period of variation. This law allows astronomers to use Cepheid variables as 'standard candles' for measuring distances in space.

Lemaître Georges Edouard 1894–1966. Belgian cosmologist who in 1927 proposed the Big Bang theory of the origin of the universe. He predicted that the entire universe was expanding, which the US astronomer Edwin Hubble confirmed. Lemaître suggested that the expansion had been started by an initial explosion, the Big Bang, a theory that is now generally accepted.

Leonov Aleksei Arkhipovich 1934– . Soviet cosmonaut. In 1965 he was the first person to walk in space, from the spacecraft *Voskhod 2*.

Leverrier Urbain Jean Joseph 1811–1877. French astronomer who predicted the existence and position of the planet Neptune, discovered in 1846.

Lovell Bernard 1913– . British radio astronomer, director until 1981 of Jodrell Bank Experimental Station (now Nuffield Radio Astronomy Laboratories).

Lowell Percival 1855–1916. US astronomer who predicted the existence of a 'Planet X' beyond Neptune, and started the search that led to the discovery of Pluto in 1930. In 1894 he founded the Lowell Observatory at Flagstaff, Arizona, where he reported seeing the apparent 'canals' on Mars previously reported by Giovanni Schiaparelli.

Messier Charles 1730–1817. French astronomer who discovered 15 comets and in 1781 published a list of 103 star clusters and nebulae. Objects on this list are given M (for Messier) numbers, which astronomers still use today, such as M1 (the Crab nebula) and M31 (the Andromeda galaxy).

Olbers Heinrich 1758–1840. German astronomer, a founder member of the ***Celestial Police***, a group of astronomers who attempted to locate a supposed 'missing planet' between Mars and Jupiter. During his search he discovered two asteroids, Pallas 1802 and Vesta 1807. Also credited to Olbers are a number of comet discoveries and a new method of calculating cometary orbits.

Oort Jan Hendrik 1900–1992. Dutch astronomer. In 1927, he calculated the mass and size of our Galaxy, the Milky Way, and the Sun's distance from its centre, from the observed movements of stars around the Galaxy's centre. In 1950 Oort proposed that comets exist in a vast swarm, now called the ***Oort cloud***, at the edge of the Solar System.

Piazzi Giuseppe 1746–1826. Italian astronomer who in 1801 identified the first asteroid, which he named Ceres. He was director of Palermo Observatory.

Ptolemy (Claudius Ptolemaeus) *c.* 100–170. Egyptian astronomer and geographer who worked in Alexandria. His *Almagest* developed the theory that Earth is the centre of the universe, with the Sun, Moon, and stars revolving around it. In 1543 the Polish astronomer Copernicus proposed an alternative to the ***Ptolemaic system***.

Ryle Martin 1918–1984. English radioastronomer. At the Mullard Radio Astronomy Observatory, Cambridge, he developed the technique of sky-mapping using 'aperture synthesis', combining smaller dish aerials to give the characteristics of one large one. His work on the distribution of radio sources in the universe brought confirmation of the Big Bang theory. He won, with Antony Hewish, the Nobel Prize for Physics 1974.

Schiaparelli Giovanni (Virginio) 1835–1910. Italian astronomer who thought he discovered canals on Mars. He studied ancient and medieval astronomy, discovered the asteroid 69 (Hesperia) April 1861, observed double stars, and revealed the connection between comets and meteors. In 1877 he was the first to draw attention to apparent linear markings on Mars, which gave rise to a controversy over whether they could be canals. These markings are now known to be optical effects and not real lines.

Shapley Harlow 1885–1972. US astronomer whose study of globular clusters showed that they were arranged in a halo around the Galaxy, and that the Galaxy was much larger than previously thought. He realized that the Sun was not at the centre of the Galaxy as then assumed, but two-thirds of the way out to the rim.

Shepard Alan (Bartlett) 1923– . US astronaut, the fifth person to walk on the Moon. He was the first American in space, as pilot of the suborbital *Mercury-Redstone 3* mission on board the *Freedom 7* capsule May 1961, and commanded the *Apollo 14* lunar landing mission 1971.

Struve Friedrich Georg Wilhelm 1793–1864. German-born Russian astronomer, a pioneer in the observation of double stars. The founder and first director (from 1839) of Pulkovo Observatory near St Petersburg, he was succeeded by his son ***Otto Wilhelm Struve*** (1819–1905). His great-grandson ***Otto Struve*** (1897–1963) left the USSR in 1921 for the USA, where he became joint director of the Yerkes and McDonald observatories 1932 and championed the notion that planetary systems were common around stars.

Tereshkova Valentina Vladimirovna 1937– . Soviet cosmonaut, the first woman to fly in space. In June 1963 she made a three-day flight in *Vostok 6*, orbiting the Earth 48 times.

Tombaugh Clyde (William) 1906– . US astronomer who discovered the planet Pluto 1930. He was an assistant at the Lowell Observatory in Flagstaff, Arizona.

Van Allen James (Alfred) 1914– . US physicist whose instruments aboard the first US satellite *Explorer 1* 1958 led to the discovery of the Van Allen belts, two zones of intense radiation around the Earth. He pioneered high-altitude research with rockets after World War II.

CHEMISTRY

Divisions

analytical chemistry branch of chemistry that deals with the determination of the chemical composition of substances. ***Qualitative analysis*** determines the identities of the substances in a given sample; ***quantitative analysis*** determines how much of a particular substance is present.

biochemistry science concerned with the chemistry of living organisms: the structure and reactions of proteins (such as enzymes), nucleic acids, carbohydrates, and lipids. Its study has led to an increased understanding of life processes, such as those by which organisms synthesize essential chemicals from food materials, store and generate energy, and pass on their characteristics through their genetic material. A great deal of medical research is concerned with the ways in which these processes are disrupted. Biochemistry also has applications in agriculture and in the food industry (for instance, in the use of enzymes).

inorganic chemistry branch of chemistry dealing with the chemical properties of the elements and their compounds, excluding the more complex covalent compounds of carbon, which are considered in organic chemistry.

organic chemistry branch of chemistry that deals with carbon compounds. Organic compounds form the chemical basis of life and are more abundant than inorganic compounds. In a typical organic compound, each carbon atom forms bonds covalently with each of its neighbouring carbon atoms in a chain or ring, and additionally with other atoms, commonly hydrogen, oxygen, nitrogen, or sulphur. Compounds containing only carbon and hydrogen are known as ***hydrocarbons***.

physical chemistry branch of chemistry concerned with examining the relationships between the chemical compositions of substances and the physical properties that they display. Most chemical reactions exhibit some physical phenomenon (change of state, temperature, pressure, or volume, or the use or production of electricity), and the measurement and study of such phenomena has led to many chemical theories and laws.

Biochemistry

amino acid water-soluble organic molecule, mainly composed of carbon, oxygen, hydrogen, and nitrogen, containing both a basic amino group (NH_2) and an acidic carboxyl (COOH) group. When two or more amino acids are joined together, they are known as peptides; proteins are made up of interacting polypeptides (peptide chains consisting of more than three amino acids) and are folded or twisted in characteristic shapes.

Many different proteins are found in the cells of living organisms, but they are all made up of the same 20 amino acids, joined together in varying combinations (although other types of amino acid do occur infrequently in nature). Eight of these, the ***essential amino acids***, cannot be synthesized by humans and must be obtained from the diet. Children need a further two amino acids that are not essential for adults. Other animals also need some preformed amino acids in their diet, but green plants can manufacture all the amino acids they need from simpler molecules, relying on energy from the Sun and minerals (including nitrates) from the soil.

ATP abbreviation for ***adenosine triphosphate***, a nucleotide molecule found in all cells. It can yield large amounts of energy, and is used to drive the thousands of biological processes needed to sustain life, growth, movement, and reproduction. Green plants use light energy to manufacture ATP as part of the process of photosynthesis. In animals, ATP is formed by the breakdown of glucose molecules, usually obtained from the carbohydrate component of a diet, in a series of reactions termed respiration. It is the driving force behind muscle contraction and the synthesis of complex molecules needed by individual cells.

carbohydrate chemical compound composed of carbon, hydrogen, and oxygen, with the basic formula $C_m(H_2O)_n$, and related compounds with the same basic structure but modified functional groups. As sugar and starch, carbohydrates form a major energy-providing part of the human diet. The simplest carbohydrates are sugars (***monosaccharides***, such as glucose and fructose, and ***disaccharides***, such as sucrose), which are soluble compounds, some with a sweet taste. When these basic sugar units are joined together in long chains or branching structures they form ***polysaccharides***, such as starch and glycogen, which often serve as food stores in living organisms. Even more complex carbohydrates are known, including chitin, which is found in the cell walls of fungi and the hard outer skeletons of insects, and cellulose, which makes up the cell walls of plants. Carbohydrates form the chief foodstuffs of herbivorous animals.

disaccharide sugar made up of two monosaccharides or simple sugars, such as glucose or fructose. Sucrose, $C_{12}H_{22}O_{11}$, or table sugar, is a disaccharide.

DNA (*deoxyribonucleic acid*) complex giant molecule that contains, in chemically coded form, all the information needed to build, control, and maintain a living organism. DNA is a ladderlike double- stranded nucleic acid that forms the basis of genetic inheritance in all organisms, except for a few viruses that have only RNA. In organisms other than bacteria it is organized into chromosomes and contained in the cell nucleus.

DNA is made up of two chains of nucleotide subunits, with each nucleotide containing either a purine (adenine or guanine) or pyrimidine (cytosine or thymine) base. The bases link up with each other (adenine linking with thymine, and cytosine with guanine) to form base pairs that connect the two strands of the DNA molecule like the rungs of a twisted ladder. The specific way in which the pairs form means that the base sequence is preserved from generation to generation.

biochemistry: chronology

***c.* 1830**	Johannes Müller discovered proteins.
1833	Anselme Payen and J F Persoz first isolated an enzyme.
1862	Haemoglobin was first crystallized.
1869	The genetic material DNA (deoxyribonucleic acid) was discovered by Friedrich Mieschler
1899	Emil Fischer postulated the 'lock-and-key' hypothesis to explain the specificity of enzyme action.
1913	Leonor Michaelis and M L Menten developed a mathematical equation describing the rate of enzyme-catalysed reactions
1915	The hormone thyroxine was first isolated from thyroid-gland tissue.
1920	The chromosome theory of heredity was postulated by Thomas H Morgan; growth hormone was discovered by Herbert McLean Evans and J A Long.
1921	Insulin was first isolated from the pancreas by Frederick Banting and Charles Best.
1926	Insulin was obtained in pure crystalline form.
1927	Thyroxine was first synthesized.
1928	Alexander Fleming discovered penicillin.
1931	Paul Karrer deduced the structure of retinol (vitamin A); vitamin D compounds were obtained in crystalline form by Adolf Windaus and Askew, independently of each other.
1932	Charles Glen King isolated ascorbic acid (vitamin C).
1933	Tadeus Reichstein synthesized ascorbic acid.
1935	Richard Kuhn and Karrer established the structure of riboflavin (vitamin B_2).
1936	Robert Williams established the structure of thiamine (vitamin B_1); biotin was isolated by Kogl and Tonnis.
1937	Niacin was isolated and identified by Conrad Arnold Elvehjem.
1938	Pyridoxine (vitamin B_6) was isolated in pure crystalline form.
1939	The structure of pyridoxine was determined by Kuhn.
1940	Hans Krebs proposed the citric acid (Krebs) cycle; Hickman isolated retinol in pure crystalline form; Williams established the structure of pantothenic acid; biotin was identified by Albert Szent-Györgyi, Vincent Du Vigneaud, and co-workers.
1941	Penicillin was isolated and characterized by Howard Florey and Ernst Chain.
1943	The role of DNA in genetic inheritance was first demonstrated by Oswald Avery, Colin MacLeod, and Maclyn McCarty.
1950	The basic components of DNA were established by Erwin Chargaff; the alpha-helical structure of proteins was established by Linus Pauling and R B Corey.
1953	James Watson and Francis Crick determined the molecular structure of DNA.
1956	Mahlon Hoagland and Paul Zamecnick discovered transfer RNA (ribonucleic acid); mechanisms for the biosynthesis of RNA and DNA were discovered by Arthur Kornberg and Severo Ochoa.
1957	Interferon was discovered by Alick Isaacs and Jean Lindemann.
1958	The structure of RNA was determined.
1960	Messenger RNA was discovered by Sydney Brenner and François Jacob.
1961	Marshall Nirenberg and Severo Ochoa determined the chemical nature of the genetic code.
1965	Insulin was first synthesized.
1966	The immobilization of enzymes was achieved by Chibata.
1968	Brain hormones were discovered by Roger Guillemin and Andrew Schally.
1975	J Hughes and Hans Kosterlitz discovered encephalins.
1976	Guillemin discovered endorphins.
1977	J Baxter determined the genetic code for human growth hormone.
1978	Human insulin was first produced by genetic engineering.
1979	The biosynthetic production of human growth hormone was announced by Howard Goodman and J Baxter of the University of California, and by D V Goeddel and Seeburg of Genentech.
1982	Louis Chedid and Michael Sela developed the first synthesized vaccine.
1983	The first commercially available product of genetic engineering (Humulin) was launched.
1985	Alec Jeffreys devised genetic fingerprinting.
1993	UK researchers introduced a healthy version of the gene for cystic fibrosis into the lungs of mice with induced cystic fibrosis, restoring normal function.

enzyme biological catalyst produced in cells, and capable of speeding up the chemical reactions necessary for life by converting one molecule (substrate) into another. Enzymes are not themselves destroyed by this process. They are large, complex proteins, and are highly specific, each chemical reaction requiring its own particular enzyme. The enzyme fits into a 'slot' (active site) in the substrate molecule, forming an enzyme–substrate complex that lasts until the substrate is altered or split, after which the enzyme can fall away. The substrate may therefore be compared to a lock, and the enzyme to the key required to open it. (See ***Life Sciences*** for more on enzymes.)

fat in the broadest sense, a mixture of lipids – chiefly triglycerides (lipids containing three fatty acid molecules linked to a molecule of glycerol). More specifically, the term refers to a lipid mixture that is solid at room temperature (20°C); lipid mixtures that are liquid at room temperature are called ***oils***. The higher the proportion of saturated fatty acids in a mixture, the harder the fat. Fats are essential constituents of food for many animals, with a calorific value twice that of carbohydrates; however, eating too much fat, especially fat of animal origin, has been linked with heart disease in humans. In many animals and plants, excess carbohydrates and proteins are converted into fats for storage. Mammals and other vertebrates store fats in specialized connective tissues (adipose tissues), which not only act as energy reserves but also insulate the body and cushion its organs.

glucose or ***dextrose*** or ***grape-sugar*** $C_6H_{12}O_6$ sugar present in the blood, and found also in honey and fruit juices. It is a source of energy for the body, being produced from other sugars and starches to form the 'energy currency' of many biochemical reactions also involving ATP. Glucose is prepared in syrup form by the hydrolysis of cane sugar or starch, and may be purified to a white crystalline powder. Glucose is a monosaccharide sugar (made up of a single sugar unit), unlike the more familiar sucrose (cane or beet sugar), which is a disaccharide (made up of two sugar units: glucose and fructose).

immunoglobulin human globulin protein that can be separated from blood and administered to confer immediate immunity on the recipient. It participates in the immune reaction as the antibody for a specific antigen (disease-causing agent). Normal immunoglobulin (gamma globulin) is the fraction of the blood serum that, in general, contains the most antibodies, and is obtained from plasma pooled from about a thousand donors. It is given for short-term (two to three months) protection when a person is at risk, mainly from hepatitis A (infectious hepatitis), or when a pregnant woman, not immunized against German measles, is exposed to the rubella virus. Specific immunoglobulins are injected when a nonimmunized person is at risk of infection from a potentially fatal disease, such as hepatitis B (serum hepatitis), rabies, or tetanus. These immunoglobulins are prepared from blood pooled from donors convalescing from the disease.

isoenzyme or ***isozyme*** one of a number of enzymes (biological catalysts) that act within the same organism on the same substrate but differ from each other in their affinity for that substrate or in their regulatory properties. Different isoenzymes are usually coded by different genes and can be separated from each other by such methods as electrophoresis.

Krebs cycle or ***citric acid cycle*** or ***tricarboxylic acid cycle*** final part of the chain of biochemical reactions by which organisms break down food using oxygen to release energy (respiration). It takes place within structures called mitochondria in the body's cells, and breaks down food molecules in a series of small steps, producing energy-rich molecules of ATP.

lipid any of a large number of esters of fatty acids, commonly formed by the reaction of a fatty acid with glycerol. They are soluble in alcohol but not in water. Lipids are the chief constituents of plant and animal waxes, fats, and oils. Phospholipids are lipids that also contain a phosphate group, usually linked to an organic base; they are major components of biological cell membranes.

metabolism the chemical processes of living organisms: a constant alternation of building up (***anabolism***) and breaking down (***catabolism***). For example, green plants build up complex organic substances from water, carbon dioxide, and mineral salts (photosynthesis); by digestion animals partially break down complex organic substances, ingested as food, and subsequently resynthesize them in their own bodies.

monosaccharide or ***simple sugar*** carbohydrate that cannot be hydrolysed (split) into smaller carbohydrate units. Examples are glucose and fructose, both of which have the molecular formula $C_6H_{12}O_6$.

nucleic acid complex organic acid made up of a long chain of nucleotides. The two types, known as DNA (deoxyribonucleic acid) and RNA (ribonucleic acid), form the basis of heredity. The nucleotides are made up of a sugar (deoxyribose or ribose), a phosphate group, and one of four purine or pyrimidine bases. The order of the bases along the nucleic acid strand contains the genetic code.

nucleotide organic compound consisting of a purine (adenine or guanine) or a pyrimidine (thymine, uracil, or cytosine) base linked to a sugar (deoxyribose or ribose) and a phosphate group. DNA and RNA are made up of long chains of nucleotides.

peptide molecule comprising two or more amino acid molecules (not necessarily different) joined by ***peptide bonds***, whereby the acid group of one acid is linked to the amino group of the other (–CO.NH). The number of amino acid molecules in the peptide is indicated by referring to it as a di-, tri-, or polypeptide (two, three, or many amino acids). Proteins are built up of interacting polypeptide chains with various types of bonds occurring between the chains. Incomplete hydrolysis (splitting up) of a protein yields a mixture of peptides, examination of which helps to determine the sequence in which the amino acids occur within the protein.

polysaccharide long-chain carbohydrate made up of hundreds or thousands of linked simple sugars (monosaccharides) such as glucose and closely related molecules. The polysaccharides are natural polymers. They either act as energy-rich food stores in plants (starch) and animals (glycogen), or have structural roles in the plant cell wall (cellulose, pectin) or the tough outer skeleton of insects and similar creatures (chitin).

protein complex, biologically important substance composed of amino acids joined by peptide bonds. Other types of bond, such as sulphur–sulphur bonds, hydrogen bonds, and cation bridges between acid sites, are responsible for creating the protein's characteristic three-dimensional structure, which may be fibrous, globular, or pleated. (See ***Life Sciences*** for more on protein.)

recombinant DNA in genetic engineering, DNA formed by splicing together genes from different sources into new combinations.

respiration biochemical process whereby food molecules are progressively broken down (oxidized) to release energy in the form of ATP. In most organisms this requires oxygen, but in some bacteria the oxidant is the nitrate or sulphate ion instead. In all higher organisms, respiration occurs in the mitochondria. Respiration is also used to mean breathing, although this is more accurately described as a form of gas exchange.

Chocolate: chemistry or psychology

Women eat more chocolate than men, with children's consumption somewhere in between. Each Briton, on average, now eats more than 7 kg/ 15 lb per year. Sales of chocolate rose during the depression in the 1930s and have remained buoyant during the current one. No one actually needs to eat chocolate, so what is so special about it?

Expert opinion is divided. Chemists have analysed chocolate and discovered several powerful chemical substances. One of these, phenylethylamine (up to 660 mg per 100 g), is a stimulant. Its chemical structure is similar to that of dopamine and adrenaline, which both occur naturally in the body. It raises the heart rate, blood pressure, and blood glucose, and generally heightens sensation. So perhaps chocolate is a sex substitute?

Chocolate also contains two other interesting chemical substances: methyl xanthine (5 mg per 100 g) and theobromine (160 mg per 100 g). These are also stimulants, chemically related to caffeine. So perhaps the effect of chocolate consumption is like drinking tea or coffee?

Carried to excess, the consumption of chocolate leads to nausea and vomiting. But what most people like is the sensation that eating chocolate produces in the mouth. This is due to cocoa butter, the vegetable fat in cocoa beans. Cocoa butter is a highly saturated fat, but has little effect on serum cholesterol levels.

Psychologists believe that obsession with chocolate is caused by social conditioning. Chocolate is comforting; it is eaten as an indulgence and often when we are already full – at Christmas, for example. Giving chocolate is a sign of social approval. Chocolate is also big business. Chocolate of all sorts, for all sorts of occasions, is heavily advertised, and the advertising is mostly directed at women and children. Unsurprisingly, sales peak at Christmas and Easter.

Whatever the explanation for chocolate addiction, it seems likely that the debate will continue as people continue to enjoy their favourite confectionery.

RNA ***ribonucleic acid*** nucleic acid involved in the process of translating the genetic material DNA into proteins. It is usually single-stranded, unlike the double-stranded DNA, and consists of a large number of nucleotides strung together, each of which comprises the sugar ribose, a phosphate group, and one of four bases (uracil, cytosine, adenine, or guanine). RNA is copied from DNA by the formation of base pairs, with uracil taking the place of thymine.

RNA occurs in three major forms, each with a different function in the synthesis of protein molecules. ***Messenger RNA*** (mRNA) acts as the template for protein synthesis. Each codon (a set of three bases) on the RNA molecule is matched up with the corresponding amino acid, in accordance with the genetic code. This process (translation) takes place in the ribosomes, which are made up of proteins and ***ribosomal RNA*** (rRNA). ***Transfer RNA*** (tRNA) is responsible for combining with specific amino acids, and then matching up a special 'anticodon' sequence of its own with a codon on the mRNA. This is how the genetic code is translated.

Although RNA is normally associated only with the process of protein synthesis, it makes up the hereditary material itself in some viruses, such as retroviruses.

steroid any of a group of cyclic, unsaturated alcohols (lipids without fatty acid components), which, like sterols, have a complex molecular structure consisting of four carbon rings. Steroids include the sex hormones, such as testosterone, the corticosteroid hormones produced by the adrenal gland, bile acids, and cholesterol. The term is commonly used to refer to anabolic steroid.

sterol any of a group of solid, cyclic, unsaturated alcohols, with a complex structure that includes four carbon rings; cholesterol is an example. Steroids are derived from sterols.

substrate a compound or mixture of compounds acted on by an enzyme. The term also refers to a substance such as agar that provides the nutrients for the metabolism of microorganisms. Since the enzyme systems of microorganisms regulate their metabolism, the essential meaning is the same.

sugar or ***sucrose*** sweet, soluble crystalline carbohydrate found in the pith of sugar cane and in sugar beet. It is a ***disaccharide*** sugar, each of its molecules being made up of two simple-sugar (***monosaccharide***) units: glucose and fructose. Sugar is easily digested and forms a major source of energy in humans, being used in cooking and in the food industry as a sweetener and, in high concentrations, as a preservative.

urea $CO(NH_2)_2$ waste product formed in the mammalian liver when nitrogen compounds are broken down. It is excreted in urine. When purified, it is a white, crystalline solid. In industry it is used to make urea-formaldehyde plastics (or resins), pharmaceuticals, and fertilizers.

vitamin any of various chemically unrelated organic compounds that are necessary in small quantities for the normal functioning of the body. Many act as coenzymes, small molecules that enable enzymes to function effectively. They are normally present in adequate amounts in a balanced diet. Deficiency of a vitamin will normally lead to a metabolic disorder ('deficiency disease'), which can be remedied by sufficient intake of the vitamin. They are generally classified as ***water-soluble*** (B and C) or ***fat-soluble*** (A, D, E, and K).

Inorganic Chemistry

ammonia NH_3 colourless, pungent-smelling gas, lighter than air and very soluble in water. It is made on an industrial scale by the Haber process, and is used mainly to produce nitrogenous fertilizers, some explosives, and nitric acid.

aqua regia mixture of three parts concentrated hydrochloric acid and one part concentrated nitric acid, which dissolves all metals except silver.

bauxite principal ore of aluminium, consisting of a mixture of hydrated aluminium oxides and hydroxides, generally contaminated with compounds of iron, which give it a red colour. To produce aluminium the ore is processed into a white powder (alumina), which is then smelted by passing a large electric current through it.

carbon nonmetallic element, symbol C, atomic number 6, relative atomic mass 12.011. It is one of the most widely distributed elements, both inorganically and organically, and occurs in combination with other elements in all plants and animals. The atoms of carbon can link with one another in rings or chains, giving rise to innumerable complex compounds. It occurs in nature (1) in the pure state in three crystalline forms of graphite, diamond, and various fullerenes; (2) as calcium carbonate ($CaCO_3$) in carbonaceous rocks such as chalk and limestone; (3) as carbon dioxide (CO_2) in the atmosphere; and (4) as hydrocarbons in the fossil fuels petroleum, coal, and natural gas. Noncrystalline forms of pure carbon include charcoal and coal. When added to steel, carbon forms a wide range of alloys. In its elemental form, it is widely used as a moderator in nuclear reactors; as colloidal graphite it is a good lubricant, which, when deposited on a surface in a vacuum, obviates photoelectric and secondary emission of electrons. The radioactive isotope C-14 (half-life 5,730 years) is widely used in archaeological dating and as a tracer in biological research. Analysis of interstellar dust has led to the discovery of discrete carbon molecules, each containing 60 carbon atoms. These C_{60} molecules have been named buckminsterfullerenes.

ferrite ceramic ferrimagnetic material. Ferrites are iron oxides to which small quantities of transition metal oxides (such as cobalt and nickel oxides) have been added. They are used in transformer cores, radio antenna, and, formerly, in computer memories.

gallium arsenide GaAs compound of gallium and arsenic that has been proposed as a rival to silicon as a semiconductor material for microprocessors. Chips made from gallium arsenide require less electric power and process data faster than those made from silicon.

gold heavy, precious, yellow, metallic element; symbol Au, atomic number 79, relative atomic mass 197.0. It is unaffected by temperature changes and is highly resistant to acids. For manufacture, gold is alloyed with another strengthening metal (such as copper or silver), its purity being measured in carats on a scale of 24. Like silver, gold is used in printed circuits and for electrical contacts because of its excellent electrical conductivity.

Gold is so soft that a single gram can be drawn into a wire 1 km/0.6 mi long. Sheets of gold can be produced that are less than 0.00013 mm/0.000005 in (400 atoms) thick.

halogen any of a group of five nonmetallic elements with similar chemical bonding properties: fluorine, chlorine, bromine, iodine, and astatine. They form a linked group in the periodic table of the elements, descending from fluorine, the most reactive, to astatine, the least reactive. They combine directly with most metals to form salts, such as common salt (NaCl). Each halogen has seven electrons in its valence shell, which accounts for the chemical similarities displayed by the group.

hydrochloric acid HCl solution of hydrogen chloride (a colourless, acidic gas) in water. The concentrated acid is about 35% hydrogen chloride and is corrosive. The acid is a typical strong, monobasic acid forming only one series of salts, the chlorides. It has many industrial uses, including recovery of zinc from galvanized scrap iron and the production of chlorine. It is also produced in the stomachs of animals for the purposes of digestion.

hydrogen colourless, odourless, gaseous, nonmetallic element, symbol H, atomic number 1, relative atomic mass 1.00797. It is the lightest of all the elements and occurs on Earth chiefly in combination with oxygen as water. Hydrogen is the most abundant element in the universe, where it accounts for 93% of the total number of atoms and 76% of the total mass. It is a component of most stars, including the Sun, whose heat and light are produced through the nuclear-fusion process that converts hydrogen into helium. When subjected to a pressure 500,000 times greater than that of the Earth's atmosphere, hydrogen becomes a solid with metallic properties, as in one of the inner zones of Jupiter. Common and industrial uses of hydrogen include the hardening of oils and fats by hydrogenation, the creation of high-temperature flames for welding, and as rocket fuel. It has been proposed as a fuel for road vehicles. Its isotopes deuterium and tritium (half-life 12.5 years) are used in nuclear weapons, and deuterons (deuterium nuclei) are used in synthesizing elements.

metal any of a class of chemical elements with certain chemical characteristics (metallic character) and physical properties: they are good conductors of heat and electricity; opaque, but reflect light well; malleable, which enables them to be cold-worked and rolled into sheets; and ductile, which permits them to be drawn into thin wires. Metallic elements compose about 75% of the 109 elements shown in the periodic table of the elements. They form alloys with each other, bases with the hydroxyl radical (OH), and replace the hydrogen in an acid to form a salt. The majority are found in nature in the combined form only, as compounds or mineral ores; about 16 of them also occur in the elemental form, as native metals. Their chemical properties are largely determined by the extent to which their atoms can lose one or more electrons and form positive ions (cations).

nitric acid or ***aqua fortis*** HNO_3 fuming acid obtained by the oxidation of ammonia or the action of sulphuric acid on potassium nitrate. It is a highly corrosive acid, dissolving most metals, and a strong oxi-

industrial chemical processes: chronology

***c.* AD 1100**	Alcohol was first distilled.
1746	John Roebuck invented the lead-chamber process for the manufacture of sulphuric acid.
1790	Nicolas Leblanc developed a process for making sodium carbonate from sodium chloride (common salt).
1827	John Walker invented phosphorus matches.
1831	Peregrine Phillips developed the contact process for the production of sulphuric acid; it was first used on an industrial scale 1875.
1834	Justus von Liebig developed melamine.
1835	Tetrachloroethene (vinyl chloride) was first prepared.
1850	Ammonia was first produced from coal gas.
1855	A technique was patented for the production of cellulose nitrate (nitrocellulose) fibres, the first artificial fibres.
1856	Henry Bessemer developed the Bessemer converter for the production of steel.
1857	William Henry Perkin set up the first synthetic-dye factory, for the production of mauveine.
1861	Ernest Solvay patented a method for the production of sodium carbonate from sodium chloride and ammonia; the first production plant was established 1863.
1862	Alexander Parkes produced the first known synthetic plastic (Parkesine, or xylonite) from cellulose nitrate, vegetable oils, and camphor; it was the forerunner of celluloid.
1864	William Siemens and Pierre Emile Martin developed the Siemens–Martin process (open-hearth method) for the production of steel.
1868	Henry Deacon invented the Deacon process for the production of chlorine by the catalytic oxidation of hydrogen chloride.
1869	Celluloid was first produced from cellulose nitrate and camphor.
1880	The first laboratory preparation of polyacrylic substances.
1886	Charles M Hall and Paul-Louis-Toussaint Héroult developed, independently of each other, a method for the production of aluminium by the electrolysis of aluminium oxide.
1891	Rayon was invented. Herman Frasch patented the Frasch process for the recovery of sulphur from underground deposits. Lindemann produced the first epoxy resins.
1894	Carl Kellner and Hamilton Castner developed, independently of each other, a method for the production of sodium hydroxide by the electrolysis of brine; collaboration gave rise to the Castner–Kellner process.
1895	The Thermit reaction for the reduction of metallic oxides to their molten metals was developed by Johann Goldschmidt.
1902	Friedrich Ostwald patented a process for the production of nitric acid by the catalytic oxidation of ammonia.
1908	Fritz Haber invented the Haber process for the production of ammonia from nitrogen and hydrogen. Heike Kamerlingh-Onnes prepared liquid helium.
1909	The first totally synthetic plastic (Bakelite) was produced by Leo Baekeland.
1912	I Ostromislensky patented the use of plasticizers, which rendered plastics mouldable.
1913	The thermal cracking of petroleum was established.
1919	Elwood Haynes patented non-rusting stainless steel.
1927	The commercial production of polyacrylic polymers began.
1930	Freons were first prepared and used in refrigeration plants. William Chalmers produced the polymer of methyl methacrylate (later marketed as Perspex).
1933	E W Fawcett and R O Gibson first produced polyethylene (polyethene) by the high-pressure polymerization of ethene.
1935	The catalytic cracking of petroleum was introduced. Triacetate film (used as base for photographic film) was developed.
1937	Wallace Carothers invented nylon. Polyurethanes were first produced .
1938	Roy Plunkett first produced polytetrafluoroethene (PTFE, marketed as Teflon).
1943	The industrial production of silicones was initiated. J R Whinfield invented Terylene.
1955	Artificial diamonds were first produced.
1959	The Du Pont company developed Lycra.
1963	Leslie Phillips and co-workers at the Royal Aircraft Establishment, Farnborough, England, invented carbon fibre.
1980	Nippon Oil patented the use of methyl-tert-butyl ether (MTBE) as a lead-free antiknock additive to petrol.
1984	About 2,500 people died in Bhopal, central India, when poisonous methyl isocyanate gas escaped from a chemical plant owned by US company Union Carbide.
1991	ICI began production of the hydrofluorocarbon HFA-134a, a substitute for CFCs in refrigerators and air-conditioning systems. Superconducting salts of buckminsterfullerene were discovered by researchers at AT & T Bell Laboratories, New Jersey, USA.
1992	Blue-light-emitting diodes based on the organic chemical poly(*p*-phenylene) were reported by Australian researchers.

Transuranic elements

atomic number	name	symbol	year discovered	source of first preparation identified	isotope	half-life of first isotope identified
Actinide series						
93	neptunium	Np	1940	irradiation of uranium-238 with neutrons	Np-239	2.35 days
94	plutonium	Pu	1941	bombardment of uranium-238 with deuterons	Pu-238	86.4 years
95	americium	Am	1944	irradiation of plutonium-239 with neutrons	Am-241	458 years
96	curium	Cm	1944	bombardment of plutonium-239 with helium nuclei	Cm-242	162.5 days
97	berkelium	Bk	1949	bombardment of americium-241 with helium nuclei	Bk-243	4.5 hours
98	californium	Cf	1950	bombardment of curium-242 with helium nuclei	Cf-245	44 minutes
99	einsteinium	Es	1952	irradiation of uranium-238 with neutrons in first thermonuclear explosion	Es-253	20 days
100	fermium	Fm	1953	irradiation of uranium-238 with neutrons in first thermonuclear explosion	Fm-235	20 hours
101	mendelevium	Md	1955	bombardment of einsteinium-253 with helium nuclei	Md-256	76 minutes
102	nobelium	No	1958	bombardment of curium-246 with carbon nuclei	No-255	2.3 secs
103	lawrencium	Lr	1961	bombardment of californium-252 with boron nuclei	Lr-257	4.3 secs
Transactinide elements						
104	unnilquadium* (also called rutherfordium or kurchatovium)	Unq	1969	bombardment of californium-249 with carbon-12 nuclei	Unq-257	3.4 secs
105	unnilpentium* (also called hahnium or nielsbohrium)	Unp	1970	bombardment of californium-249 with nitrogen-15 nuclei	Unp-260	1.6 secs
106	unnilhexium*	Unh	1974	bombardment of californium-249 with oxygen-18 nuclei	Unh-263	0.9 secs
107	unnilseptium*	Uns	1977	bombardment of bismuth-209 with nuclei of chromium-54	Uns	102 m/secs†
108	unniloctium*	Uno	1984	bombardment of lead-208 with nuclei of iron-58	Uno-265	1.8 m/secs
109	unnilennium*	Une	1982	bombardment of bismuth-209 with nuclei of iron-58	Une	3.4 m/secs

** names for elements 104-109 are as proposed by the International Union for Pure and Applied Chemistry 1980*
† m/secs = milliseconds

dizing agent. It is used in the nitration and esterification of organic substances, and in the making of sulphuric acid, nitrates, explosives, plastics, and dyes.

nitrogen colourless, odourless, tasteless, gaseous, nonmetallic element, symbol N, atomic number 7, relative atomic mass 14.0067. It forms almost 80% of the Earth's atmosphere by volume and is a constituent of all plant and animal tissues (in proteins and nucleic acids). Nitrogen is obtained for industrial use by the liquefaction and fractional distillation of air. It is used in the Haber process to make ammonia, NH_3, and to provide an inert atmosphere for certain chemical reactions. Its compounds are used in the manufacture of foods, drugs, fertilizers, dyes, and explosives.

nonmetal one of a set of elements (around 20 in total) with certain physical and chemical properties opposite to those of metals. Nonmetals accept electrons and are sometimes called electronegative elements.

oxygen colourless, odourless, tasteless, nonmetallic, gaseous element, symbol O, atomic number 8, relative atomic mass 15.9994. It is the most abundant element in the Earth's crust (almost 50% by mass), forms about 21% by volume of the atmosphere, and is present in combined form in water and many other substances. In nature it exists as a molecule composed of two atoms (O_2); single atoms of oxygen are very short-lived owing to their reactivity. Life on Earth evolved using oxygen, which is a by-product of photosynthesis and the basis for respiration in plants and animals. Oxygen is essential for combustion, and is used with ethyne (acetylene) in high-temperature oxyacetylene welding and cutting torches.

ozone O_3 highly reactive pale-blue gas with a penetrating odour. Ozone is an allotrope of oxygen, made up of three atoms of oxygen. It is formed when the molecule of the stable form of oxygen (O_2) is split by ultraviolet radiation or electrical discharge. It forms a thin layer in the upper atmosphere, which protects life on Earth from ultraviolet rays, a cause of skin cancer. At lower atmospheric levels it is an air pollutant and contributes to the greenhouse effect.

phosphate salt or ester of phosphoric acid. Incomplete neutralization of phosphoric acid gives rise to acid phosphates. Phosphates are used as fertilizers, and are required for the development of healthy root systems. They are involved in many biochemical processes, often as part of complex molecules, such as adenosine triphosphate (ATP).

plutonium silvery-white, radioactive, metallic element of the actinide series, symbol Pu, atomic number 94, relative atomic mass 239.13. It occurs in nature in minute quantities in pitchblende and other ores, but is produced in quantity only synthetically. It is one of three fissile elements (elements capable of splitting into other elements – the others are thorium and uranium), and is used as a fuel in fast-breeder reactors and in making nuclear weapons. It has a long half-life (24,000 years) during which time it remains highly toxic, and poses considerable disposal problems.

silicon brittle, nonmetallic element, symbol Si, atomic number 14, relative atomic mass 28.086. It is the second most abundant element (after oxygen) in the Earth's crust and occurs in amorphous and crystalline forms. In nature it is found only in combination with other elements, chiefly with oxygen in silica (silicon dioxide, SiO_2) and the silicates. These form the mineral quartz, which makes up most sands, gravels, and beaches. The crystalline form of silicon is used as a deoxidizing and hardening agent in steel, and has become the basis of the electronics industry because of its semiconductor properties, being used to make 'silicon chips' for microprocessors.

silver white, lustrous, precious, extremely malleable and ductile, metallic element, symbol Ag, atomic number 47, relative atomic mass 107.868. It occurs in nature in ores and as a free metal; the chief ores are sulphides, from which the metal is extracted by smelting with lead. It is one of the best metallic conductors of both heat and electricity; its most useful compounds are the chloride and bromide, which darken on exposure to light and are the basis of photographic emulsions.

sulphur brittle, pale-yellow, nonmetallic element, symbol S, atomic number 16, relative atomic mass 32.064. It occurs in three forms: two crystalline (called rhombic and monoclinic, following the arrangements of the atoms within the crystals) and one amorphous. It burns in air with a blue flame and a stifling odour. Sulphur is widely used in the manufacture of sulphuric acid (used to treat phosphate rock to make fertilizers) and in making paper, matches, gunpowder and fireworks, in vulcanizing rubber, and in medicines and insecticides. It is also a good electrical insulator.

sulphuric acid or ***oil of vitriol*** H_2SO_4 dense, viscous, colourless liquid that is extremely corrosive. It gives out heat when added to water and can cause severe burns. Sulphuric acid is used extensively in the chemical industry, in the refining of petrol, and in the manufacture of fertilizers, detergents, explosives, and dyes. It forms the acid component of car batteries.

superphosphate phosphate fertilizer made by treating apatite with sulphuric or phosphoric acid. The commercial mixture contains largely monocalcium phosphate. Single-superphosphate obtained from apatite and sulphuric acid contains 16-20% available phosphorus, as P_2O_5; triple-superphosphate, which contains 45-50% phosphorus, is made by treating apatite with phosphoric acid.

transuranic element or ***transuranium element*** chemical element with an atomic number of 93 or more – that is, with a greater number of protons in the nucleus than uranium. All transuranic elements are radioactive. Neptunium and plutonium are found in nature; the others are synthesized in nuclear reactions.

uranium hard, lustrous, silver-white, malleable and ductile, radioactive, metallic element of the actinide series, symbol U, atomic number 92, relative atomic mass 238.029. It is the most abundant radioactive element in the Earth's crust, its decay giving rise to essentially all radioactive elements in nature; its final decay product is the stable element lead. Uranium is one of three fissile elements (elements capable of splitting into other elements; the others are plutonium and thorium); the isotope uranium-235 is used as a fuel in nuclear reactors and in making nuclear weapons.

water H_2O liquid without colour, taste, or odour, an oxide of hydrogen. It is the most abundant substance on Earth, and is essential to all forms of life. Water begins to freeze at 0°C or 32°F, and to boil at 100°C or 212°F. When liquid, it is virtually incompressible; frozen, it expands by $^1/_{11}$ of its volume. It has the highest known specific heat, and acts as an efficient solvent, particularly when hot.

Organic Chemistry

alcohol any member of a group of organic chemical compounds characterized by the presence of one or more aliphatic OH (hydroxyl) groups in the molecule, and which form esters with acids. The main uses of alcohols are as solvents for gums, resins, lacquers, and varnishes; in the making of dyes; for essential oils in perfumery; and for medical substances in pharmacy. Alcohol (ethanol) is produced naturally in the fermentation process and is consumed as part of alcoholic beverages.

aldehyde any of a group of organic chemical compounds prepared by oxidation of primary alcohols, so that the OH (hydroxyl) group loses its hydrogen to give an oxygen joined by a double bond to a carbon atom (the aldehyde group, with the formula CHO).

aliphatic compound any organic chemical compound in which the carbon atoms are joined in straight chains, as in hexane (C_6H_{14}), or in branched chains, as

Types of plastic

Plastics are any of the stable synthetic materials that are fluid at some stage in their manufacture, when they can be shaped, and that later set to rigid or semi-rigid solids. Plastics today are chiefly derived from petroleum. Most are polymers, made up of long chains of molecules.

Processed by extrusion, injection-moulding, vacuum-forming and compression, plastics emerge in consistencies ranging from hard and inflexible to soft and rubbery. They replace an increasing number of natural substances, being lightweight, easy to clean, durable, and capable of being rendered very strong – for example, by the addition of carbon fibres – for building aircraft and other engineering projects.

Thermoplastics soften when warmed, then re-harden as they cool. Examples of thermoplastics include polystyrene, a clear plastic used in kitchen utensils or (when expanded into a 'foam' by gas injection) in insulation and ceiling tiles; polyethylene or polythene, used for containers and wrapping; and polyvinyl chloride (PVC), used for drainpipes, floor tiles, audio discs, shoes, and handbags.

Thermosets remain rigid once set, and do not soften when warmed. They include bakelite, used in electrical insulation and telephone receivers; epoxy resins, used in paints and varnishes, to laminate wood, and as adhesives; polyesters, used in synthetic textile fibres and, with fibreglass reinforcement, in car bodies and boat hulls; and polyurethane, prepared in liquid form as a paint or varnish, and in foam form for upholstery and in lining materials (where it may be a fire hazard). One group of plastics, the silicones, are chemically inert, have good electrical properties, and repel water. Silicones find use in silicone rubber, paints, electrical insulation materials, laminates, waterproofing for walls, stain-resistant textiles, and cosmetics.

Shape-memory polymers are plastics that can be crumpled or flattened and will resume their original shape when heated. They include transpolyisoprene and polynorbornene. The initial shape is determined by heating the polymer to over 35°C and pouring it into a metal mould. The shape can be altered with boiling water and the substance solidifies again when its temperature falls below 35°C.

Biodegradable plastics are increasingly in demand: Biopol was developed in 1990. Soil microorganisms are used to build the plastic in their cells from carbon dioxide and water (it constitutes 80% of their cell tissue). The unused parts of the microorganism are dissolved away by heating in water. The discarded plastic can be placed in landfill sites where it breaks back down into carbon dioxide and water. It costs three to five times as much as ordinary plastics to produce.

in 2-methylpentane ($CH_3CH(CH_3)\ CH_2CH_2CH_3$). Aliphatic compounds have bonding electrons localized within the vicinity of the bonded atoms. Cyclic compounds that do not have delocalized electrons are also aliphatic, as in the alicyclic compound cyclohexane (C_6H_{12}) or the heterocyclic piperidine ($C_5H_{11}N$).

alkane member of a group of hydrocarbons having the general formula C_nH_{2n+2}, commonly known as ***paraffins***. Lighter alkanes, such as methane, ethane, propane, and butane, are colourless gases; heavier ones are liquids or solids. In nature they are found in natural gas and petroleum. As alkanes contain only single covalent bonds, they are said to be saturated.

alkene member of the group of hydrocarbons having the general formula C_nH_{2n+2}, formerly known as ***olefins***. Lighter alkenes, such as ethene and propene, are gases, obtained from the cracking of oil fractions. Alkenes are unsaturated compounds, characterized by one or more double bonds between adjacent carbon atoms. They react by addition, and many useful compounds, such as poly(ethene) and bromoethane, are made from them.

alkyne member of the group of hydrocarbons with the general formula C_nH_{2n-2}, formerly known as the ***acetylenes***. They are unsaturated compounds, characterized by one or more triple bonds between adjacent carbon atoms. Lighter alkynes, such as ethyne, are gases; heavier ones are liquids or solids. The best-known alkyne is ethyne (acetylene), used in oxyacetylene cutting and welding torches.

amino acid water-soluble organic molecule, mainly composed of carbon, oxygen, hydrogen, and nitrogen, containing both a basic amine group (NH_2) and an acidic carboxyl (COOH) group. When two or more amino acids are joined together, they are known as peptides; proteins are made up of interacting polypeptides (peptide chains consisting of more than three amino acids) and are folded or twisted in characteristic shapes.

aromatic compound organic chemical compound in which some of the bonding electrons are delocalized (shared among several atoms within the molecule and not localized in the vicinity of the atoms involved in bonding). The commonest aromatic compounds have ring structures, the atoms comprising the ring being either all carbon or containing one or more different atoms (usually nitrogen, sulphur, or oxygen). Typical examples are benzene (C_6H_6) and pyridine (C_6H_5N).

buckminsterfullerene form of carbon, made up of molecules (buckyballs) consisting of 60 carbon atoms arranged in 12 pentagons and 20 hexagons to form a perfect sphere. It was named after the US

Molecular machines and buckyballs

Chemistry is all around us; everything, including ourselves, is made of chemicals. Chemistry's effects underlie change throughout the universe. As we approach a new century, our understanding of chemistry is increasing faster than ever.

Chemical synthesis

Chemists have hundreds of techniques for manipulating chemicals, from the simplest gases to complex anticancer drugs and supermolecules. In the 1960s, Elias J Corey made a breakthrough in organic (carbon-based) chemistry when he developed retrosynthesis, a powerful tool for building complex molecules from smaller, cheaper, and more readily available ones. Retrosynthesis can be used to picture a molecule like a jigsaw, working backwards to find reactive components to complete the puzzle. Modern chemists use retrosynthesis to design everything from insect antifeedants for 'greener' farming to better drugs with fewer side-effects.

Recently, one such chemical puzzle, Taxol, has received worldwide attention. Extracted from Pacific yew tree bark, it is an effective treatment for advanced forms of ovarian, breast, and other cancers, which resist traditional drugs. Retrosynthesis will help chemists design a laboratory production method for Taxol. Such a 'total' synthesis might need 25 individual chemical steps, making industrial scale-up difficult, but the payback could easily make such a process commercially viable.

Enzymes in chemistry

Traditional synthesis is powerful but often requires numerous steps, and many reactions need high temperatures and pressures to work at a useful rate. Man-made catalysts help speed up some reactions, such as the conversion of methane (natural gas) into useful products. But some are expensive and can pose disposal problems.

Chemists are turning to nature to solve such problems. Enzymes – nature's catalysts – have many advantages. They work at low temperatures using less energy. Each type only catalyses certain reactions, so by-products are reduced. This does not limit their use because over 10,000 enzymes are known and protein engineering could lead to even more.

Enzymes can distinguish between the right- and left-hand forms of a molecule. Some chemicals exist in two forms – enantiomers – with the chemical groups arranged as mirror images, like a pair of hands. The two enantiomers often interact very differently with other molecules. For example, one form of the morning sickness drug, thalidomide, is an effective tranquillizer; the other severely disturbs foetal development. Enzymes allow the chemist to determine the handedness of such reaction products.

Molecular recognition

Some researchers are working towards building 'molecular machines': tiny switches and transistors that respond to light; molecular wires and diodes that carry signals; and self-replicating systems and artificial enzymes.

To do this, they are exploiting 'molecular recognition'. Certain large molecules can 'recognize' and trap smaller molecules or ions in their cavities. A simple example is the crown ethers – simple rings of alternating carbon and oxygen atoms. The number of atoms in the ring determines its size, and this determines which chemicals the molecule will recognize. The smallest crown ether can recognize and trap lithium metal ions, but nothing larger, and could be incorporated in a sensor to detect lithium in the presence of other metal ions.

A second important property is 'self-assembly'. If the component parts of the crown ether ring are mixed in a solution containing lithium ions, the parts will spontaneously assemble around the ion to complete the ring. The lithium acts as a 'template' for the self-assembly of the ring.

Fraser Stoddart's research team at Birmingham University, UK, have recently built some long-chain compounds with cyclic molecules threaded on ring-shaped molecules, like beads on a string. They can make the 'beads' shuttle backwards and forwards between chemical groups incorporated along the chain. Once they can control this movement using an external input such as light, they will have a switch for use in molecular-scale optoelectronic computers.

Jean-Marie Lehn and colleagues at the University Louis Pasteur, France, are using cyclic rings related to crown ethers to mimic biochemical processes and to develop chemical sensors and other devices.

Julius Rebek's group at MIT, USA, have found a molecule that could help explain the early replication processes at life's origins. It acts as a template, bringing molecules together and speeding up their self-assembly. The first template catalyses the formation of a second; the two templates then separate and each catalyses the next round of assembly.

Rebek's self-replicating system is analogous to DNA replication in dividing cells. A single helical strand acts as a template for the self-assembly of the DNA base units forming a double helix. These two entwined templates then uncoil, resulting in two single-stranded templates, and so on.

The round chemistry of fullerenes

Fullerenes, or buckyballs, are the latest fascinating field of chemistry. These all-carbon compounds were first produced in the laboratory in the early 1990s. Fullerene-60 (buckminsterfullerene) is the archetypal 60-carbon spherical molecule.

Chemists and other scientists are investing vast amounts of time and money researching buckyballs, which have huge potential as everything from high-temperature superconductors to super-lubricants.

DB

architect and engineer Richard Buckminster Fuller because of its structural similarity to the geodesic dome that he designed. Buckminsterfullerene can be made into stable polymers using palladium. (See feature on buckyballs in this section.)

carboxyl group –COOH the acidic functional group that determines the properties of fatty acids (carboxylic acids) and amino acids.

ester organic compound formed by the reaction between an alcohol and an acid, with the elimination of water. Unlike salts, esters are covalent compounds.

ethanoic acid common name ***acetic acid*** CH_3CO_2H one of the simplest fatty acids (a series of organic acids). In the pure state it is a colourless liquid with an unpleasant pungent odour; it solidifies to an icelike mass of crystals at 16.7°C/62.4°F, and hence is often called glacial ethanoic acid. Vinegar contains 5% or more ethanoic acid, produced by fermentation.

ether any of a series of organic chemical compounds having an oxygen atom linking the carbon atoms of two hydrocarbon radical groups (general formula R-O-R'); also the common name for ethoxyethane $C_2H_5OC_2H_5$ (also called diethyl ether). Ethoxyethane is a colourless, volatile, inflammable liquid, slightly soluble in water, and miscible with ethanol. It is prepared by treatment of ethanol with excess concentrated sulphuric acid at 140°C/284°F. It is used as an anaesthetic by vapour inhalation and as an external cleansing agent before surgical operations. It is also used as a solvent, and in the extraction of oils, fats, waxes, resins, and alkaloids.

fatty acid or ***carboxylic acid*** organic compound consisting of a hydrocarbon chain, up to 24 carbon atoms long, with a carboxyl group (–COOH) at one end. The covalent bonds between the carbon atoms may be single or double; where a double bond occurs the carbon atoms concerned carry one instead of two hydrogen atoms. Chains with only single bonds have all the hydrogen they can carry, so they are said to be ***saturated*** with hydrogen. Chains with one or more double bonds are said to be ***unsaturated***.

functional group a small number of atoms in an arrangement that determines the chemical properties of the group and of the molecule to which it is attached (for example, the carboxyl group –COOH, or the amine group NH_2). Organic compounds can be considered as structural skeletons, with a high carbon content, with functional groups attached.

homologous series any of a number of series of organic chemicals with similar chemical properties in which members differ by a constant relative molecular mass. Alkanes (paraffins), alkenes (olefins), and alkynes (acetylenes) form such series in which members differ in mass by 14, 12, and 10 atomic mass units respectively.

hydrocarbon any of a class of chemical compounds containing only hydrogen and carbon (for example, the alkanes and alkenes). Hydrocarbons are obtained industrially, principally from petroleum and coal tar.

isomer chemical compound having the same molecular composition and mass as another, but with different physical or chemical properties owing to the different structural arrangement of its constituent atoms. For example, the organic compounds butane ($CH_3(CH_2)_2CH_3$) and methyl propane ($CH_3CH(CH_3)CH_3$) are isomers, each possessing four carbon atoms and ten hydrogen atoms but differing in the way that these are arranged with respect to each other.

ketone member of the group of organic compounds containing the carbonyl group (C=O) bonded to two atoms of carbon (instead of one carbon and one hydrogen as in aldehydes). Ketones are liquids or low-melting-point solids, slightly soluble in water. An example is propanone (acetone, CH_3COCH_3), used as a solvent.

lipid any of a large number of esters of fatty acids, commonly formed by the reaction of a fatty acid with glycerol. They are soluble in alcohol but not in water. Lipids are the chief constituents of plant and animal waxes, fats, and oils.

phenol member of a group of aromatic chemical compounds with weakly acidic properties, which are characterized by a hydroxyl (OH) group attached directly to an aromatic ring. The simplest of the phenols, derived from benzene, is also known as phenol and has the formula C_6H_5OH. It is sometimes called ***carbolic acid*** and can be extracted from coal tar. Pure phenol consists of colourless, needle-shaped crystals, which take up moisture from the atmosphere. It has a strong and characteristic smell and was once used as an antiseptic. It is, however, toxic by absorption through the skin.

polymer compound made up of a large long-chain or branching matrix composed of many repeated simple units (***monomers***). There are many polymers, both natural (cellulose, chitin, lignin) and synthetic (polyethylene and nylon, types of plastic). Synthetic polymers belong to two groups: thermosoftening and thermosetting.

polyunsaturate type of fat or oil containing a high proportion of triglyceride molecules whose fatty-acid chains contain several double bonds. By contrast, the fatty-acid chains of the triglycerides in saturated fats (such as lard) contain only single bonds. Medical evidence suggests that polyunsaturated fats, used widely in margarines and cooking fats, are less likely to contribute to cardiovascular disease than saturated fats, but there is also some evidence that they may have adverse effects on health.

saturated compound organic compound, such as propane, that contains only single covalent bonds. Saturated organic compounds can only undergo further reaction by substitution reactions, as in the production of chloropropane from propane.

tetrachloromethane or ***carbon tetrachloride*** CCl_4 chlorinated organic compound that is a very efficient solvent for fats and greases, and was at one time the main constituent of household dry-cleaning fluids and of fire extinguishers used with electrical and petrol fires. Its use became restricted after it was discovered to be carcinogenic and it has now been largely removed from educational and industrial laboratories.

unsaturated compound chemical compound in which two adjacent atoms are bonded by a double or triple covalent bond. Examples are alkenes and alkynes, where the two adjacent atoms are both carbon, and ketones, where the unsaturation exists between atoms of different elements.

Terms

absorption spectroscopy or ***absorptiometry*** technique for determining the identity or amount present of a chemical substance by measuring the amount of electromagnetic radiation the substance absorbs at specific wavelengths.

acid compound that, in solution in an ionizing solvent (usually water), gives rise to hydrogen ions (H^+ or protons). In modern chemistry, acids are defined as substances that are proton donors and accept electrons to form ionic bonds. Acids react with bases to form salts, and they act as solvents. Strong acids are corrosive; dilute acids have a sour or sharp taste, although in some organic acids this may be partially masked by other flavour characteristics. Acids are classified as monobasic, dibasic, tribasic, and so forth, according to the number of hydrogen atoms, replaceable by bases, in a molecule.

activation analysis technique used to reveal the presence and amount of minute impurities in a substance or element. A sample of a material that may contain traces of a certain element is irradiated with neutrons, as in a reactor. The gamma rays emitted by the material's radioisotope have unique energies and relative intensities, similar to the spectral lines from a luminous gas. Measurements and interpretation of the gamma-ray spectrum, using data from standard samples for comparison, provide information on the amount of impurities present.

activation energy the energy required in order to start a chemical reaction. Some elements and compounds will react together merely by bringing them into contact (spontaneous reaction). For others it is necessary to supply energy in order to start the reaction, even if there is ultimately a net output of energy. This initial energy is the activation energy.

aerogel light, transparent, highly porous material composed of more than 90% air. Such materials are formed from silica, metal oxides, and organic chemicals, and are produced by drying gels – networks of linked molecules suspended in a liquid – so that air fills the spaces previously occupied by the liquid. They are excellent heat insulators and have unusual optical, electrical, and acoustic properties. (See feature on aerogels in this section.)

alkali chemical compound classed as a base that is soluble in water. Alkalis neutralize acids and are soapy to the touch. The hydroxides of metals are alkalis; those of sodium (sodium hydroxide, NaOH) and of potassium (potassium hydroxide, KOH) being chemically powerful.

assay the determination of the quantity of a given substance present in a sample. Usually it refers to determining the purity of precious metals. The assay may be carried out by 'wet' methods, when the sample is wholly or partially dissolved in some reagent (often an acid), or by 'dry' or 'fire' methods, in which the compounds present in the sample are combined with other substances.

atom the smallest unit of matter that can take part in a chemical reaction, and which cannot be broken down chemically into anything simpler. An atom is made up of protons and neutrons in a central nucleus surrounded by electrons. The atoms of the various elements differ in atomic number, relative atomic mass, and chemical behaviour. There are 109 different types of atom, corresponding with the 109 known elements as listed in the periodic table of the elements.

atomic number or ***proton number*** the number (symbol Z) of protons in the nucleus of an atom. It is equal to the positive charge on the nucleus. In a neutral atom, it is also equal to the number of electrons surrounding the nucleus. The 109 elements are arranged in the periodic table of the elements according to their atomic number.

atomic orbital region around the nucleus of an atom (or, in a molecule, around several nuclei) in which an electron is most likely to be found. According to quantum theory, the position of an electron is uncertain; it may be found at any point. However, it is more likely to be found in some places than in others, and it is these that make up the orbital. An atom or molecule has numerous orbitals, each of which has a fixed size and shape.

base a substance that accepts protons, such as the hydroxide ion (OH^-) and ammonia (NH_3). Bases react with acids to give a salt. Those that dissolve in water are called alkalis. Inorganic bases are usually oxides or hydroxides of metals, which react with dilute acids to form a salt and water. A number of carbonates also react with dilute acids, additionally giving off carbon dioxide. Many organic compounds that contain nitrogen are bases.

boiling point for any given liquid, the temperature at which any further application of heat does not raise the temperature of the liquid, but converts it into vapour.

bond the result of the forces of attraction that hold together atoms of an element or elements to form a molecule. The principal types of bonding are ionic, covalent, metallic, and intermolecular (such as hydrogen bonding). The type of bond formed depends on the elements concerned and their electronic structure.

buffer mixture of chemical compounds chosen to maintain a steady pH. The commonest buffers consist of a mixture of a weak organic acid and one of its salts or a mixture of acid salts of phosphoric acid. The addition of either an acid or a base causes a shift in the chemical equilibrium, thus keeping the pH constant.

catalyst substance that alters the speed of, or makes possible, a chemical or biochemical reaction but remains unchanged at the end of the reaction. Enzymes are natural biochemical catalysts. In practice most catalysts are used to speed up reactions.

centrifuge apparatus that rotates at high speeds, causing substances inside it to be thrown outwards. One use is for separating mixtures of substances of different densities. A common example is the separation of the lighter plasma from the heavier blood corpuscles in certain blood tests.

chain reaction mechanism that produces very fast, exothermic reactions, as in the formation of flames

Aerogels: materials for the future

There is a new material that can be used to catch micrometeorites in space, that can replace CFC-filled insulating foams, or can be part of a detector for subatomic particles. It is also transparent, and the list of its uses is growing.

A new material is born

The story started 60 years ago, when the American chemist Samuel Kristler attempted to dry wet silica gels without shrinking them in the process. Silica gels are useful drying agents because they readily absorb moisture from the air. The problem that Kristler was trying to overcome can be seen when mud in a puddle dries out in the sun. Cracks develop and the broken surface warps. His aim was to replace the liquid within wet silica gels with air, without causing their silica skeletons to collapse. He was successful and called the new, highly porous materials 'aerogels'. Kristler found that these new materials had many unusual properties.

Ordinary glass, which consists mainly of silica, is a heavy material. Silica aerogels are full of holes encircled by strings of silica and so they are extraordinarily light: they are 90% composed of air and can even float on whisked egg white. Aerogels can be made from many different substances, as Kristler discovered during the ten years he was carrying out his pioneering work at Stanford University. He substituted alcohol for water in making his gels, which were then dried at high temperatures and pressures. This procedure was slow and potentially very dangerous, but Kristler brilliantly succeeded in preparing aerogels from alumina, iron, tungsten, and tin oxide as well as from silica, the oxide of the element silicon.

Improved production methods

Now there are much faster and safer methods of making aerogels in a few hours rather than in weeks. These were developed by a group working at the Claude Bernard University at Lyons in France, and since the mid-1980s the number of researchers working with aerogels around the world has increased dramatically.

Following an accident in 1984, when the pressure vessel used to dry the aerogels leaked enough alcohol to cause an explosion that wrecked the entire facility, scientists at BASF in Germany decided to use liquid carbon dioxide instead. This method enabled pellets of aerogels to be made. While not perfectly transparent, the pellets make excellent insulators because, like other forms of aerogel, they do not burn and can withstand temperatures up to 600°C.

Many uses for aerogels

Research into better methods of insulation received a boost during the energy crisis in the 1970s, and aerogels, because of their unique microstructure and chemical properties, are likely to be the insulators of choice in the future: they are five times more effective than expanded polystyrene.

Fast micrometeorites, which are tiny particles of interstellar debris, burn up as they enter the Earth's atmosphere. But low-density aerogels can trap them in outer space. The micrometeorites are slowed to a stop as they penetrate the porous material, which because of its transparency enables scientists to inspect them where they come to rest.

Transparent tiles made of aerogels are used at DESY, Geneva, in place of compressed gases or low-density liquids in Cherenkov detectors to detect pions, protons, and muons moving at speeds near to the speed of light.

CFCs are effectively banned after January 1996 by international agreement. Aerogels have impressive insulating properties and have already found use as insulating materials. Because they are transparent, pelleted aerogels can be sandwiched between two layers of glass, minimizing heat loss. Since the pellets also scatter light, they can provide an excellent alternative to frosted glass. A layer of aerogel also improves the performance of solar panels.

In aerogels, the air-containing pores vary between 1 and 100 nm in diameter. This is about the distance that an air molecule travels before it collides with another air molecule. So, on average, air molecules collide with each other as often as they do with the walls of pores in an aerogel in which they are trapped. This is why aerogels insulate so well.

Silica aerogels, combined with phosphors, the substances that provide the colour in colour televisions, and tiny amounts of radioactivity can provide a source of light without electricity. Aerogels prepared from organic chemicals are less brittle than those made from inorganic chemicals and some of these are good conductors of electricity. Sound travels more slowly through aerogels than it does in air. Research in this field has already led to novel applications of aerogels in ultrasonics.

JR

and explosions. The reaction begins with the formation of a single reactive molecule. This combines with an inactive molecule to form two reactive molecules. These two produce four (or more) reactive molecules; very quickly, very many reactive molecules are produced, so the reaction rate accelerates dramatically.

chemical equation method of indicating the reactants and products of a chemical reaction by using chemical symbols and formulae. A chemical equation gives two basic pieces of information: (1) the reactants (on the left-hand side) and products (right-hand side); and (2) the reacting proportions (stoichiometry) – that is, how many units of each reactant and product are involved. The equation must balance; that is, the total number of atoms of a particular element on the left-hand side must be the same as the number of atoms of that element on the right-hand side.

chemical equilibrium condition in which the products of a reversible chemical reaction are formed at the same rate at which they decompose back into the reactants, so that the concentration of each reactant and product remains constant.

chlorination treatment of water with chlorine in order to disinfect it; also, any chemical reaction in which a chlorine atom is introduced into a chemical compound.

chromatography technique for separating or analysing a mixture of gases, liquids, or dissolved substances. This is brought about by means of two immiscible substances, one of which (***the mobile phase***) transports the sample mixture through the other (***the stationary phase***). The mobile phase may be a gas or a liquid; the stationary phase may be a liquid or a solid, and may be in a column, on paper, or in a thin layer on a glass or plastic support. The components of the mixture are absorbed or impeded by the stationary phase to different extents and therefore become separated.

colligative property property that depends on the concentration of particles in a solution. Such properties include osmotic pressure, elevation of boiling point, depression of freezing point, and lowering of vapour pressure.

colloid substance composed of extremely small particles of one material (the dispersed phase) evenly and stably distributed in another material (the continuous phase). The size of the dispersed particles (1–1,000 nanometres

compound chemical substance made up of two or more elements bonded together, so that they cannot be separated by physical means. Compounds are held together by ionic or covalent bonds.

An estimated 10 million chemical compounds have been discovered; 400,000 new compounds are discovered each year.

configuration the arrangement of atoms in a molecule or of electrons in atomic orbitals.

covalent bond chemical bond produced when two atoms share one or more pairs of electrons (usually each atom contributes an electron). The bond is often represented by a single line drawn between the two atoms. Covalently bonded substances include hydrogen (H_2), water (H_2O), and most organic substances. Double bonds, seen, for example, in the alkenes, are formed when two atoms share two pairs of electrons (the atoms usually contribute a pair each); triple bonds, seen in the alkynes, are formed when atoms share three pairs of electrons. Such bonds are represented by a double or triple line, respectively, between the atoms concerned.

cracking reaction in which a large alkane molecule is broken down by heat into a smaller alkane and a small alkene molecule. The reaction is carried out at a high temperature (600°C or higher) and often in the presence of a catalyst. It is the main method of preparation of alkenes and is also used to manufacture petrol from the higher-boiling-point fractions that are obtained by fractional distillation (fractionation) of crude oil.

decomposition process whereby a chemical compound is reduced to its component substances.

detergent surface-active cleansing agent. The common detergents are made from fats (hydrocarbons) and sulphuric acid, and their long-chain molecules have a type of structure similar to that of soap molecules: a salt group at one end attached to a long hydrocarbon 'tail'. They have the advantage over soap in that they do not produce scum by forming insoluble salts with the calcium and magnesium ions present in hard water.

diffusion spontaneous and random movement of molecules or particles in a fluid (gas or liquid) from a region in which they are at a high concentration to a region in which they are at a low concentration, until a uniform concentration is achieved throughout. No mechanical mixing or stirring is involved. For instance, if a drop of ink is added to water, its molecules will diffuse until their colour becomes evenly distributed throughout. One application of diffusion is the separation of isotopes, particularly those of uranium. When uranium hexafluoride diffuses through a porous plate, the ratio of the 235 and 238 isotopes is changed slightly. With sufficient number of passages, the separation is almost complete.

dipole the uneven distribution of magnetic or electrical characteristics within a molecule or substance so that it behaves as though it possesses two equal but opposite poles or charges, a finite distance apart. The uneven distribution of electrons within a molecule composed of atoms of different electronegativities may result in an apparent concentration of electrons towards one end of the molecule and a deficiency towards the other, so that it forms a dipole consisting of apparently separated but equal positive and negative charges. A bar magnet behaves as though its magnetism were concentrated in separate north and south magnetic poles because of the uneven distribution of its magnetic field.

dissociation the process whereby a single compound splits into two or more smaller products, which may be capable of recombining to form the reactant.

distillation technique used to purify liquids or to separate mixtures of liquids possessing different boiling points. ***Simple distillation*** is used in the purification of liquids (or the separation of substances in solution from their solvents) – for example, in the production of pure water from a salt solution. The solu-

chemistry: chronology

c. 3000 BC	Egyptians were producing bronze, an alloy of copper and tin.
c. 450 BC	Greek philosopher Empedocles proposed that all substances are made up of a combination of four elements – earth, air, fire, and water – an idea that was developed by Plato and Aristotle and persisted for over 2,000 years.
c. 400 BC	Greek philosopher Democritus theorized that matter consists ultimately of tiny, indivisible particles, *atomos.*
AD 1	Gold, silver, copper, lead, iron, tin, and mercury were known.
200	The techniques of solution, filtration, and distillation were known.
7th–17th centuries	Chemistry was dominated by alchemy, the attempt to transform nonprecious metals such as lead and copper into gold. Though misguided, it led to the discovery of many new chemicals and techniques, such as sublimation and distillation.
12th century	Alcohol was first distilled in Europe.
1242	Gunpowder introduced to Europe from the Far East.
1620	Scientific method of reasoning expounded by Francis Bacon in his *Novum Organum.*
1650	Leyden University in the Netherlands set up the first chemistry laboratory.
1661	Robert Boyle defined an element as any substance that cannot be broken down into still simpler substances and asserted that matter is composed of 'corpuscles' (atoms) of various sorts and sizes, capable of arranging themselves into groups, each of which constitutes a chemical substance.
1662	Boyle described the inverse relationship between the volume and pressure of a fixed mass of gas (Boyle's law).
1697	Georg Stahl proposed the erroneous theory that substances burn because they are rich in a certain substance, called phlogiston.
1755	Joseph Black discovered carbon dioxide.
1774	Joseph Priestley discovered oxygen, which he called 'dephlogisticated air'. Antoine Lavoisier demonstrated his law of conservation of mass.
1777	Lavoisier showed air to be made up of a mixture of gases, and showed that one of these - oxygen - is the substance necessary for combustion (burning) and rusting to take place.
1781	Henry Cavendish showed water to be a compound.
1792	Alessandra Volta demonstrated the electrochemical series.
1807	Humphry Davy passed electric current through molten compounds (the process of electrolysis) in order to isolate elements, such as potassium, that had never been separated by chemical means. Jo#4ns Berzelius proposed that chemicals produced by living creatures should be termed "organic'.
1808	John Dalton published his atomic theory, which states that every element consists of similar indivisible particles – called atoms – which differ from the atoms of other elements in their mass; he also drew up a list of relative atomic masses. Joseph Gay-Lussac announced that the volumes of gases that combine chemically with one another are in simple ratios.
1811	Publication of Amedeo Avogadro's hypothesis on the relation between the volume and number of molecules of a gas, and its temperature and pressure.
1813–14	Berzelius devised the chemical symbols and formulae still used to represent elements and compounds.
1828	Franz Wöhler converted ammonium cyanate into urea – the first synthesis of an organic compound from an inorganic substance.
1832–33	Michael Faraday expounded the laws of electrolysis, and adopted the term "ion' for the particles believed to be responsible for carrying current.
1846	Thomas Graham expounded his law of diffusion.
1853	Robert Bunsen invented the Bunsen burner.
1858	Stanislao Cannizzaro differentiated between atomic and molecular weights (masses).
1861	Organic chemistry was defined by German chemist Friedrich Kekulé as the chemistry of carbon compounds.
1864	John Newlands devised the first periodic table of the elements.
1869	Dmitri Mendeleyev expounded his periodic table of the elements (based on atomic weight), leaving gaps for elements that had not yet been discovered.
1874	Jacobus van't Hoff suggested that the four bonds of carbon are arranged tetrahedrally, and that carbon compounds can therefore be three-dimensional and asymmetric.
1884	Swedish chemist Svante Arrhenius suggested that electrolytes (solutions or molten compounds that conduct electricity) dissociate into ions, atoms or groups of atoms that carry a positive or negative charge.
1894	William Ramsey and Lord Rayleigh discovered the first inert gases, argon.
1897	The electron was discovered by J J Thomson.
1901	Mikhail Tsvet invented paper chromatography as a means of separating pigments.
1909	Sören Sörensen devised the pH scale of acidity.
1912	Max von Laue showed crystals to be composed of regular, repeating arrays of atoms by studying the patterns in which they diffract X-rays.
1913–14	Henry Moseley equated the atomic number of an element with the positive charge on its nuclei, and drew up the periodic table, based on atomic number, that is used today.

***chemistry: chronology** (cont.)*

1916	Gilbert Newton Lewis explained covalent bonding between atoms as a sharing of electrons.
1927	Nevil Sidgwick published his theory of valency, based on the numbers of electrons in the outer shells of the reacting atoms.
1930	Electrophoresis, which separates particles in suspension in an electric field, was invented by Arne Tiselius.
1932	Deuterium (heavy hydrogen), an isotope of hydrogen, was discovered by Harold Urey.
1940	Edwin McMillan and Philip Abelson showed that new elements with a higher atomic number than uranium can be formed by bombarding uranium with neutrons, and synthesized the first transuranic element, neptunium.
1942	Plutonium was first synthesized by Glenn T Seaborg and Edwin McMillan.
1950	Derek Barton deduced that some properties of organic compounds are affected by the orientation of their functional groups (the study of which became known as conformational analysis).
1954	Einsteinium and fermium were synthesized.
1955	Ilya Prigogine described the thermodynamics of irreversible processes (the transformations of energy that take place in, for example, many reactions within living cells).
1962	Neil Bartlett prepared the first compound of an inert gas, xenon hexafluoroplatinate; it was previously believed that inert gases could not take part in a chemical reaction.
1965	Robert B Woodward synthesized complex organic compounds .
1981	Quantum mechanics applied to predict course of chemical reactions by US chemist Roald Hoffmann and Kenichi Fukui of Japan.
1982	Element 109, unnilennium, synthesized.
1985	Fullerenes, a new class of carbon solids made up of closed cages of carbon atoms, were discovered by Harold Kroto and David Walton at the University of Sussex, England.
1987	US chemists Donald Cram and Charles Pederson, and Jean-Marie Lehn of France created artificial molecules that mimic the vital chemical reactions of life processes.
1990	Jean-Marie Lehn, Ulrich Koert, and Margaret Harding reported the synthesis of a new class of compounds, called nucleohelicates, that mimic the double helical structure of DNA, turned inside out.

tion is boiled and the vapours of the solvent rise into a separate piece of apparatus (the condenser) where they are cooled and condensed. The liquid produced (the distillate) is the pure solvent; the non-volatile solutes (now in solid form) remain in the distillation vessel to be discarded as impurities or recovered as required. Mixtures of liquids (such as petroleum or aqueous ethanol) are separated by ***fractional distillation***, or fractionation.

elastomer any material with rubbery properties, which stretches easily and then quickly returns to its original length when released. Natural and synthetic rubbers and such materials as polychloroprene and butadiene copolymers are elastomers. The convoluted molecular chains making up these materials are uncoiled by a stretching force, but return to their original position when released because there are relatively few crosslinks between the chains.

electron stable, negatively charged elementary particle, a constituent of all atoms, and the basic particle of electricity. The electrons in each atom surround the nucleus in groupings called shells; in a neutral atom the number of electrons is equal to the number of protons in the nucleus. This electron structure is responsible for the chemical properties of the atom. A beam of electrons will undergo diffraction (scattering) and produce interference patterns in the same way as electromagnetic waves such as light; hence they may also be regarded as waves.

electronegativity the ease with which an atom can attract electrons to itself. Electronegative elements attract electrons, forming negative ions. Nonmetals such as fluorine and chlorine have the highest values of electronegativity; metals have low values.

electrophoresis powerful technique used to separate and identify chemical compounds in a mixture. By applying an electric field to a mixture of chemicals in solution, they are made to migrate at different speeds within a plastic gel or piece of filter paper. Genetic fingerprinting depends on this technique.

element substance that cannot be split chemically into simpler substances. The atoms of a particular element all have the same number of protons in their nuclei (their atomic number). Of the 109 known elements, 95 are known to occur in nature (those with atomic numbers 1–95). Those from 96 to 109 do not occur in nature and are synthesized only, produced in particle accelerators. Eighty-one of the elements are stable; all the others, which include atomic numbers 43, 61, and from 84 up, are radioactive. The elements are classified in the periodic table.

Symbols are used to denote the elements; the symbol is usually the first letter or letters of the English or Latin name (for example, C for carbon, Ca for calcium, Fe for iron, *ferrum*). The symbol represents one atom of the element.

elution washing out of an adsorbed substance from the adsorbing material; it is used, for example, in the separation processes of chromatography and electrophoresis.

emulsion a stable dispersion of a liquid in another liquid – for example, oil and water in some cosmetic lotions.

energy of reaction energy released or absorbed during a chemical reaction, also called ***enthalpy of reaction*** or ***heat of reaction***. In a chemical reaction, the energy stored in the reacting molecules is rarely

Discovery of the elements

Date	Element (symbol)	Discoverer
prehistoric knowledge	antimony (Sb)	
	arsenic (As)	
	bismuth (Bi)	
	carbon (C)	
	copper (Cu)	
	gold (Au)	
	iron (Fe)	
	lead (Pb)	
	mercury (Hg)	
	silver (Ag)	
	sulphur (S)	
	tin (Sn)	
	zinc (Zn)	
1557	platinum (Pt)	Julius Scaliger
1669	phosphorus (P)	Hennig Brand
1702	boron (B)	Wilhelm Homberg
1735	cobalt (Co)	Georg Brandt
1751	nickel (Ni)	Axel Cronstedt
1755	magnesium (Mg)	Joseph Black (isolated by Humphry Davy 1808)
1766	hydrogen (H)	Henry Cavendish
1771	fluorine (F)	Karl Scheele (isolated by Henri Moissan 1886)
1772	nitrogen (N)	Daniel Rutherford
1774	chlorine (Cl)	Karl Scheele
	manganese (Mn)	Johann Gottlieb Gahn
	oxygen (O)	Joseph Priestley and Karl Scheele, independently of each other
1778	molybdenum (Mo)	detected by Karl Scheele (isolated by Peter Jacob Hjelm 1782)
1782	tellurium (Te)	Franz Müller
1783	tungsten (W)	Juan José Elhuyar and Fausto Elhuyar
1789	uranium (U)	Martin Klaproth (isolated by Eugène Péligot 1841)
	zirconium (Zr)	Martin Klaproth
1790	titanium (Ti)	William Gregor
1794	yttrium (Y)	Johan Gadolin
1797	chromium (Cr)	Louis-Nicolas Vauquelin
1798	beryllium (Be)	Louis-Nicolas Vauquelin (isolated by Friedrich Wöhler and Antoine-Alexandre-Brutus Bussy 1828)
1801	vanadium (V)	Andrés del Rio (disputed), or Nils Sefström 1830
1801	niobium (Nb)	Charles Hatchett
1802	tantalum (Ta)	Anders Ekeberg
1803	cerium (Ce)	Jöns Berzelius and Wilhelm Hisinger, and independently by Martin Klaproth
	iridium (Ir)	Smithson Tennant
	osmium (Os)	Smithson Tennant
	palladium (Pd)	William Wollaston
	rhodium (Rh)	William Wollaston
1807	potassium (K)	Humphry Davy
	sodium (Na)	Humphry Davy
1808	barium (Ba)	Humphry Davy
	boron (B)	Humphry Davy, and independently by Joseph Gay-Lussac and Louis-Jacques Thénard
	calcium (Ca)	Humphry Davy
	strontium (Sr)	Humphry Davy
1811	iodine (I)	Bernard Courtois
1817	cadmium (Cd)	Friedrich Strohmeyer
	lithium (Li)	Johan Arfwedson
	selenium (Se)	Jöns Berzelius
1823	silicon (Si)	Jö4ns Berzelius
1824	aluminium (Al)	Hans Oersted (also attributed to Friedrich Wöhler 1827)
1826	bromine (Br)	Antoine-Jérôme Balard
1827	ruthenium (Ru)	G W Osann (isolated by Karl Klaus 1844)
1828	thorium (Th)	Jöns Berzelius
1839	lanthanum (La)	Carl Mosander
1842	erbium (Er)	Carl Mosander
1843	terbium (Tb)	Carl Mosander
1860	caesium (Cs)	Robert Bunsen and Gustav Kirchoff

the same as that stored in the product molecules. Depending on which is the greater, energy is either released (an ***exothermic reaction***) or absorbed (an ***endothermic reaction***) from the surroundings. The amount of energy released or absorbed by the quantities of substances represented by the chemical equation is the energy of reaction.

formula a representation of a molecule, radical, or ion, in which the component chemical elements are represented by their symbols. An ***empirical formula*** indicates the simplest ratio of the elements in a compound, without indicating how many of them there are or how they are combined. A ***molecular formula*** gives the number of each type of element present in one molecule. A ***structural formula*** shows the relative positions of the atoms and the bonds between them. For example, for ethanoic acid, the empirical formula is CH_2O, the molecular formula is $C_2H_4O_2$, and the structural formula is CH_3COOH.

fractional distillation or ***fractionation*** form of distillation used in industry to separate the components of a liquid mixture, for example petroleum. When the mixture is boiled, the vapours of its most volatile component rise into a vertical fractionating column where they condense to liquid form. However, as this liquid runs back down the column it is reheated to boiling point by the hot rising vapours of the next-most-volatile component and so its vapours

Date	*Element (symbol)*	*Discoverer*
1861	rubidium (Rb)	Robert Bunsen and Gustav Kirchoff
	thallium (Tl)	William Crookes (isolated by William Crookes and Claude August Lamy, independently of each other 1862)
1863	indium (In)	Ferdinand Reich and Hieronymus Richter
1868	helium (He)	Pierre Janssen
1875	gallium (Ga)	Paul Lecoq de Boisbaudran
1876	scandium (Sc)	Lars Nilson
1878	ytterbium (Yb)	Jean Charles de Marignac
1879	holmium (Ho)	Per Cleve
	samarium (Sm)	Paul Lecoq de Boisbaudran
	thulium (Tm)	Per Cleve
1885	neodymium (Nd)	Carl von Welsbach
	praseodymium (Pr)	Carl von Welsbach
1886	dysprosium (Dy)	Paul Lecoq de Boisbaudran
	gadolinium (Gd)	Paul Lecoq de Boisbaudran
	germanium (Ge)	Clemens Winkler
1894	argon (Ar)	John Rayleigh and William Ramsay
1898	krypton (Kr)	William Ramsay and Morris Travers
	neon (Ne)	William Ramsay and Morris Travers
	polonium (Po)	Marie and Pierre Curie
	radium (Ra)	Marie Curie
	xenon (Xe)	William Ramsay and Morris Travers
1899	actinium (Ac)	André Debierne
1900	radon (Rn)	Friedrich Dorn
1901	europium (Eu)	Eugène Demarçay
1907	lutetium (Lu)	Georges Urbain and Carl von Welsbach independently of each other

ascend the column once more. This boiling-condensing process occurs repeatedly inside the column, eventually bringing about a temperature gradient along its length. The vapours of the more volatile components therefore reach the top of the column and enter the condenser for collection before those of the less volatile components. In the fractional distillation of petroleum, groups of compounds (fractions) possessing similar relative molecular masses and boiling points are tapped off at different points on the column.

free radical an atom or molecule that has an unpaired electron and is therefore highly reactive. Most free radicals are very short-lived. If free radicals are produced in living organisms they can be very damaging.

freezing point for any given liquid, the temperature at which any further removal of heat will convert the liquid into the solid state. The temperature remains at this point until all the liquid has solidified. It is invariable under similar conditions of pressure – for example, the freezing point of water under standard atmospheric pressure is 0°C/32°F.

immiscible term describing liquids that will not mix with each other, such as oil and water. When two immiscible liquids are shaken together, a turbid mixture is produced. This normally forms separate layers when it is left to stand.

indicator chemical compound that changes its structure and colour in response to its environment. The commonest chemical indicators detect changes in pH (for example, litmus), or in the oxidation state of a system (redox indicators).

ion atom, or group of atoms, that is either positively charged (***cation***) or negatively charged (***anion***), as a result of the loss or gain of electrons during chemical reactions or exposure to certain forms of radiation.

ion exchange process whereby an ion in one compound is replaced by a different ion, of the same charge, from another compound. It is the basis of a type of chromatography in which the components of a mixture of ions in solution are separated according to the ease with which they will replace the ions on the polymer matrix through which they flow. Ion-exchange is used in commercial water softeners to exchange the dissolved ions responsible for the water's hardness with others that do not have this effect.

ionic bond or ***electrovalent bond*** bond produced when atoms of one element donate electrons to atoms of another element, forming positively and negatively charged ions respectively. The electrostatic attraction between the oppositely charged ions constitutes the bond. Sodium chloride (Na^+Cl^-) is a typical ionic compound.

isotope one of two or more atoms that have the same atomic number (same number of protons), but which contain a different number of neutrons, thus differing in their atomic masses. They may be stable or radioactive, naturally occurring or synthesized.

litmus dye obtained from various lichens and used in chemistry as an indicator to test the acidic or alkaline nature of aqueous solutions; it turns red in the presence of acid, and blue in the presence of alkali.

lone pair a pair of electrons in the outermost shell of an atom that are not used in bonding. In certain circumstances, they will allow the atom to bond with atoms, ions, or molecules (such as boron trifluoride, BF_3) that are deficient in electrons, forming coordinate covalent (dative) bonds in which they provide both of the bonding electrons.

mass action, law of law stating that at a given temperature the rate at which a chemical reaction takes place is proportional to the product of the active masses of the reactants. The active mass is taken to be the molar concentration of the each reactant.

periodic table of the elements

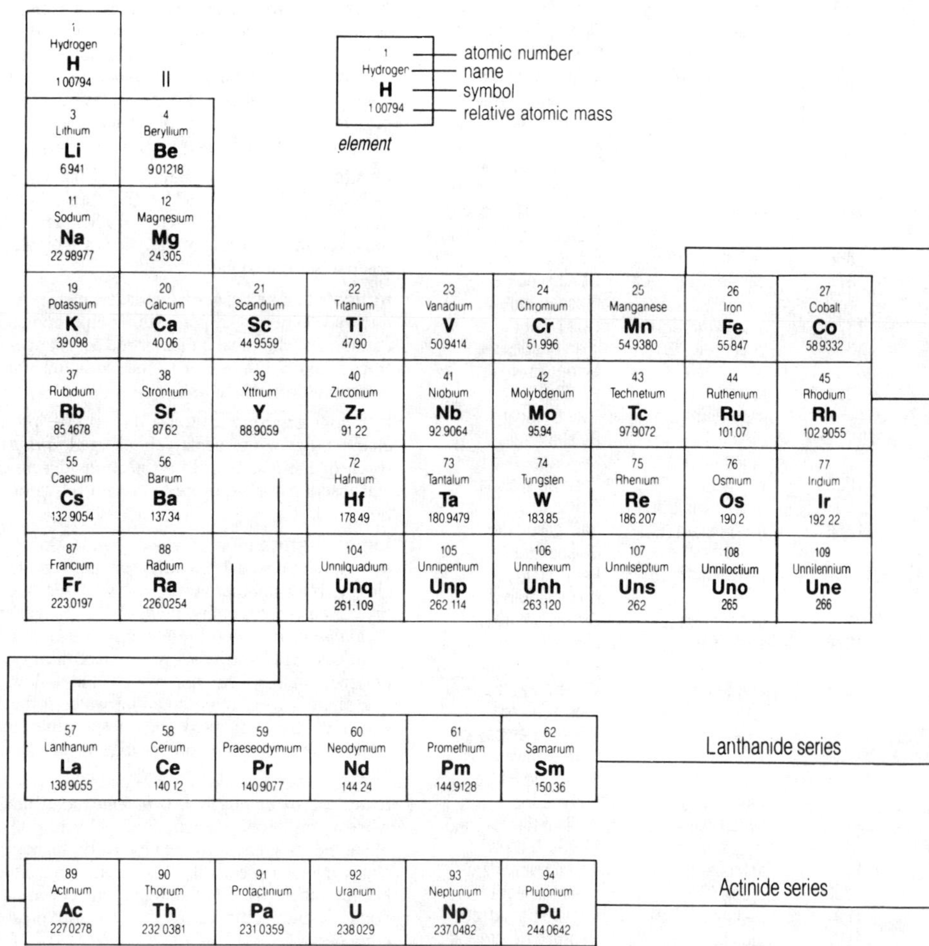

methylated spirit alcohol that has been rendered undrinkable, and is used for industrial purposes, as a fuel for spirit burners or a solvent.

mixture a substance containing two or more compounds that still retain their separate physical and chemical properties. There is no chemical bonding between them and they can be separated from each other by physical means.

molecule group of two or more atoms bonded together. A molecule of an element consists of one or more like atoms; a molecule of a compound consists of two or more different atoms bonded together. Molecules vary in size and complexity from the hydrogen molecule (H_2) to the large macromolecules of proteins. They are held together by ionic bonds, in which the atoms gain or lose electrons to form ions, or by covalent bonds, where electrons from each atom are shared in a new molecular orbital.

Most molecules are made up of small numbers of atoms but some contain rather more. For example, a molecule of aspirin contains 21 atoms. A molecule of haemoglobin, a substance found in blood, contains 758 carbon atoms, 1,203 hydrogen atoms, 195 oxygen atoms, 218 nitrogen atoms, one iron atom, and three sulphur atoms. Rubber molecules may have up to 65,000 atoms.

neutralization a process occurring when the excess acid (or excess base) in a substance is reacted with added base (or added acid) so that the resulting substance is neither acidic nor basic. In theory neutralization involves adding acid or base as required to achieve pH 7.0.

neutral solution solution of pH 7, in which the concentrations of $H^+_{(aq)}$ and $OH^-_{(aq)}$ ions are equal.

neutron one of the three chief subatomic particles (the others being the proton and the electron). Neutrons have about the same mass as protons but no electric charge, and occur in the nuclei of all atoms except hydrogen. They contribute to the mass of atoms but do not affect their chemistry, which depends on the proton or electron numbers. For

			III	IV	V	VI	VII	0
								2 Helium **He** 4 00260
			5 Boron **B** 10 81	6 Carbon **C** 12 011	7 Nitrogen **N** 14 0067	8 Oxygen **O** 15 9994	9 Fluorine **F** 18 99840	10 Neon **Ne** 20 179
			13 Aluminium **Al** 26 98154	14 Silicon **Si** 28 086	15 Phosphorus **P** 30 97376P	16 Sulphur **S** 32 06	17 Chlorine **Cl** 35 453	18 Argon **Ar** 39 948
28 Nickel **Ni** 58 70	29 Copper **Cu** 63 546	30 Zinc **Zn** 65 38	31 Gallium **Ga** 69 72	32 Germanium **Ge** 72 59	33 Arsenic **As** 74 9216	34 Selenium **Se** 78 96	35 Bromine **Br** 79 904	36 Krypton **Kr** 83 80
46 Palladium **Pd** 106 4	47 Silver **Ag** 107 868	48 Cadmium **Cd** 112 40	49 Indium **In** 114 82	50 Tin **Sn** 118 69	51 Antimony **Sb** 121 75	52 Tellurium **Te** 127 75	53 Iodine **I** 126 9045	54 Xenon **Xe** 131 30
78 Platinum **Pt** 195 09	79 Gold **Au** 196 9665	80 Mercury **Hg** 200 59	81 Thallium **Tl** 204 37	82 Lead **Pb** 207 37	83 Bismuth **Bi** 207 2	84 Polonium **Po** 210	85 Astatine **At** 211	86 Radon **Rn** 222 0176

63 Europium **Eu** 151 96	64 Gadolinium **Gd** 157 25	65 Terbium **Tb** 158 9254	66 Dysprosium **Dy** 162 50	67 Holmium **Ho** 164 9304	68 Erbium **Er** 167 26	69 Thulium **Tm** 168 9342	70 Ytterbium **Yb** 173 04	71 Lutetium **Lu** 174 97
95 Americium **Am** 243 0614	96 Curium **Cm** 247 0703	97 Berkelium **Bk** 247 0703	98 Californium **Cf** 251 0786	99 Einsteinium **Es** 252 0828	100 Fermium **Fm** 257 0951	101 Mendelevium **Me** 258.0986	102 Nobelium **No** 259 1009	103 Lawrencium **Lr** 260 1054

instance, isotopes of a single element (with different masses) differ only in the number of neutrons in their nuclei and have identical chemical properties.

oxidation the loss of electrons, gain of oxygen, or loss of hydrogen by an atom, ion, or molecule during a chemical reaction.

paraffin common name for alkane, any member of the series of hydrocarbons with the general formula C_nH_{2n+2}.

PCB abbreviation for ***polychlorinated biphenyl***.

periodic table of the elements a table of classification of the elements arranged in order by their atomic numbers. The table summarizes the major properties of the elements, which are a direct consequence of the electronic (and nuclear) structure of their atoms, and enables predictions to be made about their behaviour. There are striking similarities in the chemical properties of the elements in each of the vertical columns (called ***groups***), which are numbered I–VII and then 0 (from left to right) to reflect the number of electrons in the outermost unfilled shell and hence the maximum valency. A gradation of properties may be traced along the horizontal rows (called ***periods***). Metallic character increases across a period from right to left, and down a group. A large block of elements, between groups II and III, contains the transition elements, characterized by displaying more than one valency state.

The first periodic table was devised by Russian chemist Dmitri Mendeleyev 1869; the elements being arranged by atomic mass (rather than by atomic number in today's table) in accordance with Mendeleyev's statement 'the properties of elements are in periodic dependence upon their atomic weight'.

pH scale from 0 to 14 for measuring acidity or alkalinity. A pH of 7.0 indicates neutrality, below 7 is acid, while above 7 is alkaline. The pH of a solution can be measured by using a broad-range indicator, either in solution or as a paper strip. The colour produced by the indicator is compared

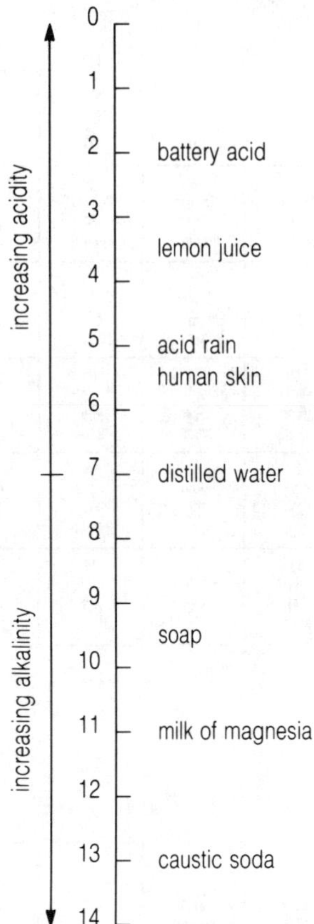

with a colour code related to the pH value. An alternative method is to use a pH meter fitted with a glass electrode.

photolysis chemical reaction that is driven by light or ultraviolet radiation. For example, the light reaction of photosynthesis (the process by which green plants manufacture carbohydrates from carbon dioxide and water) is a photolytic reaction.

polychlorinated biphenyl (PCB) any of a group of chlorinated isomers of biphenyl $(C_6H_5)_2$. They are dangerous industrial chemicals, valuable for their fire-resisting qualities. They constitute an environmental hazard because of their persistent toxicity. Since 1973 their use has been limited by international agreement.

precipitation the formation of an insoluble solid in a liquid as a result of a reaction within the liquid between two or more soluble substances. If the solid settles, it forms a ***precipitate***; if the particles of solid are very small, they will remain in suspension, forming a ***colloidal precipitate***.

proton positively charged subatomic particle, a fundamental constituent of any atomic nucleus. Its lifespan is effectively infinite. A proton carries a unit positive charge equal to the negative charge of an electron. The number of protons in the atom of an element is equal to its atomic, or proton, number.

radioactivity spontaneous alteration of the nuclei of radioactive atoms, accompanied by the emission of radiation. It is the property exhibited by the radioactive isotopes of stable elements and all isotopes of radioactive elements, and can be either natural or induced.

rate of reaction the speed at which a chemical reaction proceeds. It is usually expressed in terms of the concentration (usually in moles per litre) of a reactant consumed, or product formed, in unit time; so the units would be moles per litre per second (mol l^{-1} s^{-1}). The rate of a reaction may be affected by the concentration of the reactants, the temperature of the reactants, and the presence of a catalyst. If the reaction is entirely in the gas state, the rate is affected by pressure, and, for solids, it is affected by the particle size.

reaction the coming together of two or more atoms, ions, or molecules with the result that a chemical change takes place. The nature of the reaction is portrayed by a chemical equation.

reactivity series chemical series produced by arranging the metals in order of their ease of reaction with reagents such as oxygen, water, and acids. This arrangement aids the understanding of the properties of metals, helps to explain differences between them, and enables predictions to be made about a metal's behaviour, based on a knowledge of its position or properties.

redox reaction chemical change where one reactant is reduced and the other reactant oxidized. The reaction can only occur if both reactants are present and each changes simultaneously. For example, hydrogen reduces copper(II) oxide to copper while it is itself oxidized to water. The corrosion of iron and the reactions taking place in electric and electrolytic cells are just a few instances of redox reactions.

reduction the gain of electrons, loss of oxygen, or gain of hydrogen by an atom, ion, or molecule during a chemical reaction.

relative atomic mass the mass of an atom relative to one-twelfth the mass of an atom of carbon-12. It depends on the number of protons and neutrons in the atom, the electrons having negligible mass. If more than one isotope of the element is present, the relative atomic mass is calculated by taking an average that takes account of the relative proportions of each isotope, resulting in values that are not whole numbers. The term ***atomic weight***, although commonly used, is strictly speaking incorrect.

repellent anything of which the smell, taste, or other properties discourages nearby creatures. ***Insect repellent*** is usually a chemical substance that keeps, for example, mosquitoes at bay; natural substances include citronella, lavender oil, and eucalyptus oils. A device that emits ultrasound waves is also claimed to repel insects and small mammals. The bitter-tasting denatonium saccharide may be added to medicines to prevent consumption by children, and to plastic garbage bags to repel foraging animals.

salt any member of a group of compounds containing a positive ion (cation) derived from a metal or ammonia and a negative ion (anion) derived from an acid or nonmetal. If the negative ion has a replaceable hydrogen atom it is an ***acid salt*** (for example sodium hydrogensulphate, $NaHSO_4$; potassium phosphonate, KH_2PO_4; sodium hydrogencarbonate, $NaHCO_3$); if not, it is classed as a ***normal salt*** (for example sodium chloride, NaCl; potassium sulphate, K_2SO_4; magnesium nitrate, $Mg(NO_3)_2$). ***Common salt*** is sodium chloride. Salts have the properties typical of ionic compounds.

Crystals of common salt (NaCl) are made up of small cubes of atoms. A crystal of rock salt contains 40,000 million million million atoms in each cubic centimetre, arranged in tiny cubes 0.00000002 cm/0.000000008 in across.

solute substance that is dissolved in another substance.

solution two or more substances mixed to form a single, homogenous phase. One of the substances is the ***solvent*** and the others (***solutes***) are said to be dissolved in it. The constituents of a solution may be solid, liquid, or gaseous. The solvent is normally the substance that is present in greatest quantity; however, if one of the constituents is a liquid this is considered to be the solvent even if it is not the major substance.

solvent substance, usually a liquid, that will dissolve another substance. Although the commonest solvent is water, in popular use the term refers to low-boiling-point organic liquids, which are harmful if used in a confined space. They can give rise to respiratory problems, liver damage, and neurological complaints. Typical organic solvents are petroleum distillates (in glues), xylol (in paints), alcohols (for synthetic and natural resins such as shellac), esters (in lacquers, including nail varnish), ketones (in cellulose lacquers and resins), and chlorinated hydrocarbons (as paint stripper and dry-cleaning fluids).

standard temperature and pressure (STP) a standard set of conditions for experimental measurements, to enable comparisons to be made between sets of results. Standard temperature is 0°C and standard pressure 1 atmosphere (101,325 Pa).

strength of acids and bases the ability of acids and bases to dissociate in solution with water, and hence to produce a low or high pH respectively. A strong acid is fully dissociated in aqueous solution and has a low pH, whereas a weak acid is only partly dissociated and has a higher pH. A strong base will have a high pH, whereas a weaker base will not dissociate completely and will have a pH of nearer 7.

sublimation the conversion of a solid to vapour without passing through the liquid phase. Some substances that do not sublime at atmospheric pressure can be made to do so at low pressures. This is the principle of freeze-drying, during which ice sublimes at low pressure.

surfactant (contraction of ***surface-active agent***) substance added to a liquid in order to increase its wetting or spreading properties. Detergents are examples.

tautomerism form of isomerism (when substances have the same molecular formula) in which two interconvertible isomers are in equilibrium. It is often specifically applied to an equilibrium between the keto (–C–C=O) and enol (–C=C–OH) forms of carbonyl compounds.

triple bond three covalent bonds between adjacent atoms, as in the alkynes (–C≡C–).

universal indicator a mixture of pH indicators, used to gauge the acidity or alkalinity of a solution. Each component changes colour at a different pH value, and so the indicator is capable of displaying a range of colours, according to the pH of the test solution, from red (at pH 1) to purple (at pH 13).

valency the measure of an element's ability to combine with other elements, expressed as the number of atoms of hydrogen (or any other standard univalent element) capable of uniting with (or replacing) its atoms. The number of electrons in the outermost shell of the atom dictates the combining ability of an element.

zwitterion ion that has both a positive and a negative charge, such as an amino acid in neutral solution. For example, glycine contains both a basic amino group (NH^2) and an acidic carboxyl group (–COOH); when both these are ionized in aqueous solution, the acid group loses a proton to the amino group, and the molecule is positively charged at one end and negatively charged at the other.

Great Chemists

Arrhenius Svante August 1859–1927. Swedish scientist, the founder of physical chemistry. Born near Uppsala, he became a professor at Stockholm in 1895, and made a special study of electrolysis. He wrote *Worlds in the Making* and *Destinies of the Stars*, and in 1903 received the Nobel Prize for Chemistry. In 1905 he predicted global warming as a result of carbon dioxide emission from burning fossil fuels.

Berzelius Jöns Jakob 1779–1848. Swedish chemist who accurately determined more than 2,000 relative atomic and molecular masses. He devised (1813–14) the system of chemical symbols and formulae now in use and proposed oxygen as a reference standard for atomic masses. His discoveries include the elements cerium (1804), selenium (1817), and thorium (1828); he was the first to prepare silicon in its amorphous form and to isolate zirconium. The words ***isomerism***, ***allotropy***, and ***protein*** were coined by him.

Cannizzaro Stanislao 1826–1910. Italian chemist who revived interest in the work of Avogadro that had, in 1811, revealed the difference between atoms and molecules, and so established atomic and molecular weights as the basis of chemical calculations.

Curie Marie (born Sklodovska) 1867–1934. Polish scientist. In 1898 she reported the possible existence of a new, powerfully radioactive element in pitchblende ores. Her husband, Pierre (1859–1906) abandoned his own researches to assist her, and in the same year they announced the existence of polonium and radium. They isolated the pure elements 1902. Both scientists refused to take out a patent on their discovery and were jointly awarded the Davy Medal 1903 and the Nobel Prize for Physics 1903, with Antoine Becquerel. Marie Curie wrote a *Treatise on Radioactivity* 1910, and was awarded the Nobel Prize for Chemistry 1911.

Nobel Prize for Chemistry (1956–92)

Year	*Prizewinners*
1956	Cyril Hinshelwood (UK) and Nikoly Semenov (USSR): mechanism of chemical reactions
1957	Alexander Todd (UK): nucleotides and nucleotide coenzymes
1958	Frederick Sanger (UK): structure of proteins, especially insulin
1959	Jaroslav Heyrovský (Czechoslovakia): polarographic methods of chemical analysis
1960	Willard Libby (USA): radiocarbon dating in archaeology, geology, and geography
1961	Melvin Calvin (USA): assimilation of carbon dioxide by plants
1962	Max Perutz (UK) and John Kendrew (UK): structures of globular proteins
1963	Karl Ziegler (West Germany) and Giulio Natta (Italy): chemistry and technology of high polymers
1964	Dorothy Crowfoot Hodgkin (UK): crystallographic determination of the structures of biochemical compounds, notably penicillin and cyanocobalamin (vitamin B!12!)
1965	Robert Woodward (USA): organic synthesis
1966	Robert Mulliken (USA): molecular orbital theory of chemical bonds and structures
1967	Manfred Eigen (West Germany), Ronald Norrish (UK), and George Porter (UK): investigation of rapid chemical reactions by means of very short pulses of energy
1968	Lars Onsager (USA): discovery of reciprocal relations, fundamental for the thermodynamics of irreversible processes
1969	Derek Barton (UK) and Odd Hassel (Norway): concept and applications of conformation
1970	Luis Federico Leloir (Argentina): discovery of sugar nucleotides and their role in carbohydrate biosynthesis
1971	Gerhard Herzberg (Canada): electronic structure and geometry of molecules, particularly free radicals
1972	Christian Anfinsen (USA), Stanford Moore (USA), and William Stein (USA): amino-acid structure and biological activity of the enzyme ribonuclease
1973	Ernst Fischer (West Germany) and Geoffrey Wilkinson (UK): chemistry of organometallic sandwich compounds
1974	Paul Flory (USA): physical chemistry of macromolecules
1975	John Cornforth (Australia): stereochemistry of enzyme-catalysed reactions. Vladimir Prelog (Yugoslavia): stereochemistry of organic molecules and their reactions
1976	William N Lipscomb (USA): structure and chemical bonding of boranes (compounds of boron and hydrogen)
1977	Ilya Prigogine (USSR): thermodynamics of irreversible and dissipative processes
1978	Peter Mitchell (UK): biological energy transfer and chemiosmotic theory
1979	Herbert Brown (USA) and Georg Wittig (West Germany): use of boron and phosphorus compounds, respectively, in organic syntheses
1980	Paul Berg (USA): biochemistry of nucleic acids, especially recombinant-DNA. Walter Gilbert (USA) and Frederick Sanger (UK): base sequences in nucleic acids
1981	Kenichi Fukui (Japan) and Roald Hoffmann (USA): theories concerning chemical reactions
1982	Aaron Klug (UK): crystallographic electron microscopy: structure of biologically important nucleic-acid-protein complexes
1983	Henry Taube (USA): electron-transfer reactions in inorganic chemical reactions
1984	Bruce Merrifield (USA): chemical syntheses on a solid matrix
1985	Herbert A Hauptman (USA) and Jerome Karle (USA): methods of determining crystal structures
1986	Dudley Herschbach (USA), Yuan Lee (USA), and John Polanyi (Canada): dynamics of chemical elementary processes
1987	Donald Cram (USA), Jean-Marie Lehn (France), and Charles Pedersen (USA): molecules with highly selective structure-specific interactions
1988	Johann Deisenhofer (West Germany), Robert Huber (West Germany), and Hartmut Michel (West Germany): three-dimensional structure of the reaction centre of photosynthesis
1989	Sydney Altman (USA) and Thomas Cech (USA): discovery of catalytic function of RNA
1990	Elias James Corey (USA): new methods of synthesizing chemical compounds
1991	Richard R Ernst (Switzerland): improvements in the technology of nuclear magnetic resonance (NMR) imaging
1992	Rudolph A Marcus (USA): theoretical discoveries relating to reduction and oxidation reactions.

Dalton John 1766–1844. English chemist who proposed the theory of atoms, which he considered to be the smallest parts of matter. He produced the first list of relative atomic masses in *Absorption of Gases* 1805 and put forward the law of partial pressures of gases (Dalton's law).

Davy Humphry 1778–1829. English chemist. He discovered, by electrolysis, the metallic elements sodium and potassium in 1807, and calcium, boron, magnesium, strontium, and barium in 1808. In addition, he established that chlorine is an element and proposed that hydrogen is present in all acids. He invented the 'safety lamp' for use in mines where methane was present, enabling miners to work in previously unsafe conditions.

Domagk Gerhard 1895–1964. German pathologist, discoverer of antibacterial sulphonamide drugs. He found in 1932 that a coal-tar dye called Prontosil red contains chemicals with powerful antibacterial properties. Sulphanilamide became the first of the sulphonamide drugs, used before antibiotics were discovered to treat a wide range of conditions, including pneumonia and septic wounds. Domagk was awarded the 1939 Nobel Prize for Physiology and Medicine (which, because of Nazi opposition, he had to wait until 1947 to claim).

Faraday Michael 1791–1867. English chemist and physicist. In 1821 he began experimenting with electromagnetism, and ten years later discovered the induction of electric currents and made the first dynamo. He subsequently found that a magnetic field will rotate the plane of polarization of light. Faraday also investigated electrolysis.

Fischer Emil Hermann 1852–1919. German chemist who produced synthetic sugars and from these various enzymes. His descriptions of the chemistry of the carbohydrates and peptides laid the foundations for the science of biochemistry. Nobel prize 1902.

Gibbs Josiah Willard 1839–1903. US theoretical physicist and chemist who developed a mathematical approach to thermodynamics. His book *Vector Analysis* 1881 established vector methods in physics.

Grignard François Auguste-Victor 1871–1935. French chemist. In 1900 he discovered a series of organic compounds, the ***Grignard reagents***, that found applications as some of the most versatile reagents in organic synthesis. Members of the class contain a hydrocarbon radical, magnesium, and a halogen such as chlorine. He shared the 1912 Nobel Prize for Chemistry.

Haber Fritz 1868–1934. German chemist whose conversion of atmospheric nitrogen to ammonia opened the way for the synthetic fertilizer industry. His study of the combustion of hydrocarbons led to the commercial 'cracking' or fractional distillation of natural oil (petroleum) into its components (for example, diesel, petrol, and paraffin). In electrochemistry, he was the first to demonstrate that oxidation and reduction take place at the electrodes; from this he developed a general electrochemical theory.

Haworth Norman 1883–1950. English organic chemist who was the first to synthesize a vitamin (ascorbic acid, vitamin C) 1933, for which he shared a Nobel prize 1937.

Helmont Jean Baptiste van 1577–1644. Belgian doctor who was the first to realize that there are gases other than air, and claimed to have coined the word 'gas' (from Greek *cháos*).

Hodgkin Dorothy Crowfoot 1910– . English biochemist who analysed the structure of penicillin, insulin, and vitamin B_{12}. Hodgkin was the first to use a computer to analyse the molecular structure of complex chemicals, and this enabled her to produce three-dimensional models. She was awarded the Nobel Prize for Chemistry 1964.

Hofmann August Wilhelm von 1818–1892. German chemist who studied the extraction and exploitation of coal tar derivatives. Hofmann taught chemistry in London from 1845 until his return to Berlin in 1865.

Kekulé von Stradonitz Friedrich August 1829–1896. German chemist whose theory 1858 of molecular structure revolutionized organic chemistry. He proposed two resonant forms of the benzene ring.

Kendall Edward 1886–1972. US biochemist. In 1914 he isolated the hormone thyroxine, the active compound of the thyroid gland. He went on to work on secretions from the adrenal gland, among which he discovered a compound E, which was in fact the steroid cortisone. For this Kendall shared the 1950 Nobel Prize for Medicine with Philip Hench (1896–1965) and Tadeus Reichstein.

Kendrew John 1917– . British biochemist. Kendrew began, in 1946, the ambitious task of determining the three-dimensional structure of the major muscle protein myoglobin. This was completed in 1959 and won for Kendrew a share of the 1962 Nobel Prize for Chemistry with Max Perutz.

Kornberg Arthur 1918– . US biochemist. In 1956, Kornberg discovered the enzyme DNA-polymerase, which enabled molecules of DNA to be synthesized for the first time. For this work Kornberg shared the 1959 Nobel Prize for Medicine with Severo Ochoa.

Kuhn Richard 1900–1967. Austrian chemist. Working at Heidelberg University in the 1930s, Kuhn succeeded in determining the structures of vitamins A, B_2, and B_6. He was awarded the 1938 Nobel Prize for Chemistry, but was unable to receive it until after World War II.

Langmuir Irving 1881–1957. US scientist who invented the mercury vapour pump for producing a high vacuum, and the atomic hydrogen welding process; he was also a pioneer of the thermionic valve. In 1932 he was awarded a Nobel prize for his work on surface chemistry.

Lavoisier Antoine Laurent 1743–1794. French chemist. He proved that combustion needed only a part of the air, which he called oxygen, thereby destroying the theory of phlogiston (an imaginary 'fire element' released during combustion). With Pierre de Laplace, the astronomer and mathematician, he showed that water was a compound of oxygen and hydrogen. In this way he established the basic rules of chemical combination.

Liebig Justus, Baron von 1803–1873. German chemist, a major contributor to agricultural chemistry. He introduced the theory of radicals and discovered chloroform and chloral.

Martin Archer John Porter 1910– . British biochemist who received the 1952 Nobel Prize for Chemistry for work with Richard Synge on paper chromatography in 1944.

Mendeleyev Dmitri Ivanovich 1834–1907. Russian chemist who framed the periodic law in chemistry 1869, which states that the chemical properties of the elements depend on their relative atomic masses. This law is the basis of the periodic table of elements, in which the elements are arranged by atomic number and organized by their related groups. For this work, Mendeleyev and Lothar Meyer (who presented a similar but independent classification of the elements) received the Davy medal in 1882. From his table Mendeleyev predicted the properties of elements then unknown (gallium, scandium, and germanium).

Nernst (Walther) Hermann 1864–1941. German physical chemist. His investigations, for which he won the 1920 Nobel Prize for Chemistry, were concerned with heat changes in chemical reactions. He proposed in 1906 the principle known as the ***Nernst heat theorem*** or the third law of thermodynamics: the law states that chemical changes at the temperature of absolute zero involve no change of entropy (disorder).

Nobel Alfred Bernhard 1833–1896. Swedish chemist and engineer. He invented dynamite in 1867 and ballistite, a smokeless gunpowder, in 1889. He amassed a large fortune from the manufacture of explosives and the exploitation of the Baku oilfields in Azerbaijan, near the Caspian Sea. He left this fortune in trust for the endowment of five Nobel prizes.

Ochoa Severo 1905– . Spanish-born US biochemist. He discovered an enzyme able to assemble units of the nucleic acid RNA in 1955, while working at New York University. For his work towards the synthesis of RNA, Ochoa shared the 1959 Nobel Prize for Medicine with Arthur Kornberg.

Ostwald Wilhelm 1853–1932. German chemist who devised the Ostwald process (the oxidation of ammonia over a platinum catalyst to give nitric acid). His work on catalysts laid the foundations of the petrochemical industry. He won the Nobel Prize for Chemistry 1909.

Pauling Linus Carl 1901– . US chemist, author of fundamental work on the nature of the chemical bond and on the discovery of the helical structure of many proteins. He also investigated the properties and uses of vitamin C as related to human health. He won the Nobel Prize for Chemistry 1954. An outspoken opponent of nuclear testing, he also received the Nobel Peace Prize in 1962.

Perutz Max 1914– . Austrian-born British biochemist who shared the 1962 Nobel Prize for Chemistry with John Kendrew for work on the structure of the haemoglobin molecule.

Porter George 1920– . English chemist. From 1949 he and Ronald Norrish (1897–1978) developed the technique by which flashes of high energy are used to bring about and study extremely fast chemical reactions. He shared the 1967 Nobel Prize for Chemistry with Norrish and German chemist Manfred Eigen.

Priestley Joseph 1733–1804. English chemist and Presbyterian minister. He identified the gas oxygen 1774. In 1791 his chapel and house were sacked by a mob because of his support for the French Revolution. He emigrated to the USA 1794.

Ramsay William 1852–1916. Scottish chemist who, with Lord Rayleigh, discovered argon 1894. In 1895 Ramsay produced helium and in 1898, in cooperation with Morris Travers (1872–1961), identified neon, krypton, and xenon. In 1903, with Frederick Soddy, he noted the transmutation of radium into helium, which led to the discovery of the density and relative atomic mass of radium. Nobel prize 1904.

Raoult François 1830–1901. French chemist. In 1882, while working at the University of Grenoble, Raoult formulated one of the basic laws of chemistry. ***Raoult's law*** enables the relative molecular mass of a substance to be determined by noting how much of it is required to depress the freezing point of a solvent by a certain amount.

Scheele Karl Wilhelm 1742–1786. Swedish chemist and pharmacist. In the book *Experiments on Air and Fire* 1777, he argued that the atmosphere was composed of two gases. One, which supported combustion (oxygen), he called 'fire air', and the other, which inhibited combustion (nitrogen), he called 'vitiated air'. He thus anticipated Joseph Priestley's discovery of oxygen by two years.

Seaborg Glenn Theodore 1912– . US nuclear chemist. He was awarded a Nobel prize in 1951 for his discoveries of transuranic elements (with atomic numbers greater than that of uranium), and for production of the radio-isotope uranium-233.

Soddy Frederick 1877–1956. English physical chemist who pioneered research into atomic disintegration and coined the term isotope. He was awarded a Nobel prize 1921 for investigating the origin and nature of isotopes.

Svedberg Theodor 1884–1971. Swedish chemist. In 1924 he constructed the first ultracentrifuge, a machine that allowed the rapid separation of particles by mass. He was awarded the Nobel Prize for Chemistry 1926.

Szent-Györgyi Albert 1893–1986. Hungarian-born US biochemist who isolated vitamin C and studied the chemistry of muscular activity. He was awarded the Nobel Prize for Medicine 1937.

Tiselius Arne 1902–1971. Swedish chemist who developed a powerful method of chemical analysis known as electrophoresis. He applied his new techniques to the analysis of animal proteins. Nobel prize 1948.

Todd Alexander, Baron Todd 1907– . British organic chemist who won a Nobel prize 1957 for his work on the role of nucleic acids in genetics. He also synthesized vitamins B_1, B_{12}, and E.

Urey Harold Clayton 1893–1981. US chemist. In 1932 he isolated heavy water and discovered deuterium, for which he was awarded the 1934 Nobel Prize for Chemistry.

Vane John 1927– . British pharmacologist who discovered the wide role of prostaglandins in the human body, produced in response to illness and stress. He shared the 1982 Nobel Prize for Medicine with Sune Bergström (1916–) and Bengt Samuelson (1934–) of Sweden.

Wöhler Friedrich 1800–1882. German chemist, a student of Jöns Berzelius, who in 1828 was the first person to synthesize an organic compound (urea) from an inorganic compound (ammonium cyanate). He also devised a method 1827 that isolated the metals aluminum, beryllium, yttrium, and titanium from their ores.

Ziegler Karl 1898–1973. German organic chemist. In 1963 he shared the Nobel Prize for Chemistry with Giulio Natta (1903–1979) of Italy for his work on the chemistry and technology of large polymers. He combined simple molecules of the gas ethylene (ethene) into the long-chain plastic polyethylene (polyethene).

COMPUTING AND ELECTRONICS

How Computers Work

Despite their impressive capabilities, computers are really only able to perform the simplest of tasks: adding or multiplying two numbers together; determining whether one number is greater than another; and so on. It is their ability to perform these tasks extremely quickly and in a predefined sequence that gives them their apparent power.

At the heart of the computer is a ***central processing unit*** (CPU). The CPU is built around an ***arithmetic and logic unit*** (ALU), which performs all the basic computations. It includes a set of ***registers*** that provide limited storage for immediate data and results. The whole thing is coordinated by an internal ***clock***.

The CPU is supported by ***memory***. This is used to store large amounts of data, as well as programs (instructions). There are two main types of memory. ***Internal memory*** (or ***immediate-access memory***) is readily available to the CPU. It can be accessed very quickly, but its contents are lost when the power is removed. ***External memory*** (or ***backing storage***) is used for longer-term storage. It is provided by such devices as magnetic discs (floppy and hard discs), optical discs (such as CD-ROM), and magnetic tape. These generally provide a higher capacity than internal memory, but are considerably slower. The CPU cannot access external memory directly, so data has to be transferred to internal memory before it can be used.

The CPU communicates with external devices by means of a ***bus***. This carries data between the various types of memory, and also to and from the ***ports***, to which peripherals such as keyboards, screens, and printers are attached.

Programming

Computers have no intelligence of their own. They work by carrying out the detailed instructions provided by a programmer. The programmer's job is to break down the required task into a series of simple steps.

Programs are written in a ***programming language***, designed for the convenience of the programmer. They are then translated into ***machine code***, which the computer can execute. The translation is itself done by the computer, using a special program called a ***compiler*** (which performs the translation before the program is run) or an ***interpreter*** (which translates each part of the program as it is being executed).

Types of computer

There are four main classes of computer, corresponding roughly to their size and intended use. ***Microcomputers*** (also called ***personal computers*** or ***PCs***) are the smallest and most common, used in small businesses, at home, and in schools. They are usually single-user machines but can also be linked together to form networks so that users can share data and programs. ***Mainframes***, which can often service several hundred users simultaneously, are found in large organizations, such as national companies and government departments. ***Minicomputers*** were originally developed as smaller, cheaper, less well-equipped alternatives to mainframe computers. They may support from 10 to 200 or so users at once. The dividing line between minicomputers and mainframes has never been well defined and the advent of more powerful microcomputer-based systems that rival minicomputers has made the term even less clear. ***Supercomputers*** are capable of very high computing speeds and are used for highly complex scientific tasks, such as analysing the results of nuclear physics experiments and weather forecasting.

Computers are also classified by ***generation***. Computers of the first generation were developed in the 1940s and 1950s, and made from valves and wire circuits. Second-generation computers, emerging in the early 1960s, incorporated transistors and printed circuits. The third generation, from the late 1960s, used integrated circuits and were often sold as families of computers, such as the IBM 360 series. Fourth-generation computers are the most commonly used in the 1990s, and are based on microprocessors, large-scale integration (LSI), and sophisticated programming languages. Finally, a fifth generation is emerging, using very large-scale integration (VLSI) and parallel processors.

Uses of Computers

artificial intelligence (AI) branch of science concerned with creating computer programs that can perform actions comparable with those of an intelligent human. Current AI research covers such areas as planning (for robot behaviour), language understanding, pattern recognition, and knowledge representation.

Early AI programs, developed in the 1960s, attempted simulations of human intelligence or were aimed at general problem-solving techniques. It is now thought that intelligent behaviour depends as much on the knowledge a system possesses as on its reasoning power. Present emphasis is on knowledge-based systems, such as expert systems. Britain's largest AI laboratory is at the Turing Institute, University of Strathclyde, Glasgow. In May 1990 the first International Robot Olympics was held there, including table-tennis matches between robots of the UK and the USA.

CAD (acronym for ***computer-aided design***) the use of computers in creating and editing design drawings. CAD also allows such things as automatic testing of designs and multiple or animated three-dimensional views of designs. CAD systems are widely used in architecture, electronics, and engineering, for example in the motor-vehicle industry, where cars designed with the assistance of computers are now commonplace. A related development is CAM (computer-assisted manufacturing).

CAL (acronym for ***computer-assisted learning***) the use of computers in education and training: the computer displays instructional material to a student and asks questions about the information given; the student's answers determine the sequence of the lessons.

CAM (acronym for ***computer–aided manufacturing***) the use of computers to control production processes; in particular, the control of machine tools and robots in factories. In some factories, the whole design and production system has been automated by linking CAD (computer-aided design) to CAM.

computer game or ***video game*** any computer-controlled game in which the computer (sometimes) opposes the human player. Computer games typically employ fast, animated graphics on a VDU (visual display unit), and synthesized sound.

computer graphics use of computers to display and manipulate information in pictorial form. The output may be as simple as a pie chart, or as complex as an animated sequence in a science-fiction film, or a seemingly three-dimensional engineering blueprint. Input may be achieved by scanning an image, by drawing with a mouse or stylus on a graphics tablet, or by drawing directly on the screen with a light pen. The drawing is stored in the computer as raster graphics or vector graphics. Computer graphics are increasingly used in computer-aided design (CAD), and to generate models and simulations in engineering, meteorology, medicine and surgery, and other fields of science.

Recent developments in software mean that designers on opposite sides of the world will soon be able to work on complex three-dimensional computer models using ordinary PCs linked by telephone lines rather then powerful graphics workstations.

computer simulation representation of a real-life situation in a computer program. For example, the program might simulate the flow of customers arriving at a bank. The user can alter variables, such as the number of cashiers on duty, and see the effect. More complex simulations can model the behaviour of chemical reactions or even nuclear explosions. Computers also control the actions of machines – for example, a flight simulator models the behaviour of real aircraft and allows training to take place in safety. Computer simulations are very useful when it is too dangerous, time consuming, or simply impossible to carry out a real experiment or test.

database a structured collection of data, which may be manipulated to select and sort desired items of information. For example, an accounting system might be built around a database containing details of customers and suppliers. In larger computers, the database makes data available to the various programs that need it, without the need for those programs to be aware of how the data are stored. The term is also sometimes used for simple record-keeping systems, such as mailing lists, in which there are facilities for searching, sorting, and producing records. A collection of databases is known as a ***databank***. A database-management system (DBMS) program ensures that the integrity of the data is maintained by controlling the degree of access of the applications programs using the data.

desktop publishing (DTP) use of microcomputers for small-scale typesetting and page make-up. DTP systems are capable of producing camera-ready pages (pages ready for photographing and printing), made up of text and graphics, with text set in different typefaces and sizes. The page can be previewed on the screen before final printing on a laser printer.

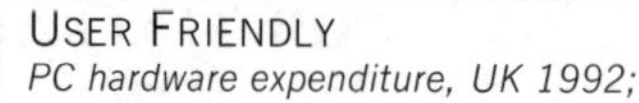

USER FRIENDLY

PC hardware expenditure, UK 1992; percentage share by industry sector

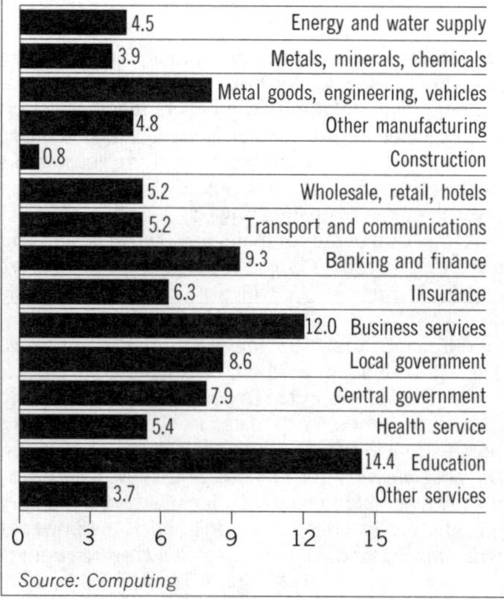

Source: Computing

electronic mail or ***E-mail*** system that enables the users of a computer network to send messages to other users. The messages are usually placed in a reserved area of backing store on a central computer until they are retrieved by the receiving user. Passwords are frequently used to prevent unauthorized access to stored messages.

expert system computer program for giving advice (such as diagnosing an illness or interpreting the law) that incorporates knowledge derived from human expertise. It is a kind of knowledge-based system containing rules that can be applied to find the solution to a problem. It is a form of artificial intelligence.

multimedia computer system that combines audio and video components to create an interactive application that uses text, sound, and graphics (still, animated, and video sequences). For example, a multimedia database of musical instruments may allow a user not only to search and retrieve text about a particular instrument but also to see pictures of it and hear it play a piece of music. Multimedia PCs are frequently fitted with CD drives because of the high storage capacity of CD-ROM discs.

point of sale in business premises, the point where a sale is transacted, for example, a supermarket checkout. In conjunction with electronic funds transfer, point of sale is part of the terminology of 'cashless shopping', enabling buyers to transfer funds directly from their bank accounts to the shop's.

simulation short for computer simulation.

speech recognition or ***voice input*** in computing, any technique by which a computer can understand ordinary speech. Spoken words are divided into 'frames', each lasting about one-thirtieth of a second, which are converted to a wave form. These are then compared with a series of stored frames to determine

Multimedia: the video game grows up

Buying a computer has never been simpler. Almost every customer, large or small, wants an IBM PC-compatible with Intel 80486SX processor, four megabytes of memory, EISA expansion bus, Super VGA colour screen and Microsoft Windows 3.1 software. There are variations – faster processors, bigger hard discs and screens, more memory – but the market has a working standard: one that has made Microsoft and Intel very rich; one that is being extended, and challenged.

Beyond the desktop

Microsoft, Intel, and numerous PC manufacturers want to expand beyond the desktop. Firms like Grid and NCR are selling battery-powered, portable 'pen-driven' computers for people who don't need a keyboard – van drivers making deliveries, or field service engineers. They can use PCs with power-saving processors and Microsoft's Windows for Pen Computing. Home users can have interactive CD players with infrared controllers and Microsoft's Modular Windows. Corporate users can have multi-processor 'servers' using Windows NT (New Technology) to replace minicomputers and small mainframes. RAID (redundant arrays of inexpensive discs) storage systems use multiple PC hard drives instead of large, expensive, mainframe discs.

Modular systems comprising PC processors and drives appeal to a market where large computers have been expensive and incompatible. Since PCs sell in large volumes, intense competition and economies of scale have driven down prices, and propagated a huge range of software. But some suppliers offer faster processors than Intel, and operating systems designed for specific tasks, without the inevitable compromises of standardization.

Many firms have produced reduced instruction set computer (RISC) processors – simpler and faster than traditional designs like Intel's x86 line. Examples include AT&T's Hobbit, DEC's Alpha, the ARM (Acorn Risc Machine), Hewlett-Packard's Precision Architecture, Mips' R4000, and Sun's Sparc (scalable processor architecture). The Sparc chip is the most popular, but the market is confusing and confused. There is a plethora of alternative operating systems exploiting these various chips. One is Go's PenPoint, which AT&T, IBM, and others are adopting for pen-driven computers and personal communicators. On minis and workstations, Unix is becoming dominant but, instead of backing the industry-standard Unix System V Release 4, several firms have developed variants, confusing the market and introducing unnecessary incompatibilities. The resulting 'Unix wars' over the last five years have provided Microsoft's NT with its opportunity. Paradoxically, the challenges to Intel and Microsoft have reinforced the PC's appeal. The slogan is: 'evolution not revolution'. When fast PCs are so cheap, why take a risk?

CD-ROM

The biggest development is CD-ROM (compact disc, read-only memory). One disc can store more than 600 megabytes of data, equivalent to 450 standard floppies or 150 million words of text. Prices are low, because the industry benefits from the R&D investment and high-volume production facilities for audio CD, with which CD-ROM is compatible.

A large operating system or suite of programs, occupying from 25 to 80 or more floppy discs, can be packed onto a single CD. 'Multimedia' programs can be produced, with digital data, sound, still and moving images on the same disc. Typical discs include dictionaries that have pictures and can say the words you look up, atlases including national anthems, and encyclopedias with moving diagrams. Computer games are also appearing on CD-ROM.

Suppliers have started 'format wars' that make the VHS–Betamax video battle look trivial. Most CD-ROMs are designed for a specific system; there are products for PCs and Apple Macintoshes, Sun workstations, Commodore Amigas (the CDTV system), Fujitsu's FM-Towns, and Sega Megadrive and NEC games consoles. There are other consumer offerings, including CD-I (compact disc–interactive) from Philips and Sony, Photo CD from Philips and Kodak, the Video Information System from Tandy and Zenith, and Sony's Electronic Book. There is also a recordable format, CD-R.

Millions of CD-ROM drives will be sold for Sega, Nintendo, and NEC games consoles, but the emerging standards are CD-I (incorporating Photo CD) and MPC, the Microsoft-backed Multimedia Personal Computer specification based on Windows 3. CD-I systems look like high-end CD players: they plug into a TV set, and can be used for audio CDs as well as multimedia programs. MPC systems are usually 386SX-based PCs upgraded with CD-ROM drive, sound card and, usually, two small stereo loudspeakers. The CD-ROM drive should be able to play 'multi-session' discs (enabling it to handle Photo CD discs, holding more than one set of pictures) and have XA (extended architecture) capabilities, to interleave sound with graphics.

The original PC was expensive, and its handling of colour graphics and sound primitive, limiting its appeal to the business market. The MPC is becoming affordable and suitable for use in homes and schools, ushering in a new age of electronic books in which people can speak, cows can moo, cartoons can be animated, and you can display the text any size you like. CDs of plays, operas and musicals can have moving video clips plus the libretto and score. Viewers will become interactive participants, making 'director's cuts' of films, steering plot-lines or choosing their own endings. Offered such power, will anyone want to resist?

JS

the most likely word. Research into speech recognition started in 1938, but the technology did not become sufficiently developed for commercial applications until the late 1980s.

spreadsheet a program that mimics a sheet of ruled paper, divided into columns and rows. The user enters values in the sheet, then instructs the program to perform some operation on them, such as totalling a column or finding the average of a series of numbers. Highly complex numerical analyses may be built up from these simple steps. Spreadsheets are widely used in business for forecasting and financial control. The first spreadsheet program, Software Arts' VisiCalc, appeared 1979. The best known include Lotus 1–2–3 and Microsoft Excel.

virtual reality advanced form of computer simulation, in which a participant has the illusion of being part of an artificial environment. The participant views the environment through two tiny television screens (one for each eye) built into a visor. Sensors detect movements of the participant's head or body, causing the apparent viewing position to change. Gloves (datagloves) fitted with sensors may be worn, which allow the participant seemingly to pick up and move objects in the environment. The technology is still under development but is expected to have widespread applications; for example, in military and surgical training, architecture, and home entertainment.

word processing storage and retrieval of written text by computer. Word-processing software packages enable the writer to key in text and amend it in a number of ways. A print-out can be obtained or the text can be sent to another person or organization on disc or via electronic mail. Word-processing packages can be used with databases or graphics packages, and desk-top publishing packages are available too.

workstation high-performance desktop computer with strong graphics capabilities, traditionally used for engineering (CAD and CAM), scientific research, and desktop publishing. Frequently based on fast RISC (reduced instruction-set computer) chips, workstations generally offer more processing power than microcomputers (although the distinction between workstations and the more powerful microcomputer models is becoming increasingly blurred). Most workstations use Unix as their operating system, and have good networking facilities.

Computer Hardware

CD-ROM (abbreviation for ***compact-disc read-only memory***) computer storage device developed from the technology of the audio compact disc. It consists of a plastic-coated metal disc, on which binary digital information is etched in the form of microscopic pits. This can then be read optically by passing a light beam over the disc. CD-ROMs typically hold about 550 megabytes of data, and are used in distributing large amounts of text and graphics, such as encyclopedias, catalogues, and technical manuals.

Standard CD-ROMs cannot have information written onto them by computer, but must be manufactured from a master. Although recordable CDs, called CD-R discs, have been developed for use as computer discs, they are as yet too expensive for widespread use. A compact disc that can be overwritten repeatedly by a computer has also been developed. The compact disc, with its enormous storage capability, may eventually replace the magnetic disc as the most common form of backing store for computers.

CD Boom

World CD-ROM and multimedia CD companies (1987–1992)

	Number of companies	*% Growth*
1987	48	-
1988	156	225.0
1989	323	107.1
1990	732	126.6
1991	1,840	151.4
1992	2,602	41.4

Source: TFPL

digitizer a device that converts an analogue video signal into a digital format so that video images can be input, stored, displayed, and manipulated by a computer. The term is sometimes used to refer to a graphics tablet.

disc or ***disk*** a common medium for storing large volumes of data (an alternative is magnetic tape). A ***magnetic disc*** is rotated at high speed in a disc-drive unit as a read/write (playback or record) head passes over its surfaces to record or read the magnetic variations that encode the data. Recently, ***optical discs***, such as CD-ROM (compact-disc read-only memory) and WORM (write once, read many times), have been used to store computer data. Data are recorded on the disc surface as etched microscopic pits and are read by a laser-scanning device. Optical discs have an enormous capacity – about 550 megabytes (million bytes) on a compact disc, and thousands of megabytes on a full-size optical disc.

Magnetic discs come in several forms: ***fixed hard discs*** are built into the disc-drive unit, occasionally stacked on top of one another. A fixed disc cannot be removed: once it is full, data must be deleted in order to free space or a complete new disc drive must be added to the computer system in order to increase storage capacity. Large fixed discs, used with mainframe and minicomputers, provide up to 3,000 megabytes. Small fixed discs for use with microcomputers typically hold 40–400 megabytes. ***Removable hard discs*** are common in minicomputer systems. The discs are contained, individually or as stacks, in a protective plastic case, and can be taken out of the drive unit and kept for later use. By swapping such discs around, a single hard-disc drive can be made to provide a potentially infinite storage capacity. However, access speeds and capacities tend to be lower that those associated with large fixed hard discs. A ***floppy disc*** (or diskette) is the most common form of backing store for microcomputers. It is much smaller in size and capacity than a hard disc, normally holding 0.5–2 megabytes of data. The floppy disc is so called because it is manufactured from thin flexible plastic coated with a magnetic material. The earliest form of floppy disc was packaged in a card case and was easily damaged; more recent versions are contained in a smaller, rigid plastic case and are much more robust. All floppy discs can be removed from the drive unit.

graphics tablet or ***bit pad*** an input device in which a stylus or cursor is moved, by hand, over a flat surface. The computer can keep track of the position of the stylus, so enabling the operator to input drawings or diagrams into the computer.

joystick an input device that signals to a computer the direction and extent of displacement of a hand-held lever. It is similar to the joystick used to control the flight of an aircraft. Joysticks are sometimes used to control the movement of a cursor across a display screen, but are much more frequently used to provide fast and direct input for moving the characters and symbols that feature in computer games. Unlike a mouse, which can move a pointer in any direction, simple games joysticks are often only capable of moving an object in one of eight different directions.

keyboard an input device resembling a typewriter keyboard, used to enter instructions and data. There are many variations on the layout and labelling of keys. Extra numeric keys may be added, as may special-purpose function keys, whose effects can be defined by programs in the computer.

light pen a device resembling an ordinary pen, used to indicate locations on a computer screen. With certain computer-aided design (CAD) programs, the light pen can be used to instruct the computer to change the shape, size, position, and colours of sections of a screen image. The pen has a photoreceptor at its tip that emits signals when light from the screen passes beneath it. From the timing of this signal and a gridlike representation of the screen in the computer memory, a computer program can calculate the position of the light pen.

memory the part of a system used to store data and programs either permanently or temporarily. There are two main types: immediate access memory and backing storage. Memory capacity is measured in bytes or, more conveniently, in kilobytes (units of 1,024 bytes) or megabytes (units of 1,024 kilobytes).

Immediate access memory, or ***internal memory***, describes the memory locations that can be addressed directly and individually by the central processing unit. It is either read-only (stored in ROM, PROM, and EPROM chips) or read/write (stored in RAM chips). Read-only memory stores information that must be constantly available and is unlikely to be changed. It is nonvolatile – that is, it is not lost when the computer is switched off. Read/write memory is volatile – it stores programs and data only while the computer is switched on.

Backing storage, or ***external memory***, is nonvolatile memory, located outside the central processing unit, used to store programs and data that are not in current use. Backing storage is provided by such devices as magnetic discs (floppy and hard discs), magnetic tape (tape streamers and cassettes), optical discs (such as CD-ROM), and bubble memory. By rapidly switching blocks of information between the backing storage and the immediate-access memory, the limited size of the immediate-access memory may be increased artificially. When this technique is used to give the appearance of a larger internal memory than physically exists, the additional capacity is referred to as virtual memory.

modem (acronym for ***modulator/demodulator***) device for transmitting computer data over telephone lines. Such a device is necessary because the digital signals produced by computers cannot, at present, be transmitted directly over the telephone network, which uses analogue signals. The modem converts the digital signals to analogue, and back again. Modems are used for linking remote terminals to central computers and enable computers to communicate with each other anywhere in the world.

mouse an input device used to control a pointer on a computer screen. It is a feature of graphical user-interface (GUI) systems. The mouse is about the size of a pack of playing cards, is connected to the computer by a wire, and incorporates one or more buttons that can be pressed. Moving the mouse across a flat surface causes a corresponding movement of the pointer. In this way, the operator can manipulate objects on the screen and make menu selections. Mice work either mechanically (with electrical contacts to sense the movement in two planes of a ball on a level surface), or optically (photoelectric cells detecting movement by recording light reflected from a grid on which the mouse is moved).

plotter or ***graph plotter*** device that draws pictures or diagrams under computer control. Plotters are often used for producing business charts, architectural plans, and engineering drawings. ***Flatbed plotters*** move a pen up and down across a flat drawing surface, whereas ***roller plotters*** roll the drawing paper past the pen as it moves from side to side.

printer an output device for producing printed copies of text or graphics. Types include the ***daisy-wheel printer***, which produces good-quality text but no graphics; the ***dot-matrix printer***, which produces text and graphics by printing a pattern of small dots; the ***ink-jet printer***, which creates text and graphics by spraying a fine jet of quick-drying ink onto the paper; and the ***laser printer***, which uses electrostatic technology very similar to that used by a photocopier to produce high-quality text and graphics.

The CD industry by sector

CD-ROM and multimedia CD companies by activity, 1992 (percentage of companies in each area)

	World	*Europe*	*UK*
Distributors	45.3	40.6	37.6
Publishers	40.7	33.7	40.7
Information providers	30.4	23.6	23.2
Software producers	16.2	11.0	19.3
System integrators	10.6	11.4	10.1
Hardware producers	6.6	3.2	12.5
Data preparation	6.0	6.3	6.7
Mastering	4.7	4.4	5.5
Replication	3.4	3.5	3.4

Source: Key Note

screen or ***monitor*** output device on which the computer displays information for the benefit of the operator. The commonest type is the cathode-ray tube (CRT), which is similar to a television screen. Portable computers often use liquid crystal display (LCD) screens. These are harder to read than CRTs, but require less power, making them suitable for battery operation.

touch screen an input device allowing the user to communicate with the computer by touching a display screen with a finger. In this way, the user can point to a required menu option or item of data. Typically, the screen is able to detect the touch either because the finger presses against a sensitive membrane or because it interrupts a grid of light beams crossing the screen surface. Touch screens are used less widely than other pointing devices such as the mouse or joystick.

VDU abbreviation for ***visual display unit*** computer terminal consisting of a keyboard for input data and a screen for displaying output. The oldest and the most popular type of VDU screen is the cathode-ray tube (CRT), which uses essentially the same technology as a television screen. Other types use plasma display technology and liquid-crystal displays.

Terms

ASCII (acronym for ***American standard code for information interchange***) a coding system in which numbers are assigned to letters, digits, and punctuation symbols. Although computers work in binary number code, ASCII numbers are usually quoted as decimal or hexadecimal numbers. For example, the decimal number 45 (binary 0101101) represents a hyphen, and 65 (binary 1000001) a capital A. The first 32 codes are used for control functions, such as carriage return and backspace.

binary number system or ***binary number code*** system of numbers to base two, using combinations of the digits 1 and 0. Codes based on binary numbers are used to represent instructions and data in all modern digital computers, the values of the binary digits (contracted to 'bits') being represented as the on/off states of switches and high/low voltages in circuits.

bit (contraction of ***bi****nary digi****t***) a single binary digit, either 0 or 1. A bit is the smallest unit of data stored in a computer; all other data must be coded into a pattern of individual bits. A byte represents sufficient computer memory to store a single character of data, and usually contains eight bits. For example, in the ASCII code system used by most microcomputers the capital letter A would be stored in a single byte of memory as the bit pattern 01000001.

boot or ***bootstrap*** the process of starting up a computer. Most computers have a small, built-in boot program that starts automatically when the computer is switched on – its only task is to load a slightly larger program, usually from a disc, which in turn loads the main operating system. In microcomputers the operating system is often held in the permanent ROM memory and the boot program simply triggers its operation.

buffer a part of the memory used to store data temporarily while it is waiting to be used. For example, a program might store data in a printer buffer until the printer is ready to print it.

byte sufficient computer memory to store a single character of data. The character is stored in the byte of memory as a pattern of bits (binary digits), using a code such as ASCII. A byte usually contains eight bits – for example, the capital letter F can be stored as the bit pattern 01000110. A single byte can specify 256 values, such as the decimal numbers from 0 to 255; in the case of a single-byte pixel (picture element), it can specify 256 different colours. Three bytes (24 bits) can specify 16,777,216 values. Computer memory size is measured in ***kilobytes*** (1,024 bytes) or ***megabytes*** (1,024 kilobytes).

chip or ***silicon chip*** another name for an ***integrated circuit***, a complete electronic circuit on a slice of silicon (or other semiconductor) crystal only a few millimetres square.

client-server architecture a system in which the mechanics of looking after data are separated from the programs that use the data. For example, the 'server' might be a central database, typically located on a large computer that is reserved for this purpose. The 'client' would be an ordinary program that requests data from the server as needed.

data facts, figures, and symbols, especially as stored in computers. The term is often used to mean raw, unprocessed facts, as distinct from information, to which a meaning or interpretation has been applied.

data compression techniques for reducing the amount of storage needed for a given amount of data. They include word tokenization (in which frequently used words are stored as shorter codes), variable bit lengths (in which common characters are represented by fewer bits than less common ones), and run-length encoding (in which a repeated value is stored once along with a count).

dedicated computer computer built into another device for the purpose of controlling or supplying information to it. Its use has increased dramatically since the advent of the microprocessor: washing machines, digital watches, cars, and video recorders all now have their own processors.

directory a list of file names, together with information that enables a computer to retrieve those files from backing storage. The computer operating system will usually store and update a directory on the backing storage to which it refers. So, for example, on each disc used by a computer a directory file will be created listing the disc's contents.

DOS (acronym for ***disc operating system***) computer operating system specifically designed for use with disc storage; also used as an alternative name for a particular operating system, MS-DOS.

emulator an item of software or firmware that allows one device to imitate the functioning of another. Emulator software is commonly used to allow one make of computer to run programs written for a different make of computer. This allows a user to select from a wider range of applications programs, and perhaps to save money by running programs designed for an expensive computer on a cheaper model.

computing: chronology

1614 John Napier invented logarithms.
1615 William Oughtred invented the slide rule.
1623 Wilhelm Schickard (1592–1635) invented the mechanical calculating machine.
1645 Blaise Pascal produced a calculator.
1672–74 Gottfried Leibniz built his first calculator, the Stepped Reckoner.
1801 Joseph-Marie Jacquard developed an automatic loom controlled by punch cards.
1820 The first mass-produced calculator, the Arithometer, was developed by Charles Thomas de Colmar (1785–1870).
1822 Charles Babbage completed his first model for the difference engine.
1830s Babbage created the first design for the analytical engine.
1890 Herman Hollerith developed the punched-card ruler for the US census.
1936 Alan Turing published the mathematical theory of computing.
1938 Konrad Zuse constructed the first binary calculator, using Boolean algebra.
1939 US mathematician and physicist J V Atanasoff (1903–   ) became the first to use electronic means for mechanizing arithmetical operations.
1943 The Colossus electronic code-breaker was developed at Bletchley Park, England. The Harvard University Mark I or Automatic Sequence Controlled Calculator (partly financed by IBM) became the first program-controlled calculator.
1946 ENIAC (acronym for electronic numerator, integrator, analyser, and computer), the first general purpose, fully electronic digital computer, was completed at the University of Pennsylvania, USA.
1948 Manchester University (England) Mark I, the first stored-program computer, was completed. William Shockley of Bell Laboratories invented the transistor.
1951 Launch of Ferranti Mark I, the first commercially produced computer. Whirlwind, the first real- time computer, was built for the US air-defence system. Grace Murray Hopper of Remington Rand invented the compiler computer program.
1952 EDVAC (acronym for electronic discrete variable computer) was completed at the Institute for Advanced Study, Princeton, USA (by John Von Neumann and others).
1953 Magnetic core memory was developed.
1958 The first integrated circuit was constructed.
1963 The first minicomputer was built by Digital Equipment (DEC). The first electronic calculator was built by Bell Punch Company.
1964 Launch of IBM System/360, the first compatible family of computers. John Kemeny and Thomas Kurtz of Dartmouth College invented BASIC (Beginner's All-purpose Symbolic Instruction Code), a computer language similar to FORTRAN.
1965 The first supercomputer, the Control Data CD6600, was developed.
1971 The first microprocessor, the Intel 4004, was announced.
1974 CLIP–4, the first computer with a parallel architecture, was developed by John Backus at IBM.
1975 Altair 8800, the first personal computer (PC), or microcomputer, was launched.
1981 The Xerox Star system, the first WIMP system (acronym for windows, icons, menus, and pointing devices), was developed. IBM launched the IBM PC.
1984 Apple launched the Macintosh computer.
1985 The Inmos T414 transputer, the first 'off-the-shelf' microprocessor for building parallel computers, was announced.
1988 The first optical microprocessor, which uses light instead of electricity, was developed.
1989 Wafer-scale silicon memory chips, able to store 200 million characters, were launched.
1990 Microsoft released Windows 3, a popular windowing environment for PCs.
1992 Philips launched the CD-I (compact disc-interactive) player, based on CD audio technology, to provide interactive multimedia programs for the home user.
1993 The Personal Digital Assistant went on sale, using a stylus for input; the PDA recognizes handwriting, which is turned into text for storage, fax transmission, or printout.

function a small part of a program that supplies a specific value – for example, the square root of a specified number, or the current date. Most programming languages incorporate a number of built-in functions; some allow programmers to write their own. A function may have one or more arguments (the values on which the function operates). A ***function key*** on a keyboard is one that, when pressed, performs a designated task, such as ending a program.

fuzzy logic a form of knowledge representation suitable for notions (such as 'hot' or 'loud') that cannot be defined precisely but which depend on their context. For example, a jug of water may be described as too hot or too cold, depending on whether it is to be used to wash one's face or to make tea. The central idea of fuzzy logic is ***probability of set membership***. For instance, referring to someone 5 ft 9 in tall, the statement 'this person is tall' (or 'this person is a member of the set of tall people') might be about 70% true if that person is a man, and about 85% true if that person is a woman. Fuzzy logic enables computerized devices to reason more like humans, responding effectively to complex messages from their control panels and sensors. For example, a vacuum cleaner launched in 1992 by

Matsushita uses fuzzy logic to adjust its sucking power in response to messages from its sensors about the type of dirt on the floor, its distribution, and its depth.

gigabyte a measure of memory capacity, equal to 1,024 megabytes. It is also used, less precisely, to mean 1,000 billion bytes.

graphical user interface (GUI) or ***WIMP*** a type of user interface in which programs and files appear as icons (small pictures), user options are selected from pull-down menus, and data are displayed in windows (rectangular areas), which the operator can manipulate in various ways. The operator uses a pointing device, typically a mouse, to make selections and initiate actions.

The concept of the graphical user interface was developed by the Xerox Corporation in the 1970s, was popularized with the Apple Macintosh computers in the 1980s, and is now available on many types of computer – most notably as Windows, an operating system for IBM PC-compatible microcomputers developed by the software company Microsoft.

hacking unauthorized access to a computer, either for fun or for malicious or fraudulent purposes. Hackers generally use microcomputers and telephone lines to obtain access. In computing, the term is used in a wider sense to mean using software for enjoyment or self-education, not necessarily involving unauthorized access.

hardware the mechanical, electrical, and electronic components of a computer system, as opposed to the various programs, which constitute software. Hardware associated with a microcomputer might include the power supply and housing of its processor unit, its circuit boards, VDU (screen), disc drive, keyboard, and printer.

hexadecimal number system number system to the base 16, used in computing. In hex (as it is commonly known) the decimal numbers 0–15 are represented by the characters 0, 1, 2, 3, 4, 5, 6, 7, 8, 9, A, B, C, D, E, F. Hexadecimal numbers are easy to convert to the computer's internal binary code and are more compact than binary numbers.

hypertext system for viewing information (both text and pictures) on a computer screen in such a way that related items of information can easily be reached. For example, the program might display a map of a country; if the user clicks (with a mouse) on a particular city, the program will display some information about that city.

image compression one of a number of methods used to reduce the amount of information required to represent an image, so that it takes up less computer memory and can be transmitted more rapidly and economically via telecommunications systems. It plays a major role in fax transmission and in videophone and multimedia systems.

information technology (IT) use of computers to produce, store, handle, and retrieve information. The machines used today are mostly microcomputers rather than mainframe computers. Word processing, databases, and spreadsheets are just some of the software packages which have revolutionized work in the office environment.

integrated circuit (IC), popularly called ***silicon chip***, a miniaturized electronic circuit produced on a single crystal, or chip, of a semiconducting material – usually silicon. It may contain many thousands of components and yet measure only 5 mm/0.2 in square and 1 mm/0.04 in thick. The IC is encapsulated within a plastic or ceramic case, and linked via gold wires to metal pins with which it is connected to a printed circuit board and the other components that make up such electronic devices as computers and calculators.

interface the point of contact between two programs or pieces of equipment. The term is most often used for the physical connection between the computer and a peripheral device, which is used to compensate for differences in such operating characteristics as speed, data coding, voltage, and power consumption. For example, a ***printer interface*** is the cabling and circuitry used to transfer data from a computer to a printer, and to compensate for differences in speed and coding.

kilobyte (K or KB) a unit of memory equal to 1,024 bytes. It is sometimes used, less precisely, to mean 1,000 bytes.

laptop computer portable microcomputer, small enough to be used on the operator's lap. It consists of a single unit, incorporating a keyboard, floppy disc or hard disc drives, and a screen. The screen often forms a lid that folds back in use. It uses a liquid-crystal or gas-plasma display, rather than the bulkier and heavier cathode-ray tubes found in most display terminals. A typical laptop computer measures about 210 × 297 mm/8.3 × 11.7 in (A4), is 5 cm/2 in thick, and weighs less than 3 kg/6 lb 9 oz.

local area network (LAN) a network restricted to a single room or building. Local area networks enable around 500 devices to be connected together.

Macintosh range of microcomputers produced by Apple Computers. The Apple Macintosh, introduced in 1984, was the first popular microcomputer with a graphical user interface. The success of the Macintosh prompted other manufacturers and software companies to create their own graphical user interfaces. Most notable of these are Microsoft Windows, which runs on IBM PC-compatible microcomputers, and OSF/Motif, from the Open Software Foundation, which is used with many Unix systems.

macro in programming, a new command created by combining a number of existing ones. For example, if

Information technology

Per capita IT expenditure in Europe, 1991

	£
Germany	1,158
France	1,077
Luxembourg	1,067
Belgium	971
Netherlands	947
Italy	943
UK	845

Source: Computer Weekly

Programming languages: a selection

Language	*Main uses*	*Description*
assembler languages	jobs needing detailed control of the hardware, fast execution, and small program sizes	fast and efficient but require considerable effort and skill
BASIC (***b***eginner's ***a***ll-purpose ***s***ymbolic ***i***nstruction ***c***ode)	in education and the home, and among nonprofessional programmers, such as engineers	easy to learn; early versions (derived from FORTRAN) lacked the features of other languages
C	systems programming; general programming	fast and efficient; widely used as a general-purpose language; especially popular among professional programmers
COBOL (***co***mmon ***b***usiness-***o***riented ***l***anguage)	business programming	strongly oriented towards data processing work; easy to learn but very verbose; widely used on mainframes
FORTRAN (***for***mula ***tran***slation)	scientific and computational work	based on mathematical formulae; popular among engineers, scientists, and mathematicians
LISP (***lis***t ***p***rocessing)	artificial intelligence	symbolic language with a reputation for being hard to learn; popular in the academic and research communities
Modula-2	systems and real-time programming; general programming	highly structured; intended to replace Pascal for 'real-world' applications
PASCAL	general-purpose language	highly structured; widely used for teaching programming in universities
PROLOG (***pro***gramming in ***log***ic)	artificial intelligence	symbolic-logic programming system, originally intended for theorem solving but now used more generally in artificial intelligence

a programming language has separate commands for obtaining data from the keyboard and for displaying data on the screen, the programmer might create a macro that performs both these tasks with one command. A ***macro key*** on the keyboard combines the effects of pressing several individual keys.

megabyte (Mb) a unit of memory equal to 1,024 kilobytes. It is sometimes used, less precisely, to mean 1 million bytes.

menu a list of options, displayed on screen, from which the user may make a choice – for example, the choice of services offered to the customer by a bank cash dispenser: withdrawal, deposit, balance, or statement. Menus are used extensively in graphical user-interface (GUI) systems, where the menu options are often selected using a pointing device called a mouse.

microprocessor complete computer central processing unit (CPU) contained on a single integrated circuit, or chip. The appearance of the first microprocessor 1971 designed by Intel for a pocket calculator manufacturer heralded the introduction of the microcomputer. The microprocessor has led to a dramatic fall in the size and cost of computers, and dedicated computers can now be found in washing machines, cars, and so on. Examples of microprocessors are the Intel 8086 family and the Motorola 68000 family.

MIDI (acronym for ***musical instruments digital interface***) standard interface that enables electronic musical instruments to be connected to a computer. A computer with a MIDI interface can input and store the sounds produced by the connected instruments, and can then manipulate these sounds in many different ways. For example, a single keystroke may change the key of an entire composition. Even a full written score for the composition may be automatically produced.

MS-DOS (abbreviation for ***Microsoft Disc Operating System***) computer operating system produced by Microsoft Corporation, widely used on microcomputers with Intel x 86 family microprocessors. A version called PC-DOS is sold by IBM specifically for its personal computers. MS-DOS and PC-DOS are usually referred to as DOS. MS-DOS first appeared 1981, and was similar to an earlier system from Digital Research called CP/M.

multitasking or ***multiprogramming*** a system in which one processor appears to run several different programs (or different parts of the same program) at the same time. All the programs are held in memory together and each is allowed to run for a certain period. For example, one program may run while other programs are waiting for a peripheral device to work or for input from an operator. The ability to multitask depends on the operating system rather than the type of computer. Unix is one of the commonest.

neural network artificial network of processors that attempts to mimic the structure of nerve cells (neurons) in the human brain. Neural networks may be electronic, optical, or simulated by computer software. A basic network has three layers of processors: an input layer, an output layer, and a 'hidden' layer

Creatures from the morph lagoon

Cinema history is full of artificially created monsters and fantasy characters, from King Kong to Roger Rabbit. Until 1990, all these were either cartoon characters or the products of model shops. Either way, those sequences had to be created a frame at a time, whether it was by drawing each frame by hand on plastic 'cels' or by stop-motion photography. *The Abyss* 1990 was the first film to be made with a character that was wholly computer-generated and animated. This was an alien water creature that sent a watery pseudopod through a ship, mimicking the faces of the humans it met.

It was the 1991 film *Terminator 2*, however, that really took computer-generated effects off the hard discs and into people's imaginations. In it, the T1000 Terminator is an invincible killing machine made of liquid metal. Flowing into different shapes, the T1000 thoroughly upstages its on-screen arch enemy, played by Arnold Schwarzenegger.

The T1000 made extensive use of a technique known as ***morphing***, the computer-handled metamorphosis of one shape or object into another: the liquid metal man, the actor Robert Patrick, the actress Linda Hamilton, a shapeless blob. This sort of effect is a direct extension of the earliest uses of computers in animation, in-betweening.

Animators of a cartoon sequence start with drawings of the characters at specific points in the action. The necessary in-between images are drawn up based on the speed at which the characters are moving and the number of images needed to fill the time – for film, 24 per second. Computers are ideal for this kind of drudgery.

Morphing adds a geometrical degree of complexity: instead of two-dimensional in-betweening, morphing is a three-dimensional transformation. To create such effects, you must first specify the beginning and end points. This means creating the objects that start and finish the transformation – in *Terminator 2*, for example, the liquid-metal man and the police-uniformed actor Robert Patrick. You begin with a wire-frame model on the computer screen that mathematically defines your object. To make the object three-dimensional, the wire frame can be extruded from a cross section or turned, as if on a lathe, to produce an evenly curved surface. This is then rendered, or filled in and shaded.

The artist must specify the object's colour, lighting colour and direction, colour and brightness of reflections, surface texture, bumps, transparency, and the object's location in space and its environment. A technique known as ray tracing calculates how the light directed at the object reaches it, with what intensity, and in what areas. From all this information, the computer calculates the colour intensity of each pixel that makes up the on-screen object. This sounds a long process, and it is: a single frame may take hours. The 50 shots (less than five minutes' worth of screen time) needed for *Terminator 2* took the special-effects house Industrial Light and Magic a year to create.

Once the beginning and end objects are created, the computer can calculate the morphing process. Even so, a great deal of traditional animation skill is needed to make the images look realistic. Often, it is the small details that count, as in a famous shot where the Terminator walks out of a fire: it is the slight flattening of its foot on the ground that makes it look so real.

Creating the objects is only the first step, however. They must be placed against the film's background, into the action. In the past, inserting models like King Kong into a shot was known as 'matte-process', and creating those shots involved rephotographing each model in front of the already filmed background sequence. This involves a loss of quality, since each time a sequence is photographed it loses sharpness – and today's special effects are complicated enough to require many 'generations' of photography. The advent of computer animation has brought with it digital compositing, which eliminates this loss of quality: the film is scanned into the computer, where the objects are superimposed, and then the finished image is converted back into film.

Predictions are, however, that the flashy morphing effects that we have seen so far will give way to more subtle uses, much as Technicolor gave way to selective use of colours. The 1992 film *Death Becomes Her*, for example, used morphing to blur the actress Meryl Streep's hand from old to young. Morphing is also useful in blurring the transition between live action and computer animation.

In addition, the constantly decreasing cost of computer power means that we are on the verge of wholly digital characters. Even some of the people working on this find the technology they are creating frightening. This goes beyond seamless editing of video or audiotapes. Imagine seeing dead politicians, such as Winston Churchill or Abraham Lincoln, giving speeches, or films starring dead or retired actors. All that is a logical extension of the technology we have today. Such movie effects will inspire even more heated arguments – and litigation – than the comparatively simple but emotive issue of musicians giving 'live' concerts by lip-synching to their own recordings.

In the end, it all comes down to light, the way we see everything. As Steve Williams, ILM's animation director for *Terminator 2*, has said, 'Reality is in a paint palette of 13 million colours.' Coordinate that, and you can create illusions that the human eye can't distinguish from reality.

WG

in between. Each processor is connected to every other in the network by a system of 'synapses'; every processor in the top layer connects to every one in the hidden layer, and each of these connects to every processor in the output layer. This means that each nerve cell in the middle and bottom layers receives input from several different sources; only when the amount of input exceeds a critical level does the cell fire an output signal.

The chief characteristic of neural networks is their ability to sum up large amounts of imprecise data and decide whether they match a pattern or not. Networks of this type may be used in developing robot vision, matching fingerprints, and analysing fluctuations in stock-market prices. However, it is thought unlikely by scientists that such networks will ever be able accurately to imitate the human brain, which is very much more complicated; it contains around 10 billion nerve cells, whereas current artificial networks contain only a few hundred processors.

notebook computer small laptop computer. Notebook computers became available in the early 1990s and, even complete with screen and hard-disc drive, are no larger than a standard A4 notebook.

operating system (OS) a program that controls the basic operation of a computer. A typical OS controls the peripheral devices, organizes the filing system, provides a means of communicating with the operator, and runs other programs. Some operating systems were written for specific computers, but some are accepted standards. These include CP/M (by Digital Research) and MS-DOS (by Microsoft) for microcomputers. Unix (developed at AT&T's Bell Laboratories) is the standard on workstations, minicomputers, and super computers; it is also used on desktop PCs and mainframes.

pixel (acronym for ***picture element***) single dot on a computer screen. All screen images are made up of a collection of pixels, with each pixel being either off (dark) or on (illuminated, possibly in colour). The number of pixels available determines the screen's resolution. Typical resolutions of microcomputer screens vary from 320 × 200 pixels to 640 × 480 pixels, but screens with 1024 × 768 pixels are now quite common for high-quality graphic (pictorial) displays.

procedure a small part of a computer program that performs a specific task, such as clearing the screen or sorting a file. A ***procedural language***, such as BASIC, is one in which the programmer describes a task in terms of how it is to be done, as opposed to a ***declarative language***, such as PROLOG, in which it is described in terms of the required result.

RISC (acronym for ***reduced instruction-set computer***) a microprocessor (processor on a single chip) that carries out fewer instructions than other (CISC) microprocessors in common use in the 1990s. Because of the low number of machine-code instructions, the processor carries out those instructions very quickly.

software a collection of programs and procedures for making a computer perform a specific task, as opposed to hardware, the physical components of a computer system. Software is created by programmers and is either distributed on a suitable medium, such as the floppy disc, or built into the computer in the form of firmware. Examples of software include operating systems, compilers, and applications programs, such as payrolls. No computer can function without some form of software.

Unix multiuser operating system designed for minicomputers but becoming increasingly popular on large microcomputers, workstations, mainframes, and supercomputers. It was developed by AT&T's Bell Laboratories in the USA during the late 1960s, using the programming language C. It could therefore run on any machine with a C compiler, so ensuring its wide portability. Its wide range of functions and flexibility have made it widely used by universities and in commercial software.

user interface the procedures and methods through which the user operates a program. These might include menus, input forms, error messages, and keyboard procedures. A graphical user interface (GUI or WIMP) is one that makes use of icons (small pictures) and allows the user to make menu selections with a mouse.

virtual memory a technique whereby a portion of the computer backing storage, or external, memory is used as an extension of its immediate-access, or internal, memory. The contents of an area of the immediate-access memory are stored on, say, a hard disc while they are not needed, and brought back into main memory when required.

virus a piece of software that can replicate itself and transfer itself from one computer to another, without the user being aware of it. Some viruses are relatively harmless, but others can damage or destroy data. They are written by anonymous programmers, often maliciously, and are spread along telephone lines or on floppy discs. Antivirus software can be used to detect and destroy well-known viruses, but new viruses continually appear and these may bypass existing antivirus programs.

wide area network a network that connects computers distributed over a wide geographical area.

window a rectangular area on the screen of a graphical user interface. A window is used to display data and can be manipulated in various ways by the computer user.

word a group of bits (binary digits) that a computer's central processing unit treats as a single working unit. The size of a word varies from one computer to another and, in general, increasing the word length leads to a faster and more powerful computer. In the late 1970s and early 1980s, most microcomputers were 8-bit machines. During the 1980s 16-bit microcomputers were introduced and 32-bit microcomputers are now available. Mainframe computers may be 32-bit or 64-bit machines.

WYSIWYG (acronym for ***what you see is what you get***) a program that attempts to display on the screen a faithful representation of the final printed output. For example, a WYSIWYG word processor would show actual page layout – line widths, page breaks, and the sizes and styles of type.

Electronics

Electronics is the branch of science that deals with the emission of electrons from conductors and semiconductors, with the subsequent manipulation of these electrons, and with the construction of electronic devices. The first electronic device was the thermionic valve, or vacuum tube, in which electrons moved in a vacuum, and led to such inventions as radio, television, radar, and the digital computer.

Replacement of valves with the comparatively tiny and reliable transistor in 1948 revolutionized electronic development. Modern electronic devices are based on minute integrated circuits (silicon chips), wafer-thin crystal slices holding tens of thousands of electronic components.

By using solid-state devices such as integrated circuits, extremely complex electronic circuits can be constructed, leading to the development of digital watches, pocket calculators, powerful microcomputers, and word processors.

adder electronic circuit in a computer or calculator that carries out the process of adding two binary numbers. A separate adder is needed for each pair of binary bits to be added. Such circuits are essential components of a computer's arithmetic and logic unit (ALU).

amplifier electronic device that magnifies the strength of a signal, such as a radio signal. The ratio of output signal strength to input signal strength is called the ***gain*** of the amplifier. As well as achieving high gain, an amplifier should be free from distortion and able to operate over a range of frequencies. Practical amplifiers are usually complex circuits, although simple amplifiers can be built from single transistors or valves.

analogue signal current or voltage that conveys or stores information, and varies continuously in the same way as the information it represents. Analogue signals are prone to interference and distortion. The bumps in the grooves of an LP (gramophone) record form a mechanical analogue of the sound information stored, which is then is converted into an electrical analogue signal by the record player's pick-up device.

analogue-to-digital converter (ADC) electronic circuit that converts an analogue signal into a digital one. Such a circuit is needed to convert the signal from an analogue device into a digital signal for input into a computer. For example, many sensors designed to measure physical quantities, such as temperature and pressure, produce an analogue signal in the form of voltage and this must be passed through an ADC before computer input and processing. A digital-to-analogue converter performs the opposite process.

bistable circuit or ***flip-flop*** simple electronic circuit that remains in one of two stable states until it receives a pulse through one of its inputs, upon which it switches, or 'flips', over to the other state. Because it is a two-state device, it can be used to store binary digits and is widely used in the integrated circuits used to build computers.

capacitor or ***condenser*** device for storing electric charge, used in electronic circuits; it consists of two or more metal plates separated by an insulating layer called a dielectric. Its ***capacitance*** is the ratio of the charge stored on either plate to the potential difference between the plates. The SI unit of capacitance is the farad, but most capacitors have much smaller capacitances, and the microfarad (a millionth of a farad) is the commonly used practical unit.

cathode the part of an electronic device in which electrons are generated. In a thermionic valve, electrons are produced by the heating effect of an applied current; in a photoelectric cell, they are produced by the interaction of light and a semiconducting material. The cathode is kept at a negative potential relative to the device's other electrodes (anodes) in order to ensure that the liberated electrons stream away from the cathode and towards the anodes.

complementary metal-oxide semiconductor (CMOS) a particular way of manufacturing integrated circuits (chips). The main advantage of CMOS chips is their low power requirement and heat dissipation, which enables them to be used in electronic watches and portable microcomputers. However, CMOS circuits are expensive to manufacture and have lower operating speeds than have circuits of the transistor–transistor logic (TTL) family.

digital a term meaning 'coded as numbers'. A digital system uses two-state, either on/off or high/low voltage pulses, to encode, receive, and transmit information. A ***digital display*** shows discrete values as numbers (as opposed to an analogue signal, such as the continuous sweep of a pointer on a dial). ***Digital electronics*** is the technology that underlies digital techniques. Low-power, miniature, integrated circuits (chips) provide the means for the coding, storage, transmission, processing, and reconstruction of information of all kinds.

digital-to-analogue converter electronic circuit that converts a digital signal into an analogue (continuously varying) signal. Such a circuit is used to convert the digital output from a computer into the analogue voltage required to produce sound from a conventional loudspeaker.

diode combination of a cold anode and a heated cathode (or the semiconductor equivalent, which incorporates a *p–n* junction). Either device allows the passage of direct current in one direction only, and so is commonly used in a rectifier to convert alternating current (AC) to direct current (DC).

DRAM (acronym for ***dynamic random-access memory***) computer memory device in the form of a silicon chip commonly used to provide the immediate-access memory of microcomputers. DRAM loses its contents unless they are read and rewritten every 2 milliseconds or so. This process is called ***refreshing*** the memory. DRAM is slower but cheaper than SRAM, an alternative form of silicon-chip memory.

EEPROM (acronym for ***electrically erasable programmable read-only memory***) computer memory that can record data and retain it indefinitely. The data can be erased with an electrical charge and new data recorded. Some EEPROM must be removed from the computer and erased and reprogrammed using a special device. Other EEPROM, called ***flash memory***, can be erased and reprogrammed without removal from the computer.

Electronics: chronology

1897 The electron was discovered by English physicist John Joseph Thomson.
1904 English physicist Ambrose Fleming invented the diode valve, which allows flow of electricity in one direction only.
1906 The triode electron valve, the first device to control an electric current, was invented by US physicist Lee De Forest.
1947 John Bardeen, William Shockley, and Walter Brattain invented the junction germanium transistor at the Bell Laboratories, New Jersey, USA.
1952 British physicist G W A Dunner proposed the integrated circuit.
1953 Jay Forrester of the Massachusetts Institute of Technology, USA, built a magnetic memory smaller than existing vacuum-tube memories.
1954 The silicon transistor was developed by Gordon Teal of Texas Instruments, USA.
1958 The first integrated circuit, containing five components, was built by US electrical physicist Jack Kilby.
1959 The planar transistor, which is built up in layers, or planes, was designed by Robert Noyce of Fairchild Semiconductor Corporation, USA.
1961 Steven Hofstein designed the field-effect transistor used in integrated circuits.
1971 The first microprocessor, the Intel 4004, was designed by Ted Hoff in the USA; it contained 2,250 components and could add two four-bit numbers in 11-millionths of a second.
1974 The Intel 8080 microprocessor was launched; it contained 4,500 components and could add two eight-bit numbers in 2.5-millionths of a second.
1979 The Motorola 68000 microprocessor was introduced; it contained 70,000 components and could multiply two 16-bit numbers in 3.2-millionths of a second.
1981 The Hewlett-Packard Superchip was introduced; it contained 450,000 components and could multiply two 32-bit numbers in 1.8-millionths of a second.
1985 The Inmos T414 transputer, the first microprocessor designed for use in parallel computers, was launched.
1988 The first optical microprocessor, which uses light instead of electricity, was developed.
1989 Wafer-scale silicon memory chips were introduced: the size of a beer mat, they are able to store 200 million characters.
1990 Memory chips capable of holding 4 million bits of information began to be mass-produced in Japan. The chips can store the equivalent of 520,000 characters, or the contents of a 16-page newspaper. Each chip contains 9 million components packed on a piece of silicon less than 15 mm long by 5 mm wide.
1992 Transistors made from high-temperature superconducting ceramics rather than semiconductors produced in Japan by Sanyo Electric. The new transistors are 10 times faster than semiconductor transistors.
1993 Intel launched the Pentium 64-bit processor with two separate integer processing units that can run in parallel, promising to be up to 10 times faster than earlier processors.

electron stable, negatively charged elementary particle; it is a constituent of all atoms, and a member of the class of particles known as leptons.

The electrons in each atom surround the nucleus in groupings called shells; in a neutral atom the number of electrons is equal to the number of protons in the nucleus. This electron structure is responsible for the chemical properties of the atom.

Electrons are the basic particles of electricity. Each carries a charge of 1.602192×10^{-19} coulomb, and all electrical charges are multiples of this quantity. A beam of electrons will undergo diffraction (scattering) and produce interference patterns in the same way as electromagnetic waves such as light; hence they may also be regarded as waves.

filter a circuit that transmits a signal of some frequencies better than others. A low-pass filter transmits signals of low frequency and direct current; a high-pass filter transmits high-frequency signals; a band-pass filter transmits signals in a band of frequencies.

gain the ratio of the amplitude of the output signal produced by an amplifier to that of the input signal. In a voltage amplifier the voltage gain is the ratio of the output voltage to the input voltage; in an inverting operational amplifier (op-amp) it is equal to the ratio of the resistance of the feedback resistor to that of the input resistor.

integrated circuit (IC), popularly called ***silicon chip***, a miniaturized electronic circuit produced on a single crystal, or chip, of a semiconducting material – usually silicon. It may contain many thousands of components and yet measure only 5 mm/0.2 in square and 1 mm/0.04 in thick. The IC is encapsulated within a plastic or ceramic case, and linked via gold wires to metal pins with which it is connected to a printed circuit board and the other components that make up such electronic devices as computers and calculators.

logic gate or ***logic circuit*** in electronics, one of the basic components used in building integrated circuits. The five basic types of gate make logical decisions based on the functions NOT, AND, OR, NAND (NOT AND), and NOR (NOT OR). With the exception of the NOT gate, each has two or more inputs.

Information is fed to a gate in the form of binary-coded input signals (logic value 0 stands for 'off' or 'low-voltage pulse', logic 1 for 'on' or 'high-voltage'), and each combination of input signals yields a specific output (logic 0 or 1). An ***OR*** gate will give a logic 1 output if one or more of its inputs receives a logic 1 signal; however, an ***AND*** gate will yield a logic 1 output only if it receives a logic 1 signal through both its inputs. The output of a ***NOT*** or ***inverter*** gate is the opposite of the signal received through its single input, and a ***NOR*** or ***NAND*** gate produces an output signal that is the opposite of the signal that would have been produced by an OR or AND gate respectively. The properties of a logic gate, or of a combination of gates, may be defined and presented in the form of a diagram called a ***truth table***, which lists the output that will be triggered by each of the possible combinations of input signals. The process has close parallels in computer programming, where it forms the basis of binary logic.

LSI (abbreviation for ***large-scale integration***) the technology that enables whole electrical circuits to be etched into a piece of semiconducting material just a few millimetres square. By the late 1960s a complete computer processor could be integrated on a single chip, or integrated circuit, and in 1971 the US electronics company Intel produced the first commercially available microprocessor. Very large-scale integration (VLSI) results in even smaller chips.

microprocessor complete computer central processing unit contained on a single integrated circuit, or chip. The appearance of the first microprocessor 1971 designed by Intel for a pocket-calculator manufacturer heralded the introduction of the microcomputer. The microprocessor has led to a dramatic fall in the size and cost of computers, and dedicated computers can now be found in washing machines, cars, and so on. Examples of microprocessors are the Intel 8086 family and the Motorola 68000 family.

operational amplifier (op-amp) type of electronic circuit that is used to increase the size of an alternating voltage signal without distorting it. Operational amplifiers are used in a wide range of electronic measuring instruments. The name arose because they were originally designed to carry out mathematical operations and solve equations.

optoelectronics branch of electronics concerned with the development of devices (based on the semiconductor gallium arsenide) that respond not only to the electrons of electronic data transmission, but also to photons.

In 1989, scientists at IBM in the USA built a gallium arsenide microprocessor ('chip') containing 8,000 transistors and four photodetectors. The densest optoelectronic chip yet produced, this can detect and process data at a speed of 1 billion bits per second.

oscillator any device producing a desired oscillation (vibration). There are many types of oscillator for different purposes, involving various arrangements of thermionic valves or components such as transistors, inductors, capacitors, and resistors. An oscillator is an essential part of a radio transmitter, generating the high-frequency carrier signal necessary for radio communication. The frequency is often controlled by the vibrations set up in a crystal (such as quartz).

p–n junction diode a two-terminal semiconductor device that allows electric current to flow in only one direction, the ***forward-bias*** direction. A very high resistance prevents current flow in the opposite, or ***reverse-bias***, direction. It is used as a rectifier, converting alternating current (AC) to direct current (DC).

semiconductor crystalline material with an electrical conductivity between that of metals (good) and insulators (poor). The conductivity of semiconductors can usually be improved by minute additions of different substances or by other factors. Silicon, for example, has poor conductivity at low temperatures, but this is improved by the application of light, heat, or voltage; hence silicon is used in transistors, rectifiers, and integrated circuits (silicon chips).

solid-state circuit electronic circuit where all the components (resistors, capacitors, transistors, and diodes) and interconnections are made at the same time, and by the same processes, in or on one piece of single-crystal silicon. The small size of this construction accounts for its use in electronics for space vehicles and aircraft.

SRAM (acronym for ***static random-access memory***) computer memory device in the form of a silicon chip used to provide immediate-access memory. SRAM is faster but more expensive than DRAM (dynamic random-access memory). DRAM loses its contents unless they are read and rewritten every 2 milliseconds or so. This process is called ***refreshing*** the memory. SRAM does not require such frequent refreshing.

thermionics branch of electronics dealing with the emission of electrons from matter under the influence of heat. The ***thermionic valve*** (electron tube), used in telegraphy and telephony and in radio and radar, is a device using space conduction by thermionically emitted electrons from an electrically heated cathode. In most applications valves have been replaced by transistors.

thyristor type of rectifier, an electronic device that conducts electricity in one direction only. The thyristor is composed of layers of semiconductor material sandwiched between two electrodes called the anode and cathode. The current can be switched on by using a third electrode called the gate. Thyristors are used to control mains-driven motors and in lighting dimmer controls.

transistor solid-state electronic component, made of semiconductor material, with three or more electrodes, that can regulate a current passing through it. A transistor can act as an amplifier, oscillator, photocell, or switch, and (unlike earlier thermionic valves) usually operates on a very small amount of power. Transistors commonly consist of a tiny sandwich of germanium or silicon, alternate layers having different electrical properties because they are impregnated with minute amounts of different impurities.

Transistors have had a great impact on the electronics industry, and thousands of millions are now made each year. They perform many of the functions of the thermionic valve, but have the advantages of greater reliability, long life, compactness, and instantaneous action, no warming-up period being necessary. They are widely used in most electronic equipment, including portable radios and televisions, computers, and satellites, and are the basis of the integrated circuit (silicon chip). They were invented at Bell Telephone Laboratories in the USA in 1948 by John Bardeen and Walter Brattain, developing the work of William Shockley.

transistor-transistor logic (TTL) the type of integrated circuit most commonly used in building electronic products. In TTL chips, the bipolar transistors are directly connected (usually collector to base). In mass-produced items, large numbers of TTL chips are commonly replaced by a small number of uncommitted logic arrays (ULAs), or logic gate arrays.

transputer a member of a family of microprocessors designed for parallel processing, developed in the UK by Inmos. In the circuits of a standard computer the processing of data takes place in sequence; in a transputer's circuits processing takes place in parallel, greatly reducing computing time for those programs that have been specifically written for it. The transputer implements a special programming language called OCCAM, which Inmos based on CSP (communicating sequential processes), developed by C A R Hoare of Oxford University Computing Laboratory.

triode three-electrode thermionic valve containing an anode and a cathode (as does a diode) with an additional negatively biased control grid. Small variations in voltage on the grid bias result in large variations in the current. The triode was commonly used in amplifiers but has now been almost entirely superseded by the transistor.

truth table in electronics, a diagram showing the effect of a particular logic gate on every combination of inputs.

uncommitted logic array (ULA) or ***gate array*** a type of semicustomized integrated circuit in which the logic gates are laid down to a general-purpose design but are not connected to each other. The interconnections can then be set in place according to the requirements of individual manufacturers. Producing ULAs may be cheaper than using a large number of TTL (transistor–transistor logic) chips or commissioning a fully customized chip.

valve or ***electron tube*** a glass tube containing gas at low pressure, which is used to control the flow of electricity in a circuit. Three or more metal electrodes are inset into the tube. By varying the voltage on one of them, called the ***grid electrode***, the current through the valve can be controlled, and the valve can act as an amplifier. Valves have been replaced for most applications by transistors. However, they are still used in high-power transmitters and amplifiers, and in some hi-fi systems.

VLSI (abbreviation for ***very large-scale integration***) in electronics, the early-1990s level of advanced technology in the microminiaturization of integrated circuits, and an order of magnitude smaller than LSI (large-scale integration).

voltage amplifier electronic device that increases an input signal in the form of a voltage or potential difference, delivering an output signal that is larger than the input by a specified ratio.

EARTH SCIENCE

The Interior of the Earth

asthenosphere division of the Earth's structure lying beneath the lithosphere, at a depth of approximately 70 km/45 mi to 260 km/160 mi. It is thought to be the soft, partially molten layer of the mantle on which the rigid plates of the Earth's surface move to produce the motions of plate tectonics.

bed single sedimentary rock unit with a distinct set of physical characteristics or contained fossils, readily distinguishable from those of beds above and below. Well-defined partings called ***bedding planes*** separate successive beds or strata.

continent any one of the seven large land masses of the Earth, as distinct from the oceans. They are Asia, Africa, North America, South America, Europe, Australia, and Antarctica. Continents are constantly moving and evolving. A continent does not end at the coastline; its boundary is the edge of the shallow continental shelf, which may extend several hundred kilometres or miles out to sea.

core the innermost part of the Earth. It is divided into an inner core, the upper boundary of which is 1,700 km/1,060 mi from the centre, and an outer core, 1,820 km/1,130 mi thick. Both parts are thought to consist of iron-nickel alloy, with the inner core being solid and the outer core being semisolid. The temperature may be 3,000°C/5,400°F.

craton or ***shield*** core of a continent, a vast tract of highly deformed metamorphic rock around which the continent has been built. Intense mountain-building periods shook these shield areas in Precambrian times before stable conditions set in.

crust the outermost part of the structure of Earth, consisting of two distinct parts, the oceanic crust and the continental crust. The ***oceanic*** crust is on average about 10 km/6.2 mi thick and consists mostly of basaltic types of rock. By contrast, the ***continental*** crust is largely made of granite and is more complex in its structure. Because of the movements of plate tectonics, the oceanic crust is in no place older than about 200 million years. However, parts of the continental crust are over 3 billion years old.

diagenesis or ***lithification*** the physical and chemical changes by which a sediment becomes a sedimentary rock. The main processes involved include compaction of the grains, and the cementing together of the grains by the growth of new minerals deposited by percolating groundwater.

earthquake shaking of the Earth's surface as a result of the sudden release of stresses built up in the Earth's crust. The study of earthquakes is called seismology. Most earthquakes occur along faults (fractures or breaks) in the crust. Plate tectonic movements generate the major proportion: as two plates move past each other they can become jammed and deformed, and a series of shock waves (seismic waves) occur when they spring free. Their force (magnitude) is measured on the Richter scale, and their effect (intensity) on the Mercalli scale. The point at which an earthquake originates is the ***seismic focus***; the point on the Earth's surface directly above this is the ***epicentre***.

Major 20th-century earthquakes

Date	*Place*	*Magnitude (Richter scale)*	*Number of deaths*
1906	San Francisco, USA	8.3	450
1908	Messina, Italy	7.5	83,000
1915	Avezzano, Italy	7.5	29,980
1920	Gansu, China	8.6	100,000
1923	Tokyo, Japan	8.3	99,330
1927	Nan-Shan, China	8.3	200,000
1932	Gansu, China	7.6	70,000
1935	Quetta, India	7.5	30,000
1939	Erzincan, Turkey	7.9	30,000
1939	Chillán, Chile	8.3	28,000
1948	USSR	7.3	110,000
1970	N Peru	7.7	66,794
1976	Tangshan, China	8.2	242,000
1978	NE Iran	7.7	25,000
1980	El Asnam, Algeria	7.3	20,000
1985	Mexico	8.1	25,000
1988	Armenia, USSR	6.9	25,000
1989	San Francisco, USA	7.1	300
1990	NW Iran	7.7	50,000

epicentre the point on the Earth's surface immediately above the seismic focus of an earthquake. Most damage usually takes place at an earthquake's epicentre. The term sometimes refers to a point directly above or below a nuclear explosion ('at ground zero').

fault fracture in the Earth's crust along which the two sides have moved as a result of differing strains in the adjacent rock bodies. Displacement of rock masses horizontally or vertically along a fault may be microscopic, or it may be massive, causing major earthquakes.

fold bend in beds or layers of rock. If the bend is arched in the middle it is called an ***anticline***; if it sags downwards in the middle it is called a ***syncline***. The line along which a bed of rock folds is called its axis. The axial plane is the plane joining the axes of successive beds.

geochemistry science of chemistry as it applies to geology. It deals with the relative and absolute abundances of the chemical elements and their isotopes in the Earth, and also with the chemical changes that accompany geologic processes.

geophysics branch of earth science using physics to study the Earth's surface, interior, and atmosphere. Studies also include winds, weather, tides, earthquakes, volcanoes, and their effects.

geothermal energy energy extracted for heating and electricity generation from natural steam, hot water, or hot dry rocks in the Earth's crust. Water is pumped down through an injection well where it passes through joints in the hot rocks. It rises to the surface through a recovery well and may be converted to steam or run through a heat exchanger. Dry steam may be directed through turbines to produce electricity. It is a important source of energy in volcanically active areas such as Iceland and New Zealand.

geyser natural spring that intermittently discharges an explosive column of steam and hot water into the air due to the build-up of steam in underground chambers. One of the most remarkable geysers is Old Faithful, in Yellowstone National Park, Wyoming, USA. Geysers also occur in New Zealand and Iceland.

intrusion mass of igneous rock that has formed by 'injection' of molten rock, or magma, into existing cracks beneath the surface of the Earth, as distinct from a volcanic rock mass which has erupted from the surface. Intrusion features include vertical cylindrical structures such as stocks, pipes, and necks; sheet structures such as dykes that cut across the strata and sills that push between them; laccoliths, which are blisters that push up the overlying rock; and batholiths, which represent chambers of solidified magma and contain vast volumes of rock.

lava molten rock that erupts from a volcano and cools to form extrusive igneous rock. It differs from magma in that it is molten rock on the surface; magma is molten rock below the surface. Lava that is high in silica is viscous and sticky and does not flow far; it forms a steep-sided conical volcano, for example Mount Fuji, Japan. Low-silica lava can flow for long distances and forms a broad flat volcano, such as Kilauea, Hawaii.

lithosphere topmost layer of the Earth's structure, forming the jigsaw of plates that take part in the movements of plate tectonics. The lithosphere comprises the crust and a portion of the upper mantle. It is regarded as being rigid and moves about on the semi-molten asthenosphere. The lithosphere is about 75 km/47 mi thick.

magma molten rock material beneath the Earth's surface from which igneous rocks are formed. Lava is magma that has reached the surface and solidified, losing some of its components on the way.

mantle intermediate zone of the Earth between the crust and the core, accounting for 82% of the Earth's volume. It is thought to consist of silicate minerals such as olivine.

Mercalli scale scale used to measure the intensity of an earthquake. It differs from the Richter scale, which measures ***magnitude***. It is named after the Italian seismologist Giuseppe Mercalli (1850–1914). Intensity is a subjective value, based on observed phenomena, and varies from place to place with the same earthquake.

metamorphism geological term referring to the changes in rocks of the Earth's crust caused by increasing pressure and temperature. The resulting rocks are metamorphic rocks. All metamorphic changes take place in solid rocks. If the rocks melt and then harden, they become igneous rocks.

Mohorovičić discontinuity also ***Moho*** or ***M-discontinuity*** boundary that separates the Earth's crust and mantle, marked by a rapid increase in the speed of earthquake waves. It follows the variations in the thickness of the crust and is found approximately 32 km/20 mi below the continents and about 10 km/6 mi below the oceans. It is named after the Yugoslav geophysicist Andrija Mohorovičić (1857–1936) who suspected its presence after analysing seismic waves from the Kulpa Valley earthquake 1909.

petrology branch of geology that deals with the study of rocks, their mineral compositions, and their origins.

Richter scale scale based on measurement of seismic waves, used to determine the magnitude of an earthquake at its epicentre. The magnitude of an earthquake differs from its intensity, measured by the Mercalli scale, which is subjective and varies from place to place for the same earthquake. The scale is named after US seismologist Charles Richter.

sial the substance of the Earth's continental crust, as distinct from the sima of the ocean crust. The name, now used rarely, is derived from ***si***lica and ***al***umina, its two main chemical constituents.

sima the substance of the Earth's oceanic crust, as distinct from the sial of the continental crust. The name, now used rarely, is derived from ***si***lica and ***ma***gnesia, its two main chemical constituents.

volcano crack in the Earth's crust through which hot magma (molten rock) and gases well up. The magma becomes known as lava when it reaches the surface. A volcanic mountain, usually cone shaped with a crater on top, is formed around the opening, or vent, by the build-up of solidified lava and ashes (rock fragments). Most volcanoes arise on plate margins, where the movements of plates generate magma or allow it to rise from the mantle beneath. However, a number are found far from plate-margin activity, on 'hot spots' where the Earth's crust is thin.

The explosion of Krakatoa, an island between Java and Sumatra in the Pacific Ocean, in 1883, was equivalent to 26 of the most powerful H-bombs ever exploded. The dense cloud of dust produced reduced the Sun's heating effect by 20%. The dust circled the world within a month, producing blazing red sunsets as far afield as London.

continent

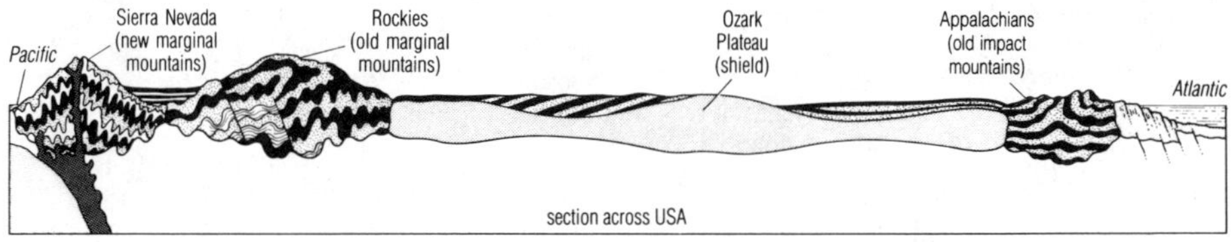

Exploring the Earth from above and below

Recent years have seen basic geology merge with other sciences to produce the all-embracing discipline of earth science and the advent of sophisticated data-gathering systems. There has been much debate amongst the scientists involved. Traditionalists maintain that the only way to study the Earth is to go out and sample it, record it, and interpret it directly. Progressives insist that the only way to a full picture of the Earth is through remote sensing and computerized assessment of the data. No matter how the science changes, there will always be room for both approaches.

Measuring the Earth

The greatest advances in remote sensing have been in distance measurement. The surface of the Earth can be measured extremely accurately, using global positioning geodesy (detecting signals from satellites by Earth-based receivers), satellite laser ranging (in which satellites reflect signals from ground transmitters back to ground receivers), and very-long-baseline interferometry, comparing signals received at ground-based receivers from distant extraterrestrial bodies. These techniques can measure distances of thousands of kilometres to accuracies of less than a centimetre. Movements of faults can be measured, as can the growth of the tectonic plates. Previously such speeds were calculated by averaging displacements measured over decades or centuries. The results show that in the oceanic crust, plate growth is steady: from 12 mm/0.5 in per year across the Mid-Atlantic Ridge to 160 mm/6.5 in per year across the East Pacific Rise. The major continental faults seem to be very irregular in their movement; the Great Rift Valley of East Africa has remained stationary for 20 years, when long-term averages suggest that it would have opened up by about 100 mm/4 in in that time.

Offshore petroleum exploration

Petroleum is society's most important raw fuel. The traditional oilfields were on land. In 1896, wells were drilled into the Summerland oilfield from piers extending from the California coast. Oilwells were sunk in the Caspian Sea, the Gulf of Mexico and Venezuela's Lake Maracaibo in the 1930s and 1940s, but only in the 1970s with the development of the North Sea and Canadian Arctic oilfields did offshore exploration really start. Even under such hostile sea conditions, wells could be drilled into the continental shelf 125 m/400 ft below sea level.

As the more accessible deposits become depleted, petroleum exploration is going into ever-deeper waters of the world's continental shelves. In 1991, Brazil, currently leading the way in offshore oil exploration, sank a production well in water 752 m/2,467 ft deep off the northeast coast. It is estimated that by the year 2000, more than 30% of the world's petroleum production will be from offshore wells.

However, the main oil reserves may lie somewhere else altogether. Accepted theory says that petroleum was formed from the remains of plant and animal matter, in the sedimentary rocks in which they were entombed. An alternative theory proposes inorganic origins for oil, from methane and hydrogen trapped when the Earth was formed in granites or metamorphic rocks, from which the oil seeps into the known traps in surrounding sedimentary basins. One team has been drilling into granite rocks in Sweden since 1987, with apparent success. Another will drill into granites in Canada in 1993, seeking vast new oil deposits in totally different geological sites from those traditionally investigated.

Climatic change

The burning of oil and other carbon-based fuels, pumping vast quantities of carbon dioxide into the atmosphere, raises the possibility of climatic change. The prospect is alarming, especially if such change is brought about by human interference with nature. However, the Earth's climate has never been stable, and human effects may be masked by natural variations. Beds of coal in Spitzbergen and glacial debris in the middle of the Australian desert attest to large-scale climate variations over hundreds of millions of years. Other studies show shorter-term variations: temperate tree fossils in Antarctica, 5° from the South Pole, and in the far north of Canada, show that climates were much warmer than now right up to the beginning of the Ice Age.

The international Pliocene Research Interpretation and Synoptic Mapping programme, begun in 1990, should produce fine details of climatic changes before the Ice Age. The Greenland Icecore project has shown that, during the Ice Age, temperatures over the ice caps varied between cold – with temperatures about 12°C lower than at present – and mild, with temperatures about 7° lower than at present. Each cold period lasted between 500 and 2,000 years, starting abruptly and ending gradually.

Several sudden, catastrophic climate changes may have been caused in the past by the impact of giant meteorites or comets. The crater of one, 214 million years old, has been found in Canada; this seems to relate to a mass extinction in the Triassic period. Scientists are still seeking remains of the meteorite believed to have wiped out the dinosaurs 65 million years ago.

DD

The Surface of the Earth

abyssal zone dark ocean region 2,000-6,000 m/ 6,500-19,500 ft deep; temperature 4°C/39°F. Three-quarters of the area of the deep ocean floor lies in the abyssal zone, which is too far from the surface for photosynthesis to take place. Some fish and crustaceans living there are blind or have their own light sources. The region above is the bathyal zone; the region below, the hadal zone.

alluvial deposit layer of broken rocky matter, or sediment, formed from material that has been carried in suspension by a river or stream and dropped as the velocity of the current changes. River plains and deltas are made entirely of alluvial deposits, but smaller pockets can be found in the beds of upland torrents.

Antarctic Circle imaginary line that encircles the South Pole at latitude 66° 32' S. The line encompasses the continent of Antarctica and the Antarctic Ocean.

anticline fold in the rocks of the Earth's crust in which the layers or beds bulge upwards to form an arch (seldom preserved intact).

aquifer any rock formation containing water. The rock of an aquifer must be porous and permeable (full of interconnected holes) so that it can absorb water. Aquifers supply artesian wells, and are actively sought in arid areas as sources of drinking and irrigation water.

archipelago group of islands, or an area of sea containing a group of islands. The islands of an archipelago are usually volcanic in origin, and they sometimes represent the tops of peaks in areas around continental margins flooded by the sea.

Arctic Circle imaginary line that encircles the North Pole at latitude 66° 32' N. Within this line there is at least one day in the summer during which the Sun never sets, and at least one day in the winter during which the Sun never rises.

artesian well well that is supplied with water rising from an underground water-saturated rock layer (aquifer). The water rises from the aquifer under its own pressure. Such a well may be drilled into an aquifer that is confined by impermeable rocks both above and below. If the water table (the top of the region of water saturation) in that aquifer is above the level of the well head, hydrostatic pressure will force the water to the surface.

badlands barren landscape cut by erosion into a maze of ravines, pinnacles, gullies and sharp-edged ridges. Areas in South Dakota and Nebraska, USA, are examples.

caldera very large basin-shaped crater. Calderas are found at the tops of volcanoes, where the original peak has collapsed into an empty chamber beneath. The basin, many times larger than the original volcanic vent, may be flooded, producing a crater lake, or the flat floor may contain a number of small volcanic cones, produced by volcanic activity after the collapse.

crater bowl-shaped depression, usually round and with steep sides. Craters are formed by explosive events such as the eruption of a volcano or by the impact of a meteorite. A caldera is a much larger feature.

delta tract of land at a river's mouth, composed of silt deposited as the water slows on entering the sea. Familiar examples of large deltas are those of the Mississippi, Ganges and Brahmaputra, Rhîne, Po, Danube, and Nile; the shape of the Nile delta is like the Greek letter *delta* Δ, and thus gave rise to the name.

desert arid area without sufficient rainfall and, consequently, vegetation to support human life. The term includes the ice areas of the polar regions (known as cold deserts). Almost 33% of the Earth's land surface is desert, and this proportion is increasing.

Largest deserts

Name/location	*area* sq m*	*sq km*
Sahara, N Africa	8,600,000	3,320,000
Arabian, SW Asia	2,330,000	900,000
Gobi, Mongolia and NE China	1,166,000	450,000
Patagonian, Argentina	673,000	260,000
Great Victoria, SW Australia	647,000	250,000
Great Basin, SW USA	492,000	190,000
Chihuahuan, Mexico	450,000	175,000
Great Sandy, NW Australia	400,000	150,000
Sonoran, SW USA	310,000	120,000
Kyzyl Kum, SW USSR	300,000	115,000
Takla Makan, N China	270,000	105,000
Kalahari, SW Africa	260,000	100,000

** desert areas are very approximate, because clear physical boundaries may not occur*

dune mound or ridge of wind-drifted sand. Loose sand is blown and bounced along by the wind, up the windward side of a dune. The sand particles then fall to rest on the lee side, while more are blown up from the windward side. In this way, a dune moves gradually downwind.

equator the ***terrestrial equator*** is the great circle whose plane is perpendicular to the Earth's axis (the line joining the poles). Its length is 40,092 km/ 24,901.8 mi, divided into 360 degrees of longitude. The equator encircles the broadest part of the Earth, and represents 0° latitude. It divides the Earth into two halves, called the northern and the southern hemispheres.

erosion wearing away of the Earth's surface, caused by the breakdown and transportation of particles of rock or soil (by contrast, weathering does not involve transportation). Agents of erosion include the sea, rivers, glaciers, and wind. Water, consisting of sea waves and currents, rivers, and rain; ice, in the form of glaciers; and wind, hurling sand fragments against exposed rocks and moving dunes along, are the most potent forces of erosion. People also contribute to erosion by bad farming practices and the cutting down of forests, which can lead to the formation of dust bowls.

fjord or ***fiord*** narrow sea inlet enclosed by high cliffs. Fjords are found in Norway, New Zealand, and western parts of Scotland. They are formed when an overdeepened U-shaped glacial valley is drowned by a rise in sea-level. At the mouth of the fjord there is a characteristic lip causing a shallowing of the water. This is due to reduced glacial erosion and the deposition of moraine at this point.

flood plain area of periodic flooding along the course of river valleys. When river discharge exceeds the capacity of the channel, water rises over the channel banks and floods the adjacent low-lying lands. As water spills out of the channel, some alluvium (silty material) will be deposited on the banks to form levees (raised river banks). This water will slowly seep into the flood plain, depositing a new layer of rich fertile alluvium as it does so. Many important floodplains, such as the inner Niger delta in Mali, occur in arid areas where their exceptional productivity has great importance for the local economy.

glacier tongue of ice, originating in mountains in snowfields above the snowline, which moves slowly downhill and is constantly replenished from its source. The scenery produced by the erosive action of glaciers is characteristic and includes glacial troughs (U-shaped valleys), corries, and arêtes. In lowlands, the laying down of moraine (rocky debris once carried by glaciers) produces a variety of landscape features.

The longest glacier in the world is the Lambert Glacier in Australian Antarctic Territory. It is up to 64 km/40 mi wide and at least 400 km/250 mi long.

ground water water collected underground in porous rock strata and soils; it emerges at the surface as springs and streams. The groundwater's upper level is called the ***water table***. Sandy or other kinds of beds that are filled with groundwater are called ***aquifers***. Recent estimates are that usable ground water amounts to more than 90% of all the fresh water on Earth; however, keeping such supplies free of pollutants entering the recharge areas is a critical environmental concern.

The water table dropped in the UK during the drought of the early 1990s; however, under cities such as London and Liverpool the water table rose because the closure of industries meant that less water was being removed.

International Date Line (IDL) imaginary line that approximately follows the 180° line of longitude. The date is put forward a day when crossing the line going west, and back a day when going east. The IDL was chosen at the International Meridian Conference 1884.

island area of land surrounded entirely by water. Islands can be formed in many ways. ***Continental islands*** were once part of the mainland, but became isolated (by tectonic movement, erosion, or a rise in sea level, for example). ***Volcanic islands***, such as Japan, were formed by the explosion of underwater volcanoes. ***Coral islands*** consist mainly of coral, built up over many years. An ***atoll*** is a circular coral reef surrounding a lagoon; atolls were formed when a coral reef grew up around a volcanic island that subsequently sank or was submerged by a rise in sea level. ***Barrier islands*** are found by the shore in shallow water, and are formed by the deposition of sediment eroded from the shoreline.

landslide sudden downward movement of a mass of soil or rocks from a cliff or steep slope. Landslides happen when a slope becomes unstable, usually because the base has been undercut or because materials within the mass have become wet and slippery.

latitude and longitude imaginary lines used to locate position on the globe. Lines of latitude are drawn parallel to the equator, with 0° at the equator and 90° at the north and south poles. Lines of longitude are drawn at right angles to these, with 0° (the Prime Meridian) passing through Greenwich, England.

meander loop-shaped curve in a river flowing across flat country. As a river flows, any curve in its course is accentuated by the current. The current is fastest on the outside of the curve where it cuts into the bank; on the curve's inside the current is slow and deposits any transported material. In this way the river changes its course across the flood plain.

meridian half a great circle drawn on the Earth's surface passing through both poles and thus through all places with the same longitude. Terrestrial longi-

latitude and longitude

Point X lies on longitude 60°W

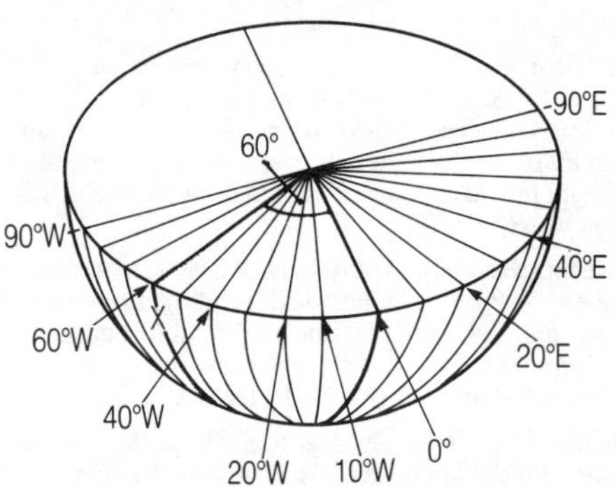

Point X lies on latitude 20°S

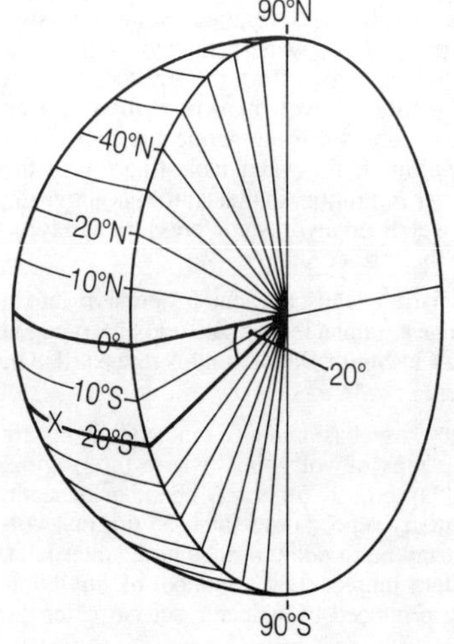

Together longitude 60°W latitude 20°S places point X on a precise position on the globe.

tudes are usually measured from the Greenwich Meridian.

moraine rocky debris or till carried along and deposited by a glacier. Material eroded from the side of a glaciated valley and carried along the glacier's edge is called lateral moraine; that worn from the valley floor and carried along the base of the glacier is called ground moraine. Rubble dropped at the foot of a melting glacier is called terminal moraine.

mountain natural upward projection of the Earth's surface, higher and steeper than a hill. The process of mountain building (orogeny) consists of volcanism, folding, faulting, and thrusting, resulting from the collision and welding together of two tectonic plates. This process deforms the rock and compresses the sediment between the two plates into mountain chains.

Highest mountains

Name	*Height* *m*	*ft*	*Location*
Everest	8,850	29,030	China–Nepal
K2	8,610	28,250	Kashmir–Jammu
Kangchenjunga	8,590	28,170	India–Nepal
Lhotse	8,500	27,890	China-Nepal
Kangchenjunga S Peak	8,470	27,800	India–Nepal
Makalu I	8,470	27,800	China–Nepal
Kangchenjunga W Peak	8,420	27,620	India–Nepal
Llotse E Peak	8,380	27,500	China–Nepal
Dhaulagiri	8,170	26,810	Nepal
Cho Oyu	8,150	26,750	China–Nepal
Manaslu	8,130	26,660	Nepal
Nanga Parbat	8,130	26,660	Kashmir–Jammu
Annapurna I	8,080	26,500	Nepal
Gasherbrum I	8,070	26,470	Kashmir–Jammu
Broad-highest	8,050	26,400	Kashmir–Jammu
Gasherbrum II	8,030	26,360	Kashmir–Jammu
Gosainthan	8,010	26,290	China
Broad-middle	8,000	26,250	Kashmir–Jammu
Gasherbrum III	7,950	26,090	Kashmir–Jammu
Annapurna II	7,940	26,040	Nepal
Nanda Devi	7,820	25,660	India
Rakaposhi	7,790	25,560	Kashmir
Kamet	7,760	25,450	India
Ulugh Muztagh	7,720	25,340	Tibet
Tirich Mir	7,690	25,230	Pakistan

** Heights are given to the nearest 10m/ft.*

peat fibrous organic substance found in bogs and formed by the incomplete decomposition of plants such as sphagnum moss. N Asia, Canada, Finland, Ireland, and other places have large deposits, which have been dried and used as fuel from ancient times. Peat can also be used as a soil additive.

permafrost condition in which a deep layer of soil does not thaw out during the summer. Permafrost occurs under periglacial conditions. It is claimed that 26% of the world's land surface is permafrost.

plain or ***grassland*** land, usually flat, upon which grass predominates. The plains cover large areas of the Earth's surface, especially between the deserts of the tropics and the rainforests of the equator, and have rain in one season only. In such regions the climate belts move north and south during the year, bringing rainforest conditions at one time and desert conditions at another. Temperate plains include the North European Plain, the High Plains of the USA and Canada, and the Russian Plain also known as the steppe.

plateau elevated area of fairly flat land, or a mountainous region in which the peaks are at the same height. An ***intermontane plateau*** is one surrounded by mountains. A ***piedmont plateau*** is one that lies between the mountains and low-lying land. A ***continental plateau*** rises abruptly from low-lying lands or the sea. Examples are the Tibetan Plateau and the Massif Central in France.

polder area of flat reclaimed land that used to be covered by a river, lake, or the sea. Polders have been artificially drained and protected from flooding by building dykes. They are common in the Netherlands, where the total land area has been increased by nearly one-fifth since AD 1200. Such schemes as the Zuider Zee project have provided some of the best agricultural land in the country.

pole either of the geographic north and south points of the axis about which the Earth rotates. The geographic poles differ from the magnetic poles, which are the points towards which a freely suspended magnetic needle will point.

In 1985, the magnetic north pole was some 350 km/ 218 mi NW of Resolute Bay, Northwest Territories, Canada. It moves northwards about 10 km/6 mi each year, although it can vary in a day about 80 km/ 50 mi from its average position. It is relocated every decade in order to update navigational charts.

It is thought that periodic changes in the Earth's core cause a reversal of the magnetic poles. Many animals, including migrating birds and fish, are believed to orientate themselves partly using the Earth's magnetic field. A permanent scientific base collects data at the South Pole.

rift valley valley formed by the subsidence of a block of the Earth's crust between two or more parallel faults. Rift valleys are steep-sided and form where the crust is being pulled apart, as at ocean ridges, or in the Great Rift Valley of E Africa.

sand loose grains of rock, sized 0.0625–2.00 mm/ 0.0025–0.08 in in diameter, consisting chiefly of quartz, but owing their varying colour to mixtures of other minerals. Sand is used in cement-making, as an abrasive, in glass-making, and for other purposes.

scarp and dip the two slopes formed when a sedimentary bed outcrops as a landscape feature. The scarp is the slope that cuts across the bedding plane; the dip is the opposite slope which follows the bedding plane. The scarp is usually steep, while the dip is a gentle slope.

sediment any loose material that has 'settled' – deposited from suspension in water, ice, or air, generally as the water current or wind speed decreases. Typical sediments are, in order of increasing coarseness, clay, mud, silt, sand, gravel, pebbles, cobbles, and boulders.

soil loose covering of broken rocky material and decaying organic matter overlying the bedrock of the

Weathering

Physical weathering	
temperature changes	weakening rocks by expansion and contraction
frost	wedging rocks apart by the expansion of water on freezing
unloading	the loosening of rock layers by release of pressure after the erosion and removal of those layers above
Chemical weathering	
carbonation	the breakdown of calcite by reaction with carbonic acid in rainwater
hydrolysis	the breakdown of feldspar into china clay by reaction with carbonic acid in rainwater
oxidation	the breakdown of iron-rich minerals due to rusting
hydration	the expansion of certain minerals due to the uptake of water

Earth's surface. Various types of soil develop under different conditions: deep soils form in warm wet climates and in valleys; shallow soils form in cool dry areas and on slopes. ***Pedology***, the study of soil, is significant because of the relative importance of different soil types to agriculture.

stalactite and stalagmite cave structures formed by the deposition of calcite dissolved in ground water. ***Stalactites*** grow downwards from the roofs or walls and can be icicle-shaped, straw-shaped, curtain-shaped, or formed as terraces. ***Stalagmites*** grow upwards from the cave floor and can be conical, fir-cone-shaped, or resemble a stack of saucers. Growing stalactites and stalagmites may meet to form a continuous column from floor to ceiling.

syncline geological term for a fold in the rocks of the Earth's crust in which the layers or beds dip inwards, thus forming a trough-like structure with a sag in the middle. The opposite structure, with the beds arching upwards, is an anticline.

topography the surface shape and aspect of the land, and its study. Topography deals with relief and contours, the distribution of mountains and valleys, the patterns of rivers, and all other features, natural and artificial, that produce the landscape.

tropics the area between the tropics of Cancer and Capricorn, defined by the parallels of latitude approximately 23°30' N and S of the equator. They are the limits of the area of Earth's surface in which the Sun can be directly overhead. The mean monthly temperature is over 20°C/68°F.

water table the upper level of ground water (water collected underground in porous rocks). Water that is above the water table will drain downwards; a spring forms where the water table cuts the surface of the ground. The water table rises and falls in response to rainfall and the rate at which water is extracted, for example, for irrigation and industry.

In many irrigated areas the water table is falling due to the extraction of water. That below N China, for example, is sinking at a rate of 1 m/3 ft a year. Regions with high water tables and dense industrialization have problems with pollution of the water table. In the USA, New Jersey, Florida, and Louisiana have water tables contaminated by both industrial wastes amd saline seepage from the ocean.

weathering process by which exposed rocks are broken down on the spot by the action of rain, frost, wind, and other elements of the weather. It differs from erosion in that no movement or transportion of the broken-down material takes place. Two types of weathering are recognized: physical (or mechanical) and chemical. They usually occur together.

Atmosphere and Ocean

barometer instrument that measures atmospheric pressure as an indication of weather. Most often used are the ***mercury barometer*** and the ***aneroid barometer***.

bathyal zone upper part of the ocean, which lies on the continental shelf at a depth of between 200 m/650 ft and 2,000 m/6,500 ft.

beach strip of land bordering the sea, normally consisting of boulders and pebbles on exposed coasts or sand on sheltered coasts. It is usually defined by the high- and low-water marks. A berm, a ridge of sand and pebbles, may be found at the farthest point that the water reaches.

Beaufort scale system of recording wind velocity, devised by Francis Beaufort 1806. It is a numerical scale ranging from 0 to 17, calm being indicated by 0 and a hurricane by 12; 13–17 indicate degrees of hurricane force.

Coriolis effect the effect of the Earth's rotation on the atmosphere and on all objects on the Earth's surface. In the northern hemisphere it causes moving objects and currents to be deflected to the right; in the southern hemisphere it causes deflection to the left. The effect is named after its discoverer, French mathematician Gaspard Coriolis (1792–1843).

cloud water vapour condensed into minute water particles that float in masses in the atmosphere. Clouds, like fogs or mists, which occur at lower levels, are formed by the cooling of air containing water vapour, which generally condenses around tiny dust particles.

Clouds are classified according to the height at which they occur and their shape. ***Cirrus*** and ***cirrostratus*** clouds occur at around 10 km/33,000 ft. Three types of cloud are found at 3–7 km/10,000–23,000 ft: cirrocumulus, altocumulus, and altostratus. ***Cirrocumulus*** clouds occur in small or large rounded tufts, sometimes arranged in the pattern called mackerel sky. ***Altocumulus*** clouds are similar, but larger, white clouds, also arranged in lines. ***Altostratus*** clouds are like heavy cirrostratus clouds and may stretch across the sky as a grey sheet. ***Stratocumulus*** clouds are generally lower, occurring at 2–6 km/6,500–20,000 ft. They are dull grey clouds that give rise to a leaden sky that may not yield rain. Two types of clouds, ***cumulus*** and ***cumulonimbus***, are placed in a special category because they are produced by daily ascending air currents, which take moisture into the cooler regions of the atmosphere.

Cloud

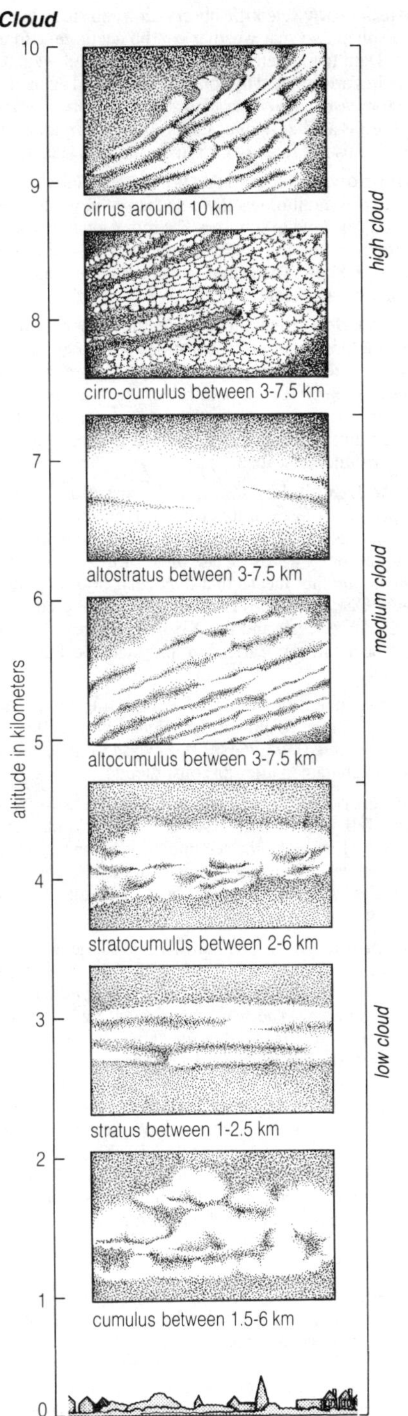

current flow of a body of water or air, or of heat, moving in a definite direction. Ocean currents are fast-flowing currents of seawater generated by the wind or by variations in water density between two areas. They are partly responsible for transferring heat from the equator to the poles and thereby evening out the global heat imbalance. There are three basic types of ocean current: ***drift currents*** are broad and slow-moving; ***stream currents*** are narrow and swift-moving; and ***upwelling currents*** bring cold, nutrient-rich water from the ocean bottom.

doldrums area of low atmospheric pressure along the equator, in the intertropical convergence zone where the NE and SE trade winds converge. The doldrums are characterized by calm or very light winds, during which there may be sudden squalls and stormy weather. For this reason the areas are avoided as far as possible by sailing ships.

drought period of prolonged dry weather. The area of the world subject to serious droughts, such as the Sahara, is increasing because of destruction of forests, overgrazing, and poor agricultural practices. In the UK, drought is defined as the passing of 15 days with less than 0.2 mm of rain.

estuary river mouth widening into the sea, where fresh water mixes with salt water and tidal effects are felt.

exosphere the uppermost layer of the atmosphere. It is an ill-defined zone above the thermosphere, beginning at about 700 km/435 mi and fading off into the vacuum of space. The gases are extremely thin, with hydrogen as the main constituent.

fog cloud that collects at the surface of the Earth, composed of water vapour that has condensed on particles of dust in the atmosphere. Cloud and fog are both caused by the air temperature falling below dew point. The thickness of fog depends on the number of water particles it contains.

front the boundary between two air masses of different temperature or humidity. A ***cold front*** marks the line of advance of a cold air mass from below, as it displaces a warm air mass; a ***warm front*** marks the advance of a warm air mass as it rises up over a cold one. Frontal systems define the weather of the mid-latitudes, where warm tropical air is constantly meeting cold air from the poles.

frost condition of the weather that occurs when the air temperature is below freezing, 0°C/32°F. Water in the atmosphere is deposited as ice crystals on the ground or exposed objects. As cold air is heavier than warm, ground frost is more common than hoar frost, which is formed by the condensation of water particles in the same way that dew collects.

greenhouse effect phenomenon of the Earth's atmosphere by which solar radiation, trapped by the Earth and re-emitted from the surface, is prevented from escaping by various gases in the air. The result is a rise in the Earth's temperature. The main greenhouse gases are carbon dioxide, methane, and chlorofluorocarbons (CFCs). Fossil-fuel consumption and forest fires are the main causes of carbon-dioxide build-up; methane is a byproduct of agriculture (rice, cattle, sheep). Water vapour is another greenhouse gas. (See ***Environment*** for more.)

gyre circular surface rotation of ocean water in each major sea (a type of current). Gyres are large and permanent, and occupy the N and S halves of the three major oceans. Their movements are dictated by the prevailing winds and the Coriolis effect. Gyres move clockwise in the northern hemisphere and anticlockwise in the southern hemisphere.

hail precipitation in the form of pellets of ice (hailstones). It is caused by the circulation of moisture in strong convection currents, usually within cumulonimbus clouds. Water droplets freeze as they are carried upwards. As the circulation continues, layers of ice are deposited around the droplets until they become too heavy to be supported by the currents and they fall as a hailstorm.

hurricane revolving storm in tropical regions, called ***typhoon*** in the N Pacific. It originates between 5° and 20° N or S of the equator, when the surface temperature of the ocean is above 27°C/80°F. A central calm area, called the eye, is surrounded by inwardly spiralling winds (anticlockwise in the northern hemisphere) of up to 320 kph/200 mph. A hurricane is accompanied by lightning and torrential rain, and can cause extensive damage. In meteorology, a hurricane is a wind of force 12 or more on the Beaufort scale. The most intense hurricane recorded in the Caribbean/Atlantic sector was Hurricane Gilbert in 1988, with sustained winds of 280 kph/175 mph and gusts of over 320 kph/200 mph.

isobar line drawn on maps and weather charts linking all places with the same atmospheric pressure (usually measured in millibars). When used in weather forecasting, the distance between the isobars is an indication of the barometric gradient.

jet stream narrow band of very fast wind (velocities of over 150 kph/95 mph) found at altitudes of 10–16 km/6–10 mi in the upper troposphere or lower stratosphere. Jet streams usually occur about the latitudes of the Westerlies (35°–60°).

lagoon coastal body of shallow salt water, usually with limited access to the sea. The term is normally used to describe the shallow sea area cut off by a coral reef or barrier islands.

lightning high-voltage electrical discharge between two charged rainclouds or between a cloud and the Earth, caused by the build-up of electrical charges. Air in the path of lightning ionizes (becomes conducting), and expands; the accompanying noise is heard as thunder. Currents of 20,000 amperes and temperatures of 30,000°C/54,000°F are common.

The upward flash of a lightning stroke can travel at up to 140,000 km/87,000 mi per second, which is nearly half the speed of light. The downward stroke of a lightning flash is much slower at 1,600 km/1,000 mi per second.

magnetic storm a sudden disturbance affecting the Earth's magnetic field, causing anomalies in radio transmissions and magnetic compasses. It is probably caused by sunspot activity.

Mediterranean climate climate characterized by hot dry summers and warm wet winters. Mediterranean zones are situated in either hemisphere on the western side of continents, between latitudes of 30° and 60°.

mesosphere layer in the Earth's atmosphere above the stratosphere and below the thermosphere. It lies between about 50 km/31 mi and 80 km/50 mi above the ground.

meteorology scientific observation and study of the atmosphere, so that weather can be accurately forecast. Data from meteorological stations and weather satellites are collated by computer at central agencies, and forecast and weather maps based on current readings are issued at regular intervals. Modern analysis can give useful forecasts for up to six days ahead.

monsoon wind pattern that brings seasonally heavy rain to S Asia; it blows towards the sea in winter and towards the land in summer. The monsoon may cause destructive flooding all over India and SE Asia from April to Sept. Thousands of people are rendered homeless each year.

ocean ridge mountain range on the seabed indicating the presence of a constructive plate margin (where tectonic plates are moving apart and magma rises to the surface). Ocean ridges, such as the Mid-Atlantic Ridge, consist of many segments offset along faults, and can rise thousands of metres above the surrounding seabed.

ocean trench deep trench in the seabed indicating the presence of a destructive margin (produced by the movements of plate tectonics). The subduction or dragging downwards of one plate of the lithosphere beneath another means that the ocean floor is pulled down. Ocean trenches are found around the edge of the Pacific Ocean and the NE Indian Ocean; minor ones occur in the Caribbean and near the Falkland Islands.

ooze sediment of fine texture consisting mainly of organic matter found on the ocean floor at depths greater than 2,000 m/6,600 ft. Several kinds of ooze exist, each named after its constituents.

rain form of precipitation in which separate drops of water fall to the Earth's surface from clouds. The drops are formed by the accumulation of fine droplets that condense from water vapour in the air. The condensation is usually brought about by rising and subsequent cooling of air.

thunderstorm severe storm of very heavy rain, thunder, and lightning. Thunderstorms are usually caused by the intense heating of the ground surface during summer. The warm air rises rapidly to form tall cumulonimbus clouds with a characteristic anvil-shaped top. Electrical charges accumulate in the clouds and are discharged to the ground as flashes of lightning. Air in the path of lightning becomes heated and expands rapidly, creating shock waves that are heard as a crash or rumble of thunder. The rough distance between an observer and a lightning flash can be calculated by timing the number of seconds between the flash and the thunder. A gap of 3 seconds represents about a kilometre; 5 seconds represents about a mile.

tornado extremely violent revolving storm with swirling, funnel-shaped clouds, caused by a rising column of warm air propelled by strong wind. A tornado can rise to a great height, but with a diameter of only a few hundred metres or yards or less. Tornadoes move with wind speeds of 160–480 kph/100–300 mph, destroying everything in their path. They are common in central USA and Australia.

trade wind prevailing wind that blows towards the equator from the northeast and southeast. Trade winds are caused by hot air rising at the equator and the consequent movement of air from north and south to take its place. The winds are deflected towards the west because of the Earth's west-to-east rotation. The unpredictable calms known as the doldrums lie at their convergence.

troposphere lower part of the Earth's atmosphere extending about 10.5 km/6.5 mi from the Earth's surface, in which temperature decreases with height to about –60°C/–76°F except in local layers of temperature inversion. The ***tropopause*** is the upper boundary of the troposphere, above which the temperature increases slowly with height within the atmosphere. All of the Earth's weather takes place within the troposphere.

tsunami (Japanese 'harbour wave') wave generated by an undersea earthquake or volcanic eruption. In the open ocean it may take the form of several successive waves, rarely in excess of a metre in height but travelling at speeds of 650–800 kph/400-500 mph. In the coastal shallows tsunamis slow down and build up, producing towering waves that can sweep inland and cause great loss of life and property.

wind the lateral movement of the Earth's atmosphere from high-pressure areas (anticyclones) to low-pressure areas (depression). Its speed is measured using an anemometer or by studying its effects on, for example, trees by using the Beaufort Scale. Although modified by features such as land and water, there is a basic worldwide system of trade winds, Westerlies, monsoons, and others.

The Developing Earth

Archaean or ***Archaeozoic*** the earliest eon of geological time; the first part of the Precambrian, from the formation of Earth up to about 2,500 million years ago. It was a time when no life existed, and with every new discovery of ancient life, its upper boundary is being pushed further back.

Cambrian period of geological time 570–510 million years ago; the first period of the Palaeozoic era. All invertebrate animal life appeared and marine algae were widespread. The earliest fossils with hard shells, such as trilobites, date from this period.

Carboniferous period of geological time 363–290 million years ago, the fifth period of the Palaeozoic era. In the USA, it is divided into two periods: the Mississippian (lower) and the Pennsylvanian (upper). Typical of the lower-Carboniferous rocks are shallow-water limestones, while upper-Carboniferous rocks have delta deposits with coal (hence the name). Amphibians were abundant and reptiles evolved during this period.

continental drift the theory that, about 250–200 million years ago, the Earth consisted of a single large continent (Pangaea), which subsequently broke apart to form the continents known today. The theory was proposed 1912 by German meteorologist Alfred Wegener, but such vast continental movements could not be satisfactorily explained until the study of plate tectonics in the 1960s.

continental drift

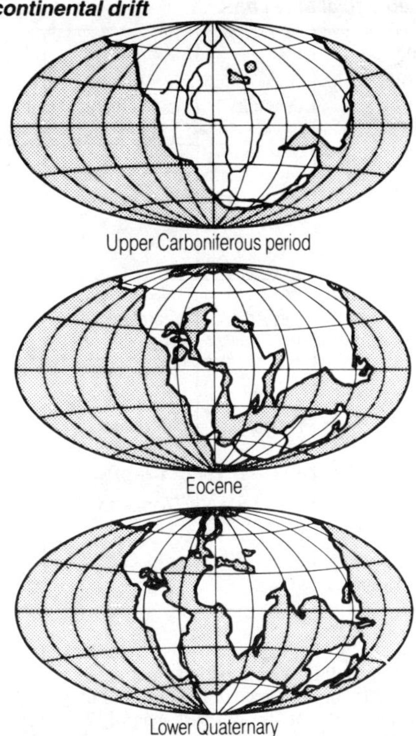

Cretaceous period of geological time 146–65 million years ago. It is the last period of the Mesozoic era, during which angiosperm (seed-bearing) plants evolved, and dinosaurs reached a peak before their almost complete extinction at the end of the period. Chalk is a typical rock type of the second half of the period.

dating science of determining the age of geological structures, rocks, and fossils, and placing them in the context of geological time. The techniques are of two types: relative dating and absolute dating. ***Relative dating*** can be carried out by identifying fossils of creatures that lived only at certain times (marker fossils), and by looking at the physical relationships of rocks to other rocks of a known age. ***Absolute dating*** is achieved by measuring how much of a rock's radioactive elements have changed since the rock was formed, using the process of radiometric dating.

Devonian period of geological time 408–360 million years ago, the fourth period of the Palaeozoic era. Many desert sandstones from North America and Europe date from this time. The first land plants flourished in the Devonian period, corals were abundant in the seas, amphibians evolved from air-breathing fish, and insects developed on land.

epoch subdivision of a geological period in the geological time scale. Epochs are sometimes given their own names (such as the Palaeocene, Eocene, Oligocene, Miocene, and Pliocene epochs comprising the Tertiary period), or they are referred to as the late, early, or middle portions of a given period (as the Late Cretaceous or the Middle Triassic epoch).

Geological time chart

Eon	Era	Period	Epoch	Millions of years ago	Life forms
	Cenozoic	Quaternary	Holocene	0.01	
			Pleistocene	1.64	humans appeared
			Pliocene	5.2	
			Miocene	23.5	
		Tertiary	Oligocene	35.5	
			Eocene	56.5	
			Palaeocene	65	mammals flourished
Phanerozoic		Cretaceous		146	heyday of dinosaurs
	Mesozoic	Jurassic		208	first birds
		Triassic		245	first mammals and dinosaurs
		Permian		290	reptiles expanded
		Carboniferous		363	first reptiles
	Palaeozoic	Devonian		409	first amphibians
		Silurian		439	first land plants
		Ordovician		510	first fish
		Cambrian		570	first fossils
(Precambrian)					
Proterozoic				3,500	earliest living things
Archaean				4,600	

era any of the major divisions of geological time, each including several periods, but smaller than an eon. The currently recognized eras all fall within the Phanerozoic eon – or the vast span of time, starting about 570 million years ago, when fossils are found to become abundant. The eras in ascending order are the Palaeozoic, Mesozoic, and Cenozoic. We are living in the Recent epoch of the Quaternary period of the Cenozoic era.

geological time time scale embracing the history of the Earth from its physical origin to the present day. Geological time is traditionally divided into eons (Phanerozoic, Proterozoic, and Archaean), which in turn are divided into eras, periods, epochs, ages, and finally chrons.

Gondwanaland or ***Gondwana*** southern land mass formed 200 million years ago by the splitting of the single world continent Pangaea. (The northern land mass was Laurasia.) It later fragmented into the continents of South America, Africa, Australia, and Antarctica, which then drifted slowly to their present positions. The baobab tree found in both Africa and Australia is a relic of this ancient land mass.

A database of the entire geology of Gondwanaland has been constructed by geologists in South Africa. The database, known as Gondwana Geoscientific Indexing Database (GO-GEOID), displays information as a map of Gondwana 155 million years ago, before the continents drifted apart.

Holocene epoch of geological time that began 10,000 years ago, the second and current epoch of the Quaternary period. The glaciers retreated, the climate became warmer, and humans developed significantly.

Iapetus Ocean or ***Proto-Atlantic*** sea that existed in early Palaeozoic times between the continent that was to become Europe and that which was to become North America. The continents moved together in the late Palaeozoic, obliterating the ocean. When they moved apart once more, they formed the Atlantic.

ice age any period of glaciation occurring in the Earth's history, but particularly that in the Pleistocene epoch, immediately preceding historic times. On the North American continent, glaciers reached as far south as the Great Lakes, and an ice sheet spread over N Europe, leaving its remains as far south as Switzerland. There were several glacial advances separated by interglacial stages during which the ice melted and temperatures were higher than today. Formerly there were thought to have been only three or four glacial advances, but recent research has shown about 20 major incidences. There is a possibility that the Pleistocene ice age is not yet over.

Major ice ages

Name	Date (years ago)
Pleistocene	1.64 million–10,000
Permo-Carboniferous	330–250 million
Ordovician	440–430 million
Verangian	615–570 million
Sturtian	820–770 million
Gnejso	940–880 million
Huronian	2,700–1,800 million

K-T boundary geologists' shorthand for the boundary between the rocks of the Cretaceous and the Tertiary periods 65 million years ago. It marks the extinction of the dinosaurs and in many places reveals a layer of iridium, possibly deposited by a meteorite that may have caused their extinction by its impact.

Laurasia northern land mass formed 200 million years ago by the splitting of the single world continent Pangaea. (The southern land mass was Gondwanaland.) It consisted of what was to become North America, Greenland, Europe, and Asia, and is believed to have broken up about 100 million years ago with the separation of North America from Europe.

mass extinction an event that produced the extinction of many species at about the same time. One notable example is the boundary between the Cretaceous and Tertiary periods (known as the K-T boundary) that saw the extinction of the dinosaurs and other big reptiles, and many of the marine invertebrates as well. Mass extinctions have taken place several times during Earth's history. The Age of Man may eventually be regarded as another.

Mesozoic era of geological time 245–65 million years ago, consisting of the Triassic, Jurassic, and Cretaceous periods. At the beginning of the era, the continents were joined together as Pangaea; dinosaurs and other giant reptiles dominated the sea and air; and ferns, horsetails, and cycads thrived in a warm climate worldwide. By the end of the Mesozoic era, the continents had begun to assume their present positions, flowering plants were dominant, and many of the large reptiles and marine fauna were becoming extinct.

Ordovician period of geological time 510–439 million years ago; the second period of the Palaeozoic era. Animal life was confined to the sea: reef-building algae and the first jawless fish are characteristic.

palaeomagnetism science of the reconstruction of the Earth's ancient magnetic field and the former positions of the continents from the evidence of ***remanent magnetization*** in ancient rocks; that is, traces left by the Earth's magnetic field in igneous rocks before they cool. Palaeomagnetism shows that the Earth's magnetic field has reversed itself – the magnetic north pole becoming the magnetic south pole, and vice versa – at approximate half-million-year intervals, with shorter reversal periods in between the major spans.

palaeontology the study of ancient life that encompasses the structure of ancient organisms and their environment, evolution, and ecology, as revealed by their fossils. The practical aspects of palaeontology are based on using the presence of different fossils to date particular rock strata and to identify rocks that were laid down under particular conditions, for instance giving rise to the formation of oil.

Palaeozoic era of geological time 570–245 million years ago. It comprises the Cambrian, Ordovician, Silurian, Devonian, Carboniferous, and Permian periods. The Cambrian, Ordovician, and Silurian constitute the Lower or Early Palaeozoic; the Devonian, Carboniferous, and Permian make up the Upper or Late Palaeozoic. The era includes the evolution of hard-shelled multicellular life forms in the sea; the invasion of land by plants and animals; and the evolution of fish, amphibians, and early reptiles. The earliest identifiable fossils date from this era.

Pangaea or ***Pangea*** single land mass, made up of all the present continents, believed to have existed between 250 and 200 million years ago; the rest of the Earth was covered by the Panthalassa ocean. Pangaea split into two land masses – Laurasia in the north and Gondwanaland in the south – which subsequently broke up into several continents. These then drifted slowly to their present positions.

Panthalassa ocean that covered the surface of the Earth not occupied by the world continent Pangaea between 250 and 200 million years ago.

Early birds

Archaeopteryx has always been regarded as the success story of evolutionary study. Since its first discovery in late Jurassic rocks in Germany in 1861, six specimens have come to light. A seventh was unearthed in the summer of 1992 and is currently being studied. As the transitional form between dinosaurs and birds, *Archaeopteryx* combines the dinosaur features of clawed hands, toothed jaws, and long bony tail, with the bird features of feathers and functioning wings. In the absence of other fossils it can be imagined that the descendants of *Archaeopteryx* gradually lost the hands, the jaws, and the tail, and became more and more like modern birds. But a few bird fossils have been unearthed in recent years, which show that the evolutionary progression is not as simple as envisaged.

Sparrow-sized *Sinornis* from the early Cretaceous of China, discovered in 1990, looked very much like a modern bird, with its stump of a tail and perching feet. It still had claws on its wings, and teeth in its jaws, and was almost a transitional form between *Archaeopteryx* and modern birds.

However, a hen-sized flightless bird from the late Cretaceous of Argentina (as yet unnamed) had a short but lizard-like tail, and wings that were too small to allow it to fly. It probably had had flying ancestors but later reverted to a ground-dwelling existence.

A late Cretaceous oddity called *Mononychus*, discovered in Mongolia in 1992, was essentially a slimly-built pheasant-sized dinosaur. But it had the legs of a wading bird and stumpy forelimbs, like degenerate bird's wings, each with a large claw at the tip. It fits into no imagined scheme of bird evolution.

It seems that after *Archaeopteryx* the birds branched out into many different lineages, most of which became extinct, leaving only the line that evolved into the modern types.

And to confuse the issue further, a contentious jumble of bones from the Triassic of Texas has been given the name *Protoavis* and is regarded by its discoverer as the earliest bird – 75 million years older than *Archaeopteryx* itself.

Permian period of geological time 290–245 million years ago, the last period of the Palaeozoic era. Its end was marked by a significant change in marine life, including the extinction of many corals and trilobites. Deserts were widespread, and terrestrial amphibians and mammal-like reptiles flourished. Cone-bearing plants (gymnosperms) came to prominence.

Phanerozoic eon in Earth history, consisting of the most recent 570 million years. It comprises the Palaeozoic, Mesozoic, and Cenozoic eras. The vast majority of fossils come from this eon, owing to the evolution of hard shells and internal skeletons. The name means 'interval of well-displayed life'.

plate tectonics theory formulated in the 1960s to explain the phenomena of continental drift and seafloor spreading, and the formation of the major physical features of the Earth's surface. The Earth's outermost layer is regarded as a jigsaw of rigid major and minor plates up to 100 km/62 mi thick, which move relative to each other, probably under the influence of convection currents in the mantle beneath. Major landforms occur at the margins of the plates, where plates are colliding or moving apart – for example, volcanoes, fold mountains, ocean trenches, and ocean ridges.

Since plate tectonics started 2,000 million years ago, the continents have travelled at about 6 cm/2.5 in per year, circling the globe at least four times, a journey of 160,000 km/100,000 mi.

Precambrian the time from the formation of Earth (4.6 billion years ago) up to 570 million years ago. Its boundary with the succeeding Cambrian period marks the time when animals first developed hard outer parts (exoskeletons) and so left abundant fossil remains. It comprises about 85% of geological time and is divided into two periods: the Archaean, in which no life existed, and the Proterozoic, in which there was life in some form.

Proterozoic eon of geological time, possible 3.5 billion to 570 million years ago, the second division of the Precambrian. It is defined as the time of simple life, since many rocks dating from this eon show traces of biological activity, and some contain the fossils of bacteria and algae.

Quaternary period of geological time that began 1.64 million years ago and is still in process. It is divided into the Pleistocene and Holocene epochs.

seafloor spreading growth of the ocean crust outwards (sideways) from ocean ridges. The concept of seafloor spreading has been combined with that of continental drift and incorporated into plate tectonics.

stratigraphy branch of geology that deals with the sequence of formation of sedimentary rock layers and the conditions under which they were formed. Its basis was developed by William Smith, a British canal engineer.

stromatolite mound produced in shallow water by mats of algae that trap mud particles. Another mat grows on the trapped mud layer and this traps another layer of mud and so on. The stromatolite grows to heights of a metre or so. They are uncommon today but their fossils are among the earliest evidence for living things — over 2,000 million years old.

tectonics the study of the movements of rocks on the Earth's surface. On a small scale tectonics involves the formation of folds and faults, but on a large scale plate tectonics deals with the movement of the Earth's surface as a whole.

Tertiary period of geological time 65–1.64 million years ago, divided into five epochs: Palaeocene, Eocene, Oligocene, Miocene, and Pliocene. During the Tertiary, mammals took over all the ecological niches left vacant by the extinction of the dinosaurs, and became the prevalent land animals. The continents took on their present positions, and climatic and vegetation zones as we know them became established. Within the geological time column the Tertiary follows the Cretaceous period and is succeeded by the Quaternary period.

Triassic period of geological time 245–208 million years ago, the first period of the Mesozoic era. The continents were fused together to form the world continent Pangaea. Triassic sediments contain remains of early dinosaurs and other reptiles now extinct. By late Triassic times, the first mammals had evolved.

ENERGY

Terms

The chief direct sources of energy are oil, coal, wood, and natural gas, and indirectly, electricity produced by the use of such fuels or derived from water power or nuclear fission. Increasing costs, and the prospect of the exhaustion of nonrenewable resources, led in the 1980s to consideration of alternative, renewable sources. These included solar power, which provides completely 'clean' energy; wind and wave power; tidal power (which, like geothermal power, is geographically limited in application); utilization of organic waste, such as chicken manure; photosynthetic power, produced by use of simple, fast-reproducing plants as fuel; and nuclear power, by fusion rather than fission.

Burning fossil fuels causes acid rain and is gradually increasing the carbon dioxide content in the atmosphere, with unknown consequences for future generations. Coal-fired power stations also release significant amounts of radioactive material, and the potential dangers of nuclear power stations are greater still. The ultimate nonrenewable but almost inexhaustible energy source would be nuclear fusion (the way in which energy is generated in the Sun), but controlled fusion is a long way off. Harnessing resources generally implies converting their energy into electrical form, because electrical energy is easy to convert to other forms and to transmit from place to place, though not to store.

biofuel any solid, liquid, or gaseous fuel produced from organic (once living) matter, either directly from plants or indirectly from industrial, commercial, domestic, or agricultural wastes. There are three main ways for the development of biofuels: the burning of dry organic wastes (such as household refuse, industrial and agricultural wastes, straw, wood, and peat); the fermentation of wet wastes (such as animal dung) in the absence of oxygen to produce biogas (containing up to 60% methane), or the fermentation of sugar cane or corn to produce alcohol; and energy forestry (producing fast-growing wood for fuel).

combined cycle generation system of electricity generation that makes use of both a gas turbine and a steam turbine. Combined cycle plants are more efficient than conventional generating plants, with an efficiency of energy conversion of around 40% (compared with under 38% for conventional plants). In combined cycle generation, the gas turbine is powered by burning gas fuel, and turns an electric generator. The exhaust gases are then used to heat water to produce steam. The steam powers a steam turbine attached to an electric generator, producing additional electricity.

combined heat and power generation (CHP generation) simultaneous production of electricity and useful heat in a power station. The heat is often in the form of hot water or steam, which can be used for local district heating or in industry. The electricity output from a CHP plant is lower than from a conventional station, but the overall efficiency of energy conversion is higher.

electricity generation and supply electricity is the most useful and most convenient form of energy, readily convertible into heat and light and used to power machines. Because electricity readily flows through wires, it can be made, or generated, in one place and distributed to anywhere it is needed. It is generated at power stations where a suitable energy source is harnessed to drive turbines that spin electricity generators. The generators produce alternating current (AC), and the producing units are generally called turboalternators. The main energy sources for electricity generation are coal, oil, water power (hydroelectricity), natural gas, and nuclear power, with limited contributions from wind, tidal, and geo-thermal power. Nuclear fuel provides the cheapest form of electricity generation in Britain, but environmental considerations may limit its future development.

Electricity is generated at power stations at about 25,000 volts, which is not a suitable voltage for long-distance transmission. For minimal power loss, transmission must take place at very high voltage (400,000 volts or more). The generated voltage is therefore increased, or stepped-up, by a transformer. The resulting high-voltage electricity is then fed into the main arteries of the grid system, an interconnected network of power stations and distribution centres covering a large area, sometimes (as in the UK) countrywide, even (as in Europe) from country to country. After transmission to a local substation, the line voltage is reduced by a step-down transformer and distributed to consumers.

fossil fuel fuel, such as coal, oil, and natural gas, formed from the fossilized remains of plants that lived hundreds of millions of years ago. Fossil fuels are a nonrenewable resource and will eventually run out. Extraction of coal and oil causes considerable environmental pollution, and burning coal contributes to problems of acid rain and the greenhouse effect.

World's smallest electric battery

An electric battery has been made from just 500,000 atoms by researchers at the University of California at Irvine. The battery, a hundredth the size of a red blood cell, was constructed using a scanning tunnelling electron microscope, which can manipulate individual atoms. The battery was made by creating two minute columns of silver atoms and two nearby columns of copper atoms on a graphite chip. When the chip is immersed in a liquid solution of copper sulphate, the tiny battery generates electricity. Too little power is generated to drive even the smallest electric motors, but different combinations of metals may increase the output.

geothermal energy energy extracted for heating and electricity generation from natural steam, hot water, or hot dry rocks in the Earth's crust. Water is pumped down through an injection well where it passes through joints in the hot rocks. It rises to the surface through a recovery well and may be converted to steam or run through a heat exchanger. Dry steam may be directed through turbines to produce electricity. It is a important source of energy in volcanically active areas such as Iceland and New Zealand.

heat pump machine, run by electricity or another power source, that cools the interior of a building by removing heat from interior air and pumping it out or, conversely, heats the inside by extracting energy from the atmosphere or from a hot-water source and pumping it in.

heat storage any means of storing heat for release later. It is usually achieved by using materials that undergo phase changes, for example, Glauber's salt and sodium pyrophosphate, which melts at 70°C/158°F. The latter is used to store off-peak heat in the home: the salt is liquefied by cheap heat during the night and then freezes to give off heat during the day. Other developments include the use of plastic crystals, which change their structure rather than melting when they are heated. They could be incorporated in curtains or clothing.

hydroelectric power (HEP) electricity generated by moving water. In a typical HEP scheme, water stored in a reservoir, often created by damming a river, is piped into water turbines, coupled to electricity generators. In pumped storage plants, water flowing through the turbines is recycled. A tidal power station exploits the rise and fall of the tides. About one-fifth of the world's electricity comes from HEP. HEP plants have prodigious generating capacities. The Grand Coulee plant in Washington State, USA, has a power output of some 10,000 megawatts. The Itaipu power station on the Paraná River (Brazil/Paraguay) has a potential capacity of 12,000 megawatts.

natural gas mixture of flammable gases found in the Earth's crust (often in association with petroleum), now one of the world's three main fossil fuels (with coal and oil). Natural gas is a mixture of hydrocarbons, chiefly methane, with ethane, butane, and propane. Before the gas is piped to storage tanks and on to consumers, butane and propane are removed and liquefied to form 'bottled gas'. Natural gas is liquefied for transport and storage, and is therefore often used where other fuels are scarce and expensive.

nuclear energy energy from the inner core or nucleus of the atom, as opposed to energy released in chemical processes, which is derived from the electrons surrounding the nucleus. ***Nuclear fission***, as in an atom bomb, is achieved by allowing a neutron to strike the nucleus of an atom of fissile material (such as uranium-235 or plutonium-239), which then splits apart to release two or three other neutrons. If the uranium-235 is pure, a chain reaction is set up when these neutrons in turn strike other nuclei. This happens very quickly, resulting in the tremendous release of energy seen in nuclear weapons. The process is controlled inside the reactor of a nuclear power plant by absorbing excess neutrons in control rods and slowing down their speed. ***Nuclear fusion*** is the process whereby hydrogen nuclei fuse to helium nuclei with an accompanying release of energy. It is a continuing reaction in the Sun and other stars. Nuclear fusion is the principle behind thermonuclear weapons (the hydrogen bomb). Attempts to harness fusion for commercial power production have so far been unsuccessful, although the Joint European Torus (or JET) laboratory at Culham, Oxfordshire, England, achieved fusion 1991.

nuclear reactor device for producing nuclear energy in a controlled manner. There are various types of reactor in use, all using nuclear fission.

In a ***gas-cooled reactor***, a circulating gas under pressure (such as carbon dioxide) removes heat from the core of the reactor, which usually contains natural uranium. The efficiency of the fission process is increased by slowing neutrons in the core by using a moderator such as carbon. The reaction is controlled

nuclear energy: chronology

1896 French physicist Henri Becquerel discovered radioactivity.
1905 In Switzerland, Albert Einstein showed that mass can be converted into energy.
1911 New Zealand physicist Ernest Rutherford proposed the nuclear model of the atom.
1919 Rutherford split the atom, by bombarding a nitrogen nucleus with alpha particles.
1939 Otto Hahn, Fritz Strassman, and Lise Meitner announced the discovery of nuclear fission.
1942 Enrico Fermi built the first nuclear reactor, in a squash court at the University of Chicago, USA.
1946 The first fast reactor, called Clementine, was built at Los Alamos, New Mexico.
1951 The Experimental Breeder Reactor, Idaho, USA, produced the first electricity to be generated by nuclear energy.
1954 The first reactor for generating electricity was built in the USSR, at Obninsk.
1956 The world's first commercial nuclear power station, Calder Hall, came into operation in the UK.
1957 The release of radiation from Windscale (now Sellafield) nuclear power station, Cumbria, England, caused 39 deaths to 1977. In Kyshym, USSR, the venting of plutonium waste caused high but undisclosed casualties (30 small communities were deleted from maps produced in 1958).
1959 Experimental fast reactor built in Dounreay, N Scotland.
1979 Nuclear-reactor accident at Three Mile Island, Pennsylvania, USA.
1986 An explosive leak from a reactor at Chernobyl, the Ukraine, resulted in clouds of radioactive material spreading as far as Sweden; 31 people were killed and thousands of square kilometres were contaminated.
1991 The first controlled and substantial production of nuclear-fusion energy (a two-second pulse of 1.7 MW) was achieved at JET, the Joint European Torus, at Culham, Oxfordshire, England.

Why dash for gas?

Coal is the fuel of the future. World reserves of oil and gas will last for about 50 years, but there is enough easily accessible coal for 300 years. If all known coal deposits were exploitable, they would last for thousands of years. So, long after the oil and gas have run out, coal will offer the world a supply of energy. Yet despite this outlook, Britain is in the process of closing down its coal industry. Why?

Three factors must be borne in mind when considering a country's energy policy, and these factors interact in a subtle way, sometimes leading to unexpected results. The factors are politics, price, and pollution.

First, politics. The troubles of the British coal industry stem from the privatization of the electricity industry. The state-owned Central Electricity Generating Board, which had previously generated and distributed electricity, was broken up by the Conservative government and replaced by a collection of privately owned companies that supplied electricity to regional electricity companies via the national grid. The regional electricity companies in turn sold the electricity to its customers.

When the generating companies were privatized in 1991, government power to influence the energy market was lost, or at least much reduced. Of course, politicians could still have influenced the operation of the market if they had so wished. However, the Conservative government of the time did not want to; they sought truly 'free markets'. Nigel Lawson, who as energy secretary and later chancellor was involved in the privatization of the electricity industry said, 'I did not think that it makes sense to have an energy policy over and above the government's overall supply-side policy to the energy sector of the economy.'

Secondly, price. The consequences of having no energy policy except the free market were soon revealed. The generating companies, Powergen and National Power, quickly saw that it was in their financial interests to build gas-fired power stations rather than coal-fired ones. They undertook the construction of 16 large gas-fired power stations, a 'dash for gas' that will result in the closure of the majority of Britain's coal mines.

The power companies chose to use gas for financial reasons. British Gas, a newly private-owned company, sold gas to the generators at prices cheaper than the cost of Britain's deep-mined coal. Furthermore, the cost of a gas-fired station is less than half the cost of an equivalent coal-fired station and a quarter the cost of a nuclear plant. Using gas meant that not only were the generators paying less for each unit of fuel burnt, but their initial capital costs and consequent financing costs were much less. The financial arguments also rule out nuclear plants, wind farms, and tidal barrages, since these operations involve high initial capital costs even if their running costs are low.

The outlook for nuclear power seems particularly grim. Nuclear power is not cheaper than that from other sources. The cost of decommissioning nuclear plants is enormous: high enough to scare away private investors when the government first tried to privatize the electricity industry. Pollution and safety is another worry, bringing in the political factor: will the public turn strongly against nuclear power? The nuclear fusion research programme would seem to have exactly the same problems lying in wait should it be a technical success.

Also, thanks to the dash for gas, the generating companies avoided the costs of meeting new European pollution laws. Before privatization, the UK government estimated that it would cost £1 billion to reduce emissions of sulphur dioxide and nitrogen oxides to levels laid down by the European Commission. The generators realized that it would be cheaper to close down the coal-burning stations and build new cleaner gas-fired stations.

The President of the Board of Trade, Michael Heseltine, told the House of Commons that the case for closing 31 of Britain's 50 pits was unanswerable. This seems to be the accountant's position, since it takes into account only the short-term cash position. It does not address the longer-term overall requirements of the country.

And the future will be here sooner than we think. British Gas is contracted to supply the electricity generators for 15 years. At current rates of consumption Britain's gas reserves will last for about 20 years. But when the gas-fired stations begin operation, reserves will be depleted much more quickly. By the end of the decade Britain's gas reserves will be exhausted. What then?

Will the 'dash for gas' of the 1990's appear shortsighted in retrospect?

PL

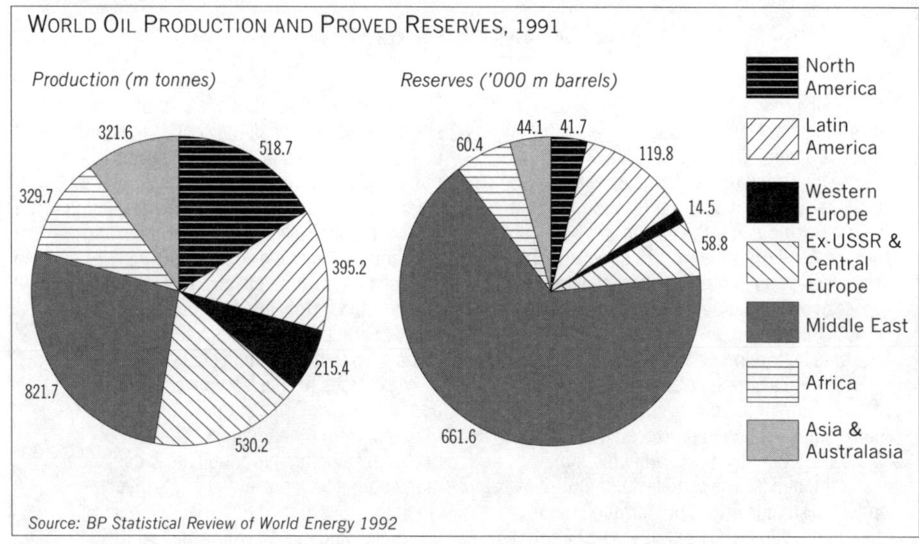

with neutron-absorbing rods made of boron. An ***advanced gas-cooled reactor*** (AGR) generally has enriched uranium as its fuel. A ***water-cooled reactor***, such as the steam-generating heavy water (deuterium oxide) reactor, has water circulating through the hot core. The water is converted to steam, which drives turbo-alternators for generating electricity. The most widely used reactor is the ***pressurized-water reactor*** (PWR), which contains a sealed system of pressurized water that is heated to form steam in heat exchangers in an external circuit. The ***fast reactor*** has no moderator and uses fast neutrons to bring about fission. It uses a mixture of plutonium and uranium oxide as fuel. When operating, uranium is converted to plutonium, which can be extracted and used later as fuel. The fast breeder is so called because it produces more plutonium than it consumes. Heat is removed from the reactor by a coolant of liquid sodium.

Public concern over the safety of nuclear reactors has been intensified by explosions and accidental release of radioactive materials. The safest system allows for the emergency cooling of a reactor by automatically flooding an overheated core with water. Other concerns about nuclear power centre on the difficulties of reprocessing nuclear fuel and disposing safely of nuclear waste, and the cost of maintaining nuclear power stations and of decommissioning them at the end of their lives.

In 1989, the UK government decided to postpone the construction of new nuclear power stations; in the USA, no new stations have been commissioned in over a decade. Rancho Seco, near Sacramento, California, was the first nuclear power station to be closed, by popular vote, in 1989. Sweden is committed to decommissioning its reactors. Some countries, such as France, are pressing ahead with their nuclear programmes. (See also ***nuclear safety*** and ***nuclear waste*** in ***Environment and Conservation***.)

petroleum or ***crude oil*** natural mineral oil, a thick greenish-brown flammable liquid found underground in permeable rocks. Petroleum consists of hydrocarbons mixed with oxygen, sulphur, nitrogen, and other elements in varying proportions. It is thought to be derived from ancient organic material that has been converted by, first, bacterial action, then heat and pressure (but its origin may be chemical also). From crude petroleum, various products are made by distillation and other processes; for example, fuel oil, petrol, kerosene, diesel, lubricating oil, paraffin wax, and petroleum jelly.

The organic material in petroleum was laid down millions of years ago (hence it is known as a fossil fuel). Petroleum is found trapped in porous reservoir rocks, such as sandstone or limestone, in anticlines and other traps below impervious rock layers. Oil may flow from wells under natural pressure, causing it to rise up the borehole, but many oil wells require pumping to bring the oil to the surface.

The exploitation of oilfields began with the first commercial well in Pennsylvania 1859. The USA led in production until the 1960s, when the Middle East outproduced other areas, their immense reserves leading to a worldwide dependence on cheap oil for transport and industry. In 1961 the Organization of the Petroleum Exporting Countries (OPEC) was established to avoid exploitation of member countries; after OPEC's price rises 1973, the International Energy Agency (IEA) was established 1974 to protect the interests of oil-consuming countries. New technologies were introduced to pump oil from offshore and from the Arctic (the Alaska pipeline) in an effort to avoid a monopoly by OPEC. Petroleum products and chemicals are used in large quantities in the manufacture of detergents, artificial fibres, plastics, insecticides, fertilizers, pharmaceuticals, toiletries, and synthetic rubber. Aviation fuel is a volatile form of petrol.

The burning of petroleum fuel is one cause of air pollution. The transport of oil can lead to catastrophes – for example, the *Torrey Canyon* tanker lost off SW England 1967, which led to an agreement by the international oil companies 1968 to pay compensation for massive shore pollution. The 1989 oil spill in Alaska from the *Exxon Valdez* damaged the area's fragile environment, despite clean-up efforts. Drilling for oil involves the risks of accidental spillage and drilling-rig accidents. The problems associated with oil have led to the various alternative energy technologies. A new kind of bacterium was developed during the 1970s in the USA, capable of 'eating' oil as a means of countering oil spills. Its creation gave rise to the so-called Frankenstein law (a ruling that allowed new forms of life created in laboratories to be patented).

renewable resource natural resource that is replaced by natural processes in a reasonable amount of time. Soil, water, forests, plants, and animals are all renewable resources as long as they are properly conserved. Solar, wind, wave, and geothermal energies are based on renewable resources.

World's largest photovoltaic solar power station

The world's largest array of photovoltaic cells at Davis, California, was plugged into the local electricity system in early 1993. The sun-powered station is made up of 9,600 modules, each of which can generate 50 W. The total output of the array is 479 kW, enough for 125 homes. The technology used in the modules relies on thin films of amorphous silicon deposited on a layer of glass titanium oxide to provide more power per dollar than other forms of photovoltaic cell.

solar energy energy derived from the Sun's radiation. The amount of energy falling on just 1 sq km/0.3861 sq mi is about 4,000 megawatts, enough to heat and light a small town. In one second the Sun gives off 13 million times more energy than all the electricity used in the USA in one year. ***Solar heaters*** have industrial or domestic uses. They usually consist of a black (heat-absorbing) panel containing pipes through which air or water, heated by the Sun, is circulated, either by thermal convection or by a pump.

Solar energy may also be harnessed indirectly using ***solar cells*** (photovoltaic cells) made of panels of semiconductor material (usually silicon), which generate electricity when illuminated by sunlight. Although it is difficult to generate a high output from solar energy compared to sources such as nuclear or fossil fuels, it is a major nonpolluting and renewable energy source used as far north as Scandinavia as well as in the SW USA and in Mediterranean countries.

A solar furnace, such as that built 1970 at Odeillo in the French Pyrénées, has thousands of mirrors to focus the Sun's rays; it produces uncontaminated intensive heat (up to 3,000°C/5,400°F) for industrial and scientific or experimental purposes. The world's first solar power station connected to a national grid opened 1991 at Adrano in Sicily. Scores of giant mirrors move to follow the Sun throughout the day, focusing the rays into a boiler. Steam from the boiler drives a conventional turbine. The plant generates up to 1 megawatt. A similar system, called Solar 1, has been built in the Mojave desert near Daggett, California, USA. It consists of 1,818 computer-controlled mirrors arranged in circles around a 91 m/300 ft central boiler tower. Advanced schemes have been proposed that would use giant solar reflectors in space to harness solar energy and beam it down to Earth in the form of microwaves. Despite their low running costs, their high installation cost and low power output have meant that solar cells have found few applications outside space probes and artificial satellites. Solar heating is, however, widely used for domestic purposes in many parts of the world.

tidal power station hydroelectric power plant that uses the 'head' of water created by the rise and fall of the ocean tides to spin the water turbines. An example is located on the estuary of the river Rance in the Gulf of St Malo, Brittany, France, which has been in use since 1966.

turbine engine in which steam, water, gas, or air is made to spin a rotating shaft by pushing on angled blades, like a fan. Turbines are among the most powerful machines. Steam turbines are used to drive generators in power stations and ships' propellers; water turbines spin the generators in hydroelectric power plants; and gas turbines (as jet engines; see jet propulsion) power most aircraft and drive machines in industry.

The high-temperature, high-pressure steam for ***steam turbines*** is raised in boilers heated by furnaces burning coal, oil, or gas, or by nuclear energy. A steam turbine consists of a shaft, or rotor, which rotates inside a fixed casing (stator). The rotor carries 'wheels' consisting of blades, or vanes. The stator has vanes set between the vanes of the rotor, which direct the steam through the rotor vanes at the optimum angle. When steam expands through the turbine, it spins the rotor by reaction. Less widely used than the reaction turbine is the ***impulse turbine***,

Hidden power

A new power unit, which generates electricity from the tides, solves the problem of large unsightly turbines, common in many alternative energy generation schemes. The new generator is out of sight, below the surface of the sea. It consists of a two-blade turbine, 4 m/13 ft across, suspended from a buoy and weighed down by two anchors. In strong currents or tides, the turbine drives a generator in a streamlined waterproof casing. When the tide turns, the turbine and generator swing round on their mooring to the optimum position. The system is intended for use where there are strong tides or currents, such as between islands and the mainland, or in the mouth of rivers. A prototype is being built for testing in Loch Linnhe, Scotland.

Energy in the UK

Production and consumption of primary fuels, 1988-92 (m tonnes of oil or oil equivalent)

Year	*Total*	*Coal*	*Petroleum*	*Natural gas*[1]	*Primary electricity*		
					Nuclear	*Natural flow hydro*[2]	
1988	229.7	61.1	114.5	39.3	13.45	1.42	
1989	206.4	59.5	91.8	38.3	15.35	1.38	
1990	205.3	55.5	91.6	42.5	14.19	1.55	
1991	211.7	56.6	91.3	47.3	15.17	1.37	
1992 (p)	211.6	51.4	94.2	47.7	16.68	1.62	
% change	–	*–9.1*	*+3.3*	*+0.8*	*+9.9*	*+18.0*	
Energy consumption (seasonally adjusted)							*Net imports*
1988	201.9	65.9	68.3	49.7	13.45	1.42	3.08
1989	204.9	64.5	70.2	50.5	15.35	1.38	3.03
1990	209.3	65.0	73.3	52.4	14.19	1.55	2.87
1991	207.0	63.1	70.8	52.7	15.17	1.37	3.94
1992 (p)	207.4	60.0	70.9	54.2	16.68	1.62	4.01
% change	*+0.2*	*–5.0*	*+0.1*	*+3.0*	*+9.9*	*+18.2*	*+1.8*

[1] *Including non-energy use and excluding gas flared or re-injected.*
[2] *Excludes generation from pumped storage stations. Including generation at wind stations.*
(p) provisional
Source: Energy Trends/DTI

which works by directing a jet of steam at blades on a rotor. Similarly there are reaction and impulse water turbines: impulse turbines work on the same principle as the water wheel and consist of sets of buckets arranged around the edge of a wheel; reaction turbines look much like propellers and are fully immersed in the water.

In a ***gas turbine*** a compressed mixture of air and gas, or vaporized fuel, is ignited, and the hot gases produced expand through the turbine blades, spinning the rotor. In the industrial gas turbine, the rotor shaft drives machines. In the jet engine, the turbine drives the compressor, which supplies the compressed air to the engine, but most of the power developed comes from the jet exhaust in the form of propulsive thrust.

water mill machine that harnesses the energy in flowing water to produce mechanical power, typically for milling (grinding) grain. Water from a stream is directed against the paddles of a water wheel to make it turn. Simple gearing transfers this motion to the millstones. The modern equivalent of the water wheel is the water turbine, used in hydro-electric power plants.

wave power power obtained by harnessing the energy of water waves. Various schemes have been advanced since 1973, when oil prices rose dramatically and an energy shortage threatened. In 1974 the British engineer Stephen Salter developed the duck – a floating boom whose segments nod up and down with the waves. The nodding motion can be used to drive pumps and spin generators. Another device, developed in Japan, uses an oscillating water column to harness wave power. However, a major breakthrough will be required if wave power is ever to contribute significantly to the world's energy needs.

windmill mill with sails or vanes that, by the action of wind upon them, drive machinery for grinding corn or pumping water, for example. Wind turbines, designed to use wind power on a large scale, usually have a propeller-type rotor mounted on a tall shell tower. The turbine drives a generator for producing electricity. The main types of traditional windmill are the ***post mill***, which is turned around a post when the direction of the wind changes, and the ***tower mill***, which has a revolving turret on top. It usually has a device (fantail) that keeps the sails pointing into the wind.

wind turbine windmill of advanced aerodynamic design connected to an electricity generator and used

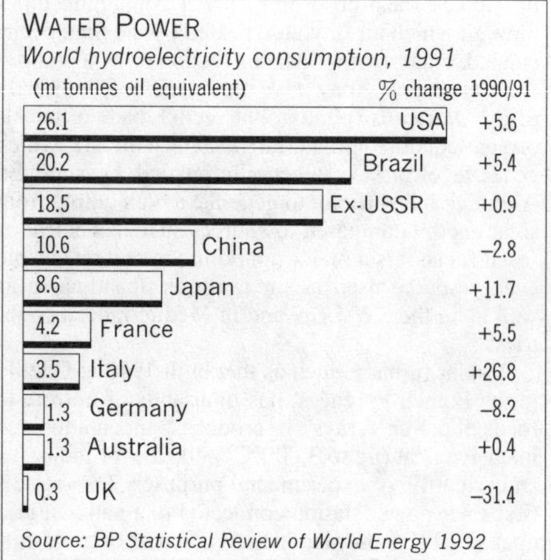

Source: BP Statistical Review of World Energy 1992

in wind-power installations. Wind turbines can be either large propeller-type rotors mounted on a tall tower, or flexible metal strips fixed to a vertical axle at top and bottom. In 1990, over 20,000 wind turbines were in use throughout the world, generating 1,600 megawatts of power.

The world's largest wind turbine is on Hawaii, in the Pacific Ocean. It has two blades 50 m/160 ft long on top of a tower 20 storeys high. An example of a propeller turbine is found at Tvind in Denmark and has an output of some 2 megawatts. Other machines use novel rotors, such as the 'egg-beater' design developed at Sandia Laboratories in New Mexico, USA. The largest wind turbine on mainland Britain is at Richborough on the Kent coast. The three-bladed turbine, which is 35 m/115 ft across, produces 1 megawatt of power. Britain's largest vertical-axis wind turbine has two 24 m/80 ft blades and began operating in Dyfed, Wales, 1990.

Worldwide, wind turbines on land produce only the energy equivalent of a single nuclear power station (such as the Sizewell nuclear station). In Britain, 300 turbines, mainly in Cornwall, the northwest, and Wales, provide enough power for 60,000 homes.

GALLUP POLL

Do you have the impression that most people in Britain support or oppose the growth of nuclear power stations? Would you say that you support or oppose the growth of nuclear power stations?

	Oct 1992		July 1988	
	Most people	Self	Most people	Self
Support	9	18	15	25
Oppose	64	62	64	63
Don't know	27	20	21	13

Source: Gallup

ENVIRONMENT AND CONSERVATION

The Natural World

balance of nature the idea that there is an inherent equilibrium in most ecosystems, with plants and animals interacting so as to produce a stable, continuing system of life on Earth. Organisms in the ecosystem are adapted to each other – for example, waste products produced by one species are used by another and resources used by some are replenished by others; the oxygen needed by animals is produced by plants while the waste product of animal respiration, carbon dioxide, is used by plants as a raw material in photosynthesis. The nitrogen cycle, the water cycle, and the control of animal populations by natural predators are other examples. The activities of human beings can, and frequently do, disrupt the balance of nature.

biodiversity (contraction of ***biological diversity***) measure of the variety of the Earth's animal, plant, and microbial species; of genetic differences within species; and of the ecosystems that support those species. Its maintenance is important for ecological stability and as a resource for research into, for example, new drugs and crops. Research suggests that biodiversity is far greater than previously realized, especially among smaller organisms – for instance, it is thought that only 1–10% of the world's bacterial species have been identified. Tropical rainforest is particularly rich in biodiversity. In the 20th century, however, the destruction of habitats is believed to have resulted in the most severe and rapid loss of diversity in the history of the planet. An international convention for the preservation of biodiversity was signed by over 100 world leaders 1992.

biological oxygen demand (BOD) the amount of dissolved oxygen taken up by microorganisms in a sample of water. Since these microorganisms live by decomposing organic matter, and the amount of oxygen used is proportional to their number and metabolic rate, BOD can be used as a measure of the extent to which the water is polluted with organic compounds.

biome broad natural assemblage of plants and animals shaped by common patterns of vegetation and climate. Examples include the tundra biome and the desert biome.

biosphere the narrow zone that supports life on our planet. It is limited to the waters of the Earth, a fraction of its crust, and the lower regions of the atmosphere.

carbon cycle sequence by which carbon circulates and is recycled through the natural world. The carbon element from carbon dioxide, released into the atmosphere by living things as a result of respiration, is taken up by plants during photosynthesis and converted into carbohydrates; the oxygen component is released back into the atmosphere. The simplest link in the carbon cycle occurs when an animal eats a plant and carbon is transferred from, say, a leaf cell to the animal body. Today, the carbon cycle is in danger of being disrupted by the increased consumption and burning of fossil fuels, and the burning of large tracts of tropical forests, as a result of which levels of carbon dioxide are building up in the atmosphere and probably contributing to the greenhouse effect.

carrying capacity the maximum number of animals of a given species that a particular area can support. When the carrying capacity is exceeded, there is insufficient food (or other resources) for the members of the population. The population may then be reduced by emigration, reproductive failure, or death through starvation.

chemical oxygen demand (COD) measure of water and effluent quality, expressed as the amount of oxygen (in parts per million) required to oxidize the reducing substances present.

climate weather conditions at a particular place over a period of time. Climate encompasses all the meteorological elements and the factors that influence them. The primary factors that determine the variations of climate over the surface of the Earth are: (a) the effect of latitude and the tilt of the Earth's axis to the plane of the orbit about the Sun (66.5°); (b) the large-scale movements of different wind belts over the Earth's surface; (c) the temperature difference between land and sea; (d) contours of the ground; and (e) location of the area in relation to ocean currents. Catastrophic variations to climate may be caused by the impact of another planetary body, or by clouds resulting from volcanic activity. The most important local or global meteorological changes brought about by human activity are those linked with ozone depleters and the greenhouse effect.

colonization the spread of species into a new habitat, such as a freshly cleared field, a new motorway verge, or a recently flooded valley. The first species to move in are called ***pioneers***, and may establish conditions that allow other animals and plants to move in (for example, by improving the condition of

Teeming marine life

Coral reef biological diversity, 1992

Location	*Coral species* (number)	*Fish species* (number)
Philippines	400	1,500
Great Barrier Reef (Australia)	350	1,500
New Caledonia	300	1,000
French Polynesia	168	800
Aqaba	150	400
Toliara (Madagascar)	147	552
Society Islands	120	633
St Gilles (Réunion)	120	258
Tadjoura (Djibouti)	65	180
Baie Possession (Réunion)	54	109
Tutia Reef (Tanzania)	52	192
Hermitage (Réunion)	30	81
Kuwait	23	85

Source: State of the World 1993/Worldwatch Institute

the soil or by providing shade). Over time a range of species arrives and the habitat matures; early colonizers will probably be replaced, so that the variety of animal and plant life present changes. This is known as succession.

community any assemblage of plants, animals, and other organisms living within a circumscribed area. Communities are usually named by reference to a dominant feature such as characteristic plant species (for example, beech-wood community), or a prominent physical feature (for example, a freshwater-pond community).

ecology study of the relationship among organisms and the environments in which they live, including all living and nonliving components. The term was coined by German biologist Ernst Haeckel (1834–1919) 1866.

Ecology may be concerned with individual organisms (for example, behavioural ecology, feeding strategies), with populations (for example, population dynamics), or with entire communities (for example, competition between species for access to resources in an ecosystem, or predator–prey relationships). Applied ecology is concerned with the management and conservation of habitats and the consequences and control of pollution.

ecosystem integrated unit consisting of the community of living organisms and the physical environment in a particular area. The relationships among species in an ecosystem are usually complex and finely balanced, and removal of any one species may be disastrous. The removal of a major predator, for example, can result in the destruction of the ecosystem through overgrazing by herbivores.

habitat localized environment in which an organism lives, and which provides for all (or almost all) of its needs. The diversity of habitats found within the Earth's ecosystem is enormous, and they are changing all the time. Many can be considered inorganic or physical; for example, the Arctic icecap, a cave, or a cliff face. Others are more complex; for instance, a woodland or a forest floor. Some habitats are so precise that they are called ***microhabitats***, such as the area under a stone where a particular type of insect lives. Most habitats provide a home for many species.

hedge or ***hedgerow*** row of closely planted shrubs or low trees, generally acting as a land division and windbreak. Hedges also serve as a source of food and as a refuge for wildlife, and provide a habitat not unlike the understorey of a natural forest.

mangrove any of several shrubs and trees, especially of the mangrove family Rhizophoraceae, found in the muddy swamps of tropical and subtropical coasts and estuaries. By sending down aerial roots from their branches, they rapidly form close-growing mangrove thickets. Their timber is impervious to water and resists marine worms. Mangrove swamps are important for stabilizing coastlines and are provide rich spawning grounds for fish and shellfish. These habitats are being destroyed in many countries.

national park land set aside and conserved for public enjoyment. The first was Yellowstone National Park, USA, established 1872. National parks include not only the most scenic places, but also places distinguished for their historic, prehistoric, or scientific interest, or for their superior recreational assets. They range from areas the size of small countries to pockets of just a few hectares.

In England and Wales under the National Park Act 1949 the Peak District, Lake District, Snowdonia, and other areas of natural beauty were designated national parks. In the UK, national parks are not wholly wilderness or conservation areas, but merely places where planning controls on development are stricter than elsewhere. They are run by National Park Authorities and financed by national government (75%) and local government (25%).

nature reserve area set aside to protect a habitat and the wildlife that lives within it, with only restricted admission for the public. A nature reserve often provides a sanctuary for rare species. The world's largest is Etosha Reserve, Namibia; area 99,520 sq km/38,415 sq mi.

niche the 'place' occupied by a species in its habitat, including all chemical, physical, and biological components, such as what it eats, the time of day at which the species feeds, temperature, moisture, the parts of the habitat that it uses (for example, trees or open grassland), the way it reproduces, and how it behaves.

It is believed that no two species can occupy exactly the same niche, because they would be in direct competition for the same resources at every stage of their life cycle.

nonrenewable resource natural resource, such as coal or oil, that takes thousands or millions of years to form naturally and can therefore not be replaced once it is consumed. The main energy sources used by humans are nonrenewable; renewable sources, such as solar, tidal, and geothermal power, have so far been less exploited.

oceanography study of the oceans, their origin, composition, structure, history, and wildlife (seabirds, fish, plankton, and other organisms). Much oceanography uses computer simulations to plot the possible movements of the waters, and many studies are carried out by remote sensing.

Oceanography involves the study of water movements – currents, waves, and tides – and the chemical and physical properties of the seawater. It deals with the origin and topography of the ocean floor – ocean trenches and ridges formed by plate tectonics, and continental shelves from the submerged portions of the continents.

The World Ocean Circulation Experiment, a seven-year project begun 1990, involves researchers from 44 countries examining the physics of the ocean and its role in the climate of the Earth. It is based at Southampton University, England.

rainforest dense forest usually found on or near the equator where the climate is hot and wet. Heavy rainfall results as the moist air brought by the converging tradewinds rises because of the heat. Over half the tropical rainforests are in Central and South America, the rest in SE Asia and Africa. They provide the bulk of the oxygen needed for plant and animal respiration. Tropical rainforest once covered 14% of the Earth's land surface, but are now being destroyed at an increasing rate as their valuable timber is harvested

Losing the battle for a greener world?

In June 1992, Rio de Janeiro in Brazil hosted probably the largest-ever meeting of heads of state, to discuss the world's environment crisis at the United Nations Conference on Environment and Development (UNCED or Earth Summit). For many people it was the 'coming of age' of environmental issues: at last, world leaders were taking ecology and conservation seriously. But reactions to the conference have been mixed; some environmental organizations lament a lost opportunity, while many politicians claim important advances.

There were two concrete results. First, many nations committed themselves to protect biological diversity ('biodiversity') in terms of ecosystems, species, and genetic variation within species. This should provide an important additional stimulus to conservation legislation in many countries. Secondly, a global climate convention committed countries to combating the impact of global warming and resulting climate changes.

There were also notable failures: the lack of agreement on a global forest convention, and the richer nations' insistence on only modest additional funding to help developing countries enact some of the UNCED proposals. Many southern politicians claimed the conference had given them new obligations without the funding to carry them out. Maurice Strong, secretary of UNCED, has suggested a global fund of $625 billion a year is needed to solve the world's environmental problems.

International trade

Despite the gains made at the Earth Summit, some people believe international trade conditions may eventually cancel these out. The GATT (General Agreement on Tariffs and Trade) negotiations have concentrated on the risks of a trade war, but current discussions may drastically reduce individual countries' power to set individual standards on environmental safety if they interfere with 'free trade'.

For example, international determination of pesticide safety (by the Codex Alimentaris committee of the Food and Agricultural Organization) may mean the forcible reintroduction of previously banned pesticides into countries such as the USA, UK, and Germany, with stricter standards than the FAO committee. Other trade agreements carry similar hidden environmental problems. In late 1992, it was suggested the European Commission might outlaw planting native wild flowers along British verges because it blocked the free trade of continental seed sources. Clearly, there is more controversy to come.

Pollution

Air pollution monitoring shows continuing deterioration in the global atmosphere. The 1991 UN survey of forest damage in Europe found 22% of trees suffering over 25% defoliation, largely because of the cocktail of air pollutants. The ozone layer in the stratosphere is still being degraded by pollutants such as chlorofluorocarbons and halons. World Meteorological Organization readings for January 1992 found average ozone levels over northern Europe 20% below normal, and those in Canada 16% below. Stratospheric ozone plays a vital role in blocking harmful radiation from the Sun; the UN estimated that a sustained 10% ozone layer loss would increase skin cancer by 26%. In the UK, the Department of the Environment has published information on reducing risks from ozone pollution following evidence of an *increase* near ground level. Here, ozone, created as a side-effect of other air pollutants, especially from road vehicles, reacting in sunlight, can damage the health of plants and animals, including humans. (Unfortunately, this near-ground ozone does not replace the effects of stratospheric ozone.)

In November 1992, timetables for phasing out ozone-depleting chemicals were agreed by the 86 nations meeting in Copenhagen. They agreed to phase out CFCs by 1996, halons by 1994, and tetrachloromethane (carbon tetrachloride) and methyl chloroform by 1996.

Disappearing forests

Conservationists' fears about tropical deforestation are broadening to include temperate and boreal (Arctic) forests. In October 1992, the World Wide Fund for Nature (WWF) estimated that up to 90% of primary temperate forests, outside Russia, had been destroyed. In temperate regions, the area under trees is currently stable or even increasing, but with rapid loss of forest quality, as plantations and intensively managed forest areas replace natural or old-growth forests. They support less wildlife than natural forests and often create problems of soil erosion and loss of water quality. In Scandinavia and Scotland, for example, natural forests have been reduced to 1% or less and are still being destroyed. Temperate forests are likely to be the scene of increasing conservation efforts in the next few years.

The International Tropical Timber Agreement is up for renegotiation in 1993. The ITTA, and the associated International Tropical Timber Organization, have been criticized for insufficient action on tropical forest loss. Also, there are demands that the Agreement be broadened to include *all* timber, including that from temperate regions. This would accord with the wishes of conservation bodies promoting plans for the certification of timber from well-managed forests, which would have a special quality label and thus command a price premium.

ND

and the land cleared for agriculture, causing problems of deforestation. By 1991 over 50% of the world's rainforest had been removed, though they still comprise about 50% of all growing wood on the planet, and harbour at least 40% of the Earth's species (plants and animals). If clearance continues at the present rate, all of the world's primary (undisturbed) rainforest will disappear or be damaged within the next 30 years.

Tropical rainforests are characterized by a great diversity of species, usually of tall broad-leafed evergreen trees, with many climbing vines and ferns, some of which are a main source of raw materials for medicines. A tropical forest, if properly preserved, can yield medicinal plants, oils (from cedar, juniper, cinnamon, sandalwood), spices, gums, resins (used in inks, lacquers, linoleum), tanning and dyeing materials, forage for animals, beverages, poisons, green manure, rubber, and animal products (feathers, hides, honey).

Other rainforests include montane, upper montane or cloud, mangrove, and subtropical. Rainforests comprise some of the most complex and diverse ecosystems on the planet and help to regulate global weather patterns. When deforestation occurs, the microclimate of the mature forest disappears; soil erosion and flooding become major problems since rainforests protect the shallow tropical soils. Clearing of the rainforests may lead to a global warming of the atmosphere, and contribute to the greenhouse effect.

renewable resource natural resource that is replaced by natural processes in a reasonable amount of time. Soil, water, forests, plants, and animals are all renewable resources as long as they are properly conserved. Solar, wind, wave, and geothermal energies are based on renewable resources.

water water covers 70% of the Earth's surface and supports all forms of Earth's life. The ***water cycle*** or ***hydrological cycle*** is the natural circulation of water through the biosphere. Water is lost from the Earth's surface to the atmosphere either by evaporation from the surface of lakes, rivers, and oceans, or through the transpiration of plants. This atmospheric water forms clouds that condense to deposit moisture on the land and sea as rain or snow. The water that collects on land flows to the ocean in streams and rivers.

Water supply in sparsely populated regions usually comes from underground water rising to the surface in natural springs, supplemented by pumps and wells. Urban sources are deep artesian wells, rivers, and reservoirs, usually formed from enlarged lakes or dammed and flooded valleys, from which water is conveyed by pipes, conduits, and aqueducts to filter beds. As water seeps through layers of shingle, gravel, and sand, harmful organisms are removed and the water is then distributed by pumping or gravitation through mains and pipes. Often other substances are added to the water, such as chlorine and fluorine; aluminium sulphate is the most widely used chemical in water treatment. In coastal desert areas, such as the Arabian peninsula, desalination plants remove salt from sea water. The Earth's water, both fresh and saline, have been polluted by industrial and domestic chemicals, many of which are toxic and others radioactive.

In 1991, the UK was taken to court for failing to meet EC drinking-water standards on nitrate and pesticide levels.

Facing water scarcity

Water-scarce countries, 1992, with projections for 2010[1]

Region/Country	*Per capita renewable water supplies* 1992 (cubic meters per person)	2010 (cubic meters per person)	*Change* (%)
Africa			
Algeria	730	500	–32
Botswana	710	420	–41
Burundi	620	360	–42
Cape Verde	500	290	–42
Djibouti	750	430	–43
Egypt	30	20	–33
Kenya	560	330	–41
Libya	160	100	–38
Mauritania	190	110	–42
Rwanda	820	440	–46
Tunisia	450	330	–27
Middle East			
Bahrain	0	0	0
Israel	330	250	–24
Jordan	190	110	–42
Kuwait	0	0	0
Qatar	40	30	–25
Saudi Arabia	140	70	–50
Syria	550	300	–45
United Arab Emirates	120	60	–50
Yemen	240	130	–46
Other			
Barbados	170	170	0
Belgium	840	870	+4
Hungary	580	570	–2
Malta	80	80	0
Netherlands	660	600	–9
Singapore	210	190	–10
Additional Countries by 2010			
Malawi	1,030	600	–42
Sudan	1,130	710	–37
Morocco	1,150	830	–28
South Africa	1,200	760	–37
Oman	1,250	670	–46
Somalia	1,390	830	–40
Lebanon	1,410	980	–30
Niger	1,690	930	–45

[1] Countries with per capita renewable water supplies of less than 1,000 cubic meters per year. Does not include water flowing in from neighbouring countries.

wetland permanently wet land area or habitat. Wetlands include areas of marsh, fen, bog, flood plain, and shallow coastal areas. Wetlands are extremely fertile. They provide warm, sheltered waters for fisheries, lush vegetation for grazing livestock, and an abundance of wildlife. Estuaries and seaweed beds are more than 16 times as productive as the open ocean.

Loss of wetlands is a worldwide environmental problem as a result of drainage for agriculture, plantation forestry, pollution, and urban expansion. There have been a number of attempts to protect wetlands through international treaties, but drainage schemes continue in many countries. Creation of new wetland areas is taking place on some nature reserves.

wilderness area of uninhabited land that has never been disturbed by humans. In the USA wilderness areas are specially designated by Congress and protected by federal agencies.

Environmental Issues and Pollutants

acid rain acidic precipitation (rain, snow, or mist), thought to be caused principally by the release into the atmosphere of sulphur dioxide (SO_2) and oxides of nitrogen. Sulphur dioxide is formed by the burning of fossil fuels, such as coal, that contain high quantities of sulphur; nitrogen oxides are contributed from various industrial activities and from car exhaust fumes.

Acid rain is linked with damage to and the death of forests and lake organisms in Scandinavia, Europe, and eastern North America. It also results in damage to buildings and statues. US and European power stations that burn fossil fuels release some 8 g/0.3 oz of sulphur dioxide and 3 g/0.1 oz of nitrogen oxides per kilowatt-hour. According to the UK Department of the Environment figures, emissions of sulphur dioxide from power stations would have to be decreased by 81% in order to arrest damage.

aerosol particles of liquid or solid suspended in a gas. Aerosol cans contain a substance such as scent or cleaner packed under pressure with a device for releasing it as a fine spray. Most aerosols used chlorofluorocarbons (CFCs) as propellants until these were found to cause destruction of the ozone layer in the stratosphere. Most so-called 'ozone-friendly' aerosols also use ozone-depleting chemicals, although they are not as destructive as CFCs.

air pollution contamination of the atmosphere caused by the discharge, accidental or deliberate, of a wide range of toxic airborne substances. Often the amount of the released substance is relatively high in a certain locality, so the harmful effects become more noticeable. The cost of preventing any discharge of pollutants into the air is prohibitive, so attempts are more usually made to reduce gradually the amount of discharge and to disperse this as quickly as possible by using a very tall chimney, or by intermittent release.

antiknock substance added to petrol to reduce knocking in car engines. It is a mixture of dibromoethane and tetraethyl lead. Its use in leaded petrol has resulted in atmospheric pollution by lead compounds. Children exposed to this form of pollution over long periods of time can suffer impaired learning ability. Unleaded petrol has been used in the USA for some years, and is increasingly popular in the UK. Leaded petrol cannot be used in cars fitted with catalytic converters.

biodegradable capable of being broken down by living organisms, principally bacteria and fungi. In biodegradable substances, such as food and sewage, the natural processes of decay lead to compaction and liquefaction, and to the release of nutrients that are then recycled by the ecosystem. Nonbiodegradable substances, such as glass, heavy metals, and most types of plastic, present serious problems of disposal.

carbon dioxide CO_2 colourless, odourless gas, slightly soluble in water and denser than air. It is produced by living things during the processes of respiration and the decay of organic matter, and plays a vital role in the carbon cycle. It is used as a coolant in its solid form (known as 'dry ice'), and in the chemical industry. Its increasing density contributes to the greenhouse effect and global warming. Britain has 1% of the world's population, yet it produces 3% of CO_2 emissions; the USA has 5% of the world's population and produces 25% of CO_2 emissions.

carbon monoxide CO colourless, odourless gas formed when carbon is oxidized in a limited supply of air. It is a poisonous constituent of car exhaust fumes, forming a stable compound with haemoglobin in the blood, thus preventing the haemoglobin from transporting oxygen to the body tissues.

catalytic converter device fitted to the exhaust system of a motor vehicle in order to reduce toxic emissions from the engine. It converts harmful exhaust products to relatively harmless ones by passing the exhaust gases over a mixture of catalysts. ***Oxidation catalysts*** (small amounts of precious palladium and platinum metals) convert hydrocarbons (unburnt fuel) and carbon monoxide into carbon dioxide and water, while ***three-way catalysts*** (platinum and rhodium metals) convert nitrogen oxide gases into nitrogen and oxygen.

Air pollution

Pollutant	*Sources*	*Effects*
sulphur dioxide SO_2	oil, coal combustion in power stations	acid rain formed, which damages plants, trees, buildings, and lakes
oxides of nitrogen NO, NO_2	high-temperature combustion in cars, and to some extent power stations	acid rain formed
lead compounds	from leaded petrol used by cars	nerve poison
carbon dioxide CO_2	oil, coal, petrol, diesel combustion	greenhouse effect
carbon monoxide CO	limited combustion of oil, coal, petrol, diesel fuels	poisonous, leads to photochemical smog in some areas
nuclear waste	nuclear power plants, nuclear weapon testing, war	radioactivity, contamination of locality, cancers, mutations, death

Over the lifetime of a vehicle, a catalytic converter can reduce hydrocarbon emissions by 87%, carbon monoxide emissions by 85%, and nitrogen oxide emissions by 62%, but will cause a slight increase in the amount of carbon dioxide emitted. Catalytic converters are standard in the USA, where a 90% reduction in pollution from cars was achieved without loss of engine performance or fuel economy.

chlorofluorocarbon (CFC) synthetic chemical that is odourless, nontoxic, nonflammable, and chemically inert. CFCs have been used as propellants in aerosol cans, as refrigerants in refrigerators and air conditioners, and in the manufacture of foam packaging. They are partly responsible for the destruction of the ozone layer. In June 1990 representatives of 93 nations, including the UK and the USA, agreed to phase out production of CFCs by the end of the 20th century.

When CFCs are released into the atmosphere, they drift up slowly into the stratosphere, where, under the influence of ultraviolet radiation from the Sun, they break down into chlorine atoms which destroy the ozone layer and allow harmful radiation from the Sun to reach the Earth's surface. CFCs can remain in the atmosphere for more than 100 years. Replacements for CFCs are being developed, and research into safe methods of destroying existing CFCs is being carried out. The European Community has agreed to ban by the end of 1995 a range of CFCs.

compost organic material decomposed by bacteria under controlled conditions to make a nutrient-rich natural fertilizer for use in gardening or farming. A well-made compost heap reaches a high temperature during the composting process, killing most weed seeds that might be present.

conservation action taken to protect and preserve the natural world, usually from pollution, overexploitation, and other harmful features of human activity. The late 1980s saw a great increase in public concern for the environment, with membership of conservation groups, such as Friends of the Earth, rising sharply. Globally the most important issues include the depletion of atmospheric ozone by the action of chlorofluorocarbons (CFCs), the build-up of carbon dioxide in the atmosphere (thought to contribute to an intensification of the greenhouse effect), and the destruction of the tropical rainforests.

In the UK the conservation debate has centred on water quality, road-building schemes, the safety of nuclear power, and animal rights.

DDT abbreviation for ***dichloro- diphenyl-trichloroethane*** ($ClC_6H_5)_2CHCHCl_2$), an insecticide discovered 1939 by Swiss chemist Paul Müller. It is useful in the control of insects that spread malaria, but resistant strains develop. DDT is highly toxic and persists in the environment and in living tissue. Its use is now banned in most countries, but it continues to be used on food plants in Latin America.

deforestation destruction of forest for timber, fuel, charcoal burning, and clearing for agriculture and extractive industries, such as mining, without planting new trees to replace those lost (reafforestation) or working on a cycle that allows the natural forest to regenerate. Deforestation causes fertile soil to be blown away or washed into rivers, leading to soil erosion, drought, flooding, and loss of wildlife. Deforestation is taking place in both tropical rainforests and temperate forests.

desertification creation of deserts by changes in climate, or by human-aided processes. The processes leading to desertification include overgrazing, destruction of forest belts, and exhaustion of the soil by intensive cultivation without restoration of fertility – all of which may be prompted by the pressures of an expanding population, by concentration in land ownership, or by other political conditions forcing people onto unsuitable land. About 135 million people are directly affected by desertification, mainly in Africa, the Indian subcontinent, and South America.

dioxin any of a family of over 200 organic chemicals, but especially 2,3,7,8-tetrachlorodibenzo-dioxin

It pays to save

Industrial water conservation and cost-effectiveness, selected companies, San Jose, California

Company	*Water use*		*Water savings (%)*	*Payback period on investment (months)*
	Before conservation	*After conservation*		
	(thousand cubic meters per year)			
IBM[1]	420	42	90	3.6
California Paper-Board Corp.	2,473	689	72	2.4
Gangi Bros. Food Processing	568	212	63	10.8
Hewlett-Packard[1]	87	42	52	3.6
Advanced Micro Devices	2,098	1,318	37	7.2[2]
Tandem Computers	125	87	30	12.0
Dyna-Craft Metal Finishing	193	140	27	2.4

[1] *Water use rates apply only to one or more processes involving conservation measures.*

[2] *Payback based only on that portion of water savings with which costs could be associated.*

Source: Worldwatch Institute, based on studies published 1990

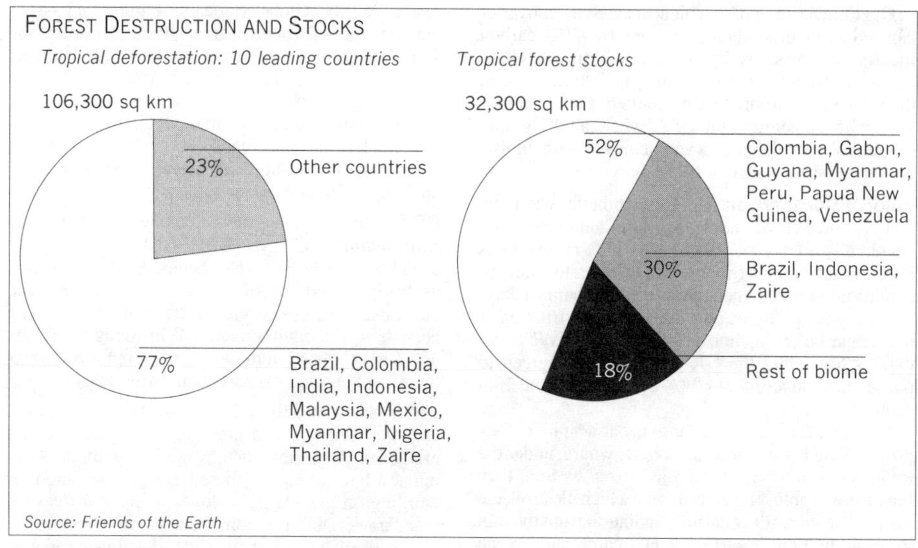

Source: Friends of the Earth

(2,3,7,8-TCDD), a highly toxic chemical that occurs, for example, as an impurity in the defoliant Agent Orange, used in the Vietnam War, and sometimes in the weedkiller 2,4,5-T. It has been associated with a disfiguring skin complaint (chloracne), birth defects, miscarriages, and cancer. UK government figures released in 1989 showed dioxin levels in breast milk 100 times higher than guidelines set for environmental dioxin.

Disasters involving accidental release of large amounts of dioxin into the environment have occurred at Seveso, Italy, and Times Beach, Missouri, USA. Small amounts of dioxins are released by the burning of a wide range of chlorinated materials (treated wood, exhaust fumes from fuels treated with chlorinated additives, and plastics) and as a side effect of some techniques of papermaking. The possibility of food becoming contaminated by dioxins in the environment has led the EC to decrease significantly the allowed levels of dioxin emissions from incinerators.

endangered species plant or animal species whose numbers are so few that it is at risk of becoming extinct. Officially designated endangered species are listed by the International Union for the Conservation of Nature (IUCN).

An example of an endangered species is the Javan rhinoceros. There are only about 50 alive today and, unless active steps are taken to promote this species' survival, it will probably be extinct within a few decades.

energy conservation methods of reducing energy use through insulation, increasing energy efficiency, and changes in patterns of use. Profligate energy use by industrialized countries contributes greatly to air pollution and the greenhouse effect when it draws on nonrenewable energy sources.

It has been calculated that increasing energy efficiency alone could reduce carbon dioxide emissions in several high-income countries by 1–2% a year. By applying existing conservation methods, UK electricity use could be reduced by 4 gigawatts by the year 2000 – the equivalent of four Sizewell nuclear power stations – according to a study by the Open University. The average annual decrease in energy consumption in relation to gross national product 1973–87 was 1.2% in France, 2% in the UK, 2.1% in the USA, and 2.8% in Japan.

Endangered species

Species	*Observation*
plants	one-quarter of the world's plants are threatened with extinction by the year 2010
amphibians	worldwide decline in numbers; half of New Zealand's frog species are now extinct
birds	three-quarters of all bird species are declining or threatened with extinction
carnivores	almost all species of cats and bears are declining in numbers
fish	one-third of North American freshwater fish are rare or endangered; half the fish species in Lake Victoria, Africa's largest lake, are close to extinction due to predation by the introduced Nile perch
invertebrates	about 100 species are lost each day due to deforestation; half the freshwater snails in the southeastern USA are now extinct or threatened; over one-quarter of Germany's invertebrates are threatened
mammals	half of Australia's mammals are threatened; 40% of mammals in France, the Netherlands, Germany, and Portugal are threatened
primates	two-thirds of primate species are threatened
reptiles	over 40% of reptile species are threatened

eutrophication excessive enrichment of rivers, lakes, and shallow sea areas, primarily by nitrate fertilizers washed from the soil by rain, by phosphates from fertilizers and detergents in municipal sewage, and by nutrients in sewage itself. These encourage the growth of algae and bacteria, which use up the oxygen in the water, thereby making it uninhabitable for fishes and other animal life.

extinction the complete disappearance of a species. In the past, extinctions are believed to have occurred because species were unable to adapt quickly enough to a naturally changing environment. Today, most extinctions are due to human activity. Some species, such as the dodo of Mauritius, the moas of New Zealand, and the passenger pigeon of North America, were exterminated by hunting. Others became extinct when their habitat was destroyed.

Mass extinctions are episodes during which whole groups of species have become extinct, the best known being that of the dinosaurs, other large reptiles, and various marine invertebrates about 65 million years ago. Another mass extinction occurred about 10,000 years ago when many giant species of mammal died out. This is known as the 'Pleistocene overkill' because their disappearance was probably hastened by the hunting activities of prehistoric humans. The greatest mass extinction occurred about 250 million years ago marking the Permian-Triassic boundary, when up to 96% of all living species became extinct. It was proposed 1982 that mass extinctions occur periodically, at approximately 26-million-year intervals.

The current mass extinction is largely due to human destruction of habitats, as in the tropical forests and coral reefs; it is far more serious and damaging than mass extinctions of the past because of the speed at which it occurs. Man-made climatic changes and pollution also make it less likely that the biosphere can recover and evolve new species to suit a changed environment. The rate of extinction is difficult to estimate, since most losses occur in the rich environment of the tropical rainforest, where the total number of existent species is not known. Conservative estimates put the rate of loss due to deforestation alone at 4,000 to 6,000 species a year. Overall, the rate could be as high as one species an hour, with the loss of one species putting those dependent on it at risk. Australia has the worst record for extinction: 18 mammals have disappeared since Europeans settled there, and 40 more are threatened.

The last mouse-eared bat (*Myotis myotis*) in the UK died 1990. This is the first mammal to have become extinct in the UK for 250 years, since the last wolf was exterminated.

firewood the principal fuel for some 2 billion people, mainly in the Third World. In principle a renewable energy source, firewood is being cut far faster than the trees can regenerate in many areas of Africa and Asia, leading to deforestation. In Mali, for example, wood provides 97% of total energy consumption, and deforestation is running at an estimated 9,000 hectares a year. The heat efficiency of firewood can be increased by use of stoves, but many people cannot afford to buy these.

fossil fuel fuel, such as coal, oil, and natural gas, formed from the fossilized remains of plants that lived hundreds of millions of years ago. Fossil fuels are a nonrenewable resource and will eventually run out. Extraction of coal and oil causes considerable environmental pollution, and burning coal contributes to problems of acid rain and the greenhouse effect.

Gaia hypothesis theory that the Earth's living and nonliving systems form an inseparable whole that is regulated and kept adapted for life by living organisms themselves. The planet therefore functions as a single organism, or a giant cell. Since life and environment are so closely linked, there is a need for humans to understand and maintain the physical environment and living things around them. The Gaia hypothesis was elaborated by British scientist James Lovelock (1919–) in the 1970s.

global warming projected imminent climate change attributed to the greenhouse effect.

green audit inspection of a company to assess the total environmental impact of its activities or of a particular product or process.

greenhouse effect phenomenon of the Earth's atmosphere by which solar radiation, trapped by the Earth and re-emitted from the surface, is prevented from escaping by various gases in the air. The result is a rise in the Earth's temperature. The main greenhouse gases are carbon dioxide, methane, and chlorofluorocarbons (CFCs). Fossil-fuel consumption and forest fires are the main causes of carbon-dioxide build-up; methane is a byproduct of agriculture (rice, cattle, sheep). Water vapour is another greenhouse gas.

The United Nations Environment Programme estimates that by 2025 average world temperatures will have risen by 1.5°C with a consequent rise of 20 cm in sea level. Low-lying areas and entire countries would be threatened by flooding and crops would be affected by the change in climate. A computer model from the British Meteorological Office predicts a warming of 2.7°C for a doubling of carbon dioxide. The concentration of carbon dioxide in the atmosphere is estimated to have risen by 25% since the Industrial Revolution, and 10% since 1950; the rate of increase is now 0.5% a year. However, predictions about global warming and its possible climatic effects are tentative and often conflict with each other.

Dubbed the 'greenhouse effect' by Swedish scientist Svante Arrhenius (1859–1927), it was first predicted 1827 by French mathematician Joseph Fourier (1768–1830).

halon organic chemical compound containing one or two carbon atoms, together with bromine and other halogens. The halons are gases and are widely used in fire extinguishers. As destroyers of the ozone layer, they are up to ten times more effective than chlorofluorocarbons (CFCs), to which they are chemically related. Levels in the atmosphere are rising by about 25% each year, mainly through the testing of fire-fighting equipment.

insulation process or material that prevents or reduces the flow of electricity, heat, or sound from one place to another. *U* ***thermal*** or ***heat insulation*** makes use of insulating materials such as fibreglass to reduce the loss of heat through the roof and walls

The race to prevent mass extinction

About a million different living species have been identified so far. Recent studies in tropical forests – where biodiversity is greatest – suggest the true figure is nearer 30 million. Most are animals, and most of those are insects. Because the tropical forests are threatened, at least half the animal species could become extinct within the next century. There have been at least five 'mass extinctions' in our planet's history; the last removed the dinosaurs 65 million years ago. The present wave of extinction is of similar scale, but hundreds of times faster.

There is conflict within the conservation movement. Some believe that *habitats* (the places where animals and plants live) should be conserved; others prefer to concentrate upon individual *species*. Both approaches have strengths and weaknesses, and they must operate in harmony.

Habitat protection

Habitat protection has obvious advantages. Many species benefit if land is preserved. Animals need somewhere to live; unless the habitat is preserved it may not be worth saving the individual animal. Habitat protection *seems* cheap; for example, tropical forest can often be purchased for only a few dollars per hectare. Only by habitat protection can we save more than a handful of the world's animals.

But there are difficulties. Even when a protected area is designated a 'national park', its animals may not be safe. All five remaining species of rhinoceros are heavily protected in the wild, but are threatened by poaching. Early in 1991, Zimbabwe had 1,500 black rhinos – the world's largest population. Patrols of game wardens shoot poachers on sight. Yet by late 1992, 1,000 of the 1,500 had been poached. In many national parks worldwide, the habitat is threatened by the local farmers' need to graze their cattle.

Computer models and field studies show that wild populations need several hundred individuals to be viable. Smaller populations will eventually go extinct in the wild, because of accidents to key breeding individuals, or epidemics. The big predators need vast areas. One tiger may command hundreds of square kilometres; a viable population needs an area as big as Wales or Holland. Only one of the world's five remaining subspecies of tiger – a population of Bengals in India – occupies an area large enough to be viable. All the rest (Indo-Chinese, Sumatran, Chinese, and Siberian) seem bound to die out. Three other subspecies have gone extinct in the past 100 years – the latest, the Javan, in the 1970s.

Mosaic

Ecologists now emphasize the concept of *mosaic.* All animals need different things from their habitat; a failure of any one is disastrous. Giant pandas feed mainly on bamboo, but give birth in old hollow trees – of which there is a shortage. Birds commonly roost in one place, but feed in special areas far way. Nature reserves must either contain all essentials for an animal's life, or else allow access to such areas elsewhere. For many animals in a reserve, these conditions are not fulfilled. Hence year by year, after reserves are created, species go extinct: a process called *species relaxation.* The remaining fauna and flora may be a poor shadow of the original.

Interest is increasing in *captive breeding,* carried out mainly by the world's 800 zoos. Their task is formidable; each captive species should include several hundred individuals. Zoos maintain such numbers through *cooperative breeding,* organized regionally and coordinated by the Captive Breeding Specialist Group or the World Conservation Union, based in Minneapolis, Minnesota. Each programme is underpinned by a studbook, showing which individuals are related to which.

Genetic diversity

Breeding for conservation is different from breeding for livestock improvement. Livestock breeders breed *uniform* creatures by selecting animals conforming to some prescribed ideal. Conservation breeders maintain *maximum genetic diversity* by encouraging every individual to breed, including those reluctant to breed in captivity; by equalizing family size, so one generation's genes are all represented in the next; and by swapping individuals between zoos, to prevent inbreeding.

Cooperative breeding programmes are rapidly diversifying; by the year 2000 there should be several hundred. They can only make a small impression on the 15 million endangered species, but they can contribute greatly to particular groups of animals, especially the land vertebrates – mammals, birds, reptiles, and amphibians. These include most of the world's largest animals, with the greatest impact on their habitats. There are 24,000 species of land vertebrate, of which 2,000 probably require captive breeding to survive. Zoos could save all 2,000; that would be a great contribution.

Captive breeding is not intended to establish 'museum' populations, but to provide a temporary 'lifeboat'. Things are hard for wild animals, but over the next few decades, despite the growing human population, it should be possible to establish more, safe national parks. Arabian oryx, California condor, black-footed ferret, red wolf, and Mauritius kestrel are among the creatures saved from extinction by captive breeding and returned to the wild. In the future, we can expect to see many more.

CT

of buildings. The U-value of a material is a measure of its ability to conduct heat – a material chosen as an insulator should therefore have a low U-value. Air trapped between the fibres of clothes acts as a thermal insulator, preventing loss of body warmth.

leaching process by which substances are washed out of the soil. Fertilizers leached out of the soil drain into rivers, lakes, and ponds and cause water pollution. In tropical areas, leaching of the soil after the destruction of forests removes scarce nutrients and can lead to a dramatic loss of soil fertility. The leaching of soluble minerals in soils can lead to the formation of distinct soil horizons as different minerals are deposited at successively lower levels.

lead heavy, soft, malleable, grey, metallic element, symbol Pb (from Latin *plumbum*). As a cumulative poison, lead enters the body from lead water pipes, lead-based paints, and leaded petrol. In humans, exposure to lead shortly after birth is associated with impaired mental health between the ages of two and four.

mercury or ***quicksilver*** heavy, silver-grey, metallic element, symbol Hg (from Latin *hydrargyrum*). Mercury is a cumulative poison that can contaminate the food chain and cause intestinal disturbance, kidney and brain damage, and birth defects in humans. (The World Health Organization's 'safe' limit for mercury is 0.5 milligrams of mercury per kilogram of muscle tissue.) The discharge into the sea by industry of organic mercury compounds such as dimethylmercury is the chief cause of mercury poisoning in the latter half of the 20th century.

nitrate any salt of nitric acid, containing the NO_3^- ion. Nitrates of various kinds are used in explosives, in the chemical industry, in curing meat, and as inorganic fertilizers. Being soluble in water, nitrate is leached out by rain into streams and reservoirs. High levels are now found in drinking water in arable areas. These may be harmful to newborn babies, and have been tentatively linked with stomach cancer. The UK current standard is 100 milligrams per litre, double the EC limits to be implemented by 1993.

nuclear safety measures to avoid accidents in the operation of nuclear reactors and in the production and disposal of nuclear weapons and of nuclear waste. There are no guarantees of the safety of any of the various methods of disposal.

nuclear accidents

1957 At Windscale (now Sellafield), Cumbria, England, fire destroyed the core of a reactor, releasing large quantities of radioactive fumes into the atmosphere.

1965 130 km/80 mi off the coast of Japan, a US Navy Skyhawk jet bomber fell off the deck of the ship *Ticonderoga*, sinking in 4,900 m/16,000 ft of water. It carried a one-megaton hydrogen bomb. The accident was only revealed in 1989.

1979 In Three Mile Island, Harrisburg, Pennsylvania, USA, a combination of mechanical and electrical failure, as well as operator error, caused a pressurized water reactor to leak radioactive matter.

1979 In Church Rock, New Mexico, USA, 380 million litres/100 million gallons of radioactive water containing uranium leaked from a pond into the Rio Purco, causing the water to become over 6,500 times as radioactive as safety standards allow for drinking water.

1986 In Chernobyl, Ukraine, there was an explosive leak, caused by overheating, from a nonpressurized boiling-water reactor, one of the largest in Europe. The resulting clouds of radioactive material spread as far as the UK; 31 people were killed in the explosion (many more are expected to die or become ill because of the long-term effects of radiation), and thousands of square kilometres of land were contaminated by fallout.

1993 In Tomsk, Siberia, Russian Federation, a tank exploded at a uranium reprocessing plant, sending a cloud of radioactive particles into the air.

The *Braer* oil spill

On 5 Jan 1993, the oil tanker *Braer* ran ashore in heavy seas on the coast of the Scottish Shetland Islands. While salvage experts watched helplessly from the cliffs, several days of intense storms broke the ship completely in two and spilled virtually the whole of its 85 thousand-tonne cargo into the surrounding sea. Huge waves and gale-force winds dispersed the oil, blowing volatile chemicals over much of the island. Hundreds of islanders experienced headaches, diarrhoea, and eczema, and 1,500 sea birds were washed ashore dead, although the total death toll may have been far higher. An exclusion zone of 1,000 sq km/400 sq mi was created, fishing within it forbidden, and the fish from salmon farms banned from sale. Salmon that would have been worth £7 million if uncontaminated has already been minced and used to feed captive mink in Norway. On shore, areas of sheep pasture are judged off limits because of contamination by storm-blown oil droplets.

The Shetland islanders now face years of legal wrangling about compensation. For many, the issue has as much to do with politics as accidents. Physically and culturally remote from the decision-making power of the government in London, the islanders have already had to fight against the risks to fisheries from the nuclear power plant on the mainland. Fears of a major oil-tanker accident had been expressed for years. Since the *Braer* accident, tankers have continued to sail within 16 km/10 mi of the islands. Isobel Mitchell, who organized a petition demanding a full public inquiry into the disaster, signed by a third of the Shetland population, said some months afterwards: 'Nothing has really changed to stop the same thing happening tomorrow.'

nuclear waste the radioactive and toxic by-products of the nuclear-energy and nuclear-weapons industries. Nuclear waste may have an active life of several thousand years. Reactor waste is of three types: ***high-level*** spent fuel, or the residue when nuclear fuel has been removed from a reactor and reprocessed; ***intermediate***, which may be long- or short-lived; and ***low-level***, but bulky, waste from reactors, which has only short-lived radioactivity. Disposal, by burial on land or at sea, has raised problems of safety, environmental pollution, and security. In absolute terms, nuclear waste cannot be safely relocated or disposed of.

About one-third of the fuel from nuclear reactors becomes spent each year. It is removed to a ***reprocessing*** plant where radioactive waste products are chemically separated from remaining uranium and plutonium, in an expensive and dangerous process. This practice increases the volume of radioactive waste more than a hundred times.

The dumping of nuclear waste at sea officially stopped 1983, when a moratorium was agreed by the members of the London Dumping Convention (a United Nations body that controls disposal of wastes at sea). Covertly, the USSR continued dumping, and deposited thousands of tonnes of nuclear waste and three faulty reactors in the sea 1964–86.

In 1990, a scientific study revealed an increased risk of leukaemia in children whose fathers had worked at Sellafield, Cumbria, England, between 1950 and 1985. Sellafield is the world's greatest discharger of radioactive waste, followed by Hanford, Washington (USA). (See feature in this section.)

oil spill oil released by damage to or discharge from a tanker or oil installation. An oil spill kills all shore life, clogging up the feathers of birds and suffocating other creatures. At sea, toxic chemicals leach into the water below, poisoning sea life. Mixed with dust, the oil forms globules that sink to the seabed, poisoning sea life there as well.

In March 1989, the *Exxon Valdez* (belonging to the Exxon Corporation) spilled oil in Alaska's Prince William Sound, covering 12,400 sq km/4,800 sq mi and killing at least 34,400 sea birds, 10,000 sea otters, and up to 16 whales. The incident led to the US Oil Pollution Act of 1990, which requires tankers operating in US waters to have double hulls. The world's largest oil spill was in the Persian Gulf in Feb 1991 as a direct result of hostilities during the Gulf War. Around 6–8 million barrels of oil were spilled, polluting 675 km/ 420 mi of Saudi coastline. In some places, the oil was 30 cm/12 in deep in the sand. In Jan 1993, the *Braer* oil tanker went aground near the Shetland Islands, discharging its 85,000-tonne cargo into the surrounding waters.

Oil spills around Britain's coasts in 1990 numbered around 791. There were 135 clean-up operations, at a cost of £2 million.

organic farming farming without the use of synthetic fertilizers (such as nitrates and phosphates), pesticides (herbicides, insecticides, and fungicides), or other agrochemicals (such as hormones, growth stimulants, or fruit regulators). (For more, see ***Food and Agriculture***.)

overfishing fishing at rates that exceed the sustained-yield cropping of fish species, resulting in a net population decline. For example, in the North Atlantic, herring has been fished to the verge of extinction and the cod and haddock populations are severely depleted. In the Third World, use of huge factory ships, often by fisheries from industrialized countries, has depleted stocks for local people who cannot obtain protein in any other way.

ozone O_3 highly reactive pale-blue gas with a penetrating odour. Ozone forms a thin layer in the upper atmosphere, which protects life on Earth from ultraviolet rays, a cause of skin cancer. At lower atmospheric levels it is an air pollutant.

Ground-level ozone can cause asthma attacks, stunted growth in plants, and corrosion of certain materials. It is produced by the action of sunlight on air pollutants, including car exhaust fumes, and is so dangerous that the US Environment Protection Agency recommends people should not be exposed for more than one hour a day to ozone levels of 120 parts per billion (ppb), while the World Health Organization recommends a lower 76–100 ppb. It is known that even at levels of 60 ppb ozone causes respiratory problems, and may cause the yields of some crops to fall.

ozone hole a continent-sized hole in the ozone layer has formed over Antarctica. It is believed that the ozone layer is depleting at a rate of about 5%

Major oil spills

Year	Place	Source	Quantity (tonnes)	Quantity (litres)
1967	off Cornwall, England	*Torrey Canyon*	107,100	
1968	off South Africa	*World Glory*		51,194,000
1972	Gulf of Oman	*Sea Star*	103,500	
1977	North Sea	Ekofisk oilfield		31,040,000
1978	off France	*Amoco Cadiz*	200,000	
1979	Gulf of Mexico	Ixtoc 1 oil well	535,000	
1979	off Trinidad and Tobago	collision of *Atlantic Empress* and *Aegean Captain*	270,000	
1983	Persian Gulf	Nowruz oilfield	540,000	
1983	off South Africa	*Castillo de Beliver*	225,000	
1989	off Alaska	*Exxon Valdez*		40,504,000
1991	Persian Gulf	oil wells in Kuwait and Iraq		130–585,000,000
1993	Shetland Islands, Scotland	*Braer*	85,000	

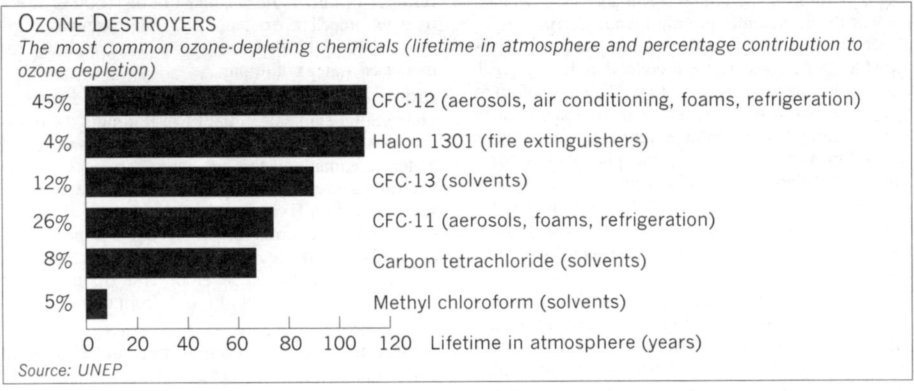

every 10 years over N Europe, with depletion extending south to the Mediterranean and southern USA. However, ozone depletion over the polar regions – 50% over the Antarctic compared with 3% over the Arctic 1989 – is the most dramatic manifestation of a general global effect. This has been caused by chemicals collectively known as ozone depleters.

ozone depleter any chemical that destroys the ozone in the stratosphere. Most ozone depleters are chemically stable compounds containing chlorine or bromine, which remain unchanged for long enough to drift up to the upper atmosphere. The best known are chlorofluorocarbons (CFCs), but many other ozone depleters are known, including halons, used in some fire extinguishers; methyl chloroform and carbon tetrachloride, both solvents; some CFC substitutes; and the pesticide methyl bromide.

packaging material, usually of metal, paper, plastic, or glass, used to protect products, make them easier to display, and as a form of advertising. Environmentalists have criticized packaging materials as being wasteful of energy and resources. In Germany from 1993, shops are obliged to take back surplus paper and plastic packaging, empty cans, toothpaste tubes, and yoghurt cartons, and a compulsory deposit is levied on certain types of packaging.

pesticide any chemical used in farming, gardening, or indoors to combat pests. Pesticides are of three main types: ***insecticides*** (to kill insects), ***fungicides*** (to kill fungal diseases), and ***herbicides*** (to kill plants, mainly those considered weeds). Pesticides cause a number of pollution problems through spray drift onto surrounding areas, direct contamination of users or the public, and as residues on food. The

The ozone hole comes closer

The atmosphere consists of a number of gases, the most important of which, from the point of view of life on Earth, is oxygen. It is a by-product of plant metabolism, it is essential to the metabolism of animals, and it also takes part in an important reaction in the stratosphere.

The oxygen molecule consists of two atoms of oxygen – written as O_2. In the stratosphere, the ultraviolet rays of the Sun can break the molecule down into individual atoms – O and O. These atoms are unstable and can attach themselves to other oxygen molecules to form molecules of ozone – oxygen with three atoms of oxygen – O_3. Under the influence of radiation from another part of the ultraviolet spectrum, the molecules of ozone can break down and unite with more free oxygen atoms to form oxygen molecules again – O_3 unites with O to produce O_2 and O_2. As a result, there is a layer in the atmosphere where ozone is continually produced and destroyed. This ozone layer lies between 15 and 50 km above the ground – with the greatest concentration at about 23 km – and is estimated to contain about 5 billion tonnes of ozone at one time. All this activity absorbs the energy of the ultraviolet light and prevents it from reaching the ground, which is a good thing as certain wavebands of ultraviolet light can cause cancers, cataracts, and decreases in crop yields.

The presence of certain other molecules, particularly of chlorine, influences the speed of these reactions – usually increasing the speed of the breakdown of the ozone. This is very noticeable in springtime in the Antarctic when chlorine from pollutants is released from the icy winter clouds. The ozone concentration is reduced here, and the still conditions cannot bring it in from elsewhere, resulting in the so-called ozone hole. It is believed that much of the chlorine responsible comes from industrial gases such as CFCs, as well as from natural sources such as volcanoes. This is becoming a worldwide problem as a thinning of the ozone layer over Europe was detected early in 1993.

safest pesticides include those made from plants, such as the insecticides pyrethrum and derris.

More potent are synthetic products, such as chlorinated hydrocarbons. These products, including DDT and dieldrin, are highly toxic to wildlife and often to human beings, so their use is now restricted by law in some areas and is declining. Safer pesticides, such as malathion, are based on organic phosphorus compounds, but they still present hazards to health. The aid organization Oxfam estimates that pesticides cause about 10,000 deaths worldwide every year. There are around 4,000 cases of acute pesticide poisoning a year in the UK.

polluter-pays principle the idea that whoever causes pollution is responsible for the cost of repairing any damage. The principle is accepted in British law but has in practice often been ignored; for example, farmers causing the death of fish through slurry pollution have not been fined the full costs of restocking the river.

pollution the harmful effect on the environment of by-products of human activity, principally industrial and agricultural processes – for example, noise, smoke, car emissions, chemical and radioactive effluents in air, seas, and rivers, pesticides, radiation, sewage, and household waste. Pollution contributes to the greenhouse effect.

In the UK in 1987, air pollution caused by carbon monoxide emission from road transport was measured at 5.26 million tonnes. California passed a law in 1990 stating that 2% of all new cars sold by 1998 must be emission free. In Feb 1990, the UK had failed to apply 21 European Community Laws on air and water pollution and faced prosecution before the European Court of Justice on 31 of the 160 EC directives in force. The existence of 1,300 toxic waste tips in the UK in 1990 posed a considerable threat for increased water pollution.

radon colourless, odourless, gaseous, radioactive, nonmetallic element, symbol Rn. Radon is the densest gas known and occurs in small amounts in spring water, streams, and the air, being formed from the natural radioactive decay of radium. The average radon radiation level found in a study of 40 British limestone caves was 2,900 becquerels per cubic metre. This compares with the National Radiological Protection Board's set level of 200 Bq per cubic metre at which removal of radon from homes is recommended.

recycling processing of industrial and household waste (such as paper, glass, and some metals and plastics) so that it can be reused. This saves expenditure on scarce raw materials, slows down the depletion of nonrenewable resources, and helps to reduce pollution.

The USA recycles only around 13% of its waste, compared to around 33% in Japan. However, all US states encourage or require local recycling programmes to be set up. By 1992, around 33% of newspapers, 22% of office paper, 64% of aluminium cans, 3% of plastic containers, and 20% of all glass bottles and jars were recycled.

Most British recycling schemes are voluntary, and rely on people taking waste items to a central collection point. However, some local authorities, such as Leeds, now ask householders to separate waste before collection, making recycling possible on a much larger scale.

Recycling

Levels of recycling of packaging waste, selected European countries, 1980–1990 (percentage of total consumption)

	Paper and cardboard			Glass			Aluminium	
	1980	1985	1989	1980	1985	1989	1989	1990
EC members								
Belgium	14.7			42.0	39.0			59.0
Denmark	25.6	31.3	29.7	53.9	55.0			40.0
France	37.0	41.3	45.7	26.0	26.1	28.5		41.0
Germany, East								
Germany, West	33.9	43.6	43.0	35.5	39.4	42.3	3.0	54.0
Greece							21.0	16.0
Ireland	15.0			7.0	8.0		2.0	19.0
Italy				25.0	38.0		8.0	48.0
Luxembourg								
Netherlands	45.5	50.3	58.4	53.0	62.0	55.2		66.0
Portugal	38.0			10.0	14.0			23.0
Spain	38.1	44.1		13.1	22.0			27.0
UK	29.0	27.0	27.0	12.0	14.0	18.0		21.0
EFTA members								
Austria				38.0	44.0		3.0	60.0
Finland	30.0	36.8		21.0	25.0			46.0
Iceland								
Liechtenstein								
Norway	21.9	21.1	23.2			10.0		34.0
Sweden	34.0	40.0			20.0	22.0	82.0	35.0
Switzerland	38.0			36.0	46.0	47.0	31.0	61.0

Source: OECD

Nuclear waste: a permanent hazard

Although it is now almost 50 years since scientists achieved controlled nuclear fission, the question of what to do about nuclear waste is as controversial as ever. Indeed, recent news about lack of control over nuclear waste in the former USSR is likely once again to raise the political temperature of this issue.

The growth of the nuclear-waste industry

Nuclear waste comes from nuclear power stations, nuclear weapons, uranium mines, and waste from medical and industrial uses of nuclear energy. It is one of the most hazardous of all waste products, because it releases dangerous forms of radiation, capable of causing a range of immediate and long-term health effects including radiation sickness, cancer, and birth defects. Some nuclear waste products can stay dangerously radioactive for many thousands of years, thus creating a disposal problem of a type and scale not met previously.

Nuclear waste can be categorised into three main types: high-, medium-, and low-level waste. The spent uranium rods from nuclear power stations are among the highest-level waste products, as are certain nuclear-weapon components. Less radioactive waste includes protective suits, cooling water used in power stations, and medical equipment.

Radiation in nuclear waste cannot be destroyed by burning or industrial processes, and people regulating nuclear waste have a choice of storing it indefinitely, releasing it into the environment in the hope that it will disperse to nontoxic levels, or, in the case of some high-level wastes, reprocessing it to remove usable fuel.

Nuclear waste in the environment

In practice, all three options are used. When nuclear power was first used, far less was known about its hazards, and large amounts of low-level waste were simply discharged into the environment, ending up in the air, in rivers and oceans, and sometimes in the soil. Since then, there has been a steady decrease in what is judged 'acceptable' levels of radiation from the point of view of human health and a consequent tightening of controls over discharges.

Unfortunately, a lot of damage has already been done. Despite some changes in regulations, low-level waste is still lost by accident or design. Evidence collected by the environmental organization Greenpeace confirmed suspicions that the Soviet navy used simply to dump reactors from nuclear submarines in Arctic seas, some of them with fuel still inside. Clusters of child leukaemias around some of the UK's nuclear facilities have caused a storm of controversy among researchers, with some believing that they point to a link with discharges of radiation, and others saying that the statistical probability of a link with the nuclear-power programme remains tenuous. Radiation from past and present uranium mines continues to cause problems in Namibia, the USA, and elsewhere.

Storing nuclear waste

Many nuclear operations now choose to store their waste, until either the radioactivity has fallen to background levels or new disposal techniques are developed. The lowest-level waste, such as radioactive test tubes or tissue paper, are buried in metal containers in shallow trenches. Some countries have built concrete storage tanks for low- and intermediate-level waste, such as that in Drigg, Cumbria, in the UK. High-level waste – for example, used fuel rods or other components of a nuclear reactor – is sometimes stored underwater until the most intense radioactivity has dissipated.

Although many methods have been suggested for the long-term storage of waste, all these have their problems. Options include burial deep underground, with the waste vitrified (encased in glass), deposited in deep-sea trenches, or buried in polar icecaps. Some nuclear scientists even suggest blasting it off into space by rocket. None of these alternatives is without serious problems. Space disposal would be extremely expensive and hazardous in case of accident. Sea dumping is banned by international treaty. Burial underground is the most favoured option at present but, given the enormous time scale involved, it is impossible for us to be sure that containers would not corrode, be displaced by earth movements, and otherwise leak their contents. Simply moving nuclear waste, by sea, air, road or rail, risks further accidents and escapes of radioactive material.

Reprocessing: the most controversial option of all

The third disposal option for high-level waste from spent fuel includes reprocessing to extract remaining uranium and also another fissionable material, plutonium. The latter can be used to make nuclear weapons or as nuclear fuel.

Reprocessing has long been favoured by the nuclear industry, partly because of greater fuel-use efficiency and partly because the close links between civilian and military nuclear programmes in many countries makes plutonium production an attractive option.

One of the best-known reprocessing facilities is Sellafield (once known as Windscale) in Cumbria, which processes nuclear waste from many parts of the world. The complex has long been the subject of intense controversy. It suffered a serious accident in 1957, and a continuing series of more minor leaks and emissions since. Although reprocessing recovers some of the most intensely radioactive material, it also produces large amounts of low-level waste, particularly cooling water and gases, which are released. Discharges from Sellafield have now made the Irish Sea the world's most radioactive ocean.

In theory, the Sellafield complex should soon be even more busy. A Thermal Oxide Reprocessing Plant (THORP) has been built, following a long public inquiry in the 1970s, and is now ready for commissioning. However, lack of interest from potential foreign customers has raised doubts about whether it will actually go ahead.

ND

reuse multiple use of a product (often a form of packaging), by returning it to the retailer, manufacturer, or processor each time. Many such returnable items are sold with a deposit which is reimbursed if the item is returned. Reuse is usually more energy- and resource-efficient than recycling unless there are large transport or cleaning costs.

sewage disposal the disposal of human excreta and other waterborne waste products from houses, streets, and factories. Conveyed through sewers to sewage works, sewage has to undergo a series of treatments to be acceptable for discharge into rivers or the sea, according to various local laws and ordinances. Raw sewage, or sewage that has not been treated adequately, is one serious source of water pollution and a cause of eutrophication.

In the industrialized countries of the West, most industries are responsible for disposing of their own wastes. Government agencies establish industrial waste-disposal standards. In most countries, sewage works for residential areas are the responsibility of local authorities. The solid waste (sludge) may be spread over fields as a fertilizer or, in a few countries, dumped at sea. A significant proportion of bathing beaches in densely populated regions have unacceptably high bacterial content, largely as a result of untreated sewage being discharged into rivers and the sea. This can, for example, cause stomach upsets in swimmers.

The use of raw sewage as a fertilizer (long practised in China) has the drawback that disease-causing microorganisms can survive in the soil and be transferred to people or animals by consumption of subsequent crops. Sewage sludge is safer, but may contain dangerous levels of heavy metals and other industrial contaminants.

slash and burn simple agricultural method whereby natural vegetation is cut and burned, and the clearing then farmed for a few years until the soil loses its fertility, whereupon farmers move on and leave the area to regrow. Although this is possible with a small, widely dispersed population, it becomes unsustainable with more people and is now a form of deforestation.

slurry form of manure composed mainly of liquids. Slurry is collected and stored on many farms, especially when large numbers of animals are kept in factory units. When slurry tanks are accidentally or deliberately breached, large amounts can spill into rivers, killing fish and causing eutrophication. Some slurry is spread on fields as a fertilizer.

Slurry spills in the UK increased enormously in the 1980s and were by 1991 running at rates of over 4,000 a year. Tighter regulations were being introduced to curb this pollution.

soil erosion the wearing away and redistribution of the Earth's soil layer. It is caused by the action of water, wind, and ice, and also by improper methods of agriculture. If unchecked, soil erosion results in the formation of deserts (desertification). It has been estimated that 20% of the world's cultivated topsoil was lost between 1950 and 1990.

If the rate of erosion exceeds the rate of soil formation (from rock and decomposing organic matter), then the land will decline and eventually become infertile. The removal of forests or other vegetation often leads to serious soil erosion, because plant roots bind soil, and without them the soil is free to wash or blow away, as in the American dust bowl. The effect is worse on hillsides, and there has been devastating loss of soil where forests have been cleared from mountainsides, as in Madagascar. Improved agricultural practices such as contour ploughing are needed to combat soil erosion. Windbreaks, such as hedges or strips planted with coarse grass, are valuable, and organic farming can reduce soil erosion by as much as 75%.

sustained-yield cropping the removal of surplus individuals from a population of organisms so that the population maintains a constant size. This usually requires selective removal of animals of all ages and both sexes to ensure a balanced population structure. Taking too many individuals can result in a population decline, as in overfishing.

unleaded petrol petrol manufactured without the addition of antiknock. It has a slightly lower octane rating than leaded petrol but has the advantage of not polluting the atmosphere with lead compounds. Many cars can be converted to running on unleaded petrol by altering the timing of the engine, and most new cars are designed to do so. Cars fitted with a catalytic converter must use unleaded fuel. The use of unleaded petrol has been standard in the USA for some years and is increasing in the UK (encouraged by a lower rate of tax than that levied on leaded petrol).

CLEANER FUEL

Top users of unleaded petrol in Europe, 1990 (unleaded petrol as percentage of market)

Use of environmentally less damaging unleaded petrol in Europe has increased greatly in recent years. Consumption of unleaded petrol more than doubled between 1988 and 1990, from 17.18m tonnes to 43.7m tonnes.

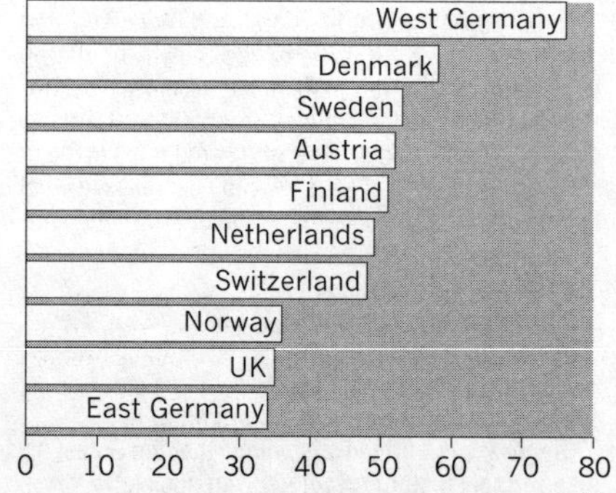

*East Germany, which had virtually no unleaded petrol in 1989, speedily revolutionized its petrol supply, following German unification, in order to come closer to West Germany's higher environmental standards.

Source: UK Petroleum Industry Association

Waldsterben (German 'forest death') tree decline related to air pollution, common throughout the industrialized world. It appears to be caused by a mixture of pollutants; the precise chemical mix varies

Which paper ...?

Ecolabelling on paper products has become big business. Over the last few years, many books, magazines, stationery, and packaging products have started carrying claims that the paper used in their manufacture is produced in ways that do not harm the environment: 'recycled', 'made from sustainable wood products', 'chlorine-free', and so on. For the consumer, the mass of information can be confusing and misleading. It is impossible to check whether forests really are being managed sustainably, for instance, and in some countries 'recycled' can be used if *any* of the pulp is recycled, so that paper brands labelled as 'recycled' may actually consist mainly of virgin wood pulp. Statements on many labels have never been verified and some manufacturers have simply added a green label to give themselves a marketing edge, without too much concern about its accuracy.

From 1993, the confusion is going to be taken out of green labelling on paper products. Within the European Community, ecolabelling legislation will tighten restrictions on claims and ensure that these reflect real changes in manufacture. In addition, the Forest Stewardship Council (FSC) is being launched as a new international body running certification schemes for environmentally and socially benign forest products. This will regulate claims and build a market for products from well-managed forests.

In the meantime, three things are particularly important. ***Chlorine-free*** means the paper has been produced in ways that do not release a range of harmful chemicals, including dioxins, into freshwater systems, and does not contain traces of these by-products. ***Recycled*** means the paper is made with at least some recycled pulp. An increasing number of labels state the percentage of recycled material, and some say 'post-consumer waste', which means waste that has been collected after use and pulped again, rather than waste. Claims about ***sustainable management*** are much more difficult to check and count for little if, for example, natural or old-growth forests are being felled to provide the timber, as is often the case in some countries.

between locations, but it includes acid rain, ozone, sulphur dioxide, and nitrogen oxides. Britain's trees are among the most badly affected in Europe.

waste materials that are no longer needed and are discarded. Examples are household waste, industrial waste (which often contains toxic chemicals), medical waste (which may contain organisms that cause disease), and nuclear waste (which is radioactive). By recycling, some materials in waste can be reclaimed for further use. In 1990, the industrialized nations generated 2 billion tonnes of waste. In the USA, 40 tonnes of solid waste are generated annually per person. In Britain, the average person throws away about ten times their own body weight in household refuse each year. Collectively, the country generates about 50 million tonnes of waste per year.

waste disposal depositing waste. Methods of waste disposal vary according to the materials in the waste and include incineration, burial at designated sites, and dumping at sea. Organic waste can be treated and reused as fertilizer. Nuclear waste and toxic waste are usually buried or dumped at sea, although this does not negate the danger.

Waste disposal is an increasing problem in the late 20th century. Environmental groups, such as Greenpeace and Friends of the Earth, are campaigning for more recycling, a change in lifestyle so that less waste (from packaging and containers to nuclear materials) is produced, and safer methods of disposal.

The industrial waste dumped every year by the UK in the North Sea includes 550,000 tonnes of fly ash from coal-fired power stations. The British government stopped North Sea dumping 1993, but dumping in the heavily polluted Irish Sea will continue. Industrial pollution is suspected of causing ecological problems, including an epidemic that killed hundreds of seals 1989. The Irish Sea receives 80 tonnes of uranium a year from phosphate rock processing, and 300 million gallons of sewage every day, 80% of it untreated or merely screened. In 1988, 80,000 tonnes of hazardous waste were imported into the UK for processing, including 6,000 tonnes of polychlorinated biphenyls.

water pollution any addition to fresh or sea water that disrupts biological processes or causes a health hazard. Common pollutants include nitrate, pesticides, and sewage, though a huge range of industrial contaminants, such as chemical by-products and residues created in the manufacture of various goods, also enter water – legally, accidentally, and through illegal dumping.

weedkiller or ***herbicide*** chemical that kills some or all plants. Selective herbicides are effective with cereal crops because they kill all broad-leaved plants without affecting grasslike leaves. Those that kill all plants include sodium chlorate, paraquat, and Agent Orange. The widespread use of weedkillers in agriculture has led to an increase in crop yield but also to pollution of soil and water supplies and killing of birds and small animals, as well as creating a health hazard for humans.

whaling the hunting of whales, largely discontinued 1986. Whales are killed for whale oil (made from the thick layer of fat under the skin called 'blubber'), used for food and cosmetics; for the large reserve of oil in the head of the sperm whale, used in the leather industry; and for ambergris, a waxlike substance from the intestines, used in making perfumes. There are synthetic substitutes for all these products. Whales are also killed for their meat, which is eaten by the Japanese and was used as pet food in the USA and Europe.

The International Whaling Commission (IWC), established 1946, failed to enforce quotas on whale killing until world concern about the possible extinction of the whale mounted in the 1970s. By the end of the 1980s, 90% of blue, fin, humpback, and sperm whales had been wiped out. Low reproduction rates mean that protected species are slow to recover. After 1986 only Iceland, Japan, Norway, and the USSR continued with limited whaling for 'scientific purposes', but Japan has been repeatedly implicated in commercial whaling, and pirates also operate. In 1990, the IWC rejected every proposal from Japan, Norway, and the USSR for further scientific whaling. Norway, Greenland, the Faroes, and Iceland formed a breakaway whaling club. In 1991, Japan held a 'final' whale feast before conforming to the regulations of the IWC. In 1993, Norway decided to flout the moratorium and resume commercial hunting of minke whales. (See box in this section.)

wildlife trade international trade in live plants and animals, and in wildlife products such as skins, horns, shells, and feathers. The trade has made some species virtually extinct, and whole ecosystems (for example, coral reefs) are threatened. Wildlife trade is to some extent regulated by CITES (the Convention on International Trade in Endangered Species).

Species almost eradicated by trade in their products include many of the largest whales, crocodiles, marine turtles, and some wild cats. Until recently, some 2 million snake skins were exported from India every year. Populations of black rhino and African elephant have collapsed because of hunting for their horns and tusks (ivory), and poaching remains a problem in cases where trade is prohibited.

Environmental Groups and Initiatives

CITES (acronym for ***Convention on International Trade in Endangered Species***) international agreement under the auspices of the IUCN with the aim of regulating trade in endangered species of animals and plants. The agreement came into force 1975 and by 1991 had been signed by 110 states. It prohibits any trade in a category of 8,000 highly endangered species and controls trade in a further 30,000 species.

Council for the Protection of Rural England countryside conservation group founded 1926 with a brief that extends from planning controls to energy policy. A central organization campaigns on national issues and 42 local groups lobby on regional matters. The ***Campaign for the Preservation of Rural Wales*** is the Welsh equivalent.

Countryside Council for Wales Welsh nature conservation body formed 1991 by the fusion of the former Nature Conservancy Council and the Welsh Countryside Commission. It is government-funded and administers conservation and land-use policies within Wales.

English Nature agency created 1991 from the division of the Nature Conservancy Council into English, Scottish, and Welsh sections. It is government-funded and responsible for designating and managing national nature reserves and other conservation areas, advising government ministers on policies, providing advice and information, and commissioning or undertaking relevant scientific research.

Environmentally Sensitive Area (ESA) scheme introduced by the UK Ministry of Agriculture 1984, as a result of EC legislation, to protect some of the most beautiful areas of the British countryside from

The wildlife trade

Reported trade in wildlife and wildlife products, 1992 (imports and exports, in thousands)

Wildlife		*Africa*	*Asia*	*Europe*	*North & Central America*	*South America*	*World*
Mammals							
Live primates	I	–	7	15	17	–	42
	E	7.8	22	3	5	3.8	43
Cat skins	I	6.7	7	116	43	1.0	175
	E	7.7	60	15	87	3.4	179
Raw ivory *(kg)*	I	14.2	505	133	26	0.1	679
	E	303.7	280	134	2	–	720
Birds							
Live parrots	I	13.2	67	196	322	6.2	606
	E	160.3	89	55	36	265.3	607
Reptiles							
Reptile skins	I	3.4	2,480	3,908	2,436	80.7	8,910
	E	359.7	4,198	1,539	930	1,900.3	8,953

I = imports
E = exports
Source: World Resources Institute

the loss and damage caused by agricultural change. The first areas to be designated ESAs are in the Pennine Dales, the North Peak District, the Norfolk Broads, the Breckland, the Suffolk River Valleys, the Test Valley, the South Downs, the Somerset Levels and Moors, West Penwith, Cornwall, the Shropshire Borders, the Cambrian Mountains, and the Lleyn Peninsula.

In these ESAs, farmers are encouraged to use traditional methods to preserve the value of the land as a wildlife habitat. A farmer who joins the scheme agrees to manage the land in this way for at least five years. In return for this agreement, the Ministry of Agriculture pays the farmer a sum that reflects the financial losses incurred as a result of reconciling conservation with commercial farming. Further ESAs were in 1993 under threat from budget cuts.

Environmental Protection Agency (EPA) US agency set up 1970 to control water and air quality, industrial and commercial wastes, pesticides, noise, and radiation. In its own words, it aims to protect 'the country from being degraded, and its health threatened, by a multitude of human activities initiated without regard to long-ranging effects upon the life-supporting properties, the economic uses, and the recreational value of air, land, and water'.

Friends of the Earth (FoE or FOE) environmental pressure group, established in the UK 1971, that aims to protect the environment and to promote rational and sustainable use of the Earth's resources. It campaigns on issues such as acid rain; air, sea, river, and land pollution; recycling; disposal of toxic wastes; nuclear power and renewable energy; the destruction of rainforests; pesticides; and agriculture. FoE has branches in 30 countries.

Green Party political party aiming to 'preserve the planet and its people', based on the premise that incessant economic growth is unsustainable. The leaderless party structure reflects a general commitment to decentralization. Green parties sprang up in W Europe in the 1970s and in E Europe from 1988. Parties in different countries are linked to one another but unaffiliated with any pressure group.

Greenpeace international environmental pressure group, founded 1971, with a policy of nonviolent direct action backed by scientific research. During a protest against French atmospheric nuclear testing in the S Pacific 1985, its ship *Rainbow Warrior* was sunk by French intelligence agents, killing a crew member.

Henry Doubleday Research Association British gardening group founded 1954 to investigate organic growing techniques. It runs the ***National Centre for Organic Gardening***, a 1-hectare/22-acre demonstration site, at Ryton-on-Dunsmore near Coventry, England. The association is named after the person who first imported Russian comfrey, a popular green-manuring crop.

International Union for Conservation of Nature (IUCN) organization established by the United Nations to promote the conservation of wildlife and habitats as part of the national policies of member states. It has formulated guidelines and established research programmes (for example, the

Whaling in the news again

The 30-year debate about the commercial killing of whales, a group of intelligent marine mammals, has flared up again, after Norway announced that it intends to resume killing minke whales, *Balaenoptera acutorostrata*, for meat.

The commercial killing of whales, for meat, blubber, whalebone (baleen filters used by many whales who feed on plankton), sperm-whale oil, and so on, has devastated many populations. For example, the blue whale *Balaenoptera musculus* is the largest animal ever to have lived on Earth, measuring up to 30 m/100 ft and weighing the equivalent of 30 elephants or 1,600 people. A favourite of whaling fleets, the blue whale was reduced from a world population of some 250,000 to under 3,000, about 1% of the population, before it was protected in 1967.

Whale hunting is controlled by the International Whaling Commission (IWC), formed 1946 and now with delegates from 38 countries. In 1982, in reponse to evidence about decline in whale populations and concern about the suffering of whales during the hunt, the IWC voted to ban commercial whaling indefinitely from 1986. (Some 'subsistence' whaling continues, by ethnic groups traditionally dependent on it, such as Alaskan Inuit, Siberian Aleut, Faroese, and Greenlanders.)

However, at the IWC meeting in 1993, Japan and Norway lobbied to resume hunting minke whales, one of the smaller species of great whale, citing evidence that populations had recovered in numbers. (Iceland had already resigned from the IWC in protest against the continued moratorium in 1991.) Arguments in favour of whaling ranged from the need for remote fishing communities to find employment, to claims that minke whales were reducing stocks of cod, and even suggestions that increases in the number of minke whales were blocking recovery of larger whales.

In the event, the IWC voted to maintain the moratorium, after sustained lobbying by environmental groups. However, Norway has decided to flout the ban, which has no legal standing outside the agreement between members of the IWC. This not only opens up commercial whaling again, but also throws the whole future of the IWC in doubt.

Meanwhile, the main economic benefits from whales today come from those living peacefully. In 1991, some 4 million people paid to watch whales in places where they pass close to shore during their migrations.

International Biological Programme) and set up advisory bodies (such as Survival Commissions). In 1980, it launched the ***World Conservation Strategy*** to highlight particular problems, designating a small number of areas ***World Heritage Sites*** to ensure their survival as unspoiled habitats (for example, Yosemite National Park in the USA, and the Simen Mountains in Ethiopia).

Montréal Protocol international agreement, signed 1987 and reviewed 1992, to stop the production of ozone-depleting chemicals by the year 2000. A controversial amendment concerns a fund established to pay for the transfer of ozone-safe technology to poor countries.

National Rivers Authority (NRA) UK government agency launched 1989. It is responsible for managing water resources, investigating and regulating pollution, and taking over flood controls and land drainage from the former ten regional water authorities of England and Wales.

National Trust British trust founded 1895 for the preservation of land and buildings of historic interest or beauty, incorporated by act of Parliament 1907. It is the largest private landowner in Britain. The National Trust for Scotland was established 1931.

Natural Environment Research Council (NERC) UK organization established by royal charter 1965 to undertake and support research in the earth sciences, to give advice both on exploiting natural resources and on protecting the environment, and to support education and training of scientists in these fields of study. Research areas include geothermal energy, industrial pollution, waste disposal, satellite surveying, acid rain, biotechnology, atmospheric circulation, and climate. Research is carried out principally within the UK but also in Antarctica and in many Third World countries. It comprises 13 research bodies.

Nature Conservancy Council (NCC) former name of UK government agency divided 1991 into English Nature, Scottish Natural Heritage, and the Countryside Council for Wales.

Scottish Natural Heritage Scottish nature conservation body formed 1991 after the break up of the national Nature Conservancy Council. It is government-funded.

Single European Act 1986 update of the Treaty of Rome (signed in 1957) that provides a legal basis for action by the European Community in matters relating to the environment. The act requires that environmental protection shall be a part of all other Community policies. Also, it allows for agreement by a qualified majority on some legislation, whereas before such decisions had to be unanimous.

site of special scientific interest (SSSI) in the UK, land that has been identified as having animals, plants, or geological features that need to be protected and conserved. From 1991, these sites were designated and administered by English Nature, Scottish Natural Heritage, and the Countryside Council for Wales.

Numbers fluctuate, but there were over 5,000 SSSIs in 1991, covering about 6% of Britain. Although SSSIs enjoy some legal protection, this does not in practice always prevent damage or destruction; during 1989, for example, 44 SSSIs were so badly damaged that they were no longer worth protecting.

Soil Association pioneer British ecological organization founded 1946, which campaigns against pesticides and promotes organic farming. It also sets the Standards for Organic Agriculture; administers and monitors the Symbol Scheme (the Symbol is a quality mark for organically grown food); researches and publishes findings on organic issues; lobbies the government for changes in agriculture; and promotes educational programmes for the general public on organic farming.

World Conservation Monitoring Centre organization established 1983, to support international programmes for conservation and sustainable development through the provision of information on the world's biological diversity. It provides information to the World Wide Fund for Nature, the World Conservation Union (IUCN), and the United Nations Environment Programme (UNEP) (*not* direct to the general public).

World Wide Fund for Nature (WWF, formerly the ***World Wildlife Fund***) international organization established 1961 to raise funds for conservation by public appeal. Projects include conservation of particular species, for example, the tiger and giant panda, and special areas, such as the Simen Mountains, Ethiopia.

GALLUP POLL: Issues

Thinking about Britain as a whole, what is the most important environmental problem facing it? If you feel that there are no serious environmental problems facing Britain, please feel free to say so.

Pollution	15
Air pollution	11
Vehicle exhausts	10
Ozone destruction	8
Water pollution	7
Nuclear waste	6
Ocean pollution	5
Pollution of lakes	5
Solid waste	5
Waste disposal	4
Industrial pollution	4
Global warming	3
Chemical pollution	2
Other	12
None	2
Don't know	15

How much, if at all, do you believe environmental problems..., a great deal, a fair amount, not very much, or not at all...:

	A great deal	A fair amount	Not very much	Not at all	Not sure/ don't know
Now affect your health?	17	37	30	15	2
Affected your health in the past – say 10 years ago?	7	20	42	25	5
Will affect the health of our children and grand-children – say over the next 25 years	47	35	8	3	7

Here is a list of environmental problems facing many communities. How serious do you consider each one to be here in your community - very serious, somewhat serious, not very serious, or not serious at all?

	Very serious	Somewhat serious	Not very serious	Not at all serious	Not sure/ don't know
Poor water quality	23	25	32	18	2
Poor air quality	21	27	31	18	3
Contaminated soil	14	20	24	22	20
Inadequate sewage, sanitation and Rubbish disposal	21	22	27	26	4
Too many people, over-crowding	14	25	30	29	2
Too much noise	17	23	34	25	2

Here is a list of environmental issues that may be affecting the world as a whole. How serious a problem do you personally believe each issue to be in the world - very serious, somewhat serious, not very serious, or not serious at all?

	Very serious	Somewhat serious	Not very serious	Not at all serious	Not sure/ don't know
Air pollution and smog	52	34	8	1	4
Pollution of rivers, lakes and oceans	72	23	3	0	1
Soil erosion, polluted land, and loss of farm-land	50	34	7	1	8
Loss of animals and plant species	60	28	6	0	6
Loss of rain forests and jungles	79	17	1	0	4
Global warming or the 'greenhouse' effect	62	25	4	1	8
Loss of ozone in the earth's atmosphere	65	22	3	1	8

Causes

Here is a list of possible causes of Britain's environmental problems. How much do you think it contributes to the environmental problem here in Britain – a great deal, a fair amount, not very much, or not at all?

	A great deal	A fair amount	Not very much	Not at all	Not sure/ don't know
Overpopulation – there are too many people using up resources	25	39	27	7	2
Our government – it does not place enough emphasis on protecting the environment	37	43	13	4	3
Waste – individuals use more resources than they need and throw away too much	60	32	4	1	2
Lack of education – people just don't know what to do to protect the environment	39	44	11	4	3
Business and industry – they care more about growth than protecting the environment	65	27	5	1	3
Technology – they way products are made uses too many resources and creates too much pollution	53	34	8	1	4

FOOD AND AGRICULTURE

Food and Drink

beer alcoholic drink made from water and malt (fermented barley or other grain), flavoured with hops. Beer contains between 1% and 6% alcohol. The medieval distinction between beer (containing hops) and ***ale*** (without hops) has now fallen into disuse and beer has come to be used strictly as a generic term including ale, stout, and lager. ***Stout*** is top fermented, but is sweet and strongly flavoured with roasted grain; ***lager*** is a light beer, bottom fermented and matured over a longer period.

biscuit small, flat, brittle cake of baked dough. The basic components of biscuit dough are weak flour and fat; other ingredients, such as eggs, sugar, chocolate, and spices, may be added to vary the flavour and texture. Originally made from slices of unleavened bread baked until hard and dry, biscuits could be stored for several years, and were a useful, though dull, source of carbohydrate on long sea voyages and military campaigns. The first biscuit factory opened in Carlisle, N England, 1815 and the UK is now Europe's largest producer and consumer of factory-made biscuits.

bread food baked from a kneaded dough or batter made with ground cereals, usually wheat, and water; many other ingredients may be added. The dough may be unleavened or raised (usually with yeast).

Leavened bread was first made in the ancient Middle East and Egypt in brick ovens similar to ceramic kilns. The yeast creates gas, making the dough rise. Traditionally bread has been made from whole grains: wheat, barley, rye and oats, ground into a meal which varied in quality. Modern manufacturing processes have changed this to optimize the profit and shorten the manufacturing time. Fermentation is speeded up using ascorbic acid and potassium bromide with fast-acting flour improvers. White bread was developed by the end of the 19th century by roller-milling, which removed the wheat germ to satisfy fashionable consumer demand, but lacking in important fibre and nutrient content. Today, some of the nutrients, such as vitamins, are removed in the processing of bread are synthetically replaced.

bulghur wheat or ***bulgar*** or ***burghul*** cracked wholewheat, made by cooking the grains, then drying and cracking them. It is widely eaten in the Middle East. Coarser bulghur may be cooked in the same way as rice; more finely ground bulghur is mixed with minced meat to make a paste that may be eaten as a dip with salad, or shaped and stuffed before being grilled or fried.

butter solid, edible yellowish fat made from whole milk. Usually by machine, the cream is churned, the buttermilk drawn off, and the butter washed, salted, and worked, to achieve an even consistency. Colour and flavouring may be added. British butter typically contains 1,300 micrograms vitamin A per 100g in summer and 500 micrograms per 100g in winter; it contains about 82% fat, 0.4% protein, and up to 16% water.

cake baked food item made from a mixture of weak flour, sugar, eggs, and fat (usually butter or margarine). Other ingredients, such as dried fruits, can be added, and pastry is sometimes used as a base. Cakes may be eaten to celebrate special occasions. The UK is Europe's biggest producer of factory-made cakes.

cereal, breakfast food prepared from the seeds of cereal crops. Some cereals require cooking (porridge oats), but most are ready to eat. Mass-marketed cereals include refined and sweetened varieties as well as whole cereals such as muesli. Whole cereals are more nutritious and provide more fibre than the refined cereals, which often have vitamins and flavourings added to replace those lost in the refining process.

cheese food made from the ***curds*** (solids) of soured milk from cows, sheep, or goats, separated from the ***whey*** (liquid), then salted, put into moulds, and pressed into firm blocks. Cheese is ripened with bacteria or surface fungi, and kept for a time to mature before eating.

There are six main types of cheese. ***Soft cheeses*** may be ripe or unripe, and include cottage cheese and high-fat soft cheeses such as Bel Paese, Camembert, and Neufchatel. ***Semi-hard cheeses*** are ripened by bacteria (Munster) or by bacteria and surface fungi (Port Salut, Gouda, St Paulin); they may also have penicillin moulds injected into them (Roquefort, Gorgonzola, blue Stilton, Wensleydale). ***Hard cheeses*** are ripened by bacteria, and include Cheddar, Cheshire, and Cucciocavallo; some have large cavities within them, such as Swiss Emmental and Gruyère. ***Very hard cheeses***, such as Parmesan and Spalen, are made with skimmed milk. ***Processed cheese*** is made with dried skim-milk powder and additives, and ***whey cheese*** is made by heat coagulation of the proteins from whey; examples are Mysost and Primost.

cider fermented drink made from the juice of the apple; in the USA, the term usually refers to unfermented (nonalcoholic) apple juice. Cider has been

Composition of cheeses

Cheese	*Fat (%)*	*Protein (%)*	*Calcium (mg)*	*Salt (mg)*	*Calories (per 100 g)*
Cheddar	32.2	25	750	700	398
Roquefort	31.5	21.5	315	–	368
Camembert	min 26	17.5	105	–	299
Emmental	28	27.5	925	710	370
processed	28	25	850	1,1150	360
cottage	0.3	17	90	290	86

made for more than 2,000 years, and for many centuries has been a popular drink in France and England, which are now its main centres of production.

cocoa and chocolate food products made from the cacao (or cocoa) bean, fruit of a tropical tree *Theobroma cacao*, now cultivated mainly in Africa. Chocolate as a drink was introduced to Europe from the New World by the Spanish in the 16th century; eating chocolate was first produced in the late 18th century.

Preparation takes place in the importing country and consists chiefly of roasting, winnowing, and grinding the nib (the edible portion of the bean). If ***cocoa*** for drinking is required, a proportion of the cocoa butter is removed by hydraulic pressure and the remaining cocoa is reduced by further grinding and sieving to a fine powder. ***Plain chocolate*** is made by removing some of the cocoa butter and adding a little sugar. It is dark and has a slightly bitter flavour. ***Milk chocolate*** a sweeter variety, made by adding condensed or powdered milk and a larger amount of sugar. In the UK, cheaper vegetable fats are widely substituted for milk, and chocolate need contain only 20% cocoa solids. ***White chocolate*** contains cocoa butter but no cocoa solids, and is flavoured with sugar and vanilla.

coffee drink made from the roasted and ground beanlike seeds found inside the red berries of any of several species of shrubs of the genus *Coffea*. It contains a stimulant, caffeine. Coffee drinking began in Arab regions in the 14th century but did not become common in Europe until 300 years later, when the first coffee houses were opened in Vienna, and soon after in Paris and London. The world's largest producers are Brazil, Colombia, and Côte d'Ivoire.

The flavour of coffee beans depends on the variety grown, the location of the plantation, and the manner in which the beans were processed; for example, Arabica beans, grown at high altitudes, are considered finer than the cheaper Robusta and Liberian varieties. Manufacturers, therefore, blend beans from a number of sources in order to achieve a consistent product.

cream the part of milk that has the highest fat content; it can be separated by centrifugation or gravity (if milk is left to stand, the upper layer will be cream, the lower layer skimmed milk). To whip cream, that is, process it to trap air bubbles, it must contain at least 30% fat. ***Clotted cream*** is made from heating double cream over a bain marie, or by floating milk and skimming off the clotted upper layer. It should contain 55% fat and 4% protein.

drink, soft drink that provides water and often sugar, in a flavoured form. Soft drinks include all kinds of carbonated drinks, such as variously flavoured colas and sodas, ginger ale, and soda water. Many fruit-flavoured drinks contain no fruit but consist of water, sugar or artificial sweetener, and synthetic flavourings.

egg the shell-covered egg of a domestic chicken, duck, or goose, or of a game bird such as quail. It is a highly nutritious food: the albumin, or egg white, of a chicken's egg is 10% protein; the yolk is 33% fat and 15% protein, and contains vitamins A, B, and D. The yolk also contains cholesterol, a fatty substance associated with heart disease.

Eggs have many uses in cooking. They can be used for thickening sauces, binding and coating crumbly foods, and raising batters and cakes; whisked egg white gives a foamy texture to soufflés and desserts; and yolk acts as an emulsifier, keeping oil in suspension in mixtures such as mayonnaise.

fibre, dietary or ***roughage*** plant material that cannot be digested by human digestive enzymes; it consists largely of cellulose, a carbohydrate found in plant cell walls. Fibre adds bulk to the gut contents, assisting the muscular contractions that force food along the intestine. A diet low in fibre causes constipation and is believed to increase the risk of developing diverticulitis, diabetes, gall-bladder disease, and cancer of the large bowel – conditions that are rare in countries where the diet contains a high proportion of unrefined cereals.

Soluble fibre consists of indigestible plant carbohydrates (such as pectins, hemicelluloses, and gums) that dissolve in water. A high proportion of the fibre in such foods as oat bran, pulses, and vegetables is of this sort.

fish flesh or roe of freshwater or saltwater fish. The nutrient composition of fish is similar to that of meat, except that there are no obvious deposits of fat. Examples of fish comparatively high in fat are salmon, mackerel, and herring. White fish such as cod, haddock, and whiting contain only 0.4–4% fat. Fish are good sources of B vitamins and iodine, and the fatty fish livers are good sources of A and D vitamins. Calcium can be obtained from fish with soft skeletons, such as sardines. Roe and caviar have a high protein content (20–25%).

Spending on food and drink

Expenditure in US$ per capita, Europe, 1991

EC members	*Food*	*Alcoholic drinks*
Belgium	2,022	344
Denmark	1,982	384
France	1,909	235
West Germany	2,128	339
East Germany	2,190	946
Greece	1,329	64
Ireland	1,429	798
Italy	2,293	139
Luxembourg	1,872	192
Netherlands	1,662	125
Portugal	1,412	61
Spain	1,443	106
UK	1,254	726
EC average	***1,825***	***335***
EFTA members		
Austria	2,072	245
Finland	2,328	427
Iceland	4,486	375
Liechtenstein	1,946	998
Norway	2,302	424
Sweden	2,162	417
EFTA total	***2,545***	***482***

Source: European Marketing Data and Statistics 1993, Euromonitor

Fat or fit?

In the last few decades, it has become accepted wisdom that diet plays a key role in health. Furthermore, it is generally understood that some foods, in particular fats, sugars, and salt, are bad if eaten in excess. This has, in turn, created a vast 'health food' market, both through speciality shops and as particular lines in almost all retailers. Now, some of the theories behind healthy eating are coming under attack.

Diseases of Western civilization

Links between diet and health were identified by a few pioneer nutritionists in the first half of the 20th century. Sir Robert McCarrison carried out a series of comparisons on populations in different parts of India and found marked contrasts in average life span, which he ascribed to different diets. Studies of people with a very different diet from that of Western society, such as the Inuit (Eskimo) people of the far north, some African tribespeople, farmers in the Himalayas, and the Japanese, found that these groups were virtually free of many of the major killer diseases of Europe and North America, including heart disease and cancer. The theory of 'diseases of Western civilization' was developed. This suggested that some factor or factors in our way of life made us particularly susceptible to a range of serious health problems that were virtually unknown in the past.

For the last few decades, much medical research has been concentrated on identifying these links. Perhaps even more importantly, their relative importance, and the interactions between various factors, have to be distinguished.

This is not as easy as it sounds. Identifying precisely why any particular person becomes ill or dies of heart disease or cancer is impossible, and research depends on complicated statistical analysis, looking at all possible factors affecting a large population and tracking down causes by a process of elimination. For example, it took years to establish links between smoking and lung cancer, and the tobacco companies continue to dispute the connection today. Yet in 1993, Sir Richard Doll, one of the main researchers on this issue, announced that his long-term study now suggested that one in two regular cigarette smokers would die ahead of time as a result of smoking.

Identifying the food connection

Links between food and health are even more difficult to pin down. Harmful factors, known or suspected, include many additives, including colourings and preservatives, agrochemical residues, microbial contaminants, natural toxins in food, and the type of food itself.

The cholesterol controversy

Over the past few years, the role of different foodstuffs in creating diseases of Western civilization have become the focus of controversy. In particular, links between cholesterol and heart disease have become increasingly well publicized. Cholesterol is a fatty substance that is important to the functioning of the body and is made in the liver. It is also provided in the diet by dairy products and meat. However, high levels in the blood are thought to contribute to hardening of the arteries, leading to heart attacks. People who are overweight often, but by no means always, have higher levels of cholesterol than thin people. Saturated fatty acids are particularly high in cholesterol.

Since heart disease is one of the major killers in Western society, reduction of cholesterol has become a preoccupation of many people. To date, advice about this has concentrated on reducing consumption of fatty meat and dairy products, with substitution of more vegetables, margarine made with polyunsaturated fats, and so on.

However, as so often in questions of diet, the case is more complicated than it seems at first. Research into links between cholesterol levels and heart disease is ambiguous, as is evidence that lowering cholesterol helps prevent heart disease. It now appears that the precise chemical form of cholesterol is important, and perhaps also the way that it reaches the body. Some people believe that diet is all-important, others that cholesterol formed as a result of stress is more significant. Some of the alternatives to a high-cholesterol diet are turning out to have problems of their own; for example, partially hydrogenated vegetable oils made from soya beans and maize are now thought to be possibly linked to development of heart disease themselves.

There is now a reaction, with people talking about the 'great cholesterol myth'. Such disdain is probably premature. There are clearly links between Western diet and both cancer and heart disease, and a range of established health problems linked with being overweight that are at least partially caused by too many fatty foods and sugars. There is also now good evidence that increasing consumption of vegetables can help prevent such problems, as can regular exercise, relaxation, and a reduction in stress. Although we may well see some modification of ideas about diet and health over the next few years, and fad solutions are unlikely to be of much use, the general principles of increasing fresh food, roughage, and vegetables, and reducing rich foods, remains a good basis for a healthy diet.

ND

flour foodstuff made by grinding starchy vegetable materials, usually cereal grains, into a fine powder. Flour may also be made from root vegetables such as potato and cassava, and from pulses such as soya beans and chick peas. The most commonly used cereal flour is wheat flour.

The properties of wheat flour depend on the strain of wheat used. Bread requires strong ('hard') flour, with a high gluten content. ***Durum flour*** also has a high gluten content, and is used for pasta. Cakes and biscuits are made from weak ('soft') flour, containing less gluten. ***Granary flour*** contains malted flakes of wheat. Wheat flour may contain varying proportions of bran (husk) and wheatgerm (embryo), ranging from 100% ***wholemeal flour*** to refined white flour, which has less than 75% of the whole grain. Much of the flour available now is bleached to whiten it; bleaching also destroys some of its vitamin content, so synthetic vitamins are added instead.

fruit in ordinary usage, any sweet, fleshy plant item, such as an orange, strawberry, or rhubarb stalk. When eaten they provide vitamins, minerals, and enzymes, but little protein.

Fruits are divided into three agricultural categories on the basis of the climate in which they grow. ***Temperate fruits*** require a cold season for satisfactory growth; the principal temperate fruits are apples, pears, plums, peaches, apricots, cherries, and soft fruits, such as strawberries. ***Subtropical fruits*** require warm conditions but can survive light frosts; they include oranges and other citrus fruits, dates, pomegranates, and avocados. ***Tropical fruits*** cannot tolerate temperatures that drop close to freezing point; they include bananas, mangoes, pineapples, papayas, and litchis.

fruit juice juice extracted from fruits, either by pressing (citrus fruits) or by spinning at high speed in a centrifuge (other fruits). Although fruit juice provides no fibre, its nutritional value is close to that of the whole fruit. Most fruit juices are transported in concentrated form, and are diluted and pasteurized before being packaged. Concentrated juices may be used as sweeteners in cooking.

herb any plant (usually a flowering plant) tasting sweet, bitter, aromatic, or pungent, used in cooking, medicine, or perfumery. Most herbs are temperate plants; they include bay, thyme, borage, mint, chives, and tarragon. Their leaves and stems release aromatic oils on being crushed, chopped, or heated, and may be used fresh, dried, or freeze-dried.

honey sweet syrup produced by honey bees from the nectar of flowers. It is stored in honeycombs and made in excess of their needs as food for the winter. Honey comprises various sugars, mainly laevulose and dextrose, with enzymes, colouring matter, acids, and pollen grains. It has antibacterial properties and was widely used in ancient Egypt, Greece, and Rome as a wound salve. It is still popular for sore throats, in hot drinks or in lozenges.

ice cream rich, creamy, frozen confectionery, made commercially from the early 20th century from various milk products, sugar, and fruit and nut flavourings, usually with additives to improve keeping qualities and ease of serving.

In the UK, the sale of ice cream made with 'non-milk' animal or vegetable fat, and with chemical additives to give colour and flavour, is permitted. Water ices and sorbets are frozen fruit juices and do not contain milk or cream. ***Sherbet*** is a frozen dessert of watered fruit juice, egg white, and sugar, like an ice, but with gelatin and milk added.

lard clarified edible pig fat. It is used in cooking and in the manufacture of margarine, soaps, and ointments. It can be heated to very high temperatures without burning.

liqueur alcoholic liquor made by infusing flavouring substances (fruits, herbs, spices) in alcohol. Specific recipes are closely guarded commercial secrets. Originally liqueurs were used as medicines and are still thought of as digestives.

macrobiotics dietary system of organically grown wholefoods. It originates in Zen Buddhism, and attempts to balance the principles of yin and yang, thought to be present in foods in different proportions.

margarine butter substitute made from animal fats and/or vegetable oils. French chemist Hippolyte Mège-Mouries invented margarine 1889. Today, margarines are usually made with vegetable oils, such as soy, corn (maize), or sunflower oil, giving a product low in saturated fats and fortified with vitamins A and D.

meat flesh of animals taken as food, in Western countries chiefly the muscle tissue of domestic cattle (beef and veal), sheep (lamb and mutton), pigs (pork), and poultry. The practice of cooking meat is at least 600,000 years old.

Beef, lamb, and mutton are termed ***red meats***; poultry, pork, and veal are termed ***white meats***. Meat has a high protein content and is a good source of B vitamins and iron; its fat tends to have a high proportion of saturated fatty acids. ***Game*** is meat obtained from wild animals and birds, such as deer, hare, grouse, pheasant, and wild duck. It has a stronger flavour than that of farm-reared animals, and is thought to be less easy to digest. Before being cooked, therefore, it is stored suspended ('hung') in a cool place to make it more tender, generally for two to eight days. ***Offal*** comprises the edible internal organs of an animal, and also its head, feet, tail, tongue, and bone marrow. It is generally cheaper than muscle tissue.

Meat is wasteful in production (the same area of grazing land would produce far greater food value in cereal crops). The main exporters are Argentina, Australia, New Zealand, Canada, the USA, and Denmark (chiefly bacon). The consumption of meat in 1989 was 111 kg/244 lb per person in the USA, 68 kg/150 lb in the UK, 30 kg/66 lb in Japan, 6 kg/13 lb in Nigeria, and 1 kg/2.2 lb in India. Research suggests that, in a healthy diet, consumption of meat (especially with a high fat content) should not exceed the Japanese level.

milk secretion of the mammary glands of female mammals, with which they suckle their young. Over 85% is water, the remainder comprising protein, fat, lactose (a sugar), calcium, phosphorus, iron, and vitamins. The milk of cows, goats, and sheep is often consumed by humans, but regular drinking of milk after infancy is principally a Western practice; for people in most of the world, milk causes flatulence and diarrhoea.

Milk composition varies among species, depending on the nutritional requirements of the young; human milk contains less protein and more lactose than that of cows. ***Skimmed milk*** is what remains when the cream has been separated from milk. It is readily dried and is available in large quantities at low prices, so it is often sent as food aid to Third World countries. ***Evaporated milk*** is milk reduced by heat until it reaches about half its volume. ***Condensed milk*** is concentrated to about a third of its original volume with added sugar.

Composition of milks

Source	*Protein (g/100ml)*	*Fat (g/100 ml)*	*Carbohydrate (g/100ml)*	*Energy Kcal/100ml*
cow	3.5	3.5	5.0	65
buffalo	4.3	7.5	4.5	105
camel	3.7	4.2	4.0	70
ewe	6.5	7.0	5.0	110
goat	3.7	5.0	4.5	75
mare	1.3	1.2	5.5	30
reindeer	10.5	22.5	2.5	250
human	1.1	6.2	7.5	70

mineral water water with mineral constituents gathered from the rocks with which it comes in contact, and classified by these into earthy, brine, and oil mineral waters; also water with artificially added minerals and, sometimes, carbon dioxide.

The most widely sold mineral water is Perrier, from the French village of Vergèze in W Provence. It is naturally carbonated, but the gas is removed at source and then used to recarbonate the water during bottling. Evian water comes from Haute-Savoie *département*, France, and Malvern water from Hereford and Worcester, England. Some mineral waters contain relatively high bacterial contaminants.

mushroom fruiting body of certain fungi, consisting of an upright stem and a spore-producing cap with radiating gills on the undersurface. Many species are inedible or even poisonous. Cultivated edible mushrooms are usually species of the genus *Agaricus*. Edible wild, or field, mushrooms include the cep *Boletus edulis*, the chanterelle *Cantharellus cibarius*, and the horn of plenty *Cratellus cornicupoides*, all woodland species; and the horse mushroom *Agaricus arvensis* and shaggy ink cap *Corpinus comatus*, found in grassland. The most prized mushrooms are truffles (various species of *Tuber*), which fruit underground, and morels (species of *Morchella*).

mustard strong-tasting condiment made from the whole, crushed, or ground seeds of the black, brown, or white mustard plants. Table mustard is most often used as an accompaniment to meat, although it can also be used in sauces and dressings, and with fish.

English mustard is made from finely milled brown and white mustard seed to which turmeric is added as a colorant. French ***Dijon mustard*** contains brown mustard seed, verjuice (the juice of unripe grapes), oil, and white wine. Other varieties are made with vinegar, and may be flavoured with herbs or garlic.

nut commonly, any edible seed or fruit with a woody shell, such as a coconut, almond, walnut, peanut (groundnut), Brazil nut, or hazelnut. The edible parts

GATT, food safety, and the environment

Delays in agreeing the current round of the General Agreement on Tariffs and Trade (GATT) have dominated the financial media for over a year. Attention has focused on disagreements between the European Community and the USA over the future of the EC's Common Agricultural Policy. Perhaps even more important, however, is the impact that GATT regulations may have on food health and safety.

In order to encourage a 'free' global market, GATT negotiators are attempting to eliminate protectionism by individual countries, such as trade barriers and state subsidies. However, GATT does not appear to distinguish very clearly between financial protectionism and restrictions introduced for social and environmental reasons.

Over the past few decades, consumer organizations have fought to improve national food standards with respect to pesticide residues, nutritional information, food contamination, and so on. Under GATT proposals, standards will be harmonized through the Codex Alimentarius Committee of the United Nations. Codex will, for example, decide which pesticides are safe to use on food, and it will become illegal for countries to ban pesticides approved by Codex. Yet Codex Committees are dominated by industry; in 1989–91, 81% of nongovernmental organizations on Codex represented industry while only 1% represented public-interest groups. If the GATT agreements go ahead, some pesticides now banned for health and environmental reasons in countries such as the UK, Germany, and the USA are almost certain to be reintroduced.

GATT negotiations have other implications for food quality. Many tuna fish are caught in nets that annually kill huge numbers of dolphins through accidentally catching and drowning them. In response to consumer pressure, many retailers are stocking tuna from sources caught in ways that do not endanger dolphins. In 1992, there was an international outcry when it was suggested that it would be illegal to sell tuna labelled as 'dolphin-safe' under the terms of GATT, because this would be a barrier to trade. Although this restriction has now apparently been relaxed, it suggests that many of the green labelling initiatives are likely to come under attack from those sections of industry that cannot match up to consumer demands for healthy food which does not damage the environment. From being a formerly obscure UN body, GATT could become the focus of much debate about food safety over the next few years.

of most nuts provide a concentrated, nutritious food, containing vitamins, minerals, and enzymes, about 50% fat, and 10–20% protein, although a few, such as chestnuts, are high in carbohydrates and have only a moderate protein content of 5%. Nuts also provide edible oils.

Most nuts are produced by perennial trees and shrubs. Whereas the majority of nuts are obtained from plantations, considerable quantities of pecans and brazil nuts are still collected from the wild.

oil, cooking any fat that is liquid at room temperature, extracted from the seeds or fruits of certain plants, and used for frying, salad dressings, and sauces and condiments such as mayonnaise and mustard. Plants used for cooking oil include sunflower, olive, maize (corn), soya, peanut, and rape. Vegetable oil is a blend of more than one type of oil. Most oils are hot-pressed and refined, a process that leaves them without smell or flavour. Cold-pressed, unrefined oils keep their flavour. Oils are generally low in cholesterol and contain a high proportion of polyunsaturated or monounsaturated fatty acids, although all except soya and corn oil become saturated when heated.

pasta food made from a dough of durum-wheat flour or semolina, water, and sometimes egg, and cooked in boiling water. Some types of Far Eastern pasta (noodles) are made from buckwheat. It is usually served with a sauce. Pasta is available either fresh or dried, and comes in a wide variety of shapes. It may be creamy yellow or coloured green with spinach or red with tomato. Pasta has been used in Italian cooking since the Middle Ages, and is now popular in many other countries.

pastry baked dough made from flour, fat, water, and salt. It makes a useful base or container for soft, moist fillings, and is widely used for tarts, pies, quiches, and pasties. Richer pastries may include eggs, yeast, or sugar, or may use ground nuts instead of flour. Types include short pastry, flaky pastry, suet crust, filo, and choux. ***Puff pastry*** is made with a higher proportion of fat. Its preparation involves repeated folding, which, with the fat, makes it flaky.

pepper aromatic spice derived from the berry of the climbing plant *Piper nigrum* native to the E Indies. The dried berries (peppercorns) may be crushed or ground to release their flavour, or may be used whole. Green peppercorns are berries that have been harvested while unripe, and dried or canned; black peppercorns are unripe berries that have been left to darken and shrivel in the sun; and white peppercorns are dried ripe berries that have had their outer husks removed. Black peppercorns are hotter but less aromatic than white peppercorns.

The mild pink peppercorns that became fashionable in the 1980s are the fruits of a different plant, a member of the poison ivy family. Chilli pepper, cayenne or red pepper and the sweet peppers used as a vegetable come from capsicums native to the New World.

potato tuberous root of the perennial plant *Solanum tuberosum*, native to the Andes of South America. One of the most versatile of foods, the potato is cultivated in many varieties, particularly in temperate regions. It is a good source of carbohydrate, fibre, and vitamin C, and also contains some protein, phosphates, and iron.

Potato varieties can be grouped according to when their tubers mature: ***new*** or ***early potatoes*** are gathered in the spring and summer, are generally small and waxy, and are suitable for boiling in their skins and canning; the larger ***maincrop potatoes*** are lifted in the autumn, are more floury in texture, and are suitable for mashing and baking, and for commercial processing into such products as frozen chips, crisps and snacks, and potato flour.

The unrelated ***sweet potato***, native to tropical America, has a sweet orange or yellow flesh and is rich in vitamin A.

pulse dried seed, such as a pea, bean, or lentil, gathered from the pod of a leguminous plant. Pulses provide a concentrated source of vegetable protein, and make a vital contribution to human diets in countries where meat is scarce, and among vegetarians.

Soya beans are the major temperate protein crop in the West; most are used for oil production or for animal feed. In Asia, most are processed into soya milk and bean curd (tofu). ***Miso*** is soya beans fermented with cereal grains, water, and salt, used in soups and sauces; ***soya sauce*** is beans fermented with salt; ***tamari*** is similar to soya sauce but stronger, having been matured for up to two years. ***Peanuts*** (groundnuts), which are not true nuts but pulses grown in underground pods, dominate pulse production in the tropical world. They yield a valuable oil and form the basis for numerous processed foods, such as peanut butter. Canned ***baked beans*** are usually a variety of haricot bean.

rice grain of *Oryza sativa*, principal cereal of the wet regions of the tropics and grown also in the Po valley of Italy and in the USA. Boiled or ground into flour, it forms the staple food of one-third of the world's population. It is rich in carbohydrate and contains 8–9% protein. Brown, or unhusked, rice has valuable B-vitamins that are lost in husking or polishing. Most of the the rice eaten in the world is, however, sold in polished form.

salt, common or ***sodium chloride*** NaCl white crystalline solid, found dissolved in sea water and as rock salt (halite) in large deposits and salt domes. Common salt is used extensively in the food industry as a preservative and for flavouring. While common salt is an essential part of our diet, some medical experts believe that excess salt can lead to high blood pressure and increased risk of heart attacks.

sauce food preparation that usually is liquid or soft, taken as a relish. Sauces may be thick or thin, hot or cold, sweet or savoury. There are sauces suitable for serving with almost any dish, ranging from the simplest vinaigrette – a cold mixture of oil, vinegar, and seasonings – to cooked sauces containing cream, wine, egg yolks, or herbs. Nutritionally sauces add little to the diet unless used in large quantities. Sugar is a major ingredient in chutney, french dressing, and tomato ketchup.

shellfish any mollusc or crustacean. Many species are eaten, including the whelk, mussel, oyster, lobster, crab, and shrimp. Shellfish are high in protein and minerals. They do not keep well, and should only be used if known to be fresh. They become tough if overcooked; some are eaten raw.

spice any aromatic vegetable substance used as a condiment and for flavouring food. Spices are mostly obtained from tropical plants, and include pepper, nutmeg, ginger, and cinnamon. They have little food value but increase the appetite and may facilitate digestion.

spirit strong alcoholic liquor, distilled from the fruit, seeds, roots, or stems of certain plants. Fruit-based spirits include Calvados (apples) and brandy (grapes); grain-based spirits include whisky (malted barley, with other grains sometimes added), gin (barley, maize, or rye), sake (rice); others include rum (sugar cane) and tequila (agave). Spirits are usually matured for several years before use; they may be drunk on their own, diluted, or iced. Sake, from Japan, is usually heated before serving.

stock liquid used as a base for soups, stews, or sauces. ***White stock*** is made from poultry or veal, and vegetables boiled together in water. ***Brown stock*** is made from red meat or bones, and vegetables, browned in fat before being boiled in water.

sugar or ***sucrose*** sweet, soluble crystalline carbohydrate, such as sucrose, glucose, fructose, maltose, and lactose. Sugar is easily digested and forms a major source of energy in humans, being used in cooking and in the food industry as a sweetener and, in high concentrations, as a preservative. A high consumption is associated with obesity and tooth decay. In the UK, sucrose may not be used in baby foods.

The main sources of sucrose sugar are tropical sugar cane *Saccharum officinarum*, which accounts for two-thirds of production, and temperate sugar beet *Beta vulgaris*. Minor quantities are produced from the sap of maple trees, and from sorghum and date palms. Raw sugar crystals obtained by heating the juice of sugar canes are processed to form brown sugars, such as Muscovado and Demerara, or refined and sifted to produce white sugars, such as granulated, caster, and icing. The syrup that is drained away from the raw sugar is molasses; it may be processed to form golden syrup or treace, or fermented to form rum. Molasses obtained from sugar beet juice is too bitter for human consumption.

sweetener any chemical that gives sweetness to food. Caloric sweeteners are various forms of sugar; noncaloric, or artificial, sweeteners are used by dieters and diabetics and provide neither energy nor bulk. Sweeteners are used to make highly processed foods attractive, whether sweet or savoury. Most of the noncaloric sweeteners do not have E numbers. Questions have been raised about the long-term health effects of several artificial sweeteners. Some are banned for baby foods and for young children: thaumatin, aspartame, acesulfame-K, sorbitol, and mannitol. Cyclamate is banned in the UK and the USA; acesulfame-K is banned in the USA.

sweets confectionery made mainly from sucrose sugar. Other ingredients include glucose, milk, nuts, fat (animal and vegetable), and fruit. Boiled-sugar

Main types of vitamins

Vitamin/chemical name	*Source*	*Established benefit*	*Deficiency symptoms*
A retinol (carotene)/ beta (converts to A in the body)	Liver, egg yolks, whole milk, butter, dark green vegetables, yellow and orange vegetables, and yellow/red fruits	prevents night blindness and xerophthalmia (a common cause of blindness among children in developing countries); helps keep the skin and mucous membranes resistant to infection	night blindness; rough skin impaired bone growth
B_1 thiamin	germ and bran of seeds, grains; yeast	prevents beri-beri; essential to carbohydrate metabolism and health of nervous system	beri-beri, Korsakov's syndrome
B_2 riboflavin	liver, milk, meat, poultry, broccoli, mushrooms	protects skin, mouth, eyes, eyelids, mucous membranes	skin disorders; failure to thrive
B_6 pyridoxine/ pantothenic acid/biotin	meat, poultry, fish, fruits, nuts, whole grains, leafy vegetables, yeast extract	helps prevent anaemia, skin lesions, nerve damage; important in the regulation of the central nervous system and in protein metabolism	dermatitis; neurological disorders
B_{12} cyanocobalamin	liver, meat, fish, eggs, dairy products, soybeans	needed to form red blood cells; helps prevent pernicious anaemia	anaemia, neurological disturbance
folic acid	green leafy vegetables, liver, peanuts; cooking and processing can cause serious losses in food	helps protect against cervical dysplasia (precancerous changes in the cells of the uterine cervix)	anaemia
C ascorbic acid	citrus fruit, green peppers, blackcurrants, strawberries, other fruits, fresh leafy vegetables, potatoes; losses occur during storage and cooking	prevents scurvy, loose teeth; fights haemorrhage; maintains collagen, a protein necessary for the formation of skin, ligaments, and bones; helps heal wounds and mend fractures, and aids in resisting some types of virus and bacterial infections	scurvy
D cholecalciferol	liver, butter, fatty fish, egg yolks, fortified milk; also produced when skin is exposed to sunlight	important for bone development; prevents rickets	rickets; osteomalacia (bone malformation)
E tocopherols	nuts, seeds, whole grains, vegetable and fish-liver oils	helps prevent retrolental fibroplasia (an eye disorder in premature infants), anaemia; helps protect red blood cells	multiple diseases produced in laboratory animals; humans, multiple symptoms follow impaired fat absorption
K phytomenadione	leafy vegetables, corn and soybean oils, liver, meat, cereals, dairy products, fruits	helps prevent haemorrhage (necessary for the formation of prothrombin, which helps blood to clot)	haemorrhagic problems
niacin	grains, meat, nuts, offal, fish	maintains the health of skin, tongue, and digestive system	pellagra

Main trace minerals

Trace minerals	*Source*	*Deficiency symptoms*
Calcium	milk and dairy products, blackstrap molasses, sardines, citrus fruits, leafy vegetables	rickets in children; osteoporosis in adults
Chromium	liver, wholemeal bread, black pepper, beer, brewer's yeast	adult-onset diabetes
Copper	green vegetables, liver, fish, oysters	anaemia; Menkes' syndrome
Fluorine	tea, seafood, fluoridated drinking water	tooth decay; possibly osteoporosis
Iodine	iodized salt, table salt, seafood, salt-water fish, seaweed	cretinism in new-born children; goitre
Iron	offal, beans, green leafy vegetables, shell-fish, egg yolk, potatoes, molasses, dried fruit	anaemia
Magnesium	nuts, whole grains, green leafy vegetables (eaten raw)	muscular weakness; insomnia; irregular heart beat
Manganese	green leafy vegetables, legumes, cereal grains, tea	not known in humans
Molybolenum	cereal grains, liver, kidney, legumes, some dark green vegetables	not known in humans
Phosphorus	milk and dairy products, bread and other cereal products, meat, poultry, fish, eggs, dried beans, and peas	bone pain; loss of appetite; muscular weakness
Potassium	vegetables, meat, milk, bran, bananas, orange juice	fatigue; muscular weakness; kidney and lung failure; irregular heart beat; in severe cases of depletion, heart failure
Selenium	meat, fish, cereal products, garlic, egg yolk	not known in man
Sodium	table salt, bread and cereal products, meat products including bacon and ham, milk	impaired acid-base balance in body fluids (very rare)
Zinc	meat and meat products, milk, bread and other cereal products, oysters, legumes	loss of appetite; impaired wound healing; impaired sexual development; stunting

sweets contain sugar, glucose, colour, and flavouring, and are boiled, cooled, and shaped. ***Chewing gum*** consists of synthetic or vegetable gum with colour, flavouring, and sometimes sweetener added. ***Toffee*** and ***caramel*** are made from sugar, glucose, animal fat, milk, and cream or vegetable fat, heated and shaped. The USA is the biggest producer of sweets, though the UK has the highest consumption, with millions of pounds spent each year on advertising.

tea beverage made by infusing the dried leaves of the evergreen shrub *Camellia sinensis*. Known in China as early as 2737 BC, tea was first brought to Europe AD 1610 and rapidly became a fashionable drink. In 1823, it was found growing wild in N India, and plantations were later established in Assam and Sri Lanka; producers today include Africa, South America, Georgia, Azerbaijan, Indonesia, and Iran.

The young leaves and shoots of the tea plant are picked every five years; once plucked, the young leaves are spread out on shelves, and allowed to wither in a current of air for 4–18 hours. ***Green teas*** (from China, Taiwan, and Japan) are steamed or heated and then rolled, dried and finally graded. ***Black teas*** (from Ceylon and India) are macerated in rolling machines, allowed to ferment and then dried and graded. Grading is carried out according to the size of leaf. For example, some Ceylon tea grades are orange pekoe, flowery pekoe, broken orange pekoe, broken pekoe, and fannings. The latter grades dominate the black teas sold in tea bags. Black tea make up 75% of the world's trade in tea. Some teas are scented with plant oils: Earl Grey, for example, is flavoured with oil of bergamot.

Many other plants are used in herbal teas; if leaves are used fresh the infusion is called a ***tisane***.

vegetable any food plant, especially leafy plants (cabbage and lettuce), roots and tubers (carrots, parsnips, and potatoes), legumes (peas, lentils, and beans), and even flowers (cauliflower, broccoli, and artichoke). Tomatoes, peppers, aubergines, and cucumbers are generally regarded as vegetables but are technically fruits. Green leafy vegetables and potatoes are good sources of vitamin C, though much is lost in cooking, and legumes are a main source of protein. Cooking softens vegetables by dissolving pectins and hemicellulose and gelatininzing starch.

vinegar sour liquid consisting of a 4% solution of acetic acid produced by the oxidation of alcohol, used to flavour food and as a preservative in pickling. ***Malt vinegar*** is brown and made from malted cereals; ***white vinegar*** is distilled from it. Other sources of vinegar include cider, wine, and honey. ***Balsamic vinegar*** is wine vinegar aged in wooden barrels.

wine alcoholic beverage, usually made from fermented grape pulp, although wines have also traditionally been made from many other fruits such as damsons and elderberries. ***Red wine*** is the product of the grape with the skin; ***white wine*** of the inner pulp of the grape. The sugar content is converted to ethyl alcohol by the yeast *Saccharomyces ellipsoideus*, which lives on the skin of the grape. The largest wine-producing countries are Italy, France, Russia, Georgia, Moldova, Armenia, and Spain.

For ***dry wine*** the fermentation is allowed to go on longer than for ***sweet*** or ***medium***; champagne (sparkling wine from the Champagne region of France) is bottled while still fermenting, but other sparkling wines are artificially carbonated. Some wines are fortified with additional alcohol obtained from various sources, and most wines contain preservatives, some of which may cause dangerous side effects. For this reason, organic wines, containing no preservatives, have recently become popular.

A ***vintage wine*** is produced during a good year (as regards quality of wine, produced by favourable weather conditions) in recognized vineyards of a particular area; France has a guarantee of origin (*appellation controlée*), as do Italy (*Denominazione di Origine Controllata*), Spain (*Denominación Controllata*), and Germany (a series of graded qualities running from *Qualitätswein* to *Beerenauslese*).

The greatest alcohol concentration that yeasts can tolerate is 16%; most wines have an alcohol content of 10–12%. Tannin in the skin imparts a bitter taste to the wine.

wine, fortified wine that has extra alcohol added to raise its alcohol content to about 20%. Fortified wines keep well because the alcohol kills the microorganisms that spoil natural wines. Port, which originates from Oporto in Portugal, is made by adding brandy to wine before fermentation is complete; sherry, originally made in Jerez in Spain, is a dry wine fortified after fermentation and later blended with sugar for sweet sherry; vermouth is flavoured with bitter herbs. Marsala, from Sicily, is fortified after fermentation and then heated gradually.

yoghurt or ***yogurt*** or ***yoghourt*** semi-solid curdlike dairy product made from milk fermented with bacteria. It was originally made by nomadic tribes of Central Asia from mare's milk in leather pouches attached to their saddles. It is drunk plain throughout the Asian and Mediterranean region, to which it spread, but honey, sugar, and fruit were added in Europe and the USA, and the product made solid and creamy, to be eaten with a spoon.

Heat-treated, homogenized milk is inoculated with a culture of *Streptococcus lactis* and *Lactobacillus bulgaricus* in equal amounts, which change the lactose in the milk to lactic acid. Acetaldehyde gives yoghurt its characteristic flavour. Commercially, fruit, flavourings, and colouring and thickening agents are added to the fermented yoghurt.

Food Technology

Food technology is the commercial processing of foodstuffs in order to render them more palatable or digestible, or to preserve them from spoilage. Food spoils because of the action of enzymes within the food that change its chemical composition, or because of the growth of bacteria, moulds, yeasts, and other microorganisms. Fatty or oily foods also suffer oxidation of the fats, giving them an unpleasant rancid flavour. Traditional forms of processing include boiling, frying, flour-milling, bread-making, yoghurt- and cheese-making, brewing, and various methods of ***food preservation***, such as salting, smoking, pickling, drying, bottling, and preserving in sugar. Modern food technology still employs traditional methods, but also uses many novel processes and additives, which allow a wider range of foodstuffs to be preserved.

additive any natural or artificial chemical added to prolong the shelf life of processed foods, alter the colour or flavour of food, or improve its nutritional value. Many additives are used and they are subject to regulation, since individuals may be affected by constant exposure even to traces of certain chemicals, and may suffer side effects ranging from headaches and hyperactivity to cancer. Additives approved for use throughout the European Community are given an official E number.

flavours are used to alter or intensify a food's taste. They may be natural or artificial, and include artificial sweeteners. They are more numerous and less controlled than other additives.

enhancers heighten the flavour or smell of foods without imparting their own taste – for example, monosodium glutamate (MSG).

colourings enhance the visual appeal of foods.

nutrients enhance food value or replace nutrients lost in processing.

preservatives slow down the rate of spoilage by controlling the growth of bacteria and fungi.

antioxidants prevent fatty foods from going rancid by inhibiting their natural oxidation.

emulsifiers and ***stabilizers*** modify the texture and consistency of food, and prevent the ingredients of a mixture from separating out.

leavening agents are substances other than yeast that lighten the texture of baked products – for example, sodium bicarbonate.

acidulants sharpen the taste of foods but may also perform a buffering function in the control of acidity.

bleaching agents whiten flours.

anticaking agents prevent powdered products from coagulating into solid lumps.

humectants control the humidity of foods by absorbing and retaining moisture.

clarifying agents are used in fruit juices, vinegars, and other fermented liquids. Gelatin is the most common.

firming agents restore the texture of vegetables that may be damaged during processing.

foam regulators may be used in beer to provide a controlled 'head' on top of the poured product.

canning preservation of food in hermetically sealed steel, aluminium, or plastic containers (cans) by the application of heat. The high temperature destroys microorganisms and enzymes, and the can's seal prevents recontamination. Beverages may also be canned to preserve the carbon dioxide that makes drinks fizzy.

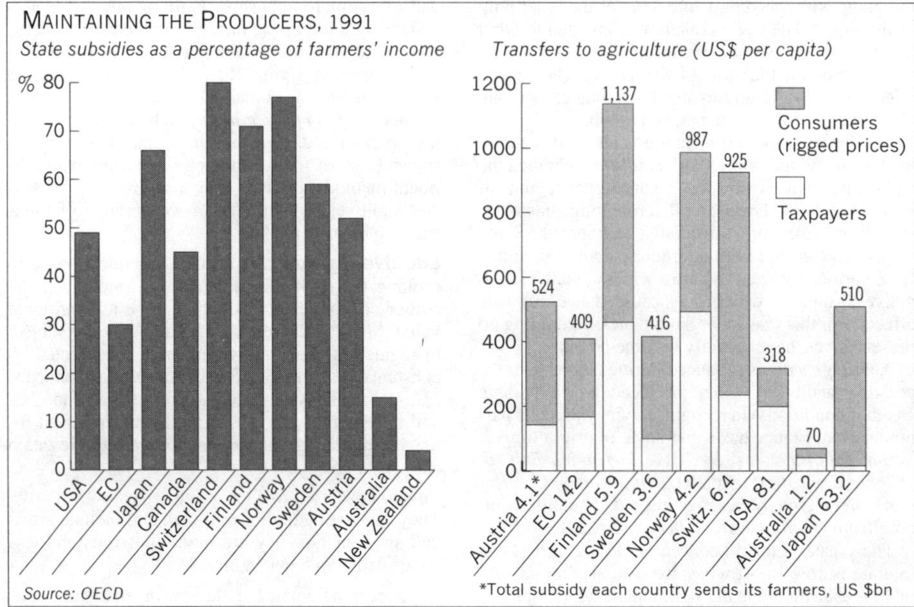

curing method of preserving meat by soaking it in salt (sodium chloride) solution, with saltpetre (sodium nitrate) added to give the meat its pink colour and characteristic taste. The nitrates in cured meats are converted to nitrites and nitrosamines by bacteria, and these are potentially carcinogenic to humans.

deep freezing method of preserving food by lowering its temperature to –18°C/0°F or below. It stops almost all spoilage processes, although there may be some residual enzyme activity in uncooked vegetables, which is why these are blanched (dipped in hot water to destroy the enzymes) before freezing. Microorganisms cannot grow or divide while frozen, but most remain alive and can resume activity once defrosted. Commercial techniques freeze foods rapidly in order to prevent the growth of large ice crystals, which would damage the food tissue on thawing.

dehydration preservation of food by reducing its moisture content by 80% or more. It inhibits the activity of moulds and bacteria, and reduces the mass and volume of foods, thereby lowering distribution costs. Products such as dried milk and instant coffee are made by spraying the liquid into a rising column of dry, heated air.

freeze-drying method of preserving food by freezing it and then placing it in a vacuum chamber so that the ice is forced out as water vapour. Many of the substances that give products such as coffee their typical flavour are volatile, and would be lost in a normal drying process because they would evaporate along with the water. In the freeze-drying process these volatile compounds do not pass into the ice that is to be sublimed, and are therefore largely retained.

hydrogenation method by which liquid oils are transformed into solid products, such as margarine. Vegetable oils contain double carbon-to-carbon bonds and are therefore examples of unsaturated compounds. When hydrogen is added to these double bonds, the oils become saturated and more solid in consistency.

irradiation method of preserving food by subjecting it to low-level gamma radiation in order to kill microorganisms. Although the process is now legal in several countries, uncertainty remains about possible long-term effects on consumers from irradiated food. The process does not make the food radioactive, but some vitamins, such as vitamin C, are destroyed and many molecular changes take place including the initiation of free radicals, which may be further changed into a range of unknown and unstable chemicals. Irradiation also eradicates the smell, taste, and poor appearance of bad or ageing food products.

pasteurization treatment of food to reduce the number of microorganisms it contains and so protect consumers from disease. Harmful bacteria are killed and the development of others is delayed. For milk, the method involves heating it to 72°C/161°F for 15 seconds followed by rapid cooling to 10°C/50°F or lower. However, the process also kills beneficial bacteria and reduces the nutritive property of milk.

pickling method of preserving food by soaking it in acetic acid (found in vinegar), which stops the growth of moulds. In sauerkraut, lactic acid, produced by bacteria, has the same effect.

puffing method of processing cereal grains. The grains are first subjected to high pressures, and then suddenly ejected into a normal atmospheric pressure, causing each grain to expand sharply. This type of process is used to make puffed wheat cereals and puffed rice cakes.

refrigeration method of preserving food by lowering its temperature to below 5°C/41°F (or below 3°C/37°F for cooked foods). It slows the processes of spoilage, but is less effective for foods with a high water content. Although a convenient form of preservation, this process cannot kill microorganisms, nor stop their growth completely, and a failure to realize its limitations causes many cases of food poisoning. Refrigerator temperatures should be checked as the efficiency of the machinery can decline with age.

smoking method of preserving fresh oily meats (such as pork and goose) or fish (such as herring and salmon). Before being smoked, the food is first salted or soaked in brine, then hung to dry. Meat is hot-smoked over a fast-burning wood fire, which is covered with sawdust, producing thick smoke and partly cooking the meat. Fish may be hot-smoked or cold-smoked over a slow-burning wood fire, which does not cook it. Modern refrigeration techniques mean that food does not need to be smoked to help it keep, so factory-smoked foods tend to be smoked just enough to give them a smoky flavour, with colours added to give them the appearance of traditionally smoked food. The smoke itself may contain harmful substances.

ultra-heat treatment (UHT) preservation of milk by raising its temperature to 132°C/269°F or more. It uses higher temperatures than pasteurization, and kills all bacteria present, giving the milk a long shelf life but altering the flavour.

Agriculture

agriculture the practice of farming, including the cultivation of the soil (for raising crops) and the raising of domesticated animals. Crops are for human nourishment, animal fodder, or commodities such as cotton and sisal. Animals are raised for wool, milk, leather, dung (as fuel), or meat. The units for managing agricultural production vary from smallholdings and individually owned farms to corporate-run farms and collective farms run by entire communities.

Agriculture developed in the Middle East and Egypt at least 10,000 years ago. Farming communities soon became the base for society in China, India, Europe, Mexico, and Peru, then spread throughout the world. Reorganization along more scientific and productive lines took place in Europe in the 18th century in response to dramatic population growth.

Mechanization made considerable progress in the USA and Europe during the 19th century. After World War II, there was an explosive growth in the use of agricultural chemicals: herbicides, insecticides, fungicides, and fertilizers. In the 1960s there was development of high-yielding species, especially in the ***green revolution*** of the Third World, and the industrialized countries began intensive farming of cattle, poultry, and pigs. In the 1980s, hybridization by genetic engineering methods and pest control by the use of chemicals and pheromones were developed. However, there was also a reaction against some forms of intensive agriculture because of the pollution and habitat destruction caused. One result of this was a growth of alternative methods, including organic farming.

overproduction The greater efficiency in agriculture achieved since the 19th century, coupled with government subsidies for domestic production in the USA and the European Community (EC), have led to the development of high stocks, nicknamed 'lakes' (wine, milk) and 'mountains' (butter, beef, grain). The overall cost of bulk transport and the potential destabilization of other economies has acted against high producers exporting their excess on a regular basis to needy countries.

agricultural revolution sweeping changes that took place in British agriculture over the period 1750–1850 in response to the increased demand for food from a rapidly expanding population. Changes of the latter half of the 18th century included the enclosure of open fields, the introduction of four-course rotation together with new fodder crops such as turnips, and the development of improved breeds of livestock.

agrochemical artificially produced chemical used in modern, intensive agricultural systems. Agrochemicals include nitrate and phosphate fertilizers, pesticides, some animal-feed additives, and pharmaceuticals. Many are responsible for pollution and almost all are avoided by organic farmers.

agronomy study of crops and soils, a branch of agricultural science. Agronomy includes such topics as selective breeding (of plants and animals), irrigation, pest control, and soil analysis and modification.

aquaculture or ***fish farming*** raising fish and shellfish (molluscs and crustaceans) under controlled con-

The world's top fishing nations

Catches in 1989 (in metric tons)

USSR	11,310,091
China	11,219,994
Japan	11,174,464
Peru	6,832,465
Chile	6,454,142
USA	5,744,318
India	3,618,919
South Korea	2,832,431
Thailand	2,822,530*
Indonesia	2,700,000*
Philippines	2,098,787*
Denmark	1,927,493
Norway	1,899,941
North Korea	1,700,100*
Canada	1,554,233
Iceland	1,504,771
Mexico	1,416,784
Spain	1,370,000
South Africa	878,580
France	875,839*
Vietnam	868,000*
Brazil	850,000
Bangladesh	832,791
UK	797,259
Ecuador	723,624
Myanmar	702,700*
Malaysia	608,967*
Poland	564,885
Italy	550,964
Morocco	520,354

** estimate*

Source: FAO

ditions in tanks and ponds, sometimes in offshore pens. It has been practised for centuries in the Far East, where Japan alone produces some 100,000 tonnes of fish a year. In the 1980s, one-tenth of the world's consumption of fish and shellfish was farmed, notably carp, catfish, trout, salmon, turbot, eel, mussels, clams, oysters, and shrimp.

artificial insemination (AI) fertilization of animals by means of introducing (by instrument) semen from a sperm bank or donor into the female reproductive tract to bring about fertilization. AI is used by animal breeders to improve stock with sperm from high-quality males.

bovine spongiform encephalopathy (BSE) or ***mad cow disease*** disease of cattle, allied to scrapie, that renders the brain spongy and may drive an animal mad. It has been identified only in the UK, where it was first diagnosed in Nov 1986 and 12,900 cases were confirmed between June 1992 and June 1993. The organism causing it is unknown, but the source of the disease has been traced to manufactured protein feed incorporating the rendered brains of scrapie-infected sheep. BSE is very similar to, and may be related to, Creutzfeld-Jakob disease and kuru, which affect humans.

cash crop crop grown solely for sale rather than for the farmer's own use; for example, coffee, cotton, and sugar beet. Many Third World countries grow cash crops to meet their debt repayments rather than grow food for their own people. The price for these crops depends on financial interests, such as those of the multinational companies and the International Monetary Fund.

cattle any large, ruminant, even-toed, hoofed mammal of the genus *Bos*, family Bovidae. Cattle are bred for meat (beef cattle) or milk (dairy cattle). Fermentation in the four-chambered stomach allows cattle to make good use of the grass that is normally the main part of the diet. There are two main types of domesticated cattle: the European breeds and the various breeds of zebu *Bos indicus*, the humped cattle of India.

The old-established beef breeds are mostly British in origin. The Hereford, for example, is the premier English breed; ideally suited to rich lowland pastures, it will also thrive on poorer land such as that found in the US Midwest and the Argentine pampas. Of the Scottish beef breeds, the Aberdeen Angus, a black and hornless variety, produces high-quality meat through intensive feeding methods. Other British breeds include the Devon, a hardy early-maturing type, and the Beef Shorthorn. Other European breeds tend to have less fat and are more suited to modern tastes. Examples include the Charolais and the Limousin from central France, and the Simmental, originally from Switzerland.

For dairying purposes, a breed raised in many countries is variously known as the Friesian, Holstein, or Black and White. It can give enormous milk yields, up to 13,000 l/3,450 gal in a single lactation, and will produce calves ideally suited for intensive beef production. Other dairying types include the Jersey and Guernsey, whose milk has a high butterfat content, and the Ayrshire, a smaller breed capable of staying outside all year.

cereal grass grown for its edible, nutrient-rich, starchy seeds. The term refers primarily to wheat, oats, rye, and barley, but may also refer to corn, millet, and rice. Cereals contain about 75% complex carbohydrates and 10% protein, plus fats and fibre (roughage). They store well. If all the world's cereal crop were consumed as whole-grain products directly by humans, everyone could obtain adequate protein and carbohydrate; however, a large proportion of cereal production in affluent nations is used as animal feed to boost the production of meat, dairy products, and eggs.

collective farm farm in which a group of farmers pool their land, domestic animals, and agricultural implements, retaining as private property enough only for the members' own requirements. The profits of the farm are divided among its members. In ***cooperative farming***, farmers retain private ownership of the land.

combine harvester or ***combine*** machine used for harvesting cereals and other crops, so called because it combines the actions of reaping (cutting the crop) and threshing (beating the ears so that the grain separates).

Common Agricultural Policy (CAP) system that allows the member countries of the European Community (EC) jointly to organize and control agricultural production within their boundaries. The objectives of the CAP were outlined in the Treaty of Rome: to increase agricultural productivity, to provide a fair standard of living for farmers and their employees, to stabilize markets, and to assure the availability of supply at a price that was reasonable to the consumer. The CAP is increasingly criticized for its role in creating overproduction, and consequent environmental damage, and for the high price of food subsidies.

crop rotation system of regularly changing the crops grown on a piece of land. The crops are grown in a particular order to utilize and add to the nutrients in the soil and to prevent the build-up of insect and fungal pests. Including a legume crop, such as peas or beans, in the rotation helps build up nitrate in the soil because the roots contain bacteria capable of fixing nitrogen from the air.

dairying the business of producing milk and milk products. It is now usual for dairy farms to concentrate on the production of milk and for factories to take over the handling, processing, and distribution of milk as well as the manufacture of dairy products. In Britain, the Milk Marketing Board (1933), to which all producers must sell their milk, forms a connecting link between farms and factories.

deer farming method of producing venison through the controlled breeding and rearing of deer on farms rather than hunting them in the wild. British deer-farming enterprises have been growing in number as more farmers seek to diversify into new sources of income. The meat is sold largely to the restaurant trade, and there is a market for the antlers and skin.

factory farming intensive rearing of poultry or animals for food, usually on high-protein foodstuffs in confined quarters. Chickens for eggs and meat, and calves for veal are commonly factory farmed. Some

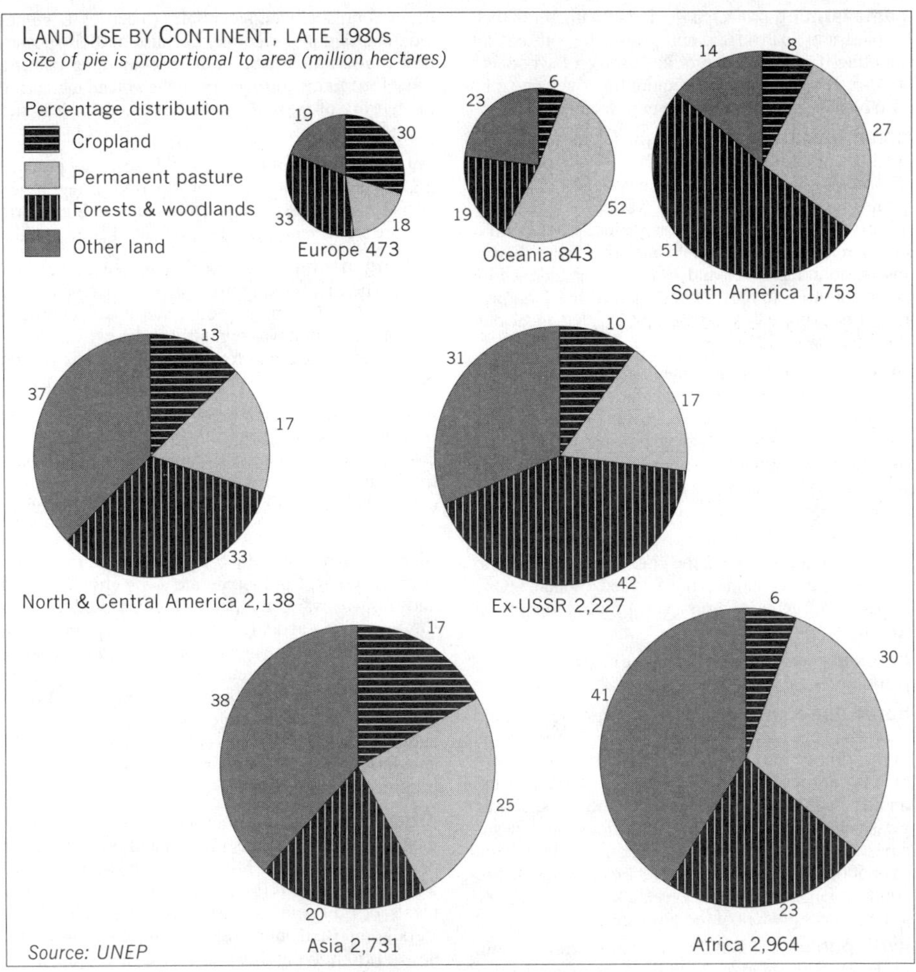

countries restrict the use of antibiotics and growth hormones as aids to factory farming, because they can persist in the flesh of the animals after they are slaughtered. Many people object to factory farming for moral as well as health reasons.

fallow land ploughed and tilled, but left unsown for a season to allow it to recuperate. In Europe, it is associated with the medieval three-field system. It is used in some modern crop rotations.

fertilizer substance containing some or all of a range of about 20 chemical elements necessary for healthy plant growth, used to compensate for the deficiencies of poor or depleted soil. Fertilizers may be ***organic***, for example farmyard manure, composts, bonemeal, blood, and fishmeal; or ***inorganic***, in the form of compounds, mainly of nitrogen, phosphate, and potash.

fibre crop plant that is grown for the fibres that can be extracted from its tissues. Temperate areas produce flax and hemp; tropical and subtropical areas produce cotton, jute, and sisal. Cotton dominates fibre-crop production.

field enclosed area of land used for farming. Twentieth-century developments in agricultural science and technology have encouraged farmers to amalgamate and enlarge their fields, often to as much as 40 hectares/100 acres.

fish farming aquaculture; the cultivation of fish and shellfish for human consumption.

foot-and-mouth disease contagious eruptive viral disease of cloven-hoofed mammals, characterized by blisters in the mouth and around the hooves. In cattle it causes deterioration of milk yield and abortions. The virus is airborne, which makes its eradication extremely difficult.

In the UK, affected herds are destroyed; inoculation is practised in Europe, and in the USA, a vaccine was developed in the 1980s.

forage crop plant that is grown to feed livestock; for example, grass, clover, and kale (a form of cabbage). Forage crops cover a greater area of the world than food crops, and grass, which dominates this group, is the world's most abundant crop, though much of it is still in an unimproved state.

game farming protected rearing of gamebirds such as pheasants, partridges, and grouse for subsequent shooting. Game farms provide plenty of woodland and brush, which the birds require for cover, and may also plant special crops for them to feed on.

green revolution popular term for the change in methods of arable farming in Third World countries. The intent is to provide more and better food for their populations, by use of crop varieties (especially wheat and rice) giving higher yields, albeit with a heavy reliance on chemicals and machinery. It was instigated in the 1940s and 1950s, but abandoned by some countries in the 1980s. Much of the food produced is exported as cash crops, so that local diet does not always improve.

harrow agricultural implement used to break up the furrows left by the plough and reduce the soil to a fine consistency or tilth, and to cover the seeds after sowing. The traditional harrow consists of spikes set in a frame; modern harrows use sets of discs.

hay preserved grass used for winter livestock feed. The grass is cut and allowed to dry in the field before being removed for storage in a barn. The optimum period for cutting is when the grass has just come into flower and contains most feed value. One hectare/2.47 acres of grass can produce up to 7.5 tonnes/7.3 tons of hay.

herbicide weedkiller; any chemical used to destroy plants or check their growth.

horticulture art and science of growing flowers, fruit, and vegetables. The growth of industrial towns in the 19th century led to the development of commercial horticulture in the form of nurseries and market gardens, pioneering methods such as glasshouses, artificial heat, herbicides, and pesticides, synthetic fertilizers, and machinery. In Britain, over 500,000 acres/200,000 hectares are devoted to commercial horticulture; vegetables account for almost three-quarters of the produce.

hydroponics cultivation of plants without soil, using specially prepared solutions of mineral salts. Beginning in the 1930s, large crops were grown by hydroponic methods, at first in California but since then in many other parts of the world.

insecticide any chemical pesticide used to kill insects. Among the most effective insecticides are synthetic organic chemicals such as DDT and dieldrin, which are chlorinated hydrocarbons. These chemicals, however, have proved persistent in the environment and are also poisonous to all animal life, including humans, and are consequently banned in many countries. Other synthetic insecticides include organic phosphorus compounds such as malathion. Insecticides prepared from plants, such as derris and pyrethrum, are safer to use but need to be applied frequently and carefully.

irrigation artificial water supply for dry agricultural areas by means of dams and channels. Drawbacks are that it tends to concentrate salts, ultimately causing infertility, and that rich river silt is retained at dams, to the impoverishment of the land and fisheries below them.

legume plant of the family Leguminosae, which has a pod containing dry seeds. The family includes peas, beans, lentils, clover, and alfalfa (lucerne). Legumes are important in agriculture because of their specialized roots, which have nodules containing bacteria capable of fixing nitrogen from the air and increasing the fertility of the soil. The edible seeds of legumes are called ***pulses***.

ley area of temporary grassland, sown to produce grazing and hay or silage for a period of one to ten years before being ploughed and cropped. Short-term leys are often incorporated in systems of crop rotation.

milking machine machine that uses suction to milk cows. The first milking machine was invented in the USA by L O Colvin in 1860. Later it was improved so that the suction was regularly released by a pulsating device, since it was found that continuous suction is harmful to cows.

monoculture farming system where only one crop is grown. In Third World countries this is often a cash crop, grown on plantations. Cereal crops in the industrialized world are also frequently grown on a monoculture basis; for example, wheat in the Canadian prairies.

oil crop plant from which vegetable oils are pressed from the seeds. Cool temperate areas grow rapeseed and linseed; warm temperate regions produce sunflowers, olives, and soya beans; tropical regions produce groundnuts (peanuts), palm oil, and coconuts. Some of the major vegetable oils, such as soya bean oil, peanut oil, and cottonseed oil, are derived from crops grown primarily for other purposes. Most vegetable oils are used as both edible oils and as ingredients in industrial products such as soaps, varnishes, printing inks, and paints.

organic farming farming without the use of synthetic fertilizers (such as nitrates and phosphates) or pesticides (herbicides, insecticides, and fungicides) or other agrochemicals (such as hormones, growth stimulants, or fruit regulators). In place of artificial fertilizers, compost, manure, seaweed, or other substances derived from living things are used (hence the name 'organic'). Growing a crop of a nitrogen-fixing plant such as lucerne, then ploughing it back into the soil, also fertilizes the ground. Pest-control methods include removal by hand, intercropping (planting with companion plants which deter pests), mechanical barriers to infestation, crop rotation, better cultivation methods, and biological control. Weeds can be controlled by hoeing, mulching (covering with manure, straw, or black plastic), or burning off. Organic farming methods produce food with minimal pesticide residues and greatly reduce pollution of the environment. They are more labour-intensive, and therefore more expensive, but use less fossil fuel. Soil structure is greatly improved by organic methods.

pesticide any chemical used in farming, gardening or indoors to combat pests. Pesticides are of three main types: ***insecticides*** (to kill insects), ***fungicides*** (to kill fungal diseases), and ***herbicides*** (to kill plants, mainly those considered weeds). Pesticides cause a number of pollution problems through spray drift onto surrounding areas, direct contamination of users or the public, and as residues on food. The safest pesticides are those made from plants, such as the insecticides pyrethrum and derris.

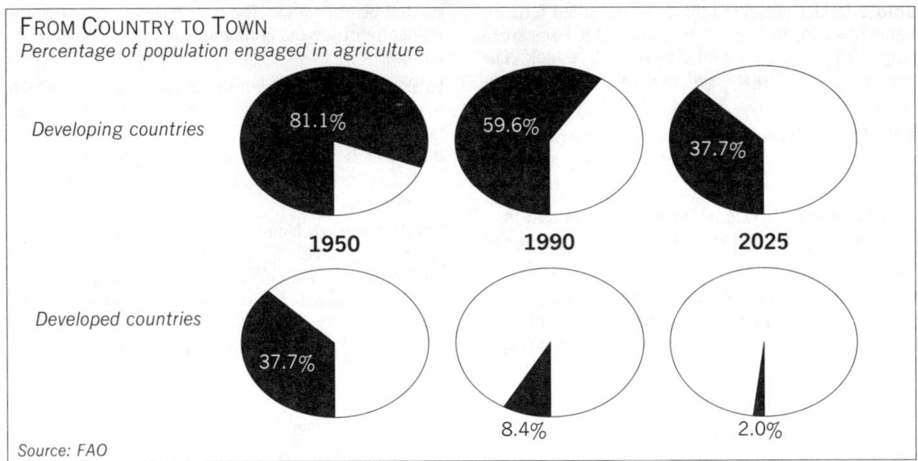

pig even-toed hoofed mammal of the family Suidae. Pigs are omnivorous, and have simple, non-ruminating stomachs and thick hides. More than 400 varieties have been bred over the centuries, many of which have all but disappeared with the development of intensive rearing systems.

The Berkshire, Chester White, Poland, China, Saddleback, Yorkshire, Duroc, and Razorback are the main surviving breeds. Modern indoor rearing methods favour the large white breeds, such as the Chester White and the originally Swedish Landrace, over coloured varieties, which tend to be hardier and can survive better outdoors. Since 1960, hybrid pigs, produced by crossing two or more breeds, have become popular for their heavy but lean carcasses.

plough agricultural implement used for tilling the soil. The plough dates from about 3500 BC, when oxen were used to pull a simple wooden blade. The modern plough consists of many 'bottoms', each comprising a curved ploughshare and angled mouldboard. The bottom is designed so that it slices into the ground and turns the soil over.

poultry domestic birds such as chickens, turkeys, ducks, and geese. Good egg-laying breeds of chicken are Leghorns, Minorcas, and Anconas; varieties most suitable for eating are Dorkings, Australorps, Brahmas, and Cornish; those useful for both purposes are Orpingtons, Rhode Island Reds, Wyandottes, Plymouth Rocks, and Jersey White Giants. Most farm poultry are hybrids, selectively crossbred for certain characteristics, including feathers and down.

Factory farming has doubled egg yields and increased the availability of poultry meat. The birds are often kept constantly in small cages, have their beaks and claws removed to prevent them from pecking their neighbours, and are given feed containing growth hormones and antibacterial drugs, which eventually make their way up the food chain to humans. Deep-litter and free-range systems account for only a small percentage of total production.

root crop plant cultivated for its swollen edible root (which may or may not be a true root). Potatoes are the major temperate root crop; the major tropical root crops are cassava, yams, and sweet potatoes. Root crops are second in importance only to cereals as human food. Roots have a high carbohydrate content, but their protein content rarely exceeds 2%. Consequently, communities relying almost exclusively upon roots may suffer from protein deficiency. Food production for a given area from roots is greater than from cereals.

scrapie fatal disease of sheep and goats that attacks the central nervous system, causing deterioration of the brain cells. It is believed to be caused by a submicroscopic organism known as a prion and may be related to bovine spongiform encephalopathy (mad cow disease).

scythe harvesting tool with long wooden handle and sharp, curving blade. It is similar to a sickle. The scythe was in common use in the Middle East and Europe from the dawn of agriculture until the early 20th century, by which time it had generally been replaced by machinery.

seed drill machine for sowing cereals and other seeds, developed by Jethro Tull (1674–1741) in England 1701. The seed is stored in a hopper and delivered by tubes into furrows in the ground. The furrows are made by a set of blades, or coulters, attached to the front of the drill. A harrow is drawn behind the drill to cover up the seeds.

sheep ruminant, even-toed, hoofed mammal of the family Bovidae. The domesticated breeds are all classified as *Ovis aries*. Various breeds of sheep are reared worldwide for meat, wool, milk, and cheese, and for rotation on arable land to maintain its fertility.

Over 50 varieties of sheep were bred in the UK, but only a small proportion are still in full commercial use. They are grouped into three principal categories. The hardy ***upland*** breeds, such as the Scottish Blackface and Welsh Mountain, are able to survive in a bleak, rugged environment. The ***shortwool*** varieties, such as the Down breeds of Hampshire and Suffolk, are well adapted to thrive on the lush grassland of lowland areas. ***Longwool*** breeds, such as the Leicesters and Border Leicesters, were originally bred for their coarse, heavy fleeces, but are now crossed with hill-sheep flocks to produce fat lambs. In 1989, there were 41 million sheep in Britain, making Britain the main producer of lambs in Europe.

silage fodder preserved through controlled fermentation in a silo, an airtight structure that presses green crops. It is used as a winter feed for livestock. The term also refers to stacked crops that may be preserved indefinitely.

subsistence farming farming when the produce is enough to feed only the farmer and family and there is no surplus to sell.

tenant farming system whereby farmers rent their holdings from a landowner in return for the use of agricultural land.

threshing agricultural process of separating cereal grains from the plant. Traditionally, the work was carried out by hand in winter months using the flail, a jointed beating stick. Today, threshing is done automatically inside the combine harvester at the time of cutting.

topsoil the upper, cultivated layer of soil, which may vary in depth from 8 to 45 cm/3 to 18 in. It contains organic matter – the decayed remains of vegetation, which plants need for active growth – along with a variety of soil organisms, including earthworms.

tractor powerful motor vehicle, commonly having large rear wheels or caterpillar tracks, used for pulling farm machinery and loads. It is usually powered by a diesel engine and has a power-takeoff mechanism for driving machinery, and a hydraulic lift for raising and lowering implements.

LIFE SCIENCES

Evolutionary Biology

adaptation any change in the structure or function of an organism that allows it to survive and reproduce more effectively in its environment. In evolution, adaptation is thought to occur as a result of random variation in the genetic make-up of organisms (produced by mutation and recombination) coupled with natural selection.

artificial selection selective breeding of individuals that exhibit the particular characteristics that a plant or animal breeder wishes to develop. In plants, desirable features might include resistance to disease, high yield (in crop plants), or attractive appearance. In animal breeding, selection has led to the development of particular breeds of cattle for improved meat production (such as the Aberdeen Angus) or milk production (such as Jerseys).

cladistics method of biological classification (taxonomy) that uses a formal step-by-step procedure for objectively assessing the extent to which organisms share particular characters, and for assigning them to taxonomic groups. Taxonomic groups (for example, species, genus, family) are termed ***clades***.

competition interaction between two or more organisms, or groups of organisms (for example, species), that use a common resource which is in short supply. Competition invariably results in a reduction in the numbers of one or both competitors, and in evolution, contributes both to the decline of certain species and to the evolution of adaptations.

convergent evolution independent evolution of similar structures in species (or other taxonomic groups) that are not closely related, as a result of living in a similar way. Thus, birds and bats have wings, not because they are descended from a common winged ancestor, but because their respective ancestors independently evolved flight.

evolution slow process of change from one form to another, as in the evolution of the universe from its formation in the Big Bang to its present state, or in the evolution of life on Earth. The current theory of the latter is called neo-Darwinism.

extinction the complete disappearance of a species. In the past, extinctions are believed to have occurred because species were unable to adapt quickly enough to a naturally changing environment. Today, most extinctions are due to human activity – hunting and habitat destruction. Conservative estimates put the rate of loss due to deforestation alone at 4,000 to 6,000 species a year. Overall, the rate could be as high as one species an hour. Those known to be at risk are called endangered species. (See *Environment* for more.)

human species, origins of evolution of humans from ancestral primates. Molecular studies put the date of the split between the human and African ape lines at 5–10 million years ago. The oldest known fossils of hominids (creatures of the human group), *Australopithecus afarensis*, found in Ethiopia and Tanzania, date from 3.5 to 4 million years ago. They may have been the ancestors of *Homo habilis*, probably the first to use stone tools. Over 1.5 million years ago, *Homo erectus*, believed by some to be descended from *H. habilis*, appeared. They were probably the first to use fire and the first to move out of Africa. Modern humans *Homo sapiens sapiens* evolved from *H. erectus* about 200,000 years ago, either in Africa or in different parts of the world at around the same time.

Lamarckism theory of evolution, now discredited, advocated during the early 19th century by French naturalist Jean Baptiste Lamarck. He believed that acquired characteristics were inherited; for example, that giraffes had lengthened their necks by stretching and passed this characteristic on to their offspring.

mutation change in the genes produced by a change in the DNA that makes up the hereditary material of all living organisms. Mutations, the raw material of evolution, result from mistakes during replication (copying) of DNA molecules. Only a few improve the organism's performance and are therefore favoured by natural selection. Mutation rates are increased by certain chemicals and by radiation.

natural selection the process whereby gene frequencies in a population change through certain individuals producing more descendants than others because they are better able to survive and reproduce

Antarctic dinosaurs

The first dinosaur remains in the continent of Antarctica have been discovered within the past year. They include the remains of a flying pterosaur, a plant-eating sauropod and a large and unusual carnivorous dinosaur with a crest and a pair of horns. The finds were made in the Transantarctic mountains, about 500 km/300 mi from the South Pole, at latitude 85 degrees south.

The animals are thought to be about 175 million years old, from the middle Jurassic period. During that period, dinosaurs evolved to their largest sizes. The carnivore is 8–9 m/20–22 ft long and is similar to dinosaurs found in South America.

Just because dinosaurs have been found in Antarctica, it does not mean that they lived under the conditions of snow and ice found there now. The remains found in the Transantarctic mountains suggest that the climate was much warmer than today. The theory of continental drift suggests that the entire continent was much further north. The dinosaurs lived and died in warm climates, and their remains have drifted with the continent to the icy wastes of the south polar region.

in their environment. The accumulated effect of natural selection is to produce adaptations such as the insulating coat of a polar bear or the spadelike forelimbs of a mole. The process is slow, relying firstly on random variation in the genes of an organism being produced by mutation and secondly on the genetic recombination of sexual reproduction. It was recognized by English naturalists Charles Darwin and Alfred Russel Wallace as the main process driving evolution.

neo-Darwinism the modern theory of evolution, built up since the 1930s by integrating 19th-century English scientist Charles Darwin's theory of evolution through natural selection with the theory of genetic inheritance founded on the work of Austrian biologist Gregor Mendel.

phylogeny historical sequence of changes that occurs in a given species during the course of its evolution. It was once erroneously associated with ontogeny (the process of development of a living organism).

punctuated equilibrium model evolutionary theory developed by Niles Eldridge and US palaeontologist Stephen Jay Gould 1972 to explain discontinuities in the fossil record. It claims that periods of rapid change alternate with periods of relative stability (stasis), and that the appearance of new lineages is a separate process from the gradual evolution of adaptive changes within a species.

saltation the idea that an abrupt genetic change can occur in an individual, which then gives rise to a new species. The idea has now been largely discredited, although the appearance of polyploid individuals (possessing three or more sets of chromosomes) can be considered an example.

species distinguishable group of organisms that resemble each other or consist of a few distinctive types, and that can all interbreed to produce fertile offspring. Species are the lowest level in the system of biological classification. Around 1.4 million species have been identified so far, of which 750,000 are insects, 250,000 are plants, and 41,000 are vertebrates.

variation difference between individuals of the same species, found in any sexually reproducing population. Variations may be almost unnoticeable in some cases, obvious in others, and can concern many aspects of the organism. Typically, variation in size, behaviour, biochemistry, or colouring may be found. The cause of the variation is genetic (that is, inherited), environmental, or usually a combination of the two. The origins of variation can be traced to the recombination of the genetic material during the formation of the gametes, and, more rarely, to mutation.

The diversity of life

Estimated number of species worldwide

	Number identified	*% of estimated total number of species*
Micro-organisms	5,800	3–27% (micro-organisms and invertebrates)
Invertebrates	1,021,000	
Plants	322,500	67–100%
Fish	19,100	83–100%
Birds	9,100	94–100%
Reptiles and amphibians	12,000	90–95% (reptiles, amphibians and mammals)
Mammals	4,000	
Total	***1,393,500***	

	Number of species	*% identified*
Low estimate of all species	4.4 million	31%
High estimate of all species	80 million	2%

This table shows the probable number of species and the extent of unidentified biological diversity worldwide. Estimates of the number of species vary widely because many species-rich ecosystems, such as tropical forests, contain unexplored and unstudied habitats, and the probable number of habitats may have been underestimated. The figures provided above are the most recent and widely accepted. The percentage values are based on the averages of a number of estimates and are intended as a guide only.

Source: WWF

Reproduction

Reproduction is any process by which a living organism produces other organisms similar to itself. There are two kinds: asexual reproduction and sexual reproduction.

asexual reproduction reproduction that does not involve the manufacture and fusion of sex cells, nor the necessity for two parents. Asexual processes include binary fission, in which the parent organism splits into two or more new organisms, and budding, in which a new organism is formed initially as an outgrowth of the parent organism. The asexual reproduction of spores, as in ferns and mosses, is also common and many plants reproduce asexually by means of runners, rhizomes, bulbs, and corms.

Asexual reproduction carries a clear advantage in that there is no need to search for a mate nor to develop complex pollinating mechanisms; every asexual organism can reproduce on its own. Asexual reproduction can therefore lead to a rapid population build-up.

In evolutionary terms, the disadvantage of asexual reproduction is that only identical individuals, or clones, are produced – there is no variation. In the field of horticulture, where standardized production is needed, this is useful, but in the wild, a population that cannot adapt to a changing environment or evolve defences against a new disease is at risk of extinction. Many asexually reproducing organisms are therefore capable of reproducing sexually as well.

binary fission asexual reproduction whereby a single-celled organism, such as the amoeba, divides into two smaller 'daughter' cells. It can also occur in a few simple multicellular organisms, such as sea anemones, producing two smaller sea anemones of equal size.

budding asexual reproduction in which an outgrowth develops from a cell to form a new individual. Most yeasts reproduce in this way. Simple invertebrates, such as hydra, can also reproduce by budding.

biology: chronology

***c.* 500 BC**	First studies of the structure and behaviour of animals, by the Greek Alcmaeon of Creton.
***c.* 450**	Hippocrates of Cos undertook the first detailed studies of human anatomy.
***c.* 350**	Aristotle laid down the basic philosophy of the biological sciences and outlined a theory of evolution.
***c.* 300**	Theophrastus carried out the first detailed studies of plants.
***c.* AD 175**	Galen established the basic principles of anatomy and physiology.
***c.* 1500**	Leonardo da Vinci studied human anatomy to improve his drawing ability and produced detailed anatomical drawings.
1628	William Harvey described the circulation of the blood and the function of the heart as a pump.
1665	Robert Hooke used a microscope to describe the cellular structure of plants.
1672	Marcello Malpighi undertook the first studies in embryology by describing the development of a chicken egg.
1677	Anthony van Leeuwenhoek greatly improved the microscope and used it to describe spermatozoa as well as many microorganisms.
1682	Nehemiah Grew published the first textbook on botany.
1736	Carolus (Carl) Linnaeus published his systematic classification of plants, so establishing taxonomy.
1768–79	James Cook's voyages of discovery in the Pacific revealed an undreamed-of diversity of living species, prompting the development of theories to explain their origin.
1796	Edward Jenner established the practice of vaccination against smallpox, laying the foundations for theories of antibodies and immune reactions.
1809	Jean-Baptiste Lamarck advocated a theory of evolution through inheritance of acquired characters.
1839	Theodor Schwann proposed that all living matter is made up of cells.
1857	Louis Pasteur established that microorganisms are responsible for fermentation, creating the discipline of microbiology.
1859	Charles Darwin published *On the Origin of Species*, expounding his theory of the evolution of species by natural selection.
1866	Gregor Mendel pioneered the study of inheritance with his experiments on peas, but achieved little recognition.
1883	August Weismann proposed his theory of the continuity of the germ plasm.
1900	Mendel's work was rediscovered and the science of genetics founded.
1935	Konrad Lorenz published the first of many major studies of animal behaviour, which founded the discipline of ethology.
1953	James Watson and Francis Crick described the molecular structure of the genetic material, DNA.
1964	William Hamilton recognized the importance of inclusive fitness, so paving the way for the development of sociobiology.
1975	Discovery of endogenous opiates (the brain's own painkillers) opened up a new phase in the study of brain chemistry.
1976	Har Gobind Khorana and his colleagues constructed the first artificial gene to function naturally when inserted into a bacterial cell, a major step in genetic engineering.
1982	Gene databases were established at Heidelberg, Germany, for the European Molecular Biology Laboratory, and at Los Alamos, USA, for the US National Laboratories.
1985	The first human cancer gene, retinoblastoma, was isolated by researchers at the Massachusetts Eye and Ear Infirmary and the Whitehead Institute, Massachusetts.
1988	The Human Genome Organization (HUGO) was established in Washington DC with the aim of mapping the complete sequence of DNA.
1991	Biosphere 2, an experiment that attempts to reproduce the world's biosphere in miniature within a sealed glass dome, was launched in Arizona, USA.
1992	Researchers at the University of California, USA, stimulated the multiplication of isolated brain cells of mice, overturning the axiom that mammalian brains cannot produce replacement cells once birth has taken place. The world's largest organism, a honey fungus with underground hyphae (filaments) spreading across 600 hectares/1,480 acres, was discovered in Washington State, USA.

In horticulture, the term is used for a technique of plant propagation whereby a bud (or scion) and a sliver of bark from one plant are transferred to an incision made in the bark of another plant (the stock). This method of grafting is often used for roses.

parthenogenesis development of an ovum (egg) without any genetic contribution from a male. Parthenogenesis is the normal means of reproduction in a few plants (for example, dandelions) and animals (for example, certain fish). Some sexually reproducing species, such as aphids, show parthenogenesis at some stage in their life cycle.

In most cases, there is no fertilization at all, but in a few, the stimulus of being fertilized by a sperm is needed to initiate development, although the male's chromosomes are not absorbed into the nucleus of the ovum. Parthenogenesis can be artificially induced in many animals (such as rabbits) by cooling, pricking, or applying acid to an egg.

sexual reproduction reproductive process in organisms that requires the union, or fertilization, of gametes (such as eggs and sperm). These are usually produced by two different individuals, although self-fertilization occurs in a few hermaphrodites such as tapeworms. Most organisms other than bacteria and cyanobacteria (blue-green algae) show some sort of sexual process. Except in some lower organisms, the gametes are of two distinct types called eggs and sperm. The organisms producing the eggs are called females, and those producing the sperm, males. The fusion of a male and a female gamete produces a ***zygote***, from which a new individual develops.

The Life Cycle

The life cycle is the sequence of developmental stages through which members of a given species pass. Most vertebrates have a simple life cycle consisting of fertilization of sex cells or gametes, a period of development as an embryo, a period of juvenile growth after hatching or birth, an adulthood including sexual reproduction, and finally death. Invertebrate life cycles are generally more complex and may involve major reconstitution of the individual's appearance (metamorphosis) and completely different styles of life. Thus dragonflies live an aquatic life as larvae and an aerial life during the adult phase. In many invertebrates and protozoa there is a sequence of stages in the life cycle, and in parasites different stages often occur in different host organisms. Plants have a special type of life cycle with two distinct phases, known as alternation of generations.

ageing the period of deterioration of the physical condition of a living organism that leads to death; in biological terms, the entire life process. Three current theories attempt to account for ageing. The first suggests that the process is genetically determined, to remove individuals that can no longer reproduce. The second suggests that it is due to the accumulation of mistakes during the replication of DNA at cell division. The third suggests that it is actively induced by pieces of DNA that move between cells, or by cancer-causing viruses; these may become abundant in old cells and induce them to produce unwanted proteins or interfere with the control functions of their DNA.

allele one of two or more alternative forms of a gene at a given position (locus) on a chromosome, caused by a difference in the DNA. Blue and brown eyes in humans are determined by different alleles of the gene for eye colour. Organisms with two sets of chromo-somes (diploids) will have two copies of each gene. If the two alleles are identical, the individual is said to be homozygous at that locus; if different, heterozygous. Some alleles show dominance over others. These mask the effect of other alleles, which are known as recessive.

alternation of generations typical life cycle of terrestrial plants and some seaweeds, in which there are two distinct forms occurring alternately: ***diploid*** (having two sets of chromosomes) and ***haploid*** (one set of chromosomes). The diploid generation produces haploid spores by meiosis (reduction cell division) and is called the sporophyte, whereas the haploid generation produces gametes (sex cells) and is called the gametophyte. The gametes fuse to form a diploid zygote which develops into a new sporophyte; thus the sporophyte and gametophyte alternate.

birth the act of producing live young from within the body of female animals. Both viviparous and ovoviviparous animals give birth to young. In viviparous animals, embryos obtain nourishment from the mother via a placenta or other means during pregnancy. In ovoviviparous animals, fertilized eggs develop and hatch in the oviduct of the mother and gain little or no nourishment from maternal tissues.

chromosome structure in a cell nucleus that carries the genes. Each chromosome consists of one very long strand of DNA, coiled and folded to produce a compact body. The point on a chromosome where a particular gene occurs is known as its locus. Most higher organisms have two copies of each chromosome (they are diploid) but some have only one (they are haploid). There are 46 chromosomes in a normal human cell.

death the cessation of all life functions, so that the molecules and structures associated with living things become disorganized and indistinguishable from similar molecules found in non-living things. When the energy for repair and replacement of complex molecules and whole cells is no longer available, large molecules such as proteins break down into simpler, soluble components. Eventually the organism partly dissolves into the soil or evaporates into the air, leaving behind skeletal material. The purpose of death may be evolutionary: individual organisms must die in order to make way for new ones, which, by virtue of sexual reproduction, may vary slightly in relation to the previous generation. Without this variation, organisms would be unable to adapt to environmental changes.

In human beings, death used to be pronounced when a person's breathing and heartbeat stopped. The advent of mechanical aids has made this point sometimes difficult to determine, and in controversial cases a person is now pronounced dead when the brain ceases to control the vital functions.

diploid having two sets of chromosomes in each cell. In sexually reproducing species, one set is derived from each parent, the gametes, or sex cells, of each parent being haploid (having only one set of chromosomes) owing to meiosis (reduction cell division).

embryo early development stage of an animal or a plant following fertilization of an ovum (egg cell) or activation of an ovum by parthenogenesis. In animals the embryo exists either within an egg (where it is nourished by food contained in the yolk) or, in mammals, in the uterus of the mother. In mammals (except marsupials), the embryo is fed through the placenta. In humans, the term 'embryo' describes the fertilized egg during its first seven weeks of existence; from the eighth week onwards it is referred to as a fetus. The plant embryo is found within the seed in higher plants.

fetus or *foetus* stage in mammalian embryo development. The human embryo is usually termed a fetus after the eighth week of development, when the limbs and external features of the head are recognizable.

fertilization in sexual reproduction, the union of two gametes (sex cells, often called egg and sperm) to produce a zygote, which combines the genetic material contributed by each parent. In self-fertilization the male and female gametes come from the same plant; in cross-fertilization they come from different plants. Self-fertilization rarely occurs in animals; usually even hermaphrodite animals cross-fertilize each other.

gamete cell that functions in sexual reproduction by merging with another gamete to form a zygote. Examples of gametes include sperm and egg cells. In most organisms, the gametes are haploid (they contain half the number of chromosomes of the parent), owing to reduction division, or meiosis.

gene unit of inherited material, encoded by a strand of DNA, and transcribed by RNA. In higher organisms, genes are located on the chromosomes. A gene is the inherited factor that consistently affects a particular character in an individual – for example, the gene for eye colour. It occurs at a particular point or locus on a particular chromosome and may have several variants or alleles, each specifying a particular form of that character – for example, blue or brown eyes. Genes do this by controlling the structure of proteins via the genetic code, as well as the amounts produced and the timing of production.

genome the full complement of genes carried by a single (haploid) set of chromosomes. The term may be applied to the genetic information carried by an individual or to the range of genes found in a given species.

genotype the particular set of alleles (variants of genes) possessed by a given organism. The term is usually used in conjunction with phenotype (physical appearance), which is the product of the genotype and all environmental effects.

germination the initial stages of growth in a seed, spore, or pollen grain. Seeds germinate when they are exposed to favourable external conditions of moisture, light, and temperature, and when any factors causing dormancy have been removed. The process begins with the uptake of water by the seed. The embryonic root, or radicle, is normally the first organ to emerge, followed by the embryonic shoot, or plumule. Food reserves, either within the endo-sperm (the nutritive tissue in the seeds of most flowering plants) or from the cotyledons (the seed leaves), are broken down to nourish the rapidly growing seedling. Germination is considered to have ended with the production of the first true leaves.

gestation in all mammals except the monotremes (duck-billed platypus and spiny anteaters), the period from the time of implantation of the embryo in the uterus to birth. This period varies among species; in humans it is about 266 days, in elephants 18–22 months, in cats about 60 days, and in some species of marsupial (such as opossum) as short as 12 days.

haploid having a single set of chromosomes in each cell. Most higher organisms are diploid – that is, they have two sets – but their gametes (sex cells) are haploid. Some plants, such as mosses, liverworts, and many seaweeds, are haploid, and male honey bees are haploid because they develop from eggs that have not been fertilized.

hermaphrodite organism that has both male and female sex organs. Hermaphroditism is the norm in species such as earthworms and snails, and is common in flowering plants. Cross-fertilization is the rule among hermaphrodites, with the parents functioning as male and female simultaneously, or as one or the other sex at different stages in their development.

heterozygous in a living organism, having two different alleles for a given trait. In homozygous organ-

Animal lifespans and gestation periods

Animal	*Gestation* *days*	*Average longevity/ maximum longevity* *years*
Ass	365	12/35.8
Baboon	187	20/35.5
Bear: black	219	18/36.8
grizzly	225	25/–
polar	240	20/34.7
Beaver	122	5/20.5
Buffalo (American)	278	15/–
Camel, Bactrian	406	12/29.5
Cat (domestic)	63	12/28
Chimpanzee	231	20/44.5
Chipmunk	31	6/8
Cow	284	15/30
Deer (white-tailed)	201	8/17.5
Dog (domestic)	61	12/20
Elephant (African)	–	35/60
Elephant (Asian)	645	40/70
Elk	250	15/26.5
Fox (red)	52	7/14
Giraffe	425	10/33.5
Goat (domestic)	151	8/18
Gorilla	257	20/39.3
Guinea pig	68	4/7.5
Hippopotamus	238	25/–
Horse	330	20/46
Kangaroo	42	7/–
Leopard	98	12/19.3
Lion	100	15/25
Monkey (rhesus)	164	15/–
Moose	240	12/–
Mouse (meadow)	21	3/–
Mouse (dom. white)	19	3/3.5
Opossum (American)	14–17	1/–
Pig (domestic)	112	10/27
Puma	90	12/19
Rabbit (domestic)	31	5/13
Rhinoceros (black)	450	15/–
Rhinoceros (white)	–	20/–
Sea lion (California)	350	12/28
Sheep (domestic)	154	12/20
Squirrel (grey)	44	10/–
Tiger	105	16/26.3
Wolf (maned)	63	5/–
Zebra (Grant's)	365	15/–
Incubation time (days)		
Chicken	21	
Duck	30	
Goose	30	
Pigeon	18	
Turkey	26	

**Longevity figures refer to animals in captivity; an animal's potential life span is rarely attained in nature.*

isms, by contrast, both chromosomes carry the same allele. In an outbreeding population (one that seeks mates from outside the family, tribe, or group), an individual organism will generally be heterozygous for some genes but homozygous for others.

homozygous in a living organism, having two identical alleles for a given trait. Individuals homozygous for a trait always breed true; that is, they produce offspring that resemble them in appearance when bred with a genetically similar individual; inbred varieties or species are homozygous for almost all traits. Recessive alleles are only expressed in the homozygous condition.

karyotype the set of chromosomes characteristic of a given species. It is described as the number, shape, and size of the chromosomes in a single cell of an organism. In humans, for example, the karyotype consists of 46 chromosomes, in mice 40, in crayfish 200, and in fruit flies 8.

larva stage between hatching and adulthood in those species in which the young have a different appearance and way of life from the adults. Examples include tadpoles (frogs) and caterpillars (butterflies and moths). Larvae are typical of the invertebrates, some of which (for example, shrimps) have two or more distinct larval stages. Among vertebrates, it is only the amphibians and some fishes that have a larval stage. The process whereby the larva changes into another stage, such as a pupa (chrysalis) or adult, is known as metamorphosis.

meiosis process of cell division in which the number of chromosomes in the cell is halved. It only occurs in eukaryotic cells (that is, not in bacteria), and is part of a life cycle that involves sexual reproduction because it allows the genes of two parents to be combined without the total number of chromosomes increasing.

metamorphosis period during the life cycle of many invertebrates, most amphibians, and some fish, during which the individual's body changes from one form to another through a major reconstitution of its tissues. For example, adult frogs are produced by metamorphosis from tadpoles, and butterflies are produced from caterpillars following metamorphosis within a pupa.

mitosis the process of cell division. The genetic material of eukaryotic cells is carried on a number of chromosomes. To control their movements during cell division so that both new cells get a full complement, a system of protein tubules, known as the spindle, organizes the chromosomes into position in the middle of the cell before they replicate. The spindle then controls the movement of chromosomes as the cell goes through the stages of division: ***interphase***, ***prophase***, ***metaphase***, ***anaphase***, and ***telophase***.

ovum (plural ***ova***) female gamete (sex cell) before fertilization. In animals it is called an egg, and is produced in the ovaries. In plants, where it is also known as an egg cell or oosphere, the ovum is produced in an ovule. The ovum is nonmotile. It must be fertilized by a male gamete before it can develop further, except in cases of parthenogenesis.

phenotype visible traits, those actually displayed by an organism. The phenotype is not a direct reflection of the genotype because some alleles are masked by the presence of other, dominant alleles. The phenotype is further modified by the effects of the environment (for example, poor nutrition stunts growth).

pollen the grains of seed plants that contain the male gametes. In angiosperms (flowering plants) pollen is produced within anthers; in most gymnosperms (cone-bearing plants) it is produced in male cones. A pollen grain is typically yellow and, when mature, has a hard outer wall. Individual species or genera of plants can be recognized from their pollen. Pollen of insect-pollinated plants is often sticky and spiny and larger than the smooth, light grains produced by wind-pollinated species.

pregnancy in humans, the period during which an embryo grows within the womb. It begins at conception and ends at birth, and the normal length is 40 weeks. Menstruation usually stops on conception. About one in five pregnancies fails, but most of these failures occur very early on, so the woman may notice only that her period is late. After the second month, the breasts become tense and tender, and the areas round the nipples become darker. Enlargement of the uterus can be felt at about the end of the third month, and thereafter the abdomen enlarges progressively. Pregnancy in animals is called gestation.

puberty stage in human development when the individual becomes sexually mature. It may occur from the age of ten upwards. The sexual organs take on their adult form and pubic hair grows. In girls, menstruation begins, and the breasts develop; in boys, the voice breaks and becomes deeper, and facial hair develops.

pupa non-feeding, largely immobile stage of some insect life cycles, in which larval tissues are broken down and adult tissues and structures are formed. In many insects, the pupa is ***exarate***, with the appendages (legs, antennae, wings) visible outside the pupal case; in butterflies and moths, it is called a chrysalis, and is ***obtect***, with the appendages developing inside the case.

replication production of copies of the genetic material DNA; it occurs during cell division. Most mutations are caused by mistakes during replication.

seed the reproductive structure of higher plants (angiosperms and gymnosperms). It develops from a fertilized ovule and consists of an embryo and a food store, surrounded and protected by an outer seed coat, called the testa. The food store is contained either in a specialized nutritive tissue, the endo sperm, or in the cotyledons of the embryo itself. In angiosperms, the seed is enclosed within a fruit, whereas in gymnosperms it is usually naked and unprotected, once shed from the female cone. After germination the seed develops into a new plant.

sperm or ***spermatozoon*** the male gamete of animals. Each sperm cell has a head capsule containing a nucleus, a middle portion containing mitochondria (which provide energy), and a long tail (flagellum).

spore small reproductive or resting body, usually consisting of just one cell. Unlike a gamete, it does not need to fuse with another cell in order to develop into a new organism. Spores are produced by the lower plants, most fungi, some bacteria, and certain protozoa. They are generally light and easily dispersed by wind movements.

The Maintenance of Life

aerobic requiring oxygen (usually dissolved in water) for the efficient release of energy contained in food molecules, such as glucose. Almost all living organisms are aerobic, plants as well as animals, except certain (anaerobic) bacteria. Aerobic reactions occur inside every cell, and most aerobic organisms die in the absence of oxygen, but certain organisms and cells, such as those found in muscle tissue, can function for short periods anaerobically.

anaerobic not requiring oxygen for the release of energy from food molecules such as glucose. Anaerobic organisms include many bacteria, yeasts, and internal parasites. ***Obligate anaerobes***, such as certain primitive bacteria, cannot function in the presence of oxygen; but ***facultative anaerobes***, like the fermenting yeasts and most bacteria, can function with or without oxygen.

autotroph any living organism that synthesizes organic substances from inorganic molecules by using light or chemical energy. Autotrophs are the ***primary producers*** in all food chains since the materials they synthesize and store are the energy sources of all other organisms. All green plants and many planktonic organisms are autotrophs, using sunlight to convert carbon dioxide and water into sugars by photosynthesis.

basal metabolic rate (BMR) amount of energy needed by an animal just to stay alive. It is measured when the animal is awake but resting, and includes the energy required to keep the heart beating, sustain breathing, repair tissues, and keep the brain and nerves functioning. Measuring the animal's con-sumption of oxygen gives an accurate value for BMR, because oxygen is needed to release energy from food.

BMR varies from one species to another, and from males to females. In humans, it is highest in children and declines with age. Disease, including mental illness, can make it rise or fall. Hormones from the thyroid gland control the BMR.

biosynthesis synthesis of organic chemicals from simple inorganic ones by living cells; for example, the conversion of carbon dioxide and water to glucose by plants during photosynthesis. Other biosynthetic reactions produce cell constituents including proteins and fats.

carnivore animal that eats other animals. Although the term is sometimes confined to those that eat the flesh of vertebrate prey, it is often used more broadly to include any animal that eats other animals, even microscopic ones. Carrion-eaters may or may not be included.

chemosynthesis method of making protoplasm (contents of a cell) using the energy from chemical reactions, in contrast to the use of light energy employed for the same purpose in photosynthesis. The process is used by certain bacteria, which can synthesize organic compounds from carbon dioxide and water using the energy from special methods of respiration.

decomposer any organism that breaks down dead matter. Decomposers play a vital role in the ecosystem by freeing important chemical substances, such as nitrogen compounds, locked up in dead organisms or excrement. They feed on some of the released organic matter, but leave the rest to filter back into the soil or pass in gas form into the atmosphere. The principal decomposers are bacteria and fungi, but earthworms and many other invertebrates are often included in this group. The nitrogen cycle relies on the actions of decomposers.

food chain sequence showing the feeding relationships between organisms in a particular ecosystem. Each organism depends on the next lowest member of the chain for its food.

Energy in the form of food is shown to be transferred from autotrophs, or producers, which are principally plants and photosynthetic microorganisms, to a series of heterotrophs, or consumers. The heterotrophs comprise the herbivores, which feed on the producers; carnivores, which feed on the herbivores; and decomposers, which break down the dead bodies and waste products of all four groups (including their own), ready for recycling.

gas exchange exchange of gases between living organisms and the atmosphere, principally oxygen and carbon dioxide.

herbivore animal that feeds on green plants (or photosynthetic single-celled organisms) or their prod-

Green cows?

Cows and other cud-chewing animals produce methane when they digest their food. And when they burp, this methane belches forth to add to the greenhouse gases in the atmosphere. In fact, nearly 3% of all the greenhouse gases are thought to come from this source.

Previous attempts to measure the methane production of cattle have consisted of putting a cow into a sealed container, so that the gas produced can be easily monitored. However, putting a cow in a small sealed area naturally alters its behaviour, so the results have not been very useful.

Now a team of scientists in Australia have started investigating methane production 'in the field'. A network of pipes is set up on either side of the test area. The pipes, up to 2 m/4 ft above ground, have tiny holes drilled into them, and gases are drawn into the pipes by an air pump. The gas is carefully analysed, and the results from the upwind side compared with the results for the downwind. The difference between the two shows how much methane the cows have produced.

The aim of the investigation is to find how methane production varies according to the feed given to the cows. The feed that produces the least methane can be said to be most environmentally friendly. We can look forward to the arrival of the truly 'green' cow.

ucts, including seeds, fruit, and nectar. The most numerous type of herbivore is thought to be the zooplankton, tiny invertebrates in the surface waters of the oceans that feed on small photosynthetic algae. Herbivores are more numerous than other animals because their food is the most abundant. They form a vital link in the food chain between plants and carnivores.

heterotroph any living organism that obtains its energy from organic substances produced by other organisms. All animals and fungi are heterotrophs, and they include herbivores, carnivores, and saprotrophs (those that feed on dead animal and plant material).

nitrogen cycle the process of nitrogen passing through the ecosystem. Nitrogen, in the form of inorganic compounds (such as nitrates) in the soil, is absorbed by plants and turned into organic compounds (such as proteins) in plant tissue. A proportion of this nitrogen is eaten by herbivores, with some of this in turn being passed on to the carnivores, which feed on the herbivores. The nitrogen is ultimately returned to the soil as excrement and when organisms die and are converted back to inorganic form by decomposers.

omnivore animal that feeds on both plant and animal material. Omnivores have digestive adaptations intermediate between those of herbivores and carnivores, with relatively unspecialized digestive systems and gut microorganisms that can digest a variety of foodstuffs.

photosynthesis process by which green plants trap light energy and use it to drive a series of chemical reactions, leading to the formation of carbohydrates. All animals ultimately depend on photosynthesis because it is the method by which the basic food (sugar) is created. For photosynthesis to occur, the plant must possess chlorophyll and must have a supply of carbon dioxide and water.

Photosynthesis by cyanobacteria was responsible for the appearance of oxygen in the Earth's atmosphere 2 billion years ago, and photosynthesis by plants maintains the oxygen level today.

respiration biochemical process whereby food molecules are progressively broken down (oxidized) to release energy in the form of ATP (the nucleotide that powers cellular reactions). In most organisms this requires oxygen, but in some bacteria the oxidant is the nitrate or sulphate ion instead. In all higher organisms, respiration occurs in the mitochondria. Respiration is also used to mean breathing, although this is more accurately described as a form of gas exchange.

The Macroscopic World

ANIMAL

or ***metazoan*** member of the kingdom Animalia, one of the major categories of living things, the science of which is ***zoology***. Animals are all heterotrophs (they obtain their energy from organic substances produced by other organisms); they have eukaryotic cells (the genetic material is contained within a distinct nucleus) bounded by a thin cell membrane rather than the thick cell wall of plants. Most animals are capable of moving around for at least part of their life cycle.

Types

Invertebrate

animal without a backbone. The invertebrates comprise over 95% of the million or so existing animal species and include sponges, coelenterates, flatworms, nematodes, annelid worms, arthropods, molluscs, echinoderms, and primitive aquatic chordates, such as sea squirts and lancelets.

annelid any segmented worm of the phylum Annelida. Annelids include earthworms, leeches, and marine worms such as lugworms. They have a distinct head and a soft body divided into segments shut off from one another by membranous partitions.

arachnid or ***arachnoid*** type of arthropod, including spiders, scorpions, and mites. They differ from insects in possessing only two main body regions, the cephalothorax and the abdomen.

arthropod member of the phylum Arthropoda; an invertebrate animal with jointed legs and a seg-

Changing orders

DNA analysis is changing the way we classify animals, and throwing new light on how they evolve. A good example is shown by recent findings concerning whale families. Researchers in Belgium and the USA have recently completed a detailed analysis of similar genes in 16 species of whales, and the results are at variance with the way these species have been traditionally classified.

Whales with teeth, such as the sperm whale and the dolphins, have previously been thought to be closely related and have been classified as such. However, comparing the DNA that codes for ribosomal RNA in whales shows that the sperm whales are more closely related to the baleen whales, which do not have teeth but which filter food from the sea. The comparison also showed that the beaked whale, which has a few teeth, is only distantly related to the other whale families.

The results were confirmed by comparison of the DNA sequence for myoglobin in different whale species. And what use is it to know? Well, it helps to fill in our understanding of how this important group evolved. One important point, for example, concerns echo-location, the ability of whales to navigate by listening to the echoes of sounds. According to traditional classification, baleen whales never had the ability to echo-locate. The new classification implies that baleen whales have evolved from species that were able to echo-locate, and have now lost the ability.

mented body with a horny or chitinous casing (exoskeleton), which is shed periodically and replaced as the animal grows. Included are arachnids such as spiders and mites, as well as crustaceans, millipedes, centipedes, and insects.

crustacean one of the class of arthropods that includes crabs, lobsters, shrimps, woodlice, and barnacles. The external skeleton is made of protein and chitin hardened with lime. Each segment bears a pair of appendages that may be modified as sensory feelers (antennae), as mouthparts, or as swimming, walking, or grasping structures.

echinoderm marine invertebrate of the phylum Echinodermata ('spiny-skinned'), characterized by five-radial symmetry. Echinoderms include starfishes (or sea stars), brittlestars, sea lilies, sea urchins, and sea cucumbers. The skeleton is external, made of a series of limy plates, and echinoderms generally move by using tube feet, small water-filled sacs that can be protruded or pulled back to the body.

flatworm invertebrate of the phylum Platyhelminthes. Some are free-living, but many are parasitic (for example, tapeworms and flukes). The body is simple and bilaterally symmetrical, with one opening to the intestine. Many are hermaphroditic (with both male and female sex organs), and practise self-fertilization.

insect any member of the class Insecta among the arthropods or jointed-legged animals. An insect's body is divided into head, thorax, and abdomen. The head bears a pair of feelers or antennae, and attached to the thorax are three pairs of legs and usually two pairs of wings. The skeleton is external and is composed of chitin. It is membranous at the joints, but elsewhere is hard. The life cycle of insects includes metamorphosis. More than 1 million species are known. Insects vary in size from 0.02 cm/0.007 in to 35 cm/13.5 in in length.

jellyfish marine invertebrate of the phylum Cnidaria (coelenterates) with an umbrella-shaped body composed of a semitransparent gelatinous substance, with a fringe of stinging tentacles. Most adult jellyfishes move freely, but during parts of their life cycle many are polyplike and attached. They feed on small animals that are paralysed by stinging cells in the jellyfishes' tentacles.

mollusc any invertebrate of the phylum Mollusca with a body divided into three parts, a head, a foot, and a visceral mass. The majority of molluscs are marine animals, but some inhabit fresh water, and a few are terrestrial. They include bivalves, mussels, octopuses, oysters, snails, slugs, and squids. The body is soft, limbless, and cold-blooded. There is no internal skeleton, but many species have a hard shell covering the body.

nematode unsegmented worm of the phylum Nematoda. Nematodes are pointed at both ends, with a tough, smooth outer skin. They include many free-living species found in soil and water, including the sea, but a large number are parasites, such as the roundworms and pinworms that live in humans, or the eelworms that attack plant roots. They differ from flatworms in that they have two openings to the gut (a mouth and an anus).

Vertebrate

any animal with a backbone. The 41,000 species of vertebrates include mammals, birds, reptiles, amphibians, and fishes. They include most of the larger animals, but in terms of numbers of species are only a tiny proportion of the world's animals. The zoological taxonomic group Vertebrata is a subgroup of the phylum Chordata.

amphibian member of the vertebrate class Amphibia, which generally spend their larval (tadpole) stage in fresh water, transferring to land at maturity (after metamorphosis) and generally returning to water to breed. Like fish and reptiles, they continue to grow throughout life, and cannot maintain a temperature greatly differing from that of their environment. The class includes caecilians (wormlike in appearance), salamanders, frogs, and toads.

bird backboned animal of the class Aves, the biggest group of land vertebrates, characterized by warm blood, feathers, wings, breathing through lungs, and egg-laying by the female. There are nearly 8,500 species of birds.

fish aquatic vertebrate that uses gills for obtaining oxygen from fresh or sea water. There are three main groups, not closely related: the bony fishes or Osteichthyes (goldfish, cod, tuna); the cartilaginous fishes or Chondrichthyes (sharks, rays); and the jawless fishes or Agnatha (hagfishes, lampreys). Most lay eggs, sometimes in vast numbers. The bony fishes constitute the majority of living fishes (about 20,000 species). The skeleton is bone, movement is controlled by mobile fins, and the body is usually covered with scales.

mammal animal characterized by having mammary glands in the female, used for suckling the young, and hair (very reduced in some species, such as whales). Mammals are divided into three groups: ***placental mammals***, where the young develop inside the uterus, receiving nourishment from the blood of the mother via the placenta; ***marsupials***, where the young are born at an early stage of development and develop further in a pouch on the mother's body; and ***monotremes***, where the young hatch from an egg outside the mother's body and are then nourished with milk. There are over 4,000 species of mammals. The smallest shrew weighs only 2 g/0.07 oz, the largest whale up to 140 tonnes.

reptile any member of a class (Reptilia) of vertebrates. They include snakes, lizards, crocodiles, turtles, and tortoises. Unlike amphibians, reptiles have hard-shelled, yolk-filled eggs that are laid on land and from which fully formed young are born. Some snakes and lizards retain their eggs and give birth to live young. Reptiles are cold-blooded, and the skin is usually covered with scales. The metabolism is slow, and in some cases (certain large snakes) intervals between meals may be months.

Systems

alimentary canal in animals, the tube through which food passes; it extends from the mouth to the anus. It is a complex organ, adapted for digestion. In human adults, it is about 9 m/30 ft long, consisting of the mouth cavity, pharynx, oesophagus, stomach, and the small and large intestines.

bone hard connective tissue comprising the skeleton of most vertebrate animals. It consists of a network of collagen fibres impregnated with mineral salts (largely calcium phosphate and calcium carbonate), a combination that gives the bone great strength, comparable in some cases with that of reinforced concrete. Enclosed within this solid matrix are bone cells, blood vessels, and nerves. The interior of the long bones of the limbs consists of a spongy matrix filled with a soft marrow that produces blood cells.

brain in higher animals, a mass of interconnected nerve cells, forming the anterior part of the central nervous system, whose activities it coordinates and controls. In vertebrates, the brain is contained by the skull. An enlarged portion of the upper spinal cord, the ***medulla oblongata***, contains centres for the control of respiration, heartbeat rate and strength, and blood pressure. Overlying this is the ***cerebellum***, which is concerned with coordinating complex muscular processes such as maintaining posture and moving limbs. The cerebral hemispheres (***cerebrum***) are paired outgrowths of the front end of the forebrain, in early vertebrates mainly concerned with the senses, but in higher vertebrates greatly developed and involved in the integration of all sensory input and motor output, and in intelligent behaviour. In the brain, nerve impulses are passed across synapses by neurotransmitters, in the same way as in other parts of the nervous system.

In mammal the cerebrum is the largest part of the brain, carrying the ***cerebral cortex***. This consists of a thick surface layer of cell bodies (grey matter), below which fibre tracts (white matter) connect various parts of the cortex to each other and to other points in the central nervous system. As cerebral complexity grows, the surface of the brain becomes convoluted into deep folds.

circulatory system system of vessels in an animal's body that transports essential substances (blood or other circulatory fluid) to and from the different parts of the body. Except for simple animals such as sponges and coelenterates (jellyfishes, sea anemones, corals), all animals have a circulatory system. Although most animals have a heart or hearts to pump the blood, normal body movements circulate the fluid in some small invertebrates. The human circulatory system contains about 96,500 km/60,000 mi of blood vessels.

muscle contractile animal tissue that produces locomotion and maintains the movement of body substances. Muscle is made of long cells that can contract to between one-half and one-third of their relaxed length. ***Striped*** muscles are activated by motor nerves under voluntary control; their ends are usually attached via tendons to bones. ***Involuntary*** or ***smooth*** muscles are controlled by motor nerves of the autonomic nervous system, and are located in the gut, blood vessels, iris, and various ducts. ***Cardiac*** muscle occurs only in the heart, and is also controlled by the autonomic nervous system.

nervous system the system of interconnected nerve cells of most invertebrates and all vertebrates. It is composed of the central and autonomic nervous systems. It may be as simple as the nerve net of coelenterates (for example, jellyfishes) or as complex as the mammalian nervous system, with a central nervous system comprising brain and spinal cord, and a peripheral nervous system connecting up with sensory organs, muscles, and glands.

How slow is a snail's pace?

Maximum speeds for a selection of animals

Animal	*mph*
Cheetah	70
Wildebeest	50
Lion	50
Quarterhorse	47.5
Elk	45
Cape hunting dog	45
Coyote	43
Grey fox	42
Hyena	40
Zebra	40
Greyhound	39.35
Whippet	35.50
Rabbit (domestic)	35
Jackal	35
Reindeer	32
Giraffe	32
White-tailed deer	30
Wart hog	30
Grizzly bear	30
Cat (domestic)	30
Human	27.89
Elephant	25
Black mamba snake	20
Wild turkey	15
Squirrel	12
Pig (domestic)	11
Chicken	9
Spider (Tegenaria atrica)	1.17
Giant tortoise	0.17
Three-toed sloth	0.15
Garden snail	0.03

Most of these measurements refer to the maximum speed registered for approximately quarter-mile distances.

Source: Natural History

skeleton the rigid or semirigid framework that supports an animal's body, protects its internal organs, and provides anchorage points for its muscles. The skeleton may be composed of bone and cartilage (vertebrates), chitin (arthropods), calcium carbonate (molluscs and other invertebrates), or silica (many protists).

It may be internal, forming an ***endoskeleton***, or external, forming an ***exoskeleton***. Another type of skeleton, found in invertebrates such as earthworms, is the ***hydrostatic skeleton***. This gains partial rigidity from fluid enclosed within a body cavity. Because the fluid cannot be compressed, contraction of one part of the body results in extension of another part, giving peristaltic motion.

PLANT

an organism that carries out photosynthesis, has cellulose cell walls and complex cells, and is immobile. A few parasitic plants have lost the ability to photosynthesize but are still considered to be plants. Plants are autotrophs, that is, they make carbohydrates from water and carbon dioxide, and are the primary producers in all food chains, so that all animal life is dependent on them. They play a vital part in the carbon cycle, removing carbon dioxide from the atmosphere and generating oxygen.

algae (singular *alga*) diverse group of plants that shows great variety of form, ranging from single-celled forms to multicellular seaweeds of considerable size and complexity. Algae can be classified into 12 divisions, largely to be distinguished by their pigmentation, including the ***green algae*** Chlorophyta, freshwater or terrestrial; ***stoneworts*** Charophyta; ***golden-brown algae*** Chrysophyta; ***brown algae*** Phaeophyta, mainly marine and including the ***kelps*** *Laminaria* and allies, the largest of all algae; ***red algae*** Rhodophyta, mainly marine and often living parasitically or as epiphytes on other algae; ***diatoms*** Bacillariophyta; ***yellow-green algae*** Xanthophyta, mostly freshwater and terrestrial; and ***blue-green algae*** Cyanophyta, of simple cell structure and without sexual reproduction, mostly freshwater or terrestrial.

angiosperm flowering plant in which the seeds are enclosed within an ovary, which ripens to a fruit. Angiosperms are divided into monocotyledons (single seed leaf in the embryo) and dicotyledons (two seed leaves in the embryo). They include the majority of flowers, herbs, grasses, and trees except conifers.

bryophyte member of the Bryophyta, a division of the plant kingdom containing three classes: the Hepaticae (liverwort), Musci (moss), and Anthocerotae (hornwort). Bryophytes are generally small, low-growing, terrestrial plants with no vascular (water-conducting) system as in higher plants. Their life cycle shows a marked alternation of generations. Bryophytes chiefly occur in damp habitats and require water for the dispersal of the male gametes (antherozoids).

gymnosperm any plant whose seeds are exposed, as opposed to the structurally more advanced angiosperms, where they are inside an ovary. The group includes conifers and related plants such as cycads and ginkgos, whose seeds develop in cones.

pteridophyte simple type of vascular plant. The pteridophytes comprise four classes: the Psilosida, including the most primitive vascular plants, found mainly in the tropics; the Lycopsida, including the club mosses; the Sphenopsida, including the horsetails; and the Pteropsida, including the ferns. They are mainly terrestrial, non-flowering plants characterized by alternation of generations. They do not produce seeds.

Systems

chlorophyll green pigment present in most plants; it is responsible for the absorption of light energy during photosynthesis. The pigment absorbs the red and blue-violet parts of sunlight but reflects the green, thus giving plants their characteristic colour.

chloroplast structure (organelle) within a plant cell containing the green pigment chlorophyll. Chloroplasts occur in most cells of the green plant that are exposed to light, often in large numbers. Typically, they are flattened and disclike, with a double membrane enclosing the stroma, a gel-like matrix. Within the stroma are stacks of fluid-containing cavities, or vesicles, where photosynthesis occurs.

flower the reproductive unit of an angiosperm or flowering plant, typically consisting of four whorls of modified leaves: sepals, petals, stamens, and carpels. These are borne on a central axis or receptacle. The many variations in size, colour, number, and arrangement of parts are closely related to the method of pollination. Flowers adapted for wind pollination typically have reduced or absent petals and sepals and long, feathery stigmas that hang outside the flower to trap airborne pollen. The petals of insect-pollinated flowers are usually conspicuous and brightly coloured.

leaf lateral outgrowth on the stem of a plant, and in most species the primary organ of photosynthesis. The chief leaf types are cotyledons (seed leaves), scale leaves (on underground stems), foliage leaves, and bracts (in the axil of which a flower is produced). Structurally the leaf is made up of mesophyll cells surrounded by the epidermis and usually, in addition, a waxy layer, termed the cuticle, which prevents excessive evaporation of water from the leaf tissues by transpiration. The epidermis is interrupted by small pores, or stomata, through which gas exchange between the plant and the atmosphere occurs.

Vine tuning

In the effort to find a drug to combat the HIV virus, many botanical samples from different parts of the world have been tested. At the United States National Cancer Institute in Maryland, over 20,000 samples from 7,000 different plants have been tested.

One of the most promising so far has been from the leaves of a woody vine found in the rainforest of Cameroon. Dried leaves from this vine were sent to the Institute in 1987, and extracts were found to have a considerable effect on the ability of HIV to kill human cells. HIV targets white blood cells, but adding the vine-leaf extract reduced the number of these cells killed by the virus.

The Institute requested further supplies to continue the testing programme. However, results from extracts taken from the new supplies all proved negative. Puzzled and disappointed, the Institute requested the original collector to return to the original site and find some of the first set of leaves. Only when the collector returned to the site was it realized that the leaves came from a previously unrecognized species of plant, related to the common jungle vine, but with a shorter petal and a slightly different shape to the leaf.

Testing with leaves from this batch looks more promising, and extracts may be ready to try on humans within two years.

root the part of a plant that is usually underground, and whose primary functions are anchorage and the absorption of water and dissolved mineral salts. Roots usually grow downwards and towards water (that is, they are positively geotropic and hydrotropic). Plants such as epiphytic orchids, which grow above ground, produce aerial roots that absorb moisture from the atmosphere. Others, such as ivy, have climbing roots arising from the stems, which serve to attach the plant to trees and walls.

The Microscopic World

archaebacteria three groups of bacteria whose DNA differs significantly from that of other bacteria (called the 'eubacteria'). All are strict anaerobes; that is, they are killed by oxygen. This is thought to indicate that the archaebacteria are related to the earliest life forms, which appeared about 4 billion years ago, when there was little oxygen in the Earth's atmosphere. Archaebacteria are found in undersea vents, hot springs, the Dead Sea, and salt pans, and have adapted to refuse dumps.

bacillus member of a group of rodlike bacteria that occur everywhere in the soil and air. Some are responsible for diseases, such as anthrax, or for causing food spoilage.

bacteria (singular *bacterium*) microscopic unicellular organisms with prokaryotic cells (lacking true nuclei). They usually reproduce by binary fission (dividing into two equal parts), and since this may occur approximately every 20 minutes, a single bacterium is potentially capable of producing 16 million copies of itself in a day. It is thought that 1–10% of the world's bacteria have been identified. Many bacteria cause disease, but certain types of bacteria are vital in many food and industrial processes, while others play an essential role in the nitrogen cycle, which maintains soil fertility.

blue-green algae or *cyanobacteria* single-celled, primitive organisms that resemble bacteria in their internal cell organization, sometimes joined together in colonies or filaments. Blue-green algae are among the oldest known living organisms and, with bacteria, belong to the kingdom Monera; remains have been found in rocks up to 3.5 billion years old. They are widely distributed in aquatic habitats, on the damp surfaces of rocks and trees, and in the soil. Some can fix nitrogen and thus are necessary to the nitrogen cycle, while others follow a symbiotic existence; for example, living in association with fungi to form lichens.

cell discrete, membrane-bound portion of living matter, the smallest unit capable of an independent existence. All living organisms consist of one or more cells, with the exception of viruses. Bacteria, protozoa, and many other microorganisms consist of single cells, whereas a human is made up of billions of cells. Essential features of a cell are the membrane, which encloses it and restricts the flow of substances in and out; the jellylike material within, often known as protoplasm; the ribosomes, which carry out protein synthesis; and the DNA, which forms the hereditary material.

coccus (plural *cocci*) member of a group of globular bacteria, some of which are harmful to humans. The cocci contain the subgroups ***streptococci***, where the bacteria associate in straight chains, and ***staphylococci***, where the bacteria associate in branched chains.

cytoplasm the part of the cell outside the nucleus. Strictly speaking, this includes all the organelles (mitochondria, chloroplasts, and so on), but often cytoplasm refers to the jellylike matter in which the organelles are embedded (correctly termed the cytosol).

eukaryote one of the two major groupings into which all organisms are divided. Included are all organisms, except bacteria and cyanobacteria (blue-green algae), which belong to the prokaryote grouping. The cells of eukaryotes possess a clearly defined nucleus, bounded by a membrane, within which DNA is formed into distinct chromosomes. Eukaryotic cells also contain mitochondria, chloroplasts, and other structures (organelles) that, together with a defined nucleus, are lacking in the cells of prokaryotes.

methanogenic bacteria one of a group of primitive bacteria (archaebacteria). They give off methane gas as a by-product of their metabolism, and are common in sewage treatment plants and hot springs, where the temperature is high and oxygen is absent.

microorganism or *microbe* living organism invisible to the naked eye but visible under a microscope. Microorganisms include viruses and single-celled organisms such as bacteria, protozoa, yeasts, and some algae. The term has no taxonomic significance in biology. The study of microorganisms is known as microbiology.

nucleus the central, membrane-enclosed part of a eukaryotic cell, containing the chromosomes.

prokaryote organism whose cells lack organelles (specialized segregated structures such as nuclei, mitochondria, and chloroplasts). Prokaryote DNA is not arranged in chromosomes but forms a coiled structure called a ***nucleoid***. The prokaryotes comprise only the ***bacteria*** and ***cyanobacteria*** (blue-green algae); all other organisms are eukaryotes.

protist single-celled organism that has a eukaryotic cell but is not a member of the plant, fungal, or animal kingdoms. The main protists are protozoa.

protozoa group of single-celled organisms without rigid cell walls. Some, such as amoeba, ingest other cells, but most are saprotrophs or parasites. The group is polyphyletic (containing organisms which have different evolutionary origins).

virus infectious particle consisting of a core of nucleic acid (DNA or RNA) enclosed in a protein shell. Viruses are acellular and able to function and reproduce only if they can invade a living cell to use the cell's system to replicate themselves. In the process, they may disrupt or alter the host cell's own DNA. The healthy human body reacts by producing an antiviral protein, interferon, which prevents the infection spreading to adjacent cells.

Viroids are even smaller than viruses; they consist of a single strand of nucleic acid with no protein coat.

Viruses are abundant in seas and lakes, with between 5 million and 250 million per millilitre of water, rising with the degree of pollution. Among diseases caused by viruses are chickenpox, common cold, herpes, influenza, rabies, smallpox, AIDS, and many plant diseases.

The New Synthesis

amino acid water-soluble organic molecule, mainly composed of carbon, oxygen, hydrogen, and nitrogen, containing both a basic amino group (NH_2) and an acidic carboxyl (COOH) group. When two or more amino acids are joined together, they are known as peptides; proteins are made up of interacting polypeptides (peptide chains consisting of more than three amino acids) and are folded or twisted in characteristic shapes.

Many different proteins are found in the cells of living organisms, but they are all made up of the same 20 amino acids, joined together in varying combinations (although other types of amino acid do occur infrequently in nature). Eight of these, the ***essential amino acids***, cannot be synthesized by humans and must be obtained from the diet. Children need a further two amino acids that are not essential for adults. Other animals also need some preformed amino acids in their diet, but green plants can manufacture all the amino acids they need from simpler molecules, relying on energy from the Sun and minerals (including nitrates) from the soil.

amylase one of a group of enzymes that break down starches into their component molecules (sugars) for use in the body. It occurs widely in both plants and animals. In humans, it is found in saliva and in pancreatic juices.

ATP abbreviation for ***adenosine triphosphate***, a nucleotide molecule found in all cells. It can yield large amounts of energy, and is used to drive the thousands of biological processes needed to sustain life, growth, movement, and reproduction. Green plants use light energy to manufacture ATP as part of the process of photosynthesis. In animals, ATP is formed by the breakdown of glucose molecules, usually obtained from the carbohydrate component of a diet, in a series of reactions termed respiration. It is the driving force behind muscle contraction and the synthesis of complex molecules needed by individual cells.

base pair the linkage of two base (purine or pyrimidine) molecules in DNA. They are found in nucleotides, and form the basis of the genetic code. One base lies on one strand of the DNA double helix, and one on the other, so that the base pairs link the two strands like the rungs of a ladder. In DNA, there are four bases: adenine and guanine (purines) and cytosine and thymine (pyrimidines). Adenine always pairs with thymine, and cytosine with guanine.

codon triplet of bases in a molecule of DNA or RNA that directs the placement of a particular amino acid during the process of protein (polypeptide) synthesis. There are 64 codons in the genetic code.

cytochrome protein responsible for part of the process of respiration by which food molecules are broken down in aerobic organisms. Cytochromes are part of the electron transport chain, which uses energized electrons to reduce molecular oxygen (O_2) to oxygen ions (O_2–). These combine with hydrogen ions (H+) to form water (H_2O), the end product of aerobic respiration. As electrons are passed from one cytochrome to another, energy is released and used to make ATP (nucleotide that powers cellular reactions).

DNA ***deoxyribonucleic acid*** complex giant molecule that contains, in chemically coded form, all the information needed to build, control, and maintain a

DNA

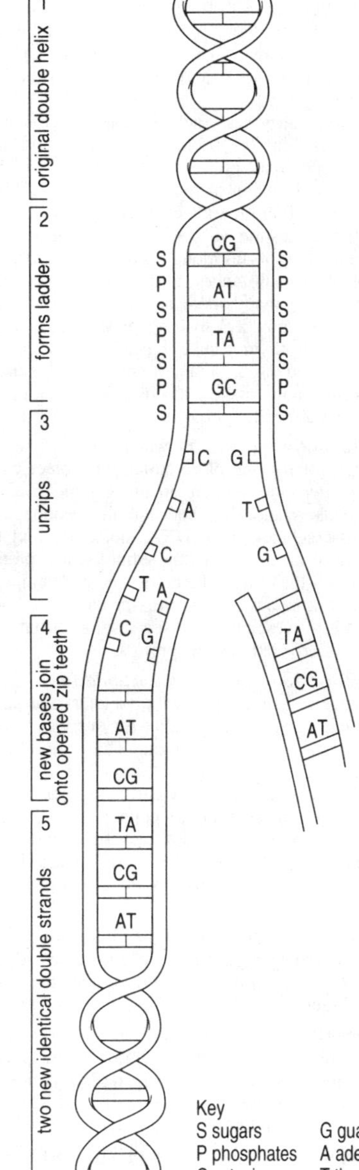

living organism. DNA is a ladderlike double-stranded nucleic acid that forms the basis of genetic inheritance in all organisms, except for a few viruses that have only RNA. In organisms other than bacteria it is organized into chromosomes and contained in the cell nucleus.

enzyme biological catalyst produced in cells, and capable of speeding up the chemical reactions necessary for life by converting one molecule (substrate) into another. Enzymes are not themselves destroyed by this process. They are large, complex proteins, and are highly specific, each chemical reaction requiring its own particular enzyme. The enzyme fits into a 'slot' (active site) in the substrate molecule, forming an enzyme-substrate complex that lasts until the substrate is altered or split, after which the enzyme can fall away. The substrate may therefore be compared to a lock, and the enzyme to the key required to open it.

Digestive enzymes include amylases (which digest starch), lipases (which digest fats), and proteases (which digest protein). Other enzymes play a part in the conversion of food energy into ATP; the manufacture of all the molecular components of the body; the replication of DNA when a cell divides; the production of hormones; and the control of movement of substances into and out of cells. Enzymes have many medical and industrial uses, from washing powders to drug production, and as research tools in molecular biology. They can be extracted from bacteria and moulds, and genetic engineering now makes it possible to tailor an enzyme for a specific purpose.

genetic code the way in which instructions for building proteins, the basic structural molecules of living matter, are 'written' in the genetic material DNA. This relationship between the sequence of bases (the subunits in a DNA molecule) and the sequence of amino acids (the subunits of a protein molecule) is the basis of heredity. The code employs codons of three bases each; it is the same in almost all organisms, except for a few minor differences recently discovered in some protozoa.

mitochondria (singular ***mitochondrion***) membrane-enclosed organelles within eukaryotic cells, containing enzymes responsible for energy production during aerobic respiration. These rodlike or spherical bodies are thought to be derived from free-living bacteria that, at a very early stage in the history of life, invaded larger cells and took up a symbiotic way of life inside. Each still contains its own small loop of DNA called mitochondrial DNA, and new mitochondria arise by division of existing ones.

molecular biology study of the molecular basis of life, including the biochemistry of molecules such as DNA, RNA, and proteins, and the molecular structure and function of the various parts of living cells.

nucleotide organic compound consisting of a purine (adenine or guanine) or a pyrimidine (thymine, uracil, or cytosine) base linked to a sugar (deoxyribose or ribose) and a phosphate group. DNA and RNA are made up of long chains of nucleotides.

operon group of genes that are found next to each other on a chromosome, and are turned on and off as an integrated unit. They usually produce enzymes that control different steps in the same biochemical pathway. Operons are found in bacteria; they are less common in higher organisms, where the control of metabolism is a more complex process.

peptide molecule comprising two or more amino acid molecules (not necessarily different) joined by ***peptide bonds***, whereby the acid group of one acid is linked to the amino group of the other (–CO.NH). The number of amino acid molecules in the peptide is indicated by referring to it as a di-, tri-, or polypeptide (two, three, or many amino acids).

protein complex, biologically important substance composed of amino acids joined by peptide bonds. Other types of bond, such as sulphur–sulphur bonds, hydrogen bonds, and cation bridges between acid sites, are responsible for creating the protein's characteristic three-dimensional structure, which may be fibrous, globular, or pleated.

Proteins are essential to all living organisms. As ***enzymes*** they regulate all aspects of metabolism. Structural proteins such as ***keratin*** and ***collagen*** make up the skin, claws, bones, tendons, and ligaments; ***muscle*** proteins produce movement; ***haemoglobin*** transports oxygen; and ***membrane*** proteins regulate the movement of substances into and out of cells.

ribosome the protein-making machinery of the cell. Ribosomes are located on the endoplasmic reticulum of eukaryotic cells, and are made of proteins and a special type of RNA, ribosomal RNA. They receive messenger RNA (copied from the DNA) and amino acids, and 'translate' the messenger RNA by using its chemically coded instructions to link amino acids in a specific order, to make a strand of a particular protein.

RNA ***ribonucleic acid*** nucleic acid involved in the process of translating the genetic material DNA into proteins. It is usually single-stranded, unlike the double-stranded DNA, and consists of a large number of nucleotides strung together, each of which comprises the sugar ribose, a phosphate group, and one of four bases (uracil, cytosine, adenine, or guanine). RNA is copied from DNA by the formation of base pairs, with uracil taking the place of thymine. Although RNA is normally associated only with the process of protein synthesis, it makes up the hereditary material itself in some viruses, such as retroviruses.

transcription in living cells, the process by which the information for the synthesis of a protein is transferred from the DNA strand on which it is carried to the messenger RNA strand involved in the actual synthesis. It occurs by the formation of base pairs when a single strand of unwound DNA serves as a template for assembling the complementary nucleotides that make up the new RNA strand.

translation the process by which proteins are synthesized in living cells. During translation, the information coded as a sequence of nucleotides in messenger RNA is transformed into a sequence of amino acids in a peptide chain. The process involves the 'translation' of the genetic code.

Genetic engineering's brave new world

The 1980s and 1990s have seen considerable advances in understanding of the structure of genes and how they work, thanks to the development of techniques for isolating and manipulating genes (recombinant DNA technology). We can determine the structure of the genetic material (DNA sequencing) and study minute quantities of DNA using PCR (polymerase chain reaction). We know more about embryogenesis (the process by which a single fertilized egg develops into a complex embryo), about the changes in the early stages of cancer, and about the basic defects in inherited diseases like cystic fibrosis, muscular dystrophy, and certain types of blindness. We also understand more of what makes healthy people different; racial differences are trivial by comparison. There have been remarkable applications of this knowledge that could not have been foreseen in the 1960s.

Large-scale production of pure proteins

Each gene is responsible for making a protein. By purifying genes and transferring them to bacterial cells, scientists can harvest large quantities of proteins that would not normally be made by bacteria. Most of the insulin for diabetics is now made in bacteria. Several hormones and enzymes, whose deficiency results in inherited diseases, are manufactured in microorganisms. Other proteins are commercially produced in this way, including the bovine enzyme, rennin, used in making 'vegetarian' cheese. Experiments are in progress to transfer genes to sheep and cattle (transgenic animals), and then purify the relevant proteins from their milk.

Genetic engineering is being used to produce vaccines. These are normally made by growing pathogens (disease-causing organisms) in animals, or in organ or tissue culture, and then harvesting the live pathogen. The inactivated (attenuated) pathogens provoke our immune system, which reacts to the coat proteins covering the pathogen. The new method transfers the gene coding for the pathogen's coat protein into harmless bacteria or viruses which then make the protein themselves. The purified protein is used to stimulate the immune system. Vaccines against, for example, foot-and-mouth disease of cattle and hepatitis B in humans are proving much safer than attenuated vaccines.

Some animal vaccines now use live non-pathogenic viruses which have, in addition to their own coat proteins, those of a pathogen. Such a modified 'friendly' virus has been successfully used to eradicate the rabies virus from populations of wild foxes in southern Belgium. The transfer of genes between viruses will play an important part in the development of new vaccines.

Crop improvement

The transfer of 'foreign' genes into plants has led to the development of crops with desirable characteristics. Species have been made resistant to weed-killers, permitting the removal of weeds without damage to the crop. A bacterial gene can be transferred, conferring resistance to caterpillars and other insects that can devastate crops, reducing the need for insecticides and their consequent environmental damage. Transgenic plants, resistant to the alfalfa mosaic virus and the tobacco ringspot virus, are also now available.

Many Third World countries depend heavily on a single crop containing storage proteins deficient in essential amino acids. By modifying the genes for these proteins, the nutritional value of the food has been greatly improved.

Genetic fingerprinting

Mini- and microsatellite DNA are types of DNA that differ so much between individuals that each person is effectively unique. Forensic scientists can determine the origin of tissue samples like blood and semen with a certainty that was previously impossible. Genetic fingerprinting has rapidly become invaluable in convicting murderers and rapists, and in eliminating suspects. Genetic fingerprints also allow relationships between people to be established, and are increasingly being used in paternity and immigration disputes.

Medical applications

The fundamental genetic changes responsible for some inherited diseases have been identified, leading to deeper understanding of the causes of disease, and to diagnostic methods. Prenatal diagnosis allows parents the opportunity to abort an affected fetus and try again for a normal baby. Similar methods have been used on eggs fertilized in the test tube, permitting implantation of normal embyos only. In certain communities, a particular inherited disease is so common that programmes of preventive medicine have been attempted. All pregnancies are screened; termination is offered to females shown to be carrying an affected fetus. Such community medicine has, for example, dramatically reduced the number of babies suffering from a blood disease in Sardinia.

Two recent projects promise exciting developments. One is human gene therapy – transferring normal genes to people with inherited diseases. Animals have been successfully treated, and after much discussion, medical approval has been granted for human trials. The other is the Human Genome Project, a huge international research effort to identify and study all 100,000 human genes. The project will take about 10 years; it should lead to deeper understanding of development and disease, and have unforeseen applications in many branches of biology. TD

New Techniques

abzyme artificially created antibody that can be used like an enzyme to accelerate reactions.

autoradiography technique for following the movement of molecules within an organism, especially a plant, by labelling with a radioactive isotope that can be traced on photographs. It is used to study photosynthesis, where the pathway of radioactive carbon dioxide can be traced as it moves through the various chemical stages.

bacteriophage virus that attacks bacteria. Such viruses are of use in genetic engineering.

biosensor device based on microelectronic circuits that can directly measure medically significant variables for the purpose of diagnosis or monitoring treatment. One such device measures the blood-sugar level using a single drop of blood, and shows the result on a liquid-crystal display within a few minutes.

biotechnology industrial use of living organisms to manufacture food, drugs, or other products. The brewing and baking industries have long relied on the yeast microorganism for fermentation purposes, while the dairy industry employs a range of bacteria and fungi to convert milk into cheeses and yoghurts. In genetic engineering, single-celled organisms with modified DNA are used to produce insulin and other drugs. Enzymes, whether extracted from cells or produced artificially, are central to most biotechnological applications.

clone group of cells or organisms arising by asexual reproduction from a single 'parent' individual. Clones therefore have exactly the same genetic make-up as the parent cell. Traditional methods of cloning have been used on plant material throughout history; they include such techniques as leaf and stem cuttings. Recent advances in biotechnology have allowed the cloning of animals.

cosmid fragment of DNA from the human genome inserted into a bacterial cell. The bacterium replicates the fragment along with its own DNA. In this way the fragments are copied for a gene library. Cosmids are characteristically 40,000 base pairs in length. The most commonly used bacterium is *Escherichia coli*. A yeast artificial chromosome works in the same way.

electron microscope instrument that produces a magnified image by using a beam of electrons instead of light rays, as in an optical microscope. An ***electron lens*** is an arrangement of electromagnetic coils that control and focus the beam. There is a fluorescent screen or a photographic plate on which the electrons form an image. The wavelength of the electron beam is much shorter than that of light, so much greater magnification and resolution (ability to distinguish detail) can be achieved. The development of the electron microscope has made possible the observation of very minute organisms, viruses, and even large molecules.

A transmission electron microscope passes the electron beam through a very thin slice of a specimen. A scanning electron microscope looks at the exterior of a specimen. A scanning transition electron microscope (STEM) can produce a magnification of 90 million times.

electroporation technique of introducing foreign DNA into pollen with a strong burst of electricity, used in creating genetically engineered plants.

fluorescence microscopy technique for examining samples under a microscope without slicing them into thin sections. Instead, fluorescent dyes are introduced into the tissue and used as a light source for imaging purposes. Fluorescent dyes can also be bonded to monoclonal antibodies and used to highlight areas where particular cell proteins occur.

gene bank collection of seeds or other forms of genetic material, such as tubers, spores, bacterial or yeast cultures, live animals and plants, frozen sperm and eggs, or frozen embryos. These are stored for possible future use in agriculture, plant and animal breeding, or in medicine, genetic engineering, or the restocking of wild habitats where species have become extinct. Gene banks will be increasingly used as the rate of extinction increases, depleting the Earth's genetic variety (biodiversity).

gene therapy curing or alleviating inherited diseases or defects by altering the DNA of some of the patient's cells by genetic engineering in a laboratory, and reintroducing the functioning cells into the body. In 1990, an engineered gene was used for the first time to treat a patient.

genetic engineering manipulation of genetic material by biochemical techniques. It is often achieved by the introduction of new DNA, usually by means of a virus or plasmid. This can be for pure research or to breed functionally specific plants, animals, or bacteria. These organisms with a foreign gene added are said to be transgenic.

In genetic engineering, the splicing and reconciliation of genes is used to increase knowledge of cell function and reproduction, but it can also achieve practical ends. For example, plants grown for food could be given the ability to fix nitrogen, found in some bacteria, and so reduce the need for expensive fertilizers, or simple bacteria could be modified to produce rare drugs. Developments in genetic engineering have led to the production of human insulin, human growth hormone, and a number of other bone-marrow stimulating hormones. New strains of animals have also been produced; a new strain of mouse was patented in the USA 1989 (the application was rejected in the European patent office). A vaccine against a sheep parasite (a larval tapeworm) has been developed by genetic engineering; most existing vaccines protect against bacteria and viruses. There is a risk that when transplanting genes between different types of bacteria (*Escherichia coli*, which lives in the human intestine, is often used) new and harmful strains might be produced. For this reason strict safety precautions are observed, and the altered bacteria are disabled in some way so they are unable to exist outside the laboratory.

genetic fingerprinting (or ***DNA fingerprinting*** or ***DNA profiling***) technique used for determining the pattern of certain parts of the genetic material DNA that is unique to each individual. Like skin fingerprinting, it can accurately distinguish humans from one another, with the exception of identical siblings

Cloning dinosaurs: how close are we?

The story is told of a mosquito preserved intact from Mesozoic times in a block of amber. The mosquito is found to contain the ingested blood of a dinosaur – its last meal. The dinosaur DNA in the blood is then cloned by scientists to produce living dinosaurs to populate a theme park. Then it all gets out of hand ...

Very dramatic. But how likely is the story?

There are many ways in which a fossil can be preserved. Most involve the total destruction of the original organic material and its replacement by minerals. The trees in Arizona's petrified forest, and the casts of seashells in limestone, are examples. However, should the original organism be completely entombed immediately after death in a sterile medium – such as oxygen-free mud in a stagnant swamp or fresh resin oozing from a tree – then some of the creature's substance may survive for a long time. Mammoths remain intact after being embedded in frozen mud, and coal is formed from the original carbon of the plants that were buried. The search for original biological material in fossils was started with the advent of precise analytical techniques in the early 1960s. Collagen, the protein substance that forms the flexible component of bone, has been found in fossil mammal remains dating from Pleistocene and Miocene times – about 1 million years ago (mya) and 5–24 mya respectively. The problem is that the amino acids that form the collagen are the same as the amino acids that exist in sediments and it is difficult to ascertain how much of the amino acid in the fossil bone is actually original and how much has leached in from outside.

Collagen is quite simple and quite sturdy compared with DNA – the organic chemical that defines the whole organism and forms the basis of the organism's growth and reproduction. DNA has been collected from the remains of recently extinct animals. The quagga – a kind of horse related to the zebra – was hunted to extinction in 1883. In 1984, scientists in Berkeley, California, were able to extract DNA from a preserved quagga skin. After a century there remained only about 1% of the DNA usually present in fresh tissue. The researchers were able to multiply this by cloning and obtain enough for experimental purposes. The procedure involved inserting a DNA fragment into the cell of a bacterium and letting the bacterium reproduce it as if it were its own. This produced enough to enable the scientists to compare the DNA structure with that of the modern mountain zebra. The difference between the two sets of DNA was so small that they could deduce that the common ancestor of the quagga and the mountain zebra must have existed between 3 and 4 mya.

The direct study of DNA from living animals is becoming increasingly useful in plotting evolution. It has recently been found that the genetic differences between the marine iguana and the land iguana of the Galapagos Islands is such that the two animals must have had a common ancestor some tens of millions of years ago. This is at odds with the knowledge that the oldest of the Galapagos islands is no more than 4 million years old. The inference is that the volcanic Galapagos Islands are continually appearing and eroding away as the oceanic plate passes over a hot spot in the Earth's mantle, and that there were islands in the area much longer ago than was first imagined.

The genetic differences between all populations of modern cheetahs, to give another example, show that they evolved from very few individuals – perhaps a single litter – some time during the last Ice Age. Seemingly the entire population of cheetahs was all but wiped out by the harsh climatic conditions of the time.

An alternative to cloning in a bacterium cell was developed in 1985. This technique is called polymerase chain reaction and involves treating the DNA sample with enzymes that promote its reproduction. This has now become important in forensic science, in obtaining enough DNA to identify decomposed bodies.

In 1992, DNA was extracted from the chloroplasts of a magnolia leaf found in 16-million-year-old lake deposits from the Miocene of Idaho, USA. The ancient lake had waters that were entirely free from oxygen, and as the leaves fell into the water they sank and were buried in a totally sterile environment. This still does not explain the preservation. Even under oxygen-free conditions moisture tends to break down organic molecules. Such a breakdown is helped by the presence of metals, and possibly the metals that were in the sediments were trapped by the acids in the muds or prevented by bacterial action from taking part in the reaction.

Then, in 1993, even older DNA fragments were discovered. These belonged to a weevil that was trapped in amber some time between 120 and 130 million years ago – during the Cretaceous period – the time of the dinosaurs.

This is all very interesting and has considerable practical application in determining evolutionary sequences and identifying murder victims – but it is still a long way from cloning dinosaurs. The only way of doing this would be to obtain a complete set of dinosaur DNA and then to insert it into the growth cell of some compatible creature, such as a bird. The original DNA of the cell would have to be destroyed, so that the cell would work as a host for the growth and reproduction of the introduced DNA. This would then develop into an embryo, and form an egg which would hatch into a young dinosaur. Such techniques have so far worked only in very simple organisms. It is quite beyond the present state of the art to do it with the higher vertebrates. In any case, we would need to start with a complete set of DNA from a dinosaur, and it is very unlikely that such delicate organic material would have survived for 65 million years in the guts of a preserved mosquito or any other environment known to geologists.

For the present the story must remain a story.

SS

Designs on life

Late in December 1992, the US Patent office granted three patents on transgenic mice. These were the first animal patents for over four years, since the Harvard onco-mouse achieved notoriety in 1988. In 1991, the European Patent Office granted a patent on the self-same mouse. The patents have once again created a furore among animal rights, religious, and farm groups, and legal battles are threatened through the next year as campaigners seek to block further animal patents. Early in 1993, European animal rights groups appealed against the onco-mouse patent.

So what are the onco-mouse and its transgenic fellows? Why do they arouse such hopes among supporters and such passions among opponents?

Transferring genes

The onco-mouse is one of many transgenic organisms. Transgenic organisms have had new genetic material transferred to them. The onco-mouse carries a human oncogene, a gene that causes the mouse to develop cancer. The gene is implanted in the mouse by genetic engineering: the gene is identified, cut from its original DNA by using enzymes that normally destroy invading viruses, and then joined into new, mouse DNA. A lot of genetic engineering is carried out with bacteria, because their cells have no nucleus, and so the DNA is easier to separate. But as techniques and knowledge progress, more and more genetic engineering is carried out on larger organisms, and mice in particular are popular. They are small and hence easy to keep, and they grow and reproduce rapidly. Above all, they are mammals, so they can be used to model and study human disease processes.

Designed to die

The onco-mouse in particular is an example of an organism designed to study a human disease. The gene causes it to develop cancer; knowing this it is possible to study not only the effect of possible cancer treatments given after the onset of the disease, but also the helpful or harmful effect of drugs administered before the disease begins. The European Patent Office decided to grant the patent on the onco-mouse because it considered the benefit to humans fighting cancer outweighed the suffering of an animal designed to die of cancer. It was a close decision; initially the EPO rejected the application.

Is it right to design an animal to develop a painful disease? The British Union for the Abolition of Vivisection points out that allowing cruelty because it is useful is allowing the end to justify the means. There has also been doubt as to the usefulness of the onco-mouse in studying cancer: screening chemicals for carcinogenic or beneficial effect still requires large numbers of mice, just as the process did before the onco-mouse.

The new patents in the USA may help to clarify the issues. One new transgenic mouse produces a human protein, beta interferon. Another is deficient in T cells and can be used to study immune deficiency. The third develops an enlarged prostate gland. All three should pass a usefulness test. The amount of pain inherent in each design is varied, but the beta interferon producer should invoke no cruelty at all.

Taking creation into our hands

But this still leaves the issue of whether humans should engineer new forms of life: and, having been thus engineered, should the results be protected by patent? The latter issue has worried small farmers, whose concern is that they will be denied access to patented 'superlivestock' and will be forced out of business by large corporations exploiting genetically engineered breeds.

There is little doubt that 'superlivestock' is a genuine possibility. Following the new US patents, there are over 180 applications pending for animals ranging from cows to fish. The situation is similar in Europe, with over 100 applications for patent awaiting attention. So far, only a few transgenic organisms have achieved patented status, but the numbers are set to grow exponentially over the next few years.

And so legislatures in both Europe and the USA will need to make up their minds. Stripped of the side issues of cruelty and accessibility, the decision will need to be taken: can we play God, and create and exploit new organisms, or is it an area in which we should not meddle?

SS

from multiple births. It can be applied to as little material as a single cell.

The technique involves isolating DNA from cells, then comparing and contrasting the sequences of component chemicals between individuals. The DNA pattern can be ascertained from a sample of skin, hair, or semen. Although differences are minimal (only 0.1% between unrelated people), certain regions of DNA, known as ***hypervariable regions***, are unique to individuals.

Genetic fingerprinting is now allowed as a means of legal identification. It is used in paternity testing, forensic medicine, and inbreeding studies. A new method that makes it possible to express the individuals' information in digital code will mean that genetic fingerprinting will now be much more accurate than before.

molecular clock use of rates of mutation in genetic material to calculate the length of time elapsed since two related species diverged from each other during evolution. The method can be based on comparisons of the DNA or of widely occurring proteins, such as haemoglobin.

Since mutations are thought to occur at a constant rate, the length of time that must have elapsed in order to produce the difference between two species can be estimated. This information can be compared with the evidence obtained from palaeontology to reconstruct evolutionary events.

protein engineering the creation of synthetic proteins designed to carry out specific tasks. For example, an enzyme may be designed to remove grease from soiled clothes and remain stable at the high temperatures in a washing machine.

restriction enzyme bacterial enzyme that breaks a chain of DNA into two pieces at a specific point; used in genetic engineering. The point along the DNA chain at which the enzyme can work is restricted to places where a specific sequence of base pairs occurs. Different restriction enzymes will break a DNA chain at different points. The overlap between the fragments is used in determining the sequence of base pairs in the DNA chain.

sequencing determining the sequence of chemical subunits within a large molecule. Techniques for sequencing amino acids in proteins were established in the 1950s, insulin being the first for which the sequence was completed. Efforts are now being made to determine the sequence of base pairs within DNA.

transgenic organism plant, animal, bacterium, or other living organism that has had a foreign gene added to it by means of genetic engineering.

yeast artificial chromosome (YAC) fragment of DNA from the human genome inserted into a yeast cell. The yeast replicates the fragment along with its own DNA. In this way the fragments are copied to be preserved in a gene library. YACs are characteristically between 250,000 and 1 million base pairs in length. A cosmid works in the same way.

MATHEMATICS

Terms

abacus method of calculating with a handful of stones on 'a flat surface' (Latin *abacus*), familiar to the Greeks and Romans, and used by earlier peoples, possibly even in ancient Babylon; it still survives in the more sophisticated bead-frame form of the Russian *schoty* and the Japanese *soroban*. The abacus has been superseded by the electronic calculator.

abscissa in coordinate geometry, the *x*-coordinate of a point – that is, the horizontal distance of that point from the vertical or *y*-axis. For example, a point with the coordinates (4, 3) has an abscissa of 3. The *y*-coordinate of a point is known as the ordinate.

algebra system of arithmetic applying to any set of non-numerical symbols (usually letters), and the axioms and rules by which they are combined or operated upon; sometimes known as ***generalized arithmetic***. It is used in many branches of mathematics, for example, matrix algebra and Boolean algebra (the latter method was first devised in the 19th century by the British mathematician George Boole and used in working out the logic for computers).

alternate angles a pair of angles that lie on opposite sides and at opposite ends of a transversal (a line that cuts two or more lines in the same plane). The alternate angles formed by a transversal of two parallel lines are equal.

altitude in geometry, the perpendicular distance from a vertex (corner) of a figure, such as a triangle, to the base (the side opposite the vertex).

angle in mathematics, the amount of turn or rotation; it may be defined by a pair of rays (half-lines) that share a common endpoint but do not lie on the same line. Angles are measured in degrees (°) or radians (rads) – a complete turn or circle being 360° or 2π rads. Angles are classified generally by their degree measures: ***acute angles*** are less than 90°; ***right angles*** are exactly 90° (a quarter turn); ***obtuse angles*** are greater than 90° but less than 180°; ***reflex angles*** are greater than 180° but less than 360°.

apex the highest point of a triangle, cone, or pyramid – that is, the vertex (corner) opposite a given base.

Arabic numerals or ***Hindu-Arabic numerals*** the symbols 0, 1, 2, 3, 4, 5, 6, 7, 8, 9, early forms of which were in use among the Arabs before being adopted by the peoples of Europe during the Middle Ages in place of Roman numerals. The symbols appear to have originated in India and probably reached Europe by way of Spain.

arc a section of a curved line or circle. A circle has three types of arc: a ***semicircle***, which is exactly half of the circle; ***minor arcs***, which are less than the semicircle; and ***major arcs***, which are greater than the semicircle.

area the size of a surface. It is measured in square units, usually square centimetres (cm^2), square metres (m^2), or square kilometres (km^2). Surface area is the area of the outer surface of a solid.

Common areas

figure	*rule for calculating area*
rectangle	length × breadth
triangle	half base length × height
parallelogram	base length × height
trapezium	average length of parallel sides × perpendicular distance between them
circle	πr^2, where r is the radius sector
	$\frac{x\pi r^2}{360}$ where x is the angle of the sector

arithmetic branch of mathematics concerned with the study of numbers and their properties. The fundamental operations of arithmetic are addition, subtraction, multiplication, and division. Raising to powers (for example, squaring or cubing a number), the extraction of roots (for example, square roots), percentages, fractions, and ratios are developed from these operations.

associative operation mathematical operation in which the outcome is independent of the grouping of the numbers or symbols concerned. For example, multiplication is associative, as $4 \times (3 \times 2) = (4 \times 3) \times 2 = 24$; however, division is not, as $12 \div (4 \div 2) = 6$, but $(12 \div 4) \div 2 = 1.5$. Compare commutative operation and distributive operation.

axis (plural ***axes***) one of the reference lines by which a point on a graph may be located. The horizontal axis is usually referred to as the *x*-axis, and the vertical axis as the *y*-axis. The term is also used to refer to the imaginary line about which an object may be said to be symmetrical (***axis of symmetry***) – for example, the diagonal of a square – or the line about which an object may revolve (***axis of rotation***).

base in mathematics, the number of different single-digit symbols used in a particular number system. In our usual (decimal) counting system of numbers (with symbols 0, 1, 2, 3, 4, 5, 6, 7, 8, 9) the base is 10. In the binary number system, which has only the symbols 1 and 0, the base is two. A base is also a number that, when raised to a particular power (that is, when multiplied by itself a particular number of times as in $10^2 = 10 \times 10 = 100$), has a logarithm equal to the power. For example, the logarithm of 100 to the base ten is 2.

In geometry, the term is used to denote the line or area on which a polygon or solid stands.

bearing the direction of a fixed point, or the path of a moving object, from a point of observation on the Earth's surface, expressed as an angle from the north. Bearings are taken by compass and are measured in degrees (°), given as three-digit numbers increasing clockwise. For instance, north is 000°, northeast is 045°, south is 180°, and southwest is 225°. True north differs slightly from magnetic north (the direction in which a compass needle points), hence NE may be denoted as 045M or 045T, depending on whether the reference line is magnetic (M) or true (T) north. True north also differs slightly from grid north since

Base

binary (base 2)	octal (base 8)	decimal (base 10)	hexadecimal (base 16)
0	0	0	0
1	1	1	1
10	2	2	2
11	3	3	3
100	4	4	4
101	5	5	5
110	6	6	6
111	7	7	7
1000	10	8	8
1001	11	9	9
1010	12	10	A
1011	13	11	B
1100	14	12	C
1101	15	13	D
1110	16	14	E
1111	17	15	F
10000	20	16	10
11111111	377	255	FF
11111010001	3721	2001	7D1

it is impossible to show a spherical Earth on a flat map.

binomial in mathematics, an expression consisting of two terms, such as $a + b$ or $a - b$.

calculus branch of mathematics that permits the manipulation of continuously varying quantities, used in practical problems involving such matters as changing speeds, problems of flight, varying stresses in the framework of a bridge, and alternating current theory. ***Integral calculus*** deals with the method of summation or adding together the effects of continuously varying quantities. ***Differential calculus*** deals in a similar way with rates of change. Many of its applications arose from the study of the gradients of the tangents to curves.

cardinal number one of the series of numbers 0, 1, 2, 3, 4, ... Cardinal numbers relate to quantity, whereas ordinal numbers (first, second, third, fourth, ...) relate to order.

chord in geometry, a straight line joining any two points on a curve. The chord that passes through the centre of a circle (its longest chord) is the diameter. The longest and shortest chords of an ellipse (a regular oval) are called the major and minor axes respectively.

circle perfectly round shape, the path of a point that moves so as to keep a constant distance from a fixed point (the centre). Each circle has a ***radius*** (the distance from any point on the circle to the centre), a ***circumference*** (the boundary of the circle), ***diameters*** (straight lines crossing the circle through the centre), ***chords*** (lines joining two points on the circumference), ***tangents*** (lines that touch the circumference at one point only), ***sectors*** (regions inside the circle between two radii), and ***segments*** (regions between a chord and the circumference).

circumference the curved line that encloses a curved plane figure, for example a circle or an ellipse. Its length varies according to the nature of the curve, and may be ascertained by the appropriate formula. The circumference of a circle is πd or $2\pi r$, where d is the diameter of the circle, r is its radius and π is the constant pi, approximately equal to 3.1416.

coefficient the number part in front of an algebraic term, signifying multiplication. For example, in the expression $4x^2 + 2xy - x$, the coefficient of x^2 is 4 (because $4x^2$ means $4 \times x^2$), that of xy is 2, and that of x is −1 (because $-1 \times x = -x$).

commutative operation an operation that is independent of the order of the numbers or symbols concerned. For example, addition is commutative: the result of adding 4 + 2 is the same as that of adding 2 + 4; subtraction is not as 4 − 2 = 2, but 2 − 4 = −2. Compare associative operation and distributive operation.

complement the set of the elements within the universal set that are not contained in the designated set. For example, if the universal set is the set of all positive whole numbers and the designated set S is the set of all even numbers, then the complement of S (denoted S') is the set of all odd numbers.

concave of a surface, curving inwards, or away from the eye. For example, a bowl appears concave when viewed from above. In geometry, a concave polygon is one that has an interior angle greater than 180°. Concave is the opposite of convex.

concentric circles two or more circles that share the same centre.

cone a solid or surface consisting of the set of all straight lines passing through a fixed point (the vertex) and the points of a circle or ellipse whose plane does not contain the vertex. A circular cone of perpendicular height, with its apex above the centre of the circle, is known as a ***right circular cone***; it is generated by rotating an isosceles triangle or framework about its line of symmetry. A right circular cone of perpendicular height h and base of radius r has a volume $V = \frac{1}{3}\pi r^2 h$. The distance from the edge of the base of a cone to the vertex is called the slant height. In a right circular cone of slant height l, the curved surface area is πrl, and the area of the base is πr^2. Therefore the total surface area $A = \pi rl + \pi r^2 = \pi r(l + r)$.

congruent having the same shape and size, as applied to two-dimensional or solid figures. With plane congruent figures, one figure will fit on top of the other exactly, though this may first require rotation and/or rotation of one of the figures.

conic section curve obtained when a conical surface is intersected by a plane. If the intersecting plane cuts both extensions of the cone, it yields a hyperbola; if it is parallel to the side of the cone, it produces a parabola. Other intersecting planes produce circles or ellipses.

constant a fixed quantity or one that does not change its value in relation to variables. For example, in the algebraic expression $y^2 = 5x - 3$, the numbers 3 and 5 are constants. In physics, certain quantities are regarded as universal constants, such as the speed of light in a vacuum.

converse the reversed order of a conditional statement; the converse of the statement 'if a, then b' is 'if *b*, then *a*'. The converse does not always hold true; for example, the converse of 'if $x = 3$, then $x^2 = 9$' is 'if $x^2 = 9$, then $x = 3$', which is not true, as x could also be -3.

convex of a surface, curving outwards, or towards the eye. For example, the outer surface of a ball appears convex. In geometry, the term is used to describe any polygon possessing no interior angle greater than 180°. Convex is the opposite of concave.

coordinate geometry or ***analytical geometry*** system of geometry in which points, lines, shapes, and surfaces are represented by algebraic expressions. In plane (two-dimensional) coordinate geometry, the plane is usually defined by two axes at right angles to each other, the horizontal x-axis and the vertical y-axis, meeting at O, the origin. A point on the plane can be represented by a pair of Cartesian coordinates, which define its position in terms of its distance along the x-axis and along the y-axis from O. These distances are respectively the x and y coordinates of the point.

Lines are represented as equations; for example, $y = 2x + 1$ gives a straight line, and $y = 3x^2 + 2x$ gives a parabola (a curve). The graphs of varying equations can be drawn by plotting the coordinates of points that satisfy their equations, and joining up the points. One of the advantages of coordinate geometry is that geometrical solutions can be obtained without drawing but by manipulating algebraic expressions. For example, the coordinates of the point of intersection of two straight lines can be determined by finding the unique values of x and y that satisfy both of the equations for the lines, that is, by solving them as a pair of simultaneous equations. The curves studied in simple coordinate geometry are the conic sections (circle, ellipse, parabola, and hyperbola), each of which has a characteristic equation.

cosine in trigonometry, a function of an angle in a right-angled triangle found by dividing the length of the side adjacent to the angle by the length of the hypotenuse (the longest side). It is usually shortened to ***cos***.

cube in geometry, a regular solid figure whose faces are all squares. It has six equal-area faces and 12 equal-length edges. If the length of one edge is l, the volume V of the cube is given by $V = l^3$ and its surface area A by $A = 6l^2$.

cuboid six-sided three-dimensional prism whose faces are all rectangles. A brick is a cuboid.

curve in geometry, the locus of a point moving according to specified conditions. The circle is the locus of all points equidistant from a given point (the centre). Other common geometrical curves are the ellipse, parabola, and hyperbola, which are also produced when a cone is cut by a plane at different angles. Many curves have been invented for the solution of special problems in geometry and mechanics — for example, the cissoid (the inverse of a parabola) and the cycloid.

cybernetics science concerned with how systems organize, regulate, and reproduce themselves, and also how they evolve and learn. In the laboratory, inanimate objects are created that behave like living systems. Applications range from the creation of electronic artificial limbs to the running of the fully automated factory where decision-making machines operate up to managerial level. Cybernetics was founded and named in 1947 by US mathematician Norbert Wiener.

cycloid in geometry, a curve resembling a series of arches traced out by a point on the circumference of a circle that rolls along a straight line. Its applications include the study of the motion of wheeled vehicles along roads and tracks.

cylinder in geometry, a tubular solid figure with a circular base. In everyday use, the term applies to a ***right cylinder***, the curved surface of which is at right angles to the base. The volume V of a cylinder is given by the formula $V = \pi r^2 h$, where r is the radius of the base and h is the height of the cylinder. Its total surface area A has the formula $A = 2\pi r(h + r)$, where $2\pi rh$ is the curved surface area, and $2\pi r^2$ is the area of both circular ends.

decimal fraction a fraction in which the denominator is any higher power of 10. Thus $^3/_{10}$, $^{51}/_{100}$, and $^{23}/_{1,000}$ are decimal fractions and are normally expressed as 0.3, 0.51, 0.023. The use of decimals greatly simplifies addition and multiplication of fractions, though not all fractions can be expressed exactly as decimal fractions. The regular use of the decimal point appears to have been introduced about 1585, but the occasional use of decimal fractions can be traced back as far as the 12th century.

degree a unit (symbol °) of measurement of an angle or arc. A circle or complete rotation is divided into 360°. A degree may be subdivided into 60 minutes (symbol '), and each minute may be subdivided in turn into 60 seconds (symbol "). ***Temperature*** is also measured in degrees, which are divided on a decimal scale.

denominator the bottom number of a fraction, so called because it ***names*** the family of the fraction. The top number, or numerator, specifies how many unit fractions are to be taken.

determinant an array of elements written as a square, and denoted by two vertical lines enclosing the array. For a 2 × 2 matrix, the determinant is given by the difference between the products of the diagonal terms. For example, the determinant of the matrix

$$\begin{pmatrix} a & b \\ c & d \end{pmatrix} = \begin{vmatrix} a & b \\ c & d \end{vmatrix} = ad - bc$$

Determinants are used to solve sets of simultaneous equations by matrix methods.

differentiation a procedure for determining the gradient of the tangent to a curve $f(x)$ at any point x.

directed number an integer with a positive (+) or negative (−) sign attached, for example +5 or −5. On a graph, a positive sign shows a movement to the right or upwards; a negative sign indicates movement downwards or to the left.

distributive operation an operation, such as multiplication, that bears a relationship to another operation, such as addition, such that $a \times (b + c) = (a \times b) + (a \times c)$. For example, $3 \times (2 + 4) = (3 \times 2) + (3 \times 4) = 18$. Multiplication may be said to be distributive over addition. Addition is not, however, distributive over multiplication because $3 + (2 \times 4) \neq (3 + 2) \times (3 + 4)$.

dodecahedron regular solid with 12 pentagonal faces and 12 vertices. It is one of the five regular polyhedra, or Platonic solids.

ellipse curve joining all points (loci) around two fixed points (foci) such that the sum of the distances from those points is always constant. The diameter passing through the foci is the major axis, and the diameter bisecting this at right angles is the minor axis. An ellipse is one of a series of curves known as conic sections. A slice across a cone that is not made parallel to, and does not pass through, the base will produce an ellipse.

epicycloid a curve resembling a series of arches traced out by a point on the circumference of a circle that rolls around another circle of a different diameter. If the two circles have the same diameter, the curve is a cardioid.

equation in mathematics, expression that represents the equality of two expressions involving constants and/or variables, and thus usually includes an equals sign (=). For example, the equation $A = \pi r^2$ equates the area A of a circle of radius r to the product πr^2. The algebraic equation $y = mx + c$ is the general one in coordinate geometry for a straight line.

If a mathematical equation is true for all variables in a given domain, it is sometimes called an identity and denoted by $\equiv$.

equilateral of a geometrical figure, having all sides of equal length. An equilateral triangle, to which the term is most often applied, has all three sides equal and all three angles equal (at 60°).

exponent or ***index*** in mathematics, a number that indicates the number of times a term is multiplied by itself; for example $x^2 = x \times x$, $4^3 = 4 \times 4 \times 4$. Exponents obey certain rules. Terms that contain them are multiplied together by adding the exponents; for example, $x^2 \times x^5 = x^7$. Division of such terms is done by subtracting the exponents; for example, $y^5 \div y^3 = y^2$. Any number with the exponent 0 is equal to 1; for example, $x^0 = 1$ and $99^0 = 1$.

exponential descriptive of a function in which the variable quantity is an exponent (a number indicating the power to which another number or expression is raised). Exponential functions and series involve the constant $e = 2.71828$.... Scottish mathematician John Napier devised natural logarithms in 1614 with e as the base.

Exponential functions are basic mathematical functions, written as e^x or exp x. ***Exponential growth*** is not constant. It applies, for example, to population growth, where the population doubles in a short time period. A graph of population number against time produces a curve that is characteristically rather flat at first but then shoots almost directly upwards.

factor a number that divides into another number exactly. For example, the factors of 64 are 1, 2, 4, 8, 16, 32, and 64. In algebra, certain kinds of polynomials (expressions consisting of several or many terms) can be factorized. For example, the factors of $x^2 + 3x + 2$ are $x + 1$ and $x + 2$, since $x^2 + 3x + 2 = (x + 1)(x + 2)$. This is called factorization.

factorial of a positive number, the product of all the whole numbers (integers) inclusive between 1 and the number itself. A factorial is indicated by the symbol '!'. Thus $6! = 1 \times 2 \times 3 \times 4 \times 5 \times 6 = 720$. Factorial zero, 0!, is defined as 1.

fractal an irregular shape or surface produced by a procedure of repeated subdivision. Generated on a computer screen, fractals are used in creating models for geographical or biological processes (for example, the creation of a coastline by erosion or accretion, or the growth of plants). The name was coined by the French mathematician Benoit Mandelbrot. Fractals are also used for computer art.

fraction a number that indicates one or more equal parts of a whole. Usually, the number of equal parts into which the unit is divided (denominator) is written below a horizontal line, and the number of parts comprising the fraction (numerator) is written above; thus $^2/_3$ or $^3/_4$. Such fractions are called ***vulgar*** or ***simple*** fractions. The denominator can never be zero.

A ***proper fraction*** is one in which the numerator is less than the denominator. An ***improper fraction*** has a numerator that is larger than the denominator, for example $^3/_2$. It can therefore be expressed as a mixed number, for example, $1^1/_2$. A ***decimal fraction*** has as its denominator a power of 10, and these are omitted by use of the decimal point and notation, for example 0.04, which is $^4/_{100}$. Fractions are also known as the ***rational numbers***, that is numbers formed by a ratio. ***Integers*** may be expressed as fractions with a denominator of 1.

function a function f is a non-empty set of ordered pairs $(x,f(x))$ of which no two can have the same first element. Hence, if $f(x) = x^2$, two ordered pairs are (−2,4) and (2,4). The set of all first elements in a function's ordered pairs is called the ***domain***; the set of all second elements is the ***range***. In the algebraic expression $y = 4x^3 + 2$, the dependent variable y is a function of the independent variable x, generally written as $f(x)$.

geometry branch of mathematics concerned with the properties of space, usually in terms of plane (two-dimensional) and solid (three-dimensional) figures. The subject is usually divided into ***pure geometry***, which embraces roughly the plane and solid geometry dealt with in Euclid's *Elements*, and ***analytical*** or ***coordinate geometry***, in which problems are solved using algebraic methods. A third, quite distinct, type includes the non-Euclidean geometries.

group a finite or infinite set of elements that can be combined by an operation; formally, a group must satisfy certain conditions. For example, the set of all integers (positive or negative whole numbers) forms a group with regard to addition because: (1) addition is associative, that is, the sum of two or more integers is the same regardless of the order in which the integers are added; (2) adding two integers gives another integer; (3) the set includes an identity element 0, which has no effect on any integer to which it is added (for example, $0 + 3 = 3$); and (4) each integer has an inverse (for instance, 7 has the inverse −7), such that the sum of an integer and its inverse is 0. ***Group theory*** is the study of the properties of groups.

helix a three-dimensional curve resembling a spring, corkscrew, or screw thread. It is generated by a line that encircles a cylinder or cone at a constant angle.

hyperbola a curve formed by cutting a right circular cone with a plane so that the angle between the plane and the base is greater than the angle between the base and the side of the cone. All hyperbolae are bounded by two asymptotes (straight lines which the hyperbola moves closer and closer to but never reaches). A hyperbola is a member of the family of curves known as conic sections.

hypotenuse the longest side of a right-angled triangle, opposite the right angle. It is of particular application in Pythagoras's theorem (the square of the hypotenuse equals the sum of the squares of the other two sides), and in trigonometry where the ratios sine and cosine are defined as the ratios opposite/hypotenuse and adjacent/hypotenuse respectively.

icosahedron (plural ***icosahedra***) regular solid with 20 equilateral (equal-sided) triangular faces. It is one of the five regular polyhedra, or Platonic solids.

infinity mathematical quantity that is larger than any fixed assignable quantity; symbol ∞. By convention, the result of dividing any number by zero is regarded as infinity.

integer any whole number. Integers may be positive or negative; 0 is an integer, and is often considered positive. Formally, integers are members of the set $Z = \{... -3, -2, -1, 0, 1, 2, 3,... \}$. Fractions, such as $^1/_2$ and 0.35, are known as non-integral numbers ('not integers').

integration a method in calculus of determining the solutions of definite or indefinite integrals. An example of a definite integral can be thought of as finding the area under a curve (as represented by an algebraic expression or function) between particular values of the function's variable. In practice, integral calculus provides scientists with a powerful tool for doing calculations that involve a continually varying quantity (such as determining the position at any given instant of a space rocket that is accelerating away from Earth). Its basic principles were discovered in the late 1660s independently by the German philosopher Leibniz and the British scientist Newton.

linear equation a relationship between two variables that, when plotted on Cartesian axes produces a straight-line graph; the equation has the general form $y = mx + c$, where m is the slope of the line represented by the equation and c is the y-intercept, or the value of y where the line crosses the y-axis in the Cartesian coordinate system. Sets of linear equations can be used to describe the behaviour of buildings, bridges, trusses, and other static structures.

locus (Latin 'place') traditionally the path traced out by a moving point, but now defined as the set of all points on a curve satisfying given conditions. For example, the locus of a point that moves so that it is always at the same distance from another fixed point is a circle; the locus of a point that is always at the same distance from two fixed points is a straight line that perpendicularly bisects the line joining them.

logarithm or ***log*** the exponent or index of a number to a specified base – usually 10. For example, the logarithm to the base 10 of 1,000 is 3 because $10^3 = 1{,}000$; the logarithm of 2 is 0.3010 because $2 = 10^{0.3010}$. Before the advent of cheap electronic calculators, multiplication and division could be simplified by being replaced with the addition and subtraction of logarithms.

For any two numbers x and y (where $x = b^a$ and $y = b^c$) $x \times y = b^a \times b^c = b^{a+c}$; hence we would add the logarithms of x and y, and look up this answer in antilogarithm tables. Tables of logarithms and antilogarithms are available that show conversions of numbers into logarithms, and vice versa. For example, to multiply 6,560 by 980, one looks up their logarithms (3.8169 and 2.9912), adds them together (6.8081), then looks up the antilogarithm of this to get the answer (6,428,800). ***Natural*** or ***Napierian logarithms*** are to the base e, an irrational number equal to approximately 2.7183.

magic square in mathematics, a square array of different numbers in which the rows, columns, and diagonals add up to the same total. A simple example employing the numbers 1 to 9, with a total of 15, is:

6	7	2
1	5	9
8	3	4

matrix a square ($n \times n$) or rectangular ($m \times n$) array of elements (numbers or algebraic variables). They are a means of condensing information about mathematical systems and can be used for, among other things, solving simultaneous linear equations and transformations.

maximum and minimum in coordinate geometry, points at which the slope of a curve representing a function changes from positive to negative (maximum), or from negative to positive (minimum). A tangent to the curve at a maximum or minimum has zero gradient. Maxima and minima can be found by differentiating the function for the curve and setting the differential to zero (the value of the slope at the turning point). For example, differentiating the function for the parabola $y = 2x^2 - 8x$ gives $dy/dx = 4x - 8$. Setting this equal to zero gives $x = 2$, so that $y = -8$ (found by substituting $x = 2$ into the parabola equation). Thus the function has a minimum at the point $(2, -8)$.

mean a measure of the average of a number of terms or quantities. The simple ***arithmetic mean*** is the average value of the quantities, that is, the sum of the quantities divided by their number. The ***weighted mean*** takes into account the frequency of the terms that are summed; it is calculated by multiplying each term by the number of times it occurs, summing the results and dividing this total by the total number of occurrences. The ***geometric mean*** of n quantities is the nth root of their product. In statistics, it is a measure of central tendency of a set of data.

modulus a number that divides exactly into the difference between two given numbers. Also, the multiplication factor used to convert a logarithm of one base to a logarithm of another base. Also, another name for absolute value.

number symbol used in counting or measuring. In mathematics, there are various kinds of numbers. The everyday number system is the decimal ('proceeding by tens') system, using the base ten. ***Real numbers*** include all rational numbers (integers, or whole numbers, and fractions) and irrational numbers (those not expressible as fractions). ***Complex numbers*** include the real and unreal numbers (real-number multiples of the square root of -1). The binary number system, used in computers, has two as its base.

The ordinary numerals, 0, 1, 2, 3, 4, 5, 6, 7, 8, and 9, give a counting system that, in the decimal system, continues 10, 11, 12, 13, and so on. These are whole numbers (integers), with fractions represented as, for example, $^1/_4$, $^1/_2$, $^3/_4$, or as decimal fractions (0.25, 0.5, 0.75). They are also ***rational numbers***. ***Irrational numbers*** cannot be represented in this way and require symbols, such as $\sqrt{2}$, π, and e. They can be expressed numerically only as the (inexact) approximations 1.414, 3.142 and 2.718 (to three places of decimals) respectively. The symbols π and e are also examples of ***transcendental numbers***, because they (unlike $\sqrt{2}$) cannot be derived by solving a polynomial equation (an equation with one variable quantity) with rational coefficients (multiplying factors). Complex numbers, which include the real numbers as well as unreal numbers, take the general form $a + bi$, where $i = \sqrt{-1}$ (that is, $i^2 = -1$), and a is the real part and bi the unreal part.

number theory the abstract study of the structure of number systems and the properties of positive integers (whole numbers). For example, the theories of factors and prime numbers fall within this area as do the work of mathematicians Giuseppe Peano (1858–1932), Pierre de Fermat, and Karl Gauss.

numerator the number or symbol that appears above the line in a vulgar fraction. For example, the numerator of 5/6 is 5. The numerator represents the fraction's dividend and indicates how many of the equal parts indicated by the denominator (number or symbol below the line) comprise the fraction.

octahedron (regular) one of the five platonic solids with eight faces each of whichis an equilateral triangle. The figure made by joining the midpoints of the faces is a perfect cube and the vertices of theoctahedron are themselves the mid points of the faces of asurrounding cube. For this reason cube and octahedron are calleddual solids.

ordinal number one of the series first, second, third, fourth, ... Ordinal numbers relate to order, whereas cardinal numbers (1, 2, 3, 4, ...) relate to quantity, or count.

ordinate in coordinate geometry, the y coordinate of a point; that is, the vertical distance of the point from the horizontal or x-axis. For example, a point with the coordinates (3,4) has an ordinate of 4.

origin the point where the x axis meets the y axis. The coordinates of the origin are (0,0).

parabola a curve formed by cutting a right circular cone with a plane parallel to the sloping side of the cone. A parabola is one of the family of curves known as conic sections. The graph of $y = x^2$ is a parabola. The corresponding solid figure, the paraboloid, is formed by rotating a parabola about its axis. It is a common shape for headlight reflectors, dish-shaped microwave and radar aerials, and radiotelescopes, since a source of radiation placed at the focus of a paraboloidal reflector is propagated as a parallel beam.

parallel lines and parallel planes straight lines or planes that always remain a constant distance from one another no matter how far they are extended. This is a principle of Euclidean geometry. Some non-Euclidean geometries, such as elliptical and hyperbolic geometry, however, reject Euclid's parallel axiom.

parallelogram a quadrilateral (four-sided plane figure) with opposite pairs of sides equal in length and parallel, and opposite angles equal. The diagonals of a parallelogram bisect each other. Its area is the product of the length of one side and the perpendicular distance between this and the opposite side. In the special case when all four sides are equal in length, the parallelogram is known as a rhombus, and when the internal angles are right angles, it is a rectangle or square.

percentage way of representing a number as a fraction of 100. Thus 45 percent (45%) equals $^{45}/_{100}$, and 45% of 20 is $^{45}/_{100} \times 20 = 9$. In general, if a quantity x changes to y, the percentage change is $100(x - y)/x$. Thus, if the number of people in a room changes from 40 to 50, the percentage increase is $(100 \times 10)/40 =$ 25%. To express a fraction as a percentage, its denominator must first be converted to 100 – for example, $^1/_8 = 12.5/100 = 12.5\%$. The use of percentages often makes it easier to compare fractions that do not have a common denominator.

perimeter or ***boundary*** line drawn around the edge of an area or shape. For example, the perimeter of a rectangle is the sum of its four sides; the perimeter of a circle is known as its ***circumference***.

permutation a specified arrangement of a group of objects. It is the arrangement of a distinct objects taken b at a time in all possible orders. It is given by $a!/(a - b)!$, where '!' stands for factorial. For example, the number of permutations of four letters taken from any group of six different letters is $6!/2! = (1 \times 2 \times 3 \times 4 \times 5 \times 6)/(1 \times 2) = 360$. The theoretical number of four-letter 'words' that can be made from an alphabet of 26 letters is $26!/22! = 358,800$.

perpendicular at a right angle; also, a line at right angles to another or to a plane. For a pair of skew lines (lines in three dimensions that do not meet), there is just one common perpendicular, which is at right angles to both lines; the nearest points on the two lines are the feet of this perpendicular.

polygon a plane (two-dimensional) figure with three or more straight-line sides. Common polygons have names which define the number of sides (for example, triangle, quadrilateral, pentagon). These are all convex polygons, having no interior angle greater than 180°. The sum of the internal angles of a polygon having n sides is given by the formula $(2n - 4) \times 90°$; therefore, the more sides a polygon has, the larger the sum of its internal angles and, in the case of a convex polygon, the more closely it approximates to a circle.

polyhedron a solid figure with four or more plane faces. The more faces there are on a polyhedron, the more closely it approximates to a sphere. Knowledge of the properties of polyhedra is needed in crystallography and stereochemistry to determine the shapes of crystals and molecules. There are only five types of regular polyhedron (with all faces the same size and shape): the tetrahedron (four equilateral triangular faces), cube (six square faces), octahedron (eight equilateral triangles), dodecahedron (12 regular pentagons) and icosahedron (20 equilateral triangles).

prime number number that can be divided only by 1 or itself, that is, having no other factors. There is an infinite number of primes, the first ten of which are 2, 3, 5, 7, 11, 13, 17, 19, 23, and 29 (by definition, the number 1 is excluded from the set of prime numbers). The number 2 is the only even prime because all other even numbers have 2 as a factor.

In 1989, researchers at Amdahl Corporation, Sunnyvale, California, calculated the largest known prime number. It has 65,087 digits, and is more than a trillion trillion trillion times as large as the previous record holder. It took over a year of computation to locate the number and prove it was a prime.

prism a solid figure whose cross section is constant in planes drawn perpendicular to its axis. A cube, for example, is a rectangular prism with all faces (bases and sides) the same shape and size. A cylinder is a prism with a circular cross section.

probability likelihood, or chance, that an event will occur, often expressed as odds, or in mathematics, numerically as a fraction or decimal. In general, the probability that n particular events will happen out of a total of m possible events is n/m. A certainty has a probability of 1; an impossibility has a probability of 0. Empirical probability is defined as the number of successful events divided by the total possible number of events.

In tossing a coin, the chance that it will land 'heads' is the same as the chance that it will land 'tails', that is, 1 to 1 or even; mathematically, this probability is expressed as $^1/_2$ or 0.5. The odds against any chosen number coming up on the roll of a fair die are 5 to 1; the probability is $^1/_6$ or 0.1666... Probability theory was developed by the French mathematicians Blaise Pascal and Pierre de Fermat in the 17th century, initially in response to a request to calculate the odds of being dealt various hands at cards. Today, probability plays a major part in the mathematics of atomic theory and finds application in insurance and statistical studies.

progression sequence of numbers each formed by a specific relationship to its predecessor. An ***arithmetic progression*** has numbers that increase or decrease by a common sum or difference (for example, 2, 4, 6, 8); a ***geometric progression*** has numbers each bearing a fixed ratio to its predecessor (for example, 3, 6, 12, 24); and a ***harmonic progression*** has numbers whose reciprocals are in arithmetical progression, for example 1, $^1/_2$, $^1/_3$, $^1/_4$.

proportion two variable quantities x and y are proportional if, for all values of x, $y = kx$, where k is a constant. This means that if x increases, y increases in a linear fashion. A graph of x against y would be a straight line passing through the origin (the point $x = 0$, $y = 0$). y is inversely proportional to x if the graph of y against $1/x$ is a straight line through the origin. The corresponding equation is $y = k/x$. Many laws of science relate quantities that are proportional.

pyramid a three-dimensional figure with triangular side-faces meeting at a common vertex (point) and with a polygon as its base. The volume V of a pyramid is given by $V = {}^1/_3Bh$, where B is the area of the base and h is the perpendicular height. Pyramids are generally classified by their bases. For example, the Egyptian pyramids have square bases, and are therefore called square pyramids. Triangular pyramids are also known as tetrahedra ('four sides').

Pythagoras' theorem in geometry, a theorem stating that in a right-angled triangle, the area of the square on the hypotenuse (the longest side) is equal to the sum of the areas of the squares drawn on the other two sides. If the hypotenuse is h units long and the lengths of the other sides are a and b, then $h^2 = a^2 + b^2$. The theorem provides a way of calculating the length of any side of a right-angled triangle if the lengths of the other two sides are known.

quadratic equation a polynomial equation of second degree (that is, an equation containing as its highest power the square of a variable, such as x^2). The general formula of such equations is $ax^2 + bx + c = 0$, in which a, b, and c are real numbers, and only the coefficient a cannot equal 0. In coordinate geometry, a quadratic function represents a parabola.

Some quadratic equations can be solved by factorization, or the values of x can be found by using the formula for the general solution

$$x = [-b \pm \sqrt{(b^2-4ac)}]/2a.$$

Depending on the value of the discriminant $b^2 - 4ac$, a quadratic equation has two real, two equal, or two complex roots (solutions). When $b^2 - 4ac < 0$, there are two distinct real roots. When $b^2 - 4ac = 0$, there are two equal real roots. When $b^2 - 4ac > 0$, there are two distinct complex roots.

radian SI unit (symbol rad) of plane angles, an alternative unit to the degree. It is the angle at the centre of a circle when the centre is joined to the two ends of an arc (part of the circumference) equal in length to the radius of the circle. There are 2π (approximately 6.284) radians in a full circle (360°). One radian is approximately 57°, and 1° is $\pi/180$ or approximately 0.0175 radians. Radians are commonly used to specify angles in polar coordinates

ratio measure of the relative size of two quantities or of two measurements (in similar units), expressed as a proportion. For example, the ratio of vowels to consonants in the alphabet is 5:21; the ratio of 500 m to 2 km is 500:2,000, or 1:4.

reciprocal the result of dividing a given quantity into 1. Thus the reciprocal of 2 is $^1/_2$; of $^2/_3$ is $^3/_2$; of x^2 is $^1/_{x^2}$ or x^{-2}.

rectangle quadrilateral (four-sided plane figure) with opposite sides equal and parallel and with each interior angle a right angle (90°). Its area A is the product of the length l and height h; that is, $A = l \times h$. A rectangle with all four sides equal is a square.

rhombus an equilateral (all sides equal) parallelogram. Its diagonals bisect each other at right angles, and its area is half the product of the lengths of the two diagonals. A rhombus whose internal angles are 90° is called a square.

right-angled triangle triangle in which one of the angles is a right angle (90°). It is the basic form of triangle for defining trigonometrical ratios (for example, sine, cosine, and tangent) and for which Pythagoras' theorem holds true. The longest side of a right-angled triangle is called the hypotenuse; its area is equal to half the product of the lengths of the two shorter sides. Any triangle constructed with its hypotenuse as the diameter of a circle, with its opposite vertex (corner) on the circumference, is a right-angled triangle. This is a fundamental theorem in geometry, first credited to the Greek mathematician Thales about 580 BC.

Roman numerals ancient European number system using symbols different from Arabic numerals (the ordinary numbers 1, 2, 3, 4, 5, and so on). The seven key symbols in Roman numerals, as represented today, are I (1), V (5), X (10), L (50), C (100), D (500) and M (1,000). There is no zero, and therefore no place-value as is fundamental to the Arabic system. The first ten Roman numerals are I, II, III, IV (or IIII), V, VI, VII, VIII, IX, and X. When a Roman symbol is preceded by a symbol of equal or greater value, the values of the symbols are added (XVI = 16). When a symbol is preceded by a symbol of less value, the values are subtracted (XL = 40). A horizontal bar over a symbol indicates a multiple of 1,000 ($\bar{X}$ = 10,000). Although addition and subtraction are fairly straightforward using Roman numerals, the absence of a zero makes other arithmetic calculations (such as multiplication) clumsy and difficult.

scalar quantity a quantity that has magnitude but no direction, as distinct from a vector quantity, which has a direction as well as a magnitude. Temperature, mass, and volume are scalar quantities.

set or ***class*** any collection of defined things (elements), provided the elements are distinct and that there is a rule to decide whether an element is a member of a set. It is usually denoted by a capital letter and indicated by curly brackets { }. For example, L may represent the set that consists of all the letters of the alphabet. The symbol $\in$ stands for 'is a member of'; thus $p \in L$ means that p belongs to the set consisting of all letters, and $4 \notin L$ means that 4 does not belong to the set consisting of all letters.

A ***finite set*** has a limited number of members, such as the letters of the alphabet; an ***infinite set*** has an unlimited number of members, such as all whole numbers; an ***empty*** or ***null set*** has no members, such as the number of people who have swum across the Atlantic Ocean, written as { } or ∅; a ***single-element set*** has only one member, such as days of the week beginning with M, written as {Monday}. ***Equal sets*** have the same members; for example, if W = {days of the week} and S = {Sunday, Monday, Tuesday, Wednesday, Thursday, Friday, Saturday}, it can be said that $W = S$. Sets with the same number of members are ***equivalent sets***. Sets with some members in common are ***intersecting sets***; for example, if R = {red playing cards} and F = {face cards}, then R and F share the members that are red face cards. Sets with no members in common are ***disjoint sets***. Sets contained within others are ***subsets***; for example, V = {vowels} is a subset of L = {letters of the alphabet}. Sets and their interrelationships are often illustrated by a Venn diagram.

significant figures the figures in a number that, by virtue of their place value, express the magnitude of that number to a specified degree of accuracy. The final significant figure is rounded up if the following digit is greater than 5. For example, 5,463,254 to three significant figures is 5,460,000; 3.462891 to four significant figures is 3.463; 0.00347 to two significant figures is 0.0035.

simultaneous equations one of two or more algebraic equations that contain two or more unknown quantities that may have a unique solution. For example, in the case of two linear equations with two unknown variables, such as (i) $x + 3y = 6$ and (ii) $3y - 2x = 4$, the solution will be those unique values of x and y that are valid for both equations. Linear simultaneous equations can be solved by using algebraic manipulation to eliminate one of the variables, coordinate geometry, or matrices.

sine in trigonometry, a function of an angle in a right-angled triangle which is defined as the ratio of the length of the side opposite the angle to the length of the hypotenuse (the longest side). Various properties in physics vary sinusoidally; that is, they can be represented diagrammatically by a sine wave (a graph obtained by plotting values of angles against the values of their sines). Examples include simple harmonic motion, such as the way alternating current (AC) electricity varies with time.

speed the rate at which an object moves. The average speed v of an object may be calculated by dividing the distance s it has travelled by the time t taken to do so, and may be expressed as:

$$v = s/t$$

The usual units of speed are metres per second or kilometres per hour. Speed is a scalar quantity in which direction of motion is unimportant (unlike the vector quantity velocity, in which both magnitude and direction must be taken into consideration).

sphere a perfectly round object with all points on its surface the same distance from the centre. This distance is the radius of the sphere. For a sphere of radius r, the volume $V = {}^4/_3\pi r^3$ and the surface area $A = 4\pi^2$.

square root a number that when squared (multiplied by itself) equals a given number. For example, the square root of 25 (written $\sqrt{25}$) is ± 5, because 5 × 5 = 25, and (−5) × (−5) = 25. As an exponent, a square root is represented by $^1/_2$, for example, $16^{1/2}$ = ± 4. Negative numbers (less than 0) do not have square roots that are real numbers. Their roots are represented by complex numbers, in which the square root of −1 is given the symbol i (that is, $\pm i^2 = -1$). Thus the square root of −4 is $\sqrt{[(-1) \times 4]} = \sqrt{-1} \times \sqrt{4} = 2i$.

standard deviation in statistics, a measure (symbol Σ or s) of the spread of data. The deviation (difference) of each of the data items from the mean is found, and their values squared. The mean value of these squares is then calculated. The standard deviation is the square root of this mean.

statistics branch of mathematics concerned with the collection and interpretation of data. For example, to determine the mean age of the children in a school, a statistically acceptable answer might be obtained by calculating an average based on the ages of a representative sample, consisting, for example, of a random tenth of the pupils from each class. Probability is the branch of statistics dealing with predictions of events.

tangent a straight line that touches a curve and gives the gradient of the curve at the point of contact. At a maximum, minimum, or point of inflection, the tangent to a curve has zero gradient. Also, in trigonometry, a function of an acute angle in a right-angled triangle, defined as the ratio of the length of the side opposite the angle to the length of the side adjacent to it; a way of expressing the gradient of a line.

tetrahedron (plural ***tetrahedra***) a polyhedron with four triangular faces; that is, a pyramid on a triangular base. A regular tetrahedron has equilateral triangles as its faces. In chemistry and crystallography, tetrahedra describe the shapes of some molecules and crystals; for example, the carbon atoms in a crystal of diamond are arranged in space as a set of interconnected regular tetrahedra.

topology branch of geometry that deals with those properties of a figure that remain unchanged even when the figure is transformed (bent, stretched) – for example, when a square painted on a rubber sheet is deformed by distorting the sheet. Topology has scientific applications, as in the study of turbulence in flowing fluids. The map of a subway system is an example of the topological representation of a network; connectivity (the way the lines join together) is preserved, but shape and size are not. The topological theory, proposed 1880, that only four colors are required in order to produce a map in which no two adjoining countries have the same color, inspired extensive research, and was proved 1972 by Kenneth Appel and Wolfgang Haken.

topology

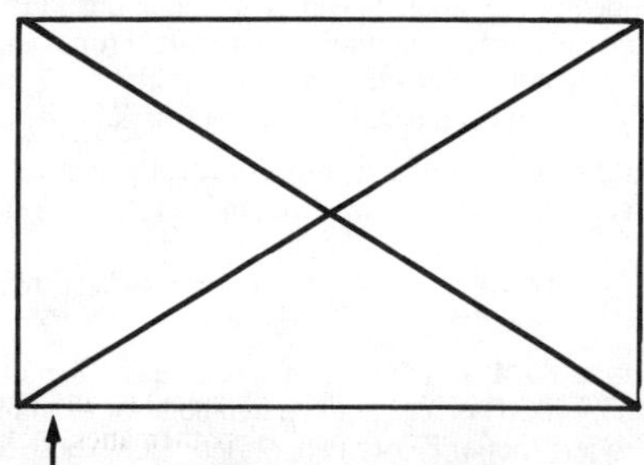

this figure is topologically equivalent to this one

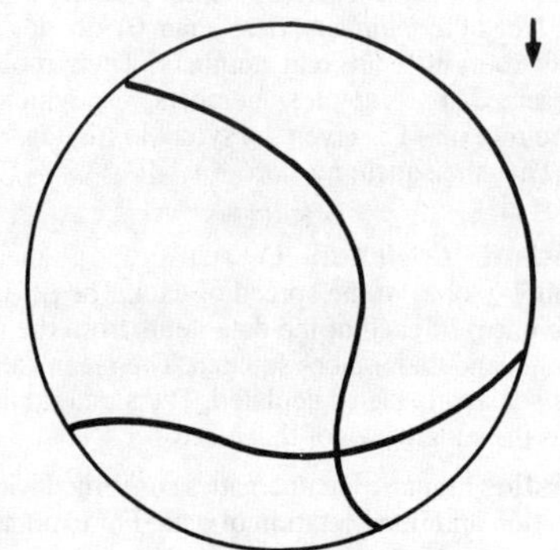

trapezium a four-sided plane figure (quadrilateral) with no two sides parallel.

triangle a three-sided plane figure, the sum of whose interior angles is 180°. Triangles can be classified by the relative lengths of their sides. A ***scalene triangle*** has no sides of equal length; an ***isosceles triangle*** has at least two equal sides; an ***equilateral triangle*** has three equal sides (and three equal angles of 60°). A ***right-angled triangle*** has one angle of 90°.

trigonometry branch of mathematics that solves problems relating to plane and spherical triangles. Its principles are based on the fixed proportions of sides for a particular angle in a right-angled triangle, the simplest of which are known as the sine, cosine, and tangent (so-called trigonometrical ratios). It is of practical importance in navigation, surveying, and simple harmonic motion in physics.

variable a changing quantity (one that can take various values), as opposed to a constant. For example, in the algebraic expression $y = 4x^3 + 2$, the variables are x and y, whereas 4 and 2 are constants.

variance in statistics, the square of the standard deviation, the measure of spread of data. Population and sample variance are denoted by Σ^2 or s^2, respectively.

vector quantity any physical quantity that has both magnitude and direction (such as the velocity or acceleration of an object) as distinct from scalar quantity (such as speed, density, or mass), which has magnitude but no direction. A vector is represented either geometrically by an arrow whose length corresponds to its magnitude and points in an appropriate direction, or by a pair of numbers written vertically and placed within brackets (xy). Vectors can be added graphically by constructing a parallelogram of vectors (such as the parallelogram of forces commonly employed in physics and engineering). In technical writing, a vector is denoted by ***bold*** type, underlined AB, or overlined AB.

velocity speed of an object in a given direction. Velocity is a vector quantity, since its direction is important as well as its magnitude (or speed).

Venn diagram a diagram representing a set or sets and the logical relationships between them. The sets are drawn as circles. An area of overlap between two circles (sets) contains elements that are common to both sets, and thus represents a third set. Circles that do not overlap represent sets with no elements in common (disjoint sets).

vertex (plural ***vertices***) a point shared by three or more sides of a solid figure; the point farthest from a figure's base; or the point of intersection of two sides of a plane figure or the two rays of an angle.

volume the space occupied by a three-dimensional solid object. A prism (such as a cube) or a cylinder has a volume equal to the area of the base multiplied by the height. For a pyramid or cone, the volume is equal to one-third of the area of the base multiplied by the perpendicular height. The volume of a sphere is equal to $^4/_3\pi r^3$, where r is the radius. Volumes of irregular solids may be calculated by the technique of integration.

triangle

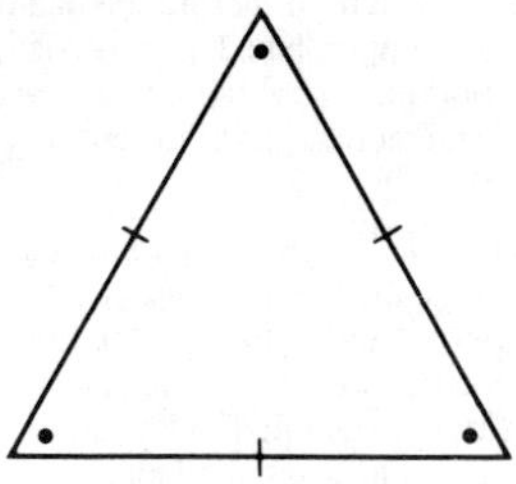

Equilateral triangle: all the sides are the same length; all the angles are equal to 60°

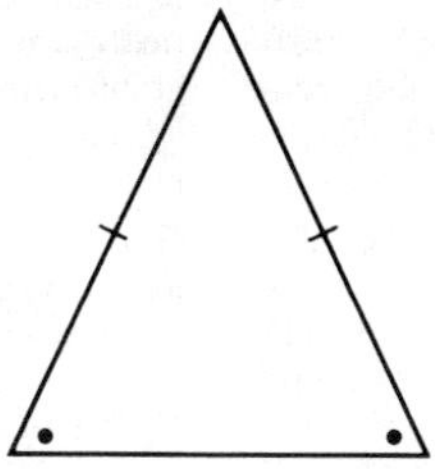

Isosceles triangle: two sides and two angles are the same

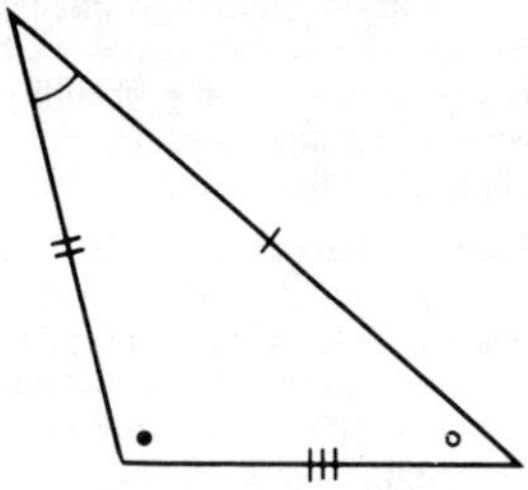

Scalene triangle: all the sides and angles are different

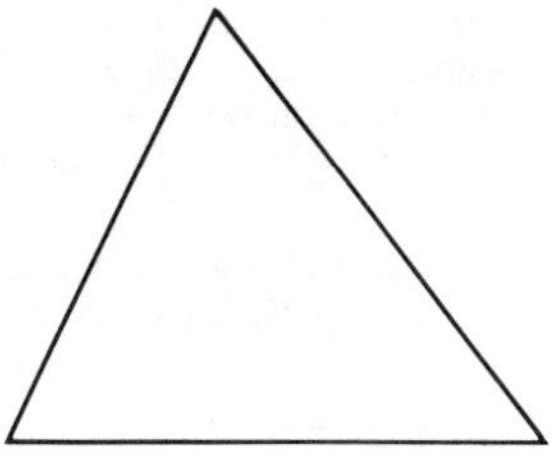

Acute-angle triangle: each angle is acute (less than 90°)

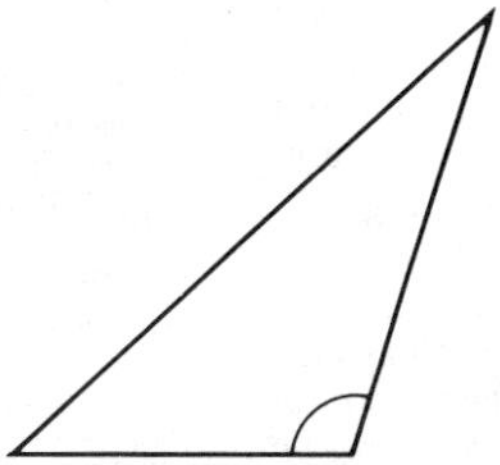

Obtuse-angle triangle: one angle is obtuse (more than 90°)

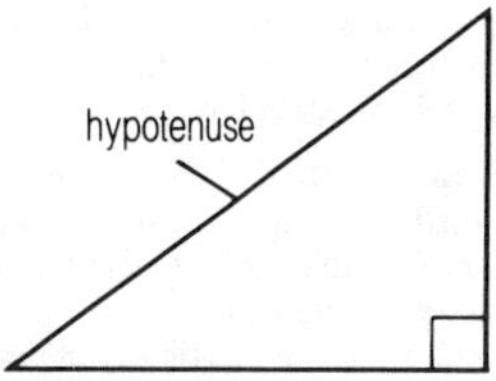

A right-angle triangle has one angle of 90°, the *hypotenuse* is the side opposite the right angle

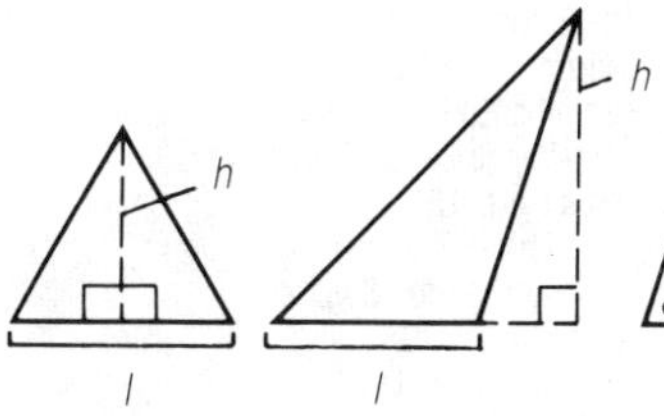

hypotenuse

h

l

Area of triangle = ½*lh*

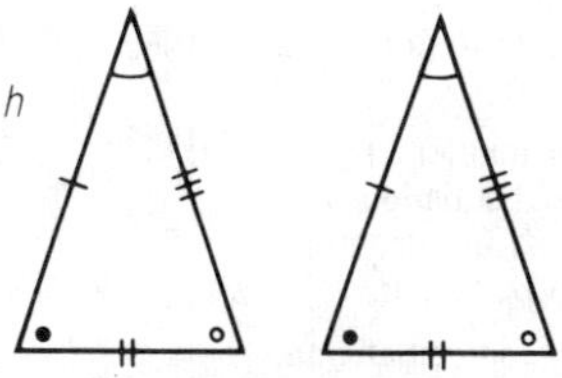

Triangles are *congruent* if corresponding sides and corresponding angles are equal

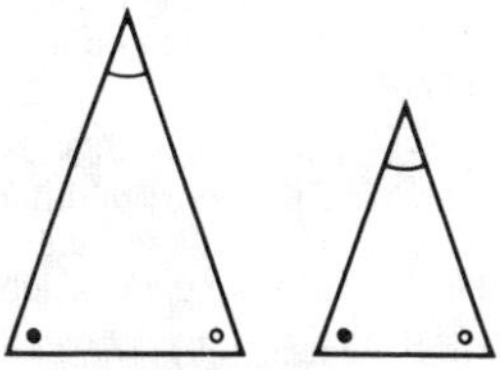

Similar triangles have corresponding angles that are equal; they therefore have the same shape

Great Mathematicians

Archimedes *c.* 287–212 BC. Greek mathematician who made major discoveries in geometry, hydro-statics, and mechanics. He formulated a law of fluid displacement (Archimedes' principle), and is credited with the invention of the Archimedes screw, a cylindrical device for raising water. This device is still used to raise water in the Nile delta.

Bernoulli Swiss family that produced many mathematicians and scientists in the 17th, 18th, and 19th centuries, in particular the brothers ***Jakob*** (1654–1705) and ***Johann*** (1667–1748). Jakob and Johann were pioneers of Leibniz's calculus. Jakob used calculus to study the forms of many curves arising in practical situations, and studied mathematical probability; ***Bernoulli numbers*** are named after him. Johann developed exponential calculus and contributed to many areas of applied mathematics, including the problem of a particle moving in a gravitational field. His son, ***Daniel*** (1700–1782) worked on calculus and probability, and in physics proposed ***Bernoulli's principle***.

Boole George 1815–1864. English mathematician whose work *The Mathematical Analysis of Logic* 1847 established the basis of modern mathematical logic, and whose ***Boolean algebra*** can be used in designing computers.

Cantor Georg 1845–1918. German mathematician who followed his work on number theory and trigonometry by considering the foundations of mathematics. He defined real numbers and produced a treatment of irrational numbers using a series of transfinite numbers. Cantor's set theory has been used in the development of topology and real function theory.

Cauchy Augustin Louis 1789–1857. French mathematician who employed rigorous methods of analysis. His prolific output included work on complex functions, determinants, and probability, and on the convergence of infinite series. In calculus, he refined the concepts of the limit and the definite integral.

Descartes René 1596–1650. French philosopher and mathematician. He believed that commonly accepted knowledge was doubtful because of the subjective nature of the senses, and attempted to rebuild human knowledge using as his foundation *cogito ergo sum* ('I think, therefore I am'). He also believed that the entire material universe could be explained in terms of mathematical physics, and founded coordinate geometry as a way of defining and manipulating geometrical shapes by means of algebraic expressions. Cartesian coordinates, the means by which points are represented in this system, are named after him. Descartes also established the science of optics, and helped to shape contemporary theories of astronomy and animal behaviour.

Eratosthenes *c.* 276–194 BC. Greek geographer and mathematician whose map of the ancient world was the first to contain lines of latitude and longitude, and who calculated the Earth's circumference with an error of about 10%. His mathematical achievements include a method for duplicating the cube, and for finding prime numbers (Eratosthenes' sieve).

Euclid *c.* 330–*c.* 260 BC. Greek mathematician, who lived in Alexandria and wrote the *Stoicheia/Elements* in 13 books, of which nine deal with plane and solid geometry and four with number theory. His great achievement lay in the systematic arrangement of previous discoveries, based on axioms, definitions, and theorems.

Euler Leonhard 1707–1783. Swiss mathematician. He developed the theory of differential equations and the calculus of variations, and worked in astronomy and optics. He was a pupil of Johann Bernoulli.

Fermat Pierre de 1601–1665. French mathematician, who with Blaise Pascal founded the theory of probability and the modern theory of numbers and who made contributions to analytical geometry. ***Fermat's last theorem*** states that equations of the form $xn + yn = zn$ where x, y, z, and n are all integers have no solutions if $n < 2$. The theorem still remains unproven (and therefore, strictly speaking, constitutes a conjecture rather than a theorem).

Fibonacci Leonardo, also known as ***Leonardo of Pisa*** *c.* 1175–*c.* 1250. Italian mathematician. He published *Liber abaci* in Pisa 1202, which was instrumental in the introduction of Arabic notation into Europe. From 1960, interest increased in ***Fibonacci numbers***, in their simplest form a sequence in which each number is the sum of its two predecessors (1, 1, 2, 3, 5, 8, 13, ..). They have unusual characteristics with possible applications in botany, psychology, and astronomy (for example, a more exact correspondence than is given by Bode's law to the distances between the planets and the Sun).

Galois Evariste 1811–1832. French mathematician who originated the theory of groups. His attempts to gain recognition for his work were largely thwarted by the French mathematical establishment, critical of his lack of formal qualifications. Galois was killed in a duel before he was 21. The night before, he had hurriedly written out his unpublished discoveries on group theory, the importance of which would come to be appreciated more and more as the 19th century progressed.

Gauss Karl Friedrich 1777–1855. German mathematician who worked on the theory of numbers, non-Euclidean geometry, and the mathematical development of electric and magnetic theory. A method of neutralizing a magnetic field, used to protect ships from magnetic mines, is called 'degaussing'.

Gödel Kurt 1906–1978. Austrian-born US mathematician and philosopher. He proved that a mathematical system always contains statements that can be neither proved nor disproved within the system; in other words, as a science, mathematics can never be totally consistent and totally complete. He worked on relativity, constructing a mathematical model of the universe that made travel back through time theoretically possible.

Hilbert David 1862–1943. German mathematician who founded the formalist school with the publication

Fields medals

Awarded every four years by the International Congress of Mathematicians

	Field medalists:
1936	Lars Ahlfors, Finland
	Jesse Douglas, USA
1950	Atle Selberg, USA
	Laurent Schwartz, France
1954	Kunihiko Kodaira, USA
	Jean-Pierre Serre, France
1958	Klaus Roth, UK
	René Thom, France
1962	Lars Hörmander, Sweden
	John Milnor, USA
1966	Michael Atiyah, UK
	Paul J Cohen, USA
	Alexander Grothendieck, France
	Stephen Smale, USA
1970	Alan Baker, UK
	Heisuke Hironaka, USA
	Sergei Novikov, USSR
	John G Thompson, USA
1974	Enrico Bombieri, Italy
	David Mumford, USA
1978	Pierre Deligne, Belgium
	Charles Fefferman, USA
	G A Margulis, USSR
	Daniel Quillen, USA
1982	Alain Connes, France
	William Thurston, USA
	S T Yau, USA
1986	Simon Donaldson, UK
	Gerd Faltings, FRG
	Michael Freedman, USA
1990	Vladimir Drinfeld, USSR
	Vaughan F R Jones, USA
	Shigefumi Mori, Japan
	Edward Witten, USA

of *Grundlagen der Geometrie/Foundations of Geometry* 1899, which was based on his idea of postulates. He attempted to put mathematics on a logical foundation through defining it in terms of a number of basic principles, which Gödel later showed to be impossible; nonetheless, his attempt greatly influenced 20th-century mathematicians.

Khwārizmī, al- Muhammad ibn- Mūsā *c.* 780–*c.* 850. Persian mathematician from Khwarizm (now Khiva, Uzbekistan), who lived and worked in Baghdad. He wrote a book on algebra, from part of whose title (*al-jabr*) comes the word 'algebra', and a book in which he introduced to the West the Hindu-Arabic decimal number system. The word 'algorithm' is a corruption of his name. He also compiled astronomical tables and was responsible for introducing the concept of zero into Arab mathematics.

Lagrange Joseph Louis 1736–1813. French mathematician. His *Mécanique analytique* 1788 applied mathematical analysis, using principles established by Newton, to such problems as the movements of planets when affected by each other's gravitational force. He presided over the commission that introduced the metric system in 1793.

Leibniz Gottfried Wilhelm 1646–1716. German mathematician and philosopher. Independently of, but concurrently with, the British scientist Isaac Newton he developed the branch of mathematics known as calculus. In his metaphysical works, such as *The Monadology* 1714, he argued that everything consisted of innumerable units, ***monads***, the individual properties of which determined each thing's past, present, and future. Monads, although independent of each other, interacted predictably; this meant that Christian faith and scientific reason need not be in conflict and that 'this is the best of all possible worlds'. His optimism is satirized in Voltaire's *Candide*.

Lobachevsky Nikolai Ivanovich 1792–1856. Russian mathematician who concurrently with, but independently of, Karl Gauss and the Hungarian János Bolyai (1802–1860), founded non-Euclidean geometry. Lobachevsky published the first account of the subject in 1829, but his work went unrecognized until Georg Riemann's system was published.

Lorenz Ludwig Valentine 1829–1891. Danish mathematician and physicist. He developed mathematical formulae to describe phenomena such as the relation between the refraction of light and the density of a pure transparent substance, and the relation between a metal's electrical and thermal conductivity and temperature.

Mandelbrot Benoit B 1924– .Polish born US scientist who coined the term ***fractal geometry*** to describe 'self-similar' shape, a motif that repeats indefinitely, each time smaller.

Markov Andrei 1856–1922. Russian mathematician, formulator of the Markov chain, an example of a stochastic (random) process.

Möbius August Ferdinand 1790–1868. German mathematician, discoverer of the Möbius strip and considered one of the founders of topology.

Napier John 1550–1617. Scottish mathematician who invented logarithms 1614 and 'Napier's bones', an early mechanical calculating device for multi-plication and division.

Newton Isaac 1642–1727. English physicist and mathematician who laid the foundations of physics as a modern discipline. He discovered the law of gravity, created calculus, discovered that white light is composed of many colours, and developed the three standard laws of motion still in use today. In 1685, he expounded his universal law of gravitation. His *Philosophiae naturalis principia mathematica*, usually referred to as *Principia*, was published in 1687, with the aid of Edmond Halley.

Pascal Blaise 1623–1662. French philosopher and mathematician. He contributed to the development of hydraulics, the calculus, and the mathematical theory of probability. ***Pascal's triangle*** is a triangular array of numbers in which each number is the sum of the pair of numbers above it. Plotted at equal distances along a horizontal axis, the numbers in the rows give the binomial probability distribution with equal probability of success and failure, such as when tossing fair coins.

Poincaré Jules Henri 1854–1912. French mathematician who developed the theory of differential equations and was a pioneer in relativity theory. He suggested that Isaac Newton's laws for the behaviour of the universe could be the exception rather than the rule. However, the calculation was so complex and time-consuming that he never managed to realize its full implication.

Pythagoras *c.* 580–500 BC. Greek mathematician and philosopher who formulated the Pythagorean theorem. Much of his work concerned numbers, to which he assigned mystical properties. For example, he classified numbers into triangular ones (1, 3, 6, 10,...), which can be represented as a triangular array, and square ones (1, 4, 9, 16,...), which form squares. He also observed that any two adjacent triangular numbers add to a square number (for example, $1 + 3 = 4$; $3 + 6 = 9$; $6 + 10 = 16$;...).

Riemann Georg Friedrich Bernhard 1826–1866. German mathematician whose system of non-Euclidean geometry, thought at the time to be a mere mathematical curiosity, was used by Einstein to develop his general theory of relativity.

Rubik Erno 1944– . Hungarian architect who invented the ***Rubik cube***, a multicoloured puzzle that can be manipulated and rearranged in only one correct way, but about 43 trillion wrong ones. Intended to help his students understand three-dimensional design, it became a fad that swept around the world.

Thales 640–546 BC. Greek philosopher and scientist. He made advances in geometry, predicted an eclipse of the Sun 585 BC, and, as a philosophical materialist, theorized that water was the first principle of all things, that the Earth floated on water, and so proposed an explanation for earthquakes. He lived in Miletus in Asia Minor.

Turing Alan Mathison 1912–1954. English mathematician and logician. In 1936 he described a 'universal computing machine' that could theoretically be programmed to solve any problem capable of solution by a specially designed machine. This concept, now called the ***Turing machine***, foreshadowed the digital computer.

Von Neumann John 1903–1957. Hungarian- born US scientist and mathematician, known for his pioneering work on computer design. He invented his 'rings of operators' (called Von Neumann algebras) in the late 1930s, and also contributed to set theory, games theory, cybernetics (with his theory of self-reproducing automata, called ***Von Neumann machines***), and the development of the atomic and hydrogen bombs.

Wiener Norbert 1894–1964. US mathematician. Best known for his book *Cybernetics* 1948, he laid the theoretical groundwork for information feedback systems. He laid the foundation of the study of stochastic processes (those dependent on random events), including Brownian movement (evidence of constant random motion of molecules).

GALLUP POLL

Suppose that the rate of inflation dropped from 20% to 15%. Which one of these results would you have expected?

32%, given four choices, correctly chose 'prices would still be rising but not as fast as before'

If you bought a raincoat in the 'summer sales' reduced from £84 to £59.50, how much would you save?

61% got the correct answer (£24.50)

From this graph showing the temperature changes on a day last summer can you say when was the hottest time of day and how hot it was then?

88% got the correct time
72% got the correct temperature

If you saw this sign in a shop which said 25% off, what would you expect to pay?

66% correctly said they would pay three quarters when there was 25% off all marked prices

Source: Gallup

PHYSICS

Terms

absolute zero lowest temperature theoretically possible, zero degrees Kelvin (0K), equivalent to −273.15°C/−459.67°F, at which molecules are motionless. Although the third law of thermodynamics indicates the impossibility of reaching absolute zero exactly, a temperature of seven-millionths of a degree above absolute zero was achieved by a team of scientists at Lancaster University, England, in June 1993. Near absolute zero, the physical properties of some materials change substantially; for example, some metals lose their electrical resistance and become superconductive.

acoustics in general, the experimental and theoretical science of sound and its transmission; in particular, that branch of the science that has to do with the phenomena of sound in a particular space such as a room or theatre.

analogue signal electric current or voltage that conveys or stores information, and varies continuously in the same way as the information it represents (unlike a digital signal). Analogue signals are prone to interference and distortion.

centre of mass or ***centre of gravity*** point in or near an object from which its total weight appears to originate and can be assumed to act. A symmetrical homogeneous object such as a sphere or cube has its centre of mass at its physical centre; a hollow shape (such as a cup) may have its centre of mass in space inside the hollow.

chain reaction nuclear fission reaction that is maintained because neutrons released by the splitting of some atomic nuclei themselves go on to split others, releasing even more neutrons. Such a reaction can be controlled (as in a nuclear reactor) by using moderators to absorb excess neutrons. Uncontrolled, a chain reaction produces a nuclear explosion (as in an atom bomb).

critical mass in nuclear physics, the minimum mass of fissile material that can undergo a continuous chain reaction. Below this mass, too many neutrons escape from the surface for a chain reaction to carry on; above the critical mass, the reaction may accelerate into a nuclear explosion.

cryogenics the science of very low temperatures (approaching absolute zero), including the production of very low temperatures and the exploitation of special properties associated with them, such as the disappearance of electrical resistance (superconductivity).

density measure of the compactness of a substance; it is equal to its mass per unit volume and is measured in kg per cubic metre/lb per cubic foot. Density is a scalar quantity. The density D of a mass m occupying a volume V is given by the formula:

$$D = m/V.$$

Relative density is the ratio of the density of a substance to that of water at 4°C.

Densities of some common substances

Solid	*Density in kg m^{-3}*
balsa wood	200
oak	700
butter	900
ice	920
ebony	120
sand (dry)	1,600
concrete	2,400
aluminium	2,700
steel	7,800
copper	8,900
lead	11,000
uranium	19,000
Liquid	
water	1,000
petrol, paraffin	800
olive oil	900
milk	1030
sea water	1,030
glycerine	1,300
Dead Sea brine	1,800
Gases at standard temperature and pressure (0° C and 1 atm)	
air	1.3
hydrogen	0.09
helium	0.18
methane	0.72
nitrogen	1.25
oxygen	1.43
carbon dioxide	1.98
propane	2.02
butane	2.65

diffraction the slight spreading of a light beam into a pattern of light and dark bands when it passes through a narrow slit or past the edge of an obstruction. A ***diffraction grating*** is aplate of glass or metal ruled with close, equidistant parallel lines used for separating a wave train such as a beam of incident light into its component frequencies (white light results in a spectrum).

digital in electronics and computing, a term meaning 'coded as numbers'. A digital system uses two- state, either on/off or high/low voltage pulses, to encode, receive, and transmit information. A ***digital display*** shows discrete values as numbers (as opposed to an analogue signal, such as the continuous sweep of a pointer on a dial). ***Digital electronics*** is the technology that underlies digital techniques. Low-power, miniature, integrated circuits (chips) provide the means for the coding, storage, transmission, processing, and reconstruction of information of all kinds.

dynamics or ***kinetics*** in mechanics, the mathematical and physical study of the behaviour of bodies under the action of forces that produce changes of motion in them.

efficiency the output of a machine (work done by the machine) divided by the input (work put into the machine), usually expressed as a percentage. Because of losses caused by friction, efficiency is always less than 100%, although it can approach this for electrical machines with no moving parts (such as a transformer).

elasticity the ability of a solid to recover its shape once deforming forces (stresses modifying its dimensions or shape) are removed. An elastic material obeys Hooke's law: that is, its deformation is proportional to the applied stress up to a certain point, called the ***elastic limit***, beyond which additional stress will deform it permanently. Elastic materials include metals and rubber; however, all materials have some degree of elasticity.

electric current the flow of electrically charged particles through a conducting circuit due to the presence of a potential difference. The current at any point in a circuit is the amount of charge flowing per second; its SI unit is the ampere (coulomb per second). Current carries electrical energy from a power supply, such as a battery of electrical cells, to the components of the circuit, where it is converted into other forms of energy, such as heat, light, or motion. It may be either direct current or alternating current.

electricity all phenomena caused by electric charge, whether static or in motion. Electric charge is caused by an excess or deficit of electrons in the charged substance, and an electric current by the movement of electrons around a circuit. Substances may be electrical conductors, such as metals, which allow the passage of electricity through them, or insulators, such as rubber, which are extremely poor conductors. Substances with relatively poor conductivities that can be improved by the addition of heat or light are known as semiconductors.

electrodynamics the branch of physics dealing with electric currents and associated magnetic forces. Quantum electrodynamics (QED) studies the interaction between charged particles and their emission and absorption of electromagnetic radiation. This field combines quantum theory and relativity theory, making accurate predictions about subatomic processes involving charged particles such as electrons and protons.

electromagnetic waves oscillating electric and magnetic fields travelling together through space at a speed of nearly 300,000 km/186,000 mi per second. The (limitless) range of possible wavelengths or frequencies of electromagnetic waves, which can be thought of as making up the ***electromagnetic spectrum***, includes radio waves, infrared radiation, visible light, ultraviolet radiation, X-rays, and gamma rays.

energy the capacity for doing work. Potential energy (PE) is energy deriving from position; thus a stretched spring has elastic PE, and an object raised to a height above the Earth's surface, or the water in an elevated reservoir, has gravitational PE. A lump of coal and a tank of petrol, together with the oxygen needed for their combustion, have chemical energy. Other sorts of energy include electrical and nuclear energy, and light and sound. Moving bodies possess kinetic energy (KE). Energy can be converted from one form to another, but the total quantity stays the same (in accordance with the conservation of energy principle). For example, as an apple falls, it loses gravitational PE but gains KE.

engine device for converting stored energy into useful work or movement. Most engines use a fuel as their energy store. The fuel is burned to produce heat energy – hence the name 'heat engine' – which is then converted into movement. Heat engines can be classified according to the fuel they use (petrol engine or diesel engine), or according to whether the fuel is burnt inside (internal combustion engine) or outside (steam engine) the engine, or according to whether they produce a reciprocating or rotary motion (turbine or Wankel engine).

entropy in thermodynamics, a parameter representing the state of disorder of a system at the atomic, ionic, or molecular level; the greater the disorder, the higher the entropy. Thus the fast-moving disordered molecules of water vapour have higher entropy than those of more ordered liquid water, which in turn have more entropy than the molecules in solid crystalline ice.

equilibrium unchanging condition in which the forces acting on a particle or system of particles (a body) cancel out, or in which energy is distributed among the particles of a system in the most probable way; or the state in which a body is at rest or moving at constant velocity. A body is in ***thermal equilibrium*** with its surroundings if no heat enters or leaves it, so that all its parts are at the same temperature as the surroundings.

field region of space in which an object exerts a force on another separate object because of certain properties they both possess. For example, there is a force of attraction between any two objects that have mass when one is in the gravitational field of the other. Other fields of force include electric fields (caused by electric charges) and magnetic fields (caused by magnetic poles), either of which can involve attractive or repulsive forces.

force any influence that tends to change the state of rest or the uniform motion in a straight line of a body. The action of an unbalanced or resultant force results in the acceleration of a body in the direction of action of the force or it may, if the body is unable to move freely, result in its deformation. Force is a vector quantity, possessing both magnitude and direction; its SI unit is the newton.

frequency the number of periodic oscillations, vibrations, or waves occurring per unit of time. The unit of frequency is the hertz (Hz), one hertz being equivalent to one cycle per second. Human beings can hear sounds from objects vibrating in the range 20–15,000 Hz. Ultrasonic frequencies are those above 15,000 Hz; infrasound is low-frequency sound.

friction the force that opposes the relative motion of two bodies in contact. The ***coefficient of friction*** is the ratio of the force required to achieve this relative motion to the force pressing the two bodies together.

fundamental constant physical quantity that is constant in all circumstances throughout the whole universe. Examples are the electric charge of an electron, the speed of light, Planck's constant, and the gravitational constant.

Fundamental constants

Constant	*Symbol*	*Value in SI units*
acceleration of free fall	g	9.80665 m s^{-2}
Avogadro's constant	N_A	$6.02252 \times 10^{23} \text{ mol}^{-1}$
Boltzmann's constant	$k = R/N_A$	$1.380622 \times 10^{-23} \text{ J K}^{-1}$
electronic charge	e	$1.602192 \times 10^{-19} \text{ C}$
electronic rest mass	m_e	$9.109558 \times 10^{-31} \text{ kg}$
Faraday's constant	F	$9.648670 \times 10^{4} \text{ C mol}^{-1}$
gas constant	R	$8.31434 \text{ J K}^{-1} \text{ mol}^{-1}$
gravitational constant	G	$6.664 \times 10^{-11} \text{ N m}^2 \text{ kg}^{-2}$
Loschmidt's number	N_L	$2.68719 \times 10^{25} \text{ m}^{-3}$
neutron rest mass	m_n	$1.67492 \times 10^{-27} \text{ kg}$
Planck's constant	h	$6.626196 \times 10^{-34} \text{ J s}$
proton rest mass	m_p	$1.672614 \times 10^{-27} \text{ kg}$
speed of light	c	$2.99792458 \times 10^{8} \text{ m s}^{-1}$
standard atmospheric pressure	P	$1.01325 \times 10^{5} \text{ Pa}$
Stefan–Boltzmann constant	Σ	$5.6697 \times 10^{-8} \text{ W m}^{-2} \text{ K}^{-4}$

grand unified theory (GUT) sought-for theory that would combine the theory of the strong nuclear force (called quantum chromodynamics) with the theory of the weak nuclear and electromagnetic forces. The search for the grand unified theory is part of a larger programme seeking a unified field theory, which would combine all the forces of nature (including gravity) within one framework.

gravity force of attraction that arises between objects by virtue of their masses. On Earth, gravity is the force of attraction between any object in the Earth's gravitational field and the Earth itself. It is regarded as one of the four fundamental forces of nature. The gravitational force is the weakest of the four forces, but it acts over great distances. The particle that is postulated as the carrier of the gravitational force is the graviton.

half-life during radioactive decay, the time in which the strength of a radioactive source decays to half its original value. In theory, the decay process is never complete and there is always some residual radioactivity. For this reason, the half-life (the time taken for 50% of the isotope to decay) is measured, rather than the total decay time. It may vary from millionths of a second to billions of years. Plutonium-239, one of the most toxic of all radioactive substances, has a half-life of about 24,000 years.

heat form of internal energy possessed by a substance by virtue of the kinetic energy in the motion of its molecules or atoms. Heat energy is transferred by conduction, convection, and radiation. It always flows from a region of higher temperature (heat intensity) to one of lower temperature. Its effect on a substance may be simply to raise its temperature, or to cause it to expand, melt (if a solid), vaporize (if a liquid), or increase its pressure (if a confined gas). Quantities of heat are usually measured in units of energy, such as joules (J) or calories (C).

hydrodynamics the science of nonviscous fluids (such as water, alcohol, and ether) in motion.

hydrostatics the branch of statics dealing with the mechanical problems of fluids in equilibrium – that is, in a static condition. Practical applications include shipbuilding and dam design.

inertia the tendency of an object to remain in a state of rest or uniform motion until an external force is applied, as stated by Isaac Newton's first law of motion.

interference the phenomenon of two or more wave motions interacting and combining to produce a resultant wave of larger or smaller amplitude (depending on whether the combining waves are in or out of phase with each other).

Interference of white light (multiwavelength) results in spectral coloured fringes; for example, the iridescent colours of oil films seen on water or soap bubbles. With monochromatic light (of a single wavelength), interference produces patterns of light and dark bands. This is the basis of holography, for example. Interference of sound waves of similar frequency produces the phenomenon of beats, often used by musicians when tuning an instrument. Interferometry can also be applied to radio waves, and is a powerful tool in modern astronomy.

kinetic theory theory describing the physical properties of matter in terms of the behaviour – principally movement – of its component atoms or molecules. The temperature of a substance is dependent on the velocity of movement of its constituent particles, increased temperature being accompanied by increased movement. A gas consists of rapidly moving atoms or molecules and, according to kinetic theory, it is their continual impact on the walls of the containing vessel that accounts for the pressure of the gas. The slowing of molecular motion as temperature falls, according to kinetic theory, accounts for the physical properties of liquids and solids, culminating in the concept of no molecular motion at absolute zero (0K/–273°C). By making various assumptions about the nature of gas molecules, it is possible to derive from the kinetic theory the various gas laws (such as Avogadro's hypothesis, Boyle's law, and Charles's law).

laser (acronym for ***light amplification by stimulated emission of radiation***) device for producing a narrow beam of light, capable of travelling over vast distances without dispersion, and of being focused to give enormous power densities (10^8 watts per cm^2 for high-energy lasers). The uses of lasers include com-

Fastest-ever laser pulses

Pulses of laser light lasting only 11 femtoseconds have been produced by US physicists: the shortest pulses of light ever generated by a laser.

What is a femtosecond? It is a millionth of a billionth of a second. Still not clear? Then consider this: light takes 1.25 seconds to travel from the Earth to the Moon but, in one femtosecond, light travels only one hundredth of the width of a human hair. This means that the record-breaking pulses are just over one-tenth of the width of a hair in length.

Generating the pulses was difficult, because short light pulses are composed of a range of wavelengths and, with a range of wavelengths, the pulse spreads out as it travels. Researchers at Washington State University in Pullman used a new type of laser to produce the 11 fs pulses, based on a sapphire crystal doped with titanium. The laser emits a wider range of wavelengths than any other laser but allows the pulses to be compressed before they leave the laser. The pulses will be used to probe high-speed events, such as chemical reactions and electron movements within molecules.

munications (a laser beam can carry much more information than can radio waves), cutting, drilling, welding, satellite tracking, medical and biological research, and surgery.

A gallium arsenide microchip, produced by IBM in 1989, contains the world's smallest lasers in the form of cylinders of semiconductor roughly one tenth of the thickness of a human hair; a million lasers can fit on a chip 1 cm/2.5 in square.

lens in optics, a piece of a transparent material, such as glass, with two polished surfaces – one concave or convex, and the other plane, concave, or convex – that modifies rays of light. A convex lens brings rays of light together; a concave lens makes the rays diverge. Lenses are essential to spectacles, microscopes, telescopes, cameras, and almost all optical instruments.

lever simple machine consisting of a rigid rod pivoted at a fixed point called the fulcrum, used for shifting or raising a heavy load or applying force in a similar way. Levers are classified into orders according to where the effort is applied, and the load-moving force developed, in relation to the position of the fulcrum.

A ***first-order*** lever has the load and the effort on opposite sides of the fulcrum; for example, a see-saw or pair of scissors. A ***second-order*** lever has the load and the effort on the same side of the fulcrum, with the load nearer the fulcrum; for example, nutcrackers or a wheelbarrow. A ***third-order*** lever has the effort nearer the fulcrum than the load, with both on the same side of it; for example, a pair of tweezers or tongs.

light electromagnetic waves in the visible range, having a wavelength from about 400 nanometres in the extreme violet to about 770 nanometres in the extreme red. Light is considered to exhibit particle and wave properties, and the fundamental particle, or quantum, of light is called the photon. The speed of light (and of all electromagnetic radiation) in a vacuum is approximately 300,000 km/186,000 mi per second, and is a universal constant denoted by *c*.

luminescence emission of light from a body when its atoms are excited by means other than raising its temperature. Short-lived luminescence is called fluorescence; longer-lived luminescence is called phosphorescence.

magnetism phenomena associated with magnetic fields. Magnetic fields are produced by moving charged particles: in electromagnets, electrons flow through a coil of wire connected to a battery; in permanent magnets, spinning electrons within the atoms generate the field.

mass the quantity of matter in a body as measured by its inertia. Mass determines the acceleration produced in a body by a given force acting on it, the acceleration being inversely proportional to the mass of the body. The mass also determines the force exerted on a body by gravity on Earth, although this attraction varies slightly from place to place. In the SI system, the base unit of mass is the kilogram.

mechanics branch of physics dealing with the motions of bodies and the forces causing these motions, and also with the forces acting on bodies in equilibrium. It is usually divided into dynamics and statics.

mirror any polished surface that reflects light; often made from 'silvered' glass (in practice, a mercury-alloy coating of glass). A plane (flat) mirror produces a same-size, erect 'virtual' image located behind the mirror at the same distance from it as the object is in front of it. A spherical concave mirror produces a reduced, inverted real image in front or an enlarged, erect virtual image behind it (as in a shaving mirror), depending on how close the object is to the mirror. A spherical convex mirror produces a reduced, erect virtual image behind it (as in a car's rear-view mirror).

Newton's laws of motion three laws that form the basis of Newtonian mechanics. (1) Unless acted upon by a net force, a body at rest stays at rest, and a moving body continues moving at the same speed in the same straight line. (2) A net force applied to a body gives it a rate of change of momentum proportional to the force and in the direction of the force. (3) When a body A exerts a force on a body B, B exerts an equal and opposite force on A; that is, to every action there is an equal and opposite reaction.

nuclear fission process whereby an atomic nucleus breaks up into two or more major fragments with the emission of two or three neutrons. It is accompanied by the release of energy in the form of gamma radiation and the kinetic energy of the emitted particles. Fission occurs spontaneously in nuclei of uranium-235, the main fuel used in nuclear reactors. However, the process can also be induced by bombarding nuclei with neutrons.

physics: chronology

c. 400 BC The first 'atomic' theory was put forward by Democritus.
c. 250 Archimedes' principle of buoyancy was established.
AD 1600 Magnetism was described by William Gilbert.
1608 Hans Lippershey invented the refracting telescope.
c. 1610 The principle of falling bodies descending to earth at the same speed was established by Galileo.
1642 The principles of hydraulics were put forward by Blaise Pascal.
1643 The mercury barometer was invented by Evangelista Torricelli.
1656 The pendulum clock was invented by Christiaan Huygens.
1662 Boyle's law concerning the behaviour of gases was established by Robert Boyle.
c. 1665 Isaac Newton put forward the law of gravity, stating that the Earth exerts a constant force on falling bodies.
1690 The wave theory of light was propounded by Christiaan Huygens.
1704 The corpuscular theory of light was put forward by Isaac Newton.
1714 The mercury thermometer was invented by Daniel Fahrenheit.
1764 Specific and latent heats were described by Joseph Black.
1771 The link between nerve action and electricity was discovered by Luigi Galvani.
c. 1787 Charles's law relating the pressure, volume, and temperature of a gas was established by Jacques Charles.
1795 The metric system was adopted in France.
1798 The link between heat and friction was discovered by Benjamin Rumford.
1800 Alessandro Volta invented the Voltaic cell.
1801 Interference of light was discovered by Thomas Young.
1808 The 'modern' atomic theory was propounded by John Dalton.
1811 Avogadro's hypothesis relating volumes and numbers of molecules of gases was proposed by Amedeo Avogadro.
1814 Fraunhofer lines in the solar spectrum were mapped by Joseph von Fraunhofer.
1815 Refraction of light was explained by Augustin Fresnel.
1819 The discovery of electromagnetism was made by Hans Oersted.
1821 The dynamo principle was described by Michael Faraday; the thermocouple was discovered by Thomas Seebeck.
1822 The laws of electrodynamics were established by André Ampère.
1824 Thermodynamics as a branch of physics was proposed by Sadi Carnot.
1827 Ohm's law of electrical resistance was established by Georg Ohm; Brownian motion resulting from molecular vibrations was observed by Robert Brown.
1829 The law of gaseous diffusion was established by Thomas Graham.
1831 Electromagnetic induction was discovered by Faraday.
1834 Faraday discovered self-induction.
1842 The principle of conservation of energy was observed by Julius von Mayer.
c. 1847 The mechanical equivalent of heat was described by James Joule.
1849 A measurement of speed of light was put forward by French physicist Armand Fizeau (1819–1896).
1851 The rotation of the Earth was demonstrated by Jean Foucault.
1858 The mirror galvanometer, an instrument for measuring small electric currents, was invented by William Thomson (Lord Kelvin).
1859 Spectrographic analysis was made by Robert Bunsen and Gustav Kirchhoff.
1861 Osmosis was discovered.
1873 Light was conceived as electromagnetic radiation by James Maxwell.
1877 A theory of sound as vibrations in an elastic medium was propounded by John Rayleigh.
1880 Piezoelectricity was discovered by Pierre Curie.
1887 The existence of radio waves was predicted by Heinrich Hertz.
1895 X-rays were discovered by Wilhelm Röntgen.
1896 The discovery of radioactivity was made by Antoine Becquerel.
1897 Joseph Thomson discovered the electron.
1899 Ernest Rutherford discovered alpha and beta rays.
1900 Quantum theory was propounded by Max Planck; the discovery of gamma rays was made by French physicist Paul-Ulrich Villard (1860–1934).
1902 Oliver Heaviside discovered the ionosphere.
1904 The theory of radioactivity was put forward by Rutherford and Frederick Soddy.
1905 Albert Einstein propounded his special theory of relativity.
1908 The Geiger counter was invented by Hans Geiger and Rutherford.
1911 The discovery of the atomic nucleus was made by Rutherford.
1913 The orbiting electron atomic theory was propounded by Danish physicist Niels Bohr.
1915 X-ray crystallography was discovered by William and Lawrence Bragg.
1916 Einstein put forward his general theory of relativity; mass spectrography was discovered by William Aston.
1924 Edward Appleton made his study of the Heaviside layer.
1926 Wave mechanics was introduced by Erwin Schrödinger.
1927 The uncertainty principle of atomic physics was established by Werner Heisenberg.

***physics: chronology** (cont.)*

1931	The cyclotron was developed by Ernest Lawrence.
1932	The discovery of the neutron was made by James Chadwick; the electron microscope was developed by Vladimir Zworykin.
1933	The positron, the antiparticle of the electron, was discovered by Carl Anderson.
1934	Artificial radioactivity was developed by Frédéric and Irène Joliot-Curie.
1939	The discovery of nuclear fission was made by Otto Hahn and Fritz Strassmann.
1942	The first controlled nuclear chain reaction was achieved by Enrico Fermi.
1956	The neutrino, an elementary particle, was discovered by Clyde Cowan and Fred Reines.
1960	The Mössbauer effect of atom emissions was discovered by Rudolf Mössbauer; the first maser was developed by US physicist Theodore Maiman (1927–).
1963	Maiman developed the first laser.
1964	Murray Gell-Mann and George Zweig discovered the quark.
1967	Jocelyn Bell (now Burnell) and Antony Hewish discovered pulsars (rapidly rotating neutron stars that emit pulses of energy).
1971	The theory of superconductivity was announced, where electrical resistance in some metals vanishes above absolute zero.
1979	The discovery of the asymmetry of elementary particles was made by US physicists James W Cronin and Val L Fitch.
1982	The discovery of processes involved in the evolution of stars was made by Subrahmanyan Chandrasekhar and William Fowler.
1983	Evidence of the existence of weakons (W and Z particles) was confirmed at CERN, validating the link between the weak nuclear force and the electromagnetic force.
1986	The first high-temperature superconductor was discovered, able to conduct electricity without resistance at a temperature of −238°C/−396°F.
1989	CERN's Large Electron Positron Collider (LEP), a particle accelerator with a circumference of 27 km/16.8 mi, came into operation.
1991	LEP experiments demonstrated the existence of three generations of elementary particles, each with two quarks and two leptons.
1992	Japanese researchers developed a material that becomes superconducting at −103°C/−153°F (about 45°C/80°F warmer than the previous record).
1993	Top quark discovered at Fermilab, the US particle physics laboratory near Chicago, USA.

nuclear fusion process whereby two atomic nuclei are fused, with the release of a large amount of energy. Very high temperatures and pressures are thought to be required in order for the process to happen. Under these conditions the atoms involved are stripped of all their electrons so that the remaining particles, which together make up plasma, can come close together at very high speeds and overcome the mutual repulsion of the positive charges on the atomic nuclei. At very close range another nuclear force will come into play, fusing the particles together to form a larger nucleus. Because fusion is accompanied by the release of large amounts of energy, methods of achieving controlled fusion are the subject of research around the world.

optics branch of physics that deals with the study of light and vision – for example, shadows and mirror images, lenses, microscopes, telescopes, and cameras. For all practical purposes light rays travel in straight lines, although Albert Einstein demonstrated that they may be 'bent' by a gravitational field. On striking a surface they are reflected or refracted with some absorption of energy, and the study of this is known as geometrical optics.

potential, electric the relative electrical state of an object. A charged conductor, for example, has a higher potential than the Earth, whose potential is taken by convention to be zero. An electric cell (battery) has a potential in relation to emf (electromotive force), which can make current flow in an external circuit. The difference in potential between two points – the potential difference – is expressed in volts; that is, a 12 V battery has a potential difference of 12 volts between its negative and positive terminals.

power the rate of doing work or consuming energy. It is measured in watts (joules per second) or other units of work per unit time.

pressure the force acting normally (at right angles) to a body per unit surface area. The SI unit of pressure is the pascal (newton per square metre), equal to 0.01 millibars. In a fluid (liquid or gas), pressure increases with depth. At the edge of Earth's atmosphere, pressure is zero, whereas at sea level atmospheric pressure due to the weight of the air above is about 100 kilopascals (1,013 millibars or 1 atmosphere). Pressure is commonly measured by means of a barometer, manometer, or Bourdon gauge.

quantum theory or ***quantum mechanics*** the theory that energy does not have a continuous range of values, but is, instead, absorbed or radiated discontinuously, in multiples of definite, indivisible units called quanta. Just as earlier theory showed how light, generally seen as a wave motion, could also in some ways be seen as composed of discrete particles (photons), quantum theory shows how atomic particles such as electrons may also be seen as having wavelike properties. Quantum theory is the basis of particle physics, modern theoretical chemistry, and the solid-state physics that describes the behaviour of the silicon chips used in computers.

radiation emission of radiant energy as particles or waves; for example, heat, light, alpha particles, and beta particles.

radioactivity spontaneous alteration of the nuclei of radioactive atoms, accompanied by the emission of radiation. It is the property exhibited by the radioactive isotopes of stable elements and all isotopes of radioactive elements, and can be either natural or induced.

radioisotope (contraction of ***radioactive isotope***) naturally occurring or synthetic radioactive form of an element. Most radioisotopes are made by bombarding a stable element with neutrons in the core of a nuclear reactor. The radiations given off by radioisotopes are easy to detect (hence their use as tracers), can in some instances penetrate substantial thicknesses of materials, and have profound effects (such as genetic mutation) on living matter. Although dangerous, radioisotopes are used in the fields of medicine, industry, agriculture, and research.

reflection the throwing back or deflection of waves, such as light or sound waves, when they hit a surface. The ***law of reflection*** states that the angle of incidence (the angle between the ray and a perpendicular line drawn to the surface) is equal to the angle of reflection (the angle between the reflected ray and a perpendicular to the surface).

refraction the bending of a wave of light, heat, or sound when it passes from one medium to another. Refraction occurs because waves travel at different velocities in different media.

relativity the theory of the relative rather than absolute character of motion and mass, and the interdependence of matter, time, and space, as developed by German physicist Albert Einstein in two phases:

special theory (1905) Starting with the premises that (1) the laws of nature are the same for all observers in unaccelerated motion, and (2) the speed of light is independent of the motion of its source, Einstein postulated that the time interval between two events was longer for an observer in whose frame of reference the events occur in different places than for the observer for whom they occur at the same place.

general theory of relativity (1915) The geometrical properties of space-time were to be conceived as modified locally by the presence of a body with mass. A planet's orbit around the Sun (as observed in three-dimensional space) arises from its natural trajectory in modified space-time; there is no need to invoke, as Isaac Newton did, a force of gravity coming from the Sun and acting on the planet. Einstein's theory predicted slight differences in the orbits of the planets from Newton's theory, which were observable in the case of Mercury. The new theory also said light rays should bend when they pass by a massive object, owing to the object's effect on local space-time. The predicted bending of starlight was observed during the eclipse of the Sun 1919, when light from distant stars passing close to the Sun was not masked by sunlight.

resistance that property of a substance that restricts the flow of electricity through it, associated with the conversion of electrical energy to heat; also the magnitude of this property. Resistance depends on many factors, such as the nature of the material, its temperature, dimensions, and thermal properties; degree of impurity; the nature and state of illumination of the surface; and the frequency and magnitude of the current. The SI unit of resistance is the ohm.

resonance rapid and uncontrolled increase in the size of a vibration when the vibrating object is subject to a force varying at its natural frequency. In a trombone, for example, the length of the air column in the instrument is adjusted until it resonates with the note being sounded. Resonance effects are also produced by many electrical circuits. Tuning a radio, for example, is done by adjusting the natural frequency of the receiver circuit until it coincides with the frequency of the radio waves falling on the aerial.

semiconductor crystalline material with an electrical conductivity between that of metals (good) and insulators (poor). The conductivity of semiconductors can usually be improved by minute additions of different substances or by other factors. Silicon, for example, has poor conductivity at low temperatures, but this is improved by the application of light, heat, or voltage; hence silicon is used in transistors, rectifiers, and integrated circuits (silicon chips).

SI units (French ***Système International d'Unités***) standard system of scientific units used by scientists worldwide. Originally proposed in 1960, it replaces the m.k.s., c.g.s., and f.p.s. systems. It is based on seven basic units: the metre (m) for length, kilogram

SI units

Quantity	*SI unit*	*Symbol*
absorbed radiation dose	gray	Gy
amount of substance	mole*	mol
electric capacitance	farad	F
electric charge	coulomb	C
electric conductance	siemens	S
electric current	ampere*	A
energy or work	joule	J
force	newton	N
frequency	hertz	Hz
illuminance	lux	lx
inductance	henry	H
length	metre*	m
luminous flux	lumen	lm
luminous intensity	candela*	cd
magnetic flux	weber	Wb
magnetic flux density	tesla	T
mass	kilogram*	kg
plane angle	radian	rad
potential difference	volt	V
power	watt	W
pressure	pascal	Pa
radiation dose equivalent	sievert	Sv
radiation exposure	roentgen	r
radioactivity	becquerel	Bq
resistance	ohm	Ω
solid angle	steradian	sr
sound intensity	decibel	dB
temperature	°Celsius	°C
temperature, thermodynamic	kelvin*	K
time	second*	s

**SI base unit*

SI prefixes

Multiple	Prefix	Symbol	Example
1,000,000,000,000,000,000 (10^{18})	exa-	E	Eg (exagram)
1,000,000,000,000,000 (10^{15})	peta-	P	PJ (petajoule)
1,000,000,000,000 (10^{12})	tera-	T	TV (teravolt)
1,000,000,000 (10^{9})	giga-	G	GW (gigawatt)
1,000,000 (10^{6})	mega-	M	MHz (megahertz)
1,000 (10^{3})	kilo-	k	kg (kilogram)
100 (10^{2})	hecto-	h	hm (hectometre)
10	deca-	da-	daN (decanewton)
1/10 (10^{-1})	deci-	d	dC (decicoulomb)
1/100 (10^{-2})	centi-	c	cm (centimetre)
1/1,000 (10^{-3})	milli-	m	mA (milliampere)
1/1,000,000 (10^{-6})	micro-	μ	μF (microfarad)
1/1,000,000,000 (10^{-9})	nano-	n	nm (nanometre)
1/1,000,000,000,000 (10^{-12})	pico-	p	ps (picosecond)
1/1,000,000,000,000,000 (10^{-15})	femto-	f	frad (femtoradian)
1/1,000,000,000,000,000,000 (10^{-18})	atto-	a	aT (attotesla)

(kg) for mass, second (s) for time, ampere (A) for electrical current, kelvin (K) for temperature, mole (mol) for amount of substance, and candela (cd) for luminosity.

sound physiological sensation received by the ear, originating in a vibration (pressure variation in the air) that communicates itself to the air, and travels in every direction, spreading out as an expanding sphere. All sound waves in air travel with a speed dependent on the temperature; under ordinary conditions, this is about 330 m/1,070 ft per second. The pitch of the sound depends on the number of vibrations imposed on the air per second, but the speed is unaffected. The loudness of a sound is dependent primarily on the amplitude of the vibration of the air.

spectroscopy study of spectra associated with atoms or molecules in solid, liquid, or gaseous phase. Spectroscopy can be used to identify unknown compounds and is an invaluable tool in science, medicine, and industry (for example, in checking the purity of drugs).

spectrum (plural ***spectra***) arrangement of frequencies or wavelengths when electromagnetic radiations are separated into their constituent parts. Visible light is part of the electromagnetic spectrum and most sources emit waves over a range of wavelengths that can be broken up or 'dispersed'; white light can be separated into red, orange, yellow, green, blue, indigo, and violet. The visible spectrum was first studied by Isaac Newton, who showed in 1672 how white light could be broken up into different colours.

states of matter forms (solid, liquid, or gas) in which material can exist. Whether a material is solid, liquid, or gas depends on its temperature and the pressure on it. The transition between states takes place at definite temperatures, called melting point and boiling point.

statics branch of mechanics concerned with the behaviour of bodies at rest and forces in equilibrium.

stress and strain in the science of materials, measures of the deforming force applied to a body (stress) and of the resulting change in its shape (strain). For a perfectly elastic material, stress is proportional to strain (Hooke's law).

surface tension the property that causes the surface of a liquid to behave as if it were covered with a weak elastic skin; this is why a needle can float on water. It is caused by the exposed surface's tendency to contract to the smallest possible area because of unequal cohesive forces between molecules at the surface. Allied phenomena include the formation of droplets, the concave profile of a meniscus, and the capillary action by which water soaks into a sponge.

temperature the state of hotness or coldness of a body, and the condition that determines whether or not it will transfer heat to, or receive heat from, another body according to the laws of thermodynamics. It is measured in degrees Celsius (before 1948 called centigrade), kelvin, or Fahrenheit.

tension reaction force set up in a body that is subjected to stress. In a stretched string or wire it exerts a pull that is equal in magnitude but opposite in direction to the stress being applied at its ends. Tension originates in the net attractive intermolecular force created when a stress causes the mean distance separating a material's molecules to become greater than the equilibrium distance. It is measured in newtons.

thermodynamics branch of physics dealing with the transformation of heat into and from other forms of energy. It is the basis of the study of the efficient working of engines, such as the steam and internal-combustion engines. The three laws of thermodynamics are (1) energy can be neither created nor destroyed, heat and mechanical work being mutually convertible; (2) it is impossible for an unaided self-acting machine to convey heat from one body to another at a higher temperature; and (3) it is impossible by any procedure, no matter how idealized, to reduce any system to the absolute zero of temperature (0K/–273°C) in a finite number of operations. Put into mathematical form, these laws have widespread applications in physics and chemistry.

ultrasound pressure waves similar in nature to sound waves but occurring at frequencies above 20,000 Hz (cycles per second), the approximate upper limit of human hearing (15–16 Hz is the lower limit). Ultrasonics is concerned with the study and practical application of these phenomena.

viscosity the resistance of a fluid to flow, caused by its internal friction, which makes it resist flowing past a solid surface or other layers of the fluid. It applies to the motion of an object moving through a fluid as well as the motion of a fluid passing by an object.

wave disturbance consisting of a series of oscillations that propagate through a medium (or space). There are two types: in a ***longitudinal wave*** (such as a sound wave) the disturbance is parallel to the wave's direction of travel; in a ***transverse wave*** (such as an electromagnetic wave) it is perpendicular. The medium only vibrates as the wave passes; it does not travel outward from the source with the waves.

weight the force exerted on an object by gravity. The weight of an object depends on its mass – the amount of material in it – and the strength of the Earth's gravitational pull, which decreases with height. Consequently, an object weighs less at the top of a mountain than at sea level. On the Moon, an object has only one-sixth of its weight on Earth, because the pull of the Moon's gravity is one-sixth that of the Earth.

work measure of the result of transferring energy from one system to another to cause an object to move. Work should not be confused with energy (the capacity to do work, which is also measured in joules) or with power (the rate of doing work, measured in joules per second).

Particle Physics

antimatter matter in which most of the attributes (such as electrical charge, magnetic moment, and spin) of elementary particles are reversed. Such particles (antiparticles) can be created in particle accelerators, such as those at CERN in Geneva, Switzerland, and at Fermilab in the USA.

baryon heavy subatomic particle made up of three indivisible elementary particles called quarks. The baryons form a subclass of the hadrons, and comprise the nucleons (protons and neutrons) and hyperons.

boson elementary particle whose spin can only take values that are whole numbers or zero. Bosons may be classified as gauge bosons (carriers of the four fundamental forces) or mesons. All elementary particles are either bosons or fermions.

electron stable, negatively charged elementary particle; it is a constituent of all atoms, and a member of the class of particles known as leptons. The electrons in each atom surround the nucleus in groupings called shells; in a neutral atom the number of electrons is equal to the number of protons in the nucleus. This electron structure is responsible for the chemical properties of the atom.

fermion subatomic particle whose spin can only take values that are half-integers, such as $^1/_2$ or $^3/_2$. Fermions may be classified as leptons, such as the electron, and baryons, such as the proton and neutron. All elementary particles are either fermions or bosons.

forces, fundamental the four fundamental interactions believed to be at work in the physical universe. There are two long-range forces: ***gravity***, which keeps the planets in orbit around the Sun, and acts between all particles that have mass; and the ***electromagnetic force***, which stops solids from falling apart, and acts between all particles with electric charge. There are two very short-range forces which operate only inside the atomic nucleus: the ***weak nuclear force***, responsible for the reactions that fuel the Sun and for the emission of beta particles from certain nuclei; and the ***strong nuclear force***, which binds together the protons and neutrons in the nuclei of atoms. The relative strengths of the four forces are: strong, 1; electromagnetic, 10^{-2}; weak, 10^{-6}; gravitational, 10^{-40}.

gauge boson or ***field particle*** any of the particles that carry the four fundamental forces of nature. Gauge bosons are elementary particles that cannot be subdivided, and include the photon, the graviton, the gluons, and the weakons.

gluon gauge boson that carries the strong nuclear force, responsible for binding quarks together to form the strongly interacting subatomic particles known as hadrons. There are eight kinds of gluon.

graviton gauge boson that is the postulated carrier of gravity.

hadron subatomic particle that experiences the strong nuclear force. Each is made up of two or three indivisible particles called quarks. The hadrons are grouped into the baryons (protons, neutrons, and hyperons) and the mesons (particles with masses between those of electrons and protons).

Higgs particle or ***Higgs boson*** postulated elementary particle whose existence would explain why particles, such as the intermediate vector boson, have mass. The current theory of elementary particles, called the standard model, cannot explain how mass arises, To overcome this difficulty, Peter Higgs (1929–) of the University of Edinburgh, Scotland, and Thomas Kibble (1932–) of Imperial College, London, England, proposed in 1964 a new particle that binds to other particles and gives them their mass. The Higgs particle has not yet been detected experimentally.

hyperon type of hadron; any of a group of highly unstable elementary particles that includes all the baryons with a mass greater than the neutron. They are all composed of three quarks. The lambda, xi, sigma, and omega particles are hyperons.

lepton any of a class of light elementary particles that are not affected by the strong nuclear force; they do not interact strongly with other particles or nuclei. The leptons are comprised of the electron, muon, and tau, and their neutrinos (the electron neutrino, muon neutrino, and tau neutrino), plus their six antiparticles.

meson unstable subatomic particle made up of two indivisible elementary particles called quarks. It has a mass intermediate between that of the electron and that of the proton, is found in cosmic radiation, and is emitted by nuclei under bombardment by very high-energy particles.

muon elementary particle similar to the electron except for its mass, which is 207 times greater than that of the electron. It has a half-life of 2 millionths of a second, decaying into electrons and neutrinos. The muon was originally thought to be a meson and is thus sometimes called a mu meson, although current opinion is that it is a lepton.

neutrino any of three uncharged elementary particles (and their antiparticles) of the lepton class, having a mass too close to zero to be measured. The most familiar type, the antiparticle of the electron neutrino, is emitted in the beta decay of a nucleus. The other two are the muon neutrino and the tau neutrino.

neutron one of the three main subatomic particles, the others being the proton and the electron. The neutron is a composite particle, being made up of three quarks, and therefore belongs to the baryon group of the hadrons. Neutrons have about the same mass as protons but no electric charge, and occur in the nuclei of all atoms except hydrogen. They contribute to the mass of atoms but do not affect their chemistry.

nucleus the positively charged central part of an atom, which constitutes almost all its mass. Except for hydrogen nuclei, which have only protons, nuclei are composed of both protons and neutrons. Surrounding the nuclei are electrons, which contain a negative charge equal to the protons, thus giving the atom a neutral charge.

photon elementary particle or 'package' (quantum) of energy in which light and other forms of electromagnetic radiation are emitted. The photon has both particle and wave properties; it has no charge, is considered massless but possesses momentum and energy. It is one of the gauge bosons, a particle that cannot be subdivided, and is the carrier of the electromagnetic force, one of the fundamental forces of nature.

proton positively charged subatomic particle, a constituent of the nucleus of all atoms. It belongs to the baryon subclass of the hadrons. A proton is extremely long-lived, with a lifespan of at least 10^{32} years. It carries a unit positive charge equal to the negative charge of an electron. Its mass is almost 1,836 times that of an electron, or 1.67×10^{-24} g. The number of protons in the atom of an element is equal to the atomic number of that element.

quantum chromodynamics (QCD) theory describing the interactions of quarks, the elementary particles that make up all hadrons (subatomic particles such as protons and neutrons). In quantum chromodynamics, quarks are considered to interact by exchanging particles called gluons, which carry the strong nuclear force, and whose role is to 'glue' quarks together. The mathematics involved in the theory is complex, and although a number of successful predictions have been made, the theory does not yet compare in accuracy with quantum electrodynamics, upon which it is modelled.

quantum electrodynamics (QED) theory describing the interaction of charged subatomic particles within electric and magnetic fields. It combines quantum theory and relativity, and considers charged particles to interact by the exchange of photons. QED is remarkable for the accuracy of its predictions – for example, it has been used to calculate the value of some physical quantities to an accuracy of ten decimal places, a feat equivalent to calculating the distance between New York and Los Angeles to within the thickness of a hair. The theory was developed by US physicists Richard Feynman and Julian Schwinger, and by Japanese physicist Sin-Itiro Tomonaga 1948.

quark elementary particle that is the fundamental constituent of all hadrons (baryons, such as neutrons and protons, and mesons). There are six types, or 'flavours': up, down, top, bottom, strange, and charm, each of which has three varieties, or 'colours': red, yellow, and blue (visual colour is not meant, although the analogy is useful in many ways). To each quark there is an antiparticle, called an antiquark.

Top quark glimpsed?

Physicists may have glimpsed the top quark, although they are slow to admit it. The top quark is the only one of the six quarks (fundamental particles that make up protons, neutrons, and other subatomic particles) that remains to be observed, and physicists have been searching for it for more than four years. If observed, the top quark will confirm the standard model that describes the behaviour of fundamental particles.

The best hope of observing the top quark is agreed to lie with the Tevatron particle accelerator at the Fermilab particle physics centre near Chicago. The Tevatron collides protons with antiprotons at high energies. Each collision produces a stream of particles including, it is hoped, the top quark. Three years ago Fermilab workers recorded a 'candidate', or particle that might be the top quark, but the evidence was inconclusive. Recently, two other candidates have been recorded. The candidates were discovered when particle detectors at Fermilab found an unusual pattern of particle tracks spiralling out of the debris produced by a proton–antiproton collision. The tracks indicated the presence of an electron, a muon, and a shower of other particles. This is precisely the pattern expected if a proton and antiproton transform into the top quark. Unfortunately, the same pattern can also be produced in other ways. A new detector, called the vertex detector, has been added which should distinguish between true top quark and other events.

So the search must go on. Fermilab scientists are right to be cautious in interpreting their results. In 1985, workers at CERN, the European particle physics laboratory near Geneva, announced the discovery of the top quark, only to be proved wrong later.

The short life of a neutron

In 1992, physicists finally agreed a value for the lifetime of the neutron. The neutron is one of the particles found in the atomic nucleus. Like most other subatomic particles, it spontaneously disintegrates, or decays, when outside the nucleus. The neutron lifetime is a measure of how long it takes for half of any sample of neutrons to decay.

Until recently, estimates of the average lifetime of the neutron varied widely. In the early 1960s, most physicists thought the neutron lifetime lay between 980 and 1040 seconds. Then a set of more accurate experiments indicated a value between 910 and 950 seconds. In the 1970s, expert opinion favoured the range between 900 and 950 seconds. In the 1980s, 870 to 910 seconds seemed to be indicated. Finally, in the early 1990s, data from several different sources converged on the now-accepted value of 889 seconds: 14 minutes 49 seconds.

Does it matter how long a neutron lives? Physicists are interested in having an exact value for the neutron lifetime because there is a relationship between the neutron lifetime and the lifetimes of other subatomic particles. If the decay rate of the neutron is known accurately the decay rate of other particles, such as the muon, can be calculated.

The neutron decays by a process called 'beta decay'. The neutron ejects an electron and an antineutrino when it decays, and turns into a proton (hydrogen nucleus). This process is responsible for some of the nuclear reactions that take place inside stars and the Sun. So astronomers need to understand neutron decay if they are to calculate the structure and energy output of the Sun and stars.

During the 1980s, cosmologists pointed out that our knowledge of the Big Bang – the explosion at the beginning of time – could be used to calculate the neutron lifetime. According to the Big Bang theory, when the Universe was about a second old, it was a seething mass of protons and neutrons. The temperature was initially very high – over 10 billion degrees. At this temperature, neutrons constantly change into protons, and vice versa. The rapid interchange of protons and neutrons produced an approximate balance between the particles. But as the Universe expanded, and the temperature dropped, there was no longer enough energy to change protons into neutrons, and the proportion of neutrons dropped. When the Universe was about 200 seconds old, the temperature had dropped to about 1 billion degrees. At this temperature, when neutrons and protons collide they combine to form nuclei, first of deuterium and then of helium-4. Once locked inside the nuclei, neutrons are stable, and have survived to the present day.

So the Big Bang theory tells us that there was a period of less than 200 seconds during which neutrons were decaying without being replaced. If neutrons had a very short lifetime, they would have all decayed during this period, and there would be no helium today. If neutrons had a very long lifetime, they would all have survived to become helium and there would be no hydrogen today. But today's Universe contains about 75% hydrogen and 25% helium. This observation has been used to calculate the lifetime of the neutron. The resulting figure – 890 seconds – was lower than many physicists thought likely even in the late 1980s.

Laboratory measurements of the neutron lifetime were successful in 1989. A team headed by Jim Byrne and Peter Dawber of Sussex University, England, monitored the decay of neutrons in a beam. They counted the number of protons produced by neutron decay at various points along the beam. To do this, the researchers had to collect the protons at various points using a device called a Penning trap.

This device is a series of electrodes sitting in the neutron beam. As protons are produced by neutron decay, they are trapped by the electric and magnetic fields between the electrodes. A typical neutron beam with 200 million neutrons passing along each square centimetre of the beam in a second will produce one proton every second. In Byrne's experiment, where 4000 million neutrons passed along the beam each second, there were just 10 decay protons produced each second. Byrne and Dawber's result was 893 $\pm$15 seconds.

Another experiment undertaken at around the same time involved watching a collection of neutrons confined in magnetic storage rings or 'bottles'. Researchers measured the number of neutrons that survived during a given period, rather than the number that decayed. This experiment provided a valuable confirmation of Byrne and Dawber's result and allowed the neutron lifetime to be calculated even more precisely.

The story ends, then, with evidence from several different sources all pointing to the same result.

PL

PRINCIPAL SUBATOMIC PARTICLES

	Group	Particle	Symbol	Charge	Mass (MeV)	Spin	Lifetime (sec)
elementary particle	quark	up	u	⅔	336	½	?
		down	d	−⅓	336	½	?
		(top)	t	(⅔)	(<600,000)	(½)	?
		bottom	b	−⅓	4,700	½	?
		strange	s	−⅓	540	½	?
		charm	c	⅔	1,500	½	?
	lepton	electron	e^-	−1	0·511	½	stable
		electron neutrino	ν_e	0	(0)	½	stable
		muon	μ^-	−1	105·66	½	2·2 × 10^{-6}
		muon neutrino	ν_μ	0	(0)	½	stable
		tau	τ^-	−1	1,784	½	3·4 × 10^{-13}
		tau neutrino	ν_τ	0	(0)	½	?
	gauge boson	photon	γ	0	0	1	stable
		graviton	g	0	(0)	2	stable
		gluon	g	0	0	1	?
		weakon	$W^\pm$	±1	81,000	1	?
			Z	0	94,000	1	?
hadron	meson	pion	π^+	1	139·57	0	2·6 × 10^{-8}
			π^0	0	134·96	0	8·3 × 10^{-17}
		kaon	K^+	1	493·67	0	1·2 × 10^{-8}
			K^0_s	0	497·67	0	8·9 × 10^{-11}
			K^0_L	0	497·67	0	5·18 × 10^{-8}
		psi	Ψ	0	3,100	1	6·3 × 10^{-2}
		upsilon	Υ	0	9,460	1	~1 × 10^{-20}
	baryon	nucleon					
		proton	p	1	938·28	½	stable
		nucleon	n	0	939·57	½	920
		hyperon					
		lambda	Λ	0	1,115·6	½	2·63 × 10^{-10}
		sigma	Σ^+	1	1,189·4	½	8·0 × 10^{-11}
			Σ^-	−1	1,197·3	½	1·5 × 10^{-10}
			Σ^0	0	1,192·5	½	5·8 × 10^{-20}
		xi	Ξ^-	−1	1,321·3	½	1·64 × 10^{-10}
			Ξ^0	0	1,314·9	½	2·9 × 10^{-10}
		omega	Ω	−1	1,672·4	$\frac{3}{2}$	8·2 × 10^{-11}

? indicates that the particle's lifetime has yet to be determined
( ) indicates that the property has been deduced but not confirmed
MeV = million electron volts

spin the intrinsic angular momentum of a subatomic particle, nucleus, atom, or molecule, which continues even when the particle comes to rest. A particle in a specific energy state has a particular spin, just as it has a particular electric charge and mass. According to quantum theory, this is restricted to discrete and indivisible values, specified by a spin quantum number. Because of its spin, a charged particle acts as a small magnet and is affected by magnetic fields.

standard model the modern theory of elementary particles and their interactions. According to the standard model, elementary particles are classified as leptons (light particles, such as electrons), hadrons (particles, such as neutrons and protons, that are formed from quarks), and gauge bosons. Leptons and hadrons interact by exchanging gauge bosons, each of which is responsible for a different fundamental force: photons mediate the electromagnetic force, which affects all charged particles; gluons mediate the strong nuclear force, which affects quarks; gravitons mediate the force of gravity; and the weakons (intermediate vector bosons) mediate the weak nuclear force.

superstring theory mathematical theory developed in the 1980s to explain the properties of elementary particles and the forces between them (in particular, gravity and the nuclear forces) in a way that combines relativity and quantum theory. In string theory, the fundamental objects in the universe are not pointlike particles but extremely small stringlike objects. These objects exist in a universe of ten dimensions, although, for reasons not yet understood, only three space dimensions and one dimension of time are discernible.

supersymmetry theory that relates the two classes of elementary particle, the fermions and the bosons. According to supersymmetry, each fermion particle has a boson partner particle, and vice versa. It has not been possible to marry up all the known fermions with the known bosons, and so the theory postulates the existence of other, as yet undiscovered fermions, such as the photinos (partners of the photons), gluinos (partners of the gluons), and gravitinos (partners of the gravitons). Using these ideas, it has become possible to develop a theory of gravity – called supergravity – that extends Albert Einstein's work and considers the gravitational, nuclear, and electromagnetic forces to be manifestations of an underlying superforce. Supersymmetry has been incorporated into the superstring theory, and appears to be a crucial ingredient in the 'theory of everything' sought by scientists.

tau elementary particle with the same electric charge as the electron but a mass nearly double that of a proton. It has a lifetime of around 3×10^{-13} seconds and belongs to the lepton family of particles: those that interact via the electromagnetic, weak nuclear, and gravitational forces, but not the strong nuclear force.

uncertainty principle or ***indeterminacy principle*** the principle that it is meaningless to speak of a particle's position, momentum, or other parameters, except as results of measurements; measuring, however, involves an interaction (such as a photon of light bouncing off the particle under scrutiny), which must disturb the particle, though the disturbance is noticeable only at an atomic scale. The principle implies that one cannot, even in theory, predict the moment-to-moment behaviour of such a system.

weakon or ***intermediate vector boson*** gauge boson that carries the weak nuclear force, one of the fundamental forces of nature. There are three types of weakon: the positive and negative W particle and the neutral Z particle.

Z particle elementary particle, one of the weakons responsible for carrying the weak nuclear force.

Great Physicists

Ampère André Marie 1775–1836. French physicist and mathematician who made many discoveries in electromagnetism and electrodynamics. He followed up the work of Danish physicist Hans Oersted (1777–1851) on the interaction between magnets and electric currents, developing a rule for determining the direction of the magnetic field associated with an electric current. The ampere is named after him.

Bohr Niels (Henrik David) 1885–1962. Danish physicist. His theoretic work produced a new model of atomic structure, now called the Bohr model, and helped establish the validity of quantum theory.

Boyle Robert 1627–1691. Irish physicist and chemist who published the seminal *The Sceptical Chymist* 1661. He formulated ***Boyle's law*** 1662.

Broglie Louis de, 7th Duc de Broglie 1892–1987. French theoretical physicist who established that all subatomic particles can be described either by particle equations or by wave equations, thus laying the foundations of wave mechanics. Nobel Prize for Physics 1929.

Carnot (Nicolas Leonard) Sadi 1796–1832. French scientist and military engineer who founded the science of thermodynamics; his pioneering work was *Reflexions sur la puissance motrice du feu/On the Motive Power of Fire*, which considered the changes that would take place in an idealized, frictionless steam engine.

Cavendish Henry 1731–1810. English physicist who discovered hydrogen (which he called 'inflammable air') 1766, and determined the compositions of water and of nitric acid.

Chadwick James 1891–1974. British physicist. In 1932, he discovered the particle in the nucleus of an atom that became known as the neutron because it has no electric charge. Nobel Prize for Physics 1935.

Curie Marie (born Sklodovska) 1867–1934. Polish scientist. In 1898 she reported the possible existence of a new, powerfully radioactive element in pitchblende ores.

Her husband, ***Pierre Curie*** (1859-1906), abandoned his own researches to assist her, and in the same year they announced the existence of polonium and radium. They isolated the pure elements 1902. They shared the Nobel Prize for Physics 1903 with Antoine Becquerel (1852–1908); Marie Curie wrote a *Treatise on Radioactivity* 1910, and was awarded the Nobel Prize for Chemistry 1911.

Dirac Paul Adrien Maurice 1902–1984. British physicist who worked out a version of quantum mechanics consistent with special relativity. The existence of the positron (positive electron) was one of its predictions. He shared the Nobel Prize for Physics 1933 with Erwin Schrödinger.

Einstein Albert 1879–1955. German-born US physicist who formulated the ***theories of relativity***, and worked on radiation physics and thermodynamics. In 1905 he published the special theory of relativity, and in 1915 issued his general theory of relativity. He received the Nobel Prize for Physics 1921.

His last conception of the basic laws governing the universe was outlined in his unified field theory, made public 1953.

Faraday Michael 1791–1867. English chemist and physicist. In 1821 he began experimenting with electromagnetism, and ten years later discovered the induction of electric currents and made the first dynamo. He subsequently found that a magnetic field will rotate the plane of polarization of light. Faraday also investigated electrolysis.

Fermi Enrico 1901–1954. Italian-born US physicist who proved the existence of new radioactive elements produced by bombardment with neutrons, and discovered nuclear reactions produced by low-energy neutrons. His theoretical work included study of the weak nuclear force, one of the fundamental forces of nature, and (with Paul Dirac) of the quantum statistics of fermion particles. Nobel prize 1938.

Feynman Richard P(hillips) 1918–1988. US physicist whose work laid the foundations of quantum electrodynamics. As a member of the committee investigating the *Challenger* space-shuttle disaster 1986, he demonstrated the lethal faults in rubber seals on the shuttle's booster rocket. For his work on the theory of radiation he shared the Nobel Prize for Physics 1965.

Nobel prize for physics

	Prizewinners
1960	Donald Glaser (USA): invention of the bubble chamber
1961	Robert Hofstadter (USA): scattering of electrons in atomic nuclei, and structure of protons and neutrons. Rudolf Mössbauer (Germany): resonance absorption of gamma radiation
1962	Lev Landau (USSR): theories of condensed matter, especially liquid helium
1963	Eugene Wigner (USA): discovery and application of symmetry principles in atomic physics. Maria Goeppert-Mayer (USA) and Hans Jensen (Germany): discovery of the shell-like structure of atomic nuclei
1964	Charles Townes (USA), Nikolai Basov (USSR), and Aleksandr Prokhorov (USSR): quantum electronics leading to construction of oscillators and amplifiers based on maser–laser principle
1965	Sin-Itiro Tomonaga (Japan), Julian Schwinger (USA), and Richard Feynman (USA): quantum electrodynamics
1966	Alfred Kastler (France): development of optical pumping, whereby atoms are raised to higher energy levels by illumination
1967	Hans Bethe (USA): theory of nuclear reactions, and discoveries concerning production of energy in stars
1968	Luis Alvarez (USA): elementary-particle physics, and discovery of resonance states, using hydrogen bubble chamber and data analysis
1969	Murray Gell-Mann (USA): classification of elementary particles, and study of their interactions
1970	Hannes Alfvén (Sweden): magnetohydrodynamics and its applications in plasma physics. Louis Néel (France): antiferromagnetism and ferromagnetism in solid-state physics
1971	Dennis Gabor (UK): invention and development of holography
1972	John Bardeen (USA), Leon Cooper (USA), and John Robert Schrieffer (USA): theory of superconductivity
1973	Leo Eskai (Japan) and Ivar Giaver (USA): tunnelling phenomena in semiconductors and superconductors. Brian Josephson (UK): theoretical predictions of the properties of a supercurrent through a tunnel barrier
1974	Martin Ryle (UK) and Antony Hewish (UK): development of radioastronomy, particularly aperture-synthesis technique, and the discovery of pulsars
1975	Aage Bohr (Denmark), Ben Mottelson (Denmark), and James Rainwater (USA): discovery of connection between collective motion and particle motion in atomic nuclei, and development of theory of nuclear structure
1976	Burton Richter (USA) and Samuel Ting (USA): discovery of the psi meson
1977	Philip Anderson (USA), Nevill Mott (UK), and John Van Vleck (USA): electronic structure of magnetic and disordered systems
1978	Pyotr Kapitza (USSR): low-temperature physics. Arno Penzias (Germany), and Robert Wilson (USA): discovery of cosmic background radiation
1979	Sheldon Glashow (USA), Abdus Salam (Pakistan), and Steven Weinberg (USA): unified theory of weak and electromagnetic fundamental forces, and prediction of the existence of the weak neutral current
1980	James W Cronin (USA) and Val Fitch (USA): violations of fundamental symmetry principles in the decay of neutral kaon mesons
1981	Nicolaas Bloemergen (USA) and Arthur Schawlow (USA): development of laser spectroscopy. Kai Siegbahn (Sweden): high-resolution electron spectroscopy
1982	Kenneth Wilson (USA): theory for critical phenomena in connection with phase transitions
1983	Subrahmanyan Chandrasekhar (USA): theoretical studies of physical processes in connection with structure and evolution of stars. William Fowler (USA): nuclear reactions involved in the formation of chemical elements in the universe
1984	Carlo Rubbia (Italy) and Simon van der Meer (Netherlands): contributions to the discovery of the W and Z particles (weakons)
1985	Klaus von Klitzing (Germany): discovery of the quantized Hall effect
1986	Erns Ruska (Germany): electron optics, and design of the first electron microscope. Gerd Binnig (Germany) and Heinrich Rohrer (Switzerland): design of scanning tunnelling microscope
1987	Georg Bednorz (Germany) and Alex Müller (Switzerland): superconductivity in ceramic materials
1988	Leon M Lederman (USA), Melvin Schwartz (USA), and Jack Steinberger (Germany): neutrino-beam method, and demonstration of the doublet structure of leptons through discovery of muon neutrino
1989	Norman Ramsey (USA): measurement techniques leading to discovery of caesium atomic clock. Hans Dehmelt (USA) and Wolfgang Paul (Germany): ion-trap method for isolating single atoms
1990	Jerome Friedman (USA), Henry Kendall (USA), and Richard Taylor (Canada): experiments demonstrating that protons and neutrons are made up of quarks
1991	Pierre-Gilles de Gennes (France): work on disordered systems including polymers and liquid crystals; development of mathematical methods for studying the behaviour of molecules in a liquid on the verge of solidifying
1992	Georges Charpak (Poland): invention and development of detectors used in high-energy physics

Galileo vindicated after 359 years

In 1633, the Inquisition condemned Galileo for propounding the theory that the Earth moves around the Sun, since it clashed with Bible teaching. However, after 359 years, the Roman Catholic Church has admitted that it was wrong. In November 1992, the Pope accepted the results of a commission of the Vatican academy of sciences set up 13 years ago to examine the case – and which has sided with Galileo's view of the Solar System. Better late than never!

Foucault Jean Bernard Léon 1819–1868. French physicist who used a pendulum to demonstrate the rotation of the Earth on its axis, and invented the gyroscope.

Gabor Dennis 1900–1979. Hungarian-born British physicist. In 1947 he invented the holographic method of three-dimensional photography. Nobel prize 1971.

Galileo properly Galileo Galilei 1564–1642. Italian mathematician, astronomer, and physicist. He developed the astronomical telescope and was the first to see sunspots, the four main satellites of Jupiter, mountains and craters on the Moon, and the appearance of Venus going through 'phases', thus proving it was orbiting the Sun. In mechanics, Galileo discovered that freely falling bodies, heavy or light, had the same, constant acceleration (although the story of his dropping cannonballs from the Leaning Tower of Pisa is questionable) and that a body moving on a perfectly smooth horizontal surface would neither speed up nor slow down.

Gell-Mann Murray 1929– . US physicist. In 1964, he formulated the theory of the quark as one of the fundamental constituents of matter. In 1969, he was awarded a Nobel prize for his work on elementary particles and their interaction.

Glashow Sheldon Lee 1932– . US particle physicist. In 1964, he proposed the existence of a fourth 'charmed' quark, and later argued that quarks must be coloured. Insights gained from these theoretical studies enabled Glashow to consider ways in which the weak nuclear force and the electromagnetic force (two of the fundamental forces of nature) could be unified as a single force now called the electroweak force. For this work he shared the Nobel Prize for Physics 1979 with Abdus Salam and Steven Weinberg.

Hawking Stephen 1942– . English physicist who has researched black holes and gravitational field theory. His books include *A Brief History of Time* 1988, in which he argues that our universe is only one small part of a 'super-universe' that has existed for ever and comprises an infinite number of universes like our own.

Heisenberg Werner Carl 1901–1976. German physicist who developed quantum theory and formulated the ***uncertainty principle***, which concerns matter, radiation, and their reactions, and places absolute limits on the achievable accuracy of measurement. Nobel prize 1932.

Hertz Heinrich 1857–1894. German physicist who studied electromagnetic waves, showing that their behaviour resembles that of light and heat waves.

Hooke Robert 1635–1703. English scientist and inventor, originator of ***Hooke's law***, and considered the foremost mechanic of his time. His inventions included a telegraph system, the spirit level, marine barometer, and sea gauge. He coined the term 'cell' in biology.

Josephson Brian 1940– . British physicist, a leading authority on superconductivity. In 1973, he shared a Nobel prize for his theoretical predictions of the properties of a supercurrent through a tunnel barrier (the Josephson effect), which led to the development of the Josephson junction.

Joule James Prescott 1818–1889. English physicist whose work on the relations between electrical, mechanical, and chemical effects led to the discovery of the first law of thermodynamics.

Kelvin William Thomson, 1st Baron Kelvin 1824–1907. Irish physicist who introduced the ***kelvin scale***, the absolute scale of temperature. His work on the conservation of energy 1851 led to the second law of thermodynamics.

Lawrence Ernest O(rlando) 1901–1958. US physicist whose invention of the cyclotron particle accelerator pioneered the production of artificial radioisotopes.

Michelson Albert Abraham 1852–1931. German-born US physicist. In conjunction with Edward Morley, he performed in 1887 the ***Michelson–Morley experiment*** to detect the motion of the Earth through the postulated ether (a medium believed to be necessary for the propagation of light). The failure of the experiment indicated the nonexistence of the ether, and led Albert Einstein to his theory of relativity. Michelson was the first American to be awarded a Nobel prize, in 1907.

Newton Isaac 1642–1727. English physicist and mathematician who laid the foundations of physics as a modern discipline. He discovered the law of gravity, created calculus, discovered that white light is composed of many colours, and developed the three standard laws of motion still in use today. During 1665–66, he discovered the binomial theorem, and differential and integral calculus, and also began to investigate the phenomenon of gravitation. In 1685, he expounded his universal law of gravitation. His *Philosophiae naturalis principia mathematica*, usually referred to as *Principia*, was published in 1687.

Ohm Georg Simon 1787–1854. German physicist who studied electricity and discovered the fundamental law that bears his name. The SI unit of electrical resistance is named after him.

Pauli Wolfgang 1900–1958. Austrian physicist who originated the ***exclusion principle***: in a given system no two fermions (electrons, protons, neutrons, or other elementary particles of half-integral spin) can be characterized by the same set of quantum numbers. He also predicted the existence of neutrinos. He was awarded a Nobel prize 1945 for his work on atomic structure.

Planck Max 1858–1947. German physicist who framed the quantum theory 1900. His research into the manner in which heated bodies radiate energy led him to report that energy is emitted only in indivisible amounts, called quanta, the magnitudes of which are proportional to the frequency of the radiation. His discovery ran counter to classical physics and is held to have marked the commencement of the modern science. Nobel Prize for Physics 1918.

Powell Cecil Frank 1903–1969. English physicist. From the 1930s he and his team at Bristol University investigated the charged subatomic particles in cosmic radiation by using photographic emulsions carried in weather balloons. This led to his discovery of the pion (pi meson) 1946, a particle whose existence had been predicted by the Japanese physicist Hideki Yukawa (1907–1981) 1935. Powell received a Nobel prize 1950.

Rutherford Ernest 1871–1937. New Zealand physicist, a pioneer of modern atomic science. His main research was in the field of radioactivity, and he discovered alpha, beta, and gamma rays. He named the nucleus, and was the first to recognize the nuclear nature of the atom. Nobel prize 1908.

Salam Abdus 1926– . Pakistani physicist. In 1967, he proposed a theory linking the electromagnetic and weak nuclear forces, also arrived at independently by Steven Weinberg. In 1979, he was the first person from his country to receive a Nobel prize, which he shared with Weinberg and Sheldon Glashow.

Schrödinger Erwin 1887–1961. Austrian physicist who advanced the study of wave mechanics (an aspect of quantum theory). He became senior professor at the Dublin Institute for Advanced Studies 1940. He shared (with Paul Dirac) a Nobel prize 1933.

Shockley William 1910–1989. US physicist and amateur geneticist who worked with John Bardeen (1908–) and Walter Brattain (1902–1987) on the invention of the transistor. They were jointly awarded a Nobel prize 1956. During the 1970s, Shockley was criticized for his claim that blacks were genetically inferior to whites in terms of intelligence.

Thomson J(oseph) J(ohn) 1856–1940. English physicist who discovered the electron. He was responsible for organizing the Cavendish atomic research laboratory at Cambridge University. His work inaugurated the electrical theory of the atom, and his elucidation of positive rays and their application to an analysis of neon led to Francis Aston's (1877–1945) discovery of isotopes. Nobel prize 1906.

Volta Alessandro 1745–1827. Italian physicist who invented the first electric cell (the voltaic pile), the electrophorus (an early electrostatic generator), and an electroscope.

Watt James 1736–1819. Scottish engineer who developed the steam engine. He made the steam engine developed by Thomas Newcomen (1663–1729) vastly more efficient by cooling the used steam in a condenser separate from the main cylinder.

Weinberg Steven 1933– . US physicist who in 1967 demonstrated, together with Abdus Salam, that the weak nuclear force and the electromagnetic force (two of the fundamental forces of nature) are variations of a single underlying force, now called the electroweak force. Weinberg and Salam shared a Nobel prize with Sheldon Glashow in 1979.

TELECOMMUNICATIONS AND VIDEO TECHNOLOGY

Telecommunications are communications over a distance, generally by electronic means. Long-distance voice communication was pioneered 1876 by Scottish–US inventor Alexander Graham Bell (1847–1922), when he invented the telephone as a result of English chemist and physicist Michael Faraday's (1791–1867) discovery of electromagnetism. Today it is possible to communicate with most countries by telephone cable, or by satellite or microwave link, with more than 100,000 simultaneous conversations and several television channels being carried by the latest satellites. Integrated Services Digital Network (ISDN) makes videophones and high-quality fax possible; the world's first large-scale centre of ISDN began operating in Japan 1988. ISDN is a system that transmits voice and image data on a single transmission line by changing them into digital signals. The chief method of relaying long-distance calls on land is microwave radio transmission.

The first mechanical telecommunications systems were the semaphore and heliograph (using flashes of sunlight), invented in the mid-19th century, but the forerunner of the present telecommunications age was the electric telegraph. The earliest practicable telegraph instrument was invented by William Cooke (1806–1879) and Charles Wheatstone (1802–1875) in Britain 1837 and used by railway companies. In the USA, Samuel Morse (1791–1872) invented a signalling code, Morse code, which is still used, and a recording telegraph, first used commercially between England and France 1851. As a result of German physicist Heinrich Hertz's (1857–1894) discoveries using electromagnetic waves, Italian inventor Guglielmo Marconi (1874–1937) pioneered a 'wireless' telegraph, ancestor of the radio. He established wireless communication between England and France 1899 and across the Atlantic 1901. The modern telegraph uses teleprinters to send coded messages along telecommunications lines. Telegraphs are keyboard-operated machines that transmit a five-unit Baudot code. The receiving teleprinter automatically prints the received message.

The drawback to long-distance voice communication via microwave radio transmission is that the transmissions follow a straight line from tower to tower, so that over the sea the system becomes impracticable. A solution was put forward 1945 by US science-fiction writer Arthur C Clarke, when he proposed a system of communications satellites in an orbit 35,900 km/22,300 mi above the equator, where they would circle the Earth in exactly 24 hours, and thus appear fixed in the sky. Such a system is now in operation internationally, by Intelsat. The satellites are called geostationary satellites (syncoms). The first to be successfully launched, by Delta rocket from Cape Canaveral, was *Syncom 2* in July 1963. Many such satellites are now in use, concentrated over heavy traffic areas such as the Atlantic, Indian, and Pacific oceans. Telegraphy, telephony, and television transmissions are carried simultaneously by high-frequency radio waves. They are beamed to the satellites from large dish antennae or Earth stations, which connect with international networks. Recent advances include the use of fibre-optic cables consisting of fine glass fibres for telephone lines instead of the usual copper cables. The telecommunications signals are transmitted along the fibres on pulses of laser light.

The first public telegraph line was laid in England between Paddington (London) and Slough 1843. In 1980, the Post Office opened its first System X (all-electronic, digital) telephone exchange in London, a method already adopted in North America. In the UK, Goonhilly (Cornwall) and Madley are the main Earth stations for satellite transmissions.

Terms

aerial or ***antenna*** conducting device that radiates or receives electromagnetic waves. The design of an aerial depends principally on the wavelength of the signal. Long waves (hundreds of metres in wavelength) may employ long wire aerials; short waves (several centimetres in wavelength) may employ rods and dipoles; microwaves may also use dipoles – often with reflectors arranged like a toast rack – or highly directional parabolic dish aerials. Because microwaves travel in straight lines, giving line-of-sight communication, microwave aerials are usually located at the tops of tall masts or towers.

amplifier electronic device that magnifies the strength of a signal, such as a radio signal. The ratio of output signal strength to input signal strength is called the ***gain*** of the amplifier. As well as achieving high gain, an amplifier should be free from distortion and able to operate over a range of frequencies. Practical amplifiers are usually complex circuits, although simple amplifiers can be built from single transistors or valves.

Top suppliers

The leading telecommunications equipment companies, ranked in order of 1991 revenues (US $bn)

1	Alcatel (France)	15.53
2	AT&T (USA)	10.34
3	Siemens (Germany)	9.88
4	Northern Telecom (Canada)	8.18
5	NEC (Japan)	6.69
6	Ericsson (Sweden)	6.67
7	Motorola (USA)	6.56
8	Fujitsu (Japan)	3.30
9	Bosch (Germany)	3.25
10	GPT (UK)	2.20
11	Italtel (Italy)	2.12
12	Philips (Netherlands)	2.09
13	Ascom (Switzerland)	1.45
14	Oki (Japan)	1.37
15	Nokia (Finland)	1.24

Source: Financial Times

No go on bug-proof cellphones

Recent cases of the eavesdropping of cellphone conversations have highlighted the need for bug-proof mobile phones. The technology is available, but it seems that powerful forces are ranged against it. One of the successes of the European electronics industry, a new all-digital cellphone system called GSM, looks like being sidelined because the security services think it is too good.

The GSM system was developed by a consortium of European manufacturers and telecommunications authorities in the mid-1980s. The system allows travellers to use the same portable phone anywhere in Europe. Furthermore, the GSM system is bug-proof. It converts speech into digital codes, which are then scrambled or encrypted using a system called A5.

The trouble is that the A5 scrambling system is too good. The American FBI is in the habit of listening in to the conversations of criminals who are using mobile phones and the new system would close down this source of information. The UK government listening post at Cheltenham, GCHQ, which monitors radio signals from around the world, also objects to the new system. As a result, the UK government has restricted the use of the new system, and insisted that the encryption system be weakened.

baud unit of electrical signalling speed equal to one pulse (one bit) per second, used in data transmission, measuring the rate at which signals are sent between electronic devices such as telegraphs and computers; 300 baud is about 300 words a minute.

cable television distribution of broadcast signals through cable relay systems. Narrow-band systems were originally used to deliver services to areas with poor regular reception; systems with wider bands, using coaxial and fibreoptic cable, are increasingly used for distribution and development of home-based interactive services.

cellular phone or ***cellphone*** mobile radio telephone, one of a network connected to the telephone system by a computer-controlled communication system. Service areas are divided into small 'cells', about 5 km/3 mi across, each with a separate low-power transmitter.

citizens' band (CB) short-range radio communication facility (around 27 MHz) used by members of the public in the USA and many European countries to talk to one another or call for emergency assistance. Use of a form of citizens' band called Open Channel (above 928 MHz) was legalized in the UK 1980.

coaxial cable electric cable that consists of a solid or stranded central conductor insulated from and surrounded by a solid or braided conducting tube or sheath. It can transmit the high-frequency signals used in television, telephone, and other telecommunications transmissions.

communications satellite relay station in space for sending telephone, television, telex, and other messages around the world. Messages are sent to and from the satellites via ground stations. Most communications satellites are in geostationary orbit, appearing to hang fixed over one point on the Earth's surface. A new generation of satellites, called ***direct broadcast satellites***, are powerful enough to transmit direct to small domestic aerials. The power for such satellites is produced by solar cells.

data communications sending and receiving data via any communications medium, such as a telephone line. The term usually implies that the data are digital (such as computer data) rather than analogue (such as voice messages). However, in the ISDN (Integrated Services Digital Network) system, all data – including voices and video images – are transmitted digitally.

data compression techniques for reducing the amount of storage needed for a given amount of data. They include word tokenization (in which frequently used words are stored as shorter codes), variable bit lengths (in which common characters are represented by fewer bits than less common ones), and run-length encoding (in which a repeated value is stored once along with a count).

digital coded as numbers. A digital system uses two-state, either on/off or high/low voltage pulses, to encode, receive, and transmit information. A ***digital display*** shows discrete values as numbers (as opposed to an analogue signal, such as the continuous sweep of a pointer on a dial).

Digital electronics is the technology that underlies digital techniques. Low-power, miniature, integrated circuits (chips) provide the means for the coding, storage, transmission, processing, and reconstruction of information of all kinds.

digital data transmission way of sending data by converting all signals (whether pictures, sounds, or words) into numeric (normally binary) codes before transmission, then reconverting them on receipt. This virtually eliminates any distortion or degradation of the signal during transmission, storage, or processing.

digital sampling electronic process used in telecommunications for transforming a constantly varying (analogue) signal into one composed of discrete units, a digital signal.

digital television any system of transmitting television programmes in digital codes. A fully digital high-definition system was demonstrated in the USA 1992.

Until the late 1980s, it was considered impossible to convert a TV signal into digital code because of the sheer amount of information needed to represent a visual image – the current British PAL system needs about 6 million bits of information each second; HDTV needs about 30 million bits each second.

High-definition TV: a confusing picture

Current television pictures in Europe are built from 625 horizontal scanning lines. On a small screen, the lines are too close together to be visible; on a large screen, especially a projected television picture, they become very noticeable. In the USA and Japan, television pictures consist of just 525 lines, and look even coarser on large screens.

Around 20 years ago, engineers with Japan's state broadcaster, NHK, started developing a system with 1,125 lines, giving a movie-quality picture. They also made the picture wider, with a 16:9 aspect ratio instead of conventional television's squarish 4:3. This is high-definition television (HDTV).

The HDTV signal contains at least four times more information than a conventional television signal, and cannot be transmitted in the channels allocated for conventional terrestrial broadcasts. Satellite transmitters have wider bandwidths, which is why Japan pushed ahead with satellite broadcasting. Satellites are now broadcasting HDTV programmes direct into Japanese homes. Shops sell receivers with widescreen picture tubes.

European confusion

In 1986, European manufacturers and broadcasters cooperated to develop a native European HDTV system. Called HD-MAC, it uses 1,250 lines, twice the current number, to facilitate compatibility with existing television sets. It is not directly compatible with the PAL sets used in most of Europe, or the SECAM sets used in France. HD-MAC builds instead on a new 625-line system called MAC.

This was invented in the early 1980s in the research laboratories of the Independent Broadcasting Authority (now privatized as National Transcommunications Ltd). Through the 1980s, other European broadcasters and electronics companies helped perfect MAC. It was intended for satellite use, and designed to bridge the gap between 'old-fashioned' 4:3 625-line pictures, new 625-line widescreen pictures, and future 1,250-line HDTV widescreen pictures.

In 1986, the EC decreed that all European satellite broadcasters must use MAC, not PAL or SECAM. The aim was to provide Europe with an elegant upgrade path to widescreen and 1,250-line television. Unfortunately, Europe split the MAC standard into incompatible variants: D-MAC for the UK and D2-MAC for France, Germany, and most other countries. This slowed development of the vital MAC receiver microchips. The EC's directive contained legal loopholes which allowed some broadcasters (including the UK's Sky and the German cable channels) to use PAL from Luxembourg's Astra satellite. In late 1992, the UK vetoed EC plans to subsidise satellite transmissions using the D2-MAC system. The veto effectively killed off MAC and HD-MAC. In February 1993, the EC said that it would not try to force broadcasters to use these systems.

Meanwhile, European broadcasters have been developing PALplus, a widescreen version of the existing PAL system. Television stations will transmit programmes in 'letterbox' format, with black borders at the top and bottom of the screen. New, widescreen television sets will expand this image to fill a full 16:9 screen, extracting signals hidden in the black borders to restore the clarity lost by expansion. The PALplus pictures still have only 625 lines, but look clearer (and wider) than existing PAL pictures.

Many people question the need for 1,250-line HDTV pictures unless the screen is very large; and screen size is limited by the difficulty of making large cathode-ray tubes. Flat-panel screens have been promised for years, but a flat screen is unlikely to match a cathode-ray tube for price, size, and performance until the next century.

Indecision on the best widescreen/HDTV system has opened up a new debate: should future television be digital, not analogue?

Digital systems

All existing television and HDTV systems are analogue-based. But the major electronics companies in Europe, Japan, and the USA have been working on digital systems. They have remained silent on this work, to protect their existing analogue investment. But the US government looks set to issue a digital standard for HDTV.

The key is data compression, which can reduce the number of digital bits needed to carry a picture by 30 or 40 times, without noticeable loss of quality. An existing television channel could carry at least one HDTV channel or several programmes of today's quality. So digital television gives viewers wider programme choice. The technology works, and should be available for domestic use by the late 1990s. Both terrestrial and satellite broadcasters can use it, creating market opportunities for a new kind of home video recorder.

Existing VCRs record pictures as analogue signals. Picture quality from the VHS and Video 8 formats has been improved by the Super-VHS and Hi 8 variants. These deliver quality matching or exceeding broadcast standards, so few users need the further improvement offered by switching to digital recording. Digital recording, however, will allow taping of a digital broadcast channel and subsequent decoding, watching either HDTV on a widescreen set or choosing between a selection of conventional-quality programmes, all taped together from the same channel.

BF

However, data-compression techniques have been developed to reduce the number of bits that need to be transmitted each second. As a result, digital technology is being developed that will offer sharper pictures on wider screens, and HDTV with image quality comparable to a cinema. A common world standard for digital TV was agreed in 1993 at a meeting of engineers representing manufacturers and broadcasters from 18 countries.

eidophor television projection system that produces pictures up to 10 m/33 ft square at sports events and rock concerts, for example. The system uses three coloured beams of light, one of each primary colour (red, blue, and green), which scan the screen. The intensity of each beam is controlled by the strength of the corresponding colour in the television picture.

electronic mail or ***E-mail*** telecommunications system that enables the users of a computer to send written messages to other users. A modem connects the computer to the telephone network, through which the signals are sent from terminal to terminal.

fax (common name for ***facsimile transmission*** or ***telefax***) the transmission of images over a telecommunications link, usually the telephone network. When placed on a fax machine, the original image is scanned by a transmitting device and converted into coded signals, which travel via the telephone lines to the receiving fax machine, where an image is created that is a copy of the original. Photographs as well as printed text and drawings can be sent. The standard transmission takes place at 4,800 or 9,600 bits of information per second.

high-definition television (HDTV) television system offering a significantly greater number of scanning lines, and therefore a clearer picture, than that provided by conventional systems. The Japanese HDTV system, or Vision as it is trade-named in Japan, uses 1,125 scanning lines and an aspect ratio of 16:9 instead of the squarish 4:3 which conventional television uses. A European HDTV system, called HD-MAC, using 1,250 lines, is under development. In the USA, fractal mathematics may be used to encode and broadcast HDTV, following a 1992 decision by the National Institute for Standards and Technology to fund a new chip to decode digitized pictures.

Integrated Services Digital Network (ISDN) internationally developed telecommunications system for sending signals in digital format along optical fibres and coaxial cable. It involves converting the 'local loop' – the link between the user's telephone (or private automatic branch exchange) and the digital telephone exchange – from an analogue system into a digital system, thereby greatly increasing the amount of information that can be carried. The first large-scale use of ISDN began in Japan 1988.

British Telecom began offering ISDN to businesses 1991, with some 47,000 ISDN-equipped lines. Its adoption in the UK is expected to stimulate the use of data-communications services such as faxing, teleshopping, and home banking. New services may include computer conferencing,where both voice and computer communications take place simultaneously, and videophones.

interactive video (IV) computer-mediated system that enables the user to interact with and control information (including text, recorded speech, or moving images) stored on video disc. IV is most commonly used for training purposes, using analogue video discs, but has wider applications with digital video systems such as CD-I (Compact Disc Interactive, from Philips and Sony) which are based on the CD-ROM format derived from audio compact discs.

loudspeaker electromechanical device that converts electrical signals into sound waves, which are radiated into the air. The most common type of loudspeaker is the ***moving-coil speaker***. Electrical signals from, for example, a radio are fed to a coil of fine wire wound around the top of a cone. The coil is surrounded by a magnet. When signals pass through it, the coil becomes an electromagnet, which by moving causes the cone to vibrate, setting up sound waves.

microphone primary component in a sound-reproducing system, whereby the mechanical energy of sound waves is converted into electrical signals by means of a transducer. One of the simplest is the telephone receiver mouthpiece, invented by Scottish-US inventor Alexander Graham Bell in 1876; other types of microphone are used with broadcasting and sound-film apparatus.

modulation the intermittent change of frequency, or amplitude, of a carrier wave, in accordance with the audio characteristics of the speaking voice, music, or other signal being transmitted. Microwave or light waves can carry digital information in pulse-code modulation; radio waves are altered for transmission with AM (amplitude modulation) or FM (frequency modulation).

Talking on the go

Usership of cellular radio telephones, Europe 1991 (per '000 inhabitants)

Austria	11.8
Belgium	4.6
Cyprus	5.2
Czechoslovakia	0.4
Denmark	31.7
Finland	51.4
France	5.9
Germany, East	–
Germany, West	5.8
Greece	–
Iceland	41.9
Ireland	7.8
Italy	7.5
Luxembourg	2.0
Malta	4.8
Netherlands	6.7
Norway	51.5
Portugal	0.9
Spain	2.0
Sweden	63.3
Switzerland	22.3
Turkey	0.6
UK	20.8

Source: Euromonitor

Telecommunications: chronology

1794 Claude Chappe in France built a long-distance signalling system using semaphore.
1839 Charles Wheatstone and William Cooke devised an electric telegraph in England.
1843 Samuel Morse transmitted the first message along a telegraph line in the USA, using his Morse code of signals – short (dots) and long (dashes).
1858 The first transatlantic telegraph cable was laid.
1876 Alexander Graham Bell invented the telephone.
1877 Thomas Edison invented the carbon transmitter for the telephone.
1878 The first telephone exchange was opened at New Haven, Connecticut.
1884 The first long-distance telephone line was installed, between Boston and New York.
1891 A telephone cable was laid between England and France.
1892 The first automatic telephone exchange was opened, at La Porte, Indiana, USA.
1894 Guglielmo Marconi pioneered wireless telegraphy in Italy, later moving to England.
1900 Reginald Fessenden in the USA first broadcast voice by radio.
1901 Marconi transmitted the first radio signals across the Atlantic.
1904 John Ambrose Fleming invented the thermionic valve.
1907 Charles Krumm introduced the forerunner of the teleprinter.
1920 Stations in Detroit and Pittsburgh, USA, began regular radio broadcasts.
1922 The BBC began its first radio transmissions, for the London station 2LO.
1932 The Post Office introduced the Telex in Britain.
1956 The first transatlantic telephone cable was laid.
1962 *Telstar* pioneered transatlantic satellite communications, transmitting live TV pictures.
1966 Charles Kao in England advanced the idea of using optical fibres for telecommunications transmissions.
1969 Live TV pictures were sent from astronauts on the Moon back to Earth.
1975 The Post Office announced Prestel, the world's first viewdata system, using the telephone lines to link a computer data bank with the TV screen.
1977 The first optical-fibre cable was installed in California.
1984 First commercial cellphone service started in Chicago, USA.
1988 International Services Digital Network (ISDN), an international system for sending signals in digital format along optical fibres and coaxial cable, launched in Japan.
1989 The first transoceanic optical-fibre cable, capable of carrying 40,000 simultaneous telephone conversations, was laid between Europe and the USA.
1991 ISDN introduced in the UK.
1992 Videophones, made possible by advances in image compression and the development of ISDN, introduced in the UK.
1993 Electronic version of the *Guardian* newspaper, for those with impaired vision, launched in the UK. The newspaper is transmitted to the user's home and printed out in braille or spoken by a speech synthesizer.

multiplexing sending several messages simultaneously along the same telephone or telegraph wire. In ***frequency-division multiplexing***, signals of different frequency, each carrying a different message, are transmitted. Electrical frequency filters separate the message at the receiving station. In ***time-division multiplexing***, the messages are broken into sections and the sections of several messages interleaved during transmission. ***Pulse-code modulation*** allows hundreds of messages to be sent simultaneously over a single link.

optical fibre very fine, optically pure glass fibre through which light can be reflected to transmit an image or information from one end to the other. Optical fibres are increasingly being used to replace copper wire in telephone cables, the messages being coded as pulses of light rather than a fluctuating electric current.

oscillator any device producing a desired oscillation (vibration). There are many types of oscillator for different purposes, involving various arrangements of thermionic valves or components such as transistors, inductors, capacitors, and resistors. An oscillator is an essential part of a radio transmitter, generating the high-frequency carrier signal necessary for radio communication. The frequency is often controlled by the vibrations set up in a crystal (such as quartz).

pulse-code modulation (PCM) form of digital modulation in which microwaves or light waves (the carrier waves) are switched on and off in pulses of varying length according to a binary code. It is a relatively simple matter to transmit data that are already in binary code, such as those used by computer, by these means. An analogue audio signal can be converted into a ***pulse-amplitude modulated*** signal (PAM) by regular sampling of its amplitude. The value of the amplitude is then converted into a binary code for transmission on the carrier wave.

radio transmission and reception of radio waves. In radio ***transmission*** a microphone converts sound waves (pressure variations in the air) into electromagnetic waves; these are picked up by a receiving aerial and fed to a loudspeaker, which converts them back into sound waves.

To carry the transmitted electrical signal, an oscillator produces a carrier wave of high frequency; different stations are allocated different transmitting carrier frequencies. A modulator superimposes the audiofrequency signal on the carrier. There are two main ways of doing this: ***amplitude modulation*** (AM), used for long- and medium-wave broadcasts, in which the strength of the carrier is made to fluctuate in time with the audio signal; and ***frequency modulation*** (FM), as used for VHF (very high frequency) broadcasts, in which the frequency of the carrier is made to fluctuate. The transmitting aerial emits the modulated electromagnetic waves, which travel outwards from it.

In radio ***reception***, a receiving aerial picks up minute voltages in response to the waves sent out by a transmitter. A tuned circuit selects a particular frequency, usually by means of a variable capacitor connected across a coil of wire. A demodulator disentangles the audio signal from the carrier, which is now discarded, having served its purpose. An amplifier boosts the audio signal for feeding to the loudspeaker. In a superheterodyne receiver, the incoming signal is mixed with an internally generated signal of fixed frequency so that the amplifier circuits can operate near their optimum frequncy.

receiver, radio component of a radio communication system that receives and processes radio waves. It detects and selects modulated radio waves by means of an aerial and tuned circuit, and then separates the transmitted information from the carrier wave by a process that involves rectification. The receiver device will usually also include the amplifiers that produce the audio signals.

scrambling circuit in radiotelephony, a transmitting circuit that renders signals unintelligible unless received by the corresponding unscrambling circuit.

signal-to-noise ratio ratio of the power of an electrical signal to that of the unwanted noise accompanying the signal. It is expressed in decibels. In general, the higher the signal-to-noise ratio, the better. For a telephone, an acceptable ratio is 40 decibels; for television, the acceptable ratio is 50 decibels.

single-sideband transmission radio-wave transmission using either the frequency band above the carrier wave frequency, or below, instead of both (as now).

superheterodyne receiver the most widely used type of radio receiver, in which the incoming signal is mixed with a signal of fixed frequency generated within the receiver circuits. The resulting signal, called the intermediate-frequency (i.f.) signal, has a frequency between that of the incoming signal and the internal signal. The intermediate frequency is near the optimum frequency of the amplifier to which the i.f. signal is passed. This arrangement ensures greater gain and selectivity. The superheterodyne system is also used in basic television receivers.

System X modular, computer-controlled, digital switching system used in telephone exchanges from 1980.

telephone instrument for communicating by voice over long distances, invented by Scottish–US inventor Alexander Graham Bell 1876. The transmitter (mouthpiece) consists of a carbon microphone, with a diaphragm that vibrates when a person speaks into it. The diaphragm vibrations compress grains of carbon to a greater or lesser extent, altering their resistance to an electric current passing through them. This sets up variable electrical signals, which travel along the telephone lines to the receiver of the person being called. There they cause the magnetism of an electromagnet to vary, making a diaphragm above the electromagnet vibrate and give out sound waves, which mirror those that entered the mouthpiece originally.

A cordless telephone is connected to a base unit by radio. It can be used at distances up to about 100 m/330 ft from the base unit.

The cost of a call

Cost of a three-minute telephone call, Jan 1993 (US $)

	*International**	*Local*
Italy	6.68	0.09
Germany	3.69	0.14
Sweden	3.66	0.08
Belgium	3.60	0.15
USA	3.42	0.08
Netherlands	3.21	0.08
Canada	3.00	–
Australia	2.94	0.17
France	2.68	0.11
UK	1.88	0.17

** To New York; except USA and Canada, to London*

Source: National Utility Services

teletext broadcast system of displaying information on a television screen. The information – typically about news items, entertainment, sport, and finance – is constantly updated. Teletext is a form of videotext, pioneered in Britain by the British Broadcasting Corporation (BBC) with Ceefax and by Independent Television with Teletext.

television (TV) reproduction at a distance by radio waves of visual images. For transmission, a TV camera converts the pattern of light it takes in into a pattern of electrical charges. This is scanned line by line by a beam of electrons from an electron gun, resulting in variable electrical signals that represent the picture. These signals are combined with a radio carrier wave and broadcast as electromagnetic waves. The TV aerial picks up the wave and feeds it to the receiver (TV set). This separates out the vision signals, which pass to a cathode-ray tube where a beam of electrons is made to scan across the screen line by line, mirroring the action of the electron gun in the TV camera. The result is a recreation of the pattern of light that entered the camera. Twenty-five pictures are built up each second with interlaced scanning in Europe (30 in North America), with a total of 625 lines in Europe (525 lines in North America and Japan); high-definition television (HDTV) offers a significantly greater number of scanning lines.

television channels In addition to transmissions received by all viewers, the 1970s and 1980s saw the growth of pay-television cable networks, which are received only by subscribers, and of devices, such as those used in the Qube system (USA), which allow the viewers' opinions to be transmitted instantaneously to the studio via a response button, so that, for example, a home viewing audience can vote in a talent competition. The number of programme channels continues to increase, following the introduction of satellite-beamed TV signals.

The big screen

A problem that has defeated technologists for many years may have been solved: how to make a TV screen large and thin enough to hang on a wall. The answer may be light-emitting plastics. These materials have been developed by scientists at Cambridge University, England, who noticed during routine investigations that some plastics glow when an electric current flows through them. One useful feature of the light-emitting plastics is that they can be painted onto a backing material. The material can then be printed with an array of transparent electrodes to transmit electrical signals through the plastic, causing it to glow. The plastic can be made to emit different colours by altering the chemical composition, so a sheet of material can be covered in clusters of red, blue, and yellow-emitting dots, or pixels, which build up a full colour picture. The light-emitting plastics could be used in television sets the size of a cinema screen. Because they are flexible, the new materials could be shaped to fit car dashboards, so dashboard instruments could incorporate them. Lightweight portable computer displays are another possibility.

history In 1873 it was realized that, since the electrical properties of the nonmetallic chemical element selenium vary according to the amount of light to which it is exposed, light could be converted into electrical impulses, making it possible to transmit such impulses over a distance and then reconvert them into light. The chief difficulty was seen to be the 'splitting of the picture' so that the infinite variety of light and shade values might be transmitted and reproduced. Mechanical devices were used at the first practical demonstration of television, given by Scottish electrical engineer John Logie Baird (1888–1946) in London 27 Jan 1926, and cathode-ray tubes were used experimentally in the UK from 1934. The world's first public television service was started from the BBC station at Alexandra Palace in N London, 2 Nov 1936. In 1990 in the UK, the average viewing time per person was 25.5 hours each week.

colour television Baird gave a demonstration of colour TV in London 1928, but it was not until Dec 1953 that the first successful system was adopted for broadcasting, in the USA. This is called the NTSC system, since it was developed by the National Television System Committee, and variations of it were developed in Europe; for example, SECAM (sequential and memory) in France and Eastern Europe, and PAL (phase alternation by line) in most of Western Europe. The three differ only in the way colour signals are prepared for transmission, the scanning rate, and the number of lines used. When there was no agreement on a universal European system 1964, in 1967 the UK, West Germany, the Netherlands, and Switzerland adopted PAL while France and the USSR adopted SECAM. In 1989, the European Community agreed to harmonize TV channels from 1991, allowing any station to show programmes anywhere in the EC.

The method of colour reproduction is related to that used in colour photography and printing. It uses the principle that any colours can be made by mixing the primary colours red, green, and blue in appropriate proportions. In colour television, the receiver reproduces only three basic colours: red, green, and blue. The effect of yellow, for example, is reproduced by combining equal amounts of red and green light, while white is formed by a mixture of all three basic colours. Signals indicate the amounts of red, green, and blue light to be generated at the receiver.

To transmit each of these three signals in the same way as the single brightness signal in black and white television would need three times the normal band width and reduce the number of possible stations and programmes to one-third of that possible with monochrome television. The three signals are therefore coded into one complex signal, which is transmitted as a more or less normal black and white signal and produces a satisfactory – or compatible – picture on black and white receivers. A fraction of each primary red, green, and blue signal is added together to produce the normal brightness, or luminance, signal. The minimum of extra colouring information is then sent by a special subcarrier signal, which is superimposed on the brightness signal. This extra colouring information corresponds to the hue and saturation of the transmitted colour, but without any of the fine detail of the picture. The impression of sharpness is conveyed only by the brightness signal, the colouring being added as a broad colour wash. The various colour systems differ only in the way in which the colouring information is sent on the subcarrier signal. The colour receiver has to amplify the complex signal and decode it back to the basic red, green, and blue signals; these primary signals are then applied to a colour cathode-ray tube.

The colour display tube is the heart of any colour receiver. Many designs of colour picture tubes have been invented; the most successful of these is known as the 'shadow mask tube'. It operates on similar electronic principles to the black and white television picture tube, but the screen is composed of a fine mosaic of over one million dots arranged in an orderly fashion. One-third of the dots glow red when bombarded by electrons, one-third glow green, and one-third blue. There are three sources of electrons, respectively modulated by the red, green, and blue signals. The tube is arranged so that the shadow mask allows only the red signals to hit red dots, the green signals to hit green dots, and the blue signals to hit blue dots. The glowing dots are so small that from a normal viewing distance the colours merge into one another and a picture with a full range of colours is seen.

video camera portable television camera that takes moving pictures electronically on magnetic tape. It produces an electrical output signal corresponding to rapid line-by-line scanning of the field of view. The output is recorded on video cassette and is played back on a television screen via a video tape recorder.

television: chronology

1878 William Crookes in England invented the Crookes tube, which produced cathode rays.
1884 Paul Nipkow in Germany built a mechanical scanning device, the Nipkow disc, a rotating disc with a spiral pattern of holes in it.
1897 Karl Ferdinand Braun, also in Germany, modified the Crookes tube to produce the ancestor of the TV receiver picture tube.
1906 Boris Rosing in Russia began experimenting with the Nipkow disc and cathode-ray tube, eventually succeeding in transmitting some crude TV pictures.
1923 Vladimir Zworykin in the USA invented the first electronic camera tube, the iconoscope.
1926 John Logie Baird demonstrated a workable TV system, using mechanical scanning by Nipkow disc.
1928 Baird demonstrated colour TV.
1929 The BBC began broadcasting experimental TV programmes using Baird's system.
1936 The BBC began regular broadcasting using Baird's system from Alexandra Palace, London.
1940 Experimental colour TV transmission began in the USA, using the present-day system of colour reproduction.
1953 Successful colour TV transmissions began in the USA.
1956 The first video tape recorder was produced in California by the Ampex Corporation.
1962 TV signals were transmitted across the Atlantic via the *Telstar* satellite.
1970 The first videodisc system was announced by Decca in Britain and AEG-Telefunken in Germany, but it was not perfected until the 1980s, when laser scanning was used for playback.
1973 The BBC and Independent Television in the UK introduced the world's first teletext systems, Ceefax and Oracle, respectively.
1975 Sony introduced their videocassette tape-recorder system, Betamax, for domestic viewers, six years after their professional U-Matic system. The UK Post Office (now British Telecom) announced their Prestel viewdata system.
1979 Matsushita in Japan developed a pocket-sized, flat-screen TV set, using a liquid-crystal display.
1986 Data broadcasting using digital techniques was developed; an enhancement of teletext was produced.
1989 The Japanese began broadcasting high-definition television; satellite television was introduced in the UK.
1990 The BBC introduced a digital stereo sound system (NICAM); MAC, a European system allowing greater picture definition, more data, and sound tracks, was introduced.
1992 All-digital high-definition television demonstrated in the USA.
1993 A worldwide standard for digital television was agreed by manufacturers and broadcasters.

video disc disc with pictures and sounds recorded on it, played back by laser. The video disc is a type of compact disc.

The video disc was originated by Scottish inventor John Logie Baird 1928, and became commercially available 1978. It is chiefly used to provide commercial films for private viewing. Most systems use a 30-cm/12-in rotating vinyl disc coated with a reflective material. Laser scanning recovers picture and sound signals from the surface where they are recorded as a spiral of microscopic pits.

video tape recorder (VTR) device for recording pictures and sound on cassettes or spools of magnetic tape. The first commercial VTR was launched 1956 for the television broadcasting industry, but from the late 1970s cheaper models developed for home use, to record broadcast programmes for future viewing and to view rented or owned video cassettes of commercial films.

Video recording works in the same way as audio tape recording: the picture information is stored as a line of varying magnetism, or track, on a plastic tape covered with magnetic material. The main difficulty – the huge amount of information needed to reproduce a picture – is overcome by arranging the video track diagonally across the tape. During recording, the tape is wrapped around a drum in a spiral fashion. The recording head rotates inside the drum. The combination of the forward motion of the tape and the rotation of the head produces a diagonal track. The audio signal accompanying the video signal is recorded as a separate track along the edge of the tape.

Two video cassette systems were introduced by Japanese firms in the 1970s. The Sony Betamax was technically superior, but Matsushita's VHS had larger marketing resources behind it and after some years became the sole system on the market. Super-VHS is an improved version of the VHS system, launched 1989, with higher picture definition and colour quality.

videotext system in which information (text and simple pictures) is displayed on a television (video) screen. There are two basic systems, known as teletext and viewdata; both require the use of a television receiver with a special decoder.

viewdata system of displaying information on a television screen in which the information is extracted from a computer data bank and transmitted via the telephone lines. It is one form of videotext. The British Post Office (now British Telecom) developed the world's first viewdata system, Prestel, 1975, and similar systems are now in widespread use in other countries. Viewdata users have access to an almost unlimited store of information, presented on the screen in the form of 'pages'.

Since viewdata uses telephone lines, it can become a two-way interactive information system, making possible, for example, home banking and shopping. In contrast, the only user input allowed by the teletext system is to select the information to be displayed.

Watch my lips

The videophone has arrived. Videophones are telephones that have a video screen attached so that users can see who they are talking to. The first video phones went on sale in Japan and the USA about five years ago. They were rudimentary devices. A video camera took a picture of whoever was using the phone. The camera signal was digitized and the digital code was used to modulate an audio signal, producing a warble like a fax signal, which was sent down the phone line at a rate of 8 kbit/s (kilobits per second). At the other end of the line, a decoder converted the signal into a black-and-white picture on a small screen, 15 cm/6 in wide. The results were not impressive. It took about five seconds to transmit a picture, during which time the user could not speak. The images were not better than those sent by a fax, and no cheaper or faster.

The latest British Telecom videophone, called Relate 2000, plugs into a normal telephone point and uses the normal telephone lines. Each device has a colour camera and a 7.5 cm/3 in liquid crystal display. About five pictures a second from the camera are converted to digital code and used to modulate an audio signal that goes down the telephone line at a rate of 14.4 kbit/s. A similar videophone has been produced by the US company AT&T; it sells at about twice the price of the BT model.

A choppy start

The performance of these videophones may disappoint some users. The picture and sound quality of a videophone depends upon the amount of data that is transmitted each second. The more data sent down the line, the bigger the screen that can be used, the better the quality of the sound, and the smoother moving images are. The new phones are necessarily a compromise between cost and quality. Conventional phone lines can only transmit enough data to support a small screen, sufficient for a view of the other person's face. They can only transmit about five images per second, so movements seen on the screen are jerky and blurred (a television set displays 25 or 30 pictures each second to produce smooth movement). The AT&T model uses a different transmission rate from the BT device – 19.2 kbit/s. This produces a slightly better picture. On both versions, the speech is of poor quality.

Help from data compression...

There are several approaches that promise better performance in the next generation of videophones. The first is the more effective use of data compression. Data compression is one of the 'hidden' technological advances. Like the microprocessor, which powered advances on many fronts but was often hidden from everyday view, data compression lies behind many communications, computing, and video advances. It is a technique for reducing the amount of data needed to represent a given amount of information. There are a variety of compression techniques, including tokenization in which frequently used signal sequences are represented by shorter codes or tokens. Using these techniques the data rate of a video signal can be drastically reduced without reducing picture quality. Both the BT and AT&T videophones use data compression techniques but further development in this area is expected.

...and from ISDN

The second approach is to make use of the Integrated Services Digital Network (ISDN), which uses optical fibres and coaxial cable, as used on a TV aerial, to carry digital signals at 64 kbit/s along a single line, about four times faster than ordinary telephone lines. Higher transmission rates, up to 384 kbit/s, can be achieved by using groups of lines. The digital data carried by these lines are ideal for transmission of videophone signals. Most industrial countries have ISDN systems and, although different standards have been adopted in different countries, most countries have electronic 'gateways', which allow signals from one country to connect with others. In Britain, 12,000 businesses have installed ISDN lines since 1991. The network should be extended to domestic subscribers within a few years. An extensive network has been installed in the Highlands and Island region of Scotland.

Connect your phone to your PC

The ISDN network has already been used to connect videophones and personal desktop computers. In these systems, the videophone image appears as a window on the computer screen. For a window occupying about one-sixth of the computer screen, a transmission rate of 645 kbit/s produces an acceptable picture. Higher transmission rates, 128 kbit/s, possible with the ISDN system, produce even better-quality pictures. BT have launched a system with a 25 cm/10 in colour-television-like screen, which transmits at 128 kbit/s. The British telecommunications company GPT also sells128 kbit/s systems with screens up to 70 cm/27 in.

PL

GALLUP POLL

Think of the many innovations we take for granted in modern life – television, telephone, aerosols, insecticides, computers, air travel, painkillers, etc. How would you summarise the influence that science and technology have had on everyday life during the past 50 years?

Enormously beneficial	43
Moderately beneficial	38
No overall benefit or harm	4
Quite harmful	9
Disastrous	2
Don't know	4

How concerned are you that your own understanding and knowledge about science and technology may be running behind the latest advance in these fields?

Very concerned	9
Concerned	32
Neither	22
Unconcerned	24
Very unconcerned	10
Don't know	3

Many people admit to being confused by new scientific achievements. Where do you feel the blame lies for this confusion?

Scientists only publish their discoveries in specialist journals/magazines	22
Scientists find it difficult to explain their achievements in simple, understandable language	34
The mass media eg TV and newspapers, don't publicise scientific achievements enough	38
People not given a thorough enough science education at school	33
None of these/don't know	8

Which one of the following risks is the most unacceptable price to pay in the name of progress?

Nuclear war	42
Radiation leaks	19
Pollution from factories/cars	15
Jobs lost through automation	14
Side-effects of drugs	6
Accidents in space	1
None of these	2

How much do you think you personally rely on science and technology in a typical day?

Not at all	7
A little	27
A great deal	55
Totally dependent	11

People have always asked big questions such as 'What is the meaning of life?'. Do you think scientists are the right people to answer such questions?

Yes	33
No	61
Don't know	6

Which one of the following would you ask to explain how life came to exist on earth?

A biologist	37
A religious leader	20
An historian	11
A philosopher	8
A parent	6
A poet or writer	1
Don't know	18

To which one of these tasks do you think scientists today should devote most effort?

Discovering cures for disease	42
Dealing with pollution, finding cleaners sources of energy	41
Developing cheaper and safer food	6
Inventing things to boost the nation's economy	4
Inventing things to make everyday life easier	2
Discovering the origins of the universe	1
Inventing new kinds of space travel	1
Experimenting to create new forms of life	0
Don't know/none of these	3

Source: Gallup

The World

History 571

Continents 596

Countries 602

HISTORY

Leaders of the Modern World (1945 to the present)

Adenauer Konrad 1876–1967. German Christian Democrat politician, chancellor of West Germany 1949–63. With the French president de Gaulle, he achieved the postwar reconciliation of France and Germany and strongly supported all measures designed to strengthen the Western bloc in Europe.

Alfonsín Foulkes Raúl Ricardo 1927– . Argentine politician, president 1983–89, leader of the moderate Radical Union Party (UCR). As president from the country's return to civilian government, he set up an investigation of the army's human-rights violations. Economic problems caused him to seek help from the International Monetary Fund and introduce austerity measures.

Allende Gossens Salvador 1908–1973. Chilean Marxist politician, president from 1970 until his death during a military coup in 1973. As president, Allende nationalized the banking and copper industries and instituted land reform, provoking the conservative elements in the country. As Chile's economy declined and strikes and disturbances supported by the US Central Intelligence Agency spread, the military staged a coup, during which Allende either was killed or committed suicide.

Amin (Dada) Idi 1926– . Ugandan politician, president 1971–79. He led the coup that deposed Milton Obote 1971, expelled the Asian community 1972, and exercised a reign of terror over his people. He fled to Libya when insurgent Ugandan and Tanzanian troops invaded the country 1979.

Andreotti Giulio 1919– . Italian Christian Democrat politician. He headed seven postwar governments: 1972–73, 1976–79 (four successive terms), and 1989–92 (two terms). In addition, he was defence minister eight times, and foreign minister five times. He was a fervent European. In 1993, Andreotti was among several high-ranking politicians under investigation for possible involvement in Italy's corruption network.

Antall Jozsef 1932– . Hungarian politician, prime minister 1990– . A former teacher and museum director, he led the centre-right Hungarian Democratic Forum (MDF) to electoral victory in April 1990, becoming Hungary's first post-communist prime minister. He has promoted gradual, and successful, privatization and encouraged inward foreign investment.

Aquino (Maria) Corazon (born Cojuangco) 1933– . President of the Philippines 1986–92. She was instrumental in the nonviolent overthrow of President Ferdinand Marcos 1986. As president, she sought to rule in a conciliatory manner, but encountered opposition from left (communist guerrillas) and right (army coup attempts), and her land reforms were seen as inadequate.

Arafat Yassir 1929– . Palestinian nationalist politician, cofounder of al-Fatah 1956 and president of the Palestine Liberation Organization (PLO) from 1969. His support for Saddam Hussein after Iraq's invasion of Kuwait 1990 weakened his international standing, but he has since been influential in Middle East peace talks.

Assad Hafez al 1930– . Syrian Ba'athist politician, president from 1971. He became prime minister after a bloodless military coup 1970, and the following year was the first president to be elected by popular vote. Having suppressed dissent, he was re-elected 1978 and 1985. He is a Shia (Alawite) Muslim.

Attlee Clement (Richard), 1st Earl 1883–1967. British Labour politician. In the coalition government during World War II he was Lord Privy Seal 1940–42, dominions secretary 1942–43, and Lord President of the Council 1943–45, as well as deputy prime minister from 1942. As prime minister 1945–51, he introduced a sweeping programme of nationalization and a whole new system of social services.

Babangida Ibrahim 1941– . Nigerian politician and soldier, president from 1985. He became head of the Nigerian army in 1983 and in 1985 led a coup against President Buhari, assuming the presidency himself. In Jan 1992, responding to calls for a return to civilian rule, he announced dates for assembly and presidential elections later in the year. Alleging fraudlent electoral practices in the first primaries Sept 1992, Babangida subsequently delayed the date for a transition to civilian rule.

Balladur Edouard 1929– . French conservative politician, prime minister from 1993. He was the protégé of France's former premier and president, Georges Pompidou, during the 1960s and 1970s. Balladur later became a top adviser to former prime minister Jacques Chirac and was finance minister 1986–88. Following strong gains by the conservatives in the 1993 French election, Balladur was strongly placed for an eventual challenge for the presidency. Balladur is a strong supporter of the European Community and of maintaining close relations between France and Germany.

Banda Hastings Kamuzu 1902– . Malawi politician, president from 1966. He led his country's independence movement and was prime minister of Nyasaland (the former name of Malawi) from 1963. He became Malawi's first president 1966 and 1971 was named president for life; his rule has been authoritarian. Despite civil unrest during 1992, he has resisted calls for free, multiparty elections.

Bandaranaike Sirimavo (born Ratwatte) 1916– . Sri Lankan politician who succeeded her husband Solomon Bandaranaike to become the world's first female prime minister, 1960–65 and 1970–77, but was expelled from parliament 1980 for abuse of her powers while in office.

Begin Menachem 1913–1992. Israeli politician. He was leader of the extremist Irgun Zvai Leumi organization in Palestine from 1942, and prime minister of Israel 1977–83, as head of the right-wing Likud party. In 1978, Begin shared a Nobel Peace Prize with President Sadat of Egypt for work on the Camp David Agreements for a Middle East peace settlement.

Ben Bella Ahmed 1916– . Algerian politician. He was leader of the National Liberation Front (FLN) from 1952, the first prime minister of independent Algeria 1962–63, and its first president 1963–65. In 1965, Ben Bella was overthrown by Col Houari Boumédienne and detained until 1979. In 1985, he founded a new party, Mouvement pour la Démocratie en Algérie, and returned to Algeria 1990 after nine years in exile.

Ben-Gurion David. Adopted name of David Gruen 1886–1973. Israeli statesman and socialist politician, one of the founders of the state of Israel, the country's first prime minister 1948–53, and again 1955–63.

Bhutto Benazir 1953– . Pakistani politician, leader of the Pakistan People's Party (PPP) from 1984 (in exile until 1986), and prime minister of Pakistan 1988–90, when the opposition manoeuvred her from office and charged her with corruption. In May 1991 new charges were brought against her. She was the first female leader of a Muslim state.

Bhutto Zulfikar Ali 1928–1979. Pakistani politician, president 1971–73; prime minister from 1973 until the 1977 military coup led by General Zia ul-Haq. In 1978, Bhutto was sentenced to death for conspiring to murder a political opponent and was hanged the following year. He was the father of Benazir Bhutto.

Bokassa Jean-Bédel 1921– . President of the Central African Republic 1966–79 and later self-proclaimed emperor 1977–79. Commander in chief from 1963, in Dec 1965, he led the military coup that gave him the presidency. On 4 Dec 1976, he proclaimed the Central African Empire and one year later crowned himself as emperor for life. He was overthrown in 1979 and was in exile until 1986. Upon his return he was sentenced to death, but this was commuted to life imprisonment in 1988.

Bolger Jim (James) Brendan 1935– . New Zealand politician and prime minister from 1990. A successful sheep and cattle farmer, Bolger was elected to parliament 1972. He held a variety of cabinet posts under Robert Muldoon's leadership 1977–84, and was an effective, if uncharismatic, leader of the opposition from March 1986, taking the National Party to electoral victory Oct 1990. His subsequent failure to honour election pledges, leading to cuts in welfare provision, led to a sharp fall in his popularity.

Botha P(ieter) W(illem) 1916– . South African politician, prime minister from 1978. Botha initiated a modification of apartheid, which later slowed in the face of Afrikaner (Boer) opposition. In 1984, he became the first executive state president. In 1989, he unwillingly resigned both party leadership and presidency after suffering a stroke, and was succeeded by F W de Klerk.

Boumédienne Houari. Adopted name of Mohammad Boukharouba 1925–1978. Algerian politician who brought the nationalist leader Ben Bella to power by a revolt 1962, and superseded him as president in 1965 by a further coup.

Boutros-Ghali Boutros 1922– . Egyptian diplomat and politician, deputy prime minister 1991–92. He worked towards peace in the Middle East in the foreign ministry posts he held 1977–91. He became secretary general of the United Nations Jan 1992, and during his first year of office had to deal with the war in Bosnia-Herzegovina and famine in Somalia.

Bourguiba Habib ben Ali 1903– . Tunisian politician, first president of Tunisia 1957–87. In 1934, he founded the Destour Socialist Party (PSD), and led Tunisia's campaign for independence from France. He became prime minister 1956, president (for life from 1974) and prime minister of the Tunisian republic 1957; he was overthrown in a bloodless coup 1987.

Brandt Willy. Adopted name of Karl Herbert Frahm 1913–1992. German socialist politician, federal chancellor (premier) of West Germany 1969–74. He played a key role in the remoulding of the Social Democratic Party (SPD) as a moderate socialist force (leader 1964–87). As mayor of West Berlin 1957–66, Brandt became internationally known during the Berlin Wall crisis 1961. Nobel Peace Prize 1971.

Brezhnev Leonid Ilyich 1906–1982. Soviet leader. A protégé of Stalin and Khrushchev, he came to power (after he and Kosygin forced Khrushchev to resign) as general secretary of the Soviet Communist Party (CPSU) 1964–82 and was president 1977–82. Domestically he was conservative; abroad the USSR was established as a military and political superpower during the Brezhnev era, extending its influence in Africa and Asia.

Brundtland Gro Harlem 1939– . Norwegian Labour politician. Environment minister 1974–76, she briefly took over as prime minister 1981, and was elected prime minister 1986 and again 1990. She chaired the World Commission on Environment and Development which produced the Brundtland Report, published as *Our Common Future* 1987. In 1992, she resigned as leader of the Norwegian Labour Party, a post she had held since 1981.

Bush George 1924– . 41st president of the USA 1989–93, a Republican. He was director of the Central Intelligence Agency (CIA) 1976-81 and US vice president 1981–89. As president, his response to the Soviet leader Gorbachev's diplomatic initiatives were initially criticized as inadequate, but his sending of US troops to depose his former ally, General Noriega of Panama, proved a popular move at home. Success in the 1991 Gulf War against Iraq further raised his standing. Domestic economic problems 1991–92 were followed by his defeat in the 1992 presidential elections by Democrat Bill Clinton.

Buthelezi Chief Gatsha 1928– . Zulu leader and politician, chief minister of KwaZulu, a black 'homeland' in the Republic of South Africa from 1970. He is the founder (1975) and president of Inkatha, a paramilitary organization for attaining a nonracial democratic political system. He has been accused of complicity in the factional violence between Inkatha and African National Congress supporters that has

Prime ministers of the United Kingdom from 1721

Term	*Name*	*Party*	*Term*	*Name*	*Party*
1721–42	Sir Robert Walpole	Whig	1868–74	W E Gladstone	Liberal
1742–43	Earl of Wilmington	Whig	1874–80	Benjamin Disraeli	Conservative
1743–54	Henry Pelham	Whig	1880–85	W E Gladstone	Liberal
1754–56	Duke of Newcastle	Whig	1885–86	Marquess of Salisbury	Conservative
1756–57	Duke of Devonshire	Whig	1886	W E Gladstone	Liberal
1757–62	Duke of Newcastle	Whig	1886–92	Marquess of Salisbury	Conservative
1762–63	Earl of Bute	Tory	1892–94	W E Gladstone	Liberal
1763–65	George Grenville	Whig	1894–95	Earl of Rosebery	Liberal
1765–66	Marquess of Rockingham	Whig	1895–1902	Marquess of Salisbury	Conservative
1767–70	Duke of Grafton	Whig	1902–05	Arthur James Balfour	Conservative
1770–82	Lord North	Tory	1905–08	Sir H Campbell-Bannerman	Liberal
1782	Marquess of Rockingham	Whig	1908–15	H H Asquith	Liberal
1782–83	Earl of Shelburne	Whig	1915–16	H H Asquith	coalition
1783	Duke of Portland	coalition	1916–22	David Lloyd George	coalition
1783–1801	William Pitt the Younger	Tory	1922–23	Andrew Bonar Law	Conservative
1801–04	Henry Addington	Tory	1923–24	Stanley Baldwin	Conservative
1804–06	William Pitt the Younger	Tory	1924	Ramsay MacDonald	Labour
1806–07	Lord Grenville	coalition	1924–29	Stanley Baldwin	Conservative
1807–09	Duke of Portland	Tory	1929–31	Ramsay MacDonald	Labour
1809–12	Spencer Perceval	Tory	1931–35	Ramsay MacDonald	national coalition
1812–27	Earl of Liverpool	Tory			
1827	George Canning	coalition	1935–37	Stanley Baldwin	national coalition
1827–28	Viscount Goderich	Tory			
1828–30	Duke of Wellington	Tory	1937–40	Neville Chamberlain	national coalition
1830–34	Earl Grey	Tory			
1834	Viscount Melbourne	Whig	1940–45	Sir Winston Churchill	coalition
1834–35	Sir Robert Peel	Whig	1945–51	Clement Attlee	Labour
1835–41	Viscount Melbourne	Whig	1951–55	Sir Winston Churchill	Conservative
1841–46	Sir Robert Peel	Conservative	1955–57	Sir Anthony Eden	Conservative
1846–52	Lord Russell	Liberal	1957–63	Harold Macmillan	Conservative
1852	Earl of Derby	Conservative	1963–64	Sir Alec Douglas-Home	Conservative
1852–55	Lord Aberdeen	Peelite	1964–70	Harold Wilson	Labour
1855–58	Viscount Palmerston	Liberal	1970–74	Edward Heath	Conservative
1858–59	Earl of Derby	Conservative	1974–76	Harold Wilson	Labour
1859–65	Viscount Palmerston	Liberal	1976–79	James Callaghan	Labour
1865–66	Lord Russell	Liberal	1979–90	Margaret Thatcher	Conservative
1866–68	Earl of Derby	Conservative	1990–	John Major	Conservative
1868	Benjamin Disraeli	Conservative			

continued to rack the townships despite his signing of a peace accord with ANC leader, Nelson Mandela, Sept 1991.

Callaghan (Leonard) James, Baron Callaghan 1912– . British Labour politician. As chancellor of the Exchequer 1964–67, he introduced corporation and capital-gains taxes, and resigned following devaluation. He was home secretary 1967–70 and prime minister 1976–79 in a period of increasing economic stress.

Campbell Kim 1947– . Canadian Progressive Conservative politician and lawyer. She succeeded Brian Mulroney as prime minister 1993, becoming the first woman to hold this office. A protégée of former prime minister Brian Mulroney, Campbell was elected to the federal House of Commons 1988 and elevated to the cabinet in 1989. In her role as defense minister 1993 she backed an unpopular decision to spend $3.7 billion on high technology helicopters for the armed forces.

Carter Jimmy (James Earl) 1924– . 39th president of the USA 1977–81, a Democrat. In 1976, he narrowly wrested the presidency from Gerald Ford. Features of his presidency were the return of the Panama Canal Zone to Panama, the Camp David Agreements for peace in the Middle East, and the Iranian seizure of US embassy hostages. He was defeated by Ronald Reagan 1980.

Castro (Ruz) Fidel 1927– . Cuban communist politician, prime minister 1959-76 and president from 1976. He led two unsuccessful coups against the right-wing Batista regime and led the revolution that overthrew the dictator 1959. He raised the standard of living for most Cubans but dealt harshly with dissenters.

Cavaco Silva Anibal 1939– . Portuguese politician, finance minister 1980–81, and prime minister and Social Democratic Party (PSD) leader from 1985. Under his leadership Portugal joined the European Community 1985 and the Western European Union 1988.

Ceauşescu Nicolae 1918–1989. Romanian politician, leader of the Romanian Communist Party (RCP), in power 1965–89. He pursued a policy line independent of and critical of the USSR. He appointed family members, including his wife ***Elena Ceauşescu***, to senior state and party posts, and governed in an increasingly repressive manner, zealously implementing schemes that impoverished the nation. The Ceauşescus were overthrown in a bloody revolutionary coup Dec 1989 and executed.

Chadli Benjedid 1929– . Algerian socialist politician, president 1979–92. An army colonel, he supported Boumédienne in the overthrow of Ben Bella 1965, and succeeded Boumédienne 1979, pursuing more moderate policies. Chadli resigned Jan 1992 following a victory for Islamic fundamentalists in the first round of assembly elections.

Chirac Jacques 1932– . French conservative politician, prime minister 1974–76 and 1986–88. He established the neo-Gaullist Rassemblement pour la République (RPR) 1976, and became mayor of Paris 1977.

Chissano Joaquim 1939– . Mozambique nationalist politician, president from 1986; foreign minister 1975–86. In Oct 1992, Chissano signed a peace accord with the leader of the rebel Mozambique National Resistance (MNR) party, bringing to an end 16 years of civil war.

Clinton Bill (William Jefferson) 1946– . 42nd president of the USA from 1993, a Democrat. He served as governor of Arkansas 1979–81, and 1983–93, establishing a liberal and progressive reputation. He became the first Democrat in the White House for 13 years. In Jan 1993, he delayed for six months an executive order to suspend the ban on homosexuals in the armed forces. In spring 1993, Congress passed his medium-term economic plan, combining spending cuts with tax increases targeted against the rich, to cut the huge federal budget deficit.

Collor de Mello Fernando 1949– . Brazilian politician, president 1990–92. As candidate of the centre-right National Reconstruction Party (PRN), he conducted the 1989 presidential campaign on a platform of rooting out government corruption and entrenched privileges. Rumours of his own past wrongdoings were rife by 1992, leading to his constitutional removal from office by a vote of impeachment in congress in Sept 1992. He resigned in Dec at the start of his trial, and was subsequently banned from public office for eight years. He was succeeded by Itamar Franco.

Craxi Bettino 1934– . Italian socialist politician, leader of the Italian Socialist Party (PSI) 1976–93, prime minister 1983–87. He has been accused of involvement in Italy's corruption network.

Dalai Lama 14th incarnation 1935– . Spiritual and temporal head of the Tibetan state until 1959, when he went into exile in protest against Chinese annexation and oppression. His people have continued to demand his return. The Dalai Lama was awarded the Nobel Peace Prize 1989 in recognition of his commitment to the nonviolent liberation of his homeland.

de Gaulle Charles André Joseph Marie 1890–1970. French general and first president of the Fifth Republic 1958–69. He organized the Free French troops fighting the Nazis 1940–44, was head of the provisional French government 1944–46, and leader of his own Gaullist party. In 1958, the national assembly asked him to form a government during France's economic recovery and to solve the crisis in Algeria. He became president at the end of 1958, having changed the constitution to provide for a presidential system, and served until 1969.

de Klerk F(rederik) W(illem) 1936– . South African National Party politician, president from 1989. He served in the cabinets of B J Vorster and P W Botha 1978–89, and replaced Botha as National Party leader Feb 1989 and as state president Aug 1989. In Feb 1990, he ended the ban on the African National Congress opposition movement and released its effective leader, Nelson Mandela. In Feb 1991, de Klerk promised the end of all apartheid legislation and a new multiracial constitution, and by June of the same year, had repealed all racially discriminating laws. In March 1992, a nationwide, whites-only referendum gave de Klerk a clear mandate to proceed with plans for major constitutional reform to end white minority rule. In Feb 1993, he and Nelson Mandela agreed to the formation of a government of national unity after free, nonracial elections in late 1993 or early 1994.

Delors Jacques 1925– . French socialist politician, finance minister 1981–84. As president of the European Commission from 1984 he has overseen significant budgetary reform and the move towards a free European Community market in 1992, with increased powers residing in Brussels.

Demirel Suleyman 1924– . Turkish politician. Leader from 1964 of the Justice Party, he was prime minister 1965–71, 1975–77, and 1979–80. He favoured links with the West, full membership in the European Community, and foreign investment in Turkish industry.

Deng Xiaoping or ***Teng Hsiao-ping*** 1904– . Chinese political leader. A member of the Chinese Communist Party (CCP) from the 1920s, he took part in the Long March 1934–36. He was in the Politburo from 1955 until ousted in the Cultural Revolution 1966–69. Reinstated in the 1970s, he gradually took power and introduced a radical economic modernization programme. He retired from the Politburo 1987 and from his last official position (as chair of State Military Commission) March 1990, but remained influential behind the scenes.

Diouf Abdou 1935– . Senegalese left-wing politician, president from 1980. He became prime minister 1970 under President Leopold Senghor and, on his retirement, succeeded him, being re-elected in 1983, 1988, and 1993. His presidency has been characterized by authoritarianism.

Dubček Alexander 1921–1992. Czechoslovak politician, chair of the federal assembly 1989–92. He was a member of the Slovak resistance movement during World War II, and became first secretary of the Communist Party 1967–69. He launched a liberalization campaign (called the Prague Spring) that was opposed by the USSR and led to the Soviet invasion of Czechoslovakia 1968. He was arrested by Soviet troops and expelled from the party 1970. In 1989, he gave speeches at prodemocracy rallies, and after the fall of the hardline regime, he was elected

Presidents of the USA

Term	*Name*	*Party*
1789–97	George Washington	Federalist
1797–1801	John Adams	Federalist
1801–09	Thomas Jefferson	Democratic-Republican
1809–17	James Madison	Democratic-Republican
1817–25	James Monroe	Democratic-Republican
1825–29	John Quincy Adams	Democratic-Republican
1829–37	Andrew Jackson	Democrat
1837–41	Martin Van Buren	Democrat
1841	William Henry Harrison	Whig
1841–45	John Tyler	Whig
1845–49	James Knox Polk	Democrat
1849-50	Zachary Taylor	Whig
1850–53	Millard Fillmore	Whig
1853–57	Franklin Pierce	Democrat
1857–61	James Buchanan	Democrat
1861–65	Abraham Lincoln	Republican
1865–69	Andrew Johnson	Democrat
1869–77	Ulysses S Grant	Republican
1877–81	Rutherford B Hayes	Republican
1881	James A Garfield	Republican
1881–85	Chester Alun Arthur	Republican
1885–89	Grover Cleveland	Democrat
1889–93	Benjamin Harrison	Republican
1893–97	Grover Cleveland	Republican
1897–1901	William McKinley	Republican
1901–09	Theodore Roosevelt	Republican
1909–13	William Howard Taft	Republican
1913–21	Woodrow Wilson	Democrat
1921–23	Warren Gamaliel Harding	Republican
1923–29	Calvin Coolidge	Republican
1929–33	Herbert C Hoover	Republican
1933–45	Franklin Delano Roosevelt	Democrat
1945–53	Harry S Truman	Democrat
1953–61	Dwight D Eisenhower	Republican
1961–63	John F Kennedy	Democrat
1963–69	Lyndon B Johnson	Democrat
1969–74	Richard M Nixon	Republican
1974–77	Gerald R Ford	Republican
1977–81	James Earl Carter	Democrat
1981–89	Ronald Reagan	Republican
1989–93	George Bush	Republican
1993–	Bill Clinton	Democrat

speaker of the National Assembly in Prague, a position to which he was re-elected 1990. He was fatally injured in a car crash Sept 1992.

Duvalier François 1907–1971. Right-wing president of Haiti 1957–71. Known as ***Papa Doc***, he ruled as a dictator, organizing the Tontons Macoutes ('bogeymen') as a private security force to intimidate and assassinate opponents of his regime. He rigged the 1961 elections in order to have his term of office extended until 1967, and in 1964, declared himself president for life. He was excommunicated by the Vatican for harassing the church, and was succeeded on his death by his son Jean-Claude Duvalier.

Duvalier Jean-Claude 1951– . Right-wing president of Haiti 1971–86. Known as ***Baby Doc***, he succeeded his father François Duvalier, becoming, at the age of 19, the youngest president in the world. He continued to receive support from the USA but was pressured into moderating some elements of his father's regime, yet still tolerated no opposition. In 1986, with Haiti's economy stagnating and with increasing civil disorder, Duvalier fled to France, taking much of the Haitian treasury with him.

Eisenhower Dwight David ('Ike') 1890–1969. 34th president of the USA 1953–60, a Republican. A general in World War II, he commanded the Allied forces in Italy 1943, then the Allied invasion of Europe, and from Oct 1944 all the Allied armies in the West. As president he promoted business interests at home and conducted the Cold War abroad. His vice president was Richard Nixon.

Ershad Hussain Mohammad 1930– . Military ruler of Bangladesh 1982–90. He became chief of staff of the Bangladeshi army 1979 and assumed power in a military coup 1982. As president from 1983, Ershad introduced a successful rural-oriented economic programme. He was re-elected 1986 and lifted martial law, but faced continuing political opposition, which forced him to resign Dec 1990. In 1991, he was formally charged with the illegal possession of arms, convicted, and sentenced to ten years' imprisonment. He received a further sentence of three years' imprisonment Feb 1992 after being convicted of corruption.

Fahd 1921– . King of Saudi Arabia from 1982, when he succeeded his half-brother Khalid. As head of government, he has been active in trying to bring about a solution to the Middle East conflicts.

Franco Francisco (Paulino Hermenegildo Teódulo Bahamonde) 1892–1975. Spanish dictator from 1939. As a general, he led the insurgent Nationalists to victory in the Spanish Civil War 1936–39, supported by Fascist Italy and Nazi Germany, and established a dictatorship. In 1942, Franco reinstated a Cortes (Spanish parliament), which in 1947, passed an act by which he became head of state for life.

Franco Itamar 1931– . Brazilian politician and president since 1992. A member of the Liberal Front Party (PFL), he had had a long, but largely low-profile, career in Brazilian politics until his elevation to head of state. Although holding fundamentally different views on economic policy, he served as vice-president to President Fernando Collor until the latter's removal from office on charges of corruption Dec 1992. Franco, whose record was clean, became interim, then full, president. Criticizing his predecessor's economic modernization policies as 'unrealistic', he promised reform with stability but his first months in office attracted widespread criticism from both supporters and opponents.

Fujimori Alberto 1939– . President of Peru from July 1990. As leader of the newly formed Cambio 90 (Change 90) he campaigned on a reformist ticket and defeated his more experienced Democratic Front opponent. With no assembly majority, and faced with increasing opposition to his policies, he imposed military rule early 1992.

Gandhi Indira (born Nehru) 1917–1984. Indian politician, prime minister of India 1966–77 and

1980–84, and leader of the Congress Party 1966–77 and subsequently of the Congress (I) party. She was assassinated 1984 by members of her Sikh bodyguard, resentful of her use of troops to clear malcontents from the Sikh temple at Amritsar.

Gandhi Mohandas Karamchand, called ***Mahatma*** ('Great Soul') 1869–1948. Indian nationalist leader. A pacifist, he led the struggle for Indian independence from the UK by advocating nonviolent noncooperation (*satyagraha*, defence of and by truth) from 1915. He was imprisoned several times by the British authorities and was influential in the nationalist Congress Party and in the independence negotiations 1947. He was assassinated by a Hindu nationalist in the violence that followed the partition of British India into India and Pakistan.

Gandhi Rajiv 1944–1991. Indian politician, prime minister from 1984 (following his mother Indira Gandhi's assassination) to Nov 1989. As prime minister, he faced growing discontent with his party's elitism and lack of concern for social issues. He was assassinated by a bomb at an election rally.

Geingob Hage Gottfried 1941– . Namibian politician and prime minister. Geingob was appointed founding director of the United Nations Institute for Namibia in Lusaka, 1975. He became the first prime minister of an independent Namibia March 1990.

Giscard d'Estaing Valéry 1926– . French conservative politician, president 1974–81. He was finance minister to de Gaulle 1962–66 and Pompidou 1969–74. As leader of the Union pour la Démocratie Française, which he formed in 1978, Giscard sought to project himself as leader of a 'new centre'.

Goh Chok Tong 1941– . Singapore politician, prime minister from 1990. A trained economist, Goh became a member of parliament for the ruling People's Action Party 1976. Rising steadily through the party ranks, he was appointed deputy prime minister 1985, and subsequently chosen by the cabinet as Lee Kuan Yew's successor, first as prime minister and from 1992 also as party leader.

González Márquez Felipe 1942– . Spanish socialist politician, leader of the Socialist Workers' Party (PSOE), prime minister from 1982. Although PSOE was re-elected in 1989 and 1993, his popularity suffered from economic upheaval and allegations of corruption.

Gorbachev Mikhail Sergeyevich 1931– . Soviet president, in power 1985–91. As general secretary of the Communist Party (CPSU) 1985–91, and president of the Supreme Soviet 1988–91, he introduced liberal reforms at home (*perestroika* and *glasnost*), proposed the introduction of multiparty democracy, and attempted to halt the arms race abroad. He became head of state 1989. He was awarded the Nobel Peace Prize 1990 but his international reputation suffered in the light of harsh state repression of nationalist demonstrations in the Baltic states. Following an abortive coup attempt by hardliners Aug 1991, international acceptance of independence for the Baltic states, and accelerated moves towards independence in other republics, Gorbachev's power base as Soviet president was greatly weakened and in Dec 1991 he resigned.

Presidents and Communist Party leaders of the USSR

Term	*Name*
Communist Party leaders	
1917–22	V I Lenin
1922–53	Joseph Stalin
1953–64	Nikita Khrushchev
1964–82	Leonid Brezhnev
1982–84	Yuri Andropov
1984–85	Konstantin Chernenko
1985–91	Mikhail Gorbachev
presidents	
1917–22	V I Lenin
1922–46	Mikhail Kalinin
1946–53	N Shvernik
1953–60	Marshal K Voroshilov
1960–64	Leonid Brezhnev
1964–65	A Mikoyan
1965–77	N Podgorny
1977–82	Leonid Brezhnev
1982–83	V Kuznetsov (acting)
1983–84	Yuri Andropov
1984	V Kuznetsov (acting)
1984–85	Konstantin Chernenko
1985	V Kuznetsov (acting)
1985–89	Andrei Gromyko
1989–91	Mikhail Gorbachev

Haughey Charles 1925– . Irish Fianna Fáil politician of Ulster descent. Dismissed 1970 from Jack Lynch's cabinet for alleged complicity in IRA gunrunning, he was afterwards acquitted. He was prime minister 1979–81, March–Nov 1982, and 1986–92, when he was replaced by Albert Reynolds.

Havel Václav 1936– . Czech dramatist and politician, president of Czechoslovakia 1989–92 and president of the Czech Republic from 1993. Havel became widely known as a human-rights activist. He was imprisoned 1979–83 and again 1989 for support of Charter 77, a human-rights manifesto. As president of Czechoslovakia he sought to preserve a united republic, but resigned in recognition of the breakup of the federation 1992. In 1993 he became president of the newly independent Czech Republic.

Hawke Bob (Robert) 1929– . Australian Labor politician, prime minister 1983–91, on the right wing of the party. He was president of the Australian Council of Trade Unions 1970–80. He announced his retirement from politics 1992.

Heath Edward (Richard George) 1916– . British Conservative politician, party leader 1965–75. As prime minister 1970–74, he took the UK into the European Community but was brought down by economic and industrial relations crises at home. He was replaced as party leader by Margaret Thatcher 1975, and became increasingly critical of her policies and her opposition to the UK's full participation in the EC. In 1990, he undertook a mission to Iraq in an attempt to secure the release of British hostages.

Hekmatyar Gulbuddin 1949– . Afghani Islamic fundamentalist guerrilla leader, prime minister from 1993. Strongly anticommunist, he resisted the takeover of Kabul by moderate mujaheddin forces

April 1992 and refused to join the interim administration, continuing to bombard the city until being driven out. A year later he became prime minister by a peace agreement.

Ho Chi Minh adopted name of Nguyen Tat Thanh 1890–1969. North Vietnamese communist politician, premier and president 1954–69. Having trained in Moscow shortly after the Russian Revolution, he headed the communist Vietminh from 1941 and fought against the French during the Indochina War 1946–54, becoming president and prime minister of the republic at the armistice. Aided by the communist bloc, he did much to develop industrial potential. He relinquished the premiership 1955, but continued as president. In the years before his death, Ho successfully led his country's fight against US-aided South Vietnam in the Vietnam War 1954–75.

Honecker Erich 1912– . German communist politician, in power 1973–89, elected chair of the council of state (head of state) 1976. He governed in an outwardly austere and efficient manner and, while favouring East–West détente, was a loyal ally of the USSR. In Oct 1989, following a wave of prodemocracy demonstrations, he was replaced as leader of the Socialist Unity Party (SED) and head of state by Egon Krenz, and in Dec expelled from the Communist Party. Following revelations of corruption during his regime, he was placed under house arrest, awaiting trial on charges of treason, corruption, and abuse of power. In 1993, he was allowed to go into exile in Chile.

Houphouët-Boigny Félix 1905– . Côte d'Ivoire right-wing politician. He held posts in French ministries, and became president of the Republic of the Ivory Coast on independence 1960, maintaining close links with France, which helped to boost an already thriving economy and encourage political stability. Pro-Western and opposed to communist intervention in Africa, Houphouët-Boigny has been strongly criticized for maintaining diplomatic relations with South Africa. He was re-elected for a seventh term 1990 in multiparty elections, amid allegations of ballot rigging and political pressure.

Hoxha Enver 1908–1985. Albanian Communist politician, the country's leader from 1954. He founded the Albanian Communist Party 1941, and headed the liberation movement 1939–44. He was prime minister 1944–54, combining with foreign affairs 1946–53, and from 1954 was first secretary of the Albanian Party of Labour. In policy he was a Stalinist and independent of both Chinese and Soviet communism.

Hun Sen 1950– . Cambodian political leader, prime minister from 1985. Originally a member of the Khmer Rouge army, he defected in 1977 to join Vietnam-based anti-Khmer Cambodian forces. His leadership has been characterized by the promotion of economic liberalization and a thawing in relations with exiled non-Khmer opposition forces as a prelude to a compromise political settlement. In Oct 1991, following a peace accord ending 13 years of civil war in Cambodia, Hun Sen agreed to rule the country in conjunction with the United Nations Transitional Authority in Cambodia (UNTAC) and representatives of the warring factions until UN-administered elections 1993.

Hussein ibn Talal 1935– . King of Jordan from 1952. By 1967, he had lost all his kingdom west of the river Jordan in the Arab-Israeli Wars, and in 1970, suppressed the Palestine Liberation Organization acting as a guerrilla force against his rule on the remaining East Bank territories. He has become a moderating force in Middle Eastern politics.

Hussein Saddam 1937– . Iraqi politician, in power from 1968, president from 1979, progressively eliminating real or imagined opposition factions as he gained increasing dictatorial control. He fought a bitter war against Iran 1980–88, with US economic aid, and dealt harshly with Kurdish rebels seeking independence, using chemical weapons against civilian populations. In 1990, he annexed Kuwait, to universal condemnation, before being driven out by a US-dominated coalition army Feb 1991. He subseqently sent the remainder of his army to crush the Kurds, bringing international charges of genocide against him and causing hundreds of thousands of Kurds to flee their homes in northern Iraq. His continued indiscriminate bombardment of Shi'ites in southern Iraq caused the UN to impose a 'no-fly zone' in the area Aug 1992. Alleging infringements of the zone, US-led warplanes bombed strategic targets in Iraq Jan 1993, forcing Hussein to back down and comply with repeated UN requests for access to inspect his arms facilities.

Iliescu Ion 1930– . Romanian president from 1990. A former member of the Romanian Communist Party (PCR) and of Nicolae Ceauşescu's government, Iliescu swept into power on Ceauşescu's fall as head of the National Salvation Front.

Jaruzelski Wojciech 1923– . Polish general, communist leader from 1981, president 1985–90. He imposed martial law for the first year of his rule, suppressed the opposition, and banned trade-union activity, but later released many political prisoners. In 1989, elections in favour of the free trade union Solidarity forced Jaruzelski to speed up democratic reforms, overseeing a transition to a new form of 'socialist pluralist' democracy and stepping down as president 1990.

Jayawardene Junius Richard 1906– . Sri Lankan politician. Leader of the United Nationalist Party from 1973, he became prime minister 1977 and the country's first president 1978–88.

Jiang Zemin 1926– . Chinese political leader, state president from 1993. He succeeded Zhao Ziyang as Communist Party leader after the Tiananmen Square massacre of 1989. Jiang is a cautious proponent of economic reform who held with unswerving adherence to the party's 'political line'.

Johnson Lyndon Baines 1908–1973. 36th president of the USA 1963–69, a Democrat. He was elected to Congress 1937–49 and the Senate 1949–60. Born in Texas, he brought critical Southern support as J F Kennedy's vice-presidential running mate 1960, and became president on Kennedy's assassination. After the Tonkin Gulf Incident, which escalated US involvement in the Vietnam War, support won by Johnson's Great Society legislation (civil rights, education, alleviation of poverty) dissipated, and he declined to run for re-election 1968.

Kádár János 1912–1989. Hungarian Communist leader, in power 1956–88, after suppressing the national uprising. As Hungarian Socialist Workers' Party (HSWP) leader and prime minister 1956–58 and 1961–65, Kádár introduced a series of market-socialist economic reforms, while retaining cordial political relations with the USSR.

Karadzic Radovan 1945– . Bosnian Serb political leader, president of the community's unofficial government 1992– . As leader, he launched the siege of Sarajevo in 1992, which escalated swiftly into a brutal civil war. Distrusted in the West and viewed as an intransigent figure, for many Bosnian Serbs he is considered a moderate.

Kaunda Kenneth (David) 1924– . Zambian politician, president 1964–91. Imprisoned in 1958–60 as founder of the Zambia African National Congress, he became in 1964 the first prime minister of Northern Rhodesia, then the first president of independent Zambia. In 1973, he introduced one-party rule. He supported the nationalist movement in Southern Rhodesia, now Zimbabwe, and survived a coup attempt 1980 thought to have been promoted by South Africa. He was elected chair of the Organization of African Unity 1987. In 1990, he was faced with wide anti-government demonstrations, leading to the acceptance of a multiparty political system. He lost the first multiparty election, in Nov 1991, to Frederick Chiluba.

Keating Paul 1954– . Australian politician, Labor Party (ALP) leader and prime minister from 1991. He was treasurer and deputy leader of the ALP 1983–91.

Kennedy John F(itzgerald) 'Jack' 1917–1963. 35th president of the USA 1961–63, a Democrat; the first Roman Catholic and the youngest person to be elected president. In foreign policy, he carried through the unsuccessful Bay of Pigs invasion of Cuba, and in 1963 secured the withdrawal of Soviet missiles from the island. His programme for reforms at home, called the ***New Frontier***, was posthumously executed by Lyndon Johnson. Kennedy was assassinated while on a visit to Dallas, Texas, on 22 Nov 1963 by Lee Harvey Oswald (1939–1963), who was within a few days shot dead by Jack Ruby (1911–1967).

Kenyatta Jomo. Assumed name of Kamau Ngengi *c.* 1894–1978. Kenyan nationalist politician, prime minister from 1963, as well as the first president of Kenya from 1964 until his death. He led the Kenya African Union from 1947 (***KANU*** from 1963) and was active in liberating Kenya from British rule.

Khaddhafi or ***Gaddafi*** or ***Qaddafi***, Moamer al 1942– . Libyan revolutionary leader. Overthrowing King Idris 1969, he became virtual president of a republic, although he nominally gave up all except an ideological role 1974. He favours territorial expansion in N Africa reaching as far as Zaire, has supported rebels in Chad, and has proposed mergers with a number of countries. His theories, based on those of the Chinese communist leader Mao Zedong, are contained in a *Green Book*.

Khasbulatov Rusian 1943– . Russian politician and chairman of the Supreme Soviet since 1991. As the Russian first vice-president, he was initially a strong supporter of Boris Yeltsin, and, after the collapse of the 1991 anti-Gorbachev coup, became chairman of the Russian Supreme Soviet. Thereafter, however, relations between Yeltsin and Khasbulatov deteriorated rapidly, the latter repeatedly trying to block the Russian leader's economic and political reforms. Khasbulatov's critics accused him of shifting his ideological ground to pursue his personal ambitions.

Khomeini Ayatollah Ruhollah 1900–1989. Iranian Shi'ite Muslim leader, born in Khomein, central Iran. Exiled for opposition to the Shah from 1964, he returned when the Shah left the country 1979, and established a fundamentalist Islamic republic. His rule was marked by a protracted war with Iraq, and suppression of opposition within Iran, executing thousands of opponents.

Khrushchev Nikita Sergeyevich 1894–1971. Soviet politician, secretary general of the Communist Party 1953–64, premier 1958–64. He emerged as leader from the power struggle following Stalin's death and was the first official to denounce Stalin, in 1956. His de-Stalinization programme gave rise to revolts in Poland and Hungary 1956. Because of problems with the economy and foreign affairs (a breach with China 1960; conflict with the USA in the Cuban missile crisis 1962), he was ousted by Leonid Brezhnev and Alexei Kosygin.

Kim Il Sung 1912– . North Korean communist politician and marshal. He became prime minister 1948 and president 1972, retaining the presidency of the Communist Workers' party. He likes to be known as the 'Great Leader' and has campaigned constantly for the reunification of Korea. His son ***Kim Jong Il*** (1942–), known as the 'Dear Leader', has been named as his successor.

Kim Young Sam 1927– . South Korean democratic politician, president from 1993. A member of the National Assembly from 1954 and president of the New Democratic Party (NDP) from 1974, he lost his seat and was later placed under house arrest because of his opposition to President Park Chung Hee. In 1983, he led a pro-democracy hunger strike but in 1987, failed to defeat Roh Tae-Woo in the presidential election. In 1990, he merged the NDP with the ruling party to form the new Democratic Liberal Party (DLP). In the Dec 1992 presidential election, he captured 42% of the national vote, and assumed office Feb 1993.

King Martin Luther Jr 1929–1968. US civil-rights campaigner, black leader, and Baptist minister. He first came to national attention as leader of the Montgomery, Alabama, bus boycott 1955, and was one of the organizers of the massive (200,000 people) march on Washington DC 1963 to demand racial equality. An advocate of nonviolence, he was awarded the Nobel Peace Prize 1964. He was assassinated in Memphis, Tennessee, by James Earl Ray (1928–).

Kohl Helmut 1930– . German conservative politician, leader of the Christian Democratic Union (CDU) from 1976, West German chancellor (prime minister) 1982–90. He oversaw the reunification of East and West Germany 1989–90 and in 1990, won a resounding victory to become the first chancellor of reunited Germany. His miscalculation of the true costs of reunification and their subsequent effects on the German economy led to a dramatic fall in his popularity.

Koivisto Mauno Henrik 1923– . Finnish politician, prime minister 1968–70 and 1979–82, and president since 1982. He gradually moved from the fringe of politics into active participation, becoming finance minister 1966–67 and prime minister 1968–72, leading a Social Democratic Party (SDP) coalition. He returned as head of government 1979–82 and then became president 1982, sharing power with Centre Party (KESK) prime minister, Esko Aho, in Finland's unusual 'dual executive'.

Kravchuk Leonid 1934– . Ukrainian politician, president from July 1990. Formerly a member of the Ukrainian Communist Party (UCP), he became its ideology chief in the 1980s. After the suspension of the UCP Aug 1991, Kravchuk became an advocate of independence and market-centred economic reform.

Landsbergis Vytautas 1932– . President of Lithuania 1990–1993. He became active in nationalist politics in the 1980s, founding and eventually chairing the anticommunist Sajudis independence movement 1988. When Sajudis swept to victory in the republic's elections March 1990, Landsbergis chaired the Supreme Council of Lithuania becoming, in effect, president. He immediately drafted the republic's declaration of independence from the USSR which, after initial Soviet resistance, was recognized Sept 1991.

Lange David (Russell) 1942– . New Zealand Labour prime minister 1983–89. Lange, a barrister, was elected to the House of Representatives 1977. Labour had a decisive win in the 1984 general election on a non-nuclear military policy, which Lange immediately put into effect, despite criticism from the USA. He introduced a free-market economic policy and was re-elected 1987. He resigned Aug 1989 over a disagreement with his finance minister.

Lee Kuan Yew 1923– . Singapore politician, prime minister 1959–90. Lee founded the anticommunist Socialist People's Action Party 1954 and entered the Singapore legislative assembly 1955. He was elected the country's first prime minister 1959, and took Singapore out of the Malaysian federation 1965. He remained in power until his resignation 1990, and was succeeded by Goh Chok Tong. Until 1992, he held on to the party leadership.

Li Peng 1928– . Chinese communist politician, a member of the Politburo from 1985, and head of government from 1987. During the pro-democracy demonstrations of 1989 he supported the massacre of students by Chinese troops in Tiananmen Square and the subsequent execution of others. He sought improved relations with the USSR prior to its demise, and has favoured maintaining firm central and party control over the economy.

Lubbers Rudolph Franz Marie (Ruud) 1939– . Dutch politician, prime minister of the Netherlands from 1982. Leader of the Christian Democratic Appeal (CDA), he is politically right of centre. He became minister for economic affairs 1973.

Lumumba Patrice 1926–1961. Congolese politician, prime minister of Zaire 1960. Imprisoned by the Belgians, but released in time to attend the conference giving the Congo independence in 1960, he led the National Congolese Movement to victory in the subsequent general election. He was deposed in a coup d'état, and murdered some months later.

Machel Samora 1933–1986. Mozambique nationalist leader, president 1975–86. Machel was active in the liberation front Frelimo from its conception 1962, fighting for independence from Portugal. He became Frelimo leader 1966, and Mozambique's first president from independence 1975 until his death in a plane crash near the South African border.

Macmillan (Maurice) Harold, 1st Earl of Stockton 1894–1986. British Conservative politician, prime minister 1957–63; foreign secretary 1955 and chancellor of the Exchequer 1955–57. In 1963, he attempted to negotiate British entry into the European Economic Community, but was blocked by French president de Gaulle. Much of his career as prime minister was spent defending the retention of a UK nuclear weapon, and he was responsible for the purchase of US Polaris missiles 1962.

Prime ministers of Australia from 1901

Term	*Name*	*Party*
1901–03	Sir Edmund Barton	Protectionist
1903–04	Alfred Deacon	Protectionist
1904–04	John Watson	Labor
1904–05	Sir G Reid	Protectionist–Free Trade coalition
1905–08	Alfred Deakin	Protectionist
1908–09	Andrew Fisher	Labor
1909–10	Alfred Deakin	Protectionist–Free Trade coalition
1910–13	Andrew Fisher	Labor
1913–14	Sir J Cook	Liberal
1914–15	Andrew Fisher	Labor
1915–23	William Morris Hughes	Labor (National Labor from 1917)
1923–29	J H Scullin	Labor
1932–39	Joseph Aloysius Lyons	United Australia–Country coalition
1939–41	R G Menzies	United Australia
1941–41	A W Fadden	Country–United Australia coalition
1941–45	John Curtin	Labor
1945	F M Forde	Labor
1945–49	J B Chifley	Labor
1949–66	R G Menzies	Liberal–Country coalition
1966–67	Harold Holt	Liberal–Country coalition
1967–68	John McEwen	Liberal–Country coalition
1968–71	J G Gorton	Liberal–Country coalition
1971–72	William McMahon	Liberal–Country coalition
1972–75	Gough Whitlam	Labor
1975–83	Malcolm Fraser	Liberal–National coalition
1983–91	Robert Hawke	Labor
1991–	Paul Keating	Labor

Major John 1943– . British Conservative politician, prime minister from Nov 1990. He was foreign secretary 1989 and chancellor of the Exchequer 1989–90. His earlier positive approach to European Community (EC) matters was hindered during 1991 by divisions within the Conservative Party. Major was returned to power in the April 1992 general election; however, he subsequently faced mounting public dissatisfaction over a range of issues, including the sudden withdrawal of the pound from the European Monetary System (EMS), a drastic pit-closure programme, and past sales of arms to Iraq. His indecisive presidency of the European Community, particularly regarding ratification of the Maastricht Treaty, was also criticized.

Makarios III 1913–1977. Cypriot politician, Greek Orthodox archbishop 1950–77. A leader of the Resistance organization EOKA, he was exiled by the British to the Seychelles 1956–57 for supporting armed action to achieve union with Greece (*enosis*). He was president of the republic of Cyprus 1960–77 (briefly deposed by a Greek military coup July–Dec 1974).

Mandela Nelson (Rolihlahla) 1918– . South African politician and lawyer, president of the African National Congress (ANC) from 1991. As organizer of the then banned ANC, he was imprisoned 1964. In prison he became a symbol of unity for the worldwide anti-apartheid movement. In Feb 1990 ,he was released, the ban on the ANC having been lifted, and he entered into negotiations with the government about a multiracial future for South Africa. In Sept 1992, Mandela and President de Klerk agreed to hasten the creation of an interim government under which reforms could take place. In Feb 1993, they agreed to the formation of a government of national unity after free, nonracial elections in late 1993 or early 1994.

Manley Michael (Norman) 1924– . Jamaican politician, leader of the socialist People's National Party from 1969, and prime minister 1972–80 and 1989–92. He resigned the premiership because of ill health March 1992 and was succeeded by P J Patterson. Manley left parliament April 1992. His father, ***Norman Manley*** (1893–1969), was the founder of the People's National Party and prime minister 1959–62.

Mao Zedong or ***Mao Tse-tung*** 1893–1976. Chinese political leader and Marxist theoretician. A founder of the Chinese Communist Party (CCP) 1921, Mao soon emerged as its leader. He organized the Long March 1934–35 and the war of liberation 1937–49, following which he established a People's Republic and communist rule in China; he headed the CCP and government until his death. His influence diminished with the failure of his 1958–60 Great Leap Forward, but he emerged dominant again during the 1966–69 Cultural Revolution. Mao adapted communism to Chinese conditions, as set out in the *Little Red Book*. Since 1978, the leadership of Deng Xiaoping has reinterpreted Maoism and criticized its policy excesses, but many of Mao's ideas remain valued.

Marcos Ferdinand 1917–1989. Filipino right-wing politician, president from 1965 to 1986, when he was forced into exile in Hawaii by a popular front led by Corazon Aquino. He was backed by the USA when in power, but in 1988, US authorities indicted him and his wife Imelda Marcos for racketeering, embezzlement.

Prime ministers of Canada from 1867

Term	*Name*	*Party*
1867–73	John A Macdonald	Conservative
1873–78	Alexander Mackenzie	Liberal
1878–91	John A Macdonald	Conservative
1891–92	John J Abbott	Conservative
1892–94	John S D Thompson	Conservative
1894–96	Mackenzie Bowell	Conservative
1896	Charles Tupper	Conservative
1896–1911	Wilfred Laurier	Liberal
1911–20	Robert L Borden	Conservative
1920–21	Arthur Meighen	Conservative
1921–26	William L M King	Liberal
1926–26	Arthur Meighen	Conservative
1926–30	William L M King	Liberal
1930–35	Richard B Bennett	Conservative
1935–48	William L M King	Liberal
1948–57	Louis S St Laurent	Liberal
1957–63	John G Diefenbaker	Conservative
1963–68	Lester B Pearson	Liberal
1968–79	Pierre E Trudeau	Liberal
1979–80	Joseph Clark	Progressive Conservative
1980–84	Pierre E Trudeau	Liberal
1984	John Turner	Liberal
1984–93	Brian Mulroney	Progressive Conservative
1993–	Kim Campbell	Progressive Conservative

Martens Wilfried 1936– . Prime minister of Belgium 1979–92, member of the Social Christian Party. He was president of the Dutch-speaking CVP 1972–79 and, as prime minister, headed several coalition governments in the period 1979–92 when he was replaced by Jean-Luc Dehaene heading a new coalition.

Masire Quett Ketumile Joni 1925– . President of Botswana from 1980. In 1962, with Seretse Khama, he founded the Botswana Democratic Party (BDP) and in 1965 was made deputy prime minister. After independence 1966, he became vice president and, on Khama's death 1980, president, continuing a policy of nonalignment. A centrist, he has helped Botswana become one of the most stable states in Africa.

Meciar Vladimir 1942– . Slovak politician, prime minister of the new state of Slovakia from January 1993. A dissident, he was expelled from the Communist Party 1970. As leader of the Movement for a Democratic Slovakia (HZDS), he sought an independent Slovak state. Meciar became prime minister of the Slovak republic 1990, within the federal system, and subsequently, the first prime minister of the new state, which formally came into being Jan 1993. With his Czech counterparts he played an important role in ensuring that the 'velvet revolution' of 1989 was translated into a similarly bloodless 'velvet divorce'.

Meir Golda 1898–1978. Israeli Labour (*Mapai*) politician. Born in Russia, she emigrated to the USA

1906, and in 1921 went to Palestine. She was foreign minister 1956–66 and prime minister 1969–74. Criticism of the Israelis' lack of preparation for the 1973 Arab-Israeli War led to election losses for Labour and, unable to form a government, she resigned.

Menem Carlos (Saul) 1935– . Argentine politician, president from 1989; leader of the Peronist (Justicialist Party) movement. As president, he introduced sweeping privatization and public spending cuts, released hundreds of political prisoners jailed under the Alfonsín regime, and sent two warships to the Gulf to assist the USA against Iraq in the 1992 Gulf War (the only Latin American country to offer support to the USA). He also improved relations with the UK.

Mengistu Haile Mariam 1937– . Ethiopian soldier and socialist politician, head of state 1977–91 (president 1987–91). He seized power in a coup and was confronted with severe problems of drought and secessionist uprisings, but survived with help from the USSR and the West until his violent overthrow.

Milosevic Slobodan 1941– . Serbian communist politician, party chief and president of Serbia from 1986; re-elected Dec 1990 in multiparty elections and again re-elected Dec 1992. Milosevic wielded considerable influence over the Serb-dominated Yugoslav federal army during the 1991–92 civil war and has continued to back Serbian militia in Bosnia-Herzegovina 1992–93, although publicly disclaiming any intention to 'carve up' the newly independent republic.

Mitterrand François 1916– . French socialist politician, president from 1981. He held ministerial posts in 11 governments 1947–58, and founded the French Socialist Party (PS) 1971. In 1985, he introduced proportional representation, allegedly to weaken the growing opposition from left and right. Since 1982, his administrations have combined economic orthodoxy with social reform.

Miyazawa Kiichi 1920– . Japanese right-wing politician. After holding a number of key government posts, he became leader of the ruling Liberal Democratic Party and prime minister Nov 1991. He was defeated June 1993 on a vote of confidence (triggered by demand for electoral reform), and resigned in July following a general election.

Mobutu Sese Seko Kuku Ngbeandu Wa Za Banga 1930– . Zairean president from 1965. He assumed the presidency in a coup, and created a unitary state under a centralized government. In 1991, opposition leaders forced Mobutu to agree formally to give up some of his powers, but the president continued to oppose constitutional reform. His decision Jan 1993 to pay his regular army with near worthless banknotes resulted in mutiny and the accidental shooting of the French ambassador by troops loyal to the president, causing French and Belgium governments to intervene and prepare to evacuate civilians. His personal wealth is estimated at $3–4 billion, and more money is spent on the presidency than on the entire social-services budget. The harshness of some of his policies and charges of corruption have attracted widespread international criticism.

Mohamad Mahathir bin 1925– . Prime minister of Malaysia from 1981 and leader of the United Malays National Organization (UMNO). His 'look east' economic policy emulates Japanese industrialization.

Moi Daniel arap 1924– . Kenyan politician, president from 1978. Leader of Kenya African National Union (KANU), he became minister of home affairs 1964, vice president 1967, and succeeded Jomo Kenyatta as president. He enjoys the support of Western governments but has been widely criticized for Kenya's poor human-rights record. From 1988, his rule became increasingly authoritarian and in 1991, in the face of widespread criticism, he promised an eventual introduction of multiparty politics. In 1992, he was elected president in the first free elections amid widespread accusations of fraud.

Mubarak Hosni 1928– . Egyptian politician, president from 1981. Vice president to Anwar Sadat from 1975, Mubarak succeeded him on his assassination. He has continued to pursue Sadat's moderate policies, and has significantly increased the freedom of the press and of political association, while trying to repress the growing Islamic fundamentalist movement.

Mugabe Robert (Gabriel) 1925– . Zimbabwean politician, prime minister from 1980 and president from 1987. He was in detention in Rhodesia for nationalist activities 1964–74, then carried on guerrilla warfare from Mozambique. As leader of ZANU he was in an uneasy alliance with Joshua Nkomo of ZAPU (Zimbabwe African People's Union) from 1976. The two parties merged 1987. His failure to anticipate and respond to the 1991–92 drought in southern Africa adversely affected his popularity.

Muldoon Robert David 1921–1992. New Zealand National Party politician, prime minister 1975–84, during which time he pursued austere economic policies such as a wage-and-price policy to control inflation. Muldoon announced his retirement from politics 1992.

Mulroney Brian 1939– . Canadian politician, Progressive Conservative Party leader from 1983, prime minister 1984–93. He achieved a landslide in the 1984 election, and won the 1988 election on a platform of free trade with the USA. Opposition to the Meech Lake agreement, a prerequisite to signing the 1982 constitution, eventually forced him, in Feb 1993, to resign the leadership of the Conservative Party, though he remained prime minister until Kim Campbell was appointed his successor in June.

Museveni Yoweri Kaguta 1945– . Ugandan general and politician, president from 1986. He led the opposition to Idi Amin's regime 1971–78 and was minister of defence 1979–80 but, unhappy with Milton Obote's autocratic leadership, formed the National Resistance Army (NRA). When Obote was ousted in a coup in 1985, Museveni entered into a brief power-sharing agreement with his successor, Tito Okello, before taking over as president. Museveni leads a broad-based coalition government.

Najibullah Ahmadzai 1947– . Afghan communist politician, state president 1986-92. A member of the Politburo from 1981, he was leader of the People's Democratic Party of Afghanistan (PDPA) from 1986. Although his government initially survived the withdrawal of Soviet troops Feb 1989, continuing pressure from the mujaheddin forces resulted in his eventual overthrow. In the spring of 1992, he was captured while attempting to flee the country and placed under United Nations protection, pending trial by an Islamic court.

Nakasone Yasuhiro 1917– . Japanese conservative politician, leader of the Liberal Democratic Party (LDP) and prime minister 1982–87. He stepped up military spending and increased Japanese participation in international affairs, with closer ties to the USA. He was forced to resign his party post May 1989 as a result of having profited from insider trading in the Recruit scandal. After serving a two-year period of atonement, he rejoined the LDP April 1991.

Narasimha Rao P(amulaparti) V(enkata) 1921– . Indian politician, prime minister of India from 1991 and Congress (I) leader. He governed the state of Andhra Pradesh as chief minister 1971–73, and served in the Congress (I) cabinets of Indira and Rajiv Gandhi as minister of external affairs 1980–85 and 1988–90 and of human resources 1985–88. He took over the party leadership after the assassination of Rajiv Gandhi. Elected prime minister the following month, he instituted a reform of the economy.

Nasser Gamal Abdel 1918–1970. Egyptian politician, prime minister 1954–56 and from 1956 president of Egypt (the United Arab Republic 1958–71). In 1952, he was the driving power behind the Neguib coup, which ended the monarchy. His nationalization of the Suez Canal 1956 led to an Anglo-French invasion and the Suez Crisis, and his ambitions for an Egyptian-led union of Arab states led to disquiet in the Middle East (and in the West). Nasser was also an early and influential leader of the nonaligned movement.

Natanyahu ('Bibi') Binjamin 1949– . Israeli right-wing politician and diplomat. As deputy foreign minister in the Likud-led government of Yitzak Shamir, he was the chief Israeli spokesperson in the 1991–92 Middle East peace talks. Having served in the Israeli embassy in Washington 1982–84 and as principal representative at the UN in New York 1984–88, he was well-equipped for this role. A persuasive television performer and a hard-line politician, he succeeded Shamir to the Likud leadership March 1993 following the party's June 1992 electoral defeat.

Nazarbayev Nursultan 1940– . President of Kazakhstan from 1990. In the Soviet period he was prime minister of the republic 1984–89 and leader of the Kazakh Communist Party 1989–91, which established itself as the independent Socialist Party of Kazakhstan (SPK) Sept 1991. He advocates free-market policies, yet enjoys the support of the environmentalist lobby. He joined the Communist Party at 22 and left it after the failed Soviet coup 1991.

Nehru Jawaharlal 1889–1964. Indian nationalist politician, prime minister from 1947. Before the partition (the division of British India into India and Pakistan), he led the socialist wing of the nationalist Congress Party, and was second in influence only to Mohandas Gandhi. He was imprisoned nine times by the British 1921–45 for political activities. As prime minister from the creation of the dominion (later republic) of India in Aug 1947, he originated the idea of nonalignment (neutrality towards major powers). His daughter was Prime Minister Indira Gandhi.

Nixon Richard (Milhous) 1913– . 37th president of the USA 1969–74, a Republican. He attracted attention as a member of the Un-American Activities Committee 1948, and was vice president to Eisenhower 1953–61. As president he was responsible for US withdrawal from Vietnam, and forged new links with China, but at home his culpability in the cover-up of the Watergate scandal and the existence of a 'slush fund' for political machinations during his re-election campaign 1972 led to his resignation 1974 when threatened with impeachment. He was granted a pardon 1974 by President Ford and turned to lecturing and writing.

Nkomo Joshua 1917– . Zimbabwean politician, vice-president from 1988. As president of ZAPU (Zimbabwe African People's Union) from 1961, he was a leader of the black nationalist movement against the white Rhodesian regime. He was a member of Robert Mugabe's cabinet 1980–82 and from 1987.

Nkrumah Kwame 1909–1972. Ghanaian nationalist politician, prime minister of the Gold Coast (Ghana's former name) 1952–57 and of newly independent Ghana 1957–60. He became Ghana's first president 1960 but was overthrown in a coup 1966. His policy of 'African socialism' led to links with the communist bloc.

Noriega Manuel (Antonio Morena) 1940– . Panamanian soldier and politician, effective ruler of Panama from 1982, as head of the National Guard, until deposed by the USA 1989. An informer for the US Central Intelligence Agency, he was known to be involved in drug trafficking as early as 1972. He enjoyed US support until 1987. In the 1989 US invasion of Panama, he was forcibly taken to the USA to stand trial. He was eventually convicted of drug trafficking and racketeering in 1992 and given a 40-year prison sentence.

Nujoma Sam 1929– . Namibian left-wing politician, president from 1990, founder and leader of SWAPO (the South-West Africa People's Organization) from 1959. He was exiled in 1960 and controlled guerrillas from Angolan bases until the first free elections were held 1989, taking office early the following year.

Nyerere Julius (Kambarage) 1922– . Tanzanian socialist politician, president 1964–85. He devoted himself from 1954 to the formation of the Tanganyika African National Union and subsequent campaigning for independence. He became chief minister 1960, was prime minister of Tanganyika 1961–62, president of the newly formed Tanganyika Republic 1962–64, and first president of Tanzania 1964–85.

Obote (Apollo) Milton 1924– . Ugandan politician who led the independence movement from 1961. He became prime minister 1962 and was president 1966–71 and 1980–85, being overthrown by first Idi Amin and then by Lt-Gen Tito Okello.

Ortega Saavedra Daniel 1945– . Nicaraguan socialist politician, head of state 1981–90. He was a member of the Sandinista Liberation Front (FSLN), which overthrew the regime of Anastasio Somoza 1979. US-sponsored Contra guerrillas opposed his government from 1982. In Feb 1990, Ortega lost the presidency to US-backed Violeta Chamorro.

Özal Turgut 1927–1993. Turkish Islamic right-wing politician, prime minister 1983–89, president 1989–93. He was responsible for improving his country's relations with Greece, but his prime objective was to strengthen Turkey's alliance with the USA. He died in office and was succeeded by Suleyman Demirel.

Palme (Sven) Olof 1927–1986. Swedish social-democratic politician, prime minister 1969–76 and 1982–86. As prime minister he carried out constitutional reforms, turning the Riksdag into a single-chamber parliament and stripping the monarch of power, and was widely respected for his support of Third World countries. He was assassinated Feb 1986.

Papandreou Andreas 1919– . Greek socialist politician, founder of the Pan-Hellenic Socialist Movement (PASOK), and prime minister 1981–89, when he became implicated in the alleged embezzlement and diversion of funds to the Greek government of $200 million from the Bank of Crete, headed by George Koskotas, and as a result lost the election. In Jan 1992, a trial cleared Papandreou of all corruption charges.

Paz (Estenssoro) Victor 1907– . President of Bolivia 1952–56, 1960–64, and 1985–89. He founded and led the Movimiento Nacionalista Revolucionario (MNR), which seized power 1952. His regime extended the vote to Indians, nationalized the country's largest tin mines, embarked on a programme of agrarian reform, and brought inflation under control.

Pérez de Cuéllar Javier 1920– . Peruvian diplomat, secretary general of the United Nations 1982–91. He raised the standing of the UN by his successful diplomacy in ending the Iran–Iraq War 1988 and securing the independence of Namibia 1989.

Perón Juan (Domingo) 1895–1974. Argentine politician, dictator 1946–55 and from 1973 until his death. His populist appeal to the poor was enhanced by the charisma and political work of his second wife Eva (Evita) Perón. After her death in 1952 his popularity waned and he was deposed in a military coup 1955. He returned from exile to the presidency 1973, but died in office 1974, and was succeeded by his third wife Isabel Perón.

Pinochet (Ugarte) Augusto 1915– . Military ruler of Chile from 1973, when a coup backed by the US Central Intelligence Agency ousted and killed President Salvador Allende. Pinochet took over the presidency and governed ruthlessly, crushing all opposition. He was voted out of power when general elections were held in Dec 1989 but remains head of the armed forces until 1997. In 1990, his attempt to reassert political influence was firmly censured by President Patricio Aylwin.

Pol Pot (also known as ***Saloth Sar***, ***Tol Saut***, and ***Pol Porth***) 1925– . Cambodian politician and leader of the Khmer Rouge communist movement that overthrew the government 1975. After widespread atrocities against the civilian population, his regime was deposed by a Vietnamese invasion 1979. Pol Pot continued to help lead the Khmer Rouge despite officially resigning from all positions in 1989.

Prime ministers of India

Term	*Name*	*Party*
1949–64	Jawaharlal Nehru	Congress
1964–66	Lal Bahadur Shastri	Congress
1966–77	Indira Gandhi	Congress (I)
1977–79	Morarji Desai	Janata
1979–80	Charan Singh	Janata/Lok Dal
1980–84	Indira Gandhi	Congress (I)
1984–89	Rajiv Gandhi	Congress (I)
1989–90	Viswanath Pratap Singh	Janata Dal
1990–91	Chandra Shekhar	Janata Dal (Socialist)
1991–	P V Narasimha Rao	Congress (I)

Rabin Yitzhak 1922– . Israeli Labour politician, prime minister 1974–77 and from 1992. Rabin was minister for defence under the conservative Likud coalition government 1984–90. His policy of favouring Palestinian self-government in the occupied territories contributed to the success of the centre-left party in the 1992 elections. Shortly after taking office he visited Egypt's President Hosni Mubarak July 1992 as the first step in negotiating an Arab-Israeli peace accord.

Rafsanjani Hojatoleslam Ali Akbar Hashemi 1934– . Iranian politician and cleric, president from 1989. When his former teacher Ayatollah Khomeini returned after the revolution of 1979–80, Rafsanjani became the speaker of the Iranian parliament and, after Khomeini's death, state president and effective political leader. He was re-elected with a reduced majority 1993.

Ramos Fidel (Eddie) 1928– . Philippine politician and president from 1992. He was Corazon Aquino's staunchest ally as defence secretary, and was later nominated her successor.

Reagan Ronald (Wilson) 1911– . 40th president of the USA 1981–89, a Republican. He was governor of California 1966–74, and a former Hollywood actor. Reagan was a hawkish and popular president. He adopted an aggressive policy in Central America, attempting to overthrow the government of Nicaragua, and invading Grenada 1983. In 1987, Irangate was investigated by the Tower Commission; Reagan admitted that USA–Iran negotiations had become an 'arms for hostages deal', but denied knowledge of resultant funds being illegally sent to the Contras in Nicaragua. He increased military spending (sending the national budget deficit to record levels), cut social programmes, introduced deregulation of domestic markets, and cut taxes. His Strategic Defense Initiative, announced 1983, proved controversial owing to the cost and unfeasibility. He was succeeded by George Bush.

Reynolds Albert 1933– . Irish politician, prime minister from 1992. He joined Fianna Fáil 1977, and held various government posts including minister for industry and commerce 1987–88 and minister of finance 1989–92. He became prime minister when

Charles Haughey was forced to resign Jan 1992, but his government was defeated on a vote of confidence Nov 1992. Subsequent elections gave no party an overall majority but, after prolonged negotiations, Reynolds succeeded in forming a Fianna Faíl–Labour coalition.

Robinson Mary 1944– . Irish Labour politician, president from 1990. She became a professor of law at 25. A strong supporter of women's rights, she has campaigned for the liberalization of Ireland's laws prohibiting divorce and abortion.

Rocard Michel 1930– . French socialist politician, prime minister 1988–91. A former radical, he joined the Socialist Party (PS) 1973, emerging as leader of its moderate social-democratic wing. He held ministerial office under President François Mitterrand 1981–85.

Sadat Anwar 1918–1981. Egyptian politician. Succeeding Nasser as president 1970, he restored morale by his handling of the Egyptian campaign in the 1973 war against Israel. In 1974, his plan for economic, social, and political reform to transform Egypt was unanimously adopted in a referendum. In 1977, he visited Israel to reconcile the two countries, and shared the Nobel Peace Prize with Israeli prime minister Menachem Begin 1978. He was assassinated by Islamic fundamentalists.

Salazar Antonio de Oliveira 1889–1970. Portuguese prime minister 1932–68 who exercised a virtual dictatorship. During World War II, he maintained Portuguese neutrality but fought long colonial wars in Africa (Angola and Mozambique) that impeded his country's economic development as well as that of the colonies.

Salinas de Gortiari Carlos 1948– . Mexican politician, president from 1988, a member of the dominant Institutional Revolutionary Party (RPI). Educated in Mexico and the USA, he taught at Harvard and in Mexico before joining the government in 1971 and thereafter held a number of posts, mostly in the economic sphere, including finance minister. He narrowly won the 1988 presidnetial election, despite allegations of fraud.

Sarney (Costa) José 1930– . Brazilian politician, member of the centre-left Democratic Movement (PMDB), president 1985–90. He was succeeded by Fernando Collor.

Schlüter Poul Holmskov 1929– . Danish right-wing politician, leader of the Conservative People's Party (KF) from 1974 and prime minister 1982–93. Having joined the KF in his youth, he trained as a lawyer and then entered the Danish parliament (Folketing) in 1964. His centre-right coalition survived the 1990 election and was reconstituted, with Liberal support. In Jan 1993, Schlüter resigned, accused of dishonesty regarding his role in an incident involving Tamil refugees. He was succeeded by Poul Nyrup Rasmussen.

Schmidt Helmut 1918– . German socialist politician, member of the Social Democratic Party (SPD), chancellor of West Germany 1974–83. As chancellor, Schmidt introduced social reforms and continued Brandt's policy of Ostpolitik. With the French president Giscard d'Estaing, he instigated annual world and European economic summits. He was a firm supporter of NATO and of the deployment of US nuclear missiles in West Germany during the early 1980s.

Shamir Yitzhak 1915– . Polish-born Israeli right-wing politician; prime minister 1983–84 and 1986–92; leader of the Likud (Consolidation Party) until 1993. He was foreign minister under Menachem Begin 1980–83, and again foreign minister in the Peres unity government 1984–86.

Shevardnadze Edvard 1928– . Georgian politician, Soviet foreign minister 1985–91, head of state of Georgia from 1992. A supporter of Gorbachev, he was first secretary of the Georgian Communist Party from 1972 and an advocate of economic reform. In 1985, he became a member of the Politburo, working for détente and disarmament. In July 1991, he resigned from the Communist Party (CPSU) and, along with other reformers and leading democrats, established the Democratic Reform Movement. In March 1992, he was chosen as chair of Georgia's ruling military council, and in Oct elected speaker of parliament.

Shushkevich Stanislav 1934– . Belarus politician, president from 1991 after the attempted Soviet coup in Moscow. He was elected to parliament as a 'reform communist' 1990 and played a key role in the creation of the Commonwealth of Independent States as the successor to the Soviet Union.

Sihanouk Norodom 1922– . Cambodian politician, king 1941–55, prime minister 1955–70, when his government was overthrown by a military coup led by Lon Nol. With Pol Pot's resistance front, he overthrew Lon Nol 1975 and again became prime minister 1975–76, when he was forced to resign by the Khmer Rouge. He returned from exile Nov 1991 under the auspices of a United Nations-brokered

Prime ministers of Japan from 1945

Term	*Name*	*Party*
1945–46	Kijurō Shidehara	coalition
1946–47	Shigeru Yoshida	Liberal
1947–48	Tetsu Katayama	coalition
1948–48	Hitoshi Ashida	Democratic
1948–54	Shigeru Yoshida	Liberal
1954–56	Ichirō Hatoyama	Liberal*
1956–57	Tanzan Ishibashi	LDP
1957–60	Nobusuke Kishi	LDP
1960–64	Hayato Ikeda	LDP
1964–72	Eisaku Satō	LDP
1972–74	Kakuei Tanaka	LDP
1974–76	Takeo Miki	LDP
1976–78	Takeo Fukuda	LDP
1978–80	Masayoshi Ohira	LDP
1980–82	Zenkō Suzuki	LDP
1982–87	Yasuhiro Nakasone	LDP
1987–89	Noboru Takeshita	LDP
1989–89	Sōsuke Uno	LDP
1989–91	Toshiki Kaifu	LDP
1991–93	Kiichi Miyazawa	LDP
1993–	Morohiro Hosokawa	JNP-led coalition

** The conservative parties merged 1955 to form the Liberal Democratic Party (LDP, Jiyū-Minshūtō).*

peace settlement to head the Supreme National Council, a new coalition comprising all Cambodia's warring factions, including the Khmer Rouge. On his return, Sihanouk called for an international trial of the leaders of the Khmer Rouge on charges of genocide.

Smith Ian (Douglas) 1919– . Rhodesian politician. He was a founder of the Rhodesian Front 1962 and prime minister 1964–79. In 1965, he made a unilateral declaration of Rhodesia's independence and, despite United Nations sanctions, maintained his regime with tenacity. In 1979, he was succeeded as prime minister by Bishop Abel Muzorewa, when the country was renamed Zimbabwe. He was suspended from the Zimbabwe parliament April 1987 and resigned in May as head of the white opposition party.

Soares Mario 1924– . Portuguese socialist politician, president from 1986. Exiled 1970, he returned to Portugal 1974, and, as leader of the Portuguese Socialist Party, was prime minister 1976–78. He resigned as party leader 1980, but in 1986 he was elected Portugal's first socialist president.

Stroessner Alfredo 1912– . Military leader and president of Paraguay 1954–89. As head of the armed forces from 1951, he seized power in a coup in 1954 sponsored by the right-wing ruling Colorado Party. Accused by his opponents of harsh repression, his regime spent heavily on the military to preserve his authority. He was ousted in an army-led coup and gained asylum in Brazil.

Suharto Raden 1921– . Indonesian politician and general. He ousted Sukarno to become president 1967. He ended confrontation with Malaysia, invaded East Timor 1975, and reached a cooperation agreement with Papua New Guinea 1979. His authoritarian rule has met with domestic opposition from the left.

Sukarno Achmed 1901–1970. Indonesian nationalist, president 1945–67. During World War II, he cooperated in the local administration set up by the Japanese, replacing Dutch rule. After the war, he became the first president of the new Indonesian republic, becoming president-for-life in 1966; he was ousted by Suharto.

Tambo Oliver 1917–1993. South African nationalist politician, in exile 1960–90, president of the African National Congress (ANC) 1977–91. Because of poor health, he was given the honorary post of national chair July 1991, and Nelson Mandela resumed the ANC presidency.

Thant, U 1909–1974. Burmese diplomat, secretary general of the United Nations 1962–71. He helped to resolve the US–Soviet crisis over the Soviet installation of missiles in Cuba, and made the controversial decision to withdraw the UN peacekeeping force from the Egypt–Israel border.

Thatcher Margaret Hilda (born Roberts), Baroness Thatcher of Kesteven 1925– . British Conservative politician, prime minister 1979–90. She was education minister 1970–74 and Conservative Party leader from 1975. In 1982, she sent British troops to recapture the Falkland Islands from Argentina. She confronted trade-union power during the miners' strike 1984–85, sold off majority stakes in many public utilities to the private sector, and reduced the influence of local government through such measures as the abolition of metropolitan councils, the control of expenditure through 'rate-capping', and the introduction of the community charge, or poll tax, from 1989. In 1990, splits in the cabinet over the issues of Europe and consensus government forced her resignation. An astute Parliamentary tactician, she tolerated little disagreement, either from the opposition or from within her own party. She was created a life peer 1992.

Tito adopted name of Josip Broz 1892–1980. Yugoslav communist politician, in power from 1945. In World War II, he organized the National Liberation Army to carry on guerrilla warfare against the German invasion 1941, and was created marshal 1943. As prime minister 1946–53 and president from 1953, he followed a foreign policy of 'positive neutralism'.

Trudeau Pierre (Elliott) 1919– . Canadian Liberal politician. He was prime minister 1968–79 and 1980–84. In 1980, having won again by a landslide on a platform opposing Québec separatism, he helped to defeat the Québec independence movement in a referendum. He repatriated the constitution from Britain 1982, but by 1984 had so lost support that he resigned.

Truman Harry S 1884–1972. 33rd president of the USA 1945–53, a Democrat. In Jan 1945, he became vice president to F D Roosevelt, and president when Roosevelt died in April that year. He used the atom bomb against Japan, launched the Marshall Plan to restore W Europe's economy, and nurtured the European Community and NATO (including the rearmament of West Germany).

Tutu Desmond (Mpilo) 1931– . South African priest, Anglican archbishop of Cape Town and general secretary of the South African Council of Churches 1979–84. One of the leading figures in the struggle against apartheid in the Republic of South Africa, he was awarded the Nobel Peace Prize 1984.

Ulbricht Walter 1893–1973. East German communist politician, in power 1960–71. He lived in exile in the USSR during Hitler's rule 1933–45. A Stalinist, he became first secretary of the Socialist Unity Party in East Germany 1950 and (as chair of the Council of State from 1960) was instrumental in the building of the Berlin Wall 1961. He established East Germany's economy and recognition outside the Eastern European bloc.

Vranitzky Franz 1937– . Austrian socialist politician, federal chancellor from 1986. A banker, he entered the political arena through the moderate, left-of-centre Socialist Party of Austria (SPÖ), and became minister of finance 1984. He succeeded Fred Sinowatz as federal chancellor 1986, heading an SPÖ–ÖVP (Austrian People's Party) coalition.

Waldheim Kurt 1918– . Austrian politician and diplomat, president 1986-92. He was secretary general of the United Nations 1972–81, having been Austria's representative there 1964–68 and 1970–71. He was elected president of Austria despite revelations that during World War II he had been an intelligence officer in an army unit responsible for transporting Jews to death camps. However, with mounting international pressure, in 1991 he announced that he would not run for re-election.

Wałesa Lech 1943– . Polish trade-union leader and president of Poland from 1990, founder of Solidarity (Solidarność) in 1980, an organization, independent of the Communist Party, which forced substantial political and economic concessions from the Polish government 1980–81 until being outlawed. During his presidency, his public standing diminished and economic problems increased. Nobel Peace Prize 1983.

Wilson (James) Harold, Baron Wilson of Rievaulx 1916– . British Labour politician, party leader from 1963, prime minister 1964–70 and 1974–76. His premiership was dominated by the issue of UK admission to membership of the European Community, the social contract (unofficial agreement with the trade unions), and economic difficulties. He was knighted 1976 and made a peer 1983.

Yeltsin Boris Nikolayevich 1931– . Russian politician, president of the Russian Soviet Federative Socialist Republic (RSFSR) 1990–91, and president of the newly independent Russian Federation from 1991. He directed the Federation's secession from the USSR and the formation of a new, decentralized confederation, the Commonwealth of Independent States (CIS), with himself as the most powerful leader. A referendum 1993 supported his policies of price deregulation and accelerated privatization, despite severe economic problems and civil unrest. He has consistently requested international aid to bring his country out of recession.

Zhao Ziyang 1918– . Chinese politician, prime minister 1980–87 and secretary of the Chinese Communist Party 1987–89. His reforms included self-management and incentives for workers and factories. He lost his secretaryship and other posts after the Tiananmen Square massacre in Beijing June 1989.

Zhelev Zhelyu 1935– . Bulgarian politician, president since 1990. He was expelled from the Bulgarian Communist Party because of his criticisms of Lenin; in 1989, he became head of the opposition movement, the Democratic Forces coalition. He was nominated, unopposed, for the presidency in 1990 after the demise of the 'reform communist' regime, and was directly elected to the post 1992. He is a proponent of market-centred economic reform and social peace.

Zhivkov Todor 1911– . Bulgarian Communist Party leader 1954–89, prime minister 1962–71, president 1971–89. His period in office was one of caution and conservatism. In 1991, he was tried for gross embezzlement.

Zia ul-Haq Mohammad 1924–1988. Pakistani general, in power from 1977 until his death, probably an assassination, in an aircraft explosion. He became army chief of staff 1976, led the military coup against Zulfikar Ali Bhutto 1977, and became president 1978. Zia introduced a fundamentalist Islamic regime and restricted political activity.

Revolutions

Revolution any rapid, far-reaching, or violent change in the political, social, or economic structure of society. It has usually been applied to different forms of political change; the American Revolution (War of Independence) where colonists broke free from their colonial ties and established a sovereign, independent state; the French Revolution, where an absolute monarchy was overthrown by opposition from inside the country and a popular rising; and the Russian Revolution, where a repressive monarchy was overthrown by those seeking to institute widespread social and economic changes in line with a socialist model. While political revolutions are often associated with violence, there are other types of change, which often have just as much impact on society. Most notable is the Industrial Revolution, a process that has imposed massive changes on economies and societies since the mid-18th century. In the 1980s, a new 'silicon' revolution can be identified, involving the increasing use of computers to undertake tasks formerly done 'by hand'.

Industrial Revolution the sudden acceleration of technical development that occurred in Europe from the late 18th century, and which transferred the balance of political power from the landowner to the industrial capitalist, and created an organized industrial working class. The great achievement of the first phase (to 1830) was the invention of the steam engine in Britain, originally developed for draining mines, but rapidly put to use in factories and in the railways. In the second phase, from 1830 to the early 20th century, the Industrial Revolution enlarged its scope from Europe to the world, with some initial exploitation of 'colonial' possessions by European powers as a preliminary to their independent development. During this period, the internal combustion engine and electricity were developed. In 1911, Rutherford split the atom and opened up the prospect of nuclear power. Electronic devices were developed, which made possible automation at such a sophisticated level that even managerial decision-making came within the capabilities of machines.

French Revolution the forcible abolition of the *Ancien Régime* 'old order of things' (feudalism and absolute monarchy) 1789–99.
1789 *5 May* the States General (an assembly of the three 'estates', nobles, clergy, and commons) met at Versailles, bent on establishing a new constitution; *17 June* National Assembly formed by the Third Estate (commons); *14 July* Bastille was taken by the mob when Louis XVI attempted repressive moves.
1791 *20 June* flight of the royal family to Varennes; 14 Sept Louis, brought back as a prisoner, accepted the new constitution.
1792 *20 April* war declared on Austria, which threatened to suppress the revolution; *10 Aug* royal palace stormed by the French mob; *21 Sept* First Republic proclaimed.
1793 *21 Jan* Louis XVI executed; *2 June* overthrow of the moderate Girondists by the Jacobins; rule of the dictatorial Committee of Public Safety; *5 Sept* the mass executions of the Terror began.
1794 *27 July* (9 Thermidor under the Revolutionary calendar) fall of Robespierre and end of the Terror;

the Directory (a body of five directors) established to hold a middle course between Royalism and Jacobinism. It ruled until Napoleon seized power in 1799.

Bastille a fortress prison in Paris, stormed by the mob at the beginning of the revolution on 14 July 1789, when it was found to contain only seven prisoners. The governor and most of the garrison were killed and the building razed.

Commune of Paris first body that took this name between 1789–94 and acted as the municipal government of Paris from the storming of the Bastille to the fall of Robespierre.

Jacobins extremist republican club founded at Versailles in 1789, which later used a former Jacobin (Dominican) friary as its headquarters in Paris. It was led by Robespierre and closed after his execution in 1794.

Girondins right wing republicans of the French Revolution whose leaders came from the Gironde *departement* of France.

Robespierre Maximilien. French politician,'the Sea Green Incorruptible'. As Jacobin leader in the National Convention, he supported the execution of Louis XVI and the overthrow of the Girondins, and as dominant member of the Committee of Public Safety, instituted the Reign of Terror in 1793. His extremist zeal made him enemies on both left and right, resulting in his overthrow and death by guillotine in July 1794.

Danton Georges Jacques. French lawyer and leading revolutionary. Influential in the early years of the revolution in Paris, he was instrumental in organizing the rising of 10 Aug 1792, which overthrew the monarchy. He also helped to instigate the revolutionary tribunal and the Committee of Public Safety in 1793. He led the Committee until July 1793 but was then superseded by Robespierre. An attempt to reassert his power failed and he was guillotined in 1794.

Marat Jean Paul 1743–1793. French revolutionary leader and journalist. He was the idol of the Paris revolutionary crowds, and was elected in 1792 to the National Convention, where he carried on a long struggle with the Girondins, ending in their overthrow in May 1793. In July he was murdered by Charlotte Corday.

revolutions of 1848 a series of revolts in various parts of Europe against monarchial rule. While some of the revolutionaries had republican ideas, many more were motivated by economic grievances. The revolution began in France and then spread to Italy, the Austrian Empire, and to Germany where the short-lived Frankfurt Parliament put forward ideas about German political unity. None of the revolutions enjoyed any lasting success, and most were violently suppressed within a few months.

Indian Mutiny (1857–58) the revolt of the Bengal Army against the British in India. The movement was confined to the north, from Bengal to the Punjab, and central India. Most support came from the army and recently dethroned princes, but in some areas it developed into a peasant rising or general revolt. Outstanding episodes were the seizure of Delhi by the rebels, and its seige and recapture by the British, and the defence of Lucknow by a British garrison. The mutiny led to the end of rule by the British East Indian Co. and its replacement by direct Crown administration.

Paris Commune the second body to bear this name. A provisional government of socialist and left-wing republicans, elected in March 1871 after an attempt by the right-wing National Assembly at Versailles to disarm the Paris National Guard, it held power until May, when the Versailles troops captured Paris and massacred at least 20,000 people. It is famous as the first socialist government in history.

Chinese Revolution a series of major political upheavals which began in 1911 with a nationalist revolt, which overthrew the Manchu imperial dynasty in 1912. Led by Sun Yat-sen (1923–25) and then by Chiang Kai-shek (1925–49), the nationalists came under increasing pressure form the growing communist movement. The 6,000 mile 'Long March' of the Chinese communists (1934–35) to escape from the nationalist forces saw Mao Zedong emerge as leader. After World War II, the conflict expanded into open civil war (1946–49) with the nationalists finally being defeated at Nanking. This effectively established communist rule in China under the leadership of Mao.

Sun Yat-sen or ***Sun Zhong Shan*** 1867–1925. Chinese revolutionary, founder of the Guomindang, and moving spirit behind the revolution of 1911 that overthrew the Manchu dynasty. He was briefly president 1912, but the reactionaries gained the ascendant, and he broke away to try to establish an independent republic in S China based in Canton. He lacked organizational ability, but his three 'people's principles' of nationalism, democracy, and social reform were influential.

Chiang Kai-shek or ***Jiang Jie Shi*** Chinese statesman. He took part in the revolution of 1911, and after the death of Sun Yat-sen was made commander-in-chief of the Guomindang armies in S China in 1925. The initial collaboration with the communists, broken in 1927, was resumed following the Xi An incident, and he nominally headed the struggle against the Japanese invaders, receiving the Japanese surrender in 1945. Civil war then resumed between communists and nationalists, and ended in the defeat of Chiang in 1949 and the limitation of his rule to Taiwan.

Mao Zedong or ***Mao Tse-Tung*** 1893–1976. Chinese statesman, the 'Great Helmsman'. Born in Hunan, he became the leader of the communists in 1927. After the rupture with the nationalists, led by Chiang Kai-shek, Mao Zedong and his troops undertook the 'Long March' of 10,000 km/6000 mi 1934–35 from SE to NW China, the prelude to his ascent to power. Again in nominal alliance with Chiang against the Japanese 1937–45, he subsequently defeated him, and proclaimed the People's Republic of China in 1949. As chairman of the Communist Party, he provided the pattern for the development of the country through the Great Leap Forward of 1959, and the Cultural Revolution of 1966 based on his thoughts contained in the 'Little Red Book'. His reputation plunged after his death, but was later somewhat restored.

Russian Revolution two revolutions of March and Nov 1917, which began with the overthrow of the Romanov Imperial dynasty and ended with the the establishment of a state run by Lenin and the Bolsheviks. The revolution of March 1917 arose in part from the repressive nature of tsarist government but primarily as a result of the mismanagement of World War I after 1914. Riots in St Petersburg led to the abdication of Tsar Nicholas II and the formation of a provisional government under Kerensky. The provisional government ruled until Oct 1917 but found its power increasingly undermined by the soldiers' and workers' soviets in Petrograd (St Petersburg) and Moscow. During this period, the Bolsheviks under Lenin's guidance, had concentrated on gaining control of the soviets and advocating an end to the war and land reform. Under the slogan 'All power to the Soviets', they staged a coup on the night of 6–7 Nov that overthrew the government. The second All-Russian Congress of Soviets, which met the following day, proclaimed itself the new government of Russia. The Bolshevik seizure of power led to peace with Germany through the Treaty of Brest-Litovsk, but also to civil war as anti-Bolshevik elements within the army attempted to seize power. The war lasted until 1920, when the Red Army, organized by Trotsky, finally overcame 'white' opposition.

Lenin Vladimir Ilich Ulyanov 1870–1924. Born 22 April 1870 at Simbinsk (Ulyanovsk), Vladimir Ilich Ulyanov was converted to Marxism in 1889 and exiled to Siberia in 1895 as a result of subversive activity. After 1900, he spent most of his time in Western Europe, emerging as the leader of the more radical Bolshevik section of Russian Social Democracy. Returning to Russia in April 1917 with German help, Lenin assumed control of the Bolshevik movement and was instrumental in organizing the coup of 6–7 Nov. From then until his death in 1924, he effectively controlled Russia, establishing Bolshevik rule and the beginnings of communism. In addition, he consolidated his position as a great Marxist theoretician, modifying traditional Marxist doctrine to fit the objective conditions prevailing in Russia, a doctrine known as Marxism-Leninism which became the basis of communist ideology.

Trotsky Leon 1879–1940. Born 7 Nov 1879 at Yanovka. Communist theorist, agitator, and collaborator with Lenin after the two met in exile in London in 1902. Trotsky was a leading member of the Bolshevik movement in 1917 and helped organize the overthrow of the provisional government. He was instrumental in building up the Red Army to the point where it could win the civil war and acted as commissioner for foreign affairs until 1924. He was ousted during the power struggle which followed Lenin's death, but he remained active in opposing Stalin's rule until he was assassinated in Aug 1940.

Cuban Revolution the overthrow of the Batista regime in Jan 1959 by Fidel Castro and the 26 July Movement. Having led abortive coups in 1953 and 1956, Castro succeeded in overthrowing Batista with a force of only 5,000 men. Politically non-aligned, Castro was increasingly forced to seek Eastern Bloc help for government as a result of US opposition, which culminated in the abortive 'Bay of Pigs' invasion of 1961, sponsored by the CIA. The missile crisis of 1962 highlighted Russian involvement in Cuba. Between 1959 and 1974, Cuba, led by Castro, his brother Raúl, and initially, Che Guevara, adopted economic and social policies based on the principles of Marxism–Leninism and relied almost exclusively on communist help. After 1974, in an attempt to stabilise the economy, Castro reintroduced incentives into society with the maxim that each 'should receive according to his work' rather than according to his need.

Castro Ruz Fidel 1927– . Cuban prime minister. Of wealthy parentage, Castro was educated at Jesuit schools and, after studying law at the University of Havana, gained a reputation through his work for poor clients. He strongly opposed the Batista dictatorship, and with his brother Raúl, took part in an unsuccessful attack on the army barracks at Santiago de Cuba in 1953. After spending some time in exile in the US and Mexico, Castro attempted a secret landing in Cuba in 1956 in which all but 11 of his supporters were killed. He eventually gathered an army of over 5,000 which overthrew Batista in 1959 and he became prime minister a few months later. He became president in 1976, and in 1979 also president of the Non-Aligned Movement. His brother Raúl was appointed minister of armed forces in 1959.

Guevara Ernesto 'Che' 1928–67. Revolutionary. Born in Argentina, he was trained as a doctor, but in 1953 left the country because of his opposition to Peron. In effecting the Cuban revolution of 1959, he was second only to Castro and his brother, but in 1965 moved on to fight against white mercenaries in the Congo, and then to Bolivia, where he was killed in an unsuccessful attempt to lead a peasant rising. His revolutionary technique using minimum resources has been influential, but his orthodox Marxism has been obscured by romanticizing disciples.

Chilean Revolution the period between 1970 and 1973 and the presidency of Salvador Allende, the world's first democratically elected Marxist head of state. Allende was brought to power in 1970 as the head of the Popular Unity alliance of socialists, communists, and radicals, a victory which owed more to the disunity of the Christian Democrat opposition than a major shift in voter preferences. Allende was committed to extensive social and economic reforms to be carried out within the existing political structure – the so-called 'peaceful road to socialism'. Nationalization of key industries and increased contacts with Eastern Bloc countries strained Chile's traditional economic relations with the USA and the West. His failure to stabilize the economy created widespread opposition; Allende was unable to fulfil the expectations of his supporters or quell the fears of his opponents about the pace of change. This led to increasing political polarization which culminated in a military coup in Sept 1973. The Allende regime was overthrown and replaced by a four-man junta led by General Pinochet.

Allende Gossens Salvador 1908– . Born in Valparaiso, Chile, Allende became a Marxist activist in the 1930s and rose to prominence as a left-wing presidential candidate in 1952, 1958, and 1964. In each election he had the support of the socialist and communist movements but was defeated by the Christian

Democrats and Nationalists. Elected in 1970 as the candidate of the Popular Front alliance, Allende never succeeded in keeping the electoral alliance together in government. His failure to solve the country's economic problems or to deal with political subversion allowed the army to stage the 1973 coup which brought about Allende's death, and those of many of his supporters.

Nicaraguan Revolution the revolt led by the FSLN (Sandinist National Liberation Front named after Augusto Cesar Sandino, killed by the National Guard in 1934) against the dictatorship established by the father of the president Anastasio 'Tacho' Somoza. The dictatorship of the Somoza family had been underwritten by US support but this was of little help in 1978–79 when the Sandinistas mounted a full scale challenge to the regime and the hated National Guard. Somoza was forced into exile and assassinated in Paraguay in 1980. Since the revolution, the Sandinistas have taken political control of the country, introducing socialist policies and receiving help from Eastern Bloc countries, while US aid has dried up. The Sandinista government has had to contend with severe economic problems and also the activities of a counter-revolutionary movement, the Contras, operating in the north of the country with US monetary and technical support.

Iranian Revolution the revolution in Iran 1979 that deposed the shah 15 Jan and led to the popular return of Ayatollah Khomeini 1 Feb. Opposition to the shah's one-party regime (introduced 1975) became so great that he was forced to quit the country, leaving the way open for Khomeini's return. Khomeini, exiled for 25 years, had led an effective campaign from France. He appointed Mehdi Bazargan as prime minister 1979–80; real power, however, remained with Khomeini's Islamic Revolutionary Council. Revolutionary forces took control of the country, and Khomeini announced the establishment of the Islamic Republic, in which a return was made to the strict observance of Muslim principles and tradition. The harshness of the Islamic codes caused increasing opposition to Khomeini's regime, which led to a power struggle after his death 1989. The more moderate Hoshemi Rafsanjani became president.

revolutions of 1989 a series of revolutions in various countries of Eastern Europe against communist rule. By 1990, most had moved from monist to pluralist political systems.

Mikhail Gorbachev's official encouragement of *perestroika* (radical restructuring), and *glasnost* (greater political openness), largely for economic reasons, unleashed a wave of simmering discontent, both within the USSR (notably in the Baltic states of Estonia, Latvia, and Lithuania, and in Belarus, the Ukraine, and Moldova) and in several East European countries. Until the late 1980s, any potentially damaging discontent, however widespread, had been kept in check by the use of, or threat of military force controlled from Moscow – as in the termination of the Prague Spring experiment 1968 in Czechoslovakia.

Bulgaria, Czechoslovakia, East Germany, Hungary, Poland, Romania, Albania, and Yugoslavia were not as 'reluctantly content' with their lot as had been supposed, though they still subscribed to a form of one-party communism. Though many of the countries achieved bloodless coups (Bulgaria, Czechoslovakia, and Hungary), some were more dramatic: Romania's 'Christmas Revolution' 1989, in which Nicolae Ceauşescu was shot, was short and bloody. East Germany's revolution witnessed the symbolic dismantling of the Berlin Wall Nov 1989, with formal unification of East and West Germany Oct 1990. In Yugoslavia, the multiparty systems established in Slovenia and Croatia led to several republics calling for secession, and fighting between Serbs and Croats in Croatia 1991.

Roman emperors 27 BC–AD 285

Reign	*Name*
Julio-Claudian emperors	
27 BC–14 AD	Augustus
14–37	Tiberius I
37–41	Caligula (Gaius Caesar)
41–54	Claudius I
54–68	Nero
68–69	Galba
Flavian emperors	
69–79	Vespasian
79–81	Titus
81–96	Domitian
the Five Good emperors	
96–98	Nerva
98–117	Trajan
117–38	Hadrian
138–61*	Antoninus Pius
161–69*	Lucius Verus

*divided voluntarily between two brothers

Reign	*Name*
despotic emperors	
161–80	Marcus Aurelius
180–92	Commodus
193	Pertinax
193	Didius Julianus
the Severi	
193–211	Septimus Severus
211–17	Caracalla
217–18	Macrinus
218–22	Elagabalus
222–35	Severus Alexander
the soldier emperors	
235–38	Maximus the Thracian
238–44	Gordian III
244–49	Philip I, the Arabian
249–51	Decius
251–53	Trebonianus Gallus
253–68	Gallienus
268–70	Claudius II
270–75	Aurelian
275–76	Tacitus
276–76	Florian
276–82	Probus
282–83	Carus
283–85	Carinus

Ottoman emperors 1280–1924

Reign	*Osmanli dynasty*
1280–1324	Osman I
1324–62	Orhan
1362–89	Murad I
1389–1402	Bayezid I, the Thunderbolt (deposed)
1402–03	Isa (claimed Anatolia)
1402–11	Suleiman (claimed Rumelia)
1409–13	Mesa (claimed Rumelia)
1413–21	Mehmed I (claimed Anatolia, 1402-13)
1421–51	Murad II (abdicated in favour of Mehmed II 1444-46)
1451–81	Mehmed II, the Conqueror
1481–1512	Bayezid II (deposed)
1512–20	Selim I, the Grim
1520–66	Suleiman I, the Magnificent
1566–74	Selim II, the Sot
1574–95	Murad III
1595–1603	Mehmed III
1603–17	Ahmed I
1617–18	Mustafa I (deposed)
1618–22	Osman II
1622–23	Mustafa I (restored; deposed)
1623–40	Murad IV
1640–48	Ibrahim (deposed)
1648–87	Mehmed IV (deposed)
1687–91	Suleiman II
1691–95	Ahmed II
1695–1703	Mustafa II (deposed)
1703–30	Ahmed III (deposed)
1730–54	Mahmud I
1754–57	Osman III
1757–74	Mustafa III
1774–89	Abdulhamid I
1789–1807	Selim III (deposed)
1807–08	Mustafa IV (deposed)
1808–39	Mahmud II
1839–61	Abdulmecid I
1861–76	Abdulaziz (deposed)
1876–76	Murad V (deposed)
1876–1909	Abdulhamid II (deposed)
1909–18	Mehmed V Resad
1918–22	Mehmed VI Vahiduddin (deposed)
1922–24	Abdulmecid II (deposed)

Holy Roman emperors

Reign	Name
Carolingian kings and emperors	
800–14	Charlemagne (Charles the Great)
814–40	Louis the Pious
840–55	Lothair I
855–75	Louis II
875–77	Charles II, the Bald
881–87	Charles III, the Fat
891–94	Guido of Spoleto
892–98	Lambert of Spoleto (co-emperor)
896–901	Arnulf (rival)
901–05	Louis III of Provence
905–24	Berengar
911–18	Conrad I of Franconia (rival)
Saxon kings and emperors	
918–36	Henry I, the Fowler
936–73	Otto I, the Great
973–83	Otto II
983–1002	Otto III
1002–24	Henry II, the Saint
Franconian (Salian) emperors	
1024–39	Conrad II
1039–56	Henry III, the Black
1056–1106	Henry IV
1077–80	Rudolf of Swabia (rival)
1081–93	Hermann of Luxembourg (rival)
1093–1101	Conrad of Franconia (rival)
1106–25	Henry V
1126–37	Lothair II
Hohenstaufen kings and emperors	
1138–52	Conrad III
1152–90	Frederick Barbarossa
1190–97	Henry VI
1198–1215	Otto IV
1198–1208	Philip of Swabia (rival)
1215–50	Frederick II
1246–47	Henry Raspe of Thuringia (rival)
1247–56	William of Holland
1250–54	Conrad IV
1254–73	no ruler (the Great Interregnum)
Rulers from various noble families	
1257–72	Richard of Cornwall (rival)
1257–73	Alfonso X of Castile (rival)
1273–91	Rudolf I, Habsburg
1292–98	Adolf I of Nassau
1298–1308	Albert I, Habsburg
1308–13	Henry VII, Luxembourg
1314–47	Louis IV of Bavaria
1314–25	Frederick of Habsburg (co-regent)
1347–78	Charles IV, Luxembourg
1378–1400	Wenceslas of Bohemia
1400	Frederick III of Brunswick
1400–10	Rupert of the Palatinate
1411–37	Sigismund, Luxembourg
Habsburg emperors	
1438–39	Albert II
1440–93	Frederick III
1493–1519	Maximilian I
1519–56	Charles V
1556–64	Ferdinand I
1564–76	Maximilian II
1576–1612	Rudolf II
1612–19	Matthias
1619–37	Ferdinand II
1637–57	Ferdinand III
1658–1705	Leopold I
1705–11	Joseph I
1711–40	Charles VI
1742–45	Charles VII of Bavaria
Habsburg-Lorraine emperors	
745–65	Francis I of Lorraine
1765–90	Joseph II
1790–92	Leopold II
1792–1806	Francis II

Ming dynasty emperors of China

Reign	Name	Born
1368–98	Hongwu	1328
1398–1402	Jianwen	1377
1402–24	Yongle	1360
1424–25	Hongxi	1378
1425–35	Xuande	1399
1435–49	Zhengtong	1427*
1449–57	Jingtai	1428
1457–64	Tianshun	1427
1464–87	Chenghua	1447
1487–1505	Hongzhi	1470
1505–21	Zhengde	1491
1521–67	Jiajing	1507
1567–72	Longqing	1537
1572–1620	Wanli	1563
1620	Taichang	1582
1620–27	Tianqi	1605
1627–44	Chongzhen	1611

** Zhengtong was deposed in 1449 and held captive. He was restored, as Tianshun, in 1457.*

Qing dynasty emperors of China

Reign	Name	Born
1644–61	Shunzhi	1638
1661–1722	Kangxi	1645
1722–35	Yongzheng	1678
1735–96	Qianlong	1711
1796–1820	Jiaqing	1760
1820–50	Daoguang	1782
1850–61	Xianfeng	1831
1861–75	Tongzhi	1856
1875–1908	Guangxu	1871
1908–12	Xuantong*	1906

** Personal name: P'u-i*

Emperors of India

Reign	Name
Mauryan emperors	
325–297 BC	Chandragupta Maurya
297–272 BC	Bindusara
272–268 BC	interregnum
268–232 BC	Asoka
232–224 BC	Dasaratha
224–215 BC	Samprati
215–202 BC	Salisuka
202–195 BC	Devavarman
195–187 BC	Satadhanvan
187–185 BC	Brihadratha
Gupta emperors	
AD 320–50	Chandragupta I
350–76	Samudragupta
376–415	Chandragupta II
415–55	Kumaragupta I
455–70	Skandagupta
470–75	Kumaragupta II
475–500	Budhagupta
500–15	Vainyagupta
515–30	Narasimhagupta
530–40	Kumaragupta III
540–50	Vishnugupta
Mogul emperors	
Great Moguls	
1526–30	Babur (Zahiruddin Muhammad)
1530–56	Humayun (Nasiruddin Muhammad)*
1556–1605	Akbar (Jalaluddin Muhammad)
1605–27	Jahangir (Nuruddin)
1627–28	Dewar Baksh
1628–58	Shah Jahan (Shihabuddin; dethroned)
1658–1707	Aurangzeb (Muhiyuddin)
lesser Moguls	
1707–07	Azam Shah
1707–12	Shah Alam I (Muhammad Mu'azzam)
1712–12	Azim-ush Shan
1712–13	Jahandar Shah (Muhammad Muizzuddin)
1713–19	Farrukh Siyar (Jalaluddin Muhammad)
1719–19	Rafi ud-Darajat (Shamsuddin)
1719–19	Rafi ud-Daula Shah Jahan II
1719–19	Nikusiyar
1719–48	Muhammad Shah (Nasiruddin)
1748–54	Ahmad Shah Bahadur (Abu al-Nasir Muhammad)
1754–60	Alamgir II (Muhammad Azizuddin)
1760–60	Shah Jahan III
1760–1806	Shah Alam II (Jalaluddin Ali Jauhar; deposed briefly in 1788)
1806–37	Akbar Shah II (Muhiyuddin)
1837–58	Bahadur Shah II (Abul al-Zafar Muhammad Sirajuddin; banished)

** Humayun was defeated 1540 and expelled from India until 1555, leaving N India under the control of Sher Shah Suri (died 1545), Islam Shah, and Sikandar Shah.*

Inca emperors

Reign	Name	Relationship
the kingdom of Cuzco		
c. 1200	Manco Capac	traditional founder of Cuzco and the Inca royal house
	Sinchi Roca	son
	Lloque Yupanqui	son
	Mayta Capac	son
	Capac Yupanqui	son
	Inca Roca	son
	Yahuar Huaca	son
	Viracocha Inca	son
the empire		
1438–71	Pachacuti	son; abdicated, died 1471
1471–93	Topa Inca	son
1493–24	Huayna Capac	son
1524–32	Huascar	son; deposed, died 1532
1532	Atahualpa	brother; deposed, died 1533 in the Spanish conquest of the Inca Empire
the Vilcabamba state		
1533	Topa Hualpa	brother
1533–45	Manco Inca	brother
1545–60	Sayri Tupac	son
1560–71	Titu Cusi Yupanqui	brother
1571–72	Tupac Amaru	brother; deposed, died 1572 in the Spanish conquest of the Vilcabamba state

Aztec emperors

Reign*	Name
1372–91	Acamapichtli (chieftain at Tenochtitlán; traditional founder of Aztec royal house)
1391–1416	Huitzilihuitl (son)
1416–27	Chimalpopoca (son)
1427–40	Itzcoatl (son of Acamapichtli)
1468–81	Axayacatl (grandson of Itzcoatl)
1481–86	Tizoc (brother)
1486–1502	Ahuitzotl (brother)
1502–20	Montezuma II, Xocoyotzin (son of Axayacatl)
1520	Cuitlahuac (brother)
1520–21	Cuauhtemoc (son of Ahuitzotl)

* Dates before 1468 are approximate.

Kings of France 751–1848

Reign	Name
Carolingian House (*Robertian House)	
751–68	Pepin the Short
768–814	Charlemagne
814–40	Louis I, the Pious
840–77	Charles I, the Bald
877–79	Louis II, the Stammerer
879–82	Louis III
879–84	Carloman
884–88	Charles II, the Fat
888–93	Eudes
893–922	Charles III, the Simple
922–23	Robert I
923–36	Rudolf*
936–54	Louis IV of Outremer
954–86	Lothair
986–87	Louis V, the Sluggard
Capetian House	
987–96	Hugh Capet
996–1031	Robert II, the Pious
1031–60	Henry I
1060–1108	Philip I
1108–37	Louis VI, the Fat
1137–80	Louis VII, the Younger
1180–1223	Philip II (Philip Augustus)
1223–26	Louis VIII, the Lion
1226–70	St Louis IX
1270–85	Philip III, the Bold
1285–1314	Philip IV, the Fair
1314–16	Louis X, the Stubborn
1316	John I
1316–22	Philip V, the Tall
1322–28	Charles IV, the Fair
House of Valois	
1328–50	Philip VI
1350–64	John II, the Good
1364–80	Charles V, the Wise
1380–1422	Charles VI, the Mad
1422–61	Charles VII, the Victorious
1461–83	Louis XI
1483–98	Charles VIII
1498–1515	Louis XII
1515–47	Francis I
1547–59	Henry II
1559–60	Francis II
1560–74	Charles IX
1574–89	Henry III
House of Bourbon	
1589–1610	Henry IV
1610–43	Louis X1II
1643–1715	Louis XIV
1715–74	Louis XV
1774–92	Louis XVI (deposed)
1792–1803	First Republic
1804–14	House of Bonaparte (First Empire)
1814–24	Louis XVIII
1824–30	Charles X (deposed)
1830–48	Louis Philippe I (deposed)

Rulers of Spain from 1516

Reign	Name
House of Habsburg	
1516–56	Charles I
1556–98	Philip II
1598–1621	Philip III
1621–65	Philip IV
1665–1700	Charles II
House of Bourbon	
1700–46	Philip V
1746–59	Ferdinand VI
1759–88	Charles III
1788–1808	Charles IV
1808	Ferdinand VII (deposed)
1808–13	Joseph Napoleon*
1813–33	Ferdinand VII (restored)
1833–68	Isabel II
1868–70	provisional government
1870–73	Amadeus I † (abdicated)
1873–74	first republic
1874–86	Alfonso XII
1886–1931	Alfonso XIII (deposed)
1931–39	second republic
1939–75	fascist state, General Francisco Franco head of state
1975–	Juan Carlos I

** House of Bonaparte*
† House of Savoy

Kings of Italy 1861–1946

Reign	Name
1861–78	Victor Emmanuel II
1878–1900	Umberto I
1900–46	Victor Emmanuel III
1946–46	Umberto II (abdicated)

House of Habsburg

Reign	Name
emperors of Austria	
1804–35	Francis (Franz) I (of Austria) and II (as Holy Roman emperor until 1806)
1835–48	Ferdinand
emperors of Austria-Hungary	
1848–1916	Franz Josef
1916–18	Charles (Karl; abdicated)

Tsars of Russia 1547–1917

Reign	*Name*
House of Rurik	
1547–84	Ivan the Terrible
1584–98	Theodore I
1598	Irina
House of Gudonov	
1598–1605	Boris Gudonov
1605	Theodore II
usurpers	
1605–06	Dimitri III
1606–10	Basil IV
1610–13	interregnum
House of Romanov	
1613–45	Michael Romanov
1645–76	Alexis
1676–82	Theodore III
1682–96	Peter I and Ivan V (brothers)
1689–1725	Peter I, the Great*
1725–27	Catherine I
1727–30	Peter II
1730–40	Anna Ivanovna
1740–41	Ivan VI
1741–62	Elizabeth
1762	Peter III
1762–96	Catherine II, the Great
1796–1801	Paul I
1801–25	Alexander I
1825–55	Nicholas I
1855–81	Alexander II
1881–94	Alexander III
1894–1917	Nicholas II

** The title of 'tsar' was replaced by 'emperor' from 1721.*

Kings and Queens of Scotland 1005–1603

(from the unification of Scotland to the union of the crowns of Scotland and England)

Reign	*Name*
Celtic kings	
1005	Malcolm II
1034	Duncan I
1040	Macbeth
1057	Malcolm III Canmore
1095	Donald Ban (restored)
1097	Edgar
1107	Alexander I
1124	David
1153	Malcolm IV
1165	William the Lion
1214	Alexander II
1249	Alexander III
1286–90	Margaret of Norway
English domination	
1292–96	John Baliol
1296–1306	annexed to England
House of Bruce	
1306	Robert I, the Bruce
1329	David II
House of Stuart	
1371	Robert II
1390	Robert III
1406	James I
1437	James II
1460	James III
1488	James IV
1513	James V
1542	Mary
1567	James VI
1603	union of crowns

English sovereigns from 900

Reign	*Name*	*Relationship*
West Saxon kings		
901–25	Edward the Elder	son of Alfred the Great
925–40	Athelstan	son of Edward I
940–46	Edmund	half-brother of Athelstan
946–55	Edred	brother of Edmund
955–59	Edwy	son of Edmund
959–75	Edgar	brother of Edwy
975–78	Edward the Martyr	son of Edgar
978–1016	Ethelred II	son of Edgar
1016	Edmund Ironside	son of Ethelred
Danish kings		
1016–35	Canute	son of Sweyn I of Denmark, who conquered England in 1013
1035–40	Harold I	son of Canute
1040–42	Hardicanute	son of Canute
West Saxon kings (restored)		
1042–66	Edward the Confessor	son of Ethelred II
1066	Harold II	son of Godwin
Norman kings		
1066–87	William I	illegitimate son of Duke Robert the Devil
1087–1100	William II	son of William I
1100–35	Henry I	son of William I
1135–54	Stephen	grandson of William II
House of Plantagenet		
1154–89	Henry II	son of Matilda (daughter of Henry I)
1189–99	Richard I	son of Henry II
1199–1216	John	son of Henry II
1216–72	Henry III	son of John
1272–1307	Edward I	son of Henry III
1307–27	Edward II	son of Edward I
1327–77	Edward III	son of Edward II
1377–99	Richard II	son of the Black Prince
House of Lancaster		
1399–1413	Henry IV	son of John of Gaunt
1413–22	Henry V	son of Henry IV
1422–61, 1470–71	Henry VI	son of Henry V
House of York		
1461–70, 1471–83	Edward IV	son of Richard, Duke of York
1483	Edward V	son of Edward IV
1483–85	Richard III	brother of Edward IV
House of Tudor		
1485–1509	Henry VII	son of Edmund Tudor, Earl of Richmond
1509–47	Henry VIII	son of Henry VII
1547–53	Edward VI	son of Henry VIII
1553–58	Mary I	daughter of Henry VIII
1558–1603	Elizabeth I	daughter of Henry VIII
House of Stuart		
1603–25	James I	great-grandson of Margaret (daughter of Henry VIII)
1625–49	Charles I	son of James I
1649–60	***the Commonwealth***	
House of Stuart (restored)		
1660–85	Charles II	son of Charles I
1685–88	James II	son of Charles I
1689–1702	William III and Mary	son of Mary (daughter of Charles I); daughter of James II
1702–14	Anne	daughter of James II
House of Hanover		
1714–27	George I	son of Sophia (granddaughter of James I)
1727–60	George II	son of George I
1760–1820	George III	son of Frederick (son of George II)
1820–30	George IV (regent 1811–20)	son of George III
1830–37	William IV	son of George III
1837–1901	Victoria	daughter of Edward (son of George III)
House of Saxe-Coburg		
1901–10	Edward VII	son of Victoria
House of Windsor		
1910–36	George V	son of Edward VII
1936	Edward VIII	son of George V
1936–52	George VI	son of George V
1952–	Elizabeth II	daughter of George VI

CONTINENTS

Continents

Africa second largest of the continents, three times the area of Europe

area 30,097,000 sq km/11,620,451 sq mi

largest cities (population over 1 million) Cairo, Algiers, Lagos, Kinshasa, Abidjan, Cape Town, Nairobi, Casablanca, El Gîza, Addis Ababa, Luanda, Dar-es Salaam, Ibadan, Douala, Mogadishu

physical dominated by a uniform central plateau comprising a southern tableland with a mean altitude of 1,070 m/3,000 ft that falls northwards to a lower elevated plain with a mean altitude of 400 m/1,300 ft. Although there are no great alpine regions or extensive coastal plains, Africa has a mean altitude of 610 m/2,000 ft, two times greater than Europe. The highest points are Mount Kilimanjaro 5,900 m/ 19,364 ft, and Mount Kenya 5,200 m/17,058 ft; the lowest point in Lac Assal in Djibouti −144 m/−471 ft. Compared with other continents, Africa has few broad estuaries or inlets and therefore has proportionately the shortest coastline (24,000 km/15,000 mi). The geographical extremities of the continental mainland are Cape Hafun in the E, Cape Almadies in the W, Ras Ben Sekka in the N, and Cape Agulhas in the S. The Sahel is a narrow belt of savanna and scrub forest which covers 700 million hectares of west and central Africa; 75% of the continents lies within the tropics

features Great Rift Valley, containing most of the great lakes of E Africa (except Lake Victoria); Atlas Mountains in NW; Drakensberg mountain range in SE; Sahara Desert (world's largest desert) in N; Namib, Kalahari, and Great Karoo deserts in S; Nile, Zaïre, Niger, Zambezi, Limpopo, Volta, and Orange rivers

products has 30% of the world's minerals including diamonds (51%) and gold (47%); produces 11% of world's crude petroleum, 58% of world's cocoa (Ivory Coast, Ghana, Cameroon, Nigeria) 23% of world's coffee (Uganda, Ivory Coast, Zaïre, Ethiopia, Cameroon, Kenya), 20% of the world's groundnuts (Senegal, Nigeria, Sudan, Zaïre), and 21% of the world's hardwood timber (Nigeria, Zaïre, Tanzania, Kenya)

population (1988) 610 million; more than double the 1960 population of 278 million, and rising to an estimated 900 million by 2000; annual growth rate 3%, (10 times greater than Europe); 27% of the world's undernourished people live in sub-Saharan Africa where an estimated 25 million are facing famine

language over 1,000 languages spoken in Africa; Niger-Kordofanian languages including Mandinke, Kwa, Lingala, Bemba, and Bantu (Zulu, Swahili, Kikuyu), spoken over half of Africa from Mauritania in the W to South Africa; Nilo-Saharan languages, including Dinka, Shilluk, Nuer, and Masai, spoken in Central Africa from the bend of the Niger river to the foothills of Ethiopia; Afro-Asiatic (Hamito-Semitic) languages, including Arabic, Berber, Ethiopian, and Amharic, N of Equator; Khoisan languages with 'click' consonants spoken in SW by Bushmen, Hottentots, and Nama people of Namibia

religion Islam in the N and on the E coast as far S as N Mozambique; animism below the Sahara, which survives alongside Christianity (both Catholic and Protestant) in many central and S areas.

Antarctica an ice-covered continent surrounding the South Pole

area 13,900,000 sq km/5,400,000 sq mi (the size of Europe and the USA combined)

physical formed of two blocs of rock with an area of about 8 million sq km/3 million sq mi, Antarctica is covered by a cap of ice that flows slowly towards its 22,400 km/14,000 mi coastline, reaching the sea in high ice cliffs. The most southerly shores are near the 78th parallel in the Ross and Weddell Seas. E Antarctica is a massive bloc of ancient rocks that surface in the Transantarctic Mountains of Victoria Land. Separated by a deep channel, W Antarctica is characterized by the mountainous regions of Graham Land, the Antarctic Peninsula, Palmer Land, and Ellsworth Land; the highest peak is Vinson Massif (5,139 m/ 16,866 ft). Little more than 1% of the land is ice-free. With an estimated volume of 24 million cu m/5.9 million cu mi, the ice-cap has a mean thickness of 1,880 m/6,170 ft and in places reaches depths of 5,000 m/16,000 ft or more. Each annual layer of snow preserves a record of global conditions, and where no melting at the surface of the bedrock has occurred the ice can be a million years old. Occupying 10% of the world's surface, the continent contains 90% of the world's ice and 70% of its fresh water. Winds are strong and temperatures are cold, particularly in the interior where temperatures can drop to −70°C/−100°F and below. Precipitation is largely in the form of snow or hoar-frost rather than rain which rarely exceeds 50 mm/2 in in a year (less than the Sahara Desert). The Antarctic ecosystem is characterized by large numbers of relatively few species of higher plants and animals, and a short food chain from tiny marine plants to whales, seals, penguins, and other sea birds. Only two species of vascular plant are known, but there are about 60 species of moss, 100 species of lichen, and 400 species of algae. The crabeater seal is the most numerous wild large mammal in the world

features Mount Erebus on Ross Island is the world's southernmost active volcano; the Ross Ice Shelf is formed by several glaciers coalescing in the Ross Sea

products cod, Antarctic icefish and krill are fished in Antarctic waters. Whaling, which began in the early 20th century ceased during the 1960s as a result of overfishing. Petroleum, coal, and minerals such as palladium and platinum exist, but their exploitation is prevented by a 50-year ban on commercial mining agreed by 39 nations in 1991

population no permanent residents; settlement limited to scientific research stations with maximum population of 2,000 to 3,000 during the summer months. Sectors of Antarctica are claimed by

Antarctic exploration

1773–7	English explorer James Cook first sailed in Antarctic seas, but exploration was difficult before the development of iron ships able to withstand ice pressure.
1819–21	Antarctica circumnavigated by Russian explorer Fabian Bellingshausen.
1823	British navigator James Weddell sailed into the sea named after him.
1841–42	Scottish explorer James Ross sighted the Great Ice Barrier named after him.
1895	Norwegian explorer Carsten Borchgrevink was one of the first landing party on the continent.
1898	Borchgrevink's British expedition first wintered in Antarctica.
1901–04	English explorer Robert Scott first penetrated the interior of the continent.
1907–08	English explorer Ernest Shackleton came within 182 km/113 mi of the Pole.
1911	Norwegian explorer Roald Amundsen reached the Pole, 14 Dec, overland with dogs.
1912	Scott reached the Pole, 18 Jan, initially aided by ponies.
1928–29	US naval officer Richard Byrd made the first flight to the Pole.
1935	US explorer Lincoln Ellsworth first flew across Antarctica.
1946–48	US explorer Finn Ronne's expedition proved the Antarctic to be one continent.
1957–58	English explorer Vivian Fuchs made the first overland crossing.
1959	Soviet expedition from the West Ice Shelf to the Pole.
1959	International Antarctic Treaty suspended all territorial claims, reserving an area south of 60°S latitude for peaceful purposes.
1961–62	Bentley Trench discovered, which suggested that there may be an Atlantic-Pacific link beneath the Continent.
1966–67	Specially protected areas established internationally for animals and plants.
1979	Fossils of ape-like humanoids resembling E Africa's Proconsul found 500 km/300 mi from the Pole.
1980	International Convention on the exploitation of resources – oil, gas, fish, and krill.
1982	First circumnavigation of Earth (2 Sept 1979–29 Aug 1982) via the Poles by English explorers Ranulph Fiennes and Charles Burton.
1990	Longest unmechanized crossing (6,100 km/3,182 mi) completed by a 6-person international team, using only skis and dogs.
1991	Antarctic Treaty imposing a 50-year ban on mining activity secured.
1992–93	Norwegian lawyer Erling Kagge skied unassisted to South Pole from Berkner Island in Weddell Sea; Ranulph Fiennes and Michael Strond crossed Antarctic continent on foot, unassisted, but had to be rescued before reaching ultimate destination of Scott's Base.

Argentina, Australia, Chile, France, the UK, Norway, and New Zealand

history following multi-national scientific cooperation in Antarctica during the International Geophysical Year of 1957–58, 12 countries signed an Antarctic Treaty with a view to promoting scientific research and keeping Antarctica free from conflict. After it came into effect 1961, a further 27 countries acceded to the treaty. In response to overfishing in Antarctic waters, the Conservation of Antarctic Marine Living Resources was agreed 1980. In 1988 the Convention on the Regulation of Antarctic Mineral Resource Activities gave any signatory the right to veto mining activity on environmental grounds. While this provided a means of regulation, environmental pressure groups felt it would not prevent commercial exploitation. In 1991 an agreement was signed extending the Antarctic Treaty and imposing a 50-year ban on mining activity.

Arctic, the that part of the northern hemisphere surrounding the North Pole; arbitrarily defined as the region lying N of the Arctic Circle (66° 32°N) or N of the tree line. There is no Arctic continent – the greater part of the region comprises the Arctic Ocean which is the world's smallest ocean. Arctic climate, fauna, and flora extend over the islands and northern edges of continental land masses that surround the Arctic Ocean (Svalbard, Iceland, Greenland, Siberia, Scandinavia, Alaska, and Canada)

physical pack ice floating on the Arctic Ocean occupies almost the entire region between the North Pole and the coasts of North America and Eurasia, covering an area that ranges in diameter from 3,000 km/1,900 mi to 4,000 km/2,500 mi. The pack-ice reaches a maximum extent in Feb when its outer limit (influenced by the cold Labrador Current and the warm Gulf Stream) varies from 50°N along the coast of Labrador to 75°N in the Barents Sea N of Scandinavia. In spring the pack-ice begins to break up into ice floes which are carried by the S-flowing Greenland Current to the Atlantic Ocean. Arctic ice is at its minimum area in August. The greatest concentration of icebergs in Arctic regions is found in Baffin Bay. They are derived from the glaciers of W Greenland, then carried along Baffin Bay and down into the N Atlantic where they melt off Labrador and Newfoundland. The Bering Straits are icebound for more than six months each year, but the Barents Sea between Scandinavia and Svalbard is free of ice and is navigable throughout the year. Arctic coastlines, which have emerged from the sea since the last Ice Age, are characterized by deposits of gravel and disintegrated rock

climate permanent ice-sheets and year-round snow cover are found in regions where average monthly temperatures remain below 0°C/32°F, but on land areas where one or more summer months have average temperatues between freezing point and 10°C/50°F, a stunted, treeless tundra vegetation is found. Mean annual temperatures range from –23°C at the North Pole to –12°C on the coast of Alaska. In winter the Sun disappears below the horizon for a time, but the cold is less severe than in parts of E

Siberia or Antarctica. During the short summer season there is a maximum of 24 hours of daylight at the summer solstice on the Artic Circle and six months constant light at the North Pole. Countries with Arctic coastlines established the International Arctic Sciences Committee in 1987 to study ozone depletion and climatic change

flora and fauna the plants of the relatively infertile Arctic tundra (lichens, mosses, grasses, cushion plants, and low shrubs) spring to life during the short summer season and remain dormant for the remaining ten months of the year. There are no annual plants, only perennials. Animal species include reindeer, caribou, musk ox, fox, hare, lemming, wolf, polar bear, seal, and walrus. There are few birds, except in summer, when insects, especially mosquitoes, are plentiful

natural resources the Arctic is rich in coal (Svalbard, Russia), oil and natural gas (Alaska, Canadian Arctic, Russia), and mineral resources, including gold, silver, copper, uranium, lead, zinc, nickel, and bauxite. Because of climatic conditions the Arctic is not suited to navigation and the exploitation of these resources. Murmansk naval base on the Kola Peninsula is the largest in the world

population there are about one million aboriginal people including the Aleuts of Alaska, North American Indians, the Lapps of Scandinavia and Russia, the Yakuts, Samoyeds, Komi, Chukchi, Tungus, and Dolgany of Russia, and the Inuit of Siberian Russia, the Canadian Arctic, and Greenland.

Asia largest of the continents, occupying one third of the total land surface of the world

area 44,000,000 sq km/17,000,000 sq mi

largest cities (population over 5 million) Tokyo, Shanghai, Osaka, Beijing, Seoul, Calcutta, Bombay, Jakarta, Bangkok, Tehran, Hong Kong, Delhi, Tianjin, Karachi

physical lying in the eastern hemisphere, Asia extends from the Arctic Circle to just over 10°S of the Equator. The Asia mainland, which forms the greater part of the Eurasian continent, lies entirely in the northern hemisphere and stretches from Cape Chelyubinsk at its N extremity to Cape Piai at the S tip of the Malay Peninsula. From Dezhneva Cape in

Arctic exploration

60,000–35,000 BC	Ancestors of the Inuit and American Indians began migration from Siberia to North America by the 'lost' landbridge of Beringia.
320 BC	Pytheas, Greek sailor contemporary with Alexander the Great, possibly reached Iceland.
9th–10th centuries AD	Vikings colonized Iceland and Greenland, which then had a much warmer climate.
***c.* 1000**	Norwegian sailor Leif Ericsson reached Baffin Island (NE of Canada) and Labrador.
1497	Genoese pilot Giovanni Caboto first sought the Northwest Passage as a trade route around North America for Henry VII of England.
1553	English navigator Richard Chancellor tried to find the Northeast Passage around Siberia and first established direct English trade with Russia.
1576	English sailor Martin Frobisher reached Frobisher Bay, but found only 'fools' gold' (iron pyrites) for Elizabeth I of England.
1594–97	Dutch navigator Willem Barents made three expeditions in search of the Northeast Passage.
1607	English navigator Henry Hudson failed to cross the Arctic Ocean, but his reports of whales started the northern whaling industry.
1670	Hudson's Bay Company started the fur trade in Canada.
1728	Danish navigator Vitus Bering passed Bering Strait.
1829–33	Scottish explorer John Ross discovered the North Magnetic Pole.
1845	Mysterious disappearance of English explorer John Franklin's expedition to the Northwest Passage stimulated further exploration.
1878–79	Swedish navigator Nils Nordenskјöld was the first European to discover the Northeast Passage.
1893–96	Norwegian explorer Fridtjof Nansen's ship *Fram* drifted across the Arctic, locked in the ice, proving that no Arctic continent existed.
1903–06	Norwegian explorer Roald Amundsen sailed through the Northwest Passage.
1909	US explorer Robert Peary, Matt Henson, and four Inuit reached the North Pole on 2 Apr.
1926	US explorer Richard Byrd and Floyd Bennett flew to the Pole on 9 May.
1926	Italian aviator Umberto Nobile and Amundsen crossed the Pole (Spitzbergen–Alaska) in the airship *Norge* on 12 May.
1954	First regular commercial flights over the short-cut polar route by Scandinavian Airlines.
1958	the US submarine *Nautilus* crossed the Pole beneath the ice.
1960	from this date a Soviet nuclear-powered icebreaker has kept open a 4,000 km/2,500 mi Asia-Europe passage along the north coast of Siberia 150 days a year.
1969	first surface crossing, by dog sled, of the Arctic Ocean (Alaska–Spitzbergen) by Wally Herbert, British Transarctic Expedition, Feb–May.
1977	The Soviet icebreaker *Arktika* made the first surface voyage to the Pole.
1982	first circumnavigation of Earth (2 Sept 1979–29 Aug 1982) via the Poles by Ranulph Fiennes and Charles Burton.
1988	Canadian and Soviet skiers attempted the first overland crossing from the USSR to Canada via the Pole.

the E, the mainland extends W over more than 165° longitude to Cape Baba in Turkey. Containing the world's highest mountains and largest inland seas, Asia can be divided into five physical units:

1) at the heart of the continent, a central triangle of plateaux at varying altitudes (Tibetan Plateau, Tarim Basin, Gobi Desert), surrounded by huge mountains chains which spread in all directions (Himalayas, Karakoram, Hindu Kush, Pamirs, Kunlun, Tien Shan, Altai);

2)the W plateaus and ranges (Elburz, Zagros, Taurus, Great Caucasus mountains) of Afghanistan, Iran, N Iraq, Armenia, and Turkey;

3) the lowlands of Turkestan and Siberia which stretch N of the central mountains to the Arctic Ocean and include large areas in which the subsoil is permanently frozen;

4) the fertile and densely populated E lowlands and river plains of Korea, China, and Indochina, and the islands of the East Indies and Japan;

5) the southern plateaux of Arabia, and the Deccan, with the fertile alluvial plains of the Euphrates, Tigris, Indus, Ganges, Brahmaputra, and Irrawaddy rivers.

In Asiatic Russia are the largest areas of coniferous forest (taiga) in the world. The climate shows great extremes and contrasts, the heart of the continent becoming bitterly cold in winter and extremely hot in summer. When the heated air over land rises, moisture-laden air from the surrounding seas flows in, bringing heavy monsoon rain to all SE Asia, China, and Japan between May and Oct

features Mount Everest at 8,872 m/29,118 ft, is the world's highest mountain; Dead Sea −394 m/−1,293 ft is the world's lowest point below sea level; rivers (over 3,200 km/2,000 mi) include Chiang Jiang (Yangtze), Huang He (Yellow River), Ob-Irtysh, Amur, Lena, Mekong, Yeni sei; lakes (over 18,000 sq km/7,000 sq mi) include Caspian Sea (the largest body of water in the world), Aral Sea, Baikal (largest freshwater lake in Eurasia), Balkhash; deserts include the Gobi, Takla Makan, Syrian Desert, Arabian Desert, Negev

products 62% of the population are employed in agriculture; Asia produces 46% of the world's cereal crops (91% of the world's rice); other crops include mangoes (India), groundnuts (India, China), 84% of the world's copra (Philippines, Indonesia), 93% of the world's rubber (Indonesia, Malaysia, Thailand), tobacco (China), flax (China, Russia), 95% of the world's jute (India, Bangladesh, China), cotton (China, India, Pakistan), silk (China, India), fish (Japan, China, Korea, Thailand); China produces 55% of the world's tungsten; 45% of the world's tin is produced by Malaysia, China, and Indonesia; Saudi Arabia is the world's largest producer of oil

population (1988) 3 billion; the world's largest, though not the fastest-growing population, amounting to more than half the total number of people in the world; between 1950 and 1990 the death rate and infant mortality were reduced by more than 60%; annual growth rate 1.7%; projected to increase to 3,550,000 by 2000

language predominantly tonal languages (Chinese, Japanese) in the E, Indo-Iranian languages (Hindi, Urdu, Persian) in S Asia, Altaic languages (Mongolian, Turkish) in W and Central Asia, Semitic languages (Arabic, Hebrew) in the SW

religion the major religions of the world had their origins in Asia – Judaism and Christianity in the Middle East, Islam in Arabia, Buddhism, Hinduism, and Sikhism in India, Confucianism in China, and Shinto in Japan.

Europe second smallest continent, occupying 8% of the Earth's surface

area 10,400,000 sq km/4,000,000 sq mi

largest cities (population over 1.5 million) Athens, Barcelona, Berlin, Birmingham, Bucharest, Budapest, Hamburg, Istanbul, Kharkov, Kiev, Lisbon, London, Madrid, Manchester, Milan, Moscow, Paris, Rome, St Petersburg, Vienna, Warsaw

physical conventionally occupying that part of Eurasia to the west of the Ural Mountains, north of the Caucasus Mountains and north of the Sea of Marmara; Europe lies entirely in the northern hemisphere between 36°N and the Arctic Ocean. About two-thirds of the continent is a great plain which covers the whole of European Russia and spreads westward through Poland to the Low Countries and the Bay of Biscay. To the north lie the Scandinavian highlands rising to 2,470 m/8,110 ft at Glittertind, in the Jotenheim Range of Norway. To the south, a series of mountain ranges stretch from east to west (Caucasus, Balkans, Carpathians, Apennines, Alps, Pyrenees, and Sierra Nevada). The most westerly point of the mainland is Cape Roca in Portugal; the most southerly location is Tarifa Point in Spain; the most northerly point on the mainland is Nordkynn, in Norway. A line from the Baltic to the Black Sea divides Europe between an eastern continental region and a western region characterized by a series of peninsulas that include Scandinavia (Norway, Sweden, and Finland), Jutland (Denmark and Germany), Iberia (Spain and Portugal), and Italy and the Balkans (Greece, Albania, Croatia, Slovenia, Bosnia-Herzegovina, Yugoslavia, Bulgaria, and European Turkey). Because of the large number of bays, inlets, and peninsulas, the coastline is longer in proportion to its size than that of any other continent. The largest islands adjacent to continental Europe are the British Isles, Novaya Zemlya, Sicily, Sardinia, Crete, Corsica, Gotland (in the Baltic Sea), and the Balearic Islands; other more distant islands associated with Europe include Iceland, Svalbard, Franz Josef Land, Madeira, the Azores, and the Canary Islands. The greater part of Europe falls within the northern temperate zone which is modified by the Gulf Stream in the northwest; Central Europe has warm summers and cold winters; the Mediterranean coast has comparatively mild winters and hot summers

features Mount Elbruz 5,642 m/18,517 ft in the Caucasus mountains is the highest peak in Europe; Mont Blanc 4,807 m/15,772 ft is the highest peak in the Alps; lakes (over 5,100 sq km/2,000 sq mi) include Ladoga, Onega, Vänern; rivers (over 800 km/500 mi) include the Volga, Danube, Dnieper Ural, Don, Pechora, Dneister, Rhine, Loire, Tagus, Ebro, Oder, Prut, Rhône

products nearly 50% of the world's cars are produced in Europe (Germany, France, Italy, Spain, Russia, Georgia, Ukraine, Latvia, Belarus, UK); the rate of fertilizer consumption on agricultural land is four times greater than that in any other continent; Europe produces 43% of the world's barley (Germany, Spain, France, UK), 41% of its rye (Poland, Germany), 31% of its oats (Poland, Germany, Sweden, France), and 24% of its wheat (France, Germany, UK, Romania); Italy, Spain, and Greece produce more than 70% of the world's olive oil

population (1985) 496 million (excluding Turkey and the ex-Soviet republics); annual growth rate 0.3%, projected population of 512 million by 2000

language mostly Indo-European, with a few exceptions, including Finno-Ugrian (Finnish and Hungarian), Basque and Altaic (Turkish); apart from a fringe of Celtic, the NW is Germanic; Letto-Lithuanian languages separate the Germanic from the Slavonic tongues of E Europe; Romance languages spread E-W from Romania through Italy and France to Spain and Portugal

religion Christianity (Protestant, Roman Catholic, Eastern Orthodox), Muslim (Turkey, Albania, Bosnia-Herzegovina, Yugoslavia, Bulgaria), Judaism.

North America third largest of the continents (including Greenland and Central America), and over twice the size of Europe

area 24,000,000 sq km/9,400,000 sq mi

largest cities (population over 1 million) Mexico City, New York, Chicago, Toronto, Los Angeles, Montreal, Guadalajara, Monterrey, Philadelphia, Houston, Guatemala City, Vancouver, Detroit, San Diego, Dallas

physical occupying the N part of the landmass of the western hemisphere between the Arctic Ocean and the tropical SE tip of the isthmus that joins Central America to South America; the northernmost point on the mainland is the tip of Boothia Peninsula in the Canadian Arctic; the northernmost point on adjacent islands is Cape Morris Jesup on Greenland; the most westerly point on the mainland is Cape Prince of Wales, Alaska; the most westerly point on adjacent islands is Attu Island in the Aleutians; the most easterly point on the mainland lies on the SE coast of Labrador; the highest point is Mount McKinley, Alaska 6,194 m/20,320 ft; the lowest point is Badwater in Death Valley −86 m/−282 ft. In Canada and the USA, the Great Plains of the interior separate mountain belts to the E (Appalachians, Laurentian Highlands) and W (Rocky Mountains, Coast Mountains, Cascade Range, Sierra Nevada). The W range extends S into Mexico as the Sierra Madre. The Mississippi river system drains from the central Great Plains into the Gulf of Mexico; low coastal plains on the Atlantic coast are indented by the Gulf of St Lawrence, Bay of Fundy, Delaware Bay, Chesapeake Bay; the St Lawrence and Great Lakes form a rough crescent (with Lake Winnipeg, Lake Athabasca, the Great Bear, and the Great Slave lakes) around the exposed rock of the great Canadian/Laurentian shield, into which Hudson Bay break from the north; Greenland (the largest island in the world next to Australia) is a high, ice-covered plateau with a deeply indented coastline of fjords

features Lake Superior (the largest body of freshwater in the world); Grand Canyon on the Colorado river; Redwood National Park, California has some of the world's tallest trees; San Andreas Fault, California; deserts: Death Valley, Mojave, Sonoran; rivers (over 1,600 km/1,000 mi) include Mississippi, Missouri, Mackenzie, Rio Grande, Yukon, Arkansas, Colorado, Saskatchewan-Bow, Columbia, Red, Peace, Snake

products with abundant resources and an ever-expanding home market, the USA's fast-growing industrial and technological strength has made it less dependent on exports and a dominant economic power throughout the continent. Canada is the world's leading producer of nickel, zinc, uranium, potash, and linseed, and the world's second largest producer of asbestos, silver, titanium, gypsum, sulphur, and molybdenum; Mexico is the world's leading producer of silver and the fourth largest oil producer; the USA is the world's leading producer of salt and the second largest producer of oil and cotton; nearly 30% of the world's beef and veal is produced in North America

population (1988) 417 million, rising to an estimated 450 million by 2000; annual growth rate from 1980 to 1985: Canada 1.08%, USA 0.88%, Mexico 2.59%, Honduras 3.39%; the native American Indian, Inuit, and Aleut peoples are now a minority within a population predominantly of European immigrant origin. Many Africans were brought in as part of the slave trade

language English predominates in Canada, USA, and Belize; Spanish is the chief language of the countries of Latin America and a sizeable minority in the USA; French is spoken by about 25% of the population of Canada, and by people of the French département of St Pierre and Miquelon; indigenous non-European minorities, including the Inuit of Arctic Canada, the Aleuts of Alaska, North American Indians, and the Maya of Central America, have their own languages and dialects

religion Christian and Jewish religions predominate; 97% of Latin Americans, 47% of Canadians, and 21% of those living in the USA are Roman Catholic.

Oceania a general term for the islands of the central and S Pacific, including Australia, New Zealand, and the E half of New Guinea; although situated in the world's largest ocean, Oceania is the smallest continent in the world in terms of land surface

area 8,500,000 sq km/3,300,000 sq mi (land area)

largest cities (population over 500,000) Sydney, Melbourne, Brisbane, Perth, Adelaide, Auckland

physical stretching from the Tropic of Cancer in the N to the S tip of New Zealand, Oceania can be broadly divided into groups of volcanic and coral islands on the basis of the ethnic origins of their inhabitants: Micronesia (Guam, Kiribati, Mariana, Marshall, Caroline Islands), Melanesia (Papua New Guinea, Vanuatu, New Caledonia, Fiji, Solomon Islands) and Polynesia (Tonga, Samoa, Line Islands, Tuvalu, French Polynesia, Pitcairn); Australia (the largest island in the world) occupies more than 90% of the land surface; the highest point is Mount Wilhelm, Papua New Guinea 4,509 m/14,793 ft; the lowest point is Lake Eyre, South Australia −16 m/−52 ft; the longest river is the Murray in SE Australia 2,590 km/1,609 mi

features the Challenger Deep in the Mariana Trench −11,034 m/−36,201 ft is the greatest known depth of sea in the world; Ayers Rock in Northern Territory, Australia is the world's largest monolith; the Great Barrier Reef is the longest coral reef in the world; Mount Kosciusko 2,229 m/7,316 ft in New South Wales, is the highest peak in Australia; Mount Cook 3,764 m/21,353 ft is the highest peak in New Zealand

products with a small home market, Oceania has a manufacturing sector dedicated to servicing domestic requirements and a large export-oriented sector 70% of which is based on exports of primary agricultural or mineral products. Australia is a major producer of bauxite, nickel, silver, cobalt, gold, iron ore, diamonds, lead, and uranium; New Caledonia is a source of cobalt, chromite, and nickel; Papua and New Guinea produces gold and copper

Agricultural products include coconuts, copra, palm oil, coffee, cocoa, phosphates (Nauru), rubber (Papua New Guinea), 40% of the world's wool (Australia, New Zealand); New Zealand and Australia are, respectively, the world's second and third largest producers of mutton and lamb; fishing and tourism are also major industries

population 26 million, rising to 30 million by 2000; annual growth rate from 1980 to 1985 1.5%; Australia accounts for 65% of the population; 1% of Australia's population are Aboriginal and 9% of the people of New Zealand are Maori

language English, French (French Polynesia, New Caledonia, Wallis and Fatuna, Vanuatu); a wide range of indigenous Aboriginal, Maori, Melanesian, Micronesian, and Polynesian languages and dialects (over 700 in Papua New Guinea) are spoken

religion predominantly Christian; 30% of the people of Tonga adhere to the Free Wesleyan Church; 70% of the people of Tokelau adhere to the Congregational Church; French overseas territories are largely Roman Catholic.

South America fourth largest of the continents, nearly twice as large as Europe, occupying 13% of the world's land surface

area 17,864,000 sq km/6,900,000 sq mi

largest cities (population over 2 million) Buenos Aires, São Paulo, Rio de Janeiro, Bogotá, Santiago, Lima, Caracas, Janeiro, Belo Horizonte

physical occupying the S part of the landmass of the western hemisphere, the South American continent stretches from Point Gallinas on the Caribbean coast of Colombia to Cape Horn at the southern tip of Horn Island which lies adjacent to Tierra del Fuego; the most southerly point on the mainland is Cape Froward on the Brunswick peninsula, S Chile; at its maximum width (5,120 km/3,200 mi) the continent stretches from Point Pariñas , Peru in the extreme W to Point Coqueiros, just N of Recife, Brazil, in the E; five-sixths of the continent lies in the southern hemisphere and two-thirds within the tropics. South America can be divided into the following physical regions:

1) the Andes mountain system which begins as three separate ranges in the N and stretches the whole length of the W coast approximately 7,200 km/4,500 mi; the highest peak is Aconcagua 6,960 m/22,834 ft; the width of the Andes ranges from 40 km/25 mi in Chile to 640 km/400 mi in Bolivia; a narrow coastal belt lies between the Andes and the Pacific Ocean;

2) the uplifted remains of the old continental mass, with interior plains at an elevation of 610–1,520 m/2,000–5,000 ft, are found in the E and NE, in the Brazilian Highlands (half the area of Brazil) and Guiana Highlands;

3) the plain of the Orinoco river is an alluvial tropical lowland lying between the Venezuelan Andes and the Guiana Highlands. The tropical Amazon Plain stretches over 3,200 km/2,000 mi from the E foothills of the Andes to the Atlantic ocean, separating the Brazilian and Guiana highlands; once an inland sea, the Amazon basin was filled with sediment and then uplifted;

5) the Pampa-Chaco plain of Argentina, Paraguay, and Bolivia occupies a former bay of the Atlantic that has been filled with sediment brought down from the surrounding highlands;

6) the Patagonian Plateau in the S consists of a series of terraces that rise from the Atlantic Ocean to the foothills of the Andes; glaciation, wind, and rain have dissected these terraces and created rugged land forms

features Lake Titicaca (world's highest navigable lake); La Paz (highest capital city in the world); Atacama Desert; Inca ruins at Machu Picchu; rivers include the Amazon (world's largest and second longest), Parana, Madeira, São Francisco, Purus, Paraguay, Orinoco, Araguaia, Negro, Uruguay

products produces 44% of the world's coffee (Brazil, Colombia), 22% of its cocoa (Brazil), 35% of its citrus fruit, meat (Argentina, Brazil), soybeans (Argentina, Brazil), cotton (Brazil), linseed (Argentina); Argentina is the world's second largest producer of sunflower seed; Brazil is the world's largest producer of bananas, its second largest producer of tin and its third largest producer of manganese, tobacco, and mangoes; Peru is the world's second largest producer of silver; Chile is the world's largest producer of copper

population (1988) 285 million, rising to 550 million by 2000; annual growth rate from 1980 to 1985 2.3%

language Spanish, Portuguese (chief language in Brazil), Dutch (Surinam), French (French Guiana), Amerindian languages; Hindi, Javanese, and Chinese spoken by descendants of Asian immigrants to Surinam and Guyana; a variety of Creole dialects spoken by those of African descent

religion 90–95% Roman Catholic; local animist beliefs among Amerindians; Hindu and Muslim religions predominate among the descendants of Asian immigrants in Surinam and Guyana.

COUNTRIES

Afghanistan

Republic of (*Jamhuria Afghanistan*)

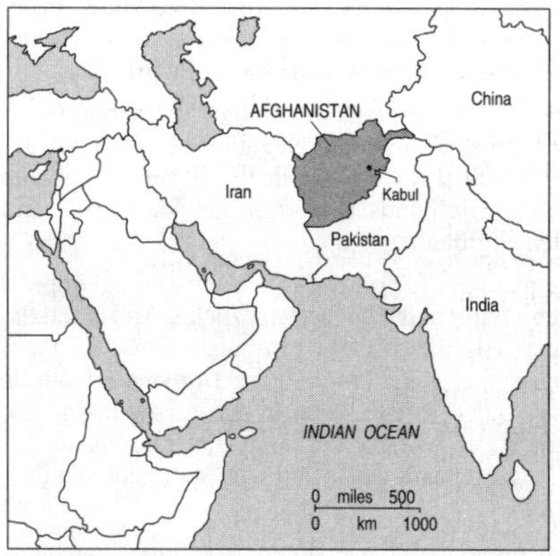

area 652,090 sq km/251,707 sq mi
capital Kabul
towns Kandahar, Herat, Mazar-i-Sharif
physical mountainous in centre and NE, plains in N and SW
environment an estimated 95% of the urban population is without access to sanitation services
features Hindu Kush mountain range (Khyber and Salang passes, Wakhan salient and Panjshir Valley), Amu Darya (Oxus) River, Helmand River, Lake Saberi
head of state Burhanuddin Rabbani from 1992
head of government Gulbuddin Hekmatyar from 1993
political system emergent democracy
political parties Homeland Party (Hezb-i-Watan, formerly People's Democratic Party of Afghanistan, PDPA) Marxist-Leninist; Hezb-i-Islami and Jamiat-i-Islami, Islamic fundamentalist mujaheddin; National Liberation Front, moderate mujaheddin
exports dried fruit, natural gas, fresh fruits, carpets; small amounts of rare minerals, karakul lamb skins, and Afghan coats
currency afgháni
population (1992) 18,052,000 (more than 5 million became refugees after 1979); growth rate 0.6% p.a.
life expectancy (1986) men 43, women 41
languages Pushtu, Dari (Persian)
religion Muslim (80% Sunni, 20% Shi'ite)
literacy men 39%, women 8% (1985 est)
GNP $3.3 bn (1985); $275 per head
GDP $1,858 million; $111 per head
chronology
1747 Afghanistan became an independent emirate.
1839–42 and 1878–80 Afghan Wars instigated by Britain to counter the threat to British India from expanding Russian influence in Afghanistan.
1919 Afghanistan recovered full independence following Third Afghan War.
1953 Lt-Gen Daud Khan became prime minister and introduced reform programme.
1963 Daud Khan forced to resign and constitutional monarchy established.
1973 Monarchy overthrown in coup by Daud Khan.
1978 Daud Khan ousted by Taraki and the PDPA.
1979 Taraki replaced by Hafizullah Amin; USSR entered country to prop up government; they installed Babrak Karmal in power. Amin executed.
1986 Replacement of Karmal as leader by Dr Najibullah Ahmadzai. Partial Soviet troop withdrawal.
1988 New non-Marxist constitution adopted.
1989 Complete withdrawal of Soviet troops; state of emergency imposed in response to intensification of civil war.
1991 US and Soviet military aid withdrawn. Mujaheddin began talks with Russians and Kabul government.
1992 April: Najibullah government overthrown. June: after a succession of short-term presidents, Burhanuddin Rabbani named interim head of state; Islamic law introduced. Sept: Hezb-i-Islami barred from government participation after shell attacks on Kabul. Dec: Rabbani elected president for two-year term by constituent assembly.
1993 Jan: renewed bombardment of Kabul by Hezbi-Islami and other rebel forces. Interim parliament appointed by constituent assembly. March: peace agreement signed between Rabbani and dissident mujaheddin leader Gulbuddin Hekmatyar, under which Hekmatyar became prime minister.

Albania

Republic of (*Republika e Shqipërisë*)

area 28,748 sq km/11,097 sq mi
capital Tiranë
towns Shkodër, Elbasan, Vlorë, chief port Durrës
physical mainly mountainous, with rivers flowing E–W, and a narrow coastal plain
features Dinaric Alps, with wild boar and wolves
head of state Sali Berisha from 1992
head of government Alexander Meksi from 1992
political system emergent democracy
political parties Democratic Party of Albania (PSDS), moderate, market-oriented; Socialist Party of Albania (PSS), ex-communist; Human Rights Union (HMU), Greek minority party

exports crude oil, bitumen, chrome, iron ore, nickel, coal, copper wire, electricity, tobacco, fruit, vegetables
currency lek
population (1992) 3,357,000; growth rate 1.9% p.a.
life expectancy men 69, women 73
languages Albanian, Greek
religion Muslim 70%, although all religion banned 1967–90
literacy 75% (1986)
GNP $2.8 bn (1986 est); $900 per head
GDP $1,313 million; $543 per head

chronology
c. 1468 Albania made part of the Ottoman Empire.
1912 Independence achieved from Turkey.
1925 Republic proclaimed.
1928–39 Monarchy of King Zog.
1939–44 Under Italian and then German rule.
1946 Communist republic proclaimed under the leadership of Enver Hoxha.
1949 Admitted into Comecon.
1961 Break with Khrushchev's USSR.
1967 Albania declared itself the 'first atheist state in the world'.
1978 Break with 'revisionist' China.
1985 Death of Hoxha.
1987 Normal diplomatic relations restored with Canada, Greece, and West Germany.
1988 Attendance of conference of Balkan states for the first time since the 1930s.
1990 One-party system abandoned; first opposition party formed.
1991 Party of Labour of Albania (PLA) won first multiparty elections; Ramiz Alia re-elected president; three successive governments formed. PLA renamed PSS.
1992 Presidential elections won by PSDS; Sali Berisha elected president. Alia and other former communist officials charged with corruption and abuse of power; totalitarian and communist parties banned.
1993 Jan: Nexhmije Hoxha, widow of Enver Hoxha, sentenced to nine years' imprisonment for misuse of government funds 1985–90.

Algeria

Democratic and Popular Republic of (*al-Jumhuriya al-Jazairiya ad-Dimuqratiya ash- Shabiya*)

area 2,381,741 sq km/919,352 sq mi
capital al-Jazair (Algiers)
towns Qacentina/Constantine; ports are Ouahran/Oran, Annaba/Bône
physical coastal plains backed by mountains in N; Sahara desert in S
features Atlas mountains, Barbary Coast, Chott Melrhir depression, Hoggar mountains
head of state Ali Kafi from 1992
head of government Belnid Absessalem from 1992
political system semi-military rule
political parties National Liberation Front (FLN), nationalist socialist; Socialist Forces Front (FSS), Berber-based
exports oil, natural gas, iron, wine, olive oil
currency dinar
population (1992) 26,401,000 (83% Arab, 17% Berber); growth rate 3.0% p.a.
life expectancy men 59, women 62
languages Arabic (official); Berber, French
religion Sunni Muslim (state religion)
literacy men 63%, women 37% (1985 est)
GDP $64.6 bn; $2,796 per head

chronology
1954 War for independence from France led by the FLN.
1962 Independence achieved from France. Republic declared. Ahmed Ben Bella elected prime minister.
1963 Ben Bella elected Algeria's first president.
1965 Ben Bella deposed by military, led by Colonel Houari Boumédienne.
1976 New constitution approved.
1978 Death of Boumédienne.
1979 Benjedid Chadli elected president. Ben Bella released from house arrest. FLN adopted new party structure.
1981 Algeria helped secure release of US prisoners in Iran.
1983 Chadli re-elected.
1988 Riots in protest at government policies; 170 killed. Reform programme introduced. Diplomatic relations with Egypt restored.
1989 Constitutional changes proposed, leading to limited political pluralism.
1990 Fundamentalist Islamic Salvation Front (FIS) won Algerian municipal and provincial elections.
1991 Dec: FIS won first round of multiparty elections.
1992 Jan: Chadli resigned; military took control of government; Mohamed Boudiaf became president; FIS leaders detained. Feb: state of emergency declared. March: FIS ordered to disband. June: Boudiaf assassinated; Ali Kafi chosen as new head of state and Belnid Absessalem as prime minister.

Andorra

Principality of (*Principat d'Andorra*)
area 468 sq km/181 sq mi
capital Andorra-la-Vella
towns Les Escaldes
physical mountainous, with narrow valleys
features the E Pyrenees, Valira River
heads of state Joan Marti i Alanis (bishop of Urgel, Spain) and François Mitterrand (president of France)
head of government Oscar Riba Reig from 1989

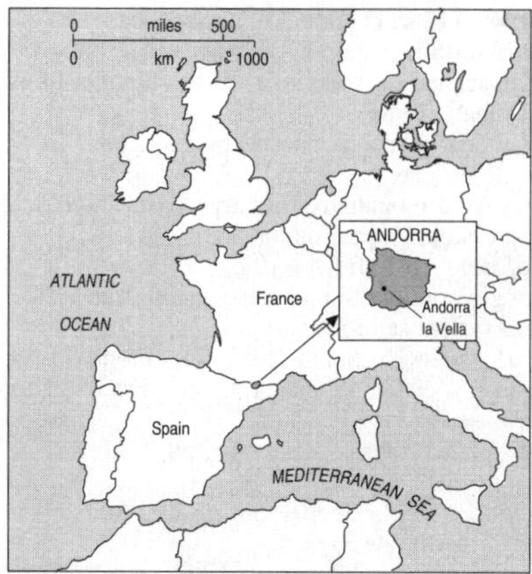

political system semi-feudal co-principality
political party Democratic Party of Andorra
exports main industries are tourism and tobacco
currency French franc and Spanish peseta
population (1992) 57,100 (30% Andorrans, 61% Spanish, 6% French)
languages Catalan (official); Spanish, French
religion Roman Catholic
literacy 100% (1987)
GDP $300 million (1985)

chronology
1278 Treaty signed making Spanish bishop and French count joint rulers of Andorra (through marriage the king of France later inherited the count's right).
1970 Extension of franchise to third-generation female and second-generation male Andorrans.
1976 First political organization (Democratic Party of Andorra) formed.
1977 Franchise extended to first-generation Andorrans.
1981 First prime minister appointed by General Council.
1982 With the appointment of an Executive Council, executive and legislative powers were separated.
1991 Links with European Community (EC) formalized.
1993 First constitution approved in a referendum.

Angola

People's Republic of (*República Popular de Angola*)

area 1,246,700 sq km/481,226 sq mi
capital and chief port Luanda
towns Lobito and Benguela, also ports; Huambo, Lubango
physical narrow coastal plain rises to vast interior plateau with rainforest in NW; desert in S
features Cuanza, Cuito, Cubango, and Cunene rivers; Cabinda enclave
head of state and government José Eduardo dos Santos from 1979
political system socialist republic
political parties People's Movement for the Liberation of Angola–Workers' Party (MPLA–PT), Marxist-Leninist; National Union for the Total Independence of Angola (UNITA); National Front for the Liberation of Angola (FNLA)
exports oil, coffee, diamonds, palm oil, sisal, iron ore, fish
currency kwanza
population (1992) 10,609,000 (largest ethnic group Ovimbundu); growth rate 2.5% p.a.
life expectancy men 40, women 44
languages Portuguese (official); Bantu dialects
religions Roman Catholic 68%, Protestant 20%, animist 12%
literacy 20%
GDP $2.7 bn; $432 per head

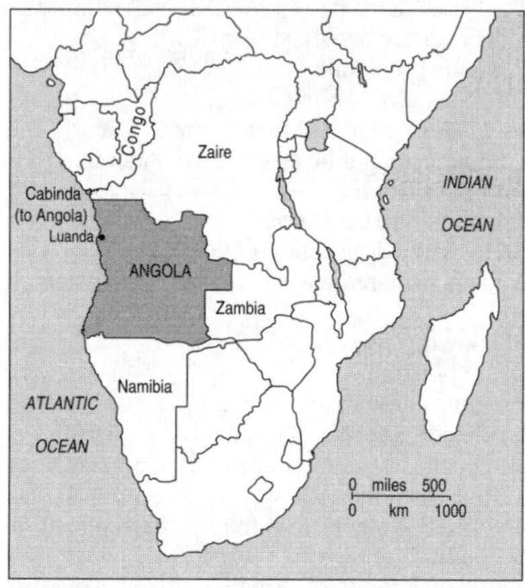

chronology
1951 Angola became an overseas territory of Portugal.
1956 First independence movement formed, the MPLA.
1961 Unsuccessful independence rebellion.
1962 Second nationalist movement formed, the FNLA.
1966 Third nationalist movement formed, UNITA.
1975 Independence achieved from Portugal. Transitional government of independence formed from representatives of MPLA, FNLA, UNITA, and Portuguese government. MPLA proclaimed People's Republic of Angola under the presidency of Dr Agostinho Neto. FNLA and UNITA proclaimed People's Democratic Republic of Angola.
1976 MPLA gained control of most of the country. South African troops withdrawn, but Cuban units remained.
1977 MPLA restructured to become MPLA–PT.
1979 Death of Neto, succeeded by José Eduardo dos Santos.
1980 UNITA guerrillas, aided by South Africa, continued raids against the Luanda government and bases of the South West Africa People's Organization (SWAPO) in Angola.
1984 South Africa promised to withdraw its forces if the Luanda government guaranteed that areas vacated would not by filled by Cuban or SWAPO units (the Lusaka Agreement).
1985 South African forces officially withdrawn.
1986 Further South African raids into Angola. UNITA continued to receive South African support.

1988 Peace treaty, providing for the withdrawal of all foreign troops, signed with South Africa and Cuba.
1989 Cease-fire agreed with UNITA broke down and guerrilla activity restarted.
1990 Peace offer by rebels. Return to multiparty politics promised.
1991 Peace agreement signed, civil war between MPLA–PT and UNITA officially ended. Amnesty for all political prisoners.
1992 MPLA–PT's general-election victory fiercely disputed by UNITA, plunging the country into renewed civil war. UNITA offered, and eventually accepted, seats in the new government, but fighting continued.
1993 MPLA–PT made power-sharing agreement with UNITA.

Antigua and Barbuda

State of

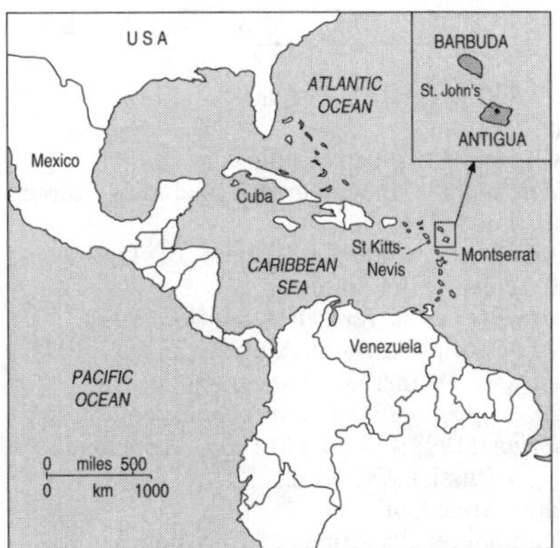

area Antigua 280 sq km/108 sq mi, Barbuda 161 sq km/62 sq mi, plus Redonda 1 sq km/0.4 sq mi
capital and chief port St John's
towns Codrington (on Barbuda)
physical low-lying tropical islands of limestone and coral with some higher volcanic outcrops; no rivers and low rainfall result in frequent droughts and deforestation
features Antigua is the largest of the Leeward Islands; Redonda is an uninhabited island of volcanic rock rising to 305 m/1,000 ft
head of state Elizabeth II from 1981, represented by governor general
head of government Vere C Bird from 1981
political system liberal democracy
political parties Antigua Labour Party (ALP), moderate, left of centre; Progressive Labour Movement (PLM), left of centre
exports sea-island cotton, rum, lobsters
currency Eastern Caribbean dollar
population (1992) 64,000; growth rate 1.3% p.a.
life expectancy 70 years
language English
media no daily newspaper; weekly papers all owned by political parties
religion Christian (mostly Anglican)
literacy 90% (1985)
GDP $173 million (1985); $2,200 per head
chronology
1493 Antigua visited by Christopher Columbus.
1632 Antigua colonized by English settlers.
1667 Treaty of Breda formally ceded Antigua to Britain.
1871–1956 Antigua and Barbuda administered as part of the Leeward Islands federation.
1967 Antigua and Barbuda became an associated state within the Commonwealth, with full internal independence.
1971 PLM won the general election by defeating the ALP.
1976 PLM called for early independence, but ALP urged caution. ALP won the general election.
1981 Independence from Britain achieved.
1983 Assisted US invasion of Grenada.
1984 ALP won a decisive victory in the general election.
1985 ALP re-elected.
1989 Another sweeping general election victory for the ALP under Vere Bird.
1991 Bird remained in power despite calls for his resignation.

Argentina

Republic of (*República Argentina*)

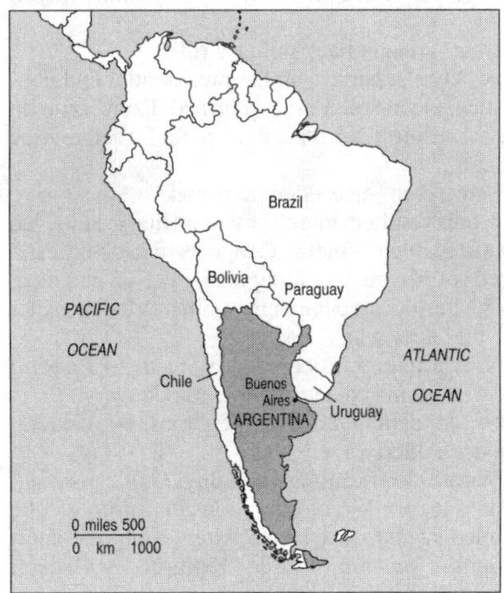

area 2,780,092 sq km/1,073,116 sq mi
capital Buenos Aires (to move to Viedma)
towns Rosario, Córdoba, Tucumán, Mendoza, Santa Fé; ports are La Plata and Bahía Blanca
physical mountains in W, forest and savanna in N, pampas (treeless plains) in E central area, Patagonian plateau in S; rivers Colorado, Salado, Paraná, Uruguay, Río de la Plata estuary
territories part of Tierra del Fuego; disputed claims to S Atlantic islands and part of Antarctica
environment an estimated 20,000 sq km/7,700 sq mi of land has been swamped with salt water
features Andes mountains, with Aconcagua the highest peak in the W hemisphere; Iguaçú Falls

head of state and government Carlos Menem from 1989
political system emergent democratic federal republic
political parties Radical Civic Union Party (UCR), moderate centrist; Justicialist Party, right-wing Peronist
exports livestock products, cereals, wool, tannin, peanuts, linseed oil, minerals (coal, copper, molybdenum, gold, silver, lead, zinc, barium, uranium); the country has huge resources of oil, natural gas, hydroelectric power
currency peso
population (1992) 33,070,000 (mainly of Spanish or Italian origin, only about 30,000 American Indians surviving); growth rate 1.5% p.a.
life expectancy men 66, women 73
languages Spanish (official); English, Italian, German, French
religion Roman Catholic (state-supported)
literacy men 96%, women 95% (1985 est)
GDP $70.1 bn (1990); $2,162 per head

chronology
1816 Independence achieved from Spain, followed by civil wars.
1946 Juan Perón elected president, supported by his wife 'Evita'.
1952 'Evita' Perón died.
1955 Perón overthrown and civilian administration restored.
1966 Coup brought back military rule.
1973 A Peronist party won the presidential and congressional elections. Perón returned from exile in Spain as president, with his third wife, Isabel, as vice president.
1974 Perón died, succeeded by Isabel.
1976 Coup resulted in rule by a military junta led by Lt-Gen Jorge Videla. Congress dissolved, and hundreds of people, including Isabel Perón, detained.
1976–83 Ferocious campaign against left-wing elements, the 'dirty war'.
1978 Videla retired. Succeeded by General Roberto Viola, who promised a return to democracy.
1981 Viola died suddenly. Replaced by General Leopoldo Galtieri.
1982 With a deteriorating economy, Galtieri sought popular support by ordering an invasion of the British-held Falkland Islands. After losing the short war, Galtieri was removed and replaced by General Reynaldo Bignone.
1983 Amnesty law passed and democratic constitution of 1853 revived. General elections won by Raúl Alfonsín and the UCR. Armed forces under scrutiny.
1984 National Commission on the Disappearance of Persons (CONADEP) reported on over 8,000 people who had disappeared during the 'dirty war' of 1976–83.
1985 A deteriorating economy forced Alfonsín to seek help from the International Monetary Fund and introduce an austerity programme.
1986 Unsuccessful attempt on Alfonsín's life.
1988 Unsuccessful army coup.
1989 Carlos Menem, of the Justicialist Party, elected president.
1990 Full diplomatic relations with the UK restored. Menem elected Justicialist Party leader. Revolt by army officers thwarted.
1992 New currency introduced.

Armenia

Republic of

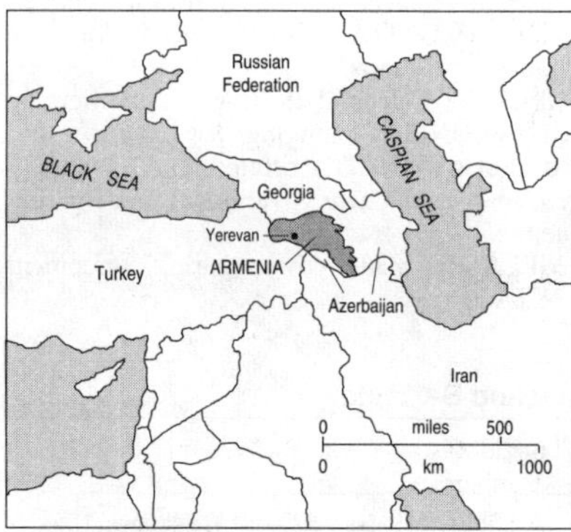

area 29,800 sq km/11,500 sq mi
capital Yerevan
towns Kumayri (formerly Leninakan)
physical mainly mountainous (including Mount Ararat), wooded
features State Academia Theatre of Opera and Ballet; Yerevan Film Studio
head of state Levon Ter-Petrossian from 1990
head of government Gagik Arutyunyan from 1991
political system emergent democracy
products copper, molybdenum, cereals, cotton, silk
population (1992) 3,426,000 (90% Armenian, 5% Azeri, 2% Russian, 2% Kurd)
language Armenian
religion traditionally Armenian Christian

chronology
1918 Became an independent republic.
1920 Occupied by the Red Army.
1936 Became a constituent republic of the USSR.
1988 Feb: demonstrations in Yerevan called for transfer of Nagorno-Karabakh from Azerbaijan to Armenian control. Dec: earthquake claimed around 25,000 lives and caused extensive damage.
1989 Jan–Nov: strife-torn Nagorno-Karabakh placed under direct rule from Moscow. Pro-autonomy Armenian National Movement founded. Nov: civil war erupted with Azerbaijan over Nagorno-Karabakh.
1990 March: Armenia boycotted USSR constitutional referendum. Aug: nationalists secured control of Armenian supreme soviet; former dissident Levon Ter-Petrossian indirectly elected president; independence declared. Nakhichevan republic affected by Nagorno-Karabakh dispute.
1991 March: overwhelming support for independence in referendum. Dec: Armenia joined new Commonwealth of Independent States; Nagorno-Karabakh declared its independence; Armenia granted diplomatic recognition by USA.
1992 Admitted into United Nations and the Conference on Security and Cooperation in Europe. Conflict over Nagorno-Karabakh worsened.

Australia

Commonwealth of

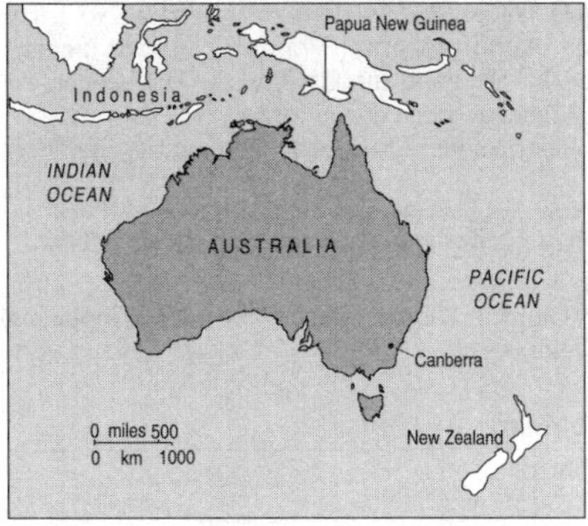

area 7,682,300 sq km/2,966,136 sq mi
capital Canberra

towns Adelaide, Alice Springs, Brisbane, Darwin, Melbourne, Perth, Sydney, Hobart, Geelong, Newcastle, Townsville, Wollongong
physical the world's smallest, flattest, and driest continent (40% lies in the tropics, one-third is desert, and one- third is marginal grazing); Great Sandy Desert; Gibson Desert; Great Victoria Desert; Simpson Desert; the Great Barrier Reef (largest coral reef in the world, stretching 2,000 km/1,250 mi off E coast of Queensland); Great Dividing Range and Australian Alps in the E (Mount Kosciusko, 2,229 m/7,136 ft, Australia's highest peak). The fertile SE region is watered by the Darling, Lachlan, Murrumbridgee, and Murray rivers; rivers in the interior are seasonal. Lake Eyre basin and Nullarbor Plain in the S
territories Norfolk Island, Christmas Island, Cocos (Keeling) Islands, Ashmore and Cartier Islands, Coral Sea Islands, Heard Island and McDonald Islands, Australian Antarctic Territory
environment an estimated 75% of Australia's northern tropical rainforest has been cleared for agriculture or urban development since Europeans first settled there in the early 19th century
features Ayers Rock; Arnhem Land; Gulf of Carpentaria; Cape York Peninsula; Great Australian Bight; unique animal species include the kangaroo, koala, platypus, wombat, Tasmanian devil, and spiny anteater; of 800 species of bird, the budgerigar, cassowary, emu, kookaburra, lyre bird, and black swan are also unique as a result of Australia's long isolation from other continents
head of state Elizabeth II from 1952, represented by governor general
head of government Paul Keating from 1991
political system federal constitutional monarchy
political parties Australian Labor Party, moderate left of centre; Liberal Party of Australia, moderate, liberal, free enterprise; National Party of Australia (formerly Country Party), centrist non-metropolitan
exports world's largest exporter of sheep, wool, diamonds, alumina, coal, lead and refined zinc ores, and mineral sands; other exports include cereals, beef, veal, mutton, lamb, sugar, nickel (world's second largest producer), iron ore; principal trade partners are Japan, the USA, and EC member states
currency Australian dollar
population (1992) 17,562,000; growth rate 1.5% p.a.
life expectancy men 75, women 80
languages English, Aboriginal languages
religions Anglican 26%, other Protestant 17%, Roman Catholic 26%
literacy 98.5.% (1988)
GDP $286.9 bn (1992)

chronology
1901 Creation of Commonwealth of Australia.
1911 Site acquired for capital at Canberra.
1927 Seat of government moved to Canberra.
1942 Statute of Westminster Adoption Act gave Australia autonomy from UK in internal and external affairs.
1944 Liberal Party founded by Robert Menzies.
1951 Australia joined New Zealand and the USA as a signatory to the ANZUS Pacific security treaty.
1966 Menzies resigned after being Liberal prime minister for 17 years, and was succeeded by Harold Holt.
1967 A referendum was passed giving Aborigines full citizenship rights.
1968 John Gorton became prime minister after Holt's death.
1971 Gorton succeeded by William McMahon, heading a Liberal–Country Party coalition.
1972 Gough Whitlam became prime minister, leading a Labor government.
1975 Senate blocked the government's financial legislation; Whitlam dismissed by the governor general, who invited Malcolm Fraser to form a Liberal–Country Party caretaker government. This action of the governor general, John Kerr, was widely criticized.
1977 Kerr resigned.
1978 Northern Territory attained self-government, with Darwin as its capital.
1983 Labor Party, returned to power under Bob Hawke, convened meeting of employers and unions to seek consensus on economic policy to deal with growing unemployment.
1986 Australia Act passed by UK government, eliminating last vestiges of British legal authority in Australia.
1988 Labor foreign minister Bill Hayden appointed governor general designate. Free-trade agreement with New Zealand signed.
1990 Hawke won record fourth election victory, defeating Liberal Party by small majority.
1991 Paul Keating became new Labor Party leader and prime minister.
1992 Keating's popularity declined as economic problems continued. Oath of allegiance to British crown abandoned.
1993 Labor Party won general election, entering fifth term of office.

Austria

Republic of (*Republik Österreich*)

area 83,500 sq km/32,374 sq mi
capital Vienna
towns Graz, Linz, Salzburg, Innsbruck
physical landlocked mountainous state, with Alps in

W and S and low relief in E where most of the population is concentrated
environment Hainburg, the largest primeval forest left in Europe, under threat from a dam project (suspended 1990)
features Austrian Alps (including Grossglockner and Brenner and Semmering passes); Lechtaler and Allgauer Alps N of river Inn; Carnic Alps on Italian border; river Danube
head of state Thomas Klestil from 1992
head of government Franz Vranitzky from 1986
political system democratic federal republic
political parties Socialist Party of Austria (SPÖ), democratic socialist; Austrian People's Party (ÖVP), progressive centrist; Freedom Party of Austria (FPÖ), moderate left of centre; United Green Party of Austria (VGÖ), conservative ecological; Green Alternative Party (ALV), radical ecological
exports lumber, textiles, clothing, iron and steel, paper, machinery and transport equipment, foodstuffs
currency schilling
population (1992) 7,857,000; growth rate 0.1% p.a.
life expectancy men 70, women 77
language German
religions Roman Catholic 85%, Protestant 6%
literacy 98% (1983)
GDP $184.7 bn (1992)

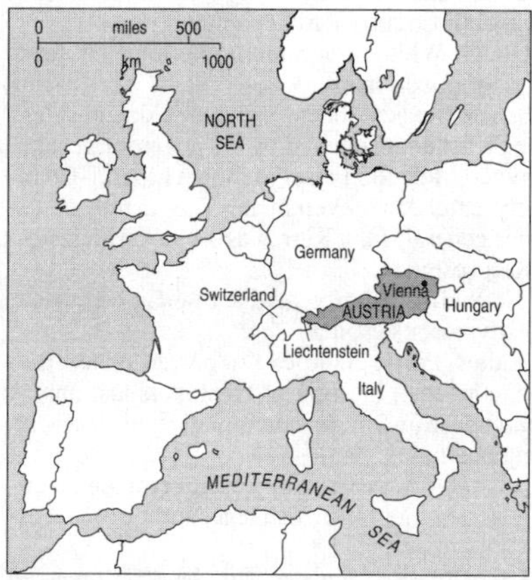

chronology
1867 Emperor Franz Josef established dual monarchy of Austria–Hungary.
1914 Archduke Franz Ferdinand assassinated by a Serbian nationalist; Austria–Hungary invaded Serbia, precipitating World War I.
1918 Habsburg empire ended; republic of Austria proclaimed.
1938 Austria incorporated into German Third Reich by Hitler (the *Anschluss*).
1945 Under Allied occupation, constitution of 1920 reinstated and coalition government formed by the SPÖ and the ÖVP.
1955 Allied occupation ended, and the independence of Austria formally recognized.
1966 ÖVP in power with Josef Klaus as chancellor.
1970 SPÖ formed a minority government, with Dr Bruno Kreisky as chancellor.
1983 Kreisky resigned and was replaced by Dr Fred Sinowatz, leading a coalition.
1986 Dr Kurt Waldheim elected president. Sinowatz resigned, succeeded by Franz Vranitzky. No party won an overall majority; Vranitzky formed a coalition of the SPÖ and the ÖVP, with ÖVP leader, Dr Alois Mock, as vice chancellor.
1989 Austria sought European Community membership.
1990 Vranitzky re-elected.
1991 Bid for EC membership endorsed by the Community.
1992 Thomas Klestil elected president, replacing Waldheim.

Azerbaijan

Republic of

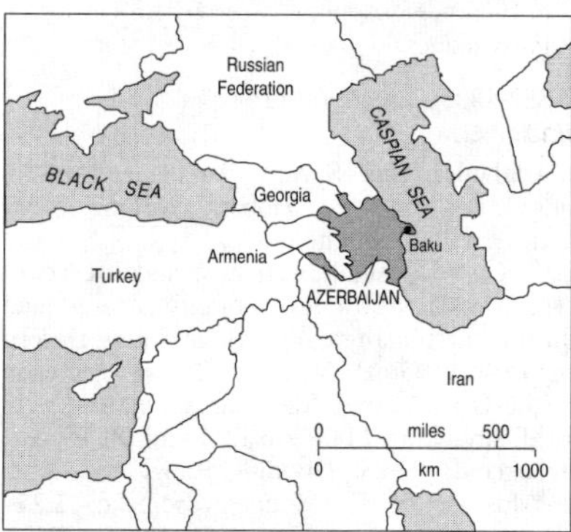

area 86,600 sq km/33,400 sq mi
capital Baku
towns Gyandzha (formerly Kirovabad), Sumgait
physical Caspian Sea; the country ranges from semi-desert to the Caucasus Mountains
head of state Geidar Aliyev from 1993
head of government to be appointed
political system emergent democracy
political parties Republican Democratic Party, ex-communist-dominated; Popular Front, democratic nationalist; Islamic Party, fundamentalist
products oil, iron, copper, fruit, vines, cotton, silk, carpets
population (1992) 7,237,000 (83% Azeri, 6% Russian, 6% Armenian)
language Turkic
religion traditionally Shi'ite Muslim

chronology
1917–18 A member of the anti-Bolshevik Transcaucasian Federation.
1918 Became an independent republic.
1920 Occupied by the Red Army.
1922–36 Formed part of the Transcaucasian Federal Republic with Georgia and Armenia.
1936 Became a constituent republic of the USSR.
1988 Riots followed Nagorno-Karabakh's request for transfer to Armenia.
1989 Jan–Nov: strife-torn Nagorno-Karabakh placed under direct rule from Moscow. Azerbaijan Popular Front established. Nov: civil war erupted with Armenia.

1990 Jan: Soviet troops dispatched to Baku to restore order. Aug: communists won parliamentary elections. Nakhichevan republic affected by Nagorno-Karabakh dispute.
1991 Aug: Azeri leadership supported attempted anti-Gorbachev coup in Moscow; independence declared. Sept: former communist Ayaz Mutalibov elected president. Dec: joined new Commonwealth of Independent States; Nagorno-Karabakh declared independence.
1992 Jan: admitted into Conference on Security and Cooperation in Europe; March: Mutalibov resigned; Azerbaijan became a member of the United Nations; accorded diplomatic recognition by the USA. June: Albulfaz Elchibey, leader of the Popular Front, elected president; renewed campaign against Armenia in the fight for Nagorno-Karabakh.
1993 Prime Minister Rakham Guseinov resigned. President Elchibey ousted, replaced by former Communist Party leader Geidar Aliyev.

Bahamas

Commonwealth of the

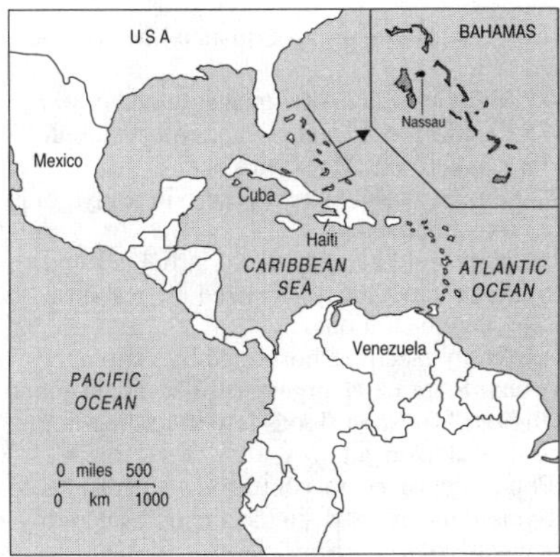

area 13,864 sq km/5,352 sq mi
capital Nassau on New Providence
towns Alice Town, Andros Town, Hope Town, Spanish Wells, Freeport, Moss Town, George Town
physical comprises 700 tropical coral islands and about 1,000 cays
features desert islands: only 30 are inhabited; Blue Holes of Andros, the world's longest and deepest submarine caves; the Exumas are a narrow spine of 365 islands
principal islands Andros, Grand Bahama, Great Abaco, Eleuthera, New Providence, Berry Islands, Biminis, Great Inagua, Acklins, Exumas, Mayaguana, Crooked Island, Long Island, Cat Island, Rum Cay, Watling (San Salvador) Island
head of state Elizabeth II from 1973, represented by governor general
head of government Hubert Ingraham from 1992
political system constitutional monarchy
political parties Progressive Liberal Party (PLP), centrist; Free National Movement (FNM), centre-left
exports cement, pharmaceuticals, petroleum products, crawfish, salt, aragonite, rum, pulpwood; over half the islands' employment comes from tourism
currency Bahamian dollar
population (1992) 264,000; growth rate 1.8% p.a.
languages English and some Creole
media three independent daily newspapers
religions 29% Baptist, 23% Anglican, 22% Roman Catholic
literacy 95% (1986)
GDP $2.7 bn (1987); $11,261 per head

chronology
1964 Independence achieved from Britain.
1967 First national assembly elections; Lynden Pindling became prime minister.
1972 Constitutional conference to discuss full independence.
1973 Full independence achieved.
1983 Allegations of drug trafficking by government ministers.
1984 Deputy prime minister and two cabinet ministers resigned. Pindling denied any personal involvement and was endorsed as party leader.
1987 Pindling re-elected despite claims of frauds.
1992 FNM led by Hubert Ingraham won absolute majority in assembly elections.

Bahrain

State of (*Dawlat al Bahrayn*)

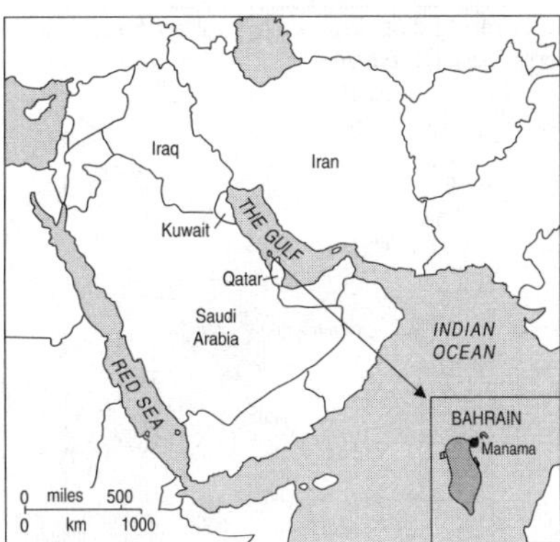

area 688 sq km/266 sq mi
capital Manama on the largest island (also called Bahrain)
towns Muharraq, Jidd Hafs, Isa Town; oil port Mina Sulman
physical 35 islands, composed largely of sand-covered limestone; generally poor and infertile soil; flat and hot
environment a wildlife park on Bahrain preserves the endangered oryx; most of the south of the island is preserved for the ruling family's falconry
features causeway linking Bahrain to mainland Saudi Arabia; Sitra island is a communications centre for the lower Persian Gulf and has a satellite-tracking station
head of state and government Sheik Isa bin Sulman al-Khalifa from 1961
political system absolute emirate
political parties none
exports oil, natural gas, aluminium, fish
currency Bahrain dinar

population (1992) 531,000 (two-thirds are nationals); growth rate 4.4% p.a.
life expectancy men 67, women 71
languages Arabic (official); Farsi, English, Urdu
religion 85% Muslim (Shi'ite 60%, Sunni 40%)
literacy men 79%, women 64% (1985 est)
GDP $3.5 bn (1987); $7,772 per head

chronology

1861 Became British protectorate.
1968 Britain announced its intention to withdraw its forces. Bahrain formed, with Qatar and the Trucial States, the Federation of Arab Emirates.
1971 Qatar and the Trucial States withdrew from the federation and Bahrain became an independent state.
1973 New constitution adopted, with an elected national assembly.
1975 Prime minister resigned and national assembly dissolved. Emir and his family assumed virtually absolute power.
1986 Gulf University established in Bahrain. A causeway was opened linking the island with Saudi Arabia.
1988 Bahrain recognized Afghan rebel government.
1991 Bahrain joined United Nations coalition that ousted Iraq from its occupation of Kuwait.

Bangladesh

People's Republic of (*Gana Prajatantri Bangladesh*) (formerly ***East Pakistan***)

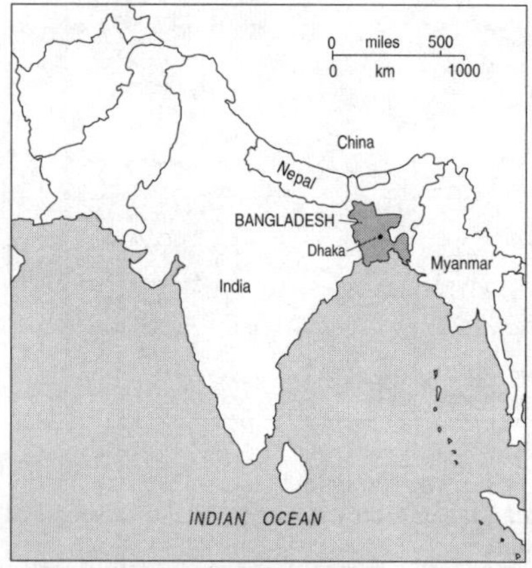

area 144,000 sq km/55,585 sq mi
capital Dhaka (formerly Dacca)
towns ports Chittagong, Khulna
physical flat delta of rivers Ganges (Padma) and Brahmaputra (Jamuna), the largest estuarine delta in the world; annual rainfall of 2,540 mm/100 in; some 75% of the land is less than 3 m/10 ft above sea level; hilly in extreme SE and NE
environment deforestation on the slopes of the Himalayas increases the threat of flooding in the coastal lowlands of Bangladesh, which are also subject to devastating monsoon storms. The building of India's Farakka Barrage has reduced the flow of the Ganges in Bangladesh and permitted salt water to intrude further inland. Increased salinity has destroyed fisheries, contaminated drinking water, and damaged forests
head of state Abdur Rahman Biswas from 1991
head of government Begum Khaleda Zia from 1991
political system emergent democratic republic
political parties Bangladesh Nationalist Party (BNP), Islamic, right of centre; Awami League, secular, moderate socialist; Jatiya Dal (National Party), Islamic nationalist
exports jute, tea, garments, fish products
currency taka
population (1992) 110,602,000; growth rate 2.17% p.a.; just over 1 million people live in small ethnic groups in the tropical Chittagong Hill Tracts, Mymensingh, and Sylhet districts
life expectancy men 50, women 52
language Bangla (Bengali)
religions Sunni Muslim 85%, Hindu 14%
literacy men 43%, women 22% (1985 est)
GDP $17.6 bn (1987); $172 per head

chronology

1947 Formed into eastern province of Pakistan on partition of British India.
1970 Half a million killed in flood.
1971 Bangladesh emerged as independent nation, under leadership of Sheik Mujibur Rahman, after civil war.
1975 Mujibur Rahman assassinated. Martial law imposed.
1976–77 Maj-Gen Zia ur-Rahman assumed power.
1978–79 Elections held and civilian rule restored.
1981 Assassination of Maj-Gen Zia.
1982 Lt-Gen Ershad assumed power in army coup. Martial law reimposed.
1986 Elections held but disputed. Martial law ended.
1987 State of emergency declared in response to opposition demonstrations.
1988 Assembly elections boycotted by main opposition parties. State of emergency lifted. Islam made state religion. Monsoon floods left 30 million homeless and thousands dead.
1989 Power devolved to Chittagong Hill Tracts to end 14-year conflict between local people and army-protected settlers.
1990 Following mass antigovernment protests, President Ershad resigned; Shahabuddin Ahmad became interim president.
1991 Feb: elections resulted in coalition government with BNP dominant. April: cyclone killed around 139,000 and left up to 10 million homeless. Sept: parliamentary government restored; Abdur Rahman Biswas elected president.

Barbados

area 430 sq km/166 sq mi
capital Bridgetown
towns Speightstown, Holetown, Oistins
physical most easterly island of the West Indies; surrounded by coral reefs; subject to hurricanes June–Nov
features highest point Mount Hillaby 340 m/1,115 ft
head of state Elizabeth II from 1966, represented by governor general Hugh Springer from 1984
head of government prime minister Erskine Lloyd Sandiford from 1987
political system constitutional monarchy
political parties Barbados Labour Party (BLP), moderate, left of centre; Democratic Labour Party (DLP),

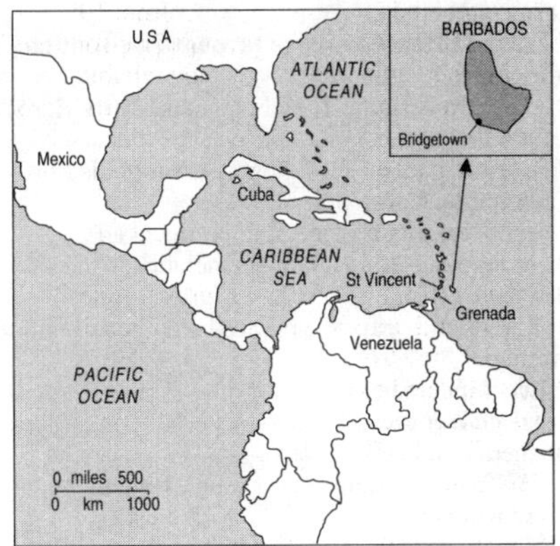

moderate, left of centre; National Democratic Party (NDP), centre
exports sugar, rum, electronic components, clothing, cement
currency Barbados dollar
population (1992) 259,000; growth rate 0.5% p.a.
life expectancy men 70, women 75
languages English and Bajan (Barbadian English dialect)
media two independent daily newspapers
religions 70% Anglican, 9% Methodist, 4% Roman Catholic
literacy 99% (1984)
GDP $1.4 bn (1987); $5,449 per head

chronology
1627 Became British colony; developed as a sugar-plantation economy, initially on basis of slavery.
1834 Slaves freed.
1951 Universal adult suffrage introduced. BLP won general election.
1954 Ministerial government established.
1961 Independence achieved from Britain. DLP, led by Errol Barrow, in power.
1966 Barbados achieved full independence within Commonwealth. Barrow became the new nation's first prime minister.
1972 Diplomatic relations with Cuba established.
1976 BLP, led by Tom Adams, returned to power.
1983 Barbados supported US invasion of Grenada.
1985 Adams died; Bernard St John became prime minister.
1986 DLP, led by Barrow, returned to power.
1987 Barrow died; Erskine Lloyd Sandiford became prime minister.
1989 New NDP opposition formed.
1991 DLP, under Erskine Sandiford, won general election.

Belarus

Republic of

area 207,600 sq km/80,100 sq mi
capital Minsk (Mensk)
towns Gomel, Vitebsk, Mogilev, Bobruisk, Grodno, Brest
physical more than 25% forested; rivers W Dvina, Dnieper and its tributaries, including the Pripet and Beresina; the Pripet Marshes in the E; mild and damp climate
environment large areas contaminated by fallout from Chernobyl
features Belovezhskaya Pushcha (scenic forest reserve)
head of state Stanislav Shushkevich from 1991
head of government Vyacheslav Kebich from 1990
political system emergent democracy
political parties Byelorussian Popular Front (Adradzhenne), moderate nationalist; Byelorussian Ecological Union (BEU); Byelorussian Social Democratic Party, moderate left of centre; Christian Democratic Union of Belarus, centrist; Communist Party, left-wing
products peat, agricultural machinery, fertilizers, glass, textiles, leather, salt, electrical goods, meat, dairy produce
currency rouble and dukat
population (1992) 10,321,000 (77% Byelorussian 'Eastern Slavs', 13% Russian, 4% Polish, 1% Jewish)
languages Byelorussian, Russian
religions Roman Catholic, Russian Orthodox, with Baptist and Muslim minorities

chronology
1918–19 Briefly independent from Russia.
1937–41 More than 100,000 people were shot in mass executions ordered by Stalin.
1941–44 Occupied by Nazi Germany.
1945 Became a founding member of the United Nations.
1986 April: fallout from the Chernobyl nuclear reactor in Ukraine contaminated a large area.
1989 Byelorussian Popular Front established as well as a more extreme nationalist organization, the Tolaka group.
1990 Sept: Byelorussian established as state language and republican sovereignty declared.
1991 April: Minsk hit by nationalist-backed general strike. Aug: declared independence from Soviet Union; CP suspended. Sept: reformist Shushkevich elected president. Dec: Commonwealth of Independent States formed in Minsk; Belarus accorded diplomatic recognition by USA.
1992 Jan: admitted into Conference on Security and Cooperation in Europe. May: protocols signed with USA agreeing to honour START disarmament treaty.

Belgium

Kingdom of (French *Royaume de Belgique*, Flemish *Koninkrijk België*)

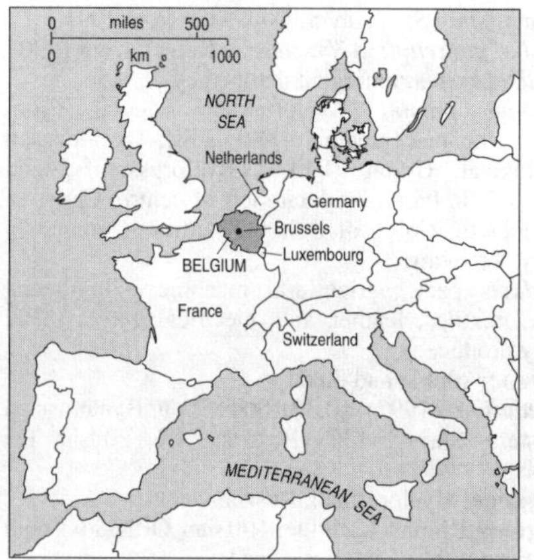

area 30,510 sq km/11,784 sq mi
capital Brussels
towns Ghent, Liège, Charleroi, Bruges, Mons, Namur, Leuven; ports are Antwerp, Ostend, Zeebrugge
physical fertile coastal plain in NW, central rolling hills rise eastwards, hills and forest in SE
environment a 1989 government report judged the drinking water in Flanders to be 'seriously substandard' and more than half the rivers and canals in that region to be in a 'very bad' condition
features Ardennes Forest; rivers Scheldt and Meuse
head of state King Baudouin from 1951
head of government Jean-Luc Dehaene from 1992
political system liberal democracy
political parties Flemish Christian Social Party (CVP), centre-left; French Social Christian Party (PSC), centre-left; Flemish Socialist Party (SP), left of centre; French Socialist Party (PS), left of centre; Flemish Liberal Party (PVV), moderate centrist; French Liberal Reform Party (PRL), moderate centrist; Flemish People's Party (VU), federalist; Flemish Green Party (Agalev); French Green Party (Ecolo)
exports iron, steel, textiles, manufactured goods, petrochemicals, plastics, vehicles, diamonds
currency Belgian franc
population (1992) 10,021,000 (comprising Flemings and Walloons); growth rate 0.1% p.a.
life expectancy men 72, women 78
languages in the N (Flanders) Flemish (a Dutch dialect, known as *Vlaams*) 55%; in the S (Wallonia) Walloon (a French dialect) 32%; bilingual 11%; German (E border) 0.6%; all are official
religion Roman Catholic 75%
literacy 98% (1984)
GDP $218.7 bn (1992)

chronology
1830 Belgium became an independent kingdom.
1914 Invaded by Germany.
1940 Again invaded by Germany.
1948 Belgium became founding member of Benelux Customs Union.
1949 Belgium became founding member of Council of Europe and NATO.
1951 Leopold III abdicated in favour of his son Baudouin.
1952 Belgium became founding member of European Coal and Steel Community.
1957 Belgium became founding member of the European Economic Community.
1971 Steps towards regional autonomy taken.
1972 German-speaking members included in the cabinet for the first time.
1973 Linguistic parity achieved in government appointments.
1974 Leo Tindemans became prime minister. Separate regional councils and ministerial committees established.
1978 Wilfried Martens succeeded Tindemans as prime minister.
1980 Open violence over language divisions. Regional assemblies for Flanders and Wallonia and a three-member executive for Brussels created.
1981 Short-lived coalition led by Mark Eyskens was followed by the return of Martens.
1987 Martens head of caretaker government after break-up of coalition.
1988 Following a general election, Martens formed a new CVP–PS–SP–PSC–VU coalition.
1992 Martens-led coalition collapsed; Jean-Luc Dehaene formed a new CVP-led coalition.
1993 Federal system adopted, based on Flanders, Wallonia, and Brussels. King Baudouin died; succeeded by his brother, Prince Albert of Liege.

Belize

(formerly ***British Honduras***)

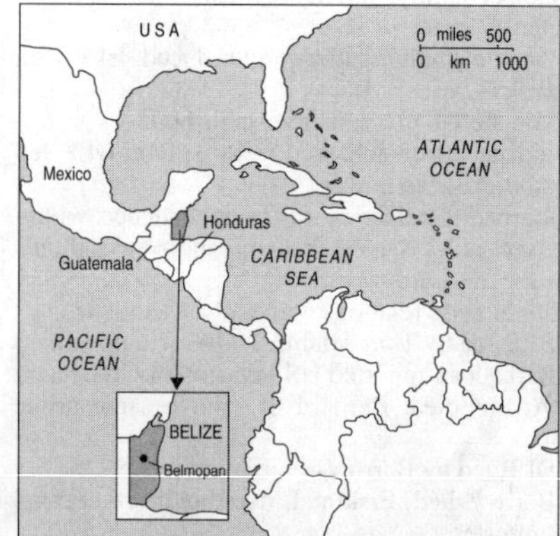

area 22,963 sq km/8,864 sq mi
capital Belmopan
towns ports Belize City, Dangriga and Punta Gorda; Orange Walk, Corozal
physical tropical swampy coastal plain, Maya Mountains in S; over 90% forested
environment since 1981 Belize has developed an extensive system of national parks and reserves to protect large areas of tropical forest, coastal mangrove, and offshore islands. Forestry has been replaced by agriculture and ecotourism, which are now the most important sectors of the economy; world's first jaguar reserve created 1986 in the Cockscomb Mountains

features world's second longest barrier reef; Maya ruins
head of state Elizabeth II from 1981, represented by governor general
head of government Manuel Esquivel from 1993
political system constitutional monarchy
political parties People's United Party (PUP), left of centre; United Democratic Party (UDP), moderate conservative
exports sugar, citrus fruits, rice, fish products, bananas
currency Belize dollar
population (1992) 196,000 (including Mayan minority in the interior); growth rate 2.5% p.a.
life expectancy (1988) 60 years
languages English (official); Spanish (widely spoken), native Creole dialects
media no daily newspaper; several independent weekly tabloids
religions Roman Catholic 60%, Protestant 35%
literacy 93% (1988)
GDP $247 million (1988); $1,220 per head

chronology
1862 Belize became a British colony.
1954 Constitution adopted, providing for limited internal self-government. General election won by George Price.
1964 Self-government achieved from the UK (universal adult suffrage introduced).
1965 Two-chamber national assembly introduced, with Price as prime minister.
1970 Capital moved from Belize City to Belmopan.
1973 British Honduras became Belize.
1975 British troops sent to defend the disputed frontier with Guatemala.
1980 United Nations called for full independence.
1981 Full independence achieved. Price became prime minister.
1984 Price defeated in general election. Manuel Esquivel formed the government. The UK reaffirmed its undertaking to defend the frontier.
1989 Price and the PUP won the general election.
1991 Diplomatic relations with Guatemala established.
1993 In general election UDP defeated PUP. Manuel Esquivel returned as prime minister.

Benin

People's Republic of (*République Populaire du Bénin*)

area 112,622 sq km/43,472 sq mi
capital Porto Novo (official), Cotonou (de facto)
towns Abomey, Natitingou, Parakou; chief port Cotonou
physical flat to undulating terrain; hot and humid in S; semiarid in N
features coastal lagoons with fishing villages on stilts; Niger River in NE
head of state and government Nicéphore Soglo from 1991
political system socialist pluralist republic
political parties Party of the People's Revolution of Benin (PRPB); other parties from 1990
exports cocoa, peanuts, cotton, palm oil, petroleum, cement, sea products

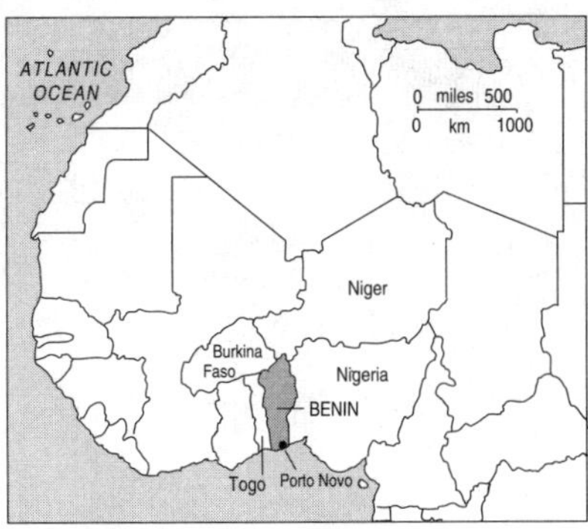

currency CFA franc
population (1992) 4,928,000; growth rate 3% p.a.
life expectancy men 42, women 46
languages French (official); Fon 47% and Yoruba 9% in south; six major tribal languages in north
religions animist 65%, Christian 17%, Muslim 13%
literacy men 37%, women 16% (1985 est)
GDP $1.6 bn (1987); $365 per head

chronology
1851 Under French control.
1958 Became self-governing dominion within the French Community.
1960 Independence achieved from France.
1960–72 Acute political instability, with switches from civilian to military rule.
1972 Military regime established by General Mathieu Kerekou.
1974 Kerekou announced that the country would follow a path of 'scientific socialism'.
1975 Name of country changed from Dahomey to Benin.
1977 Return to civilian rule under a new constitution.
1980 Kerekou formally elected president by the national revolutionary assembly.
1989 Marxist-Leninism dropped as official ideology. Strikes and protests against Kerekou's rule mounted; army deployed against protesters.
1991 Multiparty elections held. Kerekou defeated in presidential elections by Nicéphore Soglo.

Bhutan

Kingdom of (*Druk-yul*)

area 46,500 sq km/17,954 sq mi
capital Thimbu (Thimphu)
towns Paro, Punakha, Mongar
physical occupies southern slopes of the Himalayas; cut by valleys formed by tributaries of the Brahmaputra; thick forests in S
features Gangkar Punsum (7,529 m/24,700 ft) is one of the world's highest unclimbed peaks
head of state and government Jigme Singye Wangchuk from 1972
political system absolute monarchy
political parties none officially; illegal Bhutan People's Party (BPP)
exports timber, talc, fruit and vegetables, cement, distilled spirits, calcium carbide
currency ngultrum; also Indian currency
population (1992) 1,511,000; growth rate 2% p.a. (75% Ngalops and Sharchops, 25% Nepalese)

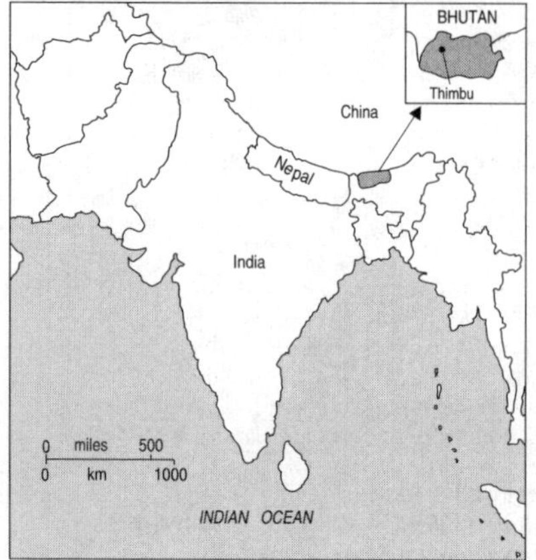

life expectancy men 44, women 43
languages Dzongkha (official, a Tibetan dialect), Sharchop, Bumthap, Nepali, and English
media one daily newspaper (*Kuensel*), published in Dzongkha, English, and Nepali editions; it gives the government's point of view
religions 75% Lamaistic Buddhist (state religion), 25% Hindu
literacy 5%
GDP $250 million (1987); $170 per head

chronology
1865 Trade treaty with Britain signed.
1907 First hereditary monarch installed.
1910 Anglo-Bhutanese Treaty signed.
1949 Indo-Bhutan Treaty of Friendship signed.
1952 King Jigme Dorji Wangchuk installed.
1953 National assembly established.
1959 4,000 Tibetan refugees given asylum.
1968 King established first cabinet.
1972 King died and was succeeded by his son Jigme Singye Wangchuk.
1979 Tibetan refugees told to take Bhutanese citizenship or leave; most stayed.
1983 Bhutan became a founding member of the South Asian Regional Association for Cooperation.
1988 King imposed 'code of conduct' suppressing Nepalese customs.
1990 Hundreds of people allegedly killed during prodemocracy demonstrations.

Bolivia

Republic of (*República de Bolivia*)

area 1,098,581 sq km/424,052 sq mi
capital La Paz (seat of government), Sucre (legal capital and seat of judiciary)
towns Santa Cruz, Cochabamba, Oruro, Potosí
physical high plateau (Altiplano) between mountain ridges (cordilleras); forest and lowlands (llano) in the E
features Andes, lakes Titicaca (the world's highest navigable lake, 3,800 m/12,500 ft) and Poopó; La Paz is world's highest capital city (3,600 m/11,800 ft)
head of state and government Gonzalo Sanchez de Lozado from 1993
political system emergent democratic republic
political parties National Revolutionary Movement (MNR), centre right; Movement of the Revolutionary Left (MIR), left of centre; Solidarity Civil Union (UCS), radical free-market; Nationalist Democratic Action (ADN), right of centre
exports tin, antimony (second largest world producer), other nonferrous metals, oil, gas (piped to Argentina), agricultural products, coffee, sugar, cotton
currency boliviano
population (1992) 7,739,000; (Quechua 25%, Aymara 17%, mestizo (mixed) 30%, European 14%); growth rate 2.7% p.a.
life expectancy men 51, women 54
languages Spanish, Aymara, Quechua (all official)
religion Roman Catholic 95% (state-recognized)
literacy men 84%, women 65% (1985 est)
GDP $4.2 bn (1987); $617 per head

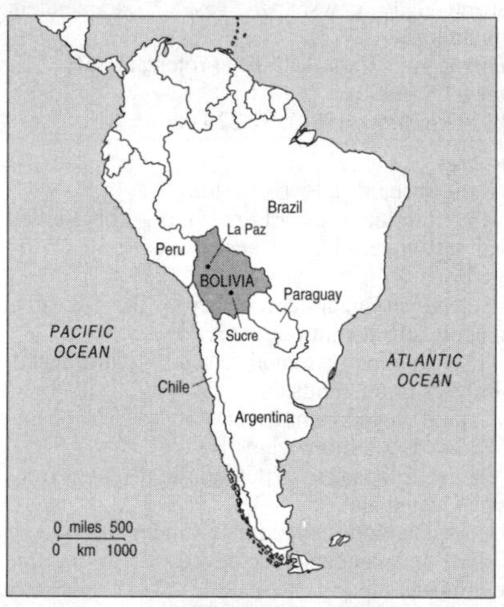

chronology
1825 Liberated from Spanish rule by Simón Bolívar; independence achieved (formerly known as Upper Peru).
1952 Dr Víctor Paz Estenssoro elected president.
1956 Dr Hernán Siles Zuazo became president.
1960 Estenssoro returned to power.
1964 Army coup led by the vice president, General René Barrientos.
1966 Barrientos became president.
1967 Uprising, led by 'Che' Guevara, put down with US help.
1969 Barrientos killed in plane crash, replaced by Vice President Siles Salinas. Army coup deposed him.
1970 Army coup put General Juan Torres González in power.
1971 Torres replaced by Col Hugo Banzer Suárez.
1973 Banzer promised a return to democratic government.
1974 Attempted coup prompted Banzer to postpone elections and ban political and trade-union activity.
1978 Elections declared invalid after allegations of fraud.
1980 More inconclusive elections followed by another coup, led by General Luis García. Allegations of corruption and drug trafficking led to cancellation of US and EC aid.

1981 García forced to resign. Replaced by General Celso Torrelio Villa.
1982 Torrelio resigned. Replaced by military junta led by General Guido Vildoso. Because of worsening economy, Vildoso asked congress to install a civilian administration. Dr Siles Zuazo chosen as president.
1983 Economic aid from USA and Europe resumed.
1984 New coalition government formed by Siles. Abduction of president by right-wing officers. The president undertook a five-day hunger strike as an example to the nation.
1985 President Siles resigned. Election result inconclusive; Dr Paz Estenssoro, at the age of 77, chosen by congress as president.
1989 Jaime Paz Zamora (MIR) elected president in power-sharing arrangement with Hugo Banzer Suárez, pledged to maintain fiscal and monetary discipline and preserve free- market policies.
1993 MNR won congressional and presidential elections.

Bosnia-Herzegovina

Republic of

area 51,129 sq km/19,745 sq mi
capital Sarajevo
towns Banja Luka, Mostar, Prijedor, Tuzla, Zenica
physical barren, mountainous country
features part of the Dinaric Alps, limestone gorges
population (1992) 4,397,000 including 44% Muslims, 33% Serbs, 17% Croats; a complex patchwork of ethnically mixed communities
head of state Alija Izetbegović from 1990
head of government Mile Akmadzic from 1992
political system emergent democracy
political parties Party of Democratic Action (SDA), Muslim-oriented; Serbian Democratic Party (SDS), Serbian nationalist; Christian Democratic Union (HDS), centrist; League of Communists, left-wing
products citrus fruits and vegetables; iron, steel, and leather goods; textiles
language Serbian variant of Serbo-Croatian
religions Sunni Muslim, Serbian Orthodox, Roman Catholic
chronology
1918 Incorporated in the future Yugoslavia.
1941 Occupied by Nazi Germany.
1945 Became republic within Yugoslav Socialist Federation.
1980 Upsurge in Islamic nationalism.
1990 Ethnic violence erupted between Muslims and Serbs. Communists defeated in multiparty elections; coalition formed by Serb, Muslim, and Croatian parties.
1991 May: Serbia–Croatia conflict spread disorder into Bosnia-Herzegovina. Aug: Serbia revealed plans to annex the SE part of the republic. Sept: Serbian enclaves established by force. Oct: 'sovereignty' declared. Nov: plebiscite by Serbs favoured remaining within Yugoslavia; Serbs and Croats established autonomous communities.
1992 Feb–March: Muslims and Croats voted overwhelmingly in favour of independence; referendum boycotted by Serbs. April: USA and EC recognized Bosnian independence. Ethnic hostilities escalated, with Serb forces occupying E and Croatian forces much of W; state of emergency declared; all- out civil war. May: admitted to United Nations. June: UN forces drafted into Sarajevo to break three-month siege of city by Serbs. Accusations of 'ethnic cleansing' being practised, particularly by Serbs. Oct: UN ban on military flights over Bosnia-Herzegovina. First British troops deployed, under UN control.
1993 UN-EC peace plan introduced, failed. USA began airdrops of food and medical supplies.

Botswana

Republic of

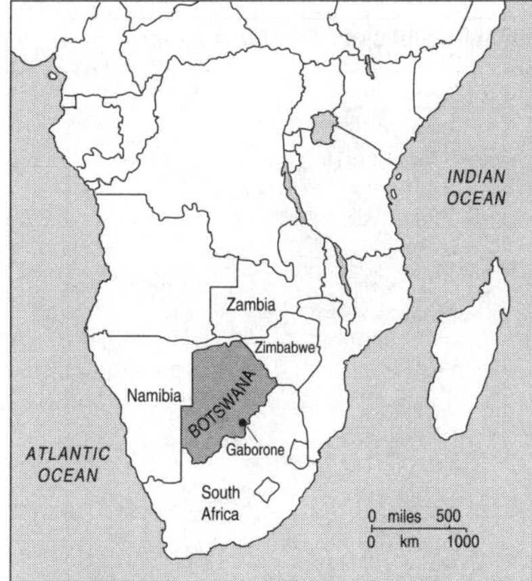

area 582,000 sq km/225,000 sq mi
capital Gaborone
towns Mahalpye, Serowe, Tutume, Francistown
physical desert in SW, plains in E, fertile lands and swamp in N
environment the Okavango Swamp is threatened by plans to develop the area for mining and agriculture
features Kalahari Desert in SW; Okavango Swamp in N, remarkable for its wildlife; Makgadikgadi salt pans in E; diamonds mined at Orapa and Jwaneng in partnership with De Beers of South Africa
head of state and government Quett Ketamile Joni Masire from 1980
political system democratic republic
political parties Botswana Democratic Party (BDP),

moderate centrist; Botswana National Front (BNF), moderate, left of centre
exports diamonds (third largest producer in world), copper, nickel, meat products, textiles
currency pula
population (1992) 1,359,000 (Bamangwato 80%, Bangwaketse 20%); growth rate 3.5% p.a.
life expectancy (1988) 59 years
languages English (official), Setswana (national)
religions Christian 50%, animist 50%
literacy (1988) 84%
GDP $2.0 bn (1988); $1,611 per head
chronology
1885 Became a British protectorate.
1960 New constitution created a legislative council.
1963 End of rule by High Commission.
1965 Capital transferred from Mafeking to Gaborone. Internal self-government achieved. Sir Seretse Khama elected head of government.
1966 Independence achieved from Britain. New constitution came into effect; name changed from Bechuanaland to Botswana; Seretse Khama elected president.
1980 Seretse Khama died; succeeded by Vice President Quett Masire.
1984 Masire re-elected.
1985 South African raid on Gaborone.
1987 Joint permanent commission with Mozambique established, to improve relations.
1989 The BDP and Masire re-elected.

Brazil

Federative Republic of (*República Federativa do Brasil*)

area 8,511,965 sq km/3,285,618 sq mi
capital Brasília
towns São Paulo, Belo Horizonte, Curitiba, Manaus, Fortaleza; ports are Rio de Janeiro, Belém, Recife, Pôrto Alegre, Salvador
physical the densely forested Amazon basin covers the northern half of the country with a network of rivers; the south is fertile; enormous energy resources, both hydroelectric (Itaipú dam on the Paraná, and Tucuruí on the Tocantins) and nuclear (uranium ores)
environment Brazil has one-third of the world's tropical rainforest. It contains 55,000 species of flowering plants (the greatest variety in the world) and 20% of all the world's bird species. During the 1980s at least 7% of the Amazon rainforest was destroyed by settlers who cleared the land for cultivation and grazing
features Mount Roraima, Xingu National Park; Amazon delta; Rio harbour
head of state and government Itamar Franco from 1992
political system emergent democratic federal republic
political parties Social Democratic Party (PDS), moderate, left of centre; Brazilian Democratic Movement Party (PMDB), centre-left; Liberal Front Party (PFL), moderate, left of centre; Workers' Party (PT), left of centre; National Reconstruction Party (PRN), centre-right
exports coffee, sugar, soya beans, cotton, textiles, timber, motor vehicles, iron, chrome, manganese, tungsten and other ores, as well as quartz crystals, industrial diamonds, gemstones; the world's sixth largest arms exporter
currency cruzado (introduced 1986; value = 100 cruzeiros, the former unit); inflation 1990 was 1,795%
population (1992) 151,381,000 (including 200,000 Indians, survivors of 5 million, especially in Rondônia and Mato Grosso, mostly living on reservations); growth rate 2.2% p.a.
life expectancy men 61, women 66
languages Portuguese (official); 120 Indian languages
religions Roman Catholic 89%; Indian faiths
literacy men 79%, women 76% (1985 est)
GDP $352 bn (1988); $2,434 per head

chronology
1822 Independence achieved from Portugal; ruled by Dom Pedro, son of the refugee King John VI of Portugal.
1889 Monarchy abolished and republic established.
1891 Constitution for a federal state adopted.
1930 Dr Getúlio Vargas became president.
1945 Vargas deposed by the military.
1946 New constitution adopted.
1951 Vargas returned to office.
1954 Vargas committed suicide.
1956 Juscelino Kubitschek became president.
1960 Capital moved to Brasília.
1961 João Goulart became president.
1964 Bloodless coup made General Castelo Branco president; he assumed dictatorial powers, abolishing free political parties.
1967 New constitution adopted. Branco succeeded by Marshal da Costa e Silva.
1969 Da Costa e Silva resigned and a military junta took over.
1974 General Ernesto Geisel became president.
1978 General Baptista de Figueiredo became president.
1979 Political parties legalized again.
1984 Mass calls for a return to fully democratic government.
1985 Tancredo Neves became first civilian president in 21 years. Neves died and was succeeded by the vice president, José Sarney.
1988 New constitution approved, transferring power from the president to the congress. Measures

announced to halt large-scale burning of Amazonian rainforest for cattle grazing.
1989 Forest Protection Service and Ministry for Land Reform abolished. International concern over how much of the Amazon has been burned. Fernando Collor (PRN) elected president Dec, pledging free-market economic policies.
1990 Government won the general election offset by mass abstentions.
1992 Collor charged with corruption and replaced by Vice President Itamar Franco.
1993 Collor indicted for 'passive corruption'. June: Collor appeared before supreme court.

Brunei

Islamic Sultanate of (*Negara Brunei Darussalam*)

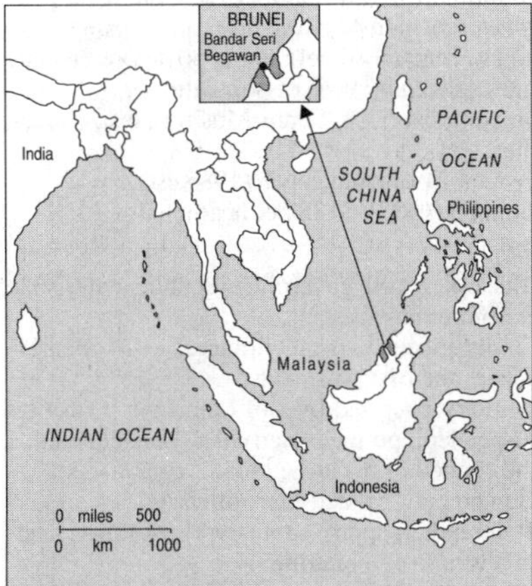

area 5,765 sq km/2,225 sq mi
capital Bandar Seri Begawan
towns Tutong, Seria, Kuala Belait
physical flat coastal plain with hilly lowland in W and mountains in E; 75% of the area is forested; the Limbang valley splits Brunei in two, and its cession to Sarawak 1890 is disputed by Brunei
features Temburong, Tutong, and Belait rivers; Mount Pagon (1,850 m/6,070 ft)
head of state and of government HM Muda Hassanal Bolkiah Mu'izzaddin Waddaulah, Sultan of Brunei, from 1968
political system absolute monarchy
political party Brunei National United Party (BNUP)
exports liquefied natural gas (world's largest producer) and oil, both expected to be exhausted by the year 2000
currency Brunei dollar
population (1992) 268,000 (65% Malay, 20% Chinese – few Chinese granted citizenship); growth rate 12% p.a.
life expectancy 74 years
languages Malay (official), Chinese (Hokkien), English
religion 60% Muslim (official)
literacy 95%
GDP $3.4 bn (1985); $20,000 per head

chronology
1888 Brunei became a British protectorate.
1941–45 Occupied by Japan.
1959 Written constitution made Britain responsible for defence and external affairs.
1962 Sultan began rule by decree.
1967 Sultan abdicated in favour of his son, Hassanal Bolkiah.
1971 Brunei given internal self-government.
1975 United Nations resolution called for independence for Brunei.
1984 Independence achieved from Britain, with Britain maintaining a small force to protect the oil- and gasfields.
1985 A 'loyal and reliable' political party, the Brunei National Democratic Party (BNDP), legalized.
1986 Death of former sultan, Sir Omar. Formation of multiethnic BNUP.
1988 BNDP banned.

Bulgaria

Republic of (*Republika Bulgaria*)

area 110,912 sq km/42,812 sq mi
capital Sofia
towns Plovdiv, Ruse; Black Sea ports Burgas and Varna
physical lowland plains in N and SE separated by mountains that cover three-quarters of the country
environment pollution has virtually eliminated all species of fish once caught in the Black Sea. Vehicle-exhaust emissions in Sofia have led to dust concentrations more than twice the medically accepted level
features key position on land route from Europe to Asia; Black Sea coast; Balkan and Rhodope mountains; Danube River in N
head of state Zhelyu Zhelev from 1990
head of government Lyuben Berov from 1992
political system emergent democratic republic
political parties Union of Democratic Forces (UDF), right of centre; Bulgarian Socialist Party (BSP), left-wing, ex-communist; Movement for Rights and Freedoms (MRF), centrist
exports textiles, leather, chemicals, nonferrous metals, timber, machinery, tobacco, cigarettes (world's largest exporter)
currency lev
population (1992) 8,985,000 (including 900,000–1,500,000 ethnic Turks, concentrated in S and NE); growth rate 0.1% p.a.

life expectancy men 69, women 74
languages Bulgarian, Turkish
religions Eastern Orthodox Christian 90%, Sunni Muslim 10%
literacy 98%
GDP $25.4 bn (1987); $2,836 per head

chronology
1908 Bulgaria became a kingdom independent of Turkish rule.
1944 Soviet invasion of German-occupied Bulgaria.
1946 Monarchy abolished and communist-dominated people's republic proclaimed.
1947 Soviet-style constitution adopted.
1949 Death of Georgi Dimitrov, the communist government leader.
1954 Election of Todor Zhivkov as Communist Party general secretary; made nation a loyal satellite of USSR.
1971 Constitution modified; Zhivkov elected president.
1985–89 Large administrative and personnel changes to government made haphazardly under Soviet stimulus.
1987 New electoral law introduced multicandidate elections.
1989 Programme of 'Bulgarianization' resulted in mass exodus of Turks to Turkey. Nov: Zhivkov ousted by Petar Mladenov. Dec: opposition parties allowed to form.
1990 April: BCP renamed Bulgarian Socialist Party (BSP). Aug: Dr Zhelyu Zhelev elected president. Nov: government headed by Andrei Lukanov resigned, replaced Dec by coalition led by Dimitur Popov.
1991 July: new constitution adopted. Oct: UDF beat BSP in general election by narrow margin; formation of first noncommunist, UDF-minority government under Filip Dimitrov.
1992 Zhelev became Bulgaria's first directly elected president. Relations with West greatly improved. Dimitrov resigned after vote of no confidence; replaced by Lyuben Berov and non-party government.

Burkina Faso

The People's Democratic Republic of (formerly *Upper Volta*)

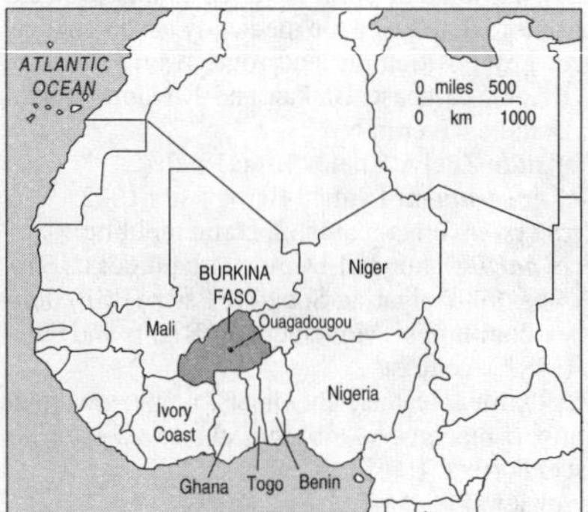

area 274,122 sq km/105,811 sq mi
capital Ouagadougou
towns Bobo-Dioulasso, Koudougou
physical landlocked plateau with hills in W and SE; headwaters of the river Volta; semiarid in N, forest and farmland in S
environment tropical savanna subject to overgrazing and deforestation
features linked by rail to Abidjan in Ivory Coast, Burkina Faso's only outlet to the sea
head of state and government Blaise Compaoré from 1987
political system transitional
political parties Organization for Popular Democracy–Workers' Movement (ODP–MT), nationalist left-wing; FP–Popular Front
exports cotton, groundnuts, livestock, hides, skins, sesame, cereals
currency CFA franc
population (1992) 9,515,000; growth rate 2.4% p.a.
life expectancy men 44, women 47
languages French (official); about 50 native Sudanic languages spoken by 90% of population
religions animist 53%, Sunni Muslim 36%, Roman Catholic 11%
literacy men 21%, women 6% (1985 est)
GDP $1.6 bn (1987); $188 per head

chronology
1958 Became a self-governing republic within the French Community.
1960 Independence from France, with Maurice Yaméogo as the first president.
1966 Military coup led by Col Lamizana. Constitution suspended, political activities banned, and a supreme council of the armed forces established.
1969 Ban on political activities lifted.
1970 Referendum approved a new constitution leading to a return to civilian rule.
1974 After experimenting with a mixture of military and civilian rule, Lamizana reassumed full power.
1977 Ban on political activities removed. Referendum approved a new constitution based on civilian rule.
1978 Lamizana elected president.
1980 Lamizana overthrown in bloodless coup led by Col Zerbo.
1982 Zerbo ousted in a coup by junior officers. Major Ouédraogo became president and Thomas Sankara prime minister.
1983 Sankara seized complete power.
1984 Upper Volta renamed Burkina Faso, 'land of upright men'.
1987 Sankara killed in coup led by Blaise Compaoré.
1989 New government party ODP–MT formed by merger of other pro-government parties. Coup against Compaoré foiled.
1991 New constitution approved. Compaoré re-elected president.
1992 Multiparty elections won by FP–Popular Front.

Burundi

Republic of (*Republika y'Uburundi*)

area 27,834 sq km/10,744 sq mi
capital Bujumbura
towns Gitega, Bururi, Ngozi, Muyinga
physical landlocked grassy highland straddling watershed of Nile and Congo
features Lake Tanganyika, Great Rift Valley

head of state and government Melchior Ndadaye from 1993
political system one-party military republic
political party Union for National Progress (UPRONA), nationalist socialist
exports coffee, cotton, tea, nickel, hides, livestock, cigarettes, beer, soft drinks; there are 500 million tonnes of peat reserves in the basin of the Akanyaru River
currency Burundi franc
population (1992) 5,657,000 (of whom 15% are the Nilotic Tutsi, still holding most of the land and political power, 1% are Pygmy Twa, and the remainder Bantu Hutu); growth rate 2.8% p.a.
life expectancy men 45, women 48
languages Kirundi (a Bantu language) and French (both official), Kiswahili
religions Roman Catholic 62%, Protestant 5%, Muslim 1%, animist 32%
literacy men 43%, women 26% (1985)
GDP $1.1 bn (1987); $230 per head

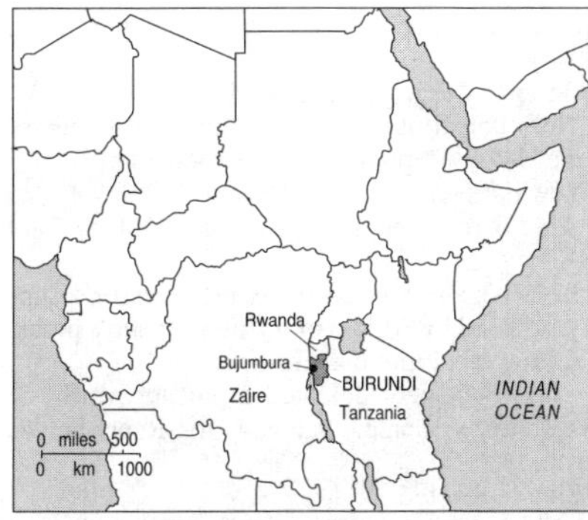

chronology
1962 Separated from Ruanda-Urundi, as Burundi, and given independence as a monarchy under King Mwambutsa IV.
1966 King deposed by his son Charles, who became Ntare V; he was in turn deposed by his prime minister, Capt Michel Micombero, who declared Burundi a republic.
1972 Ntare V killed, allegedly by the Hutu ethnic group. Massacres of 150,000 Hutus by the rival Tutsi ethnic group, of which Micombero was a member.
1973 Micombero made president and prime minister.
1974 UPRONA declared the only legal political party, with the president as its secretary general.
1976 Army coup deposed Micombero. Col Jean-Baptiste Bagaza appointed president by the Supreme Revolutionary Council.
1981 New constitution adopted, providing for a national assembly.
1984 Bagaza elected president as sole candidate.
1987 Bagaza deposed in coup Sept. Maj Pierre Buyoya headed new Military Council for National Redemption.
1988 Some 24,000 majority Hutus killed by Tutsis.
1992 New constitution approved by referendum.
1993 Melchior Ndadaye, a Hutu, elected president.

Cambodia

State of (formerly ***Khmer Republic*** 1970–76,

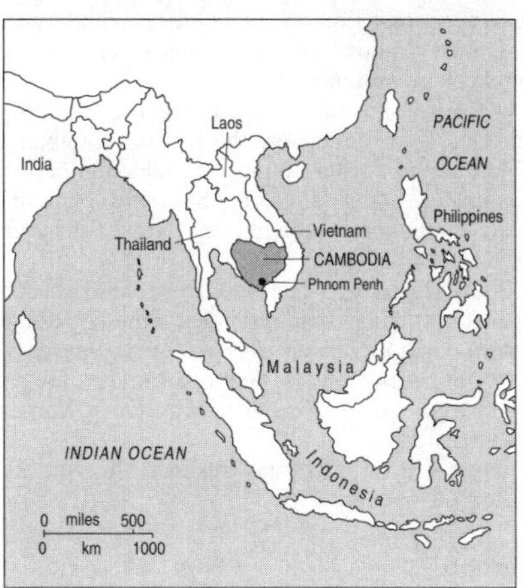

Democratic Kampuchea 1976–79, ***People's Republic of Kampuchea*** 1979–89)
area 181,035 sq km/69,880 sq mi
capital Phnom Penh
towns Battambang, the seaport Kompong Som
physical mostly flat forested plains with mountains in SW and N; Mekong River runs N–S
features ruins of ancient capital Angkor; Lake Tonle Sap
head of state Prince Norodom Sihanouk from 1991
head of government to be chosen
political system transitional
political parties Cambodian People's Party (CPP), reform socialist (formerly the communist Kampuchean People's Revolutionary Party (KPRP)); Party of Democratic Kampuchea (Khmer Rouge), ultranationalist communist; Khmer People's National Liberation Front (KPNLF), anticommunist; United Front for an Independent, Neutral, Peaceful, and Cooperative Cambodia (FUNCINPEC), moderate centrist
exports rubber, rice, pepper, wood, cattle
currency Cambodian riel
population (1992) 8,974,000; growth rate 2.2% p.a.
life expectancy men 42, women 45
languages Khmer (official), French
religion Theravāda Buddhist 95%
literacy men 78%, women 39% (1980 est)
GDP $592 mn (1987); $83 per head

chronology
1863–1941 French protectorate.
1941–45 Occupied by Japan.
1946 Recaptured by France.
1953 Independence achieved from France.
1970 Prince Sihanouk overthrown by US-backed Lon Nol.
1975 Lon Nol overthrown by Khmer Rouge.
1976–78 Khmer Rouge introduced an extreme communist programme, forcing urban groups into rural areas and bringing over 2.5 million deaths from famine, disease, and maltreatment.
1978–79 Vietnamese invasion and installation of Heng Samrin government.

1982 The three main anti-Vietnamese resistance groups formed an alliance under Prince Sihanouk.
1987 Vietnamese troop withdrawal began.
1989 Sept: completion of Vietnamese withdrawal. Nov: United Nations peace proposal rejected by Phnom Penh government.
1991 Oct: Peace agreement signed in Paris, providing for a UN Transitional Authority in Cambodia (UNTAC) to administer country in transition period in conjunction with all-party Supreme National Council; communism abandoned. Nov: Sihanouk returned as head of state.
1992 Political prisoners released; freedom of speech and party formation restored. Oct: Khmer Rouge refused to disarm in accordance with peace process. Dec: UN Security Council voted to impose limited trade embargo on area of country controlled by Khmer Rouge guerrillas.
1993 Free general elections resulted in win by FUNCINPEC over the CPP.

Cameroon

Republic of (*République du Cameroun*)

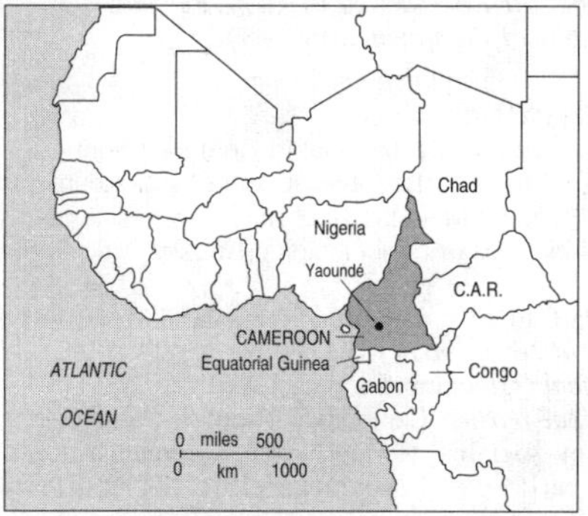

area 475,440 sq km/183,638 sq mi
capital Yaoundé
towns chief port Douala; Nkongsamba, Garova
physical desert in far north in the Lake Chad basin, mountains in W, dry savanna plateau in the intermediate area, and dense tropical rainforest in S
environment the Korup National Park preserves 1,300 sq km/500 sq mi of Africa's fast-disappearing tropical rainforest. Scientists have identified nearly 100 potentially useful chemical substances produced naturally by the plants of this forest
features Mount Cameroon 4,070 m/13,358 ft, an active volcano on the coast, W of the Adamawa Mountains
head of state and of government Paul Biya from 1982
political system emergent democratic republic
political parties Democratic Assembly of the Cameroon People (RDPC), nationalist, left of centre; Social Democratic Front (SDF), centre-left; Social Movement for New Democracy (MSND), left of centre; Union of the Peoples of Cameroon (UPC), left of centre
exports cocoa, coffee, bananas, cotton, timber, rubber, groundnuts, gold, aluminium, crude oil
currency CFA franc
population (1992) 12,662,000; growth rate 2.7% p.a.
life expectancy men 49, women 53
languages French and English in pidgin variations (official); there has been some discontent with the emphasis on French – there are 163 indigenous peoples with their own African languages
media heavy government censorship
religions Roman Catholic 35%, animist 25%, Muslim 22%, Protestant 18%
literacy men 68%, women 45% (1985 est)
GDP $12.7 bn (1987); $1,170 per head

chronology
1884 Treaty signed establishing German rule.
1916 Captured by Allied forces in World War I.
1922 Divided between Britain and France.
1946 French Cameroon and British Cameroons made UN trust territories.
1960 French Cameroon became the independent Republic of Cameroon. Ahmadou Ahidjo elected president.
1961 Northern part of British Cameroon merged with Nigeria and southern part joined the Republic of Cameroon to become the Federal Republic of Cameroon.
1966 One-party regime introduced.
1972 New constitution made Cameroon a unitary state, the United Republic of Cameroon.
1973 New national assembly elected.
1982 Ahidjo resigned and was succeeded by Paul Biya.
1983 Biya began to remove his predecessor's supporters; accused by Ahidjo of trying to create a police state. Ahidjo went into exile in France.
1984 Biya re-elected; defeated a plot to overthrow him. Country's name changed to Republic of Cameroon.
1988 Biya re-elected.
1990 Widespread public disorder. Biya granted amnesty to political prisoners.
1991 Constitutional changes made.
1992 Ruling RDPC won in first multiparty elections in 28 years. Biya's presidential victory challenged by opposition.

Canada

area 9,970,610 sq km/3,849,674 sq mi
capital Ottawa
towns Toronto, Montréal, Vancouver, Edmonton, Calgary, Winnipeg, Quebec, Hamilton, Saskatoon, Halifax
physical mountains in W, with low-lying plains in interior and rolling hills in E. Climate varies from temperate in S to arctic in N
environment sugar maples are dying in E Canada as a result of increasing soil acidification; nine rivers in Nova Scotia are now too acid to support salmon or trout reproduction
features St Lawrence Seaway, Mackenzie River; Great Lakes; Arctic Archipelago; Rocky Mountains; Great Plains or Prairies; Canadian Shield; Niagara Falls; the world's second largest country
head of state Elizabeth II from 1952, represented by governor general
head of government Kim Campell from 1993
political system federal constitutional monarchy

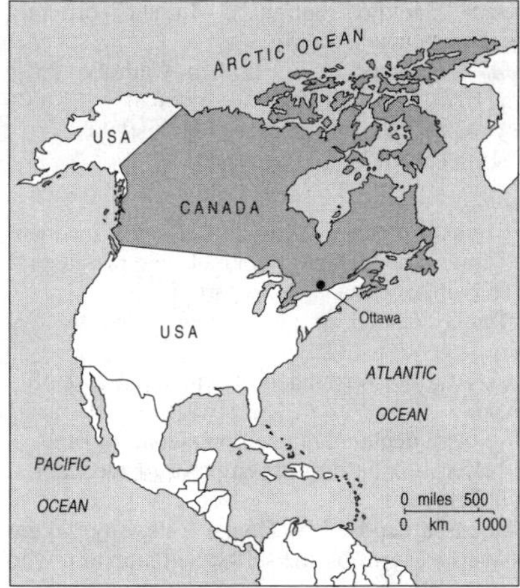

political parties Progressive Conservative Party, free-enterprise, right of centre; Liberal Party, nationalist, centrist; New Democratic Party (NDP), moderate left of centre
exports wheat, timber, pulp, newsprint, fish (salmon), furs (ranched fox and mink exceed the value of wild furs), oil, natural gas, aluminium, asbestos (world's second largest producer), coal, copper, iron, zinc, nickel (world's largest producer), uranium (world's largest producer), motor vehicles and parts, industrial and agricultural machinery, fertilizers, chemicals
currency Canadian dollar
population (1992) 27,737,000 – including 300,000 North American Indians, of whom 75% live on more than 2,000 reservations in Ontario and the four western provinces; some 300,000 Métis (people of mixed race) and 19,000 Inuit of whom 75% live in the Northwest Territories. Over half Canada's population lives in Ontario and Québec. Growth rate 1.1% p.a.
life expectancy men 72, women 79
languages English, French (both official; about 70% speak English, 20% French, and the rest are bilingual); there are also North American Indian languages and the Inuit Inuktitut
religion Roman Catholic 46%, Protestant 35%
literacy 99%
GDP $562 bn (1992)

chronology
1867 Dominion of Canada founded.
1949 Newfoundland joined Canada.
1957 Progressive Conservatives returned to power after 22 years in opposition.
1961 NDP formed.
1963 Liberals elected under Lester Pearson.
1968 Pearson succeeded by Pierre Trudeau.
1979 Joe Clark, leader of the Progressive Conservatives, formed a minority government; defeated on budget proposals.
1980 Liberals under Trudeau returned with a large majority. Québec referendum rejected demand for independence.
1982 Canada Act removed Britain's last legal control over Canadian affairs; 'patriation' of Canada's constitution.
1983 Clark replaced as leader of the Progressive Conservatives by Brian Mulroney.
1984 Trudeau retired and was succeeded as Liberal leader and prime minister by John Turner. Progressive Conservatives won the federal election with a large majority, and Mulroney became prime minister.
1988 Conservatives re-elected with reduced majority on platform of free trade with the USA.
1989 Free-trade agreement signed. Turner resigned as Liberal Party leader, and Ed Broadbent as NDP leader.
1990 Collapse of Meech Lake accord. Canada joined the coalition opposing Iraq's invasion of Kuwait.
1992 Gradual withdrawal of Canadian forces in Europe announced. Self-governing homeland for Inuit approved. Constitutional reform package, the Charlottetown agreement, rejected in national referendum.
1993 Mulroney resigned leadership of Conservative Party; Kim Campbell, the new party leader, became prime minister.

Cape Verde

Republic of (*República de Cabo Verde*)

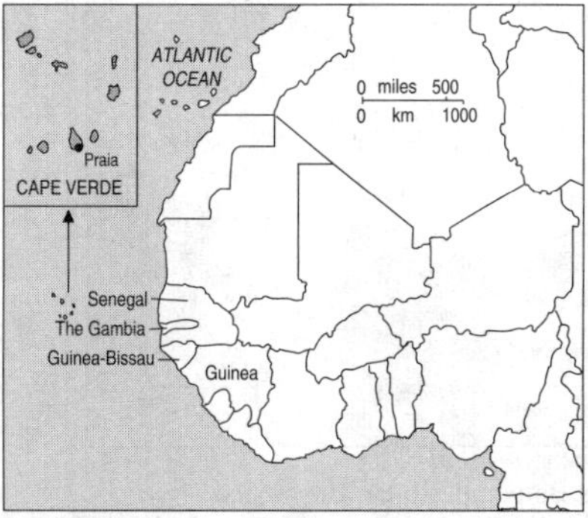

area 4,033 sq km/1,557 sq mi
capital Praia
towns Mindelo, Sal-Rei, Porto Novo
physical archipelago of ten volcanic islands 565 km/350 mi W of Senegal; the windward (Barlavento) group includes Santo Antão, São Vicente, Santa Luzia, São Nicolau, Sal, and Boa Vista; the leeward (Sotovento) group comprises Maio, São Tiago, Fogo, and Brava; all but Santa Luzia are inhabited
features strategic importance guaranteed by its domination of western shipping lanes; Sal, Boa Vista, and Maio lack water supplies but have fine beaches
head of state Mascarenhas Monteiro from 1991
head of government Carlos Viega from 1991
political system socialist pluralist state
political parties African Party for the Independence of Cape Verde (PAICV), African nationalist; Movement for Democracy (MPD)
exports bananas, salt, fish
currency Cape Verde escudo
population (1992) 346,000 (including 100,000 Angolan refugees); growth rate 1.9% p.a.
life expectancy men 57, women 61
language Creole dialect of Portuguese
religion Roman Catholic 80%

literacy men 61%, women 39% (1985)
GDP $158 million (1987); $454 per head

chronology
15th century First settled by Portuguese.
1951–74 Ruled as an overseas territory by Portugal.
1974 Moved towards independence through a transitional Portuguese–Cape Verde government.
1975 Independence achieved from Portugal. National people's assembly elected. Aristides Pereira became the first president.
1980 Constitution adopted providing for eventual union with Guinea-Bissau.
1981 Union with Guinea-Bissau abandoned and the constitution amended; became one-party state.
1991 First multiparty elections held. New party, MPD, won majority in assembly. Pereira replaced by Mascarenhas Monteiro.

Central African Republic

(*République Centrafricaine*)
area 622,436 sq km/240,260 sq mi
capital Bangui

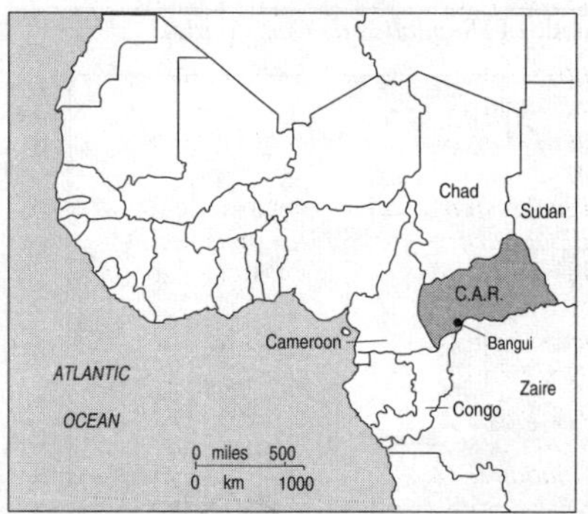

towns Berbérati, Bouar, Bossangoa
physical landlocked flat plateau, with rivers flowing N and S, and hills in NE and SW; dry in N, rainforest in SW
environment an estimated 87% of the urban population is without access to safe drinking water
features Kotto and Mbali river falls; the Oubangui River rises 6 m/20 ft at Bangui during the wet season (June– Nov)
head of state André Kolingba from 1981
head of government Enoch Derant Lakoue from 1993
political system one-party military republic
political parties Central African Democratic Assembly (RDC), nationalist; all political activity has been banned since the 1981 coup, but the main opposition groups, although passive, still exist. They are the Patriotic Front Ubangi Workers' Party (FPO-PT), the Central African Movement for National Liberation (MCLN), and the Movement for the Liberation of the Central African People (MPLC)
exports diamonds, uranium, coffee, cotton, timber, tobacco
currency CFA franc
population (1992) 2,930,000 (more than 80 ethnic groups); growth rate 2.3% p.a.
life expectancy men 41, women 45
languages Sangho (national), French (official), Arabic, Hunsa, and Swahili
religions Protestant 25%, Roman Catholic 25%, Muslim 10%, animist 10%
literacy men 53%, women 29% (1985 est)
GDP $1 bn (1987); $374 per head

chronology
1960 Central African Republic achieved independence from France; David Dacko elected president.
1962 The republic made a one-party state.
1965 Dacko ousted in military coup led by Col Bokassa.
1966 Constitution rescinded and national assembly dissolved.
1972 Bokassa declared himself president for life.
1977 Bokassa made himself emperor of the Central African Empire.
1979 Bokassa deposed by Dacko following violent repressive measures by the self-styled emperor, who went into exile.
1981 Dacko deposed in a bloodless coup, led by General André Kolingba, and an all-military government established.
1983 Clandestine opposition movement formed.
1984 Amnesty for all political party leaders announced. President Mitterrand of France paid a state visit.
1985 New constitution promised, with some civilians in the government.
1986 Bokassa returned from France, expecting to return to power; he was imprisoned and his trial started. General Kolingba re-elected. New constitution approved by referendum.
1988 Bokassa found guilty and received death sentence, later commuted to life imprisonment.
1992 Abortive debate held on political reform; multiparty elections promised but then postponed.
1993 Enoch Derant Lakoue appointed prime minister.

Chad

Republic of (*République du Tchad*)

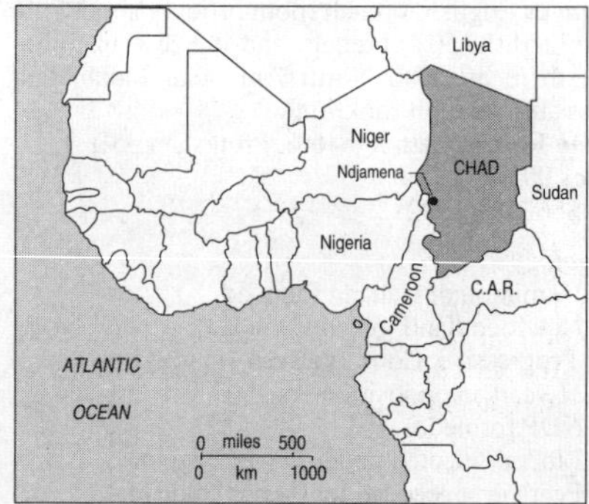

area 1,284,000 sq km/495,624 sq mi
capital Ndjamena (formerly Fort Lamy)
towns Sarh, Moundou, Abéché
physical landlocked state with mountains and part of Sahara Desert in N; moist savanna in S; rivers in S flow NW to Lake Chad
head of state Idriss Deby from 1990
head of government Fuidel Mounyar (interim) 1993

political system emergent democratic republic
political parties National Union for Independence and Revolution (UNIR), nationalist; Alliance for Democracy and Progress (RDP), centre-left; Union for Democracy and Progress (UPDT), centre-left
exports cotton, meat, livestock, hides, skins
currency CFA franc
population (1992) 5,961,000; growth rate 2.3% p.a. Nomadic tribes move N–S seasonally in search of water
life expectancy men 42, women 45
languages French, Arabic (both official), over 100 African languages spoken
religions Muslim 44% (N), Christian 33%, animist 23% (S)
literacy men 40%, women 11% (1985 est)
GDP $980 million (1986); $186 per head

chronology
1960 Independence achieved from France, with François Tombalbaye as president.
1963 Violent opposition in the Muslim north, led by the Chadian National Liberation Front (Frolinat), backed by Libya.
1968 Revolt quelled with France's help.
1975 Tombalbaye killed in military coup led by Félix Malloum. Frolinat continued its resistance.
1978 Malloum tried to find a political solution by bringing the former Frolinat leader Hissène Habré into his government but they were unable to work together.
1979 Malloum forced to leave the country; an interim government was set up under General Goukouni. Habré continued his opposition with his Army of the North (FAN).
1981 Habré now in control of half the country. Goukouni fled and set up a 'government in exile'.
1983 Habré's regime recognized by the Organization for African Unity (OAU), but in the north Goukouni's supporters, with Libya's help, fought on. Eventually a cease- fire was agreed, with latitude 16°N dividing the country.
1984 Libya and France agreed to a withdrawal of forces.
1985 Fighting between Libyan-backed and French-backed forces intensified.
1987 Chad, France, and Libya agreed on cease-fire proposed by OAU.
1988 Full diplomatic relations with Libya restored.
1989 Libyan troop movements reported on border; Habré re-elected, amended constitution.
1990 President Habré ousted in coup led by Idriss Deby. New constitution adopted.
1991 Several anti-government coups foiled.
1992 Anti-government coup foiled. Two new opposition parties approved.
1993 Fuidel Mounyar chosen as transitional prime minister pending multiparty elections.

Chile

Republic of (*República de Chile*)
area 756,950 sq km/292,257 sq mi
capital Santiago
towns Concepción, Viña del Mar, Temuco; ports Valparaíso, Antofagasta, Arica, Iquique, Punta Arenas
physical Andes mountains along E border, Atacama Desert in N, fertile central valley, grazing land and forest in S

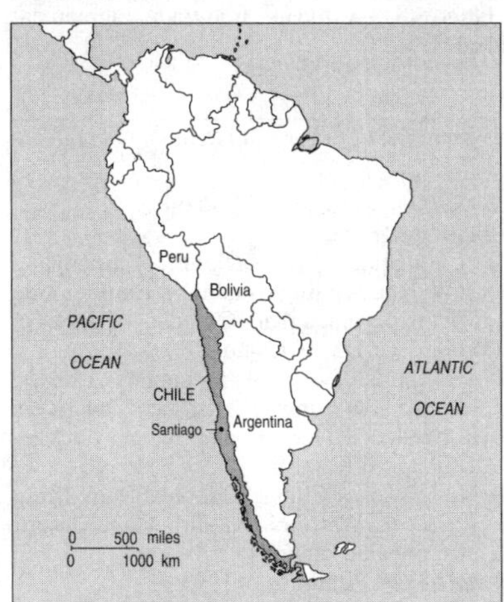

territories Easter Island, Juan Fernández Islands, part of Tierra del Fuego, claim to part of Antarctica
features Atacama Desert is one of the driest regions in the world
head of state and government Patricio Aylwin from 1990
political system emergent democratic republic
political parties Christian Democratic Party (PDC), moderate centrist; National Renewal Party (RN), right-wing
exports copper (world's leading producer), iron, molybdenum (world's second largest producer), nitrate, pulp and paper, steel products, fishmeal, fruit
currency peso
population (1992) 13,599,000 (the majority are of European origin or are mestizos, of mixed American Indian and Spanish descent); growth rate 1.6% p.a.
life expectancy men 64, women 73
language Spanish
religion Roman Catholic 89%
literacy 94% (1988)
GDP $18.9 bn (1987); $6,512 per head

chronology
1818 Achieved independence from Spain.
1964 PDC formed government under Eduardo Frei.
1970 Dr Salvador Allende became the first democratically elected Marxist president; he embarked on an extensive programme of nationalization and social reform.
1973 Government overthrown by the CIA-backed military, led by General Augusto Pinochet. Allende killed. Policy of repression began during which all opposition was put down and political activity banned.
1983 Growing opposition to the regime from all sides, with outbreaks of violence.
1988 Referendum on whether Pinochet should serve a further term resulted in a clear 'No' vote.
1989 President Pinochet agreed to constitutional changes to allow pluralist politics. Patricio Aylwin (PDC) elected president (his term would begin 1990); Pinochet remained as army commander in chief.

1990 Aylwin reached accord on end to military junta government. Pinochet censured by president.
1992 Future US–Chilean free-trade agreement announced.

China

People's Republic of (*Zhonghua Renmin Gonghe Guo*)

area 9,596,960 sq km/3,599,975 sq mi
capital Beijing (Peking)
towns Chongqing (Chungking), Shenyang (Mukden), Wuhan, Nanjing (Nanking), Harbin; ports Tianjin (Tientsin), Shanghai, Qingdao (Tsingtao), Lüda (Lü-ta), Guangzhou (Canton)
physical two-thirds of China is mountains or desert (N and W); the low-lying E is irrigated by rivers Huang He (Yellow River), Chang Jiang (Yangtze-Kiang), Xi Jiang (Si Kiang)
features Great Wall of China; Gezhouba Dam; Ming Tombs; Terracotta Warriors (Xi'ain); Gobi Desert; world's most populous country
head of state Jiang Zemin from 1993
head of government Li Peng from 1987
political system communist republic
political party Chinese Communist Party (CCP), Marxist-Leninist-Maoist
exports tea, livestock and animal products, silk, cotton, oil, minerals (China is the world's largest producer of tungsten and antimony), chemicals, light industrial goods
currency yuan
population (1992) 1,165,888,000 (the majority are Han or ethnic Chinese; the 67 million of other ethnic groups, including Tibetan, Uigur, and Zhuang, live in border areas). The number of people of Chinese origin outside China, Taiwan, and Hong Kong is estimated at 15-24 million. Growth rate 1.2% p.a.
life expectancy men 67, women 69
languages Chinese, including Mandarin (official), Cantonese, and other dialects
religions officially atheist, but traditionally Taoist, Confucianist, and Buddhist; Muslim 13 million; Catholic 3-6 million (divided between the 'patriotic' church established 1958 and the 'loyal' church subject to Rome); Protestant 3 million
literacy men 82%, women 66% (1985 est)
GDP $293.4 bn (1987); $274 per head

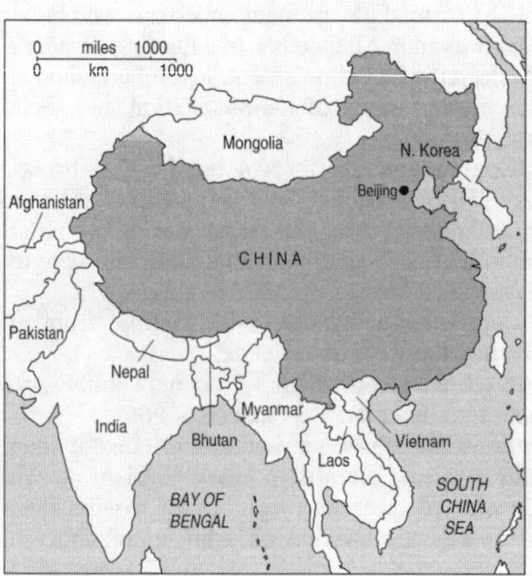

chronology
1949 People's Republic of China proclaimed by Mao Zedong.
1954 Soviet-style constitution adopted.
1956–57 Hundred Flowers Movement encouraged criticism of the government.
1958–60 Great Leap Forward commune experiment to achieve 'true communism'.
1960 Withdrawal of Soviet technical advisers.
1962 Sino-Indian border war.
1962–65 Economic recovery programme under Liu Shaoqi; Maoist 'socialist education movement' rectification campaign.
1966–69 Great Proletarian Cultural Revolution; Liu Shaoqi overthrown.
1969 Ussuri River border clashes with USSR.
1970-76 Reconstruction under Mao and Zhou Enlai.
1971 Entry into United Nations.
1972 US president Nixon visited Beijing.
1975 New state constitution. Unveiling of Zhou's 'Four Modernizations' programme.
1976 Deaths of Zhou Enlai and Mao Zedong; appointment of Hua Guofeng as prime minister and Communist Party chair. Vice Premier Deng Xiaoping in hiding. Gang of Four arrested.
1977 Rehabilitation of Deng Xiaoping.
1979 Economic reforms introduced. Diplomatic relations opened with USA. Punitive invasion of Vietnam.
1980 Zhao Ziyang appointed prime minister.
1981 Hu Yaobang succeeded Hua Guofeng as party chair. Imprisonment of Gang of Four.
1982 New state constitution adopted.
1984 'Enterprise management' reforms for industrial sector.
1986 Student prodemocracy demonstrations.
1987 Hu was replaced as party leader by Zhao, with Li Peng as prime minister. Deng left Politburo but remained influential.
1988 Yang Shangkun replaced Li Xiannian as state president. Economic reforms encountered increasing problems; inflation rocketed.
1989 Over 2,000 killed in prodemocracy student demonstrations in Tiananmen Square; international sanctions imposed.
1991 March: European Community and Japanese sanctions lifted. May: normal relations with USSR resumed. Sept: UK prime minister John Major visited Beijing. Nov: relations with Vietnam normalized.
1992 China promised to sign 1968 Nuclear Non-Proliferation Treaty. Historic visit by Japan's emperor.
1993 Jiang Zemin, Chinese Communist Party general secretary, set to replace Yang Shangkun as president.

Colombia

Republic of (*República de Colombia*)

area 1,141,748 sq km/440,715 sq mi
capital Bogotá
towns Medellín, Cali, Bucaramanga; ports Barranquilla, Cartagena, Buenaventura
physical the Andes mountains run N–S; flat coastland in W and plains (llanos) in E; Magdalena River runs N to Caribbean Sea; includes islands of Providencia, San Andrés, and Mapelo

features Zipaquira salt mine and underground cathedral; Lake Guatavita, source of the legend of 'El Dorado'
head of state and government Cesar Gaviria Trujillo from 1990
political system emergent democratic republic
political parties Liberal Party (PL), centrist; April 19 Movement (M-19); National Salvation Movement; Conservative Party, right of centre
exports emeralds (world's largest producer), coffee (world's second largest producer), cocaine (country's largest export), bananas, cotton, meat, sugar, oil, skins, hides, tobacco
currency peso
population (1992) 33,392,000 (mestizo 68%, white 20%, Amerindian 1%); growth rate 2.2% p.a.
life expectancy men 61, women 66; Indians 34
language Spanish
religion Roman Catholic 95%
literacy men 89%, women 87% (1987); Indians 40%
GDP $31.9 bn (1987); $1,074 per head

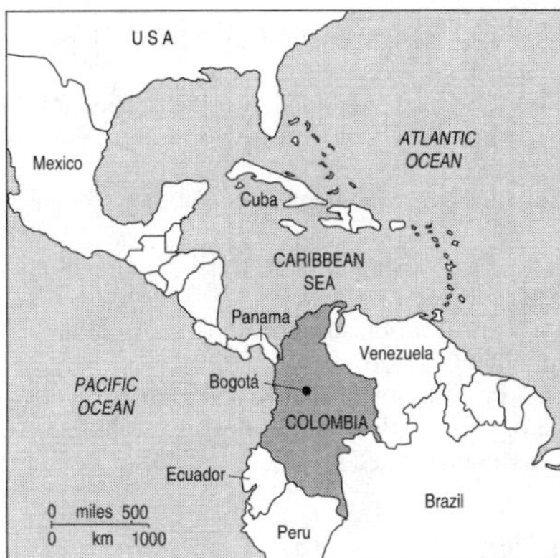

chronology
1886 Full independence achieved from Spain. Conservatives in power.
1930 Liberals in power.
1946 Conservatives in power.
1948 Left-wing mayor of Bogotá assassinated; widespread outcry.
1949 Start of civil war, 'La Violencia', during which over 250,000 people died.
1957 Hoping to halt the violence, Conservatives and Liberals agreed to form a National Front, sharing the presidency.
1970 National Popular Alliance (ANAPO) formed as a left-wing opposition to the National Front.
1974 National Front accord temporarily ended.
1975 Civil unrest because of disillusionment with the government.
1978 Liberals, under Julio Turbay, revived the accord and began an intensive fight against drug dealers.
1982 Liberals maintained their control of congress but lost the presidency. The Conservative president, Belisario Betancur, granted guerrillas an amnesty and freed political prisoners.
1984 Minister of justice assassinated by drug dealers; campaign against them stepped up.
1986 Virgilio Barco Vargas, Liberal, elected president by record margin.
1989 Drug cartel assassinated leading presidential candidate; Vargas declared antidrug war; bombing campaign by drug traffickers killed hundreds; police killed José Rodríguez Gacha, one of the most wanted cartel leaders.
1990 Cesar Gaviria Trujillo elected president. Liberals maintained control of congress.
1991 New constitution prohibited extradition of Colombians wanted for trial in other countries; several leading drug traffickers arrested. Oct: Liberal Party won general election.
1992 One of the drug cartel leaders, Pablo Escobar, escaped from prison.
1993 Escobar continued to defy government.

Comoros

Federal Islamic Republic of (*Jumhurīyat al-Qumur al- Itthādīyah al-Islāmīyah*)
area 1,862 sq km/719 sq mi
capital Moroni
towns Mutsamudu, Domoni, Fomboni
physical comprises the volcanic islands of Njazídja, Nzwani, and Mwali (formerly Grande Comore, Anjouan, Moheli); at N end of Mozambique Channel

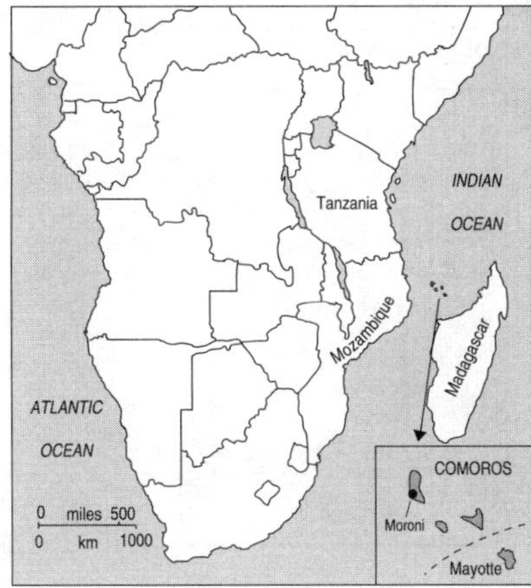

features active volcano on Njazídja; poor tropical soil
head of state Said Mohammad Djohar (interim administration) from 1989
head of government Halidi Abderamane Ibrahim from 1993
political system emergent democracy
political parties Comoran Union for Progress (Udzima), nationalist Islamic; National Union for Congolese Democracy (UNDC), left of centre; Popular Democratic Movement (MDP), centrist
exports copra, vanilla, cocoa, sisal, coffee, cloves, essential oils
currency CFA franc
population (1992) 497,000; growth rate 3.1% p.a.
life expectancy men 48, women 52
languages Arabic (official), Comorian (Swahili and Arabic dialect), Makua, French
religions Muslim (official) 86%, Roman Catholic 14%

literacy 15%
GDP $198 million (1987); $468 per head
chronology
1975 Independence achieved from France, but island of Mayotte remained part of France. Ahmed Abdallah elected president. The Comoros joined the United Nations.
1976 Abdallah overthrown by Ali Soilih.
1978 Soilih killed by mercenaries working for Abdallah. Islamic republic proclaimed and Abdallah elected president.
1979 The Comoros became a one-party state; powers of the federal government increased.
1985 Constitution amended to make Abdallah head of government as well as head of state.
1989 Abdallah killed by French mercenaries who took control of government; under French and South African pressure, mercenaries left Comoros, turning authority over to French administration and interim president Said Mohammad Djohar.
1990 Antigovernment coup foiled.
1992 Third transitional government appointed. Antigovernment coup foiled.
1993 General election failed to provide any one party with overall assembly majority. President Djohar appointed Halidi Abderamane Ibrahim prime minister.

Congo

Republic of (*République du Congo*)

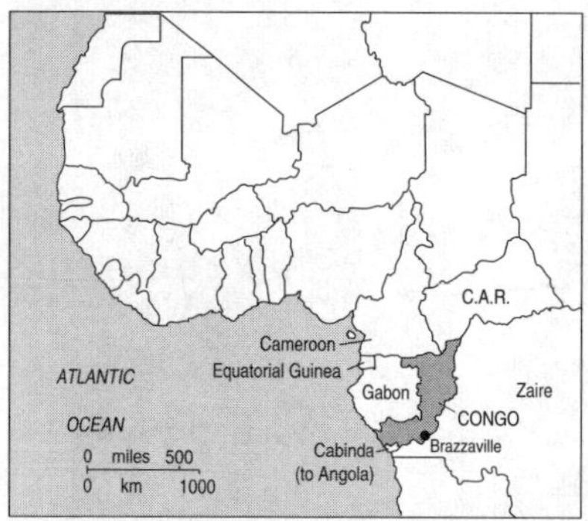

area 342,000 sq km/132,012 sq mi
capital Brazzaville
towns chief port Pointe-Noire; N'Kayi, Loubomo
physical narrow coastal plain rises to central plateau, then falls into northern basin; Zaïre (Congo) River on the border with Zaire; half the country is rainforest
environment an estimated 93% of the rural population is without access to safe drinking water
features 70% of the population lives in Brazzaville, Pointe-Noire, or in towns along the railway linking these two places
head of state and government Pascal Lissouba from 1992
political system emergent democracy
political parties Pan-African Union for Social Democracy (UPADS), moderate left of centre; Congolese Labour Party (PCT), (Marxist-Leninist ideology abandoned 1990) left-wing; Congolese Movement for Democracy and Integral Development (MCDDI), moderate centrist
exports timber, petroleum, cocoa, sugar
currency CFA franc
population (1992) 2,692,000 (chiefly Bantu); growth rate 2.6% p.a.
life expectancy men 45, women 48
languages French (official); many African languages
religions animist 50%, Christian 48%, Muslim 2%
literacy men 79%, women 55% (1985 est)
GDP $2.1 bn (1983); $500 per head
chronology
1910 Became part of French Equatorial Africa.
1960 Achieved independence from France, with Abbé Youlou as the first president.
1963 Youlou forced to resign. New constitution approved, with Alphonse Massamba-Débat as president.
1964 The Congo became a one-party state.
1968 Military coup, led by Capt Marien Ngouabi, ousted Massamba-Débat.
1970 A Marxist state, the People's Republic of the Congo, was announced, with the PCT as the only legal party.
1977 Ngouabi assassinated. Col Yhombi-Opango became president.
1979 Yhombi-Opango handed over the presidency to the PCT, who chose Col Denis Sassou-Nguessou as his successor.
1984 Sassou-Nguessou elected for another five-year term.
1990 The PCT abandoned Marxist-Leninism and promised multiparty politics.
1991 1979 constitution suspended. Country renamed the Republic of Congo.
1992 New constitution approved and multiparty elections held, giving UPADS the most assembly seats. Pascal Lissouba elected president.

Costa Rica

Republic of (*República de Costa Rica*)

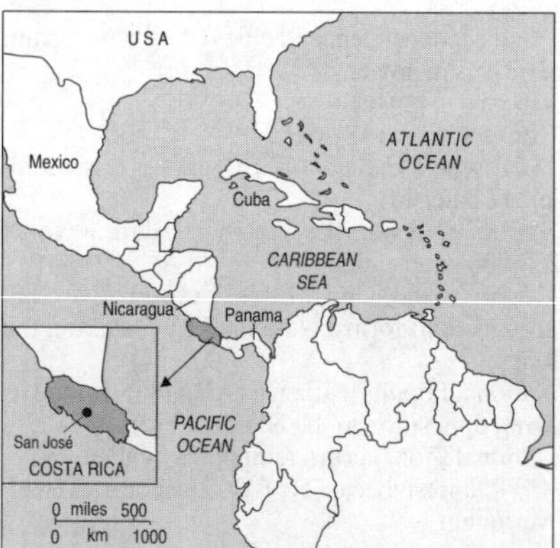

area 51,100 sq km/19,735 sq mi
capital San José
towns ports Limón, Puntarenas
physical high central plateau and tropical coasts; Costa Rica was once entirely forested, containing an estimated 5% of the Earth's flora and fauna. By 1983 only 17% of the forest remained; half of the arable

land had been cleared for cattle ranching, which led to landlessness, unemployment (except for 2,000 politically powerful families), and soil erosion; the massive environmental destruction also caused incalculable loss to the gene pool
environment one of the leading centres of conservation in Latin America, with more than 10% of the country protected by national parks, and tree replanting proceeding at a rate of 150 sq km/60 sq mi per year
features Poas Volcano; Guayabo pre-Colombian ceremonial site
head of state and government Rafael Calderón from 1990
political system liberal democracy
political parties National Liberation Party (PLN), left of centre; Christian Socialist Unity Party (PUSC), centrist coalition; ten minor parties
exports coffee, bananas, cocoa, sugar, beef
currency colón
population (1992) 3,161,000 (including 1,200 Guaymi Indians); growth rate 2.6% p.a.
life expectancy men 71, women 76
language Spanish (official)
religion Roman Catholic 95%
literacy men 94%, women 93% (1985 est)
GDP $4.3 bn (1986); $1,550 per head

chronology
1821 Independence achieved from Spain.
1949 New constitution adopted. National army abolished. José Figueres, cofounder of the PLN, elected president; he embarked on ambitious socialist programme.
1958–73 Mainly conservative administrations.
1974 PLN regained the presidency and returned to socialist policies.
1978 Rodrigo Carazo, conservative, elected president. Sharp deterioration in the state of the economy.
1982 Luis Alberto Monge (PLN) elected president. Harsh austerity programme introduced to rebuild the economy. Pressure from the USA to abandon neutral stance and condemn Sandinista regime in Nicaragua.
1983 Policy of neutrality reaffirmed.
1985 Following border clashes with Sandinista forces, a US-trained antiguerrilla guard formed.
1986 Oscar Arias Sánchez won the presidency on a neutralist platform.
1987 Arias won Nobel Prize for Peace for devising a Central American peace plan.
1990 Rafael Calderón (PUSC) elected president.

Croatia

Republic of

area 56,538 sq km/21,824 sq mi
capital Zagreb
towns chief port: Rijeka (Fiume); other ports: Zadar, Sibenik, Split, Dubrovnik
physical Adriatic coastline with large islands; very mountainous, with part of the Karst region and the Julian and Styrian Alps; some marshland
features popular sea resorts along the extensive Adriatic coastline
head of state Franjo Tudjman from 1990
head of government Nikica Valentic from 1993
political system emergent democracy
political parties Christian Democratic Union (HDZ), right-wing, nationalist; Coalition of National Agreement, centrist; Communist Party, reform-communist

products cereals, potatoes, tobacco, fruit, livestock, metal goods, textiles
currency Croatian dinar
population (1992) 4,808,000 including 75% Croats, 12% Serbs, and 1% Slovenes
language Croatian variant of Serbo-Croatian
media no official censorship but no press or TV independent of government
religions Roman Catholic (Croats); Orthodox Christian (Serbs)
GNP $7.9 bn (1990); $1,660 per head

chronology
1918 Became part of the kingdom that united the Serbs, Croats, and Slovenes.
1929 The kingdom of Croatia, Serbia, and Slovenia became Yugoslavia. Croatia continued its campaign for autonomy.
1941 Became a Nazi puppet state following German invasion.
1945 Became constituent republic of Yugoslavia.
1970s Separatist demands resurfaced. Crackdown against anti-Serb separatist agitators.
1989 Formation of opposition parties permitted.
1990 April–May: Communists defeated by Tudjman-led Croatian Democratic Union (HDZ) in first free election since 1938. Sept: 'sovereignty' declared. Dec: new constitution adopted.
1991 Feb: assembly called for Croatia's secession. March: Serb-dominated Krajina announced secession from Croatia. June: Croatia declared independence; military conflict with Serbia; internal civil war ensued. July onwards: civil war intensified. Oct: Croatia formally seceded from Yugoslavia.
1992 Jan: United Nations peace accord reached in Sarajevo; Croatia's independence recognized by the European Community. March–April: UN peacekeeping forces drafted into Croatia. April: independence recognized by USA. May: became a member of the United Nations. Aug: Tudjman directly elected president; HDZ won assembly elections. Sept: Tudjman requested withdrawal of UN forces on expiry of mandate 1993.

1993 Jan: Croatian forces launched offensive to retake parts of Serb-held Krajina, violating the 1992 UN peace accord.

Cuba

Republic of (*República de Cuba*)

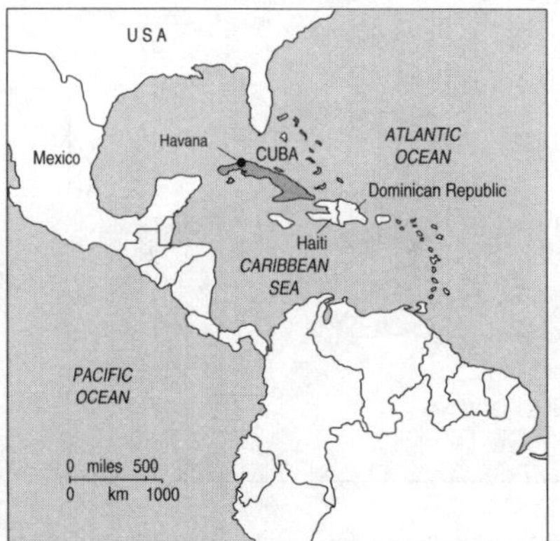

area 110,860 sq km/42,820 sq mi
capital Havana
towns Santiago de Cuba, Camagüey
physical comprises Cuba, the largest and westernmost of the West Indies, and smaller islands including Isle of Youth; low hills; Sierra Maestra mountains in SE
features 3,380 km/2,100 mi of coastline, with deep bays, sandy beaches, coral islands and reefs; more than 1,600 islands surround the Cuban mainland
head of state and government Fidel Castro Ruz from 1959
political system communist republic
political party Communist Party of Cuba (PCC), Marxist-Leninist
exports sugar, tobacco, coffee, nickel, fish
currency Cuban peso
population (1992) 10,848,000; 37% are white of Spanish descent, 51% mulatto, and 11% are of African origin; growth rate 0.6% p.a.
life expectancy men 72, women 75
language Spanish
religions Roman Catholic 85%; also Episcopalians and Methodists
literacy men 96%, women 95% (1988)
disposable national income $15.8 bn (1983); $1,590 per head

chronology
1492 Christopher Columbus landed in Cuba and claimed it for Spain.
1898 USA defeated Spain in Spanish-American War; Spain gave up all claims to Cuba.
1901 Cuba achieved independence; Tomás Estrada Palma became first president of the Republic of Cuba.
1933 Fulgencia Batista seized power.
1944 Batista retired.
1952 Batista seized power again to begin an oppressive regime.
1953 Fidel Castro led an unsuccessful coup against Batista.
1956 Second unsuccessful coup by Castro.
1959 Batista overthrown by Castro. Constitution of 1940 replaced by a 'Fundamental Law', making Castro prime minister, his brother Raúl Castro his deputy, and 'Che' Guevara his number three.
1960 All US businesses in Cuba appropriated without compensation; USA broke off diplomatic relations.
1961 USA sponsored an unsuccessful invasion at the Bay of Pigs. Castro announced that Cuba had become a communist state, with a Marxist-Leninist programme of economic development.
1962 Cuba expelled from the Organization of American States. Soviet nuclear missiles installed but subsequently removed from Cuba at US insistence.
1965 Cuba's sole political party renamed Communist Party of Cuba (PCC). With Soviet help, Cuba began to make considerable economic and social progress.
1972 Cuba became a full member of the Moscow-based Council for Mutual Economic Assistance.
1976 New socialist constitution approved; Castro elected president.
1976-81 Castro became involved in extensive international commitments, sending troops as Soviet surrogates, particularly to Africa.
1982 Cuba joined other Latin American countries in giving moral support to Argentina in its dispute with Britain over the Falklands.
1984 Castro tried to improve US–Cuban relations by discussing exchange of US prisoners in Cuba for Cuban 'undesirables' in the USA.
1988 Peace accord with South Africa signed, agreeing to withdrawal of Cuban troops from Angola.
1989 Reduction in Cuba's overseas military activities.
1991 Soviet troops withdrawn.
1992 Castro affirmed continuing support of communism.
1993 Mysterious epidemic swept the country, possibly linked to malnutrition.

Cyprus

Greek ***Republic of Cyprus*** (*Kypriakí Dimokratía*) in the south, and ***Turkish Republic of Northern Cyprus*** (*Kibris Cumhuriyeti*) in the north

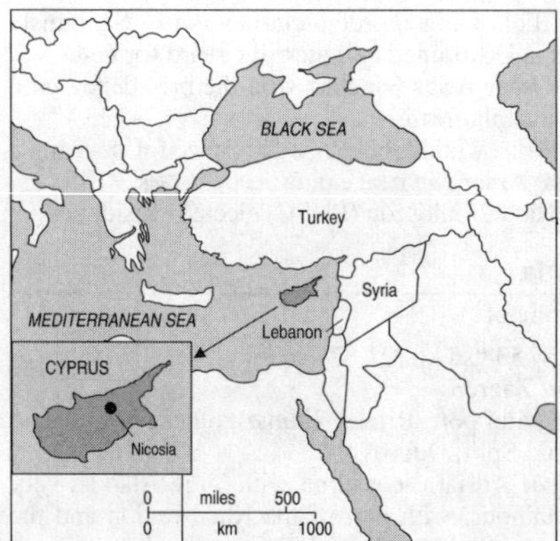

area 9,251 sq km/3,571 sq mi, 37% in Turkish hands
capital Nicosia (divided between Greeks and Turks)
towns ports Limassol, Larnaca, Paphos (Greek); Morphou, and ports Kyrenia and Famagusta (Turkish)

physical central plain between two E–W mountain ranges
features archaeological and historic sites; Mount Olympus 1,953 m/6,406 ft (highest peak); beaches
heads of state and government Glafkos Clerides (Greek) from 1993, Rauf Denktaş (Turkish) from 1976
political system democratic divided republic
political parties Democratic Front (DIKO), centre-left; Progressive Party of the Working People (AKEL), socialist; Democratic Rally (DISY), centrist; Socialist Party (EDEK), socialist; *Turkish zone*: National Unity Party (NUP), Communal Liberation Party (CLP), Republican Turkish Party (RTP), New British Party (NBP)
exports citrus, grapes, raisins, Cyprus sherry, potatoes, clothing, footwear
currency Cyprus pound and Turkish lira
population (1992) 580,000 (Greek Cypriot 78%, Turkish Cypriot 18%); growth rate 1.2% p.a.
life expectancy men 72, women 76
languages Greek and Turkish (official), English
religions Greek Orthodox 78%, Sunni Muslim 18%
literacy 99% (1984)
GDP $3.7 bn (1987); $5,497 per head

chronology
1878 Came under British administration.
1955 Guerrilla campaign began against the British for enosis (union with Greece), led by Archbishop Makarios and General Grivas.
1956 Makarios and enosis leaders deported.
1959 Compromise agreed and Makarios returned to be elected president of an independent Greek-Turkish Cyprus.
1960 Independence achieved from Britain, with Britain retaining its military bases.
1963 Turks set up their own government in northern Cyprus. Fighting broke out between the two communities.
1964 United Nations peacekeeping force installed.
1971 Grivas returned to start a guerrilla war against the Makarios government.
1974 Grivas died. Military coup deposed Makarios, who fled to Britain. Nicos Sampson appointed president. Turkish army sent to northern Cyprus to confirm Turkish Cypriots' control; military regime in southern Cyprus collapsed; Makarios returned. Northern Cyprus declared itself the Turkish Federated State of Cyprus (TFSC), with Rauf Denktaş as president.
1977 Makarios died; succeeded by Spyros Kyprianou.
1983 An independent Turkish Republic of Northern Cyprus proclaimed but recognized only by Turkey.
1984 UN peace proposals rejected.
1985 Summit meeting between Kyprianou and Denktaş failed to reach agreement.
1988 Georgios Vassiliou elected president. Talks with Denktaş began, under UN auspices.
1989 Peace talks abandoned.
1992 UN-sponsored peace talks collapsed.
1993 Democratic Rally leader Glafkos Clerides narrowly won presidential election.

Czech Republic

(Česká Republika)

area 78,864 sq km/30,461 sq mi
capital Prague

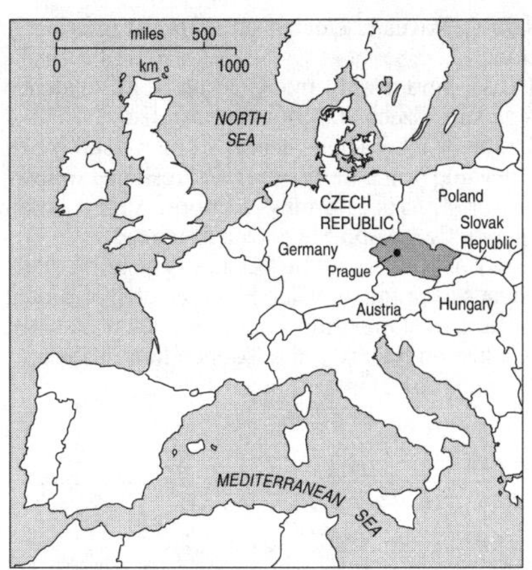

towns Brno, Ostrava, Olomouc, Liberec, Plzeň, Ustí nad Labem, Hradec Králové
physical mountainous; rivers: Morava, Labe (Elbe), Vltava (Moldau)
environment considered in 1991 to be the most polluted country in E Europe. Pollution is worst in N Bohemia, which produced 70% of Czechoslovakia's coal and 45% of its coal-generated electricity. Up to 20 times the permissible level of sulphur dioxide is released over Prague, where 75% of the drinking water fails to meet the country's health standards
features summer and winter resort areas in Western Carpathian, Bohemian, and Sudetic mountain ranges
head of state Václav Havel from 1993
head of government Václav Klaus from 1993
political system emergent democracy
political parties Civic Democratic Party (CDP), right of centre; Civic Movement (CM), left of centre; Communist Party (CPCZ), left-wing; Czechoslovak People's Party, centrist nationalist
exports machinery, vehicles, coal, iron and steel, chemicals, glass, ceramics, clothing
currency new currency based on koruna
population (1991) 10,298,700 (with German and other minorities); growth rate 0.4% p.a.
life expectancy men 68, women 75
languages Czech (official)
religions Roman Catholic (75%), Protestant, Hussite, Orthodox
literacy 100%
GDP $26,600 million (1990); $2,562 per head

chronology
1526–1918 Under Habsburg domination.
1918 Independence achieved from Austro-Hungarian Empire; Czechs joined Slovaks in forming Czechoslovakia as independent nation.
1948 Communists assumed power in Czechoslovakia.
1968 Czech Socialist Republic created under new federal constitution.
1989 Nov: pro-democracy demonstrations in Prague; new political parties formed, including Czech-based Civic Forum under Václav Havel; Communist Party stripped of powers; political parties legalized. Dec: new 'grand coalition' government formed, including former dissidents; Havel appointed state president. Amnesty granted to 22,000 prisoners; calls for USSR to withdraw troops.

1990 July: Havel re-elected president in multiparty elections.
1991 Civic Forum split into CDP and CM; evidence of increasing Czech and Slovak separatism.
1992 June: Václav Klaus, leader of the Czech-based CDP, became prime minister; Havel resigned following Slovak gains in assembly elections. Aug: creation of separate Czech and Slovak states agreed.
1993 Jan: Czech Republic became sovereign state, with Klaus as prime minister. Havel elected president of the new republic. Admitted into United Nations, Conference on Security and Cooperation in Europe, and Council of Europe.

Denmark

Kingdom of (*Kongeriget Danmark*)
area 43,075 sq km/16,627 sq mi
capital Copenhagen
towns Aarhus, Odense, Aalborg, Esbjerg, all ports
physical comprises the Jutland peninsula and about 500 islands (100 inhabited) including Bornholm in the Baltic Sea; the land is flat and cultivated; sand dunes and lagoons on the W coast and long inlets (fjords) on the E; the main island is Sjælland (Zealand), where most of Copenhagen is located (the rest is on the island of Amager)
territories the dependencies of Faeroe Islands and Greenland

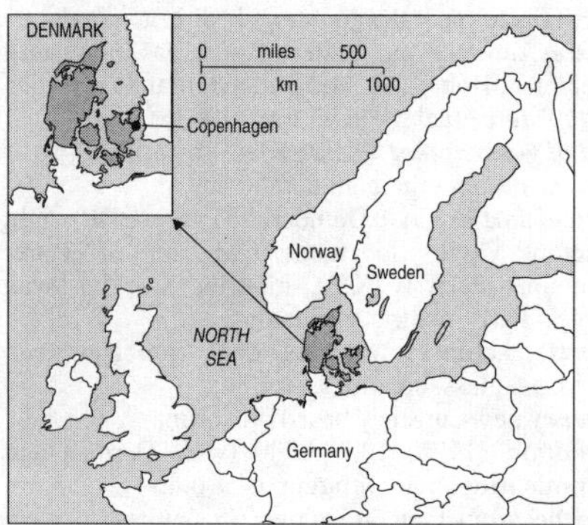

features Kronborg Castle in Helsingør (Elsinore); Tivoli Gardens (Copenhagen); Legoland Park in Sillund
head of state Queen Margrethe II from 1972
head of government Poul Nyrup Rasmussen from 1993
political system liberal democracy
political parties Social Democrats (SD), left of centre; Conservative People's Party (KF), moderate centre-right; Liberal Party (V), centre-left; Socialist People's Party (SF), moderate left-wing; Radical Liberals (RV), radical internationalist, left of centre; Centre Democrats (CD), moderate centrist; Progress Party (FP), radical antibureaucratic; Christian People's Party (KrF), interdenominational, family values
exports bacon, dairy produce, eggs, fish, mink pelts, car and aircraft parts, electrical equipment, textiles, chemicals
currency kroner
population (1992) 5,167,000; growth rate 0% p.a.
life expectancy men 72, women 78
languages Danish (official); there is a German-speaking minority
religion Lutheran 97%
literacy 99% (1983)
GDP $142.1 bn (1992)
chronology
1940–45 Occupied by Germany.
1945 Iceland's independence recognized.
1947 Frederik IX succeeded Christian X.
1948 Home rule granted for Faeroe Islands.
1949 Became a founding member of NATO.
1960 Joined European Free Trade Association (EFTA).
1972 Margrethe II became Denmark's first queen in nearly 600 years.
1973 Left EFTA and joined European Economic Community (EEC).
1979 Home rule granted for Greenland.
1985 Strong non-nuclear movement in evidence.
1990 General election; another coalition government formed.
1992 Rejection of Maastricht Treaty in national referendum.
1993 Poul Schlüter resigned; replaced by Poul Nyrup Rasmussen at head of Social Democrat-led coalition government. Second referendum approved the Maastricht Treaty after modifications.

Djibouti

Republic of (*Jumhouriyya Djibouti*)

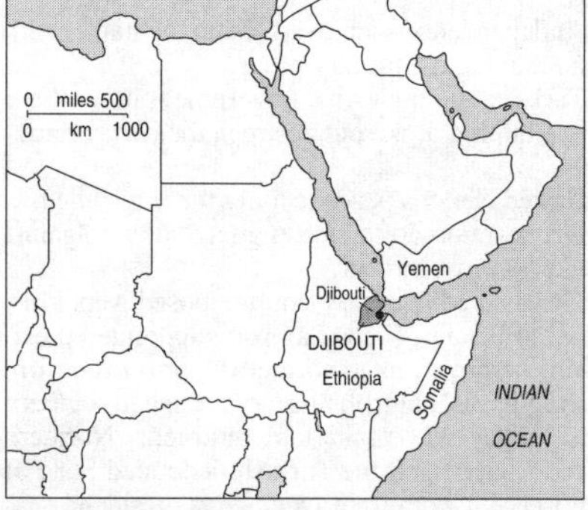

area 23,200 sq km/8,955 sq mi
capital (and chief port) Djibouti
towns Tadjoura, Obock, Dikhil
physical mountains divide an inland plateau from a coastal plain; hot and arid
features terminus of railway link with Ethiopia; Lac Assal salt lake is the second lowest point on Earth (–144 m/–471 ft)
head of state and government Hassan Gouled Aptidon from 1977
political system authoritarian nationalism
political party People's Progress Assembly (RPP), nationalist
exports acts mainly as a transit port for Ethiopia
currency Djibouti franc
population (1992) 557,000 (Issa 47%, Afar 37%, European 8%, Arab 6%); growth rate 3.4% p.a.
life expectancy 50

languages French (official), Somali, Afar, Arabic
religion Sunni Muslim
literacy 20% (1988)
GDP $378 million (1987); $1,016 per head

chronology
1884 Annexed by France as part of French Somaliland.
1967 French Somaliland became the French Territory of the Afars and the Issas.
1977 Independence achieved from France; Hassan Gouled was elected president.
1979 All political parties combined to form the People's Progress Assembly (RPP).
1981 New constitution made RPP the only legal party. Gouled re-elected. Treaties of friendship signed with Ethiopia, Somalia, Kenya, and Sudan.
1984 Policy of neutrality reaffirmed.
1987 Gouled re-elected for a third term.
1991 Amnesty International accused secret police of brutality.
1992 Djibouti elected member of UN Security Council 1993–95.
1993 Gouled re-elected for a fourth term.

Dominica

Commonwealth of

area 751 sq km/290 sq mi
capital Roseau, with a deepwater port
towns Portsmouth, Marigot
physical second largest of the Windward Islands, mountainous central ridge with tropical rainforest
features of great beauty, it has mountains of volcanic origin rising to 1,620 m/5,317 ft; Boiling Lake (an effect produced by escaping subterranean gas)
head of state Clarence Seignoret from 1983
head of government Eugenia Charles from 1980
political system liberal democracy
political parties Dominica Freedom Party (DFP), centrist; Labour Party of Dominica (LPD), left-of-centre coalition
exports bananas, coconuts, citrus, lime, bay oil
currency Eastern Caribbean dollar; pound sterling; French franc
population (1992) 71,500 (mainly black African in origin, but with a small Carib reserve of some 500); growth rate 1.3% p.a.
life expectancy men 57, women 59

language English (official), but the Dominican patois reflects earlier periods of French rule
media one independent weekly newspaper
religion Roman Catholic 80%
literacy 80%
GDP $91 million (1985); $1,090 per head

chronology
1763 Became British possession.
1978 Independence achieved from Britain. Patrick John, leader of Dominica Labour Party (DLP), elected prime minister.
1980 Dominica Freedom Party (DFP), led by Eugenia Charles, won convincing victory in general election.
1981 Patrick John implicated in plot to overthrow government.
1982 John tried and acquitted.
1985 John retried and found guilty. Regrouping of left-of-centre parties resulted in new Labour Party of Dominica (LPD). DFP, led by Eugenia Charles, re-elected.
1990 Charles elected to a third term.
1991 Integration into Windward Islands confederation proposed.

Dominican Republic

(*República Dominicana*)

area 48,442 sq km/18,700 sq mi
capital Santo Domingo
towns Santiago de los Caballeros, San Pedro de Macoris
physical comprises eastern two-thirds of island of Hispaniola; central mountain range with fertile valleys
features Pico Duarte 3,174 m/10,417 ft, highest point in Caribbean islands; Santo Domingo is the oldest European city in the western hemisphere
head of state and government Joaquín Ricardo Balaguer from 1986
political system democratic republic
political parties Dominican Revolutionary Party (PRD), moderate, left of centre; Christian Social Reform Party (PRSC), independent socialist; Dominican Liberation Party (PLD), nationalist
exports sugar, gold, silver, tobacco, coffee, nickel
currency peso
population (1992) 7,471,000; growth rate 2.3% p.a.
life expectancy men 61, women 65
language Spanish (official)

religion Roman Catholic 95%
literacy men 78%, women 77% (1985 est)
GDP $4.9 bn (1987); $731 per head

chronology
1492 Visited by Christopher Columbus.
1844 Dominican Republic established.
1930 Military coup established dictatorship of Rafael Trujillo.
1961 Trujillo assassinated.
1962 First democratic elections resulted in Juan Bosch, founder of the PRD, becoming president.
1963 Bosch overthrown in military coup.
1965 US Marines intervene to restore order and protect foreign nationals.
1966 New constitution adopted. Joaquín Balaguer, leader of PRSC, became president.
1978 PRD returned to power, with Silvestre Antonio Guzmán as president.
1982 PRD re-elected, with Jorge Blanco as president.
1985 Blanco forced by International Monetary Fund to adopt austerity measures to save the economy.
1986 PRSC returned to power, with Balaguer re-elected president.
1990 Balaguer re-elected by a small majority.

Ecuador

Republic of (*República del Ecuador*)

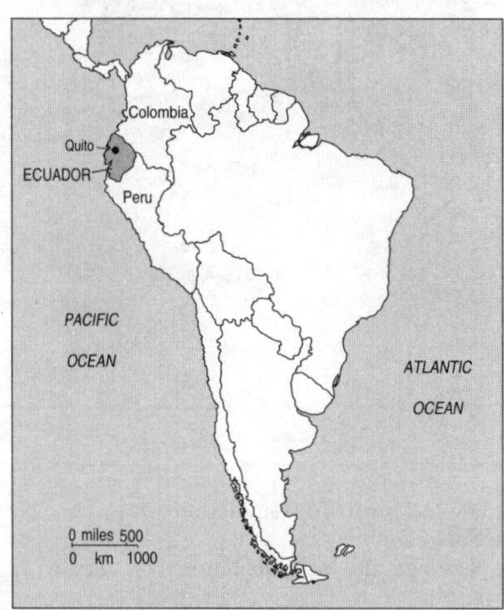

area 270,670 sq km/104,479 sq mi
capital Quito
towns Cuenca; chief port Guayaquil
physical coastal plain rises sharply to Andes Mountains, which are divided into a series of cultivated valleys; flat, low-lying rainforest in E
environment about 25,000 species became extinct 1965–90 as a result of environmental destruction
features Ecuador is crossed by the equator, from which it derives its name; Galápagos Islands; Cotopaxi is world's highest active volcano; rich wildlife in rainforest of Amazon basin
head of state and government Sixto Duran Ballen from 1992
political system emergent democracy
political parties Social Christian Party (PSC), right-wing; United Republican Party (PUR), right-of-centre coalition; Ecuadorean Roldosist Party (PRE)
exports bananas, cocoa, coffee, sugar, rice, fruit, balsa wood, fish, petroleum
currency sucre
population (1992) 10,607,000; (mestizo 55%, Indian 25%, European 10%, black African 10%); growth rate 2.9% p.a.
life expectancy men 62, women 66
languages Spanish (official), Quechua, Jivaro, and other Indian languages
religion Roman Catholic 95%
literacy men 85%, women 80% (1985 est)
GDP $10.6 bn (1987); $1,069 per head

chronology
1830 Independence achieved from Spain.
1925–48 Great political instability; no president completed his term of office.
1948–55 Liberals in power.
1956 First conservative president in 60 years.
1960 Liberals returned, with José Velasco as president.
1961 Velasco deposed and replaced by the vice president.
1962 Military junta installed.
1968 Velasco returned as president.
1972 A coup put the military back in power.
1978 New democratic constitution adopted.
1979 Liberals in power but opposed by right- and left-wing parties.
1982 Deteriorating economy provoked strikes, demonstrations, and a state of emergency.
1983 Austerity measures introduced.
1984–85 No party with a clear majority in the national congress; Febres Cordero narrowly won the presidency for the Conservatives.
1988 Rodrigo Borja Cevallos elected president for moderate left-wing coalition.
1989 Guerrilla left-wing group *Alfaro Vive, Carajo* ('Alfaro lives, damn it'), numbering about 1,000, laid down arms after nine years.
1992 PUR leader Sixto Duran Ballen elected president; PSC became largest party in congress.

Egypt

Arab Republic of (*Jumhuriyat Misr al-Arabiya*)

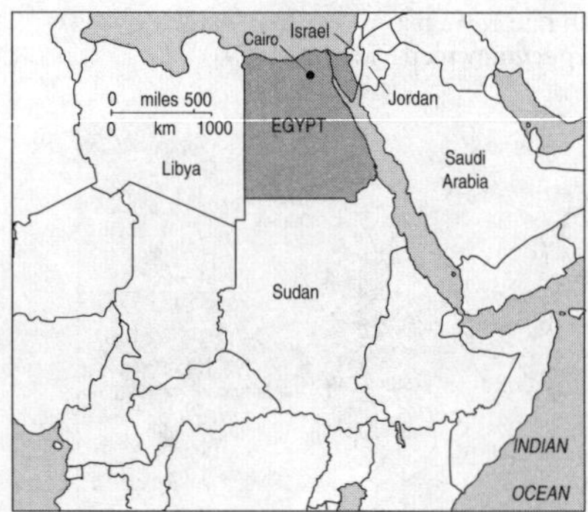

area 1,001,450 sq km/386,990 sq mi
capital Cairo
towns Gîza; ports Alexandria, Port Said, Suez, Damietta

physical mostly desert; hills in E; fertile land along Nile valley and delta; cultivated and settled area is about 35,500 sq km/13,700 sq mi
environment the building of the Aswan Dam (opened 1970) on the Nile has caused widespread salinization and an increase in waterborne diseases in villages close to Lake Nasser. A dramatic fall in the annual load of silt deposited downstream has reduced the fertility of cropland and has led to coastal erosion and the consequent loss of sardine shoals
features Aswan High Dam and Lake Nasser; Sinai; remains of ancient Egypt (pyramids, Sphinx, Luxor, Karnak, Abu Simbel, El Faiyum)
head of state and government Hosni Mubarak from 1981
political system democratic republic
political parties National Democratic Party (NDP), moderate left of centre; Socialist Labour Party, right of centre; Socialist Liberal Party, free-enterprise; New Wafd Party, nationalist
exports cotton and textiles, petroleum, fruit and vegetables
currency Egyptian pound
population (1992) 55,979,000; growth rate 2.4% p.a.
life expectancy men 57, women 60
languages Arabic (official); ancient Egyptian survives to some extent in Coptic
media there is no legal censorship, but the largest publishing houses, newspapers, and magazines are owned and controlled by the state, as is all television. Questioning of prevalent values, ideas, and social practices is discouraged
religions Sunni Muslim 95%, Coptic Christian 5%
literacy men 59%, women 30% (1985 est)
GDP $34.5 bn (1987); $679 per head

chronology
1914 Egypt became a British protectorate.
1936 Independence achieved from Britain. King Fuad succeeded by his son Farouk.
1946 Withdrawal of British troops except from Suez Canal Zone.
1952 Farouk overthrown by army in bloodless coup.
1953 Egypt declared a republic, with General Neguib as president.
1956 Neguib replaced by Col Gamal Nasser. Nasser announced nationalization of Suez Canal; Egypt attacked by Britain, France, and Israel. Cease-fire agreed because of US intervention.
1958 Short-lived merger of Egypt and Syria as United Arab Republic (UAR). Subsequent attempts to federate Egypt, Syria, and Iraq failed.
1967 Six-Day War with Israel ended in Egypt's defeat and Israeli occupation of Sinai and Gaza Strip.
1970 Nasser died suddenly; succeeded by Anwar Sadat.
1973 Attempt to regain territory lost to Israel led to fighting; cease-fire arranged by US secretary of state Henry Kissinger.
1977 Sadat's visit to Israel to address the Israeli parliament was criticized by Egypt's Arab neighbours.
1978-79 Camp David talks in the USA resulted in a treaty between Egypt and Israel. Egypt expelled from the Arab League.
1981 Sadat assassinated, succeeded by Hosni Mubarak.
1983 Improved relations between Egypt and the Arab world; only Libya and Syria maintained a trade boycott.
1984 Mubarak's party victorious in the people's assembly elections.
1987 Mubarak re-elected. Egypt readmitted to Arab League.
1988 Full diplomatic relations with Algeria restored.
1989 Improved relations with Libya; diplomatic relations with Syria restored. Mubarak proposed a peace plan.
1990 Gains for independents in general election.
1991 Participation in Gulf War on US-led side. Major force in convening Middle East peace conference in Spain.
1992 Outbreaks of violence between Muslims and Christians. Earthquake devastated Cairo.

El Salvador

Republic of (*República de El Salvador*)

area 21,393 sq km/8,258 sq mi
capital San Salvador
towns Santa Ana, San Miguel
physical narrow coastal plain, rising to mountains in N with central plateau
features smallest and most densely populated Central American country; Maya archaeological remains
head of state and government Alfredo Cristiani from 1989
political system emergent democracy
political parties Christian Democrats (PDC), anti-imperialist; National Republican Alliance (ARENA), right-wing; National Conciliation Party (PCN), right-wing; Farabundo Marti Liberation Front (FMLN), left-wing
exports coffee, cotton, sugar
currency colón
population (1992) 5,460,000 (mainly of mixed Spanish and Indian ancestry; 10% Indian); growth rate 2.9% p.a.
life expectancy men 63, women 66
languages Spanish, Nahuatl
religion Roman Catholic 97%
literacy men 75%, women 69% (1985 est)
GDP $4.7 bn (1987); $790 per head

chronology
1821 Independence achieved from Spain.

1931 Peasant unrest followed by a military coup.
1961 Following a coup, PCN established and in power.
1969 'Soccer' war with Honduras.
1972 Allegations of human-rights violations; growth of left-wing guerrilla activities. General Carlos Romero elected president.
1979 A coup replaced Romero with a military-civilian junta.
1980 Archbishop Oscar Romero assassinated; country on verge of civil war. José Duarte became first civilian president since 1931.
1981 Mexico and France recognized the guerrillas as a legitimate political force, but the USA actively assisted the government in its battle against them.
1982 Assembly elections boycotted by left-wing parties and held amid considerable violence.
1986 Duarte sought a negotiated settlement with the guerrillas.
1988 Duarte resigned.
1989 Alfredo Cristiani (ARENA) became president in rigged elections; rebel attacks intensified.
1991 United Nations-sponsored peace accord signed by representatives of the government and the socialist guerrilla group, the FMLN.
1992 Peace accord validated; FMLN became political party.

Equatorial Guinea

Republic of (*República de Guinea Ecuatorial*)

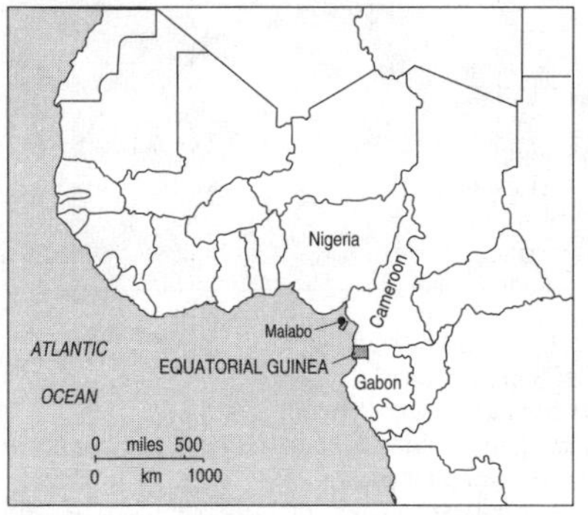

area 28,051 sq km/10,828 sq mi
capital Malabo (Bioko)
towns Bata, Mbini (Río Muni)
physical comprises mainland Río Muni, plus the small islands of Corisco, Elobey Grande and Elobey Chico, and Bioko (formerly Fernando Po) together with Annobón (formerly Pagalu)
features volcanic mountains on Bioko
head of state and government Teodoro Obiang Nguema Mbasogo from 1979
political system one-party military republic
political party Democratic Party of Equatorial Guinea (PDGE), militarily controlled
exports cocoa, coffee, timber
currency ekuele; CFA franc
population (1992) 367,000 (plus 110,000 estimated to live in exile abroad); growth rate 2.2% p.a.
life expectancy men 44, women 48
languages Spanish (official); pidgin English is widely spoken, and on Annobón (whose people were formerly slaves of the Portuguese) a Portuguese dialect; Fang and other African dialects spoken on Río Muni
religions nominally Christian, mainly Catholic, but in 1978 Roman Catholicism was banned
literacy 55% (1984)
GDP $90 million (1987); $220 per head

chronology
1778 Fernando Po (Bioko Island) ceded to Spain.
1885 Mainland territory came under Spanish rule; colony known as Spanish Guinea.
1968 Independence achieved from Spain. Francisco Macias Nguema became first president, soon assuming dictatorial powers.
1979 Macias overthrown and replaced by his nephew, Teodoro Obiang Nguema Mbasogo, who established a military regime. Macias tried and executed.
1982 Obiang elected president unopposed for another seven years. New constitution adopted.
1989 Obiang re-elected president.
1992 New constitution adopted; elections held, but president continued to nominate candidates for top government posts.

Estonia

Republic of

area 45,000 sq km/17,000 sq mi
capital Tallinn
towns Tartu, Narva, Kohtla-Järve, Pärnu
physical lakes and marshes in a partly forested plain; 774 km/481 mi of coastline; mild climate
features Lake Peipus and Narva River forming boundary with Russian Federation; Baltic islands, the largest of which is Saaremaa Island
head of state Lennart Meri from 1992
head of government Tiit Vahl from 1992
political system emergent democracy
political parties Estonian Popular Front (Rahvarinne), nationalist; Association for a Free Estonia, nationalist; Fatherland Group, right-wing; International Movement, ethnic Russian; Estonian Green Party, environmentalist
products oil and gas (from shale), wood products, flax, dairy and pig products
currency kroon
population (1992) 1,592,000 (Estonian 62%, Russian 30%, Ukrainian 3%, Byelorussian 2%)
language Estonian, allied to Finnish
religion traditionally Lutheran

chronology
1918 Estonia declared its independence. March: Soviet forces, who had tried to regain control from occupying German forces during World War I, were overthrown by German troops. Nov: Soviet troops took control after German withdrawal.
1919 Soviet rule overthrown with help of British navy; Estonia declared a democratic republic.
1934 Fascist coup replaced government.
1940 Estonia incorporated into USSR.
1941–44 German occupation during World War II.
1944 USSR regained control.
1980 Beginnings of nationalist dissent.
1988 Adopted own constitution, with power of veto on all centralized Soviet legislation. Popular Front (Rahvarinne) established to campaign for democracy. Estonia's supreme soviet (state assembly) voted to declare the republic 'sovereign' and autonomous in all matters except military and foreign affairs; rejected by USSR as unconstitutional.
1989 Estonian replaced Russian as main language.
1990 Feb: Communist Party monopoly of power abolished; multiparty system established. March: pro-independence candidates secured majority after republic elections; coalition government formed with Popular Front leader Edgar Savisaar as prime minister; Arnold Rüütel became president. May: prewar constitution partially restored.
1991 March: independence plebiscite overwhelmingly approved. Aug: full independence declared after abortive anti-Gorbachev coup; Communist Party outlawed. Sept: independence recognized by Soviet government and Western nations; admitted into United Nations and Conference on Security and Cooperation in Europe (CSCE).
1992 Jan: Savisaar resigned owing to his government's inability to alleviate food and energy shortages; new government formed by Tiit Vahl. June: New constitution approved. Sept: presidential election inconclusive; right-wing Fatherland Group did well in general election. Oct: Fatherland leader Lennart Meri chosen by parliament to replace Rüütel.

Ethiopia

People's Democratic Republic of (*Hebretesebawit Ityopia*, formerly also known as ***Abyssinia***)

area 1,221,900 sq km/471,653 sq mi
capital Addis Ababa
towns Asmara (capital of Eritrea), Dire Dawa; ports Massawa, Assab
physical a high plateau with central mountain range divided by Rift Valley; plains in E; source of Blue Nile River
environment more than 90% of the forests of the Ethiopian highlands have been destroyed since 1900
features Danakil and Ogaden deserts; ancient remains (in Aksum, Gondar, Lalibela, among others); only African country to retain its independence during the colonial period
head of state and government Meles Zenawi from 1991
political system transition to democratic socialist republic
political parties Ethiopian People's Revolutionary Democratic Front (EPRDF), nationalist, left of centre; Tigré People's Liberation Front (TPLF); Eritrean People's Liberation Front (EPLF); Ethiopian People's Democratic Movement (EPDM); Oromo People's Democratic Organization (OPDO)
exports coffee, pulses, oilseeds, hides, skins
currency birr
population (1992) 53,845,000 (Oromo 40%, Amhara 25%, Tigré 12%, Sidamo 9%); growth rate 2.5% p.a.
life expectancy 38
languages Amharic (official), Tigrinya, Orominga, Arabic
religions Sunni Muslim 45%, Christian (Ethiopian Orthodox Church, which has had its own patriarch since 1976) 40%
literacy 35% (1988)
GDP $4.8 bn (1987); $104 per head

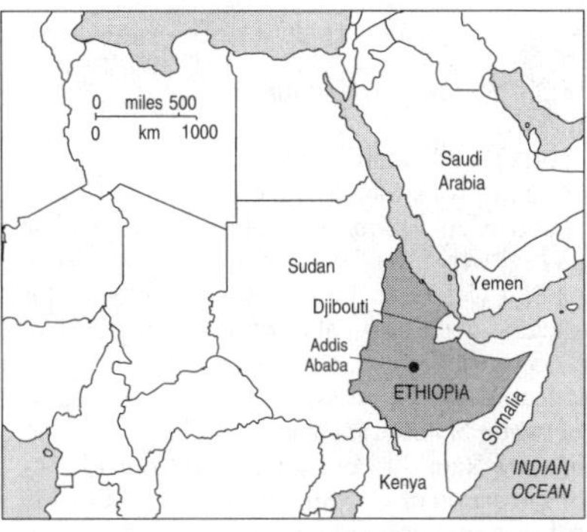

chronology
1889 Abyssinia reunited by Menelik II.
1930 Haile Selassie became emperor.
1962 Eritrea annexed by Haile Selassie; resistance movement began.
1974 Haile Selassie deposed and replaced by a military government led by General Teferi Benti. Ethiopia declared a socialist state.
1977 Teferi Benti killed and replaced by Col Mengistu Haile Mariam.
1977-79 'Red Terror' period in which Mengistu's regime killed thousands of innocent people.
1981-85 Ethiopia spent at least $2 billion on arms.
1984 WPE declared the only legal political party.
1985 Worst famine in more than a decade; Western aid sent and forcible internal resettlement programmes undertaken.
1987 New constitution adopted, Mengistu Mariam elected president. New famine; food aid hindered by guerrillas.
1988 Mengistu agreed to adjust his economic policies in order to secure IMF assistance. Influx of refugees from Sudan.
1989 Coup attempt against Mengistu foiled. Peace talks with Eritrean rebels mediated by former US president Carter reported some progress.
1990 Rebels captured port of Massawa.
1991 Mengistu overthrown; transitional government set up by EPRDF. EPLF secured Eritrea; Eritrea's right to secede recognized. Meles Zenawi elected Ethiopia's new head of state and government.
1993 Eritrean independence recognized after referendum.

Fiji

Republic of

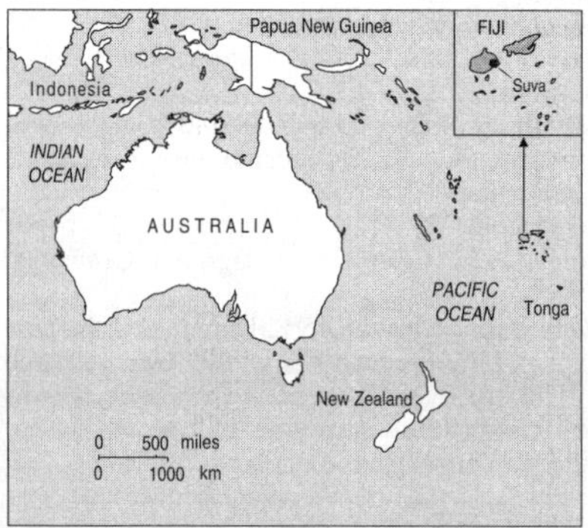

area 18,333 sq km/7,078 sq mi
capital Suva
towns ports Lautoka and Levuka
physical comprises 844 Melanesian and Polynesian islands and islets (about 110 inhabited), the largest being Viti Levu (10,429 sq km/4,028 sq mi) and Vanua Levu (5,550 sq km/2,146 sq mi); mountainous, volcanic, with tropical rainforest and grasslands
features almost all islands surrounded by coral reefs; high volcanic peaks; crossroads of air and sea services between N America and Australia
head of state Ratu Sir Penaia Ganilau from 1987
head of government Col Sitiveni Rabuka from 1992
political system democratic republic
political parties Alliance Party (AP), moderate centrist Fijian; National Federation Party (NFP), moderate left-of-centre Indian; Fijian Labour Party (FLP), left-of- centre Indian; United Front, Fijian
exports sugar, coconut oil, ginger, timber, canned fish, gold; tourism is important
currency Fiji dollar
population (1992) 748,000 (46% Fijian, holding 80% of the land communally, and 49% Indian, introduced in the 19th century to work the sugar crop); growth rate 2.1% p.a.
life expectancy men 67, women 71
languages English (official), Fijian, Hindi
religions Hindu 50%, Methodist 44%
literacy men 88%, women 77% (1980 est)
GDP $1.2 bn (1987); $1,604 per head

chronology
1874 Fiji became a British crown colony.
1970 Independence achieved from Britain; Ratu Sir Kamisese Mara elected as first prime minister.
1987 April: general election brought to power an Indian-dominated coalition led by Dr Timoci Bavadra. May: military coup by Col Sitiveni Rabuka removed new government at gunpoint; Governor General Ratu Sir Penaia Ganilau regained control within weeks. Sept: second military coup by Rabuka proclaimed Fiji a republic and suspended the constitution. Oct: Fiji ceased to be a member of the Commonwealth. Dec: civilian government restored with Rabuka retaining control of security as minister for home affairs.
1990 New constitution, favouring indigenous Fijians, introduced.
1992 General election produced coalition government; Col Rabuka named as president.

Finland

Republic of (*Suomen Tasavalta*)

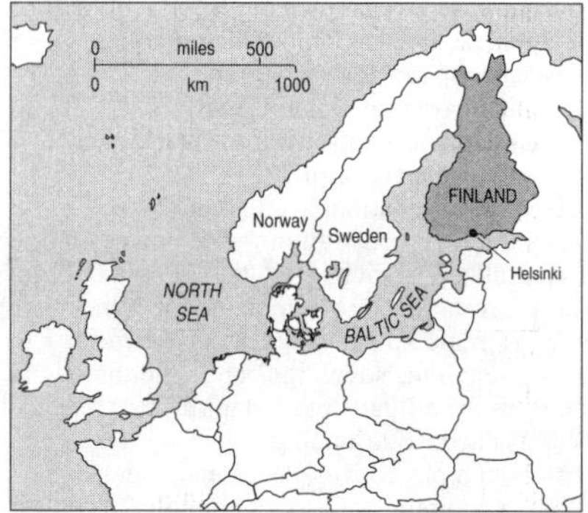

area 338,145 sq km/130,608 sq mi
capital Helsinki
towns Tampere, Rovaniemi, Lahti; ports Turku, Oulu
physical most of the country is forest, with low hills and about 60,000 lakes; one-third is within the Arctic Circle; archipelago in S; includes Åland Islands
features Helsinki is the most northerly national capital on the European continent; at the 70th parallel there is constant daylight for 73 days in summer and 51 days of uninterrupted night in winter
head of state Mauno Koivisto from 1982
head of government Esko Aho from 1991
political system democratic republic
political parties Social Democratic Party (SDP), moderate left of centre; National Coalition Party (KOK), moderate right of centre; Centre Party (KP), centrist, rural-oriented; Finnish People's Democratic League (SKDL), left-wing; Swedish People's Party (SFP), independent Swedish-oriented; Finnish Rural Party (SMP), farmers and small businesses; Democratic Alternative, left-wing; Green Party
exports metal, chemical, and engineering products (icebreakers and oil rigs), paper, sawn wood, clothing, fine ceramics, glass, furniture
currency markka
population (1992) 5,033,000; growth rate 0.5% p.a.
life expectancy men 70, women 78
languages Finnish 93%, Swedish 6% (both official), small Saami- and Russian-speaking minorities
religions Lutheran 97%, Eastern Orthodox 1.2%
literacy 99%
GDP $109.6 bn (1992)

chronology
1809 Finland annexed by Russia.
1917 Independence declared from Russia.
1920 Soviet regime acknowledged independence.
1939 Defeated by USSR in Winter War.
1941 Allowed Germany to station troops in Finland to attack USSR; USSR bombed Finland.
1944 Concluded separate armistice with USSR.
1948 Finno-Soviet Pact of Friendship, Cooperation, and Mutual Assistance signed.

1955 Finland joined the United Nations and the Nordic Council.
1956 Urho Kekkonen elected president; re-elected 1962, 1968, 1978.
1973 Trade treaty with European Economic Community signed.
1977 Trade agreement with USSR signed.
1982 Mauno Koivisto elected president; re-elected 1988.
1989 Finland joined Council of Europe.
1991 Big swing to the centre in general election. New coalition government formed.
1992 Formal application for European Community membership.

France

French Republic (*République Française*)

area (including Corsica) 543,965 sq km/209,970 sq mi
capital Paris
towns Lyons, Lille, Bordeaux, Toulouse, Nantes, Strasbourg; ports Marseille, Nice, Le Havre
physical rivers Seine, Loire, Garonne, Rhône, Rhine; mountain ranges Alps, Massif Central, Pyrenees, Jura, Vosges, Cévennes; the island of Corsica
territories Guadeloupe, French Guiana, Martinique, Réunion, St Pierre and Miquelon, Southern and Antarctic Territories, New Caledonia, French Polynesia, Wallis and Futuna
features Ardennes forest, Auvergne mountain region, Riviera, Mont Blanc (4,810 m/15,781 ft), caves of Dordogne with relics of early humans; largest W European nation
head of state François Mitterrand from 1981
head of government Edouard Balladur from 1993
political system liberal democracy
political parties Socialist Party (PS), left of centre; Rally for the Republic (RPR), neo-Gaullist conservative; Union for French Democracy (UDF), centre-right; Republican Party (RP), centre-right; French Communist Party (PCF), Marxist-Leninist; National Front, far right; Greens, environmentalist
exports fruit (especially apples), wine, cheese, wheat, cars, aircraft, iron and steel, petroleum products, chemicals, jewellery, silk, lace; tourism is very important
currency franc

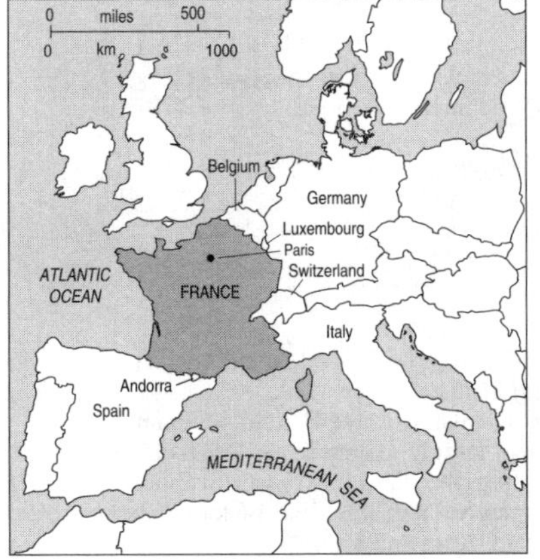

population (1992) 57,289,000 (including 4,500,000 immigrants, chiefly from Portugal, Algeria, Morocco, and Tunisia); growth rate 0.3% p.a.
life expectancy men 71, women 79
language French (regional languages include Basque, Breton, Catalan, and the Provençal dialect)
religions Roman Catholic 90%, Protestant 2%, Muslim 1%
literacy 99% (1984)
GNP $1,324.9 bn (1992)

chronology
1944-46 Provisional government headed by General Charles de Gaulle; start of Fourth Republic.
1954 Indochina achieved independence.
1956 Morocco and Tunisia achieved independence.
1957 Entry into European Economic Community.
1958 Recall of de Gaulle after Algerian crisis; start of Fifth Republic.
1959 De Gaulle became president.
1962 Algeria achieved independence.
1966 France withdrew from military wing of NATO.
1968 'May events' uprising of students and workers.
1969 De Gaulle resigned after referendum defeat; Georges Pompidou became president.
1974 Giscard d'Estaing elected president.
1981 François Mitterrand elected Fifth Republic's first socialist president.
1986 'Cohabitation' experiment, with the conservative Jacques Chirac as prime minister.
1988 Mitterrand re-elected. Moderate socialist Michel Rocard became prime minister. Matignon Accord on future of New Caledonia approved by referendum.
1989 Greens gained 11% of vote in elections to European Parliament.
1991 French forces were part of the US-led coalition in the Gulf War. Edith Cresson became prime minister; Mitterrand's popularity rating fell rapidly.
1992 March: Socialist Party humiliated in regional and local elections; Greens and National Front polled strongly. April: Cresson replaced by Pierre Bérégovoy. Sept: referendum narrowly endorsed Maastricht Treaty.
1993 Socialist Party suffered heavy defeat in National Assembly elections. Edouard Balladur appointed prime minister; 'cohabitation' government re-established.

Gabon

Gabonese Republic (*République Gabonaise*)

area 267,667 sq km/103,319 sq mi
capital Libreville
towns Port-Gentil and Owendo (ports); Masuku (Franceville)
physical virtually the whole country is tropical rainforest; narrow coastal plain rising to hilly int-erior with savanna in E and S; Ogooué River flows N–W
features Schweitzer hospital at Lambaréné; Trans-Gabonais railway
head of state and government Omar Bongo from 1967
political system emergent democracy
political parties Gabonese Democratic Party (PDG), nationalist; Morena Movement of National Recovery, left of centre

exports petroleum, manganese, uranium, timber
currency CFA franc
population (1992) 1,253,000 including 40 Bantu groups; growth rate 1.6% p.a.
life expectancy men 47, women 51
languages French (official), Bantu
religions Christian 96% (Roman Catholic 65%), small Muslim minority 1%, animist 3%
literacy men 70%, women 53% (1985 est)
GDP \$3.5 bn (1987); \$3,308 per head

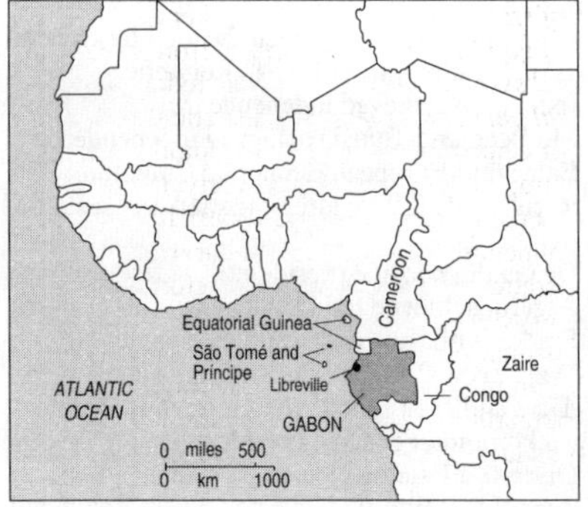

chronology
1889 Gabon became part of the French Congo.
1960 Independence from France achieved; Léon M'ba became the first president.
1964 Attempted coup by rival party foiled with French help. M'ba died; he was succeeded by his protégé Albert-Bernard Bongo.
1968 One-party state established.
1973 Bongo re-elected; converted to Islam, he changed his first name to Omar.
1986 Bongo re-elected.
1989 Coup attempt against Bongo defeated.
1990 PDG won first multiparty elections since 1964 amidst allegations of ballot-rigging.

Gambia

Republic of The

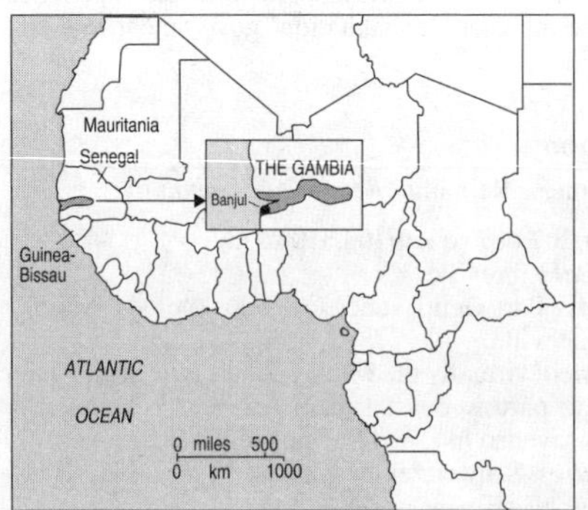

area 10,402 sq km/4,018 sq mi
capital Banjul
towns Serekunda, Bakau, Georgetown
physical banks of the river Gambia flanked by low hills
features smallest state in black Africa; stone circles; Karantaba obelisk marking spot where Mungo Park began his journey to the Niger River 1796
head of state and government Dawda K Jawara from 1970
political system liberal democracy
political parties Progressive People's Party (PPP), moderate centrist; National Convention Party (NCP), left of centre
exports groundnuts, palm oil, fish
currency dalasi
population (1992) 921,000; growth rate 1.9% p.a.
life expectancy 42 (1988 est)
languages English (official), Mandinka, Fula and other native tongues
media no daily newspaper; two official weeklies sell about 2,000 copies combined and none of the other independents more than 700
religions Muslim 90%, with animist and Christian minorities
literacy men 36%, women 15% (1985 est)
GDP \$189 million (1987); \$236 per head

chronology
1843 The Gambia became a British crown colony.
1965 Independence achieved from Britain as a constitutional monarchy within the Commonwealth, with Dawda K Jawara as prime minister.
1970 Declared itself a republic, with Jawara as president.
1972 Jawara re-elected.
1981 Attempted coup foiled with the help of Senegal.
1982 Formed with Senegal the Confederation of Senegambia; Jawara re-elected.
1987 Jawara re-elected.
1989 Confederation of Senegambia dissolved.
1990 Gambian troops contributed to the stabilizing force in Liberia.

Georgia

Republic of

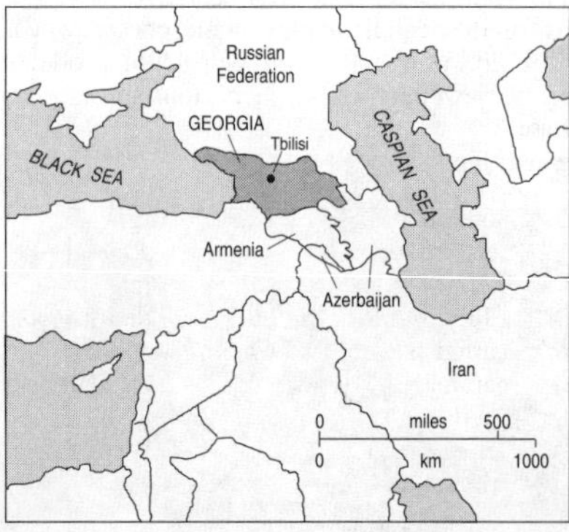

area 69,700 sq km/26,911 sq mi
capital Tbilisi
towns Kutaisi, Rustavi, Batumi, Sukhumi
physical largely mountainous with a variety of landscape from the subtropical Black Sea shores to the ice and snow of the crest line of the Caucasus; chief rivers are Kura and Rioni

features holiday resorts and spas on the Black Sea; good climate; two autonomous republics, Abkhazia and Adzharia; one autonomous region, South Ossetia
head of state Eduard Shevardnadze from 1992
head of government Tengiz Sigua from 1992
political system emergent democracy
political parties Georgian Popular Front, nationalist; Democratic National Party of Georgia, left of centre; National Independence Party, nationalist
products tea, citrus and orchard fruits, tung oil, tobacco, vines, silk, hydroelectricity
population (1992) 5,482,000 (Georgian 70%, Armenian 8%, Russian 8%, Azeri 6%, Ossetian 3%, Abkhazian 2%)
language Georgian
religion Georgian Church, independent of the Russian Orthodox Church since 1917
GNP $24,030,000 (1990); $4,410 per head

chronology
1918–21 Independent republic.
1921 Uprising quelled by Red Army and Soviet republic established.
1922–36 Linked with Armenia and Azerbaijan as the Transcaucasian Republic.
1936 Became separate republic within USSR.
1972 Drive against corruption by Georgian Communist Party (GCP) leader Eduard Shevardnadze.
1978 Outbreaks of violence by nationalists.
1981–88 Increasing demands for autonomy, spearheaded from 1988 by the Georgian Popular Front.
1989 March–April: Abkhazians demanded secession from Georgia, provoking inter-ethnic clashes. April: GCP leadership purged. July: state of emergency imposed in Abkhazia; interethnic clashes in South Ossetia. Nov: economic and political sovereignty declared.
1990 March: GCP monopoly ended. Oct: nationalist coalition triumphed in supreme-soviet elections. Nov: Zviad Gamsakhurdia became president. Dec: GCP seceded from Communist Party of USSR; calls for Georgian independence.
1991 April: declared independence. May: Gamsakhurdia popularly elected president. Aug: GCP outlawed and all relations with USSR severed. Sept: anti-Gamsakhurdia demonstrations; state of emergency declared. Dec: Georgia failed to join new Commonwealth of Independent States.
1992 Jan: Gamsakhurdia fled to Armenia; Tengiz Sigua appointed prime minister; Georgia admitted into Conference on Security and Cooperation in Europe. Eduard Shevardnadze appointed interim president. July: admitted into United Nations. Aug: fighting started between Georgian troops and Abkhazian separatists in Abkhazia in NW. Oct: Shevardnadze elected chair of new parliament. Clashes in South Ossetia and Abkhazia continued.
1993 Inflation at 1,500%.

Germany

Federal Republic of (*Bundesrepublik Deutschland*)

area 357,041 sq km/137,853 sq mi
capital Berlin
towns Cologne, Munich, Essen, Frankfurt-am-Main, Dortmund, Stuttgart, Düsseldorf, Leipzig, Dresden, Chemnitz, Magdeburg; ports Hamburg, Kiel, Cuxhaven, Bremerhaven, Rostock
physical flat in N, mountainous in S with Alps; rivers Rhine, Weser, Elbe flow N, Danube flows SE, Oder, Neisse flow N along Polish frontier; many lakes, including Müritz
environment acid rain causing *Waldsterben* (tree death) affects more than half the country's forests; industrial E Germany has the highest sulphur-dioxide emissions in the world per head of population
features Black Forest, Harz Mountains, Erzgebirge (Ore Mountains), Bavarian Alps, Fichtelgebirge, Thüringer Forest
head of state Richard von Weizsäcker from 1984
head of government Helmut Kohl from 1982
political system liberal democratic federal republic
political parties Christian Democratic Union (CDU), right of centre; Christian Social Union (CSU), right of centre; Social Democratic Party (SPD), left of centre; Free Democratic Party (FDP), liberal; Greens, environmentalist; Republicans, far right; Party of Democratic Socialism (PDS), reform-communist (formerly Socialist Unity Party: SED)
exports machine tools (world's leading exporter), cars, commercial vehicles, electronics, industrial goods, textiles, chemicals, iron, steel, wine, lignite (world's largest producer), uranium, coal, fertilizers, plastics
currency Deutschmark
population (1992) 80,293,000 (including nearly 5,000,000 'guest workers', *Gastarbeiter*, of whom 1,600,000 are Turks; the rest are Yugoslav, Italian, Greek, Spanish, and Portuguese); growth rate –0.7% p.a.
life expectancy men 68, women 74
languages German, Sorbian
religions Protestant 42%, Roman Catholic 35%
literacy 99% (1985)
GNP $1,775.1 bn (1992)

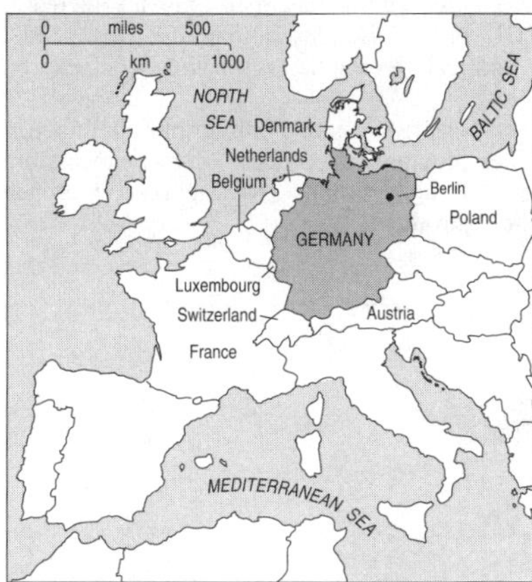

chronology
1945 Germany surrendered; country divided into four occupation zones (US, French, British, Soviet).
1948 Blockade of West Berlin.
1949 Establishment of Federal Republic under the 'Basic Law' Constitution with Konrad Adenauer as chancellor; establishment of the German Democratic Republic as an independent state.
1953 Uprising in East Berlin suppressed by Soviet troops.

1954 Grant of full sovereignty to both West Germany and East Germany.
1957 West Germany was a founder-member of the European Economic Community; recovery of Saarland from France.
1961 Construction of Berlin Wall.
1963 Retirement of Chancellor Adenauer.
1964 Treaty of Friendship and Mutual Assistance signed between East Germany and USSR.
1969 Willy Brandt became chancellor of West Germany.
1971 Erich Honecker elected SED leader in East Germany.
1972 Basic Treaty between West Germany and East Germany; treaty ratified 1973, normalizing relations between the two.
1974 Resignation of Brandt; Helmut Schmidt became chancellor.
1975 East German friendship treaty with USSR renewed for 25 years.
1982 Helmut Kohl became West German chancellor.
1987 Official visit of Honecker to the Federal Republic.
1988 Death of Franz-Josef Strauss, leader of the West German Bavarian CSU.
1989 West Germany: rising support for far right in local and European elections, declining support for Kohl. East Germany: mass exodus to West Germany began. Honecker replaced by Egon Krenz. National borders opened in Nov, including Berlin Wall. Reformist Hans Modrow appointed prime minister. Krenz replaced.
1990 March: East German multiparty elections won by a coalition led by the right-wing CDU. 3 Oct: official reunification of East and West Germany. 2 Dec: first all-German elections since 1932, resulting in a victory for Kohl.
1991 Kohl's popularity declined after tax increase. The CDU lost its Bundesrat majority to the SPD. Racist outbreaks continued with violent attacks on foreigners.
1992 Neo-Nazi riots against immigrants continued.
1993 Unemployment exceeded 7%; severe recession. Outbreaks of racist violence. Restrictions on refugee admission introduced.

Ghana

Republic of

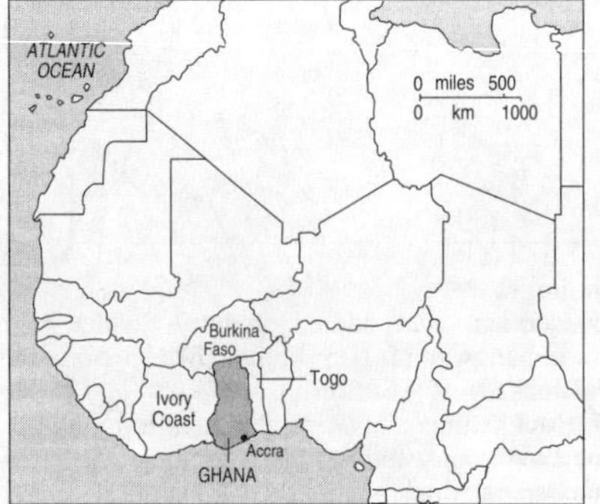

area 238,305 sq km/91,986 sq mi
capital Accra
towns Kumasi, and ports Sekondi-Takoradi, Tema
physical mostly tropical lowland plains; bisected by river Volta
environment forested areas shrank from 8.2 million sq km/3.17 million sq mi at the beginning of the 20th century to 1.9 million sq km/730,000 sq mi by 1990
features world's largest artificial lake, Lake Volta; relics of traditional kingdom of Ashanti: 32,000 chiefs and kings
head of state and government Jerry Rawlings from 1981
political system emergent democracy
exports cocoa, coffee, timber, gold, diamonds, manganese, bauxite
currency cedi
population (1992) 15,237,000; growth rate 3.2% p.a.
life expectancy men 50, women 54
languages English (official) and African languages
media all media are government-controlled and the two daily newspapers are government-owned
religion animist 38%, Muslim 30%, Christian 24%
literacy men 64%, women 43% (1985 est)
GNP $3.9 bn (1983); $420 per head
chronology
1957 Independence achieved from Britain, within the Commonwealth, with Kwame Nkrumah as president.
1960 Ghana became a republic.
1964 Ghana became a one-party state.
1966 Nkrumah deposed and replaced by General Joseph Ankrah.
1969 Ankrah replaced by General Akwasi Afrifa, who initiated a return to civilian government.
1970 Edward Akufo-Addo elected president.
1972 Another coup placed Col Acheampong at the head of a military government.
1978 Acheampong deposed in a bloodless coup led by Frederick Akuffo; another coup put Flight-Lt Jerry Rawlings in power.
1979 Return to civilian rule under Hilla Limann.
1981 Rawlings seized power again, citing the incompetence of previous governments. All political parties banned.
1989 Coup attempt against Rawlings foiled.
1992 New multiparty constitution approved. Partial lifting of ban on political parties. Nov: Rawlings won presidency in national elections.
1993 Fourth republic of Ghana formally inaugurated in Rawlings' presence.

Greece

Hellenic Republic (*Elliniki Dimokratia*)

area 131,957 sq km/50,935 sq mi
capital Athens
towns Larisa; ports Piraeus, Thessaloníki, Patras, Iráklion
physical mountainous; a large number of islands, notably Crete, Corfu, and Rhodes
environment acid rain and other airborne pollutants are destroying the Classical buildings and ancient monuments of Athens
features Corinth canal; Mount Olympus; the Acropolis; many classical archaeological sites; the Aegean and Ionian Islands

head of state Constantine Karamanlis from 1990
head of government Constantine Mitsotakis from 1990
political system democratic republic
political parties Panhellenic Socialist Movement (PASOK), democratic socialist; New Democracy Party (ND), centre-right; Democratic Renewal (DR); Communist Party; Greek Left Party
exports tobacco, fruit, vegetables, olives, olive oil, textiles, aluminium, iron, and steel
currency drachma
population (1992) 10,288,000; growth rate 0.3% p.a.
life expectancy men 72, women 76
language Greek
religion Greek Orthodox 97%
literacy men 96%, women 89% (1985)
GDP $79.2 bn (1992)

chronology
1829 Independence achieved from Turkish rule.
1912–13 Balkan Wars; Greece gained much land.
1941–44 German occupation of Greece.
1946 Civil war between royalists and communists; communists defeated.
1949 Monarchy re-established with Paul as king.
1964 King Paul succeeded by his son Constantine.
1967 Army coup removed the king; Col George Papadopoulos became prime minister. Martial law imposed, all political activity banned.
1973 Republic proclaimed, with Papadopoulos as president.
1974 Former premier Constantine Karamanlis recalled from exile to lead government. Martial law and ban on political parties lifted; restoration of the monarchy rejected by a referendum.
1975 New constitution adopted, making Greece a democratic republic.
1980 Karamanlis resigned as prime minister and was elected president.
1981 Greece became full member of European Economic Community. Andreas Papandreou elected Greece's first socialist prime minister.
1983 Five-year military and economic cooperation agreement signed with USA; ten-year economic cooperation agreement signed with USSR.
1985 Papandreou re-elected.
1988 Relations with Turkey improved. Major cabinet reshuffle after mounting criticism of Papandreou.
1989 Papandreou defeated. Tzannis Tzannetakis became prime minister; his all-party government collapsed. Xenophon Zolotas formed new unity government. Papandreou charged with corruption.
1990 New Democracy Party (ND) won half of parliamentary seats in general election but no outright majority; Constantine Mitsotakis became premier; formed new all-party government. Karamanlis re-elected president.
1992 Papandreou acquitted. Greece opposed recognition of independence of the Yugoslav breakaway republic of Macedonia.
1993 Parliament ratified the Maastricht Treaty.

Grenada

area (including the Grenadines, notably Carriacou) 340 sq km/131 sq mi
capital St George's
towns Grenville, Hillsborough (Carriacou)
physical southernmost of the Windward Islands; mountainous
features Grand-Anse beach; Annandale Falls; Great Pool volcanic crater
head of state Elizabeth II from 1974, represented by governor general
head of government Nicholas Braithwaite from 1990
political system emergent democracy
political parties New National Party (NNP), centrist; Grenada United Labour Party (GULP), nationalist, left of centre; National Democratic Congress (NDC), centrist
exports cocoa, nutmeg, bananas, mace
currency Eastern Caribbean dollar
population (1992) 90,900, 84% of black African descent; growth rate –0.2% p.a.
life expectancy 69
language English (official); some French patois spoken
religion Roman Catholic 60%
literacy 85% (1985)
GDP $139 million (1987); $1,391 per head

chronology
1974 Independence achieved from Britain; Eric Gairy elected prime minister.
1979 Gairy removed in bloodless coup led by Maurice Bishop; constitution suspended and a People's Revolutionary Government established.
1982 Relations with the USA and Britain deteriorated as ties with Cuba and the USSR strengthened.

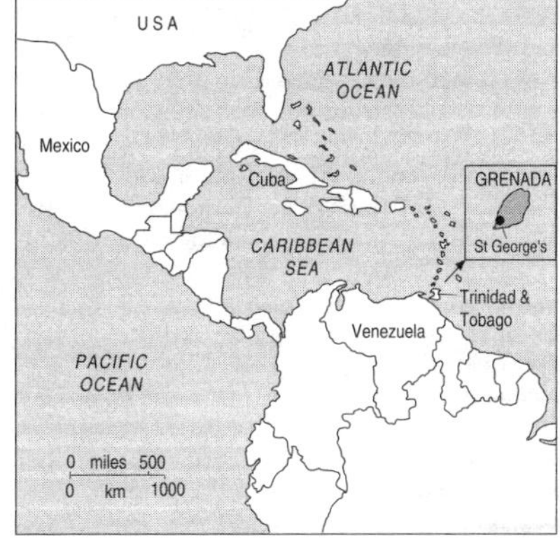

1983 After Bishop's attempt to improve relations with the USA, he was overthrown by left-wing opponents. A coup established the Revolutionary Military Council (RMC), and Bishop and three colleagues were executed. The USA invaded Grenada, accompanied by troops from other E Caribbean countries; RMC overthrown, 1974 constitution reinstated.
1984 The newly formed NNP won 14 of the 15 seats in the house of representatives and its leader, Herbert Blaize, became prime minister.
1989 Herbert Blaize lost leadership of NNP, remaining as head of government; he died and was succeeded by Ben Jones.
1990 Nicholas Braithwaite of the NDC became prime minister.
1991 Integration into Windward Islands confederation proposed.

Guatemala

Republic of (*República de Guatemala*)

area 108,889 sq km/42,031 sq mi
capital Guatemala City
towns Quezaltenango, Puerto Barrios (naval base)
physical mountainous; narrow coastal plains; limestone tropical plateau in N; frequent earthquakes
environment between 1960 and 1980 nearly 57% of the country's forest was cleared for farming
features Mayan archaeological remains, including site at Tikal
head of state and government Ramiro de Leon Carpio from 1993

political system democratic republic
political parties Guatemalan Christian Democratic Party (PDCG), Christian centre-left; Centre Party (UCN), centrist; National Democratic Cooperation Party (PDCN), centre-right; Revolutionary Party (PR), radical; Movement of National Liberation (MLN), extreme right-wing; Democratic Institutional Party (PID), moderate conservative; Solidarity Action Movement (MAS), right-wing
exports coffee, bananas, cotton, sugar, beef
currency quetzal
population (1992) 9,442,000 (Mayaquiche Indians 54%, mestizos (mixed race) 42%); growth rate 2.8% p.a. (87% of under-fives suffer from malnutrition)
life expectancy men 57, women 61
languages Spanish (official); 40% speak 18 Indian languages
religions Roman Catholic 80%, Protestant 20%
literacy men 63%, women 47% (1985 est)
GDP $7 bn (1987); $834 per head

chronology
1839 Independence achieved from Spain.
1954 Col Carlos Castillo became president in US-backed coup, halting land reform.
1963 Military coup made Col Enrique Peralta president.
1966 Cesar Méndez elected president.
1970 Carlos Araña elected president.
1974 General Kjell Laugerud became president. Widespread political violence precipitated by the discovery of falsified election returns in March.
1978 General Fernando Romeo became president.
1981 Growth of antigovernment guerrilla movement.
1982 General Angel Anibal became president. Army coup installed General Ríos Montt as head of junta and then as president; political violence continued.
1983 Montt removed in coup led by General Mejía Victores, who declared amnesty for the guerrillas.
1985 New constitution adopted; PDCG won congressional elections; Vinicio Cerezo elected president.
1989 Coup attempt against Cerezo foiled. Over 100,000 people killed and 40,000 reported missing since 1980.
1991 Jorge Serrano Elías of the Solidarity Action Movement elected president. Diplomatic relations with Belize established.
1993 President Serrano deposed; Ramiro de Leon Carpio elected president by assembly.

Guinea

Republic of (*République de Guinée*)

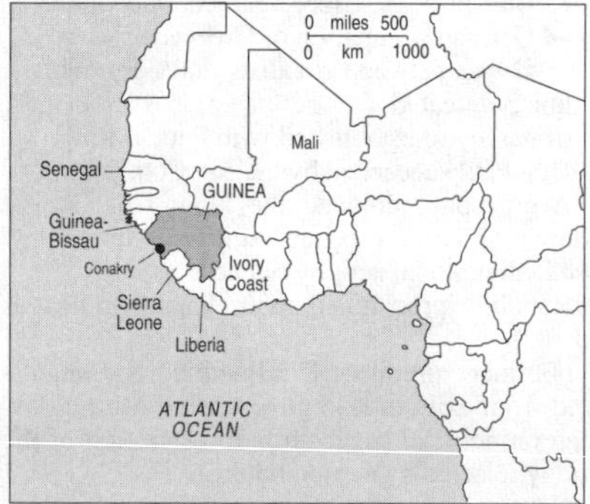

area 245,857 sq km/94,901 sq mi
capital Conakry
towns Labé, Nzérékoré, Kankan
physical flat coastal plain with mountainous interior; sources of rivers Niger, Gambia, and Senegal; forest in SE
environment large amounts of toxic waste from industrialized countries have been dumped in Guinea
features Fouta Djallon, area of sandstone plateaus, cut by deep valleys
head of state and government Lansana Conté from 1984
political system military republic
political parties none since 1984

exports coffee, rice, palm kernels, alumina, bauxite, diamonds
currency syli or franc
population (1992) 7,232,000 (chief peoples are Fulani, Malinke, Susu); growth rate 2.3% p.a.
life expectancy men 39, women 42
languages French (official), African languages
media state-owned, but some criticism of the government tolerated; no daily newspaper
religions Muslim 85%, Christian 10%, local 5%
literacy men 40%, women 17% (1985 est)
GNP $1.9 bn (1987); $369 per head

chronology
1958 Full independence achieved from France; Sékou Touré elected president.
1977 Strong opposition to Touré's rigid Marxist policies forced him to accept return to mixed economy.
1980 Touré returned unopposed for fourth seven-year term.
1984 Touré died. Bloodless coup established a military committee for national recovery, led by Col Lansana Conté.
1985 Attempted coup against Conté while he was out of the country was foiled by loyal troops.
1990 Sent troops to join the multinational force that attempted to stabilize Liberia.
1991 Antigovernment general strike by National Confederation of Guinea Workers (CNTG).

Guinea-Bissau

Republic of *(República da Guiné-Bissau)*

area 36,125 sq km/13,944 sq mi
capital Bissau

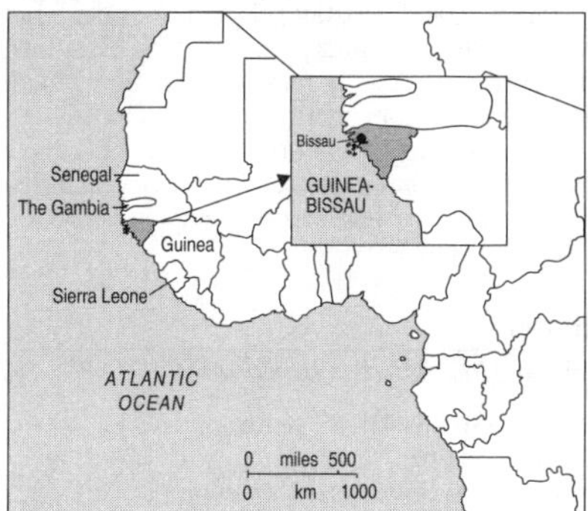

towns Mansâa, São Domingos
physical flat coastal plain rising to savanna in E
features the archipelago of Bijagós
head of state and government João Bernardo Vieira from 1980
political system emergent democracy
political party African Party for the Independence of Portuguese Guinea and Cape Verde (PAIGC), nationalist socialist
exports rice, coconuts, peanuts, fish, timber
currency peso
population (1992) 1,015,000; growth rate 2.4% p.a.
life expectancy 42; 1990 infant mortality rate was 14.8%
languages Portuguese (official), Crioulo (Cape Verdean dialect of Portuguese), African languages
religions animism 54%, Muslim 38%, Christian 8%
literacy men 46%, women 17% (1985 est)
GDP $135 million (1987); $146 per head

chronology
1956 PAIGC formed to secure independence from Portugal.
1973 Two-thirds of the country declared independent, with Luiz Cabral as president of a state council.
1974 Independence achieved from Portugal.
1980 Cape Verde decided not to join a unified state. Cabral deposed, and João Vieira became chair of a council of revolution.
1981 PAIGC confirmed as the only legal party, with Vieira as its secretary general.
1982 Normal relations with Cape Verde restored.
1984 New constitution adopted, making Vieira head of government as well as head of state.
1989 Vieira re-elected.
1991 Other parties legalized.
1992 Multiparty electoral commission established.

Guyana

Cooperative Republic of

area 214,969 sq km/82,978 sq mi
capital (and port) Georgetown
towns New Amsterdam, Mabaruma
physical coastal plain rises into rolling highlands with savanna in S; mostly tropical rainforest
features Mount Roraima; Kaietur National Park, including Kaietur Fall on the Potaro (tributary of Essequibo) 250 m/821 ft
head of state Cheddi Jagan from 1992
head of government Sam Hinds from 1992
political system democratic republic
political parties People's National Congress (PNC), Afro-Guyanan nationalist socialist; People's Progressive Party (PPP), Indian Marxist-Leninist
exports sugar, rice, rum, timber, diamonds, bauxite, shrimps, molasses
currency Guyanese dollar
population (1992) 748,000 (51% descendants of workers introduced from India to work the sugar plantations after the abolition of slavery, 30% black, 5% Amerindian); growth rate 2% p.a.
life expectancy men 66, women 71
languages English (official), Hindi, Amerindian

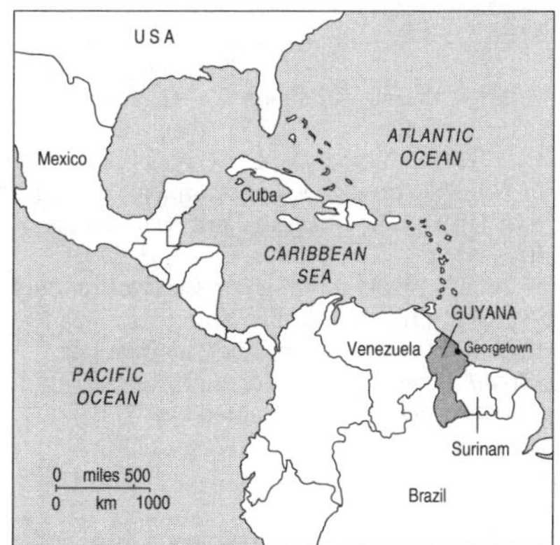

media one government-owned daily newspaper; one independent paper published three times a week, on which the government puts pressure by withholding foreign exchange for newsprint; one weekly independent in the same position. There is also legislation that restricts exchange of information between public officials, government, and the press
religions Christian 57%, Hindu 33%, Sunni Muslim 9%
literacy men 97%, women 95% (1985 est)
GNP $359 million (1987); $445 per head

chronology
1831 Became British colony under name of British Guiana.
1953 Assembly elections won by left-wing PPP; Britain suspended constitution and installed interim administration, fearing communist takeover.
1961 Internal self-government granted; Cheddi Jagan became prime minister.
1964 PNC leader Forbes Burnham led PPP–PNC coalition.
1966 Independence achieved from Britain.
1970 Guyana became a republic within the Commonwealth.
1981 Forbes Burnham became first executive president under new constitution.
1985 Burnham died; succeeded by Desmond Hoyte.
1992 PPP had decisive victory in assembly elections; Jagan became president.

Haiti

Republic of (*République d'Haïti*)

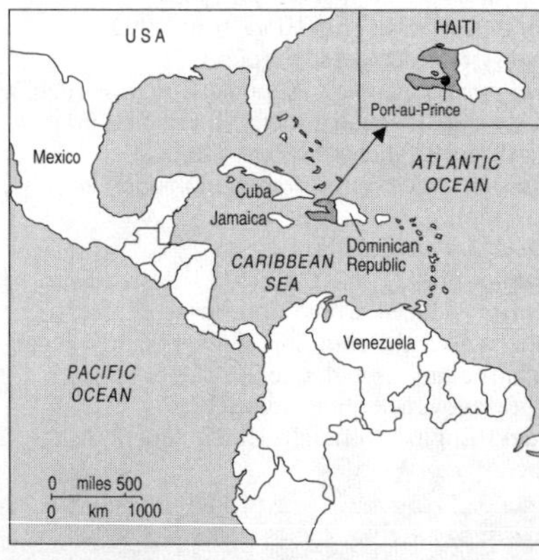

area 27,750 sq km/10,712 sq mi
capital Port-au-Prince
towns Cap-Haïtien, Gonaïves, Les Cayes
physical mainly mountainous and tropical; occupies W third of Hispaniola Island in Caribbean Sea; seriously deforested
features oldest black republic in the world; only French-speaking republic in the Americas; island of La Tortuga off N coast was formerly a pirate lair
interim head of state Joseph Nerette from 1991
head of government to be appointed (1993)
political system transitional
political party National Progressive Party (PNP), right-wing military
exports coffee, sugar, sisal, cotton, cocoa, bauxite
currency gourde
population (1992) 6,764,000; growth rate 1.7% p.a.; one of highest population densities in the world; about 1.5 million Haitians live outside Haiti (in USA and Canada); about 400,000 live in virtual slavery in the Dominican Republic, where they went or were sent to cut sugar cane
life expectancy men 51, women 54
languages French (official, spoken by literate 10% minority), Creole (spoken by 90% black majority)
religion Christian 95% of which 80% Roman Catholic, voodoo 4%
literacy men 40%, women 35% (1985 est)
GDP $2.2 bn (1987); $414 per head

chronology
1804 Independence achieved from France.
1915 Haiti invaded by USA; remained under US control until 1934.
1957 Dr François Duvalier (Papa Doc) elected president.
1964 Duvalier pronounced himself president for life.
1971 Duvalier died, succeeded by his son, Jean-Claude (Baby Doc); thousands murdered during Duvalier era.
1986 Duvalier deposed; replaced by Lt-Gen Henri Namphy as head of a governing council.
1988 Feb: Leslie Manigat became president. Namphy staged a military coup in June, but another coup in Sept led by Brig-Gen Prosper Avril replaced him with a civilian government under military control.
1989 Coup attempt against Avril foiled; US aid resumed.
1990 Opposition elements expelled; Ertha Pascal-Trouillot acting president.
1991 Jean-Bertrand Aristide elected president but later overthrown in military coup led by Brig-Gen Raoul Cedras. Efforts to reinstate Aristide failed. Joseph Nerette became interim head of state.
1992 Economic sanctions imposed since 1991 were eased by the USA but increased by the Organization of American States. Marc Bazin appointed premier.
1993 Bazin resigned.

Honduras

Republic of (*República de Honduras*)

area 112,100 sq km/43,282 sq mi
capital Tegucigalpa
towns San Pedro Sula; ports La Ceiba, Puerto Cortés
physical narrow tropical coastal plain with mountainous interior, Bay Islands
features archaeological sites; Mayan ruins at Copán
head of state and government Rafael Leonardo Callejas from 1990
political system democratic republic
political parties Liberal Party of Honduras (PLH), centre-left; National Party (PN), right-wing
exports coffee, bananas, meat, sugar, timber (including mahogany, rosewood)
currency lempira
population (1992) 4,996,000 (mestizo, or mixed, 90%; Indians and Europeans 10%); growth rate 3.1% p.a.
life expectancy men 58, women 62
languages Spanish (official), English, Indian languages

religion Roman Catholic 97%
literacy men 61%, women 58% (1985 est)
GDP $3.5 bn (1987); $758 per head

chronology
1838 Independence achieved from Spain.
1980 After more than a century of mostly military rule, a civilian government was elected, with Dr Roberto Suazo as president; the commander in chief of the army, General Gustavo Alvarez, retained considerable power.
1983 Close involvement with the USA in providing naval and air bases and allowing Nicaraguan counterrevolutionaries ('Contras') to operate from Honduras.
1984 Alvarez ousted in coup led by junior officers, resulting in policy review towards USA and Nicaragua.
1985 José Azcona elected president after electoral law changed, making Suazo ineligible for presidency.
1989 Government and opposition declared support for Central American peace plan to demobilize Nicaraguan Contras based in Honduras; Contras and their dependents in Honduras in 1989 thought to number about 55,000.
1990 Rafael Callejas (PN) inaugurated as president.
1992 Border dispute with El Salvador dating from 1861 finally resolved.

Hungary

Republic of (*Magyar Köztársaság*)

area 93,032 sq km/35,910 sq mi
capital Budapest
towns Miskolc, Debrecen, Szeged, Pécs
physical Great Hungarian Plain covers E half of country; Bakony Forest, Lake Balaton, and Transdanubian Highlands in the W; rivers Danube, Tisza, and Raba
environment an estimated 35%–40% of the population live in areas with officially 'inadmissible' air and water pollution. In Budapest lead levels have reached 30 times the maximum international standards
features more than 500 thermal springs; Hortobágy National Park; Tokay wine area
head of state Arpád Göncz from 1990
head of government József Antall from 1990
political system emergent democratic republic
political parties over 50, including Hungarian Socialist Party (HSP), left of centre; Hungarian Democratic Forum (MDF), umbrella prodemocracy grouping; Alliance of Free Democrats (SzDSz), radical free-market opposition group heading coalition with Alliance of Young Democrats, Social Democrats, and Smallholders Party, right-wing
exports machinery, vehicles, iron and steel, chemicals, fruit and vegetables
currency forint
population (1992) 10,303,000 (Magyar 92%, Romany 3%, German 2.5%; Hungarian minority in Romania has caused some friction between the two countries); growth rate 0.2% p.a.
life expectancy men 67, women 74
language Hungarian (or Magyar), one of the few languages of Europe with non-Indo-European origins; it is grouped with Finnish, Estonian, and others in the Finno-Ugric family
religions Roman Catholic 67%, other Christian denominations 25%
literacy men 99.3%, women 98.5% (1980)
GDP $26.1 bn (1987); $2,455 per head

chronology
1918 Independence achieved from Austro-Hungarian empire.
1919 A communist state formed for 133 days.
1920-44 Regency formed under Admiral Horthy, who joined Hitler's attack on the USSR.
1945 Liberated by USSR.
1946 Republic proclaimed; Stalinist regime imposed.
1949 Soviet-style constitution adopted.
1956 Hungarian national uprising; workers' demonstrations in Budapest; democratization reforms by Imre Nagy overturned by Soviet tanks, János Kádár installed as party leader.
1968 Economic decentralization reforms.
1983 Competition introduced into elections.
1987 VAT and income tax introduced.
1988 Kádár replaced by Károly Grosz. First free trade union recognized; rival political parties legalized.
1989 May: border with Austria opened. July: new four-person collective leadership of HSWP. Oct: new 'transitional constitution' adopted, founded on multiparty democracy and new presidentialist executive. HSWP changed name to Hungarian Socialist Party, with Nyers as new leader. Kádár 'retired'.

1990 HSP reputation damaged by 'Danubegate' bugging scandal. March–April: elections won by right-of-centre coalition, headed by Hungarian Democratic Forum (MDF). May: József Antall, leader of the MDF, appointed premier. Aug: Arpád Göncz elected president.
1991 Jan: devaluation of currency. June: legislation approved to compensate owners of land and property expropriated under communist government. Last Soviet troops departed. Dec: EC association pact signed.
1992 March: EC pact came into effect.

Iceland

Republic of (*Lýdveldid ísland*)

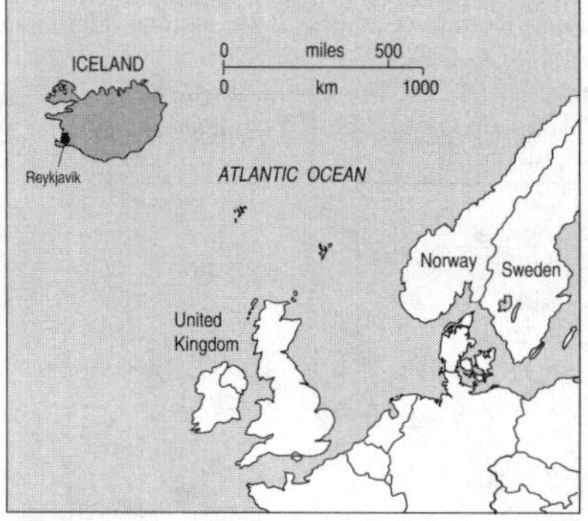

area 103,000 sq km/39,758 sq mi
capital Reykjavík
towns Akureyri, Akranes
physical warmed by the Gulf Stream; glaciers and lava fields cover 75% of the country; active volcanoes (Hekla was once thought the gateway to Hell), geysers, hot springs, and new islands created offshore (Surtsey in 1963); subterranean hot water heats 85% of Iceland's homes
features Thingvellir, where the oldest parliament in the world first met AD 930; shallow lake Mývatn (38 sq km/15 sq mi) in N
head of state Vigdís Finnbogadóttir from 1980
head of government Davíd Oddsson from 1991
political system democratic republic
political parties Independence Party (IP), right of centre; Progressive Party (PP), radical socialist; People's Alliance (PA), socialist; Social Democratic Party (SDP), moderate, left of centre; Citizens' Party, centrist; Women's Alliance, women- and family-oriented
exports cod and other fish products, aluminium, diatomite
currency krona
population (1992) 261,000; growth rate 0.8% p.a.
life expectancy men 74, women 80
language Icelandic, the most archaic Scandinavian language
religion Evangelical Lutheran 95%
literacy 99.9% (1984)
GDP $6.6 bn (1992)
chronology
1944 Independence achieved from Denmark.
1949 Joined NATO and Council of Europe.
1953 Joined Nordic Council.
1976 'Cod War' with UK.
1979 Iceland announced 320-km/200-mi exclusive fishing zone.
1983 Steingrímur Hermannsson appointed to lead a coalition government.
1985 Iceland declared itself a nuclear-free zone.
1987 New coalition government formed by Thorsteinn Pálsson after general election.
1988 Vigdís Finnbogadóttir re-elected president for a third term; Hermannsson led new coalition.
1991 Davíd Oddsson led new IP–SDP (Independence Party and Social Democratic Party) centre-right coalition, becoming prime minister in the general election.
1992 Iceland defied world ban to resume whaling industry.

India

Republic of (Hindi *Bharat*)

area 3,166,829 sq km/1,222,396 sq mi
capital Delhi
towns Bangalore, Hyderabad, Ahmedabad, Kanpur, Pune, Nagpur; ports Calcutta, Bombay, Madras
physical Himalaya mountains on N border; plains around rivers Ganges, Indus, Brahmaputra; Deccan peninsula S of the Narmada River forms plateau between Western and Eastern Ghats mountain ranges; desert in W; Andaman and Nicobar Islands, Lakshadweep (Laccadive Islands)
environment the controversial Narmada Valley Project is the world's largest combined hydroelectric irrigation scheme. In addition to displacing a million people, the damming of the holy Narmada River will submerge large areas of forest and farmland and create problems of waterlogging and salinization
features Taj Mahal monument; Golden Temple, Amritsar; archaeological sites and cave paintings (Ajanta); world's second most populous country

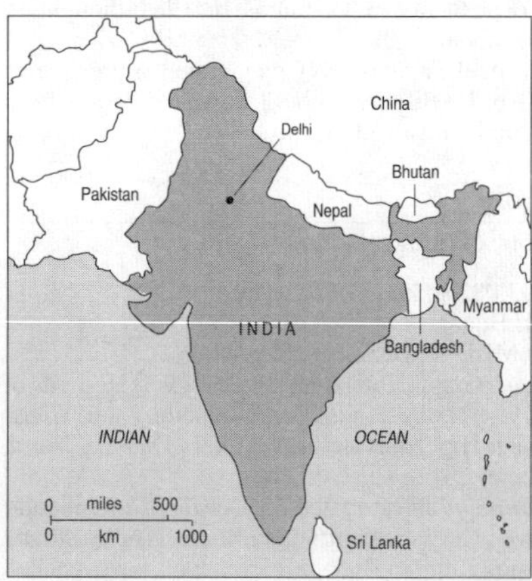

head of state Shankar Dayal Sharma from 1992
head of government P V Narasimha Rao from 1991
political system liberal democratic federal republic
political parties All India Congress Committee (I), or Congress (I), cross-caste and cross-religion, left of centre; Janata Dal, left of centre; Bharatiya Janata Party (BJP), conservative Hindu-chauvinist; Commu-

nist Party of India (CPI), pro-Moscow Marxist-Leninist; Communist Party of India–Marxist (CPI–M), West Bengal-based moderate socialist
exports tea (world's largest producer), coffee, fish, iron and steel, leather, textiles, clothing, polished diamonds
currency rupee
population 889,700,000 (920 women to every 1,000 men); growth rate 2.0% p.a.
life expectancy men 56, women 55
languages Hindi (widely spoken in N India), English, and 14 other official languages: Assamese, Bengali, Gujarati, Kannada, Kashmiri, Malayalam, Marathi, Oriya, Punjabi, Sanskrit, Sindhi, Tamil, Telugu, Urdu
media free press; government-owned broadcasting
religions Hindu 80%, Sunni Muslim 10%, Christian 2.5%, Sikh 2%
literacy men 57%, women 29% (1985 est)
GDP $220.8 bn (1987); $283 per head

chronology
1947 Independence achieved from Britain.
1950 Federal republic proclaimed.
1962 Border skirmishes with China.
1964 Death of Prime Minister Nehru. Border war with Pakistan over Kashmir.
1966 Indira Gandhi became prime minister.
1971 War with Pakistan leading to creation of Bangladesh.
1975–77 State of emergency proclaimed.
1977–79 Janata Party government in power.
1980 Indira Gandhi returned in landslide victory.
1984 Indira Gandhi assassinated; Rajiv Gandhi elected with record majority.
1987 Signing of 'Tamil' Colombo peace accord with Sri Lanka; Indian Peacekeeping Force (IPKF) sent there. Public revelation of Bofors corruption scandal.
1988 New opposition party, Janata Dal, established by former finance minister V P Singh. Voting age lowered from 21 to 18.
1989 Congress (I) lost majority in general election, after Gandhi associates implicated in financial misconduct; Janata Dal minority government formed, with V P Singh prime minister.
1990 Central rule imposed in Jammu and Kashmir. V P Singh resigned; new minority Janata Dal government formed by Chandra Shekhar. Interethnic and religious violence in Punjab and elsewhere.
1991 Central rule imposed in Tamil Nadu. Shekhar resigned; elections called for May. May: Rajiv Gandhi assassinated. June: elections resumed, resulting in a Congress (I) minority government led by P V Narasimha Rao. Separatist violence continued.
1992 Congress (I) won control of state assembly and a majority in parliament in Punjab state elections. Split in Janata Dal opposition resulted in creation of National Front coalition party (including rump of Janata Dal party). Widespread communal violence killed over 1,200 people, mainly Muslims, following destruction of a mosque in Ayodhya, N India, by Hindu extremists.
1993 Sectarian violence in Bombay left 500 dead. Rao narrowly survived a confidence vote in parliament.

Indonesia

Republic of (*Republik Indonesia*)

area 1,919,443 sq km/740,905 sq mi
capital Jakarta
towns Bandung; ports Surabaya, Semarang, Tandjungpriok
physical comprises 13,677 tropical islands, of the Greater Sunda group (including Java and Madura, part of Borneo (Kalimantan), Sumatra, Sulawesi and Belitung), and the Lesser Sundas/Nusa Tenggara (including Bali, Lombok, Sumbawa, Sumba, Flores, and Timor), as well as Malaku/Moluccas and part of New Guinea (Irian Jaya)
environment comparison of primary forest and 30-year-old secondary forest has shown that logging in Kalimantan has led to a 20% decline in tree species
head of state and government T N J Suharto from 1967
political system authoritarian nationalist republic
political parties Golkar, ruling military-bureaucrat, farmers' party; United Development Party (PPP), moderate Islamic; Indonesian Democratic Party (PDI), nationalist Christian
exports coffee, rubber, timber, palm oil, coconuts, tin, tea, tobacco, oil, liquid natural gas
currency rupiah
population (1992) 184,796,000 (including 300 ethnic groups); growth rate 2% p.a.; Indonesia has the world's largest Muslim population; Java is one of the world's most densely populated areas
life expectancy men 52, women 55
languages Indonesian (official), closely allied to Malay; Javanese is the most widely spoken local dialect
religions Muslim 88%, Christian 10%, Buddhist and Hindu 2%
literacy men 83%, women 65% (1985 est)
GDP $69.7 bn (1987); $409 per head

chronology
17th century Dutch colonial rule established.
1942 Occupied by Japan; nationalist government established.
1945 Japanese surrender; nationalists declared independence under Achmed Sukarno.
1949 Formal transfer of Dutch sovereignty.
1950 Unitary constitution established.
1963 Western New Guinea (Irian Jaya) ceded by the Netherlands.
1965–66 Attempted communist coup; General T N J Suharto imposed emergency administration, carried out massacre of hundreds of thousands.
1967 Sukarno replaced as president by Suharto.

1975 Guerrillas seeking independence for S Moluccas seized train and Indonesian consulate in the Netherlands, held Western hostages.
1976 Forced annexation of former Portuguese colony of East Timor.
1986 Institution of 'transmigration programme' to settle large numbers of Javanese on sparsely populated outer islands, particularly Irian Jaya.
1988 Partial easing of travel restrictions to East Timor. Suharto re-elected for fifth term.
1989 Foreign debt reaches $50 billion; Western creditors offer aid on condition that concessions are made to foreign companies and that austerity measures are introduced.
1991 Democracy forums launched to promote political dialogue. Massacre in East Timor.
1992 The ruling Golkar party won the assembly elections.
1993 President Suharto re-elected for sixth consecutive five-year term.

Iran

Islamic Republic of (*Jomhori-e-Islami-e-Irân*; until 1935 ***Persia***)

area 1,648,000 sq km/636,128 sq mi
capital Tehran
towns Isfahan, Mashhad, Tabriz, Shiraz, Ahvaz; chief port Abadan
physical plateau surrounded by mountains, including Elburz and Zagros; Lake Rezayeh; Dasht-Ekavir Desert; occupies islands of Abu Musa, Greater Tunb and Lesser Tunb in the Gulf
features ruins of Persepolis; Mount Demavend 5,670 m/18,603 ft
Leader of the Islamic Revolution Seyed Ali Khamenei from 1989

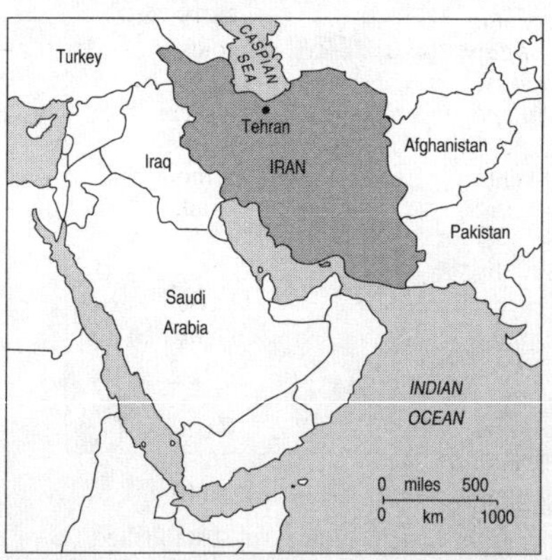

head of government Ali Akbar Hoshemi Rafsanjani from 1989
political system authoritarian Islamic republic
political party Islamic Republican Party (IRP), fundamentalist Islamic
exports carpets, cotton textiles, metalwork, leather goods, oil, petrochemicals, fruit
currency rial
population (1992) 59,570,000 (including minorities in Azerbaijan, Baluchistan, Khuzestan/Arabistan, and Kurdistan); growth rate 3.2% p.a.
life expectancy men 57, women 57
languages Farsi (official), Kurdish, Turkish, Arabic, English, French
religions Shi'ite Muslim (official) 92%, Sunni Muslim 5%, Zoroastrian 2%, Jewish, Baha'i, and Christian 1%
literacy men 62%, women 39% (1985 est)
GDP $86.4 bn (1987); $1,756 per head

chronology
1946 British, US, and Soviet forces left Iran.
1951 Oilfields nationalized by Prime Minister Muhammad Mossadeq.
1953 Mossadeq deposed and the US-backed shah, Muhammad Reza Shah Pahlavi, took full control of the government.
1975 The shah introduced single-party system.
1978 Opposition to the shah organized from France by Ayatollah Khomeini.
1979 Shah left the country; Khomeini returned to create Islamic state. Revolutionaries seized US hostages at embassy in Tehran; US economic boycott.
1980 Start of Iran–Iraq War.
1981 US hostages released.
1984 Egyptian peace proposals rejected.
1985 Fighting intensified in Iran–Iraq War.
1988 Cease-fire; talks with Iraq began.
1989 Khomeini called for the death of British writer Salman Rushdie. June: Khomeini died; Ali Khamenei elected interim Leader of the Revolution; speaker of Iranian parliament Hoshemi Rafsanjani elected president. Secret oil deal with Israel revealed.
1990 Generous peace terms with Iraq accepted. Normal relations with UK restored.
1991 Imprisoned British business executive released. Nearly one million Kurds arrived in Iran from Iraq, fleeing persecution by Saddam Hussein after the Gulf War.
1992 Pro-Rafsanjani moderates won assembly elections.
1993 President Rafsanjani re-elected, but with a smaller vote.

Iraq

Republic of (*al Jumhouriya al 'Iraqia*)

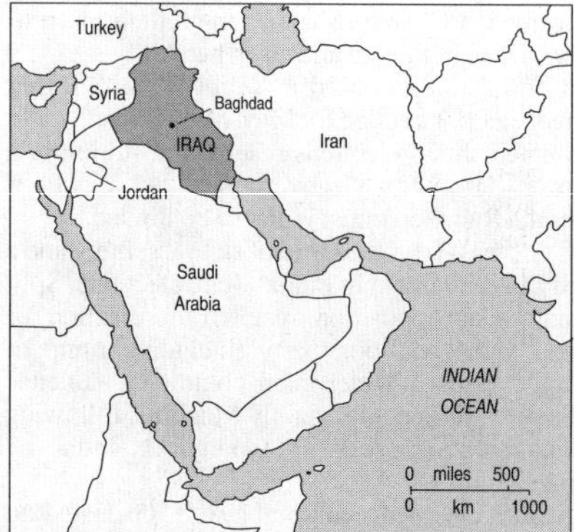

area 434,924 sq km/167,881 sq mi
capital Baghdad
towns Mosul and port of Basra
physical mountains in N, desert in W; wide valley of rivers Tigris and Euphrates NW–SE

environment a chemical-weapons plant covering an area of 65 sq km/25 sq mi, situated 80 km/50 mi NW of Baghdad, has been described by the UN as the largest toxic waste dump in the world
features reed architecture of the marsh Arabs; ancient sites of Eridu, Babylon, Nineveh, Ur, Ctesiphon
head of state and government Saddam Hussein al-Tikriti from 1979
political system one-party socialist republic
political party Arab Ba'ath Socialist Party, nationalist socialist
exports oil (prior to UN sanctions), wool, dates (80% of world supply)
currency Iraqi dinar
population (1992) 18,838,000 (Arabs 77%, Kurds 19%, Turks 2%); growth rate 3.6% p.a.
life expectancy men 62, women 63
languages Arabic (official); Kurdish, Assyrian, Armenian
religions Shi'ite Muslim 60%, Sunni Muslim 37%, Christian 3%
literacy men 68%, women 32% (1980 est)
GDP $42.3 bn (1987); $3,000 per head

chronology
1920 Iraq became a British League of Nations protectorate.
1921 Hashemite dynasty established, with Faisal I installed by Britain as king.
1932 Independence achieved from British protectorate status.
1958 Monarchy overthrown; Iraq became a republic.
1963 Joint Ba'athist-military coup headed by Col Salem Aref.
1968 Military coup put Maj-Gen al-Bakr in power.
1979 Al-Bakr replaced by Saddam Hussein.
1980 War between Iraq and Iran broke out.
1985 Fighting intensified.
1988 Cease-fire; talks began with Iran. Iraq used chemical weapons against Kurdish rebels seeking greater autonomy.
1989 Unsuccessful coup against President Hussein; Iraq launched ballistic missile in successful test.
1990 Peace treaty favouring Iran agreed. Aug: Iraq invaded and annexed Kuwait, precipitating another Gulf crisis. US forces massed in Saudi Arabia at request of King Fahd. United Nations resolutions ordered Iraqi withdrawal from Kuwait and imposed total trade ban on Iraq; UN resolution sanctioning force approved. All foreign hostages released.
1991 16 Jan: US-led forces began aerial assault on Iraq; Iraq's infrastructure destroyed by bombing. 23–28 Feb: land–sea–air offensive to free Kuwait successful. Uprisings of Kurds and Shi'ites brutally suppressed by surviving Iraqi troops. Talks between Kurdish leaders and Saddam Hussein about Kurdish autonomy. Allied troops withdrew after establishing 'safe havens' for Kurds in the north, leaving a rapid-reaction force near the Turkish border. Allies threatened to bomb strategic targets in Iraq if full information about nuclear facilities denied to UN.
1992 UN imposed a 'no-fly zone' over S Iraq to protect Shi'ites.
1993 Iraqi incursions into the 'no-fly zone' prompted US-led alliance aircraft to bomb 'strategic' targets in Iraq. USA also bombed a target in Baghdad in retaliation for an alleged plot against former president Bush, claiming that the action was taken in 'self-defence'.

Ireland

Republic of *(Eire)*

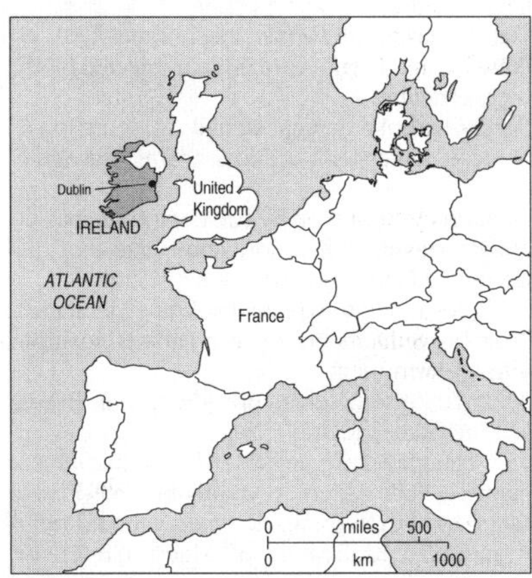

area 70,282 sq km/27,146 sq mi
capital Dublin
towns ports Cork, Dun Laoghaire, Limerick, Waterford
physical central plateau surrounded by hills; rivers Shannon, Liffey, Boyne
features Bog of Allen, source of domestic and national power; Macgillicuddy's Reeks, Wicklow Mountains; Lough Corrib, lakes of Killarney; Galway Bay and Aran Islands
head of state Mary Robinson from 1990
head of government Albert Reynolds from 1992
political system democratic republic
political parties Fianna Fáil (Soldiers of Destiny), moderate centre-right; Fine Gael (Irish Tribe), moderate centre-left; Labour Party, moderate, left of centre; Progressive Democrats, radical free-enterprise
exports livestock, dairy products, Irish whiskey, microelectronic components and assemblies, mining and engineering products, chemicals, clothing; tourism is important
currency punt
population (1992) 3,519,000; growth rate 0.1% p.a.
life expectancy men 70, women 76
languages Irish Gaelic and English (both official)
religion Roman Catholic 94%
literacy 99% (1984)
GDP $48.8 (1992)
chronology
1916 Easter Rising: nationalists against British rule seized the Dublin general post office and proclaimed a republic; the revolt was suppressed by the British army and most of the leaders were executed.
1918-21 Guerrilla warfare against British army led to split in rebel forces.
1921 Anglo-Irish Treaty resulted in creation of the Irish Free State (Southern Ireland).
1937 Independence achieved from Britain.

1949 Eire left the Commonwealth and became the Republic of Ireland.
1973 Fianna Fáil defeated after 40 years in office; Liam Cosgrave formed a coalition government.
1977 Fianna Fáil returned to power, with Jack Lynch as prime minister.
1979 Lynch resigned, succeeded by Charles Haughey.
1981 Garret FitzGerald formed a coalition.
1983 New Ireland Forum formed, but rejected by the British government.
1985 Anglo-Irish Agreement signed.
1986 Protests by Ulster Unionists against the agreement.
1987 General election won by Charles Haughey.
1988 Relations with UK at low ebb because of disagreement over extradition decisions.
1989 Haughey failed to win majority in general election. Progressive Democrats given cabinet positions in coalition government.
1990 Mary Robinson elected president; John Bruton became Fine Gael leader.
1992 Jan: Haughey resigned after losing parliamentary majority. Feb: Albert Reynolds became Fianna Fáil leader and prime minister. June: National referendum approved ratification of Maastricht Treaty. Nov: Reynolds lost confidence vote; election result inconclusive.
1993 Fianna Fáil–Labour coalition formed.

Israel

State of (*Medinat Israel*)

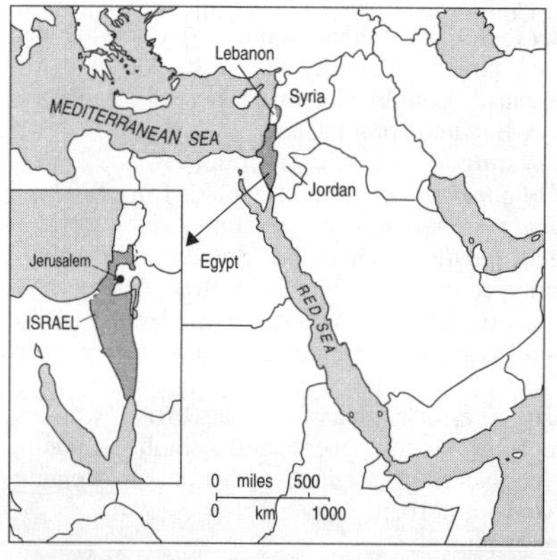

area 20,800 sq km/8,029 sq mi (as at 1949 armistice)
capital Jerusalem (not recognized by the United Nations)
towns ports Tel Aviv/Jaffa, Haifa, Acre, Eilat; Bat-Yam, Holon, Ramat Gan, Petach Tikva, Beersheba
physical coastal plain of Sharon between Haifa and Tel Aviv noted since ancient times for fertility; central mountains of Galilee, Samariq, and Judea; Dead Sea, Lake Tiberias, and river Jordan Rift Valley along the E are below sea level; Negev Desert in the S; Israel occupies Golan Heights, West Bank, and Gaza
features historic sites: Jerusalem, Bethlehem, Nazareth, Masada, Megiddo, Jericho; caves of the Dead Sea scrolls
head of state Ezer Weizman from 1993
head of government Yitzhak Rabin from 1992
political system democratic republic
political parties Israel Labour Party, moderate, left of centre; Consolidation Party (Likud), right of centre
exports citrus and other fruit, avocados, chinese leaves, fertilizers, diamonds, plastics, petrochemicals, textiles, electronics, electro-optics, precision instruments, aircraft, and missiles
currency shekel
population (1992) 5,239,000 (including 750,000 Arab Israeli citizens and over 1 million Arabs in the occupied territories); under the Law of Return 1950, 'every Jew shall be entitled to come to Israel as an immigrant'; those from the East and E Europe are Ashkenazim, and those from Mediterranean Europe (Spain, Portugal, Italy, France, Greece) and Arab N Africa are Sephardim (over 50% of the population is now of Sephardic descent). Between Jan 1990 and April 1991, 250,000 Soviet Jews emigrated to Israel. An Israeli-born Jew is a Sabra. About 500,000 Israeli Jews are resident in the USA. Growth rate 1.8% p.a.
life expectancy men 73, women 76
languages Hebrew and Arabic (official); Yiddish, European and W Asian languages
religions Israel is a secular state, but the predominant faith is Judaism 83%; also Sunni Muslim, Christian, and Druse
literacy Jewish 88%, Arab 70%
GDP $35 bn (1987); $8,011 per head

chronology
1948 Independent State of Israel proclaimed with David Ben-Gurion as prime minister; attacked by Arab nations, Israel won the War of Independence. Many displaced Arabs settled in refugee camps in the Gaza Strip and West Bank.
1952 Col Gamal Nasser of Egypt stepped up blockade of Israeli ports and support of Arab guerrillas in Gaza.
1956 Israel invaded Gaza and Sinai.
1959 Egypt renewed blockade of Israeli trade through Suez Canal.
1963 Ben-Gurion resigned, succeeded by Levi Eshkol.
1964 Palestine Liberation Organization (PLO) founded with the aim of overthrowing the state of Israel.
1967 Israel victorious in the Six-Day War. Gaza, West Bank, E Jerusalem, Sinai, and Golan Heights captured.
1968 Israel Labour Party formed, led by Golda Meir.
1969 Golda Meir became prime minister.
1973 Yom Kippur War: Israel attacked by Egypt and Syria.
1974 Golda Meir succeeded by Yitzhak Rabin.
1975 Suez Canal reopened.
1977 Menachem Begin elected prime minister. Egyptian president addressed the Knesset.
1978 Camp David talks.
1979 Egyptian-Israeli agreement signed. Israel agreed to withdraw from Sinai.
1980 Jerusalem declared capital of Israel.
1981 Golan Heights formally annexed.
1983 Peace treaty between Israel and Lebanon signed but not ratified.
1985 Formation of government of national unity with Labour and Likud ministers.
1986 Yitzhak Shamir took over from Peres under power-sharing agreement.

1987 Outbreak of Palestinian uprising (Intifada) in West Bank and Gaza.
1988 Criticism of Israel's handling of Palestinian uprising in occupied territories; PLO acknowledged Israel's right to exist.
1989 New Likud–Labour coalition government formed under Shamir. Limited progress achieved on proposals for negotiations leading to elections in occupied territories.
1990 Coalition collapsed due to differences over peace process; international condemnation of Temple Mount killings. New Shamir right-wing coalition formed.
1991 Shamir gave cautious response to Middle East peace proposals. Some Palestinian prisoners released. Peace talks began in Madrid.
1992 Jan: Shamir lost majority in Knesset when ultra-orthodox party withdrew from coalition. June: Labour Party, led by Yitzhak Rabin, won elections; coalition formed under Rabin. Aug: US-Israeli loan agreement signed. Dec: 400 Palestinians summarily expelled, in the face of international criticism.
1993 March: Ezer Weizman elected president; Binyamin Netanyahu elected leader of Likud party. July: Israel launched attacks against Hezbollah in S Lebanon. Sept: historic accord of mutual recognition agreed between Israel and PLO, to result in partial autonomy for Palestinians and phased Israeli withdrawal from parts of occupied territories

Italy

Republic of (*Repubblica Italiana*)

area 301,300 sq km/116,332 sq mi
capital Rome
towns Milan, Turin; ports Naples, Genoa, Palermo, Bari, Catania, Trieste
physical mountainous (Maritime Alps, Dolomites, Apennines) with narrow coastal lowlands; rivers Po, Adige, Arno, Tiber, Rubicon; islands of Sicily, Sardinia, Elba, Capri, Ischia, Lipari, Pantelleria; lakes Como, Maggiore, Garda
environment Milan has the highest recorded level of sulphur-dioxide pollution of any city in the world. The Po River, with pollution ten times higher than officially recommended levels, is estimated to discharge around 250 tonnes of arsenic into the sea each year

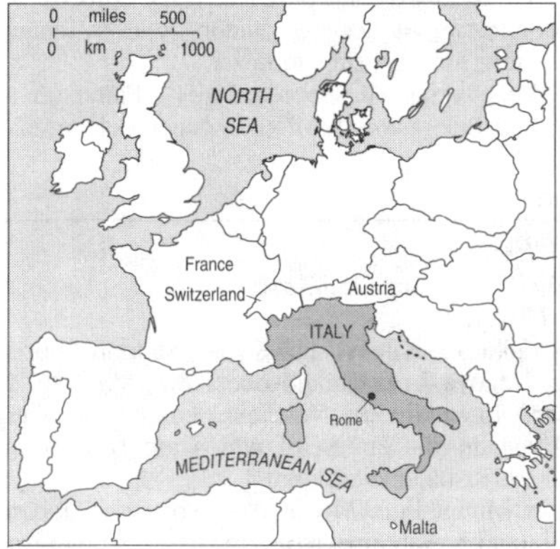

features continental Europe's only active volcanoes: Vesuvius, Etna, Stromboli; historic towns include Venice, Florence, Siena, Rome; Greek, Roman, Etruscan archaeological sites
head of state Oscar Luigi Scalfaro from 1992
head of government Carlo Azeglio Ciampi from 1993
political system democratic republic
political parties Christian Democratic Party (DC), Christian, centrist; Democratic Party of the Left (PDS), pro-European socialist; Italian Socialist Party (PSI), moderate socialist; Italian Social Movement–National Right (MSI–DN), neofascist; Italian Republican Party (PRI), social democratic, left of centre; Italian Social Democratic Party (PSDI), moderate left of centre; Liberals (PLI), right of centre
exports wine (world's largest producer), fruit, vegetables, textiles (Europe's largest silk producer), clothing, leather goods, motor vehicles, electrical goods, chemicals, marble (Carrara), sulphur, mercury, iron, steel
currency lira
population (1992) 57,103,000; growth rate 0.1% p.a.
life expectancy men 73, women 80 (1989)
languages Italian; German, French, Slovene, and Albanian minorities
religion Roman Catholic (state religion)
literacy 97% (1989)
GDP $1,223.6 bn (1992)

chronology
1946 Monarchy replaced by a republic.
1948 New constitution adopted.
1954 Trieste returned to Italy.
1976 Communists proposed establishment of broad-based, left–right government, the 'historic compromise'; rejected by Christian Democrats.
1978 Christian Democrat Aldo Moro, architect of the historic compromise, kidnapped and murdered by Red Brigade guerrillas infiltrated by Western intelligence agents.
1983 Bettino Craxi, a Socialist, became leader of broad coalition government.
1987 Craxi resigned; succeeding coalition fell within months.
1988 Christian Democrats' leader Ciriaco de Mita established a five-party coalition including the Socialists.
1989 De Mita resigned after disagreements within his coalition government; succeeded by Giulio Andreotti. De Mita lost his leadership of Christian Democrat Party; Communists formed a 'shadow government'.
1991 Referendum approved electoral reform.
1992 April: ruling coalition lost its majority in general election; President Cossiga resigned, replaced by Oscar Luigi Scalfaro in May. Giuliano Amato, deputy leader of PDS, accepted premiership. Sept: lira devalued and Italy withdrew from the Exchange Rate Mechanism.
1993 Investigation of corruption network exposed Mafia links with several notable politicians, including Craxi and Andreotti. Craxi resigned Socialist Party leadership; replaced by Giorgio Benvenutu and then Ottaviano del Turro. Referendum supported ending the proportional-representation electoral system. Amato resigned premiership; Carlo Ciampi, with no party allegiance, named as his successor.

Ivory Coast

Republic of (*République de la Côte d'Ivoire*)

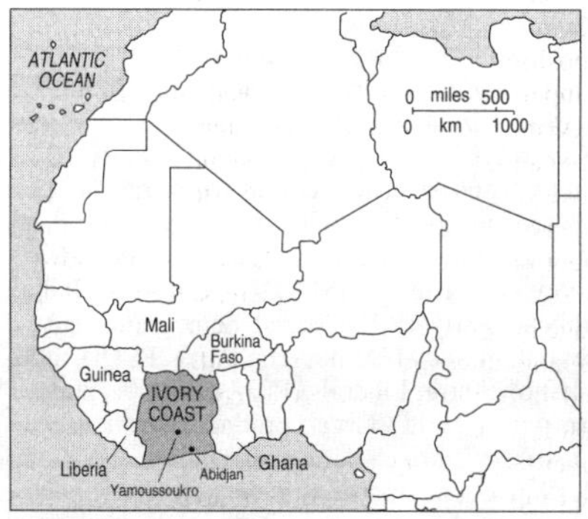

area 322,463 sq km/124,471 sq mi
capital Yamoussoukro
towns Bouaké, Daloa, Man; ports Abidjan, San-Pédro
physical tropical rainforest (diminishing as exploited) in S; savanna and low mountains in N
environment an estimated 85% of the country's forest has been destroyed by humans
features Vridi canal, Kossou dam, Monts du Toura
head of state and government Félix Houphouët-Boigny from 1960
political system emergent democratic republic
political party Democratic Party of the Ivory Coast (PDCI), nationalist, free-enterprise
exports coffee, cocoa, fish, timber, petroleum products
currency franc CFA
population (1992) 12,951,000; growth rate 3.3% p.a.
life expectancy men 52, women 55 (1989)
languages French (official), over 60 native dialects
media the government has full control of the media
religions animist 65%, Muslim 24%, Christian 11%
literacy 35% (1988)
GDP $7.6 bn (1987); $687 per head
chronology
1904 Became part of French West Africa.
1958 Achieved internal self-government.
1960 Independence achieved from France, with Félix Houphouët-Boigny as president of a one-party state.
1985 Houphouët-Boigny re-elected, unopposed.
1986 Name changed officially from Ivory Coast to Côte d'Ivoire.
1990 Houphouët-Boigny and PDCI re-elected.

Jamaica

area 10,957 sq km/4,230 sq mi
capital Kingston
towns Montego Bay, Spanish Town, St Andrew
physical mountainous tropical island
features Blue Mountains (so called because of the haze over them) renowned for their coffee; partly undersea ruins of pirate city of Port Royal, destroyed by an earthquake 1692
head of state Elizabeth II from 1962, represented by governor general
head of government P J Patterson from 1992
political system constitutional monarchy
political parties Jamaica Labour Party (JLP), moderate, centrist; People's National Party (PNP), left of centre
exports sugar, bananas, bauxite, rum, cocoa, coconuts, liqueurs, cigars, citrus
currency Jamaican dollar
population (1992) 2,445,000 (African 76%, mixed 15%, Chinese, Caucasian, East Indian); growth rate 2.2% p.a.
life expectancy men 75, women 78 (1989)
languages English, Jamaican creole
media one daily newspaper 1834–1988 (except 1973–82), privately owned; sensational evening and weekly papers
religions Protestant 55.9%, Rastafarian 5%
literacy 82% (1988)
GDP $2.9 bn; $1,187 per head (1989)

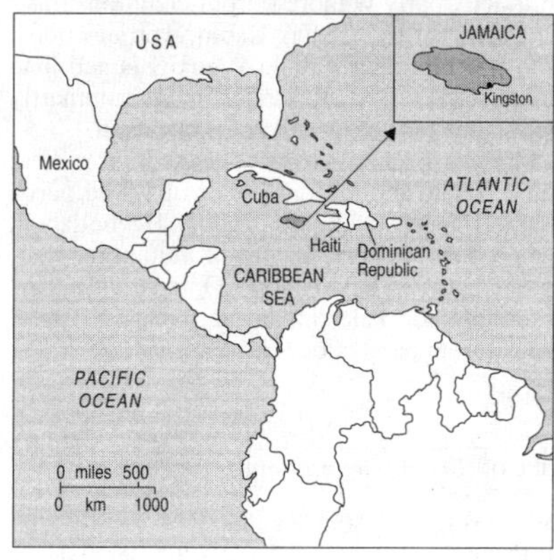

chronology
1494 Columbus reached Jamaica.
1509–1655 Occupied by Spanish.
1655 Captured by British.
1944 Internal self-government introduced.
1962 Independence achieved from Britain, with Alexander Bustamante of the JLP as prime minister.
1967 JLP re-elected under Hugh Shearer.
1972 Michael Manley of the PNP became prime minister.
1980 JLP elected, with Edward Seaga as prime minister.
1983 JLP re-elected, winning all 60 seats.
1988 Island badly damaged by Hurricane Gilbert.
1989 PNP won a decisive victory with Michael Manley returning as prime minister.
1992 Manley resigned, succeeded by P J Patterson.
1993 Landslide victory for PNP in general election.

Japan

(*Nippon*)

area 377,535 sq km/145,822 sq mi
capital Tokyo
towns Fukuoka, Kitakyushu, Kyoto, Sapporo; ports Osaka, Nagoya, Yokohama, Kobe, Kawasaki
physical mountainous, volcanic; comprises over 1,000 islands, the largest of which are Hokkaido, Honshu, Kyushu, and Shikoku
features Mount Fuji, Mount Aso (volcanic), Japan Alps, Inland Sea archipelago

head of state (figurehead) Emperor Akihito (Heisei) from 1989
head of government Morohiro Hosokawa from 1993
political system liberal democracy
political parties Liberal Democratic Party (LDP), right of centre; Social Democratic Party of Japan (SDJP), former Socialist Party, left of centre but moving towards centre; Komeito (Clean Government Party), Buddhist, centrist; Democratic Socialist Party, centrist; Japanese Communist Party (JCP), socialist; Nihon Shinto, centrist reformist; Shinsei, right-wing reformist
exports televisions, cassette and video recorders, radios, cameras, computers, robots, other electronic and electrical equipment, motor vehicles, ships, iron, steel, chemicals, textiles
currency yen
population (1992) 124,310,000; growth rate 0.5% p.a.
life expectancy men 76, women 82 (1989)
language Japanese
religions Shinto, Buddhist (often combined), Christian; 30% claim a personal religious faith
literacy 99% (1989)
GDP $3,674.5 bn (1992)

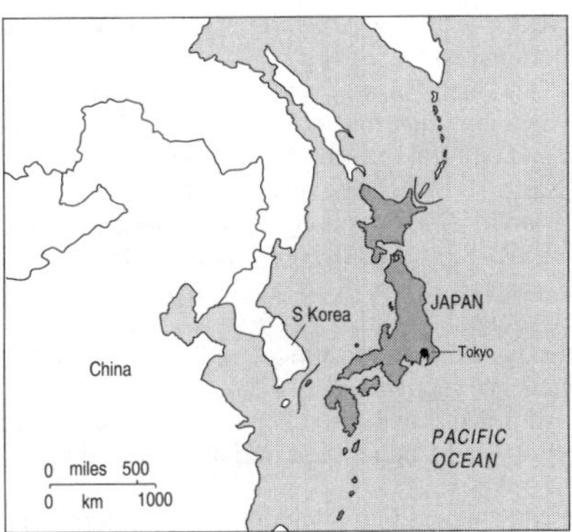

chronology
1867 End of shogun rule; executive power passed to emperor. Start of modernization of Japan.
1894–95 War with China; Formosa (Taiwan) and S Manchuria gained.
1902 Formed alliance with Britain.
1904–05 War with Russia; Russia ceded southern half of Sakhalin.
1910 Japan annexed Korea.
1914 Joined Allies in World War I.
1918 Received German Pacific islands as mandates.
1931–32 War with China; renewed 1937.
1941 Japan attacked US fleet at Pearl Harbor 7 Dec.
1945 World War II ended with Japanese surrender. Allied control commission took power. Formosa and Manchuria returned to China.
1946 Framing of 'peace constitution'. Emperor Hirohito became figurehead ruler.
1952 Full sovereignty regained.
1958 Joined United Nations.
1968 Bonin and Volcano Islands regained.
1972 Ryukyu Islands regained.
1974 Prime Minister Tanaka resigned over Lockheed bribes scandal.
1982 Yasuhiro Nakasone elected prime minister.
1985 Yen revalued.
1987 Noboru Takeshita chosen to succeed Nakasone.
1988 Recruit scandal cast shadow over government and opposition parties.
1989 Emperor Hirohito (Shōwa) died; succeeded by his son Akihito. Many cabinet ministers implicated in Recruit scandal and Takeshita resigned; succeeded by Sosuke Uno. Aug: Uno resigned after sex scandal; succeeded by Toshiki Kaifu.
1990 Feb: new house of councillors' elections won by LDP. Public-works budget increased by 50% to encourage imports.
1991 Japan contributed billions of dollars to the Gulf War and its aftermath. Kaifu succeeded by Kiichi Miyazawa.
1992 Over 100 politicians implicated in new financial scandal. Emperor Akihito made first Japanese imperial visit to China. Trade surpluses reached record levels.
1993 Worst recession of postwar era; trade surpluses, however, again reached record levels. LDP 'godfather' Shin Kanemaru charged with tax evasion. Government lost no-confidence vote over electoral reform. Miyazawa resigned. Morohiro Hosokawa chosen as prime minister. New party (Shinsei) formed from LDP faction.

Jordan

Hashemite Kingdom of (*Al Mamlaka al Urduniya al Hashemiyah*)

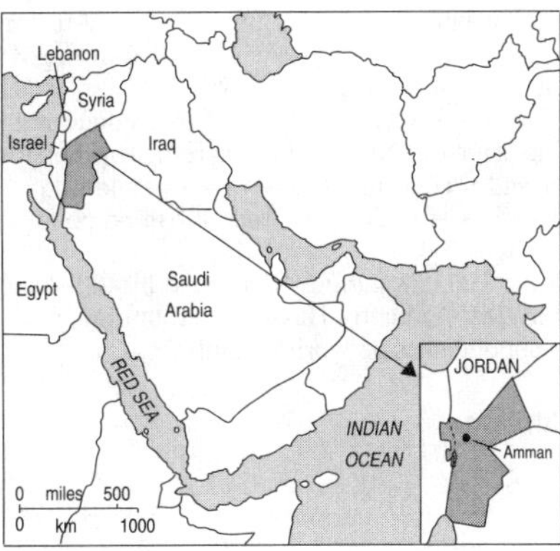

area 89,206 sq km/34,434 sq mi (West Bank 5,879 sq km/2,269 sq mi)
capital Amman
towns Zarqa, Irbid, Aqaba (the only port)
physical desert plateau in E; rift valley separates E and W banks of the river Jordan
features lowest point on Earth below sea level in the Dead Sea (–396 m/–1,299 ft); archaeological sites at Jerash and Petra
head of state King Hussein ibn Talai from 1952
head of government Abdul-Salam-al-Mujali from 1993
political system constitutional monarchy
political parties none
exports potash, phosphates, citrus, vegetables
currency Jordanian dinar
population (1992) 3,636,000; growth rate 3.6% p.a.
life expectancy men 67, women 71

languages Arabic (official), English
religions Sunni Muslim 92%, Christian 8%
literacy 71% (1988)
GDP $4.3 bn (1987); $1,127 per head (1988)

chronology
1946 Independence achieved from Britain as Transjordan.
1949 New state of Jordan declared.
1950 Jordan annexed West Bank.
1953 Hussein ibn Talai officially became king of Jordan.
1958 Jordan and Iraq formed Arab Federation that ended when the Iraqi monarchy was deposed.
1967 Israel captured and occupied West Bank. Martial law imposed.
1976 Lower house dissolved, political parties banned, elections postponed until further notice.
1982 Hussein tried to mediate in Arab-Israeli conflict.
1984 Women voted for the first time.
1985 Hussein and Yassir Arafat put forward framework for Middle East peace settlement. Secret meeting between Hussein and Israeli prime minister.
1988 Hussein announced decision to cease administering the West Bank as part of Jordan, passing responsibility to Palestine Liberation Organization, and the suspension of parliament.
1989 Prime Minister Zaid al-Rifai resigned; Hussein promised new parliamentary elections following criticism of economic policies. Riots over price increases up to 50% following fall in oil revenues. First parliamentary elections for 22 years; Muslim Brotherhood won 25 of 80 seats but exiled from government; martial law lifted.
1990 Hussein unsuccessfully tried to mediate after Iraq's invasion of Kuwait. Massive refugee problems as thousands fled to Jordan from Kuwait and Iraq.
1991 24 years of martial law ended; ban on political parties lifted.
1993 King Hussein publicly distanced himself from Iraqi leader Saddam Hussein. Abdul-Salam-al-Mujali appointed as new prime minister.

Kazakhstan

Republic of

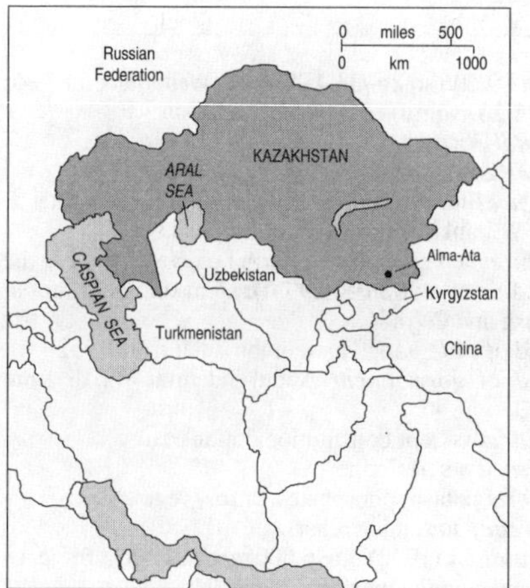

area 2,717,300 sq km/1,049,150 sq mi
capital Alma-Ata
towns Karaganda, Semipalatinsk, Petropavlovsk
physical Caspian and Aral seas, Lake Balkhash; Steppe region
features Baikonur Cosmodrome (space launch site at Tyuratam, near Baikonur)
head of state Nursultan Nazarbayev from 1990
head of government Sergey Tereshchenko from 1991
political system emergent democracy
political parties Independent Socialist Party of Kazakhstan (SPK)
products grain, copper, lead, zinc, manganese, coal, oil
population (1992) 17,008,000 (Kazakh 40%, Russian 38%, German 6%, Ukrainian 5%)
languages Russian; Kazakh, related to Turkish
religion Sunni Muslim
chronology
1920 Autonomous republic in USSR.
1936 Joined the USSR and became a full union republic.
1950s Site of Nikita Khrushchev's ambitious 'Virgin Lands' agricultural extension programme.
1960s A large influx of Russian settlers turned the Kazakhs into a minority in their own republic.
1986 Riots in Alma-Alta after Gorbachev ousted local communist leader.
1989 Nursultan Nazarbayev became leader of the Kazakh Communist Party (KCP) and instituted economic and cultural reform programmes.
1990 Nazarbayev became head of state.
1991 March: support pledged for continued union with USSR; Aug: Nazarbayev condemned attempted anti-Gorbachev coup; KCP abolished and replaced by Independent Socialist Party of Kazakhstan. Dec: joined new Commonwealth of Independent States; independence recognized by USA.
1992 Admitted into United Nations and Conference on Security and Cooperation in Europe. Trade agreement with USA.
1993 New constitution adopted, increasing the authority of the president and making Kazakh the state language.

Kenya

Republic of (*Jamhuri ya Kenya*)

area 582,600 sq km/224,884 sq mi
capital Nairobi
towns Kisumu, port Mombasa
physical mountains and highlands in W and centre; coastal plain in S; arid interior and tropical coast
environment the elephant faces extinction as a result of poaching
features Great Rift Valley, Mount Kenya, Lake Nakuru (salt lake with world's largest colony of flamingos), Lake Turkana (Rudolf), national parks with wildlife, Malindini Marine Reserve, Olduvai Gorge
head of state and government Daniel arap Moi from 1978
political system authoritarian nationalism
political parties Kenya African National Union (KANU), nationalist, centrist; National Democratic Party (NDP), centrist (launched 1991, not accepted by government)

exports coffee, tea, fruits and vegetables, petroleum products
currency Kenya shilling
population (1992) 26,985,000 (Kikuyu 21%, Luo 13%, Luhya 14%, Kelenjin 11%; Asian, Arab, European); growth rate 4.2% p.a.
life expectancy men 59, women 63 (1989)
languages Kiswahili (official), English; there are many local dialects
religions Protestant 38%, Roman Catholic 28%, indigenous beliefs 26%, Muslim 6%
literacy 50% (1988)
GDP $6.9 bn (1987); $302 per head (1988)

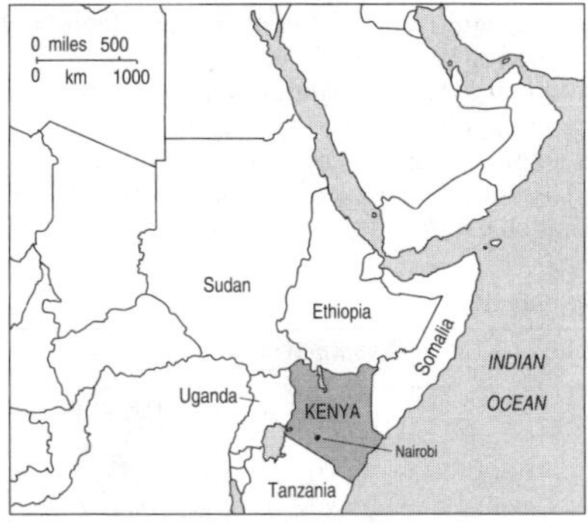

chronology
1895 British East African protectorate established.
1920 Kenya became a British colony.
1944 African participation in politics began.
1950 Mau Mau campaign began.
1953 Nationalist leader Jomo Kenyatta imprisoned by British authorities.
1956 Mau Mau campaign defeated, Kenyatta released.
1963 Achieved internal self-government, with Kenyatta as prime minister.
1964 Independence achieved from Britain as a republic within the Commonwealth, with Kenyatta as president.
1967 East African Community (EAC) formed with Tanzania and Uganda.
1977 Collapse of EAC.
1978 Death of Kenyatta. Succeeded by Daniel arap Moi.
1982 Attempted coup against Moi foiled.
1983 Moi re-elected unopposed.
1984 Over 2,000 people massacred by government forces at Wajir.
1985-86 Thousands of forest villagers evicted and their homes destroyed to make way for cash crops.
1988 Moi re-elected. 150,000 evicted from state-owned forests.
1989 Moi announced release of all known political prisoners. Confiscated ivory burned in attempt to stop elephant poaching.
1990 Despite antigovernment riots, Moi refused multiparty politics.
1991 Increasing demands for political reform; Moi promised multiparty politics.
1992 Constitutional amendment passed. Dec: Moi re-elected in first direct elections despite allegations of fraud.

Kiribati

Republic of

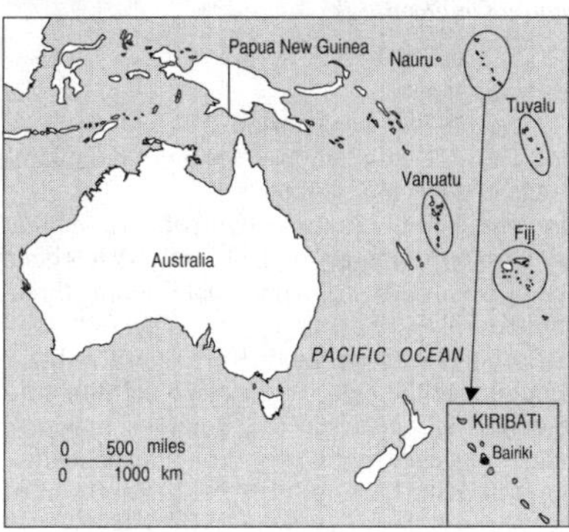

area 717 sq km/277 sq mi
capital (and port) Bairiki (on Tarawa Atoll)
physical comprises 33 Pacific coral islands: the Kiribati (Gilbert), Rawaki (Phoenix), Banaba (Ocean Island), and three of the Line Islands including Kiritimati (Christmas Island)
environment the islands are threatened by the possibility of a rise in sea level caused by global warming. A rise of approximately 30 cm/1 ft by the year 2040 will make existing fresh water brackish and undrinkable
features island groups crossed by equator and International Date Line
head of state and government Teatao Teannaki from 1991
political system liberal democracy
political parties National Progressive Party, governing faction; opposition parties: Christian Democratic Party and the Kiribati United Party
exports copra, fish
currency Australian dollar
population (1992) 74,700; growth rate 1.7% p.a.
languages English (official), Gilbertese
religions Roman Catholic 48%, Protestant 45%
literacy 90% (1985)
GDP $26 million (1987); $430 per head (1988)

chronology
1892 Gilbert and Ellice Islands proclaimed a British protectorate.
1937 Phoenix Islands added to colony.
1950s UK tested nuclear weapons on Kiritimati (formerly Christmas Island).
1962 USA tested nuclear weapons on Kiritimati.
1975 Ellice Islands separated to become Tuvalu.
1977 Gilbert Islands granted internal self-goverment.
1979 Independence achieved from Britain, within the Commonwealth, as the Republic of Kiribati, with Ieremia Tabai as president.
1982 and 1983 Tabai re-elected.
1985 Fishing agreement with Soviet state-owned company negotiated, prompting formation of Kiribati's first political party, the opposition Christian Democrats.
1987 Tabai re-elected.
1991 Tabai re-elected but not allowed under constitution to serve further term; Teatao Teannaki elected president.

Korea, North

Democratic People's Republic of (*Chosun Minchu-chui Inmin Konghwa-guk*)

area 120,538 sq km/46,528 sq mi
capital Pyongyang
towns Chongjin, Nampo, Wonsan
physical wide coastal plain in W rising to mountains cut by deep valleys in interior
environment the building of a hydroelectric dam at Kumgangsan on a tributary of the Han River has been opposed by South Korea as a potential flooding threat to central Korea
features separated from South Korea by a military demarcation line; the richer of the two Koreas in mineral resources (copper, iron ore, graphite, tungsten, zinc, lead, magnesite, gold, phosphor, phosphates)
head of state Kim Il Sung from 1972 (also head of Korean Workers' Party)
head of government Kang Song San from 1992
political system communism
political parties Korean Workers' Party (KWP), Marxist-Leninist-Kim Il Sungist (leads Democratic Front for the Reunification of the Fatherland, including North Korean Democratic Party and Religious Chungwoo Party)
exports coal, iron, copper, textiles, clothing, chemicals
currency won
population (1992) 22,227,000; growth rate 2.5% p.a.
life expectancy men 67, women 73 (1989)
language Korean
religions traditionally Buddhist, Confucian, but religious activity curtailed by the state
literacy 99% (1989)
GNP $20 bn; $3,450 per head (1988)

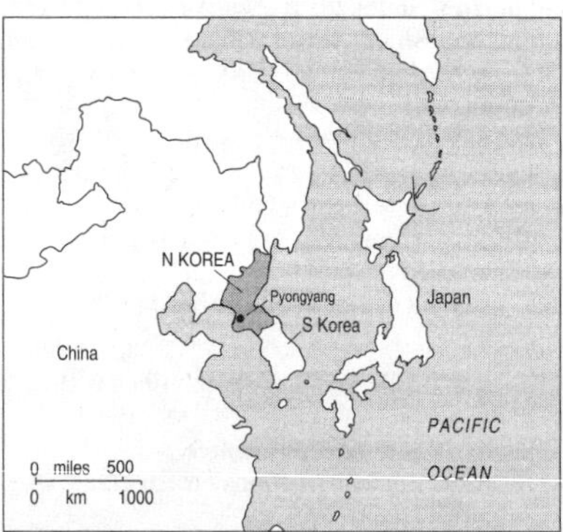

chronology
1910 Korea formally annexed by Japan.
1945 Russian and US troops entered Korea, forced surrender of Japanese, and divided the country in two. Soviet troops occupied North Korea.
1948 Democratic People's Republic of Korea declared.
1950 North Korea invaded South Korea to unite the nation, beginning the Korean War.
1953 Armistice agreed to end Korean War.
1961 Friendship and mutual assistance treaty signed with China.
1972 New constitution, with executive president, adopted. Talks took place with South Korea about possible reunification.
1980 Reunification talks broke down.
1983 Four South Korean cabinet ministers assassinated in Rangoon, Burma (Myanmar), by North Korean army officers.
1985 Increased relations with the USSR.
1989 Increasing evidence shown of nuclear-weapons development.
1990 Diplomatic contacts with South Korea and Japan suggested the beginning of a thaw in North Korea's relations with the rest of the world.
1991 Became a member of the United Nations. Signed nonaggression agreement with South Korea; agreed to ban nuclear weapons.
1992 Signed Nuclear Safeguards Agreement, allowing international inspection of its nuclear facilities. Also signed a pact with South Korea for mutual inspection of nuclear facilities. Passed legislation making foreign investment in the country attractive. Yon Hyong Muk replaced by Kang Song San.
1993 Threatened to withdraw from Nuclear Non-Proliferation Treaty.

Korea, South

Republic of Korea (*Daehan Minguk*)

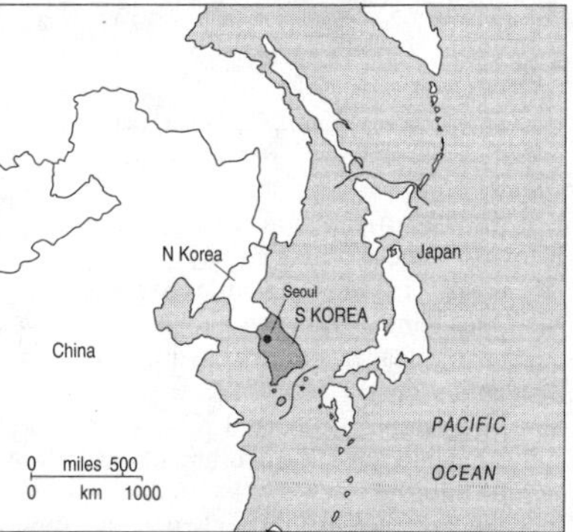

area 98,799 sq km/38,161 sq mi
capital Seoul
towns Taegu, ports Pusan, Inchon
physical southern end of a mountainous peninsula separating the Sea of Japan from the Yellow Sea
features Chomsongdae (world's earliest observatory); giant Popchusa Buddha; granite peaks of Soraksan National Park
head of state Kim Young Sam from 1992
head of government Hwang In Sung from 1993
political system emergent democracy
political parties Democratic Liberal Party (DLP), right of centre; Democratic Party, left of centre; Unification National Party (UNP), right of centre
exports steel, ships, chemicals, electronics, textiles and clothing, plywood, fish
currency won
population (1992) 43,663,000; growth rate 1.4% p.a.
life expectancy men 66, women 73 (1989)
language Korean
media freedom of the press achieved 1987; large numbers of newspapers with large circulations. It is prohibited to say anything favourable about North Korea
religions traditionally Buddhist, Confucian, and Chondokyo; Christian 28%

literacy 92% (1989)
GNP $171bn (1988); $2,180 per head (1986)

chronology
1910 Korea formally annexed by Japan.
1945 Russian and US troops entered Korea, forced surrender of Japanese, and divided the country in two. US military government took control of South Korea.
1948 Republic proclaimed.
1950-53 War with North Korea.
1960 President Syngman Rhee resigned amid unrest.
1961 Military coup by General Park Chung-Hee. Industrial growth programme.
1979 Assassination of President Park.
1980 Military takeover by General Chun Doo Hwan.
1987 Adoption of more democratic constitution after student unrest. Roh Tae Woo elected president.
1988 Former president Chun, accused of corruption, publicly apologized and agreed to hand over his financial assets to the state. Seoul hosted Summer Olympic Games.
1989 Roh reshuffled cabinet, threatened crackdown on protesters.
1990 Two minor opposition parties united with Democratic Justice Party to form ruling Democratic Liberal Party. Diplomatic relations established with the USSR.
1991 Violent mass demonstrations against the government. New opposition grouping, the Democratic Party, formed. Prime Minister Ro Jai Bong replaced by Chung Won Shik. Entered United Nations. Nonaggression and nuclear pacts signed with North Korea.
1992 DLP lost absolute majority in March general election; substantial gains made by Democratic Party and newly formed UNP, led by Chung Ju Wong. Diplomatic relations with China established. Dec: Kim Young Sam, DLP candidate, won the presidential election.
1993 Hwang In Sung appointed prime minister.

Kuwait

State of (*Dowlat al Kuwait*)

area 17,819 sq km/6,878 sq mi
capital Kuwait (also chief port)
towns Jahra, Ahmadi, Fahaheel
physical hot desert; islands of Failaka, Bubiyan, and Warba at NE corner of Arabian Peninsula
environment during the Gulf War 1990–91, 650 oil wells were set alight and about 300,000 tonnes of oil were released into the waters of the Gulf leading to pollution haze, photochemical smog, acid rain, soil contamination, and water pollution
features there are no rivers and rain is light; the world's largest desalination plants, built in the 1950s
head of state and government Jabir al-Ahmad al-Jabir al-Sabah from 1977
political system absolute monarchy
political parties none
exports oil
currency Kuwaiti dinar
population (1992) 1,190,000 (Kuwaitis 40%, Palestinians 30%); growth rate 5.5% p.a.
life expectancy men 72, women 76 (1989)
languages Arabic 78%, Kurdish 10%, Farsi 4%
religion Sunni Muslim 45%, Shi'ite minority 30%
literacy 71% (1988)
GNP $19.1 bn; $10,410 per head (1988)

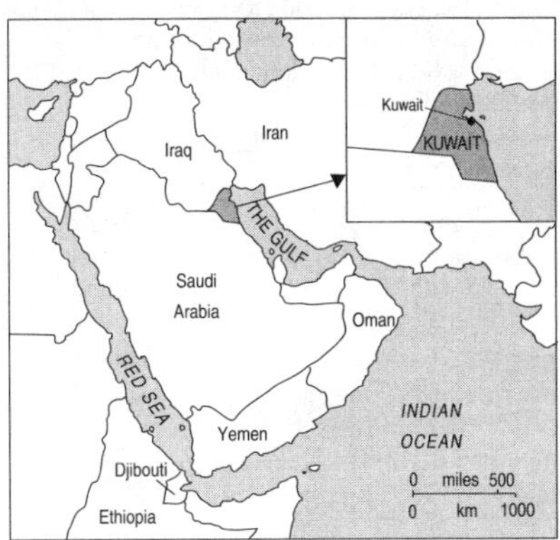

chronology
1914 Britain recognized Kuwait as an independent sovereign state.
1961 Full independence achieved from Britain, with Sheik Abdullah al-Salem al-Sabah as emir.
1965 Sheik Abdullah died; succeeded by his brother, Sheik Sabah.
1977 Sheik Sabah died; succeeded by Crown Prince Jabir.
1983 Shi'ite guerrillas bombed targets in Kuwait; 17 arrested.
1986 National assembly suspended.
1987 Kuwaiti oil tankers reflagged, received US Navy protection; missile attacks by Iran.
1988 Aircraft hijacked by pro-Iranian Shi'ites demanding release of convicted guerrillas; Kuwait refused.
1989 Two of the convicted guerrillas released.
1990 Prodemocracy demonstrations suppressed. Aug: Kuwait annexed by Iraq. Emir set up government in exile in Saudi Arabia.
1991 Feb: Kuwait liberated by US-led coalition forces; extensive damage to property and environment. New government omitted any opposition representatives. Trials of alleged Iraqi collaborators criticized.
1992 Reconstituted national assembly elected on restricted franchise, with opposition party winning majority of seats.
1993 Jan: incursions by Iraq into Kuwait again created tension; US-led air strikes reassured Kuwaitis.

Kyrgyzstan

Republic of

area 198,500 sq km/76,641 sq mi
capital Bishkek (formerly Frunze)
towns Osh, Przhevalsk, Kyzyl-Kiya, Tormak
physical mountainous, an extension of the Tian Shan range
head of state Askar Akayev from 1990
head of government Tursunbek Chyngyshev from 1991
political system emergent democracy
political parties Democratic Kyrgyzstan, nationalist reformist; Asaba (Banner) Party and Free Kyrgyzstan Party, both opposition groupings

products cereals, sugar, cotton, coal, oil, sheep, yaks, horses
population (1992) 4,533,000 (Kyrgyz 52%, Russian 22%, Uzbek 13%, Ukrainian 3%, German 2%)
language Kyrgyz, a Turkic language
religion Sunni Muslim

chronology
1917–1924 Part of an independent Turkestan republic.
1924 Became autonomous republic within USSR.
1936 Became full union republic within USSR.
1990 June: ethnic clashes resulted in state of emergency being imposed in Bishkek. Nov: Askar Akayev, founder of Democratic movement, chosen as state president.
1991 March: Kyrgyz voters endorsed maintenance of Union in USSR referendum. Aug: President Akayev condemned anti-Gorbachev attempted coup in Moscow; Kyrgyz Communist Party, which supported the coup, suspended. Oct: Akayev directly elected president. Dec: joined new Commonwealth of Independent States and independence recognized by USA.
1992 Joined the United Nations and Conference on Security and Cooperation in Europe. Supreme Soviet (parliament) renamed the Uluk Kenesh.

Laos

Lao People's Democratic Republic (*Saathiaranagroat Prachhathippatay Prachhachhon Lao*)

area 236,790 sq km/91,400 sq mi
capital Vientiane
towns Luang Prabang (the former royal capital), Pakse, Savannakhet
physical landlocked state with high mountains in E; Mekong River in W; jungle covers nearly 60% of land
features Plain of Jars, where prehistoric people carved stone jars large enough to hold a person
head of state Nouhak Phoumsavan from 1992
head of government General Khamtay Siphandon from 1991
political system communism, one-party state
political party Lao People's Revolutionary Party (LPRP) (only legal party)
exports hydroelectric power from the Mekong is exported to Thailand; timber, teak, coffee, electricity
currency new kip
population (1992) 4,409,000 (Lao 48%, Thai 14%, Khmer 25%, Chinese 13%); growth rate 2.2% p.a.
life expectancy men 48, women 51 (1989)
languages Lao (official), French
religions Theravāda Buddhist 85%, animist beliefs among mountain dwellers
literacy 45% (1991)
GNP $500 million (1987); $180 per head (1988)

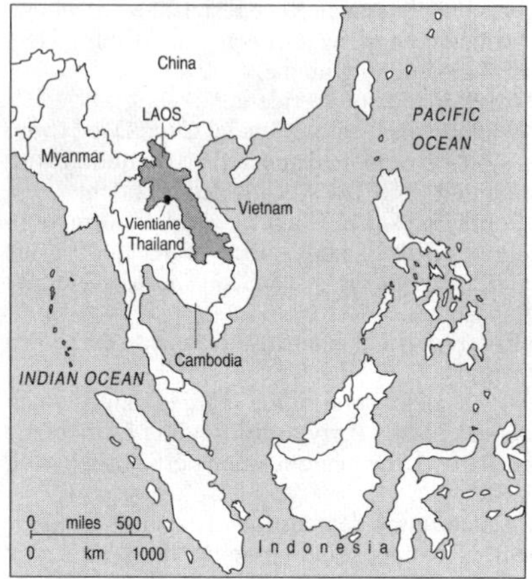

chronology
1893–1945 Laos was a French protectorate.
1945 Temporarily occupied by Japan.
1946 Retaken by France.
1950 Granted semi-autonomy in French Union.
1954 Independence achieved from France.
1960 Right-wing government seized power.
1962 Coalition government established; civil war continued.
1973 Vientiane cease-fire agreement. Withdrawal of US, Thai, and North Vietnamese forces.
1975 Communist-dominated republic proclaimed with Prince Souphanouvong as head of state.
1986 Phoumi Vongvichit became acting president.
1988 Plans announced to withdraw 40% of Vietnamese forces stationed in the country.
1989 First assembly elections since communist takeover.
1991 Constitution approved. Kaysone Phomvihane elected president. General Khamtay Siphandon named as new premier.
1992 Nov: Phomvihane died; replaced by Nouhak Phoumsavan. Dec: new national assembly created, replacing supreme people's assembly, and general election held (effectively one-party).

Latvia

Republic of

area 63,700 sq km/24,595 sq mi
capital Riga
towns Daugavpils, Liepāja, Jurmala, Jelgava, Ventspils
physical wooded lowland (highest point 312 m/1,024 ft), marshes, lakes; 472 km/293 mi of coastline; mild climate

features Western Dvina River; Riga is largest port on the Baltic after Leningrad
head of state Anatolijs Gorbunov from 1988
head of government Ivars Godmanis from 1990
political system emergent democratic republic
political parties Latvian Popular Front, nationalist; Latvian Social-Democratic Workers' Party; Latvian Way, moderate, nationalist
products electronic and communications equipment, electric railway carriages, motorcycles, consumer durables, timber, paper and woollen goods, meat and dairy products
currency Latvian rouble
population (1992) 2,685,000 (Latvian 52%, Russian 34%, Byelorussian 5%, Ukrainian 3%)
language Latvian
religions mostly Lutheran Protestant, with a Roman Catholic minority

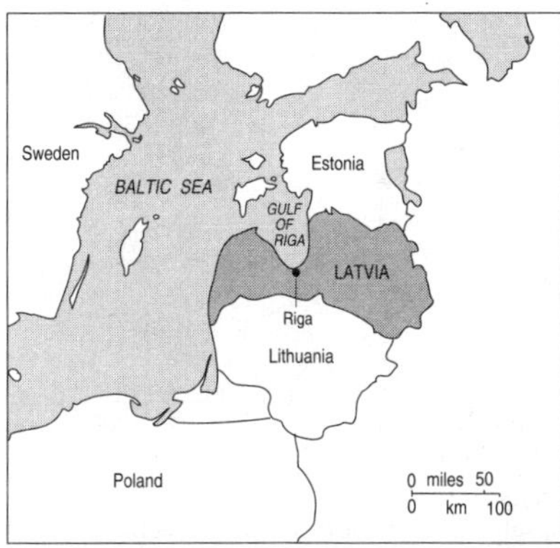

chronology
1917 Soviets and Germans contested for control of Latvia.
1918 Feb: Soviet forces overthrown by Germany. Nov: Latvia declared independence. Dec: Soviet rule restored after German withdrawal.
1919 Soviet rule overthrown by British naval and German forces May–Dec; democracy established.
1934 Coup replaced established government.
1939 German-Soviet secret agreement placed Latvia under Russian influence.
1940 Incorporated into USSR as constituent republic.
1941–44 Occupied by Germany.
1944 USSR regained control.
1980 Nationalist dissent began to grow.
1988 Latvian Popular Front established to campaign for independence. Prewar flag readopted; official status given to Latvian language.
1989 Popular Front swept local elections.
1990 Jan: Communist Party's (CP) monopoly of power abolished. March–April: Popular Front secured majority in elections. April: Latvian CP split into pro-independence and pro-Moscow wings. May: unilateral declaration of independence from USSR, subject to transitional period for negotiation.
1991 Jan: Soviet troops briefly seized key installations in Riga. March: overwhelming vote for independence in referendum. Aug: full independence declared at time of anti-Gorbachev coup; CP outlawed. Sept: independence recognized by Soviet government and Western nations; joined United Nations (UN) and Conference on Security and Cooperation in Europe.
1992 Russia began pull-out of ex-Soviet troops, to be completed 1994. July: curbing of rights of noncitizens in Latvia prompted Russia to request minority protection by UN.
1993 Latvian Way, led by former CP ideological secretary Anatolijs Gorbunov, won most seats in general election.

Lebanon

Republic of (*al-Jumhouria al-Lubnaniya*)

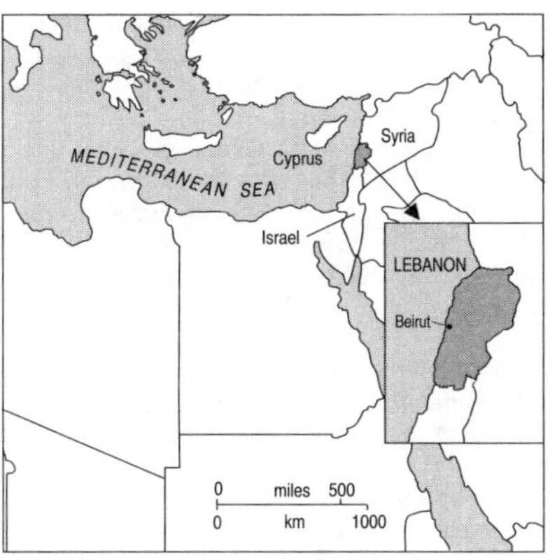

area 10,452 sq km/4,034 sq mi
capital and port Beirut
towns ports Tripoli, Tyre, Sidon
physical narrow coastal plain; Bekka valley N–S between Lebanon and Anti-Lebanon mountain ranges
features Mount Hermon; Chouf Mountains; archaeological sites at Baalbeck, Byblos, Tyre; until the civil war, the financial centre of the Middle East
head of state Elias Hrawi from 1989
head of government Rafik al-Hariri from 1992
political system emergent democratic republic
political parties Phalangist Party, Christian, radical, right-wing; Progressive Socialist Party (PSP), Druse, moderate, socialist; National Liberal Party (NLP), Maronite, centre-left; Parliamentary Democratic Front, Sunni Muslim, centrist; Lebanese Communist Party (PCL), nationalist, communist
exports citrus and other fruit, vegetables; industrial products; jewellery; clothing; metal products
currency Lebanese pound
population (1992) 2,803,000 (Lebanese 82%, Palestinian 9%, Armenian 5%); growth rate –0.1% p.a.
life expectancy men 65, women 70 (1989)
languages Arabic, French (both official), Armenian, English
religions Muslim 57% (Shiite 33%, Sunni 24%), Christian (Maronite and Orthodox) 40%, Druse 3%
literacy 75% (1989)
GNP $1.8 bn; $690 per head (1986)

chronology
1920–41 Administered under French mandate.
1944 Independence achieved.
1948–49 Lebanon joined first Arab war against Israel. Palestinian refugees settled in the south.

1964 Palestine Liberation Organization (PLO) founded in Beirut.
1967 More Palestinian refugees settled in Lebanon.
1971 PLO expelled from Jordan; established headquarters in Lebanon.
1975 Outbreak of civil war between Christians and Muslims.
1976 Cease-fire agreed; Syrian-dominated Arab deterrent force formed to keep the peace but considered by Christians as a occupying force.
1978 Israel invaded S Lebanon in search of PLO fighters. International peacekeeping force established. Fighting broke out again.
1979 Part of S Lebanon declared an 'independent free Lebanon'.
1982 Bachir Gemayel became president but was assassinated before he could assume office; succeeded by his brother Amin Gemayel. Israel again invaded Lebanon. Palestinians withdrew from Beirut under supervision of international peacekeeping force. PLO moved its headquarters to Tunis.
1983 Agreement reached for the withdrawal of Syrian and Israeli troops but abrogated under Syrian pressure.
1984 Most of international peacekeeping force withdrawn. Muslim militia took control of W Beirut.
1985 Lebanon in chaos; many foreigners taken hostage.
1987 Syrian troops sent into Beirut.
1988 Agreement on a Christian successor to Gemayel failed; he established a military government; Selim al-Hoss set up rival government; threat of partition hung over the country.
1989 Christian leader General Michel Aoun declared 'war of liberation' against Syrian occupation; Saudi Arabia and Arab League sponsored talks that resulted in new constitution recognizing Muslim majority; René Muhawad named president, assassinated after 17 days in office; Elias Hrawi named successor; Aoun occupied presidential palace, rejected constitution.
1990 Release of Western hostages began. General Aoun surrendered and legitimate government restored, with Umar Karami as prime minister.
1991 Government extended control to the whole country. Treaty of cooperation with Syria signed. More Western hostages released. General Aoun pardoned.
1992 Karami resigned as prime minister; succeeded by Rashid al-Solh. Remaining Western hostages released. General election boycotted by many Christians; pro-Syrian administration re-elected; Rafik al-Hariri became prime minister.
1993 July: Israel launched attacks on S Lebanon against Hezbollah strongholds

Lesotho

Kingdom of

area 30,355 sq km/11,717 sq mi
capital Maseru
towns Teyateyaneng, Mafeteng, Roma, Quthing
physical mountainous with plateaus, forming part of South Africa's chief watershed
features Lesotho is an enclave within South Africa
political system constitutional monarchy
head of state King Letsie III from 1990
head of government Ntsu Mokhehle from 1993
political parties Basotho National Party (BNP), traditionalist, nationalist; Basutoland Congress Party (BCP); Basotho Democratic Alliance (BDA)
exports wool, mohair, diamonds, cattle, wheat, vegetables
currency maluti
population (1992) 1,854,000; growth rate 2.7% p.a.
life expectancy men 59, women 62 (1989)
languages Sesotho, English (official), Zulu, Xhosa
religions Protestant 42%, Roman Catholic 38%
literacy 59% (1988)
GNP $408 million; $410 per head (1988)

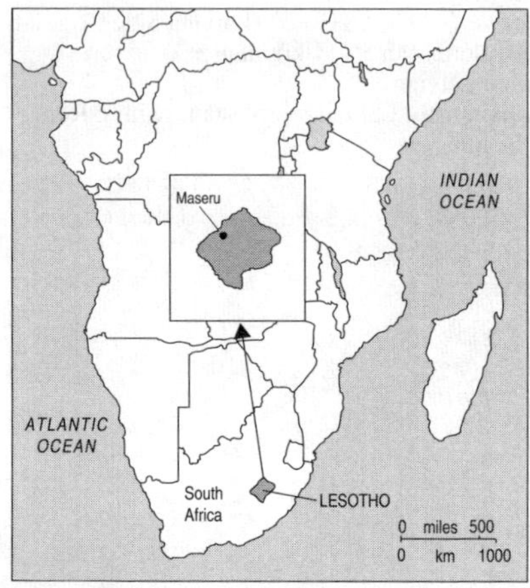

chronology
1868 Basutoland became a British protectorate.
1966 Independence achieved from Britain, within the Commonwealth, as the Kingdom of Lesotho, with Moshoeshoe II as king and Chief Leabua Jonathan as prime minister.
1970 State of emergency declared and constitution suspended.
1973 Progovernment interim assembly established; BNP won majority of seats.
1975 Members of the ruling party attacked by guerrillas backed by South Africa.
1985 Elections cancelled because no candidates opposed BNP.
1986 South Africa imposed border blockade, forcing deportation of 60 African National Congress members. General Lekhanya ousted Chief Jonathan in coup. National assembly abolished. Highlands Water Project agreement signed with South Africa.
1990 Moshoeshoe II dethroned by military council; replaced by his son Mohato as King Letsie III.
1991 Lekhanya ousted in military coup led by Col Elias Tutsoane Ramaema. Political parties permitted to operate.
1992 Ex-king Moshoeshoe returned from exile.
1993 Free elections ended military rule; Ntsu Mokhehle of BCP became prime minister.

Liberia

Republic of

area 111,370 sq km/42,989 sq mi
capital and port Monrovia
towns ports Buchanan, Greenville

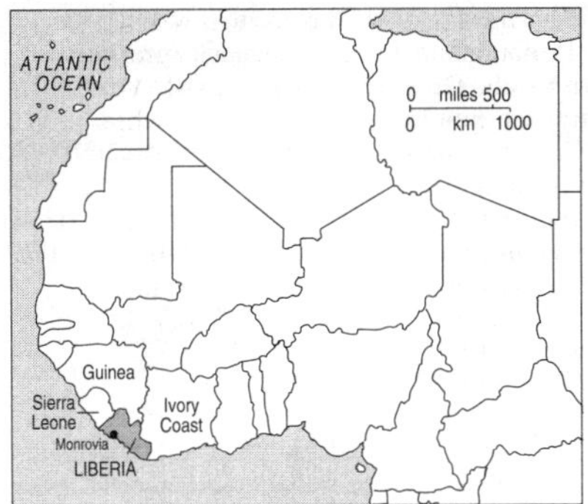

physical forested highlands; swampy tropical coast where six rivers enter the sea
features nominally the world's largest merchant navy as minimal registration controls make Liberia's a flag of convenience; the world's largest rubber plantations
head of state and government Amos Sawyer from 1990
political system emergent democratic republic
political parties National Democratic Party of Liberia (NDLP), nationalist; Liberian Action Party (LAP); Liberian Unity Party (LUP); United People's Party (UPP); Unity Party (UP)
exports iron ore, rubber (Africa's largest producer), timber, diamonds, coffee, cocoa, palm oil
currency Liberian dollar
population (1992) 2,780,000; growth rate 3% p.a.
life expectancy men 53, women 56 (1989)
languages English (official), over 20 Niger-Congo languages
media two daily newspapers, one published under government auspices, the other independent and with the largest circulation (10,000 copies)
religions animist 65%, Muslim 20%, Christian 15%
literacy men 47%, women 23% (1985 est)
GNP $973 million; $450 per head (1988)

chronology
1847 Founded as an independent republic.
1944 William Tubman elected president.
1971 Tubman died; succeeded by William Tolbert.
1980 Tolbert assassinated in coup led by Samuel Doe, who suspended the constitution and ruled through a People's Redemption Council.
1984 New constitution approved. National Democratic Party of Liberia (NDPL) founded by Doe.
1985 NDPL won decisive victory in allegedly rigged general election. Unsuccessful coup against Doe.
1990 Rebels under former government minister Charles Taylor controlled nearly entire country by July. Doe killed during a bloody civil war between rival rebel factions. Amos Sawyer became interim head of government.
1991 Amos Sawyer re-elected president. Rebel leader Charles Taylor agreed to work with Sawyer. Peace agreement failed but later revived; UN peacekeeping force drafted into republic.
1992 Monrovia under siege by Taylor's rebel forces.
1993 Peace agreement between opposing groups signed in Benin, under OAU/UN auspices.

Libya

Great Socialist People's Libyan Arab Jamahiriya (*al-Jamahiriya al-Arabiya al-Libya al-Shabiya al-Ishtirakiya al-Uzma*)
area 1,759,540 sq km/679,182 sq mi
capital Tripoli
towns ports Benghazi, Misurata, Tobruk
physical flat to undulating plains with plateaus and depressions stretch S from the Mediterranean coast to an extremely dry desert interior
environment plan to pump water from below the Sahara to the coast risks rapid exhaustion of nonrenewable supply (Great Manmade River Project)
features Gulf of Sirte; rock paintings of about 3000 BC in the Fezzan; Roman city sites include Leptis Magna, Sabratha
head of state and government Moamer al-Khaddhafi from 1969
political system one-party socialist state
political party Arab Socialist Union (ASU), radical, left-wing
exports oil, natural gas
currency Libyan dinar
population (1992) 4,447,000 (including 500,000 foreign workers); growth rate 3.1% p.a.
life expectancy men 64, women 69 (1989)
language Arabic
religion Sunni Muslim 97%
literacy 60% (1989)
GNP $20 bn; $5,410 per head (1988)

chronology
1911 Conquered by Italy.
1934 Colony named Libya.
1942 Divided into three provinces: Fezzan (under French control); Cyrenaica, Tripolitania (under British control).
1951 Achieved independence as the United Kingdom of Libya, under King Idris.
1969 King deposed in a coup led by Col Moamer al-Khaddhafi. Revolution Command Council set up and the Arab Socialist Union (ASU) proclaimed the only legal party.
1972 Proposed federation of Libya, Syria, and Egypt abandoned.
1980 Proposed merger with Syria abandoned. Libyan troops began fighting in Chad.
1981 Proposed merger with Chad abandoned.

1986 US bombing of Khaddhafi's headquarters, following allegations of his complicity in terrorist activities.
1988 Diplomatic relations with Chad restored.
1989 USA accused Libya of building a chemical-weapons factory and shot down two Libyan planes; reconciliation with Egypt.
1992 Khaddhafi under international pressure to extradite suspected Lockerbie and UTA (Union de Transports Aerians) bombers for trial outside Libya; sanctions imposed.

Liechtenstein

Principality of (*Fürstentum Liechtenstein*)

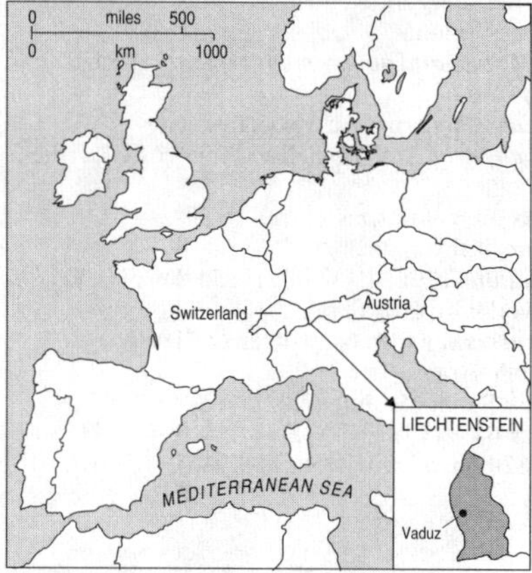

area 160 sq km/62 sq mi
capital Vaduz
towns Balzers, Schaan, Ruggell
physical landlocked Alpine; includes part of Rhine Valley in W
features no airport or railway station; easy tax laws make it an international haven for foreign companies and banks (some 50,000 companies are registered)
head of state Prince Hans Adam II from 1989
head of government Hans Brunhart from 1978
political system constitutional monarchy
political parties Fatherland Union (VU); Progressive Citizens' Party (FBP)
exports microchips, dental products, small machinery, processed foods, postage stamps
currency Swiss franc
population (1992) 29,600 (33% foreign); growth rate 1.4% p.a.
life expectancy men 78, women 83 (1989)
language German (official); an Alemannic dialect is also spoken
religions Roman Catholic 87%, Protestant 8%
literacy 100% (1989)
GNP $450 million (1986)
GDP $1 bn (1987); $32,000 per head
chronology
1342 Became a sovereign state.
1434 Present boundaries established.
1719 Former counties of Schellenberg and Vaduz constituted as the Principality of Liechtenstein.
1921 Adopted Swiss currency.
1923 United with Switzerland in a customs union.
1938 Prince Franz Josef II came to power.
1984 Prince Franz Joseph II handed over power to Crown Prince Hans Adam. Vote extended to women in national elections.
1989 Prince Franz Joseph II died; Hans Adam II succeeded him.
1990 Became a member of the United Nations (UN).
1991 Became seventh member of European Free Trade Association.

Lithuania

Republic of

area 65,200 sq km/25,174 sq mi
capital Vilnius
towns Kaunas, Klaipeda, Siauliai, Panevezys
physical central lowlands with gentle hills in W and higher terrain in SE; 25% forested; some 3,000 small lakes, marshes, and complex sandy coastline
features river Nemen; white sand dunes on Kursiu Marios lagoon
head of state Algirdas Brazauskas from 1993
head of government Adolfas Slezevicius from 1993
political system emergent democracy
political parties Sajudis (Lithuanian Restructuring Movement), nationalist; Democratic Party, centrist; Humanism and Progress Party, reformist; Social Democratic Party, left of centre; Green Party, ecological; Christian Democratic Party, right of centre; Democratic Labour Party, 'reform communist'
products heavy engineering, electrical goods, shipbuilding, cement, food processing, bacon, dairy products, cereals, potatoes
currency Lithuanian rouble
population (1992) 3,802,000 (Lithuanian 80%, Russian 9%, Polish 7%, Byelorussian 2%)
language Lithuanian
religion predominantly Roman Catholic

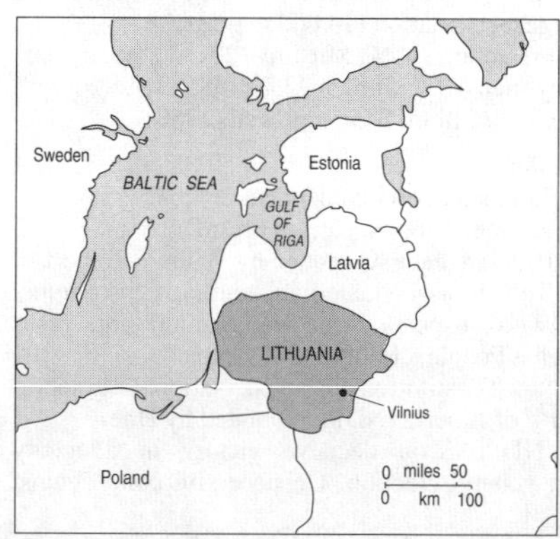

chronology
1918 Independence declared following withdrawal of German occupying troops at end of World War I; USSR attempted to regain power.
1919 Soviet forces overthrown by Germans, Poles, and nationalist Lithuanians; democratic republic established.
1920–39 Province and city of Vilnius occupied by Poles.
1926 Coup overthrew established government; Antanas Smetona became president.

1939 Secret German-Soviet agreement brought most of Lithuania under Soviet influence.
1940 Incorporated into USSR as constituent republic.
1941 Lithuania revolted against USSR and established own government. During World War II Germany again occupied the country.
1944 USSR resumed rule.
1944–52 Lithuanian guerrillas fought USSR.
1972 Demonstrations against Soviet government.
1980 Growth in nationalist dissent, influenced by Polish example.
1988 Popular front formed, the Sajudis, to campaign for increased autonomy.
1989 Lithuanian declared the state language; flag of independent interwar republic readopted. Communist Party (CP) split into pro-Moscow and nationalist wings. Communist local monopoly of power abolished.
1990 Feb: nationalist Sajudis won elections. March: Vytautas Landsbergis became president; unilateral declaration of independence resulted in temporary Soviet blockade.
1991 Jan: Albertas Shiminas became prime minister. Soviet paratroopers briefly occupied key buildings in Vilnius. Sept: independence recognized by Soviet government and Western nations; Gediminas Vagnorius elected prime minister; CP outlawed; admitted into United Nations (UN) and Conference on Security and Cooperation in Europe (CSCE).
1992 July: Aleksandras Abisala became prime minister. Nov: DLP, led by Algirdas Brazauskas, won majority vote. Dec: Bronislovas Lubys appointed prime minister.
1993 Brazauskas elected president; Adolfas Slezevicius appointed prime minister.

Luxembourg

Grand Duchy of (*Grand-Duché de Luxembourg*)

area 2,586 sq km/998 sq mi
capital Luxembourg
towns Esch-sur-Alzette, Dudelange
physical on the river Moselle; part of the Ardennes (Oesling) forest in N
features seat of the European Court of Justice, Secretariat of the European Parliament, international banking centre; economically linked with Belgium
head of state Grand Duke Jean from 1964

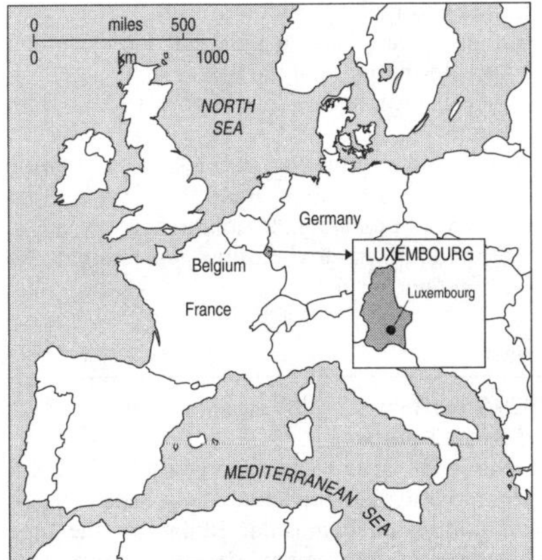

head of government Jacques Santer from 1984
political system liberal democracy
political parties Christian Social Party (PCS), moderate, left of centre; Luxembourg Socialist Workers' Party (POSL), moderate, socialist; Democratic Party (PD), centre-left; Communist Party of Luxembourg, pro-European left-wing
exports pharmaceuticals, synthetic textiles, steel
currency Luxembourg franc
population (1992) 387,000; growth rate 0% p.a.
life expectancy men 71, women 78 (1989)
languages French (official), local Letzeburgesch, German
religion Roman Catholic 97%
literacy 100% (1989)
GNP $10.4 bn (1992)

chronology
1354 Became a duchy.
1482 Under Habsburg control.
1797 Ceded, with Belgium, to France.
1815 Treaty of Vienna created Luxembourg a grand duchy, ruled by the king of the Netherlands.
1830 With Belgium, revolted against Dutch rule.
1890 Link with Netherlands ended with accession of Grand Duke Adolphe of Nassau-Weilburg.
1948 With Belgium and the Netherlands, formed the Benelux customs union.
1960 Benelux became fully effective economic union.
1961 Prince Jean became acting head of state on behalf of his mother, Grand Duchess Charlotte.
1964 Grand Duchess Charlotte abdicated; Prince Jean became grand duke.
1974 Dominance of Christian Social Party challenged by Socialists.
1979 Christian Social Party regained pre-eminence.
1991 Pact agreeing European free-trade area signed in Luxembourg.
1992 Voted in favour of ratification of Maastricht Treaty on European union.

Madagascar

Democratic Republic of (*Repoblika Demokratika n'i Madagaskar*)

area 587,041 sq km/226,598 sq mi
capital Antananarivo
towns chief port Toamasina, Antseranana, Fianarantsoa, Toliary
physical temperate central highlands; humid valleys and tropical coastal plains; arid in S
environment according to 1990 UN figures, 93% of the forest area has been destroyed and about 100,000 species have been made extinct
features one of the last places to be inhabited, it evolved in isolation with unique animals (such as the lemur, now under threat from deforestation)
head of state Albert Zafy from 1993
head of government Guy Razanamasy from 1991
political system emergent democratic republic
political parties National Front for the Defence of the Malagasy Socialist Revolution (FNDR); AKFM-Congress and AKFM-Renewal, both left of centre; Social Democratic Party (PSD), centre-left
exports coffee, cloves, vanilla, sugar, chromite, shrimps
currency Malagasy franc
population (1992) 12,804,000, mostly of Malayo-Indonesian origin; growth rate 3.2% p.a.

life expectancy men 50, women 53 (1989)
languages Malagasy (official), French, English
religions animist 50%, Christian 40%, Muslim 10%
literacy 53% (1988)
GNP $2.1 bn (1987); $280 per head (1988)

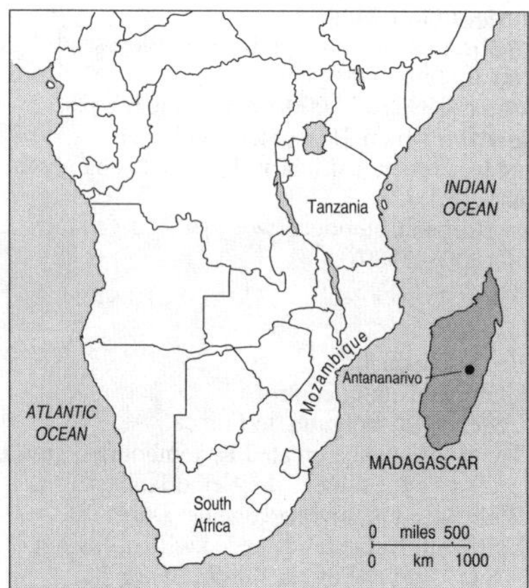

chronology
1885 Became a French protectorate.
1896 Became a French colony.
1960 Independence achieved from France, with Philibert Tsiranana as president.
1972 Army took control of the government.
1975 Martial law imposed under a national military directorate. New Marxist constitution proclaimed the Democratic Republic of Madagascar, with Didier Ratsiraka as president.
1976 Front-Line Revolutionary Organization (AREMA) formed.
1977 National Front for the Defence of the Malagasy Socialist Revolution (FNDR) became the sole legal political organization.
1980 Ratsiraka abandoned Marxist experiment.
1983 Ratsiraka re-elected, despite strong opposition from radical socialist National Movement for the Independence of Madagascar (MONIMA) under Monja Jaona.
1989 Ratsiraka re-elected for third term after restricting opposition parties.
1990 Political opposition legalized; 36 new parties created.
1991 Antigovernment demonstrations; opposition to Ratsiraka led to general strike. Ratsiraka formed new unity government.
1992 Constitutional reform approved by referendum. First multiparty elections won by Democrat coalition.
1993 Albert Zafy, leader of coalition, elected president.

Malawi

Republic of (*Malaŵi*)
area 118,000 sq km/45,560 sq mi
capital Lilongwe
towns Blantyre (largest city and commercial centre), Mzuzu, Zomba
physical landlocked narrow plateau with rolling plains; mountainous W of Lake Malawi

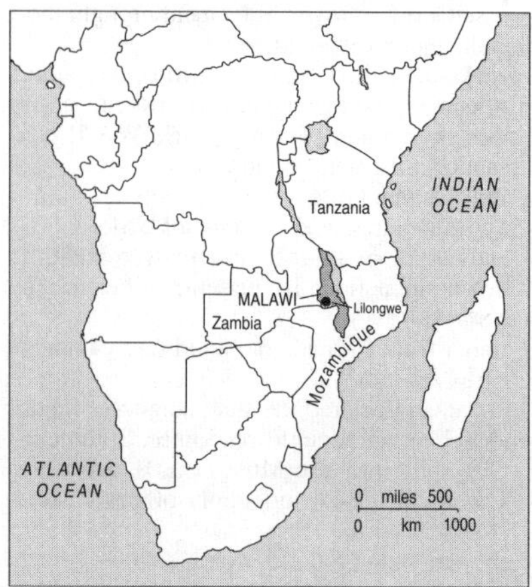

features one-third is water, including lakes Malawi, Chilara, and Malombe; Great Rift Valley; Nyika, Kasungu, and Lengare national parks; Mulanje Massif; Shire River
head of state and government Hastings Kamusu Banda from 1966 for life
political system one-party republic
political party Malawi Congress Party (MCP), multiracial, right-wing
exports tea, tobacco, cotton, peanuts, sugar
currency kwacha
population (1992) 9,484,000 (nearly 1 million refugees from Mozambique); growth rate 3.3% p.a.
life expectancy men 46, women 50 (1989)
languages English, Chichewa (both official)
religions Christian 75%, Muslim 20%
literacy 25% (1989)
GNP $1.2 bn (1987); $160 per head (1988)

chronology
1891 Became the British protectorate Nyasaland.
1964 Independence achieved from Britain, within the Commonwealth, as Malawi.
1966 Became a one-party republic, with Hastings Banda as president.
1971 Banda was made president for life.
1977 Banda released some political detainees and allowed greater freedom of the press.
1986–89 Influx of nearly a million refugees from Mozambique.
1992 Calls for multiparty politics. Countrywide industrial riots caused many fatalities. Western aid suspended over human-rights violations.
1993 Referendum overwhelmingly supported the ending of one-party rule.

Malaysia

area 329,759 sq km/127,287 sq mi
capital Kuala Lumpur
towns Johor Baharu, Ipoh, Georgetown (Penang), Kuching in Sarawak, Kota Kinabalu in Sabah
physical comprises Peninsular Malaysia (the nine Malay states – Johore, Kedah, Kelantan, Negri Sem-

bilan, Pahang, Perak, Perlis, Selangor, Trengganu – plus Malacca and Penang); and E Malaysia (Sabah and Sarawak); 75% tropical jungle; central mountain range; swamps in E
features Mount Kinabalu (highest peak in SE Asia); Niah caves (Sarawak)
head of state Rajah Azlan Muhibuddin Shah (sultan of Perak) from 1989
head of government Mahathir bin Mohamad from 1981
political system liberal democracy
political parties New United Malays' National Organization (UMNO Baru), Malay-oriented nationalist; Malaysian Chinese Association (MCA), Chinese-oriented conservative; Gerakan Party, Chinese-oriented, left of centre; Malaysian Indian Congress (MIC), Indian-oriented; Democratic Action Party (DAP), left of centre, multiracial but Chinese-dominated; Pan-Malayan Islamic Party (PAS), Islamic; Semangat '46 (Spirit of 1946), moderate, multiracial
exports pineapples, palm oil, rubber, timber, petroleum (Sarawak), bauxite
currency ringgit
population (1992) 18,630,000 (Malaysian 47%, Chinese 32%, Indian 8%, others 13%); growth rate 2% p.a.
life expectancy men 65, women 70 (1989)
languages Malay (official), English, Chinese, Indian, and local languages
religions Muslim (official), Buddhist, Hindu, local beliefs
literacy 80% (1989)
GNP $34.3 bn; $1,870 per head (1988)

chronology
1786 Britain established control.
1826 Became a British colony.
1963 Federation of Malaysia formed, including Malaya, Singapore, Sabah (N Borneo), and Sarawak (NW Borneo).
1965 Secession of Singapore from federation.
1969 Anti-Chinese riots in Kuala Lumpur.
1971 Launch of *bumiputra* ethnic-Malay-oriented economic policy.
1981 Election of Dr Mahathir bin Mohamad as prime minister.
1982 Mahathir bin Mohamad re-elected.

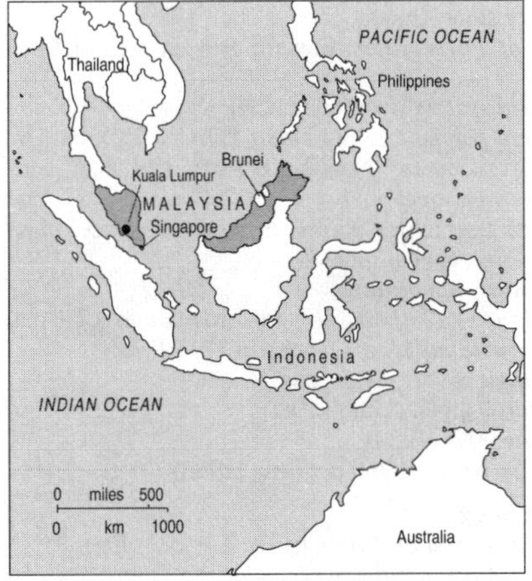

1986 Mahathir bin Mohamad re-elected.
1987 Arrest of over 100 opposition activists, including DAP leader, as Malay-Chinese relations deteriorated.
1988 Split in ruling UMNO party over Mahathir's leadership style; new UMNO formed.
1989 Semangat '46 set up by former members of UMNO including ex-premier Tunku Abdul Rahman.
1990 Mahathir bin Mohamad re-elected.
1991 New economic-growth programme launched.

Maldives

Republic of (*Divehi Jumhuriya*)

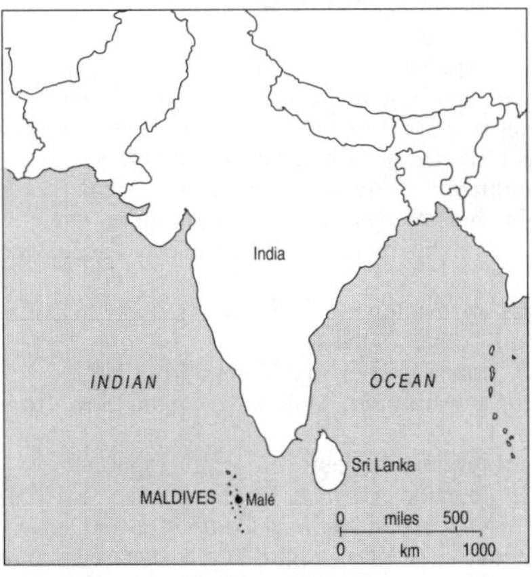

area 298 sq km/115 sq mi
capital Malé
towns Seenu
physical comprises 1,196 coral islands, grouped into 12 clusters of atolls, largely flat, none bigger than 13 sq km/5 sq mi, average elevation 1.8 m/6 ft; 203 are inhabited
environment the threat of rising sea level has been heightened by the frequency of flooding in recent years
features tourism developed since 1972
head of state and government Maumoon Abdul Gayoom from 1978
political system authoritarian nationalism
political parties none; candidates elected on the basis of personal influence and clan loyalties
exports coconuts, copra, bonito (fish related to tuna), garments
currency rufiya
population (1992) 230,000; growth rate 3.7% p.a.
life expectancy men 60, women 63 (1989)
languages Divehi (Sinhalese dialect), English
religion Sunni Muslim
literacy 36% (1989)
GNP $69 million (1987); $410 per head (1988)
chronology
1887 Became a British protectorate.
1953 Long a sultanate, the Maldive Islands became a republic within the Commonwealth.
1954 Sultan restored.
1965 Achieved full independence outside the Commonwealth.

1968 Sultan deposed; republic reinstated with Ibrahim Nasir as president.
1978 Nasir retired; replaced by Maumoon Abdul Gayoom.
1982 Rejoined the Commonwealth.
1983 Gayoom re-elected.
1985 Became a founder member of South Asian Association for Regional Cooperation (SAARC).
1988 Gayoom re-elected. Coup attempt by mercenaries, thought to have the backing of former president Nasir, was foiled by Indian paratroops.

Mali

Republic of (*République du Mali*)

area 1,240,142 sq km/478,695 sq mi
capital Bamako
towns Mopti, Kayes, Ségou, Timbuktu
physical landlocked state with river Niger and savanna in S; part of the Sahara in N; hills in NE; Senegal River and its branches irrigate the SW
environment a rising population coupled with recent droughts has affected marginal agriculture. Once in surplus, Mali has had to import grain every year since 1965
features ancient town of Timbuktu; railway to Dakar is the only outlet to the sea
head of state Alpha Oumar Konare from 1992
head of government Abdoulaye Sekou Sow from 1993
political system emergent democratic republic
political parties Alliance for Democracy in Mali (ADEMA), centrist; National Committee for Democratic Initiative (CNID), centre-left; Sudanese Union–African Democratic Rally (US–RDA), Sudanese nationalist
exports raw cotton and cotton products, peanuts, livestock, fish
currency franc CFA
population (1992) 8,464,000; growth rate 2.9% p.a.
life expectancy men 44, women 47 (1989)
languages French (official), Bambara
religions Sunni Muslim 90%, animist 9%, Christian 1%
literacy 10% (1989)
GNP $1.6 bn (1987); $230 per head (1988)

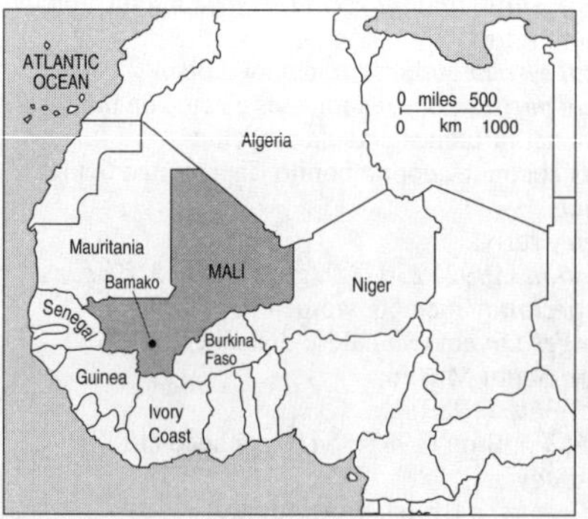

chronology
1895 Came under French rule.
1959 With Senegal, formed the Federation of Mali.
1960 Became the independent Republic of Mali, with Modibo Keita as president.
1968 Keita replaced in an army coup by Moussa Traoré.
1974 New constitution made Mali a one-party state.
1976 New national party, the Malian People's Democratic Union, announced.
1983 Agreement between Mali and Guinea for eventual political and economic integration signed.
1985 Conflict with Burkina Faso lasted five days; mediated by International Court of Justice.
1991 Demonstrations against one-party rule. Moussa Traoré ousted in a coup led by Lt-Col Amadou Toumani Toure. New multiparty constitution agreed, subject to referendum.
1992 Referendum endorsed new democratic constitution. Alliance for Democracy in Mali (ADEMA) won multiparty elections; Alpha Oumar Konare elected president.
1993 Abdoulaye Sekou Sow appointed prime minister.

Malta

Republic of (*Repubblika Ta'Malta*)

area 320 sq km/124 sq mi
capital and port Valletta
towns Rabat; port of Marsaxlokk
physical includes islands of Gozo 67 sq km/26 sq mi and Comino 2.5 sq km/1 sq mi
features occupies strategic location in central Mediterranean; large commercial dock facilities
head of state Vincent Tabone from 1989
head of government Edward Fenech Adami from 1987
political system liberal democracy
political parties Malta Labour Party (MLP), moderate, left of centre; Nationalist Party, Christian, centrist, pro-European
exports vegetables, knitwear, handmade lace, plastics, electronic equipment
currency Maltese lira
population (1990 est) 373,000; growth rate 0.7% p.a.
life expectancy men 72, women 77 (1987)
languages Maltese, English
religion Roman Catholic 98%
literacy 90% (1988)
GNP $1.6 bn; $4,750 per head (1988)

chronology
1814 Annexed to Britain by the Treaty of Paris.
1947 Achieved self-government.

1955 Dom Mintoff of the Malta Labour Party (MLP) became prime minister.
1956 Referendum approved MLP's proposal for integration with the UK. Proposal opposed by the Nationalist Party.
1958 MLP rejected the British integration proposal.
1962 Nationalists elected, with Borg Olivier as prime minister.
1964 Independence achieved from Britain, within the Commonwealth. Ten-year defence and economic-aid treaty with UK signed.
1971 Mintoff re-elected. 1964 treaty declared invalid and negotiations began for leasing the NATO base in Malta.
1972 Seven-year NATO agreement signed.
1974 Became a republic.
1979 British military base closed.
1984 Mintoff retired and was replaced by Mifsud Bonnici as prime minister and MLP leader.
1987 Edward Fenech Adami (Nationalist) elected prime minister.
1989 Vincent Tabone elected president. USA–USSR summit held offshore.
1990 Formal application made for EC membership.
1992 Nationalist Party returned to power in general election.

Mauritania

Islamic Republic of (*République Islamique de Mauritanie*)

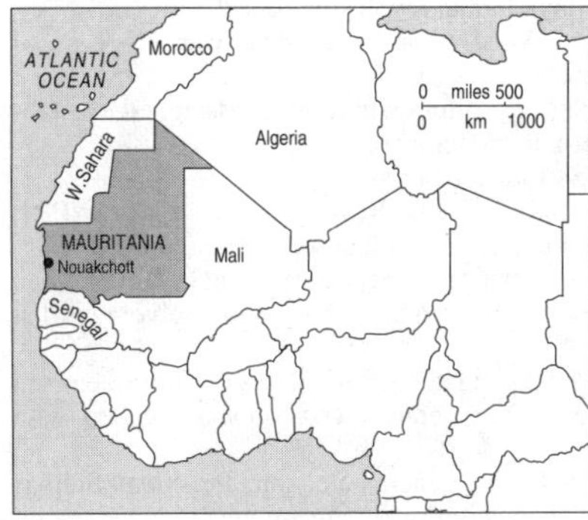

area 1,030,700 sq km/397,850 sq mi
capital Nouakchott
towns port of Nouadhibou, Kaédi, Zouérate
physical valley of river Senegal in S; remainder arid and flat
features part of the Sahara Desert; dusty sirocco wind blows in March
head of state and government Maaouia Ould Sid Ahmed Taya from 1984
political system emergent democratic republic
political parties Democratic and Social Republican Party (PRDS), centre-left, militarist; Union of Democratic Forces (UFD), centre-left; Rally for Democracy and National Unity (RDUN), centrist; Mauritian Renewal Party (PMR), centrist; Umma, Islamic fundamentalist; Socialist and Democratic Popular Front Union (UDSP), left of centre
exports iron ore, fish, gypsum
currency ouguiya
population (1992) 2,108,000 (Arab-Berber 30%, black African 30%, Haratine – descendants of black slaves, who remained slaves until 1980–30%); growth rate 3% p.a.
life expectancy men 43, women 48 (1989)
languages French (official), Hasaniya Arabic, black African languages
religion Sunni Muslim 99%
literacy 17% (1987)
GNP $843 million; $480 per head (1988)

chronology
1903 Became a French protectorate.
1960 Independence achieved from France, with Moktar Ould Daddah as president.
1975 Western Sahara ceded by Spain. Mauritania occupied the southern area and Morocco the north. Polisario Front formed in Sahara to resist the occupation by Mauritania and Morocco.
1978 Daddah deposed in bloodless coup; replaced by Mohamed Khouna Ould Haidalla. Peace agreed with Polisario Front.
1981 Diplomatic relations with Morocco broken.
1984 Haidalla overthrown by Maaouia Ould Sid Ahmed Taya. Polisario regime formally recognized.
1985 Relations with Morocco restored.
1989 Violent clashes between Mauritanians and Senegalese. Arab-dominated government expelled thousands of Africans into N Senegal; governments had earlier agreed to repatriate each other's citizens (about 250,000).
1991 Amnesty for political prisoners. Multiparty elections promised. Calls for resignation of President Taya.
1992 First multiparty elections won by ruling PRDS. Diplomatic relations with Senegal resumed.

Mauritius

Republic of

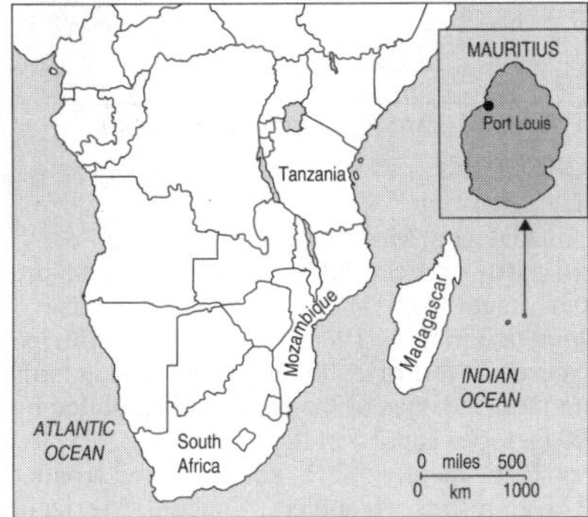

area 1,865 sq km/720 sq mi; the island of Rodrigues is part of Mauritius; there are several small island dependencies
capital Port Louis
towns Beau Bassin-Rose Hill, Curepipe, Quatre Bornes
physical mountainous, volcanic island surrounded by coral reefs
features unusual wildlife includes flying fox and ostrich; it was the home of the dodo (extinct from about 1680)

interim head of state Veerasamy Ringadoo from 1992
head of government Aneerood Jugnauth from 1982
political system liberal democratic republic
political parties Mauritius Socialist Movement (MSM), moderate socialist-republican; Mauritius Labour Party (MLP), centrist, Hindu-oriented; Mauritius Social Democratic Party (PMSD), conservative, Francophile; Mauritius Militant Movement (MMM), Marxist-republican; Rodriguais People's Organization (OPR), left of centre
exports sugar, knitted goods, tea
currency Mauritius rupee
population (1992) 1,081,000, 68% of Indian origin; growth rate 1.5% p.a.
life expectancy men 64, women 71 (1989)
languages English (official), French, creole, Indian languages
religions Hindu 51%, Christian 30%, Muslim 17%
literacy 94% (1989)
GNP $1.4 bn (1987); $1,810 per head (1988)
chronology
1814 Annexed to Britain by the Treaty of Paris.
1968 Independence achieved from Britain within the Commonwealth, with Seewoosagur Ramgoolam as prime minister.
1982 Aneerood Jugnauth became prime minister.
1983 Jugnauth formed a new party, the Mauritius Socialist Movement. Ramgoolam appointed governor general. Jugnauth formed a new coalition government.
1985 Ramgoolam died; succeeded by Veersamy Ringadoo.
1987 Jugnauth's coalition re-elected.
1990 Attempt to create a republic failed.
1991 Jugnauth's ruling MSM–MMM–OPR coalition won general election; pledge to secure republican status by 1992.
1992 Mauritius became a republic while remaining a member of the Commonwealth. Ringadoo became interim president.

Mexico

United States of (*Estados Unidos Mexicanos*)

area 1,958,201 sq km/756,198 sq mi
capital Mexico City
towns Guadalajara, Monterrey; port Veracruz
physical partly arid central highlands; Sierra Madre mountain ranges E and W; tropical coastal plains
environment during the 1980s, smog levels in Mexico City exceeded World Health Organization standards on more than 300 days of the year. Air is polluted by 130,000 factories and 2.5 million vehicles
features Rio Grande; 3,218 km/2,000 mi frontier with USA; resorts Acapulco, Cancun, Mexicali, Tijuana; Baja California, Yucatán peninsula; volcanoes, including Popocatépetl; pre-Columbian archaeological sites
head of state and government Carlos Salinas de Gortari from 1988
political system federal democratic republic
political parties Institutional Revolutionary Party (PRI), moderate, left-wing; National Action Party (PAN), moderate Christian socialist
exports silver, gold, lead, uranium, oil, natural gas, handicrafts, fish, shellfish, fruits and vegetables, cotton, machinery

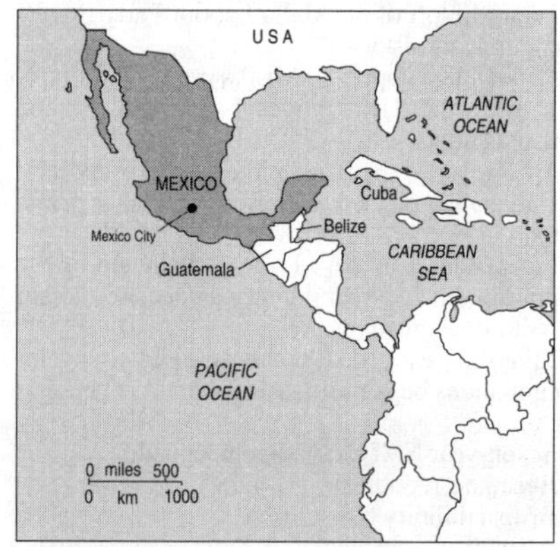

currency peso
population (1992) 84,439,000 (mixed descent 60%, Indian 30%, Spanish descent 10%); 50% under 20 years of age; growth rate 2.6% p.a.
life expectancy men 67, women 73
languages Spanish (official) 92%, Nahuatl, Maya, Mixtec
religion Roman Catholic 97%
literacy men 92%, women 88% (1989)
GNP $126 bn (1987); $2,082 per head
chronology
1821 Independence achieved from Spain.
1846–48 Mexico at war with USA; loss of territory.
1848 Maya Indian revolt suppressed.
1864–67 Maximilian of Austria was emperor of Mexico.
1917 New constitution introduced, designed to establish permanent democracy.
1983–84 Financial crisis.
1985 Institutional Revolutionary Party (PRI) returned to power. Earthquake in Mexico City.
1986 International Monetary Fund (IMF) loan agreement signed to keep the country solvent until at least 1988.
1988 PRI candidate Carlos Salinas de Gortari elected president. Debt reduction accords negotiated with USA.
1991 PRI won general election. President Salinas promised constitutional reforms.
1992 Public outrage following Guadalajara gas-explosion disaster.

Moldova

Republic of

area 33,700 sq km/13,012 sq mi
capital Chişinău (Kishinev)
towns Tiraspol, Beltsy, Bendery
physical hilly land lying largely between the rivers Prut and Dniester; northern Moldova comprises the level plain of the Beltsy Steppe and uplands; the climate is warm and moderately continental
features Black Earth region
head of state Mircea Snegur from 1989
head of government Valerin Murovsky from 1992
political system emergent democracy
political parties Moldavian Popular Front (MRF), Romanian nationalist; Gagauz-Khalky People's Movement (GKPM), Gagauz separatist

products wine, tobacco, canned goods
population (1992) 4,394,000 (Moldavian 64%, Ukrainian 14%, Russian 13%, Gagauzi 4%, Bulgarian 2%)
language Moldavian, allied to Romanian
religion Russian Orthodox

chronology
1940 Bessarabia in the E became part of the Soviet Union whereas the W part remained in Romania.
1941 Bessarabia taken over by Romania–Germany.
1944 Red army reconquered Bessarabia.
1946–47 Widespread famine.
1988 A popular front, the Democratic Movement for Perestroika, campaigned for accelerated political reform.
1989 Jan–Feb: nationalist demonstrations in Chişinău. May: Moldavian Popular Front established. July: former Communist Party deputy leader Mircea Snegur became head of state. Aug: Moldavian language granted official status, triggering clashes between ethnic Russians and Moldavians. Nov: Gagauz-Khalky People's Movement formed to campaign for Gagauz autonomy.
1990 Feb: Popular Front polled strongly in supreme soviet elections. June: economic and political sovereignty declared; renamed Republic of Moldova. Oct: Gagauzi held unauthorized elections to independent parliament; state of emergency declared after interethnic clashes. Trans-Dniester region declared its sovereignty. Nov: state of emergency declared in Trans-Dniester region after interethnic killings.
1991 March: Moldova boycotted the USSR's constitutional referendum. Aug: independence declared after abortive anti-Gorbachev coup; Communist Party outlawed. Dec: Moldova joined new Commonwealth of Independent States.
1992 Admitted into United Nations and the Conference on Security and Cooperation in Europe; diplomatic recognition granted by USA. Possible union with Romania discussed. Trans-Dniester region fighting intensified; Russian peacekeeping force reportedly deployed after talks between Moldova and Russia. Andrei Sangheli became premier.
1993 Secessionist unrest continued in Gagauz and Trans-Dniester regions.

Monaco

Principality of

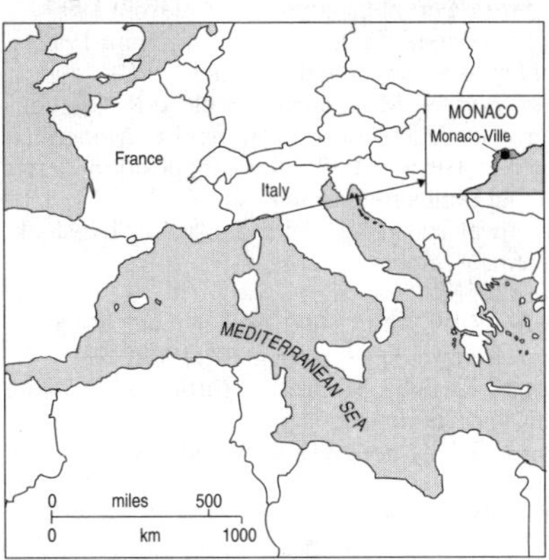

area 1.95 sq km/0.75 sq mi
capital Monaco-Ville
towns Monte Carlo, La Condamine; heliport Fontvieille
physical steep and rugged; surrounded landwards by French territory; being expanded by filling in the sea
features aquarium and oceanographic centre; Monte Carlo film festival, motor races, and casinos; world's second smallest state
head of state Prince Rainier III from 1949
head of government Jean Ausseil from 1986
political system constitutional monarchy under French protectorate
political parties National and Democratic Union (UND); Democratic Union Movement; Monaco Action; Monégasque Socialist Party
exports some light industry; economy dependent on tourism and gambling
currency French franc
population (1989) 29,000; growth rate –0.5% p.a.
languages French (official), English, Italian
religion Roman Catholic 95%
literacy 99% (1985)

chronology
1861 Became an independent state under French protection.
1918 France given a veto over succession to the throne.
1949 Prince Rainier III ascended the throne.
1956 Prince Rainier married US actress Grace Kelly.
1958 Birth of male heir, Prince Albert.
1959 Constitution of 1911 suspended.
1962 New constitution adopted.

Mongolia

State of

(***Outer Mongolia*** until 1924; ***People's Republic of Mongolia*** until 1991)

area 1,565,000 sq km/604,480 sq mi
capital Ulaanbaatar
towns Darhan, Choybalsan
physical high plateau with desert and steppe (grasslands)

features Altai Mountains in SW; salt lakes; part of Gobi Desert in SE
head of state Punsalmaagiyn Ochirbat from 1990
head of government Puntsagiyn Jasray from 1992
political system emergent democracy
political parties Mongolian People's Revolutionary Party (MPRP), reform-communist; Mongolian Democratic Party (MDP), main opposition party; Mongolian Democratic Union
exports meat and hides, minerals, wool, livestock, grain, cement, timber
currency tugrik
population (1992) 2,182,000; growth rate 2.8% p.a.
life expectancy men 63, women 67 (1989)
languages Khalkha Mongolian (official), Chinese, Russian, and Turkic languages
religion officially none (Tibetan Buddhist Lamaism suppressed 1930s)
literacy 89% (1985)
GNP $3.6 bn; $1,820 per head (1986)

chronology
1911 Outer Mongolia gained autonomy from China.
1915 Chinese sovereignty reasserted.
1921 Chinese rule overthrown with Soviet help.
1924 People's Republic proclaimed.
1946 China recognized Mongolia's independence.
1966 20-year friendship, cooperation, and mutual-assistance pact signed with USSR. Relations with China deteriorated.
1984 Yumjaagiyn Tsedenbal, effective leader, deposed and replaced by Jambyn Batmonh.
1987 Soviet troops reduced; Mongolia's external contacts broadened.
1989 Further Soviet troop reductions.
1990 Democratization campaign launched by Mongolian Democratic Union. Punsalmaagiyn Ochirbat's MPRP elected in free multiparty elections. Mongolian script readopted.
1991 Massive privatization programme launched as part of move towards a market economy. The word 'Republic' dropped from country's name. GDP declined by 10%.
1992 Jan: New constitution introduced. Economic situation worsened; GDP again declined by 10%. Puntsagiyn Jasray appointed as the new prime minister.

Morocco

Kingdom of (*al-Mamlaka al-Maghrebia*)

area 458,730 sq km/177,070 sq mi (excluding Western Sahara)
capital Rabat
towns Marrakesh, Fez, Meknès; ports Casablanca, Tangier, Agadir
physical mountain ranges NE–SW; fertile coastal plains in W
features Atlas Mountains; the towns Ceuta (from 1580) and Melilla (from 1492) are held by Spain; tunnel crossing the Strait of Gibraltar to Spain proposed 1985
head of state Hassan II from 1961
head of government Mohamed Lawrani from 1992
political system constitutional monarchy
political parties Constitutional Union (UC), right-wing; National Rally of Independents (RNI), royalist; Popular Movement (MP), moderate socialist; Istiqlal, nationalist, right of centre; Socialist Union of Popular Forces (USFP), progressive socialist; National Democratic Party (PND), moderate, nationalist
exports dates, figs, cork, wood pulp, canned fish, phosphates
currency dirham (DH)
population (1992) 26,239,000; growth rate 2.5% p.a.
life expectancy men 62, women 65 (1989)
languages Arabic (official) 75%, Berber 25%, French, Spanish
religion Sunni Muslim 99%
literacy men 45%, women 22% (1985 est)
GNP $18.7 bn; $750 per head (1988)

chronology
1912 Morocco divided into French and Spanish protectorates.
1956 Independence achieved as the Sultanate of Morocco.
1957 Sultan restyled king of Morocco.
1961 Hassan II came to the throne.
1969 Former Spanish province of Ifni returned to Morocco.
1972 Major revision of the constitution.
1975 Western Sahara ceded by Spain to Morocco and Mauritania.
1976 Guerrilla war in Western Sahara with the Polisario Front. Sahrawi Arab Democratic Republic

(SADR) established in Algiers. Diplomatic relations between Morocco and Algeria broken.
1979 Mauritania signed a peace treaty with Polisario.
1983 Peace formula for Western Sahara proposed by the Organization of African Unity (OAU); Morocco agreed but refused to deal directly with Polisario.
1984 Hassan signed an agreement for cooperation and mutual defence with Libya.
1987 Cease-fire agreed with Polisario, but fighting continued.
1988 Diplomatic relations with Algeria restored.
1989 Diplomatic relations with Syria restored.
1992 Mohamed Lawrani appointed prime minister; new constitution approved in referendum.

Mozambique

People's Republic of (*República Popular de Moçambique*)

area 799,380 sq km/308,561 sq mi
capital and chief port Maputo
towns Beira, Nampula
physical mostly flat tropical lowland; mountains in W
features rivers Zambezi, Limpopo; 'Beira Corridor' rail, road, and pipeline link with Zimbabwe
head of state and government Joaquim Alberto Chissano from 1986
political system emergent democratic republic
political parties National Front for the Liberation of Mozambique (Frelimo), Marxist-Leninist; Renamo, or Mozambique National Resistance (MNR), former rebel movement
exports prawns, cashews, sugar, cotton, tea, petroleum products, copra
currency metical (replaced escudo 1980)
population (1992) 14,842,000 (mainly indigenous Bantu peoples; Portuguese 50,000); growth rate 2.8% p.a.; nearly 1 million refugees in Malawi
life expectancy men 45, women 48 (1989)
languages Portuguese (official), 16 African languages
religions animist 60%, Roman Catholic 18%, Muslim 16%
literacy men 55%, women 22% (1985 est)
GDP $4.7 bn; $319 per head (1987)

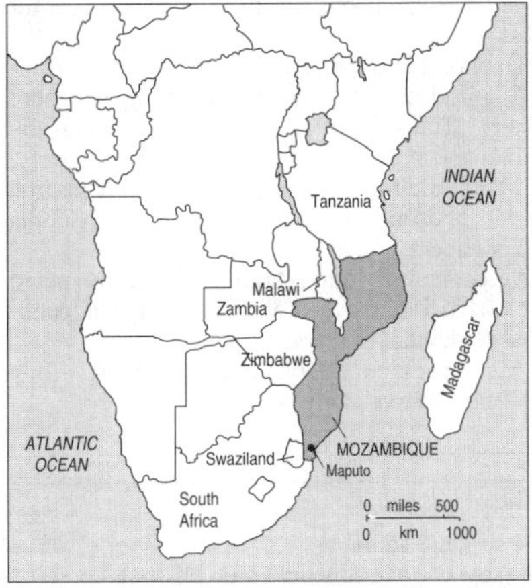

chronology
1505 Mozambique became a Portuguese colony.
1962 Frelimo (liberation front) established.
1975 Independence achieved from Portugal as a socialist republic, with Samora Machel as president and Frelimo as the sole legal party.
1977 Renamo resistance group formed.
1983 Re-establishment of good relations with Western powers.
1984 Nkomati accord of nonaggression signed with South Africa.
1986 Machel killed in air crash; succeeded by Joaquim Chissano.
1988 Tanzania announced withdrawal of its troops. South Africa provided training for Mozambican forces.
1989 Frelimo offered to abandon Marxist-Leninism; Chissano re-elected. Renamo continued attacks on government facilities and civilians.
1990 One-party rule officially ended. Partial cease-fire agreed.
1991 Peace talks resumed in Rome, delaying democratic process. Attempted antigovernment coup thwarted.
1992 Peace accord signed, but fighting continued.

Myanmar

Union of (*Thammada Myanmar Naingngandaw*) (formerly ***Burma***, until 1989)

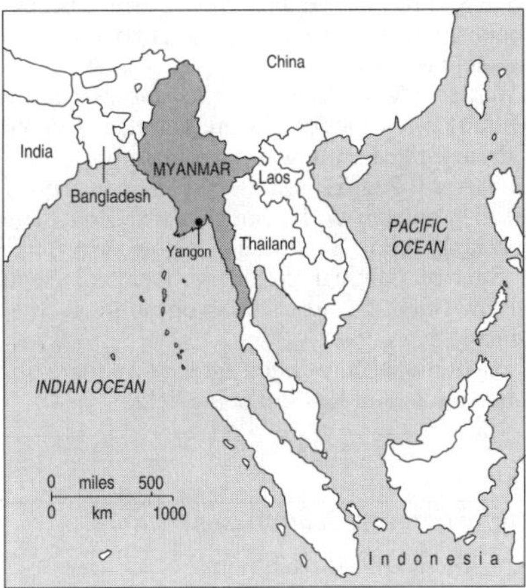

area 676,577 sq km/261,228 sq mi
capital (and chief port) Yangon (formerly Rangoon)
towns Mandalay, Moulmein, Pegu
physical over half is rainforest; rivers Irrawaddy and Chindwin in central lowlands ringed by mountains in N, W, and E
environment landslides and flooding during the rainy season (June–Sept) are becoming more frequent as a result of deforestation
features ruined cities of Pagan and Mingun
head of state and government Than Shwe from 1992
political system military republic
political parties National Unity Party (NUP), military-socialist ruling party; National League for Democracy (NLD), pluralist opposition grouping
exports rice, rubber, jute, teak, jade, rubies, sapphires
currency kyat

population (1992) 43,466,000; growth rate 1.9% p.a. (includes Shan, Karen, Ráljome, Chinese, and Indian minorities)
life expectancy men 53, women 56 (1989)
language Burmese
religions Hinayana Buddhist 85%, animist, Christian
literacy 66% (1989)
GNP $9.3 bn (1988); $210 per head (1989)

chronology
1886 United as province of British India.
1937 Became crown colony in the British Commonwealth.
1942–45 Occupied by Japan.
1948 Independence achieved from Britain. Left the Commonwealth.
1962 General Ne Win assumed power in army coup.
1973–74 Adopted presidential-style 'civilian' constitution.
1975 Opposition National Democratic Front formed.
1986 Several thousand supporters of opposition leader Suu Kyi arrested.
1988 Government resigned after violent demonstrations. General Saw Maung seized power in military coup Sept; over 1,000 killed.
1989 Martial law declared; thousands arrested including advocates of democracy and human rights. Country renamed Myanmar and capital Yangon.
1990 Landslide victory for NLD in general election was ignored by military junta; opposition leader Aung San Suu Kyi placed under house arrest. Breakaway opposition group formed 'parallel government' on rebel-held territory.
1991 Martial law and human-rights abuses continued. Military offensives continued. Suu Kyi awarded Nobel Prize for Peace but was not released.
1992 Jan–April: Pogrom against Muslim community in Arakan province, W Myanmar, carried out with army backing. April: Saw Maung replaced by Than Shwe. Several political prisoners liberated. Sept: martial law lifted, but restrictions on political freedom remained.
1993 Constitutional convention agreed on a more liberal constitution. Suu Kyi still being held.

Namibia

Republic of (formerly ***South West Africa***)

area 824,300 sq km/318,262 sq mi
capital Windhoek
towns Swakopmund, Rehoboth, Rundu
physical mainly desert
features Namib and Kalahari deserts; Orange River; Caprivi Strip links Namibia to Zambezi River; includes the enclave of Walvis Bay (area 1,120 sq km/432 sq mi)
head of state Sam Nujoma from 1990
head of government Hage Geingob from 1990
political system democratic republic
political parties South-West Africa People's Organization (SWAPO), socialist Ovambo-oriented; Democratic Turnhalle Alliance (DTA), moderate, multiracial coalition; United Democratic Front (UDF), disaffected ex-SWAPO members; National Christian Action (ACN), white conservative
exports diamonds, uranium, copper, lead, zinc
currency South African rand
population (1992) 1,512,000 (black African 85%, European 6%)
life expectancy blacks 40, whites 69
languages Afrikaans (spoken by 60% of white population), German, English (all official), several indigenous languages
religions 51% Lutheran, 19% Roman Catholic, 6% Dutch Reformed Church, 6% Anglican
literacy whites 100%, nonwhites 16%
GNP $1.6 bn; $1,300 per head (1988)

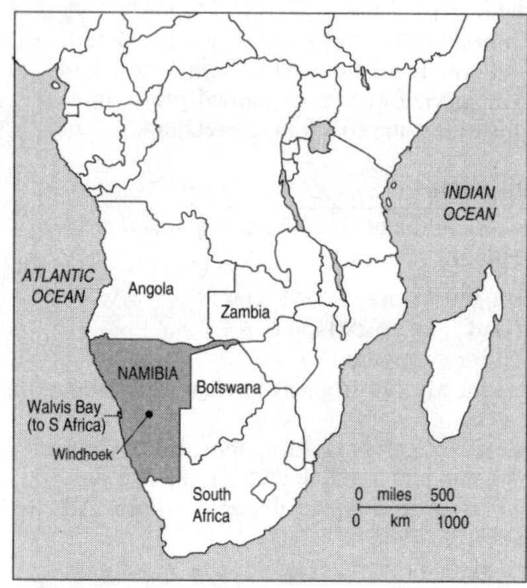

chronology
1884 German and British colonies established.
1915 German colony seized by South Africa.
1920 Administered by South Africa, under League of Nations mandate, as British South Africa.
1946 Full incorporation in South Africa refused by United Nations (UN).
1958 South-West Africa People's Organization (SWAPO) set up to seek racial equality and full independence.
1966 South Africa's apartheid laws extended to the country.
1968 Redesignated Namibia by UN.
1978 UN Security Council Resolution 435 for the granting of full sovereignty accepted by South Africa and then rescinded.
1988 Peace talks between South Africa, Angola, and Cuba led to agreement on full independence for Namibia.
1989 Unexpected incursion by SWAPO guerrillas from Angola into Namibia threatened agreed independence. Transitional constitution created by elected representatives; SWAPO dominant party.
1990 Liberal multiparty 'independence' constitution adopted; independence achieved. Sam Nujoma elected president.
1991 Agreement on joint administration of disputed port of Walvis Bay reached with South Africa, pending final settlement of dispute.
1992 Agreement on establishment of Walvis Bay Joint Administrative Body.

Nauru

Republic of (*Naoero*)

area 21 sq km/8 sq mi
capital (seat of government) Yaren District

physical tropical island country in SW Pacific; plateau encircled by coral cliffs and sandy beaches
features lies just S of equator; one of three phosphate rock islands in the Pacific
head of state and government Bernard Dowiyogo from 1989
political system liberal democracy
political party Democratic Party of Nauru (DPN), opposition to government
exports phosphates
currency Australian dollar
population (1990 est) 8,100 (mainly Polynesian; Chinese 8%, European 8%); growth rate 1.7% p.a.
languages Nauruan (official), English
religions Protestant 66%, Roman Catholic 33%
literacy 99% (1988)
GNP $160 million (1986); $9,091 per head (1985)

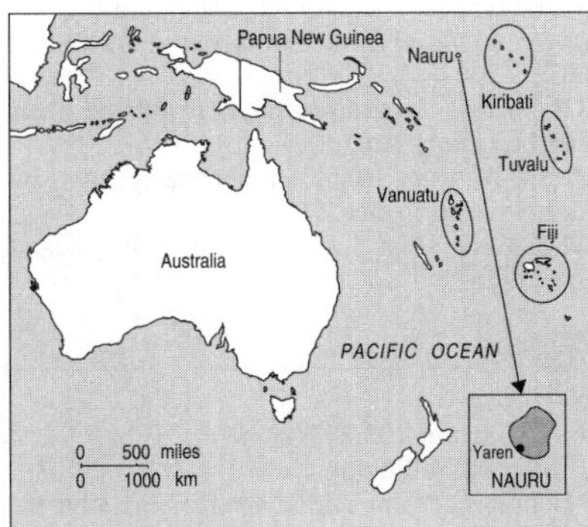

chronology
1888 Annexed by Germany.
1920 Administered by Australia, New Zealand, and UK until independence, except 1942–45, when it was occupied by Japan.
1968 Independence achieved from Australia, New Zealand, and UK with 'special member' Commonwealth status. Hammer DeRoburt elected president.
1976 Bernard Dowiyogo elected president.
1978 DeRoburt re-elected.
1986 DeRoburt briefly replaced as president by Kennan Adeang.
1987 DeRoburt re-elected; Adeang established the Democratic Party of Nauru.
1989 DeRoburt replaced by Kensas Aroi, who was later succeeded by Dowiyogo.
1992 Dowiyogo re-elected.
1993 Nauru issued lawsuit against Australian firm of solicitors for the recovery of $14 million of the island's trust fund. A claim against Australia for compensation for 60 years of environmental destruction was in progress at the International Court of Justice.

Nepal

Kingdom of (*Nepal Adhirajya*)

area 147,181 sq km/56,850 sq mi
capital Katmandu
towns Pátan, Moráng, Bhádgáon
physical descends from the Himalayan mountain range in N through foothills to the river Ganges plain in S
environment described as the world's highest rubbish dump, Nepal attracts 270,000 tourists, trekkers, and mountaineers each year. An estimated 500 kg/1,100 lb of rubbish is left by each expedition trekking or climbing in the Himalayas. Since 1952 the foothills of the Himalayas have been stripped of 40% of their forest cover
features Mount Everest, Mount Kangchenjunga; the only Hindu kingdom in the world; Lumbini, birthplace of the Buddha
head of state King Birendra Bir Bikram Shah Dev from 1972
head of government Girija Prasad Koirala from 1991
political system constitutional monarchy
political parties Nepali Congress Party (NCP), left-of-centre; United Nepal Communist Party (UNCP), Marxist-Leninist-Maoist; United Liberation Torchbearers; Democratic Front, radical republican
exports jute, rice, timber, oilseed
currency Nepalese rupee
population (1992) 19,795,000 (mainly known by name of predominant clan, the Gurkhas; the Sherpas are a Buddhist minority of NE Nepal); growth rate 2.3% p.a.
life expectancy men 50, women 49 (1989)
language Nepali (official); 20 dialects spoken
religions Hindu 90%; Buddhist, Muslim, Christian
literacy men 39%, women 12% (1985 est)
GNP $3.1 bn (1988); $160 per head (1986)

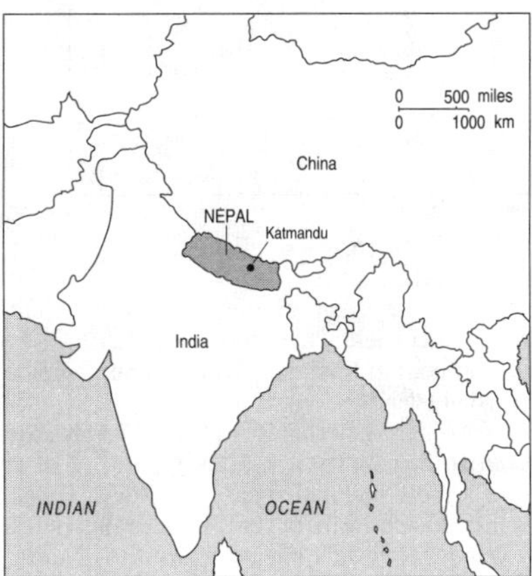

chronology
1768 Nepal emerged as unified kingdom.
1815–16 Anglo-Nepali 'Gurkha War'; Nepal became a British-dependent buffer state.
1846–1951 Ruled by the Rana family.
1923 Independence achieved from Britain.
1951 Monarchy restored.
1959 Constitution created elected legislature.
1960–61 Parliament dissolved by king; political parties banned.
1980 Constitutional referendum held following popular agitation.
1981 Direct elections held to national assembly.
1983 Overthrow of monarch-supported prime minister.
1986 New assembly elections returned a majority opposed to *panchayat* system of partyless government.

1988 Strict curbs placed on opposition activity; over 100 supporters of banned opposition party arrested; censorship imposed.
1989 Border blockade imposed by India in treaty dispute.
1990 *Panchayat* system collapsed after mass prodemocracy demonstrations; new constitution introduced; elections set for May 1991.
1991 Nepali Congress Party, led by Girija Prasad Koirala, won the general election.
1992 Communists led anti-government demonstrations in Katmandu and Pátan.

Netherlands

Kingdom of the (*Koninkrijk der Nederlanden*), popularly referred to as ***Holland***

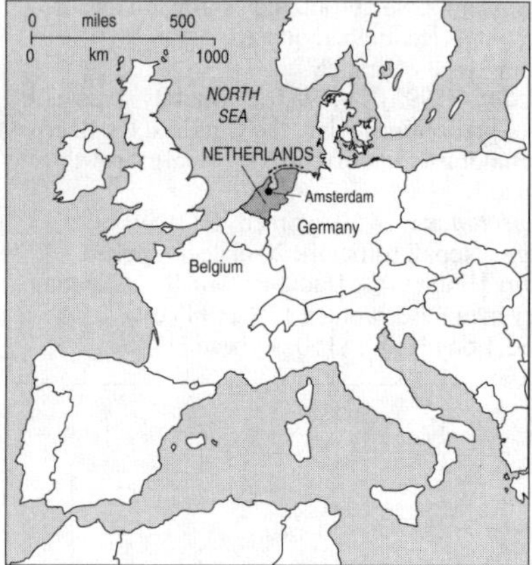

area 41,863 sq km/16,169 sq mi
capital Amsterdam
towns The Hague (seat of government), Utrecht, Eindhoven, Maastricht; chief port Rotterdam
physical flat coastal lowland; rivers Rhine, Scheldt, Maas; Frisian Islands
territories Aruba, Netherlands Antilles (Caribbean)
environment the country lies at the mouths of three of Europe's most polluted rivers, the Maas, Rhine, and Scheldt. Dutch farmers contribute to this pollution by using the world's highest quantities of nitrogen-based fertilizer per hectare/acre per year
features polders (reclaimed land) make up over 40% of the land area; dyke (*Afsluitdijk*) 32 km/20 mi long 1932 has turned the former Zuider Zee inlet into the freshwater IJsselmeer; Delta Project series of dams 1986 forms sea defence in Zeeland delta of the Maas, Scheldt, and Rhine
head of state Queen Beatrix Wilhelmina Armgard from 1980
head of government Ruud Lubbers from 1989
political system constitutional monarchy
political parties Christian Democratic Appeal (CDA), Christian, right of centre; Labour Party (PvdA), moderate, left of centre; People's Party for Freedom and Democracy (VVD), free-enterprise, centrist
exports dairy products, flower bulbs, vegetables, petrochemicals, electronics
currency guilder
population (1992) 15,163,000 (including 300,000 of Dutch-Indonesian origin absorbed 1949–64 from former colonial possessions); growth rate 0.4% p.a.
life expectancy men 74, women 81 (1989)
language Dutch
religions Roman Catholic 40%, Protestant 31%
literacy 99% (1989)
GNP $320.4 bn (1992)

chronology
1940–45 Occupied by Germany during World War II.
1947 Joined Benelux customs union.
1948 Queen Juliana succeeded Queen Wilhelmina to the throne.
1949 Became a founding member of North Atlantic Treaty Organization (NATO).
1953 Dykes breached by storm; nearly 2,000 people and tens of thousands of cattle died in flood.
1958 Joined European Economic Community.
1980 Queen Juliana abdicated in favour of her daughter Beatrix.
1981 Opposition to cruise missiles averted their being sited on Dutch soil.
1989 Prime Minister Ruud Lubbers resigned; new Lubbers-led coalition elected.
1992 Maastricht Treaty on European political and monetary union ratified.

New Zealand

Dominion of
area 268,680 sq km/103,777 sq mi
capital and port Wellington
towns Hamilton, Palmerston North, Christchurch, Dunedin; port Auckland
physical comprises North Island, South Island, Stewart Island, Chatham Islands, and minor islands; mainly mountainous
overseas territories Tokelau (three atolls transferred 1926 from former Gilbert and Ellice Islands colony); Niue Island (one of the Cook Islands, separately administered from 1903: chief town Alafi); Cook Islands are internally self-governing but share common citizenship with New Zealand; Ross Dependency in Antarctica

features Ruapehu on North Island, 2,797 m/9,180 ft, highest of three active volcanoes; geysers and hot springs of the Rotorua district; Lake Taupo (616 sq km/238 sq mi), source of Waikato River; Kaingaroa state forest. On South Island are the Southern Alps and Canterbury Plains

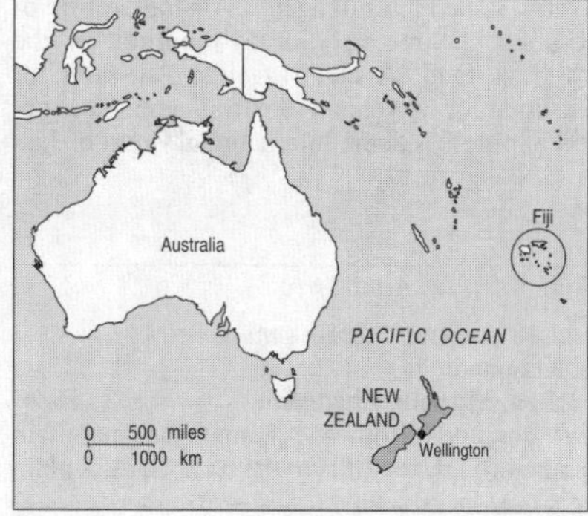

head of state Elizabeth II from 1952 represented by governor general (Catherine Tizard from 1990)
head of government Jim Bolger from 1990
political system constitutional monarchy
political parties Labour Party, moderate, left of centre; New Zealand National Party, free enterprise, centre-right; Alliance Party, left of centre, ecologists
exports lamb, beef, wool, leather, dairy products, processed foods, kiwi fruit, seeds and breeding stock, timber, paper, pulp, light aircraft
currency New Zealand dollar
population (1992) 3,481,000 (European, mostly British, 87%; Polynesian, mostly Maori, 12%); growth rate 0.9% p.a.
life expectancy men 72, women 78 (1989)
languages English (official), Maori
religions Protestant 50%, Roman Catholic 15%
literacy 99% (1989)
GNP $40.3 bn (1992)
chronology
1840 New Zealand became a British colony.
1907 Created a dominion of the British Empire.
1931 Granted independence from Britain.
1947 Independence within the Commonwealth confirmed by the New Zealand parliament.
1972 National Party government replaced by Labour Party, with Norman Kirk as prime minister.
1974 Kirk died; replaced by Wallace Rowling.
1975 National Party returned, with Robert Muldoon as prime minister.
1984 Labour Party returned under David Lange.
1985 Non-nuclear military policy created disagreements with France and the USA.
1987 National Party declared support for the Labour government's non-nuclear policy. Lange re-elected. New Zealand officially classified as a 'friendly' rather than 'allied' country by the USA because of its non-nuclear military policy.
1988 Free-trade agreement with Australia signed.
1989 Lange resigned over economic differences with finance minister (he cited health reasons); replaced by Geoffrey Palmer.
1990 Palmer replaced by Mike Moore. Labour Party defeated by National Party in general election; Jim Bolger became prime minister.
1991 Formation of amalgamated Alliance Party set to challenge two-party system.
1992 Ban on visits by US warships lifted. Referendum aproved change in voting system from 1996.

Nicaragua

Republic of (*República de Nicaragua*)

area 127,849 sq km/49,363 sq mi
capital Managua
towns León, Granada; chief ports Corinto, Puerto Cabezas, El Bluff
physical narrow Pacific coastal plain separated from broad Atlantic coastal plain by volcanic mountains and lakes Managua and Nicaragua
features largest state of Central America and most thinly populated; Mosquito Coast, Fonseca Bay, Corn Islands
head of state and government Violeta Barrios de Chamorro from 1990
political system emergent democracy
political parties Sandinista National Liberation Front (FSLN), Marxist-Leninist; Democratic Conservative Party (PCD), centrist; National Opposition Union (UNO), loose, US-backed coalition
exports coffee, cotton, sugar, bananas, meat
currency cordoba
population (1992) 4,131,000 (mestizo 70%, Spanish descent 15%, Indian or black 10%); growth rate 3.3% p.a.
life expectancy men 61, women 63 (1989)
languages Spanish (official), Indian, English
religion Roman Catholic 95%
literacy 66% (1986)
GNP $2.1 bn; $610 per head (1988)

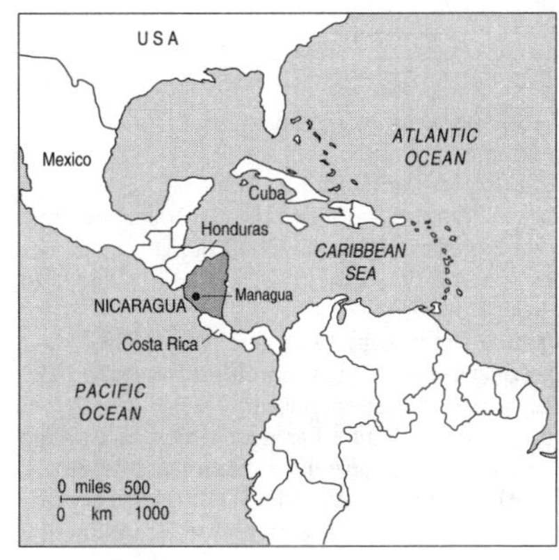

chronology
1838 Independence achieved from Spain.
1926–1933 Occupied by US marines.
1936 General Anastasio Somoza elected president; start of near-dictatorial rule by Somoza family.
1962 Sandinista National Liberation Front (FSLN) formed to fight Somoza regime.
1979 Somoza government ousted by FSLN.
1982 Subversive activity against the government by right-wing Contra guerrillas promoted by the USA. State of emergency declared.
1984 The USA mined Nicaraguan harbours.
1985 Denunciation of Sandinista government by US president Reagan. FSLN won assembly elections.
1987 Central American peace agreement cosigned by Nicaraguan leaders.
1988 Peace agreement failed. Nicaragua held talks with Contra rebel leaders. Hurricane left 180,000 people homeless.
1989 Demobilization of rebels and release of former Somozan supporters; cease-fire ended.
1990 FSLN defeated by UNO, a US-backed coalition; Violeta Barrios de Chamorro elected president. Antigovernment riots.
1991 First presidential state visit to USA for over fifty years.
1992 June: US aid suspended because of concern over role of Sandinista in Nicaraguan government. Sept: around 16,000 made homeless by earthquake.

Niger

Republic of (*République du Niger*)

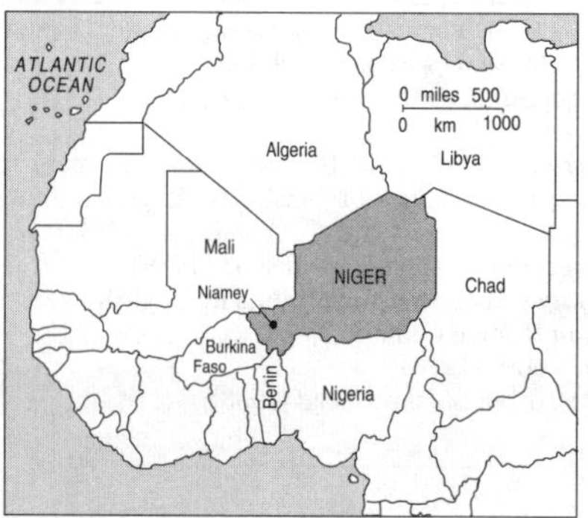

area 1,186,408 sq km/457,953 sq mi
capital Niamey
towns Zinder, Maradi, Tahoua
physical desert plains between hills in N and savanna in S; river Niger in SW, Lake Chad in SE
features part of the Sahara Desert and subject to Sahel droughts
head of state Mahamane Ousmane from 1993
head of government Mahamdou Issaufou from 1993
political system military republic
political parties Alliance for the Forces of Change (AFC), moderate left of centre; National Movement for a Development Society (MNSD), right of centre
exports peanuts, livestock, gum arabic, uranium
currency franc CFA
population (1992) 8,281,000; growth rate 2.8% p.a.
life expectancy men 48, women 50 (1989)
languages French (official), Hausa, Djerma, and other minority languages
religions Sunni Muslim 85%, animist 15%
literacy men 19%, women 9% (1985 est)
GNP $2.2 bn; $310 per head (1987)
chronology
1960 Achieved full independence from France; Hamani Diori elected president.
1974 Diori ousted in army coup led by Seyni Kountché.
1977 Cooperation agreement signed with France.
1987 Kountché died; replaced by Col Ali Saibu.
1989 Ali Saibu elected president without opposition.
1990 Multiparty politics promised.
1991 Saibu stripped of executive powers; transitional government formed.
1992 Transitional government collapsed. Referendum endorsed the adoption of multiparty politics.
1993 Mamahame Ousmane elected president in multiparty elections; Mahamdou Issaufou appointed prime minister.

Nigeria

Federal Republic of

area 923,773 sq km/356,576 sq mi
capital Abuja
towns Ibadan, Ogbomosho, Kano; ports Lagos, Port Harcourt, Warri, Calabar
physical arid savanna in N; tropical rainforest in S, with mangrove swamps along the coast; river Niger forms wide delta; mountains in SE
environment toxic waste from northern industrialized countries has been dumped in Nigeria
features harmattan (dry wind from the Sahara); rich artistic heritage, for example, Benin bronzes
head of state and government Ibrahim Babangida from 1985
political system military republic pending promised elections
political parties Social Democratic Party (SDP), left of centre; National Republican Convention (NRC), right of centre
exports petroleum (largest oil resources in Africa), cocoa, peanuts, palm oil (Africa's largest producer), cotton, rubber, tin
currency naira
population (1992) 89,666,000 (Yoruba in W, Ibo in E, and Hausa-Fulani in N); growth rate 3.3% p.a.
life expectancy men 47, women 49 (1989)
languages English (official), Hausa, Ibo, Yoruba
media all radio and television stations and almost 50% of all publishing owned by the federal government or the Nigerian states
religions Sunni Muslim 50% (in N), Christian 40% (in S), local religions 10%
literacy men 54%, women 31% (1985 est)
GNP $78 bn (1987); $790 per head (1984)

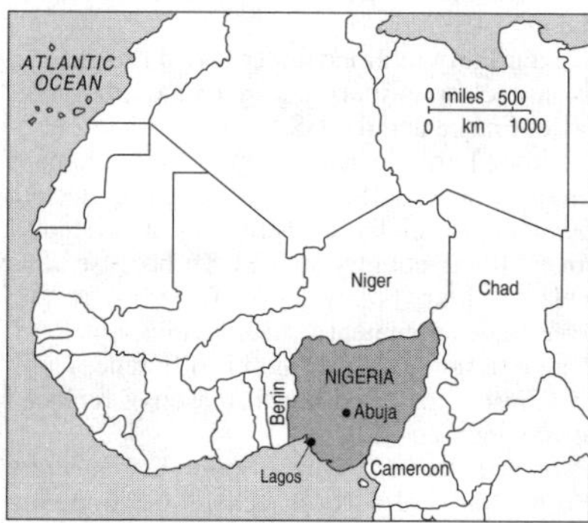

chronology
1914 N Nigeria and S Nigeria united to become Britain's largest African colony.
1954 Nigeria became a federation.
1960 Independence achieved from Britain within the Commonwealth.
1963 Became a republic, with Nnamdi Azikiwe as president.
1966 Military coup, followed by a counter-coup led by General Yakubu Gowon. Slaughter of many members of the Ibo tribe in north.
1967 Conflict over oil revenues led to declaration of an independent Ibo state of Biafra and outbreak of civil war.
1970 Surrender of Biafra and end of civil war.
1975 Gowon ousted in military coup; second coup put General Olusegun Obasanjo in power.
1979 Shehu Shagari became civilian president.
1983 Shagari's government overthrown in coup by Maj-Gen Muhammadu Buhari.

1985 Buhari replaced in a bloodless coup led by Maj-Gen Ibrahim Babangida.
1989 Two new political parties approved. Babangida promised a return to pluralist politics; date set for 1992.
1991 Nine new states created. Babangida confirmed his commitment to democratic rule for 1992.
1992 Multiparty elections won by Babangida's SDP.
1993 Results of presidential elections suspended by national commission, following complaints of ballot rigging. SDP agreed to work with NRC to form an interim government but Babangida postponed talks.

Norway

Kingdom of (*Kongeriket Norge*)

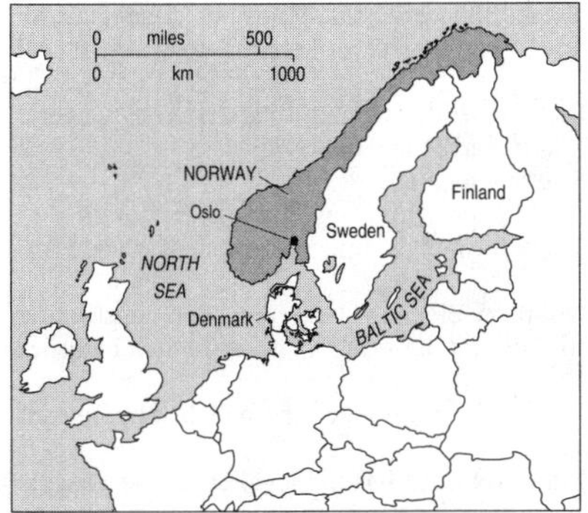

area 387,000 sq km/149,421 sq mi (includes Svalbard and Jan Mayen)
capital Oslo
towns Bergen, Trondheim, Stavanger
physical mountainous with fertile valleys and deeply indented coast; forests cover 25%; extends N of Arctic Circle
territories dependencies in the Arctic (Svalbard and Jan Mayen) and in Antarctica (Bouvet and Peter I Island, and Queen Maud Land)
environment an estimated 80% of the lakes and streams in the southern half of the country have been severely acidified by acid rain
features fjords, including Hardanger and Sogne, longest 185 km/115 mi, deepest 1,245 m/4,086 ft; glaciers in north; midnight sun and northern lights
head of state Harald V from 1991
head of government Gro Harlem Brundtland from 1990
political system constitutional monarchy
political parties Norwegian Labour Party (DNA), moderate left of centre; Conservative Party, progressive, right of centre; Christian People's Party (KrF), Christian, centre-left; Centre Party (SP), left of centre, rural-oriented
exports petrochemicals from North Sea oil and gas, paper, wood pulp, furniture, iron ore and other minerals, high-tech goods, sports goods, fish
currency krone
population (1992) 4,283,000; growth rate 0.3% p.a.
life expectancy men 73, women 80 (1989)
languages Norwegian (official); there are Saami-(Lapp) and Finnish-speaking minorities
religion Evangelical Lutheran (endowed by state) 94%
literacy 100% (1989)
GNP $113.1 bn (1992)
chronology
1814 Became independent from Denmark; ceded to Sweden.
1905 Links with Sweden ended; full independence achieved.
1940–45 Occupied by Germany.
1949 Joined North Atlantic Treaty Organization (NATO).
1952 Joined Nordic Council.
1957 King Haakon VII succeeded by his son Olaf V.
1960 Joined European Free Trade Association (EFTA).
1972 Accepted into membership of European Economic Community; application withdrawn after a referendum.
1988 Gro Harlem Brundtland awarded Third World Prize.
1989 Jan P Syse became prime minister.
1990 Brundtland returned to power.
1991 King Olaf V died; succeeded by his son Harald V.
1992 Defied whaling ban to resume whaling industry. Brundtland relinquished leadership of the Labour Party. Formal application made for EC membership.

Oman

Sultanate of (*Saltanat `Uman*)

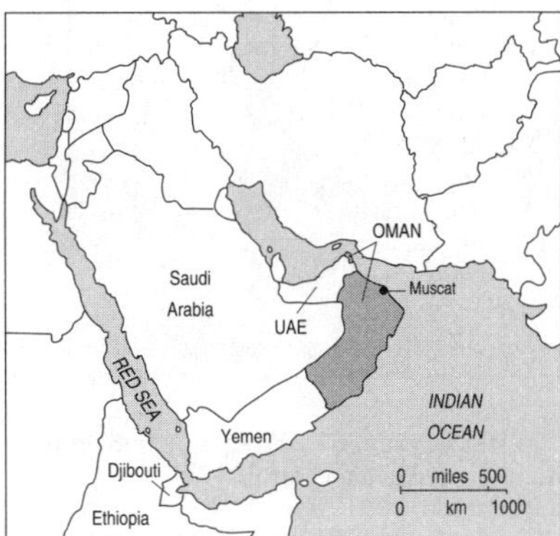

area 272,000 sq km/105,000 sq mi
capital Muscat
towns Salalah, Nizwa
physical mountains to N and S of a high arid plateau; fertile coastal strip
features Jebel Akhdar highlands; Kuria Muria islands; Masirah Island is used in aerial reconnaissance of the Arabian Sea and Indian Ocean; exclave on Musandam Peninsula controlling Strait of Hormuz
head of state and government Qaboos bin Said from 1970
political system absolute monarchy
political parties none
exports oil, dates, silverware, copper
currency rial Omani
population (1992) 1,640,000; growth rate 3.0% p.a.
life expectancy men 55, women 58 (1989)

languages Arabic (official), English, Urdu, other Indian languages
religions Ibadhi Muslim 75%, Sunni Muslim, Shi'ite Muslim, Hindu
literacy 20% (1989)
GNP $7.5 bn (1987); $5,070 per head (1988)

chronology
1951 The Sultanate of Muscat and Oman achieved full independence from Britain. Treaty of Friendship with Britain signed.
1970 After 38 years' rule, Sultan Said bin Taimur replaced in coup by his son Qaboos bin Said. Name changed to Sultanate of Oman.
1975 Left-wing rebels in south defeated.
1982 Memorandum of Understanding with UK signed, providing for regular consultation on international issues.
1985 Diplomatic ties established with USSR.
1991 Sent troops to Operation Desert Storm, as part of coalition opposing Iraq's occupation of Kuwait.

Pakistan

Islamic Republic of

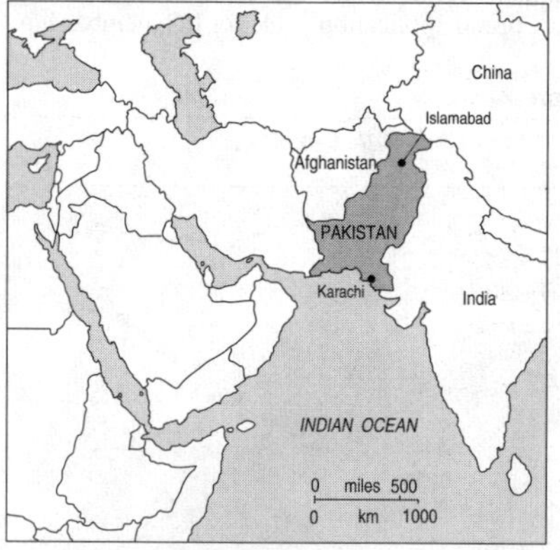

area 796,100 sq km/307,295 sq mi; one-third of Kashmir under Pakistani control
capital Islamabad
towns Karachi, Lahore, Rawalpindi, Peshawar
physical fertile Indus plain in E, Baluchistan plateau in W, mountains in N and NW
environment about 68% of irrigated land is waterlogged or suffering from salinization
features the 'five rivers' (Indus, Jhelum, Chenab, Ravi, and Sutlej) feed the world's largest irrigation system; Tarbela (world's largest earthfill dam); K2 mountain; Khyber Pass; sites of the Indus Valley civilization
head of state Wasim Sajjad
head of government Benazir Bhutto from 1993
political system emergent democracy
political parties Pakistan People's Party (PPP), moderate, Islamic, socialist; Islamic Democratic Alliance (IDA), including the Pakistan Muslim League (PML), Islamic conservative; Mohajir National Movement (MQM), Sind-based *mohajir* (Muslims previously living in India) settlers
exports cotton textiles, rice, leather, carpets
currency Pakistan rupee
population (1992) 130,129,000 (Punjabi 66%, Sindhi 13%); growth rate 3.1% p.a.
life expectancy men 54, women 55 (1989)
languages Urdu and English (official); Punjabi, Sindhi, Pashto, Baluchi, other local dialects
religions Sunni Muslim 75%, Shi'ite Muslim 20%, Hindu 4%
literacy men 40%, women 19% (1985 est)
GDP $39 bn (1988); $360 per head (1984)

chronology
1947 Independence achieved from Britain, Pakistan formed following partition of British India.
1956 Proclaimed a republic.
1958 Military rule imposed by General Ayub Khan.
1969 Power transferred to General Yahya Khan.
1971 Secession of East Pakistan (Bangladesh). After civil war, power transferred to Zulfiqar Ali Bhutto.
1977 Bhutto overthrown in military coup by General Zia ul-Haq; martial law imposed.
1979 Bhutto executed.
1981 Opposition Movement for the Restoration of Democracy formed. Islamization process pushed forward.
1985 Nonparty elections held, amended constitution adopted, martial law and ban on political parties lifted.
1986 Agitation for free elections launched by Benazir Bhutto.
1988 Zia introduced Islamic legal code, the Shari'a. He was killed in a military plane crash in Aug. Benazir Bhutto elected prime minister Nov.
1989 Pakistan rejoined the Commonwealth.
1990 Army mobilized in support of Muslim separatists in Indian Kashmir. Bhutto dismissed on charges of incompetence and corruption. Islamic Democratic Alliance (IDA), led by Nawaz Sharif, won Oct general election.
1991 Shari'a bill enacted; privatization and economic deregulation programme launched.
1992 Sept: Floods devastated north of country. Oct: Pakistan elected to UN Security Council 1993–95.
1993 Oct: Benazir Bhutto elected prime minister.

Panama

Republic of (*República de Panamá*)

area 77,100 sq km/29,768 sq mi
capital Panamá (Panama City)
towns Cristóbal, Balboa, Colón, David
physical coastal plains and mountainous interior; tropical rainforest in E and NW; Pearl Islands in Gulf of Panama
features Panama Canal; Barro Colorado Island in Gatún Lake (reservoir supplying the canal), a tropical forest reserve since 1923; Smithsonian Tropical Research Institute
head of state and government Guillermo Endara from 1989
political system emergent democratic republic
political parties Democratic Revolutionary Party (PRD), right-wing; Labour Party (PALA), right of centre; Panamanian Republican Party (PPR), right-wing; Nationalist Liberal Republican Movement

(MOLIRENA), left of centre; Authentic Panamanian Party (PPA), centrist; Christian Democratic Party (PDC), centre-left
exports bananas, petroleum products, copper, shrimps, sugar
currency balboa
population (1992) 2,515,000 (mestizo, or mixed race, 70%; West Indian 14%; European descent 10%; Indian (Cuna, Choco, Guayami) 6%); growth rate 2.2% p.a.
life expectancy men 71, women 75 (1989)
languages Spanish (official), English
religions Roman Catholic 93%, Protestant 6%
literacy 87% (1989)
GNP $4.2 bn (1988); $1,970 per head (1984)

chronology
1821 Achieved independence from Spain; joined confederacy of Gran Colombia.
1903 Full independence achieved on separation from Colombia.
1974 Agreement to negotiate full transfer of the Panama Canal from the USA to Panama.
1977 USA–Panama treaties transferred the canal to Panama, effective from 1990, with the USA guaranteeing its protection and an annual payment.
1984 Nicolás Ardito Barletta elected president.
1985 Barletta resigned; replaced by Eric Arturo del Valle.
1987 General Noriega (head of the National Guard and effective ruler) resisted calls for his removal, despite suspension of US military and economic aid.
1988 Del Valle replaced by Manuel Solis Palma. Noriega, charged with drug smuggling by the USA, declared a state of emergency.
1989 Opposition won election; Noriega declared results invalid; Francisco Rodríguez sworn in as president. Coup attempt against Noriega failed; Noriega declared head of government by assembly. 'State of war' with the USA announced. US invasion deposed Noriega; Guillermo Endara installed as president. Noriega sought asylum in Vatican embassy; later surrendered and taken to US for trial.
1991 Attempted antigovernment coup foiled. Army abolished.
1992 Noriega found guilty of drug offences. Referendum voted down overwhelmingly government's constitutional changes, including abolition of a standing army.

Papua New Guinea

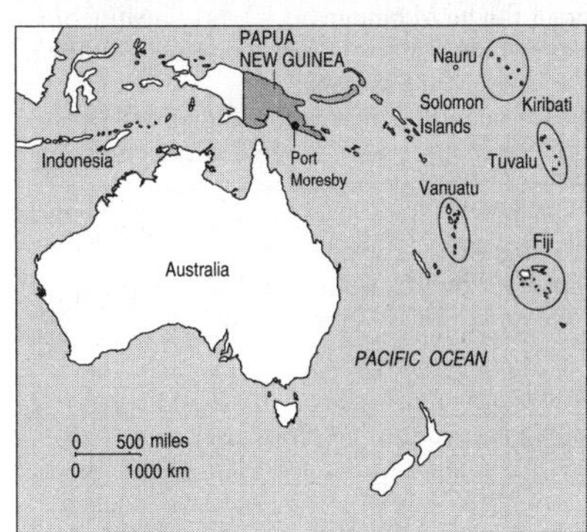

area 462,840 sq km/178,656 sq mi
capital Port Moresby (on E New Guinea)
towns Lae, Rabaul, Madang
physical mountainous; includes tropical islands of New Ireland, New Britain, and Bougainville; Admiralty Islands, D'Entrecasteaux Islands, and Louisiade Archipelago
features one of world's largest swamps on SW coast; world's largest butterfly, orchids; Sepik River
head of state Elizabeth II, represented by governor general
head of government Paias Wingti from 1992
political system liberal democracy
political parties Papua New Guinea Party (Pangu Pati: PP), urban- and coastal-oriented nationalist; People's Democratic Movement (PDM), 1985 breakaway from the PP; National Party (NP), highlands-based; Melanesian Alliance (MA), Bougainville-based autonomy; People's Progress Party (PPP), conservative
exports copra, coconut oil, palm oil, tea, copper, gold, coffee
currency kina
population (1992) 3,834,000 (Papuans, Melanesians, Negritos, various minorities); growth rate 2.6% p.a.
life expectancy men 53, women 54 (1987)
languages English (official); pidgin English, 715 local languages
religions Protestant 63%, Roman Catholic 31%, local faiths
literacy men 55%, women 36% (1985 est)
GNP $2.5 bn; $730 per head (1987)

chronology
1883 Annexed by Queensland; became the Australian Territory of Papua.
1884 NE New Guinea annexed by Germany; SE claimed by Britain.
1914 NE New Guinea occupied by Australia.
1921–42 Held as a League of Nations mandate.
1942–45 Occupied by Japan.
1975 Independence achieved from Australia, within the Commonwealth, with Michael Somare as prime minister.
1980 Julius Chan became prime minister.
1982 Somare returned to power.
1985 Somare challenged by Paias Wingti, the deputy prime minister, who later formed a five-party coalition government.

1988 Wingti defeated on no-confidence vote and replaced by Rabbie Namaliu, who established a six-party coalition government.
1989 State of emergency imposed on Bougainville in response to separatist violence.
1991 Peace accord signed with Bougainville secessionists. Economic boom as gold production doubled. Wiwa Korowi elected as new governor general. Deputy Prime Minister Ted Diro resigned, having been found guilty of corruption.
1992 April: killings by outlawed Bougainville secessionists reported. July: Wingti elected premier.

Paraguay

Republic of (*República del Paraguay*)

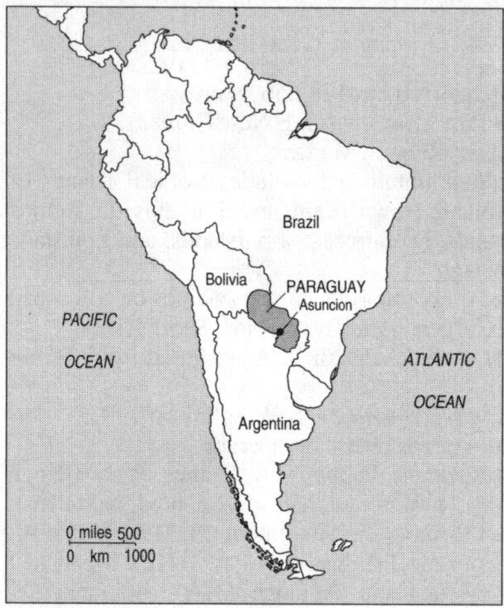

area 406,752 sq km/157,006 sq mi
capital Asunción
towns Puerto Presidente Stroessner, Pedro Juan Caballero; port Concepción
physical low marshy plain and marshlands; divided by Paraguay River; Paraná River forms SE boundary
features Itaipú dam on border with Brazil; Gran Chaco plain with huge swamps
head of state and government General Andrés Rodríguez from 1989
political system emergent democratic republic
political parties National Republican Association (Colorado Party), right of centre; Liberal Party (PL), right of centre; Radical Liberal Party (PLR), centrist
exports cotton, soya beans, timber, vegetable oil, maté
currency guaraní
population (1992) 4,519,000 (95% mixed Guarani Indian–Spanish descent); growth rate 3.0% p.a.
life expectancy men 67, women 72 (1989)
languages Spanish 6% (official), Guarani 90%
religion Roman Catholic 97%
literacy men 91%, women 85% (1985 est)
GNP $7.4 bn; $1,000 per head (1987)
chronology
1811 Independence achieved from Spain.
1865–70 War with Argentina, Brazil, and Uruguay; less than half the population survived and much territory lost.
1932–35 Territory won from Bolivia during the Chaco War.
1940–48 Presidency of General Higinio Morínigo.
1948–54 Political instability; six different presidents.
1954 General Alfredo Stroessner seized power.
1989 Stroessner ousted in coup led by General Andrés Rodríguez. Rodríguez elected president; Colorado Party won the congressional elections.
1991 Colorado Party successful in assembly elections.
1993 Colorado Party candidate Juan Carlos Wasmosy won presidential elections, to take office on 15 Aug.

Peru

Republic of (*República del Perú*)

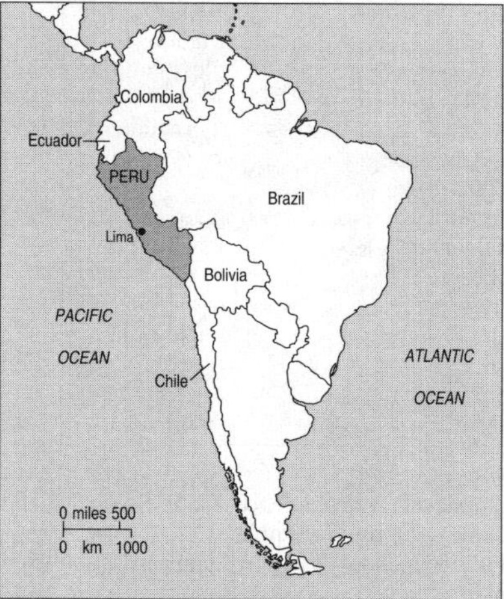

area 1,285,200 sq km/496,216 sq mi
capital Lima, including port of Callao
towns Arequipa, Iquitos, Chiclayo, Trujillo
physical Andes mountains NW–SE cover 27% of Peru, separating Amazon river-basin jungle in NE from coastal plain in W; desert along coast N–S
environment an estimated 38% of the 8,000 sq km/3,100 sq mi of coastal lands under irrigation are either waterlogged or suffering from saline water. Only half the population has access to clean drinking water
features Lake Titicaca; Atacama Desert; Nazca lines, monuments of Machu Picchu, Chan Chan, Charín de Huantar
head of state and government Alberto Fujimori from 1990
political system democratic republic
political parties American Popular Revolutionary Alliance (APRA), moderate, left-wing; United Left (IU), left-wing; Change 90, centrist
exports coca, coffee, alpaca, llama and vicuña wool, fish meal, lead (largest producer in South America), copper, iron, oil
currency new sol
population (1992) 22,454,000 (Indian, mainly Quechua and Aymara, 46%; mixed Spanish–Indian descent 43%); growth rate 2.6% p.a.
life expectancy men 61, women 66

languages Spanish 68%, Quechua 27% (both official), Aymara 3%
religion Roman Catholic 90%
literacy men 91%, women 78% (1985 est)
GNP $19.6 bn (1988); $940 per head (1984)

chronology
1824 Independence achieved from Spain.
1849–74 Some 80,000–100,000 Chinese labourers arrived in Peru to fill menial jobs such as collecting guano.
1902 Boundary dispute with Bolivia settled.
1927 Boundary dispute with Colombia settled.
1942 Boundary dispute with Ecuador settled.
1948 Army coup, led by General Manuel Odría, installed a military government.
1963 Return to civilian rule, with Fernando Belaúnde Terry as president.
1968 Return of military government in a bloodless coup by General Juan Velasco Alvarado.
1975 Velasco replaced, in a bloodless coup, by General Morales Bermúdez.
1980 Return to civilian rule, with Fernando Belaúnde as president. Sendero Luminoso ('Shining Path') Maoist guerrilla group formed.
1981 Boundary dispute with Ecuador renewed.
1985 Belaúnde succeeded by Social Democrat Alan García Pérez.
1987 President García delayed the nationalization of Peru's banks after a vigorous campaign against the proposal.
1988 García pressured to seek help from the International Monetary Fund (IMF). Sendero Luminoso increased campaign of violence.
1989 Writer Mario Vargas Llosa entered presidential race; his Democratic Front won municipal elections Nov.
1990 Alberto Fujimori defeated Vargas Llosa in presidential elections. Assassination attempt on president failed.
1992 Two coup attempts against the government failed. USA suspended humanitarian aid. Sendero Luminoso leader Abimael Guzman Reynoso was arrested and sentenced to life imprisonment after a show trial. Single-chamber legislature replaced two-chamber system.
1993 National congress voted to allow Fujimori to seek re-election in 1995.

Philippines

Republic of the (*Republika ng Pilipinas*)

area 300,000 sq km/115,800 sq mi
capital Manila (on Luzon)
towns Quezon City (Luzon), Zamboanga (Mindanao); ports Cebu, Davao (on Mindanao), and Iloilo
physical comprises over 7,000 islands; volcanic mountain ranges traverse main chain N–S; 50% still forested. The largest islands are Luzon 108,172 sq km/41,754 sq mi and Mindanao 94,227 sq km/36,372 sq mi; others include Samar, Negros, Palawan, Panay, Mindoro, Leyte, Cebu, and the Sulu group
environment cleared for timber, tannin, and the creation of fish ponds, the mangrove forest was reduced from 5,000 sq km/1,930 sq mi to 380 sq km/146 sq mi between 1920 and 1988
features Luzon, site of Clark Field, US air base used as a logistical base in Vietnam War; Subic Bay, US naval base; Pinatubo volcano (1,759 m/5,770 ft); Mindanao has active volcano Apo (2,954 m/9,690 ft) and mountainous rainforest
head of state and government Fidel Ramos from 1992
political system emergent democracy
political parties People's Power, including the PDP–Laban Party and the Liberal Party, centrist pro-Aquino; Nationalist Party, Union for National Action (UNA), and Grand Alliance for Democracy (GAD), conservative opposition groupings; Mindanao Alliance, island-based decentralist body
exports sugar, copra (world's largest producer) and coconut oil, timber, copper concentrates, electronics, clothing
currency peso
population (1992) 63,609,000 (93% Malaysian); growth rate 2.4% p.a.
life expectancy men 63, women 69 (1989)
languages Tagalog (Filipino, official); English and Spanish
religions Roman Catholic 84%, Protestant 9%, Muslim 5%
literacy 88% (1989)
GNP $38.2 bn; $667 per head (1988)

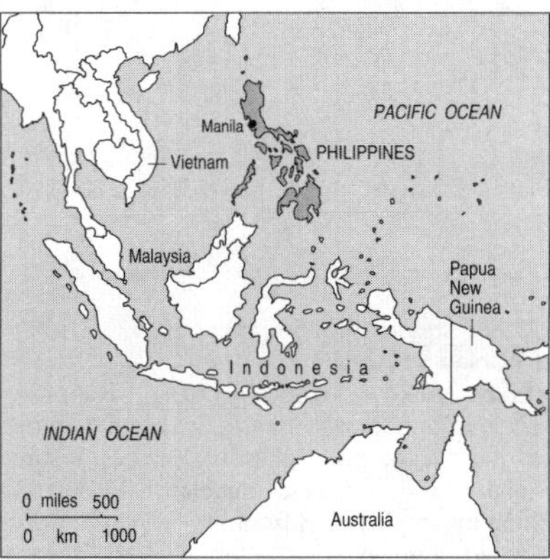

chronology
1542 Named the Philippines (Filipinas) by Spanish explorers.
1565 Conquered by Spain.
1898 Ceded to the USA after Spanish–American War.
1935 Granted internal self-government.
1942–45 Occupied by Japan.
1946 Independence achieved from USA.
1965 Ferdinand Marcos elected president.
1983 Opposition leader Benigno Aquino murdered by military guard.
1986 Marcos overthrown by Corazon Aquino's People's Power movement.
1987 'Freedom constitution' adopted, giving Aquino mandate to rule until June 1992; People's Power won majority in congressional elections. Attempted right-wing coup suppressed. Communist guerrillas active. Government in rightward swing.
1988 Land Reform Act gave favourable compensation to holders of large estates.
1989 Referendum on southern autonomy failed; Marcos died in exile; Aquino refused his burial in

Philippines. Sixth coup attempt suppressed with US aid; Aquino declared state of emergency.
1990 Seventh coup attempt survived by President Aquino.
1991 June: eruption of Mount Pinatubo, hundreds killed. USA agreed to give up Clark Field airbase but keep Subic Bay naval base for ten more years. Sept: Philippines Senate voted to urge withdrawal of all US forces. US renewal of Subic Bay lease rejected. Nov: Imelda Marcos returned.
1992 Fidel Ramos elected to replace Aquino.

Poland

Republic of (*Polska Rzeczpospolita*)

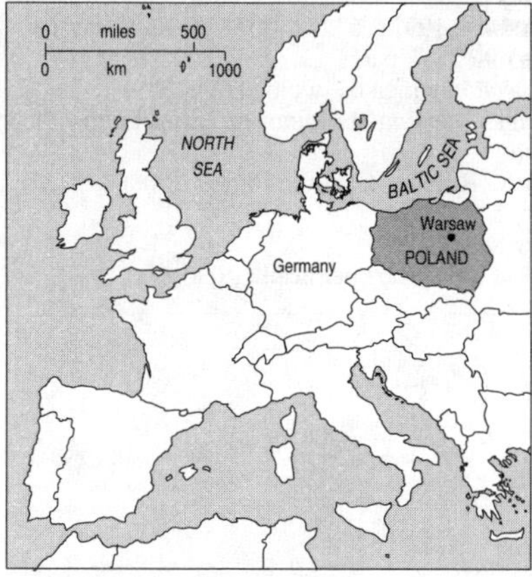

area 127,886 sq km/49,325 sq mi
capital Warsaw
towns Lódź, Kraków, Wrocław, Poznań, Katowice, Bydgoszcz, Lublin; ports Gdańsk, Szczecin, Gdynia
physical part of the great plain of Europe; Vistula, Oder, and Neisse rivers; Sudeten, Tatra, and Carpathian mountains on S frontier
environment atmospheric pollution derived from coal (producing 90% of the country's electricity), toxic waste from industry, and lack of sewage treatment have resulted in the designation of 27 ecologically endangered areas. Half the country's lakes have been seriously contaminated and three-quarters of its drinking water does not meet official health standards
features last wild European bison (only in protected herds)
head of state Lech Wałesa from 1990
head of government Hanna Suchocka from 1992
political system emergent democratic republic
political parties Democratic Union, centrist, ex-Solidarity; Democratic Left Alliance, ex-communist; Centre Alliance, right of centre, Wałesa-linked; Social Democratic Party of the Polish Republic, 1990 successor to Polish United Workers' Party (PUWP), social democratic; Union of Social Democrats, radical breakaway from PUWP formed 1990; Solidarność (Solidarity) Parliamentary Club (OKP), anticommunist coalition
exports coal, softwood timber, chemicals, machinery, ships, vehicles, meat, copper (Europe's largest producer)
currency zloty
population (1992) 38,429,000; growth rate 0.6% p.a.
life expectancy men 66, women 74 (1989)
languages Polish (official), German
media broadcasters required by law to 'respect Christian values'
religion Roman Catholic 95%
literacy 98% (1989)
GNP $276 billion (1988); $2,000 per head (1986)

chronology
1918 Poland revived as independent republic.
1939 German invasion and occupation.
1944 Germans driven out by Soviet forces.
1945 Polish boundaries redrawn at Potsdam Conference.
1947 Communist people's republic proclaimed.
1956 Poznań riots. Wladyslaw Gomułka installed as Polish United Workers' Party (PUWP) leader.
1970 Gomułka replaced by Edward Gierek after Gdańsk riots.
1980 Solidarity emerged as a free trade union following Gdańsk disturbances.
1981 Martial law imposed by General Wojciech Jaruzelski.
1983 Martial law ended.
1984 Amnesty for political prisoners.
1985 Zbigniew Messner became prime minister.
1987 Referendum on economic reform rejected.
1988 Solidarity-led strikes and demonstrations called off after pay increases. Messner resigned; replaced by the reformist Mieczysław F Rakowski.
1989 Solidarity relegalized. April: new 'socialist pluralist' constitution formed. June: widespread success for Solidarity in assembly elections, the first open elections in 40 years. July: Jaruzelski elected president. Sept: 'Grand coalition', first non-Communist government since World War II formed; economic restructuring undertaken on free-market lines; W Europe and US create $1 billion aid package.
1990 Jan: PUWP dissolved; replaced by Social Democratic Party and breakaway Union of Social Democrats. Lech Wałesa elected president; Dec: prime minister Mazowiecki resigned.
1991 Oct: Multiparty general election produced inconclusive result. Five-party centre-right coalition formed under Jan Olszewski. Treaty signed agreeing to complete withdrawal of Soviet troops.
1992 June: Olszewski ousted on vote of no confidence; succeeded by Waldemar Pawlak. July: Hanna Suchocka replaced Pawlak.
1993 14% of workforce (2.6 million) unemployed. Suchocka lost vote of confidence; general election promised for Sept 1993.

Portugal

Republic of (*República Portuguesa*)

area 92,000 sq km/35,521 sq mi (including the Azores and Madeira)
capital Lisbon
towns Coimbra; ports Pôrto, Setúbal
physical mountainous in N, plains in S
features rivers Minho, Douro, Tagus (Tejo), Guadiana; Serra da Estrêla mountains
head of state Mario Alberto Nobre Lopes Soares from 1986

head of government Aníbal Cavaco Silva from 1985
political system democratic republic
political parties Social Democratic Party (PSD), moderate left of centre; Socialist Party (PS), progressive socialist; Democratic Renewal Party (PRD), centre-left; Democratic Social Centre Party (CDS), moderate left of centre
exports wine, olive oil, resin, cork, sardines, textiles, clothing, pottery, pulpwood
currency escudo
population (1992) 9,844,000; growth rate 0.5% p.a.
life expectancy men 71, women 78 (1989)
language Portuguese
religion Roman Catholic 97%
literacy men 89%, women 80% (1985)
GNP $83.9 bn (1992)

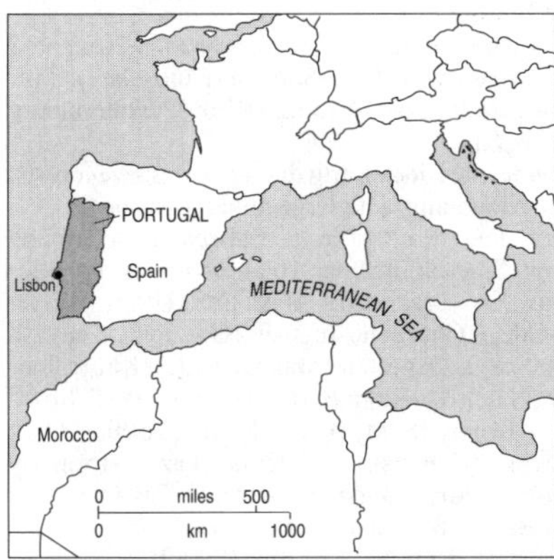

chronology
1928–68 Military dictatorship under António de Oliveira Salazar.
1968 Salazar succeeded by Marcello Caetano.
1974 Caetano removed in military coup led by General António Ribeiro de Spínola. Spínola replaced by General Francisco da Costa Gomes.
1975 African colonies became independent.
1976 New constitution, providing for return to civilian rule, adopted. Minority government appointed, led by Socialist Party leader Mario Soares.
1978 Soares resigned.
1980 Francisco Balsemão formed centre-party coalition after two years of political instability.
1982 Draft of new constitution approved, reducing powers of presidency.
1983 Centre-left coalition government formed.
1985 Aníbal Cavaco Silva became prime minister.
1986 Mario Soares elected first civilian president in 60 years. Portugal joined European Community.
1988 Portugal joined Western European Union.
1989 Constitution amended to allow major state enterprises to be denationalized.
1991 Mario Soares re-elected president; Social Democrat (PSD) majority slightly reduced in assembly elections.

Qatar

State of (*Dawlat Qatar*)

area 11,400 sq km/4,402 sq mi
capital and chief port Doha
town Dukhan, centre of oil production
physical mostly flat desert with salt flats in S
features negligible rain and surface water; only 3% is fertile, but irrigation allows self-sufficiency in fruit and vegetables; extensive oil discoveries since World War II
head of state and government Sheik Khalifa bin Hamad al-Thani from 1972
political system absolute monarchy
political parties none
exports oil, natural gas, petrochemicals, fertilizers, iron, steel
currency riyal
population (1992) 520,000 (half in Doha; Arab 40%, Indian 18%, Pakistani 18%); growth rate 3.7% p.a.
life expectancy men 68, women 72 (1989)
languages Arabic (official), English
religion Sunni Muslim 95%
literacy 60% (1987)
GNP $5.9 bn (1983); $35,000 per head

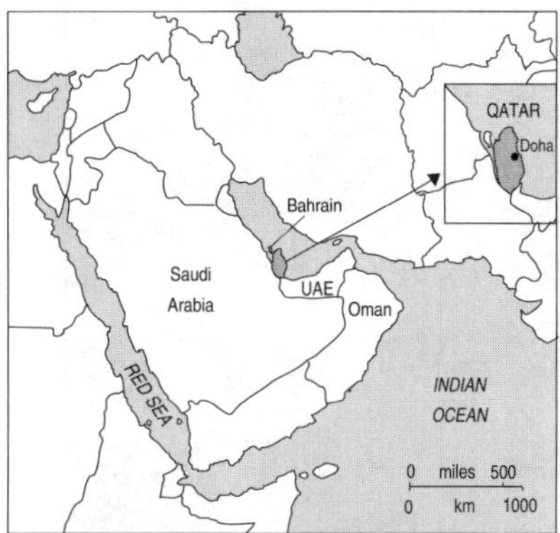

chronology
1916 Qatar became a British protectorate.
1970 Constitution adopted, confirming the emirate as an absolute monarchy.
1971 Independence achieved from Britain.
1972 Emir Sheik Ahmad replaced in bloodless coup by his cousin, Crown Prince Sheik Khalifa.
1991 Forces joined UN coalition in Gulf War against Iraq.

Romania

area 237,500 sq km/91,699 sq mi
capital Bucharest
towns Braşov, Timişoara, Cluj-Napoca, Iaşi; ports Galaţi, Constanta, Brăila
physical mountains surrounding a plateau, with river plains S and E
environment although sulphur-dioxide levels are low, only 20% of the country's rivers can provide drinkable water
features Carpathian Mountains, Transylvanian Alps; river Danube; Black Sea coast; mineral springs
head of state Ion Iliescu from 1989
head of government Nicolai Vacaroiu from 1992
political system emergent democratic republic
political parties National Salvation Front (NSF), reform socialist; Civic Alliance (CA), right of centre; Convention for Democracy, umbrella organization for right-of-centre National Liberal Party (NLP)

and ethnic-Hungarian Magyar Democratic Union (UDM)
exports petroleum products and oilfield equipment, electrical goods, cars, cereals
currency leu
population (1992) 23,332,000 (Romanians 89%, Hungarians 7.9%, Germans 1.6%); growth rate 0.5% p.a.
life expectancy men 67, women 73 (1989)
languages Romanian (official), Hungarian, German
media television is state-run; there are an estimated 900 newspapers and magazines, but only the progovernment papers have adequate distribution and printing facilities
religions Romanian Orthodox 80%, Roman Catholic 6%
literacy 98% (1988)
GNP $151 bn (1988); $6,400 per head

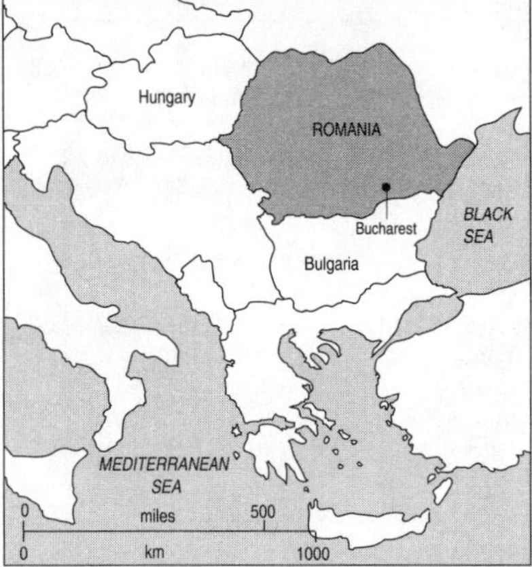

chronology
1944 Pro-Nazi Antonescu government overthrown.
1945 Communist-dominated government appointed.
1947 Boundaries redrawn. King Michael abdicated and People's Republic proclaimed.
1949 New Soviet-style constitution adopted. Joined Comecon.
1952 Second new Soviet-style constitution.
1955 Romania joined Warsaw Pact.
1958 Soviet occupation forces removed.
1965 New constitution adopted.
1974 Ceauşescu created president.
1985–86 Winters of austerity and power cuts.
1987 Workers demonstrated against austerity programme.
1988–89 Relations with Hungary deteriorated over 'systematization programme'.
1989 Announcement that all foreign debt paid off. Razing of villages and building of monuments to Ceauşescu. Communist orthodoxy reaffirmed; demonstrations violently suppressed; massacre in Timisoara. Army joined uprising; heavy fighting; bloody overthrow of Ceauşescu regime in 'Christmas Revolution'; Ceauşescu and wife tried and executed; estimated 10,000 dead in civil warfare. Power assumed by new National Salvation Front, headed by Ion Iliescu.
1990 Securitate secret police replaced by new Romanian Intelligence Service; religious practices resumed; mounting strikes and protests against effects of market economy.
1991 April: treaty on cooperation and good neighbourliness signed with USSR. Aug: privatization law passed. Sept: prime minister Petre Roman resigned following riots; succeeded by Theodor Stolojan heading a new cross-party coalition government. Dec: new constitution endorsed by referendum.
1992 Iliescu re-elected president; Nicolai Vacaroiu appointed prime minister.

Russian Federation

formerly (until 1991) Russian Soviet Federal Socialist Republic (RSFSR)
area 17,075,500 sq km/6,591,100 sq mi
capital Moscow
towns St Petersburg (Leningrad), Nizhny-Novgorod (Gorky), Rostov-on-Don, Samara (Kuibyshev), Tver (Kalinin), Volgograd, Vyatka (Kirov), Ekaterinburg (Sverdlovsk)
physical fertile Black Earth district; extensive forests; the Ural Mountains with large mineral resources
features the heavily industrialized area around Moscow; Siberia; includes 16 autonomous republics (capitals in brackets): Bashkir (Ufa); Buryat (Ulan-Ude); Checheno-Ingush (Grozny); Chuvash (Cheboksary); Dagestan (Makhachkala); Kabardino-Balkar (Nalchik); Kalmyk (Elista); Karelia (Petrozavodsk); Komi (Syktyvkar); Mari (Yoshkar-Ola); Mordovia (Saransk); Vladikavkaz (formerly Ordzhonikidze); Tatarstan (Kazan); Tuva (Kizyl); Udmurt (Izhevsk); Yakut (Yakutsk)
head of state Boris Yeltsin from 1990/91
head of government Viktor Chernomyrdin from 1992
political system emergent democracy
political parties Democratic Russia, liberal-radical, pro-Yeltsin; Congress of Civil and Patriotic Groups (CCDG), right-wing; Civic Union, right of centre; Nashi (Ours), far-right, Russian imperialist coalition; Communist (Bolshevik) Party, Stalinist-communist
products iron ore, coal, oil, gold, platinum, and other minerals, agricultural produce
currency rouble
population (1992) 149,469,000 (82% Russian, Tatar 4%, Ukrainian 3%, Chuvash 1%)
language Great Russian
religion traditionally Russian Orthodox

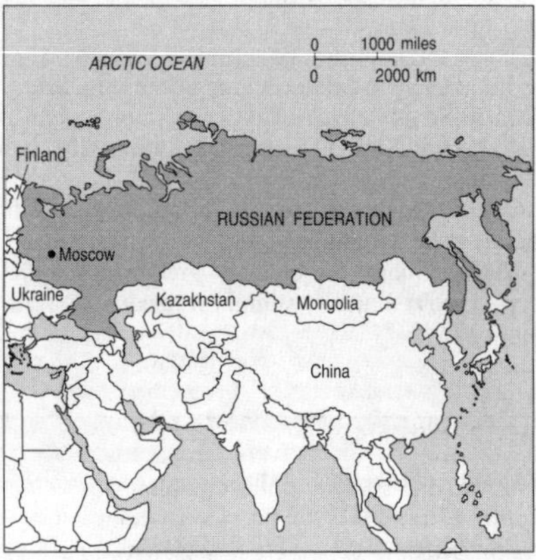

chronology
1945 Became a founding member of United Nations (UN).
1988 Aug: Democratic Union formed in Moscow as political party opposed to totalitarianism. Oct: Russian-language demonstrations in Leningrad, tsarist flag raised.
1989 March: Boris Yeltsin elected to USSR Congress of People's Deputies. Sept: conservative-nationalist Russian United Workers' Front established in Sverdlovsk.
1990 May: anticommunist May Day protests in Red Square, Moscow; Yeltsin narrowly elected RSFSR president by Russian parliament. June: economic and political sovereignty declared; Ivan Silaev became Russian prime minister. Aug: Tatarstan declared sovereignty. Dec: rationing introduced in some cities; private land ownership allowed.
1991 June: Yeltsin directly elected president under a liberal-radical banner. July: Yeltsin issued a decree to remove Communist Party cells from workplaces; sovereignty of the Baltic republics recognized by the republic. Aug: Yeltsin stood out against abortive anti-Gorbachev coup, emerging as key power-broker within Soviet Union; national guard established and pre-revolutionary flag restored. Sept: Silaev resigned as Russian premier. Nov: Yeltsin named prime minister; Soviet and Russian Communist Parties banned; Yeltsin's goverment gained control of Russia's economic assets and armed forces. Oct: Checheno-Ingush declared its independence. Dec: Yeltsin negotiated formation of new confederal Commonwealth of Independent States; Russia admitted into UN; independence recognized by USA and European Community.
1992 Jan: admitted into Conference on Security and Cooperation in Europe; assumed former USSR's permanent seat on UN Security Council; prices freed. Feb: demonstrations in Moscow and other cities as living standards plummeted. June: Yeltsin–Bush summit meeting. March: 18 out of 20 republics signed treaty agreeing to remain within loose Russian Federation; Tatarstan and Checheno-Ingush refused to sign. Dec: Victor Chernomyrdin elected prime minister; new constitution agreed in referendum. START II arms-reduction agreement signed with USA.
1993 Power struggle between Yeltsin and Congress of People's Deputies. Referendum gave vote of confidence in Yeltsin's presidency but did not support constitutional change.

Rwanda

Republic of (*Republika y'u Rwanda*)

area 26,338 sq km/10,173 sq mi
capital Kigali
towns Butare, Ruhengeri
physical high savanna and hills, with volcanic mountains in NW
features part of lake Kivu; highest peak Mount Karisimbi 4,507 m/14,792 ft; Kagera River (whose headwaters are the source of the Nile) and National Park
head of state and government Maj-Gen Juvenal Habyarimana from 1973
political system one-party military republic
political party National Revolutionary Movement for Development (MRND), nationalist, socialist

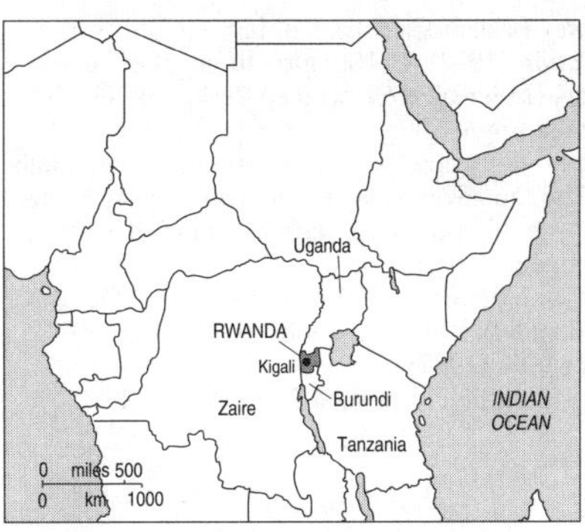

exports coffee, tea, pyrethrum
currency franc
population (1992) 7,347,000 (Hutu 90%, Tutsi 9%, Twa 1%); growth rate 3.3% p.a.
life expectancy men 49, women 53 (1989)
languages Kinyarwanda, French (official); Kiswahili
religions Roman Catholic 54%, animist 23%, Protestant 12%, Muslim 9%
literacy men 50% (1989)
GNP $2.3 bn (1987); $323 per head (1986)
chronology
1916 Belgian troops occupied Rwanda; League of Nations mandated Rwanda and Burundi to Belgium as Territory of Ruanda-Urundi.
1959 Interethnic warfare between Hutu and Tutsi.
1962 Independence from Belgium achieved, with Grégoire Kayibanda as president.
1972 Renewal of interethnic fighting.
1973 Kayibanda ousted in a military coup led by Maj-Gen Juvenal Habyarimana.
1978 New constitution approved; Rwanda remained a military-controlled state.
1980 Civilian rule adopted.
1988 Refugees from Burundi massacres streamed into Rwanda.
1990 Government attacked by Rwandan Patriotic Front (FPR), a Tutsi military-political organization based in Uganda.
1992 Peace accord with FPR.
1993 Power-sharing agreement with government repudiated by FPR. Peace accord formally signed.

St Christopher (St Kitts)–Nevis

Federation of

area 269 sq km/104 sq mi (St Christopher 176 sq km/68 sq mi, Nevis 93 sq km/36 sq mi)
capital Basseterre (on St Christopher)
towns Charlestown (largest on Nevis)
physical both islands are volcanic
features fertile plains on coast; black beaches
head of state Elizabeth II from 1983 represented by governor general
head of government Kennedy Simmonds from 1980
political system federal constitutional monarchy
political parties People's Action Movement (PAM), centre-right; Nevis Reformation Party (NRP), Nevis-separatist; Labour Party, moderate left of centre
exports sugar, molasses, electronics, clothing

currency Eastern Caribbean dollar
population (1992) 43,100; growth rate 0.2% p.a.
life expectancy men 69, women 72
language English
media no daily newspaper; two weekly papers, published by the governing and opposition party respectively – both receive advertising support from the government
religions Anglican 36%, Methodist 32%, other Protestant 8%, Roman Catholic 10% (1985 est)
literacy 90% (1987)
GNP $40 million (1983); $870 per head

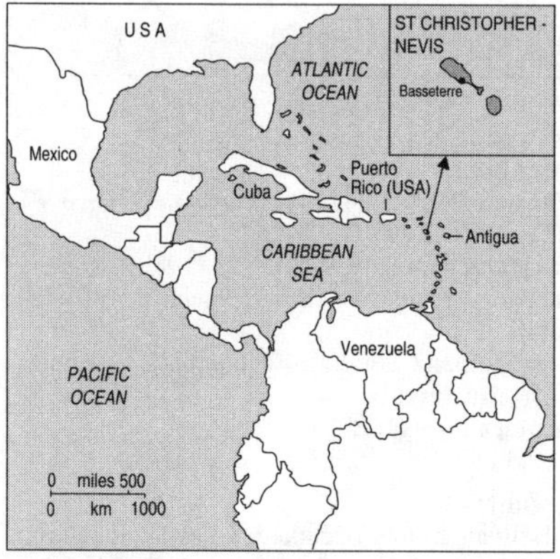

chronology
1871–1956 Part of the Leeward Islands Federation.
1958–62 Part of the Federation of the West Indies.
1967 St Christopher, Nevis, and Anguilla achieved internal self-government, within the British Commonwealth, with Robert Bradshaw, Labour Party leader, as prime minister.
1971 Anguilla returned to being a British dependency.
1978 Bradshaw died; succeeded by Paul Southwell.
1979 Southwell died; succeeded by Lee L Moore.
1980 Coalition government led by Kennedy Simmonds.
1983 Full independence achieved within the Commonwealth.
1984 Coalition government re-elected.
1989 Prime Minister Simmonds won a third successive term.

St Lucia

area 617 sq km/238 sq mi
capital Castries
towns Vieux-Fort, Soufrière
physical mountainous island with fertile valleys; mainly tropical forest
features volcanic peaks; Gros and Petit Pitons
head of state Elizabeth II from 1979, represented by governor general
head of government John Compton from 1982
political system constitutional monarchy
political parties United Workers' Party (UWP), moderate left of centre; St Lucia Labour Party (SLP), moderate left of centre; Progressive Labour Party (PLP), moderate left of centre
exports coconut oil, bananas, cocoa, copra
currency Eastern Caribbean dollar
population (1992) 135,000; growth rate 2.8% p.a.
life expectancy men 68, women 73 (1989)
languages English; French patois
media two independent biweekly newspapers
religion Roman Catholic 90%
literacy 78% (1989)
GNP $166 million; $1,370 per head (1987)

chronology
1814 Became a British crown colony following Treaty of Paris.
1967 Acquired internal self-government as a West Indies associated state.
1979 Independence achieved from Britain within the Commonwealth. John Compton, leader of the United Workers' Party (UWP), became prime minister. Allan Louisy, leader of the St Lucia Labour Party (SLP), replaced Compton as prime minister.
1981 Louisy resigned; replaced by Winston Cenac.
1982 Compton returned to power at the head of a UWP government.
1987 Compton re-elected with reduced majority.
1991 Integration with Windward Islands proposed.
1992 UWP won general election.

St Vincent and the Grenadines

area 388 sq km/150 sq mi, including islets of the Northern Grenadines 43 sq km/17 sq mi
capital Kingstown
towns Georgetown, Chateaubelair
physical volcanic mountains, thickly forested
features Mustique, one of the Grenadines, a holiday resort; Soufrière volcano
head of state Elizabeth II from 1979, represented by governor general
head of government James Mitchell from 1984
political system constitutional monarchy
political parties New Democratic Party (NDP), moderate, left of centre; St Vincent Labour Party (SVLP), moderate, left of centre
exports bananas, taros, sweet potatoes, arrowroot, copra
currency Eastern Caribbean dollar
population (1992) 109,000; growth rate –4% p.a.
life expectancy men 69, women 74 (1989)
languages English; French patois

media government-owned radio station; two privately owned weekly newspapers, subject to government pressure
religions Anglican 47%, Methodist 28%, Roman Catholic 13%
literacy 85% (1989)
GNP $188 million; $1,070 per head (1987)

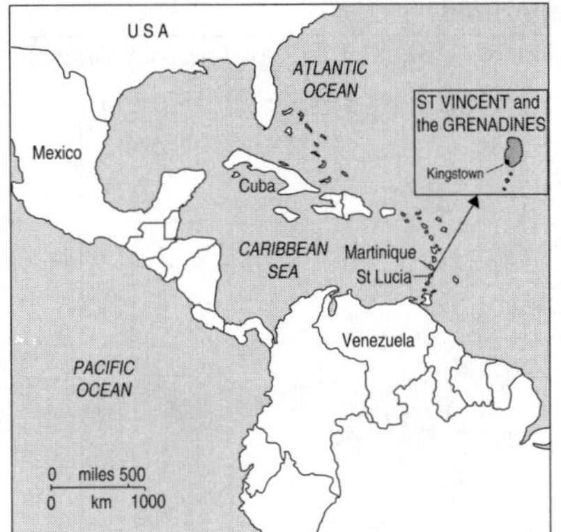

chronology
1783 Became a British crown colony.
1958–62 Part of the West Indies Federation.
1969 Achieved internal self-government.
1979 Achieved full independence from Britain, within the Commonwealth, with Milton Cato as prime minister.
1984 James Mitchell replaced Cato as prime minister.
1989 Mitchell decisively re-elected.
1991 Integration with Windward Islands proposed.

Samoa, Western

Independent State of (*Samoa i Sisifo*)

area 2,830 sq km/1,093 sq mi
capital Apia (on Upolu island)
physical comprises South Pacific islands of Savai'i and Upolu, with two smaller tropical islands and islets; mountain ranges on main islands
features lava flows on Savai'i
head of state King Malietoa Tanumafili II from 1962
head of government Tofilau Eti Alesana from 1988
political system liberal democracy
political parties Human Rights Protection Party (HRPP), led by Tofilau Eti Alesana; the Va'ai Kolone Group (VKG); Christian Democratic Party (CDP), led by Tupua Tamasese Efi. All 'parties' are personality-based groupings
exports coconut oil, copra, cocoa, fruit juice, cigarettes, timber
currency talà
population (1992) 160,000; growth rate 1.1% p.a.
life expectancy men 64, women 69 (1989)
languages English, Samoan (official)
religions Protestant 70%, Roman Catholic 20%
literacy 90% (1989)
GNP $110 million (1987); $520 per head

chronology
1899–1914 German protectorate.
1920–61 Administered by New Zealand.
1959 Local government elected.

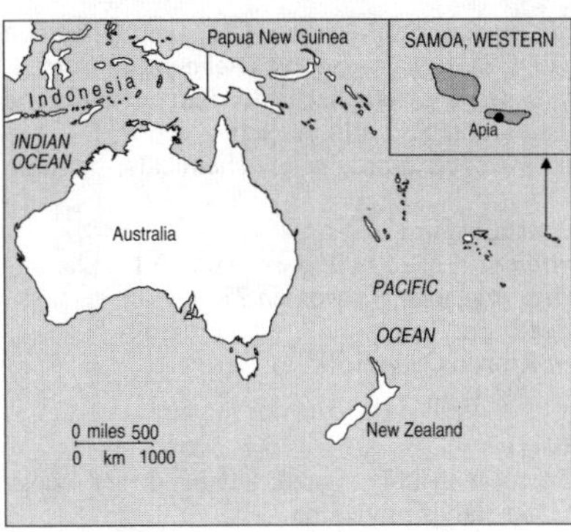

1961 Referendum favoured independence.
1962 Independence achieved within the Commonwealth, with Fiame Mata Afa Mulinu'u as prime minister.
1975 Mata Afa died.
1976 Tupuola Taisi Efi became first nonroyal prime minister.
1982 Va'ai Kolone became prime minister; replaced by Tupuola Efi. Assembly failed to approve budget; Tupuola Efi resigned; replaced by Tofilau Eti Alesana.
1985 Tofilau Eti resigned; head of state invited Va'ai Kolone to lead the government.
1988 Elections produced a hung parliament, with first Tupuola Efi as prime minister and then Tofilau Eti Alesana.
1990 Universal adult suffrage introduced.
1991 Tofilau Eti Alesana re-elected. Fiame Naome became first woman in cabinet.

San Marino

Republic of (*Repubblica di San Marino*)

area 61 sq km/24 sq mi
capital San Marino
towns Serravalle (industrial centre)
physical on the slope of Mount Titano
features surrounded by Italian territory; one of the world's smallest states
heads of state and government two captains regent, elected for a six-month period
political system direct democracy

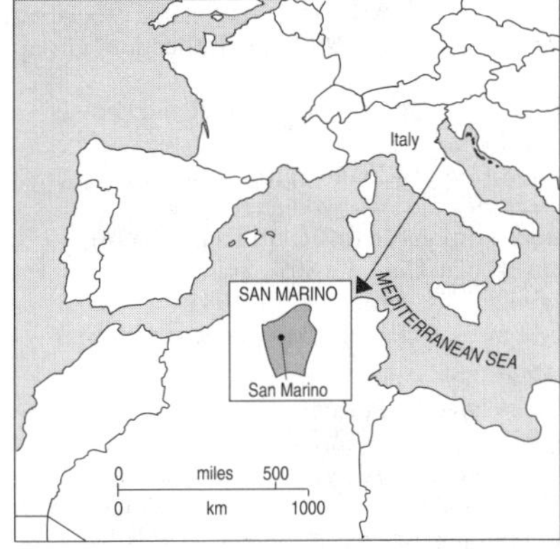

political parties San Marino Christian Democrat Party (PDCS), right of centre; Democratic Progressive Party (PDP), Socialist Unity Party (PSU), and Socialist Party (PSS), all three left of centre
exports wine, ceramics, paint, chemicals, building stone
currency Italian lira
population (1992) 23,600; growth rate 0.1% p.a.
life expectancy men 70, women 77
language Italian
religion Roman Catholic 95%
literacy 97% (1987)

chronology
1862 Treaty with Italy signed; independence recognized under Italy's protection.
1947–86 Governed by a series of left-wing and centre-left coalitions.
1986 Formation of Communist and Christian Democrat 'grand coalition'.
1992 Joined the United Nations.

São Tomé e Príncipe

Democratic Republic of

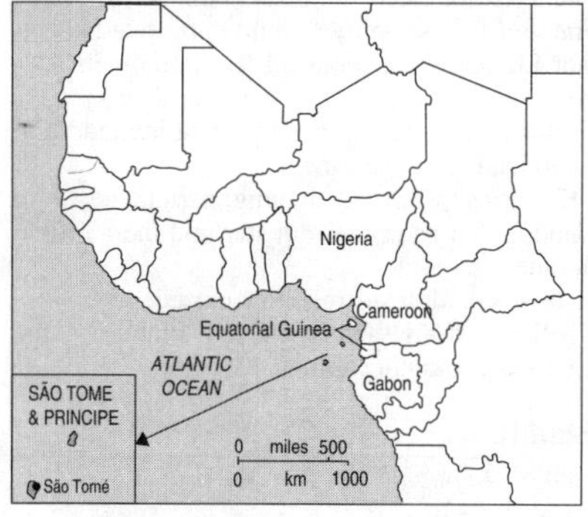

area 1,000 sq km/386 sq mi
capital São Tomé
towns Santo Antonio, Santa Cruz
physical comprises two main islands and several smaller ones, all volcanic; thickly forested and fertile
head of state and government Miguel Trovoada from 1991
political system emergent democratic republic
political parties Movement for the Liberation of São Tomé e Príncipe (MLSTP), nationalist socialist; Democratic Convergence Party–Reflection Group (PCD–EM), centre-left
exports cocoa, copra, coffee, palm oil and kernels
currency dobra
population (1992) 126,000; growth rate 2.5% p.a.
life expectancy men 62, women 62
languages Portuguese (official), Fang (Bantu)
religions Roman Catholic 80%, animist
literacy men 73%, women 42% (1981)
GNP $32 million (1987); $384 per head (1986)

chronology
1471 Discovered by Portuguese.
1522–1973 A province of Portugal.
1973 Achieved internal self-government.
1975 Independence achieved from Portugal, with Manuel Pinto da Costa as president.
1984 Formally declared a nonaligned state.
1987 Constitution amended.
1988 Unsuccessful coup attempt against da Costa.
1990 New constitution approved.
1991 First multiparty elections held; Miguel Trovoada replaced Pinto da Costa.

Saudi Arabia

Kingdom of (*al-Mamlaka al-'Arabiya as-Sa'udiya*)

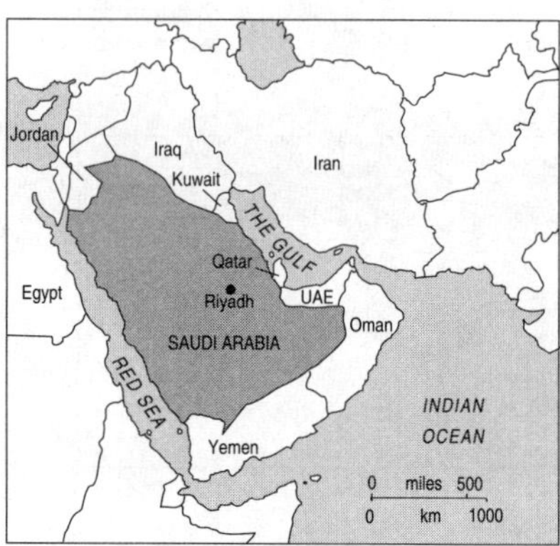

area 2,200,518 sq km/849,400 sq mi
capital Riyadh
towns Mecca, Medina, Taif; ports Jidda, Dammam
physical desert, sloping to the Persian Gulf from a height of 2,750 m/9,000 ft in the W
environment oil pollution caused by the Gulf War 1990–91 has affected 460 km/285 mi of the Saudi coastline, threatening desalination plants and damaging the wildlife of saltmarshes, mangrove forest, and mudflats
features Nafud Desert in N and the Rub'al Khali (Empty Quarter) in S, area 650,000 sq km/250,000 sq mi; with a ban on women drivers, there are an estimated 300,000 chauffeurs
head of state and government King Fahd Ibn Abdul Aziz from 1982
political system absolute monarchy
political parties none
exports oil, petroleum products
currency rial
population (1992) 15,267,000 (16% nomadic); growth rate 3.1% p.a.
life expectancy men 64, women 67 (1989)
language Arabic
religion Sunni Muslim; there is a Shi'ite minority
literacy men 34%, women 12% (1980 est)
GNP $70 bn (1988); $6,170 per head (1988)

chronology
1926–32 Territories of Nejd and Hejaz united and kingdom established.
1953 King Ibn Saud died and was succeeded by his eldest son, Saud.
1964 King Saud forced to abdicate; succeeded by his brother, Faisal.
1975 King Faisal assassinated; succeeded by his half-brother, Khalid.
1982 King Khalid died; succeeded by his brother, Crown Prince Fahd.

1987 Rioting by Iranian pilgrims caused 400 deaths in Mecca; diplomatic relations with Iran severed.
1990 Iraqi troops invaded and annexed Kuwait and massed on Saudi Arabian border. King Fahd called for help from US and UK forces.
1991 King Fahd provided military and financial assistance in Gulf War. Calls from religious leaders for 'consultative assembly' to assist in government of kingdom. Saudi Arabia attended Middle East peace conference.
1992 Formation of a 'consultative council' seen as possible move towards representative government.

Senegal

Republic of (*République du Sénégal*)

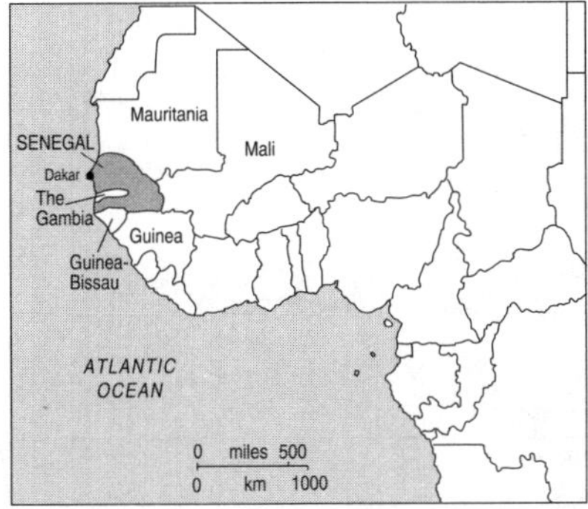

area 196,200 sq km/75,753 sq mi
capital (and chief port) Dakar
towns Thiès, Kaolack
physical plains rising to hills in SE; swamp and tropical forest in SW
features river Senegal; the Gambia forms an enclave within Senegal
head of state and government Abdou Diouf from 1981
political system emergent socialist democratic republic
political parties Senegalese Socialist Party (PS), democratic socialist; Senegalese Democratic Party (PDS), left of centre
exports peanuts, cotton, fish, phosphates
currency franc CFA
population (1992) 7,691,000; growth rate 3.1% p.a.
life expectancy men 51, women 54 (1989)
languages French (official); African dialects are spoken
religions Muslim 80%, Roman Catholic 10%, animist
literacy men 37%, women 19% (1985 est)
GNP $2 bn (1987); $380 per head (1984)

chronology
1659 Became a French colony.
1854–65 Interior occupied by French.
1902 Became a territory of French West Africa.
1959 Formed the Federation of Mali with French Sudan.
1960 Independence achieved from France, but withdrew from the federation. Léopold Sédar Senghor, leader of the Senegalese Progressive Union (UPS), became president.
1966 UPS declared the only legal party.
1974 Pluralist system re-established.
1976 UPS reconstituted as Senegalese Socialist Party (PS). Prime Minister Abdou Diouf nominated as Senghor's successor.
1980 Senghor resigned; succeeded by Diouf. Troops sent to defend Gambia.
1981 Military help again sent to Gambia.
1982 Confederation of Senegambia came into effect.
1983 Diouf re-elected. Post of prime minister abolished.
1988 Diouf decisively re-elected.
1989 Violent clashes between Senegalese and Mauritanians in Dakar and Nouakchott killed more than 450 people; over 50,000 people repatriated from both countries. Senegambia federation abandoned.
1991 Constitutional changes outlined.
1992 Diplomatic links with Mauritania re-established.
1993 Diouf re-elected.

Seychelles

Republic of

area 453 sq km/175 sq mi
capital Victoria (on Mahé island)
towns Cascade, Port Glaud, Misere
physical comprises two distinct island groups, one concentrated, the other widely scattered, totalling over 100 islands and islets
features Aldabra atoll, containing world's largest tropical lagoon; the unique 'double coconut' (*coco de mer*); tourism is important
head of state and government France-Albert René from 1977
political system one-party socialist republic
political party Seychelles People's Progressive Front (SPPF), nationalist socialist
exports copra, cinnamon
currency Seychelles rupee
population (1992) 71,000; growth rate 2.2% p.a.
life expectancy 66 years (1988)
languages creole (Asian, African, European mixture) 95%, English, French (all official)
religion Roman Catholic 90%
literacy 80% (1989)
GNP $175 million; $2,600 per head (1987)

chronology
1744 Became a French colony.
1794 Captured by British.

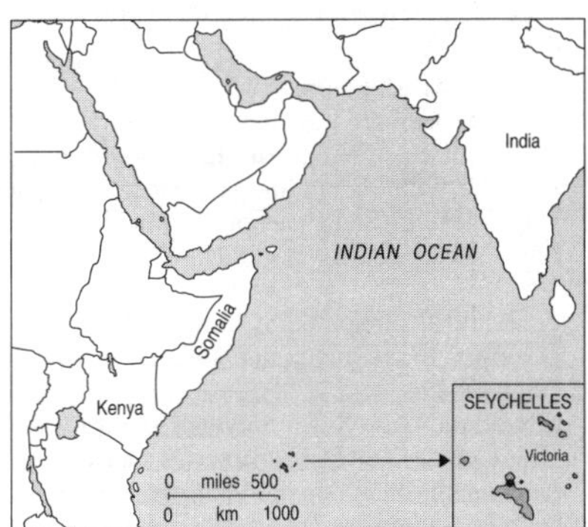

1814 Ceded by France to Britain; incorporated as a dependency of Mauritius.
1903 Became a separate British colony.
1975 Internal self-government agreed.
1976 Independence achieved from Britain as a republic within the Commonwealth, with James Mancham as president.
1977 France-Albert René ousted Mancham in an armed coup and took over presidency.
1979 New constitution adopted; Seychelles People's Progressive Front (SPPF) sole legal party.
1981 Attempted coup by South African mercenaries thwarted.
1984 René re-elected.
1987 Coup attempt foiled.
1989 René re-elected.
1991 Multiparty politics promised.
1992 Mancham returned from exile. Constitutional commission elected; constitutional reform received insufficient support in referendum.
1993 René defeated Mancham in multi-party presidential elections.

Sierra Leone

Republic of
area 71,740 sq km/27,710 sq mi
capital Freetown
towns Koidu, Bo, Kenema, Makeni
physical mountains in E; hills and forest; coastal mangrove swamps
features hot and humid climate (3,500 mm/138 in rainfall p.a.)
head of state and government military council headed by Capt Valentine Strasser from 1992
political system transitional
political parties All People's Congress (APC), moderate socialist; United Front of Political Movements (UNIFORM), centre-left
exports palm kernels, cocoa, coffee, ginger, diamonds, bauxite, rutile
currency leone
population (1992) 4,373,000; growth rate 2.5% p.a.
life expectancy men 41, women 47 (1989)
languages English (official), local languages
media no daily newspapers; 13 weekly papers, of which 11 are independent but only one achieves sales of over 5,000 copies
religions animist 52%, Muslim 39%, Protestant 6%, Roman Catholic 2% (1980 est)
literacy men 38%, women 21% (1985 est)
GNP $965 million (1987); $320 per head (1984)
chronology
1808 Became a British colony.
1896 Hinterland declared a British protectorate.
1961 Independence achieved from Britain within the Commonwealth, with Milton Margai, leader of Sierra Leone People's Party (SLPP), as prime minister.
1964 Milton succeeded by his half-brother, Albert Margai.
1967 Election results disputed by army, who set up a National Reformation Council and forced the governor general to leave.
1968 Army revolt made Siaka Stevens, leader of the All People's Congress (APC), prime minister.
1971 New constitution adopted, making Sierra Leone a republic, with Stevens as president.
1978 APC declared only legal party. Stevens sworn in for another seven-year term.
1985 Stevens retired; succeeded by Maj-Gen Joseph Momoh.
1989 Attempted coup against President Momoh foiled.
1991 Referendum endorsed multiparty politics.
1992 Military take-over; President Momoh fled. National Provisional Ruling Council (NPRC) established under Capt Valentine Strasser.

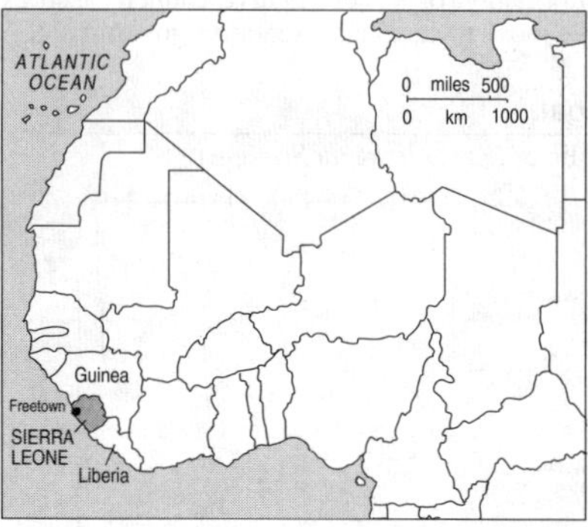

Singapore

Republic of
area 622 sq km/240 sq mi
capital Singapore City
towns Jurong, Changi
physical comprises Singapore Island, low and flat, and 57 small islands
features Singapore Island is joined to the mainland by causeway across Strait of Johore; temperature range 21°–34°C/69°–93°F
head of state Ong Teng Cheong from 1993
head of government Goh Chok Tong from 1990
political system liberal democracy with strict limits on dissent
political parties People's Action Party (PAP), conservative; Workers' Party (WP), socialist; Singapore Democratic Party (SDP), liberal pluralist

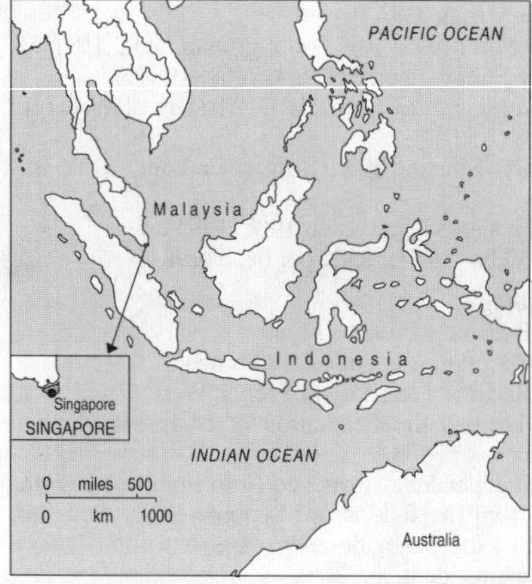

exports electronics, petroleum products, rubber, machinery, vehicles
currency Singapore dollar
population (1992) 2,792,000 (Chinese 75%, Malay 14%, Tamil 7%); growth rate 1.2% p.a.
life expectancy men 71, women 77 (1989)
languages Malay (national tongue), Chinese, Tamil, English (all official)
religions Buddhist, Taoist, Muslim, Hindu, Christian
literacy men 93%, women 79% (1985 est)
GDP $19.9 bn (1987); $7,616 per head

chronology
1819 Singapore leased to British East India Company.
1858 Placed under crown rule.
1942 Invaded and occupied by Japan.
1945 Japanese removed by British forces.
1959 Independence achieved from Britain; Lee Kuan Yew became prime minister.
1963 Joined new Federation of Malaysia.
1965 Left federation to become an independent republic.
1984 Opposition made advances in parliamentary elections.
1986 Opposition leader convicted of perjury and prohibited from standing for election.
1988 Ruling conservative party elected to all but one of available assembly seats; increasingly authoritarian rule.
1990 Lee Kuan Yew resigned as prime minister; replaced by Goh Chok Tong.
1991 PAP and Goh Chok Tong re-elected.
1992 Lee Kuan Yew surrendered PAP leadership to Goh Chok Tong.
1993 Ong Teng Cheong chosen as president.

Slovakia

Slovak Republic (*Slovenská Republika*)

area 49,035 sq km/18,940 sq mi
capital Bratislava
towns Košice, Nitra, Prešov, Banská Bystrica
physical W range of the Carpathian Mountains including Tatra and Beskids in N; Danube plain in S; numerous lakes and mineral springs
features fine beech and oak forests with bears and wild boar

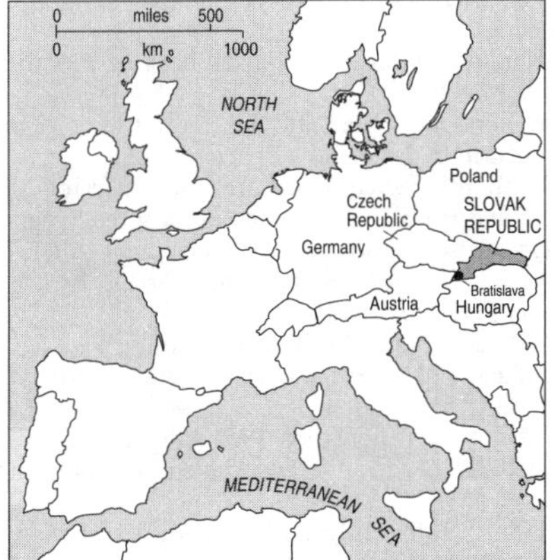

head of state Michal Kovak from 1993
head of government Vladimir Meciar from 1993
political system emergent democracy
political parties Civic Democratic Union (CDU), centre-left; Movement for a Democratic Slovakia (HZDS), centre-left, nationalist; Christian Democratic Movement (KDH), right of centre; Slovak National Party, nationalist; Party of the Democratic Left, left-wing, ex-communist; Coexistence and Hungarian Christian Democratic Movement, both representing Hungarian minority
exports iron ore, copper, mercury, magnesite, armaments, chemicals, textiles, machinery
currency new currency based on koruna
population (1991) 5,268,900 (with Hungarian and other minorities); growth rate 0.4% p.a.
life expectancy men 68, women 75
languages Slovak (official)
religions Roman Catholic (over 50%), Lutheran, Reformist, Orthodox
literacy 100%
GDP $10,000 million (1990); $1,887 per head

chronology
1918 Independence achieved from Austro-Hungarian Empire; Slovaks joined Czechs in forming Czechoslovakia as independent nation.
1948 Communists assumed power in Czechoslovakia.
1968 Slovak Socialist Republic created under new federal constitution.
1989 Prodemocracy demonstrations in Bratislava; new political parties formed, including Slovak-based People Against Violence (PAV); Communist Party stripped of powers. Dec: new government formed, including former dissidents; political parties legalized; Václav Havel appointed president.
1991 Evidence of increasing Slovak separatism. March: PAV splinter group formed under Slovak premier Vladimir Meciar. April: Meciar dismissed, replaced by Jan Carnogursky; pro-Meciar rallies held in Bratislava.
1992 March: PAV renamed Civic Democratic Union (CDU). June: Havel resigned following Slovak gains in assembly elections. Aug: agreement on creation of separate Czech and Slovak states.
1993 Jan: Slovak Republic became sovereign state, with Meciar, leader of the MFDS, as prime minister. Feb: Michal Kovak became president. June: Slovakia gained membership of Council of Europe.

Slovenia

Republic of

area 20,251 sq km/7,817 sq mi
capital Ljubljana
towns Maribor, Kranj, Celji; chief port: Koper
physical mountainous; Sava and Drava rivers
head of state Milan Kucan from 1990
head of government Janez Drnovsek from 1992
political system emergent democracy
political parties Christian Democratic Party, right of centre; People's Party, right of centre; Liberal Democratic Party, left of centre; Democratic Party, left of centre
products grain, sugarbeet, livestock, timber, cotton and woollen textiles, steel, vehicles

currency tolar
population (1992) 1,985,000 (Slovene 91%, Croat 3%, Serb 2%)
languages Slovene, resembling Serbo-Croat, written in Roman characters
religion Roman Catholic

chronology
1918 United with Serbia and Croatia.
1929 The kingdom of Serbs, Croats, and Slovenes took the name of Yugoslavia.
1945 Became a constituent republic of Yugoslav Socialist Federal Republic.
mid-1980s The Slovenian Communist Party liberalized itself and agreed to free elections. Yugoslav counterintelligence (KOV) began repression.
1989 Jan: Social Democratic Alliance of Slovenia launched as first political organization independent of Communist Party. Sept: constitution changed to allow secession from federation.
1990 April: nationalist DEMOS coalition secured victory in first multiparty parliamentary elections; Milan Kucan became president. July: sovereignty declared. Dec: independence overwhelmingly approved in referendum.
1991 June: independence declared; 100 killed after federal army intervened; cease-fire brokered by European Community (EC). July: cease-fire agreed between federal troops and nationalists. Oct: withdrawal of Yugoslav army completed. Dec: DEMOS coalition dissolved.
1992 Jan: EC recognized Slovenia's independence. April: Janez Drnovsek appointed prime minister; independence recognized by USA. May: admitted into United Nations and Conference on Security and Cooperation in Europe. Dec: Liberal Democrats and Christian Democrats won assembly elections; Kucan re-elected president.
1993 Drnovsek re-elected prime minister.

Solomon Islands

area 27,600 sq km/10,656 sq mi
capital Honiara (on Guadalcanal)
towns Gizo, Yandina
physical comprises all but the northernmost islands (which belong to Papua New Guinea) of a Melanesian archipelago stretching nearly 1,500 km/900 mi. The largest is Guadalcanal (area 6,500 sq km/2,510 sq mi); others are Malaita, San Cristobal, New Georgia, Santa Isabel, Choiseul; mainly mountainous and forested
features rivers ideal for hydroelectric power
head of state Elizabeth II represented by governor general
head of government Francis Billy Hilly from 1993
political system constitutional monarchy
political parties People's Alliance Party (PAP), centre-left; Solomon Islands United Party (SIUPA), right of centre
exports fish products, palm oil, copra, cocoa, timber
currency Solomon Island dollar
population (1992) 339,000 (Melanesian 95%, Polynesian 4%); growth rate 3.9% p.a.
life expectancy men 66, women 71
languages English (official); there are some 120 Melanesian dialects
religions Anglican 34%, Roman Catholic 19%, South Sea Evangelical 17%
literacy 60% (1989)
GNP $141 million; $420 per head (1987)

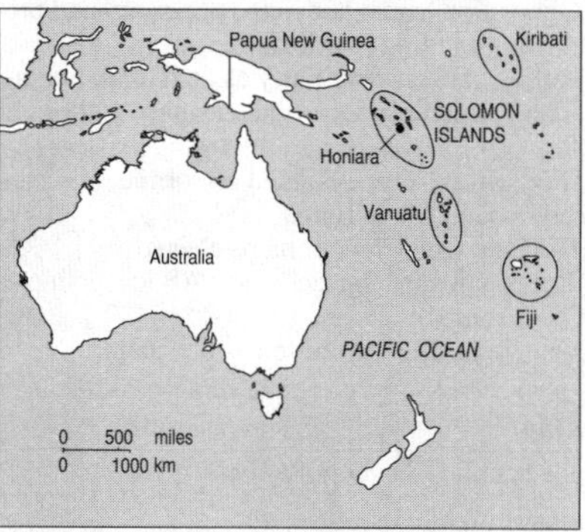

chronology
1893 Solomon Islands placed under British protection.
1978 Independence achieved from Britain within the Commonwealth, with Peter Kenilorea as prime minister.
1981 Solomon Mamaloni of the People's Progressive Party (PPP) replaced Kenilorea as prime minister.
1984 Kenilorea returned to power, heading a coalition government.
1986 Kenilorea resigned after allegations of corruption; replaced by his deputy, Ezekiel Alebua.
1988 Kenilorea elected deputy prime minister. Joined Vanuatu and Papua New Guinea to form the Spearhead Group, aiming to preserve Melanesian cultural traditions and secure independence for the French territory of New Caledonia.
1989 Solomon Mamaloni, now leader of the People's Action Party (PAP), elected prime minister; formed PAP-dominated coalition.
1990 Mamaloni resigned as PAP party leader, but continued as head of a government of national unity.
1993 Francis Billy Hilly, an independent politician, elected prime minister.

Somalia

Somali Democratic Republic (*Jamhuriyadda Dimugradiga Somaliya*)

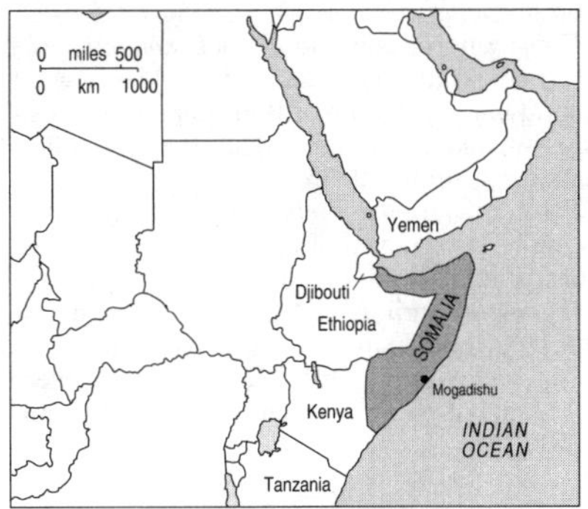

area 637,700 sq km/246,220 sq mi
capital Mogadishu
towns Hargeisa, Kismayu, port Berbera
physical mainly flat, with hills in N
environment destruction of trees for fuel and by grazing livestock has led to an increase in desert area
features occupies a strategic location on the Horn of Africa
head of state and government Ali Mahdi Mohammed from 1991
political system one-party socialist republic
political party Somali Revolutionary Socialist Party (SRSP), nationalist, socialist
exports livestock, skins, hides, bananas, fruit
currency Somali shilling
population (1992) 7,872,000 (including 350,000 refugees in Ethiopia and 50,000 in Djibouti); growth rate 3.1% p.a.
life expectancy men 53, women 53 (1989)
languages Somali, Arabic (both official), Italian, English
religion Sunni Muslim 99%
literacy 40% (1986)
GNP $1.5 bn; $290 per head (1987)

chronology
1884–87 British protectorate of Somaliland established.
1889 Italian protectorate of Somalia established.
1960 Independence achieved from Italy and Britain.
1963 Border dispute with Kenya; diplomatic relations broken with Britain.
1968 Diplomatic relations with Britain restored.
1969 Army coup led by Maj-Gen Mohamed Siad Barre; constitution suspended, Supreme Revolutionary Council set up; name changed to Somali Democratic Republic.
1978 Defeated in eight-month war with Ethiopia. Armed insurrection began in north.
1979 New constitution for socialist one-party state adopted.
1982 Antigovernment Somali National Movement formed. Oppressive countermeasures by government.
1987 Barre re-elected president.
1989 Dissatisfaction with government and increased guerrilla activity in north.
1990 Civil war intensified. Constitutional reforms promised.
1991 Mogadishu captured by rebels; Barre fled; Ali Mahdi Mohammed named president; free elections promised. Secession of NE Somalia, as the Somaliland Republic, announced. Cease-fire signed, but later collapsed. Thousands of casualties as a result of heavy fighting in capital.
1992 Relief efforts to ward off impending famine severely hindered by unstable political situation; relief convoys hijacked by 'warlords'. Dec: UN peacekeeping troops, mainly US Marines, sent in to protect relief operations; dominant warlords agreed truce.
1993 March: leaders of armed factions agreed to federal system of government, based on 18 autonomous regions. June: US-led UN forces destroyed headquarters of warlord Gen Mohammad Farah Aidid, following killing of Pakistani peacekeeping troops.

South Africa

Republic of (*Republiek van Suid-Afrika*)

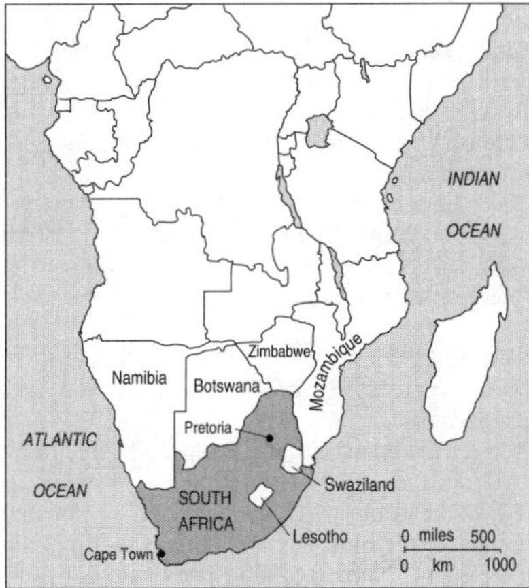

area 1,223,181 sq km/472,148 sq mi (includes Walvis Bay and independent black homelands)
capital and port Cape Town (legislative), Pretoria (administrative), Bloemfontein (judicial)
towns Johannesburg; ports Durban, Port Elizabeth, East London
physical southern end of large plateau, fringed by mountains and lowland coastal margin
territories Marion Island and Prince Edward Island in the Antarctic
features Drakensberg Mountains, Table Mountain; Limpopo and Orange rivers; the Veld and the Karoo; part of Kalahari Desert; Kruger National Park
head of state and government F W de Klerk from 1989
political system racist, nationalist republic, restricted democracy
political parties White: National Party (NP), right of centre, racist; Conservative Party of South Africa (CPSA), extreme right, racist; Democratic Party (DP), left of centre, multiracial. Coloureds: Labour Party of South Africa, left of centre; People's Congress Party, right of centre. Indian: National People's Party, right of centre; Solidarity Party, left of centre

exports maize, sugar, fruit, wool, gold (world's largest producer), platinum, diamonds, uranium, iron and steel, copper; mining and minerals are largest export industry, followed by arms manufacturing
currency rand
population (1992) 32,063,000 (73% black: Zulu, Xhosa, Sotho, Tswana; 18% white: 3% mixed, 3% Asian); growth rate 2.5% p.a.
life expectancy whites 71, Asians 67, blacks 58
languages Afrikaans and English (both official), Bantu
religions Dutch Reformed Church 40%, Anglican 11%, Roman Catholic 8%, other Christian 25%, Hindu, Muslim
literacy whites 99%, Asians 69%, blacks 50% (1989)
GNP $81 bn; $1,890 per head (1987)

chronology
1910 Union of South Africa formed from two British colonies and two Boer republics.
1912 African National Congress (ANC) formed.
1948 Apartheid system of racial discrimination initiated by Daniel Malan, leader of National Party (NP).
1955 Freedom Charter adopted by ANC.
1958 Malan succeeded as prime minister by Hendrik Verwoerd.
1960 ANC banned.
1961 South Africa withdrew from Commonwealth and became a republic.
1962 ANC leader Nelson Mandela jailed.
1964 Mandela, Walter Sisulu, Govan Mbeki, and five other ANC leaders sentenced to life imprisonment.
1966 Verwoerd assassinated; succeeded by B J Vorster.
1976 Soweto uprising.
1977 Death in custody of Pan African Congress activist Steve Biko.
1978 Vorster resigned and was replaced by Pieter W Botha.
1984 New constitution adopted, giving segregated representation to Coloureds and Asians and making Botha president. Nonaggression pact with Mozambique signed but not observed.
1985 Growth of violence in black townships.
1986 Commonwealth agreed on limited sanctions. US Congress voted to impose sanctions. Some major multinational companies closed down their South African operations.
1987 Government formally acknowledged the presence of its military forces in Angola.
1988 Botha announced 'limited constitutional reforms'. South Africa agreed to withdraw from Angola and recognize Namibia's independence as part of regional peace accord.
1989 Botha gave up NP leadership and state presidency. F W de Klerk became president. ANC activists released; beaches and public facilities desegregated. Elections held in Namibia to create independence government.
1990 ANC ban lifted; Nelson Mandela released from prison. NP membership opened to all races. ANC leader Oliver Tambo returned. Daily average of 35 murders and homicides recorded.
1991 Mandela and Zulu leader Mangosuthu Buthelezi urged end to fighting between ANC and Inkatha. Mandela elected ANC president. Revelations of government support for Inkatha threatened ANC cooperation. De Klerk announced repeal of remaining apartheid laws. South Africa readmitted to international sport; USA lifted sanctions. PAC and Buthelezi withdrew from negotiations over new constitution.
1992 Constitution leading to all-races majority rule approved by whites-only referendum. Massacre of civilians at black township of Boipatong near Johannesburg by Inkatha, aided and abetted by police, threatened constitutional talks.
1993 Feb: de Klerk and Nelson Mandela agreed to formation of government of national unity after free elections. Buthelezi not consulted; he opposed such an arrangement. April: ANC leader Chris Hani assassinated by white extremist. July: riots followed announcement of April 1994 date for nonracial elections. Victims of political violence since 1990 numbered 9,000.

Spain

(España)

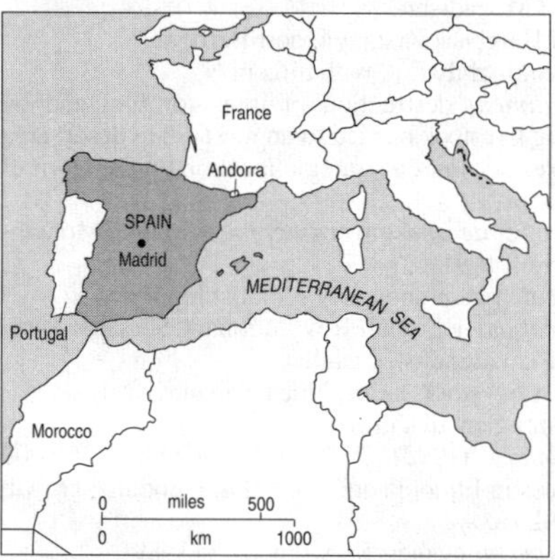

area 504,750 sq km/194,960 sq mi
capital Madrid
towns Zaragoza, Seville, Murcia, Córdoba; ports Barcelona, Valencia, Cartagena, Málaga, Cádiz, Vigo, Santander, Bilbao
physical central plateau with mountain ranges; lowlands in S
territories Balearic and Canary Islands; in N Africa: Ceuta, Melilla, Alhucemas, Chafarinas Is, Peñón de Vélez
features rivers Ebro, Douro, Tagus, Guadiana, Guadalquivir; Iberian Plateau (Meseta); Pyrenees, Cantabrian Mountains, Andalusian Mountains, Sierra Nevada
head of state King Juan Carlos I from 1975
head of government Felipe González Márquez from 1982
political system constitutional monarchy
political parties Socialist Workers' Party (PSOE), democratic socialist; Popular Alliance (AP), centre-right; Christian Democrats (DC), centrist; Liberal Party (PL), left of centre
exports citrus fruits, grapes, pomegranates, vegetables, wine, sherry, olive oil, canned fruit and fish, iron ore, cork, vehicles, textiles, petroleum products, leather goods, ceramics

currency peseta
population (1992) 39,085,000; growth rate 0.2% p.a.
life expectancy men 74, women 80 (1989)
languages Spanish (Castilian, official), Basque, Catalan, Galician, Valencian, Majorcan
religion Roman Catholic 99%
literacy 97% (1989)
GNP $573.7 bn (1992)

chronology
1936–39 Civil war; General Francisco Franco became head of state and government; fascist party Falange declared only legal political organization.
1947 General Franco announced restoration of the monarchy after his death, with Prince Juan Carlos as his successor.
1975 Franco died; succeeded as head of state by King Juan Carlos I.
1978 New constitution adopted with Adolfo Suárez, leader of the Democratic Centre Party, as prime minister.
1981 Suárez resigned; succeeded by Leopoldo Calvo Sotelo. Attempted military coup thwarted.
1982 Socialist Workers' Party (PSOE), led by Felipe González, won a sweeping electoral victory. Basque separatist organization (ETA) stepped up its guerrilla campaign.
1985 ETA's campaign spread to holiday resorts.
1986 Referendum confirmed NATO membership. Spain joined the European Economic Community.
1988 Spain joined the Western European Union.
1989 PSOE lost seats to hold only parity after general election. Talks between government and ETA collapsed and truce ended.
1992 ETA's 'armed struggle' resumed. European Community's Maastricht Treaty ratified.
1993 Allegations of corruption within PSOE. González narrowly won general election and formed a new minority government, including independents in his cabinet.

Sri Lanka

Democratic Socialist Republic of (*Prajathanrika Samajawadi Janarajaya Sri Lanka*) (until 1972 ***Ceylon***)

area 65,600 sq km/25,328 sq mi
capital (and chief port) Colombo
towns Kandy; ports Jaffna, Galle, Negombo, Trincomalee
physical flat in N and around the coast; hills and mountains in S and central interior
features Adam's Peak (2,243 m/7,538 ft); ruined cities of Anuradhapura, Polonnaruwa
head of state Dingiri Banda Wijetumya from 1993
head of government to be appointed (1993)
political system liberal democratic republic
political parties United National Party (UNP), right of centre; Sri Lanka Freedom Party (SLFP), left of centre; Democratic United National Front (DUNF), centre-left; Tamil United Liberation Front (TULF), Tamil autonomy; Eelam People's Revolutionary Liberation Front (EPLRF), Indian-backed Tamil-secessionist 'Tamil Tigers'
exports tea, rubber, coconut products, graphite, sapphires, rubies, other gemstones
currency Sri Lanka rupee
population (1992) 17,464,000 (Sinhalese 74%, Tamils 17%, Moors 7%); growth rate 1.8% p.a.
life expectancy men 67, women 72 (1989)
languages Sinhala, Tamil, English
religions Buddhist 69%, Hindu 15%, Muslim 8%, Christian 7%
literacy 87% (1988)
GNP $7.2 bn; $400 per head (1988)

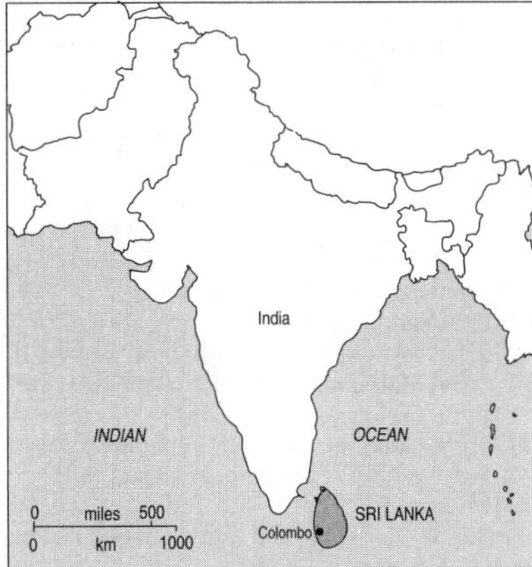

chronology
1802 Ceylon became a British colony.
1948 Ceylon achieved independence from Britain within the Commonwealth.
1956 Sinhala established as the official language.
1959 Prime Minister Solomon Bandaranaike assassinated.
1972 Socialist Republic of Sri Lanka proclaimed.
1978 Presidential constitution adopted by new government headed by Junius Jayawardene of the UNP.
1983 Tamil guerrilla violence escalated; state of emergency imposed.
1987 President Jayawardene and Indian prime minister Rajiv Gandhi signed Colombo Accord. Violence continued despite cease-fire policed by Indian troops.
1988 Left-wing guerrillas campaigned against Indo-Sri Lankan peace pact. Prime Minister Ranasinghe Premadasa elected president.
1989 Premadasa became president; D B Wijetumya, prime minister. Leaders of the TULF and the banned Sinhala extremist People's Liberation Front (JVP) assassinated.
1990 Indian peacekeeping force withdrawn. Violence continued.
1991 March: defence minister Ranjan Wijeratne assassinated; Sri Lankan army killed 2,552 Tamil Tigers at Elephant Pass. Oct: impeachment motion against President Premadasa failed. Dec: new party, the Democratic United National Front (DUNF), formed by former members of the UNP.
1992 35 Tamil civilians massacred by Sinhalese soldiers.
1993 DUNF leader assassinated; DUNF and SLFP leaders held the government responsible. President Premadasa assassinated; succeeded by Prime Minister Wijetumya.

Sudan

Democratic Republic of (*Jamhuryat es-Sudan*)

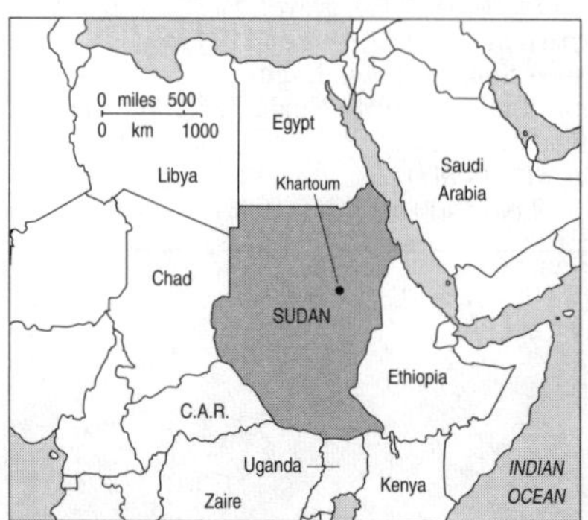

area 2,505,800 sq km/967,489 sq mi
capital Khartoum
towns Omdurman, Juba, Wadi Medani, al-Obeid, Kassala, Atbara, al-Qadarif, Kosti; chief port Port Sudan
physical fertile valley of river Nile separates Libyan Desert in W from high rocky Nubian Desert in E
environment the building of the Jonglei Canal to supply water to N Sudan and Egypt threatens the grasslands of S Sudan
features Sudd swamp; largest country in Africa
head of state and government General Omar Hassan Ahmed el-Bashir from 1989
political system military republic
political parties New National Umma Party (NNUP), Islamic, nationalist; Democratic Unionist Party (DUP), moderate, nationalist; National Islamic Front, Islamic, nationalist
exports cotton, gum arabic, sesame seed, peanuts, sorghum
currency Sudanese pound
population (1992) 29,971,000; growth rate 2.9% p.a.
life expectancy men 51, women 55 (1989)
languages Arabic 51% (official), local languages
religions Sunni Muslim 73%, animist 18%, Christian 9% (in south)
literacy 30% (1986)
GNP $8.5 bn (1988); $330 per head (1988)
chronology
1820 Sudan ruled by Egypt.
1885 Revolt led to capture of Khartoum by self-proclaimed Mahdi.
1896-98 Anglo-Egyptian offensive led by Lord Kitchener subdued revolt.
1899 Sudan administered as an Anglo-Egyptian condominium.
1955 Civil war between Muslim north and non-Muslim south broke out.
1956 Sudan achieved independence from Britain and Egypt as a republic.
1958 Military coup replaced civilian government with Supreme Council of the Armed Forces.
1964 Civilian rule reinstated.
1969 Coup led by Col Gaafar Mohammed Nimeri established Revolutionary Command Council (RCC); name changed to Democratic Republic of Sudan.
1970 Union with Egypt agreed in principle.
1971 New constitution adopted; Nimeri confirmed as president; Sudanese Socialist Union (SSU) declared only legal party.
1972 Proposed Federation of Arab Republics, comprising Sudan, Egypt, and Syria, abandoned. Addis Ababa conference proposed autonomy for southern provinces.
1974 National assembly established.
1983 Nimeri re-elected. Shari'a (Islamic law) introduced.
1985 Nimeri deposed in a bloodless coup led by General Swar al-Dahab; transitional military council set up. State of emergency declared.
1986 More than 40 political parties fought general election; coalition government formed.
1987 Virtual civil war with Sudan People's Liberation Army (SPLA).
1988 Al-Mahdi formed a new coalition. Another flare-up of civil war between north and south created tens of thousands of refugees. Floods made 1.5 million people homeless. Peace pact signed with SPLA.
1989 Sadiq al-Mahdi overthrown in coup led by General Omar Hassan Ahmed el-Bashir.
1990 Civil war continued with new SPLA offensive.
1991 Federal system introduced, with division of country into nine states.
1993 March: SPLA leaders John Garang and Riek Machar announced unilateral cease-fire in ten years' war with government in Khartoum. April: peace talks began between government and two factions of the SPLA.

Surinam

Republic of (*Republiek Suriname*)

area 163,820 sq km/63,243 sq mi
capital Paramaribo
towns Nieuw Nickerie, Brokopondo, Nieuw Amsterdam
physical hilly and forested, with flat and narrow coastal plain
features Suriname River
head of state and government Ronald Venetiaan from 1991
political system emergent democratic republic
political parties Party for National Unity and Solidarity (KTPI)*, Indonesian, left of centre; Surinam National Party (NPS)*, Creole, left of centre; Progressive Reform Party (VHP)*, Indian, left of centre; New Front for Democracy (NF)* members of Front for Democracy and Development (FDD)
exports alumina, aluminium, bauxite, rice, timber
currency Surinam guilder
population (1990 est) 408,000 (Hindu 37%, Creole 31%, Javanese 15%); growth rate 1.1% p.a.
life expectancy men 66, women 71 (1989)
languages Dutch (official), Sranan (creole), English, others
religions Christian 30%, Hindu 27%, Muslim 20%
literacy 65% (1989)
GNP $1.1 bn (1987); $2,920 per head (1985)
chronology
1667 Became a Dutch colony.
1954 Achieved internal self-government as Dutch Guiana.
1975 Independence achieved from the Netherlands, with Dr Johan Ferrier as president and Henck Arron

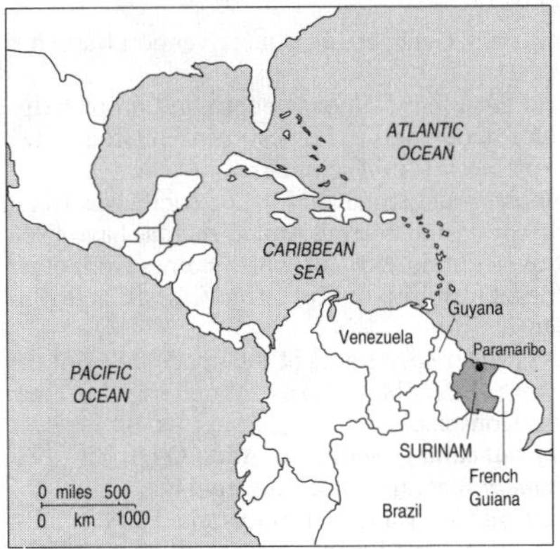

as prime minister; 40% of the population emigrated to the Netherlands.
1980 Arron's government overthrown in army coup; Ferrier refused to recognize military regime; appointed Dr Henk Chin A Sen to lead civilian administration. Army replaced Ferrier with Dr Chin A Sen.
1982 Army, led by Lt Col Desi Bouterse, seized power, setting up a Revolutionary People's Front.
1985 Ban on political activities lifted.
1986 Antigovernment rebels brought economic chaos to Surinam.
1987 New constitution approved.
1988 Ramsewak Shankar elected president.
1989 Bouterse rejected peace accord reached by President Shankar with guerrilla insurgents, vowed to continue fighting.
1990 Shankar deposed in army coup.
1991 Johan Kraag became interim president. New Front for Democracy won assembly majority. Ronald Venetiaan elected president.
1992 Peace accord with guerrilla groups.

Swaziland

Kingdom of (*Umbuso weSwatini*)

area 17,400 sq km/6,716 sq mi
capital Mbabane
towns Manzini, Big Bend
physical central valley; mountains in W (Highveld); plateau in E (Lowveld and Lubombo plateau)
features landlocked enclave between South Africa and Mozambique
head of state and government King Mswati III from 1986
political system near-absolute monarchy
political party Imbokodvo National Movement (INM), nationalist monarchist
exports sugar, canned fruit, wood pulp, asbestos
currency lilangeni
population (1992) 826,000; growth rate 3% p.a. ***life expectancy*** men 47, women 54 (1989)
languages Swazi 90%, English (both official)
religions Christian 57%, animist
literacy men 70%, women 66% (1985 est)
GNP $539 million; $750 per head (1987)

chronology
1903 Swaziland became a special High Commission territory.
1967 Achieved internal self-government.
1968 Independence achieved from Britain, within the Commonwealth, as the Kingdom of Swaziland, with King Sobhuza II as head of state.
1973 The king suspended the constitution and assumed absolute powers.
1978 New constitution adopted.
1982 King Sobhuza died; his place was taken by one of his wives, Dzeliwe, until his son, Prince Makhosetive, reached the age of 21.
1983 Queen Dzeliwe ousted by another wife, Ntombi.
1984 After royal power struggle, it was announced that the crown prince would become king at 18.
1986 Crown prince formally invested as King Mswati III.
1987 Power struggle developed between advisory council Liqoqo and Queen Ntombi over accession of king. Mswati dissolved parliament; new government elected with Sotsha Dlamini as prime minister.
1991 Calls for democratic reform.
1992 Mswati dissolved parliament, assuming 'executive powers'.

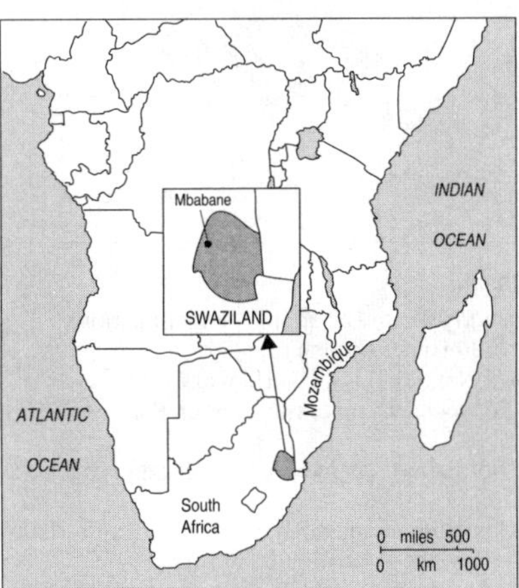

Sweden

Kingdom of (*Konungariket Sverige*)

area 450,000 sq km/173,745 sq mi
capital Stockholm
towns Göteborg, Malmö, Uppsala, Norrköping, Västerås
physical mountains in W; plains in S; thickly forested; more than 20,000 islands off the Stockholm coast
environment of the country's 90,000 lakes, 20,000 are affected by acid rain; 4,000 are so severely acidified that no fish are thought to survive in them
features lakes, including Vänern, Vättern, Mälaren, Hjälmaren; islands of Öland and Gotland; wild elk
head of state King Carl XVI Gustaf from 1973
head of government Carl Bildt from 1991
political system constitutional monarchy
political parties Social Democratic Labour party (SAP), moderate, left of centre; Moderate Party, right of centre; Liberal Party, centre-left; Centre Party, centrist; Christian Democratic Party, Christian,

centrist; Left (Communist) Party, European, Marxist; Green, ecological
exports aircraft, vehicles, ballbearings, drills, missiles, electronics, petrochemicals, textiles, furnishings, ornamental glass, paper, iron and steel
currency krona
population (1992) 8,673,000 (including 17,000 Saami [Lapps] and 1.2 million immigrants from Turkey, Yugoslavia, Greece, Iran, Finland and other Nordic countries); growth rate 0.1% p.a.
life expectancy men 74, women 81 (1989)
languages Swedish; there are Finnish- and Saami-speaking minorities
religion Lutheran (official) 95%
literacy 99% (1989)
GNP $245.8 bn (1992)

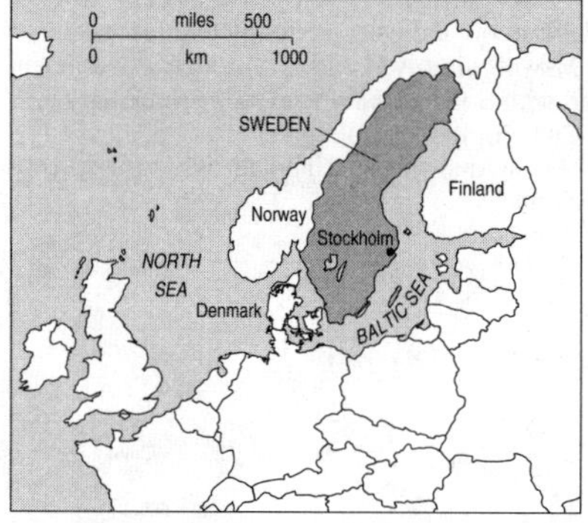

chronology
12th century United as an independent nation.
1397–1520 Under Danish rule.
1914–45 Neutral in both world wars.
1951–76 Social Democratic Labour Party (SAP) in power.
1969 Olof Palme became SAP leader and prime minister.
1971 Constitution amended, creating a single-chamber Riksdag, the governing body.
1975 Monarch's last constitutional powers removed.
1976 Thorbjörn Fälldin, leader of the Centre Party, became prime minister, heading centre-right coalition.
1982 SAP, led by Palme, returned to power.
1985 SAP formed minority government, with Communist support.
1986 Olof Palme murdered. Ingvar Carlsson became prime minister and SAP party leader.
1988 SAP re-elected with reduced majority; Green Party gained representation in Riksdag.
1990 SAP government resigned.
1991 Formal application for European Community (EC) membership submitted. Election defeat for SAP; Carlsson resigned. Coalition government formed; Carl Bildt became new prime minister.
1992 Cross-party collaboration to solve economic problems.

Switzerland

Swiss Confederation (German ***Schweiz***, French ***Suisse***, Romansch ***Svizzera***)
area 41,300 sq km/15,946 sq mi
capital Bern
towns Zürich, Geneva, Lausanne; river port Basel (on the Rhine)
physical most mountainous country in Europe (Alps and Jura mountains); highest peak Dufourspitze 4,634 m/15,203 ft in Apennines
environment an estimated 43% of coniferous trees, particularly in the central Alpine region, have been killed by acid rain, 90% of which comes from other countries. Over 50% of bird species are classified as threatened
features winter sports area of the upper valley of the river Inn (Engadine); lakes Maggiore, Lucerne, Geneva, Constance
head of state and government Adolf Ogi from 1993
government federal democratic republic
political parties Radical Democratic Party (FDP), radical, centre-left; Social Democratic Party (SPS), moderate, left of centre; Christian Democratic Party (PDC), Christian, moderate, centrist; People's Party (SVP), centre-left; Liberal Party (PLS), federalist, centre-left; Green Party, ecological
exports electrical goods, chemicals, pharmaceuticals, watches, precision instruments, confectionery
currency Swiss franc
population (1992) 6,911,000; growth rate 0.2% p.a.
life expectancy men 74, women 82 (1989)
languages German 65%, French 18%, Italian 12%, Romansch 1% (all official)
religions Roman Catholic 50%, Protestant 48%
literacy 99% (1989)
GNP $240.5 bn (1992)

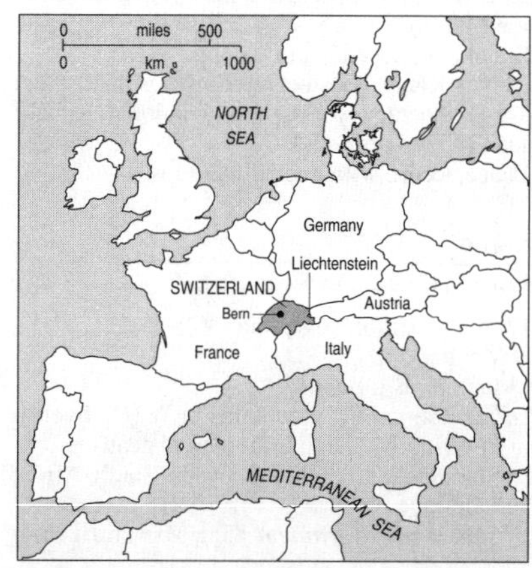

chronology
1648 Became independent of the Holy Roman Empire.
1798–1815 Helvetic Republic established by French revolutionary armies.
1847 Civil war resulted in greater centralization.
1874 Principle of the referendum introduced.
1971 Women given the vote in federal elections.
1984 First female cabinet minister appointed.
1986 Referendum rejected proposal for membership of United Nations.
1989 Referendum supported abolition of citizen army and military service requirements.

1991 18-year-olds allowed to vote for first time in national elections. Four-party coalition remained in power.
1992 René Felber elected president with Adolf Ogi as vice president. Closer ties with European Community rejected in national referendum.
1993 Ogi replaced Felber as head of state.

Syria

Syrian Arab Republic (*al- Jamhuriya al-Arabya as-Suriya*)

area 185,200 sq km/71,506 sq mi
capital Damascus
towns Aleppo, Homs, Hama; chief port Latakia
physical mountains alternate with fertile plains and desert areas; Euphrates River
features Mount Hermon, Golan Heights; crusader castles (including Krak des Chevaliers); Phoenician city sites (Ugarit), ruins of ancient Palmyra
head of state and government Hafez al-Assad from 1971
political system socialist republic
political parties National Progressive Front (NPF), pro-Arab, socialist; Communist Action Party, socialist
exports cotton, cereals, oil, phosphates, tobacco
currency Syrian pound
population (1992) 12,471,000; growth rate 3.5% p.a.
life expectancy men 67, women 69 (1989)
languages Arabic 89% (official), Kurdish 6%, Armenian 3%
religions Sunni Muslim 74%; ruling minority Alawite, and other Islamic sects 16%; Christian 10%
literacy men 76%, women 43% (1985 est)
GNP $17 bn (1986); $702 per head

chronology
1946 Achieved full independence from France.
1958 Merged with Egypt to form the United Arab Republic (UAR).
1961 UAR disintegrated.
1967 Six-Day War resulted in the loss of territory to Israel.
1970–71 Syria supported Palestinian guerrillas against Jordanian troops.
1971 Following a bloodless coup, Hafez al-Assad became president.
1973 Israel consolidated its control of the Golan Heights after the Yom Kippur War.
1976 Substantial numbers of troops committed to the civil war in Lebanon.
1978 Assad re-elected.
1981–82 Further military engagements in Lebanon.
1982 Islamic militant uprising suppressed; 5,000 dead.
1984 Presidents Assad and Gemayel approved plans for government of national unity in Lebanon.
1985 Assad secured the release of 39 US hostages held in an aircraft hijacked by extremist Shi'ite group, Hezbollah. Assad re-elected.
1987 Improved relations with USA and attempts to secure the release of Western hostages in Lebanon.
1989 Diplomatic relations with Morocco restored. Continued fighting in Lebanon; Syrian forces reinforced in Lebanon; diplomatic relations with Egypt restored.
1990 Diplomatic relations with Britain restored.
1991 Syria fought against Iraq in Gulf War. President Assad agreed to US Middle East peace plan. Assad re-elected president.
1993 Syria joined Iraq and other Arab countries in boycotting UN treaty outlawing production and use of chemical weapons.

Taiwan

Republic of China (*Chung Hua Min Kuo*)

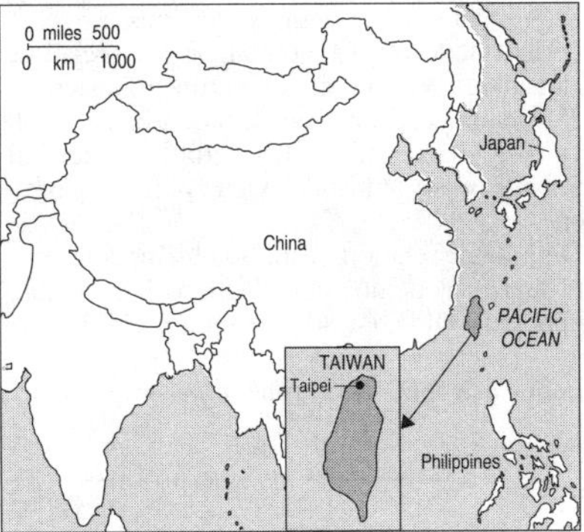

area 36,179 sq km/13,965 sq mi
capital Taipei
towns ports Kaohsiung, Keelung
physical island (formerly Formosa) off People's Republic of China; mountainous, with lowlands in W
environment industrialization has taken its toll: an estimated 30% of the annual rice crop is dangerously contaminated with mercury, cadmium, and other heavy metals
features Penghu (Pescadores), Jinmen (Quemoy), Mazu (Matsu) islands
head of state Lee Teng-hui from 1988
head of government Lien Chan from 1993
political system emergent democracy
political parties Nationalist Party of China (Kuomintang: KMT), anticommunist, Chinese nationalist; Democratic Progressive Party (DPP), centrist-pluralist, pro-self-determination grouping; Workers' Party (Kuntang), left of centre
exports textiles, steel, plastics, electronics, foodstuffs
currency New Taiwan dollar

population (1992) 20,727,000 (Taiwanese 84%, mainlanders 14%); growth rate 1.4% p.a.
life expectancy 70 men, 75 women (1986)
languages Mandarin Chinese (official); Taiwan, Hakka dialects
religions officially atheist; Taoist, Confucian, Buddhist, Christian
literacy 90% (1988)
GNP $119.1 bn; $6,200 per head (1988)

chronology
1683 Taiwan (Formosa) annexed by China.
1895 Ceded to Japan.
1945 Recovered by China.
1949 Flight of Nationalist government to Taiwan after Chinese communist revolution.
1954 US-Taiwanese mutual defence treaty.
1971 Expulsion from United Nations.
1972 Commencement of legislature elections.
1975 President Chiang Kai-shek died; replaced as Kuomintang leader by his son, Chiang Ching-kuo.
1979 USA severed diplomatic relations and annulled 1954 security pact.
1986 Democratic Progressive Party (DPP) formed as opposition to the nationalist Kuomintang.
1987 Martial law lifted; opposition parties legalized; press restrictions lifted.
1988 President Chiang Ching-kuo died; replaced by Taiwanese-born Lee Teng-hui.
1989 Kuomintang won assembly elections.
1990 Formal move towards normalization of relations with China. Hau Pei-tsun became prime minister.
1991 President Lee Teng-hui declared end to state of civil war with China. Constitution amended. Kuomintang won landslide victory in assembly elections.
1992 Diplomatic relations with South Korea broken. Dec: in first fully democratic elections Kuomintang lost support to DPP but still secured a majority of seats.
1993 Lien Chan appointed prime minister.

Tajikistan

Republic of

area 143,100 sq km/55,251 sq mi
capital Dushanbe
towns Khodzhent (formerly Leninabad), Kurgan-Tyube, Kulyab
physical mountainous, more than half of its territory lying above 3,000 m/10,000 ft; huge mountain glaciers, which are the source of many rapid rivers
features Pik Kommunizma (Communism Peak); health resorts and mineral springs
head of state Akbasho Iskandrov from 1992
head of government Abdumalik Abdullajanov from 1992
political system emergent democracy
political parties Socialist (formerly Communist) Party of Tajikistan (SPT); Democratic Party; Islamic Revival Party
products fruit, cereals, cotton, cattle, sheep, silks, carpets, coal, lead, zinc, chemicals, oil, gas
population (1992) 5,568,000 (Tajik 63%, Uzbek 24%, Russian 8%, Tatar 1%, Kyrgyz 1%, Ukrainian 1%)
language Tajik, similar to Farsi (Persian)
religion Sunni Muslim

chronology
1921 Part of Turkestan Soviet Socialist Autonomous Republic.
1929 Became a constituent republic of USSR.
1990 Ethnic Tajik-Armenian conflict in Dushanbe resulted in rioting against Communist Party of Tajikistan (TCP); state of emergency and curfew imposed.
1991 Jan: curfew lifted in Dushanbe. March: maintenance of Soviet Union endorsed in referendum. Aug: President Makhkamov forced to resign after failed anti-Gorbachev coup; TCP broke links with Moscow. Sept: declared independence; Rakhman Nabiyev elected president; TCP renamed Socialist Party of Tajikistan; state of emergency declared. Dec: joined new Commonwealth of Independent States.
1992 Jan: admitted into Conference for Security and Cooperation in Europe. Nabiyev temporarily ousted; state of emergency lifted. Feb: joined the Muslim Economic Cooperation Organization. March: admitted into United Nations; US diplomatic recognition achieved. May: coalition government formed. Sept: Nabiyev forced to resign; replaced by Akbasho Iskandrov; Abdumalik Abdullajanov became prime minister.
1993 Civil war between the forces of the country's communist former rulers and Islamic and prodemocracy groups continued to rage.

Tanzania

United Republic of (*Jamhuri ya Muungano wa Tanzania*)

area 945,000 sq km/364,865 sq mi
capital Dodoma (since 1983)
towns Zanzibar Town, Mwanza; chief port and former capital Dar es Salaam
physical central plateau; lakes in N and W; coastal plains; lakes Victoria, Tanganyika, and Niasa
environment the black rhino faces extinction as a result of poaching
features comprises islands of Zanzibar and Pemba; Mount Kilimanjaro, 5,895 m/19,340 ft, the highest peak in Africa; Serengeti National Park, Olduvai Gorge; Ngorongoro Crater, 14.5 km/9 mi across, 762 m/2,500 ft deep

head of state and government Ali Hassan Mwinyi from 1985
political system one-party socialist republic
political party Revolutionary Party of Tanzania (CCM), African, socialist
exports coffee, cotton, sisal, cloves, tea, tobacco, cashew nuts, diamonds
currency Tanzanian shilling
population (1992) 25,809,000; growth rate 3.5% p.a.
life expectancy men 49, women 54 (1989)
languages Kiswahili, English (both official)
religions Muslim 35%, Christian 35%, traditional 30%
literacy 85% (1987)
GNP $4.9 bn; $258 per head (1987)

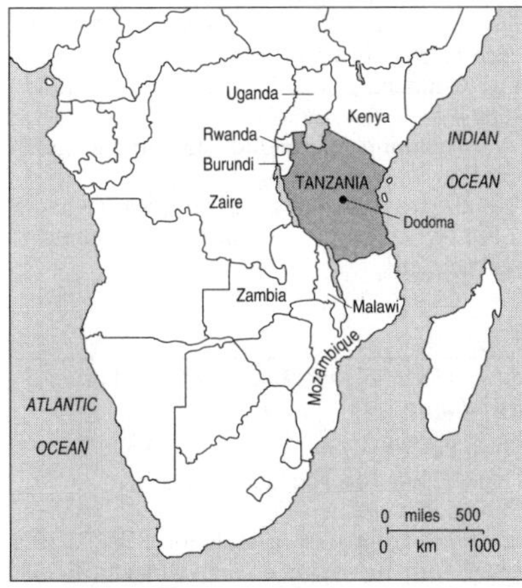

chronology
16th–17th centuries Zanzibar under Portuguese control.
1890–1963 Zanzibar became a British protectorate.
1920–46 Tanganyika administered as a British League of Nations mandate.
1946–62 Tanganyika came under United Nations (UN) trusteeship.
1961 Tanganyika achieved independence from Britain, within the Commonwealth, with Julius Nyerere as prime minister.
1962 Tanganyika became a republic with Nyerere as president.
1964 Tanganyika and Zanzibar became the United Republic of Tanzania with Nyerere as president.
1967 East African Community (EAC) formed. Nyerere comitted himself to building a socialist state (the Arusha Declaration).
1977 Revolutionary Party of Tanzania (CCM) proclaimed the only legal party. EAC dissolved.
1978 Ugandan forces repulsed after crossing into Tanzania.
1979 Tanzanian troops sent to Uganda to help overthrow the president, Idi Amin.
1985 Nyerere retired from presidency but stayed on as CCM leader; Ali Hassan Mwinyi became president.
1990 Nyerere surrendered CCM leadership; replaced by President Mwinyi.
1992 CCM agreed to abolish one-party rule. East African cooperation pact with Kenya and Uganda to be re- established.

Thailand

Kingdom of (*Prathet Thai* or *Muang-Thai*)

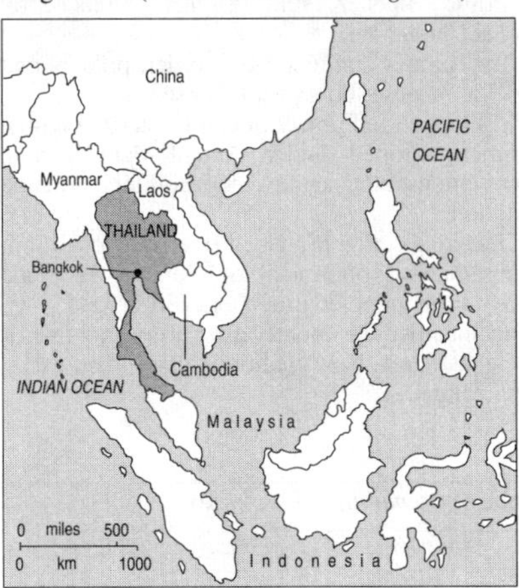

area 513,115 sq km/198,108 sq mi
capital and chief port Bangkok
towns Chiangmai, Nakhon Sawan river port
physical mountainous, semi-arid plateau in NE, fertile central region, tropical isthmus in S
environment tropical rainforest was reduced to 18% of the land area 1988 (from 93% in 1961); logging was banned by the government 1988
features rivers Chao Phraya, Mekong, Salween; ancient ruins of Sukhothai and Ayurrhaya
head of state King Bhumibol Adulyadej from 1946
head of government Chuan Leekpai from 1992
political system military-controlled emergent democracy
political parties New Aspiration Party; Samakkhi Tham (Justice and Unity) Party, right of centre, airforce-linked; Palang Dharma, anti-corruption; Social Action Party (Kij Sangkhom), right of centre; Thai Nation (Chart Thai), conservative, pro-business; Liberal Democratic Party
exports rice, textiles, rubber, tin, rubies, sapphires, maize, tapioca
currency baht
population (1992) 56,801,000 (Thai 75%, Chinese 14%); growth rate 2% p.a.
life expectancy men 62, women 68 (1989)
languages Thai and Chinese (both official); regional dialects
religions Buddhist 95%, Muslim 4%
literacy 89% (1988)
GNP $52 bn (1988); $771 per head (1988)
chronology
1782 Siam absolutist dynasty commenced.
1896 Anglo-French agreement recognized Siam as independent buffer state.
1932 Constitutional monarchy established.
1939 Name of Thailand adopted.
1941-44 Japanese occupation.
1947 Military seized power in coup.
1972 Withdrawal of Thai troops from South Vietnam.
1973 Military government overthrown.
1976 Military reassumed control.
1980 General Prem Tinsulanonda assumed power.

1983 Civilian government formed; martial law maintained.
1988 Prime Minister Prem resigned; replaced by Chatichai Choonhavan.
1989 Thai pirates continued to murder, pillage, and kidnap Vietnamese 'boat people' at sea.
1991 Military seized power in coup. Interim civilian government formed under Anand Panyarachun. 50,000 demonstrated against new military-oriented constitution.
1992 General election produced five-party coalition; the subsequent appointment of General Suchinda Kraprayoon as premier provoked widespread riots, and Suchinda fled the country after army shooting of 100 demonstrators. New coalition government led by Chuan Leekpai.

Togo

Republic of (*République Togolaise*)

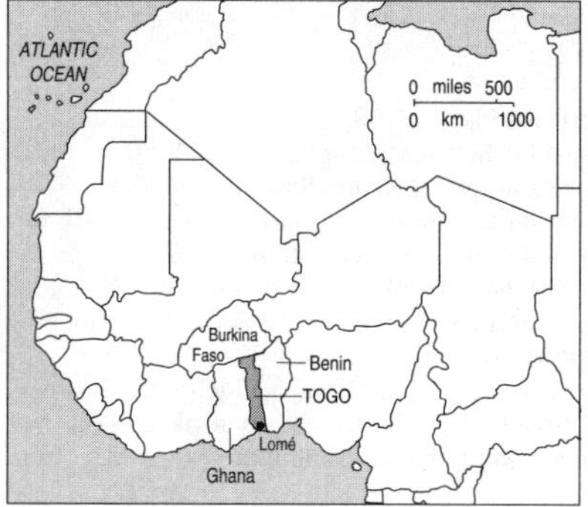

area 56,800 sq km/21,930 sq mi
capital Lomé
towns Sokodé, Kpalimé
physical two savanna plains, divided by range of hills NE–SW; coastal lagoons and marsh
environment the homes of thousands of people in Keto were destroyed by coastal erosion as a result of the building of the Volta dam
features Mono Tableland, Oti Plateau, Oti River
head of state Etienne Gnassingbé Eyadéma from 1967
head of government Jospeh Kokou Koffigoh from 1991
political system transitional
political parties Rally of the Togolese People (RPT), centrist nationalist; Alliance of Togolese Democrats (ADT), left of centre; Togolese Movement for Democracy (MDT), left of centre
exports phosphates, cocoa, coffee, coconuts
currency franc CFA
population (1992) 3,701,000; growth rate 3% p.a.
life expectancy men 53, women 57 (1989)
languages French (official), Ewe, Kabre
religions animist 46%, Catholic 28%, Muslim 17%, Protestant 9%
literacy men 53%, women 28% (1985 est)
GNP $1.3 bn (1987); $240 per head (1985)
chronology
1885–1914 Togoland was a German protectorate until captured by Anglo-French forces.
1922 Divided between Britain and France under League of Nations mandate.
1946 Continued under United Nations trusteeship.
1956 British Togoland integrated with Ghana.
1960 French Togoland achieved independence from France as the Republic of Togo with Sylvanus Olympio as head of state.
1963 Olympio killed in a military coup. Nicolas Grunitzky became president.
1967 Grunitzky replaced by Lt-Gen Etienne Gnassingbé Eyadéma in bloodless coup.
1973 Assembly of Togolese People (RPT) formed as sole legal political party.
1975 EEC Lomé convention signed in Lomé, establishing trade links with developing countries.
1979 Eyadéma returned in election. Further EEC Lomé convention signed.
1986 Attempted coup failed.
1991 Eyadéma legalized opposition parties. National conference elected Joseph Kokou Koffigoh head of interim government; troops loyal to Eyadéma failed to reinstate him.
1992 Overwhelming referendum support for multiparty politics.
1993 Feb: all-party talks to avoid civil war began in France but were suspended after disagreements among participants.

Tonga

Kingdom of (*Pule'anga Fakatu'i 'o Tonga*) or ***Friendly Islands***

area 750 sq km/290 sq mi
capital Nuku'alofa (on Tongatapu island)
towns Pangai, Neiafu
physical three groups of islands in SW Pacific, mostly coral formations, but actively volcanic in W
features of 170 islands in the Tonga group, 36 are inhabited
head of state King Taufa'ahau Tupou IV from 1965
head of government Baron Vaea from 1991
political system constitutional monarchy
political parties none
currency Tongan dollar or pa'anga
population (1992) 97,300; growth rate 2.4% p.a.
life expectancy men 69, women 74 (1989)
languages Tongan (official), English
religions Wesleyan 47%, Roman Catholic 14%, Free Church of Tonga 14%, Mormon 9%, Church of Tonga 9%
literacy 93% (1988)
GNP $65 million (1987); $430 per head

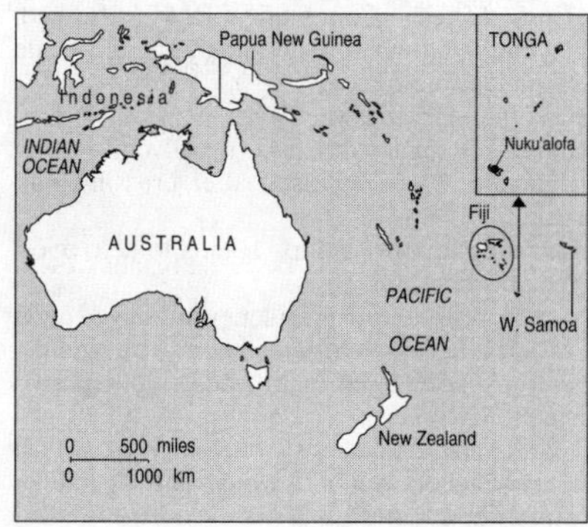

chronology
1831 Tongan dynasty founded by Prince Taufa'ahau Tupou.
1900 Became a British protectorate.
1965 Queen Salote died; succeeded by her son, King Taufa'ahau Tupou IV.
1970 Independence achieved from Britain within the Commonwealth.
1990 Three prodemocracy candidates elected. Calls for reform of absolutist power.

Trinidad and Tobago

Republic of

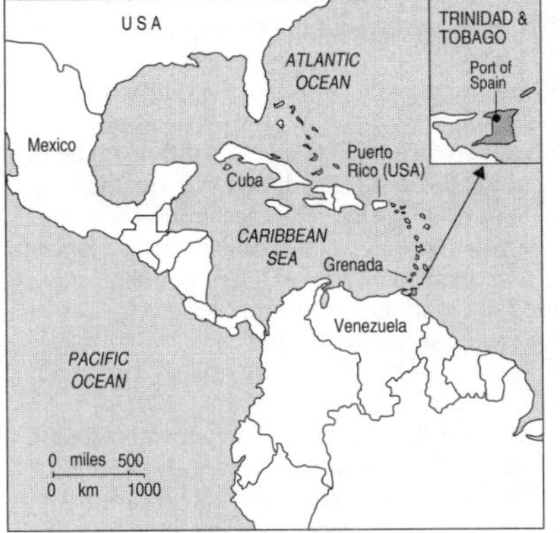

area Trinidad 4,828 sq km/1,864 sq mi and Tobago 300 sq km/116 sq mi
capital Port-of-Spain
towns San Fernando, Arima, Scarborough (Tobago)
physical comprises two main islands and some smaller ones; coastal swamps and hills E–W
features Pitch Lake, a self-renewing source of asphalt used by 16th-century explorer Walter Raleigh to repair his ships
head of state Noor Hassanali from 1987
head of government Patrick Manning from 1991
political system democratic republic
political parties National Alliance for Reconstruction (NAR), nationalist, left of centre; People's National Movement (PNM), nationalist, moderate, centrist
exports oil, petroleum products, chemicals, sugar, cocoa
currency Trinidad and Tobago dollar
population (1992) 1,261,000 (African descent 40%, Indian 40%, European 16%, Chinese and others 2%), 1.2 million on Trinidad; growth rate 1.6% p.a.
life expectancy men 68, women 72 (1989)
languages English (official), Hindi, French, Spanish
media freedom of press guaranteed by constitution and upheld by government; there are two independent morning newspapers and several weekly tabloids
religions Roman Catholic 32%, Protestant 29%, Hindu 25%, Muslim 6%
literacy 97% (1988)
GNP $4.5 bn; $3,731 per head (1987)

chronology
1888 Trinidad and Tobago united as a British colony.
1956 People's National Movement (PNM) founded.
1959 Achieved internal self-government, with PNM leader Eric Williams as chief minister.
1962 Independence achieved from Britain, within the Commonwealth, with Williams as prime minister.
1976 Became a republic, with Ellis Clarke as president and Williams as prime minister.
1981 Williams died and was succeeded by George Chambers, with Arthur Robinson as opposition leader.
1986 National Alliance for Reconstruction (NAR), headed by Arthur Robinson, won general election.
1987 Noor Hassanali became president.
1990 Attempted antigovernment coup defeated.
1991 General election saw victory for PNM, with Patrick Manning as prime minister.

Tunisia

Tunisian Republic (*al-Jumhuriya at-Tunisiya*)

area 164,150 sq km/63,378 sq mi
capital and chief port Tunis
towns ports Sfax, Sousse, Bizerta
physical arable and forested land in N graduates towards desert in S
features fertile island of Jerba, linked to mainland by causeway (identified with island of lotus-eaters); Shott el Jerid salt lakes; holy city of Kairouan, ruins of Carthage
head of state and government Zine el-Abidine Ben Ali from 1987
political system emergent democratic republic
political party Constitutional Democratic Rally (RCD), nationalist, moderate, socialist
exports oil, phosphates, chemicals, textiles, food, olive oil
currency dinar
population (1992) 8,413,000; growth rate 2% p.a.
life expectancy men 68, women 71 (1989)
languages Arabic (official), French
media publications must be authorized; the offence of defamation is used to protect members of the government from criticism
religion Sunni Muslim 95%; Jewish, Christian
literacy men 68%, women 41% (1985 est)
GNP $9.6 bn (1987); $1,163 per head (1986)

chronology
1883 Became a French protectorate.
1955 Granted internal self-government.

1956 Independence achieved from France as a monarchy, with Habib Bourguiba as prime minister.
1957 Became a republic with Bourguiba as president.
1975 Bourguiba made president for life.
1985 Diplomatic relations with Libya severed.
1987 Bourguiba removed Prime Minister Rashed Sfar and appointed Zine el-Abidine Ben Ali. Ben Ali declared Bourguiba incompetent and seized power.
1988 Constitutional changes towards democracy announced. Diplomatic relations with Libya restored.
1989 Government party, RDC, won all assembly seats in general election.
1991 Opposition to US actions during the Gulf War. Crackdown on religious fundamentalists.

Turkey

Republic of (*Türkiye Cumhuriyeti*)

area 779,500 sq km/300,965 sq mi
capital Ankara
towns ports Istanbul and Izmir
physical central plateau surrounded by mountains
environment only 0.3% of the country is protected by national parks and reserves compared with a global average of 7% per country
features Bosporus and Dardanelles; Mount Ararat; Taurus Mountains in SW (highest peak Kaldi Dağ, 3,734 m/12,255 ft); sources of rivers Euphrates and Tigris in E; archaeological sites include Çatal Hüyük, Ephesus, and Troy; rock villages of Cappadocia; historic towns (Antioch, Iskenderun, Tarsus)
head of state Suleyman Demirel from 1993
head of government Tansu Ciller from 1993
political system democratic republic
political parties Motherland Party (ANAP), Islamic, nationalist, right of centre; Social Democratic Populist Party (SDPP), moderate, left of centre; True Path Party (TPP), centre-right
exports cotton, yarn, hazelnuts, citrus, tobacco, dried fruit, chromium ores
currency Turkish lira
population (1992) 58,584,000 (Turkish 85%, Kurdish 12%); growth rate 2.1% p.a.
life expectancy men 63, women 66 (1989)
languages Turkish (official), Kurdish, Arabic
religion Sunni Muslim 98%
literacy men 86%, women 62% (1985)
GNP $112.5 bn (1992)
chronology
1919–22 Turkish War of Independence provoked by Greek occupation of Izmir. Mustafa Kemal (Atatürk), leader of nationalist congress, defeated Italian, French, and Greek forces.
1923 Treaty of Lausanne established Turkey as independent republic under Kemal. Westernization began.
1950 First free elections; Adnan Menderes became prime minister.
1960 Menderes executed after military coup by General Cemal Gürsel.
1965 Suleyman Demirel became prime minister.
1971 Army forced Demirel to resign.
1973 Civilian rule returned under Bulent Ecevit.
1974 Turkish troops sent to protect Turkish community in Cyprus.
1975 Demirel returned to head of a right-wing coalition.
1978 Ecevit returned, as head of coalition, in the face of economic difficulties and factional violence.
1979 Demeril returned. Violence grew.
1980 Army took over, and Bulent Ulusu became prime minister. Harsh repression of political activists attracted international criticism.
1982 New constitution adopted.
1983 Ban on political activity lifted. Turgut Özal became prime minister.
1987 Özal maintained majority in general election.
1988 Improved relations and talks with Greece.
1989 Turgut Özal elected president; Yildirim Akbulut became prime minister. Application to join European Community (EC) rejected.
1991 Mesut Yilmaz became prime minister. Turkey sided with UN coalition against Iraq in Gulf War. Conflict with Kurdish minority continued. Coalition government formed under Suleyman Demirel after inconclusive election result.
1992 Earthquake claimed thousands of lives.
1993 Özal died and was succeeded by Demirel. Tansu Ciller became first female prime minister.

Turkmenistan

Republic of

area 488,100 sq km/188,406 sq mi
capital Ashkhabad
towns Chardzhov, Mary (Merv), Nebit-Dag, Krasnovodsk
physical some 90% of land is desert including the Kara Kum 'Black Sands' desert (area 310,800 sq km/120,000 sq mi)
features on the edge of the Kara Kum desert is the Altyn Depe, 'golden hill', site of a ruined city with a ziggurat, or stepped pyramid; river Amu Darya; rich deposits of petroleum, natural gas, sulphur, and other industrial raw materials
head of state Saparmurad Niyazov from 1991
head of government Sakhat Muradov from 1992
political system socialist pluralist
products silk, karakul, sheep, astrakhan fur, carpets, chemicals, rich deposits of petroleum, natural gas, sulphur, and other industrial raw materials
population (1992) 3,859,000 (Turkmen 72%, Russian 10%, Uzbek 9%, Kazakh 3%, Ukrainian 1%)
language West Turkic, closely related to Turkish
religion Sunni Muslim

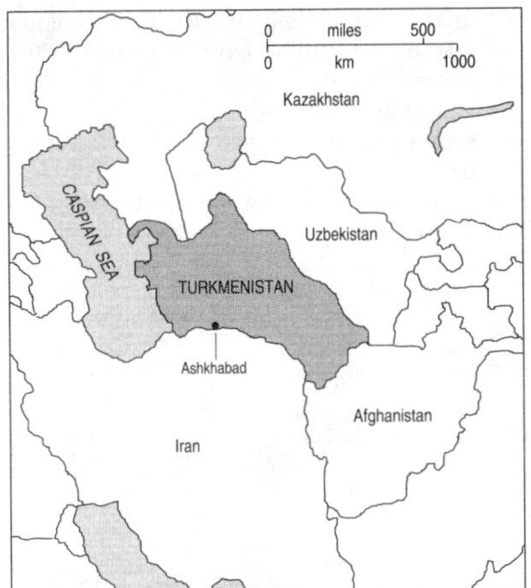

chronology
1921 Part of Turkestan Soviet Socialist Autonomous Republic.
1925 Became a constituent republic of USSR.
1990 Aug: economic and political sovereignty declared.
1991 Jan: Communist Party leader Sakhat Niyazov became state president. March: endorsed maintenance of the Union in USSR referendum. Aug: Niyazov initially supported attempted anti-Gorbachev coup. Oct: independence declared. Dec: joined new Commonwealth of Independent States.
1992 Jan: admitted into Conference for Security and Cooperation in Europe. Feb: joined the Muslim Economic Cooperation Organization. March: admitted into United Nations; US diplomatic recognition achieved. May: new constitution adopted. Nov–Dec: 60-member assembly popularly elected with Sakhat Muradov as prime minister.

Tuvalu

South West Pacific State of (formerly ***Ellice Islands***)

area 25 sq km/9.5 sq mi
capital Funafuti
physical nine low coral atolls forming a chain of 579 km/650 mi in the SW Pacific

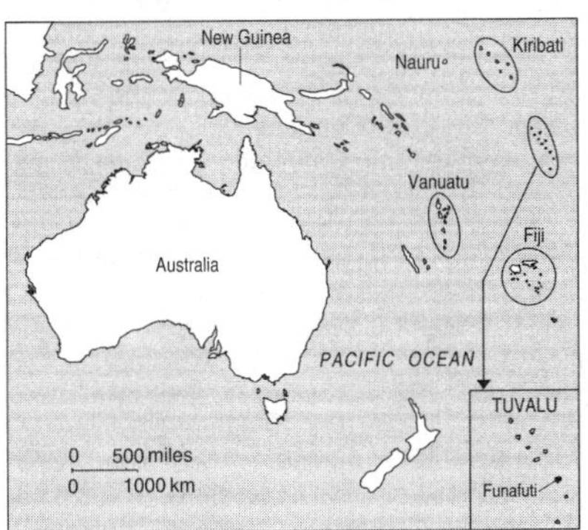

features maximum height above sea level 6 m/20 ft; coconut palms are main vegetation
head of state Elizabeth II from 1978, represented by governor general
head of government Bikenibeu Paeniu from 1989
political system liberal democracy
political parties none; members are elected to parliament as independents
exports copra, handicrafts, stamps
currency Australian dollar
population (1992) 9,500 (Polynesian 96%); growth rate 3.4% p.a.
life expectancy 60 men, 63 women (1989)
languages Tuvaluan, English
religion Christian (Protestant)
literacy 96% (1985)
GDP (1983) $711 per head

chronology
1892 Became a British protectorate forming part of the Gilbert and Ellice Islands group.
1916 The islands acquired colonial status.
1975 The Ellice Islands were separated from the Gilbert Islands.
1978 Independence achieved from Britain, within the Commonwealth, with Toaripi Lauti as prime minister; reverted to former name Tuvalu.
1981 Dr Tomasi Puapua replaced Lauti as premier.
1986 Islanders rejected proposal for republican status.
1989 Bikenibeu Paeniu elected new prime minister.

Uganda

Republic of

area 236,600 sq km/91,351 sq mi
capital Kampala
towns Jinja, M'Bale, Entebbe, Masaka
physical plateau with mountains in W; forest and grassland; arid in NE
features Ruwenzori Range (Mount Margherita, 5,110 m/16,765 ft); national parks with wildlife (chimpanzees, crocodiles, Nile perch to 70 kg/160 lb); Owen Falls on White Nile where it leaves Lake Victoria; Lake Albert in W
head of state and government Yoweri Museveni from 1986
political system emergent democratic republic
political parties National Resistance Movement (NRM), left of centre; Democratic Party (DP), centre-left; Conservative Party (CP), centre-right; Uganda People's Congress (UPC), left of centre; Uganda Freedom Movement (UFM), left of centre
exports coffee, cotton, tea, copper
currency Uganda new shilling
population (1992) 17,194,000 (largely the Baganda, after whom the country is named; also Langi and Acholi, some surviving Pygmies); growth rate 3.3% p.a.
life expectancy men 49, women 51 (1989)
languages English (official), Kiswahili, Luganda, and other African languages
religions Roman Catholic 33%, Protestant 33%, Muslim 16%, animist
literacy men 70%, women 45% (1985 est)
GNP $3.6 bn (1987); $220 per head

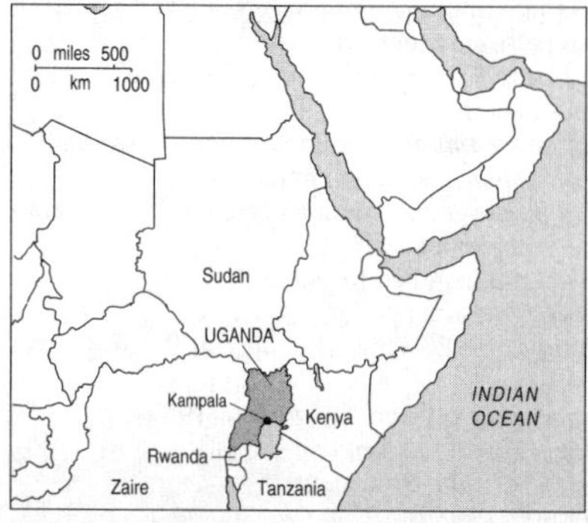

chronology
1962 Independence achieved from Britain, within the Commonwealth, with Milton Obote as prime minister.
1963 Proclaimed a federal republic with King Mutesa II as president.
1966 King Mutesa ousted in coup led by Obote, who ended the federal status and became executive president.
1969 All opposition parties banned after assassination attempt on Obote.
1971 Obote overthrown in army coup led by Maj-Gen Idi Amin Dada; ruthlessly dictatorial regime established; nearly 49,000 Ugandan Asians expelled; over 300,000 opponents of regime killed.
1978 Amin forced to leave country by opponents backed by Tanzanian troops. Provisional government set up with Yusuf Lule as president. Lule replaced by Godfrey Binaisa.
1978–79 Fighting broke out against Tanzanian troops.
1980 Binaisa overthrown by army. Elections held and Milton Obote returned to power.
1985 After opposition by National Resistance Army (NRA), and indiscipline in army, Obote ousted by Brig Tito Okello; power-sharing agreement entered into with NRA leader Yoweri Museveni.
1986 Agreement ended; Museveni became president, heading broad-based coalition government.
1992 Announcement made that East African cooperation pact with Kenya and Tanzania would be revived.

Ukraine

area 603,700 sq km/233,089 sq mi
capital Kiev
towns Kharkov, Donetsk, Odessa, Dnepropetrovsk, Lugansk (Voroshilovgrad), Lviv (Lvov), Mariupol (Zhdanov), Krivoi Rog, Zaporozhye
physical Russian plain; Carpathian and Crimean Mountains; rivers: Dnieper (with the Dnieper dam 1932), Donetz, Bug
features Askaniya-Nova Nature Reserve (established 1921); health spas with mineral springs
head of state Leonid Kravchuk from 1990
head of government Leonid Kuchma from 1992
political system emergent democracy
political party Ukrainian People's Movement (Rukh), umbrella nationalist grouping, with three leaders
products grain, coal, oil, various minerals
currency grivna
population (1992) 52,135,000 (Ukrainian 73%, Russian 22%, Byelorussian 1%, Russian-speaking Jews 1% – some 1.5 million have emigrated to the USA, 750,000 to Canada)
language Ukrainian (Slavonic)
famous people Ivan Kotlyarevsky and Taras Shevchenko
religions traditionally Ukrainian Orthodox; also Ukrainian Catholic

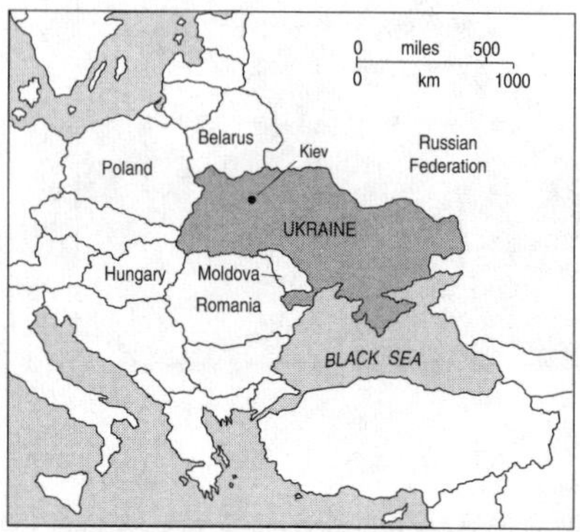

chronology
1918 Independent People's Republic proclaimed.
1920 Conquered by Soviet Red Army.
1921 Poland alloted charge of W Ukraine.
1932–33 Famine caused the deaths of more than 7.5 million people.
1939 W Ukraine occupied by Red Army.
1941–44 Under Nazi control; Jews massacred at Babi Yar; more than 5 million Ukrainians and Ukrainian Jews deported and exterminated.
1944 Soviet control re-established.
1945 Became a founder member of the United Nations.
1946 Ukrainian Uniate Church proscribed and forcibly merged with Russian Orthodox Church.
1986 April: Chernobyl nuclear disaster.
1989 Ukrainian People's Movement (Rukh) established. Ban on Ukrainian Uniate Church lifted.
1990 July: voted to proclaim sovereignty; former Communist Party (CP) leader Leonid Kravchuk indirectly elected president; sovereignty declared.
1991 Aug: demonstrations against the abortive anti-Gorbachev coup; independence declared, pending referendum; CP activities suspended. Oct: voted to create independent army. Dec: Kravchuk popularly elected president; independence overwhelmingly endorsed in referendum; joined new Commonwealth of Independent States; independence acknowledged by USA and European Community.
1992 Jan: admitted into Conference on Security and Cooperation in Europe (CSCE); pipeline deal with Iran to end dependence on Russian oil; prices freed. Feb: prices 'temporarily' re-regulated. March: agreed tactical arms shipments to Russia suspended. May: Crimean sovereignty declared, but subsequently rescinded. Aug: joint control of Black Sea fleet agreed with Russia. Oct: Leonid Kuchma became prime minister. Production declined by 20% during 1992.
1993 Inflation at 35% a month in early part of year; budget deficit at 44% of GDP. Kuchma resigned but was reinstated.

United Arab Emirates

(UAE) (*Ittihad al-Imarat al-Arabiyah*) federation of the emirates of Abu Dhabi, Ajman, Dubai, Fujairah, Ras al Khaimah, Sharjah, Umm al Qaiwain

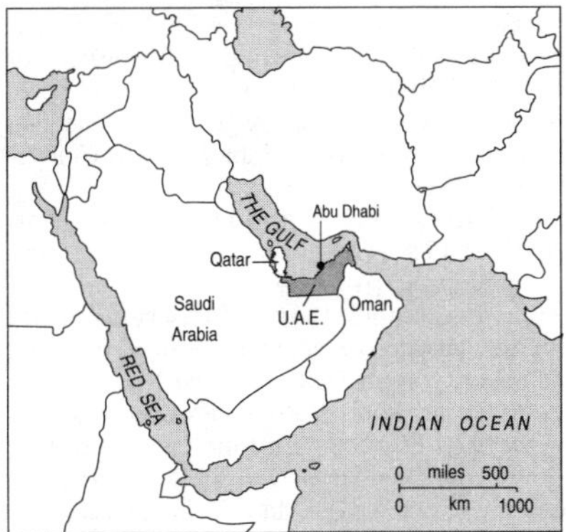

total area 83,657 sq km/32,292 sq mi
capital Abu Dhabi
towns (chief port) Dubai
physical desert and flat coastal plain; mountains in E
features linked by dependence on oil revenues
head of state and of government Sheik Sultan Zayed bin al-Nahayan of Abu Dhabi from 1971
political system absolutism
political parties none
exports oil, natural gas, fish, dates
currency UAE dirham
population (1992) 1,989,000 (10% nomadic); growth rate 6.1% p.a.
life expectancy men 68, women 72 (1989)
languages Arabic (official), Farsi, Hindi, Urdu, English
religions Muslim 96%, Christian, Hindu
literacy 68% (1989)
GNP $22 bn (1987); $11,900 per head

chronology
1952 Trucial Council established.
1971 Federation of Arab Emirates formed; later dissolved. Six Trucial States formed United Arab Emirates, with ruler of Abu Dhabi, Sheik Zayed, as president.
1972 The seventh state, Ras al Khaimah, joined the federation.
1976 Sheik Zayed threatened to relinquish presidency unless progress towards centralization became more rapid.
1985 Diplomatic and economic links with USSR and China established.
1987 Diplomatic relations with Egypt restored.
1990–91 Iraqi invasion of Kuwait opposed; UAE fights with UN coalition.
1991 Bank of Commerce and Credit International (BCCI), controlled by Abu Dhabi's ruler, collapsed.

United Kingdom

of Great Britain and Northern Ireland (UK)

area 244,100 sq km/94,247 sq mi
capital London
towns Birmingham, Glasgow, Leeds, Sheffield, Liverpool, Manchester, Edinburgh, Bradford, Bristol, Belfast, Newcastle-upon-Tyne, Cardiff
physical became separated from European continent about 6000 BC; rolling landscape, increasingly mountainous towards the N, with Grampian Mountains in Scotland, Pennines in N England, Cambrian Mountains in Wales; rivers include Thames, Severn, and Spey
territories Anguilla, Bermuda, British Antarctic Territory, British Indian Ocean Territory, British Virgin Islands, Cayman Islands, Falkland Islands, Gibraltar, Hong Kong (until 1997), Montserrat, Pitcairn Islands, St Helena and Dependencies (Ascension, Tristan da Cunha), Turks and Caicos Islands
environment an estimated 67% (the highest percentage in Europe) of forests have been damaged by acid rain
features milder climate than N Europe because of Gulf Stream; considerable rainfall. Nowhere more than 120 km/74.5 mi from sea; indented coastline, various small islands
head of state Elizabeth II from 1952
head of government John Major from 1990
political system liberal democracy
political parties Conservative and Unionist Party, right of centre; Labour Party, moderate left of centre; Social and Liberal Democrats, centre-left; Scottish National Party (SNP), Scottish nationalist; Plaid Cymru (Welsh Nationalist Party), Welsh nationalist; Official Ulster Unionist Party (OUP), Northern Ireland moderate right of centre; Democratic Unionist Party (DUP), Northern Ireland, right of centre; Social Democratic Labour Party (SDLP), Northern Ireland, moderate left of centre; Ulster People's Unionist Party (UPUP), Northern Ireland, militant right of centre; Sinn Féin, Northern Ireland, pro-united Ireland; Green Party, ecological
exports cereals, rape, sugar beet, potatoes, meat and meat products, poultry, dairy products, electronic and telecommunications equipment, engineering equipment and scientific instruments, oil and gas, petrochemicals, pharmaceuticals, fertilizers, film and television programmes, aircraft
currency pound sterling
population (1992) 57,561,000 (81.5% English, 9.6% Scottish, 1.9% Welsh, 2.4% Irish, 1.8% Ulster); growth rate 0.1% p.a.

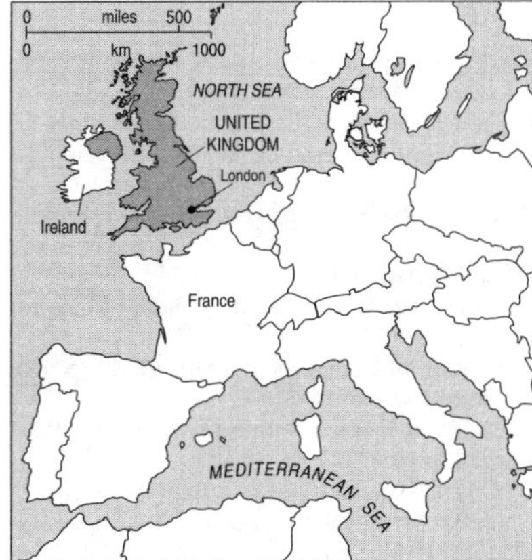

religion Christian (55% Protestant, 10% Roman Catholic); Muslim, Jewish, Hindu, Sikh
life expectancy men 72, women 78 (1989)
languages English, Welsh, Gaelic
literacy 99% (1989)
GNP $1,040.5 bn (1992)

chronology
1707 Act of Union between England and Scotland under Queen Anne.
1721 Robert Walpole unofficially first prime minister, under George I.
1783 Loss of North American colonies that form USA; Canada retained.
1801 Act of Ireland united Britain and Ireland.
1819 Peterloo massacre: cavalry charged a meeting of supporters of parliamentary reform.
1832 Great Reform Bill became law, shifting political power from upper to middle class.
1838 Chartist working-class movement formed.
1846 Corn Laws repealed by Robert Peel.
1851 Great Exhibition in London.
1867 Second Reform Bill, extending the franchise, introduced by Disraeli and passed.
1906 Liberal victory; programme of social reform.
1911 Powers of House of Lords curbed.
1914 Irish Home Rule Bill introduced.
1914-18 World War I.
1916 Lloyd George became prime minister.
1920 Home Rule Act incorporated NE of Ireland (Ulster) into the United Kingdom of Great Britain and Northern Ireland.
1921 Ireland, except for Ulster, became a dominion (Irish Free State, later Eire, 1937).
1924 First Labour government led by Ramsay MacDonald.
1926 General Strike.
1931 Coalition government; unemployment reached 3 million.
1939 World War II began.
1940 Winston Churchill became head of coalition government.
1945 Labour government under Clement Attlee; welfare state established.
1951 Conservatives under Winston Churchill defeated Labour.
1956 Suez Crisis.
1964 Labour victory under Harold Wilson.
1970 Conservatives under Edward Heath defeated Labour.
1972 Parliament prorogued in Northern Ireland; direct rule from Westminster began.
1973 UK joined European Economic Community.
1974 Three-day week, coal strike; Wilson replaced Heath.
1976 James Callaghan replaced Wilson as prime minister.
1977 Liberal–Labour pact.
1979 Victory for Conservatives under Margaret Thatcher.
1981 Formation of Social Democratic Party (SDP). Riots occurred in inner cities.
1982 Unemployment over 3 million. Falklands War.
1983 Thatcher re-elected.
1984-85 Coal strike, the longest in British history.
1986 Abolition of metropolitan counties.
1987 Thatcher re-elected for third term.
1988 Liberals and most of SDP merged into the Social and Liberal Democrats, leaving a splinter SDP. Inflation and interest rates rose.
1989 The Green Party polled 2 million votes in the European elections.
1990 Riots as poll tax introduced in England. Troops sent to the Persian Gulf following Iraq's invasion of Kuwait. British hostages held in Iraq, later released. Britain joined European exchange rate mechanism (ERM). Thatcher replaced by John Major as Conservative leader and prime minister.
1991 British troops took part in US-led war against Iraq under United Nations umbrella. Severe economic recession and rising unemployment.
1992 Recession continued. April: Conservative Party won fourth consecutive general election, but with reduced majority. John Smith replaced Neil Kinnock as Labour leader. Sept: sterling devalued and UK withdrawn from ERM. Oct: drastic pit-closure programme encountered massive public opposition; subsequently reviewed. Major's popularity at unprecedentedly low rating. Nov: Maastricht Treaty on European union ratified. Revelations of past arms sales to Iraq implicated senior government figures, including the prime minister.
1993 Recession continued. The Conservatives were knocked into third place in a by-election and the chancellor of the Exchequer was replaced. The Conservative Party was criticized for accepting large, often undisclosed sums from foreign donors after one of them, charged with fraud, jumped bail.

United States of America

area 9,368,900 sq km/3,618,770 sq mi
capital Washington DC
towns New York, Los Angeles, Chicago, Philadelphia, Detroit, San Francisco, Washington, Dallas, San Diego, San Antonio, Houston, Boston, Baltimore, Phoenix, Indianapolis, Memphis, Honolulu, San José
physical topography and vegetation from tropical (Hawaii) to arctic (Alaska); mountain ranges parallel with E and W coasts; the Rocky Mountains separate rivers emptying into the Pacific from those flowing into the Gulf of Mexico; Great Lakes in N; rivers

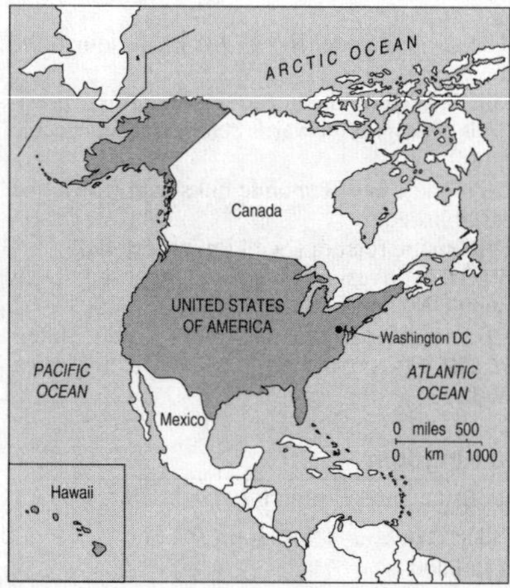

include Hudson, Mississippi, Missouri, Colorado, Columbia, Snake, Rio Grande, Ohio
environment the USA produces the world's largest quantity of municipal waste per person (850 kg/ 1,900 lb)
features see individual states
territories the commonwealths of Puerto Rico and Northern Marianas; the federated states of Micronesia; Guam, the US Virgin Islands, American Samoa, Wake Island, Midway Islands, Marshall Islands, Belau, and Johnston and Sand Islands
head of state and government Bill Clinton from 1993
political system liberal democracy
political parties Democratic Party, liberal centre; Republican Party, centre-right
currency US dollar
population (1992) 255,414,000 (white 80%, black 12%, Asian/Pacific islander 3%, American Indian, Inuit, and Aleut 1%, Hispanic [included in above percentages] 9%); growth rate 0.9% p.a.
life expectancy men 72, women 79 (1989)
languages English, Spanish
religions Christian 86.5% (Roman Catholic 26%, Baptist 19%, Methodist 8%, Lutheran 5%), Jewish 1.8%, Muslim 0.5%, Buddhist and Hindu less than 0.5%
literacy 99% (1989)
GNP $5,880.7 bn (1990)

chronology
1776 Declaration of Independence.
1787 US constitution drawn up.
1789 Washington elected as first president.
1803 Louisiana Purchase.
1812-14 War with England, arising from commercial disputes caused by Britain's struggle with Napoleon.
1819 Florida purchased from Spain.
1836 The battle of the Alamo, Texas, won by Mexico.
1841 First wagon train left Missouri for California.
1846 Mormons, under Brigham Young, founded Salt Lake City, Utah.
1846-48 Mexican War resulted in cession to USA of Arizona, California, part of Colorado and Wyoming, Nevada, New Mexico, Texas, and Utah.
1848-49 California gold rush.
1860 Lincoln elected president.
1861-65 Civil War between North and South.
1865 Slavery abolished. Lincoln assassinated.
1867 Alaska bought from Russia.
1890 Battle of Wounded Knee, the last major battle between American Indians and US troops.
1898 War with Spain ended with the Spanish cession of Philippines, Puerto Rico, and Guam; it was agreed that Cuba be independent. Hawaii annexed.
1917-18 USA entered World War I.
1919-1921 Wilson's 14 Points became base for League of Nations.
1920 Women achieved the vote.
1924 American Indians made citizens by Congress.
1929 Wall Street stock-market crash.
1933 F D Roosevelt's New Deal to alleviate the Depression put into force.
1941-45 The Japanese attack on Pearl Harbor Dec 1941 precipitated US entry into World War II.
1945 USA ended war in the Pacific by dropping atom bombs on Hiroshima and Nagasaki, Japan.
1950–53 US involvement in Korean War. McCarthy anticommunist investigations (HUAC) became a 'witch hunt'.
1954 Civil Rights legislation began with segregation ended in public schools.
1957 Civil Rights bill on voting.
1958 First US satellite in orbit.
1961 Abortive CIA-backed invasion of Cuba at the Bay of Pigs.
1963 President Kennedy assassinated; L B Johnson assumed the presidency.
1964–68 'Great Society' civil-rights and welfare measures in the Omnibus Civil Rights bill.
1964–75 US involvement in Vietnam War.
1965 US intervention in Dominican Republic.
1969 US astronaut Neil Armstrong was the first human on the Moon.
1973 OPEC oil embargo almost crippled US industry and consumers. Inflation began.
1973–74 Watergate scandal began in effort to re-elect Richard Nixon and ended just before impeachment; Nixon resigned as president; replaced by Gerald Ford, who 'pardoned' Nixon.
1975 Final US withdrawal from Vietnam.
1979 US–Chinese diplomatic relations normalized.
1979-80 Iranian hostage crisis; relieved by Reagan concessions and released on his inauguration day Jan 1981.
1981 Space shuttle mission was successful.
1983 US invasion of Grenada.
1986 'Irangate' scandal over secret US government arms sales to Iran, with proceeds to antigovernment Contra guerrillas in Nicaragua.
1987 Reagan and Gorbachev (for USSR) signed intermediate-range nuclear forces treaty. Wall Street stock- market crash caused by programme trading.
1988 USA became world's largest debtor nation, owing $532 billion. George Bush elected president.
1989 Bush met Gorbachev at Malta, end to Cold War declared; large cuts announced for US military; USA invaded Panama; Noriega taken into custody.
1990 Bush and Gorbachev met again. Nelson Mandela freed in South Africa, toured USA. US troops sent to Middle East following Iraq's invasion of Kuwait.
1991 Jan–Feb: US-led assault drove Iraq from Kuwait in Gulf War. US support was given to the USSR during the dissolution of communism and the recognition of independence of the Baltic republics. July: Strategic Arms Reduction Treaty (START) signed at US–Soviet summit in Moscow. Nov: Bush co-hosted Middle East peace conference in Spain.
1992 Bush's popularity slumped as economic recession continued. Widespread riots in Los Angeles. Nov: Bill Clinton won presidential elections for the Democrats; independent candidate Ross Perot won nearly 20% of votes.
1993 Jan: Clinton inaugurated. He delayed executive order to suspend ban on homosexuals in the armed forces. Feb: medium-term economic plan passed by Congress to cut federal budget deficit. July: air strike on Baghdad, Iraq.

Uruguay

Oriental Republic of (*República Oriental del Uruguay*)

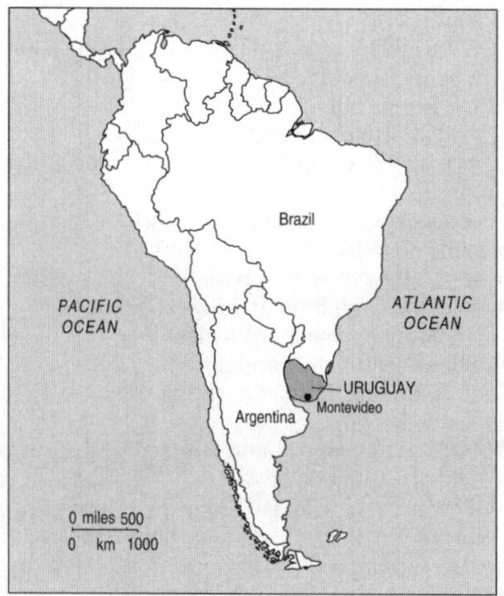

area 176,200 sq km/68,031 sq mi
capital Montevideo
towns Salto, Paysandú
physical grassy plains (pampas) and low hills
features rivers Negro, Uruguay, Río de la Plata
head of state and government Luis Lacalle Herrera from 1989
political system democratic republic
political parties Colorado Party (PC), progressive, centre-left; National (Blanco) Party (PN), traditionalist, right of centre; Amplio Front (FA), moderate, left-wing
exports meat and meat products, leather, wool, textiles
currency nuevo peso
population (1992) 3,130,000 (Spanish, Italian; mestizo, mulatto, black); growth rate 0.7% p.a.
life expectancy men 68, women 75 (1989)
language Spanish
media the Ministry of Defence controls broadcasting licences; press heavily dependent on official advertising. Four national and two Montevideo daily papers, combined circulation 500,000 copies per week (1993); all proprietors associated with political parties
religion Roman Catholic 66%
literacy 96% (1984)
GNP $7.5 bn; $2,470 per head (1988)

chronology
1825 Independence declared from Brazil.
1836 Civil war.
1930 First constitution adopted.
1966 Blanco party in power, with Jorge Pacheco Areco as president.
1972 Colorado Party returned, with Juan Maria Bordaberry Arocena as president.
1976 Bordaberry deposed by army; Dr Méndez Manfredini became president.
1984 Violent antigovernment protests after ten years of repressive rule.
1985 Agreement reached between the army and political leaders for return to constitutional government. Colorado Party won general election; Dr Julio Maria Sanguinetti became president.
1986 Government of national accord established under President Sanguinetti's leadership.
1989 Luis Lacalle Herrera elected president.

Uzbekistan

Republic of

area 447,400 sq km/172,741 sq mi
capital Tashkent
towns Samarkand, Bukhara, Namangan
physical oases in the deserts; rivers: Amu Darya, Syr Darya; Fergana Valley; rich in mineral deposits
features more than 20 hydroelectric plants; three natural gas pipelines
head of state Islam Karimov from 1990
head of government Abdul Hashim Mutalov from 1991
political system socialist pluralist
political parties National Democratic (formerly Communist) Party, reform-socialist; Democratic Party, tolerated opposition
products rice, dried fruit, vines (all grown by irrigation); cotton, silk
population (1992) 21,363,000 (Uzbek 71%, Russian 8%, Tajik 5%, Kazakh 4%)
language Uzbek, a Turkic language
religion Sunni Muslim

chronology
1921 Part of Turkestan Soviet Socialist Autonomous Republic.
1925 Became constituent republic of the USSR.
1944 Some 160,000 Meskhetian Turks forcibly transported from their native Georgia to Uzbekistan by Stalin.
1989 Tashlak, Yaipan, and Ferghana were the scenes of riots in which Meskhetian Turks were attacked; 70 killed and 850 wounded.
1990 June: economic and political sovereignty declared; former Uzbek Communist Party (UCP) leader Islam Karimov became president.
1991 March: Uzbek supported 'renewed federation' in USSR referendum. Aug: anti-Gorbachev coup in Moscow initially accepted by President Karimov; later, Karimov resigned from Soviet Communist

Party (CPSU) Politburo; UCP broke with CPSU; pro-democracy rallies dispersed by militia; independence declared. Dec: joined new Commonwealth of Independent States.
1992 Jan: admitted into Conference on Security and Cooperation in Europe; violent food riots in Tashkent. March: joined the United Nations; US diplomatic recognition achieved.

Vanuatu

Republic of (*Ripablik Blong Vanuatu*)

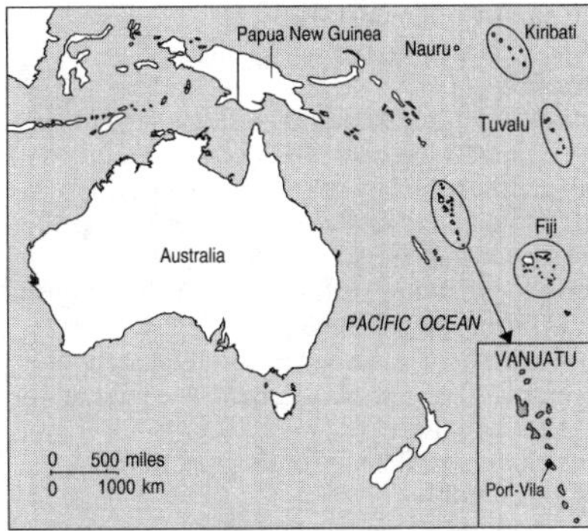

area 14,800 sq km/5,714 sq mi
capital Vila (on Efate)
towns Luganville (on Espíritu Santo)
physical comprises around 70 islands, including Espíritu Santo, Malekula, and Efate; densely forested, mountainous
features three active volcanoes
head of state Fred Timakata from 1989
head of government Maxime Carlot from 1991
political system democratic republic
political parties Union of Moderate Parties (UMP), Francophone centrist; Vanuatu National United Party (VNUP), formed by Walter Lini; Vanua'aku Pati (VP), Anglophone centrist; Melanesian Progressive Party (MPP), Melanesian centrist; Fren Melanesian Party
exports copra, fish, coffee, cocoa
currency vatu
population (1992) 154,000 (90% Melanesian); growth rate 3.3% p.a.
life expectancy men 67, women 71 (1989)
languages Bislama 82%, English, French (all official)
literacy 53%
religions Presbyterian 40%, Roman Catholic 16%, Anglican 14%, animist 15%
GDP $125 million (1987); $927 per head

chronology
1906 Islands jointly administered by France and Britain.
1975 Representative assembly established.
1978 Government of national unity formed, with Father Gerard Leymang as chief minister.
1980 Revolt on the island of Espíritu Santo delayed independence but it was achieved within the Commonwealth, with George Kalkoa (adopted name Sokomanu) as president and Father Walter Lini as prime minister.
1988 Dismissal of Lini by Sokomanu led to Sokomanu's arrest for treason. Lini reinstated.
1989 Sokomanu sentenced to six years' imprisonment; succeeded as president by Fred Timakata.
1991 Lini voted out by party members; replaced by Donald Kalpokas. General election produced UMP–VNUP coalition under Maxime Carlot.

Vatican City State

(*Stato della Città del Vaticano*)

area 0.4 sq km/109 acres
physical forms an enclave in the heart of Rome, Italy
features Vatican Palace, official residence of the pope; basilica and square of St Peter's; churches in and near Rome, the pope's summer villa at Castel Gandolfo; the world's smallest state
head of state and government John Paul II from 1978
political system absolute Catholicism
currency Vatican City lira; Italian lira
population (1985) 1,000
languages Latin (official), Italian
religion Roman Catholic

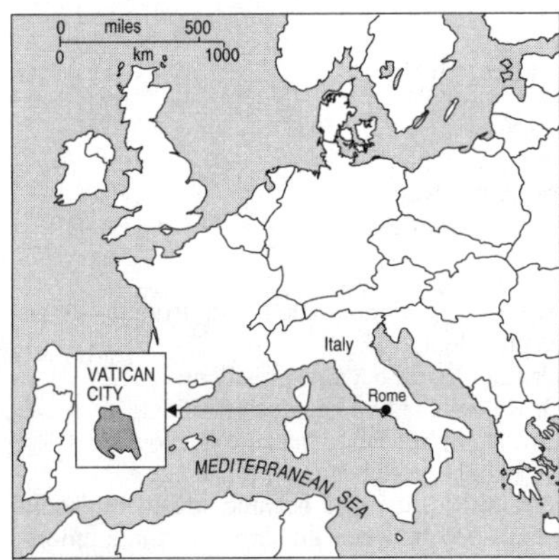

chronology
1929 Lateran Treaty recognized sovereignty of the pope.
1947 New Italian constitution confirmed the sovereignty of the Vatican City State.
1978 John Paul II became the first non-Italian pope for more than 400 years.
1985 New concordat signed under which Roman Catholicism ceased to be Italy's state religion.

Venezuela

Republic of (*República de Venezuela*)

area 912,100 sq km/352,162 sq mi
capital Caracas
towns Barquisimeto, Valencia; port Maracaibo
physical Andes Mountains and Lake Maracaibo in NW; central plains (llanos); delta of river Orinoco in E; Guiana Highlands in SE
features Angel Falls, world's highest waterfall
head of state and of government (interim) Ramon José Velasquez Mujica from 1993
government federal democratic republic
political parties Democratic Action Party (AD), moderate left of centre; Social Christian Party

(COPEI), Christian centre-right; Movement towards Socialism (MAS), left of centre
exports coffee, timber, oil, aluminium, iron ore, petrochemicals
currency bolívar
population (1992) 20,184,000 (mestizos 70%, white (Spanish, Portuguese, Italian) 20%, black 9%, Amerindian 2%); growth rate 2.8% p.a.
life expectancy men 67, women 73 (1989)
religions Roman Catholic 96%, Protestant 2%
languages Spanish (official), Indian languages 2%
literacy 88% (1989)
GNP $47.3 bn (1988); $2,629 per head (1985)

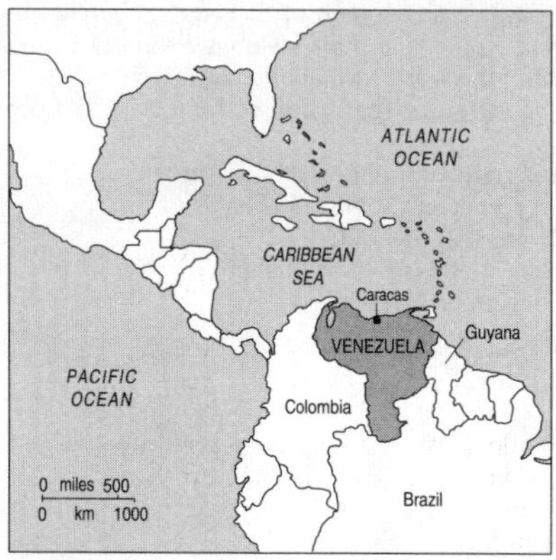

chronology
1961 New constitution adopted, with Rómulo Betancourt as president.
1964 Dr Raúl Leoni became president.
1969 Dr Rafael Caldera became president.
1974 Carlos Andrés Pérez became president.
1979 Dr Luis Herrera became president.
1984 Dr Jaime Lusinchi became president; social pact established between government, trade unions, and business; national debt rescheduled.
1987 Widespread social unrest triggered by inflation; student demonstrators shot by police.
1988 Carlos Andrés Pérez elected president. Payments suspended on foreign debts (increase due to drop in oil prices).
1989 Economic austerity programme enforced by $4.3 billion loan from International Monetary Fund. Price increases triggered riots; 300 people killed. Feb: martial law declared. May: General strike. Elections boycotted by opposition groups.
1991 Protests against austerity programme continued.
1992 Attempted anti-government coups failed. Pérez promised constitutional changes.
1993 Pérez resigned, accused of corruption; Ramon José Velasquez succeeded him as interim head of state pending elections.

Vietnam

Socialist Republic of (*Công Hòa Xã Hôi Chu Nghĩa Viêt Nam*)

area 329,600 sq km/127,259 sq mi
capital Hanoi
towns ports Ho Chi Minh City (formerly Saigon), Da Nang, Haiphong
physical Red River and Mekong deltas, centre of cultivation and population; tropical rainforest; mountainous in N and NW
environment during the Vietnam War an estimated 2.2 million hectares/5.4 million acres of forest were destroyed. The country's National Conservation Strategy is trying to replant 500 million trees each year
features Karst hills of Halong Bay, Cham Towers
head of state Le Duc Anh from 1992
head of government Vo Van Kiet from 1991
political system communism
political party Communist Party
exports rice, rubber, coal, iron, apatite
currency dong
population (1992) 69,052,000 (750,000 refugees, majority ethnic Chinese left 1975–79, some settled in SW China, others fled by sea – the 'boat people' – to Hong Kong and elsewhere); growth rate 2.4% p.a.
life expectancy men 62, women 66 (1989)
languages Vietnamese (official), French, English, Khmer, Chinese, local languages
media independent newspapers prohibited by law 1989; central government approval is required for appointment of editors
religions Buddhist, Taoist, Confucian, Christian
literacy 78% (1989)
GNP $12.6 bn; $180 per head (1987)

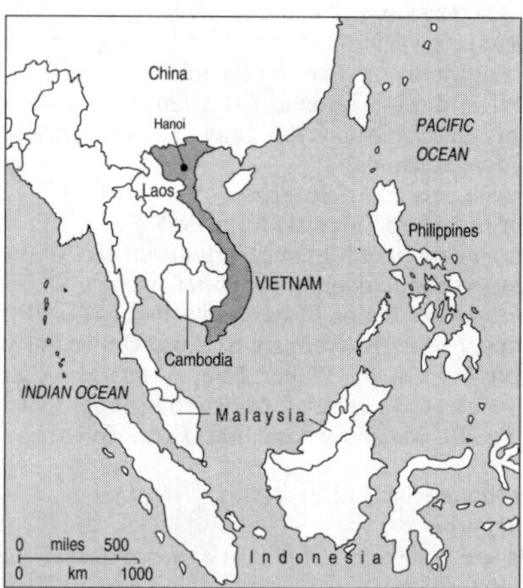

chronology
1945 Japanese removed from Vietnam at end of World War II.
1946 Commencement of Vietminh war against French.
1954 France defeated at Dien Bien Phu. Vietnam divided along 17th parallel.
1964 US troops entered Vietnam War.
1973 Paris cease-fire agreement.
1975 Saigon captured by North Vietnam.
1976 Socialist Republic of Vietnam proclaimed.
1978 Admission into Comecon. Vietnamese invasion of Cambodia.
1979 Sino-Vietnamese border war.
1986 Retirement of 'old guard' leaders.
1987–88 Over 10,000 political prisoners released.
1988–89 Troop withdrawals from Cambodia continued.

1989 'Boat people' leaving Vietnam murdered and robbed at sea by Thai pirates. Troop withdrawal from Cambodia completed. Hong Kong forcibly repatriated some Vietnamese refugees.
1991 Vo Van Kiet replaced Do Muoi as prime minister. Cambodia peace agreement signed. Relations with China normalized.
1992 Sept: Le Duc Anh elected president. Dec: relations with South Korea normalized; USA eased 30-year-old trade embargo.

Yemen

Republic of (*al Jamhuriya al Yamaniya*)

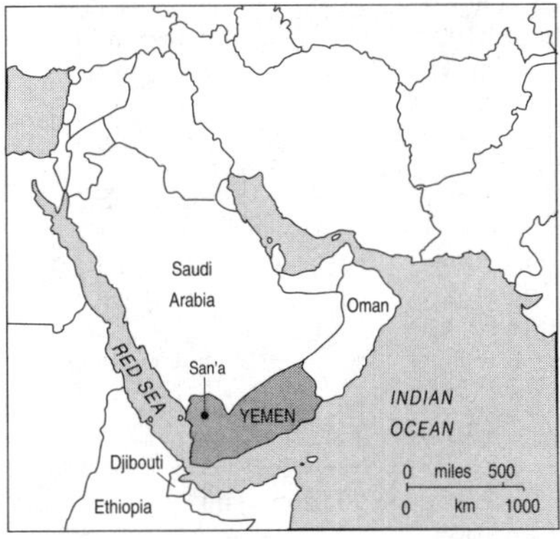

area 531,900 sq km/205,367 sq mi
capital San'a
towns Ta'iz; and chief port Aden
physical hot moist coastal plain, rising to plateau and desert
features once known as *Arabia felix* because of its fertility, includes islands of Perim (in strait of Bab-el-Mandeb, at S entrance to Red Sea), Socotra, and Kamaran
head of state Ali Abdullah Saleh from 1990
head of government Haydar Abu Bakr al-Attas from 1993
political system emergent democratic republic
political parties Yemen Socialist Party (YSP), Democratic Unionist Party, National Democratic Front, Yemen Reform Group, General People's Congress
exports cotton, coffee, grapes, vegetables
currency rial
population (1992) 12,147,000; growth rate 2.7% p.a.
life expectancy men 47, women 50
language Arabic
religions Sunni Muslim 63%, Shi'ite Muslim 37%
literacy men 20%, women 3% (1985 est)
GNP $4.9 bn (1983); $520 per head

chronology
1918 Yemen became independent.
1962 North Yemen declared the Yemen Arab Republic (YAR), with Abdullah al-Sallal as president. Civil war broke out between royalists and republicans.
1967 Civil war ended with the republicans victorious. Sallal deposed and replaced by Republican Council. The People's Republic of South Yemen was formed.
1970 People's Republic of South Yemen renamed People's Democratic Republic of Yemen.
1971–72 War between South Yemen and the YAR; union agreement signed but not kept.
1974 Ibrahim al-Hamadi seized power in North Yemen and Military Command Council set up.
1977 Hamadi assassinated and replaced by Ahmed ibn Hussein al-Ghashmi.
1978 Constituent people's assembly appointed in North Yemen and Military Command Council dissolved. Ghashmi killed by envoy from South Yemen; succeeded by Ali Abdullah Saleh. War broke out again between the two Yemens. South Yemen president deposed and Yemen Socialist Party (YSP) formed.
1979 Cease-fire agreed with commitment to future union.
1983 Saleh elected president of North Yemen for a further five-year term.
1984 Joint committee on foreign policy for the two Yemens met in Aden.
1985 Ali Nasser re-elected secretary general of the YSP in South Yemen; removed his opponents. Three bureau members killed.
1986 Civil war in South Yemen; Ali Nasser dismissed. New administration under Haydar Abu Bakr al-Attas.
1988 President Saleh re-elected in North Yemen.
1989 Draft constitution for single Yemen state published.
1990 Border between two Yemens opened; countries formally united 22 May as Republic of Yemen.
1991 New constitution approved.
1992 Anti-government riots.
1993 General People's Congress won most seats in general elections but no overall majority; coalition government formed, led by Haydar Abu Bakr al-Attas.

Yugoslavia

area 88,400 sq km/34,100 sq mi
capital Belgrade
towns Kraljevo, Leskovac, Pristina, Novi Sad, Titograd
head of state Zoran Lilic from 1993
head of government Radoje Kontic from 1993
political system socialist pluralist republic
political parties Socialist Party of Serbia, ex-communist; Serbian Renaissance Movement, pro-monarchist; Democratic Party, Serbia-based, liberal, free market; Montenegro League of Communists; Democratic Coalition of Muslims; Alliance of Reform Forces, Montenegro-based; Internal Macedonian Revolutionary Organization–Democratic Party for Macedonian National Unity (VMRO–DMPNE), Macedonian nationalist; Macedonian League of Communists
exports machinery, electrical goods, chemicals, clothing, tobacco
currency dinar
population (1992) 10,394,000 (Serb 53%, Albanian 15%, Macedonian 11%, Montenegrin 5%, Muslim 3%, Croat 2%)
life expectancy men 69, women 75 (1989)
languages Serbian variant of Serbo-Croatian, Macedonian, Slovenian
religion Eastern Orthodox 41% (Serbs), Roman Catholic 12% (Croats), Muslim 3%
literacy 90% (1989)
GNP $154.1 bn; $6,540 per head (1988)

chronology
1918 Creation of Kingdom of the Serbs, Croats, and Slovenes.
1929 Name of Yugoslavia adopted.
1941 Invaded by Germany.
1945 Yugoslav Federal Republic formed under leadership of Tito; communist constitution introduced.
1948 Split with USSR.
1953 Self-management principle enshrined in constitution.
1961 Nonaligned movement formed under Yugoslavia's leadership.
1974 New constitution adopted.
1980 Tito died; collective leadership assumed power.
1987 Threatened use of army to curb unrest.
1988 Economic difficulties: 1,800 strikes, 250% inflation, 20% unemployment. Ethnic unrest in Montenegro and Vojvodina; party reshuffled and government resigned.
1989 Reformist Croatian Ante Marković became prime minister. 29 died in ethnic riots in Kosovo province, protesting against Serbian attempt to end autonomous status of Kosovo and Vojvodina; state of emergency imposed. May: inflation rose to 490%; tensions with ethnic Albanians rose.
1990 Multiparty systems established in Serbia and Croatia.
1991 June: Slovenia and Croatia declared independence, resulting in clashes between federal and republican armies; Slovenia accepted European Community (EC)-sponsored peace pact. Fighting continued in Croatia; repeated calls for cease-fires failed. Dec: President Stipe Mesic and Prime Minister Ante Marković resigned.
1992 Jan: EC-brokered cease-fire established in Croatia; EC and USA recognized Slovenia's and Croatia's independence. Bosnia-Herzegovina and Macedonia declared independence. April: Bosnia-Herzegovina recognized as independent by EC and USA amid increasing ethnic hostility; bloody civil war ensued. New Federal Republic of Yugoslavia (FRY) proclaimed by Serbia and Montenegro but not recognized externally. May: Western ambassadors left Belgrade. International sanctions imposed against Serbia and Montenegro. Hostilities continued. Jun: Dobrica Cosic became president. Jul: Milan Panic became prime minister. Sept: UN membership suspended. Dec: Slobodan Milosevic re-elected Serbian president; Panic removed from office in vote of no confidence.
1993 Cosic removed from office by Yugoslav parliament; replaced by Zoran Lilic. Radoje Kontic became prime minister.

Zaire

Republic of (*République du Zaíre*) (formerly ***Congo***)

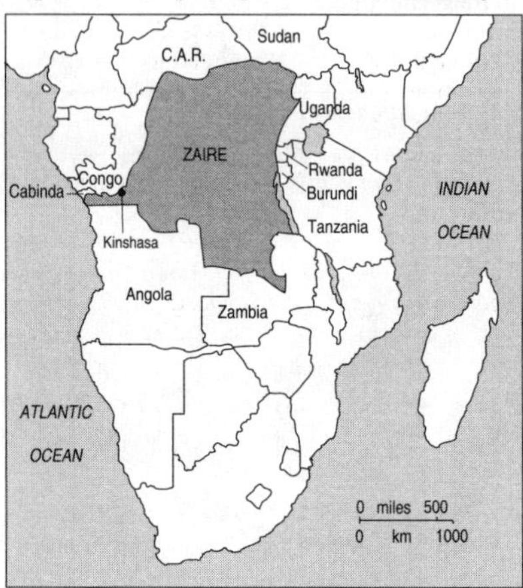

area 2,344,900 sq km/905,366 sq mi
capital Kinshasa
towns Lubumbashi, Kananga, Kisangani; ports Matadi, Boma
physical Zaïre River basin has tropical rainforest and savanna; mountains in E and W
features lakes Tanganyika, Mobutu Sese Seko, Edward; Ruwenzori mountains
head of state Mobutu Sese Seko Kuku Ngbendu wa Zabanga from 1965
head of government Faustin Birindwa from 1993
political system socialist pluralist republic
political parties Popular Movement of the Revolution (MPR), African socialist; numerous new parties registered 1991
exports coffee, copper, cobalt (80% of world output), industrial diamonds, palm oil
currency zaïre
population (1992) 41,151,000; growth rate 2.9% p.a.
life expectancy men 51, women 54 (1989)
languages French (official), Swahili, Lingala, other African languages; over 300 dialects
religions Christian 70%, Muslim 10%
literacy men 79%, women 45% (1985 est)
GNP $5 bn (1987); $127 per head

chronology
1908 Congo Free State annexed to Belgium.
1960 Independence achieved from Belgium as Republic of the Congo. Civil war broke out between central government and Katanga province.
1963 Katanga war ended.
1967 New constitution adopted.
1970 Col Mobutu elected president.
1971 Country became the Republic of Zaire.
1972 The Popular Movement of the Revolution (MPR) became the only legal political party. Katanga province renamed Shaba.

1974 Foreign-owned businesses and plantations seized by Mobutu and given in political patronage.
1977 Original owners of confiscated properties invited back. Mobutu re-elected; Zairians invaded Shaba province from Angola, repulsed by Belgian paratroopers.
1978 Second unsuccessful invasion from Angola.
1988 Potential rift with Belgium avoided.
1990 Mobutu announced end of ban on multiparty politics, following internal dissent.
1991 Multiparty elections promised. Sept: after antigovernment riots, Mobutu agreed to share power with opposition; Etienne Tshisekedi appointed premier. Oct: Tshisekedi dismissed.
1992 Aug: Tshisekedi reinstated against Mobutu's wishes; interim opposition parliament formed. Oct: renewed rioting.
1993 Jan: army mutiny; France and Belgium prepared to evacuate civilians. March: Tshisekedi dismissed by Mobutu, replaced by Faustin Birindwa, but Tshisekedi still considered himself in office.

Zambia

Republic of

area 752,600 sq km/290,579 sq mi
capital Lusaka
towns Kitwe, Ndola, Kabwe, Chipata, Livingstone, Kasama
physical forested plateau cut through by rivers
features Zambezi River, Victoria Falls, Kariba Dam
head of state and government Frederick Chiluba from 1991
political system socialist pluralist republic
political parties United National Independence Party (UNIP), African socialist; Movement for Multiparty Democracy (MMD); National Democratic Alliance (Nada)
exports copper, cobalt, zinc, emeralds, tobacco, lead
currency kwacha
population (1992) 8,303,000; growth rate 3.3% p.a.
life expectancy men 54, women 57 (1989)
language English (official); Bantu dialects
religions Christian 66%, animist, Hindu, Muslim
literacy 54% (1988)
GNP $2.1 bn (1987); $304 per head (1986)

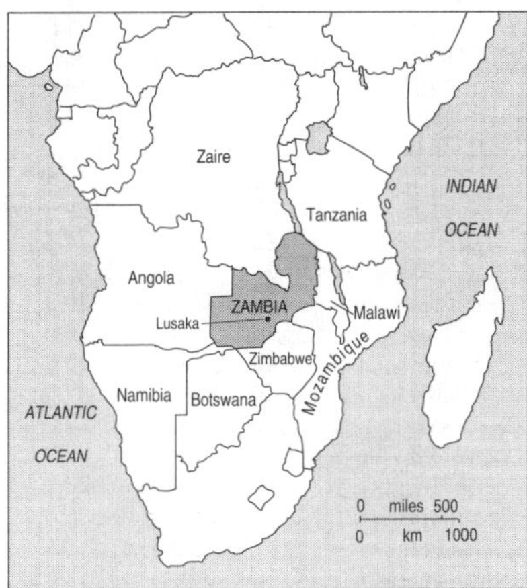

chronology
1899–1924 As Northern Rhodesia, under administration of the British South Africa Company.
1924 Became a British protectorate.
1964 Independence achieved from Britain, within the Commonwealth, as the Republic of Zambia with Kenneth Kaunda as president.
1972 United National Independence Party (UNIP) declared the only legal party.
1976 Support for the Patriotic Front in Rhodesia declared.
1980 Unsuccessful coup against President Kaunda.
1985 Kaunda elected chair of the African Front Line States.
1987 Kaunda elected chair of the Organization of African Unity (OAU).
1988 Kaunda re-elected unopposed for sixth term.
1990 Multiparty system announced for 1991.
1991 Movement for Multiparty Democracy won landslide election victory; Frederick Chiluba became president.
1992 Food and water shortages caused by severe drought.

Zimbabwe

Republic of

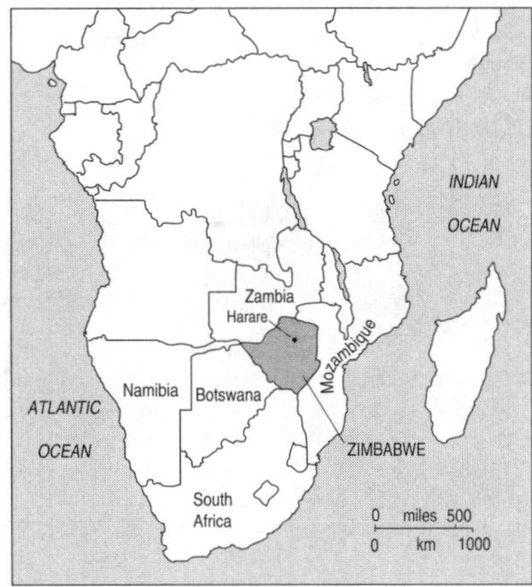

area 390,300 sq km/150,695 sq mi
capital Harare
towns Bulawayo, Gweru, Kwekwe, Mutare, Hwange
physical high plateau with central high veld and mountains in E; rivers Zambezi, Limpopo
features Hwange National Park, part of Kalahari Desert; ruins of Great Zimbabwe
head of state and government Robert Mugabe from 1987
political system effectively one-party socialist republic
political party Zimbabwe African National Union–Patriotic Front (ZANU–PF), African socialist; Forum Party, moderate centrist
exports tobacco, asbestos, cotton, coffee, gold, silver, copper
currency Zimbabwe dollar
population (1992) 9,871,000 (Shona 80%, Ndbele 19%; about 100,000 whites); growth rate 3.5% p.a.
life expectancy men 59, women 63 (1989)
languages English (official), Shona, Sindebele

religions Christian, Muslim, Hindu, animist
literacy men 81%, women 67% (1985 est)
GNP $5.5 bn (1988); $275 per head (1986)

chronology
1889–1923 As Southern Rhodesia, under administration of British South Africa Company.
1923 Became a self-governing British colony.
1961 Zimbabwe African People's Union (ZAPU) formed, with Joshua Nkomo as leader.
1962 ZAPU declared illegal.
1963 Zimbabwe African National Union (ZANU) formed, with Robert Mugabe as secretary general.
1964 Ian Smith became prime minister. ZANU banned. Nkomo and Mugabe imprisoned.
1965 Smith declared unilateral independence.
1966–68 Abortive talks between Smith and UK prime minister Harold Wilson.
1974 Nkomo and Mugabe released.
1975 Geneva conference set date for constitutional independence.
1979 Smith produced new constitution and established a government with Bishop Abel Muzorewa as prime minister. New government denounced by Nkomo and Mugabe. Conference in London agreed independence arrangements (Lancaster House Agreement).
1980 Independence achieved from Britain, with Robert Mugabe as prime minister and Rev Canaan Banana as president.
1981 Rift between Mugabe and Nkomo.
1982 Nkomo dismissed from the cabinet, leaving the country temporarily.
1984 ZANU–PF party congress agreed to create a one-party state in future.
1985 Relations between Mugabe and Nkomo improved. Troops sent to Matabeleland to suppress rumoured insurrection; 5,000 civilians killed.
1986 Joint ZANU–PF rally held amid plans for merger.
1987 White-roll seats in the assembly were abolished. President Banana retired; Mugabe combined posts of head of state and prime minister with the title executive president.
1988 Nkomo returned to the cabinet and was appointed vice president.
1989 Opposition party, the Zimbabwe Unity Movement, formed by Edgar Tekere; draft constitution drawn up, renouncing Marxism–Leninism; ZANU and ZAPU formally merged.
1990 ZANU–PF re-elected. State of emergency ended. Opposition to creation of one-party state.
1992 United Front formed to oppose ZANU–PF. March: Mugabe declared dire drought and famine situation a national disaster

City limits

Urban population growth, 1990–2000

	1990		2000		1990–2000
	Urban population	*Urban population/ total population*	*Urban population*	*Urban population/ total population*	*Growth*
	millions	*%*	*millions*	*%*	*millions*
World	2,282.4	43	2,962.1	48	679.7
Developing countries	1,401.4	34	1,993.7	40	592.3
Africa	205.5	32	322.1	38	116.6
Algeria	12.9	52	19.5	60	6.6
Ivory Coast	4.9	40	8.0	47	3.1
Egypt	23.0	44	30.0	46	7.0
Kenya	5.7	24	11.1	32	5.4
Nigeria	38.2	35	63.9	43	25.7
Zaire	10.5	28	15.8	31	5.3
Latin America	315.5	72	400.6	77	71.1
Bolivia	3.7	51	5.2	58	1.5
Brazil	112.1	75	140.8	82	28.7
Mexico	61.3	73	79.7	78	18.4
Peru	15.0	70	19.6	75	4.6
Asia	974.3	31	1,370.0	37	395.7
Bangladesh	18.7	16	33.1	23	14.4
China	302.2	26	451.7	35	149.5
India	216.1	26	290.9	29	74.8
Indonesia	53.1	29	79.5	37	26.4
Pakistan	37.8	32	58.6	38	20.8
Philippines	26.7	43	37.2	49	10.5
Thailand	12.1	22	17.7	29	5.6
Developed countries	880.9	73	968.4	76	87.5
Australia	14.6	85	16.8	86	2.2
United States	188.1	75	213.3	78	25.2
Europe	373.4	73	401.4	77	28.0
Japan	95.3	77	101.1	79	5.8

Source: World Urbanisation Prospects 1992, United Nations, New York, 1993

APPENDICES

Conversion tables 719

Temperature scales 720

Currency exchange rates 721

Time zones and relative times 723

Islamic calendar 724

Jewish calendar 725

Christian festivals and holy days 726

Movable Christian feasts 726

Hindu festivals 727

Buddhist festivals 727

National holidays 728

Wedding anniversaries 734

Birthstones 734

Signs of the zodiac 734

Index 735

Conversion tables

To convert from imperial to metric	Multiply by	Multiply by	To convert from metric to imperial
Length			
inches	25.4	0.039,37	millimetres
feet	0.3048	3.2808	metres
yards	0.9144	1.0936	metres
furlongs	0.201	4.971	kilometres
miles	1.6093	0.6214	kilometres
Area			
square inches	6.4516	0.1550	square centimetres
square feet	0.0929	10.7639	square metres
square yards	0.8361	1.1960	square metres
square miles	2.5900	0.3861	square kilometres
acres	4046.86	0.000,247	square metres
acres	0.4047	2.47105	hectares
hectares	0.001	1,000	square kilometres
Volume, capacity			
cubic inches	16.3871	0.0610	cubic centimetres
cubic feet	0.02832	35.3134	cubic metres
cubic yards	0.7646	1.3079	cubic metres
fluid ounces	28.4131	0.0352	millilitres
pints	0.5683	1.760	litres
quarts	1.1365	0.88	litres
imperial gallons	4.54609	0.21997	litres
US gallons	3.7854	0.2642	litres
Mass/weight			
ounces	28.3495	0.03527	grams
pounds	0.4536	2.2046	kilograms
stone (14 lb)	6.3503	0.1575	kilograms
tons (imperial)	1016.05	0.00098	kilograms
tons (US)	907.2	0.001	kilograms
tons (imperial)	0.9842	1.0161	tonnes
tons (US)	0.9072	1.102	tonnes
Speed			
miles per hour	1.6093	0.6214	kilometres per hour
feet per second	0.3048	3.2808	metres per second
Force			
pound force	4.448	0.2248	newton
kilogram force	9.8096	0.1019	newton
Pressure			
pounds per square inch	6.894,76	0.1450	kilopascals
tons per square inch	15.4443	0.0647	megapascals
atmospheres	101,325	0.000,009,86	newtons per square metre
atmospheres	14.69	0.068	pounds per square inch
Energy			
calorie	4.186	0.238	joule
kilowatt hour	3,600,000	0.000,000,277	joule
Power			
horsepower	0.7457	1.341	kilowatts
Fuel consumption			
miles per gallon	0.3540	2.825	kilometres per litre
miles per US gallon	0.4251	2.3521	kilometres per litre
gallons per mile	2.8248	0.3540	litres per kilometre
US gallons per mile	2.3521	0.4251	litres per kilometre

Temperature scales

The freezing point and boiling point of water are 0°C and 100°C on the Celsius (centigrade) scale (100 degrees), and 32°F and 212°F on the Fahrenheit scale (180 degrees). So Celsius and Fahrenheit temperatures can be converted as follows:

$C = (F - 32) \times {}^{100}/_{180}$

$F = (C \times {}^{180}/_{100}) + 32$

Table of equivalent temperatures

°C	°F	°C	°F	°C	°F	°C	°F
100	212.0	70	158.0	40	104.0	10	50.0
99	210.2	69	156.2	39	102.2	9	48.2
98	208.4	68	154.4	38	100.4	8	46.4
97	206.6	67	152.6	37	98.6	7	44.6
96	204.8	66	150.8	36	96.8	6	42.8
95	203.0	65	149.0	35	95.0	5	41.0
94	201.2	64	147.2	34	93.2	4	39.2
93	199.4	63	145.4	33	91.4	3	37.4
92	197.6	62	143.6	32	89.6	2	35.6
91	195.8	61	141.8	31	87.8	1	33.8
90	194.0	60	140.0	30	86.0	0	32.0
89	192.2	59	138.2	29	84.2	–1	30.2
88	190.4	58	136.4	28	82.4	–2	28.4
87	188.6	57	134.6	27	80.6	–3	26.6
86	186.8	56	132.8	26	78.8	–4	24.8
85	185.0	55	131.0	25	77.0	–5	23.0
84	183.2	54	129.2	24	75.2	–6	21.2
83	181.4	53	127.4	23	73.4	–7	19.4
82	179.6	52	125.6	22	71.6	–8	17.6
81	177.8	51	123.8	21	69.8	–9	15.8
80	176.0	50	122.0	20	68.0	–10	14.0
79	174.2	49	120.2	19	66.2	–11	12.2
78	172.4	48	118.4	18	64.4	–12	10.4
77	170.6	47	116.6	17	62.6	–13	8.6
76	168.8	46	114.8	16	60.8	–14	6.8
75	167.0	45	113.0	15	59.0	–15	5.0
74	165.2	44	111.2	14	57.2	–16	3.2
73	163.4	43	109.4	13	55.4	–17	1.4
72	161.6	42	107.6	12	53.6	–18	–0.4
71	159.8	41	105.8	11	51.8	–19	–2.2

World currency exchange rates (as of 6 August 1993)

Country	*Currency*	*£ sterling*
Afghanistan	afgháni	1576.05
Albania	lek	165.11
Algeria	dinar	29.73
Andorra	French franc	8.92
	Spanish peseta	209.54
Angola	kwanza	6004.30
Antigua	East Caribbean dollar	4.05
Argentina	austral	1.50
Aruba	florin	2.69
Australia	Australian dollar	2.20
Austria	schilling	18.06
Azores	port escudo	260.00
Bahamas	Bahamian dollar	1.50
Bahrain	Bahrain dinar	0.57
Bangladesh	taka	59.53
Barbados	Barbados dollar	3.02
Belgium	Belgian franc	54.26
Belize	Belize dollar	3.00
Benin	CFA franc	445.83
Bermuda	Bermudian dollar	1.50
Bhutan	ngultrum	47.10
Bolivia	boliviano	6.45
Botswana	pula	3.72
Bouvet Island	Norwegian krone	11.10
Brazil	cruzeiro	112.39
Brunei	Brunei dollar	2.42
Bulgaria	lev	40.96
Burkina Faso	CFA franc	445.83
Burundi	Burundi franc	349.23
Cambodia	Cambodian riel	5253.50
Cameroon	CFA franc	445.83
Canada	Canadian dollar	1.94
Cape Verde	Cape Verde escudo	111.37
Cayman Islands	Cayman Island dollar	1.28
Central African Republic	CFA franc	445.83
Chad	CFA franc	445.83
Chile	Chilean peso (m)	609.51
	Chilean peso (o)	643.04
China	Renminbi yuan	8.65
Colombia	Colombian peso	1203.53
Commonwealth of Ind States	rouble	1478.48
Comoros	CFA franc	445.83
Congo	CFA franc	445.83
Costa Rica	colón	213.52
Côte d'Ivoire	CFA franc	445.83
Cuba	Cuban peso	1.98
Cyprus	Cyprus pound	2.90
Czech Republic	koruna	44.73
Denmark	Danish kroner	10.18
Djibouti	Djibouti franc	267.42
Dominica	East Caribbean dollar	4.05
Dominican Republic	Dominican peso	19.51
Ecuador	sucre(d)	2919.44
	sucre(o)	2776.85
Egypt	Egyptian pound	5.01
El Salvador	colón	13.11
Equatorial Guinea	CFA franc	445.83
Estonia	kroon	20.40
Ethiopia	Ethiopian birr	4.50
Faeroe Islands	Danish kroner	10.18
Falkland Islands	Falkland pound	2.25
Fiji Islands	Fiji dollar	2.28
Finland	markka	8.69
French Pacific Islands	CFP Franc	162.12
France	French franc	8.92
French Guiana	French franc	8.92
Gabon	CFA franc	445.83
Gambia	dalasi	13.57
Germany	Deutschmark	2.56
Ghana	cedi	975.65
Gibraltar	Gibraltar pound	2.25
Greece	drachma	358.36
Greenland	Danish krone	10.18
Grenada	East Caribbean dollar	4.05
Guadaloupe	local franc	8.92
Guam	US dollar	1.50
Guatemala	quetzal	8.61
Guinea	Guinea franc	1219.25
Guinea-Bissau	Guinea-Bissau peso	7505.00
Guyana	Guyanese dollar	189.13
Haiti	gourde	18.01
Honduras	lempira	10.24
Hong Kong	Hong Kong dollar	11.64
Hungary	forint	143.60
Iceland	Icelandic krona	107.89
India	Indian rupee	47.10
Indonesia	rupiah	3143.39
Iran	Iranian riyal	2377.58
Iraq	Iraqi dinar	0.47
Irish Republic	punt	2.10
Israel	shekel	4.19
Italy	lira	2394.09
Jamaica	Jamaican dollar	36.02
Japan	yen	156.73
Jordan	Jordanian dinar	1.04
Kenya	Kenyan shilling	98.43
Kiribati	Australian dollar	2.20
Korea, North	won	3.23
Korea, South	won	1210.56
Kuwait	Kuwaiti dinar	0.45
Laos	new kip	1080.72
Lebanon	Lebanese pound	2593.72
Lesotho	maluti	5.06
Liberia	Liberian dollar	1.50
Libya	Libyan dinar	0.45
Liechtenstein	Swiss franc	2.25
Lithuania	Lita	6.00
Luxembourg	Luxembourg franc	54.26
Macao	pataca	12.02
Madagascar	Malagasy franc	2922.82
Malawi	kwacha	6.66
Malaysia	ringgit	3.83
Maldive Islands	rufiya	17.97
Mali Republic	CFA franc	445.83
Malta	Maltese lira	3.83
Martinique	local franc	8.92
Mauritania	ougiya	170.83
Mauritius	Mauritius rupee	27.27
Mexico	Mexican peso	12.17
Monaco	French franc	8.92
Mongolia	tugrik	600.40
Montserrat	East Caribbean dollar	4.05

World currency exchange rates (as of 6 August 1993) *(cont.)*

Country	*Currency*	*£ sterling*
Morocco	dirham	14.03
Mozambique	metical	5905.90
Myanmar	kyat	9.21
Namibia	South African rand	5.06
Nauru Island	Australian dollar	2.20
Nepal	Nepalese rupee	68.84
Netherlands	guilder	2.88
Netherlands Antilles	Antillian guilder	2.69
New Zealand	New Zealand dollar	2.72
Nicaragua	gold cordoba	9.26
Niger Republic	CFA franc	445.83
Nigeria	naira	37.52
Norway	Norwegian krone	11.10
Oman	Omani rial	0.58
Pakistan	Pakistan rupee	44.73
Panama	balboa	1.50
Papua New Guinea	kina	1.46
Paraguay	guaraní	2619.24
Peru	new sol	3.09
Philippines	peso	41.88
Pitcairn Islands	New Zealand dollar	2.72
Poland	zloty	27403.76
Portugal	escudo	260.00
Puerto Rico	US dollar	1.50
Qatar	Qatar riyal	5.51
Réunion Islands	French franc	8.92
Romania	leu	1205.30
Rwanda	Rwandan franc	173.01
St Christopher	East Caribbean dollar	4.05
St Helena	pound sterling	2.25
St Lucia	East Caribbean dollar	4.05
St Pierre	French franc	8.92
St Vincent	East Caribbean dollar	4.05
San Marino	Italian lira	2394.09
São Tomé e Principe	dobra	360.24
Saudi Arabia	Saudi riyal	5.63
Senegal	CFA franc	445.83
Seychelles	Seychelles rupee	7.83
Sierra Leone	leone	825.55
Singapore	dollar	2.42
Solomon Islands	Solomon Island dollar	4.77
Somali Republic	Somali shilling	3932.62
South Africa	rand(c)	5.06
	rand(g)	6.96
Spain	peseta	209.54
Sri Lanka	Sri Lanka rupee	73.17
Sudan Republic	Sudanese pound	195.13
	diner	19.51
Surinam	Surinam guilder	2.68
Swaziland	lilangeni	5.06
Sweden	krona	12.04
Switzerland	Swiss franc	2.25
Syria	Syrian pound	32.27
Taiwan	New Taiwan dollar	40.42
Tanzania	Tanzanian shilling	688.15
Thailand	baht	37.82
Togo Republic	CFA franc	445.83
Tonga Islands	pa'anga	2.20
Trinidad and Tobago	Trinidad and Tobago dollar	8.31
Tunisia	Tunisian dinar	1.52
Turkey	Turkish lira	17455.34
Turks and Caicos Islands	US dollar	1.50
Tuvalu	Australian dollar	2.20
Uganda	new shilling	1794.16
Ukraine	karbovanets	8645.76
United Arab Emirates	UAE dirham	5.51
United Kingdom	pound sterling	1
United States	US dollar	1.50
Uruguay	nuevo peso	6.00
Vanuatu	vatu	181.62
Vatican City State	lira	2394.09
Venezuela	bolívar	139.22
Vietnam	dong	15933.11
Virgin Islands, British	US dollar	1.50
Virgin Islands, US	US dollar	1.50
Western Samoa	taia	3.86
Yemen, Republic of	Yemini dinar	0.69
	Yemini riyal	24.77
Yugoslavia	New Yugoslav dinar	20.41
Zaire Republic	zaire	6906101.00
Zambia	kwacha	108.35
Zimbabwe	Zimbabwe dollar	9.94

Abbreviations: (c) commercial rate; (d) controlled rate; (g) financial rate; (m) market rate; (o) official rate.

Data supplied by Bank of America, Economics Department, London Trading Centre

*Time zones and relative times **

At 12.00 noon, Greenwich Mean Time (GMT), the standard time elsewhere around the world is as follows:

Abu Dhabi	16.00	Dublin	12.00	Oslo	13.00
Accra	12.00	Florence	13.00	Ottawa	07.00
Addis Ababa	15.00	Frankfurt	13.00	Panama City	07.00
Adelaide	21.30	Gdansk	13.00	Paris	13.00
Alexandria	14.00	Geneva	13.00	Perth	20.00
Algiers	13.00	Gibraltar	13.00	Port Said	14.00
Amman	14.00	Hague, The	13.00	Prague	13.00
Amsterdam	13.00	Harare	14.00	Quebec	07.00
Anchorage	02.00	Havana	07.00	Rangoon	18.30
Ankara	14.00	Helsinki	14.00	Rawalpindi	17.00
Athens	14.00	Ho Chi Minh City	19.00	Reykjavik	12.00
Auckland	24.00	Hobart	22.00	Rio de Janeiro	09.00
Baghdad	15.00	Hong Kong	20.00	Riyadh	15.00
Bahrain	15.00	Istanbul	14.00	Rome	13.00
Bangkok	19.00	Jakarta	19.00	San Francisco	04.00
Barcelona	13.00	Jerusalem	14.00	Santiago	08.00
Beijing	20.00	Johannesburg	14.00	Seoul	21.00
Beirut	14.00	Karachi	17.00	Shanghai	20.00
Belgrade	13.00	Kiev	15.00	Singapore	20.00
Berlin	13.00	Kuala Lumpur	20.00	Sofia	14.00
Berne	13.00	Kuwait	15.00	St Petersburg	15.00
Bogota	07.00	Kyoto	21.00	Stockholm	13.00
Bombay	17.30	Lagos	13.00	Sydney	22.00
Bonn	13.00	Le Havre	13.00	Taipei	20.00
Brazzaville	13.00	Lima	07.00	Tashkent	18.00
Brisbane	22.00	Lisbon	12.00	Tehran	15.30
Brussels	13.00	Los Angeles	04.00	Tel Aviv	14.00
Bucharest	14.00	Luanda	13.00	Tenerife	12.00
Budapest	13.00	Luxembourg	13.00	Tokyo	21.00
Buenos Aires	09.00	Lyon	13.00	Toronto	07.00
Cairo	14.00	Madras	17.30	Tripoli	13.00
Calcutta	17.30	Madrid	13.00	Tunis	13.00
Canberra	22.00	Manila	20.00	Valparaiso	08.00
Cape Town	14.00	Marseille	13.00	Vancouver	04.00
Caracas	08.00	Mecca	15.00	Vatican City	13.00
Casablanca	12.00	Melbourne	22.00	Venice	13.00
Chicago	06.00	Mexico City	06.00	Vienna	13.00
Cologne	13.00	Milan	13.00	Vladivostok	22.00
Colombo	17.30	Minsk	15.00	Volgograd	16.00
Copenhagen	13.00	Monrovia	11.00	Warsaw	13.00
Dacca	18.00	Montevideo	09.00	Washington	07.00
Damascus	14.00	Montreal	07.00	Wellington	24.00
Dar es Salaam	15.00	Moscow	15.00	Winnipeg	06.00
Darwin	21.30	Munich	13.00	Yokohama	21.00
Delhi	17.30	Nairobi	15.00	Zagreb	13.00
Denver	05.00	New Orleans	06.00	Zurich	13.00
Djakarta	20.00	New York	07.00		
Dubai	16.00	Nicosia	14.00		

** The surface of the earth is divided into 24 time zones. Each zone represents 15° of longitude or 1 hour of time. Countries to the east of London and the Greenwich meridian are ahead of Greenwich Mean Time (GMT) and countries to the west are behind. The time indicated in the table above is fixed by law and is called standard time. Use of daylight saving time (such as British Summer Time) varies widely.*

Islamic calendar

The Islamic calendar is reckoned from the year of the *hijra*, or flight of Muhammad from Mecca to Medina. The corresponding date in the Julian calendar is 16 July AD 622. The years are purely lunar, and consist of 12 months with alternately 29 or 30 days, plus one extra day at the end of the 12th month (Dhul- Hijja) in leap years, which occur at stated intervals in each cycle of 30 years.

Islamic calendar 1414–1415 (June 1993–June 1995)

The beginning of the month in the Islamic calendar depends on the visibility of the new moon; therefore dates may differ from those stated here

Hijrah month	*1414 AH*	*1415 AH*
1 Muharram	20 June 1993	9 June 1994
1 Safar	20 July 1993	9 July 1994
1 Rabi'a I	18 Aug 1993	7 Aug 1994
1 Rabi'a II	17 Sept 1993	6 Sept 1994
1 Jumada I	16 Oct 1993	5 Oct 1994
1 Jumada II	15 Nov 1993	4 Nov 1994
1 Rajab	14 Dec 1993	4 Dec 1994
1 Sha'ban	13 Jan 1994	2 Jan 1995
1 Ramadan	11 Feb 1994	31 Jan 1995
1 Shawwal	13 March 1994	2 March 1995
1 Dhul-Qi'da	11 April 1994	31 March 1995
1 Dhul-Hijja	11 May 1994	30 April 1995
Important days	*1414 AH*	*1415 AH*
Hijrah New Year	20 June 1993	9 June 1994
Ashura'	29 June 1993	18 June 1994
Birthday of the prophet Muhammad	29 Aug 1993	18 Aug 1994
Lailat-ul-Isra'wal Mi'raj	8 Jan 1994	29 Dec 1994
Lailat-ul-Bara'h	26 Jan 1994	15 Jan 1995
Ramadan	11 Feb 1994	31 Jan 1995
Lailat-ul-Qadr	8 March 1994	25 Feb 1995
Eid-ul-Fitr	13 March 1994	2 March 1995
Arafat	19 May 1994	8 May 1995
Eid-ul-Adha	20 May 1994	9 May 1995

AH – *anno Hegirae*, the Muslim era

Jewish calendar

The Jewish calendar is a complex combination of lunar and solar cycles, varied by considerations of religious observance. A year may have 12 or 13 months, each of which normally alternates between 29 and 30 days; the New Year (Rosh Hashanah) falls between 5 Sept and 5 Oct. The calendar dates from the hypothetical creation of the world (taken as 7 Oct 3761 BC). Some say that the Jewish calendar as used today was formalized in AD 358 by Rabbi Hillel II; others that this occurred later. A Jewish year is one of the following six types:

Minimal Common	353 days
Regular Common	354 days
Full Common	355 days
Minimal Leap	383 days
Regular Leap	384 days
Full Leap	385 days

Jewish calendar 5754 and 5755 (Sept 1993–Sept 1995)

Jewish month	*AM 5754*	*AM 5755*
1 Tishri	16 Sept 1993	6–7 Sept 1994
1 Marcheshvan	16 Oct 1993	5–6 Oct 1994
1 Kislev	15 Nov 1993	4 Nov 1994
1 Tebet	15 Dec 1993	3–4 Dec 1994
1 Shebat	13 Jan 1994	2 Jan 1995
1 Adar*	12 Feb 1994	1 Feb/3 March 1995
1 Nisan	13 March 1994	1 April 1995
1 Iyar	12 April 1994	1 May 1995
1 Sivan	11 May 1994	30 May 1995
1 Tammuz	10 June 1994	10 June 1995
1 Av	9 July 1994	28 July 1995
1 Elul	8 Aug 1994	27 Aug 1995

Jewish fasts and festivals

Date in Jewish calendar	*Fast/festival*	*Date in 1994*
1–2 Tishri	Rosh Hashanah (New Year)	6–7 Sept
3 Tishri	Fast of Gedaliah*	8 Sept
10 Tishri	Yom Kippur (Day of Atonement)	15 Sept
15–21 Tishri	Succot (Feast of Tabernacles)	20–26 Sept
22 Tishri	Shemini Atzeret	27 Sept
23 Tishri	Simchat Torah	28 Sept
25 Kislev	Hanukkah (Dedication of the Temple) begins	28 Nov–5 Dec
10 Tebet	Fast of Tevet	13 Dec
13 Adar	Fast of Esther†	24 Feb
14 Adar	Purim	25 Feb
15 Adar	Shushan Purim	26 Feb
14 Nisan	Taanit Behorim (Fast of the Firstborn)	24 March
15–22 Nisan	Pesach (Passover)	27 March–3 April
27 Nisan	Yom Ha-Shoah (Holocaust Day)	8 April
4 Lyar	Yom Ha'Zikharon (Remembrance Day)	13 April
5 Lyar	Yom Ha'Atzmaut (Independence Day)	14 April
18 Lyar	33rd Day of Counting the Omer	29 April
28 Lyar	Yom Yerushalayim (Jerusalem Day)	9 May
6–7 Sivan	Shavuot (Festival of Weeks)	16–17 May
17 Tammuz	Fast of 17 Tammuz**	26 June
9 Av	Fast of 9 Av**	17 July

* *Ve-Adar in leap years.*

** *If these dates fall on the sabbath the fast is kept on the following day.*

† *This fast is observed on 11 Adar (or 11 Ve-Adar in leap years) if 13 Adar falls on a sabbath.*

AM – *anno mundi*, in the year of the world

Christian festivals and holy days

1 January	The naming of Jesus The Circumcision of Christ The Solemnity of Mary Mother of God
6 January	Epiphany
25 January	The Conversion of St Paul
2 February	The Presentation of Christ in the Temple
19 March	St Joseph of Nazareth, husband of the Blessed Virgin Mary
25 March	The Annunciation of Our Lord to the Blessed Virgin Mary
25 April	St Mark the Evangelist
1 May	St Philip and St James, Apostles
14 May	St Matthias the Apostle
31 May	The Visitation of the Blessed Virgin Mary
11 June	St Barnabas the Apostle
24 June	The Birth of St John the Baptist
29 June	St Peter and St Paul, Apostles
3 July	St Thomas the Apostle
22 July	St Mary Magdalen
25 July	St James the Apostle
6 August	The Transfiguration of our Lord
24 August	St Bartholomew the Apostle
1 September	New Year (Eastern Orthodox Church)
8 September	The Nativity of the Blessed Virgin Mary
14 September	The Exaltation of the Holy Cross
21 September	St Matthew the Apostle
29 September	St Michael and All Angels (Michaelmas)
18 October	St Luke the Evangelist
28 October	St Simon and St Jude, Apostles
1 November	All Saints
21 November	Presentation of the Blessed Virgin Mary in the Temple
30 November	St Andrew the Apostle
8 December	The Immaculate Conception of the Blessed Virgin Mary
25 December	Christmas
26 December	St Stephen the first Martyr
27 December	St John the Evangelist
28 December	The Holy Innocents

Movable Christian feasts 1994–2025

	Ash Wednesday	Easter Day	Ascension Day	Pentecost (Whit Sunday)	Advent Sunday
1994	16 Feb	3 April	12 May	22 May	27 Nov
1995	1 March	16 April	25 May	4 June	3 Dec
1996	21 Feb	7 April	16 May	26 May	1 Dec
1997	12 Feb	30 March	8 May	18 May	30 Nov
1998	25 Feb	12 April	21 May	31 May	29 Nov
1999	17 Feb	4 April	13 May	23 May	28 Nov
2000	8 March	23 April	1 June	11 June	3 Dec
2001	28 Feb	15 April	24 May	3 June	2 Dec
2002	13 Feb	31 March	9 May	19 May	1 Dec
2003	5 March	20 April	29 May	8 June	30 Nov
2004	25 Feb	11 April	20 May	30 May	28 Nov
2005	9 Feb	27 March	5 May	15 May	27 Nov
2006	1 March	16 April	25 May	4 June	3 Dec
2007	21 Feb	8 April	17 May	27 May	2 Dec
2008	6 Feb	23 March	1 May	11 May	30 Nov
2009	25 Feb	12 April	21 May	31 May	29 Nov
2010	17 Feb	4 April	13 May	23 May	28 Nov
2011	9 March	24 April	2 June	12 June	27 Nov
2012	22 Feb	8 April	17 May	27 May	2 Dec
2013	13 Feb	31 March	9 May	19 May	1 Dec
2014	5 March	20 April	29 May	8 June	30 Nov
2015	18 Feb	5 April	14 May	24 May	29 Nov
2016	10 March	27 March	5 May	15 May	27 Nov
2017	1 March	16 April	25 May	4 June	3 Dec
2018	14 Feb	1 April	10 May	20 May	2 Dec
2019	6 March	21 April	30 May	9 June	1 Dec
2020	26 Feb	12 April	21 May	31 May	29 Nov
2021	17 Feb	4 April	13 May	23 May	28 Nov
2022	2 March	17 April	26 May	5 June	27 Nov
2023	22 Feb	9 April	18 May	28 May	3 Dec
2024	14 Feb	31 March	9 May	19 May	1 Dec
2025	5 March	20 April	29 May	8 June	30 Nov

Advent Sunday is the fourth Sunday before Christmas Day
Ash Wednesday is the first day of Lent, and falls in the seventh week before Easter
Holy Week is the week before Easter Day, and includes Palm Sunday, Maundy Thursday, Good Friday, and Easter Eve.
Ascension Day is 40 days after Easter Day.
Pentecost (Whit Sunday) is seven weeks after Easter Day.
Trinity Sunday is eight weeks after Easter Day.

Hindu festivals

January	Makar Sankranti/Til Sankranti/ Lohri, Pongal, Kumbha Mela at Prayag (every 12 years)
January–February	Vasanta Panchami/Shri Panchami/Saraswati Puja, Bhogali Bihu, Mahashivratri
20 February	Ramakrishna Utsav
February–March	Holi
March–April	Ugadi, Basora, Rama Navami, Hanuman Jayanti
April	Vaisakhi
April–May	Akshaya Tritiya, Chittrai
May–June	Ganga Dasa-hara, Nirjala Ekadashi, Snan-yatra
June–July	Ratha-yatra/Jagannatha, Ashadhi Ekadashi/Toli Ekadashi
July–August	Teej, Naga Panchami, Raksha Bandhan/Shravana Purnima/ Salono/Rakhi Purnima
August–September	Onam, Ganesha Chaturthi, Janamashtami/Krishna Jayanti
September–October	Mahalaya/Shraddha/Pitri Paksha/Kanagat, Navaratri/ Durga Puja/Dassehra, Lakshmi Puja
2 October	Gandhi Jayanti
October–November	Divali/Deepavali Chhath, Karttika Ekadashi/Devuthna Ekadashi/Tulsi Ekadashi Karttika Purnima/Tripuri Purnima, Hoi, Skanda Shasti
November–December	Vaikuntha Ekadashi, Lakshmi Puja (Orissa)

Buddhist festivals

Myanmar	
16–17 April	New Year
May–June	The Buddha's Birth, Enlightenment and Death
July	The Buddha's First Sermon Beginning of the Rains Retreat
October	End of the Rains Retreat
November	Kathina Ceremony
China	
June–August	Summer Retreat
August	Festival of Hungry Ghosts; Gautama Buddha's Birth; Kuan-Yin
Sri Lanka	
13 April	New Year
May–June	The Buddha's Birth, Enlightenment and Death
June–July	Establishment of Buddhism in Sri Lanka
July	The Buddha's First Sermon
July–August	Procession of the Month of Asala
September	The Buddha's First Visit to Sri Lanka
December–January	Arrival of Sanghamitta
Thailand	
13–16 April	New Year
May	The Buddha's Enlightenment
May–June	The Buddha's Cremation
July–October	Rains Retrear
October	End of the Rains Retreat
November	Kathina Ceremony; Festival of Lights
February	All Saints' Day
Tibet	
February	New Year
May	The Buddha's Birth, Enlightenment and Death
June	Dzamling Chisang
June–July	The Buddha's First Sermon
October	The Buddha's Descent from Tushita
November	Death of Tsongkhapa
January	The Conjunction of Nine Evils and the Conjunction of Ten Virtues

National holidays[1]

	Jan	*Feb*	*March*	*April*	*May*	*June*	*July*	*Aug*
Afghanistan				27	1			19
Albania	1, 11				1			
Algeria	1				1	19	5	
Andorra	1, 6	19			1	24		15
Angola	1	4			1			
Argentina	1				1, 25	10, 20	9	17
Australia	1			25				
Austria	1, 6				1			15
Bahamas	1						10	
Bahrain	1							
Bangladesh		21	26		1		1	
Barbados	1							
Belgium	1				1		21	15
Belize	1		9		1, 24			
Benin	1, 16			1	1			
Bhutan					2	2	21	
Bolivia	1				1			6
Botswana	1, 2							
Brazil	1			21	1			
Brunei	1	23			31		15	
Bulgaria	1				1, 24			
Burkina Faso	1, 3				1			4, 15
Burundi	1				1		1	15
Cameroon	1	11			1, 20			15
Canada	1						1	
Cape Verde	1, 20		8		1	1		
Central African Republic	1		29		1	1		13, 15
Chad	1				1, 25	7		11
Chile	1				1, 21	29		15
China	1				1			
Colombia	1, 6				1	29	20	7, 15
Congo	1		18		1		31	13–15
Costa Rica	1		19	11	1	29	25	2, 15
Côte d'Ivoire	1				1			15
Cuba	1				1		25	
Cyprus	1, 6		25		1			
Czechoslovakia	1, 2				1, 9			
Denmark	1					5		
Djibouti	1				1	27		
Dominica	1				1			
Dominican Republic	1, 6, 21, 26	27			1			16
Ecuador	1				1	30	24	10
Egypt	7			25	1	18	1, 23	
El Salvador	1				1	29, 30		
England and Wales	1							
Equatorial Guinea	1				1	5		3
Ethiopia	7, 19		2	6	1			
Fiji	1							
Finland	1				1			
France	1				1, 8		14	14, 15
Gabon	1		12		1			17
Gambia	1	1, 18			1			15
German Federal Republic	1				1	17		

[1] Chart excludes ex-USSR republics and Baltic states.

Sept	Oct	Nov	Dec	Variable[2]
				Ad (3), Ar, As, ER(3), NY (Hindu), PB, R
		28,29		
		1		Ad, As, ER, NY (Muslim), PB
8		1, 4	8, 25, 26	A, CC, EM, GF, WM
17		11	10, 25	
	12		8, 25, 31	GF, HT
			25, 26	EM, GF, HS
	26	1	8, 24, 25, 26	A, CC, EM, WM
			25, 26	
			16	Ad(3), As(2), ER(3), NY (Muslim), PB
		7	16, 25, 31	Ad(3), ER(3), NY (Bengali), PB, etc
		30	25, 26	EM, GF, WM, Kadooment (Aug), May Hol, United Nations (Oct)
		1, 11	25	A, EM, WM; May, Aug, Nov BH; regional hol (July/Sept)
10, 21	12	19	25, 26	EM, GF, HS
	26	30	25, 31	Ad, ER
		11–13	17	
		1	25	C(2), CC, GF
30			25, 26	A, EM, GF, HS; President's Day (July); PH July, Oct
7	12	2, 15	25	C(2), CC, GF, HS, HT
			25	Ad, ER(2), GF, NY (Chinese, Muslim), PB, R, Mi'raj (March–April), Koran (May)
9		7		
		1	25	A, Ad, EM, ER, PB, WM
18		1	25	A
			25	A, Ad, ER, GF
		11	25, 26	EM, GF, Labour (Sept), Thanksgiving (Oct), Victoria (May)
12			24, 25	GF
1		1	1, 25	A, EM, WM
		1, 28	25	Ad, EM, ER, PB
11, 18, 19	12	1	8, 25, 31	GF, HS
	1			Spring Fest (4) (Jan/Feb)
	12	1, 15	8, 25, 30, 31	A, CC, GF, HT, St Joseph (March), Sacred Heart (June)
		1	25, 31	
15	12		8, 25	CC, GF, HS, HT
		1	24, 25, 31	A, Ad, EM, ER, GF, WM
	10			
	28, 29		25, 26	Ad, EM, ER, GF, HS, PB
			24, 25, 26, 31	EM
			24, 25, 26	A, EM, GF, HT, WM, General Prayer (April/May)
			25	Ad(2), ER(2), NY (Muslim), PB, Mi'raj (March/April)
		3, 4	25, 26	C(2), EM, GF, WM, Aug Monday
24			25	CC, GF
	9, 12	2, 3	6, 25, 31	C(2), GF, HT
	6			Ad(2), Ar, ER(2), NY (Muslim), PB, Ps, ES (E Orth), Sham El-Nessim (April/May)
15	12	2, 5	24, 25, 30, 31	GF, HT, AW, San Salvador (4)
				EM, GF; BH Early May, Late May, Aug
	12		10, 25	CC, GF, Constitution (Aug)
12, 27				Ad, ER, NY (Ethiopian, Sept), PB, Ethiopian GF and Easter
	12		25, 26	D, EM, GF, HS, PB, Aug BH, Queen's b'day (June), Pr Charles' b'day (Nov)
	31	1	6, 24, 25, 26, 31	A, EM, GF, Midsummer Eve and Day (June), Twelfthtide (Jan), Whit (May/June)
	31	1, 11	24, 25, 31	A, EM, GF, HS, WM, Ascension Eve, Whit Hol Eve, Law of 20 Dec 1906, Law of 23 Dec 1904
		1	25	Ad, EM, ER, WM
			25	Ad, As, ER(2), GF, PB
			24, 25, 26	A, EM, GF, WM, Day of Penance (Nov)

[2] For abbreviation key see end of chart. Numbers in brackets refer to number of days devoted to the holiday.

National holidays *(cont.)*

	Jan	*Feb*	*March*	*April*	*May*	*June*	*July*	*Aug*	*Sept*
Ghana	1		6		1	4	1		
Greece	1, 6		25		1			15	
Grenada	1, 2	7			1			3, 4	
Guatemala	1				1	30	1		15
Guinea	1			3	1			15	
Guyana	1	23			1			1	
Haiti	1, 2			14	1			15	
Honduras	1			14	1				15
Hungary	1			4	1			20	
Iceland	1				1	17			
India	1, 26				1	30		15	
Indonesia	1							17	
Iran		11	20, 21	1, 2		5			
Iraq	1, 6	8	21		1		14, 17		
Ireland	1		17						
Israel	1				14				
Italy	1, 6			25				14, 15	
Jamaica	1				23			5	
Japan	1, 2, 3, 15	11	21	29	3, 5				15, 23
Jordan	1				1, 25	10		11	
Kenya	1				1	1			
Korea, South	1, 2, 3		1, 10	5	5	6	17	15	
Kuwait	1	25, 26, 27							
Lebanon	1	9			1			15	
Lesotho	1		12, 21		2				
Liberia	1	11	15	12	14		26	24	
Libya			2, 8, 28			11	23		1
Liechtenstein	1, 6	2	19		1			15	
Luxembourg	1				1	23		15	
Madagascar	1		29		1	26		15	
Malawi	1		3		14		6		
Malaysia	1				1	3		31	
Maldives	1						26, 27		
Mali	1, 20				1, 25				22
Malta	1		31		1			15	
Mauritania	1				1, 25		10		
Mauritius	1, 2		12		1				
Mexico	1	5	21		1, 5				1, 16
Monaco	1, 27				1, 8		14	15	3
Mongolia	1, 2		8		1		10, 11, 12		
Morocco	1		3		1, 23		9	14	
Mozambique	1	3		7	1	25			7, 25
Myanmar	4	12	2, 27	1	1		19		
Nauru	1, 31				17		1		
Nepal	11	19							
Netherlands	1			30	5				
New Zealand	1, 2	6		25					
Nicaragua	1				1		19		14, 15
Niger	1			15	1			3	
Nigeria	1				1				
Northern Ireland			17						
Norway	1				1, 17				
Oman									

Oct	*Nov*	*Dec*	*Variable*
		25, 26, 31	EM, GF, HS
28		25, 26	GF, EM, WM, Mon in Lent
25		25, 26	CC, EM, GF, WM
12, 20	1	24, 25, 31	GF, HS, HT
2	1	25	Ad, EM, ER, PB
		25, 26	Ad, D, EM, GF, PB, Phagwah (March), Caribbean (July)
17, 24	1, 2, 18	5, 25	A, C, CC, GF
3, 12, 21		25, 31	GF, HT
	7	25, 26	EM
		25, 26	A, EM, GF, HT, WM, First Day of Summer, Aug Hol Mon
2		25, 31	NY (Parsi, Aug)
		25	A, AD, ER(2), GF, NY (Icaka, March; Muslim), PB, Ascension of Prophet (March/April), Waisak (May)
			Ad, As, ER, PB, Prophet's Mission (April), Birth of 12th Imam (April/May) Martyrdom of Imam Ali (May), Death of Imam Jaffar Sadegh (June/July), Birth of Imam Reza (July), Eid-E-Ghadir (Aug), Death of Prophet and Martyrdom of Imam Hassan (Oct/Nov)
			Ad(4), As, ER(3), NY (Muslim), PB
		25, 26	EM, GF, Aug Hol, Oct Hol, Christmas Hol
			NY (Jewish, Sept/Oct), Purim (March), First Day of Passover (April), Last Day of Passover (April), Pentecost (May/June), Fast of Av (July/Aug), Day of Atonement (Oct), Feast of Tabernacles (Oct)(2)
	1	8, 25, 26	EM
20		25, 26	AW, EM, GF
10	3	23	
	14	25	Ad(4), R, ER(4), NY (Muslim), PB
20		12, 25, 26	EM, GF, ER(3) 26 GF, HS, EM, Youth (Aug)
1, 3, 9		25	NY (Chinese, Jan/Feb), Lord Buddha's Birthday (May), Moon Fest (Sept/Oct)
			Ad(3), ER(3), NY (Muslim), PB, Ascension of Prophet (March/April), Standing on Mt Ararat (Aug)
	1, 22	25	Ad(3), As, EM, GF, ER(3), NY (Muslim), PB
4		25, 26	A, EM, GF, Family (July), National Sports (Oct)
	29	25	Decoration (March), National Fast and Prayer (April), Thanksgiving (Nov)
7			Ad(4), ER(3), PB
	1	8, 24, 25, 26, 31	A, C, CC, EM, GF, WM
	1, 2	25, 26, 31	A, EM, WM, Shrove Mon
	1	25 , 30	A, EM, GF, WM
17		22, 25, 26	EM, GF, HS
		25	Ad, D, ER(2), NY (Chinese, Jan/Feb; Muslim), PB, Wesak
	11, 12		Ad(4), ER(3), NY (Muslim), PB, R(2), Huravee (Feb), Martyrs (April), National (Oct/Nov)(2)
	19	25	Ad, ER, PB, Prophet's Baptism (Nov)
		13, 25	GF
	28		Ad, ER, NY (Muslim), PB
	1	25	Ad, D, ER, PB, Chinese Spring Fest (Feb)
12	2, 20	12, 25, 31	HT, GF
	1, 11, 19	8, 25	EM, WM
	7		
	6, 18		Ad(2), ER(2), NY (Muslim), PB
		25	
1		25	NY (Burmese), Thingyan (April)(4), End Buddhist Lent, full moon days
27		25, 26	EM, GF, Easter Tue
	8	16, 29	NY (Sinhala/Tamil, April), Maha Shivarata (Feb/March)
		25, 26	A, EM, GF, WM
		25, 26	EM, GF, Queen's b'day (June), Labour (Oct)
		8, 25	GF, HT
		18, 25	Ad, ER, PB
1		25, 26	Ad(2), EM, ER(2), GF, PB
		25, 26, 29	BH early May, late May, July, Aug
		25, 26	A, EM, GF, HT, WM
	18, 19	31	Ad(5), ER(4), NY (Muslim), PB, Lailat al-Miraj (March/April)

***National holidays** (cont.)*

	Jan	*Feb*	*March*	*April*	*May*	*June*	*July*	*Aug*	*Sept*
Pakistan			23		1		1	14	6, 11
Panama	1, 9				1				
Papua New Guinea	1							15	16
Paraguay	1	3	1		1, 14, 15	12		15, 25	29
Peru	1				1	29, 30	28	30	
Philippines	1				1	12	4		
Poland	1				1		22		
Portugal	1			25	1	10		15	
Qatar									3
Romania	1, 2				1, 2			23	
Rwanda	1, 28				1		1, 5	1, 15	25
St Christopher and Nevis	1								19
St Lucia	1, 2	22			1				
St Vincent and the Grenadines	1, 22								
São Tomé and Principe	1	3			1		12		6, 30
Saudi Arabia									23
Scotland	1, 2								
Senegal	1	1		4	1			15	
Seychelles	1, 2				1	5, 29		15	
Sierra Leone	1			19					
Singapore	1				1			9	
Solomon Islands	1						7		
Somalia	1				1	26	1		
South Africa	1			6	31				
Spain	1, 6		19		1			15	
Sri Lanka	14	4			1, 22	30			
Sudan	1		3	6					
Suriname	1	25			1		1		
Swaziland	1			25			22		6
Sweden	1, 6				1				
Switzerland	1							1, 15	
Syria	1		8	17	1, 6		23		1
Taiwan	1, 2, 3		29	5			1		28
Tanzania	1, 12	5			1		7		
Thailand	1			6, 13	1, 5		1	12	
Togo	1, 13, 24			24, 27	1			15	
Tonga	1			25	5	4	4		
Trinidad and Tobago	1					19		1, 31	24
Tunisia	1, 18		20	9	1	1, 2	25	3, 13	3
Turkey	1			23	19			30	
Uganda	1			1	1				
United Arab Emirates	1							6	
USA	1, 21						4		
Uruguay	1			19	1, 18	19	18	25	
Vanuatu	1		5		1		30	15	
Venezuela	1, 6		19	19	1	24, 29	5, 24	15	
Western Samoa	1, 2			25	1, 2, 3				
Yemen Arab Republic					1				26
Yemen People's Democratic Republic	1		8		1	22			26
Yugoslavia	1, 2				1, 2		4		
Zaire	1, 4				1, 20	24, 30		1	
Zambia	1				1, 25				
Zimbabwe	1			18, 19	1, 25			11, 12	

Abbreviations used for variable holidays are as follows:

A Ascension Thursday
Ad Eid-ul-Adha
Ar Arafa
As Ashora
AW Ash Wednesday
BH Bank holiday
C Carnival (before Christian Lent, unless specified)
CC Corpus Christi
D Diwali, Deepavali

Oct	Nov	Dec	Variable
	9	25, 31	Ad(3), As(2), ER(3), PB, R
11, 12	3, 4, 28	8, 25	C(2), GF
		25, 26	EM, GF, HS, Queen's b'day (June), Remembrance (July)
12	1	8, 25, 31	CC, GF, HT
8	1	8, 25, 31	GF, HT
	1, 30	25, 30, 31	GF, HT
	1	25, 26	CC, EM
5	1	1, 8, 24, 25	C, CC, GF
		31	Ad(4), ER(4)
26	1	25	A, EM, WM
		25, 26, 31	EM, GF, WM, Labour (May), Queen's b'day (June), Aug Mon
		13, 25, 26	C, CC, EM, GF, WM, Emancipation (Aug), Thanksgiving (Oct)
27		25, 26	C (July), EM, GF, WM, Labour (May), Caricom (July), Emancipation (Aug)
		21, 25	
			Ad(7), ER(4)
		25, 26	GF, Early May, Late May, Summer BH (Aug)
	1	25	Ad , EM, ER, NY (Muslim), PB, WM
	1	8, 25	CC, GF, HS
		25, 26	Ad, EM, ER, GF, PB
		25	Ad, D, ER, GF, NY (Chinese, Jan/Feb)(2), Vesak
		25, 26	EM, GF, HS, WM, Queen's b'day (June)
21, 22			Ad(2), ER(2), PB
10		16, 25, 26	A, GF, Family (March/April)
12	1	6, 8, 25	CC, GF, HS, HT
		25, 31	Ad, D, ER, GF, NY (Sinhala, Tamil, April), PB, Maha Sivarathri (Feb/March), Full Moon (monthly)
		25	Ad(5), ER(5), NY (Muslim), PB, Sham al-Naseem (April/May)
	25	25, 26	EM, ER, GF, Holi (March)
24		25, 26	A, EM, GF, Commonwealth (March)
	1	24, 25, 26, 31	A, EM, GF, WM, Midsummer Eve and Day (June)
	1	24, 25, 26	A, CC, EM, GF, WM
6		25	Ad(3), ER(4), ES, NY (Muslim), PB
10, 25, 31	12	25	NY (Chinese, Jan/Feb), Dragon Boat Fest (June), Mid-Autumn Fest (Sept/Oct)
		9, 25	Ad, EM, ER(2), GF, PB
23		5, 10, 31	ER, Makha Bucha (Feb), Visakha Bucha (May), Buddhist Lent (July)
	1	25	A, Ad, ER
	4	4, 25, 26	EM, GF
		25, 26	CC, EM, GF, WM
15			Ad(2), ER(2), NY (Muslim), PB
29			Ad(4), ER(3)
9		25, 26	EM, ER, GF, HS
		2, 3	Ad(3), ER(4), NY (Muslim), PB, Mi'raj (March/April)
	11	25	Washington's b'day (Feb), Memorial (May), Labor (Sept), Discoverers' (Oct), Thanksgiving (Nov)
12	2	25	C(2), GF, HT, Mon- Wed of Holy Week
		25, 26	A, EM, GF, Constitution (Oct), Unity (Nov)
12	1	8, 25	A, C(2), CC, GF, HT
12		25, 26	EM, GF, HS
			Ad(5), ER(4), NY (Muslim), PB
14		30	Ad(3), ER(2), NY (Muslim), PB
	29, 30, 31		People's Uprising (July)
14, 27	17, 24	25	
24		25	GF, HS, Youth (March), Heroes (July), Unity (July), Farmers (Aug)
		25, 26	EM, GF

Abbreviations *(cont.)*

EM	Easter Monday	HS	Holy Saturday	PH	Public holiday
ER	End of Ramadan	HT	Holy Thursday	PS	Palm Sunday
ES	Easter Sunday	NY	New Year	R	First day of Ramadan
GF	Good Friday	PB	Prophet's Birthday	WM	Whit Monday

Wedding anniversaries

In many Western countries, different wedding anniversaries have become associated with gifts of different materials. There is variation between countries.

Anniversary	*Material*
1st	cotton
2nd	paper
3rd	leather
4th	fruit, flowers
5th	wood
6th	sugar
7th	copper, wool
8th	bronze, pottery
9th	pottery, willow
10th	tin
11th	steel
12th	silk, linen
13th	lace
14th	ivory
15th	crystal
20th	china
25th	silver
30th	pearl
35th	coral
40th	ruby
45th	sapphire
50th	gold
55th	emerald
60th	diamond
70th	platinum

Birthstones

Month	*Stone*	*Quality*
January	garnet	constancy
February	amethyst	sincerity
March	bloodstone	courage
April	diamond	innocence and lasting love
May	emerald	success and hope
June	pearl	health and purity
July	ruby	love and contentment
August	agate	married happiness
September	sapphire	wisdom
October	opal	hope
November	topaz	fidelity
December	turquoise	harmony

Signs of the zodiac

Spring		
Aries	The Ram	21 March–20 April
Taurus	The Bull	21 April–21 May
Gemini	The Twins	22 May–21 June
Summer		
Cancer	The Crab	22 June–23 July
Leo	The Lion	24 July–23 Aug
Virgo	The Virgin	24 Aug–23 Sept
Autumn		
Libra	The Balance	24 Sept–23 Oct
Scorpio	The Scorpion	24 Oct–22 Nov
Sagittarius	The Archer	23 Nov–21 Dec
Winter		
Capricorn	The Goat	22 Dec–20 Jan
Aquarius	The Water Bearer	21 Jan–19 Feb
Pisces	The Fishes	20 Feb–20 March

INDEX

a cappella 341
Aalto, Alvar 296
abacus 530
Abbott, Berenice 361
ABC (American Broadcasting Company) 138
Abe, Kobo 38
aberration of starlight 405
Abkhazi 143
ABM *see* antiballistic missile
aboriginal religion 171
Aborigine, Australian 143
abortion 82
abortion pill 82
Abraham 183
abscissa 530
absolute dating 379, 380
absolute monarchy 158
absolute war 242
absolute zero 543
absolutism 158
absorption spectroscopy 425
Abstract Expressionism 313
Absurd, Theatre of the 365
Abu Bakr 183
Abú Nuwás, Hasan ibn Háni 317
abyssal zone 457
abzyme 526
Academy Awards 328
accelerator mass spectrometry (AMS) 379
accessory 123
accomplice 123
Achilles tendon 86
acid 425
acid rain 259, 478
acne 91
acoustics 341, 543
acquittal 123
act of God 123
Act of Parliament 123
activation analysis 425
activation energy 425
acupressure 106
acupuncture 103
acute rheumatism 98
Adam, Robert 296
Adam, William 296
Adams, Ansel 361
Adams, John Couch 411
Adamson, Robert 357
adaptation 511
added value 255
adder, in electronics 450
additive 503
Adenauer, Konrad 571
adenoids 86
adenosine triphosphate 414, 523
Adi Granth 182
adjective 154
adjournment 123
admiral 235
adobe 292
adoption 123
adrenal gland 86
adult education 74
adultery 123
adverb 154
adverse variance 255
advertising
  expenditure, European 140
  expenditure, UK 138
  restrictions, European television 141
Advertising Standards Authority (ASA) 142
advocate 123
Aegean civilizations, art of 301
aerial 559
aerial archaeology 379
aerial photography 379
aerial reconnaissance 379
aerobic 517
aerogel 425, 426
aeroplane 226
aerosol 478
Aeschylus 368
AEW (airborne early warning) system 238
affidavit 123
affirmative action 160
Afghanistan 25, 27, 602
Africa 596
African Development Bank 283
African religions 171
African traditional dance 337
Afrikaans language 143
Afro-Asiatic languages 143
Agassi, Andre 15
ageing 514
Agence France-Presse 138
agoraphobia 89
Agostini, Giacomo 210
agricultural revolution 505
agriculture 505-10
  agricultural subsidies 504
  population engaged in 509
agrochemical 505
agronomy 505
aid, development 274
Aidid, Mohammed 22, 24
AIDS (acquired immune deficiency syndrome) 15, 19, 91, 92, 93, 100, 101, 103
Ainu 143
air force 235
air pollutants 476
air pollution 478
air transport 226-9
aircraft carrier 242, 248
airship 228
Airy, George Biddell 411
Alamein, El, Battles of 243
Alaska 36
Albania 602
albedo 405
Albee, Edward 368
Alberti, Leon Battista 296
alcohol 421
alcoholism 91
aldehyde 421
Aldrin, Edwin 411
Alexander II 31
Alexander the Great 35
Alexander technique 104
Alexeev, Vasiliy 210
Alfonsín Foulkes, Raúl Ricardo 571
Alfred, King 30
algae 521
algebra 530
Algeria 13, 14, 603
Algol 401
Algonquin 143
Algonquin Radio Observatory 408
Ali 183
Ali, Muhammad 210
alibi 123
alien 123
alimentary canal 86, 519
alimony 123
aliphatic compound 421
alkali 425
alkane 421
alkene 421
alkyne 421
All England Netball Association 225
allele 514
Allen, Woody 327
Allende Gossens, Salvador 571, 588
allergen 82
allergy 82
alliance 160
Allied Mobile Force (AMF) 235
Allies, the 235
Allitt, Beverly 28
alluvial deposit 457
Alma-Tadema, Lawrence 310
Alpha Centauri 401
alpha share 255
Altdorfer, Albrecht 307
Alter, Simha 38
alternation of generations 514
alternative medicine 103-6
altitude 530
Altman, Robert 327
alto 341
ALU 439
Alzheimer's disease 91
Amateur Fencing Association 224
Amateur Rowing Association 225
Amateur Swimming Federation of Great Britain 225
Amato, Giuliano 13, 27
Amazon Pact 108
ambassador 160
American ballet 337
American War of Independence 30, 36
Ames Research Center 390
Amhara 143
Amin Dada, Idi 571
amino acid 414, 422, 523
ammonia 418
amnesty 124
Amnesty International 121
amniocentesis 82
amortization 255
Ampère, André Marie 555
amphibian 519
amplifier 449, 559
Amritsar 184
Amundsen, Roald 35
amylase 523
anabolic steroid 101
anaemia 91
anaerobic 517
anaesthetic 101
analgesic 101
analogue signal 449, 543
analogue-to-digital converter (ADC) 450
analytical chemistry 414
analytical geometry 532
anarchism 158
Anaximander 411
ANC (African National Congress) 13, 16, 17, 19, 23, 26
Andean Group 108
Andersen, Hans Christian 317
Anderson, Brett 8
Anderson, Marian 38

Andorra 603
Andre, Carl 314
Andrea del Sarto 306
Andreotti, Giulio 25, 571
Andrews, Dana 39
Andromeda galaxy 401
angina pectoris 92
angiosperm 521
angle 530
angling 188
Anglo-Australian Telescope 410
Anglo-Chinese War 33
Angola 19, 22, 24, 36, 604
animals 518-20
  classification 518
  lifespans 515
  patents 528
Annamese 143
Anne, Queen of England 34
annelid 518
Annenberg, Walter 9
annual accounts 255
annual general meeting (AGM) 255
annual percentage rate (APR) 255
anorexia 89
Anouilh, Jean 368
Antail, Jozsef 571
Antarctic 511
  Circle 457
  Treaty 108
Antarctica 596-7
antenna 559
anthem 341
anthropology 379
anti-inflammatory 102
antiballistic missile (ABM) 235, 241
antibiotic 101
antibody 86
anticline 454, 457
antidepressant 102
Antigua and Barbuda 605
antiknock 478
antimatter 551
antiseptic 102
antiviral 102
Antonello da Messina 306
Antonioni, Michelangelo 327
anxiety 89
Anyaoko, Chief Emeka 119
aorta 86
Aouita, Said 210
apartheid 160
aperture 358
apex 530
aphelion 405
apogee 405
Apollo asteroid 395
Apollo project 390
apoplexy 99
apostrophe 154
appeal 124
appendicitis 92
Apple computer 267, 268
applied kinesiology 104
applied materials 270
aqua fortis 418
aqua regia 418
aquaculture 505
aquifer 457
Aquino, Corazón 571
Arab Common Market 283
Arab League 108
Arab Maghreb Union 108
Arab Monetary Fund 283
Arab-Israeli peace talks 18, 21, 25
Arab-Israeli Wars 243
Arabic numerals 530
Arabs 143
arachnid 518
Arafat, Yassir 571
arbitrageur 255
arbitration 124
Arbus, Diane 361
arc 530
arc minute 406
arc second 406
arch 290
Archaean 463
archaebacteria 522
archaeology 379-89
  chronology 386
  historical 383
archaeomagnetic dating 379
Archaeopteryx 465
Archaeozoic 463
archaeozoology 379
Archaic art 302
archery 188
Archigram 296
Archimedes 539
archipelago 457
architectural orders 292
architecture 289-300
  biographies 296-300
  history 289
  terms 290-2
Arctic 597-8
Arctic Circle 457
area, in mathematics 530
Arecibo 408
Argentina 21, 31, 605
aria 341
Ariane 390
Ariel 390
Ariosto, Ludovico 317
Aristarchus of Samos 411
Aristophanes 368
arithmetic 530
Armani, Giorgio 69
Armenia 606
Armenian 143
Armistice Day 235
armour 235
armoured personnel carrier 248
arms control 160
arms trade 235, 236
Armstrong, Louis 348
Armstrong, Neil Alden 411
army 235
Army Sport Control Board 225
Arnhem, Battle of 245
aromatherapy 104
aromatic compound 422
Arp, Hans 313
Arras, Battle of 245
arrest 124
Arrhenius, Svante August 435
arson 124
art 301-16
  15th and 16th centuries 306-7
  17th century 307-13
  18th century 308
  20th century 311, 315
  ancient 301-16
  auction sale prices 311, 313, 314
  patronage 304
  sale of works left in trust 310
Art Nouveau 290
Artaud, Antonin 368
artery 86
artesian well 457
arthritis 92
arthropod 518
articles of association 255
artifact 379
artificial insemination 506
artificial intelligence (AI) 439
artificial selection 511
artillery 235
Asante 143
Ascher, Zika 39
ASCII 444
asexual reproduction 512
Ashanti 143
Ashdown, Battle of 30
Ashdown, Paddy 3, 16
Ashe, Arthur 39, 210
Ashikaga period 316
Asia 598-9
Asia-Pacific Economic Cooperation Conference (APEC) 108
Asian Development Bank 283
Asian and Pacific Council (ASPAC) 108
Asoka 183
aspirin 102
Assad, Hafez al 571
assault 124
assault ship 248
assay 425
assemblage 379
asset 255
Assisted Places Scheme 74
Associated Press (AP) 138
Association of South East Asian Nations (ASEAN) 108
associative operation 530
asterisk 154
asteroid 395
asthenosphere 454
asthma 92
Astra satellite 139
astrological diagnosis 104
astrometry 406
astronaut 390
astronautics 390
Astronomers Royal 411
astronomical unit 406
astronomy 390-413
  biographies 411-13
  chronology 393
  technical terms 405-8
astrophotography 406
Asturias, Miguel Angel 317
Asuka period 316
Atget, Eugne 361
atherosclerosis 92
athletics 188
Atlantic, Battle of the 245
Atlee, Clement 571
atmosphere 460-3
atom 425
atom bomb 34
atomic absorption spectrometry 379
atomic number 425
atomic orbital 425
atomic weight 434
atonality 341
ATP 414, 523
atrium 290
Attorney General 124
attribute, in archaeology 379
Atwood, Margaret 317
audit 255
auger 379
Auger, Arleen 40
Augustine, Saint 183
aura diagnosis 104
Aurenche, Jean 40
aurora (australis; borealis) 395
Austen, Jane 317
Australia 13, 607
  prime ministers 579
Australia Telescope 408
Austria 14, 607
authoritarianism 158
autochrome 358
autogenics 104
autoimmunity 92
autonomy 160
autoradiography 526
autos sacramentales 365
autotroph 517
avant-garde dance 337

Avedon, Richard 361
AWACS 235
Axel Springer 141
axis 530
Ayckbourn, Alan 368
Aymara 143
Azerbaijan 26, 608
Azerbaijani 143
Azeri 143
AZT *see* zidovudine
Aztec emperors 592

Baade, Walter 411
Babangida, Ibrahim 571
Baccalaurat 74
Bach, Johann Sebastian 344
Bach flower healing 104
bacillus 522
back pain 92
Bacon, Francis 314
bacteria 522
bacteriophage 526
bad debt 255
badlands 457
badminton 189
BAFTA 329
bagatelle 341
Baha'i 178
Bahamas 16, 609
Bahrain 609
bail 124
bailey 290
Bailey, David 361
Baily's beads 396
Baker, James 14
balance of payments 274
balance sheet 255
Balboa, Vasco 35
Balchen, Bernt 37
Baldwin, James 317
baleen whales 518
Balla, Giacomo 312
Balladur, Edouard 25, 571
Ballesteros, Seve(riano) 210
ballet 337-9
ballistic missile 249
balloon 228
  hot-air 228
ballot 160
Balzac, Honoré de 317
Banco Central Hispano (BCH) 265
Banda, Hastings Kamuzu 571
Bandaranaike, Sirimavo 571
Bangladesh 610
bank 274
Bank of Commerce and Credit International 24
Bank of England 17, 18, 23, 24, 283
Bank for International Settlements 283
bankruptcy 255
Bannister, Roger 32, 210
baptism 180
bar 341
Bar, the 134
bar mitzvah 181
Barbados 610
barbershop 341
Barcelona 16
baritone 341
Barker, Howard 368
Barlach, Ernst 314
Barnard's star 401
barometer 460
Baroque architecture 289
Baroque art 307
barrister 124
Barry, Charles 296
Bartók, Béla 344
baryon 551
basal metabolic rate 517
base
  in chemistry 425
  in mathematics 530, 531
base lending rate 255
base pair 523
baseball 190
Baselitz, Georg 314
Bashkir 144
Bashō 317
BASIC 449
basilica 290
Basinger, Kim 335
basketball 190
Basque 144
bass 341
Bastille 587
BAT Industries 265
Bataan 245
Bates eyesight training 104
bathyal zone 460
battalion 235
battleship 235, 242
baud 560
Baudelaire, Charles Pierre 317
Bauhaus 312
bauxite 418
Baylis, Lilian 368
bayonet 248
Bazin, Marc 13
BBC *see* British Broadcasting Corporation
beach 460
Beach Boys, the 348
bear, on stock exchange 255
bearing 530
beat music 348
Beatles, the 348
Beaton, Cecil 361
Beaufort scale 460
bebop 348
Beckenbauer, Franz 210
Becker, Andrew 30
Becker, Boris 211
Beckett, Samuel 368
bed, in earth science 454
beer 494
Beethoven, Ludwig van 344
Begin, Menachem 571
behaviour therapy 90
bel canto 341
Belarus 611
Belgium 612
Belize 612
Bellini, Giovanni 306
Bellow, Saul 317
belly dancing 339
Belorussian 144
Ben Bella, Ahmed 572
Ben-Gurion, David 572
Benares 185
Bender, Lee 72
Benelux 108
Bengali 144
Benin 613
Bérégovoy, Pierre 40
Berg, Alban 344
Bergman, Ingmar 327
Bergman, Ingrid 334
Berkoff, Steven 368
Berlage, Hendrikus 296
Berlin Film Festival 329
Berlin Wall 244
Berlioz, (Louis) Hector 344
Bernini, Giovanni Lorenzo 296, 307
Bernoulli family 539
Bernstein, Sidney Lewis, Lord 41
Berry, Chuck 348
Bertelsmann 141
Berzelius, Jöns Jakob 435
Bessel, Friedrich Wilhelm 411
Best, George 211
Beta Persei 401
beta share 255
beta-blocker 102
bhangra 348
Bhil 144
Bhutan 613
Bhutto, Benazir 572
Bhutto, Zulfikar Ali 572
Biba 72
Bible 182
bicycle 231
Biffen, John 3
Big Bang 274, 401, 553
big-band jazz 348
bigamy 124
Biggs, Ronnie 8
Bihari 144
bill of exchange 255
bill of lading 255
billiards 190
binary fission 512
binary number system 444
binary star 403
binary weapon 248
binomial 531
biochemic tissue salts therapy 104
biochemistry 414-18
  chronology 415
biodegradable 478
biodiversity 474, 476
bioenergetics 104
biofeedback 104
biofuel 467
biological oxygen demand 474
biological warfare 235
biology, chronology 513
biome 474
biosensor 526
biosphere 474
biosynthesis 517
biotechnology 526
bird 519
  fossils 465
birth 514
birth rites 180
birthstones 734
biscuit 494
bistable circuit 449
bit 444
black hole 403, 404
blackmail 124
Blake, William 309, 317
Blanco, Serge 211
blasphemy 124
blindness 92
blockade 160
Blondin, Charles 33
blood 86
  poisoning 92
  pressure 82
blue chip 256
blue-green algae 522
blues, in music 348
boarding schools 74
bobsleighing 190
Boccaccio, Giovanni 317
Boccioni, Umberto 312
Bode, Johann Elert 411
Bodhidharma 183
Body art 314
Boff, Leonardo 10
Bohm, David 41
Bohr, Niels Henrik David 555
boiling point 425
Bokassa, Jean-Bédel 572
Boleyn, Anne 33
Bolger, Jim 572
Bolivia 614
Böll, Heinrich 317
Bologna, Giovanni 306
Bolshevik Revolution 36
bomb 236
bond
  in chemistry 425
  in economics 256
Bond, Edward 6, 12, 368
bone 520
bone marrow 86
Bonnard, Pierre 311

Bono 8, 10
boogie-woogie 348
book imports, USA 322
book production 318
Booker Prize 320
Boole, George 539
boot, in computing 444
Booth, William 33
Border, Alan 211
Borg, Bjorn 211
Borges, Jorge Luis 317
Borromini, Francesco 296
Borsellino, Paolo 14
borstal institution 134
Bosch, Hieronymous 306
bosing 379
Bosnia-Herzegovina 113, 162, 239, 615
peace talks 25
boson 551
Boston Massacre 31
Botha, P W 572
Botham, Ian 211
Botswana 615
Botticelli, Sandro 305
Bottomley, Virginia 12
Boucher, François 308
Boucicault, Dion(ysus) Larner 368
Boumédienne, Houari 572
Bourdelle, Emile-Antoine 314
Bourguiba, Habib ben Ali 572
Bourke-White, Margaret 361
Boutros-Ghali, Boutros 23, 24, 114, 115, 572
bovine spongiform encephalopathy 506
Bowe, Riddick 29
Bowie, David 12, 348
bowls 191
boxing 191
Boycott, Geoffrey 211
Boyle, Robert 555
Bradley, James 411
Bradley, Omar Nelson 245
Bradman, Donald George 212
Brady, Matthew B 361
Braer oil spill 483
Brahe, Tycho 411
Brahms, Johannes 344
brain 86, 520
Bramah, Joseph 32
Bramante, Donato 296
Branagh, Kenneth 368
Branch Davidians 24, 27, 179
Brancusi, Constantin 314
brand leader 256
Brandt, Bill 361
Brandt, Willy 41, 572
Branson, Richard 8, 226
Braque, Georges 312
Brassäi 362
Brazauskas, Algirdas 24
Brazil 616
bread 494
breakeven point 256
breathalyzer 124
Brecht, Bertolt 368
Breton, André 313
Brezhnev, Leonid 572
brick 292
bridge 292
brief 124
brigade 237
Bristow, Eric 212
Britain, Battle of 245
British Aerospace 269
British Airways 19, 23, 226
British Amateur Boxing Association 224
British Amateur Gymnastics Association 224
British Amateur Weightlifters' Association 225
British Amateur Wrestling Association 225
British Association of Sport and Medicine 225
British Athletic Federation 224
British Badminton Olympic Committee 224
British Baseball Federation 224
British Bobsleigh Association 224
British Broadcasting Corporation (BBC) 138
British Canoe Union 224
British Coal 27
British Coal Company 18, 21
British Commonwealth 119-21
British Cycling Federation 224
British Equestrian Federation 224
British Handball Association 225
British Ice Hockey Association 225
British and Irish Basketball Federation 224
British Judo Association 225
British Karate Federation 225
British Olympic Association 224
British Olympic Table Tennis Committee 225
British Orienteering Federation 225
British Ski Federation 225
British Taekwondo Control Board 225
British Tenpin Bowling Association 225
British Union for the Abolition of Vivisection 528
British Volleyball Association 225
British Water Ski Federation 225
Britten, Benjamin 344
Broadcasting Complaints Commission 142
Broadcasting Standards Council 142
Broglie, Louis de 555
broker 256
bronchitis 92
bronchus 86
Brontë, Anne 318
Brontë, Charlotte 318
Brontë, Emily Jane 318
Brontë, Patrick Branwell 318
Bronze Age 379
art 315
Bronzino, Agnolo 306
Brook, Peter 20, 369
Brown, Barbara 104
Brown, James 349
Brown & Williamson 265
brown dwarf 403
Bruckner, (Joseph) Anton 344
Bruegel, Pieter the Elder 306
Brundtland, Gro Harlem 572
Brunei 617
Brunelleschi, Filippo 296, 305
Brutalism 290
Bryant, David 212
Bryer, David 5
bryophyte 521
BSkyB 138
Büchner, Georg 369
buckminsterfullerene 423
buckyball 423
Buddha 183
Buddhism 171, 181, 185
Buddhist art 315
Buddhist festivals 727
budding 512
Budge, Donald 212
budget 256
buffer 444
buffer mixture 425
building and construction 292-6
building projects, UK 293
Bulgaria 617
Bulge, Battle of the 245
bulghur wheat 494
bulimia 89
bull, on stock exchange 256
Buñuel, Luis 327
burden of proof 124
burglary 124
Burkina Faso 618
Burkitt, Denis Parsons 42
burlesque 365
Burlington, Richard Boyle 296
Burman 144
Burns, Robert 318
Burundi 618
bus, in computing 439
Bush, Barbara 4
Bush, George 4, 5, 13, 15, 22, 572
Bushman 144
business 255-73
news 264-9
terms 255-64
Buthelezi, Chief Gatsha 572
butoh dance 339
butter 494
Butterfield, William 296
buttress 290
Byelorussia *see* Belarus
Byrd, Richard 37
Byrds, the 349
Byron, George Gordon 318
byte 444
Byzantine architecture 289
Byzantine art 304

cabaret 365
cabinet 160
Cable News Network 138
cable television 560
cadence 341
cadenza 341
Caesarean section 82
Cahn, Sammy 42
Caine, Michael 12
Cajun 349
cake 494
calculator 32
calculus 531
Calcutt report 23
Calder, Alexander 314
caldera 457
calendars 724-5
call 256
Callaghan, James 573
Callas, Maria 33
Callisto 396
calotype 358
calypso 349
Cambodia 20, 21, 23, 32, 619
Cambrian 463
camcorder 358
camera 358
camera obscura 358

Cameron, Julia Margaret 362
Cameroon 620
Camoëns (Camões), Lús Vaz de 318
Campaign for Nuclear Disarmament (CND) 121
Campbell, Kim 4, 573
Campese, David 212
Campin, Robert 306
Camus, Albert 318
Canada 16, 21, 24, 28, 620
 prime ministers 580
Canaletto, Antonio 309
Canary Wharf 265
cancer 92
candidiasis 99
Cannes Film Festival 329
canning 503
Cannizzaro, Stanislao 435
Cannon, Annie Jump 411
canoeing 191
canon, in music 341
Canova, Antonio 308
cantata 341
cantilever 290
Cantinflas 43
Cantor, Georg 539
Cao Chan (T'sao Chan) 318
Capa, Robert 362
capacitor 450
capacity 256
Cape Canaveral 390
Cape Verde 621
capital 274
 employed 256
 expenditure 256
 flight 256
Capital Cities/ABC 138
capital punishment 124, 137
Caporetto 245
Capra, Frank 327
capriccio 341
captive breeding 482
car 231
 chronology 232
 sales 270
 top producers 231
Caravaggio, Michelangelo Merisi da 307
carbohydrate 414
carbolic acid 421
carbon 418
carbon cycle 474
carbon dioxide 478
carbon monoxide 478
carbon tetrachloride 424
Carboniferous 463
carboxyl group 424
carboxylic acid 424
cardiac asthma 92
Cardin, Pierre 69
cardinal number 531
care order 125
Carey, George 9
Caribbean Community and Common Market (CARICOM) 108
Carlton Communications, the 265
Carné, Marcel 327
carnivore 517
Carnot, Sadi 555
Carracci, Annibale 307
carrier warfare 237
Carroll, Lewis 318
carrying capacity 474
Carson, Willie 212
cartel 256
Carter, Jimmy 573
Cartier, Jacques 34
Cartier-Bresson, Henri 362
Cartland, Barbara 6
caryatid 290
cash crop 506
cash flow 256
Caslavska, Vera 212
Cassini, Giovanni Domenico 411
Cassini space probe 390
Cassino 245
Casson, Hugh 296
Castagno, Andrea del 305
castle 290
Castro Ruz, Fidel 573, 587
catalyst 425
catalytic converter 478
cataract 93
cathedral 290
cathode 450
cattle 506
Cauchy, Augustin Louis 540
Cavaco Silva, Anibal 573
cave art 385
Cavendish, Henry 555
Caxton, William 36
CBC (Canadian Broadcasting Corporation) 138
CBS (Columbia Broadcasting System) 138
CD (compact disc) 349, 439
 boon 442
 costs 349
 industry 443
 top 10 350
CD-I (compact disc-interactive) 441
CD-ROM 439, 441, 442
Ceauşescu, Nicolae 573
celestial mechanism 406
celestial sphere 406
cell 522
Cellini, Benvenuto 307
cellular phone 560
Celtic burials 388
Celtic languages 144
cement 293
Central African Republic 622
Central American Common Market 283
Central Command 237
Central Council of Physical Recreation 225
central processing unit (CPU) 439
centre of gravity 543
centre of mass 543
centrifuge 425
Cepheid variable 403
cereal 494, 506
Ceres 396
CERN 108, 552
Cervantes Saavedra, Miguel de 318
cervical smear 82
Cézanne, Paul 311
CFC *see* chlorofluorocarbon
Chad 622
Chadli, Benjedid 574
Chadwick, James 555
Chagall, Marc 313
chain reaction 425, 543
chamber music 341
Chambers, William 296
Chandrasekhar, Subrahmanyan 411
Chaplin, Charlie 37, 327
Chardin, Jean-Baptiste Siméon 308
charge-coupled device (CCD) 406
Charlemagne 37
Charles II, King of England 36
Charles, Ray 349
Charlton, Bobby 212
Charteris, Leslie 43
château 290
Chaucer, Geoffrey 318
cheese 494
Chekhov, Anton Pavlovich 369
chemical equation 427
chemical equilibrium 427
chemical oxygen demand (COD) 474
chemical synthesis 423
chemical warfare 237
chemical weapons 23
chemistry 414-70
 chronology 428-9
 Nobel Prize for 436
chemosynthesis 517
chemotherapy 82
Chernobyl 32
Chiang Kai-shek 587
chickenpox 93
child abuse 125
child mortality 95
Chile 623
 Chilean Revolution 588-9
China 16, 18, 19, 20, 35, 624
 art 315
 Ming dynasty 591
 Qing dynasty 591
 religions 182, 185
 Revolution 587
Chinese 144
chip 444
Chirac, Jacques 574
Chiron 396
chiropractic 104
Chissano, Joaquim 574
chlorination 427
chlorine-free paper 489
chlorofluorocarbon (CFC) 479, 485
chlorophyll 521
chloroplast 521
chocolate 417, 495
cholesterol 496
Chopin, Frederic 344
chord 531
Christian, Fletcher 32
Christianity 173, 185
 feasts and festivals 726
Christie, Linford 213
Christo 314
Christopher, Warren 23
chromatography 427
chromosome 514
chromosphere 396
chronic fatigue syndrome 96
Chuang 144
church 290
Church of England 20, 21
Churchill, Caryl 369
Churchill, Winston 8
Chuvash 144
Ciampi, Carlo Azeglio 26
Cibachrome 358
cider 494
Cidrerie Stassen 269
cine camera 358
cinema 327-36
 chronology 330
 UK box office takings 331
circle 531
circulatory system 520
circumcision 180
circumference 531
circus 365
cirrhosis 93
CIS *see* Commonwealth of Independent States
CITES 490
Citizens Advice Bureau (CAB) 134
citizens' band 560
citizenship 160
citric acid cycle 416
city technology college (CTC) 74
civil defence 237
civil disobedience 125

civil law 125
civil service 166
Civil Service Sports Council 225
civil war 242
cladding 293
cladistics 511
Clapton, Eric 350
Clark, Alan 3, 7
Clark, David 8
Clark, Jim 213
Clark, Ossie 72
Clarke, Kenneth 3, 4, 28
Classic FM 139
Classical architecture 289
Classical art 302-4
Clausewitz, Karl von 245
claustrophobia 90
Clay Pigeon Shooting Association 225
clef, in music 341
Clemente, Francesco 315
client-server architecture 444
climate 474
climatic change 456
clinical ecology 104
clinical psychology 90
Clinton, Bill 4, 11, 14, 19, 22, 24, 26, 165, 352, 574
Clive, Robert 33
cloister 290
clone 526, 527
clothes and fashion 69-73
  designers 69-73
  spending on 69
cloud 460
Clouet, François 307
Clouet, Jean 307
CNN (Cable News Network) 138
coal 469
coal mines 26
coalition 160
Coates, Nigel 296
coaxial cable 560
Cobb, Ty(rus) Raymond 213
coccus 522
cocoa 495
coda 341
codeine 102
codon 523
Coe, Sebastian 213
coeducation 74
coefficient 531
coffee 495
cognitive archaeology 380
cognitive therapy 90
COIN (counter insurgency) 237
Cold War 244
Coleman, Ornette 350
Coleman, Pat 9
collagen 527
collective bargaining 274
collective farm 506
collectivism 158
college of higher education 74
colligative property 427
colloid 427
Collor de Mello, Fernando 18, 574
Colombia 15, 18, 19, 624
Colombo Plan 283
colon 154
colonization 474
colonnade 290
coloratura 341
colour therapy 105
Coltrane, John 350
Columbus, Christopher 19, 32, 34, 36
column 290
Comaneci, Nadia 213
combine harvester 506
combined cycle generation 467
combined heat and power generation 467
combined pill 103
Comecon 283
comedy 365
comet 396, 397, 402, 456
comma 154
commando 237
Comme des Garçons 69, 70
commedia dell'arte 365
commissioner for oaths 125
committal proceedings 125
Committee of Permanent Representatives (EC) 114
commodity 256
commodity markets 256
Common Agricultural Policy (CAP) 111, 499, 506
common law 125
Commonwealth, British 119-21
Commonwealth of Independent States (CIS) 28, 108, 174
communications satellite 390, 560
communism 158
Communist International 31
community architecture 291
community charge 279
commutative operation 531
Comoros 625
company, army 237
company, business term 256
comparative advantage 274
competition 511
compiler 439
complement 531
complementary metal-oxide semiconductor 450
Composite order 290, 291
compost 479
compound 427
comprehensive schools 74
compulsory purchase 125
computer 439-49
  chronology 445
  games 440
  generation 439
  graphics 303, 440
  hardware 442-4
  information, misuse 226
  memory 439, 443
  menu 447
  personal (PC) 439
  police, use by 123, 126
  simulation 440
  software 449
  terms 444-9
  uses for, generally 439-42
computer-aided design (CAD) 439
computer-aided manufacturing (CAM) 440
computer-assisted learning (CAL) 439
computer-generated effects 448
computerized axial tomography (CAT) 380
concave 531
concentric circle 531
Conceptualism 314
concerto 341
concrete 293
condenser 450
conductive education 74
cone 531
Conference on Security and Cooperation in Europe (CSCE) 108
conferences, international 242-3
configuration 427
confirmation 181
Confucianism 174
Confucius 183
Congo 626
Congreve, William 369
congruent 531
conic section 531
conjunction
  in astronomy 406
  in grammar 154
Conley, Rosemary 10
Connolly, Maureen 213
Connors, Jimmy 213
Conrad, Joseph 318
Conran, Jasper 69
conscription 237
consent, age of 125
conservation 474-93
  architectural 291
conservatism 158
Constable, John 309
constants 531
  fundamental 545
constellation 403
constitution 161
Constructivism 312
consumer 256
  protection of 125
  sovereignty 256
consumer durables 256
consumption 100, 274
contact improvisation 339
contemporary art 314
contempt of court 125
context, in archaeology 380
continental drift 463
continents 454, 596-601
contraceptive 82
contract archaeology 380
contract of employment 125
contralto 341
convergent evolution 511
converse 531
conversion tables 719
convertible loan stock 256
convex 532
convulsion 82
Cook, Captain James 30, 34
Cooper, Samuel 308
Coopers & Lybrand 271
coordinate geometry 532
coordinated universal time (UTC) 408
Copernicus, Nicolaus 411
Coplaca 270
Coppola, Francis Ford 328
Copt 145
copyright 127
coral reef 474
core 380, 454
Corinthian order 290, 291
Coriolis effect 460
cornea 86
Corneille, Pierre 369
corona 396
coroner 127
Corot, Jean-Baptiste Camille 309
corporal punishment 127
corporate strategy 257
corps 237
cortex 86
corticosteroid 102
cosine 532
cosmic background radiation 403
cosmid 526
cosmology 406
Cosmos 390
cost of living 274
cost of sales 257
cost-benefit analysis 257

cost-push inflation 274
Costa Rica 626
Costello, Elvis 6, 350
cot death 93
council 161
Council of the Entente 109
Council of Europe 109
Council of Ministers (EC) 112, 114
Council for the Protection of Rural England 490
counterpoint 341
country and western music 350
Countryside Council for Wales 490
county court 134
coup d'état 161
Courbet, Gustave 309
Courrèges, André 69
Court, Margaret 214
Court of Appeal 134
court martial 127
court order 129
Court of Protection 134
covalent bond 427
Coward, Noel 369
cracking, in chemistry 427
Cranach, Lucas the Elder 307
cranium 86
crater 396, 457
craton 454
Craxi, Bettino 21, 574
cream 495
credit 274
creditor 257
creole language 145
crescent 396
Cretaceous 463
Crichton, Michael 8
cricket 192
Crimean War 35
Criminal Injuries Compensation Board 134
Criminal Investigation Department (CID) 134
criminal law 127
critical mass 543
critical path analysis 257
Croat 145, 214
Croatia 15, 113, 627
Cromwell, Oliver 36
crop improvement 525
crop rotation 506
Crosby, Bing 350
cross-dating 380
crowding out 274
crown court 134
Crown Prosecution Service 134
crude oil 470
Cruelty, Theatre of 365
cruise missile 249
crust 454
crustacean 519
Cruyff, Johann 214
cryogenics 543
crystal therapy 105
Cuba 628
  Cuban Revolution 588
Cuban Missile Crisis 36
cube 312, 532
cuboid 532
cults 179
cultural anthropology 380
cultural resource management (CRM) 380
cumulative preference shares 257
Cunningham, Imogen 362
cupping 105
Curie, Marie 435, 555
Curie, Pierre 555
curing, preservation by 504
curling 193
currency 275
  exchange rates 276, 721-2
current, in earth sciences 461
current asset 257
current liability 257
current ratio 257
curriculum 74
curtain wall 291
curve 532
custody 127
Cuyp, Aelbert 308
cybernetics 532
cycling 193
cycloid 532
cylinder 532
Cyprus 34, 628
cystic fibrosis 93
cystitis 94
cytochrome 523
cytoplasm 522
Czech 13, 22
Czech Republic 629
Czechoslovakia 14, 22

D-day 245
da Gama, Vasco 32
Dachau 32
Dada 312
Daguerre, Louis 30, 362
daguerrotype 358
dairying 506
Dalai Lama 574
Dali, Salvador 313
Dalton, John 436
dam 293
damages, legal 127
dance 337-40
  chronology 338-9
Danka Business Systems 269
Dante Alighieri 319
Danton, Georges Jacques 587
Danube Commission 109
Dariganga 145
Darío, Rubén 319
Dark Ages, art of the 304
dark matter 403
darts 194
data 444
  communications 560
  compression 444, 560, 567
database 440
dating
  archaeology 380
  geological 463
Daumier, Honoré 309
David, Jacques-Louis 308
David Dunlap Observatory 408
Davis, Miles 350
Davis, Steve 214
Davy, Humphry 436
dawn raid 257
Dawson, Les 43
daycare 76
DDT 479
de Chirico, Giorgio 313
De Clercq, Willy 3
de Filippo, Eduardo 369
de Gaulle, Charles 30, 37, 245, 574
de Klerk, F W 17, 19, 21, 25, 574
de Mille, Cecil B(lount) 328
de Sica, Vittorio 329
de la Tour, Georges 307
deafness 94
Dean, Christopher 224
Dearing, Ron 75
death 514
death rites 181
debenture 258
debt 258
  international debt crisis 275
Debussy, (Achille) Claude 344
deception, in warfare 237
decimal fraction 532
Declaration of the Rights of Man 35
declination 406
decomposer 517
decomposition 427
deconstruction
  in architecture 290
  in fashion 70
decree absolute 128
decree nisi 128
dedicated computer 444
deed 128
deed poll 128
deep freezing 504
deer farming 506
defamation 128
defence, in law 128
defence spending 244
defendant 128
deferred share 258
deficit financing 275
Defoe, Daniel 319
defoliation 476
deforestation 476, 479, 480
Degas, Edgar 310
degree 532
dehydration 504
Deimos 396
Delacroix, Eugène 309
Delaunay, Robert 312
Delors, Jacques 113, 574
delta 457
Delta Force 237
Delta rocket 390
delusion 90
demand-pull inflation 275
dementia 94
Demirel, Suleyman 574
Demjanjuk, John 13
democracy 158
Dempsey, Jack 214
dendrochronology 381
Deng Xiaoping 574
Denmark 630
denominator 532
density 543
Denys, Jean-Baptiste 33
deoxyribonucleic acid *see* DNA
depreciation 258
depression 90
Derain, André 312
Derby winners 199
deregulation 275
dermatitis 94
dermatology 82
dermatosis 94
dervish dance 340
Descartes, René 540
desert 457
Desert Shield, Operation 245
Desert Storm, Operation 245
desertification 479
designer drugs 94
desktop publishing (DTP) 440
destroyer 237
détente 161
detergent 427
determinant 532
Dettingen, Battle of 33
devaluation 275
developed countries 509
developing, in photography 358
developing countries 509
Devonian 463
Di Maggio, Joe 214
diabetes 94
diagenesis 454
Diaghilev, Sergei 337
dialectical materialism 159
dialysis 82

diamond ring effect 396
diarrhoea 94
diatonic 341
Diaz, Bartholomew 30
Dickens, Charles 319
Dickens, Monica Enid 44
dictatorship 161
Diebenkorn, Richard 44
diet 496
Diet of Worms 32
dietetics 105
differentiation 532
diffraction 543
diffusion 381, 427
digital 450, 543, 560
digital data transmission 560
digital sampling 560
digital television 560
digital-to-analogue converter 450
digitizer 442
Dinka 145
dinosaur 465, 511, 527
diode 450
Diouf, Abdou 574
dioxin 479
diploid 514
diplomacy 161
dipole 4573
Dirac, Paul Adrien Maurice 555
Dire Straits 350
direct democracy 158
directed number 532
director 258
Director of Public Prosecutions 128
directory, in computing 444
disaccharide 414, 417
disarmament 238
disc 439
disco music 350
diseconomies of scale 258
disinvestment 275
disk 442
Disney, Walt 329
dissident 161
dissociation 427
distance learning 76
distances by air 820-1
distillation 427
distributive operation 532
diversification 258
dividend 258
diving 194
division, military 238
divorce 128
Dixieland jazz 350
Djibouti 630
DNA (deoxyribonucleic acid) 414, 523, 526, 527
  fingerprinting 126, 525, 526
  profiling 126, 526
  sequencing 525
dodecahedron 533
Dogon 145
Doisneau, Robert 362
Dolce, Domenico 69
Dolce e Gabbana 69, 72
doldrums 461
Domagk, Gerhard 436
Domenichino 307
Domi, Tanya 11
Dominica 631
Dominican Republic 631
Dominion Astrophysical Observatory 408
Donatello 305
Donellan, Declan 369
Dongxiang 145
Dönitz, Karl 245
Donne, John 319
Doors, the 350
Doric order 290, 291
DOS (disc operating system) 444
Dos Passos, John 319
Dostoievsky, Fyodor Mikhailovich 319
double star 403
Douglas Home, William 44
Dow Jones 142
Dow Jones Index 275
Down's syndrome 94
dowsing 381
Drake, Francis 31, 37
DRAM 450
Dresdner Bank 268
Dreyer, Carl Theodor 329
drink 494-503
drought 259, 461
drugs 101-3
  dependence on 90
  misuse of 94
Dryden, John 32
Dubček, Alexander 45, 574
Duccio 305
Duchamp, Marcel 313
dune 457
Dunkirk 245
Dunlop, J B 231
Duras, Marguerite 319
Dürer, Albrecht 306
Duvalier, François 575
Duvalier, Jean-Claude 575
Dvorák, Antonin (Leopold) 344
dye-transfer print 358
Dylan, Bob 33, 351
dynamic random-access memory (DRAM) 450
dynamics 543
dyslexia 90
E-mail *see* electronic mail
ear 86
Earle, Sylvia 12
early warning systems 238
earnings, as economic term 258
Earth, the 396
  development of 463-6
  interior of 454-5
  measuring 456
  surface of 457-60
Earth art 314
earth science 454-66
Earth Summit 13, 476
earthquake 17, 19, 22, 454
easement 128
East Germany 265
Eastern art 315-16
Eastern European Mutual Assistance Pact 111
Eastman Kodak 267
EC *see* European Community
ecclesiastical law 128
echinoderm 519
echo-locate 518
Eckstine, Billy (William Clarence) 45
eclipse 397
eclipsing binary 403
ecliptic 406
ecolabelling 489
ecology 475
Ecomax (UK) 267
Economic Commission for Africa (ECA) 119
Economic Commission for Europe (ECE) 119
Economic Commission for Latin America (ECLA) 119
Economic Commission for Western Asia (ECWA) 119
Economic Community of Central African States (CEEAC) 109
Economic Community of West African States (ECOWAS) 109
Economic Cooperation Organization (ECO) 109
economic growth 275
Economic and Social Commission for Asia and the Pacific (ESCAP) 119
Economic and Social Committee (EC) 114
Economic and Social Council (UN) 115
economics, international 274-85
  terms 274-82
economies of scale 258
ecosystem 475
Ecuador 17, 632
eczema 94
Edberg, Stefan 17, 214
Eddington, Arthur Stanley 411
Edo period 316
education 74-81
  costs 74
  expenditure 74
  terms 74-80
Education Reform Act 75
Edwards, Gareth 214
Edwards Air Force Base 390
EEPROM 450
Effelsberg, radio telescope 408
efficiency, in physics 543
egalitarianism 158
egg 495
Eggleston, William 362
Egypt 20, 632
Egyptian 19, 24
Egyptian art 301
Ehrlich, Paul 82
eidophor 562
Einstein, Albert 555
Eisenhower, Dwight 575
Eisenstein, Sergei Mikhailovich 329
El Greco 307
El Salvador 633
elasticity 544
elastomer 429
electric battery 467
electric current 544
electricity 467, 471, 544
electroconvulsive therapy (ECT) 90
electrocrystal diagnosis 105
electrodynamics 544
electrolysis, in archaeology 381
electromagnetic waves 544
electron 429, 451, 551
  microscope 526
  spin resonance (ESR) 381
  tube 453
electronegativity 429
Electronic Book 441
electronic funds transfer 258
electronic mail (E mail) 440, 562
electronics 450-3
  chronology 451
electrophoresis 427
electroporation 526
electrostatic document analysis (ESDA) 126
electrovalent bond 431
elements 429
  discovery of 430-1
  periodic table 433
Eleven Plus examination 76
Elgar, Edward 344
Eliot, George 319
Eliot, T S 319
Elizabeth II, Queen of Great Britain 119

Ellington, Duke 351
Elliott, Denholm Mitchell 45
ellipse 533
Ellis, Perry 70
elongation 406
elution 429
embryo 514
employment law 128
EMS *see* European Monetary System
emulator 444
emulsion 429
Encke's comet 397
encore 341
end-use certificate, in shipping 258
endangered species 480
Endeavour, space shuttle 23
endogenous endocrinotherapy 105
endometriosis 94
endoscopy 82
Energia 390
energy 467-511, 544
  conservation 480
  nuclear 468
  of reaction 429
  solar 471
  in the UK 472
engine 544
England
  art in 307-9
  sovereigns 595
English Lacrosse Union 225
English language, common spelling errors 157
English legal system 128
English Nature 490
enhanced radiation weapon 249
Enso-Gutzeit 265
enthalpy of reaction 430
entropy 544
environment and conservation 474-93
environmental groups 490-1
  issues, generally 480
environmental archaeology 381
Environmental Protection Agency, US 491
Environmentally Sensitive Area (ESA) 490
enzyme 415, 524
eolith 381
epicentre 454
epicycloid 533
epilepsy 94
epoch 463
Epstein, Jacob 314
equal opportunities 128, 258
equation 533
equator 457
Equatorial Guinea 634
equestrianism 194
equilateral 533
equilibrium 544
equinox 406
equity 128, 258
era 464
Eratosthenes 540
Eritrea 26, 28
ERM *see* Exchange Rate Mechanism
Ernst & Young 271
Eros, asteroid 397
erosion 457
Ershad, Hussain Mohammad 575
erythrocyte 88
escape velocity 406
Escobar, Pablo 15
escrow 128
ester 424
Estes, Richard 314
Estonia 14, 634
Estonian 145
estuary 461
ethanoic acid 424
ether 424
Ethiopia 635
ethnic cleansing 15, 161
ethnic groups 143-54
ethnoarchaeology 381
ethnography 381
ethnology 381
Etruscan art 302
étude 341
Euclid 540
eukaryote 522
Euler, Leonhard 540
Euripides 369
Eurobond 258
EuroDisney 272
Europa, moon 398
Europe 599-600
  conventional forces in 13
  European Atomic Energy Commission (EURATOM) 111
  European Bank for Reconstruction and Development (EBRD) 283
  European Broadcasting Union (EBU) 138
  European Coal and Steel Community (ECSC) 111
  European Commission 112, 114
    presidents 112
  European Common Market 111
  European Community (EC) 16, 18, 19, 20, 21, 22, 23, 28, 111-14, 122
    aims 112
    budget 112
    CAP *see* Common Agricultural Policy
    Committee of Permanent Representatives 114
    Council of Ministers 112, 114
    directives 259
    EMS *see* European Monetary System
    ERM *see* Exchange Rate Mechanism
    legislation 132
    members 112
    quality standards 259
    Treaty of European Unity 13, 24, 28
European Court of Human Rights 134
European Court of Justice 111, 134
European defence expenditure and personnel 249
European Economic Community (EEC) 111
European Free Trade Association (EFTA) 109, 284
European Investment Bank (EIB) 111
European Monetary System (EMS) 15, 17, 19, 111, 113, 284
European Parliament 114
European Southern Observatory 408
European Space Agency (ESA) 109, 390
eutrophication 481
Evans, Arthur 31
Evans, Geraint Llewellyn 46
Evans, Walker 362
Evert, Chris 215
evidence 126
evolution 511
evolutionary biology 511-12
excavation, archaeological 381
Exchange Rate Mechanism (ERM) 15, 17, 19, 23, 269, 284
exchange rate policy 276
exchange rates 276, 721-2
excise duty 276
exclamation mark 154
exclusion principle 557
executive director 258
executor 128
exobiology 406
exosphere 461
expenditure, health 83, 86
experience curve 258
experimental archaeology 381
expert system 440
exploration
  Antarctic 597
  Arctic 598
  offshore petroleum 456
Explorer satellites 390
explosive 238
exponent 533
exponential 533
export 276
export markets 276
exposure meter 358
Expressionism 312
external economies of scale 258
extinction 481, 482, 511
extradition 128
extraterrestrial life 19
Eyck, Aldo van 296
eye 86
Eyre, Richard 12, 369

f-number 358
factor 533
factorial 533
factoring 258
factory farming 506
Fahd, King of Saudi Arabia 575
Faldo, Nick 215
Falklands War 245-6
Fallopian tube 86
fallout 238
fallow 507
Fang 145
Faraday, Michael 437, 555
farce 365
Farhi, Nicole 70
Farrell, Terry 296
Farsi 145
fascism 158
fashion 69-73
fasting 105
fat 415, 496
fat-soluble 417
fatty acid 424
Faul, Denis 10
Faulkner, William 319
fault 454
faunal dating 381
Fauvism 311
favourable variance 258
Fawkes, Guy 30, 36
fax 562
Federal Reserve System 284
federalism 161
Fellini, Frederico 329
fencing 195
Fenton, Roger 362
Fermat, Pierre de 540
Fermi, Enrico 555
fermion 551
Ferranti 268
Ferrari, Enzo 215
ferrite 418
Ferruzzi-Montedison 273

fertilization 514
fertilizer 507
fetus 514
Feydeau, Georges 369
Feynman, Richard 555
Fiat 272
Fibonacci, Leonardo 540
fibre, dietary 495
fibre crop 507
field
  in agriculture 507
  in physics 544
field marshal 238
Field medalists 540
field particle 551
field survey 382
Fielding, Henry 319
Fiennes, Ranulph Twistleton-Wykeham 7
Fiji 636
film, photographic 358
film awards 329
film directors 327
filter 451
finale 341
Financial Times Index 258, 276
financial year 258
Fininvest 140
Finland 636
Finney, Tom 215
Finno-Ugric language group 145
Fiorentino, Rosso 306
Firdawsi, Mansûr Abu'l Qâsim 319
firearm 238
firewood 481
fiscal policy 276
Fischer, Bobby 17, 20
Fischer, Emil Hermann 437
fish 495, 519
fish farming 505, 507
fishing nations 505
fission-track dating 382
Fittipaldi, Emerson 29
Fitzgerald, Ella 351
Fitzgerald, F Scott 320
fixed costs 258
fixed hard disc 442
fjord 457
flamenco 340
Flamsteed, John 412
flatworm 519
Flaubert, Gustave 320
flight, chronology 227
flip-flop 450
flood plain 458
floppy disc 439, 442
Florence 305
flour 497
flower 521
fluorescence microscopy 526
Fo, Dario 369
focus 360
foetus 514
fog 461
fold 454
folk dance 340
Fon 145
food 494-503
Food and Agriculture Organization (FAO) 115
food chain 517
food and drink, spending on 495
food poisoning 94
food technology 503-5
Foot, Michael 12
foot-and-mouth disease 507
football
  American 195
  Australian rules 197
  Gaelic 197
  World Cup 195-6
Football Association 195, 224
forage crop 507
force 544
Ford, John 329, 371
Ford (Europe) 272
Fordism 259
foreclosure 128
forensic science 126
forest, deforestation 476, 479, 480
forgery 128
Forman, Milos 5
formula 430
Forté, Lord 9
fossil fuels 467, 481
Foster, Norman 297
Foucault, Jean Bernard Léon 557
Fouquet, Jean 307
Fowler, Gerald (Gerry) 46
Fowler, Norman 3, 11
Fox, George 36
Fra Angelico 305
fractal 533
fraction 533
fractional distillation 430
fractionation 430
Fragonard, Jean-Honoré 308
France 15, 16, 28, 34, 35, 637
  art in 307-9
  French Revolution 586
  kings 593
franchise 259
franchise auction, broadcasting 139
Franck, César Auguste 344
Franco, Francisco 575
Franco, Itamar 18, 575
Francome, John 215
fraud 128
free radical 431
free-enterprise economy 276
free-market economy 276
freehold 128
freeze-drying 504
freezing point 431
frequency 544
fresco painting 305
fret, in music 341
friction 544
Friedrich, Caspar David 309
Friel, Brian 371
Friends of the Earth (FoE) 491
frigate 238
fringe theatre 365
Frink, Dame Elizabeth 47
front 461
frost 461
Frost, Major General John 47
fruit 497
fruit juice 497
Fuchs, Klaus 246
fuel economy 230
fuel-air explosive 249
fugue 341
Fujimori, Alberto 575
Fujitsu 270
Fulani 145
full stop 156
Fuller, Buckminster 297
Fuller, John Frederick Charles 246
fullerene 423
function 445, 533
functional group 424
fundamental constant 544, 545
funk dance music 351
further education colleges 76
Fuseli, Henry 309
future 259
futures market 259
Futurism 312
fuzzy logic 445
Fyffes 270
Fyodorov, Boris 4

G7 *see* Group of Seven
Gabbana, Stefano 69
Gabo, Naum 312
Gabon 637
Gabor, Dennis 557
Gagarin, Yuri 412
Gaia hypothesis 481
gain 451
Gainsborough, Thomas 309
galaxies 401-4
galaxy 403
Galileo Galilei 557
Galileo spacecraft 390
Galinski, Heinz 47
gall bladder 86
Galla 145
Galle, Johann Gottfried 412
Galliano, John 70
Gallipoli 246
gallium arsenide 418
gallstone 82
Gallup poll
  armed forces 251
  economics and business 285-358
  education 81
  environment and conservation 492-3
  health and medicine 106-7
  law 136-7
  mathematics 542
  media 142
  nuclear power stations 473
  politics 169-70
  religion 187
  telecommunications and video technology 568
Galois, Evariste 538
Galtieri, Leopoldo 246
Gambia 638
game farming 508
gamelan 341
gamete 515
Gance, Abel 331
Ganda 145
Gandhi, Indira 575
Gandhi, Mahatma 31, 576
Gandhi, Rajiv 576
Ganic, Ejup 10
Gannett 142
Ganymede, moon 398
García Márquez, Gabriel 320
garden city 291
gargoyle 291
gas 469
gas exchange 517
Gascoigne, Paul 215
gastroenteritis 95
GATT *see* General Agreement on Tariffs and Trade
Gaudí, Antonio 297
Gaudier-Brzeska, Henri 314
gauge boson 551
Gauguin, Paul 311
Gaultier, Jean-Paul 71
Gauss, Karl Friedrich 538
Gavaskar, Sunil Manohar 215
GCSE (General Certificate of Secondary Education) 76
gearing, financial 259
Gehry, Frank 297
Geingob, Hage Gottfried 576
Gell-Mann, Murray 557
Gemini project 391
gene 515
gene bank 526

gene therapy 89, 526
general, military rank 238
General Agreement on Tariffs and Trade (GATT) 115, 284, 499
Générale des Eaux 259
Genet, Jean 371
genetic code 524
genetic fingerprinting 126, 525, 526
genetics 84
 genetic code 524
 genetic engineering 525, 526, 528
Geneva Convention 129
Genocide Convention 129
genome 515
genotype 515
genre pictures 308
geochemistry 454
geodesic dome 291
geological time chart 464
geometry 533
geophysics 454
Georgetown, Declaration of 242
Georgia 14, 16, 18, 638
Georgian 145
geostationary orbit 406
geosynchronous orbit 406
geothermal energy 454, 468
Gerber, Paul 12
geriatrics 82
Géricault, Theodore 309
German measles 95
Germanic languages 145
Germany 15, 19, 28, 639
 art in 306, 309
germination 515
Gershwin, George 351
Gerson therapy 105
gestation 515
 periods 515
geyser 455
Ghana 19, 640
Ghazzali, al- 183
Ghiberti, Lorenzo 305
Ghirlandaio, Domenico del 305
Giacometti, Alberto 314
Gibbs, James 297
Gibbs, Josiah Williard 437
Gide, André 320
gigabyte 446
Gilbert, Cass 297
Gillespie, Dizzy 48, 351
Gillette 270
gilt-edged securities 276
Giorgione 306
Giotto 305
Giotto space probe 391, 395
Girondins 587
Giscard d'Estaing, Valéry 576
Gish, Lillian 48
glacier 458
glandular fever 95
Glashow, Sheldon Lee 557
glasnost 161
glaucoma 95
Glenn, John Herschel 412
global warming 481
globular cluster 403
glucose 416
gluon 551
GmbH 260
Gobind Singh 183
Godard, Jean-Luc 331
Goddard Space Flight Center 391
Gödel, Kurt 538
Goethe, Johann Wolfgang von 320, 371
Gogol, Nikolai 320
Goh Chok Tong 576
gold 418
golden share 260
Golding, William Gerald 48
Goldoni, Carlo 371
golf 197
Gond 145
Gondwana 464
Gondwanaland 464
González Márquez, Felipe 576
Gonzalez, Julio 314
Gooch, Graham 6, 215
Goodman, Benny 351
Gorbachev, Mikhail 576
Gordon, Kim 11
Gorecki, Henryk 12
gospel music 351
Gothic Classicism 305
Gothic style 289, 304
gout 95
government, UK 166-9
Gower, David 216
Goya (y Lucientes), Francisco de 309
Grace, W G 216
Graf, Steffi 15, 216
Graham, Martha 340
grammar 154, 155
grammar schools 76
Grand National 27
Grand National Archery Society 224
grand unified theory 545
grant-maintained schools 76
graphical user interface 446
graphics tablet 443
Grass, Günter 320
grassland 459
gravitational lens 406
graviton 551
gravity 406, 545
Grazinian 145
Great Britain Luge Association 225
Great Britain Olympic Hockey Board 225
Great Britain Target Shooting Federation 225
Greek art 302
Green, Lucinda 216
green audit 481
green belt 291
Green Party 491
green revolution 508
Greene, Graham 320
greenhouse effect 461, 481
greenmail 260
Greenpeace 491
Greenwich Mean Time (GMT) 407
Gregorian chant 341
Grenada 641
Gretzky, Wayne 216
grey market 260
greyhound racing 198
grid system 383
Grieg, Edvard 344
grievous bodily harm (GBH) 129
Griffith, D W 331
Griffith-Joyner, Delorez Florence 216
Grignard, François Auguste-Victor 437
Grimshaw, Nicholas 297
Gropius, Walter 297
gross 260
gross domestic product (GDP) 276
gross national product (GNP) 276
Grotowski, Jerzy 372
ground proximity warning systems (GPWS) 228
ground water 458
group 533
Group of Eight 109
Group of Rio 109
Group of Seven (G7) 14, 26, 109
 GNP/GDP in 275
Grünewald, Mathias 307
grunge
 fashion 70, 72
 music 351
Grupo Andino 108
Guaraní 145
Guardi, Francesco 309
Guatemala 642
Gudmundsdottir, Björk 11
Guernica 313
guerrilla 238
guerrilla war 242
Guevara, Ernesto 'Che' 588
Guinea 642
Guinea-Bissau 643
Gujarati 146
Gulf Cooperation Council (GCC) 109
Gulf War 246
Gunn, David 26
Gurkha 240
Guru Granth Sahib 182
Guthrie, Tyrone 372
Guthrie, Woody 351
Guyana 643
gymnastics 198
gymnosperm 521
gynaecology 82
Gypsy 150
gyre 461

ha-ha 291
Haber, Fritz 437
habitat 475
habitat protection 482
Habsburg, House of 593
Hachette 141
hacking 446
Hadlee, Richard John 216
hadron 551
haematology 82
haemophilia 95
haemorrhoids 95
Hâfiz, Sham al-Din Muhammad 321
Hahnemann, Samuel 105
hail 462
hair 87
hair analysis 105
Haiti 13, 14, 644
Hale, George Ellery 412
half-life 545
Hall, Peter 372
Halley, Edmond 412
Halley's comet 398
halogen 418
halon 481
Hals, Frans 308
Hamilton, Archie 3
Hamilton, Richard 314
Hamito-Semitic languages 143
Hamnett, Katharine 71
Han 146
Han dynasty art 315
handball 198
Handel, Georg Frederic 344
Hands, Terry 5
Hani, Chris 26, 49
Hanley, Ellery 216
Hanson, Duane 314
haploid 515
hard disc 439
hardcore rock music 351
Hardy, Thomas 321
Hare, David 372
Hariri, Rafik 18
harmonics 342
Harrier 249
harrow 508
Hattersley, Roy 11
Haughey, Charles 576
Hausa 146
Haussmann, Georges Eugène 297

Havel, Václav 5, 14, 576
Hawke, Bob 576
Hawkes, Christopher 49
Hawking, Stephen 557
Hawkins, Coleman 351
Hawks, Howard 331
Hawksmoor, Nicholas 297
Haworth, Norman 437
hay 508
hay fever 95
Haydn, Franz Joseph 345
Hayes, Helen 50
hazardous chemicals 20
HD-MAC 561
headache 102
health 82-107
 education 76
 expenditure 83
 screening 85
hearsay evidence 129
Hearst, William Randolph 140
heart 87
heart attack 95
heart disease 84
heartburn 95
heat 545
 pump 468
 storage 468
Heath, Edward 8, 9, 10, 576
heavy metal 351
hedgerow 475
Hei Ku T'ou 154
Hei-I 154
Heian period 316
Heine, Heinrich 321
Heinrich Bauer 141
Heisenberg, Werner 557
Hekmatyar, Gulbuddin 576
helicopter 228
heliopause 398
heliosphere 398
helix 534
Hellenistic art 302
Helmont, Jean Baptiste van 437
Helsinki Conference 243
Hemingway, Ernest 321
Hendrix, Jimi 351
Hendry, Stephen 217
Henry Doubleday Research Association 491
hepatitis 95
Hepburn, Audrey 50
herb 497
herbalism 105
herbicide 508
herbivore 517
hermaphrodite 515
hernia 95
herpes 95
Hersant 141
Herschel, John Frederick William 412
Herschel, William 412
Hertz, Heinrich 557
Hertzsprung-Russell diagram 407
Heseltine, Michael 11, 18
heterotroph 518
heterozygous 515
Hewish, Antony 412
Hewlett-Packard 267
hexadecimal number system 446
Hick, Graeme 217
Higgs boson 551
high-definition television (HDTV) 561, 562
higher education 76
Hilbert, David 538
Hill, David Octavius 362
Hill, Graham 217
Hilliard, Nicholas 307
Hindi language 146
Hindu art 315
Hindu festivals 727
Hindu-Arabic numerals 530
Hinduism 174, 182, 187
Hine, Lewis 362
hip-hop 351
Hipparchus 412
Hipparcos satellite 391
Hiroshima 246
Hirst, Damien 6
history 571-95
Hitchcock, Alfred 331
Hitler, Adolf 30, 31
HIV (human immunodeficiency virus) 15, 19, 91, 92, 100, 102, 103, 521
 worldwide statistics 92
Hmong 146
Ho Chi Minh 577
hoard 383
Hobbs, Jack 217
hockey 198
Hockney, David 7
Hodgkin, Dorothy Crowfoot 437
Hoechst 269
Hofmann, August Wilhelm von 437
Hogarth, William 309
Holbein, Hans 307
Holiday, Billie 351
holistic medicine 105
Holley, Robert William 50
Holly, Buddy 351
Holocene 464
Holy Roman emperors 591
home service force (HSF) 240
Homer 321
homicide 129
homo erectus 148
homo sapiens 148
homoeopathy 105
homologous series 424
homozygous 516
Honduras 644
Honecker, Erich 14, 22, 577
honey 497
Hong Kong 18, 19, 20, 163
Hooch, Pieter de 308
Hooke, Robert 557
Hooke's law 557
Horace 321
hormone 87
hormone-replacement therapy (HRT) 83
horse racing 199
Horszowski, Mieczyslaw 51
horticulture 508
Hosking, Eric 362
hospice 83
hospital beds 99
hostage 13, 29
Houphouët-Boigny, Félix 577
House of Habsburg 593
house music 353
Houston, Whitney 11
hovercraft 233
Howard, Ebenezer 297
Howe, Gordie 217
Hoxha, Enver 577
Hoxne treasure hoard 384
Hoyle, Fred(erick) 412
HP Bulmer 269
Hrawi, Elias 18
Hubble, Edwin Powell 412
Hubble Space Telescope 391
Hubble's constant 407
Hubble's law 407
Hugo, Victor 321
Hui 147
human body 86-9
Human Genome Project 19
human rights groups 119, 121-2
Human Rights Watch 121
human species, origins of 511
human-resource management 260
humanism, in art 306
Hun Sen 577
Hungary 645
hurling 200
hurricane 16, 462
Hussein, ibn Talal 577
Hussein, Saddam 22, 577
Huston, Angelica 331
Huston, John 331
Huston, Walter 331
Hutton, Len 217
Hutu 147
Huxley, Aldous 321
hydrocarbon 424
hydrochloric acid 418
hydrodynamics 545
hydroelectric power 468
hydrofoil boat 233
hydrogen 418
hydrogen bomb 240
hydrogenation 504
hydrophobia 98
hydroponics 508
hydrostatics 545
hydrotherapy 105
hyperactivity 90
hyperbola 534
hyperinflation 276
hyperon 551
hypertension 96
hypertext 446
hyphen 155
hypnosis 90
hypnotherapy 105
hypo 360
hypotenuse 534
hypothermia 96
hysterectomy 83
hysteria 90

Iapetus Ocean 464
Iban 147
IBM 23, 271
Ibo 147
Ibsen, Henrik 372
Icarus, asteroid 398
ICBM (intercontinental ballistic missile) 240
Ice Ages 464
ice cream 497
Ice Cube 5, 12
ice hockey 200
Iceland 3, 646
icosahedron 534
Ifugao 147
Igbo 147
Iliescu, Ion 577
illegitimacy 129
image compression 446
IMF *see* International Monetary Fund
immiscible 431
immunization 83
immunoassays 126
immunoglobulin 416
Imperial Chemical Industries (ICI) 267
imperial conversion tables 719
imperialism 159
import 276
import control 278
impotence 96
Impressionism 310, 311
imprisonment, cost of 136
impromptu 342
in vitro fertilization (IVF) 83
Inca emperors 592
incendiary bomb 249
inclination, in astronomy 407
income tax 278
incomes policy 278
incontinence 96
incubation time 515

indemnity 129
indentures 128
independent schools 76
Independent Television Commission (ITC) 138
indeterminacy principle 555
index of a number 533
India 20, 22, 26, 646
Emperors 592
Indian Mutiny 587
prime ministers 583
Indian art 315
Indian languages 147
indicator 431
indie music 353
indirect cost 260
indirect tax 260
individualism 159
Indo-European languages 147, 153
Indonesia 22, 647
Industrial Revolution 586
industrial tribunal 260
inertia 545
INF (intermediate nuclear forces) 243
infection 96
infectious disease 84
inferior planet 398
infinity 534
inflammation 83
inflation 278
inflection 156
influenza 96
information technology (IT) 446
Ingham, Bernard 9
Ingres, Jean-Auguste Dominique 309
initiation rites 181
injunction 129
Inkatha 17
Inns of Court 134
inorganic chemistry 418-21
inquest 129
Inquisition 557
insect 519
insecticide 508
insider trading 260
insolvency 260
instruments, unusual classical 342
insulation 481
insulin 102
integer 534
integrated circuit (IC) 444, 446, 451
Integrated Services Digital Network (ISDN) 562, 567
integration 534
Intelsat 391
Inter-American development Bank 284
intercontinental ballistic missile (ICBM) 240
interest 278
interface 446
interference 545
Intermediate Nuclear Forces Treaty 243
intermediate vector boson 555
intermezzo 342
internal economies of scale 260
internal-combustion engine 233
International Atomic Energy Agency (IAEA) 117
International Bank for Reconstruction and Development (IRBD) 117, 285
International Civil Aviation Organization (ICAO) 117
International Court of Justice 115, 134
International Date Line 458
International Development Association (IDA) 117, 285
International Finance Corporation (IFC) 117
International Fund for Agricultural Development (IFAD) 117
International Labour Organization (ILO) 117
International Maritime Organization (IMO) 118
International Monetary Fund (IMF) 118, 284
International Red Cross 15
International Telecommunication Union (ITU) 118
International Union for the Conservation of Nature (IUCN) 491
International Whaling Commission 29
International Whaling Commission (IWC) 491
interplanetary matter 398
Interpol 134
interstellar molecules 403
intestacy 129
intrauterine device 83
intrusion 455
Inuit 147
inventory 260
invertebrates 518-19
investment 260
investment trust 260
invisible trade 278
Io, moon 398
ion 431
Ionesco, Eugène 372
ion exchange 431
ionic bond 431
Ionic order 290, 291
ionization therapy 105
Iqbāl, Muhammad 321
IRA 13, 21, 25, 26, 27, 28, 294
Iran 28, 648
Iranian Revolution 589
Iraq 14, 15, 16, 22, 26, 28, 648
IRAS (Infrared Astronomy Satellite) 391
Ireland, Republic of 19
iridology 105
iris of the eye 86
Iron Age 383
irradiation 504
irrigation 508
ISDN 567
Ishiguro, Kazuo 321
Islam 175
Islamic architecture 289
Islamic calendar 724
Islamic Conference Organization (ICO) 109
island 458
islets of Langerhans 88
ISO 360
isobar 462
isoenzyme 416
isomer 424
isotope 431
isotopic analysis 384
Isozaki, Arata 297
Israel 13, 14, 18, 21, 23, 25, 650
issued capital 260
Italy 13, 18, 25, 26, 651
art in 307, 308
kings 592
ITAR-TASS (Information Telegraph Agency of Russia) 138
Ivory Coast 652
Ivy League 76
Iwo Jima 246
Izetbegovic, Alija 22

Jackson, Betty 71
Jackson, Michael 353
Jacobins 587
Jacobs, Marc 70
Jagger, Mick 10
Jainism 176, 182
Jamaica 652
James, Baroness 9
James, Henry 321
Janáček, Leoš 345
Jansky, Karl Guthe 412
Japan 27, 28, 652
Japanese art 316
Jaruzelski, Wojciech 577
Jat 147
jaundice 96
Javanese 147
Jayawardene, Junius Richard 577
jazz 348-57
Jehovah's Witness 178
Jellicoe, Geoffrey 297
jellyfish 519
Jencks, Charles 297
Jenkins, David 4, 11
Jenkins, Roy (Lord Jenkins of Hillhead) 9
Jennings, Humphrey 333
Jerusalem 184
Jesus 184
jet propulsion 228
Jet Propulsion Laboratory 391
jet stream 462
jetfoil 233
Jewish calendar 725
Jiang, Zemin 577
job enrichment 260
Jodrell Bank 408
Johns, Jasper 314
Johnson, Ben 26
Johnson, Jack 217
Johnson, Lyndon B 577
Johnson, Philip 297
Johnson, Samuel 321
Johnson Space Center 391
joint, anatomical term 88
joint venture 261
Jōmon period 316
Jones, Bobby 217
Jones, Inigo 297
Jones, Steve 12
Jonson, Ben 372
Jordan 26, 653
Joseph, Helen 51
Josephson, Brian 557
Joule, James Prescot 557
Joyce, James 321
joystick, computer 443
Judaism 176, 182, 187
judge 129
judicial review 129
judiciary 161
judo 200
junk bond 261
Jupiter 399
jurisprudence 129
jury 129
just-in-time (JIT) 261
justice 137
Jutland, Battle of 246
juvenile offender 129

K-T boundary 464
Kádár, János 578
kaaba 185
kabuki 365
Kafi, Ali 14
Kafka, Franz 321

Kahn, Louis 297
Kālidāsa 321
Kamakura period 316
Kamiya, Joseph 104
Kanarese 147
Kandinsky, Wassily 312
Kannada 147
Kantor, Tadeusz 372
Karadzic, Radovan 5, 22, 162, 578
Karan, Donna 71, 72
karaoke 353
Karen 147
Karsh, Yousuf 362
karyotype 516
Kaunda, Kenneth 578
Kawakubo, Rei 69, 70
Kazakh 147
Kazakhstan 654
Kazan, Elia 372
Keating, Paul 23, 25, 578
Keats, John 321
Kechua 150
Keck Telescope 408
Keifer, Anslem 314
Kekulé von Stradonitz, Fredrich August 437
Kelly, Petra Karin 52
Kelvin, William Thomson 557
Kemptner, Thomas 13
Kendall, Edward 437
Kendrew, John 437
Kennedy, John F 578
Kennedy, Nigel 7
Kennedy Space Center 391
Kenya 654
Kenyatta, Jomo 578
Kenzo Takada 71
Kerouac, Jack 321
Kertész, André 362
ketone 424
key 342
key-results analysis 261
keyboard, computer 443
Khaddafi, Moamer al 578
Khan, Imran 218
Khan, Jahangir 218
Khasbulatov, Ruslan 578
Khe Sanh 246
Khmer 147
Khmer Rouge 160
Khoikhoi 147
Khoisan 147
Khomeini, Ayatollah Ruhollah 578
Khrushchev, Nikita 578
Khwārizmā, Muhammad ibn Mūsāc al- 541
kidney 88
Kikuyu 147
kilobyte (KB) 446
Kim Il Sung 578
Kim Young Sam 578
kindergarten 77
kinetic theory 545
King, Albert 52
King, Billie Jean 218
King, Lord 8
King, Martin Luther 578
King's Counsel 130
Kinnock, Neil 15
Kipling, Rudyard 321
Kirchner, Ernst Ludwig 312
Kirghiz 147
Kiribati 655
Kitt Peak National Observatory 409
Klammer, Franz 218
Klaus, Vaclav 13, 14
Klee, Paul 313
Klein, Calvin 71
Klein, Roland 71
Klestil, Thomas 14
Kmer 147
Kobarid 246
Kofun period 316
Kohl, Helmut 113, 578
Koivisto, Mauno Henrik 579
Komatsu 270
Koon, Stacey 5
Koran 182
Korbut, Olga 218
Korea, North 656
Korea, South 657
Koresh, David 24, 27, 53
Kornberg, Arthur 437
Koudelka, Josef 362
Kourou 391
KPMG Peat Marwick 271
Kravchuk, Leonid 579
Krebs cycle 416
Kristiansen, Ingrid 218
Kroger, Helen 53
Kubrick, Stanley 333
Kuhn, Richard 437
Kuiper belt 399
Kung 149
Kurd 149
Kurosawa, Akira 333
Kuwait 18, 657
Kyrgyzstan 657
L-dopa 103
La Fontaine, Jean de 322
Labett, John 271
Labour Party 15
Lacroix, Christian 71
lacrosse 200
Lafontaine, Oskar 322
Lagerfeld, Karl 71
lagoon 462
Lagrange, Joseph Louis 541
Lagrangian points 399
Lahnda 149
laissez faire 278
Lamaism 171
lamarckism 511
Lamont, Norman 3, 5, 9, 12, 15, 20, 25, 28
LAN 446
Land, Erwin Herbert 362
Land art 314
Land Registry 135
land rights 144
land use by continent 507
Landsat 391
Landsbergis, Vyutautus 579
landscape archaeology 384
landslide 458
Lang, Fritz 333
Lang, Helmut 70
Lange, David Russell 579
Lange, Dorothea 362
Langmuir, Irving 437
languages 143-54
Lao Tzu 184
Laos 658
Laplace, Pierre Simon, Marquis de 412
Lapp 151
laptop computer 446, 449
larceny 130
lard 498
larva 516
laryngitis 96
Las Campanas Observatory 409
Lasdun, Denys 297
laser 545
 disc 303
 guidance systems 236
 pulses 546
Latimer, Clare 23
Latin American Economic System (LAES) 110
Latin American Integration Association (ALADI) 110
latitude 458
Latvia 658
Latvian 149
Latynina, Larissa Semyonovna 218
Lauda, Niki 36, 218
Laurasia 464
Lauren, Ralph 71
lava 455
Laver, Rod(ney) George 218
Lavoisier, Antoine Laurent 437
law 123-37
Law Commission 135
law courts 135
law lords 130
Lawn Tennis Association 225
Lawrence, D H 322
Lawrence, Ernest 557
Le Corbusier 298
Le Gray, Gustave 362
Le Pen, Jean-Marie 9
leaching 483
lead 483
leaders of the modern world 571-86
leaf 521
Lean, David 333
learning curve 261
leasehold 130
Leavitt, Henrietta Swan 412
Lebanese Civil War 32
Lebanon 13, 21, 23, 26, 659
Lebrun, Charles 307
Ledoux, Claude-Nicolas 298
Lee, Spike 5
Lee Kuan Yew 579
Lee-Potter, Jeremy 3
Leekpai, Chuan 17
left wing 161
legacy 130
legal action 123
legal aid 130
legal institutions 134
legal terms 123-34
legume 508
Leibniz, Gottfried Wilhelm 541
Leibovitz, Annie 363
Leighton, Frederic, Lord 310
Lely, Peter 308
Lemaître, Georges Edouard 412
Lenin, Vladimir Ilyich 588
Lennon, John 353
lens 86
 in optics 546
Leonard, Sugar Ray 219
Leonardo da Vinci 305
Leonov, Aleksei Arkhipovich 412
Leopardi, Giacomo 322
lepton 551
Lesotho 660
Lethaby, William Richard 298
Lettish 149
leukaemia 96
lever 546
leveraged buyout 261
Leverrier, Urbain Jean Joseph 412
Levi, Primo 322
Lewis, Carl 219
Lewis, Lennox 219
Lewis, Sinclair 322
ley 508
Lhasa 152
Li Peng 579
Li Po 322
libel 130
liberal democracy 158
liberalism 159
Liberia 660
libretto 342
Libya 661
licensing laws 130
Lichtenstein, Roy 314
Lick Observatory 409

Liddell Hart, Basil 246
Liebig, Justus, Baron von 437
Liechtenstein 662
lied, in music 342
lien 130
life sciences 511-29
LIFFE 284
Liggett Group 265
light 546
light pen 443
light year 407
light-emitting plastics 565
lightning 462
Lillee, Dennis 219
Lilley, Peter 3, 13
Limbourg brothers 305
limited company 261
limited liability 261
limited war 242
linear equation 534
Lineker, Gary 219
lipid 416, 424
Lippershey, Hans 35
liqueur 498
liquidation 261
Lissitsky, El 312
listed building 291
Lister, Joseph 102
Liszt, Franz 345
literacy 76
lithosphere 455
Lithuania 18, 24, 662
Lithuanian 149
litmus 431
Littlewood, Joan 372
liver 88
Lloyd's of London 266, 268
loan 261
Lobachevsky, Nikolai Ivanovich 541
lobby 161
local area network (LAN) 446
local government 161
Local Group 403
Locarno Pact 37
lockjaw 99
locus 534
logarithm 534
logic circuit 451
logic gate 451
Lolo 154
Lomé Convention 110
London, Jack 322
London International Financial Futures Exchange (LIFFE) 284
lone pair 431
Long, Richard 314
longitude 458
Lopez, Nancy 219
Lorca, Federico Garćia 322, 372
Lord Advocate 130
Lord Chancellor 130
Lorenz, Ludwig Valentine 541
Lorenzetti, Ambrogio 305
Lorrain, Claude 307
loss 261
loudspeaker 562
Louis, Joe 219
Lovell, Bernard 412
Lowell, Percival 412
Lowell Observatory 409
Lubbers, Rudolph Franz Marie (Ruud) 579
Luftwaffe 240
luminescence 546
luminosity 407
Lumumba, Patrice 579
lunar eclipse 398
lung 88
Luther, Martin 184
Lutyens, Edwin Landseer 298
Lutz, Hermann 5
Luxembourg 663
lymph node 88
Lysippus 302

Maastricht Treaty 13, 20, 25, 28, 112-13
McAlpine, Lord 11
McBride, Willie John 219
McClintock, Barbara 55
McCullin, Donald 363
Mcdonald Observatory 409
McEnroe, John 219
McGrath, John 372
Machado de Assis, Joaquim Maria 322
Machel, Samora 579
machine code, computer 439
machine gun 249
MacKenzie, Lewis 10
Mackintosh, Charles Rennie 298
Macmillan, Harold, 579
McMillan, Keith 7
MacMillan, Kenneth 53
macro 446
macrobiotics 498
Madagascar 663
Madonna 6, 353
madrigal 342
Magellan, space probe 391
Magellanic Clouds 403
magic square 534
magistrate 130
magistrates' court 135
magma 455
magnet schools 77
magnet therapy 105
magnetic disc 442
magnetic storm 462
magnetism 546
magnetometer 384
magnetosphere 399
magnitude 407
Magritte, René 313
Mahābhārata 182
Mahavira 184
Mahāyāna Buddhism 171
Mahler, Gustav 345
Mahratta 149
Maimonides 184
mainframe computer 439
maintenance payment 130
Major, John 3, 7, 9, 12, 113, 580
Makarios III 580
Makua 149
Malagasy 149
malaria 96, 97
Malawi 664
Malayalam 149
Malaysia 664
Malcolm X 3
Maldives 665
Malevich, Kasimir 312
Mali 666
malnutrition 83
malpractice 130
Malta 666
Mamet, David 372
mammal 519
mammography 83
Man Ray 363
management accounting 261
management buyout 261
management information system 261
managing director 261
mandate 161
Mandela, Nelson 17, 580
Mandelbrot, Benoit B 541
Manet, Edouard 310
mangrove 475
manic depression 90
manifesto 161
Mankiewicz, Joseph 54
Manley, Michael 580
Mann, Thomas 322
Mannerism 306
manoeuvre 240
Mansell, Nigel 220
manslaughter 130
Mansoor, Mallikarjun 54
Mantegna, Andrea 306
mantle 455
Mantle, Mickey 220
Manzoni, Alessandro 322
Mao Zedong 580, 587
Maoism 159
Maori 149
Mapplethorpe, Robert 363
Maradona, Diego 10, 220
Marat, Jean Paul 587
Maratha 149
Marc, Franc 312
Marciano, Rocky 220
Marcos, Ferdinand 580
margarine 498
Margiela, Martin 70, 71
Mariner spacecraft 391
Marines 240
Marinetti, Filippo 312
maritime law 130
market
  capitalization 261
  economy 278
  forces 278
  segment 261
  share 261
Markov, Andrei 541
Marley, Bob 353
Marlowe, Christopher 372
Marne, Battles of the 246
marriage rites 181
Mars 399
Mars Observer 18
Marshall, Thurgood 54
Marshall Space Flight Center 391
Martens, Wilfried 580
martial law 130
Martin, Archer John Porter 437
Martini, Simone 305
Marxism 159
Masaccio 305
Masai 149
Masire, Quett Ketumile Joni 580
Maskell, Dan 55
masonry 293
masque 366
mass, in physics 546
mass action, law of 431
mass extinction 465
Masson, André 313
material culture 384
Mates, Michael 11
mathematics 539-42
  awards 540
  biographies 539-42
  terms 530-9
Matisse, Henri 311
matrix 534
Matthews, Stanley 220
Matura, Mustapha 372
Mauna Kea 409
Maupassant, Guy de 322
Mauritania 667
Mauritius 667
Maximilian I 30
Maxwell, Robert 138
Maxwell Communications 138
Méliès, Georges 333
mean, in mathematics 534
meander 458
measles 96
meat 498
Mecca 185
mechanics 546
mechanized infantry combat vehicle 249
Meciar, Vladimir 580
media 138-42
media conglomerates 140-2

media watchdogs 142
medicine 82-107
Medina 185
Mediterranean climate 462
medulla 86
megabyte 447
megavitamin therapy 105
Meier, Richard 298
Meiji period 316
meiosis 516
Meir, Golda 580
Meiselas, Susan 363
melanoma 97
Mellor, David 17
melodrama 366
melody 342
Melville, Herman 322
Memlinc, Hans 306
memorandum of association 261
Mende 149
Mendeleyev, Dmitri Ivanovich 437
Mendelsohn, Erich 298
Mendelssohn, Felix 345
Menem, Carlos Saul 581
Mengistu, Haile Mariam 581
meningitis 97
mental handicap 90
Mercalli scale 455
mercenary 240
Merckx, Eddie 220
Mercosur 110
mercury 483
Mercury, planet 399
mergers 261
meridian 458
Mesolithic 384
meson 551
mesosphere 462
Mesozoic 465
Messiaen, Olivier 345
Messier, Charles 413
metabolism 416
metal 418
metal detector 384
metallographic examination 384
metamorphism 455
metamorphosis 516
meteor 399
meteorite 399, 456
meteorology 462
methanogenic bacteria 522
Metheny, Pat 7
methylated spirit 432
metre, in music 342
metric conversion tables 719
Mexico 668
Meyerhold, Vsevolod 372
mezzanine 291
mezzo-soprano 342
Miandad, Javed 220
Michelangelo 306
Michelson, Albert Abraham 557
Michelson-Morley experiment 557
microcomputer 439
microorganism 522
microphone 562
microprocessor 447, 452
Microsoft 267, 269
microwear analysis 384
middle C 342
Middle Ages, art of the 304
Middle East
peace talks 21, 25, 27, 28
MIDI 447
Mies van der Rohe, Ludwig 298
mifepristone 86, 103
migraine 97
Migration Period art 304
military equipment 248-50
military terms 235-42
militia 161
milk 498
milking machine 508
milks, composition of 498
Milky Way 23, 403
Miller, Arthur 373
Miller, Glenn 354
Millet, Jean-François 309
Milligan, Spike 6
Mills Cross 409
Milosevic, Slobodan 22, 27, 581
Milton, John 322
mime 366
minaret 291
mine 249
mineral water 498
minerals, trace 502
minesweeper 240
Ming dynasty 315, 591
Mingus, Charles 354
minicomputer 439
Minimalism 314
minipill 103
Minoan civilization 301
minor, in law 130
minority interest 262
Minority Rights Group 121
minuet 343
Mir space station 391
Mira 403
miracle play 366
Miró, Joan 313
mirror 546
misericord 291
Mishima, Yukio 323
missile systems and technology 228, 249
Missoni, Ottavio 71
Missoni, Rosia 71
mitochondria 524
mitochondrial DNA 148
mitosis 516
Mitsubishi Motors 272
Mitterrand, François 8, 25, 581
mixed-ability teaching 77
mixture, chemical 432
Miyake, Issey 71
Miyazawa, Kiichi 21, 26, 581
Mnouchkine, Ariane 373
mobile phone 560
mobilization 240
Möbius, August Ferdinand 541
Mobutu, Sese-Seko-Kuku Ngbeandu-Wa-ZaBanga 6, 23, 581
modem 443
modern dance 340
Modernism 290
Modigliani, Amedeo 314
Modotti, Tina 363
modular course 77
modulation 343, 562
module 293
modulus 534
Mogul art 316
Mohamad, Mahathir bin 581
Mohammed *see* Muhammad
Moholy-Nagy, Laszlo 363
Mohorovičič discontinuity 455
Moi, Daniel Arap 581
Moldavian 149
Moldova 668
molecular biology 524
molecular clock 528
molecular machines 423
molecular recognition 423
molecule 432
Molière (Jean-Baptiste Poquelin) 373
mollusc 519
Momoyama period 316
Mon 149
Monaco 28, 669
Mondrian, Piet 312
Monet, Claude 310
monetarism 278
monetary policy 279
money 279
Mongolia 669
monitor, in computing 444
Monk, Thelonius 354
monoculture 508
monomer 424
Monopolies and Mergers Commission 284
monopoly 279
monopsony 279
monorail 231
monosaccharide 416, 417
monsoon 462
Montaigne, Michel Eyquem de 323
Montana, Claude 71
Montana, Joe 220
Montenegro 27, 28
Monteverdi, Claudio 345
Montgomery 246
Montréal Protocol 492
Moon, the 399
Moon probe 392
Moonies 180
Moore, Bobby 55, 221
Moore, Charles 298
Moore, Henry 314
moraine 459
morality play 366
Mordvin 149
Moreau, Gustave 311
Mormon 178
Morocco 670
morphing 448
Morris, William 310
Morrison, Van 354
Morrissey 5
mortar bomb 249
mosaic
in art 304
in ecology 482
Moses 184
Mossi 149
motor neuron disease 97
motorcycle 233
motorcycle racing 201
motoring law 130
Moulinex (SA) 271
Mount Wilson 409
mountain 459
mouse, computer 443
movement, in music 343
Mozambique 15, 18, 21, 671
Mozart, Wolfgang Amadeus 345
MRBM (medium range ballistic missile) 240
MS *see* multiple sclerosis
MS-DOS (Microsoft Disc Operating System) 447
MTV Europe 264
Mubarak, Hosni 14, 581
Mugabe, Robert 581
Mugler, Thierry 71
Muhammad 184
Muir, Jean 71
Muldoon, Robert David 581
Mullard Radio Astronomy Observatory 409
Müller, Heiner 373
Mulroney, Brian 24, 581
multicultural education 77
multimedia 440, 441
multinational corporation 262
Multiple Mirror Telescope 410
multiple sclerosis (MS) 97
multiplexing 563
multiplier 279
multiprogramming 447

multitasking 447
mumps 97
Munch, Edvard 311
Munda 149
Munkácsi, Martin 363
muon 551
murder 130
Murdoch, Rupert 141
Murillo, Bartolomee Estebán 308
Muromachi period 316
muscle 88, 520
muscular dystrophy 97
Museveni, Yoweri Kaguta 581
mushroom 498
music 341-57
music hall 366
music therapy 105
musical 366
musical comedy 366
musical instruments digital interface (MIDI) 447
Musil, Robert 323
Muslims 182, 187
Mussorgsky, Modest Petrovich 345
mustard 498
mutation 511
Muybridge, Eadweard 363
myalgic encephalitis *see* ME
myalgic encephalitis (ME) 96, 98
Myanmar 671
Mycenean civilization 301
mystery play 366

Nabis, The 311
Nabokov, Vladimir 323
Nadar 363
nadir 407
Nadir, Asil 11, 28
Naga 149
Nahuatl 150
Naipaul, V S 323
Naipaul, Shiva(dhar) 323
Najibullah, Ahmadzai 581
Nakasone, Yasuhiro 582
Namath, Joe 221
Namibia 672
Namuth, Hans 363
Nanak 184
napalm 249
Napier, John 541
Narasimha Rao, P V 24, 582
NASA (National Aeronautics and Space Administration) 19, 30, 392
Nash, John 298
Nash, Paul 313
Nasser, Gamal Abdel 34, 582
Natanyahu, Binjamin 582
Natchez 150
National Curriculum 75, 77
national debt 279
national holidays 728-33
national insurance 262
national park 475
National Rivers Authority 492
National Skating Association of Great Britain 225
National Trust 492
National Union of Mineworkers 27
National Union of Rail, Maritime and Transport Workers (RMT) 27
national vocational qualification (NVQ) 77
nationalism 159
nationalization 163
NATO *see* North Atlantic Treaty Organization
Natural Environment Research Council (NERC) 492
natural gas 468
natural selection 511
Nature Conservancy Council (NCC) 492
nature reserve 475
naturopathy 105
Nauru 672
Navajo 150
Navratilova, Martina 221
navy 240
Nazarbayev, Nursultan 582
NBC (National Broadcasting Company) 140
NBC (nuclear, biological and chemical warfare) 240
Neanderthal 148
nebula 403
negative/positive image 360
negligence, in law 131
Negrillo 150
Nehru, Jawaharlal 582
neighbourhood watch 131
Nellist, David 8
nematode 519
Neo-Classical architecture 289
neo-Darwinism 512
Neo-Expressionism 314
Neo-Gothic architecture 289
neo-nazism 159
Neo-Plasticism 312
neofascism 159
Neolithic 384
Nepal 673
Neptune 35, 399
Nernst, (Walther) Hermann 438
Neruda, Pablo 323
nerve 88
Nervi, Pier Luigi 298
nervous breakdown 90
nervous system 520
Nestlé 267
net 262
net assets 262
net current assets 262
net worth 262
netball 202
Netherlands 674
neural network 440, 447
neurosis 90
Neutra, Richard Joseph 298
neutral solution 432
neutralization 432
neutrino 552
neutron 432, 552, 553
neutron bomb 241
neutron star 404
New Age music 354
New Archaeology 384
new catechism, the 182
New Technology Telescope 410
New Wave music 354
New Zealand 674
newly industrialized countries (NICs) 279
News International/News Corporation 141
Newton, Isaac 541, 557
Newton's laws of motion 546
Nicaragua 675
  Nicaraguan Revolution 589
niche, in ecology 475
Nicholson, Jack 4
Nicklaus, Jack 221
Nielsen, Carl 345
Niemeyer, Oscar 298
Niger 676
Niger-Congo languages 150
Nigeria 676
Nightingale, Florence 83
Nintendo 441
nitrate 483
nitric acid 418
nitrogen 420
nitrogen cycle 518
Nixon, Richard Milhous 582
Nkomo, Joshua 582
Nkrumah, Kwame 582
Nnova (Noh) 366
Nobel, Alfred Bernhard 438
Nobel prize
  chemistry 436
  literature 320
  physics 556
nocturne 343
Nolan, Sidney Robert 56
nonexecutive director 262
nonmetal 420
nonrenewable resources 475
nonvoting share 262
Noriega, Manuel 15, 582
North America 600
North American Free Trade Agreement 21
North American indigenous religions 177
North Atlantic Cooperation Council 110, 240
North Atlantic Treaty Organization (NATO) 14, 26, 110, 240
North Korea 25
North Star 404
Northern Ireland 16, 20, 21, 28
Norway 677
notebook, computer 449
noun 156
nova 404
Nuba 150
nuclear
  accidents 32, 483
  energy 468
  fission 468, 546
  fusion 548
  proliferation 244
  reactor 468-70
  safety 483
  testing 15
  warfare 240-1
  waste 484, 487
nucleic acid 416
nucleotide 416, 524
nucleus
  in biology 552
  in physics 522
Nujoma, Sam 582
number 534
number theory 535
numerator 535
Nureyev, Rudolf 56
nursery school 77, 78
nursing 83
nut 498
nutation 407
nutrition 83
Nutter, Tommy 57
Nyanja 150
Nyerere, Julius 582

oath 131
obelisk 291
Obote, Milton 582
obscenity law 131
observatories 408-11
obsession 90
obstetrics 83, 84
O'Casey, Sean 373
occultation 399

ocean 460-3
  ridge 462
  trench 462
Oceania 600-1
oceanography 475
Ochoa, Severo 438
octahedron 535
Odets, Clifford 373
oesophagus 88
offshore petroleum exploration 456
Ohm, Georg Simon 557
oil 470-1
  spills 483, 484
  world production 470
oil, food and agriculture 499, 508
Okinawa 246
Olbers, Heinrich 413
Olbers' paradox 404
Olbrich, Joseph Maria 298
Old Bailey 135
Oldfield, Bruce 71
Oldfield, Harry 105
oligopoly 279
Olivier, Laurence 373
Oman 677
omnivore 518
oncology 83
oncomouse 528
O'Neill, Eugene 373
Oort, Jan Hendrik 57, 413
Oort cloud 399
ooze 462
Op art 314
OPEC *see* Organization of Petroleum Exporting Countries
Open College 77
Open University 77
opera 343
operating system 449
operational amplifier 452
operetta 343, 366
operon 524
ophthalmology 83
Ophuls, Marcel 333
Ophuls, Max 333
opposition, in astronomy 407
optical disc 442
optical fibre 563
optics 548
opting out, schools 78
option 262
optoelectronics 452
opus 343
oratorio 343
orbit 407
orchestra 343, 347
orchestration 343
order, in architecture 291
orders, of animals 518
ordinal number 535
ordinary share 262
ordinate 535
ordination of women 172
Ordovician 465
organic farming 484
Organisation Commune Africaine et Mauricienne (OCAM) 110
Organization of African Unity (OAU) 110
Organization of American States (OAS) 110
Organization of Arab Petroleum Exporting Countries (OAPEC) 110
Organization of Central American States (ODECA) 110
Organization for Economic Cooperation and Development (OECD) 110, 284
Organization of Petroleum Exporting Countries (OPEC) 17, 30, 110, 285
orienteering 202
origin, in geometry 535
Orion nebula 404
Oriya 150
Oromo 150
Orphism 312
Ortega Saavedra, Daniel 582
orthochromatic 360
Orthodox Church 173
orthopaedics 83
Orton, Joe 373
Orwell, George 323
Osborne, John 373
oscillating universe 404
oscillator 452, 563
osteoarthritis 92, 98
osteopathy 105
osteoporosis 98
Ostrovsky, Alexander 373
Ostwald, Wilhelm 438
otitis 98
Ottoman emperors 590
ovary 88
overfishing 484
overheads 262
overture 343
Ovid 323
oviduct 86
ovum 516
Owen, David, Lord 5, 18, 113
Owens, Jesse 221
Oxfam 121
oxidation 433
oxygen 420
oxytocin 103
Ozal, Turgut 57, 583
Ozbek, Rifat 71
ozone 26, 421, 484
  depleter 485
  hole 484, 485
  layer 20, 476
Ozu, Yasujiro 333

p-n junction diode 452
p/e ratio 262
pacemaker 83
packaging 485
paediatrics 83
pageant 366
pain 83
Pakistan 17, 26, 678
palaeobotany 386
Palaeolithic 386
palaeomagnetism 465
palaeontology 387, 465
Palaeozoic 465
Palestinians 18, 21, 23, 25, 26, 27
Palestrina, Giovanni Perluigi da 345
Palikur 150
Palladio, Andrea 298
Palme, (Sven) Olof 583
Palmer, Arnold 221
Palomar, Mount 409
Panama 678
panchromatic film 360
pancreas 88
panel painting 305
Pangaea 465
Panic, Milan 5, 14, 15, 21
Panthalassa 465
pantheon 291
pantomime 367
Paolozzi, Eduardo 314
pap test 82
Papandreou, Andreas 583
paper 489
Papua New Guinea 679
parabola 535
paracetamol 103
paraffin 433
Paraguay 21, 27, 680
parallax 407
parallel lines 535
parallelogram 535
paralysis agitans 98
paranoia 90
paraplegia 83
parathyroid 88
parent-teacher association (PTA) 78
Paris, treaties of 243
Paris Commune 587
Parker, Charlie 354
Parkes 410
Parkinson, Norman 363
Parkinson's disease 98
parliament 163
parole 131
parsec 407
part of speech 156
participle 156
particle physics 551-5
party, in law 131
Pascal, Blaise 541
Pasolini, Pier Paolo 334
Passchendaele 246
pasta 499
Pasternak, Boris Leonidovich 323
pasteurization 504
pastry 499
patent 131, 262
Pathan 150
pathenogenesis 513
Patriot missile 249
Patten, Chris 18, 19, 163
Patten, John 3, 75
Patton, George 246
Paul, Saint 184
Pauli, Wolfgang 557
Pauling, Linus Carl 438
Pawlak, Waldemar 13
Paxton, Joseph 298
PAYE 262
Paz (Estenssoro), Victor 583
Paz, Octavio 323
PBS (Public Broadcasting System) 140
PC *see* personal computer
peace dividend 244
Pearl Harbor, Battle of 247
Pearson 141
peat 459
pediatrics 83
pediment 291
pedology 460
Pei, Ieoh Ming 298
Pelé 221
pelvic girdle 88
pelvis 88
penal institution 134
penicillin 103
penis 88
Penn, Irving 363
pepper 499
peptide 416, 524
percentage 535
perestroika 163
Pérez, Carlos Andreas 28
Pérez de Cuéllar, Javier 115, 583
performance art 314
performance-related pay 262
perigee 407
perihelion 407
perimeter 535
period 156
periodic table of the elements 433
periscope 250
peristyle 291
perjury 131
Perkins, Anthony 58
permafrost 459
Permian 466
permutation 535
Perón, Juan 583
Perot, Ross 4, 14, 18, 165
perpendicular 535

Perrault, Charles 323
Perrier 498
Perseids 402
Persian 147
personal computer (PC) 439
perspective 305
pertussis 101
Peru 680
Perutz, Max 438
perverting the course of justice 131
Pessoa, Fernando 323
pesticide 485, 508
Petrarch (Petrarca), Francesco 323
petrol, unleaded 488
petroleum 470
petrology 455
pH scale 433
Phanerozoic 466
pharynx 88
phase 407
phenol 424
phenotype 516
Philippines 139, 681
phobia 90
Phobos 399
phosphate 421
phosphate analysis 387
Photo CD 441
Photo Realism 314
photogram 360
photography 358-64
  biographies 354-64
  chronology 359-60
  terms 358-9
photojournalism 358
photolysis 434
photon 552
photosphere 399
photosynthesis 518
phthisis 100
phylogeny 512
physical anthropology 387
physical chemistry 414
physics 543-58
physiotherapy 83
piano nobile 291
Piazzi, Giuseppe 413
Picasso, Pablo 312
picketing 131
pickling 504
Piero della Francesca 305
Pietro da Cortona 307
pig 509
Piggott, Lester 221
piggy-back export scheme 262
Pike, Magnus Alfred 58
pill, the 82, 103
Pinochet (Ugarte), Augusto 583
Pinter, Harold 373
Pioneer space probes 392
Pirandello, Luigi 373
Piranesi, Giovanni Battista 299, 309
Pisano, Giovanni and Nicola 305
Piscator, Erwin 373
Pissarro, Camille 310
pixel 449
placebo 103
Plaidy, Jean 58
plain, in earth sciences 459
plaintiff 131
Planchon, Roger 374
Planck, Max 37, 558
planet 399
planetarium 410
planetary nebula 404
planets 400
plants 520-2
Plaskett's Star 404
plastic, types of 422
plate tectonics 466
plateau 459
Platini, Michel 222
platoon 241
Plesetsk 392
plotter 443
plough 509
pluralism 159
Pluto 400
plutonium 421
pneumatic tyres 231
pneumonia 98
poaching 131
Poe, Edgar Allan 323
Poincaré, Jules Henri 541
point 156
point-of-sale system 440
pointillism 311
poison 85
poison pill 262
Pol Pot 583
Poland 13, 14, 682
Polaris 404
Polaroid camera 360
polder 459
pole 459
Pole Star 404
police 131
Police Complaints Authority 135
poliomyelitis 98
poll tax 279
Pollaiuolo 305
pollen 516
pollen analysis 387
Pollock, Jackson 313
polluter pays principle 486
pollution 259, 476, 478-90
polo 202
polychlorinated biphenyl 433, 434
polygon 535
polyhedron 535
Polykleitos 302
polymer 424
polysaccharide 416
polytechnic 78, 80
polyunsaturate 424
Pontormo 306
Pop art 314
pop music 354
Pope, Alexander 323
popes, dates of 183
population, urban 716
port, in computing 439
Porter, Cole 354
Porter, Edwin Stanton 334
Porter, George 438
portico 291
Portugal 682
Post-Impressionism 310
Post-Modernism 290
postnatal depression 90
postviral fatigue syndrome 96
potassium-argon dating 387
potato 500
Potemkin 33
potential, electric 548
Potiguara 150
Potter, Dennis 6
poultry 509
Pound, Ezra 323
Poussin, Nicolas 307
Powell, Cecil Frank 558
Powell, Michael 334
Powell, Tim 8
power 548
power of attorney 131
Praxiteles 302
Pre-Raphaelites 310
Precambrian 466
precedent 131
precession 407
precipitation 434, 462
prefabricated building 295
preference share 262
Preferential Trade Area for Eastern and Southern African States (PTA) 110
pregnancy 516
prehistoric art 301, 385
prehistory 387
prelude 343
Premadasa, Ranasinghe 27, 59
prematurity 85
premedication 103
premenstrual tension (PMT) 98
premier 163
premium price 262
preparatory school 79
preposition 156
president 163
Presley, Elvis 354
Press Complaints Commission 142
press media 138-42
pressure 548
prestressed concrete 295
price elasticity of demand 262
Price Waterhouse 271
price/earnings ratio 262
pricing strategy 262
Priestley, Joseph 438
primary education 79
primary fuels, production and consumption 472
Primaticcio, Francesco 307
prime minister 163
prime number 536
prime rate 262
Prince 354
printer 443
prism 536
prison 136
prisoner of war 241
prisoners, numbers of 136
privacy legislation 142
private school 79
privatization 163, 279
Prix Goncourt 320
probability 536
probate 131
probation 131
procedure, in computing 449
procurator fiscal 132
productivity 280
profit 263
profit and loss account 263
profit-sharing 263, 280
programming, computer 439
programming languages 439, 449, 462
progression 536
progressive education 79
prokaryote 522
Prokofiev, Sergey 345
PROLOG 449
prominence 400
pronoun 157
propaganda 163
proper motion 407
prophylaxis 85
proportional 536
prosecution 132
Prost, Alain 222
prostate gland 88
protectionism 499
protein 416, 524
protein engineering 529
Proterozoic 466
Protestantism 173
protist 522
Proto-Atlantic 464
protohistory 387
proton 434, 552
proton number 425
Proton rocket 392
protozoa 522
Proust, Marcel 323
provost 132
Proxima Centauri 404
proxy 132
psionic medicine 105
psoriasis 98
psychedelic rock music 355
psychiatry 91

psychic healing 106
psychoanalysis 91
psychological disorders 89-91
psychology 91
psychosis 91
psychotherapy 91
psychotic disorder 91
pteridophyte 521
Ptolemy 413
puberty 516
public inquiry 132
public relations 263
public school 79
public-sector borrowing requirement (PSBR) 280
public-sector debt repayment (PSDR) 280
Pucci, Emilio 59
Puccini, Giacomo 345
puerperal fever 98
puffing 504
Pugin, Augustus Welby Northmore 299
Pulitzer Prize 320
pulsar 404, 405
pulse 500
pulse-code modulation (PCM) 563
pulsed high frequency (PHF) 105
punctuated equilibrium model 512
punctuation 157
Punjabi 150
punk rock 355
pupa 516
pupil, of eye 86
puppet theatre 367
Purcell, Henry 345
pure proteins 525
purge 163
Pushkin, Aleksandr 324
put option 263
Pygmy 150
pylon 295
Pynchon, Thomas 324
pyramid 291, 536
Pythagoras 541
Pythagoras' theorem 536

Qatar 683
Qing dynasty 315, 591
quadratic equation 536
qualitative analysis 414
quality circle 263
quality control 263
quality of life 280
Quant, Mary 72
quantitative analysis 414
quantity theory of money 280
quantum
  mechanics 548
  theory 548
quantum chromodynamics (QCD) 552
quantum electrodynamics (QED) 552
quark 552
quarter session 132
quasar 405
Quaternary 466
Quayle, Dan 9
Quechua 150
Queen's Counsel 130, 132
question mark 157
Quichua 150
quicksilver 483

Rabelais, François 324
rabies 98
Rabin, Yitzhak 13, 14, 15, 25, 583
Race Walking Association 225
Rachmaninov, Sergei 345
Racine, Jean 374
radian 536
radiation 549
radio 563
radio galaxy 405
radio telescope 410
radioactivity 434, 549
radiocarbon dating 387
radioisotope 549
radionics 105
radiotherapy 85
radon 486
Rafsanjani, Hojatoleslam Ali Akbar Hashemi 583
ragga 355
ragtime 355
raï music 355
rail transport 229-31
rain 462
rainbow alliance 163
rainforest 475
Rajneesh meditation 178
RAM (random access memory) 443
Rāmāyana 182
Rambert, Marie 337
Ramos, Fidel 13, 583
Ramsay, William 438
rangefinder 360
Raoult, François 438
rap music 355
rape 132, 137
Raphael (Raffaello Sanzio) 306
Rapid Reaction Force (RRF) 241
Rarotonga Treaty 111
Rastafarianism 178
rate of reaction 434
rate of return 263
ratio 536
Ravel, (Joseph) Maurice 345
Rawlings, Jerry 19
Ray, Satyajit 334
ray tracing 448
RCS Editore 141
reaction 434
reactivity series 434
Reagan, Ronald 583
Realism, in art 309
receiver, in law 132, 263
receiver, radio 564
recession 280
in Europe 277
reciprocal 536
recombinant DNA 416
reconnaissance 241
rectangle 536
recycling 486, 489
Red Army 241
red blood cell 88
Red Crescent 121
Red Cross 21, 27, 121
Red or Dead 72
red dwarf 405
red giant 405
red shift 407
redeemable preference share 263
Redon, Odilon 311
redox reaction 434
Redstone rocket 392
reduction 434
redundancy rights 132
Reed, Carol 334
Reed, Lou 355
Reed/Elsevier 140
Rees-Mogg, Lord William 7, 8, 12
referendum 163
reflection 549
reflex camera 360
reflexology 106
refraction 549
refrigeration 504
refugee 164
reggae 355
regiment 241
regional conflicts, current 247
Reichian therapy 106
Reinhardt, Max 374
relative atomic mass 434
relative dating 387
relativity, theory of 549
relaxation therapy 106
relief organizations 119, 121-2
religious
  festivals 185-7
  figures 183-4
  movements 178-80
  rites of passage 180-1
  traditions 171-8
remand 132
remanent magnetization 465
Rembrandt van Rijn 308
remedial education 79
remission 85
remix 355
remote sensing 387, 456
remotely piloted vehicle (RPV) 250
removable hard disc 442
Renaissance architecture 289
Renault 270
renewable resource 471, 477
Renger-Patzsch, Albert 363
Reni, Guido 307
Reno, Janet 7
Renoir, Jean 334
Renoir, Pierre-Auguste 310
repellent 434
replication 516
reply, right of 132
reprieve 132
reproduction 512-14
reptile 519
requiem 343
rescue archaeology 387
research and development (R&D) 263
reserve currency 280
resistance 549
resistivity survey 387
resonance 549
respiration 416, 518
restriction enzyme 529
resuscitation 85
retail price index 280
retina 86
retrovirus 85
reuse 488
Reuters 140
revaluation 275
revenge tragedy 368
revenue 263
reverse takeover 263
revolutions 586-9
  of 1848 587
  of 1989 589
revue 367
Reynolds, Albert 10, 19, 22, 583
Reynolds, Joshua 309
Reynoso, Abimael Guzman 17
rhapsody 343
rheumatic fever 98
rheumatoid arthritis 92
Rhodes, Wilfred 222
rhombus 536
rhythm 343
rhythm and blues 355
rib 88
Ribera, José 307
ribonucleic acid *see* RNA
ribosome 524
rice 500
Rice, Peter 59
Richards, Gordon 222
Richards, Viv 222
Richardson, Samuel 324
Richmond, John 72

Richter scale 455
Ridley, Nicholas 60
Riemann, Georg Friedrich Bernhard 541
Rietveld, Gerrit 312
Rifkind, Malcolm 13, 15
rifle 250
rift valley 459
right ascension 408
right wing 164
right-angled triangle 537
rights issue 263
Rigil Kent 401
Riina, Salvatore 23
Riley, Bridget 314
Rilke, Rainer Maria 324
Rimbaud, Arthur 324
Rimsky-Korsakov, Nikolay Andreyevich 274
RISC (reduced instruction set computer) 449
risk capital 263
RNA (ribonucleic acid) 417, 524
Roach, Hal 60
road transport 231-3
Roberts, Gareth 7
Robespierre, Maximilien 587
Robinson, Mary 584
Robinson, Smokey 355
Rocard, Michel 584
rock art 380, 385
rock and roll 355
rocket 229, 392
Rococo architecture 289
Rococo art 308
Rodchenko, Alexander 363
Rodin, Auguste 311
Rodnina, Irina 222
Rogers, Richard 299
Rolfing 106
Rolling Stones 355
ROM (read-only memory) 443
Roman Catholicism 20, 173, 557
Roman empire
 art 302, 304
 emperors 590
 Hoxne treasure hoard 384
roman numerals 537
Romance languages 150
Romanesque architecture 289
Romanesque art 304
Romania 683
Romano, Giulio 306
Romantic art 309
Romantic ballet 337
Romany 150
Rommel, Erwin 247
rondo 343
root 522
root crop 509
roots music 357
ROSAT 392
Rossellini, Isabella 334
Rossellini, Roberto 334
Rossetti, Dante Gabriel 310
Rossini, Gioacchino 346
Rosso, Giovanni Battista 306
Roth, Christian Francis 70
Rothko, Mark 313
Rothschild Group 268
Rouault, Georges 312
Rousseau, Jean-Jacques 324
Rousseau, Theodore 309
rowing 203
Royal Air Force 241
Royal British Legion 241
Royal Dutch/Shell Group 267, 270
Royal Greenwich Observatory 410
Royal Marines 241
Royal Yachting Association 225
RTE (Radio Telefis Eireann) 140
rubella 95, 98
Rubens, Peter Paul 308
Rubik, Erno 541
rugby 203
Ruisdael, Jacob van 308
rule of law 132
Runcie, Lord 7
rupture 95
Rushdie, Salman 8
Russia 14, 18, 23, 24, 28
 Russian Revolution 588
 Tsars 594
Russian 151
Russian Federation 684
Russian Ilyushin 269
Russo-Japanese War 247
Ruth, Babe 223
Rutherford, Ernest 558
Rwanda 685
Ryle, Martin 413

Saami 151
Saarinen, Eero 299
Saarinen, Eliel 299
Sabin, Albert Bruce 60
Sadat, Anwar 584
St Christopher (St Kitts) Nevis 685
Saint Group 269
St Lucia 686
St Vincent and the Grenadines 686
Saint-Denis, Michel 374
Saint-Laurent, Yves 72
Saint-Saëns, (Charles) Camille 346
Salam, Abdus 558
Salazar, Antonio de Oliviera 584
sales promotion 264
Salinas de Gortiari, Carlos 584
Salinger, J D 324
salsa 355
salt 434, 500
SALT (Strategic Arms Limitation Talks) 243
saltation 512
salvage archaeology 387
Salvation Army 33
Salyut space station 393
Sam, Kim Young 21
Samerec 270
Samoa, Western 687
Sampras, Pete 17
San Marino 687
Sanchez Vicario, Arantxa 17
sanction 164
sand 459
Sander, August 363
Sané Pierre 6
Sant'Elia, Antonio 299
São Tomé e Principe 688
Sargent, Claire 4
Sarney (Costa), José 584
Sartre, Jean-Paul 324
satellite 393, 400, 401
satellite town 291
saturated compound 424
Saturn 400
Saturn rocket 394
sauce 500
Saudi Arabia 688
Saudi Aramco 270
Save the Children Fund 122
savings 280
Sawchuk, Terry 223
Say's law 280
scabies 98
scalar quantity 537
scale, in music 343
Scalfaro, Oscar Luigi 26
scanning electron microscope 126
Scargill, Arthur 4
scarp and dip 459
Scheele, Karl Wilhelm 438
Schering 269
scherzo 343
Schiaparelli, Giovanni (Virginio) 413
Schiller, Johann Christoph Friedrich von 374
Schinkel, Karl Friedrich 299
schizophrenia 91
Schlürwe, Poul Holmskov 584
Schmidt, Helmut 584
Schmidt Telescope 410
Schmitt-Rotluff, Karl 312
Schnabel, Julian 314
Schoenberg, Arnold 346
School of Fontainebleau 307
Schrödinger, Erwin 558
Schubert, Franz 346
Schuessler, W H 104
Schultz, Johannes 104
Schumann, Robert 346
Schwarzkopf, H Norman 247
sciatica 98
Scientology 180
Scopas 302
Scorsese, Martin 334
Scotland, Kings and Queens of 594
Scots law 132
Scott, (George) Gilbert 299
Scott, Walter 324
Scottish Amateur Athletic Association 225
Scottish Amateur Boxing Association 225
Scottish Amateur Swimming Association 225
Scottish Natural Heritage 492
scrambling circuit 564
scrapie 509
screen 444
scrip issue 264
Scud missile 250
Scudamore, Peter 223
sculpture 311
scythe 509
Sea Dayak *see* Iban
sea transport 233-48
Seaborg, Glenn Theodore 438
seafloor spreading 466
Sears Roebuck 273
seaside bathing 535-6
SECAM 561
secondary education 79
Secretariat (UN) 115
Securities and Exchange Commission (SEC) 285
Securities and Investment Board 285
Security Council *see* UN
sediment 459
seed 516
seed drill 509
Sega Megadrive 441
Seles, Monica 15, 17, 27, 223
self-sufficiency 280
Sellafield 487
Selwyn Gummer, John 9
semicolon 157
semiconductor 452, 549
Semtex 250
Senegal 689
senile dementia 91, 94
Senna, Ayrton 223
septicaemia 98
sequencing 529
sequestrator 264

Serbia 27, 28
Serbo-Croatian 151
serenade 343
seriation 387
Serlio, Sebastiano 299
services, armed 241
set 537
settlement out of court 132
Seurat, Georges 311
Sevastopol 247
Seventh Day Adventist 180
Severini, Gino 312
sewage disposal 488
sexual reproduction 513
Seychelles 689
Seyfert galaxy 405
Shakespeare, William 324, 374
Shamir, Yitzhak 13, 584
Shankara 184
SHAPE (Supreme Headquarters Allied Powers Europe) 241
Shapley, Harlow 413
shareholder 264
Shaw, George Bernard 374
Shaw, (Richard) Norman 299
Shawn, William 61
sheep 509
Shelley, Percy Bysshe 324
shellfish 500
Shepard, Alan (Bartlett) 413
Shepard, Sam 374
Shephard, Gillian 25
Sheridan, Richard Brinsley 375
sheriff 132
Shevardnadze, Edvard 14, 584
shiatsu 106
shield 454
Shi'ite Muslims 175
Shilton, Peter 223
shingles 98
Shining Path 17
Shinto 177
shinty 204
shipping 233-4
shock 98
Shockley, William 558
Shoemaker, Willie 223
Shona 151
Short, Nigel 7
short takeoff and landing (STOL) craft 226
shorthand 36
Shoshow trialwa period 316
Shostakovich, Dmitry 347
show trial 132
Shuskevich, Stanislaw 584
Shuster, Joseph (Joe) 61
shuttle diplomacy 164
SI units 549, 550
sial 455
Sibelius, Jean 347
sick building syndrome 292
sickle-cell disease 99
Siddhanta 182
sidereal period 408
Siding Spring Mountain 410
Siemens Nixdorf 270
Sierra Leone 690
signal-to-noise ratio 563
Sihanouk, Norodom 15, 584
Sikhism 177, 182, 187
silage 510
silicon 421
silver 421
sima 455
Simon, (Marvin) Neil 375
Simon, Paul 355
simulation 440
simultaneous equation 537
Sinai 247
Sinan 299
Sinatra, Frank 355
Sindhi 151
sine 537
Singapore 690
Singer, Isaac Bashevis 324
Single European Act 492
single-lens reflex 360
singles, top 10 355
singularity, in astronomy 408
Sinhalese 151
Sino-Japanese Wars 247
Sino-Tibetan languages 151
sinusitis 99
Siskind, Aaron 363
Sisley, Alfred 310
site 387
site catchment analysis (SCA) 387
site exploration territory (SET) 387
site of special scientific interest (SSSI) 492
skating 204
skeleton 520
skiing 204
skull 88
Skylab 394
skyscraper 292
slash and burn 488
slaughterhouse 508
Slav 151
Slavonic languages 151
SLBM (submarine launched ballistic missile) 241
Slovakia 13, 22, 691
Slovene 151
Slovenia 113, 691
slump 280
slurry 488
Sluter, Claus 306
small arms 250
smart weapons 250
Smetana, Bedřich 347
Smirke, Robert 299
Smith, David 314
Smith, Ian Douglas 585
Smith, John 3, 15, 18, 24
Smith, Paul 72
Smith, Robert 9
Smiths, the 356
Smithson, Alison 299
Smithson, Peter 299
smoking, food 505
snooker 205
Soane, John 299
Soares, Mario 4, 585
Sobers, Gary 223
soca 356
soccer 195
Social Chapter 24, 28
social costs and benefits 282
social democracy 158
socialism 159
Soddy, Frederick 438
sodium chloride 500
soft drink 495
softball 205
soil 459
  erosion 488
Soil Association 492
solar
  eclipse 398
  energy 471
  spicules 400
  system 400
  wind 400
solar flare 400
solicitor 132
solid-state circuit 452
Solomon Islands 692
solstice 408
solute 435
solution 435
solvency 264
solvent 435
Solzhenitsyn, Alexander 324
Somalia 16, 17, 20, 22, 23, 24, 25, 693
sonata 343
sondage 388
Sondheim, Stephen 356
Song dynasty art 315
Sony 267
Sophocles 375
soprano 343
Soros, George 8, 10
Sotho 151
soul music 356
sound 550
sound therapy 106
South Africa 13, 14, 15, 16, 19, 21, 23, 25, 693
South African Astronomical Observatory 410
South America 601
indigenous religions 178
South Asian Association for Regional Cooperation 111
South Korea 16
South Korean 21
South Pacific Bureau for Economic Cooperation (SPEC) 111
South Pacific Commission (SPC) 111
South Pacific Forum (SPF) 111
Southeast Asia Treaty Organization (SEATO) 111
Southern African Development Coordination Conference (SADCC) 111
sovereignty 164
Soviet Army 241
Soyinka, Wole 324
Soyuz 394
space adaptation syndrome 394
space exploration 390-5
  budgets 390, 391
  main launches 392
  UK expenditure 391
space shuttle 394
space sickness 394
space suit 394
space-frame 295
Spacelab 394
Spain 16, 28, 694
  art in 307, 309
  rulers 593
Spanish cave art 380
Spassky, Boris 17, 20
spastic 85
Special Air Service (SAS) 241
special education 79
species 512
speckle interferometry 408
Spector, Phil 356
spectrographic analysis 388
spectroscopy 550
spectrum 550
speech recognition 440
speed, of animals 520
speed, in mathematics 537
Speer, Albert 299
Spenser, Edmund 324
sperm 516
sperm whale 518
spermatozoon 516
spermicide 85
sphere 537
spice 500
Spielberg, Steven 334
spin 554

spina bifida 99
spinal cord 89
spirit, alcoholic 500
spiritual healing 106
Spitz, Mark Andrew 35, 223
Spock, Benjamin 12
spore 516
sport
  biographies 210-24
  events and records 188-210
  governing bodies 224-5
spreadsheet 264, 442
Springsteen, Bruce 356
Sputnik 35, 394
square root 537
squash, in sport 205
SRAM 452
Sri Lanka 695
stadium rock 356
stag, in business 264
stagflation 282
stakeholder 264
stalactite 460
stalagmite 460
Stalingrad 248
Stallone, Sylvester 10
standard deviation 537
standard model 554
Standard and Poor's Stock Price Index 264
standard temperature and pressure (STP) 435
Stanislavsky, Konstantin Sergeivich 375
star cluster 405
Star Wars 241-2
Starforth Hill, Ian 12
Stark, Dame Freya 61
starlight, aberration of 405
stars 401-5
START *see* Strategic Arms Reduction Treaty
state, as political term 164
states of matter 550
static random-access memory 452
statics, in physics 550
statistics 537
steady-state theory 405
stealth technology 250
steel band 356
Steen, Jan 308
Steichen, Edward 363
Stein, Peter 375
Steinbeck, John 325
Stendhal 325
step-trenching 388
sterilization 85
Sternberg, Josef von 334
Sterne, Laurence 325
steroid 103, 417
Stevenson, Robert Louis 325
Stewart, Jackie 223
Stieglitz, Alfred 364
still-life painting 308
Stirling, James 299
stock, in nutrition 500
stock exchange 282
Stockhausen, Karlheinz 347
Stockley, Des 11
stocks and shares 264
STOL (short takeoff and landing) craft 226
stomach 89
Stone Age 388
stop-loss insurance 268
Stoppard, Tom 375
Storey, Helen 70, 72
Stouffer Hotel Holdings 267
Strand, Paul 364
Strasberg, Lee 375
Strategic Arms Limitation Talks (SALT) 243
Strategic Arms Reduction Treaty (START) 13, 22, 243
Strategic Defense Initiative (SDI) 241-2
stratigraphy 388, 466
Strauss, Johann 347
Strauss, Richard 347
Stravinsky, Igor 347
streaming 79
strength of acids and bases 435
stress, in medicine 91
stress and strain, in science of materials 550
Strindberg, August 375
Stroessner, Alfredo 585
Stroheim, Erich von 335
stroke 99
stromatolite 466
Struebig, Heinrich 13
Struve, Friedrich Georg Wilhelm 413
Stubbs, George 309
student finance 79
students, statistics 76
Sturges, Preston 335
sublimation 435
submarine 234, 242
subpoena 132
subsidies to farmers 504
subsistence farming 510
substrate 417
Suchocka, Hanna 14
sucrose 417
Sudan 696
sudden infant death syndrome (SIDS) 93
Suez Canal 34
Sufism 175, 176
sugar 417, 500
Suharto, President 25
Suharto, Raden 585
suite 343
Sukarno, Achmed 585
Sullivan, Louis Henry 299
sulphur 421
sulphuric acid 421
summit conference 164
summons 132
Sun 400, *see also*, solar
Sun Ra 62
Sun Yat-Sen 587
Sundanese 151
Sunni Muslims 175, 176
sunspot 401
Super Realism 314
supercomputer 439
superconductor 423
superheterodyne receiver 564
superior planet 401
superlubricant 423
supernova 404, 405
superphosphate 421
superstring theory 554
supersymmetry 554
supply curve 264
suprarenal gland 86
Suprematism 312
Supremes, the 356
surface tension 550
surfactant 435
surfing 206
surgery 84
Surinam 696
Surrealism 313
Survival International 122
sustainable management 489
sustained-yield cropping 488
Svedberg, Theodor 438
Swahili 151
Swaziland 697
Sweden 19, 697
sweetener, artificial 500
sweets 500
Swift, Jonathan 325
swimming 206
swing music 356
Switzerland 698
SWOT analysis 264
Symbolism 311
symphonic poem 343
symphony 343
syncline 454, 460
syncopation 343, 356
Synge, J M 375
synodic period 408
syphilis 99
Syria 26, 699
System X 563
Szent-Görgyi, Albert 438

table tennis 207
Tadzhik 151
Tagalog 151
tagging, electronic 132
Tagore, Rabindranath 325
Taiwan 699
Tajik 151
Tajikistan 700
takeover 264
Talaing 149
Talbot, William Henry Fox 364
tallest structures 295
Talmud 182
Tambo, Oliver 62, 585
Tamil 151
Tang dynasty art 315
Tange, Kenzo 299
tangent 538
tank 242
Tanzania 700
Taoism 178
tap dancing 340
Tarkovsky, Andrei 335
Tartar 152
TASM (tactical air-to-surface missile) 250
Tatar 152
Tati, Jacques 335
Tatlin, Vladimir 312
tau 555
tautomerism 435
Taylor Woodrow 272
TB 100
Tchaikovsky, Pyotr Il'yich 347
tea 502
teacher training 79
tectonics 466
tektite 401
telecommunications 559-68
  chronology 563
  equipment companies 559
telephone 564
telephone tapping 132
telephoto lens 361
telescope 410
teletext 564
television 564
  chronology 566
  media 138-42
Telstar 394
Telugu 152
temperature 550
  scales 720
tempo 343
tenant farming 510
tennis, lawn 207
Tennyson, Alfred 325
tenor 343
tension 550
Tereshkova, Valentina Vladimirovna 413
Terminator 2 448
terrestrial equator 400
Territorial Army 240, 242
terrorism 164
Terry, (John) Quinlan 299
Tertiary 466
tertiary college 79
TESSA (tax-exempt special savings account) 264

testing for schools 75
testis 89
tetanus 99
Tetra Laval 265
tetrachloromethane 424
tetrahedron 538
Tevatron particle 552
Thackeray, William Makepeace 325
Thai 152
Thailand 17, 701
Thales 541
thanatology 106
Thant, U 585
Thatcher, Margaret 5, 585
Thatcherism 159
thaumatrope 361
theatre 365-76
  awards 367
  biographies 368-76
  chronology 370-1
  genres 365-8
theft 133
theocracy 159
Theravāda Buddhism 171
Thermal Oxide Reprocessing Plant (THORP) 487
thermionics 452
thermodynamics 550
thermoluminescence 388
thin-layer chromatography 126
thin-section analysis 388
Third Age 79
Thompson, Daley 224
Thompson, Emma 6, 327
Thomson, J J 558
Three Age System 388
threshing 510
throat 89
thrombosis 99
thrush 99
thunderstorm 462
thyristor 452
thyroid 89
Tibet 28, 152
Tibetan 152
tidal power station 471
tides 471
Tiepolo, Giovanni Battista 308
Tigré 152
Tigrinya 152
timbre 343
time zones 723
Time-Warner 141
Tinguely, Jean 314
Tintoretto, Jacopo 306
Tipitaka 182
Tirpitz, Alfred von 248
Tiselius, Arne 438
Titan 401
Titan rocket 394
Titanic 35
Titian 306
Tito 585
TLR (twin-lens reflex) camera 361
Todd, Alexander, Baron Todd 438
Todd, Ann 63
Togo 702
Tokugawa 316
Tolstoy, Leo Nikolaievich 325
Tombaugh, Clyde (William) 413
tomography 85
tonality 344
Tonga 702
tongue 89
Tonkin Gulf Incident 248
topography 460
topology 538
topsoil 510
Torah 182
tornado 462
torpedo 250
tort 133
Torvill, Jayne 224
total war 242
totalitarianism 159
Tottenham Three 133
touch screen 444
Touche Ross 271
Toulouse-Lautrec, Henri de 311
town planning 292
toxic shock syndrome 99
toxic waste 22
toxin 85
trace element analysis 389
trace minerals 502
trachea 89
tractor 510
trade barrier 499
trade cycle 282
trade union 164
trade wind 462
trading account 264
tragedy 367
trampolining 208
tramway 231
transcendental meditation 180
transcription 524
transfer orbit 408
transfusion 85
transgenic organism 528, 529
transistor 452
transistor-transistor logic (TTL) 453
transit 408
translation, in cells 524
transparency 361
transplant 85
transputer 453
transuranic elements 420, 421
trapezium 538
trauma 85
travel sickness 99
treason 133
treasure trove 133, 384
Treasury bill 282
treaties, peace 242-3
Treaty of European Union 13, 24, 28
trespass 133
Treurnicht, Andries 63
trial 133
triangle 538, 539
Triassic 466
tribunal 133
tricarboxylic acid cycle 416
Trident submarine 15
trigonometry 538
Trinidad and Tobago 703
triode 453
triple bond 435
trolleybus 231
tropical deforestation 476
tropical diseases 100
tropics 460
tropopause 463
troposphere 463
Trotsky, Leon 30, 588
Trotskyism 159
Trudeau, Pierre (Elliott) 585
Truffaut, François 335
Trujillo, Gaviria 19
Truman, Harry S 585
trust 133
Trusteeship Council (UN) 115
truth table 453
tsunami 463
Tswana 153
Tuareg 153
tuberculosis (TB) 100
Tudjman, Franjo 15
Tumim, Stephen 7
tumour 85
Tunisia 703
tunnel 295
turbine 471
Turgenev, Ivan 325
Turing, Alan 541
Turkey 704
Turkmenistan 28, 704
Turkoman 153
Turner, Joseph Mallord William 309
turnover 264
Tuscan order 290, 291
Tutsi 153
Tutu, Desmond 585
Tuvalu 705
Twa 153
Twain, Mark 325
typhoon 462
typology 389
tyre 231
Tyson, Mike 224
Tzara, Tristan 312

U-2 250
U-boat 251
Uccello, Paolo 305
Uganda 705
Uigur 153
Ukraine 706
Ukrainian 153
Ulbricht, Walter 585
ultraheat treatment (UHT) of food 505
ultrasound 85, 550
Ulysses space probe 394
uncertainty principle 555, 557
uncommitted logic array (ULA) 453
underwater reconnaissance 389
unemployment 16, 21, 25, 282
Unification Church (Moonies) 180
unilateralism 164
Unilever 268
Union of Socialist Soviet Republics (USSR), leaders of 576
unit trust 264
Unitarianism 180
United Arab Emirates (UAE) 707
United Kingdom
  prime ministers 573
United Kingdom Infrared Telescope 410
United Kingdom (UK) 15, 16, 28, 707
United Nations (UN) 16, 23, 114-22
  in Bosnia-Herzegovina 24, 25, 27, 239
  Centre for Human Settlements (UNCHS) 118
  Children's Emergency Fund (UNICEF) 114, 118
  Conference on Environment and Development 476
  Conference on Trade and Development (UNCTAD) 118
  Development Programme (UNDP) 118, 119
  Disaster Relief Coordinator (UNDRO) 118
  Economic and Social Council 115
  Educational, Scientific and Cultural Organisation (UNESCO) 118
  Environmental Programme (UNEP) 118
  Fund for Population